P9-DXR-727

The Middle Ages · SIMPSON

The Sixteenth Century · GREENBLATT / LOGAN

The Early Seventeenth Century
MAUS

The Restoration and the Eighteenth Century
NOGGLE

The Romantic Period · LYNCH

The Victorian Age · ROBSON

The Twentieth and Twenty-First Centuries
RAMAZANI

THE NORTON ANTHOLOGY OF

ENGLISH

LITERATURE

TENTH EDITION

VOLUME B

THE SIXTEENTH CENTURY
AND
THE EARLY SEVENTEENTH CENTURY

George M. Logan
SENIOR FELLOW OF MASSEY COLLEGE IN THE UNIVERSITY OF TORONTO
JAMES CAPPON PROFESSOR OF ENGLISH EMERITUS, QUEEN'S UNIVERSITY

Deidre Shauna Lynch
ERNEST BERNBAUM PROFESSOR OF LITERATURE AND PROFESSOR OF ENGLISH, HARVARD UNIVERSITY

Katharine Eisaman Maus
JAMES BRANCH CABELL PROFESSOR OF ENGLISH, UNIVERSITY OF VIRGINIA

James Noggle
PROFESSOR OF ENGLISH AND MARION BUTLER McLEAN PROFESSOR
IN THE HISTORY OF IDEAS, WELLESLEY COLLEGE

Jahan Ramazani
UNIVERSITY PROFESSOR AND EDGAR F. SHANNON PROFESSOR OF ENGLISH,
UNIVERSITY OF VIRGINIA

Catherine Robson
PROFESSOR OF ENGLISH, NEW YORK UNIVERSITY

James Simpson
DOUGLAS P. AND KATHERINE B. LOKER PROFESSOR OF ENGLISH, HARVARD UNIVERSITY

M. H. Abrams, *Founding Editor*
LATE OF CORNELL UNIVERSITY

THE NORTON ANTHOLOGY OF

ENGLISH

LITERATURE

TENTH EDITION

Stephen Greenblatt, *General Editor*

COGAN UNIVERSITY PROFESSOR OF THE HUMANITIES

HARVARD UNIVERSITY

VOLUME B

THE SIXTEENTH CENTURY AND
THE EARLY SEVENTEENTH CENTURY

Stephen Greenblatt   Katharine Eisaman Maus
George Logan

W · W · NORTON & COMPANY
NEW YORK · LONDON

W. W. Norton & Company has been independent since its founding in 1923, when William Warder Norton and Mary D. Herter Norton first published lectures delivered at the People's Institute, the adult education division of New York City's Cooper Union. The firm soon expanded its program beyond the Institute, publishing books by celebrated academics from America and abroad. By midcentury, the two major pillars of Norton's publishing program—trade books and college texts—were firmly established. In the 1950s, the Norton family transferred control of the company to its employees, and today—with a staff of four hundred and a comparable number of trade, college, and professional titles published each year—W. W. Norton & Company stands as the largest and oldest publishing house owned wholly by its employees.

Copyright © 2018, 2012, 2006, 2000, 1993, 1990, 1986, 1979, 1974, 1968, 1962 by W. W. Norton & Company, Inc.
All rights reserved
Printed in the United States of America

Editors: Julia Reidhead and Marian Johnson
Assistant Editor, Print: Rachel Taylor
Manuscript Editors: Michael Fleming, Katharine Ings, Candace Levy
Media Editor: Carly Fraser Doria
Assistant Editor, Media: Ava Bramson
Marketing Manager, Literature: Kimberly Bowers
Managing Editor, College Digital Media: Kim Yi
Production Manager: Sean Mintus
Text design: Jo Anne Metsch
Art director: Rubina Yeh
Photo Editor: Nelson Colon
Permissions Manager: Megan Jackson Schindel
Permissions Clearing: Nancy J. Rodwan
Cartographer: Adrian Kitzinger
Composition: Westchester Book Company
Manufacturing: LSC Crawfordsville

Since this page cannot legibly accommodate all the copyright notices, the Permissions Acknowledgments constitute an extension of the copyright page.

ISBN: 978-0-393-60303-3

W. W. Norton & Company, Inc., 500 Fifth Avenue, New York, NY 10110
wwnorton.com

W. W. Norton & Company Ltd., 15 Carlisle Street, London W1D 3BS

1 2 3 4 5 6 7 8 9 0

Contents*

PREFACE xxiii

ACKNOWLEDGMENTS xxxiii

The Sixteenth Century (1485–1603)

INTRODUCTION 3

TIMELINE 34

JOHN SKELTON (ca. 1460–1529)   36
  Mannerly Margery Milk and Ale 37
  With lullay, lullay, like a child 38
  The Tunning of Elinour Rumming 39
    Secundus Passus 39

SIR THOMAS MORE (1478–1535)   41
  Utopia 44
    Thomas More to Peter Giles 44
    Book I 47
    Book II 69
    Thomas More to His Friend Peter Giles 117

SIR THOMAS WYATT THE ELDER (1503–1542)   118
  The long love that in my thought doth harbor 120
    Petrarch, Rima 140 121
  Whoso list to hunt 121
    Petrarch, Rima 190 121
  Farewell, Love 122
  I find no peace 122
    Petrarch, Rima 134 123
  My galley 123
    Petrarch, Rima 189 124
  Divers doth use 124
  What vaileth truth? 124

*Additional readings are available on the NAEL Archive (digital.wwnorton.com/englishlit10abc).

Madam, withouten many words 125
They flee from me 125
The Lover Showeth How He Is Forsaken of Such as He
    Sometime Enjoyed 126
My lute, awake! 127
Forget not yet 128
Blame not my lute 128
Stand whoso list 129
Who list his wealth and ease retain 130
Mine own John Poins 131

HENRY HOWARD, EARL OF SURREY (1517–1547)   133
The soote season 134
        Petrarch, Rima 310 135
Love, that doth reign and live within my thought 135
Alas! so all things now do hold their peace 136
        Petrarch, Rima 164 136
Th'Assyrians' king, in peace with foul desire 136
So cruel prison how could betide 137
Wyatt resteth here, that quick could never rest 138
O happy dames, that may embrace 140
Martial, the things for to attain 141
The Fourth Book of Virgil 141
        [Dido in Love] 141

                    FAITH IN CONFLICT   143
THE ENGLISH BIBLE: 1 Corinthians 13   145
From Tyndale's Translation 146
From The Geneva Bible 146
From The Douay-Rheims Version 148
From The Authorized (King James) Version 148
WILLIAM TYNDALE: The Obedience of a Christian Man   149
[The Forgiveness of Sins] 149
[Scriptural Interpretation] 150
THOMAS MORE: A Dialogue Concerning Heresies   151
From Book 1, Chapter 28 151
JOHN CALVIN: The Institution of Christian Religion   153
From Book 3, Chapter 21 153
ANNE ASKEW: From The First Examination of Anne Askew   156
JOHN FOXE: Acts and Monuments   159
[The Death of Anne Askew] 160
BOOK OF COMMON PRAYER: From The Form of
Solemnization of Matrimony   161
BOOK OF HOMILIES: From An Homily Against
Disobedience and Willful Rebellion   164

RICHARD HOOKER: Of the Laws of Ecclesiastical Polity   167
  Book 1, Chapter 3 168
    [On the Several Kinds of Law, and on the Natural Law] 168
ROBERT SOUTHWELL: The Burning Babe   170

ROGER ASCHAM (1515–1568)   171
  The Schoolmaster 172
    The First Book for the Youth 172
      [Teaching Latin] 172
      [The Italianate Englishman] 173

SIR THOMAS HOBY (1530–1566)   176
  Castiglione's The Courtier 176
    Book 1, Sections 25–26 176
      [Grace] 176
    Book 4, Sections 49–73 178
      [The Ladder of Love] 178

WOMEN IN POWER   193

MARY I (MARY TUDOR)   194
  Letter to Henry VIII 195
  From An Ambassadorial Dispatch to the Holy Roman Emperor,
    Charles V: The Coronation of Mary I 196
  The Oration of Queen Mary in the Guildhall, on the First of
    February, 1554 198
LADY JANE GREY   199
  Roger Ascham's Schoolmaster 200
    [A Talk with Lady Jane] 200
  From A Letter of the Lady Jane to M. H., late chaplain to the duke of
    Suffolk her father 202
  A Letter of the Lady Jane, Sent unto Her Father 205
  A Prayer of the Lady Jane 205
  A Second Letter to Her Father 207
  Foxe's Acts and Monuments 207
    The Words and Behavior of the Lady Jane upon the Scaffold 207
MARY, QUEEN OF SCOTS   208
  From Casket Letter Number 2 210
  A Letter to Elizabeth I, May 17, 1568 212
  From Narrative of the Execution of the Queen of Scots 214
ELIZABETH I   221
  Verses Written with a Diamond 222

From The Passage of Our Most Dread Sovereign Lady Queen Elizabeth
through the City of London to Westminster on the Day before Her
Coronation 223
Speech to the House of Commons, January 28, 1563 225
From A Speech to a Joint Delegation of Lords and Commons,
November 5, 1566 226
From A Letter to Mary, Queen of Scots, February 24, 1567 229
The doubt of future foes 230
On Monsieur's Departure 230
A Letter to Robert Dudley, Earl of Leicester, February 10, 1586 231
A Letter to Sir Amyas Paulet, August 1586 232
A Letter to King James VI of Scotland, February 14, 1587 232
Verse Exchange between Elizabeth and Sir Walter Ralegh 233
Speech to the Troops at Tilbury 234
The "Golden Speech" 235

EDMUND SPENSER (1552?–1599)   238
The Shepheardes Calender 241
    To His Booke 241
    October 242
The Faerie Queene 247
    A Letter of the Authors 249
    Book 1 253
    Book 2 406
        Summary 406
        Canto 12 406
            [The Bower of Bliss] 406
    Book 3 418
        Summary 418
        Canto 6 418
            [The Garden of Adonis] 418
        Cantos 7–10 Summary 431
        Canto 11 432
        Canto 12 445
    Mutabilitie Cantos 457
Amoretti *and* Epithalamion 486
    Amoretti
        1 ("Happy ye leaves when as those lilly hands")   487
        34 ("Lyke as a ship that through the Ocean wyde")   487
        37 ("What guyle is this, that those her golden tresses")   488
        54 ("Of this worlds Theatre in which we stay")   488
        64 ("Coming to kisse her lyps [such grace I found])"   488
        65 ("The doubt which ye misdeeme, fayre love, is vaine")   489
        67 ("Lyke as a huntsman after weary chace")   489
        68 ("Most glorious Lord of Lyfe, that on this day")   489

74 ("Most happy letters fram'd by skilfull trade") 490
75 ("One day I wrote her name upon the strand") 490
79 ("Men call you fayre, and you doe credit it") 491
Epithalamion 491

AN ELIZABETHAN MISCELLANY 502

RICHARD TOTTEL: Songs and Sonnets 504
The Printer to the Reader 504
ANNE VAUGHAN LOCKE: A Meditation of a Penitent Sinner 505
4 ("Have mercy, Lord, have mercy") 505

GEORGE GASCOIGNE 506
And if I did, what then? 506
The Lullaby of a Lover 507
Woodmanship 508
FULKE GREVILLE: Caelica 512
69 ("When all this All doth pass from age to age") 512
82 ("You that seek what life is in death") 512
100 ("In night when colors all to black are cast") 513
THOMAS LODGE 513
Pluck the fruit and taste the pleasure 513
Phyllis 35 ("I hope and fear, I pray and hold my peace") 514
HENRY CONSTABLE: Diana 515
4.1 ("Needs must I leave, and yet needs must I love") 515
6.2 ("To live in hell, and heaven to behold") 515

SAMUEL DANIEL: Delia 516
9 ("If this be love, to draw a weary breath") 516
32 ("But love whilst that thou may'st be loved again") 517
33 ("When men shall find thy flower, thy glory, pass") 517
MICHAEL DRAYTON: Idea 517
To the Reader of These Sonnets 518
5 ("Nothing but 'No' and 'I' and 'I' and 'No'?") 518
6 ("How many paltry, foolish, painted things") 518
8 ("There's nothing grieves me, but that age should haste") 519
50 ("As in some countries far remote from hence") 519
61 ("Since there's no help, come, let us kiss and part") 519

JOHN DAVIES OF HEREFORD: The Scourge of Folly 520
"If there were (oh!) an Hellespont of cream" 520
THOMAS CAMPION 521
My sweetest Lesbia 521
I care not for these ladies 522
When to her lute Corinna sings 522
When thou must home to shades of underground 523
Jack and Joan, they think no ill 523
Now winter nights enlarge 524

Never love unless you can 525
There is a garden in her face 525

SIR WALTER RALEGH (1552–1618) 526

The Nymph's Reply to the Shepherd 527
What is our life? 527
[Sir Walter Ralegh to His Son] 528
The Lie 528
Farewell, false love 530
Methought I saw the grave where Laura lay 531
Nature, that washed her hands in milk 531
[The Author's Epitaph, Made by Himself] 532
From The discovery of the large, rich, and beautiful Empire
    of Guiana 533
The History of the World 536
    [Conclusion: On Death] 536

JOHN LYLY (1554–1606) 536

Euphues: The Anatomy of Wit 537
    [Euphues Introduced] 537

SIR PHILIP SIDNEY (1554–1586) 539

The Countess of Pembroke's Arcadia 541
    Book 2, Chapter 1 541
The Defense of Poesy 546
Astrophil and Stella 586
    1 ("Loving in truth, and fain in verse my love to show") 586
    2 ("Not at first sight, nor with a dribbèd shot") 587
    5 ("It is most true that eyes are formed to serve") 587
    6 ("Some lovers speak, when they their muses entertain") 588
    7 ("When Nature made her chief work, Stella's eyes") 588
    9 ("Queen Virtue's court, which some call Stella's face") 588
    10 ("Reason, in faith thou art well served") 589
    15 ("You that do search for every purling spring") 589
    16 ("In nature apt to like when I did see") 589
    18 ("With what sharp checks I in myself am shent") 590
    20 ("Fly, fly, my friends, I have my death-wound, fly") 590
    21 ("Your words, my friend [right healthful caustics], blame") 591
    27 ("Because I oft, in dark abstracted guise") 591
    28 ("You that with allegory's curious frame") 591
    31 ("With how sad steps, O Moon, thou climb'st the skies") 592
    33 ("I might [unhappy word], O me, I might") 592
    34 ("Come, let me write. 'And to what end?'") 592
    37 ("My mouth doth water, and my breast doth swell") 593
    39 ("Come, Sleep, O Sleep, the certain knot of peace") 593
    41 ("Having this day my horse, my hand, my lance") 594
    45 ("Stella oft sees the very face of woe") 594

47 ("What, have I thus betrayed my liberty?") 594
49 ("I on my horse, and Love on me doth try") 595
52 ("A strife is grown between Virtue and Love") 595
53 ("In martial sports I had my cunning tried") 595
54 ("Because I breathe not love to every one") 596
56 ("Fie, school of Patience, fie, your lesson is") 596
61 ("Oft with true sighs, oft with uncallèd tears") 597
69 ("O joy, too high for my low style to show") 597
71 ("Who will in fairest book of Nature know") 597
72 ("Desire, though thou my old companion art") 598
74 ("I never drank of Aganippe well") 598
81 ("O kiss, which dost those ruddy gems impart") 598
Fourth Song ("Only joy, now here you are") 599
87 ("When I was forced from Stella ever dear") 600
89 ("Now that of absence the most irksome night") 600
91 ("Stella, while now by Honor's cruel might") 601
94 ("Grief, find the words; for thou hast made my brain") 601
Eleventh Song ("Who is it that this dark night") 602
106 ("O absent presence, Stella is not here") 603
108 ("When Sorrow [using mine own fire's might]") 603

MARY (SIDNEY) HERBERT, COUNTESS OF PEMBROKE
(1562–1621)   604
Psalm 52 605
Psalm 119: O 606
Psalm 139 606

THE WIDER WORLD   609
Hakluyt's Dedicatory Epistle to The Principal Navigations, 1589   612
Leo Africanus on the North Africans, 1526   616
An English Traveler's Guide to the North Africans, 1547   620
A Voyage to Equatorial Africa, 1554   622
A Voyage to the Arctic, 1577, with Reflections on Racial Difference 626
Witherington and Lister's Voyage to West Africa and South America,
    1586–87   634
Amadas and Barlowe's Voyage to Virginia, 1584   639
Hariot's Report on Virginia, 1585   643
A Gift for the Sultan, 1599   649
The General History of the Turks, 1603   654

CHRISTOPHER MARLOWE (1564–1593)   658
Hero and Leander 659
The Passionate Shepherd to His Love 678
Doctor Faustus 679
        The Tragical History of Doctor Faustus 680
        The Two Texts of Doctor Faustus 716

WILLIAM SHAKESPEARE (1564–1616)   718

Sonnets 722

1 ("From fairest creatures we desire increase") 723
3 ("Look in thy glass and tell the face thou viewest") 723
12 ("When I do count the clock that tells the time") 724
15 ("When I consider every thing that grows") 724
18 ("Shall I compare thee to a summer's day?") 724
19 ("Devouring Time, blunt thou the lion's paws") 725
20 ("A woman's face with Nature's own hand painted") 725
23 ("As an unperfect actor on the stage") 726
29 ("When, in disgrace with Fortune and men's eyes") 726
30 ("When to the sessions of sweet silent thought") 726
33 ("Full many a glorious morning have I seen") 727
35 ("No more be grieved at that which thou hast done") 727
55 ("Not marble nor the gilded monuments") 727
60 ("Like as the waves make towards the pebbled shore") 728
62 ("Sin of self-love possesseth all mine eye") 728
65 ("Since brass, nor stone, nor earth, nor boundless sea") 728
71 ("No longer mourn for me when I am dead") 729
73 ("That time of year thou may'st in me behold") 729
74 ("But be contented; when that fell arrest") 729
80 ("O, how I faint when I of you do write") 730
85 ("My tongue-tied muse in manners holds her still") 730
87 ("Farewell: thou art too dear for my possessing") 730
93 ("So shall I live supposing thou art true") 731
94 ("They that have power to hurt and will do none") 731
97 ("How like a winter hath my absence been") 732
98 ("From you have I been absent in the spring") 732
105 ("Let not my love be called idolatry") 732
106 ("When in the chronicle of wasted time") 733
107 ("Not mine own fears, nor the prophetic soul") 733
110 ("Alas, 'tis true I have gone here and there") 733
116 ("Let me not to the marriage of true minds") 734
126 ("O thou, my lovely boy, who in thy power") 734
127 ("In the old age black was not counted fair") 735
128 ("How oft when thou, my music, music play'st") 735
129 ("Th' expense of spirit in a waste of shame") 735
130 ("My mistress' eyes are nothing like the sun") 736
135 ("Whoever hath her wish, thou hast thy *Will*") 736
138 ("When my love swears that she is made of truth") 736
144 ("Two loves I have of comfort and despair") 737
146 ("Poor soul, the center of my sinful earth") 737
147 ("My love is as a fever, longing still") 738
152 ("In loving thee thou know'st I am forsworn") 738

Twelfth Night 739
Othello 803

The Early Seventeenth Century (1603–1660)

INTRODUCTION 891

TIMELINE 918

JOHN DONNE (1572–1631)   920
    Songs and Sonnets 923
            The Flea 923
            The Good-Morrow 923
            Song ("Go and catch a falling star") 924
            The Undertaking 925
            The Sun Rising 926
            The Indifferent 927
            The Canonization 927
            Song ("Sweetest love, I do not go") 929
            Air and Angels 930
            Break of Day 930
            A Valediction: Of Weeping 931
            Love's Alchemy 932
            A Nocturnal upon Saint Lucy's Day, Being the Shortest Day 932
            The Bait 934
            The Apparition 935
            A Valediction: Forbidding Mourning 935
            The Ecstasy 936
            The Funeral 938
            The Blossom 939
            The Relic 940
            A Lecture upon the Shadow 941
        Elegy 16. On His Mistress 942
        Elegy 19. To His Mistress Going to Bed 943
        Satire 3 944
        Sappho to Philaenis 947
        An Anatomy of the World: The First Anniversary 949
        Holy Sonnets 960
                1 ("Thou hast made me, and shall thy work decay?") 960
                5 ("I am a little world made cunningly") 961
                7 ("At the round earth's imagined corners, blow") 961
                9 ("If poisonous minerals, and if that tree") 962
                10 ("Death, be not proud, though some have callèd thee") 962
                11 ("Spit in my face ye Jews, and pierce my side") 962
                13 ("What if this present were the world's last night?") 963
                14 ("Batter my heart, three-personed God; for you") 963
                17 ("Since she whom I loved hath paid her last debt") 964
                18 ("Show me, dear Christ, thy spouse so bright and clear") 964
                19 ("Oh, to vex me, contraries meet in one") 965
        Good Friday, 1613. Riding Westward 965

A Hymn to Christ, at the Author's Last Going into Germany 966
Hymn to God My God, in My Sickness 967
A Hymn to God the Father 968
Devotions upon Emergent Occasions 969
  Meditation 4 969
  Meditation 17 970
  From Expostulation 19 971
From Death's Duel 973

IZAAK WALTON (1593–1683)   974
  The Life of Dr. John Donne 976
    [Donne on His Deathbed] 976

AEMILIA LANYER (1569–1645)   980
  Salve Deus Rex Judaeorum 981
    To the Doubtful Reader 981
    To the Queen's Most Excellent Majesty 981
    To the Virtuous Reader 982
    Eve's Apology in Defense of Women 983
  The Description of Cookham 986

BEN JONSON (1572–1637)   991
  Volpone, or The Fox 994
  Epigrams 1089
    To My Book 1089
    On Something, That Walks Somewhere 1090
    To William Camden 1090
    On My First Daughter 1091
    To John Donne 1091
    On Giles and Joan 1091
    On My First Son 1092
    On Lucy, Countess of Bedford 1092
    To Lucy, Countess of Bedford, with Mr. Donne's Satires 1093
    To Sir Thomas Roe 1093
    Inviting a Friend to Supper 1094
    On Gut 1095
    Epitaph on S. P., a Child of Queen Elizabeth's Chapel 1095
  The Forest 1096
    To Penshurst 1096
    Song: To Celia 1098
    To Heaven 1099
  Underwood 1099
    From A Celebration of Charis in Ten Lyric Pieces 1099
      4. Her Triumph 1099
    A Sonnet, to the Noble Lady, the Lady Mary Wroth 1100
    My Picture Left in Scotland 1101

To the Immortal Memory and Friendship of That Noble Pair,
    Sir Lucius Cary and Sir H. Morison 1101
Queen and Huntress 1105
To the Memory of My Beloved, The Author, Mr. William Shakespeare 1106
Ode to Himself 1108

MARY WROTH (1587–1651?)   1110
  The Countess of Montgomery's Urania 1112
    From The First Book 1112
    Song ("Love what art thou? A vain thought") 1115
  Pamphilia to Amphilanthus 1116
    1 ("When night's black mantle could most darkness prove") 1116
    16 ("Am I thus conquered? Have I lost the powers") 1117
    25 ("Like to the Indians scorched with the sun") 1117
    28 Song ("Sweetest love, return again") 1117
    39 ("Take heed mine eyes, how you your looks do cast") 1118
    40 ("False hope which feeds but to destroy, and spill") 1118
    64 ("Love like a juggler comes to play his prize") 1119
    68 ("My pain, still smothered in my grievèd breast") 1119
    74 Song ("Love a child is ever crying") 1120
    From A Crown of Sonnets Dedicated to Love 1120
       77 ("In this strange labyrinth how shall I turn?") 1120
    103 ("My muse now happy, lay thyself to rest") 1121

JOHN WEBSTER (1580?–1625?)   1121
  The Duchess of Malfi 1122

    GENDER RELATIONS: CONFLICT AND COUNSEL   1198

JOSEPH SWETNAM: *From* The Arraignment of Lewd, Idle, Froward
  and Unconstant Women   1200
RACHEL SPEGHT: *From* A Muzzle for Melastomus   1202
WILLIAM GOUGE: *From* Of Domestical Duties   1205

    INQUIRY AND EXPERIENCE   1211

SIR FRANCIS BACON   1212
  Essays 1213
    Of Truth 1213
    Of Marriage and Single Life 1214
    Of Great Place 1216
    Of Superstition 1218
    Of Plantations 1219
    Of Negotiating 1221
    Of Masques and Triumphs 1222
    Of Studies [1597 version] 1223
    Of Studies [1625 version] 1224

The Advancement of Learning 1225
    [The Abuses of Language] 1225
From Novum Organum 1227
The New Atlantis 1231
    [Solomon's House] 1231
WILLIAM HARVEY: *From* Anatomical Exercises . . . Concerning
  the Motion of the Heart and Blood   1236
ROBERT BURTON   1239
  The Anatomy of Melancholy 1240
    From Love Melancholy 1240
SIR THOMAS BROWNE   1246
  Religio Medici 1247
    From Part 1 1247
    From Part 2 1254

GEORGE HERBERT (1593–1633)   1255
  The Temple 1257
    The Altar 1257
    Redemption 1258
    Easter 1258
    Easter Wings 1259
    Affliction (1) 1260
    Prayer (1) 1261
    Jordan (1) 1262
    Church Monuments 1262
    The Windows 1263
    Denial 1263
    Virtue 1264
    Man 1265
    Jordan (2) 1266
    Time 1267
    The Bunch of Grapes 1268
    The Pilgrimage 1268
    The Holdfast 1269
    The Collar 1270
    The Pulley 1271
    The Flower 1271
    The Forerunners 1273
    Discipline 1274
    Death 1275
    Love (3) 1275

HENRY VAUGHAN (1621–1695)   1276
  Poems 1277
    A Song to Amoret 1277

Silex Scintillans 1278
    Regeneration 1278
    The Retreat 1280
    Silence, and Stealth of Days! 1281
    Corruption 1282
    Unprofitableness 1283
    The World 1283
    They Are All Gone into the World of Light! 1285
    Cock-Crowing 1286
    The Night 1288
    The Waterfall 1289

RICHARD CRASHAW (ca. 1613–1649)   1290
  The Delights of the Muses 1291
    Music's Duel 1291
  Steps to the Temple 1295
    To the Infant Martyrs 1295
    I Am the Door 1295
    On the Wounds of Our Crucified Lord 1296
    Luke 11.[27] 1296
  Carmen Deo Nostro 1297
    In the Holy Nativity of Our Lord God: A Hymn Sung
      as by the Shepherds 1297
    To the Noblest & best of Ladies, the Countess of Denbigh 1300
    The Flaming Heart 1302

ROBERT HERRICK (1591–1674)   1306
  Hesperides 1307
    The Argument of His Book 1307
    Upon the Loss of His Mistresses 1307
    The Vine 1308
    Dreams 1308
    Delight in Disorder 1308
    His Farewell to Sack 1309
    Corinna's Going A-Maying 1310
    To the Virgins, to Make Much of Time 1312
    The Hock Cart, or Harvest Home 1312
    How Roses Came Red 1314
    Upon the Nipples of Julia's Breast 1314
    Upon Jack and Jill. Epigram 1314
    To Marigolds 1315
    His Prayer to Ben Jonson 1315
    The Bad Season Makes the Poet Sad 1315
    The Night-Piece, to Julia 1316
    Upon His Verses 1316
    His Return to London 1316
    Upon Julia's Clothes 1317

Upon Prue, His Maid 1317
To His Book's End 1317
Noble Numbers 1318
To His Conscience 1318
Another Grace for a Child 1318

THOMAS CAREW (1595–1640)   1318
An Elegy upon the Death of the Dean of Paul's, Dr. John Donne 1319
To Ben Jonson 1321
A Song ("Ask me no more where Jove bestows") 1323
To Saxham 1323
A Rapture 1325

RICHARD LOVELACE (1618–1657)   1329
Lucasta 1329
To Lucasta, Going to the Wars 1329
The Grasshopper 1330
To Althea, from Prison 1331
Love Made in the First Age. To Chloris 1332

KATHERINE PHILIPS (1632–1664)   1333
A Married State 1334
Upon the Double Murder of King Charles 1335
Friendship's Mystery, To My Dearest Lucasia 1336
To Mrs. M. A. at Parting 1337
On the Death of My First and Dearest Child, Hector Philips 1338

ANDREW MARVELL (1621–1678)   1339
The Coronet 1341
Bermudas 1341
A Dialogue Between the Soul and Body 1342
The Nymph Complaining for the Death of Her Fawn 1344
To His Coy Mistress 1346
The Definition of Love 1348
The Picture of Little T. C. in a Prospect of Flowers 1349
The Mower Against Gardens 1350
Damon the Mower 1351
The Mower to the Glowworms 1353
The Mower's Song 1353
The Garden 1354
An Horatian Ode 1356
Upon Appleton House 1361

CRISIS OF AUTHORITY   1384

REPORTING THE NEWS   1384
The Moderate, No. 28 1386
[The Trial of King Charles I, the first day] 1386

A Perfect Diurnal of Some Passages in Parliament, No. 288 1388
    [The Execution of Charles I] 1388
POLITICAL WRITING   1392
  ROBERT FILMER: *From* Patriarcha   1393
  JOHN MILTON: *From* The Tenure of Kings and Magistrates   1396
  GERRARD WINSTANLEY: *From* A New Year's Gift Sent to the
    Parliament and Army   1399
  THOMAS HOBBES: *From* Leviathan   1405
WRITING THE SELF   1417
  LUCY HUTCHINSON:
  Memoirs of the Life of Colonel John Hutchinson   1418
    [Charles I and Henrietta Maria] 1419
  EDWARD HYDE, EARL OF CLARENDON:
  The History of the Rebellion   1421
    [The Character of Oliver Cromwell] 1421
  LADY ANNE HALKETT: The Memoirs   1424
    [Springing the Duke] 1425
  DOROTHY WAUGH: *From* A Relation Concerning
    Dorothy Waugh's Cruel Usage by the Mayor of Carlisle   1428

THOMAS TRAHERNE (1637–1674)   1430
  Centuries of Meditation 1430
    From The Third Century 1430
  Wonder 1431
  On Leaping over the Moon 1433

MARGARET CAVENDISH (1623–1673)   1434
  Poems and Fancies 1435
    The Poetess's Hasty Resolution 1435
    The Hunting of the Hare 1436
  From A True Relation of My Birth, Breeding, and Life 1438
  From The Description of a New World, Called The Blazing World 1441

JOHN MILTON (1608–1674)   1447
  Poems 1451
    On the Morning of Christ's Nativity 1451
    On Shakespeare 1459
    L'Allegro 1459
    Il Penseroso 1463
    Lycidas 1467
  The Reason of Church Government Urged Against Prelaty 1474
    [Plans and Projects] 1474
  From Areopagitica 1479

Sonnets 1489
    How Soon Hath Time 1489
    On the New Forcers of Conscience under the Long Parliament 1490
    To the Lord General Cromwell, May 1652 1491
    When I Consider How My Light Is Spent 1492
    On the Late Massacre in Piedmont 1492
    Methought I Saw My Late Espousèd Saint 1493
Paradise Lost 1493
Samson Agonistes 1728

APPENDIXES   A1
General Bibliography A3
Literary Terminology A11
Geographic Nomenclature A32
British Money A34
The British Baronage A39
    The Royal Lines of England and Great Britain A42
Religions in Great Britain A45
Illustration: The Universe According to Ptolemy A50
Illustration: A London Playhouse of Shakespeare's Time A51

PERMISSIONS ACKNOWLEDGMENTS A53

INDEX A55

Preface to the Tenth Edition

For centuries the study of literature has occupied a central place in the Humanities curriculum. The power of great literature to reach across time and space, its exploration of the expressive potential of language, and its ability to capture the whole range of experiences from the most exalted to the everyday have made it an essential part of education. But there are significant challenges to any attempt to derive the full measure of enlightenment and pleasure from this precious resource. In a world in which distraction reigns, savoring works of literature requires quiet focus. In a society in which new media clamor for attention, attending to words on the page can prove difficult. And in a period obsessed with the present at its most instantaneous, it takes a certain effort to look at anything penned earlier than late last night.

The Norton Anthology of English Literature is designed to meet these challenges. It is deeply rewarding to enter the sensibility of a different place, to hear a new voice, to be touched by an unfamiliar era. It is critically important to escape the narrow boundaries of our immediate preoccupations and to respond with empathy to lives other than our own. It is moving, even astonishing, to feel that someone you never met is speaking directly to you. But for any of this to happen requires help. The overarching goal of the Norton Anthology—as it has been for over fifty-five years and ten editions—is to help instructors energize their classrooms, engage their students, and bring literature to life.* At a time when the Humanities are under great pressure, we are committed to facilitating the special joy that comes with encountering significant works of art.

The works anthologized in these six volumes generally form the core of courses designed to introduce students to English literature. The selections reach back to the earliest moments of literary creativity in English, when the language itself was still molten, and extend to some of the most recent experiments, when, once again, English seems remarkably fluid and open. That openness—a recurrent characteristic of a language that has never been officially regulated and that has constantly renewed itself—helps to account for the sense of freshness that characterizes the works brought together here.

One of the joys of literature in English is its spectacular abundance. Even within the geographical confines of England, Scotland, Wales, and

---

* For more on the help we offer and how to access it, see "Additional Resources for Instructors and Students," p. xxx.

Ireland, where the majority of texts in this collection originated, one can find more than enough distinguished and exciting works to fill the pages of this anthology many times over. But English literature is not confined to the British Isles; it is a global phenomenon. This border-crossing is not a consequence of modernity alone. It is fitting that among the first works here is *Beowulf*, a powerful epic written in the Germanic language known as Old English about a singularly restless Scandinavian hero. *Beowulf's* remarkable translator in *The Norton Anthology of English Literature*, Seamus Heaney, was one of the great contemporary masters of English literature— he was awarded the Nobel Prize for Literature in 1995—but it would be potentially misleading to call him an "English poet" for he was born in Northern Ireland and was not in fact English. It would be still more misleading to call him a "British poet," as if the British Empire were the most salient fact about the language he spoke and wrote in or the culture by which he was shaped. What matters is that the language in which Heaney wrote is English, and this fact links him powerfully with the authors assembled in these volumes, a linguistic community that stubbornly refuses to fit comfortably within any firm geographical or ethnic or national boundaries. So too, to glance at other authors and writings in the anthology, in the twelfth century, the noblewoman Marie de France wrote her short stories in an Anglo-Norman dialect at home on both sides of the channel; in the sixteenth century William Tyndale, in exile in the Low Countries and inspired by German religious reformers, translated the New Testament from Greek and thereby changed the course of the English language; in the seventeenth century Aphra Behn touched readers with a story that moves from Africa, where its hero is born, to South America, where Behn herself may have witnessed some of the tragic events she describes; and early in the twentieth century Joseph Conrad, born in Ukraine of Polish parents, wrote in eloquent English a celebrated novella whose ironic vision of European empire gave way by the century's end to the voices of those over whom the empire, now in ruins, had once hoped to rule: the Caribbean-born Claude McKay, Louise Bennett, Derek Walcott, Kamau Brathwaite, V. S. Naipaul, and Grace Nichols; the African-born Chinua Achebe, J. M. Coetzee, Ngũgĩ Wa Thiong'o, and Chimamanda Ngozi Adichie; and the Indian-born A. K. Ramanujan and Salman Rushdie.

A vital literary culture is always on the move. This principle was the watchword of M. H. Abrams, the distinguished literary critic who first conceived *The Norton Anthology of English Literature,* brought together the original team of editors, and, with characteristic insight, diplomacy, and humor, oversaw seven editions. Abrams wisely understood that new scholarly discoveries and the shifting interests of readers constantly alter the landscape of literary history. To stay vital, the anthology, therefore, would need to undergo a process of periodic revision, guided by advice from teachers, as well as students, who view the anthology with a loyal but critical eye. As with past editions, we have benefited from detailed information on the works actually assigned and suggestions for improvements from 273 reviewers. Their participation has been crucial as the editors grapple with the task of strengthening the selection of more traditional texts while adding texts that reflect the expansion of the field of English studies.

With each edition, *The Norton Anthology of English Literature* has offered a broadened canon without sacrificing major writers and a selection of complete longer texts in which readers can immerse themselves. Perhaps the most emblematic of these great texts are the epics *Beowulf* and *Paradise Lost*. Among the many other complete longer works in the Tenth Edition are *Sir Gawain and the Green Knight* (in Simon Armitage's spectacular translation), Sir Thomas More's *Utopia*, Sir Philip Sidney's *Defense of Poesy*, William Shakespeare's *Twelfth Night* and *Othello*, Samuel Johnson's *Rasselas*, Aphra Behn's *Oroonoko*, Jonathan Swift's *Gulliver's Travels*, Laurence Sterne's *A Sentimental Journey through France and Italy*, Charles Dickens's *A Christmas Carol*, Robert Louis Stevenson's *The Strange Case of Dr. Jekyll and Mr. Hyde*, Rudyard Kipling's *The Man Who Would Be King*, Joseph Conrad's *Heart of Darkness*, Virginia Woolf's *Mrs. Dalloway*, James Joyce's *Portrait of the Artist as a Young Man*, Samuel Beckett's *Waiting for Godot*, Harold Pinter's *The Dumb Waiter*, and Tom Stoppard's *Arcadia*. To augment the number of complete longer works instructors can assign, and—a special concern—better to represent the achievements of novelists, the publisher is making available the full list of Norton Critical Editions, more than 240 titles, including such frequently assigned novels as Jane Austen's *Pride and Prejudice*, Mary Shelley's *Frankenstein*, Charles Dickens's *Hard Times*, and Chinua Achebe's *Things Fall Apart*. A Norton Critical Edition may be included with either package (volumes A, B, C and volumes D, E, F) or any individual volume at a discounted price (contact your Norton representative for details).

We have in this edition continued to expand the selection of writing by women in several historical periods. The sustained work of scholars in recent years has recovered dozens of significant authors who had been marginalized or neglected by a male-dominated literary tradition and has deepened our understanding of those women writers who had managed, against considerable odds, to claim a place in that tradition. The First Edition of the Norton Anthology included 6 women writers; this Tenth Edition includes 84, of whom 13 are newly added and 10 are reselected or expanded. Poets and dramatists whose names were scarcely mentioned even in the specialized literary histories of earlier generations—Aemilia Lanyer, Lady Mary Wroth, Margaret Cavendish, Mary Leapor, Anna Letitia Barbauld, Charlotte Smith, Letitia Elizabeth Landon, Mary Elizabeth Coleridge, Mina Loy, and many others—now appear in the company of their male contemporaries. There are in addition four complete long prose works by women— Aphra Behn's *Oroonoko*, Eliza Haywood's *Fantomina*, Jane Austen's *Love and Friendship*, and Virginia Woolf's *Mrs. Dalloway*—along with selections from such celebrated fiction writers as Maria Edgeworth, Jean Rhys, Katherine Mansfield, Doris Lessing, Margaret Atwood, Kiran Desai, Zadie Smith, and new authors Hilary Mantel and Chimamanda Ngozi Adichie.

Building on an innovation introduced in the First Edition, the editors have expanded the array of topical clusters that gather together short texts illuminating the cultural, historical, intellectual, and literary concerns of each of the periods. We have designed these clusters with three aims: to make them lively and accessible, to ensure that they can be taught effectively in a class meeting or two, and to make clear their relevance to the surrounding works of literature. Hence, for example, in the Sixteenth Century, a new cluster, "The Wider World," showcases the English fascination with narratives of adventure, exploration, trade, and reconnaissance. New in the Eighteenth Century, "Print Culture and the Rise of the Novel" offers statements on the emergence of what would become English literature's most popular form as well as excerpts from *Robinson Crusoe* and *Evelina*. And in the Romantic Period, a new cluster on "The Romantic Imagination and the 'Oriental Nations'" joins contemporary discussion of the literature of those nations with selections from William Beckford's *Vathek* and Byron's *The Giaour*, among other texts. Across the volumes the clusters provide an exciting way to broaden the field of the literary and to set masterpieces in a wider cultural, social, and historical framework

Now, as in the past, cultures define themselves by the songs they sing and the stories they tell. But the central importance of visual media in contemporary culture has heightened our awareness of the ways in which songs and stories have always been closely linked to the images that societies have fashioned and viewed. The Tenth Edition of *The Norton Anthology of English Literature* features fifty-six pages of color plates (in seven color inserts) and more than 120 black-and-white illustrations throughout the volumes, including six new maps. In selecting visual material—from the Sutton Hoo treasure of the seventh century to Yinka Shonibare's *Nelson's Ship in a Bottle* in the twenty-first century—the editors sought to provide images that conjure up, whether directly or indirectly, the individual writers in each section; that relate specifically to individual works in the anthology; and that shape and illuminate the culture of a particular literary period. We have tried to choose visually striking images that will interest students and provoke discussion, and our captions draw attention to important details and cross-reference related texts in the anthology.

Period-by-Period Revisions

The Middle Ages. Edited by James Simpson, this period, huge in its scope and immensely varied in its voices, continues to offer exciting surprises. The heart of the Anglo-Saxon portion is the great epic *Beowulf*, in the acclaimed translation by Seamus Heaney. Now accompanied by a map of England at the time, the Anglo-Saxon texts include the haunting poems "Wulf and Eadwacer" and "The Ruin" as well as an intriguing collection of Anglo-Saxon riddles. These new works join verse translations of the *Dream of the Rood*, the *Wanderer*, and *The Wife's Lament*. An Irish Literature selection features a tale from *The Tain* and a group of ninth-century lyrics. The Anglo-Norman section—a key bridge between the Anglo-Saxon period and the time of Chaucer—offers a new pairing of texts about the tragic story of Tristan and Ysolt; an illuminating cluster on the Romance, with three stories by Marie de France (in award-winning translations); and *Sir Orfeo*, a comic version of the Orpheus and Eurydice story. The Middle English section centers, as always, on Chaucer, with a generous selection of tales and poems glossed and annotated so as to heighten their accessibility. Simon Armitage's brilliant verse translation of *Sir Gawain and the Green Knight* appears once again, and we offer newly modernized versions both of Thomas Hoccleve's *My Complaint*, a startlingly personal account of the speaker's attempt to reenter society after a period of mental instability, and of the playfully ironic and spiritually moving *Second Shepherds' Play*. "Talking Animals," a delightful new cluster, presents texts by Marie de France, Chaucer, and Robert Henryson that show how medieval writers used animals in stories that reveal much about humankind.

The Sixteenth Century, edited by Stephen Greenblatt and George Logan, features eight extraordinary longer texts in their entirety: More's *Utopia* (with two letters from More to Peter Giles); Book 1 of Spenser's *Faerie Queene* and, new to this edition, the posthumously published *Mutabilitie Cantos*, which arguably offer some of Spenser's finest poetry; Marlowe's *Hero and Leander* and *Doctor Faustus*, Sidney's *Defense of Poesy*; and Shakespeare's *Twelfth Night* and *Othello*, which has been added to the Tenth Edition by instructor request. Two exciting new topical clusters join the section. "An Elizabethan Miscellany" is a full, richly teachable grouping of sixteenth-century poems in English, by writers from George Gascoigne to Michael Drayton to Thomas Campion, among others, and provides access the period's explosion of lyric genius. "The Wider World" showcases the English Renaissance fascination with narratives of adventure, exploration, trade, and reconnaissance. Ranging from Africa to the Muslim East to the New World, the texts are compelling reading in our contemporary global context and offer particularly suggestive insights into the world of Shakespeare's *Othello*.

The Early Seventeenth Century. At the heart of this period, edited by Katharine Eisaman Maus, is John Milton's *Paradise Lost*, presented in its entirety. New to the Tenth Edition are the Arguments to each book, which are especially helpful for students first reading this magnificent, compelling epic. Along with Milton's "Lycidas" and *Samson Agonistes*, which is new to this edition, other complete longer works include John Donne's *Satire 3* and *The Anatomy of the World: The First Anniversary*; Aemilia Lanyer's country-house poem "The Description of Cookham"; Ben Jonson's *Volpone* and the moving Cary-Morison ode; and John Webster's tragedy *The Duchess of Malfi*. Generous selections from Donne, Mary Wroth, George Herbert, Katherine Philips, Andrew Marvell, and others, as well as the clusters "Inquiry and Experience," "Gender Relations," and "Crisis of Authority," together make for an exciting and thorough representation of the period.

The Restoration and the Eighteenth Century. The impressive array of complete longer texts in this period, edited by James Noggle, includes Dryden's *Absalom and Achitophel* and *MacFlecknoe*; Aphra Behn's *Oroonoko* (now with its dedicatory epistle); Congreve's comedy *The Way of the World*; Swift's *Gulliver's Travels* (newly complete, with illustrations from the first edition); Pope's *Essay on Criticism*, *The Rape of the Lock*, and *Epistle to Dr. Arbuthnot*; Gay's *Beggar's Opera*; Eliza Haywood's novella of sexual role-playing, *Fantomina*; Hogarth's graphic satire "Marriage A-la-Mode"; Johnson's *Vanity of Human Wishes* and *Rasselas*; Laurence Sterne's *A Sentimental Journey through France and Italy* (new to this edition); Gray's "Elegy Written in a Country Churchyard"; and Goldsmith's "The Deserted Village." An exciting new topical cluster, "Print Culture and the Rise of the Novel," with selections by Daniel Defoe, Henry Fielding, Samuel Richardson, Frances Burney, Clara Reeve, and others, enables readers to explore the origins of English literature's most popular form.

The Romantic Period. Edited by Deidre Shauna Lynch, this period again offers many remarkable additions. Chief among them are two topical clusters: "Romantic Literature and Wartime," which, through texts by Godwin, Wordsworth, Coleridge, Barbauld, Byron, De Quincey, and others, explores the varied ways in which war's violence came home to English literature; and "The Romantic Imagination and the 'Oriental Nations,'" which shows how English writers of the late eighteenth and early nineteenth centuries looked eastward for new, often contradictory themes of cultural identity and difference and for "exotic" subjects that were novel and enticing to the English audience. Also new to this period are poems by Barbauld, Robinson, Charlotte Smith, Wordsworth, Shelley, Hemans, and Landon. We are excited to include an excerpt from *The History of Mary Prince, a West Indian Slave*—the first slave narrative by a woman. John Clare, the increasingly appreciated "natural poet," receives four new texts.

The Victorian Age, edited by Catherine Robson, offers an impressive array of complete longer works. New to the prose selections is Charles Dickens's *A Christmas Carol,* complete with its original illustrations. Dickens's celebrated tale, which entertains at the same time that it deals brilliantly with matters social, economic, and spiritual, joins Robert Louis Stevenson's *The Strange Case of Dr. Jekyll and Mr. Hyde,* Arthur Conan Doyle's *The Speckled Band,* Elizabeth Gaskell's *The Old Nurse's Story,* and Rudyard Kipling's *The Man Who Would Be King.* Authors with significant longer poems include Elizabeth Barrett Browning, Alfred, Lord Tennyson, Robert Browning, Dante Gabriel Rossetti, Christina Rossetti, Algernon Charles Swinburne, and Gerard Manley Hopkins. Plays include Oscar Wilde's *The Importance of Being Earnest* and George Bernard Shaw's controversial drama on prostitution, *Mrs Warren's Profession.* And, continuing the tradition of enabling readers to grapple with the period's most resonant and often fiercely contentious issues, the Tenth Edition offers an exciting new cluster, "Beacons of the Future? Education in Victorian Britain," which brings together powerful reflections by John Stuart Mill and others, government reports on the nature of education, and illuminating excerpts from *Hard Times, Alice's Adventures in Wonderland, Tom Brown's School Days,* and *Jude the Obscure.*

The Twentieth and Twenty-First Centuries. The editor, Jahan Ramazani, continues his careful revision of this, the most rapidly changing period in the anthology. Once again its core is three modernist masterpieces: Virginia Woolf's *Mrs. Dalloway,* James Joyce's *Portrait of the Artist as a Young Man,* and Samuel Beckett's *Waiting for Godot,* all complete. These works are surrounded by a dazzling array of other fiction and drama. New to the Tenth Edition are the recent recipient of the Nobel Prize for Literature, Kazuo Ishiguro, along with Hilary Mantel, Caryl Phillips, and Chimamanda Ngozi Adichie. Their works join Joseph Conrad's *Heart of Darkness,* Harold Pinter's

The Dumb Waiter, Tom Stoppard's *Arcadia*, and stories by D. H. Lawrence, Katherine Mansfield, Jean Rhys, Doris Lessing, Nadine Gordimer, Kiran Desai, and Zadie Smith. A generous representation of poetry centers on substantial selections from Thomas Hardy, William Butler Yeats, and T. S. Eliot, and extends out to a wide range of other poets, from A. E. Housman, Wilfred Owen, and W. H. Auden to Philip Larkin, Derek Walcott, and Seamus Heaney. Two new poets, frequently requested by our readers, join the anthology: Anne Carson and Simon Armitage; and there are new poems by Yeats, Heaney, Geoffrey Hill, and Carol Ann Duffy. Visual aids have proved very helpful in teaching this period, and new ones include facsimile manuscript pages of poems by Isaac Rosenberg and Wilfred Owen, plus five new maps, which illustrate, among other things, the dramatic changes in the British Empire from 1891 to the late twentieth century, the movement of peoples to and from England during this time, and the journeys around London of the central characters in Woolf's *Mrs. Dalloway*. Linton Kwesi Johnson, Bernardine Evaristo, Patience Agbabi, and Dajlit Nagra join Claude McKay, Louise Bennett, Kamau Brathwaite, Ngũgĩ Wa Thiong'o, M. NourbeSe Philip, Salman Rushdie, and Grace Nichols in the much-praised cluster "Nation, Race, and Language"—together they bear witness to the global diffusion of English, the urgency of issues of nation and identity, and the rich complexity of literary history.

Editorial Procedures and Format

The Tenth Edition adheres to the principles that have always characterized *The Norton Anthology of English Literature*. Period introductions, head-notes, and annotations are designed to enhance students' reading and, without imposing an interpretation, to give students the information they need to understand each text. The aim of these editorial materials is to make the anthology self-sufficient, so that it can be read anywhere—in a coffeeshop, on a bus, under a tree.

The *Norton Anthology of English Literature* prides itself on both the scholarly accuracy and the readability of its texts. To ease students' encounter with some works, we have normalized spelling and capitalization in texts up to and including the Romantic period—for the most part they now follow the conventions of modern English. We leave unaltered, however, texts in which such modernizing would change semantic or metrical qualities. From the Victorian period onward, we have used the original spelling and punctuation. We continue other editorial procedures that have proved useful in the past. After each work, we cite the date of first publication on the right; in some instances, this date is followed by the date of a revised edition for which the author was responsible. Dates of composition, when they differ from those of publication and when they are known, are provided on the left. We use square brackets to indicate titles supplied by the editors for the convenience of readers. Whenever a portion of a text is omitted, we indicate that omission with three asterisks. If the omitted portion is important for following the plot or argument, we provide a brief summary within the text or in a footnote. Finally, we have reconsidered annotations throughout and increased the number of marginal glosses for archaic, dialect, or unfamiliar words.

The Tenth Edition includes the useful "Literary Terminology" appendix, a quick-reference alphabetical glossary with examples from works in the anthology. We have also updated the General Bibliography that appears in the print volumes, as well as the period and author bibliographies, which appear online, where they can be easily searched and updated.

Additional Resources for Instructors and Students

The idea that a vital literary culture is always on the move applies not only to the print anthology but also to the resources that accompany it. For the Tenth Edition, we have added exciting new resources and improved and updated existing resources to make them more useful and easy to find.

We are pleased to launch the new NAEL Archive site, found at digital. wwnorton.com/englishlit10abc (for volumes A, B, C) and digital.wwnorton .com/englishlit10def (for volumes D, E, F). This searchable and sortable site contains thousands of resources for students and instructors in one centralized place at no additional cost. Following are some highlights:

- A series of twenty brand-new video modules designed to enhance classroom presentation of the literary works. These videos, conceived of and narrated by the anthology editors, bring various texts from the anthology to life by providing a closer look at a rarely seen manuscript, visiting a place of literary significance, or offering a conversation with a living writer.
- Over 1,000 additional readings from the Middle Ages to the turn of the twentieth century, edited, glossed, and annotated to the scholarly standards and with the sensitivity to classroom use for which the Norton Anthology is renowned. Teachers who wish to add to the selections in the print anthology will find numerous exciting works, including Wycherley's *The Country Wife*, Joanna Baillie's "A Mother to Her Waking Infant," and Edward Lear's "The Jumblies." In addition, there are many fascinating topical clusters—"The First Crusade: Sanctifying War," "Genius," and "The Satanic and Byronic Hero," to name only a few—all designed to draw readers into larger cultural contexts and to expose them to a wide spectrum of voices.
- Hundreds of images—maps, author portraits, literary places, and manuscripts—available for student browsing or instructor download for in-class presentation.
- Several hours of audio recordings.
- Annotated bibliographies for all periods and authors in the anthology.

The NAEL Archive also provides a wealth of teaching resources that are unlocked on instructor log-in:

- "Quick read" summaries, teaching notes, and discussion questions for every work in the anthology, from the much-praised *Teaching with The Norton Anthology of English Literature: A Guide for Instructors* by Naomi Howell (University of Exeter), Philip Schwyzer (University of Exeter), Judyta Frodyma (University of Northern British Columbia), and Sondra Archimedes (University of California–Santa Cruz).

- Downloadable PowerPoints featuring images and audio for in-class presentation

In addition to the wealth of resources in the NAEL Archive, Norton offers a downloadable coursepack that allows instructors to easily add high-quality Norton digital media to online, hybrid, or lecture courses—all at no cost. Norton Coursepacks work within existing learning management systems; there's no new system to learn, and access is free and easy. Content is customizable and includes over seventy-four reading-comprehension quizzes, short-answer questions with suggested answers, links to the video modules, and more.

The editors are deeply grateful to the hundreds of teachers worldwide who have helped us to improve *The Norton Anthology of English Literature*. A list of the instructors who replied to a detailed questionnaire follows, under Acknowledgments. The editors would like to express appreciation for their assistance to Lara Bovilsky (University of Oregon), Gordon Braden (University of Virginia), Dympna Callaghan (Syracuse University), Ariel Churchill (Harvard University), Joseph Connors (Harvard University), Taylor Cowdery (University of North Carolina at Chapel Hill), Maria Devlin (Harvard University), Lars Engel (University of Tulsa), James Engell (Harvard University), Aubrey Everett (Harvard University), Kevis Goodman (University of California, Berkeley), Alexander Gourlay (Rhode Island School of Design), John Hale (University of Otago), Stephen Hequembourg (University of Virginia),Seth Herbst (United States Military Academy, West Point), Rhema Hokama (Singapore University of Technology and Design), Jean Howard (Columbia University), Robert Irvine (University of Edinburgh), Thomas Keirstead (University of Toronto), Mario Menendez (Harvard University), John Miller (University of Virginia), Peter Miller (University of Virginia), A. J. Odasso (Wellesley College, Robert Pinsky (Boston University), Will Porter (Harvard University), Mark Rankin (James Madison University), Josephine Reece (Harvard University), Jessica Rosenberg (University of Miami), Suparna Roychoudhury (Mount Holyoke College), Peter Sacks (Harvard University), Ray Siemens (University of Victoria), Kim Simpson (University of Southampton), Bailey Sincox (Harvard University), Ramie Targoff (Brandeis University), Misha Teramura (Reed College), Gordon Teskey (Harvard University), Katie Trumpener (Yale University), Paul Westover (Brigham Young University), Katy Woodring (Harvard University), and Faye Zhang (Harvard University).

We also thank the many people at Norton, an employee-owned publishing house with a commitment to excellence, who contributed to the Tenth Edition. In planning this edition, Julia Reidhead served, as she has done in the past, as our wise and effective collaborator. In addition, we are now working with Marian Johnson, literature editor and managing editor for college books, a splendid new collaborator who has helped us bring the Tenth Edition to fruition. With admirable equanimity and skill, Carly Frasier Doria, electronic media editor and course guide editor, fashioned the new video modules and brought together the dazzling array of web resources and other pedagogical aids. We also have debts of gratitude to Katharine Ings,

Candace Levy, and Michael Fleming, manuscript editors; Kimberly Bowers, marketing manager for literature; Sean Mintus, senior production manager; Megan Jackson Schindel and Nancy Rodwan, permissions; Jo Anne Metsch, designer; Nelson Colon, photo editor; and Rachel Taylor and Ava Bramson, assistant editor and assistant media editor, respectively. All these friends provided the editors with indispensable help in meeting the challenge of representing the unparalleled range and variety of English literature.

STEPHEN GREENBLATT

Acknowledgments

The editors would like to express appreciation and thanks to the hundreds of teachers who provided reviews:

Michel Aaij (Auburn University at Montgomery), Jerry J. Alexander (Presbyterian College), Sarah Alexander (The University of Vermont), Marshall N. Armintor (University of North Texas), Marilyn Judith Atlas (Ohio University), Alison Baker (California State Polytechnic University, Pomona), Reid Barbour (University of North Carolina, Chapel Hill), Jessica Barnes-Pietruszynski (West Virginia State University), Jessica Barr (Eureka College), Chris Barrett (Louisiana State University), Craig Barrette (Brescia University), Carol Beran (St. Mary's College), Peter Berek (Amherst College), David Bergman (Towson University), Scott Black (University of Utah), William R. "Beau" Black III (Weatherford College), Justin Blessinger (Dakota State University), William E. Bolton (La Salle University), Wyatt Bonikowski (Suffolk University), Rebecca Bossie (University of Texas at El Paso), Bruce Brandt (South Dakota State University), Heather Braun (University of Akron), Mark Brown (University of Jamestown), Logan D. Browning (Rice University), Monica Brzezinski Potkay (College of William and Mary), Rebecca Bushnell (University of Pennsylvania), Claire Busse (La Salle University), Thomas Butler (Eastern Kentucky University), Jim Casey (Arcadia University), Susan P. Cerasano (Colgate University), Maria Chappell (University of Georgia), Brinda Charry (Keene State College), Susannah Chewning (Union County College), Lin Chih-hsin (National Chengchi University), Kathryn Chittick (Trent University), Nora Corrigan (Mississippi University for Women), David Cowart (University of South Carolina), Catherine Craft-Fairchild (University of St. Thomas), Susan Crisafulli (Franklin College), Jenny Crisp (Dalton State College), Ashley Cross (Manhattan College), James P. Crowley (Bridgewater State University), Susie Crowson (Del Mar College), Rebecca Crump (Louisiana State University), Cyrus Mulready (SUNY New Paltz), Lisa Darien (Hartwick College), Sean Dempsey (University of Arkansas), Anthony Ding (Grossmont Community College), Lorraine Eadie (Hillsdale College), Schuyler Eastin (San Diego Christian College), Gary Eddy (Winona State University), J. Craig Eller (Louisburg College), Robert Ellison (Marshall University), Nikolai Endres (Western Kentucky University), Robert Epstein (Fairfield University), Richard Erable (Franklin College), Simon C. Estok (Sungkyunkwan University), Michael Faitell (Mohawk Valley Community College), Jonathan Farina (Seton Hall University), Tyler Farrell (Marquette University), Jennifer

Feather (The University of North Carolina Greensboro), Annette Federico (James Madison University), Kerstin Feindert (Cosumnes River College), Maryanne Felter (Cayuga Community College), Benjamin Fischer (Northwest Nazarene University), Matthew Fisher (University of California, Los Angeles), Chris Fletcher (North Central University), Michael J. Flynn (The University of North Dakota), James E. Foley (Worcester State University), Walter C. Foreman (University of Kentucky), Ann Frank Wake (Elmhurst College), Michael D. Friedman (University of Scranton), Lee Garver (Butler University), Paul L. Gaston (Kent State University), Sara E. Gerend (Aurora University), Avilah Getzler (Grand View University), Edward Gieskes (University of South Carolina), Elaine Glanz (Immaculata University), Adam Golaski (Brown University), Rachel Goldberg (Northeastern CPS), Augusta Gooch (University of Alabama–Huntsville), Nathan Gorelick (Utah Valley University), Robert Gorsch (Saint Mary's College of California), Carey Goyette (Clinton Community College), Richard J. Grande (Pennsylvania State University–Abington), David A. Grant (Columbus State Community College), Sian Griffiths (Weber State University), Ann H. Guess (Alvin Community College), Audley Hall (NorthWest Arkansas Community College), Jenni Halpin (Savannah State University), Brian Harries (Concordia University Wisconsin), Samantha Harvey (Boise State University), Raychel Haugrud Reiff (University of Wisconsin–Superior), Erica Haugtvedt (The Ohio State University), Mary Hayes (University of Mississippi), Joshua R. Held (Indiana University, Bloomington), Roze Hentschell (Colorado State University), Erich Hertz (Siena College), Natalie Hewitt (Hope International University), Lisa Hinrichsen (University of Arkansas), Lorretta Holloway (Framingham State University), Catherine Howard (University of Houston), Chia-Yin Huang (Chinese Culture University), Sister Marie Hubert Kealy (Immaculata University), Elizabeth Hutcheon (Huntingdon College), Peter Hyland (Huron University College, Western University), Eileen Jankowski (Chapman University), Alan Johnson (Idaho State University), Brian Jukes (Yuba College), Kari Kalve (Earlham College), Parmita Kapadia (Northern Kentucky University), Deborah Kennedy (Saint Mary's University), Mark Kipperman (Northern Illinois University), Cindy Klestinec (Miami University–Ohio), Neal W. Kramer (Brigham Young University), Kathryn Laity (College of Saint Rose), Jameela Lares (University of Southern Mississippi), Caroline Levine (University of Wisconsin–Madison), Melinda Linscott (Idaho State University), Janet Madden (El Camino College), Gerald Margolis (Temple University), Elizabeth Mazzola (The City College of New York), Keely McCarthy (Chestnut Hill College), Cathryn McCarthy Donahue (College of Mount Saint Vincent), Mary H. McMurran (University of Western Ontario), Josephine A. McQuail (Tennessee Technological University), Brett Mertins (Metropolitan Community College), Christian Michener (Saint Mary's University), Brook Miller (University of Minnesota, Morris), Kristine Miller (Utah State University), Jacqueline T. Miller (Rutgers University), Richard J. Moll (University of Western Ontario), Lorne Mook (Taylor University), Rod Moore (Los Angeles Valley College), Rory Moore (University of California, Riverside), Grant Moss (Utah Valley University), Nicholas D. Nace (Hampden-Sydney College), Jonathan Naito (St. Olaf College), Mary Nelson (Dallas Baptist University), Mary Anne Nunn (Central Connecticut State University), John O'Brien (University of Virginia),

Onno Oerlemans (Hamilton College), Michael Oishi (Leeward Community College), Sylvia Pamboukian (Robert Morris University), Adam Parkes (University of Georgia), Michelle Parkinson (University of Wisconsin–River Falls), Geoffrey Payne (Macquarie University), Anna Peak (Temple University), Dan Pearce (Brigham Young University–Idaho), Christopher Penna (University of Delaware), Zina Petersen (Brigham Young University), Kaara L. Peterson (Miami University of Ohio), Keith Peterson (Brigham Young University–Hawaii), Professor Maggie Piccolo (Rowan University), Ann Pleiss Morris (Ripon College), Michael Pogach (Northampton Community College), Matthew Potolsky (The University of Utah), Miguel Powers (Fullerton College), Gregory Priebe (Harford Community College), Jonathan Purkiss (Pulaski Technical College), Kevin A. Quarmby (Oxford College of Emory University), Mark Rankin (James Madison University), Tawnya Ravy (The George Washington University), Joan Ray (University of Colorado, Colorado Springs), Helaine Razovsky (Northwestern State University of Louisiana), Vince Redder (Dakota Wesleyan University), Elizabeth Rich (Saginaw Valley State University), Patricia Rigg (Acadia University), Albert J. Rivero (Marquette University), Phillip Ronald Stormer (Culver-Stockton College), Kenneth Rooney (University College Cork, Ireland), David Ruiter (University of Texas at El Paso), Kathryn Rummell (California Polytechnic State University), Richard Ruppel (Chapman University), Jonathan Sachs (Concordia University), David A. Salomon (Russell Sage College), Abigail Scherer (Nicholls State University), Roger Schmidt (Idaho State University), William Sheldon (Hutchinson Community College), Christian Sheridan (Bridgewater College), Nicole Sidhu (East Carolina University), Lisa Siefker Bailey (Indiana University–Purdue University Columbus), Samuel Smith (Messiah College), Cindy Soldan (Lakehead University), Diana Solomon (Simon Fraser University), Vivasvan Soni (Northwestern University), Timothy Spurgin (Lawrence University), Felicia Jean Steele (The College of New Jersey), Carole Lynn Stewart (Brock University), Judy Suh (Duquesne University), Dean Swinford (Fayetteville State University), Allison Symonds (Cecil College), Brenda Tuberville (Rogers State University), Verne Underwood (Rogue Community College), Janine Utell (Widener University), Paul Varner (Abilene Christian University), Deborah Vause (York College of Pennsylvania), Nicholas Wallerstein (Black Hills State University), Rod Waterman (Central Connecticut State University), Eleanor Welsh (Chesapeake College), Paul Westover (Brigham Young University), Christopher Wheatley (The Catholic University of America), Miranda Wilcox (Brigham Young University), Brett D. Wilson (College of William & Mary), Lorraine Wood (Brigham Young University), Nicholas A. Wright (Marist College), Michael Wutz (Weber State University).

THE NORTON ANTHOLOGY OF

ENGLISH

LITERATURE

TENTH EDITION

VOLUME B

The Sixteenth Century
and
The Early Seventeenth Century

The Sixteenth Century 1485–1603

1485: Accession of Henry VII inaugurates the Tudor dynasty
1509: Accession of Henry VIII
1517: Martin Luther's Wittenberg Theses; beginning of the Reformation
1534: Henry VIII declares himself head of the English church
1557: Publication of Tottel's *Songs and Sonnets*, containing poems by Sir Thomas Wyatt; Henry Howard, earl of Surrey; and others
1558: Accession of Elizabeth I
1576: Building of The Theater, the first permanent structure in England for the presentation of plays
1588: Defeat of the Spanish Armada
1603: Death of Elizabeth I and accession of James I, the first of the Stuart kings

The ancient Roman poet Virgil characterized Britain as a wild, remote place set apart from all the world, and it must still have seemed so in the early sixteenth century to the inhabitants of cities like Venice, Madrid, and Paris. To be sure, some venturesome Continental travelers crossed the Channel and visited London, Oxford, or Cambridge, bringing home reports of bustling markets, impressive universities, and ambitious nobles vying for position at an increasingly powerful royal court. But these visitors were but a trickle compared with the flood of wealthy young Englishmen (and, to a lesser extent, Englishwomen) who embarked at the first opportunity for the Continent. English travelers were virtually obliged to learn some French, Italian, or Spanish, for

The Life and Death of Sir Henry Unton (detail), anonymous, ca. 1597. For more information about this painting, see the color insert in this volume.

they would encounter very few people who knew their language. On returning home, they would frequently wear foreign fashions—much to the disgust of moralists—and would pepper their speech with foreign phrases.

At the beginning of the sixteenth century, the English language had almost no prestige abroad, and there were those at home who doubted that it could serve as a suitable medium for serious, elevated, or elegant discourse. It is no accident that one of the first works in this selection of English Renaissance literature, Thomas More's *Utopia*, was not written in English: More, who began his great book in 1515 when he was on a diplomatic mission in the Netherlands, was writing for an international intellectual community, and as such his language of choice was Latin. His work quickly became famous throughout Europe, but it was not translated into English until the 1550s. Evidently, neither More himself nor the London printers and booksellers thought it imperative to publish a vernacular *Utopia*. Yet by the century's end there were signs of a great increase in what we might call linguistic self-confidence, signs that at least some contemporary observers were aware that something extraordinary was happening to their language. Though in 1600 England still remained somewhat peripheral to the Continent, English had been fashioned into an immensely powerful expressive medium, one whose cadences in the works of Marlowe, Shakespeare, and the translators of the Bible continue after more than four centuries to thrill readers.

How did it come about that by the century's end so many remarkable poems, plays, and prose works were written in English? The answer lies in part in the spectacular creativity of a succession of brilliant writers, the best of whom are represented in these pages. Still, a vital literary culture is the product of a complex process, involving thousands of more modest, half-hidden creative acts sparked by a wide range of motives, some of which we will briefly explore.

THE COURT AND THE CITY

The development of the English language in the sixteenth century is linked at least indirectly to the consolidation and strengthening of the English state. Preoccupied by violent clashes between the thuggish feudal retainers of rival barons, the English, through most of the fifteenth century, had rather limited time and inclination to cultivate rhetorical skills. The social and economic health of the nation had been severely damaged by the so-called Wars of the Roses, a vicious, decades-long struggle for royal power between the noble houses of York and Lancaster. The struggle was resolved by the establishment of the Tudor dynasty, which ruled England from 1485 to 1603. The family name derives from Owen Tudor, an ambitious Welshman who himself had no claim to the throne but who married Catherine of Valois, widow of the Lancastrian king Henry V. Their grandson, the earl of Richmond, who also inherited Lancastrian blood on his mother's side, became the first Tudor monarch: he won the crown by leading the army that defeated and killed the reigning Yorkist king, Richard III, at the battle of Bosworth Field. The victorious Richmond, crowned King Henry VII in 1485, promptly consolidated his rather shaky claim to the throne by marrying Elizabeth of the house of York, hence effectively uniting the two rival factions.

England's barons, impoverished and divided by the dynastic wars, could not effectively oppose the new power of the Crown, and the leaders of the Church also generally supported royal power. The wily Henry VII was therefore able to counter the multiple and competing power structures characteristic of feudal society and to impose a much stronger central authority and order on the nation. Initiated by the first Tudor sovereign, this consolidation progressed throughout the sixteenth century; by the reign of the last Tudor—Henry's granddaughter, Elizabeth I—though the ruler still needed the consent of Parliament on crucial matters (including the all-important one of levying taxes), the royal court had concentrated in itself much of the nation's power.

The court was a center of culture as well as power: court entertainments such as theater and masque (a sumptuous, elaborately costumed performance of dance, song, and poetry); court fashions in dress and speech; court tastes in painting, music, and poetry—all shaped the taste and the imagination of the country as a whole. Culture and power were not, in any case, easily separable in Tudor England. In a society with no freedom of speech as we understand it and with relatively limited means of mass communication, important public issues were often aired indirectly, through what we might now regard as entertainment, and lyrics that to us seem slight and nonchalant could serve as carefully designed manifestations of rhetorical agility by aspiring courtiers.

Whereas in the Middle Ages noblemen, ruling over semi-independent fiefdoms, had guarded their power by keeping their distance from London and the king, in the Tudor era the route to power lay in proximity to the royal body. (One of the coveted positions in the court of Henry VIII was Groom of the Stool, "close stool" being the Tudor term for toilet.) The monarch's chief ministers and favorites were the primary channels through which patronage was dispensed to courtiers who competed for offices in the court, the government bureaucracies, the royal household, the army, the church, and the universities or who sought titles, grants of land, leases, or similar favors. But if proximity held out the promise of wealth and power, it also harbored danger. Festive evenings with the likes of the ruthless Henry VIII were not occasions for relaxation. The court fostered paranoia, and an attendant obsession with secrecy, spying, duplicity, and betrayal.

Tudor courtiers were torn between the need to protect themselves and the equally pressing need to display themselves. For lessons in the art of intrigue, many no doubt turned to Machiavelli's notorious *Il Principe* (The Prince), with its cool guidance on how power may be gained and kept. For advice on the cultivation and display of the self, they could resort to the still more influential *Il Cortegiano* (The Courtier) by Count Baldassare Castiglione. It was particularly important, Castiglione wrote, to conceal the effort that lay behind elegant accomplishments, so that they would seem natural. In this anxious atmosphere, courtiers became highly practiced at crafting and deciphering graceful words with double or triple meanings. Poets had much to learn from courtiers, the Elizabethan critic George Puttenham observed; indeed many of the best poets in the period, Sir Thomas Wyatt, Sir Philip Sidney, Sir Walter Ralegh, and others, *were* courtiers.

If court culture fostered performances for a small coterie audience, other forces in Tudor England pulled toward a more public sphere. Markets expanded significantly, international trade flourished, and cities throughout the realm experienced a rapid surge in size and importance. London's population in particular soared, from 60,000 in 1520, to 120,000 in 1550, to 375,000 a century later, making it the largest and fastest-growing city not only in England but in all of Europe. Every year in the first half of the seventeenth century about 10,000 people migrated to London from other parts of England—wages in London tended to be around 50 percent higher than in the rest of the country—and it is estimated that one in eight English people lived in London at some point in their lives. Elderly Londoners in the 1590s could barely recognize the city of their childhood; London's boom was one factor among many contributing to the sense of a culture moving at increasing velocity away from its historical roots.

About a decade before Henry VII won his throne, the art of printing from movable metal type, a German invention, had been introduced into England by William Caxton (ca. 1422–1491), who had learned and practiced it in the Low Countries. Though reliable statistics are impossible to come by, literacy seems to have increased during the fifteenth century and still more during the sixteenth, when Protestantism encouraged a direct encounter with the Bible. Printing made books cheaper and more plentiful, providing more opportunity to read and more incentive to learn. The greater availability of books may also have reinforced the trend toward silent reading, a practice that gradually transformed what had been a communal experience into a more intimate encounter with a text.

Yet it would be a mistake to imagine these changes as sudden and dramatic. Manuscripts retained considerable prestige among the elite; throughout the sixteenth century and well into the seventeenth, court poets in particular were wary of the "stigma of print" that might mark their verse as less exclusive. Although Caxton, who was an author and a translator as well as a printer, introduced printed books, he attempted to cater to courtly tastes by translating works whose tone was more medieval than modern. Fascination with the old chivalric code of behavior is reflected as well in the jousts and tournaments that continued at court for a century, long after gunpowder had rendered them obsolete. As often in an age of alarming novelty, many people looked back to an idealized past. Indeed the great innovations of the Tudor era—intellectual, governmental, and religious—were all presented, at the time, as attempts to restore lost links with ancient traditions.

RENAISSANCE HUMANISM

During the fifteenth century a few English clerics and government officials had journeyed to Italy and had seen something of the extraordinary cultural and intellectual movement flourishing in the city-states there. That movement, generally known as the Renaissance, involved a rebirth of letters and arts stimulated by the recovery of texts and artifacts from classical antiquity, the development of techniques such as linear perspective, and the creation of powerful new aesthetic practices based on classical models. It also unleashed new ideas and new social, political, and economic forces that gradually displaced the spiritual and communal values of the Middle Ages. To Renaissance intellectuals and artists, the achievements of the pagan philosophers of ancient Greece and Rome came to seem more compelling than the subtle distinctions drawn by medieval Christian theologians. In the brilliant, intensely competitive, and vital world of Leonardo da Vinci and Michelangelo, the submission of the human spirit to penitential discipline gave way to unleashed curiosity, individual self-assertion, and a powerful conviction that man was the measure of all things. Yet the superb human figure placed at the center of the Renaissance worldview was also seen as remarkably malleable. "We have made thee neither of heaven nor of earth, neither mortal nor immortal," God tells Adam, in the Florentine Pico della Mirandola's *Oration on the Dignity of Man* (1486), "so that with freedom of choice and with honor, as though the maker and molder of thyself, thou mayest fashion thyself in whatever shape thou shalt prefer." "As though the maker and molder of thyself": this vision of self-fashioning may be glimpsed in the poetry of Petrarch, the sculpture of Donatello, and the statecraft of Lorenzo de' Medici. But in England it was not until Henry VII's reign brought some measure of political stability that the Renaissance could take root, and it was not until the accession of Henry VIII that it began to flower.

This flowering, when it occurred, came not, as in Italy, in painting, sculpture, and architecture. It came rather in the intellectual program and literary vision known as humanism. More's *Utopia* (1516), with its dream of human existence entirely transformed by a radical change in institutional arrangements, is an extreme instance of a general humanist interest in education: in England and elsewhere, humanism was bound up with struggles over the purposes of education and curriculum reform. The great Dutch humanist Erasmus, who spent some time in England and developed a close friendship with More, was a leader in the assault on what he and others regarded as a hopelessly narrow and outmoded intellectual culture based on scholastic hairsplitting and a dogmatic adherence to the philosophy of Aristotle. English humanists, including John Colet (who, as dean of St. Paul's Cathedral, recast its grammar school on humanist principles), Roger Ascham (tutor to Princess Elizabeth), and Sir Thomas Elyot, wrote treatises on education to promote the kind of learning they regarded as the most suitable preparation for public service. That education—predominantly male and conducted by tutors in wealthy families or in grammar schools—was still ordered according to the subjects of the medieval *trivium* (grammar, logic, and rhetoric) and *quadrivium* (arithmetic, geometry, astronomy, and music), but its focus shifted from training for the Church to the general acquisition of "literature," in the sense both of literacy and of cultural knowledge. For some of the more intellectually ambitious humanists, that knowledge extended to ancient Greek, whose enthusiastic adherents began to challenge the entrenched preeminence of Latin.

Still, at the core of the curriculum remained the study of Latin, the mastery of which was in effect a prolonged male puberty rite involving pain as well as pleasure. Though some educators counseled mildness, punishment was an established part of the pedagogy of the age, and even gifted students could rarely escape recurrent flogging. The purpose was to train the sons of the nobility and gentry to speak and write good Latin, the language of diplomacy, of the professions, and of all higher learning. Their sisters were always educated at home or in other noble houses. They chiefly learned modern languages, religion, music, and needlework, but they very seldom received the thorough training in the ancient languages and classical literature so central to the dominant culture. Through this training, Elizabethan schoolmasters sought to impart facility and rhetorical elegance, but the books their students laboriously pored over were not considered mere exhibitions of literary style: from the *Sententiae Pueriles* (Maxims for Children) for beginners on up through the dramatists Terence, Plautus, and Seneca; the poets Virgil and Horace; and the orator Cicero, the classics were also studied for the moral, political, and philosophical truths they contained. Though originating in pagan times, those truths could, in the opinion of many humanists, be reconciled to the moral vision of Christianity. The result, perplexing for some modern readers, is that pagan gods and goddesses flourish on the pages of even such a devoutly Christian poem as Edmund Spenser's *Faerie Queene*.

Humanists committed to classical learning were faced with the question of whether to write their own works in Latin or in English. To many learned men, influenced both by the humanist exaltation of the classical languages and by the characteristic Renaissance desire for eternal fame, the national languages seemed relatively unstable and ephemeral. Intellectuals had long shared a pan-European world of scientific inquiry, so that works by such English scientists as William Gilbert, William Harvey, and Francis Bacon easily joined those by Nicolaus Copernicus, Johannes Kepler, and Andreas Vesalius in the common linguistic medium of Latin. But throughout Europe

Tudor schoolroom. In this woodcut from the sixteenth century, the pupils sit on "forms," or benches, with few if any desks. As an early school statute explains, "When they have to write, let them use their knees for a table." All the lessons, for the different age groups, are taught in the same room: the younger boys (left) are learning their letters, while the students at the upper right are studying music. The schoolmaster, seated, holds a birch, while the usher, or assistant master, is beating a student. The windows of the schoolroom are set high in the walls, to cut down on distractions. Next to the far pillar is an hourglass used in marking time for various lessons. The school's valuable books are kept in a locked chest, behind the schoolmaster.

nationalism and the expansion of the reading public were steadily strengthening the power and allure of the vernaculars. The famous schoolmaster Richard Mulcaster (ca. 1530–1611), Spenser's teacher, captured this emergent sense of national identity in singing the praises of his native tongue:

> Is it not indeed a marvelous bondage, to become servants to one tongue for learning's sake the most of our time, with loss of most time, whereas we may have the very same treasure in our own tongue, with the gain of more time? our own bearing the joyful title of our liberty and freedom, the Latin tongue remembering us of our thralldom and bondage? I love Rome, but London better; I favor Italy, but England more; I honor the Latin, but I worship the English.

These two impulses—humanist reverence for the classics and English pride in the vernacular language—gave rise to many distinguished translations throughout the century: Homer's *Iliad* and *Odyssey* by George Chapman, Plutarch's *Lives of the Noble Grecians and Romans* by Sir Thomas North, and Ovid's *Metamorphoses* by Arthur Golding. Translators also sought to make available in English the most notable literary works in the modern languages: Castiglione's *Il Cortegiano* by Sir Thomas Hoby, Ariosto's *Orlando furioso* (Orlando mad) by Sir John Harington, and Montaigne's *Essais* by John Florio. The London book trade of the sixteenth century was a thoroughly international affair.

THE REFORMATION

There had long been serious ideological and institutional tensions in the religious life of England, but officially, at least, England in the early sixteenth century had a single religion, Catholicism, whose acknowledged head was the pope in Rome. For its faithful adherents the Roman Catholic Church was the central institution in their lives, a universal and infallible guide to human existence from cradle to grave and on into the life to come. They were instructed by its teachings, corrected by its discipline, sustained by its sacraments, and comforted by its promises. At Mass, its most sacred ritual, the congregation could witness a miracle, as the priest held aloft the Host and uttered the words that transformed the bread and wine into the body and blood of God incarnate. A vast system of confession, pardons, penance, absolution, indulgences, sacred relics, and ceremonies gave the unmarried male clerical hierarchy great power, at once spiritual and material, over their largely illiterate flock. The Bible, the liturgy, and most of the theological discussions were in Latin, which few laypeople could understand; however, religious doctrine and spirituality were mediated to them by the priests, by beautiful church art and music, and by the liturgical ceremonies of daily life—festivals, holy days, baptisms, marriages, exorcisms, and funerals.

Several of the key doctrines and practices of the Catholic Church had been challenged in fourteenth-century England by the teachings of John Wycliffe and his followers, known as Lollards. But the heretical challenge had been ruthlessly suppressed, and the embers of dissent lay largely dormant until they were ignited once again in Germany by Martin Luther, an Augustinian monk and a professor of theology at the University of Wittenberg. What began in November 1517 as an academic disputation grew with

The Pope as Antichrist. In this satirical woodcut, the pope, riding the seven-headed
Beast of the Apocalypse, holds in his hand a banner on which he urges his followers to be
traitors and kill their princes. His message, carried by three froglike devils, flies into the
gaping mouths of a knight, a bishop, and a monk. The devils are a reference to Revelation
16.13: "And I saw three unclean spirits like frogs come out of the mouth of the dragon,
and out of the mouth of the beast, and out of the mouth of the false prophet." From *Fierie
Tryall of God's Saints* (1611; author unknown).

amazing speed into a bitter, far-reaching, and bloody revolt that forever rup-
tured the unity of Western Christendom.

When Luther rose up against the ancient church, he did so in the name
of private conscience enlightened by a personal reading of the Scriptures. A
person of formidable intellectual energy, eloquence, and rhetorical violence, Luther charged that the pope and his hierarchy were the servants of
Satan and that the Church had degenerated into a corrupt, worldly conspiracy designed to bilk the credulous and subvert secular authority. Salvation
depended on destroying this conspiracy and enabling all of the people to
regain direct access to the word of God by means of vernacular translations
of the Bible. The common watchwords of the Reformation, as the movement
Luther sparked came to be known, were *sola scriptura* and *sola fide*: only the
Scriptures (not the Church or tradition or the clerical hierarchy) have authority in matters of religion and should determine what an individual must
believe and practice; only the faith of the individual (not good works or the
scrupulous observance of religious rituals) can effect a Christian's salvation.

These tenets, heretical in the eyes of the Catholic Church, spread and
gathered force, especially in northern Europe, where major leaders like the
Swiss pastor Ulrich Zwingli in Zurich and the French theologian John Calvin
in Geneva, elaborating various and sometimes conflicting doctrinal principles, organized the populace to overturn the existing church and established new institutional structures. In England, however, the Reformation
began less with popular discontent and theological disputation than with
dynastic politics and royal greed. Henry VIII, who had received from Pope
Leo X the title Defender of the Faith for writing a diatribe against Luther,

craved a legitimate son to succeed to the throne, and his queen, Catherine of Aragon, failed to give him one. (Catherine had borne six children, but only a daughter, Mary, survived infancy.) After lengthy negotiations, the pope, under pressure from Catherine's powerful Spanish family, refused to grant the king the divorce he sought in order to marry Anne Boleyn.

A series of momentous events followed, as England lurched away from the Church of Rome. In 1531 Henry forced the entire clergy of England to beg pardon for having usurped royal authority in the administration of canon law (the law that governed such matters as divorce). Two years later Henry's marriage to Catherine was officially declared null and void and Anne Boleyn was crowned queen. The king was promptly excommunicated by the pope, Clement VII. In the following year, a parliamentary Act of Succession required an oath from all adult male subjects confirming the new dynastic settlement. Thomas More and John Fisher, the bishop of Rochester, were among the small number who refused. The Act of Supremacy, passed later in the year, formally declared the king to be "Supreme Head of the Church in England" and again required an oath to this effect. In 1535 and 1536 further acts made it treasonous to refuse the oath of royal supremacy or, as More had tried to do, to remain silent. The first victims were three Carthusian monks who rejected the oath—"How could the king, a layman," said one of them, "be Head of the Church of England?"—and in May 1535 were duly hanged, drawn, and quartered. A few weeks later Fisher and More were convicted and beheaded. Between 1536 and 1539, under the direction of Henry's powerful secretary of state, Thomas Cromwell, England's monasteries were suppressed. Their vast wealth was seized by the Crown and transferred, by either gift or sale, to the king's followers.

Royal defiance of the authority of Rome was a key element in the Reformation but did not by itself constitute the establishment of Protestantism in England. On the contrary, in the same year that Fisher and More were martyred for their adherence to Roman Catholicism, twenty-five Protestants, members of a sect known as Anabaptists, were burned for heresy on a single day. Through most of his reign, Henry remained an equal-opportunity persecutor, pitiless to Catholics loyal to Rome and hostile to many of those who espoused Reformation ideas, though these ideas, aided greatly by the printing press, gradually established themselves on English soil.

Upon Henry's death, in 1547, his son, Edward (by his third wife, Jane Seymour), came to the throne. Both the ten-year-old Edward and his successive Protectors, the dukes of Somerset and Northumberland, were staunch Protestants, and reformers hastened to transform the English Church accordingly. During Edward's brief reign, Thomas Cranmer, the archbishop of Canterbury, formulated the forty-two articles of religion that became the core of Anglican orthodoxy and wrote the first *Book of Common Prayer*, which was officially adopted in 1549 as the basis of English worship services.

The sickly Edward died in 1553, only six years after his accession to the throne, and was succeeded by his half-sister Mary (Henry VIII's daughter by his first wife, Catherine), who immediately took steps to return her kingdom to Roman Catholicism. Though she was unable to get Parliament to agree to return Church lands seized under Henry VIII, she restored the Catholic Mass, once again affirmed the authority of the pope, and put down a rebellion that sought to depose her. Seconded by her ardently Catholic husband, Philip II, king of Spain, she initiated a series of religious persecutions that earned her (from her enemies) the name Bloody Mary. Hundreds of Protestants took refuge abroad in cities like Calvin's Geneva; almost three hundred less-fortunate Protestants were condemned as heretics and burned at the stake. Yet for thousands of English men and women, Mary's reign came as a liberation; the rapid restoration of old Catholic ornaments to parish churches all over England indicates that they had not in fact been confiscated or destroyed as ordered, but simply hidden away, in hopes of better times.

Mary died childless in 1558, and her younger half-sister, Elizabeth, became queen. Elizabeth's succession had been by no means assured. For if Protestants regarded as invalid Henry VIII's marriage to Catherine and hence deemed Mary illegitimate, so Catholics regarded as invalid his marriage to Anne Boleyn and hence deemed *her* daughter illegitimate. Henry himself seemed to support both views; only three years after divorcing Catherine he beheaded Anne on charges of treason and adultery and urged Parliament to invalidate the marriage. Moreover, though during her sister's reign Elizabeth outwardly complied with the official Catholic religious observances, Mary and her advisers rightly suspected her of Protestant leanings, and the young princess's life was in grave danger. Poised and circumspect, Elizabeth warily evaded the traps that were set for her. When she ascended the throne, her actions were scrutinized for some indication of the country's future course. During her coronation procession, when a girl in an allegorical pageant presented her with a Bible in English translation—banned under Mary's reign—Elizabeth kissed the book, held it up reverently, and laid it to her breast. By this simple yet profound (and carefully choreographed) gesture, Elizabeth signaled England's return to the Reformation.

Many English men and women, of all classes, remained loyal to the old Catholic faith, but English authorities under Elizabeth moved steadily, if cautiously, toward ensuring at least an outward conformity to the official Protestant settlement. Recusants, those who refused to attend regular Sunday services in their parish churches, were heavily fined. Anyone who wished to receive a university degree, to be ordained as a priest in the Church of England, or to be named as an officer of the state had to swear an oath to the royal supremacy. Bishops were directed to investigate whether parish clergy had, as commanded, "removed, abolished, and destroyed" all images that were judged to be superstitious. Commissioners were sent throughout the land to confirm that religious services were following the officially approved liturgy and to investigate any reported backsliding into Catholic practice or, alternatively, any attempts to introduce reforms more radical than the queen and her bishops had chosen to embrace. For the Protestant exiles who streamed back were eager not only to undo the damage Mary had done but also to carry the Reformation much further than it had gone. A minority, who would come to be known as Puritans, sought to dismantle the church hierarchy, to purge the calendar of folk customs deemed pagan and the church service of ritual practices deemed superstitious, to dress the clergy in simple garb, and to smash "idolatrous" statues, crucifixes, and altarpieces. Throughout her long reign, however, Elizabeth remained cautiously conservative and determined to hold religious zealotry in check.

In the space of a single lifetime, England had gone officially from Roman Catholicism, to Catholicism under the supreme headship of the English king, to a guarded Protestantism, to a more radical Protestantism, to a renewed and aggressive Roman Catholicism, and finally to Protestantism again. Each of these shifts was accompanied by danger, persecution, and death. It was enough to make people wary. Or skeptical. Or extremely agile.

A FEMALE MONARCH IN A MALE WORLD

In the last year of Mary's reign, the Scottish Calvinist minister John Knox thundered against what he called "the monstrous regiment of women." After the Protestant Elizabeth came to the throne the following year, Knox and his religious brethren were less inclined to denounce all female rulers, but in England, as elsewhere in Europe, there remained a widespread conviction that women were unsuited to wield power over men. Many men seem to have regarded the capacity for rational thought as exclusively male; women, they assumed, were led only by their passions. While gentlemen mastered the arts of rhetoric and warfare, gentlewomen were expected to display the virtues of silence and good housekeeping. Among upper-class males, the will to dominate others was acceptable and indeed admired; the same will in women was condemned as a grotesque and dangerous aberration.

Apologists for the queen countered these prejudices by appealing to historical precedent and legal theory. History offered inspiring examples of just female rulers, notably Deborah, the biblical prophetess who had judged Israel. In the legal sphere, Crown lawyers advanced the theory of "the king's two bodies." As England's crowned head, Elizabeth's person was mystically divided between her mortal "body natural" and the immortal "body politic." While the queen's natural body was inevitably subject to the failings of human flesh, the body politic was timeless and perfect. In political terms, therefore, Elizabeth's sex was a matter of no consequence, a thing indifferent.

Elizabeth, who had received a fine humanist education and an extended, dangerous lesson in the art of survival, made it immediately clear that she intended to rule in more than name only. She assembled a group of trustworthy advisers, foremost among them William Cecil (later created Lord Burghley), but she insisted on making many of the crucial decisions herself. Like many Renaissance monarchs, Elizabeth was drawn to the idea of royal absolutism, the theory that ultimate power was quite properly concentrated in her person and indeed that God had appointed her to be His deputy in the kingdom. Opposition to her rule, in this view, was not only a political act but also a kind of impiety, a blasphemous grudging against the will of God. Supporters of absolutism contended that God commands obedience even to manifestly wicked rulers whom He has sent to punish the sinfulness of humankind. Such arguments were routinely made in speeches and political tracts and from the pulpits of churches, where they were incorporated into the *Book of Homilies* that clergymen were required to read out to their congregations.

In reality, Elizabeth's power was not absolute. The government had a network of spies, informers, and *agents provocateurs*, but it lacked a standing army, a national police force, an efficient system of communication, and an extensive bureaucracy. Above all, the queen had limited financial resources and needed to turn periodically to an independent and often recalcitrant Parliament, which by long tradition had the sole right to levy taxes and to grant subsidies. Members of the House of Commons were elected from their boroughs, not appointed by the monarch, and though the queen had considerable influence over their decisions, she could by no means dictate policy. Under these constraints, Elizabeth ruled through a combination of adroit political maneuvering and imperious command, all the while enhancing her authority in the eyes of both court and country by means of an extraordinary cult of love.

"We all loved her," Elizabeth's godson Sir John Harington wrote, with just a touch of irony, a few years after the queen's death, "for she said she loved us." Ambassadors, courtiers, and parliamentarians all submitted to Elizabeth's cult of love, in which the queen's gender was transformed from a potential liability into a significant asset. Those who approached her generally did so on their knees and were expected to address her with the most extravagant compliments; she in turn spoke, when it suited her to do so, in a comparable language of love. The court moved in an atmosphere of romance, with music, dancing, plays, and the elaborate, fancy-dress entertainments called masques. The queen adorned herself in dazzling clothes and rich jewels. When she went on one of her summer "progresses," ceremonial journeys through her land, she looked like an exotic, sacred image in a religious cult of love, and her noble hosts virtually bankrupted themselves to lavish upon her the costliest pleasures. England's leading artists, such as the poet Edmund Spenser and the painter Nicholas Hilliard, enlisted themselves in the celebration of Elizabeth's mystery, likening her to the goddesses of mythology and the heroines of the Bible: Diana, Astraea, Cynthia, Deborah. The cultural sources of the cult of Elizabeth were both secular (her courtiers could pine for her as the cruelly chaste mistress celebrated in Petrarchan love poetry) and sacred (the veneration that under Catholicism had been due to the Virgin Mary could now be directed toward England's semidivine queen).

There was a sober, even grim aspect to these poetical fantasies: Elizabeth was brilliant at playing off one dangerous faction against another, now turning her gracious smiles on one favorite, now honoring his hated rival, now suddenly looking elsewhere and raising an obscure upstart to royal favor. And when she was disobeyed or when she felt that her prerogatives had been challenged, she was capable of an anger that, as Harington put it, "left no doubtings whose daughter she was." Thus when Sir Walter Ralegh, one of the queen's glittering favorites, married without her knowledge and consent, he found himself promptly imprisoned in the Tower of London. Or when the Protestant polemicist John Stubbes ventured to publish a pamphlet stridently denouncing the queen's proposed marriage to the French Catholic duke of Anjou, Stubbes and his publisher were arrested and had their right hands chopped off. (After receiving the blow, the now prudent Stubbes lifted his hat with his remaining hand and cried, "God save the Queen!")

THE KINGDOM IN DANGER

Beset by Catholic and Protestant extremists, Elizabeth contrived to forge a moderate compromise that enabled her realm to avert the massacres and civil wars that poisoned France and other countries on the Continent. But menace was never far off, and there were continual fears of conspiracy, rebellion,

Armada Portrait. This portrait of Queen Elizabeth, painted ca. 1588–89, is attributed to George Gower. Through the windows to the left and right can be glimpsed the arrival and then the defeat of the Spanish Armada, wrecked in violent storms. The queen, glowing with the pearls that symbolized her chastity, rests her hand on a globe, her fingers in effect claiming the Americas for her empire.

and assassination. Suspicion swirled around Elizabeth's second cousin Mary, Queen of Scots, who had been driven from her own kingdom in 1568 and had taken refuge in England. The presence, under a kind of house arrest, of a Catholic queen with a plausible claim to the English throne was the source of widespread anxiety and helped generate recurrent rumors of plots. Some of these were real enough, others imaginary, still others fabricated by the secret agents of the government's intelligence service under the direction of Sir Francis Walsingham. Fears of Catholic conspiracies intensified greatly after Spanish imperial armies invaded the Netherlands to stamp out Protestant rebels (1567), after the St. Bartholomew's Day Massacre of Protestants (Huguenots) in France (1572), and after the assassination of Europe's other major Protestant leader, William of Orange (1584).

The queen's life seemed to be in even greater danger after Pope Gregory XIII's proclamation in 1580 that the assassination of the great heretic Elizabeth (who had been excommunicated a decade before) would not constitute a mortal sin. The immediate effect of the proclamation was to make life more difficult for English Catholics, most of whom were loyal to the queen but who fell under grave suspicion. Suspicion was heightened by the clandestine presence of English Jesuits, trained at seminaries abroad and smuggled back into England to serve the Roman Catholic cause. When, after several botched conspiracies had been disclosed, Elizabeth's spymaster Walsingham unearthed another assassination plot, in the correspondence between the Queen of Scots and the Catholic Anthony Babington, the wretched Mary's fate was sealed. After a public display of vacillation and perhaps with genuine regret, Elizabeth signed the death warrant, and her cousin was beheaded.

The long-anticipated military confrontation with Catholic Spain was now unavoidable. Elizabeth learned that Philip II, her former brother-in-law and one-time suitor, was preparing to send an enormous fleet against her island realm. The Armada was to sail first to the Netherlands, where a Spanish army would be waiting to embark and invade England. Barring its way was England's small fleet of well-armed and highly maneuverable fighting vessels, backed up by ships from the merchant navy. The Invincible Armada reached English waters in July 1588, only to be routed in one of the most famous and decisive naval battles in European history. Then, in what many viewed as an act of God on behalf of Protestant England, the Spanish fleet was dispersed and all but destroyed by violent storms.

As England braced itself to withstand the land invasion that never materialized, Elizabeth appeared in person to review a detachment of soldiers assembled at Tilbury, on the Thames estuary. Dressed in a white gown and a silver breastplate, she declared that though some among her councilors had urged her not to appear before a large crowd of armed men, she would never fail to trust the loyalty of her faithful and loving subjects. Nor did she fear the Spanish armies. "I know I have the body but of a weak and feeble woman," Elizabeth declared, "but I have the heart and stomach [i.e., valor] of a king, and of a king of England too." In this celebrated, carefully publicized speech, Elizabeth displayed many of her most memorable qualities: her self-consciously theatrical command of grand public occasions, her subtle blending of magniloquent rhetoric and the language of love, her strategic appropriation of traditionally masculine qualities, and her great personal courage. "We princes," she once remarked, "are set on stages in the sight and view of all the world."

THE ENGLISH AND OTHERNESS

In 1485, most English people would have devoted little thought to their national identity. If asked to describe their sense of belonging, they would probably have spoken of the international community of Christendom and of their local region, such as Kent or Cornwall. The extraordinary events of the Tudor era, from the encounter with the New World to the break with Rome, made many people newly aware and proud of their Englishness. At the same time, they began to perceive those who lay outside the national community in new (and often negative) ways. Like most national communities, the English defined themselves largely in terms of what or who they were not. In the wake of the Reformation, the most prominent "others" were those who had until recently been more or less the same—that is, the Catholics of western Christendom. But other groups were also instrumental in the project of English self-definition.

Elizabethan London had a large population of resident aliens, mainly artisans and merchants and their families, from Portugal, Italy, Spain, Germany, and above all, France and the Netherlands. Many of these people were Protestant refugees, and they were accorded some legal and economic protection by the government. But they were not always welcome to the local populace. Throughout the sixteenth century, London was the site of repeated demonstrations and, on occasion, bloody riots against the communities of foreign artisans, who were accused of taking jobs away from Englishmen. There was widespread hostility as well toward the Welsh, the Scots, and above all the Irish, whom the English had for centuries been struggling unsuccessfully to subdue. The kings of England claimed to be rulers of Ireland, but in reality they effectively controlled only a small area known as the Pale, extending north from Dublin. The great majority of the Irish population remained stubbornly Catholic and, despite endlessly reiterated English repression, burning of villages, destruction of crops, seizure of land, and massacres, incorrigibly independent.

Medieval England's Jewish population, the recurrent object of persecution, extortion, and massacre, had been officially expelled by King Edward I in 1290—the earliest such mass expulsion in Europe—but Elizabethan England harbored a tiny number of Jews or Jewish converts to Christianity. They were the objects of suspicion and hostility. Elizabethans appear to have been fascinated by Jews and Judaism but quite uncertain whether the terms referred to a people, a foreign nation, a set of strange practices, a living faith, a defunct religion, a villainous conspiracy, or a messianic inheritance. Protestant Reformers brooded deeply on the Hebraic origins of Christianity; government officials ordered the arrest of those "suspected to be Jews"; villagers paid pennies to itinerant fortune-tellers who claimed to be descended from Abraham or masters of kabbalistic mysteries; and London playgoers enjoyed the spectacle of the downfall of the wicked Barabas in Christopher Marlowe's *The Jew of Malta* and the forced conversion of Shylock in Shakespeare's *The Merchant of Venice*. Jews were not officially permitted to resettle in England until the middle of the seventeenth century, and even then their legal status was ambiguous.

Sixteenth-century England also had a small African population, whose skin color was the subject of pseudoscientific speculation and theological debate. Some Elizabethans believed that Africans' blackness resulted from the climate of the regions where they lived, where, as one traveler put it, they were "so scorched and vexed with the heat of the sun, that in many places they curse it when it riseth." Others held that blackness was a curse inherited from their forefather Cush, the son of Ham (who had, according to Genesis, wickedly exposed the nakedness of his drunken father, Noah). George Best, a proponent of this theory of inherited skin color, reported that "I myself have seen an Ethiopian as black as coal brought into England, who taking a fair English woman to wife, begat a son in all respects as black as the father was, although England were his native country, and an English woman his mother: whereby it seemeth this blackness proceedeth rather of some natural infection of that man."

As the word *infection* suggests, Elizabethans frequently regarded blackness as a physical defect, though the black people who lived in England and Scotland throughout the sixteenth century were also treated as exotic curiosities. At his marriage to Anne of Denmark, James VI of Scotland (the son of Mary, Queen of Scots; as James I of England, he succeeded Elizabeth, in 1603) entertained his bride and her family by commanding four naked black youths to dance before him in the snow. (The youths died of exposure shortly afterward.) In 1594, in the festivities celebrating the baptism of James's son, a "Black-Moor" entered pulling an elaborately decorated chariot that was, in the

Etching of a black woman, 1645, by Wenceslaus Hollar. The Bohemian-born Hollar lived and worked for most of his career in Antwerp and in London. He drew portraits of many men and women, including this sympathetic depiction of a black woman, probably a servant.

original plan, supposed to be pulled by a lion. In England there was a black trumpeter in the courts of Henry VII and Henry VIII, while Elizabeth had at least two black servants, one an entertainer, the other a page. Africans became increasingly fashionable as servants in aristocratic and gentle households in the last decades of the sixteenth century.

Some of these Africans were almost certainly slaves, though the legal status of slavery in England was ambiguous. In Cartwright's Case (1569), the court ruled "that England was too Pure an Air for Slaves to breathe in," but there is evidence that black slaves were owned in Elizabethan and Jacobean England. Moreover, by the mid-sixteenth century the English had become involved in the profitable trade that carried African slaves to the New World. In 1562 John Hawkins embarked on his first slaving voyage, transporting some three hundred Africans from the Guinea coast to Hispaniola, where they were sold for ten thousand pounds. Elizabeth is reported to have said that this venture was "detestable, and would call down the Vengeance of Heaven upon the Undertakers." Nevertheless, she invested profitably in Hawkins's subsequent voyages and loaned him ships.

Elizabeth also invested in other enterprises that combined aggressive nationalism and the pursuit of profit. In 1493 the pope had divided the New World between the Spanish and the Portuguese by drawing a line from pole to pole (hence Brazil speaks Portuguese today and the rest of Latin America speaks Spanish): the English were not in the picture. But by the end of Edward VI's reign, the Company of Merchant Adventurers had been founded, and Englishmen had begun to explore Asia and North America. Some of these adventurers turned to piracy, preying on Spanish ships that were returning laden with wealth extracted from Spain's New World possessions. (The pope had ruled that the native peoples were human beings—and hence could be converted to Christianity—but the ruling did nothing to prevent their enslavement and brutal exploitation.) English acts of piracy soon became a private undeclared war, with the queen and her courtiers covertly investing in the raids but accepting no responsibility for them. The greatest of many astounding exploits was the voyage of Francis Drake (1577–80): he sailed through the Strait of Magellan, pillaged Spanish towns on the

Pacific, reached as far north as San Francisco, crossed to the Philippines, and returned around the Cape of Good Hope; he came back with a million pounds in treasure, and his investors earned a dividend of 5,000 percent. Queen Elizabeth knighted him on the deck of his ship, *The Golden Hind*.

WRITERS, PRINTERS, AND PATRONS

The association between literature and print, so natural to us, was less immediate in the sixteenth century. Poetry in particular frequently circulated in manuscript, copied by reader after reader into personal anthologies—commonplace books—or reproduced by professional scribes for a fee. The texts that have come down to us in printed form often bear an uncertain relation to authorial manuscripts, and were frequently published only posthumously. The career of professional writer in sixteenth-century England was almost impossible: there was no such thing as author's copyright, no royalties paid to an author according to the sales of his book, and virtually no notion that anyone could make a decent living through the creation of works of literature. Writers sold their manuscripts to the printer or bookseller outright, for what now seem like ridiculously low prices. The churchyard of St. Paul's Cathedral in London was lined with booksellers' shops: dissolved chantries were taken over by bookshops in the 1540s, church officials leased out their residences near the church's north door to members of the Stationers' Company (the guild whose members had the exclusive right to own printing presses), and eventually bookstores two stories high and more filled the bays between the cathedral's buttresses. St. Paul's was the main center of business in the capital, with the church itself serving as a meeting place, and its columns as bulletin boards; publishers would post there, and elsewhere in the city, the title pages of new books as advertisements. Those title pages listed the wholesaler for the work, but customers could have bought popular books at most of the shops in St. Paul's Yard. The publishing business was not entirely contained in that busy space. Some stationers were only printers, merely working as contractors for publishers, and their printshops were located all over the city, often in the owner's residence.

Freedom of the press did not exist. Before Elizabeth's reign, state control of printed books was poorly organized, although licensing efforts had been under way since 1538. In 1557, however, the Stationers' Company received its charter, and became responsible for the licensing of books. Two years later, the government commanded the stationers to license only books that had been approved by either six privy councilors or the archbishop of Canterbury and the bishop of London. Despite these seemingly strict regulations, "scandalous, malicious, schismatical, and heretical" works were never effectively suppressed. Though there were occasional show trials and horrendous punishments—the printer William Carter was hanged for treason in 1584 because he had published a Catholic pamphlet; the Protestant separatists John Penry, Henry Barrow, and John Greenwood were executed in 1593 under a statute that made it a capital offense to "devise and write, print or set forth, any manner of book . . . letter, or writing containing false, seditious, and slanderous matter to the defamation of the Queen's Majesty"—active censorship was not as frequent or thorough as we might expect.

The censors largely focused their attention on works of history, which often had political implications for the present, and on religious treatises. In this, they shared the public's taste. Plays and secular poetry occasionally sold well (Shakespeare's *Henry IV, Part 1* was printed 7 times in 25 years), but they could not compete with publishing blockbusters such as *The Plain Man's Pathway* (16 editions in 25 years), let alone *The Psalms in English Meter* (published 124 times between 1583 and 1608). Publishers were largely interested in profit margins, and the predominance of devotional texts among the surviving books from the period attests to their greater marketability. The format in which works of literature were usually published is also telling. We normally find plays and poetry in quartos (or octavos), small volumes that had four (or eight) pages printed on each side of a sheet that was then folded twice (or three times) and stitched together with other such folded sheets to form the book. The more imposing folio format (in which the paper was folded only once, at two pages per side of a sheet) tended to be reserved not just for longer works but for those regarded as meriting especially respectful treatment. In 1577, Raphael Holinshed's massive history *The Chronicles of England, Scotlande, and Irelande* appeared in a woodcut-illustrated folio; ten years later, a second edition was published, again in the large format. In contrast, Edmund Spenser's huge poem *The Faerie Queene* was printed as a quarto both in 1590 and in 1596. A decade after his death, though, as the poet's reputation grew, his epic appeared again (1609), this time as a folio.

Elizabethan writers of exalted social standing, like the earl of Surrey or Sir Philip Sidney, thought of themselves as courtiers, statesmen, and landowners; poetry was for them an indispensable social grace and a deeply pleasurable, exalted form of play. Writers of lower rank, such as Samuel Daniel and Michael Drayton, sought careers as civil servants, secretaries, tutors, and clerics; they might take up more or less permanent residence in a noble household or, more casually, offer their literary work to actual or prospective patrons, in the hope of protection, career advancement, or financial reward. Ambitious authors eager to rise from threadbare obscurity often looked to the court for livelihood, notice, and encouragement, but their great expectations generally proved chimerical. "A thousand hopes, but all nothing," wailed John Lyly, alluding to his long wait for the office of Master of the Revels, "a hundred promises but yet nothing."

Financial rewards for writing prose or poetry came mostly in the form of gifts from wealthy patrons, who sought to enhance their status and gratify their vanity through the achievements and lavish praises of their clients. Some Elizabethan patrons, though, were well-educated humanists motivated by aesthetic interests, and with them, patronage extended beyond financial support to the creation of lively literary and intellectual circles. Poems by Daniel, Ben Jonson, Aemilia Lanyer, and others bear witness to the sustaining intelligence and sophistication, as well as the generosity, of their benefactors. But the experience of Robert Greene is perhaps equally revealing: the fact that he had sixteen different patrons for seventeen books suggests that he did not find much favor or support from any one of them. Indeed, a practice grew up of printing off several dedications to be inserted into particular copies of a book so that an impecunious author could deceive each of several patrons into thinking that he or she was the uniquely fortunate person to be honored by the volume.

In addition to the court and great families as dispensers of patronage, the city of London and the two universities also had a substantial impact on the period's literature. London was the center of the book trade, the nursery of a fledgling middle-class reading public, and, most important, the home of the public theaters. Before Elizabeth's time, the universities were mainly devoted to educating the clergy, and that remained an important part of their function. But in the second half of the century, the sons of the gentry and the aristocracy were going in increasing numbers to the universities and the Inns of Court (law schools), not to take religious orders or to practice law but to prepare for public service or the management of their estates. Other, less affluent students, such as Marlowe and Spenser, attended Oxford or Cambridge on scholarship. A group of graduates, including Thomas Nashe, Robert Greene, and George Peele, enlivened the literary scene in London in the 1590s, but the precarious lives of these so-called "university wits" testify to the difficulties they encountered in their quixotic attempt to survive by their writing skill. The diary of Philip Henslowe, a leading theatrical manager, has entry after entry showing university graduates in prison or in debt or at best eking out a miserable existence patching plays.

Women had no access to grammar schools, the universities, or the Inns of Court. While Protestantism, with its emphasis on reading Scripture, certainly helped improve female literacy in the sixteenth century, girls were rarely encouraged to pursue their studies. Indeed, while girls were increasingly taught to read, they were not necessarily taught to write, for the latter skill in women was considered to be at the very least useless, at the worst dangerous. When the prominent humanist Sir Thomas Smith thought of how he should describe his country's social order, he declared that "we do reject women, as those whom nature hath made to keep home and to nourish their family and children, and not to meddle with matters abroad, nor to bear office in a city or commonwealth." Then, with a kind of nervous glance over his shoulder, he made an exception of those few in whom "the blood is respected, not the age nor the sex": for example, the queen. Every piece of writing by a woman from this period is a triumph over nearly impossible odds.

TUDOR STYLE: ORNAMENT, PLAINNESS, AND WONDER

Renaissance literature is the product of a rhetorical culture, a culture steeped in the arts of persuasion and trained to process complex verbal signals. (The contemporary equivalent would be the ease with which we deal with complex visual signals, effortlessly processing such devices as fade-out, montage, crosscutting, and morphing.) In 1512, Erasmus published a work called *De copia* that taught its readers how to cultivate "copiousness," verbal richness, in discourse. The work obligingly provides, as a sample, a list of 144 different ways of saying "Thank you for your letter."

In Renaissance England, certain syntactic forms or patterns of words known as "figures" (also called "schemes") were shaped and repeated to confer beauty or heighten expressive power. Figures were usually known by their Greek and Latin names, though in an Elizabethan rhetorical manual, *The Arte of English Poesie*, George Puttenham made a valiant if short-lived attempt to give them English equivalents, such as "Hyperbole, or the

Overreacher" and "Ironia, or the Dry Mock." Those who received a grammar-school education throughout Europe at almost any point between the Roman Empire and the eighteenth century probably knew by heart the names of up to one hundred such figures, just as they knew by heart their multiplication tables. According to one scholar's count, William Shakespeare knew and made use of about two hundred.

As certain grotesquely inflated Renaissance texts attest, lessons from *De copia* and similar rhetorical guides could encourage prolixity and verbal self-display. Elizabethans had a taste for elaborate ornament in language as in clothing, jewelry, and furniture, and if we are to appreciate their accomplishments, it helps to set aside the modern preference, particularly in prose, for unadorned simplicity and directness. When, in one of the age's most fashionable works of prose fiction, John Lyly wishes to explain that the vices of his young hero, Euphues, are tarnishing his virtues, he offers a small flood of synonymous images: "The freshest colors soonest fade, the teenest [i.e., keenest] razor soonest turneth his edge, the finest cloth is soonest eaten with moths." Lyly's multiplication of balanced rhetorical figures sparked a small literary craze known as "Euphuism," which was soon ridiculed by Shakespeare and others for its formulaic excesses. Yet the multiplication of figures was a source of deep-rooted pleasure in rhetorical culture, and most of the greatest Renaissance writers used it to extraordinary effect. Consider, for example, the succession of images in Shakespeare's sonnet 73:

> That time of year thou mayst in me behold
> When yellow leaves, or none, or few, do hang
> Upon those boughs which shake against the cold,
> Bare ruined choirs, where late the sweet birds sang.
> In me thou seest the twilight of such day
> As after sunset fadeth in the west;
> Which by and by black night doth take away,
> Death's second self that seals up all in rest.
> In me thou seest the glowing of such fire
> That on the ashes of his youth doth lie,
> As the deathbed whereon it must expire,
> Consumed with that which it was nourished by.
>> This thou perceiv'st, which makes thy love more strong,
>> To love that well, which thou must leave ere long.

What seems merely repetitious in Lyly here becomes a subtle, poignant amplification of the perception of decay, through the succession of images from winter (or late fall) to twilight to the last glow of a dying fire. Each of these images is in turn sensitively explored, so that, for example, the season is figured by bare boughs that shiver, as if they were human, and then these anthropomorphized tree branches in turn are figured as the ruined choirs of a church where services were once sung. No sooner is the image of singers in a church choir evoked than these singers are instantaneously transmuted back into the songbirds who, in an earlier season, had sat upon the boughs, while these sweet birds in turn conjure up the poet's own vanished youth. And this nostalgic gaze extends, at least glancingly, to the chancels of the Catholic abbeys reduced to ruins by Protestant iconoclasm and the dissolution of the monasteries. All of this within the first four lines: here and elsewhere Shakespeare, along with other poets of his time, contrives to freight the small compass and tight formal constraints of the sonnet—fourteen lines of rhymed iambic pentameter—with remarkable emotional intensity, psychological nuance, and imagistic complexity. The effect is what Christopher Marlowe called "infinite riches in a little room."

Elizabethans were certainly capable of admiring plainness of speech—in *King Lear* Shakespeare contrasts the severe directness of the virtuous Cordelia to the "glib and oily art" of her wicked sisters—and such poets as George Gascoigne, Thomas Nashe, and, in the early seventeenth century, Ben Jonson wrote restrained, aphoristic, moralizing lyrics in a plain style whose power depends precisely on the avoidance of richly figurative verbal pyrotechnics. This power is readily apparent in the wintry spareness of Nashe's "A Litany in Time of Plague," with its grim refrain:

> Wit with his wantonness
> Tasteth death's bitterness;
> Hell's executioner
> Hath no ears for to hear
> What vain art can reply.
> I am sick, I must die.
>   Lord, have mercy on us!

Here the linguistic playfulness beloved by Elizabethan culture is scorned as an ineffectual "vain art" to which the executioner, death, is utterly indifferent.

But here and in other plain-style poetry, the somber, lapidary effect depends on a tacit recognition of the allure of the suppleness, grace, and sweet harmony that the dominant literary artists of the period so assiduously cultivated. Poetry, writes Puttenham, is "more delicate to the ear than prose is, because it is more current and slipper upon the tongue [i.e., flowing and easily pronounced], and withal tunable and melodious, as a kind of Music, and therefore may be termed a musical speech or utterance." The sixteenth century was an age of superb vocal music. The renowned composers William Byrd, Thomas Morley, John Dowland, and others scarcely less distinguished, wrote a rich profusion of madrigals (part songs for two to eight voices, unaccompanied) and airs (songs for solo voice, generally accompanied by the lute). These works, along with hymns, popular ballads, rounds, catches, and other forms of song, enjoyed immense popularity, not only in the royal court, where musical skill was regarded as an important accomplishment, and in aristocratic households, where professional musicians were employed as entertainers, but also in less exalted social circles. In his *Plain and Easy Introduction to Practical Music* (1597), Morley tells a story of social humiliation at a failure to perform that suggests that a well-educated Elizabethan was expected to be able to sight sing. Even if this is an exaggeration in the interest of book sales, there is evidence of impressively widespread musical literacy, a literacy reflected in a splendid array of music for the lute, viol, recorder, harp, and virginal as well as vocal music.

Many sixteenth-century poems were written to be set to music, but even those that were not often aspire in their metrical and syllabic virtuosity to the complex pleasures of madrigals or to the sweet fluency of airs. In poetry and music, as in gardens, architecture, and dance, Elizabethans had a taste for elaborate, intricate, but perfectly regular designs. They admired form, valued the artist's manifest control of the medium, and took pleasure in the highly patterned surfaces of things. Modern responses to art often evidence a suspicion of surfaces, impatience with order, the desire to rip away the mask to discover a hidden core of experiential truth: these responses are far less evident in Renaissance aesthetics than is a delight in pattern. Indeed many writers of the time expressed the faith that the universe itself had in its basic construction the beauty, concord, and harmonious order of a poem or a piece of music. "The world is made by Symmetry and proportion," wrote Thomas Campion, who was both a poet and a composer, "and is in that respect compared to Music, and Music to Poetry." The design of an exquisite work of art is deeply linked in this view to the design of the cosmos.

Such an emphasis on conspicuous pattern might seem to encourage an art as stiff as the starched ruffs that ladies and gentlemen wore around their necks, but the period's fascination with order was conjoined with a profound interest in persuasively conveying the movements of the mind and heart. Syntax in the sixteenth century was looser, more flexible than our own and punctuation less systematic. If the effect is sometimes confusing, it also enabled writers to follow the twists and turns of thought or perception. Consider, for example, Roger Ascham's account, in his book on archery, of a day in which he saw the wind blowing the new-fallen snow:

> That morning the sun shone bright and clear, the wind was whistling aloft, and sharp according to the time of the year. The snow in the highway lay loose and trodden with horse feet: so as the wind blew, it took the loose snow with it, and made it so slide upon the snow in the field which was hard and crusted by reason of the frost overnight, that thereby I might see very well, the whole nature of the wind as it blew that day. And I had a great delight and pleasure to mark it, which maketh me now far better to remember it. Sometime the wind would be not past two yards broad, and so it would carry the snow as far as I could see. Another time the snow would blow over half the field at once. Sometime the snow would tumble softly, by and by it would fly wonderful fast. And this I perceived also, that the wind goeth by streams and not whole together. . . . And that which was the most marvel of all, at one time two drifts of snow flew, the one of the West into the East, the other out of the North into the East: And I saw two winds by reason of the snow the one cross over the other, as it had been two highways. . . . The more uncertain and deceivable the wind is, the more heed must a wise Archer give to know the guiles of it.

What is delightful here is not only the author's moment of sharpened perception but his confidence that this moment—a glimpse of baffling complexity and uncertainty—can be captured in the restless succession of sentences and then neatly summed up in the pithy conclusion. (This effect parallels that of the couplet that sums up the complexities of a Shakespearean sonnet.) A similar confidence emanates from Sir Walter Ralegh's deeply melancholy, deeply ironic apostrophe to Death at the close of *The History of the World*, written when he was a prisoner in the Tower of London:

> O eloquent, just, and mighty Death! Whom none could advise, thou hast persuaded; what none hath dared, thou hast done; and whom all the world hath flattered, thou only hast cast out of the world and despised;

> thou hast drawn together all the far-stretched greatness, all the pride, cruelty, and ambition of man, and covered it all over with these two narrow words: *Hic jacet!* [Here lies]

Death is triumphant here, but so is Ralegh's eloquent, just, and mighty language.

The sense of *wonder* that animates both of these exuberant prose passages—as if the world were being seen clearly and distinctly for the first time—characterizes much of the period's poetry as well. The mood need not always be solemn. One can sense laughter, for example, rippling just below the surface of Marlowe's admiring description of the beautiful maiden Hero's boots:

> Buskins of shells all silvered usèd she,
> And branched with blushing coral to the knee,
> Where sparrows perched, of hollow pearl and gold,
> Such as the world would wonder to behold;
> Those with sweet water oft her handmaid fills;
> Which, as she went, would chirrup through the bills.

Seashells were beloved by Renaissance collectors because their intricate designs, functionally inexplicable, seemed the works of an ingenious, infinitely playful craftsman. Typically, the shells did not simply stand by themselves in cabinets but were gilded or silvered and then turned into other objects: cups, miniature ships, or, in Marlowe's fantasy, boots further decorated with coral and mechanical sparrows made of conspicuously precious materials and designed, as he puts it deliciously, to "chirrup." The poet knows perfectly well that the boots would be implausible footwear in the real world, but he invites us into an imaginary world of passion, a world in which the heroine's costume includes a skirt "whereon was many a stain, / Made with the blood of wretched lovers slain" and a veil of "artificial flowers and leaves, / Whose workmanship both man and beast deceives." The veil reflects an admiration for an art of successful imitation—after all, bees are said to look in vain for honey amid the artificial flowers—but it is cunning illusion rather than realism that excites Marlowe's wonder. Renaissance poetry is interested not in representational accuracy but in the magical power of exquisite workmanship to draw its readers into fabricated worlds.

In his *Defense of Poesy*, the most important work of literary criticism in sixteenth-century England, Sidney claims that this magical power is also a moral power. All other arts, he argues, are subjected to fallen, imperfect nature, but the poet alone is free to range "within the zodiac of his own wit" and create a second nature, superior to the one we are condemned to inhabit: "Her world is brazen, the poets only deliver a golden." The poet's golden world in this account is not an escapist fantasy; it is a model to be emulated in actual life, an ideal to be brought into reality as completely as possible. It is difficult to say, of course, how seriously this project of realization was taken—though the circumstances of Sidney's own death suggest that he may have been attempting to enact on the battlefield an ideal image of Protestant chivalry. A didactic role for poetry is, in any case, urged not by Sidney alone but by most Elizabethan poets. Human sinfulness has corrupted life, robbing it of the sweet wholesomeness that it had once possessed in Eden, but poetry can mark the way back to a more virtuous and fulfilled existence. And not only mark the way: poetry, Sidney and others argue, has a unique persuasive force that shatters inertia and impels readers toward the good they glimpse in its ravishing lines.

This force, attributed to the energy and vividness of figurative language, made poetry a fitting instrument not only for such high-minded enterprises as moral exhortation, prayer, and praise and for such uplifting narratives as the legends of religious and national heroes but also for such verbal actions as cursing, lamenting, flattering, and seducing. The almost inexhaustible range of motives was given some order by literary conventions that functioned as shared cultural codes, enabling poets to elicit particular responses from readers and to relate their words to other times, other languages, and other cultures. Among the most prominent of the clusters of conventions in the period were those that defined the major literary modes (or "kinds," as Sidney terms them): pastoral, heroic, lyric, satiric, elegiac, tragic, and comic. They helped shape subject matter, attitude, tone, and values, and in some cases—sonnet, verse epistle, epigram, funeral elegy, and masque, to name a few—they also governed formal structure, meter, style, length, and occasion. We can glimpse some of the ways in which these literary codes worked by looking briefly at two that are, for modern readers, among the least familiar: pastoral and heroic.

The conventions of the pastoral mode present a world inhabited by shepherds and shepherdesses who are concerned not just to tend their flocks but to fall in love and to engage in friendly singing contests. The mode celebrated leisure, humility, and contentment, exalting the simple country life over the city and its business, the military camp and its violence, the court and its burdens of rule. Pastoral motifs could be deployed in different genres. Pastoral songs commonly expressed the joys of the shepherd's life or his disappointment in love. Pastoral dialogues between shepherds might conceal serious, satiric comment on abuses in the great world under the guise of homely, local concerns. There were pastoral funeral elegies, pastoral dramas, pastoral romances (prose fiction), and even pastoral episodes within epics. The most famous pastoral poem of the period is Marlowe's "The Passionate Shepherd to His Love," an erotic invitation whose promise of gold buckles, coral clasps, and amber studs serves to remind us that, however much it sings of naive innocence, the mode is ineradicably sophisticated and urban.

With its rustic characters, simple concerns, and modest scope, the pastoral mode was regarded as situated at the opposite extreme from heroic, with its values of honor, martial courage, loyalty, leadership, and endurance, and its glorification of a nation or people. The chief genre here was the epic, typically a long, ambitious poem in the high style, based on a heroic story from the nation's distant past and imitating Homer and Virgil in structure and motifs. Renaissance poets throughout Europe undertook to honor their nations and their vernacular languages by writing this most prestigious kind of poetry. In sixteenth-century England the major success in heroic poetry is Spenser's *Faerie Queene*. Yet the success of *The Faerie Queene* owes much to the fact that the poem is a generic hybrid, in which the conventions of classical epic mingle with those of romance, medieval allegory, pastoral, satire, mythological narrative, comedy, philosophical meditation, and many others in a strange, wonderful blend. The spectacular mixing of genres in Spenser's poem is only an extreme instance of a general Elizabethan indifference to the generic purity admired by writers, principally on the Continent, who adhered to Aristotle's *Poetics*. Where such neoclassicists attempted to observe rigid stylistic boundaries, English poets tended to approach the different genres in the spirit of Sidney's inclusivism: "if severed they be good, the conjunction cannot be hurtful."

THE ELIZABETHAN THEATER

If Sidney welcomed the experimental intertwining of genres in both poetry and prose—and his own *Arcadia*, a prose romance incorporating both pastoral and heroic elements, confirms that he did—there was one place where he found it absurd: the theater. He condemned the conjunction of high and low characters in "mongrel" tragicomedies that mingled "kings and clowns." Moreover, in the spirit of neoclassical advocacy of the "dramatic unities," Sidney disliked the ease with which the action on the bare stage ("where you shall have Asia of the one side, and Afric of the other") violated the laws of time and space. "Now you shall have three ladies walk to gather flowers," he writes in *The Defense of Poesy*, "and then we must believe the stage to be a garden. By and by we hear news of shipwreck in the same place: and then we are to blame if we accept it not for a rock." The irony is that this mocking account, written probably in 1579, anticipates by a few years the stupendous achievements of Marlowe and Shakespeare, whose plays joyously break every rule that Sidney thought it essential to observe.

A permanent, freestanding public theater in England dates only from Shakespeare's own lifetime. A London playhouse, the Red Lion, is first mentioned in 1567, and James Burbage's playhouse, The Theater, was built in 1576. But it is quite misleading to identify English drama exclusively with the new, specially constructed playhouses, for in fact there was a rich and vital theatrical tradition in England stretching back for centuries. Townspeople in late medieval England mounted elaborate cycles of plays (sometimes called "mystery plays") depicting the great biblical stories, from the creation of the world to Christ's Passion and its miraculous aftermath. Many of these plays have been lost, but those that survive include magnificent and complex works of art. At once civic and religious festivals, the cycles continued to be performed into the reign of Elizabeth, but their close links to popular Catholic piety led Protestant authorities in the later sixteenth century to suppress them.

Early English theater was not restricted to these annual festivals. Performers acted in town halls and the halls of guilds and aristocratic mansions, on scaffolds erected in town squares and marketplaces, on pageant wagons in the streets, and in innyards. By the fifteenth century, and probably earlier, there were organized companies of players traveling under noble patronage. Such companies earned a precarious living providing amusement, while enhancing the prestige of the patron whose livery they wore and whose protection they enjoyed. (Otherwise, by statutes enjoining productive labor, actors without another, ordinary trade could have been classified as vagabonds and whipped or branded.) This practice explains why the professional acting companies of Shakespeare's time, including Shakespeare's own, attached themselves to a nobleman and were technically his servants (the Lord Chamberlain's Men, the Lord Admiral's Men, etc.), even though virtually all their time was devoted to entertaining the public, from whom most of their income derived.

The "Long View" of London, 1647, by Wenceslaus Hollar. In this detail from Hollar's engraving of London, one can glimpse, on the south bank of the Thames, the Globe Theater and an arena for bearbaiting. The labels were accidentally transposed in the original: the Globe is the round structure on the left.

Before the construction of the public theaters, the playing companies often performed short plays called "interludes" that were, in effect, staged dialogues on religious, moral, and political themes. Henry Medwall's *Fulgens and Lucrece* (ca. 1490–1501), for example, pits a wealthy but dissolute nobleman against a virtuous public servant of humble origins, while John Heywood's *The Play of the Weather* (ca. 1525–33) stages a debate among social rivals, including a gentleman, a merchant, a forest ranger, and two millers. The structure of such plays reflects the training in argumentation that students received in Tudor schools and, in particular, the sustained practice in examining both sides of a difficult question. Some of Shakespeare's amazing ability to look at critical issues from multiple perspectives may be traced back to this practice and the dramatic interludes it helped to inspire.

Another major form of theater that flourished in England in the fifteenth century and continued on into the sixteenth was the morality play, a dramatization of the spiritual struggle of the Christian soul. As *Everyman* (included in Volume A, "The Middle Ages") demonstrates, these dramas derived their power from the poignancy and terror of an individual's encounter with death. Often this somber power was supplemented by the extraordinary comic vitality of the evil character, or Vice.

If such plays sound more than a bit like sermons, it is because they were. The Church was a profoundly different institution from the theater, but its professionals shared some of the same rhetorical skills. It would be grossly misleading to regard churchgoing and playgoing as comparable entertainments, but clerical attacks on the theater sometimes make it sound as if ministers thought themselves to be in direct competition with professional players. The players, for their part, were generally too discreet to present themselves in a similar light, yet they almost certainly understood their craft as relating to sermons, with an uneasy blend of emulation and rivalry. When, in 1610, the theater manager Philip Rosseter was reported to have declared that plays were as good as sermons, he was summoned before the bishop of London to recant; but Rosseter had said no more than what many players must have privately thought.

By the later sixteenth century, many churchmen, particularly those with Puritan leanings, were steadfastly opposed to the theater, but some early Protestant Reformers, such as John Bale, tried their hand at writing plays. Thomas Norton, who with a fellow lawyer, Thomas Sackville, wrote the first English tragedy in blank verse, *Gorboduc, or Ferrex and Porrex* (1561), was also a translator of the great Reformer John Calvin. There is no evidence that Norton felt a tension between his religious convictions and his theatrical interests, nor was his play a private exercise. The five-act tragedy, a grim vision of Britain descending into civil war, was performed at the Inner Temple (one of London's law schools) and subsequently acted before the queen.

Gorboduc was closely modeled on the works of the Roman playwright Seneca, and Senecan influence—including violent plots, resounding rhetorical speeches, and ghosts thirsting for blood—remained pervasive in the Elizabethan theater, giving rise to the subgenre of revenge tragedy, in which a wronged protagonist plots and executes revenge, destroying himself (or herself) in the process. An early, highly influential example is Thomas Kyd's *Spanish Tragedy* (1592), and, despite its unprecedented psychological complexity, Shakespeare's *Hamlet* clearly participates in this kind. A related but distinct kind is the villain tragedy, in which the protagonist is blatantly evil: in his *Poetics*, Aristotle had advised against attempting to use a wicked person as the hero of a tragedy, but Shakespeare's *Richard III* and *Macbeth* amply justify the general English indifference to classical rules. Some Elizabethan tragedies, such as the fine *Arden of Feversham* (whose author is unknown), are concerned not with the fall of great men but with domestic violence; others, such as Christopher Marlowe's *Tamburlaine*, are concerned with "overreachers," larger-than-life heroes who challenge the limits of human possibility. Certain tragedies in the period, such as *Richard III*, intersect with another Elizabethan genre, the history play, in which dramatists staged the great events, most often conspiracies, rebellions, and wars, of the nation. Not all of the events commemorated in history plays were tragic, but they tend to circle back again and again to the act that epitomized what for this period was the ultimate challenge to authority: the killing of a king. When the English cut off the head of their king in 1649, they were performing a deed which they had been rehearsing, literally, for most of a century.

English schoolboys would read and occasionally perform comedies by the great Roman playwrights Plautus and Terence. Shortly before mid-century a schoolmaster, Nicholas Udall, used these as a model for a comedy in English, *Ralph Roister Doister*. At about the same time, another comedy, *Gammar Gurton's Needle*, which put vivid, native English material into classical form, was amusing the students at Cambridge. From the classical models English playwrights derived some elements of structure and content: plots based on intrigue, division into acts and scenes, and type characters such as the rascally servant and the *miles gloriosus* (cowardly braggart soldier). The latter type appears in *Ralph Roister Doister* and is a remote ancestor of Shakespeare's Sir John Falstaff in the two parts of *Henry IV* and *The Merry Wives of Windsor*.

Early plays such as *Gorboduc* and *Ralph Roister Doister* are rarely performed or read today, and with good reason. In terms of both dramatic structure and style, they are comparatively crude. Take, for example, this clumsy expression of passionate love by the title character in *Cambyses, King of Persia*, a popular play written around 1560 by a Cambridge graduate, Thomas Preston:

> For Cupid he, that eyeless boy, my heart hath so enflamed
> With beauty, you me to content the like cannot be named;
> For since I entered in this place and on you fixed mine eyes,
> Most burning fits about my heart in ample wise did rise.
> The heat of them such force doth yield, my corpse they scorch, alas!
> And burns the same with wasting heat as Titan doth the grass.
> And sith this heat is kindled so and fresh in heart of me,
> There is no way but of the same the quencher you must be.

Around 1590, an extraordinary change overcame the English drama, transforming it almost overnight into a vehicle for unparalleled poetic and dramatic expression. Many factors contributed to this transformation, but probably the chief was the eruption onto the scene of Christopher Marlowe. Compare Preston's couplets, written in a meter called "fourteeners," with the lines in Marlowe's *Doctor Faustus* (ca. 1592–93) with which Faustus greets the conjured figure of Helen of Troy:

> Was this the face that launched a thousand ships,
> And burnt the topless towers of Ilium?
> Sweet Helen, make me immortal with a kiss:
> Her lips sucks forth my soul, see where it flies!
> Come Helen, come, give me my soul again.
> Here will I dwell, for heaven be in these lips,
> And all is dross that is not Helena! (Scene 12, lines 81–87)

Marlowe has created and mastered a theatrical language—a superb unrhymed iambic pentameter, or blank verse—far more expressive than anything that anyone accustomed to the likes of Preston could have imagined.

Play-acting, whether of tragedies, comedies, or any of the other Elizabethan genres, took its place alongside other forms of public expression and entertainment as well. Perhaps the most important, from the perspective of the theater, were music and dance, because these were directly and repeatedly incorporated into plays. Moreover, virtually all plays in the period, including Shakespeare's, apparently ended with a dance. Brushing off the theatrical gore and changing their expressions from woe to pleasure, the actors in plays like *Doctor Faustus* and *King Lear* would presumably have received the audience's applause and then bid for a second round by performing a stately pavane or a lively jig.

Plays, music, and dancing were by no means the only shows in town. There were jousts, tournaments, royal entries, religious processions, pageants in honor of newly installed civic officials or ambassadors arriving from abroad; wedding masques, court masques, and costumed entertainments known as Disguisings or Mummings; juggling acts, fortune-tellers, exhibitions of swordsmanship, mountebanks, folk healers, storytellers, magic shows; bearbaiting, bullbaiting, cockfighting, and other blood sports; folk festivals such as Maying, the Feast of Fools, Carnival, and Whitsun Ales. For several years, Elizabethan Londoners were delighted by a trained animal—Banks's Horse—that could, it was thought, do arithmetic and answer questions. And there was always the grim but compelling spectacle of public shaming, mutilation, and execution.

Most English towns had stocks and whipping posts. Drunks, fraudulent merchants, adulterers, and quarrelers could be placed in carts or mounted backward on asses and paraded through the streets for crowds to jeer and throw refuse at. Women accused of being scolds could be publicly muzzled by an iron device called a brank or tied to a "cucking stool" and dunked in the river. Convicted criminals could have their ears cut off, their noses slit, their foreheads branded. Public beheadings and hangings were common. In the worst cases, felons were sentenced to be "hanged by the neck, and being alive cut down, and your privy members to be cut off, and your bowels to be taken out of your belly and there burned, you being alive." In the dismemberment with which Marlowe's *Doctor Faustus* ends, the audience

Scold's bridle, or brank. First recorded in Scotland, the scold's bridle was a device to humiliate and torture women who were regarded as "riotous" or "troublesome" in speech. The metal gag was designed to inflict maximum pain if the victim attempted to speak. In England, unruly women were also humiliated by being dragged through the streets in chairs known as "cucking stools," to be dunked.

was witnessing the theatrical equivalent of the execution of criminals and traitors that they could have also watched in the flesh, as it were, nearby.

Doctor Faustus was performed by the Lord Admiral's Men at the Rose Theater, one of four major public playhouses that by the mid-1590s were feverishly competing for crowds of spectators. These playhouses (including Shakespeare's famous Globe Theater, which opened in 1599) each accommodated some two thousand spectators and generally followed the same design: they were oval in shape, with an unroofed yard in the center where stood the groundlings (apprentices, servants, and others of the lower classes) and three rising tiers around the yard for men and women able to pay a higher price for places to sit and a roof over their heads. A large platform stage jutted out into the yard, surrounded on three sides by spectators (see the conjectural drawing of an Elizabethan playhouse in the appendices to this volume). These financially risky ventures relied on admission charges—it was an innovation of this period to have money advanced in the expectation of pleasure rather than offered to servants afterward as a reward—and counted on habitual playgoing fueled by a steady supply of new plays. The public playhouses were all located outside the limits of the city of London and, accordingly, beyond the jurisdiction of the city authorities, who were generally hostile to dramatic spectacles. Eventually, indoor theaters, artificially lighted and patronized by a more select audience, were also built inside the city, secured under conditions that would allow them some protection from those who wished to shut them down.

Why should what we now regard as one of the undisputed glories of the age have aroused so much hostility? One answer, curiously enough, is traffic: plays drew large audiences, and nearby residents objected to the crowds, the noise, and the crush of carriages. Other, more serious concerns were public health and crime. It was thought that many diseases, including the dreaded bubonic plague, were spread by noxious odors, and the packed playhouses were obvious breeding grounds for infection. (Patrons often tried to protect themselves by sniffing nosegays or stuffing cloves in their nostrils.) The large crowds drew pickpockets, cutpurses, and other scoundrels. On one memorable afternoon a pickpocket was caught in the act and tied for the duration of the play to one of the posts that held up the canopy above the stage. The theater was, moreover, a well-known haunt of prostitutes and, it was alleged, a place where innocent maids were seduced and respectable matrons corrupted. It was darkly rumored that "chambers and secret places" adjoined the theater galleries, and in any case, taverns, disreputable inns, and brothels were close at hand.

There were other charges as well. Plays were performed in the afternoon and therefore drew people, especially the young, away from their work. They were schools of idleness, luring apprentices from their trades, law students from their studies, housewives from their kitchens, and potentially pious souls from the sober meditations to which they might otherwise devote themselves. Moralists warned that the theaters were nests of sedition, and religious polemicists, especially Puritans, obsessively focusing on the use of boy actors to play the female parts, charged that theatrical transvestism excited illicit sexual desires, both heterosexual and homosexual.

But the playing companies had powerful allies, including Queen Elizabeth herself, and continuing popular support. One theater historian has estimated that between the late 1560s and 1642, when the playhouses were shut down by the English Civil War, well over fifty million visits were paid to the London theater, an astonishing figure for a city that had, by our standards, a very modest population. Plays were performed without the scene breaks and intermissions to which we are accustomed; there was no scenery and few props, but costumes were usually costly and elaborate. The players formed what would now be called repertory companies—that is, they filled the roles of each play from members of their own group, not employing outsiders. They performed a number of different plays on consecutive days, and the principal actors were shareholders in the profits of the company. Boys were apprenticed to actors just as they were apprenticed to master craftsmen in the guilds; they took the women's parts in plays until their voices changed. The plays might be bought for the company from freelance writers, or as in Shakespeare's company, the group might include an actor-playwright who could supply it with some (though by no means all) of its plays. The script remained the property of the company, but a popular play was eagerly sought by the printers, and the companies, which generally tried to keep their plays from appearing in print, sometimes had trouble guarding their rights. The editors of the earliest collected edition of Shakespeare, the First Folio (1623), complained about the prior publication of "divers stolen and surreptitious copies" of his plays, "maimed and deformed by the frauds and stealths of injurious imposters."

SURPRISED BY TIME

All of the ways we cut up time into units are inevitably distortions. The dividing line between centuries was not, as far as we can tell, a highly significant one for people in the Renaissance, and many of the most important literary careers cross into the seventeenth century without a self-conscious moment of reflection. But virtually everyone must have been aware, by the end of the 1590s, that the long reign of England's Queen Elizabeth was nearing its end, and this impending closure occasioned considerable anxiety. Childless, the last of her line, Elizabeth had steadfastly refused to name a successor. She continued to make brilliant speeches, to receive the extravagant compliments of her flatterers, and to exercise her authority—in 1601, she had her favorite, the headstrong earl of Essex, executed for attempting to raise an insurrection. But, as her seventieth birthday approached, she was clearly, as Ralegh put it, "a lady surprised by time." She suffered from bouts of ill health and melancholy; her godson Sir John Harington was dismayed to see her pacing through the rooms of her palace, striking at the tapestries with a sword. Her more astute advisers—among them Lord Burghley's son, Sir Robert Cecil, who had succeeded his father as her principal councillor—secretly entered into correspondence with the likeliest claimant to the throne, James VI of Scotland. Though the English queen had executed his Catholic mother, Mary, Queen of Scots, the Protestant James had continued to exchange polite letters with Elizabeth. It was at least plausible, as officially claimed, that in her dying breath, on March 24, 1603, Elizabeth designated James as her successor. A jittery nation that had feared a possible civil war at her death lit bonfires to welcome its new king. But in just a very few years, the English began to express nostalgia for the rule of "Good Queen Bess" and to look back on her reign as a magnificent high point in the history and culture of their nation.

THE SIXTEENTH CENTURY

TEXTS	CONTEXTS
	1485 Accession of Henry VII inaugurates Tudor dynasty
	ca. 1504 Leonardo da Vinci paints the *Mona Lisa*
ca. 1505–07 Amerigo Vespucci, *New World* and *Four Voyages*	**1508–12** Michelangelo paints Sistine Chapel ceiling
	1509 Death of Henry VII; accession of Henry VIII
1511 Desiderius Erasmus, *Praise of Folly*	
	1513 James IV of Scotland killed at Battle of Flodden; succeeded by James V
1516 Thomas More, *Utopia*. Ludovico Ariosto, *Orlando furioso*	
ca. 1517 John Skelton, "The Tunning of Elinour Rumming"	**1517** Martin Luther's Ninety-Five Theses; beginning of the Reformation in Germany
	1519 Cortés invades Mexico. Magellen begins his voyage around the world
1520s–30s Thomas Wyatt's poems circulating in manuscript	**1521** Pope Leo X names Henry VIII "Defender of the Faith"
1525 William Tyndale's English translation of the New Testament	
1528 Baldassare Castiglione, *The Courtier*	
	1529–32 More is Lord Chancellor
1532 Niccolò Machiavelli, *The Prince* (written 1513)	**1532–34** Henry VIII divorces Catherine of Aragon to marry Anne Boleyn; Elizabeth I born; Henry declares himself head of the Church of England
	1535 More beheaded
1537 John Calvin, *The Institution of Christian Religion*	**1537** Establishment of Calvin's theocracy at Geneva
	1542 Roman Inquisition. James V of Scotland dies; succeeded by infant daughter, Mary
1543 Copernicus, *On the Revolution of the Spheres*	
1547 *Book of Homilies*	**1547** Death of Henry VIII; accession of Protestant Edward VI
1549 *Book of Common Prayer*	
	1553 Death of Edward VI; failed attempt to put Protestant Lady Jane Grey on throne; accession of Catholic Queen Mary, daughter of Catherine of Aragon
	1555–56 Archbishop Cranmer and former bishops Latimer and Ridley burned at the stake
1557 Tottel's *Songs and Sonnets* (printing poems by Wyatt, Surrey, and others)	
	1558 Mary dies; succeeded by Protestant Elizabeth I

TEXTS	CONTEXTS
1563 John Foxe, *Acts and Monuments*	
1565 Thomas Norton and Thomas Sackville, *Gorboduc*, first English blank-verse tragedy (acted in 1561)	
1567 Arthur Golding, translation of Ovid's *Metamorphoses*	**1567–68** Mary, Queen of Scots, forced to abdicate; succeeded by her son James VI; Mary imprisoned in England
	1570 Elizabeth I excommunicated by Pope Pius V
	1572 St. Bartholomew's Day Massacre of French Protestants
	1576 James Burbage's playhouse, The Theater, built in London
	1577–80 Drake's circumnavigation of the globe
1578 John Lyly, *Euphues*	
1579 Edmund Spenser, *The Shepheardes Calender*	
1580 Montaigne, *Essais*	
	1583 Irish rebellion crushed
	1584–87 Sir Walter Ralegh's earliest attempts to colonize Virginia
	1586–87 Mary, Queen of Scots, tried for treason and executed
ca. 1587–90 Marlowe's *Tamburlaine* acted. Shakespeare begins career as actor and playwright	
1588 Thomas Hariot, *A Brief and True Report of . . . Virginia*	**1588** Failed invasion of the Spanish Armada
1589 Richard Hakluyt, *The Principal Navigations . . . of the English Nation*	
1590 Sir Philip Sidney, *Arcadia* (posthumously published); Spenser, *The Faerie Queene*, Books 1–3	
1591 Sidney, *Astrophil and Stella* published	
ca. 1592 John Donne's earliest poems circulating in manuscript	
1595 Sidney, *The Defense of Poesy* published	**1595** Ralegh's voyage to Guiana
1596 Spenser, *The Faerie Queene*, Books 4–6 (with Books 1–3)	
1598 Ben Jonson, *Every Man in His Humor*	
	1599 Globe Theater opens
	1603 Elizabeth I dies; succeeded by James VI of Scotland (as James I), inaugurating the Stuart dynasty

JOHN SKELTON
ca. 1460–1529

John Skelton was not a tame poet. There was something wild about him that continues to provoke, baffle, and fascinate readers. It is difficult to fit the varied pieces of his life together: gifted rhetorician, translator, Latin tutor to the young prince who became Henry VIII, disgruntled courtier, political pamphleteer, visionary, biting satirist, and ordained priest. He was also the major English poet of the first quarter of the sixteenth century, with the title of poet laureate from both Oxford and Cambridge. His poetic achievement, remarkable though it is, is equally difficult to place; as C. S. Lewis observes, Skelton had "no real predecessors and no important disciples" in the history of English verse. His poetry draws, to be sure, on a long tradition of medieval anticlerical satire and carnivalesque parody, but Skelton brings to his mature works a fresh, often extremely eccentric voice.

His early works were more routinely conventional—ornate compliments, dutiful elegies, occasional verses, and the like—but in a satire written at the end of the fifteenth century, *The Bowge of Court* (available in the NAEL Archive), Skelton gave unusually powerful expression to the anxiety of living in the dangerous, viciously competitive precincts of royal power. (The poem's main character is called "Dread.") A few years later, whether self-exiled or sent away by his enemies, Skelton was living far from the court: about 1503 he became the rector of the parish church at Diss, in Norfolk, where he remained for some eight years. By 1512 he had returned to court, having been appointed *orator regius*, or "the king's orator." He moved to a house in the sanctuary of Westminster Abbey in 1518 and shortly thereafter, in a series of satires including *Speak, Parrot; Colin Clout;* and *Why Come Ye Not to Court?* (1521–22), began vituperative attacks on Cardinal Wolsey, the great prelate-statesman. Wolsey had Skelton briefly imprisoned but released him and promptly hired his services for himself.

Skelton's poems gain their most startling effects by mixing high and low styles and by playing bawdy and scatological verbal games with some of his culture's most respected and authoritative texts: the ancient classics, the poetry of Chaucer, the canonical works of logic and rhetoric taught at Oxford and Cambridge, and even the Catholic liturgy. The latter games were not necessarily sacrilegious—for the Catholic Church, before the challenge of the Reformation, was capable of tolerating a wide range of expression—but they seem deliberately risk-taking, provocative, and obstreperous, an impression heightened by the way they are written. In the satires, Skelton rejects the ornate rhetorical devices and aureate language that characterized his period's most ambitious poetry; he writes in short rhymed lines, having from two to five beats, and the lines can keep on rhyming helter-skelter until the resources of the language give out. To many of his poems, with their aggressive and restless energies, this strange verse form is singularly appropriate. "The Tunning of Elinour Rumming" is, for example, a wonderfully clattering, apparently disordered portrait of an alewife, and the "skeltonics," as this way of writing has come to be called, contribute to the effect of disorder. The voice of the narrator of the satires has a breathless urgency that was much admired by twentieth-century poets, while to contemporary ears, its attention to detail, madcap rhymes, and brash tone are strikingly reminiscent of rap.

The English Reformation, which was set in motion shortly after Skelton's death, would drastically alter the context in which his work was received. English Protestants later in the century had trouble knowing what to make of the "rude railing rhymer," as the Elizabethan critic George Puttenham called Skelton. On the one hand, his satires of Cardinal Wolsey made him ripe for inclusion (with Langland and others) in the honor roll of supposedly proto-Protestant poets. Yet on the other hand, as a foul-mouthed and frivolous priest, Skelton could serve equally well as an emblem of the alleged corruption of the Catholic clergy. He also became associated with various tales and jests that seemed nostalgically to recall the innocence and "merriment" of pre-Reformation England. (In one of these, Skelton proudly ascends the pulpit to show off his naked illegitimate baby to his astonished parishioners.) For English society, as for English poetry, Skelton quickly came to represent the path not taken.*

Mannerly Margery Milk and Ale[1]

	Aye, beshrew° you, by my fay,°	*curse / faith*
	These wanton clerks[2] be nice° alway,	*foolish*
	Avaunt, avaunt, my popagay![3]	
	"What, will ye do nothing but play?"	
5	Tilly vally straw,[4] let be I say!	
	Gup,[5] Christian Clout, gup, Jack of the Vale!	
	With Mannerly Margery milk and ale.	
	"By God, ye be a pretty pode,°	*toad*
	And I love you an whole cartload."	
10	Straw, James Foder, ye play the fode,°	*deceiver, flatterer*
	I am no hackney° for your rod:°	*horse / riding*
	Go watch a bull, your back is broad!	
	Gup, Christian Clout, gup, Jack of the Vale!	
	With Mannerly Margery milk and ale.	
15	Ywis° ye deal uncourteously;	*truly*
	What, would ye frumple° me? now fie!	*rumple, tumble*
	"What, and ye shall not be my pigsny?"[6]	
	By Christ, ye shall not, no hardily:	
	I will not be japed° bodily!	*tricked, deceived*
20	Gup, Christian Clout, gup, Jack of the Vale!	
	With Mannerly Margery milk and ale.	
	"Walk forth your way, ye cost me naught;	
	Now have I found that° I have sought:	*that which*
	The best cheap flesh that ever I bought."	
25	Yet, for his love that hath all wrought,	
	Wed me, or else I die for thought.°	*i.e., of distress*
	Gup, Christian Clout, your breath is stale!	
	With Mannerly Margery milk and ale!	

* In addition to *The Bowge of Court*, the NAEL Archive includes an excerpt from *Colin Clout*, with the author's own account of "skeltonics," as well as two additional short poems.
1. The poem is a song for three voices. The seducer's lines are in quotation marks; Margery sings the rest, except the chorus, which is sung by a bass.
2. Educated men: students, scholars, clergymen.
3. Popinjay, parrot—i.e., vain fellow.
4. An exclamation of impatience: Nonsense!
5. "Go on!" (usually addressed to horses).
6. Pig's eye. Here used as a (rough) term of endearment.

Gup, Christian Clout, gup, Jack of the Vale!
30 With Mannerly Margery milk and ale.

ca. 1495   1523

With lullay, lullay, like a child

With lullay, lullay, like a child,
Thou sleepest too long, thou art beguiled.°   *deceived*
"My darling dear, my daisy flower,
Let me," quod° he, "lie in your lap."   *quoth*
5   "Lie still," quod she, "my paramour,°   *lover*
Lie still, hardily,° and take a nap."   *confidently*
His head was heavy, such was his hap,°   *fortune, lot*
All drowsy dreaming, drowned in sleep,
That of his love he took no keep.°   *care*
10 With hey lullay, lullay, like a child,
Thou sleepest too long, thou art beguiled.

With ba, ba, ba! and bas,[1] bas, bas!
She cherished him, both cheek and chin,
That he wist° never where he was;   *knew*
15 He had forgotten all deadly sin.
He wanted wit[2] her love to win,
He trusted her payment and lost all his prey;
She left him sleeping and stale° away,   *stole*
With hey lullay, lullay, like a child,
20 Thou sleepest too long, thou art beguiled.

The rivers rowth,° the waters wan,   *rough*
She sparèd not to wet her feet;
She waded over, she found a man
That halsèd° her heartily and kissed her sweet—   *embraced*
25 Thus after her cold she caught a heat.
"My lief,"° she said, "routeth° in his bed;   *lover / snores*
Ywis° he hath an heavy head."   *truly*
With hey lullay, lullay, like a child,
Thou sleepest too long, thou art beguiled.

30 What dreamest thou, drunkard, drowsy pate?°   *head*
Thy lust and liking[3] is from thee gone.
Thou blinkard blowboll,[4] thou wakest too late:
Behold thou liest, luggard,° alone!   *sluggard*
Well may thou sigh, well may thou groan,
35 To deal with her so cowardly.
Ywis, pole-hatchet, she bleared thine eye.[5]

1495–1500   1527

---

1. Kiss. "Ba": the "by" of *lullaby*.
2. Lacked sufficient intelligence.
3. Your pleasure and enjoyment.

4. Blink-eyed drunkard.
5. Deceived you. "Pole-hatchet": a soldier who carried a poleax.

From The Tunning of Elinour Rumming[1]

Secundus Passus[2]

Some have no money
That thither comey,
For their ale to pay;
That is a shrewd array!°   *sorry state of affairs*
5 Elinour sweared, "Nay,
Ye shall not bear away
My ale for nought,
By Him that me bought."
With, "Hey, dog, hey,
10 Have these hogs away!"
With, "Get me a staff,
The swine eat my draff!°   *refuse, dregs*
Strike the hogs with a club,
They have drunk up my swilling-tub!"° *tub for stirring*
15 For, be there never so much prese,° *crowd*
These swine go to the high dese;[3]
The sow with her pigs;
The boar his tail wrigs,°   *wriggles*
His rump also he frigs°   *rubs*
20 Against the high bench!
With, "Fo, there is a stench!
Gather up, thou wench;
Seest thou not what is fall?°   *has fallen*
Take up dirt° and all,   *dung*
25 And bear out of the hall:
God give it ill preving°   *ill success*
Cleanly as evil cheving!"°   *bad luck*
  But let us turn plain
There° we left° again.   *where / left off*
30 For as ill a patch° as that   *poor piece of ground*
The hens run in the mash-fat;°   *mixing vat*
For they go to roost
Straight over the ale-joust,°   *ale pot*
And dung, when it comes,
35 In the ale tuns.°   *barrels*
Then Elinour taketh
The mash-bowl, and shaketh
The hens' dung away,
And skommeth° it in a tray   *skims*
40 Whereas the yeast is,
With her mangy fistis,°   *fists*
And sometime she blens
The dung of her hens
And the ale together;

---

1. This rowdy poem—whose heroine really did keep an alehouse in Surrey—recounts Elinour's brewing practices ("tunning") and the social life in her establishment.
2. *Second Section* (Latin).
3. Go to the dais; i.e., take the best place.

45 And saith, "Gossip,° come hither,   *friend*
This ale shall be thicker,
And flower° the more quicker;   *froth*
For I may tell you,
I learned it of a Jew,
50 When I began to brew,
And I have found it true;
Drink now while it is new;
And ye may it brook,[4]
It shall make you look
55 Younger than ye be,
Years two or three,
For ye may prove it by me.
Behold," she said, "and see
How bright I am of ble!°   *complexion*
60 Ich° am not cast away,   *I*
That can my husband say,
When we kiss and play
In lust and in liking;
He calleth me his whiting,[5]
65 His mulling and his miting,
His nobs° and his cony,°   *dear / bunny*
His sweeting and his honey,
With, 'Bas,° my pretty bonny,   *kiss*
Thou art worth good° and money!'   *goods*
70 Thus make I my falyre fonny,°   *make my fellow foolish*
Till that he dream and dronny,°   *laze*
For after all our sport,
Then will he rout° and snort;   *snore*
Then sweetly together we lie
75 As two pigs in a sty."
  To cease meseemeth best,
And of this tale to rest,
And for to leave this letter,°   *text, subject*
Because it is no better,
80 And because it is no sweeter;
We will no farther rhyme
Of it at this time,
But we will turn plain
Where we left again.[6]

1517?   ca. 1545

---

4. If you can tolerate it.
5. A small white fish—here a term of endearment, like "mulling" (meaning unclear) and "miting" (mite) in line 65.
6. I.e., go back to where we left off.

SIR THOMAS MORE
1478–1535

Sir Thomas More is one of the most brilliant, compelling, and disturbing figures of the English Renaissance. He has been the hero of people who, given the chance, would (and on occasion did) tear each other apart: the Catholic Church in 1935 made him a saint; leading Communists celebrated his book *Utopia* as a forerunner of their plan to abolish private property; and middle-class liberals have admired his vision of free public education, careers open to talents, and freedom of thought. But at the same time each of these groups has been deeply troubled by aspects of More's life and writings: the Catholic bishops of sixteenth-century Spain and Portugal placed *Utopia* on their list of prohibited books; Karl Marx reserved his most bitter scorn for those impractical socialists he branded as "utopian"; and liberals have noticed uneasily that More embraced the idea of the forced labor camp. Robert Bolt's play (and film) *A Man for All Seasons* celebrates More for his steadfast probity and humanity, while a pair of recent novels—Hilary Mantel's *Wolf Hall* and *Bring Up the Bodies* (books also adapted for the stage and television)—depicts him as a dangerous, wily fanatic.

More was born in London, the son of a prominent lawyer. As a boy he served as a page in the grand household of the archbishop of Canterbury, John Morton, who was also King Henry VII's lord chancellor. It is reported that at Christmastime, when wandering actors would perform plays at the archbishop's palace, young More would step in among the players and improvise a part for himself. This early talent for improvisation characterized More throughout his life, as did a lingering sense that he was never quite at home in any of the parts he played. (In the famous portrait of More by Hans Holbein the Younger—included in the color insert in this volume— More may well have been wearing a hair shirt under his rich robe of office.)

He studied at Oxford and at the Inns of Court, but he did not automatically follow in his father's footsteps. He was torn between a career as a lawyer, with its promise of wealth and access to power, and a life of religious devotion. For some four years, according to one of his early biographers, he lived as a layman among the ascetic monks in London's Charterhouse, but deciding that he wanted to marry, he turned toward a secular career in public affairs. Still, amid his law practice, his position as an undersheriff of London, his participation in Parliament and on the king's council, his service in diplomatic and commercial negotiations, and ultimately his three tumultuous years as lord chancellor, More constantly showed signs of reserving some part of himself for other realms. One of those realms was his growing family, to whom he was a devoted and loving father, but he himself spoke of his familial concerns as a kind of business that took him away from the life of the mind. Shortly after the completion of his law studies, he gave a series of public lectures on Saint Augustine's monumental work *The City of God*, and theological and moral arguments continued to fascinate him until his death. He also had a passion for Greek and Latin literature, a passion he shared with his close friend Desiderius Erasmus of Rotterdam (ca. 1466–1536), the greatest humanist scholar of the Northern Renaissance.

Erasmus and More shared not only the profound classical learning that lay at the heart of the humanist movement but also an ardent Christian piety, a suspicion of scholastic hairsplitting, a delight in rhetoric, a taste for the ancient satirist Lucian, and a lively interest in experimental, unsettling wit. For Erasmus this interest bore fruit in his most enduring work, *The Praise of Folly* (1511), which he completed as a guest in More's London house and dedicated to him. For More, the love of playful, subversive wit culminated in *Utopia*, which he began in 1515 while in the Netherlands on a diplomatic mission for Henry VIII and finished the next year. Both works, written in Latin and quickly circulated among humanists throughout Europe, are daring intellectual games that call into question the period's most cherished assumptions.

Utopia displays the strong influence of Plato's *Republic*, in its radically communalistic reimagining of society, but it was also shaped by more contemporary influences: monastic communities, which forbade private property and required everyone to labor; emerging market societies, with their emphasis on education and social mobility over hereditary privilege and their dislike of the old warrior aristocracy; the recurrent outcries of peasant rebels demanding a more just distribution of wealth; and explicitly, Amerigo Vespucci's published accounts of his voyages to the newly discovered lands across the Atlantic Ocean. Those voyages disclosed a whole world organized on principles utterly unlike those that governed European societies, a world seemingly free of the inequality, economic exploitation, dynastic squabbles, and legal chicanery that More observed everywhere around him.

Vespucci's letters, part sober reportage, part wild fantasy, helped More imagine an alternative to the world he inhabited. Book II of *Utopia* (the part of the work More composed first) describes in detail the laws and customs of a country that bears some striking physical resemblances to England. But, in other ways, how unlike England it is! The abolition of money and private property has prevented any neurotic attachment to goods and status, and the parasitic classes—nobles, lawyers, idle priests, rapacious soldiers—have been eliminated. In Utopia, a well-ordered political democracy, education is free and universal. Instead of the misery of oppressed peasants, there are prosperous collective farms. Instead of stench and suffering in crowded, crooked streets, there are gleaming, rational cities, with free hospitals and child care. Because everyone works, no one is overburdened; and there is ample time for all citizens to pursue the arts of peace and the pleasures of the mind and the body.

The picture of England in Book I of *Utopia*—beggars in the streets, convicted petty thieves hanging from the gibbets, hungry farmers displaced from lands fenced off for more profitable sheep rearing, cynical flatterers encouraging the king to embark on imperialistic wars—makes the sharpest contrast imaginable with the ordered and peaceable state described in Book II. Yet Book I is not, or not directly, a call for revolutionary social reform. It is, rather, a meditation, in the form of a dialogue, on the question of whether intellectuals should involve themselves in politics. The two speakers in the dialogue are a traveler named Raphael Hythloday and someone named Thomas More, who closely resembles but perhaps should not be identified precisely with the real More. More argues that Hythloday, with his extraordinary learning, experience, and high principles, should offer his services as a councillor to one of the great monarchs of Europe. Hythloday counters that kings, who want only flattery from their councillors, would never dream of adopting the radical policies, such as the abandonment of warfare and the abolition of private property, which alone might lead to a good society. In the dialogue, Hythloday is the aloof idealist, unwilling to dirty his hands in a pointless cause; More is the sincere pragmatist, prepared to compromise with the system and seek to change it from within rather than give up on any possibility of action. In Book I, the debate between Hythloday and More has no clear winner; but not long after completing *Utopia*, the real Thomas More entered the council of Henry VIII.

Book II, Hythloday's narrative of his visit to Utopia, is also in some sense a dialogue, a complex, often ambiguous meditation on the nature of the ideal commonwealth. The dialogue form not only allows the actual Thomas More some rhetorical cover for caustic critiques in both books of the social policy of his own country but also encourages the reader to register the disturbing underside of More's island commonwealth: Utopia is a society that rests on slavery, including enslavement for social deviance. There is no variety in dress or housing or cityscape, and no privacy. Citizens are encouraged to value pleasure, but they are constantly monitored, lest their pursuit of pleasure pass the strict bounds set by "nature" or "reason." There are constitutional guarantees of freedom of thought and toleration of religious diversity, but people who fail to believe in divine providence and the afterlife are regarded as subhuman and, accordingly, not treated as citizens. The Utopians officially despise war, but they nevertheless appear to fight a good many of them. It is very difficult to gauge More's attitude toward his imaginary commonwealth; perhaps he himself could not have said with any absolute certainty what it was.

If there is deep ambivalence in More's attitude toward Utopia, there is no comparable ambivalence in the other great work he wrote at approximately the same time, *The History of King Richard III*. (A celebrated passage—on Tudor England's favorite fallen woman—is included in the NAEL Archive.) In More's influential account, Richard III, the last Yorkist king, was an unmitigated monster, twisted in mind and body, subtle, hypocritical, and murderous. This account, obviously appealing to the Tudors, whose dynasty was founded on Richard's overthrow, was incorporated verbatim into several sixteenth-century chronicles and so came down to Shakespeare, whose *Richard III* (ca. 1592) fixed the portrait of Richard as a deformed, homicidal tyrant.

More wrote *Utopia* in Latin, for an international audience of humanist intellectuals; he wrote *Richard III*, which he left unfinished, in both Latin and English versions. The English text, in prose of great energy and suppleness, suggests that he was, in this highly charged vernacular account of the recent past, thinking of a different readership, more national in scope and interests. In his subsequent works, he continued to address both audiences on the matters that most concerned him, but he never repeated the mode of either playful speculation or historical narrative. Instead he focused on theology, moral philosophy, and religious controversy. (A characteristic excerpt is included in "Faith in Conflict," pp. 151–53.) Though his wit and irony are everywhere evident in these writings, they are yoked to the service of an increasingly desperate struggle.

The struggle was against Lutheranism, which began to make inroads into England precisely during the period of More's rise to great power. More, an ardent Catholic, hated the central tenets of the Protestant Reformation and fought its adherents with every means at his disposal, including book burnings, imprisonment, and execution. As Henry VIII's confidant and, finally, lord chancellor (1529–32), he played for a time a significant role in the war on heresy, but he resigned his high office when the king, seeking a divorce in order to marry Anne Boleyn, broke with the Roman Catholic Church. When More was required to take the oath for the Act of Succession, acknowledging that the rightful claim to the throne would lie with Henry's children by Anne, and to state his approval of the Act of Supremacy, affirming that the king rather than the pope was the supreme head of the Church in England, he declined. He attempted to remain silent, but the king treated his silence as a refusal and deemed this refusal to be treason. Against the pleadings of his family, More maintained his silence, choosing, as he put it, "to die the king's good servant, but God's first." In 1535 he was beheaded. Four hundred years later he was canonized by the Catholic Church as Saint Thomas More.

Utopia[1]

CONCERNING THE BEST
STATE OF A COMMONWEALTH
AND THE NEW ISLAND
OF UTOPIA

A Truly Golden Handbook
No Less Beneficial Than Entertaining
by the Most Distinguished and Eloquent Author
THOMAS MORE
Citizen and Undersheriff[2] of the Famous City
of London

Thomas More to Peter Giles,[3] Greetings

My very dear Peter Giles, I am almost ashamed to be sending you after nearly a year this little book about the Utopian commonwealth, which I'm sure you expected in less than six weeks. For, as you were well aware, I faced no problem in finding my materials, and had no reason to ponder the arrangement of them. All I had to do was repeat what you and I together heard Raphael[4] describe. There was no occasion, either, for labor over the style, since what he said, being extempore and informal, couldn't be couched in fancy terms. And besides, as you know, he's a man not so well versed in Latin as in Greek; so that my language would be nearer the truth, the closer it approached to his casual simplicity. Truth in fact is the only quality at which I should have aimed, or did aim, in writing this book.

I confess, friend Peter, that having all these materials ready to hand left hardly anything at all for me to do. Otherwise, thinking through a topic like this from scratch and disposing it in proper order might have demanded no little time and work even if a man were not entirely deficient in talent and learning. And then if the matter had to be set forth with eloquence, not just factually, there's no way I could have done that, however hard I worked, for however long a time. But now when I was relieved of all these problems, over which I could have sweated forever, there was nothing for me to do but simply write down what I had heard. Well, little as it was, that task was rendered almost impossible by my many other obligations. Most of my day is given to the law—pleading some cases, hearing others, compromising

---

1. More coined the word "Utopia" from Greek *ou* ("not")+*topos* ("place"): "Noplace"; perhaps with a pun on *eu*+*topos*, "Happy" or "Fortunate" Place. The book was written in Latin and published— elaborately titled, as below—on the European continent under the supervision of More's friend the great Dutch humanist Desiderius Erasmus (ca. 1466–1536). This translation is by Robert M. Adams, as published in the Norton Critical Edition of *Utopia* (3rd ed., 2011), with revisions by George M. Logan.
2. As an undersheriff, More's principal duty was to serve as a judge in the Sheriff's Court, a city

court that heard a wide variety of cases.
3. Giles (ca. 1486–1533) was both a humanistic scholar and a practical man of affairs, city clerk of Antwerp. Erasmus had recommended him and More to each other, and they met in Antwerp in the summer of 1515 (see pp. 47–48); *Utopia* seems to have originated in conversations between them. In the first edition of the book, this letter is called its Preface.
4. I.e., the fictitious character Raphael Hythloday. His given name associates him with the archangel Raphael, traditionally a guide and healer.

others, and deciding still others. I have to visit this man because of his official position and that man because of his business; and so almost the whole day is devoted to other people's business and the rest to my own; and then for myself—that is, my studies—there's nothing left.

For when I get home, I have to talk with my wife, chatter with my children, and consult with the servants. All these matters I consider part of my business, since they have to be done, unless a man wants to be a stranger in his own house. Besides, you are bound to bear yourself as agreeably as you can toward those whom nature or chance or your own choice has made the companions of your life. But of course you mustn't spoil them with your familiarity, or by overindulgence turn the servants into your masters. And so, amid these concerns, the day, the month, and the year slip away.

What time do I find to write, then? especially since I still have taken no account of sleeping or even of eating, to which many people devote as much time as to sleep itself, which consumes almost half of our lives.[5] My own time is only what I steal from sleeping and eating. It isn't very much, but it's something, and so I've finally been able to finish *Utopia*, even though belatedly, and I'm sending it to you now. I hope, my dear Peter, that you'll read it over and let me know if you find anything that I've overlooked. Though I'm not really afraid of having forgotten anything important—I wish my judgment and learning were up to my memory, which isn't half bad—still, I don't feel so sure of it that I would swear I've missed nothing.

For my servant John Clement[6] has raised a great doubt in my mind. As you know, he was there with us, for I always want him to be present at conversations where there's profit to be gained. (And one of these days I expect we'll get a fine crop of learning from this young sprout, who's already made excellent progress in Greek as well as Latin.) Anyhow, as I recall matters, Hythloday said the bridge over the Anyder at Amaurot[7] was five hundred yards long; but my John says that is two hundred yards too much—that in fact the river is not more than three hundred yards wide there. So I beg you, consult your memory. If your recollection agrees with his, I'll yield to the two of you, and confess myself mistaken. But if you don't recall the point, I'll follow my own memory and keep my present figure. For, as I've taken particular pains to avoid having anything false in the book, so, if anything is in doubt, I'd rather say something untrue than tell a lie. In short, I'd rather be honest than clever.

But the whole matter can easily be cleared up if you'll ask Raphael about it—either face to face or else by letter. And I'm afraid you must do this anyway, because of another problem that has cropped up—whether through my fault, or yours, or Raphael's, I'm not sure. For it didn't occur to us to ask, nor to him to say, in what area of the New World Utopia is to be found. I wouldn't have missed hearing about this for a sizable sum of money, for I'm quite ashamed not to know even the name of the ocean where this island

---

5. More's 16th-century biographer Thomas Stapleton says he slept four or five hours a night, rising at 2 A.M.
6. Clement (d. 1572) had entered More's household by 1514, as servant and pupil. He later became a respected physician.

7. From Greek: "made dark or dim." "Hythloday": its first root is surely Greek *hythlos*, "nonsense"; the second part is probably from *daiein*, "to distribute"—hence, together, "nonsense-peddler." "Anyder": waterless (also from Greek).

lies about which I've written so much. Besides, there are various people here, and one in particular, a devout man and a professor of theology, who very much wants to go to Utopia. His motive is not by any means idle curiosity, a hankering after new sights, but rather a desire to foster and further the growth of our religion, which has made such a happy start there. To do this properly, he has decided to arrange to be sent there by the pope, and even to be named bishop to the Utopians. He feels no particular scruples about applying for this post, for he considers it a holy ambition, arising not from motives of glory or gain, but simply from religious zeal.[8]

Therefore I beg you, my dear Peter, to get in touch with Hythloday—in person if you can, or by letters if he's gone—and make sure that my work contains nothing false and omits nothing true. It would probably be just as well to show him the book itself. If I've made a mistake, there's nobody better qualified to correct me; but even he cannot do it, unless he reads over my book. Besides, you will be able to discover in this way whether he's pleased or annoyed that I have written the book. If he has decided to write out his own story himself, he may not want me to do so; and I should be sorry, too, if, in publicizing the Utopian commonwealth, I had robbed him and his story of the flower of novelty.

But to tell the truth, I'm still of two minds as to whether I should publish the book at all. For the tastes of mortals are so various, the tempers of some are so severe, their minds so ungrateful, their judgments so foolish, that there seems no point in publishing something, even if it's intended for their advantage, that they will receive only with contempt and ingratitude. Better simply to follow one's own natural inclinations, lead a merry life, and ignore the vexing problems of publication. Most people know nothing of learning; many despise it. The clod rejects as too difficult whatever isn't cloddish. The pedant dismisses as mere trifling anything that isn't stuffed with obsolete words. Some readers approve only of ancient authors; many men like only their own writing. Here's a man so solemn he won't allow a shadow of levity, and there's one so insipid of taste that he can't endure the salt of a little wit. Some dullards dread satire as a man bitten by a rabid dog dreads water;[9] some are so changeable that they like one thing when they're seated and another when they're standing.

These people lounge around the taverns, and as they swill their ale pass judgment on the intelligence of writers. With complete assurance they condemn every author by his writings, just as they think best, plucking each one, as it were, by the beard. But they themselves remain safe and, as the proverb has it, out of harm's way. No use trying to lay hold of them; they're shaved so close, there's not so much as a hair of their heads to catch them by.

Finally, some people are so ungrateful that even though they're delighted with a work, they don't like the author any better because of it. They are like rude guests who, after they have stuffed themselves with a splendid dinner, go off, carrying their full bellies homeward without a word of thanks to the host who invited them. A fine task, providing at your own

---

8. Tradition has it that this zealous theologian was Rowland Phillips, warden of Merton College, Oxford. But there is no real support for the identification, and the passage may be wholly fabricated.

9. A late-stage symptom of rabies, which gives the disease its other name, hydrophobia.

expense a banquet for men of such finicky palates and such various tastes, who will remember and reward you with such thanks!

At any rate, my dear Peter, will you take up with Hythloday the points I spoke of? After I've heard from him, I'll take a fresh look at the whole matter. But since I've already taken the pains to write up the subject, it's too late to be wise. In the matter of publication, I hope we can have Hythloday's approval; after that, I'll follow the advice of my friends—and especially yours. Farewell, my dear Peter Giles. My regards to your excellent wife. Love me as you have always done; I am more fond of you than ever.

THE BEST STATE OF A COMMONWEALTH
A DISCOURSE BY THE EXTRAORDINARY
RAPHAEL HYTHLODAY
AS RECORDED BY THE NOTED THOMAS MORE
CITIZEN AND UNDERSHERIFF OF LONDON
THE FAMOUS CITY OF GREAT BRITAIN

Book I

The most invincible king of England, Henry, the eighth of that name, a prince adorned with the royal virtues beyond any other, had recently some differences of no slight import with Charles, the most serene prince of Castille,[1] and sent me into Flanders as his spokesman to discuss and settle them. I was companion and associate to that incomparable man Cuthbert Tunstall,[2] whom the king has recently created master of the rolls, to everyone's great satisfaction. I will say nothing in praise of this man, not because I fear the judgment of a friend might be questioned, but because his integrity and learning are greater than I can describe and too well known everywhere to need my commendation—unless I would, according to the proverb, "light up the sun with a lantern."

Those appointed by the prince to deal with us, all excellent men, met us at Bruges by prearrangement. Their head and leader was the mayor of Bruges, a most distinguished person. But their main speaker and guiding spirit was Georgius de Theimseke, the provost of Cassel, a man eloquent by nature as well as by training, very learned in the law, and most skillful in diplomatic affairs through his ability and long practice. After we had met several times, certain points remained on which we could not come to agreement; so they adjourned the meetings and went to Brussels for some days to learn their prince's pleasure.

Meanwhile, since my business required it, I went to Antwerp.[3] Of those who visited me while I was there, no one was more welcome than Peter Giles.

---

1. Later (1519), as Charles V, he became the Holy Roman Emperor. By 1515 he had already (at age fifteen) inherited the Low Countries, and he was soon to become king of Spain. The matters in dispute between him and Henry VIII concerned especially the trade in English wool.
2. An admired scholar and influential cleric, Tunstall (1474–1559) was appointed ambassador to Brussels in May 1515 and a year later became master of the rolls (principal clerk of the Chancery Court).
3. Antwerp and Brussels are about equidistant (sixty miles) from Bruges.

He was a native of Antwerp, a man of high reputation, already appointed to a good position and worthy of the very best: I hardly know whether the young man is more distinguished in learning or in character. Apart from being cultured, virtuous, and courteous to all, with his intimates he is so open-hearted, affectionate, loyal, and sincere that you would be hard-pressed to find anywhere a man comparable to him in all the points of friendship. No one is more modest or more frank; none better combines simplicity with wisdom. His conversation is so pleasant, and so witty without malice, that the ardent desire I felt to see again my native country, my wife, and my children (from whom I had been separated more than four months) was much eased by his agreeable company and delightful talk.

One day after I had heard mass at Nôtre Dame, the most beautiful and most popular church in Antwerp, I was about to return to my quarters when I happened to see him talking with a stranger, a man of quite advanced years. The stranger had a sunburned face, a long beard, and a cloak hanging loosely from his shoulders; from his appearance and dress, I took him to be a ship's captain. When Peter saw me, he approached and greeted me. As I was about to return his greeting, he drew me aside, and, indicating the stranger, said, "Do you see that fellow? I was just on the point of bringing him to you."

"He would have been very welcome on your behalf," I answered.

"And on his own too, if you knew him," said Peter, "for there is no mortal alive today can tell you so much about unknown peoples and lands; and I know that you're always greedy for such information."

"In that case," said I, "my guess wasn't a bad one, for at first glance I supposed he was a skipper."

"Then you're far off the mark," he replied, "for his sailing has not been like that of Palinurus, but more that of Ulysses, or rather of Plato.[4] This man, who is named Raphael—his family name is Hythloday—knows a good deal of Latin, and is particularly learned in Greek. He studied Greek more than Latin because his main interest is philosophy, and in that field he found that the Romans have left us nothing very valuable except certain works of Seneca and Cicero.[5] Being eager to see the world, he left to his brothers the patrimony to which he was entitled at home (he is a native of Portugal) and took service with Amerigo Vespucci.[6] He was Vespucci's constant companion on the last three of his four voyages, accounts of which are now common reading everywhere; but on the last voyage, he did not return home with the commander. After much persuasion and expostulation he got Amerigo's permission to be one of the twenty-four men who were left in a fort at the farthest point of the last voyage.[7] Being marooned in this way was altogether agreeable to him, as he was more anxious to pursue his travels than afraid of death. He would often say, 'The man who has no grave is covered by the sky,'

---

4. Palinurus—Aeneas's pilot, who dozed over his steering oar and fell overboard (*Aeneid* 5.833ff.)—is an exemplar of the careless traveler; Ulysses, of the person who learns from traveling; and Plato (who made trips to Sicily and Egypt), of the person who travels to learn.

5. The great orator Cicero (106–43 B.C.E.), though not a philosopher, in his writings rehearsed at length the views of the various philosophical schools. Seneca (ca. 4 B.C.E.–65 C.E.) was the foremost Roman Stoic philosopher.

6. The Florentine explorer was sponsored first by the king of Spain and later by the king of Portugal and was reputed to have made four trips to the New World, starting in 1497. Accounts of his voyages published in the opening years of the 16th century were widely circulated and made his exploits more famous than the more substantial explorations of Columbus and Cabot.

7. Reputedly at Cape Frio, east of present-day Rio de Janeiro.

and 'The road to heaven is the same length from all places.'[8] Yet this frame of mind would have cost him dear, if God had not been gracious to him. After Vespucci's departure, he traveled through many countries with five companions from the garrison. At last, by strange good fortune, he got, via Ceylon, to Calicut, where he opportunely found some Portuguese ships; and so, beyond anyone's expectation, he returned to his own country."[9]

When Peter had told me this, I thanked him for his great kindness in wishing to introduce me to a man whose conversation he hoped I would enjoy, and then I turned to Raphael. After we had greeted each other and exchanged the usual civilities of strangers upon their first meeting, we all went off to my house. There in the garden we sat down on a bench covered with turf, to talk together.

He told us that when Vespucci sailed away, he and his companions who had stayed behind in the fort often met with the people of the countryside, and by ingratiating speeches gradually won their friendship. Before long they came to dwell with them safely and even affectionately. The prince (I have forgotten his name and that of his country) also gave them his favor, furnishing Raphael and his five companions not only with ample provisions but with means for traveling—rafts when they went by water, wagons when they went by land. In addition, he sent with them a most trusty guide, who was to conduct them to other princes to whom he heartily recommended them. After many days' journey, he said, they came to towns and cities, and to commonwealths that were both very populous and not badly governed.

To be sure, under the equator and as far on both sides of the line as the sun moves, there lie vast empty deserts, scorched with perpetual heat. The whole region is desolate and squalid, grim and uncultivated, inhabited by wild beasts, serpents, and also by men no less wild and dangerous than the beasts themselves. But as you go on, conditions gradually grow milder. The sun is less fierce, the earth greener, the creatures less savage. At last you reach people, cities, and towns which not only trade among themselves and with their neighbors but even carry on commerce by sea and land with remote countries. After that, he said, they were able to visit different lands in every direction, for he and his companions were welcome as passengers aboard any ship about to make a journey.

The first vessels they saw were flat-bottomed, he said, with sails made of stitched papyrus-reeds or wicker, or elsewhere of leather. Farther on, they found ships with pointed keels and canvas sails, in every respect like our own.[1] The seamen were not unskilled in managing wind and water; but they were most grateful to him, Raphael said, for showing them the use of the compass, of which they had been ignorant. For that reason, they had formerly sailed with great timidity, and only in summer. Now they have such trust in the compass that they no longer fear winter at all, and tend to be overconfident rather than cautious. There is some danger that through their imprudence this device, which they thought would be so advantageous to them, may become the cause of much mischief.

8. Both these dicta have classical sources: the epic poet Lucan (Seneca's nephew), *Pharsalia* 7.819; and Cicero, *Tusculan Disputations* 1.43.104.
9. Thus becoming the first circumnavigator of the globe. (Magellan's men completed the trip in 1522.) Calicut is a seaport on the west coast of India.
1. As a matter of fact, the indigenous peoples of South America, when they traveled by water, used canoes made from hollowed logs. In general, More's depiction is fanciful.

It would take too long to repeat all that Raphael told us he had observed in each place, nor would it make altogether for our present purpose. Perhaps on another occasion we shall tell more about the things that are most profitable, especially the wise and sensible institutions that he observed among the civilized nations. We asked him many eager questions about such things, and he answered us willingly enough. We made no inquiries, however, about monsters, for nothing is less new or strange than they are. Scyllas, ravenous Celaenos, man-eating Lestrygonians,[2] and that sort of monstrosity you can hardly avoid, but well and wisely trained citizens you will hardly find anywhere. While he told us of many ill-considered usages in these new-found nations, he also described quite a few other customs from which our own cities, nations, races, and kingdoms might take example in order to correct their errors. These I shall discuss in another place, as I said. Now I intend to relate only what he told us about the customs and institutions of the Utopians,[3] first recounting the conversation that led him to speak of that commonwealth. Raphael had been talking very sagely about the faulty arrangements and also the wise institutions found in that hemisphere and this (many of both sorts in each), speaking as shrewdly about the manners and governments of each place he had visited as though he had lived there all his life. Peter was amazed.

"My dear Raphael," he said, "I'm surprised that you don't enter some king's service; for I don't know of a single prince who wouldn't be eager to employ you. Your learning and your knowledge of various countries and peoples would entertain him, while your advice and your supply of examples would be very helpful in the council chamber. Thus you might advance your own interests and be useful at the same time to all your relatives and friends."

"I am not much concerned about my relatives and friends," he replied, "because I consider that I have already done my duty by them. While still young and healthy, I distributed among my relatives and friends the possessions that most men do not part with till they are old and sick (and then only reluctantly, because they can no longer keep them). I think they should be content with this gift of mine, and not expect that for their sake I should enslave myself to any king whatever."

"Well said," Peter replied; "but I do not mean that you should be in servitude to any king, only in his service."

"The difference is only a matter of one syllable," said Raphael.

"All right," said Peter, "but whatever you call it, I do not see any other way in which you can be so useful to your friends or to the general public, in addition to making yourself happier."

"Happier indeed!" exclaimed Raphael. "Would a way of life so absolutely repellent to my spirit make my life happier? As it is now, I live as I please, and I fancy very few courtiers, however splendid, can say that. As a matter of fact, there are so many men soliciting favors from the powerful that it will be no great loss if they have to do without me and a couple of others like me."

---

2. Scylla and the Lestrygonians were Homeric bogeys: the former, a six-headed sea monster (*Odyssey* 12.73ff.); the latter, giant cannibals (*Odyssey* 10.80ff.). Celaeno, one of the Harpies (birds with women's faces), appears in the *Aeneid* (3.209ff.).
3. As J. H. Hexter argues (*More's "Utopia": The*

Biography of an Idea [1952], pp. 18–21), it is almost certain that at this point More opened a seam in the original version of *Utopia*—which evidently included only the account of the Utopian commonwealth (now Book II) and the opening pages of what is now Book I—to insert the additions that constitute the remainder of Book I.

Then I said, "It is clear, my dear Raphael, that you seek neither wealth nor power, and indeed I value and revere a man of such a disposition as much as I do the mightiest persons in the world. Yet I think if you would devote your time and energy to public affairs, you would do a thing worthy of a generous and philosophical nature, even if you did not much like it. You could best perform such a service by joining the council of some great prince and inciting him to just and noble actions (as I'm sure you would): for a people's welfare or misery flows in a stream from their prince, as from a never-failing spring. Your learning is so full, even if it weren't combined with experience, and your experience is so great, even apart from your learning, that you would be an extraordinary counselor to any king in the world."

"You are twice mistaken, my dear More," he replied, "first in me and then in the situation itself. I don't have the capacity you ascribe to me, and if I had it in the highest degree, the public would still not be any better off if I exchanged my contemplative leisure for this kind of action. In the first place, most princes apply themselves to the arts of war, in which I have neither ability nor interest, instead of to the good arts of peace. They are generally more set on acquiring new kingdoms by hook or by crook than on governing well those they already have. Moreover, the counselors of kings are all so wise already that they need no advice from anyone else (or at least that's the way they see it). At the same time, they approve and even flatter the most absurd statements of favorites through whose influence they seek to stand well with the prince. It is only natural, of course, that each man should think his own opinions best: the crow loves his fledgling, and the ape his cub.

"Now in a court composed of people who envy everyone else and admire only themselves, if a man should suggest something he had read of in other ages or seen in practice elsewhere, the other counselors would think their reputation for wisdom was endangered and they would look like simpletons, unless they could find fault with his proposal. If all else failed, they would take refuge in some remark like this: 'The way we're doing it was good enough for our ancestors, and I only hope we're as wise as they were.' And with this deep thought they would take their seats, as though they had said the last word on the subject—implying, of course, that it would be a very dangerous matter if anyone were found to be wiser in any point than his ancestors were. As a matter of fact, we have no misgivings about neglecting the best examples they have left us; but if something better is proposed, we eagerly seize upon the excuse of reverence for times past and cling to it desperately. Such proud, obstinate, ridiculous judgments I have encountered many times, and once even in England."

"What!" I said. "Were you ever in my country?"

"Yes," he answered, "I spent several months there. It was not long after the revolt of the Cornishmen against the king had been put down, with the miserable slaughter of the rebels.[4] During my stay I was deeply beholden to the reverend father John Cardinal Morton,[5] archbishop of Canterbury, and in

---

4. Angered by the greedy taxation of Henry VII, an army of Cornishmen marched on London in 1497 but were defeated at the Battle of Blackheath.
5. Morton (1420–1500) was a distinguished prelate, statesman, and administrator. More's father, following a custom of the age, sent his son to serve as a page for two years (1490–92) in the cardinal's household; the seventy-year-old Morton is said to have been so impressed with the twelve-year-old More that he arranged for his education at Oxford.

addition at that time lord chancellor of England. He was a man, my dear Peter (for More knows about him, and can tell what I'm going to say), as much respected for his wisdom and virtue as for his authority. He was of medium height, not bent over despite his years; his looks inspired respect rather than fear. In conversation, he was not forbidding, though serious and grave. When suitors came to him on business, he liked to test their spirit and presence of mind by speaking to them sharply, though not rudely. He liked to uncover these qualities, which were those of his own nature, as long as they were not carried to the point of effrontery; and he thought such men were best qualified to carry on business. His speech was polished and pointed; his knowledge of the law was great; he had an incomparable understanding and a prodigious memory, for he had improved extraordinary natural abilities by study and practice. At the time when I was in England, the king relied heavily on his advice, and he seemed the chief support of the nation as a whole. He had been taken from school to court when scarcely more than a boy, had devoted all his life to important business, and had acquired from weathering violent changes of fortune and many great perils a supply of practical wisdom, which is not soon lost when so purchased.

"One day when I was dining with him, there was present a layman, learned in the laws of your country, who for some reason took occasion to praise the rigid execution of justice then being practiced upon thieves. They were being executed everywhere, he said, with as many as twenty at a time being hanged on a single gallows. And then he declared that he could not understand how so many thieves sprang up everywhere, when so few of them escaped hanging. I ventured to speak freely before the cardinal, and said, 'There is no need to wonder: this way of punishing thieves goes beyond the call of justice, and is not, in any case, for the public good. The penalty is too harsh in itself, yet it isn't an effective deterrent. Simple theft[6] is not so great a crime that it ought to cost a man his life, yet no punishment however severe can withhold those from robbery who have no other way to eat. In this matter not only you in England but a good part of the world seem to imitate bad schoolmasters, who would rather whip their pupils than teach them. Severe and terrible punishments are enacted against theft, when it would be much better to enable every man to earn his own living, instead of being driven to the awful necessity of stealing and then dying for it.'

"'Oh, we've taken care of that,' said the fellow. 'There are the trades and there is farming, by which men may make a living unless they choose deliberately to be rogues.'

"'Oh no you don't,' I said, 'you won't get out of it that way. We may disregard for the moment the cripples who come home from foreign and civil wars, as lately from the Cornish battle and before that from your wars with France. These men, who have lost limbs in the service of king and country, are too badly crippled to follow their old trades, and too old to learn new ones. But since wars occur only from time to time, let us, I say, disregard these men, and consider what happens every day. There are a great many noblemen who live idly like drones off the labor of others, their tenants whom they bleed white by constantly raising their rents. (This is the only

6. Theft is "simple" when not accompanied by violence or intimidation.

instance of their tightfistedness, because they are prodigal in everything else, ready to spend their way to the poorhouse.) These noblemen drag around with them a great train of idle servants,[7] who have never learned any trade by which they could earn a living. As soon as their master dies, or they themselves fall ill, they are promptly turned out of doors, for lords would rather support idlers than invalids, and the son is often unable to maintain as big a household as his father had, at least at first. Those who are turned off soon set about starving, unless they set about stealing. What else can they do? Then when a wandering life has left their health impaired and their clothes threadbare, when their faces look pinched and their garments tattered, men of rank will not care to engage them. And country people dare not do so, for they don't have to be told that one who has been raised softly to idle pleasures, who has been used to swaggering about with sword and buckler, is likely to look down on the whole neighborhood and despise everybody else as beneath him. Such a man can't be put to work with spade and mattock; he will not serve a poor man faithfully for scant wages and sparse diet.'

" 'But we ought to encourage these men in particular,' said the lawyer. 'In case of war the strength and power of our army depend on them, because they have a bolder and nobler spirit than workmen and farmers have.'

" 'You may as well say that thieves should be encouraged for the sake of wars,' I answered, 'since you will never lack for thieves as long as you have men like these. In fact thieves don't make bad soldiers, and soldiers turn out to be pretty good robbers—so nearly are these two ways of life related. But the custom of keeping too many retainers is not peculiar to this nation; it is common to almost all of them. France suffers from an even more grievous plague. Even in peacetime—if you can call it peace—the whole country is crowded with foreign mercenaries, imported on the same principle that you've given for your noblemen keeping idle servants.[8] Wise fools think that the public safety depends on having ready a strong army, preferably of veteran soldiers. They think inexperienced men are not reliable, and they sometimes hunt out pretexts for war, just so they may have trained soldiers and experienced cutthroats—or, as Sallust neatly puts it, that "hand and spirit may not grow dull through lack of practice."[9] But France has learned to her cost how pernicious it is to feed such beasts. The examples of the Romans, the Carthaginians, the Syrians,[1] and many other peoples show the same thing; for not only their governments but their fields and even their cities were ruined more than once by their own standing armies. Besides, this preparedness is unnecessary: not even the French soldiers, practiced in arms from their cradles, can boast of having often got the best of your raw recruits.[2] I shall say no more on this point, lest I seem to flatter present

7. Some of these were household servants; others were the last vestiges of the private armies by which, under feudalism, every lord was followed.
8. Charles VII of France (reigned 1422–61) had tried to establish a national army, but his successors reverted to mercenaries, mostly Swiss infantrymen.
9. Paraphrasing the *Catiline* (16.3) of the Roman historian Sallust (86–35 B.C.E.).
1. The Romans and Carthaginians both had to

fight servile wars against gladiators and mercenaries. The victimizers of the Syrians that Hythloday has in mind are probably the Mamelukes, a military caste of foreign extraction that ruled, from the 13th century to the early 16th, a state that included much of the Middle East.
2. Past English victories over the French included Crécy (1346), Poitiers (1356), and Henry V's triumph at Agincourt (1415).

company. At any rate, neither your town workmen nor your rough farm laborers—except for those whose physiques aren't suited for strength or boldness, or whose spirits have been cowed by inability to feed their families—seem to be much afraid of fighting the idle attendants of noblemen. So you need not fear that retainers, once strong and vigorous (for that's the only sort noblemen deign to corrupt), but now soft and flabby because of their idle, effeminate life, would be weakened if they were taught practical crafts to earn their living, and trained to manly labor. Anyway, I cannot think it's in the public interest to maintain for the emergency of war such a vast multitude of people who trouble and disturb the peace. You never have war unless you choose it, and peace is always more to be considered than war. Yet this is not the only circumstance that makes thieving necessary. There is another one, which, I believe, applies more especially to you Englishmen.'

"'What is that?' asked the cardinal.

"'Your sheep,' I replied, 'that used to be so meek and eat so little. Now they have become so greedy and fierce that they devour human beings themselves, as I hear.[3] They devastate and depopulate fields, houses, and towns. For in whatever parts of the land the sheep yield the softest and most expensive wool, there the nobility and gentry, yes, and even some abbots—holy men—are not content with the old rents that the land yielded to their predecessors. Living in idleness and luxury, without doing any good to society, no longer satisfies them; they have to do positive harm. For they leave no land free for the plow: they enclose every acre for pasture; they destroy houses and abolish towns, keeping only the churches, and those for sheep-barns. And as if enough of your land were not already wasted on woods and game-preserves, these worthy men turn all human habitations and cultivated fields back to wilderness. Thus one greedy, insatiable glutton, a frightful plague to his native country, may enclose many thousand acres of land within a single hedge. The tenants are dismissed; some are stripped of their belongings by trickery or brute force, or, wearied by constant harassment, are driven to sell them. By hook or by crook these miserable people—men, women, husbands, wives, orphans, widows, parents with little children, whole families (poor but numerous, since farming requires many hands)—are forced to move out. They leave the only homes familiar to them, and they can find no place to go. Since they cannot afford to wait for a buyer, they sell for a pittance all their household goods, which would not bring much in any case. When that little money is gone (and it's soon spent in wandering from place to place), what remains for them but to steal, and so be hanged—justly, you'd say!—or to wander and beg? And yet if they go tramping, they are jailed as idle vagrants. They would be glad to work, but they can find no one who will hire them. There is no need for farm labor, in which they have been trained, when there is no land left to be planted. One herdsman or shepherd can look after a flock of beasts large enough to stock an area that would require many hands if it were plowed and harvested.

3. This vivid image introduces Hythloday's treatment of the social dislocation brought about by "enclosure"—the gradual amalgamation and fencing, over a period extending from the 12th century to the 19th, of the open fields of the feudal system: one incentive to the practice was the increasing profitability of the wool trade.

"'This enclosing has had the effect of raising the price of food in many places. In addition, the price of raw wool has risen so much that poor people who used to make cloth are no longer able to buy it, and so great numbers are forced from work to idleness. One reason is that after the enlarging of the pasture-land, a murrain killed a great number of sheep—as though God were punishing greed by sending a plague upon the animals, which in justice should have fallen on the owners! But even if the number of sheep should increase greatly, their price will not fall a penny. The reason is that the wool trade, though it can't be called a monopoly, because it isn't in the hands of one single person, is concentrated in few hands (an oligopoly, you might say), and these so rich that the owners are never pressed to sell until they have a mind to, and that is only when they can get their price.

"'For the same reason other kinds of livestock also are priced exorbitantly, the more so because with so many farmhouses being pulled down, and farming in a state of decay, there are not enough people to look after the breeding of animals. These rich men will not breed other animals as they do lambs, but buy them lean and cheap, fatten them in their own pastures, and then sell them at a high price. I don't think the full impact of this bad system has yet been felt. We know these dealers raise prices where the fattened animals are sold. But when, over a period of time, they keep buying beasts from other localities faster than they can be bred, then as the supply gradually diminishes where they are purchased, a severe shortage is bound to ensue. So your island, which seemed especially fortunate in this matter, will be ruined by the crass avarice of a few. For the high food prices cause everyone to dismiss as many retainers as he can from his household; and what, I ask, can these men do, but rob or beg? And a man of courage is more likely to steal than to cringe.

"'To make this hideous poverty and scarcity worse, they exist side by side with wanton luxury.[4] Not only the servants of noblemen, but tradespeople, even some farmers, and people of every social rank are given to ostentatious dress and gluttonous greed. Look at the eating houses, the bawdy houses, and those other places just as bad, the wine bars and alehouses. Look at all the crooked games of chance, dice, cards, backgammon, tennis, bowling, and quoits, in which money slips away so fast. Don't all these lead their habitués straight to robbery? Banish these blights, make those who have ruined farmhouses and villages restore them, or hand them over to someone who will rebuild. Restrict the right of the rich to buy up anything and everything, and then to exercise a kind of monopoly. Let fewer people be brought up in idleness. Let agriculture be restored and the wool manufacture revived as an honest trade, so there will be useful work for the whole crowd of those now idle—whether those whom poverty has already made into thieves, or those whom vagabondage and habits of lazy service are converting, just as surely, into the robbers of the future.

"'If you do not find a cure for these evils, it is futile to boast of your justice in punishing theft. Your policy may look superficially like justice, but in

4. Luxurious living was not, in fact, characteristic of the reign of the parsimonious Henry VII (when Hythloday is supposed to be addressing Cardinal Morton). More is projecting onto the earlier period, perhaps unconsciously, a kind of extravagant display that began in 1509 with the accession of Henry VIII.

reality it is neither just nor practical. If you allow young folk to be abominably brought up and their characters corrupted, little by little, from childhood; and if then you punish them as grownups for committing crimes to which their early training has inclined them, what else is this, I ask, but first making them thieves and then punishing them for it?'

"As I was speaking thus, the lawyer had made ready his answer, choosing the usual style of disputants who are better at summing up than at replying, and who like to show off their memory. So he said to me, 'You have talked very well for a stranger, but you have heard about more things than you have been able to understand correctly. I will make the matter clear to you in a few words. First, I will summarize what you have said; then I will show how you have been misled by ignorance of our customs; finally, I will demolish all your arguments and reduce them to rubble. And so to begin where I promised, on four points you seemed to me—'

"'Hold your tongue,' said the cardinal, 'for you won't be finished in a few words, if this is the way you start. We will spare you the trouble of answering now, and reserve the pleasure of your reply till our next meeting, which will be tomorrow, if your affairs and Raphael's permit it. Meanwhile, my dear Raphael, I am eager to hear why you think theft should not be punished with death, or what other punishment you think would be more in the public interest. For I'm sure even you don't think it should go unpunished entirely. Even as it is, the fear of death does not restrain evildoers; once they were sure of their lives, as you propose, what force or fear could restrain them? They would look on a lighter penalty as an open invitation to commit more crimes—it would be like offering them a reward.'

"'It seems to me, most kind and reverend father,' I said, 'that it's altogether unjust to take someone's life for taking money. Nothing in the world that fortune can bestow is equal in value to a human life. If they say the thief suffers not for the money, but for violation of justice and transgression of laws, then this extreme justice should really be called extreme injury.[5] We ought not to approve of these fierce Manlian edicts[6] that invoke the sword for the smallest violations. Neither should we accept the Stoic view that considers all crimes equal,[7] as if there were no difference between killing a man and taking a coin from him. If equity means anything, there is no proportion or relation at all between these two crimes. God has said, "Thou shalt not kill"; shall we kill so readily for the theft of a bit of small change? Perhaps it will be argued that God's commandment against killing does not apply where human law allows it. But then what prevents men from making other laws in the same way—perhaps even laws legalizing rape, adultery, and perjury? God has taken from each person the right not only to kill another, but even to kill himself. If mutual consent to human laws on manslaughter entitles men freely to exempt their agents from divine law and allows them to kill those condemned by human decrees where God has given no precedent, what is this but preferring the law of man to the law of God? The result will be that in every situation men will decide for themselves how far it suits

---

5. Echoing the classical adage *summum ius, summa iniuria*, long cited in discussions of equity.
6. Proverbially strict, like those imposed by the Roman consul Titus Manlius in the 4th century

B.C.E. Manlius executed his own son for disobeying one of them.
7. This view was actually maintained by some of the ancient Stoic philosophers.

them to observe the laws of God. The law of Moses was harsh and severe, as for an enslaved and stubborn people, but it punished theft with a fine, not death.[8] Let us not think that in his new law of mercy, where he rules us with the tenderness of a father, God has given us greater license to be cruel to one another.

"'These are the reasons why I think it is wrong to put thieves to death. But surely everybody knows how absurd and even harmful to the public welfare it is to punish theft and murder alike. If theft carries the same penalty as murder, the thief will be encouraged to kill the victim whom otherwise he would only have robbed. When the punishment is the same, murder is safer, since one conceals both crimes by killing the witness. Thus while we try to terrify thieves with extreme cruelty, we really invite them to kill the innocent.

"'As for the usual question of what more suitable punishment can be found, in my judgment it would be much easier to find a better one than a worse. Why should we question the value of the punishments long used by the Romans, who were most expert in the arts of government? They condemned those convicted of heinous crimes to work, shackled, for life, in stone quarries and mines. But of all the alternatives, I prefer the method which I observed in my Persian travels, among the people commonly called the Polylerites.[9] They are a sizable nation, not badly governed, free and subject only to their own laws, except that they pay annual tribute to the Persian king. Living far from the sea, they are nearly surrounded by mountains. Being contented with the products of their own land, which is by no means unfruitful, they do not visit other nations, nor are they much visited. According to their ancient customs, they do not try to enlarge their boundaries, and easily protect themselves behind their mountains by paying tribute to their overlord. Thus they have no wars and live in a comfortable rather than a showy manner, more contented than renowned or glorious. Indeed, I think they are hardly known by name to anyone but their next-door neighbors.

"'In their land, whoever is found guilty of theft must make restitution to the owner, not (as elsewhere) to the prince; they think the prince has no more right to the stolen goods than the thief. If the stolen property has disappeared, its value is repaid from the thief's possessions. Whatever remains of those is handed over to his wife and children, while the thief himself is sentenced to hard labor.

"'Unless their crimes were compounded with atrocities, thieves are neither imprisoned nor shackled, but go freely and unconstrained about their work on public projects. If they shirk and do their jobs slackly, they are not chained, but they are whipped. If they work hard, they are treated without any indignities, except that at night after roll call they are locked up in their dormitories. Apart from constant work, they undergo no discomfort in living. As they work for the public good, they are decently fed out of the public stores, though arrangements vary from place to place. In some districts they are supported by alms. Unreliable as this support may seem, the Polylerites are so compassionate that no way is found more rewarding. In other places, public revenues are set aside for their support, or a special tax is levied on

8. The Mosaic law is that spelled out in the first verses of Exodus 22. It provides various penalties for theft, but nowhere death. This is contrasted with the "new law" of Christ, under which England is supposed to be operating.
9. From Greek: "the People of Much Nonsense."

every individual for their use; and sometimes they do not do public work, but anyone in need of workmen can go to the market and hire some of them by the day at a set rate, a little less than that for free men. If they are lazy, it is lawful to whip them. Thus they never lack for work, and each one of them brings a little profit into the public treasury beyond the cost of his keep.

"'They are all dressed in clothes of the same distinctive color. Their hair is not shaved but trimmed close about the ears,[1] and the tip of one ear is cut off. Their friends are allowed to give them food, drink, or clothing, as long as it is of the proper color; but to give them money is death, both to the giver and to the taker. It is just as serious a crime for any free man to take money from them for any reason whatever; and it is also a capital crime for any of these slaves (as the condemned are called) to carry weapons. In each district of the country they are required to wear a special badge. It is a capital crime to throw away the badge, to go beyond one's own district, or to talk with a slave of another district. Plotting escape is no more secure than escape itself: it is death for any other slave to know of a plot to escape, and slavery for a free man. On the other hand, there are rewards for informers— money for a free man, freedom for a slave, and for both of them pardon and amnesty. Thus it can never be safer for them to persist in an illicit scheme than to renounce it.

"'Such are their laws and policies in this matter. It is clear how mild and practical they are, for the aim of the punishment is to destroy vices and save men. The criminals are treated so that they become good of necessity, and for the rest of their lives they atone for the wrong they have done before. There is so little danger of relapse that travelers going from one part of the country to another think slaves the most reliable guides, changing them at the boundary of each district. The slaves have no means of committing robbery, since they are unarmed, and any money in their possession is evidence of a crime. If caught, they would be punished, and there is no hope of escape anywhere. Since every bit of a slave's clothing is unlike the usual clothing of the country, how could a slave escape, unless he fled naked? Even then his cropped ear would give him away. Might not the slaves form a conspiracy against the government? Perhaps. But the slaves of one district could hardly expect to succeed unless they first involved in their plot the slave-gangs of many other districts. And that is impossible, since they are not allowed to meet or talk together or even to greet one another. No one would risk a plot when they all know joining is so dangerous to the participant and betrayal so profitable to the informer. Besides, no one is quite without hope of gaining his freedom eventually if he accepts his punishment in the spirit of obedience and patience, and gives promise of future good conduct. Indeed, every year some are pardoned as a reward for their submissive behavior.'

"When I had finished this account, I added that I saw no reason why this system could not be adopted even in England, and with much greater advan-

1. At this point in the text, the early editions have a marginal gloss—in translation, "Yet nowadays the servants of noblemen think such a haircut quite handsome." This is one of a series of some two hundred glosses, which were supplied by Peter Giles after Erasmus shared More's manuscript with him. The glosses range in length from a single word to a full sentence and provide a valuable record of the response to *Utopia* (especially to Book II, where they are heavily concentrated) by a particularly well-positioned member of the humanist audience for it. The present edition includes a selection of the more pungent glosses, as footnotes.

tage than the 'justice' which my legal antagonist had praised so highly. But the lawyer replied that such a system could never be established in England without putting the commonwealth in serious peril. And so saying, he shook his head, made a wry face, and fell silent. And all the company sided with him.

"Then the cardinal remarked, 'It is not easy to guess whether this scheme would work well or not, since nobody has yet tried it out. But perhaps when the death sentence has been passed on a thief, the king might reprieve him for a time without right of sanctuary,[2] and thus see how the plan worked. If it turned out well, then he might establish it by law; if not, he could execute immediate punishment on the man formerly condemned. This would be neither less nor more unjust than if the condemned man had been put to death at once, and the experiment would involve no risk. I think vagabonds too might be treated this way, for though we have passed many laws against them, they have had no real effect as yet.'

"When the cardinal had concluded, they all began praising enthusiastically ideas which they had received with contempt when I suggested them; and they particularly liked the idea about vagabonds, because it was the cardinal's addition.

"I don't know whether it is worthwhile telling what followed, because it was silly, but I'll tell it anyhow, for there's no harm in it, and it bears on our subject. There was a hanger-on standing around, who was so good at playing the fool that you could hardly tell him from the real thing. He was constantly making jokes, but so awkwardly that we laughed more at him than at them; yet sometimes a rather clever thing came out, confirming the old proverb that a man who throws the dice often will sooner or later make a lucky cast. One of the company happened to say that in my speech I had taken care of the thieves, and the cardinal had taken care of the vagabonds, so now all that was left to do was to take care of the poor whom sickness or old age had reduced to poverty and kept from earning a living.

"'Leave that to me,' said the fool, 'and I'll set it right at once. These are people I'm eager to get out of my sight, having been so often vexed with them and their woeful complaints. No matter how pitifully they beg for money, they've never whined a single penny out of my pocket. They can't win with me: either I don't want to give them anything, or I haven't anything to give them. Now they're getting wise; they know me so well, they don't waste their breath, but let me pass without a word or a hope—no more, by heaven, than if I were a priest. But I would make a law sending all these beggars to Benedictine monasteries, where the men could become lay brothers,[3] as they're called, and the women could be nuns.'

"The cardinal smiled and passed it off as a joke; the rest took it seriously. But a certain friar, a theologian, took such pleasure in this jest at the expense of priests and monks that he too began to make merry, though generally he was grave to the point of sourness. 'Even so, you will not get rid of the beggars,' he began, 'unless you take care of us friars[4] too.'

2. In earlier days almost any criminal could take sanctuary in any church and be safe from the law. By More's time the privilege had been considerably abridged.

3. Men who lived and worked in monasteries (mostly performing menial tasks) but who were not admitted to clerical orders.

4. Members of a mendicant (begging) order, as opposed to monks, who live, and labor, in a cloister.

" 'You have been taken care of already,' retorted the fool. 'The cardinal provided for you splendidly when he said vagabonds should be arrested and put to work, for you friars are the greatest vagabonds of all.'

"When the company, watching the cardinal closely, saw that he admitted this jest like the other, they all took it up with vigor—except for the friar. He, as you can easily imagine, was stung by the vinegar,[5] and flew into such a rage that he could not keep from abusing the fool. He called him a knave, a slanderer, a sneak, and a 'son of perdition,'[6] quoting the meanwhile terrible denunciations from Holy Scripture. Now the joker began to jest in earnest, for he was clearly on his own ground.

" 'Don't get angry, good friar,' he said, 'for it is written, "In your patience possess ye your souls." '[7]

"In reply, the friar said, and I quote his very words, 'I am not angry, you gallows-bird, or at least I do not sin, for the psalmist says, "Be ye angry, and sin not." '[8]

"At this point the cardinal gently cautioned the friar to calm down, but he answered: 'No, my lord, I speak only from righteous zeal, as I ought to. For holy men have had great zeal. That is why Scripture says, "the zeal of thine house hath eaten me up,"[9] and we sing in church, "those who mocked Elisha as he went up to the house of God, felt the zeal of the baldhead,"[1] just as this mocker, this rascal, this guttersnipe may very well feel it.'

" 'Perhaps you mean well,' said the cardinal, 'but you would act in a holier, and certainly in a wiser way, if you didn't set your wit against a fool's wit and try to spar with a buffoon.'

" 'No, my lord,' he replied, 'I would not act more wisely. For Solomon himself, the wisest of men, said, "Answer a fool according to his folly,"[2] and that's what I'm doing now. I am showing him the pit into which he will fall if he does not take care. For if the many mockers of Elisha, who was only one bald man, felt the effects of his zeal, how much more effect shall be felt by a single mocker of many friars, who include a great many baldheads! And besides, we have a papal bull,[3] by which all who mock us are excommunicated.'

"When the cardinal saw there was no end to the matter, he nodded to the fool to leave, and turned the conversation to another subject. Soon after, he rose from table, and, going to hear petitioners, dismissed us.

"Look, my dear More, what a long story I have inflicted on you. I would be quite ashamed, if you had not yourself asked for it, and seemed to listen as if you did not want any part to be left out. Though I ought to have related this conversation more concisely, I did feel bound to recount it, so you might see how those who rejected what I said at first approved of it immediately afterward, when they saw the cardinal did not disapprove. In fact they went so far in their flattery that they indulged and almost took seriously ideas

---

5. Alluding to a phrase in Horace's *Satires* 1.7.32: *italo perfusus aceto*, "soaked in Italian vinegar."
6. John 17.12; 2 Thessalonians 2.3.
7. Luke 21.19.
8. Psalms 4.4. The Vulgate Bible translates as *Irascimini* ("Be angry") the Hebrew word that is rendered as "Stand in awe" in the King James Version.
9. Psalms 69.9.
1. Some children mocked Elisha, son of Elijah the

prophet, for his baldness; but he called two bears out of the woods, and they tore the bad children to pieces (2 Kings 23–24). The friar quotes a hymn that was based on this cautionary tale.
2. Proverbs 26.5. But compare the previous verse: "Answer not a fool according to his folly, lest thou also be like unto him."
3. A formal papal document, named after the seal (Latin *bulla*) that authenticated it.

that he tolerated only as the jesting of a fool. From this episode you can see how little courtiers would value me or my advice."

To this I answered, "You have given me great pleasure, my dear Raphael, for everything you've said has been both wise and witty. As you spoke, I seemed to be a child and in my own native land once more, through the pleasant recollection of that cardinal in whose court I was brought up as a lad. Dear as you are to me on other accounts, you cannot imagine how much dearer you are because you honor his memory so highly. Still, my friend Raphael, I don't give up my former opinion: I think if you could overcome your aversion to court life, your advice to a prince would be of the greatest advantage to the public welfare. This, after all, is the chief duty of every good man, including you. Your friend Plato thinks that commonwealths will become happy only when philosophers become kings or kings become philosophers.[4] No wonder we are so far from happiness, when philosophers do not condescend even to assist kings with their counsels."

"They are not so ungracious," Raphael replied, "but that they would gladly do it; in fact, they have already done it in a great many published books, if the rulers would only read their good advice. But doubtless Plato was right in foreseeing that unless kings became philosophical themselves, they would never take the advice of real philosophers, drenched as they are and infected with false values from boyhood on. Plato certainly had this experience with Dionysius of Syracuse.[5] If I proposed wise laws to some king, and tried to root out of his soul the seeds of evil and corruption, don't you suppose I would be either banished forthwith, or treated with scorn?

"Imagine, if you will, that I am at the court of the king of France.[6] Suppose I were sitting in his royal council, meeting in secret session with the king himself presiding, and all the cleverest councillors were hard at work devising a set of crafty machinations by which the king might keep hold of Milan, recover Naples, which has proved so slippery;[7] then overthrow the Venetians and subdue all Italy; next add Flanders, Brabant, and the whole of Burgundy to his realm, besides some other nations he has in mind to invade. One man urges him to make an alliance with the Venetians for just as long as the king finds it convenient—perhaps to develop a common strategy with them, and even allow them some of the loot, which can be recovered later when things work out according to plan. While one recommends hiring German mercenaries, his neighbor proposes paying the Swiss to stay neutral.[8] A fourth voice suggests soothing the offended divinity of the emperor with an offering of gold.[9] Still another, who is of a different mind, thinks a settlement should be made with the king of Aragon, and that, to cement the

4. Plato, *Republic* 5.473.

5. Plato is reported to have made three visits to Syracuse (in Sicily), where his attempts to reform the tyrant Dionysius the Elder, and later his son Dionysius the Younger, were notoriously unsuccessful.

6. At the time of writing, Francis I; at the time of Hythloday's supposed visit to England, either Charles VIII (d. 1498) or Louis XII (d. 1515). All three were would-be imperialists with hereditary claims to Milan and Naples, and all three bogged down in the intricacies of Italian political intrigue.

7. A marginal gloss at this point says, "Indirectly

he discourages the French from seizing Italy." France gained Milan in 1499, lost it in 1512, and regained it at the Battle of Marignano in September 1515. Naples was won in 1495, lost in 1496, won again in 1501, and lost again in 1504. But, as Hythloday goes on to suggest, French territorial ambitions in the period extended almost limitlessly.

8. Among foot soldiers for hire, the Swiss ranked first, the Germans second.

9. Maximilian of Austria, Holy Roman Emperor, had grandiose schemes (he even dreamed of being pope) but little money. He was always accessible to a bribe.

peace, he should be allowed to take Navarre[1] from its proper ruler. Meanwhile, someone suggests snaring the prince of Castile into a marriage alliance—a first step would be to buy up some nobles of his court with secret pensions.[2]

"The hardest problem of all is what to do about England. They all agree that peace should be made, and that the alliance, which is weak at best, should be strengthened as much as possible; but while the English are being treated as friends, they should also be suspected as enemies. And so the Scots must be kept in constant readiness, poised to attack the English in case they stir ever so little.[3] Also a banished nobleman with some pretensions to the English throne must be secretly encouraged (there are treaties against doing it openly), and in this way pressure can be brought to bear on the English king, and a ruler kept in check who can't really be trusted.[4]

"Now in a meeting like this one, where so much is at stake, where so many brilliant men are competing to think up intricate strategies of war, what if an insignificant fellow like me were to get up and advise going on another tack entirely? Suppose I said the king should leave Italy alone and stay at home, because the single kingdom of France all by itself is almost too much for one man to govern well, and the king should not dream of adding others to it? Then imagine I told about the decrees of the Achorians,[5] who live off the island of Utopia toward the southeast. Long ago, these people went to war to gain another realm for their king, who had inherited an ancient claim to it through marriage. When they had conquered it, they soon saw that keeping it was going to be as hard as getting it had been. The seeds of war were constantly sprouting, their new subjects were continually rebelling or being attacked by foreign invaders, the Achorians had to be constantly at war for them or against them, and they saw no hope of ever being able to disband their army. In the meantime, they were being heavily taxed, money flowed out of their kingdom, their blood was being shed for the advantage of others, and peace was no closer than it had ever been. The war corrupted their own citizens by encouraging lust for robbery and murder; and the laws fell into contempt because their king, distracted with the cares of two kingdoms, could give neither one his proper attention.

"When they saw that the list of these evils was endless, the Achorians took counsel together and very courteously offered their king his choice of keeping whichever of the two kingdoms he preferred, because he couldn't rule them both. They were too numerous a people, they said, to be ruled by half a king; and they added that a man would not even hire a muledriver, if he had to divide his services with somebody else. The worthy king was thus obliged to be content with his own realm and give his new one to a friend, who before long was driven out.

---

1. A small independent enclave astride the Pyrenees, long disputed between Spain and France.
2. The future emperor Charles V was a great matrimonial and diplomatic catch. (Before he was twenty, he had been engaged ten times.) The question of a French marriage that would unite the two greatest Continental and Catholic powers was continually in the air.

3. The Scots, as traditional enemies of England, were traditional allies of France.
4. The French had in fact supported various pretenders to the English throne—most recently, Richard de la Pole, the inheritor of the Yorkist claim.
5. The name arises from Greek *a* ("without") and *chora* ("place"): "the People without a Country."

"Finally, suppose I told the French king's council that all this warmongering, by which so many different nations were kept in turmoil as a result of one man's connivings, would exhaust his treasury and demoralize his people, and yet in the end come to nothing, through some mishap or other.[6] And therefore he should look after his ancestral kingdom, improve it as much as he could, cultivate it in every conceivable way. He should love his people and be loved by them; he should live among them, govern them kindly, and let other kingdoms alone, since his own is big enough, if not too big, for him. How do you think, my dear More, the other councillors would take this speech of mine?"

"Not very well, I'm sure," said I.

"Well, let's go on," he said. "Suppose the councillors of some other king are discussing various schemes for raising money to fill his treasury. One man recommends increasing the value of money when the king pays his debts and devaluing it when he collects his revenues.[7] Thus he can discharge a huge debt with a small payment, and collect a large sum when only a small one is due him. Another suggests a make-believe war, so that money can be raised under pretext of carrying it on; then, when the money is in, he can conclude a ceremonious peace treaty—which the deluded common people will attribute to the piety of their prince and his careful compassion for the lives of his subjects.[8] Another councillor calls to mind some old motheaten laws, antiquated by long disuse, which no one remembers being made and consequently everyone has transgressed. By imposing fines for breaking these laws, the king will get great sums of money, as well as credit for upholding law and order, since the whole procedure can be made to look like justice.[9] Another recommendation is that he forbid under particularly heavy fines a lot of practices that are contrary to the public interest; afterward, he can dispense with his own rules for large sums of money. Thus he pleases the people and makes a double profit, one from the heavy fines imposed on lawbreakers, and the other from selling dispensations. Meanwhile he seems careful of his people's welfare, since it is plain he will not allow private citizens to do anything contrary to the public interest, except for a huge price.

"Another councillor proposes that he work on the judges so that they will decide every case in favor of the king. They should be summoned to court often, and invited to debate his affairs in the royal presence. However unjust his claims, one or another of the judges, whether from love of contradiction, or desire to seem original, or simply to serve his own interest, will be bound to find some way of twisting the law in the king's favor. If the judges can be brought to differ, then the clearest matter in the world will be obscured, and the truth itself brought into question. The king is given leverage to interpret the law as he will, and everyone else will acquiesce from shame or fear. The judges will have no hesitation about supporting the

6. Francis I lost Milan in 1520 (i.e., four years after More wrote this passage) and, in a catastrophic effort to regain it in 1525, was defeated and taken prisoner by Charles V.

7. Both Henry VII and (after *Utopia* was written) Henry VIII fiddled with the English currency in ways like those suggested here.

8. Something like this happened in 1492, when

Henry VII not only pretended war with France on behalf of Brittany and levied taxes for the war (which was hardly fought) but collected a bribe from Charles VIII for not fighting it.

9. This had been common practice under Henry VII, whose ministers Empson and Dudley scratched up many forgotten laws for strictly mercenary purposes.

royal interest, for there are always plenty of pretexts for giving judgment in favor of the king. Either equity is on his side, or the letter of the law happens to make for him, or the words of the law can be twisted into obscurity—or, if all else fails, he can appeal above the law to the royal prerogative, which is a never-failing argument with judges who know their 'duty.'

"Then all the councillors agree with the famous maxim of Crassus: a king can never have too much gold, because he must maintain an army.[1] Further, that a king, even if he wants to, can do no wrong, for all property belongs to the king, and so do his subjects themselves; a man owns nothing but what the king, in his goodness, sees fit to leave him. The king should in fact leave his subjects as little as possible, because his own safety depends on keeping them from growing insolent with wealth and freedom. For riches and liberty make people less patient to endure harsh and unjust commands, whereas meager poverty blunts their spirits, makes them docile, and grinds out of the oppressed the lofty spirit of rebellion.

"Now at this point, suppose I were to get up again and declare that all these counsels are both dishonorable and ruinous to the king? Suppose I said his honor and his safety alike rest on the people's resources rather than his own? Suppose I said that the people choose a king for their own sake, not for his, so that by his efforts and troubles they may live in comfort and safety? This is why, I would say, it is the king's duty to take more care of his people's welfare than of his own, just as it is the duty of a shepherd who cares about his job to feed his sheep rather than himself.[2]

"They are absolutely wrong when they say that the people's poverty safeguards public peace—experience shows the contrary. Where will you find more squabbling than among beggars? Who is more eager for revolution than the man who is most discontented with his present position? Who is more reckless about creating disorder than the man who knows he has nothing to lose and thinks he may have something to gain? If a king is so hated or despised by his subjects that he can rule them only by mistreatment, plundering, confiscation, and pauperization of his people, then he'd do much better to abdicate his throne—for under these circumstances, though he keeps the name of authority, he loses all the majesty of a king. A king has no dignity when he exercises authority over beggars, only when he rules over prosperous and happy subjects. This was certainly what that noble and lofty spirit Fabricius[3] meant when he said he would rather be a ruler of rich men than be rich himself.

"A solitary ruler who enjoys a life of pleasure and self-indulgence while all about him are grieving and groaning is acting like a jailer, not a king. Just as an incompetent doctor can cure his patient of one disease only by throwing him into another, so it's an incompetent king who can rule his

1. Adapted from Cicero, *On Moral Obligation* 1.8.25. Crassus was a rich Roman who joined with Pompey and Caesar to form the First Triumvirate, which dominated Rome from 60 B.C.E. to Crassus's death seven years later. Legend has it that he died when a Parthian general, after defeating and capturing Crassus at the Battle of Carrhae, disproved his maxim by pouring molten gold down his throat.

2. This metaphor is one of the great commonplaces. Ezekiel 34.2 reads: "Woe be to the shepherds of Israel that do feed themselves! should not the shepherds feed the flocks?"

3. Gaius Fabricius Luscinus, who took part in the wars against Pyrrhus, king of Epirus (280–275 B.C.E.). The saying attributed to him here was actually coined by his colleague Manius Curius Dentatus, but it is quite in his spirit.

people only by depriving them of all life's pleasures. Such a king openly confesses that he does not know how to rule free men.

"A king of this stamp should correct his own sloth or arrogance, because these are the vices that cause people to hate or despise him. Let him live on his own income without wronging others, and limit his spending to his income. Let him curb crime, and by wise training of his subjects keep them from misbehavior, instead of letting it breed and then punishing it. Let him not suddenly revive antiquated laws, especially if they have been long forgotten and never missed. And let him never take money as a fine when a judge would regard an ordinary subject as a low fraud for claiming it.

"Suppose I should then describe for them the law of the Macarians,[4] a people who also live not far from Utopia? On the day that their king first assumes office, he must take an oath confirmed by solemn ceremonies that he will never have in his treasury at any one time more than a thousand pounds in gold, or its equivalent in silver. They say this law was made by an excellent king, who cared more for his country's prosperity than for his own wealth; he established it as a barrier against any king heaping up so much money as to impoverish his people.[5] He thought this sum would enable the king to put down rebellions or repel hostile invasions, but would not tempt him into aggressive adventures. His law was aimed chiefly at keeping the king in check, but he also wanted to ensure an ample supply of money for the daily business transactions of the citizens. Besides, a king who has to distribute all his excess money to the people will not be much disposed to seek out opportunities for extortion. Such a king will be both a terror to evildoers and beloved by the good.—Now, don't you suppose if I set such ideas before men strongly inclined to the contrary, they would turn deaf ears to me?"

"Stone deaf, indeed, there's no doubt about it," I said, "and no wonder! To tell you the truth, I don't think you should offer advice or thrust on people ideas of this sort, that you know will not be listened to. What good can it do? When your listeners are already prepossessed against you and firmly convinced of opposite opinions, how can you win over their minds with such out-of-the-way speeches? This academic philosophy is quite agreeable in the private conversation of close friends, but in the councils of kings, where grave matters are being authoritatively decided, there is no place for it."

"That is just what I was saying," Raphael replied. "There is no place for philosophy in the councils of kings."

"Yes, there is," I said, "but not for this school philosophy which supposes that every topic is suitable for every occasion. There is another philosophy that is better suited for political action, that takes its cue, adapts itself to the drama in hand, and acts its part neatly and appropriately. This is the philosophy for you to use. Otherwise, when a comedy of Plautus is being played,[6] and the household slaves are cracking trivial jokes together, you propose to come on stage in the garb of a philosopher and repeat Seneca's speech to Nero from the *Octavia*.[7] Wouldn't it be better to take a silent role than to say

4. From Greek *makarios*, "blessed," "happy."
5. Once again More glances at the previous English monarch, Henry VII, who died the richest prince in Christendom and probably the most hated. He combined unscrupulous greed with skinflint stinginess.

6. Most of the plays of the Roman comic dramatist Plautus (ca. 250–184 B.C.E.) involve low intrigue: needy young men, expensive prostitutes, senile moneybags, and clever slaves, in predictable combinations.
7. The Latin tragedy *Octavia* involves Seneca

something wholly inappropriate, and thus turn the play into a tragicomedy? You pervert and ruin a play when you add irrelevant speeches, even if they are better than the original. So go through with the drama in hand as best you can, and don't spoil it all simply because you happen to think of a play by someone else that would be better.

"That's how things go in the commonwealth, and in the councils of princes. If you cannot pluck up bad ideas by the root, if you cannot cure long-standing evils as completely as you would like, you must not therefore abandon the commonwealth. Don't give up the ship in a storm because you cannot hold back the winds. And don't force strange ideas on people who you know have set their minds on a different course from yours. You must strive to influence policy indirectly, handle the situation tactfully, and thus what you cannot turn to good, you may at least make as little bad as possible. For it is impossible to make everything good unless you make all men good, and that I don't expect to see for a long time to come."

"The only result of this," he answered, "will be that while I try to cure others of madness, I'll be raving along with them myself. If I am to speak the truth, I will simply have to talk in the way I have described. For all I know, it may be the business of a philosopher to tell lies, but it certainly isn't mine. Though my advice may be repugnant and irksome to the king's councillors, I don't see why they should consider it eccentric to the point of folly. What if I told them the kind of thing that Plato advocates in his republic, or that the Utopians actually practice in theirs? However superior those institutions might be (and as a matter of fact they are), yet here they would seem inappropriate, because private property is the rule here, and there all things are held in common.

"People who have made up their minds to rush headlong down the opposite road are never pleased with someone who calls them back and tells them they are on the wrong course. But, apart from that, what did I say that could not and should not be said anywhere and everywhere? If we dismiss as out of the question and absurd everything which the perverse customs of men have made to seem alien to us, we shall have to set aside most of the commandments of Christ, even in a community of Christians. Yet he forbade us to dissemble them, and even ordered that what he had whispered to his disciples should be preached openly from the housetops.[8] Most of his teachings differ more radically from the common customs of mankind than my discourse did. But preachers, like the crafty fellows they are, have found that people would rather not change their lives to conform to Christ's rule, and so, just as you suggest, they have accommodated his teaching to the way people live, as if it were a leaden yardstick.[9] At least in that manner they can get the two things to correspond in some way or other. The only real thing they accomplish that I can see is to make people feel more secure about doing evil.

"And this is all that I could accomplish in the councils of princes. For either I would have different ideas from the others, and that would come to

---

as a character and was long thought to have been written by him. In the speech More refers to (lines 440–592), Seneca lectures Nero on the abuses of power.
8. Matthew 10.27; Luke 12.3.
9. A flexible measuring rod of lead was particu-

larly helpful in constructing the many curved moldings used in a kind of building associated, in antiquity, with the Greek isle of Lesbos. This "Lesbian rule" became proverbial as a metaphor for adaptable moral standards.

the same thing as having no ideas at all, or else I would agree with them, and that, as Mitio says in Terence, would merely confirm them in their madness.[1] When you say I should 'influence policy indirectly,' I simply don't know what you mean; remember, you said I should try hard to handle the situation tactfully, and what can't be made good I should try to make as little bad as possible. In a council, there is no way to dissemble, no way to shut your eyes to things. You must openly approve the worst proposals, and consent to the most vicious policies. A man who went along only halfheartedly even with the worst decisions would immediately get himself a name as a spy and perhaps a traitor. How can one individual do any good when he is surrounded by colleagues who would more readily corrupt the best of men than do any reforming of themselves? Either they will seduce you by their evil ways or, if you keep yourself honest and innocent, you will be made a screen for the knavery and folly of others. Influencing policy indirectly! You wouldn't have a chance.

"This is why Plato in a very fine comparison declares that wise men are right in keeping clear of public business.[2] They see the people swarming through the streets and getting soaked with rain, and they cannot persuade them to go indoors and get out of the wet. They know if they go out themselves, they can do no good but only get drenched with the rest. So they stay indoors and are content to keep at least themselves dry, since they cannot remedy the folly of others.

"But as a matter of fact, my dear More, to tell you what I really think, as long as you have private property, and as long as money is the measure of all things, it is scarcely ever possible for a commonwealth to be just or happy. For justice cannot exist where all the best things in life are held by the worst people; nor can anyone be happy where property is limited to a few, since even those few are always uneasy, and the many are utterly wretched.

"So I reflect on the wonderfully wise and sacred institutions of the Utopians, who are so well governed with so few laws. Among them virtue has its reward, yet everything is shared equally, and everyone lives in plenty. I contrast them with the many other nations, which are constantly passing new ordinances and yet can never order their affairs satisfactorily. In these other nations, whatever a man can get he calls his own private property; but all the mass of laws old and new don't enable him to secure his own, or defend it, or even distinguish it from someone else's property—as is shown by innumerable and interminable lawsuits, fresh ones every day. When I consider all these things, I become more sympathetic to Plato and do not wonder that he declined to make laws for any people who refused to share their goods equally.[3] Wisest of men, he saw easily that the one and only road to the welfare of all lies through the absolute equality of goods. I doubt whether such equality can ever be achieved where property belongs to individuals. However abundant goods may be, when everyone tries to get as much as he can for his own exclusive use, a handful of men end up sharing the whole pile,

1. The allusion is to a comedy—*The Brothers* (lines 145–47)—by the Roman playwright Terence (ca. 190–159 B.C.E.).
2. *Republic* 6.496.
3. Diogenes Laertius (3rd century C.E.) reports that the Arcadians and Thebans united to build a great city and asked Plato to be its legislator. He made communism a condition of his going there, and when the inhabitants would not consent, he declined their offer (*Lives of Eminent Philosophers* 3.23).

and the rest are left in poverty. The result generally is two sorts of people whose fortunes ought to be interchanged: the rich are rapacious, wicked, and useless, while the poor are unassuming, modest men who work hard, more for the benefit of the public than of themselves.

"Thus I am wholly convinced that unless private property is entirely done away with, there can be no fair or just distribution of goods, nor can the business of mortals be happily conducted. As long as private property remains, by far the largest and the best part of the human race will be oppressed by a heavy and inescapable burden of cares and anxieties. This load, I admit, may be lightened to some extent, but I maintain it cannot be entirely removed. Laws might be made that no one should own more than a certain amount of land or receive more than a certain income. Or laws might be passed to prevent the prince from becoming too powerful and the populace too unruly. It might be made unlawful for public offices to be solicited, or put up for sale, or made burdensome for the officeholder by great expense. Otherwise, officials are tempted to get their money back by fraud or extortion, and only rich men can afford to accept positions which ought to be held by the wise. Laws of this sort, I agree, may have as much effect as poultices continually applied to sick bodies that are past cure. The social evils I mentioned may be alleviated and their effects mitigated for a while, but so long as private property remains, there is no hope at all of effecting a cure and restoring society to good health. While you try to cure one part, you aggravate the disease in other parts. Suppressing one symptom causes another to break out, since you cannot give something to one person without taking it away from someone else."[4]

"But I don't see it that way," I replied. "It seems to me that people cannot possibly live well where all things are in common. How can there be plenty of commodities where every man stops working? The hope of gain will not spur him on; he will rely on others, and become lazy. If men are driven by need, and yet cannot legally protect what they have gained, what can follow but continual bloodshed and turmoil, especially when respect for magistrates and their authority has been lost? I for one cannot conceive of authority existing among men who are equal to one another in every respect."[5]

"I'm not surprised," said Raphael, "that you think of it this way, since you have no idea, or only a false idea, of such a commonwealth. But you should have been with me in Utopia, and seen with your own eyes their manners and customs as I did—for I lived there more than five years, and would never have left, if it had not been to make that new world known to others. If you had seen them, you would frankly confess that you had never seen a people well governed anywhere but there."

"You will have a hard time persuading me," said Peter Giles, "that people in that new land are better governed than in the world we know. Our minds are not inferior to theirs, and our governments, I believe, are older. Long experience has helped us develop many conveniences of life, and by good luck we have discovered many other things which human ingenuity could never have hit upon."

4. Plato also employs the metaphor of societal disease, and of the statesman as physician (*Republic* 4.425E–426A; *Statesman* 297E–298E; Epistle 7, 330C–331A).

5. These objections to communism derive from the critique of the *Republic* in Aristotle's *Politics* 2.1–5.

"As for the relative ages of the governments," Raphael replied, "you might judge more accurately if you had read their histories. If we believe these records, they had cities before there were even people here. What ingenuity has discovered or chance hit upon could have turned up just as well in one place as the other. For the rest, I believe that even if we surpass them in natural intelligence, they leave us far behind in their diligence and zeal to learn.

"According to their chronicles, they had heard nothing of ultra-equatorials (that's their name for us) until we arrived, except that once, some twelve hundred years ago, a ship which a storm had blown toward Utopia was wrecked on their island. Some Romans and Egyptians were cast ashore, and never departed. Now note how the Utopians profited, through their diligence, from this one chance event. They learned every single useful art of the Roman empire either directly from their guests or indirectly from hints and surmises on which they based their own investigations. What benefits from the mere fact that on a single occasion some Europeans landed there! If a similar accident has hitherto brought anyone here from their land, the incident has been completely forgotten, as it will perhaps be forgotten in time to come that I was ever in their country. From one such accident they made themselves masters of all our useful inventions, but I suspect it will be a long time before we accept any of their institutions which are better than ours. This willingness to learn is, I think, the really important reason for their being better governed and living more happily than we do, though we are not inferior to them in brains or resources."

"Then let me implore you, my dear Raphael," said I, "to describe that island to us. Do not try to be brief, but explain in order everything relating to their land, their rivers, towns, people, manners, institutions, laws—everything, in short, that you think we would like to know. And you can take it for granted that we want to know everything that we don't know yet."

"There's nothing I'd rather do," he replied, "for these things are fresh in my mind. But it will take quite some time."

"In that case," I said, "let's first go to lunch. Afterward, we shall have all the time we want."

"Agreed," he said. So we went in and had lunch. Then we came back to the same spot, and sat down on the bench. I ordered my servants to take care that no one should interrupt us. Peter Giles and I urged Raphael to keep his promise. When he saw that we were attentive and eager to hear him, he sat silent and thoughtful a moment, and then began as follows.

Book II

[THE GEOGRAPHY OF UTOPIA][1]

The island of the Utopians is two hundred miles across in the middle part, where it is widest, and is nowhere much narrower than this except toward the two ends, where it gradually tapers. These ends, drawn toward one

---

1. The early editions of *Utopia* include, in Book II, eight section headings. These help in locating the treatment of particular topics in Hythloday's rather sprawling discourse, but since in several instances the headings identify only the *initial* topic of a section, they can also be misleading. In the present edition, they are supplemented by additional headings, enclosed in brackets to identify them as editorial insertions.

VTOPIAE INSVLAE TABVLA.

Woodcut map of Utopia, by Ambrosius Holbein (brother of the more famous Hans Holbein the Younger). This map appeared in the two 1518 editions.

another as if in a five-hundred-mile circle, make the island crescent-shaped, like a new moon.[2] Between the horns of the crescent, which are about eleven miles apart, the sea enters and spreads into a broad bay. Being sheltered from the wind by the surrounding land, the bay is never rough, but quiet and smooth instead, like a big lake. Thus nearly the whole inner coast is one great harbor, across which ships pass in every direction, to the great advantage of the people. What with shallows on one side and rocks on the

---

2. The island is similar to England in size, though not at all in shape.

other, the entrance into the bay is perilous. Near the middle of the channel, there is one rock that rises above the water, and so presents no danger in itself; on top of it a tower has been built, and there a garrison is kept. Since the other rocks lie underwater, they are very dangerous to navigation. The channels are known only to the Utopians, so hardly any strangers enter the bay without one of their pilots; and even they themselves could not enter safely if they did not direct their course by some landmarks on the coast. If these landmarks were shifted about, the Utopians could easily lure to destruction an enemy fleet coming against them, however big it was.

On the outer side of the island there are likewise occasional harbors; but the coast is rugged by nature, and so well fortified that a few defenders could beat off the attack of a strong force. They say (and the appearance of the place confirms this) that their land was not always an island. But Utopus, who conquered the country and gave it his name (it had previously been called Abraxa),[3] and who brought its rude and uncouth inhabitants to such a high level of culture and humanity that they now excel in that regard almost every other people, also changed its geography. After winning the victory at his first landing, he cut a channel fifteen miles wide where their land joined the continent, and caused the sea to flow around the country. He put not only the natives to work at this task, but all his own soldiers too, so that the vanquished would not think the labor a disgrace. With the work divided among so many hands, the project was finished quickly, and the neighboring peoples, who at first had laughed at his folly, were struck with wonder and terror at his success.

There are fifty-four cities on the island, all spacious and magnificent, identical in language, customs, institutions, and laws. So far as the location permits, all of them are built on the same plan and have the same appearance. The nearest are twenty-four miles apart, and the farthest are not so remote that a person cannot go on foot from one to the other in a day.

Once a year each city sends three of its old and experienced citizens to Amaurot to consider affairs of common interest to the island. Amaurot lies at the navel of the land, so to speak, and is convenient to every other district, so it acts as a capital. Every city has enough ground assigned to it so that at least twelve miles of farm land are available in every direction, though where the cities are farther apart, they have much more land.[4] No city wants to enlarge its boundaries,[5] for the inhabitants consider themselves good tenants rather than landlords. At proper intervals all over the countryside they have built houses and furnished them with farm equipment. These houses are inhabited by citizens who come to the country by turns. No rural household has fewer than forty men and women in it, besides two slaves bound to the land. A master and mistress, serious and mature persons, are in charge of each household. Over every thirty households is placed a single phylarch.[6] Each year twenty persons from each household move back to the city, after

---

3. The Greek Gnostic Basilides (2nd century c.e.) postulated 365 heavens and called the highest of them Abraxas. The Greek letters that constitute the word have numerical equivalents summing to 365, but what it actually *means* is unknown.

4. Each consisting of a central metropolis and the surrounding countryside, the Utopian cities

recall the ancient Greek city-states.

5. Marginal gloss: "But today this is the curse of all countries." Although Utopia exists in the present, the glosses repeatedly refer to it as if it belonged to the distant past, like classical Greece and Rome.

6. From Greek *phylarchos*, "ruler of a tribe."

completing a two-year stint in the country. In their place, twenty others are sent out from town, to learn farm work from those who have already been in the country for a year and are therefore better skilled in farming. They, in turn, will teach those who come the following year. If all were equally unskilled in farm work, and new to it, they might harm the crops out of ignorance. This custom of alternating farm workers is the usual procedure, so that no one will have to do such hard work unwillingly for more than two years; but many of them, who take a natural pleasure in farm life, are allowed to stay longer.

The farm workers till the soil, feed the animals, hew wood, and take it to the city by land or by water, as is more convenient. They breed an enormous number of chickens by a marvelous method. The farmers, not hens, hatch the eggs, by keeping them in a warm place at an even temperature. As soon as they come out of the shell, the chicks recognize the humans, follow them around, and are devoted to them instead of to their mothers.

They raise very few horses, and those full of mettle, which they keep only to exercise the young people in the art of horsemanship.[7] For all the work of plowing and hauling they use oxen, which they agree are inferior to horses over the short haul, but which can hold out longer under heavy burdens, are less subject to disease (as they suppose), and can be kept with less cost and trouble. Moreover, when oxen are too old for work, they can be used for meat.

Grain they use only to make bread.[8] They drink wine, apple or pear cider, or simple water, which they sometimes boil with honey or licorice, of which they have an abundance. Although they know very well, down to the last detail, how much food each city and its surrounding district will consume, they produce much more grain and cattle than they need for themselves, and share the surplus with their neighbors. Whatever goods the folk in the country need which cannot be produced there, they request of the town magistrates, and since there is nothing to be paid or exchanged, they get what they want without any trouble. They generally go to town once a month in any case, for the feast day. When harvest time approaches, the phylarchs in the country notify the town magistrates how many hands will be needed. Crews of harvesters come just when they're wanted, and in one day of good weather they can usually get in the whole crop.

THEIR CITIES, ESPECIALLY AMAUROT

If you know one of their cities, you know them all, for they're exactly alike, except where geography itself makes a difference. So I'll describe one of them, and no matter which. But what one rather than Amaurot, the most worthy of all?—since its eminence is acknowledged by the other cities, which send representatives to the annual meeting there; besides which, I know it best, because I lived there for five full years.

Well, then, Amaurot lies up against a gently sloping hill; the town is almost square in shape. From a little below the crest of the hill, it runs down about two miles to the river Anyder, and then spreads out along the river bank for a

---

7. In fact, horses had long been extinct in the New World, before Europeans imported them.

8. I.e., they don't, like the English, use it to make beer and ale.

somewhat greater distance. The Anyder rises from a small spring about eighty miles above Amaurot, but other streams flow into it, two of them being pretty big, so that, as it runs past Amaurot, the river has grown to a width of five hundred yards. It continues to grow even larger until at last, sixty miles farther along, it is lost in the ocean. In all this stretch between the sea and the city, and also for some miles above the city, the river is tidal, ebbing and flowing every six hours with a swift current.[9] When the tide comes in, it fills the whole Anyder with salt water for about thirty miles, driving the fresh water back. Even above that, for several miles farther, the water is brackish; but a little higher up, as it runs past the city, the water is always fresh, and when the tide ebbs, the river runs clean and sweet all the way to the sea.

The two banks of the river at Amaurot are linked by a bridge, built not on wooden piles but on remarkable stone arches. It is placed at the upper end of the city, farthest removed from the sea, so that ships can sail along the entire length of the city quays without obstruction. There is also another stream, not particularly large, but very gentle and pleasant, which gushes from the hill on which the city is situated, flows down through the center of town, and into the Anyder. The inhabitants have walled around the source of this river, which takes its rise a little outside the town, and joined it to the town proper so that if they should be attacked, the enemy would not be able to cut off the stream or divert or poison it. Water from the stream is carried by tile piping into various sections of the lower town. Where the terrain makes this impractical, they collect rain water in cisterns, which serve just as well.

The town is surrounded by a thick, high wall, with many towers and bastions. On three sides it is also surrounded by a dry ditch, broad and deep and filled with thorn hedges; on its fourth side the river itself serves as a moat. The streets are conveniently laid out for use by vehicles and for protection from the wind. Their buildings are by no means shabby; unbroken rows of houses face each other across the streets along the whole block. The streets are twenty feet wide.[1] Behind each row of houses—at the center of every block and extending the full length of the street—there are large gardens.

Every house has a door to the street and another to the garden. The doors, which are made with two leaves, open easily and swing shut automatically, letting anyone enter who wants to—so there is nothing private anywhere. Every ten years, they change houses by lot. The Utopians are very fond of these gardens of theirs. They raise vines, fruits, herbs, and flowers, so well cared for and flourishing that I have never seen any gardens more productive or elegant than theirs. They keep interested in gardening, partly because they delight in it, and also because of the competition between different blocks, which challenge one another to produce the best gardens. Certainly you will not easily find anything else in the whole city more useful or more pleasant to the citizens. And this gives reason to think that the founder of the city paid particular attention to the siting of these gardens.

They say that in the beginning the whole city was planned by Utopus himself, but that he left to posterity matters of adornment and improvement

9. Many of the details of Amaurot—its situation on a tidal river, its stone bridge (next paragraph), though not the location of that bridge—are reminiscent of London.
1. Lavish, by 16th-century standards.

such as could not be perfected in one man's lifetime. Their records began 1,760 years ago with the conquest of the island, have been diligently compiled, and are carefully preserved. From these it appears that the first houses were low, like cabins or peasant huts, built out of any sort of timber, with mud-plastered walls and pointed roofs thatched with straw. But now their houses are all three stories high and handsomely constructed; the fronts are faced with fieldstone, quarried rock, or brick, over rubble construction. The roofs are flat, and are covered with a kind of plaster that is cheap but fireproof, and more weather-resistant even than lead.[2] Glass (which is plentiful there) is used in windows to keep out the weather;[3] and they also use thin linen cloth treated with oil or gum so that it lets in more light and keeps out more wind.

THEIR OFFICIALS

Once a year, every group of thirty households elects an official, formerly called the syphogrant,[4] but now called the phylarch. Over every group of ten syphogrants with their households there is another official, once called the tranibor but now known as the head phylarch. All the syphogrants, two hundred in number, elect the governor. They take an oath to choose the man they think best qualified; and then by secret ballot they elect the governor from among four men nominated by the people of the four sections of the city. The governor holds office for life, unless he is suspected of aiming at a tyranny. Though the tranibors are elected annually, they are not changed for light or casual reasons. All their other officials hold office for a single year only.

The tranibors meet to consult with the governor every other day, and more often if necessary: they discuss affairs of state, and settle any disputes between private parties (there are very few), acting as quickly as possible.[5] The tranibors always invite two syphogrants to the senate chamber, different ones every day. There is a rule that no decision can be made on a matter of public business unless it has been discussed in the senate on three separate days. It is a capital offense to make plans about public business outside of the senate or the popular assembly. The purpose of these rules, they say, is to prevent the governor and the tranibors from conspiring together to alter the government and enslave the people. Therefore all matters which are considered important are first laid before the assembly of the syphogrants. They talk the matter over with the households they represent, debate it with one another, then report their recommendation to the senate. Sometimes a question is brought before the general council of the whole island.

The senate also has a standing rule never to discuss a matter on the day when it is first introduced; all new business is deferred to the next meeting.[6] They do this so that a man will not blurt out the first thought that occurs to

---

2. Used in More's time to roof important buildings.

3. During More's day in England window glass was not common; oiled cloth and lattices of wicker or wood were more frequent.

4. The word appears to be constructed from Greek *sophos* ("wise")—or perhaps *sypheos* ("of the sty")—plus *gerontes* ("old men"). The etymology for "tranibor" (below) seems to be *traneis* or *tranos* ("clear," "plain," "distinct") plus *boros* ("devouring," "gluttonous"). There is no explanation of why Hythloday consistently uses the "older" form of the titles.

5. Marginal gloss: "A quick ending to disputes, which now are endlessly and deliberately prolonged."

6. Marginal gloss: "Would that the same rule prevailed in our modern councils."

him, and then devote all his energies to defending those foolish impulses, instead of considering impartially the public good. They know that some men would rather jeopardize the general welfare than admit to having been heedless and shortsighted—so perverse and preposterous is their sense of pride. They should have had enough foresight at the beginning to speak with prudence rather than haste.

THEIR OCCUPATIONS

Agriculture is the one occupation at which everyone works, men and women alike, with no exceptions. They are trained in it from childhood, partly in the schools, where they learn theory, and partly through field trips to nearby farms, which make something like a game of practical instruction. On these trips they not only watch the work being done, but frequently pitch in and get a workout by doing the jobs themselves.

Besides farm work (which, as I said, everybody performs), each person is taught a particular trade of his own, such as wool-working, linen-making, masonry, metal-work, or carpentry. There is no other craft that is practiced by any considerable number of them.[7] Throughout the island people wear, and throughout their lives always wear, the same style of clothing, except for the distinction between the sexes, and between married and unmarried persons. Their clothing is attractive, does not hamper bodily movement, and serves for warm as well as cold weather; what is more, each household makes its own.

Every person (and this includes women as well as men) learns a second trade, besides agriculture. As the weaker sex, women practice the lighter crafts, such as working in wool or linen; the heavier jobs are assigned to the men. As a rule, the son is trained to his father's craft, for which most feel a natural inclination. But if anyone is attracted to another occupation, he is transferred by adoption into a family practicing the trade he prefers. Both his father and the authorities make sure that he is assigned to a grave and responsible householder. After someone has learned one trade, if he wants to learn another he gets the same permission. When he has learned both, he pursues whichever he likes better, unless the city needs one more than the other.

The chief and almost the only business of the syphogrants is to manage matters so that no one sits around in idleness, and assure that everyone works hard at his trade. But no one has to exhaust himself with endless toil from early morning to late at night, as if he were a beast of burden. Such wretchedness, really worse than slavery, is the common lot of workmen almost everywhere except Utopia.[8] Of the day's twenty-four hours, the Utopians devote only six to work. They work three hours before noon, when they go to lunch. After lunch they rest for a couple of hours, then go to work for another three hours. Then they have supper, and at eight o'clock (counting the first hour after noon as one) they go to bed, and sleep eight hours.

7. Would not considerable numbers also be employed making such things as pottery, harnesses, bread, and books, as well as in mining and the merchant marine? Presumably all the professionals—doctors, for example—are drawn from the class of scholars (see p. 77).

8. E.g., in England a law of 1514–15 required workmen to be present at the workplace from daybreak to nightfall in fall and winter and from 5 A.M. to between 7 and 8 P.M. in spring and summer. (There were breaks for meals and, in summer, for a brief afternoon nap.)

The other hours of the day, when they are not working, eating, or sleeping, are left to each person's individual discretion, provided that free time is not wasted in roistering or sloth but used properly in some chosen occupation. Generally these periods are devoted to intellectual activity. For they have an established custom of giving daily public lectures before dawn;[9] attendance at these lectures is required only of those who have been specially chosen to devote themselves to learning, but a great many other people, both men and women, choose voluntarily to attend. Depending on their interests, some go to one lecture, some to another. But if anyone would rather devote his spare time to his trade, as many do who don't care for the intellectual life, this is not discouraged; in fact, such persons are commended as especially useful to the commonwealth.

After supper, they devote an hour to recreation, in their gardens in summer, or during winter in the common halls where they have their meals. There they either play music or amuse themselves with conversation. They know nothing about gambling with dice, or other such foolish and ruinous games.[1] They do play two games not unlike chess. One is a battle of numbers, in which one number captures another. The other is a game in which the vices fight a battle against the virtues. The game is ingeniously set up to show how the vices oppose one another, yet combine against the virtues; then, what vices oppose what virtues, how they try to assault them openly or undermine them insidiously; how the defenses of the virtues can break the strength of the vices or skillfully elude their plots; and finally, by what means one side or the other gains the victory.[2]

But in all this, you may get a wrong impression, if we don't go back and consider one point more carefully. Because they allot only six hours to work, you might think the necessities of life would be in scant supply. This is far from the case. Their working hours are ample to provide not only enough but more than enough of the necessities and even the conveniences of life. You will easily appreciate this if you consider how large a part of the population in other countries exists without doing any work at all. In the first place, hardly any of the women, who are a full half of the population, work;[3] or, if they do, then as a rule their husbands lie snoring in bed. Then there is a great lazy gang of priests and so-called religious.[4] Add to them all the rich, especially the landlords, who are commonly called gentlemen and nobles. Include with them their retainers, that mob of swaggering bullies. Finally, reckon in with these the sturdy and lusty beggars who go about feigning some disease as an excuse for their idleness. You will certainly find that the things which satisfy our needs are produced by far fewer hands than you had supposed.

And now consider how few of those who do work are doing really essential things. For where money is the standard of everything, many vain, superfluous trades are bound to be carried on simply to satisfy luxury and

9. Renaissance universities got under way early: first lecture was between 5 and 7 A.M.
1. Marginal gloss: "But now dicing is the sport of princes."
2. Moral games of this general character were popular with Renaissance educators.
3. A strange statement, since in More's time most women selected, prepared, and cooked the family

food; did the family laundry; performed a thousand other routine tasks of domestic drudgery; and were responsible for taking care of the children. In Utopia too they are responsible for at least some of these duties—cooking, childcare—in addition to practicing a craft and taking their turn at farmwork.
4. I.e., members of the various religious orders.

licentiousness. Suppose the multitude of those who now work were limited to a few trades, and set to producing just those commodities that nature really requires. They would be bound to produce so much that prices would drop and the workmen would be unable to gain a living. But suppose again that all the workers in useless trades were put to useful ones, and that all the idlers (who now guzzle twice as much as the workingmen who make what they consume) were assigned to productive tasks—well, you can easily see how little time would be enough and more than enough to produce all the goods that human needs and conveniences require—yes, and human pleasure too, as long as it's true and natural pleasure.

The experience of Utopia makes this perfectly apparent. In each city and its surrounding countryside barely five hundred of those men and women whose age and strength make them fit for work are exempted from it.[5] Among these are the syphogrants, who by law are free not to work; yet they don't take advantage of the privilege, preferring to set a good example to their fellow citizens. Some others are permanently exempted from work so that they may devote themselves to study, but only on the recommendation of the priests[6] and through a secret vote of the syphogrants. If any of these scholars disappoints their hopes, he becomes a workman again. On the other hand, it happens from time to time that a craftsman devotes his leisure so earnestly to study, and makes such progress as a result, that he is relieved of manual labor and promoted to the class of learned men. From this class of scholars are chosen ambassadors, priests, tranibors, and the governor himself, who used to be called Barzanes, but in their modern tongue is known as Ademus.[7] Since almost all the rest of the population is neither idle nor occupied in useless trades, it is easy to see why they produce so much in so short a working day.

Apart from all this, in several of the necessary crafts their way of life requires less total labor than does that of people elsewhere. In other countries, building and repairing houses requires the constant work of many men, because what a father has built, his thriftless heir lets fall into ruin; and then his successor has to repair, at great expense, what could easily have been maintained at a very small charge. Further, when a man has built a splendid house at vast cost, someone else may think he has finer taste, let the first house fall to ruin, and then build another one somewhere else for just as much money. But among the Utopians, where everything has been well ordered and the commonwealth properly established, building a brand-new home on a new site is a rare event. They are not only quick to repair damage, but foresighted in preventing it. The result is that their buildings last for a very long time with minimal repairs; and the carpenters and masons sometimes have so little to do that they are set to hewing timber and cutting stone in case some future need for it should arise.

---

5. I.e., are exempted from manual labor. As Hythloday proceeds to explain, in each city those exempted include the 200 syphogrants and the class of scholars, from which is chosen the other exempted individuals: the twenty tranibors, the governor, ambassadors, and the thirteen (p. 110) priests.

6. Who are in charge of the education of children (p. 111).
7. Marginal gloss: "Only the learned hold public office." "Ademus": from Greek for "Without People." "Barzanes": "Son of Zeus" (Hebrew—bar—plus Greek).

Consider, too, how little labor their clothing requires. Their work clothes are unpretentious garments made of leather, which last seven years. When they go out in public, they cover these rough working-clothes with a cloak. Throughout the entire island, these cloaks are of the same color, which is that of natural wool.[8] As a result, they not only need less wool than people in other countries, but what they do need is less expensive. Even so, they use linen cloth most, because it requires least labor. They like linen cloth to be white and wool cloth to be clean; but they put no price on fineness of texture. Elsewhere a man may not be satisfied with four or five woolen cloaks of different colors and as many silk shirts; or if he's a clotheshorse, even ten are not enough. But there everyone is content with a single cloak, and generally wears it for two years. There is no reason at all why he should want any others, for if he had them, he would not be better protected against the cold, nor would he appear in any way better dressed.

Since there is an abundance of everything, as a result of everyone working at useful trades and the trades requiring less work, they sometimes assemble great numbers of people to work on the roads, if any of them need repairing. And when there is no need even for this sort of work, then the officials very often proclaim a shorter workday, since they never force their citizens to perform useless labor. The chief aim of their constitution is that, whenever public needs permit, all citizens should be free to withdraw as much time as possible from the service of the body and devote themselves to the freedom and culture of the mind. For in that, they think, is the real happiness of life.

SOCIAL RELATIONS

Now I must explain how the citizens behave toward one another, the nature of their social relations, and how they distribute their goods within the society.

Each city, then, consists of households, the households consisting generally of blood-relations. When the women grow up and are married, they move into their husbands' households. On the other hand, male children and after them grandchildren remain in the family, and are subject to the oldest member, unless his mind has started to fail, in which case the next oldest takes his place. To keep the cities from becoming too large or too small, they take care that there should be no more than six thousand households in each (exclusive of the surrounding countryside), each family containing between ten and sixteen adults.[9] They do not, of course, try to regulate the number of minor children in a family. The limit on adults is easily observed by transferring individuals from a household with too many into a household with not enough. Likewise if a city has too many people, the extra persons serve to make up a shortage of population in other cities. And if the population throughout the entire island exceeds the quota, they enroll citizens out of

8. In a letter to Erasmus of ca. December 4, 1516, More identifies this garment as the habit of a Franciscan friar.

9. If an average household includes thirteen adults, and there are 6,000 households per city (not counting those on the surrounding farms), then there are about 78,000 adults per city; allow-

ing for children and slaves, the total population must be well in excess of 100,000, making every Utopian city larger than all but the greatest European cities of the time. Whether More actually made these calculations (or whether there is really much point in making them) is another matter.

every city and plant a colony under their own laws on the mainland near them, wherever the natives have plenty of unoccupied and uncultivated land. Those natives who want to live with the Utopian settlers are taken in. When such a merger occurs, the two peoples gradually and easily blend together, sharing the same way of life and customs, much to the advantage of both. For by their policies the Utopians make the land yield an abundance for all, though previously it had seemed too poor and barren even to support the natives. But if the natives will not join in living under their laws, the Utopians drive them out of the land they claim for themselves, and if they resist make war on them. They think it is perfectly justifiable to make war on people who leave their land idle and waste, yet forbid the use of it to others who, by the law of nature, ought to be supported from it.

If for any reason one of their cities shrinks so sharply in population that it cannot be made up from other cities without bringing them too under proper strength, the numbers are restored by bringing people back from the colonies. This has happened only twice, they say, in their whole history, both times as a result of a frightful plague. They would rather that their colonies disappeared than that any of the cities on their island should get too small.

But to return to their manner of living. The oldest of every household, as I said, is the ruler. Wives are subject to their husbands, children to their parents, and generally the younger to their elders.[1] Every city is divided into four equal districts, and in the middle of each district is a market for all kinds of commodities. Whatever each household produces is brought here and stored in warehouses, each kind of goods in its own place. Here the head of each household looks for what he or his family needs, and carries off what he wants without any sort of payment or compensation. Why should anything be refused him? There is plenty of everything, and no reason to fear that anyone will claim more than he needs. Why would anyone be suspected of asking for more than is needed, when everyone knows there will never be any shortage? Fear of want, no doubt, makes every living creature greedy and rapacious—and, in addition, man develops these qualities out of sheer pride, pride which glories in getting ahead of others by a superfluous display of possessions. But this kind of vice has no place whatever in the Utopian way of life.

Next to the marketplace of which I just spoke are the food markets, where people bring all sorts of vegetables, fruit, and bread. Fish, meat, and poultry are also brought there from designated places outside the city, where running water can carry away all the blood and refuse. Bondsmen do the slaughtering and cleaning in these places: citizens are not allowed to do such work. The Utopians feel that slaughtering our fellow creatures gradually destroys the sense of compassion, which is the finest sentiment of which our human nature is capable. Besides, they don't allow anything dirty or filthy to be brought into the city, lest the air become tainted by putrefaction and thus infectious.

1. Utopian women enjoy considerably more equality with men than did their 16th-century European counterparts, but Utopian social relations as a whole exhibit the same patriarchal structure that had always been prevalent in Europe and was sanctioned in classical and biblical texts (e.g., Aristotle, *Politics* 1.12.1–2; Ephesians 5.22–6.4) as well as in many later ones.

Each block has its own spacious halls, equally distant from one another, and each known by a special name. In these halls live the syphogrants. Thirty families are assigned to each hall, to take their meals in common[2]—fifteen live on one side of the hall, fifteen on the other. The stewards of all the halls meet at a fixed time in the market and get food according to the number of persons for whom each is responsible.

But first consideration goes to the sick, who are cared for in public hospitals. Every city has four of these, built at the city limits, slightly outside the walls, and spacious enough to appear like little towns. The hospitals are large for two reasons: so that the sick, however numerous they may be, will not be packed closely and uncomfortably together, and also so that those who have a contagious disease, such as might pass from one to the other, may be isolated. The hospitals are well ordered and supplied with everything needed to cure the patients, who are nursed with tender and watchful care. Highly skilled physicians are in constant attendance. Consequently, though nobody is sent there against his will, there is hardly anyone in the city who would not rather be treated for an illness at the hospital than at home.

When the hospital steward has received the food prescribed for the sick by their doctors, the best of the remainder is fairly divided among the halls according to the number in each, except that special regard is paid to the governor, the high priest, and the tranibors, as well as to ambassadors and foreigners, if there are any. In fact, foreigners are very few; but when they do come, they have certain furnished houses assigned to them.

At the hours of lunch and supper, a brazen trumpet summons the entire syphogranty to assemble in their hall, except for those who are bedridden in the hospitals or at home. After the halls have been served with their quotas of food, nothing prevents an individual from taking food home from the marketplace. They realize that no one would do this without good reason. For while it is not forbidden to eat at home, no one does it willingly, because it is not thought proper; and besides, it would be stupid to take the trouble of preparing a worse meal at home when there is an elegant and sumptuous one near at hand in the hall.

In this hall, slaves do all the particularly dirty and heavy work. But planning the meal, as well as preparing and cooking the food, is carried out by the women alone, with each family taking its turn. Depending on their number, they sit down at three or more tables. The men sit with their backs to the wall, the women on the outside, so that if a woman has a sudden qualm or pain, such as occasionally happens during pregnancy, she may get up without disturbing the others and go off to the nurses.

A separate dining room is assigned to the nurses and infants, with a plentiful supply of cradles, clean water, and a warm fire. Thus the nurses may lay the infants down, or remove their swaddling clothes and let them refresh themselves by playing freely before the fire. Each child is nursed by its own mother, unless death or illness prevents. When that happens, the wives of the syphogrants quickly find a nurse. The problem is not difficult. Any

2. The institution of the common messes has precedents in ancient Sparta and in the designs for an ideal commonwealth by Plato (*Republic* 3.416E) and Aristotle (*Politics* 7.10.10). It has also been a feature of other communities with a utopian bent, e.g., the Israeli kibbutzim.

woman who can, gladly volunteers for the job, since everyone applauds her kindness and the child itself regards its nurse as its natural mother.

Children under the age of five sit together in the nursery. All other minors, both boys and girls up to the age of marriage, either wait on table or, if not old and strong enough for that, stand by in absolute silence. Both groups eat whatever is handed to them by those sitting at the table, and have no other set time for their meals.

The syphogrant with his wife sits at the middle of the first table, in the highest part of the dining hall. This is the place of greatest honor, and from this table, which is placed crosswise to the others, the whole gathering can be seen. Two of the eldest sit with them, for they always sit in groups of four; if there is a church in the district, the priest and his wife sit with the syphogrant, so as to preside.[3] On both sides of them sit younger people, next to them older people again, and so through the hall: those of about the same age sit together, yet are mingled with others of a different age. The reason for this, as they explain it, is that the dignity of the aged, and the respect due them, may restrain the younger people from improper freedom of words and gestures, since nothing said or done at table can pass unnoticed by the old, who are present on every side.

Dishes of food are not served down the tables in order from top to bottom, but all the old persons, who are seated in conspicuous places, are served with the best food; and then equal shares are given to the rest. The old people, as they feel inclined, give their neighbors a share of those delicacies which are not plentiful enough to be served to everyone. Thus due respect is paid to seniority, yet everyone enjoys some of the benefits.

They begin every lunch and supper with some reading on a moral topic,[4] but keep it brief lest it become a bore. Taking that as an occasion, the elders introduce proper topics of conversation, which they try not to make gloomy or dull. They never monopolize the conversation with long monologues, but are eager to hear what the young people say. In fact, they deliberately draw them out, in order to discover the natural temper and quality of each one's mind, as revealed in the freedom of mealtime talk.

Their lunches are light, their suppers rather more elaborate, because lunch is followed by work, supper by rest and a night's sleep, which they think particularly helpful to good digestion. No evening meal passes without music, and the dessert course is never scanted; during the meal, they burn incense and scatter perfume, omitting nothing which will make the occasion festive. For they are somewhat inclined to think that no kind of pleasure is forbidden, provided harm does not come of it.

This is the pattern of life in the city; but in the country, where they are farther removed from neighbors, they all eat in their own homes. No family lacks for food, since, after all, whatever the city-dwellers eat comes originally from those in the country.

---

3. Marginal gloss: "Priest before prince. But now even bishops act as servants to royalty."
4. Humanists were fond of this social custom, the origins of which were part monastic, part classical.

THE TRAVELS [AND TRADE] OF THE UTOPIANS

Anyone who wants to visit friends in another city, or simply to see the place itself, can easily obtain permission from his syphogrant and tranibor, unless for some special reason he is needed at home. They travel together in groups, taking a letter from the governor granting leave to travel and fixing a day of return. They are given a wagon and a public slave to drive the oxen and look after them, but unless women are in the company they dispense with the wagon as an unnecessary bother. Wherever they go, though they take nothing with them, they never lack for anything, because they are at home everywhere. If they stay more than a day in one place, each one practices his trade there, and is kindly received by his fellow artisans.

Anyone who takes upon himself to leave his district without permission, and is caught without the governor's letter, is treated with contempt, brought back as a runaway, and severely punished. If he is bold enough to try it a second time, he is made a slave. Anyone who wants to stroll about and explore the extent of his own district is not prevented, provided he first obtains his father's permission and his wife's consent. But wherever he goes in the countryside, he gets no food until he has completed either a morning's or an afternoon's stint of work. On these terms, he may go where he pleases within his own district, yet be just as useful to the city as if he were at home.

So you see there is no chance to loaf or any pretext for evading work; there are no wine bars or alehouses or brothels, no chances for corruption, no hiding places, no spots for secret meetings. Because they live in the full view of all, they are bound to be either working at their usual trades or enjoying their leisure in a respectable way. Such customs must necessarily result in plenty of life's good things, and since they share everything equally, it follows that no one can ever be reduced to poverty or forced to beg.

In the senate at Amaurot (to which, as I said before, three representatives come every year from each city), they survey the island to find out where there are shortages and surpluses, and promptly satisfy one district's shortage with another's surplus. These are outright gifts; those who give receive nothing in return from those to whom they give. Though they give freely to one city, asking nothing in return, they get freely from another to which they gave nothing; and thus the whole island is like a single family.

After they have accumulated enough for themselves—and this they consider to be a full two-years' store, because next year's crop is always uncertain—then they export their surpluses to other countries: great quantities of grain, honey, wool, flax, timber, scarlet and purple dyestuffs, hides, wax, tallow, and leather, as well as livestock. One-seventh of their cargo they give freely to the poor of the importing country, and the rest they sell at moderate prices. In exchange they receive not only such goods as they lack at home (in fact, about the only important thing they lack is iron) but immense quantities of silver and gold. They have been carrying on trade for a long time now, and have accumulated a greater supply of the precious metals than you would believe possible. As a result, they now care very little whether they sell for cash or on credit, and most payments to them actually take the form of promissory notes. However, in all such transactions, they never trust individuals but insist that the foreign city become officially responsible. When the day of payment comes, the city collects the money due from private debtors, puts it into the treasury, and enjoys the use of it till the Utopians claim payment. Most of it, in fact, is never claimed. The Utopians think it hardly right to take what they don't need away from people who do need it. But if they need to lend some part of the money to another nation, then they call it in—as they do also when they must wage war. This is the only reason that they keep such an immense treasure at home, as a protection against extreme peril or sudden emergency. They use it above all to hire, at extravagant rates of pay, foreign mercenaries, whom they would much rather risk in battle than their own citizens. They know very well that for large enough sums of money many of the enemy's soldiers can themselves be bought off or set at odds with one another, either secretly or openly.[5]

[THEIR ATTITUDE TO GOLD AND SILVER]

For this reason, therefore, they have accumulated a vast treasure; but they do not keep it like a treasure. I'm really quite ashamed to tell you how they do keep it, because you probably won't believe me. I would not have believed it myself if someone had just told me about it; but I was there, and saw it with my own eyes. It is a general rule that the more different anything is from what people are used to, the harder it is to accept. But, considering that all their other customs are so unlike ours, a sensible judge will perhaps not be surprised that they treat gold and silver quite differently from the way we do. After all, they never do use money among themselves, but keep it only for a contingency which may or may not actually arise. So in the meanwhile they take care that no one shall overvalue gold and silver, of which money is made, beyond what the metals themselves deserve. Anyone can see, for example, that iron is far superior to either; men could not live without iron, by heaven, any more than without fire or water. But Nature granted to gold and silver no function with which we cannot easily dispense. Human folly has made them precious because they are rare. In contrast, Nature, like a most indulgent mother, has placed the best things out in the open, like air, water, and the earth itself; but vain and unprofitable things she has hidden away in remote places.

If in Utopia gold and silver were kept locked up in some tower, foolish heads among the common people might concoct a story that the governor and senate were out to cheat ordinary folk and get some advantage for themselves. They might indeed put the gold and silver into plate-ware and such handiwork, but then in case of necessity the people would not want to give up such articles, on which they had begun to fix their hearts, only to melt them down for soldiers' pay. To avoid all these inconveniences, they thought of a plan which conforms with their institutions as clearly as it contrasts with our own. Unless one has actually seen it working, their plan may seem incredible, because we prize gold so highly and are so careful about protecting it. While they eat from pottery dishes and drink from glass cups, well made but inexpensive, their chamber pots and all their humblest vessels, for use in the common halls and even in private homes, are made of gold and silver.[6] The chains and heavy fetters of slaves are also made of these metals.

---

5. Marginal gloss: "Better to avoid war by bribery or guile than to wage it with great loss of human blood."

6. Marginal gloss: "O magnificent scorn for gold!" Vespucci had reported Native Americans' indifference to gold and gems.

Finally, criminals who are to bear the mark of some disgraceful act are forced to wear golden rings in their ears and on their fingers, golden chains around their necks, and even golden headbands. Thus they hold gold and silver up to scorn in every conceivable way. As a result, if they had to part with their entire supply of these metals, which other nations give up with as much agony as if they were being disemboweled, the Utopians would feel it no more than the loss of a penny.

They pick up pearls by the seashore, and diamonds and garnets from certain cliffs, but never go out of set purpose to look for them. If they happen to find some, they polish them and give them to the children, who, when they are small, feel proud and pleased with such gaudy decorations. But after, when they grow a bit older, and notice that only babies like such toys, they lay them aside. Their parents don't have to say anything; the children simply put these trifles away out of shame, just as our children when they grow up put away their marbles, baubles, and dolls.

These customs so different from those of other people produce quite different attitudes: this never became clearer to me than it did in the case of the Anemolian[7] ambassadors, who came to Amaurot while I was there. Because they came to discuss important business, the national council had assembled ahead of time, three citizens from each city. The ambassadors from nearby nations, who had visited Utopia before and knew something of their customs, understood that fine clothing was not respected in that land, silk was despised, and gold a badge of contempt; therefore they always came in the very plainest of their clothes. But the Anemolians, who lived farther off and had had fewer dealings with the Utopians, had heard only that they all dressed alike and very simply; so they took for granted that their hosts had nothing to wear that they didn't put on. Being themselves rather more proud than wise, they decided to dress as resplendently as the very gods, and dazzle the eyes of the poor Utopians by the glitter of their garb.

Consequently the three ambassadors made a grand entry with a suite of a hundred attendants, all in clothing of many colors, and most in silk. Being noblemen at home, the ambassadors were arrayed in cloth of gold, with heavy gold chains on their necks, gold earrings, gold rings on their fingers, and sparkling strings of pearls and gems on their caps. In fact, they were decked out in all the articles which in Utopia are used to punish slaves, shame wrongdoers, or entertain infants. It was a sight to see how they strutted when they compared their finery with the dress of the Utopians, who had poured out into the streets to see them pass. But it was just as funny to see how wide they fell of the mark, and how far they were from getting the consideration they wanted and expected. Except for a very few Utopians who for some special reason had visited foreign countries, all the onlookers considered this pomp and splendor a mark of disgrace. They therefore bowed to the humblest of the party as lords, and took the ambassadors, because of their golden chains, to be slaves, passing them by without any reverence at all. You might have seen children, who had themselves thrown away their

7. From Greek *anemolios,* "windy." The story of the Anemolian ambassadors owes much to "Nigrinus," a dialogue by the Syrian satirist Lucian (2nd century C.E.) in which a rich Roman makes a fool of himself by stalking around Athens in a purple robe. More and Erasmus had published a volume of Latin translations of Lucian (who wrote in Greek) in 1506.

pearls and gems, nudge their mothers when they saw the ambassadors' jeweled caps, and say:

"Look at that big lummox, mother, who's still wearing pearls and jewels as if he were a little boy!"

But the mother, in all seriousness, would answer:

"Hush, son, I think he is one of the ambassadors' fools."

Others found fault with the golden chains as useless, because they were so flimsy any slave could break them, and so loose that he could easily shake them off and run away whenever he wanted, footloose and fancy-free. But after the ambassadors had spent a couple of days among the Utopians, they saw the immense amounts of gold which were as thoroughly despised there as they were prized at home. They saw too that more gold and silver went into making the chains and fetters of a single runaway slave than into costuming all three of them. Somewhat ashamed and crestfallen, they put away all the finery in which they had strutted so arrogantly, especially after they had talked with the Utopians enough to learn their customs and opinions.

[THEIR PHILOSOPHY]

The Utopians marvel that any mortal can take pleasure in the dubious sparkle of a little jewel or bright gemstone, when he has a star, or the sun itself, to look at. They are amazed at the foolishness of any man who considers himself a nobler fellow because he wears clothing of specially fine wool. No matter how delicate the thread, they say, a sheep wore it once, and still was nothing but a sheep.[8] They are surprised that gold, a useless commodity in itself, is everywhere valued so highly that man himself, who for his own purposes conferred this value on it, is considered far less valuable than the gold. They do not understand why a dunderhead with no more brains than a post, and who is as depraved as he is foolish, should command a great many wise and good men simply because he happens to have a great pile of gold. Yet if this master should lose his money to the lowest rascal in his household (as can happen by chance, or through some legal trick—for the law can produce reversals as violent as Fortune herself), he would promptly become the servant of his servant, as if he were personally attached to the coins, and a mere appendage to them.[9] Even more than this, the Utopians are appalled at those people who practically worship a rich man, though they neither owe him anything nor are obligated to him in any way. What impresses them is simply that the man is rich. Yet all the while they know he is so mean and grasping that as long as he lives not a single penny out of that great mound of money will ever come their way.

These and the like attitudes the Utopians have picked up partly from their upbringing, since the institutions of their commonwealth are completely opposed to such folly, and partly from instruction and their reading of good books. For though not many people in each city are excused from labor and assigned to scholarship full-time (these are persons who from childhood have given evidence of excellent character, unusual intelligence, and devotion to learning), every child gets an introduction to good literature, and throughout

8. Echoing Lucian's "Demonax" (sect. 41).
9. Alongside this passage and obviously applying to several sentences in it, a marginal gloss proclaims, "How much wiser are the Utopians than the ruck of Christians!"

their lives a large part of the people, men and women alike, spend their leisure time in reading.

They study all the branches of learning in their native tongue, which is not deficient in terminology or unpleasant in sound, and adapts itself as well as any to the expression of thought. Just about the same language is spoken throughout that entire area of the world, though elsewhere it is corrupted to various degrees.

Before we came there, the Utopians had never so much as heard about a single one of those philosophers[1] whose names are so celebrated in our part of the world. Yet in music, dialectic, arithmetic, and geometry they have found out just about the same things as our great men of the past. But while they equal the ancients in almost all subjects, they are far from matching the inventions of our modern logicians.[2] In fact they have not discovered even one of those elaborate rules about restrictions, amplifications, and suppositions which our own young men study in the *Little Logicbook*.[3] They are so far from being able to speculate on "second intentions" that not one of them was able to see "man-in-general,"[4] though I pointed straight at him with my finger, and he is, as you well know, bigger than any giant, maybe even a colossus. On the other hand, they have learned to plot expertly the courses of the stars and the movements of the heavenly bodies. They have devised a number of different instruments by which they compute with the greatest exactness the course and position of the sun, the moon, and the other stars that are visible in their area of the sky. As for the conjunctions and oppositions of the planets, and that whole deceitful business of divination by the stars, they have never so much as dreamed of it.[5] From long experience in observation, they are able to forecast rains, winds, and other changes in the weather. But as to the causes of the weather, of the tides in the sea and its saltiness, and the origins and nature of the heavens and the earth, they have various opinions. They agree with our ancient philosophers on some matters, but on others, just as the ancients disagreed with one another, so the Utopians differ from all the ancients and yet reach no consensus among themselves.

In matters of moral philosophy, they carry on the same arguments as we do. They inquire into the nature of the good, distinguishing goods of the body from goods of the mind and external goods.[6] They ask whether the name of "good" may be applied to all three, or applies only to goods of the mind. They discuss virtue and pleasure, but their chief concern is what to think of human happiness, and whether it consists of one thing or of more. On this point, they seem overly inclined to the view of those who think that all or most human happiness consists of pleasure.[7] And what is more surpris-

---

1. As the next sentence indicates, the idea of "philosophy" here is the old, broad one that encompasses learning in general (the sense that survives in the title Doctor of Philosophy).
2. The Scholastic philosophers, constantly deprecated by humanists.
3. Probably the *Parva logicalia*, a textbook of logic by Peter of Spain, later Pope John XXI (d. 1277).
4. Man conceived of as a "universal." "Second intentions": in Scholastic discourse, purely abstract conceptions, derived from "first intentions" (the direct apprehensions of things). The

sentence is typical of the way humanists liked to ridicule, in the name of common sense, the Scholastics' abstractions.
5. Marginal gloss: "Yet these astrologers are revered by Christians to this day."
6. This threefold classification of goods is associated especially with Aristotle (*Nicomachean Ethics* 1.8.2, *Politics* 7.1.3–4).
7. I.e., the Utopians' primary affinity in moral philosophy is with the hedonistic school founded by Epicurus (341–271 B.C.E.). Cf. Vespucci on the Native Americans: "I deem their manner of life to

ing, they seek support for this comfortable opinion from their religion, which is serious and strict, indeed almost stern and forbidding. For they never discuss happiness without joining to their philosophic rationalism certain principles drawn from religion. Without these religious principles, they think that reason by itself is weak and defective in its efforts to investigate true happiness.

Their religious principles are of this nature: that the soul of man is immortal, and by God's goodness born for happiness; that after this life, rewards are appointed for our virtues and good deeds, punishments for our sins. Though these are indeed religious beliefs, they think that reason leads us to believe and accept them. And they add unhesitatingly that if these beliefs were rejected, no one would be so stupid as not to feel that he should seek pleasure, regardless of right and wrong. His only care would be to keep a lesser pleasure from standing in the way of a greater one, and to avoid pleasures that are inevitably followed by pain.[8] They think you would have to be actually crazy to pursue harsh and painful virtue, give up the pleasures of life, and suffer pain from which you can expect no advantage. For if there is no reward after death, you have no compensation for having passed your entire existence without pleasure, that is, miserably.

To be sure, they believe happiness is found, not in every kind of pleasure, but only in good and honest pleasure. Virtue itself, they say, draws our nature to this kind of pleasure, as to the supreme good. There is an opposed school which declares that virtue is itself happiness.[9]

They define virtue as living according to nature;[1] and God, they say, created us to that end. When an individual obeys the dictates of reason in choosing one thing and avoiding another, he is following nature. Now the first rule of reason is to love and venerate the Divine Majesty to whom we owe our existence and our capacity for happiness. The second rule of nature is to lead a life as free of anxiety and as full of joy as possible, and to help all one's fellow men toward that end. The most hard-faced eulogist of virtue and the grimmest enemy of pleasure, while they invite us to toil and sleepless nights and self-laceration, still admonish us to relieve the poverty and misfortune of others as best we can. It is especially praiseworthy, they tell us, when we provide for our fellow creatures' comfort and welfare. Nothing is more humane (and humanity is the virtue most proper to human beings) than to relieve the misery of others and, by removing all sadness from their lives, restore them to enjoyment, that is, pleasure. Well, if this is the case, why doesn't nature equally invite us to do the same thing for ourselves? Either a joyful life (that is, one of pleasure) is a good thing, or it isn't. If it isn't, then you should not help anyone to it—indeed, you ought to take it away from everyone you can, as being harmful and deadly to them. But if such a life is good, and if we are supposed, indeed obliged, to help others to it, why shouldn't we first of all seek it for ourselves, to whom we owe no less charity

---

be Epicurean." Contrary to popular opinion, however, Epicurus himself did not mean, by the pursuit of pleasure, mere undiscriminating sensual indulgence: like the Utopians, he placed primary emphasis on the pleasures of a virtuous, rational life.

8. These rules for choosing among pleasures are attributed to Epicurus (Diogenes Laertius, *Lives of Eminent Philosophers* 10.129).

9. This is the position of the Stoics, who asserted that virtue constitutes happiness whether or not it leads to pleasure.

1. Another Stoic precept.

than to anyone else? When nature prompts you to be kind to your neighbors, she does not mean that you should be cruel and merciless to yourself.[2] Thus they say that nature herself prescribes for us a joyous life, in other words, pleasure, as the goal of our actions; and living according to her prescriptions is to be defined as virtue. But as nature bids mortals to make one another's lives merrier, to the extent that they can, so she warns us constantly not to seek our own advantage in ways that cause misfortune to our fellows. And the reason for this is an excellent one; for no one is placed so far above the rest that he is nature's sole concern: she cherishes alike all those living beings to whom she has granted the same form.

Consequently, the Utopians maintain that one should not only abide by private agreements but also obey all those public laws which control the distribution of vital goods, such as are the very substance of pleasure. Any such laws, provided they have been properly promulgated by a good king, or ratified by a people free of force and fraud, should be observed; and as long as they are observed, to pursue your own interests is prudent; to pursue the public interest as well is pious; but to pursue your own pleasure by depriving others of theirs is unjust. On the other hand, deliberately to decrease one's own pleasure in order to augment that of others is a work of humanity and benevolence which never fails to reward the doer over and above his sacrifice. You may be repaid for your kindness; and in any case you are conscious of having done a good deed. Your mind draws more joy from recalling the affection and good will of those whom you have benefited than your body would have drawn pleasure from the things you gave up. Finally, they believe (as religion easily persuades a well-disposed mind to believe) that God will recompense us, for surrendering a brief and transitory pleasure here, with immense and neverending joy in heaven. And so they conclude, after carefully considering and weighing the matter, that all our actions and the virtues exercised within them look toward pleasure and happiness as their ultimate end.

By pleasure they understand every state or movement of body or mind in which we find delight in accordance with the behests of nature. They are right in adding that the desire must accord with nature. By simply following our senses and right reason[3] we may discover what is pleasant by nature: it is a delight that does not injure others, that does not preclude a greater pleasure, and that is not followed by pain. But a pleasure which is against nature, and which men call "delightful" only by the emptiest of fictions (as if one could change the real nature of things just by changing their names), does not, they hold, really make for happiness; in fact, they say it often precludes happiness. And the reason is that men whose minds are filled with false ideas of pleasure have no room left for true and genuine delight. As a matter of fact, there are a great many things which have no genuine sweetness in them but are for the most part actually bitter, yet which, through the perverse enticements of evil desires, are considered very great pleasures, and even included among the supreme goals of life.

---

2. Marginal gloss: "But now some people cultivate pain as if it were the essence of religion, rather than incidental to performance of a pious duty or the result of natural necessity—and thus to be borne, not pursued."

3. The power, thought to have been implanted by God in all humankind, to apprehend truth and moral law; conscience.

Among the devotees of this false pleasure, they include those whom I mentioned before, the people who think themselves finer fellows because they wear finer clothes. These people are twice mistaken: first in thinking their clothes better than anyone else's, and then in thinking themselves better because of their clothes. As far as a garment's usefulness goes, what does it matter if it was woven of fine thread or coarse? Yet they act as if they were set apart by Nature herself, rather than their own fantasies; they strut about, and put on airs. Because they have a fancy suit, they think themselves entitled to honors they would never have expected if they were dressed in homespun, and they grow indignant if someone passes them by without showing special respect.

It is the same kind of absurdity to be pleased by empty, ceremonial honors. What true and natural pleasure can you get from someone's bent knee or bared head? Will the creaks in your own knees be eased thereby, or the madness in your head? The phantom of false pleasure is illustrated by others who run mad with delight over their own blue blood, plume themselves on their nobility, and applaud themselves for all their rich ancestors (the only ancestors that count nowadays), and especially for all their ancient family estates. Even if they don't have the shred of an estate themselves, or if they've squandered every penny of their inheritance, they don't consider themselves a bit less noble.

In the same class the Utopians put those people I described before who are mad for jewelry and gems, and think themselves divinely happy if they find a good specimen, especially of the sort that happens to be fashionable in their country at the time—for stones vary in value from one market to another. The collector will not make an offer for a stone till it's taken out of its gold setting, and even then he will not buy unless the dealer guarantees and gives security that it is a true and genuine stone. What he fears is that his eyes will be deceived by a counterfeit. But if you consider the matter, why should a counterfeit give any less pleasure, when your eyes cannot distinguish it from a real gem? Both should be of equal value to you—as they would be, in fact, to a blind man.[4]

What about those who pile up money not because they want to do anything with the heap, but so they can sit and look at it? Is that true pleasure they experience, or aren't they simply cheated by a show of pleasure? Or what of those with the opposite vice, who hide away gold they will never use and perhaps never even see again? In their anxiety to hold onto it, they actually lose it. For what else happens when you deprive yourself, and perhaps other people too, of a chance to use your gold, by burying it in the ground? And yet when you've hidden your treasure away, you exult over it as if your mind were now free to rejoice. Suppose someone stole it, and you died ten years later, knowing nothing of the theft. During all those ten years, what did it matter whether the money was stolen or not? In either case, it was equally useless to you.

To these false and foolish pleasures they add gambling, which they have heard about, though they've never tried it, as well as hunting and hawking. What pleasure can there be, they wonder, in throwing dice on a table? If

---

4. In *The Praise of Folly*, Erasmus tells a story about More giving his young wife some false gems, which he passed off as being real and highly valuable.

there were any pleasure in the action, wouldn't doing it over and over again quickly make one tired of it? What pleasure can there be in listening to the barking and yelping of dogs—isn't that rather a disgusting noise? Is there any more pleasure felt when a dog chases a hare than when a dog chases a dog? If what you like is fast running, there's plenty of that in both cases; they're just about the same. But if what you really want is slaughter, if you want to see a living creature torn apart under your eyes—you ought to feel nothing but pity when you see the little hare fleeing from the hound, the weak creature tormented by the stronger, the fearful and timid beast brutalized by the savage one, the harmless hare killed by the cruel dog. The Utopians, who regard this whole activity of hunting as unworthy of free men, have assigned it accordingly, to their butchers, who, as I said before, are all slaves.[5] In their eyes, hunting is the lowest thing even butchers can do. In the slaughterhouse, their work is more useful and honest, since there they kill animals only from necessity; but the hunter seeks merely his own pleasure from the killing and mutilating of some poor little creature. Even in beasts, taking such relish in the sight of death reveals, in the Utopians' opinion, a cruel disposition, or else one that has become so through the constant practice of such brutal pleasures.

Common opinion considers these activities, and countless others like them, to be pleasures; but the Utopians say flatly they have nothing at all to do with real pleasure, since there's nothing naturally pleasant about them. They often please the senses, and in this they are like pleasure, but that does not alter their basic nature. The enjoyment doesn't arise from the experience itself, but only from the perverse habits of the mob, as a result of which they mistake the bitter for the sweet, just as pregnant women, whose taste has been turned awry, sometimes think pitch and tallow taste sweeter than honey. A person's taste may be similarly depraved by disease or by custom, but that does not change the nature of pleasure, or of anything else.

They distinguish several different classes of true pleasure, some being pleasures of the mind and others pleasures of the body. Those of the mind are knowledge and the delight which rises from contemplating the truth, also the gratification of looking back on a well-spent life and the unquestioning hope of happiness to come.

Pleasures of the body they also divide into two classes. The first is that which fills the senses with immediate delight. Sometimes this happens when bodily organs that have been weakened by natural heat are restored with food and drink; sometimes it happens when we eliminate some excess in the body, as when we move our bowels, generate children, or relieve an itch somewhere by rubbing or scratching it. Now and then pleasure arises, not from restoring a deficiency or discharging an excess, but from something that excites our senses with a hidden but unmistakable force, and attracts them to itself. Such is the power of music.

The second kind of bodily pleasure they describe as nothing but the calm and harmonious state of the body, its state of health when undisturbed by any disorder. Health itself, when not oppressed by pain, gives pleasure, without any external excitement at all. Even though it appeals less directly to the

---

5. Marginal gloss: "Yet today this is the chosen art of our court-divinities."

senses than the gross gratifications of eating and drinking, many consider this to be the greatest pleasure of all. Most of the Utopians regard it as the foundation and basis of all the pleasures, since by itself alone it can make life peaceful and desirable, whereas without it there is no possibility of any other pleasure. Mere absence of pain, without positive health, they regard as insensibility, not pleasure.

Some have maintained that a stable and tranquil state of health is not really a pleasure, on the grounds that the presence of health cannot be felt except through some external stimulus.[6] The Utopians (who have considered the matter thoroughly) long ago rejected this opinion. On the contrary, they nearly all agree that health is crucial to pleasure. Since pain is inherent in disease, they argue, and pain is the bitter enemy of pleasure, just as disease is the enemy of health, then pleasure must be inherent in quiet good health. You may say pain is not the disease itself, simply an accompanying effect; but they argue that that makes no difference, since the effect is the same either way. For whether health is itself a pleasure or is merely the cause of pleasure (as fire is the cause of heat), the fact remains that those who have stable health must also have pleasure.

When we eat, they say, what happens is that health, which was starting to fade, takes food as its ally in the fight against hunger. While our health gains strength, the simple process of returning vigor gives us pleasure and refreshment. If our health feels delight in the struggle, will it not rejoice when the victory has been won? When at last it is restored to its original strength, which was its aim all through the conflict, will it at once become insensible, and fail to recognize and embrace its own good? The idea that health cannot be felt they consider completely wrong. Every man who's awake, they say, feels that he's in good health—unless he isn't. Is anyone so torpid and dull that he won't admit health is delightfully agreeable to him? And what is delight except pleasure under another name?

Of all the different pleasures, they seek primarily those of the mind, and prize them most highly. The foremost mental pleasure, they believe, arises from the practice of the virtues and the consciousness of a good life. Among the pleasures of the body, they give the first place to health. As for eating and drinking and other delights of that sort, they consider them desirable, but only for the sake of health. They are not pleasant in themselves, but only as ways to withstand the insidious attacks of sickness. A wise man would rather escape sickness altogether than have a good cure for it; he would rather prevent pain than find a palliative for it. And so it would be better not to need this kind of pleasure at all than to be assuaged by it.

Anyone who thinks happiness consists of this sort of pleasure must confess that his ideal life would be one spent in an endless round of hunger, thirst, and itching, followed by eating, drinking, scratching, and rubbing. Who can fail to see that such an existence is not only disgusting but miserable? These pleasures are certainly the lowest of all, as they are the most adulterate— for they never occur except in connection with the pains that are their contraries. Hunger, for example, is linked to the pleasure of eating, and far from equally, since the pain is sharper and lasts longer; it precedes the pleasure,

---

6. This is, especially, the position of Plato, e.g., *Republic* 9.583C–585A.

and ends only when the pleasure ends with it. So the Utopians think pleasures of this sort should not be much valued, except insofar as they are necessary to life. Yet they enjoy these pleasures too, and acknowledge gratefully the kindness of Mother Nature, who coaxes her children with allurements and cajolery to do what in any case they must do from necessity. How wretched life would be if the daily diseases of hunger and thirst had to be overcome by bitter potions and drugs, like some other diseases that afflict us less often!

Beauty, strength, and agility, as special and pleasant gifts of nature, they joyfully accept. The pleasures of sound, sight, and smell they also pursue as the special seasonings of life, recognizing that nature intended these delights to be the particular province of man. No other kind of animal admires the shape and loveliness of the universe, or enjoys odors, except in the way of searching for food, or distinguishes harmonious from dissonant sounds. But in all their pleasures, the Utopians observe this rule, that the lesser pleasure must not interfere with the greater, and that no pleasure shall carry pain with it as a consequence. If a pleasure is dishonorable, they think it will inevitably lead to pain.

Moreover, they think it is crazy for a man to despise beauty of form, to impair his own strength, to grind his energy down to lethargy, to exhaust his body with fasts, to ruin his health, and to scorn all other natural delights, unless by so doing he can better serve the welfare of others or the public good. Then indeed he may expect a greater reward from God. But otherwise for a man to inflict pain on himself does no one any good. He gains, perhaps, the empty and shadowy reputation of virtue; and no doubt he hardens himself against fantastic adversities which may never occur. But such a person the Utopians consider absolutely crazy—cruel to himself, as well as most ungrateful to Nature—as if, to avoid being in her debt, he rejects all her gifts.

This is the way they think about virtue and pleasure. Human reason, they believe, can attain to no surer conclusions than these, unless a revelation from heaven should inspire men with holier notions. In all this, I have no time now to consider whether they are right or wrong, and don't feel obliged to do so. I have undertaken only to describe their principles, not to defend them. But of this I am sure, that whatever you think of their ideas, there is not a more excellent people or a happier commonwealth anywhere in the whole world.

In body they are nimble and lively, and stronger than you would expect from their stature, though they're by no means tiny. Their soil is not very fertile, nor their climate of the best, but they protect themselves against the weather by temperate living, and improve their soil by industry, so that nowhere do grain and cattle flourish more plentifully, nowhere are people more vigorous, and liable to fewer diseases. There you can see not only that they do all the things farmers usually do to improve poor soil by hard work and technical knowledge, but you can see a forest which they uprooted with their own hands and moved to another site. They did this not so much for the sake of better growth but to make transport easier, by having wood closer to the sea, the rivers, or the cities themselves. For grain is easier than wood to carry by land over a long distance.

[THEIR DELIGHT IN LEARNING]

The people in general are easygoing, cheerful, clever, and like their leisure. When they must, they can stand heavy labor, but otherwise they are not very fond of it. In intellectual pursuits, they are tireless. When they heard from us about the literature and learning of the Greeks (for we thought there was nothing in Latin, except the historians and poets, that they would value), it was wonderful to behold how eagerly they sought to be instructed in Greek. We therefore began to study a little of it with them, at first more to avoid seeming lazy than out of any expectation that they would profit by it. But after a short trial, their diligence convinced us that our efforts would not be wasted. They picked up the forms of the letters so easily, pronounced the language so aptly, memorized it so quickly, and began to recite so accurately that it seemed like a miracle. Most of our pupils were established scholars, of course, picked for their unusual ability and mature minds; and they studied with us, not just of their own free will, but at the command of the senate.[7] Thus in less than three years they had perfect control of the language and could read the best authors fluently, unless the text was corrupt. I have a feeling they picked up Greek more easily because it was somewhat related to their own tongue. Though their language resembles Persian in most respects, I suspect their race descends from the Greeks, because their language retains some vestiges of Greek in the names of cities and in official titles.

Before leaving on the fourth voyage, I placed on board, instead of merchandise, a good-sized packet of books; for I had resolved not to return at all rather than come home soon. Thus they received from me most of Plato's works and more of Aristotle's, as well as Theophrastus's book *On Plants*, though the latter, I'm sorry to say, was somewhat mutilated.[8] During the voyage I carelessly left it lying around, a monkey got hold of it, and from sheer mischief ripped out a few pages here and there and tore them up. Of the grammarians they have only Lascaris, for I did not take Theodorus with me, nor any dictionary except that of Hesychius; and they have Dioscorides.[9] They are very fond of Plutarch's writings, and delighted with the witty persiflage of Lucian.[1] Among the poets they have Aristophanes, Homer, and Euripides, together with Sophocles in the small typeface of the Aldine edition.[2] Of the historians they possess Thucydides and Herodotus, as well as Herodian.[3]

As for medical books, a comrade of mine named Tricius Apinatus brought with him some small treatises by Hippocrates, and the *Microtechne* of

---

7. Marginal gloss: "But now clods and blockheads are assigned to learning, while the best minds are corrupted by pleasures."
8. Theophrastus, Aristotle's pupil, was studied in the Renaissance not as a quaint curiosity but because his views were still current in botany.
9. Dioscorides (1st century C.E.) wrote a treatise on drugs and herbs that was printed in 1544. The Renaissance scholars Constantine Lascaris and Theodore of Gaza wrote grammars of Greek. The Greek dictionary of Hesychius of Alexandria (5th century C.E.) was published in 1514.
1. The Syrian-born ironist who was admired, translated, and imitated by both More and Erasmus (see p. 84, n. 7). The writings of Plutarch (ca.

46–ca. 120 C.E.) referred to presumably include his *Moral Essays* as well as his *Parallel Lives* of eminent Greeks and Romans.
2. The first printed edition of Sophocles was that of Aldus Manutius in 1502. The house of Aldus, established in Venice toward the end of the 15th century, was not only the first establishment to print Greek texts in Greek type but was responsible for some of the best-designed books in the history of the art.
3. Thucydides and Herodotus (both 5th century B.C.E.) are the preeminent Greek historians. Herodian (ca. 175–250 C.E.) wrote a history of the Roman emperors of the 2nd and 3rd centuries.

a b c d e f g h i k l m n o p q r s t u x y

ⓄⒽⓂⓈⒼⒼⓈⒼⓆⒸⒽⓈⒶ⅃⌐Ⓒ⌐ⒼⒾⒽⒾⒼⒼⒼⒶ

TETRASTICHON VERNACVLA VTO-
PIENSIVM LINGVA.

Vtopos   ha   Boccas   peula   chama.

ⒽⒾ⅃⌐⅃ⒽⒼⓄ Ⓖ⅃ⓂⓂⒽⒼ ⌐ⒼⒼⒼⓄ ⓄⒼⓄⒶⓄ

polta   chamaan

⌐⅃ⒼⒾⓄ ⓄⒼⓄⒶⓄⓄ⅃.

Bargol   he   maglomi   baccan

ⒼⓄⒾⒼ⅃Ⓖ ⒼⒼ ⒶⓄⒼⒼ⅃ⒶⓂ ⒼⓄⓂⓂⓄ⅃

foma   gymnofophaon

Ⓖ⅃ⒶⓄ ⒼⒼⒶ⅃⅃Ⓖ⅃⌐ⒼⓄ⅃.

Agrama   gymnofophon   labarem

ⓄⒼⒾⓄⒶⓄ ⒼⒼⒶ⅃⅃Ⓖ⅃⌐Ⓖ⅃⅃ ⒼⓄⒼⓄⒾⒼⒶ

bacha   bodamilomin

ⒼⓄⓂⒼⓄ Ⓖ⅃ⓄⓄⒶⓆⒼ⅃ⒶⓆ⅃.

Voluala   barchin   heman   la

Ⓖ⅃ⒼⒼⓄⒼⓄ ⒼⓄⒾⓂⒼⒶ⅃ ⒼⒼⒶⓄ⅃ ⒼⓄ

lauoluola   dramme   pagloni.

ⒼⓄⒼ⅃ⒼⒼ⅃ⒼⓄ ⒼⒾⓄⒶⒶⒼ ⌐ⓄⒼⒼ⅃⅃Ⓐ.

HORVM VERSVVM AD VERBVM HAEC
EST SENTENTIA.

Vtopus me dux ex non infula fecit infulam.
Vna ego terrarum omnium abſq; philoſophia.
Ciuitatem philoſophicam expreſſi mortalibus.
Libenter impartio mea, non grauatim accipio meliora.

b ;

This sample of the Utopian language, which first appeared in the earliest edition of More's book (1516), reveals affinities with Greek and Latin and has enough internal consistency to suggest that it was worked out with care (evidently by Peter Giles). The stilted Latin quatrain at the end, which purports to be a literal translation, can itself be translated as follows: "Me, once a peninsula, Utopus the king made an island. / Alone among all nations, and without complex abstractions, / I set before men's eyes the philosophical city. / What I give is free; what is better I am not slow to take from others."

Galen.[4] They were delighted to have these books. Even though there's hardly a country in the world that needs doctors less, medicine is nowhere held in greater honor: they consider it one of the finest and most useful parts of philosophy. They think that when, with the help of philosophy, they explore the secrets of nature they are gratifying not only themselves but the author and maker of nature. They suppose that, like other artists, he created this beautiful mechanism of the world to be admired—and by whom, if not by man, who is alone in being able to appreciate so great a thing? Therefore he is bound to prefer a careful observer and sensitive admirer of his work before one who, like a brute beast, looks on the grand spectacle with a stupid and blockish mind.

Once stimulated by learning, the minds of the Utopians are wonderfully quick to seek out those various arts which make life more agreeable. Two inventions, to be sure, they owe to us: the art of printing and the manufacture of paper. At least they owe these arts partly to us, though partly to their own ingenuity. While we were showing them the Aldine editions of various works, we talked about papermaking and how letters are printed, though without going into detail, for none of us had had any practical experience of either skill. But with great sharpness of mind they immediately grasped the basic principles. While previously they had written only on vellum, bark, and papyrus, they now undertook to make paper and to print with type. Their first attempts were not altogether successful, but with practice they soon mastered both arts. They became so proficient that, if they had texts of the Greek authors, they would soon have no lack of volumes; but as they have no more than those I mentioned, they have contented themselves with reprinting each in thousands of copies.

Any sightseer coming to their land who has some special intellectual gift, or who has traveled widely and seen many countries, is sure of a warm welcome, for they love to hear what is happening throughout the world. This is why we were received so kindly. Few merchants, however, go there to trade. What could they import except iron—or else gold and silver, which everyone would rather bring home than send abroad? As for the export trade, the Utopians prefer to do their own transportation, rather than invite strangers to do it. By carrying their own cargos they are able to learn more about foreign countries on all sides, and keep up their skill in navigation.

SLAVES[5]

The only prisoners of war the Utopians enslave are those captured in wars they fight themselves. The children of slaves are not automatically enslaved,[6]

---

4. Hippocrates (5th century B.C.E.) and Galen (2nd century C.E.) were the most influential Greek medical writers. The *Microtechne* is a medieval summary of Galen's ideas. The name Tricius Apinatus (like Hythloday) is a learned joke: in classical Italy, Trica and Apina were extinct towns whose names, taken together, were proverbial for trifling, worthless things.
5. The institution of slavery—with prisoners of war (civilians as well as combatants) as a major source of the slaves—was ubiquitous in the ancient world, including the Greek and Roman civilizations that Utopia resembles in various

ways. In Europe, slavery declined in the Middle Ages, being replaced as a source of labor by feudal serfdom, in which individuals were bound to the land rather than to a particular owner. Chattel slavery, however, revived strongly in the European colonies in the New World: the enslavement of Native Americans began with the earliest settlements, in the 1490s, and the first African slaves were imported in 1502.
6. This fact sharply distinguishes Utopian slavery from both classical and early modern slavery and medieval serfdom.

nor are slaves obtained from foreign countries. Their slaves are either their own citizens, enslaved for some heinous offense, or else foreigners who were condemned to death in their own land. Most are of the latter sort. Sometimes the Utopians buy them at a very modest rate, more often they ask for them, get them for nothing, and bring them home in considerable numbers. Both kinds of slaves are kept constantly at work, and are always fettered. But the Utopians deal with their own people more harshly than with the others, feeling that their crimes are worse and deserve stricter punishment because they had an excellent education and the best of moral training, yet still couldn't be restrained from wrongdoing. A third class of slaves consists of hardworking penniless drudges from other nations who voluntarily choose to become slaves in Utopia. Such people are treated well, almost as well as citizens, except that they are given a little extra work, on the score that they're used to it. If one of them wants to leave, which seldom happens, no obstacles are put in his way, nor is he sent off emptyhanded.

[SUICIDE AND EUTHANASIA]

As I said before, the sick are carefully tended, and nothing is neglected in the way of medicine or diet which might cure them. Everything possible is done to mitigate the pain of those who are suffering from incurable diseases; and visitors do their best to console them by sitting and talking with them. But if the disease is not only incurable but excruciatingly and constantly painful, then the priests and public officials come and urge the invalid not to endure such agony any longer. They remind him that he is now unfit for any of life's duties, a burden to himself and to others; he has really outlived his own death. They tell him he should not let the disease prey on him any longer, but now that life is simply torture, he should not hesitate to die but should rely on hope for something better. Since life has become a mere prison cell, where he is bitterly tormented, he should free himself, or let others free him, from the rack of living. This would be a wise act, they say, since for him death would put an end not to pleasure but to agony. In addition, he would be obeying the advice of the priests, who are the interpreters of God's will; which ensures that it would be a holy and pious act.[7]

Those who have been persuaded by these arguments either starve themselves to death or, having been put to sleep, are freed from life without any sensation of dying. But they never force this step on a man against his will; nor, if he decides against it, do they lessen their care of him. Under these circumstances, when death is advised by the authorities, they consider self-destruction honorable. But the suicide, who takes his own life without the approval of priests and senate, they consider unworthy either of earth or fire, and throw his body, unburied and disgraced, into a bog.

[MARRIAGE AND DIVORCE]

Women do not marry till they are eighteen, nor men till they are twenty-two. Premarital intercourse, if discovered and proved, brings severe punishment

---

7. In ancient Rome, suicide was regarded as an honorable way out of deep personal or political difficulties, but neither suicide nor euthanasia has ever been acceptable in Catholic Christianity. Cf. Hythloday's earlier reference to God's prohibition of suicide (p. 56).

on both man and woman, and the guilty parties are forbidden to marry during their whole lives, unless the governor by his pardon remits the sentence. In addition both the father and mother of the household where the offense occurred suffer public disgrace for having been remiss in their duty. The reason they punish this offense so severely is that they suppose few people would join in married love—with confinement to a single partner, and all the petty annoyances that married life involves—unless they were strictly restrained from a life of promiscuity.

In choosing marriage partners, they solemnly and seriously follow a custom which seemed to us foolish and absurd in the extreme. Whether she is a widow or a virgin, the woman is shown naked to the suitor by a responsible and respectable matron; and similarly, some respectable man presents the suitor naked to the woman.[8] We laughed at this custom and called it absurd; but they were just as amazed at the folly of all other peoples. When men go to buy a colt, where they are risking only a little money, they are so suspicious that, though the beast is almost bare, they won't close the deal until the saddle and blanket have been taken off, lest there be a hidden sore underneath. Yet in the choice of a mate, which may cause either delight or disgust for the rest of their lives, people are completely careless. They leave all the rest of her body covered up with clothes and estimate the attractiveness of a woman from a mere handsbreadth of her person, the face, which is all they can see. And so they marry, running great risk of bitter discord, if something in either's person should offend the other. Not all people are so wise as to concern themselves solely with character; and even the wise appreciate physical beauty, as a supplement to the virtues of the mind. There's no question but that deformity may lurk under clothing, serious enough to make a man hate his wife when it's too late to be separated from her. If some disfiguring accident occurs after marriage, each person must bear his own fate; but beforehand everyone should be legally protected from deception.

There is extra reason for them to be careful, because in that part of the world they are the only people who practice monogamy. Their marriages are seldom terminated except by death, though they do allow divorce for adultery or for intolerably offensive behavior. A husband or wife who is the aggrieved party in such a divorce is granted permission by the senate to remarry, but the guilty party is considered disreputable and is permanently forbidden to take another mate.[9] They absolutely forbid a husband to put away his wife against her will and without any fault on her part, just because of some bodily misfortune; they think it cruel that a person should be abandoned when most in need of comfort; and they add that old age, since it not only entails disease but is actually a disease itself, needs more than a precarious fidelity.

It happens occasionally that a married couple cannot get along, and have both found other persons with whom they hope to live more harmoniously. After getting the approval of the senate, they may then separate by mutual consent and contract new marriages. But such divorces are allowed only after the senators and their wives have carefully investigated the case. They allow divorce only very reluctantly, because they know that husbands and

8. Marginal gloss: "Not very modest, but not so imprudent, either."
9. In Europe, the Catholic Church allowed separation in cases of adultery but did not allow even the aggrieved party to remarry.

wives will find it hard to settle down together if each has in mind that a new marriage is easily available.

They punish adulterers with the strictest form of slavery. If both parties were married, they are both divorced, and the injured parties may marry one another, if they want, or someone else. But if one of the injured parties continues to love such an undeserving spouse, the marriage may go on, providing the innocent person chooses to share in the labor to which the slave is condemned. And sometimes it happens that the repentance of the guilty and the devotion of the innocent party move the governor to pity, so that he restores both to freedom. But a second conviction of adultery is punished by death.

[PUNISHMENTS AND REWARDS; CUSTOMS AND LAWS]

No other crimes carry fixed penalties; the senate sets specific penalties for each particular misdeed, as it is considered atrocious or venial. Husbands chastise their wives, and parents their children, unless the offense is so serious that public punishment is called for. Generally, the gravest crimes are punished by slavery, for they think this deters offenders just as much as getting rid of them by immediate capital punishment, and is more beneficial to the commonwealth. In addition, slaves contribute more by their labor than by their death, and they are permanent and visible reminders that crime does not pay. If the slaves rebel against their condition, then, like savage beasts which neither bars nor chains can tame, they are finally put to death. But if they are patient, they are not left altogether without hope. When subdued by long hardships, if they show by their behavior that they regret the crime more than the punishment, their slavery is lightened or remitted altogether, sometimes by the governor's pardon, sometimes by popular vote.

Attempted seduction is subject to the same penalty as seduction itself. They think that a crime clearly and deliberately attempted is as bad as one committed, and that failure should not confer advantages on a criminal who did all he could to succeed.

They are very fond of fools, and think it contemptible to insult them.[1] There is no prohibition against enjoying their foolishness, and they even regard this as beneficial to the fools. If anyone is so serious and solemn that the foolish behavior and comic patter of a clown do not amuse him, they don't entrust him with the care of such a person, for fear that a man who gets not only no use from a fool but not even any amusement—a fool's only gift—will not treat him kindly.

To mock a person for being deformed or crippled is considered ugly and disfiguring, not to the victim but to the mocker, who stupidly reproaches the cripple for something he cannot help.

They think it a sign of a weak and sluggish character to neglect one's natural beauty, but they consider cosmetics a detestable affectation. From experience they have learned that no physical beauty recommends a wife to her husband so effectually as goodness and respect. Though some men are captured by beauty alone, none are held except by virtue and compliance.

---

1. More's household included a fool, Henry Patenson.

As they deter people from crime by penalties, so they incite them to virtue by public honors. They set up in the marketplace statues of distinguished men who have served their country well, thinking thereby to preserve the memory of their good deeds and to spur on the citizens to emulate the glory of their ancestors.

Any man who campaigns for a public office is disqualified for all of them. They live together harmoniously, and the public officials are never arrogant or unapproachable. Instead, they are called "fathers," and that is the way they behave. Because the officials never extort respect from the people against their will, the people respect them spontaneously, as they should. Not even the governor is distinguished from his fellow citizens by a robe or crown; he is known only by a sheaf of grain he carries, just as the high priest is distinguished by a wax candle borne before him.[2]

They have very few laws, and their training is such that they need no more. The chief fault they find with other nations is that, even with infinite volumes of laws and interpretations, they cannot manage their affairs properly. They think it completely unjust to bind people by a set of laws that are too many to be read and too obscure for anyone to understand. As for lawyers, a class of men whose trade it is to manipulate cases and multiply quibbles, they exclude them entirely.[3] They think it is better for each man to plead his own case, and say the same thing to the judge that he would tell his lawyer. This makes for less ambiguity, and readier access to the truth. A man speaks his mind without tricky instructions from a lawyer, and the judge examines each point carefully, taking pains to protect simple folk against the false accusations of the crafty. It is hard to find this kind of plain dealing in other countries, where they have such a multitude of incomprehensibly intricate laws. But in Utopia everyone is a legal expert. For the laws are very few, as I said, and they consider the most obvious interpretation of any law to be the fairest. As they see things, all laws are promulgated for the single purpose of teaching every man his duty. Subtle interpretations teach very few, since hardly anybody is able to understand them, whereas the more simple and apparent sense of the law is open to everyone. If laws are not clear, they are useless; for simpleminded men (and most men are of this sort, and need to be told where their duty lies), there might as well be no laws at all as laws which can be interpreted only by devious minds after endless disputes. The dull common man cannot understand this legal chicanery, and couldn't even if he studied it his whole life, since he has to earn a living in the meantime.

[FOREIGN RELATIONS]

Some of the Utopians' free and independent neighbors (many of whom were previously liberated by them from tyranny), having learned to admire Utopian virtues, have made a practice of asking the Utopians to supply magistrates for them. Some of these magistrates serve one year, others five. When their service is over, they bring them home with honor and praise, and take back new ones to their country. These peoples seem to have settled on an

---

2. Grain and candle evidently symbolize the special function of each ruler: to ensure prosperity and to provide spiritual vision.

3. Marginal gloss: "The useless crowd of lawyers." More was, of course, one himself.

excellent scheme to safeguard the commonwealth. Since the welfare or ruin of a commonwealth depends on the character of its officials, where could they make a more prudent choice than among Utopians, who cannot be tempted by money? For money is useless to them when they go home, as they soon must, and they can have no partisan or factional feelings, since they are strangers in the city over which they rule. Wherever they take root in men's minds, these two evils, greed and faction, are the destruction of all justice—and justice is the strongest bond of any society. The Utopians call these people who have borrowed magistrates from them their *allies*; others whom they have benefited they call simply *friends*.

While other nations are constantly making treaties, breaking them, and renewing them, the Utopians never make any treaties at all. If nature, they say, doesn't bind man adequately to his fellow man, will an alliance do so? If a man scorns nature herself, is there any reason to think he will care about mere words? They are confirmed in this view by the fact that in that part of the world, treaties and alliances between kings are not generally observed with much good faith.

In Europe, of course, the dignity of treaties is everywhere kept sacred and inviolable, especially in those regions where the Christian religion prevails. This is partly because the kings are all so just and virtuous, partly also because of the reverence and fear that everyone feels toward the popes.[4] Just as the popes themselves never promise anything which they do not most conscientiously perform, so they command all other princes to abide by their promises in every way. If someone declines to do so, they compel him to obey by means of pastoral censure and sharp reproof. The popes rightly declare that it would be particularly disgraceful if people who are specifically called "the faithful" acted in bad faith.

But in that new world, which is as distant from ours in customs and way of life as in the distance the equator puts between us, nobody trusts treaties. The greater the formalities, the more numerous and solemn the oaths, the sooner the treaty will be broken. The rulers will easily find some defect in the wording of it, which often enough they deliberately inserted themselves. No treaty can be made so strong and explicit that a government will not be able to worm out of it, breaking in the process both the treaty and its own word. If such craft, deceit, and fraud were practiced in private contracts, the politicians would raise a great outcry against both parties, calling them sacrilegious and worthy of the gallows. Yet the very same politicians think themselves clever fellows when they give this sort of advice to kings. As a consequence, people are apt to think that justice is a humble, plebeian virtue, far beneath the majesty of kings. Or else they conclude that there are two kinds of justice, one which is only for the common herd, a lowly justice that creeps along the ground, hedged in everywhere and encumbered with chains; and the other, which is the justice of princes, much more free and majestic, so that it can do anything it wants and nothing it doesn't want.

This royal practice of keeping treaties badly there is, I suppose, the reason the Utopians don't make any; doubtless if they lived here in Europe they would change their minds. However, they think it a bad idea to make trea-

---

4. In fact the crowned heads of Europe and the popes alike were ruthless and casual violators of treaties.

ties at all, even if they are faithfully observed. A treaty implies that people who are separated by some natural obstacle as slight as a hill or a brook are joined by no bond of nature; it assumes that they are born rivals and enemies, and are right in aiming to destroy one another except insofar as a treaty restrains them. Moreover, they see that treaties do not really promote friendship; for both parties still retain the right to prey upon one another to whatever extent incautious drafting has left the treaty without sufficient provisions against it. The Utopians think, on the other hand, that no one should be considered an enemy who has done you no harm, that the fellowship of nature is as good as a treaty, and that men are united more firmly by good will than by pacts, by their hearts than by their words.

MILITARY PRACTICES

They despise war as an activity fit only for beasts, yet practiced more by man than by any other creature. Unlike almost every other people in the world, they think nothing so inglorious as the glory won in battle. Yet on certain fixed days, men and women alike carry on vigorous military training, so they will be fit to fight should the need arise. But they go to war only for good reasons: to protect their own land, to protect their friends from an invading army, or to liberate an oppressed people from tyranny and servitude. Out of human sympathy, they not only protect their friends from present danger but sometimes avenge previous injuries; they do this, however, only if they themselves have previously been consulted, have approved the cause, and have demanded restitution in vain. Then and only then they think themselves free to declare war. They take this final step not only when their friends have been plundered but also, and even more fiercely, when their friends' merchants have been subjected to extortion in another country, either on the pretext of laws unjust in themselves or through the perversion of good laws.

This and no other was the cause of the war which the Utopians waged a little before our time on behalf of the Nephelogetes against the Alaopolitans.[5] Under pretext of right, a wrong (as they saw it) had been inflicted on some Nephelogete traders residing among the Alaopolitans. Whatever the rights and wrongs of the quarrel, it developed into a fierce war, into which, apart from the hostile forces of the two parties themselves, the neighboring nations poured their efforts and resources. Some prosperous nations were ruined completely, others badly shaken. One trouble led to another, and in the end the Alaopolitans were crushed and reduced to slavery (since the Utopians weren't involved on their own account) by the Nephelogetes—a people who, before the war, had not been remotely comparable in power to their rivals.

So severely do the Utopians punish wrong done to their friends, even in matters of mere money; but they are not so strict in enforcing their own rights. When they are cheated out of their goods, so long as no bodily harm is done, their anger goes no further than cutting off trade relations with that nation till restitution is made. The reason is not that they care more for their allies' citizens than for their own, but simply this: when the merchants

---

5. "People Born from the Clouds" versus "Citizens of a Country without People."

of their friends are cheated, it is their own property that is lost, but when the Utopians lose something, it comes from the common stock, and is bound to be in plentiful supply at home; otherwise they wouldn't have been exporting it. Hence no one individual even notices the loss. So small an injury, which affects neither the life nor the livelihood of any of their own people, they consider it cruel to avenge by the deaths of many soldiers. On the other hand, if one of their own is maimed or killed anywhere, whether by a government or by a private citizen, they first send envoys to look into the circumstances; then they demand that the guilty persons be surrendered; and if that demand is refused, they are not to be put off, but at once declare war. If the guilty persons are surrendered, their punishment is death or slavery.

The Utopians are not only troubled but ashamed when their forces gain a bloody victory, thinking it folly to pay too high a price even for the best goods. But if they overcome the enemy by skill and cunning, they exult mightily, celebrate a public triumph, and raise a monument as for a hard-won victory. They think they have really acted with manly virtue when they have won a victory such as no animal except man could have won—a victory achieved by strength of understanding. Bears, lions, boars, wolves, dogs, and other wild beasts fight with their bodies, they say; and most of them are superior to us in strength and ferocity; but we outdo them all in shrewdness and rationality.

The only thing they aim at, in going to war, is to secure what would have prevented the declaration of war, if the enemy had conceded it beforehand. Or if they cannot get that, they try to take such bitter revenge on those who have provoked them that they will be afraid ever to do it again. These are their chief aims, which they try to achieve quickly, yet in such a way as to avoid danger rather than to win fame and glory.

As soon as war is declared, therefore, they have their secret agents simultaneously post many placards, each marked with their official seal, in the most conspicuous places throughout the enemy territory. In these proclamations they promise immense rewards to anyone who will kill the enemy's king. They offer smaller but still very substantial sums for killing any of a list of other individuals whom they name. These are the persons whom they regard as most responsible, after the king, for plotting aggression against them. The reward for an assassin is doubled for anyone who succeeds in bringing in one of the proscribed men alive. The same reward, plus a guarantee of personal safety, is offered to any one of the proscribed men who turns against his comrades. As a result, the enemies of the Utopians quickly come to suspect everyone, particularly one another; and the many perils of their situation lead to panic. They know perfectly well that many of them, including their princes, have been betrayed by those in whom they placed complete trust—so effective are bribes as an incitement to crime. Knowing this, the Utopians are lavish in their promises of bounty. Being well aware of the risks their agents must run, they make sure that the payments are in proportion to the peril; thus they not only offer, but actually deliver, enormous sums of gold, as well as large landed estates in very secure locations on the territory of their friends.

Everywhere else in the world, this process of bidding for and buying the life of an enemy is condemned as the cruel villainy of a degenerate mind; but the Utopians consider it good policy, both wise and merciful. In the first place, it enables them to win tremendous wars without fighting any actual battles; and in the second place it enables them, by the sacrifice of a few guilty men, to spare the lives of many innocent persons who would have died in battle, some on their side, some on the enemy's. They pity the mass of the enemy's soldiers almost as much as their own citizens, for they know common people do not go to war of their own accord, but are driven to it by the madness of princes.

If assassination does not work, they sow the seeds of dissension in enemy ranks by inciting the prince's brother or some other member of the nobility to scheme for the crown. If internal discord dies down, they try to rouse up neighboring peoples against the enemy by reviving forgotten claims to dominion, of which kings always have an ample supply.

When they promise their resources to help in a war, they send money very freely, but commit their own citizens only sparingly. They hold their own people dear, and value them so highly that they would not willingly exchange one of their citizens for an enemy's prince. Since they keep their gold and silver for the purpose of war alone, they spend it without hesitation; after all, they will continue to live just as well even if they expend the whole sum. Besides the wealth they have at home, they have a vast treasure abroad, since, as I said before, many nations owe them money. So they hire mercenary soldiers from all sides, especially the Zapoletes.[6]

These people live five hundred miles to the east of Utopia, and are rude, rough, and fierce. The forests and mountains where they are bred are the kind of country they like: tough and rugged. They are a hard race, capable of standing heat, cold, and drudgery, unacquainted with any luxuries, careless of what houses they live in or what they wear; they don't till the fields but raise cattle instead. Most of them survive by hunting and stealing. These people are born for battle and are always eager for a fight; they seek one out at every opportunity. Leaving their own country in great numbers, they offer themselves for cheap hire to anyone in need of warriors. The only art they know for earning a living is the art of taking life.

They fight with great courage and incorruptible loyalty for the people who pay them, but they will not bind themselves to serve for any fixed period of time. If someone, even the enemy, offers them more money tomorrow, they will take his side; and day after tomorrow, if a trifle more is offered to bring them back, they'll return to their first employers. Hardly a war is fought in which a good number of them are not engaged on both sides. It happens every day that men who are united by ties of blood and have served together in friendship, but who are now separated into opposing armies, meet in battle. Forgetful of kinship and comradeship alike, they furiously run one another through, driven to mutual destruction for no other reason than that they were hired for paltry pay by opposing princes. They care so much about money that they can easily be induced to change sides for an increase of only a penny a day. They have picked up the habit of avarice, but none of the profit; for what they earn by shedding blood, they quickly squander on debauchery of the most squalid sort.

Because the Utopians give higher pay than anyone else, these people are ready to serve them against any enemy whatever. And the Utopians, who seek

---

6. "Busy sellers." The Zapoletes resemble the Swiss, who produced the best and most feared mercenaries of Europe (a remnant still survives as the Swiss Guard in the Vatican).

out the best possible men for proper uses, hire these, the worst possible men, for improper uses. When the situation requires, they thrust the Zapoletes into the positions of greatest danger by offering them immense rewards. Most of them never come back to collect their pay, but the Utopians faithfully pay off those who do survive, to encourage them to try it again. As for how many Zapoletes get killed, the Utopians never worry about that, for they think they would deserve very well of all mankind if they could exterminate from the face of the earth that entire disgusting and vicious race.

Besides the Zapoletes, they employ as auxiliaries the soldiers of the people for whom they have taken up arms, and then squadrons of their other friends. Last, they add their own citizens, including some man of known bravery to command the entire army. In addition, they appoint two substitutes for him, who hold no rank as long as he is safe. But if the commander is captured or killed, the first of these two substitutes becomes his successor, and in case of a mishap to him, the other. Thus, though the accidents of war cannot be foreseen, they make sure that the whole army will not be disorganized through the loss of their leader.

In each city, soldiers are chosen from those who have volunteered. No one is forced to fight abroad against his will, because they think a man who is naturally fearful will act weakly at best, and may even spread panic among his comrades. But if their own country is invaded, they call everyone to arms, posting the fearful (as long as they are physically fit) on shipboard among braver men, or here and there along fortifications, where there is no place to run away. Thus shame at failing their countrymen, desperation at the immediate presence of the enemy, and the impossibility of flight often combine to overcome their fear, and they make a virtue out of sheer necessity.

Just as no man is forced into a foreign war against his will, so women are allowed to accompany their men on military service if they want to—not only not forbidden, but encouraged and praised for doing so. Each goes with her husband to the front, and stands shoulder to shoulder with him in the line of battle; in addition, they place around a man his children and blood- or marriage-relations, so that those who by nature have most reason to help one another may be closest at hand for mutual aid. It is a matter of great reproach for either partner to come home without the other, or for a son to return after losing a parent. The result is that if the enemy stands his ground, the hand-to-hand fighting is apt to be long and bitter, ending only when everyone is dead.

As I observed, they take every precaution to avoid having to fight in person, so long as they can bring the war to an end with mercenaries. But when they are forced to take part in battle, they are as bold in the struggle as they were prudent in avoiding it while they could. In the first charge they are not fierce, but gradually as the fighting goes on they grow more determined, putting up a steady, stubborn resistance. Their spirit is so strong that they will die rather than yield ground. They are certain that everyone at home will be provided for, and they have no worries about the future of their families (and that sort of worry often daunts the boldest courage); so their spirit is exalted and unconquerable. Their skill in the arts of war gives them extra confidence; also from childhood they have been trained in sound principles of conduct (which their education and the good institutions of their commonwealth reinforce); and that too adds to their courage. They don't hold life so cheap that they throw it away recklessly, nor so dear as to grasp it avidly at the price of shame, when duty bids them give it up.

At the height of the battle, a band of the bravest young men, who have taken a special oath, devote themselves to seeking out the opposing general. They attack him directly, they lay secret traps for him, they hit at him from near and far. A long and continuous supply of fresh men keep up the assault as the exhausted drop out. In the end, they rarely fail to kill or capture him, unless he takes to flight.

When they win a battle, it never ends in a massacre, for they would much rather take prisoners than cut throats. They never pursue fugitives without keeping one line of their army drawn up under the colors. They are so careful of this that if they win the victory, with this last reserve force (supposing the rest of their army has been beaten), they would rather let the enemy army escape than pursue fugitives with their own ranks in disorder. They remember what has happened more than once to themselves: that when the enemy seemed to have the best of the day, had routed the main Utopian force and, exulting in their victory, had scattered to pursue the fugitives, a few Utopians held in reserve and watching their opportunity have suddenly attacked the dispersed and scattered enemy at the very moment when he felt safe and had lowered his guard. Thereby they changed the fortune of the day, snatched certain victory out of the enemy's hands, and, though conquered themselves, conquered their conquerors.

It is not easy to say whether they are more crafty in laying ambushes or more cautious in avoiding those laid for them. Sometimes they seem to be on the point of breaking and running when that is the last thing they have in mind; but when they really are ready to retreat, you would never guess it. If they are outnumbered, or if the terrain is unsuitable, they shift their ground silently by night or slip away from the enemy by some stratagem. Or if they have to withdraw by day, they do so gradually, and in such good order that they are as dangerous to attack then as if they were advancing. They fortify their camps very carefully with a deep, broad ditch all around them, the earth being thrown inward to make a wall; the work is done not by workmen but by the soldiers themselves with their own hands. The whole army pitches in, except for an armed guard posted around the rampart to prevent a surprise attack. With so many hands at work, they complete great fortifications, enclosing wide areas with unbelievable speed.

The armor they wear is strong enough to protect them from blows, but does not prevent easy movement of the body; in fact, it doesn't interfere even with their swimming, and part of their military training consists of swimming in armor. For long-range fighting they use arrows, which they fire with great force and accuracy, and from horseback as well as on foot. At close quarters they use not swords but battle-axes, which because of their sharp edge and great weight are lethal weapons, whether used in slashing or thrusting. They are very skillful in inventing machines of war, but conceal them with the greatest care, since if they were made known before they were needed, they might be more ridiculous than useful. Their first consideration in designing them is to make them easy to move and aim.[7]

7. The military devices of the Utopians represent a patchwork of notions from the common knowledge of the day. Their camps are fortified like Roman ones. Their reliance on archery links them with the

When the Utopians make a truce with the enemy, they observe it religiously, and will not break it even if provoked. They do not ravage the enemy's territory or burn his crops; indeed, so far as possible, they avoid any trampling of the fields by men or horses, thinking they may need the grain themselves later on. Unless he is a spy, they injure no unarmed man. When cities are surrendered to them, they keep them intact; even when they have stormed a place, they do not plunder it, but put to death the men who prevented surrender, enslave the other defenders, and do no harm to the civilians. If they find any inhabitants who recommended surrender, they give them a share in the property of the condemned, and present their auxiliaries with the rest; for the Utopians themselves never take any booty.

After a war is ended, they collect the cost of it, not from the allies for whose sake they undertook it, but from the conquered. They take as indemnity not only money, which they set aside to finance future wars, but also landed estates, from which they may enjoy forever a substantial annual income. They now have revenues of this sort in many different countries, acquired little by little in various ways, till it now amounts to over seven hundred thousand ducats a year.[8] As managers of these estates, they send abroad some of their own citizens to serve as collectors of revenue. Though they live on the properties in grand style and conduct themselves like great lords, plenty of income is still left over to be put in the public treasury, unless they choose to give the conquered nation credit. They often do the latter, until they happen to need the money, and even then it's rare for them to call in the entire debt. Some of the estates are given, as I've already described, to those who have risked great dangers on their behalf.

If any prince takes up arms and prepares to invade their land, they immediately attack him in full force outside their own borders. They are most reluctant to wage war on their own soil, and no necessity could ever compel them to admit foreign auxiliaries onto their island.

THE RELIGIONS OF THE UTOPIANS

There are different forms of religion throughout the island, and even in individual cities. Some worship as a god the sun, others the moon, and still others one of the planets. There are some who worship a man of past ages who was conspicuous either for virtue or glory; they consider him not only a god but the supreme god. The vast majority, however, and these by far the wisest, believe nothing of the sort: they believe in a single power, unknown, eternal, infinite, inexplicable, beyond the grasp of the human mind, and diffused throughout the universe, not physically, but in influence. Him they call their parent, and to him alone they attribute the origin, increase, progress, changes, and ends of all things; they do not offer divine honors to any other.

English, whose archers had played key roles in the famous victories over the French at Crécy and Agincourt—though the Utopians' skill in shooting arrows from horseback recalls the ancient Parthians and Scythians. Their "machines" are presumably like Roman dart hurlers, battering rams, and stone throwers, but the emphasis on their portability probably reflects contemporary experience with cannon, which were extremely hard to drag over the muddy roads of the time.

8. Gold coins of this name were minted by several European states. Four ducats of Venice, Burgundy, or Hungary were roughly equivalent to an English pound, and the pound itself was worth several hundred times its value today. The point is that the Utopians' annual income from the estates is huge.

Though the other sects of the Utopians differ from this main group in various particular doctrines, they agree with them in this single head, that there is one supreme power, the maker and ruler of the universe, whom they all call in their native language Mithra.[9] Different people define him differently, and each supposes the object of his worship is that one and only nature to whose divine majesty, by the consensus of all nations, the creation of all things is attributed. But gradually they are coming to forsake this mixture of superstitions, and to unite in that one religion which seems more reasonable than any of the others. And there is no doubt that the other religions would have disappeared long ago, had not various unlucky accidents that befell certain Utopians who were thinking about changing their religion been interpreted, out of fear, as signs of divine anger, not chance, as if the deity who was being abandoned were avenging an insult against himself.

But after they had heard from us the name of Christ, and learned of his teachings, his life, his miracles, and the no less marvelous constancy of the many martyrs whose blood, freely shed, has drawn many nations far and near into the Christian fellowship, you would not believe how eagerly they assented to it, either through the mysterious inspiration of God, or because Christianity seemed very like the religion already prevailing among them. But I think they were also much influenced by the fact that Christ approved a communal way of life for his disciples, and that among the truest communities of Christians the practice still prevails.[1] Whatever the reason, no small number of them chose to join our communion, and received the holy water of baptism. By that time, two of our group had died, and among us four survivors there was, I am sorry to say, no priest; so, though they received the other sacraments, they still lack those which in our religion can be administered only by priests.[2] They do, however, understand what these are, and earnestly desire them. In fact, they dispute vigorously whether a man chosen from among themselves could legitimately assume the functions of a priest without the dispatch of a Christian bishop. Though they seemed on the point of selecting such a person, they had not yet done so when I left.

Those who have not accepted Christianity make no effort to restrain others from it, nor do they criticize new converts to it. While I was there, only one of the Christians was interfered with. As soon as he was baptized, he took upon himself to preach the Christian religion publicly, with more zeal than discretion. We warned him not to do so, but he soon worked himself up to a pitch where he not only set our religion above the rest but condemned all others as profane in themselves, leading their impious and sacrilegious followers to the hell-flames they richly deserved. After he had been going on in this style for a long time, they arrested him. He was tried on a charge, not of despising their religion, but of creating a public disorder, convicted, and sentenced to exile. For it is one of their oldest rules that no man's religion, as such, shall be held against him.

---

9. In ancient Persian religion, Mithra (or Mithras) was the spirit of light.
1. The communist practice of the early Christians is described in Acts 2.44–45 and 4.32–35. Many monastic and ascetic orders still made a practice of abolishing private property for their members.
2. Of the seven Catholic sacraments, only baptism and matrimony can be conferred by laymen. Priests are created by ordination by a bishop (cf. below).

Utopus had heard that before his arrival the inhabitants were continually quarreling over religious matters. In fact, he found it was easy to conquer the country because the different sects were too busy fighting one another to oppose him. As soon as he had gained the victory, therefore, he decreed that everyone could cultivate the religion of his choice, and strenuously proselytize for it too, provided he did so quietly, modestly, rationally, and without bitterness toward others. If persuasion failed, no one was allowed to resort to abuse or violence. Anyone who fights wantonly about religion is punished by exile or enslavement.

Utopus laid down these rules not simply for the sake of peace, which he saw was in danger of being destroyed by constant quarrels and implacable hatreds, but also for the sake of religion itself. In matters of religion, he was not at all quick to dogmatize, because he suspected that God perhaps likes diverse and manifold forms of worship and has therefore deliberately inspired different people with different views. On the other hand, he was quite sure that it was arrogant folly for anyone to enforce conformity with his own beliefs on everyone else by means of threats or violence.[3] He supposed that if one religion is really true and the rest false, the true one will sooner or later emerge and prevail by its own natural strength, provided only that men consider the matter reasonably and moderately. But if they try to decide these matters by fighting and rioting, since the worst men are always the most headstrong, the best and holiest religion in the world will be crowded out by blind superstitions, like grain choked out of a field by thorns and briars. So he left the whole matter open, allowing each individual to choose what he would believe. The only exception he made was a solemn and strict law against any person who should sink so far below the dignity of human nature as to think that the soul perishes with the body, or that the universe is ruled by mere chance rather than divine providence.

Thus the Utopians all believe that after this life vices are to be punished and virtue rewarded; and they consider that anyone who denies this proposition is not even one of the human race, since he has degraded the sublimity of his own soul to the base level of a beast's wretched body. Still less will they count him as one of their citizens, since he would openly despise all the laws and customs of society, if not prevented by fear. Who can doubt that a man who has nothing to fear but the law, and no hope of life beyond the grave, will do anything he can to evade his country's laws by craft or break them by violence, in order to gratify his own private greed? Therefore a person who holds such views is offered no honors, entrusted with no offices, and given no public responsibility; he is universally regarded as low and torpid. Yet they do not afflict him with punishments, because they are persuaded that no one can choose to believe by a mere act of the will. They do not compel him by threats to dissemble his views, nor do they tolerate in the matter any deceit or lying, which they detest as next door to deliberate

---

3. This was not the attitude More took a decade after *Utopia*, when, the Reformation schism having begun, he was involved in the prosecution of Protestant heretics, sometimes to the death. In the *Dialogue Concerning Heresies* (1529), he wrote that "if it were now doubtful and ambiguous whether the church of Christ were in the right rule of doctrine or not, then were it very necessary to give them all good audience that could and would anything dispute on either party for it or against it, to the end that if we were now in a wrong way, we might leave it and walk in some better." Utopia was in this hypothetical situation; England, in More's view, was not.

malice. The man may not argue with the common people in behalf of his opinion; but in the presence of the priests and other important persons, in private, they not only permit but encourage it. For they are confident that in the end his madness will yield to reason.

There are some others, in fact no small number of them, who err in the opposite direction, in supposing that animals too have immortal souls,[4] though not comparable to ours in excellence, nor destined to equal felicity. These people are not thought to be evil, their opinion is not thought to be wholly unreasonable, and so they are not interfered with.

Almost all the Utopians are absolutely convinced that human bliss after death will be enormous; thus they lament every individual's sickness, but mourn over a death only if the person was torn from life anxiously and unwillingly. Such behavior they take to be a very bad sign, as if the soul, despairing and conscious of guilt, dreaded death through a secret premonition of punishments to come. Besides, they suppose God can hardly be well pleased with the coming of one who, when he is summoned, does not come gladly but is dragged off reluctantly and against his will. Such a death fills the onlookers with horror, and they carry the corpse out to burial in melancholy silence. There, after begging God to have mercy on his spirit and to pardon his infirmities, they commit his body to the earth. But when someone dies blithely and full of good hope, they do not mourn for him but carry the body cheerfully away, singing and commending the dead man's soul to God. They cremate him in a spirit more of reverence than of grief, and erect a column on which the dead man's honors are inscribed. After they have returned home, they talk of his character and deeds, and no part of his life is mentioned more frequently or more gladly than his joyful death.

They think that recollecting the dead person's goodness helps the living to behave virtuously and is also the most acceptable form of honor to the dead. For they think that dead people are actually present among us, and hear what we say about them, though through the dullness of human sight they are invisible to our eyes. Given their state of bliss, the dead must be able to travel freely where they please, and it would be unkind of them to cast off every desire of revisiting their friends, to whom they had been bound by mutual affection and charity during their lives. Like all other good things, they think that after death charity is increased rather than decreased in good men; and thus they believe the dead come frequently among the living, to observe their words and actions. Hence they go about their business the more confidently because of their trust in such protectors; and the belief that their forefathers are physically present keeps them from any secret dishonorable deed.

Fortune-telling and other vain forms of superstitious divination, such as other peoples take very seriously, they have no part of and consider ridiculous. But they venerate miracles which occur without the help of nature, considering them direct and visible manifestations of the divine power. Indeed, they report that miracles have frequently occurred in their country. Sometimes in great and dangerous crises they pray publicly for a miracle, which they then anticipate with great confidence, and obtain.

---

4. These Utopians resemble the ancient Pythagoreans, who, as a facet of their doctrine of the transmigration of souls, conceded them to animals.

They think that the contemplation of nature, and the sense of reverence arising from it, are acts of worship to God. There are some people, however, and not just a few of them, who from religious motives reject learning and pursue no studies; but none of them is the least bit idle. Constant dedication to the offices of charity, these people think, will increase their chances of happiness after death; and so they are always busy in the service of others. Some tend the sick; others repair roads, clean ditches, rebuild bridges, dig turf, sand, or stones; still others fell trees and cut them up, and transport wood, grain, or other commodities into the cities by wagon. They work for private citizens as well as for the public, and work even harder than slaves. They undertake with cheery good will any task that is so rough, hard, and dirty that most people refuse to tackle it because of the toil, boredom, and frustration involved. While constantly engaged in heavy labor themselves, they secure leisure for others, and yet they claim no credit for it. They do not criticize the way other people live, nor do they boast of their own doings. The more they put themselves in the position of slaves, the more highly they are honored by everyone.

These people are of two sects. The first are celibates who abstain not only from sex but also from eating meat, and some of them from any sort of animal food whatever. They reject all the pleasures of this life as harmful, and look forward only to the joys of the life to come, which they hope to deserve by hard labor and all-night vigils. As they hope to attain it soon, they are cheerful and active in the here and now. The other kind are just as fond of hard work, but prefer to marry. They don't despise the comforts of marriage, but think that, as their duty to nature requires work, so their duty to their country requires them to beget children. They avoid no pleasure unless it interferes with their labor, and gladly eat meat, precisely because they think it makes them stronger for any sort of heavy work. The Utopians regard the second sort as more sensible, but the first sort as holier. If they claimed to prefer celibacy to marriage, and a hard life to a comfortable one, on grounds of reason alone, the Utopians would think them absurd. But since these men claim to be motivated by religion, the Utopians respect and revere them. There is no subject on which they are warier of jumping to conclusions than in this matter of religion. These then are the men whom in their own language they call Buthrescas, a term which may be translated as "the especially religious."

Their priests are of great holiness, and therefore very few. In each city, there are no more than thirteen, one for each church. In case of war, seven of them go out with the army, and seven substitutes are appointed to fill their places for the time being. When the regular priests come back, the substitutes return to their former posts—that is, they serve as assistants to the high priest, until one of the regular thirteen dies, and then one of them succeeds to his position. The high priest is, of course, in authority over all the others. Priests are elected, just like all other officials, by secret popular vote, in order to avoid partisan feeling. After election they are ordained by the college of priests.

They preside over divine worship, attend to religious matters, and act as censors of public morality. For a man to be summoned before them and scolded for not living an honorable life is considered a great disgrace. As the duty of the priests is simply to counsel and advise, so correcting and punishing offenders is the duty of the governor and the other officials, though the priests do exclude from divine service persons whom they find to be extraordinarily wicked. Hardly any punishment is more dreaded than this; the excommunicate incurs great disgrace, and is tortured by the fear of damnation. Not even his body is safe for long, for unless he quickly convinces the priests of his repentance he will be seized and punished by the senate for impiety.

The priests are entrusted with teaching the children and young people.[5] Instruction in morality and virtue is considered just as important as the accumulation of learning. From the very first they try to instill in the pupils' minds, while they are still young and tender, principles which will be useful to preserve the commonwealth. What is planted in the minds of children lives on in the minds of adults, and is of great value in strengthening the commonwealth: the decline of society can always be traced to vices which arise from wrong attitudes.

Women are not debarred from the priesthood, but only a widow of advanced years is ever chosen, and it doesn't happen often. The wives of the male priests are the very finest women in the whole country.

No official in Utopia is more honored than the priest. Even if one of them commits a crime, he is not brought into a court of law, but left to God and his own conscience. They think it is wrong to lay human hands on a man, however guilty, who has been specially consecrated to God as a holy offering, so to speak. This custom is the easier for them to observe because their priests are very few and very carefully chosen. Besides, it rarely happens that a man selected for his goodness and raised to high dignities wholly because of his moral character will fall into corruption and vice. And even if such a thing should happen, human nature being as changeable as it is, no great harm is to be feared, because the priests are so few and have no power beyond that which derives from their good reputation. In fact, the reason for having so few priests is to prevent the order, which the Utopians now esteem so highly, from being cheapened by numbers.[6] Besides, they think it would be hard to find many men qualified for a dignity for which merely ordinary virtues are not sufficient.

Their priests are esteemed no less highly abroad than at home, which can be seen from the following fact: Whenever their armies join in battle, the Utopian priests are to be found, a little removed from the fray but not far, wearing their sacred vestments and down on their knees. With hands raised to heaven, they pray first of all for peace, and then for victory to their own side, but without much bloodshed on either hand.[7] Should their side be victorious, they rush among the combatants and restrain the rage of their own men against the enemy. If any of the enemy see these priests and call to them, it is enough to save their lives; to touch the flowing robes of a priest will save all their property from confiscation. This custom has brought them such veneration among all peoples, and given them such genuine authority, that they have saved the Utopians from the rage of the enemy as often as

---

5. Presumably the priests only *supervise* the teaching: there are only thirteen of them per city, whereas each city is home to thousands of children.

6. Marginal gloss: "But what a crowd of them we have!"

7. Marginal gloss: "O priests far holier than our own!"

they have protected the enemy from Utopians. Instances of this are well known. Sometimes when the Utopian line has buckled, when the field was lost, and the enemy was rushing in to kill and plunder, the priests have intervened to stop the carnage and separate the armies, and an equitable peace has been concluded. There was never anywhere a tribe so fierce, cruel, and barbarous as not to hold their persons sacrosanct and inviolable.

The Utopians celebrate the first and last days of every month, and likewise of each year, as feast days. They divide the year into months which they measure by the orbit of the moon, just as they measure the year itself by the course of the sun. In their language, the first days are known as the Cynemerns and the last days as the Trapemerns, which is to say "First-feasts" and "Last-feasts."[8] Their churches are beautifully constructed, finely adorned, and large enough to hold a great many people. This is a necessity, since churches are so few. Their interiors are all rather dark, not from architectural ignorance but from deliberate policy; for the priests think that in bright light the congregation's thoughts will go wandering, whereas a dim light tends to concentrate the mind and encourage devotion.

Though there are various religions in Utopia, all of them, even the most diverse, agree in the main point, which is worship of the divine nature; they are like travelers going to one destination by different roads. So nothing is seen or heard in the churches that does not square with all the creeds. If any sect has a special rite of its own, that is celebrated in a private house; the public service is ordered by a ritual which in no way derogates from any of the private services. Therefore in the churches no image of the gods is to be seen, so that each person may be free to form his own image of God according to his own religion, in any shape he pleases. They do not invoke God by any name except Mithra. Whatever the nature of the divine majesty may be, they all agree to refer to it by that single word, and their prayers are so phrased as to accommodate the beliefs of all the different sects.

On the evening of the "Last-feast" they meet in their churches, and while still fasting they thank God for their prosperity during that month or year which is just ending. Next day, which is "First-feast," they all flock to the churches in the morning, to pray for prosperity and happiness in the month or year which is just beginning. On the day of "Last-feast," in the home before they go to church, wives kneel before their husbands and children before their parents, to confess their various sins of commission or of negligence and beg forgiveness for their offenses. Thus if any cloud of anger or resentment has arisen in the family, it is dispersed, and they can attend divine services with clear and untroubled minds—for they consider it sacrilege to worship with a rankling conscience. If they are conscious of hatred or anger toward anyone, they do not take part in divine services till they have been reconciled and have cleansed their hearts, for fear of some swift and terrible punishment.

As they enter the church, they separate, men going to the right side and women to the left.[9] Then they take their seats so that the males of each household are placed in front of the head of that household, while the women-

8. The Greek coinage *Trapemerns* actually means "turning-days"; *Cynemerns* means "dog-days" (or perhaps "starting-days").

9. Separation of the sexes in church had been customary since the early Christian centuries.

folk are directly in front of the mother of the family. In this way they ensure that everyone's behavior in public is supervised by the same person whose authority and discipline direct him at home. They take great care that the young are everywhere placed in the company of their elders. For if children were trusted to the care of other children, they might spend in childish foolery the time they should devote to developing a religious fear of the gods, which is the greatest and almost the only incitement to virtue.

They do not slaughter animals in their sacrifices, and do not think that a merciful God, who gave life to all creatures precisely so that they might live, will be gratified with the shedding of blood. They burn incense, scatter perfumes, and display a great number of candles—not that they think these practices profit the divine nature in any way, any more than human prayers do; but they like this harmless kind of worship. They feel that sweet smells, lights, and other such rituals elevate the mind and lift it with a livelier devotion toward the adoration of God.

When they go to church, the people all wear white. The priest wears robes of various colors, wonderful for their workmanship and decoration, though not of materials as costly as one would suppose. The robes have no gold embroidery nor any precious stones, but are decorated with the feathers of different birds so skillfully woven together that the value of the handiwork far exceeds the cost of the most precious materials.[1] Also, certain symbolic mysteries are hidden in the patterning of the feathers on the robes, the meaning of which is carefully handed down among the priests. These messages serve to remind them of God's benefits toward them, and consequently of the devotion they owe to God, as well as of their duty to one another.

As the priest in his robes appears from the vestibule, the people all fall to the ground in reverence. The stillness is so complete that the scene strikes one with awe, as if a divinity were actually present. After remaining in this posture for some time, they rise at a signal from the priest. Then they sing hymns to the accompaniment of musical instruments, most of them quite different in shape from those in our part of the world. Many of them produce sweeter tones than ours, but others are not even comparable. In one respect, however, they are beyond doubt far ahead of us, because all their music, both vocal and instrumental, renders and expresses natural feelings and perfectly matches the sound to the subject. Whether the words of the hymn are supplicatory, cheerful, troubled, mournful, or angry, the music represents the meaning through the contour of the melody so admirably that it penetrates and inspires the minds of the ardent hearers. Finally, the priest and the people together recite certain fixed forms of prayer, so composed that what they all repeat in unison each individual can apply to himself.

In these prayers, the worshipers acknowledge God to be the creator and ruler of the universe and the author of all good things. They thank God for benefits received, and particularly for the divine favor which placed them in the happiest of commonwealths and inspired them with religious ideas which they hope are the truest. If they are wrong in this, and if there is some sort of society or religion more acceptable to God, they pray that he will, in his goodness, reveal it to them, for they are ready to follow wherever he

---

1. Perhaps related to Vespucci's observation that the Native Americans' wealth "consists of feathers of many-hued birds . . . and of many other things to which we attach no value."

leads. But if their form of society is the best and their religion the truest, then they pray that God will keep them steadfast, and bring other mortals to the same way of life and the same religious faith—unless, indeed, there is something in this variety of religions which delights his inscrutable will.

Then they pray that after an easy death God will receive each of them to himself, how soon or how late it is not for them to say. But if God's divine majesty so please, they ask to be brought to him soon, even by the hardest possible death, rather than be kept away from him longer, even by the most fortunate of earthly lives. When this prayer has been said, they prostrate themselves on the ground again; then after a little while they rise and go to lunch. The rest of the day they pass in games and military training.

Now I have described to you as accurately as I could the structure of that commonwealth which I consider not only the best but indeed the only one that can rightfully claim that name. In other places men talk very liberally of the commonwealth, but what they mean is simply their own wealth; in Utopia, where there is no private business, everyone zealously pursues the public business. And in both places people are right to act as they do. For among us, even though the commonwealth may flourish, there are very few who do not know that unless they make separate provision for themselves, they may perfectly well die of hunger. Bitter necessity, then, forces them to think that they must look out for themselves rather than for others, that is, for the people. But in Utopia, where everything belongs to everybody, no one need fear that, so long as the public warehouses are filled, anyone will ever lack for anything he needs. For the distribution of goods is not niggardly; in Utopia no one is poor, there are no beggars, and though no one owns anything, everyone is rich.

For what can be greater riches than to live joyfully and peacefully, free from all anxieties, and without worries about making a living? No man is bothered by his wife's querulous entreaties about money, no man fears poverty for his son, or struggles to scrape up a dowry for his daughter. Everyone can feel secure of his own livelihood and happiness, and of his whole family's as well: wife, sons, grandsons, great-grandsons, great-great-grandsons, and that whole long line of descendants that gentlefolk are so fond of contemplating. Indeed, even those who once worked but can no longer do so are cared for just as well as those who are still working.

Now here I'd like to see anyone try to compare this equity of the Utopians with the so-called justice that prevails among other peoples—among whom let me perish if I can discover the slightest scrap of justice or fairness. What kind of justice is it when a nobleman or a goldsmith or a moneylender, or someone else who makes his living by doing either nothing at all or something completely useless to the commonwealth, gets to live a life of luxury and grandeur, while in the meantime a laborer, a carter, a carpenter, or a farmer works so hard and so constantly that even a beast of burden could scarcely endure it? Although this work of theirs is so necessary that no commonwealth could survive a year without it, they earn so meager a living and lead such miserable lives that beasts of burden would really seem to be better off. Beasts do not have to work every minute, and their food is not much worse; in fact they like it better. And besides, they do not have to worry about their future. But workingmen not only have to sweat and suffer without present reward, but agonize over the prospect of a penniless old age. Their daily wage is inadequate even for their present needs, so there is no possible chance of their saving toward the future.

Now isn't this an unjust and ungrateful commonwealth? It lavishes rich rewards on so-called gentry, goldsmiths, and the rest of that crew, who don't work at all or are mere parasites, purveyors of empty pleasures. And yet it makes no provision whatever for the welfare of farmers and colliers, laborers, carters, and carpenters, without whom the commonwealth would simply cease to exist. After society has taken the labor of their best years, when they are worn out by age and sickness and utter destitution, then the thankless commonwealth, forgetting all their sleepless nights and great services, throws them out to die a miserable death. What is worse, the rich constantly try to grind out of the poor part of their meager wages, not only by private swindling but by public laws. Before, it appeared to be unjust that people who deserve most from the commonwealth should receive least; but now, by promulgating law, they have palmed injustice off as "legal." When I run over in my mind the various commonwealths flourishing today, so help me God, I can see in them nothing but a conspiracy of the rich, who are fattening up their own interests under the name and title of the commonwealth.[2] They invent ways and means to hang onto whatever they have acquired by sharp practice, and then they scheme to oppress the poor by buying up their toil and labor as cheaply as possible. These devices become law as soon as the rich, speaking for the commonwealth—which, of course, includes the poor as well—say they must be observed.

And yet, when these insatiably greedy and evil men have divided among themselves all the goods which would have sufficed for the entire people, how far they remain from the happiness of the Utopian republic, which has abolished not only money but with it greed! What a mass of trouble was cut away by that one step! What a multitude of crimes was pulled up by the roots! Everyone knows that if money were abolished, fraud, theft, robbery, quarrels, brawls, altercations, seditions, murders, treasons, poisonings, and a whole set of crimes which are avenged but not prevented by the hangman would at once die out. If money disappeared, so would fear, anxiety, worry, toil, and sleepless nights. Even poverty, the one condition which seems more than anything else to need money for its relief, would die away if money were entirely abolished.

Consider, if you will, this example. Take a barren year of failed harvests, when many thousands of people have been carried off by famine. If at the end of the scarcity the barns of the rich were searched, I dare say positively that enough grain would be found in them to have kept all those who died of starvation and disease from even realizing that a shortage ever existed—if only it had been divided among them. So easily might people get the necessities of life if that cursed money, that marvelous invention which is supposed to provide access to them, were not in fact the only barrier to our getting what we need to live. Even the rich, I'm sure, understand this. They must

2. Marginal gloss: "Reader, note well!" In the text at this point, More may be alluding to the judgment of Saint Augustine in *The City of God* 4.4: "Take away justice, and what are kingdoms but great robber-bands?" As a young man, More had given a series of public lectures on Augustine's book.

know that it's better to have enough of what we really need than an abundance of superfluities, much better to escape from our many present troubles than to be burdened with great masses of wealth. And in fact I have no doubt that every man's perception of where his true interest lies, along with the authority of Christ our Savior (whose wisdom could not fail to recognize the best, and whose goodness would not fail to counsel it), would long ago have brought the whole world to adopt Utopian laws, if it were not for one single monster, the prime plague and begetter of all others—I mean Pride.

Pride measures her advantages not by what she has but by what others lack. Pride would not condescend even to be made a goddess, if there were no wretches for her to sneer at and domineer over. Her good fortune is dazzling only by contrast with the miseries of others, her riches are valuable only as they torment and tantalize the poverty of others. Pride is a serpent from hell that twines itself around the hearts of men; and it acts like a suckfish[3] in holding them back from choosing a better way of life.

Pride is too deeply fixed in human nature to be easily plucked out. So I am glad that the Utopians at least have been lucky enough to achieve this commonwealth, which I wish all mankind would imitate. The institutions they have adopted have made their community most happy, and, as far as anyone can tell, capable of lasting forever. Now that they have rooted up the seeds of ambition and faction at home, along with most other vices, they are in no danger from internal strife, which alone has been the ruin of many cities that seemed secure. As long as they preserve harmony at home, and keep their institutions healthy, the Utopians can never be overcome or even shaken by all the envious princes of neighboring countries, who have often attempted their ruin, but always in vain.

When Raphael had finished his story, I was left thinking that not a few of the customs and laws he had described as existing among the Utopians were quite absurd. These included their methods of waging war, their religious practices, as well as other customs of theirs, but my chief objection was to the basis of their whole system, that is, their communal living and their moneyless economy. This one thing alone takes away all the nobility, magnificence, splendor, and majesty which (in the popular view) are the true ornaments and glory of any commonwealth. But I saw Raphael was tired with talking, and I was not sure he could take contradiction in these matters, particularly when I remembered what he had said about certain people who were afraid they might not appear wise unless they found out something to criticize in the ideas of others. So with praise for the Utopian way of life and his account of it, I took him by the hand and led him in to supper. But first I said that we would find some other time for thinking of these matters more deeply, and for talking them over in more detail. And I still hope such an opportunity will present itself someday.

Meanwhile, though he is a man of unquestionable learning, and highly experienced in the ways of the world, I cannot agree with everything he

3. A fish (the remora) with a suction plate atop its head, by which it attaches itself to the underbelly of larger fishes or the hulls of ships. Impressed by the tenacity of its grip, the ancients fabled that it could stop ships in their courses.

said. Yet I freely confess there are very many things in the Utopian commonwealth that in our own societies I would wish rather than expect to see.

1515–16   1516

Thomas More to His Friend Peter Giles, Warmest Greetings[1]

My dear Peter, I was absolutely delighted with the judgment of that very sharp fellow you recall, who posed this dilemma about my *Utopia*: if the story is put forward as fact, he said, then I see a number of absurdities in it; but if it's fiction, then it seems to me that in various respects More's usual good judgment is at fault. I suspect this fellow of being learned, and I see that he's a friend; but whoever he is, I'm much obliged to him. By this frank opinion of his, he has pleased me more than anyone else since the book was published.

For in the first place, either out of fondness for me or for the work itself, he seems to have borne up under the burden of reading the book all the way through—and that not perfunctorily or hastily, the way priests read the divine office—those, at least, who read it at all.[2] No, he read slowly and attentively, noting all the particular points. Then, having singled out certain matters for criticism, and not very many, as a matter of fact, he gives careful and considered approval to the rest. And finally, in the very expressions he uses to criticize me, he implies higher praises than some of those who have put all their energies into compliment. It's easy to see what a high opinion he has of me, when he expresses disappointment over reading something imperfect or inexact—whereas I don't expect, in treating so many different matters, to be able to say more than a few things which aren't totally ridiculous.

Still, I'd like to be just as frank with him as he was with me; and, in fact, I don't see why he should think himself so acute (so "sharp-sighted," as the Greeks would say) just because he's discovered some absurdities in the institutions of Utopia, or caught me putting forth some half-baked ideas about the constitution of a republic. Aren't there any absurdities elsewhere in the world? And did any one of the philosophers who've offered a pattern of a society, a ruler, or even a private household set down everything so well that nothing ought to be changed? Actually, if it weren't for the great respect I retain for certain highly distinguished names, I could easily produce from each of them a number of notions which I can hardly doubt would be universally condemned as absurd.

But when he wonders whether *Utopia* is fact or fiction, then I find *his* judgment, in turn, sorely at fault. I do not deny that if I'd decided to write about a commonwealth, and a tale of this sort had occurred to me, I might have spread a little fiction, like so much honey, over the truth, to make it more acceptable. But I would certainly have tempered the fiction a little, so that, while it deceived the common folk, I gave hints to the more learned

---

1. This second letter of More to Giles appeared only in the second edition of *Utopia* (Paris, 1517), where it immediately follows Book II. The letter praises a supposedly perspicacious critique of *Utopia* by a "very sharp fellow," whose identity is unknown—if indeed More didn't simply invent him.

2. Priests read the "divine office"—the daily round of prescribed prayers to be recited at set hours—with varying degrees of enthusiasm, according to More.

which would enable them to see what I was about. So, if I'd done nothing but give special names to the governor, the river, the city, and the island, which hinted to the learned that the island was nowhere, the city a phantom, the river waterless, and that the governor had no people,[3] that would not have been hard to do, and would have been far more clever than what I actually did. Unless I had a historian's devotion to fact, I am not so stupid as to have used those barbarous and senseless names of Utopia, Anyder, Amaurot, and Ademus.

Still, my dear Giles, I see some people are so suspicious that what we simple-minded and credulous fellows have written down of Hythloday's account can hardly find any credence at all with these circumspect and sagacious persons. I'm afraid my personal reputation, as well as my authority as a historian, may be threatened by their skepticism; so it's a good thing that I can defend myself by saying, as Terence's Mysis says about Glycerium's boy, to confirm his legitimacy, "Praise be to God there were some free women present at his birth."[4] And so it was a good thing for me that Raphael told his story not just to you and me, but to a great many perfectly respectable and serious-minded men. Whether he told them more things, and more important things, I don't know; but I'm sure he told them no fewer and no less important things than he told us.

Well, if these doubters won't believe such witnesses, let them consult Hythloday himself, for he is still alive. I heard only recently from some travelers coming out of Portugal that on the first of last March he was as healthy and vigorous a man as he ever was. Let them get the truth from him—dig it out of him with questions, if they want. I only want them to understand that I'm responsible for my own work, and my own work alone, not for anyone else's credibility.

Farewell, my dearest Peter, to you, your charming wife, and your clever little girl—to all, my wife sends her very best wishes.

1517

3. This is of course precisely what the names do mean.

4. *The Lady of Andros*, lines 770–71.

SIR THOMAS WYATT THE ELDER
1503–1542

Thomas Wyatt made his career in the shifting, dangerous currents of Renaissance courts, whose power struggles, sexual intrigues, and sophisticated tastes shaped his remarkable achievements as a poet. Educated at St. John's College, Cambridge, Wyatt entered the service of Henry VIII, becoming clerk of the king's jewels, a member of diplomatic missions to France and the Low Countries, and, in 1537–39, ambassador to Spain at the court of the Holy Roman Emperor, Charles V.

The years he spent abroad as a diplomat had a significant impact on his writing, imbuing it with the spirit of Continental Renaissance poetry and especially of its great fourteenth-century master Francesco Petrarca (Petrarch). Diplomacy, with its veiled threats, rhetorical manipulation, and cynical role-playing, may have had a more indirect impact as well, reinforcing the lessons in self-presentation and self-concealment that Wyatt would have received at the English court.

Life in the orbit of the ruthless, unpredictable Henry VIII was competitive and risky. When, in the late 1530s, Wyatt wrote to his son of the "thousand dangers and hazards, enmities, hatreds, prisonments, despites [insults], and indignations" he had faced, he was not exaggerating. He probably came closest to the executioner's ax when in 1536 he was imprisoned in the Tower of London along with several others accused of having committed adultery with the queen, Anne Boleyn. As his poem "Who list his wealth and ease retain" suggests, Wyatt may have watched from his cell the execution of the queen and her alleged lovers; but he himself was spared, as he was spared a few years later, when he was again imprisoned in the Tower, on charges of high treason brought by his enemies at court. His death, at the age of thirty-nine, came from a fever.

It is not surprising, given his career, that many of Wyatt's poems, including his satires and his psalm translations, express an intense longing for "steadfastness" and an escape from the corruption, anxiety, and duplicity of the court. The praise, in his verse epistle to John Poins, of a quiet retired life in the country and the harsh condemnation of courtly hypocrisy derive from his own experience. But the eloquent celebration of simplicity and truthfulness can itself be a cunning strategy. Wyatt was a master of the game of poetic self-display. Again and again he represents himself as a plain-speaking and steadfast man, betrayed by the "doubleness" of a fickle mistress or the instability of fortune. At this distance it is impossible to know how much this account corresponds to reality, but we can admire, as Wyatt's contemporaries did, the rhetorical deftness of the performance.

In a move with momentous consequences for English poetry, Wyatt introduced into English the sonnet, a fourteen-line poem in iambic pentameter with a complex, intertwining rhyme scheme and the development of one or more sustained metaphors or "conceits." For the most part, he took his subject matter from Petrarch's sonnets, but his rhyme schemes make a significant departure. Petrarch's sonnets consist of an "octave," rhyming *abba abba*, followed, after a turn (*volta*) in the sense, by a "sestet" with various rhyme schemes (such as *cd cd cd* and *cde cde*) that have in common their avoidance of a rhyming couplet at the end. Wyatt employs the Petrarchan octave, but his most common sestet scheme is *cddc ee*: the Petrarchan sonnet was already beginning to change into the characteristic "English" structure for the sonnet, three quatrains and a closing couplet.

In his freest translations of Petrarchan sonnets, such as "Whoso list to hunt," Wyatt tends to turn the idealizing of the woman into disillusionment and complaint. For the lover in Petrarch's poems, love is an ongoing, transcendent experience, extending beyond the boundaries of life itself; for the lover in Wyatt's poems, it is all too transient and embittering. The tone of bitterness carries over to many poems less closely linked to Italian and French models, poems with short stanzas and refrains that associate them with the native English song tradition. Some of Wyatt's songs, to be sure, strike a note of jaunty independence, often tinged with misogyny; but melancholy complaint is rarely very distant. Perhaps the poem that most brilliantly captures his blend of passion, anger, cynicism, longing, and pain is "They flee from me."

Wyatt never published a collection of his own poems, and very few of them appeared in print during his lifetime. Carefully crafted pieces in an elaborate and sometimes risky erotic chess game, many of them may have been designed for specific social occasions, to be recited or sometimes set to music and sung to the accompaniment of a lute. In addition to such oral performances, the poems were written out, exchanged, and circulated in manuscript, both within a small, exclusive circle of friends and among those beyond the court who were eager to enjoy the latest poetic fashions.

Contemporaries clearly took pleasure in staging and savoring the drama of sexual relations: the Devonshire Manuscript, one of the chief sources for Wyatt's verse, collects a variety of poetic perspectives on courtship. The miscellany contains not only several male-authored poems in a female voice but also a number of poems probably written by women, along with many more transcribed by female hands. Wyatt was writing within a larger game of courtly poetry in which women played key roles.

In 1557 (fifteen years after Wyatt's death), 97 poems attributed to him were included by the printer Richard Tottel among the 271 poems in his miscellany, *Songs and Sonnets*. (For more on Tottel and his book, see, in "Elizabethan Miscellany," pp. 502–05.) By the time this collection was published, Wyatt's deliberately rough, vigorous, and expressive metrical practice was felt to be crude, and Tottel (or perhaps some intermediary) smoothed out the versification. We reprint "They flee from me" both in Tottel's "improved" version and in the version found in the Egerton Manuscript, which contains poems in Wyatt's own hand and corrections he made to scribal copies of his poems. Unlike the Egerton Manuscript (E. MS.), the Devonshire Manuscript (D. MS.) was apparently not in the poet's possession, but some of its texts seem earlier than Egerton's, and it furnishes additional poems, as do the Blage Manuscript (B. MS.) and the Arundel Manuscript (A. MS.).

In the following selections we have indicated the manuscript from which each of the poems derives and divided the poems into three generic groups: sonnets, other lyrics, and finally a satire. Within each of the first two groups, the poems are printed in the order in which they appear in the manuscripts. There is no reason to think that this is a chronological ordering.*

The long love that in my thought doth harbor[1]

> The long love that in my thought doth harbor,
> And in mine heart doth keep his residence,
> Into my face presseth with bold pretense
> And therein campeth, spreading his banner.[2]
> 5 She that me learneth° to love and suffer   *teaches me*
> And will that my trust and lust's negligence[3]
> Be reined by reason, shame, and reverence,
> With his hardiness taketh displeasure.
> Wherewithal° unto the heart's forest he fleeth,   *because of which*
> 10 Leaving his enterprise with pain and cry,
> And there him hideth, and not appeareth.
> What may I do, when my master feareth,
> But in the field with him to live and die?
> For good is the life ending faithfully.

E. MS.

---

* For the Italian originals of the Petrarchan sonnets translated here, as well as additional poems by Wyatt, see the NAEL Archive. For a broad grouping of 16th-century poems, see "An Elizabethan Miscellany," below.

1. Wyatt's version of poem 140 of Petrarch's *Rime sparse* (Scattered Rhymes); his younger friend the earl of Surrey also translated it (p. 135).

2. I.e., the speaker's blush. The first four lines of this sonnet introduce the "conceit" (elaborately sustained metaphor) of Love as a warrior who, "with bold pretense" (i.e., making bold claim), flaunts his presence by means of the "banner." Elaborate metaphors of this kind are common in Petrarchan (and Elizabethan) love poetry, and often, as in this instance, an entire sonnet will turn on a single conceit.

3. I.e., my open and careless revelation of my love.

Petrarch, Rima 140

A MODERN PROSE TRANSLATION[4]

Love, who lives and reigns in my thought and keeps his principal seat in my heart, sometimes comes forth all in armor into my forehead, there camps, and there sets up his banner.

She who teaches us to love and to be patient, and wishes my great desire, my kindled hope, to be reined in by reason, shame, and reverence, at our boldness is angry within herself.

Wherefore Love flees terrified to my heart, abandoning his every enterprise, and weeps and trembles; there he hides and no more appears outside.

What can I do, when my lord is afraid, except stay with him until the last hour? For he makes a good end who dies loving well.

Whoso list to hunt[1]

Whoso list° to hunt, I know where is an hind,°		*cares / female deer*
But as for me, alas, I may no more.		
The vain travail° hath wearied me so sore,°		*labor / sorely, seriously*
I am of them that farthest cometh behind.		
5 Yet may I, by no means, my wearied mind		
Draw from the deer, but as she fleeth afore,		
Fainting I follow. I leave off, therefore,		
Since in a net I seek to hold the wind.		
Who list her hunt, I put him out of doubt,°		*assure him*
10 As well as I, may spend his time in vain.		
And graven with diamonds in letters plain		
There is written, her fair neck round about,		
"*Noli me tangere*, for Caesar's I am,		
And wild for to hold, though I seem tame."		

E. MS.

Petrarch, Rima 190

A MODERN PROSE TRANSLATION

A white doe on the green grass appeared to me, with two golden horns, between two rivers, in the shade of a laurel, when the sun was rising in the unripe season.

---

4. This and the prose translations of Rime 190, 134, and 189 are by Robert K. Durling.
1. An adaptation of Petrarch's Rima 190, perhaps influenced by commentators on Petrarch, who said that *Noli me tangere quia Caesaris sum* ("Touch me not, for I am Caesar's") was inscribed on the collars of Caesar's hinds, which were then set free and were presumably safe from hunters. Wyatt's sonnet is usually supposed to refer to Anne Boleyn, in whom Henry VIII became interested in 1526.

Her look was so sweet and proud that to follow her I left every task, like the miser who as he seeks treasure sweetens his trouble with delight.

"Let no one touch me," she bore written with diamonds and topazes around her lovely neck. "It has pleased my Caesar to make me free."

And the sun had already turned at midday; my eyes were tired by looking but not sated, when I fell into the water, and she disappeared.

Farewell, Love

Farewell, Love, and all thy laws forever,
Thy baited hooks shall tangle me no more;
Senec and Plato call me from thy lore,
To perfect wealth my wit for to endeavor.[1]
5   In blind error when I did persever,
Thy sharp repulse, that pricketh aye° so sore,   *always*
Hath taught me to set in trifles no store,°   *value*
And 'scape forth since liberty is lever.°   *more pleasing, dearer*
Therefore farewell, go trouble younger hearts,
10   And in me claim no more authority;
With idle youth go use thy property,[2]
And thereon spend thy many brittle darts.°   *arrows*
For hitherto though I have lost all my time,
Me lusteth° no longer rotten boughs to climb.   *I care*

E. MS.

I find no peace[1]

I find no peace, and all my war is done,
I fear and hope, I burn and freeze like ice,
I fly above the wind, yet can I not arise,
And naught I have, and all the world I seize on.
5   That° looseth nor locketh holdeth me in prison,   *that which*
And holdeth me not, yet can I 'scape nowise;
Nor letteth me live nor die at my devise,°   *my own will*
And yet of death it giveth me occasion.
Without eyen° I see, and without tongue I plain;°   *eyes / complain*

1. I.e., "Senec" (Seneca, the Roman moral philosopher and tragedian) and Plato call him to educate his mind ("wit") to perfect well-being ("wealth").

2. Do what you characteristically do.
1. Translated from Petrarch's Rima 134. For Thomas Lodge's adaptation of the same sonnet, see p. 514.

10   I desire to perish, and yet I ask health;
I love another, and thus I hate myself;
I feed me in sorrow, and laugh in all my pain.
Likewise displeaseth me both death and life,
And my delight is causer of this strife.

E. MS.

Petrarch, Rima 134

A MODERN PROSE TRANSLATION

Peace I do not find, and I have no wish to make war; and I fear and hope, and burn and am of ice; and I fly above the heavens and lie on the ground; and I grasp nothing and embrace all the world.

One has me in prison who neither opens nor locks, neither keeps me for his own nor unties the bonds; and Love does not kill and does not unchain me, he neither wishes me alive nor frees me from the tangle.

I see without eyes, and I have no tongue and yet cry out; and I wish to perish and I ask for help; and I hate myself and love another.

I feed on pain, weeping I laugh; equally displeasing to me are death and life. In this state am I, Lady, on account of you.

My galley[1]

My galley charged° with forgetfulness[2]		*freighted*
Thorough° sharp seas, in winter nights doth pass		*through*
'Tween rock and rock; and eke° mine enemy, alas,		*also*
That is my lord, steereth with cruelness;		
5 And every oar a thought in readiness,		
As though that death were light in such a case.[3]		
An endless wind doth tear the sail apace°		*swiftly*
Of forced sighs and trusty fearfulness.°		*fear to trust*
A rain of tears, a cloud of dark disdain,		
10 Hath done the wearied cords great hinderance;		
Wreathed° with error and eke with ignorance.		*twisted*
The stars be hid that led me to this pain.		
Drowned is reason that should me consort,°		*accompany*
And I remain despairing of the port.		

E. MS.

---

1. Translated from Petrarch's Rima 189. For Edmund Spenser's adaptation of the same poem, see p. 487.

2. I.e., obliviousness of everything except love.
3. As though my destruction would not matter much.

Petrarch, Rima 189

A MODERN PROSE TRANSLATION

My ship laden with forgetfulness passes through a harsh sea, at midnight, in winter, between Scylla and Charybdis,[4] and at the tiller sits my lord, rather my enemy;

each oar is manned by a ready, cruel thought that seems to scorn the tempest and the end; a wet, changeless wind of sighs, hopes, and desires breaks the sail;

a rain of weeping, a mist of disdain wet and loosen the already weary ropes, made of error twisted up with ignorance.

My two usual sweet stars are hidden; dead among the waves are reason and skill; so that I begin to despair of the port.

Divers doth use

    Divers doth use,[1] as I have heard and know,
    When that to change their ladies do begin,
    To mourn and wail, and never for to lin,°   *cease*
    Hoping thereby to pease° their painful woe.   *appease, relieve*
5   And some there be, that when it chanceth so
    That women change and hate where love hath been,
    They call them false and think with words to win
    The hearts of them which otherwhere doth grow.
    But as for me, though that by chance indeed
10 Change hath outworn the favor that I had,
    I will not wail, lament, nor yet be sad,
    Nor call her false that falsely did me feed,
    But let it pass, and think it is of kind°   *nature*
    That often° change doth please a woman's mind. *frequent*

D. MS.

What vaileth truth?[1]

    What vaileth° truth? or by it to take pain,   *avails*
    To strive by steadfastness for to attain.
    To be just and true and flee from doubleness;

---

4. The monster and the whirlpool that threaten Odysseus's ship on either side of the Strait of Messina, in *Odyssey* 12.
1. Are accustomed. "Divers": the adjective ("various," "sundry"), not the noun; i.e., various other men.
1. A rondeau: a difficult French verse form in which the unrhymed refrain "rounds" back to the opening words, and the rest of the poem uses only two rhyme sounds.

Sithens all° alike, where ruleth craftiness,   *since exactly*
5   Rewarded is both false and plain?
Soonest he speedeth° that most can feign;   *succeeds*
True-meaning heart is had in disdain.
Against deceit and doubleness,
    What vaileth truth?

10 Deceived is he by crafty train°   *treachery*
That meaneth no guile and doth remain
Within the trap without redress.°   *remedy*
But for° to love, lo, such a mistress,   *except*
Whose cruelty nothing can refrain,°   *restrain*
15   What vaileth truth?

E. MS.

Madam, withouten many words

Madam, withouten many words,
Once,° I am sure, ye will or no.   *sometime*
And if ye will, then leave your bordes,°   *jests*
And use your wit° and show it so.   *mind*

5 And with a beck ye shall me call.
And if of one that burneth alway
Ye have any pity at all,
Answer him fair with yea or nay.

If it be yea, I shall be fain.°   *glad*
10 If it be nay, friends as before.
Ye shall another man obtain,
And I mine own and yours no more.

E. MS.

They flee from me

They flee from me, that sometime did me seek
With naked foot stalking° in my chamber.   *walking softly*
I have seen them gentle, tame, and meek
That now are wild and do not remember
5 That sometime they put themself in danger
To take bread at my hand; and now they range,
Busily seeking with a continual change.

Thanked be fortune it hath been otherwise
Twenty times better; but once in special,
10 In thin array, after a pleasant guise,

When her loose gown from her shoulders did fall,
And she me caught in her arms long and small,°   *slender*
Therewithal° sweetly did me kiss   *with that*
And softly said, "Dear heart, how like you this?"

15   It was no dream, I lay broad waking.
But all is turned, thorough° my gentleness,   *through*
Into a strange fashion of forsaking;
And I have leave to go, of her goodness,
And she also to use newfangleness.°   *fickleness*
20   But since that I so kindely[1] am served,
I fain would° know what she hath deserved.   *would like to*

E. MS.

The Lover Showeth How He Is Forsaken of Such as He Sometime Enjoyed

[THEY FLEE FROM ME]

They flee from me, that sometime did me seek
With naked foot stalking within my chamber.
Once have I seen them gentle, tame, and meek
That now are wild and do not once remember
5   That sometime they have put themselves in danger
To take bread at my hand; and now they range,
Busily seeking in continual change.

Thankèd be fortune, it hath been otherwise
Twenty times better; but once especial,
10   In thin array, after a pleasant guise,
When her loose gown did from her shoulders fall,
And she me caught in her arms long and small,
And therewithal so sweetly did me kiss
And softly said, "Dear heart, how like you this?"

15   It was no dream, for I lay broad awaking.
But all is turned now, through my gentleness,
Into a bitter fashion of forsaking;
And I have leave to go, of her goodness,
And she also to use newfangleness.
20   But since that I unkindly so am served,
How like you this? What hath she now deserved?

TOTTEL, 1557

---

1. Naturally (from *kind*: "nature," but with an ironic suggestion of the modern meaning of "kindly"). In Wyatt's spelling, the word should presumably be pronounced as three syllables.

My lute, awake!

My lute, awake! Perform the last
Labor that thou and I shall waste,
And end that I have now begun:
For when this song is sung and past,
5   My lute be still, for I have done.

As to be heard where ear is none,
As lead to grave in marble stone,[1]
My song may pierce her heart as soon.
Should we then sigh or sing or moan?
10   No, no, my lute, for I have done.

The rocks do not so cruelly
Repulse the waves continually
As she my suit and affectïon.
So that I am past remedy,
15   Whereby my lute and I have done.

Proud of the spoil that thou hast got
Of simple hearts, thorough° Love's shot,   *through*
By whom, unkind, thou hast them won,
Think not he hath his bow forgot,
20   Although my lute and I have done.

Vengeance shall fall on thy disdain
That makest but game on earnest pain.
Think not alone under the sun
Unquit° to cause thy lovers plain,°   *unrevenged / to complain*
25   Although my lute and I have done.

Perchance thee lie[2] withered and old
The winter nights that are so cold,
Plaining in vain unto the moon.
Thy wishes then dare not be told.
30   Care then who list,° for I have done.   *likes*

And then may chance thee to repent
The time that thou hast lost and spent
To cause thy lovers sigh and swoon.
Then shalt thou know beauty but lent,
35   And wish and want as I have done.

Now cease, my lute. This is the last
Labor that thou and I shall waste,
And ended is that we begun.

---

1. I.e., when sound may be heard with no ear to
hear it or when soft lead is able to carve ("grave")
hard marble.
2. Perhaps it may befall you to lie.

Now is this song both sung and past;
40 My lute be still, for I have done.

E. MS.

Forget not yet

Forget not yet the tried intent
Of such a truth° as I have meant,   *fidelity*
My great travail so gladly spent,
    Forget not yet.

5 Forget not yet when first began
The weary life ye know since when,
The suit,° the service[1] none tell can,   *pursuit, wooing*
    Forget not yet.

Forget not yet the great essays,°   *trials*
10 The cruel wrong, the scornful ways,
The painful patience in denays,°   *denials, refusals*
    Forget not yet.

Forget not yet, forget not this,
How long ago hath been and is
15 The mind that never meant amiss,
    Forget not yet.

Forget not then thine own approved,
The which so long hath thee so loved,
Whose steadfast faith yet never moved,
20   Forget not this.

D. MS.

Blame not my lute

Blame not my lute, for he must sound
Of this or that as liketh° me: *pleases*
For lack of wit° the lute is bound   *intelligence*
To give such tunes as pleaseth me.
5 Though my songs be somewhat strange,
And speaks such words as touch thy change,°   *unfaithfulness*
    Blame not my lute.

My lute, alas, doth not offend,
Though that perforce° he must agree   *of necessity*

---

1. Actions of a lover, often called the lady's "servant."

10 To sound such tunes as I intend
To sing to them that heareth me.
Then though my songs be somewhat plain,
And toucheth some that use to feign,[2]
Blame not my lute.

15 My lute and strings may not deny,
But as I strike they must obey:
Break not them then so wrongfully,
But wreak° thyself some wiser way.   *avenge*
And though the songs which I indite°   *write*
20 Do quit thy change[3] with rightful spite,
Blame not my lute.

Spite asketh° spite, and changing change,   *calls for*
And falsèd faith must needs be known;
The fault so great, the case so strange,
25 Of right it must abroad be blown.
Then since that by thine own desert
My songs do tell how true thou art,
Blame not my lute.

Blame but thyself, that hast misdone
30 And well deservèd to have blame;
Change thou thy way so evil begun,
And then my lute shall sound that same.
But if till then my fingers play
By thy desert their wonted° way,   *accustomed*
35 Blame not my lute.

Farewell, unknown, for though thou break
My strings in spite with great disdain,
Yet have I found out for thy sake
Strings for to string my lute again.
40 And if perchance this foolish rhyme
Do make thee blush at any time,
Blame not my lute.

D. MS.

Stand whoso list[1]

Stand whoso list° upon the slipper° top   *cares to / slippery*
Of court's estates,° and let me here rejoice   *high positions*
And use me quiet without let or stop,[2]

---

2. And comment on some who are accustomed
to deceive.
3. Requite your unfaithfulness.
1. A translation of Seneca, *Thyestes*, lines 391–
403. For a literal translation of this famous passage, and other verse translations of it, see the
NAEL Archive.
2. Comport myself quietly without hindrance or
impediment.

Unknown in court, that hath such brackish[3] joys.
5 In hidden place so let my days forth pass
That when my years be done withouten noise,
I may die aged after the common trace.°   way
For him death grippeth right hard by the crop°   throat
That is much known of other, and of himself, alas,
10 Doth die unknown, dazed, with dreadful° face.   fearful

A. MS.

Who list his wealth and ease retain[1]

Who list° his wealth° and ease retain,   desires / well-being
Himself let him unknown contain.[2]
Press not too fast in at that gate
Where the return stands by disdain:
5 For sure, *circa regna tonat.*[3]

The high mountains are blasted oft
When the low valley is mild and soft.
Fortune with Health stands at debate.[4]
The fall is grievous from aloft.
10 And sure, *circa regna tonat.*

These bloody days have broken my heart.
My lust,° my youth did then depart,   pleasure
And blind desire of estate.°   status
Who hastes to climb seeks to revert.°   fall back
15 Of truth, *circa regna tonat.*

The Bell Tower showed me such sight
That in my head sticks day and night.
There did I learn out of a grate,°   barred window
For all favor, glory, or might,[5]
20 That yet *circa regna tonat.*

By proof,° I say, there did I learn: experience
Wit helpeth not defense to yerne,
Of innocence to plead or prate.[6]
Bear low°, therefore, give God the stern,[7]   be humble
25 For sure, *circa regna tonat.*

B. MS.

3. Spoiled by mixture, as of seawater with fresh.
1. This poem was almost certainly written at the time of Wyatt's imprisonment in 1536, during which he witnessed from the Bell Tower the execution of Anne Boleyn.
2. I.e., let him keep himself unknown.
3. "He [i.e., Jupiter] thunders around thrones" (Seneca, *Phaedra*, line 1140). The first two stanzas of Wyatt's poem paraphrase lines from that

play. "The return stands by disdain": i.e., "you will be disdained as you make your (forced) exit."
4. I.e., fortune and well-being are always at odds.
5. I.e., whatever one's favor, glory, or might.
6. I.e., intelligence does not help one earn ("yerne") a defense, [nor does it help] to plead or prattle about one's innocence.
7. Let God do the steering.

Mine own John Poins[1]

Mine own John Poins, since ye delight to know
The cause why that homeward I me draw
(And flee the press of courts, whereso they go,
Rather than to live thrall under the awe
5   Of lordly looks) wrapped within my cloak,
To will and lust° learning to set a law;   *desire*
It is not for because I scorn or mock
The power of them to whom Fortune hath lent
Charge over us, of right to strike the stroke.[2]
10   But true it is that I have always meant
Less to esteem them than the common sort,
Of outward things that judge in their intent,
Without regard what doth inward resort.
I grant sometime that of glory the fire
15   Doth touch my heart; me list not to report
Blame by honor, and honor to desire.[3]
But how may I this honor now attain,
That cannot dye the color black a liar?[4]
My Poins, I cannot frame my tune to feign,
20   To cloak the truth for praise, without desert,
Of them that list° all vice for to retain.   *desire*
I cannot honor them that sets their part
With Venus and Bacchus all their life long,[5]
Nor hold my peace of° them although I smart.   *concerning*
25   I cannot crouch nor kneel nor do so great a wrong
To worship them like God on earth alone
That are as wolves these sely° lambs among.   *innocent*
I cannot with my words complain and moan
And suffer naught,° nor smart without complaint,   *wickedness*
30   Nor turn the word that from my mouth is gone;
I cannot speak and look like a saint,
Use wiles for wit° and make deceit a pleasure,   *wisdom*
And call craft° counsel, for profit still to paint;°   *craftiness / deceive*
I cannot wrest the law to fill the coffer,
35   With innocent blood to feed myself fat,
And do most hurt where most help I offer.
I am not he that can allow° the state°   *approve / exaltation*
Of high Caesar and damn Cato[6] to die,
That with his death did 'scape out of the gate

---

1. Poins was a friend of Wyatt's. This verse epistle of informal satire is based on the tenth satire of the Italian Luigi Alamanni but is personalized and Anglicized in detail by Wyatt. It was apparently written during his banishment from court, in 1536. Lines 1–52 of the poem are missing from the authoritative Egerton Manuscript and are here supplied from the Devonshire Manuscript.
2. I.e., my retirement from court is not because I scorn the powerful, or their prerogatives of rule and punishment. But I esteem them less than do the "common sort" of people, who judge by externals only (lines 10–13).
3. I.e., I do not wish to attack honor or to call dishonorable desire honorable.
4. I.e., cannot pretend that black is not black.
5. I.e., I cannot honor those who devote their lives to Venus (goddess of love) and Bacchus (god of drinking).
6. Cato the Younger, the famous Roman patriot who committed suicide rather than submit to Caesar.

40 From Caesar's hands, if Livy[7] do not lie,
And would not live where liberty was lost,
So did his heart the common weal apply.[8]
I am not he such eloquence to boast
To make the crow singing as the swan,
45 Nor call the lion of coward beasts the most,
That cannot take a mouse as the cat can;
And he that dieth for hunger of the gold,
Call him Alexander,[9] and say that Pan
Passeth° Apollo in music many fold;[1]   *surpasses*
50 Praise Sir Thopas for a noble tale,
And scorn the story that the Knight told;[2]
Praise him for counsel that is drunk of ale;
Grin when he laugheth that beareth all the sway,°   *power*
Frown when he frowneth, and groan when he is pale;
55 On other's lust° to hang both night and day—   *wishes*
None of these points would ever frame in me;°   *appeal to me*
My wit° is naught:° I cannot learn the way;   *intellect / worthless*
And much the less of things that greater be,
That asken help of colors of device°   *tricks of rhetoric*
60 To join the mean with each extremity:
With the nearest virtue to cloak alway the vice,
And, as to purpose likewise it shall fall,[3]
To press the virtue that it may not rise;
As drunkenness, good fellowship to call;
65 The friendly foe, with his double face,
Say he is gentle and courteous therewithal;°   *besides*
And say that favel° hath a goodly grace   *flattery*
In eloquence; and cruelty to name
Zeal of justice, and change in time and place;[4]
70 And he that suffereth offense° without blame,   *allows offenses*
Call him pitiful,° and him true and plain   *compassionate*
That raileth reckless° to every man's shame;   *recklessly*
Say he is rude° that cannot lie and feign,   *uneducated*
The lecher a lover, and tyranny
75 To be the right of a prince's reign.
I cannot, I: no, no, it will not be.
This is the cause that I could never yet
Hang on their sleeves that weigh, as thou mayst see,
A chip of chance more than a pound of wit.
80 This maketh me at home to hunt and hawk
And in foul weather at my book to sit;
In frost and snow then with my bow to stalk.
No man doth mark° whereso I ride or go.   *note*
In lusty leas° at liberty I walk,   *pleasant fields*

---

7. **Titus Livius** (59 B.C.E.–17 C.E.), the great Roman historian.
8. So much did he devote himself to the common good.
9. Compare him to Alexander the Great with his towering ambition.
1. According to classical mythology, the music of the nature god Pan was far inferior to that of

Apollo, patron of music and art.
2. The silly tale of Sir Thopas, in *The Canterbury Tales*, is told by Chaucer himself, until the Host forces him to stop. *The Knight's Tale* is the most courtly and dignified of the tales.
3. I.e., as will also be opportune.
4. I.e., to miscall cruelty zeal for justice, and to rationalize it by appeals to altered circumstances.

85   And of these news I feel nor weal nor woe,
Save that a clog doth hang yet at my heel.[5]
No force° for that, for it is ordered so   *no matter*
That I may leap both hedge and dike full well.
I am not now in France, to judge the wine,
90   With sav'ry sauce the delicates° to feel;   *delicacies*
Nor yet in Spain, where one must him incline,
Rather than to be, outwardly to seem.
I meddle not with wits that be so fine;
Nor Flanders' cheer[6] letteth° not my sight to deem   *hinders*
95   Of black and white, nor taketh my wit away
With beastliness they, beasts, do so esteem.
Nor am I not where Christ is given in prey
For money, poison, and treason—at Rome[7]
A common practice, usèd night and day.
100   But here I am in Kent and Christendom,
Among the Muses, where I read and rhyme;
Where if thou list, my Poins, for to come,
Thou shalt be judge how I do spend my time.

D. MS., E. MS.

5. I.e., I feel neither happiness nor unhappiness about current political affairs, except that a "clog" (i.e., his confinement on parole to his estate) keeps me from traveling far. Note that *news* is a plural in Elizabethan English.
6. I.e., the drinking for which, in the 16th century, Flemings were notorious.
7. In *Tottel's Miscellany,* published in the reign of the Catholic Queen Mary, these lines were altered as follows: "where *truth* is given in prey / For money, poison, and treason—*of some.*"

HENRY HOWARD, EARL OF SURREY
1517–1547

The ax that decapitated Surrey at the age of thirty had been hanging over his head for much of his life. In the court of Henry VIII, it was dangerous to be a potential claimant to the throne, and Surrey was descended from kings on both sides of his family. He was brought up at Windsor Castle as the close companion of Henry VIII's illegitimate son, the duke of Richmond, who married Surrey's sister. As the eldest son of the duke of Norfolk, the chief bulwark of the old Catholic aristocracy against the rising tide of "new men" and the reformed religion, Surrey was the heir not only to the Howard family's great wealth but also to their immense pride, their sense at once of noble privilege and of obligation. Like his father and grandfather, he was a brave and able soldier, serving in Henry VIII's French wars as "Lieutenant General of the King on Sea and Land." He was also repeatedly imprisoned for rash behavior, on one occasion for striking a courtier, on another for wandering through the streets of London breaking the windows of sleeping townspeople. In 1541 Surrey used his family connections—his first cousin, Catherine Howard, was queen—to secure the release from the Tower of his close friend the poet Thomas Wyatt, who had been accused of treason. But a year later, Catherine Howard was executed for adultery, like Anne Boleyn before her. Power returned to the rival family of the former queen Jane Seymour, who had died in childbirth giving a son and heir to the aging Henry VIII. Surrey's situation was already precarious, and his vocal opposition to the Seymours, with their strong Protestant leanings, sealed his fate. Convicted of treason, he had the grim distinction of being Henry's last victim.

Poets and critics of the later sixteenth century, fascinated by Surrey's noble rank and his tragic fate, routinely praised him as one of the very greatest English poets. The full title of Tottel's influential miscellany, published in 1557 (ten years after Surrey's death), is *Songs and Sonnets Written by the Right Honorable Lord Henry Howard Late Earl of Surrey and Other*. The principal "other" here is his older friend Wyatt, with whose poetry Surrey's is closely linked. Poets who circulated their verse in manuscript in a courtly milieu, the two shared a passion for French and Italian poetry, especially for Petrarch's sonnets. Surrey established a form for these that was used by Shakespeare and that has become known as the English sonnet: three quatrains and a couplet, all in iambic pentameter and rhyming *abab cdcd efef gg*. Even more significant, he was the first English poet to publish in blank verse— unrhymed iambic pentameter—a verse form so popular in the succeeding centuries that it has come to seem almost indigenous to the language. The work in which he used his "strange meter," as the publisher called it, was a translation of part of Virgil's *Aeneid*. Managing the five-stress line with exceptional skill, Surrey initiated the rhythmic fluency that distinguishes so many Elizabethan lyrics. It is striking that his two great literary innovations, the English sonnet and blank verse, should emerge in the same period that saw radical upheavals in traditional religious and social life. It is possible that he was drawn to Virgil's epic because it offered a model of continuity in the face of disaster. Aeneas cannot prevent the fall of Troy, but he goes on to establish a new world without abandoning his old values.

As a conventional love poet Surrey is not very convincing: in 1593 Thomas Nashe wrote sardonically that Surrey "was more in love with his own curious forming fancy" than with this mistress's face. His verse comes alive when he writes about his deep male friendships ("So cruel prison" and the moving epitaph he published on Wyatt), or imagines himself as a woman longing for her absent man ("O happy dames"), or employs his new sonnet form in a savage attack on the "womanish delight" of an unmanly king ("Th'Assyrians' king").

Our selections from Surrey are divided into three groups: sonnets; lyric and reflective poems; classical translations.*

The soote season[1]

> The soote° season, that bud and bloom forth brings,   *sweet, fragrant*
> With green hath clad the hill and eke° the vale.   *also*
> The nightingale with feathers new she sings;
> The turtle to her make° hath told her tale.   *turtledove to her mate*
> 5   Summer is come, for every spray now springs.
> The hart hath hung his old head on the pale;°   *fence, paling*
> The buck in brake° his winter coat he flings;   *thicket*
> The fishes float with new repairèd scale;

---

* For additional lyrics by Surrey, as well as two other excerpts from his partial translation of Virgil's *Aeneid* and the Italian originals of the Petrarchan sonnets translated here, see the NAEL Archive. For more on Richard Tottel and his *Songs and Sonnets*, see, in "An Elizabethan Miscellany," pp. 502–05.

1. This poem is a free adaptation of Petrarch's Rima 310, one of the sonnets written after the death of the poet's beloved.

The adder all her slough° away she slings;   *cast-off skin*
10   The swift swallow pursueth the fliès small;
The busy bee her honey now she mings.°   *mingles*
Winter is worn, that was the flowers' bale.°   *harm*
And thus I see among these pleasant things,
Each care decays, and yet my sorrow springs.

1557

Petrarch, Rima 310

A MODERN PROSE TRANSLATION[2]

Zephyrus returns and leads back the fine weather and the flowers
and the grass, his sweet family, and chattering Procne and weeping Philomena,[3] and Spring, all white and vermilion;

the meadows laugh and the sky becomes clear again, Jupiter is
gladdened looking at his daughter,[4] the air and the waters and the
earth are full of love, every animal takes counsel again to love.

But to me, alas, come back heavier sighs, which she draws from
my deepest heart, she who carried off to Heaven the keys to it;

and the singing of little birds, and the flowering of meadows,
and virtuous gentle gestures in beautiful ladies are a wilderness
and cruel, savage beasts.

Love, that doth reign and live within my thought[1]

Love, that doth reign and live within my thought,
And built his seat within my captive breast,
Clad in the arms wherein with me he fought,
Oft in my face he doth his banner rest.
5   But she that taught me love and suffer pain,
My doubtful hope and eke° my hot desire   *also*
With shamefast° look to shadow and refrain,°   *modest / restrain*
Her smiling grace converteth straight to ire.
And coward Love then to the heart apace°   *at once*
10   Taketh his flight, where he doth lurk and plain,°   *complain*
His purpose lost, and dare not show his face.
For my lord's guilt thus faultless bide° I pain,   *endure*
Yet from my lord shall not my foot remove:
Sweet is the death that taketh end by love.

1557

2. This and the prose translation of Rima 164
are by Robert K. Durling.
3. The swallow and the nightingale, respectively.
Zephyrus is the west wind.
4. Jupiter and his daughter Venus are here the

planets, in favorable astrological relation.
1. Cf. Surrey's version of Petrarch's Rima 140
with Wyatt's translation of the same original
(pp. 120–21; with a modern prose translation).

Alas! so all things now do hold their peace[1]

Alas! so all things now do hold their peace,
Heaven and earth disturbèd in no thing.
The beasts, the air, the birds their song do cease;
The nightès chare[2] the stars about doth bring;
5 Calm is the sea, the waves work less and less.
So am not I, whom love, alas, doth wring,
Bringing before my face the great increase
Of my desires, whereat I weep and sing,
In joy and woe, as in a doubtful ease:
10 For my sweet thoughts sometime do pleasure bring,
But by and by° the cause of my disease[3]   *immediately*
Gives me a pang that inwardly doth sting,
When that I think what grief it is, again,
To live, and lack the thing should rid my pain.

1557

Petrarch, Rima 164

A MODERN PROSE TRANSLATION

Now that the heavens and the earth and the wind are silent, and
sleep reins in the beasts and the birds, Night drives her starry car
about, and in its bed the sea lies without a wave,

I am awake, I think, I burn, I weep; and she who destroys me is
always before me, to my sweet pain: war is my state, full of sorrow
and suffering, and only thinking of her do I have any peace.

Thus from one clear living fountain alone spring the sweet and the
bitter on which I feed; one hand alone heals me and pierces me.

And that my suffering may not reach an end, a thousand times a
day I die and a thousand am born, so distant am I from health.

Th'Assyrians' king,[1] in peace with foul desire

Th'Assyrians' king, in peace with foul desire
And filthy lust that stained his regal heart,
In war, that should set princely hearts afire,
Vanquished did yield for want° of martial art.   *lack*
5 The dint of swords from° kisses seemèd strange,   *after*
And harder than his lady's side, his targe;°   *shield*

---

1. Adapted from Petrarch's Rima 164.
2. From Italian *carro* (the Great Bear).
3. Dis-ease, i.e., discomfort.

1. The legendary Sardanapalus was often cited
as an example of degenerate kingship. Surrey's
poem may allude to Henry VIII.

From glutton feasts to soldier's fare, a change,
His helmet, far above a garland's charge.[2]
Who scace° the name of manhood did retain,   *scarcely*
10   Drenchèd in sloth and womanish delight,
Feeble of sprite,° unpatient° of pain,   *spirit / impatient*
When he had lost his honor and his right
(Proud, time of wealth; in storms, appalled with dread),[3]
Murdered himself, to show some manful deed.[4]

1557

So cruel prison how could betide[1]

So cruel prison how could betide,[2] alas,
As proud Windsor, where I in lust° and joy   *pleasure*
With a king's son my childish° years did pass   *youthful*
In greater feast than Priam's sons of Troy?[3]

5   Where each sweet place returns a taste full sour:
The large green courts, where we were wont to hove,°   *linger*
With eyes cast up unto the Maidens' Tower,
And easy sighs, such as folk draw in love.

The stately sales,° the ladies bright of hue,   *halls*
10   The dances short, long tales of great delight,
With words and looks that tigers could but rue,[4]
Where each of us did plead the other's right.

The palm play° where, dispoilèd° for the game,   *handball / stripped*
With dazed eyes oft we by gleams of love
15   Have missed the ball and got sight of our dame,
To bait° her eyes, which kept the leads[5] above.   *attract, as in fishing*

The graveled ground, with sleeves° tied on the helm,   *ladies' favors*
On foaming horse, with swords and friendly hearts,
With cheer° as though the one should overwhelm,   *countenance*
20   Where we have fought and chasèd oft with darts.°   *spears*

With silver drops the meads yet spread[6] for ruth,°   *pity*
In active games of nimbleness and strength,
Where we did strain, trailèd by swarms of youth,
Our tender limbs that yet shot up in length.

2. I.e., a far heavier burden than a garland.
3. I.e., he was arrogant in good times but overcome with dread in times of trouble.
4. Sardanapalus committed suicide by casting himself into a fire in which he had first burned up his treasure.
1. In the summer of 1537 Surrey was imprisoned at Windsor Castle for striking another courtier. The poem recalls his boyhood stay there (1530–32) with Henry Fitzroy, illegitimate son of Henry VIII.
2. I.e., how could there happen to be.
3. Priam, king of Troy in the *Iliad*, had fifty sons.
4. Take pity on, despite tigers' legendary fierceness.
5. Who was on the lead-covered roof.
6. I.e., when the dew, like tears, was still on the meadows.

25 The secret groves which oft we made resound
Of pleasant plaint and of our ladies' praise,
Recording soft what grace° each one had found,   *favor*
What hope of speed,° what dread of long delays.   *success*

The wild forest, the clothèd holts° with green,   *wooded hills*
30 With reins availed° and swift ybreathèd horse,   *slackened*
With cry of hounds and merry blasts° between,   *i.e., of the horn*
Where we did chase the fearful hart a force.[7]

The void° walls eke° that harbored us each night,   *empty / also*
Wherewith, alas, revive within my breast
35 The sweet accord, such sleeps as yet delight,
The pleasant dreams, the quiet bed of rest,

The secret thoughts imparted with such trust,
The wanton° talk, the divers change of play,   *playful*
The friendship sworn, each promise kept so just,
40 Wherewith we passed the winter nights away.

And with this thought, the blood forsakes my face,
The tears berain my cheeks of deadly hue,
The which as soon as sobbing sighs, alas,
Upsuppèd have, thus I my plaint renew:

45 "O place of bliss, renewer of my woes,
Give me accompt,° where is my noble fere,[8]   *account*
Whom in thy walls thou didst each night enclose,
To other lief,° but unto me most dear."   *dear*

Each stone, alas, that doth my sorrow rue,°   *pity*
50 Returns thereto a hollow sound of plaint.
Thus I alone, where all my freedom grew,
In prison pine with bondage and restraint.

And with remembrance of the greater grief
To banish the less, I find my chief relief.

1537   1557

Wyatt resteth here, that quick could never rest

Wyatt resteth here, that quick° could never rest,   *alive*
Whose heavenly gifts, increasèd by disdain[1]
And virtue, sank the deeper in his breast:
Such profit he by envy could obtain.

---

7. I.e., to run it down.
8. Companion. Henry Fitzroy had died the year before, aged seventeen.

1. Hostility (equivalent to "envy" in line 4). I.e., he could turn hostility toward him to his advantage.

5 A head where wisdom mysteries° did frame,   *subtle meanings*
   Whose hammers beat still in that lively brain
   As on a stith,° where that some work of fame   *anvil*
   Was daily wrought to turn to Britain's gain.

   A visage stern and mild, where both did grow
10 Vice to contemn,° in virtue to rejoice;   *despise*
   Amid great storms whom grace assurèd so
   To live upright and smile at fortune's choice.

   A hand that taught what might be said in rhyme,
   That reft° Chaucer the glory of his wit[2]—   *bereft*
15 A mark the which, unperfited° for time,   *unperfected*
   Some may approach, but never none shall hit.

   A tongue that served in foreign realms his king;
   Whose courteous talk to virtue did inflame
   Each noble heart: a worthy guide to bring
20 Our English youth by travail° unto fame.   *labor*

   An eye whose judgment none affect° could blind,   *no partiality*
   Friends to allure and foes to reconcile,
   Whose piercing look did represent a mind
   With virtue fraught, reposèd, void of guile.

25 A heart where dread yet never so impressed
   To hide the thought that might the truth advance;
   In neither fortune loft nor yet repressed[3]
   To swell in wealth° or yield unto mischance.   *well-being*

   A valiant corpse[4] where force and beauty met,
30 Happy°—alas, too happy, but° for foes;   *fortunate / if not*
   Lived and ran the race that Nature set,
   Of manhood's shape, where she the mold did lose.[5]

   But to the heavens that simple° soul is fled,   *innocent*
   Which left, with such as covet Christ to know,
35 Witness of faith[6] that never shall be dead,
   Sent for our health,° but not receivèd so.   *welfare*

   Thus for our guilt, this jewel have we lost;
   The earth his bones, the heavens possess his ghost.°   *spirit*

1542   1542

---

2. Genius. I.e., Wyatt (supposedly) replaced Chaucer as England's greatest poet.
3. I.e., neither overly elated by good fortune nor downcast by bad.
4. Body (not, as now, a dead one).

5. A conventional praise—that Nature, in creating someone, made a masterpiece and then lost the pattern.
6. I.e., which left with Christians ("such as covet Christ to know") a testimony of faith.

O happy dames, that may embrace[1]

O happy dames,° that may embrace   *wives*
The fruit of your delight,
Help to bewail the woeful case
And eke° the heavy plight   *also*
5 Of me, that wonted° to rejoice   *was accustomed*
The fortune of my pleasant choice:
Good ladies, help to fill my mourning voice.

In ship, freight° with rememberance   *loaded*
Of thoughts and pleasures past,
10 He sails that hath in governance
My life while it will last;
With scalding sighs, for lack of gale,
Futhering his hope, that is his sail,
Toward me, the sweet port of his avail.°   *destination*

15 Alas, how oft in dreams I see
Those eyes that were my food,
Which sometime so delighted me,
That yet they do me good;
Wherewith I wake with his return,
20 Whose absent flame did make me burn:
But when I find the lack, Lord how I mourn!

When other lovers in arms across°   *embracing*
Rejoice their chief delight,
Drowned in tears to mourn my loss
25 I stand the bitter night
In my window, where I may see
Before the winds how the clouds flee.
Lo, what a mariner love hath made me!

And in green waves when the salt flood
30 Doth rise by rage of wind,
A thousand fancies in that mood
Assail my restless mind.
Alas, now drencheth° my sweet foe,[2]   *drowns*
That with the spoil° of my heart did go *plunder, booty*
35 And left me; but, alas, why did he so?

And when the seas wax calm again,
To chase from me annoy,°   *distress*

1. The speaker is a woman. The poem was probably written for Surrey's wife, from whom he was separated while on military duty in France in the 1540s.
2. A conventional expression for a loved one, going back to medieval love poetry.

My doubtful hope doth cause me plain,°   *to complain*
So dread cuts off my joy.
40   Thus is my wealth° mingled with woe,   *happiness*
And of each thought a doubt doth grow:
Now he comes! Will he come? Alas, no, no!

1557

Martial, the things for to attain[1]

Martial, the things for to attain
The happy life be these, I find:
The riches left, not got with pain;
The fruitful ground, the quiet mind;

5   The equal friend; no grudge nor strife;
No charge° of rule, nor governance;   *burden*
Without disease the healthy life;
The household of continuance;°   *long duration*

The mean diet, no delicate fare;
10   Wisdom joined with simplicity;
The night dischargèd of all care,
Where wine may bear no sovereignty;

The chaste wife, wise, without debate;°   *strife*
Such sleeps as may beguile° the night;   *charm away*
15   Contented with thine own estate;
Neither wish death nor fear his might.

1547

From The Fourth Book of Virgil[1]

[DIDO IN LOVE]

Unhappy Dido burns, and in her rage°   *passion*
Throughout the town she wand'reth up and down,
Like to the stricken hind with shaft[2] in Crete
Throughout the woods, which chasing with his darts°   *arrows*
90   Aloof,° the shepherd smiteth at unwares°   *at a distance / without warning*
And leaves unwist° in her the thirling° head,   *unknown / piercing*

1. A translation of an epigram (10.47) by the
Roman poet Martial (ca. 40–104 C.E.). The theme,
a glorification of "the mean estate" (the modest,
moderate life), is very common in literature of
this period.

1. Surrey translated Books 2 and 4 of Virgil's
Aeneid. In this excerpt, Dido, the widowed queen
of Carthage, suffers the pangs of undeclared love
for her guest Aeneas.
2. I.e., like a deer shot with an arrow.

That through the groves and launds° glides in her flight;   *glades*
Amid whose side the mortal° arrow sticks.   *deadly*
　　Aeneas now about the walls she leads,
95　The town prepared and Carthage wealth to show.
Off'ring to speak, amid her voice, she whists.°   *falls silent*
And when the day gan fail, new feasts she makes;
The Troys'° travails to hear anew she lists,°   *Trojans' / wants*
Enragèd all,° and stareth in his face   *wholly impassioned*
100　That tells the tale. And when they were all gone,
And the dim moon doth eft° withhold the light,   *again*
And sliding stars provokèd unto sleep,
Alone she mourns within her palace void,
And sets her down on her forsaken bed;
105　And absent him she hears, when he is gone,
And seeth eke.° Oft in her lap she holds   *also*
Ascanius,[3] trapped by his father's form,
So to beguile the love° cannot be told.   *the love that*

1554

---

3. Aeneas's son; Dido is captivated ("trapped") by the boy's likeness to his father.

Faith in Conflict

When, in the late 1520s, the Catholic authorities of England tried to burn all copies of William Tyndale's English translation of the New Testament, they were attempting to stop the spread of what they viewed as a dangerous new plague of heresies. The plague was the Protestant Reformation, a movement opposed to crucial aspects of both the belief system and the institutional structure of Roman Catholicism.

The movement had been launched by the German theologian Martin Luther, who in 1517 challenged the authority of the pope and attacked several key doctrines of the Catholic Church. According to Luther, the Church, with its elaborate hierarchical structure centered in Rome, its rich monasteries and convents, and its enormous political influence, had become a hopelessly corrupt conspiracy of venal priests who manipulated popular superstitions to enrich themselves and amass worldly power. Luther began by vehemently attacking the sale of indulgences—certificates promising the remission of punishments to be suffered in the afterlife by souls sent to Purgatory to expiate their sins before being allowed into heaven. Purgatory, he argued, had no foundation in Scripture, which in his view was the only legitimate source of religious truth (*sola scriptura*). Christians would be saved not by scrupulously following the ritual practices fostered by the Catholic Church—observing fast days, reciting the ancient Latin prayers, endowing chantries to say prayers for the dead, invoking the protection of individual saints, and so on—and not even by the performance of good deeds, but by faith and faith alone (*sola fide*).

This challenge spread and gathered force, especially in northern Europe, where major leaders like the French theologian Calvin (who, after his break with Catholicism, established a theocracy in Geneva) transformed religious institutions and elaborated various and sometimes conflicting doctrinal principles. Calvin, whose thought came to be particularly influential in England and Scotland, emphasized the obligation of governments to implement God's will in the world. He advanced too the doctrine of predestination, by which, as he put it, "God adopts some to hope of life and sentences others to eternal death." God's "secret election" of the saved troubled Calvin, but his study of the Scriptures had led him to conclude that "only a small number, out of an incalculable multitude, should obtain salvation." Some Christians found this idea horrifying. How, they asked, could a loving creator condemn the great majority of his creatures to an eternity of torment? And was it not possible for humans to avert the severe decree through virtuous actions? But for Calvin predestination was a mystery bound up with faith, confidence, and an active engagement in the fashioning of a Christian community.

The Reformation had a direct and powerful impact on those realms where it gained control. Monasteries were sacked, their possessions seized by princes or sold off to the highest bidder; monks and nuns, expelled from their cloisters, were encouraged to break their vows of chastity and find spouses, as Luther and his wife, a former nun, had done. In the great cathedrals and in hundreds of smaller churches and chapels, the elaborate altarpieces, bejeweled crucifixes, crystal reliquaries holding the bones of saints, venerated statues, and paintings were attacked as "idols." Condemned for their Catholic doctrinal content and accused of violating the biblical prohibition on the making of "graven images," they were often defaced or destroyed. Protestant congregations continued, for the most part, to celebrate the most sacred Christian ritual, the Eucharist, or Lord's Supper, but they did so in a profoundly different spirit from the Catholic Church, more as commemoration than as miracle, and the service was conducted not in the old liturgical Latin but in the vernacular.

The Reformation was at first vigorously resisted in England. Protestant writings were seized by officials of the Church and the state and burned. Protestants who made their views known were persecuted—driven to flee the country or arrested, put on trial, and burned at the stake. But the situation changed drastically after Henry decided to seek a divorce from his first wife, Catherine of Aragon, to marry Anne Boleyn. When the Roman Catholic Church, under pressure from Catherine's powerful family, refused to grant the divorce, Henry defied papal authority, declared himself head of the Church in England, seized the wealth of the monasteries, and unleashed Protestant energies, including fierce bursts of iconoclasm. On most doctrinal questions, however, Henry remained an orthodox Catholic, and in the latter part of his reign his clerical authorities renewed the persecution of Protestants.

The turn toward the Reformation was more decisive in the reign (1547–53) of Henry's heir, Edward VI; and the attempt by Edward's successor, Mary (daughter of Catherine of Aragon), to reimpose Roman Catholicism as the national religion came to an end with her death, in 1558. The long reign (1558–1603) of Henry's daughter by Anne Boleyn, Elizabeth I, firmly established Protestantism as the faith of the Church of England. Reformation doctrine shaped the vernacular liturgy eloquently formulated in the officially sanctioned *Book of Common Prayer* and was reinforced in the series of homilies, or sermons, that ministers were commanded to deliver to their parishioners.

The Reformation did not spread quickly or easily among the mass of the English population. Like Henry VIII himself, most English people in the decades after the break with Rome were far from being full-fledged Protestants. Emotional attachment to the traditional religion ran deep, as did resentment of an aggressively intolerant Protestant officialdom. From the 1530s to the end of the century, a significant number of individuals, including Thomas More and the Jesuit Robert Southwell, were prepared to die for the old faith. Many more, though still a small minority, stubbornly rejected the new orthodoxy, absenting themselves from Protestant worship; these recusants, as they were known, were subjected to fines and sometimes worse punishments. A much greater number conformed in public but remained largely untouched by Protestant doctrine.

Though Protestantism and Catholicism were exposed, under different regimes, to brutal persecution, both faiths proved impossible to eradicate. In large part this tenacity arose from the passionate, often suicidal heroism of men and women who felt that their soul's salvation depended on the precise character of their Christianity and who consequently embraced martyrdom rather than repudiate their beliefs. It arose too from a mid-fifteenth-century technological innovation that made it extremely difficult to suppress unwelcome ideas: the printing press. Early Protestants quickly grasped that with a few clandestine presses they could defy the Catholic authorities and flood the country with their texts. "How many printing presses there be in the world," wrote the Protestant polemicist and martyrologist John Foxe, "so many blockhouses there be against the high castle" of the pope in Rome, "so that either the pope must abolish knowledge and printing or printing at length will root him out." By the century's end, it was the Catholics, as well as the more radical Protestants—known as Puritans—who were using the clandestine press to propagate their beliefs in the face of official persecution.

THE ENGLISH BIBLE

Protestant insistence that true belief must be based on the Holy Scriptures alone made the translation and dissemination of the Bible in English and other vernacular languages a matter of utmost urgency. Before the Reformation, the Roman Catholic Church had not always and everywhere opposed vernacular translations of the Bible, but it generally preferred that the populace encounter the Scriptures through the interpretations of its priests, trained to read the Latin translation known as the Vulgate. In times of great conflict this preference for clerical mediation hardened into outright prohibition of vernacular translation and into persecution and book burning. The late fourteenth-century English translation associated with John Wycliffe was vehemently attacked as heretical, and its suppression led to an edict banning any unauthorized attempt to translate the Bible into English. Throughout the fifteenth century no authorization was granted.

It was in the face of such fierce opposition that zealous Protestants all over Europe set out to put the Bible into the hands of the laity. A remarkable translation of the New Testament by an English Lutheran named William Tyndale was printed on the Continent and smuggled into England in 1526; Tyndale's translation of the Pentateuch, the first five books of the Hebrew Bible, followed in 1530. Many copies of these translations were seized and destroyed, as was the translator himself, but the printing press made it extremely difficult for authorities to eradicate books for which there was a passionate demand.

Tyndale's translation of the Bible was completed by an associate, Miles Coverdale, whose rendering of the Psalms proved to be particularly influential. Their joint labor was the basis for the Great Bible (1539), a copy of which was ordered to be placed in every church in the kingdom. Four years later, as Henry VIII sought to halt the tide of reform, a law was passed forbidding women, craftsmen, servants, and laborers from reading the Bible either in public or in private. Yet at this stage it was already too late to get the Scriptures out of the hands of the populace. Though there would be further opposition in years to come—innumerable Bibles were printed under Edward VI, only to be burned during the reign of his half-sister Mary—the English Bible was a force that could not be suppressed, and it became, in its various forms, the single most important book of the sixteenth century.

Marian persecution was indirectly responsible for what would become the most scholarly Protestant English Bible, the translation known as the Geneva Bible, prepared, with extensive, learned, and often fiercely polemical marginal notes, by English exiles in Calvin's Geneva and widely diffused in England after Elizabeth came to the throne. In addition, Elizabethan church authorities ordered a careful revision of the Great Bible, and this version, known as the Bishops' Bible, was the one read in the churches. The success of the Geneva Bible in particular prompted those Elizabethan Catholics who now in turn found themselves in exile to bring out a vernacular translation of their own, the Douay-Rheims version, to counter the Protestant readings and glosses.

After Elizabeth's death, in 1603, King James I and his bishops ordered that a revised translation of the entire Bible be undertaken by a group of forty-seven scholars. The result, published in 1611, was the Authorized Version, more popularly known as the King James Bible. This translation, whose diction and rhythms have had an immense influence on English literature, continues to be read and treasured.

In the passage selected here, 1 Corinthians 13, Tyndale's use of the word *love,* echoed by the Geneva Bible, is set against the Catholic *charity.* The latter term gestures toward the religious doctrine of works, against the Protestant insistence on salvation by faith alone. It is a sign of the conservative, moderate Protantism of the King James Version that it too opts for *charity.*

1 Corinthians 13

From *Tyndale's Translation*

Though I spake with the tongues of men and angels, and yet had no love, I were even as sounding brass: or as a tinkling cymbal. And though I could prophesy, and understood all secrets, and all knowledge: yea, if I had all faith, so that I could move mountains out of their places, and yet had no love, I were nothing. And though I bestowed all my goods to feed the poor, and though I gave my body even that I burned, and yet had no love, it profiteth me nothing.

Love suffereth long, and is courteous. Love envieth not. Love doth not forwardly,[1] swelleth not, dealeth not dishonestly, seeketh not her own, is not provoked to anger, thinketh not evil, rejoiceth not in iniquity: but rejoiceth in the truth, suffereth all things, believeth all things, hopeth all things, endureth in all things. Though that prophesying fail, other[2] tongues shall cease, or knowledge vanish away, yet love falleth never away.

For our knowledge is unperfect and our prophesying is unperfect. But when that which is perfect is come, then that which is unperfect shall be done away. When I was a child, I spake as a child, I understood as a child, I imagined as a child. But as soon as I was a man, I put away childishness. Now we see in a glass, even in a dark[3] speaking: but then shall we see face to face. Now I know unperfectly: but then shall I know even as I am known. Now abideth faith, hope, and love, even these three: but the chief of these is love.

1525, 1535

From *The Geneva Bible*

Though I speak with the tongues of men and Angels, and have not love, I am as sounding brass, or a tinkling cymbal. And though I had the gift of prophecy, and knew all secrets and all knowledge, yea, if I had all faith, so that I could remove mountains, and had not love, I were nothing. And though I feed the poor with all my goods, and though I give my body, that I be burned, and have not love, it profiteth me nothing. Love suffereth long: it is bountiful: love envieth not: love doth not boast itself: it is not puffed up: It disdaineth not: it seeketh not her own things: it is not provoked to anger: it thinketh not evil: It rejoiceth not in iniquity, but rejoiceth in the truth: It suffereth all things: it believeth all things: it hopeth all things: it endureth all things. Love doth never fall away, though that prophesyings be abolished, or the tongues cease, or knowledge vanish away. For we know in part, and we prophesy in part. But when that which is perfect is come, then that which is in part shall be abolished. When I was a child, I spake as a child, I understood as a child, I thought as a child: but when I became a man, I put away childish things. For now we see through a glass darkly:[4] but then shall we see face to face. Now I know in part: but then shall I know even as I am known. And now abideth faith, hope, and love, even these three: but the chiefest of these is love.

1560, 1602

---

1. Perversely, evilly.
2. Or.
3. Obscure, unclear. "Glass": mirror. The meta-phor of indirect, imperfect sight seems to derive from Plato's Allegory of the Cave (*Republic* 7).
4. By means of a mirror, obscurely.

not the eie, I am not of the body, is it therefore not of the bodie?

17 If the whole bodie were an eie, where were
the hearing? If the whole were hearing,
where were the smelling?

18 But now hath God disposed the members euery one of them in the bodie at his
owne pleasure.

19 For if they were all one member, where
were the bodie?

20 But now are there many members, yet
but m one bodie.

21 And the eye cannot say vnto the hande, I
haue no neede of thee: nor the heade againe
to the feete, I haue no neede of you.

22 Yea, much rather those members of the
bodie, which seeme to be n more feeble, are
necessarie.

23 And vpon those members of the bodie,
which we thinke most vnhonest, put wee
more o honestie on: and our vncomely partes
haue more comelines on.

24 For our comely partes neede it not: but
God hath tempered the bodie together, and
hath giuen the more honour to that part
which lacked,

25 Least there should be any diuision in the
bodie: but that the members should p haue
the same care one for another.

26 Therefore if one member suffer, all suffer
with it: if one member be had in honour,
all the members reioyce with it.

27 Now ye are the body of Christ, and members q for your part.

28 * And God hath ordeyned some in the
Church: as first Apostles, secondly Prophets,
thirdly teachers, then them that do miracles: after that, the giftes of healing, r helpers, gouernours, diuersitie of tongues.

29 Are all Apostles? are all Prophets? are all
teachers?

30 Are al doers of miracles? haue al the gifts
of healing? do all speake with tongues? do
all interpret?

31 But s desire you the best giftes, and I will
yet shew you a more excellent way.

CHAP. XIII.
*Because loue is the fountaine and rule of edifying the Church, he set-
teth forth the nature, office and prayse therof.*

1 Though I speake with the tongues of
men and a Angels, and haue not loue, I
am as sounding brasse, or a tinke-
ling cymball.

2 And though I had the gift of prophecie,
and knewe all secretes and all knowledge,
yea, if I had b all fayth, so that I could re-
moue * mountaines and had not loue, I
were nothing.

3 And though I feede the poore with all
my goodes, and though I giue my bodie,
that I be burned, and haue not loue, it profiteth me nothing.

4 Loue suffereth long: it is bountifull: loue
enuieth not: loue doeth not boast it selfe: it
is not puffed vp:

5 It disdayneth not: it seeketh not her owne

thinges: it is not prouoked to anger: it
thinketh not euill:

6 It reioyceth not in iniquitie, but reioyceth
in the trueth:

7 It suffreth al things: it beleueth c al things:
it hopeth al things: it endureth d all things.

8 Loue doeth neuer fall away, though that
prophecyings be abolished, or the tongues
cease, or knowledge vanish away.

9 For e we know f in part, and we f prophecie in part.

10 But when that which is perfect, is come,
then that which is in part, shall be abolished.

11 When I was a childe, I spake as a childe,
I vnderstoode as a childe, I thought as a
childe: but when I became a man, I put a-
way childish things.

12 For now we see g through a glasse darke-
ly: but then shall we see face to face. Nowe
I know in part: but then shall I knowe e-
uen as I am known.

13 And nowe abideth fayth, hope and loue,
euen these three: but the h chiefest of these is
loue.

CHAP. XIIII.

*The exhorteth to loue, commendeth the gift of tongues, and other spi-
rituall giftes, But chiefly prophecying. 19 He commandeth women to keepe silence in the church, 40 And sheweth what good order ought to be obserued in the church.*

1 Follow after loue, and couet spirituall
giftes, & rather that ye may a prophecie.

2 For he that speaketh a strange tongue,
speaketh not vnto men, but vnto God: for
no man b heareth him: howbeit in the c spirit
he speaketh secret things.

3 But he that prophecieth, speaketh vnto
men to edifying, and to exhortation, and to
comfort.

4 He that speaketh strange language, edifi-
eth him selfe: but he that prophecieth, edi-
fieth the Church.

5 I would that ye all spake strange languages, but rather that yee prophecied: for
greater is hee that prophecieth, then hee
that speaketh diuers tongues, except he expound it, that the Church may receyue edi-
fication.

6 And nowe, brethren, if I come vnto you
speaking diuers tongues, what shall I profite you, except I speake to you, either by
e reuelation, or by knowledge, or by prophecying, or by doctrine?

7 Moreouer things without life which giue
a sound, whether it be a f pipe or an harpe,
except they make a distinctio in the sounds,
howe shall it be knowen what is pyped or
harped?

8 And also if the trumpet giue an vncer-
taine sounde, who shall prepare him selfe to
battel?

9 So likewise you, by the tongue, except ye
vtter wordes that haue signification, howe
shall it be vnderstand what is spoken? for
ye shall speake in the g aire.

10 There are so many kindes of voyces (as
it commeth to passe) in the world, and none
of them s is domme.

11 Except

Nn.iiii.

A page from the Geneva Bible, with commentary; 1583 edition. The Geneva Bible includes elaborate marginal notes, often with a sharply Protestant inflection. Some Elizabethan Catholics may have detected such a perspective in one note's anticipation of a redeemed state "where we shal neither nede scholes nor teachers."

From *The Douay-Rheims Version*

If I speak with the tongues of men and of Angels, and have not charity,[5] I am become as sounding brass, or a tinkling cymbal. And if I should have prophecy, and knew all mysteries, and all knowledge, and if I should have all faith so that I could remove mountains, and have not charity, I am nothing. And if I should distribute all my goods to be meat[6] for the poor, and if I should deliver my body so that I burn, and have not charity, it doth profit me nothing.

Charity is patient, is benign: charity envieth not, dealeth not perversely: is not puffed up, is not ambitious, seeketh not her own, is not provoked to anger, thinketh not evil: rejoiceth not upon iniquity, but rejoiceth with the truth: suffereth all things, believeth all things, hopeth all things, beareth all things. Charity never falleth away: whether prophecies shall be made void, or tongues shall cease, or knowledge shall be destroyed. For in part we know, and in part we prophesy. But when that shall come that is perfect, that shall be made void that is in part. When I was a little one, I spake as a little one, I understood as a little one, I thought as a little one. But when I was made a man, I did away the things that belonged to a little one. We see now by a glass in a dark sort: but then face to face. Now I know in part: but then I shall know as also I am known. And now there remain faith, hope, charity, these three, but the greater of these is charity.

1582

From *The Authorized (King James) Version*

Though I speak with the tongues of men and of angels, and have not charity, I am become as sounding brass, or a tinkling cymbal. And though I have the gift of prophecy, and understand all mysteries, and all knowledge; and though I have all faith, so that I could remove mountains, and have no charity, I am nothing. And though I bestow all my goods to feed the poor, and though I give my body to be burned, and have not charity, it profiteth me nothing. Charity suffereth long, and is kind; charity envieth not; charity vaunteth not itself, is not puffed up, doth not behave itself unseemly, seeketh not her own, is not easily provoked, thinketh no evil; rejoiceth not in iniquity, but rejoiceth in the truth; beareth all things, believeth all things, hopeth all things, endureth all things. Charity never faileth: but whether there be prophecies, they shall fail; whether there be tongues, they shall cease; whether there be knowledge, it shall vanish away. For we know in part, and we prophesy in part. But when that which is perfect is come, then that which is in part shall be done away. When I was a child, I spake as a child, I understood as a child, I thought as a child: but when I became a man, I put away childish things. For now we see through a glass, darkly; but then face to face: now I know in part; but then shall I know even as also I am known. And now abideth faith, hope, charity, these three; but the greatest of these is charity.

1611

5. From Latin *caritas*, love; but also carrying the modern sense.   6. Food (in general).

WILLIAM TYNDALE

Educated at Oxford, William Tyndale (ca. 1490–1536) became a lecturer at Cambridge, where he was associated with a group of humanist scholars who met regularly at the White Horse Inn. Having become convinced that salvation depended on direct access to the word of God, he sought support to undertake a translation of the Bible into English, but English church authorities, concerned about the spread of heresies, blocked this project. In 1524 Tyndale went to Germany, where with the financial assistance of wealthy London merchants, he completed a translation of the New Testament the following year. Deeply influenced by the writings of Martin Luther and other reformers, he also wrote a series of doctrinal and polemical works, such as *The Obedience of a Christian Man* (1528), that eloquently express the Protestant hope of salvation through faith alone and reject the principles and practices of Roman Catholicism. Because of their vitriolic assaults on the Catholic Church, Protestants like Tyndale were often accused of fomenting rebellion. *The Obedience of a Christian Man* attempts to answer the charge by insisting on the subject's absolute secular obligation to obey the king. At Anne Boleyn's urging, Henry VIII read it and is reported to have remarked that "this is a book for me and for all kings to read." Notwithstanding this supposed endorsement, English Catholic authorities during Henry's reign managed to lure Tyndale into a trap and had him executed in Vilvorde, Flanders.

From The Obedience of a Christian Man

[THE FORGIVENESS OF SINS]

* * * For sin we through fragility never so oft, yet as soon as we repent and come into the right way again, and unto the testament[1] which God hath made in Christ's blood, our sins vanish away as smoke in the wind, and as darkness at the coming of light; or as thou castest a little blood, or milk, into the main sea: insomuch that whosoever goeth about to make satisfaction for his sins to God-ward,[2] saying in his heart, This much have I sinned, this much will I do again; or this-wise will I live to make amends withal; or this will I do, to get heaven withal; the same is an infidel, faithless, and damned in his deed-doing, and hath lost his part in Christ's blood; because he is disobedient unto God's testament, and setteth up another of his own imagination, unto which he will compel God to obey. If we love God, we have a commandment to love our neighbor also, as saith John in his epistle;[3] and if we have offended him, to make him amends; or if we have not wherewith, to ask him forgiveness, and to do and suffer all things for his sake, to win him

---

1. Covenant. "Fragility": frailty, moral weakness.
2. I.e., in his relationship to God.
3. "If a man say, I love God, and hateth his brother, he is a liar: for he that loveth not his brother whom he hath seen, how can he love God whom he hath not seen? And this commandment have we from him, That he who loveth God love his brother also" (1 John 4.20–21).

to God, and to nourish peace and unity. But to God-ward Christ is an ever-lasting satisfaction, and ever sufficient.[4]

[SCRIPTURAL INTERPRETATION]

Thou shalt understand, therefore, that the Scripture hath but one sense, which is the literal sense. And that literal sense is the root and ground of all, and the anchor that never faileth, whereunto if thou cleave, thou canst never err or go out of the way. And if thou leave the literal sense, thou canst not but go out of the way. Neverthelater,[5] the Scripture useth proverbs, similitudes, riddles, or allegories, as all other speeches do; but that which the proverb, similitude, riddle, or allegory signifieth, is ever the literal sense, which thou must seek out diligently: as in the English we borrow words and sentences of one thing, and apply them unto another, and give them new significations. We say, "Let the sea swell and rise as high as he will, yet hath God appointed how far he shall go": meaning that the tyrants shall not do what they would, but that only which God hath appointed them to do. "Look ere thou leap": whose literal sense is, "Do nothing suddenly, or without advisement." "Cut not the bough that thou standest upon": whose literal sense is, "Oppress not the commons"; and is borrowed of hewers. When a thing speedeth[6] not well, we borrow speech, and say, "The bishop hath blessed it"; because that noth-ing speedeth well that they meddle withal. If the porridge be burned too, or the meat over-roasted, we say, "The bishop hath put his foot in the pot," or "The bishop hath played the cook"; because the bishops burn whom they lust,[7] and whosoever displeaseth them. "He is a pontifical fellow"; that is, proud and stately. "He is popish"; that is, superstitious and faithless.

* * *

Beyond all this, when we have found out the literal sense of the Scripture by the process of the text, or by a like text of another place, then go we, and as the Scripture borroweth similitudes of worldly things, even so we again borrow similitudes or allegories of the Scripture, and apply them to our pur-poses; which allegories are no sense of the Scripture, but free things besides the Scripture, and altogether in the liberty of the Spirit. * * * This allegory proveth nothing, neither can do. For it is not the Scripture, but an ensample[8] or a similitude borrowed of the Scripture, to declare a text or a conclusion of the Scripture more expressly, and to root it and grave[9] it in the heart. For a similitude, or an ensample, doth print a thing much deeper in the wits of a man than doth a plain speaking, and leaveth behind him as it were a sting to prick him forward, and to awake him withal. Moreover, if I could not prove with an open[1] text that which the allegory doth express, then were the alle-gory a thing to be jested at, and of no greater value than a tale of Robin Hood.

1527, 1528

---

4. To the ecclesiastical commissioners who examined Tyndale's works in 1530, this passage was clearly heretical. One of the commissioners, Sir Thomas More, lambasted it as constituting an encouragement to sin because it made obtain-ing forgiveness seem such an easy matter.

5. Nevertheless.
6. Succeeds, prospers.
7. Whomever they please.
8. Example.
9. Engrave.
1. Plain, clear.

THOMAS MORE

As early as 1521, when he became Henry VIII's "theological councillor," Thomas More had played an important role in the official campaign against Luther. Initially writing as the king's surrogate in doctrinal polemics conducted in Latin, by 1529, when he became lord chancellor of England, More had become deeply immersed in the anti-Protestant campaign in his own right. His extremely energetic contributions included written attacks, in English, on Tyndale's Bible translations and other prohibited books and extended to active persecution of those defined as heretics. A few years earlier, in *Utopia*, More had imagined a state that would tolerate a diversity of religious convictions, but that view had vanished in the face of actual dissent. "I find that breed of men absolutely loathsome," More wrote to his friend Erasmus; "I want to be as hateful to them as anyone can possibly be." During his tenure as lord chancellor, several Protestants were imprisoned in More's own house while he tried to persuade them to recant views unacceptable to Roman Catholic orthodoxy, and six people were burned at the stake for heresy. If More was willing to kill in defense of the Christian consensus in which he fervently believed, he also proved himself willing in the end to die for his belief.

More had two principal quarrels with Lutheranism: (1) he objected to Luther's denial that Christians could contribute toward their own salvation through their good works, and (2) he objected to Luther's view of biblical interpretation. For Luther, Scripture preceded and ideally determined the form of the Church; for More, the Church preceded and determined the interpretation of Scripture.

In *A Dialogue Concerning Heresies* (1529), More broaches both issues. Departing from the head-on, vituperative attacks of his Latin works, More here adopts a different approach: his interlocutor in the *Dialogue* is a young man on friendly terms with More, but infatuated with Protestant ideas. More's aim seems less to attack Luther directly than, by using wit and cajolery as well as dialectic, to dissuade English men and women from embracing Protestantism.

The selection printed here tackles the fundamental issues of biblical interpretation. Who decides on the meaning of Scripture: the Church or individual readers? More's interlocutor is in no doubt: Scripture is for the most part entirely plain; individual readers have no trouble interpreting it. More strongly counters such simple faith in the plain and literal sense. Everything, he argues (in a passage playing with the consonance of "goose" and "gloss"), requires a commentary. Even to compare one text with another is to gloss it, and any translation of the Bible is itself inevitably a gloss. If commentary is always necessary, then some stable ground for establishing authority over that commentary also becomes necessary. For More that ground is the Catholic Church, whose authority is established by the many centuries of its continued existence and by the consensus of the Church's Councils. More casts the young Lutheran's position as that of a single opinionated reader perversely resisting the "common faith" of Christendom.

From A Dialogue Concerning Heresies

From Book 1, Chapter 28: * * * *proving the authority of the old interpreters and the infallible authority of the Church* * * *

"* * * in somewhat, ye say, ye will believe the Church, but not in all. In anything beside Scripture ye will not, nor in the interpretation of Scripture ye will not; and so, where ye said that ye believe the Church in somewhat, in very deed ye believe the Church in right nought. For wherein will ye believe it, if ye believe it not in the interpretation of Scripture? For as touching the text, ye believe the Scripture self, and not the Church."

"Methinketh," quod[1] he, "the text is good enough and plain enough, needing no gloss[2] if it be well considered, and every part compared with other."

"Hard it were," quod I, "to find anything so plain that it should need no gloss at all."

"In faith," quod he, "they make a gloss to some texts that be as plain as it is that twice two make four."

"Why," quod I, "needeth that no gloss at all?"

"I trow[3] so," quod he. "Or else the devil is on it."

"Iwis,"[4] quod I, "and yet though ye would believe one that would tell you that twice two ganders made always four geese, yet ye would be advised[5] ere ye believed him that would tell you that twice two geese made always four ganders. For therein might ye be deceived. And him would ye not believe at all, that would tell you that twice two geese would always make four horse."

"Tut," quod he, "this is a merry[6] matter. They must be all the twice twain always of one kind. But geese and horse be of diverse."

"Well," quod I, "then every man that is neither goose nor horse seeth that there is one gloss yet.[7] But now," quod I, "the geese and the ganders be both of one kind, and yet twice two geese make not always four ganders."

"A sweet matter," quod he. "Ye wot[8] what I mean well enough."

"I think I do," quod I. "But I think if ye bring it forth it will make another gloss to your text, as plain as your text is; and[9] ye will in all Holy Scripture have no gloss at all. And yet will ye have collation made of one text with another, and show how they may be agreed together[1]—as though all that were no gloss."

"Yea," quod he, "but would you that we should believe the Church if it set a gloss that will in no wise[2] agree with the text, but that it appeareth plainly that the text, well considered, saith clean the contrary?"

"To whom doth that appear," quod I, "so plainly, when it appeareth one to you, and to the whole Church another?"

"Yet if I see it so," quod he, "though holy doctors and all the whole Church would tell me the contrary, methinketh I were no more bounden to believe them all, that the Scripture meaneth as they take it, than if they would all tell me that a thing were white which I see myself is black."

"Of late," quod I, "ye would believe the Church in something. And now not only ye would believe it in nothing, but also whereas God would the Church should be your judge, ye would now be judge over the Church. And ye will by your wit[3] be judge whether the Church, in the understanding of Holy Scripture that God hath written to His Church, do judge aright or err. As for your white and black, never shall it be that ye shall see the thing black that all other shall see white. But ye may be sure that if all other see it white, and ye take it for black, your eyen[4] be sore deceived. For the Church will not, I think, agree to call it other than it seemeth to them. And

---

1. Quoth, said.
2. Interpretation, commentary.
3. Believe.
4. Certainly.
5. Warned.
6. Frivolous.
7. Still.

8. Know.
9. Whereas.
1. Reconciled.
2. Way.
3. Intellect.
4. Eyes.

much marvel were it, if ye should in Holy Scripture see better than the old holy doctors and Christ's whole Church."

* * *

1528–29   1529

JOHN CALVIN

Born to middle-class parents in Picardy, France, and trained as a lawyer, Calvin (1509–1564) was steeped in the Greek and Latin learning associated with Renaissance humanism. He acquired as well a knowledge of Hebrew, so that he was powerfully equipped to respond to the call, from Erasmus and others, for a study of the Bible in its original languages. Drawn increasingly toward Protestantism, Calvin left Catholic France for Switzerland, where he eventually became the dominant figure in Geneva, establishing a stern theocratic rule. Through his voluminous writings, he also became the principal theologian of the Protestant Reformation, exercising immense influence in England and Scotland as well as on the Continent. His major work, revised in successive Latin and French editions and widely translated, is *The Institution of Christian Religion*. The passage printed here is from Calvin's famous, troubling account of the doctrine of predestination, according to which God has determined before the foundation of the world whom he will save and whom he will damn, regardless of the merits or defects of these individuals. The good deeds that a virtuous person does in life are a sign of divine election, not a means to secure it. The translation, closely adhering to the Latin original, is by Thomas Norton (1532–1584), a lawyer and member of Parliament and, with Thomas Sackville, the author of the earliest English tragedy in blank verse, *Gorboduc*—first performed in the same year (1561) that Norton's translation of Calvin appeared.

From The Institution of Christian Religion, written in Latin by Master John Calvin, and translated into English according to the author's last edition

From *Book 3, Chapter 21*
Of the eternal election, whereby God hath predestinate some to salvation, and other some to destruction

But now whereas the covenant of life[1] is not equally preached to all men, and with them to whom it is preached it doth not either equally or continually find like place,[2] in this diversity the wondrous depth of the judgment of God appeareth. For neither is it any doubt but that this diversity also serveth the free choice of God's eternal election.[3] If it be evident that it is wrought by the will of God that salvation is freely offered to some, and other some are

1. Promise of salvation.   3. Choice; i.e., of whom to save.
2. Consideration.

debarred from coming to it, here by and by[4] arise great and hard questions which cannot otherwise be discussed than if the godly minds have that certainly stablished which they ought to hold[5] concerning election and predestination. This is (as many think) a cumbersome[6] question: because they think nothing to be less reasonable than of the common multitude of men some to be foreordained to salvation, other some to destruction. But how they wrongfully encumber themselves shall afterward be evident by the framing of the matter together.[7] Beside that in the very same darkness which maketh men afraid, not only the profitableness of this doctrine but also the most sweet fruit showeth forth itself. We shall never be clearly persuaded, as we ought to be, that our salvation floweth out of the fountain of the free mercy of God, till his eternal election be known to us, which by this comparison brightly setteth forth the grace of God, that he doth not without difference adopt all into the hope of salvation,[8] but giveth to some that which he denieth to other. How much the ignorance of this principle diminisheth of the glory of God, how much it withdraweth from true humility, it is plain to see.

✳ ✳ ✳

They which shut the gates, that none may be bold to come to the tasting of this doctrine, do no less wrong to men than to God: because neither shall any other thing suffice to humble us as we ought to be, neither shall we otherwise feel from our heart how much we are bound[9] to God. Neither yet is there any otherwhere the upholding stay of sound affiance,[1] as Christ himself teacheth, which to deliver us from all fear, and to make us unvanquishable among so many dangers, ambushes, and deadly battles, promiseth that whatsoever he hath received of[2] his Father to keep shall be safe.[3] Whereof we gather that they shall with continual trembling be miserable, whosoever they be that know not themselves to be the proper possession of God; and therefore that they do very ill provide both for themselves and for all the faithful, which, in being blind at these three profits which we have touched,[4] would wish the whole foundation of our salvation to be quite taken from among us. Moreover, hereby the Church appeareth unto us, which otherwise (as Bernard rightly teacheth)[5] were not possible to be found nor to be known among creatures, because both ways in marvelous wise[6] it lieth hidden: within the bosom of blessed predestination, and within the mass of miserable damnation.

But ere I enter into the matter itself, I must beforehand in two sorts speak to two sorts of men.[7] That the entreating[8] of predestination, whereas of itself it is somewhat cumbersome, is made very doubtful, yea, and dangerous, the curiousness of men is the cause: which can by no stops be refrained from wandering into forbidden compasses,[9] and climbing up on high; which,

---

4. Immediately.
5. Believe. "Stablished": established.
6. Troublesome.
7. I.e., from the following discussion.
8. He does not extend the hope of salvation equally to all.
9. Obliged.
1. Trust, faith. "Stay": support.
2. From.
3. "My sheep hear my voice, and I know them, and they follow me: And I give unto them eternal life; and they shall never perish, neither shall any man pluck them out of my hand. My Father,

which gave them me, is greater than all; and no man is able to pluck them out of my Father's hand" (John 10.27–29).
4. I.e., God's free mercy, God's glory, and our true humility.
5. Saint Bernard of Clairvaux (1090–1153), in his *Sermons on the Song of Songs*.
6. In a marvelous fashion.
7. I must first speak in two different ways about two sorts of men.
8. Treating, discussing.
9. Places.

if it may, will leave to God no secret which it will not search and turn over. Into this boldness and importunacy[1] forasmuch as we commonly see many to run headlong, and among those some that are otherwise not evil men, here is fit occasion to warn them what is in this behalf[2] the due measure of their duty. First, therefore, let them remember that when they inquire upon predestination, they pierce into the secret closets[3] of the wisdom of God: whereinto if any man too carelessly and boldly break in, he shall both not attain wherewith to satisfy his curiousness, and he shall enter into a maze whereof he shall find no way to get out again. For neither is it meet[4] that man should freely search those things which God hath willed to be hidden in himself, and to turn over from very eternity the height of wisdom,[5] which he willed to be honored and not to be conceived, that by it also he mought[6] be marvelous unto us. Those secrets of his will which he hath determined to be opened unto us, he hath disclosed in his Word: and he hath determined, so far as he foresaw to pertain to us and to be profitable for us.[7]

✳ ✳ ✳

There be other which, when they have a will to remedy this evil,[8] do command all mention of predestination to be in a manner buried: at the least they teach men to flee from every manner of questioning thereof as from a rock. Although the moderation of these men be herein worthily to be praised, that they judge that mysteries should be tasted of with such sobriety, yet because they descend too much beneath the mean,[9] they little prevail with the wit of man, which doth not lightly suffer[1] itself to be restrained. Therefore, that in this behalf also we may keep a right end,[2] we must return to the Word of the Lord, in which we have a sure rule of understanding. For the Scripture is the school of the Holy Ghost, in which as nothing is left out which is both necessary and profitable to be known, so nothing is taught but that which is behoveful[3] to learn. Whatsoever therefore is uttered in the Scripture concerning predestination, we must beware that we debar not the faithful from it, lest we should seem either enviously[4] to defraud them of the benefit of their God or to blame and accuse the Holy Ghost, who hath published those things which it is in any wise[5] profitable to be suppressed.

✳ ✳ ✳

That, therefore, which the Scripture clearly showeth, we say that God by eternal and unchangeable counsel hath once appointed whom in time to come he would take to salvation, and on the other side whom he would condemn to destruction. This counsel as touching the elect,[6] we say to be grounded upon his free mercy, without any respect of[7] the worthiness of man: but whom he appointeth to damnation, to them by his judgment (which

<hr>

1. Pertinacity, stubborn persistence.
2. In this regard.
3. Inner chambers.
4. Fitting.
5. And to search out from eternity itself the sublimest wisdom.
6. Might. "Conceived": understood.
7. I.e., God has let us know, in the Scriptures, as much about these matters as he foresaw would be useful for us to know.
8. I.e., the audacious attempt to learn more

about predestination than Scripture teaches.
9. I.e., fall short of the appropriate middle ground ("mean").
1. Permit. "Wit": intellect.
2. Keep within proper bounds.
3. Useful, advantageous.
4. Out of jealously; maliciously.
5. In any way.
6. Those predestined to salvation.
7. Regard toward.

is indeed just and irreprehensible but also incomprehensible) the entry of life is foreclosed. Now in the elect we set vocation to be the testimony[8] of election; and then justification[9] to be another sign of the manifest showing of it, till they come to glory, wherein is the fulfilling of it. But as by vocation and election God marketh his elect, so by shutting out the reprobate[1] either from the knowledge of his name or from the sanctification of his spirit, he doth as it were by these marks open what judgment abideth[2] for them. * * *

1561

8. Evidence. "Vocation": a calling; a predisposition to the religious life.
9. The state of being justified; i.e., freed from the penalty of sin and accounted righteous by God. The underlying Scriptural text for this passage is

Romans 8.30: "whom he did predestinate, them he also called: and whom he called, them he also justified: and whom he justified, them he also glorified."
1. Those predestined to damnation.
2. Waits. "Open": reveal.

ANNE ASKEW

I n the 1540s, Henry VIII sought to return the English Church to a basically Catholic doctrinal position, and Protestants were subjected to persecution. The outspoken Protestant Anne Askew (1521–1546) was called in for questioning in 1545; the next year, she was tortured on the rack and burned at the stake. Askew's accounts of her two examinations were smuggled out of England by the reformer John Bale, who published them in Germany (1546–47). The texts were later incorporated into John Foxe's *Acts and Monuments* (1563).

Vivid first-person accounts like Askew's were intended to bear witness to the astonishing courage and determination of a small group of ardent Protestants, men and women alike, who were willing to die for their convictions. (When the political tides shifted, there were comparable Catholic figures who endured similar trials for their faith.) Though obedience to authority was widely inculcated in Tudor England and though women in particular were expected to be submissive, social norms could be upended by religious conviction. By the time of the examinations Askew describes, she had already repeatedly defied her Catholic husband, who denounced her publicly and had her arrested. Even when showed the instruments of torture, she refused to name any of her associates or to recant her beliefs.

The theological controversies over the Eucharist, for which Askew and her companions along with many other Protestants and Catholics were willing to lay down their lives, require some explanation. Catholic doctrine held that sacraments properly performed were independent of the spiritual condition either of the priest or of the worshiper. Hence, for example, if the formula of consecration of the bread and wine was correctly spoken by a properly ordained priest, the miraculous transubstantiation of the Host into the body and blood of Christ would occur, whether or not the priest or the communicant was in a state of grace. Indeed, some Catholic theologians argued that because the bread had objectively been transformed into the body of God even a mouse nibbling on a consecrated host would be receiving Christ's flesh. In contrast, Protestants argued that the efficacy of certain key religious sacraments, including the Lord's Supper, depended on the spiritual state of the minister and the congregant. An evil priest, in this conception, would not only be damning himself (as Catholics also believed) but would be turning the Lord's Supper into the Devil's Supper.

From The First Examination of Anne Askew

To satisfy your expectation, good people (sayeth she), this was my first examination in the year of our Lord 1545, and in the month of March. First, Christopher Dare examined me at Saddlers' Hall, being one of the quest,[1] and asked if I did not believe that the sacrament hanging over the altar[2] was the very body of Christ really. Then I demanded[3] this question of him: wherefore Saint Stephen was stoned to death.[4] And he said he could not tell. Then I answered that no more would I assoil[5] his vain question.

Secondly, he said that there was a woman which did testify that I should read[6] how God was not in temples made with hands. Then I showed him the seventh and the seventeenth chapters of the Acts of the Apostles, what Stephen and Paul had said therein.[7] Whereupon he asked me how I took those sentences.[8] I answered that I would not throw pearls among swine,[9] for acorns were good enough.

Thirdly, he asked me wherefore I said that I had rather to read five lines in the Bible than to hear five masses in the temple. I confessed that I said no less. Not for the dispraise of either the Epistle or Gospel, but because the one did greatly edify me and the other[1] nothing at all. As Saint Paul doth witness in the fourteenth chapter of his first Epistle to the Corinthians, whereas he doth say: "If the trumpet giveth an uncertain sound, who will prepare himself to the battle?"

Fourthly, he laid unto my charge that I should say: "If an ill[2] priest ministered, it was the Devil and not God." My answer was that I never spake such thing. But this was my saying: "That whatsoever he were which ministered unto me, his ill conditions could not hurt my faith, but in spirit I received nevertheless the body and blood of Christ." He asked me what I said concerning confession. I answered him my meaning, which was as Saint James sayeth, that every man ought to knowledge[3] his faults to other, and the one to pray for the other.

Sixthly, he asked me what I said to the king's book.[4] And I answered him that I could say nothing to it, because I never saw it.

Seventhly, he asked me if I had the spirit of God in me. I answered if I had not, I was but reprobate or cast away. Then he said he had sent for a priest to examine me, which was there at hand. The priest asked me what I said to the sacrament of the altar.[5] And required much to know therein my meaning. But I desired him again to hold me excused concerning that matter. None other answer would I make him, because I perceived him a papist.[6]

1. Inquest. "Saddlers' Hall": belonging to the guild of saddle makers.
2. The holy wafers were sometimes held in a hanging vessel in the shape of a dove, symbolizing the Holy Ghost.
3. Asked.
4. Stephen was martyred in Jerusalem after proclaiming that God "dwelleth not in temples made with hands" and accusing the priests of the temple of resisting the Holy Ghost and persecuting the prophets (Acts 7.48–60).
5. Resolve.
6. Would teach.
7. Acts 17.24 repeats the assertion of Acts 7 that God does not dwell in temples built by human hands.
8. Interpreted those pronouncements.
9. Matthew 7.6.
1. "The one . . . the other": i.e., the Bible . . . the mass.
2. Wicked.
3. Acknowledge. James 5.16.
4. *A Necessary Doctrine and Erudition for Any Christian Man* (1543), with a preface by the king, sought to put a brake on reformers' "sinister understanding of Scripture, presumption, arrogancy, carnal liberty, and contention," by affirming a number of basically Catholic positions.
5. The Eucharist.
6. Follower of the pope; i.e., Roman Catholic.

Eighthly, he asked me if I did not think that private masses did help souls departed.[7] And [I] said it was great idolatry to believe more in them than in the death which Christ died for us. Then they had me thence unto my lord mayor and he examined me, as they had before, and I answered him directly in all things as I answered the quest afore. Besides this, my lord mayor laid one thing unto my charge which was never spoken of[8] me but of them. And that was whether a mouse eating the host received God or no. This question did I never ask, but indeed they asked it of me, whereunto I made them no answer, but smiled. Then the bishop's chancellor rebuked me and said that I was much to blame for uttering the Scriptures. For Saint Paul (he said) forbade women to speak or to talk of the word of God. I answered him that I knew Paul's meaning as well as he, which is, 1 Corinthians 14, that a woman ought not to speak in the congregation by the way of teaching. And then I asked him how many women he had seen go into the pulpit and preach? He said he never saw none. Then I said he ought to find no fault in poor women, except[9] they had offended the law. Then my lord mayor commanded me to ward.[1] I asked him if sureties[2] would not serve me, and he made me short answer, that he would take none.

Then was I had to the Counter,[3] and there remained eleven days, no friend admitted to speak with me. But in the meantime there was a priest sent to me which said that he was commanded of the bishop to examine me and to give me good counsel, which he did not. But first he asked me for what cause I was put in the Counter. And I told him I could not tell. Then he said it was great pity that I should be there without cause, and concluded that he was very sorry for me.

Secondly, he said it was told him that I should deny the sacrament of the altar. And I answered him again that, that[4] I had said, I had said. Thirdly, he asked me if I were shriven.[5] I told him, so that I might have one of these three, that is to say, Doctor Crome, Sir William, or Huntingdon,[6] I was contented, because I knew them to be men of wisdom. "As for you or any other I will not dispraise, because I know ye not."

Then he said, "I would not have you think but that I or another that shall be brought you shall be as honest as they. For if we were not, ye may be sure, the king would not suffer us to preach."

Then I answered by the saying of Solomon, "By communing with the wise, I may learn wisdom: But by talking with a fool, I shall take scathe"[7] (Proverbs 1).

Fourthly, he asked me, if the host should fall and a beast did eat it, whether the beast did receive God or no. I answered, "Seeing ye have taken the pains to ask this question, I desire you also to assoil[8] it yourself. For I will not do it, because I perceive ye come to tempt me." And he said it was against the order of schools that he which asked the question should answer it. I told him I was but a woman and knew not the course of schools.[9] Fifthly, he asked me if I

---

7. By shortening their time in Purgatory.
8. By.
9. Unless.
1. Imprisonment.
2. Guarantors of good behavior.
3. A London prison.
4. What.

5. Absolved after confessing to a priest.
6. Reformist preachers. "So": if.
7. Injury.
8. Answer.
9. Rules governing Catholic theological debates; scholastic procedures.

intended to receive the sacrament at Easter or no. I answered that else I were no Christian woman, and that I did rejoice that the time was so near at hand. And then he departed thence with many fair words.

✳   ✳   ✳

In the meanwhile he commanded his archdeacon to common[1] with me, who said unto me, "Mistress, wherefore are ye accused and thus troubled here before the bishop?"

To whom I answered again and said, "Sir, ask, I pray you, my accusers, for I know not as yet."

Then took he my book out of my hand and said, "Such books as this hath brought you to the trouble you are in. Beware," sayeth he, "beware, for he that made this book and was the author thereof was an heretic, I warrant you, and burnt in Smithfield."[2]

Then I asked him if he were certain and sure that it was true that[3] he had spoken. And he said he knew well the book was of John Frith's making.[4] Then I asked him if he were not ashamed for to judge of the book before he saw it within, or yet knew the truth thereof. I said also that such unadvised and hasty judgment is token apparent of a very slender wit.[5] Then I opened the book and showed it to him. He said he thought it had been another, for he could find no fault therein. Then I desired him no more to be so unadvisedly rash and swift in judgment, till he thoroughly knew the truth; and so he departed from me. ✳ ✳ ✳

1546–47, 1563

1. Converse.
2. Smithfield Market, just outside the London city walls, was a site of public executions until the 17th century.
3. What.
4. The reformer John Frith was executed in 1533. *A Book Made by John Frith, Prisoner in the Tower of London, Answering unto Master More's Letter . . . Concerning the Sacrament of the Body and Blood of Christ,* published in that year, was reissued in revised form in 1546, a few weeks before Askew was executed.
5. Shallow mind.

JOHN FOXE

When the Catholic Mary Tudor became queen, in 1553, and began to persecute Protestants, John Foxe (1516–1587), who had been a fellow at Oxford University and had served as a tutor to the children of noble families, fled to the Continent. The book for which he became famous was already under way: the first version (Strasbourg, 1554) was in Latin and dealt with the persecutions suffered by the early reformers, particularly Wycliffe and John Hus. But his book grew and grew as Foxe received from England and Scotland accounts of the persecutions, including hideous tortures, being inflicted on the Protestants there. When Elizabeth came to the throne, in 1558, Foxe returned at once to England, and there he translated his Latin volume, adding to it hundreds of stories of the Marian martyrs (many based on eyewitness testimony, some on hearsay and rumor). The English edition was first published in 1563; often called "Foxe's Book of Martyrs," its title was *Acts and Monuments of these latter and perilous days, touching matters of the church, wherein are comprehended and described the great persecution and horrible troubles that have been wrought and practiced by the Romish prelates from the year of Our Lord a thousand to the time now present.*

Foxe saw life as an apocalyptic struggle between good and evil, Christ and Antichrist. Immediately and enormously popular, his book is a compendium of memoirs, stories, personal letters, court records, and the like, rendering the words, acts, and sufferings of some hundreds of martyrs in graphic—if often fictionalized—detail. The final version of the book (1583) is massive—more than six thousand folio pages, containing four million words. Though vehemently criticized by Catholics for its polemical distortions and errors, it helped shape for generations of men and women across the broad social spectrum a sense of collective identity and destiny. Apart from fanning the flames of anti-Catholic feeling, Foxe had an immense influence on English nationalism. His stories—from the medieval crypto-Protestants burned for heresy to the Protestant martyrs who passed through the fiery trials of the Marian persecutions—portrayed England as the land of a new chosen people, destined to lead the way toward the kingdom of God on earth. Foxe's second edition (1570) was placed, by government order, in churches throughout England.*

From Acts and Monuments

[THE DEATH OF ANNE ASKEW]

Hitherto we have entreated of[1] this good woman; now it remaineth that we touch somewhat as touching her end and martyrdom. She being born of such stock and kindred that she might have lived in great wealth and prosperity, if she would rather have followed the world than Christ, but now she was so tormented, that she could neither live long in so great distress, neither yet by the adversaries be suffered[2] to die in secret. Wherefore the day of her execution was appointed, and she brought into Smithfield[3] in a chair, because she could not go on her feet, by means[4] of her great torments. When she was brought unto the stake she was tied by the middle with a chain that held up her body. When all things were thus prepared to the fire, the king's letters of pardon were brought, whereby to offer her safeguard of her life if she would recant, which she would neither receive neither[5] yet vouchsafe once to look upon. Shaxton[6] also was there present, who, openly that day recanting his opinions, went about with a long oration to cause her also to turn, against whom she stoutly resisted. Thus she being troubled so many manner of ways, and having passed through so many torments, having now ended the long course of her agonies, being compassed in with flames of fire, as a blessed sacrifice unto God, she slept in the Lord, in anno[7] 1546, leaving behind her a singular example of Christian constancy for all men to follow.

1563

---

* For Foxe's account of the execution of Lady Jane Grey, see the section "Women in Power." For his account of the burning of Nicholas Ridley (bishop of London) and Hugh Latimer (former bishop of Worcester), see the NAEL Archive.
1. Treated, discussed.
2. Allowed.
3. See p. 159, n. 2.
4. Because.
5. Nor.
6. Nicholas Shaxton, formerly bishop of Salisbury.
7. The year.

The burning of Thomas Cranmer, from Foxe's *Acts and Monuments*. Cranmer, archbishop of Canterbury, was arrested, tried for treason, and burned at the stake in front of Balliol College, Oxford, on March 21, 1556. Here he stretches his right hand into the fire, since that hand had been responsible for writing (or at least signing) a recantation of his Protestant faith, an apostasy that he repudiated just before his execution. The image also shows Cranmer crying out, "Lord, receive my spirit," traditionally said to be part of the dying words of the first Christian martyr, Saint Stephen.

BOOK OF COMMON PRAYER

The Protestant attack on Catholic rituals and the demand for worship in the vernacular led during the reign of Edward VI to the preparation of an English liturgical book, authorized to be the official and only text for public worship in England. Initiated by the Act of Uniformity in 1549, the work's principal architect was Thomas Cranmer (1489–1556). Cranmer, the archbishop of Canterbury, was at first careful to translate and shape the old Latin liturgy into a moderate, occasionally ambiguous compromise between Catholic and Protestant positions. His thorough revision in 1552 put the *Book of Common Prayer* much more decisively into the Protestant camp. Banned by the Catholic Mary Tudor, during whose reign Cranmer was executed, the *Book of Common Prayer* was restored, with small revisions, by Elizabeth and has remained the basis of Anglican worship ever since. Cranmer was, among his other accomplishments, a brilliant prose stylist, and the cadences of his book have had a profound influence on the English language. The selection, part of the marriage service, is from the version used during the reign of Elizabeth.

From The Book of Common Prayer and Administration of the Sacraments and Other Rites and Ceremonies in the Church of England

From *The Form of Solemnization of Matrimony*

* * * At the day appointed for solemnization of matrimony, the persons to be married shall come into the body of the church with their friends and neighbors. And there the priest shall thus say:

Dearly beloved friends, we are gathered together here in the sight of God, and in the face of his congregation, to join together this man and this woman in holy matrimony, which is an honorable estate,[1] instituted of God in paradise, in the time of man's innocency, signifying unto us the mystical union that is betwixt Christ and his church:[2] which holy estate Christ adorned and beautified with his presence and first miracle that he wrought in Cana of Galilee,[3] and is commended of Saint Paul to be honorable among all men,[4] and therefore is not to be enterprised[5] nor taken in hand unadvisedly, lightly, or wantonly, to satisfy men's carnal lusts and appetites, like brute beasts that have no understanding; but reverently, discreetly, advisedly, soberly, and in the fear of God, duly considering the causes for the which matrimony was ordained. One was, the procreation of children, to be brought up in the fear and nurture of the Lord, and praise of God. Secondly, it was ordained for a remedy against sin, and to avoid fornication, that such persons as have not the gift of continency might marry, and keep themselves undefiled members of Christ's body.[6] Thirdly, for the mutual society, help, and comfort that the one ought to have of the other, both in prosperity and adversity: into the which holy estate these two persons present come now to be joined. Therefore if any man can show any just cause why they may not lawfully be joined together, let him now speak, or else hereafter forever hold his peace.

And also speaking to the persons that shall be married, he shall say:

I require and charge you (as you will answer at the dreadful day of judgment, when the secrets of all hearts shall be disclosed) that if either of you do know any impediment why ye may not be lawfully joined together in matrimony, that ye confess it. For be ye well assured, that so many as be coupled together otherwise than God's word doth allow are not joined together by God, neither is their matrimony lawful.

At which day of marriage, if any man do allege and declare any impediment why they may not be coupled together in matrimony by God's law or the laws of this realm; and will be bound, and sufficient sureties with

---

1. State, condition.
2. Cf. Ephesians 5.31–32: "For this cause shall a man leave his father and mother, and shall be joined unto his wife, and they two shall be one flesh. This is a great mystery: but I speak concerning Christ and the church."

3. He changed water into wine (John 2.1–11).
4. "Marriage is honorable in all, and the bed undefiled: but whoremongers and adulterers God will judge" (Hebrews 13.4).
5. Undertaken.
6. The church.

him, to the parties, or else put in a caution,[7] to the full value of such charges as the persons to be married doth sustain, to prove his allegation: then the solemnization must be deferred unto such time as the truth be tried. If no impediment be alleged, then shall the curate[8] say unto the man,

N.[9] Wilt thou have this woman to thy wedded wife, to live together after God's ordinance in the holy estate of matrimony? Wilt thou love her, comfort her, honor and keep her, in sickness and in health? And forsaking all other, keep thee only to her, so long as you both shall live?

The man shall answer,
I will.
Then shall the priest say to the woman,

N. Wilt thou have this man to thy wedded husband, to live together after God's ordinance in the holy estate of matrimony? Wilt thou obey him and serve him, love, honor, and keep him, in sickness and in health, and forsaking all other, keep thee only unto him, so long as you both shall live?

The woman shall answer,
I will.
Then shall the minister say,

Who giveth this woman to be married unto this man?

And the minister receiving the woman at her father or friend's hands, shall cause the man to take the woman by the right hand, and so either to give their troth[1] to other. The man first saying:

I N. take thee N. to my wedded wife, to have and to hold from this day forward, for better, for worse, for richer, for poorer, in sickness and in health, to love and to cherish, till death us depart,[2] according to God's holy ordinance: and thereto I plight thee my troth.

Then shall they loose their hands, and the woman taking again the man by the right hand shall say:

I N. take thee N. to my wedded husband, to have and to hold from this day forward, for better, for worse, for richer, for poorer, in sickness and in health, to love, cherish, and to obey, till death us depart, according to God's holy ordinance: and thereto I give thee my troth.

Then shall they again loose their hands, and the man shall give unto the woman a ring, laying the same upon the book with the accustomed duty[3] to the priest and clerk. And the priest taking the ring, shall deliver it unto the man, to put it upon the fourth finger of the woman's left hand. And the man taught by the priest shall say:

---

7. Surety.
8. A clergyman who has charge of a parish.
9. Name; i.e., the minister inserts the man's given name here.

1. Truth; i.e., pledge.
2. Part.
3. Payment. "Book": Bible.

With this ring I thee wed: with my body I thee worship: and with all my worldly goods I thee endow. In the name of the Father, and of the Son, and of the Holy Ghost. Amen.

Then the man leaving the ring upon the fourth finger of the woman's left hand, the minister shall say:

O eternal God, creator and preserver of all mankind, giver of all spiritual grace, the author of everlasting life: send thy blessing upon these thy servants, this man and this woman, whom we bless in thy name; that as Isaac and Rebecca lived faithfully together,[4] so these persons may surely perform and keep the vow and covenant betwixt them made, whereof this ring given and received is a token and pledge, and may ever remain in perfect love and peace together, and live according unto thy laws: through Jesus Christ our Lord. Amen.

Then shall the priest join their right hands together, and say:

Those whom God hath joined together, let no man put asunder.[5]

Then shall the minister speak unto the people:

Forasmuch as N. and N. have consented together in holy wedlock, and have witnessed the same before God and this company, and thereto have given and pledged their troth, either to other, and have declared the same by giving and receiving of a ring, and by joining of hands: I pronounce that they be man and wife together. In the name of the Father, and of the Son, and of the Holy Ghost. Amen.

And the minister shall add this blessing:

God the Father, God the Son, God the Holy Ghost, bless, preserve, and keep you: the Lord mercifully with his favor look upon you, and so fill you with all spiritual benediction and grace that you may so live together in this life that in the world to come you may have life everlasting. Amen.

1559

4. In Genesis 24–27.   5. From Mark 10.9.

BOOK OF HOMILIES

The first Protestant archbishop of Canterbury, Thomas Cranmer, was responsible in 1547 for the publication of the *Book of Homilies*. Hoping to curb the influence of "ignorant preachers" and fearing the spread of unauthorized beliefs, Cranmer brought together twelve sermons that were, by royal and ecclesiastical decree, to be read over and over, in the order in which they were set forth, in parish churches throughout the realm. The *Homilies*, revised and reissued during the reign of Elizabeth, are political as well as religious documents. As the "Homily Against Disobedience" (added in 1570 in the aftermath of a Catholic uprising the preceding year) amply demonstrates, the intention was to teach the English people "to honor

God and to serve their king with all humility and subjection, and godly and honestly to behave themselves toward all men." Artfully crafted and tirelessly reiterated, these sermons would have been familiar to almost everyone in the latter half of the sixteenth century.

From An Homily Against Disobedience and Willful Rebellion

* * * How horrible a sin against God and man rebellion is cannot possibly be expressed according unto the greatness thereof. For he that nameth rebellion nameth not a singular, or one only sin, as is theft, robbery, murder, and such-like, but he nameth the whole puddle and sink[1] of all sins against God and man, against his prince, his country, his countrymen, his parents, his children, his kinfolks, his friends, and against all men universally: all sins, I say, against God and all men heaped together nameth he that nameth rebellion. For concerning the offense of God's majesty, who seeth not that rebellion riseth first by contempt of God and of his holy ordinances and laws, wherein he so straitly[2] commandeth obedience, forbiddeth disobedience and rebellion?[3] And besides the dishonor done by rebels unto God's holy name by their breaking of the oath made to their prince with the attestation of God's name and calling of his majesty to witness, who heareth not the horrible oaths and blasphemies of God's holy name that are used daily amongst rebels, that is either amongst them or heareth the truth of their behavior? Who knoweth not that rebels do not only themselves leave all works necessary to be done upon workdays undone, whiles they accomplish their abominable work of rebellion, and do compel others that would gladly be well occupied to do the same, but also how rebels do not only leave the sabbath day of the Lord unsanctified, the temple and church of the Lord unresorted unto, but also do by their works of wickedness most horribly profane and pollute the sabbath day, serving Satan, and by doing of his work making it the devil's day instead of the Lord's day? Besides that they compel good men that would gladly serve the Lord assembling in his temple and church upon his day, as becometh the Lord's servants, to assemble and meet armed in the field to resist the fury[4] of such rebels. Yea, and many rebels, lest they should leave any part of God's commandments in the first table of his law[5] unbroken or any sin against God undone, do make rebellion for the maintenance of their images and idols, and of their idolatry committed or to be committed by them, and, in despite of God, cut and tear in sunder his Holy Word, and tread it under their feet, as of late ye know was done.[6]

1. Cesspool.
2. Strictly.
3. Romans 13.1–2: "Let every soul be subject unto the higher powers. For there is no power but of God: the powers that be are ordained of God. Whosoever therefore resisteth the power, resisteth the ordinance of God: and they that resist shall receive to themselves damnation."
4. Violence.
5. The first of the two "tables" (tablets) of stone on

which God wrote the Ten Commandments (Deuteronomy 5.22): those on the first table specify our obligations to God, those on the second (see the following paragraph) our obligations to one another.
6. These enormities were purportedly perpetrated by the Catholic rebels who, in the winter of 1569, rose in the north of England against Queen Elizabeth and in support of her Catholic cousin, Mary, Queen of Scots (who had been imprisoned in England since May 1568).

As concerning the second table of God's law, and all sins that may be committed against man, who seeth not that they be all contained in rebellion? For first, the rebels do not only dishonor their prince, the parent of their country, but also do dishonor and shame their natural parents, if they have any, do shame their kindred and friends, disherit[7] and undo forever their children and heirs. Thefts, robberies, and murders, which of all sins are most loathed of most men, are in no men so much, nor so perniciously and mischievously, as in rebels. For the most arrant thieves and cruelest murderers that ever were, so long as they refrain from rebellion, as they are not many in number, so spreadeth their wickedness and damnation unto a few: they spoil[8] but a few, they shed the blood but of few in comparison. But rebels are the cause of infinite robberies and murders of great multitudes, and of those also whom they should defend from the spoil and violence of other; and, as rebels are many in number, so doth their wickedness and damnation spread itself unto many. And if whoredom and adultery amongst such persons as are agreeable to such wickedness are (as they indeed be) most damnable, what are the forcible oppressions[9] of matrons and men's wives, and the violating and deflowering of virgins and maids, which are most rife with rebels; how horrible and damnable, think you, are they? Now, besides that rebels, by breach of their faith given and oath made to their prince, be guilty of most damnable perjury, it is wondrous to see what false colors and feigned causes, by slanderous lies made upon their prince and the counselers, rebels will devise to cloak their rebellion withal, which is the worst and most damnable of all false-witness-bearing that may be possible. For what should I speak of coveting or desiring of other men's wives, houses, lands, goods, and servants in rebels, who by their wills would leave unto no man anything of his own?

Thus you see that all God's laws are by rebels violated and broken, and that all sins possible to be committed against God or man be contained in rebellion: which sins, if a man list[1] to name by the accustomed names of the seven capital or deadly sins, as pride, envy, wrath, covetousness, sloth, gluttony, and lechery, he shall find them all in rebellion, and amongst rebels. For first, as ambition and desire to be aloft, which is the property of pride, stirreth up many men's minds to rebellion, so cometh it of a luciferian pride and presumption that a few rebellious subjects should set themselves up against the majesty of their prince, against the wisdom of the counselors, against the power and force of all nobility, and the faithful subjects and people of the whole realm. As for envy, wrath, murder, and desire of blood, and covetousness of other men's goods, lands, and livings, they are the inseparable accidents of all rebels, and peculiar properties[2] that do usually stir up wicked men unto rebellion. Now such as by riotousness, gluttony, drunkenness, excess of apparel, and unthrifty[3] games have wasted their own goods unthriftily, the same are most apt unto and most desirous of rebellion, whereby they trust to come by other men's goods unlawfully and violently. And where other

---

7. Disinherit.
8. Despoil, plunder.
9. Rapes.
1. Wants.

2. Distinctive characteristics. "Inseparable accidents": unavoidable accompaniments.
3. Dissolute.

gluttons and drunkards take too much of such meats and drinks as are served to tables, rebels waste and consume in short space all corn in barns, fields, or elsewhere, whole graners,[4] whole storehouses, whole cellars, devour whole flocks of sheep, whole droves of oxen and kine.[5] And as rebels that are married, leaving their own wives at home, do most ungraciously, so much more do unmarried men than any stallions or horses, being now by rebellion set at liberty from correction of laws which bridled them before, which abuse by force other men's wives and daughters, and ravish virgins and maidens most shamefully, abominably, and damnably. Thus all sins, by all names that sins may be named, and by all means that all sins may be committed and wrought, do all wholly upon heaps follow rebellion, and are to be found all together amongst rebels.

1570

4. Granaries. "Corn": grain.   5. Cattle.

RICHARD HOOKER

Out of the long and bitter controversy over the government of the church in sixteenth-century England emerged one literary masterpiece. It is a work in eight books called *Of the Laws of Ecclesiastical Polity* (that is, the governmental system of the church). The author was the Oxford-educated Richard Hooker (1554–1600), a scholar and minister. In 1585 Hooker was master of the Temple (in modern terms, dean of a law school); one of his subordinates was a Puritan intellectual named Walter Travers. Between them a contentious debate developed on the burning question of how the church should be governed. The Puritan view was that no organization or authority in the church was valid unless it was based clearly and specifically on the Bible; the whole hierarchical system of the English Church, with its deacons, priests, bishops, and archbishops, was accordingly wrong, along with its liturgy and most of its rituals. The position Hooker undertook to defend was that the Scriptures, or divine revelation, are not the only guide given to Christians for organizing and administering the church. Another guide is the law of nature, also divinely given, but which can be discerned by the use of human reason unassisted by revelation.

In the book that grew out of his controversy with Travers, Hooker explained how the law of nature affords principles that justify the existing organization and practices of the English Church. Book 1 of *Ecclesiastical Polity* deals with law in general and the several kinds of law; it pictures the entire universe, and also human society, as founded on reason and operating under various natural and divine laws. Book 2 deals with the nature, authority, and adequacy of Scripture. Books 3 to 5 explain and defend the rites, ceremonies, worship, and government of the English Church. Books 6, 7, and 8 deal with various embodiments of authority, legitimate and illegitimate—elders, bishops, kings, and popes.

Hooker was a close and effective reasoner; avoiding the fiery invective or impassioned rhetoric that characterized most disputants of his time, he wrote in a calm, reasonable, and judicious manner. His defense of existing ecclesiastical practices went back to fundamental principles, to a philosophy of nature and our place in it, to the subordination of the individual to a larger community and to God. It is this worldview, set forth in what is perhaps the period's most sonorous and quietly elegant prose, that makes *Ecclesiastical Polity* of enduring interest.*

From Of the Laws of Ecclesiastical Polity

From *Book 1, Chapter 3*

[ON THE SEVERAL KINDS OF LAW, AND ON THE NATURAL LAW]

I am not ignorant that by law eternal the learned for the most part do understand the order, not which God hath eternally purposed himself in all his works to observe, but rather that which with himself he hath set down as expedient to be kept by all his creatures, according to the several[1] conditions wherewith he hath indued them. They who thus are accustomed to speak apply the name of *Law* unto that only rule of working which superior authority imposeth; whereas we, somewhat more enlarging the sense thereof, term any kind of rule or canon whereby actions are framed[2] a law. Now that law, which as it is laid up in the bosom of God they call *eternal*, receiveth according unto the different kinds of things which are subject unto it different and sundry kinds of names. That part of it which ordereth natural agents,[3] we call usually *nature's* law; that which angels do clearly behold, and without any swerving observe, is a law *celestial* and heavenly; the law of *reason* that which bindeth creatures reasonable in this world, and with which by reason they may most plainly perceive themselves bound; that which bindeth them, and is not known but by special revelation from God, *divine* law; *human* law, that which, out of the law either of reason or of God, men probably[4] gathering to be expedient, they make it a law. All things, therefore, which are as they ought to be, are conformed unto *this second law eternal*, and even those things which to this *eternal* law are not conformable are notwithstanding in some sort ordered by *the first eternal law*. For what good or evil is there under the sun, what action correspondent to or repugnant unto the law which God hath imposed upon his creatures, but in or upon it God doth work according to the law which himself hath eternally purposed to keep, that is to say, the *first law eternal?* So that a twofold law eternal being thus made, it is not hard to conceive how they both take place in all things. Wherefore to come to the law of nature, albeit thereby we sometimes mean that manner of working which God hath set for each created thing to keep, yet forasmuch as those things are termed most properly natural agents, which keep the law of their kind[5] unwittingly, as the heavens and elements of the world, which can do no otherwise than they do, and forasmuch as we give unto intellectual natures the name of voluntary agents, that so we may distinguish them from the other, expedient it will be that we sever[6] the law of nature observed by the one from that which the other is tied unto. Touching the former, their strict keeping of

---

* For several additional excerpts from *Ecclesiastical Polity*, see the NAEL Archive.
1. Different.
2. Directed.
3. Referring to the mineral, vegetable, and animal

agents, traditionally distinguished from human agents by their lack of rationality.
4. Plausibly.
5. Species, nature.
6. Distinguish.

one tenure statute[7] and law is spoken of by all, but hath in it more than men have as yet attained to know, or perhaps ever shall attain, seeing the travail of wading herein is given of God to the sons of men, that perceiving how much the least thing in the world hath in it more than the wisest are able to reach unto, they may by this means learn humility. Moses in describing the work of creation attributeth speech unto God: "God said, Let there be light, Let there be a firmament; Let the waters under the heaven be gathered together into one place; Let the earth bring forth; Let there be lights in the firmament of heaven."[8] Was this only the intent of Moses, to signify the greatness of God's power by the easiness of his accomplishing such effects without travail, pain, or labor? Surely it seemeth that Moses had herein besides this a further purpose: namely, first to teach that God did not work as a necessary, but a voluntary, agent, intending beforehand and decreeing with himself that which did outwardly proceed from him; secondly, to show that God did then institute a law natural to be observed by creatures, and therefore according to the manner of laws, the institution thereof is described as being established by solemn injunction. His commanding those things to be which are, and to be in such sort as they are, to keep that tenure and course which they do, importeth[9] the establishment of nature's law. This world's first creation, and the preservation since of things created, what is it but only so far forth a manifestation by execution, what the eternal law of God is concerning things natural? And as it cometh to pass in a kingdom rightly ordered, that after a law is once published, it presently[1] takes effect far and wide, all states[2] framing themselves thereunto; even so let us think it fareth[3] in the natural course of the world: since the time that God did first proclaim the edicts of his law upon it, heaven and earth have hearkened unto his voice, and their labor hath been to do his will. He made a law for the rain. He gave his decree unto the sea, that the waters should not pass his commandment.[4]

Now if Nature should intermit[5] her course and leave altogether, though it were but for a while, the observation of her own laws; if those principal and mother elements of the world, whereof all things in this lower world are made, should lose the qualities which now they have; if the frame of that heavenly arch erected over our heads should loosen and dissolve itself; if celestial spheres should forget their wonted[6] motions and by irregular volubility[7] turn themselves any way as it might happen; if the prince of the lights of heaven, which now as a giant doth run his unwearied course, should as it were through a languishing faintness begin to stand[8] and to rest himself; if the moon should wander from her beaten way, the times and seasons of the year blend themselves by disordered and confused mixture, the winds breathe out their last gasp, the clouds yield no rain, the earth be defeated[9] of heavenly influence, the fruits of the earth pine away as children at the withered breasts of their mother no longer able to yield them relief, what would

---

7. Decree establishing the domains of the various creatures and the conditions of service by which they hold these domains.
8. Genesis 1.3, 6, 9, 11, 14. In this period, Moses was generally assumed to be the author of the Book of Genesis.
9. Signifies, implies.
1. Immediately.

2. Classes.
3. Happens.
4. Proverbs 8.29. "Pass": overstep.
5. Interrupt.
6. Accustomed.
7. Revolution, rotation.
8. Stand still.
9. Deprived.

become of man himself, whom these things now do all serve? See we not plainly that obedience of creatures unto the law of nature is the stay[1] of the whole world? Notwithstanding with nature it cometh sometimes to pass as with art. Let Phidias[2] have rude[3] and obstinate stuff to carve, though his art do that[4] it should, his work will lack that beauty which otherwise in fitter matter it might have had. He that striketh an instrument with skill may cause notwithstanding a very unpleasant sound, if the string whereon he striketh chance to be uncapable of harmony. In the matter whereof natural things consist, that of Theophrastus taketh place:[5] "much of it is oftentimes such as will by no means yield to receive that impression which were best and most perfect." Which defect in the matter of things natural, they who gave themselves unto the contemplation of nature among the heathen observed often; but the true original cause thereof divine malediction,[6] laid for the sin of man upon those creatures which God had made for the use of man. This, being an article of that saving truth which God hath revealed unto his church, was above the reach of their[7] merely natural[8] capacity and understanding. But howsoever these swervings[9] are now and then incident into[1] the course of nature, nevertheless so constantly the laws of nature are by natural agents observed, that no man denieth but those things which nature worketh are wrought either always or for the most part after one and the same manner. * * *

1593

1. Mainstay, support.
2. The greatest of ancient Greek sculptors (5th century B.C.E.).
3. Rough, undressed (i.e., unprepared).
4. What.
5. I.e., "that remark of Theophrastus carries weight." Theophrastus was a Greek writer of the 3rd century B.C.E., a follower of Aristotle and inventor of the species of essay called the "char-

acter," which portrayed a type of person in concise form.
6. God's curse in Eden, which fell not only on sinful humankind but on the earth as well.
7. I.e., the ancient pagans'.
8. I.e., unaided by revelation.
9. Deviations.
1. Likely to happen in.

ROBERT SOUTHWELL

Robert Southwell (1561–1595), the younger son of a prominent Roman Catholic family, went to the English seminary for Catholics at Douai, France, in his youth, then to Rome, where he entered the Society of Jesus (the Jesuits). In 1586 he returned to England to minister to English Catholics. His mission was a dangerous one because of laws that proscribed Roman Catholic worship and banished priests; in 1592 he was apprehended, imprisoned, tortured, and, three years later, executed as a traitor in the usual grisly manner—by being hanged, disemboweled, and then beheaded. Southwell wrote a good deal of religious prose and verse; the most famous of his lyrics is "The Burning Babe." Ben Jonson told his friend William Drummond of Hawthornden that if he had written "The Burning Babe" he would have been content to destroy many of his own poems.

The Burning Babe

As I in hoary winter's night stood shivering in the snow,
Surprised I was with sudden heat which made my heart to glow;
And lifting up a fearful eye to view what fire was near,
A pretty babe all burning bright did in the air appear;
5 Who, scorchèd with excessive heat, such floods of tears did shed
As though his floods should quench his flames which with his tears
      were fed.
"Alas," quoth he, "but newly born in fiery heats I fry,°   *burn*
Yet none approach to warm their hearts or feel my fire but I!
My faultless breast the furnace is, the fuel wounding thorns,
10 Love is the fire, and sighs the smoke, the ashes shame and scorns;
The fuel justice layeth on, and mercy blows the coals,
The metal in this furnace wrought are men's defilèd souls,
For which, as now on fire I am to work them to their good,
So will I melt into a bath to wash them in my blood."
15 With this he vanished out of sight and swiftly shrunk away,
And straight[1] I callèd unto mind that it was Christmas day.

1602

---

1. Straightaway, immediately.

ROGER ASCHAM
1515–1568

When she heard of the death of her former tutor and Latin Secretary, Queen Elizabeth is said to have exclaimed, "I would rather have cast ten thousand pounds in the sea than parted from my Ascham." Educated at St. John's College, Cambridge, one of the great centers of humanism in England, Ascham passionately believed in the study of the Greek and Latin classics, not merely for erudition and aesthetic pleasure but for guidance in moral values and in political activity. He corresponded widely in Latin with learned men on the Continent, but eager to influence his countrymen, whether they read Latin or not, he wrote several important books in English, including *Toxophilus*, a dialogue in praise of archery with the traditional English longbow, and *A Report and Discourse of the State of Germany*, based on his experience as secretary to the English ambassador there in 1550–53. His most famous work in English was *The Schoolmaster*, published two years after his death.

    The Schoolmaster eloquently opposes the widespread use of corporal punishment in schools. Instilling a love of learning, rather than a fear of physical pain, inspires young children to excel in their studies. Ascham advocates "double translation" as the most effective way of acquiring a sound Latin style: students would translate a passage from Latin to English and then, without consulting the Latin original, translate the English back into Latin; they would then compare their version with the author's. The approach thus downplays rote learning of the rules of grammar and emphasizes instead a sense of style.

In the hands of a pedant, Ascham's method (which included discouraging students from speaking Latin, for fear that everyday life would corrupt the linguistic purity of classical antiquity) could, like so many other educational reforms, harden into a rigid frame into which individuals are hammered. But his ultimate goal was not a sterile miming but an ethical and aesthetic fashioning of the self. Deeply fearing what he called the "divorce between the tongue and the heart," he believed that education should teach a person to conjoin language and values in the achievement of what *The Schoolmaster* calls "decorum." Ascham's most despairing vision of a society without this moral decorum comes in his account of a brief trip to Italy, which he viewed as an evil seductress, luring unwitting Englishmen away from their ethical and religious values.*

From The Schoolmaster

From *The First Book for the Youth*

[TEACHING LATIN]

There is a way, touched in the first book of Cicero *De oratore*,[1] which, wisely brought into schools, truly taught, and constantly used, would not only take wholly away this butcherly fear in making of Latins[2] but would also, with ease and pleasure and in short time, as I know by good experience, work a true choice and placing of words, a right ordering of sentences, an easy understanding of the tongue, a readiness to speak, a facility to write, a true judgment both of his own and other men's doings, what tongue soever he doth use.

The way is this. After the three concordances[3] learned, as I touched before, let the master read unto him the epistles of Cicero gathered together and chosen out by Sturmius[4] for the capacity of children.

First, let him teach the child, cheerfully and plainly, the cause and matter[5] of the letter; then, let him construe[6] it into English so oft as the child may easily carry away the understanding of it; lastly, parse[7] it over perfectly. This done thus, let the child, by and by,[8] both construe and parse it over again so that it may appear that the child doubteth in nothing that his master taught him before. After this, the child must take a paper book and, sitting in some place where no man shall prompt him, by himself, let him translate into English his former lesson. Then, showing it to his master, let the master take from him his Latin book, and, pausing an hour at the least, then let the child translate his own English into Latin again in another paper book. When the child bringeth it turned into Latin, the master must compare it with Tully's[9] book and lay them both together, and where the child doth well,

* Another excerpt from *The Schoolmaster*—on Ascham's last conversation with Lady Jane Grey—is found on pp. 200–201. For an excerpt from Ascham's *Toxophilus*, see the NAEL Archive.

1. Cicero's *On the Orator* (55 B.C.E.) consists of three parts, or books.
2. I.e., in Latin composition.
3. Agreement of noun and adjective, verb and noun, relative with antecedent.

4. Johannes Sturm (1507–1589), German scholar and educator.
5. Occasion and content.
6. Translate.
7. Give a grammatical analysis.
8. Immediately.
9. Common English name for Marcus Tullius Cicero.

either in choosing or true placing of Tully's words, let the master praise him and say, "Here ye do well." For I assure you, there is no such whetstone to sharpen a good wit and encourage a will to learning as is praise.

But if the child miss, either in forgetting a word, or in changing a good with a worse, or misordering the sentence, I would not have the master either frown or chide with him, if the child have done his diligence and used no truantship therein. For I know by good experience that a child shall take more profit of two faults gently warned of than of four things rightly hit. For then the master shall have good occasion to say unto him:

> N[omen],[1] Tully would have used such a word, not this; Tully would have placed this word here, not there; would have used this case, this number, this person, this degree, this gender; he would have used this mood, this tense, this simple rather than this compound; this adverb here, not there; he would have ended the sentence with this verb, not with that noun or participle, etc.

In these few lines I have wrapped up the most tedious part of grammar and also the ground of almost all the rules that are so busily taught by the master, and so hardly[2] learned by the scholar, in all common schools, which after this sort[3] the master shall teach without all error, and the scholar shall learn without great pain, the master being led by so sure a guide, and the scholar being brought into so plain and easy a way. And therefore we do not contemn[4] rules, but we gladly teach rules, and teach them more plainly, sensibly, and orderly than they be commonly taught in common schools. For when the master shall compare Tully's book with his scholar's translation, let the master, at the first, lead and teach his scholar to join the rules of his grammar book with the examples of his present lesson, until the scholar by himself be able to fetch out of his grammar every rule for every example, so as the grammar book be ever in the scholar's hand and also used of him, as a dictionary, for every present use. This is a lively and perfect way of teaching of rules, where the common way, used in common schools, to read the grammar alone by itself, is tedious for the master, hard for the scholar, cold and uncomfortable to them both.

Let your scholar be never afraid to ask you any doubt,[5] but use discreetly the best allurements ye can to encourage him to the same, lest his overmuch fearing of you drive him to seek some misorderly shift,[6] as to seek to be helped by some other book, or to be prompted by some other scholar, and so go about to beguile you much, and himself more.

[THE ITALIANATE ENGLISHMAN]

* * * But I am afraid that overmany of our travelers into Italy do not eschew the way to Circe's court but go[7] and ride and run and fly thither; they make great haste to come to her; they make great suit[8] to serve her; yea, I could point out some with my finger that never had[9] gone out of England but only

---

1. Name (Latin). The teacher will substitute the child's name.
2. With such difficulty.
3. Method.
4. Disdain.
5. Question.

6. Subterfuge.
7. Walk. Circe was an enchantress in Homer's *Odyssey* who changed men into swine and other animals.
8. Petition.
9. Would never have.

to serve Circe in Italy. Vanity and vice and any license to ill-living in England was counted stale and rude[1] unto them. And so, being mules and horses before they went, returned very[2] swine and asses home again; yet everywhere very foxes with subtle and busy heads and, where they may, very wolves with cruel malicious hearts. A marvelous monster which for filthiness of living, for dullness to learning himself, for wiliness in dealing with others, for malice in hurting without cause, should carry at once in one body the belly of a swine, the head of an ass, the brain of a fox, the womb of a wolf. If you think we judge amiss and write too sore against you, hear what the Italian saith of the Englishman, what the master reporteth of the scholar, who uttereth plainly what is taught by him and what is learned by you, saying, *Inglese italianato è un diavolo incarnato*; that is to say, "You remain men in shape and fashion but become devils in life and condition." This is not the opinion of one, for some private spite, but the judgment of all in a common proverb which riseth of that learning and those manners which you gather in Italy—a good schoolhouse of wholesome doctrine, and worthy masters of commendable scholars, where the master had rather defame himself for his teaching than not shame his scholar for his learning: a good nature of the master, and fair conditions of the scholars. And now choose you, you Italian Englishmen, whether you will be angry with us for calling you monsters, or with the Italians for calling you devils, or else with your own selves, that take so much pains and go so far to make yourselves both. If some yet do not well understand what is an Englishman Italianated, I will plainly tell him: he that by living and traveling in Italy bringeth home into England out of Italy the religion, the learning, the policy,[3] the experience, the manners[4] of Italy. That is to say, for religion, papistry[5] or worse; for learning, less, commonly, than they carried out with them; for policy, a factious heart, a discoursing head, a mind to meddle in all men's matters; for experience, plenty of new mischiefs never known in England before; for manners, variety of vanities and change of filthy living. These be the enchantments of Circe brought out of Italy to mar men's manners in England: much by example of ill life but more by precepts of fond[6] books, of late translated out of Italian into English, sold in every shop in London, commended by honest titles the sooner to corrupt honest manners, dedicated overboldly to virtuous and honorable personages, the easilier to beguile simple and innocent wits. It is pity that those which have authority and charge to allow and disallow books to be printed be no more circumspect herein than they are. Ten sermons at Paul's Cross[7] do not so much good for moving men to true doctrine as one of those books do harm with enticing men to ill-living. Yea, I say farther, those books tend not so much to corrupt honest living as they do to subvert true religion. More papists be made by your merry books of Italy than by your earnest books of Louvain.[8] And because our great physicians do wink at the matter and make no count[9] of this sore, I, though not

---

1. Unrefined.
2. True.
3. Politics.
4. Morals.
5. Catholicism.
6. Foolish.
7. An outdoor pulpit near St. Paul's Cathedral

where important and eloquent ministers preached.
8. Town in Belgium noted in the 16th century for its Catholic university, especially the theological faculty.
9. Account. "Wink at": shut their eyes to, connive at.

admitted one of their fellowship, yet having been many years a prentice to God's true religion, and trust to continue a poor journeyman therein all days of my life, for the duty I owe and love I bear both to true doctrine and honest living, though I have no authority to amend the sore myself, yet I will declare my good will to discover[1] the sore to others.

St. Paul saith that sects and ill opinions be the works of the flesh and fruits of sin.[2] This is spoken no more truly for the doctrine than sensibly for the reason. And why? For ill-doings breed ill-thinkings, and of corrupted manners spring perverted judgments. And how? There be in man two special[3] things: man's will, man's mind. Where will inclineth to goodness the mind is bent to truth; where will is carried from goodness to vanity the mind is soon drawn from truth to false opinion. And so the readiest way to entangle the mind with false doctrine is first to entice the will to wanton living. Therefore, when the busy and open[4] papists abroad could not by their contentious books turn men in England fast enough from truth and right judgment in doctrine, then the subtle[5] and secret papists at home procured bawdy books to be translated out of the Italian tongue, whereby overmany young wills and wits, allured to wantonness, do now boldly contemn all severe books that sound to[6] honesty and godliness. In our forefathers' time, when papistry as a standing pool covered and overflowed all England, few books were read in our tongue, saving certain books of chivalry, as they said, for pastime and pleasure, which, as some say, were made in monasteries by idle monks or wanton canons; as one for example, *Morte Darthur*,[7] the whole pleasure of which book standeth in two special points—in open manslaughter and bold bawdry; in which book those be counted the noblest knights that do kill most men without any quarrel and commit foulest adulteries by subtlest shifts:[8] as Sir Lancelot with the wife of King Arthur his master, Sir Tristram with the wife of King Mark his uncle, Sir Lamorak with the wife of King Lot that was his own aunt. This is good stuff for wise men to laugh at or honest men to take pleasure at. Yet I know when God's Bible was banished the court and *Morte Darthur* received into the prince's chamber.[9] * * *

1570

1. Reveal.
2. Galatians 5.19–21.
3. I.e., peculiar to the human species.
4. Meddlesome and openly declared.
5. Deceitful.
6. Treat of. "Severe": serious.

7. Sir Thomas Malory's collection of Arthurian romances.
8. Stratagems.
9. Referring to the prohibition of the Protestant translations of the Bible during the reign of the Catholic Queen Mary I (1553–58).

SIR THOMAS HOBY
1530–1566

One of the most influential books of the Renaissance was *Il Cortegiano* (The Courtier), published in 1528 in Italian by Count Baldassare Castiglione (1478–1529) and soon translated into all the major European languages. The English translation, by the humanist and diplomat Sir Thomas Hoby, was not published until 1561 but had been written earlier, probably during the reign of Queen Mary (1553–58), when Hoby lived abroad as a Protestant exile.

Castiglione's book describes, by means of four fictitious dialogues—on successive evenings, among actual men and women living at the court of the duke of Urbino in the years 1504–08—the qualities of the ideal courtier. Supreme among these qualities is grace, the mysterious attribute that renders a person's speech and actions not merely impressive or accomplished but persuasive, touching, and beautiful. Though few people are born with grace, it is possible to acquire it by the mastery of certain techniques. In a famous passage, one of *The Courtier's* speakers, Count Lodovico Canossa, defines the most important of these techniques as *sprezzatura* or, as Hoby translates it, "recklessness." *Sprezzatura* is in fact close to the opposite of recklessness, as we ordinarily understand the term; it is a device for manipulating appearances and masking all the tedious memorizing of lines and secret rehearsals that underlie successful social performances. There is a paradox here, still evident in many social settings: success requires the painstaking mastery of complex codes of behavior, yet there is no surer recipe for failure than to be seen (like Malvolio in *Twelfth Night*) to be trying too hard.

The most famous passage in *The Courtier* presents an elegant version of an ideal of love that ultimately derives from Plato's *Symposium*. In the ancient Greek original, dating from the late fourth century B.C.E., that ideal is principally focused on the love of men for beautiful boys; in Castiglione's dialogue, the poet and scholar Peter Bembo recasts it as both heterosexual and Christian. Bembo declares that love is not the mere gratification of the senses but is the yearning of the soul after beauty, which is finally identical with the eternal good, as perceived by such holy visionaries as Saint Francis and Saint Paul. Love properly understood is, therefore, a kind of ladder by which the soul progresses from lower to higher things. As he pursues his theme, Bembo becomes more and more enraptured and ends with a vision of the soul ravished by heavenly beauty, purged of the flesh, and admitted to the feast of the angels. One of the spirited ladies in the court, Emilia Pia, plucks his garment and gently reminds him that he also has a body.*

From Castiglione's *The Courtier*

From *Book 1, Sections 25–26*

[GRACE]

"* * * Perhaps I am able to tell you what a perfect Courtier ought to be, but not to teach you how ye should do to be one. Notwithstanding, to fulfill your request in what I am able, although it be (in manner) in a proverb that

---

* Additional excerpts from Bembo's discourse can be found in the NAEL Archive.

Grace[1] is not to be learned, I say unto you, whoso mindeth to be gracious or to have a good grace in the exercises of the body (presupposing first that he be not of nature unapt) ought to begin betimes, and to learn his principles of cunning[2] men. The which thing how necessary a matter Philip, king of Macedonia,[3] thought it, a man may gather in that his will was that Aristotle, so famous a philosopher, and perhaps the greatest that ever hath been in the world, should be the man that should instruct Alexander, his son, in the first principles of letters. And of men whom we know nowadays, mark how well and with what a good grace Sir Galeazzo Sanseverino, master of the horse to the French king, doth all exercises of the body; and that because, besides the natural disposition of person that is in him, he hath applied all his study to learn of cunning men, and to have continually excellent men about him, and, of every one, to choose the best of that they have skill in. For as in wrestling, in vaulting, and in learning to handle sundry kind of weapons he hath taken for his guide our Master Peter Mount, who (as you know) is the true and only master of all artificial[4] force and sleight, so in riding, in jousting, and in every other feat, he hath always had before his eyes the most perfectest that hath been known to be in those professions.

"He therefore that will be a good scholar, beside the practicing of good things, must evermore set all his diligence to be like his master, and, if it were possible, change himself into him. And when he hath had some entry,[5] it profiteth him much to behold sundry men of that profession; and, governing himself with that good judgment that must always be his guide, go about to pick out, sometime of one and sometime of another, sundry matters. And even as the bee in the green meadows flieth always about the grass choosing out flowers, so shall our Courtier steal this grace from them that to his seeming have it, and from each one that parcel[6] that shall be most worthy praise. And not do as a friend of ours whom you all know, that thought he resembled much King Ferdinand the Younger, of Aragon, and regarded not to resemble him in any other point but in the often lifting up his head, wrying, therewithal,[7] a part of his mouth, the which custom the king had gotten by infirmity. And many such there are that think they do much, so they resemble a great man in somewhat, and take many times the thing in him that worst becometh him.

"But I, imagining with myself often times how this grace cometh, leaving apart such as have it from above, find one rule that is most general which in this part (methink) taketh place[8] in all things belonging to a man, in word or deed, above all other. And that is to eschew as much as a man may, and as a sharp and dangerous rock, *Affectation* or curiosity,[9] and, to speak a new word, to use in everything a certain Recklessness, to cover art[1] withal, and seem whatsoever he doth and sayeth to do it without pain, and, as it were, not

---

1. *Grace* had a wide range of meanings for Elizabethans, and many puns were made on the word. It refers especially to a natural, easy manner, and also to that favor of God that can be neither earned nor deserved. "In manner": in the manner of; almost.
2. Knowing. "Betimes": early.
3. Philip II (ca. 382–336 B.C.E.), the father of Alexander the Great.
4. Artful, skillful.

5. Introduction.
6. Aspect. "To his seeming": in his opinion.
7. Twisting awry, moreover.
8. Precedence.
9. Overfastidiousness.
1. Artifice. "Recklessness": care-lessness; i.e., nonchalance. The Italian word, whose sense Hoby's translation does not clearly convey, is *sprezzatura*: a natural, easy grace.

minding[2] it. And of this do I believe grace is much derived, for in rare matters and well brought to pass every man knoweth the hardness of them, so that a readiness therein maketh great wonder. And contrariwise to use force and, as they say, to hale by the hair, giveth a great disgrace and maketh everything, how great soever it be, to be little esteemed. Therefore that may be said to be a very[3] art that appeareth not to be art; neither ought a man to put more diligence in anything than in covering it, for in case it be open, it loseth credit clean, and maketh a man little set by.[4] And I remember that I have read in my days that there were some most excellent orators which among other their cares enforced themselves to make every man believe that they had no sight[5] in letters, and dissembling their cunning, made semblant[6] their orations to be made very simply, and rather as nature and truth made them than study and art, the which if it had been openly known would have put a doubt in the people's mind, for fear lest he beguiled them. You may see then how to show art and such bent[7] study taketh away the grace of everything. * * *"

From *Book 4, Sections 49–73*

[THE LADDER OF LOVE]

Then the Lord Gaspar:[8] "I remember," quoth he, "that these lords yester-night, reasoning of the Courtier's qualities, did allow him to be a lover; and in making rehearsal[9] of as much as hitherto hath been spoken, a man may pick out a conclusion that the Courtier which with his worthiness and credit must incline his prince to virtue[1] must in manner of necessity be aged, for knowledge cometh very seldom-time before years, and specially in matters that be learned with experience. I cannot see, when he is well drawn[2] in years, how it will stand well with him to be a lover, considering, as it hath been said the other night, love frameth not with[3] old men, and the tricks that in young men be gallantness, courtesy, and preciseness[4] so acceptable to women, in them are mere follies and fondness[5] to be laughed at, and purchase him that useth them hatred of women and mocks of others. Therefore, in case this your Aristotle, an old Courtier, were a lover and practiced the feats that young lovers do, as some that we have seen in our days, I fear me he would forget to teach his prince; and peradventure boys would mock him behind his back, and women would have none other delight in him but to make him a jesting-stock."

Then said the Lord Octavian:[6] "Since all the other qualities appointed to the Courtier are meet[7] for him, although he be old, methink we should not then bar him from this happiness to love."

---

2. Noticing.
3. True.
4. Lightly regarded. "Clean": entirely.
5. Skill, insight.
6. Pretended.
7. Assiduous.
8. Gaspar Pallavicino, whose attitude in the dialogue is usually that of the misogynist. For an uncut version of the discussion that ensues on his remarks here, see the NAEL Archive.
9. Reviewing.

1. The courtier's role in counseling his prince had been discussed in the preceding part of Book 4.
2. Advanced.
3. Is not suitable to.
4. Excessive neatness.
5. Foolishness. "In them": i.e., in old men.
6. Ottaviano Fregoso, a soldier, later doge of Genoa.
7. Suitable.

"Nay rather," quoth the Lord Gaspar, "to take this love from him is a perfection over and above, and a making him to live happily out of misery and wretchedness."

* * *

Then M. Peter[8] after a while's silence, somewhat settling himself as though he should entreat upon a weighty matter, said thus: "My lords, to show that old men may love not only without slander, but otherwhile[9] more happily than young men, I must be enforced to make a little discourse to declare what love is, and wherein consisteth the happiness that lovers may have. Therefore I beseech you give the hearing with needfulness, for I hope to make you understand that it were not unfitting for any man here to be a lover, in case he were fifteen or twenty years elder than M. Morello."[1]

And here, after they had laughed awhile, M. Peter proceeded: "I say, therefore, that according as it is defined of the wise men of old time, love is nothing else but a certain coveting to enjoy beauty;[2] and forsomuch as coveting longeth for nothing but for things known, it is requisite that knowledge go evermore before coveting, which of his own nature willeth the good, but of himself is blind and knoweth it not. Therefore hath nature so ordained that to every virtue[3] of knowledge there is annexed a virtue of longing. And because in our soul there be three manner ways to know, namely, by sense, reason, and understanding:[4] of sense ariseth appetite or longing, which is common to us with brute beasts; of reason ariseth election or choice, which is proper[5] to man; of understanding, by the which man may be partner with angels, ariseth will. Even as therefore the sense knoweth not but sensible matters and that which may be felt, so the appetite or coveting only desireth the same; and even as the understanding is bent but to behold things that may be understood, so is that will only fed with spiritual goods. Man of nature endowed with reason, placed, as it were, in the middle between these two extremities, may, through his choice inclining to sense or reaching to understanding, come nigh to the coveting sometime of the one, sometime of the other part. In these sorts therefore may beauty be coveted; the general name whereof may be applied to all things, either natural or artificial, that are framed in good proportion and due temper,[6] as their nature beareth. But speaking of the beauty that we mean, which is only it that appeareth in bodies, and especially in the face of man, and moveth this fervent coveting which we call love, we will term it an influence of the heavenly bountifulness, the which for all it stretcheth over all things that be created (like the light of the sun), yet when it findeth out a face well proportioned, and framed with a certain lively agreement of several colors, and set forth with lights and shadows, and with an orderly distance and limits of lines, thereinto it distilleth itself and appeareth most well favored, and decketh out and lighteneth the subject where it shineth with a marvelous grace and

8. Pietro Bembo (1470–1547), poet, Platonist, grammarian, and historian, later a cardinal. He undertakes to prove that it is suitable for an older courtier to be (in a special sense) a lover.
9. Sometimes.
1. Morello da Ortona, a courtier and musician. "In case": even if.
2. The definition derives from Plato's *Sympo-*

sium.
3. Power.
4. Direct intellectual apprehension, without need of reasoning. "Manner": kinds of.
5. Distinctive.
6. The right mixture or combination of elements. Bembo's definition of beauty, as of love, derives from Plato.

glistering,[7] like the sunbeams that strike against beautiful plate of fine gold wrought and set with precious jewels, so that it draweth unto it men's eyes with pleasure, and piercing through them imprinteth himself in the soul, and with an unwonted sweetness all to-stirreth[8] her and delighteth, and setting her on fire maketh her to covet him.

* * *

"Do you believe, M. Morello," quoth then Count Lewis,[9] that beauty is always so good a thing as M. Peter Bembo speaketh of?"

"Not I, in good sooth," answered M. Morello. "But I remember rather that I have seen many beautiful women of a most ill inclination, cruel and spiteful, and it seemeth that, in a manner, it happeneth always so, for beauty maketh them proud, and pride, cruel."

Count Lewis said, smiling: "To you perhaps they seem cruel, because they content you not with it that you would have. But cause M. Peter Bembo to teach you in what sort old men ought to covet beauty, and what to seek at their ladies' hands, and what to content themselves withal; and in not passing out of these bounds ye shall see that they shall be neither proud nor cruel, and will satisfy you with what you shall require."

M. Morello seemed then somewhat out of patience, and said: "I will not know the thing that toucheth[1] me not. But cause you to be taught how the young men ought to covet this beauty that are not so fresh and lusty as old men be."

Here Sir Frederick,[2] to pacify M. Morello and to break their talk, would not suffer Count Lewis to make answer, but interrupting him said: "Perhaps M. Morello is not altogether out of the way in saying that beauty is not always good, for the beauty of women is many times cause of infinite evils in the world—hatred, war, mortality, and destruction, whereof the razing of Troy[3] can be a good witness; and beautiful women for the most part be either proud and cruel, as is said, or unchaste; but M. Morello would find no fault with that. There be also many wicked men that have the comeliness of a beautiful countenance, and it seemeth that nature hath so shaped them because they may be the readier to deceive, and that this amiable look were like a bait that covereth the hook."

Then M. Peter Bembo: "Believe not," quoth he, "but[4] beauty is always good."

Here Count Lewis, because he would return again to his former purpose, interrupted him and said: "Since M. Morello passeth[5] not to understand that which is so necessary for him, teach it me, and show me how old men may come by this happiness of love, for I will not care to be counted old, so it may profit me."

M. Peter Bembo laughed, and said: "First will I take the error out of these gentlemen's mind, and afterward will I satisfy you also." So beginning

---

7. Glittering, sparkling.
8. Moves violently. In this passage, "it" and "him" refer to beauty, "her" to the soul.
9. Lodovico Canossa, who had earlier discoursed on grace.
1. Concerns.
2. Federico Fregoso, later archbishop of Salerno.

3. The destruction of Troy by the Greeks, celebrated in Homer's *Iliad*, was caused by the Trojan Paris's abduction of Helen, the most beautiful woman in the world.
4. I.e., anything but that.
5. Cares.

afresh: "My Lords," quoth he, "I would not that with speaking ill of beauty, which is a holy thing, any of us as profane and wicked should purchase him the wrath of God. Therefore, to give M. Morello and Sir Frederick warning, that they lose not their sight, as Stesichorus did—a pain most meet[6] for whoso dispraiseth beauty—I say that beauty cometh of God and is like a circle, the goodness whereof is the center. And therefore, as there can be no circle without a center, no more can beauty be without goodness. Whereupon doth very seldom an ill[7] soul dwell in a beautiful body. And therefore is the outward beauty a true sign of the inward goodness, and in bodies this comeliness is imprinted, more and less, as it were, for a mark of the soul, whereby she is outwardly known; as in trees, in which the beauty of the buds giveth a testimony of the goodness of the fruit. And the very same happeneth in bodies, as it is seen that palmisters[8] by the visage know many times the conditions and otherwhile the thoughts of men. And, which is more, in beasts also a man may discern by the face the quality of the courage,[9] which in the body declareth itself as much as it can. Judge you how plainly in the face of a lion, a horse, and an eagle, a man shall discern anger, fierceness, and stoutness; in lambs and doves, simpleness and very innocency; the crafty subtlety in foxes and wolves; and the like, in a manner, in all other living creatures. The foul,[1] therefore, for the most part be also evil, and the beautiful good. Therefore it may be said that beauty is a face pleasant, merry, comely, and to be desired for goodness; and foulness a face dark, uglesome,[2] unpleasant, and to be shunned for ill. And in case you will consider all things, you shall find that whatsoever is good and profitable hath also evermore the comeliness of beauty. Behold the state of this great engine of the world,[3] which God created for the health and preservation of everything that was made: the heaven round beset with so many heavenly lights; and in the middle the earth environed with the elements and upheld with the very weight of itself; the sun, that compassing about[4] giveth light to the whole, and in winter season draweth to the lowermost sign,[5] afterward by little and little climbeth again to the other part; the moon, that of him taketh her light, according as she draweth nigh or goeth farther from him; and the other five stars[6] that diversely keep the very same course. These things among themselves have such force by the knitting together of an order so necessarily framed that, with altering them any one jot, they should all be loosed and the world would decay. They have also such beauty and comeliness that all the wits men have cannot imagine a more beautiful matter.

"Think now of the shape of man, which may be called a little world, in whom every parcel of his body is seen to be necessarily framed by art and not by hap,[7] and then the form altogether most beautiful, so that it were a hard matter to judge whether the members (as the eyes, the nose, the mouth, the ears, the arms, the breast, and in like manner the other parts) give either more profit to the countenance and the rest of the body, or comeliness. The

6. Fitting. Stesichorus: "a notable poet which lost his sight for writing against Helena, and recanting, had his sight restored him again" [Hoby's note].
7. Evil.
8. Fortune-tellers.
9. Heart.
1. Ugly.

2. Horribly ugly (apparently first used by Hoby).
3. Mechanism of the universe.
4. Revolving.
5. Of the zodiac.
6. I.e., the five other planets then known: Mercury, Venus, Mars, Jupiter, and Saturn.
7. By skill rather than by chance.

like may be said of all other living creatures. Behold the feathers of fowls, the leaves and boughs of trees, which be given them of nature to keep them in their being, and yet have they withal a very great sightliness. Leave nature, and come to art. What thing is so necessary in sailing vessels as the forepart, the sides, the main yards, the mast, the sails, the stern, oars, anchors, and tacklings? All these things notwithstanding are so well-favored in the eye that unto whoso beholdeth them they seem to have been found out as well for pleasure as for profit. Pillars and great beams uphold high buildings and palaces, and yet are they no less pleasureful unto the eyes of the beholders than profitable to the buildings. When men began first to build, in the middle of temples and houses they reared the ridge of the roof, not to make the works to have a better show, but because the water might the more commodiously avoid[8] on both sides; yet unto profit there was forthwith adjoined a fair sightliness, so that if, under the sky where there falleth neither hail nor rain, a man should build a temple without a reared ridge, it is to be thought that it could have neither a sightly show nor any beauty. Besides other things, therefore, it giveth a great praise to the world in saying that it is beautiful. It is praised in saying the beautiful heaven, beautiful earth, beautiful sea, beautiful rivers, beautiful woods, trees, gardens, beautiful cities, beautiful churches, houses, armies. In conclusion, this comely and holy beauty is a wondrous setting out of everything. And it may be said that good and beautiful be after a sort one self[9] thing, especially in the bodies of men; of the beauty whereof the nighest cause, I suppose, is the beauty of the soul; the which, as a partner of the right and heavenly beauty, maketh sightly and beautiful whatever she toucheth, and most of all if the body where she dwelleth be not of so vile a matter that she cannot imprint in it her property.[1] Therefore beauty is the true monument and spoil[2] of the victory of the soul, when she with heavenly influence beareth rule over material and gross nature, and with her light overcometh the darkness of the body. It is not, then, to be spoken that beauty maketh women proud or cruel, although it seem so to M. Morello. Neither yet ought beautiful women to bear the blame of that hatred, mortality, and destruction which the unbridled appetites of men are the cause of. I will not now deny but it is possible also to find in the world beautiful women unchaste; yet not because beauty inclineth them to unchaste living, for it rather plucketh them from it, and leadeth them into the way of virtuous conditions, through the affinity that beauty hath with goodness; but otherwhile[3] ill bringing-up, the continual provocations of lovers' tokens,[4] poverty, hope, deceits, fear, and a thousand other matters overcome the steadfastness, yea, of beautiful and good women; and for these and like causes may also beautiful men become wicked."

Then said the Lord Cesar:[5] "In case the Lord Gaspar's saying be true of yesternight, there is no doubt but the fair women be more chaste than the foul."

"And what was my saying?" quoth the Lord Gaspar.

The Lord Cesar answered: "If I do well bear in mind, your saying was that the women that are sued to always refuse to satisfy him that sueth to them,

---

8. Escape.
9. Same.
1. Attribute, quality.
2. Reward, trophy.

3. Sometimes.
4. Gifts.
5. Cesar Gonzaga, cousin of Castiglione.

but those that are not sued to, sue to others. There is no doubt but the beautiful women have always more suitors, and be more instantly laid at[6] in love, than the foul. Therefore the beautiful always deny, and consequently be more chaste than the foul, which, not being sued to, sue unto others."

M. Peter Bembo laughed, and said: "This argument cannot be answered to."

Afterward he proceeded: "It chanceth also, oftentimes, that as the other senses, so the sight is deceived and judgeth a face beautiful which indeed is not beautiful. And because in the eyes and in the whole countenance of some woman a man beholdeth otherwhile a certain lavish wantonness painted, with dishonest flickerings,[7] many, whom that manner delighteth because it promiseth them an easiness to come by the thing that they covet, call it beauty; but indeed it is a cloaked un-shamefastness,[8] unworthy of so honorable and holy a name."

M. Peter Bembo held his peace, but those lords still were earnest upon him to speak somewhat more of this love and of the way to enjoy beauty aright, and at the last, "Methink," quoth he, "I have showed plainly enough that old men may love more happily than young, which was my drift;[9] therefore it belongeth not to me to enter any farther."

Count Lewis answered: "You have better declared the unluckiness of young men than the happiness of old men, whom you have not as yet taught what way they must follow in this love of theirs; only you have said that they must suffer themselves to be guided by reason, and the opinion of many is that it is unpossible for love to stand with reason."

Bembo notwithstanding sought to make an end of reasoning, but the duchess[1] desired him to say on, and he began thus afresh: "Too unlucky were the nature of man, if our soul, in which this so fervent coveting may lightly[2] arise, should be driven to nourish it with that only which is common to her with beasts, and could not turn it to the other noble part,[3] which is proper to her. Therefore, since it is so your pleasure, I will not refuse to reason upon this noble matter. And because I know myself unworthy to talk of the most holy mysteries of Love, I beseech him to lead my thought and my tongue so that I may show this excellent Courtier how to love contrary to the wonted[4] manner of the common ignorant sort; and even as from my childhood I have dedicated all my whole life unto him, so also now that my words may be answerable to the same intent, and to the praise of him. I say, therefore, that since the nature of man in youthful age is so much inclined to sense, it may be granted the Courtier, while he is young, to love sensually; but in case afterward also, in his riper years, he chance to be set on fire with this coveting of love, he ought to be good and circumspect, and heedful that he beguile not himself to be led willfully into the wretchedness that in young men deserveth more to be pitied than blamed, and contrariwise in old men more to be blamed than pitied. Therefore when an amiable coun-

---

6. Persistently urged.
7. Hints of lewdness.
8. Immodesty.
9. Purpose. In a passage omitted above, Bembo had argued that old men, whose senses have cooled, find it easier than young men to be guided in love by reason and can therefore more easily avoid the miseries that, he argues, inevit-

ably follow from sensual love.
1. Elisabetta Gonzaga, duchess of Urbino, the presiding figure in the life of the court and in these dialogues.
2. Easily, readily.
3. I.e., reason.
4. Accustomed.

tenance of a beautiful woman cometh in his sight, that is accompanied with noble conditions and honest[5] behaviors, so that, as one practiced in love, he wotteth well that his hue[6] hath an agreement with hers, as soon as he is aware that his eyes snatch that image and carry it to the heart, and that the soul beginneth to behold it with pleasure, and feeleth within herself the influence that stirreth her and by little and little setteth her in heat, and that those lively spirits[7] that twinkle out through the eyes put continually fresh nourishment to the fire, he ought in this beginning to seek a speedy remedy and to raise up reason, and with her to fence the fortress of his heart, and to shut in such wise[8] the passages against sense and appetites that they may enter neither with force nor subtle practice.[9] Thus, if the flame be quenched, the jeopardy is also quenched. But in case it continue or increase, then must the Courtier determine, when he perceiveth he is taken, to shun throughly[1] all filthiness of common love, and so enter into the holy way of love with the guide of reason, and first consider that the body where that beauty shineth is not the fountain from whence beauty springeth, but rather because beauty is bodiless and, as we have said, an heavenly shining beam, she loseth much of her honor when she is coupled with that vile subject[2] and full of corruption: because the less she is partner thereof, the more perfect she is, and, clean sundered from it, is most perfect. And as a man heareth not with his mouth, nor smelleth with his ears, no more can he also in any manner wise enjoy beauty, nor satisfy the desire that she stirreth up in our minds, with feeling, but with the sense unto whom beauty is the very butt to level at,[3] namely, the virtue[4] of seeing. Let him lay aside, therefore, the blind judgment of the sense, and enjoy with his eyes the brightness, the comeliness, the loving sparkles, laughters, gestures, and all the other pleasant furnitures[5] of beauty, especially with hearing the sweetness of her voice, the tunableness[6] of her words, the melody of her singing and playing on instruments (in case the woman beloved be a musician); and so shall he with most dainty food feed the soul through the means of these two senses which have little bodily substance in them and be the ministers of reason, without entering farther toward the body with coveting unto any longing otherwise than honest. Afterward, let him obey, please, and honor with all reverence his woman, and reckon her more dear to him than his own life, and prefer all her commodities[7] and pleasures before his own, and love no less in her the beauty of the mind than of the body. Therefore let him have a care not to suffer her to run into any error, but with lessons and good exhortations seek always to frame her to modesty, to temperance, to true honesty, and so to work that there may never take place in her other than pure thoughts and far wide from all filthiness of vices. And thus in sowing of virtue in the garden of that mind, he shall also gather the fruits of most beautiful conditions, and savor them with a marvelous good relish. And this shall be the right engendering and imprinting of beauty in beauty, the which some hold opinion to be the end[8] of love. In this manner shall our Courtier

---

5. Virtuous (as also several times in the following pages). "Conditions": personal qualities.
6. Aspect. "Wotteth": knows.
7. Vital, animating powers. Cf. p. 186, n. 2.
8. In such a way.
9. Treachery.
1. Thoroughly.

2. I.e., the body.
3. Target to aim at.
4. Power.
5. Ornaments.
6. Musical quality.
7. Conveniences.
8. Goal.

be most acceptable to his lady, and she will always show herself toward him tractable, lowly,[9] and sweet in language, and as willing to please him as to be beloved of him; and the wills of them both shall be most honest and agreeable, and they consequently shall be most happy."

Here M. Morello: "The engendering," quoth he, "of beauty in beauty aright were the engendering of a beautiful child in a beautiful woman; and I would think it a more manifest token a great deal that she loved her lover, if she pleased him with this than with the sweetness of language that you speak of."

M. Peter Bembo laughed, and said: "You must not, M. Morello, pass your bounds. I may tell you it is not a small token that a woman loveth when she giveth unto her lover her beauty, which is so precious a matter; and by the ways that be a passage to the soul (that is to say, the sight and the hearing) sendeth the looks of her eyes, the image of her countenance, and the voice of her words, that pierce into the lover's heart and give a witness of her love."

M. Morello said: "Looks and words may be, and oftentimes are, false witnesses. Therefore whoso hath not a better pledge of love, in my judgment he is in an ill assurance. And surely I looked[1] still that you would have made this woman of yours somewhat more courteous and free toward the Courtier than my Lord Julian[2] hath made his; but meseemeth ye be both of the property[3] of those judges that, to appear wise, give sentence against their own."

Bembo said: "I am well pleased to have this woman much more courteous toward my Courtier not young than the Lord Julian's is to the young; and that with good reason, because mine coveteth but honest matters, and therefore may the woman grant him them all without blame. But my Lord Julian's woman, that is not so assured of the modesty of the young man, ought to grant him the honest matters only, and deny him the dishonest. Therefore more happy is mine, that hath granted him whatsoever he requireth, than the other, that hath part granted and part denied. And because[4] you may moreover the better understand that reasonable love is more happy than sensual, I say unto you that selfsame things in sensual ought to be denied otherwhile, and in reasonable granted; because in the one they be honest, and in the other dishonest. Therefore the woman, to please her good lover, besides the granting him merry countenances, familiar and secret talk, jesting, dallying, hand-in-hand, may also lawfully and without blame come to kissing, which in sensual love, according to the Lord Julian's rules, is not lawful. For since a kiss is a knitting together both of body and soul, it is to be feared lest the sensual lover will be more inclined to the part of the body than of the soul; but the reasonable lover wotteth well that although the mouth be a parcel[5] of the body, yet is it an issue for the words that be the interpreters of the soul, and for the inward breath, which is also called the soul; and therefore hath a delight to join his mouth with the woman's beloved with a kiss, not to stir him to any unhonest desire, but because he feeleth that that bond is the opening of an entry to the souls, which, drawn with a coveting the one of the other, pour themselves by turn the one into the other's body,

---

9. Modest.
1. Expected.
2. Giuliano de' Medici, younger son of Lorenzo the Magnificent. In Book 3, discussing the ideal courtier's female counterpart, he expresses the opinions alluded to here.
3. Nature.
4. So that.
5. Part.

and be so mingled together that each of them hath two souls, and one alone, so framed of them both, ruleth, in a manner, two bodies. Whereupon a kiss may be said to be rather a coupling together of the soul than of the body, because it hath such force in her that it draweth her unto it, and, as it were, separateth her from the body. For this do all chaste lovers covet a kiss as a coupling of souls together. And therefore Plato,[6] the divine lover, saith that in kissing his soul came as far as his lips to depart out of the body. And because the separating of the soul from the matters of the sense, and the thorough coupling of her with matters of understanding, may be betokened by a kiss, Solomon saith[7] in his heavenly book of ballads, 'Oh that he would kiss me with a kiss of his mouth,' to express the desire he had that his soul might be ravished through heavenly love to the beholding of heavenly beauty in such manner that, coupling herself inwardly with it, she might forsake the body."

They stood all hearkening heedfully to Bembo's reasoning, and after he had stayed[8] a while and saw that none spake, he said: "Since you have made me to begin to show our not-young Courtier this happy love, I will lead him yet somewhat farther forwards; because to stand still at this stay were somewhat perilous for him, considering, as we have oftentimes said, the soul is most inclined to the senses, and for all[9] reason with discourse chooseth well, and knoweth that beauty not to spring of the body, and therefore setteth a bridle to the unhonest desires, yet to behold it always in that body doth oftentimes corrupt the right judgment. And where no other inconvenience ensueth upon it, one's absence from the wight[1] beloved carrieth a great passion with it; because the influence of that beauty when it is present giveth a wondrous delight to the lover and, setting his heart on fire, quickeneth and melteth certain virtues in a trance and congealed in the soul, the which, nourished with the heat of love, flow about and go bubbling nigh the heart, and thrust out through the eyes those spirits which be most fine vapors made of the purest and clearest part of the blood, which receive the image of beauty[2] and deck it with a thousand sundry furnitures. Whereupon the soul taketh a delight, and with a certain wonder is aghast, and yet enjoyeth she it, and, as it were, astonied[3] together with the pleasure, feeleth the fear and reverence that men accustomably have toward holy matters, and thinketh herself to be in paradise. The lover, therefore, that considereth only the beauty in the body loseth this treasure and happiness as soon as the woman beloved with her departure leaveth the eyes without their brightness, and consequently the soul as a widow without her joy. For since beauty is far off, that influence of love setteth not the heart on fire, as it did in presence. Whereupon the pores be dried up and withered, and yet doth the remembrance of beauty somewhat stir those virtues of the soul in such wise that they seek to scatter abroad the spirits, and they, finding the ways closed up, have no issue, and still they seek to get out, and so with those shootings enclosed prick the soul and torment her bitterly, as young children when in

6. Plato's discussion of love in *The Symposium*.
7. Song of Solomon 1.2. "Betokened": symbolized.
8. Paused.
9. "For all": although.
1. Person.

2. Love "melts" certain elements ("virtues") that were before "congealed," releasing the vital blood "spirits" that take in the image of beauty through the eyes.
3. Stunned.

their tender gums they begin to breed teeth. And hence come the tears, sighs, vexations, and torments of lovers; because the soul is always in affliction and travail and, in a manner, waxeth wood,[4] until the beloved beauty cometh before her once again, and then she is immediately pacified and taketh breath, and, throughly bent to it, is nourished with most dainty food, and by her will would never depart from so sweet a sight. To avoid, therefore, the torment of this absence, and to enjoy beauty without passion, the Courtier by the help of reason must full and wholly call back again the coveting of the body to beauty alone, and, in what he can, behold it in itself simple and pure, and frame it within his imagination sundered from all matter, and so make it friendly and loving to his soul, and there enjoy it, and have it with him day and night, in every time and place, without mistrust ever to lose it; keeping always fast in mind that the body is a most diverse[5] thing from beauty, and not only not increaseth but diminisheth the perfection of it. In this wise shall our not-young Courtier be out of all bitterness and wretchedness that young men feel, in a manner continually, as jealousies, suspicions, disdains, angers, desperations, and certain rages full of madness, whereby many times they be led into so great error that some do not only beat the women whom they love, but rid themselves out of their life. He shall do no wrong to the husband, father, brethren, or kinsfolk of the woman beloved. He shall not bring her in slander. He shall not be in case with[6] much ado otherwhile to refrain his eyes and tongue from discovering his desires to others. He shall not take thought[7] at departure or in absence, because he shall evermore carry his precious treasure about with him shut fast within his heart. And besides, through the virtue of imagination, he shall fashion within himself that beauty much more fair than it is indeed. But among these commodities the lover shall find another yet far greater, in case he will take this love for a stair, as it were, to climb up to another far higher than it. The which he shall bring to pass, if he will go and consider with himself what a strait bond it is to be always in the trouble to behold the beauty of one body alone. And therefore, to come out of this so narrow a room,[8] he shall gather in his thought by little and little so many ornaments that, meddling[9] all beauties together, he shall make a universal concept, and bring the multitude of them to the unity of one alone, that is generally spread over all the nature of man. And thus shall he behold no more the particular beauty of one woman, but an universal, that decketh out all bodies. Whereupon, being made dim with this greater light, he shall not pass upon[1] the lesser, and, burning in a more excellent flame, he shall little esteem it that[2] he set great store by at the first. This stair of love, though it be very noble and such as few arrive at it, yet is it not in this sort to be called perfect, forsomuch as where the imagination is of force to make conveyance, and hath no knowledge but through those beginnings that the senses help her withal, she is not clean purged from gross darkness; and therefore, though she do consider that universal beauty in sunder and in itself alone, yet doth she not well and clearly discern it, nor without some doubtfulness, by reason of the

---

4. Mad, crazy.
5. Very different.
6. In the situation of having.
7. Be distressed.

8. Space.
9. Mingling.
1. Concern himself with.
2. I.e., the thing that.

agreement that the fancies have with the body. Wherefore such as come to this love are like young birds almost flush,[3] which for all they flutter a little their tender wings, yet dare they not stray far from the nest, nor commit themselves to the wind and open weather. When our Courtier, therefore, shall be come to this point, although he may be called a good and happy lover, in respect of them that be drowned in the misery of sensual love, yet will I not have him to set his heart at rest, but boldly proceed farther, following the highway, after his guide[4] that leadeth him to the point of true happiness. And thus, instead of going out of his wit[5] with thought, as he must do that will consider the bodily beauty, he may come into his wit to behold the beauty that is seen with the eyes of the mind, which then begin to be sharp and through-seeing when the eyes of the body lose the flower of their sightliness.

"Therefore the soul, rid of vices, purged with the studies of true philosophy, occupied in spiritual, and exercised in matters of understanding, turning her to the beholding of her own substance, as it were raised out of a most deep sleep, openeth the eyes that all men have and few occupy,[6] and seeth in herself a shining beam of that light which is the true image of the angel-like beauty partened[7] with her, whereof she also partneth with the body a feeble shadow; therefore, waxed blind about earthly matters, is made most quick of sight about heavenly. And otherwhile,[8] when the stirring virtues of the body are withdrawn alone through earnest beholding, either[9] fast bound through sleep, when she is not hindered by them, she feeleth a certain privy[1] smell of the right angel-like beauty, and, ravished with the shining of that light, beginneth to be inflamed, and so greedily followeth after, that in a manner she waxeth drunken and beside herself, for coveting to couple herself with it, having found, to her weening,[2] the footsteps of God, in the beholding of whom, as in her happy end, she seeketh to settle herself. And therefore, burning in this most happy flame, she ariseth to the noblest part of her, which is the understanding, and there, no more shadowed with the dark night of earthly matters, seeth the heavenly beauty; but yet doth she not for all that enjoy it altogether perfectly, because she beholdeth it only in her particular[3] understanding, which cannot conceive the passing[4] great universal beauty; whereupon, not throughly satisfied with this benefit, love giveth unto the soul a greater happiness. For like as through the particular beauty of one body he guideth her to the universal beauty of all bodies, even so in the last degree of perfection through particular understanding he guideth her to the universal understanding. Thus the soul kindled in the most holy fire of heavenly love fleeth to couple herself with the nature of angels, and not only clean forsaketh sense, but hath no more need of the discourse of reason, for, being changed into an angel, she understandeth all things that may be understood; and without any veil or cloud she seeth the main sea of the pure heavenly beauty, and receiveth it into her, and enjoyeth that sovereign happiness that cannot be comprehended of the senses. Since, therefore, the beauties which we daily see with these our dim eyes in bodies

3. Fledged, fit to fly.
4. I.e., reason.
5. Mind, intellect.
6. Use.
7. Shared.
8. Sometimes.

9. Or.
1. Intimate.
2. Thinking, opinion.
3. Individual.
4. Surpassing.

subject to corruption, that nevertheless be nothing else but dreams and most thin shadows of beauty, seem unto us so well favored and comely that oftentimes they kindle in us a most burning fire, and with such delight that we reckon no happiness may be compared to it that we feel otherwhile through the only look[5] which the beloved countenance of a woman casteth at us; what happy wonder, what blessed abashment, may we reckon that to be that taketh the souls which come to have a sight of the heavenly beauty? What sweet flame, what sweet incense, may a man believe that to be which ariseth of the fountain of the sovereign and right beauty? Which is the origin of all other beauty, which never increaseth nor diminisheth, always beautiful, and of itself, as well on the one part as on the other, most simple, only like itself, and partner of none other, but in such wise beautiful that all other beautiful things be beautiful because they be partners of the beauty of it.

"This is the beauty unseparable from the high bounty which with her voice calleth and draweth to her all things; and not only to the endowed with understanding giveth understanding, to the reasonable reason, to the sensual sense and appetite to live, but also partaketh with plants and stones, as a print of herself, stirring, and the natural provocation of their properties.[6] So much, therefore, is this love greater and happier than others, as the cause that stirreth it is more excellent. And therefore, as common fire trieth gold and maketh it fine, so this most holy fire in souls destroyeth and consumeth whatsoever is mortal in them, and relieveth and maketh beautiful the heavenly part, which at the first by reason of the sense was dead and buried in them. This is the great fire in the which, the poets write, that Hercules was burned on the top of the mountain Oeta,[7] and, through that consuming with fire, after his death was holy and immortal. This is the fiery bush of Moses;[8] the divided tongues of fire;[9] the inflamed chariot of Elias;[1] which doubleth grace and happiness in their souls that be worthy to see it, when they forsake this earthly baseness and flee up into heaven. Let us, therefore, bend all our force and thoughts of soul to this most holy light, which showeth us the way which leadeth to heaven; and after it, putting off the affections we were clad withal at our coming down, let us climb up the stairs which at the lowermost step have the shadow of sensual beauty, to the high mansion place where the heavenly, amiable, and right beauty dwelleth, which lieth hid in the innermost secrets of God, lest unhallowed eyes should come to the sight of it; and there shall we find a most happy end for our desires, true rest for our travails, certain remedy for miseries, a most healthful medicine for sickness, a most sure haven in the troublesome storms of the tempestuous sea of this life.

"What tongue mortal is there then, Oh most holy Love, that can sufficiently praise thy worthiness? Thou most beautiful, most good, most wise,

---

5. Through the look alone.
6. I.e., motion ("stirring") and, as we would say, their natural instincts.
7. "A mountain between Thessalia and Macedonia where is the sepulcher of Hercules" [Hoby's note].
8. "And the angel of the Lord appeared unto . . . [Moses] in a flame of fire out of the midst of a bush: and he looked, and, behold, the bush burned with fire, and the bush was not consumed" (Exodus 3.2).

9. "And there appeared unto them [i.e., the Apostles] cloven tongues like as to fire, and it sat upon each of them. And they were all filled with the Holy Ghost, and began to speak with other tongues, as the Spirit gave them utterance" (Acts 2.3–4).
1. The prophet Elijah. "And it came to pass, as they still went on, and talked, that, behold, there appeared a chariot of fire, and horses of fire, and parted them both asunder; and Elijah went up by a whirlwind into heaven" (2 Kings 2.11).

art derived of the unity of heavenly beauty, goodness, and wisdom, and therein dost thou abide, and unto it through it, as in a circle, turnest about. Thou the most sweet bond of the world, a mean betwixt heavenly and earthly things, with a bountiful temper bendest the high virtues[2] to the government of the lower, and turning back the minds of mortal men to their beginning, couplest them with it. Thou with agreement bringest the elements in one, and stirrest nature to bring forth that which ariseth and is born for the succession of the life.[3] Thou bringest severed matters into one, to the unperfect givest perfection, to the unlike likeness, to enmity amity, to the earth fruits, to the sea calmness, to the heaven lively light. Thou art the father of true pleasures, of grace, peace, lowliness, and goodwill, enemy to rude wildness and sluggishness—to be short, the beginning and end of all goodness. And forsomuch as thou delightest to dwell in the flower of beautiful bodies and beautiful souls, I suppose that thy abiding-place is now here among us, and from above otherwhile showest thyself a little to the eyes and minds of them that be worthy to see thee. Therefore vouchsafe, Lord, to hearken to our prayers, pour thyself into our hearts, and with the brightness of thy most holy fire lighten our darkness, and, like a trusty guide in this blind maze, show us the right way; reform the falsehood of the senses, and after long wandering in vanity give us the right and sound joy. Make us to smell those spiritual savors that relieve the virtues of the understanding, and to hear the heavenly harmony so tunable that no discord of passion take place any more in us. Make us drunken with the bottomless fountain of contentation that always doth delight and never giveth fill, and that giveth a smack[4] of the right bliss unto whoso drinketh of the running and clear water thereof. Purge with the shining beams of thy light our eyes from misty ignorance, that they may no more set by[5] mortal beauty, and well perceive that the things which at the first they thought themselves to see be not indeed, and those that they saw not, to be in effect. Accept our souls that be offered unto thee for a sacrifice. Burn them in the lively flame that wasteth[6] all gross filthiness, that after they be clean sundered from the body they may be coupled with an everlasting and most sweet bond to the heavenly beauty. And we, severed from ourselves, may be changed like right lovers into the beloved, and, after we be drawn from the earth, admitted to the feast of the angels, where, fed with immortal ambrosia and nectar,[7] in the end we may die a most happy and lively death, as in times past died the fathers of old time, whose souls with most fervent zeal of beholding, thou didst hale from the body and coupledst them with God."

When Bembo had hitherto spoken with such vehemency that a man would have thought him, as it were, ravished and beside himself, he stood still without once moving, holding his eyes toward heaven as astonied; when the Lady Emilia,[8] which together with the rest gave most diligent ear to this talk, took him by the plait of his garment and plucking him a little, said: "Take heed, M. Peter, that these thoughts make not your soul also to forsake the body."

2. Powers.
3. I.e., for the perpetuation of life.
4. Taste.
5. Set store by.
6. Consumes.

7. The food and drink of the gods in classical mythology.
8. Emilia Pia, a widow living at court, the faithful companion of the duchess Elisabetta and the mistress of ceremonies of the discussions.

"Madam," answered M. Peter, "it should not be the first miracle that love hath wrought in me."

Then the Duchess and all the rest began afresh to be instant[9] upon M. Bembo that he would proceed once more in his talk, and everyone thought he felt in his mind, as it were, a certain sparkle of that godly love that pricked him, and they all coveted to hear farther; but M. Bembo: "My Lords," quoth he, "I have spoken what the holy fury of love hath, unsought for, indited[1] to me; now that, it seemeth, he inspireth me no more, I wot not what to say. And I think verily that Love will not have his secrets discovered any farther, nor that the Courtier should pass the degree that his pleasure is I should show him, and therefore it is not perhaps lawful to speak any more in this matter."

"Surely," quoth the Duchess, "if the not-young Courtier be such a one that he can follow this way which you have showed him, of right he ought to be satisfied with so great a happiness, and not to envy the younger."

Then the Lord Cesar Gonzaga: "The way," quoth he, "that leadeth to this happiness is so steep, in my mind, that I believe it will be much ado to get to it."

The Lord Gaspar said: "I believe it be hard to get up for men, but unpossible for women."

The Lady Emilia laughed, and said: "If you fall so often to offend us, I promise you you shall be no more forgiven."

The Lord Gaspar answered: "It is no offense to you in saying that women's souls be not so purged from passions as men's be, nor accustomed in beholdings,[2] as M. Peter hath said is necessary for them to be that will taste of the heavenly love. Therefore it is not read that ever woman hath had this grace; but many men have had it, as Plato, Socrates, Plotinus,[3] and many other, and a number of our holy fathers, as Saint Francis, in whom a fervent spirit of love imprinted the most holy seal of the five wounds.[4] And nothing but the virtue[5] of love could hale up Saint Paul the Apostle to the sight of those secrets which is not lawful for man to speak of; nor show Saint Stephen the heavens open."[6]

Here answered the Lord Julian: "In this point men shall nothing pass women, for Socrates himself doth confess that all the mysteries of love which he knew were oped unto him by a woman, which was Diotima.[7] And the angel that with the fire of love imprinted the five wounds in Saint Francis hath also made some women worthy of the same print in our age. You must remember, moreover, that Saint Mary Magdalen[8] had many faults forgiven her, because she loved much; and perhaps with no less grace than Saint Paul was she many times through angelic love haled up to the third heaven. And

---

9. Insistent.
1. Dictated. "Fury": frenzy; enthusiasm of one possessed as by a god.
2. Contemplations.
3. Plotinus (205–270 C.E.) was the founder of the Neoplatonic philosophical school of late antiquity—the tradition revived by Bembo and, especially, his predecessor the great Florentine philosopher Marsilio Ficino (1433–1499).
4. Saint Francis of Assisi (1182–1226) is supposed to have received the stigmata, marking on his body the five wounds of Jesus on the Cross.
5. Power.

6. Before being stoned to death, Saint Stephen, the first Christian martyr, said, "Behold, I see the heavens opened, and the Son of man standing on the right hand of God" (Acts 7.56). Saint Paul's vision of the "third heaven" is in 2 Corinthians 12.2–4.
7. In Plato's *Symposium*, Socrates claims that a wise woman, Diotima, taught him his philosophy of love. "Oped": opened, disclosed.
8. Traditionally though baselessly regarded as a converted prostitute, she became one of Jesus's most faithful followers.

many other, as I showed you yesterday more at large, that for love of the name of Christ have not passed upon[9] life, nor feared torments, nor any other kind of death how terrible and cruel ever it were. And they were not, as M. Peter will have his Courtier to be, aged, but soft and tender maidens, and in the age when he saith that sensual love ought to be borne withal[1] in men."

The Lord Gaspar began to prepare himself to speak, but the Duchess: "Of this," quoth she, "let M. Peter be judge, and the matter shall stand to his verdict, whether women be not as meet[2] for heavenly love as men. But because the plead[3] between you may happen be too long, it shall not be amiss to defer it until tomorrow."

"Nay, tonight," quoth the Lord Cesar Gonzaga.

"And how can it be tonight?" quoth the Duchess.

The Lord Cesar answered: "Because it is day already," and showed her the light that began to enter in at the clefts of the windows. Then every man arose upon his feet with much wonder, because they had not thought that the reasonings had lasted longer than the accustomed wont, saving only that they were begun much later, and with their pleasantness had deceived so the lords' minds that they wist[4] not of the going away of the hours. And not one of them felt any heaviness of sleep in his eyes, the which often happeneth when a man is up after his accustomed hour to go to bed. When the windows then were opened on the side of the palace that hath his prospect toward the high top of Mount Catri, they saw already risen in the east a fair morning like unto the color of roses, and all stars voided,[5] saving only the sweet governess of the heaven, Venus, which keepeth the bounds of the night and the day, from which appeared to blow a sweet blast that, filling the air with a biting cold, began to quicken the tunable notes of the pretty birds among the hushing woods of the hills at hand. Whereupon they all, taking their leave with reverence of the Duchess, departed toward their lodgings without torch, the light of the day sufficing.

And as they were now passing out at the great chamber door, the Lord General[6] turned him to the Duchess and said: "Madam, to take up the variance between the Lord Gaspar and the Lord Julian, we will assemble this night with the judge sooner than we did yesterday."

The Lady Emilia answered: "Upon condition that in case my Lord Gaspar will accuse women, and give them, as his wont is, some false report, he will also put us in surety to stand to trial:[7] for I reckon him a wavering starter."[8]

1561

---

9. Cared for.
1. Put up with.
2. Fitted.
3. Controversy.
4. Knew.
5. Vanished.
6. Francesco Maria della Rovere, nephew and adopted heir of the duke.
7. I.e., he must give us some pawn ("surety") to guarantee that he will answer the charge of falsely accusing women. "Wont": habit.
8. I.e., one who is likely to "start"—suddenly desert his post.

Women in Power

Tudor England was a patriarchal society. Though in practice many women had more influence and authority than official doctrine acknowledged, that doctrine affirmed the subordination of women in public, private, economic, and spiritual life. Sermon writers and moralists cited alleged scriptural, medical, moral, historical, and philosophical "proofs" of male superiority and urged women to be chaste, silent, and obedient. These urgings could be enforced. Public ridicule was heaped on husbands perceived to be dominated by their wives, and women perceived to be scolds were on occasion brutally punished with a "brank": a metal cage for the head, with a built-in gag.

Yet from 1553 to 1603 England experienced five uninterrupted decades of female rule. What effect did this unprecedented experience have on the society's discourse of gender relations? The answer would seem to be, precious little. Though women governed the realm, Tudor men, with very few exceptions, clung to and reiterated their misogynistic views. And none of the women introduced in this section showed either an interest in improving the lot of less privileged women in their society or a sense of solidarity with their powerful female peers. Two of them, Mary Tudor and Elizabeth, signed the death warrants of the two others, Jane Grey and Mary Stuart. In addition, Mary Tudor probably came close to having her half-sister, Elizabeth, executed, and Mary Stuart plotted her cousin Elizabeth's assassination. These women are fascinating because they found themselves thrust into positions of almost unbelievable complexity, challenge, and danger. That one of them—Elizabeth I—not only flourished but also managed to use to her advantage the fact that she was a woman is one of the age's great stories.

Before the Reformation, some learned and ambitious women found within convents scope for both literary expression and the exercise of authority. With the dissolution of the monasteries under Henry VIII, that option was closed, and as Protestantism gathered strength, the emphasis on marriage further narrowed for women the possibilities of an independent life. Nonetheless, many Tudor women ran households and businesses; others played prominent roles in city life and were influential in regional politics and church appointments. Protestant insistence on Scripture as the crucial guide to faith also placed a sharply increased emphasis on literacy, which contributed, over the course of the sixteenth century, to a gradual increase in the number of women writers.

If public affirmations of male superiority continued, condemnations of the female sex could not, under Elizabeth, be quite so sweeping or absolute as in previous times. When the prominent humanist Sir Thomas Smith thought of how he should describe his country's social order, he declared that "we do reject women, as those whom nature hath made to keep home and to nourish their family and children, and not to meddle with matters abroad, nor to bear office in a city or commonwealth." Then, with a kind of nervous glance over his shoulder, he made an exception of those few in whom "the blood is respected, not the age nor the sex"—for example, the queen.

Even at the top, however, women could not easily escape being defined by their marital status, sexual behavior, and reproductive potential. Such was the case for Jane Grey, matched to Guildford Dudley as a move in a dangerous political game; for Mary Tudor, with her marriage to a foreign king and her phantom pregnancies; and for Mary Stuart, with her string of disastrous marriages and reputed sexual liaisons. Imagining how the careers of these contemporary women appeared in the eyes of Elizabeth helps explain her choice to remain unwed.

MARY I (MARY TUDOR)

Mary Tudor (1516–1558) was the only surviving child of Henry VIII's first wife, Catherine of Aragon. The king saw his daughter as a useful bargaining chip in international diplomacy—at the age of six she was engaged to be married to her cousin Charles V, the Holy Roman Emperor and England's chief ally against France—but balked at the thought of leaving his kingdom to a female heir. Blaming Catherine for failing to produce a son, he determined to seek a divorce. The pope's refusal to grant it precipitated the Protestant Reformation in England.

In the years immediately following the royal divorce and the break with Rome, Mary had good reason to believe that her life was in danger. When she refused to take the Oaths of Succession and Supremacy (affirming, respectively, the invalidity of her parents' marriage and her father's supreme authority over the English Church), Henry came close to having her arrested for treason. At length, her own Catholic councillors prevailed on her to sign the oaths rather than lose her life. Sparing her no humiliation, the Privy Council insisted that she add a postscript acknowledging that Henry VIII's marriage to her mother had been "incestuous and unlawful," thus effectively declaring herself a bastard. In his will, however, Henry VIII left Mary second in line for the throne, after her younger half-brother, Edward.

Harassed for harboring priests and attending Mass during Edward's reign, Mary very nearly did not survive the attempt, at its end, to establish as successor the Protestant Jane Grey. But when, somewhat surprisingly, Protestants as well as Catholic's rallied firmly to Mary's cause, she ascended the throne, and Jane Grey and her supporters went to the scaffold. The early eagerness of Protestants to accept Henry VIII's legitimate heir as their queen, regardless of her religion, diminished sharply when it became clear that Mary intended to marry a foreign ruler, Philip II of Spain. (Eleven years her junior, Philip was the son of her childhood fiancé, Charles V.) Sir Thomas Wyatt, son of the poet of the same name, led an uprising in January 1554 to prevent the match. Urged to flee, Mary instead went to the Guildhall in London and made a forceful speech that garnered popular support.

Wyatt's rebellion was subdued a week later, but there would never thereafter be real peace between Mary and her subjects. Her determination to restore the Catholic religion was probably welcomed by the majority, but there was no hope of avoiding confrontation with committed Protestants, and Mary did not attempt to avoid it. Between the beginning of 1555 and the end of her reign in 1558, she had 283 Protestants, from famous bishops to village zealots, executed for heresy. The immediate popular response of horror and resentment, which would soon solidify into the lurid historical legend of "Bloody Mary," had less to do with the number of executions than with the nature of the charge and with the grisly method employed. In reality both Henry VIII and Elizabeth executed many more people in the course of their reigns than did Mary. But Henry and Elizabeth, who were disposed to treat religious dissent as treason, typically had their victims executed as traitors—that is, hanged or beheaded. The pious Mary attempted to stamp out heresy and had *her* victims burned at the stake.

Impelled to marry for political reasons, Mary seemed to fall genuinely in love with her husband, who, however, did not reciprocate her feelings. On two occasions in her reign, she believed and announced herself to be with child, but both were phantom pregnancies. The melancholy from which she had always suffered intensified in the later years of her reign, when she grappled with bitter disappointments: many of her subjects incorrigibly heretical, her husband aloof and usually absent, her body apparently incapable of child-bearing. In 1558 Mary died, leaving the throne to her Protestant half-sister. The two royal half-sisters are buried in a single tomb in Westminster Abbey.

Letter to Henry VIII

To the King's Most Gracious Highness, my father:[1]

Most humbly prostrate before the feet of Your Most Excellent Majesty, your most humble, faithful, and obedient subject, which hath so extremely offended Your Most Gracious Highness that my heavy and fearful heart dare not presume to call you father, ne[2] Your Majesty hath any cause by my deserts, saving the benignity of your most blessed nature doth surmount all evils, offenses, and trespasses, and is ever merciful and ready to accept the penitent calling for grace in any convenient time. Having received this Thursday at night certain letters from Mr. Secretary,[3] as well advising me to make my humble submission immediately to yourself, which because I durst not without your gracious license presume to do before, I lately sent unto him, as signifying that your most merciful heart and fatherly pity had granted me your blessing, with condition that I should persevere in that I had commenced and begun, and that I should not eftsoons[4] offend Your Majesty by the denial or refusal of any such articles and commandments as it may please Your Highness to address unto me for the perfect trial of mine heart and inward affection. For the perfect declaration of the bottom of my heart and stomach,[5] first, I knowledge[6] myself to have most unkindly and unnaturally offended Your Most Excellent Highness, in that I have not submitted myself to your most just and virtuous laws, and for mine offense therein, which I must confess were in me a thousandfold more grievous than they could be in any other living creature, I put myself wholly and entirely to your gracious mercy; at whose hands I cannot receive that punishment for the same[7] that I have deserved. Secondly, to open my heart to Your Grace in these things which I have hitherto refused to condescend[8] unto, and have now written with mine own hand, sending the same to Your Highness herewith; I shall never beseech Your Grace to have pity and compassion of me, if ever you shall perceive that I shall privily or apertly[9] vary or alter from one piece of that I have written and subscribed, or refuse to confirm, ratify, or declare the same where Your Majesty shall appoint me. Thirdly, as I have and

---

1. After the execution of Anne Boleyn on May 19, 1536, Mary thought that she would quickly be restored to her father's favor. Henry, though, persisted in the demand that he had been making of her for several years: that she acknowledge in writing his supremacy over the English Church, as well as the invalidity of his marriage to her mother. In the weeks after Anne's beheading, Mary's continuing refusal to comply with this demand infuriated Henry to the point that he threatened her (not for the first time) with death. Finally, lambasted by Henry's secretary and principal adviser Thomas Cromwell, who had supported her until the king's rage made him fear for his own safety, and urged to submit even by her Spanish allies, Mary yielded, signing the prescribed articles on a Thursday night in June (either the 15th or the 22nd) and writing her father this supplicatory letter (which may have been drafted by Cromwell).

2. Nor.
3. Cromwell.
4. Again.
5. The stomach, like the heart, often designated the inward seat of thought and feeling.
6. Acknowledge.
7. I.e., for my offense.
8. Consent.
9. Secretly or openly.

shall, knowing your excellent learning, virtue, wisdom, and knowledge, put my soul into your direction, and, by the same, hath and will, in all things, from henceforth direct my conscience, so my body I do wholly commit to your mercy and fatherly pity; desiring no state, no condition, nor no manner degree of living, but such as Your Grace shall appoint unto me; knowledging and confessing that my state cannot be so vile as either the extremity of justice would appoint unto me, or as mine offenses have required and deserved. And whatsoever Your Grace shall command me to do, touching any of these points, either for things past, present, or to come, I shall as gladly do the same, as Your Majesty can command me. Most humbly therefore, beseeching your mercy, most gracious sovereign lord and benign father, to have pity and compassion of your miserable and sorrowful child, and with the abundance of your inestimable goodness so to overcome my iniquity towards God, Your Grace, and your whole realm, as I may feel some sensible[1] token of reconciliation, which, God is my judge, I only desire, without other respect.[2] To Whom I shall daily pray for the preservation of Your Highness, with the Queen's Grace,[3] and that it may please Him to send you issue. From Hunsdon, this Thursday, at 11 of the clock at night.

> Your Grace's most humble and
> obedient daughter and handmaid,
> Mary

1536   1830

From An Ambassadorial Dispatch to the Holy Roman Emperor, Charles V: The Coronation of Mary I[1]

Your Highness's own cousin,[2] Queen Mary, now wears the crown of this kingdom. She was crowned on the first day of this month,[3] with the pomp and ceremonies customary here, which are far grander than elsewhere, as I shall briefly show; and according to the rites of the old religion.[4] On the eve of her coronation-day, the queen was removed from the Tower and castle of London to Westminster Palace, where the sovereigns of England are by custom wont to reside in London. She was accompanied by the earls, lords, gentlemen, ambassadors, and officers, all dressed in rich garments. The queen was carried in an open litter covered with brocade. Two coaches followed her: the Lady Elizabeth and the Lady of Cleves[5] rode in one; some of the ladies of the court in the other. The streets were hung with tapestries and strewn with grass and flowers; and many triumphal arches were erected along her way. The next day, coronation-day, the queen went from the Hall

---

1. Evident. "As": so that.
2. Regard.
3. Jane Seymour, whom Henry had married on May 30 (eleven days after the execution of Anne Boleyn).
1. Translated from Spanish, in *Calendar of State Papers, Spanish*, vol. 5, pt. 1.
2. Mary and Charles were first cousins.

3. October 1553.
4. I.e., Catholicism.
5. Anne of Cleves, the German noblewoman who had been Henry VIII's fourth wife, was the only one of the six still alive in 1553. Henry had had the marriage annulled after seven months, but Anne had remained in England. "Lady Elizabeth" is Mary's half-sister, the future Elizabeth I.

of Parliament and Justice to the church,[6] in procession with the bishops and priests in full canonical dress, the streets being again covered with flowers and decked with stuffs.[7] She mounted a scaffolding that was erected at the church for this purpose, and showed herself to the people. The queen's coronation was proclaimed to them and the question asked of them if they were willing to accept her as their queen. All answered: Yes; and the ordinary ceremonies were then gone through, the queen making an offering of silver and silken stuffs. The bishop of Winchester, who officiated, gave her the scepter and the orb, fastened on the spurs, and girt her with the sword; he received the oath, and she was twice anointed and crowned with three crowns. The ceremonies lasted from ten in the morning till five o'clock in the afternoon. She was carried from the church to the Parliament Hall, where a banquet was prepared. The queen sat on a stone chair[8] covered with brocade,which they say was carried off from Scotland in sign of a victory, and was once used by the kings of Scotland at their crowning; she rested her feet upon two of her ladies, which is also a part of the prescribed ceremonial, and ate thus. She was served by the earls and lords, Knights of the Order[9] and officers, each one performing his own special office. The meats[1] were carried by the Knights of the Bath. These knights are made by the kings on the eve of their coronation and at no other time; and their rank is inferior to the other order. The queen instituted twenty fresh ones. They are called Knights of the Bath because they plunge naked into a bath with the king and kiss his shoulder. The queen being a woman, the ceremony was performed for her by the earl of Arundel, her great master of the household. The earl marshal and the lord steward[2] directed the ceremonies mounted on horseback in the great hall. When the banquet was over, an armed knight rode in upon a Spanish horse and flung down his glove,[3] while one of the kings-of-arms[4] challenged anyone who opposed the queen's rights to pick up the glove and fight the champion in single combat. The queen gave him a gold cup, as it is usual to do. Meanwhile the earls, vassals, and councillors paid homage to her, kissing her on the shoulder; and the ceremonies came to an end without any of the interruptions or troubles that were feared on the part of the Lutherans, who would rejoice in upsetting the queen's reign. They were feared especially because of the Lady Elizabeth, who does not feel sincerely the oath she took at the coronation; she has had intelligence with the king of France, which has been discovered.[5] A remedy is to be sought at the convocation of the estates,[6] which is to take place on the fifth of this month: Elizabeth is to be declared a bastard, having been born during the lifetime of Queen Catherine, mother of the queen. The affairs of the

6. I.e., from Westminster Hall to Westminster Abbey.
7. Pieces of cloth.
8. The coronation throne—not itself stone, but having the Stone of Scone (taken from Scotland by Edward I in 1292) encased in its seat.
9. The Order of the Garter.
1. Food in general (not just animal flesh).
2. The earl of Arundel was both the lord steward and the lord great master of the household. The earl marshal was the duke of Norfolk.
3. I.e., threw down the gauntlet. The challenge

by the "king's champion" (a hereditary office) was a part of the coronation ritual until 1821.
4. The title of the three chief heralds of the College of Arms.
5. There is, at least now, no evidence of Elizabeth's conniving with the French king. "Intelligence": communication.
6. I.e., Parliament. Statutes declaring both Mary and Elizabeth illegitimate were already in place; Parliament nullified those pertaining to Mary, but left unrepealed the ones concerning Elizabeth.

kingdom are unsettled because the vassals and people are prone to scandal, and seekers after novelties; they are strange and troublesome folk.

* * *

1553   1916

The Oration of Queen Mary in the Guildhall, on the First of February, 1554[1]

I am come unto you in mine own person, to tell you that which already you see and know; that is, how traitorously and rebelliously a number of Kentishmen have assembled themselves against both us and you. Their pretense (as they said at the first) was for a marriage determined for us: to the which, and to all the articles thereof, ye have been made privy. But since,[2] we have caused certain of our Privy Council to go again unto them, and to demand the cause of this their rebellion: and it appeared then unto our said council that the matter of the marriage seemed to be but a Spanish cloak to cover their pretended purpose against our religion; for that[3] they arrogantly and traitorously demanded to have the governance of our person, the keeping of the Tower,[4] and the placing of our councillors.

Now, loving subjects, what I am, ye right well know. I am your queen, to whom at my coronation, when I was wedded to the realm and laws of the same (the spousal ring whereof I have on my finger, which never hitherto was, nor hereafter shall be, left off), you promised your allegiance and obedience unto me. And that I am the right and true inheritor of the crown of this realm of England, I take all Christendom to witness. My father, as ye all know, possessed the same regal state, which now rightly is descended unto me: and to him always ye showed yourselves most faithful and loving subjects; and therefore I doubt not, but ye will show yourselves likewise to me, and that ye will not suffer a vile traitor to have the order and governance of our person, and to occupy our estate,[5] especially being so vile a traitor as Wyatt is; who most certainly, as he hath abused mine ignorant subjects which be on his side, so doth he intend and purpose the destruction of you, and spoil[6] of your goods. And this I say to you, on the word of a prince: I cannot tell how naturally the mother loveth the child, for I was never the mother of any; but certainly, if a prince and governor may as naturally and earnestly love her subjects, as the mother doth the child, then assure yourselves that I, being your lady and mistress, do as earnestly and as tenderly

1. When, in the early months of Mary's reign, it became clear that she intended to marry the heir to the Spanish throne (the future Philip II, son of her cousin Charles V), discontent broke into insurrection. In late January 1554, a sizable army led by the Kentishman Sir Thomas Wyatt II began an advance on London. In the crisis, Mary went to the Guildhall and made this rousing speech to the assembled Londoners. They rallied to her side, and when Wyatt reached the city he found an unreceptive populace. The uprising collapsed, and he and other rebel leaders were executed. The version of Mary's speech given here was printed, with grudging admiration, by the Protestant martyrologist John Foxe, in his *Acts and Monuments* (see p. 159).
2. Subsequently.
3. Because.
4. I.e., the Tower of London.
5. Position.
6. Despoliation, pillage.

love and favor you. And I, thus loving you, cannot but think that ye as heartily and faithfully love me; and then I doubt not but we shall give these rebels a short and speedy overthrow.

As concerning the marriage, ye shall understand that I enterprised not the doing thereof without advice, and that by the advice of all our Privy Council, who so considered and weighed the great commodities[7] that might ensue thereof, that they not only thought it very honorable, but also expedient, both for the wealth[8] of our realm and also of all you our subjects. And as touching myself, I assure you, I am not so bent to my will, neither so precise nor affectionate,[9] that either for mine own pleasure I would choose where I lust,[1] or that I am so desirous as needs[2] I would have one. For God, I thank him, to whom be the praise therefore, I have hitherto lived a virgin, and doubt nothing[3] but with God's grace am able so to live still. But if, as my progenitors have done before, it might please God that I might leave some fruit of my body behind me to be your governor, I trust ye would not only rejoice thereat, but also I know it would be to your great comfort. And certainly, if I either did think or know that this marriage were to the hurt of any of you my commons, or to the impeachment[4] of any part or parcel of the royal state of this realm of England, I would never consent thereunto, neither would I ever marry while I lived. And on the word of a queen I promise you that if it shall not probably[5] appear to all the nobility and commons in the high court of Parliament that this marriage shall be for the high benefit and commodity of the whole realm, then I will abstain from marriage while I live.

And now, good subjects, pluck up your hearts, and like true men stand fast against these rebels, both our enemies and yours, and fear them not; for I assure you, I fear them nothing at all. And I will leave with you my Lord Howard and my lord treasurer,[6] who shall be assistants with the mayor for your defense.

1554   1563

7. Benefits.
8. Well-being.
9. Nor so fastidious nor willful.
1. Where I please.
2. So full of desire that it is necessary.
3. Not at all.

4. Injury; discrediting.
5. Plausibly.
6. Sir William Paulet, marquis of Winchester. "My Lord Howard": William Howard, earl of Warwick.

LADY JANE GREY

J ane Grey (1537–1554) was unlucky in her parents, the duke and duchess of Suffolk. They were, by her own account, impossible to please, subjecting her to taunts, threats, and physical abuse whenever she made a minor error in performance or deportment. Much worse for Jane, her mother was a granddaughter of Henry VII with a distant but plausible claim to the English throne. This fact, more than any action of her own, determined the course of Jane's life and death.

In 1553 England was ruled in name by the boy-king Edward VI, but in reality by John Dudley, duke of Northumberland, who as Protector (regent) stood at the head of an aggressively Protestant regime. With Edward's health in decline and his Catholic half-sister Mary next in line to the throne, Protestant nobles feared for their future and for England's. For Northumberland, Jane Grey's bloodline offered an elegant solution. Aged fifteen, Lady Jane was married to Northumberland's son, Guildford Dudley. Within six weeks of the marriage, Edward VI was dead, having named Jane Grey as his successor. The Privy Council, pressured by Northumberland, denounced Mary Tudor as a bastard and declared Jane queen of England.

Jane's reign lasted a mere nine days, July 9–18. For the first seventy-two hours, there seemed some hope of success; even the hostile ambassadors of Catholic powers were ready to hail Jane as queen. But the nobility and the common people, Protestant as well as Catholic, soon began to shift their allegiance to Mary, who at the time downplayed her religion. Personal connections to Mary's household and local grievances, along with Catholic sympathies, motivated much of the gentry to rally around her. Within weeks Northumberland was defeated, arrested, and executed. Jane, who had briefly reigned from the Tower of London, was now made prisoner there. The victorious Mary initially had no intention of executing Jane or her young husband, who, she recognized, had been no more than pawns in their parents' political games. But in January 1554 the duke of Suffolk joined in an ill-fated rebellion intended to reinstate his daughter on the throne. Mary's councillors convinced her that Jane would pose a danger as long as she remained alive. On the morning of February 12, 1554, Jane watched from a Tower window as her husband, Guildford, went to his public execution; within an hour she too had been beheaded, privately, on Tower Green.

Jane Grey was never really a woman in power. Her ability to command her own destiny, let alone that of others, was hardly greater when she was queen of England than when she was prisoner in the Tower. Yet it is clear from her writings and the testimony of others that Jane possessed a firm, even fiery will. In her brief stint as queen, she shocked her controllers by refusing to allow Guildford to take the title of king and rule jointly with her, and again by insisting that Northumberland, rather than her father, Suffolk, should lead her forces against Mary. Her will was harnessed to a militant and unshakable Protestantism; from an early age she mocked Catholic beliefs. In the Tower, where a politic conversion to Catholicism might well have saved her life, she instead wrote a violent and soon public letter to her onetime tutor Thomas Harding, who had converted, lambasting him as a "seed of Satan." Yet far from being an ignorant bigot, Jane was, though dead at sixteen, among the most learned women of her century; she had mastered Latin and Greek and was a student of Hebrew. She rivaled Elizabeth in intellectual brilliance and—to her fatal cost—exceeded her greatly in religious fervor.

From Roger Ascham's *Schoolmaster*[1]

[A TALK WITH LADY JANE]

* * * One example whether love or fear doth work more in a child for virtue and learning I will gladly report; which may be heard with some pleasure and followed with more profit. Before I went into Germany,[2] I came to

1. On Ascham—the preeminent humanist educational theorist of mid-16th-century England—see p. 171.
2. In 1550, as secretary of the English ambassador to the emperor Charles V. So Lady Jane was thirteen at the time of the conversation Ascham recounts.

Broadgate in Leicestershire to take my leave of that noble Lady Jane Grey, to whom I was exceeding much beholding. Her parents, the duke and the duchess, with all the household, gentlemen and gentlewomen, were hunting in the park. I found her in her chamber reading *Phaedon Platonis*[3] in Greek, and that with as much delight as some gentleman would read a merry tale in Boccaccio.[4] After salutation and duty done, with some other talk, I asked her why she would lose[5] such pastime in the park. Smiling she answered me, "Iwis,[6] all their sport in the park is but a shadow to that pleasure that I find in Plato. Alas, good folk, they never felt what true pleasure meant." "And how came you, madam," quoth I, "to this deep knowledge of pleasure, and what did chiefly allure you unto it, seeing not many women, but very few men, have attained thereunto?" "I will tell you," quoth she, "and tell you a truth which perchance ye will marvel at. One of the greatest benefits that ever God gave me is that he sent me so sharp and severe parents and so gentle a schoolmaster. For when I am in presence either of father or mother, whether I speak, keep silence, sit, stand, or go,[7] eat, drink, be merry or sad, be sewing, playing, dancing, or doing anything else, I must do it, as it were, in such weight, measure, and number even so perfectly as God made the world, or else I am so sharply taunted, so cruelly threatened, yea, presently sometimes, with pinches, nips, and bobs,[8] and other ways which I will not name for the honor I bear them,[9] so without measure misordered, that I think myself in hell till time come that I must go to Master Aylmer,[1] who teacheth me so gently, so pleasantly, with such fair allurements to learning, that I think all the time nothing whilst I am with him. And when I am called from him, I fall on weeping, because whatsoever I do else but learning is full of grief, trouble, fear, and whole misliking unto me. And thus my book hath been so much my pleasure, and bringeth daily to me more pleasure and more, that in respect of it all other pleasures in very deed be but trifles and troubles unto me." I remember this talk gladly, both because it is so worthy of memory and because also it was the last talk that ever I had, and the last time that ever I saw, that noble and worthy lady.

1570

---

3. Plato's dialogue *Phaedo*, which recounts the last hours of Socrates and affirms the immortality of the soul.
4. Boccaccio's *Decameron* (1348–53), a collection of one hundred "merry," sometimes licentious, tales, not translated into English in Ascham's time.
5. Miss, forgo.
6. Truly.

7. Walk.
8. Raps, blows. "Presently": on the spot.
9. Her parents.
1. John Aylmer (1521–1594). As a schoolboy he attracted the notice of Jane's father, who provided for his education at Cambridge and appointed him tutor to his daughters. In 1577 Queen Elizabeth made him bishop of London.

From A Letter of the Lady Jane to M. H., late chaplain to the duke of Suffolk her father, and then fallen from the truth of God's most Holy Word[1]

So oft as I call to mind the dreadful and fearful saying of God, "That he which layeth hold upon the plough, and looketh back, is not meet for the kingdom of heaven,"[2] and, on the other side, the comfortable[3] words of our Savior Christ to all those that, forsaking themselves, do follow him, I cannot but marvel at thee, and lament thy case, which seemed sometime to be the lively member of Christ, but now the deformed imp[4] of the devil; sometime the beautiful temple of God, but now the stinking and filthy kennel of Satan; sometime the unspotted spouse of Christ, but now the unshamefaced paramour of Antichrist; sometime my faithful brother, but now a stranger and apostate; sometime a stout Christian soldier, but now a cowardly runaway. Yea, when I consider these things, I cannot but speak to thee, and cry out upon thee, thou seed of Satan, and not of Judah,[5] whom the devil hath deceived, the world hath beguiled, and the desire of life subverted, and made thee of a Christian an infidel. Wherefore hast thou taken the testament of the Lord in thy mouth? Wherefore hast thou preached the law and the will of God to others? Wherefore hast thou instructed others to be strong in Christ, when thou thyself dost now so shamefully shrink, and so horribly abuse the testament and law of the Lord? when thou thyself preachest not to steal, yet most abominably stealest, not from men but from God, and, committing most heinous sacrilege, robbest Christ thy Lord of his right members, thy body and thy soul, and choosest rather to live miserably with shame to the world, than to die and gloriously with honor to reign with Christ, in whom even in death is life? Why dost thou now show thyself most weak, when indeed thou oughtest to be most strong? The strength of a fort is unknown before the assault: but thou yieldest thy hold before any battery be made.

O wretched and unhappy man, what art thou, but dust and ashes? and wilt thou resist thy maker that fashioned thee and framed thee? Wilt thou now forsake Him that called thee from the custom gathering among the Romish Antichristians,[6] to be an ambassador and messenger of his eternal word? He that first framed thee, and since thy first creation and birth preserved thee, nourished, and kept thee, yea, and inspired thee with the spirit of knowledge (I cannot say of grace), shall he not now possess thee? Darest thou deliver up thyself to another, being not thine own, but his? How canst thou, having knowledge, or how darest thou neglect the law of the Lord and follow the vain traditions of men, and whereas thou hast been a public professor of his name, become now a defacer of his glory? Wilt thou refuse the true God, and worship the invention of man, the golden calf, the whore of

1. Taken from the 2nd edition (1570) of John Foxe's *Acts and Monuments* (see p. 159). In a subsequent edition, "M. H." is identified as "Master Harding"—the eminent theologian Thomas Harding, who was one of Lady Jane's tutors. Like many other English clergymen, Harding had renounced his Protestantism after Mary I made clear her determination to restore Catholicism.

Jane wrote to him from her prison in the Tower.
2. Luke 9.62. "Meet": fit.
3. Comforting.
4. Offshoot.
5. Patriarch of the biblical kingdom of the Hebrews.
6. In the late 1540s, Harding had studied in Catholic Italy.

Lady Jane Grey. Dating from the 1590s and by an unknown artist, this oil painting on oak panel has been claimed to represent Jane Grey, though the claim has been contested. Scratched lines across the painting suggest that the work might have been the victim of an iconoclastic attack.

Babylon,[7] the Romish religion, the abominable idol, the most wicked Mass? Wilt thou torment again, rend and tear the most precious body of our Savior Christ, with thy bodily and fleshly teeth?[8] Wilt thou take upon thee to offer up any sacrifice unto God for our sins, considering that Christ offered up himself, as Paul saith, upon the cross, a lively sacrifice once for all? Can neither the punishment of the Israelites (which, for their idolatry, they so oft received), nor the terrible threatenings of the prophets, nor the curses of God's own mouth, fear thee to honor any other god than him? Dost thou so regard Him that spared not his dear and only son for thee, so diminishing, yea, utterly extinguishing his glory, that thou wilt attribute the praise and honor due unto him to the idols, "which have mouths and speak not, eyes and see not, ears and hear not";[9] which shall perish with them that made them?

* * *

7. Revelation 17–19. Protestants often identified her with the Church of Rome. "The golden calf": the idol fashioned by the Israelites while Moses was on Mount Sinai receiving the Ten Commandments (Exodus 32).
8. Alluding to the bitter controversy over transubstantiation: Catholic doctrine holds that although the bread and wine of the Eucharist retain their normal appearance, they are miraculously transformed into the actual body and blood of Christ; Protestants believe that the identification is symbolic rather than substantive.
9. Psalms 115.

Return, return again into Christ's war, and, as becometh a faithful warrior, put on that armor that St. Paul teacheth to be most necessary for a Christian man.[1] And above all things take to you the shield of faith, and be you provoked by Christ's own example to withstand the devil, to forsake the world, and to become a true and faithful member of his mystical body, who spared not his own body for our sins.

Throw down yourself with the fear of his threatened vengeance for this so great and heinous an offense of apostasy; and comfort yourself, on the other part, with the mercy, blood, and promise of him that is ready to turn unto you whensoever you turn unto him. Disdain not to come again with the lost son,[2] seeing you have so wandered with him. Be not ashamed to turn again with him from the swill of strangers[3] to the delicates of your most benign and loving Father, acknowledging that you have sinned against heaven and earth: against heaven, by staining the glorious name of God and causing his most sincere and pure word to be evil-spoken-of through you; against earth, by offending so many of your weak brethren, to whom you have been a stumbling-block through your sudden sliding. Be not abashed to come home again with Mary,[4] and weep bitterly with Peter,[5] not only with shedding the tears of your bodily eyes, but also pouring out the streams of your heart—to wash away, out of the sight of God, the filth and mire of your offensive fall. Be not abashed to say with the publican,[6] "Lord be merciful unto me a sinner."

Last of all, let the lively remembrance of the last day[7] be always before your eyes, remembering the terror that such shall be in at that time, with the runagates[8] and fugitives from Christ, which, setting more by the world than by heaven, more by their life than by him that gave them life, did shrink, yea did clean fall away, from him that forsook not them; and, contrariwise, the inestimable joys prepared for them that, fearing no peril nor dreading death, have manfully fought and victoriously triumphed over all power of darkness, over hell, death, and damnation, through their most redoubted[9] captain, Christ, who now stretcheth out his arms to receive you, ready to fall upon your neck and kiss you, and, last of all, to feast you with the dainties and delicates of his own precious blood: which undoubtedly, if it might stand with his determinate purpose, he would not let[1] to shed again, rather than you should be lost. To whom, with the Father and the Holy Ghost, be all honor, praise, and glory everlasting. Amen.

> Be constant, be constant; fear not for pain:
> Christ hath redeemed thee, and heaven is thy gain.

1553–54   1563, 1570

---

1. Ephesians 6.11–18.
2. The Prodigal Son (Luke 15.10–32).
3. The Prodigal journeyed into a "far country," where, having "wasted his substance with riotous living," he "would fain have filled his belly with the husks that the swine did eat."
4. Christ's follower Mary Magdalene, long regarded (though without substantive basis in the Gospels) as a repentant sinner.
5. After thrice denying Christ, Peter wept bitterly for his apostasy (Matthew 26.75; Luke 22.62).
6. Luke 18.13. "Publican": in Christ's parable of the Pharisee and the publican (tax collector—agent of the hated Roman occupiers), the latter humbles himself before God and is forgiven.
7. Judgment Day.
8. Runaways; i.e., apostates.
9. Reverenced; dreaded.
1. Hesitate.

A Letter of the Lady Jane, Sent unto her Father[1]

Father, although it hath pleased God to hasten my death by you, by whom my life should rather have been lengthened; yet can I so patiently take it, as I yield God more hearty thanks for shortening my woeful days than if all the world had been given into my possession, with life lengthened at my own will. And albeit I am well assured of your impatient dolors, redoubled manifold ways, both in bewailing your own woe and especially, as I hear, my unfortunate state, yet, my dear father (if I may without offense rejoice in my own mishaps), meseems in this I may account myself blessed, that washing my hands with the innocency of my fact,[2] my guiltless blood may cry before the Lord, Mercy, mercy to the innocent! And yet, though I must needs acknowledge that, being constrained and, as you wot well enough, continually assayed,[3] in taking upon me I seemed to consent,[4] and therein grievously offended the queen and her laws: yet do I assuredly trust that this mine offense towards God is so much the less in that, being in so royal estate as I was, mine enforced honor never agreed with mine innocent heart. And thus, good father, I have opened unto you the state wherein I presently stand; whose death at hand, although to you perhaps it may seen right woeful, to me there is nothing that can be more welcome than from this vale of misery to aspire to that heavenly throne of all joy and pleasure with Christ our savior. In whose steadfast faith (if it may be lawful for the daughter so to write to the father) the Lord that hitherto hath strengthened you so continue you that at the last we may meet in heaven with the Father, the Son, and the Holy Ghost.[5]

1554   1570

A Prayer of the Lady Jane[1]

O Lord, thou God and Father of my life, hear me, poor and desolate woman, which flieth unto thee only, in all troubles and miseries. Thou, O Lord, art the only defender and deliverer of those that put their trust in thee: and therefore I, being defiled with sin, encumbered with affliction, unquieted with troubles, wrapped in cares, overwhelmed with miseries, vexed with temptations, and grievously tormented with the long imprisonment of this vile mass of clay, my sinful body, do come unto thee, O merciful Savior,

---

1. Written shortly before her execution and later published in Foxe's *Acts and Monuments* (see p. 159). Lady Jane's father, the duke of Suffolk, had been pardoned by Mary I for his involvement in the attempt to put Jane on the throne following the death of Edward VI; Jane herself, though remaining in custody, also had good hopes of being pardoned. But when Suffolk joined in the insurrection of January 1554 against Mary, the queen decided that both must die. Suffolk was executed eleven days after his daughter, on February 23.

2. Actions. Jane had had to be coerced to accept the crown in July 1553 and was in no way involved in the later uprising.
3. Assailed; i.e., browbeaten. "Wot": know.
4. I.e., though I accepted the crown only under intense pressure, nonetheless, by accepting it at all I apparently consented to Mary's displacement.
5. As Foxe noted, this final sentence amounts to an admonition that Suffolk not renounce his Protestantism.
1. Also written shortly before her death.

craving thy mercy and help, without the which so little hope of deliverance is left that I may utterly despair of any liberty.

Albeit it is expedient, that, seeing our life standeth upon trying,[2] we should be visited sometime with some adversity, whereby we might both be tried whether we be of thy flock or no, and also know thee and ourselves the better, yet thou, that saidst thou wouldst not suffer us to be tempted above our power,[3] be merciful unto me now, a miserable wretch, I beseech thee; which with Solomon[4] do cry unto thee, humbly desiring thee that I may neither be too much puffed up with prosperity, neither too much pressed down with adversity, lest I, being too full, should deny thee, my God, or being too low brought, should despair and blaspheme thee, my Lord and Savior.

O merciful God, consider my misery, best known unto thee; and be thou now unto me a strong tower of defense, I humbly require[5] thee. Suffer me not to be tempted above my power, but either be thou a deliverer unto me out of this great misery, either[6] else give me grace patiently to bear thy heavy hand and sharp correction. It was thy right hand that delivered the people of Israel out of the hands of Pharaoh, which for the space of four hundred years did oppress them and keep them in bondage. Let it, therefore, likewise seem good to thy fatherly goodness to deliver me, sorrowful wretch (for whom thy son Christ shed his precious blood on the cross), out of this miserable captivity and bondage wherein I am now.

How long wilt thou be absent? forever? O Lord, hast thou forgotten to be gracious, and hast thou shut up thy loving-kindness in displeasure? Wilt thou be no more entreated? Is thy mercy clean gone forever, and thy promise come utterly to an end for evermore?[7] Why dost thou make so long tarrying? Shall I despair of thy mercy, O God? Far be that from me. I am thy workmanship, created in Christ Jesu: give me grace, therefore, to tarry thy leisure, and patiently to bear thy works; assuredly knowing that as thou canst, so thou wilt deliver me when it shall please thee, nothing doubting or mistrusting thy goodness towards me; for thou knowest better what is good for me than I do: therefore do with me in all things what thou wilt, and plague me what way thou wilt. Only in the meantime, arm me, I beseech thee, with thy armor,[8] that I may stand fast, my loins being girded about with verity, having on the breastplate of righteousness and shod with the shoes prepared by the gospel of peace; above all things, taking to me the shield of faith, wherewith I may be able to quench all the fiery darts of the wicked, and taking the helmet of salvation and the sword of the spirit, which is thy most holy Word: praying always with all manner of prayer and supplication, that I may refer myself wholly to thy will, abiding thy pleasure and comforting myself in those troubles that it shall please thee to send me; seeing such troubles be profitable for me, and seeing I am assuredly persuaded that it cannot be but well, all that thou doest.

---

2. Trial.
3. 1 Corinthians 10.13.
4. Proverbs 30.7–9.
5. Ask.

6. Or.
7. Psalms 77.8.
8. The allegorical armor of Ephesians 6.11–18. The ensuing passage closely echoes these verses.

Hear me, O merciful Father, for His sake whom thou wouldst should be a sacrifice for my sins: to whom with thee and the Holy Ghost, be all honor and glory. Amen.

1554   1563

A Second Letter to Her Father[1]

The Lord comfort your grace, and that in his Word, wherein all creatures only are to be comforted. And though it hath pleased God to take away two of your children,[2] yet think not, I most humbly beseech your grace, that you have lost them, but trust that we, by losing this mortal life, have won an immortal life. And I for my part, as I have honored your grace in this life, will pray for you in another life. Your grace's humble daughter,

Jane Dudley

1554   1850

From Foxe's *Acts and Monuments*[1]

The Words and Behavior of the Lady Jane upon the Scaffold

These are the words that the Lady Jane spake upon the scaffold, at the hour of her death. First, when she mounted upon the scaffold, she said to the people standing thereabout, "Good people, I am come hither to die, and by a law I am condemned to the same. The fact[2] against the queen's highness was unlawful, and the consenting thereunto by me; but, touching the procurement and desire thereof by me, or on my behalf, I do wash my hands thereof in innocency before God and the face of you, good Christian people, this day." And therewith she wrung her hands, wherein she had her book.[3] Then said she, "I pray you all, good Christian people, to bear me witness that I die a true Christian woman, and that I do look to be saved by no other mean but only by the mercy of God,[4] in the blood of his only Son Jesus Christ; and I confess that when I did know the word of God I neglected the same, loved myself and the world; and therefore this plague and punishment is happily and worthily happened unto me for my sins; and yet I thank God of his goodness that he hath thus given me a time and respite to repent. And now, good people, while I am alive, I pray you assist me with your prayers."[5] And then, kneeling down, she turned her to Feckenham,[6] saying, "Shall I

---

1. Lady Jane inscribed this farewell message in a prayer book, now in the British Library.
2. I.e., his daughter and son-in-law.
1. On the Protestant martyrologist John Foxe (1516–1587), see p. 159.
2. Act.
3. Prayer book.
4. Asserting the Protestant doctrine of salvation by faith alone.
5. Implicitly challenging the Catholic doctrine of the efficacy of prayers for the *dead*.
6. John de Feckenham, Queen Mary's confessor, who at her behest had tried unsuccessfully, in Lady Jane's last days, to convert her to Catholicism. A gifted and tolerant man, Feckenham was later put in charge of Mary's project of restoring the Benedictine monastery of Westminster Abbey, where he thus became the last abbot.

say this psalm?" And he said, "Yea." Then said she the psalm of *Miserere mei Deus*[7] in English, in most devout manner, throughout to the end; and then she stood up, and gave her maiden, Mistress Ellen, her gloves and handkerchief, and her book to Master Brydges.[8] And then she untied her gown, and the hangman pressed upon her to help her off with it;[9] but she, desiring him to let her alone, turned towards her two gentlewomen, who helped her off therewith, and also with her frau's paste[1] and neckerchief, giving her a fair handkerchief to knit about her eyes.

Then the hangman kneeled down and asked her forgiveness, whom she forgave most willingly. Then he willed her to stand upon the straw;[2] which doing, she saw the block. Then she said, "I pray you, dispatch me quickly." Then she kneeled down, saying, "Will you take it off before I lay me down?" And the hangman said, "No, madam." Then tied she the kerchief about her eyes, and feeling for the block she said, "What shall I do? Where is it? Where is it?" One of the standers-by guiding her thereunto, she laid her head down upon the block, and then stretched forth her body and said, "Lord, into thy hands I commend my spirit";[3] and so finished her life, in the year of our Lord God 1554, the twelfth day of February.

1563

7. Psalm 51, which opens "Have mercy upon me, O God."
8. Sir John Brydges, lieutenant of the Tower.
9. The victim's adornments were part of the executioner's fee.

1. A type of elaborate headdress worn by married women.
2. Strewn about the execution block to soak up some of the blood.
3. Echoing Christ's dying words, Luke 23.46.

MARY, QUEEN OF SCOTS

Mary Stuart (1542–1587) was born on December 8, and within a week, following the death of her father, King James V, she had inherited the throne of Scotland. She has always been remembered as the "Queen of Scots," though she spent very few years in Scotland, never spoke its language as easily as French, and was forced to abdicate at the age of twenty-four.

Determined to foil the ambitions of Henry VIII, who sought to force a union between England and Scotland by having Mary married to his own son, Edward, Mary's guardians sent her at the age of five to the court of France, where she would be brought up. At age fifteen she married Francis, the French dauphin, who became king in 1559. A year later, Francis II died, and at the age of eighteen Mary returned to her own kingdom, Scotland, a land she could barely remember. As a Catholic woman coming to rule over a patriarchal society in which militant Protestantism was gathering force, Mary could hardly hope for a unanimously warm welcome. Her own subsequent decisions destroyed whatever chance she may have had of enjoying a peaceful reign. In 1565 she married her vain and erratic cousin, Henry Stewart, Lord Darnley, with whom she was soon deeply unhappy. In 1566 Darnley was implicated in the murder of Mary's secretary, David Rizzio, who was rumored to be her lover. In 1567 Darnley was murdered in turn, certainly with the connivance of the powerful James Hepburn, earl of Bothwell. Soon Mary was married to Bothwell, though her own will in the matter remains unclear. The scandal of this marriage alienated many of her supporters and helped provoke an uprising of the Scottish nobility. Mary was imprisoned at Lochleven Castle and forced to abdicate in favor of her one-year-old son, James. Though she escaped, she failed to rally the Scottish people to her side, and in 1568 she fled across the border into England, where she appealed for help from her cousin Elizabeth.

The arrival on English soil of the twenty-five-year-old Queen of Scots was not welcome news to the Protestant queen and her wary advisers. As a descendant of Henry VII with a good claim to the English throne, Mary was seen to be a dangerous and destabilizing presence. She was immediately taken prisoner and remained so until her execution at the age of forty-four. She was tried in England in 1568–69 on the charge of murdering her second husband. At this point her Scottish accuser produced the notorious Casket Letters, which had supposedly been discovered in a silver casket seized from an associate of Bothwell's. The casket, it was said, contained eight letters and twelve sonnets, all in French, testifying (if they are authentic) to an adulterous relationship with Bothwell and, more ambiguously, to Mary's involvement in the murder of Darnley. Mary herself was not permitted to inspect the letters, which were withdrawn shortly after being displayed in court and subsequently disappeared, though not before translations of them had been made into English and Scots. The result of the trial was inconclusive; Elizabeth declared that nothing had been proven that would make her "conceive an evil opinion of her good sister"; yet she continued to keep Mary prisoner, moving her from one place of confinement to another for the next nineteen years.

Mary quickly became the focus for the aspirations of discontented Catholics at home and abroad. She conspired with these adherents by means of secret messages, written in ciphers or in invisible ink on white taffeta, smuggled in and out of her prison hidden in such things as beer barrels. The conspiracies were monitored, and to some extent even engineered, by Elizabeth's spymaster, Francis Walsingham, who was setting a trap for the Queen of Scots and English Catholics generally. In 1586 Mary was found to be in communication with a young Englishman named Anthony Babington, who was plotting to assassinate Elizabeth and place Mary on the throne. Babington and his coconspirators were drawn and quartered, their heads displayed on Tower Bridge. Though she insisted that, as the sovereign queen of another country, she could not be charged with treason against England's queen, Mary was convicted as a traitor and sentenced to death. Elizabeth vacillated for some time over carrying out the sentence, worrying about the reaction abroad and about the precedent involved in executing a monarch. Eventually she was prevailed upon to sign the death warrant, and Mary was beheaded on February 8, 1587. A week later, Elizabeth wrote to the orphaned James VI of Scotland, lamenting the "miserable accident, which far contrary to my meaning hath befallen."

Many of the words that seem to speak to us most eloquently of Mary's self and circumstances are not in fact her own. Throughout her life, Mary encountered no shortage of people—some who were admirers and others deadly foes—who were eager to seize control of her voice. The controversy over the Casket Letters thus crystallizes the more general problem of locating the "real" Mary Stuart. It will probably never be possible to prove with certainty whether the letters are products of Mary's own hand or cunning forgeries designed to incriminate her, and indeed it is this impossibility that lends them much of their fascination, opening them up for the endless play of interpretation. Yet if the interpretation of the Casket Letters has become a kind of intellectual game, it began as a matter of life or death. If Mary was in one respect a text with many authors, she was also a singular woman inhabiting a body that, on the orders of another woman, was at last cut in two.

From Casket Letter Number 2[1]

* * * This day I have wrought[2] till two of the clock upon this bracelet, to put the key in the cleft[3] of it, which is tied with two laces. I have had so little time that it is very ill,[4] but I will make a fairer; and in the meantime take heed that none of those that be here do see it: for all the world would know it, for I have made it in haste in their presence. I go to my tedious talk.[5] You make me dissemble so much that I am afraid thereof with horror; and you make me almost to play the part of a traitor. Remember that if it were not for obeying you, I had rather be dead;[6] my heart bleedeth for it. To be short, he will not come[7] but with condition that I shall promise to be with him as heretofore at bed and board,[8] and that I shall forsake him no more; and upon my word[9] he will do whatsoever I will, and will come, but he hath prayed me to tarry till after tomorrow. * * * But now, to make him trust me, I must feign something unto him; and therefore when he desired me to promise that when he should be whole[1] we should make but one bed, I told him (feigning to believe his fair promises) [that if he][2] did not change his mind between this time and that, I was contented, so as[3] he would say nothing thereof: for (to tell it between us two) the lords wished no ill to him,[4] but did fear lest (considering the threatenings which he made in case we did agree together) he would make them feel the small account[5] they have made of him, and that he would persuade me to pursue some of them; and for this respect should be in jealousy if at one instant,[6] without their knowledge, I did break a game made to the contrary in their presence.[7] And he said unto me, very pleasant and merry, "Think you that they do the more esteem you therefore? But I am glad that you talk to me of the lords. I hear[8] that you desire now that we shall live a happy life—for if it were otherwise, it could not be but greater inconvenience should happen to us both than you think. But I will do now whatsoever you will have me do, and will love all those that you shall love, so as you make them to love me also. For, so as they seek not my life, I love them all equally."

---

1. The English translation was made shortly after the French originals of the Casket Letters were produced at Mary's first trial in England (1568–69).
2. Worked.
3. I.e., lock.
4. Badly made.
5. I.e., with Darnley. He was lying ill (probably from syphilis, though smallpox was given out as the cause) at Glasgow; Mary had joined him there.
6. I.e., than play the traitor.
7. I.e., to Craigmillar Castle, outside Edinburgh. "To be short": in short.
8. I.e., to live again with him as husband and wife.

9. I.e., if I give my word to do this.
1. Well.
2. The manuscript of the English translation has a tear at this point; the missing words have been inferred from the contemporary Scottish translation.
3. Provided that.
4. Darnley—weak, arrogant, and vicious—had many bitter enemies among the other Scottish lords.
5. Make them suffer for the low estimate.
6. Suddenly. "Respect": reason.
7. At their urging, Mary had authorized a confederacy of nobles to find a way for her to divorce Darnley. "Game": undertaking.
8. I.e., I am convinced.

Thereupon I have willed this bearer to tell you many pretty[9] things; for I have too much to write, and it is late, and I trust him, upon your word. To be short, he[1] will go anywhere upon my word. Alas! and I never deceived anybody; but I remit[2] myself wholly to your will. And send me word what I shall do, and whatever happen to me, I will obey you. Think also if you will not find some invention more secret, by physic,[3] for he is to take physic at Craigmillar, and the baths also, and shall not come forth of[4] long time. To be short, for that that[5] I can learn, he hath great suspicion, and yet nevertheless trusteth upon my word, but not to tell me as yet anything. Howbeit, if you will that I shall *avow*[6] him, I will know all of him; but I shall never be willing[7] to beguile one who putteth his trust in me. Nevertheless, you may do all.[8] And do not esteem me the less therefore, for you are the cause thereof; for, for my own revenge, I would not do it.

He giveth me certain charges[9] (and those strong) of that that I fear: even to say that his faults be published, but there be that commit some secret faults and fear not to have them spoken of so loudly, and that there is speech of great and small. And even touching the Lady Reres,[1] he said, "God grant that she serve you to your honor," and that men may not think, nor he neither, that mine own power was not in myself,[2] seeing I did refuse his offers. To conclude, for a surety he mistrusteth us of that that you know,[3] and for his life. But in the end, after I had spoken two or three good words to him, he was very merry and glad. I have not seen him this night, for ending[4] your bracelet; but I can find no clasps for it. It is ready thereunto,[5] and yet I fear lest it should bring you ill hap, or that it should be known if you were hurt.[6] Send me word whether you will have it, and more money,[7] and when I shall return, and how far I may speak. * * *

He hath sent to me, and prayeth me to see him rise tomorrow in the morning early. To be short, this bearer shall declare unto you the rest; and if I shall learn anything, I will make every night a memorial[8] thereof. He shall tell you the cause of my stay.[9] Burn this letter, for it is too dangerous; neither is there anything well said in it, for I think upon nothing but upon grief if you be at Edinburgh.[1]

Now if to please you, my dear life, I spare neither honor, conscience, nor hazard, nor greatness, take it in good part, and not according to the

---

9. Small(er). "This bearer": the bearer of the letter.
1. I.e., Darnley.
2. Submit.
3. Medicine (i.e., a poisoned drink). "Invention": contrivance. If Mary wrote this sentence, it shows her complicit in the plot to murder Darnley, who was in fact strangled—and the house he was occupying at Kirk O'Field, just outside Edinburgh, blown up—on the night of February 9–10, 1567.
4. For a.
5. As far as.
6. Assure him by taking a vow. "Howbeit": however.
7. I.e., without reluctance.
8. I.e., you may command me in all things.
9. Admonitions. The idea seems to be that Darnley hinted that he might reveal Mary's secrets.

1. She was acting as wet nurse to Mary's son, James (later James VI of Scotland and, in 1603, James I of England).
2. I.e., that I was not acting of my own will.
3. The thing that you know about. "For a surety": for certain.
4. Because I was finishing.
5. Apart from that.
6. Recognized if you were wounded (and thus powerless to conceal the bracelet). "Ill hap": misfortune.
7. I.e., whether you want more money.
8. Memorandum.
9. Delay.
1. The Scottish translation makes this clause the beginning of a new sentence, which says, in effect, "If you are in Edinburgh when you receive this, send me word soon."

interpretation of your false brother-in-law,[2] to whom I pray you give no credit against the most faithful lover that ever you had, or shall have.

See not also her whose feigned tears you ought not more to regard than the true travails which I endure to deserve her place, for obtaining of which, against my own nature I do betray those that could let[3] me. God forgive me, and give you, my only friend,[4] the good luck and prosperity that your humble and faithful lover doth wish unto you: who hopeth shortly to be another thing unto you, for the reward of my pains. I have not made[5] one word, and it is very late, although I should never be weary in writing to you, yet will I end, after kissing of your hands. Excuse my evil[6] writing, and read it over twice. Excuse also that [I scribbled,[7] for I had yesternight no paper, when I took the paper of a memorial.[8] . . . Remember your friend, and write unto her, and often. Love me al[ways, as I shall do you].[9]

1567   1571

A Letter to Elizabeth I, May 17, 1568[1]

Madam my good sister,[2] I believe you are not ignorant how long certain of my subjects, whom from the least of my kingdom I have raised to be the first, have taken upon themselves to involve me in trouble, and to do what it appears they had in view from the first. You know how they purposed to seize me and the late king my husband, from which attempt it pleased God to protect us, and to permit us to expel them from the country, where, at your request, I again afterwards received them; though, on their return, they committed another crime, that of holding me a prisoner, and killing in my presence a servant of mine, I being at the time in a state of pregnancy.[3] It again pleased God that I should save myself from their hands; and, as above said, I not only pardoned them, but even received them into favor. They, however, not yet satisfied with so many acts of kindness, have, on the contrary, in spite of their promises, devised, favored, subscribed to, and aided in a crime[4] for the purpose of charging it falsely upon me, as I hope fully to make you understand. They have, under this pretence, arrayed themselves

2. Presumably the brother of Bothwell's wife, Jean Gordon, who in turn is presumably the person referred to in the following sentence.
3. Prevent.
4. Lover.
5. Possibly "reade"—in which case the meaning is "I have not read over a word."
6. Poor.
7. Words torn off the English manuscript here; reading inferred from the Scottish translation.
8. She apologizes for having had to use paper already used for memoranda.
9. Again words torn from the English manuscript are inferred from the Scottish translation. The latter continues with what seem to be the memoranda—to herself or perhaps to the bearer of the letter—mentioned earlier: "Remember zow [you] of the purpois of the Lady Reres. Of the Inglismen. Of his mother. Of the Erle of Argyle. Of the Erle Bothwell. Of the ludgeing [lodging]

in Edinburgh."
1. This letter (translated from the French by Agnes Strickland) was written just after Mary, in flight from her Scottish enemies, made her fateful crossing into England. Its account of her troubles is, though not exaggerated, inevitably one-sided. In 1565, Mary's ill-advised marriage to her cousin Lord Darnley had upset the power structure of the nation's factious and violent nobility. A group of nobles rebelled against her, led by Mary's illegitimate half-brother James Stewart, earl of Moray, who had previously been her key supporter and adviser.
2. Fellow queen.
3. The servant was David Rizzio, Mary's secretary and confidant. At the time of his murder, Mary was six months pregnant with her only child, the future King James VI. She omits the fact that Darnley was involved in the murder.
4. The murder of Darnley.

against me, accusing me of being ill-advised, and pretending a desire of seeing me delivered from bad counsels, in order to point out to me the things that required reformation. I, feeling myself innocent, and desirous to avoid the shedding of blood, placed myself in their hands, wishing to reform what was amiss.[5] They immediately seized and imprisoned me. When I upbraided them with a breach of their promise, and requested to be informed why I was thus treated, they all absented themselves. I demanded to be heard in council, which was refused me. In short, they have kept me without any servants, except two women, a cook, and a surgeon; and they have threatened to kill me, if I did not sign an abdication of my crown, which the fear of immediate death caused me to do,[6] as I have since proved before the whole of the nobility, of which I hope to afford you evidence.

After this, they again laid hold of me in parliament, without saying why, and without hearing me; forbidding, at the same time, every advocate to plead for me; and, compelling the rest to acquiesce in their unjust usurpation of my rights, they have robbed me of everything I had in the world, not permitting me either to write or to speak, in order that I might not contradict their false inventions.

At last, it pleased God to deliver me,[7] when they thought of putting me to death, that they might make more sure of their power, though I repeatedly offered to answer any thing they had to say to me, and to join them in the punishment of those who should be guilty of any crime. In short, it pleased God to deliver me, to the great content of all my subjects, except Moray, Morton, the Humes, Glencairn, Mar, and Sempill, to whom, after that my whole nobility was come from all parts, I sent to say that, notwithstanding their ingratitude and unjust cruelty employed against me, I was willing to invite them to return to their duty, and to offer them security of their lives and estates, and to hold a parliament for the purpose of reforming every thing. I sent twice. They seized and imprisoned my messengers, and made proclamation, declaring traitors all those who should assist me, and guilty of that odious crime. I demanded that they should name one of them, and I would give him up, and begged them, at the same time, to deliver to me such as should be named to them. They seized upon my officer and my proclamation. I sent to demand a safe-conduct for my Lord Boyd, in order to treat of an accommodation, not wishing, as far as I might be concerned, for any effusion of blood. They refused, saying that those who had not been true to their regent and to my son, whom they denominate king, should leave me and put themselves at their disposal, a thing at which the whole nobility were greatly offended.

Seeing, therefore, that they were only a few individuals, and that my nobility were more attached to me than ever, I was in hope that, in course of time, and under your favor, they would be gradually reduced; and, seeing that they said they would either retake me or all die, I proceeded toward Dumbarton,[8]

5. Unhappy about the elevation of Bothwell to the position of Mary's consort (she had married him three months after Darnley's murder, in which he was well known to have been the principal conspirator), the nobles brought an army against the royal couple in June 1567. With their own forces melting away, Bothwell escaped, and Mary surrendered herself to the nobles.

6. In late July. Her infant son was then crowned king on July 29, in a Protestant church. Moray became regent.

7. Mary escaped from captivity on May 2, 1568.

8. In the west of Scotland. The royal army passed near Glasgow, in a deliberate attempt to draw Moray's army, which was smaller, into battle.

passing at the distance of two miles from them, my nobility accompanying me, marching in order of battle between them and me; which they seeing, sallied forth, and came to cut off my way and take me. My people seeing this, and moved by that extreme malice of my enemies, with a view to check their progress, encountered them without order, so that, though they were twice their number, their sudden advance caused them so great a disadvantage that God permitted them to be discomfited, and several killed and taken; some of them were cruelly put to death when taken on their retreat. The pursuit was immediately interrupted, in order to take me on my way to Dumbarton; they stationed people in every direction, either to kill or take me. But God through his infinite goodness has preserved me, and I escaped to my Lord Herries's,[9] who, as well as other gentlemen, have come with me into your country,[1] being assured that, hearing the cruelty of my enemies, and how they have treated me, you will, conformably to your kind disposition and the confidence I have in you, not only receive me for the safety of my life but also aid and assist me in my just quarrel; and I shall solicit other princes to do the same. I entreat you to send to fetch me as soon as you possibly can,[2] for I am in a pitiable condition, not only for a queen, but for a gentlewoman; for I have nothing in the world but what I had on my person when I made my escape, traveling across the country the first day, and not having since ever ventured to proceed except in the night, as I hope to declare before you, if it pleases you to have pity, as I trust you will, upon my extreme misfortune; of which I will forbear complaining, in order not to importune you, and pray to God that he may give to you a happy state of health and long life, and to me patience, and that consolation which I expect to receive from you, to whom I present my humble commendations. From Workington, the 17th of May.

> Your most faithful and affectionate good
> sister, and cousin, and escaped prisoner,
> Mary R.[3]

1568   1844

From Narrative of the Execution of the Queen of Scots. In a Letter to the Right Honorable Sir William Cecil[1]

It may please your lordship to be advertised[2] that, according as your honor gave me in command, I have here set down in writing the true order and manner of the execution of the Lady Mary, late queen of Scots, the 8th of February last, in the great hall within the castle of Fotheringhay,[3] together

---

9. Herries was a magnate of southwestern Scotland, which remained strongly Catholic.
1. Crossing the Solway Firth in a fishing boat, Mary and twenty supporters landed in the Cumberland port of Workington on May 16, 1568.
2. Elizabeth never granted Mary an audience; two days after arriving in England, she was conducted to Carlisle Castle, where her nineteen years of English captivity began.
3. A royal signature: "R."="Regina" (Latin for "Queen").

1. Elizabeth's lord high treasurer and principal minister. The author of the letter (of which there are various versions extant) was Robert Wingfield, Cecil's nephew, sent by him to report on the execution.
2. Informed.
3. In Northamptonshire. Mary had been moved to Fotheringhay in September 1586 and was there tried and convicted of treason against Elizabeth (though she was not Elizabeth's subject).

with relation of all such speeches and actions spoken and done by the said queen or any others, and all other circumstances and proceedings concerning the same, from and after the delivery of the said Scottish queen to Thomas Andrews, Esquire, high sheriff for Her Majesty's county of Northampton, unto the end of the said execution: as followeth.

It being certified the 6th of February last to the said queen, by the right honorable the earl of Kent, the earl of Shrewsbury, and also by Sir Amyas Paulet and Sir Drue Drury, her governors,[4] that she was to prepare herself to die the 8th of February next, she seemed not [to] be in any terror, for aught that appeared by any her outward gesture or behavior (other than marveling she should die), but rather with smiling cheer and pleasing countenance digested and accepted the said admonition of preparation to her (as she said) unexpected execution, saying that her death should be welcome unto her, seeing Her Majesty was so resolved, and that that soul were too too far unworthy the fruition of joys of heaven forever, whose body would not in this world be content to endure the stroke of the executioner for a moment. And that spoken, she wept bitterly and became silent.

The said 8th day of February being come, and time and place appointed for the execution, the said queen, being of stature tall, of body corpulent, round-shouldered, her face fat and broad, double-chinned, and hazel-eyed, her borrowed hair auburn, her attire was this. On her head she had a dressing of lawn edged with bone lace,[5] a pomander chain[6] and an *Angus Dei* about her neck,[7] a crucifix in her hand, a pair of beads at her girdle,[8] with a silver cross at the end of them. A veil of lawn fastened to her caul,[9] bowed out with wire and edged round about with bone lace. Her gown was of black satin painted, with a train and long sleeves to the ground, set with acorn buttons of jet trimmed with pearl, and short sleeves of satin black cut,[1] with a pair of sleeves of purple velvet whole under them. Her kirtle[2] whole, of figured black satin, and her petticoat skirts of crimson velvet, her shoes of Spanish leather with the rough side outward, a pair of green silk garters, her nether stockings[3] worsted colored watchet,[4] clocked[5] with silver, and edged on the tops with silver, and next her leg a pair of jersey[6] hose, white, etc. Thus apparelled, she departed her chamber, and willingly bended her steps towards the place of execution.

As the commissioners and divers other knights were meeting the queen coming forth, one of her servants, called Melvin,[7] kneeling on his knees to his queen and mistress, wringing his hands and shedding tears, used these words unto her: "Ah, Madam, unhappy me: what man on earth was ever before the messenger of so important sorrow and heaviness as I shall be,

---

4. Keepers. The earls of Kent and Shrewsbury were sent by the royal council to oversee the execution. Paulet had been Mary's principal custodian since January 1585; Drury joined him in his charge in November 1586.
5. Lace that is woven with bobbins made of bone. "Lawn": fine linen.
6. Pomander is a mixture of aromatic substances; a small bag of it was sometimes suspended from a necklace.
7. A medallion bearing the figure of a lamb: an emblem of Christ. From *"Agnus Dei"* ("Lamb of God"; Latin), a part of the Mass beginning with those words.

8. Belt. "Beads": rosary beads.
9. Close-fitting cap.
1. Slashed, to reveal the contrasting-colored sleeves beneath.
2. Outer petticoat.
3. "Nether stockings" means simply "stockings." ("Nether" = "of the legs.")
4. Light blue.
5. Embroidered.
6. Worsted.
7. Sir Andrew Melville.

when I report that my good and gracious queen and mistress is beheaded in England?" This said, tears prevented him of further speaking. Whereupon the said queen, pouring forth her dying tears, thus answered him: "My good servant, cease to lament, for thou hast cause rather to joy than to mourn. For now shalt thou see Mary Stuart's troubles receive their long-expected end and determination. For know (said she), good servant, all the world is but vanity, and subject still to more sorrow than a whole ocean of tears can bewail. But I pray thee (said she), carry this message from me, that I die a true woman to my religion, and like a true queen of Scotland and France. But God forgive them (said she) that have long desired my end and thirsted for my blood, as the hart doth for the water brooks. Oh God (said she), thou that art the author of truth, and truth itself, knowest the inward chamber of my thought, how that I was ever willing that England and Scotland should be united together. Well (said she), commend me to my son, and tell him that I have not done anything prejudicial to the state and kingdom of Scotland"; and so resolving[8] herself again into tears, said, "Good Melvin, farewell"; and with weeping eyes and her cheeks all besprinkled with tears as they were, kissed him, saying once again, "Farewell, good Melvin, and pray for thy mistress and queen."

And then she turned herself unto the lords, and told them she had certain requests to make unto them. One was, for certain money to be paid to Curle, her servant. Sir Amyas Paulet, knowing of that money, answered to this effect, "it should." Next, that her poor servants might have that with quietness[9] which she had given them by her will, and that they might be favorably entreated,[1] and to send them safely into their countries. "To this (said she) I conjure[2] you." Last, that it would please the lords to permit her poor distressed servants to be present about her at her death, that their eyes and hearts may see and witness how patiently their queen and mistress would endure her execution, and so make relation, when they came into their country, that she died a true constant Catholic to her religion. Then the earl of Kent did answer thus: "Madam, that which you have desired cannot conveniently be granted. For if it should, it were to be feared lest some of them, with speeches or other behavior, would both be grievous to Your Grace and troublesome and unpleasing to us and our company, whereof we have had some experience. For if such an access might be allowed, they would not stick to put some superstitious trumpery in practice, and if it were but dipping their handkerchiefs in Your Grace's blood, whereof it were very unmeet[3] for us to give allowance."

"My lord," said the queen of Scots, "I will give my word, although it be but dead, that they shall not deserve any blame in any the actions you have named. But alas, poor souls, it would do them good to bid their mistress farewell; and I hope your mistress" (meaning the queen), "being a maiden queen, will vouchsafe in regard of[4] womanhood that I shall have some of my own people about me at my death: and I know Her Majesty hath not given

---

8. Dissolving.
9. Without contestation.
1. Treated.

2. Earnestly entreat.
3. Unfitting.
4. For the sake of.

you any such strait[5] charge or commission but that you might grant me a request of far greater courtesy than this is, if I were a woman of far meaner calling[6] than the queen of Scots." And then, perceiving that she could not obtain her request without some difficulty, burst out into tears, saying, "I am cousin to your queen, and descended from the blood royal of Henry the Seventh, and a married queen of France, and an anointed queen of Scotland." Then, upon great consultation had betwixt the two earls and the others in commission, it was granted to her what she instantly[7] before earnestly entreated, and desired her to make choice of six of her best-beloved men and women. Then of her men she chose Melvin, her apothecary, her surgeon, and one old man more;[8] and of her women, those two which did lie in her chamber. Then, with an unappalled countenance, without any terror of the place, the persons, or the preparations, she came out of the entry into the hall, stepped up to the scaffold, being two foot high and twelve foot broad, with rails round about, hanged and covered with black, with a low stool, long fair cushion, and a block covered also with black. The stool brought her, she sat down. The earl of Kent stood on the right hand, the earl of Shrewsbury on the other, other knights and gentlemen stood about the rails. The commission for her execution was read (after silence made) by Mr. Beale, clerk of the council;[9] which done, the people with a loud voice said, "God save the Queen!" During the reading of this commission, the said queen was very silent, listening unto it with so careless a regard as if it had not concerned her at all, nay, rather with so merry and cheerful a countenance as if it had been a pardon from Her Majesty for her life; and withal[1] used such a strangeness in her words as if she had not known any of the assembly, nor had been anything seen[2] in the English tongue.

Then Mr. Doctor Fletcher, dean of Peterborough,[3] standing directly before her without[4] the rails, bending his body with great reverence, uttered the exhortation following:

"Madam, the Queen's Most Excellent Majesty (whom God preserve long to reign over us), having (notwithstanding this preparation for the execution of justice justly to be done upon you for your many trespasses against her sacred person, state, and government) a tender care over your soul, which presently departing out of your body must either be separated in the true faith in Christ or perish forever, doth for Jesus Christ offer unto you the comfortable[5] promises of God, wherein I beseech Your Grace, even in the bowels of Jesus Christ,[6] to consider these three things:

"First, your state past, and transitory glory;

"Secondly, your condition present, of death;

"Thirdly, your estate to come, either in everlasting happiness or perpetual infelicity.

---

5. Strict.
6. Far lower station.
7. Importunely.
8. Her aged porter, Didier.
9. I.e., the royal council.
1. As well.
2. At all fluent.

3. I.e., of the Anglican cathedral there.
4. Outside.
5. Comforting, reassuring.
6. "In the bowels of Jesus Christ": in the name of Christ's pity. The bowels were regarded as the seat of pity and compassion.

"For the first, let me speak to Your Grace with David the King: Forget, Madam, yourself, and your own people, and your father's house; forget your natural birth, your regal and princely dignity: so shall the King of Kings have pleasure in your spiritual beauty, etc.[7]

"Madam, even now, Madam, doth God Almighty open you a door into a heavenly kingdom; shut not therefore this passage by the hardening of your heart, and grieve not the Spirit of God, which may seal your hope to a day of redemption."

The queen three or four times said unto him, "Mr. Dean, trouble not yourself nor me: for know that I am settled in the ancient Catholic and Roman religion, and in defense thereof, by God's grace, I mind to spend my blood."

Then said Mr. Dean, "Madam, change your opinion, and repent you of your former wickedness. Settle your faith only upon this ground, that in Christ Jesus you hope to be saved." She answered again and again, with great earnestness, "Good Mr. Dean, trouble yourself not anymore about this matter, for I was born in this religion, have lived in this religion, and am resolved to die in this religion."

Then the earls, when they saw how far uncomfortable[8] she was to hear Mr. Dean's good exhortation, said, "Madam, we will pray for Your Grace with Mr. Dean, that you may have your mind lightened with the true knowledge of God and his word."

"My lords," answered the queen, "if you will pray with me, I will even from my heart thank you, and think myself greatly favored by you; but to join in prayer with you in your manner, who are not of one[9] religion with me, it were a sin, and I will not."

Then the lords called Mr. Dean again, and bade him say on, or what he thought good else. The dean kneeled and prayed. * * *[1]

All the assembly, save the queen and her servants, said the prayer after Mr. Dean as he spake it, during which prayer the queen sat upon her stool, having her *Agnus Dei*, crucifix, beads, and an office[2] in Latin. Thus furnished with superstitious trumpery, not regarding what Mr. Dean said, she began very fastly[3] with tears and a loud voice to pray in Latin, and in the midst of her prayers, with overmuch weeping and mourning, slipped off her stool, and kneeling presently said diverse other Latin prayers. Then she rose, and kneeled down again, praying in English for Christ's afflicted church, an end of her troubles, for her son, and for the Queen's Majesty, to God for forgiveness of the sins of them in this island: she forgave her enemies with all her heart, that had long sought her blood. This done, she desired all saints to make intercession for her to the Savior of the World, Jesus Christ. Then she began to kiss her crucifix and to cross herself, saying these words: "Even as thy arms, oh Jesu Christ, were spread here upon the cross, so receive me into the arms of mercy." Then the two executioners kneeled down unto her, desiring her to forgive them her death. She answered, "I forgive you with all

---

7. The dean paraphrases Psalms 45.10–11, a passage addressed to the bride of a king: "forget also thine own people, and thy father's house; So shall the king greatly desire thy beauty."
8. Unwilling.
9. The same.

1. The dean prays at considerable length, beseeching God to wash away Mary's "blindness and ignorance of heavenly things."
2. Prayer book.
3. Steadfastly.

my heart. For I hope this death shall give an end to all my troubles." They, with her two women helping, began to disrobe her, and then she laid the crucifix upon the stool. One of the executioners took from her neck the *Agnus Dei*, and she laid hold of it, saying she would give it to one of her women, and, withal, told the executioner that he should have money for it.[4] Then they took off her chain. She made herself unready[5] with a kind of gladness, and, smiling, putting on a pair of sleeves with her own hands, which the two executioners before had rudely[6] put off, and with such speed as if she had longed to be gone out of the world.

During the disrobing of this queen, she never altered her countenance, but smiling said she never had such grooms before to make her unready, nor ever did put off her clothes before such a company. At length, unattired and unapparelled to her petticoat and kirtle, the two women burst out into a great and pitiful shrieking, crying, and lamentation, crossed themselves, and prayed in Latin. The queen turned towards them: "Ne criez vous; j'ai promis pour vous";[7] and so crossed and kissed them, and bade them pray for her.

Then with a smiling countenance she turned to her menservants, Melvin and the rest, crossed them, bade them fare well, and pray for her to the last.

One of the women having a Corpus Christi cloth,[8] lapped[9] it up three-corner-wise and kissed it, and put it over the face of her queen, and pinned it fast upon the caul of her head. Then the two women departed. The queen kneeled down upon the cushion resolutely, and without any token of fear of death, said aloud in Latin the Psalm *"In te, Domine, confido."*[1] Then, groping for the block, she laid down her head, putting her chain over her back with both her hands, which, holding there still,[2] had been cut off, had they not been espied.

Then she laid herself upon the block most quietly, and stretching out her arms and legs cried out: *"In manus tuas, Domine, commendo spiritum meum,"*[3] three or four times.

At last, while one of the executioners held her straitly[4] with one of his hands, the other gave two strokes with an axe before he did cut off her head, and yet left a little gristle behind.

She made very small noise, no part stirred from the place where she lay. The executioners lifted up the head, and bade God save the Queen. Then her dressing of lawn fell from her head,[5] which appeared as gray as if she had been threescore and ten years old,[6] polled[7] very short. Her face much altered, her lips stirred up and down almost a quarter of an hour after her head was cut off. Then said Mr. Dean: "So perish all the Queen's enemies!" The earl of

---

4. A condemned person's adornments were normally perquisites of the executioner.
5. Undressed.
6. Roughly.
7. "Don't make an outcry; I promised you wouldn't."
8. The veil (also known as the "pyx cloth") that covered the vessel holding the consecrated Host the Communion. "Corpus Christi": the body of Christ (Latin).
9. Folded.

1. Psalms 10 (Vulgate), 11 (King James): "In the Lord put I my trust."
2. I.e., if her hands had remained there.
3. Luke 13.46: "Father, into thy hands I commend my spirit": the words of Christ on the Cross.
4. Tightly.
5. That is, her headcovering and auburn wig came off in the executioner's hand.
6. She was actually forty-four.
7. Cut.

The execution of Mary, Queen of Scots. Though this watercolor image was not painted until some years after Mary's execution, it reflects eyewitness accounts. The minister depicted is likely Dr. Richard Fletcher, dean of Peterborough, who was so nervous that he stammered and never actually delivered his sermon because he was interrupted by Mary herself. Mary wears a Corpus Christi cloth around her head as a blindfold. On the stool beside her is a prayer book, and in her hands a crucifix. Her gentlewomen stand weeping to the left of the scaffold, which is covered in black cloth. On the far left of the image is a bonfire, for burning any cloth or other items with Mary's blood on them so that they could not serve as Catholic relics after her death.

Kent came to the dead body, and with a loud voice said, "Such end happen to all the Queen's and Gospel's enemies." One of the executioners, plucking off her garters, espied her little dog, which was crept under her clothes, which would not be gotten forth but with force, and afterwards would not depart from the dead corpse, but came and laid between her head and shoulders: a thing much noted. The dog, imbrued in her blood, was carried away and washed, as all things else were that had any blood, save those things which were burned. The executioners were sent away with money for their fees, not having any one thing that belonged unto her. Afterwards everyone was commanded forth of the hall, saving[8] the sheriff and his men, who carried her up into a great chamber made ready for the surgeons to embalm her; and there she was embalmed.

And thus I hope (my very good lord) I have certifieth Your Honor of all actions, matters, and circumstances as did proceed from her or any other at her death: wherein I dare promise unto your good lordship (if not in some better or worse words than were spoken I am somewhat mistaken), in matter I have not in any whit offended.[9] Howbeit,[1] I will not so justify my duty

---

8. Except. "Forth of": out of.
9. I.e., though I may not have gotten the speeches word-for-word, I promise that my account is completely accurate in substance.
1. However.

herein but that[2] many things might well have been omitted, as not worthy noting. Yet because it is your lordship's fault to desire to know all, and so I have certified all, it is an offense pardonable. So, resting at Your Honor's further commandment, I take my leave this 11th of February, 1587.

Your Honor's in all humble service to command,
R. W.

1587   1843

2. I.e., I will concede that.

ELIZABETH I

Elizabeth I (1533–1603), queen of England from 1558 to her death, set her mark indelibly on the age that has come to bear her name. Endowed with intelligence, courage, eloquence, and a talent for self-display, she managed to survive and flourish in a world that would easily have crushed a weaker person. Her birth was a disappointment to her father, Henry VIII, who had hoped for a male heir to the throne, and her prospects were further dimmed when her mother, Anne Boleyn, was executed a few years later on charges of adultery and treason. By an act of Parliament she was ruled illegitimate. At six years old, observers noted, Elizabeth had as much gravity as if she had been forty.

Under distinguished tutors, including the Protestant humanist Roger Ascham, the young princess received a rigorous education, with training in classical and modern languages, history, rhetoric, theology, and moral philosophy. Her own religious orientation was also Protestant, which put her in great danger during the reign of her Catholic older half-sister, Mary. Imprisoned in the Tower of London, interrogated and constantly spied upon, Elizabeth steadfastly professed innocence, loyalty, and a pious abhorrence of heresy. Upon Mary's death, she ascended the throne and quickly made clear that the official religion of the land would be Protestantism.

When she came to the throne, at twenty-five, speculation about a suitable match, already widespread, intensified. It remained for decades at a fever pitch, for the stakes were high. If Elizabeth died childless, the Tudor line would come to an end. The nearest heir was her cousin Mary, Queen of Scots, a Catholic whose claim was supported by France and by the papacy, and whose penchant for sexual and political intrigue soon confirmed the worst fears of English Protestants. The obvious way to avert the nightmare was for Elizabeth to marry and produce an heir, and the pressure on her to do so was intense.

More than the royal succession hinged on the question of the queen's marriage; Elizabeth's perceived eligibility was a vital factor in the complex machinations of international diplomacy. A dynastic marriage between the queen of England and a foreign ruler could forge an alliance sufficient to alter the balance of power in Europe. The English court hosted a steady stream of ambassadors from kings and princelings eager to win the hand of the royal maiden, and Elizabeth played her romantic part with exemplary skill, sighing and spinning the negotiations out for months and even years. Most probably, she never meant to marry any of her numerous foreign (and domestic) suitors. "She is determined," a shrewd Spanish observer wrote to his king, at the moment that Elizabeth ascended to the throne, "to be governed by no one." Marriage would have meant the end of her independence as well as the end of the complex diplomatic game by which she played off one power against another. One day she would seem to be on the verge of accepting a proposal; the next, she would vow never to forsake her virginity. "She is a princess," the French ambassador remarked, "who can act any part she pleases." Ultimately she refused all offers and declared repeatedly that she was wedded to her country.

In the face of deep skepticism about the ability of any woman to rule, Elizabeth strategically blended imperiousness with an elaborate cult of love. Quickly making it clear that she would not be a figurehead, she gathered around her an able group of advisers, but she held firmly to the reins of power, subtly manipulating factional disputes, conducting diplomacy, and negotiating with an often contentious Parliament. Her courtiers and advisers, on their knees, approached the queen, glittering in jewels and gorgeous gowns, and addressed her in extravagant terms that conjoined romantic passion and religious veneration. Artists and poets celebrated her in mythological guise—as Diana, the chaste goddess of the moon; Astraea, the goddess of justice; Gloriana, the queen of the fairies. Though she could suddenly veer, whenever she chose, toward bluntness and anger, Elizabeth often contrived to transform the language of politics into the language of love. "We all loved her," her godson John Harington wrote, "for she said she loved us."

Throughout her life, Elizabeth took pride in her command of languages (she spoke fluent French and Italian and read Latin and Greek) and in her felicity of expression. Her own writing includes carefully crafted letters and speeches on several state occasions; a number of prayers; prose and verse translations, including works of Horace, Seneca, Plutarch, Boethius, Calvin, and the French Protestant Queen Margaret of Navarre; and a few original poems. The original poems known to be hers deal with actual events in her life. They show her to have been an exceptionally agile, poised, and self-conscious writer, a gifted role-player fully in control of the rhetorical as well as political situation in which she found herself. The texts printed here, occasionally altered in light of variant versions, are from *Elizabeth I: Collected Works*, ed. Leah Marcus, Janel Mueller, and Mary Beth Rose (2000).*

Verses Written with a Diamond

In her imprisonment at Woodstock, these verses she wrote with her diamond in a glass window:[1]

> Much suspected by[2] me,
> Nothing proved can be.
>   Quod[3] Elizabeth the prisoner

1554–55   1563

---

* For a painting of the queen in procession, see the color insert in this volume.
1. This is the heading given to the verses in John Foxe's *Acts and Monuments*. After the insurrection of January 1554 against Mary I, Elizabeth was imprisoned in the Tower of London. Extensive interrogation and investigation yielded against her no firm evidence of treason, but she was transferred to the royal manor at Woodstock in Oxfordshire and held there in close custody for a year.
2. About.
3. Quoth, said.

From The Passage of Our Most Dread Sovereign Lady Queen Elizabeth through the City of London to Westminster on the Day before Her Coronation[1]

* * * Her grace, by holding up her hands and merry countenance to such as stood far off, and most tender and gentle language to those that stood nigh to her grace, did declare herself no less thankfully to receive her people's goodwill than they lovingly offered it unto her. To all that wished her grace well she gave hearty thanks, and to such as bade God save her grace she said again,[2] God save them all, and thanked them with all her heart. So that on either side there was nothing but gladness, nothing but prayer, nothing but comfort. The queen's majesty rejoiced marvelously to see it so exceedingly showed toward her grace which all good princes have ever desired: I mean, so earnest love of subjects, so evidently declared even to her grace's own person being carried in the midst of them. The people, again, were wonderfully ravished with welcoming answers and gestures of their princess, like to the which they had before tried at her first coming to the Tower from Hatfield.[3] This her grace's loving behavior, preconceived in the people's heads, upon these considerations was thoroughly confirmed, and indeed implanted a wonderful hope in them touching her worthy government in the rest of her reign. For in all her passage she did not only show her most gracious love toward the people in general, but also privately. If the baser personages had either offered her grace any flowers or such like as a signification of their goodwill, or moved to her any suit, she most gently, to the common rejoicing of all the lookers-on and private comfort of the party, stayed her chariot[4] and heard their requests. So that if a man should say well, he could not better term the City of London that time than a stage wherein was showed the wonderful spectacle of a noble-hearted princess toward her most loving people and the people's exceeding comfort in beholding so worthy a sovereign and hearing so princelike a voice. * * *

Out at the windows and penthouses of every house did hang a number of rich and costly banners and streamers, till her grace came to the upper end of Cheap.[5] And there, by appointment, the right worshipful Master Ranulph Cholmley, recorder[6] of the City, presented to the queen's majesty a purse of crimson satin richly wrought with gold, wherein the City gave unto the queen's majesty a thousand marks[7] in gold, as Master Recorder did declare briefly unto the queen's majesty, whose words tended to this end: that the lord mayor, his brethren, and commonality of the City, to declare their

---

1. By Richard Mulcaster (ca. 1530–1611), who became a well-known authority on the education of children. Elizabeth had succeeded to the throne upon the death of Mary I on November 17, 1558, but her coronation did not take place until January 15, 1559. By long-established custom, the ceremonies began the day before the coronation itself, with the ruler being conducted across the city in procession from the Tower of London to Westminster. See the account of Mary's coronation procession on p. 196.
2. I.e., said in reply.
3. Elizabeth had set out from the royal manor at Hatfield (in Hertfordshire) to London on November 23.
4. Wearing a robe made of gold and silver cloth, trimmed with ermine, and overlaid with gold lace, Elizabeth rode in a litter trimmed to the ground with gold damask.
5. Also known as Cheapside or Westcheap: the chief market street in London. (The name derives from the Old English word for "market.")
6. Senior law officer.
7. The mark was valued at two-thirds of a pound sterling, and the pound was worth far more than at present—so this was a very large gift.

gladness and goodwill towards the queen's majesty, did present her grace with that gold, desiring her grace to continue their good and gracious queen and not to esteem the value of the gift, but the mind of the givers. The queen's majesty with both her hands took the purse and answered to him again marvelous pithily, and so pithily that the standers-by, as they embraced entirely her gracious answer, so they marveled at the couching thereof, which was in words, truly reported these:

> I thank my lord mayor, his brethren, and you all. And whereas your request is that I should continue your good lady and queen, be ye ensured that I will be as good unto you as ever queen was to her people. No will in me can lack, neither do I trust shall there lack any power. And persuade yourselves that for the safety and quietness of you all I will not spare, if need be, to spend my blood. God thank you all.

Which answer of so noble an hearted princess, if it moved a marvelous shout and rejoicing, it is nothing to be marveled at, since both the heartiness thereof was so wonderful, and the words so jointly[8] knit.

But because princes be set in their seat by God's appointing and therefore they must first and chiefly tender[9] the glory of Him from whom their glory issueth, it is to be noted in her grace that forsomuch as God hath so wonderfully placed her in the seat of government over this realm, she in all doings doth show herself most mindful of His goodness and mercy showed unto her. And amongst all other, two principal signs thereof were noted in this passage. First in the Tower, where her grace, before she entered her chariot, lifted up her eyes to heaven and said:

> O Lord, almighty and everlasting God, I give Thee most hearty thanks that Thou hast been so merciful unto me as to spare me to behold this joyful day. And I acknowledge that Thou hast dealt as wonderfully and as mercifully with me as Thou didst with Thy true and faithful servant Daniel, Thy prophet, whom Thou deliveredst out of the den from the cruelty of the greedy and raging lions.[1] Even so was I overwhelmed and only by Thee delivered. To Thee (therefore) only be thanks, honor, and praise forever, amen.

The second was the receiving of the Bible at the Little Conduit[2] in Cheap. For when her grace had learned that the Bible in English[3] should there be offered, she thanked the City therefor, promised the reading thereof most diligently, and incontinent[4] commanded that it should be brought. At the receipt whereof, how reverently did she with both her hands take it, kiss it, and lay it upon her breast, to the great comfort of the lookers-on! God will undoubtedly preserve so worthy a prince, which at His honor so reverently taketh her beginning. For this saying is true and written in the book of truth: he that first seeketh the kingdom of God shall have all other things cast unto him.[5]

---

8. Concordantly.
9. Have regard to.
1. Daniel 6.16–23.
2. The smaller of two lead pipe water conduits situated at the west end of Cheap Street.

3. In contrast to the Latin Bibles of the restored Catholicism of Mary's reign.
4. Immediately.
5. Matthew 6.33.

Now, therefore, all English hearts and her natural people must needs praise God's mercy, which hath sent them so worthy a prince, and pray for her grace's long continuance amongst us.

1559   1559

Speech to the House of Commons, January 28, 1563[1]

Williams,[2] I have heard by you the common request of my Commons, which I may well term (methinketh) the whole realm, because they give, as I have heard, in all these matters of Parliament their common consent to such as be here assembled. The weight and greatness of this matter might cause in me, being a woman wanting both wit[3] and memory, some fear to speak and bashfulness besides, a thing appropriate to my sex. But yet the princely seat and kingly throne wherein God (though unworthy) hath constituted me, maketh these two causes to seem little in mine eyes, though grievous perhaps to your ears, and boldeneth me to say somewhat in this matter, which I mean only to touch but not presently to answer. For this so great a demand[4] needeth both great and grave advice. I read of a philosopher whose deeds upon this occasion I remember better than his name[5] who always when he was required to give answer in any hard question of school points would rehearse over his alphabet before he would proceed to any further answer therein, not for that he could not presently have answered, but have his wit the riper and better sharpened to answer the matter withal.[6] If he, a common man, but[7] in matters of school took such delay the better to show his eloquent tale, great cause may justly move me in this, so great a matter touching the benefits of this realm and the safety of you all, to defer mine answer till some other time, wherein I assure you the consideration of my own safety (although I thank you for the great care that you seem to have thereof) shall be little in comparison of that great regard that I mean to have of the safety and surety of you all. And although God of late seemed to touch me rather like one that He chastised than one that He punished, and though death possessed almost every joint of me,[8] so as I wished then that the feeble thread of life, which lasted (methought) all too long, might by Clotho's hand[9] have quietly been cut off, yet desired I not then life (as I have some witnesses here) so much for mine own safety, as for yours. For I know that in exchanging of this reign I should have enjoyed a better reign where residence is perpetual.

---

1. Because a secure royal succession depended on Elizabeth's marrying and producing an heir, Parliament had been concerned about her single state from the beginning of her reign. The Commons raised the matter with her (not for the first time) in January 1563; the speech printed here is a later, written version of her extemporaneous response.
2. Thomas Williams, speaker of the Parliament.
3. Intellect.
4. Question.

5. According to the *Moral Essays* of Plutarch (ca. 46–ca. 120 C.E.), the philosopher was Athenodorus.
6. By that means.
7. Merely.
8. Elizabeth had nearly died of smallpox the past October.
9. Clotho is one of the three Fates of classical mythology, who spin and eventually cut the thread of each individual life.

There needs no boding of my bane.[1] I know now as well as I did before that I am mortal. I know also that I must seek to discharge myself of that great burden that God hath laid upon me; for of them to whom much is committed, much is required.[2] Think not that I, that in other matters have had convenient[3] care of you all, will in this matter touching the safety of myself and you all be careless. For I know that this matter toucheth me much nearer than it doth you all, who if the worst happen can lose but your bodies. But if I take not that convenient care that it behoveth me to have therein, I hazard to lose both body and soul. And though I am determined in this so great and weighty a matter to defer mine answer till some other time because I will not in so deep a matter wade with so shallow a wit, yet have I thought good to use these few words, as well to show you that I am neither careless nor unmindful of your safety in this case, as I trust you likewise do not forget that by me you were delivered whilst you were hanging on the bough ready to fall into the mud—yea, to be drowned in the dung; neither[4] yet the promise which you have here made concerning your duties and due obedience, wherewith, I assure you, I mean to charge[5] you, as, further, to let you understand that I neither mislike any of your requests herein, nor the great care that you seem to have of the surety and safety of yourselves in this matter.

Lastly, because I will discharge[6] some restless heads in whose brains the needless hammers beat with vain judgment that I should mislike this their petition, I say that of the matter and sum thereof I like and allow very well. As to the circumstances, if any be, I mean upon further advice further to answer. And so I assure you all that though after my death you may have many stepdames, yet shall you never have any a more mother than I mean to be unto you all.

1563   1921

From A Speech to a Joint Delegation of Lords and Commons, November 5, 1566[1]

* * * Was I not born in the realm? Were my parents born in any foreign country? Is there any cause I should alienate myself from being careful over this country? Is not my kingdom here? Whom have I oppressed? Whom have I enriched to others' harm? What turmoil have I made in this commonwealth, that I should be suspected to have no regard to the same? How have

1. Prognosticating of my death.
2. Luke 12.48.
3. Befitting.
4. Nor. "Mud . . . dung": harsh characterizations of the Roman Catholicism that Mary I had been restoring to England.
5. Exhort.
6. Disabuse.
1. The birth on June 19, 1566, of a son—James— to Mary, Queen of Scots, imparted new urgency to the concern about Elizabeth's unmarried state.

Mary was Elizabeth's second cousin and, in the absence of any child of Elizabeth's own, had a strong claim to be her heir; Mary's male child would have an even stronger one. On November 5, a delegation of sixty members of the Lords and Commons met with Elizabeth, to urge her to marry and also to establish formally the line of succession. After the meeting, a member of the delegation wrote down Elizabeth's impromptu response.

I governed since my reign? I will be tried by envy itself.[2] I need not to use many words, for my deeds do try me.

Well, the matter whereof they[3] would have made their petition, as I am informed, consisteth in two points: in my marriage and in the limitation of the succession of the crown, wherein my marriage was first placed as for manner[4] sake. I did send them answer by my Council I would marry, although of mine own disposition I was not inclined thereunto. But that was not accepted nor credited, although spoken by their prince. And yet I used so many words that I could say no more. And were it not now I had spoken those words, I would never speak them again. I will never break the word of a prince spoken in public place, for my honor[5] sake. And therefore I say again I will marry as soon as I can conveniently, if God take not him away with whom I mind to marry, or myself, or else some other great let[6] happen. I can say no more except[7] the party were present. And I hope to have children; otherwise I would never marry. A strange order of petitioners, that will make a request and cannot be otherwise ascertained[8] but by the prince's word, and yet will not believe it when it is spoken! But they, I think, that moveth the same will be as ready to mislike him with whom I shall marry as they are now to move it, and then it will appear they nothing meant it. I thought they would have been rather ready to have given me thanks than to have made any new request for the same. There hath been some that have, ere this, said unto me they never required more than that they might once hear me say I would marry. Well, there was never so great a treason but might be covered under as fair a pretense.

The second point was the limitation of the succession of the crown, wherein was nothing said for my safety, but only for themselves. A strange thing that the foot should direct the head in so weighty a cause, which cause hath been so diligently weighed by us for that[9] it toucheth us more than them. I am sure there was not one of them that ever was a second person,[1] as I have been, and have tasted of the practices against my sister, who I would to God were alive again. I had great occasions to hearken to their motions,[2] of whom some of them are of the Common House. But when friends fall out truth doth appear, according to the old proverb, and were it not for my honor, their knavery should be known. There were occasions in me at that time: I stood in danger of my life, my sister was so incensed against me. I did differ from her in religion and I was sought for divers ways; and so shall never be my successor.

I have conferred before this time with those that are well learned and have asked their opinions touching the limitation of succession, who have been silent—not that by their silence after lawlike manner[3] they have seemed to assent to it, but that indeed they could not tell what to say, considering the great peril to the realm and most danger to myself. But now the matter

---

2. I.e., envy itself could not fault my governance.
3. Parliament, which had planned to submit a written petition to the queen.
4. Manners'.
5. Honor's.
6. Hindrance. At the time, there were negotiations for a possible match with Archduke Charles of Austria.

7. Unless.
8. Assured.
9. Because.
1. Next in line to the throne, as Elizabeth had been under her half-sister, Mary I.
2. To pay heed to their doings.
3. In accordance with the legal maxim (that silence implies consent).

must needs go trimly and pleasantly, when the bowl runneth all on the one side.[4] And alas, not one amongst them all would answer for us, but all their speeches was for the surety[5] of their country. They would have twelve or fourteen limited in succession, and the mo[6] the better. And those shall be of such uprightness and so divine as in them shall be divinity itself. Kings were wont to honor philosophers, but if I had such[7] I would honor them as angels, that should have such piety in them that they would not seek where they are the second to be the first, and where the third to be the second, and so forth.

It is said I am no divine.[8] Indeed, I studied nothing else but divinity till I came to the crown, and then I gave myself to the study of that which was meet[9] for government, and am not ignorant of stories wherein appeareth what hath fallen out for[1] ambition of kingdoms, as in Spain, Naples, Portingal,[2] and at home. And what cocking[3] hath been between the father and the son for the same! You would have a limitation of succession. Truly if reason did not subdue will in me, I would cause you to deal in it, so pleasant a thing it should be unto me. But I stay[4] it for your benefit; for if you should have liberty to treat of it, there be so many competitors—some kinsfolk, some servants, and some tenants; some would speak for their master, and some for their mistress, and every man for his friend—that it would be an occasion of a greater charge than a subsidy.[5] And if my will did not yield to reason, it should be that thing I would gladly desire, to see you deal in it.

Well, there hath been error—I say not errors, for there were too many in the proceeding in this matter. But we will not judge that these attempts were done of any hatred to our person, but even for lack of good foresight. I do not marvel though *Domini Doctores*[6] with you, my lords, did so use themselves therein, since after my brother's[7] death they openly preached and set forth that my sister and I were bastards.[8] Well, I wish not the death of any man, but only this I desire: that they which have been the practitioners herein may before their deaths repent the same and show some open confession of their faults, whereby the scabbed[9] sheep may be known from the whole. As for my own part, I care not for death, for all men are mortal; and though I be a woman, yet I have as good a courage answerable to my place as ever my father had. I am your anointed queen. I will never be by violence constrained to do anything. I thank God I am indeed endued with such qualities that if I were turned out of the realm in my petticoat, I were able to live in any place of Christendom.

* * *

1566   1949

4. A metaphorical extension of the preceding clause: in the game of bowls, the ball has a flat place: rolled unskillfully, it wobbles, bounces, and prematurely stops; rolled well ("all on the one side"), it runs smoothly.
5. Security.
6. More.
7. I.e., such virtuous potential successors.
8. Theologian.
9. Relevant to. Elizabeth's claim that before ascending the throne she studied nothing but theology is an exaggeration, but it is true that she had devoted much effort to the subject, as evidenced by her translations of several religious works.
1. Happened as a result of.

2. Portugal.
3. Cockfighting: strife, contention.
4. Stop.
5. I.e., it would cost more than a tax. Subsidies were tax levies granted to the sovereign to meet special expenses.
6. The Doctors of the Lord: her derisive Latin term for the bishops who had supported the petition in the House of Lords.
7. Edward VI's.
8. Presumably in support of the claim of Lady Jane Grey to the throne (see p. 199).
9. Infected with scab (the skin disease also known as scabies).

From A Letter to Mary, Queen of Scots, February 24, 1567[1]

Madame:

My ears have been so deafened and my understanding so grieved and my heart so affrighted to hear the dreadful news of the abominable murder of your mad husband and my killed cousin[2] that I scarcely yet have the wits to write about it. And inasmuch as my nature compels me to take his death in the extreme, he being so close in blood, so it is that I will boldly tell you what I think of it. I cannot dissemble that I am more sorrowful for you than for him. O madame, I would not do the office of faithful cousin or affectionate friend if I studied rather to please your ears than employed myself in preserving your honor. However, I will not at all dissemble what most people are talking about: which is that you will look through your fingers at[3] the revenging of this deed, and that you do not take measures that touch those who have done as you wished, as if the thing had been entrusted in a way that the murderers felt assurance in doing it.[4] Among the thoughts in my heart I beseech you to want no such thought to stick at this point. Through all the dealings of the world I never was in such miserable haste to lodge and have in my heart such a miserable opinion of any prince as this would cause me do. Much less will I have such of her to whom I wish as much good as my heart is able to imagine or as you were able a short while ago to wish. However, I exhort you, I counsel you, and I beseech you to take this thing so much to heart that you will not fear to touch even him whom you have nearest to you[5] if the thing touches him, and that no persuasion will prevent you from making an example out of this to the world: that you are both a noble princess and a loyal wife. I do not write so vehemently out of doubt that I have, but out of the affection that I bear you in particular. For I am not ignorant that you have no wiser counselors than myself. Thus it is that, when I remember that our Lord had one Judas out of twelve, and I assure myself that there could be no one more loyal than myself, I offer you my affection in place of this prudence.

*　*　*

1567   1900

---

1. Written after news reached Elizabeth of the murder of Henry Stuart, Lord Darnley, the arrogant and erratic Scottish nobleman whom Mary had ill-advisedly married in 1565.
2. Darnley, like Mary, was Elizabeth's second cousin and a potential claimant to the throne of England.
3. Wink at.

4. Because Mary and Darnley had been estranged, there were immediately rumors that she had been complicit in his murder.
5. Evidently an allusion to James Hepburn, earl of Bothwell, whom Mary married (under much-disputed circumstances) three months after Darnley's death, although Bothwell was known to have been one of the chief conspirators in the murder.

The doubt of future foes[1]

The doubt° of future foes exiles my present joy,   *fear*
And wit° me warns to shun such snares as threatens mine   *intelligence*
    annoy.[2]
For falsehood now doth flow, and subjects' faith doth ebb,[3]
Which should not be, if reason ruled or wisdom weaved the web.
5   But clouds of toys° untried do cloak aspiring minds,   *tricks*
Which turns to rain of late repent, by course of changèd winds.[4]
The top of hope supposed, the root of rue° shall be,   *regret*
And fruitless all their grafted guile,[5] as shortly you shall see.
Their dazzled eyes with pride, which great ambition blinds,
10   Shall be unsealed° by worthy wights° whose foresight   *opened / men*
    falsehood finds.
The daughter of debate,[6] that discord aye° doth sow,   *continually*
Shall reap no gain where former rule[7] still° peace hath taught   *stable*
    to grow.
No foreign banished wight shall anchor in this port:
Our realm brooks no seditious sects—let them elsewhere resort.
15   My rusty sword through rest[8] shall first his edge employ
To poll their tops[9] who seek such change or gape for future joy.
            Vivat Regina[1]

ca. 1571   1589

On Monsieur's Departure[1]

I grieve and dare not show my discontent,
I love and yet am forced to seem to hate,
I do, yet dare not say I ever meant,
I seem stark mute but inwardly do prate.°   *chatter*
5   I am and not, I freeze and yet am burned,
        Since from myself another self I turned.

My care is like my shadow in the sun,
Follows me flying, flies when I pursue it,
Stands and lies by me, doth what I have done.[2]

1. The poem concerns Mary, Queen of Scots, who in 1568 sought refuge in England from her rebellious subjects.
2. I.e., threaten to do me harm ("annoy").
3. I.e., the tide of faith (loyalty) is ebbing, yielding to the rising tide of falsehood.
4. Clouds of tricks not yet tested or detected hide the "aspiring minds" of ambitious foes, but those clouds will turn at last into rains of repentance.
5. The deception ("guile") grafted into them will not bear fruit.
6. Strife. Mary Stuart also was sometimes called "Mother of Debate," because she was constantly the focus of conspiracies and plots.
7. Either the reign of Henry VIII or that of Edward VI, which established the Reformation in England.
8. Sword rusty from disuse.
9. Strike off their heads.
1. Long live the queen (Latin).
1. The heading, present in a 17th-century manuscript, identifies the occasion of this poem as the breaking off of marriage negotiations between Elizabeth and the French duke of Anjou, in 1582.
2. Does everything I do.

10   His too familiar care[3] doth make me rue° it.   *regret*
       No means I find to rid him from my breast,
       Till by the end of things it be suppressed.

       Some gentler passion slide into my mind,
       For I am soft and made of melting snow;
15   Or be more cruel, love, and so be kind.
       Let me or° float or sink, be high or low.   *either*
       Or let me live with some more sweet content,
       Or die and so forget what love e'er° meant.   *ever*

ca. 1582   1823

A Letter to Robert Dudley, Earl of Leicester, February 10, 1586[1]

How contemptuously we conceive ourselves to have been used by you, you shall by this bearer[2] understand: whom we have expressly sent unto you to charge you withal. We could never have imagined (had we not seen it fall out[3] in experience) that a man raised up by ourself and extraordinarily favored by us, above any other subject of this land, would have in so contemptible a sort broken our commandment in a cause that so greatly toucheth us in honor. Whereof although you have showed yourself to make but little account in so most undutiful a sort, you may not therefore think that we have so little care of the reparation thereof as we mind to pass so great a wrong in silence unredressed. And therefore our express pleasure and commandment is that, all delays and excuses laid apart, you do presently upon the duty of your allegiance obey and fulfill whatsoever the bearer hereof shall direct you to do in our name.[4] Whereof fail you not, as you will answer the contrary at your uttermost peril.

1586   1935

3. I.e., my own care, which he caused.

1. Leicester (ca. 1532–1588) had been the queen's greatest favorite from the beginning of her reign and was for a time her suitor and possibly lover. Sent to the Netherlands to assist the revolt of the Dutch Protestants against Spanish rule, however, he incurred her rage by accepting, without her permission, the offer of the Dutch to make him their absolute governor. They had been without a leader since the assassination of William of Orange, in 1584, and had offered Elizabeth herself the sovereignty of the United Provinces (which she declined) the preceding summer.

2. Sir Thomas Heneage, one of Elizabeth's most trusted courtiers.

3. Happen.

4. Heneage was instructed to direct Leicester to resign the governorship immediately. Though it was several months before Leicester did so, Elizabeth was by April already addressing him fondly again.

A Letter to Sir Amyas Paulet, August 1586[1]

Amyas, my most careful and faithful servant,

God reward thee treblefold in the double for thy most troublesome charge[2] so well discharged. If you knew, my Amyas, how kindly, besides dutifully, my careful[3] heart accepts your double labors and faithful actions, your wise orders and safe regards performed in so dangerous and crafty[4] a charge, it would ease your troubles' travail and rejoice your heart. In which I charge you to carry this most nighest thought: that I cannot balance in any weight of my judgment the value that I prize you at. And suppose no treasure to countervail[5] such a faith, and condemn me in that behalf which I never committed if I reward not such deserts. Yea, let me lack when I have most need if I acknowledge not such a merit with a reward *non omnibus datum.*[6]

But let your wicked mistress know how, with hearty sorrow, her vile deserts compels these orders; and bid her, from me, ask God forgiveness for her treacherous dealing towards the saver of her life many years, to the intolerable peril of her own.[7] And yet not content with so many forgivenesses, must fall again so horribly, far passing a woman's thought, much more a princess', instead of excusing, whereof not one can serve, it being so plainly confessed by the actors[8] of my guiltless death. Let repentance take place; and let not the fiend possess her so as her best part be lost, which I pray with hands lifted up to Him that may both save and spill,[9] with my loving adieu and prayer for thy long life.

> Your most assured and loving sovereign in heart,
> by good desert induced, *Elizabeth Regina.*

1586   1854

A Letter to King James VI of Scotland, February 14, 1587

My dear brother,[1]

I would you knew though not felt the extreme dolor that overwhelms my mind for that miserable accident,[2] which far contrary to my meaning hath befallen. I have now sent this kinsman of mine,[3] whom ere now it hath

---

1. Paulet was the keeper of Mary, Queen of Scots. In 1586 a number of her supporters, led by Anthony Babington, plotted to murder Elizabeth and place Mary on the throne. The plot was discovered, and the plotters were executed in September. Mary, who had been complicit with them, was placed under stricter confinement, and then tried for treason.
Elizabeth's letter to Paulet circulated widely in manuscript: to her contemporaries, it was evidently the single best-known of the queen's letters.
2. Duty, responsibility.
3. Full of care.
4. Requiring skill.
5. To be equal in value to.
6. Not given to all (Latin).

7. I.e., Elizabeth's own life.
8. I.e., the conspirators.
9. Destroy.
1. Fellow ruler.
2. I.e., the execution, six days before, of James's mother, Mary, Queen of Scots. In the aftermath of the Babington plot, Elizabeth decided to have Mary tried and convicted of treason—legally an outrageous charge, since she was not a subject of England. Mary was sentenced to death, and Elizabeth, after much vacillation, signed the warrant for her execution. Once the sentence had been carried out, however, the queen went to great lengths to exculpate herself, even in her own mind, from responsibility for her cousin's death.
3. Sir Robert Carey, related to Elizabeth on her mother's side.

pleased you to favor, to instruct you truly of that which is too irksome for my pen to tell you. I beseech you that—as God and many more know—how innocent I am in this case, so you will believe me that if I had bid aught I would have bid by it.[4] I am not so base minded that fear of any living creature or prince should make me afraid to do that[5] were just or, done, to deny the same. I am not of so base a lineage nor carry so vile a mind; but as not to disguise fits most a king, so will I never dissemble my actions but cause them show even as I meant them. Thus assuring yourself of me that, as I know this was deserved, yet if I had meant it I would never lay it on others' shoulders, no more will I not damnify[6] myself that thought it not. The circumstance it may please you to have of this bearer. And for your part, think you have not in the world a more loving kinswoman nor a more dear friend than myself, nor any that will watch more carefully to preserve you and your estate.[7] And who shall otherwise persuade you, judge them more partial to others than you. And thus in haste, I leave to trouble you, beseeching God to send you a long reign. The 14 of February, 1587.

Your most assured, loving sister and cousin,
Elizabeth R.

1587   1834

Verse Exchange between Elizabeth and Sir Walter Ralegh[1]

[RALEGH TO ELIZABETH]

Fortune hath taken away my love,
My life's joy and my soul's heaven above.
Fortune hath taken thee away, my princess,
My world's joy and my true fantasy's mistress.

5   Fortune hath taken thee away from me;
Fortune hath taken all by taking thee.
Dead to all joys, I only live to woe:
So is Fortune become my fantasy's foe.

In vain, my eyes, in vain ye waste your tears;
10   In vain, my sights,° the smoke of my despairs,   *sighs (?)*
In vain you search the earth and heaven above.
In vain you search, for Fortune keeps my love.

Then will I leave my love in Fortune's hand;
Then will I leave my love in worldlings' band,°   *bond*
15   And only love the sorrows due to me—
Sorrow, henceforth, that shall my princess be—

---

4. I.e., if I had commanded her death, I would have abided by my decision. "Bid" is a form of the past participle of both *bid* and *bide*.)
5. I.e., the thing that.
6. Wrong.
7. Position.

1. This exchange, which exemplifies the poetic banter that sometimes passed between the queen and her favorites, took place about 1587, when Ralegh believed that the rapid rise of the earl of Essex in Elizabeth's favor entailed a diminution of his own standing with her.

And only joy that Fortune conquers kings.
Fortune, that rules the earth and earthly things,
Hath taken my love in spite of virtue's might:
20   So blind a goddess did never virtue right.

With wisdom's eyes had but blind Fortune seen,
Then had my love, my love forever been.
But love, farewell—though Fortune conquer thee,
No fortune base nor frail shall alter me.

[ELIZABETH TO RALEGH]

Ah, silly Pug,[2] wert thou so sore afraid?
Mourn not, my Wat,[3] nor be thou so dismayed.
It passeth fickle Fortune's power and skill
To force my heart to think thee any ill.
5   No Fortune base, thou sayest, shall alter thee?
And may so blind a witch so conquer me?
No, no, my Pug, though Fortune were not blind,
Assure thyself she could not rule my mind.
Fortune, I know, sometimes doth conquer kings,
10   And rules and reigns on earth and earthly things,
But never think Fortune can bear the sway
If virtue watch, and will her not obey.
Ne° chose I thee by fickle Fortune's rede,°   *nor / decision*
Ne she shall force me alter with such speed
15   But if[4] to try this mistress' jest with thee.[5]
Pull up thy heart, suppress thy brackish tears,
Torment thee not, but put away thy fears.
Dead to all joys and living unto woe,
Slain quite by her that ne'er gave wise men blow,
20   Revive again and live without all dread,
The less afraid, the better thou shalt speed.°   *succeed*

ca. 1587   ca. 1600?

Speech to the Troops at Tilbury[1]

My loving people, I have been persuaded by some that are careful of[2] my
safety, to take heed how I committed myself to armed multitudes, for fear
of treachery. But I tell you that I would not desire to live to distrust my
faithful and loving people. Let tyrants fear! I have so behaved myself that,

2. An endearment, which Elizabeth used as her pet name for Ralegh.
3. Short for Walter.
4. Unless I do it.
5. Since "thee" has nothing to rhyme with, and since the line is hard to construe, it seems likely that there is a line missing before or after this one.
1. Delivered by Elizabeth on August 9, 1588, to the land forces assembled at Tilbury (in Essex) to repel the anticipated invasion of the Spanish Armada, a fleet of warships sent by Philip II. The Armada was defeated at sea and never reached England, a miraculous deliverance and sign of God's special favor to Elizabeth and to England, in the general view.
2. Anxious about.

under God, I have placed my chiefest strength and safeguard in the loyal hearts and goodwill of my subjects. Wherefore I am come among you at this time but for my recreation and pleasure, being resolved in the midst and heat of the battle to live and die amongst you all,[3] to lay down for my God and for my kingdom and for my people mine honor and my blood even in the dust. I know I have the body but of a weak and feeble woman; but I have the heart and stomach of a king, and of a king of England too[4]—and take foul scorn that Parma[5] or any prince of Europe should dare to invade the borders of my realm. To the which, rather than any dishonor shall grow by me, I myself will venter[6] my royal blood; I myself will be your general, judge, and rewarder of your virtue in the field. I know that already for your forwardness you have deserved rewards and crowns,[7] and I assure you in the word of a prince you shall not fail of them. In the meantime, my lieutenant general[8] shall be in my stead, than whom never prince commanded a more noble or worthy subject; not doubting but by your concord in the camp and valor in the field, and your obedience to myself and my general, we shall shortly have a famous victory over these enemies of my God and of my kingdom.

1588   1654

The "Golden Speech"

The "Golden Speech"   A speech to Elizabeth's last Parliament, delivered November 30, 1601, and here given as recorded by one of the members. The designation "Golden Speech" stems from the headnote to a version of the speech printed near the end of the Puritan interregnum (1659?): "This speech ought to be set in letters of gold, that as well the majesty, prudence, and virtue of this royal queen might in general most exquisitely appear, as also that her religious love and tender respect which she particularly and constantly did bear to her Parliament in unfeigned sincerity might (to the shame and perpetual disgrace and infamy of some of her successors) be nobly and truly vindicated."

The royal prerogatives included the right to grant or sell "letters patent," which gave the recipient monopoly control of some branch of commerce. (Sir Walter Ralegh, for example, was given the exclusive right, for a period of thirty years, to license all taverns.) Discontent with the monopolies—which had resulted in higher prices for a wide range of commodities, including such basic ones as salt and starch—came to a head in the Parliament of 1601. Under parliamentary pressure (and in return for a subsidy granted to her treasury), Elizabeth agreed to revoke some of the most obnoxious patents and to allow the courts to rule freely on charges brought against the holders of others. She invited members of Parliament who wished to offer thanks for this largesse to come to her in a body, and on November 30 received about 150 of them at Whitehall Palace. After effusive remarks by the

---

3. In another version of the speech (based, like this one, on an auditor's memory), the sentence up to this point reads: "And therefore I am come amongst you, as you see at this time, not for my recreation and disport, but being resolved in the midst and heat of the battle to live or die amongst you all."
4. An allusion to the concept of the king's (or queen's) two bodies, the one natural and mortal, the other an ideal and enduring political con-

struct. "Stomach": valor.
5. Alessandro Farnese, duke of Parma, allied with the king of Spain and expected to join with him in the invasion of England.
6. Venture, risk.
7. The crown was an English coin. "Forwardness": eagerness.
8. The earl of Leicester led the English troops. Elizabeth's great and powerful favorite, he died just a month later.

speaker of the House of Commons (Sir John Croke), the queen responded more or less as recorded here. (Elizabeth revised the speech for publication; and none of the surviving versions of it—which differ considerably—was printed earlier than about 1628.)

The "Golden Speech"[1]

Mr. Speaker, we have heard your declaration and perceive your care of our estate,[2] by falling into the consideration of a grateful acknowledgment of such benefits as you have received; and that your coming is to present thanks unto us, which I accept with no less joy than your loves can have desire to offer such a present.

I do assure you that there is no prince that loveth his subjects better, or whose love can countervail[3] our loves. There is no jewel, be it of never so rich a price, which I set before this jewel—I mean your loves. For I do more esteem it than any treasure or riches: for that we know how to prize, but love and thanks I count unvaluable.[4] And though God hath raised me high, yet this I count the glory of my crown, that I have reigned with your loves. This makes me that I do not so much rejoice that God hath made me to be a queen, as to be a queen over so thankful a people. Therefore I have cause to wish nothing more than to content the subjects, and that is a duty which I owe. Neither do I desire to live longer days than that I may see your prosperity, and that is my only desire. And as I am that person that still,[5] yet under God, hath delivered you, so I trust, by the almighty power of God, that I shall be His instrument to preserve you from envy, peril, dishonor, shame, tyranny, and oppression, partly by means of your intended helps, which we take very acceptable because it manifesteth the largeness of your loves and loyalties unto your sovereign.

Of myself I must say this: I never was any greedy, scraping grasper, nor a strait, fast-holding prince, nor yet a waster. My heart was never set on worldly goods, but only for my subjects' good. What you bestow on me, I will not hoard it up, but receive it to bestow on you again. Yea, my own properties I account yours to be expended for your good, and your eyes shall see the bestowing of all for your good. Therefore render unto them from me, I beseech you, Mr. Speaker, such thanks as you imagine my heart yieldeth but my tongue cannot express.

Mr. Speaker, I would wish you and the rest to stand up, for I shall yet trouble you with longer speech.[6]

Mr. Speaker, you give me thanks, but I doubt[7] me that I have more cause to thank you all than you me; and I charge you to thank them of the Lower House[8] from me. For had I not received a knowledge from you, I might have fallen into the lapse of an error only for lack of true information.

---

1. We print only the words of the queen, omitting various interpolations as well as the opening remarks by the speaker of the Parliament.
2. Rank, position.
3. Match.
4. Invaluable.
5. Continually.
6. Up to this point, the assemblage had been kneeling.
7. Fear.

Since I was queen yet did I never put my pen to any grant but that upon pretext and semblance made unto me, it was both good and beneficial to the subject in general, though a private profit to some of my ancient servants who had deserved well. But the contrary being found by experience, I am exceedingly beholding to such subjects as would move the same at the first.[9] And I am not so simple to suppose but that there be some of the Lower House whom these grievances never touched; and for them I think they speak out of zeal to their countries[1] and not out of spleen or malevolent affection, as being parties grieved. And I take it exceedingly gratefully from them, because it gives us to know that no respects or interests had moved them other than the minds they bear to suffer[2] no diminution of our honor and our subjects' love unto us, the zeal of which affection, tending to ease my people and knit their hearts unto me, I embrace with a princely care.

For above all earthly treasures I esteem my people's love, more than which I desire not to merit. That my grants should be grievous to my people and oppressions to be privileged under color[3] of our patents, our kingly dignity shall not suffer it. Yea, when I heard it I could give no rest unto my thoughts until I had reformed it.[4] Shall they (think you) escape unpunished that have thus oppressed you and have been respectless of their duty and regardless of our honor? No, no, Mr. Speaker, I assure you were it not more for conscience' sake than for any glory or increase of love that I desire, these errors, troubles, vexations, and oppressions done by these varlets and low persons (not worthy the name of subjects) should not escape without condign punishment. But I perceive they dealt with me like physicians who, ministering a drug, make it more acceptable by giving it a good aromatical savor; or when they give pills, do gild them all over.

I have ever used[5] to set the Last Judgment Day before my eyes and so to rule as I shall be judged, to answer before a higher Judge. To whose judgment seat I do appeal that never thought was cherished in my heart that tended not unto my people's good. And now if my kingly bounties have been abused and my grants turned to the hurts of my people, contrary to my will and meaning, or if any in authority under me have neglected or perverted what I have committed to them, I hope God will not lay their culps[6] and offenses to my charge. Who, though there were danger in repealing our grants, yet what danger would I not rather incur for your good than I would suffer them still to continue?

I know the title of a king is a glorious title, but assure yourself that the shining glory of princely authority hath not so dazzled the eyes of our understanding but that we well know and remember that we also are to yield an account of our actions before the great Judge. To be a king and wear a crown is more glorious to them that see it than it is pleasant to them that bear it.

8. The House of Commons.
9. I.e., those members of the House of Commons who had raised the issue of monopolies in previous sessions.
1. Their constituents.
2. Permit. "Minds": intentions.
3. Pretext.

4. In fact Elizabeth was extremely slow to respond to the grievances, which had, for example, previously been raised in the Parliament of 1597.
5. Been accustomed.
6. Sins.

For myself, I was never so much enticed with the glorious name of a king or royal authority of a queen as delighted that God hath made me His instrument to maintain His truth and glory, and to defend this kingdom (as I said) from peril, dishonor, tyranny, and oppression.

There will never queen sit in my seat with more zeal to my country, care to my subjects, and that will sooner with willingness venture her life for your good and safety, than myself. For it is not my desire to live nor reign longer than my life and reign shall be for your good. And though you have had and may have many princes more mighty and wise sitting in this seat, yet you never had or shall have any that will be more careful and loving.

Shall I ascribe anything to myself and my sexly[7] weakness? I were not worthy to live then, and of all most unworthy of the mercies I have had from God, who hath ever yet given me a heart which yet never feared any foreign or home enemy. I speak it to give God the praise as a testimony before you, and not to attribute anything unto myself. For I, O Lord, what am I, whom practices and perils past should not fear?[8] O, what can I do, that I should speak for any glory? God forbid!

This, Mr. Speaker, I pray you deliver unto the House, to whom heartily recommend me. And so I commit you all to your best fortunes and further counsels. And I pray you, Mr. Comptroller, Mr. Secretary,[9] and you of my council, that before these gentlemen depart into their countries,[1] you bring them all to kiss my hand.

1601   1601 (in a summary version)

7. Characteristic of my sex. "Ascribe": attribute.
8. Frighten. "Practices": treacherous schemes.
9. William Knollys, earl of Banbury, and Robert

Cecil, earl of Salisbury.
1. Districts.

EDMUND SPENSER
1552?–1599

E dmund Spenser set out, consciously and deliberately, to become the great English poet of his age. In a culture in which most accomplished poetry was written by those who were, or at least professed to be, principally interested in something else— advancement at court, diplomacy, statecraft, or the Church—Spenser's ambition was altogether remarkable, and it is still more remarkable that he succeeded in reaching his goal. Unlike such poets as Wyatt, Surrey, and Sidney, born to privilege and social distinction, Spenser was born—in London, probably in 1552—to parents of modest means and station. He nonetheless received an impressive education, first at the Merchant Taylors' School, under its demanding, humanist headmaster, Richard Mulcaster, and then at Pembroke College, Cambridge, where he was enrolled as a "sizar," or poor scholar. In the Puritan environment of Cambridge, where the popular preacher Thomas Cartwright was beginning to make the authorities uneasy, Spenser began as a poet by translating some poems for a volume of anti-Catholic propaganda. He also began his friendship with Gabriel Harvey, an eccentric Cambridge don, humanist, and pamphleteer. Their correspondence shows they shared a passionate and patriotic interest in the reformation of English verse. In a 1580 letter to Harvey, Spenser demanded, "Why a God's name may not we, as else the Greeks, have the kingdom of our own language?"

After receiving the B.A. degree in 1573 and the M.A. in 1576, Spenser served as personal secretary and aide to several prominent men, including both Dr. John Young, bishop of Rochester, and Robert Dudley, earl of Leicester and the queen's principal favorite. During his employment in Leicester's household, Spenser came to know Sir Philip Sidney and his friend Sir Edward Dyer, courtiers who sought to promote a new English poetry. Spenser's contribution to the movement was *The Shepheardes Calender*, published in 1579 and dedicated to Sidney.

In *The Shepheardes Calender* Spenser used a deliberately archaic language, partly in homage to Chaucer, whose work he praised as a "well of English undefiled," and partly to achieve a rustic effect, in keeping with the feigned simplicity of pastoral poetry's shepherd singers. Sidney did not entirely approve, and another contemporary, Ben Jonson, growled that Spenser "writ no language." In the eighteenth century Samuel Johnson described the language of *The Shepheardes Calender* as "studied barbarity." Johnson's characterization is, in a way, quite accurate, for Spenser was attempting to conjure up a native English style to which he could wed the classical mode of the pastoral. Moreover, because pastoral was traditionally viewed as the prelude in a great poet's career, Spenser was also in effect announcing his extravagant ambition to become England's national poet.

Spenser was a prolific and daring experimenter: the poems of *The Shepheardes Calender* use no fewer than thirteen different metrical schemes. In his later poems, he went on to make further innovations: the special rhyme scheme of the Spenserian sonnet, the remarkably beautiful adaptation of the Italian *canzone* forms for the *Epithalamion* and *Prothalamion*, and the great Spenserian stanza of *The Faerie Queene* (eight iambic pentameters followed by a six-foot line, rhymed *ababbcbcc*) are the best known. Spenser is sometimes called "the poet's poet," because so many later English poets learned the art of versification from him. In the nineteenth century alone his influence may be seen in Shelley's *Revolt of Islam*, Byron's *Childe Harold's Pilgrimage*, Keats's *Eve of St. Agnes*, and Tennyson's *The Lotus-Eaters*.

The year after the publication of *The Shepheardes Calender*, Spenser went to Ireland as secretary and aide to Lord Grey of Wilton, lord deputy of Ireland. Although the poet tried continually to obtain appointments in England (which he revisited on several occasions) and to secure the patronage of the queen, he lived in Ireland nearly to the end of his life, holding various minor government posts and hence participating actively in the English struggle against those who resisted their colonial authority. The grim realities of that struggle—massacres, the burning of miserable hovels and of crops with the deliberate intention of starving the inhabitants, the forced relocation of whole communities, the manipulation of treason charges to facilitate the seizure of lands, the endless repetition of acts of military "justice" calculated to intimidate and break the spirit—may be glimpsed in distorted and on occasion direct form throughout Spenser's writings, along with dreamlike depictions of the beauty of the Irish landscape. Those writings include an anonymously published political tract, *A View of the Present State of Ireland*, which was unusual in its time both for its genuine fascination with Irish culture and for the ruthlessness of the policies it prescribed.

Spenser's attitudes toward Ireland and his conduct there raise difficult questions concerning the relationship between literature and colonialism. Are the harsh policies of the *View* echoed, allegorically, in *The Faerie Queene?* What does it mean to admire a poet who might, by modern standards, be judged a war criminal (as his master, Lord Grey, was judged to be, even by notoriously brutal Elizabethan standards)? Does Spenser use his Irish vantage point to launch daring criticisms of Queen Elizabeth and the English form of government? In addition to sharpening racial chauvinism, the experience of Ireland seems to have given English settlers a new perspective on events back home. As one of Spenser's contemporaries remarked, words that would be considered treasonous in England were common table talk among the Irish settlers.

Spenser was rewarded for his efforts in Ireland with a castle and 3,028 acres of expropriated land at Kilcolman, in the province of Munster. There he was visited by another colonist and poet, the powerful and well-connected Sir Walter Ralegh, to whom Spenser showed the great chivalric epic on which he was at work. With Ralegh's influential backing, Spenser traveled to England and published, in 1590, the first three books of *The Faerie Queene*, which made a strong bid for the queen's favor and patronage. He was rewarded with a handsome pension of £50 a year for life, though the queen's principal councillor, Lord Burghley, is said to have grumbled that it was a lot for a song. Soon after, Spenser published a volume of poems called *Complaints*; a pastoral called *Colin Clouts Come Home Againe* (1595), commenting on the courtiers and ladies at the center of English court life at the time of his 1590 visit; his sonnet cycle, *Amoretti*; and two wedding poems, *Prothalamion*, celebrating the double marriage of aristocratic sisters, and *Epithalamion,* celebrating the poet's own marriage to Elizabeth Boyle. The six-book *Faerie Queene* was published in 1596, with some revisions in the first part and a changed ending to Book 3 to provide a bridge to the added books; the two so-called Mutabilitie Cantos and two stanzas of a third canto—perhaps part of an intended seventh book—appeared posthumously, in the 1609 edition.

In 1598, there was an uprising in Munster, and rebels burned down the house in which Spenser lived. The poet fled with his wife; their newborn baby is said to have died in the flames. Spenser was sent to England with messages from the besieged English garrison. He died in Westminster on January 13, 1599, and was buried near his beloved Chaucer in what is now called the Poets' Corner of Westminster Abbey.

Spenser cannot be put into neatly labeled categories. He is steeped in both Neoplatonism and Aristotelianism. His work is mystical, but also earthy and practical. He is a lover and celebrator of physical beauty, yet also a profound analyst of good and evil in all their perplexing shapes and complexities. A staunch Protestant, influenced by Puritanism, he portrayed the Roman Catholic Church as a demonic villain in *The Faerie Queene*, and yet his understanding of faith and of sin owes much to Catholic thinkers. He is a poet of sensuous images yet also something of an iconoclast, deeply suspicious of the power of images (material and verbal) to turn into idols. He is an idealist, drawn to courtesy, gentleness, and exquisite moral refinement, yet also a celebrant of English nationalism, empire, and martial power. He is the author of the most memorable literary idealization of Elizabeth I, yet he fills his poem with coded criticisms of the queen. He is in some ways a backward-looking poet who paid homage to Chaucer, used archaic language, and compared his own age unfavorably with the feudal past. Yet as British epic poet and poet-prophet, he points forward to the poetry of the Romantics and especially to Milton, who himself paid homage to the "sage and serious" Spenser as "a better teacher than Scotus or Aquinas."

Because it was a deliberate choice on Spenser's part that his language should seem antique, his poetry is always printed in the original spelling and punctuation; a few of the most confusing punctuation marks have, however, been altered in the present text, and we have sometimes added diacritical marks to indicate pronunciation. Spenser also spells words variably, in such a way as to suggest rhymes to the eye or to suggest etymologies (often incorrect ones). This inconsistency in his spellings is typical of his time; in the sixteenth century people even varied the spelling of their own names.*

---

* For additional poetry by Spenser—"Aprill" from *The Shepheardes Calender,* four more sonnets from the *Amoretti* (nos. 15, 35, 59, 70), "A Hymne in Honour of Beautie," and, from *The Faerie Queene,* the Cave of Mammon canto from Book 2 and extensive excerpts from Book 3—see the NAEL Archive.

The Shepheardes Calender   Pastoral poetry—with its odd idea of shepherds among their flocks piping on their flutes and singing beautiful songs of love, sadness, and complaint—was an influential classical form whose most famous practitioners were the Alexandrian poet Theocritus (third century B.C.E.) and the Roman poet Virgil (first century B.C.E.). The singers of the pastoral, or eclogue, were depicted as simple rustics who inhabited a world in which human beings and nature lived in harmony, but the form was always essentially urban and elite: in his series of twelve eclogues, Spenser, a Londoner, was self-consciously assuming a highly conventional literary role. That role enabled him at once to lay claim to the prestige of classical poetry and to insist on his native Englishness, insistently signaled by the deliberately archaic, pseudo-Chaucerian language. The rustic mask also allowed Spenser, in certain of the eclogues, to make sharply satirical comments on religious and political issues of his day, such as Elizabeth's suppression of Puritan clergy in the Church of England, and to reflect on his own marginal social position.

The eclogues of *The Shepheardes Calender* are titled for the months of the year. Each is prefaced by an illustrative woodcut representing the characters and theme of the poem and picturing in the clouds the dominant sign of the zodiac for that month, and each is accompanied by a commentary ascribed to "E. K.," who also wrote an introductory epistle to the work as a whole. E. K., who has not been identified but must have been someone close to Spenser (or, in the opinion of some, Spenser himself), trumpets the arrival of a "new poet" whose skills are conspicuously displayed in the sequence of poems. *October* deals with the place of poetry and the responsibility of the poet in the world, an important theme throughout the *Calender* and in much of Spenser's work.

From The Shepheardes Calender

To His Booke

　　Goe little booke:[1] thy selfe present,
　As child whose parent is unkent:°
　To him that is the president°
　Of noblesse and of chevalree,
5　And if that Envie barke at thee,
　As sure it will, for succoure° flee
　　Under the shadow of his wing,[2]
　And askèd, who thee forth did bring,
　A shepheards swaine° saye did thee sing,
10　All as his straying flocke he fedde:
　And when his honor has thee redde,°
　Crave pardon for my hardyhedde.°
　　But if that any aske thy name,
　Say thou wert base° begot with blame:
15　For thy° thereof thou takest shame.
　And when thou art past jeopardee,
　Come tell me, what was sayd of mee:
　And I will send more after thee.
　　　　　IMMERITO.°

unknown
pattern

aid

boy

seen
boldness

lowly
therefore

unworthy

---

1. A deliberate echo of Chaucer's line "Go litel bok, go litel myn tragedye" (*Troilus and Criseyde* 5.1786).

2. I.e., the protective sponsorship of Sir Philip Sidney, to whom this poem dedicates the book.

October[3]

Aegloga decima[4]

ARGUMENT

In Cuddie[5] is set out the perfecte paterne of a Poete, which finding no maintenaunce of his state and studies, complayneth of the comtempte of Poetrie, and the causes thereof: Specially having bene in all ages, and even amongst the most barbarous alwayes of singular accounpt[6] and honor, and being indede so worthy and commendable an arte: or rather no arte, but a divine gift and heavenly instinct not to bee gotten by laboure and learning, but adorned with both: and poured into the witte by a certaine *enthousiasmos* and celestiall inspiration, as the Author hereof els where at large discourseth, in his booke called the English Poete,[7] which booke being lately come to my hands, I mynde[8] also by Gods grace upon further advisement to publish.

PIERS   CUDDIE

Cuddie, for shame hold up thy heavye head,
And let us cast with what delight to chace,

---

3. When *The Shepheardes Calender* was published, in 1579, each of the twelve eclogues was followed by a commentary (called a "Glosse") by the mysterious E. K., which contained explications of difficult or archaic words, together with learned discussions of—and disagreements with—Spenser's ideas, imagery, and poetics. Designed to appear authoritative, the commentaries in fact often serve to complicate the process of interpretation. To give the reader some sense of them, we have included several of the individual notes from the "October" Glosse.

4. Tenth Eclogue. An eclogue ("aeglogue") is a short pastoral poem in the form of a dialogue or soliloquy. Spenser's spelling is based on a false etymology (*aix*, "goat" + *logos*, "speech"), signifying, according to E. K., "Goteheards tales." For this eclogue, E. K. identifies as sources Theocritus's *Idyl* 16, which reproves the tyrant Hiero of Syracuse for his neglect of poets, and also Bap-

tista Spagnuoli (1448–1516), called Mantuan (the fifth eclogue). The illustration portrays Cuddie (left) holding a pipe and crowned with a laurel wreath (emblems of a poet). He talks with his fellow shepherd, Piers, in a pastoral landscape, with the court in the background. The astrological sign for October, Scorpio, is at the top of the picture.

5. E. K. queries "whether by Cuddie be specified the authour selfe, or some other," noting that in "August" he was introduced as singing a song "of Colins making. So that some doubt, that the persons be different." It may be that Cuddie and Piers, along with Colin, present different aspects of Spenser the poet.

6. Esteem.

7. *The English Poete* is evidently a lost work by Spenser. *"Enthousiasmos"*: inspiration. The Greek word originally meant "possessed by a god."

8. Intend.

And weary thys long lingring Phoebus race.[9]
Whilome thou wont[1] the shepheards laddes to leade,
5 In rymes, in ridles, and in bydding base:[2]
Now they in thee, and thou in sleepe art dead.

CUDDIE

Piers, I have pypèd erst° so long with payne,°   *up to now / care*
That all mine Oten reedes[3] bene rent° and wore: *torn*
And my poore Muse hath spent her sparèd° store,   *saved up*
10 Yet little good hath got, and much lesse gayne.
Such pleasaunce makes the Grashopper so poore,
And ligge so layd,[4] when Winter doth her straine.°   *constrain*

The dapper° ditties, that I wont[5] devise,   *pretty*
To feede youthes fancie, and the flocking fry,[6]
15 Delighten much: what I the bett for thy?[7]
They han° the pleasure, I a sclender prise.°   *have / meager reward*
I beate the bush, the byrds to them doe flye:
What good thereof to Cuddie can arise?

PIERS

Cuddie, the prayse is better, then° the price,   *than*
20 The glory eke° much greater then the gayne: *also*
O what an honor is it, to restraine
The lust° of lawlesse youth with good advice:[8]   *desires*
Or pricke° them forth with pleasaunce of thy vaine°   *spur / talent*
Whereto thou list° their traynèd° willes entice.   *desire / ensnared*

25 Soone as thou gynst° to sette thy notes in frame,   *begin*
O how the rurall routes° to thee doe cleave: *crowds*
Seemeth thou dost their soule of sence bereave,[9]
All as the shepheard, that did fetch his dame
From Plutoes balefull bowre withouten leave:
30 His musicks might the hellish hound did tame.[1]

CUDDIE

So praysen babes the Peacoks spotted traine,
And wondren at bright Argus blazing eye:[2]

9. I.e., let us see how we may pass this long day
pleasantly.
1. Formerly you were accustomed.
2. A popular game; here, perhaps a poetry contest.
3. The shepherd's pipe, symbol of pastoral
poetry.
4. I.e., lie so subdued. The reference is to the fable
of the industrious ant who laid up supplies for
winter, and the carefree grasshopper who did not.
5. Am accustomed to.
6. "A bold Metaphore, forced from the spawning
fishes. For the multitude of young fish be called
the frye" [E. K.].
7. I.e., how am I the better for that?
8. E. K. compares these lines with *The Laws* 1,
in which Plato declares "that the first invention
of Poetry was of very vertuous intent."

9. I.e., hypnotize them. E. K. cites Plato and
Pythagoras for the theory that the mind is made
of "a certaine harmonie and musicall nombers,"
and gives several examples of music's irresistible
power over the emotions.
1. In classical mythology, the three-headed dog
Cerberus guards the entrance to Hades. But he
let pass Orpheus, "of whom is sayd, that by his
excellent skil in Musick and Poetry, he recovered
his wife Eurydice from hell" [E. K.]; i.e., from
"Plutoes balefull bowre."
2. E. K. alludes to the myth of Argus of the hundred eyes, who, set by Juno to guard Io, Jupiter's
current paramour, was lulled asleep by Mercury's
music and then killed. Juno placed his eyes in the
tail of her bird, the peacock, whose splendor elic-
its the praises even of "babes."

But who rewards him ere° the more for thy?° *at all / therefore*
Or feedes him once the fuller by a graine?
35 Sike° prayse is smoke, that sheddeth° in the skye, *such / is dispersed*
Sike words bene wynd, and wasten soone in vayne.

PIERS

Abandon then the base and viler clowne,° *rustic*
Lyft up thy selfe out of the lowly dust:
And sing of bloody Mars,[3] of wars, of giusts.° *jousts*
40 Turne thee to those, that weld° the awful° crowne, *bear / awesome*
To doubted° Knights, whose woundlesse[4] armour rusts, *dreaded*
And helmes unbruzèd waxen° dayly browne. *grow*

There may thy Muse display her fluttryng wing,
And stretch her selfe at large from East to West:[5]
45 Whither thou list° in fayre Elisa rest, *choose*
Or if thee please in bigger notes to sing,
Advaunce° the worthy whome shee loveth best, *extol*
That first the white beare to the stake did bring.[6]

And when the stubborne stroke of stronger stounds,° *efforts*
50 Has somewhat slackt[7] the tenor of thy string:
Of love and lustihead tho° mayst thou sing, *pleasure then*
And carrol lowde, and leade the Myllers rownde,[8]
All° were Elisa one of thilke same ring.[9] *although*
So mought our Cuddies name to Heaven sownde.

CUDDIE

55 Indeede the Romish Tityrus,[1] I heare,
Through his Mecaenas left his Oaten reede,
Whereon he earst° had taught his flocks to feede, *formerly*
And laboured lands to yield the timely eare,
And eft° did sing of warres and deadly drede,° *afterward / danger*
60 So as the Heavens did quake his verse to here.[2]

But ah Mecaenas is yclad in claye,
And great Augustus long ygoe is dead:
And all the worthies liggen° wrapt in leade, *lie*

---

3. Roman god of war.
4. "Unwounded in warre, doe rust through long peace" [E. K.].
5. E. K. explains this "poeticall metaphore" as indicating the heroic subjects available to Cuddie if he wishes to "showe his skill in matter of more dignitie, then [i.e., than] is the homely Aeglogue." These include "our most gratious soveraign, whom (as before) he calleth Elisa," and also the "noble and valiaunt men" who deserve his praise and have been his patrons.
6. "He meaneth (as I guesse) the most honorable and renowmed the Erle of Leycester" [E. K.]. Leicester's device was the bear and ragged staff.
7. "That is when thou chaungest thy verse from stately discourse, to matter of more pleasaunce

and delight" [E. K.].
8. "A kind of daunce" [E. K.].
9. A "company of dauncers" [E. K.].
1. "Wel knowen to be Virgile, who by Mecaenas means was brought into the favour of the Emperor Augustus, and by him moved to write in loftier kinde, then he erst had doen" [E. K.]. Maecenas ("Mecaenas") was Virgil's patron.
2. "In these three verses are the three severall workes of Virgile intended. For in teaching his flocks to feede, is meant his Aeglogues. In labouring of lands, is hys Georgiques. In singing of wars and deadly dreade, is his divine Aeneis figured" [E. K.]. The *Georgics* ("Georgiques") is Virgil's idealizing poem about farm life.

That matter made for Poets on to play:
65 For ever, who in derring doe[3] were dreade,°   *held in awe*
The loftie verse of hem° was lovèd aye.[4]   *them*

But after vertue gan for age to stoupe,
And mighty manhode brought a bedde of° ease:[5]   *to bed by*
The vaunting Poets found nought worth a pease,°   *pea*
70 To put in preace° among the learned troupe.   *present for competition*
Tho° gan the streames of flowing wittes to cease,   *then*
And sonnebright honour pend in shamefull coupe.[6]

And if that any buddes of Poesie,
Yet of the old stocke gan to shoote agayne:
75 Or° it mens follies mote° be forst to fayne,°   *either / must / feign*
And rolle with rest in rymes of rybaudrye:°   *ribaldry*
Or as it sprong, it wither must agayne:
Tom Piper makes us better melodie.[7]

PIERS

O pierlesse Poesye, where is then thy place?
80 If nor in Princes pallace thou doe sitt:
(And yet is Princes pallace the most fitt)
Ne brest of baser birth[8] doth thee embrace.
Then make thee winges of thine aspyring wit,°   *mind*
And, whence thou camst, flye backe to heaven apace.

CUDDIE

85 Ah Percy it is all to° weake and wanne,   *too*
So high to sore,° and make so large a flight: *soar*
Her peecèd pyneons bene not so in plight,
For Colin fittes such famous flight to scanne:[9]
He, were he not with love so ill bedight,°   *afflicted*
90 Would mount as high, and sing as soote° as Swanne.[1]   *sweet*

PIERS

Ah fon,° for love does teach him climbe so hie,   *fool*
And lyftes him up out of the loathsome myre:
Such immortall mirrhor,[2] as he doth admire,
Would rayse ones mynd above the starry skie.

---

3. "In manhoode and chevalrie" [E. K.].
4. "He sheweth the cause, why Poetes were wont be had in such honor of noble men; that is, that by them their worthines and valor shold through theyr famous Posies be commended to al posterities" [E. K.].
5. "He sheweth the cause of contempt of Poetry to be idlenesse and basenesse of mynd" [E. K.].
6. Coop, cage. I.e., poets found nothing worthy to write of, and the spirit of heroic achievement (sun-bright honor) found expression neither in deeds nor in song.
7. "An Ironicall Sarcasmus, spoken in derision of these rude wits, whych make more account of a ryming rybaud, then of skill grounded upon learning and judgment" [E. K.].
8. "The meaner sort of men" [E. K.].
9. Cuddie explains that the imperfect, patched wings ("peecèd pyneons") of his own poetic powers are not in condition, but that it is proper for ("fittes") Colin to attempt ("scanne") such a high poetic flight.
1. "It is sayd of the learned that the swan a little before hir death, singeth most pleasantly" [E. K.].
2. "Beauty, which is an excellent object of Poeticall spirites" [E. K.].

95 And cause a caytive corage[3] to aspire,
  For lofty love doth loath a lowly eye.

CUDDIE

All otherwise the state of Poet stands,
For lordly love is such a Tyranne fell:°   *fierce*
That where he rules, all power he doth expell.
100 The vaunted verse a vacant head demaundes,
  Ne wont with crabbèd care the Muses dwell:
  Unwisely weaves, that takes two webbes in hand.[4]

Who ever casts° to compasse° weightye prise,   *tries / attain*
And thinks to throwe out thondring words of threate:
105 Let powre in lavish cups and thriftie bitts of meate,
  For Bacchus fruite is frend to Phoebus wise.[5]
  And when with Wine the braine begins to sweate,
  The nombers° flowe as fast as spring doth ryse.   *verses*

Thou kenst° not Percie howe the ryme should rage.   *knowest*
110 O if my temples were distaind° with wine,   *stained*
  And girt in girlonds of wild Yvie[6] twine,
  How I could reare the Muse on stately stage,
  And teache her tread aloft in buskin[7] fine,
  With queint Bellona[8] in her equipage.°   *equipment; retinue*

115 But ah my corage cooles ere it be warme,
  For thy,° content us in thys humble shade: *therefore*
  Where no such troublous tydes° han us assayde,°   *times / assaulted*
  Here we our slender pipes may safely charme.[9]

PIERS

And when my Gates shall han their bellies layd:[1]
120 *Cuddie* shall have a Kidde to store his farme.

Cuddies Embleme

Agitante calescimus illo &c.[2]

---

3. "A base and abject minde" [E. K.].
4. I.e., the Muses are not accustomed ("wont") to dwell with those afflicted by love ("crabbèd care"); he is an unwise weaver who takes two pieces of cloth ("webbes") in hand at once.
5. I.e., let him pour lavish drink but take only a little food, for wine ("Bacchus fruite") promotes poetry ("Phoebus"—Apollo—is the god of poetry).
6. Worn by followers of Bacchus. "He seemeth here to be ravished with a Poetical furie. For (if one rightly mark) the numbers rise so ful, and the verse groweth so big, that it seemeth he hath forgot the meanenesse of shepheards state and stile" [E. K.].
7. Buskins are boots worn by actors in classical

tragedies—hence a symbol for tragedy.
8. "Strange Bellona; the goddesse of battaile, that is Pallas" [E. K.]. Pallas Athena, the Greek goddess of wisdom, is not normally identified with Bellona, the Roman goddess of war.
9. "Temper and order" [E.K.].
1. I.e., when my goats bear their young.
2. The Latin line, of which Spenser gives the first three words, is from Ovid's *Fasti* 6.5: "There is a god within us; it is from his stirring that we feel warm." E. K. comments, "Hereby is meant, as also in the whole course of this Aeglogue, that Poetry is a divine instinct and unnatural rage passing the reache of comen reason."

The Faerie Queene

In a letter to Sir Walter Ralegh, appended to the first, 1590 edition of *The Faerie Queene*, Spenser describes his exuberant, multifaceted poem as an allegory—an extended metaphor or "dark conceit"—and invites us to interpret the characters and adventures in its several books in terms of the particular virtues and vices they enact or come to embody. Thus the Redcrosse Knight in Book 1 is the knight of Holiness (and also Saint George, the patron saint of England); Sir Guyon in Book 2 is the knight of Temperance; the female knight Britomart in Book 3 is the knight of Chastity ("chastity" here meaning chaste love leading to marriage). The heroes of Books 4, 5, and 6 represent Friendship, Justice, and Courtesy. The poem's general end, Spenser writes, is "to fashion a gentleman or noble person in vertuous and gentle discipline," and the individual moral qualities, taken together, constitute the ideal human being.

However, Spenser's allegory is not as simple as the letter to Ralegh might suggest, and the fashioning of identity proves to be anything but straightforward. Far from being the static embodiments of abstract moral precepts, the knights have a surprisingly complex, altogether human relation to their allegorical identities, identities into which they grow only through painful trial and error in the course of their adventures. These adventures repeatedly take the form of mortal combat with sworn enemies—hence the Redcrosse Knight of Holiness smites the "Saracen" (that is, Muslim) Sansfoy (literally, "Without faith")—but the enemies are revealed more often than not to be weirdly dissociated aspects of the knights themselves: when he encounters Sansfoy, Redcrosse has just been faithless to his lady, Una, and his most dangerous enemy ultimately proves to be his own despair. Accordingly, the meaning of the various characters, episodes, and places is richly complex, revealed to us (and to the characters themselves) only by degrees.

The complexity is heightened by the inclusion, in addition to the moral allegory, of a historical allegory to which Spenser calls attention, in the letter to Ralegh, by observing that both the Faerie Queene and another character, Belphoebe, are representations of Queen Elizabeth. (In fact, they are only two among many oblique representations of Elizabeth.) Throughout the poem there is a dense network of allusions to events, issues, and particular persons in England and the rest of the British Isles—for example, the queen's rival Mary, Queen of Scots, the Spanish Armada, the English Reformation, the controversies over religious images, and the bitter colonial struggles against Irish rebellion. Some of Spenser's characters are identified by conventional symbols and attributes that would have been obvious to readers of his time. For example, they would know immediately that a woman who wears a miter and scarlet clothes and who dwells near the river Tiber represents (in one sense at least) the Roman Catholic Church, which had often been identified by Protestant preachers with the Whore of Babylon in the Book of Revelation. Marginal notes jotted in early copies of *The Faerie Queene* suggest, however, that there was no consensus among Spenser's contemporaries about the precise historical referents of other of the poem's myriad figures. (Sir Walter Ralegh's wife, Bess, for example, seems to have identified many of the virtuous female characters as allegorical representations of herself.) Spenser's poem may be enjoyed as a fascinating story with multiple meanings, a story that works on several levels at once and continually eludes the full and definitive allegorical explanation it constantly promises to deliver.

The poem is also an epic. In moving from *The Shepheardes Calender* to *The Faerie Queene*, Spenser deliberately fashioned himself after the great Roman poet Virgil, who began his poetic career with pastoral poetry and moved on to his epic poem, the *Aeneid*. Spenser was acutely conscious that poets elsewhere in Europe, such as Ariosto and Tasso in Italy and Camoens in Portugal, had already produced works modeled on Virgil's, in celebration of their respective nations. In drawing on the British legends of Saint George and King Arthur, weaving together classical and medieval sources, and adapting whole episodes from Ariosto and Tasso, Spenser was providing his country with the epic it had lacked.

Like Virgil, Spenser is deeply concerned with the dangerous struggles and painful renunciations required to attain the highest goals. The heroic deeds of his brave knights are the achievements of individual aristocratic men and women, not the triumphs of armies or communities united in serving a common purpose, not even the triumph of the virtually invisible royal court of Gloriana, the Faerie Queene. Yet, taken together, the disjointed adventures of these solitary warriors constitute in Spenser's fervent vision the glory of Britain, the collective memory of its heroic past, and the promise of a still more glorious future. And if the Faerie Queene herself is consigned to the margins of the poem that bears her name, she nonetheless is the symbolic embodiment of a shared national destiny, a destiny that reaches beyond mere political success to participate in the ultimate, millennial triumph of good over evil.

If *The Faerie Queene* is thus an epic celebration of Queen Elizabeth, the Protestant faith, and the English nation, it is also a chivalric romance, full of jousting knights and damsels in distress, dragons, witches, enchanted trees, wicked magicians, giants, dark caves, shining castles, and "paynims" (with French names). A clear, pleasant stream may be dangerous to drink from because to do so produces loss of strength. A pious hermit may prove to be a cunningly disguised villain. Houses, castles, and gardens are often places of education and challenge or of especially dense allegorical significance, as if they possessed special, half-hidden keys to the meaning of the books in which they appear. As a romance, Spenser's poem is designed to produce wonder, to enthrall its readers with sprawling plots, marvelous adventures, heroic characters, ravishing descriptions, and esoteric mysteries.

In addition to enthralling its readers, the poem habitually entraps, misleads, and deludes them. Like Spenser's protagonists, readers are constantly in danger of mistaking hypocritical evil for good, or cunningly disguised foulness for true beauty. *The Faerie Queene* demands vigilance from its readers, and many passages must be reread in light of what follows after. In some sections, such as the dialogue between Redcrosse and Despaire (Book 1, canto 9), the repeated use of pronouns instead of proper names can lead to confusion as to who is speaking; the effect is intentional, for the promptings of evil are not always easy to disentangle from the voice of conscience.

The whole of *The Faerie Queene* is written in a remarkable nine-line stanza of closely interlocking rhymes (*ababbcbcc*), the first eight lines each with five stresses (iambic pentameter) and the final line with six stresses (iambic hexameter or alexandrine). The stanza gives the work a certain formal regularity, but the various books are composed on quite different structural principles. Book 1 is almost entirely self-contained; it has been called a miniature epic in itself, centering on the adventures of one principal hero, Redcrosse, who at length achieves the quest he undertakes at Una's behest: killing the dragon who has imprisoned her parents and thereby winning her as his bride. The spiritual allegory is similarly self-contained; it presents the Christian struggling heroically against many evils and temptations—doctrinal error, hypocrisy, the Seven Deadly Sins, and despair—to some of which he succumbs before finally emerging triumphant. It shows him separated from the one true faith and, aided by interventions of divine grace, at length reunited with it. Then it treats his purgation from sin, his education in the House of Holiness, and his final salvation. By contrast, the structure of Book 3 is more romancelike, with its multiplicity of principal characters (who present, allegorically, several varieties of chaste and unchaste love), its interwoven stories, its heightened attention to women, and its conspicuous lack of closure.

Spenser had outlined a plan for an immense poem twelve or even twenty-four books in length, but he died long before he could bring this project anywhere near completion. To some degree a lack of closure characterizes all of *The Faerie Queene*, including the more self-contained of the six finished books, and it is fitting that there survives the fragment of another book, the cantos of Mutabilitie, in which Spenser broods on the tension in nature between systematic order and ceaseless change (see pp. 457–86). The poem as a whole is built around principles that pull tautly against one another: a commitment to a life of constant struggle and a profound longing for rest; a celebration of human heroism and a perception of ineradicable human sinfulness; a vision of evil as a terrifyingly potent force and a vision of evil as mere emptiness and filth; a faith in the supreme value of visionary art and a recurrent suspicion that art is dangerously allied to graven images and deception. That Spenser's knights never quite reach the havens they seek may reflect irresolvable tensions to which we owe much of the power and beauty of this great, unfinished work.

FROM THE FAERIE QUEENE

A Letter of the Authors[1]

EXPOUNDING HIS WHOLE INTENTION IN THE COURSE OF THIS WORKE: WHICH FOR THAT IT GIVETH GREAT LIGHT TO THE READER, FOR THE BETTER UNDERSTANDING IS HEREUNTO ANNEXED

To the Right noble, and Valorous, Sir Walter Raleigh knight, Lo. Wardein of the Stanneryes,[2] and her Majesties liefetenaunt of the County of Cornewayll

Sir knowing how doubtfully all Allegories may be construed, and this booke of mine, which I have entituled the *Faery Queene*, being a continued Allegory, or darke conceit,[3] I have thought good as well for avoyding of gealous opinions and misconstructions, as also for your better light in reading thereof, (being so by you commanded,) to discover unto you the general intention and meaning, which in the whole course thereof I have fashioned, without expressing of any particular purposes or by-accidents[4] therein occasioned. The generall end therefore of all the booke is to fashion a gentleman or noble person in vertuous and gentle[5] discipline: Which for that I conceived shoulde be most plausible and pleasing, being coloured with an historicall fiction, the which the most part of men delight to read, rather for variety of matter, then for profite of the ensample:[6] I chose the historye of King Arthure, as most fitte for the excellency of his person, being made famous by many mens former workes, and also furthest from the daunger of envy, and suspition of present time.[7] In which I have followed all the antique Poets historicall,[8] first

1. The Letter was appended—not prefixed—to the 1590 edition of the poem. (It was omitted from the 1596 edition.) We follow the common practice of printing it as a "preface" to the work.
2. I.e., the mining districts of Cornwall and Devon. "Lo.": Lord.
3. Obscure or difficult poetic figure.
4. Secondary matters.
5. Pertaining to a gentleman. "Fashion": (1) to represent; (2) to educate.
6. Example. "Then": than.
7. I.e., free from current political controversy.
8. I.e., epic.

Homere, who in the Persons of Agamemnon and Ulysses hath ensampled a good governour and a vertuous man, the one in his *Ilias*, the other in his *Odysseis*: then Virgil, whose like intention was to doe in the person of Aeneas: after him Ariosto comprised them both in his Orlando: and lately Tasso dissevered them againe, and formed both parts in two persons, namely that part which they in Philosophy call Ethice, or vertues of a private man, coloured in his Rinaldo: The other named Politice in his Godfredo.[9] By ensample of which excellente Poets, I labour to pourtraict in Arthure, before he was king, the image of a brave knight, perfected in the twelve private morall vertues, as Aristotle hath devised,[1] the which is the purpose of these first twelve bookes: which if I finde to be well accepted, I may be perhaps encouraged, to frame the other part of polliticke vertues in his person, after that hee came to be king. To some I know this Methode will seeme displeasaunt, which had rather have good discipline[2] delivered plainly in way of precepts, or sermoned at large, as they use, then thus clowdily enwrapped in Allegoricall devises. But such, me seeme, should be satisfide with the use of these dayes, seeing all things accounted by their showes,[3] and nothing esteemed of, that is not delightfull and pleasing to commune sence.[4] For this cause is Xenophon preferred before Plato, for that the one in the exquisite depth of his judgment, formed a Commune welth such as it should be, but the other in the person of Cyrus and the Persians fashioned a governement such as might best be:[5] So much more profitable and gratious is doctrine by ensample, then by rule. So have I laboured to doe in the person of Arthure: whome I conceive after his long education by Timon, to whom he was by Merlin delivered to be brought up, so soone as he was borne of the Lady Igrayne, to have seene in a dream or vision the Faery Queen, with whose excellent beauty ravished, he awaking resolved to seeke her out, and so being by Merlin armed, and by Timon throughly[6] instructed, he went to seeke her forth in Faerye land. In that Faery Queene I meane glory in my generall intention, but in my particular I conceive the most excellent and glorious person of our soveraine the Queene, and her kingdome in Faery land. And yet in some places els, I doe otherwise shadow[7] her. For considering she beareth two persons, the one of a most royall Queene or Empresse, the other of a most vertuous and beautifull Lady, this latter part in some places I doe express in Belphoebe, fashioning her name according to your owne excellent conceipt of Cynthia,[8] (Phoebe and Cynthia being both names of Diana.) So in the person of Prince Arthure I sette forth magnificence in particular, which vertue for that (according to Aristotle and the rest) it is the perfection of all

---

9. Torquato Tasso (1544–1595) published his chivalric romance *Rinaldo* in 1562 and completed the epic *Gerusalemme liberata* (centered on the heroic figure of Count Godfredo) in 1575. Lodovico Ariosto (1474–1533) was author of the epic romance *Orlando furioso*, first published in 1516.
1. Though Aristotle distinguished between private and public virtues, he did not devise lists of twelve of each. Spenser was in fact relying on more modern philosophers—his friend Lodowick Bryskett and the Italian Alessandro Piccolomini. That

Spenser contemplated (as he proceeds to indicate) a poem four times as long as the six books we now have rather staggers the imagination.
2. Teaching.
3. I.e., judged according to their appearances.
4. The notions of the many.
5. The allusion is to Plato's *Republic* and Xenophon's *Cyropaedia*.
6. Thoroughly.
7. Picture, portray.
8. Ralegh's poem *The Ocean to Cynthia* praised Queen Elizabeth.

the rest,[9] and conteineth in it them all, therefore in the whole course I mention the deedes of Arthure applyable to that vertue, which I write of in that booke. But of the xii. other vertues, I make xii. other knights the patrones, for the more variety of the history. Of which these three bookes contayn three, The first of the knight of the Redcrosse, in whome I expresse Holynes: The seconde of Sir Guyon, in whome I sette forth Temperaunce: The third of Britomartis a Lady knight, in whome I picture Chastity. But because the beginning of the whole worke seemeth abrupte and as depending upon other antecedents,[1] it needs that ye know the occasion of these three knights severall adventures. For the Methode of a Poet historical is not such, as of an Historiographer.[2] For an Historiographer discourseth of affayres orderly as they were donne, accounting as well the times as the actions, but a Poet thrusteth into the middest,[3] even where it most concerneth him, and there recoursing to the thinges forepaste,[4] and divining of thinges to come, maketh a pleasing Analysis of all. The beginning therefore of my history, if it were to be told by an Historiographer, should be the twelfth booke, which is the last, where I devise that the Faery Queene kept her Annuall feaste xii. dayes, uppon which xii. severall dayes, the occasions of the xii. severall adventures hapned, which being undertaken by xii. severall knights, are in these xii books severally handled and discoursed. The first was this. In the beginning of the feaste, there presented him selfe a tall clownishe[5] younge man, who falling before the Queen of Faeries desired a boone (as the manner then was) which during that feast she might not refuse: which was that hee might have the atchievement of any adventure, which during that feaste should happen: that being graunted, he rested him on the floore, unfitte through his rusticity for a better place. Soone after entred a faire Ladye in mourning weedes, riding on a white Asse, with a dwarfe behind her leading a warlike steed, that bore the Armes of a knight, and his speare in the dwarfes hand. Shee falling before the Queene of Faeries, complayned that her father and mother an ancient King and Queene, had bene by an huge dragon many years shut up in a brasen Castle, who thence suffred them not to yssew:[6] and therefore besought the Faery Queene to assygne her some one of her knights to take on him that exployt. Presently[7] that clownish person upstarting, desired that adventure: whereat the Queene much wondering, and the Lady much gainesaying, yet he earnestly importuned his desire. In the end the Lady told him that unlesse that armour which she brought, would serve him (that is the armour of a Christian man specified by Saint Paul v. Ephes.[8]) that he could not succeed in that enterprise, which being forthwith put upon him with dewe furnitures[9] thereunto, he seemed the goodliest man in

9. For Aristotle, magnanimity ("magnificence" in Spenser)—greatness of soul—is the ultimate virtue.
1. Earlier events.
2. Historian.
3. Referring to the critical dictum that epic should begin, as the Roman poet Horace said, in medias res—"in the middle of things" (Art of Poetry, lines 147–48).
4. Past.
5. Rustic-looking.

6. Come forth.
7. Immediately.
8. Ephesians 6.11, "Put on the whole armor of God, that ye may be able to stand against the wiles of the devil." The parts (verses 14 to 17) are loins girt about with truth, breastplate of righteousness, feet shod with the gospel of peace, shield of faith "wherewith ye shall be able to quench all the fiery darts of the wicked," helmet of salvation, and "sword of the Spirit, which is the word of God."
9. Suitable equipment.

al that company, and was well liked of the Lady. And eftesoones[1] taking on him knighthood, and mounting on that straunge Courser, he went forth with her on that adventure: where beginneth the first booke, vz.

A gentle knight was pricking on the playne. &c.

The second day ther came in a Palmer[2] bearing an Infant with bloody hands, whose Parents he complained to have bene slayn by an Enchaunteresse called Acrasia: and therfore craved of the Faery Queene, to appoint him some knight, to performe that adventure, which being assigned to Sir Guyon, he presently went forth with that same Palmer: which is the beginning of the second booke and the whole subject thereof. The third day there came in, a Groome who complained before the Faery Queene, that a vile Enchaunter called Busirane had in hand a most faire Lady called Amoretta, whom he kept in most grievous torment, because she would not yield him the pleasure of her body. Whereupon Sir Scudamour the lover of that Lady presently tooke on him that adventure. But being unable to performe it by reason of the hard Enchauntments, after long sorrow, in the end met with Britomartis, who succoured him, and reskewed his love.

But by occasion hereof, many other adventures are intermedled, but rather as Accidents, then intendments.[3] As the love of Britomart, the overthrow of Marinell, the misery of Florimell, the vertuousnes of Belphoebe, the lasciviousnes of Hellenora, and many the like.

Thus much Sir, I have briefly overronne[4] to direct your understanding to the wel-head of the History, that from thence gathering the whole intention of the conceit,[5] ye may as in a handfull gripe al the discourse, which otherwise may happily[6] seeme tedious and confused. So humbly craving the continuaunce of your honorable favour towards me, and th' eternall establishment of your happines, I humbly take leave.

23. January, 1589[7]
Yours most humbly affectionate.
ED. SPENSER.

---

1. Forthwith.
2. Pilgrim.
3. I.e., there are episodes that are not part of these principal stories.
4. Run through, summarized.

5. Conception.
6. Perhaps.
7. The date is actually 1590, because until England adopted the Gregorian calendar in 1752, the new year began on March 25.

The First Booke of The Faerie Queene

Contayning
The Legende of the
Knight of the Red Crosse, or
Of Holinesse

1

Lo I the man, whose Muse whilome did maske,
  As time her taught, in lowly Shepheards weeds,[1]
  Am now enforst a far unfitter taske,
  For trumpets sterne to chaunge mine Oaten reeds,[2]
  And sing of Knights and Ladies gentle° deeds;   *noble*
  Whose prayses having slept in silence long,[3]
  Me, all too meane,° the sacred Muse areeds°   *low / counsels*
  To blazon° broad emongst her learned throng: *proclaim*
Fierce warres and faithfull loves shall moralize[4] my song.

2

Helpe then, O holy Virgin chiefe of nine,[5]
  Thy weaker° Novice to performe thy will,   *too weak*
  Lay forth out of thine everlasting scryne°   *a chest for papers*
  The antique rolles, which there lye hidden still,
  Of Faerie knights and fairest Tanaquill,°   *i.e., Gloriana*
  Whom that most noble Briton Prince[6] so long
  Sought through the world, and suffered so much ill,
  That I must rue° his undeserved wrong: *pity*
O helpe thou my weake wit, and sharpen my dull tong.

3

And thou most dreaded impe° of highest Jove,   *offspring*
  Faire Venus sonne,° that with thy cruell dart   *Cupid*
  At that good knight so cunningly didst rove,°   *shoot*
  That glorious fire it kindled in his hart,
  Lay now thy deadly Heben° bow apart,   *ebony*
  And with thy mother milde come to mine ayde:
  Come both, and with you bring triumphant Mart,[7]
  In loves and gentle jollities arrayd,
After his murdrous spoiles and bloudy rage allayd.

4

And with them eke,° O Goddesse heavenly bright,   *also*
  Mirrour of grace and Majestie divine,

---

1. Garb. The poet appeared before ("whilome") as a writer of humble pastoral (i.e., *The Shepheardes Calender*). These lines are imitated from the verses prefixed to Renaissance editions of Virgil's *Aeneid*.
2. To write heroic poetry, of which the trumpet is a symbol, instead of pastoral poetry symbolized by the humble shepherd's pipe ("Oaten reeds").
3. This and the preceding line are imitated from the opening of Ariosto's *Orlando furioso*.
4. Provide subjects for moralizing.
5. Scholars have debated whether the reference is to Clio, the Muse of history, or to Calliope, the Muse of epic.
6. I.e., Arthur, named in canto 9, stanza 6.
7. Mars, god of war and lover of Venus.

Great Lady of the greatest Isle, whose light
Like Phoebus lampe throughout the world doth shine,
Shed thy faire beames into my feeble eyne,°   *eyes*
And raise my thoughts too humble and too vile,°   *lowly*
To thinke of that true glorious type[8] of thine,
The argument° of mine afflicted stile:° *subject / humble work*
The which to heare, vouchsafe, O dearest dred° a-while. *object of awe*

Canto 1

The Patron of true Holinesse,
Foule Errour doth defeate:
Hypocrisie him to entrappe,
Doth to his home entreate.

I

A Gentle Knight was pricking° on the plaine,   *spurring*
 Ycladd[9] in mightie armes and silver shielde,
 Wherein old dints of deepe wounds did remaine,
 The cruell markes of many a bloudy fielde;
 Yet armes till that time did he never wield:
 His angry steede did chide his foming bitt,
 As much disdayning to the curbe to yield:
 Full jolly° knight he seemd, and faire did sitt,   *gallant*
As one for knightly giusts° and fierce encounters fitt. *jousts, tourneys*

2

But on his brest a bloudie Crosse he bore,
 The deare remembrance of his dying Lord,
 For whose sweete sake that glorious badge he wore,
 And dead as living ever him adored:[1]
 Upon his shield the like was also scored,°   *incised*
 For soveraine[2] hope, which in his helpe he had:
 Right faithfull true[3] he was in deede and word,
 But of his cheere[4] did seeme too solemne sad;°   *grave*
Yet nothing did he dread, but ever was ydrad.° *dreaded, feared*

3

Upon a great adventure he was bond,
 That greatest Gloriana to him gave,
 That greatest Glorious Queene of Faerie Lond,
 To winne him worship,° and her grace to have,   *honor*

8. I.e., Gloriana is the "type" (prefiguration) of
Queen Elizabeth.
9. Imitating Chaucerian English, Spenser sometimes uses the prefix *y* as the sign of a past participle.
1. A compressed reference to Revelation 1.18:
"I am he that liveth, and was dead; and, behold,

I am alive for evermore."
2. Having greatest power (often applied to medical remedies).
3. Compare Revelation 19.11: "And I saw heaven
opened, and behold a white horse; and he that
sat upon him was called Faithful and True."
4. Facial expression; mood.

Which of all earthly things he most did crave;
And ever as he rode, his hart did earne° *yearn*
To prove his puissance° in battell brave *might*
Upon his foe, and his new force to learne;
Upon his foe, a Dragon horrible and stearne.

4

A lovely Ladie rode him faire beside,
Upon a lowly Asse more white then° snow, *than*
Yet she much whiter, but the same did hide
Under a vele, that wimpled° was full low, *lying in folds*
And over all a blacke stole° she did throw, *long robe*
As one that inly° mournd: so was she sad, *inwardly*
And heavie sat upon her palfrey slow:
Seemèd in heart some hidden care she had,
And by her in a line° a milke white lambe she lad. *on a leash*

5

So pure an innocent, as that same lambe,
She was in life and every vertuous lore,
And by descent from Royall lynage came
Of ancient Kings and Queenes, that had of yore
Their scepters stretcht from East to Westerne shore,
And all the world in their subjection held;
Till that infernall feend with foule uprore
Forwasted° all their land, and them expeld: *laid waste*
Whom to avenge, she had this Knight from far compeld.° *summoned*

6

Behind her farre away a Dwarfe did lag,
That lasie seemd in being ever last,
Or wearièd with bearing of her bag
Of needments at his backe. Thus as they past,
The day with cloudes was suddeine overcast,
And angry Jove an hideous storme of raine
Did poure into his Lemans⁵ lap so fast,
That every wight° to shrowd° it did constrain, *creature / take shelter*
And this faire couple eke° to shroud themselves were fain.° *also / eager*

7

Enforst to seeke some covert° nigh at hand, *cover, shelter*
A shadie grove not far away they spide,
That promist ayde the tempest to withstand:
Whose loftie trees yclad with sommers pride,
Did spred so broad, that heavens light did hide,
Not perceable° with power of any starre: *penetrable*

5. His lover's, i.e., the earth's.

And all within were pathes and alleies wide,
  With footing worne, and leading inward farre:
Faire harbour that them seemes; so in they entred arre.

8

And foorth they passe, with pleasure forward led,
  Joying to heare the birdes sweete harmony,
  Which therein shrouded from the tempest dred,°   *fearful*
  Seemd in their song to scorne the cruell sky.
  Much can° they prayse the trees, so straight and hy,   *did*
  The sayling[6] Pine, the Cedar proud and tall,
  The vine-prop Elme, the Poplar never dry,
  The builder Oake, sole king of forrests all,
The Aspine good for staves, the Cypresse funerall.°   *funereal*

9

The Laurell, meed° of mightie Conquerours   *reward*
  And Poets sage, the Firre that weepeth still,[7]
  The Willow worne of forlorne Paramours,
  The Eugh° obedient to the benders will,   *yew*
  The Birch for shaftes, the Sallow° for the mill,   *willow*
  The Mirrhe sweete bleeding in the bitter wound,
  The warlike Beech, the Ash for nothing ill,
  The fruitfull Olive, and the Platane° round,   *plane tree*
The carver Holme,[8] the Maple seeldom inward sound.

10

Led with delight, they thus beguile the way,
  Untill the blustring storme is overblowne;
  When weening° to returne, whence they did stray,   *thinking*
  They cannot finde that path, which first was showne,
  But wander too and fro in wayes unknowne,
  Furthest from end then, when they neerest weene,
  That makes them doubt, their wits be not their owne:
  So many pathes, so many turnings seene,
That which of them to take, in diverse doubt they been.

11

At last resolving forward still to fare,
  Till that some end they finde or° in or out,   *either*
  That path they take, that beaten seemed most bare,
  And like to lead the labyrinth about°   *out of*
  Which when by tract° they hunted had throughout, *track; tracing*
  At length it brought them to a hollow cave,
  Amid the thickest woods. The Champion stout

---

6. Either because pine was used for ships or because of the tree's soaring height.
7. I.e., exudes resin continuously. Spenser in these stanzas imitates Chaucer's catalog of trees in the *Parliament of Fowls*; the convention goes back to Ovid.
8. Holly or holm oak, both suitable for carving.

Eftsoones° dismounted from his courser brave,   *at once*
And to the Dwarfe a while his needlesse spere[9] he gave.

12

"Be well aware,"° quoth then that Ladie milde,   *watchful*
  "Least suddaine mischiefe° ye too rash provoke: *misfortune*
  The danger hid, the place unknowne and wilde,
  Breedes dreadfull doubts: Oft fire is without smoke,
  And perill without show: therefore your stroke
  Sir knight with-hold, till further triall made."
  "Ah Ladie," said he, "shame were to revoke°   *draw back*
  The forward footing for° an hidden shade: *because of*
Vertue gives her selfe light, through darkenesse for to wade."

13

"Yea but," quoth she, "the perill of this place
  I better wot then° you, though now too late   *know than*
  To wish you backe returne with foule disgrace,
  Yet wisedome warnes, whilest foot is in the gate,
  To stay the stepe, ere forcèd to retrate.
  This is the wandring wood, this Errours den,
  A monster vile, whom God and man does hate:
  Therefore I read° beware." "Fly fly," quoth then   *advise*
The fearefull Dwarfe: "this is no place for living men."

14

But full of fire and greedy hardiment,°   *boldness*
  The youthfull knight could not for ought° be staide,   *anything*
  But forth unto the darksome hole he went,
  And lookèd in: his glistring° armor made   *shining*
  A litle glooming light, much like a shade,
  By which he saw the ugly monster plaine,
  Halfe like a serpent horribly displaide,
  But th' other halfe did womans shape retaine,
Most lothsom, filthie, foule, and full of vile disdaine.[1]

15

And as she lay upon the durtie ground,
  Her huge long taile her den all overspred,
  Yet was in knots and many boughtes° upwound,   *coils*
  Pointed with mortall sting. Of her there bred
  A thousand yong ones, which she dayly fed,
  Sucking upon her poisonous dugs, eachone
  Of sundry shapes, yet all ill favorèd:
  Soone as that uncouth° light upon them shone,   *unfamiliar*
Into her mouth they crept, and suddain all were gone.

---

9. Needless because the spear is used only on horseback.
1. Loathsomeness. The description echoes both classical and biblical monsters (cf. Revelation 9.7–10).

16

Their dam upstart, out of her den efrraide,°   *alarmed*
  And rushèd forth, hurling her hideous taile
  About her cursèd head, whose folds displaid°   *extended*
  Were stretcht now forth at length without entraile.°   *coiling*
  She lookt about, and seeing one in mayle
  Armèd to point,° sought backe to turne againe;   *i.e., completely*
  For light she hated as the deadly bale,°   *injury*
  Ay wont° in desert darknesse to remain,   *ever accustomed*
Where plaine none might her see, nor she see any plaine.

17

Which when the valiant Elfe[2] perceived, he lept
  As Lyon fierce upon the flying pray,
  And with his trenchand° blade her boldly kept   *cutting*
  From turning backe, and forcèd her to stay:
  Therewith enraged she loudly gan to bray,
  And turning fierce, her speckled taile advaunst;
  Threatning her angry sting, him to dismay:°   *defeat*
  Who nought aghast, his mightie hand enhaunst:°   *lifted up*
The stroke down from her head unto her shoulder glaunst.

18

Much daunted with that dint,° her sence was dazd,   *blow*
  Yet kindling rage, her selfe she gathered round,
  And all attonce her beastly body raizd
  With doubled forces high above the ground:
  Tho° wrapping up her wrethèd sterne° arownd,   *then / tail*
  Lept fierce upon his shield, and her huge traine°   *tail*
  All suddenly about his body wound,
  That hand or foot to stirre he strove in vaine:
God helpe the man so wrapt in Errours endlesse traine.

19

His Lady sad to see his sore constraint,
  Cride out, "Now now Sir knight, shew what ye bee,
  Add faith unto your force, and be not faint:
  Strangle her, else she sure will strangle thee."
  That when he heard, in great perplexitie,[3]
  His gall did grate[4] for griefe° and high disdaine,   *wrath*
  And knitting all his force got one hand free,
  Wherewith he grypt her gorge° with so great paine,   *throat*
That soone to loose her wicked bands did her constraine.

---

2. I.e., knight of Faerie Land.
3. In both the usual sense and the sense of "entangled condition."

4. I.e., his gallbladder (considered the seat of anger) was violently disturbed.

20

Therewith she spewd out of her filthy maw
   A floud of poyson horrible and blacke,
   Full of great lumpes of flesh and gobbets raw,
   Which stunck so vildly, that it forst him slacke
   His grasping hold, and from her turne him backe:
   Her vomit full of bookes and papers was,[5]
   With loathly frogs and toades, which eyes did lacke,
   And creeping sought way in the weedy gras:
Her filthy parbreake° all the place defilèd has.[6]   *vomit*

21

As when old father Nilus° gins to swell   *the Nile River*
   With timely° pride above the Aegyptian vale,   *in season*
   His fattie° waves do fertile slime outwell,°   *rich / pour forth*
   And overflow each plaine and lowly dale:
   But when his later spring gins to avale,°   *subside*
   Huge heapes of mudd he leaves, wherein there breed
   Ten thousand kindes of creatures, partly male
   And partly female of his fruitfull seed;
Such ugly monstrous shapes elswhere may no man reed.°   *see*

22

The same so sore annoyed° has the knight,   *injuriously affected*
   That welnigh chokèd with the deadly stinke,
   His forces faile, ne° can no longer fight.   *nor*
   Whose corage when the feend perceived to shrinke,
   She pourèd forth out of her hellish sinke[7]
   Her fruitfull cursèd spawne of serpents small,
   Deformèd monsters, fowle, and blacke as inke,
   Which swarming all about his legs did crall,
And him encombred sore, but could not hurt at all.

23

As gentle Shepheard in sweete even-tide,
   When ruddy Phoebus° gins to welke° in west,   *the sun / sink*
   High on an hill, his flocke to vewen wide,
   Markes° which do byte their hasty supper best;   *observes*
   A cloud of combrous° gnattes do him molest,   *encumbering*
   All striving to infixe their feeble stings,
   That from their noyance he no where can rest,
   But with his clownish° hands their tender wings   *rustic*
He brusheth oft, and oft doth mar their murmurings.

---

5. Alluding (at one level) to books and pamphlets of Catholic propaganda, notably attacks on Queen Elizabeth.
6. Revelation 16.13: "And I saw three unclean spirits like frogs come out of the mouth of the dragon, and out of the mouth of the beast, and out of the mouth of the false prophet."
7. Cesspool (i.e., her womb or organ of excretion).

24

Thus ill bestedd,° and fearful more of shame,   *situated*
   Then of the certaine perill he stood in,
   Halfe furious unto his foe he came,
   Resolved in minde all suddenly to win,
   Or soone to lose, before he once would lin;°   *cease*
   And strooke at her with more then manly force,
   That from her body full of filthie sin
   He raft° her hatefull head without remorse;   *cut away*
A streame of cole black bloud forth gushèd from her corse.°   *corpse*

25

Her scattred brood, soone as their Parent deare
   They saw so rudely° falling to the ground,   *with great force*
   Groning full deadly, all with troublous feare,
   Gathred themselves about her body round,
   Weening° their wonted entrance to have found   *thinking*
   At her wide mouth: but being there withstood
   They flockèd all about her bleeding wound,
   And suckèd up their dying mothers blood,
Making her death their life, and eke° her hurt their good.   *also*

26

That detestable sight him much amazde,°   *stunned*
   To see th'unkindly Impes° of heaven accurst,   *unnatural offspring*
   Devoure their dam; on whom while so he gazd,
   Having all satisfide their bloudy thurst,
   Their bellies swolne he saw with fulnesse burst,
   And bowels gushing forth: well worthy end
   Of such as drunke her life, the which them nurst;
   Now needeth him no lenger° labour spend,   *longer*
His foes have slaine themselves, with whom he should contend.

27

His Ladie seeing all, that chaunst, from farre
   Approcht in hast to greet° his victorie,   *congratulate*
   And said, "Faire knight, borne under happy starre,
   Who see your vanquisht foes before you lye;
   Well worthy be you of that Armorie,°   *armor*
   Wherein ye have great glory wonne this day,
   And prooved your strength on a strong enimie,
   Your first adventure: many such I pray,
And henceforth ever wish, that like succeed it may."

28

Then mounted he upon his Steede againe,
   And with the Lady backward sought to wend;°   *go*
   That path he kept, which beaten was most plaine,

Ne ever would to any by-way bend,
But still did follow one unto the end,
The which at last out of the wood them brought.
So forward on his way (with God to frend)°   *with God as friend*
He passèd forth, and new adventure sought;
Long way he travelèd, before he heard of ought.°   *aught, anything*

29

At length they chaunst to meet upon the way
  An agèd Sire, in long blacke weedes yclad,[8]
  His feete all bare, his beard all hoarie° gray,   *silvery*
  And by his belt his booke he hanging had;
  Sober he seemde, and very sagely sad,°   *grave*
  And to the ground his eyes were lowly bent,
  Simple in shew,° and voyde of malice bad,   *show*
  And all the way he prayèd, as he went,
And often knockt his brest, as one that did repent.

30

He faire the knight saluted, louting° low,   *bowing*
  Who faire him quited,° as that courteous was: *responded*
  And after askèd him, if he did know
  Of straunge adventures, which abroad did pas.
  "Ah my deare Sonne," quoth he, "how should, alas,
  Silly° old man, that lives in hidden cell,   *simple*
  Bidding his beades° all day for his trespas,   *saying his prayers*
  Tydings of warre and worldly trouble tell?
With holy father sits not with such things to mell.[9]

31

"But if of daunger which hereby doth dwell,
  And homebred evill ye desire to heare,
  Of a straunge man I can you tidings tell,
  That wasteth° all this countrey farre and neare."   *lays waste to*
  "Of such," said he, "I chiefly do inquere,
  And shall you well reward to shew the place,
  In which that wicked wight his dayes doth weare.°   *spend*
  For to all knighthood it is foule disgrace,
That such a cursèd creature lives so long a space."

32

"Far hence," quoth he, "in wastfull° wildernesse   *desolate*
  His dwelling is, by which no living wight°   *creature*
  May ever passe, but thorough° great distresse."   *through*
  "Now," sayd the Lady, "draweth toward night,
  And well I wote, that of your later° fight   *recent*

8. Dressed in long black garments.
9. I.e., it is not fitting for a holy hermit to meddle ("mell") with such things.

Ye all forwearied be: for what so strong,
But wanting° rest will also want of might?   *lacking*
The Sunne that measures heaven all day long,
At night doth baite° his steedes the Ocean waves emong.   *feed; refresh*

33

"Then with the Sunne take Sir, your timely rest,
And with new day new worke at once begin:
Untroubled night they say gives counsell best."
"Right well Sir knight ye have advisèd bin,"
Quoth then that agèd man; "the way to win
Is wisely to advise:° now day is spent;   *take thought*
Therefore with me ye may take up your In°   *lodging*
For this same night." The knight was well content.
So with that godly father to his home they went.

34

A little lowly Hermitage it was,
Downe in a dale, hard by° a forests side,   *close to*
Far from resort° of people, that did pas   *access*
In travell to and froe: a little wyde°   *apart*
There was an holy Chappell edifyde,°   *built*
Wherein the Hermite dewly wont° to say   *was accustomed*
His holy things° each morne and eventyde: *prayers*
Thereby a Christall streame did gently play,
Which from a sacred fountaine wellèd forth alway.

35

Arrivèd there, the little house they fill,
Ne looke for entertainement,° where none was: *elegant provision*
Rest is their feast, and all things at their will;
The noblest mind the best contentment has.
With faire discourse the evening so they pas:
For that old man of pleasing wordes had store,
And well could file° his tongue as smooth as glas;   *polish*
He told of Saintes and Popes, and evermore
He strowd an *Ave-Mary*[1] after and before.

36

The drouping Night thus creepeth on them fast,
And the sad humour° loading their eye liddes,   *heavy moisture*
As messenger of Morpheus[2] on them cast
Sweet slombring deaw, the which to sleepe them biddes.
Unto their lodgings then his guestes he riddes:°   *leads*
Where when all drownd in deadly sleepe° he findes,   *sleep like death*
He to his study goes, and there amiddes

---

1. Hail Mary (Latin); i.e., a Catholic prayer.
2. Here (as often) Morpheus, the classical god of
dreams, is conflated with his father, Somnus, god
of sleep.

His Magick bookes and artes of sundry kindes,
He seekes out mighty charmes, to trouble sleepy mindes.

37

Then choosing out few wordes most horrible
  (Let none them read), thereof did verses frame,°   *make*
  With which and other spelles like terrible,
  He bade awake blacke Plutoes griesly Dame,[3]
  And cursèd heaven, and spake reprochfull shame
  Of highest God, the Lord of life and light;
  A bold bad man, that dared to call by name
  Great Gorgon,[4] Prince of darknesse and dead night,
At which Cocytus quakes, and Styx is put to flight.

38

And forth he cald out of deepe darknesse dred
  Legions of Sprights,° the which like little flyes[5]   *spirits*
  Fluttring about his ever damnèd hed,
  A-waite whereto their service he applyes,
  To aide his friends, or fray° his enimies: *frighten*
  Of those he chose out two, the falsest twoo,
  And fittest for to forge true-seeming lyes;
  The one of them he gave a message too,
The other by him selfe staide other worke to doo.

39

He making speedy way through spersèd° ayre,   *dispersed*
  And through the world of waters wide and deepe,
  To Morpheus house doth hastily repaire.
  Amid the bowels of the earth full steepe,
  And low, where dawning day doth never peepe,
  His dwelling is; there Tethys° his wet bed   *the wife of Ocean*
  Doth ever wash, and Cynthia[6] still° doth steepe   *continually*
  In silver deaw his ever-drouping hed,
Whiles sad° Night over him her mantle black doth spred. *sober*

40

Whose double gates he findeth lockèd fast,
  The one faire framed of burnisht Yvory,
  The other all with silver overcast;
  And wakefull dogges before them farre do lye,
  Watching to banish Care their enimy,
  Who oft is wont° to trouble gentle Sleepe.   *accustomed*
  By them the Sprite doth passe in quietly,

3. Proserpine, as patron of witchcraft and wife of Pluto, god of the underworld.
4. Demogorgon, in some myths the progenitor of all the gods, so powerful that the mention of his name causes hell's rivers (Styx and Cocytus) to tremble.
5. The simile associates him with Beelzebub (Lord of Flies), the name given to "the prince of the devils."
6. Diana, as goddess of the moon.

And unto Morpheus comes, whom drownèd deepe
In drowsie fit he findes: of nothing he takes keepe.°   *notice*

41

And more, to lulle him in his slumber soft,
  A trickling streame from high rocke tumbling downe
  And ever-drizling raine upon the loft,°   *aloft, above*
  Mixt with a murmuring winde, much like the sowne°   *sound*
  Of swarming Bees, did cast him in a swowne:°   *swoon*
  No other noyse, nor peoples troublous cryes,
  As still° are wont t'annoy the wallèd towne,   *always*
  Might there be heard: but carelesse° Quiet lyes,   *free from care*
Wrapt in eternall silence farre from enemyes.[7]

42

The messenger approching to him spake,
  But his wast° wordes returnd to him in vaine: *wasted*
  So sound he slept, that nought mought° him awake.   *might*
  Then rudely he him thrust, and pusht with paine,°   *effort*
  Whereat he gan to stretch: but he againe
  Shooke him so hard, that forcèd him to speake.
  As one then in a dreame, whose dryer braine[8]
  Is tost with troubled sights and fancies° weake,   *fantasies*
He mumbled soft, but would not all his silence breake.

43

The Sprite then gan more boldly him to wake,
  And threatned unto him the dreaded name
  Of Hecate:° whereat he gan to quake,   *queen of Hades*
  And lifting up his lumpish° head, with blame   *heavy*
  Halfe angry askèd him, for what° he came.   *why*
  "Hither," quoth he, "me Archimago[9] sent,
  He that the stubborne Sprites can wisely tame,
  He bids thee to him send for his intent
A fit false dreame, that can delude the sleepers sent."°   *senses*

44

The God obayde, and calling forth straight way
  A diverse° dreame out of his prison darke,   *diverting, distracting*
  Delivered it to him, and downe did lay
  His heavie head, devoide of carefull carke,°   *anxious concerns*
  Whose sences all were straight benumbd and starke.[1]
  He backe returning by the Yvorie dore,[2]

---

7. Spenser is imitating descriptions of the caves of Morpheus in Chaucer (*Book of the Duchess*, lines 153–77) and of Somnus in Ovid (*Metamorphoses* 11.592–632).
8. According to the old physiology, elderly people and other light sleepers had too little moisture in the brain.
9. The name can be construed as meaning both "archmagician" and "architect of images."
1. Immediately ("straight") benumbed and paralyzed.
2. According to Homer (*Odyssey* 19.562–67) and Virgil (*Aeneid* 6.893–96), false dreams come through Sleep's ivory gate, true dreams through his gate of horn.

Remounted up as light as chearefull Larke,
And on his litle winges the dreame he bore
In hast unto his Lord, where he him left afore.

45

Who all this while with charmes and hidden artes,
Had made a Lady of that other Spright,
And framed of liquid ayre her tender partes
So lively,° and so like in all mens sight,   *lifelike*
That weaker° sence it could have ravisht° quight: *too weak / entranced*
The maker selfe for all his wondrous witt,
Was nigh beguilèd° with so goodly sight: *deceived*
Her all in white he clad, and over it
Cast a blacke stole, most like to seeme for Una³ fit.°   *fitting*

46

Now when that ydle dreame was to him brought
Unto that Elfin knight he bad him fly,
Where he slept soundly void of evill thought
And with false shewes abuse his fantasy,°   *imagination*
In sort as° he him schoolèd privily: *in the way that*
And that new creature borne without her dew,°   *unnaturally*
Full of the makers guile, with usage sly
He taught to imitate that Lady trew,
Whose semblance she did carrie under feignèd hew.°   *form*

47

Thus well instructed, to their worke they hast
And comming where the knight in slomber lay
The one upon his hardy head him plast,°   *placed*
And made him dreame of loves and lustfull play,
That nigh his manly hart did melt away,
Bathèd in wanton blis and wicked joy:
Then seemèd him his Lady by him lay,
And to him playnd,° how that false wingèd boy°   *complained / Cupid*
Her chast hart had subdewd, to learne Dame pleasures toy.°   *lustful play*

48

And she her selfe of beautie soveraigne Queene,
Faire Venus seemde unto his bed to bring
Her, whom he waking evermore did weene°   *think*
To be the chastest flowre, that ay° did spring   *ever*
On earthly braunch, the daughter of a king,
Now a loose Leman° to vile service bound: *paramour*
And eke° the Graces seemèd all to sing,   *also*

---

3. Her name means "one, unity." Elizabethan readers would know the Latin phrase *Una Vera Fides* (One True Faith) and also the proverb "Truth is one."

Hymen iô Hymen, dauncing all around,
Whilst freshest Flora her with Yvie girlond crownd.[4]

49

In this great passion of unwonted° lust,   *unaccustomed*
   Or wonted feare of doing ought amis,
   He started up, as seeming to mistrust°   *suspect*
   Some secret ill, or hidden foe of his:
   Lo there before his face his Lady is,
   Under blake stole hyding her bayted hooke,
   And as halfe blushing offred him to kis,
   With gentle blandishment and lovely° looke,   *loving*
Most like that virgin true, which for her knight him took.

50

All cleane dismayd to see so uncouth° sight,   *strange; unseemly*
   And halfe enragèd at her shamelesse guise,
   He thought have slaine her in his fierce despight:°   *indignation*
   But hasty heat tempring with sufferance° wise,   *patience*
   He stayde his hand, and gan himselfe advise
   To prove his sense, and tempt° her faignèd truth.   *test*
   Wringing her hands in wemens pitteous wise,
   Tho can° she weepe, to stirre up gentle ruth,°   *then did / pity*
Both for her noble bloud, and for her tender youth.

51

And said, "Ah Sir, my liege Lord and my love,
   Shall I accuse the hidden cruell fate,
   And mightie causes wrought in heaven above,
   Or the blind God, that doth me thus amate,°   *dismay*
   For° hopèd love to winne me certaine hate?   *instead of*
   Yet thus perforce° he bids me do, or die.   *forcibly*
   Die is my dew:[5] yet rew° my wretched state   *pity*
   You, whom my hard avenging destinie
Hath made judge of my life or death indifferently.°   *impartially*

52

"Your owne deare sake forst me at first to leave
   My Fathers kingdome," There she stopt with teares;
   Her swollen hart her speach seemd to bereave,°   *deprive her of*
   And then againe begun, "My weaker yeares
   Captived to fortune and frayle worldly feares,
   Fly to your faith for succour and sure ayde:
   Let me not dye in languor° and long teares."   *sorrow*

---

4. The Three Graces of classical mythology were personifications of grace and beauty; here they sing a call to the pleasures of the marriage bed (Hymen was god of marriage). In the March eclogue of *The Shepheardes Calender,* E. K. glossed Flora as "the Goddesse of flowres, but indede (as saith Tacitus) a famous harlot."
5. I.e., I deserve to die.

"Why Dame," quoth he, "what hath ye thus dismayd?
What frayes° ye, that were wont to comfort me affrayd?"   *frightens*

53

"Love of your selfe," she said, "and deare° constraint   *dire*
   Lets me not sleepe, but wast the wearie night
   In secret anguish and unpittied plaint,
   Whiles you in carelesse sleepe are drownèd quight."
   Her doubtfull words made that redoubted[6] knight
   Suspect her truth: yet since no'untruth he knew,
   Her fawning love with foule disdainefull spight
   He would not shend,° but said, "Deare dame I rew,   *reject*
That for my sake unknowne such griefe unto you grew.

54

"Assure your selfe, it fell not all to ground;
   For all so deare as life is to my hart,
   I deeme your love, and hold me to you bound;
   Ne let vaine feares procure your needlesse smart,°   *pain*
   Where cause is none, but to your rest depart."
   Not all content, yet seemd she to appease°   *cease*
   Her mournefull plaintes, beguilèd of her art,°   *foiled in her cunning*
   And fed with words, that could not chuse° but please,   *choose*
So slyding softly forth, she turnd° as to her ease.   *returned*

55

Long after lay he musing at her mood,
   Much grieved to thinke that gentle Dame so light,°   *frivolous; wanton*
   For whose defence he was to shed his blood.
   At last dull wearinesse of former fight
   Having yrockt a sleepe his irkesome[7] spright,
   That troublous dreame gan freshly tosse his braine,
   With bowres and beds, and Ladies deare delight:
   But when he saw his labour all was vaine,
With that misformèd spright[8] he backe returnd againe.

Canto 2

The guilefull great Enchaunter parts
The Redcrosse Knight from Truth:
Into whose stead faire falshood steps,
And workes him wofull ruth.°   *mischief*

1

By this the Northerne wagoner[9] had set
   His seven fold teame behind the stedfast starre,[1]

---

6. Dreaded, but also "doubting again." "Doubt-full": fearful; also questionable, arousing doubt.
7. Tired, but also troublesome.
8. I.e., with the spirit impersonating Una.

9. The constellation Boötes, the plowman, who drives a wagon composed of the seven bright stars of Ursa Major (the Big Dipper).
1. The North Star.

That was in Ocean waves yet never wet,
  But firme is fixt, and sendeth light from farre
  To all, that in the wide deepe wandring arre:
  And chearefull Chaunticlere[2] with his note shrill
  Had warnèd once, that Phoebus fiery carre[3]
  In hast was climbing up the Easterne hill,
Full envious that night so long his roome° did fill.   *place*

2

When those accursèd messengers of hell,
  That feigning dreame, and that faire-forgèd Spright
  Came to their wicked maister, and gan tell
  Their bootelesse° paines, and ill succeeding night: *useless*
  Who all in rage to see his skilfull might
  Deluded° so, gan threaten hellish paine   *foiled*
  And sad Proserpines wrath, them to affright.
  But when he saw his threatning was but vaine,
He cast about, and searcht his balefull° bookes againe.   *deadly*

3

Eftsoones° he tooke that miscreated faire,   *immediately*
  And that false other Spright, on whom he spred
  A seeming body of the subtile° aire,   *rarefied*
  Like a young Squire, in loves and lusty-hed
  His wanton dayes that ever loosely led,
  Without regard of armes and dreaded fight:
  Those two he tooke, and in a secret bed,
  Covered with darknesse and misdeeming° night,   *misleading*
Them both together laid, to joy in vaine delight.

4

Forthwith he runnes with feignèd faithfull hast
  Unto his guest, who after troublous sights
  And dreames, gan now to take more sound repast,°   *rest*
  Whom suddenly he wakes with fearefull frights,
  As one aghast with feends or damnèd sprights,
  And to him cals, "Rise rise unhappy Swaine,°   *youth; rustic*
  That here wex° old in sleepe, whiles wicked wights   *grow*
  Have knit themselves in Venus shamefull chaine;
Come see, where your false Lady doth her honour staine."

5

All in amaze he suddenly up start
  With sword in hand, and with the old man went;
  Who soone him brought into a secret part,
  Where that false couple were full closely ment°   *mingled*
  In wanton lust and lewd embracèment:

---

2. I.e., Chanticleer; generic name for a rooster.   3. Chariot of the sun god, Phoebus Apollo.

Which when he saw, he burnt with gealous fire,
The eye of reason was with rage yblent,°   blinded
And would have slaine them in his furious ire,
But hardly° was restreinèd of° that agèd sire.   with difficulty / by

6

Returning to his bed in torment great,
    And bitter anguish of his guiltie sight,[4]
He could not rest, but did his stout heart eat,[5]
And wast his inward gall with deepe despight,°   malice
Yrkesome° of life, and too long lingring night.   tired
    At last faire Hesperus[6] in highest skie
    Had spent his lampe, and brought forth dawning light,
    Then up he rose, and clad him hastily;
The Dwarfe him brought his steed: so both away do fly.

7

Now when the rosy-fingred Morning faire,
    Weary of aged Tithones[7] saffron bed,
Had spred her purple robe through deawy aire,
And the high hils Titan° discoverèd,°   the sun / revealed
The royall virgin shooke off drowsy-hed,
    And rising forth out of her baser° bowre,   too lowly
    Lookt for her knight, who far away was fled,
    And for her Dwarfe, that wont° to wait each houre: was accustomed
Then gan she waile and weepe, to see that woefull stowre.°   affliction

8

And after him she rode with so much speede
    As her slow beast could make; but all in vaine:
For him so far had borne his light-foot steede,
Prickèd with wrath and fiery fierce disdaine,°   indignation
That him to follow was but fruitlesse paine;
    Yet she her weary limbes would never rest,
    But every hill and dale, each wood and plaine
    Did search, sore grievèd in her gentle brest,
He so ungently left her, whom she lovèd best.

9

But subtill° Archimago, when his guests   cunning
    He saw divided into double parts,
And Una wandring in woods and forrests,
Th' end of his drift,° he praisd his divelish arts   plot
That had such might over true meaning harts;
    Yet rests not so, but other meanes doth make,
    How he may worke unto her further smarts:°   pains

4. Suggesting guilt in both the sight and the
seer.
5. Proverbially, jealousy is a monster that eats
the heart.

6. The morning star.
7. Tithonus is the husband of Aurora, goddess of
the dawn.

For her he hated as the hissing snake,
And in her many troubles did most pleasure take.

10

He then devisde himselfe how to disguise;
 For by his mightie science° he could take   *knowledge*
 As many formes and shapes in seeming wise,°   *in appearance*
 As ever Proteus⁶ to himselfe could make:
 Sometime a fowle, sometime a fish in lake,
 Now like a foxe, now like a dragon fell,°   *fierce*
 That of himselfe he oft for feare would quake,
 And oft would flie away. O who can tell
The hidden power of herbes, and might of Magicke spell?

11

But now seemde best, the person to put on
 Of that good knight, his late beguilèd guest:
 In mighty armes he was yclad anon,
 And silver shield: upon his coward brest
 A bloudy crosse, and on his craven crest
 A bounch of haires discolourd diversly:°   *variously colored*
 Full jolly° knight he seemde, and well addrest,° *gallant / armed*
 And when he sate upon his courser free,°   *high-spirited*
Saint George himself ye would have deemèd him to be.

12

But he the knight, whose semblaunt° he did beare,   *likeness*
 The true Saint George was wandred far away,
 Still flying from° his thoughts and gealous feare; *because of*
 Will was his guide, and griefe led him astray.
 At last him chaunst to meete upon the way
 A faithlesse Sarazin⁷ all armed to point,°   *completely*
 In whose great shield was writ with letters gay
 Sans foy:⁸ full large of limbe and every joint
He was, and carèd not for God or man a point.°   *at all*

13

He had a faire companion of his way,
 A goodly Lady clad in scarlot red,
 Purfled° with gold and pearle of rich assay,⁹   *decorated*
 And like a Persian mitre on her hed
 She wore, with crownes and owches° garnishèd, *brooches*
 The which her lavish lovers to her gave;¹

6. A sea god who could change his shape at will (*Odyssey* 4.398–424).
7. Saracen; i.e., a Muslim, especially the foes of the Christian knights in the Crusades to the Holy Land; sometimes used generically of any non-Christian.
8. Without faith, faithless (French).
9. Proven of rich value.
1. The lady's garb associates her with the biblical Whore of Babylon (Revelation 17.3–4): "And I saw a woman sit upon a scarlet coloured beast, full of names of blasphemy, having seven heads and ten horns. And the woman was arrayed in purple and scarlet colour, and decked with gold and precious stones and pearls, having a golden cup in her hand full of abominations and filthiness of her fornication."

Her wanton° palfrey² all was overspred   *unruly, frisky*
  With tinsell trappings, woven like a wave,
Whose bridle rung with golden bels and bosses brave.°   *handsome studs*

14

With faire disport° and courting dalliaunce   *diversion*
  She intertainde her lover all the way:
  But when she saw the knight his speare advaunce,
  She soone left off her mirth and wanton play,
  And bad her knight addresse him to the fray:
  His foe was nigh at hand. He prickt with pride
  And hope to winne his Ladies heart that day,
  Forth spurrèd fast: adowne his coursers side
The red bloud trickling staind the way, as he did ride.

15

The knight of the Redcrosse when him he spide,
  Spurring so hote with rage dispiteous,°   *cruel*
  Gan fairely couch° his speare, and towards ride: *lower*
  Soone meete they both, both fell° and furious,   *fierce*
  That daunted° with their forces hideous,   *dazed*
  Their steeds do stagger, and amazèd° stand,   *stunned*
  And eke° themselves too rudely rigorous,°   *also / violent*
  Astonied° with the stroke of their owne hand,   *stunned*
Do backe rebut,° and each to other yeeldeth land.   *recoil*

16

As when two rams stird with ambitious pride,
  Fight for the rule of the rich fleecèd flocke,
  Their hornèd fronts so fierce on either side
  Do meete, that with the terrour of the shocke
  Astonied both, stand sencelesse as a blocke,
  Forgetfull of the hanging° victory: *in the balance*
  So stood these twaine, unmovèd as a rocke,
  Both staring fierce, and holding idely
The broken reliques of their former cruelty.

17

The Sarazin sore daunted with the buffe
  Snatcheth his sword, and fiercely to him flies;
  Who well it wards,° and quyteth° cuff with cuff: *fends off / requites, repays*
  Each others equall puissaunce envies,°   *power seeks to rival*
  And through their iron sides with cruell spies°   *looks*
  Does seeke to perce: repining courage yields
  No foote to foe. The flashing fier flies
  As from a forge out of their burning shields,
And streames of purple bloud new dies the verdant fields.

---

2. Riding horse (as distinguished from a warhorse); often, as here, a small saddle horse for a woman.

18

"Curse on that Crosse," quoth then the Sarazin,
  "That keepes thy body from the bitter fit;°   *death pangs*
  Dead long ygoe I wote° thou haddest bin,   *know*
  Had not that charme from thee forwarnèd° it: *prevented*
  But yet I warne thee now assurèd° sitt,   *securely*
  And hide thy head." Therewith upon his crest°   *helmet*
  With rigour° so outrageöus he smitt,   *violence*
  That a large share it hewd out of the rest,
And glauncing downe his shield, from blame him fairely blest.[3]

19

Who thereat wondrous wroth, the sleeping spark
  Of native vertue° gan eftsoones° revive,   *strength / again*
  And at his haughtie helmet making mark,°   *taking aim*
  So hugely° stroke, that it the steele did rive,   *mightily*
  And cleft his head. He tumbling downe alive,
  With bloudy mouth his mother earth did kis,
  Greeting his grave: his grudging° ghost did strive   *complaining*
  With the fraile flesh; at last it flitted is,
Whither the soules do fly of men, that live amis.

20

The Lady when she saw her champion fall,
  Like the old ruines of a broken towre,
  Staid not to waile his woefull funerall,°   *death*
  But from him fled away with all her powre;
  Who after her as hastily gan scowre,°   *scurry*
  Bidding the Dwarfe with him to bring away
  The Sarazins shield, signe of the conqueroure.
  Her soone he overtooke, and bad to stay,
For present cause was none of dread her to dismay.[4]

21

She turning backe with ruefull° countenaunce,   *pitiable*
  Cride, "Mercy mercy Sir vouchsafe to show
  On silly° Dame, subject to hard mischaunce,   *helpless*
  And to your mighty will." Her humblesse low
  In so ritch weedes° and seeming glorious show,   *clothes*
  Did much emmove his stout heroicke heart,
  And said, "Deare dame, your suddein overthrow
  Much rueth° me; but now put feare apart,   *grieves*
And tell, both who ye be, and who that tooke your part."

22

Melting in teares, then gan she thus lament;
  "The wretched woman, whom unhappy howre

---

3. Preserved him from harm.   4. I.e., there was no reason for her to be afraid.

Hath now made thrall° to your commandèment,   *slave*
Before that angry heavens list to lowre,°   *chose to frown*
And fortune false betraide me to your powre,
Was (O what now availeth that I was!)
Borne the sole daughter of an Emperour,
He that the wide West under his rule has,
And high hath set his throne, where Tiberis doth pas.[5]

23

"He in the first flowre of my freshest age,
   Betrothèd me unto the onely haire°   *heir*
Of a most mighty king, most rich and sage;[6]
Was never Prince so faithfull and so faire,
Was never Prince so meeke and debonaire;°   *gracious*
But ere my hopèd day of spousall shone,
My dearest Lord fell from high honours staire,
   Into the hands of his accursèd fone,°   *foes*
And cruelly was slaine, that shall I ever mone.

24

"His blessèd body spoild of lively breath,
   Was afterward, I know not how, convaid°   *carried away*
And fro° me hid: of whose most innocent death   *from*
When tidings came to me unhappy maid,
O how great sorrow my sad soule assaid.°   *afflicted*
Then forth I went his woefull corse to find,
And many yeares throughout the world I straid,
   A virgin widow, whose deepe wounded mind
With love, long time did languish as the striken hind.°   *deer*

25

"At last it chauncèd this proud Sarazin
   To meete me wandring, who perforce° me led   *by violence*
With him away, but yet could never win
The fort, that Ladies hold in soveraigne dread.° *utmost reverence*
There lies he now with foule dishonour dead,
Who whiles he livde, was callèd proud Sans foy,
The eldest of three brethren, all three bred
   Of one bad sire, whose youngest is Sans joy,
And twixt them both was borne the bloudy bold Sans loy.[7]

26

"In this sad plight, friendlesse, unfortunate,
   Now miserable I Fidessa° dwell,   *Faithful*

---

5. The Tiber River runs through Rome. The lady is hence associated with the Catholic Church. Her father, she says, is ruler of the west—but Una's father had the rule of both east *and* west (canto 1, stanza 5); historically, the true church once embraced east and west.
6. The lady claims to have been betrothed to Christ, bridegroom of the Church (Matthew 9.15).
7. Without law; lawless.

Craving of you in pitty of my state,
To do none° ill, if please ye not do well."   *no*
He in great passion all this while did dwell,°   *continue*
More busying his quicke eyes, her face to view,
Then his dull eares, to heare what she did tell;
And said, "Faire Lady hart of flint would rew
The undeservèd woes and sorrowes, which ye shew.

27

"Henceforth in safe assuraunce may ye rest,
  Having both found a new friend you to aid,
  And lost an old foe, that did you molest:
  Better new friend than an old foe is° said."   *it is*
  With chaunge of cheare° the seeming simple maid   *countenance*
  Let fall her eyen, as shamefast° to the earth,   *as if modestly*
  And yeelding soft, in that she nought gain-said,°   *objected*
  So forth they rode, he feining° seemely merth,   *simulating*
And she coy lookes: so dainty they say maketh derth.[8]

28

Long time they thus together traveilèd,
  Till weary of their way, they came at last,
  Where grew two goodly trees, that faire did spred
  Their armes abroad, with gray mosse overcast,
  And their greene leaves trembling with every blast,°   *breeze*
  Made a calme shadow far in compasse round:
  The fearefull Shepheard often there aghast
  Under them never sat, ne wont° there sound   *nor was accustomed to*
His mery oaten pipe, but shund th'unlucky ground.

29

But this good knight soone as he them can° spie,   *did*
  For the coole shade him thither hastly got:
  For golden Phoebus now ymounted hie,
  From fiery wheeles of his faire chariot
  Hurlèd his beame so scorching cruell hot,
  That living creature mote° it not abide;   *might*
  And his new Lady it endurèd not.
  There they alight, in hope themselves to hide
From the fierce heat, and rest their weary limbs a tide.°   *time*

30

Faire seemely pleasaunce° each to other makes,   *courtesy*
  With goodly purposes° there as they sit: *courteous conversation*
  And in his falsèd° fancy he her takes   *deceived*
  To be the fairest wight° that livèd yit;   *creature*
  Which to expresse, he bends° his gentle wit,°   *applies / mind*

---

8. A proverb meaning that disdainfulness makes one more to be coveted; here, that coyness creates unsatisfied desire.

And thinking of those braunches greene to frame
A girlond for her dainty forehead fit,
He pluckt a bough; out of whose rift there came
Small drops of gory bloud, that trickled downe the same.

31

Therewith a piteous yelling voyce was heard,
  Crying, "O spare with guilty hands to teare
  My tender sides in this rough rynd° embard,°   *bark / imprisoned*
  But fly, ah fly far hence away, for feare
  Least° to you hap, that happened to me heare,   *lest*
  And to this wretched Lady, my deare love,
  O too deare love, love bought with death too deare."
  Astond° he stood, and up his haire did hove,°   *stunned / rise*
And with that suddein horror could no member move.

32

At last whenas the dreadfull passiön
  Was overpast, and manhood well awake,
  Yet musing at the straunge occasiön,
  And doubting much his sence, he thus bespake;
  "What voyce of damnèd Ghost from Limbo[9] lake,
  Or guilefull spright wandring in empty aire,
  Both which fraile men do oftentimes mistake,°   *mislead*
  Sends to my doubtfull eares these speaches rare,°   *strange*
And ruefull plaints, me bidding guiltlesse bloud to spare?"

33

Then groning deepe, "Nor° damnèd Ghost," quoth he,   *neither*
  "Nor guilefull sprite to thee these wordes doth speake,
  But once a man Fradubio,[1] now a tree,
  Wretched man, wretched tree; whose nature weake,
  A cruell witch her cursèd will to wreake,
  Hath thus transformed, and plast in open plaines,
  Where Boreas° doth blow full bitter bleake,   *the north wind*
  And scorching Sunne does dry my secret vaines:
For though a tree I seeme, yet cold and heat me paines."

34

"Say on Fradubio then, or° man, or tree,"   *whether*
  Quoth then the knight, "by whose mischievous arts
  Art thou misshapèd thus, as now I see?
  He oft finds med'cine, who his griefe imparts;°   *expresses*
  But double griefs afflict concealing harts,
  As raging flames who striveth to suppresse."
  "The author then," said he, "of all my smarts,

---

9. A region of hell, traditionally the abode of the unbaptized.
1. *Fra* (Italian "in" or "brother") + *dubbio* ("doubt").

The motif of a man imprisoned in a tree derives from Virgil (*Aeneid* 3.27–42) and is used by Ariosto (*Orlando furioso* 6.26–53).

Is one Duessa[2] a false sorceresse,
That many errant° knights hath brought to wretchednesse. *wandering*

35

"In prime of youthly yeares, when corage hot
  The fire of love and joy of chevalree
  First kindled in my brest, it was my lot
  To love this gentle Lady, whom ye see,
  Now not a Lady, but a seeming tree;
  With whom as once I rode accompanyde,
  Me chauncèd of a knight encountred bee,
  That had a like faire Lady by his syde,
Like a faire Lady, but did fowle Duessa hyde.

36

"Whose forgèd beauty he did take in hand,°   *he maintained*
  All other Dames to have exceeded farre,
  I in defence of mine did likewise stand,
  Mine, that did then shine as the Morning starre:
  So both to battell fierce arraungèd arre,
  In which his harder fortune was to fall
  Under my speare: such is the dye° of warre: *hazard*
  His Lady left as a prise martiäll,°   *spoil of battle*
Did yield her comely person, to be at my call.

37

"So doubly loved of Ladies unlike° faire,   *diversely*
  Th'one seeming such, the other such indeede,
  One day in doubt I cast° for to compare,   *determined*
  Whether° in beauties glorie did exceede;   *which one (of two)*
  A Rosy girlond was the victors meede:°   *reward*
  Both seemde to win, and both seemde won to bee,
  So hard the discord was to be agreede.
  Fraelissa[3] was as faire, as faire mote bee,
And ever false Duessa seemde as faire as shee.

38

"The wicked witch now seeing all this while
  The doubtfull ballaunce equally to sway,
  What not by right, she cast to win by guile,
  And by her hellish science° raisd streight way   *magic*
  A foggy mist, that overcast the day,
  And a dull blast, that breathing on her face,
  Dimmed her former beauties shining ray,
  And with foule ugly forme did her disgrace:
Then was she° faire alone, when none was faire in place.[4]   *Duessa*

---

2. Double Being. *Due* (Italian "two") + *esse*
(Latin "being").

3. Frailty (Italian *Fralezza*).
4. When nobody else was fair.

39

"Then cride she out, 'Fye, fye, deformèd wight,
   Whose borrowed beautie now appeareth plaine
   To have before bewitchèd all mens sight;
   O leave her soone, or let her soone be slaine.'
   Her lothly visage viewing with disdaine,
   Eftsoones° I thought her such, as she me told,   *presently*
   And would have kild her; but with faignèd paine,
   The false witch did my wrathfull hand withhold;
So left her, where she now is turnd to treën mould.°   *the form of a tree*

40

"Thens forth I tooke Duessa for my Dame,
   And in the witch unweeting° joyd long time,   *unknowingly*
   Ne ever wist,° but that she was the same,   *knew*
   Till on a day (that day is every Prime,[5]
   When Witches wont° do penance for their crime)   *are accustomed to*
   I chaunst to see her in her proper hew,°   *in her own shape*
   Bathing her selfe in origane and thyme:[6]
   A filthy foule old woman I did vew,
That ever to have toucht her, I did deadly rew.°   *regret*

41

"Her neather partes misshapen, monstruous,
   Were hidd in water, that I could not see,
   But they did seeme more foule and hideous,
   Then° womans shape man would beleeve to bee.   *than*
   Thens forth from her most beastly companie
   I gan refraine, in minde to slip away,
   Soone as appeard safe opportunitie:
   For danger great, if not assured decay°   *destruction*
I saw before mine eyes, if I were knowne to stray.

42

"The divelish hag by chaunges of my cheare°   *demeanor*
   Perceived my thought, and drownd in sleepie night,
   With wicked herbes and ointments did besmeare
   My bodie all, through charmes and magicke might,
   That all my senses were bereavèd quight:°   *quite*
   Then brought she me into this desert waste,
   And by my wretched lovers side me pight,°   *planted*
   Where now enclosd in wooden wals full faste,[7]
Banisht from living wights, our wearie dayes we waste."

---

5. Spring; or the first appearance of the new moon.
6. Oregano and thyme were used to cure scabs and itching.
7. I.e., imprisoned within the trees.

43

"But how long time," said then the Elfin knight,
  "Are you in this misformèd house to dwell?"
"We may not chaunge," quoth he, "this evil plight,
Till we be bathèd in a living well;[8]
That is the terme prescribèd by the spell."
"O how," said he, "mote° I that well out find, *might*
That may restore you to your wonted well?"° *well-being*
"Time and suffisèd fates to former kynd
Shall us restore,[9] none else from hence may us unbynd."

44

The false Duessa, now Fidessa hight,° *called*
  Heard how in vaine Fradubio did lament,
  And knew well all was true. But the good knight
  Full of sad feare and ghastly dreriment,° *gloom*
  When all this speech the living tree had spent,
  The bleeding bough did thrust into the ground,
  That from the bloud he might be innocent,
  And with fresh clay did close the wooden wound:
Then turning to his Lady, dead with feare her found.

45

Her seeming dead he found with feignèd feare,
  As all unweeting of that well she knew,[1]
  And paynd himselfe with busie care to reare
  Her out of carelesse° swowne. Her eylids blew *unconscious*
  And dimmèd sight with pale and deadly hew° *deathlike appearance*
  At last she up gan lift: with trembling cheare
  Her up he tooke, too simple and too trew,
  And oft her kist. At length all passèd feare,[2]
He set her on her steede, and forward forth did beare.

Canto 3

Forsaken Truth long seekes her love,
  And makes the Lyon mylde,
Marres° blind Devotions mart,° and fals *spoils / trade*
  In hand of leachour° vylde. *lecher*

I

Nought is there under heav'ns wide hollownesse,° *concavity*
  That moves more deare compassïon of mind,
  Then beautie brought t'unworthy° wretchednesse *undeserved*

---

8. With allusion to John 4.14, the "well of water springing up into everlasting life."
9. I.e., time and the satisfaction of the fates alone can restore us to our former human nature.

1. I.e., pretending ignorance of what she knew well.
2. I.e., having overcome all fear.

Through envies snares or fortunes freakes° unkind: *sudden changes*
I, whether lately through her brightnesse blind,
Or through alleageance and fast fealtie,
Which I do owe unto all woman kind,
Feele my heart perst° with so great agonie,   *pierced*
When such I see, that all for pittie I could die.

2

And now it is empassionèd° so deepe,   *moved*
  For fairest Unas sake, of whom I sing,
  That my fraile eyes these lines with teares do steepe,
  To thinke how she through guilefull handeling,°   *treatment*
  Though true as touch,° though daughter of a king,   *touchstone*
  Though faire as ever living wight was faire,
  Though nor in word nor deede ill meriting,
Is from her knight divorcèd° in despaire   *separated*
And her due loves derived° to that vile witches share. *diverted*

3

Yet she most faithfull Ladie all this while
  Forsaken, wofull, solitarie mayd
  Farre from all peoples prease,° as in exile,   *press, crowd*
  In wildernesse and wastfull° deserts strayd,   *desolate*
  To seeke her knight; who subtilly betrayd
  Through that late vision, which th'Enchaunter wrought,
  Had her abandond. She of nought affrayd,
  Through woods and wastnesse° wide him daily sought; *wilderness*
Yet wishèd tydings none° of him unto her brought.   *no one*

4

One day nigh wearie of the yrkesome way,
  From her unhastie° beast she did alight,   *slow*
  And on the grasse her daintie limbes did lay
  In secret shadow,° farre from all mens sight: *shade*
  From her faire head her fillet she undight,[3]
  And laid her stole aside. Her angels face
  As the great eye of heaven shynèd bright,
  And made a sunshine in the shadie place;
Did never mortall eye behold such heavenly grace.

5

It fortunèd° out of the thickest wood   *chanced*
  A ramping° Lyon rushèd suddainly,   *raging*
  Hunting full greedie after salvage blood;°   *wild game*
  Soone as the royall virgin he did spy,
  With gaping mouth at her ran greedily,
  To have attonce° devoured her tender corse;°   *at once / body*

---

3. She took off her headband.

But to the pray when as he drew more ny,
His bloudie rage asswagèd with remorse,
And with the sight amazd, forgat his furious forse.

6

In stead thereof he kist her wearie feet,
And lickt her lilly hands with fawning tong,
As° he her wrongèd innocence did weet.°   *as if / understand*
O how can beautie maister the most strong,
And simple truth subdue avenging wrong?
Whose yeelded pride and proud submissiön,
Still dreading death, when she had markèd long,
Her hart gan melt in great compassiön,
And drizling teares did shed for pure affectiön.

7

"The Lyon Lord of everie beast in field,"
Quoth she, "his princely puissance° doth abate,   *power*
And mightie proud to humble weake does yield,
Forgetfull of the hungry rage, which late
Him prickt, in pittie of my sad estate:°   *condition*
But he my Lyon, and my noble Lord,
How does he find in cruell hart to hate
Her that him loved, and ever most adord,
As the God of my life? why hath he me abhord?"

8

Redounding° teares did choke th'end of her plaint,   *overflowing*
Which softly ecchoed from the neighbour wood;
And sad to see her sorrowfull constraint°   *affliction*
The kingly beast upon her gazing stood;
With pittie calmd, downe fell his angry mood.
At last in close hart shutting up her paine,
Arose the virgin borne of heavenly brood,°   *parentage*
And to her snowy Palfrey got againe,
To seeke her strayèd Champion, if she might attaine.°   *overtake*

9

The Lyon would not leave her desolate,
But with her went along, as a strong gard
Of her chast person, and a faithfull mate
Of her sad troubles and misfortunes hard:
Still° when she slept, he kept both watch and ward,°   *always / guard*
And when she wakt, he waited diligent,
With humble service to her will prepard:
From her faire eyes he tooke commaundèment,
And ever by her lookes conceivèd her intent.

10

Long she thus traveilèd through deserts wyde,
　By which she thought her wandring knight shold pas,
　Yet never shew° of living wight espyde;　　　　　　　　　　　*show*
　Till that at length she found the troden gras,
　In which the tract° of peoples footing was,　　　　　　　　　*track*
　Under the steepe foot of a mountaine hore;°　　　　　　　　*gray*
　The same she followes, till at last she has
　A damzell spyde slow footing her before,[4]
That on her shoulders sad° a pot of water bore.　　　　　　　*heavy*

11

To whom approching she to her gan call,
　To weet,° if dwelling place were nigh at hand;　　　　　　　*know*
　But the rude° wench her answered nought at all,　　*impolite; ignorant*
　She could not heare, nor speake, nor understand;[5]
　Till seeing by her side the Lyon stand,
　With suddaine feare her pitcher downe she threw,
　And fled away: for never in that land
　Face of faire Ladie she before did vew,
And that dread Lyons looke her cast in deadly° hew.　　　　*deathlike*

12

Full fast she fled, ne ever lookt behynd,
　As if her life upon the wager lay,°　　　　　　　　　　*were at stake*
　And home she came, whereas her mother blynd
　Sate in eternall night: nought could she say,
　But suddaine catching hold, did her dismay
　With quaking hands, and other signes of feare:
　Who full of ghastly fright and cold affray,°　　　　　　　*terror*
　Gan shut the dore. By this arrivèd there
Dame Una, wearie Dame, and entrance did requere.°　　　*request*

13

Which when none yeelded, her unruly Page
　With his rude° clawes the wicket° open rent,　　　　　*rough / door*
　And let her in; where of his cruell rage
　Nigh dead with feare, and faint astonishment,[6]
　She found them both in darkesome corner pent;°　　　　　*huddled*
　Where that old woman day and night did pray
　Upon her beades° devoutly penitent;　　　　　　　　　　*rosary*
　Nine hundred *Pater nosters* every day,
And thrise nine hundred *Aves* she was wont to say.[7]

---

4. I.e., walking slowly ahead of her.
5. Cf. Mark 4.11–12: "unto them that are without, all these things are done in parables: That seeing they may see, and not perceive; and hearing they may hear, and not understand."
6. I.e., fainting with amazement.
7. Her prayers are the Lord's Prayer ("Our Father") and the Hail Mary.

14

And to augment her painefull pennance more,
    Thrise every weeke in ashes she did sit,
    And next her wrinkled skin rough sackcloth wore,[8]
    And thrise three times did fast from any bit:°   *food*
    But now for feare her beads she did forget.
    Whose needlesse dread for to remove away,
    Faire Una framèd words and count'nance fit:
    Which hardly° doen, at length she gan them pray,   *with difficulty*
That in their cotage small, that night she rest her may.[9]

15

The day is spent, and commeth drowsie night,
    When every creature shrowded is in sleepe;
    Sad Una downe her laies in wearie plight,
    And at her feet the Lyon watch doth keepe:
    In stead of rest, she does lament, and weepe
    For the late° losse of her deare lovèd knight,   *recent*
    And sighes, and grones, and evermore does steepe
    Her tender brest in bitter teares all night,
All night she thinks too long, and often lookes for light.

16

Now when Aldeboran was mounted hie
    Above the shynie Cassiopeias chaire,[1]
    And all in deadly sleepe did drownèd lie,
    One knockèd at the dore, and in would fare;°   *come*
    He knockèd fast,° and often curst, and sware,   *insistently*
    That readie entrance was not at his call:
    For on his backe a heavy load he bare
    Of nightly stelths and pillage severall,[2]
Which he had got abroad by purchase° criminall.   *acquisition*

17

He was to weete° a stout and sturdie thiefe,   *in fact*
    Wont to robbe Churches of their ornaments,
    And poore mens boxes[3] of their due reliefe,
    Which given was to them for good intents;
    The holy Saints of their rich vestiments
    He did disrobe, when all men carelesse slept,
    And spoild the Priests of their habiliments,°   *vestments*
    Whiles none the holy things in safety kept;
Then he by cunning sleights in at the window crept.

---

8. Sackcloth and ashes are symbols of penitence and, like the rosary beads and prayers in stanza 13, are associated with Catholicism.
9. I.e., that she might rest herself.
1. The star Aldebaran, in the constellation Tau-rus, mounts over the constellation Cassiopeia.
2. I.e., he carried the booty gained from nightly thefts and various kinds of pillage.
3. A box for alms for the poor.

18

And all that he by right or wrong could find,
   Unto this house he brought, and did bestow
   Upon the daughter of this woman blind,
   Abessa daughter of Corceca[4] slow,
   With whom he whoredome usd, that few did know,
   And fed her fat with feast of offerings,
   And plentie, which in all the land did grow;
   Ne sparèd he to give her gold and rings:
And now he to her brought part of his stolen things.

19

Thus long the dore with rage and threats he bet,°   *beat*
   Yet of those fearefull women none durst rize,
   The Lyon frayèd them, him in to let:[5]
   He would no longer stay him to advize,°   *consider*
   But open breakes the dore in furious wize,°   *manner*
   And entring is; when that disdainfull° beast   *indignant*
   Encountring fierce, him suddaine doth surprize,
   And seizing° cruell clawes on trembling brest,   *fastening*
Under his Lordly foot him proudly hath supprest.

20

Him booteth not resist,[6] nor succour° call,   *help*
   His bleeding hart is in the vengers hand,
   Who streight° him rent in thousand peeces small,   *immediately*
   And quite dismembred hath: the thirstie land
   Drunke up his life; his corse left on the strand.°   *ground*
   His fearefull friends weare out the wofull night,
   Ne dare to weepe, nor seeme to understand
   The heavie hap,° which on them is alight,°   *lot / fallen*
Affraid, least to themselves the like mishappen might.[7]

21

Now when broad day the world discovered° has,   *revealed*
   Up Una rose, up rose the Lyon eke,°   *also*
   And on their former journey forward pas,
   In wayes unknowne, her wandring knight to seeke,
   With paines farre passing that long wandring Greeke,
   That for his love refusèd deitie;[8]
   Such were the labours of this Lady meeke,
   Still seeking him, that from her still did flie,
Then furthest from her hope, when most she weenèd nie.°   *believed near*

---

4. Blind heart. Abessa's name comes from "abbess," also *ab+esse* (Latin): "from being"; i.e., without substance.
5. I.e., neither of the women dared rise to let him in because the lion terrified ("frayed") them.

6. It does him no good to resist.
7. I.e., lest the same thing might happen amiss ("mishappen") to them.
8. Odysseus, who rejected immortality and the love of the nymph Calypso for his wife, Penelope.

22

Soone as she parted thence, the fearefull twaine,
  That blind old woman and her daughter deare
  Came forth, and finding Kirkrapine° there slaine,   *church robber*
  For anguish great they gan to rend their heare,
  And beat their brests, and naked flesh to teare.
  And when they both had wept and wayld their fill,
  Then forth they ranne like two amazèd deare,
  Halfe mad through malice, and revenging will,°   *desire of revenge*
To follow her, that was the causer of their ill.

23

Whom overtaking, they gan loudly bray,
  With hollow howling, and lamenting cry,
  Shamefully at her rayling all the way,
  And her accusing of dishonesty,°   *unchastity*
  That was the flowre of faith and chastity;
  And still amidst her rayling, she[9] did pray,
  That plagues, and mischiefs, and long misery
  Might fall on her, and follow all the way,
And that in endlesse error° she might ever stray.   *wandering*

24

But when she saw her prayers nought prevaile,
  She backe returnèd with some labour lost;
  And in the way as she did weepe and waile
  A knight her met in mighty armes embost,°   *encased*
  Yet knight was not for all his bragging bost,°   *boast*
  But subtill Archimag, that Una sought
  By traynes° into new troubles to have tost: *tricks*
  Of that old woman tydings he besought,
If that of such a Ladie she could tellen ought.[1]

25

Therewith she gan her passion to renew,
  And cry, and curse, and raile, and rend her heare,°   *hair*
  Saying, that harlot she too lately knew,
  That causd her shed so many a bitter teare,
  And so forth told the story of her feare:
  Much seemèd he to mone her haplesse chaunce,
  And after for that Ladie did inquere;
  Which being taught, he forward gan advaunce
His fair enchaunted steed, and eke his charmèd launce.

9. Corceca. (Abessa cannot speak.)
1. Anything. I.e., if she could tell anything about such a lady.

26

Ere long he came, where Una traveild slow,
  And that wilde Champion wayting° her besyde: *attending*
  Whom seeing such, for dread he durst not show
  Himselfe too nigh at hand, but turnèd wyde
  Unto an hill; from whence when she him spyde,
  By his like seeming shield, her knight by name
  She weend it was, and towards him gan ryde:
  Approching nigh, she wist° it was the same,   *believed*
And with faire fearefull humblesse° towards him shee came. *humility*

27

And weeping said, "Ah my long lackèd Lord,
  Where have ye bene thus long out of my sight?
  Much fearèd I to have bene quite abhord,
  Or ought° have done, that ye displeasen might,   *aught*
  That should as death unto my deare hart light:[2]
  For since mine eye your joyous sight did mis,
  My chearefull day is turnd to chearelesse night,
  And eke my night of death the shadow is;
But welcome now my light, and shining lampe of blis."

28

He thereto meeting[3] said, "My dearest Dame,
  Farre be it from your thought, and fro my will,
  To thinke that knighthood I so much should shame,
  As you to leave, that have me lovèd still,
  And chose in Faery court of meere° goodwill,   *pure*
  Where noblest knights were to be found on earth:
  The earth shall sooner leave her kindly° skill   *natural*
  To bring forth fruit, and make eternall derth,°   *desert*
Then I leave you, my liefe,° yborne of heavenly berth. *beloved*

29

"And sooth to say, why I left you so long,
  Was for to seeke adventure in strange place,
  Where Archimago said a felon strong
  To many knights did daily worke disgrace;
  But knight he now shall never more deface:°   *discredit*
  Good cause of mine excuse; that mote° ye please   *may*
  Well to accept, and evermore embrace
  My faithfull service, that by land and seas
Have vowd you to defend, now then your plaint appease."° *cease*

---

2. I.e., be as a deathblow to my loving heart. ("Deare" can also mean heavy or sore.)
3. Answering in like manner.

30

His lovely° words her seemd due recompence   *loving*
   Of all her passèd paines: one loving howre
   For many yeares of sorrow can dispence:°   *make amends*
   A dram of sweet is worth a pound of sowre:
   She has forgot, how many a wofull stowre°   *trouble*
   For him she late endured; she speakes no more
   Of past: true is, that true love hath no powre
   To looken backe; his eyes be fixt before.
Before her stands her knight, for whom she toyld so sore.

31

Much like, as when the beaten marinere,
   That long hath wandred in the Ocean wide,
   Oft soust° in swelling Tethys[4] saltish teare,   *soaked*
   And long time having tand his tawney hide
   With blustring breath of heaven, that none can bide,
   And scorching flames of fierce Orions hound,[5]
   Soone as the port from farre he has espide,
   His chearefull whistle merrily doth sound,
And Nereus crownes with cups;[6] his mates him pledg° around.   *toast*

32

Such joy made Una, when her knight she found;
   And eke th'enchaunter joyous seemd no lesse,
   Then the glad marchant, that does vew from ground
   His ship farre come from watrie wildernesse,
   He hurles out vowes, and Neptune oft doth blesse:
   So forth they past, and all the way they spent
   Discoursing of her dreadfull late distresse,
   In which he askt her, what the Lyon ment:
Who told her all that fell in journey as she went.[7]

33

They had not ridden farre, when they might see
   One pricking° towards them with hastie heat,   *spurring*
   Full strongly armd, and on a courser free,°   *eager to charge*
   That through his fiercenesse fomèd all with sweat,
   And the sharpe yron° did for anger eat,   *bit*
   When his hot ryder spurd his chauffèd° side;   *chafed; heated*
   His looke was sterne, and seemèd still to threat
   Cruell revenge, which he in hart did hyde,
And on his shield Sans loy in bloudie lines was dyde.

---

4. The wife of Ocean; here, the ocean itself.
5. Sirius, the dog star, symbolizing hot weather (the dog days).
6. Nereus, a benevolent sea god, to whom the mariner in gratitude makes libations.
7. I.e., she told all that had befallen her on her journey.

34

When nigh he drew unto this gentle payre
  And saw the Red-crosse, which the knight did beare,
  He burnt in fire, and gan eftsoones° prepare   *immediately*
  Himselfe to battell with his couchèd° speare.   *leveled*
  Loth was that other, and did faint° through feare,   *lose heart*
  To taste th'untryed dint° of deadly steele;   *blow*
  But yet his Lady did so well him cheare,
  That hope of new good hap° he gan to feele;   *fortune*
So bent° his speare, and spurnd⁸ his horse with yron heele.   *lowered*

35

But that proud Paynim° forward came so fierce,   *pagan*
  And full of wrath, that with his sharp-head speare
  Through vainely crossèd shield⁹ he quite did pierce,
  And had his staggering steede not shrunke for feare,
  Through shield and bodie eke he should him beare:°   *thrust*
  Yet so great was the puissance° of his push,   *force*
  That from his saddle quite he did him beare:
  He tombling rudely° downe to ground did rush,   *violently*
And from his gorèd wound a well of bloud did gush.

36

Dismounting lightly from his loftie steed,
  He to him lept, in mind to reave° his life,   *take*
  And proudly said, "Lo there the worthie meed°   *recompense*
  Of him, that slew Sansfoy with bloudie knife;
  Henceforth his ghost freed from repining strife,
  In peace may passen over Lethe¹ lake,
  When mourning altars purgd° with enemies life,   *cleansed*
  The blacke infernall Furies² doen aslake:°   *appease*
Life from Sansfoy thou tookst, Sansloy shall from thee take."

37

Therewith in haste his helmet gan unlace,
  Till Una cride, "O hold that heavie hand,
  Deare Sir, what ever that thou be in place:°   *whoever you are*
  Enough is, that thy foe doth vanquisht stand
  Now at thy mercy: Mercie not withstand:
  For he is one the truest knight alive,³
  Though conquered now he lie on lowly land,°   *i.e., low on the ground*
  And whilest him fortune favourd, faire did thrive
In bloudie field: therefore of life him not deprive."

8. Spurred.
9. The cross on Archimago's shield was false and did not give him the protection the Redcrosse knight received in his fight with Sansfoy (see canto 2, stanza 18).
1. The river of forgetfulness in Hades (but Styx, the river at hell's entrance, would seem more appropriate here; see canto 5, stanza 10).
2. Spirits of discord and revenge.
3. I.e., do not withhold mercy, for he is the one truest knight.

38

Her piteous words might° not abate his rage,   *could*
   But rudely rending up his helmet, would
   Have slaine him straight: but when he sees his age,
   And hoarie head of Archimago old,
   His hastie hand he doth amazèd hold,
   And halfe ashamèd, wondred at the sight:
   For the old man well knew he, though untold,[4]
   In charmes and magicke to have wondrous might,
Ne ever wont° in field, ne in round lists[5] to fight.   *accustomed*

39

And said, "Why Archimago, lucklesse syre,
   What doe I see? what hard mishap is this,
   That hath thee hither brought to taste mine yre?
   Or thine the fault, or mine the error is,
   In stead of foe to wound my friend amis?"
   He answered nought, but in a traunce still lay,
   And on those guilefull dazèd eyes of his
   The cloud of death did sit. Which doen away,°   *when the swoon passed*
He left him lying so, ne would no lenger stay.

40

But to the virgin comes, who all this while
   Amasèd stands, her selfe so mockt° to see   *deceived*
   By him, who has the guerdon° of his guile,   *reward*
   For so misfeigning her true knight to bee:
   Yet is she now in more perplexitie,°   *trouble*
   Left in the hand of that same Paynim bold,
   From whom her booteth not° at all to flie;   *is of no use*
   Who by her cleanly° garment catching hold,   *pure*
Her from her Palfrey pluckt, her visage to behold.

41

But her fierce servant full of kingly awe°   *awesomeness*
   And high disdaine,° whenas his soveraine Dame   *indignation*
   So rudely handled by her foe he sawe,
   With gaping jawes full greedy at him came,
   And ramping° on his shield, did weene° the same   *rearing / intend*
   Have reft away with his sharpe rending clawes:
   But he was stout, and lust did now inflame
   His corage more, that from his griping pawes
He hath his shield redeemed,° and foorth his swerd he drawes.   *recovered*

---

4. I.e., without needing to be told.   5. Enclosures for fighting tournaments.

42

O then too weake and feeble was the forse
   Of salvage beast, his puissance to withstand:
   For he was strong, and of so mightie corse,°   *body*
   As ever wielded speare in warlike hand,
   And feates of armes did wisely° understand.   *skillfully*
   Eftsoones he percèd through his chaufèd° chest   *angry*
   With thrilling° point of deadly yron brand,°   *penetrating / blade*
   And launcht° his Lordly hart: with death opprest   *pierced*
He roared aloud, whiles life forsooke his stubborne brest.

43

Who now is left to keepe the forlorne maid
   From raging spoile° of lawlesse victors will?   *plunder*
   Her faithfull gard removed, her hope dismaid,
   Her selfe a yeelded pray to save or spill.°   *destroy*
   He now Lord of the field, his pride to fill,
   With foule reproches, and disdainfull spight
   Her vildly° entertaines, and will or nill,   *basely*
   Beares her away upon his courser light:[6]
Her prayers nought prevaile; his rage is more of might.

44

And all the way, with great lamenting paine,
   And piteous plaints she filleth his dull° eares,   *deaf*
   That stony hart could riven have in twaine,
   And all the way she wets with flowing teares:
   But he enraged with rancor, nothing heares.
   Her servile beast° yet would not leave her so,   *the palfrey*
   But followes her farre off, ne ought° he feares, *aught; anything*
   To be partaker of her wandring woe,
More mild in beastly kind,° then that her beastly foe.   *nature*

Canto 4

To sinfull house of Pride, Duessa
*   guides the faithfull knight,*
Where brothers death to wreak° Sansjoy   *avenge*
*   doth chalenge him to fight.*

I

Young knight, what ever that dost armes professe,
   And through long labours huntest after fame,
   Beware of fraud, beware of ficklenesse,
   In choice, and change of thy deare lovèd Dame,

6. Quickly. I.e., he treats her basely and quickly bears her away, willing or not, on his horse.

Least thou of her beleeve too lightly blame,[7]
And rash misweening° doe thy hart remove: *misjudgment*
For unto knight there is no greater shame,
Then lightnesse and inconstancie in love;
That doth this Redcrosse knights ensample° plainly prove.   *example*

2

Who after that he had faire Una lorne,°   *forsaken*
Through light misdeeming° of her loialtie,   *misjudging*
And false Duessa in her sted had borne,°   *taken as companion*
Called Fidess', and so supposd to bee;
Long with her traveild, till at last they see
A goodly building, bravely garnishèd,°   *adorned*
The house of mightie Prince it seemd to bee:
And towards it a broad high way[8] that led,
All bare through peoples feet, which thither traveilèd.

3

Great troupes of people traveild thitherward
Both day and night, of each degree and place,°   *rank*
But few returnèd, having scapèd hard,°   *with difficulty*
With balefull° beggerie, or foule disgrace,   *wretched*
Which ever after in most wretched case,
Like loathsome lazars,° by the hedges lay.   *lepers*
Thither Duessa bad him bend his pace:°   *direct his steps*
For she is wearie of the toilesome way,
And also nigh consumèd is the lingring day.

4

A stately Pallace built of squarèd bricke,
Which cunningly was without morter laid,
Whose wals were high, but nothing strong, nor thick,
And golden foile° all over them displaid,   *thin layer of gold*
That purest skye with brightnesse they dismaid:°   *outdid*
High lifted up were many loftie towres,
And goodly galleries farre over laid,°   *placed above*
Full of faire windowes, and delightfull bowres;
And on the top a Diall told the timely howres.[9]

5

It was a goodly heape° for to behould,   *building*
And spake the praises of the workmans wit;°   *skill*
But full great pittie, that so faire a mould°   *structure*
Did on so weake foundation ever sit:
For on a sandie hill,[1] that still did flit,°   *shift*

---

7. [...]ou too readily believe accusations about
her.
8. [...]d is the way, that leadeth to destruction"
(M[...]w 7.13).

9. A sundial measured the hours of the day.
1. Matthew 7.26–27: "A foolish man . . . built his
house upon the sand: And the rain descended,
and the floods came, and the winds blew, and

And fall away, it mounted was full hie,
That every breath of heaven shakèd it:
And all the hinder parts, that few could spie,
Were ruinous and old, but painted cunningly.

6

Arrivèd there they passèd in forth right;
  For still° to all the gates stood open wide,   *always*
  Yet charge of them was to a Porter hight°   *committed*
  Cald Malvenù,[2] who entrance none denide:
  Thence to the hall, which was on every side
  With rich array and costly arras dight:[3]
  Infinite sorts of people did abide
  There waiting long, to win the wishèd sight
Of her, that was the Lady of that Pallace bright.

7

By them they passe, all gazing on them round,
  And to the Presence[4] mount; whose glorious vew
  Their frayle amazèd senses did confound:
  In living Princes court none ever knew
  Such endlesse richesse, and so sumptuous shew;°   *show*
  Ne° Persia selfe, the nourse° of pompous pride   *nor / breeding ground*
  Like ever saw. And there a noble crew
  Of Lordes and Ladies stood on every side,
Which with their presence faire, the place much beautifide.

8

High above all a cloth of State° was spred,   *canopy*
  And a rich throne, as bright as sunny day,
  On which there sate most brave embellishèd°   *handsomely clad*
  With royall robes and gorgeous array,
  A mayden Queene, that shone as Titans° ray,   *the sun's*
  In glistring gold, and peerelesse pretious stone:
  Yet her bright blazing beautie did assay°   *attempt*
  To dim the brightnesse of her glorious throne,
As envying her selfe, that too exceeding shone.

9

Exceeding shone, like Phoebus fairest childe,
  That did presume° his fathers firie wayne,°   *usurp / chariot*
  And flaming mouthes of steedes unwonted° wilde   *unusually*
  Through highest heaven with weaker° hand to rayne;   *too weak*
  Proud of such glory and advancement vaine,
  While flashing beames do daze his feeble eyen,°   *eyes*

---

beat upon that house; and it fell: and great was
the fall of it."
2. Unwelcome. In courtly love allegories, the
porter is often called Bienvenu or Bel-accueil

(Welcome).
3. Decorated with costly wall hangings.
4. Presence chamber, where a sovereign receives
guests.

He leaves the welkin° way most beaten plaine,   *heavenly*
 And rapt° with whirling wheeles, inflames the skyen, *carried away*
With fire not made to burne, but fairely for to shyne.[5]

10

So proud she shynèd in her Princely state,
 Looking to heaven; for earth she did disdayne,
 And sitting high; for lowly° she did hate: *lowliness*
 Lo underneath her scornefull feete, was layne
 A dreadfull Dragon with an hideous trayne,°   *tail*
 And in her hand she held a mirrhour bright,[6]
 Wherein her face she often vewèd fayne,°   *with pleasure*
 And in her selfe-loved semblance tooke delight;
For she was wondrous faire, as any living wight.

11

Of griesly° Pluto she the daughter was,   *horrid*
 And sad Proserpina the Queene of hell;
 Yet did she thinke her pearelesse worth to pas° *surpass*
 That parentage, with pride so did she swell,
 And thundring Jove, that high in heaven doth dwell,
 And wield° the world, she claymèd for her syre, *govern*
 Or if that any else did Jove excell:
 For to the highest she did still aspyre,
Or if ought° higher were then that, did it desyre. *anything*

12

And proud Lucifera men did her call,
 That made her selfe a Queene, and crownd to be,
 Yet rightfull kingdome she had none at all,
 Ne heritage of native soveraintie,
 But did usurpe with wrong and tyrannie
 Upon the scepter, which she now did hold:
 Ne ruld her Realmes with lawes, but pollicie,° *political cunning*
 And strong advizement of six wisards old,
That with their counsels bad her kingdome did uphold.

13

Soone as the Elfin knight in presence came,
 And false Duessa seeming Lady faire,
 A gentle Husher,° Vanitie by name   *usher*
 Made rowme, and passage for them did prepaire:
 So goodly° brought them to the lowest staire *graciously*
 Of her high throne, where they on humble knee
 Making obeyssance,° did the cause declare, *submission*

---

5. Phaëthon tried to drive the chariot of his father, Phoebus, the sun god, but set the skies on fire and fell.

6. Pride and figures associated with her in Renaissance literature and art often hold a mirror, emblematic of self-love.

Why they were come, her royall state to see,
To prove° the wide report of her great Majestee.   *verify*

14

With loftie eyes, halfe loth to looke so low,
  She thankèd them in her disdainefull wise,°   *manner*
  Ne other grace vouchsafèd them to show
  Of Princesse worthy, scarse them bad° arise.   *bade*
  Her Lordes and Ladies all this while devise°   *make ready*
  Themselves to setten forth to straungers sight:
  Some frounce° their curlèd haire in courtly guise,   *frizzle*
  Some prancke° their ruffes, and others trimly dight°   *pleat / arrange*
Their gay attire: each others greater pride does spight.[7]

15

Goodly they all that knight do entertaine,
  Right glad with him to have increast their crew:
  But to Duess' each one himselfe did paine
  All kindnesse and faire courtesie to shew;
  For in that court whylome° her well they knew: *formerly*
  Yet the stout Faerie mongst the middest° crowd   *thickest*
  Thought all their glorie vaine in knightly vew,
  And that great Princesse too exceeding prowd,
That to strange° knight no better countenance° allowd.   *stranger / favor*

16

Suddein upriseth from her stately place
  The royall Dame, and for her coche doth call:
  All hurtlen° forth and she with Princely pace,   *rush*
  As faire Aurora in her purple pall,[8]
  Out of the East the dawning day doth call:
  So forth she comes: her brightnesse brode° doth blaze;   *abroad*
  The heapes of people thronging in the hall,
  Do ride° each other, upon her to gaze: *climb up on*
Her glorious glitterand° light doth all mens eyes amaze.   *glittering*

17

So forth she comes, and to her coche does clyme,
  Adornèd all with gold, and girlonds gay,
  That seemd as fresh as Flora° in her prime,   *the goddess of flowers*
  And strove to match, in royall rich array,
  Great Junos golden chaire,° the which they say   *chariot*
  The Gods stand gazing on, when she does ride
  To Joves high house through heavens bras-pavèd way
  Drawne of faire Pecocks, that excell in pride,
And full of Argus eyes their tailes dispredden wide.[9]

---

7. Each despises the others' greater pride.
8. Goddess of dawn, in her crimson robe ("purple pall").

9. Peacocks, with their tails outspread ("dispredden wide"), are a symbol of pride. The hundred-eyed monster Argus was set by Juno to watch Io,

18

But this was drawne of six unequall beasts,
   On which her six sage Counsellours did ryde,
   Taught to obay their bestiall beheasts,°   *bidding*
   With like conditions to their kinds applyde:[1]
   Of which the first, that all the rest did guyde,
   Was sluggish Idlenesse the nourse of sin;
   Upon a slouthfull Asse he chose to ryde,
   Arayd in habit blacke, and amis thin,[2]
Like to an holy Monck, the service to begin.

19

And in his hand his Portesse° still he bare,   *breviary, prayer book*
   That much was worne, but therein little red,
   For of devotion he had little care,
   Still drownd in sleepe, and most of his dayes ded;
   Scarse could he once uphold his heavie hed,
   To looken, whether it were night or day:
   May seeme the wayne° was very evill led,   *chariot*
   When such an one had guiding of the way,
That knew not, whether right he went, or else astray.

20

From worldly cares himselfe he did esloyne,°   *withdraw*
   And greatly shunnèd manly exercise,
   From every worke he chalengèd essoyne,°   *claimed exemption*
   For contemplation sake: yet otherwise,
   His life he led in lawlesse riotise;°   *riotous conduct*
   By which he grew to grievous malady;
   For in his lustlesse° limbs through evill guise° *feeble / living*
   A shaking fever raignd continually:
Such one was Idlenesse, first of this company.

21

And by his side rode loathsome Gluttony,
   Deformèd creature, on a filthie swyne,
   His belly was up-blowne with luxury,°   *indulgence*
   And eke° with fatnesse swollen were his eyne,° *also / eyes*
   And like a Crane his necke was long and fyne,[3]
   With which he swallowd up excessive feast,
   For want whereof poore people oft did pyne;°   *starve*

---

one of Jupiter's loves. When Mercury killed Argus, his eyes were put in the peacock's tail feathers.
1. I.e., each bestial rider gave commands to its beast appropriate to its particular nature: the beasts and riders are suited to each other. This procession of the Seven Deadly Sins—of which Pride is queen—had a long tradition in medieval art and literature (see also Marlowe, *Dr. Faustus*,

scene 5, lines 272–328).
2. Idleness wears the gown ("habit") and hood or amice ("amis") of a monk. Traditionally, Idleness led the procession of the deadly sins.
3. Thin. The crane is a common symbol of gluttony because its long, thin neck allows extended pleasure in swallowing.

And all the way, most like a brutish beast,
He spuèd up his gorge,[4] that° all did him deteast.   *so that*

22

In greene vine leaves he was right fitly clad;
   For other clothes he could not weare for heat,
   And on his head an yvie girland had,[5]
   From under which fast trickled downe the sweat:
   Still as he rode, he somewhat° still did eat,   *something*
   And in his hand did beare a bouzing° can,   *drinking*
   Of which he supt so oft, that on his seat
   His dronken corse° he scarse upholden can,   *body*
In shape and life more like a monster, then° a man.   *than*

23

Unfit he was for any worldly thing,
   And eke unhable once° to stirre or go,°   *at all / walk*
   Not meet° to be of counsell to a king,   *fit*
   Whose mind in meat and drinke was drownèd so,
   That from his friend he seldome knew his fo:
   Full of diseases was his carcas blew,
   And a dry dropsie through his flesh did flow,
   Which by misdiet daily greater grew:
Such one was Gluttony, the second of that crew.

24

And next° to him rode lustfull Lechery,   *just after*
   Upon a bearded Goat,[6] whose rugged° haire,   *shaggy*
   And whally° eyes (the signe of gelosy,°)   *glaring / jealousy*
   Was like the person selfe, whom he did beare:
   Who rough, and blacke, and filthy did appeare,
   Unseemely man to please faire Ladies eye;
   Yet he of Ladies oft was lovèd deare,
   When fairer faces were bid standen by:°   *away*
O who does know the bent of womens fantasy?°   *caprice, whim*

25

In a greene gowne he clothèd was full faire,
   Which underneath did hide his filthinesse,
   And in his hand a burning hart he bare,
   Full of vaine follies, and new fangleness:°   *fickleness*
   For he was false, and fraught with ficklenesse,
   And learnèd had to love with secret lookes,
   And well could daunce, and sing with ruefulnesse,°   *pathos*
   And fortunes tell, and read in loving bookes,[7]
And thousand other wayes, to bait his fleshly hookes.

---

4. Vomited up what he had swallowed.
5. He resembles the drunken satyr Silenus, foster father of Bacchus, god of wine. Ivy is sacred to Bacchus.
6. Traditional symbol of lust.
7. Either manuals on the art of love (e.g., Ovid's *Ars Amatoria*) or more ordinary erotica.

26

Inconstant man, that lovèd all he saw,
   And lusted after all, that he did love,
   Ne would his looser° life be tide to law,   *lustful*
   But joyd weake wemens hearts to tempt and prove°   *try*
   If from their loyall loves he might them move;
   Which lewdnesse fild him with reprochfull paine
   Of that fowle evill, which all men reprove,°   *i.e., syphilis*
   That rots the marrow, and consumes the braine:
Such one was Lecherie, the third of all this traine.

27

And greedy Avarice by him did ride,
   Upon a Camell loaden all with gold;[8]
   Two iron coffers hong on either side,
   With precious mettall full, as they might hold,
   And in his lap an heape of coine he told;°   *counted*
   For of his wicked pelfe° his God he made,   *money*
   And unto hell him selfe for money sold;
   Accursèd usurie was all his trade,
And right and wrong ylike in equall ballaunce waide.[9]

28

His life was nigh unto deaths doore yplast,[1]
   And thread-bare cote, and cobled° shoes he ware,   *roughly mended*
   Ne scarse good morsell all his life did tast,
   But both from backe and belly still did spare,
   To fill his bags, and richesse to compare;°   *acquire*
   Yet chylde ne° kinsman living had he none   *nor*
   To leave them to; but thorough° daily care   *through*
   To get, and nightly feare to lose his owne,
He led a wretched life unto him selfe unknowne.

29

Most wretched wight, whom nothing might suffise,
   Whose greedy lust° did lacke in greatest store,°   *desire / plenty*
   Whose need had end, but no end covetise,
   Whose wealth was want, whose plenty made him pore,
   Who had enough, yet wishèd ever more;
   A vile disease, and eke in foote and hand
   A grievous gout tormented him full sore,
   That well he could not touch, nor go,° nor stand: *walk*
Such one was Avarice, the fourth of this faire band.

---

8. The camel as a symbol of avarice is based on Matthew 19.24: "It is easier for a camel to go through the eye of a needle, than for a rich man to enter into the kingdom of God."

9. I.e., he made no distinction between right and wrong.

1. Avarice was proverbially associated with old age.

30

And next to him malicious Envie rode,
 Upon a ravenous wolfe, and still° did chaw   *continually*
 Betweene his cankred° teeth a venemous tode,   *infected*
 That all the poison ran about his chaw;°   *jaw*
 But inwardly he chawèd his owne maw°   *entrails*
 At neighbours wealth, that made him ever sad;
 For death it was, when any good he saw,
 And wept, that cause of weeping none he had,
But when he heard of harme, he wexèd° wondrous glad. *waxed, grew*

31

All in a kirtle of discolourd say[2]
 He clothèd was, ypainted full of eyes;
 And in his bosome secretly there lay
 An hatefull Snake,[3] the which his taile uptyes
 In many folds, and mortall sting implyes.°   *enfolds*
 Still as he rode, he gnasht his teeth, to see
 Those heapes of gold with griple Covetyse,°   *grasping Avarice*
 And grudgèd at the great felicitie
Of proud Lucifera, and his owne companie.

32

He hated all good workes and vertuous deeds,
 And him no lesse, that any like did use,°   *perform*
 And who with gracious bread the hungry feeds,
 His almes for want of faith he doth accuse;[4]
 So every good to bad he doth abuse:°   *twist*
 And eke the verse of famous Poets witt
 He does backebite, and spightfull poison spues
 From leprous mouth on all, that ever writt:
Such one vile Envie was, that fifte in row did sitt.

33

And him beside rides fierce revenging Wrath,
 Upon a Lion, loth for to be led;
 And in his hand a burning brond° he hath,   *sword*
 The which he brandisheth about his hed;
 His eyes did hurle forth sparkles fiery red,
 And starèd sterne on all, that him beheld,
 As ashes pale of hew and seeming ded;
 And on his dagger still° his hand he held,   *always*
Trembling through hasty rage, when choler° in him sweld. *anger*

---

2. Robe or gown of many-colored cloth.
3. Traditional attribute of envy.
4. Envy perversely discounts others' good works
by attributing them to a selfish motive: the desire
to compensate (in God's eyes) for lack of faith.

34

His ruffin° raiment all was staind with blood,   *disorderly*
 Which he had spilt, and all to rags yrent,°   *torn*
 Through unadvisèd rashnesse woxen wood,°   *grown insane*
 For of his hands he had no governement,°   *control*
 Ne cared for° bloud in his avengement:° *minded / vengeance*
 But when the furious fit was overpast,
 His cruell facts° he often would repent;   *actions*
 Yet wilfull man he never would forecast,
How many mischieves should ensue his heedlesse hast.[5]

35

Full many mischiefes follow cruell Wrath;
 Abhorrèd bloudshed, and tumultuous strife,
 Unmanly murder, and unthrifty scath,[6]
 Bitter despight,° with rancours rusty knife,   *malice*
 And fretting griefe the enemy of life;
 All these, and many evils moe° haunt ire,° *more / anger*
 The swelling Splene,[7] and Frenzy raging rife,
 The shaking Palsey, and Saint Fraunces fire:[8]
Such one was Wrath, the last of this ungoldly tire.°   *train*

36

And after all, upon the wagon beame
 Rode Sathan,° with a smarting whip in hand,   *Satan*
 With which he forward lasht the laesie teme,
 So oft as Slowth° still in the mire did stand.   *Idleness*
 Huge routs° of people did about them band,   *crowds*
 Showting for joy, and still before their way
 A foggy mist had covered all the land;
 And underneath their feet, all scattered lay
Dead sculs and bones of men, whose life had gone astray.

37

So forth they marchen in this goodly sort,°   *company*
 To take the solace° of the open aire,   *pleasure*
 And in fresh flowring fields themselves to sport;
 Emongst the rest rode that false Lady faire,
 The fowle Duessa, next unto the chaire
 Of proud Lucifera, as one of the traine:
 But that good knight would not so nigh repaire,° *approach*
 Him selfe estraunging from their joyaunce° vaine, *festivity*
Whose fellowship seemd far unfit for warlike swaine.° *young man*

---

5. I.e., he never would foresee ("forecast") the calamities his careless haste caused.
6. I.e., inhuman murder and destructive harm.
7. In Renaissance physiology, the spleen was regarded as the seat of ill-humor.
8. Presumably Saint Anthony's fire: erysipelas, or the flaming itch; appropriate to Wrath.

38

So having solacèd themselves a space
 With pleasaunce of the breathing° fields yfed,   *emitting fragrance*
 They backe returnèd to the Princely Place;
 Whereas an errant knight in armes ycled,°   *clad*
 And heathnish shield, wherein with letters red
 Was writ Sans joy, they new arrivèd find:
 Enflamed with fury and fiers hardy-hed,°   *hardihood*
 He seemd in hart to harbour thoughts unkind,
And nourish bloudy vengeaunce in his bitter mind.

39

Who when the shamèd shield[9] of slaine Sans foy
 He spied with that same Faery champions page,°   *i.e., the dwarf*
 Bewraying° him, that did of late destroy   *revealing*
 His eldest brother, burning all with rage
 He to him leapt, and that same envious gage°   *envied prize*
 Of victors glory from him snatcht away:
 But th'Elfin knight, which ought that warlike wage,[1]
 Disdaind to loose the meed° he wonne in fray,°   *reward / battle*
And him rencountring° fierce, reskewd the noble pray. *encountering*

40

Therewith they gan to hurtlen° greedily,   *rush together*
 Redoubted battaile ready to darrayne,°   *contest*
 And clash their shields, and shake their swords on hy,
 That with their sturre° they troubled all the traine; *tumult*
 Till that great Queene upon eternall paine
 Of high displeasure, that ensewen° might,   *ensue*
 Commaunded them their fury to refraine,
 And if that either to that shield had right,
In equall lists[2] they should the morrow next it fight.

41

"Ah dearest Dame," quoth then the Paynim° bold,   *pagan*
 "Pardon the errour of enragèd wight,°   *creature; man*
 Whom great griefe made forget the raines to hold
 Of reasons rule, to see this recreant° knight,   *cowardly*
 No knight, but treachour° full of false despight° *traitor / disdain*
 And shamefull treason, who through guile° hath slayn *deceit*
 The prowest° knight, that ever field did fight,   *bravest*
 Even stout Sans foy (O who can then refrayn?)
Whose shield he beares renverst, the more to heape disdayn.

---

9. Carrying a shield upside down, with the heraldic arms reversed, was a great insult (see stanza 41, line 9).

1. The knight (Redcrosse) who owned ("ought") that spoil of war ("warlike wage").
2. I.e., in impartial formal combat.

42

"And to augment the glorie of his guile,
  His° dearest love the faire Fidessa loe   *i.e., Sansfoy's*
  Is there possessèd of³ the traytour vile,
  Who reapes the harvest sowen by his foe,
  Sowen in bloudy field, and bought with woe:
  That° brothers hand shall dearely well requight   *that act*
  So be, O Queene, you equall favour showe."⁴
  Him litle answerd th'angry Elfin knight:
He never meant with words, but swords to plead his right.

43

But threw his gauntlet as a sacred pledge,
  His cause in combat the next day to try:
  So been they parted both, with harts on edge,
  To be avenged each on his enimy.
  That night they pas in joy and jollity,
  Feasting and courting both in bowre and hall;⁵
  For Steward was excessive Gluttonie,
  That of his plenty pourèd forth to all;
Which doen,° the Chamberlain⁶ Slowth did to rest them call.   *done*

44

Now whenas darkesome night had all displayd
  Her coleblacke curtein over brightest skye,
  The warlike youthes on dayntie° couches layd,   *fine*
  Did chace away sweet sleepe from sluggish eye,
  To muse on meanes of hopèd victory.
  But whenas Morpheus⁷ had with leaden mace
  Arrested all that courtly company,
  Up-rose Duessa from her resting place,
And to the Paynims lodging comes with silent pace.

45

Whom broad awake she finds, in troublous fit,°   *troubled mood*
  Forecasting, how his foe he might annoy,°   *injure*
  And him amoves° with speaches seeming fit: *arouses*
  "Ah deare Sans joy, next dearest to Sans foy,
  Cause of my new griefe, cause of my new joy,
  Joyous, to see his ymage in mine eye,
  And greeved, to thinke how foe did him destroy,
  That was the flowre of grace and chevalrye;
Lo his Fidessa to thy secret faith I flye."

---

3. Possessed by (i.e., sexually).
4. I.e., if, O Queen, you show impartiality ("equall favour").
5. I.e., feasting in hall, courting in bowers (inner apartments, bedrooms).

6. The court attendant in charge of the bed-chambers.
7. Here, the god of sleep (cf. canto 1, stanza 36, n. 2).

46

With gentle wordes he can° her fairely° greet,   *did / courteously*
 And bad say on the secret of her hart.
 Then sighing soft, "I learne that litle sweet
 Oft tempred is," quoth she, "with muchell° smart: *much*
 For since my brest was launcht with lovely dart[8]
 Of deare Sansfoy, I never joyèd howre,°   *for an hour*
 But in eternall woes my weaker° hart   *too weak*
 Have wasted, loving him with all my powre,
And for his sake have felt full many an heavie stowre.°   *grief*

47

"At last when perils all I weenèd past,
 And hoped to reape the crop of all my care,
 Into new woes unweeting° I was cast,   *unknowing*
 By this false faytor,° who unworthy ware°   *imposter / wore*
 His worthy shield, whom he with guilefull snare
 Entrappèd slew, and brought to shamefull grave.
 Me silly° maid away with him he bare,   *helpless*
 And ever since hath kept in darksome cave,
For that I would not yeeld, that° to Sans foy I gave.   *what*

48

"But since faire Sunne hath sperst° that lowring clowd,   *dispersed*
 And to my loathèd life now shewes some light,
 Under your beames I will me safely shroud,°   *take shelter*
 From dreaded storme of his disdainfull spight:
 To you th'inheritance belongs by right
 Of brothers prayse, to you eke longs° his love.   *belongs*
 Let not his love, let not his restlesse spright°   *ghost*
 Be unrevenged, that calles to you above
From wandring Stygian[9] shores, where it doth endlesse move."

49

Thereto said he, "Faire Dame be nought dismaid
 For sorrowes past; their griefe is with them gone:
 Ne yet of present perill be affraid;
 For needlesse feare did never vantage° none,   *aid*
 And helplesse hap it booteth not to mone.[1]
 Dead is Sans-foy, his vitall° paines are past,   *living*
 Though greevèd ghost for vengeance deepe do grone:
 He lives, that shall him pay his dewties° last,   *rites*
And guiltie Elfin bloud shall sacrifice in hast."

8. I.e., since my breast was pierced with the arrow of love.
9. I.e., from wandering on the banks of the river Styx, in Hades.
1. I.e., it does not help to moan over that which is beyond help ("helplesse hap").

50

"O but I feare the fickle freakes,"° quoth shee, *unpredictable tricks*
 "Of fortune false, and oddes of armes[2] in field."
"Why dame," quoth he, "what oddes can ever bee,
Where both do fight alike, to win or yield?"
"Yea but," quoth she, "he beares a charmèd shield,
And eke enchaunted armes, that none can perce,
Ne none can wound the man, that does them wield."
 "Charmd or enchaunted," answerd he then ferce,° *fiercely*
"I no whit reck,[3] ne you the like need to reherce.° *recount*

51

"But faire Fidessa, sithens° fortunes guile, *since*
 Or enimies powre hath now captivèd you,
Returne from whence ye came, and rest a while
Till morrow next, that I the Elfe subdew,
And with Sans-foyes dead dowry you endew."[4]
"Ay me, that is a double death," she said,
"With proud foes sight my sorrow to renew:
Where ever yet I be, my secrete aid
Shall follow you." So passing forth she him obaid.

Canto 5

*The faithfull knight in equall field
subdewes his faithlesse foe,
Whom false Duessa saves, and for
his cure to hell does goe.*

1

The noble hart, that harbours vertuous thought,
 And is with child of° glorious great intent, *pregnant with*
Can never rest, untill it forth have brought
Th'eternall brood of glorie excellent:[5]
Such restlesse passion did all night torment
The flaming corage° of that Faery knight, *heart; mind*
Devizing, how that doughtie° turnament *worthy*
 With greatest honour he atchieven might;
Still did he wake, and still did watch for dawning light.

2

At last the golden Orientall gate
 Of greatest heaven gan to open faire,
And Phoebus[6] fresh, as bridegrome to his mate,

---

2. Advantage of superior arms.
3. I do not care at all.
4. I.e., endow you with the legacy of the dead Sansfoy.
5. That good must be manifested in action, not in mere intent, is an important Renaissance commonplace.
6. I.e., the sun. Cf. Psalms 19.4–5: "In them hath he set a Tabernacle for the sun, Which is as a bridegroom coming out of his chamber."

Came dauncing forth, shaking his deawie haire:
And hurld his glistring beames through gloomy aire.
Which when the wakeful Elfe perceived, streight way
He started up, and did him selfe prepaire,
In sun-bright armes, and battailous° array: *warlike*
For with that Pagan proud he combat will that day.

3

And forth he comes into the commune hall,
 Where earely waite him many a gazing eye,
 To weet° what end to straunger knights may fall.° *learn / befall*
 There many Minstrales maken melody,
 To drive away the dull melancholy,
 And many Bardes, that to the trembling chord
 Can tune their timely° voyces cunningly,   *measured*
 And many Chroniclers, that can record
Old loves, and warres for ladies doen° by many a Lord.[7] *done*

4

Soone after comes the cruell Sarazin,°   *Saracen*
 In woven maile all armèd warily,
 And sternly lookes at him, who not a pin
 Does care for looke of living creatures eye.
 They bring them wines of Greece and Araby,
 And daintie spices fetcht from furthest Ynd,°   *India*
 To kindle heat of courage privily:°   *within*
 And in the wine a solemne oth they bynd
T'observe the sacred lawes of armes, that are assynd.

5

At last forth comes that far renowmèd Queene,
 With royall pomp and Princely majestie;
 She is ybrought unto a palèd° greene,   *fenced*
 And placèd under stately canapee,°   *canopy*
 The warlike feates of both those knights to see.
 On th'other side in all mens open vew
 Duessa placèd is, and on a tree
Sans-foy his shield is hangd with bloudy hew:
Both those the lawrell girlonds[8] to the victor dew.

6

A shrilling trompet sownded from on hye,
 And unto battaill bad° them selves addresse: *bade*
 Their shining shieldes about their wrestes° they tye, *wrists*
 And burning blades about their heads do blesse,° *brandish*
 The instruments of wrath and heavinesse:°   *rage*

---

7. Minstrels play the music on their instruments, bards sing the words, chroniclers—historians, epic poets—write of love and war.

8. Laurel wreaths were awarded to the victor of a joust.

With greedy force each other doth assayle,
And strike so fiercely, that they do impresse
Deepe dinted furrowes in the battred mayle;
The yron walles to ward their blowes are weake and fraile.[9]

7

The Sarazin was stout,° and wondrous strong,   *bold*
 And heapèd blowes like yron hammers great:
 For after bloud and vengeance he did long.
 The knight was fiers,° and full of youthly heat: *high-spirited*
 And doubled strokes, like dreaded thunders threat:
 For all for prayse and honour he did fight.
 Both stricken strike, and beaten both do beat,
 That from their shields forth flyeth firie light,
And helmets hewen deepe, shew marks of eithers might.

8

So th'one for wrong, the other strives for right:
 As when a Gryfon[1] seizèd° of his pray,   *in possession*
 A Dragon fiers encountreth in his flight,
 Through widest ayre making his ydle° way,   *casual*
 That would his rightfull ravine° rend away: *plunder*
 With hideous horrour both together smight,
 And souce° so sore, that they the heavens affray:° *strike / startle*
 The wise Southsayer° seeing so sad sight, *soothsayer*
Th'amazèd vulgar tels of warres and mortall fight.

9

So th'one for wrong, the other strives for right,
 And each to deadly shame would drive his foe:
 The cruell steele so greedily doth bight
 In tender flesh, that streames of bloud down flow,
 With which the armes, that earst° so bright did show, *at first*
 Into a pure vermillion now are dyde:
 Great ruth° in all the gazers harts did grow, *pity*
 Seeing the gorèd woundes to gape so wyde,
That victory they dare not wish to either side.

10

At last the Paynim chaunst to cast his eye,
 His suddein° eye, flaming with wrathfull fyre, *darting*
 Upon his brothers shield, which hong thereby:
 Therewith redoubled was his raging yre,° *anger*
 And said, "Ah wretched sonne of wofull syre,
 Doest thou sit wayling by black Stygian lake° *the river Styx*
 Whilest here thy shield is hangd for victors hyre,° *reward*

---

9. I.e., their armor is too frail to withstand such blows.
1. A legendary monster, half-eagle, half-lion.

And sluggish german² doest thy forces slake,°   *slacken*
To after-send his foe, that him may overtake?

11

"Goe caytive° Elfe, him quickly overtake,   *servile*
  And soone redeeme from his long wandring woe;
  Goe guiltie ghost, to him my message make,
  That I his shield have quit° from dying foe."   *rescued*
  Therewith upon his crest he strokè him so,
  That twise he reelèd, readie twise to fall;
  End of the doubtfull battell deemèd tho°   *then*
  The lookers on,³ and lowd to him gan call
The false Duessa, "Thine the shield, and I, and all."

12

Soone as the Faerie heard his Ladie speake,
  Out of his swowning dreame he gan awake,
  And quickning° faith, that earst was woxen° weake,   *life-restoring / grown*
  The creeping deadly cold away did shake:
  Tho moved with wrath, and shame, and Ladies sake,°   *regard*
  Of all attonce he cast° avengd to bee,   *determined*
  And with so'exceeding furie at him strake,
  That forcèd him to stoupe upon his knee;
Had he not stoupèd so, he should have cloven bee.

13

And to him said, "Goe now proud Miscreant,°   *misbeliever*
  Thy selfe thy message doe° to german deare,   *give*
  Alone he wandring thee too long doth want:
  Goe say, his foe thy shield with his doth beare."
  Therewith his heavie hand he high gan reare,
  Him to have slaine; when loe a darkesome clowd
  Upon him fell: he no where doth appeare,
  But vanisht is. The Elfe him cals alowd,
But answer none receives: the darknes him does shrowd.⁴

14

In haste Duessa from her place arose,
  And to him running said, "O prowest° knight,   *bravest*
  That ever Ladie to her love did chose,
  Let now abate the terror of your might,
  And quench the flame of furious despight,°   *anger*
  And bloudie vengeance; lo th'infernall powres
  Covering your foe with cloud of deadly night,

2. Kinsman; here, brother.
3. I.e., the onlookers then thought this would end the battle, heretofore in doubt.
4. The device of a god rescuing a hero in danger by hiding him in a cloud has parallels in *Iliad* 3.380, *Aeneid* 5.810–12, and *Gerusalemme liberata* 7.44–45.

Have borne him hence to Plutoes balefull bowres.°   *i.e., Hades*
The conquest yours, I yours, the shield, and glory yours."

15

Not all so satisfide, with greedie eye
  He sought all round about, his thirstie blade
  To bath in bloud of faithlesse enemy;
  Who all that while lay hid in secret shade:
  He standes amazèd, how he thence should fade.
  At last the trumpets Triumph sound on hie,
  And running Heralds humble homage made,
  Greeting him goodly° with new victorie,   *respectfully*
And to him brought the shield, the cause of enmitie.

16

Wherewith he goeth to that soveraine Queene,
  And falling her before on lowly knee,
  To her makes present of his service seene;°   *proved*
  Which she accepts, with thankes, and goodly gree,°   *favor*
  Greatly advauncing° his gay chevalree.   *extolling*
  So marcheth home, and by her takes the knight,
  Whom all the people follow with great glee,
  Shouting, and clapping all their hands on hight,°   *aloud*
That all the aire it fils, and flyes to heaven bright.

17

Home is he brought, and laid in sumptuous bed:
  Where many skilfull leaches° him abide,°   *doctors / attend*
  To salve° his hurts, that yet still freshly bled.   *anoint*
  In wine and oyle they wash his woundès wide,
  And softly can embalme° on every side.   *carefully did anoint*
  And all the while, most heavenly melody
  About the bed sweet musicke did divide,°   *descanted*
  Him to beguile of° griefe and agony: *divert from*
And all the while Duessa wept full bitterly.

18

As when a wearie traveller that strayes
  By muddy shore of broad seven-mouthèd Nile,
  Unweeting° of the perillous wandring wayes,   *unaware*
  Doth meet a cruell craftie Crocodile,
  Which in false griefe hyding his harmefull guile,
  Doth weepe full sore, and sheddeth tender teares:[5]
  The foolish man, that pitties all this while
  His mournefull plight, is swallowed up unwares,°   *unexpectedly*
Forgetfull of his owne, that mindes anothers cares.

---

5. Medieval bestiaries popularized the legend of the hypocritical crocodile's tears.

19

So wept Duessa untill eventide,
   That shyning lampes in Joves high house were light:[6]
   Then forth she rose, ne lenger° would abide,   *longer*
   But comes unto the place, where th'Hethen knight
   In slombring swownd nigh voyd of vitall spright,[7]
   Lay covered with inchaunted cloud all day:
   Whom when she found, as she him left in plight,[8]
   To wayle his woefull case she would not stay,
But to the easterne coast of heaven makes speedy way.

20

Where griesly° Night, with visage deadly sad,   *grim, horrible*
   That Phoebus chearefull face durst never vew,
   And in a foule blacke pitchie mantle clad,
   She findes forth comming from her darkesome mew,°   *den*
   Where she all day did hide her hated hew.°   *shape; color*
   Before the dore her yron charet° stood,   *chariot*
   Alreadie harnessèd for journey new;
   And cole blacke steedes yborne of hellish brood,
That on their rustie bits did champ, as° they were wood.°   *as if / mad*

21

Who when she saw Duessa sunny bright,
   Adorned with gold and jewels shining cleare,°   *brightly*
   She greatly grew amazèd at the sight,
   And th'unacquainted° light began to feare: *unfamiliar*
   For never did such brightnesse there appeare,
   And would have backe retyred to her cave,
   Untill the witches speech she gan to heare,
   Saying, "Yet O thou dreaded Dame, I crave
Abide,° till I have told the message, which I have."   *stay*

22

She stayd, and foorth Duessa gan proceede,
   "O thou most auncient Grandmother of all,[9]
   More old then Jove, whom thou at first didst breede,
   Or that great house of Gods caelestiall,
   Which wast begot in Daemogorgons hall,
   And sawst the secrets of the world unmade,°   *before it was made*
   Why suffredst thou thy Nephewes° deare to fall   *grandsons*
   With Elfin sword, most shamefully betrade?
Lo where the stout Sansjoy doth sleepe in deadly shade.

6. I.e., when ("that") the stars came out.
7. Nearly ("nigh") devoid of life.
8. I.e., in the same desperate state in which she had left him.

9. By tradition, Night was eldest of the gods, existing before the world was formed and the Olympian gods were begotten in the hall of Demogorgon (Chaos).

23

"And him before, I saw with bitter eyes
 The bold Sansfoy shrinke underneath his speare;
 And now the pray of fowles in field he lyes,
 Nor wayld of friends, nor laid on groning beare,[1]
 That whylome° was to me too dearely deare.   *formerly*
 O what of Gods then boots it° to be borne,   *is it worth*
 If old Aveugles sonnes so evill heare?[2]
 Or who shall not great Nightès children scorne,
When two of three her Nephews are so fowle forlorne?° *wretchedly lost*

24

"Up then, up dreary Dame, of darknesse Queene,
 Go gather up the reliques° of thy race,   *remnants*
 Or else goe them avenge, and let be seene,
 That dreaded Night in brightest day hath place,
 And can the children of faire light deface."°   *destroy*
 Her feeling speeches some compassion moved
 In hart, and chaunge in that great mothers face:
 Yet pittie in her hart was never proved°   *known*
Till then: for evermore she hated, never loved.

25

And said, "Deare daughter rightly may I rew
 The fall of famous children borne of mee,
 And good successes, which their foes ensew:°   *attend*
 But who can turne the streame of destinee,
 Or breake the chayne of strong necessitee,
 Which fast is tyde to Joves eternall seat?[3]
 The sonnes of Day he favoureth, I see,
 And by my ruines thinkes to make them great:
To make one great by others losse, is bad excheat.° *exchange*

26

"Yet shall they not escape so freely all;
 For some shall pay the price of others guilt:
 And he the man that made Sansfoy to fall,
 Shall with his owne bloud price° that he hath spilt. *pay for*
 But what art thou, that telst of Nephews kilt?"
 "I that do seeme not I, Duessa am,"
 Quoth she, "how ever now in garments gilt,
 And gorgeous gold arayd I to thee came:
Duessa I, the daughter of Deceipt and Shame."

---

1. Bier attended by mourners (thus "groning").
2. I.e., are so badly thought of. Aveugle (Blind) is the son of Night and father of Sansfoy, Sansjoy, and Sansloy.

3. The golden chain that binds the entire universe. The image goes back as far as Homer (*Iliad* 8.18–27).

27

Then bowing downe her agèd backe, she kist
   The wicked witch, saying; "In that faire face
   The false resemblance of Deceipt, I wist°   *knew*
   Did closely° lurke; yet so true-seeming grace   *secretly*
   It carried, that I scarse in darkesome place
   Could it discerne, though I the mother bee
   Of falshood, and root of Duessaes race.
   O welcome child, whom I have longd to see,
And now have seene unwares.° Lo now I go with thee."   *unexpectedly*

28

Then to her yron wagon she betakes,
   And with her beares the fowle welfavourd witch:
   Through mirkesome° aire her readie way she makes.   *murky; dense*
   Her twyfold Teme,[4] of which two blacke as pitch,
   And two were browne, yet each to each unlich,°   *unlike*
   Did softly swim away, ne ever stampe,
   Unlesse she chaunst their stubborne mouths to twitch;
   Then foming tarre,° their bridles they would champe,   *black froth*
And trampling the fine element,° would fiercely rampe.°   *the air / rear up*

29

So well they sped, that they be come at length
   Unto the place, whereas the Paynim lay,
   Devoid of outward sense, and native strength,
   Coverd with charmèd cloud from vew of day,
   And sight of men, since his late° luckelesse fray.   *recent*
   His cruell wounds with cruddy° bloud congealed,   *clotted*
   They binden up so wisely,° as they may,   *skillfully*
   And handle softly, till they can be healed:
So lay him in her charet, close in night concealed.

30

And all the while she stood upon the ground,
   The wakefull dogs did never cease to bay,
   As giving warning of th'unwonted° sound,   *unusual*
   With which her yron wheeles did them affray,
   And her darke griesly° looke them much dismay;   *horrid*
   The messenger of death, the ghastly Owle
   With drearie shriekes did also her bewray;°   *reveal*
   And hungry Wolves continually did howle,
At her abhorrèd face, so filthy and so fowle.

31

Thence turning backe in silence soft they stole,
   And brought the heavie corse° with easie pace   *body*

4. Twofold team of horses.

To yawning gulfe of deepe Avernus hole.[5]
By that same hole an entrance darke and bace
With smoake and sulphure hiding all the place,
Descends to hell: there creature never past,
That backe returnèd without heavenly grace;
But dreadfull Furies, which their chaines have brast,°   *burst*
And damnèd sprights sent forth to make ill° men aghast.   *evil*

32

By that same way the direfull dames doe drive
   Their mournefull charet, fild° with rusty blood,   *defiled*
   And downe to Plutoes house are come bilive:°   *quickly; alive*
   Which passing through, on every side them stood
   The trembling ghosts with sad amazèd mood,
   Chattring their yron teeth, and staring wide
   With stonie eyes; and all the hellish brood
   Of feends infernall flockt on every side,
To gaze on earthly wight, that with the Night durst ride.

33

They pas the bitter waves of Acheron,
   Where many soules sit wailing woefully,
   And come to fiery flood of Phlegeton,[6]
   Whereas the damnèd ghosts in torments fry,
   And with sharpe shrilling shriekes doe bootlesse° cry,   *without avail*
   Cursing high Jove, the which them thither sent.
   The house of endlesse paine is built thereby,
   In which ten thousand sorts of punishment
The cursèd creatures doe eternally torment.

34

Before the threshold dreadfull Cerberus[7]
   His three deformèd heads did lay along,°   *at full length*
   Curlèd with thousand adders venemous,
   And lillèd° forth his bloudie flaming tong: *lolled*
   At them he gan to reare his bristles strong,
   And felly gnarre,° untill dayes enemy   *savagely snarl*
   Did him appease; then downe his taile he hong
   And suffered them to passen quietly:
For she in hell and heaven had power equally.

35

There was Ixion turnèd on a wheele,
   For daring tempt the Queene of heaven to sin;
   And Sisyphus an huge round stone did reele°   *roll*
   Against an hill, ne° might from labour lin;°   *nor / cease*

5. In classical mythology Avernus is hell, where Pluto (stanza 32) reigns.
6. Acheron and Phlegeton are rivers in hell.

7. The three-headed dog that guards hell. Stanzas 31–35 recall Aeneas's descent into hell (Virgil, *Aeneid* 6.200, 239–40).

There thirstie Tantalus hong by the chin;
And Tityus fed a vulture on his maw;°   *liver*
Typhoeus joynts were strechèd on a gin,°   *rack*
Theseus condemned to endlesse slouth° by law, *sloth*
And fifty sisters water in leake vessels draw.[8]

36

They all beholding worldly° wights in place,° *mortal / there*
Leave off their worke, unmindfull of their smart,° *pain*
To gaze on them; who forth by them doe pace,
Till they be come unto the furthest part:
Where was a Cave ywrought by wondrous art,
Deepe, darke, uneasie,° dolefull, comfortlesse, *lacking ease*
In which sad Aesculapius° farre a part   *god of medicine*
Emprisond was in chaines remedilesse,° *beyond any remedy*
For that Hippolytus rent corse° he did redresse.° *body / cure*

37

Hippolytus a jolly° huntsman was,   *gallant*
That wont° in charet chace the foming Bore; *used to*
He all his Peeres in beautie did surpas,
But Ladies love as losse of time forbore:
His wanton stepdame[9] lovèd him the more,
But when she saw her offred sweets refused
Her love she turnd to hate, and him before
His father fierce of treason false accused,
And with her gealous° termes his open eares abused. *arousing jealousy*

38

Who all in rage his Sea-god syre° besought, *Poseidon (Neptune)*
Some cursèd vengeance on his sonne to cast:
From surging gulf two monsters straight° were brought, *immediately*
With dread whereof his chasing steedes aghast,
Both charet swift and huntsman overcast.
His goodly corps on ragged cliffs yrent,°   *torn*
Was quite dismembred, and his members chast
Scattered on every mountaine, as he went,
That of Hippolytus was left no moniment.[1]

39

His cruell stepdame seeing what was donne,
Her wicked dayes with wretched knife did end,
In death avowing th'innocence of her sonne.

---

8. Ixion was being punished for attempting to seduce Juno; Sisyphus, for refusing to pray to the gods; Tantalus, for stealing the gods' nectar; Tityus, for his attempted assault on Apollo's mother, Leto; the monster Typhoeus, for creating destructive winds; Theseus, for stealing Persephone from Hades; and the fifty daughters of King Danaus, for having killed their husbands on their wedding night. Tantalus stood chin-deep in water that receded whenever he tried to drink— hence he is "thirstie." Ovid, Virgil, and Homer are Spenser's sources here.
9. Phaedra, the wife of his father, Theseus.
1. I.e., no trace of identity.

Which hearing his rash Syre, began to rend
His haire, and hastie tongue, that did offend:
Tho° gathering up the relicks of his smart[2]   *then*
By Dianes meanes, who was Hippolyts frend,
Them brought to Aesculape, that by his art
Did heale them all againe, and joynèd every part.

40

Such wondrous science in mans wit to raine
When Jove avizd,° that could the dead revive,   *discovered*
And fates expirèd[3] could renew againe,
Of endlesse life he might him not deprive,
But unto hell did thrust him downe alive,
With flashing thunderbolt ywounded sore:
Where long remaining, he did alwaies strive
Himselfe with salves to health for to restore,
And slake the heavenly fire, that raged evermore.

41

There auncient Night arriving, did alight
From her nigh wearie waine,[4] and in her armes
To Aesculapius brought the wounded knight:
Whom having softly disarayd of armes,
Tho gan to him discover° all his harmes,   *reveal*
Beseeching him with prayer, and with praise,
If either salves, or oyles, or herbes, or charmes
A fordonne° wight from dore of death mote raise,   *undone*
He would at her request prolong her nephews daies.

42

"Ah Dame," quoth he, "thou temptest me in vaine,
To dare the thing, which daily yet I rew,
And the old cause of my continued paine
With like attempt to like end to renew.
Is not enough, that thrust from heaven dew[5]
Here endlesse penance for one fault I pay,
But that redoubled crime with vengeance new
Thou biddest me to eeke?° Can Night defray°   *increase / appease*
The wrath of thundring Jove, that rules both night and day?"

43

"Not so," quoth she; "but sith° that heavens king   *since*
From hope of heaven hath thee excluded quight,
Why fearest thou, that canst not hope for thing,°   *anything*
And fearest not, that more thee hurten might,
Now in the powre of everlasting Night?

2. I.e., his son's remains, which caused his grief.
3. The completed term of life as fixed by the Fates.
4. I.e., the horses of Night's chariot ("waine") are nearly exhausted.
5. The proper ("dew") place for a god.

Goe to then, O thou farre renowmèd sonne
Of great Apollo, shew thy famous might
In medicine, that else° hath to thee wonne   *already*
Great paines, and greater praise, both never to be donne."°   *ended*

44

Her words prevaild: And then the learnèd leach°   *doctor*
His cunning hand gan to his wounds to lay,
And all things else, the which his art did teach:
Which having seene, from thence arose away
The mother of dread darknesse, and let stay
Aveugles sonne there in the leaches cure,°   *care*
And backe returning tooke her wonted° way,   *accustomed*
To runne her timely race,° whilst Phoebus pure   *her nightly journey*
In westerne waves his wearie wagon did recure.°   *refresh*

45

The false Duessa leaving noyous° Night,   *harmful*
Returnd to stately pallace of dame Pride;
Where when she came, she found the Faery knight
Departed thence, albe° his woundès wide   *although*
Not throughly heald, unreadie were to ride.
Good cause he had to hasten thence away;
For on a day his wary Dwarfe had spide,
Where in a dongeon deepe huge numbers lay
Of caytive° wretched thrals,° that waylèd night and day. *captive / slaves*

46

A ruefull sight, as could be seene with eie;
Of whom he learnèd had in secret wise
The hidden cause of their captivitie,
How mortgaging their lives to Covetise,
Through wastfull° Pride, and wanton Riotise,   *causing desolation*
They were by law of that proud Tyrannesse[6]
Provokt with Wrath, and Envies false surmise,
Condemnèd to that Dongeon mercilesse,
Where they should live in woe, and die in wretchednesse.

47

There was that great proud king of Babylon[7]
That would compell all nations to adore,
And him as onely God to call upon,
Till through celestiall doome° throwne out of dore,   *judgment*
Into an Oxe he was transformed of yore:
There also was king Croesus,[8] that enhaunst°   *exalted*
His heart too high through his great riches store;

---

6. Lucifera. The noble sinners named in stanzas
47–50 exemplify a theme common in Renaissance morality, the fall of princes.

7. Nebuchadnezzar (Daniel 3–4).
8. King of Lydia, famous for his riches.

And proud Antiochus,[9] the which advaunst
His cursèd hand gainst God, and on his altars daunst.°   *danced*

48

And them long time before, great Nimrod was,
  That first the world with sword and fire warrayd;°   *ravaged*
  And after him old Ninus[1] farre did pas°   *surpass*
  In princely pompe, of° all the world obayd;   *by*
  There also was that mightie Monarch layd
  Low under all, yet above all in pride,
  That name of native° syre did fowle upbrayd,   *natural*
  And would as Ammons sonne be magnifide,
Till scornd of God and man a shamefull death he dide.[2]

49

All these together in one heape were throwne,
  Like carkases of beasts in butchers stall.
  And in another corner wide° were strowne   *lying apart*
  The antique ruines of the Romaines fall:
  Great Romulus the Grandsyre of them all,
  Proud Tarquin, and too lordly Lentulus,
  Stout Scipio, and stubborne Hanniball,
  Ambitious Sylla, and sterne Marius,
High Caesar, great Pompey, and fierce Antonius.[3]

50

Amongst these mighty men were wemen mixt,
  Proud wemen, vaine, forgetfull of their yoke:°   *duty*
  The bold Semiramis,° whose sides transfixt   *wife of Ninus*
  With sonnes owne blade, her fowle reproches spoke;
  Faire Sthenoboea,[4] that her selfe did choke
  With wilfull cord, for wanting° of her will;   *lacking*
  High minded Cleopatra, that with stroke
  Of Aspes sting her selfe did stoutly° kill: *bravely*
And thousands moe the like, that did that dongeon fill.

51

Besides the endlesse routs° of wretched thralles,   *crowds*
  Which thither were assembled day by day,
  From all the world after their wofull falles,

9. King of Syria, who desecrated the Jewish temple of Jerusalem (1 Maccabees 1.20–24).
1. In classical mythology, Ninus was founder of Nineveh, archetype of the wicked city (see the Book of Jonah). Nimrod, identified as the first tyrant, caused the Tower of Babel to be built in defiance of God (Genesis 10.9–10, 11.1–9).
2. The reference is to Alexander the Great, whose "shamefull death" came ten days after he fell ill at a drinking party. The son of Philip II of Macedon, Alexander was occasionally worshiped as the son of Jupiter Ammon.
3. Romulus was the founder of Rome; Tarquin, a Roman tyrant; Lentulus, a conspirator with Catiline to overthrow the Republic; Scipio, a Roman general, conqueror of Carthage; Hannibal, a Carthaginian general; Sulla, a Roman civil war general; Marius, Sulla's rival. The figures in the final line are Julius Caesar, Pompey the Great, and Mark Antony.
4. Queen of King Proteus of Argos; she lusted after her brother-in-law Bellerophon.

Through wicked pride, and wasted wealthes decay.
But most of all, which in that Dongeon lay
Fell from high Princes courts, or Ladies bowres,
Where they in idle pompe, or wanton play,
Consumèd had their goods, and thriftlesse howres,
And lastly throwne themselves into these heavy stowres.°   *disasters*

52

Whose case wheneas the carefull° Dwarfe had tould,   *wary*
And made ensample of their mournefull sight
Unto his maister, he no lenger would
There dwell in perill of like painefull plight,
But early rose, and ere that dawning light
Discovered had the world to heaven wyde,
He by a privie Posterne° tooke his flight,   *secret back door*
That of no envious eyes he mote be spyde:
For doubtlesse death ensewd, if any him descryde.°   *descried, observed*

53

Scarse could he footing find in that fowle way,
For many corses, like a great Lay-stall°   *burial place; rubbish heap*
Of murdred men which therein strowèd lay,
Without remorse, or decent funerall:
Which all through that great Princesse pride did fall
And came to shamefull end. And them beside
Forth ryding underneath the castell wall,
A donghill of dead carkases he spide,
The dreadfull spectacle of that sad house of Pride.[5]

Canto 6

From lawlesse lust by wondrous grace
    fayre Una is releast:
Whom salvage° nation does adore,   *wild; of the woods*
    and learnes her wise beheast.°   *bidding*

1

As when a ship, that flyes faire under saile,
An hidden rocke escapèd hath unwares,°   *unexpectedly*
That lay in waite her wrack for to bewaile,[6]
The Marriner yet halfe amazèd stares
At perill past, and yet in doubt ne dares
To joy at his foole-happie oversight:°   *lucky ignorance*
So doubly is distrest twixt joy and cares
The dreadlesse° courage of this Elfin knight,   *fearless*
Having escapt so sad ensamples in his sight.

---

5. Named in the argument of canto 4, but in the poem itself, only now, after we have been shown what the name means.

6. I.e., cause the shipwreck and thereby cause it to be bewailed.

2

Yet sad he was that his too hastie speed
  The faire Duess' had forst him leave behind;
  And yet more sad, that Una his deare dreed°   *object of reverence*
  Her truth had staind with treason so unkind;°   *unnatural*
  Yet crime in her could never creature find,
  But for his love, and for her owne selfe sake,
  She wandred had from one to other Ynd,[7]
  Him for to seeke, ne ever would forsake,
Till her unwares the fierce Sansloy did overtake.

3

Who after Archimagoes fowle defeat,
  Led her away into a forrest wilde,
  And turning wrathfull fire to lustfull heat,
  With beastly sin thought her to have defilde,
  And made the vassall of his pleasures vilde.°   *vile*
  Yet first he cast by treatie,° and by traynes,°   *persuasion / tricks*
  Her to perswade, that stubborne fort to yilde:
  For greater conquest of hard love he gaynes,
That workes it to his will, then° he that it constraines.°   *than / forces*

4

With fawning wordes he courted her a while,
  And looking lovely,° and oft sighing sore,   *lovingly*
  Her constant hart did tempt with diverse guile:
  But wordes, and lookes, and sighes she did abhore,
  As rocke of Diamond stedfast evermore.[8]
  Yet for to feed his fyrie lustfull eye,
  He snatcht the vele, that hong her face before;
  Then gan her beautie shine, as brightest skye,
And burnt his beastly hart t'efforce° her chastitye.   *violate*

5

So when he saw his flatt'ring arts to fayle,
  And subtile engines bet from batteree,[9]
  With greedy force he gan the fort assayle,
  Whereof he weend° possessèd soone to bee,   *thought*
  And win rich spoile of ransackt chastetee.
  Ah heavens, that do this hideous act behold,
  And heavenly virgin thus outragèd see,
  How can ye vengeance just so long withhold,
And hurle not flashing flames upon that Paynim bold?

7. I.e., she would have wandered from the East
to the West Indies.
8. The diamond, because of its hardness, was an

emblem of fidelity.
9. I.e., beaten ("bet") from their fruitless assault
("batteree") on her unmovable virtue.

6

The pitteous maiden carefull° comfortlesse,   *full of cares*
  Does throw out thrilling° shriekes, and shrieking cryes,   *piercing*
  The last vaine helpe of womens great distresse,
  And with loud plaints importuneth the skyes,
  That molten starres do drop like weeping eyes;
  And Phoebus flying so most shamefull sight,
  His blushing face in foggy cloud implyes,°   *buries*
  And hides for shame. What wit of mortall wight
Can now devise to quit a thrall° from such a plight?   *release a captive*

7

Eternall providence exceeding° thought,   *transcending*
  Where none appeares can make her selfe a way:
  A wondrous way it for this Lady wrought,
  From Lyons clawes to pluck the gripèd° pray.   *grasped*
  Her shrill outcryes and shriekes so loud did bray,
  That all the woodes and forestes did resownd;
  A troupe of Faunes and Satyres[1] far away
  Within the wood were dauncing in a rownd,
Whiles old Sylvanus[2] slept in shady arber sownd.

8

Who when they heard that pitteous strainèd voice,
  In hast forsooke their rurall meriment,
  And ran towards the far rebownded° noyce,   *re-echoed*
  To weet,° what wight so loudly did lament.   *learn*
  Unto the place they come incontinent:°   *immediately*
  Whom when the raging Sarazin espide,
  A rude, misshapen, monstrous rablement,
  Whose like he never saw, he durst not bide,
But got his ready steed, and fast away gan ride.

9

The wyld woodgods arrivèd in the place,
  There find the virgin dolefull desolate,
  With ruffled rayments, and faire blubbred° face,   *flooded with tears*
  As her outrageous foe had left her late,°   *shortly before*
  And trembling yet through feare of former hate;
  All stand amazèd at so uncouth° sight,   *strange*
  And gin to pittie her unhappie state,
  All stand astonied° at her beautie bright,   *stupified*
In their rude° eyes unworthie° of so wofull plight.   *rustic / undeserving*

---

1. Woodland deities with men's bodies above the waist and goats' bodies below, noted for their sensuality.

2. Roman god of the woods, who is traditionally associated with fauns.

10

She more amazed, in double dread doth dwell;
    And every tender part for feare does shake:
    As when a greedie Wolfe through hunger fell°   *fierce*
    A seely° Lambe farre from the flocke does take,   *innocent*
    Of whom he meanes his bloudie feast to make,
    A Lyon spyes fast running towards him,
    The innocent pray in hast he does forsake,
    Which quit° from death yet quakes in every lim   *rescued*
With chaunge of feare, to see the Lyon looke so grim.°   *savage*

11

Such fearefull fit assaid° her trembling hart,   *assailed*
    Ne word to speake, ne joynt to move she had:
    The salvage° nation feele her secret smart,   *wild; uncivilized*
    And read her sorrow in her count'nance sad;
    Their frowning forheads with rough hornes yclad,
    And rusticke horror° all a side doe lay,   *rough, rugged looks*
    And gently grenning,° shew a semblance° glad   *grinning / an appearance*
    To comfort her, and feare to put away,
Their backward bent knees teach her humbly to obay.[3]

12

The doubtfull Damzell dare not yet commit
    Her single person to their barbarous truth,[4]
    But still twixt feare and hope amazd does sit,
    Late learnd° what harme to hastie trust ensu'th: *recently taught*
    They in compassion of her tender youth,
    And wonder of her beautie soveraine,°   *supreme*
    Are wonne with pitty and unwonted ruth,°   *unaccustomed pity*
    And all prostrate upon the lowly plaine,
Do kisse her feete, and fawne on her with count'nance faine.°   *glad*

13

Their harts she ghesseth by their humble guise,°   *appearance*
    And yieldes her to extremitie of time;[5]
    So from the ground she fearelesse doth arise,
    And walketh forth without suspect° of crime: *suspicion*
    They all as glad, as birdes of joyous Prime,°   *springtime*
    Thence lead her forth, about her dauncing round,
    Shouting, and singing all a shepheards ryme,
    And with greene braunches strowing all the ground,
Do worship her, as Queene, with olive girlond cround.

---

3. I.e., teach their knees, bent backward like a
goat's, to obey her.
4. I.e., her solitary self to their wild allegiance
("barbarous truth").
5. I.e., necessity of the time.

14

And all the way their merry pipes they sound,
　　That all the woods with doubled Eccho ring,
　　And with their hornèd feet do weare the ground,
　　Leaping like wanton kids in pleasant Spring.
　　So towards old Sylvanus they her bring;
　　Who with the noyse awakèd, commeth out,
　　To weet° the cause, his weake steps governing,　　　　*learn*
　　And agèd limbs on Cypresse stadle° stout,　　　　　　*staff*
And with an yvie twyne his wast is girt about.

15

Far off he wonders, what them makes so glad,
　　Or Bacchus merry fruit they did invent,[6]
　　Or Cybeles franticke rites[7] have made them mad;
　　They drawing nigh, unto their God present
　　That flowre of faith and beautie excellent.
　　The God himselfe vewing that mirrhour rare,[8]
　　Stood long amazd, and burnt in his intent;[9]
　　His owne faire Dryope now he thinkes not faire,
And Pholoe fowle, when her to this he doth compaire.[1]

16

The woodborne people fall before her flat,
　　And worship her as Goddesse of the wood;
　　And old Sylvanus selfe bethinkès not,° what　　　*cannot decide*
　　To thinke of wight so faire, but gazing stood,
　　In doubt to deeme her borne of earthly brood;
　　Sometimes Dame Venus selfe he seemes to see,
　　But Venus never had so sober mood;
　　Sometimes Diana he her takes to bee,
But misseth bow, and shaftes, and buskins° to her knee.　　*soft boots*

17

By vew of her he ginneth to revive
　　His ancient love, and dearest Cyparisse,[2]
　　And calles to mind his pourtraiture alive,[3]
　　How faire he was, and yet not faire to° this,　　　*compared to*
　　And how he slew with glauncing dart amisse
　　A gentle Hynd, the which the lovely boy
　　Did love as life, above all worldly blisse;
　　For griefe whereof the lad n'ould° after joy,　　　*would not*
But pynd away in anguish and selfe-wild annoy.°　　*self-willed suffering*

6. I.e., whether ("or") they did find ("invent")
wine grapes.
7. Orgiastic dances in worship of Cybele, goddess of the powers of nature.
8. I.e., Una, in the sense that she is a paragon, a
perfect reflection of heavenly faith and beauty.
9. Glowed with intense concentration.

1. Dryope and Pholoe were nymphs loved by Faunus and Pan. For Spenser, the names *Faunus,
Pan,* and *Sylvanus* were apparently interchangeable.
2. A fair youth, beloved of Sylvanus, turned into
a cypress tree.
3. I.e., his appearance when alive.

18

The wooddy Nymphes, faire Hamadryades[4]
  Her to behold do thither runne apace,
  And all the troupe of light-foot Naiades,°   *water nymphs*
  Flocke all about to see her lovely face:
  But when they vewèd have her heavenly grace,
  They envie her in their malitious mind,
  And fly away for feare of fowle disgrace:
  But all the Satyres scorne their woody kind,°   *woodborn race*
And henceforth nothing faire, but her on earth they find.

19

Glad of such lucke, the luckelesse lucky maid,
  Did her content to please their feeble eyes,
  And long time with that salvage people staid,
  To gather breath in many miseries.
  During which time her gentle wit she plyes,
  To teach them truth, which worshipt her in vaine,
  And made her th'Image of Idolatryes;[5]
  But when their bootlesse° zeale she did restraine   *useless*
From her own worship, they her Asse would worship fayn.°   *willingly*

20

It fortunèd a noble warlike knight
  By just occasion to that forrest came,
  To seeke his kindred, and the lignage right,°   *true*
  From whence he took his well deservèd name:
  He had in armes abroad wonne muchell° fame,   *great*
  And fild far landes with glorie of his might,
  Plaine, faithfull, true, and enimy of shame,
  And ever loved to fight for Ladies right,
But in vaine glorious frayes° he litle did delight.   *frays, fights*

21

A Satyres sonne yborne in forrest wyld,
  By straunge adventure as it did betyde,°   *happen*
  And there begotten of a Lady myld,
  Faire Thyamis the daughter of Labryde,[6]
  That was in sacred bands of wedlocke tyde
  To Therion,[7] a loose unruly swayne;
  Who had more joy to raunge the forrest wyde,
  And chase the salvage beast with busie payne,°   *painstaking care*
Then serve his Ladies love, and wast° in pleasures vayne.   *live idly*

---

4. Spirits of trees, whose lives ended when the tree they inhabited died.
5. The idol of their idolatries.
6. The name means "turbulence." Thyamis means "passion."
7. The name means "wild beast."

22

The forlorne mayd did with loves longing burne,
  And could not lacke° her lovers company,   *be without*
  But to the wood she goes, to serve her turne,
  And seeke her spouse, that from her still° does fly,   *always*
  And followes other game and venery:[8]
  A Satyre chaunst her wandring for to find,
  And kindling coles of lust in brutish eye,
  The loyall links of wedlocke did unbind,
And made her person thrall unto his beastly kind.

23

So long in secret cabin there he held
  Her captive to his sensuall desire,
  Till that with timely° fruit her belly sweld,   *ripening*
  And bore a boy unto that salvage sire:
  Then home he suffred her for to retire,°   *return*
  For ransome leaving him the late borne childe;
  Whom till to ryper yeares he gan aspire,°   *grow up*
  He noursled° up in life and manners wilde,   *reared*
Emongst wild beasts and woods, from lawes of men exilde.

24

For all he taught the tender ymp,° was but   *child*
  To banish cowardize and bastard° feare;   *base*
  His trembling hand he would him force to put
  Upon the Lyon and the rugged Beare,
  And from the she Beares teats her whelps to teare;
  And eke° wyld roring Buls he would him make   *also*
  To tame, and ryde their backes not made to beare;
  And the Robuckes[9] in flight to overtake,
That every beast for feare of him did fly and quake.

25

Thereby so fearelesse, and so fell° he grew,   *fierce*
  That his owne sire and maister of his guise°   *teacher of his behavior*
  Did often tremble at his horrid vew,°   *rough appearance*
  And oft for dread of hurt would him advise,
  The angry beasts not rashly to despise,
  Nor too much to provoke; for he would learne°   *teach*
  The Lyon stoup to him in lowly wise,
  (A lesson hard) and make the Libbard° sterne   *leopard*
Leave roaring, when in rage he for revenge did earne.°   *yearn*

26

And for to make his powre approvèd° more,   *demonstrated*
  Wyld beasts in yron yokes he would compell;

---

8. Hunting; also sexual play.   9. A species of deer noted for its speed.

The spotted Panther, and the tuskèd Bore,
The Pardale° swift, and the Tigre cruell;   *female leopard*
The Antelope, and Wolfe both fierce and fell;°   *savage*
And them constraine in equall teme[1] to draw.
Such joy he had, their stubborne harts to quell,
And sturdie courage tame with dreadfull aw,
That his beheast they fearèd, as a tyrans law.

27

His loving mother came upon a day
  Unto the woods, to see her little sonne;
And chaunst unwares° to meet him in the way,   *unexpectedly*
After his sportes, and cruell pastime donne,
When after him a Lyonesse did runne,
  That roaring all with rage, did lowd requere°   *demand*
  Her children deare, whom he away had wonne:°   *seized*
  The Lyon whelpes she saw how he did beare,
And lull in rugged armes, withouten childish feare.

28

The fearefull Dame all quakèd at the sight,
  And turning backe, gan fast to fly away,
Untill with love revokt° from vaine affright,   *recalled*
She hardly° yet perswaded was to stay,   *with difficulty*
And then to him these womanish words gan say;
  "Ah Satyrane,[2] my dearling, and my joy,
  For love of me leave off this dreadfull play;
To dally thus with death, is no fit toy,
Go find some other play-fellowes, mine own sweet boy."

29

In these and like delights of bloudy game
  He traynèd was, till ryper yeares he raught,°   *reached*
And there abode, whilst any beast of name
Walkt in that forest, whom he had not taught
To feare his force: and then his courage haught°   *high*
  Desird of forreine foemen to be knowne;
  And far abroad for straunge adventures sought:
In which his might was never overthrowne,
But through all Faery lond his famous worth was blown.°   *spread*

30

Yet evermore it was his manner faire,
  After long labours and adventures spent,
Unto those native woods for to repaire,°   *return*
To see his sire and ofspring° auncient.   *origin*
And now he thither came for like intent;

---

1. Side by side, yoked together in a team.   2. I.e., like a satyr.

Where he unwares the fairest Una found,
Straunge Lady, in so straunge habiliment,°   *attire*
Teaching the Satyres, which her sat around,
Trew sacred lore, which from her sweet lips did redound.° *flow*

31

He wondred at her wisedome heavenly rare,
 Whose like in womens wit he never knew;
 And when her curteous deeds he did compare,
 Gan her admire, and her sad sorrowes rew,°   *pity*
 Blaming of Fortune, which such troubles threw,
 And joyd to make proofe of her crueltie
 On gentle Dame, so hurtlesse,° and so trew: *harmless*
 Thenceforth he kept her goodly company,
And learnd her discipline° of faith and veritie. *teachings*

32

But she all vowd° unto the Redcrosse knight, *entirely promised*
 His wandring perill closely° did lament,   *secretly*
 Ne in this new acquaintaunce could delight,
 But her deare° heart with anguish did torment, *loving*
 And all her wit in secret counsels spent,
 How to escape. At last in privie wise°   *privately*
 To Satyrane she shewèd her intent;
 Who glad to gain such favour, gan devise,
How with that pensive Maid he best might thence arise.° *depart*

33

So on a day when Satyres all were gone,
 To do their service to Sylvanus old,
 The gentle virgin left behind alone
 He led away with courage stout and bold.
 Too late it was, to Satyres to be told,
 Or ever hope recover her againe:
 In vaine he seekes that having cannot hold.
 So fast he carried her with carefull paine,° *painstaking care*
That they the woods are past, and come now to the plaine.

34

The better part now of the lingring day,
 They traveild had, when as they farre espide
 A wearie wight forwandring° by the way, *wandering far and wide*
 And towards him they gan in hast to ride,
 To weet of newes, that did abroad betide,
 Or tydings of her knight of the Redcrosse.
 But he them spying, gan to turne aside,
 For feare as seemd, or for some feignèd losse;° *pretended harm*
More greedy they of newes, fast towards him do crosse.

35

A silly° man, in simple weedes forworne,°   *simple / worn out*
 And soild with dust of the long drièd way;
 His sandales were with toilesome travell torne,
 And face all tand with scorching sunny ray,
 As° he had traveild many a sommers day,   *as if*
 Through boyling sands of Arabie and Ynde;°   *India*
 And in his hand a Jacobs staffe,° to stay   *pilgrim's staff*
 His wearie limbes upon: and eke behind,
His scrip° did hang, in which his needments he did bind.   *bag*

36

The knight approching nigh, of him inquerd
 Tydings of warre, and of adventures new;
 But warres, nor new adventures none he herd.
 Then Una gan to aske, if ought° he knew,   *aught, anything*
 Or heard abroad of that her champion trew,
 That in his armour bare a croslet° red.   *small cross*
 "Aye me, Deare dame," quoth he, "well may I rew
 To tell the sad sight, which mine eies have red:°   *beheld*
These eyes did see that knight both living and eke ded."

37

That cruell word her tender hart so thrild,°   *pierced*
 That suddein cold did runne through every vaine,
 And stony horrour all her sences fild
 With dying fit,° that downe she fell for paine. *deathlike swoon*
 The knight her lightly° rearèd up againe,   *quickly*
 And comforted with curteous kind reliefe:
 Then wonne from death, she bad him tellen plaine
 The further processe° of her hidden griefe;   *account*
The lesser pangs can beare, who hath endured the chiefe.

38

Then gan the Pilgrim thus, "I chaunst this day,
 This fatall day, that shall I ever rew,°   *rue, regret*
 To see two knights in travell on my way
 (A sory° sight) arraunged° in battell new,   *grievous / drawn up*
 Both breathing vengeaunce, both of wrathfull hew:
 My fearefull flesh did tremble at their strife,
 To see their blades so greedily imbrew,[3]
 That drunke with bloud, yet thristed after life:
What more? the Redcrosse knight was slaine with Paynim knife."

39

"Ah dearest Lord," quoth she, "how might that bee,
 And he the stoutest° knight, that ever wonne?"° *bravest; strongest / fought*

3. Soak themselves in blood.

"Ah dearest dame," quoth he, "how might I see
The thing, that might not be, and yet was donne?"
"Where is," said Satyrane, "that Paynims sonne,
That him of life, and us of joy hath reft?"
"Not far away," quoth he, "he hence doth wonne°   *stay*
Foreby° a fountaine, where I late him left   *close by*
Washing his bloudy wounds, that through° the steele were cleft." *by*

40

Therewith the knight thence marchèd forth in hast,
 Whiles Una with huge heavinesse° opprest,   *grief*
 Could not for sorrow follow him so fast;
 And soone he came, as he the place had ghest,
 Whereas that Pagan proud him selfe did rest,
 In secret shadow by a fountaine side:
 Even he it was, that earst° would have supprest° *before / violated*
 Faire Una: whom when Satyrane espide,
With fowle reprochfull words he boldly him defide.

41

And said, "Arise thou cursèd Miscreaunt,°   *infidel*
 That hast with knightlesse guile and trecherous train[4]
 Faire knighthood fowly shamed, and doest vaunt°   *boast*
 That good knight of the Redcrosse to have slain:
 Arise, and with like treason now maintain°   *defend*
 Thy guilty wrong, or else thee guilty yield."
 The Sarazin this hearing, rose amain,°   *at once*
 And catching up in hast his three square° shield, *triangular*
And shining helmet, soone him buckled to the field.

42

And drawing nigh him said, "Ah misborne Elfe,[5]
 In evill houre thy foes thee hither sent,
 Anothers wrongs to wreake upon thy selfe:
 Yet ill thou blamest me, for having blent°   *stained*
 My name with guile and traiterous intent;
 That Redcrosse knight, perdie,° I never slew, *by God (pardieu)*
 But had he beene, where earst his armes were lent,
 Th'enchaunter vaine his errour should not rew:
But thou his errour shalt, I hope now proven trew."[6]

43

Therewith they gan, both furious and fell,°   *fierce*
 To thunder blowes, and fiersly to assaile
 Each other bent° his enimy to quell,°   *determined / kill*

---

4. Deceit. "Knightlesse": unknightly.
5. Base-born knight of Faerie Land ("Elfe").
6. I.e., had Redcrosse been wearing his arms, the
enchanter Archimago would not have to regret his
error in fighting me. But you will now repeat that
error and that regret.

That with their force they perst° both plate and maile,   *pierced*
And made wide furrowes in their fleshes fraile,
That it would pitty° any living eie.   *bring pity to*
Large floods of bloud adowne their sides did raile:°   *flow*
But floods of bloud could not them satisfie:
Both hungred after death: both chose to win, or die.

44

So long they fight, and fell revenge pursue,
   That fainting° each, themselves to breathen let,   *weakening*
   And oft refreshèd, battell oft renue:
   As when two Bores with rancling malice met,
   Their gory sides fresh bleeding fiercely fret,°   *tear*
   Til breathlesse both them selves aside retire,
   Where foming wrath, their cruell tuskes they whet,
   And trample th'earth, the whiles they may respire;
Then backe to fight againe, new breathèd and entire.°   *fresh*

45

So fiersly, when these knights had breathèd once,
   They gan to fight returne, increasing more
   Their puissant° force, and cruell rage attonce,   *mighty*
   With heapèd strokes more hugely, then before,
   That with their drerie° wounds and bloudy gore   *gory*
   They both deformèd,° scarsely could be known.   *disfigured*
   By this sad Una fraught° with anguish sore,   *burdened*
   Led with their noise, which through the aire was thrown,
Arrived, where they in erth their fruitles bloud had sown.

46

Whom all so soone as that proud Sarazin
   Espide, he gan revive the memory
   Of his lewd lusts, and late attempted sin,
   And left the doubtfull° battell hastily,   *undecided*
   To catch her, newly offred to his eie:
   But Satyrane with strokes him turning, staid,
   And sternely bad him other businesse plie,°   *take on*
   Then° hunt the steps of pure unspotted Maid: *than*
Wherewith he all enraged, these bitter speaches said.

47

"O foolish faeries sonne, what furie mad
   Hath thee incenst, to hast thy dolefull fate?
   Were it not better, I that Lady had,
   Then that thou hadst repented it too late?
   Most sencelesse man he, that himselfe doth hate,
   To love another. Lo then for thine ayd
   Here take thy lovers token on thy pate."
   So they to fight; the whiles the royall Mayd
Fled farre away, of that proud Paynim sore afrayd.

48

But that false Pilgrim, which that leasing° told,   *lie*
   Being in deed old Archimage, did stay
   In secret shadow, all this to behold,
   And much rejoycèd in their bloudy fray:
   But when he saw the Damsell passe away
   He left his stond,° and her pursewd apace,   *place*
   In hope to bring her to her last decay.°   *i.e., her death*
   But for to tell her lamentable cace,
And eke° this battels end, will need another place.[7]   *also*

Canto 7

The Redcrosse knight is captive made
By Gyaunt proud opprest,°   *overwhelmed*
Prince Arthur meets with Una great-
ly with those newes distrest.

1

What man so wise, what earthly wit so ware,°   *wary*
   As to descry° the crafty cunning traine,°   *perceive / guile*
   By which deceipt doth maske in visour° faire,   *a mask*
   And cast her colours dyèd deepe in graine,[8]
   To seeme like Truth, whose shape she well can faine,°   *feign, imitate*
   And fitting gestures to her purpose frame,
   The guiltlesse man with guile to entertaine?°   *engage*
   Great maistresse of her art was that false Dame,
The false Duessa, clokèd with Fidessaes name.

2

Who when returning from the drery Night,
   She fownd not in that perilous house of Pryde,
   Where she had left, the noble Redcrosse knight,
   Her hopèd pray, she would no lenger bide,
   But forth she went, to seeke him far and wide.
   Ere long she fownd, whereas° he wearie sate,   *where*
   To rest him selfe, foreby° a fountaine side,   *beside*
   Disarmèd all of yron-coted Plate,
And by his side his steed the grassy forage ate.

3

He feedes upon the cooling shade, and bayes°   *bathes*
   His sweatie forehead in the breathing wind,
   Which through the trembling leaves full gently playes
   Wherein the cherefull birds of sundry kind
   Do chaunt sweet musick, to delight his mind:

---

7. In fact Spenser never tells how the battle ended. But Satyrane reappears in Book 3.

8. I.e., Deceit disposes her colors, thoroughly dyed, so as to seem like Truth.

The Witch approaching gan him fairely° greet,   *courteously*
And with reproch of carelesnesse° unkind   *indifference*
Upbrayd, for leaving her in place unmeet,°   *unfitting*
With fowle words tempring° faire, soure gall with hony sweet. *mingling*

4

Unkindnesse past, they gan of solace treat,°   *pleasure speak*
And bathe in pleasaunce of the joyous shade,
Which shielded them against the boyling heat,
And with greene boughes decking a gloomy glade,
About the fountaine like a girlond made;
Whose bubbling wave did ever freshly well,
Ne ever would through fervent° sommer fade:°   *hot / dry up*
The sacred Nymph, which therein wont° to dwell,   *was accustomed*
Was out of Dianes favour, as it then befell.

5

The cause was this: one day when Phoebe[9] fayre
With all her band was following the chace,°   *hunt*
This Nymph, quite tyred with heat of scorching ayre
Sat downe to rest in middest of the race:
The goddesse wroth° gan fowly her disgrace,   *angered*
And bad the waters, which from her did flow,
Be such as she her selfe was then in place.°   *there*
Thenceforth her waters waxèd dull and slow,
And all that drunke thereof, did faint and feeble grow.

6

Hereof this gentle knight unweeting° was,   *ignorant*
And lying downe upon the sandie graile,°   *gravel*
Drunke of the streame, as cleare as cristall glas;
Eftsoones° his manly forces gan to faile,   *immediately*
And mightie strong was turnd to feeble fraile.
His chaunged powres at first themselves not felt,
Till crudled° cold his corage° gan assaile,   *congealing / vigor*
And chearefull° bloud in faintnesse chill did melt,   *lively*
Which like a fever fit through all his body swelt.°   *raged*

7

Yet goodly court he made still to his Dame,
Pourd out in loosnesse[1] on the grassy grownd,
Both carelesse of his health, and of his fame:°   *reputation*
Till at the last he heard a dreadfull sownd,
Which through the wood loud bellowing, did rebownd,
That all the earth for terrour seemed to shake,
And trees did tremble. Th'Elfe therewith astownd,°   *amazed*

---

9. I.e., Diana, goddess of the moon and of chastity.

1. Spread out in lewdness ("loosnesse"); sexually expended.

Upstarted lightly° from his looser make,[2]   *quickly*
And his unready weapons gan in hand to take.

8

But ere he could his armour on him dight,°   *put on*
  Or get his shield, his monstrous enimy
  With sturdie steps came stalking in his sight,
  An hideous Geant horrible and hye,
  That with his talnesse seemd to threat the skye,
  The ground eke° gronèd under him for dreed;°   *also / dread*
  His living like saw never living eye,
  Ne durst behold: his stature did exceed
The hight of three the tallest sonnes of mortall seed.

9

The greatest Earth his uncouth° mother was,   *vile; strange*
  And blustring Aeolus his boasted sire,[3]
  Who with his breath, which through the world doth pas,
  Her hollow womb did secretly inspire,°   *breathe into*
  And fild her hidden caves with stormie yre,°   *ire, anger*
  That she conceived; and trebling the dew time,
  In which the wombes of women do expire,°   *bring forth*
  Brought forth this monstrous masse of earthly slime,
Puft up with emptie wind, and fild with sinfull crime.

10

So growen great through arrogant delight
  Of th'high descent, whereof he was yborne,
  And through presumption of his matchlesse might,
  All other powres and knighthood he did scorne,
  Such now he marcheth to this man forlorne,°   *abandoned*
  And left to losse:° his stalking steps are stayde°   *destruction / supported*
  Upon a snaggy Oke,[4] which he had torne
  Out of his mothers bowelles, and it made
His mortall° mace, wherewith his foemen he dismayde.[5]   *death-dealing*

11

That when the knight he spide, he gan advance
  With huge force and insupportable mayne,°   *irresistible power*
  And towardes him with dreadfull fury praunce;°   *strut*
  Who haplesse,° and eke hopelesse, all in vaine   *unlucky*
  Did to him pace, sad battaile to darrayne,°   *engage*
  Disarmd, disgrast, and inwardly dismayde,
  And eke so faint in every joynt and vaine,
  Through that fraile° fountaine, which him feeble made, *enfeebling*
That scarsely could he weeld his bootlesse° single blade.   *useless*

---

2. Too licentious ("looser") companion.
3. Aeolus was keeper of the winds. The giant's descent from Earth and Wind links him to earthquakes.

4. I.e., he uses as walking stick a knotty ("snaggy") oak tree.
5. In its usual sense, but also "dis-made, dissolved."

12

The Geaunt strooke so maynly° mercilesse,   *mightily*
 That could have overthrowne a stony towre,
 And were not heavenly grace, that him did blesse,
 He had beene pouldred° all, as thin as flowre: *powdered*
 But he was wary of that deadly stowre,°   *peril*
 And lightly° lept from underneath the blow: *quickly*
 Yet so exceeding was the villeins powre,
 That with the wind it did him overthrow,
And all his sences stound,° that still he lay full low. *stunned*

13

As when that divelish yron Engin° wrought   *i.e., cannon*
 In deepest Hell, and framd by Furies skill,
 With windy Nitre and quick Sulphur fraught,[6]
 And ramd with bullet round, ordaind to kill,
 Conceiveth fire, the heavens it doth fill
 With thundring noyse, and all the ayre doth choke,
 That none can breath, nor see, nor heare at will,
 Through smouldry cloud of duskish stincking smoke,
That th'onely breath him daunts,[7] who hath escapt the stroke.

14

So daunted when the Geaunt saw the knight,
 His heavie hand he heavèd up on hye,
 And him to dust thought to have battred quight,
 Untill Duessa loud to him gan crye;
 "O great Orgoglio,[8] greatest under skye,
 O hold thy mortall hand for Ladies sake,
 Hold for my sake, and do him not to dye,° *do not cause him to die*
 But vanquisht thine eternall bondslave make,
And me thy worthy meed unto thy Leman take."[9]

15

He hearkned, and did stay° from further harmes, *refrain*
 To gayne so goodly guerdon,° as she spake: *reward*
 So willingly she came into his armes,
 Who her as willingly to grace° did take,   *favor*
 And was possessèd of his new found make.° *mate*
 Then up he tooke the slombred° sencelesse corse, *unconscious*
 And ere he could out of his swowne awake,
 Him to his castle brought with hastie forse,
And in a Dongeon deepe him threw without remorse.

6. Filled ("fraught") with gunpowder ("Nitre" and "Sulphur").
7. I.e., so that the blast or smell alone ("onely") overcomes him.
8. Pride, haughtiness, disdain (Italian).
9. I.e., take me, your worthy reward, as your mistress.

16

From that day forth Duessa was his deare,
   And highly honourd in his haughtie eye,
   He gave her gold and purple pall° to weare,   *crimson robe of royalty*
   And triple crowne set on her head full hye,[1]
   And her endowd with royall majestye:
   Then for to make her dreaded more of men,
   And peoples harts with awfull terrour tye,°   *bind*
   A monstrous beast ybred in filthy fen°   *marsh*
He chose, which he had kept long time in darksome den.

17

Such one it was, as that renowmèd Snake
   Which great Alcides in Stremona slew,
   Long fostred in the filth of Lerna lake,[2]
   Whose many heads out budding ever new,
   Did breed° him endlesse labour to subdew: *cause*
   But this same Monster much more ugly was;
   For seven great heads out of his body grew,
   An yron brest, and backe of scaly bras,
And all embrewd° in bloud, his eyes did shine as glas.   *stained*

18

His tayle was stretchèd out in wondrous length,
   That to the house of heavenly gods it raught,°   *reached*
   And with extorted powre, and borrowed strength,
   The ever-burning lamps° from thence it brought,   *stars*
   And prowdly threw to ground, as things of nought;
   And underneath his filthy feet did tread
   The sacred things, and holy heasts foretaught.[3]
   Upon this dreadfull Beast with sevenfold head
He set the false Duessa, for more aw and dread.

19

The wofull Dwarfe, which saw his maisters fall,
   Whiles he had keeping of his grasing steed,
   And valiant knight become a caytive° thrall,   *captive*
   When all was past, tooke up his forlorne weed,°   *abandoned garment*
   His mightie armour, missing most at need;
   His silver shield, now idle maisterlesse;
   His poynant° speare, that many made to bleed,   *sharp*
   The ruefull moniments° of heavinesse,°   *memorials / grief*
And with them all departes, to tell his great distresse.

1. Duessa is attired like the Whore of Babylon in Revelation 17.3–4. The triple crown is that of the papacy (see canto 2, stanzas 13 and 22).
2. The nine-headed Lernean hydra slain by Hercules (Alcides). Orgoglio's seven-headed monster recalls the red dragon of Revelation 12.3–9: "behold a great red dragon, having seven heads and ten horns, and seven crowns upon his heads. And his tail drew the third part of the stars of heaven, and did cast them to the earth . . . [he is] that old serpent, called the Devil, and Satan, which deceiveth the whole world." Many Protestants associated the Beast with the Roman Church.
3. Doctrines ("holy heasts") previously taught.

20

He had not travaild long, when on the way
   He wofull Ladie, wofull Una met,
   Fast flying from the Paynims greedy pray,°   *clutch*
   Whilest Satyrane him from pursuit did let:°   *prevent*
   Who when her eyes she on the Dwarfe had set,
   And saw the signes, that deadly tydings spake,
   She fell to ground for sorrowfull regret,°   *grief*
   And lively breath her sad brest did forsake,
Yet might her pitteous hart be seene to pant and quake.

21

The messenger of so unhappie newes
   Would faine° have dyde: dead was his hart within,   *gladly*
   Yet outwardly some little comfort shewes:
   At last recovering hart, he does begin
   To rub her temples, and to chaufe° her chin,   *chafe, rub*
   And every tender part does tosse and turne:
   So hardly he the flitted life does win,
   Unto her native prison to retourne:[4]
Then gins her grievèd ghost° thus to lament and mourne.   *spirit*

22

"Ye dreary instruments of dolefull sight,
   That doe this deadly spectacle behold,
   Why do ye lenger° feed on loathèd light,   *longer*
   Or liking find to gaze on earthly mould,[5]
   Sith° cruell fates the carefull° threeds unfould,   *since / intricate*
   The which my life and love together tyde?
   Now let the stony dart of senselesse cold°   *i.e., death*
   Perce to my hart, and pas through every side,
And let eternall night so sad sight fro me hide.

23

"O lightsome day, the lampe of highest Jove,
   First made by him,[6] mens wandring wayes to guyde,
   When darknesse he in deepest dongeon drove,
   Henceforth thy hated face for ever hyde,
   And shut up heavens windowes shyning wyde:
   For earthly sight can nought but sorrow breed,
   And late° repentance, which shall long abyde.   *too late*
   Mine eyes no more on vanitie shall feed,
But seelèd up with death, shall have their deadly meed."°   *reward of death*

---

4. I.e., with such difficulty ("so hardly") he persuades ("does win") the life back to her body ("native prison").
5. I.e., or find it pleasure to gaze on earthly form ("mould").
6. An allusion to Genesis 1.3: "And God said, Let there be light: and there was light."

24

Then downe againe she fell unto the ground;
  But he her quickly rearèd up againe:
  Thrise did she sinke adowne in deadly swownd,
  And thrise he her revived with busie paine:°   *care*
  At last when life recovered had the raine,°   *rule*
  And over-wrestled his strong enemie,
  With foltring° tong, and trembling every vaine,   *faltering*
  "Tell on," quoth she, "the wofull Tragedie,
The which these reliques° sad present unto mine eie.   *remains*

25

"Tempestuous fortune hath spent all her spight,
  And thrilling° sorrow throwne his utmost dart;   *piercing*
  Thy sad tongue cannot tell more heavy plight,
  Then that I feele, and harbour in mine hart:
  Who hath endured the whole, can beare each part.
  If death it be, it is not the first wound,
  That launchèd° hath my brest with bleeding smart.   *pierced*
  Begin, and end the bitter balefull stound;°   *time (of sorrow)*
If lesse, then that° I feare, more favour I have found."   *than what*

26

Then gan the Dwarfe the whole discourse° declare,   *story*
  The subtill traines° of Archimago old;   *wiles*
  The wanton loves of false Fidessa faire,
  Bought with the bloud of vanquisht Paynim bold:
  The wretched payre transformed to treen mould;°   *shape of a tree*
  The house of Pride, and perils round about;
  The combat, which he with Sansjoy did hould;
  The lucklesse conflict with the Gyant stout,
Wherein captived, of life or death he stood in doubt.

27

She heard with patience all unto the end,
  And strove to maister sorrowfull assay,°   *affliction*
  Which greater grew, the more she did contend,
  And almost rent her tender hart in tway;°   *two*
  And love fresh coles unto her fire did lay:
  For greater love, the greater is the losse.
  Was never Ladie lovèd dearer day,[7]
  Then she did love the knight of the Redcrosse;
For whose deare sake so many troubles her did tosse.

28

At last when fervent sorrow slakèd was,
  She up arose, resolving him to find

---

7. I.e., there was never a lady who loved life ("day") more dearly than she loved Redcrosse.

Alive or dead: and forward forth doth pas,
All° as the Dwarfe the way to her assynd:°   *just / showed*
And evermore in constant carefull° mind   *full of care; sorrowful*
She fed her wound with fresh renewèd bale;°   *anguish*
Long tost with stormes, and bet° with bitter wind,   *beaten*
High over hils, and low adowne the dale,
She wandred many a wood, and measurd many a vale.

29

At last she chauncèd by good hap to meet
A goodly knight, faire marching by the way
Together with his Squire, arayèd meet:°   *properly*
His glitterand° armour shinèd farre away,   *glittering*
Like glauncing° light of Phoebus brightest ray;   *flashing*
From top to toe no place appearèd bare,
That deadly dint° of steele endanger may: *stroke*
Athwart his brest a bauldrick[8] brave° he ware,   *splendid*
That shynd, like twinkling stars, with stons most pretious rare.

30

And in the midst thereof one pretious stone
Of wondrous worth, and eke of wondrous mights,°   *powers*
Shapt like a Ladies head, exceeding shone,
Like Hesperus° emongst the lesser lights,°   *evening star / stars*
And strove for to amaze the weaker sights;
Thereby his mortall blade full comely hong
In yvory sheath, ycarved with curious slights;°   *designs*
Whose hilts were burnisht gold, and handle strong
Of mother pearle, and buckled with a golden tong.°   *pin*

31

His haughtie helmet, horrid° all with gold,   *bristling*
Both glorious brightnesse, and great terrour bred;
For all the crest a Dragon did enfold
With greedie pawes, and over all did spred
His golden wings: his dreadfull hideous hed
Close couchèd on the bever,° seemed to throw   *visor*
From flaming mouth bright sparkles fierie red,
That suddeine horror to faint harts did show;
And scaly tayle was stretcht adowne his backe full low.

32

Upon the top of all his loftie crest,°   *top of helmet*
A bunch of haires discolourd° diversly,   *dyed*
With sprincled pearle, and gold full richly drest,
Did shake, and seemed to daunce for jollity,
Like to an Almond tree ymounted hye

8. Sash worn over the shoulder to support the sword.

On top of greene Selinis[9] all alone,
With blossomes brave bedeckèd daintily;
Whose tender locks do tremble every one
At every little breath, that under heaven is blowne.

33

His warlike shield all closely covered was,
  Ne might of mortall eye be ever seene;
  Not made of steele, nor of enduring bras,
  Such earthly mettals soone consumèd bene:°   *i.e., been: be, are*
  But all of Diamond perfect pure and cleene°   *clear*
  It framèd was, one massie entire mould,[1]
  Hewen out of Adamant rocke with engines° keene,   *tools*
  That point of speare it never percen could,
Ne dint° of direfull sword divide the substance would.   *blow*

34

The same to wight° he never wont disclose,   *creature*
  But° when as monsters huge he would dismay,   *except*
  Or daunt unequall armies of his foes,
  Or when the flying heavens he would affray;[2]
  For so exceeding shone his glistring ray,
  That Phoebus golden face it did attaint,°   *make dim*
  As when a cloud his beames doth over-lay;
  And silver Cynthia° wexèd pale and faint,   *the moon*
As when her face is staynd with magicke arts constraint.[3]

35

No magicke arts hereof had any might,
  Nor bloudie wordes of bold Enchaunters call,
  But all that was not such, as seemd in sight,
  Before that shield did fade, and suddeine fall:
  And when him list° the raskall routes° appall,   *wanted to / unruly mobs*
  Men into stones therewith he could transmew,°   *change*
  And stones to dust, and dust to nought at all;
  And when him list the prouder lookes subdew,
He would them gazing blind, or turne to other hew.°   *form*

36

Ne let it seeme, that credence this exceedes,
  For he that made the same, was knowne right well
  To have done much more admirable° deedes.   *marvelous*
  It Merlin was, which whylome° did excell   *formerly*
  All living wightes in might of magicke spell:
  Both shield, and sword, and armour all he wrought

9. Town associated with the palm awarded to victors (Virgil, *Aeneid* 3.705).
1. The shield was made of one solid piece of diamond, unflawed, unpierceable, translucent.

2. I.e., when he would frighten ("affray") the revolving constellations.
3. Magicians were said to be able to cause an eclipse of the moon.

For this young Prince,[4] when first to armes he fell;°   *came*
But when he dyde, the Faerie Queene it brought
To Faerie lond, where yet it may be seene, if sought.

37

A gentle° youth, his dearely lovèd Squire   *noble*
  His speare of heben° wood behind him bare,   *ebony*
  Whose harmefull head, thrice heated in the fire,
  Had riven many a brest with pikehead° square;°   *spearhead / stout*
  A goodly person, and could menage° faire   *control*
  His stubborne steed with curbèd canon bit,[5]
  Who under him did trample as the aire,
  And chauft,° that any on his backe should sit;   *fretted*
The yron rowels° into frothy fome he bit.   *ends of the bit*

38

When as this knight nigh to the Ladie drew,
  With lovely court° he gan her entertaine;   *kind courtesy*
  But when he heard her answers loth, he knew
  Some secret sorrow did her heart distraine:°   *afflict*
  Which to allay, and calme her storming paine,
  Faire feeling words he wisely gan display,°   *pour forth*
  And for her humour fitting purpose faine,[6]
  To tempt° the cause it selfe for to bewray;°   *invite / reveal*
Wherewith emmoved, these bleeding words she gan to say.

39

"What worlds delight, or joy of living speach
  Can heart, so plunged in sea of sorrowes deepe,
  And heapèd with so huge misfortunes, reach?
  The carefull° cold beginneth for to creepe,   *afflicting*
  And in my heart his yron arrow steepe,
  Soone as I thinke upon my bitter bale:°   *grief*
  Such helplesse harmes yts better hidden keepe,
  Then rip up° griefe, where it may not availe,   *than lay open*
My last left comfort is, my woes to weepe and waile."

40

"Ah Ladie deare," quoth then the gentle knight,
  "Well may I weene,° your griefe is wondrous great;   *suppose*
  For wondrous great griefe groneth in my spright,°   *spirit*
  Whiles thus I heare you of your sorrowes treat.
  But wofull Ladie let me you intrete,
  For to unfold the anguish of your hart:
  Mishaps are maistred by advice discrete,

4. The reference to Merlin indicates that the prince is Arthur (who had been mentioned in the canto's prefatory quatrain). In the *Letter to Ralegh*, he is identified with "magnificence," understood as the perfection of all the virtues and containing them all.
5. A smooth, round bit.
6. I.e., suited his manner to her mood.

And counsell mittigates the greatest smart;
Found never helpe, who never would his hurts impart."[7]

41

"O but," quoth she, "great griefe will not be tould,
  And can more easily be thought, then said."
"Right so"; quoth he, "but he, that never would,
  Could never: will to might gives greatest aid."[8]
"But grief," quoth she, "does greater grow displaid,°   *when revealed*
  If then it find not helpe, and breedes despaire."
"Despaire breedes not," quoth he, "where faith is staid."°   *firm*
"No faith so fast," quoth she, "but flesh does paire."°   *impair*
"Flesh may empaire," quoth he, "but reason can repaire."

42

His goodly reason, and well guided speach
  So deepe did settle in her gratious thought,
That her perswaded to disclose the breach,°   *wound*
  Which love and fortune in her heart had wrought,
And said; "Faire Sir, I hope good hap° hath brought   *fortune*
  You to inquire the secrets of my griefe,
Or° that your wisedome will direct my thought,   *either*
  Or that your prowesse can me yield reliefe:
Then heare the storie sad, which I shall tell you briefe.

43

"The forlorne° Maiden, whom your eyes have seene   *forsaken*
  The laughing stocke of fortunes mockeries,
Am th'only daughter of a King and Queene,
  Whose parents deare, whilest equall destinies
Did runne about,[9] and their felicities
  The favourable heavens did not envy,
Did spread their rule through all the territories,
  Which Phison and Euphrates floweth by,
And Gehons golden waves doe wash continually.[1]

44

"Till that their cruell cursèd enemy,
  An huge great Dragon horrible in sight,
Bred in the loathly lakes of Tartary,°   *Tartarus (hell)*
  With murdrous ravine,° and devouring might   *destruction*
Their kingdome spoild,° and countrey wasted quight: *plundered*
  Themselves, for feare into his jawes to fall,
He forst to castle strong to take their flight,

---

7. I.e., he never found help who would not tell
his sorrows.
8. I.e., he that fails to will something cannot do
it: willing gives the greatest help to one's power
("might").

9. I.e., while the impartial fates ran their course.
1. Phison, Euphrates, and Gehon, along with
the Tigris, were the rivers of the Garden of Eden
(Genesis 2.11–14).

Where fast embard° in mightie brasen wall,　　　　　　　*imprisoned*
He has them now foure yeres besiegd to make them thrall.

45

"Full many knights adventurous and stout
　　Have enterprizd that Monster to subdew;
　　From every coast° that heaven walks about,　　　　　*land*
　　Have thither come the noble Martiall crew,
　　That famous hard atchievements still pursew,
　　Yet never any could that girlond win,
　　But all still shronke,° and still he greater grew:　　　*quailed*
All they for want of faith, or guilt of sin,
The pitteous pray of his fierce crueltie have bin.

46

"At last yledd° with farre reported praise,　　　　　　*led*
　　Which flying fame throughout the world had spread,
　　Of doughtie° knights, whom Faery land did raise,　　*brave*
　　That noble order hight° of Maidenhed,[2]　　　　　*called*
　　Forthwith to court of Gloriane I sped,
　　Of Gloriane great Queene of glory bright,
　　Whose kingdomes seat Cleopolis[3] is red,°　　　　　*named*
　　There to obtaine some such redoubted knight,
That Parents deare from tyrants powre deliver might.

47

"It was my chance (my chance was faire and good)
　　There for to find a fresh unprovèd° knight,　　　　　*untried*
　　Whose manly hands imbrewed in guiltie blood
　　Had never bene,[4] ne ever by his might
　　Had throwne to ground the unregarded° right:　　*unrespected*
　　Yet of his prowesse proofe he since hath made
　　(I witnesse am) in many a cruell fight;
　　The groning ghosts of many one dismaide°　　　　*defeated*
Have felt the bitter dint° of his avenging blade.　　　*blow*

48

"And ye the forlorne reliques of his powre,
　　His byting sword, and his devouring speare,
　　Which have endurèd many a dreadfull stowre,°　　*conflict*
　　Can speake his prowesse, that did earst° you beare,　*before*
　　And well could rule: now he hath left you heare,
　　To be the record of his ruefull losse,
　　And of my dolefull disaventurous deare:°　　*sad unfortunate dear one*
　　O heavie record of the good Redcrosse,
Where have you left your Lord, that could so well you tosse?°　*handle*

2. The type or analogue of the Order of the Garter.
Its emblem shows Saint George killing the dragon,
and its star is the Red Cross.

3. The name means "famous city."
4. I.e., his strong hands had never been guiltily
stained ("imbrewed") with blood.

49

"Well hopèd I, and faire beginnings had,
  That he my captive langour should redeeme,[5]
  Till all unweeting,° an Enchaunter bad   *unknowing*
  His sence abusd, and made him to misdeeme°   *misjudge*
  My loyalty, not such as it did seeme;
  That rather death desire, then such despight.[6]
  Be judge ye heavens, that all things right esteeme,°   *judge rightly*
  How I him loved, and love with all my might,
So thought I eke of him, and thinke I thought aright.

50

"Thenceforth me desolate he quite forsooke,
  To wander, where wilde fortune would me lead,
  And other bywaies he himselfe betooke,
  Where never foot of living wight did tread,
  That brought not backe the balefull body dead;° *i.e., who was not killed*
  In which him chauncèd false Duessa meete,
  Mine onely foe, mine onely deadly dread,[7]
  Who with her witchcraft and misseeming° sweete, *false appearance*
Inveigled him to follow her desires unmeete.°   *improper*

51

"At last by subtill sleights she him betraid
  Unto his foe, a Gyant huge and tall,
  Who him disarmèd, dissolute,° dismaid,   *enfeebled*
  Unwares surprisèd and with mightie mall°   *club*
  The monster mercilesse him made to fall,
  Whose fall did never foe before behold;
  And now in darkesome dungeon, wretched thrall,
  Remedilesse, for aie[8] he doth him hold;
This is my cause of griefe, more great, then may be told."

52

Ere she had ended all, she gan to faint:°   *grow weak; lose heart*
  But he her comforted and faire bespake,
  "Certès,° Madame, ye have great cause of plaint, *certainly*
  That stoutest heart, I weene, could cause to quake.
  But be of cheare, and comfort to you take:
  For till I have acquit° your captive knight,   *freed*
  Assure your selfe, I will you not forsake."
  His chearefull words revived her chearelesse spright,
So forth they went, the Dwarfe them guiding ever right.

---

5. I.e., relieve my state, captive to sadness.
6. I.e., I, who prefer death to such treachery ("despight").
7. I.e., the only object of my mortal fear.
8. I.e., forever ("for aie") without hope of rescue ("remedilesse").

Canto 8

Faire virgin to redeeme her deare
brings Arthur to the fight:
Who slayes the Gyant, wounds the beast,
and strips Duessa quight.

1

Ay me, how many perils doe enfold
  The righteous man, to make him daily fall?
  Were not, that heavenly grace doth him uphold,
  And stedfast truth acquite° him out of all.   *deliver*
  Her love is firme, her care continuall,
  So oft as he through his owne foolish pride,
  Or weakesse is to sinfull bands° made thrall: *bonds*
  Else should this Redcrosse knight in bands have dyde,
For whose deliverance she this Prince doth thither guide.

2

They sadly traveild thus, untill they came
  Nigh to a castle builded strong and hie:
  Then cryde the Dwarfe, "lo yonder is the same,
  In which my Lord my liege doth lucklesse lie,
  Thrall to that Gyants hatefull tyrannie:
  Therefore, deare Sir, your mightie powres assay."°   *put to trial*
  The noble knight alighted by and by°   *immediately*
  From loftie steede, and bad the Ladie stay,
To see what end of fight should him befall that day.

3

So with the Squire, th'admirèr of his might,
  He marchèd forth towards that castle wall;
  Whose gates he found fast shut, ne living wight
  To ward° the same, nor answere commers call.   *guard*
  Then tooke that Squire an horne of bugle° small,   *wild ox*
  Which hong adowne his side in twisted gold,
  And tassels gay. Wyde wonders over all°   *everywhere*
  Of that same hornes great vertues° weren told,[9]   *powers*
Which had approvèd° bene in uses manifold.   *demonstrated*

4

Was never wight, that heard that shrilling sound,
  But trembling feare did feele in every vaine;
  Three miles it might be easie heard around,
  And Ecchoes three answered it selfe againe:
  No false enchauntment, nor deceiptfull traine°   *snare*
  Might once abide the terror of that blast,

---

9. Marvelous tales ("Wyde wonders") told of the horn connect it with the horn of the legendary French hero Roland and the ram's horn of Joshua, with which he razed the walls of Jericho (Joshua 6.5).

But presently° was voide and wholly vaine: *at once*
  No gate so strong, no locke so firme and fast,
But with that percing noise flew open quite, or brast.°   *burst*

5

The same before the Geants gate he blew,
  That all the castle quakèd from the ground,
  And every dore of freewill open flew.
  The Gyant selfe dismaièd with that sownd,
  Where he with his Duessa dalliance° fownd,   *amorous play*
  In hast came rushing forth from inner bowre,
  With staring° countenance sterne, as one astownd,   *glaring*
  And staggering steps, to weet, what suddein stowre° *disturbance*
Had wrought that horror strange, and dared his dreaded powre.

6

And after him the proud Duessa came,
  High mounted on her manyheaded beast,
  And every head with fyrie tongue did flame,
  And every head was crownèd on his creast,
  And bloudie mouthèd with late cruell feast.
  That when the knight beheld, his mightie shild
  Upon his manly arme he soone addrest,°   *made ready*
  And at him fiercely flew, with courage fild,
And eger greedinesse° through every member thrild. *eagerness for battle*

7

Therewith the Gyant buckled him to fight,
  Inflamed with scornefull wrath and high disdaine,°   *indignation*
  And lifting up his dreadfull club on hight,
  All armed with ragged snubbes° and knottie graine,   *snags*
  Him thought at first encounter to have slaine.
  But wise and warie was that noble Pere,°   *peer*
  And lightly leaping from so monstrous maine,°   *force*
  Did faire° avoide the violence him nere;   *quite*
It booted nought, to thinke, such thunderbolts to beare.[1]

8

Ne shame he thought to shunne so hideous might:
  The idle° stroke, enforcing furious way,   *useless*
  Missing the marke of his misaymèd sight
  Did fall to ground, and with his° heavie sway°   *its / force*
  So deepely dinted in the driven clay,
  That three yardes deepe a furrow up did throw:
  The sad earth wounded with so sore assay,°   *assault*
  Did grone full grievous underneath the blow,
And trembling with strange feare, did like an earthquake show.

---

1. I.e., it was useless to think of withstanding such blows.

9

As when almightie Jove in wrathfull mood,
 To wreake° the guilt of mortall sins is bent,°   *punish / disposed*
 Hurles forth his thundring dart with deadly food,°   *hatred (feud)*
 Enrold in flames, and smouldring dreriment,°   *smothering darkness*
 Through riven cloudes and molten firmament;
 The fierce threeforkèd engin° making way,   *weapon*
 Both loftie towres and highest trees hath rent,
 And all that might his angrie passage stay,
And shooting in the earth, casts up a mount of clay.

10

His boystrous° club, so buried in the ground,   *massive*
 He could not rearen up againe so light,°   *easily*
 But that the knight him at avantage found,
 And whiles he strove his combred clubbe to quight[2]
 Out of the earth, with blade all burning bright
 He smote off his left arme, which like a blocke
 Did fall to ground, deprived of native might;
 Large streames of bloud out of the trunckèd stocke° *truncated stump*
Forth gushèd, like fresh water streame from riven rocke.[3]

11

Dismaièd with so desperate deadly wound,
 And eke° impatient of unwonted paine,[4]   *also*
 He loudly brayd with beastly yelling sound,
 That all the fields rebellowèd againe;
 As great a noyse, as when in Cymbrian[5] plaine
 An heard of Bulles, whom kindly° rage doth sting,   *natural*
 Do for the milkie mothers want complaine,[6]
 And fill the fields with troublous bellowing,
The neighbour woods around with hollow murmur ring.

12

That when his deare Duessa heard, and saw
 The evill stownd, that daungerd her estate,[7]
 Unto his aide she hastily did draw
 Her dreadfull beast, who swolne with bloud of late
 Came ramping° forth with proud presumpteous gate,° *rearing / gait*
 And threatned all his heads like flaming brands.°   *torches*
 But him the Squire made quickly to retrate,
 Encountring fierce with single° sword in hand,   *only*
And twixt him and his Lord did like a bulwarke stand.

---

2. Strove to release his encumbered club.
3. Cf. Exodus 17.6, where Moses smites the rock and water flows forth.
4. I.e., unable to bear ("impatient of") this unfamiliar ("unwonted") pain.
5. Jutland, once called the Cimbric peninsula.
6. I.e., mourn the cows' absence.
7. I.e., the peril ("stownd") that endangered her state.

13

The proud Duessa full of wrathfull spight,
  And fierce disdaine, to be affronted so,
    Enforst her purple° beast with all her might   *scarlet*
    That stop° out of the way to overthroe,   *obstacle*
    Scorning the let° of so unequall foe: *hindrance*
  But nathemore° would that courageous swayne   *never the more*
  To her yeeld passage, gainst his Lord to goe,
  But with outrageous° strokes did him restraine,   *exceedingly fierce*
And with his bodie bard the way atwixt them twaine.

14

Then tooke the angrie witch her golden cup,
  Which still° she bore, replete with magick artes;[8]   *always*
    Death and despeyre did many thereof sup,
    And secret poyson through their inner parts,
    Th'eternall bale° of heavie wounded harts;   *woe*
  Which after charmes and some enchauntments said,
  She lightly sprinkled on his weaker° parts;   *too weak*
  Therewith his sturdie courage soone was quayd,°   *quelled*
And all his senses were with suddeine dread dismayd.

15

So downe he fell before the cruell beast,
  Who on his necke his bloudie clawes did seize,
    That life nigh crusht out of his panting brest:
    No powre he had to stirre, nor will to rize.
    That when the carefull° knight gan well avise,°   *watchful / observe*
  He lightly° left the foe, with whom he fought,   *quickly*
  And to the beast gan turne his enterprise;
  For wondrous anguish in his hart it wrought,
To see his lovèd Squire into such thraldome° brought.   *slavery*

16

And high advauncing° his bloud-thirstie blade,   *lifting up*
  Stroke one of those deformèd heads so sore,[9]
    That of his puissance° proud ensample made;   *strength*
    His monstrous scalpe° downe to his teeth it tore   *skull*
    And that misformèd shape mis-shapèd more:
  A sea of bloud gusht from the gaping wound,
  That her gay garments staynd with filthy gore,
  And overflowèd all the field around;
That over shoes[1] in bloud he waded on the ground.

---

8. Alludes to the golden cup of the woman in Revelation 17.4, which is "full of abominations and filthiness of her fornication"; the chalice of the Roman Church; and the cup of Circe, the sorceress who turned men into beasts (in *Odyssey* 10).
9. "I saw one of his [i.e., the beast's] heads as it were wounded to death" (Revelation 13.3).
1. I.e., deeply immersed.

17

Thereat he roarèd for exceeding paine,
 That to have heard, great horror would have bred,°   *produced*
 And scourging th'emptie ayre with his long traine,°   *tail*
 Through great impatience of his grievèd hed[2]
 His gorgeous ryder from her loftie sted°   *place*
 Would have cast downe, and trod in durtie myre,
 Had not the Gyant soone her succourèd;°   *aided*
 Who all enraged with smart° and franticke yre,°   *pain / anger*
Came hurtling in full fierce, and forst the knight retyre.

18

The force, which wont° in two to be disperst,   *used*
 In one alone left hand[3] he now unites,
 Which is through rage more strong then both were erst;°   *before*
 With which his hideous club aloft he dites,°   *raises*
 And at his foe with furious rigour° smites,   *violence*
 That strongest Oake might seeme to overthrow:
 The stroke upon his shield so heavie lites,
 That to the ground it doubleth him full low:
What mortall wight could ever beare so monstrous blow?

19

And in his fall his shield, that covered was,
 Did loose his vele° by chaunce, and open flew: *its covering*
 The light whereof, that heavens light did pas,°   *surpass*
 Such blazing brightnesse through the aier threw,
 That eye mote not the same endure to vew.
 Which when the Gyaunt spyde with staring eye,
 He downe let fall his arme, and soft withdrew
 His weapon huge, that heavèd was on hye
For to have slaine the man, that on the ground did lye.

20

And eke the fruitfull-headed° beast, amazed   *many-headed*
 At flashing beames of that sunshiny shield,
 Became starke blind, and all his senses dazed,
 That downe he tumbled on the durtie field,
 And seemed himselfe as conquerèd to yield.
 Whom when his maistresse proud perceived to fall,
 Whiles yet his feeble feet for faintnesse reeld,
 Unto the Gyant loudly she gan call,
"O helpe Orgoglio, helpe, or else we perish all."

---

2. I.e., through inability to endure ("impatience") his afflicted ("grievèd") head.   3. I.e., in the one hand left to him.

21

At her so pitteous cry was much amooved
  Her champion stout, and for to ayde his frend,°   *lover*
  Againe his wonted° angry weapon prooved:°   *usual / tried*
  But all in vaine: for he has read his end
  In that bright shield, and all their forces spend
  Themselves in vaine: for since that glauncing° sight,   *flashing*
  He hath no powre to hurt, nor to defend;
  As where th'Almighties lightning brond° does light,   *firebrand*
It dimmes the dazèd eyen, and daunts the senses quight.

22

Whom when the Prince, to battell new addrest,
  And threatning high his dreadfull stroke did see,
  His sparkling blade about his head he blest,°   *brandished*
  And smote off quite his right leg by the knee,
  That downe he tombled; as an agèd tree,
  High growing on the top of rocky clift,
  Whose hartstrings with keene steele nigh hewen be,
  The mightie trunck halfe rent, with ragged rift°   *split*
Doth roll adowne the rocks, and fall with fearefull drift.°   *impact*

23

Or as a Castle rearèd high and round,
  By subtile engins and malitious slight[4]
  Is underminèd from the lowest ground,
  And her foundation forst,° and feebled quight,   *shattered*
  At last downe falles, and with her heapèd hight
  Her hastie ruine does more heavie make,
  And yields it selfe unto the victours might;
  Such was this Gyaunts fall, that seemed to shake
The stedfast globe of earth, as° it for feare did quake.   *as if*

24

The knight then lightly° leaping to the pray,   *quickly*
  With mortall steele him smot againe so sore,
  That headlesse his unweldy bodie lay,
  All wallowd in his owne fowle bloudy gore,
  Which flowèd from his wounds in wondrous store.°   *abundance*
  But soone as breath out of his breast did pas,
  That huge great body, which the Gyaunt bore,
  Was vanisht quite, and of that monstrous mas
Was nothing left, but like an emptie bladder was.

4. Clever machines of war ("engins") and evil strategy.

25

Whose grievous fall, when false Duessa spide,
　　Her golden cup she cast unto the ground,
　　And crownèd mitre[5] rudely° threw aside;　　　　　　　*violently*
　　Such percing griefe her stubborne hart did wound,
　　That she could not endure that dolefull stound,°　　　　*sorrow*
　　But leaving all behind her, fled away:
　　The light-foot Squire her quickly turned around,
　　And by hard meanes enforcing her to stay,
So brought unto his Lord, as his deservèd pray.

26

The royall Virgin, which beheld from farre,
　　In pensive° plight, and sad perplexitie,　　　　　　　*anxious*
　　The whole achievement of this doubtfull warre,[6]
　　Came running fast to greet his victorie,
　　With sober gladnesse, and myld modestie,
　　And with sweet joyous cheare° him thus bespake;　　*countenance*
　　"Faire braunch of noblesse, flowre of chevalrie,
　　That with your worth the world amazèd make,
How shall I quite° the paines, ye suffer for my sake?　　*requite*

27

"And you° fresh bud of vertue springing fast,　　　*i.e., the Squire*
　　Whom these sad eyes saw nigh unto deaths dore,
　　What hath poore Virgin for such perill past,
　　Wherewith you to reward? Accept therefore
　　My simple selfe, and service evermore;
　　And he that high does sit, and all things see
　　With equall° eyes, their merites to restore,°　　*impartial / reward*
　　Behold what ye this day have done for mee,
And what I cannot quite,° requite with usuree.°　　*repay / interest*

28

"But sith° the heavens, and your faire handeling°　　*since / conduct*
　　Have made you maister of the field this day,
　　Your fortune maister eke with governing,[7]
　　And well begun end all so well, I pray,
　　Ne let that wicked woman scape away;
　　For she it is, that did my Lord bethrall,
　　My dearest Lord, and deepe in dongeon lay,
　　Where he his better dayes hath wasted all.[8]
O heare, how piteous he to you for ayd does call."

---

5. An allusion to the pope's triple tiara.
6. I.e., the final outcome, which had been in doubt, of this battle.
7. Secure your good fortune also by prudent man-agement.
8. I.e., he has consumed ("wasted") there his best days.

29

Forthwith he gave in charge unto his Squire,
  That scarlot whore to keepen carefully;
  Whiles he himselfe with greedie° great desire   *eager*
  Into the Castle entred forcibly,
  Where living creature none he did espye;
  Then gan he lowdly through the house to call:
  But no man cared to answere to his crye.
  There raignd a solemne silence over all,
Nor voice was heard, nor wight was seene in bowre or hall.

30

At last with creeping crooked pace forth came
  An old old man, with beard as white as snow,
  That on a staffe his feeble steps did frame,°   *support*
  And guide his wearie gate° both too and fro: *gait*
  For his eye sight him failèd long ygo,
  And on his arme a bounch of keyes[9] he bore,
  The which unusèd, rust did overgrow:
  Those were the keyes of every inner dore,
But he could not them use, but kept them still in store.

31

But very uncouth° sight was to behold,   *strange*
  How he did fashion his untoward° pace,   *awkward*
  For as he forward mooved his footing old,
  So backward still was turned his wrincled face,
  Unlike to men, who ever as they trace,°   *walk*
  Both feet and face one way are wont to lead.
  This was the auncient keeper of that place,
  And foster father of the Gyant dead;
His name Ignaro° did his nature right aread.°   *Ignorance / declare*

32

His reverend haires and holy gravitie
  The knight much honord, as beseemèd well,°   *seemed proper*
  And gently° askt, where all the people bee,   *courteously*
  Which in that stately building wont to dwell.
  Who answerd him full soft, he could not tell.
  Againe he askt, where that same knight was layd,
  Whom great Orgoglio with his puissaunce fell°   *fierce power*
  Had made his caytive° thrall; againe he sayde,   *captive*
He could not tell: ne ever other answere made.

33

Then askèd he, which way he in might pas:
  He could not tell, againe he answerèd.

---

9. Alluding to "the keys of the kingdom of heaven" (Matthew 16.19). See also Matthew 23.13 and Luke 11.52.

Thereat the curteous knight displeasèd was,
   And said, "Old sire, it seemes thou hast not red°   *recognized*
   How ill it sits with° that same silver hed   *suits*
   In vaine to mocke, or mockt in vaine to bee:
   But if thou be, as thou art pourtrahèd
   With natures pen, in ages grave degree,
Aread° in graver wise, what I demaund° of thee."   *answer / ask*

34

His answere likewise was, he could not tell.
   Whose sencelesse speach, and doted° ignorance   *foolish*
   When as the noble Prince had markèd well,
   He ghest his nature by his countenance,
   And calmd his wrath with goodly temperance.
   Then to him stepping, from his arme did reach
   Those keyes, and made himselfe free enterance.
   Each dore he opened without any breach;°   *forcing*
There was no barre to stop, nor foe him to empeach.°   *hinder*

35

There all within full rich arayd he found,
   With royal arras° and resplendent gold,   *tapestry*
   And did with store of every thing abound,
   That greatest Princes presence° might behold.   *person*
   But all the floore (too filthy to be told)
   With bloud of guiltlesse babes, and innocents trew,[1]
   Which there were slaine, as sheepe out of the fold,
   Defilèd was, that dreadfull was to vew,
And sacred ashes over it was strowèd° new.   *strewn*

36

And there beside of marble stone was built
   An Altare, carved with cunning imagery,[2]
   On which true Christians bloud was often spilt,
   And holy Martyrs often doen to dye,°   *put to death*
   With cruell malice and strong tyranny:
   Whose blessed sprites from underneath the stone
   To God for vengeance cryde continually,[3]
   And with great griefe were often heard to grone,
That hardest heart would bleede, to heare their piteous mone.

37

Through every rowme he sought, and every bowr,
   But no where could he find that wofull thrall:
   At last he came unto an yron doore,

1. Probably alluding to Herod's massacre of the Innocents (Matthew 2.16), who were traditionally viewed as the first martyrs for Christ.
2. Skillfully wrought images.
3. "And when he had opened the fifth seal, I saw under the altar the souls of them that were slain for the word of God, and for the testimony which they held: And they cried with a loud voice, saying, How long, O Lord, holy and true, dost thou not judge and avenge our blood on them that dwell on the earth?" (Revelation 6.9–10).

That fast was lockt, but key found not at all
Emongst that bounch, to open it withall;
But in the same a little grate was pight,°   *placed*
Through which he sent his voyce, and lowd did call
With all his powre, to weet,° if living wight   *learn*
Were housèd therewithin, whom he enlargen° might.   *set free*

38

Therewith an hollow, dreary, murmuring voyce
  These piteous plaints and dolours° did resound;   *laments*
  "O who is that, which brings me happy choyce
  Of death,[4] that here lye dying every stound,°   *moment*
  Yet live perforce in balefull° darkenesse bound?   *evil*
  For now three Moones have changèd thrice their hew,°   *shape*
  And have beene thrice hid underneath the ground,
Since I the heavens chearefull face did vew,
O welcome thou, that doest of death bring tydings trew."

39

Which when that Champion heard, with percing point
  Of pitty deare° his hart was thrillèd° sore,   *extreme / pierced*
  And trembling horrour ran through every joynt,
  For ruth° of gentle knight so fowle forlore:°   *pity / grievously lost*
  Which shaking off, he rent° that yron dore,   *burst open*
  With furious force, and indignation fell;°   *fierce*
  Where entred in, his foot could find no flore,
But all a deepe descent, as darke as hell,
That breathèd ever forth a filthie banefull smell.

40

But neither darkenesse fowle, nor filthy bands,°   *bonds*
  Nor noyous° smell his purpose could withhold,   *noxious*
  (Entire° affection hateth nicer° hands)   *perfect / too fastidious*
  But that with constant zeale, and courage bold,
  After long paines and labours manifold,
  He found the meanes that Prisoner up to reare;
  Whose feeble thighes, unhable to uphold
His pinèd° corse, him scarse to light could beare,   *wasted*
A ruefull spectacle of deathe and ghastly drere.°   *sorrow, wretchedness*

41

His sad dull eyes deepe sunck in hollow pits,
  Could not endure th'unwonted° sunne to view;   *unaccustomed*
  His bare thin cheekes for want of better bits,°   *food*
  And empty sides deceivèd° of their dew,   *cheated*
  Could make a stony hart his hap to rew;°   *to pity his lot*
  His rawbone armes, whose mighty brawnèd bowrs°   *brawny muscles*

---

4. I.e., the chance or right to choose death.

Were wont to rive steele plates, and helmets hew,
Were cleane consumed, and all his vitall powres
Decayd, and all his flesh shronk up like withered flowres.

42

Whom when his Lady saw, to him she ran
  With hasty joy: to see him made her glad,
  And sad to view his visage pale and wan,
  Who earst° in flowres of freshest youth was clad.   *formerly*
  Tho° when her well of teares she wasted° had,   *then / expended*
  She said, "Ah dearest Lord, what evill starre
  On you hath fround, and pourd his influence bad,
  That of your selfe ye thus berobbèd arre,
And this misseeming hew° your manly looks doth marre?   *unseemly*
                                                                  appearance

43

"But welcome now my Lord, in wele° or woe,   *weal, well-being*
  Whose presence I have lackt to long a day;
  And fie on Fortune mine avowèd foe,
  Whose wrathfull wreakes° them selves do now alay.   *punishments*
  And for these wrongs shall treble penaunce pay
  Of treble good: good growes of evils priefe."[5]
  The chearelesse man, whom sorrow did dismay,°   *unnerve*
  Had no delight to treaten° of his griefe;   *speak*
His long endurèd famine needed more reliefe.

44

"Faire Lady," then said that victorious knight,°   *i.e., Arthur*
  "The things, that grievous were to do, or beare,
  Them to renew,° I wote,° breeds no delight;   *recall / know*
  Best musicke breeds delight in loathing eare:
  But th'onely good, that growes of passèd feare,
  Is to be wise, and ware° of like agein.   *wary*
  This dayes ensample hath this lesson deare
  Deepe written in my heart with yron pen,
That blisse may not abide in state of mortall men.

45

"Henceforth sir knight, take to you wonted strength,
  And maister these mishaps with patient might;
  Loe° where your foe lyes stretcht in monstrous length,   *look*
  And loe that wicked woman in your sight,
  The roote of all your care, and wretched plight,
  Now in your powre, to let her live, or dye."
  "To do her dye," quoth Una, "were despight,[6]

---

5. I.e., Fortune will now make amends for his wrongs with triple benefits, as good comes from evils endured ("priefe").

6. I.e., to cause her to die would be spiteful.

And shame t'avenge so weake an enimy;
But spoile° her of her scarlot robe, and let her fly."   *despoil, strip*

46

So as she bad, that witch they disaraid,
  And robd of royall robes, and purple pall,°   *scarlet cloak*
  And ornaments that richly were displaid;
  Ne sparèd they to strip her naked all.
  Then when they had despoild her tire° and call,°   *robe / caul, headdress*
  Such as she was, their eyes might her behold,
  That her misshapèd parts did them appall,
  A loathly, wrinckled hag, ill favoured, old,
Whose secret filth good manners biddeth not be told.

47

Her craftie head was altogether bald,
  And as in hate of honorable eld,°   *age*
  Was overgrowne with scurfe° and filthy scald;[7]   *scabs*
  Her teeth out of her rotten gummes were feld,°   *fallen*
  And her sowre breath abhominably smeld;
  Her drièd dugs,° like bladders lacking wind,   *breasts*
  Hong downe, and filthy matter from them weld;°   *welled*
  Her wrizled° skin as rough, as maple rind,   *wrinkled*
So scabby was, that would have loathd° all womankind.   *revolted*

48

Her neather parts, the shame of all her kind,°   *i.e., womankind*
  My chaster° Muse for shame doth blush to write;   *too chaste*
  But at her rompe she growing had behind
  A foxes taile, with dong all fowly dight;°   *covered*
  And eke her feete most monstrous were in sight;
  For one of them was like an Eagles claw,
  With griping talaunts armd to greedy fight,
  The other like a Beares uneven° paw: *rough*
More ugly shape yet never living creature saw.[8]

49

Which when the knights beheld, amazd they were,
  And wondred at so fowle deformèd wight.
  "Such then," said Una, "as she seemeth here,
  Such is the face of falshood, such the sight
  Of fowle Duessa, when her borrowed light
  Is laid away, and counterfesaunce° knowne."   *deceit*
  Thus when they had the witch disrobèd quight,
  And all her filthy feature° open showne,   *form*
They let her goe at will, and wander wayes unknowne.

---

7. A scabby disease of the scalp.
8. The passage alludes to Revelation 17.16: "these shall hate the whore, and shall make her desolate and naked." The animals associated with Duessa were emblematic: foxes of cunning, eagles and bears of rapacity, cruelty, and brutality.

50

She flying fast from heavens hated face,
  And from the world that her discovered° wide,   *exposed to view*
  Fled to the wastfull° wildernesse apace,   *desolate*
  From living eyes her open shame to hide,
  And lurkt in rocks and caves long unespide.
  But that faire crew° of knights, and Una faire   *company*
  Did in that castle afterwards abide,
  To rest them selves, and weary powres repaire,
Where store they found of all, that dainty° was and rare.   *precious*

Canto 9

His loves and lignage° Arthur tells: *lineage*
  The knights knit friendly bands:°   *bonds*
Sir Trevisan flies from Despayre,
  Whom Redcrosse knight withstands.

1

O goodly golden chaine,[9] wherewith yfere°   *together*
  The vertues linkèd are in lovely wize:°   *manner*
  And noble minds of yore allyèd were,
  In brave poursuit of chevalrous emprize,°   *adventure*
  That none did others safety despize,°   *disregard*
  Nor aid envy° to him, in need that stands,   *begrudge*
  But friendly each did others prayse devize
  How to advaunce with favourable hands,
As this good Prince redeemd the Redcrosse knight from bands.

2

Who when their powres, empaird through labour long,
  With dew repast° they had recurèd° well,   *rest / restored*
  And that weake captive wight now wexèd° strong,   *waxed, grown*
  Them list° no lenger there at leasure dwell,   *they cared*
  But forward fare, as their adventures fell,
  But ere they parted, Una faire besought
  That straunger knight his name and nation tell;
  Least° so great good, as he for her had wrought,   *lest*
Should die unknown, and buried be in thanklesse thought.

3

"Faire virgin," said the Prince, "ye me require
  A thing without the compas of° my wit: *beyond the reach of*
  For both the lignage and the certain Sire,
  From which I sprong, from me are hidden yit.°   *still*
  For all so soone as life did me admit

---

9. The golden chain of love or concord that binds the world and the human race together (cf. canto 5, stanza 25, n. 3).

Into this world, and shewèd heavens light,
  From mothers pap I taken was unfit:°   *i.e., not yet weaned*
  And streight delivered to a Faery knight,
To be upbrought in gentle thewes° and martiall might.   *manners*

4

"Unto old Timon[1] he me brought bylive,°   *immediately*
  Old Timon, who in youthly yeares hath beene
  In warlike feates th'expertest man alive,
  And is the wisest now on earth I weene;
  His dwelling is low in a valley greene,
  Under the foot of Rauran mossy hore,°   *gray*
  From whence the river Dee as silver cleene°   *pure*
  His tombling billowes rolls with gentle rore:[2]
There all my dayes he traind me up in vertuous lore.

5

"Thither the great Magicien Merlin came,
  As was his use,° ofttimes to visit me: *custom*
  For he had charge my discipline° to frame,°   *education / direct*
  And Tutours nouriture° to oversee.   *tutor's upbringing*
  Him oft and oft I askt in privitie,
  Of what loines and what lignage I did spring:
  Whose aunswere bad me still assurèd bee,
  That I was sonne and heire unto a king,
As time in her just terme° the truth to light should bring." *due course*

6

"Well worthy impe,"° said then the Lady gent,° *offspring / gentle*
  "And Pupill fit for such a Tutours hand.
  But what adventure, or what high intent
  Hath brought you hither into Faery land,
  Aread° Prince Arthur,[3] crowne of Martiall band?" *declare*
  "Full hard it is," quoth he, "to read° aright   *discern*
  The course of heavenly cause, or understand
  The secret meaning of th'eternall might,
That rules mens wayes, and rules the thoughts of living wight.

7

"For whither he through fatall deepe foresight,[4]
  Me hither sent, for cause to me unghest,°   *unknown*
  Or that fresh bleeding wound, which day and night
  Whilome° doth rancle in my riven° brest, *all the while / torn*
  With forcèd fury following his behest,°   *its command*

1. The name means "honor."
2. The hill Rauran is in Wales. The river Dee flows in, and forms part of the boundary of, Wales. The Tudors (Queen Elizabeth's family) were originally Welsh, and the legends of Arthur had their beginnings in the Celtic mythology of early Wales.

3. Arthur had been named in the quatrains that precede cantos 7 and 8, but not previously in the body of the text.
4. I.e., whether God ("th'eternall might") sent me here through foresight ordained by fate ("fatall").

Me hither brought by wayes yet never found,
You to have helpt I hold my selfe yet blest."
"Ah curteous knight," quoth she, "what secret wound
Could ever find,° to grieve the gentlest hart on ground?"   *succeed*

8

"Deare Dame," quoth he, "you sleeping sparkes awake,
    Which troubled once, into huge flames will grow,
    Ne ever will their fervent fury slake
    Till living moysture into smoke do flow,
    And wasted° life do lye in ashes low.   *consumed*
    Yet sithens° silence lesseneth not my fire,   *since*
    But told it flames, and hidden it does glow,
    I will revele, what ye so much desire:
Ah Love, lay downe thy bow, the whiles I may respire.°   *take breath*

9

"It was in freshest flowre of youthly yeares,
    When courage first does creepe in manly chest,
    Then first the coale of kindly° heat appeares   *natural*
    To kindle love in every living brest;
    But me had warnd old Timons wise behest,
    Those creeping flames by reason to subdew,
    Before their rage grew to so great unrest,
    As miserable lovers use° to rew,   *are accustomed*
Which still wex° old in woe, whiles woe still wexeth new.   *grow*

10

"That idle name of love, and lovers life,
    As° losse of time, and vertues enimy   *as being*
    I ever scornd, and joyd to stirre up strife,
    In middest of their mournfull Tragedy,
    Ay° wont to laugh, when them I heard to cry,   *always*
    And blow the fire, which them to ashes brent:°   *burned*
    Their God himselfe, grieved at my libertie,
    Shot many a dart at me with fiers intent,
But I them warded all with wary government.[5]

11

"But all in vaine: no fort can be so strong,
    Ne fleshly brest can armèd be so sound,
    But will at last be wonne with battrie° long,   *siege*
    Or unawares at disavantage found;
    Nothing is sure, that growes on earthly ground:
    And who most trustes in arme of fleshly might,
    And boasts, in beauties chaine not to be bound,

5. I.e., self-control. The descriptions here of Cupid's archery and of the siege of the castle of chastity (in the next stanza) have many echoes from the medieval courtly love tradition.

Doth soonest fall in disaventrous° fight,   *disastrous*
And yeeldes his caytive° neck to victours most° despight.   *captive / greatest*

12

"Ensample make of him your haplesse joy,°   *i.e., Redcrosse*
  And of my selfe now mated,° as ye see;   *overcome*
  Whose prouder° vaunt that proud avenging boy   *too proud*
  Did soone pluck downe, and curbd my libertie.
  For on a day prickt° forth with jollitie   *spurred*
  Of looser° life, and heat of hardiment,°   *too loose / boldness*
  Raunging the forest wide on courser° free,   *warhorse*
  The fields, the floods, the heavens with one consent
Did seeme to laugh on me, and favour mine intent.

13

"For-wearied° with my sports, I did alight   *utterly wearied*
  From loftie steed, and downe to sleepe me layd;
  The verdant° gras my couch did goodly dight,°   *green / make*
  And pillow was my helmet faire displayd:
  Whiles every sence the humour sweet embayd,[6]
  And slombring soft my hart did steale away,
  Me seemèd, by my side a royall Mayd
  Her daintie limbes full softly down did lay:
So faire a creature yet saw never sunny day.

14

"Most goodly glee° and lovely blandishment° *entertainment / compliment*
  She to me made, and bad me love her deare,
  For dearely sure her love was to me bent,°   *given*
  As when just time expirèd[7] should appeare.
  But whether dreames delude, or true it were,
  Was never hart so ravisht with delight,
  Ne living man like words did ever heare,
  As she to me delivered all that night;
And at her parting said, She Queene of Faeries hight.[8]

15

"When I awoke, and found her place devoyd,°   *empty*
  And nought but pressèd gras, where she had lyen,
  I sorrowed all so much, as earst° I joyd,   *previously*
  And washèd all her place with watry eyen.
  From that day forth I loved that face divine;
  From that day forth I cast° in carefull° mind, *resolved / care-filled*
  To seeke her out with labour, and long tyne,°   *hardship*

6. I.e., while the dew ("humour") of sleep pervaded ("embayd") every sense.
7. A fitting length of time having passed.
8. Was called. In the background are many folk-tales and ballads of a hero bewitched by a fairy. Spenser's Letter to Ralegh identifies Gloriana allegorically with glory and with Queen Elizabeth.

And never vowd° to rest, till her I find,   *vowed never*
Nine monethes I seeke in vaine yet ni'll° that vow unbind."   *will not*

16

Thus as he spake, his visage wexèd pale,
  And chaunge of hew great passion did bewray;°   *reveal*
  Yet still he strove to cloke his inward bale,°   *grief*
  And hide the smoke, that did his fire display,
  Till gentle Una thus to him gan say;
  "O happy Queene of Faeries, that hast found
  Mongst many, one that with his prowesse may
  Defend thine honour, and thy foes confound:
True Loves are often sown, but seldom grow on ground."

17

"Thine, O then," said the gentle Redcrosse knight,
  "Next to that Ladies love shalbe the place,
  O fairest virgin, full of heavenly light,
  Whose wondrous faith, exceeding earthly race,
  Was firmest fixt in mine extremest case.°   *plight*
  And you, my Lord, the Patrone° of my life,   *protector*
  Of that great Queene may well gaine worthy grace:
  For onely worthy you through prowes priefe° *demonstration of prowess*
Yf living man mote° worthy be, to be her liefe."°   *may / love*

18

So diversly discoursing of their loves,
  The golden Sunne his glistring° head gan shew,   *glittering*
  And sad remembraunce now the Prince amoves,
  With fresh desire his voyage to pursew:
  Als° Una earnd° her traveill to renew.   *also / yearned*
  Then those two knights, fast friendship for to bynd,
  And love establish each to other trew,
  Gave goodly gifts, the signes of gratefull mynd,
And eke as pledges firme, right hands together joynd.

19

Prince Arthur gave a boxe of Diamond sure,°   *true*
  Embowd° with gold and gorgeous ornament,   *bound*
  Wherein were closd few drops of liquor pure,
  Of wondrous worth, and vertue° excellent,   *power*
  That any wound could heale incontinent:°   *immediately*
  Which to requite, the Redcrosse knight him gave
  A booke, wherein his Saveours testament
  Was writ with golden letters rich and brave;°   *splendid*
A worke of wondrous grace, and able soules to save.

20

Thus beene they parted, Arthur on his way
　　To seeke his love, and th'other for to fight
　　With Unas foe, that all her realme did pray.°   *prey on*
　　But she now weighing the decayèd plight,
　　And shrunken synewes of her chosen knight,
　　Would not a while her forward course pursew,
　　Ne bring him forth in face of dreadfull fight,
　　Till he recovered had his former hew:°   *appearance*
For him to be yet weake and wearie well she knew.

21

So as they traveild, lo they gan espy
　　An armèd knight towards them gallop fast,
　　That seemèd from some fearèd foe to fly,
　　Or other griesly thing, that him agast.°   *terrified*
　　Still° as he fled, his eye was backward cast,   *continually*
　　As if his feare still followed him behind;
　　Als flew his steed, as he his bands had brast,°   *broken*
　　And with his wingèd heeles did tread the wind,
As he had beene a fole of Pegasus his kind.[9]

22

Nigh as he drew, they might° perceive his head   *could*
　　To be unarmd, and curld uncombèd heares
　　Upstaring° stiffe, dismayd with uncouth° dread;   *bristling / strange*
　　Nor drop of bloud in all his face appeares
　　Nor life in limbe: and to increase his feares,
　　In fowle reproch° of knighthoods faire degree,°   *disgrace / condition*
　　About his neck an hempen rope he weares,
　　That with his glistring armes does ill agree;
But he of rope or armes has now no memoree.

23

The Redcrosse knight toward him crossèd fast,
　　To weet,° what mister° wight was so dismayd: *learn / kind of*
　　There him he finds all sencelesse and aghast,
　　That of him selfe he seemd to be afrayd;
　　Whom hardly° he from flying forward stayd,   *with difficulty*
　　Till he these wordes to him deliver might;
　　"Sir knight, aread° who hath ye thus arayd,   *declare*
　　And eke from whom make ye this hasty flight:
For never knight I saw in such misseeming° plight."   *unseemly*

9. I.e., as if he had been a foal of a horse like Pegasus, the flying horse of classical mythology.

24

He answerd nought at all, but adding new
  Feare to his first amazment, staring wide
  With stony eyes, and hartlesse hollow hew,[1]
  Astonisht stood, as one that had aspide
  Infernall furies, with their chaines untide.
  Him yet againe, and yet againe bespake
  The gentle knight; who nought to him replide,
  But trembling every joynt did inly quake,
And foltring tongue at last these words seemd forth to shake.

25

"For Gods deare love, Sir knight, do me not stay;
  For loe he comes, he comes fast after mee."
  Eft° looking backe would faine have runne away;   *again*
  But he him forst to stay, and tellen free
  The secret cause of his perplexitie:°   *distress*
  Yet nathemore° by his bold hartie speach,   *not at all*
  Could his bloud-frosen hart emboldned bee,
  But through his boldnesse rather feare did reach,
Yet forst, at last he made through silence suddein breach.

26

"And am I now in safetie sure," quoth he,
  "From him, that would have forcèd me to dye?
  And is the point of death now turnd fro mee,
  That I may tell this haplesse history?"°   *story of misfortune*
  "Feare nought:" quoth he, "no daunger now is nye."
  "Then shall I you recount a ruefull cace,"°   *pitiable event*
  Said he, "the which with this unlucky eye
  I late beheld, and had not greater grace
Me reft° from it, had bene partaker of the place.[2]   *carried*

27

"I lately chaunst (Would I had never chaunst)
  With a faire knight to keepen companee,
  Sir Terwin[3] hight,° that well himselfe advaunst   *named*
  In all affaires, and was both bold and free,
  But not so happie as mote happie bee:
  He loved, as was his lot, a Ladie gent,°   *gentle*
  That him againe° loved in the least degree: *in return*
  For she was proud, and of too high intent,°   *mind*
And joyd to see her lover languish and lament.

---

1. I.e., with blanched, bloodless countenance.
2. I.e., shared the same fate.
3. His name may connote weariness or fatigue ("terwyn").

28

"From whom returning sad and comfortlesse,°   *desolate*
    As on the way together we did fare,
    We met that villen (God from him me blesse°)   *defend*
    That cursèd wight, from whom I scapt whyleare,°   *a while before*
    A man of hell, that cals himselfe Despaire;[4]
    Who first us greets, and after faire areedes°   *tells*
    Of tydings strange, and of adventures rare:
    So creeping close, as Snake in hidden weedes,
Inquireth of our states, and of our knightly deedes.

29

"Which when he knew, and felt our feeble harts
    Embost° with bale,° and bitter byting griefe,   *exhausted / sorrow*
    Which love had launchèd° with his deadly darts,   *pierced*
    With wounding words and termes of foule repriefe,°   *insult, scorn*
    He pluckt from us all hope of due reliefe,
    That earst° us held in love of lingring life;   *formerly*
    Then hopelesse hartlesse, gan the cunning thiefe
    Perswade us die, to stint° all further strife: *end*
To me he lent this rope, to him a rustie° knife.   *i.e., bloodstained*

30

"With which sad instrument of hastie death,
    That wofull lover, loathing lenger° light,   *longer*
    A wide way made to let forth living breath.
    But I more fearefull, or more luckie wight,
    Dismayd with that deformèd dismall sight,
    Fled fast away, halfe dead with dying feare:°   *fear of death*
    Ne yet assur'd of life by you, Sir knight,
    Whose like infirmitie like chaunce may beare:
But God you never let his charmèd speeches heare."[5]

31

"How may a man," said he, "with idle speach
    Be wonne, to spoyle° the Castle of his health?"   *destroy*
    "I wote," quoth he, "whom triall° late did teach,   *experience*
    That like would not[6] for all this worldes wealth:
    His subtill tongue, like dropping honny, mealt'th°   *melts*
    Into the hart, and searcheth every vaine,
    That ere one be aware, by secret stealth
    His powre is reft,° and weaknesse doth remaine.   *taken by force*
O never Sir desire to try° his guilefull traine."°   *test / treachery*

---

4. Despair is the ultimate Christian sin, denying the possibility of divine mercy and grace.
5. I.e., may God never let you hear his mesmer-izing ("charmèd") speeches.
6. I.e., would not do the like again.

32

"Certès,"° said he, "hence shall I never rest,   *surely*
   Till I that treachours art have heard and tride;
   And you Sir knight, whose name mote° I request,   *might*
   Of grace° do me unto his cabin° guide."   *favor / cave*
"I that hight° Trevisan,"[7] quoth he, "will ride   *am called*
   Against my liking backe, to doe you grace:°   *a favor*
   But nor for gold nor glee[8] will I abide
   By you, when ye arrive in that same place;
For lever° had I die, then° see his deadly face."   *rather / than*

33

Ere long they come, where that same wicked wight
   His dwelling has, low in an hollow cave,
   Farre underneath a craggie clift ypight,°   *placed*
   Darke, dolefull, drearie, like a greedie grave,
   That still° for carrion carcases doth crave: *continually*
   On top whereof aye° dwelt the ghastly Owle,[9]   *ever*
   Shrieking his balefull note, which ever drave
   Farre from that haunt all other chearefull fowle;
And all about it wandring ghostes did waile and howle.

34

And all about old stockes° and stubs of trees,   *stumps*
   Whereon nor fruit, nor leafe was ever seene,
   Did hang upon the ragged rocky knees;°   *crags*
   On which had many wretches hangèd beene,
   Whose carcases were scattered on the greene,
   And throwne about the cliffs. Arrivèd there,
   That bare-head knight for dread and dolefull teene,°   *grief*
   Would faine° have fled, ne durst approachen neare,   *gladly*
But th' other forst him stay, and comforted in feare.

35

That darkesome cave they enter, where they find
   That cursèd man, low sitting on the ground,
   Musing full sadly in his sullein° mind;   *morose*
   His griesie° lockes, long growen, and unbound,   *gray*
   Disordred hong about his shoulders round,
   And hid his face; through which his hollow eyne
   Lookt deadly dull, and starèd as astound;°   *as if stunned*
   His raw-bone cheekes through penurie and pine,°   *starvation*
Were shronke into his jawes, as° he did never dine.   *as if*

---

7. The meaning is uncertain, but may be "flight" or "dread."

8. Beauty. I.e., not for anything in the world.

9. Traditionally a messenger of death.

36

His garment nought but many ragged clouts,°   *scraps*
  With thornes together pind and patchèd was,
  The which his naked sides he wrapt abouts;
  And him beside there lay upon the gras
  A drearie corse,° whose life away did pas,   *bloody corpse*
  All wallowd in his owne yet luke-warme blood,
  That from his wound yet wellèd fresh alas;
  In which a rustie knife fast fixèd stood,
And made an open passage for the gushing flood.

37

Which piteous spectacle, approving° trew   *confirming*
  The wofull tale that Trevisan had told,
  When as the gentle Redcrosse knight did vew,
  With firie zeale he burnt in courage bold,
  Him to avenge, before his bloud were cold,
  And to the villein said, "Thou agèd damnèd wight,
  The author of this fact,° we here behold,   *deed*
  What justice can but judge against thee right,
With thine owne bloud to price° his bloud, here shed in sight?" *pay for*

38

"What franticke fit," quoth he, "hath thus distraught
  Thee, foolish man, so rash a doome° to give?   *judgment*
  What justice ever other judgement taught,
  But he should die, who merites not to live?
  None else to death this man despayring drive,°   *drove*
  But his owne guiltie mind deserving death.
  Is then unjust to each his due to give?
  Or let him die, that loatheth living breath?
Or let him die at ease, that liveth here uneath?°   *in hardship*

39

"Who travels by the wearie wandring way,
  To come unto his wishèd home in haste,
  And meetes a flood, that doth his passage stay,
  Is not great grace to helpe him over past,
  Or free his feet, that in the myre sticke fast?
  Most envious man, that grieves at neighbours good,
  And fond,° that joyest in the woe thou hast,   *foolish*
  Why wilt not let him passe, that long hath stood
Upon the banke, yet wilt thy selfe not passe the flood?

40

"He there does now enjoy eternall rest
  And happie ease, which thou doest want and crave,
  And further from it daily wanderest:
  What if some litle paine the passage have,

That makes fraile flesh to feare the bitter wave?
Is not short paine well borne, that brings long ease,
And layes the soule to sleepe in quiet grave?
Sleepe after toyle, port after stormie seas,
Ease after warre, death after life does greatly please."[1]

41

The knight much wondred at his suddeine wit,°   *quick intelligence*
And said, "The terme of life is limited,
Ne may a man prolong, nor shorten it;
The souldier may not move from watchfull sted,[2]
Nor leave his stand, untill his Captaine bed."°   *commands*
"Who life did limit by almightie doome,"
Quoth he, "knowes best the termes establishèd;
And he, that points the Centonell his roome,°   *station*
Doth license him depart at sound of morning droome.[3]

42

"Is not his deed, what ever thing is donne,
In heaven and earth? did not he all create
To die againe? all ends that was begonne.
Their times in his eternall booke of fate
Are written sure, and have their certaine° date.   *fixed*
Who then can strive with strong necessitie,
That holds the world in his still chaunging state,
Or shunne the death ordaynd by destinie?
When houre of death is come, let none aske whence, nor why.

43

"The lenger° life, I wote° the greater sin,   *longer / know*
The greater sin, the greater punishment:
All those great battels, which thou boasts to win,
Through strife, and bloud-shed, and avengement,
Now praysd, hereafter deare° thou shalt repent: *bitterly*
For life must life, and bloud must bloud repay.[4]
Is not enough thy evill life forespent?°   *already spent*
For he, that once hath missèd the right way,
The further he doth goe, the further he doth stray.

44

"Then do no further goe, no further stray,
But here lie downe, and to thy rest betake,
Th'ill to prevent, that life ensewen may.[5]
For what hath life, that may it lovèd make,

---

1. Despaire's arguments on behalf of suicide as against a painful life are derived, like those of Hamlet in his third soliloquy (*Hamlet* 3.1.58–90), principally from Seneca, Marcus Aurelius, other ancient Stoics, and Old Testament statements on divine justice.

2. The sentry post assigned him.
3. Drum, with a pun on *doom*.
4. An echo of Genesis 9.6: "Whoso sheddeth man's blood, by man shall his blood be shed."
5. I.e., to prevent the evil that will ensue in the rest of your life.

And gives not rather cause it to forsake?
Feare, sicknesse, age, losse, labour, sorrow, strife,
Paine, hunger, cold, that makes the hart to quake;
And ever fickle fortune rageth rife,°   *widely*
All which, and thousands mo° do make a loathsome life.   *more*

45

"Thou wretched man, of death hast greatest need,
    If in true ballance thou wilt weigh thy state:
    For never knight, that darèd warlike deede,
    More lucklesse disaventures° did amate:°   *mishaps / daunt*
    Witnesse the dongeon deepe, wherein of late
    Thy life shut up, for death so oft did call;
    And though good lucke prolongèd hath thy date,°   *span of life*
    Yet death then, would the like mishaps forestall,
Into the which hereafter thou maiest happen fall.°   *happen to fall*

46

"Why then doest thou, O man of sin, desire
    To draw thy dayes forth to their last degree?
    Is not the measure of thy sinfull hire°   *service to sin*
    High heapèd up with huge iniquitie,
    Against the day of wrath,° to burden thee?   *Judgment Day*
    Is not enough that to this Ladie milde
    Thou falsèd° hast thy faith with perjurie,°   *betrayed / oath-breaking*
    And sold thy selfe to serve Duessa vilde,°   *vile*
With whom in all abuse thou hast thy selfe defilde?

47

"Is not he just, that all this doth behold
    From highest heaven, and beares an equall° eye?   *impartial*
    Shall he thy sins up in his knowledge fold,°   *cover up*
    And guiltie be of thine impietie?
    Is not his law, Let every sinner die:[6]
    Die shall all flesh? what then must needs be donne,
    Is it not better to doe willinglie,
    Then linger, till the glasse° be all out ronne?   *hourglass*
Death is the end of woes: die soone, O faeries sonne."

48

The knight was much enmovèd with his speach,
    That as a swords point through his hart did perse,
    And in his conscience made a secret breach,°   *wound*
    Well knowing true all, that he did reherse,°   *recount*
    And to his fresh remembrance did reverse°   *bring back*
    The ugly vew of his deformèd crimes,

---

6. Despaire cites only half of the Scripture verse: "The wages of sin is death; but the gift of God is eternal life through Jesus Christ our Lord" (Romans 6.23).

That all his manly powres it did disperse,
As he were charmèd with inchaunted rimes,
That oftentimes he quakt, and fainted° oftentimes.   *lost heart*

49

In which amazement, when the Miscreant°   *misbeliever*
Perceivèd him to waver weake and fraile,
Whiles trembling horror did his conscience dant,°   *daunt*
And hellish anguish° did his soule assaile,   *i.e., fear of hell*
To drive him to despaire, and quite to quaile,°   *be dismayed*
He shewed him painted in a table° plaine,   *picture*
The damnèd ghosts, that doe in torments waile,
And thousand feends that doe them endlesse paine
With fire and brimstone, which for ever shall remaine.

50

The sight whereof so throughly him dismaid,
That nought but death before his eyes he saw,
And ever burning wrath before him laid,
By righteous sentence of th'Almighties law:
Then gan the villein him to overcraw,°   *exult over*
And brought unto him swords, ropes, poison, fire,
And all that might him to perdition draw;
And bad him choose, what death he would desire:
For death was due to him, that had provokt Gods ire.

51

But when as none of them he saw him take,
He to him raught° a dagger sharpe and keene,   *reached*
And gave it him in hand: his hand did quake,
And tremble like a leafe of Aspin greene,
And troubled bloud through his pale face was seene
To come, and goe with tydings from the hart,
As it a running messenger had beene.
At last resolved to worke his finall smart,°   *pain*
He lifted up his hand, that backe againe did start.

52

Which when as Una saw, through every vaine
The crudled° cold ran to her well of life,°   *congealing / heart*
As in a swowne: but soone relived° againe,   *revived*
Out of his hand she snatcht the cursèd knife,
And threw it to the ground, enragèd rife,°   *deeply*
And to him said, "Fie, fie, faint harted knight,
What meanest thou by this reprochfull° strife?   *deserving reproach*
Is this the battell, which thou vauntst to fight
With the fire-mouthèd Dragon, horrible and bright?

53

"Come, come away, fraile, feeble, fleshly wight,
　Ne let vaine words bewitch thy manly hart,
　Ne divelish thoughts dismay thy constant spright.°   *spirit*
　In heavenly mercies hast thou not a part?
　Why shouldst thou then despeire, that chosen[7] art?
　Where justice growes, there grows eke° greater grace,   *also*
　The which doth quench the brond° of hellish smart,   *firebrand*
　And that accurst hand-writing[8] doth deface.°   *blot out*
Arise, Sir knight arise, and leave this cursèd place."

54

So up he rose, and thence amounted° streight.   *mounted his horse*
　Which when the carle° beheld, and saw his guest   *churl*
　Would safe depart, for° all his subtill sleight,   *in spite of*
　He chose an halter° from among the rest,   *noose*
　And with it hung himselfe, unbid° unblest.   *unprayed for*
　But death he could not worke himselfe thereby;
　For thousand times he so himselfe had drest,°   *made ready*
　Yet nathelesse it could not doe° him die,   *make*
Till he should die his last, that is eternally.

Canto 10

*Her faithfull knight faire Una brings
to house of Holinesse,
Where he is taught repentance, and
the way to heavenly blesse.°*   *bliss*

I

What man is he, that boasts of fleshly might,
　And vaine assurance of mortality,°   *mortal life*
　Which all so soone, as it doth come to fight,
　Against spirituall foes, yeelds by and by,°   *immediately*
　Or from the field most cowardly doth fly?
　Ne let the man ascribe it to his skill,
　That thorough° grace hath gainèd victory.   *through*
　If any strength we have, it is to ill,
But all the good is Gods, both power and eke° will.[9]   *also*

---

7. Cf. 2 Thessalonians 2.13: "God hath from the beginning chosen you to salvation through sanctification of the Spirit and belief of the truth." This is one of several similar passages in the epistles of Saint Paul that form the basis of the theological doctrine of predestination.
8. An echo of Colossians 2.14: "Blotting out the handwriting of ordinances [i.e., the Old Testament Law] that was against us, which was con-trary to us, and took it out of the way, nailing it to his cross."
9. "For by grace are ye saved through faith; and that not of yourselves: it is the gift of God: Not of works, lest any man should boast" (Ephesians 2.8–9); "it is God which worketh in you both to will and to do of his good pleasure" (Philippians 2.13).

2

By that, which lately hapned, Una saw,
    That this her knight was feeble, and too faint;
    And all his sinews woxen weake and raw,°   unready
    Through long enprisonment, and hard constraint,°   affliction
    Which he endurèd in his late restraint,
    That yet he was unfit for bloudie fight:
    Therefore to cherish° him with diets daint,°   foster / choice
    She cast° to bring him, where he chearen° might,   resolved / be cheered
Till he recovered had his° late decayèd plight.   i.e., from his

3

There was an auntient house not farre away,
    Renowmd throughout the world for sacred lore,
    And pure unspotted life: so well they say
    It governd was, and guided evermore,
    Through wisedome of a matrone grave and hore;°   hoar, venerable
    Whose onely joy was to relieve the needes
    Of wretched soules, and helpe the helpelesse pore:
    All night she spent in bidding of her bedes,°   saying prayers
And all the day in doing good and godly deedes.

4

Dame Caelia° men did her call, as thought   Heavenly
    From heaven to come, or thither to arise,
    The mother of three daughters, well upbrought
    In goodly thewes,° and godly exercise:°   habits / deeds
    The eldest two most sober, chast, and wise,
    Fidelia and Speranza virgins were,
    Though spousd,° yet wanting° wedlocks solemnize;[1] betrothed / lacking
    But faire Charissa to a lovely fere°   loving mate
Was linckèd, and by him had many pledges dere.[2]

5

Arrivèd there, the dore they find fast lockt;
    For it was warely watchèd night and day,
    For feare of many foes: but when they knockt,
    The Porter opened unto them streight way:
    He was an agèd syre, all hory gray,
    With lookes full lowly cast, and gate° full slow,   gait
    Wont° on a staffe his feeble steps to stay,   accustomed
    Hight Humilta.° They passe in stouping low;   called Humility
For streight and narrow was the way, which he did show.[3]

---

1. Solemnization.
2. I.e., many children. The daughters' names mean Faith, Hope, and Charity; cf. the three Saracens: Sansfoy, Sansjoy, and Sansloy. This canto draws heavily on scriptural references, especially 1 Corinthians 13.13: "And now abideth faith, hope, charity, these three; but the greatest of these is charity." Many aspects of the House of Holiness oppose their counterparts in the House of Pride (canto 4).
3. Alluding to Matthew 7.13–14: see stanza 10, n. 9.

6

Each goodly thing is hardest to begin,
  But entred in a spacious court they see,
  Both plaine, and pleasant to be walkèd in,
  Where them does meete a francklin[4] faire and free,
  And entertaines with comely courteous glee,
  His name was Zele,° that him right well became,   *Zeal*
  For in his speeches and behaviour hee
  Did labour lively to expresse the same,
And gladly did them guide, till to the Hall they came.

7

There fairely them receives a gentle Squire,
  Of milde demeanure, and rare courtesie,
  Right cleanly clad in comely sad° attire;   *sober*
  In word and deede that shewed great modestie,
  And knew his good° to all of each degree,   *proper respect*
  Hight Reverence. He them with speeches meet°   *fitting*
  Does faire entreat; no courting nicetie,[5]
  But simple true, and eke unfainèd sweet,
As might become a Squire so great persons to greet.

8

And afterwards them to his Dame he leades,
  That agèd Dame, the Ladie of the place:
  Who all this while was busie at her beades:
  Which doen, she up arose with seemely grace,
  And toward them full matronely[6] did pace.
  Where when that fairest Una she beheld,
  Whom well she knew to spring from heavenly race,
  Her hart with joy unwonted° inly sweld,°   *unaccustomed / swelled*
As feeling wondrous comfort in her weaker eld.°   *too weak age*

9

And her embracing said, "O happie earth,
  Whereon thy innocent feet doe ever tread,
  Most vertuous virgin borne of heavenly berth,
  That to redeeme thy woefull parents head,
  From tyrans rage, and ever-dying dread,°   *constant fear of death*
  Hast wandred through the world now long a day°   *many a long day*
  Yet ceasest not thy wearie soles to lead,
  What grace hath thee now hither brought this way?
Or doen° thy feeble feet unweeting° hither stray?   *do / unwittingly*

4. Freeholder, landowner.
5. He treats them courteously ("faire"); no courtly affectation ("nicetie").

6. Like a matron, i.e., a woman in charge of an establishment.

10

"Strange thing it is an errant° knight to see   *wandering*
   Here in this place, or any other wight,
   That hither turnes his steps. So few there bee,
   That chose the narrow path, or seeke the right:
   All keepe the broad high way, and take delight
   With many rather for to go astray,
   And be partakers of their evill plight,
   Then with a few to walke the rightest way;[7]
O foolish men, why haste ye to your owne decay?"

11

"Thy selfe to see, and tyred limbs to rest,
   O matrone sage," quoth she, "I hither came,
   And this good knight his way with me addrest,°   *directed*
   Led with thy prayses and broad-blazèd fame,
   That up to heaven is blowne."[8] The auncient Dame
   Him goodly greeted in her modest guise,
   And entertaynd them both, as best became,
   With all the court'sies,° that she could devise,   *courtesies*
Ne wanted ought,° to shew her bounteous or wise.   *nor lacked anything*

12

Thus as they gan of sundry things devise,°   *talk*
   Loe two most goodly virgins came in place,
   Ylinkèd arme in arme in lovely wise,°   *loving fashion*
   With countenance demure, and modest grace,
   They numbred even steps and equall pace:
   Of which the eldest, that Fidelia hight,
   Like sunny beames threw from her Christall face,
   That could have dazd° the rash beholders sight,   *dazzled*
And round about her head did shine like heavens light.

13

She was araièd° all in lilly white,   *arrayed*
   And in her right hand bore a cup of gold,
   With wine and water[9] fild up to the hight,
   In which a Serpent[1] did himselfe enfold,
   That horrour made to all, that did behold;
   But she no whit did chaunge her constant mood:°   *expression*
   And in her other hand she fast did hold

---

7. An echo of Matthew 7.13–14: "Broad is the way, that leadeth to destruction, and many there be which go in thereat: . . . strait is the gate, and narrow is the way, which leadeth unto life, and few there be that find it."
8. I.e., your praises and fame are widely celebrated ("blazèd"), reaching ("blowne") up to heaven.
9. Signifies the sacrament of Communion.
1. A symbol of the crucified Christ (of whom the serpent lifted up by Moses, Numbers 21.9, is a recognized "type" or prefiguration).

A booke,[2] that was both signd and seald with blood,
Wherein darke° things were writ, hard to be understood.[3]   *obscure*

14

Her younger sister, that Speranza hight,
    Was clad in blew, that her beseemèd° well;   *suited*
    Not all so chearefull seemèd she of sight,°   *in appearance*
    As was her sister; whether dread° did dwell,   *fear*
    Or anguish in her hart, is hard to tell:
    Upon her arme a silver anchor[4] lay,
    Whereon she leanèd ever, as befell:°   *as was fitting*
    And ever up to heaven, as she did pray,
Her stedfast eyes were bent, ne swarvèd other way.

15

They seeing Una, towards her gan wend,°   *walk*
    Who them encounters° with like courtesie;   *meets*
    Many kind speeches they betwene them spend,
    And greatly joy each other well to see:
    Then to the knight with shamefast° modestie   *humble*
    They turne themselves, at Unas meeke request,
    And him salute with well beseeming glee;°   *appropriate joy*
    Who faire them quites,° as him beseemèd best,   *requites*
And goodly gan discourse of many a noble gest.°   *deed*

16

Then Una thus; "But she your sister deare,
    The deare Charissa where is she become?°   *gone to*
    Or wants° she health, or busie is elsewhere?"   *is lacking*
    "Ah no," said they, "but forth she may not come:
    For she of late is lightned of her wombe,
    And hath encreast the world with one sonne more,[5]
    That her to see should be but troublesome."
    "Indeede," quoth she, "that should her trouble sore,
But thankt be God, that her encrease so evermore."[6]

17

Then said the agèd Caelia, "Deare dame,
    And you good Sir, I wote° that of your toyle,   *know*
    And labours long, through which ye hither came,
    Ye both forwearied° be: therefore a whyle   *utterly weary*
    I read° you rest, and to your bowres recoyle."[7]   *counsel*
    Then callèd she a Groome, that forth him led
    Into a goodly lodge, and gan despoile°   *disrobe*

2. I.e., the New Testament.
3. See 2 Peter 3.16, which notes that in the epistles of the apostle Paul "are some things hard to be understood."
4. The iconographic symbol of hope.

5. Charity, the fruitful virtue, is often depicted as a mother with many children.
6. I.e., God be thanked, who continually increases her thus.
7. Retire to your rooms.

Of puissant armes, and laid in easie° bed;   *comfortable*
His name was meeke Obedience rightfully arèd.°   *understood*

18

Now when their wearie limbes with kindly° rest,   *natural*
  And bodies were refresht with due repast,°   *repose*
  Faire Una gan Fidelia faire request,
  To have her knight into her schoolehouse plaste,°   *placed*
  That of her heavenly learning he might taste,
  And heare the wisedome of her words divine.
  She graunted, and that knight so much agraste,°   *favored*
  That she him taught celestiall discipline,°   *instruction*
And opened his dull eyes, that light mote in them shine.

19

And that her sacred Booke, with bloud° ywrit,   *i.e., the blood of Christ*
  That none could read, except she did them teach,
  She unto him disclosèd every whit,°   *bit*
  And heavenly documents° thereout did preach,   *doctrines*
  That weaker wit° of man could never reach,   *too weak mind*
  Of God, of grace, of justice, of free will,
  That wonder was to heare her goodly speach:
  For she was able, with her words to kill,
And raise againe to life the hart, that she did thrill.°   *pierce*

20

And when she list° poure out her larger spright,°   *chose to / greater power*
  She would commaund the hastie Sunne to stay,
  Or backward turne his course from heavens hight;
  Sometimes great hostes of men she could dismay,
  Dry-shod to passe, she parts the flouds in tway;°   *two*
  And eke huge mountaines from their native seat
  She would commaund, themselves to beare away,
  And throw in raging sea with roaring threat.
Almightie God her gave such powre, and puissance great.[8]

21

The faithfull knight now grew in litle space,°   *time*
  By hearing her, and by her sisters lore,
  To such perfection of all heavenly grace,
  That wretched world he gan for to abhore,[9]
  And mortall life gan loath, as thing forelore,°   *doomed*
  Greeved with remembrance of his wicked wayes,
  And prickt with anguish of his sinnes so sore,

---

8. Joshua made the sun stand still (Joshua 10.12); Hezekiah made it turn backward (2 Kings 20.10). With 300 men Gideon was victorious over the Midianite hosts (Judges 7.7). Moses led the Israelites through the parted waters of the Red Sea (Exodus 14.21–31). Faith, said Christ, can move mountains (Matthew 21.21). All these are miracles of faith.
9. I.e., he began to abhor the world.

That he desirde to end his wretched dayes:
So much the dart of sinfull guilt the soule dismayes.

22

But wise Speranza gave him comfort sweet,
   And taught him how to take assurèd hold
   Upon her silver anchor, as was meet;
   Else had his sinnes so great, and manifold
   Made him forget all that Fidelia told.
   In this distressèd doubtfull° agonie,   *fearful*
   When him his dearest Una did behold,
   Disdeining life, desiring leave to die,
She found her selfe assayld with great perplexitie.°   *distress*

23

And came to Caelia to declare her smart,°   *pain*
   Who well acquainted with that commune° plight,   *common*
   Which sinfull horror° workes in wounded hart,   *horror of sin*
   Her wisely comforted all that she might,
   With goodly counsell and advisement right;
   And streightway sent with carefull diligence,
   To fetch a Leach,° the which had great insight   *doctor*
   In that disease of grievèd° consciënce,   *distressed*
And well could cure the same; His name was Patiënce.

24

Who comming to that soule-diseasèd knight,
   Could hardly° him intreat, to tell his griefe: *with difficulty*
   Which knowne, and all that noyd° his heavie spright   *troubled*
   Well searcht,° eftsoones° he gan apply reliefe   *probed / immediately*
   Of salves and med'cines, which had passing priefe,[1]
   And thereto added words of wondrous might:
   By which to ease he him recurèd briefe,°   *restored quickly*
   And much asswaged the passion° of his plight,   *suffering*
That he his paine endured, as seeming now more light.

25

But yet the cause and root of all his ill,
   Inward corruption, and infected sin,[2]
   Not purged nor heald, behind remainèd still,
   And festring sore did rankle yet within,
   Close° creeping twixt the marrow and the skin.   *secretly*
   Which to extirpe,° he laid him privily   *extirpate*
   Downe in a darkesome lowly place farre in,
   Whereas° he meant his corrosives to apply,   *where*
And with streight° diet tame his stubborne malady.   *strict*

---

1. Which had extraordinary power.   2. Apparently, the effects of original sin.

26

In ashes and sackcloth[3] he did array
   His daintie corse,° proud humors[4] to abate,   *handsome body*
   And dieted with fasting every day,
   The swelling of his wounds to mitigate,
   And made him pray both earely and eke late:
   And ever as superfluous flesh did rot
   Amendment readie still at hand did wayt,
   To pluck it out with pincers firie whot,°   *hot*
That soone in him was left no one corrupted jot.

27

And bitter Penance with an yron whip,
   Was wont him once to disple° every day: *discipline*
   And sharpe Remorse his hart did pricke and nip,
   That drops of bloud thence like a well did play;
   And sad Repentance usèd to embay°   *bathe*
   His bodie in salt water smarting sore,
   The filthy blots of sinne to wash away.[5]
   So in short space they did to health restore
The man that would not live, but earst° lay at deathes dore.   *formerly*

28

In which his torment often was so great,
   That like a Lyon he would cry and rore,
   And rend his flesh, and his owne synewes eat.
   His own deare Una hearing evermore
   His ruefull shriekes and gronings, often tore
   Her guiltlesse garments, and her golden heare,
   For pitty of his paine and anguish sore;
   Yet all with patience wisely she did beare;
For well she wist, his crime could else be never cleare.°   *cleansed*

29

Whom thus recovered by wise Patiënce,
   And trew Repentance they to Una brought:
   Who joyous of his curèd consciënce,
   Him dearely kist, and fairely° eke besought   *courteously*
   Himselfe to chearish,° and consuming thought   *cheer; cherish*
   To put away out of his carefull° brest.   *care-full*
   By this° Charissa, late° in child-bed brought,   *by this time / recently*
   Was woxen° strong, and left her fruitfull nest;   *grown*
To her faire Una brought this unacquainted guest.

---

3. Symbols of penitence.
4. I.e., the bodily fluids that conduce to pride. In Renaissance physiology, the proportions of the various fluids ("humors") determine one's temperament.

5. "Wash me throughly from mine iniquity, and cleanse me from my sin" (Psalms 51.2).

30

She was a woman in her freshest age,
   Of wondrous beauty, and of bountie° rare,   *goodness*
   With goodly grace and comely personage,°   *appearance*
   That was on earth not easie to compare;°   *rival*
   Full of great love, but Cupids wanton snare
   As hell she hated, chast in worke and will;
   Her necke and breasts were ever open bare,
   That ay° thereof her babes might sucke their fill;   *ever*
The rest was all in yellow robes arayèd still.[6]

31

A multitude of babes about her hong,
   Playing their sports, that joyd her to behold,
   Whom still she fed, whiles they were weake and young,
   But thrust them forth° still, as they wexèd old: *i.e., weaned them*
   And on her head she wore a tyre° of gold,   *headdress*
   Adornd with gemmes and owches° wondrous faire,   *jewels*
   Whose passing° price uneath° was to be told; *surpassing / scarcely*
   And by her side there sate a gentle paire
Of turtle doves,[7] she sitting in an yvorie chaire.

32

The knight and Una entring, faire her greet,
   And bid her joy of that her happie brood;
   Who them requites with court'sies seeming meet,°   *appropriate*
   And entertaines with friendly chearefull mood.
   Then Una her besought, to be so good,
   As in her vertuous rules to schoole her knight,
   Now after all his torment well withstood,
   In that sad° house of Penaunce, where his spright   *solemn*
Had past° the paines of hell, and long enduring night. *passed through*

33

She was right joyous of her just request,
   And taking by the hand that Faeries sonne,
   Gan him instruct in every good behest,°   *command*
   Of love, and righteousness, and well to donne,° *i.e., right action*
   And wrath, and hatred warely° to shonne,   *warily*
   That drew on men Gods hatred, and his wrath,
   And many soules in dolours° had fordonne:° *misery / destroyed*
   In which when him she well instructed hath,
From thence to heaven she teacheth him the ready° path. *direct*

---

6. Always. Her yellow (saffron) robe is the color of marriage, fertility, and maternity. Her chaste, fruitful love (Christian *agape*) is opposed to "Cupid's wanton snare" (*eros*).
7. Emblem of true love and faithful marriage.

34

Wherein his weaker° wandring steps to guide,   *too weak*
  An auncient matrone she to her does call,
  Whose sober lookes her wisedome well describe:°   *made known*
  Her name was Mercie, well knowne over all,
  To be both gratious, and eke liberall:
  To whom the carefull charge of him she gave,
  To lead aright, that he should never fall
  In all his wayes through this wide worldès wave,°   *expanse*
That Mercy in the end his righteous soule might save.

35

The godly Matrone by the hand him beares°   *leads*
  Forth from her° presence, by a narrow way,   *i.e., Charissa's*
  Scattred with bushy thornes, and ragged breares,°   *briers*
  Which still before him she removed away,
  That nothing might his ready passage stay:°   *hinder*
  And ever when his feet encombred were,
  Or gan to shrinke, or from the right to stray,
  She held him fast, and firmely did upbeare,
As carefull Nourse her child from falling oft does reare.

36

Eftsoones unto an holy Hospitall,°   *hospice*
  That was fore° by the way, she did him bring,   *close*
  In which seven Bead-men° that had vowèd all   *men of prayer*
  Their life to service of high heavens king
  Did spend their dayes in doing godly thing:
  Their gates to all were open evermore,
  That by the wearie way were traveiling,
  And one sate wayting ever them before,
To call in commers-by, that needy were and pore.[8]

37

The first of them that eldest was, and best,°   *chiefest*
  Of all the house had charge and governement,
  As Guardian and Steward of the rest:
  His office° was to give entertainement   *duty*
  And lodging, unto all that came, and went:
  Not unto such, as could him feast againe,°   *host in return*
  And double quite,° for that he on them spent,   *repay*
  But such, as want of harbour° did constraine:°   *shelter / afflict*
Those for Gods sake his dewty was to entertaine.

---

8. I.e., one beadsman sat in front of the gates, to call in needy wayfarers.

38

The second was as Almner[9] of the place,
 His office was, the hungry for to feed,
 And thristy give to drinke, a worke of grace:
 He feard not once him selfe to be in need,
 Ne cared to hoord for those, whom he did breede:°   *i.e., his children*
 The grace of God he layd up still in store,
 Which as a stocke° he left unto his seede;°   *resource / children*
 He had enough, what need him care for more?
And had he lesse, yet some he would give to the pore.

39

The third had of their wardrobe custodie,
 In which were not rich tyres,° nor garments gay,   *attire*
 The plumes of pride, and wings of vanitie,
 But clothes meet to keepe keene could° away,   *cold*
 And naked nature seemely° to aray;   *decently*
 With which bare wretched wights he dayly clad,
 The images of God in earthly clay;
 And if that no spare clothes to give he had,
His owne coate he would cut, and it distribute glad.

40

The fourth appointed by his office was,
 Poore prisoners to relieve with gratious ayd,
 And captives to redeeme with price of bras,°   *payment of money*
 From Turkes and Sarazins, which them had stayd;°   *held captive*
 And though they faultie were, yet well he wayd,°   *considered*
 That God to us forgiveth every howre
 Much more then that, why° they in bands° were layd, *for which / bonds*
 And he that harrowd hell[1] with heavie stowre,°   *assault*
The faultie° soules from thence brought to his heavenly bowre. *sinful*

41

The fift had charge sicke persons to attend,
 And comfort those, in point of death which lay;
 For them most needeth comfort in the end,
 When sin, and hell, and death do most dismay
 The feeble soule departing hence away.
 All is but lost, that living we bestow,°   *store up*
 If not well ended at our dying day.
 O man have mind of that last bitter throw;°   *throes of death*
For as the tree does fall, so lyes it ever low.[2]

---

9. An almoner distributed charity (*alms*) to the poor.
1. Christ, who journeyed to hell to deliver those good people who lived before his time, according to a story popular in the Middle Ages. It originated in the apocryphal gospel of Nicodemus (cf. *Piers Plowman*, Passus 18).
2. "In the place where the tree falleth, there it shall be" (Ecclesiastes 11.3).

42

The sixt had charge of them now being dead,
 In seemely sort their corses to engrave,°   *bodies to bury*
 And deck with dainty flowres their bridall bed,
 That to their heavenly spouse° both sweet and brave° *i.e., Christ / fair*
 They might appeare, when he their soules shall save.
 The wondrous workemanship of Gods owne mould,[3]
 Whose face he made, all beasts to feare,° and gave   *frighten*
 All in his hand,[4] even dead we honour should.
Ah dearest God me graunt, I dead be not defould.°   *defiled*

43

The seventh now after death and buriall done,
 Had charge the tender Orphans of the dead
 And widowes ayd, least° they should be undone: *lest*
 In face of judgement° he their right would plead,   *i.e., in court*
 Ne ought° the powre of mighty men did dread   *nor at all*
 In their defence, nor would for gold or fee°   *bribe*
 Be wonne their rightfull causes downe to tread:
 And when they stood in most necessitee,
He did supply their want, and gave them ever free.[5]

44

There when the Elfin knight arrivèd was,
 The first and chiefest of the seven, whose care
 Was guests to welcome, towardes him did pas:
 Where seeing Mercie, that his steps up bare,°   *supported*
 And alwayes led, to her with reverence rare°   *uncommon*
 He humbly louted° in meeke lowlinesse,   *bowed*
 And seemely welcome for her did prepare:
 For of their order she was Patronesse,
Albe° Charissa were their chiefest founderesse.   *although*

45

There she awhile him stayes, him selfe to rest,
 That to the rest more able he might bee:
 During which time, in every good behest°   *command*
 And godly worke of Almes and charitee
 She him instructed with great industree;
 Shortly therein so perfect he became,
 That from the first unto the last degree,
 His mortall life he learnèd had to frame
In holy righteousnesse, without rebuke or blame.

3. The human body is God's own image ("mould") and a "mould" of God's making (see Genesis 1.26–30, 2.7).
4. "And the fear of you and the dread of you shall be upon every beast of the earth, and upon every fowl of the air, upon all that moveth upon the earth, and upon all the fishes of the sea; into your hand are they delivered" (Genesis 9.2).
5. Always freely. The seven beadsmen here correspond to, and perform, the seven works of charity, or corporal mercy: lodging the homeless, feeding the hungry, clothing the naked, redeeming the captive, comforting the sick, burying the dead, and succoring the orphan.

46

Thence forward by that painfull way they pas,
  Forth to an hill, that was both steepe and hy;
  On top whereof a sacred chappell was,
  And eke a litle Hermitage thereby,
  Wherein an agèd holy man did lye,°   *live*
  That day and night said his devotiön,
  Ne other worldly busines did apply;[6]
  His name was heavenly Contemplatiön;
Of God and goodnesse was his meditatiön.

47

Great grace that old man to him given had;
  For God he often saw from heavens hight,
  All° were his earthly eyen both blunt° and bad,   *although / dim*
  And through great age had lost their kindly° sight,   *natural*
  Yet wondrous quick and persant° was his spright,°   *piercing / spirit*
  As Eagles eye, that can behold the Sunne:[7]
  That hill they scale with all their powre and might,
  That his frayle thighes nigh° wearie and fordonne°   *almost / exhausted*
Gan faile, but by her helpe the top at last he wonne.

48

There they do finde that godly agèd Sire,
  With snowy lockes adowne his shoulders shed,
  As hoarie frost with spangles doth attire
  The mossy braunches of an Oke halfe ded.
  Each bone might through his body well be red,°   *seen*
  And every sinew seene through° his long fast: *because of*
  For nought he cared his carcas long unfed;
  His mind was full of spirituall repast,
And pynèd° his flesh, to keepe his body low° and chast.   *starved / weak*

49

Who when these two approching he aspide,
  At their first presence grew agrievèd sore,[8]
  That forst him lay his heavenly thoughts aside;
  And had he not that Dame respected more,°   *greatly*
  Whom highly he did reverence and adore,
  He would not once have movèd for the knight.
  They him saluted standing far afore;°   *away*
  Who well them greeting, humbly did requight,°   *respond*
And askèd, to what end they clomb° that tedious height.   *had climbed*

50

"What end," quoth she, "should cause us take such paine,
  But that same end, which every living wight

---

6. I.e., he did not attend to any worldly activities.
7. The eagle able to gaze directly at the sun is the symbol of Saint John the Divine, whose visions are recorded in Revelation.
8. I.e., he was at first sorely grieved at their arrival.

Should make his marke,° high heaven to attaine?　　　　*goal*
Is not from hence the way, that leadeth right
To that most glorious house, that glistreth° bright　　　*glistens*
With burning starres, and everliving fire,
Whereof the keyes are to thy hand behight°　　　　　*entrusted*
By wise Fidelia? she doth thee require,
To shew it to this knight, according° his desire."　　　*granting*

51

"Thrise happy man," said then the father grave,
　"Whose staggering steps thy° steady hand doth lead,　　*i.e., Mercy's*
And shewes the way, his sinfull soule to save.
Who better can the way to heaven aread°　　　　　*direct*
Then thou thy selfe, that was both borne and bred
In heavenly throne, where thousand Angels shine?
Thou doest the prayers of the righteous sead°　　　　*seed*
Present before the majestie divine,
And his avenging wrath to clemencie incline.

52

"Yet since thou bidst, thy pleasure shalbe donne.
　Then come thou man of earth,[9] and see the way,
That never yet was seene of Faeries sonne,
That never leads the traveiler astray,
But after labours long, and sad delay,
Brings them to joyous rest and endlesse blis.
But first thou must a season fast and pray,
Till from her bands the spright assoilèd° is,　　　*spirit released*
And have her strength recured° from fraile infirmitis."　*recovered*

53

That done, he leads him to the highest Mount;
　Such one, as that same mighty man° of God,　　　*Moses*
That bloud-red billowes like a wallèd front
On either side disparted° with his rod,　　　　*parted asunder*
Till that his army dry-foot through them yod,°　　　*went*
Dwelt fortie dayes upon; where writ in stone
With bloudy letters by the hand of God,
The bitter doome of death and balefull mone[1]
He did receive, whiles flashing fire about him shone.

54

Or like that sacred hill, whose head full hie,
　Adornd with fruitfull Olives all arownd,

9. An allusion to humankind's formation from the dust of the earth (Genesis 2.7) and also to the knight's name (see stanza 66 and n. 4).
1. I.e., the Ten Commandments ("bloudy letters") carried with them the judgment ("doome") of death and pain, causing sorrowful moans ("balefull mone").

Is, as it were for endlesse memory
Of that deare Lord, who oft thereon was fownd,
For ever with a flowring girlond crownd:
Or like that pleasaunt Mount, that is for ay°   *forever*
Through famous Poets verse each where° renownd,   *everywhere*
On which the thrise three learned Ladies play
Their heavenly notes, and make full many a lovely lay.[2]

55

From thence, far off he unto him did shew
A litle path, that was both steepe and long,
Which to a goodly Citie led his vew;
Whose wals and towres were builded high and strong
Of perle and precious stone,[3] that earthly tong
Cannot describe, nor wit of man can tell;
Too high a ditty° for my simple song;   *subject*
The Citie of the great king hight° it well,   *is called*
Wherein eternall peace and happinesse doth dwell.

56

As he thereon stood gazing, he might° see   *could*
The blessed Angels to and fro descend
From highest heaven, in gladsome companee,
And with great joy into that Citie wend,°   *proceed*
As commonly° as friend does with his frend.[4]   *familiarly*
Whereat he wondred much, and gan enquere,
What stately building durst so high extend
Her loftie towres unto the starry sphere,
And what unknowen nation there empeopled were.°   *dwelt*

57

"Faire knight," quoth he, "Hierusalem that is,
The new Hierusalem, that God has built
For those to dwell in, that are chosen his,
His chosen people purged from sinfull guilt,
With pretious bloud, which cruelly was spilt
On cursèd tree, of that unspotted lam,[5]
That for the sinnes of all the world was kilt:
Now are they Saints all in that Citie sam,°   *together*
More deare unto their God, then younglings to their dam."[6]

---

2. Song. The mountain is successively compared to Mount Sinai, where Moses, after parting the "bloud-red billowes" (stanza 53) of the Red Sea, received the tablets of the Ten Commandments; to the Mount of Olives, associated with Christ; and to Mount Parnassus, where the Nine Muses of art and poetry dwelt.
3. Cf. Revelation 21.10–21.
4. Cf. Jacob's ladder, which "reached to heaven; and behold the angels of God ascending and descending on it" (Genesis 28.12).
5. Christ (the lamb of God), whose death on the Cross ("cursèd tree") purged the guilt of sin from "His chosen people."
6. Than offspring to their mother. The New Jerusalem is described in Revelation 21–22; cf. "the nations of them which are saved shall walk in the light of it" (21.24).

58

"Till now," said then the knight, "I weenèd° well,   *supposed*
 That great Cleopolis,[7] where I have beene,
 In which that fairest Faerie Queene doth dwell,
 The fairest Citie was, that might be seene;
 And that bright towre all built of christall cleene,°   *clear*
 Panthea,[8] seemd the brightest thing, that was:
 But now by proofe° all otherwise I weene;   *experience*
 For this great Citie that[9] does far surpas,
And this bright Angels towre quite dims that towre of glas."

59

"Most trew," then said the holy agèd man;
 "Yet is Cleopolis for earthly frame,°   *structure*
 The fairest peece,° that eye beholden can: *masterpiece*
 And well beseemes° all knights of noble name, *becomes*
 That covet in th'immortall booke of fame
 To be eternizèd, that same to haunt,°   *frequent*
 And doen their service to that soveraigne Dame,
 That glorie does to them for guerdon° graunt: *reward*
For she is heavenly borne, and heaven may justly vaunt.[1]

60

"And thou faire ymp,° sprong out from English race, *youth*
 How ever now accompted° Elfins sonne,   *accounted*
 Well worthy doest thy service for her grace,°   *favor*
 To aide a virgin desolate foredonne.°   *undone*
 But when thou famous victorie hast wonne,
 And high emongst all knights hast hong thy shield,
 Thenceforth the suit° of earthly conquest shonne,° *pursuit / shun*
 And wash thy hands from guilt of bloudy field:
For bloud can nought but sin, and wars but sorrowes yield.

61

"Then seeke this path, that I to thee presage,° *show prophetically*
 Which after all to heaven shall thee send;
 Then peaceably thy painefull° pilgrimage   *laborious*
 To yonder same Hierusalem do bend,
 Where is for thee ordaind a blessèd end:
 For thou emongst those Saints, whom thou doest see,
 Shalt be a Saint, and thine owne nations frend
 And Patrone: thou Saint George shalt callèd bee,
Saint George of mery England, the signe of victoree."[2]

---

7. City of Fame; in the historical allegory, London or Westminster.
8. Reminiscent of the temple of glass in Chaucer's *House of Fame;* perhaps intended to allude to Westminster Abbey as pantheon of the English great.
9. I.e., the New Jerusalem far surpasses Cleopolis ("that").
1. I.e., may justly boast ("vaunt") that heaven is her home.
2. Spenser's conception of Saint George, patron saint of England, draws on the *Legenda Aurea*

62

"Unworthy wretch," quoth he, "of so great grace,
 How dare I thinke such glory to attaine?"
"These that have it attaind, were in like cace,"
Quoth he, "as wretched, and lived in like paine."
"But deeds of armes must I at last be faine,°   *content (to leave)*
And Ladies love to leave so dearely bought?"
"What need of armes, where peace doth ay° remaine,"   *ever*
Said he, "and battailes none are to be fought?
As for loose° loves are° vaine, and vanish into nought." *wanton / i.e., they are*

63

"O let me not," quoth he, "then turne againe
 Backe to the world, whose joyes so fruitlesse are;
But let me here for aye in peace remaine,
Or streight way on that last long voyage fare,°   *travel*
That nothing may my present hope empare."°   *impair*
"That may not be," said he, "ne maist thou yit
Forgo that royall maides bequeathèd care,°   *charge*
Who did her cause into thy hand commit,
Till from her cursèd foe thou have her freely quit."° *released*

64

"Then shall I soone," quoth he, "so God me grace,
 Abet° that virgins cause disconsolate,   *maintain*
And shortly backe returne unto this place
To walke this way in Pilgrims poore estate.
But now aread,° old father, why of late   *declare*
Didst thou behight° me borne of English blood,   *call*
Whom all a Faeries sonne doen nominate?"°   *name*
"That word shall I," said he, "avouchen° good,   *prove*
Sith° to thee is unknowne the cradle of thy brood.³ *since*

65

"For well I wote,° thou springst from ancient race   *know*
 Of Saxon kings, that have with mightie hand
And many bloudie battailes fought in place°   *there*
High reard their royall throne in Britane land,
And vanquisht them,° unable to withstand: *i.e., the ancient Britons*
From thence a Faerie thee unweeting reft,°   *secretly stole*
There as thou slepst in tender swadling band,
And her base Elfin brood° there for thee left.   *offspring*
Such men do Chaungelings call, so chaungd by Faeries theft.

(*The Golden Legend*, a medieval manual of
ecclesiastical lore, translated into English by William Caxton in 1487) and on pictures, tapestries,
pageants, and folklore.
3. The place from which your race derives.

66

"Thence she thee brought into this Faerie lond,
  And in an heapèd furrow did thee hyde,
  Where thee a Ploughman all unweeting fond,°   *inadvertently found*
  As he his toylesome teme° that way did guyde,   *team of oxen*
  And brought thee up in ploughmans state to byde,
  Whereof Georgos he thee gave to name;[4]
  Till prickt° with courage, and thy forces pryde,   *spurred*
  To Faery court thou cam'st to seeke for fame,
And prove thy puissaunt° armes, as seemes thee best became."[5] *powerful*

67

"O holy Sire," quoth he, "how shall I quight°   *repay*
  The many favours I with thee have found,
  That hast my name and nation red° aright,   *declared*
  And taught the way that does to heaven bound?"°   *go*
  This said, adowne he lookèd to the ground,
  To have returnd, but dazèd° were his eyne,   *dazzled*
  Through passing° brightnesse, which did quite confound *surpassing*
  His feeble sence, and too exceeding shyne.
So darke are earthly things compard to things divine.

68

At last whenas° himselfe he gan to find,°   *when / recover*
  To Una back he cast him to retire;°   *resolved to return*
  Who him awaited still with pensive° mind.   *anxious*
  Great thankes and goodly meed° to that good syre,   *gift*
  He thence departing gave for his paines hyre.°   *reward*
  So came to Una, who him joyd to see,
  And after litle rest, gan him desire,
  Of her adventure mindfull for to bee.
So leave they take of Caelia, and her daughters three.

Canto 11

The knight with that old Dragon fights
two dayes incessantly:
The third him overthrowes, and gayns
most glorious victory.

1

High time now gan it wex° for Una faire,   *grow*
  To thinke of those her captive Parents deare,
  And their forwasted kingdome to repaire:[6]
  Whereto whenas they now approachèd neare,
  With hartie° words her knight she gan to cheare,   *bold*

---

4. I.e., as a name. "Georgos": farmer (Greek); cf. Virgil's *Georgics*, on farming.
5. As best suited you.
6. I.e., to restore their kingdom, laid waste (by the dragon).

And in her modest manner thus bespake;
"Deare knight, as deare, as ever knight was deare,
That all these sorrowes suffer for my sake,
High heaven behold the tedious toyle, ye for me take.

2

"Now are we come unto my native soyle,
And to the place, where all our perils dwell;
Here haunts that feend,° and does his dayly spoyle,   *fiend*
Therefore henceforth be at your keeping well,°   *be well on your guard*
And ever ready for your foeman fell.°   *fierce*
The sparke of noble courage now awake,
And strive your excellent selfe to excell;
That shall ye evermore renowmèd make,
Above all knights on earth, that batteill undertake."

3

And pointing forth, "lo yonder is," said she,
"The brasen towre in which my parents deare
For dread of that huge feend emprisond be,
Whom I from far see on the walles appeare,
Whose sight my feeble soule doth greatly cheare:
And on the top of all I do espye
The watchman wayting tydings glad to heare,
That O my parents might I happily
Unto you bring, to ease you of your misery."

4

With that they heard a roaring hideous sound,
That all the ayre with terrour fillèd wide,
And seemd uneath° to shake the stedfast ground.   *almost*
Eftsoones° that dreadfull Dragon they espide,   *immediately*
Where stretcht he lay upon the sunny side
Of a great hill, himselfe like a great hill.
But all so soone, as he from far descride
Those glistring armes, that heaven with light did fill,
He rousd himselfe full blith,° and hastned them untill.°   *joyfully / toward*

5

Then bad° the knight his Lady yede° aloofe,   *bade / go*
And to an hill her selfe withdraw aside,
From whence she might behold that battailles proof°   *outcome*
And eke° be safe from daunger far descryde:°   *also / observed from afar*
She him obayd, and turnd a little wyde.°   *aside*
Now O thou sacred Muse, most learnèd Dame,
Faire ympe° of Phoebus, and his agèd bride,[7]   *child*
The Nourse of time, and everlasting fame,
That warlike hands ennoblest with immortall name;

7. I.e., Mnemosyne (memory), mother of the Muses.

6

O gently come into my feeble brest,
  Come gently, but not with that mighty rage,
  Wherewith the martiall troupes thou doest infest,°   *arouse*
  And harts of great Heroes doest enrage,
  That nought their kindled courage may aswage,°   *allay*
  Soone as thy dreadfull trompe° begins to sownd;   *trumpet*
  The God of warre with his fiers equipage°   *military equipment*
  Thou doest awake, sleepe never he so sownd,
And scarèd nations doest with horrour sterne astown.°   *appall*

7

Faire Goddesse lay that furious fit° aside,   *strain*
  Till I of warres and bloudy Mars do sing,[8]
  And Briton fields with Sarazin° bloud bedyde,°   *Saracen / dyed*
  Twixt that great faery Queene and Paynim° king,   *pagan*
  That with their horrour heaven and earth did ring,
  A worke of labour long, and endlesse prayse:
  But now a while let downe that haughtie string,
  And to my tunes thy second tenor rayse,[9]
That I this man of God his godly armes may blaze.°   *proclaim*

8

By this the dreadfull Beast drew nigh to hand,
  Halfe flying, and halfe footing° in his hast,   *walking*
  That with his largenesse measurèd much land,
  And made wide shadow under his huge wast;°   *girth*
  As mountaine doth the valley overcast.
  Approching nigh, he rearèd high afore
  His body monstrous, horrible, and vast,
  Which to increase his wondrous greatnesse more,
Was swolne with wrath, and poyson, and with bloudy gore.

9

And over, all with brasen scales was armd,
  Like plated coate of steele, so couchèd neare,°   *placed so closely*
  That nought mote perce,[1] ne might his corse° be harmd   *body*
  With dint of sword, nor push of pointed speare;
  Which as an Eagle, seeing pray appeare,
  His aery Plumes doth rouze,° full rudely dight,°   *shake / ruggedly arrayed*
  So shakèd he, that horrour was to heare,
  For as the clashing of an Armour bright,
Such noyse his rouzèd scales did send unto the knight.

---

8. Perhaps a reference to a projected but unwritten book of *The Faerie Queene*.
9. The high-pitched ("haughtie") mode would be appropriate to a large-scale epic war; a lower pitch ("second tenor") suits this present battle.
1. Nothing might pierce.

10

His flaggy° wings when forth he did display,   *drooping*
    Were like two sayles, in which the hollow wynd
    Is gathered full, and worketh speedy way:
    And eke the pennes, that did his pineons bynd,
    Were like mayne-yards, with flying canvas lynd,²
    With which whenas him list° the ayre to beat,   *he chose*
    And there by force unwonted° passage find,   *unaccustomed*
    The cloudes before him fled for terrour great,
And all the heavens stood still amazèd with his threat.

11

His huge long tayle wound up in hundred foldes,
    Does overspred his long bras-scaly backe,
    Whose wreathèd boughts° when ever he unfoldes,   *coils*
    And thicke entangled knots adown does slacke,
    Bespotted as with shields° of red and blacke,   *scales*
    It sweepeth all the land behind him farre,
    And of three furlongs³ does but litle lacke;
    And at the point two stings in-fixèd arre,
Both deadly sharpe, that sharpest steele exceeden farre.

12

But stings and sharpest steele did far exceed°   *i.e., were far exceeded by*
    The sharpnesse of his cruell rending clawes;
    Dead was it sure, as sure as death in deed,°   *in its effect*
    What ever thing does touch his ravenous pawes,
    Or what within his reach he ever drawes.
    But his most hideous head my toung to tell
    Does tremble: for his deepe devouring jawes
    Wide gapèd, like the griesly° mouth of hell,   *horrid*
Through which into his darke abisse all ravin° fell.   *prey; booty*

13

And that° more wondrous was, in either jaw   *what*
    Three ranckes of yron teeth enraungèd° were,   *arranged*
    In which yet trickling bloud and gobbets raw°   *chunks of unswallowed food*
    Of late° devourèd bodies did appeare,   *recently*
    That sight thereof bred cold congealèd feare:
    Which to increase, and all at once to kill,
    A cloud of smoothering smoke and sulphur seare°   *burning*
    Out of his stinking gorge° forth steemèd still,   *maw*
That all the ayre about with smoke and stench did fill.

2. I.e., the ribs of his wings were like the massive   affixed.
spars (main yards) to which a ship's mainsail is   3. I.e., three-eighths of a mile.

14

His blazing eyes, like two bright shining shields,
　Did burne with wrath, and sparkled living fyre;
　As two broad Beacons, set in open fields,
　Send forth their flames farre off to every shyre,°　　　　*shire*
　And warning give, that enemies conspyre,
　With fire and sword the region to invade;
　So flamed his eyne° with rage and rancorous yre:°　　*eyes / ire, anger*
　But farre within, as in a hollow glade,
Those glaring lampes were set, that made a dreadfull shade.

15

So dreadfully he towards him did pas,
　Forelifting up aloft his speckled brest,
　And often bounding on the brusèd gras,
　As for great joyance of his newcome guest.
　Eftsoones he gan advance his haughtie crest,
　As chauffèd° Bore his bristles doth upreare,　　　　*angry*
　And shoke his scales to battell readie drest;°　　　*prepared*
　That made the Redcrosse knight nigh quake for feare,
As bidding bold defiance to his foeman neare.

16

The knight gan fairely couch° his steadie speare,　　*level*
　And fiercely ran at him with rigorous° might:　　*violent*
　The pointed steele arriving rudely° theare,　　　*roughly*
　His harder hide would neither perce, nor bight,
　But glauncing by forth passèd forward right;
　Yet sore amovèd with so puissant push,
　The wrathfull beast about him turnèd light,°　　*quickly*
　And him so rudely passing by, did brush
With his long tayle, that horse and man to ground did rush.

17

Both horse and man up lightly rose againe,
　And fresh encounter towards him addrest:
　But th'idle° stroke yet backe recoyld in vaine,　*useless*
　And found no place his° deadly point to rest.　　*its*
　Exceeding rage enflamed the furious beast,
　To be avengèd of so great despight;°　　　*outrage*
　For never felt his imperceable brest
　So wondrous force, from hand of living wight;
Yet had he proved° the powre of many a puissant knight.　*tested*

18

Then with his waving wings displayèd wyde,
　Himselfe up high he lifted from the ground,
　And with strong flight did forcibly divide
　The yielding aire, which nigh° too feeble found　　*nearly*

Her flitting° partes, and element unsound,°   *moving / weak*
To beare so great a weight: he cutting way
With his broad sayles, about him soarèd round:
At last low stouping with unweldie sway,°   *ponderous force*
Snatcht up both horse and man, to beare them quite away.

19

Long he them bore above the subject plaine,°   *i.e., the ground below*
  So farre as Ewghen° bow a shaft may send,   *yewen, of yew*
  Till struggling strong did him at last constraine,
  To let them downe before his flightès end:
  As hagard° hauke presuming to contend   *untamed*
  With hardie fowle, above his hable might,°   *able power*
  His wearie pounces° all in vaine doth spend,   *claws*
  To trusse° the pray too heavie for his flight;   *seize*
Which comming downe to ground, does free it selfe by fight.

20

He so disseizèd of his gryping grosse,[4]
  The knight his thrilant° speare againe assayd   *piercing*
  In his bras-plated body to embosse,°   *plunge*
  And three mens strength unto the stroke he layd;
  Wherewith the stiffe beame quakèd, as affrayd,
  And glauncing from his scaly necke, did glyde
  Close under his left wing, then broad displayd.
  The percing steele there wrought a wound full wyde,
That with the uncouth° smart the Monster lowdly cryde.   *unfamiliar*

21

He cryde, as raging seas are wont° to rore,   *accustomed*
  When wintry storme his wrathfull wreck° does threat,   *ruin*
  The rolling billowes beat the ragged shore,
  As° they the earth would shoulder° from her seat,   *as if / push*
  And greedie gulfe° does gape, as he would eat   *i.e., the sea*
  His neighbour element° in his revenge: *i.e., earth*
  Then gin the blustring brethren° boldly threat,   *the winds*
  To move the world from off his stedfast henge,°   *axis*
And boystrous battell make, each other to avenge.°   *take vengeance on*

22

The steely head stucke fast still in his flesh,
  Till with his cruell clawes he snatcht the wood,
  And quite a sunder broke. Forth flowèd fresh
  A gushing river of blacke goarie° blood,   *clotted*
  That drownèd all the land, whereon he stood;
  The stream thereof would drive a water-mill.
  Trebly augmented was his furious mood

---

4. Freed from his formidable grip.

With bitter sense of his deepe rooted ill,°   *injury*
That flames of fire he threw forth from his large nosethrill.°   *nostril*

23

His hideous tayle then hurlèd he about,
  And therewith all enwrapt the nimble thyes°   *thighs*
  Of his froth-fomy steed, whose courage stout
  Striving to loose the knot, that fast him tyes,
  Himselfe in streighter° bandes too rash implyes,[5]   *tighter*
  That to the ground he is perforce° constraynd   *of necessity*
  To throw his rider: who can° quickly ryse   *did*
  From off the earth, with durty bloud distaynd,°   *defiled*
For that reprochfull fall right fowly he disdaynd.°   *resented*

24

And fiercely tooke his trenchand° blade in hand,   *sharp*
  With which he stroke so furious and so fell,°   *fiercely*
  That nothing seemd the puissance could withstand:
  Upon his crest the hardned yron fell,
  But his more hardned crest was armd so well,
  That deeper dint therein it would not make;[6]
  Yet so extremely did the buffe° him quell,°   *blow / dismay*
  That from thenceforth he shund the like to take,
But when he saw them come, he did them still forsake.°   *avoid*

25

The knight was wrath to see his stroke beguyld,°   *foiled*
  And smote againe with more outrageous might;
  But backe againe the sparckling steele recoyld,
  And left not any marke, where it did light;
  As if in Adamant rocke it had bene pight.°   *struck against*
  The beast impatient of his smarting wound,
  And of so fierce and forcible despight,°   *powerful injury*
  Thought with his wings to stye° above the ground;   *mount*
But his late wounded wing unserviceable found.

26

Then full of griefe and anguish vehement,
  He lowdly brayd, that like was never heard,
  And from his wide devouring oven sent
  A flake of fire, that flashing in his beard,
  Him all amazd, and almost made affeard;
  The scorching flame sore swingèd° all his face,   *singed*
  And through his armour all his bodie seard,
  That he could not endure so cruell cace,°   *plight; suit of armor*
But thought his armes to leave, and helmet to unlace.

---

5. I.e., too quickly entangles.   6. I.e., it could not make a deep gash there.

27

Not that great Champion of the antique world,°   *i.e, Hercules*
   Whom famous Poetes verse so much doth vaunt,
   And hath for twelve huge labours high extold,
   So many furies and sharpe fits did haunt,
   When him the poysoned garment did enchaunt
   With Centaures bloud, and bloudie verses charmed,
   As did this knight twelve thousand dolours° daunt,   *pains*
   Whom fyrie steele now burnt, that earst° him armed,   *formerly*
That erst him goodly armed, now most of all him harmed.[7]

28

Faint, wearie, sore, emboylèd,° grievèd, brent°   *boiled; enraged / burned*
   With heat, toyle, wounds, armes, smart, and inward fire
   That never man such mischiefes° did torment;   *misfortunes*
   Death better were, death did he oft desire,
   But death will never come, when needes require.
   Whom so dismayd when that his foe beheld,
   He cast to suffer° him no more respire,°   *allow / live*
   But gan his sturdie sterne° about to weld,°   *tail / lash*
And him so strongly stroke, that to the ground him feld.

29

It fortunèd (as faire it then befell)
   Behind his backe unweeting,° where he stood,   *unnoticed*
   Of auncient time there was a springing well,
   From which fast trickled forth a silver flood,
   Full of great vertues,° and for med'cine good.   *powers*
   Whylome,° before that cursèd Dragon got   *formerly*
   That happie land, and all with innocent blood
   Defyld those sacred waves, it rightly hot°   *was called*
The Well of Life,[8] ne yet his vertues had forgot.

30

For unto life the dead it could restore,
   And guilt of sinfull crimes cleane wash away,
   Those that with sicknesse were infected sore,
   It could recure, and agèd long decay
   Renew, as one were borne that very day.
   Both Silo this, and Jordan did excell,
   And th'English Bath, and eke the german Spau,

7. Redcrosse's fire baptism is compared with the burning shirt of Nessus, which killed Hercules. His "twelve huge labours" are paralleled to the knight's "twelve thousand dolours."
8. An allusion to Revelation 22.1–2: "And he showed me a pure river of water of life, clear as crystal, proceeding out of the throne of God and of the Lamb. In the midst of the street of it, and on either side of the river, was the tree of life, which bare twelve manner of fruits, and yielded her fruit every month: and the leaves of the tree were for the healing of the nations."

Ne can Cephise, nor Hebrus match this well:
Into the same the knight backe overthrowen, fell.[9]

31

Now gan the golden Phoebus for to steepe
  His fierie face in billowes of the west,
  And his faint steedes watred in Ocean deepe,
  Whiles from their journall° labours they did rest,   *daily*
  When that infernall Monster, having kest°   *cast*
  His wearie foe into that living well,
  Can° high advaunce his broad discoloured brest,   *did*
  Above his wonted pitch,° with countenance fell,°   *height / sinister*
And clapt his yron wings, as victor he did dwell.°   *remain*

32

Which when his pensive° Ladie saw from farre,   *anxious*
  Great woe and sorrow did her soule assay,°   *assail*
  As weening° that the sad end of the warre,   *thinking*
  And gan to highest God entirely° pray,   *earnestly*
  That fearèd chaunce° from her to turne away;   *fate*
  With folded hands and knees full lowly bent
  All night she watcht, ne once adowne would lay
  Her daintie limbs in her sad dreriment,°   *dismal condition*
But praying still did wake, and waking did lament.

33

The morrow next gan early to appeare,
  That° Titan° rose to runne his daily race;   *when / the sun god*
  But early ere the morrow next gan reare
  Out of the sea faire Titans deawy face,
  Up rose the gentle virgin from her place,
  And lookèd all about, if she might spy
  Her lovèd knight to move° his manly pace: *i.e., moving*
  For she had great doubt of his safety,
Since late she saw him fall before his enemy.

34

At last she saw, where he upstarted brave
  Out of the well, wherein he drenchèd lay;
  As Eagle fresh out of the Ocean wave,
  Where he hath left his plumes all hoary gray,
  And deckt himselfe with feathers youthly gay,
  Like Eyas hauke° up mounts unto the skies,   *unfledged hawk*
  His newly budded pineons to assay,°   *test*

9. The Well of Life, with its powers of renewal, is successively compared with waters of the Bible, of England and Europe, and of classical antiquity. In the pool of Siloam ("Silo"), a blind man was cured by Christ (John 9.7). Water of the river Jordan cured Naaman of leprosy (2 Kings 5.14) and Christ was baptized therein (Matthew 3.16). The towns of Bath and Spa ("Spau") were famed for their medicinal waters. Cephise and Hebrus, in Greece, were rivers noted for purifying and healing powers.

And marveiles at himselfe, still as he flies:
So new this new-borne knight to battell new did rise.

35

Whom when the damnèd feend so fresh did spy,
  No wonder if he wondred at the sight,
  And doubted, whether his late enemy
  It were, or other new supplièd knight.
  He, now to prove° his late renewèd might,   *try*
  High brandishing his bright deaw-burning blade,
  Upon his crested scalpe so sore did smite,
  That to the scull a yawning wound it made:
The deadly dint° his dullèd senses all dismaid.   *blow*

36

I wote° not, whether the revenging steele   *know*
  Were hardnèd with that holy water dew,
  Wherein he fell, or sharper edge did feele,
  Or his baptizèd hands now greater° grew;   *stronger*
  Or other secret vertue° did ensew;   *power*
  Else never could the force of fleshly arme,
  Ne molten mettall in his bloud embrew:°   *plunge*
  For till that stownd° could never wight him harme,   *moment*
By subtilty, nor slight,° nor might, nor mighty charme.   *trickery*

37

The cruell wound enragèd him so sore,
  That loud he yellèd for exceeding paine;
  As hundred ramping° Lyons seemed to rore,   *rearing*
  Whom ravenous hunger did thereto constraine:
  Then gan he tosse aloft his stretchèd traine,°   *tail*
  And therewith scourge the buxome° aire so sore,   *yielding*
  That to his force to yeelden it was faine;°   *obliged*
  Ne ought his sturdie strokes might stand afore,[1]
That high trees overthrew, and rocks in peeces tore.

38

The same advauncing high above his head,
  With sharpe intended° sting so rude° him smot,   *extended / roughly*
  That to the earth him drove, as stricken dead,
  Ne living wight would have him life behot:[2]
  The mortall sting his angry needle shot
  Quite through his shield, and in his shoulder seasd,
  Where fast it stucke, ne would there out be got:
  The griefe° thereof him wondrous sore diseasd,°   *pain / afflicted*
Ne might his ranckling paine with patience be appeasd.

---

1. I.e., neither could anything ("ought") stand
before his violent ("sturdie") strokes.

2. Promised. I.e., no one would have thought he
could survive the blow.

39

But yet more mindfull of his honour deare,
 Then° of the grievous smart, which him did wring,°   *than / torment*
 From loathèd soile he can° him lightly reare,   *did*
 And strove to loose the farre infixèd sting:
 Which when in vaine he tryde with struggeling,
 Inflamed with wrath, his raging blade he heft,°   *heaved*
 And strooke so strongly, that the knotty string
 Of his huge taile he quite a sunder cleft,
Five joynts thereof he hewd, and but the stump him left.

40

Hart cannot thinke, what outrage,° and what cryes,   *violent clamor*
 With foule enfouldred[3] smoake and flashing fire,
 The hell-bred beast threw forth unto the skyes,
 That all was coverèd with darknesse dire:
 Then fraught° with rancour, and engorgèd° ire,   *filled / swollen*
 He cast at once him to avenge for all,
 And gathering up himselfe out of the mire,
 With his uneven wings did fiercely fall
Upon his sunne-bright shield, and gript it fast withall.

41

Much was the man encombred with his hold,
 In feare to lose his weapon in his paw,
 Ne wist° yet, how his talents° to unfold;   *knew / talons*
 Nor harder was from Cerberus[4] greedie jaw
 To plucke a bone, then from his cruell claw
 To reave° by strength the gripèd gage° away: *seize / prize*
 Thrise he assayd° it from his foot to draw,   *tried*
 And thrise in vaine to draw it did assay,
It booted nought to thinke, to robbe him of his pray.

42

Tho° when he saw no power might prevaile,   *then*
 His trustie sword he cald to his last aid,
 Wherewith he fiercely did his foe assaile,
 And double blowes about him stoutly laid,
 That glauncing fire out of the yron plaid;
 As sparckles from the Andvile° use to fly,   *anvil*
 When heavie hammers on the wedge are swaid;°   *struck*
 Therewith at last he forst him to unty°   *loosen*
One of his grasping feete, him to defend thereby.

43

The other foot, fast fixèd on his shield,
 Whenas no strength, nor stroks mote° him constraine   *might*

---

3. Black as a thundercloud.   4. The dog that guards the mouth of Hades.

To loose, ne yet the warlike pledge to yield,
He smot thereat with all his might and maine,°   *strength*
That nought so wondrous puissance might sustaine;
Upon the joynt the lucky steele did light,
And made such way, that hewd it quite in twaine;
The paw yet missèd not his minisht° might,   *lessened*
But hong still on the shield, as it at first was pight.°   *placed*

44

For griefe° thereof, and divelish despight,   *pain*
From his infernall fournace forth he threw
Huge flames, that dimmèd all the heavens light,
Enrold in duskish smoke and brimstone blew;
As burning Aetna⁵ from his boyling stew°   *cauldron*
Doth belch out flames, and rockes in peeces broke,
And ragged ribs of mountaines molten new
Enwrapt in coleblacke clouds and filthy smoke,
That all the land with stench, and heaven with horror choke.

45

The heate whereof, and harmefull pestilence
So sore him noyd,° that forst him to retire   *troubled*
A little backward for his best defence,
To save his bodie from the scorching fire,
Which he from hellish entrailes did expire.°   *breathe out*
It chaunst (eternall God that chaunce did guide)
As he recoylèd backward, in the mire
His nigh forwearied° feeble feet did slide,   *exhausted*
And downe he fell, with dread of shame sore terrifide.

46

There grew a goodly tree him faire beside,
Loaden with fruit and apples rosie red,
As they in pure vermilion had beene dide,
Whereof great vertues over all were red:°   *everywhere were told*
For happie life to all, which thereon fed,
And life eke everlasting did befall:
Great God it planted in that blessed sted°   *place*
With his almightie hand, and did it call
The Tree of Life, the crime of our first fathers fall.⁶

47

In all the world like was not to be found,
Save in that soile, where all good things did grow,

---

5. Mount Etna, an active volcano in Sicily.
6. Genesis 2.9 describes the Tree of Life and also the Tree of Knowledge of Good and Evil, both of which God planted in the Garden of Eden. The "crime of our first fathers fall" is that Adam, in

eating of the second and being banished from Eden, separated himself—and (according to Christian doctrine) his descendants—from the first. The Tree of Life appears again in the New Jerusalem (Revelation 22.2).

And freely sprong out of the fruitfull ground,
As incorrupted Nature did them sow,
Till that dread Dragon all did overthrow.
Another like faire tree eke grew thereby,
Whereof who so did eat, eftsoones° did know   *soon after*
Both good and ill: O mornefull memory:
That tree through one mans fault hath doen us all to dy.°   *i.e., killed us*

48

From that first tree forth flowd, as from a well,
A trickling streame of Balme, most soveraine°   *powerful for cures*
And daintie deare,° which on the ground still fell,   *precious*
And overflowèd all the fertill plaine,
As it had deawèd bene with timely° raine: *seasonable*
Life and long health that gratious° ointment gave,   *full of grace*
And deadly woundes could heale, and reare° againe   *raise*
The senselesse corse appointed° for the grave.   *made ready*
Into that same he fell: which did from death him save.[7]

49

For nigh thereto the ever damnèd beast
Durst not approch, for he was deadly made,°   *i.e., a child of death*
And all that life preservèd, did detest:
Yet he it oft adventured° to invade.   *attempted*
By this the drouping day-light gan to fade,
And yeeld his roome° to sad succeeding° night,   *its place / following after*
Who with her sable mantle gan to shade
The face of earth, and wayes of living wight,
And high her burning torch set up in heaven bright.

50

When gentle Una saw the second fall
Of her deare knight, who wearie of long fight,
And faint through losse of bloud, moved not at all,
But lay as in a dreame of deepe delight,
Besmeard with pretious Balme, whose vertuous might
Did heale his wounds, and scorching heat alay,[8]
Againe she stricken was with sore affright,
And for his safetie gan devoutly pray;
And watch the noyous° night, and wait for joyous day.   *noxious*

51

The joyous day gan early to appeare,
And faire Aurora from the deawy bed
Of agèd Tithone gan her selfe to reare,[9]

---

7. The healing balm flowing from the Tree of Life is understood to be Christ's blood, shed to redeem humankind from eternal damnation.
8. Cf. Revelation 2.7: "To him that overcometh will I give to eat of the tree of life" and 2.11: "He that overcometh shall not be hurt of the second death" (i.e., the eternal death, of the soul).
9. Aurora is goddess of the dawn. Tithonus is her husband ("agèd" because he was granted everlasting life without everlasting youth).

With rosie cheekes, for shame as blushing red;
Her golden lockes for haste were loosely shed
About her eares, when Una her did marke
Clymbe to her charet,° all with flowers spred,   *chariot*
From heaven high to chase the chearelesse darke;
With merry note her loud salutes the mounting larke.

52

Then freshly up arose the doughtie° knight,   *valiant*
All healèd of his hurts and woundès wide,
And did himselfe to battell readie dight;°   *prepare*
Whose early foe awaiting him beside
To have devourd, so soone as day he spyde,
When now he saw himselfe so freshly reare,
As if late fight had nought him damnifyde,°   *injured*
He woxe° dismayd, and gan his fate to feare;   *grew*
Nathlesse° with wonted° rage he him advauncèd neare. *nevertheless / usual*

53

And in his first encounter, gaping wide,
He thought attonce him to have swallowed quight,
And rusht upon him with outragious pride;
Who him r'encountring fierce, as hauke in flight,
Perforce rebutted° backe. The weapon bright   *drove*
Taking advantage of his open jaw,
Ran through his mouth with so importune° might,   *violent*
That deepe emperst his darksome hollow maw,°   *throat*
And back retyrd,[1] his life bloud forth with all did draw.

54

So downe he fell, and forth his life did breath,
That vanisht into smoke and cloudès swift;
So downe he fell, that th'earth him underneath
Did grone, as feeble so great load to lift;
So downe he fell, as an huge rockie clift,
Whose false° foundation waves have washt away,   *insecure*
With dreadfull poyse° is from the mayneland rift,° *falling weight / split*
And rolling downe, great Neptune doth dismay;
So downe he fell, and like an heapèd mountaine lay.

55

The knight himselfe even trembled at his fall,
So huge and horrible a masse it seemed;
And his deare Ladie, that beheld it all,
Durst not approch for dread, which she misdeemed,°   *misjudged*
But yet at last, when as the direfull feend
She saw not stirre, off-shaking vaine affright,
She nigher drew, and saw that joyous end:

1. I.e., on being drawn back.

Then God she praysd, and thankt her faithfull knight,
That had atchiev'd so great a conquest by his might.

Canto 12

*Faire Una to the Redcrosse knight
betrouthèd is with joy:
Though false Duessa it to barre
her false sleights doe imploy.*

1

Behold I see the haven nigh at hand,
  To which I meane my wearie course to bend;
  Vere the maine shete, and beare up with the land,[2]
  The which afore is fairely to be kend,°   *recognized*
  And seemeth safe from stormes, that may offend;
  There this faire virgin wearie of her way
  Must landed be, now at her journeyes end:
  There eke° my feeble barke° a while may stay,   *also / ship*
Till merry° wind and weather call her thence away.   *favorable*

2

Scarsely had Phoebus in the glooming East°   *i.e., dawn*
  Yet harnessèd his firie-footed teeme,
  Ne reard above the earth his flaming creast,°   *crest*
  When the last deadly smoke aloft did steeme,
  That signe of last outbreathèd life did seeme
  Unto the watchman on the castle wall;
  Who thereby dead that balefull° Beast did deeme,   *evil*
  And to his Lord and Ladie lowd gan call,
To tell, how he had seene the Dragons fatall fall.

3

Uprose with hastie joy, and feeble speed
  That agèd Sire, the Lord of all that land,
  And lookèd forth, to weet,° if true indeede   *know*
  Those tydings were, as he did understand,
  Which whenas true by tryall he out fond,
  He bad° to open wyde his brazen gate,   *bade*
  Which long time had bene shut, and out of hond° *straightaway*
  Proclaymèd joy and peace through all his state;
For dead now was their foe, which them forrayèd late.[3]

4

Then gan triumphant Trompets sound on hie,
  That sent to heaven the ecchoed report

---

2. Release the mainsail line and sail toward the
land. The nautical metaphor echoes many classical authors and Chaucer's *Troilus and Criseyde*
(2.1–7).
3. Had recently ravaged.

Of their new joy, and happie victorie
   Gainst him, that had them long opprest with tort,°   *wrong*
   And fast imprisonèd in siegèd fort.
   Then all the people, as in solemne feast,
   To him assembled with one full consort,°   *all together*
   Rejoycing at the fall of that great beast,
From whose eternall bondage now they were releast.

5

Forth came that auncient Lord and agèd Queene,
   Arayd in antique robes downe to the ground,
   And sad habiliments right well beseene;[4]
   A noble crew about them waited round
   Of sage and sober Peres,° all gravely gownd;   *peers*
   Whom farre before did march a goodly band
   Of tall young men, all hable armes to sownd,[5]
   But now they laurell braunches bore in hand;
Glad signe of victorie and peace in all their land.

6

Unto that doughtie Conquerour they came,
   And him before themselves prostrating low,
   Their Lord and Patrone° loud did him proclame,   *defender*
   And at his feet their laurell boughes did throw.
   Soone after them all dauncing on a row
   The comely virgins came, with girlands dight,°   *adorned*
   As fresh as flowres in medow greene do grow,
   When morning deaw upon their leaves doth light:
And in their hands sweet Timbrels° all upheld on hight.   *tambourines*

7

And them before, the fry° of children young   *crowd*
   Their wanton° sports and childish mirth did play,   *playful*
   And to the Maydens sounding tymbrels sung
   In well attunèd notes, a joyous lay,°   *song*
   And made delightfull musicke all the way,
   Untill they came, where that faire virgin stood;
   As faire Diana° in fresh sommers day   *goddess of the hunt*
   Beholds her Nymphes, enraunged° in shadie wood,   *ranged*
Some wrestle, some do run, some bathe in christall flood.

8

So she beheld those maydens meriment
   With chearefull vew; who when to her they came,
   Themselves to ground with gratious humblesse° bent,   *humility*
   And her adored by honorable name,°   *with titles of honor*
   Lifting to heaven her everlasting fame:

---

4. I.e., sober, appropriate ("right well beseene")   5. Able to fight with weapons.
attire.

Then on her head they set a girland greene,
And crownèd her twixt earnest and twixt game:°   *i.e., half in fun*
Who in her selfe-resemblance well beseene,[6]
Did seeme such, as she was, a goodly maiden Queene.

9

And after all, the raskall many° ran,   *rabble throng*
  Heapèd together in rude rablement,°   *confusion*
  To see the face of that victorious man:
  Whom all admirèd,° as from heaven sent,   *wondered at*
  And gazd upon with gaping wonderment.
  But when they came, where that dead Dragon lay,
  Stretcht on the ground in monstrous large extent,
  The sight with idle° feare did them dismay,   *baseless*
Ne durst approch him nigh, to touch, or once assay.°   *venture to*

10

Some feard, and fled; some feard and well it faynd;°   *concealed*
  One that would wiser seeme, then all the rest,
  Warnd him not touch, for yet perhaps remaynd
  Some lingring life within his hollow brest,
  Or in his wombe might lurke some hidden nest
  Of many Dragonets,° his fruitfull seed;   *young dragons*
  Another said, that in his eyes did rest
  Yet sparckling fire, and bad thereof take heed;
Another said, he saw him move his eyes indeed.

11

One mother, when as her foolehardie chyld
  Did come too neare, and with his talants° play,   *talons*
  Halfe dead through feare, her litle babe revyld,°   *scolded*
  And to her gossips° gan in counsell° say;   *women friends / private*
  "How can I tell, but that his talants may
  Yet scratch my sonne, or rend his tender hand?"
  So diversly themselves in vaine they fray;°   *frighten*
  Whiles some more bold, to measure him nigh stand,
To prove° how many acres he did spread of land.   *determine*

12

Thus flockèd all the folke him round about,
  The whiles that hoarie° king, with all his traine,   *gray-haired*
  Being arrivèd, where that champion stout
  After his foes defeasance° did remaine,   *defeat*
  Him goodly greetes, and faire does entertaine,
  With princely gifts of yvorie and gold,
  And thousand thankes him yeelds for all his paine.
  Then when his daughter deare he does behold,
Her dearely doth imbrace, and kisseth manifold.°   *many times*

---

6. I.e., looking appropriately like herself.

13

And after to his Pallace he them brings,
  With shaumes, and trompets, and with Clarions[7] sweet;
  And all the way the joyous people sings,
  And with their garments strowes the pavèd street:
  Whence mounting up, they find purveyance° meet   *provisions*
  Of all, that royall Princes court became,°   *suited*
  And all the floore was underneath their feet
  Bespred with costly scarlot of great name,°   *i.e., famous scarlet cloth*
On which they lowly sit, and fitting purpose frame.[8]

14

What needs me tell their feast and goodly guize,°   *behavior*
  In which was nothing riotous nor vaine?
  What needs of daintie dishes to devize,°   *talk*
  Of comely° services, or courtly trayne?° *becoming / assembly*
  My narrow leaves cannot in them containe
  The large discourse° of royall Princes state. *i.e., full description*
  Yet was their manner then but bare and plaine:
  For th'antique world excesse and pride did hate;
Such proud luxurious pompe is swollen up but late.° *just recently*

15

Then when with meates and drinkes of every kinde
  Their fervent appetites they quenchèd had,
  That auncient Lord gan fit occasion finde,
  Of straunge adventures, and of perils sad,°   *grave*
  Which in his travell him befallen had,
  For to demaund° of his renowmèd guest: *inquire*
  Who then with utt'rance grave, and count'nance sad,
  From point to point,° as is before exprest, *from first to last*
Discourst his voyage long, according° his request. *granting*

16

Great pleasure mixt with pittifull° regard,   *sympathetic*
  That godly King and Queene did passionate,° *i.e., feel and express*
  Whiles they his pittifull° adventures heard,   *deserving pity*
  That oft they did lament his lucklesse state,
  And often blame the too importune° fate,   *severe*
  That heapd on him so many wrathfull wreakes:° *vengeful injuries*
  For never gentle knight, as he of late,
  So tossèd was in fortunes cruell freakes;°   *whims*
And all the while salt teares bedeawd the hearers cheaks.

7. Trumpet calls. "Shaumes": the shawm was the medieval and Renaissance predecessor of the oboe.
8. Make seemly conversation.

17

Then said that royall Pere in sober wise:
  "Deare Sonne, great beene the evils, which ye bore
  From first to last in your late enterprise,
  That I note,° whether prayse, or pitty more: *know not*
  For never living man, I weene,° so sore   *think*
  In sea of deadly daungers was distrest;
  But since now safe ye seisèd° have the shore,   *reached*
  And well arrivèd are (high God be blest),
Let us devize° of ease and everlasting rest."   *think*

18

"Ah dearest Lord," said then that doughty knight,
  "Of ease or rest I may not yet devize;
  For by the faith, which I to armes have plight,°   *pledged*
  I bounden am streight° after this emprize,°   *immediately / enterprise*
  As that your daughter can ye well advize,
  Backe to returne to that great Faerie Queene,
  And her to serve six yeares in warlike wize,°   *manner*
  Gainst that proud Paynim king, that workes her teene:° *sorrow*
Therefore I ought° crave pardon, till I there have beene."[9] *must*

19

"Unhappie falles that hard necessitie,"
  Quoth he, "the troubler of my happie peace,
  And vowèd foe of my felicitie;
  Ne° I against the same can justly preace:°   *nor / press, contend*
  But since that band° ye cannot now release,   *obligation*
  Nor doen undo (for vowes may not be vaine),[1]
  Soone as the terme of those six yeares shall cease,
  Ye then shall hither backe returne againe,
The marriage to accomplish vowd betwixt you twain.

20

"Which for my part I covet to performe,
  In sort as° through the world I did proclame,   *even as*
  That who so kild that monster most deforme,°   *hideous*
  And him in hardy battaile overcame,
  Should have mine onely daughter to his Dame,°   *wife*
  And of my kingdome heire apparaunt bee:
  Therefore since now to thee perteines° the same,   *belongs*
  By dew desert of noble chevalree,
Both daughter and eke kingdome, lo I yield to thee."

9. The final Christian triumph, the marriage of Christ and the true Church, will be achieved only at the end of time. Meanwhile, the struggle against evil (and the Roman Church) continues. 1. I.e., you cannot undo what is done ("doen"), for vows may not be (made) vain.

21

Then forth he callèd that his daughter faire,
  The fairest Un' his onely daughter deare,
  His onely daughter, and his onely heyre;
  Who forth proceeding with sad° sober cheare,°   *grave / countenance*
  As bright as doth the morning starre appeare
  Out of the East, with flaming lockes bedight,°   *bedecked*
  To tell that dawning day is drawing neare,
  And to the world does bring long wishèd light;
So faire and fresh that Lady shewd her selfe in sight.

22

So faire and fresh, as freshest flowre in May;
  For she had layd her mournefull stole[2] aside,
  And widow-like sad wimple° throwne away,   *veil*
  Wherewith her heavenly beautie she did hide,
  Whiles on her wearie journey she did ride;
  And on her now a garment she did weare,
  All lilly white, withoutten spot, or pride,°   *ornament*
  That seemed like silke and silver woven neare,°   *tightly*
But neither silke nor silver therein did appeare.[3]

23

The blazing brightnesse of her beauties beame,
  And glorious light of her sunshyny face[4]
  To tell, were as to strive against the streame.
  My ragged rimes are all too rude and bace,
  Her heavenly lineaments for to enchace.°   *adorn*
  Ne wonder; for her owne deare lovèd knight,
  All° were she dayly with himselfe in place,   *although*
  Did wonder much at her celestiall sight:
Oft had he seene her faire, but never so faire dight.°   *arrayed*

24

So fairely dight, when she in presence came,
  She to her Sire made humble reverence,
  And bowèd low, that her right well became,
  And added grace unto her excellence:
  Who with great wisdome, and grave eloquence
  Thus gan to say. But eare° he thus had said,   *ere*
  With flying speede, and seeming great pretence,°   *purpose*
  Came running in, much like a man dismaid,
A Messenger with letters, which his message said.

2. Her black robe (canto 1, stanza 4).
3. "The marriage of the Lamb is come, and his wife hath made herself ready. And to her was granted that she should be arrayed in fine linen, clean and white: for the fine linen is the righ-teousness of saints" (Revelation 19.7–8).
4. Revelation 21.9, 11 describes the New Jerusalem as "the bride, the Lamb's wife . . . her light was like unto a stone most precious."

25

All in the open hall amazèd stood,
  At suddeinnesse of that unwarie° sight,   *unexpected*
  And wondred at his breathlesse hastie mood.
  But he for nought would stay his passage right°   *direct*
  Till fast° before the king he did alight;   *close*
  Where falling flat, great humblesse he did make,
  And kist the ground, whereon his foot was pight;°   *placed*
  Then to his hands that writ° he did betake,°   *document / deliver*
Which he disclosing, red thus, as the paper spake.

26

"To thee, most mighty king of Eden faire,
  Her greeting sends in these sad lines addrest,
  The wofull daughter, and forsaken heire
  Of that great Emperour of all the West;
  And bids thee be advizèd for the best,
  Ere thou thy daughter linck in holy band
  Of wedlocke to that new unknowen guest:
  For he already plighted his right hand
Unto another love, and to another land.

27

"To me sad mayd, or rather widow sad,
  He was affiauncèd long time before,
  And sacred pledges he both gave, and had,
  False erraunt knight, infamous, and forswore:
  Witnesse the burning Altars, which° he swore,   *by which*
  And guiltie heavens of° his bold perjury,   *i.e., and heavens polluted by*
  Which though he hath polluted oft of yore,
  Yet I to them for judgement just do fly,
And them conjure° t'avenge this shamefull injury.   *implore*

28

"Therefore since mine he is, or° free or bond,°   *whether / bound*
  Or false or trew, or living or else dead,
  Withhold, O soveraine Prince, your hasty hond°   *hand*
  From knitting league with him, I you aread;°   *advise*
  Ne wene° my right with strength adowne to tread,   *think*
  Through weakenesse of my widowhed, or woe:
  For truth is strong, her rightfull cause to plead,
  And shall find friends, if need requireth soe,
So bids thee well to fare, Thy neither friend, nor foe, Fidessa."

29

When he these bitter byting words had red,
  The tydings straunge did him abashèd make,
  That still he sate long time astonishèd
  As in great muse,° ne word to creature spake.   *amazement*

At last his solemne silence thus he brake,
With doubtfull eyes fast fixèd on his guest:
"Redoubted° knight, that for mine onely sake[5]   *honored*
Thy life and honour late adventurest,
Let nought be hid from me, that ought to be exprest.

30

"What meane these bloudy vowes, and idle threats,
 Throwne out from womanish impatient mind?
 What heavens? what altars? what enragèd heates
 Here heapèd up with termes of love unkind,°   *unnatural*
 My conscience cleare with guilty bands° would bind? *bonds of guilt*
 High God be witnesse, that I guiltlesse ame.
 But if your selfe, Sir knight, ye faultie° find,   *guilty*
 Or wrappèd be in loves of former Dame,
With crime do not it cover, but disclose the same."

31

To whom the Redcrosse knight this answere sent,
 "My Lord, my King, be nought hereat dismayd,
 Till well ye wote by grave intendiment,°   *serious investigation*
 What woman, and wherefore doth me upbrayd
 With breach of love, and loyalty betrayd.
 It was in my mishaps, as hitherward
 I lately traveild, that unwares I strayd
 Out of my way, through perils straunge and hard;
That day should faile me, ere I had them all declard.

32

"There did I find, or rather I was found
 Of this false woman, that Fidessa hight,°   *is called*
 Fidessa hight the falsest Dame on ground,
 Most false Duessa, royall richly dight,
 That easie was t'invegle weaker° sight: *deceive too weak*
 Who by her wicked arts, and wylie skill,
 Too false and strong for earthly skill or might,
 Unwares me wrought unto her wicked will,
And to my foe betrayd, when least I fearèd ill."

33

Then steppèd forth the goodly royall Mayd,
 And on the ground her selfe prostrating low,
 With sober countenaunce thus to him sayd:
 "O pardon me, my soveraigne Lord, to show
 The secret treasons, which of late I know
 To have bene wroght by that false sorceresse.
 She onely she it is, that earst° did throw   *formerly*

---

5. For my sake alone.

This gentle knight into so great distresse,
That death him did awaite in dayly wretchednesse.

34

"And now it seemes, that she subornèd hath
  This craftie messenger with letters vaine,
  To worke new woe and improvided scath,°   *unexpected harm*
  By breaking of the band° betwixt us twaine;   *bond*
  Wherein she usèd hath the practicke paine°   *treacherous skill*
  Of this false footman, clokt with simplenesse,
  Whom if ye please for to discover plaine,
Ye shall him Archimago find, I ghesse,
The falsest man alive; who tries° shall find no lesse."   *investigates*

35

The king was greatly movèd at her speach,
  And all with suddein indignation fraight,°   *filled*
  Bad° on that Messenger rude° hands to reach.   *bade / harsh*
  Eftsoones° the Gard, which on his state did wait,   *immediately*
  Attacht° that faitor° false, and bound him strait: *arrested / impostor*
  Who seeming sorely chauffèd° at his band,   *angered*
  As chainèd Beare, whom cruell dogs do bait,
  With idle force did faine° them to withstand,   *feign*
And often semblaunce made to scape out of their hand.

36

But they him layd full low in dungeon deepe,
  And bound him hand and foote with yron chains.
  And with continuall watch did warely° keepe;   *vigilantly*
  Who then would thinke, that by his subtile trains°   *tricks*
  He could escape fowle death or deadly paines?[6]
  Thus when that Princes wrath was pacifide,
  He gan renew the late forbidden banes,[7]
  And to the knight his daughter deare he tyde,
With sacred rites and vowes for ever to abyde.

37

His owne two hands the holy knots did knit,
  That none but death for ever can devide;
  His owne two hands, for such a turne° most fit,   *act*
  The housling° fire did kindle and provide,   *sacramental*
  And holy water thereon sprinckled wide;[8]
  At which the bushy Teade° a groome did light,   *nuptial torch*
  And sacred lampe in secret chamber hide,

---

6. "And he laid hold on the dragon, that old serpent, which is the Devil, and Satan, and bound him a thousand years, And cast him into the bottomless pit, and shut him up, and set a seal upon him, that he should deceive the nations no more, till the thousand years should be fulfilled: and after that he must be loosed a little season" (Revelation 20.2–3).

7. Banns; i.e., proclamation or public notice of an intended marriage. Una and Redcrosse are now betrothed; the consummation of their marriage is postponed.

8. Marriages in ancient times were solemnized with sacramental fire and water.

Where it should not be quenchèd day nor night,
For feare of evill fates, but burnen ever bright.

38

Then gan they sprinckle all the posts with wine,
  And made great feast to solemnize that day;
  They all perfumde with frankencense divine,
  And precious odours fetcht from far away,
  That all the house did sweat with great aray:
  And all the while sweete Musicke did apply
  Her curious° skill, the warbling notes to play,   *intricate*
  To drive away the dull Melancholy;
The whiles one sung a song of love and jollity.

39

During the which there was an heavenly noise
  Heard sound through all the Pallace pleasantly,
  Like as it had bene many an Angels voice,
  Singing before th'eternall majesty,
  In their trinall triplicities[9] on hye;
  Yet wist° no creature, whence that heavenly sweet°   *knew / delight*
  Proceeded, yet each one felt secretly°   *inwardly*
  Himselfe thereby reft of his sences meet,°   *proper*
And ravishèd with rare impression in his sprite.[1]

40

Great joy was made that day of young and old,
  And solemne feast proclaimd throughout the land,
  That their exceeding merth may not be told:
  Suffice it heare by signes to understand
  The usuall joyes at knitting of loves band.
  Thrise happy man the knight himselfe did hold,
  Possessèd of his Ladies hart and hand,
  And ever, when his eye did her behold,
His heart did seeme to melt in pleasures manifold.

41

Her joyous presence and sweet company
  In full content he there did long enjoy,
  Ne wicked envie, ne vile gealosy
  His deare delights were able to annoy:
  Yet swimming in that sea of blisfull joy,
  He nought forgot, how he whilome° had sworne,   *formerly*
  In case he could[2] that monstrous beast destroy,

9. The nine angelic orders, divided into three groups of three, the whole hierarchy corresponding to the nine spheres of the universe. The music heard in this stanza is the music of the spheres, not audible on earth since the Fall.
1. Spirit. "Let us be glad and rejoice, and give honour to him: for the marriage of the Lamb is come" (Revelation 19.7). In Revelation, the marriage of Christ and the New Jerusalem signals the general redemption.
2. If he were able to.

Unto his Faerie Queene backe to returne:
The which he shortly did, and Una left to mourne.

42

Now strike your sailes ye jolly Mariners,
  For we be come unto a quiet rode,°   *harbor*
  Where we must land some of our passengers,
  And light this wearie vessell of her lode.
  Here she a while may make her safe abode,
  Till she repairèd have her tackles spent,°   *worn out*
  And wants supplide. And then againe abroad
  On the long voyage whereto she is bent:
Well may she speede and fairely finish her intent.

From The Second Booke of The Faerie Queene

Contayning
The Legend of Sir Guyon,
or
Of Temperaunce

Summary   In Book 2, Sir Guyon represents and becomes the virtue of Temperance, which requires moderation, self-control, and sometimes abstinence in regard to anger, sex, greed, ambition, and the whole spectrum of passions, desires, pleasures, and material goods. In his climactic adventure, he visits and destroys the Bower of Bliss of the witch Acrasia.

From *Canto 12*

[THE BOWER OF BLISS][3]

42

Thence passing forth, they[4] shortly do arrive,
  Whereas the Bowre of Blisse was situate;
  A place pickt out by choice of best alive,°   *the best living artisans*
  That natures worke by art can imitate:
  In which what ever in this worldly state
  Is sweet, and pleasing unto living sense,
  Or that may dayntiest fantasie aggrate,°   *please, satisfy*
  Was pourèd forth with plentifull dispence,°   *liberality*
And made there to abound with lavish affluence.

---

3. The Bower of Bliss, perhaps the most famous of Spenser's symbolic places, has been variously interpreted. Some critics emphasize its aspects of sterility and artifice; others, its seductive and threatening eroticism and idolatry akin to that associated, in Spenser's time, with the New World and Ireland.

4. I.e., Guyon and a character called the Palmer, who is his guide throughout Book 2 (and who is usually thought to represent reason). Pilgrims to the Holy Land were called palmers in token of the palm leaves they often brought back.

43

Goodly it was enclosèd round about,
   Aswell their entred guests to keepe within,
   As those unruly beasts to hold without;[5]
   Yet was the fence thereof but weake and thin;
   Nought feard their force, that fortilage° to win,[6]   *fortress*
   But wisedomes powre, and temperaunces might,
   By which the mightiest things efforcèd bin:°   *are compelled*
   And eke° the gate was wrought of substaunce light,   *also*
Rather for pleasure, then° for battery or fight.   *than*

44

Yt framèd° was of precious yvory,   *made*
   That seemd a worke of admirable wit;°   *marvelous skill*
   And therein all the famous history
   Of Jason and Medaea was ywrit;
   Her mighty charmes, her furious loving fit,
   His goodly conquest of the golden fleece,
   His falsèd° faith, and love too lightly flit,°   *violated / altering*
   The wondred° Argo, which in venturous peece[7]   *admired*
First through the Euxine seas bore all the flowr of Greece.[8]

45

Ye might° have seene the frothy billowes fry°   *could / foam*
   Under the ship, as thorough° them she went,   *through*
   That seemd the waves were into yvory,
   Or yvory into the waves were sent;
   And other where the snowy substaunce sprent°   *sprinkled*
   With vermell,° like the boyes bloud therein shed,[9]   *vermilion*
   A piteous spectacle did represent,
   And otherwhiles° with gold besprinkelèd;   *elsewhere*
Yt seemd th'enchaunted flame, which did Creüsa wed.[1]

46

All this, and more might in that goodly gate
   Be red; that ever open stood to all,
   Which thither came: but in the Porch there sate
   A comely personage of stature tall,
   And semblaunce° pleasing, more then naturall,   *appearance*
   That travellers to him seemd to entize;
   His looser° garment to the ground did fall,   *too loose*

5. Just outside the Bower, Guyon and the Palmer had encountered "many beasts, that roard outrageously, / As if that hungers point, or Venus sting / Had them enraged" (stanza 39). The Palmer had used the magical power of his staff to turn their aggression into cringing fear.
6. I.e., it was not at all feared that the physical force of the beasts could breach that fortress.
7. I.e., adventurous vessel.
8. Jason, in his ship the *Argo*, sought the Golden Fleece of the king of Colchis; the sorceress Medea, the king's daughter, fell in love with him and used "her mighty charmes" to help him obtain it.
9. The blood of Absyrtus, Medea's younger brother, whose body she cut into pieces and scattered to delay her father's pursuit.
1. Jason later deserted Medea for Creüsa. In revenge, Medea gave her a dress that burst into flame when she put it on; the flame consumed and thus "wed" her.

And flew about his heeles in wanton wize,°   *unruly fashion*
Not fit for speedy pace, or manly exercize.

47

They in that place him Genius° did call: *presiding spirit*
  Not that celestiall powre, to whom the care
  Of life, and generatiön of all
  That lives, pertaines in charge particulare,[2]
  Who wondrous things concerning our welfare,
  And strange phantomes° doth let us oft forsee,   *visions*
  And oft of secret ill bids us beware:
  That is our Selfe,[3] whom though we do not see,
Yet each doth in him selfe it well perceive to bee.

48

Therefore a God him sage Antiquity
  Did wisely make,[4] and good Agdistes call:
  But this same[5] was to that quite contrary,
  The foe of life, that good envyes° to all,   *grudges*
  That secretly doth us procure° to fall,   *cause*
  Through guilefull semblaunts,° which he makes us see.   *illusions*
  He of this Gardin had the governall,°   *management*
  And Pleasures porter was devizd° to bee,   *appointed*
Holding a staffe in hand for more formalitee.

49

With diverse flowres he daintily was deckt,
  And strowèd round about, and by his side
  A mighty Mazer bowle[6] of wine was set,
  As if it had to him bene sacrifide;°   *consecrated*
  Wherewith all new-come guests he gratifide:
  So did he eke Sir Guyon passing by:
  But he his idle curtesie defide,
  And overthrew his bowle disdainfully;
And broke his staffe, with which he charmèd semblants sly.[7]

50

Thus being entred, they behold around
  A large and spacious plaine, on every side
  Strowed with pleasauns,° whose faire grassy ground   *pleasure grounds*
  Mantled with greene, and goodly beautifide
  With all the ornaments of Floraes° pride,   *goddess of flowers*
  Wherewith her mother Art, as halfe in scorne

2. I.e., not Agdistes (see next stanza), the god of generation. The true Agdistes appears in the Garden of Adonis canto of Book 3 (canto 6, stanzas 31–33).
3. I.e., the daemon, or indwelling divine power, that directs the course of our lives.
4. I.e., the wise ancients were right to declare this power a god.
5. I.e., the Genius of the Bower.
6. A drinking cup of maple.
7. Raised deceitful apparitions. The rod and bowl are traditional emblems of enchantment (cf. Duessa's cup, Book 1, canto 8, stanza 14).

Of niggard° Nature, like a pompous bride *stingy*
  Did decke her, and too lavishly adorne,
When forth from virgin bowre she comes in th'early morne.

51

Thereto the Heavens alwayes Joviall,[8]
  Lookt on them lovely,° still° in stedfast state, *lovingly / always*
  Ne° suffred storme nor frost on them to fall, *nor*
  Their tender buds or leaves to violate,
  Nor scorching heat, nor cold intemperate
  T'afflict the creatures, which therein did dwell,
  But the milde aire with season moderate
  Gently attempred, and disposd so well,
That still it breathèd forth sweet spirit° and holesome smell. *breath*

52

More sweet and holesome, then° the pleasaunt hill *than*
  Of Rhodope, on which the Nimphe, that bore
  A gyaunt babe, her selfe for griefe did kill;
  Or the Thessalian Tempe, where of yore
  Faire Daphne Phoebus hart with love did gore;
  Or Ida, where the Gods lov'd to repaire,° *resort*
  When ever they their heavenly bowres forlore;° *deserted*
  Or sweet Parnasse, the haunt of Muses faire;[9]
Or Eden selfe, if ought° with Eden mote compaire. *aught, anything*

53

Much wondred Guyon at the faire aspect
  Of that sweet place, yet suffred no delight
  To sincke into his sence, nor mind affect,
  But passèd forth, and lookt still forward right,° *straight ahead*
  Bridling his will, and maistering his might:
  Till that he came unto another gate,
  No gate, but like one, being goodly dight° *arrayed*
  With boughes and braunches, which did broad dilate° *spread out*
Their clasping armes, in wanton wreathings intricate.

54

So fashionèd a Porch with rare device,° *design*
  Archt over head with an embracing vine,
  Whose bounches hanging downe, seemed to entice
  All passers by, to tast their lushious wine,
  And did themselves into their hands incline,
  As freely offering to be gatherèd:

8. Serene and beneficent, as influenced by the planet Jupiter.
9. The nymph Rhodope, who had a "gyaunt babe," Athos, by Neptune, was turned into a mountain. Daphne, another nymph, charmed Apollo so much that he pursued her until she prayed for aid and was turned into a laurel tree. Mount Ida was the scene of the rape of Ganymede by Jupiter, the judgment of Paris, and the gods' vantage point for viewing the Trojan War. Mount Parnassus is the home of the Muses.

Some deepe empurpled as the Hyacine,°   *hyacinth*
Some as the Rubine,° laughing sweetly red,   *ruby*
Some like faire Emeraudes, not yet well ripenèd.

55

And them amongst, some were of burnisht gold,
 So made by art, to beautifie the rest,
 Which did themselves emongst the leaves enfold,
 As lurking from the vew of covetous guest,
 That the weake bowes,° with so rich load opprest, *boughs*
 Did bowe adowne, as over-burdenèd.
 Under that Porch a comely dame did rest,
 Clad in faire weedes,° but fowle disorderèd, *garments*
And garments loose, that seemd unmeet for womanhed.[1]

56

In her left hand a Cup of gold she held,
 And with her right the riper° fruit did reach, *overripe*
 Whose sappy liquor, that with fulnesse sweld,
 Into her cup she scruzd,° with daintie breach° *squeezed / crushing*
 Of her fine fingers, without fowle empeach,° *injury*
 That so faire wine-presse made the wine more sweet:
 Thereof she usd to give to drinke to each,
 Whom passing by she happenèd to meet:
It was her guise,° all Straungers goodly so to greet. *custom*

57

So she to Guyon offred it to tast;
 Who taking it out of her tender hond,
 The cup to ground did violently cast,
 That all in peeces it was broken fond,° *found*
 And with the liquor stainèd all the lond:° *land*
 Whereat Excesse° exceedingly was wroth, *i.e., the "comely dame"*
 Yet no'te° the same amend, ne yet withstond, *knew not how to*
 But suffered° him to passe, all° were she loth; *allowed / although*
Who nought regarding her displeasure forward goth.

58

There the most daintie Paradise on ground,
 It selfe doth offer to his sober eye,
 In which all pleasures plenteously abound,
 And none does others happinesse envye:
 The painted° flowres, the trees upshooting hye, *brightly colored*
 The dales for shade, the hilles for breathing space,
 The trembling groves, the Christall° running by; *clear stream*
 And that, which all faire workes doth most aggrace,° *add grace to*
The art, which all that wrought, appearèd in no place.

---

1. Unfitting for womanhood.

59

One would have thought (so cunningly, the rude,
 And scornèd parts were mingled with the fine)
That nature had for wantonesse ensude°   *playfulness imitated*
Art, and that Art at nature did repine;°   *complain*
So striving each th'other to undermine,
 Each did the others worke more beautifie;
So diff'ring both in willes, agreed in fine:°   *in the end*
 So all agreed through sweete diversitie,
This Gardin to adorne with all varietie.

60

And in the midst of all, a fountaine stood,
 Of richest substaunce, that on earth might bee,
So pure and shiny, that the silver flood
 Through every channell running one might see;
Most goodly it with curious imageree
 Was over-wrought,° and shapes of naked boyes, *embellished (excessively)*
Of which some seemd with lively jollitee,
 To fly about, playing their wanton toyes,°   *sports*
Whilest others did them selves embay° in liquid joyes. *bathe*

61

And over all, of purest gold was spred,
 A trayle of yvie in his native hew:
For the rich mettall was so colourèd,
 That wight,° who did not well avis'd° it vew, *person / carefully*
Would surely deeme it to be yvie trew:
 Low his lascivious armes adown did creepe,
That themselves dipping in the silver dew,
 Their fleecy flowres they tenderly did steepe,
Which° drops of Christall seemd for wantones to weepe. *on which*

62

Infinit streames continually did well
 Out of this fountaine, sweet and faire to see,
The which into an ample laver° fell,   *basin*
 And shortly grew to so great quantitie,
That like a little lake it seemd to bee;
 Whose depth exceeded not three cubits[2] hight,
That through the waves one might the bottom see,
 All pav'd beneath with Jaspar shining bright,
That seemd the fountaine in that sea did sayle upright.

63

And all the margent° round about was set,   *border*
 With shady Laurell trees, thence to defend° *ward off*

---

2. One cubit is about twenty inches; thus the depth is no more than five feet.

The sunny beames, which on the billowes bet,°   *beat*
And those which therein bathèd, mote offend.°   *might harm*
As Guyon hapned by the same to wend,°   *pass*
Two naked Damzelles he therein espyde,
Which therein bathing, seemèd to contend,
And wrestle wantonly, ne car'd to hyde,
Their dainty parts from vew of any, which them eyde.

64

Sometimes the one would lift the other quight
  Above the waters, and then downe againe
  Her plong,° as over maisterèd by might,   *plunge*
  Where both awhile would coverèd remaine,
  And each the other from to rise° restraine;   *rising*
  The whiles their snowy limbes, as through a vele,°   *veil*
  So through the Christall waves appearèd plaine:
  Then suddeinly both would themselves unhele,°   *uncover*
And th'amarous sweet spoiles° to greedy eyes revele.   *booty, plunder*

65

As that faire Starre, the messenger of morne,[3]
  His deawy face out of the sea doth reare:
  Or as the Cyprian goddess,[4] newly borne
  Of th'Oceans fruitfull froth,° did first appeare: *foam*
  Such seemèd they, and so their yellow heare
  Christalline humour° droppèd downe apace.   *clear water*
  Whom such when Guyon saw, he drew him neare,
  And somewhat gan relent his earnest pace,
His stubborne brest gan secret pleasaunce to embrace.

66

The wanton Maidens him espying, stood
  Gazing a while at his unwonted guise;°   *unaccustomed behavior*
  Then th'one her selfe low duckèd in the flood,
  Abasht, that her a straunger did avise:°   *see*
  But th'other rather higher did arise,
  And her two lilly paps° aloft displayd,   *breasts*
  And all, that might his melting hart entise
  To her delights, she unto him bewrayed:°   *revealed*
The rest hid underneath, him more desirous made.

67

With that, the other likewise up arose,
  And her faire lockes, which formerly were bownd
  Up in one knot, she low adowne did lose:°   *loosen*

---

3. Unless "his" in the next line is to be taken as neuter, it implies that the reference is not to Venus but to Phosphorus (or Heophorus), the minor male divinity sometimes identified with the morning star.

4. Venus, one of whose principal shrines was on the island of Cyprus.

Which flowing long and thick, her cloth'd arownd,
 And th'yvorie in golden mantle gownd:
 So that faire spectacle from him was reft,°   *taken*
 Yet that, which reft it, no lesse faire was fownd:
 So hid in lockes and waves from lookers theft,
Nought but her lovely face she for his looking left.

68

Withall she laughèd, and she blusht withall,
 That blushing to her laughter gave more grace,
 And laughter to her blushing, as did fall:°   *as it happened*
 Now when they spide the knight to slacke his pace,
 Them to behold, and in his sparkling° face   *animated*
 The secret signes of kindled lust appeare,
 Their wanton meriments they did encreace,
 And to him beckned, to approch more neare,
And shewd him many sights, that courage cold could reare.

69

On which when gazing him the Palmer saw,
 He much rebukt those wandring eyes of his,
 And counseld well, him forward thence did draw.
 Now are they come nigh to the Bowre of blis
 Of her fond° favorites so nam'd amis: *enamored; foolish*
 When thus the Palmer; "Now Sir, well avise;°   *take care*
 For here the end of all our travell[5] is:
 Here wonnes° Acrasia,[6] whom we must surprise,   *dwells*
Else she will slip away, and all our drift despise."°   *plan set at nought*

70

Eftsoones° they heard a most melodious sound,   *immediately*
 Of all that mote delight a daintie eare,
 Such as attonce might not on living ground,
 Save in this Paradise, be heard elswhere:
 Right hard it was, for wight,° which did it heare,   *person*
 To read,° what manner musicke that mote bee: *discern*
 For all that pleasing is to living eare,
 Was there consorted in one harmonee,
Birdes, voyces, instruments, windes, waters, all agree.

71

The joyous birdes shrouded in chearefull shade,
 Their notes unto the voyce attempred° sweet;   *attuned*
 Th'Angelicall soft trembling voyces made
 To th'instruments divine respondence meet:°   *fitting*
 The silver sounding instruments did meet°   *join*
 With the base[7] murmure of the waters fall:

5. Travel or travail. "End": conclusion or goal.
6. Intemperance (from Greek).

7. Low-pitched; also punning on the moral sense
of the word.

The waters fall with difference discreet,°   *distinct variation*
Now soft, now loud, unto the wind did call:
The gentle warbling wind low answerèd to all.

72

There, whence that Musick seemèd heard to bee,
  Was the faire Witch her selfe[8] now solacing,°   *taking pleasure*
  With a new Lover, whom through sorceree
  And witchcraft, she from farre did thither bring:
  There she had him now layd a slombering,
  In secret shade, after long wanton joyes:
  Whilst round about them pleasauntly did sing
  Many faire Ladies, and lascivious boyes,
That ever mixt their song with light licentious toyes.°   *amorous play*

73

And all that while, right over him she hong,
  With her false° eyes fast fixèd in his sight,   *deceitful*
  As seeking medicine, whence she was stong,°   *stung*
  Or greedily depasturing° delight: *feeding on*
  And oft inclining downe with kisses light,
  For feare of waking him, his lips bedewd,
  And through his humid° eyes did sucke his spright,°   *moist / spirit*
  Quite molten into lust and pleasure lewd;
Wherewith she sighèd soft, as if his case she rewd.°   *pitied*

74

The whiles some one did chaunt this lovely lay:[9]
  "Ah see, who so faire thing doest faine° to see,   *delight*
  In springing flowre the image of thy day;
  Ah see the Virgin Rose, how sweetly shee
  Doth first peepe forth with bashfull modestee,
  That fairer seemes, the lesse ye see her may;
  Lo see soone after, how more bold and free
  Her barèd bosome she doth broad display;
Loe see soone after, how she fades, and falles away.

75

"So passeth, in the passing of a day,
  Of mortall life the leafe, the bud, the flowre,
  Ne more doth flourish after first decay,
  That earst° was sought to decke both bed and bowre,   *formerly*
  Of many a Ladie, and many a Paramowre:°   *lover*

8. Acrasia bears many resemblances to the classical Circe (in *Odyssey* 10 as well as the more witchlike and seductive figure in Ovid's *Metamorphoses* 14) and also to the enchantresses of Italian romance who derive from Circe: Acratia in Trissino's *L'Italia liberata* and Armida in Tasso's *Gerusalemme liberata*. Much of the description in this scene is imitated from Tasso's account of the garden of Armida.

9. The song ("lay") of stanzas 74 and 75 imitates that in *Gerusalemme liberata* 16.14–15. This is a classic statement of the *carpe florem* (or *carpe diem*) theme—pick the flower of youth before it fades.

Gather therefore the Rose, whilest yet is prime,°   *(its) springtime*
For soone comes age, that will her pride deflowre:
Gather the Rose of love, whilest yet is time,
Whilest loving thou mayst lovèd be with equal crime."

76

He ceast, and then gan all the quire of birdes
  Their diverse notes t'attune unto his lay,
  As in approvance of his pleasing words.
  The constant paire[1] heard all, that he did say,
  Yet swarvèd not, but kept their forward way,
  Through many covert groves, and thickets close,
  In which they creeping did at last display°   *discover*
  That wanton Ladie, with her lover lose,°   *loose, wanton*
Whose sleepie head she in her lap did soft dispose.

77

Upon a bed of Roses she was layd,
  As faint through heat, or dight to° pleasant sin,   *ready for*
  And was arayd, or rather disarayd,
  All in a vele of silke and silver thin,
  That hid no whit her alablaster skin,
  But rather shewd more white, if more might bee:
  More subtile web Arachne° cannot spin,   *the spider*
  Nor the fine nets, which oft we woven see
Of scorchèd deaw, do not in th'aire more lightly flee.°   *float*

78

Her snowy brest was bare to readie spoyle
  Of hungry eies, which n'ote° therewith be fild,   *could not*
  And yet through languor of her late sweet toyle,
  Few drops, more cleare then Nectar, forth distild,
  That like pure Orient perles[2] adowne it trild,°   *trickled*
  And her faire eyes sweet smyling in delight,
  Moystened their fierie beames,[3] with which she thrild°   *pierced*
  Fraile harts, yet quenchèd° not; like starry light   *quenched, killed*
Which sparckling on the silent waves, does seeme more bright.

79

The young man sleeping by her, seemd to bee
  Some goodly swayne of honorable place,°   *rank*
  That certès° it great pittie was to see   *certainly*
  Him his nobilitie so foule deface;°   *disgrace*
  A sweet regard,° and amiable grace,   *demeanor*
  Mixèd with manly sternnesse did appeare
  Yet sleeping, in his well proportioned face,

---

1. I.e., Guyon and the Palmer.
2. Lustrous pearls of the East.
3. Eyes—particularly those of lovers—were believed to emit beams of light or of the animating "spirits"; i.e., rarefied fluids thought to permeate the blood and bodily organs.

And on his tender lips the downy heare
Did now but freshly spring, and silken blossomes beare.

80

His warlike armes, the idle instruments
  Of sleeping praise,° were hong upon a tree,   *worthiness*
  And his brave° shield, full of old moniments,°   *splendid / marks of honor*
  Was fowly ra'st,° that none the signes might see;   *erased*
  Ne for them, ne for honour carèd hee,
  Ne ought,° that did to his advauncement tend,   *aught, anything*
  But in lewd loves, and wastfull luxuree,°   *licentiousness*
  His dayes, his goods, his bodie he did spend:
O horrible enchantment, that him so did blend.°   *blind*

81

The noble Elfe,[4] and carefull Palmer drew
  So nigh them, minding nought, but° lustfull game,   *heedful only of*
  That suddein forth they on them rusht, and threw
  A subtile net, which onely for the same
  The skilfull Palmer formally° did frame.[5]   *expressly*
  So held them under fast, the whiles the rest
  Fled all away from feare of fowler shame.
  The faire Enchauntresse, so unwares opprest,°   *surprised*
Tryde all her arts, and all her sleights, thence out to wrest.

82

And eke° her lover strove: but all in vaine;   *also*
  For that same net so cunningly was wound,
  That neither guile, nor force might it distraine.°   *tear*
  They tooke them both, and both them strongly bound
  In captive bandes,° which there they readie found: *bonds*
  But her in chaines of adamant[6] he tyde;
  For nothing else might keepe her safe and sound;° *i.e., unable to escape*
  But Verdant° (so he hight°) he soone untyde,   *Green / was called*
And counsell sage in steed° thereof to him applyde.   *instead*

83

But all those pleasant bowres and Pallace brave,°   *splendid*
  Guyon broke downe, with rigour pittilesse;
  Ne ought their goodly workmanship might save
  Them from the tempest of his wrathfulnesse,
  But that their blisse he turn'd to balefulnesse:°   *distress*
  Their groves he feld, their gardins did deface,
  Their arbers spoyle, their Cabinets° suppresse,   *bowers*
  Their banket° houses burne, their buildings race,° *banquet / raze*
And of the fairest late,° now made the fowlest place.   *lately*

---

4. Knight of Faerie Land, here, Guyon.
5. The episode recalls the capture of Venus and her lover Mars in a net cunningly set around his marriage bed by Venus's husband, Vulcan, the blacksmith god (*Odyssey* 8.272–84).
6. Steel or some other extremely hard substance.

84

Then led they her away, and eke that knight
   They with them led, both sorrowfull and sad:
   The way they came, the same retourn'd they right,
   Till they arrivèd, where they lately had
   Charm'd those wild-beasts, that rag'd with furie mad.[7]
   Which now awaking, fierce at them gan fly,
   As in their mistresse reskew, whom they lad;°   *led*
   But them the Palmer soone did pacify.
Then Guyon askt, what meant those beastes, which there did ly.

85

Said he, "These seeming beasts are men indeed,
   Whom this Enchauntresse hath transformèd thus,
   Whylome° her lovers, which her lusts did feed,   *formerly*
   Now turnèd into figures hideous,
   According to their mindes like monstruous."[8]
   "Sad end," quoth he, "of life intemperate,
   And mournefull meed° of joyes delicious: *reward*
   But Palmer, if it mote thee so aggrate,°   *please*
Let them returnèd be unto their former state."

86

Streight way he with his vertuous° staffe them strooke,   *powerful*
   And streight° of beasts they comely men became;   *immediately*
   Yet being men they did unmanly looke,
   And starèd ghastly, some for inward shame,
   And some for wrath, to see their captive Dame:
   But one aboye the rest in speciäll,
   That had an hog beene late, hight° Grille[9] by name,   *called*
   Repinèd° greatly, and did him miscall,°   *complained / revile*
That had from hoggish forme him brought to naturall.

87

Said Guyon, "See the mind of beastly man,
   That hath so soone forgot the excellence
   Of his creation, when he life began,
   That now he chooseth, with vile difference,°   *preference*
   To be a beast, and lacke intelligence."
   To whom the Palmer thus, "The donghill kind
   Delights in filth and foule incontinence:
   Let Grill be Grill, and have his hoggish mind,
But let us hence depart, whilest wether serves and wind."

---

7. See above, stanza 43, n. 5.
8. Even as their own minds were similarly monstrous. Circe changed Odysseus's companions into animals, but Odysseus had a charm to release them.

9. According to one of Plutarch's dialogues, a man named Gryllus ("fierce," "cruel"), having been changed into a hog by Circe, refused to be restored to human form by Odysseus.

From The Third Booke of The Faerie Queene

Containing
The Legend of Britomartis,[1]
or
Of Chastitie

Summary   The third book of *The Faerie Queene* is a multifaceted exploration of the virtue of chastity, which is, for Spenser, closely bound up with the power of love. The principal character is the lady knight Britomart, on a quest to find her destined beloved, the knight Artegall. Her adventures are braided together with those of many others, including the twins Belphoebe and Amoret, whose miraculous conception and birth is related at the opening of canto 6. The infant Belphoebe is adopted by the goddess Diana; Amoret is taken up by the goddess Venus and brought to the Garden of Adonis, Spenser's most remarkable allegorical vision of erotic union and procreation.

From *Canto 6*

[THE GARDEN OF ADONIS]

The birth of faire Belphoebe and
Of Amoret is told.
The Gardins of Adonis fraught°   *filled*
With pleasures manifold.

1

Well may I weene,° faire Ladies, all this while   *suppose*
    Ye wonder, how this noble Damozell°   *i.e., Belphoebe*
    So great perfections did in her compile,°   *gather together*
    Sith° that in salvage° forests she did dwell,   *since / wild*
    So farre from court and royall Citadell,
    The great schoolmistresse of all curtesy:
    Seemeth° that such wild woods should far expell   *it would seem*
    All civill° usage and gentility,   *polite*
And gentle sprite deforme with rude rusticity.

2

But to this faire Belphoebe in her berth
    The heavens so favourable were and free,°   *generous*
    Looking with myld aspect upon the earth,
    In th'Horoscope of her nativitee,
    That all the gifts of grace and chastitee
    On her they pourèd forth of plenteous horne;[2]

---

1. The name comes from the pseudo-Virgilian poem *Ciris* (lines 295–305), where Britomartis is a goddess associated with Diana, the chaste goddess of the moon. For Spenser, her name suggests the (false) etymology *Brito* ("Britoness") + *Mart*

("Mars," god of war).
2. Horn of plenty, cornucopia. The planets were in favorable relationship ("myld aspect") at her birth; the combination of Jupiter ("Jove") and Venus was thought to be especially fortunate.

Jove laught on Venus from his soveraigne see,°   *throne*
And Phoebus with faire beames did her adorne,
And all the Graces rockt her cradle being borne.

3

Her berth was of the wombe of Morning dew,[3]
  And her conception of the joyous Prime,°   *springtime*
  And all her whole creation did her shew
  Pure and unspotted from all loathly crime,
  That is ingenerate in fleshly slime.[4]
  So was this virgin borne, so was she bred,°   *nourished*
  So was she traynèd up from time to time,°   *at all times*
  In all chast vertue, and true bounti-hed°   *goodness*
Till to her dew perfection she was ripenèd.

4

Her mother was the faire Chrysogonee,[5]
  The daughter of Amphisa,[6] who by race
  A Faerie was, yborne of high degree,
  She bore Belphoebe, she bore in like cace
  Faire Amoretta in the second place:
  These two were twinnes, and twixt them two did share
  The heritage of all celestiall grace.
  That all the rest it seem'd they robbèd bare
Of bountie,° and of beautie, and all vertues rare.   *goodness*

5

It were a goodly° storie, to declare,   *pleasant*
  By what straunge accident° faire Chrysogone   *happening*
  Conceived these infants, and how them she bare,
  In this wild forrest wandring all alone,
  After she had nine moneths fulfild and gone:
  For not as other wemens commune brood,
  They were enwombèd in the sacred throne
  Of her chaste bodie, nor with commune food,
As other wemens babes, they suckèd vitall blood.

6

But wondrously they were begot, and bred
  Through influence of th'heavens fruitfull ray,[7]
  As it in antique bookes is mentionèd.
  It was upon a Sommers shynie day,

---

3. An echo of Psalms 110.3 (Book of Common Prayer): "The dew of thy birth is of the womb of the morning," taken to refer to the conception and birth of Christ.
4. Like Christ or the Virgin, she is said to be free of original sin, which is innate ("ingenerate") in human flesh.

5. Golden-born (Greek), alluding to the myth of Danaë, who conceived when Jove visited her as a shower of gold.
6. Of double nature (Greek).
7. I.e., an emanation from the heavens; continuing the analogue to the Virgin's miraculous conception of Christ.

When Titan[8] faire his beamès did display,
    In a fresh fountaine, farre from all mens vew,
    She bathed her brest, the boyling heat t'allay;
    She bathed with roses red, and violets blew,
And all the sweetest flowres, that in the forrest grew.

7

Till faint through irkesome° wearinesse, adowne   *burdensome*
    Upon the grassie ground her selfe she layd
    To sleepe, the whiles a gentle slombring swowne°   *deep sleep*
    Upon her fell all naked bare displayd;
    The sunne-beames bright upon her body playd,
    Being through former bathing mollifide,°   *softened*
    And pierst into her wombe, where they embayd°   *steeped*
    With so sweet sence° and secret power unspide,   *sensation*
That in her pregnant flesh they shortly fructifide.°   *bore fruit*

8

Miraculous may seeme to him, that reades
    So straunge ensample of conceptiön;
    But reason teacheth that the fruitfull seades
    Of all things living, through impressiön
    Of the sunbeames in moyst complexiön,
    Doe life conceive and quickned are by kynd:°   *nature*
    So after Nilus° inundatiön,   *the Nile's*
    Infinite shapes of creatures men do fynd,
Informèd in° the mud, on which the Sunne hath shynd.[9]   *formed within*

9

Great father he of generatiön
    Is rightly cald, th'author of life and light;
    And his faire sister for creatiön
    Ministreth matter fit, which tempred right
    With heate and humour,° breedes the living wight.[1]   *bodily fluid*
    So sprong these twinnes in wombe of Chrysogone,
    Yet wist° she nought thereof, but sore affright,°   *knew / afraid*
    Wondred to see her belly so upblone,
Which still increast, till she her terme had full outgone.

10

Whereof conceiving shame and foule disgrace,
    Albe° her guiltlesse consciënce her cleard,   *albeit*
    She fled into the wildernesse a space,°   *for a time*
    Till that unweeldy burden she had reard,°   *brought forth*
    And shund dishonor, which as death she feard:

8. The sun. The first Greek sun god, Helios, was descended from the Titans.
9. The theory that life was spontaneously generated by the sun's influence on the moist earth is drawn from Ovid and Lucretius.

1. Creature. The moon (the sun's "sister") is thought to furnish ("ministreth") matter for the creation of life through its control of mortal bodies, especially women's.

Where wearie of long travell,[2] downe to rest
  Her selfe she set, and comfortably cheard;[3]
  There a sad° cloud of sleepe her overkest,°   *heavy / overcast*
And seizèd every sense with sorrow sore opprest.

II

It fortunèd,° faire Venus having lost   *chanced*
  Her little sonne, the wingèd god of love,
  Who for some light° displeasure, which him crost,°   *trivial / thwarted*
  Was from her fled, as flit as ayerie Dove,[4]
  And left her blisfull bowre of joy above,
  (So from her often he had fled away,
  When she for ought° him sharpely did reprove,   *aught; anything*
  And wandred in the world in strange aray,°   *attire*
Disguiz'd in thousand shapes, that none might him bewray.°) *discover*

12

Him for to seeke, she left her heavenly hous,
  The house of goodly formes and faire aspects,[5]
  Whence all the world derives the glorious
  Features of beautie, and all shapes select,°   *choice*
  With which high God his workmanship hath deckt;°   *adorned*
  And searchèd every way, through which his wings
  Had borne him, or° his tract° she mote° detect: *ere / track / might*
  She promist kisses sweet, and sweeter things
Unto the man, that of him tydings to her brings.

13

First she him sought in Court, where most he used
  Whylome° to haunt,° but there she found him not;   *formerly / resort*
  But many there she found, which sore accused
  His falsehood, and with foule infamous blot
  His cruell deedes and wicked wyles did spot:°   *vilify*
  Ladies and Lords she every where mote heare
  Complayning, how with his empoysned shot
  Their wofull harts he wounded had whyleare,°   *a while before*
And so had left them languishing twixt hope and feare.

14

She then the Citties sought from gate to gate,
  And every one did aske, did he him see;
  And every one her answerd, that too late
  He had him seene, and felt the crueltie
  Of his sharpe darts and whot artillerie;°   *hot weapons*
  And every one threw forth reproches rife°   *numerous*
  Of his mischievous deedes, and said, That hee

2. Also travail (labor; i.e., that of childbirth).
3. I.e., weary of her long travels she sat down to rest and was cheered by that comfort.
4. Venus's bird. Venus's search for the lost Cupid
is based on a Greek poem by Moschus (2nd century B.C.E.), often imitated in the Renaissance.
5. Astrological aspects of the planet Venus.

Was the disturber of all civill life,
The enimy of peace, and author of all strife.

15

Then in the countrey she abroad him sought,
   And in the rurall cottages inquired,
   Where also many plaints to her were brought,
   How he their heedlesse harts with love had fyred,
   And his false venim through their veines inspyred;°   *breathed*
   And eke° the gentle shepheard swaynes,° which sat   *also / lovers*
   Keeping their fleecie flockes, as they were hyred,
   She sweetly heard complaine, both how and what
Her sonne had to them doen; yet she did smile thereat.

16

But when in none of all these she him got,
   She gan avize,° where else he mote him hyde: *consider*
   At last she her bethought, that she had not
   Yet sought the salvage° woods and forrests wyde,   *wild*
   In which full many lovely Nymphes abyde,
   Mongst whom might be, that he did closely lye,
   Or that the love of some of them him tyde:°   *bound*
   For thy° she thither cast° her course t'apply,   *therefore / resolved*
To search the secret haunts of Dianes company.

17

Shortly unto the wastefull° woods she came,   *desolate*
   Whereas she found the Goddesse with her crew,
   After late chace of their embrewèd° game,   *bloodstained*
   Sitting beside a fountaine in a rew,°   *row*
   Some of them washing with the liquid dew
   From off their dainty limbes the dustie sweat,
   And soyle which did deforme their lively hew;
   Others lay shaded from the scorching heat;
The rest upon her person gave attendance great.[6]

18

She having hong upon a bough on high
   Her bow and painted quiver, had unlaste°   *unlaced*
   Her silver buskins° from her nimble thigh,   *boots*
   And her lancke loynes° ungirt, and brests unbraste,   *slender waist*
   After her heat the breathing cold to taste;
   Her golden lockes, that late in tresses bright
   Embreaded were for hindring of her haste,[7]
   Now loose about her shoulders hong undight,°   *unbound*
And were with sweet Ambrosia° all besprinckled light.   *perfume*

---

6. This episode alludes to the myth of Actaeon, who angered the virgin goddess Diana by surprising her in her bath; she transformed him into a stag, and he was torn apart by his own hounds.
7. I.e., her golden locks were braided ("embreaded"), lest they should hinder her swiftness.

19

Soone as she Venus saw behind her backe,
    She was ashamed to be so loose surprized,
    And woxe° halfe wroth against her damzels slacke,   *waxed, grew*
    That had not her thereof before avized,[8]
    But suffred her so carelesly disguized°   *undressed*
    Be overtaken. Soone her garments loose
    Upgath'ring, in her bosome she comprized,°   *drew together*
    Well as she might, and to the Goddesse rose,
Whiles all her Nymphes did like a girlond her enclose.

20

Goodly° she gan faire Cytherea[9] greet,   *courteously*
    And shortly askèd her, what cause her brought
    Into that wildernesse for her unmeet,°   *unsuitable*
    From her sweete bowres, and beds with pleasures fraught:
    That suddein change she strange adventure° thought.   *chance*
    To whom halfe weeping, she thus answerèd,
    That she her dearest sonne Cupido sought,
    Who in his frowardnesse° from her was fled;   *stubbornness*
That she repented sore, to have him angerèd.

21

Thereat Diana gan to smile, in scorne
    Of her vaine plaint, and to her scoffing sayd;
    "Great pittie sure, that ye be so forlorne°   *bereft*
    Of your gay sonne, that gives ye so good ayd
    To your disports: ill mote ye bene apayd."[1]
    But she was more engrievèd, and replide;
    "Faire sister, ill beseemes it to upbrayd
    A dolefull heart with so disdainfull pride;
The like that mine, may be your paine another tide.°   *time*

22

"As you in woods and wanton wildernesse
    Your glory set, to chace the salvage beasts,
    So my delight is all in joyfulnesse,
    In beds, in bowres, in banckets,° and in feasts: *banquets*
    And ill becomes you with your loftie creasts,°   *helmets*
    To scorne the joy, that Jove is glad to seeke;
    We both are bound to follow heavens beheasts,
    And tend our charges° with obeisance meeke: *duties*
Spare, gentle sister, with reproch my paine to eeke.°   *augment*

8. I.e., she was half-angered at her nymphs, who
were remiss in not warning her (of Venus's presence).
9. Venus, so named in allusion to her emergence

from the sea near the island of Cythera.
1. I.e., your son aids you in your bad sports; may
you be repaid in kind by this ill trick he plays
on you.

23

"And tell me, if that ye my sonne have heard,
    To lurk emongst your Nymphes in secret wize;
    Or keepe their cabins: much I am affeard,   *caves*
    Least° he like one of them him selfe disguize,   *lest*
    And turne his arrowes to their exercize:[2]
    So may he long himselfe full easie hide:
    For he is faire and fresh in face and guize,
    As any Nymph (let not it be envyde.°)"   *begrudged*
So saying every Nymph full narrowly she eyde.

24

But Phoebe° therewith sore was angerèd,   *another name for Diana*
    And sharply said; "Goe Dame, goe seeke your boy,
    Where you him lately left, in Mars his bed;[3]
    He comes not here, we scorne his foolish joy,
    Ne lend we leisure to his idle toy:°   *game*
    But if I catch him in this company,
    By Stygian lake I vow, whose sad annoy°   *grievous affliction*
    The Gods doe dread,[4] he dearely shall abye:°   *suffer*
Ile clip his wanton wings, that he no more shall fly."

25

Whom when as Venus saw so sore displeased,
    She inly° sory was, and gan relent,°   *inwardly / soften*
    What she had said: so her she soone appeased,
    With sugred words and gentle blandishment,[5]
    Which as a fountaine from her sweet lips went,
    And wellèd goodly forth, that in short space
    She was well pleasd, and forth her damzels sent,
    Through all the woods, to search from place to place,
If any tract° of him or tydings they mote trace.   *track*

26

To search the God of love, her Nymphes she sent
    Throughout the wandring forrest every where:
    And after them her selfe eke° with her went   *also*
    To seeke the fugitive, both farre and nere.
    So long they sought, till they arrivèd were
    In that same shadie covert,° whereas lay   *thicket*
    Faire Crysogone in slombry traunce whilere:° *a while before*
    Who in her sleepe (a wondrous thing to say)
Unwares had borne two babes, as faire as springing° day. *dawning*

2. I.e., he may shoot his arrows disguised as one of Diana's hunting nymphs (also, he may shoot at them, causing them to fall in love).
3. Referring to Venus's love affair with Mars.

4. An oath sworn on the river Styx even the gods feared to break.
5. In making peace with her opposite, Venus here enacts one of her traditional roles, Concord.

27

Unwares she them conceived, unwares she bore:
   She bore withouten paine, that° she conceived   *what*
   Withouten pleasure: ne her need° implore   *nor did she need to*
   Lucinaes[6] aide: which when they both perceived,
   They were through wonder nigh of sense bereaved,
   And gazing each on other, nought bespake:
   At last they both agreed, her seeming grieved°   *oppressed (with sleep)*
   Out of her heavy swowne not to awake,
But from her loving side the tender babes to take.

28

Up they them tooke, each one a babe uptooke,
   And with them carried, to be fosterèd;
   Dame Phoebe to a Nymph her babe betooke,°   *gave in charge*
   To be upbrought in perfect Maydenhed,°   *virginity*
   And of her selfe her name Belphoebe red:°   *called*
   But Venus hers thence farre away convayd,
   To be upbrought in goodly womanhed,
   And in her litle loves stead, which was strayd,
Her Amoretta[7] cald, to comfort her dismayd.

29

She brought her to her joyous Paradize,
   Where most she wonnes,° when she on earth does dwel.   *dwells*
   So faire a place, as Nature can devize:
   Whether in Paphos, or Cytheron hill,
   Or it in Gnidus be, I wote not well;[8]
   But well I wote° by tryall,° that this same   *know / experience*
   All other pleasant places doth excell,
   And callèd is by her lost lovers name,
The Gardin of Adonis,[9] farre renowmd by fame.

30

In that same Gardin all the goodly flowres,
   Wherewith dame Nature doth her beautifie,
   And decks the girlonds° of her paramoures,°   *garlands / lovers*
   Are fetcht: there is the first seminarie°   *seedbed*
   Of all things, that are borne to live and die,
   According to their kindes.° Long worke it were,   *species*
   Here to account° the endlesse progenie   *recount*
   Of all the weedes,° that bud and blossome there;   *plants*
But so much as doth need, must needs be counted° here.   *recounted*

---

6. Lucina is another name for Juno (or sometimes Diana) as goddess of childbirth.
7. Because she takes the place of Cupid (Amor),
she is named Amoretta, "a little love."

8. These are all shrines of Venus.
9. The beautiful young hunter Adonis, passionately loved by Venus, was, in the standard version
of the myth, killed by a boar.

31

It sited° was in fruitfull soyle of old,   *placed*
 And girt in with two walles on either side;
 The one of yron, the other of bright gold,
 That none might thorough breake, nor over-stride:
 And double gates it had, which opened wide,
 By which both in and out men moten° pas;   *might*
 Th'one faire and fresh, the other old and dride:
 Old Geniüs[1] the porter of them was,
Old Geniüs, the which a double nature has.

32

He letteth in, he letteth out to wend,°   *go*
 All that to come into the world desire;
 A thousand thousand naked babes attend
 About him day and night, which doe require,
 That he with fleshly weedes would them attire:[2]
 Such as him list,° such as eternall fate   *as he chooses*
 Ordainèd hath, he clothes with sinfull mire,° *earth*
 And sendeth forth to live in mortall state,
Till they againe returne backe by the hinder gate.

33

After that they againe returnèd beene,
 They in that Gardin planted be againe;
 And grow afresh, as° they had never seene   *as if*
 Fleshly corruptiön, nor mortall paine.
 Some thousand yeares so doen they there remaine;
 And then of him are clad with other hew,°   *form*
 Or sent into the chaungefull world againe,
 Till thither they returne, where first they grew:
So like a wheele around they runne from old to new.[3]

34

Ne° needs there Gardiner to set, or sow,   *neither*
 To plant or prune: for of their owne accord
 All things, as they created were, doe grow,
 And yet remember well the mightie word,
 Which first was spoken by th'Almightie lord,
 That bad them to increase and multiply:[4]
 Ne° doe they need with water of the ford,° *nor / stream*
 Or of the clouds to moysten their roots dry;
For in themselves eternall moisture they imply.° *contain*

---

1. God of generation and so of the natural processes birth and death. The Garden of Adonis is a myth of Spenser's devising.
2. I.e., the souls in their preexistent state ("naked babes") request to be clothed with flesh.

3. The original source for Spenser's myth of cyclic generation and reincarnation is Plato's *Republic* 10 (the myth of Er).
4. "And God said unto them, Be fruitful, and multiply, and replenish the earth" (Genesis 1.28).

35

Infinite shapes of creatures there are bred,
 And uncouth° formes, which none yet ever knew,   *strange*
 And every sort is in a sundry° bed   *separate*
 Set by it selfe, and ranckt in comely rew:°   *row*
 Some fit for reasonable soules t'indew,[5]
 Some made for beasts, some made for birds to weare,
 And all the fruitfull spawne of fishes hew°   *shape*
 In endlesse rancks along enraungèd° were,   *arranged*
That seem'd the Oceän could not containe them there.

36

Daily they grow, and daily forth are sent
 Into the world, it to replenish more;
 Yet is the stocke not lessenèd, nor spent,
 But still remaines in everlasting store,°   *abundance*
 As it at first created was of yore.
 For in the wide wombe of the world there lyes,
 In hatefull darkenesse and in deepe horrore,
 An huge eternall Chaos,[6] which supplyes
The substances of natures fruitfull progenyes.

37

All things from thence doe their first being fetch,
 And borrow matter, whereof they are made,
 Which when as forme and feature it does ketch,°   *take*
 Becomes a bodie and doth then invade°   *enter*
 The state of life,[7] out of the griesly° shade.   *ghastly*
 That substance° is eterne, and bideth so,   *matter*
 Ne when the life decayes, and forme does fade,
 Doth it consume,° and into nothing go,   *is it destroyed*
But chaungèd is, and often altred to and fro.

38

The substance is not chaunged, nor alterèd,
 But th'only forme° and outward fashiön;   *except only the form*
 For every substance is conditionèd
 To change her hew,° and sundry formes to don,   *appearance*
 Meet° for her temper and complexiön: *suited*
 For formes are variable and decay,
 By course of kind,° and by occasiön;   *nature*
 And that faire flowre of beautie fades away,
As doth the lilly fresh before the sunny ray.

---

5. I.e., some of these shapes are fit for humans to assume. An echo of 1 Corinthians 15.39: "All flesh is not the same flesh: but there is one kind of flesh of men, another flesh of beasts, another of fishes, and another of birds."
6. The shapeless primeval matter that, in both classical and Christian traditions, supplies the material for all created things (see, e.g., Ovid, *Metamorphoses* 1.5–20, and Genesis 1–2).
7. An Aristotelian idea: living beings consist of matter animated and shaped by a form or soul.

39

Great enimy to it, and to all the rest,
   That in the Gardin of Adonis springs,
   Is wicked Time, who with his scyth addrest,°   *armed*
   Does mow the flowring herbes and goodly things,
   And all their glory to the ground downe flings,
   Where they doe wither, and are fowly mard:°   *marred*
   He flyes about, and with his flaggy° wings   *drooping*
   Beates downe both leaves and buds without regard,
Ne ever pittie may relent° his malice hard.   *soften*

40

Yet pittie often did the gods relent,
   To see so faire things mard, and spoylèd quight:°   *quite*
   And their great mother Venus did lament
   The losse of her deare brood, her deare delight;
   Her hart was pierst with pittie at the sight,
   When walking through the Gardin, them she spyde,
   Yet no'te° she find redresse for such despight.°   *could not / wrong*
   For all that lives, is subject to that law:
All things decay in time, and to their end do draw.

41

But were it not, that Time their troubler is,
   All that in this delightfull Gardin growes,
   Should happie be, and have immortall blis:
   For here all plentie, and all pleasure flowes,
   And sweet love gentle fits° emongst them throwes,   *i.e., fits of passion*
   Without fell° rancor, or fond° gealosie;   *fierce / foolish*
   Franckly each paramour his leman knowes,[8]
   Each bird his mate, ne any does envie
Their goodly meriment, and gay felicitie.

42

There is continuall spring, and harvest there[9]
   Continuall, both meeting at one time:
   For both the boughes doe laughing blossomes beare,
   And with fresh colours decke the wanton Prime,°   *spring*
   And eke attonce the heavy trees they clime,
   Which seeme to labour under their fruits lode:
   The whiles the joyous birdes make their pastime
   Emongst the shadie leaves, their sweet abode,
And their true loves without suspition° tell abrode.   *fear*

---

8. Openly each lover has intercourse with ("knowes") his mistress.
9. The coincidence of spring and autumn is char-acteristic of unfallen nature in Eden; other fea-tures of this description are drawn from a common literary topic, the *locus amoenus* (pleasant place).

43

Right in the middest of that Paradise,
    There stood a stately Mount,[1] on whose round top
    A gloomy° grove of mirtle trees[2] did rise,   *dark, shady*
    Whose shadie boughes sharpe steele did never lop,
    Nor wicked beasts their tender buds did crop,
    But like a girlond compassèd the hight,
    And from their fruitfull sides sweet gum did drop,
    That all the ground with precious deaw bedight,°   *bedecked*
Threw forth most dainty odours, and most sweet delight.

44

And in the thickest covert of that shade,
    There was a pleasant arbour, not by art,
    But of the trees owne inclination° made,   *inclining*
    Which knitting their rancke° braunches part to part,   *dense*
    With wanton yvie twyne entrayld athwart,[3]
    And Eglantine, and Caprifole° emong,   *honeysuckle*
    Fashiond above within their inmost part,
    That nether Phoebus beams could through them throng,°   *press*
Nor Aeolus° sharp blast could worke them any wrong.   *god of winds*

45

And all about grew every sort° of flowre,   *species*
    To which sad lovers were transformd of yore;
    Fresh Hyacinthus, Phoebus paramoure,
    And dearest love,[4]
    Foolish Narcisse, that likes the watry shore,
    Sad Amaranthus, made a flowre but late,°   *only recently*
    Sad Amaranthus, in whose purple gore
    Me seemes I see Amintas wretched fate,
To whom sweet Poets verse hath given endlesse date.[5]

46

There wont° faire Venus often to enjoy   *was accustomed*
    Her deare Adonis joyous company,
    And reape sweet pleasure of the wanton boy;
    There yet, some say, in secret he does ly,
    Lappèd in flowres and pretious spycery,°   *spices*
    By her hid from the world, and from the skill°   *knowledge*
    Of Stygian Gods,[6] which doe her love envy;

---

1. With allusion to the *mons veneris*.
2. Myrtle trees were sacred to Venus.
3. I.e., with luxuriant ivy entwined among them.
4. This quatrain is damaged—in rhyme pattern as well as in the truncated fourth line.
5. The purple Amaranthus is a symbol of immortality; the Greek name means "unfading." By one poetic account, Amintas died for the love of Phillis and was transformed into the Amaranthus. Hyacinth and Narcissus were also transformed into flowers and thereby eternized.
6. Gods of the underworld (e.g., Pluto, Hecate, the Furies, Charon), who have a claim on Adonis because, in the usual formulation of the myth, he was killed by the boar.

But she her selfe, when ever that she will,
Possesseth° him, and of his sweetnesse takes her fill.   *i.e., sexually*

47

And sooth° it seemes they say: for he may° not   *truth / can*
   For ever die, and ever buried bee
   In balefull night, where all things are forgot;
   All° be he subject to mortalitie,   *although*
   Yet is eterne in mutabilitie,
   And by succession made perpetuall,
   Transformèd oft, and chaungèd diverslie:
   For him the Father of all formes they call;[7]
Therefore needs mote° he live, that living gives to all.   *must*

48

There now he liveth in eternall blis,
   Joying° his goddesse, and of her enjoyd: *enjoying*
   Ne feareth he henceforth that foe of his,
   Which with his cruell tuske him deadly cloyd:°   *gored*
   For that wilde Bore, the which him once annoyd,°   *injured*
   She firmely hath emprisonèd for ay,°   *forever*
   That her sweet love his malice mote° avoyd,   *might*
   In a strong rocky Cave, which is they say,
Hewen underneath that Mount, that none him losen° may.   *set free*

49

There now he lives in everlasting joy,
   With many of the Gods in company,
   Which thither haunt,° and with the wingèd boy   *frequent*
   Sporting himselfe in safe felicity:
   Who when he[8] hath with spoiles° and cruelty   *plundering*
   Ransackt the world, and in the wofull harts
   Of many wretches set his triumphes hye,
   Thither resorts, and laying his sad darts°   *arrows*
Aside, with faire Adonis playes his wanton parts.

50

And his true love faire Psyche with him playes,[9]
   Faire Psyche to him lately reconcyld,
   After long troubles and unmeet upbrayes,[1]
   With which his mother Venus her revyld,°   *reviled*
   And eke himselfe her cruelly exyld:
   But now in stedfast love and happy state
   She with him lives, and hath him borne a chyld,

7. Adonis imposes successive forms on enduring substance and thereby brings living creatures into being.
8. Cupid, now restored to Venus.
9. Suggests, as well, sexual play. Cupid abandoned Psyche when she disobeyed his command not to look on his face; she became his bride, and immortal, after enduring many severe trials imposed by Venus. The myth was often read as an allegory of the soul's trials in this life before it gains heaven.
1. Unfitting upbraidings or scoldings.

So he surpassèd his sex masculine,
   In beastly use that I did ever find;
   Whom when as Britomart beheld behind
   The fearefull boy so greedily pursew,
   She was emmovèd in her noble mind,
   T'employ her puissaunce° to his reskew,   *power*
And prickèd° fiercely forward, where she him did vew.   *spurred*

5

Ne was Sir Satyrane her far behinde,
   But with like fiercenesse did ensew° the chace: *follow*
   Whom when the Gyaunt saw, he soone resinde°   *resigned*
   His former suit, and from them fled apace;
   They after both, and boldly bad him bace,°   *challenged him*
   And each did strive the other to out-goe,
   But he them both outran a wondrous space,
   For he was long, and swift as any Roe,°   *female deer*
And now made better speed, t'escape his fearèd foe.

6

It was not Satyrane, whom he did feare,
   But Britomart the flowre of chastity;
   For he the powre of chast hands might not beare,
   But alwayes did their dread encounter fly:
   And now so fast his feet he did apply,°   *direct*
   That he has gotten to a forrest neare,
   Where he is shrowded in security.
   The wood they enter, and search every where,
They searchèd diversely,° so both divided were.   *in different directions*

7

Faire Britomart so long him followèd,
   That she at last came to a fountaine sheare,°   *clear*
   By which there lay a knight all wallowèd°   *lying prostrate*
   Upon the grassy ground, and by him neare
   His haberjeon,° his helmet, and his speare;   *coat of mail*
   A little off, his shield was rudely throwne,
   On which the wingèd boy° in colours cleare   *Cupid*
   Depeincted° was, full easie to be knowne,   *depicted*
And he thereby, where ever it in field was showne.[8]

8

His face upon the ground did groveling° ly,   *prone*
   As if he had bene slombring in the shade,
   That the brave Mayd would not for courtesy,
   Out of his quiet slomber him abrade,°   *arouse*
   Nor seeme too suddeinly him to invade:°   *intrude on*

---

8. The knight's shield implies that he is the Sir Scudamore (Italian *scudo* + *amore*: "shield of love")
mentioned in the prefatory quatrain.

Still° as she stood, she heard with grievous throb   *ever*
Him grone, as if his hart were peeces made,
And with most painefull pangs to sigh and sob,
That pitty did the Virgins hart of patience rob.

9

At last forth breaking into bitter plaintes
  He said, "O soveraigne Lord that sit'st on hye,
  And raignst in blis emongst thy blessèd Saintes,
  How suffrest thou such shamefull cruelty,
  So long unwreakèd° of thine enimy?   *unrevenged*
  Or hast thou, Lord, of good mens cause no heed?
  Or doth thy justice sleepe, and silent ly?
  What booteth° then the good and righteous deed,   *what is the use of*
If goodnesse find no grace, nor righteousnesse no meed?°   *reward*

10

"If good find grace, and righteousnesse reward,
  Why then is Amoret in caytive band,°   *captive bond*
  Sith° that more bounteous° creature never fared   *since / virtuous*
  On foot, upon the face of living land?
  Or if that heavenly justice may withstand
  The wrongfull outrage of unrighteous men,
  Why then is Busirane⁹ with wicked hand
  Suffred,° these seven monethes day in secret den   *permitted*
My Lady and my love so cruëlly to pen?

11

"My Lady and my love is cruelly pend
  In dolefull darkenesse from the vew of day,
  Whilest deadly torments do her chast brest rend,
  And the sharpe steele doth rive° her hart in tway,°   *cut / two*
  All for° she Scudamore will not denay.°   *because / deny*
  Yet thou vile man, vile Scudamore art sound,
  Ne° canst her ayde, ne° canst her foe dismay;°   *neither / nor / defeat*
  Unworthy wretch to tread upon the ground,
For whom so faire a Lady feeles so sore a wound."

12

There an huge heape of singulfes° did oppresse   *sobs*
  His strugling soule, and swelling throbs empeach°   *hinder*
  His foltring toung with pangs of drerinesse,°   *anguish*
  Choking the remnant of his plaintife speach,
  As if his dayes were come to their last reach.
  Which when she heard, and saw the ghastly fit,
  Threatning into his life to make a breach,

---

9. His name associates him with Busiris, an Egyptian king famous for his cruelty and identified with the Pharaoh of Exodus; hence he is a symbol of tyranny.

Both with great ruth° and terrour she was smit,   *pity*
Fearing least° from her cage the wearie soule would flit.   *lest*

13

Tho° stooping downe she him amovèd° light;   *then / touched*
  Who therewith somewhat starting, up gan looke,
  And seeing him behind a straunger knight,
  Whereas no living creature he mistooke,°   *thought to be*
  With great indignaunce he that sight forsooke,
  And downe againe himselfe disdainefully
  Abjecting, th'earth with his faire forhead strooke:
  Which the bold Virgin seeing, gan apply
Fit medcine to his griefe, and spake thus courtesly.

14

"Ah gentle knight, whose deepe conceivèd griefe
  Well seemes t'exceede the powre of patiënce,
  Yet if that heavenly grace some good reliefe
  You send, submit you to high providence,
  And ever in your noble hart prepense,°   *consider before*
  That all the sorrow in the world is lesse,
  Then vertues might, and values° confidence,   *valor's*
  For who nill° bide the burden of distresse,   *will not*
Must not here thinke to live: for life is wretchednesse.

15

"Therefore, faire Sir, do comfort to you take,
  And freely read,° what wicked felon so   *tell*
  Hath outraged you, and thrald° your gentle make.° *enslaved / beloved*
  Perhaps this hand may helpe to ease your woe,
  And wreake° your sorrow on your cruell foe,   *revenge*
  At least it faire endevour will apply."
  Those feeling wordes so neare the quicke° did goe,   *heart*
  That up his head he rearèd easily,°   *readily*
And leaning on his elbow, these few wordes let fly.

16

"What boots it plaine, that cannot be redrest,[1]
  And sow vaine sorrow in a fruitlesse eare,
  Sith powre of hand, nor skill of learnèd brest,
  Ne worldly price cannot redeeme my deare,
  Out of her thraldome° and continuall feare?   *slavery*
  For he the tyraunt, which her hath in ward°   *in his power*
  By strong enchauntments and blacke Magicke leare,°   *lore*
  Hath in a dungeon deepe her close embard,
And many dreadfull feends hath pointed° to her gard.   *appointed*

---

1. What is the use of complaining for what cannot be helped?

17

"There he tormenteth her most terribly,
 And day and night afflicts with mortall paine,
 Because to yield him love she doth deny,
 Once to me yold,° not to be yold againe:[2]   *yielded*
 But yet by torture he would her constraine
 Love to conceive in her disdainfull brest;
 Till so she do, she must in doole° remaine,   *dole, pain*
 Ne may by living meanes be thence relest:
What boots it then to plaine, that cannot be redrest?"

18

With this sad hersall° of his heavy stresse,° *rehearsal; tale / affliction*
 The warlike Damzell was empassiond sore,
 And said, "Sir knight, your cause is nothing lesse,
 Then° is your sorrow, certès if not more;[3]   *than*
 For nothing so much pitty doth implore,
 As gentle Ladies helplesse misery.
 But yet, if please ye listen to my lore,°   *teaching*
 I will with proofe of last extremity,[4]
Deliver her fro thence, or with her for you dy."

19

"Ah gentlest° knight alive," said Scudamore,   *noblest*
 "What huge heroicke magnanimity[5]
 Dwels in thy bounteous brest? what couldst thou more,
 If she were thine, and thou as now am I?
 O spare thy happy dayes, and them apply
 To better boot,° but let me dye, that ought;   *use*
 More is more losse: one is enough to dy."
 "Life is not lost," said she, "for which is bought
Endlesse renowm, that more then death is to be sought."

20

Thus she at length perswaded him to rise,
 And with her wend,° to see what new successe   *go*
 Mote° him befall upon new enterprise;   *might*
 His armes, which he had vowed to disprofesse,° *renounce*
 She gathered up and did about him dresse,° *array*
 And his forwandred° steed unto him got: *wandered away*
 So forth they both yfere° make their progresse, *together*
 And march not past the mountenaunce of a shot,
Till they arrived, whereas their purpose they did plot.[6]

---

2. Scudamore's courtship and winning of Amoret as his love was recounted in canto 4, stanza 10.
3. I.e., certainly ("certès") your cause is worthy of your great sorrow, or even more.
4. I.e., at the extreme peril of my life.

5. Nobility of mind, which produces the highest virtues and the greatest deeds.
6. I.e., they went no farther than the distance of a bow shot before they arrived at the place they purposed to go.

21

There they dismounting, drew their weapons bold
   And stoutly° came unto the Castle gate;   *bravely*
   Whereas no gate they found, them to withhold,
   Nor ward° to wait at morne and evening late,   *guard*
   But in the Porch, that did them sore amate,°   *dismay*
   A flaming fire, ymixt with smouldry smoke,
   And stinking Sulphure, that with griesly° hate   *horrid*
   And dreadfull horrour did all entraunce choke,
Enforcèd them their forward footing to revoke.°   *draw back*

22

Greatly thereat was Britomart dismayd,
   Ne in that stownd wist,[7] how her selfe to beare;
   For daunger vaine it were, to have assayd°   *attempted*
   That cruell element, which all things feare,
   Ne none can suffer to approchen neare:
   And turning backe to Scudamour, thus sayd;
   "What monstrous enmity provoke° we heare,   *challenge*
   Foolhardy as th'Earthes children, the which made
Battell against the Gods?[8] so we a God invade.

23

"Daunger without discretion to attempt,
   Inglorious and beastlike is: therefore Sir knight,
   Aread° what course of you is safest dempt,°   *declare / deemed*
   And how we with our foe may come to fight."
   "This is," quoth he, "the dolorous despight,°   *evil*
   Which earst° to you I playnd:° for neither may *earlier / complained of*
   This fire be quencht by any wit or might,
   Ne yet by any meanes remov'd away,
So mighty be th'enchauntments, which the same do stay.° *maintain*

24

"What is there else, but cease these fruitlesse paines,
   And leave me to my former languishing?
   Faire Amoret must dwell in wicked chaines,
   And Scudamore here dye with sorrowing."
   "Perdy° not so," said she, "for shamefull thing   *truly*
   It were t'abandon noble chevisaunce,°   *chivalric enterprise*
   For shew of perill, without venturing:
   Rather let try extremities of chaunce,
Then enterprisèd prayse for dread to disavaunce."[9]

7. I.e., nor in that trouble ("stownd") did she
know ("wist") what to do.
8. I.e., we are like the Titans who dared to do
battle against the Olympian gods.

9. I.e., it is better to chance extreme danger than
retreat from praiseworthy enterprises because of
fear.

25

Therewith resolv'd to prove her utmost might,
  Her ample shield she threw before her face,
  And her swords point directing forward right,
  Assayld the flame, the which eftsoones° gave place,   *immediately*
  And did it selfe divide with equall space,°   *equally on both sides*
  That through she passèd; as a thunder bolt
  Perceth the yielding ayre, and doth displace
  The soring clouds into sad showres ymolt;°   *melted*
So to her yold° the flames, and did their force revolt.° *yielded / turn back*

26

Whom whenas Scudamour saw past the fire,
  Safe and untoucht, he likewise gan assay,°   *attempt*
  With greedy will, and envious desire,
  And bad° the stubborne flames to yield him way: *bade*
  But cruell Mulciber° would not obay   *god of fire*
  His threatfull pride, but did the more augment
  His mighty rage, and with imperious sway°   *power*
  Him forst (maulgre)° his fiercenesse to relent,° *nevertheless / give way*
And backe retire, all scorcht and pitifully brent.

27

With huge impatiënce he inly swelt,°   *inwardly burned*
  More for great sorrow, that he could not pas,
  Then for the burning torment, which he felt,
  That with fell woodnesse he effiercèd was,[1]
  And wilfully him throwing on the gras,
  Did beat and bounse° his head and brest full sore;   *thump*
  The whiles the Championesse now entred has
  The utmost° rowme, and past the formest° dore *outermost / foremost*
The utmost rowme, abounding with all precious store.°   *goods*

28

For round about, the wals yclothèd were
  With goodly arras° of great majesty,   *tapestries*
  Woven with gold and silke so close and nere,°   *tight*
  That the rich metall lurkèd privily,°   *secretly*
  As faining° to be hid from envious eye;   *enjoying*
  Yet here, and there, and every where unwares°   *unexpectedly*
  It shewd it selfe, and shone unwillingly;
  Like a discolourd° Snake, whose hidden snares   *multicolored*
Through the greene gras his long bright burnisht backe declares.

29

And in those Tapets° weren fashionèd   *tapestries*
  Many faire pourtraicts, and many a faire feate,

---

1. I.e., he was maddened with fierce fury.

And all of love, and all of lusty-hed,
As seemèd by their semblaunt did entreat;[2]
And eke° all Cupids warres they did repeate,°   *also / recount*
And cruell battels, which he whilome° fought   *formerly*
Gainst all the Gods, to make his empire great;
Besides the huge massacres, which he wrought
On mighty kings and kesars,° into thraldome brought.   *caesars*

30

Therein was writ,° how often thundring Jove   *woven*
  Had felt the point of his hart-percing dart,
  And leaving heavens kingdome, here did rove
  In straunge disguize, to slake his scalding smart;
  Now like a Ram, faire Helle to pervart,
  Now like a Bull, Europa to withdraw:[3]
  Ah, how the fearefull Ladies tender hart
  Did lively° seeme to tremble, when she saw   *lifelike*
The huge seas under her t'obay her servaunts° law.   *lover's*

31

Soone after that into a golden showre
  Him selfe he chaunged faire Danaë to vew,
  And through the roofe of her strong brasen towre
  Did raine into her lap an hony dew,[4]
  The whiles her foolish garde, that little knew
  Of such deceipt, kept th'yron dore fast bard,
  And watcht, that none should enter nor issew;°   *go out*
  Vaine was the watch, and bootlesse° all the ward,   *useless*
Whenas the God to golden hew him selfe transfard.[5]

32

Then was he turnd into a snowy Swan,
  To win faire Leda to his lovely° trade:[6]   *loving*
  O wondrous skill, and sweet wit° of the man,   *ingenuity*
  That her in daffadillies sleeping made,
  From scorching heat her daintie limbes to shade:
  Whiles the proud Bird ruffing° his fethers wyde,   *ruffling*
  And brushing° his faire brest, did her invade;   *preening*
  She slept, yet twixt her eyelids closely° spyde,   *secretly*
How towards her he rusht, and smilèd at his pryde.°   *sexual desire*

33

Then shewd it, how the Thebane Semelee
  Deceived of gealous Juno, did require

2. I.e., the pictures ("pourtraicts") seemed, by their appearance ("semblaunt"), to treat entirely of deeds of love and merriment ("lusty-hed").
3. A golden ram (not specifically identified in legend as Jove) came to carry away ("pervart") Helle from the fury of her stepmother, Ino. Jove assumed the shape of a bull to seduce Europa and carried her over the seas.
4. In another part of the tapestry ("soone after") Jove is shown as a shower of gold, impregnating Danaë.
5. Transmuted himself into golden form.
6. Jove became a swan to seduce Leda.

To see him in his soveraigne majestee,
Armd with his thunderbolts and lightning fire,
Whence dearely she with death bought her desire.[7]
But faire Alcmena better match did make,
Joying his love in likenesse more entire;
Three nights in one, they say, that for her sake
He then did put, her pleasures lenger° to partake.[8]   *longer*

34

Twise was he seene in soaring Eagles shape,
   And with wide wings to beat the buxome° ayre,   *yielding*
   Once, when he with Asterie did scape,
   Againe, when as the Trojane boy so faire
   He snatcht from Ida hill, and with him bare:[9]
   Wondrous delight it was, there to behould,
   How the rude Shepheards after him did stare,
   Trembling through feare, least° down he fallen should,   *lest*
And often to him calling, to take surer hould.

35

In Satyres shape Antiopa he snatcht:
   And like a fire, when he Aegin' assayd:
   A shepheard, when Mnemosyne he catcht:
   And like a Serpent to the Thracian mayd.[1]
   Whiles thus on earth great Jove these pageaunts° playd,   *tricks*
   The wingèd boy did thrust into° his throne,   *usurped*
   And scoffing, thus unto his mother sayd,
   "Lo now the heavens obey to me alone,
And take me for their Jove, while Jove to earth is gone."

36

And thou, faire Phoebus, in thy colours bright
   Wast there enwoven, and the sad distresse,
   In which that boy thee plongèd, for despight,
   That thou bewrayedst° his mothers wantonnesse,   *revealed*
   When she with Mars was meynt° in joyfulnesse: *mingled, joined*
   For thy° he thrild° thee with a leaden dart,   *therefore / pierced*
   To love faire Daphne, which thee lovèd lesse:[2]
   Lesse she thee loved, then° was thy just desart,   *than*
Yet was thy love her death, and her death was thy smart.°   *pain*

7. Juno tricked Semele into having Jove visit her in all his glory. She was burned to death by his lightning and thunderbolts.
8. Jove visited Alcmena in the likeness of her husband, Amphitryon, and made that one night the length of three.
9. Asterie changed herself into a quail to avoid Jove's advances, but he captured her as an eagle; in that form he also snatched Ganymede, who became cupbearer to the gods.

1. Jove came as a satyr to Antiope; in fire to Aegina; as a shepherd to Mnemosyne, goddess of memory (who bore the Nine Muses); and as a serpent to Proserpina, "the Thracian mayd."
2. Two stories are combined: Apollo's punishment for revealing Venus's adultery with Mars was "the sad distresse" of doting on Leucothoe; later he chased Daphne, who escaped by metamorphosis into a laurel tree. Cupid's lead-tipped arrows produce unhappiness in love.

37

So lovedst thou the lusty° Hyacinct,   *handsome*
  So lovedst thou the faire Coronis deare:
Yet both are of° thy haplesse hand extinct,   *by*
Yet both in flowres do live, and love thee beare,
The one a Paunce, the other a sweet breare:[3]
For griefe whereof, ye mote have lively° seene   *lifelike*
The God himselfe rending his golden heare,
And breaking quite his gyrlond° ever greene,   *garland*
With other signes of sorrow and impatient teene.°   *grief*

38

Both for those two, and for his owne deare sonne,
  The sonne of Climene he did repent,
Who bold to guide the charet of the Sunne,
Himselfe in thousand peeces fondly rent,[4]
And all the world with flashing fier brent;
So like, that all the walles did seeme to flame.
Yet cruell Cupid, not herewith content,
Forst him eftsoones° to follow other game,   *soon after*
And love a Shepheards daughter for his dearest Dame.

39

He lovèd Isse for his dearest Dame,
  And for her sake her cattell fed a while,
And for her sake a cowheard vile° became,   *lowly*
The servant of Admetus cowheard vile,
Whiles that from heaven he sufferèd exile.[5]
Long were to tell each other lovely fit,°   *amorous passion*
Now like a Lyon, hunting after spoile,
Now like a Stag, now like a faulcon flit:°   *fleet*
All which, in that faire arras was most lively writ.

40

Next unto him was Neptune[6] picturèd,
  In his divine resemblance wondrous lyke:
His face was rugged, and his hoarie° hed   *gray*
Droppèd with brackish° deaw; his three-forkt Pyke   *salty*
He stearnly shooke, and therewith fierce did stryke
The raging billowes, that on every syde
They trembling stood, and made a long broad dyke,°   *trench*

3. Apollo accidentally killed his lover Hyacinth at a game of quoits and transformed him into a flower ("paunce," pansy); he killed Coronis out of jealousy, but her transformation to a sweetbriar seems to be Spenser's invention.
4. Foolishly tore apart. Phaëthon, son of Apollo and Climene, extracted permission to drive the chariot of the Sun through the heavens; unable to control the horses, he killed himself and almost burned up the world.
5. Two stories are combined: Apollo disguising himself as a shepherd to gain Isse, and serving Admetus, king of Pheres in Thessaly, as a cowherd.
6. The god of the sea; here portrayed with his trident ("three-forkt Pyke") and riding in a chariot ("charet") drawn by a team of four sea horses ("Hippodames").

That his swift charet might have passage wyde,
Which foure great Hippodames did draw in temewise tyde.°   *harnessed*

41

His sea-horses did seeme to snort amayne,°   *violently*
  And from their nosethrilles° blow the brynie streame,   *nostrils*
  That made the sparckling waves to smoke agayne,
  And flame with gold, but the white fomy creame,
  Did shine with silver, and shoot forth his beame.
  The God himselfe did pensive seeme and sad,
  And hong adowne his head, as° he did dreame: *as if*
  For privy° love his brest empiercèd had,   *secret*
Ne ought but deare Bisaltis[7] ay° could make him glad.   *ever*

42

He lovèd eke° Iphimedia deare,   *also*
  And Aeolus faire daughter Arne hight,°   *called*
  For whom he turnd him selfe into a Steare,°   *steer*
  And fed on fodder, to beguile° her sight.   *deceive*
  Also to win Deucalions daughter bright,°   *beautiful*
  He turnd him selfe into a Dolphin fayre;[8]
  And like a wingèd horse he tooke his flight,
  To snaky-locke Medusa to repayre,°   *resort*
On whom he got faire Pegasus, that flitteth in the ayre.[9]

43

Next Saturne was, (but who would ever weene,°   *think*
  That sullein Saturne ever weend° to love?   *was minded*
  Yet love is sullein,° and Saturnlike seene,   *melancholy*
  As he did for Erigone it prove,)
  That to a Centaure did him selfe transmove.
  So prooved it eke that gracious° God of wine,   *graceful*
  When for to compasse° Philliras hard love,   *gain*
  He turnd himselfe into a fruitfull vine,
And into her faire bosome made his grapes decline.[1]

44

Long were to tell the amorous assayes,°   *assaults*
  And gentle pangues, with which he° makèd meeke   *i.e., Cupid*
  The mighty Mars, to learne his wanton playes:
  How oft for Venus, and how often eek°   *also*
  For many other Nymphes he sore did shreek,
  With womanish teares, and with unwarlike smarts,°   *pains*

---

7. In Greek myth it was Bisaltes's daughter Theophane who made Neptune happy: he made love to her in the form of a ram.
8. Neptune came to Iphimedia as a flowing river, to Arne as a steer, and to Deucalion's daughter Melantho as a dolphin.
9. Neptune's ravishment of Medusa in Minerva's temple caused her hair to be turned into snakes;

she gave birth to the winged horse Pegasus.
1. Hang down. Saturn, associated with melancholy, is not usually portrayed as a lover. Spenser here transposes two myths: Saturn loved Philyra ("Philliras") not Erigone, from which union came the centaur Chiron; Bacchus ("God of wine") tricked Erigone with a false bunch of grapes.

Privily° moystening his horrid° cheek.   *secretly / bristly*
There was he painted full of burning darts,°   *arrows*
And many wide woundes launchèd° through his inner parts.   *torn*

45

Ne did he spare (so cruell was the Elfe)
  His owne deare mother, (ah why should he so?)
Ne did he spare sometime to pricke himselfe,
That he might tast the sweet consuming woe,
Which he had wrought to many others moe.°   *more*
But to declare the mournfull Tragedyes,
And spoiles,° wherewith he all the ground did strow,   *plunder*
More eath° to number, with how many eyes   *easy*
High heaven beholds sad lovers nightly theeveryes.[2]

46

Kings Queenes, Lords Ladies, Knights and Damzels gent°   *gentle*
  Were heaped together with the vulgar sort,
And mingled with the raskall rablement,°   *rabble, masses*
Without respect of person or of port,°   *position*
To shew Dan° Cupids powre and great effort:°   *master / strength*
And round about a border was entrayld,°   *woven*
Of broken bowes and arrowes shivered° short,   *splintered*
And a long bloudy river through them rayld,°   *flowed*
So lively and so like, that living sence it fayld.[3]

47

And at the upper end of that faire rowme,
  There was an Altar built of pretious stone,
Of passing° valew, and of great renowme,   *surpassing*
On which there stood an Image all alone,
Of massy° gold, which with his owne light shone;   *solid*
And wings it had with sundry colours dight,°   *adorned*
More sundry colours, then the proud Pavone°   *peacock*
Beares in his boasted fan, or Iris° bright,   *goddess of the rainbow*
When her discolourd[4] bow she spreds through heaven bright.

48

Blindfold he was, and in his cruell fist
  A mortall° bow and arrowes keene did hold,   *deadly*
With which he shot at randon, when him list,°   *when it pleased him*
Some headed with sad lead, some with pure gold;[5]
(Ah man beware, how thou those darts behold)
A wounded Dragon[6] under him did ly,
Whose hideous tayle his left foot did enfold,

2. I.e., it would be easier to number the stars ("eyes") that watch lovers' nightly exploits ("theeveryes"; i.e., thieveries) than the tragedies caused by love.
3. I.e., so animated and so lifelike that it deceived ("fayld") the senses of those looking on.

4. Multicolored.
5. Cupid, by tradition blindfolded, shoots at random ("randon"). His leaden arrows cause unhappiness in love; his golden arrows, happiness.
6. Traditionally a guard, symbolic of vigilance.

And with a shaft was shot through either eye,
That no man forth might draw, ne no man remedye.

49

And underneath his feet was written thus,
  Unto the Victor of the Gods this bee:
And all the people in that ample hous
Did to that image bow their humble knee,
And oft committed fowle Idolatree.
That wondrous sight faire Britomart amazed,
Ne seeing could her wonder satisfie,
But ever more and more upon it gazed,
The whiles the passing° brightnes her fraile sences dazed.   surpassing

50

Tho° as she backward° cast her busie eye,   then / i.e., behind the statue
  To search each secret of that goodly sted,°   place
Over the dore thus written she did spye
Be bold: she oft and oft it over-red,
Yet could not find what sence it figurèd:
But what so were therein or° writ or ment,   either
She was no whit thereby discouragèd
From prosecuting of her first intent,
But forward with bold steps into the next roome went.

51

Much fairer, then° the former, was that roome,   than
  And richlier by many partes arayd:[7]
For not with arras made in painefull° loome,   painstaking
But with pure gold it all was overlayd,
Wrought with wilde Antickes,[8] which their follies playd,
In the rich metall, as° they living were: as if
A thousand monstrous formes therein were made,
Such as false love doth oft upon him weare,
For love in thousand monstrous formes doth oft appeare.

52

And all about, the glistring° walles were hong   glittering
  With warlike spoiles, and with victorious prayes,°   prizes
Of mighty Conquerours and Captaines strong,
Which were whilome° captivèd in their dayes   formerly
To cruell love, and wrought their owne decayes:
Their swerds and speres were broke, and hauberques[9] rent;
And their proud girlonds of tryumphant bayes[1]
Troden in dust with fury insolent,
To shew the victors might and mercilesse intent.

---

7. I.e., much ("by many partes") more richly decorated ("arayd").
8. Grotesque statues.

9. Coats of mail. "Swerds": swords.
1. Wreaths of laurel ("bayes") were traditionally
awarded to great military conquerors.

53

The warlike Mayde beholding earnestly
  The goodly ordinance° of this rich place,   *ordnance, military supplies*
  Did greatly wonder, ne could satisfie
  Her greedy eyes with gazing a long space,
  But more she mervaild that no footings trace,°   *trace of footprints*
  Nor wight appear'd, but wastefull° emptinesse,   *uninhabited*
  And solemne silence over all that place:
  Straunge thing it seem'd, that none was to possesse
So rich purveyance,° ne them keepe with carefulnesse.   *furnishings*

54

And as she lookt about, she did behold,
  How over that same dore was likewise writ,
  Be bold, be bold, and every where *Be bold*,
  That much she muz'd, yet could not cónstrue it
  By any ridling skill, or commune wit.°   *common sense*
  At last she spyde at that roomes upper end,
  Another yron dore, on which was writ,
  Be not too bold; whereto though she did bend
Her earnest mind, yet wist not what it might intend.°   *mean*

55

Thus she there waited untill eventyde,
  Yet living creature none she saw appeare:
  And now sad° shadowes gan the world to hyde,   *somber*
  From mortall vew, and wrap in darkenesse dreare;
  Yet nould° she d'off her weary armes, for feare   *would not*
  Of secret daunger, ne let sleepe oppresse
  Her heavy eyes with natures burdein deare,
  But drew her selfe aside in sickernesse,°   *safety*
And her welpointed weapons did about her dresse.[2]

Canto 12

*The maske[3] of Cupid, and th'enchaunted
  Chamber are displayd,
Whence Britomart redeemes faire
  Amoret, through charmes decayd.°*   *wasted away*

I

Tho° when as chearelesse Night ycovered had   *then*
  Faire heaven with an universall cloud,

---

2. Her well-appointed (and/or sharp) weapons she drew ("did dresse") about her.
3. This episode resembles a court masque (elaborate dramatic presentation) with allegorical personages and emblematic clothing and props. It is also a "Triumph" (ceremonial victory parade) of

Cupid, who is preceded and followed by the allegorical qualities that attend on his reign and who displays Amoret as the spoils of his victory, the victim of the attitudes toward love which he promotes.

That every wight dismayd with darknesse sad,°   *sober*
In silence and in sleepe themselves did shroud,
She heard a shrilling Trompet sound aloud,
Signe of nigh° battell, or got° victory;   *approaching / achieved*
Nought therewith daunted was her courage proud,
But rather stird to cruell° enmity,   *fierce*
Expecting° ever, when some foe she might descry.°   *waiting / perceive*

2

With that, an hideous storme of winde arose,
With dreadfull thunder and lightning atwixt,
And an earth-quake, as if it streight° would lose° *immediately / loosen*
The worlds foundations from his centre fixt;
A direfull stench of smoke and sulphure mixt
Ensewd, whose noyance° fild the fearefull sted,°   *annoyance / place*
From the fourth houre of night untill the sixt;[4]
Yet the bold Britonesse was nought ydred,
Though much emmoved, but stedfast still perseverèd.

3

All suddenly a stormy whirlwind blew
Throughout the house, that clappèd° every dore,   *slammed*
With which that yron wicket° open flew,   *door*
As° it with mightie levers had bene tore: *as if*
And forth issewd, as on the ready flore
Of some Theatre, a grave personage,
That in his hand a branch of laurell bore,
With comely haveöur° and count'nance sage,   *pleasing bearing*
Yclad in costly garments, fit for tragicke Stage.

4

Proceeding to the midst, he still did stand,
As if in mind he somewhat had to say,
And to the vulgar° beckning with his hand,   *groundlings*
In signe of silence, as to heare a play,
By lively actiöns he gan bewray°   *reveal*
Some argument of matter passionèd;
Which doen, he backe retyrèd soft away,
And passing by, his name discoverèd,°   *revealed*
Ease, on his robe in golden letters cypherèd.[5]

5

The noble Mayd, still standing all this vewd,
And merveild at his strange intendiment;°   *purpose*
With that a joyous fellowship issewd

4. Night begins at 6 P.M., so these effects take place from 10 P.M. to midnight, when the masque begins.
5. I.e., by pantomime he indicates that the subject ("argument") of the masque concerns pas-sion. The part of presenter is taken by Ease, suggesting that it predisposes to lechery. Similarly, Idleness leads the procession of the Seven Deadly Sins (Book 1, canto 4, stanzas 18–20).

Of Minstrals, making goodly meriment,
With wanton Bardes, and Rymers impudent,
All which together sung full chearefully
A lay° of loves delight, with sweet concent:°   *song / harmony*
After whom marcht a jolly company,
In manner of a maske, enrangèd orderly.[6]

6

The whiles a most delirious harmony,
 In full straunge notes was sweetly heard to sound,
 That the rare sweetnesse of the melody
 The feeble senses wholly did confound,
 And the fraile soule in deepe delight nigh dround:
 And when it ceast, shrill trompets loud did bray,
 That their report° did farre away rebound,   *echo*
 And when they ceast, it gan againe to play,
The whiles the maskers marchèd forth in trim aray.

7

The first was Fancy,[7] like a lovely boy,
 Of rare aspect, and beautie without peare;°   *peer, equal*
 Matchable either to that ympe of Troy,[8]
 Whom Jove did love, and chose his cup to beare,
 Or that same daintie lad, which was so deare
 To great Alcides,[9] that when as he dyde,
 He wailèd womanlike with many a teare,
 And every wood, and every valley wyde
He fild with Hylas name; the Nymphes eke° Hylas cryde. *also*

8

His garment neither was of silke nor say,°   *fine wool*
 But painted plumes, in goodly order dight,°   *placed*
 Like as the sunburnt Indians° do aray *Native Americans*
 Their tawney bodies, in their proudest plight:°   *attire*
 As those same plumes, so seemd he vaine and light,
 That by his gate° might easily appeare;   *gait*
 For still° he far'd as dauncing in delight,   *ever*
 And in his hand a windy° fan did beare, *causing wind*
That in the idle aire he mov'd still here and there.

9

And him beside marcht amorous Desyre,
 Who seemd of riper yeares, then th'other Swaine,°   *lover*
 Yet was that other swayne this elders syre,
 And gave him being, commune to them twaine:

6. As here, most masques had twelve mas-quers, forming six couples. The love song at the processional is performed by musicians ("Min-strals") and poets of varying quality ("Bardes" and "Rymers").

7. The mind's power to produce images that are often misleading or false.
8. Ganymede, as in canto 11, stanza 34.
9. Hercules, whose beloved Hylas was drowned.

His garment was disguisèd very vaine,[1]
And his embrodered Bonet sat awry;
Twixt both his hands few sparkes he close did straine,°   *clasp*
Which still he blew, and kindled busily,
That soone they life conceiv'd, and forth in flames did fly.

10

Next after him went Doubt, who was yclad
In a discolour'd° cote, of straunge disguyse,   *multicolored*
That at his backe a brode Capuccio had,
And sleeves dependant Albanese-wyse:[2]
He lookt askew with his mistrustfull eyes,
And nicely° trode, as° thornes lay in his way,   *cautiously / as if*
Or that the flore to shrinke he did avyse,
And on a broken reed he still did stay
His feeble steps, which shrunke, when hard theron he lay.[3]

11

With him went Daunger, clothed in ragged weed,°   *garment*
Made of Beares skin, that him more dreadfull made,
Yet his owne face was dreadfull, ne did need,
Straunge horrour, to deforme his griesly shade;
A net in th'one hand, and a rustie blade[4]
In th'other was, this Mischiefe, that Mishap;
With th'one his foes he threatned to invade,°   *attack*
With th'other he his friends ment to enwrap:
For whom he could not kill, he practizd° to entrap.   *plotted*

12

Next him was Feare, all arm'd from top to toe,
Yet thought himselfe not safe enough thereby,
But feard each shadow moving to and fro,
And his owne armes when glittering he did spy,
Or clashing heard, he fast away did fly,
As ashes pale of hew, and wingyheeld;[5]
And evermore on Daunger fixt his eye,
Gainst whom he alwaies bent° a brasen shield,   *turned*
Which his right hand unarmèd fearefully did wield.

13

With him went Hope in rancke, a handsome Mayd,
Of chearefull looke and lovely to behold;

---

1. I.e., Desire seems older than Fancy, but Fancy is in fact his father; he was dressed fantastically ("disguisèd very vaine").
2. Hanging down in Albanian (i.e., Scottish: Albany is a dukedom in Scotland) fashion—as in academic gowns. His hood ("Capuccio") resembles that of a Capuchin monk.
3. I.e., he trod with great precision and care ("nicely") as if thorns lay in his path or as if he perceived ("did avyse") the floor to give way ("shrinke"). His cane was a broken reed, which collapsed ("shrunke") when he leaned on it.
4. Danger's face was terrifying, needing nothing external ("straunge") to further deform his horrid ("griesly") appearance. His net and bloodstained ("rustie") knife indicate the kinds of perils he signifies.
5. I.e., he was pale as ashes and fled as if his heels had wings.

In silken samite° she was light arayd,   *a rich silk*
And her faire lockes were woven up in gold;
She alway smyld, and in her hand did hold
An holy water Sprinckle,[6] dipt in deowe,°   *water (dew)*
With which she sprinckled favours manifold,
On whom she list,° and did great liking sheowe, *pleased*
Great liking unto many, but true love to feowe.° *few*

14

And after them Dissemblance, and Suspect[7]
 Marcht in one rancke, yet an unequall paire:
 For she was gentle, and of milde aspect,
 Courteous to all, and seeming debonaire,°   *gracious*
 Goodly adornèd, and exceeding faire:
 Yet was that all but painted, and purloynd,° *stolen*
 And her bright° browes were deckt with borrowed haire: *lovely*
 Her deedes were forgèd, and her words false coynd,
And alwaies in her hand two clewes° of silke she twynd. *balls*

15

But he was foule, ill favourèd, and grim,
 Under his eyebrowes looking still askaunce;° *sideways*
 And ever as Dissemblance laught on him,
 He lowrd° on her with daungerous° eyeglaunce; *scowled / threatening*
 Shewing his nature in his countenance;
 His rolling eyes did never rest in place,
 But walkt° each where, for feare of hid mischaunce, *moved*
 Holding a lattice° still before his face,   *screen*
Through which he still did peepe, as forward he did pace.

16

Next him went Griefe, and Fury matcht yfere;° *together*
 Griefe all in sable sorrowfully clad,
 Downe hanging his dull head, with heavy chere,° *countenance*
 Yet inly being more, then° seeming sad: *than*
 A paire of Pincers in his hand he had,
 With which he pinchèd people to the hart,
 That from thenceforth a wretchèd life they lad,° *led*
 In wilfull languor° and consuming smart,° *pining / pain*
Dying each day with inward wounds of dolours dart.° *grief's arrow*

17

But Fury was full ill appareilèd
 In rags, that naked nigh° she did appeare, *nearly*
 With ghastly lookes and dreadfull drerihed;° *wretchedness*
 For from her backe her garments she did teare,
 And from her head oft rent her snarlèd heare:
 In her right hand a firebrand she did tosse° *brandish*

---

6. Aspergillum, a brush to sprinkle holy water. 7. Dissimulation and Suspicion.

About her head, still roming here and there;
  As a dismayèd° Deare in chace embost,°   *panic-stricken / hard-pressed*
Forgetfull of his safety, hath his right way lost.

18

After them went Displeasure and Pleasance,
  He looking lompish° and full sullein sad,°   *dejected / morose*
  And hanging downe his heavy countenance;
  She chearefull fresh and full of joyance glad,
  As if no sorrow she ne felt ne drad;
  That evill matchèd paire they seemd to bee:
  An angry Waspe th'one in a viall had,
  Th'other in hers an hony-lady Bee;[8]
Thus marchèd these six couples forth in faire degree.°   *order*

19

After all these there marcht a most faire Dame,
  Led of two grysie° villeins, th'one Despight,   *grim*
  The other clepèd° Cruelty by name:[9]   *called*
  She dolefull Lady, like a dreary Spright,°   *spirit*
  Cald by strong charmes out of eternall night,
  Had deathes owne image figurd in her face,
  Full of sad signes, fearefull to living sight;
  Yet in that horror shewd a seemely grace,
And with her feeble feet did move a comely pace.

20

Her brest all naked, as net° ivory,   *pure*
  Without adorne° of gold or silver bright,   *adornment*
  Wherewith the Craftesman wonts it beautify,[1]
  Of her dew honour was despoylèd quight,
  And a wide wound therein (O ruefull sight)
  Entrenchèd deepe with knife accursèd keene,
  Yet freshly bleeding forth her fainting spright,
  (The worke of cruell hand) was to be seene,
That dyde in sanguine° red her skin all snowy cleene.   *bloody*

21

At that wide orifice her trembling hart
  Was drawne forth, and in silver basin layd,
  Quite through transfixèd° with a deadly dart,   *pierced*
  And in her bloud yet steeming fresh embayd:°   *steeped*
  And those two villeins, which her steps upstayd,
  When her weake feete could scarcely her sustaine,
  And fading vitall powers gan to fade,

---

8. Honeybee or honey-laden bee.
9. Typical attributes of the lady in the world of courtly love and love sonnets: her "cruelty" causes her to reject her lover with scorn ("despight").
1. I.e., without the jewels that usually beautify her breast.

Her forward still with torture did constraine,
And evermore encreasèd her consuming paine.

22

Next after her the wingèd God himselfe°   *Cupid*
 Came riding on a Lion ravenous,
 Taught to obay the menage° of that Elfe, *horsemanship*
 That man and beast with powre imperious
 Subdeweth to his kingdome tyrannous:
 His blindfold eyes he bad° a while unbind, *bade*
 That his proud spoyle of that same dolorous
 Faire Dame he might behold in perfect kind;° *clearly*
Which seene, he much rejoycèd in his cruell mind.

23

Of which full proud, himselfe up rearing hye,
 He lookèd round about with sterne disdaine;
 And did survay his goodly company:
 And marshalling the evill ordered traine,° *retinue*
 With that the darts which his right hand did straine,° *clasp*
 Full dreadfully he shooke that all did quake,
 And clapt on hie his coulourd wingès twaine,
 That all his many° it affraide did make: *company*
Tho blinding° him againe, his way he forth did take. *then blindfolding*

24

Behinde him was Reproch, Repentance, Shame;
 Reproch the first, Shame next, Repent behind:
 Repentance feeble, sorrowfull, and lame:
 Reproch despightfull, carelesse,² and unkind;
 Shame most ill favourd, bestiall, and blind:
 Shame lowrd,° Repentance sigh'd, Reproch did scould; *scowled*
 Reproch sharpe stings, Repentance whips entwind,
 Shame burning brond-yrons° in her hand did hold: *branding irons*
All three to each unlike, yet all made in one mould.

25

And after them a rude confusèd rout° *crowd*
 Of persons flockt, whose names is hard to read:° *distinguish*
 Emongst them was sterne Strife, and Anger stout,° *fierce*
 Unquiet Care, and fond° Unthriftihead, *foolish*
 Lewd° Losse of Time, and Sorrow seeming dead, *base*
 Inconstant Chaunge, and false Disloyaltie,
 Consuming Riotise,° and guilty Dread *debauchery*
 Of heavenly vengeance, faint Infirmitie,
Vile Povertie, and lastly Death with infamie.

---

2. I.e., full of scorn, careless of where his attacks fall.

26

There were full many moe° like maladies,   *more*
   Whose names and natures I note readen well;°   *I cannot well interpret*
   So many moe, as there be phantasies
   In wavering wemens wit, that none can tell,°   *count*
   Or paines in love, or punishments in hell;
   All which disguizèd marcht in masking wise,
   About the chamber with that Damozell,
And then returnèd, having marchèd thrise,
Into the inner roome, from whence they first did rise.

27

So soone as they were in, the dore streight way
   Fast lockèd, driven with that stormy blast,
   Which first it opened; and bore all away.
   Then the brave Maid, which all this while was plast°   *placed*
   In secret shade, and saw both first and last,
   Issewèd° forth, and went unto the dore,   *came*
   To enter in, but found it lockèd fast:
   It vaine she thought with rigorous uprore°   *violent force*
For to efforce, when charmes had closèd it afore.

28

Where force might not availe, there sleights and art
   She cast° to use, both fit for hard emprize;°   *resolved / enterprise*
   For thy° from that same roome not to depart   *therefore*
   Till morrow next, she did her selfe avize,°   *counsel*
   When that same Maske againe should forth arize.
   The morrow next appeard with joyous cheare,
   Calling men to their daily exercize,
   Then she, as morrow fresh, her selfe did reare
Out of her secret stand,° that day for to out weare.   *standing place*

29

All that day she outwore in wandering,
   And gazing on that Chambers ornament,
   Till that againe the second evening
   Her covered with her sable vestiment,
   Wherewith the worlds faire beautie she hath blent:°   *obscured*
   Then when the second watch[3] was almost past,
   That brasen dore flew open, and in went
   Bold Britomart, as she had late forecast,°   *planned*
Neither of idle shewes, nor of false charmes aghast.°   *terrified*

30

So soone as she was entred, round about
   She cast her eies, to see what was become

---

3. From 9 P.M. to midnight.

Of all those persons, which she saw without:
But lo, they streight° were vanisht all and some,   *immediately*
Ne living wight she saw in all that roome,
Save that same woefull Ladie, both whose hands
Were bounden fast, that did her ill become,
And her small wast girt round with yron bands,
Unto a brasen pillour, by the which she stands.

31

And her before the vile Enchaunter sate,
  Figuring straunge characters of his art,
  With living bloud he those characters wrate,°   *wrote*
  Dreadfully dropping from her dying hart,
  Seeming transfixèd with a cruell dart,
  And all perforce° to make her him to love.   *by force*
  Ah who can love the worker of her smart?
  A thousand charmes he formerly did prove;°   *try*
Yet thousand charmes could not her stedfast heart remove.

32

Soone as that virgin knight he saw in place,
  His wicked bookes in hast he overthrew,
  Not caring his long labours to deface,[4]
  And fiercely ronning to that Lady trew,
  A murdrous knife out of his pocket drew,
  The which he thought, for villeinous despight,°   *cruelty*
  In her tormented bodie to embrew:°   *plunge*
  But the stout° Damzell to him leaping light,   *fierce*
His cursèd hand withheld, and maisterèd his might.

33

From her, to whom his fury first he ment,°   *directed*
  The wicked weapon rashly° he did wrest,°   *suddenly / turned*
  And turning to her selfe his fell intent,
  Unwares° it strooke into her snowie chest,   *without warning*
  That little drops empurpled her faire brest.
  Exceeding wroth therewith the virgin grew,
  Albe° the wound were nothing deepe imprest,   *although*
  And fiercely forth her mortall blade she drew,
To give him the reward for such vile outrage dew.

34

So mightily she smote him, that to ground
  He fell halfe dead; next stroke him should have slaine,
  Had not the Lady, which by him stood bound,
  Dernely° unto her callèd to abstaine,   *dismally*
  From doing him to dy. For else her paine
  Should be remedilesse, sith° none but hee,   *since*

4. I.e., he did not care if he ruined the spells he had labored over.

Which wrought it, could the same recure° againe.   *heal*
  Therewith she stayd her hand, loth stayd to bee;
For life she him envyde,° and long'd revenge to see.   *begrudged*

35

And to him said, "Thou wicked man, whose meed°   *reward*
  For so huge mischiefe, and vile villany
  Is death, or if that ought° do death exceed,   *aught, anything*
  Be sure, that nought may save thee from to dy,
  But if that thou this Dame doe presently
  Restore unto her health, and former state;[5]
  This doe and live, else die undoubtedly."
He glad of life, that lookt for death but late,°   *just recently*
Did yield himselfe right willing to prolong his date.°   *term of life*

36

And rising up, gan streight to overlooke°   *look over*
  Those cursèd leaves, his charmes backe to reverse;
  Full dreadfull things out of that balefull booke
  He red, and measured many a sad verse,[6]
  That horror gan the virgins hart to perse,°   *pierce*
  And her faire locks up starèd° stiffe on end,   *stood*
  Hearing him those same bloudy lines reherse;°   *say over again*
  And all the while he red, she did extend
Her sword high over him if ought he did offend.

37

Anon she gan perceive the house to quake,
  And all the dores to rattel round about;
  Yet all that did not her dismaièd make,
  Nor slacke her threatfull hand for daungers dout,[7]
  But still with stedfast eye and courage stout
  Abode,° to weet° what end would come of all.   *waited / learn*
  At last that mightie chaine, which round about
  Her tender waste was wound, adowne gan fall,
And that great brasen pillour broke in peeces small.

38

The cruell steele, which thrild° her dying hart,   *pierced*
  Fell softly forth, as of his owne accord,
  And the wyde wound, which lately did dispart°   *divide*
  Her bleeding brest, and riven bowels gor'd,
  Was closèd up, as it had not bene bor'd,
  And every part to safety full sound,
  As she were never hurt, was soone° restor'd: *immediately*

---

5. I.e., you deserve death or, if possible, something worse than death, and nothing will save you from death ("to dy") unless ("But if") you immediately ("presently") restore this lady.

6. I.e., he pronounced in proper meter many distressing verses (incantations).

7. I.e., nor relax her threatening hand for fear of danger.

Tho° when she felt her selfe to be unbound,   *then*
And perfect hole, prostrate she fell unto the ground.

39

Before Faire Britomart, she fell prostrate,
  Saying, "Ah noble knight what worthy meed°   *reward*
  Can wretched Lady, quit° from wofull state,   *released*
  Yield you in liew of° this your gratious deed?   *in return for*
  Your vertue selfe her owne reward shall breed,
  Even immortall praise, and glory wyde,
  Which I your vassall, by your prowesse freed,
  Shall through the world make to be notifyde,
And goodly well advaunce, that goodly well was tryde."[8]

40

But *Britomart* uprearing her from ground,
  Said, "Gentle Dame, reward enough I weene°   *think*
  For many labours more, then° I have found,   *than*
  This, that in safety now I have you seene,
  And meane° of your deliverance have beene: *means*
  Henceforth faire Lady comfort to you take,
  And put away remembrance of late teene;°   *pain*
  In stead thereof know, that your loving Make,°   *mate*
Hath no lesse griefe endurèd for your gentle sake."

41

She much was cheard to heare him mentiönd,
  Whom of all living wights she lovèd best.
  Then laid the noble Championesse strong hond
  Upon th'enchaunter, which had her distrest
  So sore, and with foule outrages opprest:
  With that great chaine, wherewith not long ygo
  He bound that pitteous Lady prisoner, now relest,°   *released*
  Himselfe she bound, more worthy to be so,
And captive with her led to wretchednesse and wo.

42

Returning backe, those goodly roomes, which erst°   *before*
  She saw so rich and royally arayd,
  Now vanisht utterly, and cleane subverst°   *overturned*
  She found, and all their glory quite decayd,°   *destroyed*
  That sight of such a chaunge her much dismayd.
  Thence forth descending to that perlous° Porch,   *perilous*
  Those dreadfull flames she also found delayd,°   *allayed*
  And quenchèd quite, like a consumèd torch,
That erst° all entrers wont so cruelly to scorch.   *previously*

---

8. I.e., as your vassal I will make known ("notifyde") throughout the world and extol ("advaunce") your virtue, which was so fully tested ("tryde").

43

More easie issew now, then entrance late
  She found: for now that fainèd° dreadfull flame,   *feigned*
  Which chokt the porch of that enchaunted gate,
  And passage bard to all, that thither came,
  Was vanisht quite, as it were not the same,
  And gave her leave at pleasure forth to passe.
  Th'Enchaunter selfe, which all that fraud did frame,
  To have efforst° the love of that faire lasse,   *enforced*
Seeing his worke now wasted deepe engrievèd was.

44

But when the victoresse arrivèd there,
  Where late she left the pensife° Scudamore,   *sad; anxious*
  With her owne trusty Squire,[9] both full of feare,
  Neither of them she found where she them lore:°   *left*
  Thereat her noble hart was stonisht sore;
  But most faire Amoret, whose gentle spright
  Now gan to feede on hope, which she before
  Conceivèd had, to see her owne deare knight,
Being thereof beguyld was fild with new affright.

45

But he sad man, when he had long in drede
  Awayted there for Britomarts returne,
  Yet saw her not nor signe of her good speed,°   *success*
  His expectation to despaire did turne,
  Misdeeming[1] sure that her those flames did burne;
  And therefore gan advize° with her old Squire,   *consult*
  Who her deare nourslings losse no lesse did mourne,
  Thence to depart for further aide t'enquire:
Where let them wend at will, whilest here I doe respire.[2]

1590, 1596

---

9. Her nurse, Glauce, is her squire.
1. Mistakenly thinking.
2. Take a breath, rest from my labors. In the 1590 edition, Book 3, and the poem, ended with the happy reunion of Scudamour and Amoret in a passionate embrace:

> Lightly he clipt her twixt his armès twaine,
>   And streightly did embrace her body bright,
>   Her body, late the prison of sad paine,
>   Now the sweet lodge of love and deare
>   delight:

> But she faire Lady overcommen quight
> Of huge affection, did in pleasure melt,
> And in sweete ravishment pourd out her
>   spright:
> No word they spake, nor earthly thing they
>   felt,
> But like two senceles stocks in long
>   embracement dwelt.

But in the 1596 edition Spenser made a bridge to his three added books by replacing the earlier ending with stanzas 43–45, as given here.

Mutabilitie Cantos   In 1609, in an edition of *The Faerie Queene* published ten years after Spenser's death, two cantos and a two-stanza fragment of a third one appeared for the first time. If they actually are, as their editor's note suggests, part of an uncompleted book of the poem, centered on the virtue of constancy, they constitute a longer digression from the main story than any in the other books. The cantos give Spenser's reflections on change and permanence in the world—a subject that fascinated and disturbed him and his contemporaries. How is it possible to secure any stable meaning in a world that is forever in flux? Where can beauty and truth be found in the midst of relentless strife? In a great trial scene, the Goddess of Nature rules against Mutabilitie in favor of Jove's principle of underlying order. But in the moving two-stanza fragment, the poet discloses his longing for eternal rest in the changeless realm of heaven.

Two Cantos of *Mutabilitie*:

Which, both for Forme and Matter, appeare to be parcell of some following Booke of the Faerie Queene

(∵)

Under the Legend
of
Constancie.

Canto 6

Proud Change (not pleasd, in mortall things,
  beneath the Moone, to raigne)[1]
Pretends,° as well of Gods, as Men   claims
  to be the Soveraine.

I

What man that sees the ever-whirling wheele
  Of Change, the which all mortall things doth sway,°   rule
But that therby doth find, and plainly feele,
How Mutability in them doth play
  Her cruell sports, to many mens decay?°   destruction
Which that to all may better yet appeare,
  I will rehearse° that whylome° I heard say,   relate / formerly
How she at first her selfe began to reare,
Gainst all the Gods, and th'empire sought from them to beare.

2

But first, here falleth fittest to unfold
  Her antique race and linage ancient,
As I have found it registred of old,
  In Faery Land mongst records permanent:

---

1. The old cosmology held that change occurred only in the sublunary realm.

She was, to weet,° a daughter by descent   *to wit, in fact*
Of those old Titans,[2] that did whylome strive
With Saturnes sonne for heavens regiment.°   *rule*
Whom, though high Jove of kingdome did deprive,
Yet many of their stemme° long after did survive.   *race*

3

And many of them, afterwards obtained
  Great power of Jove, and high authority;
  As Hecate,[3] in whose almighty hand,
  He plac't all rule and principality,
  To be by her disposèd diversly,
  To Gods, and men, as she them list° divide: *chose to*
  And drad° Bellona,[4] that doth sound on hie   *dreaded*
  Warres and allarums unto Nations wide,
That makes both heaven and earth to tremble at her pride.

4

So likewise did this Titanesse aspire,
  Rule and dominion to her selfe to gaine;
  That as a Goddesse, men might her admire,°   *wonder at*
  And heavenly honours yield, as to them twaine.[5]
  And first, on earth she sought it to obtaine;
  Where she such proofe and sad° examples shewed   *grievous*
  Of her great power, to many ones great paine,
  That not men onely (whom she soone subdewed)
But eke° all other creatures, her bad dooings rewed.°   *also / rued*

5

For, she the face of earthly things so changed,
  That all which Nature had establisht first
  In good estate,° and in meet° order ranged,   *condition / fitting*
  She did pervert,° and all their statutes burst: *overturn*
  And all the worlds faire frame (which none yet durst
  Of Gods or men to alter or misguide)
  She altered quite, and made them all accurst
  That God had blest; and did at first provide
In that still° happy state for ever to abide.   *continually*

6

Ne° shee the lawes of Nature onely brake,   *nor*
  But eke of Justice, and of Policie;°   *government*
  And wrong of right, and bad of good did make,
  And death for life exchangèd foolishlie:

2. The Titans were the sons and daughters of sky and earth; their king was Cronus (Time). Jove, Cronus's son, dethroned him and established the rule of the gods. But some descendants of the original Titans, such as Prometheus and Hecate, survived. Spenser invents another, a Titaness called Mutabilitie.

3. A goddess of Hades but also often associated with the powerful and generally benevolent goddess Artemis (in Rome, Diana). Her name is pronounced *HEK-a-tee.*
4. Roman goddess of war.
5. Those two; i.e., Hecate and Bellona.

Since which, all living wights° have learned to die, *creatures*
And all this world is woxen° daily worse. *grown*
O pittious worke of Mutabilitie!
By which, we all are subject to that curse,
And death in stead of life have suckèd from our Nurse.° *i.e., Nature*

7

And now, when all the earth she thus had brought
 To her behest,° and thrallèd to her might, *bidding*
 She gan to cast° in her ambitious thought, *resolve*
 T'attempt° the empire of the heavens hight, *attack*
 And Jove himselfe to shoulder from his right.
 And first, she past the region of the ayre,
 And of the fire,⁶ whose substance thin and slight,
 Made no resistance, ne could her contraire,° *withstand*
But ready passage to her pleasure did prepaire.

8

Thence, to the Circle of the Moone⁷ she clambe,
 Where Cynthia⁸ raignes in everlasting glory,
 To whose bright shining palace straight she came,
 All fairely deckt with heavens goodly story;⁹
 Whose silver gates (by which there sate an hory
 Old aged Sire, with hower-glasse in hand,
 Hight° Tyme) she entred, were he liefe or sory:¹ *called*
 Ne staide till she the highest stage° had scand,° *level / mounted to*
Where Cynthia did sit, that never still did stand.° *remain*

9

Her sitting on an Ivory throne shee found,
 Drawne of two steeds, th'one black, the other white,
 Environd with tenne thousand starres around,
 That duly her attended day and night;
 And by her side, there ran her Page, that hight
 Vesper, whom we the Evening-starre intend:° *call*
 That with his Torche, still twinkling like twylight,
 Her lightened all the way where she should wend,° *journey*
And joy to weary wandring travailers did lend:

10

That when the hardy Titanesse beheld
 The goodly building of her Palace bright,
 Made of the heavens substance, and up-held
 With thousand Crystall pillors of huge hight,
 Shee gan to burne in her ambitious spright,° *spirit*
 And t'evnie her that in such glorie raigned.

---

6. The highest sublunary region.
7. The transparent sphere that, in the Ptolemaic cosmology, revolved around the earth, carrying the moon along. (The sun, the other known planets, and, collectively, the fixed stars were similarly carried by *their* spheres.)

8. Cynthia, Diana, or Phoebe, the moon goddess, often associated with Queen Elizabeth.
9. I.e., the constellations.
1. I.e., whether he liked it or not.
2. Soon, she resolved.

Eftsoones she cast[2] by force and tortious° might, *wrongful*
  Her to displace; and to her selfe to have gained
The kingdome of the Night, and waters by her wained.° *drawn*

11

Boldly she bid the Goddesse downe descend,
  And let her selfe into that Ivory throne;
  For, shee her selfe more worthy thereof wend,° *weened, thought*
  And better able it to guide alone:
  Whether to men, whose fall she did bemone,
  Or unto Gods, whose state she did maligne,° *envy*
  Or to th'infernall Powers, her need give lone
  Of her faire light, and bounty most benigne,
Her selfe of all that rule shee deemèd most condigne.° *worthy*

12

But shee that had to her that soveraigne seat
  By highest Jove assigned, therein to beare
  Nights burning lamp, regarded not her threat,
  Ne yielded ought for favour or for feare;
  But with sterne countenaunce and disdainfull cheare,° *aspect*
  Bending her hornèd browes,[3] did put her back:
  And boldly blaming her for comming there,
  Bade her attonce from heavens coast to pack,° *depart*
Or at her perill bide the wrathfull Thunders wrack.° *destruction*

13

Yet nathemore° the Giantesse forbare: *not at all*
  But boldly preacing-on,° raught forth her hand *advancing*
  To pluck her downe perforce° from off her chaire; *by force*
  And there-with lifting up her golden wand,
  Threatned to strike her if she did with-stand.
  Where-at the starres, which round about her blazed,
  And eke the Moones bright wagon,° still did stand, *chariot*
  All beeing with so bold attempt amazed,
And on her uncouth habit[4] and sterne looke still gazed.

14

Meane-while, the lower World, which nothing knew
  Of all that chauncèd here, was darkned quite;
  And eke the heavens, and all the heavenly crew
  Of happy wights, now unpurvaide° of light, *deprived*
  Were much afraid, and wondred at that sight;
  Fearing least° Chaos broken had his chaine, *lest*
  And brought againe on them eternall night:

3. Cynthia's bent brows are the horns of the crescent moon.
4. Strange behavior.
5. In the Ptolemaic system the sphere of Mercury was next beyond that of the moon. In mythology Mercury was the messenger of the gods. In stanza 19, his Greek name, Hermes, is used. "Chaos": in Greek mythology, the first created being—the scarcely personified, profoundly unordered primordial soup.

But chiefely Mercury, that next doth raigne,[5]
Ran forth in haste, unto the king of Gods to plaine.°   *complain*

15

All ran together with a great out-cry,
   To Joves faire Palace, fixt in heavens hight;
   And beating at his gates full earnestly,
   Gan call to him aloud with all their might,
   To know what meant that suddaine lack of light.
   The father of the Gods when this he heard,
   Was troubled much at their so strange affright,
   Doubting least° Typhon[6] were againe upreared,   *fearing that*
Or other his old foes, that once him sorely feared.°   *frightened*

16

Eftsoones the sonne of Maia° forth he sent   *i.e., Mercury*
   Downe to the Circle of the Moone, to knowe
   The cause of this so strange astonishment,
   And why shee did her wonted° course forslowe;°   *accustomed / delay*
   And if that any were on earth belowe
   That did with charmes or Magick her molest,
   Him to attache,° and downe to hell to throwe: *seize*
   But, if from heaven it were, then to arrest
The Author, and him bring before his presence prest.°   *immediately*

17

The wingd-foot God, so fast his plumes did beat,
   That soone he came where-as the Titanesse
   Was striving with faire Cynthia for her seat:
   At whose strange sight, and haughty hardinesse,°   *boldness*
   He wondred much, and fearèd her no lesse.
   Yet laying feare aside to doe his charge,°   *assigned task*
   At last, he bade her (with bold stedfastnesse)
   Ceasse to molest the Moone to walke at large,[7]
Or come before high Jove, her dooings to discharge.°   *account for*

18

And there-with-all, he on her shoulder laid
   His snaky-wreathèd Mace,[8] whose awfull power
   Doth make both Gods and hellish fiends affraid:
   Where-at the Titanesse did sternely lower,°   *scowl*
   And stoutly answered, that in evill hower
   He from his Jove such message to her brought,
   To bid her leave faire Cynthias silver bower;
   Sith° shee his Jove and him esteemèd nought,   *since*
No more then° Cynthia's selfe; but all their kingdoms sought.   *than*

---

6. A giant who had rebelled against Jove.
7. I.e., stop interfering with the moon's free movement.

8. I.e., the caduceus, Mercury's rod, which could bring spirits from the underworld.

19

The Heavens Herald staid not to reply,
    But past away, his doings to relate
    Unto his Lord; who now in th'highest sky,
    Was placed in his principall Estate,°   *position of state*
    With all the Gods about him congregate:
    To whom when Hermes had his message told,
    It did them all exceedingly amate,°   *dismay*
    Save Jove; who, changing nought his count'nance bold,
Did unto them at length these speeches wise unfold;

20

"Harken to mee awhile yee heavenly Powers;
    Ye may remember since th'Earths cursèd seed
    Sought to assaile the heavens eternall towers,
    And to us all exceeding feare did breed:
    But how we then defeated all their deed,
    Yee all doe knowe, and them destroied quite;
    Yet not so quite, but that there did succeed
    An off-spring of their bloud, which did alite
Upon the fruitfull earth, which doth us yet despite.°   *disdain*

21

"Of that bad seed is this bold woman bred,
    That now with bold presumption doth aspire
    To thrust faire Phoebe[9] from her silver bed,
    And eke our selves from heavens high Empire,
    If that her might were match to her desire:
    Wherefore, it now behoves us to advise°   *consider*
    What way is best to drive her to retire;
    Whether by open force, or counsell wise,
Areed° ye sonnes of God, as best ye can devise."   *advise*

22

So having said, he ceast; and with his brow
    (His black eye-brow, whose doomefull dreaded beck[1]
    Is wont to wield° the world unto his vow,°   *sway / will*
    And even the highest Powers of heaven to check)
    Made signe to them in their degrees to speake:
    Who straight gan cast[2] their counsell grave and wise.
    Mean-while, th'Earths daughter, thogh she nought did reck[3]
    Of Hermes message; yet gan now advise,
What course were best to take in this hot bold emprize.°   *enterprise*

---

9. The moon as the twin sister of Phoebus Apollo, the sun god.
1. I.e., his awesome nod of judgment.
2. Deliver. "Straight": straightaway.
3. Care. "Earths daughter": i.e., Mutabilitie.

23

Eftsoones she thus resolved; that whil'st the Gods
 (After returne of Hermes Embassie)
 Were troubled, and amongst themselves at ods,
 Before they could new counsels re-allie,°   *form again*
 To set upon them in that extasie;°   *astonishment*
 And take what fortune time and place would lend:
 So, forth she rose, and through the purest sky
 To Joves high Palace straight cast° to ascend,   *resolved*
To prosecute her plot: Good on-set boads good end.

24

Shee there arriving, boldly in did pass;
 Where all the Gods she found in counsell close,°   *secret*
 All quite unarmed, as then their manner was.
 At sight of her they suddaine all arose,
 In great amaze,° ne wist° what way to chose.   *bewilderment / knew*
 But Jove, all fearelesse, forc't them to aby;°   *remain*
 And in his soveraine throne, gan straight dispose°   *arrange*
 Himselfe more full of grace and Majestie,
That mote encheare° his friends, and foes mote terrifie.   *cheer*

25

That, when the haughty Titanesse beheld,
 All° were she fraught with pride and impudence,   *although*
 Yet with the sight thereof was almost queld;
 And inly quaking, seemed as° reft of sense,   *as if*
 And voyd of speech in that drad° audience;   *dread*
 Until that Jove himself, her selfe bespake:
 "Speake thou fraile woman, speake with confidence,
 Whence art thou, and what doost thou here now make?°   *intend*
What idle errand hast thou, earths mansion to forsake?"

26

Shee, halfe confusèd with his great commaund,
 Yet gathering spirit of her natures pride,
 Him boldly answered thus to his demaund:
 "I am a daughter, by the mothers side,
 Of her that is Grand-mother magnifide°   *glorified*
 Of all the Gods, great Earth, great Chaos child:[4]
 But by the fathers (be it not envide°)   *begrudged*
 I greater am in bloud (whereon I build°)   *base my claim*
Then all the Gods, though wrongfully from heaven exiled.

27

"For, Titan (as ye all acknowledge must)
 Was Saturnes elder brother by birth-right;

---

4. Earth is the offspring of Chaos, in Hesiod and later mythologies.

Both, sonnes of Uranus: but by unjust
And guilefull meanes, through Corybantes slight,° *trickery*
The younger thrust the elder from his right:[5]
Since which, thou Jove, injuriously° hast held *wrongfully*
The Heavens rule from Titans sonnes by might;
And them to hellish dungeons downe hast feld:
Witnesse ye Heavens the truth of all that I have teld."

28

Whil'st she thus spake, the Gods that gave good eare
 To her bold words, and markèd well her grace,
 Beeing of stature tall as any there
 Of all the Gods, and beautifull of face,
 As any of the Goddesses in place,° *present*
 Stood all astonied, like a sort° of Steeres; *herd*
 Mongst whom, some beast of strange and forraine race,
 Unwares° is chaunc't, far straying from his peeres: *unexpectedly*
So did their ghastly gaze bewray° their hidden feares. *reveal*

29

Till having pauzed awhile, Jove thus bespake;
 "Will never mortall thoughts ceasse to aspire,
 In this bold sort, to Heaven claime to make,
 And touch celestiall seates with earthly mire?
 I would have thought, that bold Procrustes[6] hire,° *reward*
 Or Typhons fall, or proud Ixions paine,
 Or great Prometheus, tasting of our ire,
 Would have suffized, the rest for to restraine;
And warned all men by their example to refraine:

30

"But now, this off-scum of that cursèd fry,° *brood*
 Dare to renew the like bold enterprize,
 And chalenge° th'heritage of this our skie; *lay claim to*
 Whom what should hinder, but that we likewise
 Should handle as the rest of her allies,
 And thunder-drive to hell?" With that, he shooke
 His Nectar-deawèd locks,[7] with which the skyes
 And all the world beneath for terror quooke,° *quaked*
And eft° his burning levin-brond[8] in hand he tooke. *then*

5. In this variant myth, Titan, eldest son of Uranus, abdicated in favor of his younger brother Saturn on condition that Saturn would eat all his own male children, thus assuring the succession would eventually revert to Titan's line. When Jove was born to Rhea, Saturn's wife, she gave Saturn a stone to swallow instead of the baby, and her attendants, the Corybantes, beat on their shields to drown out the baby's cries. Eventually Jove deposed his father.
6. Procrustes was a robber who waylaid strangers and made them fit his bed by cutting or stretching them. (Spenser includes him among those punished by Jove, though the standard version of the myth has Theseus in that role.) Typhon was a hundred-headed monster overthrown by Jove. Ixion tried to seduce Jove's wife and was punished by being bound to a wheel of fire in hell. Prometheus stole fire from heaven and gave it to humankind, for which Jove punished him by chaining him to a cliff where an eagle fed on his liver, which grew back every night.
7. I.e., his locks were sprinkled with a fragrant balm. "Nectar" more often referred to the drink of the gods.
8. Lightning bolt.

31

But, when he lookèd on her lovely face,
  In which, faire beames of beauty did appeare,
  That could the greatest wrath soone turne to grace
  (Such sway° doth beauty even in Heaven beare)   *power*
  He staide his hand: and having changed his cheare,°   *mood*
  He thus againe in milder wise began;
  "But ah! if Gods should strive with flesh yfere,°   *together*
  Then shortly should the progeny of Man
Be rooted out, if Jove should doe still° what he can: *always*

32

"But thee faire Titans child, I rather weene,°   *suppose*
  Through some vaine errour or inducement light,°   *slight*
  To see that° mortall eyes have never seene;   *that which*
  Or through ensample° of thy sisters might,   *example*
  Bellona; whose great glory thou doost spight,°   *envy*
  Since thou hast seene her dreadfull power belowe,
  Mongst wretched men (dismaide with her affright)⁹
  To bandie Crownes, and Kingdomes to bestowe:
And sure thy worth, no lesse then hers doth seem to showe.

33

"But wote° thou this, thou hardy Titanesse,   *know*
  That not the worth of any living wight
  May challenge ought in Heavens interesse,¹
  Much lesse the Title of old Titans Right:
  For, we by Conquest of our soveraine might,
  And by eternall doome of Fates decree,
  Have wonne the Empire of the Heavens bright;
  Which to our selves we hold, and to whom wee
Shall worthy deeme partakers of our blisse to bee.

34

"Then ceasse thy idle claime thou foolish gerle,
  And seeke by grace and goodnesse to obtaine
  That place from which by folly Titan fell;
  There-to thou maist perhaps, if so thou faine°   *desire*
  Have Jove thy gratious Lord and Soveraigne."
  So, having said, she thus to him replide;
  "Ceasse Saturnes sonne, to seeke by proffers vaine
  Of idle hopes t'allure mee to thy side,
For to betray my Right, before I have it tride.

---

9. Through fear of her.
1. I.e., no living person, however worthy, can claim any title to power or authority in heaven.

35

"But thee, O Jove, no equall° Judge I deeme   *impartial*
   Of my desert, or of my dewfull° Right;   *due*
   That in thine owne behalfe maist partiall seeme:
   But to the highest him, that is behight°   *called*
   Father of Gods and men by equall might;[2]
   To weet, the God of Nature, I appeale."
   There-at Jove wexèd° wroth, and in his spright°   *waxed, grew / spirit*
   Did inly grudge, yet did it well conceale;
And bade Dan Phoebus Scribe[3] her Appellation° seale.   *appeal*

36

Eftsoones the time and place appointed were,
   Where all, both heavenly Powers, and earthly wights,
   Before great Natures presence should appeare,
   For triall of their Titles and best Rights:
   That was, to weet, upon the highest hights
   Of Arlo-hill[4] (Who knowes not Arlo-hill?)
   That is the highest head (in all mens sights)
   Of my old father Mole, whom Shepheards quill
Renowmèd hath with hymnes fit for a rurall skill.

37

And, were it not ill fitting for this file,[5]
   To sing of hilles and woods, mongst warres and Knights,
   I would abate the sternenesse of my stile,
   Mongst these sterne stounds° to mingle soft delights;   *clashes*
   And tell how Arlo through Dianaes spights
   (Beeing of old the best and fairest Hill
   That was in all this holy-Islands[6] hights)
   Was made the most unpleasant, and most ill.°   *evil*
Meane while, O Clio, lend Calliope[7] thy quill.

38

Whylome,° when Ireland florishèd in fame   *formerly*
   Of wealths and goodnesse, far above the rest
   Of all that beare the British Islands name,
   The Gods then used[8] (for pleasure and for rest)
   Oft to resort there-to, when seemed them best:
   But none of all there-in more pleasure found,
   Then Cynthia;[9] that is soveraine Queene profest°   *acknowledged*

---

2. I.e., who is called father of gods and humans, with equal authority over both. Androgynous Nature is here male, but in the following canto female.

3. Evidently Spenser makes Phoebus Apollo the secretary ("Scribe") of the gods because he is the god of poetry.

4. I.e., Galtymore, a peak of the mountain range Spenser calls "my old father Mole," near Kilcolman Castle, where he lived in Ireland. The last two lines of the stanza refer to Spenser's praise of Mole in his pastoral eclogue *Colin Clouts Come Home Againe.*

5. Thread (of the story).

6. Ireland is called the "holy-Island" because, according to legend, Christianity first found a foothold there and thence spread to the rest of the British Isles.

7. Calliope is the muse of epic poetry. Clio is the muse of history.

8. Were accustomed to.

9. I.e., as Diana, goddess of forests, fond of hunting.

Of woods and forrests, which therein abound,
Sprinkled with wholsom waters, more then most on ground.

39

But mongst them all, as fittest for her game,°   *recreation*
   Either for chace of beasts with hound or boawe,
   Or for to shroude in shade from Phoebus flame,
   Or bathe in fountaines that doe freshly flowe,
   Or° from high hilles, or from the dales belowe,   *either*
   She chose this Arlo; where shee did resort
   With all her Nymphes enrangèd on° a rowe,   *arranged in*
   With whom the woody Gods did oft consort:°   *i.e., sexually*
For, with the Nymphes, the Satyres love to play and sport.[1]

40

Amongst the which, there was a Nymph that hight
   Molanna; daughter of old father Mole,
   And sister unto Mulla,[2] faire and bright:
   Unto whose bed false Bregog whylome stole,
   That Shepheard Colin dearely did condole,°   *keenly bewailed*
   And made her lucklesse loves well knowne to be.
   But this Molanna, were she not so shole,°   *shallow*
   Were no lesse faire and beautifull then shee:
Yet as she is, a fairer flood may no man see.

41

For, first, she springs out of two marble Rocks,
   On which, a grove of Oakes high mounted growes,
   That as a girlond seemes to deck the locks
   Of som faire Bride, brought forth with pompous[3] showes
   Out of her bowre,° that many flowers strowes: *chamber*
   So, through the flowry Dales she tumbling downe,
   Through many woods, and shady coverts° flowes   *thickets*
   (That on each side her silver channell crowne)
Till to the Plaine she come, whose Valleyes shee doth drowne.

42

In her sweet streames, Diana usèd oft
   (After her sweatie chace and toilesome play)
   To bathe her selfe; and after, on the soft
   And downy grasse, her dainty limbes to lay
   In covert° shade, where none behold her may: *secret*
   For, much she hated sight of living eye.
   Foolish God Faunus, though full many a day

---

1. Nymphs in Greek mythology were minor female deities of streams, springs, trees, and other parts of nature. Satyrs were minor male gods of the woods, given to drinking and sensual pleasure. The Romans identified them with their goat-footed fauns; hence "Faunus" (stanza 42) and "Faune" (stanza 46).
2. The river Awbeg, whose joining with the river Bregog is told in *Colin Clouts Come Home Againe*. The Molanna is the shallow, rocky river Behanna.
3. Magnificent.

He saw her clad, yet longèd foolishly
To see her naked mongst her Nymphes in privity.[4]

43

No way he found to compasse° his desire,   *accomplish*
  But to corrupt Molanna, this her maid,
  Her to discover° for some secret hire:°   *reveal / reward*
  So, her with flattering words he first assaid;
  And after, pleasing gifts for her purvaid,°   *provided*
  Queene-apples,[5] and red Cherries from the tree,
  With which he her allurèd and betraid,
  To tell what time he might her Lady see
When she her selfe did bathe, that he might secret° bee.   *hidden*

44

There-to hee promist, if she would him pleasure
  With this small boone, to quit° her with a better;   *requite*
  To weet, that where-as she had out of measure
  Long loved the Fanchin, who by nought did set her,[6]
  That he would undertake, for this to get her
  To be his Love, and of him likèd well:
  Besides all which, he vowed to be her debter
  For many moe° good turnes then he would tell;   *more*
The least of which, this little pleasure should excell.

45

The simple maid did yield to him anone;°   *at once*
  And eft him placèd where he close[7] might view
  That° never any saw, save onely one;   *that which*
  Who, for his hire to so foole-hardy dew,°   *due*
  Was of his hounds devoured in Hunters hew.[8]
  Tho,° as her manner was on sunny day,   *then*
  Diana, with her Nymphes about her, drew
  To this sweet spring; where, doffing her array,
She bathed her lovely limbes, for Jove a likely pray.°   *proper prey*

46

There Faunus saw that pleasèd much his eye,
  And made his hart to tickle° in his brest,   *be thrilled*
  That for great joy of some-what he did spy,
  He could him not containe in silent rest;
  But breaking forth in laughter, loud profest
  His foolish thought. A foolish Faune indeed,
  That couldst not hold thy selfe so° hidden blest,   *thus*

4. Privacy. Spenser here adapts the classical story of Actaeon with local Irish geographical references. Actaeon while hunting happened to see Diana bathing; he was turned into a stag and pursued and killed by his own hounds.
5. Noted for their redness and early ripening.

6. I.e., who cared nothing for her. Fanchin is the river Funsheon.
7. Secretly; close up.
8. I.e., as a due reward to one so foolhardy, he was devoured by his hunting dogs in the slaughter ("hew") that follows a hunt.

But wouldest needs thine owne conceit[9] areed.°   *make known*
Babblers unworthy been of so divine a meed.°   *reward*

47

The Goddesse, all abashèd with that noise,
  In haste forth started from the guilty brooke;
  And running straight where-as she heard his voice,
  Enclosed the bush about, and there him tooke,
  Like darrèd[1] Larke; not daring up to looke
  On her whose sight before so much he sought.
  Thence, forth they drew him by the hornes, and shooke
  Nigh all to peeces, that they left him nought;°   *good for nothing*
And then into the open light they forth him brought.

48

Like as an huswife, that with busie care
  Thinks of her Dairie to make wondrous gaine,
  Finding where-as some wicked beast unware°   *unexpected*
  That breakes into her Dayr'house, there doth draine
  Her creaming pannes, and frustrate all her paine;°   *effort*
  Hath in some snare or gin° set close behind,   *trap*
  Entrappèd him, and caught into her traine,°   *snare*
  Then thinkes what punishment were best assigned,
And thousand deathes deviseth in her vengefull mind:

49

So did Diana and her maydens all
  Use silly Faunus, now within their baile:°   *power, custody*
  They mocke and scorne him, and him foule miscall;°   *revile*
  Some by the nose him pluckt, some by the taile,
  And by his goatish beard some did him haile:°   *pull*
  Yet he (poore soule) with patience all did beare;
  For, nought against their wils might countervaile:°   *avail*
  Ne ought he said what ever he did heare;
But hanging downe his head, did like a Mome° appeare.   *fool*

50

At length, when they had flouted him their fill,
  They gan to cast° what penaunce him to give.   *consider*
  Some would have gelt° him, but that same would spill[2]   *castrated*
  The Wood-gods breed, which must for ever live:
  Others would through the river him have drive,°   *forced to go*
  And duckèd deepe: but that seemed penaunce light;
  But most agreed and did this sentence give,
  Him in Deares skin to clad; and in that plight,°   *condition*
To hunt him with their hounds, him selfe save how hee might.

---

9. Thought; vanity or pride.   2. Destroy.
1. Paralyzed with fear.

51

But Cynthia's selfe, more angry then the rest,
   Thought not enough, to punish him in sport,
   And of her shame to make a gamesome° jest;   *sportive*
   But gan examine him in straighter° sort,   *stricter*
   Which of her Nymphes, or other close consort,°   *secret confederate*
   Him thither brought, and her to him betraid?
   He, much affeard, to her confessèd short,°   *soon*
   That 'twas Molanna which her so bewraid.°   *betrayed*
Then all attonce their hands upon Molanna laid.

52

But him (according as they had decreed)
   With a Deeres-skin they covered, and then chast
   With all their hounds that after him did speed;
   But he more speedy, from them fled more fast
   Then any Deere: so sore him dread aghast.°   *terrified*
   They after followed all with shrill out-cry,
   Shouting as they the heavens would have brast:°   *burst*
   That all the woods and dales where he did flie,
Did ring againe, and loud reeccho to the skie.

53

So they him followed till they weary were;
   When, back returning to Molann' againe,
   They, by commaund'ment of Diana, there
   Her whelmed with stones.[3] Yet Faunus (for her paine)°   *trouble*
   Of her belovèd Fanchin did obtaine,
   That her he would receive unto his bed.
   So now her waves passe through a pleasant Plaine,
   Till with the Fanchin she her selfe doe wed,
And (both combined) themselves in one faire river spred.

54

Nath'lesse,° Diana, full of indignatiön,   *nonetheless*
   Thence-forth abandond her delicious brooke;
   In whose sweet streame, before that bad occasiön,
   So much delight to bathe her limbes she tooke:
   Ne onely her,° but also quite forsooke   *i.e., the brook*
   All those faire forrests about Arlo hid,
   And all that Mountaine, which doth over-looke
   The richest champian that may else be rid,[4]
And the faire Shure,[5] in which are thousand Salmons bred.

---

3. This overwhelming with stones accounts for the shallowness of the river, mentioned in stanza 40.

4. The richest plain to be seen anywhere.
5. The river Suir.

55

Them all, and all that she so deare did way,°   *esteem*
  Thence-forth she left; and parting from the place,
  There-on an heavy haplesse curse did lay,
  To weet, that Wolves, where she was wont to space,°   *roam*
  Should harboured be, and all those Woods deface,
  And Thieves should rob and spoile[6] that Coast° around.   *region*
  Since which, those Woods, and all that goodly Chase,[7]
  Doth to this day with Wolves and Thieves abound:
Which too-too true that lands in-dwellers since have found.

Canto 7

   Pealing,° from Jove, to Natur's Bar,   *appealing*
     bold Alteration° pleades   *i.e., Mutabilitie*
   Large° Evidence: but Nature soone   *copious*
     her righteous Doome areads.[8]

I

Ah! whither doost thou now thou greater° Muse[9]   *very great*
  Me from these woods and pleasing forrests bring?
  And my fraile spirit (that dooth oft refuse
  This too high flight, unfit for her weake wing)
  Lift up aloft, to tell of heavens King
  (Thy soveraine Sire)[1] his fortunate successe,
  And victory, in bigger° noates to sing,   *louder*
  Which he obtained against that Titanesse,
That him of heavens Empire sought to dispossesse.

2

Yet sith° I needs must follow thy behest,   *since*
  Doe thou my weaker° wit with skill inspire,   *too weak*
  Fit for this turne;° and in my feeble brest   *task*
  Kindle fresh sparks of that immortall fire,
  Which learnèd minds inflameth with desire
  Of heavenly things: for, who but thou alone,
  That art yborne of heaven and heavenly Sire,
  Can tell things doen in heaven so long ygone;
So farre past memory of man that may be knowne.

3

Now, at the time that was before agreed,
  The Gods assembled all on Arlo hill;
  As well those that are sprung of heavenly seed,
  As those that all the other world° doe fill,   *i.e., the earth*

---

6. Despoil.
7. Hunting ground.
8. Proclaims her righteous judgment.
9. Calliope, though possibly Clio. See canto 6,

stanza 37 and n. 7.
1. Jove fathered the Muses on the Titaness Mnemosyne (Memory).

And rule both sea and land unto their will:
Onely th'infernall Powers might not appeare;
Aswell for horror of their count'naunce ill,
As for th'unruly fiends which they did feare;[2]
Yet Pluto and Proserpina were present there.[3]

4

And thither also came all other creatures,
    What-ever life or motion doe retaine,
    According to their sundry kinds of features;
    That Arlo scarsly could them all containe;
    So full they fillèd every hill and Plaine:
    And had not Natures Sergeant (that is Order)
    Them well disposèd by his busie paine,°   *care*
    And raungèd° farre abroad in every border,   *arranged*
They would have causèd much confusion and disorder.

5

Then forth issewed (great goddesse) great dame Nature,
    With goodly port° and gracious Majesty;   *bearing*
    Being far greater and more tall of stature
    Then any of the gods or Powers on hie:
    Yet certes° by her face and physnomy,°   *certainly / countenance*
    Whether she man or woman inly were,
    That could not any creature well descry:
    For, with a veile that wimpled° every where,   *covered in folds*
Her head and face was hid, that mote to none appeare.

6

That some doe say was so by skill devized,
    To hide the terror of her uncouth hew,°   *strange appearance*
    From mortall eyes that should be sore agrized;°   *terrified*
    For that her face did like a Lion shew,
    That eye of wight could not indure to view:
    But others tell that it so beautious was,
    And round about such beames of splendor threw,
    That it the Sunne a thousand times did pass,°   *surpass*
Ne° could be seene, but° like an image in a glass.   *nor / except*

7

That well may seemen true: for, well I weene
    That this same day, when she on Arlo sat,°   *i.e., in judgment*
    Her garment was so bright and wondrous sheene,°   *shining*
    That my fraile wit cannot devize to what
    It to compare, nor finde like stuffe° to that,   *fabric*
    As those three sacred Saints, though else most wise,
    Yet on mount Thabor quite their wits forgat,

2. Meaning either that the infernal powers controlled the fiends by fear or that the heavenly and
earthly powers feared *them*.
3. King and queen of the Underworld.

When they their glorious Lord in strange disguise
Transfigured sawe; his garments so did daze° their eyes.[4]   *dazzle*

8

In a fayre Plaine upon an equall° Hill,   *level-topped*
  She placèd was in a paviliön;
  Not such as Craftes-men by their idle° skill   *vain*
  Are wont for Princes states° to fashiön: *canopied thrones*
  But th'earth her self of her owne motiön,
  Out of her fruitfull bosome made to growe
  Most dainty trees; that, shooting up anon,°   *at once*
  Did seeme to bow their bloosming° heads full lowe,   *blossoming*
For homage unto her, and like a throne did shew.°   *appear*

9

So hard it is for any living wight,
  All her array and vestiments to tell,
  That old Dan° Geffrey (in whose gentle spright   *Master, Sir*
  The pure well head of Poesie did dwell)
  In his *Foules parley* durst not with it mel,°   *meddle*
  But it transferd° to Alane, who he thought   *referred*
  Had in his *Plaint of kindes* described it well:[5]
  Which who will read set forth so as it ought,
Go seek he out that Alane where he may be sought.

10

And all the earth far underneath her feete
  Was dight° with flowres, that voluntary grew   *decked*
  Out of the ground, and sent forth odours sweet,
  Tenne thousand mores° of sundry sent and hew,   *plants*
  That might delight the smell, or please the view:
  The which, the Nymphes, from all the brooks thereby
  Had gathered, which they at her foot-stoole threw;
  That richer seemed then any tapestry,
That Princes bowres adorne with painted imagery.

11

And Mole[6] himself, to honour her the more,
  Did deck himself in freshest faire attire,
  And his high head, that seemeth alwaies hore°   *hoary*
  With hardned frosts of former winters ire,
  He with an Oaken girlond now did tire,°   *attire*
  As if the love of some new Nymph late seene,
  Had in him kindled youthfull fresh desire,
  And made him change his gray attire to greene;
Ah gentle Mole! such joyance hath thee well beseene.[7]

4. Peter, James, and John saw Jesus transfigured on a mountain (traditionally Mount Tabor, in Galilee). See Matthew 17.1–8.
5. Chaucer, in his *Parliament of Fowls*, lines 316–18, refers to Alain de Lille's *De Planctu Naturae* as Aleyn's *Pleynt of Kynde* (Complaint of Nature).
6. See canto 6, stanza 36 and n. 4.
7. Well becomes you.

12

Was never so great joyance since the day,
   That all the gods whylome assembled were,
   On Haemus hill in their divine array,
   To celebrate the solemne° bridall cheare,   *sacred*
   Twixt Peleus, and dame Thetis[8] pointed° there;   *appointed*
   Where Phoebus self, that god of Poets hight,
   They say did sing the spousall hymne full cleere,
   That all the gods were ravisht with delight
Of his celestiall song, and Musicks wondrous might.

13

This great Grandmother of all creatures bred
   Great Nature, ever young yet full of eld,°   *age*
   Still° mooving, yet unmovèd from her sted;°   *always / place*
   Unseene of any, yet of all beheld;
   Thus sitting in her throne as I have teld,
   Before her came dame Mutabilite;
   And being lowe before her presence feld,°   *prostrated*
   With meek obaysance and humilitie,
Thus gan her plaintif Plea, with words to amplifie;

14

"To thee O greatest goddesse, onely° great,   *uniquely*
   An humble suppliant loe, I lowely fly
   Seeking for Right, which I of thee entreat;
   Who Right to all dost deale indifferently,°   *impartially*
   Damning all Wrong and tortious° Injurie,   *wrongful*
   Which any of thy creatures doe to other
   (Oppressing them with power, unequally)°   *unjustly*
   Sith of them all thou are the equall° mother, *impartial*
And knittest each to each, as brother unto brother.

15

"To thee therefore of this same Jove I plaine,
   And of his fellow gods that faine° to be,   *feign*
   That challenge° to themselves the whole worlds raign; *claim*
   Of which, the greatest part is due to me,
   And heaven it selfe by heritage in Fee:° *absolute possession*
   For, heaven and earth I both alike do deeme,°   *adjudge*
   Sith heaven and earth are both alike to thee;
   And, gods no more then men thou doest esteeme:
For, even the gods to thee, as men to gods do seeme.

16

"Then weigh, O soveraigne goddesse, by what right
   These gods do claime the worlds whole soverainty;

---

8. Mortal king and sea goddess, the parents of Achilles. Haemus is a mountain in Thrace. (But in the standard accounts the wedding is said to have taken place on Mount Pelion, in Greece.)

And that° is onely dew unto thy might   *that which*
  Arrogate to themselves ambitiously:
  As for the gods owne principality,°   *sovereignty*
  Which Jove usurpes unjustly; that to be
  My heritage, Jove's self cannot deny,
  From my great Grandsire Titan, unto mee,
Derived by dew descent; as is well knowen to thee.

17

"Yet mauger° Jove, and all his gods beside,   *despite*
  I doe possesse the worlds most regiment;°   *rule*
  As, if ye please it into parts divide,
  And every parts inholders° to convent,°   *inhabitants / convene*
  Shall to your eyes appeare incontinent.°   *at once*
  And first,[9] the Earth (great mother of us all)
  That only° seems unmoved and permanent,   *alone*
  And unto Mutability not thrall;
Yet is she changed in part, and eeke° in generall.   *also*

18

"For, all that from her springs, and is ybredde,
  How-ever fayre it flourish for a time,
  Yet see we soone decay; and, being dead,
  To turne again unto their earthly slime:
  Yet, out of their decay and mortall crime,[1]
  We daily see new creatures to arize;
  And of their Winter spring another Prime,°   *spring*
  Unlike in forme, and changed by strange disguise:
So turne they still about, and change in restlesse wise.

19

"As for her tenants; that is, man and beasts,
  The beasts we daily see massacred dy,
  As thralls and vassalls unto mens beheasts:
  And men themselves doe change continually,
  From youth to eld, from wealth to poverty,
  From good to bad, from bad to worst of all.
  Ne doe their bodies only flit and fly:
  But eeke their minds (which they immortal call)
Still change and vary thoughts, as new occasions fall.

20

"Ne is the water in more constant case;
  Whether those same on high, or these belowe.[2]
  For, th'Ocean moveth stil, from place to place;

---

9. In what follows, Mutabilitie argues the ubiquity of change in each of the traditional four elements (cf. stanza 25): earth, water, air, and fire. The most notable sources are Ovid, *Metamorphoses* 15, and Lucretius, *De Rerum Natura* 5.

1. I.e., death and disintegration.
2. As in Genesis 1.7, where God divides "the waters which were under the firmament from the waters which were above the firmament."

And every River still doth ebbe and flowe:
Ne any Lake, that seems most still and slowe,
Ne Poole so small, that can his smoothnesse holde,
When any winde doth under heaven blowe;
With which, the clouds are also tost and rolled;
Now like great Hills; and, streight, like sluces, them unfold.[3]

21

"So likewise are all watry living wights
  Still tost, and turnèd, with continuall change,
  Never abyding in their stedfast plights.°   *conditions*
  The fish, still floting,° doe at randon° range,   *swimming / random*
  And never rest; but evermore exchange
  Their dwelling places, as the streames them carrie:
  Ne have the watry foules a certaine grange,°   *abode*
  Wherein to rest, ne in one stead° do tarry;   *place*
But flitting still doe flie, and still their places vary.

22

"Next is the Ayre: which who feels not by sense
  (For, of all sense it is the middle meane[4])
  To flit still? and, with subtill influence°   *flowing*
  Of his thin spirit, all creatures to maintaine,
  In state of life? O weake life! that does leane
  On thing so tickle° as th'unsteady ayre;   *uncertain; changeable*
  Which every howre is changed, and altred cleane°   *altogether*
  With every blast that bloweth fowle or faire:
The faire doth it prolong; the fowle doth it impaire.

23

"Therein the changes infinite beholde,
  Which to her creatures every minute chaunce;
  Now, boyling hot: streight, friezing deadly cold:
  Now, faire sun-shine, that makes all skip and daunce:
  Streight, bitter storms and balefull countenance,
  That makes them all to shiver and to shake:
  Raync, hayle, and snowe do pay them sad penance,
  And dreadfull thunder-claps (that make them quake)
With flames and flashing lights that thousand changes make.

24

"Last is the fire: which, though it live for ever,
  Ne can be quenchèd quite;° yet, every day,   *entirely*
  We see his parts, so soone as they do sever,
  To lose their heat, and shortly to decay;
  So, makes himself his owne consuming pray.
  Ne any living creatures doth he breed:
But all, that are of others bredd, doth slay;

---

3. Open. "Streight": immediately.   4. The conductor or medium.

And, with their death, his cruell life dooth feed;
Nought leaving, but their barren ashes, without seede.

25

"Thus, all these fower° (the which the ground-work bee   *four*
    Of all the world, and of all living wights)
    To thousand sorts of Change we subject see:
    Yet are they changed (by other wondrous slights°)   *devices*
    Into themselves,° and lose their native mights;   *into one another*
    The Fire to Aire, and th'Ayre to Water sheere,°   *clear*
    And Water into Earth: yet Water fights
    With Fire, and Aire with Earth approaching neere:
Yet all are in one body, and as one appeare.

26

"So, in them all raignes Mutabilitie;
    How-ever these, that Gods themselves do call,
    Of them doe claime the rule and soveranty:
    As, Vesta, of the fire aethereall;
    Vulcan, of this, with us so usuall;
    Ops,⁵ of the earth; and Juno of the Ayre;
    Neptune, of Seas; and Nymphes, of Rivers all.
    For, all those Rivers to me subject are:
And all the rest, which they usurp, be all my share.

27

"Which to approven° true, as I have told,   *prove*
    Vouchsafe, O goddesse, to thy presence call
    The rest which doe the world in being hold:
    As, times and seasons of the yeare that fall:
    Of all the which, demand° in generall,   *ask*
    Or judge thy selfe, by verdit° of thine eye,   *verdict*
    Whether to me they are not subject all."
    Nature did yeeld thereto; and by-and-by,°   *immediately*
Bade Order call them all, before her Majesty.

28

So, forth issewed the Seasons of the yeare;
    First, lusty° Spring, all dight in leaves of flowres   *vigorous*
    That freshly budded and new bloosmes° did beare   *blossoms*
    (In which a thousand birds had built their bowres
    That sweetly sung, to call forth Paramours°):   *lovers*
    And in his hand a javelin he did beare,
    And on his head (as fit for warlike stoures)°   *encounters*
    A guilt° engraven morion° he did weare;   *gilded / helmet*
That as some did him love, so others did him feare.

5. Roman goddess of plenty and fertility, who   above the air. Vulcan, the blacksmith god, rules
rules over earth. Vesta, goddess of the hearth, is   over earthly fire ("this, with us so usuall").
assigned by Spenser to rule over the fire that is

29

Then came the jolly Sommer, being dight
  In a thin silken cassock° coloured greene,   *cloak*
  That was unlynèd all, to be more light:
  And on his head a girlond well beseene[6]
  He wore, from which as he had chauffèd° been   *heated*
  The sweat did drop; and in his hand he bore
  A boawe and shaftes, as he in forrest greene
  Had hunted late the Libbard° or the Bore,   *leopard*
And now would bathe his limbes, with labor heated sore.°   *severely*

30

Then came the Autumne all in yellow clad,
  As though he joyèd in his plentious store,
  Laden with fruits that made him laugh, full glad
  That he had banisht hunger, which to-fore°   *formerly*
  Had by the belly oft him pinchèd sore.
  Upon his head a wreath that was enrold°   *enfolded*
  With eares of corne,° of every sort he bore: *grain*
  And in his hand a sickle he did holde,
To reape the ripened fruits the which the earth had yold.°   *yielded*

31

Lastly, came Winter cloathèd all in frize.[7]
  Chattering his teeth for cold that did him chill,
  Whil'st on his hoary beard his breath did freese;
  And the dull drops that from his purpled bill°   *nose*
  As from a limbeck° did adown distill.   *alembic*
  In his right hand a tippèd° staffe he held,   *i.e., with metal*
  With which his feeble steps he stayèd still:°   *continually*
  For, he was faint with cold, and weak with eld;
That scarse his loosèd limbes he hable was to weld.°   *wield; i.e., move*

32

These, marching softly,° thus in order went,   *slowly*
  And after them, the Monthes all riding came;
  First, sturdy° March[8] with brows full sternly bent,   *stern; surly*
  And armèd strongly, rode upon a Ram,
  The same which over Hellespontus swam:[9]
  Yet in his hand a spade he also hent,°   *grasped*
  And in a bag all sorts of seeds ysame,°   *together*
  Which on the earth he strowèd as he went,
And fild her womb with fruitfull hope of nourishment.

---

6. Seen to look well; attractive.
7. A coarse woolen cloth.
8. In the Julian calendar (used in England until 1752), the year began on March 25.
9. A ram, sometimes identified as Jove in one of

the many forms he took for purposes of ravishment or seduction (see Book 3, canto 11, stanza 30 and n. 3), carried Helle through the air. But she fell off into a body of water that has since borne her name: the Hellespont.

33

Next came fresh Aprill full of lustyhed,°   *vigor*
  And wanton as a Kid whose home new buds:
  Upon a Bull he rode, the same which led
  Europa floting through th'Argolick fluds:[1]
  His homes were gilden all with golden studs,
  And garnishèd with garlonds goodly dight
  Of all the fairest flowres and freshest buds
Which th'earth brings forth, and wet he seemed in sight.
With waves, through which he waded for his loves delight.

34

Then came faire May, the fayrest mayd on ground,
  Deckt all with dainties of her seasons pryde,
  And throwing flowres out of her lap around:
  Upon two brethrens shoulders she did ride,
  The twinnes of Leda;[2] which on eyther side
  Supported her like to their soveraine Queene.
  Lord! how all creatures laught, when her they spide,
  And leapt and daunc't as they had ravisht° beene!   *enraptured*
And Cupid selfe about her fluttred all in greene.

35

And after her, came jolly June, arrayd
  All in greene leaves, as he a Player[3] were;
  Yet in his time, he wrought° as well as playd,   *worked*
  That by his plough-yrons° mote right well appeare: *ploughshares*
  Upon a Crab he rode, that him did beare
  With crooked crawling steps an uncouth pase,
  And backward yode,° as Bargemen° wont to fare   *went / rowers*
  Bending their force contrary to their face,
Like that ungracious crew which faines demurest grace.[4]

36

Then came hot July boyling like to fire,
  That all his garments he had cast away:
  Upon a Lyon raging yet with ire
  He boldly rode and made him to obay:
  It was the beast that whylome did forray°   *ravage*
  The Nemaean forrest, till th'Amphytrionide[5]
  Him slew, and with his hide did him array;
  Behinde his back a sithe,° and by his side   *scythe*
Under his belt he bore a sickle[6] circling wide.

1. The Argolic Gulf of the Aegean Sea. The bull was Jupiter in disguise. He swam with Europa from the ancient Middle Eastern city of Tyre to Crete, off the southern coast of the continent that was supposedly named after her.
2. Castor and Pollux (the zodiacal sign of Gemini). Each month brings its zodiacal sign to the conference.
3. Actor. Actors appearing as wild or savage men were attired in leafy costumes.
4. Like those who, in excessive and false politeness, walk backward as they leave a room.
5. I.e., Hercules, whose mother was the wife of King Amphitryon (though his father was Jupiter). Strangling the supernaturally powerful lion that had terrorized the region of Nemea in Greece was the first of Hercules' Twelve Labors.
6. July both mows (with his scythe) and reaps.

37

The sixth was August, being rich arrayd
  In garment all of gold downe to the ground:
  Yet rode he not, but led a lovely Mayd
  Forth by the lilly hand, the which was cround
  With eares of corne, and full her hand was found;
  That was the righteous Virgin,[7] which of old
  Lived here on earth, and plenty made abound;
  But, after Wrong was loved and Justice solde,
She left th'unrighteous world and was to heaven extold.°   raised

38

Next him, September marchèd eeke on foote;
  Yet was he heavy laden with the spoyle
  Of harvests riches, which he made his boot,°   booty
  And him enricht with bounty of the soyle:
  In his one hand, as fit for harvests toyle,
  He held a knife-hook; and in th'other hand
  A paire of waights, with which he did assoyle°   determine
  Both more and lesse, where it in doubt did stand,
And equall° gave to each as Justice duly scanned.°   equitably / judged

39

Then came October full of merry glee:
  For, yet his noule was totty of the must,[8]
  Which he was treading in the wine-fats see,[9]
  And of the joyous oyle, whose gentle gust°   taste
  Made him so frollick and so full of lust:°   lustiness
  Upon a dreadful Scorpion he did ride,
  The same which by Dianaes doom° unjust   judgment
  Slew great Orion:[1] and eeke by his side
He had his ploughing share, and coulter[2] ready tyde.

40

Next was November, he full grosse and fat,
  As fed with lard, and that right well might seeme;
  For, he had been a fatting° hogs of late,   fattening
  That yet his browes with sweat, did reek and steem,
  And yet the season was full sharp° and breem;°   rough / cold
  In planting eeke he took no small delight:
  Whereon he rode, not easie was to deeme;°   determine
  For it a dreadfull Centaure was in sight,
The seed of Saturne, and faire Naïs, Chiron[3] hight.

---

7. Astraea, the goddess of justice. After leaving earth—in despair—she became the constellation Virgo.
8. I.e., his head was unsteady from the new wine.
9. Wine vats' sea.
1. According to one myth Orion boasted that he could kill anything that came from the earth.

Indignant at his arrogance Diana sent a scorpion that stung and killed him.
2. The iron blade of a plow, which makes a vertical cut in the soil. It is then sliced horizontally by the plowshare.
3. He was stellified as the zodiacal sign Sagittarius.

41

And after him, came next the chill December:
　Yet he through merry feasting which he made,
　And great bonfires, did not the cold remember;
　His Saviours birth his mind so much did glad:
　Upon a shaggy-bearded Goat he rade,°　　　　　　　　　　*rode*
　The same wherewith Dan Jove in tender yeares,
　They say, was nourisht by th'Idaean mayd;[4]
　And in his hand a broad deepe boawle he beares;
Of which, he freely drinks an health to all his peeres.

42

Then came old January, wrappèd well
　In many weeds° to keep the cold away;　　　　　　　　　*clothes*
　Yet did he quake and quiver like to quell,°　　　　　　　*perish*
　And blowe his nayles to warme them if he may:
　For, they were numbd with holding all the day
　An hatchet keene, with which he fellèd wood,
　And from the trees did lop the needlesse spray:°　　　　*twigs*
　Upon an huge great Earth-pot steane[5] he stood;
From whose wide mouth, there flowèd forth the Romane floud.[6]

43

And lastly, came cold February, sitting
　In an old wagon, for he could not ride;
　Drawne of two fishes° for the season fitting,　　　　　*i.e., Pisces*
　Which through the flood before[7] did softly slyde
　And swim away: yet had he by his side
　His plough and harnesse fit to till the ground,
　And tooles to prune the trees, before the pride°　　　　*splendor*
　Of hasting Prime° did make them burgein° round:　　*spring / bud*
So past the twelve Months forth, and their dew places found.

44

And after these, there came the Day, and Night,
　Riding together both with equall pase,
　Th'one on a Palfrey° blacke, the other white;　　　　*saddle horse*
　But Night had covered her uncomely face
　With a blacke veile, and held in hand a mace,
　On top whereof the moon and stars were pight,°　　　　*placed*
　And sleep and darknesse round about did trace:°　　　*go*
　But Day did beare, upon his scepters hight,
The goodly Sun, encompast all with beamès bright.

---

4. The nymph Amalthea, of Mount Ida in Crete.
Jove was saved by his mother, Rhea, from being
eaten by Cronus, his father. He was brought up
in Crete and suckled by a goat identified with the
zodiacal sign Capricorn.

5. Urn; here standing for the constellation
Aquarius.
6. I.e., the Tiber River.
7. I.e., the water flowing from Aquarius's urn.

45

Then came the Howres, faire daughters of high Jove,
   And timely[8] Night, the which were all endewed
   With wondrous beauty fit to kindle love;
   But they were Virgins all, and love eschewed,
   That might forslack[9] the charge to them fore-shewed
   By mighty Jove; who did them Porters make
   Of heavens gate (whence all the gods issued)
   Which they did dayly watch, and nightly wake°   *guard*
By even turnes, ne ever did their charge forsake.

46

And after all came Life, and lastly Death;
   Death with most grim and griesly visage seene,
   Yet is he nought but parting of the breath;
   Ne ought to see, but like a shade to weene,°   *conceive*
   Unbodièd, unsouled, unheard, unseene.
   But Life was like a faire young lusty boy,
   Such as they faine Dan Cupid to have beene,
   Full of delightfull health and lively joy,
Deckt all with flowres, and wings of gold fit to employ.

47

When these were past, thus gan the Titanesse:
   "Lo, mighty mother, now be judge and say,
   Whether in all thy creatures more or lesse
   Change doth not raign and beare the greatest sway:
   For, who sees not, that Time on all doth pray?°   *prey*
   But Times do change and move continually.
   So nothing here long standeth in one stay:
   Wherefore, this lower world who can deny
But to be subject still° to Mutabilitie?"   *always*

48

Then thus gan Jove: "Right true it is, that these
   And all things else that under heaven dwell
   Are chaunged of Time, who doth them all disseise°   *deprive*
   Of being: But, who is it (to me tell)
   That Time himselfe doth move and still compell
   To keepe his course? Is not that namely wee
   Which poure that vertue° from our heavenly cell,   *power*
   That moves them all, and makes them changèd be?
So them we gods doe rule, and in them also thee."

8. Temporal, belonging to time; in contrast to "high Jove," who is immortal.
9. Cause (them) to neglect.

49

To whom, thus Mutability: "The things
  Which we see not how they are moved and swayd,
  Ye may attribute to your selves as Kings,
  And say they by your secret powre are made:
  But what we see not, who shall us perswade?
  But were they so, as ye them faine to be,
  Moved by your might, and ordred by your ayde;
  Yet what if I can prove, that even yee
Your selves are likewise changed, and subject unto mee?

50

"And first, concerning her that is the first,[1]
  Even you faire Cynthia, whom so much ye make
  Joves dearest darling, she was bred and nurst
  On Cynthus hill,[2] whence she her name did take:
  Then is she mortall borne, how-so° ye crake;°   *howsoever / brag*
  Besides, her face and countenance every day
  We changèd see, and sundry forms partake,
  Now hornd, now round, now bright, now brown° and gray: *dark*
So that 'as changefull as the Moone' men use° to say.   *are accustomed*

51

"Next, Mercury, who though he lesse appeare
  To change his hew, and alwayes seeme as one;
  Yet, he his course doth altar every yeare,
  And is of late far out of order gone:[3]
  So Venus eeke, that goodly Paragone,°   *model of excellence*
  Though faire all night, yet is she darke all day;
  And Phoebus self, who lightsome is alone,°   *alone is radiant*
  Yet is he oft eclipsed by the way,°   *in his course*
And fills the darkned world with terror and dismay.

52

"Now Mars that valiant man is changèd most:
  For, he some times so far runs out of square,
  That he his way doth seem quite to have lost,
  And cleane without° his usuall sphere to fare;   *outside*
  That even these Star-gazers stonisht are
  At sight thereof, and damne their lying bookes:
  So likewise, grim Sir Saturne oft doth spare°   *restrain*
  His sterne aspect,[4] and calme his crabbèd° lookes: *harsh*
So many turning cranks° these have, so many crookes.   *twists*

---

1. The moon is first because its orbit is closest to the earth.
2. Mount Cynthus, on the Greek isle Delos.
3. The actual orbits of Mercury and the other planets were not accurately predictable by the Ptolemaic (earth-centric) astronomical model.

4. Punning on the astrological sense of "aspect" as the relative position of planets, which supposedly affects their influence. Saturn often runs so far out of his course that his generally baleful influence is lessened.

53

"But you Dan Jove, that only constant are,
  And King of all the rest, as ye do clame,
  Are you not subject eeke to this misfare?°   *going astray*
  Then let me aske you this withouten blame,
  Where were ye borne? some say in Crete by name,
  Others in Thebes, and others other-where;
  But wheresoever they comment° the same,   *devise*
  They all consent that ye begotten were,
And borne here in this world, ne other[5] can appeare.

54

"Then are ye mortall borne, and thrall to me,
  Unless the kingdome of the sky yee make°   *claim to be*
  Immortall, and unchangeable to bee;
  Besides, that power and vertue[6] which ye spake,
  That ye here worke, doth many changes take,
  And your owne natures change: for, each of you
  That vertue have, or° this, or that to make,   *either*
  Is checkt and changèd from his nature trew,
By others opposition or obliquid view.[7]

55

"Besides, the sundry motions of your Spheares,[8]
  So sundry waies and fashions as clerkes° faine,   *learned men*
  Some in short space, and some in longer yeares;
  What is the same but alteration plaine?
  Onely the starrie skie[9] doth still remaine:°   *remains constant*
  Yet do the Starres and Signes therein still move,
  And even it self is moved, as wizards saine.°   *wise men say*
  But all that moveth, doth mutation love:
Therefore both you and them to me I subject prove.

56

"Then since within this wide great Universe
  Nothing doth firme and permanent appeare,
  But all things tost and turned by transverse:°   *turned away*
  What then should let,° but I aloft should reare   *hinder*
  My Trophee, and from all, the triumph beare?
  Now judge then (O thou greatest goddesse trew!)
  According as thy selfe doest see and heare,
  And unto me addoom that° is my dew;   *judge that which*
That is the rule of all, all being ruled by you."

5. Nor anything else.
6. Power; i.e., the paired words are synonymous.
7. Referring to the fundamental idea of astrology: that each planet has a "vertue" (power) that it sheds on earth, but that the effect depends on its position and the position of other planets. "Opposition" and "obliquity" are technical terms for the relative position of celestial bodies. "Obliquid" (found only here) is a coinage from *oblique*, presumably for the sake of the meter.
8. See canto 6, stanza 8, n. 7.
9. The crystalline sphere that bore all the fixed stars, beyond the spheres of the moon, sun, and planets.

57

So having ended, silence long ensewed,
    Ne° Nature to or fro¹ spake for a space,   *nor*
    But with firme eyes affixt, the ground still viewed.
    Meane while, all creatures, looking in her face,
    Expecting° th'end of this so doubtfull case,   *awaiting*
    Did hang in long suspence what would ensew,
    To whether° side should fall the soveraigne place: *which*
    At length, she looking up with chearefull view,
The silence brake, and gave her doome in speeches° few.   *phrases*

58

"I well consider all that ye have sayd,
    And find that all things steadfastnes doe hate
    And changèd be: yet being rightly wayd°   *weighed*
    They are not changèd from their first estate;°   *state, condition*
    But by their change their being doe dilate:²
    And turning to themselves at length againe,
    Doe worke their owne perfection so by fate:
    Then over them Change doth not rule and raigne;
But they raigne over change, and doe their states maintaine.

59

"Cease therefore daughter further to aspire,
    And thee content thus to be ruled by me:
    For thy decay° thou seekst by thy desire;   *downfall*
    But time shall come that all shall changèd bee,
    And from thenceforth, none no more change shall see."³
    So was the Titaness put downe and whist,°   *silenced*
    And Jove confirmed in his imperiall see.°   *throne*
    Then was that whole assembly quite dismist,
And Natur's selfe did vanish, whither no man wist.°   *knew*

The 8 Canto, unperfite.°   *unfinished*

1

When I bethinke me on that speech whyleare,°   *earlier*
    Of Mutability, and well it way:°   *weigh, consider*
    Me seemes, that though she all unworthy were
    Of the Heav'ns Rule; yet very sooth to say,
    In all things else she beares the greatest sway.
    Which makes me loath this state of life so tickle,°   *uncertain; changeable*
    And love of things so vaine to cast away;
    Whose flowring pride, so fading and so fickle,
Short Time shall soon cut down with his consuming sickle.

---

1. For or against.
2. Expand, as they fulfill their natures.
3. Cf. 1 Corinthians 15.51, 54: "we shall all be changed. . . . when this corruptible shall have put on incorruption, and this mortal shall have put on immortality, then shall be brought to pass the saying that is written, Death is swallowed up in victory."

2

Then gin° I thinke on that which Nature sayd,   *begin*
　　Of that same time when no more Change shall be,
　　But stedfast rest of all things firmely stayd
　　Upon the pillours of Eternity,
　　That is contrayr to° Mutabilitie: *the opposite of*
　　For, all that moveth, doth in Change delight:
　　But thence-forth all shall rest eternally
　　With Him that is the God of Sabbaoth hight:
O that great Sabbaoth God, graunt me that Sabaoths sight.[4]

1609

Amoretti *and* Epithalamion

In the early 1590s the widowed Spenser wooed and won Elizabeth Boyle, whom he married in 1594. The next year he published a small volume that included the sonnet sequence *Amoretti* ("little loves" or "little cupids") and the *Epithalamion*. Several of the sonnets explicitly address an "Elizabeth," and the volume's subtitle, "Written not long since," suggests that these poems, taken together, are a portrait of Spenser's recent courtship and marriage. It was unusual to write sonnets about a happy and successful love; traditionally, the sonneteer's love was for someone painfully inaccessible. Spenser rehearses some of the conventional motifs of frustration and longing, but his cycle of polished, eloquent poems leads toward joyous possession. Thus, for example, in sonnet 67 ("Lyke as a huntsman after weary chace"), he transforms a Petrarchan lament into a vision of unexpected fulfillment.

Spenser's great celebration of this fulfillment is the *Epithalamion*. A learned poet, he was acutely conscious that he was writing within a tradition: an epithalamion is a wedding song whose Greek name conveys that it was sung on the threshold of the bridal chamber. The genre, which goes back at least as far as Sappho (ca. 612 B.C.E.), was widely practiced by the Roman poets, particularly Catullus, and imitated in the Renaissance. Its elements typically include an invocation of the Muses, followed by a celebratory description of the procession of the bride, the religious rites, the singing and dancing at the wedding party, the preparations for the wedding night, and the sexual consummation of the marriage.

In long, flowing stanzas, Spenser follows these conventions closely, adapting them with exquisite delicacy to his small-town Irish setting and native folklore. But his first stanza announces a major innovation: "So I unto myselfe alone will sing." Traditionally, the poet of an epithalamion was an admiring observer, a kind of master of ceremonies; by combining the roles of poet and bridegroom, Spenser transforms a genial social performance into a passionate lyric utterance. Equally remarkable innovations are the complex stanza form, for which no direct model has been discovered, and the still more complex overall structure. That structure is a triumph of symbolic patterning; the more scholars have studied it, the more elaborate the order they seem to have uncovered. To cite only the most obvious examples, the poem's twenty-four stanzas represent the twenty-four hours of the day, while its 365 long lines (lines of five or more iambic feet) correspond to the number of days in a year. The subtle and rich poetic structure conjures up not only a single day of celebration but also, beyond this particular event, an orderly, harmonious universe,

---

4. Spenser here confuses, perhaps intentionally, the Hebrew word for "armies, hosts" (*Sabaoth*) with that for "rest" (*Sabbath*).

with an underlying pattern of coherence and regularity. If the *Epithalamion* goes to remarkable lengths to affirm this pattern, it is perhaps because it also registers so insistently all that threatens the enduring happiness of wedded love and indeed of human life itself. The greatest threat is the force over which the poem exercises its greatest power: time.

From Amoretti

1

Happy ye leaves[1] when as those lilly hands,
 Which hold my life in their dead doing° might,   *killing*
 Shall handle you and hold in loves soft bands,°   *bonds*
 Lyke captives trembling at the victors sight.
5 And happy lines, on which with starry light,
 Those lamping° eyes will deigne sometimes to look   *flashing*
 And reade the sorrowes of my dying spright,°   *spirit*
 Written with teares in harts close° bleeding book.   *secret*
 And happy rymes bath'd in the sacred brooke
10 Of Helicon[2] whence she derivèd is,
 When ye behold that Angels blessèd looke,
 My soules long lackèd foode, my heavens blis.
Leaves, lines, and rymes, seeke her to please alone,
 Whom if ye please, I care for other none.

34[3]

Lyke as a ship that through the Ocean wyde,
 By conduct of some star doth make her way,
 Whenas a storme hath dimd her trusty guyde,
 Out of her course doth wander far astray:
5 So I whose star, that wont° with her bright ray   *was accustomed*
 Me to direct, with cloudes is overcast,
 Doe wander now in darknesse and dismay,
 Through hidden perils round about me plast.°   *placed*
 Yet hope I well, that when this storme is past
10 My Helice[4] the lodestar° of my lyfe   *guiding star*
 Will shine again, and looke on me at last,
 With lovely light to cleare my cloudy grief.
Till then I wander carefull° comfortlesse,   *full of cares*
 In secret sorow and sad pensivenesse.

---

1. I.e., of the book: pages.
2. The "sacred brooke" is Hippocrene, which flows from Mount Helicon, the mountain sacred to the Muses.
3. An adaptation of Petrarch's Rima 189. See pp. 123–24 for Sir Thomas Wyatt's verse transla-tion of the sonnet, as well as a modern prose translation of it. The Italian original is included in the NAEL Archive.
4. A name for the Big Dipper (after the nymph who, in classical mythology, was transformed into it).

37

What guyle is this, that those her golden tresses,
    She doth attyre under a net of gold:
    And with sly° skill so cunningly them dresses,   *clever*
    That which is gold or heare,° may scarse be told?   *hair*
5 Is it that mens frayle eyes, which gaze too bold,
    She may entangle in that golden snare:
    And being caught may craftily enfold
    Theyr weaker harts, which are not wel aware?°   *wary*
Take heed therefore, myne eyes, how ye doe stare
10   Henceforth too rashly on that guilefull net,
    In which if ever ye entrappèd are,
    Out of her bands ye by no means shall get.
Fondnesse° it were for any being free,   *foolishness*
    To covet fetters, though they golden bee.

54

Of this worlds Theatre in which we stay,
    My love like the Spectator ydly sits
    Beholding me that all the pageants° play,   *dramatic scenes*
    Disguysing diversly my troubled wits.
5 Sometimes I joy when glad occasion fits,
    And mask in myrth lyke to a Comedy:
    Soone after when my joy to sorrow flits,
    I waile and make my woes a Tragedy.
Yet she beholding me with constant° eye,   *unmoved*
10   Delights not in my merth nor rues my smart:°   *pities my hurt*
    But when I laugh she mocks, and when I cry
    She laughes and hardens evermore her hart.
What then can move her? if nor merth nor mone,°   *moan*
    She is no woman, but a sencelesse stone.

64[5]

Comming to kisse her lyps (such grace I found)
    Me seemd I smelt a gardin of sweet flowres
    That dainty odours from them threw around,
    For damzels fit to decke their lovers bowres.
5 Her lips did smell lyke unto Gillyflowers,°   *carnations*
    Her ruddy cheeks lyke unto Roses red;
    Her snowy browes lyke budded Bellamoures,[6]
    Her lovely eyes like Pincks but newly spred,
Her goodly bosome lyke a Strawberry bed,
10   Her neck lyke to a bounch of Cullambynes;
    Her brest lyke lillyes, ere theyr leaves be shed,
    Her nipples lyke yong blossomd Jessemynes.°   *jasmines*

---

5. Much of the imagery of this sonnet is imitated from the Song of Solomon 4.10–16.
6. Unidentified flower, evidently white.

Such fragrant flowres doe give most odorous smell,
But her sweet odour did them all excell.

65

The doubt which ye misdeeme,° fayre love, is vaine,   *misconceive*
   That fondly° feare to loose your liberty,   *foolishly*
   When loosing one, two liberties ye gayne,
   And make him bond° that bondage earst° dyd fly.   *bound / formerly*
5 Sweet be the bands, the which true love doth tye,
   Without constraynt or dread of any ill:
   The gentle birde feels no captivity
   Within her cage, but singes and feeds her fill.
There pride dare not approch, nor discord spill°   *destroy*
10   The league twixt them, that loyal love hath bound;
   But simple truth and mutuall good will
   Seekes with sweet peace to salve each others wound.
There fayth° doth fearlesse dwell in brasen° towre,   *fidelity / brass*
   And spotlesse pleasure builds her sacred bowre.

67[7]

Lyke as a huntsman after weary chace,
   Seeing the game from him escapt away,
   Sits downe to rest him in some shady place,
   With panting hounds beguilèd° of their pray: *deluded*
5 So after long pursuit and vaine assay,°   *attempt*
   When I all weary had the chace forsooke,
   The gentle deare returnd the selfe-same way,
   Thinking to quench her thirst at the next° brooke.   *nearby*
There she beholding me with mylder looke,
10   Sought not to fly, but fearelesse still did bide:
   Till I in hand her yet halfe trembling tooke,
   And with her owne goodwill hir fyrmely tyde.
Strange thing me seemd to see a beast so wyld,
   So goodly wonne with her owne will beguyld.[8]

68

Most glorious Lord of lyfe, that on this day,°   *i.e., Easter*
   Didst make thy triumph over death and sin:
   And having harrowd hell,[9] didst bring away
   Captivity thence captive[1] us to win:
5 This joyous day, deare Lord, with joy begin,
   And grant that we for whom thou diddest dye

---

7. An imitation of Petrarch's Rima 190, but with a very different ending. Cf. Sir Thomas Wyatt's adaptation ("Whoso list to hunt") of the same sonnet, and the prose translation of the Petrarchan original appended to it, on pp. 121–22. For the Italian original, see the NAEL Archive.

8. Entrapped; won over.
9. In the apocryphal Gospel of Nicodemus, Christ descended into hell and led out into Paradise the righteous who had lived before his time.
1. A biblical phrase, as in Judges 5.12 and Ephesians 4.8.

Being with thy deare blood clene washt from sin,
  May live for ever in felicity.
And that thy love we weighing worthily,°   *valuing properly*
10   May likewise love thee for the same againe:
  And for thy sake that all lyke deare didst buy,[2]
  With love may one another entertayne.°   *sustain*
So let us love, deare love, lyke as we ought,
  Love is the lesson which the Lord us taught.[3]

74

Most happy letters fram'd by skilfull trade,°   *practice*
  With which that happy name° was first desynd: *i.e., Elizabeth*
The which three times thrise happy hath me made,
  With guifts of body, fortune and of mind.
5 The first my being to me gave by kind,°   *nature*
  From mothers womb deriv'd by dew descent,
The second is my sovereigne Queene most kind,
  That honour and large richesse to me lent.°   *bestowed*
The third my love, my lives last ornament,
10   By whom my spirit out of dust was raysed:
  To speake her prayse and glory excellent,
  Of all alive most worthy to be praysed.
Ye three Elizabeths for ever live,
  That three such graces did unto me give.

75

One day I wrote her name upon the strand,°   *shore*
  But came the waves and washèd it away:
Agayne I wrote it with a second hand,
  But came the tyde, and made my paynes his pray.°   *prey*
5 "Vayne man," sayd she, "that doest in vaine assay,°   *attempt*
  A mortall thing so to immortalize,
For I my selve shall lyke to this decay,
  And eek° my name bee wypèd out lykewize."   *also*
"Not so," quod° I, "let baser things devize°   *said / contrive*
10   To dy in dust, but you shall live by fame:
  My verse your vertues rare shall eternize,
  And in the heavens wryte your glorious name.
Where whenas death shall all the world subdew,
  Our love shall live, and later life renew."

2. I.e., Christ bought all people at the same great cost.

3. Cf. John 15.12: "This is my commandment, That ye love one another, as I have loved you."

79

Men call you fayre, and you doe credit° it,   *believe*
    For that your selfe ye dayly such doe see:
    But the trew fayre,° that is the gentle wit,°   *beauty / intelligence*
    And vertuous mind, is much more praysd of° me.   *by*
5   For all the rest, how ever fayre it be,
    Shall turne to nought and loose that glorious hew:°   *form*
    But onely that is permanent and free
    From frayle corruption, that doth flesh ensew.°   *outlast*
That is true beautie: that doth argue° you   *prove*
10   To be divine and borne of heavenly seed:
    Deriv'd from that fayre Spirit,° from whom al true   *i.e., God*
    And perfect beauty did at first proceed.
He onely fayre, and what he fayre hath made:
    All other fayre, lyke flowres, untymely fade.

                                      1595

Epithalamion

Ye learnèd sisters° which have oftentimes   *the Muses*
Beene to me ayding, others to adorne:[1]
Whom ye thought worthy of your gracefull rymes,
That even the greatest did not greatly scorne
5   To heare theyr names sung in your simple layes,°   *songs*
But joyèd in theyr prayse.
And when ye list° your owne mishaps to mourne,   *chose*
Which death, or love, or fortunes wreck did rayse,
Your string could soone to sadder tenor° turne,   *mood*
10 And teach the woods and waters to lament
Your dolefull dreriment.°   *sorrow*
Now lay those sorrowfull complaints aside,
And having all your heads with girland crownd,
Helpe me mine owne loves prayses to resound,
15 Ne° let the same of° any be envide: *nor / by*
So Orpheus did for his owne bride,[2]
So I unto my selfe alone will sing,
The woods shall to me answer and my eccho ring.

Early before the worlds light giving lampe,
20 His golden beame upon the hils doth spred,
Having disperst the nights unchearefull dampe,
Doe ye awake, and with fresh lustyhed°   *vigor*
Go to the bowre° of my belovèd love,   *bedchamber*
My truest turtle dove,

---

1. To write poems in praise of others.
2. Orpheus, archetype of the poet in classical antiquity, was famous for his love for his wife, Eurydice.

25   Bid her awake; for Hymen³ is awake,
       And long since ready forth his maske to move,
       With his bright Tead⁴ that flames with many a flake,°   *spark*
       And many a bachelor to waite on him,
       In theyr fresh garments trim.
30   Bid her awake therefore and soone her dight,°   *dress*
       For lo the wishèd day is come at last,
       That shall for al the paynes and sorrowes past,
       Pay to her usury° of long delight: *interest*
       And whylest she doth her dight,
35   Doe ye to her of joy and solace° sing,   *pleasure*
       That all the woods may answer and your Eccho ring.

       Bring with you all the Nymphes that you can heare°   *can hear you*
       Both of the rivers and the forrests greene:
       And of the sea that neighbours to her neare,
40   Al with gay girlands goodly wel beseene.°   *beautified*
       And let them also with them bring in hand,
       Another gay girland
       For my fayre love of lillyes and of roses,
       Bound truelove wize° with a blew silke riband.   *i.e., in a love knot*
45   And let them make great store° of bridale poses,°   *abundance / posies*
       And let them eeke° bring store of other flowers   *also*
       To deck the bridale bowers.
       And let the ground whereas° her foot shall tread,   *where*
       For feare the stones her tender foot should wrong
50   Be strewed with fragrant flowers all along,
       And diapred lyke the discolorèd mead.⁵
       Which done, doe at her chamber dore awayt,
       For she will waken strayt,°   *straightaway*
       The whiles doe ye this song unto her sing,
55   The woods shall to you answer and your Eccho ring.

       Ye Nymphes of Mulla⁶ which with careful heed,
       The silver scaly trouts doe tend full well,
       And greedy pikes which use° therein to feed,   *are accustomed*
       (Those trouts and pikes all others doo excell)
60   And ye likewise which keepe the rushy lake,°   *bordered by rushes*
       Where none doo fishes take,
       Bynd up the locks the which hang scatterd light,
       And in his waters which your mirror make,
       Behold your faces as the christall bright,
65   That when you come whereas° my love doth lie,   *where*
       No blemish she may spie.
       And eke ye lightfoot mayds which keepe the deere,⁷
       That on the hoary° mountayne use to towre,⁸   *gray; venerable*
       And the wylde wolves which seeke them to devoure,

---

3. The god of marriage, who leads a "maske" or procession at weddings.
4. A ceremonial torch, associated with marriages since classical times.
5. Ornamented like the many-colored meadow.

6. A river near Spenser's home in Ireland.
7. All wild animals, kept by the woodland nymphs.
8. A falconry term meaning to occupy heights.

70 With your steele darts° doo chace from comming neer, *spears*
  Be also present heere,
  To helpe to decke her and to help to sing,
  That all the woods may answer and your eccho ring.

  Wake now my love, awake; for it is time,
75 The Rosy Morne long since left Tithones bed,[9]
  All ready to her silver coche° to clyme, *coach*
  And Phoebus° gins° to shew his glorious hed. *the sun god / begins*
  Hark how the cheerefull birds do chaunt theyr laies
  And carroll of loves praise.
80 The merry Larke hir mattins° sings aloft, *morning prayers*
  The thrush replyes, the Mavis descant[1] playes,
  The Ouzell shrills, the Ruddock[2] warbles soft,
  So goodly all agree with sweet consent,° *harmony*
  To this dayes merriment.
85 Ah my deere love why doe ye sleepe thus long,
  When meeter° were that ye should now awake, *more fitting*
  T'awayt the comming of your joyous make,° *mate*
  And hearken to the birds lovelearnèd song,
  The deawy leaves among.
90 For they of joy and pleasance to you sing,
  That all the woods them answer and theyr eccho ring.

  My love is now awake out of her dreame,
  And her fayre eyes like stars that dimmèd were
  With darksome cloud, now shew° theyr goodly beams *show*
95 More bright then° Hesperus° his head doth rere. *than / evening star*
  Come now ye damzels, daughters of delight,
  Helpe quickly her to dight,° *attire*
  But first come ye fayre houres[3] which were begot
  In Joves sweet paradice, of Day and Night,
100 Which doe the seasons of the yeare allot,
  And al that ever in this world is fayre
  Doe make and still° repayre. *continuously*
  And ye three handmayds of the Cyprian Queene,[4]
  The which doe still adorne her beauties pride,
105 Helpe to addorne my beautifullest bride:
  And as ye her array, still throw betweene° *at intervals*
  Some graces to be seene,
  And as ye use° to Venus, to her sing, *are accustomed*
  The whiles the woods shal answer and your eccho ring.

9. See Song of Solomon 2.10–13: "Rise up, my love, my fair one, and come away. For, lo, the winter is past, the rain is over and gone; The flowers appear on the earth; the time of the singing of birds is come." In classical myth, Tithonus is the aged husband of Aurora, the dawn.
1. A melody or counterpoint written above a musical theme—a soprano obbligato.
2. The European robin. "Mavis": the song thrush. "Ouzell": the blackbird (which sings in England). The birds' concert is a convention of medieval love poetry.
3. The Hours, or Horae, are Olympian deities who attend to natural growth and to social order. They were traditionally the daughters of Jove and the Titaness Themis, but in the Mutabilitie Cantos of *The Faerie Queene* (above, p. 482), Spenser says Jove fathered them on Night.
4. Venus. "Three handmayds": the Graces, representing brightness, joy, and bloom.

110 Now is my love all ready forth to come,
Let all the virgins therefore well awayt,
And ye fresh boyes that tend upon her groome
Prepare your selves; for he is comming strayt.°   *straightaway*
Set all your things in seemely good aray°   *order*
115 Fit for so joyfull day,
The joyfulst day that ever sunne did see.
Faire Sun, shew forth thy favourable ray,
And let thy lifull° heat not fervent° be   *life-giving / hot*
For feare of burning her sunshyny face,
120 Her beauty to disgrace.°   *mar*
O fayrest Phoebus, father of the Muse,[5]
If ever I did honour thee aright,
Or sing the thing, that mote° thy mind delight,   *might*
Doe not thy servants simple boone° refuse,   *request*
125 But let this day let this one day be myne,
Let all the rest be thine.
Then I thy soverayne prayses loud wil sing,
That all the woods shal answer and theyr eccho ring.

Harke how the Minstrels gin to shrill aloud
130 Their merry Musick that resounds from far,
The pipe, the tabor,° and the trembling Croud,[6]   *small drum*
That well agree withouten breach or jar.°   *discord*
But most of all the Damzels doe delite,
When they their tymbrels° smyte,   *tambourines*
135 And thereunto doe daunce and carrol sweet,
That all the sences they doe ravish quite,
The whyles the boyes run up and downe the street,
Crying aloud with strong confusèd noyce,
As if it were one voyce.
140 Hymen[7] iô Hymen, Hymen they do shout,
That even to the heavens theyr shouting shrill
Doth reach, and all the firmament doth fill,
To which the people standing all about,
As in approvance doe thereto applaud
145 And loud advaunce her laud,°   *praise*
And evermore they Hymen Hymen sing,
That all the woods them answer and theyr eccho ring.

Loe where she comes along with portly° pace,   *stately*
Lyke Phoebe from her chamber of the East,
150 Arysing forth to run her mighty race,[8]
Clad all in white, that seemes° a virgin best.   *beseems, suits*
So well it her beseems that ye would weene°   *think*
Some angell she had beene.

5. Phoebus Apollo, god of the sun, was also god of
music and poetry, but he was not normally regarded
as the father of the Nine Muses (Zeus was).
6. Primitive fiddle. Spenser here designates Irish,
not classical, instruments and music for the classical masque or ballet.

7. The name of the classical god of marriage,
used as a conventional exclamation at weddings
in ancient Greece.
8. Phoebe is the moon, a virgin like the bride;
the reference to her anticipates the night.

Her long loose yellow locks lyke golden wyre,
155 Sprinckled with perle, and perling flowres a tweene,[9]
Doe lyke a golden mantle her attyre,
And being crownèd with a girland greene,
Seeme lyke some mayden Queene.
Her modest eyes abashèd to behold
160 So many gazers, as on her do stare,
Upon the lowly ground affixèd are.
Ne dare lift up her countenance too bold,
But blush to heare her prayses sung so loud,
So farre from being proud.
165 Nathlesse doe ye still loud her prayses sing,
That all the woods may answer and your eccho ring.

Tell me ye merchants daughters did ye see
So fayre a creature in your towne before,
So sweet, so lovely, and so mild as she,
170 Adornd with beautyes grace and vertues store,°   *abundance*
Her goodly eyes lyke Saphyres shining bright,
Her forehead yvory white,
Her cheekes lyke apples which the sun hath rudded,°   *made red*
Her lips lyke cherryes charming men to byte,
175 Her brest like to a bowle of creame uncrudded,°   *uncurdled*
Her paps° lyke lyllies budded,   *breasts*
Her snowie necke lyke to a marble towre,
And all her body like a pallace fayre,
Ascending uppe with many a stately stayre,
180 To honors seat and chastities sweet bowre.[1]
Why stand ye still ye virgins in amaze,
Upon her so to gaze,
Whiles ye forget your former lay to sing,
To which the woods did answer and your eccho ring.

185 But if ye saw that which no eyes can see,
The inward beauty of her lively spright,°   *living spirit, soul*
Garnisht with heavenly guifts of high degree,
Much more then would ye wonder at that sight,
And stand astonisht lyke to those which red°   *saw*
190 Medusaes mazeful hed.[2]
There dwels sweet love and constant chastity,
Unspotted fayth° and comely womanhood,   *fidelity*
Regard of honour and mild modesty,
There vertue raynes as Queene in royal throne,
195 And giveth lawes alone.
The which the base° affections doe obay,   *lower*
And yeeld theyr services unto her will,
Ne thought of thing uncomely ever may

---

9. Between. "Perling": winding.
1. The head, where the higher faculties are. The catalog of qualities is a convention in love poetry (cf. Song of Solomon 4–8).

2. Medusa, one of the Gorgons, had serpents instead of hair (hence a "mazeful hed"): the effect on beholders was to turn them to stone.

Thereto approch to tempt her mind to ill.
200 Had ye once seene these her celestial threasures,
And unrevealèd pleasures,
Then would ye wonder and her prayses sing,
That all the woods should answer and your Echo ring.

Open the temple gates unto my love,
205 Open them wide that she may enter in,[3]
And all the postes adorne as doth behove,[4]
And all the pillours deck with girlands trim,
For to recyve this Saynt with honour dew,
That commeth in to you.
210 With trembling steps and humble reverence,
She commeth in, before th'almighties vew,
Of her ye virgins learne obedience,
When so ye come into those holy places,
To humble your proud faces:
215 Bring her up to th'high altar, that she may
The sacred ceremonies there partake,
The which do endless matrimony make,
And let the roring° Organs loudly play   *i.e., resounding*
The praises of the Lord in lively notes,
220 The whiles with hollow° throates   *i.e., fully open*
The Choristers the joyous Antheme sing,
That all the woods may answere and theyr eccho ring.

Behold whiles she before the altar stands
Hearing the holy priest that to her speakes
225 And blesseth her with his two happy hands,
How the red roses flush up in her cheekes,
And the pure snow with goodly vermill° stayne,   *vermilion*
Like crimsin dyde in grayne,°   *fast color*
That even th'Angels which continually,
230 About the sacred Altare doe remaine,
Forget their service and about her fly,
Ofte peeping in her face that seemes more fayre,
The more they on it stare.
But her sad° eyes still° fastened on the ground,   *serious / ever*
235 Are governèd with goodly modesty,
That suffers° not one looke to glaunce awry,   *permits*
Which may let in a little thought unsownd.°   *flawed*
Why blush ye love to give to me your hand,
The pledge of all our band?°   *bond, tie*
240 Sing ye sweet Angels, Alleluya sing,
That all the woods may answere and your eccho ring.

Now al is done; bring home the bride againe,
Bring home the triumph of our victory,
Bring home with you the glory of her gaine,[5]

---

3. Cf. Psalms 24.7: "Lift up your heads, O ye gates; and be ye lift up, ye everlasting doors; and the King of glory shall come in."
4. As is proper. The doorposts were trimmed for weddings in classical times, and the custom was often referred to in classical and later love poetry.
5. I.e., the glory of gaining her.

245 With joyance bring her and with jollity.
    Never had man more joyfull day then this,
    Whom heaven would heape with blis.
    Make feast therefore now all this live long day,
    This day for ever to me holy is,
250 Poure out the wine without restraint or stay,°   *limit*
    Poure not by cups, but by the belly° full,   *wineskin*
    Poure out to all that wull,°   *want it*
    And sprinkle all the postes and wals with wine,
    That they may sweat, and drunken be withall.
255 Crowne ye God Bacchus° with a coronall,°   *god of wine / garland*
    And Hymen also crowne with wreathes of vine,
    And let the Graces daunce unto the rest;
    For they can doo it best:
    The whiles the maydens doe theyr carroll sing,
260 To which the woods shall answer and theyr eccho ring.

    Ring ye the bels, ye young men of the towne,
    And leave your wonted° labors for this day: *usual*
    This day is holy; doe ye write it downe,
    That ye for ever it remember may.
265 This day the sunne is in his chiefest hight,
    With Barnaby the bright,[6]
    From whence declining daily by degrees,
    He somewhat loseth of his heat and light,
    When once the Crab[7] behind his back he sees.
270 But for this time it ill ordainèd was,
    To chose the longest day in all the yeare,
    And shortest night, when longest fitter weare:
    Yet never day so long, but late° would passe.   *at last*
    Ring ye the bels, to make it weare away,
275 And bonefiers° make all day,   *bonfires*
    And daunce about them, and about them sing:
    That all the woods may answer, and your eccho ring.

    Ah when will this long weary day have end,
    And lende me leave to come unto my love?
280 How slowly do the houres theyr numbers[8] spend?
    How slowly does sad Time his feathers move?[9]
    Hast° thee O fayrest Planet to thy home   *haste*
    Within the Westerne fome:
    Thy tyred steedes long since have need of rest.[1]
285 Long though it be, at last I see it gloome,°   *begin to darken*
    And the bright evening star with golden creast°   *crest*
    Appeare out of the East.
    Fayre childe of beauty, glorious lampe of love

---

6. Saint Barnabas's Day, at the time of the summer solstice.
7. The constellation Cancer between Gemini and Leo. The sun, passing through the zodiac, leaves the Crab behind toward the end of July.
8. I.e., the number of minutes or the numbers depicted on a clock.
9. In traditional iconography, Time is winged.
1. The sun's chariot completes its daily course in the western sea ("fome").

That all the host of heaven in rankes doost lead,
290 And guydest lovers through the nightès dread,
How chearefully thou lookest from above,
And seemst to laugh atweene thy twinkling light
As joying in the sight
Of these glad many which for joy doe sing,
295 That all the woods them answer and theyr echo ring.

Now ceasse ye damsels your delights forepast;°   *previous*
Enough is it, that all the day was youres:
Now day is doen, and night is nighing° fast: *approaching*
Now bring the Bryde into the brydall boures.
300 Now night is come, now soone her disaray,°   *undress*
And in her bed her lay;
Lay her in lillies and in violets,
And silken courteins over her display,°   *spread*
And odourd° sheetes, and Arras° coverlets.   *perfumed / tapestry*
305 Behold how goodly my faire love does ly
In proud humility;
Like unto Maia,[2] when as Jove her tooke,
In Tempe,[3] lying on the flowry gras,
Twixt sleepe and wake, after she weary was,
310 With bathing in the Acidalian brooke.[4]
Now it is night, ye damsels may be gon,
And leave my love alone,
And leave° likewise your former lay to sing: *cease*
The woods no more shall answere, nor your echo ring.

315 Now welcome night, thou night so long expected,
That long daies labour doest at last defray,°   *pay for*
And all my cares, which cruell love collected,
Hast sumd° in one, and cancellèd[5] for aye:°   *combined / forever*
Spread thy broad wing over my love and me,
320 That no man may us see,
And in thy sable° mantle us enwrap,   *black*
From feare of perrill and foule horror free.
Let no false treason seeke us to entrap,
Nor any dread disquiet once annoy°   *interfere with*
325 The safety of our joy:
But let the night be calme and quietsome,
Without tempestuous storms or sad afray:°   *fear*
Lyke as when Jove with fayre Alcmena[6] lay,
When he begot the great Tirynthian groome:
330 Or lyke as when he with thy selfe[7] did lie,
And begot Majesty.

---

2. The eldest and most beautiful of the seven daughters of Atlas. (They were stellified as the Pleiades.) Jove fathered Mercury on her.
3. The Vale of Tempe in Thessaly (not, however, traditionally the site of Jove's encounter with Maia).
4. Associated with Venus.
5. Annulled or rendered void (as with a debt); compensated for.
6. The mother of Hercules ("the great Tirynthian groome"). Jove made that first night last as long as three.
7. Night. This is Spenser's own myth.

And let the mayds and yongmen cease to sing:
Ne let the woods them answer, nor theyr Eccho ring.

Let no lamenting cryes, nor dolefull teares,
335   Be heard all night within nor yet without:
Ne let false whispers, breeding hidden feares,
Breake gentle sleepe with misconceivèd dout.°   *groundless fear*
Let no deluding dreames, nor dreadful sights
Make sudden sad affrights;
340   Ne let housefyres, nor lightnings helpelesse° harmes,   *without remedy*
Ne let the Pouke,[8] nor other evill sprights,
Ne let mischivous witches with theyr charmes,
Ne let hob Goblins, names whose sence we see not,
Fray° us with things that be not.   *terrify*
345   Let not the shriech Oule, nor the Storke be heard:
Nor the night Raven that still° deadly yels,[9]   *always*
Nor damnèd ghosts cald up with mighty spels,
Nor griesly° vultures make us once affeard: *horrid*
Ne let th'unpleasant Quyre of Frogs still croking
350   Make us to wish theyr choking.
Let none of these theyr drery accents sing;
Ne let the woods them answer, nor theyr eccho ring.

But let stil Silence trew night watches keepe,
That sacred peace may in assurance rayne,
355   And tymely Sleep, when it is tyme to sleepe,
May poure his limbs forth on your pleasant playne,
The whiles an hundred little wingèd loves,°   *cupids (or amoretti)*
Like divers fethered doves,
Shall fly and flutter round about your bed,
360   And in the secret darke, that none reproves,
Their prety stealthes shal worke, and snares shal spread
To filch away sweet snatches of delight,
Conceald through covert night.
Ye sonnes of Venus, play your sports at will,
365   For greedy pleasure, carelesse of your toyes,°   *amorous dallying*
Thinks more upon her paradise of joyes,
Then° what ye do, albe it° good or ill.   *than / albeit, although*
All night therefore attend your merry play,
For it will soone be day:
370   Now none doth hinder you, that say or sing,
Ne will the woods now answer, nor your Eccho ring.

Who is the same, which at my window peepes?
Or whose is that faire face, that shines so bright,
Is it not Cinthia,[1] she that never sleepes,
375   But walkes about high heaven al the night?

8. Puck, Robin Goodfellow—here more powerful and evil than Shakespeare made him in *A Midsummer Night's Dream*.
9. The owl and the night raven were birds of ill omen. The stork, in Chaucer's *Parliament of Fowls*, is called an avenger of adultery.
1. Cynthia (or Diana) is goddess of the moon.

O fayrest goddesse, do thou not envy
My love with me to spy:
For thou likewise didst love, though now unthought,°   *not thought of*
And for a fleece of woll,° which privily,   *wool*
380   The Latmian shephard² once unto thee brought,
His pleasures with thee wrought.
Therefore to us be favorable now;
And sith° of wemens labours thou hast charge,³   *since*
And generation goodly dost enlarge,
385   Encline thy will t'effect our wishfull vow,
And the chast wombe informe° with timely seed,   *give life to*
That may our comfort breed:
Till which we cease our hopefull hap° to sing,   *fortune we hope for*
Ne let the woods us answer, nor our Eccho ring.

390   And thou great Juno, which with awful° might   *awesome*
The lawes of wedlock still dost patronize,°   *watch over*
And the religion° of the faith first plight°   *sanctity / pledged*
With sacred rites hast taught to solemnize:
And eeke° for comfort often callèd art   *also*
395   Of women in their smart,°   *(labor) pains*
Eternally bind thou this lovely band,°   *bond*
And all thy blessings unto us impart.
And thou glad Genius,⁴ in whose gentle hand,
The bridale bowre and geniall bed remaine,
400   Without blemish or staine,
And the sweet pleasures of theyr loves delight
With secret ayde doest succour° and supply,   *help*
Till they bring forth the fruitfull progeny,
Send us the timely fruit of this same night.
405   And thou fayre Hebe,⁵ and thou Hymen free,
Grant that it may so be.
Til which we cease your further prayse to sing,
Ne any woods shall answer, nor your Eccho ring.

And ye high heavens, the temple of the gods,
410   In which a thousand torches flaming bright
Doe burne, that to us wretched earthly clods,
In dreadful darknesse lend desirèd light;
And all ye powers which in the same remayne,
More then we men can fayne,°   *imagine*
415   Poure out your blessing on us plentiously,
And happy influence upon us raine,
That we may raise a large posterity,
Which from the earth, which they may long possesse,
With lasting happinesse,
420   Up to your haughty° pallaces may mount,   *lofty*
And for the guerdon° of theyr glorious merit   *reward*

2. Endymion, beloved of the moon. The "fleece of woll," however, comes from another story— that of Pan's enticement of the moon.
3. Diana is, as Lucina, patroness of births. The "labours" are, of course, those of childbirth.

4. God of generation and birth. "Geniall": having both the usual sense and the sense of *generative*, puns on his name.
5. Goddess of youth and freedom.

May heavenly tabernacles there inherit,
Of blessèd Saints for to increase the count.
So let us rest, sweet love, in hope of this,
425 And cease till then our tymely joyes to sing,
The woods no more us answer, nor our eccho ring.

Song made in lieu of many ornaments,
With which my love should duly have bene dect,°   *adorned*
Which cutting off through hasty accidents,
430 Ye would not stay your dew time to expect,°   *await*
But promist both to recompens,
Be unto her a goodly ornament,
And for short time an endlesse moniment.[6]

1595

---

6. The envoy (brief final stanza addressed to the poem itself) is traditionally apologetic in tone: the poem is offered as a substitute for presents ("ornaments") that did not arrive in time for the wedding. But this elaborate poem is itself a "goodly ornament," for it stands as a timeless monument of art to the passing day that it celebrates.

An Elizabethan Miscellany

In 1557, near the end of the reign of Queen Mary, an English publisher who specialized in the printing of law books undertook a project that lay outside of his ordinary sphere. He brought out a book of poems. The act does not sound particularly daring, but the publisher, Richard Tottel, knew that he was taking a commercial risk. The poems were not all by a single celebrated author, nor did they have the special air of authority conferred by classical antiquity. Moreover, they were not long romances, like Chaucer's celebrated *Troilus and Criseyde*, or ambitious philosophical and moral allegories. Rather this was a collection of short poems by a range of writers, many of whom were contemporaries or near-contemporaries. In England there had been nothing quite like this in print before. The book, titled *Songs and Sonnets*, has become known as *Tottel's Miscellany*.

In the fourteenth century Chaucer had demonstrated that English was a fit medium for a magnificent long narrative poem, but it was not as clear to everyone that the language was well suited for short lyrics, the kind of intense, compressed poetry made most famous by Sappho in Greek and by Catullus and Propertius in Latin. On the Continent Chaucer's contemporary Petrarch (Francesco Petrarca, 1304–1374) had brilliantly fashioned a way in his native Italian to rival the greatest of these ancient poets. Composed over a period of four decades, Petrarch's *Rime sparse* (Scattered Rhymes) consisted of a loosely unified sequence of 366 poems. Blending elements of classical Roman poetry with medieval courtly traditions, the poet created a representation, unprecedented in intensity and psychological nuance, of his unrequited love for a young woman named Laura and for all she came to symbolize for him.

Petrarch's lyrics tirelessly, even obsessively, teased out the lover's emotional states, figuring his passion as a ravishment, a deadly wound, a hunt, a form of bondage, or a storm at sea and depicting his beloved as an angel, a mortal enemy, a sun, a bejeweled idol, a flower, a milk-white deer, the epitome of all virtue or the source of all pain. The poet deployed these and other metaphors most often in sonnets, an elegant fourteen-line rhymed form that enabled him to hold each image or idea up for careful attention, elaboration, and interrogation, while at the same time conveying great emotional force.

Though Petrarch was acclaimed in his lifetime as a scholar and as a Latin poet, it was not until after his death that the massive influence of his vernacular love poems spread across Europe. In England it was only in the sixteenth century, with translations and adaptations by Sir Thomas Wyatt (d. 1542), Henry Howard, earl of Surrey (d. 1547), and others at the court of Henry VIII, that the *Rime sparse* began to exercise their full shaping force. This force was reflected in *Tottel's Miscellany*, which for the first time in print demonstrated to a larger reading public that the English tongue was capable of doing in lyric poetry—"small parcels," as Tottel put it—what had been done so brilliantly in Greek, Latin, and Italian.

Tottel's title page called particular attention to the earl of Surrey, the most socially prestigious of the poets assembled in his volume. It was not social rank alone, however, that earned Surrey this special notice: along with Wyatt, whom Tottel also heavily featured in his pages, Surrey was a supremely gifted poet whose achievement fully deserved to be singled out for praise. In this anthology they merit their own separate sections. But the idea of the *Miscellany* extended beyond showcasing these exceptionally talented courtiers. It was English lyric poetry itself that had, the collection suggested, come of age. It was high time for it to move from the relatively closed, elite world of manuscript circulation to the more public realm of the printed book.

Tottel's venture helped shape the poetic achievements of the next generation, a generation represented in the selection of lyrics that follows here. A great commercial as well as critical success, the *Miscellany* inspired in the decades that ensued an array of imitators with fetching titles like *The Paradise of Dainty Devices, A Gorgeous Gallery of Gallant Inventions, The Arbor of Amorous Devices, The Passionate Pilgrim, The Phoenix Nest,* and *England's Helicon.* What these miscellanies together manifest is an astonishingly widespread literary skill, the product of a culture in which the ability to write poems was part of a larger cultural competence, akin to knowing how to move gracefully, how to carry a tune, how to speak eloquently. Men and women—not everyone, of course, but a much larger cohort than we have come to expect in our own social world—were expected to have at least some facility in making and reciting verses. Tudor monarchs and their glittering courtiers, sober bureaucrats, hardworking law students, fashionable ladies, country gentlemen, parsons and parsons' wives, soldiers, saints, schoolchildren, and schoolmasters—all tried their hands at making metaphors, counting syllables, and shaping words into pleasing patterns of sound and meaning.

The principal testing ground in Tudor culture was not individual but social: poems were objects embedded in a world of civil conversation. Their creators generally depicted themselves as engaged in such acts as praising and blaming, inviting, commemorating, excusing, persuading, warning, insulting, lamenting, and—if possible—seducing. Poetry was an exercise in conspicuous self-display. The "Englishing" of Petrarch was a particularly significant element in this display, since the Italian poet had crafted such a rich rhetoric of emotional performance and mastered in the sonnet the perfect vehicle for all of its twists and turns. With variations in its rhyme scheme, the sonnet form played a central role in Elizabethan poetry.

The poems assembled here in "An Elizabethan Miscellany" include several sonnets that reflect Petrarch's great influence. His characteristic depiction of the lover's solitude and melancholy, for example, is perfectly mirrored in Samuel Daniel's "If this be love, to draw a weary breath"; his typical yoking of opposites, as a way to describe the tormenting experience of passion, is directly imitated in Henry Constable's "To live in hell, and heaven to behold." From their reading of miscellanies like Tottel's, Elizabethans knew what a lover, or at least a lover in verse, was supposed to sound like. When at the beginning of *Romeo and Juliet* Shakespeare wishes to depict the conventional pangs of love—before the tragedy takes a drastic turn toward the radically unconventional—he gives his hero the familiar oxymoronic lament of the Petrarchan lover: "Feather of lead, bright smoke, cold fire, sick health" (1.1.175).

But the very familiarity of what Sir Philip Sidney's Astrophil called "poor Petrarch's long deceased woes" posed a problem for English Renaissance poets: though they understood themselves to be the heirs of an impressive poetic achievement, they needed to make it seem that they were not merely following in the footsteps of the Italian master or of anyone else. Strategies for doing so included the direct repudiation most famously exemplified in Shakespeare's "My mistress' eyes are nothing like the sun" (Sonnet 130). But there were many other, less direct means of marking a distance from Petrarch and hence of creating the impression of a distinct, individual voice. Michael Drayton pushes the trope of the lady's cruelty to a wildly sadistic extreme ("As in some countries far remote from hence"): his mistress becomes a surgeon participating in a fiendish ritual of torture. The wonderfully inventive Thomas Campion takes the conventional description of the lady's face as a garden "Where roses and white lilies grow" and introduces into it an unexpected note, the voice of a street vendor crying "Cherry ripe!" In another of the Campion lyrics gathered here ("I care not for these ladies"), the lover jauntily rejects the whole stance of pining after an inaccessible, high-born mistress and opts instead for a "nut-brown lass" who "never will say no."

Important though he was, Petrarch was by no means the only model for English poets in the sixteenth century, the sonnet was not their only form, and romantic love was not their only subject. As this miscellany suggests, they developed a broad array of forms, attitudes, and styles. Hence we have the Calvinist Anne Locke praying to her stern God for mercy, George Gascoigne writing a wry lullaby to his penis, Thomas Lodge urging his readers to "Pluck the fruit and taste the pleasure," Michael Drayton imagining his mistress as a crone with hair "Like grizzled moss upon some aged tree," and Fulke Greville brooding on the end of the world ("When all this All doth pass from age to age").

Some scholars, trying to make sense of this bewildering array, have proposed that there were two main currents: an "ornate style," deriving from Petrarch and other Continental poets, and a "plain style," emerging from such native sources as popular prayers, ballads, riddles, aphorisms, didactic poems, and the like. Poets of the ornate style favored elaborate schemes of ornamentation and rhetorical display; plain-style poets opted for simplicity, severity, and directness. The ornate style, whose supreme masters in England were Sidney and Edmund Spenser, has attracted more critical admiration. C. S. Lewis termed it "Golden," as opposed to plain-style "Drab." But champions of the plain style, most notably the twentieth-century critics Yvor Winters and J. V. Cunningham, have argued that such plain-style poets as Sir Walter Ralegh or Fulke Greville deserve far more attention than they have received. Winters went so far as to claim that Gascoigne, particularly for his "Woodman-ship," deserved to be ranked among the greatest of English Renaissance poets.

The distinction between ornate and plain styles may be of use in making the poems included in this miscellany seem less miscellaneous. But it is worth recalling that Thomas Wyatt, whose poetry was so central to *Tottel's Miscellany*, wrote poems that exemplify both styles and indeed that the boundaries between them are often quite fluid. It is one of the delights of English Renaissance poetry to find plainness rearing its closely cropped head in the midst of golden ornament, and metaphorical elaboration weaving its way into sober severity.

RICHARD TOTTEL

The son of a fishmonger, Richard Tottel (1528–1593) became a successful and wealthy printer in London by gaining exclusive rights to print legal books. His success came not only from connections to the legal world but also from his innovation as a printer: his anthology of lyric poetry, *Songs and Sonnets* (1557), prominently featuring work by Thomas Wyatt and Henry Howard, earl of Surrey, was the first of its kind in England and became widely imitated. In the same year he published the first collected edition of the English works of Thomas More and Surrey's translation of two books of Virgil's *Aeneid* (one of which had first been published about 1554), the earliest English poetry in blank verse.

From Songs and Sonnets, Written by the Right Honorable Lord Henry Howard, Late Earl of Surrey, and Other

The Printer to the Reader

That to have well written in verse, yea and in small parcels, deserveth great praise, the works of divers Latins, Italians, and other do prove sufficiently. That our tongue is able in that kind to do as praiseworthily as the rest, the honorable style of the noble earl of Surrey and the weightiness of the deep-witted Sir Thomas Wyatt the Elder's verse, with several graces in sundry good English writers, do show abundantly. It resteth[1] now, gentle reader, that thou

1. Remains.

think it not evil done to publish, to the honor of the English tongue and for profit of the studious of English eloquence, those works which the ungentle hoarders-up of such treasure have heretofore envied thee. And for this point, good reader, thine own profit and pleasure, in these presently and in mo[2] hereafter, shall answer for my defense. If, perhaps, some mislike the stateliness of style removed from the rude skill of common ears, I ask help of the learned to defend their learned friends, the authors of this work. And I exhort the unlearned by reading to learn to be more skillful and to purge that swinelike grossness that maketh the sweet marjoram not to smell to their delight.

1557

2. More.

ANNE VAUGHAN LOCKE

Born to parents who served in the court of Henry VIII, Anne Vaughan Locke (ca. 1530–ca. 1590) received a privileged education in languages and became deeply involved in the Protestant Reformation, living among English exiles in Calvinist Geneva during the reign of Mary I and later exerting her influence in England, in part by translating religious works and writing her own. Her verse paraphrase of Psalm 51 is arguably the first English sonnet sequence as well as an early example of the Protestant devotional lyric that led to the religious poetry of John Donne and George Herbert.

From A Meditation of a Penitent Sinner

Sonnet 4 (main sequence)

Have mercy, Lord, have mercy: for I know
How much I need thy mercy in this case.
The horror of my guilt doth daily grow,
And, growing, wears[1] my feeble hope of grace.
5   I feel and suffer in my thrallèd[2] breast
Secret remorse and gnawing of my heart.
I feel my sin, my sin that hath oppressed
My soul with sorrow and surmounting smart.[3]
Draw me to mercy: for so oft as I
10   Presume to mercy to direct my sight,
My Chaos[4] and my heap of sin doth lie
Between me and thy mercy's shining light.
Whatever way I gaze about for grace,
My filth and fault are ever in my face.°   *sight*

1560

1. I.e., wears down, weakens.
2. Enthralled, enslaved (to sin).
3. Exceeding pain.
4. Alluding to the "great gulf" (in Latin, *chaos*) stretching between heaven and hell; see Luke 16.26. In classical mythology, Chaos is vaguely personified as a primordial deity.

GEORGE GASCOIGNE

The son of a respectable country gentleman, George Gascoigne (1534/5–1577) lived a turbulent life. Having squandered his inheritance in an attempt to cut a figure at court, he failed both as a lawyer and as a soldier and was perennially in search of occupation and patronage. Serving as part of this search, his writing, which included courtly entertainments, plays, literary criticism, moral tracts, a hunting treatise, military reportage, and a brilliant work of prose fiction as well as many poems, won him considerable esteem. But the esteem was not unmixed—some of his work was criticized as obscene—and Gascoigne seems to have died, as he lived, in financial straits.

And if I did, what then?[1]

"And if I did, what then?
Are you aggrieved therefore?
The sea hath fish for every man,
And what would you have more?"

5   Thus did my mistress once
Amaze° my mind with doubt,   *stupefy; perplex*
And popped a question, for the nonce,°   *on purpose; expressly*
To beat my brains about.

Whereto I thus replied,
10 "Each fisherman can wish
That all the sea at every tide
Were his alone to fish.

"And so did I (in vain);
But since it may not be,
15 Let such° fish there as find the gain,   *such men*
And leave the loss for me.

"And with such luck and loss,
I will content myself,
Till tides of turning time may toss
20 Such fishers on the shelf.°   *to one side*

"And when they stick on sands,
That every man may see,

---

1. This poem appears at the end of Gascoigne's evidently autobiographical novella, *The Adventures of Master F. J.* (which mixes prose and verse throughout); it is occasioned by a conversation between F. J. and his mistress, the wife of his host in Italy. F. J. accuses her of betraying him with her male secretary, "and she . . . denied it, until at last being still urged with such evident tokens [i.e., clear proofs] as he alleged, she gave him this bone to gnaw upon: And if I did so (quoth she), what then? Whereunto F. J. made none answer, but departed. . . . And when he was in place solitary, he compiled these following [verses], for a final end of the matter."

15 His eyes have been so usèd for to range,
     That now God knows they be both dim and dark.
     For proof he bears the note° of folly now,   *mark*
     Who shot sometimes to hit Philosophy,[5]
     And ask you why? forsooth I make avow,
20 Because his wanton wits went all awry.
     Next that, he shot to be a man of law,
     And spent some time with learnèd Littleton,[6]
     Yet in the end he provèd but a daw,°   *jackdaw, i.e., fool*
     For law was dark° and he had quickly done.   *obscure*
25 Then could he wish Fitzherbert such a brain
     As Tully[7] had, to write the law by art,
     So that with pleasure, or with little pain,
     He might perhaps have caught a truant's part.[8]
     But all too late, he most misliked the thing
30 Which most might help to guide his arrow straight;
     He winkèd[9] wrong, and so let slip the string,
     Which cast him wide, for all his quaint conceit.°   *clever thought*
     From thence he shot to catch a courtly grace,[1]
     And thought even there to wield the world at will,
35 But, out alas, he much mistook the place,
     And shot awry at every rover° still.   *random mark*
     The blazing baits which draw the gazing eye
     Unfeathered there his first affectiön;°   *inclination*
     No wonder then although° he shot awry,   *that*
40 Wanting° the feathers of discretiön.   *not having*
     Yet more than them, the marks of dignity
     He much mistook, and shot the wronger way,
     Thinking the purse of prodigality
     Had been best mean to purchase such a prey.
45 He thought the flattering face which fleereth still,°   *always smiles*
     Had been full fraught with all fidelity,
     And that such words as courtiers use at will
     Could not have varied from the verity.
     But when his bonnet buttonèd with gold,
50 His comely cap beguarded° all with gay,   *ornamented*
     His bombast° hose, with linings manifold,   *stuffed*
     His knit silk stocks° and all his quaint array,   *stockings*
     Had picked his purse of all the Peter-pence,[2]
     Which might have paid for his promotiön,
55 Then (all too late) he found that light° expense   *careless*
     Had quite quenched out the court's devotiön.
     So that since then the taste of misery
     Hath been always full bitter in his bit,°   *i.e., in his mouth*
     And why? forsooth because he shot awry,
60 Mistaking still the marks which others hit.

---

5. I.e., he formerly studied philosophy and then (lines 21ff.) law.
6. Author (like Fitzherbert, line 25) of a standard law text.
7. Marcus Tullius Cicero (whose exemplary prose style Gascoigne wishes Fitzherbert had had the wherewithal to emulate).
8. Been able to play truant.
9. Aimed (with one eye closed).
1. I.e., he next attempted to become a courtier.
2. I.e., money—from "Peter's pence," a tax formerly levied by the Roman church.

But now behold what mark the man doth find:
He shoots to be a soldier in his age;
Mistrusting all the virtues of the mind,
He trusts the power of his personage.
65 As though long limbs led by a lusty heart
Might yet suffice to make him rich again;
But Flushing frays[3] have taught him such a part
That now he thinks the wars yield no such gain.
And sure I fear, unless your lordship deign
70 To train him yet into some better trade,
It will be long before he hit the vein
Whereby he may a richer man be made.
He cannot climb as other catchers° can,   *huntsmen*
To lead a charge before himself be led.
75 He cannot spoil° the simple sakeless° man,   *despoil / poor innocent*
Which is content to feed him with his bread.
He cannot pinch° the painful soldier's pay,   *stint*
And shear° him out his share in ragged sheets,   *dole*
He cannot stoop to take a greedy prey
80 Upon his fellows groveling in the streets.
He cannot pull the spoil from such as pill,°   *pillage*
And seem full angry at such foul offense,
Although the gain content his greedy will,
Under the cloak of contrary pretence:
85 And nowadays, the man that shoots not so,
May shoot amiss, even as your woodman doth:
But then you marvel why I let them go,
And never shoot, but say farewell forsooth:
Alas, my lord, while I do muse hereon,
90 And call to mind my youthful years misspent,
They give me such a bone to gnaw upon,
That all my senses are in silence pent.
My mind is rapt in contemplatiön,
Wherein my dazzled eyes only behold
95 The black hour of my constellatiön[4]
Which framèd me so luckless on the mold.°   *on earth*
Yet therewithal I cannot but confess
That vain presumption makes my heart to swell,
For thus I think, not all the world (I guess)
100 Shoots bet than I, nay some shoots not so well.
In Aristotle somewhat did I learn,
To guide my manners° all by comeliness,°   *behavior / decency*
And Tully taught me somewhat to discern
Between sweet speech and barbarous rudeness.
105 Old Parkins, Rastell, and Dan Bracton's° books   *authors of law books*
Did lend me somewhat of the lawless law;
The crafty courtiers with their guileful looks
Must needs put some experience in my maw:°   *stomach*
Yet cannot these with many mast'ries moe°   *many more skills*

---

3. I.e., fighting in the Low Countries.
4. The unlucky alignment of planets at my birth.

110 Make me shoot straight at any gainful prick,°   *bull's-eye*
Where some that never handled such a bow
Can hit the white or touch it near the quick,
Who can nor speak nor write in pleasant wise,
Nor lead their life by Aristotle's rule,[5]
115 Nor argue well on questions that arise,
Nor plead a case more than my lord mayor's mule,
Yet can they hit the marks that I do miss,
And win the mean° which may the man maintain.   *means*
Now when my mind doth mumble upon this,
120 No wonder then although I pine for° pain: *because of*
And whiles mine eyes behold this mirror thus,
The herd goeth by, and farewell gentle does:
So that your lordship quickly may discuss°   *declare*
What blinds mine eyes so oft (as I suppose).
125 But since my Muse can to my lord rehearse°   *relate*
What makes me miss, and why I do not shoot,
Let me imagine in this worthless verse,
If right before me, at my standing's° foot   *hunter's station*
There stood a doe, and I should strike her dead,
130 And then she prove a carrion carcass too,
What figure might I find within my head,
To scuse the rage which ruled me so to do?
Some might interpret with plain paraphrase,
That lack of skill or fortune led the chance,
135 But I must otherwise expound the case;
I say Jehovah did this doe advance,
And made her bold to stand before me so,
Till I had thrust mine arrow to her heart,
That by the sudden° of her overthrow   *suddenness*
140 I might endeavor to amend my part
And turn mine eyes that they no more behold
Such guileful marks as seem more than they be:
And though they glister° outwardly like gold,   *glisten*
Are inwardly like brass, as men may see:
145 And when I see the milk hang in her teat,
Methinks it saith, old babe, now learn to suck,
Who in thy youth couldst never learn the feat
To hit the whites which live with all good luck.
Thus have I told my lord (God grant in season)
150 A tedious tale in rhyme, but little reason.
          Haud ictus sapio.[6]

1573

---

5. I.e., the rule of moderation. Aristotle regarded each virtue as the mean between two extremes.
6. Even though struck down, I have not learned wisdom (Latin).

FULKE GREVILLE

The wealthy Fulke Greville, Lord Brooke (1554–1628), was educated at Cambridge, traveled widely on the Continent, served in Parliament, and was a successful courtier under Elizabeth I, James I, and Charles I. Never married, he wrote some conventional love poetry addressed to a woman he called Caelica, but his most passionate expressions of love were for his friend Sir Philip Sidney, whose death, in 1586, he never ceased to mourn. In addition to a number of somberly powerful, brooding short poems, Greville wrote long philosophical verse treatises, several politically charged closet dramas, and a moving biography of Sidney. The end of Greville's life was grimly in keeping with his general pessimism: he was fatally stabbed by a long-time servant who then killed himself.

From Caelica

69

When all this All doth pass from age to age,
And revolution in a circle turn,[1]
Then heavenly justice doth appear like rage,
The caves do roar, the very seas do burn,
5   Glory grows dark, the sun becomes a night,
    And makes this great world feel a greater might.

When Love doth change his seat from heart to heart,
And worth about the wheel of Fortune goes,
Grace is diseased, desert seems overthwart,°   *thwarted; obstructed*
10 Vows are forlorn,° and truth doth credit° lose,   *abandoned / credence*
    Chance then gives law, Desire must be wise,
    And look more ways than one, or lose her eyes.

My age of joy is past, of woe begun,
Absence my presence is, strangeness my grace,[2]
15 With them that walk against me, is my sun:
The wheel is turned, I hold° the lowest place.   *occupy*
    What can be good to me since my love is,
    To do me harm, content to do amiss?

82

You that seek what life is in death,
Now find it air that once was breath.
New names unknown, old names gone:

---

1. Referring to the ancient theory of the Great Year, in which the completion of an entire revolution of the universe ("this All") marks the transition, with cataclysmic events, from one epoch ("age") to the next. For a modern version, cf. William Butler Yeats, "The Second Coming" and "Two Songs from a Play."
2. Instead of favor ("grace"), I now find aloofness ("strangeness").

Till time end bodies, but souls none.
5   Reader! then make time while you be
     But° steps to your eternity.   *only*

100

In night when colors all to black are cast,
Distinction lost, or gone down with the light,
The eye a watch to inward senses placed,
Not seeing, yet still having power of sight,

5   Gives vain alarums to the inward sense,
     Where fear stirred up with witty tyranny°   *i.e., of imaginings*
     Confounds all powers and thorough self-offense°   *through self-injury*
     Doth forge and raise impossibility:

Such as in thick depriving darknesses
10   Proper reflections of the error be,
     And images of self-confusednesses,
     Which hurt imaginations only see;
        And from this nothing seen tells news of devils,
        Which but expressions be of inward evils.

ca. 1580–1600   1633

THOMAS LODGE

L ondon-born Thomas Lodge (1558–1625) was educated at Oxford, studied law,
and eventually became a physician. He sailed in 1591 on a disastrous voyage to the
New World, which he was fortunate to survive. In a career complicated by his lifelong
Catholicism in a time of persecution, he tried his hand at writing poems, literary
tracts, plays, translations, and prose fictions (one of which became the source of
Shakespeare's *As You Like It*).

Pluck the fruit and taste the pleasure[1]

Pluck the fruit and taste the pleasure,
   Youthful lordings,° of delight,   *gentlemen*
Whilst occasion gives you seizure,[2]
   Feed your fancies and your sight:
5   After death when you are gone,
        Joy and pleasure is there none.

---

1. One of several poems interspersed in Lodge's   *of Robert, Second Duke of Normandy.*
romance *The Famous, True, and Historical Life*   2. While you have the opportunity to seize it.

Here on earth no thing is stable,
　　Fortune's changes well are known,
Whilst as youth doth then enable,
10　Let your seeds of joy be sown:
　　After death when you are gone,
　　Joy and pleasure is there none.

Feast it freely with your lovers,
　　Blithe and wanton sweets do fade,
15　Whilst that lovely Cupid hovers
　　Round about this lovely shade:
　　Sport it freely one to one,
　　After death is pleasure none.

Now the pleasant spring allureth,
20　And both place and time invites:
Out alas,[3] what heart endureth
　　To disclaim° his sweet delights?　　　　renounce; relinquish
　　After death when we are gone,
　　Joy and pleasure is there none.

1591

From Phyllis

Sonnet 35[1]

I hope and fear, I pray and hold my peace,
Now freeze my thoughts, and straight° they fry again,　　*immediately*
I now admire° and straight my wonders cease,　　　　　　*wonder*
I loose my bonds, and yet myself restrain.
5　This likes° me most that leaves me discontent,　　　*pleases*
My courage serves,[2] and yet my heart doth fail,
My will doth climb, whereas my hopes are spent,°　*drowned; exhausted*
I laugh at Love, yet when he comes I quail.
The more I strive, the duller bide I still,[3]
10　I would be thralled,° and yet my freedom love,　　*enslaved*
I would redress, yet hourly feed mine ill,°　　　　　*injury*
I would repine, and dare not once reprove.
　　And for° my love I am bereft of power,　　　　*because of*
　　And strengthless strive my weakness to devour.°　*destroy*

1593

---

3. "Out" simply intensifies "alas."
1. Adapted from Petrarch's Rima 134 (see pp. 122–23).
2. Fulfills its duty, acts as it should. "Courage":

etymologically, the word means "heart" (ultimately deriving from Latin *cor*).
3. I.e., the more sluggish I remain.

HENRY CONSTABLE

Henry Constable (1562–1613) was the second English poet, after Sidney, to publish a Petrarchan sonnet sequence. He also wrote many theological tracts and disputations. Born to a wealthy Protestant family, he converted to Catholicism, giving up his inheritance and putting himself at risk in attempts to convert King James I and to argue for the toleration of Catholics.

From Diana[1]

Decade 4, Sonnet 1

Needs must I leave, and yet needs must I love.
In vain my wit° doth paint in verse my woe;   *skill*
Disdain in thee, despair in me, doth show
How by my wit I do my folly prove:
5 All this my heart from love can never move.
Love is not in my heart, no, Lady, no,
My heart is love itself: till I forgo
My heart, I never can my love remove.
How shall I, then, leave love? I do intend
10 Not to crave grace,[2] but yet to wish it still;
Not to praise thee, but beauty to commend,
And so by beauty's praise, praise thee I will:
For as my heart is love, love not in me,
So beauty thou,[3] beauty is not in thee.

Decade 6, Sonnet 2[4]

To live in hell, and heaven to behold,
To welcome life and die a living death,
To sweat with heat and yet be freezing cold,
To grasp at stars and lie the earth beneath;
5 To tread a maze that never shall have end,
To burn in sighs and starve[5] in daily tears,
To climb a hill and never to descend,
Giants to kill, and quake at childish fears;

1. The very name that Constable gives his beloved—Diana, the chaste hunter goddess of classical mythology—suggests how little chance he (like the smitten narrators of other sonnet sequences, beginning with Petrarch) has of success.
2. I.e., the lady's favor.
3. In the same way, you *are* beauty.
4. This sonnet is found only in the second, 1594(?) edition of Constable's sequence and may not be by him at all: there is no manuscript copy linking the poem to Constable, and the title page of the edition describes it as containing "The excellent conceitful Sonnets of H. C. Augmented with divers Quatorzains [14-line poems] of honorable and learned personages." Whoever wrote the poem, it represents a durably popular kind of paradoxical sonnet ultimately traceable to Petrarch's Rima 134 (see pp. 122–23), and is based directly on a sonnet by the 16th-century French poet Philippe Desportes, *Diane* 1.29.
5. Die slowly (not necessarily of hunger).

To pine for food, and watch° th' Hesperian tree,[6]   *watch over*
10   To thirst for drink, and nectar still to draw,[7]
       To live accursed, whom men hold blest to be,
       And weep those wrongs which never creature saw:°   *experienced*
   If this be love, if love in these be founded,
   My heart is love, for these in it are grounded.°   *firmly fixed*

1594?

6. In Greek mythology, this tree, which bore golden apples, was guarded by the Hesperides (daughters, according to some, of Atlas) and the dragon Ladon. Its fruit would not actually be of any use as food.
7. And always to drink nectar (in classical myth, the delicious, immortality-conferring drink of the gods).

SAMUEL DANIEL

A poet, playwright, historian, and translator, Samuel Daniel (1562/3–1619) was a member of the circle of Mary Sidney, countess of Pembroke, and he later held various offices in the household of James I's queen, Anne of Denmark. He wrote tragedies, court masques, a historical epic, a prose history of England, a defense of rhyme, several fine verse epistles, a verse dialogue on the purpose of writing poetry, a popular "complaint" poem in which the ghost of a king's mistress laments her fate, and one of the best Elizabethan sonnet sequences, *Delia*.

From Delia

9[1]

   If this be love, to draw a weary breath,
   Paint on floods, till the shore, cry to the air,[2]
   With downward looks still° reading on the earth   *always*
   The sad memorials of my love's despair;
5   If this be love, to war against my soul,
   Lie down to wail, rise up to sigh and grieve me,
   The never-resting stone of care to roll,[3]
   Still to complain my griefs, and none relieve me;
      If this be love, to clothe me with dark thoughts,
10   Haunting untrodden paths to wail apart,
   My pleasures, horror; music, tragic notes,

1. Like the preceding sonnet by Constable, this one is adapted from Desportes, *Diane* 1.29. "Delia": in classical mythology, one of the epithets of the goddess Diana, deriving from her birthplace, the island of Delos. In giving the name to the woman he celebrates, Daniel follows the Roman love poet Tibullus (ca. 55–19 B.C.E.).
2. A series of pointless activities: painting on water, tilling the seashore . . .
3. The line—like the poem's entire list of pointless, unending labors—alludes to the myth of Sisyphus, who, having offended the gods, is punished in the underworld by having to roll a large stone to the top of a hill—a task he can never complete, because just as the stone nears the summit it always slips from his grasp and rolls to the bottom again.

Tears in my eyes and sorrow at my heart;
    If this be love, to live a living death—
    Oh then love I, and draw this weary breath.

32

But love whilst that thou may'st be loved again,°   *in return*
Now whilst thy May hath filled thy lap with flowers;
Now whilst thy beauty bears° without a stain;   *endures*
Now use thy summer smiles ere winter lours.
5   And whilst thou spread'st unto the rising sun,
The fairest flower that ever saw the light,
Now joy thy time before thy sweet be done,
And Delia, think thy morning must have night,
    And that thy brightness sets at length to west,
10 When thou wilt close up that which now thou showest:
And think the same becomes° thy fading best,   *suits*
Which then shall hide it most, and cover lowest.
    Men do not weigh° the stalk for that it was,   *value*
    When once they find her flower, her glory pass.

33

When men shall find thy flower, thy glory, pass,
And thou, with careful° brow sitting alone,   *full of care; sorrowful*
Receivèd hast this message from thy glass,°   *looking glass*
That tells thee truth, and says that all is gone,
5   Fresh shalt thou see in me the wounds thou madest,
Though spent thy flame, in me the heat remaining:
I that have loved thee thus before thou fadest,
My faith shall wax,° when thou art in thy waning.   *fidelity shall increase*
    The world shall find this miracle in me,
10 That fire can burn when all the matter's spent;
Then, what my faith hath been thyself shall see,
And that thou wast unkind thou may'st repent.
    Thou may'st repent that thou hast scorned my tears,
    When winter snows upon thy golden hairs.

1592

MICHAEL DRAYTON

The son of a Warwickshire butcher or tanner, Michael Drayton (1563–1631) had a long and productive career as a professional writer. He collaborated on plays, wrote scriptural paraphrases, pastorals, satires, odes, poetic epistles, verse legends, and a historical epic. His masterpiece is *Poly-Olbion*, a fifteen-thousand-line historical-geographical poem celebrating all the counties of England and Wales. He contributed as well to the period's vogue for sonnets, publishing a sequence of fifty-one sonnets called *Idea's Mirror* (1594), which, following substantial revision, he republished as *Idea*.

From Idea

To the Reader of These Sonnets

Into these loves° who but° for passion looks,   *i.e., love poems / only*
At this first sight here let him lay them by
And seek elsewhere, in turning other books
Which better may his labor satisfy.
5 No farfetched sigh shall ever wound my breast,
Love from mine eye a tear shall never wring,
Nor in *Ah me's* my whining sonnets dressed;
A libertine, fantasticly[1] I sing.
My verse is the true image of my mind,
10 Ever in motion, still° desiring change;   *always*
And as thus to variety inclined,
So in all humors° sportively I range;   *manners; fancies*
    My muse is rightly of the English strain,
    That cannot long one fashion entertain.

1599, 1619

5

Nothing but "No" and "I"[2] and "I" and "No"?
How falls it out° so strangely you reply?   *how does it happen*
I tell ye (fair), I'll not be answered so,
With this affirming "No," denying "I."
5 I say, "I love"; you slightly° answer, "I."   *indifferently; carelessly*
I say, "You love"; you pule me out[3] a "No."
I say, "I die"; you echo me with "I."
"Save me," I cry; you sigh me out a "No."
Must Woe and I have nought but "No" and "I"?
10 No I am I, if I no more can have.
Answer no more: with silence make reply,
And let me take myself what I do crave.
    Let "No" and "I" with I and you be so,
    Then answer "No" and "I" and "I" and "No."

1599, 1619

6

How many paltry, foolish, painted things,
That now in coaches trouble every street,
Shall be forgotten, whom no poet sings,
Ere they be well wrapped in their winding sheet?°   *shroud*
5 Where° I to thee eternity shall give,   *whereas*
When nothing else remaineth of these days;
And queens hereafter shall be glad to live

---

1. Capriciously. "Libertine": one who follows his (or her) own inclinations.
2. Here and throughout, punning on the homonym *aye* (yes). Especially in the sonnet's final couplet, a nearly limitless number of interpretations can be produced by varying the punctuation—including the quotation marks, all of which are editorial—and letting the mind play freely with the homonyms.
3. Querulously answer me with.

Upon the alms of thy superfluous praise.
Virgins and matrons, reading these my rhymes,
10 Shall be so much delighted with thy story
That they shall grieve they lived not in these times,
To have seen thee, their sex's only glory:
    So shalt thou fly above the vulgar° throng,   *common*
    Still to survive in my immortal song.

1619

8

There's nothing grieves me, but that° age should haste, *but the possibility that*
That° in my days I may not see thee old;   *with the result that*
That where those two clear, sparkling eyes are placed,
Only two loopholes then I might behold;
5 That lovely archèd, ivory, polished brow
Defaced with wrinkles that I might but see;
Thy dainty hair, so curled and crispèd now,
Like grizzled moss upon some agèd tree;
Thy cheek, now flush with roses, sunk and lean;
10 Thy lips, with age as any wafer thin;
Thy pearly teeth out of thy head so clean,°   *entirely*
That when thou feed'st, thy nose shall touch thy chin.
    These lines that now thou scorn'st, which should delight thee,
    Then would I make thee read, but to despite° thee.   *spite*

1619

50

As in some countries far remote from hence,
The wretched creature destinèd to die,
Having the judgment due to his offense,
By surgeons begg'd their art° on him to try,   *skill*
5 Which° on the living work without remorse,   *who*
First make incision on each mast'ring vein,°   *major blood vessel*
Then stanch the bleeding, then transpierce the corse,° *pierce through the body*
And with their balms recure° the wounds again,   *heal*
Then poison, and with physic° him restore,   *medical treatment*
10 Not that they fear the hopeless man to kill,
But their experience to increase the more:
Ev'n so my mistress works upon my ill,°   *illness (i.e., love's pangs)*
    By curing me and killing me each hour
    Only to show her beauty's sov'reign power.

1605

61

Since there's no help, come, let us kiss and part.
Nay, I have done, you get no more of me,
And I am glad, yea glad with all my heart
That thus so cleanly I myself can free.

5   Shake hands forever, cancel all our vows,
And when we meet at any time again,
Be it not seen in either of our brows
That we one jot of former love retain.
Now at the last gasp of love's latest breath,
10 When, his pulse failing, Passion speechless lies,
When Faith° is kneeling by his bed of death,   *faithfulness*
And Innocence is closing up his eyes;
    Now if thou would'st, when all have given him over,°   *given up on him*
    From death to life thou might'st him yet recover.

1619

JOHN DAVIES OF HEREFORD

Always associated in print with his birthplace in order to avoid confusion with a contemporary poet of the same name, John Davies of Hereford (1564/5–1618) later moved to London to work as a writing master, for which he was renowned, tutoring members of the nobility in penmanship. At the same time, he produced scores of poems, including ambitious religious and moral treatises, love sonnets, satires, eclogues, and his best-known work, a collection of epigrams (in the sense of short, pointed poems), many of them addressed to the era's most prominent writers.

From The Scourge of Folly

If there were (oh!) an Hellespont of cream

The author loving these homely meats specially, viz., cream, pancakes, buttered pippin pies[1] (laugh, good people), and tobacco, writ to that worthy and virtuous gentlewoman whom he calleth mistress, as followeth:

    If there were (oh!) an Hellespont[2] of cream
    Between us, milk-white mistress, I would swim
    To you, to show to both my love's extreme,
    Leander-like[3]—yea, dive from brim to brim.
5   But met I with a buttered pippin pie
    Floating upon't, that would I make my boat,
    To waft me to you without jeopardy,
    Though seasick I might be while it did float.
    Yet if a storm should rise, by night or day,
10   Of sugar snows and hail of caraways,[4]

1. Apple pies. "Meats": foods (not just flesh meats).
2. The ancient name for the Dardanelles, the strait linking the Aegean Sea and the Sea of Marmara. One to five miles wide, it divides Europe from Asia.
3. According to a late-classical legend, Leander swam the Hellespont to reach his ladylove, Hero. See Marlowe's *Hero and Leander* (p. 659).
4. Caraway seeds; here, in sweets.

Then, if I found a pancake in my way,[5]
It, like a plank, should bring me to your quays:[6]
Which having found, if they tobacco kept,
The smoke should dry me well, before I slept.

1611

5. On my route.
6. Or "keys": banks or landing stages, lying along-side water or projecting into it, for loading or unloading ships. Here, alluding to the breasts of his "milk-white mistress."

THOMAS CAMPION

After three years at Cambridge, Thomas Campion (1567–1620) studied law before finally settling on medicine. A composer, a writer of court masques, and a poet, he wrote his first poetic compositions in Latin, and he remained interested in the possibility of applying the classical principles of quantitative versification to English. His most memorable achievements arose from the fact that he was both poet and composer: his aim, he wrote, was "to couple my words and notes lovingly together."

My sweetest Lesbia[1]

My sweetest Lesbia, let us live and love,
And though the sager sort our deeds reprove,
Let us not weigh° them: heav'n's great lamps do dive   heed
Into their west, and straight° again revive,   at once
5   But soon as once set is our little light,
Then must we sleep one ever-during° night.   everlasting

If all would lead their lives in love like me,
Then bloody swords and armor should not be;
No drum nor trumpet peaceful sleeps should move,°   disturb
10   Unless alarm° came from the camp of love.   the call to arms
But fools do live, and waste their little light,
And seek with pain their ever-during night.

When timely death my life and fortune ends,
Let not my hearse° be vexed with mourning friends,   bier
15   But let all lovers, rich in triumph, come
And with sweet pastimes grace my happy tomb;
And Lesbia, close up thou my little light,
And crown with love my ever-during night.

1601

1. Imitated and partly translated from a poem by Catullus (87–ca. 54 B.C.E.), the Latin lyric poet who often celebrated the charms of Lesbia in his verses. This and the three lyrics that follow appeared, with musical settings, in *A Book of Airs*, which contains Campion's first work as a composer.

I care not for these ladies

I care not for these ladies
That must be wooed and prayed;
Give me kind Amaryllis,[1]
The wanton country[2] maid.
5 Nature art° disdaineth;   *artifice*
Her beauty is her own.
    Her when we court and kiss,
    She cries "Forsooth,° let go!"   *Truly!*
    But when we come where comfort is,
10   She never will say no.

If I love Amaryllis,
She gives me fruit and flowers;
But if we love these ladies,
We must give golden showers.
15 Give them gold that sell love,
Give me the nut-brown° lass   *i.e., sun-tanned*
    Who when we court and kiss,
    She cries "Forsooth, let go!"
    But when we come where comfort is,
20   She never will say no.

These ladies must have pillows,
And beds by strangers wrought.°   *i.e., imported*
Give me a bower of willows,
Of moss and leaves unbought,
25 And fresh Amaryllis,
With milk and honey fed,
    Who when we court and kiss,
    She cries "Forsooth, let go!"
    But when we come where comfort is,
30   She never will say no.

                                                              1601

When to her lute Corinna sings

When to her lute Corinna[1] sings,
Her voice revives the leaden° strings,   *i.e., heavy*
And doth in highest notes appear
As any challenged° echo clear;   *aroused*
5 But when she doth of mourning speak,
Ev'n with her sighs the strings do break.

1. In classical and later pastoral poetry, a conventional name for a shepherdess.
2. Probably with an obscene pun.
1. A classical name: (1) a female Greek poet (whose work survives only in fragments); (2) Ovid's pseudonymous—and probably fictitious—mistress in his collection of erotic poems, the *Amores*. "Lute": a stringed instrument somewhat like a guitar.

And as her lute doth live or die,
Led by her passion, so must I:
For when of pleasure she doth sing,
10   My thoughts enjoy a sudden spring;
But if she doth of sorrow speak,
Ev'n from my heart the strings do break.

1601

When thou must home to shades of underground

When thou must home to shades of underground,[1]
And there arrivèd, a new admirèd guest,
The beauteous spirits do engirt° thee round,   *gird, encircle*
White Iope, blithe Helen,[2] and the rest,
5   To hear the stories of thy finished love
From that smooth tongue whose music hell can move,

Then wilt thou speak of banqueting delights,
Of masques[3] and revels which sweet youth did make,
Of tourneys and great challenges of knights,
10   And all these triumphs[4] for thy beauty's sake:
When thou hast told these honors done to thee,
Then tell, O tell, how thou didst murther me.

1601

Jack and Joan, they think no ill[1]

Jack and Joan, they think no ill,
But loving live, and merry still;°   *always*
Do their weekdays' work, and pray
Devotely° on the holyday;   *devoutly*
5   Skip and trip it° on the green,   *caper; dance*
And help to choose the summer queen;
Lash out,° at a country feast,   *squander*
Their silver penny with the best.

Well can they judge of nappy° ale,   *heady, strong*
10   And tell at large a winter tale;[2]
Climb up to the apple loft,
And turn the crabs° till they be soft.   *crab apples (roasting)*

---

1. The classical abode of the dead, Hades.
2. Helen of Troy. Iope is another famously beautiful woman of classical mythology. In a passage that Campion has in mind here, the Roman love poet Propertius (ca. 50–after 16 B.C.E.) includes her in a list (2.28.49–56) of lovely women now among the dead.
3. See the Literary Terminology appendix in this volume.
4. Public festivities—especially, jousting tournaments.
1. This poem appears in Campion's *Two Books of Airs* (no date given).
2. An idle tale, old wives' tale (as in Shakespeare's *The Winter's Tale*).

Tib[3] is all the father's joy,
And little Tom the mother's boy.
15 All their pleasure is content;
And care, to pay their yearly rent.[4]

Joan can call by name her cows,
And deck her windows with green boughs;
She can wreaths and tutties° make,   *nosegays*
20 And trim with plums a bridal cake.
Jack knows what brings gain or loss,
And his long flail[5] can stoutly toss;
Makes the hedge, which others[6] break,
And ever thinks what he doth speak.[7]

25 Now you courtly dames and knights,
That study only strange[8] delights,
Though you scorn the homespun gray,
And revel in your rich array;
Though your tongues dissemble deep,
30 And can your heads from danger keep;
Yet, for all your pomp and train,[9]
Securer lives the silly° swain.   *simple; lowly*

1613?

Now winter nights enlarge

Now winter nights enlarge
The number of their hours,
And clouds their storms discharge
Upon the airy towers.
5 Let now the chimneys blaze
And cups o'erflow with wine,
Let well-tuned words amaze
With harmony divine.
Now yellow waxen lights
10 Shall wait on honey Love,
While youthful revels, masques,° and courtly sights   *masked balls*
Sleep's leaden spells remove.

This time doth well dispense
With[1] lovers' long discourse;
15 Much speech hath some defense,
Though beauty no remorse.
All do not all things well:
Some measures[2] comely° tread,   *pleasing*

---

3. Used as a typical name for a woman or girl of lower social status.
4. I.e., their only care is to pay their rent.
5. A long-handled wooden tool for thrashing grain.
6. Aristocrats, while hunting on horseback.
7. I.e., always says what he truly thinks.

8. With the connotation of "foreign," "from elsewhere." "Study": devote (yourselves) to.
9. (1) Attendants; (2) guile.
1. "Dispense / With": permit, allow.
2. Dances; also poetic rhythms. "Some": i.e., some people.

Some knotted riddles tell,
20   Some poems smoothly read.
The Summer hath his joys,
    And Winter his delights;
Though Love and all his pleasures are but toys,°   *trifles*
    They shorten tedious nights.

1617

Never love unless you can[1]

Never love unless you can
Bear with all the faults of man:
Men sometimes will jealous be,
Though but little cause they see,
5   And hang the head, as discontent,
    And speak what straight° they will repent.   *immediately*

Men that but one saint adore
Make a show of love to more:
Beauty must be scorned in none,
10   Though but truly served in one;
    For what is courtship but disguise?
    True hearts may have dissembling eyes.

Men when their affairs° require   *business*
Must a while themselves retire:°   *withdraw*
15   Sometimes hunt, and sometimes hawk,
And not ever sit and talk.
    If these and suchlike you can bear,
    Then like, and love, and never fear.

1617

There is a garden in her face[1]

There is a garden in her face,
Where roses and white lilies grow;
    A heav'nly paradise is that place,
Wherein all pleasant fruits do flow.[2]
5   There cherries grow, which none may buy
    Till "Cherry ripe!"[3] themselves do cry.

Those cherries fairly do enclose
Of orient° pearl a double row;   *lustrous; precious*

---

1. This and the following poem appeared in *The Third and Fourth Book of Airs* (no date given, but almost certainly published in 1617).
1. Before Campion published this poem, it had appeared in song settings by two other composers.
2. Abound—as in the biblical Promised Land, "flowing with milk and honey" (Exodus 3.8).
3. A familiar cry of London street vendors.

Which when her lovely laughter shows,
10 They look like rosebuds filled with snow.
Yet them nor° peer nor prince can buy,   *neither*
Till "Cherry ripe!" themselves do cry.

Her eyes like angels watch° them still;   *guard*
Her brows like bended bows do stand,
15 Threatening with piercing frowns to kill
All that attempt with eye or hand
Those sacred cherries to come nigh,
Till "Cherry ripe!" themselves do cry.

1605, 1606, 1617

SIR WALTER RALEGH
1552–1618

The brilliant and versatile Sir Walter Ralegh was a soldier, courtier, philosopher, explorer and colonist, student of science, historian, and poet. Born to West Country gentry of modest means, Ralegh amassed great wealth thanks to his position at court, leading him to be denounced by some as a social upstart and hated by others as a rapacious monopolist. He fought ruthlessly in Ireland and Cádiz, directed the colonization of Virginia, made the smoking of tobacco fashionable in England, brought Spenser from Ireland to the English court, conducted scientific experiments, led a 1595 expedition to Guiana (now a part of Venezuela) in an unsuccessful effort to find gold, and urged England to challenge Spanish dominance in the New World. He was known for his violent temper, his dramatic sense of life, his extravagant dress, his skepticism in religious matters, his bitter hatred of Spain, and his great favor with Queen Elizabeth. In 1592, she suspended this favor and briefly imprisoned him when he seduced, and then married, one of her ladies-in-waiting. His long, remorseful poem to the queen, *The Ocean to Cynthia*, survived in manuscript fragments, one of more than five hundred lines. His best-known shorter poems include the reply to Marlowe's "Passionate Shepherd" and "The Lie," an attack on social classes and institutions that itself provoked many replies. While he seems to have embraced the manuscript circulation of his poems at court, his active resistance to appearing as a poet in print—in one case he forced a printer to recall a volume and paste a slip of paper over his initials—makes it very difficult to put the copies that circulated in manuscript in any reliably chronological order.

After Elizabeth's death, in 1603, King James suspected Ralegh of conniving against his accession to the English throne and threw him into the Tower of London on trumped-up charges of treason. During the long years that followed, Ralegh undertook to write the vast *History of the World*, beginning with the Creation, emphasizing the providential punishment of evil princes, and projecting a treatment of English history—although not of recent events, because, he declared, he who follows truth too closely at the heels might get kicked in the teeth. The work was to have been dedicated to Henry, Prince of Wales, Ralegh's most powerful friend and supporter, who declared, "Only my father would keep such a bird in a cage." But Henry died in 1612, and the dispirited Ralegh broke off his narrative at 168 B.C.E. He remained in the Tower for the rest of his life, save for an ill-fated second expedition to Guiana, in 1617, which again failed to discover gold but succeeded in infuriating the Spanish by storming one of their settlements. Bowing to Spanish pressure, James had Ralegh executed on the old treason charge.*

The Nymph's Reply to the Shepherd[1]

If all the world and love were young,
And truth in every shepherd's tongue,
These pretty pleasures might me move
To live with thee and be thy love.

5 Time drives the flocks from field to fold
When rivers rage and rocks grow cold,
And Philomel° becometh dumb;   *the nightingale*
The rest complains of cares to come.

The flowers do fade, and wanton fields
10 To wayward winter reckoning yields;°   *renders an account*
A honey tongue, a heart of gall,
Is fancy's spring, but sorrow's fall.

Thy gowns, thy shoes, thy beds of roses,
Thy cap, thy kirtle,° and thy posies°   *dress / bouquets*
15 Soon break, soon wither, soon forgotten—
In folly ripe, in reason rotten.

Thy belt of straw and ivy buds,
Thy coral clasps and amber studs,
All these in me no means can move
20 To come to thee and be thy love.

But could youth last and love still breed,
Had joys no date° nor age no need,   *ending*
Then these delights my mind might move
To live with thee and be thy love.

                                        1600

What is our life?

What is our life? a play of passion;
Our mirth the music of division;[1]
Our mothers' wombs the tiring-houses[2] be
Where we are dressed for this short comedy.
5 Heaven the judicious sharp spectator is

---

* See the NAEL Archive for Ralegh's poem beginning "As you came from the holy land of Walsinghame" and for excerpts from his account of the battle between the *Revenge* and a Spanish fleet.

1. Cf. Marlowe, "The Passionate Shepherd to His Love," p. 678.
1. A rapid melodic passage; or the music between the acts of a play.
2. Dressing rooms in an Elizabethan theater.

That sits and marks still who doth act amiss;
Our graves that hide us from the searching sun
Are like drawn curtains when the play is done.
Thus march we, playing, to our latest rest,
10   Only we die in earnest—that's no jest.

                                        1612

[Sir Walter Ralegh to His Son][1]

Three things there be that prosper up apace
And flourish, whilst they grow asunder far,
But on a day, they meet all in one place,
And when they meet, they one another mar;
5   And they be these: the wood, the weed,° the wag.   *i.e., hemp*
The wood is that which makes the gallow tree;
The weed is that which strings the hangman's bag;[2]
The wag, my pretty knave, betokeneth° thee.   *signifies*
Mark well, dear boy, whilst these assemble not,
10   Green springs the tree, hemp grows, the wag is wild,
But when they meet, it makes the timber rot,
It frets the halter,° and it chokes the child.   *tightens the noose*
    Then bless thee, and beware, and let us pray
    We part not with thee at this meeting day.

ca. 1600

The Lie

Go, soul, the body's guest,
    Upon a thankless errand;
Fear not to touch° the best;   *speak of; censure*
    The truth shall be thy warrant.
5   Go, since I needs must die,
    And give the world the lie.[1]

Say to the court, it glows
    And shines like rotten wood;°   *i.e., with phosphorescence*
Say to the church, it shows
10   What's good, and doth no good.
If church and court reply,
    Then give them both the lie.

Tell potentates they live
    Acting by others' action;
15   Not loved unless they give,

---

1. The sonnet has this title in one of the manuscripts in which it appears.
2. I.e., when woven into rope, the hemp secures the hangman's hood ("bag") to the condemned person's neck.

1. "Give the lie": accuse of lying.

Not strong but by a faction.
If potentates reply,
Give potentates the lie.

Tell men of high condition,
20   That manage the estate,°   *state*
Their purpose is ambition,
  Their practice only hate.
And if they once reply,
  Then give them all the lie.

25 Tell them that brave it° most,   *live ostentatiously*
  They beg for more by spending,
Who, in their greatest cost,
  Seek nothing but commending.°   *i.e., others' approval*
And if they make reply,
30   Then give them all the lie.

Tell zeal it wants° devotion;   *lacks*
  Tell love it is but lust;
Tell time it is but motion;
  Tell flesh it is but dust.
35 And wish them not reply,
  For thou must give the lie.

Tell age it daily wasteth;°   *decays*
  Tell honor how it alters;
Tell beauty how she blasteth;°   *withers away*
40   Tell favor how it falters.
And as they shall reply,
  Give every one the lie.

Tell wit° how much it wrangles   *intellect*
  In tickle points of niceness;°   *in trivial distinctions*
45 Tell wisdom she entangles
  Herself in overwiseness.
And when they do reply,
  Straight give them both the lie.

Tell physic° of her boldness;°   *medicine / presumption*
50   Tell skill it is pretension;
Tell charity of coldness;
  Tell law it is contention.
And as they do reply,
  So give them still the lie.

55 Tell fortune of her blindness;
  Tell nature of decay;
Tell friendship of unkindness;
  Tell justice of delay.
And if they will reply,
60   Then give them all the lie.

  Tell arts[2] they have no soundness,
   But vary by esteeming;[3]
  Tell schools[4] they want profoundness,
   And stand too much on seeming.
65 If arts and schools reply,
   Give arts and schools the lie.

  Tell faith° it's fled the city;   *faithfulness, fidelity*
   Tell how the country erreth;
  Tell manhood shakes off pity;
70 Tell virtue least preferreth.°   *advances*
  And if they do reply,
   Spare not to give the lie.

  So when thou hast, as I
   Commanded thee, done blabbing,°   *revealing secrets*
75 Although to give the lie
   Deserves no less than stabbing,
  Stab at thee he that will,
   No stab thy soul can kill.

ca. 1592   1608

Farewell, false love

  Farewell, false love, the oracle° of lies, *i.e., authoritative source*
  A mortal foe and enemy to rest;
  An envious boy, from whom all cares arise,
  A bastard vile, a beast with rage possessed;
5 A way of error, a temple full of treason,
  In all effects contrary unto reason.

  A poisoned serpent covered all with flowers,
  Mother of sighs and murtherer° of repose,   *murderer*
  A sea of sorrows from whence are drawn such showers
10 As moisture lends to every grief that grows;
  A school of guile, a net of deep deceit,
  A gilded hook that holds a poisoned bait.

  A fortress foiled° which reason did defend,   *overthrown*
  A siren song, a fever of the mind,
15 A maze wherein affection finds no end,
  A raging cloud that runs before the wind,
  A substance like the shadow of the sun,
  A goal of grief for which the wisest run.

  A quenchless fire, a nurse of trembling fear,
20 A path that leads to peril and mishap;

---

2. The Seven Liberal Arts, basis of the academic curriculum.
3. I.e., seem good or bad according to different tastes or judgments.
4. The various philosophical traditions.

A true retreat of sorrow and despair,
An idle boy that sleeps in pleasure's lap,
A deep distrust of that which certain seems,
A hope of that which reason doubtful deems.

25 Sith° then thy trains° my younger years betrayed,   *since / tricks*
And for my faith° ingratitude I find,   *faithfulness*
And sith repentance hath my wrongs bewrayed°   *revealed*
Whose course was ever contrary to kind°—   *nature*
False love, desire, and beauty frail, adieu!
30 Dead is the root whence all these fancies grew.

1588

Methought I saw the grave where Laura lay[1]

Methought I saw the grave where Laura lay,
Within that temple where the vestal° flame   *celebrating virginity*
Was wont° to burn; and passing by that way   *accustomed*
To see that buried dust of living fame,
5 Whose tomb fair Love and fairer Virtue kept,
All suddenly I saw the Fairy Queen;
At whose approach the soul of Petrarch wept,
And from thenceforth those graces° were not seen,   *i.e., Love and Virtue*
For they this Queen attended; in whose stead
10 Oblivion laid him down on Laura's hearse.°   *grave*
Hereat the hardest stones were seen to bleed,
And groans of buried ghosts the heavens did pierce;
    Where Homer's sprite[2] did tremble all for grief,
    And cursed th' access° of that celestial thief.[3]   *accession*

1590

Nature, that washed her hands in milk

Nature, that washed her hands in milk,
    And had forgot to dry them,
Instead of earth took snow and silk,
    At Love's request to try them,
5   If she a mistress could compose
    To please Love's fancy out of those.

Her eyes he would should be of light,
    A violet breath, and lips of jelly;
Her hair not black, nor overbright,

---

1. A commendatory sonnet to the first three books of *The Faerie Queene,* by Ralegh's friend Spenser. Laura was the lady celebrated in the sonnets of Petrarch (1304–1374).
2. The spirit of Homer. Ralegh is giving extrava-gant praise to Spenser's poem as an epic, the type of poem Homer wrote.
3. The queen, stealing Laura's fame, or Spenser, stealing Homer's.

10 And of the softest down her belly;
 As for her inside he'd have it
 Only of wantonness° and wit.   *playfulness*

 At Love's entreaty such a one
   Nature made, but with her beauty
15 She hath framed a heart of stone;
   So as Love, by ill destiny,
 Must die for her whom Nature gave him,
 Because her darling would not save him.

 But Time (which Nature doth despise,
20   And rudely gives her love the lie,
 Makes Hope a fool, and Sorrow wise)
   His hands do neither wash nor dry;
 But being made of steel and rust,
 Turns snow and silk and milk to dust.

25 The light, the belly, lips, and breath,
   He dims, discolors, and destroys;
 With those he feeds but fills not death,
   Which sometimes were the food of joys.
 Yea, Time doth dull each lively wit,
30 And dries all wantonness with it.

 Oh, cruel Time! which takes in trust
   Our youth, our joys, and all we have,
 And pays us but with age and dust;
   Who in the dark and silent grave
35 When we have wandered all our ways
 Shuts up the story of our days.

1902

[The Author's Epitaph, Made by Himself][1]

 Even such is time, which takes in trust
 Our youth, our joys, and all we have,
 And pays us but with age and dust;
 Who in the dark and silent grave,
5 When we have wandered all our ways,
 Shuts up the story of our days:
 And from which earth, and grave, and dust
 The Lord shall raise me up, I trust.

1628

1. The final stanza of the preceding poem, recast as a farewell to life. The 17th-century story, which may be true, was that Ralegh inscribed the poem in his Bible the night before his execution.

From The discovery of the large, rich, and beautiful Empire of Guiana, with a relation of the great and golden city of Manoa (which the Spaniards call El Dorado)[1]

* * * When we were come to the tops of the first hills of the plains adjoining to the river, we beheld that wonderful breach of waters which ran down Caroni:[2] and might from that mountain see the river how it ran in three parts, above twenty miles off, and there appeared some ten or twelve overfalls in sight, every one as high over the other as a church tower, which fell with that fury, that the rebound of water made it seem as if it had been all covered over with a great shower of rain: and in some places we took it at the first for a smoke that had risen over some great town. For mine own part, I was well persuaded from thence to have returned, being a very ill footman,[3] but the rest were all so desirous to go near the said strange thunder of waters as they drew me on by little and little till we came into the next valley, where we might better discern the same. I never saw a more beautiful country nor more lively prospects,[4] hills so raised here and there over the valleys, the river winding into divers branches, the plains adjoining without bush or stubble, all fair green grass, the ground of hard sand easy to march on either for horse or foot, the deer crossing in every path, the birds towards the evening singing on every tree with a thousand several[5] tunes, cranes and herons of white, crimson, and carnation perching in the river's side, the air fresh with a gentle easterly wind, and every stone that we stooped to take up promised either gold or silver by his complexion.

* * *

I will promise these things that follow, which I know to be true. Those that are desirous to discover and to see many nations may be satisfied within this river,[6] which bringeth forth so many arms and branches leading to several countries and provinces, above 2000 miles east and west, and 800 miles south and north, and of these, the most either rich in gold or in other merchandises. The common soldier shall here fight for gold, and pay himself, instead of pence, with plates of half a foot broad, whereas he breaketh his bones in other wars for provant[7] and penury. Those commanders and chieftains that shoot at honor and abundance shall find there more rich and beautiful cities, more temples adorned with golden images, more sepulchers filled with treasure, than either Cortez found in Mexico, or Pizarro in Peru: and the shining glory of this conquest will eclipse all those so far extended beams of the Spanish nation. There is no country which yieldeth more pleasure to the inhabitants, either for those common delights of hunting, hawking, fishing, fowling, or the rest, than Guiana doth.

1. Ralegh had reports from several Spaniards of the unexplored kingdom of Guiana ("Land of Waters"; now a part of Venezuela). Lying between the Orinoco and Amazon rivers, the kingdom supposedly included the city the Spaniards called El Dorado—The Golden City. Ralegh led an expedition to Guiana in 1595, and the following year published an account of it, which was reprinted in 1598–1600 in Richard Hakluyt's massive collection *The Principal Navigations, Voyages, Traffics, and Discoveries of the English Nation*. For an engraving from Ralegh's report, see p. 804.
2. A tributary River of the Orinoco. Intrigued by reports of its waterfalls and the country above them, Ralegh led a small group to explore the region.
3. Poor walker.
4. Striking vistas.
5. Different.
6. The Orinoco.
7. Rations. "Plates": plate metal.

* * * Both for health, good air, pleasure, and riches I am resolved it cannot be equalled by any region either in the east or west. Moreover, the country is so healthful, as of an hundred persons and more (which lay without shift most sluttishly,[8] and were every day almost melted with heat in rowing and marching, and suddenly wet again with great showers, and did eat of all sorts of corrupt fruits, and made meals of fresh fish without seasoning, of tortugas, of lagartos[9] or crocodiles, and of all sorts good and bad, without either order or measure, and besides lodged in the open air every night) we lost not any one, nor had one ill disposed to my knowledge, nor found any calentura, or other of those pestilent diseases which dwell in all hot regions, and so near the equinoctial line.[1]

Where there is store[2] of gold, it is in effect needless to remember other commodities for trade: but it hath, towards the south part of the river, great quantities of brazil-wood, and diverse berries that dye a most perfect crimson and carnation. * * * All places yield abundance of cotton, of silk, of balsam, and of those kinds most excellent and never known in Europe, of all sorts of gums, of Indian pepper: and what else the countries may afford within the land, we know not, neither had we time to abide the trial,[3] and search. The soil besides is so excellent and so full of rivers, as it will carry sugar, ginger, and all those other commodities which the West Indies have.

The navigation is short, for it may be sailed with an ordinary wind in six weeks, and in the like time back again.

* * *

Guiana is a country that hath yet her maidenhead, never sacked, turned, nor wrought,[4] the face of the earth hath not been torn, nor the virtue and salt of the soil spent by manurance,[5] the graves have not been opened for gold, the mines not broken with sledges,[6] nor their images pulled down out of their temples. It hath never been entered by any army of strength, and never conquered or possessed by any Christian prince. It is besides so defensible, that if two forts be builded in one of the provinces which I have seen, the flood[7] setteth in so near the bank, where the channel also lieth, that no ship can pass up but within a pike's length[8] of the artillery, first of the one, and afterwards of the other. * * *

* * * Guiana hath but one entrance by the sea (if it hath that) for any vessels of burden: so as whosoever shall first possess it, it shall be found unaccessible for any enemy, except he come in wherries,[9] barges, or canoes, or else in flat-bottomed boats, and if he do offer to enter it in that manner, the woods are so thick two hundred miles together upon the rivers of such entrance, as a mouse cannot sit in a boat unhit from the bank. By land it is more impossible to approach, for it hath the strongest situation of any region under the sun, and is so environed with impassable mountains on every side, as it is impossible to victual[1] any company in the passage: which hath been well proved by the Spanish nation, who since the conquest of Peru have never

---

8. Who idled without initiative most carelessly.
9. Alligators. "Without seasoning": i.e., as preservative. "Tortugas": tortoises.
1. Equator. "Calentura": a tropical disease that causes hallucinations.
2. Abundance.
3. To wait to find out.
4. Quarried or mined. "Turned": tilled.

5. I.e., the fertility of the soil has not been exhausted by cultivation ("manurance").
6. Sledgehammers.
7. Tide.
8. The pike was a long-shafted infantry weapon.
9. Rowboats.
1. Provision.

left five years free from attempting this empire, or discovering some way into it, and yet of three and twenty several gentlemen, knights, and noblemen there was never any that knew which way to lead an army by land, or to conduct ships by sea, anything near the said country. Orellana, of whom the river of Amazones taketh name, was the first, and Don Antonio de Berreo[2] (whom we displanted) the last: and I doubt much, whether he himself or any of his yet know the best way into the said empire.

* * *

The West Indies were first offered Her Majesty's grandfather[3] by Columbus, a stranger, in whom there might be doubt[4] of deceit, and besides it was then thought incredible that there were such and so many lands and regions never written of before. This empire is made known to Her Majesty by her own vassal, and by him that oweth to her more duty than an ordinary subject, so that it shall ill sort with the many graces and benefits which I have received, to abuse Her Highness, either with fables or imaginations. The country is already discovered, many nations won to Her Majesty's love and obedience, and those Spaniards which have latest and longest labored about the conquest, beaten out, discouraged and disgraced, which among these nations were thought invincible. Her Majesty may in this enterprise employ all those soldiers and gentlemen that are younger brethren, and all captains and chieftains that want employment, and the charge[5] will be only the first setting out in victualing and arming them: for after the first or second year I doubt not but to see in London a contractation house[6] of more receipt for Guiana, than there is now in Seville for the West Indies.

And I am resolved that if there were but a small army afoot in Guiana, marching towards Manoa the chief city of Inca, he[7] would yield to Her Majesty by composition[8] so many hundred thousand pounds yearly, as should both defend all enemies abroad and defray all expenses at home, and that he would besides pay a garrison of three or four thousand soldiers very royally to defend him against other nations. * * * For whatsoever prince shall possess it shall be greatest, and if the king of Spain enjoy it, he will become unresistible. Her Majesty hereby shall confirm and strengthen the opinions of all nations as touching[9] her great and princely actions. * * *

To speak more at this time, I fear would be but troublesome: I trust in God, this being true, will suffice, and that he which is King of all Kings and Lord of Lords will put it into her heart which is Lady of Ladies to possess it; if not, I will judge those men worthy to be kings thereof, that by her grace and leave will undertake it of themselves.[1]

1596, 1599

2. One of Ralegh's informants, a captured Spanish officer at Trinidad. Francisco de Orellana (ca. 1490–ca. 1546), a Spanish soldier, was the first explorer of the Amazon.
3. Henry VII. In 1488 Bartholomew Columbus petitioned Henry to sponsor his brother Christopher in an attempt to find a new route to the (East) Indies, by sailing west. The king declined, so Christopher sought the sponsorship of Queen Isabella of Spain.
4. Fear.
5. Cost. "Younger brethren": likely recruits

because without patrimony. "Want": lack.
6. Place for receiving the goods contracted to be sent back to the investors who would finance the Guiana expedition.
7. The Inca, the supposed ruler of Guiana and its chief city, Manoa. "Resolved": convinced.
8. Treaty.
9. Concerning.
1. Despite all Ralegh's enticements and admonitions, Queen Elizabeth declined to support his proposal for the conquest of Guiana.

From The History of the World

[CONCLUSION: ON DEATH]

It is * * * Death alone that can suddenly make man to know himself. He tells the proud and insolent that they are but abjects,[1] and humbles them at the instant; makes them cry, complain, and repent; yea, even to hate their fore-passed happiness. He takes the account[2] of the rich, and proves him a beggar, a naked beggar, which hath interest in nothing but in the gravel that fills his mouth. He holds a glass[3] before the eyes of the most beautiful, and makes them see therein their deformity and rottenness, and they acknowledge it.

O eloquent, just, and mighty Death! Whom none could advise, thou hast persuaded; what none hath dared, thou hast done; and whom all the world hath flattered, thou only hast cast out of the world and despised; thou hast drawn together all the far-stretched greatness, all the pride, cruelty, and ambition of man, and covered it all over with these two narrow words: *Hic jacet!*[4]

1614

1. Castoffs.
2. Estimate, measure.
3. Mirror.
4. Here lies (Latin); often carved on tombstones.

JOHN LYLY
1554–1606

John Lyly was the grandson of William Lily, the author of the standard Latin grammar that every English schoolboy studied. After receiving the M.A. degree at Oxford, Lyly went to London, where his prose romance *Euphues* (1578) enjoyed an instant success. Subsequently, he wrote several elegant, sophisticated plays acted at court by the children's companies, and served several terms as a member of Parliament, though his hopes of obtaining a lucrative court appointment, such as Master of the Revels, were disappointed.

The title *Euphues*, taken from the name of that book's hero, is Greek for "of good natural parts, graceful, witty"; the subtitle, *Anatomy of Wit*, means something like "analysis of the mental faculties." The plot of the work involves a young man who leaves university for the carnal temptations of the city, falls in love, betrays his best friend, is in turn betrayed, repents, and thereafter ladles out great quantities of moral wisdom. But the story of the repentant prodigal is distinctly secondary to the prose style, which has come to be known as Euphuism and which greatly influenced a generation of writers eager to follow the fashion the book established. The style has two distinctive features: an elaborately patterned sentence structure based on comparison and antithesis; and a wealth of ornament, including proverbs, incidents from history and poetry, and fanciful similes drawn from contemporary science, classical texts, or the author's own imagination. Euphuism became a rage for a while, especially at court. The style may have been particularly popular among court women: the publisher of Lyly's *Six Court Comedies*, in 1632, informed his readers that "all our ladies were then his [Euphues's or Lyly's] scholars, and the beauty in court who could not parley Euphuism was as little regarded as she which now there speaks not French." When its vogue began to wane, Euphuism was criticized by Sidney, parodied by Shakespeare, and mocked by Thomas Nashe and Ben Jonson. Although it did not last, Lyly's highly self-conscious, overwrought style is an example of the Elizabethan fascination with ornate language and artifice.*

From Euphues: The Anatomy of Wit

[EUPHUES INTRODUCED]

There dwelt in Athens a young gentleman of great patrimony, and of so comely a personage, that it was doubted[1] whether he were more bound to Nature for the lineaments of his person, or to Fortune for the increase of his possessions. But Nature impatient of comparisons, and as it were disdaining a companion or copartner in her working, added to this comeliness of his body such a sharp capacity of mind, that not only she proved Fortune counterfeit, but was half of that opinion that she herself was only current.[2] This young gallant, of more wit[3] than wealth, and yet of more wealth than wisdom, seeing himself inferior to none in pleasant conceits,[4] thought himself superior to all in honest conditions, insomuch that he deemed himself so apt to all things, that he gave himself almost to nothing, but practicing of those things commonly which are incident to these sharp wits, fine phrases, smooth quipping, merry taunting, using jesting without mean,[5] and abusing mirth without measure. As therefore the sweetest rose hath his prickle, the finest velvet his brack,[6] the fairest flower his bran,[7] so the sharpest wit hath his wanton will, and the holiest head his wicked way. And true it is that some men write and most men believe, that in all perfect shapes, a blemish bringeth rather a liking every way to the eyes, than a loathing any way to the mind. Venus had her mole in her cheek which made her more amiable: Helen[8] her scar on her chin which Paris called *cos amoris,* the whetstone of love. Aristippus his wart, Lycurgus[9] his wen: So likewise in the disposition of the mind, either virtue is over-shadowed with some vice, or vice overcast with some virtue. Alexander valiant in war, yet given to wine. Tully eloquent in his glozes, yet vainglorious: Solomon wise, yet too too wanton: David holy but yet an homicide:[1] none more witty than Euphues, yet at the first none more wicked. The freshest colors soonest fade, the teenest[2] razor soonest turneth his edge, the finest cloth is soonest eaten with moths, and the cambric sooner stained than the coarse canvas: which appeared well in

---

* For Lyly's sonnet "Cupid and my Campaspe played," see the NAEL Archive.
1. Doubtful, uncertain.
2. Genuine.
3. Intellect.
4. Witty expressions.
5. Moderation.
6. Break, flaw.
7. Husk.
8. The Greek queen whom Paris abducted to Troy: the most beautiful woman in the world.
9. The legendary lawgiver of Sparta. Aristippus

was a disciple of Socrates and traditionally the founder of the Cyrenaic school of philosophy, which taught that life's goal is pleasure.
1. The biblical King David loved Bathsheba and had her husband, Uriah, killed so he could marry her. Alexander the Great killed his friend Clitus in a drunken brawl. Tully (Marcus Tullius Cicero) was the great Roman orator, famous for his "glozes" (flattering speeches). Solomon, David's son, was famous both for his wisdom and for his many wives.
2. Keenest.

this Euphues, whose wit being like wax apt to receive any impression, and having the bridle in his own hands, either to use the rein or the spur, disdaining counsel, leaving his country, loathing his old acquaintance, thought either by wit to obtain some conquest, or by shame to abide[3] some conflict, and leaving the rule of reason, rashly ran unto destruction. Who preferring fancy before friends, and his present humor[4] before honor to come, laid reason in water being too salt for his taste, and followed unbridled affection, most pleasant for his tooth.[5] When parents have more care how to leave their children wealthy than wise, and are more desirous to have them maintain the name than the nature of a gentleman; when they put gold into the hands of youth, where they should put a rod under their girdle,[6] when instead of awe they make them past grace, and leave them rich executors of goods, and poor executors of godliness, then is it no marvel that the son, being left rich by his father's will, become retchless by his own will.[7]

It hath been an old-said saw,[8] and not of less truth than antiquity, that wit is the better if it be the dearer bought: as in the sequel of this history[9] shall most manifestly appear. It happened this young imp[1] to arrive at Naples (a place of more pleasure than profit, and yet of more profit than piety), the very walls and windows whereof shewed it rather to be the Tabernacle of Venus than the Temple of Vesta.[2]

There was all things necessary and in readiness that might either allure the mind to lust or entice the heart to folly, a court more meet[3] for an atheist than for one of Athens, for Ovid than for Aristotle, for a graceless lover than for a godly liver: more fitter for Paris than Hector, and meeter for Flora than Diana.[4]

Here my youth (whether for weariness he could not, or for wantonness would not, go any further) determined to make his abode: whereby it is evidently seen that the fleetest fish swalloweth the delicatest bait, that the highest soaring hawk traineth[5] to the lure, and that the wittiest sconce[6] is inveigled with the sudden view or alluring vanities.

Here he wanted[7] no companions which courted him continually with sundry kinds of devices, whereby they might either soak[8] his purse to reap commodity, or soothe his person to win credit, for he had guests and companions of all sorts.

There frequented to this lodging and mansion house as well the spider to suck poison of his fine wit as the bee to gather honey, as well the drone as the dove, the fox as the lamb, as well Damocles[9] to betray him as Damon[1] to be true to him: yet he behaved himself so warily, that he singled his game[2] wisely. He could easily discern Apollo's music from Pan his pipe,[3] and Venus's beauty

---

3. Stand firm in.
4. Whimsy.
5. Taste. "Affection": passion.
6. I.e., whip them. ("Girdle": belt.)
7. Appetite, the opposite of reason. "Retchless": reckless.
8. Saying, proverb.
9. Rest of this story.
1. Novice.
2. Symbolizing chastity, in contrast to Venus.
3. Fitting.
4. Diana was the goddess of chastity. Ovid was famous for his love poems, Aristotle for his profound philosophical works. Paris was the lover of Helen, in contrast to his brother Hector, a great Trojan soldier. Flora was a fertility goddess whose annual celebrations were noted for lasciviousness.

5. Is attracted to.
6. Head, brain.
7. Lacked.
8. Drain.
9. Famous as a flatterer of Dionysius, who gave him a gorgeous banquet but made him sit with a sword suspended over his head by a single hair, to show how dangerous eminence is.
1. Famous in classical legend as the friend of Pythias, so loyal to him that he offered to be executed in his place.
2. Separated his target animal from the herd—that is, made distinctions.
3. In classical myth, Apollo's music was much superior to that which the wood-god Pan produced on his pipes.

from Juno's bravery,[4] and the faith of Laelius[5] from the flattery of Aristippus, he welcomed all but trusted none, he was merry but yet so wary that neither the flatterer could take advantage to entrap him in his talk nor the wisest any assurance of his friendship: who being demanded of[6] one what countryman he was, he answered, "What countryman am I not? If I be in Crete, I can lie, if in Greece I can shift, if in Italy I can court it:[7] if thou ask whose son I am also, I ask thee whose son I am not. I can carouse with Alexander, abstain with Romulus, eat with the Epicure, fast with the Stoic, sleep with Endymion, watch with Chrysippus,"[8] using these speeches and other like. An old gentleman in Naples seeing his pregnant wit,[9] his eloquent tongue somewhat taunting, yet with delight, his mirth without measure yet not without wit, his sayings vainglorious yet pithy, began to bewail his nurture and to muse at his nature, being incensed against the one as most pernicious, and enflamed with the other as most precious: for he well knew that so rare a wit would in time either breed an intolerable trouble or bring an incomparable treasure to the common weal:[1] at the one he greatly pitied, at the other he rejoiced.

1578

4. Splendid attire.
5. Laelius was famous as the faithful friend of Scipio Africanus the Younger.
6. Asked by.
7. Inhabitants of the island of Crete early had a reputation as liars. Lyly is elaborating or inventing when he says that the Greeks "shift" (practice or live by deceit) and that the Italians "court it" (behave in a courtly manner).
8. Chrysippus was a celebrated Stoic philosopher, so devoted to study that he would "watch" (stay up all night) with his books. Romulus was

the legendary founder and first king of Rome. Exposed as an infant with his twin brother, Remus, he was rescued and suckled by a she-wolf and became a symbol of abstinence. The followers of Epicurus (Epicureans) were thought to care for nothing but pleasure. The austere Stoics venerated duty. Endymion was a youth in Greek legend renowned for his beauty and his eternal sleep on Mount Latmus, where the moon goddess fell in love with him.
9. Fertile mind.
1. Commonwealth.

SIR PHILIP SIDNEY
1554–1586

S ir Philip Sidney's face was "spoiled with pimples," Ben Jonson remarked in 1619, wryly distancing himself from the virtual cult that had arisen in the years after Sidney's death. Knight, soldier, poet, friend, and patron, Sidney seemed to most Elizabethans to embody all the traits of character and personality they admired: he was Castiglione's perfect courtier come to life. When he was killed in battle in the Low Countries at the age of thirty-two, fighting for the Protestant cause against the hated Spanish, all England mourned. Stories, possibly apocryphal, began immediately to circulate about his gallantry on the battlefield—grievously wounded, he gave his water to a dying foot soldier with the words "Thy necessity is yet greater than mine"—and about his astonishing self-composure as he himself lay dying: suffering from his putrifying, gangrenous wound, Sidney composed a song and had it sung by his deathbed. When his corpse was brought back to England for burial, the spectacular funeral procession, one of the most elaborate ever staged, almost bankrupted his father-in-law, Francis Walsingham, the wealthy head of Queen Elizabeth's secret service.

Philip Sidney's father was Sir Henry Sidney, thrice lord deputy (governor) of Ireland, and his mother was a sister of Robert Dudley, earl of Leicester, the most spectacular and powerful of all the queen's favorites. He entered Shrewsbury School in 1564, at the age of ten, on the same day as Fulke Greville, who became his lifelong friend and his biographer. Greville wrote of Sidney, "though I lived with him and knew him from a child, yet I never knew him other than a man—with such staidness of mind, lovely and familiar gravity, as carried grace and reverence above greater years." He attended Oxford but left without taking a degree and completed his education by extended travels on the Continent. There he met many of the most important people of the time, from kings and queens to philosophers, theologians, and poets. In France he witnessed the Massacre of St. Bartholomew's Day, which began in Paris on August 24, 1572, and raged through France for more than a month, as Catholic mobs incited by Queen Catherine de Médicis slaughtered perhaps fifty thousand Huguenots (French Protestants). This experience undoubtedly strengthened Sidney's ardent Protestantism, which had been inculcated by his family background and education. In an intense correspondence with his mentor, the Burgundian humanist reformer Hubert Languet, he brooded on how he could help save Europe from what he viewed as the Roman Catholic menace.

Languet and his associates clearly hoped that this brilliant and wonderfully well-connected young Englishman would be able to steer royal policy toward active intervention in Europe's wars of religion. Yet when he returned to England, Sidney found the direct path to heroic action blocked by the caution and hard-nosed realism of Queen Elizabeth and her principal advisers. Though she sent him on some modest diplomatic missions, the queen clearly regarded the zealous young man with considerable skepticism. As a prominent courtier with literary interests, Sidney actively encouraged authors such as Edward Dyer, Greville, and, most important, Edmund Spenser, who dedicated *The Shepheardes Calender* to him as "the president [chief exemplar] of noblesse and of chevalree." But he clearly longed to be something more than an influential patron of letters. In 1580 his Protestant convictions led him publicly to oppose Queen Elizabeth's projected marriage to the Catholic duke of Anjou. The queen, who hated interference with her diplomatic maneuvers, angrily dismissed Sidney from the court.

He retired to Wilton, the estate of his beloved and learned sister, Mary Herbert, countess of Pembroke, and there he wrote a long, elaborate epic romance in prose, called *Arcadia*. Sidney's claim, made with studied nonchalance, that the work was casually tossed off for his sister's private entertainment is belied by its considerable literary, political, and moral ambitions, qualities that were reinforced and intensified in the extensive revisions he began to make to it in 1582. Our selection is from this revised version, termed by scholars the *New Arcadia*.

In addition to *Arcadia*, which inspired many imitations, including the *Urania* of Sidney's niece, Lady Mary Wroth, two other influential works by Sidney have had still more lasting importance. One of these, *The Defense of Poesy*, is the major work of literary criticism produced in the English Renaissance. In this long essay Sidney eloquently defends poetry (his term for all imaginative literature) against its attackers and, in the process, greatly exalts the role of the poet, the freedom of the imagination, and the moral value of fiction. Perhaps Sidney's finest literary achievement is *Astrophil and Stella* (Starlover and Star), the first of the great Elizabethan sonnet cycles. The principal focus of these sonnets is not a sequence of events or an unfolding relationship. Rather, they explore the lover's state of mind and soul, the contradictory impulses, intense desires, and frustrations that haunt him.

In his guise as a Petrarchan sonneteer, Sidney repeatedly insists that the thought of his beloved drives all more mundane matters from his mind. Yet a number of the sonnets betray a continuing preoccupation with matters of politics and foreign policy. Neither love nor literature could distract Sidney for long from what he took to be his destined role. In 1585 he tried to join Sir Francis Drake's West Indian expedition but was prevented by the queen; instead, she appointed him governor of Flushing in the Netherlands, where as a volunteer and knight-errant he engaged in several vicious skirmishes in the war against Spain. At Zutphen on September 13, 1586, leading a charge against great odds, Sidney was wounded in the thigh, shortly after he had thrown away his thigh armor in an ill-fated chivalric gesture. He died after lingering for twenty-six days.

Sidney called poetry his "unelected vocation," and in keeping with the norms of his class, he did not publish any of his major literary works himself. His ambition, continually thwarted, was to be a man of action whose deeds would affect his country's destiny. Yet he was the author of the most ambitious work of prose fiction, the most important piece of literary criticism, and the most influential sonnet cycle of the Elizabethan Age.*

The Countess of Pembroke's Arcadia   Sidney wrote his epic romance in two forms which scholars have dubbed the *Old Arcadia* and the *New Arcadia*. Shortly after the *Old Arcadia* was completed, in five "books," Sidney began to recast and greatly expand it, but broke off in mid-sentence and left the revision unfinished. This revised fragment, almost three books, is known as the *New Arcadia*; it was published posthumously, in 1590. In 1593 Sidney's sister, the countess of Pembroke, herself a gifted writer, made some small changes to the *New Arcadia* and the last two books of the *Old*, stitched them together, and published them as a single text. (The complete *Old Arcadia*, as Sidney had left it in manuscript, was not rediscovered and published until the twentieth century.) Both Sidney's original version and his revision are full of oracles, princes in disguise, mistaken identity, melodramatic incidents, and tangled love situations, but the *New Arcadia* has a much more labyrinthine, interwoven plot, as well as a more consistently elevated tone of moral and heroic high seriousness. Some episodes are of political interest, and Sidney clearly put into the work more of his serious thought on statecraft (the responsibilities of a king or queen, the evils of rebellion, and the duties of ministers, judges, and advisers of state) than his description of the *Arcadia* as mere entertainment suggests. Many poems—pastoral eclogues and songs—are interspersed throughout the narrative; they represent Sidney's experiments with diverse lyric kinds and verse forms.

Before the chapter included here, Pyrocles, prince of Macedon, has fallen in love with Philoclea, daughter of Basilius and Gynecia, the king and queen of Arcadia. To gain entrance to the royal household, he has disguised himself as a woman, the Amazon Zelmane. To his dismay, though, both Basilius and Gynecia (who sees through his disguise) have fallen in love with him.

From The Second Book of the Countess of Pembroke's Arcadia

Chapter 1

In these pastoral pastimes[1] a great number of days were sent to follow their flying predecessors, while the cup of poison[2] (which was deeply tasted of this noble company) had left no sinew of theirs without mortally searching into it; yet never manifesting his venomous work, till once that the night (parting away angry that she could distill no more sleep into the eyes of lovers) had no sooner given place to the breaking out of the morning light and

---

* For additional excerpts from the *Arcadia*, see the NAEL Archive.
1. The reference is to the elaborate entertain-

ment, featuring a series of pastoral songs, that had concluded Book 1.
2. I.e., love.

the sun bestowed his beams upon the tops of the mountains, but that the woeful Gynecia (to whom rest was no ease) had left her loathed lodging and gotten herself into the solitary places those deserts[3] were full of, going up and down with such unquiet motions as a grieved and hopeless mind is wont to bring forth. There appeared unto the eyes of her judgment the evils she was like to run into, with ugly infamy waiting upon them: she felt the terrors of her own conscience; she was guilty of a long exercised virtue which made this vice the fuller of deformity. The uttermost of the good she could aspire unto was a mortal wound to her vexed spirits; and lastly, no small part of her evils was that she was wise to see her evils. Insomuch that, having a great while thrown her countenance ghastly about her[4] (as if she had called all the powers of the world to be witness of her wretched estate), at length casting up her watery eyes to heaven:

"O sun," said she, "whose unspotted light directs the steps of mortal mankind, art thou not ashamed to impart the clearness of thy presence to such a dust-creeping worm as I am? O you heavens, which continually keep the course allotted unto you, can none of your influences prevail so much upon the miserable Gynecia as to make her preserve a course so long embraced by her? O deserts, deserts, how fit a guest am I for you, since my heart can people you with wild ravenous beasts, which in you are wanting! O virtue, where dost thou hide thyself? What hideous thing is this which doth eclipse thee? Or is it true that thou wert never but a vain name and no essential thing, which hast thus left thy professed servant when she had most need of thy lovely presence? O imperfect proportion of reason, which can too much foresee and too little prevent! Alas, alas," said she, "if there were but one hope for all my pains or but one excuse for all my faultiness! But wretch that I am, my torment is beyond all succor, and my evil-deserving doth exceed my evil fortune. For nothing else did my husband take this strange resolution to live so solitarily, for nothing else have the winds delivered this strange guest to my country, for nothing else have the destinies reserved my life to this time, but that only I, most wretched I, should become a plague to myself and a shame to womankind. Yet if my desire, how unjust soever it be, might take effect, though a thousand deaths followed it and every death were followed with a thousand shames, yet should not my sepulcher receive me without some contentment. But alas, though sure I am that Zelmane is such as can answer my love, yet as sure I am that this disguising must needs come for some foretaken conceit.[5] And then, wretched Gynecia, where canst thou find any small ground-plot for hope to dwell upon? No, no, it is Philoclea his heart is set upon; it is my daughter I have borne to supplant me. But if it be so, the life I have given thee, ungrateful Philoclea, I will sooner with these hands bereave thee of than my birth[6] shall glory she hath bereaved me of my desires. In shame there is no comfort but to be beyond all bounds of shame."

Having spoken thus, she began to make a piteous war with her fair hair, when she might hear not far from her an extremely doleful voice, but so suppressed with a kind of whispering note that she could not conceive the words distinctly. But as a lamentable tune is the sweetest music to a woeful mind,

---

3. Uninhabited regions. In consequence of an oracle, Basilius has taken the royal family to live in "a certain forest which he calleth his desert."
4. "Thrown . . . her": looked about her in a fright-

ful manner.
5. With some prior purpose.
6. Offspring.

she drew thither near-away[7] in hope to find some companion of her misery; and as she paced on she was stopped with a number of trees so thickly placed together that she was afraid she should, with rushing through, stop the speech of the lamentable party which she was so desirous to understand. And therefore sitting her down as softly as she could (for she was now in distance to hear) she might first perceive a lute excellently well played upon, and then the same doleful voice accompanying it with these verses:

> In vain, mine eyes, you labor to amend
>   With flowing tears your fault of hasty sight;
> Since to my heart her shape you so did send,
>   That her I see, though you did lose your light.
>
> In vain, my heart, now you with sight are burned,
>   With sighs you seek to cool your hot desire;
> Since sighs, into mine inward furnace turned,
>   For bellows serve to kindle more the fire.
>
> Reason in vain, now you have lost my heart,
>   My head you seek, as to your strongest fort;
> Since there mine eyes have played so false a part,
>   That to your strength your foes have sure resort.
>   Then since in vain I find were all my strife,
>   To this strange death I vainly yield my life.

The ending of the song served but for a beginning of new plaints, as if the mind, oppressed with too heavy a burden of cares, was fain to discharge itself of all sides and, as it were, paint out the hideousness of the pain in all sorts of colors. For the woeful person (as if the lute had evil[8] joined with the voice) threw it to the ground with suchlike words:

"Alas, poor lute, how much art thou deceived to think that in my miseries thou could'st ease my woes, as in my careless[9] times thou wast wont to please my fancies! The time is changed, my lute, the time is changed; and no more did my joyful mind then receive everything to a joyful consideration than my careful[1] mind now makes each thing taste like the bitter juice of care. The evil is inward, my lute, the evil is inward; which all thou dost doth serve but to make me think more freely of, and the more I think, the more cause I find of thinking, but less of hoping. And alas, what is then thy harmony but the sweetmeats of sorrow? The discord of my thoughts, my lute, doth ill agree to the concord of thy strings; therefore be not ashamed to leave thy master, since he is not afraid to forsake himself."

And thus much spoken, instead of a conclusion was closed up with so hearty a groaning that Gynecia could not refrain to show herself, thinking such griefs could serve fitly for nothing but her own fortune. But as she came into the little arbor of this sorrowful music, her eyes met with the eyes of Zelmane, which was the party that thus had indicted herself of misery, so that either of them remained confused with a sudden astonishment, Zelmane fearing lest she had heard some part of those complaints which she had risen up that morning early of purpose to breathe out in secret to

---

7. Near to it.
8. Badly.

9. Carefree.
1. Full of care.

herself. But Gynecia a great while stood still with a kind of dull amazement, looking steadfastly upon her. At length returning to some use of herself, she began to ask Zelmane what cause carried her so early abroad. But, as if the opening of her mouth to Zelmane had opened some great floodgate of sorrow whereof her heart could not abide the violent issue, she sank to the ground with her hands over her face, crying vehemently, "Zelmane, help me, O Zelmane have pity on me!"

Zelmane ran to her, marveling what sudden sickness had thus possessed her; and beginning to ask her the cause of her pain and offering her service to be employed by her, Gynecia opening her eyes wildly upon her, pricked with the flames of love and the torments of her own conscience, "O Zelmane, Zelmane," said she, "dost thou offer me physic,[2] which art my only poison? Or wilt thou do me service, which hast already brought me into eternal slavery?"

Zelmane then knowing well at what mark she shot, yet loth to enter into it, "Most excellent lady," said she, "you were best retire yourself into your lodging, that you the better may pass this sudden fit."

"Retire myself?" said Gynecia, "If I had retired myself into myself when thou (to me unfortunate guest) camest to draw me from myself, blessed had I been, and no need had I had of this counsel. But now, alas, I am forced to fly to thee for succor whom I accuse of all my hurt, and make thee judge of my cause, who art the only author of my mischief."

Zelmane the more astonished, the more she understood her, "Madam," said she, "whereof do you accuse me that I will not clear myself? Or wherein may I stead[3] you that you may not command me?"

"Alas!" answered Gynecia, "What shall I say more? Take pity of me, O Zelmane, but not as Zelmane, and disguise not with me in words, as I know thou dost in apparel."

Zelmane was much troubled with that word, finding herself brought to this strait. But as she was thinking what to answer her, they might see old Basilius pass hard by them without ever seeing them, complaining likewise of love very freshly, and ending his complaint with this song, love having renewed both his invention and voice:

> Let not old age disgrace my high desire,
>   O heavenly soul in human shape contained:
> Old wood inflamed doth yield the bravest[4] fire,
>   When younger doth in smoke his virtue[5] spend.
>
> Ne let white hairs which on my face do grow
>   Seem to your eyes of a disgraceful hue,
> Since whiteness doth present the sweetest show,[6]
>   Which makes all eyes do homage unto you.
>
> Old age is wise and full of constant truth;
>   Old age well stayed from ranging humor[7] lives;
> Old age hath known whatever was in youth;

---

2. Medicine.
3. Be of use to.
4. Most splendid.

5. Power.
6. Appearance.
7. Caprice. "Stayed": settled.

> Old age o'ercome, the greater honor gives.
> And to old age since you yourself aspire,
> Let not old age disgrace my high desire.

Which being done, he looked very curiously[8] upon himself, sometimes fetching a little skip as if he had said his strength had not yet forsaken him.

But Zelmane, having in this time gotten some leisure to think for an answer, looking upon Gynecia as if she thought she did her some wrong, "Madam," said she, "I am not acquainted with those words of disguising; neither is it the profession of an Amazon; neither are you a party with whom it is to be used. If my service may please you, employ it, so long as you do me no wrong in misjudging of me."

"Alas, Zelmane," said Gynecia, "I perceive you know full little how piercing the eyes are of a true lover. There is no one beam of those thoughts you have planted in me but is able to discern a greater cloud than you do go in. Seek not to conceal yourself further from me, nor force not the passion of love into violent extremities."

Now was Zelmane brought to an exigent,[9] when the king, turning his eyes that way through the trees, perceived his wife and mistress[1] together; so that framing the most lovely[2] countenance he could, he came straightway towards them, and at the first word, thanking his wife for having entertained Zelmane, desired her she would now return into the lodge, because he had certain matters of estate[3] to impart to the Lady Zelmane. The queen, being nothing troubled with jealousy in that point, obeyed the king's commandment, full of raging agonies, and determinately bent[4] that as she would seek all loving means to win Zelmane, so she would stir up terrible tragedies rather than fail of her intent. And so went she from them to the lodge-ward;[5] with such a battle in her thoughts and so deadly an overthrow given to her best resolutions that even her body (where the field was fought) was oppressed withal, making a languishing sickness wait upon the triumph of passion,[6] which the more it prevailed in her, the more it made her jealousy watchful both over her daughter and Zelmane, having ever one of them entrusted to her own eyes.[7]

But as soon as Basilius was rid of his wife's presence, falling down on his knees, "O lady," said he, "which hast only had the power to stir up again those flames which had so long lain dead in me, see in me the power of your beauty, which can make old age come to ask counsel of youth, and a prince unconquered to become a slave to a stranger. And when you see that power of yours, love that at least in me, since it is yours, although of me you see nothing to be loved."

"Worthy prince," answered Zelmane, taking him up from his kneeling, "both your manner and your speech are so strange unto me as I know not how to answer it better than with silence."

"If silence please you," said the king, "it shall never displease me, since my heart is wholly pledged to obey you. Otherwise, if you would vouchsafe mine ears such happiness as to hear you, they shall convey your words to such a mind which is with the humblest degree of reverence to receive them."

---

8. Carefully, attentively.
9. Crisis.
1. I.e., the woman who rules his heart.
2. Loving.
3. State.

4. Resolutely determined.
5. Toward the lodge.
6. Attend upon passion's victory procession.
7. Always having one of them in her sight.

"I disdain not to speak to you, mighty prince," said Zelmane, "but I disdain to speak to any matter which may bring my honor into question."

And therewith, with a brave counterfeited scorn she departed from the king, leaving him not so sorry for his short answer as proud in himself that he had broken[8] the matter. And thus did the king, feeding his mind with those thoughts, pass great time in writing verses and making more of himself than he was wont to do, that, with a little help, he would have grown into a pretty kind of dotage.

But Zelmane, being rid of this loving but little loved company, "Alas," said she, "poor Pyrocles, was there ever one but I that had received wrong and could blame nobody, that having more than I desire, am still in want of that I would?[9] Truly, love, I must needs say thus much on thy behalf: thou hast employed my love there where all love is deserved, and for recompense hast sent me more love than ever I desired. But what wilt thou do, Pyrocles? Which way canst thou find to rid thee of thy intricate troubles? To her whom I would be known to, I live in darkness; and to her am revealed from whom I would be most secret. What shift[1] shall I find against the diligent love of Basilius? What shield against the violent passions of Gynecia? And if that be done, yet how am I the nearer to quench the fire that consumes me? Well, well, sweet Philoclea, my whole confidence must be builded in thy divine spirit, which cannot be ignorant of the cruel wound I have received by you."

1578–83   1593

The Defense of Poesy

In 1579 Sidney found himself the unwilling dedicatee of a small book titled *The School of Abuse*. Its author, the playwright-turned-moralist Stephen Gosson, attacked poets and actors from a rigidly pious perspective that called into question the morality of any fiction making. Sidney may have shared in the author's militant Protestantism, but he took a very different, more sympathetic and more complex view of the poet's art. He did not specifically answer Gosson's polemic, but he must have had it in mind when he composed, perhaps in the same year, a major piece of critical prose that was published after his death under two titles, *The Defense of Poesy* and *An Apology for Poetry*. Probably written in 1579 though not published until 1595, *The Defense of Poesy* is an eloquent argument for the dignity, social efficacy, and moral value of imaginative literature in verse or prose.

Sidney gives this argument the underlying form of a classical oration, as if he were a lawyer in ancient Rome defending his client against defamatory accusations. The great masters of Roman rhetoric, Cicero and Quintilian, prescribed a set structure for such orations, and as our footnotes indicate in detail, Sidney adapts his defense to this structure.

Sidney responds to old charges against poetic fictions—charges of irresponsibility and unreality—that had been revived in his own time most strenuously by Puritan moralists. In a graceful, if strikingly paradoxical, rhetorical performance, the *Defense* argues both that the poet, liberated from the world, is free to range "within the zodiac of his own wit" and that poetry actively intervenes in the world and transforms it for the better. After a slyly self-deprecating introduction, Sidney points out the antiquity of poetry, its prestige in the biblical and classical worlds, and its universality; also, he

8. Broached.
9. Of the thing I desire.

1. Evasion, stratagem.

cites the names given to poets—*vates*, or "prophet," by the Romans and *poietes*, or "maker," by the Greeks—as evidence of their ancient dignity. But he bases his defense essentially on the special status of the poetic imagination. While all arts, from astronomy to music to medicine, depend ultimately on nature as their object, poetry, he claims, is uniquely free: "Only the poet, disdaining to be tied to any such subjection, lifted up with the vigor of his own invention, doth grow in effect another nature."

This freedom, Sidney argues, enables the poet to present virtues and vices in a livelier and more affecting way than nature does, teaching, delighting, and moving the reader at the same time. The poet is superior to both the philosopher and the historian, because he is more concrete than the one and more universal than the other. The *Defense* also refutes Plato's charge that poets are liars, by arguing that the poet "nothing affirms, and therefore never lieth," and it denies as well the Platonic claim that poetry arouses base desires. Tragedy, for example, "openeth the greatest wounds," in Sidney's account, "and showeth forth the ulcers that are covered with tissue," thereby making "kings fear to be tyrants." Surveying the English literary scene of his own century, Sidney finds little to praise except for Surrey's lyrics, the moralizing verse narratives of the popular mid-century collection *A Mirror for Magistrates*, and Spenser's *Shepheardes Calender*; the drama he faults for "mingling kings and clowns" and for unrealistic distortions of time and space. (The great, sprawling plays of Marlowe and Shakespeare, plays that triumphantly violated many of Sidney's cherished principles, lay just ahead.) The *Defense* ends with a mock conjuration and a playful curse, reminders of the magical power of poetry, a power that lurks beneath both Sidney's idealism and his didacticism.

The Defense of Poesy

[THE LESSONS OF HORSEMANSHIP]

When the right virtuous Edward Wotton and I were at the Emperor's court together,[1] we gave ourselves to learn horsemanship of John Pietro Pugliano, one that with great commendation had the place of an esquire[2] in his stable. And he, according to the fertileness of the Italian wit, did not only afford us the demonstration of his practice, but sought to enrich our minds with the contemplations therein which he thought most precious. But with none I remember mine ears were at that time more laden, than when (either angered with slow payment, or moved with our learner-like admiration) he exercised his speech in the praise of his faculty.[3] He said soldiers were the noblest estate of mankind, and horsemen the noblest of soldiers. He said they were the masters of war and ornaments of peace, speedy goers and strong abiders, triumphers both in camps and courts. Nay, to so unbelieved a point he proceeded, as that no earthly thing bred such wonder to a prince as to be a good horseman—skill of government was but a *pedanteria*[4] in comparison. Then would he add certain praises, by telling what a peerless beast the horse was, the only serviceable courtier without flattery, the beast

1. Sidney and Edward Wotton (1548–1626), an English courtier and diplomat, became good friends at the court of Maximilian II (the Holy Roman Emperor) in Vienna in 1574–75. "Right virtuous": most virtuous.
   Wittily shaping his defense of literature as a judicial oration (a trial lawyer's speech) according to the pattern laid down in classical and Renaissance rhetorical theory, Sidney opens with an

exordium: a brief section designed to put the audience into a receptive frame of mind and, especially, to make it well disposed toward the speaker.
2. Equerry, an officer in charge of the horses and stables of a noble house.
3. Profession.
4. Pedantry, narrow and overly detailed knowledge, of use only to schoolmasters. "Prince": ruler.

of most beauty, faithfulness, courage, and such more, that if I had not been a piece of a logician[5] before I came to him, I think he would have persuaded me to have wished myself a horse.[6] But thus much at least with his no few words he drave into me, that self-love is better than any gilding[7] to make that seem gorgeous wherein ourselves be parties. Wherein, if Pugliano's strong affection[8] and weak arguments will not satisfy you, I will give you a nearer example of myself, who (I know not by what mischance) in these my not old years and idlest times having slipped into the title of a poet, am provoked to say something unto you in the defense of that my unelected vocation, which if I handle with more good will than good reasons, bear with me, since the scholar is to be pardoned that followeth the steps of his master.[9] And yet I must say that, as I have more just cause to make a pitiful[1] defense of poor poetry, which from almost the highest estimation of learning is fallen to be the laughingstock of children, so have I need to bring some more available[2] proofs: since the former[3] is by no man barred of his deserved credit, the silly[4] latter hath had even the names of philosophers used to the defacing of it, with great danger of civil war among the Muses.

[POETRY'S HISTORICAL IMPORTANCE]

And first, truly, to all them that, professing learning, inveigh against poetry may justly be objected that they go very near to ungratefulness, to seek to deface that which, in the noblest nations and languages that are known, hath been the first light-giver to ignorance, and first nurse, whose milk by little and little enabled them to feed afterwards of tougher knowledges.[5] And will they now play the hedgehog that, being received into the den, drave out his host? Or rather the vipers, that with their birth kill their parents?[6]

Let learned Greece in any of his manifold sciences[7] be able to show me one book before Musaeus, Homer, and Hesiod,[8] all three nothing else but poets. Nay, let any history be brought that can say any writers were there before them, if they were not men of the same skill, as Orpheus, Linus,[9] and some other are named, who, having been the first of that country that made pens deliverers of their knowledge to the posterity, may justly challenge to be called their fathers in learning: for not only in time they had this priority (although in itself antiquity be venerable) but went before them, as causes to draw with their charming sweetness the wild untamed wits to an admiration of knowledge. So, as Amphion was said to move stones with his poetry to build Thebes,[1] and Orpheus to be listened to by beasts, indeed, stony and

---

5. I.e., if I had not had some skill in logic.
6. With an allusion to the root meaning of Sidney's given name, from Greek *phil+hippos*, "horse-lover."
7. With a pun on "gelding." "Drave": drove.
8. Feeling; partiality.
9. I.e., Pugliano.
1. Compassionate.
2. Effective.
3. I.e., horsemanship.
4. Weak, poor.
5. In a judicial oration, the second section is the *narratio*: a brief overview of the facts of the case. Sidney substitutes a short history of poetry and an investigation of its essential nature as inferred from the etymology of Latin and Greek words for "poet."

6. According to an ancient tradition, vipers eat their way out of their mother's womb, killing her. The ungrateful hedgehog is from a pseudo-Aesopic fable. The idea that poets were the earliest teachers descends from classical antiquity.
7. Branches of knowledge.
8. Musaeus was a mythical Greek poet, thought to have preceded Homer and Hesiod (both ca. 8th century B.C.E.). He was conflated with a much later (5th century C.E.) poet of the same name who wrote a brief epic on Hero and Leander (cf. p. 659).
9. In Greek myth, Linus was the teacher of Orpheus, the archetypal poet and musician.
1. Usually the mythological Amphion is said to have accomplished this feat with the music of his harp.

beastly people; so among the Romans were Livius Andronicus and Ennius.[2] So in the Italian language the first that made it aspire to be a treasure-house of science were the poets Dante, Boccaccio, and Petrarch. So in our English were Gower and Chaucer,[3] after whom, encouraged and delighted with their excellent fore-going, others have followed, to beautify our mother tongue, as well in the same kind as in other arts.

This did so notably show itself, that the philosophers of Greece durst not a long time appear to the world but under the masks of poets. So Thales, Empedocles, and Parmenides sang their natural philosophy in verses; so did Pythagoras and Phocylides their moral counsels; so did Tyrtaeus in war matters, and Solon[4] in matters of policy: or rather they, being poets, did exercise their delightful vein in those points of highest knowledge, which before them lay hid to the world. For that wise Solon was directly a poet it is manifest, having written in verse the notable fable of the Atlantic Island, which was continued by Plato.[5] And truly even Plato whosoever well considereth shall find that in the body of his work, though the inside and strength were philosophy, the skin, as it were, and beauty depended most of poetry: for all standeth upon[6] dialogues, wherein he feigneth many honest burgesses of Athens to speak of such matters that, if they had been set on the rack, they would never have confessed them, besides his poetical describing the circumstances of their meetings, as the well ordering of a banquet, the delicacy of a walk, with interlacing mere tales, as Gyges' ring[7] and others, which who knoweth not to be flowers of poetry did never walk into Apollo's[8] garden.

And even historiographers (although their lips sound of things done, and verity be written in their foreheads) have been glad to borrow both fashion[9] and, perchance, weight of the poets. So Herodotus entitled his history by the name of the nine Muses; and both he and all the rest that followed him either stale[1] or usurped of poetry their passionate describing of passions, the many particularities of battles, which no man could affirm; or, if that be denied me, long orations put in the mouths of great kings and captains, which it is certain they never pronounced.[2]

So that truly neither philosopher nor historiographer could at the first have entered into the gates of popular judgments if they had not taken a great passport of poetry, which in all nations at this day where learning flourisheth not, is plain to be seen; in all which they have some feeling of poetry.

---

2. Ennius (239–169 B.C.E.) authored a verse history of Rome. Livius Andronicus (3rd century B.C.E.) was a Greek writer taken to Rome as a prisoner of war; he was credited with having there become the first poet to write in Latin.
3. Evidently Sidney thought the late-14th-century poets Chaucer and John Gower the earliest English writers worth mentioning—corresponding, in English literary culture, to the great Italian writers Dante (ca. 1265–1321), Petrarch (1304–1374), and Boccaccio (1313–1375).
4. Solon and the others listed here were legendary wise men of early Greece (7th–5th centuries B.C.E.) to whom various surviving fragments of verse were attributed. The first five men were associated with science ("natural philosophy") or moral philosophy. Tyrtaeus's poetry inspired the Spartans to martial exploits. Solon was the great political reformer of early Athens.
5. Plato wrote about the sunken continent Atlan-

tis in his dialogue *Timaeus*. Solon's poem on the subject is lost.
6. Is constructed on; depends on.
7. *Republic* 2.359–60 relates the shepherd Gyges's descent to the underworld and his theft there of a ring that conferred invisibility. Sidney's argument is that Plato's dialogues rely on poetry, because they include fictional elements. Cf. his later assertion that "feigning"—fiction—is a defining element of poetry: p. 554.
8. Apollo is the Greek god of poetry (among other things).
9. Form. "Historiographers": writers of history.
1. Stole. Herodotus (5th century B.C.E.) was the first great Greek historian. After his own time, his *Histories* were divided into nine books named for the nine Muses.
2. Fictitious accounts of battles and speeches were conventional in classical historiography and Renaissance humanists' histories emulating it.

In Turkey, besides their law-giving divines, they have no other writers but poets.[3] In our neighbor country Ireland, where truly learning goes very bare, yet are their poets held in a devout reverence. Even among the most barbarous and simple Indians, where no writing is, yet have they their poets who make and sing songs, which they call *areytos*,[4] both of their ancestors' deeds and praises of their gods: a sufficient probability that, if ever learning come among them, it must be by having their hard dull wits softened and sharpened with the sweet delights of poetry—for until they find a pleasure in the exercises of the mind, great promises of much knowledge will little persuade them that know not the fruits of knowledge. In Wales, the true remnant of the ancient Britons, as there are good authorities to show the long time they had poets, which they called bards, so through all the conquests of Romans, Saxons, Danes, and Normans, some of whom did seek to ruin all memory of learning from among them, yet do their poets even to this day last; so as it is not more notable in soon beginning than in long continuing.

[THE POET AS PROPHET AND CREATOR]

But since the authors of most of our sciences were the Romans, and before them the Greeks, let us a little stand upon their authorities, but even so far as to see what names they have given unto this now scorned skill.

Among the Romans a poet was called *vates*, which is as much as a diviner, foreseer, or prophet, as by his conjoined words *vaticinium* and *vaticinari*[5] is manifest: so heavenly a title did that excellent people bestow upon this heart-ravishing knowledge. And so far were they carried into the admiration thereof, that they thought in the chanceable hitting upon any such verses great foretokens of their following fortunes were placed. Whereupon grew the word of *Sortes Virgilianae*,[6] when by sudden opening Virgil's book they lighted upon any verse of his making, whereof the histories of the emperors' lives are full: as of Albinus,[7] the governor of our island, who in his childhood met with this verse

Arma amens capio nec sat rationis in armis[8]

and in his age performed it. Which, although it were a very vain and godless superstition, as also it was to think spirits were commanded by such verses— whereupon this word charms, derived of *carmina*,[9] cometh—so yet serveth it to show the great reverence those wits[1] were held in; and altogether not without ground, since both the oracles of Delphos and Sibylla's prophecies[2] were wholly delivered in verses. For that same exquisite observing of number and measure in the words, and that high flying liberty of conceit[3] proper to the poet, did seem to have some divine force in it.

---

3. In the Ottoman Empire in Sidney's time, poetry was more highly developed than prose, but it is a great exaggeration to say the Turks had no writers other than their poets and their "law-giving divines" (the *mufti*).
4. Poems (accompanied by music and dancing) of the indigenous Haitians, celebrating ancestral valor.
5. "Prophecy" and "to prophesy."
6. Virgilian lots; i.e., accepting as prophecy a line of Virgil chosen by random ("changeable") opening of the *Aeneid*.

7. Roman governor of Britain, declared emperor by his troops in 193 C.E. but defeated and killed four years later.
8. Frantic, I take up arms, yet there is little purpose in arms (*Aeneid* 2.314).
9. Songs, poems.
1. Talented people (i.e., the poets).
2. The Pythia (priestess) at Delphi in Greece proclaimed Apollo's oracles. Sibylla (Sibyl) was a general name given to various prophetesses in Greek and Roman culture.
3. Imaginative conception.

And may not I presume a little further, to show the reasonableness of this word *vates*, and say that the holy David's[4] Psalms are a divine poem? If I do, I shall not do it without the testimony of great learned men, both ancient and modern. But even the name of Psalms will speak for me, which being interpreted, is nothing but songs; then that it is fully written in meter, as all learned Hebricians agree, although the rules be not yet fully found;[5] lastly and principally, his handling his prophecy, which is merely[6] poetical: for what else is the awaking his musical instruments, the often and free changing of persons, his notable *prosopopoeias*,[7] when he maketh you, as it were, see God coming in His majesty, his telling of the beasts' joyfulness and hills leaping, but a heavenly poesy, wherein almost[8] he showeth himself a passionate lover of that unspeakable and everlasting beauty to be seen by the eyes of the mind, only cleared by faith? But truly now having named him, I fear me I seem to profane that holy name, applying it to poetry, which is among us thrown down to so ridiculous an estimation. But they that with quiet judgments will look a little deeper into it, shall find the end and working of it such as, being rightly applied, deserveth not to be scourged out of the Church of God.

But now let us see how the Greeks named it, and how they deemed of it. The Greeks called him a "poet," which name hath, as the most excellent, gone through other languages. It cometh of this word *poiein*, which is, to make: wherein, I know not whether by luck or wisdom, we Englishmen have met with the Greeks in calling him a maker:[9] which name, how high and incomparable a title it is, I had rather were known by marking the scope of other sciences than by any partial[1] allegation.

There is no art delivered to mankind that hath not the works of nature for his principal object, without which they[2] could not consist, and on which they so depend, as they become actors and players, as it were, of what nature will have set forth. So doth the astronomer look upon the stars, and, by that he seeth, set down what order nature hath taken therein. So doth the geometrician and arithmetician in their diverse sorts of quantities. So doth the musician in times tell you which by nature agree,[3] which not. The natural philosopher thereon[4] hath his name, and the moral philosopher standeth upon[5] the natural virtues, vices, or passions of man; and follow nature (saith he) therein, and thou shalt not err. The lawyer saith what men have determined; the historian what men have done. The grammarian speaketh only of the rules of speech; and the rhetorician and logician, considering what in nature will soonest prove and persuade, thereon give artificial rules, which still are compassed within the circle of a question according to the proposed matter.[6] The physician weigheth[7] the nature of man's body, and the nature of

---

4. The biblical King David, commonly identified in the Renaissance as author of the Book of Psalms in its entirety.
5. Many Renaissance scholars who knew some Hebrew ("Hebricians") thought the Psalms were written in verse forms approximating classical Greek and Latin meters.
6. Entirely.
7. Personifications. "Changing of persons": shifts in narrative perspective, between first- and third-person expressions.
8. Indeed. "Poesy": art of making poetry.
9. A common word for *poet* in 16th-century

England. "Met with": agreed with.
1. Biased. "Marking": noting.
2. The several arts. The following argument owes much to the *Poetics* (1561) of the Renaissance Italian theorist Julius Caesar Scaliger.
3. Which rhythms are naturally consonant.
4. I.e., from nature. "Natural philosopher": scientist.
5. Takes as subject matter.
6. The rules of those arts ("artificial rules") are always limited in their application to questions pertaining to the subject at hand.
7. Considers.

things helpful or hurtful unto it. And the metaphysic, though it be in the second and abstract notions, and therefore be counted supernatural,[8] yet doth he indeed build upon the depth of nature. Only the poet, disdaining to be tied to any such subjection, lifted up with the vigor of his own invention, doth grow in effect another nature, in making things either better than nature bringeth forth, or, quite anew, forms such as never were in nature, as the Heroes, Demigods, Cyclops, Chimeras, Furies,[9] and suchlike: so as he goeth hand in hand with nature, not enclosed within the narrow warrant of her gifts, but freely ranging only within the zodiac of his own wit.[1] Nature never set forth the earth in so rich tapestry as divers poets have done; neither with so pleasant rivers, fruitful trees, sweet-smelling flowers, nor whatsoever else may make the too much loved earth more lovely. Her world is brazen, the poets only deliver a golden.[2]

But let those things alone, and go to man—for whom as the other things are, so it seemeth in him her uttermost cunning is employed—and know whether she have brought forth so true a lover as Theagenes, so constant a friend as Pylades, so valiant a man as Orlando, so right a prince as Xenophon's Cyrus,[3] so excellent a man every way as Virgil's Aeneas. Neither let this be jestingly conceived, because the works of the one be essential, the other in imitation or fiction;[4] for any understanding knoweth the skill of each artificer standeth in that *idea* or fore-conceit[5] of the work, and not in the work itself. And that the poet hath that *idea* is manifest, by delivering them forth in such excellency as he had imagined them. Which delivering forth also is not wholly imaginative, as we are wont[6] to say by them that build castles in the air; but so far substantially it worketh, not only to make a Cyrus, which had been but a particular excellency as nature might have done, but to bestow a Cyrus upon the world to make many Cyruses, if they will learn aright why and how that maker made him.

Neither let it be deemed too saucy a comparison to balance the highest point of man's wit with the efficacy of nature; but rather give right honor to the heavenly Maker of that maker, who having made man to His own likeness, set him beyond and over all the works of that second nature:[7] which in nothing he showeth so much as in poetry, when with the force of a divine breath he bringeth things forth surpassing her doings—with no small arguments to the incredulous[8] of that first accursed fall of Adam, since our erected wit maketh us know what perfection is, and yet our infected will[9] keepeth us from reaching unto it. But these arguments will by few be understood, and by fewer granted. This much (I hope) will be given me, that the Greeks with some probability of reason gave him[1] the name above all names of learning.

---

8. Outside the physical world—entirely mental. "Metaphysic": metaphysician.

9. Avenging deities who punish crimes both in this world and after death. "Heroes": in the Greek sense, part human, part divine. "Cyclops": one-eyed giants (the correct plural is "Cyclopes") in Homer's *Odyssey*. "Chimeras": fire-breathing monsters with lion's head, goat's body, and serpent's tail.

1. Intellect.

2. A reference to the classical tradition of "The Four Ages of Man," the idea that the world has declined from the first and perfect Golden Age, through the Silver, Brass (or Bronze), and Iron ages. "Her": Nature's.

3. Cyrus the Great of Persia, exemplary hero of Xenophon's prose romance, the *Cyropaedia* (4th century B.C.E.). Theagenes, hero of Heliodorus's Greek romance, *Aethiopica* (3rd or 4th century C.E.). Pylades, friend of the Greek hero Orestes. Orlando, hero especially of Ariosto's *Orlando furioso* (1516).

4. The works of nature are real ("essential"); those of the poet are fiction.

5. Imaginative plan; conception.

6. Accustomed. "Imaginative": fanciful.

7. Physical nature.

8. I.e., skeptics.

9. Will corrupted in the Fall by original sin.

1. I.e., poesy.

Now let us go to a more ordinary opening[2] of him, that the truth may be the more palpable: and so I hope, though we get not so unmatched a praise as the etymology of his names will grant, yet his very description, which no man will deny, shall not justly be barred from a principal commendation.

[DEFINITION AND CLASSIFICATION OF POETRY]

Poesy therefore is an art of imitation, for so Aristotle termeth it in the word *mimesis*[3]—that is to say, a representing, counterfeiting, or figuring forth—to speak metaphorically, a speaking picture—with this end, to teach and delight.[4]

Of this have been three general kinds. The chief, both in antiquity and excellency, were they that did imitate the unconceivable excellencies of God. Such were David in his Psalms; Solomon in his Song of Songs, in his Ecclesiastes, and Proverbs; Moses and Deborah in their Hymns;[5] and the writer of Job: which, beside other, the learned Emanuel Tremellius and Franciscus Junius[6] do entitle the poetical part of the Scripture. Against these none will speak that hath the Holy Ghost in due holy reverence. (In this kind, though in a full wrong divinity, were Orpheus, Amphion, Homer in his Hymns,[7] and many other, both Greeks and Romans.) And this poesy must be used by whosoever will follow St. James's counsel in singing psalms when they are merry;[8] and I know is used with the fruit of comfort by some, when, in sorrowful pangs of their death-bringing sins, they find the consolation of the never-leaving goodness.

The second kind is of them that deal with matters philosophical, either moral, as Tyrtaeus, Phocylides, Cato;[9] or natural, as Lucretius and Virgil's *Georgics*; or astronomical, as Manilius and Pontanus; or historical, as Lucan:[1] which who mislike, the fault is in their judgment quite out of taste, and not in the sweet food of sweetly uttered knowledge.

But because this second sort is wrapped within the fold of the proposed subject, and takes not the course of his own invention, whether they properly be poets or no let grammarians dispute, and go to the third, indeed right[2] poets, of whom chiefly this question ariseth: betwixt whom and these second

2. Analysis or explanation.
3. *Poetics* 1.2. The third part of a judicial oration is the *propositio*—as Thomas Elyot explains it in *The Art of Rhetoric* (1553), "a pithy sentence, comprehending in a small room the sum of the whole matter." This is followed by the *divisio*, in which the subject is divided into its parts and the orator clarifies which of these are in dispute.
4. The primary authorities for the commonplace notions that a poem is a "speaking picture" and that the end of poetry is "to teach and delight" are, respectively, Plutarch (ca. 46–ca. 120 C.E.), especially in *How to Study Poetry* 17–18, and Horace (65–8 B.C.E.), *Art of Poetry*, lines 343–44. The compounded definition, and the threefold classification of poets that follows, stem from Scaliger.
5. See Exodus 15.1–18, Deuteronomy 32.1–44, Judges 5.
6. Two scholars who published a Protestant Latin translation of the Bible, in 1579.
7. The Homeric Hymns are a collection of ancient Greek poems addressed to various gods and formerly attributed to Homer. Similarly,

Orpheus (the archetypal poet of Greek mythology) was thought to be the author of a group of poems that expound the beliefs of a Greek mystery-religion. The lyre-playing of Amphion (a son of Zeus) moved stones to form themselves into the walls of Thebes.
8. "Is any merry? let him sing psalms" (James 5.13).
9. The Roman Marcus Cato was the author of *Disticha de moribus*, an immensely popular collection, in verse and prose, of moral maxims. Tyrtaeus and Phocylides are among the Greek poets Sidney has previously mentioned.
1. Lucan wrote *De bello civili* (On the Civil War; also known as the *Pharsalia*), an epic poem on the struggle between Caesar and Pompey. Lucretius wrote a philosophical poem, *De rerum natura* (On the Nature of Things). Virgil's *Georgics* exalts the life and work of the farmer. Manilius wrote a long poem titled *Astronomica*. The 15th-century Italian writer Pontanus—the only post-classical poet in this list—was the author of another celebrated astronomical poem, *Urania*.
2. Justly entitled to the name.

is such a kind of difference as betwixt the meaner[3] sort of painters, who counterfeit only such faces as are set before them, and the more excellent, who having no law but wit, bestow that in colors upon you which is fittest for the eye to see: as the constant though lamenting look of Lucretia, when she punished in herself another's fault,[4] wherein he painteth not Lucretia, whom he never saw, but painteth the outward beauty of such a virtue. For these third[5] be they which most properly do imitate to teach and delight, and to imitate borrow nothing of what is, hath been, or shall be; but range, only reined with learned discretion, into the divine consideration of what may be and should be. These be they that, as the first and most noble sort may justly be termed *vates*, so these are waited on in the excellentest languages and best understandings with[6] the fore-described name of poets. For these indeed do merely[7] make to imitate, and imitate both to delight and teach; and delight, to move men to take that goodness in hand, which without delight they would fly as from a stranger; and teach, to make them know that goodness where-unto they are moved—which being the noblest scope to which ever any learning was directed, yet want[8] there not idle tongues to bark at them.

These be subdivided into sundry more special denominations. The most notable be the heroic,[9] lyric, tragic, comic, satiric, iambic, elegiac,[1] pastoral, and certain others, some of these being termed according to the matter they deal with, some by the sorts of verses they liked best to write in; for indeed the greatest part of poets have appareled their poetical inventions in that numbrous[2] kind of writing which is called verse—indeed but appareled, verse being but an ornament and no cause to poetry, since there have been many most excellent poets that never versified, and now swarm many versi-fiers that need never answer to the name of poets. For Xenophon, who did imitate so excellently as to give us *effigiem iusti imperii*, the portraiture of a just empire, under the name of Cyrus (as Cicero saith of him), made therein an absolute heroical poem. So did Heliodorus in his sugared invention of that picture of love in Theagenes and Chariclea; and yet both these wrote in prose: which I speak to show that it is not rhyming and versing that maketh a poet—no more than a long gown maketh an advocate,[3] who though he pleaded in armor should be an advocate and no soldier. But it is that feigning notable images of virtues, vices, or what else, with that delightful teaching, which must be the right describing note[4] to know a poet by; although indeed the senate of poets hath chosen verse as their fittest raiment, meaning, as in matter they passed all in all,[5] so in manner to go beyond them: not speaking (table-talk fashion or like men in a dream) words as they chanceably fall from the mouth, but peising[6] each syllable of each word by just proportion according to the dignity of the subject.

---

3. Lower.
4. A notable exemplar of chastity and honor, the Roman matron Lucretia committed suicide after being raped by the son of King Tarquinius Superbus. "Wit": creative imagination.
5. I.e., the right poets.
6. Only. "Waited on . . . with": distinguished by.
7. Lack. "Scope": aim.
8. Epic.
9. Two genres are named after their Greek and

Latin verse forms. "Iambic": associated with directly vituperative poetry (as distinguished from the irony of satire). "Elegiac": poetry written in the "elegiac couplet," which was used especially for reflective, lamenting, or erotic poetry.
2. I.e., in numbers, poetic meters.
3. Lawyer.
4. The true distinguishing characteristics.
5. All others, in all respects.
6. Weighing.

[POETRY VERSUS PHILOSOPHY AND HISTORY]

Now therefore it shall not be amiss first to weigh this latter sort of poetry by his works, and then by his parts; and if in neither of these anatomies he be condemnable, I hope we shall obtain a more favorable sentence.[7]

This purifying of wit—this enriching of memory, enabling of judgment, and enlarging of conceit[8]—which commonly we call learning, under what name soever it come forth, or to what immediate end soever it be directed, the final end is to lead and draw us to as high a perfection as our degenerate souls, made worse by their clayey lodgings, can be capable of.

This, according to the inclination of the man, bred many-formed[9] impressions. For some that thought this felicity principally to be gotten by knowledge, and no knowledge to be so high or heavenly as acquaintance with the stars, gave themselves to astronomy; others, persuading themselves to be demigods if they knew the causes of things, became natural and supernatural philosophers; some an admirable delight drew to music; and some the certainty of demonstration to the mathematics. But all, one and other, having this scope: to know, and by knowledge to lift up the mind from the dungeon of the body to the enjoying his own divine essence.

But when by the balance of experience it was found that the astronomer, looking to the stars, might fall in a ditch,[1] that the inquiring philosopher might be blind in himself, and the mathematician might draw forth a straight line with a crooked heart, then lo, did proof, the overruler of opinions, make manifest that all these are but serving sciences, which, as they have each a private[2] end in themselves, so yet are they all directed to the highest end of the mistress-knowledge, by the Greeks called *architectonike*,[3] which stands (as I think) in the knowledge of a man's self, in the ethic and politic consideration, with the end of well-doing and not of well-knowing only—even as the saddler's next[4] end is to make a good saddle, but his further end to serve a nobler faculty, which is horsemanship, so the horseman's to soldiery, and the soldier not only to have the skill, but to perform the practice of a soldier. So that, the ending end of all earthly learning being virtuous action, those skills that most serve to bring forth that have a most just title to be princes over all the rest.

Wherein, if we can, show we the poet's nobleness, by setting him before his other competitors. Among whom as principal challengers step forth the moral philosophers, whom, methinketh, I see coming towards me with a sullen gravity, as though they could not abide vice by daylight, rudely clothed for to witness outwardly their contempt of outward things, with books in their hands against glory, whereto they set their names, sophistically[5] speaking against subtlety, and angry with any man in whom they see the foul fault of anger. These men casting largess as they go, of definitions, divisions, and distinctions,[6] with a scornful interrogative do soberly ask whether it be

---

7. Judgment. "Works": effects. "Anatomies": analyses. Here Sidney moves to the central and longest part of the judicial oration, the *confirmatio* or *examinatio*, in which the speaker develops the arguments in support of his (or her) position.
8. Conceptual power. "Wit": intellect; understanding. "Enabling": strengthening.
9. Manifold. "Inclination": natural disposition.

1. As Plato (*Theatatus* 174) reported of the philosopher and astronomer Thales.
2. Particular.
3. The "chief art," to which all others are subordinate. The term is Aristotle's (*Ethics* 1.1).
4. Nearest.
5. Subtly.
6. I.e., bountiful gifts of scholastic terms and arguments.

possible to find any path so ready to lead a man to virtue as that which teacheth what virtue is; and teach it not only by delivering forth his very being, his causes and effects, but also by making known his enemy, vice, which must be destroyed, and his cumbersome[7] servant, passion, which must be mastered; by showing the generalities that containeth it, and the specialities that are derived from it; lastly, by plain setting down how it extendeth itself out of the limits of a man's own little world to the government of families and maintaining of public societies.

The historian scarcely giveth leisure to the moralist to say so much, but that he, laden with old mouse-eaten records, authorizing himself[8] (for the most part) upon other histories, whose greatest authorities are built upon the notable foundation of hearsay; having much ado to accord differing writers and to pick truth out of their partiality;[9] better acquainted with a thousand years ago than with the present age, and yet better knowing how this world goeth than how his own wit runneth; curious for antiquities and inquisitive of novelties; a wonder to young folks and a tyrant in table talk, denieth, in a great chafe,[1] that any man for teaching of virtue and virtuous actions is comparable to him. "I am *testis temporum, lux veritatis, vita memoriae, magistra vitae, nuntia vetustatis.*"[2] "The philosopher," saith he, "teacheth a disputative virtue, but I do an active. His virtue is excellent in the dangerless Academy of Plato, but mine showeth forth her honorable face in the battles of Marathon, Pharsalia, Poitiers, and Agincourt.[3] He teacheth virtue by certain abstract considerations, but I only bid you follow the footing of them that have gone before you. Old-aged experience goeth beyond the fine-witted philosopher, but I give the experience of many ages. Lastly, if he make the songbook, I put the learner's hand to the lute; and if he be the guide, I am the light." Then would he allege you innumerable examples, confirming story by stories, how much the wisest senators and princes have been directed by the credit of history, as Brutus, Alphonsus of Aragon,[4] and who not, if need be? At length the long line of their disputation maketh a point[5] in this, that the one giveth the precept, and the other[6] the example.

Now whom shall we find (since the question standeth for the highest form in the school of learning) to be moderator?[7] Truly, as me seemeth, the poet; and if not a moderator, even the man that ought to carry the title from them both, and much more from all other serving sciences. Therefore compare we the poet with the historian and with the moral philosopher; and if he go beyond them both, no other human skill can match him. For as for the divine,[8] with all reverence it is ever to be excepted, not only for having his scope as far beyond any of these as eternity exceedeth a moment, but even for passing[9]

7. Obstructive; troublesome.
8. Basing his authority.
9. Bias. "Accord": reconcile.
1. Temper.
2. "I am the witness of times, the light of truth, the life of memory, the teacher of life, the messenger of antiquity" (Cicero, *De oratore* 2.9.36).
3. At Poitiers (1356) and Agincourt (1415), the English defeated the French. At Marathon, the Greeks defeated the Persians (490 B.C.E.). At Pharsalia, Caesar defeated Pompey (48 B.C.E.).
4. Alfonso V of Aragon (1396–1458) carried the histories of Livy and Caesar into battle with him.

Marcus Brutus was inspired to rise up against Caesar by the history of his great republican ancestor, Junius Brutus, who expelled the Tarquin kings.
5. Comes to a full stop.
6. The historian. "The one": the philosopher.
7. Judge, arbitrator. Sidney images the rival claims of philosophy and history as a formal academic disputation—a standard exercise at the time—engaging the top class ("highest form") in the "school of learning."
8. The theologian.
9. Surpassing.

each of these in themselves. And for the lawyer, though *Ius*[1] be the daughter of Justice, and justice the chief of virtues, yet because he seeketh to make men good rather *formidine poenae* than *virtutis amore;*[2] or, to say righter, doth not endeavor to make men good, but that their evil hurt not others; having no care, so he be a good citizen, how bad a man he be: therefore as our wickedness maketh him[3] necessary, and necessity maketh him honorable, so is he not in the deepest truth to stand in rank with these[4] who all endeavor to take naughtiness away and plant goodness even in the secretest cabinet[5] of our souls. And these four are all that any way deal in that consideration of men's manners,[6] which being the supreme knowledge, they that best breed it deserve the best commendation.

The philosopher, therefore, and the historian are they which would win the goal, the one by precept, the other by example. But both, not having both, do both halt.[7] For the philosopher, setting down with thorny arguments the bare rule, is so hard of utterance and so misty to be conceived, that one that hath no other guide but him shall wade in him till he be old before he shall find sufficient cause to be honest.[8] For his knowledge standeth so upon the abstract and general, that happy[9] is that man who may understand him, and more happy that can apply what he doth understand. On the other side, the historian, wanting[1] the precept, is so tied, not to what should be but to what is, to the particular truth of things and not to the general reason of things, that his example draweth no necessary consequence, and therefore a less fruitful doctrine.

Now doth the peerless poet perform both: for whatsoever the philosopher saith should be done, he giveth a perfect picture of it in someone by whom he presupposeth it was done, so as he coupleth the general notion with the particular example. A perfect picture I say, for he yieldeth to the powers of the mind an image of that whereof the philosopher bestoweth but a wordish description, which doth neither strike, pierce, nor possess the sight of the soul so much as that other doth. For as in outward things, to a man that had never seen an elephant or a rhinoceros, who should tell him most exquisitely[2] all their shapes, color, bigness, and particular marks, or of a gorgeous palace the architecture, with declaring the full beauties, might well make the hearer able to repeat, as it were by rote, all he had heard, yet should never satisfy his inward conceit[3] with being witness to itself of a true lively knowledge; but the same man, as soon as he might see those beasts well painted, or that house well in model, should straightways grow, without need of any description, to a judicial[4] comprehending of them: so no doubt the philosopher with his learned definitions—be it of virtue, vices, matters of public policy or private government[5]—replenisheth the memory with many infallible grounds of wisdom, which, notwithstanding, lie dark before the imaginative and judging power, if they be not illuminated or figured forth[6] by the speaking picture of poesy.

1. Law (Latin).
2. Through fear of punishment than love of virtue. The distinction is from Horace, *Epistles* 1.16.52–53.
3. I.e., the lawyer.
4. Moral philosopher, historian, and poet.
5. Most private chamber. "Naughtiness": wickedness.
6. Moral conduct.

7. Limp (having, after all, only one leg each).
8. Virtuous.
9. Fortunate.
1. Not having.
2. Discriminatingly.
3. Conception.
4. Judicious.
5. Individual conduct (as opposed to "public policy").
6. Given form or shape.

Tully[7] taketh much pains, and many times not without poetical helps, to make us know the force love of our country hath in us. Let us but hear old Anchises speaking in the midst of Troy's flames, or see Ulysses in the fullness of all Calypso's delights bewail his absence from barren and beggarly Ithaca.[8] Anger, the Stoics said, was a short madness:[9] let but Sophocles bring you Ajax on a stage, killing or whipping sheep and oxen, thinking them the army of Greeks,[1] with their chieftains Agamemnon and Menelaus, and tell me if you have not a more familiar insight into anger than finding in the schoolmen his *genus* and difference.[2] See whether wisdom and temperance in Ulysses and Diomedes, valor in Achilles, friendship in Nisus and Euryalus,[3] even to an ignorant man carry not an apparent shining;[4] and, contrarily, the remorse of conscience in Oedipus, the soon repenting pride in Agamemnon, the self-devouring cruelty in his father Atreus, the violence of ambition in the two Theban brothers, the sour-sweetness of revenge in Medea;[5] and, to fall lower, the Terentian Gnatho and our Chaucer's Pandar[6] so expressed that we now use their names to signify their trades: and finally, all virtues, vices, and passions so in their own natural seats laid to the view, that we seem not to hear of them, but clearly to see through them.

But even in the most excellent determination of goodness, what philosopher's counsel can so readily direct a prince, as the feigned Cyrus in Xenophon; or a virtuous man in all fortunes, as Aeneas in Virgil; or a whole commonwealth, as the way of Sir Thomas More's *Utopia*? I say the way, because where Sir Thomas More erred, it was the fault of the man and not of the poet, for that way of patterning a commonwealth was most absolute,[7] though he perchance hath not so absolutely performed it. For the question is, whether the feigned image of poetry or the regular instruction of philosophy hath the more force in teaching: wherein if the philosophers have more rightly showed themselves philosophers than the poets have attained to the high top of their profession, as in truth

> Mediocribus esse poetis,
> Non dii, non homines, non concessere columnae;[8]

it is, I say again, not the fault of the art, but that by few men that art can be accomplished.

Certainly, even our Savior Christ could as well have given the moral commonplaces of uncharitableness and humbleness as the divine narration of

---

7. A common English name for Cicero (Marcus Tullius Cicero).
8. All the charms of the lovely nymph Calypso, and the promise of immortality with her, could not make Odysseus forget his home on the Greek isle of Ithaca (*Odyssey* 5.149–224). Anchises, the father of Aeneas, laments his destroyed homeland in *Aeneid* 2.638–49.
9. The formulation is Horace's (*Epistles* 1.2.62).
1. In fact, Sophocles's *Ajax* does not portray its protagonist's mad actions on the stage but has them reported by Menelaus (lines 1052–61).
2. In the logic of the Scholastic philosophers ("schoolmen"), "differences" are the attributes that distinguish among the species in a genus.
3. All are figures in the story of the Trojan War, as recounted in the *Iliad* and, for the faithful friends Nisus and Euryalus, the *Aeneid* (9.176–449).
4. An evident splendor.

5. All are figures from Greek and Roman tragedy. "The two Theban brothers": Eteocles and Polynices, twin sons of Oedipus, who killed each other in battle. (For Atreus—the father of Agamemnon, leader of the Greeks against Troy—see p. 560, n. 1).
6. The common noun *pander* derives from Pandarus, the go-between in Chaucer's *Troilus and Criseyde*. Similarly, Gnatho—a figure in the *Eunuch* of the Roman comic dramatist Terence—became a type-name for a fawning parasite.
7. Perfect. Sidney approves of More's casting a work of political philosophy as an account of a voyage to a fictional country, but he does not want to be thought of as endorsing all features of the Utopian commonwealth (especially, one surmises, its communism).
8. "That poets be middling, neither gods, nor men, nor booksellers ever allowed" (Horace, *Art of Poetry* 372–73).

Dives and Lazarus; or of disobedience and mercy, as that heavenly discourse of the lost child and the gracious father;[9] but that His through-searching wisdom knew the estate[1] of Dives burning in hell, and of Lazarus in Abraham's bosom, would more constantly (as it were) inhabit both the memory and judgment. Truly, for myself, meseems I see before mine eyes the lost child's disdainful prodigality, turned to envy a swine's dinner: which by the learned divines are thought not historical acts,[2] but instructing parables.

For conclusion, I say the philosopher teacheth, but he teacheth obscurely, so as the learned only can understand him, that is to say, he teacheth them that are already taught; but the poet is the food for the tenderest stomachs, the poet is indeed the right popular philosopher, whereof Aesop's tales give good proof: whose pretty allegories, stealing under the formal[3] tales of beasts, make many, more beastly than beasts, begin to hear the sound of virtue from these dumb speakers.

But now may it be alleged that if this imagining of matters be so fit for the imagination, then must the historian needs surpass, who bringeth you images of true matters; such as indeed were done, and not such as fantastically or falsely may be suggested to have been done. Truly, Aristotle himself, in his discourse of poesy, plainly determineth this question, saying that poetry is *philosophoteron* and *spoudaioteron*, that is to say, it is more philosophical and more studiously serious than history.[4] His reason is, because poesy dealeth with *katholou*, that is to say, with the universal consideration, and the history with *kathekaston*, the particular: now, saith he, the universal weighs what is fit to be said or done, either in likelihood or necessity (which the poesy considereth in his imposed names), and the particular only marks whether Alcibiades did, or suffered, this or that.[5] Thus far Aristotle: which reason of his (as all his) is most full of reason. For indeed, if the question were whether it were better to have a particular act truly or falsely set down, there is no doubt which is to be chosen, no more than whether you had rather have Vespasian's[6] picture right as he was, or, at the painter's pleasure, nothing resembling. But if the question be for your own use and learning, whether it be better to have it set down as it should be, or as it was, then certainly is more doctrinable[7] the feigned Cyrus in Xenophon than the true Cyrus in Justin, and the feigned Aeneas in Virgil than the right Aeneas in Dares Phrygius:[8] as to a lady that desired to fashion her countenance to the best grace, a painter should more benefit her to portrait a most sweet face, writing Canidia upon it, than to paint Canidia as she was, who, Horace sweareth, was full ill-favored.[9]

9. The Prodigal Son (Luke 15.11–32); for the parable of the rich Dives and the beggar Lazarus, see Luke 16.19–31.
1. Condition.
2. Records.
3. I.e., in the form of.
4. *Poetics* 9.
5. Alcibiades, an Athenian politician and disciple of Socrates, died in 404 B.C.E.—twenty years before Aristotle's birth. Sidney's summary of Aristotle's passage is accurate, with the important exception that he imposes the notion that Aristotelian universals have a morally prescriptive

force, weighing "what is *fit* to be said or done." Aristotle says only that "by a universal statement I mean one as to what such or such a kind of man will probably or necessarily say or do."
6. Vespasian was emperor of Rome 69–79 C.E.
7. Instructive.
8. Mentioned in the *Iliad*, Dares Phrygius was the supposed author of an eyewitness account of the Trojan War. Justin was a Roman historian of the 2nd or 3rd century C.E. who wrote an abridgment of a now-lost universal history by one Trogus.
9. For the lost looks of the witch Canidia, see Horace, *Epodes* 5.

If the poet do his part aright, he will show you in Tantalus, Atreus,[1] and suchlike, nothing that is not to be shunned; in Cyrus, Aeneas, Ulysses, each thing to be followed; where the historian, bound to tell things as things were, cannot be liberal (without he will be poetical) of a perfect pattern, but, as in Alexander or Scipio himself,[2] show doings, some to be liked, some to be misliked. And then how will you discern what to follow but by your own discretion, which you had without reading Quintus Curtius? And whereas a man may say, though in universal consideration of doctrine the poet prevaileth, yet that the history,[3] in his saying such a thing was done, doth warrant a man more in that he shall follow[4]—the answer is manifest: that, if he stand upon that was (as if he should argue, because it rained yesterday, therefore it should rain today), then indeed hath it some advantage to a gross conceit;[5] but if he know an example only informs a conjectured likelihood, and so go by reason,[6] the poet doth so far exceed him[7] as he is to frame his example to that which is most reasonable (be it in warlike, politic, or private matters), where the historian in his bare "was" hath many times that which we call fortune to overrule the best wisdom. Many times he must tell events whereof he can yield no cause; or, if he do, it must be poetically.

For that a feigned example hath as much force to teach as a true example (for as for to move, it is clear, since the feigned may be tuned to the highest key of passion), let us take one example wherein an historian and a poet did concur. Herodotus and Justin do both testify that Zopyrus, King Darius' faithful servant, seeing his master long resisted by the rebellious Babylonians, feigned himself in extreme disgrace of his king: for verifying of which, he caused his own nose and ears to be cut off, and so flying to the Babylonians was received, and for his known valor so sure credited, that he did find means to deliver them over to Darius.[8] Much like matter doth Livy record of Tarquinius and his son. Xenophon excellently feigneth such another stratagem performed by Abradatas in Cyrus' behalf. Now would I fain know, if occasion be presented unto you to serve your prince by such an honest dissimulation, why you do not as well learn it of Xenophon's fiction as of the other's verity; and truly so much the better, as you shall save your nose by the bargain: for Abradatas did not counterfeit so far. So then the best of the historian is subject to the poet; for whatsoever action, or faction, whatsoever counsel, policy, or war stratagem the historian is bound to recite, that may the poet (if he list)[9] with his imitation make his own, beautifying it both for further teaching and more delighting, as it please him: having all, from Dante's heaven to his hell, under the authority of his pen.

1. Figures from Greek mythology. In one version of his story, Tantalus served up his son at a banquet for the gods; similarly, his grandson Atreus served his brother's children to him.
2. Alexander the Great was often represented—for example, by the Roman historian Quintus Curtius—as having been corrupted by power; and even Scipio Africanus—the conqueror of Hannibal and one of the most unreservedly admired Romans—was, in his later years, accused of political misconduct. "Cannot be liberal . . . of": is not at liberty to give.
3. The historian. "Doctrine": instruction.
4. I.e., provides more reliable assurance as to what course one should follow.
5. I.e., to a person of undiscriminating intelligence.

6. I.e., if a person is sufficiently sophisticated to understand that reason is a better guide than example.
7. I.e., the historian.
8. Darius I was king of Persia 521–486 B.C.E. The story of his faithful servant Zopyrus was told in Herodotus's Histories 3.153–60 and repeated in Justin's Histories 1.10. Somewhat similar stories (see the two following sentences) are recounted by the Roman historian Livy (concerning the last of the Tarquin kings and his son) in From the Foundation of the City 1.53–54 and in Xenophon's Cyropaedia 6.1.38–44, 6.3.14–20 (though about Cyrus and one Araspas—not, as Sidney has it, Abradatas).
9. Likes.

Which if I be asked what poets have done so, as I might well name some, so yet say I, and say again, I speak of the art, and not of the artificer.

Now, to that which commonly is attributed to the praise of history, in respect of the notable learning is got by marking the success,[1] as though therein a man should see virtue exalted and vice punished—truly that commendation is particular to poetry, and far off from history. For indeed poetry ever sets virtue so out in her best colors, making Fortune her well-waiting handmaid, that one must needs be enamored of her. Well may you see Ulysses in a storm,[2] and in other hard plights; but they are but exercises of patience and magnanimity, to make them shine the more in the near-following prosperity. And of the contrary part, if evil men come to the stage, they ever go out (as the tragedy writer[3] answered to one that misliked the show of such persons) so manacled as they little animate folks to follow them. But the history, being captived to the truth of a foolish world, is many times a terror[4] from well-doing, and an encouragement to unbridled wickedness. For see we not valiant Miltiades[5] rot in his fetters? The just Phocion[6] and the accomplished Socrates put to death like traitors? The cruel Severus[7] live prosperously? The excellent Severus[8] miserably murdered? Sulla and Marius[9] dying in their beds? Pompey and Cicero[1] slain then when they would have thought exile a happiness? See we not virtuous Cato driven to kill himself,[2] and rebel Caesar so advanced that his name yet, after 1600 years, lasteth in the highest honor? And mark but even Caesar's own words of the aforenamed Sulla (who in that only did honestly, to put down his dishonest tyranny), *literas nescivit*, as if want of learning caused him to do well.[3] He meant it not by[4] poetry, which, not content with earthly plagues, deviseth new punishments in hell for tyrants, nor yet by philosophy, which teacheth *occidendos esse*;[5] but no doubt by skill in history, for that indeed can afford you Cypselus, Periander, Phalaris, Dionysius,[6] and I know not how many more of the same kennel, that speed[7] well enough in their abominable injustice of usurpation.

I conclude, therefore, that he[8] excelleth history, not only in furnishing the mind with knowledge, but in setting it forward to that which deserveth to be called and accounted good: which setting forward, and moving to well-doing, indeed setteth the laurel crown upon the poets as victorious, not only of the historian, but over the philosopher, howsoever in teaching it may be questionable.[9]

For suppose it be granted (that which I suppose with great reason may be denied) that the philosopher, in respect of his methodical proceeding, doth

---

1. Outcome.
2. In *Odyssey* 5.291ff.
3. Euripides (as reported by Plutarch, *How to Study Poetry* 4).
4. I.e., a deterrent.
5. Athenian general and architect of victory at Marathon over the Persians, later imprisoned by the Athenians.
6. Athenian general and statesman executed for treason because he opposed ill-advised opposition to Athens' Macedonian conquerors.
7. Emperor Lucius Septimius Severus, noted for ruthlessness.
8. Emperor Alexander Severus, a reformer slain by his troops.
9. Political rivals who brought unrest and destruction to Rome for two decades.

1. The great orator, killed at Mark Antony's command. Pompey the Great, defeated by Caesar at Pharsalia and slain in Egypt.
2. Cato the Younger committed suicide after his party failed to defeat Caesar.
3. When Sulla resigned ("put down") his dictatorship, Caesar joked that he was illiterate (*literas nescivit*), since he left the *dictatura* (which means both "dictatorship" and "dictation") to others.
4. With reference to.
5. They [tyrants] must be killed.
6. Four famous tyrants of the classical world: the first two were from Corinth, Phalaris was from Agrigentum, and Dionysus the Elder was from Syracuse.
7. Succeed.
8. I.e., poetry.
9. Arguable.

teach more perfectly than the poet, yet do I think that no man is so much *philophilosophos*[1] as to compare the philosopher in moving with the poet. And that moving is of a higher degree than teaching, it may by this appear, that it is well nigh both the cause and effect of teaching. For who will be taught, if he be not moved with desire to be taught? And what so much good doth that teaching bring forth (I speak still of moral doctrine) as that it moveth one to do that which it doth teach? For, as Aristotle saith, it is not *gnosis* but *praxis*[2] must be the fruit. And how *praxis* cannot be, without being moved to practice, it is no hard matter to consider.

The philosopher showeth you the way, he informeth you of the particularities, as well of the tediousness of the way, as of the pleasant lodging you shall have when your journey is ended, as of the many by-turnings that may divert you from your way. But this is to no man but to him that will read him, and read him with attentive studious painfulness;[3] which constant desire whosoever hath in him, hath already passed half the hardness of the way, and therefore is beholding to the philosopher but for the other half. Nay truly, learned men have learnedly thought that where once reason hath so much overmastered passion as that the mind hath a free desire to do well, the inward light each mind hath in itself is as good as a philosopher's book; since in nature[4] we know it is well to do well, and what is well, and what is evil, although not in the words of art which philosophers bestow upon us; for out of natural conceit[5] the philosophers drew it. But to be moved to do that which we know, or to be moved with desire to know, *hoc opus, hic labor est.*[6]

Now therein of all sciences (I speak still of human,[7] and according to the human conceit) is our poet the monarch. For he doth not only show the way, but giveth so sweet a prospect into the way, as will entice any man to enter into it. Nay, he doth, as if your journey should lie through a fair vineyard, at the first give you a cluster of grapes, that full of that taste, you may long to pass further. He beginneth not with obscure definitions, which must blur the margin with interpretations and load the memory with doubtfulness; but he cometh to you with words set in delightful proportion, either accompanied with, or prepared for, the well enchanting skill of music; and with a tale forsooth he cometh unto you, with a tale which holdeth children from play, and old men from the chimney corner. And, pretending no more, doth intend the winning of the mind from wickedness to virtue—even as the child is often brought to take most wholesome things by hiding them in such other as have a pleasant taste, which, if one should begin to tell them the nature of *aloes* or *rhabarbarum*[8] they should receive, would sooner take their physic at their ears than at their mouth.[9] So is it in men (most of which are childish in the best things, till they be cradled in their graves): glad will they be to hear the tales of Hercules, Achilles, Cyrus, Aeneas; and, hearing them, must needs hear the right description of wisdom, valor, and justice; which, if they had been barely, that is to say philosophically, set out, they would swear they be brought to school again.

---

1. A lover of philosophers.
2. Not knowing but doing (*Ethics* 1.3).
3. Painstaking effort.
4. Considering that by nature.
5. Natural understanding, as opposed to the philosophers' special vocabulary ("words of art").
6. This is the task, this is the work to be done

(Virgil, *Aeneid* 6.129).
7. As opposed to divine. "Sciences": branches of learning.
8. Two bitter purgatives: aloe and rhubarb.
9. I.e., would rather have their ears boxed than take the medicine.

That imitation whereof poetry is hath the most conveniency[1] to nature of all other, insomuch that, as Aristotle saith, those things which in themselves are horrible, as cruel battles, unnatural monsters, are made in poetical imitation delightful.[2] Truly, I have known men that even with reading *Amadis de Gaule*[3] (which God knoweth wanteth much of a perfect poesy) have found their hearts moved to the exercise of courtesy, liberality, and especially courage. Who readeth Aeneas carrying old Anchises on his back, that wisheth not it were his fortune to perform so excellent an act? Whom doth not these words of Turnus move, the tale of Turnus having planted his image in the imagination,

> Fugientem haec terra videbit?
> Usque adeone mori miserum est?[4]

Where the philosophers, as they scorn to delight, so much they be content little to move—saving wrangling whether *virtus*[5] be the chief or the only good, whether the contemplative or the active life do excell—which Plato and Boethius well knew, and therefore made Mistress Philosophy very often borrow the masking raiment of poesy.[6] For even those hard-hearted evil men who think virtue a school name, and know no other good but *indulgere genio*,[7] and therefore despise the austere admonitions of the philosopher, and feel not the inward reason they stand upon, yet will be content to be delighted—which is all the good-fellow poet seemeth to promise—and so steal[8] to see the form of goodness (which seen they cannot but love) ere themselves be aware, as if they took a medicine of cherries.

Infinite proofs of the strange effects of this poetical invention might be alleged; only two shall serve, which are so often remembered as I think all men know them. The one of Menenius Agrippa,[9] who, when the whole people of Rome had resolutely divided themselves from the senate, with apparent show of utter ruin, though he were (for that time) an excellent orator, came not among them upon trust of figurative speeches or cunning insinuations, and much less with far-fet[1] maxims of philosophy, which (especially if they were Platonic) they must have learned geometry before they could well have conceived;[2] but forsooth he behaves himself like a homely and familiar poet. He telleth them a tale, that there was a time when all the parts of the body made a mutinous conspiracy against the belly, which they thought devoured the fruits of each other's labor; they concluded they would let so unprofitable a spender starve. In the end, to be short (for the tale is notorious, and as notorious that it was a tale), with punishing the belly they plagued themselves. This applied by him wrought such effect in the people,

---

1. Congruity; suitability.
2. *Poetics* 4.
3. A chivalric romance of Spanish origin, which became extremely popular in a French translation.
4. *Aeneid* 12.645–46: "Shall this land see Turnus in flight? Is it so bad a thing to die?" The Italian king Turnus is Aeneas's worthy rival, killed by the epic hero in the poem's closing lines. Aeneas carries his father, Anchises, away from burning Troy in 2.705 ff.
5. Virtue. "Saving": except. The (satiric) point is that wrangling over standard philosophical questions is unlikely to move anyone other than the wrangling philosophers themselves.

6. For Plato's use of "poetry" (i.e., fiction), see p. 549. The *Consolation of Philosophy* of Boethius (476–524 C.E.) is cast as a dialogue between himself and Lady Philosophy, and alternates prose and verse.
7. To follow one's natural inclination.
8. I.e., come accidentally.
9. Roman consul in 503 B.C.E. The story of his parable was first related by Livy, *From the Foundation of the City* 2.32.
1. Farfetched.
2. A medieval tradition held that over the door of Plato's Academy was written: "No man untaught in geometry should enter."

as I never read that only words brought forth but then[3] so sudden and so good an alteration; for upon reasonable conditions a perfect reconcilement ensued. The other is of Nathan the prophet, who, when the holy David had so far forsaken God as to confirm adultery with murder,[4] when he was to do the tenderest office of a friend in laying his own shame before his eyes, sent by God to call again so chosen a servant, how doth he it but by telling of a man whose beloved lamb was ungratefully[5] taken from his bosom? The application most divinely true, but the discourse itself feigned; which made David (I speak of the second and instrumental cause[6]) as in a glass see his own filthiness, as that heavenly psalm of mercy[7] well testifieth.

By these, therefore, examples and reasons, I think it may be manifest that the poet, with that same hand of delight, doth draw the mind more effectually than any other art doth. And so a conclusion[8] not unfitly ensue: that, as virtue is the most excellent resting place for all worldly learning to make his end of, so poetry, being the most familiar[9] to teach it, and most princely to move towards it, in the most excellent work is the most excellent workman.

[THE POETIC KINDS]

But I am content not only to decipher him[1] by his works (although works, in commendation or dispraise, must ever hold a high authority), but more narrowly will examine his parts; so that (as in a man) though all together may carry a presence full of majesty and beauty, perchance in some one defectous piece[2] we may find blemish.

Now in his parts, kinds, or species (as you list[3] to term them), it is to be noted that some poesies have coupled together two or three kinds, as the tragical and comical, whereupon is risen the tragi-comical. Some, in the manner, have mingled prose and verse, as Sannazzaro and Boethius.[4] Some have mingled matters heroical and pastoral. But that cometh all to one in this question, for, if severed they be good, the conjunction cannot be hurtful. Therefore, perchance forgetting some and leaving some as needless to be remembered, it shall not be amiss in a word to cite the special kinds, to see what faults may be found in the right use of them.

Is it then the Pastoral poem which is misliked? (For perchance where the hedge is lowest[5] they will soonest leap over.) Is the poor pipe[6] disdained, which sometime out of Meliboeus' mouth can show the misery of people under hard lords or ravening soldiers, and again, by Tityrus, what blessedness is derived to them that lie lowest from the goodness of them that sit highest;[7] sometimes, under the pretty tales of wolves and sheep, can include the whole considerations of wrong-doing and patience; sometimes show that conten-

---

3. Except on that occasion. "Only words": words alone.
4. By killing the husband of his mistress, Bathsheba. For the deed, and Nathan's rebuke, see 2 Samuel 11–12.
5. Cruelly.
6. The *first* cause was God's intention to bring David to repentance.
7. Psalm 51, in which David pleads for God's mercy. "Glass": mirror.
8. I.e., to the argument weighing poetry by its "works" (cf. p. 555).
9. Congenial, suitable. "End": aim, objective.
1. I.e., poetry.

2. Defective part.
3. May choose.
4. Like Boethius's *Consolation of Philosophy* (see p. 563, n. 6), Jacopo Sannazaro's pastoral romance *Arcadia* (1502), which greatly influenced Sidney's own *Arcadia*, mixed prose and verse.
5. Pastoral was considered the humblest kind of poetry, written in the lowest style.
6. The shepherd's oaten flute, symbol of pastoral poetry.
7. In Virgil's first eclogue, Meliboeus laments the seizure of his land, while Tityrus rejoices that his lands were protected by the emperor.

tions for trifles can get but a trifling victory: where perchance a man may see that even Alexander and Darius, when they strave who should be cock of this world's dunghill, the benefit they got was that the after-livers may say

> Haec memini et victum frustra contendere Thirsin:
> Ex illo Corydon, Corydon est tempore nobis.[8]

Or is it the lamenting Elegiac; which in a kind heart would move rather pity than blame; who bewails with the great philosopher Heraclitus[9] the weakness of mankind and the wretchedness of the world; who surely is to be praised, either for compassionate accompanying just causes of lamentations or for rightly painting out how weak be the passions of woefulness?[1] Is it the bitter but wholesome Iambic[2] who rubs the galled mind, in making shame the trumpet of villainy, with bold and open crying out against naughtiness?[3] Or the Satiric, who

> Omne vafer vitium ridenti tangit amico;[4]

who sportingly never leaveth till he make a man laugh at folly, and at length ashamed, to laugh at himself, which he cannot avoid without avoiding the folly; who, while

> circum praecordia ludit,[5]

giveth us to feel how many headaches a passionate life bringeth us to; how, when all is done,

> Est Ulubris, animus si nos non deficit aequus?[6]

No, perchance it is the Comic, whom naughty play-makers and stage-keepers have justly made odious. To the arguments of abuse I will answer after. Only this much now is to be said, that the comedy is an imitation of the common errors of our life, which he representeth in the most ridiculous and scornful sort that may be, so as it is impossible that any beholder can be content to be such a one. Now, as in geometry the oblique must be known as well as the right, and in arithmetic the odd as well as the even, so in the actions of our life who seeth not the filthiness of evil wanteth[7] a great foil to perceive the beauty of virtue. This doth the comedy handle so in our private and domestical matters as with hearing it we get as it were an experience what is to be looked for of a niggardly Demea, of a crafty Davus, of a flattering Gnatho, of a vainglorious Thraso;[8] and not only to know what effects are to be expected, but to know who be such, by the signifying badge given them by the comedian.[9] And little reason hath any man to say that men

---

8. "This I remember, and how Thyrsis, vanquished, strove in vain. / From that day it is Corydon, Corydon with us" (Virgil, *Eclogue* 7.69–70). I.e., the great victory of Alexander the Great over Darius of Persia comes to the same thing as Corydon's victory over Thyrsis in a singing contest.
9. Ancient Greek philosopher who wept at human folly. "Who": i.e., which.
1. Sidney restricts the elegiac to lamentations; classical poets used elegiac meter for this purpose but also in poems treating love and other topics.
2. Iambic trimeter was first used by Greek poets for direct attacks (as opposed to the wit and ironic indirection that mark satire).
3. Wickedness.
4. Persius (*Satires* 1.116) on the satire of Horace, who "probes every fault while making his friends

laugh."
5. "He plays with the very vitals [of his target]" (Persius, *Satires* 1.117).
6. "It is at Ulubrae, if a well-balanced mind does not fail us" (an adaptation of Horace, *Epistles* 1.11.30). Ulubrae was a proverbially uninspiring town surrounded by marshes.
7. Is lacking. "Who": whoever.
8. Type characters in the Roman comedies of Terence (195–159 B.C.E.), respectively, the harsh father, clever servant, parasite, and braggart. Terence and Plautus (251–184 B.C.E.) were the chief classical models for comedy for the Renaissance. "Niggardly": stingy.
9. Writer of comedies. "Signifying badge": i.e., stereotypical features of looks, dress, or behavior.

learn the evil by seeing it so set out, since, as I said before, there is no man living but, by the force truth hath in nature, no sooner seeth these men play their parts, but wisheth them *in pistrinum;*[1] although perchance the sack of his own faults lie so hidden behind his back that he seeth not himself dance the same measure;[2] whereto yet nothing can more open his eyes than to find his own actions contemptibly set forth.

So that the right use of comedy will (I think) by nobody be blamed; and much less of the high and excellent Tragedy, that openeth the greatest wounds, and showeth forth the ulcers that are covered with tissue;[3] that maketh kings fear to be tyrants, and tyrants manifest their tyrannical humors;[4] that, with stirring the affects of admiration[5] and commiseration, teacheth the uncertainty of this world, and upon how weak foundations gilden roofs are builded; that maketh us know

> Qui sceptra saevus duro imperio regit
> Timet timentes; metus in auctorem redit.[6]

But how much it can move, Plutarch yieldeth a notable testimony of the abominable tyrant Alexander Pheraeus,[7] from whose eyes a tragedy, well made and represented, drew abundance of tears, who without all pity had murdered infinite numbers, and some of his own blood: so as he, that was not ashamed to make matters for tragedies, yet could not resist the sweet violence of a tragedy. And if it wrought no further good in him, it was that he, in despite of himself, withdrew himself from hearkening to that which might mollify his hardened heart. But it is not the tragedy they do mislike; for it were too absurd to cast out so excellent a representation of whatsoever is most worthy to be learned.

Is it the Lyric[8] that most displeaseth, who with his tuned lyre and well-accorded voice giveth praise, the reward of virtue, to virtuous acts; who gives moral precepts, and natural problems;[9] who sometimes raiseth up his voice to the height of the heavens, in singing the lauds[1] of the immortal God? Certainly, I must confess my own barbarousness, I never heard the old song of Percy and Douglas[2] that I found not my heart moved more than with a trumpet; and yet is it sung but by some blind crowder,[3] with no rougher voice than rude style; which, being so evil appareled in the dust and cobwebs of that uncivil age, what would it work trimmed in the gorgeous eloquence of Pindar?[4] In Hungary I have seen it the manner at all feasts, and other such meetings, to have songs of their ancestors' valor, which that right soldierlike nation think one of the chiefest kindlers of brave courage. The incomparable Lacedemonians[5] did not only carry that kind of music ever

---

1. Mill used for punishment of Roman slaves.
2. In a fable of Aesop, a sack filled with one's own faults is carried (out of sight) on the back, while one filled with the faults of others is carried in front.
3. Rich fabrics.
4. Natures or dispositions, as thought to be influenced by the balance of four chief bodily fluids, or humors—blood, phlegm, choler, and bile.
5. Awe. "Affects": feelings.
6. "He who rules his people with a harsh government / Fears those who fear him; the fear returns upon its author" (Seneca, *Oedipus*, lines 705–6).
7. Plutarch records that this cruel tyrant wept at the sufferings of Hecuba and Andromache in

Euripides' *Trojan Women.* Ashamed to be seen weeping, he abruptly left the theater.
8. Here defined as poetry concerned chiefly with praise and sung (originally) to musical accompaniment.
9. Discussions of problems of natural philosophy (the study of nature).
1. Praises.
2. "The Ballad of Chevy Chase."
3. Fiddler.
4. The odes of Pindar (518–after 446 B.C.E.), the most exalted lyric poetry of Greece, celebrated victors in athletic games. "That uncivil age": the Middle Ages.
5. Spartans, incomparable in fighting.

with them to the field, but even at home, as such songs were made, so were they all content to be singers of them—when the lusty men were to tell what they did, the old men what they had done, and the young what they would do. And where a man may say that Pindar many times praiseth highly victories of small moment, matters rather of sport than virtue; as it may be answered, it was the fault of the poet, and not of the poetry, so indeed the chief fault was in the time and custom of the Greeks, who set those toys[6] at so high a price that Philip of Macedon reckoned a horserace won at Olympus among his three fearful felicities.[7] But as the unimitable Pindar often did, so is that kind most capable and most fit to awake the thoughts from the sleep of idleness to embrace honorable enterprises.

There rests the Heroical[8]—whose very name (I think) should daunt all backbiters: for by what conceit[9] can a tongue be directed to speak evil of that which draweth with him no less champions than Achilles, Cyrus, Aeneas, Turnus, Tydeus, and Rinaldo?[1]—who doth not only teach and move to a truth, but teacheth and moveth to the most high and excellent truth; who maketh magnanimity and justice shine through all misty fearfulness and foggy desires; who, if the saying of Plato and Tully be true, that who could see virtue would be wonderfully ravished with the love of her beauty—this man[2] sets her out to make her more lovely in her holiday apparel, to the eye of any that will deign not to disdain until they understand. But if anything be already said in the defense of sweet poetry, all concurreth to the maintaining the heroical, which is not only a kind, but the best and most accomplished kind of poetry. For, as the image of each action stirreth and instructeth the mind, so the lofty image of such worthies most inflameth the mind with desire to be worthy, and informs with counsel how to be worthy. Only let Aeneas be worn in the tablet of your memory, how he governeth himself in the ruin of his country; in the preserving his old father, and carrying away his religious ceremonies;[3] in obeying God's commandment to leave Dido, though not only all passionate kindness, but even the human consideration of virtuous gratefulness, would have craved other of him; how in storms, how in sports, how in war, how in peace, how a fugitive, how victorious, how besieged, how besieging, how to strangers, how to allies, how to enemies, how to his own; lastly, how in his inward self, and how in his outward government—and I think, in a mind not prejudiced with a prejudicating humor,[4] he will be found in excellency fruitful, yea, even as Horace saith,

melius Chrysippo et Crantore.[5]

But truly I imagine it falleth out with these poet-whippers, as with some good women, who often are sick, but in faith they cannot tell where; so the name of poetry is odious to them, but neither his cause nor effects, neither

---

6. Trifles.
7. Plutarch records that Philip received three awesome tidings in one day: that his general was victorious in battle, that his wife had borne a son, and that his horse had won a race at Olympia (not, as Sidney mistakenly says, Olympus).
8. I.e., epic. "Rests": remains.
9. Conception.
1. In the Renaissance Italian Ariosto's *Orlando furioso* and his compatriot Tasso's *Gerusalemme liberata.* "Tydeus": in the Roman poet Statius's epic, *Thebaid.*

2. I.e., the epic poet.
3. Sacred objects, household gods. After fleeing Troy, Aeneas and his men stayed for a time in Carthage, whose queen, Dido, became Aeneas's lover. She killed herself when Aeneas (at Jupiter's command) sailed away to accomplish his fate, the founding of the Roman Empire.
4. Disposition.
5. In *Epistles* 1.2.4, Horace praises Homer as a "better [teacher] than Chrysippus [a great Stoic philosopher] and Crantor [a commentator on Plato]."

the sum that contains him, nor the particularities descending from him, give any fast[6] handle to their carping dispraise.

Since then poetry is of all human learning the most ancient and of most fatherly antiquity, as from whence other learnings have taken their beginnings; since it is so universal that no learned nation doth despise it, nor barbarous nation is without it; since both Roman and Greek gave such divine names unto it, the one of prophesying, the other of making, and that indeed that name of making is fit for him, considering that where all other arts retain themselves within their subject, and receive, as it were, their being from it, the poet only bringeth his own stuff, and doth not learn a conceit out of a matter, but maketh matter for a conceit; since neither his description nor end containing any evil, the thing described cannot be evil; since his effects be so good as to teach goodness and to delight the learners; since therein (namely in moral doctrine, the chief of all knowledges) he doth not only far pass the historian but, for instructing, is well nigh comparable to the philosopher, for moving leaves him behind him; since the Holy Scripture (wherein there is no uncleanness) hath whole parts in it poetical, and that even our Savior Christ vouchsafed to use the flowers of it; since all his kinds are not only in their united forms but in their severed dissections fully commendable; I think (and think I think rightly) the laurel crown appointed for triumphant captains doth worthily (of all other learnings) honor the poet's triumph.

[ANSWERS TO CHARGES AGAINST POETRY]

But because we have ears as well as tongues, and that the lightest reasons that may be will seem to weigh greatly, if nothing be put in the counterbalance, let us hear and, as well as we can, ponder what objections be made against this art, which may be worthy either of yielding or answering.[7]

First, truly I note not only in these *misomousoi*, poet-haters, but in all that kind of people who seek a praise by dispraising others, that they do prodigally spend a great many wandering words in quips and scoffs, carping and taunting at each thing which, by stirring the spleen,[8] may stay the brain from a through-beholding[9] the worthiness of the subject. Those kind of objections, as they are full of a very idle easiness,[1] since there is nothing of so sacred a majesty but that an itching tongue may rub itself upon it, so deserve they no other answer but, instead of laughing at the jest, to laugh at the jester. We know a playing wit can praise the discretion of an ass, the comfortableness of being in debt, and the jolly commodities of being sick of the plague.[2] So of the contrary side, if we will turn Ovid's verse

Ut lateat virtus proximitate mali,[3]

that good lie hid in nearness of the evil, Agrippa will be as merry in showing the vanity of science[4] as Erasmus was in the commending of folly. Neither shall any man or matter escape some touch of these smiling railers.

6. Firm.
7. The sixth part of a judicial oration is the *refutatio*, which, as Thomas Wilson's *Art of Rhetoric* says, is (or attempts to be) "a dissolving or wiping away of all such reasons as make against us."
8. Regarded as the seat of laughter.
9. Thorough consideration of.
1. An empty glibness.

2. Sidney gives several examples of the subjects of mock encomia popular in the classical world and among Renaissance humanists; the greatest of these encomia is Erasmus's *Praise of Folly*.
3. *Art of Love* 2.662 (translated just below).
4. Referring to the German scholar Cornelius Agrippa's *Of the Uncertainty and Vanity of the Sciences and the Arts* (1530).

But for Erasmus and Agrippa, they had another foundation than the superficial part would promise. Marry,[5] these other pleasant faultfinders, who will correct the verb before they understand the noun, and confute others' knowledge before they confirm their own—I would have them only remember that scoffing cometh not of wisdom. So as the best title in true English they get with their merriments is to be called good fools; for so have our grave forefathers ever termed that humorous kind of jesters.

But that which giveth greatest scope to their scorning humor[6] is rhyming and versing. It is already said[7] (and, as I think, truly said), it is not rhyming and versing that maketh poesy. One may be a poet without versing, and a versifier without poetry. But yet, presuppose it were inseparable (as indeed it seemeth Scaliger judgeth),[8] truly it were an inseparable commendation. For if *oratio* next to *ratio*, speech next to reason, be the greatest gift bestowed upon mortality,[9] that cannot be praiseless which doth most polish that blessing of speech; which considers each word, not only (as a man may say) by his most forcible quality, but by his best measured quantity,[1] carrying even in themselves a harmony—without,[2] perchance, number, measure, order, proportion be in our time grown odious. But lay aside the just praise it hath, by being the only fit speech for music (music, I say, the most divine striker of the senses), thus much is undoubtedly true, that if reading be foolish without remembering, memory being the only treasure of knowledge,[3] those words which are fittest for memory are likewise most convenient for knowledge. Now, that verse far exceedeth prose in the knitting up of memory, the reason is manifest: the words (besides their delight, which hath a great affinity to memory) being so set as one cannot be lost but the whole work fails; which accusing itself, calleth the remembrance back to itself, and so most strongly confirmeth it. Besides, one word so, as it were, begetting another, as, be it in rhyme or measured verse, by the former a man shall have a near guess to the follower. Lastly, even they that have taught the art of memory have showed nothing so apt for it as a certain room divided into many places well and thoroughly known.[4] Now, that hath the verse in effect perfectly, every word having his natural seat, which seat must needs make the word remembered. But what needeth more, in a thing so known to all men? Who is it that ever was a scholar that doth not carry away some verses of Virgil, Horace, or Cato,[5] which in his youth he learned, and even to his old age serve him for hourly lessons? But the fitness it hath for memory is notably proved by all delivery of arts: wherein for the most part, from grammar to logic, mathematics, physic, and the rest, the rules chiefly necessary to be borne away are compiled in verses.[6] So that, verse being in itself sweet and orderly, and being best for memory, the only handle of knowledge, it must be in jest that any man can speak against it.

---

5. Interjection expressing surprise or indignation. It is a euphemistic variant of "Mary" (the Virgin).
6. Disposition.
7. See p. 554.
8. *Poetics* 1.2. (For Scaliger, see p. 551, n. 2.)
9. I.e., reason and speech are the primary distinguishing characteristics of human beings (a commonplace originating in the classical era).
1. I.e., by its accent ("quality") and its duration ("quantity").
2. Unless.
3. Proverbial.

4. Standard systems for memorization involved associating the items to be remembered with particular features of imagined rooms.
5. Referring to the *Distichs of Cato*, which had for centuries been an immensely popular school text of moral advice, most of it embodied in distichs (verse couplets).
6. This pedagogical practice—which still survives in bits and pieces such as alphabet songs—was widespread in the Middle Ages and Renaissance. "Physic": medicine.

Now then go we to the most important imputations laid to the poor poets.[7] For aught I can yet learn, they are these. First, that there being many other more fruitful knowledges, a man might better spend his time in them than in this. Secondly, that it is the mother of lies. Thirdly, that it is the nurse of abuse, infecting us with many pestilent desires; with a siren's sweetness drawing the mind to the serpent's tail of sinful fancies (and herein, especially, comedies give the largest field to ear,[8] as Chaucer saith); how, both in other nations and in ours, before poets did soften us, we were full of courage, given to martial exercises, the pillars of manlike liberty, and not lulled asleep in shady idleness with poets' pastimes. And lastly, and chiefly, they cry out with open mouth as if they had overshot Robin Hood, that Plato banished them out of his commonwealth.[9] Truly, this is much, if there be much truth in it.

First, to the first.[1] That a man might better spend his time, is a reason indeed; but it doth (as they say) but *petere principium*.[2] For if it be as I affirm, that no learning is so good as that which teacheth and moveth to virtue; and that none can both teach and move thereto so much as poetry: then is the conclusion manifest that ink and paper cannot be to a more profitable purpose employed. And certainly, though a man should grant their first assumption, it should follow (methinks) very unwillingly, that good is not good because better is better. But I still and utterly deny that there is sprung out of earth a more fruitful knowledge.

To the second, therefore, that they should be the principal liars, I will answer paradoxically, but truly, I think truly, that of all writers under the sun the poet is the least liar, and, though he would,[3] as a poet can scarcely be a liar. The astronomer, with his cousin the geometrician, can hardly escape,[4] when they take upon them to measure the height of the stars. How often, think you, do the physicians lie, when they aver things good for sicknesses, which afterwards send Charon a great number of souls drowned in a potion[5] before they come to his ferry? And no less of the rest which take upon them to affirm. Now, for the poet, he nothing affirms, and therefore never lieth. For, as I take it, to lie is to affirm that to be true which is false. So as the other artists,[6] and especially the historian, affirming many things, can, in the cloudy knowledge of mankind, hardly escape from many lies. But the poet (as I said before) never affirmeth. The poet never maketh any circles[7] about your imagination, to conjure you to believe for true what he writes. He citeth not authorities of other histories, but even for his entry[8] calleth the sweet Muses to inspire into him a good invention; in truth, not laboring to tell you what is or is not, but what should or should not be. And therefore, though he recount things not true, yet because he telleth them not for true,

---

7. All four of these major charges against poetry are traceable to classical antiquity and continued, in Sidney's time, to be principal items of the stock in trade of imaginative literature's detractors; and many of the points Sidney makes in rebuttal had been made by its previous defenders.
8. To plow ("Knight's Tale," line 28).
9. Plato argued that most sorts of poets would be banished from an ideal commonwealth, because they stir up unworthy emotions and because their imitations are far removed from truth (*Republic* 10.595–608).

1. First objection.
2. Beg the question—i.e., simply *presuppose* a conclusion on the matter in question.
3. Even if he wished to.
4. I.e., can hardly avoid lying.
5. I.e., killed by medicine. Charon, in classical myth, is the ferryman who takes the souls of the dead across the river Styx in the underworld.
6. Practitioners of the liberal arts.
7. As a magician does in conjuring spirits.
8. In his opening lines.

he lieth not—without we will say that Nathan lied in his speech before-alleged to David:[9] which as a wicked man durst scarce say, so think I none so simple would say that Aesop lied in the tales of his beasts; for who thinks that Aesop wrote it for actually true were well worthy to have his name chronicled among the beasts he writeth of. What child is there, that, coming to a play, and seeing *Thebes* written in great letters upon an old door,[1] doth believe that it is Thebes? If then a man can arrive to that child's age to know that the poets' persons and doings are but pictures what should be, and not stories what have been, they will never give the lie to[2] things not affirmatively but allegorically and figuratively written. And therefore, as in history, looking for truth, they may go away full fraught with falsehood, so in poesy, looking but for fiction, they shall use the narration but as an imaginative ground-plot of a profitable invention.[3] But hereto is replied, that the poets give names to men they write of, which argueth a conceit of an actual truth, and so, not being true, proves a falsehood. And doth the lawyer lie, then, when under the names of *John-a-stiles* and *John-a-nokes*[4] he puts his case? But that is easily answered. Their naming of men is but to make their picture the more lively, and not to build any history: painting men, they cannot leave men nameless. We see we cannot play at chess but that we must give names to our chessmen; and yet, methinks, he were a very partial champion of truth that would say we lied for giving a piece of wood the reverend title of a bishop. The poet nameth Cyrus or Aeneas no other way than to show what men of their fames, fortunes, and estates should do.

Their third is, how much it abuseth men's wit,[5] training it to wanton sinfulness and lustful love: for indeed that is the principal, if not only, abuse I can hear alleged. They say, the comedies rather teach than reprehend amorous conceits. They say the lyric is larded with passionate sonnets; the elegiac weeps the want of his mistress; and that even to the heroical, Cupid hath ambitiously climbed.[6] Alas, Love, I would thou couldst as well defend thyself as thou canst offend others. I would those on whom thou dost attend could either put thee away, or yield good reason why they keep thee. But grant love of beauty to be a beastly fault (although it be very hard, since only man, and no beast, hath that gift to discern beauty); grant that lovely name of Love to deserve all hateful reproaches (although even some of my masters the philosophers spent a good deal of their lamp-oil in setting forth the excellency of it);[7] grant, I say, whatsoever they will have granted, that not only love, but lust, but vanity, but (if they list) scurrility, possesseth many leaves of the poets' books; yet think I, when this is granted, they will find their sentence may with good manners put the last words foremost, and not say that poetry abuseth man's wit, but that man's wit abuseth poetry.

For I will not deny but that man's wit may make poesy, which should be *eikastiké* (which some learned have defined: figuring forth good things), to be

---

9. For Nathan's parable, see p. 564. "Without": unless.
1. Thebes is the setting of several classical tragedies.
2. Accuse of lying.
3. I.e., readers will find that poetry's fictions are actually the foundation ("ground-plot") on which are erected "profitable invention[s]"—that is (as earlier), verbal "pictures [of] what should be."

4. John (who lives) at the stile and John (who lives) at the oak: fictitious names—equivalent to our John and Jane Doe—used in legal proceedings.
5. Mind.
6. I.e., epic is infused with eroticism, as in the Italian romance epics—and in Sidney's own contribution to that genre, *Arcadia*. "Want": lack.
7. Plato, for one, in the *Symposium* and the *Phaedrus*.

phantastiké[8] (which doth, contrariwise, infect the fancy with unworthy objects), as the painter, that should give to the eye either some excellent perspective or some fine picture, fit for building or fortification, or containing in it some notable example (as Abraham sacrificing his son Isaac, Judith killing Holofernes, David fighting with Goliath),[9] may leave those, and please an ill-pleased eye with wanton shows of better hidden matters.[1] But what, shall the abuse of a thing make the right use odious? Nay truly, though I yield that poesy may not only be abused, but that being abused, by the reason of his sweet charming force, it can do more hurt than any other army of words: yet shall it be so far from concluding that the abuse should give reproach to the abused, that, contrariwise, it is a good reason that whatsoever, being abused, doth most harm, being rightly used (and upon the right use each thing conceiveth his title[2]), doth most good. Do we not see the skill of physic, the best rampire[3] to our often-assaulted bodies, being abused, teach poison, the most violent destroyer? Doth not knowledge of law, whose end is to even and right all things, being abused, grow the crooked fosterer of horrible injuries? Doth not (to go to the highest) God's word abused breed heresy, and His name abused become blasphemy? Truly, a needle cannot do much hurt, and as truly (with leave of ladies be it spoken), it cannot do much good: with a sword thou mayst kill thy father, and with a sword thou mayst defend thy prince and country. So that, as in their calling poets fathers of lies they said nothing, so in this their argument of abuse they prove the commendation.

They allege herewith, that before poets began to be in price[4] our nation had set their hearts' delight upon action, and not imagination: rather doing things worthy to be written, than writing things fit to be done. What that before-time was, I think scarcely Sphinx can tell, since no memory is so ancient that hath not the precedent of poetry. And certain it is that, in our plainest homeliness, yet never was the Albion[5] nation without poetry. Marry, this argument, though it be leveled against poetry, yet is it indeed a chainshot[6] against all learning, or bookishness, as they commonly term it. Of such mind were certain Goths, of whom it is written that, having in the spoil of a famous city taken a fair library, one hangman[7] (belike fit to execute the fruits of their wits), who had murdered a great number of bodies, would have set fire in it: no, said another very gravely, take heed what you do, for while they are busy about these toys, we shall with more leisure conquer their countries.[8] This indeed is the ordinary doctrine of ignorance, and many words sometimes I have heard spent in it. But because this reason is generally against all learning as well as poetry, or rather, all learning but poetry; because it were too large a digression to handle it, or at least too

---

8. Plato's distinction, *Sophist* 236: *eikastiké*: making likenesses; *phantastiké*: making fantasies.
9. For Abraham and Isaac, see Genesis 21–22. For David and Goliath, see 1 Samuel 17. The story of the Israelite Judith decapitating the Assyrian general Holofernes while he lay in a drunken stupor is in Chapters 10–13 of the Book of Judith—a book included in the Roman Catholic and Eastern Orthodox versions of the Old Testament but excluded from the Hebrew Bible and relegated to the Apocrypha by Protestants.
1. Matters better to remain hidden. "Ill-pleased eye": eye pleased by evil sights.
2. Receives its justification.
3. Rampart; defense.

4. Honor, esteem.
5. Ancient name for Britain.
6. Two cannon balls linked by a chain, to do maximum damage.
7. Here used as a term of general abuse, equivalent to "villain."
8. This story of the Goths (a Germanic tribe)—relating to their sack of Athens in 267 C.E.—derives from the continuation of the *Roman History* of Dio Cassius. Sidney's near-contemporary Montaigne also records the story, in "Of Pedantry" (*Essays* 1.25)—though he deploys it in *support* of the view that book learning and martial prowess are inversely related.

superfluous (since it is manifest that all government of action is to be gotten by knowledge, and knowledge best by gathering many knowledges, which is reading), I only, with Horace, to him that is of that opinion

jubeo stultum esse libenter;[9]

for as for poetry itself, it is the freest from this objection.

For poetry is the companion of camps.[1] I dare undertake, Orlando Furioso[2] or honest King Arthur will never displease a soldier; but the quiddity of *ens* and *prima materia*[3] will hardly agree with a corslet;[4] and therefore, as I said in the beginning, even Turks and Tartars are delighted with poets. Homer, a Greek, flourished before Greece flourished. And if to a slight conjecture a conjecture may be opposed, truly it may seem, that as by him their learned men took almost their first light of knowledge, so their active men received their first motions of courage. Only Alexander's example[5] may serve, who by Plutarch is accounted of such virtue that Fortune was not his guide but his footstool; whose acts speak for him, though[6] Plutarch did not: indeed the phoenix of warlike princes. This Alexander left his schoolmaster, living Aristotle, behind him, but took dead Homer with him.[7] He put the philosopher Callisthenes to death for his seeming philosophical, indeed mutinous, stubbornness, but the chief thing he was ever heard to wish for was that Homer had been alive.[8] He well found he received more bravery of mind by the pattern of Achilles than by hearing the definition of fortitude. And therefore, if Cato misliked Fulvius for carrying Ennius with him to the field,[9] it may be answered that, if Cato misliked it, the noble Fulvius liked it, or else he had not done it; for it was not the excellent Cato Uticensis[1] (whose authority I would much more have reverenced), but it was the former, in truth a bitter punisher of faults (but else a man that had never well sacrificed to the Graces:[2] he misliked and cried out against all Greek learning, and yet, being eighty years old, began to learn it, belike fearing that Pluto[3] understood not Latin). Indeed, the Roman laws allowed no person to be carried to the wars but he that was in the soldiers' roll; and therefore, though Cato misliked his unmustered person, he misliked not his work.[4] And if he had, Scipio Nasica, judged by common consent the best Roman,[5] loved him. Both the other

---

9. "I bid him be a fool as much as he likes" (adapting *Satires* 1.1.63).
1. I.e., military encampments.
2. See p. 552, n. 3.
3. The essential nature of "being" and "first matter"—terms in Scholastic philosophy.
4. Body armor.
5. I.e., the example of Alexander the Great alone. Plutarch's estimate of him is in his *Lives* and, in his *Moral Essays*, the two tracts *On the Fortune or the Virtue of Alexander*. "Motions": promptings.
6. Even if.
7. Plutarch, *Life of Alexander* 8, says Alexander (who had Aristotle as his tutor) took the *Iliad* with him everywhere.
8. Plutarch, *How a Man may Become Aware of His Progress in Virtue* 16. Callisthenes, Aristotle's relative, and both a philosopher and a historian, accompanied Alexander on his expedition to India.
9. The Roman general Fulvius took the poet Ennius (see p. 549, n. 2) with him on a military expedition to Greece. The stern moralist Cato the Elder (234–149 B.C.E.) disapproved. The story was

often repeated by poetry's detractors.
1. Cato of Utica (great-grandson of Cato the Elder), hugely admired as the epitome of Roman Stoic virtue.
2. I.e., he was not a cultured person. (The three Graces were sister deities who personified grace and beauty.) "Else": otherwise.
3. God of the underworld (whither Cato, at eighty, was soon bound). To undermine the authority of this prestigious enemy of poetry, Sidney does not scruple to employ *argumentum ad hominem* and mockery (as also with Plato, in the following paragraph). The story of Cato's late acquisition of Greek is from Plutarch's *Life* (2).
4. A different explanation for Cato's objection to Ennius's accompanying Fulvius: it was against Roman law for an "unmustered" person (i.e., one not formally enrolled as a soldier) to go on a military mission. But one cannot logically draw from that fact the conclusion that Cato did not dislike Ennius's poetry.
5. The Roman Senate so judged him, in 204 B.C.E. (Livy, *From the Foundation of the City* 29.14).

Scipio brothers, who had by their virtues no less surnames than of Asia and Afric,[6] so loved him that they caused his body to be buried in their sepulture. So as Cato's authority, being but against his person, and that answered with so far greater than himself, is herein of no validity.

But now indeed my burden is great; now Plato's name is laid upon me, whom, I must confess, of all philosophers I have ever esteemed most worthy of reverence, and with good reason: since of all philosophers he is the most poetical.[7] Yet if he will defile the fountain out of which his flowing streams have proceeded, let us boldly examine with what reasons he did it. First, truly, a man might maliciously object that Plato, being a philosopher, was a natural enemy of poets. For indeed, after the philosophers had picked out of the sweet mysteries of poetry the right discerning true points of knowledge, they forthwith putting it in method, and making a school-art of that which the poets did only teach by a divine delightfulness, beginning to spurn at their guides, like ungrateful prentices,[8] were not content to set up shops for themselves, but sought by all means to discredit their masters; which by the force of delight being barred them, the less they could overthrow them, the more they hated them. For indeed, they found for Homer seven cities strave who should have him for their citizen; where many cities banished philosophers as not fit members to live among them.[9] For only repeating certain of Euripides' verses, many Athenians had their lives saved of the Syracusans, where the Athenians themselves thought many philosophers unworthy to live.[1] Certain poets, as Simonides and Pindar, had so prevailed with Hiero the First that of a tyrant they made him a just king; where Plato could do so little with Dionysius that he himself of a philosopher was made a slave.[2] But who should do thus,[3] I confess, should requite the objections made against poets with like cavilations[4] against philosophers; as likewise one should do that should bid one read *Phaedrus* or *Symposium* in Plato, or the discourse of love in Plutarch, and see whether any poet do authorize abominable filthiness, as they do.[5] Again, a man might ask out of what commonwealth Plato did banish them: in sooth, thence where he himself alloweth community of women[6]—so as belike this banishment grew not for effeminate wantonness, since little should poetical sonnets be hurtful, when a man might have what woman he listed.[7] But I honor philosophical instructions, and bless the wits which bred them: so as they be not abused, which is likewise stretched to poetry.

---

6. Scipio Africanus (granted that cognomen as conqueror of Hannibal) and Scipio Asiaticus (conqueror of the Seleucid emperor Antiochus III, in Asia Minor). Cousins (not brothers) of Scipio Nasica, both were patrons of Ennius.
7. See p. 549.
8. Apprentices.
9. Among the several philosophers banished from their native cities were Empedocles and Protagoras. Cicero's oration on behalf of the poet Archias (8.19) is one of the sources for the claim that seven cities competed for Homer.
1. Whatever the Athenians may have "thought," the only philosopher they are known to have executed is Socrates (though the sophist Prodicus of Ceos was sometimes said to have been executed with him). Plutarch's *Life of Nicias* (29) says that many members of an Athenian army defeated by the army of Syracuse were afterward spared because of the Sicilians' love for the writings of the Athenians' compatriot Euripides.
2. Plato visited the Syracusan tyrant Dionysius I, but fell out with him and, according to legend, was through his contrivances sold into slavery (from which he was rescued by friends). By contrast, the poets Simonides (556–468 B.C.E.) and Pindar enjoyed the patronage of Dionysius's predecessor Hiero I, whose court was a center of art and literature.
3. Anyone who would argue in this (ad hominem) fashion—as Sidney has, of course, just done (and proceeds to do again, in the following).
4. Faultfinding.
5. Parts of Plato's dialogues *Phaedrus* and *Symposium*, and of Plutarch's dialogue *On Love*, exalt male homosexual love.
6. In *Republic* 5, Plato has Socrates argue that the ruling class in his ideal commonwealth would share all things, including women, communally.
7. Pleased.

St. Paul himself (who yet, for the credit of poets, twice citeth poets, and one of them by the name of "their prophet") setteth a watchword upon philosophy[8]—indeed upon the abuse. So doth Plato upon the abuse, not upon poetry. Plato found fault that the poets of his time filled the world with wrong opinions of the gods, making light tales of that unspotted essence, and therefore would not have the youth depraved with such opinions.[9] Herein may much be said. Let this suffice: the poets did not induce such opinions, but did imitate those opinions already induced. For all the Greek stories can well testify that the very religion of that time stood upon many and many-fashioned gods, not taught so by the poets, but followed according to their nature of imitation. Who list may read in Plutarch the discourses of Isis and Osiris, of the cause why oracles ceased, of the divine providence,[1] and see whether the theology of that nation stood not upon such dreams, which the poets indeed superstitiously observed—and truly (since they had not the light of Christ) did much better in it than the philosophers, who, shaking off superstition, brought in atheism. Plato, therefore (whose authority I had much rather justly construe than unjustly resist), meant not in general of poets, in those words of which Julius Scaliger saith *Qua authoritate barbari quidam atque hispidi abuti velint ad poetas e republica exigendos*,[2] but only meant to drive out those wrong opinions of the Deity (whereof now, without further law,[3] Christianity hath taken away all the hurtful belief) perchance (as he thought) nourished by the then esteemed poets. And a man need go no further than to Plato himself to know his meaning: who, in his dialogue called *Ion*, giveth high and rightly divine commendation unto poetry.[4] So as Plato, banishing the abuse, not the thing; not banishing it, but giving due honor unto it, shall be our patron, and not our adversary. For indeed I had much rather (since truly I may do it) show their mistaking of Plato (under whose lion's skin they would make an ass-like braying against poesy)[5] than go about to overthrow his authority; whom the wiser a man is, the more just cause he shall find to have in admiration; especially since he attributeth unto poesy more than myself do,[6] namely, to be a very inspiring of a divine force, far above man's wit, as in the forenamed dialogue is apparent.

Of the other side, who would show the honors have been by the best sort of judgments granted them, a whole sea of examples would present themselves: Alexanders, Caesars, Scipios, all favorers of poets; Laelius, called the Roman Socrates, himself a poet, so as part of *Heautontimorumenos* in Terence was supposed to be made by him;[7] and even the Greek Socrates, whom Apollo confirmed to be the only wise man, is said to have spent part of his

8. A word of warning against philosophy (in Colossians 2.8). "Their prophet": see Titus 1.12. Paul's other citation of poets comes in Acts 17.28.
9. This is Plato's objection to poetry in *Republic* 2, and Sidney answers it well. But he entirely ignores the far more profound objection in 10.595–608, where Plato argues that artistic mimesis in general is at the "third remove" (597) from the true nature of things (being an imitation of the physical world, which is itself a poor imitation of the realm of the Platonic Forms) and that poetry in particular has "no serious value or claim to truth" (608).
1. Sidney gives English versions of the titles of three of Plutarch's *Moral Essays*.
2. "Which authority certain barbarians and uncivilized persons seek to misuse in order to have poets banned from the state" (*Poetics* 1.2).

3. Without further ado.
4. In the *Ion*, Plato argues that poets are divinely inspired. The argument is now regarded as ironic, but in Sidney's day it was taken seriously.
5. Referring to Aesop's fable of the ass masquerading as a lion.
6. Cf. pp. 550–51, where Sidney, departing from the main trend of 16th-century poetics, avoids claiming that any poetry other than that of the Bible is divinely inspired.
7. Gaius Laelius (2nd century B.C.E.) was an orator and intellectual much admired by Cicero, who compared him to Socrates and noted that many people ascribed the plays of Terence in whole or in part to him. In the prologues to *Heauton timorumenos* (The Self-Tormentor) and *The Brothers*, Terence himself hints at his debts to Laelius.

old time in putting Aesop's fables into verses.[8] And therefore, full evil should it become his scholar Plato to put such words in his master's mouth against poets. But what need more? Aristotle writes the Art of Poesy; and why, if it should not be written? Plutarch teacheth the use to be gathered of them; and how, if they should not be read? And who reads Plutarch's either history or philosophy[9] shall find he trimmeth both their garments with guards[1] of poesy. But I list not to defend poesy with the help of his underling historiography. Let it suffice to have showed it is a fit soil for praise to dwell upon; and what dispraise may be set upon it is either easily overcome or transformed into just commendation.

So that, since the excellencies of it may be so easily and so justly confirmed, and the low-creeping objections so soon trodden down: it not being an art of lies, but of true doctrine;[2] not of effeminateness, but of notable stirring of courage; not of abusing man's wit, but of strengthening man's wit; not banished, but honored by Plato: let us rather plant more laurels for to engarland the poets' heads (which honor of being laureate, whereas besides them only triumphant captains were, is a sufficient authority to show the price they ought to be held in) than suffer the ill-savored breath of such wrong-speakers once to blow upon the clear springs of poesy.

[POETRY IN ENGLAND]

But since I have run so long a career[3] in this matter, methinks, before I give my pen a full stop, it shall be but a little more lost time to inquire why England, the mother of excellent minds, should be grown so hard a stepmother to poets, who certainly in wit[4] ought to pass all other, since all only proceedeth from their wit, being indeed makers of themselves, not takers of others.[5] How can I but exclaim

Musa, mihi causas memora, quo numine laeso?[6]

Sweet poesy, that hath anciently had kings, emperors, senators, great captains, such as, besides a thousand others, David, Adrian, Sophocles, Germanicus, not only to favor poets, but to be poets;[7] and of our nearer times can present for her patrons a Robert, king of Sicily, the great King Francis of France, King James of Scotland; such cardinals as Bembus and Bibbiena; such famous preachers and teachers as Beza and Melanchthon; so learned philosophers as Fracastorius and Scaliger; so great orators as Pontanus and Muretus; so piercing wits as George Buchanan;[8] so grave counsellors as,

---

8. According to Plato, *Phaedo* 60, and Plutarch, *How to Study Poetry* 16. Apollo confirmed Socrates to be the wisest of men through his oracle at Delphi.
9. I.e., either Plutarch's *Parallel Lives* (of notable Greeks and Romans) or his *Moral Essays*.
1. Ornamental borders.
2. Teaching.
3. Course.
4. Intellect.
5. Rhetorical theory allowed for a *digressio* following the *refutatio*, and Sidney's lengthy digression—on the very pertinent topic of why English poetry is, in his time, in such poor repute—has itself the form of an oration, comprising a narration, proposition (see later: "the very true cause of our wanting estimation is

want of desert": we lack esteem because we don't *deserve* it), division (into "matter" and "words"), and confirmation.
6. The beginning of the invocation of the *Aeneid* (1.8): "Tell me, O Muse, the cause: by what offense to the deity?"
7. Four military leaders who wrote poetry: the biblical King David, the Roman emperor Hadrian, the tragedian Sophocles (who in 440 B.C.E. was appointed a general for Athens in its war against Samos), and Germanicus (15 B.C.E.–19 C.E.), commander of the Roman troops against the Germans.
8. The kings are Robert II of Anjou, Francis I, and probably James I. The cardinals are Pietro Bembo (who figures in Castiglione's *Courtier*: see pp. 176, 179ff.) and Bernardo Dovizi, cardinal of Bibbiena, in Italy. The preachers are Théodore

beside many, but before all, that Hôpital of France,[9] than whom (I think) that realm never brought forth a more accomplished judgment, more firmly builded upon virtue: I say these, with numbers of others, not only to read others' poesies, but to poetize for others' reading—that poesy, thus embraced in all other places, should only find in our time a hard welcome in England, I think the very earth lamenteth it, and therefore decketh our soil with fewer laurels than it was accustomed.[1] For heretofore poets have in England also flourished, and, which is to be noted, even in those times when the trumpet of Mars did sound loudest.[2] And now that an overfaint quietness should seem to strew the house[3] for poets, they are almost in as good reputation as the mountebanks at Venice.[4] Truly even that, as of the one side it giveth great praise to poesy, which like Venus (but to better purpose) had rather be troubled in the net with Mars than enjoy the homely quiet of Vulcan:[5] so serves it for a piece of a reason why they are less grateful[6] to idle England, which now can scarce endure the pain of a pen.

Upon this necessarily followeth that base men with servile wits undertake it, who think it enough if they can be rewarded of the printer. And so as Epaminondas is said with the honor of his virtue to have made an office, by his exercising it, which before was contemptible, to become highly respected;[7] so these men, no more but setting their names to it, by their own disgracefulness disgrace the most graceful poesy. For now, as if all the Muses were got with child to bring forth bastard poets, without any commission they do post over the banks of Helicon,[8] till they make the readers more weary than post-horses;[9] while in the meantime they

Queis meliore luto finxit praecordia Titan[1]

are better content to suppress the outflowings of their wit than, by publishing them, to be accounted knights of the same order. But I that, before ever I durst aspire unto the dignity, am admitted into the company of the paper-blurrers, do find the very true cause of our wanting estimation is want of desert—taking upon us to be poets in despite of Pallas.[2]

Now, wherein we want desert were a thankworthy labor to express; but if I knew, I should have mended myself. But I, as I never desired the title, so have I neglected the means to come by it. Only, overmastered by some thoughts, I yielded an inky tribute unto them. Marry, they that delight in poesy itself

---

de Bèze and Philip Melanchthon, both professors of Greek who became important Protestant reformers. The philosophers are Girolamo Fracastorio, author of medical and scientific works (some of them in verse) and Scaliger (see p. 551, n. 2). The orators are Giovanni Pontano, diplomat and writer, and Marc-Antoine Muret, humanist scholar and poet. Buchanan was an eminent Scottish humanist and Latin poet.
9. Michel de l'Hôpital, chancellor of France.
1. I.e., England now has fewer poets (whose success is traditionally rewarded with a laurel crown) than in the past.
2. I.e., when England had its most notable wars.
3. I.e., prepare a welcome, by strewing fresh rushes (a standard floor covering).
4. Venice's notorious quick-tongued hucksters of quack medicines and other trifles. For a wonderful simulation, see Ben Jonson's *Volpone* 2.2 (p. 1018).
5. Venus was caught in adultery with Mars by her

husband, the blacksmith god Vulcan, who concealed a net under the bed and then hoisted the amorous couple into the air *in flagrante delicto* (*Odyssey* 8.266–366).
6. Agreeable.
7. The Theban general Epaminondas (d. 362 B.C.E.) conferred dignity on the office of telearch (chief street cleaner).
8. Like many others, Sidney confuses Mount Helicon (sacred to the Muses) with Hippocrene—a fountain on it said to have been created by the hoof of Pegasus, the winged horse of poetic flight. "Post": ride fast.
9. Used in relay by postal couriers or kept for hire, thus often ridden to exhaustion.
1. "Whose hearts the Titan [Prometheus] has made of better clay" (Juvenal, *Satires* 14.35).
2. I.e., without wisdom (of which Pallas Athena is goddess). "Wanting estimation": lacking esteem.

should seek to know what they do, and how they do; and especially look themselves in an unflattering glass of reason, if they be inclinable unto it. For poesy must not be drawn by the ears; it must be gently led, or rather it must lead—which was partly the cause that made the ancient-learned affirm it was a divine gift, and no human skill: since all other knowledges lie ready for any that hath strength of wit. A poet no industry can make, if his own genius be not carried into it; and therefore it is an old proverb, *orator fit, poeta nascitur.*[3]

Yet confess I always that as the fertilest ground must be manured, so must the highest-flying wit have a Daedalus[4] to guide him. That Daedalus, they say, both in this and in other, hath three wings to bear itself up into the air of due commendation: that is, art, imitation, and exercise.[5] But these, neither artificial rules nor imitative patterns, we much cumber ourselves withal. Exercise indeed we do, but that very forebackwardly: for where we should exercise to know, we exercise as having known; and so is our brain delivered of much matter which never was begotten by knowledge. For there being two principal parts, matter to be expressed by words and words to express the matter, in neither we use art or imitation rightly. Our matter is *quodlibet*[6] indeed, though wrongly performing Ovid's verse,

Quicquid conabor dicere, versus erit;[7]

never marshaling it into any assured rank, that almost the readers cannot tell where to find themselves.

Chaucer, undoubtedly, did excellently in his *Troilus and Criseyde*; of whom, truly, I know not whether to marvel more, either that he in that misty time could see so clearly, or that we in this clear age go so stumblingly after him. Yet had he great wants,[8] fit to be forgiven in so reverent an antiquity. I account the *Mirror of Magistrates* meetly[9] furnished of beautiful parts, and in the earl of Surrey's lyrics many things tasting of a noble birth, and worthy of a noble mind. The *Shepherds' Calendar*[1] hath much poetry in his eclogues, indeed worthy the reading, if I be not deceived. (That same framing of his style to an old rustic language I dare not allow, since neither Theocritus in Greek, Virgil in Latin, nor Sannazzaro in Italian did affect it.[2]) Besides these I do not remember to have seen but few (to speak boldly) printed that have poetical sinews in them; for proof whereof, let but most of the verses be put in prose, and then ask the meaning, and it will be found that one verse did but beget another, without ordering at the first what should be at the last; which becomes a confused mass of words, with a tingling[3] sound of rhyme, barely accompanied with reason.

Our tragedies and comedies (not without cause cried out against), observing rules neither of honest civility nor skillful poetry—excepting *Gorboduc*[4]

---

3. An orator is made; a poet is born.
4. In classical mythology, a great artificer, who invented wings of wax for himself and his son, Icarus. Ignoring his father's instructions, Icarus flew too close to the sun, melted his wings, and fell into the sea. "Manured": cultivated.
5. The tripartite prescription for mastery advocated especially in rhetorical theory.
6. What you will.
7. "Whatever I try to say will turn to verse" (Ovid, *Tristia* 4.10.26).
8. Deficiencies.
9. Properly. *The Mirror for Magistrates* (first

edition 1559) was a large collection of poems on the downfall of princes and other notables.
1. Spenser's first major work (1579), a set of pastoral poems ("eclogues") dedicated to Sidney (see p. 241 and n. 2). For Surrey, see p. 133.
2. I.e., none of the great models for pastoral poetry offered a precedent for Spenser's archaic diction. This is, however, not strictly true of Theocritus and Virgil.
3. Tinkling.
4. Senecan tragedy by Thomas Sackville and Thomas Norton (1561): the earliest English tragedy written in blank verse. "Honest civility": decency.

(again, I say, of those that I have seen), which notwithstanding as it is full of stately speeches and well-sounding phrases, climbing to the height of Seneca's style,[5] and as full of notable morality, which it doth most delightfully teach, and so obtain the very end of poesy, yet in truth it is very defectuous in the circumstances, which grieveth me, because it might not remain as an exact model of all tragedies. For it is faulty both in place and time, the two necessary companions of all corporal actions. For where the stage should always represent but one place, and the uttermost time presupposed in it should be, both by Aristotle's precept and common reason, but one day, there is both many days, and many places, inartificially[6] imagined.

But if it be so in *Gorboduc*, how much more in all the rest, where you shall have Asia of the one side and Afric of the other, and so many other underkingdoms that the player, when he cometh in, must ever begin with telling where he is, or else the tale will not be conceived? Now you shall have three ladies walk to gather flowers: and then we must believe the stage to be a garden. By and by we hear news of shipwreck in the same place: and then we are to blame if we accept it not for a rock. Upon the back of that comes out a hideous monster with fire and smoke: and then the miserable beholders are bound to take it for a cave. While in the meantime two armies fly in, represented with four swords and bucklers: and then what hard heart will not receive it for a pitched field?[7]

Now, of time they are much more liberal: for ordinary it is that two young princes fall in love; after many traverses,[8] she is got with child, delivered of a fair boy; he is lost, groweth a man, falls in love, and is ready to get another child; and all this in two hours' space: which, how absurd it is in sense, even sense may imagine, and art hath taught, and all ancient examples justified— and at this day, the ordinary players in Italy will not err in. Yet will some bring in an example of *Eunuchus* in Terence, that containeth matter of two days,[9] yet far short of twenty years. True it is, and so was it to be played in two days, and so fitted to the time it set forth. And though Plautus have in one place done amiss,[1] let us hit with him, and not miss with him.

But they will say: How then shall we set forth a story which containeth both many places and many times? And do they not know that a tragedy is tied to the laws of poesy, and not of history; not bound to follow the story, but having liberty either to feign a quite new matter or to frame the history to the most tragical conveniency? Again, many things may be told which cannot be showed, if they know the difference betwixt reporting and representing. As, for example, I may speak (though I am here) of Peru, and in speech digress from that to the description of Calicut; but in action I cannot represent it without Pacolet's horse;[2] and so was the manner the ancients took, by some *Nuntius*[3] to recount things done in former time or other place. Lastly, if they

---

5. The highly declamatory and relentlessly moralizing Roman tragedies of Seneca (ca. 4 B.C.E.—65 C.E.) were models of the grand tragic style in the Renaissance.
6. Inartistically. Sidney here voices the Renaissance commonplace (erroneously derived from Aristotle's *Poetics*) that tragedies should observe the "three unities": of time (one day), place (one locale), and action (one plot). Aristotle insisted only on unity of action (though he does observe that most tragedies take place within a twenty-four-hour span: *Poetics* 5).

7. Battle. "Bucklers": shields.
8. Difficulties, mishaps.
9. In point of fact, the action of Terence's *Eunuch* takes place in a single day. Sidney is probably confusing it with another of Terence's plays, *The Self-Tormentor*.
1. Plautus's *Captives* does not fulfill the unity of time.
2. A flying horse in the French romance *Valentine and Orson* (1489). Calicut (Kozhikode) is a seaport on the southwest coast of India.
3. Messenger.

will represent a history, they must not (as Horace saith) begin *ab ovo*;[4] but they must come to the principal point of that one action which they will represent.

By example this will be best expressed. I have a story of young Polydorus,[5] delivered for safety's sake, with great riches, by his father Priam to Polymnestor, king of Thrace, in the Trojan war time; he, after some years, hearing the overthrow of Priam, for to make the treasure his own, murdereth the child; the body of the child is taken up by Hecuba;[6] she, the same day, findeth a sleight[7] to be revenged most cruelly of the tyrant. Where now would one of our tragedy writers begin, but with the delivery of the child? Then should he sail over into Thrace, and so spend I know not how many years, and travel numbers of places. But where doth Euripides? Even with the finding of the body, leaving the rest to be told by the spirit of Polydorus. This need no further to be enlarged; the dullest wit may conceive it.

But besides these gross absurdities, how all their plays be neither right tragedies nor right comedies, mingling kings and clowns, not because the matter so carrieth it, but thrust in the clown by head and shoulders to play a part in majestical matters with neither decency nor discretion,[8] so as neither the admiration and commiseration, nor the right sportfulness,[9] is by their mongrel tragi-comedy obtained. I know Apuleius[1] did somewhat so, but that is a thing recounted with space of time, not represented in one moment; and I know the ancients have one or two examples of tragi-comedies, as Plautus hath *Amphitruo*;[2] but, if we mark them well, we shall find that they never, or very daintily, match hornpipes[3] and funerals. So falleth it out that, having indeed no right comedy, in that comical part of our tragedy, we have nothing but scurrility, unworthy of any chaste ears, or some extreme show of doltishness, indeed fit to lift up a loud laughter, and nothing else: where the whole tract of a comedy should be full of delight, as the tragedy should be still maintained in a well-raised admiration.

But our comedians think there is no delight without laughter; which is very wrong, for though laughter may come with delight, yet cometh it not of delight, as though delight should be the cause of laughter; but well may one thing breed both together. Nay, rather in themselves they have, as it were, a kind of contrariety: for delight we scarcely do but in things that have a conveniency[4] to ourselves or to the general nature; laughter almost ever cometh of things most disproportioned to ourselves and nature. Delight hath a joy in it, either permanent or present. Laughter hath only a scornful tickling.

For example, we are ravished with delight to see a fair woman, and yet are far from being moved to laughter; we laugh at deformed creatures, wherein certainly we cannot delight. We delight in good chances, we laugh at mischances: we delight to hear the happiness of our friends, or country, at which he were worthy to be laughed at that would laugh; we shall, contrarily, laugh sometimes to find a matter quite mistaken and go down the hill against the

---

4. From the beginning; literally, from the egg (*Art of Poetry*, line 147).
5. In Euripides' *Hecuba*.
6. Priam and Hecuba were king and queen of Troy.
7. Trick, contrivance.
8. Sidney regards English tragicomedy as violating the rhetorical precept of *decorum*. But earlier (p. 564) he had, in principle, approved of mixed genres. "Decency": appropriateness.

9. Effect proper to comedy, as "admiration and commiseration" are proper to tragedy.
1. Roman author of *The Golden Ass*, a satirical romance (2nd century C.E.).
2. *Amphitruo* is tragicomic only in that it contains gods and heroes; otherwise it is pure comedy.
3. Merry tunes for country dances. "Mark them well": inspect them carefully. "Daintily": reluctantly.
4. Agreement, correspondence.

bias[5] in the mouth of some such men—as for the respect of them one shall be heartily sorry, he cannot choose but laugh, and so is rather pained than delighted with laughter.

Yet deny I not but that they may go well together. For as in Alexander's picture well set out we delight without laughter, and in twenty mad antics we laugh without delight; so in Hercules, painted with his great beard and furious countenance, in a woman's attire, spinning at Omphale's commandment,[6] it breedeth both delight and laughter: for the representing of so strange a power in love procureth delight, and the scornfulness of the action stirreth laughter. But I speak to this purpose, that all the end of the comical part be not upon such scornful matters as stir laughter only, but, mixed with it, that delightful teaching which is the end of poesy. And the great fault even in that point of laughter, and forbidden plainly by Aristotle,[7] is that they stir laughter in sinful things, which are rather execrable than ridiculous, or in miserable, which are rather to be pitied than scorned. For what is it to make folks gape at a wretched beggar and a beggarly clown; or, against law of hospitality, to jest at strangers, because they speak not English so well as we do? What do we learn, since it is certain

> Nil habet infelix paupertas durius in se,
> Quam quod ridiculos homines facit?[8]

But rather, a busy loving courtier and a heartless threatening Thraso;[9] a self-wise-seeming schoolmaster; an awry-transformed traveler. These, if we saw walk in stage names, which we play naturally,[1] therein were delightful laughter, and teaching delightfulness—as in the other, the tragedies of Buchanan[2] do justly bring forth a divine admiration.

But I have lavished out too many words of this play matter. I do it because, as they are excelling parts of poesy, so is there none so much used in England, and none can be more pitifully abused; which, like an unmannerly daughter showing a bad education, causeth her mother Poesy's honesty[3] to be called in question.

Other sort of poetry almost have we none, but that lyrical kind of songs and sonnets: which, Lord, if He gave us so good minds, how well it might be employed, and with how heavenly fruit, both private and public, in singing the praises of the immortal beauty: the immortal goodness of that God who giveth us hands to write and wits to conceive; of which we might well want words, but never matter; of which we could turn our eyes to nothing, but we should ever have new-budding occasions. But truly many of such writings as come under the banner of unresistible love, if I were a mistress, would never persuade me they were in love: so coldly they apply fiery speeches, as men that had rather read lovers' writings—and so caught up certain swelling phrases which hang together like a man that once told my father that the wind was at northwest and by south, because he would be sure to name winds enough—than that in truth they feel those passions, which easily (as

---

5. End in unexpected disaster, as when in the game of bowls a slope deflects the ball from its course, or "bias."
6. Hercules, infatuated with Omphale, queen of Lydia, submitted to be dressed as her female slave and to spin wool.
7. In *Poetics* 5.
8. "Unfortunate poverty has in itself no thing

harder to bear than that it makes men ridiculous" (Juvenal, *Satires* 3.152–53).
9. See p. 565 and n. 8.
1. In real life.
2. George Buchanan (1506–1582), influential Scottish humanist and poet.
3. Virtue.

I think) may be bewrayed by that same forcibleness or *energia*[4] (as the Greeks call it) of the writer. But let this be a sufficient though short note, that we miss the right use of the material point[5] of poesy.

Now, for the outside of it, which is words, or (as I may term it) diction, it is even well worse. So is that honey-flowing matron Eloquence apparelled, or rather disguised, in a courtesan-like painted affectation: one time, with so far-fet words that may seem monsters but must seem strangers to any poor Englishman; another time, with coursing of a letter, as if they were bound to follow the method of a dictionary; another time, with figures and flowers extremely winter-starved.[6] But I would this fault were only peculiar to versifiers, and had not as large possession among prose-printers; and (which is to be marveled) among many scholars; and (which is to be pitied) among some preachers. Truly I could wish, if at least I might be so bold to wish a thing beyond the reach of my capacity, the diligent imitators of Tully and Demosthenes (most worthy to be imitated) did not so much keep Nizolian paperbooks of their figures and phrases,[7] as by attentive translation (as it were) devour them whole, and make them wholly theirs: for now they cast sugar and spice upon every dish that is served to the table—like those Indians, not content to wear earrings at the fit and natural place of the ears, but they will thrust jewels through their nose and lips, because they will be sure to be fine.[8] Tully, when he was to drive out Catiline, as it were with a thunderbolt of eloquence, often used the figure of repetition, as *Vivit. Vivit? Imo in senatum venit, etc.*[9] Indeed, inflamed with a well-grounded rage, he would have his words (as it were) double out of his mouth, and so do that artificially which we see men in choler[1] do naturally. And we, having noted the grace of those words, hale them in sometimes to a familiar epistle, when it were too too much choler to be choleric. How well store of *similiter cadences* doth sound with the gravity of the pulpit,[2] I would but invoke Demosthenes' soul to tell, who with a rare daintiness[3] useth them. Truly they have made me think of the sophister that with too much subtlety would prove two eggs three, and though he might be counted a sophister, had none for his labor.[4] So these men bringing in such a kind of eloquence, well may they obtain an opinion of a seeming finesse,[5] but persuade few—which should be the end of their finesse. Now for similitudes, in certain printed discourses, I think all herbarists, all stories of beasts, fowls, and fishes are rifled up, that they come in multitudes to wait upon any of our conceits;[6] which certainly is as

---

4. A rhetorical term, glossed by Sidney as he introduces it. "Bewrayed": manifested.
5. I.e., the (subject) matter.
6. Sidney criticizes three abuses: exotic ("far-fet": far-fetched) borrowings from other languages; excessive alliteration ("coursing of a letter"); and sterile ("winter-starved") figurative language.
7. Commonplace books of phrases from classical rhetoricians (among whom Cicero ["Tully"] and Demosthenes were supreme), named after the Italian scholar Marius Nizolius, who in 1535 had published *Thesaurus Ciceronianus*. In place of the slavish imitation that was all too common, Sidney advocates true *absorption* of the great classical models ("attentive translation": studious transference, appropriation) and imitation with discretion.
8. Sidney had read or heard about New World indigenes whose piercings seemed "unnatural" to him (i.e., different from European practices).

9. In Cicero's famous first oration against the Roman senator Catiline—who had attempted a coup against the Republic—he marvels that Catiline still "lives. Lives? Even comes into the Senate."
1. Anger. "Artificially": through art.
2. Again Sidney expresses disapproval of the affectations of elaborate rhetoric—in this case, the excessive use ("store": abundance) of similar endings ("*similiter cadences*"), including similar rhythms or rhyme at the ends of successive phrases.
3. Good taste.
4. A familiar story of a logic chopper ("sophister") who proved two eggs to be three—here is one, and there are two, and one and two make three—and who for his pains was awarded the third egg.
5. Good taste.
6. Conceptions; here perhaps also with the sense of elaborate sustained comparisons.

absurd a surfeit to the ears as is possible.[7] For the force of a similitude not being to prove anything to a contrary disputer, but only to explain to a willing hearer, when that is done, the rest is a most tedious prattling, rather over-swaying the memory from the purpose whereto they were applied, than any whit informing the judgment, already either satisfied or by similitudes not to be satisfied. For my part, I do not doubt, when Antonius and Crassus, the great forefathers of Cicero in eloquence, the one (as Cicero testifieth of them)[8] pretended not to know art, the other not to set by it, because with a plain sensibleness they might win credit[9] of popular ears (which credit is the nearest step to persuasion, which persuasion is the chief mark[1] of oratory), I do not doubt (I say) but that they used these knacks very sparingly; which who doth generally use, any man may see doth dance to his own music, and so be noted by the audience more careful to speak curiously[2] than to speak truly. Undoubtedly (at least to my opinion undoubtedly), I have found in divers smally learned courtiers a more sound style than in some professors of learning; of which I can guess no other cause, but that the courtier, following that which by practice he findeth fittest to nature, therein (though he know it not) doth according to art, though not by art: where the other, using art to show art, and not to hide art[3] (as in these cases he should do), flieth from nature, and indeed abuseth art.

But what? Methinks I deserve to be pounded[4] for straying from poetry to oratory. But both have such an affinity in the wordish consideration,[5] that I think this digression will make my meaning receive the fuller understanding: which is not to take upon me to teach poets how they should do, but only, finding myself sick among the rest, to show some one or two spots of the common infection grown among the most part of writers, that, acknowledging ourselves somewhat awry, we may bend to the right use both of matter and manner: whereto our language giveth us great occasion, being indeed capable of any excellent exercising of it. I know some will say it is a mingled language.[6] And why not so much the better, taking the best of both the other? Another will say it wanteth grammar. Nay truly, it hath that praise, that it wants not grammar:[7] for grammar it might have, but it needs it not, being so easy in itself, and so void of those cumbersome differences of cases, genders, moods, and tenses, which I think was a piece of the Tower of Babylon's curse,[8] that a man should be put to school to learn his mother tongue. But for the uttering sweetly and properly the conceits of the mind (which is the end of speech), that hath it equally with any other tongue in the world; and is particularly happy in compositions[9] of two or three words together, near the

7. Sidney mocks the "euphuistic" style associated with John Lyly's popular romance *Euphues* (1578; see p. 537), whose affectations included an abundance of similes drawn from (often false) natural history.
8. *On the Orator* 2.1. Lucius Crassus (d. 91 B.C.E.) and Marcus Antonius (d. 87 B.C.E.—the grandfather of Cleopatra's Mark Antony) are speakers in this dialogue and are lauded by Cicero in the prefaces to the second and third of its three books.
9. Credence, trust.
1. Aim.
2. Elaborately.
3. Alluding to the proverb "It is art to hide art."
4. Impounded, like a stray animal.

5. In matters of diction.
6. Mingling, especially, words from French and Latin with those of Anglo-Saxon origin.
7. "Wanteth grammar . . . wants not grammar": lacks grammar . . . does not require grammar. English, of course, has grammar. But its grammar was not, at the time, elaborately systematized and studied, like Greek and Latin grammar.
8. Elizabethans identified Babel—where, according to Genesis 11.1–9, God stymied human overreaching by instituting a confounding variety of languages—with Babylon.
9. Compounds. (Sidney's use of them is one of the most distinctive and attractive features of his style.) "Happy": fortunate.

Greek, far beyond the Latin, which is one of the greatest beauties can be in a language.

Now of versifying there are two sorts, the one ancient, the other modern: the ancient marked the quantity of each syllable, and according to that framed his verse; the modern, observing only number[1] (with some regard of the accent), the chief life of it standeth in that like sounding of the words, which we call rhyme. Whether of these be the more excellent, would bear many speeches: the ancient (no doubt) more fit for music, both words and time observing quantity, and more fit lively to express diverse passions, by the low or lofty sound of the well-weighed syllable; the latter likewise, with his rhyme, striketh a certain music to the ear, and, in fine,[2] since it doth delight, though by another way, it obtains the same purpose: there being in either sweetness, and wanting[3] in neither majesty. Truly the English, before any vulgar[4] language I know, is fit for both sorts. For, for the ancient, the Italian is so full of vowels that it must ever be cumbered with elisions; the Dutch[5] so, of the other side, with consonants, that they cannot yield the sweet sliding, fit for a verse; the French in his whole language hath not one word that hath his accent in the last syllable saving two, called *antepenultima*; and little more hath the Spanish, and therefore very gracelessly may they use dactyls.[6] The English is subject to none of these defects. Now for the rhyme,[7] though we do not observe quantity, yet we observe the accent very precisely, which other languages either cannot do, or will not do so absolutely. That *caesura*, or breathing place in the midst of the verse, neither Italian nor Spanish have, the French and we never almost fail of. Lastly, even the very rhyme itself, the Italian cannot put it in the last syllable, by the French named the masculine rhyme, but still[8] in the next to the last, which the French call the female, or the next before that, which the Italians term *sdrucciola*. The example of the former is *buono: suono*, of the *sdrucciola* is *femina: semina*. The French, of the other side, hath both the male, as *bon: son*, and the female, as *plaise: taise*, but the *sdrucciola* he hath not: where the English hath all three, as *due: true, father: rather, motion: potion*[9]—with much more which might be said, but that already I find the triflingness of this discourse is much too much enlarged.

[CONCLUSION]

So that since the ever-praiseworthy Poesy is full of virtue-breeding delightfulness, and void of no gift that ought to be in the noble name of learning;[1] since the blames laid against it are either false or feeble; since the cause why it is not esteemed in England is the fault of poet-apes,[2] not poets; since, lastly, our tongue is most fit to honor poesy, and to be honored by poesy;

---

1. Classical "quantity" meant the length or duration of syllables. Moderns simply count the "number" of syllables.
2. In conclusion.
3. Lacking.
4. Vernacular.
5. The term referred to the languages both of the Low Countries and of Germany.
6. See (as for *caesura*, below) the Literary Terminology appendix to this volume.
7. I.e., rhymed verse as opposed to "ancient" (i.e., quantitative) verse. Because of the accent pat-

terns in French and Spanish, those languages cannot make good use of this poetic foot.
8. Always.
9. Pronounced with three syllables, accented on the first.
1. This final paragraph constitutes the *peroratio* of Sidney's judicial oration: though it includes a brief recapitulation of arguments, the main function of the peroration is, like that of the exordium, to work on the audience's feelings, leaving it well-disposed toward the speaker and the speaker's client.
2. False poets, who mimic ("ape") the real ones.

I conjure you all that have had the evil luck to read this ink-wasting toy of mine, even in the name of the nine Muses, no more to scorn the sacred mysteries of poesy; no more to laugh at the name of poets, as though they were next inheritors to fools; no more to jest at the reverent title of a rhymer; but to believe, with Aristotle, that they were the ancient treasurers of the Grecians' divinity; to believe, with Bembus, that they were first bringers-in of all civility; to believe, with Scaliger, that no philosopher's precepts can sooner make you an honest man than the reading of Virgil; to believe, with Clauserus, the translator of Cornutus, that it pleased the heavenly Deity, by Hesiod[3] and Homer, under the veil of fables, to give us all knowledge, logic, rhetoric, philosophy natural and moral, and *quid non?*;[4] to believe, with me, that there are many mysteries contained in poetry, which of purpose were written darkly, lest by profane wits it should be abused; to believe, with Landino,[5] that they are so beloved of the gods that whatsoever they write proceeds of a divine fury;[6] lastly, to believe themselves, when they tell you they will make you immortal by their verses. Thus doing, your name shall flourish in the printers' shops; thus doing, you shall be of kin to many a poetical preface; thus doing, you shall be most fair, most rich, most wise, most all, you shall dwell upon superlatives; thus doing, though you be *libertino patre natus*,[7] you shall suddenly grow *Herculea proles*,[8]

Si quid mea carmina possunt;[9]

thus doing, your soul shall be placed with Dante's Beatrice, or Virgil's Anchises.[1] But if (fie of such a but) you be born so near the dull-making cataract of Nilus that you cannot hear the planet-like[2] music of poetry; if you have so earth-creeping a mind that it cannot lift itself up to look to the sky of poetry, or rather, by a certain rustical disdain, will become such a mome as to be a Momus[3] of poetry; then, though I will not wish unto you the ass's ears of Midas,[4] nor to be driven by a poet's verses, as Bubonax[5] was, to hang himself, nor to be rhymed to death, as is said to be done in Ireland;[6] yet thus much curse I must send you, in the behalf of all poets, that while you live, you live in love, and never get favor for lacking skill of a sonnet;[7] and, when you die, your memory die from the earth for want of an epitaph.

ca. 1579   1595

---

3. Early Greek poet whose *Theogony* recounts myths of the birth and warfare of the gods and the origin of the world. For Aristotle, cf. *Metaphysics* 3.4.12. For Bembus (Pietro Bembo), see p. 576, 2nd n. 8. For Scaliger, see p. 551, n. 2. Conrad Clauser was a German scholar who translated a Greek treatise by Cornutus, a Stoic pedagogue of Nero's time.
4. What not?
5. Christoforo Landino, Florentine humanist who developed this argument in his edition of Dante's *Divine Comedy* (1481).
6. Divinely inspired frenzy.
7. Born of a freed-slave father (Horace, *Satires* 1.6.6).
8. Offspring of Hercules.
9. If my songs are of any avail (*Aeneid* 9.446).
1. I.e., in Paradise with Dante's beloved or in the

Elysian Fields with Aeneas's honored father.
2. Resembling the music of the spheres, most beautiful of all music. According to Cicero (*Dream of Scipio* 5), the noise of the waterfalls in the upper Nile deafened those who lived nearby.
3. God of ridicule, son of Night; hence, a critic. "Mome": dunce.
4. He was given ass's ears because he preferred Pan's music to Apollo's (Ovid, *Metamorphoses* 11.146–79).
5. Bupalus, an ancient Greek sculptor who, according to an apocryphal story, hanged himself when his works were satirized by the poet Hipponax. Sidney fuses the two names.
6. Irish bards were thought to be able to cause death with their rhymed charms.
7. Because you are unable to write a sonnet.

Astrophil and Stella   Sidney was a jealous protector of his privacy. "I assure you before God," he had written once in an angry letter to his father's private secretary, Molyneux, "that if ever I know you do so much as read any letter I write to my father, without his commandment or my consent, I will thrust my dagger into you. And trust to it, for I speak it in earnest." Yet in *Astrophil and Stella* he seems to hold up a mirror to every nuance of his emotional being. For its original coterie audience, Sidney's sonnet sequence must have been an elaborate game of literary masks, psychological risk taking, and open secrets. The loosely linked succession of 108 sonnets and eleven songs, with its dazzling display of technical virtuosity, provides tantalizing glimpses of identifiable characters and, still more, a sustained and remarkably intimate portrait of the poet's inner life.

Much biographical speculation has centered on Sidney's ambiguous relationship with Penelope Devereux, the supposed original of Stella. A marriage between the two had been proposed in 1576 and was talked about for some years, but in 1581 she married Lord Robert Rich, and two years later Sidney also married. (At their high social rank, marriages were negotiated in the interests of the powerful families involved, not of the individuals.) Some of the sonnets contain sly puns on the name *Rich*, and it seems likely that there are autobiographical elements in the shadowy narrative sketched by the work. At the same time, however, the "plot" of the sequence, full of trials, setbacks, much suffering on the part of the lover and occasional encouragement on the part of the lady, is highly conventional, derived from Petrarch and his many Italian, French, and Spanish imitators.

Poets in this tradition undertook to produce an anatomy of love, displaying its shifting and often contradictory states: hope and despair, tenderness and bitterness, exultation and modesty, bodily desire and spiritual transcendence. Petrarch had deployed a series of ingenious metaphors to describe these states, but by Sidney's time the metaphors—love as a freezing fire, the beloved's glance as an arrow striking the lover's heart, and so forth—had through endless repetition become familiar and predictable, less a revelation than a role. Sidney, in the role of Astrophil, protests that he uses no standard conventional phrases, that his verse is original and comes from his heart. This protest is itself conventional, and yet Sidney manages to infuse his sonnets with an extraordinary vigor and freshness. Certain of the sonnets have, within their narrow fourteen-line bounds, the force of the drama: "Fly, fly, my friends, I have my death-wound, fly" or "What, have I thus betrayed my liberty?" Others, in their grappling with insistent desire, have the probing, psychological resonance of private confession: "With what sharp checks I in myself am shent" or "Who will in fairest book of Nature know." Still others ask crucial questions about the whole project of self-representation: "Stella oft sees the very face of woe." Virtually all of them manifest the exceptional *energia*—forcibleness—that Sidney, in *The Defense of Poesy*, says is the key ingredient of good love poetry.

From Astrophil and Stella

1[1]

Loving in truth, and fain° in verse my love to show,	*desirous*
That the dear She might take some pleasure of my pain,	
Pleasure might cause her read, reading might make her know,	
Knowledge might pity win, and pity grace obtain,	

---

1. One of six sonnets in the sequence written in hexameters.

5   I sought fit words to paint the blackest face of woe,
Studying inventions fine, her wits to entertain,
Oft turning others' leaves, to see if thence would flow
Some fresh and fruitful showers upon my sunburned brain.
    But words came halting forth, wanting Invention's stay;[2]
10 Invention, Nature's child, fled step-dame Study's blows,
And others' feet still° seemed but strangers in my way.   *continually*
Thus great with child to speak, and helpless in my throes,
  Biting my truant pen, beating myself for spite,
  "Fool," said my Muse to me, "look in thy heart and write."

2

Not at first sight, nor with a dribbèd[3] shot
  Love gave the wound, which while I breathe will bleed,
  But known worth did in mine[4] of time proceed,
Till by degrees it had full conquest got.
5   I saw and liked, I liked but lovèd not,
  I loved, but straight did not[5] what Love decreed;
  At length to Love's decrees, I, forced, agreed,
Yet with repining° at so partial° lot.   *complaining / unfair*
  Now even that footstep of lost liberty
10 Is gone, and now like slave-born Muscovite,[6]
  I call it praise to suffer tyranny;
  And now employ the remnant of my wit°   *mind*
    To make myself believe that all is well,
    While with a feeling skill I paint my hell.

5

It is most true that eyes are formed to serve
  The inward light,° and that the heavenly part   *i.e., reason, understanding*
  Ought to be king, from whose rules who do swerve,
Rebels to Nature, strive for their own smart.°   *pain*
5   It is most true, what we call Cupid's dart
An image is, which for ourselves we carve;
And, fools, adore in temple of our heart,
Till that good god make church and churchman starve.[7]
  True, that true beauty virtue is indeed,
10 Whereof this beauty can be but a shade,°   *shadow*
  Which elements with mortal mixture[8] breed;
  True, that on earth we are but pilgrims made,

2. I.e., lacking the support of Invention, his words moved haltingly.
3. Ineffectual or at random.
4. Tunnel dug to undermine a besieged fortress.
5. Did not immediately do.
6. Inhabitant of Muscovy, Russian principality ruled from Moscow; 16th-century travel books describe Muscovites as contented slaves.
7. Die (not necessarily of hunger). The concessions made in the argument are to Neoplatonic and Christian doctrines opposed to romantic love. Neoplatonic theory held that physical beauty is only a shadow of inner virtue, which is at one with the true, transcendent, and immortal Idea of Beauty. For a highly influential exposition of this theory, see the excerpts from Book 4 of Castiglione's *The Courtier*, pp. 176, 179ff.
8. Physical beauty is a mixture of the four elements (earth, air, water, and fire) and is therefore mortal.

And should in soul up to our country move:
True, and yet true that I must *Stella* love.

6

Some lovers speak, when they their muses entertain,
Of hopes begot by fear, of wot° not what desires,   *know*
Of force of heavenly beams infusing hellish pain,
Of living deaths, dear wounds, fair storms, and freezing fires.[9]
5   Some one his song in Jove and Jove's strange tales attires,
Bordered with bulls and swans, powdered with golden rain;[1]
Another humbler wit to shepherd's pipe retires,
Yet hiding royal blood full oft in rural vein.[2]
    To some a sweetest plaint a sweetest style affords,[3]
10   While tears pour out his ink, and sighs breathe out his words,
His paper pale Despair, and Pain his pen doth move.
    I can speak what I feel, and feel as much as they,
    But think that all the map of my state I display,
When trembling voice brings forth that I do Stella love.

7

When Nature made her chief work, Stella's eyes,
In color black why wrapped she beams so bright?
Would she in beamy° black, like painter wise,   *radiant*
Frame daintiest luster, mixed of shades and light?
5   Or did she else that sober hue devise,
In object° best to knit and strength° our sight,   *with purpose / strengthen*
Lest if no veil those brave° gleams did disguise,   *splendid*
They sun-like should more dazzle than delight?
    Or would she her miraculous power show,
10   That whereas black seems beauty's contrary,
She even in black doth make all beauties flow?
    Both so and thus: she, minding° Love should be   *remembering*
    Placed ever there, gave him this mourning weed,°   *funeral garb*
To honor all their deaths, who for her bleed.

9

Queen Virtue's court, which some call Stella's face,
    Prepared by Nature's chiefest furniture,[4]
    Hath his front° built of alablaster° pure;   *i.e., Stella's forehead / alabaster*
Gold is the covering of that stately place.
5   The door, by which sometimes comes forth her grace,
    Red porphir[5] is, which lock of pearl makes sure;
    Whose porches rich (which name of cheeks endure),

9. Conventional Petrarchan oxymorons.
1. Jove courted Europa in the shape of a bull; Leda, as a swan; and Danaë, as a golden shower. "Bordered": the emendation "Broadred" (embroidered) has been proposed.
2. I.e., in pastoral allegory. By convention, a pastoral poet pipes his songs on an oaten or reed pipe.
3. Parodying the overuse of the word *sweet* in love complaints, with allusion to the very musical *dolce stil nuovo* (sweet new style) associated with Dante and his Italian contemporaries.
4. The best materials Nature furnishes.
5. Porphyry, an ornamental red or purple stone.

Marble mixed red and white do interlace.
    The windows now through which this heavenly guest
10 Looks o'er the world, and can find nothing such
Which dare claim from those lights the name of best,
Of touch[6] they are that without touch doth touch,
    Which Cupid's self from Beauty's mine did draw:
    Of touch they are, and poor I am their straw.

10

Reason, in faith thou art well served, that still
Wouldst brabbling° be with sense and love in me: *quarreling*
I rather wished thee climb the Muses' hill,[7]
Or reach the fruit of Nature's choicest tree,[8]
5   Or seek heaven's course, or heaven's inside to see.
Why shouldst thou toil our thorny soil to till?
Leave sense, and those which sense's objects be;
Deal thou with powers of thoughts, leave love to will.
    But thou wouldst needs fight both with love and sense,
10 With sword of wit,° giving wounds of dispraise,   *intellect*
Till downright blows did foil thy cunning fence:°   *swordplay*
For soon as they strake° thee with Stella's rays,   *struck*
    Reason thou kneel'dst, and offeredst straight° to prove   *straightaway*
    By reason good, good reason her to love.

15

You that do search for every purling° spring   *murmuring*
    Which from the ribs of old Parnassus[9] flows,
    And every flower,[1] not sweet perhaps, which grows
Near therabout, into your poesy[2] wring;
5 You that do dictionary's method bring
    Into your rhymes, running in rattling rows;
    You that poor Petrarch's long-deceasèd woes
With new-born sighs and denizened wit° do sing: *naturalized ingenuity*
    You take wrong ways, those far-fet° helps be such   *far-fetched*
10 As do bewray a want of inward touch,[3]
And sure at length stolen goods do come to light.
    But if (both for your love and skill) your name
    You seek to nurse at fullest breasts of Fame,
Stella behold, and then begin to indite.°   *compose, write*

16

In nature apt to like when I did see
    Beauties, which were of many carats fine,

---

6. Glossy black stone (lignite or jet) able to attract light bodies such as straw by static electricity.
7. Mount Helicon in Greece, sacred to the Nine Muses—a symbol of poetic inspiration.
8. The Tree of Knowledge.

9. Mountain near Delphi in Greece, sacred to the Muses.
1. Also, poetic figures ("flowers of rhetoric").
2. Also, a nosegay (posy).
3. Reveal a lack of innate talent.

My boiling sprites° did thither soon incline,   *spirits*
And, Love, I thought that I was full of thee:
5 But finding not those restless flames in me,
    Which others said did make their souls to pine,
    I thought those babes of some pin's hurt did whine,
By my love judging what love's pain might be.
    But while I thus with this young lion[4] played,
10 Mine eyes (shall I say cursed or blessed) beheld
Stella; now she is named, need more be said?
In her sight I a lesson new have spelled:
    I now have learned love right, and learned even so,
    As who by being poisoned doth poison know.

18

With what sharp checks° I in myself am shent,°   *rebukes / shamed*
    When into Reason's audit I do go,
    And by just counts myself a bankrout° know   *bankrupt*
Of all those goods, which heaven to me hath lent:
5 Unable quite to pay even Nature's rent,
    Which unto it by birthright I do owe;
    And which is worse, no good excuse can show,
But that my wealth I have most idly spent.
    My youth doth waste, my knowledge brings forth toys,[5]
10 My wit° doth strive those passions to defend,   *intellect*
Which for reward spoil it with vain annoys.°   *troubles*
I see my course to lose myself doth bend:°   *turn*
    I see and yet no greater sorrow take,
    Than that I lose no more for Stella's sake.

20

Fly, fly, my friends, I have my death-wound, fly;
See there that boy, that murth'ring° boy, I say,   *murdering*
Who like a thief hid in dark bush doth lie
Till bloody bullet get him wrongful prey.
5   So tyran° he no fitter place could spy,   *tyrant*
    Nor so fair level° in so secret stay,°   *aim / stopping place*
    As that sweet black° which veils the heav'nly eye;   *i.e., pupil*
There himself with his shot he close° doth lay.   *secretly*
    Poor passenger,° pass now thereby I did,   *passerby*
10 And stayed, pleased with the prospect of the place,
While that black hue from me the bad guest hid:
    But straight I saw motions of lightning grace,
    And then descried° the glist'ring° of his dart;°   *saw / glittering / arrow*
    But ere I could fly thence, it pierced my heart.

---

4. In a popular fable, a shepherd raised a lion cub that, while young, was a pet for his children but when grown destroyed all his flocks.
5. Trifles; i.e., these poems.

21

Your words, my friend (right healthful caustics),[6] blame
   My young mind marred, whom Love doth windlass° so,   *ensnare*
   That mine own writings like bad servants show
My wits quick in vain thoughts, in virtue lame;
5 That Plato I read for nought, but if° he tame   *unless*
   Such coltish gyres,[7] that to my birth I owe
   Nobler desires, least° else that friendly foe,   *lest*
Great Expectation, wear a train of shame.
   For since mad March great promise made of me,
10 If now the May of my years much decline,
What can be hoped my harvest time will be?
Sure you say well; your wisdom's golden mine
   Dig deep with learning's spade; now tell me this:
   Hath this world ought° so fair as Stella is?   *aught, anything*

27

Because I oft, in dark abstracted guise,
   Seem most alone in greatest company,
   With dearth of words, or answers quite awry,
To them that would make speech of speech arise,
5 They deem, and of their doom° the rumor flies,   *judgment*
   That poison foul of bubbling pride doth lie
   So in my swelling breast that only I°   *that I do nothing but*
Fawn on myself, and others do despise.
   Yet pride, I think, doth not my soul possess,
10 Which looks too oft in his unflatt'ring glass;°   *mirror*
But one worse fault, ambition, I confess,
   That makes me oft my best friends overpass,°   *pass by, ignore*
   Unseen, unheard, while thought to highest place
   Bends all his powers, even unto Stella's grace.°   *beauty, elegance; favor*

28

You that with allegory's curious frame°   *intricate contrivance*
   Of others' children changelings use° to make,   *are accustomed*
   With me those pains for God's sake do not take:
I list not° dig so deep for brazen fame.   *I don't care to*
5 When I say Stella, I do mean the same
   Princess of beauty for whose only sake
   The reins of love I love, though never slake,°   *slack*
And joy therein, though nations count it shame.
   I beg no subject to use eloquence,[8]
10 Nor in hid ways to guide philosophy;

---

6. Caustic substances for burning away diseased tissue.
7. Wild circles, like those of a young horse; there is a probable reference to Plato's story of the char-ioteer Reason reining in the horses of Passion (*Phaedrus* 254).
8. I.e., I don't ask for a topic simply as an excuse to display my rhetorical skills.

Look at my hands for no such quintessence,[9]
But know that I in pure simplicity
   Breathe out the flames which burn within my heart,
   Love only reading unto me this art.

31

With how sad steps, O Moon, thou climb'st the skies,
   How silently, and with how wan a face!
   What, may it be that even in heavenly place
That busy archer° his sharp arrows tries?   *Cupid*
5 Sure, if that long-with-love-acquainted eyes
   Can judge of love, thou feel'st a lover's case;
   I read it in thy looks: thy languished grace,
To me that feel the like, thy state descries.°   *reveals*
   Then even of fellowship, O Moon, tell me,
10 Is constant love deemed there but want of wit?°   *lack of intelligence*
Are beauties there as proud as here they be?
Do they above love to be loved, and yet
   Those lovers scorn whom that love doth possess?
   Do they call virtue there ungratefulness?[1]

33[2]

I might (unhappy word), O me, I might,
And then would not, or could not, see my bliss:
Till now, wrapped in a most infernal night,
I find how heav'nly day, wretch, I did miss.
5   Heart, rent° thyself, thou dost thyself but right: *rend, tear*
No lovely Paris made thy Helen his;[3]
No force, no fraud robbed thee of thy delight;
Nor Fortune of thy fortune author is;
   But to myself myself did give the blow,
10 While too much wit° (forsooth°) so troubled me,   *cleverness / truly*
That I respects for both our sakes must show:[4]
And yet could not by rising morn foresee
   How fair a day was near. O punished eyes,
   That I had been more foolish, or more wise!

34

Come, let me write. "And to what end?" To ease
   A burdened heart. "How can words ease, which are
   The glasses° of thy daily vexing care?"   *mirrors*
Oft cruel fights well pictured forth do please.

---

9. The mysterious "fifth element" of matter (supplementary to earth, air, fire, and water), which alchemists labored to extract.
1. I.e., is the lady's ingratitude considered virtue in heaven (as here)? Also, is the lover's virtue (fidelity) considered distasteful in heaven (as here)?
2. The sonnet seems to allude to the abortive

scheme to betroth Sidney to Penelope Devereux in 1576, when she was thirteen, he twenty-one.
3. I.e., Astrophil did not lose Stella to a more attractive rival, as Menelaus lost Helen of Troy to Paris.
4. I.e., he thought he was acting in the best interests of both.

5   "Art° not ashamed to publish thy disease?"   *are you*
     Nay, that may breed my fame, it is so rare.
     "But will not wise men think thy words fond ware?"°   *foolish trinkets*
Then be they close,[5] and so none shall displease.
     "What idler thing, than speak and not be hard?"°   *heard*
10 What harder thing than smart,° and not to speak?   *feel pain*
Peace, foolish wit;° with wit my wit is marred.   *reason; intellect*
Thus while I write I doubt° to write, and wreak° *hesitate; fear / avenge*
     My harms on Ink's poor loss: perhaps some find
     Stella's great powers, that so confuse my mind.

37

My mouth doth water, and my breast doth swell,
     My tongue doth itch, my thoughts in labor be:
     Listen then, lordings, with good ear to me,
For of my life I must a riddle tell.
5   Towards Aurora's court a nymph doth dwell,[6]
     Rich in all beauties which man's eye can see,
     Beauties so far from reach of words, that we
Abase her praise, saying she doth excel:
     Rich in the treasure of deserved renown,
10 Rich in the riches of a royal heart,
Rich in those gifts which give th' eternal crown;
Who though most rich in these and every part
     Which make the patents[7] of true worldly bliss,
     Hath no misfortune, but that Rich she is.

39

Come, Sleep, O Sleep, the certain knot of peace,
The baiting place[8] of wit,° the balm of woe,   *mind*
The poor man's wealth, the prisoner's release,
Th' indifferent° judge between the high and low;   *impartial*
5   With shield of proof[9] shield me from out the prease° *press, throng*
Of those fierce darts Despair at me doth throw:
O make in me those civil wars to cease;
I will good tribute pay if thou do so.
     Take thou of me smooth pillows, sweetest bed,
10 A chamber deaf to noise and blind to light,
A rosy garland, and a weary head:[1]
And if these things, as being thine by right,
     Move not thy heavy grace, thou shalt in me
     Livelier° than elsewhere Stella's image see.   *more lifelike*

5. Let them (my words) be kept private.
6. Aurora (the dawn) has her court in the east. Penelope Devereux Rich, the original of Stella, dwelt in Essex, one of the eastern counties. Sidney puns on her married name throughout this sonnet.

7. Grants, titles to possession.
8. Resting place on a journey.
9. Proven strength.
1. The offer of gifts to Morpheus, god of sleep, is a poetic convention. A likely source is Chaucer's *Book of the Duchess*, lines 240–69.

41

Having this day my horse, my hand, my lance
   Guided so well that I obtained the prize,
   Both by the judgment of the English eyes
And of some sent from that sweet enemy France;[2]
5 Horsemen my skill in horsemanship advance;[3]
   Townfolks my strength; a daintier° judge applies   *more discerning*
   His praise to sleight,[4] which from good use° doth rise;   *experience*
Some lucky wits impute it but to chance;
   Others, because of both sides I do take
10 My blood from them who did excel in this,[5]
Think Nature me a man of arms did make.
   How far they shoot awry! The true cause is,
     Stella looked on, and from her heavenly face
     Sent forth the beams which made so fair my race.[6]

45

Stella oft sees the very face of woe
   Painted in my beclouded stormy face,
   But cannot skill to° pity my disgrace,°   *is unable to / misfortune*
Not though thereof the cause herself she know.[7]
5 Yet hearing late a fable which did show,
   Of lovers never known, a grievous case,
   Pity thereof gate° in her breast such place   *got*
That, from that sea derived, tears' spring did flow.
   Alas, if fancy,° drawn by imaged things,   *fantasy*
10 Though false, yet with free scope more grace° doth breed   *favor*
Than servant's wrack, where new doubts honor brings,[8]
   Then think, my dear, that you in me do read
     Of lover's ruin some sad tragedy:
     I am not I; pity the tale of me.

47

What, have I thus betrayed my liberty?
   Can those black beams such burning marks° engrave   *brands of slavery*
   In my free side? or am I born a slave,
Whose neck becomes° such yoke of tyranny?   *is suited to*
5 Or want I sense to feel my misery?
   Or sprite,° disdain of such disdain to have?   *spirit*
   Who for long faith, though daily help I crave,
May get no alms but scorn of beggary.[9]

2. Sidney took part in several jousting tournaments between 1579 and 1585 with French spectators present, but the one in May 1581 was devised specifically to entertain French commissioners.
3. I.e., put forward as the reason for my triumph.
4. Skill, dexterity.
5. Sidney's father and grandfather and his maternal uncles, the earls of Leicester and Warwick,

were frequent participants in tournaments.
6. Course in a tournament.
7. I.e., even though she knows she herself is the cause of it.
8. I.e., than the ruin of her lover ("servant"), caused by the new scruples ("doubts") her honor brings up.
9. I.e., scorn for [my] begging.

Virtue awake! Beauty but beauty is;
10 I may, I must, I can, I will, I do
Leave following that which it is gain to miss.
Let her go. Soft, but here she comes. Go to,[1]
    Unkind, I love you not. O me, that eye
Doth make my heart give to my tongue the lie.°   contradict my tongue

49

I on my horse, and Love on me doth try
    Our horsemanships, while by strange work I prove
    A horseman to my horse, a horse to Love;
And now man's wrongs in me, poor beast, descry.°   discover
5 The reins wherewith my rider doth me tie
    Are humbled thoughts, which bit of reverence move,
    Curbed in with fear, but with gilt boss° above   gold stud
Of hope, which makes it seem fair to the eye.
    The wand° is will; thou, Fancy, saddle art,[2]   whip
10 Girt fast by Memory; and while I spur
My horse, he spurs with sharp desire my heart;
    He sits me fast,° however I do stir,   tightly
    And now hath made me to his hand so right
That in the manage[3] myself takes delight.

52

A strife is grown between Virtue and Love,
    While each pretends° that Stella must be his: claims
    Her eyes, her lips, her all, saith Love, do this,
Since they do wear his badge,[4] most firmly prove.
5 But Virtue thus that title doth disprove:
    That Stella (O dear name) that Stella is
    That virtuous soul, sure heir of heavenly bliss;
Not this fair outside, which our hearts doth move.
    And therefore, though her beauty and her grace
10 Be Love's indeed, in Stella's self he may
By no pretence claim any manner° place.   kind of
Well, Love, since this demur° our suit[5] doth stay,°   objection / stop
    Let Virtue have that Stella's self; yet thus,
    That Virtue but° that body grant to us.   only

53

In martial sports I had my cunning° tried,   skill
    And yet to break more staves° did me address;   lances
    While with the people's shouts, I must confess,
Youth, luck, and praise even filled my veins with pride.
5 When Cupid having me his slave descried°   discerned

---

1. An emphatic expression, like "I tell you."
2. I.e., you, Fancy (imagination), are the saddle.
3. Training or handling of a horse.

4. Device or livery worn to identify someone's (here, Cupid's) servants.
5. Courtship, in addition to the legal meaning.

In Mars's livery,[6] prancing in the press,°   *throng*
    "What now, Sir Fool," said he, "I would no less;[7]
Look here, I say." I looked, and Stella spied,
    Who hard by° made a window send forth light.   *nearby*
10 My heart then quaked, then dazzled were mine eyes,
One hand forgot to rule,° th' other to fight.   *govern the horse*
Nor trumpets' sound I heard, nor friendly cries;
    My foe came on, and beat the air for me,[8]
    Till that her blush taught me my shame to see.

54

Because I breathe not love to every one,
    Nor do not use set colors for to wear,[9]
    Nor nourish special locks of vowèd hair,[1]
Nor give each speech a full point[2] of a groan,
5   The courtly nymphs, acquainted with the moan
    Of them who in their lips Love's standard° bear,   *ensign*
    "What, he?" say they of me, "now I dare swear
He cannot love; no, no, let him alone!"
    And think so still, so[3] Stella know my mind.
10 Profess indeed I do not Cupid's art;
But you, fair maids, at length this true shall find,
    That his right badge[4] is but worn in the heart:
    Dumb swans, not chatt'ring pies,° do lovers prove;[5]   *magpies*
    They love indeed, who quake to say they love.

56

Fie, school of Patience, fie, your lesson is
    Far far too long to learn it without book:°   *i.e., by memory*
    What, a whole week without one piece of look,[6]
And think I should not your large precepts miss?°   *forget*
5   When I might read those letters fair of bliss,
    Which in her face teach virtue, I could brook°   *bear*
    Somewhat thy leaden counsels, which I took
As of a friend that meant not much amiss.
    But now that I, alas, do want° her sight,   *lack*
10 What, dost thou think that I can ever take
In thy cold stuff a phlegmatic° delight?   *sluggish*
    No, Patience, if thou wilt my good, then make
    Her come and hear with patience my desire,
    And then with patience bid me bear my fire.

---

6. Cf. sonnet 52, lines 1–4, and note. Dressed in armor for the tournament, Astrophil is wearing the "livery" of Mars, god of war.
7. I.e., I want no less [service from you].
8. Struck the empty air instead of me.
9. Am not accustomed to wear colors associated with a particular woman.

1. I.e., lovelocks: long, flowing locks characteristic of amorous courtiers.
2. Final punctuation, period.
3. Go on thinking so, provided only that.
4. True badge, livery.
5. Prove to be (true) lovers.
6. Without the briefest glimpse of her.

61

Oft with true sighs, oft with uncallèd tears,
Now with slow words, now with dumb eloquence
I Stella's eyes assail, invade her ears;
But this at last is her sweet-breathed defense:
5   That who indeed infelt affection bears,
So captives to his saint both soul and sense
That, wholly hers, all selfness° he forbears;   *concern with self*
Thence his desires he learns, his life's course thence.
    Now since her chaste mind hates this love in me,
10   With chastened mind I straight must shew° that she   *show*
Shall quickly me from what she hates remove.
    O Doctor[7] Cupid, thou for me reply,
    Driven else° to grant by angel's sophistry   *otherwise*
That I love not, without I leave to love.°   *unless I stop loving*

69

O joy, too high for my low style to show,
    O bliss, fit for a nobler state than me!
    Envy, put out thine eyes, least° thou do see   *lest*
What oceans of delight in me do flow.
5   My friend, that oft saw through all masks my woe,
    Come, come, and let me pour myself on thee:
    Gone is the winter of my misery;
My spring appears; O see what here doth grow.
    For Stella hath, with words where faith doth shine,
10   Of her high heart given me the monarchy:
I, I, O I may say that she is mine.
    And though she give but thus conditionly
    This realm of bliss, while virtuous course I take,
    No kings be crowned but° they some covenants[8] make.   *unless*

71

Who will in fairest book of Nature know
    How Virtue may best lodged in beauty be,
    Let him but learn of Love to read in thee,
Stella, those fair lines, which true goodness show.
5   There shall he find all vices' overthrow,
    Not by rude force, but sweetest sovereignty
    Of reason, from whose light those night-birds[9] fly;
That inward sun in thine eyes shineth so.
    And not content to be Perfection's heir
10   Thyself, dost strive all minds that way to move,
Who mark° in thee what is in thee most fair.[1]   *perceive*

7. In the sense of eminently learned scholar.
8. Solemn coronation oaths taken by English monarchs, promising to protect the laws and the people.
9. The owl, for example, was an emblem of various vices.
1. I.e., her virtue, which is fairer even than her beauty.

So while thy beauty draws the heart to love,
    As fast° thy Virtue bends that love to good;   *at the same rate*
    "But, ah," Desire still cries, "give me some food."

72

Desire, though thou my old companion art,
    And oft so clings to my pure Love that I
    One from the other scarcely can descry,°   *distinguish*
While each doth blow the fire of my heart,
5 Now from thy fellowship I needs must part:
    Venus is taught with Dian's[2] wings to fly;
    I must no more in thy sweet passions lie;
Virtue's gold now must head my Cupid's dart.
    Service and honor, wonder with delight,
10 Fear to offend, will worthy to appear,[3]
Care shining in mine eyes, faith in my sprite:°   *spirit*
These things are left me by my only dear.
    But thou, Desire, because thou wouldst have all,
    Now banished art. But yet alas how shall?

74

I never drank of Aganippe well,[4]
Nor ever did in shade of Tempe[5] sit;
And Muses scorn with vulgar° brains to dwell;   *common*
Poor layman I, for sacred rites unfit.
5 Some do I hear of poets' fury° tell,   *inspiration*
But God wot,° wot not what they mean by it;   *knows*
And this I swear by blackest brook of hell,[6]
I am no pick-purse of another's wit.
    How falls it then that with so smooth an ease
10 My thoughts I speak, and what I speak doth flow
In verse, and that my verse best wits doth please?
Guess we the cause. "What, is it thus?" Fie no.
    "Or so?" Much less. "How then?" Sure thus it is:
    My lips are sweet, inspired with Stella's kiss.[7]

81

O kiss, which dost those ruddy gems impart,
Or° gems, or fruits of new-found Paradise,   *either*
Breathing all bliss and sweet'ning to the heart,
Teaching dumb lips a nobler exercise!
5 O kiss, which souls, even souls, together ties

2. Diana, goddess of the moon and patron of chastity. Venus, goddess of beauty and love, mother of Cupid.
3. The phrase can mean either "the wish to appear worthy" or "desire that is worthy to appear [i.e., not shameful]."
4. The fountain at the foot of Mount Helicon in Greece, sacred to the Muses.
5. Valley beside Mount Olympus, sacred to Apollo, the god of poetry.
6. The most binding of all oaths were those sworn by the river Styx.
7. A kiss he stole from Stella when he caught her napping (Song 2).

By links of Love, and only Nature's art,
How fain° would I paint thee to all men's eyes,   *gladly*
Or of thy gifts at least shade out° some part.   *sketch*
    But she forbids, with blushing words she says
10   She builds her fame on higher-seated praise.
But my heart burns, I cannot silent be.
    Then since (dear life) you fain would have me peace,[8]
    And I, mad with delight, want wit[9] to cease,
Stop you my mouth with still still kissing me.

Fourth Song[1]

    Only joy, now here you are,
    Fit to hear and ease my care;
    Let my whispering voice obtain
    Sweet reward for sharpest pain:
5   Take me to thee, and thee to me.
    "No, no, no, no, my dear, let be."

    Night hath closed all in her cloak,
    Twinkling stars love-thoughts provoke,
    Danger hence good care doth keep,
10   Jealousy itself doth sleep:
    Take me to thee, and thee to me.
    "No, no, no, no, my dear, let be."

    Better place no wit can find,
    Cupid's yoke to loose or bind;
15   These sweet flowers on fine bed, too,
    Us in their best language woo:
    Take me to thee, and thee to me.
    "No, no, no, no, my dear, let be."

    This small light the moon bestows
20   Serves thy beams but to disclose,
    So to raise my hap° more high;   *good fortune*
    Fear not else, none can us spy:
    Take me to thee, and thee to me.
    "No, no, no, no, my dear, let be."

25   That you heard was but a mouse,
    Dumb sleep holdeth all the house;
    Yet asleep methinks they say,
    "Young folks, take time while you may."
    Take me to thee, and thee to me.
30   "No, no, no, no, my dear, let be."

    Niggard° Time threats, if we miss   *stingy*
    This large offer of our bliss,

8. You want me to be silent.
9. Lack the mental faculties.
1. Like Petrarch, Sidney intersperses songs (eleven of them, in various verse forms) in his sequence. Some of them incorporate Stella's voice. This song appears between sonnets 85 and 86.

Long stay° ere he grant the same;   *wait*
Sweet, then, while each thing doth frame,°   *serve*
35   Take me to thee, and thee to me.
"No, no, no, no, my dear, let be."

Your fair mother is abed,
Candles out, and curtains spread;
She thinks you do letters write:
40   Write, but first let me indite:°   *dictate*
Take me to thee, and thee to me.
"No, no, no, no, my dear, let be."

Sweet, alas, why strive you thus?
Concord better fitteth us.
45   Leave to Mars the force of hands;
Your power in your beauty stands:
Take me to thee, and thee to me.
"No, no, no, no, my dear, let be."

Woe to me, and do you swear
50   Me to hate? But I forbear.°   *desist*
Cursèd be my destines° all,   *fates*
That brought me so high to fall:
Soon with my death I will please thee.
"No, no, no, no, my dear, let be."

87

When I was forced from Stella ever dear,
Stella, food of my thoughts, heart of my heart,
Stella, whose eyes make all my tempests clear,
By iron laws of duty to depart,
5   Alas, I found that she with me did smart:°   *suffer*
I saw that tears did in her eyes appear;
I saw that sighs her sweetest lips did part,
And her sad words my sadded sense did hear.
    For me, I wept to see pearls scattered so,
10   I sighed her sighs, and wailèd for her woe,
Yet swam in joy, such love in her was seen.
    Thus while th' effect most bitter was to me,
    And nothing than the cause more sweet could be,
I had been° vexed, if vexed I had not been.   *i.e., would have been*

89²

Now that of absence the most irksome night
    With darkest shade doth overcome my day,
    Since Stella's eyes, wont° to give me my day,   *accustomed*
Leaving my hemisphere, leave me in night,

---

2. A sonnet with only two rhyme words, *night* and *day*.

5   Each day seems long, and longs for long-stayed° night,   *long-delayed*
     The night, as tedious, woos th' approach of day;
     Tired with the dusty toils of busy day,
Languished with horrors of the silent night,
Suffering the evils both of the day and night,
10   While no night is more dark than is my day,
Nor no day hath less quiet than my night,
     With such bad mixture of my night and day
That, living thus in blackest winter night,
     I feel the flames of hottest summer day.

91

Stella, while now by Honor's cruel might
     I am from° you, light of my life, mis-led,   *away from*
     And that fair you, my sun, thus overspread
With absence' veil, I live in Sorrow's night,
5   If this dark place yet shew,° like candlelight,   *show*
     Some beauty's piece,[3] as amber-colored head,
     Milk hands, rose cheeks, or lips more sweet, more red,
Or seeing jets,[4] black, but in blackness bright,
     They please I do confess, they please mine eyes;
10   But why? because of you they models be;
Models such be wood-globes of glist'ring° skies.[5]   *glittering*
Dear, therefore be not jealous over me,
     If you hear that they seem my heart to move:
     Not them, O no, but you in them I love.

94

Grief, find the words; for thou hast made my brain
     So dark with misty vapors which arise
     From out thy heavy mold,° that in-bent° eyes   *earth / inward-turned*
Can scarce discern the shape of mine own pain.
5   Do thou, then (for thou canst), do thou complain
     For[6] my poor soul, which now that sickness tries°   *experiences*
     Which even to sense, sense of itself denies,[7]
Though harbingers[8] of Death lodge there his train.
     Or if thy love of plaint° yet mine forbears,[9]   *complaint, lamentation*
10 As of a caitiff worthy so to die,
Yet wail thyself,° and wail with causeful° tears,   *for yourself / well-founded*
That though in wretchedness thy life doth lie,
Yet grow'st more wretched than thy nature bears,
By being placed in such a wretch as I.

---

3. Some beauties in other women.
4. I.e., jet-black eyes.
5. Wooden globes of the heavens, with painted constellations and planets.
6. "Complain / For": lament on behalf of.

7. I.e., his soul, sick unto death, is incapable of expression, cut off from the use of the senses.
8. Those sent in advance to find lodgings for a royal retinue ("train").
9. Nonetheless declines to make mine.

Eleventh Song[1]

"Who is it that this dark night
Underneath my window plaineth?"[2]
It is one who from thy sight
Being (ah) exiled, disdaineth
5 Every other, vulgar° light.   *common*

"Why, alas, and are you he?
Be not yet those fancies changèd?"
Dear, when you find change in me,
Though from me you be estrangèd,
10 Let my change to ruin be.

"Well, in absence this will die;
Leave° to see, and leave to wonder."   *cease*
Absence sure will help, if I
Can learn how myself to sunder
15 From what in my heart doth lie.

"But time will these thoughts remove:
Time doth work what no man knoweth."
Time doth as the subject prove;[3]
With time still° th' affection groweth   *ever*
20 In the faithful turtledove.

"What if you new beauties see;
Will not they stir new affection?"
I will think they pictures be,
Image-like of saint's perfection,
25 Poorly counterfeiting thee.

"But your reason's purest light,
Bids you leave such minds to nourish."[4]
Dear, do reason no such spite:
Never doth thy beauty flourish
30 More than in my reason's sight.

"But the wrongs love bears will make
Love at length leave undertaking."
No, the more fools it do shake,
In a ground of so firm making,
35 Deeper still they drive the stake.

"Peace, I think that some give ear:
Come no more, lest I get anger."[5]
Bliss, I will my bliss forbear,

1. This last song, a dialogue between Astrophil and Stella, is located between sonnets 104 and 105.
2. Complains (in song) of his love woes.
3. Things change in time according to their natures.
4. Stop indulging such thoughts.
5. The meaning is either "incur anger" or, perhaps, "become angry"—in any case, a threat designed to make Astrophil go away.

Fearing, sweet, you to endanger,
40   But my soul shall harbor there.

"Well, begone, begone I say,
  Lest that Argus'6 eyes perceive you."
O unjustest Fortune's sway,°   *power*
Which can make me thus to leave you,
45   And from louts to run away.

106

O absent presence, Stella is not here;
  False flattering Hope, that with so fair a face
  Bare me in hand,° that in this orphan place   *deceived me*
Stella, I say my Stella, should appear.
5 What say'st thou now? Where is that dainty cheer°   *countenance; food*
  Thou told'st mine eyes should help their famished case?
  But thou art gone, now that self-felt disgrace
Dost make me most to wish thy comfort near.
  But here I do store° of fair ladies meet,   *abundance*
10   Who may with charm of conversation sweet
Make in my heavy mold° new thoughts to grow: *earth*
  Sure they prevail as much with me, as he
  That bade his friend, but then new-maimed, to be
Merry with him, and not think of his woe.

108[7]

When Sorrow (using mine own fire's might)
  Melts down his lead into my boiling breast,
  Through that dark furnace to my heart oppressed
There shines a joy from thee, my only light;
5 But soon as thought of thee breeds my delight,
  And my young soul flutters to thee, his nest,
  Most rude Despair, my daily unbidden guest,
Clips straight° my wings, straight wraps me in his night,   *immediately*
  And makes me then bow down my head and say,
10 "Ah, what doth Phoebus'° gold that wretch avail,   *god of the sun*
Whom iron doors do keep from use of day?"
So strangely (alas) thy works in me prevail,
  That in my woes for thee thou art my joy,
  And in my joys for thee my only annoy.°   *trouble, pain*

1582?   1591, 1598

---

6. The hundred-eyed monster set by Juno to guard Io, a mistress of Jupiter whom Juno had transformed into a cow.

7. In many sonnet sequences, as here, the final poem brings no resolution.

MARY (SIDNEY) HERBERT,
COUNTESS OF PEMBROKE
1562–1621

When her brother, the celebrated courtier and author Philip Sidney, died, in 1586, Mary Sidney, the countess of Pembroke, became the custodian not only of his writings but also of his last name. Though her marriage in 1577 to Henry Herbert, the second earl of Pembroke, represented a great social advance for her family—her offspring would no longer be members of the gentry but rather would be among the nation's tiny hereditary nobility—yet throughout her life the countess of Pembroke held onto her identity as a Sidney.

She had good reason to do so. The Sidneys were celebrated for their generous support of poets, clergymen, alchemists, naturalists, scientists, and musicians. The Pembroke country estate, Wilton, quickly became a gathering place for thinkers who enjoyed the countess's patronage and shared her staunch Protestant convictions and her literary interests. Books, pamphlets, and scores of poems were dedicated to her in the 1590s and thereafter, as well as to her brother Robert (whose country house, Penshurst, is praised in a well-known poem by Ben Jonson). Nicholas Breton and Samuel Daniel in particular benefited from her support, as did her niece, goddaughter, and frequent companion, Mary Wroth.

In one of the dedicatory poems to *Salve Deus Rex Judaeorum*, Aemilia Lanyer praises Mary Sidney not only for her generosity toward poets but also for those "works that are more deep and more profound." These include her translation of Robert Garnier's neoclassical French tragedy *Antonius* and a translation of the religious tract *A Discourse of Life and Death* by the French Protestant Philippe de Mornay. Her translation of Petrarch's *Triumph of Death* was the first in English to maintain the original *terza rima* (a particularly challenging rhyme scheme for an English versifier). Although translation was considered an especially appropriate genre for women to work in, it is a mistake to assume that Mary Sidney's efforts as a poet are merely derivative: Elizabethans understood that translation offered the opportunity not only for the display of linguistic and technical skills but also for the indirect expression of personal and political concerns. Mary Sidney also expressed these concerns more directly: among her original poems was a powerful elegy for her brother Philip and a short pastoral entertainment for Queen Elizabeth.

Mary Sidney was best known for having prepared a composite edition of Philip Sidney's *Arcadia* and for contributing the larger number (107) of the verse translations of the 150 biblical psalms that her brother had begun. Her very free renderings re-create the psalms as English poems, using an amazing variety of stanzaic and metrical patterns and some strikingly effective images. Widely circulated in manuscript, this influential collection was an important bridge between the many metrical paraphrases of psalms in this period and the works of the great religious lyric poets of the seventeenth century, especially George Herbert. Donne's poem *Upon the Translation of the Psalms by Sir Philip Sidney and the Countess of Pembroke His Sister* testifies to that importance: "They tell us *why*, and teach us *how* to sing."*

---

* For Mary Sidney's elegy on Sir Philip Sidney, her translation of Psalm 58, and the King James Bible version of the psalms printed here, see the NAEL Archive.

Psalm 52

Tyrant, why swell'st thou thus,
    Of mischief vaunting?
Since help from God to us
    Is never wanting.

5 Lewd° lies thy tongue contrives,   *vile*
    Loud lies it soundeth;
Sharper than sharpest knives
    With lies it woundeth.

Falsehood thy wit° approves,   *mind*
10   All truth rejected:
Thy will all vices loves,
    Virtue neglected.

Not words from cursèd thee,
    But gulfs° are pourèd;   *abysses, yawning chasms*
15 Gulfs wherein daily be
    Good men devourèd.

Think'st thou to bear it° so?   *bear it off, triumph*
    God shall displace thee;
God shall thee overthrow,
20   Crush thee, deface° thee.   *destroy*

The just shall fearing see
    These fearful chances,
And laughing shoot at thee
    With scornful glances.

25 Lo, lo, the wretched wight,°   *creature*
    Who, God disdaining,
His mischief made his might,
    His guard his gaining.°   *riches*

I as an olive tree
30   Still green shall flourish:
God's house the soil shall be
    My roots to nourish.

My trust on his true love
    Truly attending,
35 Shall never thence remove,
    Never see ending.

Thee will I honor still,
    Lord, for this justice;
There fix my hopes I will
40   Where thy saints' trust is.

Thy saints trust in thy name,
Therein they joy them:
Protected by the same,
Nought° can annoy° them.   *nothing / harm*

Psalm 119: O[1]

Oh, what a lantern, what a lamp of light
     Is thy pure Word to me
To clear my paths and guide my goings right!
          I sware,° and swear again,   *swore*
5   I of the statutes will observer be,
          Thou° justly dost ordain.   *which thou*

The heavy weights of grief oppress me sore:°   *sorely, severely*
     Lord, raise me by thy Word,
As thou to me didst promise heretofore.
10   And this unforcèd praise
     I for an off'ring bring, accept, O Lord,
          And show to me thy ways.

What if my life lie naked[2] in my hand,
     To every chance exposed?
15   Should I forget what thou dost me command?
          No, no, I will not stray
     From thy edicts, though round about enclosed
          With snares the wicked lay.

Thy testimonies, as mine heritage,
205   I have retainèd still,
And unto them my heart's delight engage—
          My heart which still doth bend,
     And only bend to do what thou dost will,
          And do it to the end.

Psalm 139

O Lord, in me there lieth nought
     But to thy search revealèd lies:
          For when I sit
          Thou markest it;°   *you note it*

---

1. The 176 lines of Psalm 119 are divided into twenty-two sections of eight verses each, with the sections headed by, and their initial verses beginning with, successive letters of the Hebrew alphabet. Mary Sidney adopts the analogous procedure in English and also uses a different stanzaic form for each of the twenty-two sections.

2. I.e., exposed to danger.

5   No less thou notest when I rise;
      Yea, closest closet° of my thought   *most secret private chamber*
      Hath open windows to thine eyes.

    Thou walkest with me when I walk;
      When to my bed for rest I go,
10   I find thee there,
        And everywhere:
      Not youngest thought in me doth grow,
    No, not one word I cast° to talk   *resolve*
      But yet unuttered thou dost know.

15   If forth I march, thou goest before,
      If back I turn, thou com'st behind:
        So forth nor back
        Thy guard I lack,
      Nay, on me too thy hand I find.
20   Well I thy wisdom may adore,
      But never reach with earthy mind.

    To shun thy notice, leave thine eye,
      O whither might I take my way?
        To starry sphere?
25   Thy throne is there.
      To dead men's undelightsome stay?°   *place*
    There is thy walk, and there to lie
      Unknown° in vain I should assay.°   *(to thee) / attempt*

    O sun, whom light nor flight can match,
30   Suppose thy lightful flightful wings
        Thou lend to me,
        And I could flee
      As far as thee the ev'ning brings:
    Even led to west he would me catch,
35   Nor should I lurk° with western things.   *hide*

    Do thou thy best, O secret night,
      In sable veil to cover me:
        Thy sable veil
        Shall vainly fail;
40   With day unmasked my night shall be,
    For night is day and darkness light,
      O father of all lights, to thee.

    Each inmost piece in me is thine:
      While yet I in my mother dwelt,
45   All that me clad
        From thee I had.
      Thou in my frame° hast strangely dealt: *form*
    Needs in my praise thy works must shine,
      So inly them my thoughts have felt.

50 Thou, how my back was beam-wise laid,
   And raft'ring of my ribs, dost know;
          Know'st every point
          Of bone and joint,
   How to this whole these parts did grow,
55 In brave° embroid'ry fair arrayed,   *splendid*
   Though wrought in shop both dark and low.

Nay, fashionless, ere form I took,
   Thy all and more beholding eye
          My shapeless shape
60   Could not escape:
   All these, with times appointed by,[1]
   Ere one had being, in the book
      Of thy foresight enrolled did lie.

My God, how I these studies prize,
65   That do thy hidden workings show!
          Whose sum is such
          No sum so much:
   Nay, summed as° sand they sumless grow.   *like*
   I lie to sleep, from sleep I rise,
70   Yet still° in thought with thee I go.   *always*

My God, if thou but one[2] wouldst kill,
   Then straight would leave my further chase[3]
          This cursèd brood
          Inured to blood,
75   Whose graceless taunts at thy disgrace
   Have aimèd oft, and hating still
      Would with proud lies thy truth outface.°   *defy*

Hate not I them, who thee do hate?
   Thine, Lord, I will the censure be.[4]
80   Detest I not
          The cankered knot
   Whom I against thee banded see?
   O Lord, thou know'st in highest rate
      I hate them all as foes to me.

85 Search me, my God, and prove my heart,
   Examine me, and try° my thought;   *test*
          And mark in me
          If ought° there be   *aught, anything*
   That hath with cause their anger wrought.
90 If not (as not) my life's each part,
   Lord, safely guide from danger brought.

ca. 1595   1823

---

1. With appropriate times indicated (for each
step of the work of creation).
2. Only one (wicked man).

3. Then immediately [the wicked] would stop
pursuing me.
4. I.e., I leave it to you to censure them.

The Wider World

Othello first captured Desdemona's attention, he recalls, by telling her his "traveler's history,"

> Wherein of antars [caves] vast and deserts idle,
> Rough quarries, rocks, and hills whose heads touch heaven,
> It was my hint to speak—such was my process—
> And of the cannibals that each other eat,
> The anthropophagi, and men whose heads
> Do grow beneath their shoulders. (1.3.139–44)

The Venetian heiress was not the only person in the period who found such stories thrilling. In the sixteenth century, narratives of adventure, exploration, trade, and reconnaissance proliferated throughout western Europe and circulated widely both in manuscript and in print. The public's interest in them was not entirely new. Shakespeare probably found his more exotic details in *Mandeville's Travels*, an immensely popular fourteenth-century text still read throughout the Renaissance. Columbus took a copy with him on his first voyage, and even a century later, though skepticism about the book's wilder claims had begun to grow, Sir Walter Ralegh in what is now Venezuela continued to be on the lookout for "men whose heads / Do grow beneath their shoulders."*

But in the wake of Columbus's epochal encounter and the voyages that followed, there was a flood of new reports about places and peoples whose existence had been hitherto unknown. At stake was far more than idle curiosity. With Muslim powers in control of the key eastern Mediterranean ports and trade routes, Europeans had long been searching for an alternative route to the spices and silks of the East. Columbus believed that he had discovered such a route—he initially thought he had reached islands off the coast of India or China—but disappointment that he had not done so was assuaged, especially after the conquest of the Aztec and Inca Empires, by the enormous quantity of gold, silver, and pearls that the treasure fleets began to carry back to Spain. The major European states strengthened their fleets, supplied them with ordnance, recruited armies and navies, and fiercely competed with one another in laying claim to potentially lucrative overseas territories.

But the New World was not the only site of contest. The Mediterranean had long been the locus of commercial and military struggles, with islands like Sicily, Cyprus, Malta, and Rhodes particularly vulnerable to attempted invasion by one or another European power and by the Muslim states of Turkey and North Africa. Competition existed as well along the coasts of Africa, where access to trade in gold, ivory, and slaves had aroused the greed of merchants and their royal protectors. Wherever there was the promise of gain—in Russia, Scandinavia, Poland, and elsewhere—there were diplomatic maneuverings and trade agreements. In such a constantly shifting scene, traditional allies could suddenly become dangerous rivals; conversely, bitter enemies could forge convenient alliances.

From their position of relative isolation—a Protestant island-nation at the geographical margins of Europe—the English in the sixteenth century proved themselves to be remarkably energetic players in this increasingly global competition. Though they failed to equal the astonishing Spanish and Portuguese enterprises of

---

* For an engraving of these strange men, see below, p. 804.

exploration and conquest, the range of sixteenth-century English naval and overland ventures is extraordinary. In 1496 John Cabot, a Venetian tradesman living in Bristol, was granted a license by Henry VII to sail on a voyage of exploration and the following year, with his son Sebastian, reached northern North America, making landfall on Newfoundland or perhaps Nova Scotia. Anthony Jenkinson, working for the Muscovy Company, met Czar Ivan the Terrible in Russia, traveled from Moscow to Bukhara, and then embarked on a further expedition, to Persia; Sir Martin Frobisher explored bleak Baffin Island in search of a Northwest Passage to the Orient; Sir John Davis explored the west coast of Greenland and discovered the Falkland Islands off the coast of Argentina; Ralph Fitch made it all the way to Goa and Siam; Sir John Hawkins made large profits for himself and his investors (including the queen) by carrying shiploads of black slaves from West Africa for sale in the Caribbean; Philip Amadas and Arthur Barlowe led an expedition, financed by Sir Walter Ralegh, to Virginia; Ralegh himself ventured up the Orinoco delta in search of the mythical land of El Dorado. In a three-year voyage from 1577 to 1580, Sir Francis Drake circumnavigated the globe on his ship *The Golden Hind*, laying claim to California on behalf of the queen, and a few years later Drake's astonishing feat of navigation was repeated by a ship commanded by Thomas Cavendish.

Accounts of these and many other exploits were collected by a clergyman, geographer, and tireless promoter of empire, Richard Hakluyt (1552?–1616), and published as *The principal navigations, voiages, traffiques, and discoveries of the English Nation* (1589; expanded three-volume edition 1598–1600). Hakluyt writes that he was incited to undertake his huge editorial labors during a stay in France, where he heard "other nations miraculously extolled for their discoveries and notable enterprises by sea, but the English of all others for their sluggish security and continual neglect of the like attempts, either ignominiously reported or exceedingly condemned." His response was to assemble the records of English voyages "to the most remote and farthest distant quarters of the earth."

Hakluyt's focus was by no means exclusively on voyages to the New World. The perilous enterprise in which he hoped "the English nation" would prevail was global in its scope and required an almost limitless curiosity. It was as critically important, he believed, for his countrymen to learn about Muscovy as about Cuba; as vital to English interests to chart the coast around Sierra Leone as around Virginia; as useful to collect infor-

The title page of the first modern atlas, Abraham Ortelius's 1570 *Theatrum orbis terrarum* (Theater of the World), features allegorical figures of the known continents, with Europe as a queen enthroned at the top; Asia as an oriental princess holding an incense burner; half-clad Africa with a sprig of balsam; and naked America as an Amazonian warrior holding a severed head.

mation on China as on Brazil. There were strong xenophobic currents in English society, and a belligerent insistence on the absolute truth of Protestant Christianity. But Hakluyt understood that his nation's success in the competitive, often violent struggle to explore, chart, and exploit the natural and human resources of the globe depended on the enterprise of assembling as much reliable information as possible, preferably from eyewitness sources.

To be of full use, both for England's practical endeavors and for the general goal of understanding the world, that information would have to reach beyond physical geography to the social practices and beliefs, including religious beliefs, of alien peoples. Hence, for example, Sir Walter Ralegh sent the deeply impressive intellectual Thomas Hariot to observe the Algonkian natives of Virginia and to describe in detail their technology, society, and conceptions of the world. Hariot's ethnographic observations were supplemented by beautiful watercolors by the talented artist and cartographer John White. (One of these watercolors is reproduced in the color insert in this volume.)

The Algonkians were entirely new to the English and therefore aroused particular curiosity, but a comparable attention extended to parts of the world that were at least partially known and to peoples traditionally regarded as mortal enemies. In 1600 a protégé of Hakluyt, John Pory, undertook to translate and publish the *Geographical History of Africa* (completed in 1526) by "John Leo Africanus," a Muslim-born traveler whose vivid descriptions were widely regarded as a crucial resource for understanding that entire continent. Also around the turn of the seventeenth century, Thomas Dallam and Richard Knolles wrote accounts of the Ottoman Empire that manifested a more nuanced and ambivalent attitude to the great and fearsome Islamic power than might be expected. Popular plays on the Elizabethan stage continued to feature parodic versions of the Muslim enemy, but Queen Elizabeth's foreign policy envisaged the possibility of an alliance with rulers in Turkey and Morocco against the Spanish, and English readers could for the first time in this period begin to find reasonably detailed accounts not only of the Sultan's court and the organization of his state but also of Islam.

"To seek new worlds for gold, for praise, for glory," as Ralegh characterized the enterprises he and his contemporaries undertook, was not for the faint of heart: Drake, Cavendish, Frobisher, and Hawkins all died at sea, as did huge numbers of those who sailed under their command. Elizabethans who were sensible enough to stay at home could have material glimpses of their fellow countrymen's far-reaching voyages. Expeditions brought back native plants and their products (including tomatoes, pineapples, chocolate, and tobacco), animals, cultural artifacts, and, on occasion, samples of the native peoples themselves, most often seized against their will. There were exhibitions in London of a kidnapped Eskimo with his kayak and of Virginians with their canoes. Most of these miserable captives, violently uprooted and vulnerable to European diseases, quickly perished, but even in death they were evidently valuable property: while the English will not give one small coin "to relieve a lame beggar," one of the characters in *The Tempest* wryly remarks, "they will lay out ten to see a dead Indian" (2.2.30–31).

But the principal way in which stay-at-homes encountered the rapidly expanding world was through eyewitness accounts of the kind we present here. These accounts were not, on the whole, rhetorically ornate. Travelers' tales had an ancient and well-deserved reputation for self-inflation, exaggeration, and outright mendacity, and consequently Elizabethan writers strove for the effect of factual directness, simplicity, and trustworthiness. As ever more narratives of voyages to remote places circulated, Elizabethan readers evidently became more discriminating in sorting out truth from fable. In his first edition Hakluyt included *Mandeville's Travels*, but he quietly dropped it from the second edition.

Yet the encounters described in many of the reports printed in Hakluyt and elsewhere were so remarkable, calling into question so many of Elizabethan culture's rooted assumptions about human behavior, that even in their sober just-the-facts style they often convey the mingled wonder, fear, and longing that characterize the most extravagant literary romances. The greatest Elizabethan writer of romance, Edmund Spenser, acknowledged the affinity between reported truth and apparent fable in defending his Faerie Land against anyone who might complain that it was unreal:

> But let that man with better sense advise,
>   That of the world least part to us is read:
>   And daily how through hardy enterprise
>   Many great regions are discoverèd,
>   Which to late age were never mentionèd.
>   Who ever heard of th'Indian Peru?
>   Or who in venturous vessel measurèd
>   The Amazons' huge river, now found true?
> Or fruitfullest Virginia who did ever view?
>
> (*The Faerie Queene*, Book 2, Proem)

HAKLUYT'S DEDICATORY EPISTLE TO *THE PRINCIPAL NAVIGATIONS*, 1589

Educated at Westminster School and at Christ Church College, Oxford, Richard Hakluyt (1552?–1616) was an ordained minister in the Church of England. He is famous for his tireless efforts as a writer and editor to promote the English settlement of North America and to chronicle English maritime achievements. His major work was a monumental collection published as *The principal navigations, voiages, traffiques and discoveries of the English nation, made by sea or over-land, to the remote and farthest distant quarters of the earth*. The work assembled a vast array of texts ranging from a description of King Arthur's purported conquests in the sixth century to eyewitness accounts of contemporary voyages of exploration in the Americas, Africa, and Asia. In the dedicatory epistle to Sir Francis Walsingham, Hakluyt recalls the moment when as a boy he first was seized with what became his lifelong fascination with the literature of travel. Apart from travel to Paris, where he served for a time as chaplain to the English ambassador, he himself never set out on any of the voyages whose records he was instrumental in preserving and printing.

From To the Right Honorable Sir Francis Walsingham,[1] Knight, principal secretary to Her Majesty, chancellor of the duchy of Lancaster, and one of Her Majesty's most honorable privy council

Right honorable, I do remember that being a youth and one of Her Majesty's scholars at Westminster,[2] that fruitful nursery, it was my hap to visit the chamber of M[aster] Richard Hakluyt, my cousin, a gentleman of the Middle Temple,[3] well known unto you, at a time when I found lying open upon his board[4] certain books of cosmography, with an universal map. He, seeing me somewhat curious in the view thereof, began to instruct my ignorance by showing me the division of the earth into three parts after the old account,[5] and then, according to the latter and better distribution, into more; he pointed with his wand[6] to all the known seas, gulfs, bays, straits, capes, rivers, empires, kingdoms, dukedoms, and territories of each part, with declaration also of their special commodities and particular wants, which by the benefit of traffic[7] and intercourse of merchants are plentifully supplied. From the map he brought me to the Bible, and, turning to the 107th Psalm, directed me to the twenty-third and twenty-fourth verses, where I read that they which go down to the sea in ships and occupy[8] by the great waters, they see the works of the Lord and his wonders in the deep, etc. Which words of the prophet, together with my cousin's discourse (things of high and rare delight to my young nature), took in me so deep an impression that I constantly resolved if ever I were preferred to the university, where better time and more convenient place might be ministered for these studies, I would by God's assistance prosecute that knowledge and kind of literature, the doors whereof (after a sort) were so happily opened before me.

According to which my resolution, when, not long after, I was removed to Christ Church[9] in Oxford, my exercises of duty first performed, I fell to my intended course, and by degrees read over whatsoever printed or written discoveries and voyages I found extant either in the Greek, Latin, Italian, Spanish, Portugal, French, or English languages, and in my public lectures was the first that produced and showed both the old imperfectly composed and the new lately reformed maps, globes, spheres, and other instruments of this art for demonstration in the common schools, to the singular pleasure and general contentment of my auditory. In continuance of time, and by reason principally of my insight in this study, I grew familiarly acquainted with the chiefest captains at sea, the greatest merchants, and the best mariners of our nation; by which means having

1. Elizabeth I's secretary of state, Walsingham (ca. 1532–1590) was also her spymaster.
2. The famous preparatory school founded by Henry VIII in the precinct of Westminster Abbey.
3. One of the four Inns of Court—the legal societies of London, which educated all English lawyers and provided many of them with their chambers.
4. Table.
5. Medieval maps of the world showed its land mass divided into Asia, Europe, and Africa.
6. Rod or stick (not a magic one).
7. Trade.
8. Do business.
9. Christ Church College.

gotten somewhat more than common knowledge, I passed at length the narrow seas into France with Sir Edward Stafford, Her Majesty's careful and discreet ligier,[1] where, during my five years' abode with him in his dangerous and chargeable[2] residency in Her Highness' service, I both heard in speech and read in books other nations miraculously extolled for their discoveries and notable enterprises by sea, but the English of all others for their sluggish security[3] and continual neglect of the like attempts, especially in so long and happy a time of peace, either ignominiously reported or exceedingly condemned; which singular opportunity if some other people our neighbors had been blessed with, their protestations are often and vehement, they would far otherwise have used. * * * Thus both hearing and reading the obloquy of our nation, and finding few or none of our own men able to reply herein, and, further, not seeing any man to have care to recommend[4] to the world the industrious labors and painful travels of our countrymen; for stopping the mouths of the reproachers, myself being the last winter returned from France with the honorable the Lady Sheffield, for her passing[5] good behavior highly esteemed in all the French court, determined notwithstanding all difficulties to undertake the burden of that work wherein all others pretended either ignorance or lack of leisure or want of sufficient argument,[6] whereas (to speak truly) the huge toil and the small profit to ensue were the chief causes of the refusal. I call the work a burden in consideration that these voyages[7] lay so dispersed, scattered, and hidden in several hucksters' hands[8] that I now wonder at myself to see how I was able to endure the delays, curiosity,[9] and backwardness of many from whom I was to receive my originals.* * *

To harp no longer upon this string, and to speak a word of that just commendation which our nation do indeed deserve, it cannot be denied but as in all former ages they have been men full of activity, stirrers abroad, and searchers of the remote parts of the world, so in this most famous and peerless government of Her Most Excellent Majesty, her subjects through the special assistance and blessing of God in searching the most opposite corners and quarters of the world and, to speak plainly, in compassing[1] the vast globe of the earth more than once, have excelled all the nations and people of the earth. For which of the kings of this land before Her Majesty had their banners ever seen in the Caspian Sea? Which of them hath ever dealt with the emperor of Persia, as Her Majesty hath done, and obtained for her merchants large and loving privileges? Who ever saw, before this regiment,[2] an English ligier in the stately porch of the grand signior[3] at Constantinople? Who ever found English consuls and agents at Tripoli in Syria, at Aleppo,[4] at Babylon, at Balsara, and,

---

1. Ambassador—in Paris, where Hakluyt was Stafford's chaplain.
2. Important.
3. Complacency.
4. Commend.
5. Surpassingly.
6. Subject matter.
7. I.e., the written accounts of the voyages.

8. I.e., in various places from which they were unlikely to be recovered.
9. Whims.
1. Circumnavigating.
2. Reign.
3. The sultan of Turkey. "Porch": i.e., the Sublime Porte; the sultan's court or palace.
4. Like Tripoli, a city in Syria.

which is more, who ever heard of Englishman at Goa[5] before now? What English ships did heretofore ever anker in the mighty River of Plate,[6] pass and repass the unpassable (in former opinion) Strait of Magellan,[7] range along the coast of Chile, Peru, and all the back side of Nova Hispania[8] further than any Christian ever passed, traverse the mighty breadth of the South Sea, land upon the Luzones[9] in despight of the enemy, enter into alliance, amity, and traffic with the princes of the Moluccas[1] and the Isle of Java, double the famous Cape of Bona Speranza,[2] arrive at the Isle of Santa Helena,[3] and last of all return home most richly laden with the commodities of China, as the subjects of this now flourishing monarchy have done?

Lucius Florus in the very end of his history *De gestis Romanorum*[4] recordeth as a wonderful miracle that the Seres (which I take to be the people of Cathay, or China) sent ambassadors to Rome to entreat friendship, as moved with the fame of the majesty of the Roman Empire. And have not we as good cause to admire that the kings of the Moluccas and Java Major[5] have desired the favor of Her Majesty and the commerce and traffic of her people? Is it not as strange that the born naturals of Japan and the Philippines are here to be seen, agreeing with our climate, speaking our language, and informing us of the state of their eastern habitations? For mine own part, I take it as a pledge of God's further favor both to us and to them: to them especially, unto whose doors I doubt not in time shall be by us carried the incomparable treasure of the truth of Christianity and of the gospel, while we use and exercise common trade with their merchants. * * *

Now whereas I have always noted your wisdom to have had a special care of the honor of Her Majesty, the good reputation of our country, and the advancing of navigation, the very walls of this our island, as the oracle is reported to have spoken of the sea forces of Athens;[6] and whereas I acknowledge in all dutiful sort how honorably both by your letter and speech I have been animated in this and other my travels, I see myself bound to make presentment of this work to yourself, as the fruits of your own encouragements and the manifestation both of my unfeigned service to my prince and country and of my particular duty to your honor; which I have done with the less suspicion either of not satisfying the world or of not answering your own expectation, in that according to your order it hath passed the sight

---

5. Capital of the Portuguese colony in India. Balsara is another Indian city.
6. The Rio de la Plata (River of Silver), the large estuary between present-day Argentina and Uruguay.
7. The strait, notoriously difficult to navigate, between mainland South America and Tierra del Fuego.
8. New Spain: loosely used of South and Central America as a whole. Chile and Peru occupy much of its "back side" (western side), reached by the Strait of Magellan.
9. The Philippines, held by Spain.
1. The Spice Islands, an Indonesian archipelago.
2. The Cape of Good Hope, near the southern

tip of Africa.
3. A South Atlantic island about twelve hundred miles west of Africa, later best known as the place of exile of Napoleon Bonaparte.
4. *On the Deeds of the Romans*. Florus's work (2nd century C.E.), a history of Rome from its founding to the age of Augustus, is now usually known as the *Epitome of All the Wars during Seven Hundred Years*.
5. The Indonesian island of Java.
6. In 480 B.C.E., the Delphic Oracle prophesied that Athens could be saved from the Persian invaders by a "wall of wood." The Athenian politician and general Themistocles interpreted this—correctly, as it turned out—as referring to the wooden ships of the Athenian navy.

and party also the censure of the learned physician M[aster] Doctor James,[7] a man many ways very notably qualified.

And thus beseeching God, the giver of all true honor and wisdom, to increase both these blessings in you, with continuance of health, strength, happiness, and whatsoever good thing else yourself can wish, I humbly take my leave. London, the seventeenth of November.

Your honor's most humble
always to be commanded,
Richard Hakluyt

1589   1589, 1598–1600

7. Nothing more is known about this acquaintance of Hakluyt's.

LEO AFRICANUS ON THE NORTH AFRICANS, 1526

Born in Muslim Granada, al-Hasan ibn Muhammad al-Wazzan al-Fasi (1494–1554), as he was named at birth, was a boundary crosser throughout his life. Raised and educated in Morocco, he traveled widely in North Africa on diplomatic and other business. Captured by Spanish pirates in 1518, he was enslaved and then, when his masters realized his importance, sent to Rome, where he was presented to Pope Leo X. There he converted to Christianity and was given the name Giovanni Leone (John Leo), to which the pope, serving as his godfather, added the last name de' Medici. In 1526 he completed his long, important book on Africa, which was in manuscript circulation before it was printed in a best-selling Italian edition in 1550 and subsequently in French, Latin, and English translations. Leo's vision of Africa—a view notable for its complexity, ambiguity, and richness—had a major impact on European understanding of the continent's geography and peoples. His book's impact on Shakespeare's *Othello* has been most often remarked, but its influence extends well beyond that play.

From A Geographical History of Africa, Written in Arabic and Italian by John Leo a Moor, born in Granada and brought up in Barbary.[1] * * * Translated and collected by John Pory.

From *The commendable actions and virtues of the Africans*

Those Arabians which inhabit in Barbary or upon the coast of the Mediterranean Sea are greatly addicted unto the study of good arts and sciences; and those things which concern their law and religion are esteemed by them in the first place. Moreover, they have been heretofore most studious

1. Old name for the Arab countries along the coast of North Africa west of Egypt. Leo grew up in Morocco.

of the mathematics, of philosophy, and of astrology:[2] but these arts * * * were four hundred years ago utterly destroyed and taken away by the chief professors of their law.[3] The inhabitants of cities do most religiously observe and reverence those things which appertain unto their religion: yea they honor those doctors and priests of whom they learn their law as if they were petty gods. Their churches they frequent very diligently, to the end they may repeat certain prescript[4] and formal prayers; most superstitiously persuading themselves that the same day wherein they make their prayers it is not lawful for them to wash certain of their members, whenas at other times they will wash their whole bodies. * * *

Moreover, those which inhabit Barbary are of great cunning and dexterity for building and for mathematical inventions, which a man may easily conjecture by their artificial[5] works. Most honest people they are, and destitute of all fraud and guile; not only embracing all simplicity and truth but also practicing the same throughout the whole course of their lives, albeit certain Latin authors which have written of the same regions are far otherwise of opinion. Likewise they are most strong and valiant people, especially those which dwell upon the mountains. They keep their covenant most faithfully, insomuch that they had rather die than break promise. No nation in the world is so subject unto jealousy, for they will rather leese their lives than put up[6] any disgrace in the behalf of their women. So desirous they are of riches and honor that therein no other people can go beyond them. They travel, in a manner, over the whole world to exercise traffic.[7] For they are continually to be seen in Egypt, in Ethiopia, in Arabia, Persia, India, and Turkey: and whithersoever they go, they are most honorably esteemed of: for none of them will profess any art[8] unless he hath attained unto great exactness and perfection therein. They have always been much delighted with all kind of civility and modest behavior, and it is accounted heinous among them for any man to utter in company any bawdy or unseemly word. They have always in mind this sentence[9] of a grave author: "Give place to thy superior." If any youth, in presence of his father, his uncle, or any other of his kindred doth sing or talk aught of love matters, he is deemed to be worthy of grievous punishment. Whatsoever lad or youth there lighteth by chance into any company which discourseth of love, no sooner heareth nor understandeth what their talk tendeth unto but immediately he withdraweth himself from among them. These are the things which we thought most worthy of relation as concerning the civility, humanity, and upright dealing of the Barbarians:[1] let us now proceed unto the residue.

2. At the time, all practical applications of astronomical knowledge (e.g., forecasting tides) and not, as later, only the supposed art ("judicial astrology") of foretelling human affairs by interpreting the motions of heavenly bodies. "Philosophy": presumably in the old, broad sense that encompasses all the liberal arts, including the sciences ("*natural philosophy*").
3. The great scientific and cultural flourishing of the Islamic Golden Age of the 7th to 13th centuries C.E. ended for a number of reasons, including successive waves of invasions, beginning in the 13th century, of Arab lands by Mongols, Christians, and Turks—with attendant destruction of cultural

institutions such as libraries and schools—but also including the rise of currents of Islamic religious and legal thought not favoring rationalistic inquiry. "Professors": professed authorities (not just professors in the modern sense).
4. Prescribed.
5. Artfully made.
6. Put up with, endure. "Leese": lose.
7. I.e., to carry on trade. "In a manner": as one might say.
8. Craft; skill.
9. Maxim.
1. People of Barbary.

Those Arabians which dwell in tents, that is to say, which bring up cattle,[2] are of a more liberal and civil disposition: to wit, they are, in their kind, as devout, valiant, patient, courteous, hospital, and as honest in life and conversation,[3] as any other people. They be most faithful observers of their word and promise, insomuch that the people which, before, we said to dwell in the mountains are greatly stirred up with emulation of their virtues. Howbeit the said mountainers both for learning, for virtue, and for religion are thought much inferior to the Numidians,[4] albeit they have little or no knowledge at all in natural philosophy. They are valiant, and exceeding lovers and practicers of all humanity.[5] Also the Moors and Arabians inhabiting Libya are somewhat civil of behavior, being plain dealers, void of dissimulation, favorable to strangers, and lovers of simplicity. Those which we before named white or tawny Moors[6] are most steadfast in friendship, as likewise they indifferently[7] and favorably esteem of other nations: and wholly endeavor themselves in this one thing, namely, that they may lead a most pleasant and jocund life. Moreover, they maintain most learned professors of liberal arts and such men as are most devout in their religion. Neither is there any people in all Africa that lead a more happy and honorable life.

What vices the foresaid Africans are subject unto

Never was there any people or nation so perfectly endued with virtue but that they had their contrary faults and blemishes. Now therefore let us consider whether the vices of the Africans do surpass their virtues and good parts. Those which we named the inhabitants of the cities of Barbary are somewhat needy and covetous, being also very proud and high-minded,[8] and wonderfully addicted unto wrath; insomuch that (according to the proverb) they will deeply engrave in marble any injury be it never so small, and will in no wise blot it out of their remembrance. So rustical[9] they are and void of good manners that scarcely can any stranger obtain their familiarity and friendship. Their wits are but mean,[1] and they are so credulous that they will believe matters impossible which are told them. So ignorant are they of natural philosophy that they imagine all the effects and operations of nature to be extraordinary and divine. They observe no certain order of living nor of laws. Abounding exceedingly with choler,[2] they speak always with an angry and loud voice. Neither shall you walk in the daytime in any of their streets but you shall see commonly two or three of them together by the ears.[3] By nature they are a vile and base people, being no better accounted of by their governors[4] than if they were

2. Livestock generally (not just cows).
3. Behavior. "Kind": nature. "Hospital": hospitable.
4. *Numidia* was the long-surviving Roman name for the part of North Africa that roughly corresponds to modern Algeria and Tunisia.
5. Kindness, benevolence.
6. Leo had earlier distinguished between black Africans and the lighter-complexioned peoples of North Africa.

7. Impartially.
8. Haughty.
9. Boorish.
1. Inferior.
2. Bile, an overabundance of which was thought, in the old physiology, to produce an irascible temperament.
3. I.e., Fighting.
4. Rulers.

dogs. They have neither judges nor lawyers, by whose wisdom and counsel they ought to be directed. They are utterly unskillful in trades of merchandise, being destitute of bankers and moneychangers: wherefore a merchant can do nothing among them in his absence, but is himself constrained to go in person whithersoever his wares are carried. No people under heaven are more addicted unto covetise[5] than this nation; neither is there (I think) to be found among them one of an hundred who for courtesy, humanity, or devotion's sake will vouchsafe any entertainment[6] upon a stranger. Mindful they have always been of injuries, but most forgetful of benefits. Their minds are perpetually possessed with vexation and strife, so that they will seldom or never show themselves tractable to any man; the cause whereof is supposed to be for that[7] they are so greedily addicted unto their filthy lucre that they never could attain unto any kind of civility or good behavior.

The shepherds of that region live a miserable, toilsome, wretched, and beggarly life: they are a rude[8] people and (as a man may say) born and bred to theft, deceit, and brutish manners. Their young men may go a-wooing to divers maids, till such time as they have sped of[9] a wife. Yea the father of the maid most friendly welcometh her suitor, so that I think scarce any noble or gentleman among them can choose a virgin for his spouse; albeit so soon as any woman is married she is quite forsaken of all her suitors, who then seek out other new paramours for their liking. Concerning their religion, the greater part of these people are neither Mohammedans, Jews, nor Christians; and hardly shall you find so much as a spark of piety in any of them. They have no churches at all nor any kind of prayers, but being utterly estranged from all godly devotion they lead a savage and beastly life: and if any man chanceth to be of a better disposition (because they have no lawgivers nor teachers among them),[1] he is constrained to follow the example of other men's lives and manners.

All the Numidians, being most ignorant of natural, domestical, and commonwealth matters,[2] are principally addicted unto treason, treachery, murder, theft, and robbery. This nation, because it is most slavish, will right gladly accept of any service among the Barbarians, be it never so vile or contemptible. For some will take upon them to be dung-farmers, others to be scullions, some others to be ostlers[3] and suchlike servile occupations. Likewise the inhabitants of Libya live a brutish kind of life, who neglecting all kinds of good arts and sciences do wholly apply their minds unto theft and violence. Never as yet had they any religion, any laws, or any good form of living, but always had, and ever will have, a most miserable and distressed life. There cannot any treachery or villainy be invented so damnable which for lucre's sake they dare not attempt. They spend all their days either in most lewd practices, or in hunting, or else in warfare; neither wear they any shoes nor garments. The Negroes likewise lead a beastly kind of

---

5. Covetousness.
6. Hospitality.
7. Because.
8. Uncivilized.
9. Succeeded in acquiring. "Divers": various.
1. The idea is that, in the absence of lawgivers

and teachers, good dispositions can occur only by chance.
2. Matters of the common good.
3. Stablemen. "Dung-farmers": those contracted to remove dung and refuse. "Scullions": kitchen servants.

life, being utterly destitute of the use of reason, of dexterity, of wit,[4] and of all arts. Yea they so behave themselves as if they had continually lived in a forest among wild beasts. They have great swarms of harlots among them, whereupon a man may easily conjecture their manner of living; except their conversation[5] perhaps be somewhat more tolerable who dwell in the principal towns and cities: for it is like that they are somewhat more addicted[6] to civility.

1526   1600

4. Intellect. "Dexterity": here, mental adroit-   5. Behavior.
ness.   6. Accustomed. "Like": likely.

AN ENGLISH TRAVELER'S GUIDE
TO THE NORTH AFRICANS, 1547

Andrew Borde (or Boorde) (ca. 1490–1549) was a physician, a traveler, and the author of books on medicine and on astronomy. *The First Book of the Introduction of Knowledge* (1547) describes the customs and manners of various nations, from the English and their neighbors to the Moors, the Turks, the Egyptians, and the Jews. For each nation Borde includes a satirical description in verse and a few phrases in the local language.

From The First Book of the Introduction of Knowledge

[THE MOORS WHICH DO DWELL IN BARBARY]

I am a black Moor born in Barbary;[1]
Christian men for money oft doth me buy.
If I be unchristened, merchants do not care,
They buy me in markets, be I never so bare.
Yet will I be a good diligent slave,
Although I do stand in stead[2] of a knave.
I do gather figs, and with some I wipe my tail:
To be angry with me, what shall it avail?

Barbary is a great country, and plentiful of fruit, wine, and corn.[3] The inhabitors be called the Moors. There be white Moors and black Moors. They be infidels and unchristened. There be many Moors brought into Christendom, into great cities and towns, to be sold. And Christian men do buy them, and they will be diligent, and will do all manner of service.

1. North Africa west of Egypt.   3. Grain (in general).
2. In the place of.

A **Moor**. From Cesare Vacellio, *Degli habiti* (1590).

But they be set most commonly to vile things. They be called slaves. They do gather grapes and figs, and with some of the figs they will wipe their tail, and put them in the frail.[4] They have great lips, and knotted hair, black and curled. Their skin is soft, and there is nothing white but their teeth and the white of the eye. When a merchant or any other man do buy them, they be not all of one price, for some be better cheap than some; they be sold after as they can work and do their business. When they do die, they be cast into the water, or on a dunghill, that dogs and pies[5] and crows may eat them, except some of them that be christened: they be buried. They do keep much of Mohammed's law, as the Turks do. They have now a great captain called Barbarossa[6] which is a great warrior. They doth harm, divers times, to the Genoese, and to Provence and Languedoc, and other countries that do border on them, and for they will come over the straits, steal pigs, and geese, and other things.

Whoso will speak any Moorish,[7] English and Moorish doth follow.

One. two. three. four. five. six. seven.
    Wada. attennin. talate. orba. camata. sette. saba.
eight. nine. ten. eleven. twelve. thirteen.
    camene. tessa. asshera. habasshe. atanasshe. telatasshe.
fourteen. fifteen. sixteen. seventeen.
    arbatasshe. camatasshe. setatasshe. sabatashe.
eighteen. nineteen. twenty. one and twenty, etc.
    tematasshe. tyssatasshe. essherte. wahadaessherte, etc.

Good morrow.
    Sabaskyr.
Give me some bread and milk and cheese.
    Atteyne gobbis, leben, juben.
Give me wine, water, flesh, fish, and eggs.
    Atteyne nebet, moy, laghe, semek, beyet.

4. Basket made of rushes.
5. Magpies.
6. The Turk Khayr-al-Din (d. 1546), known to Europeans as Barbarossa ("Redbeard" in Italian), ruled Algiers and was a notorious pirate who later became admiral-in-chief of the Ottoman Empire.
7. This "Moorish" is a poorly transcribed dialect of Arabic.

Much good do it you.
Sahagh.
You be welcome.
Marrehababack.
I thank you.
Erthar lake heracke.
Good night.
Mesalkyr.

1542   1547

A VOYAGE TO EQUATORIAL AFRICA, 1554

A Cambridge graduate whose professional interests included chemistry and alchemy, Richard Eden (ca. 1520–1576) is best known as a translator of works on the New World and as an early promoter of English overseas ventures. His translation of Peter Martyr's *Decades of the New World or West India* (1555), the first widely available account of the Americas in English, presented Spanish imperialism as a model for the English to emulate. To depict English exploration as a viable competitor to that of the Spanish and Portuguese, Eden appended to his translation reports of two recent English voyages to Africa, along with his own prefatory material. Drawing heavily on traditional cosmographical works as well as eyewitness narratives, Eden laid out a standard and influential description of Africa and its inhabitants, a description in which the mythical Prester John and "people without heads, called Blemines, having their eyes and mouth in their breast," coexist with the very real inhabitants of Guinea with whom the Englishmen interact and whom they bring back to England as slaves.

From The second voyage to Guinea, * * * in the year 1554, the Captain whereof was Master John Lok[1]

[A DESCRIPTION OF AFRICANS]

* * * It is to be understood that the people which now inhabit the regions of the coast of Guinea and the middle parts of Africa, as Libya the inner and Nubia,[2] with divers other great and large regions about the same, were in old time called Ethiops and Nigritae, which we now call Moors, Moo-

1. Lok (a great-great-great-uncle of the philosopher John Locke) commanded three ships that left London in October 1554 for a trading voyage to Africa. The expedition reached the Saharan coast of West Africa in late November and sailed south and east to the Gulf of Guinea—the northeasternmost expanse of the South Atlantic Ocean, lying along the underside of the great bend in the conti-

nent's west coast. The expedition traded eastwardly along the coast until mid-February, when it turned toward home; the ships reached London in early June 1555, bearing a cargo of gold, pepper, elephants' tusks, the skull of one particularly large elephant, and five black slaves.
2. A region along the Nile, now in southern Egypt and northern Sudan.

rens,[3] or Negroes, a people of beastly living, without a God, law, religion, or commonwealth, and so scorched and vexed with the heat of the sun that in many places they curse it when it riseth. Of the regions and people about the inner Libya (called Libya interior), Gemma Frisius[4] writeth thus:

Libya interior is very large and desolate, in the which are many horrible wildernesses and mountains replenished[5] with diverse kinds of wild and monstrous beasts and serpents. First, from Mauretania or Barbary toward the south is Getulia,[6] a rough and savage region whose inhabitants are wild and wandering people. After these follow the people called Melanogetuli and Pharusii, which wander in the wilderness, carrying with them great gourds of water. The Ethiopians called Nigritae occupy a great part of Africa, and are extended to the West Ocean.[7] Southward also they reach to the river Nigris, whose nature agreeth with the river of Nilus, forasmuch as it is increased and diminished at the same time, and bringeth forth the like beasts as the crocodile.[8] By reason whereof, I think this to be the same river which the Portugals call Senaga,[9] for this river is also of the same nature. It is furthermore marvelous and very strange that is said of this river: and this is that on the one side thereof the inhabitants are of high stature and black, and on the other side of brown or tawny color and low stature; which thing also our men confirm to be true.[1]

There are also other people of Libya called Garamantes, whose women are common:[2] for they contract no matrimony, neither have respect to chastity. * * * But to speak somewhat more of Ethiopia: although there are many nations of people so named, yet is Ethiopia chiefly divided into two parts, whereof the one is called Ethiopia under Egypt, a great and rich region. To this pertaineth the Island Meroe,[3] embraced round about with the streams of the river Nilus. In this island, women reigned in old time. Josephus writeth that it was sometime called Saba, and that the queen of Saba came from thence to Jerusalem to hear the wisdom of Solomon.[4] From hence toward the east reigneth the * * * Christian Emperor Prester John, whom some call Papa Johannes and other say that he is called Pean Juan (that is) Great John, whose empire reacheth far beyond Nilus and is extended to the coasts of the Red Sea and Indian Sea.[5] * * * About this region inhabit the

3. A variant of *Moors*, from French. "Ethiops": the term was applied not just to inhabitants of Ethiopia but generally to black Africans—as was "Nigritae," the classical Latin name of a tribe living on the banks of the Nigris (or Niger) River in Ethiopia.
4. A Dutch polymath from whose Latin work *On the Elements of Astronomy and Cosmography* (1530) Eden adapted the following three paragraphs.
5. Stocked.
6. A large desert region in North Africa south of the Atlas Mountains, bordering the Sahara. "Mauretania": the old name for the Mediterranean coast of what is now Morocco. "Barbary": the name for the Arab countries along the coast of North Africa west of Egypt. Eden, though, appears to have regarded the two terms as synonymous.
7. I.e., the Atlantic off northwestern Africa.
8. Like the Nile (in Latin, *Nilus*), the Nigris floods annually. Crocodiles were thought to generate spontaneously through the action of sunlight on

Nile mud.
9. The Senegal River in West Africa, often wrongly supposed to be connected to the Nigris or Niger.
1. This discovery was made, by the Portuguese, in 1445 near the mouth of the Senegal, where the trees end and the Sahara Desert begins.
2. I.e., held in common. The Garamantes, a people of the Sahara, developed an advanced civilization, in the period 500 B.C.E.–700 C.E.
3. A Sudanese region bounded by three rivers. Its eponymous city, on the east bank of the Nile, was the capital of the ancient kingdom of Kush.
4. The story of the queen of Sheba's visit to Solomon is told in 1 Kings 10.1–13. The identification, by the Romano-Jewish historian Titus Flavius Josephus (1st century C.E.), of Sheba with the ancient African kingdom of Saba is highly suspect.
5. The legendary Christian ruler Prester John, much written of in the Middle Ages, was sometimes said to have been king of Ethiopia.

people called Clodi, Risophagi, Babylonii, Axiunitae, Molili, and Molibae. After these is the region called Troglodytica,[6] whose inhabitants dwell in caves and dens: for these are their houses, and the flesh of serpents their meat, as writeth Pliny and Diodorus Siculus.[7] They have no speech, but rather a grinning and chattering. There are also people without heads, called Blemines, having their eyes and mouth in their breast. Likewise Strucophagi and naked Ganphantantes. Satyrs[8] also, which have nothing of men but only shape. Moreover, Oripei, great hunters. Mennones also, and the region of Smyrnophora, which bringeth forth myrrh. After these is the region of Azania, in which many elephants are found. A great part of the other regions of Africa that are beyond the equinoctial line are now ascribed to the kingdom of Melinde, whose inhabitants are accustomed to traffic[9] with the nations of Arabia, and their king is joined in friendship with the king of Portugal, and payeth tribute to Prester John.

The other Ethiope, called Ethiopia interior * * *, is not yet known for the greatness[1] thereof, but only by the seacoasts. * * * Furthermore, the Ethiopians called Rhapsii and Anthropophagi,[2] that are accustomed to eat man's flesh, inhabit the regions near unto the mountains called Montes Lunae (that is) the Mountains of the Moon.[3] * * *

Some write that Africa was so named by the Grecians, because it is without cold. For the Greek letter alpha or "A" signifieth privation, void, or without, and "Phrice" signifieth cold.[4] For indeed although in the stead of winter they have a cloudy and tempestuous season, yet is it not cold but rather smothering hot, with hot showers of rain also, and somewhere[5] such scorching winds that, what by one means and other, they seem at certain times to live as it were in furnaces, and, in manner,[6] already halfway in Purgatory or Hell. Gemma Frisius writeth that in certain parts of Africa, as in Atlas the Greater,[7] the air in the night season is seen shining, with many strange fires and flames rising, in manner, as high as the moon: and that in the element are sometime heard, as it were, the sound of pipes, trumpets, and drums: which noises may perhaps be caused by the vehement and sundry motions of such fiery exhalations in the air, as we see the like in many experiences[8] wrought by fire, air, and wind.

* * *

6. A region along the west coast of the Red Sea. Its name is from the Greek for "hole dwellers."

7. Diodorus of Sicily (1st century B.C.E.) wrote a universal history (most of which is lost). The Roman Pliny the Elder (1st century C.E.) wrote a massive encyclopedia, *Natural History*, now best known for its occasional excursions into *un*natural history, such as its accounts of the headless Blemines (or Blemmyes) and some of the other extraordinary races described by Eden. The great Greek historian Herodotus (5th century B.C.E.) also supplied some wonders of this kind, and such reports became commonplaces of travel writing, proliferating in later times by way of popular works like *The Travels of Sir John Mandeville* (14th century).

8. In classical mythology, satyrs were minor woodland deities whose form was partly human and partly bestial.

9. Trade. "Equinoctial": equatorial.

1. Size.

2. Man-eaters; also from Pliny. Othello says that Desdemona was fascinated by his life story, which included encounters with "the cannibals that of each other eat, / The anthropophagi, and men whose heads / Do grow beneath their shoulders" (1.3.142–44).

3. A legendary mountain range thought to contain the headwaters of the Nile.

4. One of many false etymologies common in the period. The actual origin of the word *Africa* is uncertain.

5. In some places.

6. As it were.

7. The interior range of the Atlas Mountains, rising from the Sahara.

8. Occurrences.

Many things more our men saw and considered in this voyage, worthy to be noted, whereof I have thought good to put some in memory, that the reader may as well take pleasure in the variety of things, as knowledge of the history. Among other things, therefore, touching the manners and nature of the people, this may seem strange, that their princes and noblemen use to pounce[9] and raise their skins with pretty knots in divers forms, as it were branched damask, thinking that to be a decent[1] ornament. And albeit they go in manner[2] all naked, yet are many of them, and especially their women, in manner laden with collars, bracelets, hoops, and chains, either of gold, copper, or ivory. * * *

They are very wary people in their bargaining, and will not lose one spark[3] of gold of any value. They use weights and measures, and are very circumspect in occupying[4] the same. They that shall have to do with them must use them gently: for they will not traffic or bring in any wares if they be evil used.[5] At the first voyage that our men had into these parts, it so chanced that at their departure from the first place where they did traffic, one of them either stole a musk cat or took her away by force, not mistrusting[6] that that should have hindered their bargaining in another place whither they intended to go. But for all the haste they could make with full sails, the fame of their misusage so prevented[7] them that the people of that place also, offended thereby, would bring in no wares: insomuch that they were enforced either to restore the cat or pay for her at their price, before they could traffic there.

* * *

Many things more might be said of the manners of the people, and of the wonders and monstrous things that are engendered in Africa. But it shall suffice to have said thus much of such things as our * * * men saw.

* * *

Among other things that chanced to them in this voyage, this is worthy to be noted, that whereas they sailed thither in seven weeks, they could return in no less space than twenty weeks. The cause whereof they say to be this: That about the coast of Cabo Verde[8] the wind is ever in the east, by reason whereof they were enforced to sail far out of their course into the main ocean to find the wind at the west to bring them home. There died of our men at this last voyage about twenty and four, whereof many died at their return into the clime of the cold regions, as between the Islands of Azores[9] and England. They brought with them certain black slaves, whereof some were tall and strong men and could well agree with our meats[1] and drinks. The cold and moist air doth somewhat offend[2] them. Yet doubtless men that are born in hot regions may better abide the cold than men that are

---

9. Tattoo. "Use to": are accustomed to.
1. Becoming. "Branched damask": a fabric woven with elaborate designs and figures.
2. "In manner": here the meaning is "very nearly."
3. Bit.
4. Using.
5. Treated badly. "Gently": courteously.
6. Not suspecting. "Musk cat": civet cat, which secretes musk used for perfumery.

7. Preceded; outstripped.
8. Cape Verde, lying on the coast of Senegal, the westernmost point of the African continent.
9. An archipelago in the Atlantic 850 miles west of Portugal, claimed and settled by the Portuguese in the 15th century.
1. I.e., solid food—not just flesh.
2. Displease.

born in cold regions may abide heat, forasmuch as vehement heat resolveth[3] the radical moisture of men's bodies, as cold constraineth and preserveth the same.[4]

1555   1555, 1577, 1589, 1598–1600

3. Disperses; dissolves.
4. The idea is that excessive heat dries out the body's "radical" (i.e., fundamental) moisture and thus upsets the balance of the four humors (bodily fluids: blood, phlegm, bile, and the mythical black bile) that, in premodern physiology, was regarded as the key to good health.

A VOYAGE TO THE ARCTIC, 1577, WITH REFLECTIONS ON RACIAL DIFFERENCE

Educated at Eton, George Best (ca. 1555–1584), a navigator, took part in the latter two of the three voyages led by Martin Frobisher to discover a northwest passage to China—a purpose displaced, over time, by that of finding gold in the eastern Canadian arctic. In his account of all three voyages, *A true discourse of the late voyages of discovery, for the finding of a passage to Cathay*, Best contextualized his narrative of encounter with the Inuit peoples by appending a treatise on the causes of racial difference. His view, relying on observations drawn from English expeditions to West Africa, reflects a wider shift in theories of human difference away from explanations centered on climate and toward those based on heredity: as Best puts it, blackness is caused not by a particular geographical location but by "the curse and natural infection of blood." The expeditions to Meta Incognita ("the Unknown Boundary," now Baffin Island) failed to find the Northwest Passage, and the promising-looking ore they shipped back home proved to contain only fool's gold. The several Inuit whom Frobisher had kidnapped caused a sensation in England, but soon died of disease. Best himself was killed in a duel.

From A true discourse of the late voyages of discovery, for the finding of a passage to Cathay, by the northwest, under the conduct of Martin Frobisher, General: Before which, as a necessary preface, is prefixed a twofold discourse containing certain reasons to prove all parts of the world habitable

From *Experiences and reasons of the sphere, to prove all parts of the world habitable and thereby to confute the position of the five zones*[1]

First, it may be gathered by experience of our Englishmen in Anno 1553. For Captain Wyndham made a voyage with merchandise to Guinea[2] and entered

1. The five geographical zones, demarcated by lines of latitude, are the North and South Frigid Zones, the North and South Temperate Zones, and the Torrid Zone. Long-standing theory held that only the temperate zones were habitable. Best undertakes to refute this view, especially with respect to the Torrid Zone. "Position": proposition.
2. The European name for the part of the west

so far within the Torrida Zona that he was in three or four degrees of the equinoctial,[3] and his company, abiding there certain months, returned with gain.

Also the Englishmen made another voyage very prosperous and gainful, anno 1554,[4] to the coasts of Guinea, within 3 degrees of the equinoctial. And yet it is reported of a truth[5] that all the tract from Cape de las Palmas trending by Cape de Tres Puntas,[6] alongst by Benin, unto the Isle of St. Thomas (which is perpendicular under the equinoctial),[7] all that whole bay is more subject to many blooming and smothering heats, with infectious and contagious airs, than any other place in all Torrida Zona:[8] and the cause thereof is some accidents in the land.[9] For it is most certain that mountains, seas, woods, and lakes, etc., may cause, through their sundry kind of situation, sundry strange and extraordinary effects, which the reason of the clime otherwise would not give.[1] I mention these voyages of our Englishmen not so much to prove that Torrida Zona may be, and is, inhabited, as to show their readiness in attempting long and dangerous navigations. We also among us in England have black Moors,[2] Ethiopians, out of all parts of Torrida Zona, which after a small continuance[3] can well endure the cold of our country; and why should not we as well abide the heat of their country? * * *

And * * * by the experience of sundry men, yea thousands, travelers and merchants, to the East and West Indies in many places both directly under and hard by the equinoctial, they with one consent affirm that it aboundeth in the middle of Torrida Zona with all manner of grain, herbs, grass, fruit, wood, and cattle[4] that we have here, and thousands other sorts, far more wholesome, delectable, and precious than any we have in these northern climates, as very well shall appear to him that will read the histories and navigations of such as have traveled Arabia, India intra and extra Gangem,[5] the Islands Moluccae, America,[6] etc., which all lie about the middle of the Burning Zone, where it is truly reported that the great herbs, as are radish, lettuce, coleworts, borage,[7] and such like, do wax ripe, greater, more savory and delectable in taste than ours, within sixteen days after the seed is sown.[8] * * * And to be short, all they that have been there with one consent affirm that there are the goodliest green meadows and plains, the fairest

---

coast of Africa extending from Sierra Leone to Benin. "Captain Wyndham": Thomas Wyndham (1508–1554) led three trading voyages to Africa. For an account of his disastrous conduct of the final one—the voyage Best refers to here—see the NAEL Archive. The phrase "returned with gain" (below) glosses over a great deal.
3. The equator.
4. See p. 622.
5. As a fact; truly.
6. The Cape of the Palms (in the far southeast of what is now Liberia) and Cape Three Points (in modern Ghana) are headlands on the northern coast of the Gulf of Guinea (on which, see p. 622, n. 1). "Trending by": skirting.
7. I.e., lies directly under the celestial equator (the plane of which bisects the globe at the terrestrial equator). The island is west of modern Gabon.
8. The Torrid Zone encircles the middle swath of the globe, extending from the Tropic of Cancer to the Tropic of Capricorn.

9. Irregular features in the landscape.
1. I.e., would otherwise be unexpected in such a region.
2. Black Africans (not necessarily Muslims); often, as here, synonymous with "Ethiopians" (a term that was also used loosely). By the 17th century, the adjective and noun were often fused into "Blackmore" or "Blackamore."
3. Stay.
4. Livestock generally (not just cows).
5. India within the Ganges and without (Latin). European geographers traditionally divided India into two regions: west and east of the great river.
6. Here referring to the parts of the Americas that lie in the Torrid Zone. Moluccae is Indonesian Maluku, also known as the Moluccas or the Spice Islands.
7. A plant used in various comforting or stimulating drinks (cordials). "Coleworts": cabbages.
8. Best continues with other examples of the incredible fecundity of the Torrid Zone.

mountains covered with all sorts of trees and fruits, the fairest valleys, the goodliest pleasant fresh rivers stored with infinite kind of fishes, the thickest woods, green and bearing fruit all the whole year, that are in all the world. And as for gold, silver, and all other kind of metals, all kind of spices and delectable fruits, both for delicacy[9] and health, are there in such abundance as hitherto they have been thought to have been bred nowhere else but there. And in conclusion, it is now thought that nowhere else but under the equinoctial,[1] or not far from thence, is the earthly Paradise, and the only place of perfection in this world.

* * *

Others again imagine the Middle Zone[2] to be extreme hot because the people of Africa, especially the Ethiopians, are so coal black and their hair like wool curled short, which blackness and curled hair they suppose to come only by the parching heat of the sun, which how it should be possible I cannot see: for even under the equinoctial in America and in the East Indies and in the Islands Moluccae the people are not black, but tawny and white, with long hair uncurled as we have, so that if the Ethiopians' blackness came by the heat of the sun, why should not those Americans and Indians also be as black as they, seeing the sun is equally distant from them both, they abiding in one parallel?[3] * * *

Therefore to return again to the black Moors, I myself have seen an Ethiopian as black as a coal brought into England, who taking a fair English woman to wife begat a son in all respects as black as the father was, although England were his native country and an English woman his mother: whereby it seemeth this blackness proceedeth rather of some natural infection of that man,[4] which was so strong that neither the nature of the clime, neither[5] the good complexion of the mother concurring,[6] could anything alter: and therefore we cannot impute it to the nature of the clime. And for a more fresh[7] example, our people of Meta Incognita (of whom and for whom this discourse is taken in hand) that were brought this last year into England[8] were all generally of the same color that many nations be lying in the midst of the Middle Zone. And this their color was not only in the face, which was subject to sun and air, but also in their bodies, which were still[9] covered with garments as ours are, yea the very sucking child of twelve months' age had his skin of the very same color that most have under the equinoctial, which thing cannot proceed by reason of the clime, for that they are at least ten degrees more towards the north than we in England are; no, the sun never cometh near their zenith by forty degrees: for in effect, they are within three or four degrees of that which they call the Frozen Zone,[1] and, as I said, forty degrees from the Burning Zone: whereby it followeth that there is some other cause than the climate or the sun's perpendicular reflection that should cause the Ethiopians' great blackness. And the most probable cause,

9. Delectation.
1. I.e., somewhere along the equator.
2. The Torrid Zone.
3. In the same parallel of latitude.
4. I.e., the father.
5. Nor.
6. Combining.
7. More recent.

8. On their second voyage, Frobisher's men kidnapped several Inuit, whom they took with them back to England. For Best's account of Baffin Island and its inhabitants, see p. 630.
9. Always.
1. I.e., within a few degrees of the Arctic Circle. "They": i.e., geographers.

to my judgment, is that this blackness proceedeth of some natural infection of the first inhabitants of that country, and so all the whole progeny of[2] them descended are still polluted with the same blot of infection. Therefore it shall not be far from our purpose to examine the first original of these black men, and how by a lineal descent they have hitherto continued thus black.

It manifestly and plainly appeareth by Holy Scripture that after the general inundation and overflowing of the earth there remained no more men alive but Noah and his three sons, Shem, Ham, and Japheth, who only[3] were left to possess and inhabit the whole face of the earth: therefore all the sundry descents that until this present day have inhabited the whole earth must needs come of the offspring either of Shem, Ham, or Japheth, as the only sons of Noah, who all three being white, and their wives also, by course of nature should have begotten and brought forth white children. But the envy of our great and continual enemy the wicked spirit[4] is such that, as he could not suffer our old father Adam to live in the felicity and angelic state wherein he was first created, but, tempting him, sought and procured his ruin and fall: so again, finding at this flood none but a father and three sons living, he so caused one of them to transgress and disobey his father's commandment that after him all his posterity should be accursed. The fact[5] of disobedience was this: When Noah at the commandment of God had made the ark and entered therein, and the floodgates of heaven were opened so that the whole face of the earth, every tree and mountain, was covered with abundance of water, he straitly commanded his sons and their wives that they should with reverence and fear behold the justice and mighty power of God, and that during the time of the flood while they remained in the ark they should use continency and abstain from carnal copulation with their wives: and many other precepts he gave unto them, and admonitions touching the justice of God in revenging sin, and his mercy in delivering them, who nothing deserved it.[6] Which good instructions and exhortations notwithstanding, his wicked son Ham disobeyed, and being persuaded that the first child born after the flood (by right and law of nature) should inherit and possess all the dominions of the earth, he, contrary to his father's commandment, while they were yet in the ark used company[7] with his wife and craftily went about thereby to disinherit the offspring of his other two brethren: for the which wicked and detestable act, as an example for[8] contempt of Almighty God and disobedience to parents, God would a son should be born whose name was Cush, who not only itself but all his posterity after him should be so black and loathsome that it might remain a spectacle of disobedience to all the world. And of this black

2. From.
3. Alone. The biblical account of Noah, his sons, and the Flood is in Genesis 6–10.
4. Satan.
5. Act. In Genesis 9:20–27, the curse on Ham's posterity results from his having seen his drunken father naked. (After he told Shem and Japheth, they modestly re-covered Noah, walking backward into his tent so as not to see him.) Best gives a different version of the story—a version with no biblical warrant. Although the biblical passage says nothing about blackness, in later centuries Ham's

descendants were commonly thought to be the Africans, their blackness the mark of the curse, and the Genesis passage, in which Noah condemns Ham's son to be "a servant of servants . . . unto his brethren," a justification for their enslavement.
6. Who (Noah and his family) did not at all (he said) deserve such mercy.
7. A euphemism for having sex.
8. As a cautionary example of the consequences of.

and cursed Cush came all these black Moors which are in Africa: for after the water was vanished from off the face of the earth and that the land was dry, Shem chose that part of the land to inhabit in which now is called Asia, and Japheth had that which now is called Europa, wherein we dwell, and Africa remained for Ham and his black son Cush, and was called Chamesis[9] after the father's name, being perhaps a cursed, dry, sandy, and unfruitful ground fit for such a generation to inhabit in.

Thus you see that the cause of the Ethiopians' blackness is the curse and natural infection of blood and not the distemperature[1] of the climate; which also may be proved by this example, that these black men are found in all parts of Africa, as well without the Tropics as within, even unto Capo de Buona Speranza[2] southward, where, by reason of the sphere, should be the same temperature that is in Sicilia, Morea, and Candia,[3] where all be of very good complexions. Wherefore I conclude that the blackness proceedeth not of the hotness of the clime but, as I said, of the infection of blood, and therefore this their arguments gathered of the Africans' blackness is not able to destroy the temperature[4] of the Middle Zone.

* * *

From *A true report of such things as happened in the second voyage of Captain Frobisher pretended for the discovery of a new passage to Cathay, China, and the East India by the northwest. Ann. Dom. 1577*

* * * God having blessed us with so happy a landfall,[5] we bare into the straits which run in next hand, and somewhat further up to the northward, and came as near the shore as we might for the ice, and upon the eighteenth day of July our general taking the goldfiners[6] with him, attempted to go on shore with a small rowing pinnace, upon the small island where the ore was taken up, to prove whether there were any store[7] thereof to be found, but he could not get in all that island a piece so big as a walnut, where the first was found. But our men which sought the other islands thereabouts found them all to have good store of the ore, whereupon our general with these good tidings returned aboard about ten of the clock at night, and was joyfully welcomed of the company with a volley of shot. He brought eggs, fowls, and a young seal aboard, which the company had killed ashore, and having found upon those islands gins[8] set to catch fowl, and sticks new cut, with other things, he well perceived that not long before some of the country people had resorted thither.

Having therefore found those tokens of the people's access in those parts, and being in his first voyage well acquainted with their subtle and cruel disposition, he provided well for his better safety, and on Friday the nineteenth of July in the morning early, with his best company of gentlemen and sol-

9. Best uses the alternate form *Cham* for "Ham," which fits well with "Chamesis," a name for Ethiopia.
1. Intemperateness, severity.
2. The Cape of Good Hope, at the southern extremity of the continent.
3. Crete. Morea is the Peloponnesian peninsula, the southernmost part of mainland Greece.
4. Temperate climate.
5. At what is now called Frobisher Bay, a deep

inlet in southeastern Baffin Island. Frobisher thought it was a strait—the entrance to the Northwest Passage.
6. Refiners of gold. The main purpose of Frobisher's second and third voyages was to seek out gold mines.
7. Abundance. "Pinnace": light vessel attending on a larger ship. "Taken up": i.e., during the previous year's voyage.
8. Snares.

diers, to the number of forty persons, went on shore, as well to discover[9] the inland and habitation of the people as also to find out some fit harbor for our ships. And passing towards the shore with no small difficulty by reason of the abundance of ice which lay alongst the coast so thick together that hardly any passage through them might be discovered, we arrived at length upon the main of Hall's greater island,[1] and found there also as well as in the other small islands good store of the ore. And leaving his boats here with sufficient guard, we passed up into the country about two English miles, and recovered the top of a high hill, on the top whereof our men made a column or cross of stones heaped up of a good height together in good sort, and solemnly sounded a trumpet, and said certain prayers kneeling about the ensign, and honored the place by the name of Mount Warwick, in remembrance of the Right Honorable the Lord Ambrose Dudley, Earl of Warwick,[2] whose noble mind and good countenance[3] in this, as in all other good actions, gave great encouragement and good furtherance. This done, we retired our companies, not seeing anything here worth further discovery, the country seeming barren and full of ragged mountains, and in most parts covered with snow.

And thus marching towards our boats, we espied certain of the country people on the top of Mount Warwick with a flag wafting[4] us back again and making great noise, with cries like the mowing of bulls, seeming greatly desirous of conference with us: whereupon the general being therewith better acquainted, answered them again with the like cries, whereat and with the noise of our trumpets they seemed greatly to rejoice, skipping, laughing, and dancing for joy. And hereupon we made signs unto them, holding up two fingers, commanding two of our men to go apart from our companies, whereby they might do the like. So that forthwith two of our men and two of theirs met together a good space from company, neither party having their weapons about them. Our men gave them pins and points[5] and such trifles as they had. And they likewise bestowed on our men two bow cases and such things as they had. They earnestly desired our men to go up into their country, and our men offered them like kindness aboard our ships, but neither part (as it seemed) admitted or trusted the other's courtesy. Their manner of traffic is thus: they do use to[6] lay down of their merchandise upon the ground so much as they mean to part withal, and so looking that the other party with whom they make trade should do the like, they themselves do depart, and then if they do like of their mart they come again, and take in exchange the other's merchandise; otherwise if they like not, they take their own and depart. The day being thus well-near spent, in haste we retired our companies into our boats again, minding forthwith to search alongst the coast for some harbor fit for our ships: for the present necessity thereof was much, considering that all this while they lay off and on between the two lands, being continually subject as well to great danger of fleeting ice, which environed them, as to the sudden flaws[7] which the coast seemeth much subject unto. But when the people perceived our departure,

9. Explore.
1. Named, the preceding year, after the captain of one of Frobisher's ships.
2. Dudley (1528?–1590), a man distinguished in public service both civil and martial, was the chief promoter of Frobisher's explorations.
3. Support.
4. Beckoning.
5. Laces.
6. Are accustomed to. "Traffic": trade.
7. Squalls.

with great tokens of affection they earnestly called us back again, following us almost to our boats: whereupon our general taking his master[8] with him, who was best acquainted with their manners, went apart unto two of them, meaning, if they could lay sure hold upon them, forcibly to bring them aboard, with intent to bestow certain toys[9] and apparel upon the one, and so to dismiss him with all arguments[1] of courtesy, and retain the other for an interpreter. The general and his master being met with their two companions together, after they had exchanged certain things the one with the other, one of the savages for lack of better merchandise cut off the tail of his coat (which is a chief ornament among them) and gave it unto our general for a present. But he presently upon a watchword given with his master suddenly laid hold upon the two savages. But the ground underfoot being slippery with the snow on the side of the hill, their handfast failed, and their prey escaping ran away and lightly recovered their bow and arrows, which they had hid not far from them behind the rocks. And being only two savages in sight, they so fiercely, desperately, and with such fury assaulted and pursued our general and his master, being altogether unarmed, and not mistrusting[2] their subtlety, that they chased them to their boats, and hurt the general in the buttock with an arrow, who the rather speedily fled back because they suspected a greater number behind the rocks. Our soldiers (which were commanded before to keep their boats) perceiving the danger, and hearing our men calling for shot, came speedily to rescue, thinking there had been a greater number. But when the savages heard the shot of one of our calivers[3] (and yet having first bestowed their arrows), they ran away, our men speedily following them. But a servant of my Lord of Warwick, called Nicholas Conger, a good footman, and uncumbered with any furniture,[4] having only a dagger at his back, overtook one of them, and being a Cornishman and a good wrestler, showed his companion such a Cornish trick that he made his sides ache against the ground for a month after. And so being stayed, he was taken alive and brought away, but the other escaped. Thus with their strange and new prey our men repaired to their boats, and passed from the main to a small island of a mile compass, where they resolved to tarry all night; for even now a sudden storm was grown so great at sea that by no means they could recover[5] their ships. And here every man refreshed himself with a small portion of victuals which was laid into the boats for their dinners, having neither eat nor drunk all the day before. But because they knew not how long the storm might last, nor how far off the ships might be put to sea, nor whether they should ever recover them again or not, they made great spare of their victuals, as it greatly behooved them: for they knew full well that the best cheer[6] the country could yield them was rocks and stones, a hard food to live withal, and the people more ready to eat them than to give them wherewithal to eat. And thus keeping very good watch and ward, they lay there all night upon hard cliffs of snow and ice, both wet, cold, and comfortless.

*   *   *

8. Ship's captain.
9. Trifles.
1. Tokens.
2. Suspecting.

3. Light muskets.
4. Equipment.
5. Get back to.
6. Provisions.

Upon the mainland over against the Countess's Island[7] we discovered and beheld to our great marvel the poor caves and houses of those country people, which serve them (as it should seem) for their winter dwellings, and are made two fathom[8] underground, in compass round like to an oven, being joined fast one by another, having holes like to a fox or cony berry,[9] to keep and come together. They undertrenched these places with gutters, so that the water falling from the hills above them may slide away without their annoyance: and are seated commonly in the foot of a hill, to shield them better from the cold winds, having their door and entrance ever open towards the south. From the ground upward they build with whales' bones, for lack of timber, which bending one over another are handsomely compacted in the top together, and are covered over with sealskins, which, instead of tiles, fence them from the rain. In which house they have only one room, having the one half of the floor raised with broad stones a foot higher than the other, whereon strewing moss, they make their nests to sleep in. They defile these dens most filthily with their beastly feeding, and dwell so long in a place (as we think) until, their sluttishness loathing them,[1] they are forced to seek a sweeter air and a new seat, and are (no doubt) a dispersed and wandering nation, as the Tartarians,[2] and live in hordes and troops without any certain abode, as may appear by sundry circumstances of our experience.

Here our captive, being ashore with us to declare the use of such things as we saw, stayed himself alone behind the company, and did set up five small sticks round in a circle one by another, with one small bone placed just in the midst of all: which thing when one of our men perceived, he called us back to behold the matter, thinking that he had meant some charm or witchcraft therein. But the best conjecture we could make thereof was that he would thereby his countrymen should understand that for our five men which they betrayed[3] the last year (whom he signified by the five sticks) he was taken and kept prisoner, which he signified by the bone in the midst. For afterwards when we showed him the picture of his countryman which the last year was brought into England (whose counterfeit[4] we had drawn, with boat and other furniture, both as he was in his own, and also in English apparel), he was upon the sudden much amazed thereat, and beholding advisedly the same with silence a good while, as though he would strain courtesy whether[5] should begin the speech (for he thought him no doubt a lively[6] creature), at length began to question with him, as with his companion, and, finding him dumb and mute, seemed to suspect him, as one disdainful, and would with a little help have grown into choler[7] at the matter, until at last, by feeling and handling, he found him but a deceiving picture. And then with great noise and cries ceased not wondering, thinking that we could make men live or die at our pleasure.

And thereupon calling the matter to his remembrance, he gave us plainly to understand by signs that he had knowledge of the taking of our five men the last year, and confessing the manner of each thing, numbered the five

---

7. Named after the countess of Warwick.
8. Twelve feet.
9. Rabbit burrow.
1. Their squalor becoming unbearable to them.
2. Tartars—a people of Central Asia.

3. I.e., captured.
4. Likeness.
5. Which of them.
6. Living.
7. Anger.

men upon his five fingers and pointed unto a boat in our ship which was like unto that wherein our men were betrayed: and when we made him signs that they were slain and eaten, he earnestly denied, and made signs to the contrary.

1578, 1598–1600

WITHERINGTON AND LISTER'S VOYAGE TO WEST AFRICA AND SOUTH AMERICA, 1586–87

I n his *Principal Navigations*, Hakluyt published an account written by "John Sarracoll, merchant," of a voyage financed by the earl of Cumberland in 1586–87. Two ships, under the command of Robert Witherington and Christopher Lister, set out with a combined crew of two hundred men. At sea they joined forces with two other English ships. Abandoning an initial plan to sail along the coast of Spain in search of "some good prize to have sent home to my lord," they sailed to the west coast of Africa to load up with food and supplies before crossing the Atlantic. In his account of Sierra Leone, Sarracoll describes the English destruction of a town whose beauty and cleanliness had greatly impressed the men. The fleet, whose ultimate destination had been the Pacific, reached the coast of South America, but severe storms, violent skirmishes both with the Portuguese colonists and with the native peoples, and shortage of food and water forced them to return to England.

The voyage set out by the right honorable the earl of Cumberland in the year 1586. Intended for the South Sea, but performed no farther than the latitude of 44 degrees to the south of the equinoctial.[1] Written by Master John Sarracoll, merchant in the same voyage.

The 26th day of June, in the year 1586 and in the 28th year of the queen's majesty's reign, we departed from Gravesend in two ships: the admiral,[2] called the *Red Dragon*, and the other the bark *Clifford*, the one of the burden[3] of 260 tons, with 130 men, and the other of the burden of 130 tons, with 70 men. The captain of the admiral was Master Robert Witherington, of the vice-admiral Master Christopher Lister, both being furnished out at the costs and charges of the right honorable the earl of Cumberland, having for their masters[4] two brethren, the one John Anthony, and the other William Anthony.

---

1. Equator.
2. I.e., the principal ship, called the admiral because it carries the fleet commander. Graves-

end is a seaport on the lower Thames.
3. Carrying capacity.
4. Pilots.

The 24th of July we came into the sound of Plymouth, and being there constrained by westerly winds to stay till the 17th of August, we then departed with another ship also for our rear admiral, called the *Roe*, whereof Master Hawes was captain, and a fine pinnace also, called the *Dorothy*, which was Sir Walter Ralegh's. We four being out in the sea, met the 20th of August with 16 sails of hulks in the Sleeve,[5] who named themselves to be men of Hamborough,[6] laden and come from Lisbon. Our admiral hailed their admiral with courteous words, willing him to strike his sails, and to come aboard to him only to know some news of the country, but he refused to do so, only struck his flag and took it in. The vice-admiral of the hulks, being ahead, would neither strike flag nor sail, but passed on without budging, whereupon our admiral lent him a piece of ordnance,[7] which they repaid double, so that we grew to some little quarrel; whereupon one of the sternmost hulks, being as I suppose more afraid than hurt, struck amain.[8] Our admiral, being near him, laid him aboard and entered with certain of his men, how many I know not, for that we were giving chase to the windermost[9] men, thinking our admiral would have come up again to us, to have made them all to have struck: but the weather growing to be very thick and foggy, with small rain, he came not up but kept with another of the hulks, which Captain Hawes had boarded and kept all night, and took out of her some provision that they best liked. They learned of the men that were in the hulk that there were 7 hulks laden in Lisbon with Spaniards' goods, and because their lading was very rich, they were determined to go about Ireland,[1] and so they let her go again like a goose with a broken wing.

The next day after being the 21st day, we espied 5 sails more, which lay along to the eastwards; but by reason of the night, which then was near at hand, we could hardly come to them. Yet at last we hailed one of the biggest of them, and they told us that they were all of Hamborough: but another said she was of Denmark, so that indeed they knew neither what to say nor what to do. Our admiral being more desirous to follow his course than to linger by chasing the hulks, called us from pursuing them with his trumpet and a piece of ordnance, or else we would have seen what they had been and wherewith they had been laden.

The 22nd day because of contrary wind we put into Dartmouth[2] all four of us, and tarried there seven days.

The 29th we departed thence and put out to sea and began our voyage, thinking at the first to have run along the coast of Spain, to see if we could have met with some good prize to have sent home to my lord: but our captain thought it not the best course at the last, but rather kept off in the sea from the coast. And upon Saturday the 17th of September we fell with the coast of Barbary,[3] and the 18th haled in with the road of Santa Cruz.[4] The 21st day we fell with one of the islands of the Canaries, called Fuerteventura. In running alongst this island, we espied upon a hill by the waterside

---

5. The English Channel; the fleet is making its way west around the south coast of England. "Hulks": large unwieldy ships.
6. Hamburg.
7. I.e., fired a cannon at the ship, or across its bows.
8. Hastily lowered its sails.
9. Farthest to windward.

1. Evidently they regarded the circuitous route home as being safer than a direct one.
2. Seaport in Devon.
3. North Africa west of Egypt.
4. City on Tenerife, one of the Canary Islands. "Haled in with the road": sailed into the sheltered anchorage (roadstead).

one waving with a white flag, whereupon we manned both our boats and sent them towards the shore, to understand what news. They found them to be two ragged knaves and one horseman, and they told us that Lanzarote was taken and spoiled[5] in August by the Turks: when we saw they had nothing else to say, we left them and proceeded on our course, and fell again with the coast of Barbary.

The 25th day of September about 10 of the clock we fell with Rio del Oro, standing just under our Tropic:[6] we anchored in the mouth of it in 8 fathom; the entrance of it is about 2 leagues[7] over. And the next day our captain, with the boat, searched the river, and found it to be as broad 14 or 15 leagues up as at the entry of it, but found no town nor habitation, saving that there came down two poor men, and one of them spake good Spanish, and told our captain that certain Frenchmen used to come thither, and laded some ox hides and goats' hides, but other commodity there was none. We departed thence the 27th day, and the last day of the month being calm, we went aboard our general[8] and there consented to go for Sierra Leone, to wood and water. * * *

The 21st of October we fell with land upon the coast of Guinea.

* * *

The 23rd day, being Sunday, we came to an anchor in the bay of fresh water, and going ashore with our boat, we spake with a Portugal, who told us that not far off there were Negroes inhabiting, and that in giving to the king a botija[9] of wine and some linen cloth, he would suffer us to water and wood at our pleasure. But our captains thinking it not good to give anything for that which they might take freely, landed, and certain of our men with them, whereupon the Portugal and the Negroes ran all away into the woods. Then we returned again into our boats, and presently went and landed in another place, thinking to have fetcht a walk, and so to come to our boats again. But wandering through a little wood, we were suddenly and unawares upon a town of the Negroes, whereupon they struck up their drum, giving withal a great shout, and off went their arrows as thick as hail. We were in number about 30 calivers,[1] and 20 with our weapons, which we also let fly into the woods among them, and what hurt we did, we know not.

Then we returned to our boats and took wood and water at our pleasure, and reasonable store of fish, and amongst the rest we haled[2] up a great foul monster, whose head and back were so hard that no sword could enter it: but being thrust in under the belly in divers places, and much wounded, he bowed a sword in his mouth, as a man would do a girdle[3] of leather about his hand, and likewise the iron of a boar spear. He was in length about nine foot, and had nothing in his belly but a certain quantity of small stones, to the value of a pottle.[4]

---

5. Despoiled, plundered. Lanzarote is another of the Canary Islands.
6. The Tropic of Cancer. The Rio del Oro (River of Gold) is the Niger River, Africa's third longest, which discharges into the Atlantic at the Gulf of Guinea.
7. A league is about three miles. A fathom is six feet.

8. I.e., the admiral—the flagship.
9. Earthenware jug.
1. Soldiers armed with light muskets of that name.
2. Drew.
3. Belt. "Bowed": bent.
4. I.e., the amount that would fill a tankard (approximately half a gallon).

The fourth of November we went on shore to a town of the Negroes, which stood on the southeast side of the harbor about a saker[5] shot from the road, which we found to be but lately built: it was of about two hundred houses, and walled about with mighty great trees, and stakes so thick that a rat could hardly get in or out. But as it chanced, we came directly upon a port[6] which was not shut up, where we entered with such fierceness that the people fled all out of the town, which we found to be finely built after their fashion, and the streets of it so intricate that it was difficult for us to find the way out that we came in at. We found their houses and streets so finely and cleanly kept that it was an admiration[7] to us all, for that neither in the houses nor streets was so much dust to be found as would fill an eggshell. We found little in their houses except some mats, gourds, and some earthen pots. Our men at their departure set the town on fire, and it was burnt (for the most part of it) in a quarter of an hour, the houses being covered with reed and straw.

After this we searched the country about it, where we found in divers plains good store of rice in stacks, which our men did beat out, and brought aboard in the husk, to the quantity of 14 or 15 tons in both our ships.

The 17th day of November we departed from Sierra Leone, directing our course for the Straits of Magellan.[8] In this harbor divers of our men fell sick of a disease in the belly, which for the time was extreme, but (God be thanked) it was but of small continuance. We found also in divers places of the woods images set upon pins,[9] with divers things before them, as eggs, meal, rice, round shot of stones, and divers other things, such as the barbarous people had to offer up.

*　*　*

The second day of January we had a little sight of land,[1] being about the height of 28 degrees to the southward of the line.[2]

The 4th day we fell with the shore high and bold, being in 30 degrees and a tierce,[3] little more or less. All of it to the northward was a highland, but to the southward it did presently fail, and was a very low land, and all sandy. About six leagues from the shore we sounded and had about fifteen or sixteen fathom water, and black sandy ooze. We thought to have gone to the shore and to have watered, but we could not discern any good harbor, and therefore we cast off to seaward again.

The 12th day we found ourselves in 32 degrees and 27 minutes. From the day of the Nativitie of Christ till the 13th day of this month, although the sun was very near unto us, yet we found no want of winds, but variable as in England, and not so hot but that a man's shoulders might well disgest a frieze[4] gown and his belly the best Christmas cheer in England; yet we for our parts had no want, but such as might content honest men.

The tenth day being about 8 leagues from the shore, and a little short of the River of Plate,[5] it was my good hap to espy a sail, which was a small

5. A type of small cannon.
6. Gate.
7. A wonder.
8. Between mainland South America and Tierra del Fuego.
9. Posts.
1. I.e., of South America.

2. The equator.
3. A third.
4. A kind of coarse woolen cloth. "Disgest": a variant spelling of "digest"; here, to "swallow," "stomach."
5. The Rio de la Plata (River of Silver), an estuary between modern Uruguay and Argentina. Buenos Aires is on its southwestern shore.

Portugal bound for the river, to a town called Santa Fe: and from thence by horse and carts the merchants and part of their goods were to be transported into Peru. This ship, being about the burden of 45 or 50 tons, we took that day about three of the clock, wherein there was for master or pilot an Englishman called Abraham Cocke, born in Leigh.[6] We examined him and the rest concerning the state of the river, and they told us that there were in the river five towns, some of 70 households and some of more. The first town was about 50 leagues up the river, called Buenos Aires, the rest some 40, some 50 leagues one from another, so that the uppermost town, called Tucamán, is 230 leagues from the entrance of the river. In these towns is great store of corn, cattle, wine, and sundry fruits, but no money of gold or silver: they make a certain kind of slight cloth, which they give in truck of[7] sugar, rice, marmalade, and sucket,[8] which were the commodities that this ship had.

They had aboard also 45 Negroes, whereof every one in Peru yieldeth 400 ducats[9] apiece, and besides these, there were, as passengers in her, two Portugal women and a child.

The 11th day we espied another sail, which was the consort of this Portugal, and to him also we gave chase, and took him the same day. He was of the burden of the other, and had in him good store of sugar, marmalade, and suckets, with divers other things, which we noted down [in] our book. In this ship also we found about 35 Negro women and four or five friars, of which one was an Irish man of the age of three or four and twenty years, and two Portugal women also, which were born in the River of Janeiro.[1] Both these ships were bought in Brazil, by a young man which was factor[2] for the bishop of Tucamán; and the friars were sent for by that bishop to possess a new monastery, which the bishop was then abuilding. The books, beads,[3] and pictures in her cost (as one of the Portugals confessed) above 1000 ducats.

Of these ships we learned that Master John Drake, who went in consort with Master Fenton, had his bark cast away a little short of the River of Plate, where they were taken captives by the savages, all saving them which were slain in the taking. The savages kept them for a time, and used them very hardly, yet at the last John Drake and Richard Fairweather, and two or three more of their company with them got a canoe and escaped, and came to the first town of the Spaniards. Fairweather is married in one of the towns, but John Drake was carried to Tucamán by the pilot of this ship, and was living and in good health the last year. Concerning this voyage of the Portugals, they told us that it was the third voyage that was made into the River of Plate these 30 years.

The 12th of January we came to Seal Island, and the 14th day to the Green Island, where going in we found hard aboard the main[4] 8 fathom, 7, and 6, and never less than five fathom. There lies a ledge of rocks in the fair way, betwixt the island and the main, so that you must be sure to borrow hard aboard[5] the main and leave the ledge on the larboard side.

---

6. There are several English towns of this name.
7. In trade for. "Slight": thin.
8. Fruit preserved in sugar.
9. Gold coins of this name were minted by several European nations. Four hundred ducats is a very large sum.

1. The Rio de Janeiro (River of January).
2. Agent.
3. Rosaries.
4. "Hard aboard the main": close to the mainland.
5. "Borrow hard aboard": approach closely to.

One of the Portugals which we carried along with us in our ship seemed to be a man of experience, and I entered into speech with him concerning the state of the river. He told me that the town of Buenos Aires is from the Green Island about seventy leagues, standing on the south side of the river, and from thence to Santa Fe is 100 leagues, standing on the same side also. At which town their ships do discharge all their goods into small barks, which row and tow up the river to another town called Ascension,[6] which is from Santa Fe 150 leagues, where the boats discharge on shore, and so pass all the goods by carts and horses to Tucamán, which is in Peru.

* * *

1589, 1598–1600

6. Ascunción, in Paraguay.

AMADAS AND BARLOWE'S VOYAGE TO VIRGINIA, 1584

The first English voyage to Virginia was commanded by Philip Amadas and Arthur Barlowe. The two captains had been sent forth by Sir Walter Ralegh to discover territories in North America suitable for colonization. In Barlowe's account, which was published in Hakluyt's *Principal Navigations*, they encountered a people living very close to the blessed state of the inhabitants of the Golden Age celebrated by classical poets like Ovid, a state of simplicity, honesty, generosity, and, at least with respect to the English, peace. All the same, when a group of Algonkian hunters suddenly return home, the English colonists immediately reach for their weapons.

From The First Voyage Made to Virginia

The second of July we found shoal water, which smelt so sweetly and was so strong a smell as if we had been in the midst of some delicate garden abounding with all kind of odoriferous flowers, by which we were assured that the land could not be far distant. And keeping good watch and bearing but slack sail, the fourth of the same month we arrived upon the coast, which we supposed to be a continent and firm land, and we sailed along the same 120 English miles before we could find any entrance, or river issuing into the sea. The first that appeared unto us we entered, though not without some difficulty, and cast anchor three harquebus-shot[1] within the haven's mouth, on the left hand of the same. And after thanks given to God for our safe arrival thither, we manned our boats, and went to view the land next adjoining and to take possession of the same in the right of the queen's

1. The harquebus was a heavy but portable firearm.

most excellent Majesty, as rightful queen and princess of the same, and after delivered the same over to your use, according to Her Majesty's grant and letters patents,[2] under Her Highness's Great Seal. Which being performed according to the ceremonies used in such enterprises, we viewed the land about us, being whereas we first landed very sandy and low towards the waterside, but so full of grapes as the very beating and surge of the sea overflowed them. Of which we found such plenty, as well there as in all places else, both on the sand and on the green soil on the hills, as in the plains, as well on every little shrub, as also climbing towards the tops of high cedars, that I think in all the world the like abundance is not to be found. And myself having seen those parts of Europe that most abound, find such difference as were incredible to be written.

We passed from the seaside towards the tops of those hills next adjoining, being but of mean[3] height, and from thence we beheld the sea on both sides, to the north and to the south, finding no end any of both ways. This land lay stretching itself to the west, which after we found to be but an island of twenty leagues long and not above six miles broad. Under the bank or hill whereon we stood, we beheld the valleys replenished with goodly cedar trees, and having discharged our harquebus-shot, such a flock of cranes (the most part white) arose under us, with such a cry redoubled by many echoes, as if an army of men had shouted all together.

This island had many goodly woods, and full of deer, conies,[4] hares, and fowl, even in the midst of summer, in incredible abundance. The woods are not such as you find in Bohemia, Moscovia, or Hyrcania,[5] barren and fruitless, but the highest and reddest cedars of the world, far bettering the cedars of the Azores, of the Indies, or of Lybanus,[6] pines, cypress, sassafras, the lentisk or the tree that beareth the mastic,[7] the tree that beareth the rind of black cinnamon, of which Master Winter brought from the Straits of Magellan, and many other of excellent smell and quality.[8]

We remained by the side of this island two whole days before we saw any people of the country. The third day we espied one small boat rowing towards us, having in it three persons. This boat came to the land's side, four harquebus-shot from our ships; and there two of the people remaining, the third came along the shore side towards us, and we being then all within board, he walked up and down upon the point of the land next unto us. Then the master and the pilot of the admiral,[9] Simon Ferdinando, and the captain, Philip Amadas, myself, and others, rowed to the land; whose coming this fellow attended, never making any show of fear or doubt. And after he had spoken of many things not understood by us, we brought him, with his own good liking, aboard the ships, and gave him a shirt, a hat, and some other things, and made him taste of our wine and our meat,[1] which he liked very well. And after having viewed both barks he departed and went to his

2. Documents issued by the sovereign granting certain rights to the bearer. "Your use": i.e., Ralegh's.
3. Moderate.
4. Rabbits.
5. A region near the Caspian Sea. "Moscovia": Muscovy, the principality of Moscow; often applied to Russia in general.
6. Lebanon.

7. Resin exuded from the bark of *Pistacia lentiscus* ("the lentisk"), supposed to have medicinal value.
8. Michael Drayton drew on this passage for his "Ode to the Virginian Voyage" (in the NAEL Archive), which praises "The cedar reaching high / To kiss the sky, / The cypress, pine, / And useful sassafras."
9. Flagship.
1. Food in general (not necessarily flesh).

own boat again, which he had left in a little cove or creek[2] adjoining. As soon as he was two bow-shot into the water he fell to fishing, and in less than half an hour he had laden his boat as deep as it could swim,[3] with which he came again to the point of the land, and there he divided his fish into two parts, pointing one part to the ship and the other to the pinnace.[4] Which, after he had (as much as he might) requited the former benefits received, he departed out of our sight.

The next day there came unto us divers boats, and in one of them the king's brother, accompanied with forty or fifty men, very handsome and goodly people, and in their behavior as mannerly and civil as any of Europe. His name was Granganimeo, and the king is called Wingina; the country, Wingandacoa (and now, by Her Majesty, Virginia).[5] The manner of his coming was in this sort: he left his boats all together, as the first man did, a little from the ships by the shore, and came along to the place over against the ships, followed with forty men. When he came to the place, his servants spread a long mat upon the ground, on which he sat down, and at the other end of the mat four others of his company did the like. The rest of his men stood round about him somewhat afar off. When we came to the shore to him, with our weapons, he never moved from his place, nor any of the other four, nor never mistrusted any harm to be offered from us; but, sitting still, he beckoned us to come and sit by him, which we performed. And, being set, he made all signs of joy and welcome, striking on his head and his breast and afterwards on ours, to show we were all one, smiling and making show the best he could of all love and familiarity. After he had made a long speech unto us we presented him with divers things, which he received very joyfully and thankfully. None of his company durst speak one word all the time; only the four which were at the other end spake one in the other's ear very softly.

The king is greatly obeyed, and his brothers and children reverenced. The king himself in person was at our being there sore wounded in a fight which he had with the king of the next country, called Wingiana, and was shot in two places through the body, and once clean through the thigh, but yet he recovered. By reason whereof, and for that[6] he lay at the chief town of the country, being six days' journey off, we saw him not at all.

After we had presented this his brother with such things as we thought he liked, we likewise gave somewhat to the other that sat with him on the mat. But presently he arose and took all from them and put it into his own basket, making signs and tokens that all things ought to be delivered unto him, and the rest were but his servants and followers. A day or two after this we fell to trading with them, exchanging some things that we had for chamois, buff,[7] and deer skins. When we showed him all our packet of merchandise, of all things that he saw a bright tin dish most pleased him, which he presently took up and clapt it before his breast, and after made a hole in the brim thereof and hung it about his neck, making signs that it would defend him against his enemies' arrows. For those people maintain a deadly

2. Inlet.
3. I.e., float.
4. Light vessel attending on a larger ship. "Pointing": appointing, assigning.
5. I.e., in honor of ("by") Elizabeth, as the "Virgin Queen."
6. Because.
7. Buffalo-hide leather.

and terrible war with the people and king adjoining. We exchanged our tin dish for twenty skins, worth twenty crowns or twenty nobles;[8] and a copper kettle for fifty skins, worth fifty crowns. They offered us good exchange for our hatchets and axes, and for knives, and would have given anything for swords; but we would not depart[9] with any.

* * *

We found the people most gentle, loving, and faithful, void of guile and treason, and such as live after the manner of the Golden Age.[1] The people only care how to defend themselves from the cold in their short winter, and to feed themselves with such meat as the soil affordeth; their meat is very well sodden,[2] and they make broth very sweet and savory. Their vessels are earthen pots, very large, white, and sweet; their dishes are wooden platters of sweet timber. Within the place where they feed was their lodging, and within that their idol which they worship, of which they speak incredible things. While we were at meat, there came in at the gates two or three men with their bows and arrows from hunting, whom when we espied we began to look one towards another, and offered[3] to reach our weapons. But as soon as she[4] espied our mistrust, she was very much moved, and caused some of her men to run out, and take away their bows and arrows and break them, and withal beat the poor fellows out of the gate again. When we departed in the evening and would not tarry all night, she was very sorry, and gave us into our boat our supper half-dressed,[5] pots and all, and brought us to our boat's side, in which we lay all night, removing the same a pretty[6] distance from the shore. She perceiving our jealousy[7] was much grieved, and sent divers men and thirty women to sit all night on the bank's side by us, and sent us into our boats fine mats to cover us from the rain, using very many words to entreat us to rest in their houses. But because we were few men, and if we had miscarried the voyage had been in very great danger, we durst not adventure anything, although there was no cause of doubt.[8] For a more kind and loving people there cannot be found in the world, as far as we have hitherto had trial.[9]

* * *

We brought home also two of the savages, being lusty[1] men, whose names were Wanchese and Manteo.

1589

---

8. "Crowns" and "nobles" are gold coins (see the appendix "British Money").
9. Part.
1. Drayton's "Ode" picks up on this reference to the Golden Age.
2. Boiled.
3. Moved.

4. The wife of Granganimeo, the king's brother.
5. Half-prepared.
6. Considerable.
7. Suspicion.
8. Fear.
9. Experience.
1. Vigorous.

HARIOT'S REPORT ON VIRGINIA, 1585

Thomas Hariot (1560–1621), mathematician, astronomer, and surveyor in the service of Sir Walter Ralegh, was observing sunspots and using a telescope at about the same time as Galileo; he also made important discoveries in algebra. He accompanied Sir Richard Grenville's expedition to Virginia in 1585 and wrote an account of it intended to promote colonization. He describes the geography, climate, vegetation, wildlife, and especially, inhabitants of the New World, about whom the English were intensely curious. Reports had begun to circulate in England about tensions with the Algonkian Indians, on whom the colonists were almost completely dependent for food, and Hariot's brief ethnographic observations sketch the grounds for reassurance that the natives "are not to be feared."

From A brief and true report of the new-found land of Virginia[1]

Of the commodities there found and to be raised,
as well merchantable as others

OF THE NATURE AND MANNERS OF THE PEOPLE

It resteth[2] I speak a word or two of the natural inhabitants, their natures and manners, leaving large discourse thereof until time more convenient hereafter: now only so farforth as that you may know how that they in respect of troubling our inhabiting and planting[3] are not to be feared, but that they shall have cause both to fear and love us that shall inhabit with them.

They are a people clothed with loose mantles made of deerskins, and aprons of the same round about their middles, all else naked, of such a difference of statures only as we in England,[4] having no edge tools or weapons of iron or steel to offend us withal, neither know they how to make any. Those weapons that they have are only bows made of witch hazel and arrows of reeds, flat-edged truncheons also of wood about a yard long, neither have they anything to defend themselves but targets[5] made of barks, and some armors made of sticks wickered together with thread.

Their towns are but small, and near the seacoast but few, some containing but ten or twelve houses, some twenty; the greatest that we have seen hath been but of thirty houses. If they be walled, it is only done with barks of trees made fast to stakes, or else with poles only fixed upright, and close one by another.

Their houses are made of small poles, made fast at the tops in round form after the manner as is used in many arbories in our gardens of England; in most towns, covered with barks, and in some with artificial[6] mats made of

---

1. For an account of the *first* expedition to Virginia, see Philip Amadas and Arthur Barlowe, on p. 639. One of the illustrations from Hariot's *Report* is reproduced in the color insert in this volume.
2. Remains that.
3. Establishing colonies.
4. I.e., the variability of height among them is similar to that among the English.
5. Shields.
6. Manufactured (i.e., woven). "Arbories": orchards.

Algonkian Weroans. In 1590, Hariot's *Brief and True Report* was reprinted, in Frankfurt, by Theodor de Bry, who added copperplate engravings based on watercolors by the expedition's highly skilled artist and mapmaker, John White. This engraving depicts two Algonkian Weroans, or great lords, with their weapons. For one of White's remarkable watercolors, see the color insert.

long rushes, from the tops of the houses down to the ground. The length of them is commonly double to the breadth; in some places they are but twelve and sixteen yards long, and in other some we have seen, of four-and-twenty.

In some places of the country, one only town belongeth to the government of a *wiroans* or chief lord, in other some two or three, in some six, eight, and more. The greatest wiroans that yet we had dealing with had but eighteen towns in his government and able to make[7] not above seven or eight hundred fighting men at the most. The language of every government is different from any other, and the further they are distant, the greater is the difference.

Their manner of wars amongst themselves is either by sudden surprising one another, most commonly about the dawning of the day, or moonlight, or else by ambushes or some subtle devices. Set battles are very rare, except it fall out where there are many trees, where either part may have some hope of defense, after the delivery of every arrow, in leaping behind some or other.

If there fall out any wars between us and them, what their fight is likely to be, we having advantages against them so many manner of ways, as by our discipline, our strange weapons and devices else, especially ordnance[8] great and small, it may easily be imagined: by the experience we have had in some places, the turning up of their heels against us in running away was their best defense.

---

7. Muster.   8. Artillery.

In respect of us they are a people poor, and for want of skill and judgment in the knowledge and use of our things do esteem our trifles before things of greater value. Notwithstanding, in their proper[9] manner (considering the want of such means as we have) they seem very ingenious. For although they have no such tools nor any such crafts, sciences, and arts as we, yet in those things they do, they show excellency of wit.[1] And by how much they upon due consideration shall find our manner of knowledges and crafts to exceed theirs in perfection, and speed for doing or execution, by so much the more is it probable that they should desire our friendship and love, and have the greater respect for pleasing and obeying us. Whereby may be hoped, if means of good government be used, that they may in short time be brought to civility and the embracing of true religion.

Some religion they have already, which although it be far from the truth, yet being as it is, there is hope it may be the easier and sooner reformed.

They believe that there are many gods, which they call *mantóac*, but of different sorts and degrees, one only chief and great god, which hath been from all eternity. Who, as they affirm, when he purposed to make the world, made first other gods of a principal order to be as means and instruments to be used in the creation and government to follow, and after, the sun, moon, and stars as petty gods, and the instruments of the other order more principal. First, they say, were made waters, out of which by the gods was made all diversity of creatures that are visible or invisible.

For mankind, they say a woman was made first, which, by the working of one of the gods, conceived and brought forth children. And in such sort, they say, they had their beginning. But how many years or ages have passed since, they say they can make no relation, having no letters[2] nor other such means as we to keep records of the particularities of times past, but only tradition from father to son.

They think that all the gods are of human shape, and therefore they represent them by images in the forms of men, which they call *kewasowok*; one alone is called *kewas*: them they place in houses appropriate, or temples, which they call *machicomuck*, where they worship, pray, sing, and make many times offering unto them. In some machicomuck we have seen but one kewas, in some two, and in other some three. The common sort think them to be also gods.

They believe also the immortality of the soul, that after this life as soon as the soul is departed from the body, according to the works it hath done, it is either carried to heaven, the habitacle[3] of gods, there to enjoy perpetual bliss and happiness, or else to a great pit or hole, which they think to be in the furthest parts of their part of the world toward the sunset, there to burn continually. The place they call *Popogusso*.

For the confirmation of this opinion, they told me two stories of two men that had been lately dead and revived again. The one happened, but few years before our coming into the country, of a wicked man, which having been dead and buried, the next day the earth of the grave being seen to move, was taken up again; who made declaration where his soul had been— that is to say, very near entering into Popogusso, had not one of the gods saved him and gave him leave to return again and teach his friends what

9. Own.
1. Intelligence.
2. Writing.
3. Habitation.

they should do to avoid that terrible place of torment. The other happened in the same year we were there, but in a town that was sixty miles from us, and it was told me for strange news that one being dead, buried, and taken up again as the first, showed that although his body had lain dead in the grave, yet his soul was alive and had traveled far in a long broad way, on both sides whereof grew most delicate and pleasant trees, bearing more rare and excellent fruits than ever he had seen before or was able to express, and at length came to most brave[4] and fair houses, near which he met his father that had been dead before, who gave him great charge to go back and show his friends what good they were to do to enjoy the pleasures of that place, which when he had done he should after come again.

What subtlety[5] soever be in the wiroances and priests, this opinion worketh so much in many of the common and simple sort of people that it maketh them have great respect to their governors, and also great care what they do, to avoid torment after death and to enjoy bliss; although notwithstanding there is punishment ordained for malefactors, as stealers, whoremongers, and other sorts of wicked-doers, some punished with death, some with forfeitures, some with beating, according to the greatness of the facts.[6]

And this is the sum of their religion, which I learned by having special familiarity with some of their priests. Wherein they were not so sure grounded, nor gave such credit to their traditions and stories, but through conversing with us they were brought into great doubts of their own,[7] and no small admiration of ours, with earnest desire in many to learn more than we had means, for want of perfect utterance in their language, to express.

Most things they saw with us, as mathematical instruments, sea compasses, the virtue of the lodestone[8] in drawing iron, a perspective glass whereby was showed many strange sights, burning glasses,[9] wildfire,[1] works, guns, books, writing and reading, spring-clocks that seem to go of themselves, and many other things that we had, were so strange unto them, and so far exceeded their capacities to comprehend the reason and means how they should be made and done, that they thought they were rather the works of gods than of men, or at the leastwise they had been given and taught us of the gods. Which made many of them to have such opinion of us, as that if they knew not the truth of God and religion already, it was rather to be had from us whom God so specially loved, than from a people that were so simple as they found themselves to be in comparison of us. Whereupon greater credit was given unto that we spoke of concerning such matters.

Many times and in every town where I came, according as I was able, I made declaration of the contents of the Bible, that therein was set forth the true and only God and his mighty works, that therein was contained the true doctrine of salvation through Christ, with many particularities of miracles and chief points of religion, as I was able then to utter, and thought fit for the time. And although I told them the book materially and of itself was not of any such virtue as I thought they did conceive, but only the doctrine therein contained, yet would many be glad to touch it, to embrace it, to kiss

4. Fine, splendid.
5. Sophistication.
6. Deeds. "Forfeitures": fines.
7. I.e., of their own religion.
8. Magnet. "Virtue": power.
9. Concave mirrors used to concentrate the

sun's rays. "Perspective glass": an early telescope Hariot had devised.
1. A composition of highly flammable substances, easy to ignite and very difficult to extinguish, used in warfare.

it, to hold it to their breasts and heads, and stroke over all their body with it, to show their hungry desire of that knowledge which was spoken of.

The wiroans with whom we dwelt, called Wingina, and many of his people would be glad many times to be with us at our prayers, and many times call upon us both in his own town, as also in others whither he sometimes accompanied us, to pray and sing psalms, hoping thereby to be partaker of the same effects which we by that means also expected.

Twice this Wiroans was so grievously sick that he was like to die, and as he lay languishing, doubting of any help by his own priests and thinking he was in such danger for offending us and thereby our God, sent for some of us to pray and be a means to our God that it would please him either that he might live, or after death dwell with him in bliss; so likewise were the requests of many others in the like case.

On a time also when their corn began to wither by reason of a drought which happened extraordinarily, fearing that it had come to pass by reason that in something they had displeased us, many would come to us and desire us to pray to our God of England that he would preserve their corn, promising that when it was ripe we also should be partakers of the fruit.

There could at no time happen any strange sickness, losses, hurts, or any other cross[2] unto them, but that they would impute to us the cause or means thereof, for offending or not pleasing us. One other rare and strange accident,[3] leaving others, will I mention before I end, which moved the whole country that either knew or heard of us to have us in wonderful admiration.

There was no town where we had any subtle device practiced against us, we leaving it unpunished or not revenged (because we sought by all means possible to win them by gentleness), but that within a few days after our departure from every such town the people began to die very fast, and many in short space, in some towns about twenty, in some forty, and in one six score, which in truth was very many in respect of[4] their numbers. This happened in no place that we could learn, but where we had been, where they used some practice against us, and after such time. The disease also was so strange that they neither knew what it was nor how to cure it, the like by report of the oldest men in the country never happened before, time out of mind—a thing specially observed by us, as also by the natural inhabitants themselves. Insomuch that when some of the inhabitants which were our friends, and especially the wiroans Wingina, had observed such effects in four or five towns to follow their wicked practices, they were persuaded that it was the work of our God through our means, and that we by him might kill and slay whom we would without weapons, and not come near them. And thereupon when it had happened that they had understanding that any of their enemies had abused us in our journeys, hearing that we had wrought no revenge with our weapons, and fearing upon some cause the matter should so rest, did come and entreat us that we would be a means to our God that they, as others that had dealt ill with us, might in like sort die, alleging how much it would be for our credit and profit, as also theirs, and hoping furthermore that we would do so much at their requests in respect of the friendship we professed them.

---

2. Affliction.
3. Occurrence.

4. In proportion to.

Whose entreaties although we showed that they were ungodly, affirming that our God would not subject himself to any such prayers and requests of men—that indeed all things have been and were to be done according to his good pleasure as he had ordained, and that we to show ourselves his true servants ought rather to make petition for the contrary, that they with them might live together with us, be made partakers of his truth, and serve him in righteousness, but notwithstanding in such sort that we refer that, as all other things, to be done according to his divine will and pleasure, and as by his wisdom he had ordained to be best—yet because the effect fell out so suddenly and shortly after according to their desires, they thought nevertheless it came to pass by our means, and that we in using such speeches unto them did but dissemble the matter, and therefore came unto us to give us thanks in their manner, that although we satisfied them not in promise, yet in deeds and effect we had fulfilled their desires.

This marvelous accident in all the country wrought so strange opinions of us that some people could not tell whether to think us gods or men, and the rather because that all the space of their sickness there was no man of ours known to die, or that was specially sick: they noted also that we had no women amongst us, neither that we did care for any of theirs.

Some therefore were of opinion that we were not born of women, and therefore not mortal, but that we were men of an old generation many years past, then risen again to immortality.

Some would likewise seem to prophesy that there were more of our generation yet to come, to kill theirs and take their places, as some thought the purpose was, by[5] that which was already done. Those that were immediately to come after us they imagined to be in the air, yet invisible and without bodies, and that they by our entreaty and for the love of us did make the people to die in that sort as they did, by shooting invisible bullets into them.

To confirm this opinion, their physicians (to excuse their ignorance in curing the disease) would not be ashamed to say, but earnestly make the simple people believe, that the strings of blood that they sucked out of the sick bodies were the strings wherewithal the invisible bullets were tied and cast. Some also thought that we shot them ourselves out of our pieces[6] from the place where we dwelt, and killed the people in any town that had offended us as we listed,[7] how far distant from us soever it were. And other some said that it was the special work of God for our sakes (as we ourselves have cause in some sort to think no less, whatsoever some do or may imagine to the contrary), specially some astrologers, knowing of the eclipse of the sun which we saw the same year before in our voyage thitherward, which unto them appeared very terrible; and also of a comet which began to appear but a few days before the beginning of the said sickness. But to exclude them from being the special causes of so special an accident, there are further reasons than I think fit at this present to be alleged. These their opinions I have set down the more at large, that it may appear unto you that there is good hope they may be brought through discreet dealing and government to the embracing of the truth, and consequently to honor, obey, fear, and love us.

---

5. Judging by.
6. Firearms.

7. As we pleased.

And although some of our company towards the end of the year showed themselves too fierce in slaying some of the people in some towns, upon causes that of our part might easily enough have been borne withal, yet notwithstanding, because it was on their part justly deserved, the alteration of their opinions generally and for the most part concerning us is the less to be doubted.[8] And whatsoever else they may be, by carefulness of ourselves need nothing at all to be feared.

1588, 1589, 1590

8. Feared.

A GIFT FOR THE SULTAN, 1599

Born in Lancashire, Thomas Dallam (1575–1630?) apprenticed at the Blacksmiths' Company of London and eventually became the preeminent organ builder in England, constructing elaborate, self-playing instruments automated by clockwork. After hearing him perform at Whitehall, Elizabeth I commissioned one of these magnificent organs from Dallam and sent him to present it to Mehmed III, the Ottoman Sultan, in Istanbul. By this extraordinary gift she hoped to facilitate a diplomatic mission designed to expand commercial ties with the Turks. In a diary uncovered only in the nineteenth century, Dallam describes his journey through the eastern Mediterranean, his performance at the imperial palace before the Sultan and his court, and even an illicit glimpse into the Sultan's harem. Dallam's encounters with his Muslim hosts along the way are often tense—he momentarily fears that, as he performs, his head will be sliced off by the Sultan—but they are marked by a mutual fascination. Though he was enthusiastic about his experience of what seemed to him "another world," Dallam politely refused the Sultan's entreaties to remain at his court, instead returning to England with a much-enhanced reputation.

From A brief relation of my travel from the royal city of London towards the Straits of Mare Mediterraneum,[1] and what happened by the way

The 25[th of June] we saw afar off the famous island called the Rhodes, the which in times past hath been kept by Christian knights, but now inhabited by Turks.[2]

* * *

1. Dallam's voyage took him through the Strait of Gibraltar at the western end of the Mediterranean Sea ("Mare Mediterraneum"; Latin); the Dardanelles Strait linking the Aegean Sea to the Sea of Marmara; and finally to Constantinople, at the southern end of the Bosporus Strait.

2. The Isle of Rhodes—in the southeastern Aegean Sea, off the coast of Turkey—was conquered by forces of the Knights Hospitaller (a Roman Catholic military order) in 1309 and controlled by them as the Knights of Rhodes until it fell to a Turkish siege, in 1522.

Coming to an anchor near unto the walls of the town, there we found in the road[3] a galleon of the Great Turk's, the biggest ship he hath, about one thousand ton, a very cart,[4] a ship of no strength; yet was she richly laden, and came from Alexandria.

We were no sooner come to an anchor but the Turks began to come aboard us, so that the very first day there came aboard us not so few as five hundred rude Turks, and likewise every day that we stayed there they ceased not.

The next day * * * the Captain Pasha, governor of the town,[5] being gone abroad * * * on some great business, the Chia[6] his deputy, who for the time was Captain, he, with the chiefest men of the town, came aboard our ship, and she was trimmed up in as handsome manner as we could for the time. Our gunroom[7] was one of the fairest rooms in the ship, and pleasant to come into. In the gunroom I had a pair of virginals,[8] the which our Master Gunner, to make the better show, desired me to set them open. When the Turks and Jews came in and saw them, they wondered what it should be; but when I played on them, then they wondered more. Divers[9] of them would take me in their arms and kiss me, and wish that I would dwell with them.

* * *

The twentieth day [of August], being Monday, we began to look into our work;[1] but when we opened our chests we found that all gluing work was clean decayed, by reason that it had lain above six months in the hold of our ship, which was but newly built, so that the extremity of the heat in the hold of the ship, with the working of the sea and the hotness of the country, was the cause that all gluing failed; likewise divers of my metal pipes were bruised and broken.

When our Ambassador, Mr. William Aldridge,[2] and other gentlemen see in what case it was in, they were all amazed, and said that it was not worth iid.[3] My answer unto our Ambassador and to Mr. Aldridge at this time I will omit; but when Mr. Aldridge heard what I said, he told me that if I did make it perfect he would give me, of his own purse, 15li.;[4] so about my work I went.

* * *

The Grand Seignior,[5] being seated in his chair of state, commanded silence. All being quiet, and no noise at all, the present began to salute the Grand

---

3. Roadstead, harbor. Dallam spells it "Roode" and calls the island "the Roodes," suggesting he misunderstood the etymology of its name (which is actually from a Greek word of uncertain origin).
4. A mere transport vessel.
5. I.e., of the *city* of Rhodes. "Pasha": the title given to high-ranking officers of the Ottoman Empire.
6. Transliterating a Turkish word.
7. In warships, the compartment occupied by the gunner and his mates.
8. A virginal is a small, portable keyboard instrument of the harpsichord family, set in a box or case. A single one was often called a "pair of virginals," perhaps referring to instruments with two registers.

9. Several.
1. The English ship having arrived at Constantinople on the 15th, Dallam and those assisting him now turned to reassembling the organ—which had been disassembled and packed away for the voyage—for presentation to the Sultan.
2. The Ambassador was Sir Henry Lello. William Aldridge was the English consul at Chios, an island off the Turkish coast of the Aegean Sea.
3. Twopence (d. is from Latin *denarius*, a small Roman coin). "Case": condition. "Amazed": stunned; confounded.
4. "li.": pound(s) (from the Latin *libra*); now written as £.
5. Sultan Mehmed III, to whom the organ was presented (August 25).

Seignior; for when I left it I did allow a quarter of an hour for his coming thither. First the clock struck 22; then the chime of 16 bells went off, and played a song of 4 parts.[6] That being done, two personages which stood upon two corners of the second story, holding two silver trumpets in their hands, did lift them to their heads and sounded a tantara.[7] Then the music went off,[8] and the organ played a song of 5 parts twice over. In the top of the organ, being 16 foot high, did stand a holly bush full of blackbirds and thrushes, which at the end of the music did sing and shake their wings. Divers other motions there was which the Grand Seignior wondered at. Then the Grand Seignior asked the Coppagaw[9] if it would ever do the like again. He answered that it would do the like again at the next hour. Quoth he:[1] "I will see that." In the meantime the Coppagaw, being a wise man, and doubted whether I had so appointed it or no, for he knew that it would go of itself but 4 times in 24 hours, so he came unto me, for I did stand under the house side,[2] where I might hear the organ go, and he asked me if it would go again at the end of the next hour; but I told him that it would not, for I did think the Grand Seignior would not have stayed so long by it; but if it would please him, that when the clock had struck he would touch a little pin with his finger, which before I had showed him, it would go at any time. Then he said that he would be as good as his word to the Grand Seignior. When the clock began to strike again, the Coppagaw went and stood by it; and when the clock had struck 23, he touched that pin, and it did the like as it did before. Then the Grand Seignior said it was good. He sat very near unto it, right before the keys, where a man should play on it by hand. He asked why those keys did move when the organ went and nothing did touch them. He told him that by those things it might be played on at any time. Then the Grande Seignior asked him if he did know any man that could play on it. He said, "No, but he that came with it could, and he is here without the door." "Fetch him hither," quoth the Grand Seignior, "and let me see how he doth it." Then the Coppagaw opened that door which I went out at, for I stood near unto it. He came and took me by the hand, smiling upon me; but I bid my dragoman[3] ask him what I should do, or whither I should go. He answered that it was the Grand Seignior's pleasure that I should let him see me play on the organ. So I went with him. When I came within the door, that which I did see was very wonderful unto me. I came in directly upon the Grand Seignior's right hand, some 16 of my paces from him, but he would not turn his head to look upon me. He sat in great state, yet the sight of him was nothing in comparison of the train[4] that stood behind him, the sight whereof did make me almost to think that I was in another world. The Grand Seignior sat still, beholding the present which was before him, and I stood dazzling my eyes with looking upon his people that stood behind him, the which was four hundred persons in number. Two hundred of them were his principal pages, the youngest of them 16 years of age, some 20,

6. I.e., in four-part counterpoint.
7. Fanfare or flourish of trumpets.
8. Sounded.
9. Literally, "Gatekeeper"; a high official who evidently controlled access to the Sultan's person. Earlier Dallam had explained that the Coppagaw is "the Grand Seignoir's secretary," where "secretary" (ultimately from Latin *secretum*,

"secret") has its old sense of one entrusted with private or secret matters.
1. The Grand Seignior.
2. Dallam, not having been allowed into the royal presence, was listening from outside.
3. Interpreter.
4. Retinue.

and some 30. They were appareled in rich cloth of gold made in gowns to the midleg; upon their heads little caps of cloth of gold and some cloth of tissue;[5] great pieces of silk about their waists instead of girdles; upon their legs Cordovan buskins,[6] red. Their heads were all shaven, saving[7] that behind their ears did hang a lock of hair like a squirrel's tail; their beards shaven, all saving their upper lips. Those 200 were all very proper[8] men, and Christians born.

The third hundred were dumb men, that could neither hear nor speak, and they were likewise in gowns of rich cloth of gold and Cordovan buskins; but their caps were of violet velvet, the crown of them made like a leather bottle, the brims divided into five peaked corners. Some of them had hawks in their fists.[9]

The fourth hundred were all dwarfs, big-bodied men but very low of stature. Every dwarf did wear a scimitar by his side, and they were also appareled in gowns of cloth of gold.

☆   ☆   ☆

When I had stood almost one quarter of an hour beholding this wonderful sight, I heard the Grand Seignior speak unto the Coppagaw, who stood near unto him. Then the Coppagaw came unto me and took my cloak from about me and lay it down upon the carpets, and bid me go and play on the organ; but I refused to do so, because the Grand Seignior sat so near the place where I should play that I could not come at it but I must needs turn my back towards him and touch his knee with my breeches,[1] which no man, in pain of death, might do, saving only the Coppagaw. So he smiled, and let me stand a little. Then the Grand Seignior spoke again, and the Coppagaw, with a merry countenance, bid me go with a good courage, and thrust me on. When I came very near the Grand Seignior, I bowed my head as low as my knee, not moving my cape, and turned my back right towards him, and touched his knee with my breeches.

He sat in a very rich chair of state, upon his thumb a ring with a diamond in it half an inch square, a fair scimitar by his side, a bow, and a quiver of arrows.

He sat so right behind me that he could not see what I did; therefore he stood up, and his Coppagaw removed his chair to one side, where he might see my hands; but, in his rising from his chair he gave me a thrust forwards, which he could not otherwise do, he sat so near me; but I thought he had been drawing his sword to cut off my head.

I stood there playing such thing as I could until the clock struck, and then I bowed my head as low as I could, and went from him with my back towards him. As I was taking of my cloak, the Coppagaw came unto me and bid me stand still and let my cloak lie; when I had stood a little while, the Coppagaw bid me go and cover the keys of the organ; then I went close to the Grand Seignior again, and bowed myself, and then I went backwards to my

---

5. Rich multicolored cloth, often interwoven with gold or silver.
6. Boots made of leather from Cordova, Spain. "Girdles": belts.
7. Except.
8. Handsome.

9. The deaf-mutes' services to the Sultan included strangling nineteen of his brothers and half-brothers; they were executed because they were potential rivals for his throne.
1. Pants extending to just below the knees.

cloak. When the company saw me do so they seemed to be glad, and laughed. Then I saw the Grand Seignior put his hand behind him full of gold, which the Coppagaw received, and brought unto me forty and five pieces of gold called chickers,[2] and then was I put out again where I came in, being not a little joyful of my good success.[3]

* * *

The 12 [October], being Friday, I was sent for to the court, and also the Sunday and Monday following, to no other end but to show me the Grand Seignior's privy chambers,[4] his gold and silver, his chairs of state; and he that showed me them would have me to sit down in one of them, and then to draw that sword out of the sheath with the which the Grand Seignior doth crown his king.[5]

When he had showed me many other things which I wondered at, then, crossing through a little square court paved with marble, he pointed me to go to a grate in a wall, but made me a sign that he might not go thither himself. When I came to the grate the wall was very thick, and grated on both the sides with iron very strongly; but through that grate I did see thirty of the Grand Seignior's concubines that were playing with a ball in another court. At the first sight of them I thought they had been young men, but when I saw the hair of their heads hang down on their backs, platted[6] together with a tassel of small pearl hanging in the lower end of it, and by other plain tokens, I did know them to be women, and very pretty ones indeed.

They wore upon their heads nothing but a little cap of cloth of gold, which did but cover the crown of her head; no bands about their necks, nor anything but fair chains of pearl and a jewel hanging on their breast, and jewels in their ears; their coats were like a soldier's mandilion,[7] some of red satin and some of blue and some of other colors, and girded like a lace of contrary color.[8] They wore breeches of scammatie, a fine cloth made of cotton wool, as white as snow and as fine as lawn;[9] for I could discern the skin of their thighs through it. These breeches came down to their midleg; some of them did wear fine Cordovan buskins, and some had their legs naked, with a gold ring on the small of her leg; on her foot a velvet pantofle[1] 4 or 5 inches high. I stood so long looking upon them that he which had showed me all this kindness began to be very angry with me. He made a wry mouth, and stamped with his foot to make me give over looking; the which I was very loath to do, for that sight did please me wondrous well.

Then I went away with this adjemoglan[2] to the place where we left my dragoman or interpreter, and I told my interpreter that I had seen 30 of the Grand Seignior's concubines. But my interpreter advised me that by no

2. A variant of "sequins," Italian gold coins whose name was also applied to Turkish coins more properly called "sultanins."
3. Although Mehmed III valued the organ, his son and successor, Ahmed I, did not: he had it destroyed.
4. The Sultan's private quarters.
5. I.e., of one of the constituent kingdoms of his empire.
6. Plaited, braided.

7. A loose coat or cloak.
8. Edged with ornamental braid of a contrasting color.
9. A kind of linen, resembling cambric.
1. A cork-soled, high-heeled shoe.
2. Son of a stranger (literal translation); either a prisoner of war or a captive Christian taken when young. At the Sultan's court adjemoglans performed various servile offices considered beneath the dignity of a Turk.

means I should speak of it whereby any Turk might hear of it; for if it were known to some Turks, it would [be] present[3] death to him that showed me them. He durst not look upon them himself. Although I looked so long upon them, they saw not me, neither[4] all that while looked towards that place. If they had seen me, they would all have come presently thither to look upon me, and have wondered as much at me, or how I came thither, as I did to see them.

1599–1600   1893

3. Immediate.   4. Nor.

THE GENERAL HISTORY
OF THE TURKS, 1603

Richard Knolles (ca. 1545–1610) slaked the growing thirst in late Elizabethan England for information about the Islamic world when he published *The General History of the Turks* (1603), the first major description of the Ottoman Empire in English. Shakespeare likely used it as a source for *Othello*, and, two centuries later, Lord Byron credited "Old Knolles" with "the Oriental coloring which is observed in my poetry." The situation Knolles depicts is one of Ottoman superiority over Christian Europe, reflecting the geopolitical anxiety felt by Europeans throughout the sixteenth century and after. To Knolles, the Turks are "the scourge of God and present terror of the world." However, this alarmist frame belies both his enormous volume's careful consideration of Turkish society from eastern sources and his frequent admiration for Ottoman success.

From The general history of the Turks, from the first beginning
of that nation to the rising of the Ottoman family

From *The author's induction to the Christian reader
unto the history of the Turks following*

The long and still declining state of the Christian commonweal, with the utter ruin and subversion of the Empire of the East[1] and many other most glorious kingdoms and provinces of the Christians, never to be sufficiently lamented, might with the due consideration thereof worthily move even a right stony heart to ruth:[2] but therewith also to call to remembrance the dishonor done unto the blessed name of our Savior Christ Jesus, the desolation of his Church here militant upon earth,[3] the dreadful danger daily threatened unto the poor remainder thereof, the millions of souls cast headlong

1. The Eastern Roman Empire (later known as the Byzantine Empire), which was severed from the collapsing Western Empire in the 4th century c.e., endured until 1453, when its capital, Constantinople (formerly Byzantium and now Istan-bul), fell to a Turkish siege.
2. Pity.
3. In Christian theology, the "Church Militant" is the community of all living Christians, considered as fighting against evil.

into eternal destruction, the infinite numbers of woeful Christians (whose grievous groanings under the heavy yoke of infidelity[4] no tongue is able to express), with the carelessness of the great for the redress thereof, might give just cause unto any good Christian to sit down and with the heavy Prophet to say, as he did of Jerusalem, "O how hath the Lord darkened the daughter of Zion in his wrath? and cast down from heaven unto the earth the beauty of Israel, and remembered not his footstool in the day of his wrath?"[5]

All which miseries (with many others so great, as greater there can none be) the prince of darkness and author of all mischief[6] hath by the persecuting princes of all ages, and ancient heretics, his ministers, labored from time to time to bring upon the Church of God, to the obscuring of his blessed name and utter subversion of his most sacred word; but yet by none, no not by them all together, so much prevailed as by the false Prophet *Mahomet*, born in an

The title page of Richard Knolles's *General History of the Turks* (1603) was engraved by Laurence Johnson and features a European on the left and an Ottoman Turk on the right. Neither the Christian nor the Muslim is given precedence over the other.

unhappy[7] hour, to the great destruction of mankind: whose most gross and blasphemous doctrine first fantasied by himself in Arabia, and so by him obtruded unto the world; and afterwards by the Saracen Caliphs[8] (his seduced successors), with greater forces maintained, was by them together with their empire dispersed over a great part of the face of the earth, to the

---

4. I.e., of a "heathen" realm; here, the Islamic Ottoman Empire.
5. Lamentations (2.1), where the mournful ("heavy") prophet Jeremiah bewailed the destruction of Jerusalem by the Babylonians, in 586 B.C.E.
6. Satan.
7. Unlucky. "*Mahomet*": a variant spelling of Muhammad, the Arab prophet through whom the Qu'ran was revealed and the religion of Islam established (7th century C.E.).
8. "Caliph" (from the Arabic word for "successor"—i.e., to Muhammad): the term for the temporal and spiritual head of Islam. "Saracen": generic term (used by Christians) for "Muslim." In what follows, Knolles briefly surveys successive Muslim realms in the millennium leading up to his own time. After Muhammad's death (632 C.E.), his successors under the Rashidun Caliphate (632–661) oversaw a rapid expansion of territory through conquests from the Arabian Peninsula into the

regions north of Arabia and west into North Africa. The Umayyad Caliphate (661–750) extended Muslim territory as far as the Iberian Peninsula in the west and India in the east. The long-lived Abbasid Caliphate (750–1517) oversaw a great flourishing of science, commerce, and culture in a Golden Age centered in Baghdad. The slow decline of the Abbasids allowed for the rise of other Islamic powers, including the Seljuk Turks in the 11th century and finally the Ottoman Empire, which, established by Osman I at the end of the 13th century, claimed the caliphate and eventually grew to encompass western Asia, southeastern Europe (including Greece and the Balkans), coastal areas on both sides of the Red Sea, the Horn of Africa, Egypt, and the rest of coastal North Africa as far as eastern Morocco. Although entering a long, gradual decline in the later 16th century, the empire was still very much a threat to eastern Europe at century's end.

unspeakable ruin and destruction of the Christian religion and state especially in Asia and Africa, with some good part of Europe also. But the unity
of this great Mahometan monarchy being once dissolved, and it divided
into many kingdoms, and so after the manner of worldly things drawing
unto the fatal period[9] of itself, in process of time became of far less force
than before and so less dreadful unto the Christian princes of the West, by
whom these Saracens were again expulsed out of all the parts of Europe
excepting one corner of Spain, which they yet held within the remembrance
of our fathers, until that by their victorious forces they were thence at
length happily removed also, after that they had possessed the same about
the space of seven hundred years.[1]

In this declination of the Saracens (the first champions of the Mahometan superstition, who, though they had lost much, yet held many great
kingdoms both in Asia and Africa, taken for the most part from the Christians) arise the Turks, an obscure and base people, before scarce known
unto the world, yet fierce and courageous, who by their valor first aspired
unto[2] the kingdom of Persia, with diverse other large provinces: from whence
they were about an hundred threescore and ten years after again expulsed
by the Tartars and enforced to retire themselves into the lesser Asia:[3] where
taking the benefit of the discord of the Christian princes of the East and the
carelessness of the Christians in general, they in some good measure
repaired their former losses again and maintained the state of a kingdom at
Iconium[4] in Cilicia (now of them called Caramania), holding in their subjection the greater part of that fruitful country, still seeking to gain from the
Christians what they had before lost unto the Tartars.

But this kingdom of the Turks declining also, by the dismembering of the
same, there stept up among the Turks in Bithynia[5] one *Osman* or *Ottoman*,
of the *Oguzian* tribe or family, a man of great spirit and valor who by little
and little growing up amongst the rest of his countrymen and other[6] the
effeminate Christians on that side of Asia, at last like another *Romulus*[7]
took upon him the name of a Sultan or King, and is right worthily accounted
the first founder of the mighty Empire of the Turks: which, continued by
many descents directly in the line of himself even unto Mahomet the third
of that name, who now reigneth,[8] is from a small beginning become the
greatest terror of the world, and holding in subjection many great and mighty
kingdoms in Asia, Europe, and Africa is grown to that height of pride as that
it threateneth destruction unto the rest of the kingdoms of the earth; laboring with nothing more than with the weight of itself. In the greatness
whereof is swallowed up both the name and empire of the Saracens, the

9. The fated end (of its allotted time).
1. The *Reconquista* ("Reconquest"; Spanish), a
series of campaigns by Christian states against
the Muslims (Moors) who had controlled territory on the Iberian Peninsula since the 8th
century, ended in 1492, with the fall of the
Moorish stronghold of Granada, on the southern
coast.
2. Attained. Knolles here overviews the Seljuk
Empire (1037–1194) and the secessionist Seljuk
realm that, for a while, survived its fall, the Sul-

tanate of Rûm (1077–1243).
3. Asia Minor. Tartars are the native inhabitants
of the region of central Asia extending eastward
from the Caspian Sea.
4. Latin name for the city of Konya, in Turkey's
Central Anatolia region.
5. A region adjoining the Bosporus and the Black
Sea.
6. Also. "Growing up": rising.
7. The legendary eponymous founder of Rome.
8. Sultan Mehmed III reigned 1595–1603.

glorious empire of the Greeks,[9] the renowned kingdoms of Macedonia, Peloponnesus, Epirus, Bulgaria, Serbia, Bosnia, Armenia, Cyprus, Syria, Egypt, Judea, Tunis, Algiers, Media, Mesopotamia, with a great part of Hungary, as also of the Persian kingdom, and all those churches and places so much spoken of in Holy Scripture (the Romans only excepted);[1] and in brief, so much of Christendom as far exceedeth that which is thereof at this day left. So that at this present if you consider the beginning, progress, and perpetual felicity of this the Ottoman Empire, there is in this world nothing more admirable[2] or strange; if the greatness and luster thereof, nothing more magnificent or glorious; if the power and strength thereof, nothing more dreadful or dangerous: which wondering at nothing but at the beauty of itself, and drunk with the pleasant wine of perpetual felicity, holdeth all the rest of the world in scorn, thundering out nothing but still blood and war, with a full persuasion in time to rule over all, prefining[3] unto itself no other limits than the uttermost bounds of the earth, from the rising of the sun unto the going down of the same. * * *

By civil discord the noble country of Graecia perished,[4] whenas the father rising against the son, and the son against the father, and brother against brother, they to the mutual destruction of themselves called in the Turk, who like a greedy lion lurking in his den lay in wait for them all. So perished the kingdoms of Bulgaria, Serbia, Bosnia, and Epirus, with the famous islands of the Rhodes and Cyprus,[5] betrayed as it were by the Christian princes their neighbors, by whom they might have easily been relieved. * * *

By these and such like means is this barbarous empire (of[6] almost nothing) grown to that height of majesty and power as that it hath in contempt all the rest, being itself not inferior in greatness and strength unto the greatest monarchies that ever yet were upon the face of the earth, the Roman Empire only excepted. Which how far it shall yet farther spread, none knoweth but he that holdeth in his hand all the kingdoms of the earth and with his word boundeth in the raging of the sea, so that it cannot further pass. * * *

1603

9. The Byzantine Empire—a Greek empire in the senses that its lingua franca was Greek rather than Latin and its culture Greek rather than Roman. The list of kingdoms that follows includes several that had not existed since ancient times.
1. I.e., Rome, whose Christians are addressed in Paul's Epistle to the Romans, is the only place spoken of in Acts of the Apostles or the Pauline epistles that has not fallen to the Turks.
2. More to be wondered at.
3. Setting; envisaging. "Persuasion": assurance, conviction (that it will, "in time[,] . . . rule over all").
4. Most of Greece fell to the Turks in the decades after the fall of Constantinople (1453). Throughout the Balkans, Turkish conquest was facilitated by internecine struggles among the Christian states, some of which even formed short-sighted alliances with the Turks against their neighbors.
5. The setting of Acts 2–5 of Othello, Cyprus had come under Turkish control in 1570. Shakespeare's sources for the play may have included Knolles's account of the Battle of Lepanto (1571, off western Greece), in which the Christian "Holy League," including Venice, defeated an Ottoman fleet and thus prevented Turkish expansion into the western Mediterranean (though leaving Cyprus in Ottoman hands).
6. Beginning from.

CHRISTOPHER MARLOWE
1564–1593

The son of a Canterbury shoemaker, Christopher Marlowe was born two months before William Shakespeare. In 1580 he went to Corpus Christi College, Cambridge, on a scholarship that was ordinarily awarded to students preparing for the ministry. He held the scholarship for the maximum time, six years, but did not take holy orders. Instead, he began to write plays. When he applied for his Master of Arts degree in 1587, the university was about to deny it to him on the ground that he intended to go abroad to join the dissident English Catholics at Rheims. But the Privy Council intervened and requested that because Marlowe had done the queen "good service" he be granted his degree at the next commencement. "It is not Her Majesty's pleasure," the government officials added, "that anyone employed as he had been in matters touching the benefit of his country should be defamed by those that are ignorant in the affairs he went about." Although much sensational information about Marlowe has been discovered in modern times, we are still largely "ignorant in the affairs he went about." The likeliest possibility is that he served as a spy or an agent provocateur against English Catholics who were conspiring to overthrow the Protestant regime.

Before he left Cambridge, Marlowe had written his tremendously successful play *Tamburlaine* and perhaps also, in collaboration with his younger Cambridge contemporary Thomas Nashe, the tragedy of *Dido, Queen of Carthage*. *Tamburlaine* dramatizes the exploits of a fourteenth-century Mongol warrior who rose from humble origins to conquer a huge territory that extended from the Black Sea to Delhi. In some sixteenth-century chronicles, Tamburlaine is represented as God's scourge, the instrument of divine wrath. In Marlowe's play there are few if any glimpses of a transcendent design. His hero is the vehicle for the expression of boundless energy and ambition, the impulse to strive ceaselessly for absolute dominance. Tamburlaine's conquests are achieved not only by force of arms but also by his extraordinary mastery of language, his "high astounding terms." The English theater audience had never before heard such resonant, immensely energetic blank verse. The great period of Elizabethan drama was launched by what Ben Jonson called "Marlowe's mighty line."

From the time of his first theatrical success, when he was twenty-three, Marlowe had only six years to live. It is remarkable how much he managed to accomplish in so brief and turbulent a time. (Had Shakespeare died in the same year, we would scarcely remember him.) In 1589 Marlowe was involved in a brawl with one William Bradley, in which the poet Thomas Watson intervened and killed Bradley. Both poets were jailed, but Watson got off on a plea of self-defense, and Marlowe was released. In 1591 Marlowe was living in London with the playwright Thomas Kyd, who later, under torture, gave information to the Privy Council accusing him of atheism and treason. On May 30, 1593, an informer named Richard Baines submitted a note to the council that, on the evidence of Marlowe's own alleged utterances, branded him with atheism, sedition, and homosexuality. Four days later, at an inn in the London suburb of Deptford, Marlowe was killed by a dagger thrust, purportedly in an argument over the bill. Modern scholars have discovered that the murderer and the others present in the room at the inn had connections to the world of spies, double agents, and swindlers to which Marlowe himself was in some way linked. Those who were arrested in connection with the murder were briefly held and then quietly released.

On the bare surface, Marlowe's tragic vision seems for the most part religiously and socially conventional. Tamburlaine at last suffers divine retribution and death at the end of the sequel, *Tamburlaine Part II*; the central character of *The Jew of Malta* is a monstrous anti-Semitic caricature; *Doctor Faustus* and *Edward II* (which treats the tragic fate of a homosexual king) demonstrate the destruction that awaits those who rebel against God or violate the official moral order. Yet there is a force at work in these plays that relentlessly questions and undermines conventional morality. The crime for which Tamburlaine is apparently struck down is the burning of the Muslim Qur'an; the Jew of Malta turns out to be, if anything, less ruthless and hypocritical than his Christian counterparts; and Edward II's life of homoerotic indulgence seems innocent in comparison with the cynical and violent dealings of the corrupt rebels who turn against him. In a way that goes far beyond the demands of moral instruction, Marlowe seems to revel in the depiction of flamboyant transgression, physical abjection, and brutal punishment. Whether as a radical pursuit of absolute liberty or as an expression of sheer destructive negativity, Marlowe's plays, written in the turbulent years before his murder at the age of twenty-nine, have continued to fascinate and disturb readers and audiences.

Hero and Leander

Marlowe's mythological poem is a free and original treatment of a classic tale about two ill-fated lovers. The story derives from a version by the Alexandrian poet Musaeus (ca. fifth century C.E.), but in its blend of poignancy and irony *Hero and Leander* is closer to that of the Roman poet Ovid, who briefly recounts the story in two epistles of his *Heroides* and who refers to it in one of his *Elegies*, which Marlowe translated.

Hero and Leander is a rich and elusive poem: it is comic, decorative, cruel; now swiftly narrative, now digressive; playful and yet, in a light way, philosophical. Filled with free-floating erotic energy, both heterosexual and homosexual, it at once celebrates the power of language and calls attention to its irresponsibility and deceptiveness. The characters are evidently not intended to be consistent or psychologically credible; they inhabit a world of fancy, of strange contrasts between innocence and the wild riot of amorous intrigues among the gods that is Ovid's subject matter. Hero is paradoxically a nun vowed to chastity and a devotee of Venus, the love goddess; Leander is both a sharp, sophisticated seducer and a sexual innocent. The deadpan asides, with their irony, hyperbole, and cynicism mingling with exuberant delight in the body's instinctual freedom, heighten the poem's elusiveness, its cunning evasion of all fixed categories.

Hero and Leander cannot be precisely dated. Marlowe's translations of Ovid, to which the poem is closely related in spirit, are generally thought to be work of the later 1580s. But, alternatively, Marlowe may have been participating in a vogue for brief erotic epics (epyllia, as they are sometimes called) that dates from the early 1590s, when Shakespeare composed his contribution to the genre, *Venus and Adonis*. What is most striking, in either case, is the capacity for innovation. Just as Marlowe's plays displayed an unprecedented dramatic power in their blank verse, *Hero and Leander* manifested for the first time the sophisticated eloquence and tonal range of the heroic couplet.

Marlowe left his poem unfinished; George Chapman, the playwright and translator of Homer, undertook to complete it. Chapman's moralizing, weightily philosophical continuation, which divides the poem into "sestiads" (named after Sestos, where Hero lived), was published in 1598, shortly after Marlowe's fragment. The work is printed here without Chapman's additions.

Hero and Leander

On Hellespont,[1] guilty of true-loves'° blood,   *sweethearts'*
In view and opposite, two cities stood,
Sea-borderers, disjoined by Neptune's might;
The one Abydos, the other Sestos hight.°   *called*
5   At Sestos Hero dwelt; Hero the fair,
Whom young Apollo courted for her hair,
And offered as a dower his burning throne,
Where she should sit for men to gaze upon.
The outside of her garments were of lawn,[2]
10 The lining purple silk, with gilt stars drawn;
Her wide sleeves green, and bordered with a grove
Where Venus in her naked glory strove
To please the careless and disdainful eyes
Of proud Adonis, that before her lies;[3]
15 Her kirtle° blue, whereon was many a stain,   *long dress*
Made with the blood of wretched lovers slain.[4]
Upon her head she ware a myrtle wreath,
From whence her veil reached to the ground beneath.
Her veil was artificial flowers and leaves,
20 Whose workmanship both man and beast deceives;
Many would praise the sweet smell as she passed,
When 'twas the odor which her breath forth cast;
And there for honey, bees have sought in vain,
And, beat from thence, have lighted there again.
25 About her neck hung chains of pebble-stone,
Which, lightened° by her neck, like diamonds shone.   *illuminated*
She ware no gloves, for neither sun nor wind
Would burn or parch her hands, but to her mind°   *as she wished*
Or° warm or cool them, for they took delight   *either*
30 To play upon those hands, they were so white.
Buskins° of shells all silvered usèd she,   *boots*
And branched with blushing coral to the knee,
Where sparrows perched, of hollow pearl and gold,
Such as the world would wonder to behold;
35 Those with sweet water oft her handmaid fills,
Which, as she went,° would chirrup through the bills.   *walked*
Some say, for her the fairest Cupid pined,
And looking in her face, was strooken blind.
But this is true: so like was one the other,
40 As he imagined Hero was his mother;°   *i.e., Venus*
And oftentimes into her bosom flew,
About her naked neck his bare arms threw,
And laid his childish head upon her breast,

---

1. The Dardanelles, in Turkey, a strait that forms part of the boundary between Europe and Asia.
2. A kind of fine linen or thin cambric.
3. Venus's love for the young hunter Adonis and his death in a boar hunt are recounted by Ovid, and by Shakespeare in *Venus and Adonis*.
4. The extravagant claim is made that many "wretched lovers" had committed suicide at her feet because Hero would not have them.

And with still° panting rocked, there took his rest.   *continual*
45   So lovely fair was Hero, Venus' nun,[5]
      As Nature wept, thinking she was undone,
      Because she took more from her than she left
      And of such wondrous beauty her bereft;
      Therefore, in sign her° treasure suffered wrack,°   *i.e., Nature's / destruction*
50   Since Hero's time hath half the world been black.
      Amorous Leander, beautiful and young
      (Whose tragedy divine Musaeus[6] sung),
      Dwelt at Abydos; since him dwelt there none
      For whom succeeding times make greater moan.
55   His dangling tresses that were never shorn,
      Had they been cut and unto Colchos[7] borne,
      Would have allured the vent'rous youth of Greece
      To hazard more than for the Golden Fleece.
      Fair Cynthia° wished his arms might be her sphere;°   *the moon / orbit*
60   Grief makes her pale, because she moves not there.
      His body was as straight as Circe's wand;[8]
      Jove might have sipped out nectar from his hand.
      Even as delicious meat is to the taste,
      So was his neck in touching, and surpassed
65   The white of Pelops' shoulder.[9] I could tell ye
      How smooth his breast was, and how white his belly,
      And whose immortal fingers did imprint
      That heavenly path, with many a curious dint,°   *exquisite indentation*
      That runs along his back; but my rude° pen   *crude*
70   Can hardly blazon forth the loves of men,
      Much less of powerful gods; let it suffice
      That my slack° muse sings of Leander's eyes,   *dull*
      Those orient° cheeks and lips, exceeding his   *shining*
      That leapt into the water for a kiss
75   Of his own shadow,° and despising many,   *reflection*
      Died ere he could enjoy the love of any.[1]
      Had wild Hippolytus[2] Leander seen,
      Enamored of his beauty had he been;
      His presence made the rudest peasant melt,
80   That in the vast uplandish country dwelt;
      The barbarous Thracian soldier, moved with nought,
      Was moved with him, and for his favor sought.
      Some swore he was a maid in man's attire,
      For in his looks were all that men desire:
85   A pleasant smiling cheek, a speaking° eye,   *expressive*
      A brow for love to banquet royally;

5. The connotations of these two words are contradictory. Hero is a maiden in attendance at the temple of Venus, who is, of course, the goddess of physical love.
6. The author of the Greek poem on which *Hero and Leander* is remotely based. Though he lived in late antiquity (ca. 5th century c.e.), he was sometimes confused with a legendary early Musaeus, supposed son of Orpheus; hence Marlowe calls him "divine."

7. The country in Asia where the Argonauts ("the vent'rous youth of Greece"; line 57) found the Golden Fleece.
8. The wand with which Circe, in the *Odyssey*, turned men into beasts.
9. Pelops, according to Ovid, had a shoulder of ivory.
1. An allusion to Narcissus.
2. Like Adonis, he preferred hunting to love.

And such as knew he was a man, would say,
"Leander, thou art made for amorous play;
Why art thou not in love, and loved of° all?   by
90   Though thou be fair, yet be not thine own thrall."°   captive
     The men of wealthy Sestos every year,
For his sake whom their goddess held so dear,
Rose-cheeked Adonis, kept a solemn feast.
Thither resorted many a wandering guest
95   To meet their loves; such as had none at all
Came lovers home from this great festival;
For every street, like to a firmament,
Glistered° with breathing stars, who, where they went,   glittered
Frighted the melancholy earth, which deemed
100 Eternal heaven to burn, for so it seemed
As if another Phaëton³ had got
The guidance of the sun's rich chariot.
But far above the loveliest, Hero shined,
And stole away th' enchanted gazer's mind;
105 For like sea nymphs' inveigling harmony,
So was her beauty to the standers by.
Nor that night-wandering pale and watery star°   the moon
(When yawning dragons draw her thirling⁴ car°   chariot
From Latmos' mount⁵ up to the gloomy sky,
110 Where, crowned with blazing light and majesty,
She proudly sits) more over-rules° the flood°   rules over / tide
Than she the hearts of those that near her stood.
Even as when gaudy nymphs pursue the chase,°   hunt
Wretched Ixion's shaggy-footed race,⁶
115 Incensed with savage heat, gallop amain
From steep pine-bearing mountains to the plain,
So ran the people forth to gaze upon her,
And all that viewed her were enamored on her.
And as in fury of a dreadful fight,
120 Their fellows being slain or put to flight,
Poor soldiers stand with fear of death dead-strooken,
So at her presence all, surprised and tooken,
Await the sentence of her scornful eyes;
He whom she favors lives, the other dies.
125 There might you see one sigh, another rage,
And some, their violent passions to assuage,
Compile sharp satires; but alas, too late,
For faithful love will never turn to hate.
And many, seeing great princes were denied,
130 Pined as they went, and thinking on her, died.
On this feast day, oh, cursèd day and hour!
Went Hero thorough° Sestos, from her tower   through

---

3. A son of the sun god, he drove his father's
chariot erratically across the sky and almost
burned up the world.
4. Flying like a spear.
5. The mountain where the moon visited her

lover, Endymion.
6. The centaurs, fathered by Ixion on a cloud. For
his presumption in loving Juno, Ixion was chained
to a wheel, hence "wretched."

To Venus' temple, where unhappily,
As after chanced, they did each other spy.
135 So fair a church as this had Venus none;
The walls were of discolored° jasper stone, *many-colored*
Wherein was Proteus[7] carved, and o'erhead
A lively° vine of green sea-agate spread, *lifelike*
Where, by one hand, light-headed Bacchus[8] hung,
140 And with the other, wine from grapes out-wrung.
Of crystal shining fair the pavement was;
The town of Sestos called it Venus' glass;° *looking glass*
There might° you see the gods in sundry shapes, *could*
Committing heady° riots, incest, rapes: *passionate; violent*
145 For know that underneath this radiant floor
Was Danaë's[9] statue in a brazen tower,
Jove slyly stealing from his sister's[1] bed
To dally with Idalian Ganymed,[2]
And for his love Europa bellowing loud,[3]
150 And tumbling with the rainbow in a cloud;[4]
Blood-quaffing Mars heaving the iron net
Which limping Vulcan and his Cyclops set;[5]
Love kindling fire to burn such towns as Troy;
Sylvanus weeping for the lovely boy[6]
155 That now is turned into a cypress tree,
Under whose shade the wood-gods love to be.
And in the midst a silver altar stood;
There Hero sacrificing turtles'[7] blood,
Vailed° to the ground, veiling her eyelids close, *bowed down*
160 And modestly they opened as she rose;
Thence flew love's arrow with the golden head,[8]
And thus Leander was enamorèd.
Stone still he stood, and evermore he gazed,
Till with the fire that from his countenance blazed,
165 Relenting Hero's gentle heart was strook;
Such force and virtue° hath an amorous look. *power*
    It lies not in our power to love or hate,
For will in us is overruled by fate.
When two are stripped, long ere the course° begin *race*
170 We wish that one should lose, the other win;
And one especially do we affect° *fancy*
Of two gold ingots, like in each respect.
The reason no man knows, let it suffice,
What we behold is censured° by our eyes. *judged*
175 Where both deliberate, the love is slight;

---

7. A sea god, who could change his shape at will.
8. God of wine and revelry.
9. Imprisoned in a tower, Danaë was visited by Jove in the form of a shower of gold.
1. I.e., Juno's. She was Jove's wife.
2. Ganymede was a beautiful youth whom Jove kidnapped from Mount Ida, hence "Idalian."
3. To abduct Europa, Jove took the form of a bull.
4. Jove as Jupiter Pluvius, god of rain, frolicking with Iris, goddess of the rainbow. But no such tryst is found in classical mythology.
5. Vulcan used a net to trap Venus (his wife) and Mars, "blood-quaffing" god of war, in the act of love. "Cyclops": probably plural; members of this one-eyed race worked as Vulcan's assistants.
6. Cyparissus, beloved of the wood god Sylvanus.
7. Turtledoves, symbolic of constancy in love.
8. The "golden head" of some of Cupid's arrows produced love; he had others, of lead, that produced dislike.

Who ever loved, that loved not at first sight?[9]
    He kneeled, but unto her devoutly prayed.
Chaste Hero to herself thus softly said,
"Were I the saint he worships, I would hear him,"
180 And as she spake those words, came somewhat near him.
He started up; she blushed as one ashamed,
Wherewith Leander much more was inflamed.
He touched her hand; in touching it she trembled:
Love deeply grounded hardly° is dissembled.   *with difficulty*
185 These lovers parlèd° by the touch of hands;   *spoke*
True love is mute, and oft amazèd stands.
Thus while dumb signs their yielding hearts entangled,
The air with sparks of living fire was spangled,
And Night, deep drenched in misty Acheron,[1]
190 Heaved up her head, and half the world upon
Breathed darkness forth. (Dark night is Cupid's day.)
And now begins Leander to display
Love's holy fire, with words, with sighs and tears,
Which like sweet music entered Hero's ears,
195 And yet at every word she turned aside
And always cut him off as he replied.
At last, like to a bold sharp sophister,[2]
With cheerful hope thus he accosted° her: *addressed*
    "Fair creature, let me speak without offense;
200 I would my rude° words had the influence   *rough*
To lead thy thoughts as thy fair looks do mine;
Then shouldst thou be his prisoner, who is thine.
Be not unkind and fair—misshapen stuff°   *persons*
Are of behavior boisterous and rough.
205 O shun me not, but hear me ere you go;
God knows I cannot force° love, as you do.   *compel*
My words shall be as spotless as my youth,
Full of simplicity and naked truth.
This sacrifice, whose sweet perfume descending
210 From Venus' altar to your footsteps bending,°   *turning*
Doth testify that you exceed her far
To whom you offer and whose nun you are.
Why should you worship her? Her you surpass
As much as sparkling diamonds flaring° glass.   *glaring*
215 A diamond set in lead his worth retains;
A heavenly nymph, beloved of human swains,°   *youths*
Receives no blemish but ofttimes more grace;
Which makes me hope, although I am but base—
Base in respect of° thee, divine and pure—   *in comparison with*
220 Dutiful service may thy love procure;
And I in duty will excel all other,
As thou in beauty dost exceed Love's mother.°   *Venus*

9. Shakespeare quotes this famous line in *As You Like It* (3.5.83).
1. One of the rivers of Hades.
2. A sophist is a person skilled in arguments, especially specious ones.

Nor heaven, nor thou, were made to gaze upon;
As heaven preserves all things, so save thou one.
225 A stately builded ship, well rigged and tall,
The ocean maketh more majestical:
Why vowest thou then to live in Sestos here,
Who on Love's seas more glorious wouldst appear?
Like untuned golden strings all women are,
230 Which, long time lie untouched, will harshly jar.³
Vessels of brass, oft handled, brightly shine;
What difference betwixt the richest mine°   ore
And basest mold,° but use? for both not used   earth
Are of like worth. Then treasure is abused
235 When misers keep it; being put to loan,
In time it will return us two for one.
Rich robes themselves and others do adorn;
Neither themselves nor others, if not worn.
Who builds a palace and rams up the gate
240 Shall see it ruinous and desolate.
Ah, simple Hero, learn thyself to cherish;
Lone women, like to empty houses, perish.
Less sins the poor rich man that starves himself
In heaping up a mass of drossy pelf,°   wealth
245 Than such as you: his golden earth remains,
Which after his decease some other gains.
But this fair gem, sweet in the loss alone,
When you fleet hence can be bequeathed to none.
Or if it could, down from th' enameled° sky   many-colored
250 All heaven would come to claim this legacy,
And with intestine° broils the world destroy   internal, civil
And quite confound Nature's sweet harmony.
Well therefore by the gods decreed it is,
We human creatures should enjoy that bliss.
255 One is no number;⁴ maids are nothing then
Without the sweet society of men.
Wilt thou live single still? One shalt thou be,
Though never-singling Hymen⁵ couple thee.
Wild savages, that drink of running springs,
260 Think water far excels all earthly things;
But they that daily taste neat° wine despise it.   undiluted
Virginity, albeit° some highly prize it,   although
Compared with marriage, had you tried them both,
Differs as much as wine and water doth.
265 Base bullion for the stamp's sake⁶ we allow:°   approve
Even so for men's impression do we you;
By which alone, our reverend fathers⁷ say,
Women receive perfection every way.

---

3. I.e., instruments not played will be out of tune
and harsh.
4. A traditional concept, going back to Aristotle.
5. God of marriage. "Never-singling": i.e., one

who never separates, but always joins.
6. For the impression that makes metal ("bullion") into a coin.
7. Ancient philosophers, like Aristotle.

This idol which you term Virginity,
270 Is neither essence,° subject to the eye,   *something real*
    No, nor to any one exterior sense,
    Nor hath it any place of residence,
    Nor is 't of earth or mold° celestial,   *form*
    Or capable of any form at all.
275 Of that which hath no being do not boast:
    Things that are not at all are never lost.
    Men foolishly do call it virtuous:
    What virtue is it that is born with us?[8]
    Much less can honor be ascribed thereto:
280 Honor is purchased by the deeds we do.
    Believe me, Hero, honor is not won
    Until some honorable deed be done.
    Seek you for chastity, immortal fame,
    And know that some have wronged Diana's name?[9]
285 Whose name is it, if she be false or not,
    So she be fair, but some vile tongues will blot?
    But you are fair, aye me! so wondrous fair,
    So young, so gentle, and so debonair,°   *gracious*
    As Greece will think, if thus you live alone,
290 Some one or other keeps you as his own.
    Then, Hero, hate me not, nor from me fly
    To follow swiftly-blasting° infamy.   *-blighting*
    Perhaps thy sacred priesthood makes thee loath.
    Tell me, to whom madest thou that heedless oath?"
295   "To Venus," answered she, and as she spake,
    Forth from those two tralucent cisterns° brake   *i.e., translucent eyes*
    A stream of liquid pearl, which down her face
    Made milk-white paths whereon the gods might trace°   *go*
    To Jove's high court. He thus replied: "The rites
300 In which Love's beauteous empress most delights
    Are banquets, Doric music,[1] midnight revel,
    Plays, masques, and all that stern age counteth evil.
    Thee as a holy idiot doth she scorn;
    For thou, in vowing chastity, hast sworn
305 To rob her name and honor, and thereby
    Commit'st a sin far worse than perjury—
    Even sacrilege against her Deity,
    Through regular and formal purity.
    To expiate which sin, kiss and shake hands;
310 Such sacrifice as this Venus demands."
    Thereat she smiled and did deny him so
    As, put° thereby, yet might he hope for mo.°   *put off / more*
    Which makes him quickly reinforce his speech
    And her in humble manner thus beseech:

---

8. I.e., a virtue is not a virtue unless it is acquired.
9. I.e., no fame for chastity is secure. Even Diana, goddess of chastity, has been slandered.

1. A solemn, military mode. Leander would more appropriately have said "Lydian" (as in Milton's "L'Allegro," line 136); Lydian music was soft and sensual.

315 "Though neither gods nor men may thee deserve,
Yet for her sake whom you have vowed to serve,
Abandon fruitless, cold Virginity,
The gentle Queen of Love's sole enemy.
Then shall you most resemble Venus' nun,
320 When Venus' sweet rites are performed and done.
Flint-breasted Pallas[2] joys in single life,
But Pallas and your mistress are at strife.
Love, Hero, then, and be not tyrannous,
But heal the heart that thou hast wounded thus,
325 Nor stain thy youthful years with avarice;[3]
Fair fools delight to be accounted nice.°   *shy, reluctant*
The richest corn° dies, if it be not reaped;   *grain*
Beauty alone is lost, too warily kept."
     These arguments he used, and many more,
330 Wherewith she yielded, that was won before.
Hero's looks yielded, but her words made war:
Women are won when they begin to jar.°   *dispute*
Thus, having swallowed Cupid's golden hook,
The more she strived, the deeper was she strook.
335 Yet, evilly° feigning anger, strove she still   *badly*
And would be thought to grant against her will.
So having paused a while, at last she said:
"Who taught thee rhetoric to deceive a maid?
Aye me, such words as these should I abhor,
340 And yet I like them for the orator."
     With that, Leander stooped to have embraced her,
But from his spreading arms away she cast her,
And thus bespake him: "Gentle youth, forbear
To touch the sacred garments which I wear.
345   "Upon a rock, and underneath a hill,
Far from the town, where all is whist° and still,   *silent*
Save that the sea, playing on yellow sand,
Sends forth a rattling murmur to the land,
Whose sound allures the golden Morpheus[4]
350 In silence of the night to visit us,
My turret stands, and there, God knows, I play
With Venus' swans and sparrows[5] all the day.
A dwarfish beldame° bears me company,   *old hag*
That hops about the chamber where I lie
355 And spends the night, that might be better spent,
In vain discourse and apish° merriment.   *silly*
Come thither." As she spake this, her tongue tripped,
For unawares "Come thither" from her slipped;
And suddenly her former color changed
360 And here and there her eyes through anger ranged.

2. Athena, a rival goddess, usually portrayed in armor.
3. I.e., by hoarding the treasure of her beauty.
4. God of sleep. "Golden slumbers" was a common expression.
5. Venus was often portrayed in a chariot drawn by swans, and sparrows were associated with her because of their traditionally reputed lechery.

And like a planet, moving several° ways,[6]   *different*
At one self° instant, she, poor soul, assays,°   *one and the same / tries*
Loving, not to love at all, and every part
Strove to resist the motions of her heart;
365 And hands so pure, so innocent, nay, such
As might have made heaven stoop to have a touch,
Did she uphold to Venus, and again
Vowed spotless chastity, but all in vain.
Cupid beat down her prayers with his wings;
370 Her vows above the empty air he flings.
All deep enraged, his sinewy° bow he bent,   *strong*
And shot a shaft that burning from him went,
Wherewith she, strooken, looked so dolefully
As made Love sigh to see his tyranny.
375 And as she wept, her tears to pearl he turned,
And wound them on his arm, and for her mourned.
Then towards the palace of the Destinies,°   *the Fates*
Laden with languishment and grief, he flies,
And to those stern nymphs humbly made request
380 Both might enjoy each other and be blessed.
But with a ghastly dreadful countenance,
Threatening a thousand deaths at every glance,
They answered Love, nor would vouchsafe° so much *grant*
As one poor word, their hate to him was such.
385 Harken a while, and I will tell you why:
Heaven's wingèd herald, Jove-born Mercury,
The selfsame day that he asleep had laid
Enchanted Argus,[7] spied a country maid
Whose careless hair, instead of pearl t' adorn it,
390 Glistered with dew, as one that seemed to scorn it;[8]
Her breath as fragrant as the morning rose,
Her mind pure, and her tongue untaught to glose.° *deceive*
Yet proud she was, for lofty pride that dwells
In towered courts is oft in shepherds' cells,°   *huts*
395 And too-too well the fair vermilion knew,
And silver tincture of her cheeks, that drew
The love of every swain.° On her, this god   *rustic*
Enamored was, and with his snaky rod[9]
Did charm her nimble feet and made her stay;
400 The while upon a hillock down he lay,
And sweetly on his pipe began to play,
And with smooth speech, her fancy to assay,°   *test*
Till in his twining arms he locked her fast,
And then he wooed with kisses, and at last,
405 As shepherds do, her on the ground he laid,
And tumbling in the grass, he often strayed
Beyond the bounds of shame, in being bold

6. In Ptolemaic astronomy each planet moved in its own orbit or sphere but was also carried along in the motion of the surrounding spheres.
7. Mercury (or Hermes), the messenger god with winged feet, put to sleep Argus, the hundred-eyed monster whom Juno had placed as a guard over Io, with whom her husband, Jupiter, was in love. The myth that follows is Marlowe's invention.
8. I.e., pearl or other jewelry.
9. The caduceus (now the symbol of medicine).

To eye those parts which no eye should behold;
And, like an insolent commanding lover,
410 Boasting his parentage, would needs discover
The way to new Elysium;[1] but she,
Whose only dower was her chastity,
Having striven in vain, was now about to cry
And crave the help of shepherds that were nigh.
415 Herewith he stayed his fury,° and began   passion
To give her leave to rise. Away she ran;
After went Mercury, who used such cunning
As she, to hear his tale, left off her running.
Maids are not won by brutish force and might,
420 But speeches full of pleasure and delight.
And knowing Hermes[2] courted her, was glad
That she such loveliness and beauty had
As could provoke his liking, yet was mute,
And neither would deny nor grant his suit.
425 Still vowed he love; she, wanting° no excuse   lacking
To feed him with delays, as women use,°   as women usually do
Or thirsting after immortality
(All women are ambitious naturally),
Imposed upon her lover such a task
430 As he ought not perform, nor yet she ask.
A draft of flowing nectar she requested,
Wherewith the king of gods and men is feasted.
He, ready to accomplish what she willed,
Stole some from Hebe (Hebe Jove's cup filled)
435 And gave it to his simple rustic love,
Which being known (as what is hid from Jove?)
He inly stormed and waxed more furious
Than for the fire filched by Prometheus,
And thrusts him down from heaven. He, wandering here,
440 In mournful terms,° with sad and heavy cheer,°   condition / countenance
Complained to Cupid. Cupid, for his sake,
To be revenged on Jove did undertake;
And those on whom heaven, earth, and hell relies
(I mean the adamantine[3] Destinies)
445 He wounds with love and forced them equally
To dote upon deceitful Mercury.
They offered him the deadly fatal knife
That shears the slender threads of human life;[4]
At his fair feathered feet the engines° laid   contrivances
450 Which th' earth from ugly Chaos' den upweighed.[5]
These he regarded not, but did entreat

1. In classical mythology, the paradisal home of the favored dead; also known as the Islands of the Blessed.
2. Marlowe uses the names Mercury and Hermes interchangeably, according to the requirements of meter.
3. Of extreme hardness (so called because the Destinies'—or Fates'—decrees were irrevocable).

4. According to classical mythology, the Fates spun and cut the thread that measures each life.
5. The Fates also controlled the supports that had held up ("upweighed") the earth since it arose out of Chaos, the yawning abyss from which all things came.

That Jove, usurper of his father's seat,
Might presently° be banished into hell   *immediately*
And agèd Saturn in Olympus dwell.
455 They granted what he craved,° and once again   *requested*
Saturn and Ops began their golden reign.
Murder, rape, war, lust, and treachery
Were with Jove closed in Stygian empery.°   *realm*
But long this blessèd time continued not;
460 As soon as he his wishèd purpose got,
He, reckless of his promise, did despise
The love of th' everlasting Destinies.
They seeing it, both Love and him abhorred,
And Jupiter unto his place restored.[6]
465 And but that Learning, in despite of Fate,
Will mount aloft and enter heaven gate,
And to the seat of Jove itself advance,
Hermes had slept in hell with Ignorance.
Yet as a punishment they added this,
470 That he and Poverty should always kiss.[7]
And to this day is every scholar poor;
Gross gold from them runs headlong to the boor.°   *ignorant clod*
Likewise the angry sisters, thus deluded,
To venge themselves on Hermes, have concluded
475 That Midas' brood[8] shall sit in Honor's chair,
To which the Muses' sons are only heir.
And fruitful wits° that inaspiring[9] are   *minds*
Shall discontent run into regions far;
And few great lords in virtuous deeds shall joy,
480 But be surprised with° every garish toy,°   *captivated by / trifle*
And still° enrich the lofty servile clown,°   *ever / ignorant person*
Who, with encroaching guile, keeps learning down.
Then muse not° Cupid's suit no better sped,   *i.e., don't be surprised*
Seeing in their loves the Fates were injurèd.
485   By this, sad Hero, with love unacquainted,
Viewing Leander's face, fell down and fainted.
He kissed her and breathed life into her lips,
Wherewith, as one displeased, away she trips.
Yet as she went, full often looked behind,
490 And many poor excuses did she find
To linger by the way, and once she stayed

---

6. The story in lines 451–64 may be summarized as follows: Mercury scorns the gifts offered by the Fates but asks instead that Jove be dethroned (Jove had overthrown his father, Saturn, who ruled heaven during the Golden Age). Mercury persuades the Fates to reverse this revolution, so Saturn and his wife, Ops, return to Olympus and Jove is thrust down into "Stygian empery" (line 458), or Hades. During the Golden Age there was no murder, rape, war, lust, or treachery; these came in with Jove, so when he is sent to Hades they go with him. But this second Golden Age did not last long, because once he got what he wanted, Mercury forgot the Destinies and they restored Jove.

7. Mercury, the god of learning, would have slept in hell with Ignorance were it not that Learning is so divine that it always mounts up, even to heaven, the "seat of Jove." But it was not beyond the Fates' power to make Learning and Poverty go together, which they decreed in revenge for Mercury's neglect.

8. The rich, because everything Midas touched turned to gold; also the stupid, because Midas, judging a musical contest between Apollo and Pan, preferred the latter, against all sensible opinion.

9. Not ambitious for riches or power.

And would have turned again, but was afraid
In offering parley to be counted light.°   *immodest*
So on she goes, and in her idle flight
495   Her painted fan of curlèd plumes let fall,
Thinking to train° Leander therewithal.   *entice*
He, being a novice, knew not what she meant,
But stayed, and after her a letter sent,
Which joyful Hero answered in such sort
500   As he had hope to scale the beauteous fort
Wherein the liberal Graces[1] locked their wealth,
And therefore to her tower he got by stealth.
Wide open stood the door; he need not climb,
And she herself before the pointed° time   *appointed*
505   Had spread the board,° with roses strewed the room,   *set the table*
And oft looked out, and mused° he did not come.   *wondered*
At last he came; O who can tell the greeting
These greedy lovers had at their first meeting?
He asked, she gave, and nothing was denied;
510   Both to each other quickly were affied.°   *engaged*
Look how° their hands, so were their hearts united,   *just as*
And what he did, she willingly requited.
(Sweet are the kisses, the embracements sweet,
When like desires and affections meet,
515   For from the earth to heaven is Cupid raised,
Where fancy is in equal balance peised.°)   *weighed*
Yet she this rashness suddenly repented
And turned aside and to herself lamented,
As if her name and honor had been wronged
520   By being possessed of him for whom she longed.
Ay, and she wished, albeit not from her heart,
That he would leave her turret and depart.
The mirthful god of amorous pleasure smiled
To see how he this captive nymph beguiled,°   *deceived*
525   For hitherto he did but fan the fire
And kept it down that it might mount the higher.
Now waxed she jealous° lest his love abated,   *possessively fearful*
Fearing her own thoughts made her to be hated.
Therefore unto him hastily she goes
530   And, like light Salmacis,[2] her body throws
Upon his bosom where, with yielding eyes,
She offers up herself a sacrifice
To slake his anger, if he were displeased.
O what god would not therewith be appeased?
535   Like Aesop's cock,[3] this jewel he enjoyed,
And as a brother with his sister toyed,
Supposing nothing else was to be done,
Now he her favor and good will had won.
But know you not that creatures wanting sense°   *lacking intelligence*

---

1. Three goddesses, embodying aspects of beauty.
2. An amorous nymph in Ovid's *Metamorphoses*.
3. In Aesop's fable, a cock, scratching in the barnyard, uncovers a jewel but prefers a barley corn.

540 By nature have a mutual appetence,[4]
And wanting organs to advance a step,
Moved by love's force, unto each other leap?
Much more in subjects having intellect
Some hidden influence breeds like effect.
545 Albeit Leander, rude° in love and raw,   *untutored*
Long dallying with Hero, nothing saw
That might delight him more, yet he suspected
Some amorous rites or other were neglected.
Therefore unto his body, hers he clung;
550 She, fearing on the rushes[5] to be flung,
Strived with redoubled strength; the more she strived,
The more a gentle, pleasing heat revived,
Which taught him all that elder lovers know.
And now the same gan so to scorch and glow,
555 As, in plain terms, yet cunningly,° he craved° it.   *skillfully / asked for*
(Love always makes those eloquent that have it.)
She, with a kind of granting, put him by it,
And, ever as he thought himself most nigh it,
Like to the tree of Tantalus,[6] she fled,
560 And, seeming lavish, saved her maidenhead.
Ne'er king more sought to keep his diadem
Than Hero this inestimable gem.
Above our life we love a steadfast friend;
Yet, when a token of great worth we send,
565 We often kiss it, often look thereon,
And stay the messenger that would be gone.
No marvel then, though Hero would not yield
So soon to part from that she dearly held.
Jewels being lost are found again, this never;
570 'Tis lost but once, and once lost, lost forever.
    Now had the Morn espied her lover's steeds,[7]
Whereat she starts, puts on her purple weeds,°   *clothes*
And, red for anger that he stayed so long,
All headlong throws herself the clouds among.
575 And now Leander, fearing to be missed,
Embraced her suddenly, took leave, and kissed;
Long was he taking leave, and loath to go,
And kissed again, as lovers use° to do.   *are accustomed*
Sad Hero wrung him by the hand and wept,
580 Saying, "Let your vows and promises be kept."
Then, standing at the door, she turned about,
As loath to see Leander going out.
And now the sun that through th' horizon peeps,
As pitying these lovers, downward creeps,
585 So that in silence of the cloudy night,
Though it was morning, did he take his flight.

4. Attraction, as iron to a magnet.
5. Reeds used as carpeting in Elizabethan homes.
6. Punished in Hades by constantly reaching for
fruit from a tree that eluded him and by trying to
drink water that also escaped him.
7. The horses that pull the chariot of the sun.

But what the secret trusty night concealed,
Leander's amorous habit° soon revealed.   *dress*
With Cupid's myrtle[8] was his bonnet° crowned;   *hat*
590   About his arms the purple riband° wound   *ribbon*
Wherewith she wreathed her largely spreading hair;
Nor could the youth abstain but he must wear
The sacred ring wherewith she was endowed
When first religious chastity she vowed;
595   Which made his love through Sestos to be known,
And thence unto Abydos sooner blown
Than he could sail, for incorporeal Fame,
Whose weight consists in nothing but her name,
Is swifter than the wind, whose tardy plumes
600   Are reeking water and dull earthly fumes.[9]
Home when he came, he seemed not to be there,
But like exilèd air thrust from his sphere,
Set in a foreign place, and straight from thence,
Alcides-like,[1] by mighty violence
605   He would have chased away the swelling main°   *sea*
That him from her unjustly did detain.
Like as the sun in a diameter[2]
Fires and inflames objects removèd far,
And heateth kindly, shining lat'rally,[3]
610   So beauty sweetly quickens° when 'tis nigh,   *gives life*
But being separated and removed,
Burns where it cherished, murders where it loved.
Therefore, even as an index to a book,
So to his mind was young Leander's look.
615   O none but gods have power their love to hide:
Affection by the count'nance is descried.°   *revealed*
The light of hidden fire itself discovers,
And love that is concealed betrays° poor lovers.   *gives away*
His secret flame apparently° was seen;   *openly*
620   Leander's father knew where he had been,
And for the same mildly rebuked his son,
Thinking to quench the sparkles new begun.
But love, resisted once, grows passionate,
And nothing more than counsel lovers hate.
625   For as a hot, proud horse highly disdains
To have his head controlled, but breaks the reins,
Spits forth the ringled° bit, and with his hooves   *with rings at the ends*
Checks° the submissive ground; so he that loves,   *stamps*
The more he is restrained, the worse he fares.
630   What is it now but mad Leander dares?[4]

8. A plant sacred to Venus or Cupid, symbolic of
love.
9. I.e., are mist and smoke.
1. Like Hercules, with brute force. ("Alcides" is a
patronymic of Hercules, deriving from his step-
grandfather, Alcaeus.)
2. I.e., shining straight down at noon.

3. I.e., when it is lower in the sky. The idea is
that the sun, paradoxically, causes harm only
when it appears to be farthest away (at the zenith).
Beauty, Marlowe goes on to claim, works the
same way.
4. I.e., what is there now Leander dares not do?

"O Hero, Hero!" thus he cried full oft,
And then he got him to a rock aloft,
Where, having spied her tower, long stared he on 't
And prayed the narrow toiling Hellespont
635 To part in twain, that he might come and go;
But still the rising billows answered "No!"
With that he stripped him to the ivory skin,
And crying, "Love, I come!" leapt lively in.
Whereat the sapphire-visaged god° grew proud,[5]   *Neptune, god of the sea*
640 And made his capering Triton[6] sound aloud;
Imagining that Ganimed,[7] displeased,
Had left the heavens, therefore on him seized.
Leander strived; the waves about him wound
And pulled him to the bottom, where the ground
645 Was strewed with pearl, and in low coral groves
Sweet singing mermaids sported with their loves
On heaps of heavy gold and took great pleasure
To spurn in careless sort° the shipwreck treasure;   *manner*
For here the stately azure palace stood
650 Where kingly Neptune and his train° abode.   *attendants*
The lusty god embraced him, called him love,
And swore he never should return to Jove.
But when he knew it was not Ganimed,
For under water he was almost dead,
655 He heaved him up, and looking on his face,
Beat down the bold waves with his triple mace,[8]
Which mounted up, intending to have kissed him,
And fell in drops like tears because they missed him.
Leander being up, began to swim,
660 And, looking back, saw Neptune follow him;
Whereat aghast, the poor soul gan to cry,
"O let me visit Hero ere I die!"
The god put Helle's bracelet[9] on his arm,
And swore the sea should never do him harm.
665 He clapped his plump cheeks, with his tresses played,
And, smiling wantonly, his love bewrayed.°   *revealed*
He watched his arms, and as they opened wide,
At every stroke betwixt them he would slide
And steal a kiss, and then run out and dance
670 And, as he turned, cast many a lustful glance
And throw him gaudy toys to please his eye,
And dive into the water and there pry
Upon his breast, his thighs, and every limb,
And up again and close beside him swim,
675 And talk of love. Leander made reply,
"You are deceived; I am no woman, I."

---

5. The primary sense is probably "became sexually aroused."
6. A subordinate sea god who blew on a conch shell.
7. See p. 663, n. 2.
8. The three-pronged fork carried by Neptune.

9. Helle was the daughter of King Athamas of Thebes. To escape a cruel stepmother, she fled on a winged, golden-fleeced ram but fell off into the Hellespont, which was named for her. Marlowe apparently invented the detail of the bracelet.

Thereat smiled Neptune, and then told a tale
How that a shepherd, sitting in a vale,
Played with a boy so lovely fair and kind,
680 As for his love both earth and heaven pined;
That of the cooling river durst not drink,
Lest water nymphs should pull him from the brink;
And when he sported in the fragrant lawns,
Goat-footed satyrs and up-staring fawns[1]
685 Would steal him thence. Ere half this tale was done
"Ay me!" Leander cried, "th' enamored sun
That now should shine on Thetis' glassy bower[2]
Descends upon my radiant Hero's tower.
O that these tardy arms of mine were wings!"
690 And as he spake, upon the waves he springs.
Neptune was angry that he gave no ear,
And in his heart revenging malice bare.
He flung at him his mace, but as it went
He called it in, for love made him repent.
695 The mace returning back, his own hand hit,
As meaning to be venged for darting it.
When this fresh bleeding wound Leander viewed,
His color went and came, as if he rued°   *regretted*
The grief° which Neptune felt. In gentle breasts   *pain*
700 Relenting thoughts, remorse, and pity rests;
And who have hard hearts and obdurate minds
But vicious, harebrained, and illit'rate hinds?°   *rustics*
The god, seeing him with pity to be moved,
Thereon concluded that he was beloved.
705 (Love is too full of faith, too credulous,
With folly and false hope deluding us.)
Wherefore Leander's fancy to surprise,°   *i.e., to capture his love*
To the rich ocean for gifts he flies.
'Tis wisdom to give much; a gift prevails
710 When deep persuading oratory fails.
By this° Leander, being near the land,   *by this time*
Cast down his weary feet and felt the sand.
Breathless albeit he were, he rested not
Till to the solitary tower he got,
715 And knocked and called; at which celestial noise
The longing heart of Hero much more joys
Than nymphs and shepherds when the timbrel° rings,   *tambourine*
Or crooked[3] dolphin when the sailor sings.
She stayed not for her robes, but straight arose
720 And, drunk with gladness, to the door she goes;
Where, seeing a naked man, she screeched for fear
(Such sights as this to tender maids are rare)
And ran into the dark herself to hide.

1. Woodland spirits, who prophesied by looking
up to the heavens.
2. I.e., the sea. Thetis was a sea nymph, mother
of the hero Achilles.

3. "Crooked" because of the undulating path of
the dolphin in the water. The musician Arion
was saved from drowning by a dolphin charmed
by his music.

Rich jewels in the dark are soonest spied.
725 Unto her was he led, or rather drawn
By those white limbs which sparkled through the lawn.°   *fine linen*
The nearer that he came, the more she fled,
And, seeking refuge, slipped into her bed.
Whereon Leander sitting, thus began,
730 Through numbing cold, all feeble, faint, and wan:
   "If not for love, yet, love, for pity's sake
Me in thy bed and maiden bosom take;
At least vouchsafe° these arms some little room,   *grant*
Who, hoping to embrace thee, cheerly° swum.   *gladly*
735 This head was beat with many a churlish billow,
And therefore let it rest upon thy pillow."
Herewith affrighted Hero shrunk away
And in her lukewarm place Leander lay;
Whose lively heat, like fire from heaven fet,°   *fetched*
740 Would animate gross clay, and higher set
The drooping thoughts of base declining souls
Than dreary° Mars° carousing nectar bowls.   *bloody / god of war*
His hands he cast upon her like a snare;
She, overcome with shame and sallow fear,
745 Like chaste Diana when Actaeon[4] spied her,
Being suddenly betrayed, dived down to hide her,
And as her silver body downward went,
With both her hands she made the bed a tent,
And in her own mind thought herself secure,
750 O'ercast with dim and darksome coverture.
And now she lets him whisper in her ear,
Flatter, entreat, promise, protest, and swear;
Yet ever as he greedily assayed°   *tried*
To touch those dainties, she the Harpy[5] played,
755 And every limb did, as a soldier stout,
Defend the fort and keep the foeman out.
For though the rising ivory mount he scaled,
Which is with azure circling lines empaled,°   *surrounded*
Much like a globe (a globe may I term this,
760 By which love sails to regions full of bliss),
Yet there with Sisyphus[6] he toiled in vain,
Till gentle parley did the truce obtain.[7]
Wherein Leander on her quivering breast,
Breathless spoke something, and sighed out the rest;
765 Which so prevailed, as he, with small ado,
Enclosed her in his arms and kissed her, too.

4. A hunter who happened on Diana bathing. She turned him into a stag, and he was killed by his own hounds.
5. A monster, half-bird, half-woman, who snatches away banquets in Virgil's *Aeneid* and Shakespeare's *Tempest*.
6. Condemned in Hades endlessly to roll a stone uphill.
7. In both the authoritative early printings of the poem (1598), the lines here numbered 775–84 follow at this point (i.e., they precede the lines here numbered 763–74). Like almost all modern editors, though, we have adopted the rearrangement first made in 1910 by Tucker Brooke, in his edition of Marlowe's *Works*. The original order, Brooke thought, did not make good sense; he hypothesized that two sheets of Marlowe's manuscript had been accidentally reversed by the time (five years after his death) the poem was printed. Students may, though, want to read the passage both ways and make up their own minds as to which order is preferable.

And every kiss to her was as a charm,
And to Leander as a fresh alarm,°   *call to battle*
So that the truce was broke, and she, alas,
770 Poor silly° maiden, at his mercy was.   *innocent*
Love is not full of pity, as men say,
But deaf and cruel, where he means to prey.
Even as a bird which in our hands we wring
Forth plungeth and oft flutters with her wing,
775 She trembling strove; this strife of hers, like that
Which made the world,⁸ another world begat
Of unknown joy. Treason was in her thought,
And cunningly to yield herself she sought.
Seeming not won, yet won she was, at length.
780 (In such wars women use but half their strength.)
Leander now, like Theban Hercules,
Entered the orchard of th' Hesperides,
Whose fruit none rightly can describe but he
That pulls or shakes it from the golden tree.⁹
785 And now she wished this night were never done,
And sighed to think upon th' approaching sun,
For much it grieved her that the bright daylight
Should know the pleasure of this blessèd night,
And them like Mars and Erycine¹ displayed,
790 Both in each other's arms chained as they laid.
Again she knew not how to frame her look
Or speak to him who in a moment took
That which so long so charily° she kept;   *carefully*
And fain° by stealth away she would have crept   *gladly*
795 And to some corner secretly have gone,
Leaving Leander in the bed alone.
But as her naked feet were whipping out,
He on the sudden clinged her so about
That mermaid-like unto the floor she slid:
800 One half appeared, the other half was hid.
Thus near the bed she blushing stood upright;
And from her countenance behold ye might
A kind of twilight break, which through the hair,
As from an orient° cloud, glims° here and there,   *bright / gleams*
805 And round about the chamber this false morn
Brought forth the day before the day was born.
So Hero's ruddy cheek Hero betrayed,
And her all naked to his sight displayed,
Whence his admiring eyes more pleasure took
810 Than Dis² on heaps of gold fixing his look.
By this Apollo's golden harp began
To sound forth music to the Ocean,

---

8. The Greek philosopher Empedocles held that creation was the result of love and strife acting in opposition to each other and alternately ruling the universe.
9. One of Hercules' labors was to get the golden apples of the Hesperides, guarded by a dragon.

Hercules was born in Thebes.
1. A name for Venus, who was caught in bed with Mars by her husband, Vulcan, who enmeshed them in a fine chain net.
2. Pluto, god of the underworld and of wealth.

Which watchful Hesperus[3] no sooner heard
But he the day's bright-bearing car prepared,
815 And ran before, as harbinger of light,
And with his flaring beams mocked ugly Night
Till she, o'ercome with anguish, shame, and rage,
Danged° down to hell her loathsome carriage.   *hurled*
           Desunt nonnulla.°   *something is lacking*

1598

The Passionate Shepherd to His Love[1]

Come live with me and be my love,
And we will all the pleasures prove°   *test, experience*
That valleys, groves, hills, and fields,
Woods, or steepy mountain yields.

5 And we will sit upon the rocks,
Seeing the shepherds feed their flocks,
By shallow rivers to whose falls
Melodious birds sing madrigals.

And I will make thee beds of roses
10 And a thousand fragrant posies,°   *bouquets (also of poems)*
A cap of flowers, and a kirtle°   *dress*
Embroidered all with leaves of myrtle;

A gown made of the finest wool
Which from our pretty lambs we pull;
15 Fair linèd slippers for the cold,
With buckles of the purest gold;

A belt of straw and ivy buds,
With coral clasps and amber studs:
And if these pleasures may thee move,
20 Come live with me, and be my love.

The shepherd swains shall dance and sing
For thy delight each May morning:
If these delights thy mind may move,
Then live with me and be my love.

1599, 1600

---

3. The evening star; one would expect Lucifer, the morning star.
1. This pastoral lyric of invitation is one of the most famous of Elizabethan songs, and a few lines from it are sung in Shakespeare's *Merry Wives of Windsor.* Many poets have written replies to it, the best known of which is by Sir Walter Ralegh (p. 527).

Doctor Faustus

Marlowe's major dramas, *Tamburlaine*, *The Jew of Malta*, and *Doctor Faustus*, all portray heroes who passionately seek power—the power of rule, the power of money, and the power of knowledge, respectively. Each of the heroes, like the playwright himself, is an overreacher, striving to get beyond the conventional boundaries established to contain the human will.

Unlike Tamburlaine, whose aim and goal is "the sweet fruition of an earthly crown," or Barabas, the Jew of Malta, who lusts for "infinite riches in a little room," Faustus seeks the mastery and voluptuous pleasure that come from forbidden knowledge. To achieve his goal Faustus must make—or chooses to make—a bargain with Lucifer. This is an old folklore motif, but it would have been taken seriously in a time when belief in the reality of devils was almost universal. The story's power over its original audience is vividly suggested by the numerous accounts of uncanny events at performances of the play: strange noises in the theater or extra devils who suddenly appeared among the actors onstage, causing panic.

In the opening soliloquy, Marlowe's Faustus bids farewell to each of his studies—logic, medicine, law, and divinity—as things he has mastered and found unfulfilling. He turns instead to black magic, but the devil exacts a fearful price in exchange: the eternal damnation of Faustus's soul. Whether Faustus freely chooses to pay this price, in order to acquire hidden knowledge, or whether he is predestined to do so, is unclear. Renaissance theologians fiercely debated the question of fate versus free will, and their arguments are reflected in the play. Faustus's fall is caused by the same pride and ambition that caused the fall of the angels in heaven and of humankind in the Garden of Eden. But it is characteristic of Marlowe that he makes this catastrophic aspiration nonetheless a magnificent human venture.

The immediate source of the play is a German narrative called, in its English translation, *The History of the Damnable Life and Deserved Death of Doctor John Faustus*. That source supplies Marlowe's drama with the scenes of horseplay and low practical joking that contrast so markedly with the passages of huge ambition. It is quite possible that these comic scenes are the work of a collaborator; but no other Elizabethan could have written the first scene (with its brilliant representation of the insatiable aspiring mind of the hero), the ecstatic address to Helen of Troy, or the searing scene of Faustus's last hour. And though compared with these celebrated passages the comic scenes often seem crude, they too contribute to the overarching vision of Faustus's fate: the half-trivial, half-daring exploits, the alternating states of bliss and despair, the questions that are not answered and the answers that bring no real satisfaction, the heroic wanderings that lead nowhere.

Marlowe's play exists in two very different forms: the A text (1604) and the much longer B text (1616). Even the earlier version dates from some fifteen years after the play was actually written and contains later interpolations. The B text almost certainly incorporates additions by other hands and was also revised to conform to the severe censorship statutes of 1606. We use Roma Gill's edition, based on the A text. Following the play are parallel versions of a key scene that will enable the reader to compare the two texts.

The Tragical History of Doctor Faustus

DRAMATIS PERSONAE[1]

CHORUS	THREE SCHOLARS
DR. JOHN FAUSTUS	GOOD ANGEL
WAGNER, *his servant, a student*	EVIL ANGEL
VALDES ⎫	MEPHASTOPHILIS
CORNELIUS ⎰ *his friends, magicians*	LUCIFER
BELZEBUB	*Spirits presenting*
OLD MAN	THE SEVEN DEADLY SINS
CLOWN	PRIDE
ROBIN ⎫ *ostlers at an inn*	COVETOUSNESS
RAFE ⎰	WRATH
VINTNER	ENVY
HORSE-COURSER	GLUTTONY
THE POPE	SLOTH
THE CARDINAL OF LORRAINE	LECHERY
CHARLES V, EMPEROR OF	ALEXANDER THE GREAT *and his*
GERMANY	PARAMOUR
A KNIGHT *at the* EMPEROR'S *court*	HELEN OF TROY
DUKE OF VANHOLT	
DUCHESS OF VANHOLT	ATTENDANTS, FRIARS, *and* DEVILS

Prologue

[*Enter* CHORUS.][2]

CHORUS   Not marching now in fields of Thrasimene,
Where Mars[3] did mate° the Carthaginians,   *join with*
Nor sporting in the dalliance of love,
In courts of kings where state° is overturned,   *political power*
5   Nor in the pomp of proud audacious deeds,
Intends our Muse to vaunt his heavenly verse:
Only this (Gentlemen) we must perform,
The form of Faustus' fortunes good or bad.
To patient judgments we appeal our plaud,°   *applause*
10   And speak for Faustus in his infancy:
Now is he born, his parents base of stock,
In Germany, within a town called Rhodes;[4]
Of riper years to Wittenberg[5] he went,
Whereas° his kinsmen chiefly brought him up.   *where*
15   So soon he profits in divinity,°   *theology*
The fruitful plot of scholarism graced,
That shortly he was graced with doctor's name,[6]

---

1. There is no list of characters in the A text. The one here is an editorial construction.
2. A single actor who recited a prologue to an act or a whole play, and occasionally delivered an epilogue.
3. God of war. The battle of Lake Trasimene (217 B.C.E.) was one of the Carthaginian leader Hannibal's great victories.

4. Roda, or Stadtroda, in Germany.
5. The famous university where Martin Luther studied, as did Shakespeare's Hamlet and Horatio.
6. The lines play on two senses of *graced*: he so (1) adorned the place ("plot") of scholarship— i.e., the university—that shortly he was (2) honored with a doctor's degree.

Excelling all whose sweet delight disputes[7]
In heavenly matters of theology.
20 Till, swollen with cunning,° of a self-conceit,   *knowledge*
His waxen wings did mount above his reach,
And melting heavens conspired his overthrow.[8]
For falling to a devilish exercise,
And glutted more with learning's golden gifts,
25 He surfeits upon cursed necromancy:°   *black magic*
Nothing so sweet as magic is to him,
Which he prefers before his chiefest bliss.[9]
And this the man[1] that in his study sits.   [*Exit.*]

SCENE 1

[*Enter* FAUSTUS *in his study.*]
FAUSTUS   Settle thy studies, Faustus, and begin
To sound the depth of that thou wilt profess:
Having commenced, be a divine in show,[2]
Yet level° at the end of every art,   *aim*
5 And live and die in Aristotle's works.
Sweet *Analytics*,[3] 'tis thou hast ravished me.
Bene disserere est finis logices.[4]
Is to dispute well logic's chiefest end?
Affords this art no greater miracle?
10 Then read no more, thou hast attained the end;
A greater subject fitteth Faustus' wit.°   *intellect*
Bid *on kai me on*[5] farewell; Galen[6] come:
Seeing, *ubi desinit philosophus, ibi incipit medicus.*[7]
Be a physician, Faustus, heap up gold,
15 And be eternized for some wondrous cure.
Summum bonum medicinae sanitas:[8]
The end of physic° is our body's health.   *medicine*
Why Faustus, hast thou not attained that end?
Is not thy common talk found aphorisms?[9]
20 Are not thy bills° hung up as monuments,   *prescriptions*
Whereby whole cities have escaped the plague,
And thousand desperate maladies been eased?
Yet art thou still but Faustus, and a man.
Couldst thou make men to live eternally,
25 Or, being dead, raise them to life again,

---

7. Referring to formal disputations, academic exercises that occupied the place now held by examinations.
8. In Greek myth, Icarus flew too near the sun on wings of feathers and wax made by his father, Daedalus; the wax melted, and he fell into the sea and drowned.
9. The salvation of his soul.
1. Apparently a cue for the Chorus to draw aside the curtain to the enclosed space at the rear of the stage.
2. In external appearance. "Commenced": grad-uated, i.e., received the doctor's degree.
3. The title of two treatises on logic by Aristotle.
4. To carry on a disputation well is the end [or purpose] of logic (Latin).
5. Being and not being (Greek); here standing for philosophical studies in general.
6. The supreme ancient authority on medicine (2nd century C.E.).
7. Where the philosopher leaves off the phys-ician begins (Latin).
8. The Latin is translated in the following line.
9. I.e., generally accepted wisdom.

Then this profession were to be esteemed.
Physic farewell! Where is Justinian?[1]
Si una eademque res legatur duobus,
Alter rem alter valorem rei, etc.[2]
30 A pretty case of paltry legacies.
Exhereditare filium non potest pater nisi . . .[3]
Such is the subject of the Institute
And universal Body of the Law:
This study fits a mercenary drudge
35 Who aims at nothing but external trash!
Too servile and illiberal for me.
When all is done, divinity is best.
Jerome's Bible,[4] Faustus, view it well:
Stipendium peccati mors est:[5] ha! *Stipendium, etc.*
40 The reward of sin is death? That's hard.
Si pecasse negamus, fallimur, et nulla est in nobis veritas:[6]
If we say that we have no sin,
We deceive ourselves, and there's no truth in us.
Why then belike° we must sin,   *in all likelihood*
45 And so consequently die.
Ay, we must die an everlasting death.
What doctrine call you this? *Che sarà, sarà:*
What will be, shall be? Divinity, adieu!
These metaphysics° of magicians   *occult lore*
50 And necromantic books are heavenly!
Lines, circles, schemes, letters, and characters!
Ay, these are those that Faustus most desires.
O what a world of profit and delight,
Of power, of honor, of omnipotence
55 Is promised to the studious artisan![7]
All things that move between the quiet° poles   *unmoving*
Shall be at my command: emperors and kings
Are but obeyed in their several° provinces,   *separate*
Nor can they raise the wind, or rend the clouds;
60 But his dominion that exceeds in this
Stretcheth as far as doth the mind of man:
A sound magician is a mighty god.
Here, Faustus, try thy brains to gain a deity.
    [*Enter* WAGNER.]
Wagner, commend me to my dearest friends,
65 The German Valdes and Cornelius,

---

1. Roman emperor and authority on law (483–565 C.E.). The Latin passages that follow paraphrase Justinian's *Institutiones*, a manual included in his *Corpus Iuris* (Body of the Law); cf. lines 32–33).
2. If something is bequeathed to two persons, one shall have the thing itself, the other something of equal value.
3. A father cannot disinherit his son unless . . .
4. The Latin translation, or Vulgate, of Saint Jerome (ca. 340–420 C.E.).
5. Romans 6.23. But Faustus reads only part of the Scripture verse: "For the wages of sin is death; but the gift of God is eternal life through Jesus Christ our Lord."
6. I John 1.8 (translated in the following two lines).
7. A practitioner of an art; here, necromancy.

Request them earnestly to visit me.
WAGNER   I will, sir.   [*Exit.*]
FAUSTUS   Their conference will be a greater help to me
Than all my labors, plod I ne'er so fast.
[*Enter the* GOOD ANGEL *and the* EVIL ANGEL.]
70   GOOD ANGEL   O Faustus, lay that damnèd book aside,
And gaze not on it, lest it tempt thy soul
And heap God's heavy wrath upon thy head:
Read, read the Scriptures; that is blasphemy.
EVIL ANGEL   Go forward, Faustus, in that famous art,
75   Wherein all nature's treasury is contained:
Be thou on earth as Jove[8] is in the sky,
Lord and commander of these elements.   [*Exeunt.*]
FAUSTUS   How am I glutted with conceit° of this!   *filled with the idea*
Shall I make spirits fetch me what I please,
80   Resolve me of all ambiguities,
Perform what desperate° enterprise I will?   *reckless*
I'll have them fly to India for gold,
Ransack the ocean for orient pearl,[9]
And search all corners of the new-found world
85   For pleasant fruits and princely delicates.
I'll have them read me strange philosophy,
And tell the secrets of all foreign kings;
I'll have them wall all Germany with brass,
And make swift Rhine circle fair Wittenberg;[1]
90   I'll have them fill the public schools[2] with silk,
Wherewith the students shall be bravely° clad.   *splendidly*
I'll levy soldiers with the coin they bring,
And chase the Prince of Parma[3] from our land,
And reign sole king of all our provinces.
95   Yea, stranger engines for the brunt of war
Than was the fiery keel at Antwerp's bridge,[4]
I'll make my servile spirits to invent.
Come German Valdes and Cornelius,
And make me blest with your sage conference.
[*Enter* VALDES *and* CORNELIUS.]
100   Valdes, sweet Valdes, and Cornelius,
Know that your words have won me at the last
To practise magic and concealèd° arts;   *i.e., occult*
Yet not your words only, but mine own fantasy,°   *imagination*
That will receive no object[5] for my head,
105   But ruminates on necromantic skill.

8. God—a common substitution in Elizabethan drama.
9. Pearl of Orient—the especially lustrous pearl from the seas around India.
1. Wittenberg is in fact on the Elbe River.
2. The university lecture rooms.
3. The duke of Parma, the Spanish governor-general of the Low Countries from 1579 to 1592.

In 1588 he commanded the Spanish Armada in its failed attempt to invade England.
4. A reference to the burning ship sent by the Protestant Netherlanders in 1585 against the barrier on the river Scheldt that Parma had built as a part of the blockade of Antwerp.
5. That will pay no attention to physical reality.

Philosophy is odious and obscure,
Both law and physic are for petty wits;
Divinity is basest of the three,
Unpleasant, harsh, contemptible, and vile.
110 'Tis magic, magic that hath ravished me.
Then, gentle friends, aid me in this attempt,
And I, that have with concise syllogisms
Graveled° the pastors of the German church   *confounded*
And made the flowering pride of Wittenberg
115 Swarm to my problems⁶ as the infernal spirits
On sweet Musaeus when he came to hell,⁷
Will be as cunning as Agrippa was,
Whose shadows made all Europe honor him.⁸
VALDES   Faustus, these books, thy wit,° and our experience   *intellect*
120 Shall make all nations to canonize us.
As Indian Moors⁹ obey their Spanish lords,
So shall the spirits of every element
Be always serviceable to us three.
Like lions shall they guard us when we please,
125 Like Almaine rutters° with their horsemen's staves,   *German horsemen*
Or Lapland giants trotting by our sides;
Sometimes like women, or unwedded maids,
Shadowing° more beauty in their airy brows   *harboring*
Than in the white breasts of the Queen of Love.
130 From Venice shall they drag huge argosies,°   *merchant ships*
And from America the golden fleece
That yearly stuffs old Philip's treasury,¹
If learnèd Faustus will be resolute.
FAUSTUS   Valdes, as resolute am I in this
135 As thou to live, therefore object it not.²
CORNELIUS   The miracles that magic will perform
Will make thee vow to study nothing else.
He that is grounded in astrology,
Enriched with tongues,° well seen° in minerals,   *languages / expert*
140 Hath all the principles magic doth require:
Then doubt not, Faustus, but to be renowned
And more frequented° for this mystery°   *visited / craft*
Than heretofore the Delphian oracle.³
The spirits tell me they can dry the sea,
145 And fetch the treasure of all foreign wrecks,
Ay, all the wealth that our forefathers hid

6. Questions posed for public academic disputation.
7. Musaeus was a legendary singer, supposed son of Orpheus; it was, however, Orpheus who charmed the denizens of hell with his music.
8. Cornelius Agrippa, German author of *The Vanity and Uncertainty of Arts and Sciences* (1530), was popularly believed to have had the power of calling up the "shadows" or shades of the dead.
9. Dark-skinned Native Americans. ("India" in

the period could refer to either the East Indies or the West Indies.)
1. Comparing the treasures Philip II of Spain received from the Americas to the Golden Fleece taken, in Greek mythology, from Colchis by Jason and the Argonauts. (Evidently the Venetian argosies put Marlowe in mind of Jason's ship, the *Argo*.)
2. I.e., do not make an issue of my resolve.
3. The oracle of Apollo at Delphi in Greece.

Within the massy° entrails of the earth.   *massive*
Then tell me, Faustus, what shall we three want?°   *lack*
FAUSTUS   Nothing, Cornelius. O this cheers my soul!
150   Come, show me some demonstrations magical,
That I may conjure in some lusty° grove,   *pleasant*
And have these joys in full possessiön.
VALDES   Then haste thee to some solitary grove,
And bear wise Bacon's and Abanus'⁴ works,
155   The Hebrew Psalter, and New Testament;
And whatsoever else is requisite
We will inform thee ere our conference cease.
CORNELIUS   Valdes, first let him know the words of art,⁵
And then, all other ceremonies learned,
160   Faustus may try his cunning by himself.
VALDES   First I'll instruct thee in the rudiments,
And then wilt thou be perfecter° than I.   *more accomplished*
FAUSTUS   Then come and dine with me, and after meat
We'll canvass every quiddity° thereof: *essential feature*
165   For ere I sleep, I'll try what I can do.
This night I'll conjure,° though° I die therefore.   *call up spirits / even if*
[*Exeunt.*]

SCENE 2

[*Enter two* SCHOLARS.]
1 SCHOLAR   I wonder what's become of Faustus, that was wont to
make our schools ring with *sic probo.*⁶
2 SCHOLAR   That shall we know; for see, here comes his boy.⁷
[*Enter* WAGNER.]
1 SCHOLAR   How now, sirra,⁸ where's thy master?
5   WAGNER   God in heaven knows.
2 SCHOLAR   Why, dost not thou know?
WAGNER   Yes I know, but that follows not.
1 SCHOLAR   Go to,⁹ sirra, leave your jesting, and tell us where he is.
WAGNER   That follows not necessary by force of argument, that you,
10   being licentiates,¹ should stand upon't; therefore acknowledge
your error, and be attentive.
2 SCHOLAR   Why, didst thou not say thou knew'st?
WAGNER   Have you any witness on't?
1 SCHOLAR   Yes, sirra, I heard you.
15   WAGNER   Ask my fellow if I be a thief.²
2 SCHOLAR   Well, you will not tell us.
WAGNER   Yes sir, I will tell you; yet if you were not dunces you would
never ask me such a question. For is not he *corpus naturale*? And is

---

4. Roger Bacon, the 13th-century friar and scientist popularly thought to be a magician, and
Pietro d'Abano, 13th-century alchemist.
5. I.e., the technical terms.
6. Thus I prove; a phrase in scholastic disputation.
7. In this case, a poor student acting as a servant

to earn his living.
8. A variant of "sir," used condescendingly.
9. Come on!
1. Graduate students.
2. I.e., the testimony of your companion ("fellow")
is worth no more than one thief's testimony for
another.

not that *mobile*?[3] Then wherefore should you ask me such a question? But that I am by nature phlegmatic,[4] slow to wrath and prone
to lechery—to love I would say—it were not for you to come within
forty foot of the place of execution,[5] although I do not doubt to see
you both hanged the next sessions.[6] Thus having triumphed over
you, I will set my countenance like a precisian,[7] and begin to speak
thus: Truly, my dear brethren, my master is within at dinner with
Valdes and Cornelius, as this wine, if it could speak, it would
inform your worships. And so the Lord bless you, preserve you, and
keep you, my dear brethren, my dear brethren.   [*Exit.*]

1 SCHOLAR   Nay then, I fear he is fallen into that damned art, for
which they two are infamous through the world.

2 SCHOLAR   Were he a stranger, and not allied to me, yet should I
grieve for him. But come, let us go and inform the rector,[8] and see
if he by his grave counsel can reclaim him.

1 SCHOLAR   O but I fear me nothing can reclaim him.

2 SCHOLAR   Yet let us try what we can do.   [*Exeunt.*]

SCENE 3

[*Enter* FAUSTUS *to conjure.*]

FAUSTUS   Now that the gloomy shadow of the earth,
Longing to view Orion's drizzling look,[9]
Leaps from th'antarctic world unto the sky,
And dims the welkin° with her pitchy breath,   *sky*
Faustus, begin thine incantations,
And try if devils will obey thy hest,°   *command*
Seeing thou hast prayed and sacrificed to them.
Within this circle[1] is Jehovah's name,
Forward and backward anagrammatized;
Th'bbreviated names of holy saints,
Figures of every adjunct[2] to the heavens,
And characters of signs and erring stars,[3]
By which the spirits are enforced to rise.
Then fear not Faustus, but be resolute,
And try the uttermost magic can perform.
Sint mihi dei Acherontis propitii! Valeat numen triplex Jehovae!
Ignei, aerii, aquatici, terreni spiritus salvete! Orientis princeps, Bel-
zebub[4] *inferni ardentis monarcha, et Demogorgon,*[5] *propitiamus vos*

---

3. *Corpus naturale et mobile* (matter natural and
movable) was a scholastic definition of the subject
matter of physics. Wagner is here parodying the
language of learning at the university.
4. Dominated by the phlegm, one of the four
humors (bodily fluids) whose relative proportions
were thought to determine a person's physical
and psychological qualities.
5. I.e., if I were not slow to anger, it would be
fatally dangerous for you to come near me.
6. Sittings of a court.
7. Puritan. The rest of his speech is in the style of
the Puritans.
8. The head of a German university.
9. The constellation Orion appears at the begin-

ning of winter. The phrase is a reminiscence of
Virgil.
1. The magic circle drawn on the ground, within
which the magician would be safe from the spirits he conjured.
2. Heavenly body thought to be joined to the solid
firmament of the sky.
3. The moving planets. "Characters of signs": signs
of the zodiac and the planets.
4. Lord of the Flies; an ancient Phoenician
deity. In Matthew 12.24 he is called "the prince
of the devils."
5. In Renaissance versions of classical mythology, a mysterious primeval god.

ut appareat et surgat Mephastophilis. Quid tu moraris? Per Jehovam,
20 *Gehennam, et consecratam aquam quam nunc spargo, signumque*
   crucis quod nunc facio, et per vota nostra, ipse nunc surgat nobis
   dicatus Mephastophilis.[6]
       [*Enter a* DEVIL.]
   I charge thee to return and change thy shape,
   Thou art too ugly to attend on me;
25 Go and return an old Franciscan friar,
   That holy shape becomes a devil best.   [*Exit* DEVIL.]
   I see there's virtue° in my heavenly words!   *power*
   Who would not be proficient in this art?
   How pliant is this Mephastophilis,
30 Full of obedience and humility,
   Such is the force of magic and my spells.
   Now Faustus, thou art conjurer laureate°   *preeminent*
   That canst command great Mephastophilis.
   Quin redis, Mephastophilis, fratris imagine![7]
       [*Enter* MEPHASTOPHILIS.]
35 MEPHASTOPHILIS   Now Faustus, what would'st thou have me do?
   FAUSTUS   I charge thee wait upon me whilst I live,
   To do whatever Faustus shall command,
   Be it to make the moon drop from her sphere,
   Or the ocean to overwhelm the world.
40 MEPHASTOPHILIS   I am a servant to great Lucifer,
   And may not follow thee without his leave;
   No more than he commands must we perform.
   FAUSTUS   Did not he charge thee to appear to me?
   MEPHASTOPHILIS   No, I came now hither of mine own accord.
45 FAUSTUS   Did not my conjuring speeches raise thee? Speak!
   MEPHASTOPHILIS   That was the cause, but yet *per accidens,*[8]
   For when we hear one rack[9] the name of God,
   Abjure° the Scriptures, and his savior Christ,   *repudiate*
   We fly in hope to get his glorious soul;
50 Nor will we come unless he use such means
   Whereby he is in danger to be damned:
   Therefore the shortest cut for conjuring
   Is stoutly to abjure the Trinity,
   And pray devoutly to the prince of hell.
55 FAUSTUS   So Faustus hath already done, and holds this principle:
   There is no chief but only Belzebub,
   To whom Faustus doth dedicate himself.
   This word damnation terrifies not him,

---

6. Faustus's Latin conjures the devils: "May the gods of the lower regions favor me! Farewell to the Trinity! Hail, spirits of fire, air, water, and earth! Prince of the East, Belzebub, monarch of burning hell, and Demogorgon, we pray to you that Mephastophilis may appear and rise. What are you waiting for? By Jehovah, Gehenna, and the holy water that I now sprinkle, and the sign of the cross that I now make, and by our vows, may Mephastophilis himself now rise to serve us."
7. Return, Mephastophilis, in the shape of a friar.
8. The immediate, not ultimate, cause.
9. Torture; here, by anagrammatizing.

For he confounds hell in Elysium:
60   His ghost be with the old philosophers.[1]
But leaving these vain trifles of men's souls,
Tell me, what is that Lucifer thy lord?
MEPHASTOPHILIS   Arch-regent and commander of all spirits.
FAUSTUS   Was not that Lucifer an angel once?
65   MEPHASTOPHILIS   Yes Faustus, and most dearly loved of God.
FAUSTUS   How comes it then that he is prince of devils?
MEPHASTOPHILIS   O, by aspiring pride and insolence,
For which God threw him from the face of heaven.
FAUSTUS   And what are you that live with Lucifer?
70   MEPHASTOPHILIS   Unhappy spirits that fell with Lucifer,
Conspired against our God with Lucifer,
And are forever damned with Lucifer.
FAUSTUS   Where are you damned?
MEPHASTOPHILIS   In hell.
75   FAUSTUS   How comes it then that thou art out of hell?
MEPHASTOPHILIS   Why this is hell, nor am I out of it.
Think'st thou that I, who saw the face of God,
And tasted the eternal joys of heaven,
Am not tormented with ten thousand hells
80   In being deprived of everlasting bliss?[2]
O Faustus, leave these frivolous demands,°   questions
Which strike a terror to my fainting soul.
FAUSTUS   What, is great Mephastophilis so passionate
For being deprivèd of the joys of heaven?
85   Learn thou of Faustus manly fortitude,
And scorn those joys thou never shalt possess.
Go bear these tidings to great Lucifer:
Seeing Faustus hath incurred eternal death
By desp'rate thoughts against Jove's deity,
90   Say he surrenders up to him his soul,
So° he will spare him four and twenty years,   on condition that
Letting him live in all voluptuousness,
Having thee ever to attend on me,
To give me whatsoever I shall ask,
95   To tell me whatsoever I demand,
To slay mine enemies and aid my friends,
And always be obedient to my will.
Go, and return to mighty Lucifer,
And meet me in my study at midnight
100   And then resolve me of thy master's mind.[3]
MEPHASTOPHILIS   I will, Faustus.   [Exit.]
FAUSTUS   Had I as many souls as there be stars,
I'd give them all for Mephastophilis.

1. Faustus considers hell to be the Elysium of the classical philosophers, not the Christian hell of torment.
2. This is the punishment of loss of God's pres-ence, which is supposed to be the greatest torment of hell.
3. I.e., give me his decision.

By him I'll be great emperor of the world,
105 And make a bridge through the moving air
To pass the ocean with a band of men;
I'll join the hills that bind the Afric shore,
And make that land continent to° Spain,   *connected to*
And both contributory to my crown.
110 The emperor° shall not live but by my leave,   *i.e., Holy Roman Emperor*
Nor any potentate of Germany.
Now that I have obtained what I desire,
I'll live in speculation° of this art   *contemplation*
Till Mephastophilis return again.   [*Exit.*]

SCENE 4

[*Enter* WAGNER *and the* CLOWN.[4]]

WAGNER   Sirra boy,[5] come hither.

CLOWN   How, boy? Zounds, boy! I hope you have seen many boys
with such pickadevants as I have. Boy, quotha![6]

WAGNER   Tell me, sirra, hast thou any comings in?[7]

5 CLOWN   Ay, and goings out too; you may see else.[8]

WAGNER   Alas poor slave, see how poverty jesteth in his nakedness!
The villain is bare, and out of service,[9] and so hungry that I know
he would give his soul to the devil for a shoulder of mutton, though
it were blood raw.

10 CLOWN   How, my soul to the devil for a shoulder of mutton though
'twere blood raw? Not so good, friend; by'rlady,[1] I had need have it
well roasted, and good sauce to it, if I pay so dear.

WAGNER   Well, wilt thou serve me, and I'll make thee go like *qui mihi
discipulus?*[2]

15 CLOWN   How, in verse?

WAGNER   No, sirra; in beaten silk and stavesacre.[3]

CLOWN   How, how, knavesacre?[4] Ay, I thought that was all the land
his father left him! Do ye hear, I would be sorry to rob you of your
living.

20 WAGNER   Sirra, I say in stavesacre.

CLOWN   Oho, oho, stavesacre! Why then belike, if I were your man,
I should be full of vermin.

WAGNER   So thou shalt, whether thou be'st with me or no. But sirra,
leave your jesting, and bind yourself presently unto me for seven
25 years, or I'll turn all the lice about thee into familiars,[5] and they
shall tear thee in pieces.

---

4. Not a court jester (as in some of Shakespeare's plays) but an older stock character, a rustic buffoon.
5. God's wounds; an oath.
6. Says he. The point of the clown's retort is that he is a man and wears a beard. "Pickadevants": small, pointed beards.
7. Income, but the clown then puns on the literal meaning.
8. I.e., if you don't believe me.
9. Out of a job.

1. By Our Lady; an oath.
2. You who are my pupil (the opening phrase of a poem on how students should behave, from Lily's *Latin Grammar*, ca. 1509). Wagner means "like a proper servant of a learned man."
3. A preparation from delphinium seeds, used for killing vermin.
4. Wordplay, here and in the following lines.
5. Familiar spirits, demons. "Bind yourself": i.e., as apprentice. "Presently": immediately.

CLOWN   Do you hear, sir? You may save that labor: they are too familiar with me already—zounds, they are as bold with my flesh as if
they had paid for my meat and drink.
30 WAGNER   Well, do you hear, sirra? Hold, take these guilders.[6]
CLOWN   Gridirons; what be they?
WAGNER   Why, French crowns.[7]
CLOWN   'Mass, but for the name of French crowns a man were as
good have as many English counters![8] And what should I do with
35 these?
WAGNER   Why, now, sirra, thou art at an hour's warning whensoever
or wheresoever the devil shall fetch thee.
CLOWN   No, no, here take your gridirons again.
WAGNER   Truly I'll none of them.
40 CLOWN   Truly but you shall.
WAGNER   Bear witness I gave them him.
CLOWN   Bear witness I give them you again.
WAGNER   Well, I will cause two devils presently to fetch thee away.
Baliol[9] and Belcher!
45 CLOWN   Let your Baliol and your Belcher come here, and I'll knock[1]
them, they were never so knocked since they were devils! Say I
should kill one of them, what would folks say? "Do ye see yonder
tall fellow in the round slop?[2] He has killed the devil!" So I should
be called "Killdevil" all the parish over.
        [Enter two DEVILS, and the CLOWN runs up and down crying.]
50 WAGNER   Baliol and Belcher, spirits, away!   [Exeunt DEVILS.]
CLOWN   What, are they gone? A vengeance on them! They have vile
long nails. There was a he devil and a she devil. I'll tell you how you
shall know them: all he devils has horns,[3] and all she devils has
clefts and cloven feet.
55 WAGNER   Well, sirra, follow me.
CLOWN   But do you hear? If I should serve you, would you teach me
to raise up Banios and Belcheos?
WAGNER   I will teach thee to turn thyself to anything, to a dog, or a
cat, or a mouse, or a rat, or anything.
60 CLOWN   How! A Christian fellow to a dog or a cat, a mouse or a rat?
No, no, sir, if you turn me into anything, let it be in the likeness of
a little pretty frisking flea, that I may be here, and there, and everywhere. O I'll tickle the pretty wenches' plackets![4] I'll be amongst
them, i'faith.[5]
65 WAGNER   Well, sirra, come.
CLOWN   But do you hear, Wagner . . . ?
WAGNER   How? Baliol and Belcher!
CLOWN   O Lord I pray, sir, let Banio and Belcher go sleep.

6. Coins. "Hold": here.
7. The coins, legal tender in England at this
period, were easily counterfeited.
8. Worthless tokens. "'Mass": by the Mass.
9. Probably a corruption of Belial.
1. Beat.

2. Baggy pants. "Tall": fine.
3. Traditional mark both of devils and of cuckolded husbands.
4. Slits in garments—but with an obvious sexual
allusion.
5. In faith; an oath.

WAGNER   Villain, call me Master Wagner; and let thy left eye be dia-
70   metarily fixed upon my right heel, with *quasi vestigias nostras insis-*
       tere.[6]   [*Exit.*]
CLOWN   God forgive me, he speaks Dutch fustian![7] Well, I'll follow
       him, I'll serve him; that's flat.   [*Exit.*]

SCENE 5

[*Enter* FAUSTUS *in his study.*]
FAUSTUS   Now Faustus, must thou needs be damned,
       And canst thou not be saved.
       What boots° it then to think of God or heaven?   *avails*
       Away with such vain fancies, and despair,
5   Despair in God, and trust in Belzebub.
       Now go not backward: no, Faustus, be resolute;
       Why waverest thou? O, something soundeth in mine ears:
       "Abjure this magic, turn to God again."
       Ay, and Faustus will turn to God again.
10   To God? He loves thee not:
       The god thou servest is thine own appetite,
       Wherein is fixed the love of Belzebub.
       To him I'll build an altar and a church,
       And offer lukewarm blood of newborn babes.
       [*Enter* GOOD ANGEL *and* EVIL.]
15 GOOD ANGEL   Sweet Faustus, leave that execrable° art.   *accursed*
FAUSTUS   Contrition, prayer, repentance: what of them?
GOOD ANGEL   O they are means to bring thee unto heaven.
EVIL ANGEL   Rather illusions, fruits of lunacy,
       That makes men foolish that do trust them most.
20 GOOD ANGEL   Sweet Faustus, think of heaven, and heavenly things.
EVIL ANGEL   No, Faustus, think of honor and of wealth.   [*Exeunt.*]
FAUSTUS   Of wealth!
       Why, the signory° of Emden[8] shall be mine,   *lordship*
       When Mephastophilis shall stand by me.
25   What god can hurt thee, Faustus? Thou art safe,
       Cast no more doubts. Come, Mephastophilis,
       And bring glad tidings from great Lucifer.
       Is't not midnight? Come, Mephastophilis:
       Veni, veni, Mephastophile![9]
       [*Enter* MEPHASTOPHILIS.]
30   Now tell, what says Lucifer thy lord?
MEPHASTOPHILIS   That I shall wait on Faustus whilst he lives,
       So° he will buy my service with his soul.   *provided that*
FAUSTUS   Already Faustus hath hazarded that for thee.
MEPHASTOPHILIS   But Faustus, thou must bequeath it solemnly,
35   And write a deed of gift with thine own blood,

---

6. A pedantic way of saying "Follow my footsteps." "Diametarily": diametrically.
7. Gibberish.

8. A wealthy German trade center.
9. Come, come, Mephastophilis!

> For that security° craves great Lucifer.   *guarantee*
> If thou deny it, I will back to hell.
>
> FAUSTUS   Stay, Mephastophilis, and tell me,
> What good will my soul do thy lord?
>
> 40 MEPHASTOPHILIS   Enlarge his kingdom.
>
> FAUSTUS   Is that the reason he tempts us thus?
>
> MEPHASTOPHILIS   *Solamen miseris socios habuisse doloris.*[1]
>
> FAUSTUS   Have you any pain that tortures others?
>
> MEPHASTOPHILIS   As great as have the human souls of men.
>
> 45   But tell me Faustus, shall I have thy soul?
> And I will be thy slave and wait on thee,
> And give thee more than thou hast wit to ask.
>
> FAUSTUS   Ay Mephastophilis, I give it thee.
>
> MEPHASTOPHILIS   Then stab thine arm courageously,
>
> 50   And bind thy soul, that at some certain day
> Great Lucifer may claim it as his own,
> And then be thou as great as Lucifer.
>
> FAUSTUS   Lo Mephastophilis, for love of thee,
> I cut my arm, and with my proper° blood   *own*
>
> 55   Assure my soul to be great Lucifer's,
> Chief lord and regent of perpetual night.
> View here the blood that trickles from mine arm,
> And let it be propitious for my wish.
>
> MEPHASTOPHILIS   But Faustus, thou must write it
>
> 60   In manner of a deed of gift.
>
> FAUSTUS   Ay, so I will; but, Mephastophilis,
> My blood congeals and I can write no more.
>
> MEPHASTOPHILIS   I'll fetch thee fire to dissolve it straight.   [*Exit.*]
>
> FAUSTUS   What might the staying of my blood portend?
>
> 65   Is it unwilling I should write this bill?°   *contract*
> Why streams it not, that I may write afresh:
> "Faustus gives to thee his soul"? Ah, there it stayed!
> Why should'st thou not? Is not thy soul thine own?
> Then write again: "Faustus gives to thee his soul."
>
>   [*Enter* MEPHASTOPHILIS *with a chafer° of coals.*]   *a portable grate*
>
> 70 MEPHASTOPHILIS   Here's fire, come Faustus, set it on.
>
> FAUSTUS   So, now the blood begins to clear again.
> Now will I make an end immediately.
>
> MEPHASTOPHILIS   O what will not I do to obtain his soul!
>
> FAUSTUS   *Consummatum est,*[2] this bill is ended,
>
> 75   And Faustus hath bequeathed his soul to Lucifer.
> But what is this inscription on mine arm?
> *Homo fuge.*° Whither should I fly?   *O man, fly*
> If unto God, he'll throw me down to hell.
> My senses are deceived, here's nothing writ;
>
> 80   I see it plain, here in this place is writ,
> *Homo fuge!* Yet shall not Faustus fly.

1. Misery loves company.
2. It is finished. A blasphemy, because these are the words of Christ on the Cross (John 19.30).

MEPHASTOPHILIS   I'll fetch him somewhat to delight his mind.   [*Exit.*]
      [*Enter with* DEVILS, *giving crowns and rich apparel to* FAUSTUS,
      and dance, and then depart.]
FAUSTUS   Speak, Mephastophilis, what means this show?
MEPHASTOPHILIS   Nothing, Faustus, but to delight thy mind withal,
85   And to show thee what magic can perform.
FAUSTUS   But may I raise up spirits when I please?
MEPHASTOPHILIS   Ay, Faustus, and do greater things than these.
FAUSTUS   Then there's enough for a thousand souls!
      Here, Mephastophilis, receive this scroll,
90   A deed of gift of body and of soul:
      But yet conditionally, that thou perform
      All articles prescribed between us both.
MEPHASTOPHILIS   Faustus, I swear by hell and Lucifer
      To effect all promises between us made.
95   FAUSTUS   Then hear me read them. On these conditions following:
      First, that Faustus may be a spirit[3] *in form and substance.*
      Secondly, that Mephastophilis shall be his servant, and at his
      command.
      Thirdly, that Mephastophilis shall do for him, and bring him whatso-
100   *ever.*
      Fourthly, that he shall be in his chamber or house invisible.
      Lastly, that he shall appear to the said John Faustus at all times, in
      what form or shape soever he please.
      I, John Faustus of Wittenberg, doctor, by these presents,[4] *do give*
105   *both body and soul to Lucifer, Prince of the East, and his minister*
      Mephastophilis; and furthermore grant unto them that, four and
      twenty years being expired, the articles above-written inviolate, full
      power to fetch or carry the said John Faustus, body and soul, flesh,
      blood, or goods, into their habitation wheresoever.
110   *By me John Faustus.*
MEPHASTOPHILIS   Speak, Faustus: do you deliver this as your deed?
FAUSTUS   Ay, take it; and the devil give thee good on't.
MEPHASTOPHILIS   Now, Faustus, ask what thou wilt.
FAUSTUS   First will I question with thee about hell:
115   Tell me, where is the place that men call hell?
MEPHASTOPHILIS   Under the heavens.
FAUSTUS   Ay, but whereabouts?
MEPHASTOPHILIS   Within the bowels of these elements,
      Where we are tortured and remain for ever.
120   Hell hath no limits, nor is circumscribed
      In one self place; for where we are is hell,
      And where hell is, there must we ever be.
      And to conclude, when all the world dissolves,
      And every creature shall be purified,
125   All places shall be hell that is not heaven.
FAUSTUS   Come, I think hell's a fable.

---

3. I.e., have the supernatural powers of a spirit.   4. Legal articles.

MEPHASTOPHILIS   Ay, think so still, till experience change thy mind.

FAUSTUS   Why? think'st thou then that Faustus shall be damned?

MEPHASTOPHILIS   Ay, of necessity, for here's the scroll
130   Wherein thou hast given thy soul to Lucifer.

FAUSTUS   Ay, and body too; but what of that?
Think'st thou that Faustus is so fond° to imagine   foolish
That after this life there is any pain?
Tush, these are trifles and mere old wives' tales.

MEPHASTOPHILIS   But Faustus, I am an instance to prove the
135   contrary:
For I am damned, and am now in hell.

FAUSTUS   How, now in hell? Nay, and this be hell, I'll willingly be
damned here! What? walking, disputing, etc. . . . But leaving off
this, let me have a wife, the fairest maid in Germany, for I am
140   wanton and lascivious, and cannot live without a wife.

MEPHASTOPHILIS   How, a wife? I prithee Faustus, talk not of a wife.[5]

FAUSTUS   Nay sweet Mephastophilis, fetch me one, for I will have
one.

MEPHASTOPHILIS   Well, thou wilt have one; sit there till I come.
145   I'll fetch thee a wife in the devil's name.   [Exit.]
        [Enter with a DEVIL dressed like a woman, with fireworks.]

MEPHASTOPHILIS   Tell, Faustus, how dost thou like thy wife?

FAUSTUS   A plague on her for a hot whore!

MEPHASTOPHILIS   Tut, Faustus, marriage is but a ceremonial toy;
If thou lovest me, think no more of it.
150   I'll cull thee out the fairest courtesans
And bring them every morning to thy bed:
She whom thine eye shall like, thy heart shall have,
Be she as chaste as was Penelope,[6]
As wise as Saba,[7] or as beautiful
155   As was bright Lucifer before his fall.
Hold, take this book, peruse it thoroughly:
The iterating° of these lines brings gold;   repeating
The framing° of this circle on the ground   drawing
Brings whirlwinds, tempests, thunder and lightning.
160   Pronounce this thrice devoutly to thyself,
And men in armor shall appear to thee,
Ready to execute what thou desirest.

FAUSTUS   Thanks, Mephastophilis, yet fain would I have a book
wherein I might behold all spells and incantations, that I might
165   raise up spirits when I please.

MEPHASTOPHILIS   Here they are in this book.   [There turn to them.]

FAUSTUS   Now would I have a book where I might see all characters
and planets of the heavens, that I might know their motions and
dispositions.[8]

---

5. Mephastophilis cannot produce a wife for Faustus because marriage is a sacrament.
6. The wife of Ulysses, famed for chastity and fidelity.
7. The queen of Sheba, who tested Solomon's wisdom with "hard questions" (1 Kings 10).
8. Relationships to other planets. "Characters": occult symbols.

170 MEPHASTOPHILIS   Here they are too.   [*Turn to them.*]

FAUSTUS   Nay, let me have one book more, and then I have done,
    wherein I might see all plants, herbs, and trees that grow upon the
    earth.

MEPHASTOPHILIS   Here they be.

175 FAUSTUS   O thou art deceived!

MEPHASTOPHILIS   Tut, I warrant⁹ thee.   [*Turn to them.*]

FAUSTUS   When I behold the heavens, then I repent,
    And curse thee, wicked Mephastophilis,
    Because thou hast deprived me of those joys.

180 MEPHASTOPHILIS   Why Faustus,
    Think'st thou that heaven is such a glorious thing?
    I tell thee 'tis not half so fair as thou,
    Or any man that breathes on earth.

FAUSTUS   How prov'st thou that?

185 MEPHASTOPHILIS   It was made for man, therefore is man more excellent.

FAUSTUS   If it were made for man, 'twas made for me:
    I will renounce this magic, and repent.
        [*Enter* GOOD ANGEL *and* EVIL ANGEL.]

GOOD ANGEL   Faustus, repent, yet° God will pity thee.   *still*

EVIL ANGEL   Thou art a spirit,° God cannot pity thee.   *evil spirit, devil*

190 FAUSTUS   Who buzzeth in mine ears I am a spirit?
    Be I a devil, yet God may pity me.
    Ay, God will pity me if I repent.

EVIL ANGEL   Ay, but Faustus never shall repent.   [*Exeunt.*]

FAUSTUS   My heart's so hardened I cannot repent!

195   Scarce can I name salvation, faith, or heaven,
    But fearful echoes thunders in mine ears,
    "Faustus, thou are damned"; then swords and knives,
    Poison, guns, halters,° and envenomed steel   *hangman's nooses*
    Are laid before me to dispatch myself:

200   And long ere this I should have slain myself,
    Had not sweet pleasure conquered deep despair.
    Have I not made blind Homer sing to me
    Of Alexander's¹ love, and Oenon's death?
    And hath not he that built the walls of Thebes

205   With ravishing sound of his melodious harp,²
    Made music with my Mephastophilis?
    Why should I die then, or basely despair?
    I am resolved! Faustus shall ne'er repent.
    Come, Mephastophilis, let us dispute again,

210   And argue of divine astrology.
    Tell me, are there many heavens above the moon?
    Are all celestial bodies but one globe,

---

9. Assure.
1. Alexander is another name for Paris, the lover of Oenone; later he deserted her and abducted Helen, causing the Trojan War. Oenone refused to heal the wounds Paris received in battle, and when he died of them, she killed herself in remorse.
2. The legendary musician Amphion, whose harp caused stones, of themselves, to form the walls of Thebes.

As is the substance of this centric earth?[3]

MEPHASTOPHILIS   As are the elements, such are the spheres,
215   Mutually folded in each other's orb.
And, Faustus, all jointly move upon one axletree
Whose terminè° is termed the world's wide pole,   *end*
Nor are the names of Saturn, Mars, or Jupiter
Feigned, but are erring stars.[4]

220   FAUSTUS   But tell me, have they all one motion, both *situ et tempore?*[5]

MEPHASTOPHILIS   All jointly move from east to west in four-and-
twenty hours upon the poles of the world, but differ in their
motion upon the poles of the zodiac.[6]

FAUSTUS   Tush, these slender trifles Wagner can decide!
225   Hath Mephastophilis no greater skill?
Who knows not the double motion of the planets?
The first is finished in a natural day, the second thus: as Saturn in
thirty years; Jupiter in twelve; Mars in four; the Sun, Venus, and
Mercury in a year; the Moon in twenty-eight days. Tush, these are
230   freshmen's suppositions. But tell me, hath every sphere a dominion or *intelligentia?*[7]

MEPHASTOPHILIS   Ay.

FAUSTUS   How many heavens or spheres are there?

MEPHASTOPHILIS   Nine: the seven planets, the firmament, and the
235   empyreal heaven.[8]

FAUSTUS   Well, resolve me then in this question: why have we not
conjunctions, oppositions,[9] aspects, eclipses, all at one time, but
in some years we have more, in some less?

MEPHASTOPHILIS   *Per inaequalem motum respectu totius.*[1]

240   FAUSTUS   Well, I am answered. Tell me who made the world?

MEPHASTOPHILIS   I will not.

FAUSTUS   Sweet Mephastophilis, tell me.

MEPHASTOPHILIS   Move° me not, for I will not tell thee.   *urge*

FAUSTUS   Villain, have I not bound thee to tell me anything?

245   MEPHASTOPHILIS   Ay, that is not against our kingdom; but this is.
Think thou on hell, Faustus, for thou art damned.

FAUSTUS   Think, Faustus, upon God, that made the world.

MEPHASTOPHILIS   Remember this.   *[Exit.]*

FAUSTUS   Ay, go accursèd spirit, to ugly hell,
250   'Tis thou hast damned distressèd Faustus' soul:
Is't not too late?

3. Faustus asks whether all the apparently different heavenly bodies really form "one globe" like the
earth. Mephastophilis answers that like the elements, which are separate but combined, the heavenly bodies are separate but their spheres are
enfolded, and they move (according to the ancient
Ptolemaic cosmology) on a single axle.
4. It is appropriate to give individual names to
Saturn, Mars, Jupiter, and the other planets—
which are called wandering, or "erring" stars. The
fixed stars were in the eighth sphere (the firmament, or crystalline sphere).
5. In position and in time.

6. The common axletree on which all the spheres
revolve.
7. An angel, or intelligence, thought to be the
source of motion in each sphere.
8. The ninth sphere was the immovable empyrean.
9. When two planets are most remote from each
other. "Conjunctions": the apparent joinings of
two planets. These are two of the planetary
"aspects" (relative positions) that figure in
astrology.
1. Because of their unequal movements in
respect of the whole.

[*Enter* GOOD ANGEL *and* EVIL.]

EVIL ANGEL   Too late.

GOOD ANGEL   Never too late, if Faustus will repent.

EVIL ANGEL   If thou repent, devils shall tear thee in pieces.

255 GOOD ANGEL   Repent, and they shall never raze° thy skin.   graze

[*Exeunt.*]

FAUSTUS   Ah Christ my Savior! seek to save
Distressèd Faustus' soul!

[*Enter* LUCIFER, BELZEBUB, *and* MEPHASTOPHILIS.]

LUCIFER   Christ cannot save thy soul, for he is just.
There's none but I have interest in the same.

260 FAUSTUS   O who art thou that look'st so terrible?

LUCIFER   I am Lucifer, and this is my companion prince in hell.

FAUSTUS   O Faustus, they are come to fetch away thy soul!

LUCIFER   We come to tell thee thou dost injure us.
Thou talk'st of Christ, contrary to thy promise.

265 Thou should'st not think of God; think of the devil,
And his dam² too.

FAUSTUS   Nor will I henceforth: pardon me in this,
And Faustus vows never to look to heaven,
Never to name God, or to pray to him,

270 To burn his Scriptures, slay his ministers,
And make my spirits pull his churches down.

LUCIFER   Do so, and we will highly gratify thee. Faustus, we are
come from hell to show thee some pastime; sit down, and thou
shalt see all the Seven Deadly Sins³ appear in their proper shapes.

275 FAUSTUS   That sight will be as pleasing unto me as Paradise was to
Adam, the first day of his creation.

LUCIFER   Talk not of Paradise, nor creation, but mark this show;
talk of the devil and nothing else. Come away.

[*Enter the* SEVEN DEADLY SINS.]

Now Faustus, examine them of their several names and disposi-

280 tions.

FAUSTUS   What art thou, the first?

PRIDE   I am Pride: I disdain to have any parents. I am like to Ovid's
flea, I can creep into every corner of a wench: sometimes like a
periwig,⁴ I sit upon her brow; or like a fan of feathers, I kiss her lips.

285 Indeed I do—what do I not! But fie, what a scent⁵ is here? I'll not
speak another word, except the ground were perfumed and covered
with cloth of arras.⁶

FAUSTUS   What art thou, the second?

COVETOUSNESS   I am Covetousness, begotten of an old churl⁷ in an

290 old leathern bag; and might I have my wish, I would desire that this

---

2. Mother. "The devil and his dam" was a common colloquial expression.
3. Pride, avarice, lust, anger, gluttony, envy, and sloth, called deadly because they lead to spirtual death. All other sins are said to grow out of them (cf. the procession of the Seven Deadly Sins in Spenser's *The Faerie Queene*, Book 1, canto 4, stanzas 16–37).

4. Wig. "Ovid's flea": a salacious medieval poem "Carmen de pulice" (Song of the Flea) was attributed to Ovid.
5. Stink.
6. Arras in Flanders exported fine cloth used for tapestry hangings. "Except": unless.
7. Miser.

house, and all the people in it, were turned to gold, that I might lock you up in my good chest. O my sweet gold!

FAUSTUS What art thou, the third?

WRATH I am Wrath. I had neither father nor mother: I leaped out of
295 a lion's mouth when I was scarce half an hour old, and ever since I have run up and down the world with this case[8] of rapiers, wounding myself when I had nobody to fight withal. I was born in hell— and look to it, for some of you[9] shall be my father.

FAUSTUS What art thou, the fourth?

300 ENVY I am Envy, begotten of a chimney-sweeper and an oyster-wife. I cannot read, and therefore wish all books were burnt; I am lean with seeing others eat—O that there would come a famine through all the world, that all might die, and I live alone; then thou should'st see how fat I would be! But must thou sit and I stand? Come down,
305 with a vengeance!

FAUSTUS Away, envious rascal! What art thou, the fifth?

GLUTTONY Who, I sir? I am Gluttony. My parents are all dead, and the devil a penny they have left me but a bare pension, and that is thirty meals a day and ten bevers[1]—a small trifle to suffice nature.
310 O, I come of a royal parentage: my grandfather was a gammon[2] of bacon, my grandmother a hogshead of claret wine; my godfathers were these: Peter Pickled-Herring, and Martin Martlemas-Beef.[3] O but my godmother! She was a jolly gentlewoman, and well-beloved in every good town and city; her name was Mistress Margery
315 March-Beer.[4] Now, Faustus, thou hast heard all my progeny;[5] wilt thou bid me to supper?

FAUSTUS No, I'll see thee hanged; thou wilt eat up all my victuals.

GLUTTONY Then the devil choke thee!

FAUSTUS Choke thyself, Glutton. What art thou, the sixth?

320 SLOTH I am Sloth; I was begotten on a sunny bank, where I have lain ever since—and you have done me great injury to bring me from thence. Let me be carried thither again by Gluttony and Lechery. I'll not speak another word for a king's ransom.

FAUSTUS What are you, Mistress Minx, the seventh and last?

325 LECHERY Who, I sir? I am one that loves an inch of raw mutton better than an ell of fried stockfish;[6] and the first letter of my name begins with Lechery.

LUCIFER Away! To hell, to hell!   [*Exeunt the* SINS.]
Now Faustus, how dost thou like this?

330 FAUSTUS O this feeds my soul!

LUCIFER Tut, Faustus, in hell is all manner of delight.

FAUSTUS O might I see hell, and return again, how happy were I then!

---

8. Pair.
9. I.e., some in the audience.
1. Snacks.
2. The lower side of pork, including the leg.
3. Meat, salted to preserve it during the winter, was prepared around Martinmas (November 11).

4. A rich ale, made in March.
5. Lineage.
6. Dried cod, associated with sexual coldness and impotence. "Mutton": frequently a bawdy term in Elizabethan English; here, the penis. "Ell": forty-five inches.

LUCIFER Thou shalt; I will send for thee at midnight. In meantime,
335 take this book, peruse it thoroughly, and thou shalt turn thyself
into what shape thou wilt.
FAUSTUS Great thanks, mighty Lucifer; this will I keep as chary[7] as
my life.
LUCIFER Farewell, Faustus; and think on the devil.
340 FAUSTUS Farewell, great Lucifer; come, Mephastophilis.
[*Exeunt* OMNES.]

SCENE 6

[*Enter* ROBIN *the ostler[8] with a book in his hand.*]
ROBIN O this is admirable! here I ha' stolen one of Doctor Faustus'
conjuring books, and i'faith I mean to search some circles[9] for my
own use: now will I make all the maidens in our parish dance at
my pleasure stark naked before me, and so by that means I shall
5 see more than ere I felt or saw yet.
[*Enter* RAFE *calling* ROBIN.]
RAFE Robin, prithee come away, there's a gentleman tarries[1] to have
his horse, and he would have his things rubbed and made clean.
He keeps such a chafing[2] with my mistress about it, and she has
sent me to look thee out. Prithee, come away.
10 ROBIN Keep out, keep out; or else you are blown up, you are dismembered, Rafe. Keep out, for I am about a roaring[3] piece of work.
RAFE Come, what dost thou with that same book? Thou canst not
read!
ROBIN Yes, my master and mistress shall find that I can read—he
15 for his forehead,[4] she for her private study. She's born to bear with
me,[5] or else my art fails.
RAFE Why Robin, what book is that?
ROBIN What book? Why the most intolerable[6] book for conjuring
that ere was invented by any brimstone devil.
20 RAFE Canst thou conjure with it?
ROBIN I can do all these things easily with it: first, I can make thee
drunk with 'ipocrase[7] at any tavern in Europe for nothing, that's
one of my conjuring works.
RAFE Our master parson says that's nothing.
25 ROBIN True, Rafe! And more, Rafe, if thou hast any mind to Nan
Spit, our kitchen maid, then turn her and wind her to thy own
use, as often as thou wilt, and at midnight.
RAFE O brave Robin! Shall I have Nan Spit, and to mine own use?
On that condition I'll feed thy devil with horsebread as long as he
30 lives, of free cost.[8]

---

7. Carefully.
8. Hostler, stablehand.
9. Magicians' circles, but with a sexual innuendo.
1. Is waiting.
2. Scolding.
3. Dangerous.
4. I.e., Robin intends to give his master horns—
cuckold him.
5. I.e., bear his weight, or bear him a child.
6. Irresistible.
7. Robin's pronunciation of "hippocras," a spiced wine.
8. Free of charge. "Horsebread": fodder.

ROBIN No more, sweet Rafe; let's go and make clean our boots which lie foul upon our hands, and then to our conjuring in the devil's name. [*Exeunt.*]

CHORUS 2

[*Enter* WAGNER *solus.*]
WAGNER   Learned Faustus,
   To know the secrets of astronomy
   Graven in the book of Jove's high firmament,
   Did mount himself to scale Olympus'[9] top.
5   Being seated in a chariot burning bright,
   Drawn by the strength of yokèd dragons' necks.
   He now is gone to prove cosmography,[1]
   And, as I guess, will first arrive at Rome
   To see the pope, and manner of his court,
10   And take some part of holy Peter's feast,[2]
   That to this day is highly solemnized. [*Exit* WAGNER.]

SCENE 7

[*Enter* FAUSTUS *and* MEPHASTOPHILIS.]
FAUSTUS   Having now, my good Mephastophilis,
   Passed with delight the stately town of Trier,[3]
   Environed round with airy mountain tops,
   With walls of flint, and deep entrenchèd lakes,°   *moats*
5   Not to be won by any conquering prince;
   From Paris next, coasting° the realm of France,   *traversing*
   We saw the river Main fall into Rhine,
   Whose banks are set with groves of fruitful vines;
   Then up to Naples, rich Campania,
10   With buildings fair and gorgeous to the eye,
   The streets straight forth, and paved with finest brick,
   Quarters the town in four equivalents;
   There saw we learned Maro's[4] golden tomb,
   The way° he cut, an English mile in length,   *tunnel*
15   Thorough° a rock of stone in one night's space.   *through*
   From thence to Venice, Padua, and the rest,
   In midst of which a sumptuous temple° stands   *St. Mark's in Venice*
   That threats the stars with her aspiring top.
   Thus hitherto hath Faustus spent his time.
20   But tell me now, what resting place is this?
   Hast thou, as erst° I did command,   *earlier*
   Conducted me within the walls of Rome?
MEPHASTOPHILIS   Faustus, I have; and because we will not be unprovided, I have taken up his holiness' privy chamber[5] for our use.

---

9. The home of the gods in Greek mythology.
1. To test the accuracy of maps.
2. Saint Peter's feast is June 29.
3. Treves (in Prussia).
4. Virgil's. In medieval legend the Roman poet

Virgil was considered a magician whose powers produced a tunnel on the promontory of Posilippo at Naples, near his tomb.
5. Private quarters.

25 FAUSTUS I hope his holiness will bid us welcome.

MEPHASTOPHILIS Tut, 'tis no matter, man, we'll be bold with his good
cheer.[6]
And now, my Faustus, that thou may'st perceive
What Rome containeth to delight thee with,
30   Know that this city stands upon seven hills
That underprop the groundwork of the same;
Just through the midst runs flowing Tiber's stream,
With winding banks, that cut it in two parts;
Over the which four stately bridges lean,
35   That makes safe passage to each part of Rome.
Upon the bridge called Ponte Angelo
Erected is a castle passing[7] strong,
Within whose walls such store of ordnance are
And double cannons, framed of carvèd brass,
40   As match the days within one complete year—
Besides the gates and high pyramides°   *obelisks*
Which Julius Caesar brought from Africa.

FAUSTUS Now by the kingdoms of infernal rule,
Of Styx, Acheron, and the fiery lake
45   Of ever-burning Phlegethon,[8] I swear
That I do long to see the monuments
And situation of bright-splendent Rome.
Come therefore, let's away.

MEPHASTOPHILIS Nay, Faustus, stay. I know you'd fain see the pope,
50   And take some part of holy Peter's feast,
Where thou shalt see a troop of bald-pate friars,
Whose *summum bonum*[9] is in belly-cheer.

FAUSTUS Well, I am content to compass[1] then some sport,
And by their folly make us merriment.
55   Then charm me that I may be invisible, to do what I please
unseen of any whilst I stay in Rome.

MEPHASTOPHILIS [*casts a spell on him*] So Faustus, now do what
thou wilt, thou shalt not be discerned.
    [*Sound a sennet;*[2] *enter the* POPE *and the* CARDINAL OF LORRAINE
    to the banquet, with FRIARS *attending.*]

POPE My lord of Lorraine, will't please you draw near?

60 FAUSTUS Fall to; and the devil choke you and[3] you spare.

POPE How now, who's that which spake? Friars, look about.

1 FRIAR Here's nobody, if it like[4] your holiness.

POPE My lord, here is a dainty dish was sent to me from the bishop
of Milan.

65 FAUSTUS I thank you, sir. [*Snatch it.*]

---

6. Entertainment.
7. Surpassingly. Actually the castle is on the
bank, not the bridge.
8. Classical names for rivers of the underworld.
9. The greatest good; often refers to God.

1. Take part in.
2. A set of notes on the trumpet or cornet.
3. If. "Fall to": start eating.
4. Please.

POPE How now, who's that which snatched the meat from me? Will no man look? My lord, this dish was sent me from the cardinal of Florence.

FAUSTUS You say true? I'll have't. [*Snatch it.*]

70 POPE What, again! My lord, I'll drink to your grace.

FAUSTUS I'll pledge[5] your grace. [*Snatch the cup.*]

LORRAINE My lord, it may be some ghost newly crept out of purgatory come to beg a pardon of your holiness.

POPE It may be so; friars, prepare a dirge[6] to lay the fury of this ghost.

75 Once again my lord, fall to. [*The* POPE *crosseth himself.*]

FAUSTUS What, are you crossing of your self? Well, use that trick no more, I would advise you.
     [*Cross again.*]

FAUSTUS Well, there's the second time; aware[7] the third! I give you fair warning.
     [*Cross again, and* FAUSTUS *hits him a box of the ear, and they all run away.*]

80 Come on, Mephastophilis, what shall we do?

MEPHASTOPHILIS Nay, I know not; we shall be cursed with bell, book, and candle.[8]

FAUSTUS How! Bell, book, and candle; candle, book, and bell, Forward and backward, to curse Faustus to hell.

85 Anon you shall hear a hog grunt, a calf bleat, and an ass bray, Because it is St. Peter's holy day.
     [*Enter all the* FRIARS *to sing the Dirge.*]

1 FRIAR Come brethren, let's about our business with good devotion.
     [*Sing this.*]
     Cursed be he that stole away His Holiness' meat from the table.
     Maledicat Dominus.[9]

90 Cursed be he that struck His Holiness a blow on the face.
     Maledicat Dominus.
     Cursed be he that took Friar Sandelo a blow on the pate.
     Maledicat Dominus.
     Cursed be he that disturbeth our holy dirge.

95 *Maledicat Dominus.*
     Cursed be he that took away His Holiness' wine.
     Maledicat dominus.
          Et omnes sancti.[1] Amen.
     [*Beat the* FRIARS, *and fling fireworks among them, and so Exeunt.*]

SCENE 8

[*Enter* ROBIN *and* RAFE *with a silver goblet.*]

ROBIN Come, Rafe, did not I tell thee we were forever made by this Doctor Faustus' book? *Ecce signum!*[2] Here's a simple purchase for horsekeepers: our horses shall eat no hay as long as this lasts.

---

5. Toast.
6. A requiem mass. But what actually follows is a litany of curses.
7. Beware.
8. The traditional paraphernalia for cursing and excommunication.
9. May the Lord curse him.
1. And all the saints (also curse him).
2. Behold the proof.

[*Enter the* VINTNER.]

RAFE　But Robin, here comes the vintner.

5　ROBIN　Hush, I'll gull³ him supernaturally! Drawer,⁴ I hope all is paid; God be with you. Come, Rafe.

VINTNER　Soft, sir, a word with you. I must yet have a goblet paid from you ere you go.

ROBIN　I, a goblet, Rafe? I, a goblet? I scorn you: and you are but a
10　etc.⁵ . . . I, a goblet? Search me.

VINTNER　I mean so, sir, with your favor.　[*Searches* ROBIN.]

ROBIN　How say you now?

VINTNER　I must say somewhat to your fellow; you, sir!

RAFE　Me, sir? Me, sir? Search your fill. Now sir, you may be ashamed
15　to burden honest men with a matter of truth.

VINTNER　[*searches* RAFE]　Well, t'one of you hath this goblet about you.

ROBIN　You lie, drawer; 'tis afore me. Sirra you, I'll teach ye to impeach⁶ honest men: [*to* RAFE] stand by. [*to the* VINTNER] I'll scour
20　you for a goblet—stand aside, you were best—I charge you in the name of Belzebub—look to the goblet, Rafe!

VINTNER　What mean you, sirra?

ROBIN　I'll tell you what I mean: [*he reads*] *Sanctobulorum Periphrasticon*—nay, I'll tickle you, vintner—look to the goblet,
25　Rafe—*Polypragmos Belseborams framanto pacostiphos tostis Mephastophilis, etc.*⁷ . . .

　　　　[*Enter* MEPHASTOPHILIS: *sets squibs*⁸ *at their backs: they run about.*]

VINTNER　*O nomine Domine!*⁹ What mean'st thou, Robin? Thou hast no goblet.

RAFE　*Peccatum peccatorum!*¹ Here's thy goblet, good vintner.

30　ROBIN　*Misericordia pro nobis!*² What shall I do? Good devil, forgive me now, and I'll never rob thy library more.

　　　　[*Enter to them* MEPHASTOPHILIS.]

MEPHASTOPHILIS　Vanish, villains, th'one like an ape, another like a bear, the third an ass, for doing this enterprise.　[*Exit* VINTNER.]
　　Monarch of hell, under whose black survey
35　Great potentates do kneel with awful fear;
　　Upon whose altars thousand souls do lie;
　　How am I vexèd with these villains' charms!
　　From Constantinople am I hither come,
　　Only for pleasure of these damnèd slaves.

40　ROBIN　How, from Constantinople? You have had a great journey! Will you take sixpence in your purse to pay for your supper, and be gone?

3. Trick.
4. Wine drawer.
5. The actor might ad lib abuse at this point.
6. Accuse.
7. Dog-Latin, as Robin attempts to conjure from Faustus's book.
8. Firecrackers. Evidently Mephastophilis is

onstage only long enough to set off the firecrackers and is not seen by Robin, Rafe, or the vintner. He then reenters at line 32.
9. In the name of the Lord. The Latin invocations are used in swearing.
1. Sin of sins!
2. Have mercy on us!

MEPHASTOPHILIS   Well, villains, for your presumption, I transform
thee into an ape, and thee into a dog; and so begone!   [*Exit.*]

45   ROBIN   How, into an ape? That's brave:³ I'll have fine sport with the
boys; I'll get nuts and apples enow.⁴

RAFE   And I must be a dog.

ROBIN   I'faith, thy head will never be out of the potage⁵ pot.

[*Exeunt.*]

CHORUS 3

[*Enter* CHORUS.⁶]

CHORUS   When Faustus had with pleasure ta'en the view
Of rarest things, and royal courts of kings,
He stayed his course, and so returnèd home;
Where such as bare his absence but with grief—
5   I mean his friends and nearest companions—
Did gratulate his safety with kind words.
And in their conference of what befell,
Touching his journey through the world and air,
They put forth questions of astrology,
10   Which Faustus answered with such learnèd skill
As they admired and wondered at his wit.
Now is his fame spread forth in every land:
Amongst the rest the emperor is one,
Carolus the Fifth,⁷ at whose palace now
15   Faustus is feasted 'mongst his noblemen.
What there he did in trial° of his art   demonstration
I leave untold: your eyes shall see performed.   [*Exit.*]

SCENE 9

[*Enter* EMPEROR, FAUSTUS, *and a* KNIGHT, *with Attendants.*]

EMPEROR   Master Doctor Faustus, I have heard strange report of thy
knowledge in the black art, how that none in my empire, nor in the
whole world, can compare with thee for the rare effects of magic.
They say thou hast a familiar spirit, by whom thou canst accom-
5   plish what thou list! This therefore is my request: that thou let me
see some proof of thy skill, that mine eyes may be witnesses to confirm what mine ears have heard reported. And here I swear to thee,
by the honor of mine imperial crown, that whatever thou dost, thou
shalt be in no ways prejudiced or endamaged.

10   KNIGHT [*aside*]   I'faith, he looks much like a conjuror.

FAUSTUS   My gracious sovereign, though I must confess myself far
inferior to the report men have published, and nothing answerable
to⁸ the honor of your imperial majesty, yet for that love and duty
binds me thereunto, I am content to do whatsoever your majesty
15   shall command me.

---

3. Splendid.
4. Enough.
5. Porridge.
6. I.e., Wagner.

7. The Holy Roman Emperor Charles V (reigned
1519–56).
8. Not at all deserving of.

EMPEROR   Then Doctor Faustus, mark what I shall say. As I was
sometime solitary set within my closet,[9] sundry thoughts arose
about the honor of mine ancestors—how they had won by prowess
such exploits, got such riches, subdued so many kingdoms, as we
20   that do succeed, or they that shall hereafter possess our throne,
shall (I fear me) never attain to that degree of high renown and
great authority. Amongst which kings is Alexander the Great,[1]
chief spectacle of the world's pre-eminence:
The bright shining of whose glorious acts
25   Lightens the world with his reflecting beams;
As when I hear but motion° made of him,   *mention*
It grieves my soul I never saw the man.
If therefore thou, by cunning of thine art,
Canst raise this man from hollow vaults below,
30   Where lies entombed this famous conqueror,
And bring with him his beauteous paramour,[2]
Both in their right shapes, gesture, and attire
They used to wear during their time of life,
Thou shalt both satisfy my just desire
35   And give me cause to praise thee whilst I live.
FAUSTUS   My gracious lord, I am ready to accomplish your request,
so far forth as by art and power of my spirit I am able to perform.
KNIGHT [*aside*]   I'faith, that's just nothing at all.
FAUSTUS   But, if it like your grace, it is not in my ability to present
40   before your eyes the true substantial bodies of those two deceased
princes, which long since are consumed to dust.
KNIGHT [*aside*]   Ay, marry,[3] master doctor, now there's a sign of
grace in you, when you will confess the truth.
FAUSTUS   But such spirits as can lively resemble Alexander and his
45   paramour shall appear before your grace, in that manner that they
best lived in, in their most flourishing estate:[4] which I doubt not
shall sufficiently content your imperial majesty.
EMPEROR   Go to, master doctor, let me see them presently.[5]
KNIGHT   Do you hear, master doctor? You bring Alexander and his
50   paramour before the emperor!
FAUSTUS   How then, sir?
KNIGHT   I'faith, that's as true as Diana turned me to a stag.
FAUSTUS   No sir; but when Actaeon died, he left the horns[6] for you!
Mephastophilis, begone.   [*Exit* MEPHASTOPHILIS.]
55   KNIGHT   Nay, and[7] you go to conjuring I'll be gone.   [*Exit* KNIGHT.]
FAUSTUS   I'll meet with you anon[8] for interrupting me so. Here they
are, my gracious lord.

---

9. Private chamber.
1. The emperor traces his ancestry to the world
conqueror (356–323 B.C.E.).
2. Probably Roxana, Alexander's wife.
3. To be sure.
4. Condition.
5. Immediately.
6. Horns were traditionally a sign of the cuck-

olded husband (cf. Scene 6, lines 14–15).
"Actaeon": the hunter of classical legend who happened to see the goddess Diana bathing. For punishment he was changed into a stag; he was then
chased and killed by his own hounds.
7. If.
8. Shortly. "Meet with": be revenged on.

[*Enter* MEPHASTOPHILIS *with* ALEXANDER *and his* PARAMOUR.]

EMPEROR Master doctor, I heard this lady, while she lived, had a
wart or mole in her neck; how shall I know whether it be so or no?

60 FAUSTUS Your highness may boldly go and see.
    [*The* EMPEROR *examines the lady's neck.*]

EMPEROR Sure, these are no spirits, but the true substantial bodies
of those two deceased princes.
                    [*Exit* ALEXANDER (*and his* PARAMOUR).]

FAUSTUS Will't please your highness now to send for the knight
that was so pleasant with me here of late?

65 EMPEROR One of you call him forth.
    [*Enter the* KNIGHT *with a pair of horns on his head.*]
How now, sir knight? Why, I had thought thou hadst been a bachelor, but now I see thou hast a wife that not only gives thee horns
but makes thee wear them! Feel on thy head.

KNIGHT Thou damnèd wretch and execrable° dog,   *detestable*
70 Bred in the concave of some monstrous rock,
How dar'st thou thus abuse a gentleman?
Villain, I say, undo what thou hast done.

FAUSTUS O not so fast, sir, there's no haste but good.[9] Are you
remembered[1] how you crossed me in my conference with the
75 emperor? I think I have met with you for it.

EMPEROR Good master doctor, at my entreaty release him; he hath
done penance sufficient.

FAUSTUS My gracious lord, not so much for the injury he offered me
here in your presence, as to delight you with some mirth, hath Faus-
80 tus worthily requited this injurious knight; which being all I desire,
I am content to release him of his horns. And, sir knight, hereafter
speak well of scholars: Mephastophilis, transform him straight.[2]
Now, my good lord, having done my duty, I humbly take my leave.

EMPEROR Farewell, master doctor; yet ere you go, expect from me a
85 bounteous reward.
                    [*Exit* EMPEROR (*and his* ATTENDANTS).]

FAUSTUS Now, Mephastophilis, the restless course
That time doth run with calm and silent foot,
Shortening my days and thread of vital life,
Calls for the payment of my latest years;
90 Therefore, sweet Mephastophilis, let us make haste to Wittenberg.

MEPHASTOPHILIS What, will you go on horseback or on foot?

FAUSTUS Nay, till I am past this fair and pleasant green, I'll walk on
foot.

SCENE 10

[*Enter a* HORSE-COURSER.[3]]

HORSE-COURSER I have been all this day seeking one Master Fustian: 'Mass,[4] see where he is! God save you, master doctor.

---

9. A proverb: no point hurrying, unless it's to
good effect.
1. Have you forgotten.
2. Immediately.

3. Horse trader, traditionally a sharp bargainer
or cheat.
4. By the Mass. "Fustian": the horse-courser's
comic mistake for Faustus's name.

FAUSTUS   What, horse-courser: you are well met.

HORSE-COURSER   Do you hear, sir; I have brought you forty dollars[5]
for your horse.

FAUSTUS   I cannot sell him so: if thou lik'st him for fifty, take him.

HORSE-COURSER   Alas sir, I have no more. I pray you speak for me.

MEPHASTOPHILIS   I pray you let him have him; he is an honest fellow, and he has a great charge[6]—neither wife nor child.

FAUSTUS   Well, come, give me your money; my boy will deliver him
to you. But I must tell you one thing before you have him: ride him
not into the water at any hand.[7]

HORSE-COURSER   Why sir, will he not drink of all waters?

FAUSTUS   O yes, he will drink of all waters, but ride him not into the
water. Ride him over hedge or ditch, or where thou wilt, but not
into the water.

HORSE-COURSER   Well sir. Now am I made man forever: I'll not
leave my horse for forty! If he had but the quality of hey ding ding,
hey ding ding,[8] I'd make a brave living on him! He has a buttock
as slick as an eel. Well, God b'y,[9] sir; your boy will deliver him me.
But hark ye sir, if my horse be sick, or ill at ease, if I bring his
water[1] to you, you'll tell me what it is?

[*Exit* HORSE-COURSER.]

FAUSTUS   Away, you villain! What, dost think I am a horse-doctor?
What art thou, Faustus, but a man condemned to die?
Thy fatal time° doth draw to final end.   *time allotted by fate*
Despair doth drive distrust unto my thoughts.
Confound these passions with a quiet sleep:
Tush, Christ did call the thief upon the cross.[2]
Then rest thee, Faustus, quiet in conceit.°   *in mind*

[*Sleep in his chair.*]
[*Enter* HORSE-COURSER *all wet, crying.*]

HORSE-COURSER   Alas, alas, Doctor Fustian, quotha?[3] 'Mass, Doctor Lopus[4] was never such a doctor! H'as given me a purgation,
h'as purged me of forty dollars! I shall never see them more. But
yet, like an ass as I was, I would not be ruled by him; for he bade
me I should ride him into no water. Now I, thinking my horse had
had some rare quality that he would not have had me known of, I,
like a vent'rous[5] youth, rid him into the deep pond at the town's
end. I was no sooner in the middle of the pond, but my horse vanished away, and I sat upon a bottle[6] of hay, never so near drowning
in my life! But I'll seek out my doctor, and have my forty dollars
again, or I'll make it the dearest[7] horse. O, yonder is his snipper-
snapper![8] Do you hear, you hey-pass,[9] where's your master?

5 Common German coins.
6. Burden.
7. On any account.
8. I.e., he wishes his horse were a stallion, not a
gelding, so he could put him to stud.
9. Good-bye (contracted from "God be with you").
1. Urine.
2. In Luke 23.39–43 one of the two thieves crucified with Jesus is promised paradise. "Tush": a
scoffing exclamation.

3. He said.
4. In February 1594 Roderigo Lopez, the queen's
personal physician, was executed for plotting to
poison her. Obviously Marlowe, who died in 1593,
did not write the line.
5. Adventurous.
6. Bundle.
7. Most expensive.
8. Insignificant youth; a whipper-snapper.
9. A conjurer's phrase.

MEPHASTOPHILIS   Why, sir, what would you? You cannot speak with him.

HORSE-COURSER   But I will speak with him.

45 MEPHASTOPHILIS   Why, he's fast asleep; come some other time.

HORSE-COURSER   I'll speak with him now, or I'll break his glasswindows[1] about his ears.

MEPHASTOPHILIS   I tell thee, he has not slept this eight nights.

HORSE-COURSER   And he have not slept this eight weeks I'll speak
50   with him.

MEPHASTOPHILIS   See where he is, fast asleep.

HORSE-COURSER   Ay, this is he; God save ye, master doctor, master doctor, master Doctor Fustian, forty dollars, forty dollars for a bottle of hay!

55 MEPHASTOPHILIS   Why, thou seest he hears thee not.

HORSE-COURSER   So ho ho; so ho ho.[2] [Halloo in his ear.] No, will you not wake? I'll make you wake ere I go. [Pull him by the leg, and pull it away.] Alas, I am undone! What shall I do?

FAUSTUS   O my leg, my leg! Help, Mephastophilis! Call the officers!
60   My leg, my leg!

MEPHASTOPHILIS   Come villain, to the constable.

HORSE-COURSER   O Lord, sir! Let me go, and I'll give you forty dollars more.

MEPHASTOPHILIS   Where be they?

65 HORSE-COURSER   I have none about me: come to my ostry[3] and I'll give them you.

MEPHASTOPHILIS   Begone quickly!

[HORSE-COURSER runs away.]

FAUSTUS   What, is he gone? Farewell he: Faustus has his leg again, and the horse-courser—I take it—a bottle of hay for his labor!
70   Well, this trick shall cost him forty dollars more.

[Enter WAGNER.]

How now, Wagner, what's the news with thee?

WAGNER   Sir, the duke of Vanholt[4] doth earnestly entreat your company.

FAUSTUS   The duke of Vanholt! An honorable gentleman, to whom
75   I must be no niggard of my cunning.[5] Come, Mephastophilis, let's away to him.   [Exeunt.]

SCENE 11

[FAUSTUS and MEPHASTOPHILIS return to the stage. Enter to them the DUKE and the DUCHESS; the DUKE speaks.]

DUKE   Believe me, master doctor, this merriment hath much pleased me.

FAUSTUS   My gracious lord, I am glad it contents you so well: but it may be, madam, you take no delight in this; I have heard that

---

1. Spectacles.
2. The huntsman's cry, when he sights the quarry.
3. Hostelry, inn.
4. The duchy of Anhalt, in central Germany.
5. I.e., must generously display my skill.

5 great-bellied[6] women do long for some dainties or other—what is
it, madam? Tell me, and you shall have it.

DUCHESS   Thanks, good master doctor; and for I see your courteous
intent to pleasure me, I will not hide from you the thing my heart
desires. And were it now summer, as it is January and the dead of
10 winter, I would desire no better meat than a dish of ripe grapes.

FAUSTUS   Alas madam, that's nothing! Mephastophilis, begone! [*Exit*
MEPHASTOPHILIS.] Were it a greater thing than this, so it would
content you, you should have it. [*Enter* MEPHASTOPHILIS *with the*
grapes.] Here they be, madam; will't please you taste on them?

15 DUKE   Believe me, master doctor, this makes me wonder above the
rest: that being in the dead time of winter, and in the month of
January, how you should come by these grapes?

FAUSTUS   If it like[7] your grace, the year is divided into two circles over
the whole world, that when it is here winter with us, in the contrary
20 circle it is summer with them, as in India, Saba,[8] and farther countries in the east; and by means of a swift spirit that I have, I had
them brought hither, as ye see. How do you like them, madam;
be they good?

DUCHESS   Believe me, master doctor, they be the best grapes that ere
25 I tasted in my life before.

FAUSTUS   I am glad they content you so, madam.

DUKE   Come, madam, let us in, where you must well reward this
learned man for the great kindness he hath showed to you.

DUCHESS   And so I will, my lord; and whilst I live, rest beholding for
30 this courtesy.

FAUSTUS   I humbly thank your grace.

DUKE   Come, master doctor, follow us, and receive your reward.

[*Exeunt.*]

CHORUS 4

[*Enter* WAGNER *solus.*]

WAGNER   I think my master means to die shortly,
For he hath given to me all his goods.
And yet methinks, if that death were near,
He would not banquet, and carouse, and swill
5 Amongst the students, as even now he doth,
Who are at supper with such belly-cheer°   *gluttony*
As Wagner ne'er beheld in all his life.
See where they come: belike the feast is ended.   [*Exit.*]

SCENE 12

[*Enter* FAUSTUS (*and* MEPHASTOPHILIS), *with two or three*
SCHOLARS.]

1 SCHOLAR   Master Doctor Faustus, since our conference about
fair ladies, which was the beautifulest in all the world, we have

---

6. Pregnant.
7. Please.

8. The biblical kingdom of Sheba, in southwestern Arabia.

determined with ourselves that Helen of Greece was the admira-
blest lady that ever lived. Therefore, master doctor, if you will do
us that favor as to let us see that peerless dame of Greece, whom
all the world admires for majesty, we should think ourselves much
beholding unto you.

FAUSTUS Gentlemen, for that I know your friendship is unfeigned,
And Faustus' custom is not to deny
The just requests of those that wish him well,
You shall behold that peerless dame of Greece,
No otherways for pomp and majesty
Than when Sir Paris crossed the seas with her
And brought the spoils to rich Dardania.°   Troy
Be silent then, for danger is in words.
[*Music sounds, and* HELEN *passeth over the stage.*]

2 SCHOLAR Too simple is my wit to tell her praise,
Whom all the world admires for majesty.

3 SCHOLAR No marvel though the angry Greeks pursued
With ten years' war the rape° of such a queen,   abduction
Whose heavenly beauty passeth all compare.

1 SCHOLAR Since we have seen the pride of Nature's works
And only paragon of excellence,
Let us depart; and for this glorious deed
Happy and blest be Faustus evermore.

FAUSTUS Gentlemen, farewell; the same I wish to you.
[*Exeunt* SCHOLARS.]
[*Enter an* OLD MAN.]

OLD MAN Ah Doctor Faustus, that I might prevail
To guide thy steps unto the way of life,
By which sweet path thou may'st attain the goal
That shall conduct thee to celestial rest.
Break heart, drop blood, and mingle it with tears,
Tears falling from repentant heaviness°   grief
Of thy most vile and loathsome filthiness,
The stench whereof corrupts the inward soul
With such flagitious° crimes of heinous sins,   villainous
As no commiseration may expel
But mercy, Faustus, of thy savior sweet,
Whose blood alone must wash away thy guilt.

FAUSTUS Where art thou, Faustus? Wretch, what hast thou done!
Damned art thou, Faustus, damned; despair and die!
Hell calls for right, and with a roaring voice
Says, "Faustus, come: thine hour is come!"
[MEPHASTOPHILIS *gives him a dagger.*]
And Faustus will come to do thee right.

OLD MAN Ah stay, good Faustus, stay thy desperate steps!
I see an angel hovers o'er thy head
And with a vial full of precious grace
Offers to pour the same into thy soul!
Then call for mercy, and avoid despair.

FAUSTUS Ah my sweet friend, I feel thy words

To comfort my distressèd soul;
50   Leave me awhile to ponder on my sins.
OLD MAN   I go, sweet Faustus; but with heavy cheer,°   *heavy heart*
   Fearing the ruin of thy hopeless soul.   *[Exit.]*
FAUSTUS   Accursèd Faustus, where is mercy now?
   I do repent, and yet I do despair:
55   Hell strives with grace for conquest in my breast!
   What shall I do to shun the snares of death?
MEPHASTOPHILIS   Thou traitor, Faustus: I arrest thy soul
   For disobedience to my sovereign lord.
   Revolt,[9] or I'll in piecemeal tear thy flesh.
60 FAUSTUS   Sweet Mephastophilis, entreat thy lord
   To pardon my unjust presumptiön;
   And with my blood again I will confirm
   My former vow I made to Lucifer.
MEPHASTOPHILIS   Do it then quickly, with unfeignèd heart,
65   Lest greater danger do attend thy drift.°   *intent*
FAUSTUS   Torment, sweet friend, that base and crooked age°   *aged man*
   That durst° dissuade me from thy Lucifer,   *dared to*
   With greatest torments that our hell affords.
MEPHASTOPHILIS   His faith is great, I cannot touch his soul,
70   But what I may afflict his body with
   I will attempt—which is but little worth.
FAUSTUS   One thing, good servant, let me crave of thee,
   To glut the longing of my heart's desire:
   That I might have unto° my paramour   *for*
75   That heavenly Helen which I saw of late,
   Whose sweet embracings may extinguish clean
   These thoughts that do dissuade me from my vow,
   And keep mine oath I made to Lucifer.
MEPHASTOPHILIS   Faustus, this, or what else thou shalt desire,
80   Shall be performed in twinkling of an eye.
      [Enter HELEN.]
FAUSTUS   Was this the face that launched a thousand ships,
   And burnt the topless[1] towers of Ilium?°   *Troy*
   Sweet Helen, make me immortal with a kiss:
   Her lips sucks forth my soul, see where it flies!
85   Come Helen, come, give me my soul again.
   Here will I dwell, for heaven be in these lips,
   And all is dross that is not Helena!
      [Enter OLD MAN.]
   I will be Paris, and for love of thee,
   Instead of Troy shall Wittenberg be sacked;
90   And I will combat with weak Menelaus,°   *Helen's husband*
   And wear thy colors on my plumèd crest;
   Yea, I will wound Achilles in the heel,[2]

---

9. Turn back (to your allegiance to Lucifer).
1. Immeasurably high; matchless.

2. Achilles could be wounded only in his heel—
where he was shot by Paris.

And then return to Helen for a kiss.
O thou art fairer than the evening air
95 Clad in the beauty of a thousand stars,
Brighter art thou than flaming Jupiter
When he appeared to hapless Semele;[3]
More lovely than the monarch of the sky
In wanton Arethusa's azured arms;[4]
100 And none but thou shalt be my paramour.

[*Exeunt* (FAUSTUS *and* HELEN).]

OLD MAN   Accursèd Faustus, miserable man,
That from thy soul exclud'st the grace of heaven
And fliest the throne of His tribunal seat!

[*Enter the* DEVILS.]

Satan begins to sift me with his pride,[5]
105 As in this furnace God shall try my faith.
My faith, vile hell, shall triumph over thee!
Ambitious fiends, see how the heavens smiles
At your repulse, and laughs your state° to scorn.   *royal power*
Hence hell, for hence I fly unto my God.

[*Exeunt.*]

SCENE 13

[*Enter* FAUSTUS *with the* SCHOLARS.]

FAUSTUS   Ah gentlemen!

1 SCHOLAR   What ails Faustus?

FAUSTUS   Ah my sweet chamber-fellow, had I lived with thee, then
had I lived still;[6] but now I die eternally. Look, comes he not, comes
5   he not?

2 SCHOLAR   What means Faustus?

3 SCHOLAR   Belike he is grown into some sickness by being over-
solitary.

1 SCHOLAR   If it be so, we'll have physicians to cure him; 'tis but a
10   surfeit:[7] never fear, man.

FAUSTUS   A surfeit of deadly sin, that hath damned both body and
soul.

2 SCHOLAR   Yet Faustus, look up to heaven; remember God's mercies are infinite.

15 FAUSTUS   But Faustus' offense can ne'er be pardoned! The serpent
that tempted Eve may be saved, but not Faustus. Ah gentlemen,
hear me with patience, and tremble not at my speeches, though
my heart pants and quivers to remember that I have been a student here these thirty years—O would I had never seen Witten-
20   berg, never read book—and what wonders I have done, all
Wittenberg can witness—yea, all the world; for which Faustus

---

3. A Theban girl, loved by Jupiter and destroyed
by the fire of his lightning when he appeared to
her in his full splendor.
4. Arethusa was the nymph of a fountain, as well
as the fountain itself; she excited the passion of

the river god Alpheus, who was by some accounts
related to the sun.
5. To test me with his strength.
6. Always.
7. Indigestion caused by overeating.

hath lost both Germany and the world—yea, heaven itself—
heaven, the seat of God, the throne of the blessed, the kingdom of
joy; and must remain in hell forever—hell, ah, hell forever! Sweet
25   friends, what shall become of Faustus, being in hell forever?

3 SCHOLAR   Yet Faustus, call on God.

FAUSTUS   On God, whom Faustus hath abjured? On God, whom
Faustus hath blasphemed? Ah, my God—I would weep, but the
devil draws in my tears! Gush forth blood, instead of tears—yea,
30   life and soul! O, he stays my tongue! I would lift up my hands, but
see, they hold them, they hold them!

ALL   Who, Faustus?

FAUSTUS   Lucifer and Mephastophilis! Ah gentlemen, I gave them
my soul for my cunning.

35   ALL   God forbid!

FAUSTUS   God forbade it indeed, but Faustus hath done it: for the
vain pleasure of four-and-twenty years hath Faustus lost eternal
joy and felicity. I writ them a bill[8] with mine own blood, the date
is expired, the time will come, and he will fetch me.

40   1 SCHOLAR   Why did not Faustus tell us of this before, that divines
might have prayed for thee?

FAUSTUS   Oft have I thought to have done so, but the devil threatened to tear me in pieces if I named God, to fetch both body and
soul if I once gave ear to divinity; and now 'tis too late. Gentlemen,
45   away, lest you perish with me!

2 SCHOLAR   O what shall we do to save Faustus?

3 SCHOLAR   God will strengthen me. I will stay with Faustus.

1 SCHOLAR   Tempt not God, sweet friend, but let us into the next
room, and there pray for him.

50   FAUSTUS   Ay, pray for me, pray for me; and what noise soever ye
hear, come not unto me, for nothing can rescue me.

2 SCHOLAR   Pray thou, and we will pray, that God may have mercy
upon thee.

FAUSTUS   Gentlemen, farewell. If I live till morning, I'll visit you; if
55   not, Faustus is gone to hell.

ALL   Faustus, farewell.   [*Exeunt* SCHOLARS.]
         [*The clock strikes eleven.*]

FAUSTUS   Ah Faustus,
      Now hast thou but one bare hour to live,
      And then thou must be damned perpetually.
60   Stand still, you ever-moving spheres of heaven,
      That time may cease, and midnight never come.
      Fair Nature's eye, rise, rise again, and make
      Perpetual day, or let this hour be but
      A year, a month, a week, a natural day,
65   That Faustus may repent and save his soul.
      O lente, lente currite noctis equi![9]

---

8. Document.
9. Slowly, slowly run, O horses of the night (adapted from a line in Ovid's *Amores*).

The stars move still, time runs, the clock will strike,
The devil will come, and Faustus must be damned.
O I'll leap up to my God! Who pulls me down?
70 See, see where Christ's blood streams in the firmament!°   sky
One drop would save my soul, half a drop: ah my Christ—
Ah, rend not my heart for naming of my Christ;
Yet will I call on him—O spare me, Lucifer!
Where is it now? 'Tis gone: and see where God
75 Stretcheth out his arm, and bends his ireful brows!
Mountains and hills, come, come and fall on me,
And hide me from the heavy wrath of God.
No, no?
Then will I headlong run into the earth:
80 Earth, gape! O no, it will not harbor me.
You stars that reigned at my nativity,
Whose influence hath allotted death and hell,
Now draw up Faustus like a foggy mist
Into the entrails of yon laboring cloud,
85 That when you vomit forth into the air
My limbs may issue from your smoky mouths,
So that my soul may but ascend to heaven.[1]
    [*The watch strikes.*]
Ah, half the hour is past: 'twill all be past anon.°   shortly
O God, if thou wilt not have mercy on my soul,
90 Yet for Christ's sake, whose blood hath ransomed me,
Impose some end to my incessant pain:
Let Faustus live in hell a thousand years,
A hundred thousand, and at last be saved.
O no end is limited to damnèd souls!
95 Why wert thou not a creature wanting° soul?   lacking
Or why is this immortal that thou hast?
Ah, Pythagoras' *metempsychosis*[2]—were that true,
This soul should fly from me, and I be changed
Unto some brutish beast:
100 All beasts are happy, for when they die,
Their souls are soon dissolved in elements;
But mine must live still° to be plagued in hell.   always
Cursed be the parents that engendered me!
No, Faustus, curse thy self, curse Lucifer,
105 That hath deprived thee of the joys of heaven.
    [*The clock striketh twelve.*]
O it strikes, it strikes! Now body, turn to air,
Or Lucifer will bear thee quick° to hell.   alive
    [*Thunder and lightning.*]
O soul, be changed into little water drops
And fall into the ocean, ne'er be found.

---

1. Faustus wants to be drawn up into a cloud, which would compact his body into a thunderbolt so that his soul, thus purified, might ascend to heaven.

2. Pythagoras's doctrine of the transmigration of souls.

110 My God, my God, look not so fierce on me!
　　　　[*Enter* DEVILS.]
Adders and serpents, let me breathe awhile!
Ugly hell gape not! Come not, Lucifer!
I'll burn my books—ah, Mephastophilis!

　　　　　　　　　　　　　　　[*Exeunt with him.*]

Epilogue

　　　[*Enter* CHORUS.]
Cut is the branch that might have grown full straight,
And burnèd is Apollo's laurel bough,[3]
That sometime grew within this learnèd man.
Faustus is gone! Regard his hellish fall,
5　Whose fiendful fortune° may exhort the wise　　　　　*devilish fate*
Only to wonder at[4] unlawful things:
Whose deepness doth entice such forward wits°　　　*aspiring minds*
To practice more than heavenly power permits.

　　　　　　　　　　　　　　　[*Exit.*]

　　　Terminat hora diem, terminat author opus.[5]

　　　　　　　　　　　　　　　1604, 1616

---

3. The laurel crown of Apollo symbolizes (among other things) learning and wisdom.
4. Be content simply to observe with awe.
5. The hour ends the day, the author ends his work. This motto was probably added by the printer.

The Two Texts of *Doctor Faustus* The following excerpts enable readers to compare a sample passage (from Scene 12) of the A text (1604) with the corresponding passage of the B text (1616). (On the two texts, see p. 679.) Here the
differences in tone and content in the two versions of the Old Man's speech may signal different attitudes toward the finality of Faustus's damnation.

Doctor Faustus, A Text

[*Enter an* OLD MAN.]

OLD MAN Ah Doctor Faustus, that I might prevail
  To guide thy steps unto the way of life,
  By which sweet path thou may'st attain the goal
  That shall conduct thee to celestial rest.
5 Break heart, drop blood, and mingle it with tears,
  Tears falling from repentant heaviness°   *grief*
  Of thy most vile and loathsome filthiness,
  The stench whereof corrupts the inward soul
  With such flagitious° crimes of heinous sins   *villainous*
10 As no commiseration may expel
  But mercy, Faustus, of thy savior sweet,
  Whose blood alone must wash away thy guilt.
FAUSTUS Where art thou, Faustus? Wretch, what hast thou done!
  Damned art thou, Faustus, damned; despair and die!
15 Hell calls for right, and with a roaring voice
  Says, "Faustus, come: thine hour is come!"
      [MEPHASTOPHILIS *gives him a dagger.*]
  And Faustus will come to do thee right.
OLD MAN Ah stay, good Faustus, stay thy desperate steps!
  I see an angel hovers o'er thy head
20 And with a vial full of precious grace
  Offers to pour the same into thy soul!
  Then call for mercy, and avoid despair.
FAUSTUS Ah my sweet friend, I feel thy words
  To comfort my distressèd soul;
25 Leave me awhile to ponder on my sins.
OLD MAN I go, sweet Faustus; but with heavy cheer,° *heavy heart*
  Fearing the ruin of thy hopeless soul.   [*Exit.*]
FAUSTUS Accursèd Faustus, where is mercy now?
  I do repent, and yet I do despair:
30 Hell strives with grace for conquest in my breast!
  What shall I do to shun the snares of death?
MEPHASTOPHILIS Thou traitor, Faustus: I arrest thy soul
  For disobedience to my sovereign lord.
  Revolt,[1] or I'll in piecemeal tear thy flesh.

---

1. Turn back (to your allegiance to Lucifer).

Doctor Faustus, B Text

[*Enter an* OLD MAN.]
OLD MAN   O gentle Faustus, leave this damnèd art,
   This magic that will charm thy soul to hell
   And quite bereave thee of salvatiön.
   Though thou hast now offended like a man,
5   Do not persèver° in it like a devil.   *persevere*
   Yet, yet, thou hast an amiable° soul,   *worthy of (divine) love*
   If sin by custom grow not into nature.
   Then, Faustus, will repentance come too late;
   Then thou art banished from the sight of heaven.
10   No mortal can express the pains of hell.
   It may be this my exhortatiön
   Seems harsh and all unpleasant; let it not,
   For, gentle son, I speak it not in wrath
   Or envy of° thee, but in tender love   *ill will toward*
15   And pity of thy future misery.
   And so have hope that this my kind rebuke,
   Checking° thy body, may amend thy soul.   *rebuking*
FAUSTUS   Where art thou, Faustus? Wretch, what hast thou done?
   Hell claims his right, and with a roaring voice
20   Says, "Faustus, come; thine hour is almost come";
   And Faustus now will come to do thee right.
      [MEPHOSTOPHILIS *gives him a dagger.*]
OLD MAN   O stay, good Faustus, stay thy desperate steps.
   I see an angel hover o'er thy head,
   And with a vial full of precious grace
25   Offers to pour the same into thy soul.
   Then call for mercy and avoid despair.
FAUSTUS   O friend, I feel thy words
   To comfort my distressèd soul.
   Leave me a while to ponder on my sins.
30 OLD MAN   Faustus, I leave thee, but with grief of heart,
   Fearing the enemy of thy hapless soul.   [*Exit.*]
FAUSTUS   Accursèd Faustus, wretch, what hast thou done?
   I do repent, and yet I do despair.
   Hell strives with grace for conquest in my breast.
35   What shall I do to shun the snares of death?
MEPHOSTOPHILIS   Thou traitor, Faustus, I arrest thy soul
   For disobedience to my sovereign lord.
   Revolt,[1] or I'll in piecemeal tear thy flesh.

---

1. Turn back (to your allegiance to Lucifer).

WILLIAM SHAKESPEARE
1564–1616

William Shakespeare was born in the small market town of Stratford-on-Avon in April (probably April 23) 1564. His father, a successful glovemaker, land-owner, moneylender, and dealer in agricultural commodities, was elected to several important posts in local government but later suffered financial and social reverses, possibly as a result of adherence to the Catholic faith. Shakespeare almost certainly attended the free Stratford grammar school, where he would have acquired a rea-sonably impressive education, including a respectable knowledge of Latin, but he did not proceed to Oxford or Cambridge. There are legends about Shakespeare's youth but no documented facts. Some scholars are tempted to associate him with "William Shakeshafte," a young actor attached to a recusant Catholic circle in Lancashire around 1581; one of Shakespeare's former Stratford schoolmasters belonged to this circle. But the first unambiguous record we have of his life after his christening is that of his marriage, in 1582, at age eighteen, to Anne Hathaway, eight years his senior. A daughter, Susanna, was born six months later, in 1583, and twins, Hamnet and Judith, in 1585. We possess no information about his activities for the next seven years, but by 1592 he was in London as an actor and apparently already well known as a playwright, for a rival dramatist, Robert Greene, refers to him resent-fully in A Groatsworth of Wit as "an upstart crow, beautified with our feathers."

At this time, there were several companies of professional actors in London and in the provinces. What links Shakespeare had with one or more of them before 1592 is conjectural, but we do know of his long and fruitful connection, established by 1594, with the most successful troupe, the Lord Chamberlain's Men, who later, when James I came to the throne, became the King's Men. Shakespeare not only acted with this company but eventually became a leading shareholder and the principal playwright. Then as now, making a living in the professional theater was not easy: competition among the repertory companies was stiff, civic officials and religious moralists regarded playacting as a sinful, time-wasting nuisance and tried to ban it altogether, government officials exercised censorship over the contents of the plays, and periodic outbreaks of bubonic plague led to temporary closing of the London theaters. But Shakespeare's company, which included some of the most famous actors of the day, nonetheless thrived and in 1599 began to perform in the Globe, a fine, open-air theater that the company built for itself on the south bank of the Thames. The company also performed frequently at court and, after 1608, at Blackfriars, an indoor London the-ater. Already by 1597 Shakespeare had so prospered that he was able to purchase New Place, a handsome house in Stratford; he could now call himself a gentleman, as his father had (probably with the financial assistance of his successful playwright son) been granted a coat of arms the previous year. Shakespeare's wife and daughters (his son, Hamnet, having died in 1596) resided in Stratford, while the playwright, living in rented rooms in London, pursued his career. Shortly after writing The Tempest (ca. 1611), he retired from direct involvement in the theater and returned to Stratford. In March 1616, he signed his will; he died a month later, leaving the bulk of his estate to his daughter Susanna. To his wife of thirty-four years, he left "my second best bed."

Shakespeare began his career as a playwright, probably in the early 1590s, by writing comedies and history plays. The earliest of these histories (in which he may have had one or more collaborators), generally based on accounts of English kings written by Raphael Holinshed and other sixteenth-century chroniclers, seem theatrically vital but crude, as does an early attempt at tragedy, *Titus Andronicus*. But Shakespeare quickly moved on to create by the later 1590s a sequence of profoundly searching and ambitious history plays—*Richard II*, the first and second parts of *Henry IV*, and *Henry V*—which together explore the death throes of feudal England and the birth of the modern nation-state ruled by a charismatic monarch. In the same years he wrote a succession of romantic comedies (*The Merchant of Venice, The Merry Wives of Windsor, Much Ado About Nothing, As You Like It, Twelfth Night*) whose poetic richness and emotional complexity remain unmatched.

Twelfth Night was probably written in the same year as *Hamlet* (ca. 1601), which initiated an outpouring of great tragic dramas: *Othello, King Lear, Macbeth, Antony and Cleopatra*, and *Coriolanus*. These plays, written from 1601 to 1607, seem to mark a major shift in sensibility, an existential and metaphysical darkening that many readers think must have originated in personal anguish. Whatever the truth of this speculation—and we have no direct, personal testimony either to support or to undermine it—there appears to have occurred in the same period a shift as well in Shakespeare's comic sensibility. The comedies written between 1601 and 1604, *Troilus and Cressida, All's Well That Ends Well*, and *Measure for Measure*, are sufficiently different from the earlier comedies—more biting in tone, more uneasy with comic conventions, more ruthlessly questioning of the values of the characters and the resolutions of the plots—to have led some modern scholars to classify them as "problem plays" or "dark comedies." Another group of plays, among the last that Shakespeare wrote, seem similarly to define a distinct category. *Pericles, Cymbeline, The Winter's Tale*, and *The Tempest*, written between 1608 and 1611, when Shakespeare had developed a remarkably fluid, dreamlike sense of plot and a poetic style that could veer, apparently effortlessly, from the tortured to the ineffably sweet, are now commonly known as the "romances." These plays share an interest in the moral and emotional life less of the adolescents who dominate the earlier comedies than of their parents. The romances are deeply concerned with patterns of loss and recovery, suffering and redemption, despair and renewal. They have seemed to many critics to constitute a self-conscious conclusion to a career that opened with histories and comedies and passed through the dark and tormented tragedies. In a few of the late plays, he worked, as he apparently had at the beginning of his professional life, with collaborators. Perhaps he thought of himself as handing over his vocation to a new generation.

Shakespeare evinced no interest in preserving for posterity the sum of his writings, let alone in clarifying the chronology of his works or in specifying which plays he wrote alone and which with collaborators. He wrote plays for performance by his company, and his scripts existed in his own handwritten manuscripts or in scribal copies, in playhouse promptbooks, and probably in pirated texts based on shorthand reports of a performance or on reconstructions from memory by an actor or a spectator. None of these manuscript versions has survived. Eighteen of his plays were published during his lifetime in the small-format, inexpensive books called quartos; to these were added eighteen other plays, never before printed, in the large, expensive folio volume of *Mr. William Shakespeares Comedies, Histories, & Tragedies* (1623), published seven years after his death. This First Folio, edited by two of his friends and fellow actors, John Heminges and Henry Condell, is prefaced by a poem of Ben Jonson's, in which Shakespeare is hailed, presciently, as "not of an age, but for all time."

That Shakespeare is "for all time" does not mean that he did not also belong to his own age. It is possible to see where Shakespeare adapted the techniques of his contemporaries and where, crucially, he differed from them. Shakespeare rarely invented the plots of his dramas, preferring to work, often quite closely, with stories he found ready-made in histories, novellas, narrative poems, or other plays. The religious mystery plays and the allegorical morality plays still popular during his childhood taught him that dramas worth seeing must get at something central to the

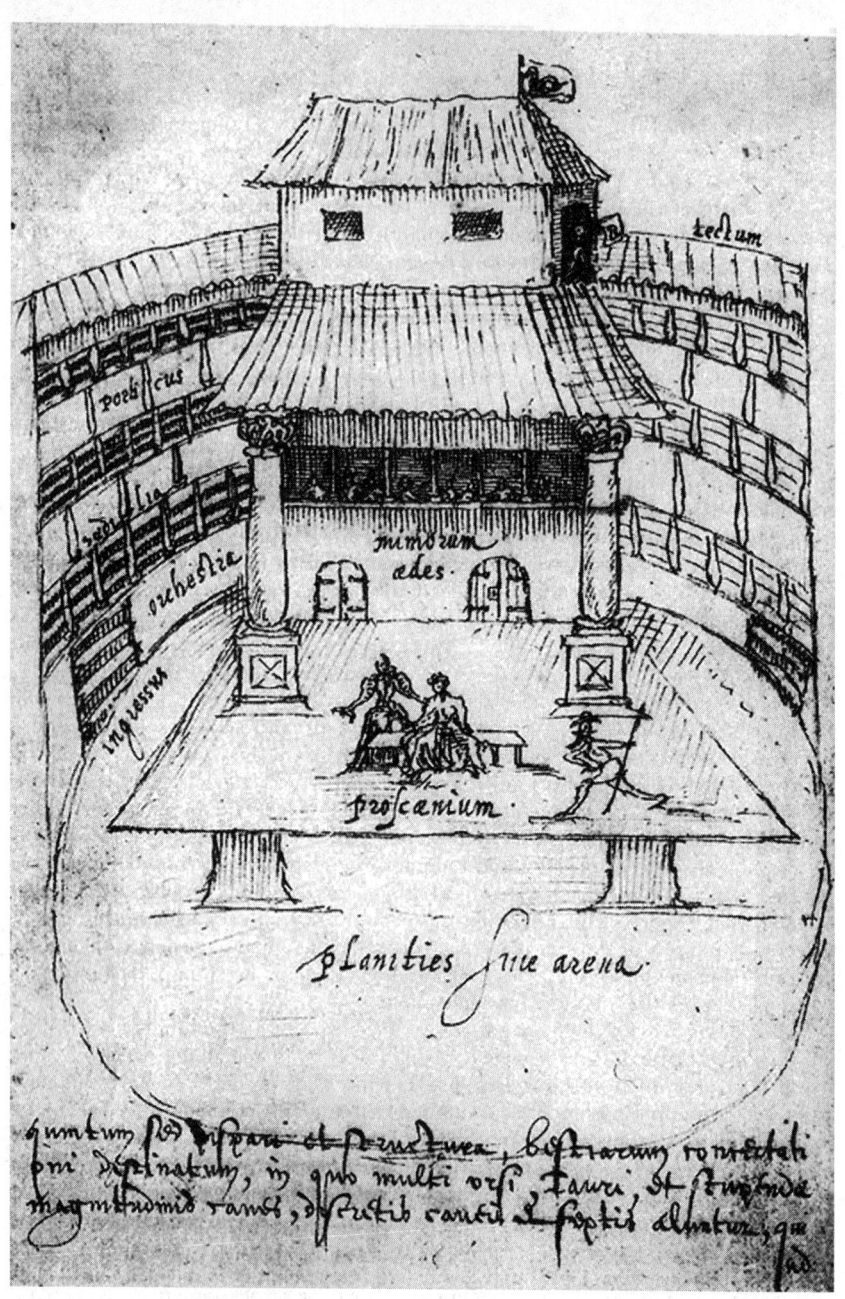

Sketch of the Swan Theater. This drawing by Arend van Buchell (ca. 1596), based on the observations of Johannes De Witt, shows features of a public playhouse in Shakespeare's time. Resembling the courtyard of an Elizabethan inn, the Swan had three galleries for the audience, and probably additional room for audience members in the gallery at the back of the stage, above the tiring-house (dressing room). The stage itself had two doors for players' entrances and exits, and the roof over the stage was supported by pillars. The flag flying from the roof signals that a play is to be performed that day, and a trumpeter announces the beginning of the performance (though the sketch shows a performance already under way). De Witt labeled parts of the sketch using Latin names derived from the Roman theater.

human condition, that they should embody as well as narrate the crucial actions, and that they could reach not only a coterie of the educated elite but also the great mass of ordinary people. From these and other theatrical models, Shakespeare learned how to construct plays around the struggle for the soul of a protagonist, how to create theatrically compelling and subversive figures of wickedness, and how to focus attention on his characters' psychological, moral, and spiritual lives as well as on their outward behavior.

The authors of the morality plays thought they could enhance the broad impact they sought to achieve by stripping their characters of all incidental distinguishing traits and getting to their essences. They believed that their audiences would thereby not be distracted by the irrelevant details of individual identities. Shakespeare grasped that the spectacle of human destiny was in fact vastly more compelling when it was attached not to generalized abstractions but to particular people, people whom he realized with an unprecedented intensity of individuation: not Youth but Viola, not Everyman but Lear. No other writer of his time was able to create and enter into the interior worlds of so many characters, conveying again and again a sense of unique and irreducible selfhood. In the plays of Shakespeare's brilliant contemporary Marlowe, the protagonist overwhelms virtually all of the other characters; in Shakespeare, by contrast, even relatively minor characters—Maria in *Twelfth Night*, for example, or Emilia in *Othello*—make astonishingly powerful claims on the audience's attention. The Romantic critic William Hazlitt observed that Shakespeare had the power to multiply himself marvelously. His plays convey the sense of an inexhaustible imaginative generosity.

Shakespeare was singularly alert to the fantastic vitality of the English language. His immense vocabulary bears witness to an uncanny ability to absorb terms from a wide range of pursuits and to transform them into intimate registers of thought and feeling. He had a seemingly boundless capacity to generate metaphors, and he was virtually addicted to wordplay. Double meanings, verbal echoes, and submerged associations ripple through every passage, deepening the reader's enjoyment and understanding, though sometimes at the expense of a single clear sense. The eighteenth-century critic Samuel Johnson complained with some justice that the quibble, the pun, was "the fatal Cleopatra for which Shakespeare lost the world and was content to lose it." For the power that continually discharges itself throughout his plays and poems, at once constituting and unsettling everything it touches, is the polymorphous power of language.

Anachronism is rarely a concern for Shakespeare. His ancient Romans throw their caps into the air and use Christian oaths: to this extent he pulled everything he touched into his contemporary existence. But at the same time he was not a social realist; other writers in this period are better at conveying the precise details of the daily lives of shoemakers, alchemists, and judges. The settings of his plays are rarely realistic representations of particular historical times and places; instead, like "Illyria" in *Twelfth Night*, they function as imaginative displacements into alternative worlds that remain strangely familiar.

Though on occasion he depicts ghosts, demons, and other supernatural figures, the universe Shakespeare conjures up seems resolutely human-centered and secular: the torments and joys that most deeply matter are found in this world, not in the next. Attempts to claim him for one or another religious system have proven unconvincing, as have attempts to assign him a specific political label. Activists and ideologues of all political stripes have viewed him as an ally: he has been admiringly quoted by kings and by revolutionaries, by fascists, liberal democrats, socialists, republicans, and communists. At once an agent of civility and an agent of subversion, Shakespeare seems to have been able to view society simultaneously as an insider and as an outsider. His plays can be interpreted and performed—with deep conviction and compelling power—in utterly contradictory ways. The centuries-long accumulation of these interpretations and performances, far from exhausting Shakespeare's aesthetic appeal, seems only to have enhanced its perennial freshness.*

Sonnets

In Elizabethan England aristocratic patronage, with the money, protection, and prestige it alone could provide, was probably a professional writer's most important asset. This patronage, or at least Shakespeare's quest for it, is most visible in his dedication, in 1593 and 1594, of his narrative poems, *Venus and Adonis* and *The Rape of Lucrece*, to the wealthy young nobleman Henry Wriothesley, earl of Southampton. What return the poet got for his exquisite offerings is unknown. We do know that among wits and gallants the narrative poems won Shakespeare a fine reputation as an immensely stylish and accomplished poet. This reputation was enhanced as well by manuscript circulation of his sonnets, which were mentioned admiringly in print more than ten years before they were published, in 1609 (apparently without his personal supervision and perhaps without his consent).

Shakespeare's sonnets are quite unlike the other sonnet sequences of his day, notably in his almost unprecedented choice of a beautiful young man (rather than a lady) as the principal object of praise, love, and idealizing devotion and in his portrait of a dark, sensuous, and sexually promiscuous mistress (rather than the usual chaste and aloof blond beauty). Nor are the moods confined to what the Renaissance thought were those of the despairing Petrarchan lover: they include delight, pride, melancholy, shame, disgust, and fear. Shakespeare's sequence suggests a story, although the details are vague, and there is even doubt whether the sonnets as published are in an order established by the poet himself. Certain motifs are evident: an introductory series (1 to 17) celebrates the beauty of a young man and urges him to marry and beget children who will bear his image. The subsequent long sequence (18 to 126), passionately focused on the beloved young man, develops as a dominant motif the transience and destructive power of time, countered only by the force of love and the permanence of poetry. The remaining sonnets focus chiefly on the so-called Dark Lady as an alluring but degrading object of desire. Some sonnets (like 144) intimate a love triangle involving the speaker, the male friend, and the woman; others take note of a rival poet (sometimes identified as George Chapman or Christopher Marlowe). The biographical background of the sonnets has inspired a mountain of speculation, but very little of it has any factual support.

Though there are many variations, Shakespeare's most frequent rhyme scheme in the sonnets is *abab cdcd efef gg*. This so-called Shakespearean pattern often (though not always) calls attention to three distinct quatrains (each of which may develop a separate metaphor), followed by a closing couplet that may either confirm or pull sharply against what has gone before. Startling shifts in direction may occur in lines other than the closing ones; consider, for example, the twists and turns in the opening lines of sonnet 138: "When my love swears that she is made of truth, / I do believe her, though I know she lies." Shakespeare's sonnets as a whole are strikingly intense, conveying a sense of high psychological and moral stakes. They are also remarkably dense, written with a daunting energy, concentration, and compression. Often the main idea of the poem may be grasped quickly, but the precise movement of thought and feeling, the links among the shifting images, the syntax, tone, and rhetorical structure prove immensely challenging. These are poems that famously reward rereading.[†]

---

* For additional writings by Shakespeare—including the full text of *The First Part of King Henry IV*, a collection of songs from the plays, five additional sonnets (nos. 56, 104, 118, 121, 124), and the philosophical poem "The Phoenix and the Turtle"—see the NAEL Archive. See the color insert in this volume for the "Chandos" portrait of Shakespeare and a portrait of Henry Wriothesley, third earl of Southampton and the dedicatee of Shakespeare's two narrative poems and, possibly, of his sonnets.
† For a broad grouping of other 16th-century poems, especially love lyrics, see "An Elizabethan Miscellany" on p. 502.

Sonnets

To the Only Begetter of
These Ensuing Sonnets
Mr. W. H. All Happiness
and That Eternity
Promised
By
Our Ever-Living Poet
Wisheth
The Well-Wishing
Adventurer in
Setting Forth
T. T.[1]

1

From fairest creatures we desire increase,
That thereby beauty's rose might never die,
But as the riper should by time decease,
His tender heir might bear his memory;
5   But thou, contracted[2] to thine own bright eyes,
Feed'st thy light's flame with self-substantial[3] fuel,
Making a famine where abundance lies,
Thyself thy foe, to thy sweet self too cruel.
Thou that art now the world's fresh ornament
10   And only[4] herald to the gaudy spring,
Within thine own bud buriest thy content[5]
And, tender churl,[6] mak'st waste in niggarding.°   *hoarding*
    Pity the world, or else this glutton be,
    To eat the world's due, by the grave and thee.[7]

3

Look in thy glass° and tell the face thou viewest   *mirror*
Now is the time that face should form another,
Whose fresh repair° if now thou not renewest,   *state*
Thou dost beguile° the world, unbless some mother.   *cheat*
5   For where is she so fair whose uneared° womb   *unplowed*
Disdains the tillage of thy husbandry?
Or who is he so fond° will be the tomb   *foolish*

1. This odd dedication bears the initials of the publisher, Thomas Thorpe. The W. H. addressed here may or may not be the male friend addressed in sonnets 1 to 126. Leading candidates for that role are Henry Wriothesley, earl of Southampton, the dedicatee of *Venus and Adonis* (1593) and *The Rape of Lucrece* (1594), and William Herbert, earl of Pembroke, a dedicatee of the First Folio. But there is no hard evidence to support these or other suggested identifications of the male friend or of the so-called Dark Lady; these sonnet personages may or may not have had real-life counterparts.
    Since all the sonnets save two were first published in 1609, we do not repeat the date after each one. Numbers 138 and 144 were first published in 1599, in a verse miscellany called *The Passionate Pilgrim*.
2. Betrothed; also, withdrawn into.
3. Of your own substance.
4. Principal, with overtones of single, solitary.
5. What you contain (potential for fatherhood), also what would content you (marriage and fatherhood).
6. Gentle boor (an oxymoron).
7. "This . . . thee": be a glutton by causing what is owed to the world (your posterity) to be consumed by the grave and within yourself.

Of his self-love, to stop posterity?
Thou art thy mother's glass, and she in thee
10 Calls back the lovely April of her prime;
So thou through windows of thine age shalt see,
Despite of wrinkles, this thy golden time.
　　But if thou live rememb'red not to be,[8]
　　Die single, and thine image dies with thee.

12

When I do count the clock that tells the time
And see the brave° day sunk in hideous night,　　　　　*splendid*
When I behold the violet past prime
And sable curls all silvered o'er with white,
5 When lofty trees I see barren of leaves,
Which erst° from heat did canopy the herd　　　　　*formerly*
And summer's green all girded up in sheaves
Borne on the bier with white and bristly beard:
Then of thy beauty do I question make°　　　　　*speculate*
10 That thou among the wastes of time must go,
Since sweets and beauties do themselves forsake,
And die as fast as they see others grow,
　　And nothing 'gainst Time's scythe can make defense
　　Save breed,° to brave° him when he takes thee hence.　　　*offspring / defy*

15

When I consider every thing that grows
Holds° in perfection but a little moment;　　　　　*remains*
That this huge stage presenteth nought but shows[9]
Whereon the stars in secret influence comment;[1]
5 When I perceive that men as plants increase,
Cheered and checked[2] even by the selfsame sky,
Vaunt[3] in their youthful sap, at height decrease,
And wear their brave state out of memory;[4]
Then the conceit° of this inconstant stay　　　　　*conception*
10 Sets you most rich in youth before my sight,
Where wasteful Time debateth[5] with Decay
To change your day of youth to sullied° night,　　　*soiled, blackened*
　　And all in war with Time for love of you,
　　As he takes from you, I ingraft[6] you new.

18

Shall I compare thee to a summer's day?
Thou art more lovely and more temperate:
Rough winds do shake the darling buds of May,
And summer's lease hath all too short a date;
5 Sometime too hot the eye of heaven shines,

8. But if you live to be forgotten.
9. (1) Appearances, (2) performances.
1. I.e., the stars secretly affect human actions.
2. Encouraged and reproached or stopped.
3. Exult, display themselves.

4. Wear their showy splendor out and are forgotten.
5. (1) Fights, (2) joins forces.
6. Renew by grafting; implant beauty again (by my verse).

And often is his gold complexion dimmed;
And every fair from fair sometime declines,
By chance or nature's changing course untrimmed.[7]
But thy eternal summer shall not fade,
10 Nor lose possession of that fair thou ow'st;° *ownest*
Nor shall death brag thou wander'st in his shade,
When in eternal lines to time thou grow'st:° *are grafted*
   So long as men can breathe or eyes can see,
   So long lives this,[8] and this gives life to thee.

19

Devouring Time, blunt thou the lion's paws,
And make the earth devour her own sweet brood;
Pluck the keen teeth from the fierce tiger's jaws,
And burn the long-lived phoenix in her blood;[9]
5 Make glad and sorry seasons as thou fleet'st,
And do whate'er thou wilt, swift-footed Time,
To the wide world and all her fading sweets,
But I forbid thee one most heinous crime:
O carve not with thy hours my love's fair brow,
10 Nor draw no lines there with thine antique[1] pen;
Him in thy course untainted[2] do allow,
For beauty's pattern to succeeding men.
   Yet do thy worst, old Time: despite thy wrong,
   My love shall in my verse ever live young.

20

A woman's face with Nature's own hand painted[3]
Hast thou, the master mistress of my passion;[4]
A woman's gentle heart but not acquainted
With shifting change as is false women's fashion;
5 An eye more bright than theirs, less false in rolling,° *roving*
Gilding the object whereupon it gazeth;
A man in hue all hues[5] in his controlling,
Which steals men's eyes and women's souls amazeth.
And for a woman wert thou first created,
10 Till Nature as she wrought thee fell a-doting,[6]
And by addition me of thee defeated,
By adding one thing to my purpose nothing.
   But since she pricked[7] thee out for women's pleasure,
   Mine be thy love, and thy love's use[8] their treasure.

---

7. Stripped of gay apparel.
8. I.e., the poem. The boast of immortality for one's verse was a convention going back to the Greek and Roman classics.
9. In full vigor of life (a hunting term). The phoenix was a mythical bird that lived five hundred years, then died in flames to rise again from its ashes.
1. (1) Old, (2) fantastic (antic).
2. (1) Undefiled, (2) untouched by a weapon (a term from jousting).

3. I.e., not made up with cosmetics.
4. (1) Strong feeling, (2) poem.
5. "Hue" probably means appearance or form. In the first edition, "hues" is spelled *"Hews,"* which some have taken as indicating a pun on a proper name. It has also been suggested that "man in" is a copyist's or compositor's misreading of "maiden."
6. (1) Crazy, (2) infatuated.
7. Marked, with obvious sexual pun.
8. (1) Sexual enjoyment, (2) interest (as in usury).

23

As an unperfect actor on the stage
Who with his fear is put besides° his part,　　　　　　　　　　*forgets*
Or some fierce thing replete with too much rage
Whose strength's abundance weakens his own heart,
5　So I, for fear of trust,° forget to say　　　　　　　　*lack of confidence*
The perfect ceremony of love's rite,[9]
And in mine own love's strength seem to decay,
O'er-charged° with burden of mine own love's might.　　　*overweighed*
O let my books be then the eloquence
10　And dumb presagers° of my speaking breast,　　　　　*mute presenters*
Who plead for love, and look for recompense
More than that tongue that more hath more expressed.[1]
　　O learn to read what silent love hath writ;
　　To hear with eyes belongs to love's fine wit.°　　　　　*intelligence*

29

When, in disgrace° with Fortune and men's eyes,　　　　　*disfavor*
I all alone beweep my outcast state,
And trouble deaf heaven with my bootless° cries,　　　　　*futile*
And look upon myself and curse my fate,
5　Wishing me like to one more rich in hope,
Featured like him, like him with friends possessed,[2]
Desiring this man's art° and that man's scope,°　　　　*skill / ability*
With what I most enjoy contented least;
Yet in these thoughts myself almost despising,
10　Haply I think on thee, and then my state[3]
(Like to the lark at break of day arising
From sullen earth) sings hymns at heaven's gate;
　　For thy sweet love remembered such wealth brings
　　That then I scorn to change my state with kings.

30

When to the sessions[4] of sweet silent thought
I summon up remembrance of things past,
I sigh the lack of many a thing I sought,
And with old woes new wail° my dear time's waste:　　　*bewail anew*
5　Then can I drown an eye (unused to flow)
For precious friends hid in death's dateless° night,　　　*endless*
And weep afresh love's long since canceled woe,
And moan th' expense° of many a vanished sight:　　　　*loss*
Then can I grieve at grievances foregone,°　　　　　　　*former*
10　And heavily from woe to woe tell° o'er　　　　　　　　*count*
The sad account of fore-bemoanèd moan,
Which I new pay as if not paid before.

9. The first edition has "right," suggesting love's due as well as love's ritual ("rite").
1. More than that (rival) speaker who has more often said more.
2. I.e., I wish I had one man's looks, another man's friends.
3. Condition, state of mind; but in line 14 there is a pun on *state* meaning chair of state, throne.
4. Sittings of court. "Summon up" (next line) continues the metaphor.

But if the while I think on thee, dear friend,
All losses are restored and sorrows end.

33

Full many a glorious morning have I seen
Flatter the mountain tops with sovereign eye,°   *sunlight*
Kissing with golden face the meadows green,
Gilding pale streams with heavenly alchemy;
5   Anon° permit the basest° clouds to ride   *(but) soon / darkest*
With ugly rack° on his celestial face,   *cloudy mask*
And from the forlorn world his visage hide,
Stealing unseen to west with this disgrace.
Even so my sun one early morn did shine
10   With all triumphant splendor on my brow;
But out, alack,° he was but one hour mine;   *alas*
The region° cloud hath masked him from me now.   *high*
    Yet him for this my love no whit disdaineth:
    Suns of the world may stain° when heaven's sun staineth.   *darken*

35

No more be grieved at that which thou hast done:
Roses have thorns, and silver fountains mud.
Clouds and eclipses stain° both moon and sun,   *dim*
And loathsome canker° lives in sweetest bud.   *rose worm*
5   All men make faults, and even I in this,
Authorizing thy trespass with compare,°   *comparisons*
Myself corrupting, salving thy amiss,°   *palliating your offense*
Excusing thy sins more than thy sins are;
For to thy sensual fault I bring in sense°—   *i.e., reason*
10   Thy adverse party is thy advocate—
And 'gainst myself a lawful plea commence.
Such civil war is in my love and hate
    That I an accessory needs must be
    To that sweet thief which sourly robs from me.

55

Not marble nor the gilded monuments
Of princes shall outlive this powerful rhyme;
But you shall shine more bright in these contents
Than unswept stone, besmeared with sluttish time.[5]
5   When wasteful war shall statues overturn,
And broils° root out the work of masonry,   *battles*
Nor Mars his° sword nor war's quick fire shall burn   *neither Mars's*
The living record of your memory.
'Gainst death and all-oblivious enmity[6]
10   Shall you pace forth; your praise shall still find room
Even in the eyes of all posterity

---

5. I.e., than in a stone tomb or effigy that slov-
enly time wears away and covers with dust.

6. The enmity of oblivion, of being forgotten.

That wear this world out to the ending doom.°   *Judgment Day*
   So, till the judgment that yourself arise,[7]
   You live in this, and dwell in lovers' eyes.

60

Like as the waves make towards the pebbled shore,
So do our minutes hasten to their end;
Each changing place with that which goes before,
In sequent toil all forwards do contend.[8]
5   Nativity, once in the main° of light,   *broad expanse*
   Crawls to maturity, wherewith being crowned,
   Crooked° eclipses 'gainst his glory fight,   *pernicious*
   And Time that gave doth now his gift confound.
   Time doth transfix the flourish[9] set on youth,
10   And delves the parallels[1] in beauty's brow,
   Feeds on the rarities of nature's truth,
   And nothing stands but for his scythe to mow.
      And yet to times in hope° my verse shall stand,   *future times*
      Praising thy worth, despite his cruel hand.

62

Sin of self-love possesseth all mine eye,
And all my soul, and all my every part;
And for this sin there is no remedy,
It is so grounded inward in my heart.
5   Methinks no face so gracious° is as mine,   *pleasing*
   No shape so true,° no truth of such account,   *perfect*
   And for myself mine own worth do define
   As° I all other° in all worths surmount.   *as if / others*
   But when my glass° shows me myself indeed,   *mirror*
10   Beated and chapped with tanned antiquity,
   Mine own self-love quite contrary° I read;   *differently*
   Self so self-loving were iniquity.
      'Tis thee, my self,° that for° myself I praise,   *you, my other self / as*
      Painting my age with beauty of thy days.

65

Since[2] brass, nor stone, nor earth, nor boundless sea,
But sad mortality o'ersways their power,
How with this rage° shall beauty hold a plea,   *destructive power*
Whose action is no stronger than a flower?
5   O how shall summer's honey breath hold out
   Against the wrackful° siege of batt'ring days,   *destructive*
   When rocks impregnable are not so stout,
   Nor gates of steel so strong, but Time decays?
   O fearful meditation! Where, alack,

---

7. Until you rise from the dead on Judgment Day.
8. Toiling and following each other, all struggle to move forward.
9. Destroy the embellishment. To "flourish" is also to blossom.
1. Digs the parallel furrows (wrinkles).
2. I.e., since there is neither.

10 Shall Time's best jewel from Time's chest³ he hid?
 Or what strong hand can hold his swift foot back?
 Or who his spoil° of beauty can forbid?   *ravaging*
  O none, unless this miracle have might,
  That in black ink my love may still shine bright.

71

No longer mourn for me when I am dead
Than you shall hear the surly sullen bell⁴
Give warning to the world that I am fled
From this vile world, with vilest worms to dwell.
5 Nay, if you read this line, remember not
The hand that writ it; for I love you so,
That I in your sweet thoughts would be forgot,
If thinking on me then should make you woe.
O, if, I say, you look upon this verse
10 When I perhaps compounded am with clay,
Do not so much as my poor name rehearse,°   *repeat*
But let your love even with my life decay;
  Lest the wise world should look into your moan,
  And mock you with me after I am gone.

73

That time of year thou may'st in me behold
When yellow leaves, or none, or few, do hang
Upon those boughs which shake against the cold,
Bare ruined choirs,⁵ where late° the sweet birds sang.   *lately*
5 In me thou seest the twilight of such day
As after sunset fadeth in the west;
Which by and by black night doth take away,
Death's second self that seals up all in rest.
In me thou seest the glowing of such fire
10 That on the ashes of his youth doth lie,
As the deathbed whereon it must expire,
Consumed with that which it was nourished by.⁶
  This thou perceiv'st, which makes thy love more strong,
  To love that well, which thou must leave ere long.

74

But be contented; when that fell⁷ arrest
Without all bail shall carry me away,
My life hath in this line some interest,⁸
Which for memorial still° with thee shall stay.   *always*
5 When thou reviewest this, thou dost review

---

3. I.e., from being coffered up by Time.
4. The bell was tolled to announce the death of a member of the parish—one stroke for each year of his or her life.
5. The part of a church where divine service was sung.

6 Choked by the ashes of that which once nourished its flame.
7. Cruel. Hamlet says, "this fell sergeant / Death is strict in his arrest" (5.2.278–79).
8. Share, participation. "In this line": i.e., in this poetry.

The very part was° consecrate to thee.   *which was*
The earth can have but earth, which is his due;
My spirit is thine, the better part of me.
So then thou hast but lost the dregs of life,
10   The prey of worms, my body being dead,
The coward conquest of a wretch's knife,[9]
Too base of° thee to be rememberèd.   *by*
    The worth of that is that which it contains,[1]
    And that is this, and this with thee remains.

80

O, how I faint° when I of you do write,   *get discouraged*
Knowing a better spirit[2] doth use your name,
And in the praise thereof spends all his might,
To make me tongue-tied, speaking of your fame!
5   But since your worth, wide as the ocean is,
The humble as° the proudest sail doth bear,   *as well as*
My saucy bark,° inferior far to his,   *impudent boat*
On your broad main° doth willfully° appear.   *waters / boldly*
Your shallowest help will hold me up afloat
10   Whilst he upon your soundless° deep doth ride;   *bottomless*
Or, being wrecked, I am a worthless boat,
He of tall building[3] and of goodly pride.°   *magnificence*
    Then if he thrive and I be cast away,
    The worst was this: my love was my decay.

85

My tongue-tied muse in manners holds her still°   *tactfully says nothing*
While comments of° your praise, richly compiled,   *commentaries in*
Reserve thy character° with golden quill   *hoard up your features*
And precious phrase by all the muses filed.°   *polished*
5   I think good thoughts whilst other° write good words,   *others*
And like unlettered clerk still cry "Amen"
To every hymn[4] that able spirit affords°   *offers*
In polished form of well-refinèd pen.
Hearing you praised I say "'Tis so, 'tis true,"
10   And to the most° of praise add something more;   *highest*
But that is in my thought,° whose love to you,   *i.e., is unspoken*
Though words come hindmost, holds his rank before.°   *before all others*
    Then others for the breath of words respect,°   *regard*
    Me for my dumb thoughts, speaking in effect.°   *in reality*

87

Farewell: thou art too dear[5] for my possessing,
And like enough thou know'st thy estimate.°   *value*

---

9. Death's weapon (like Time's scythe).
1. I.e., the only value of the body is that it contains the spirit.
2. A rival poet. See the headnote, p. 722.
3. Tall, strong build.

4. "Like . . . hymn": like an illiterate parish clerk reflexively approve ("cry 'Amen'" after) every poem ("hymn") of praise.
5. (1) Expensive, (2) beloved.

The charter° of thy worth gives thee releasing;[6]   *deed; contract for property*
My bonds in thee are all determinate.°   *expired*
5 For how do I hold thee but by thy granting,
  And for that riches where is my deserving?
  The cause of this fair gift in me is wanting,°   *absent*
  And so my patent° back again is swerving.[7]   *title*
  Thy self thou gav'st, thy own worth then not knowing,
10 Or me, to whom thou gav'st it, else mistaking;°   *i.e., overestimating*
  So thy great gift, upon misprision growing,°   *based on error*
  Comes home again, on better judgment making.[8]
    Thus have I had thee as a dream doth flatter:
    In sleep a king, but waking no such matter.

93

So shall I live supposing thou art true,
Like a deceivèd husband; so love's face°   *appearance*
May still seem love to me, though altered new—
Thy looks with me, thy heart in other place.
5 For there can live no hatred in thine eye;
  Therefore in that I cannot know thy change.
  In many's looks the false heart's history
  Is writ in moods[9] and frowns and wrinkles strange:°   *unaccustomed*
  But heaven in thy creation did decree
10 That in thy face sweet love should ever dwell;
  Whate'er thy thoughts or thy heart's workings be,
  Thy looks should nothing thence but sweetness tell.
    How like Eve's apple doth thy beauty grow°   *become*
    If thy sweet virtue answer not thy show![1]

94

They that have power to hurt and will do none,
That do not do the thing they most do show,[2]
Who, moving others, are themselves as stone,
Unmovèd, cold, and to temptation slow;
5 They rightly do inherit heaven's graces
  And husband nature's riches from expense;[3]
  They are the lords and owners of their faces,
  Others but stewards of their excellence.
  The summer's flower is to the summer sweet,
10 Though to itself it only live and die,[4]
  But if that flower with base infection meet,
  The basest weed outbraves° his dignity: *surpasses*
    For sweetest things turn sourest by their deeds;
    Lilies that fester smell far worse than weeds.

---

6. Releases you (from love's bonds).
7. I.e., reverting to you.
8. I.e., when you realize your error.
9. Moody expressions.
1. Does not correspond to your appearance.

2. Seem to do, or seem capable of doing.
3. I.e., they do not squander nature's gifts.
4. Even if it lives and dies in apparent isolation (unpollinated).

97

How like a winter hath my absence been
From thee, the pleasure of the fleeting year!
What freezings have I felt, what dark days seen!
What old December's bareness everywhere!
5 And yet this time removed[5] was summer's time,
The teeming autumn, big with rich increase,
Bearing the wanton burthen of the prime,[6]
Like widowed wombs after their lords' decease.
Yet this abundant issue° seemed to me   *outgrowth*
10 But hope of orphans and unfathered fruit;
For summer and his pleasures wait° on thee,   *attend*
And, thou away, the very birds are mute;
    Or, if they sing, 'tis with so dull a cheer°   *such a dismal mood*
    That leaves look pale, dreading the winter's near.

98

From you have I been absent in the spring,
When proud-pied[7] April, dressed in all his trim,
Hath put a spirit of youth in everything,
5 That heavy Saturn° laughed and leapt with him.   *god of melancholy*
Yet nor° the lays° of birds, nor the sweet smell   *neither / songs*
Of different flowers in odor and in hue
Could make me any summer's story tell,
Or from their proud lap pluck them where they grew;
Nor did I wonder at° the lily's white,   *admire*
10 Nor praise the deep vermilion in the rose;
They were but sweet, but figures° of delight,   *merely emblems*
Drawn after you, you pattern of all those.
    Yet seemed it winter still, and, you away,
    As with your shadow I with these did play.

105

Let not my love be called idolatry,
Nor my belovèd as an idol show,
Since all alike my songs and praises be
To one, of one, still° such, and ever so.   *continually*
5 Kind is my love today, tomorrow kind,
Still constant in a wondrous excellence.
Therefore my verse, to constancy confined,
One thing expressing, leaves out difference.°   *variety*
"Fair, kind, and true" is all my argument,°   *theme*
10 "Fair, kind, and true" varying to other words,
And in this change is my invention spent,[8]
Three themes in one, which wonderous scope affords.

5. I.e., when I was absent.
6. Spring, which has engendered the lavish crop ("wanton burthen") that autumn is now left to bear.

7. Magnificent in many colors.
8. And in varying the words alone my inventiveness is expended.

Fair, kind, and true have often lived alone,°   *separately*
Which three till now never kept seat° in one.   *dwelt permanently*

106

When in the chronicle of wasted° time   *past*
I see descriptions of the fairest wights,°   *persons*
And beauty making beautiful old rhyme
In praise of ladies dead and lovely knights,
5   Then, in the blazon[9] of sweet beauty's best,
Of hand, of foot, of lip, of eye, of brow,
I see their antique pen would have expressed
Even such a beauty as you master now.
So all their praises are but prophecies
10   Of this our time, all you prefiguring;
And, for they looked but with divining eyes,[1]
They had not skill enough your worth to sing:
    For we, which now behold these present days,
    Have eyes to wonder, but lack tongues to praise.

107

Not mine own fears, nor the prophetic soul
Of the wide world dreaming on things to come,[2]
Can yet the lease of my true love control,
Supposed as forfeit to a confined doom.[3]
5   The mortal moon hath her eclipse endured,
And the sad augurs mock their own presage;[4]
Incertainties now crown themselves assured,
And peace[5] proclaims olives of endless age.
Now with the drops of this most balmy time
10   My love looks fresh, and death to me subscribes,°   *submits*
Since, spite of him, I'll live in this poor rhyme,
While he insults o'er dull and speechless tribes:
    And thou in this shalt find thy monument,
    When tyrants' crests and tombs of brass are spent.°   *wasted away*

110

Alas, 'tis true I have gone here and there
And made myself a motley° to the view,   *fool, jester*
Gored[6] mine own thoughts, sold cheap what is most dear,
Made old offenses of affections° new.   *passions*

9. Catalog of excellencies.
1. Because ("for") they were able only ("but") to foresee prophetically.
2. This sonnet refers to contemporary events and the prophecies, common in Elizabethan almanacs, of disaster.
3. I.e., can yet put an end to my love, which I thought doomed to early forfeiture.
4. The "mortal moon" is probably Queen Elizabeth; her "eclipse" could be either her death (March 1603) or, perhaps, her "climacteric" year, her sixty-third (thought meaningful because the product of two "significant" numbers, 7 and 9), which ended in September 1596. The sober astrologers ("sad augurs") now ridicule their own predictions ("presage") of catastrophe, because they turned out to be false.
5. Perhaps referring to the peace treaty signed with Spain by Elizabeth's successor, James I, or, if the sonnet refers to the time of Elizabeth's climacteric, to an earlier treaty between England and France.
6. Wounded, pierced.

5 Most true it is that I have looked on truth°   *fidelity*
  Askance and strangely;[7] but, by all above,
  These blenches° gave my heart another youth,   *turnings aside*
  And worse essays[8] proved thee my best of love.
  Now all is done, have what shall have no end:
10 Mine appetite I never more will grind°   *whet*
  On newer proof,° to try° an older friend,   *experiences / test*
  A god in love, to whom I am confined.
    Then give me welcome, next my heaven the best,[9]
    Even to thy pure and most most loving breast.

116

  Let me not to the marriage of true minds
  Admit impediments;[1] love is not love
  Which alters when it alteration finds,
  Or bends with the remover to remove:
5 O, no, it is an ever-fixèd mark,[2]
  That looks on tempests and is never shaken;
  It is the star to every wand'ring bark,
  Whose worth's unknown, although his height[3] be taken.
  Love's not Time's fool,° though rosy lips and cheeks   *plaything*
10 Within his[4] bending sickle's compass come;
  Love alters not with his brief hours and weeks,
  But bears it out even to the edge of doom.°   *brink of Judgment Day*
    If this be error and upon me proved,
    I never writ, nor no man ever loved.

126[5]

  O thou, my lovely boy, who in thy power
  Dost hold Time's fickle glass,[6] his sickle, hour;°   *hourglass*
  Who hast by waning grown and therein show'st°   *i.e., in contrast*
  Thy lovers withering as thy sweet self grow'st;
5 If Nature (sovereign mistress over wrack°)   *destruction*
  As thou goest onwards still will pluck thee back,
  She keeps thee to this purpose, that her skill
  May Time disgrace and wretched minutes kill.
  Yet fear her, O thou minion° of her pleasure,   *darling*
10 She may detain, but not still° keep, her treasure!   *always*
    Her audit° (though delayed) answered must be,   *accounting*
    And her quietus° is to render° thee.   *settlement / surrender*

---

7. Obliquely or asquint, and coldly (like a stranger).

8. Trials of worse relationships.

9. I.e., the next best thing to the Christian heaven.

1. From the Anglican marriage service: "If either of you do know any impediment why ye may not be lawfully joined together . . ."

2. Seamark, such as a lighthouse or a beacon.

3. The star's value is incalculable, although its altitude may be known and used for navigation.

4. Time's (as also in line 11).

5. This poem—not a sonnet but six couplets—is an envoy (a closing summary or commentary) marking the end of the sequence addressed to a beloved young man (see the headnote) and formally signaling a change in tone and subject matter in the remaining sonnets.

6. Mirror, fickle because as the subject ages, the mirror reflects a changed image.

127

In the old age black was not counted fair,[7]
Or, if it were, it bore not beauty's name;
But now is black beauty's successive heir,[8]
And beauty slandered with a bastard shame:°   *declared illegitimate*
5   For since each hand hath put on nature's power,
Fairing the foul with art's false borrowed face,°   *i.e., with cosmetics*
Sweet beauty hath no name, no holy bower,[9]
But is profaned, if not lives in disgrace.
Therefore my mistress' brows are raven black,
10   Her eyes so suited,° and they mourners seem   *i.e., also black*
At° such who, not born fair, no beauty lack,[1]   *for*
Sland'ring creation with a false esteem:
    Yet so they mourn, becoming of° their woe,   *gracing*
    That every tongue says beauty should look so.

128

How oft when thou, my music, music play'st
Upon that blessèd wood[2] whose motion sounds
With thy sweet fingers when thou gently sway'st°   *govern*
The wiry concord that mine ear confounds,[3]
5   Do I envỳ those jacks[4] that nimble leap
To kiss the tender inward of thy hand,
Whilst my poor lips, which should that harvest reap,
At the wood's boldness by thee blushing stand.
To be so tickled they would change their state[5]
10   And situation[6] with those dancing chips,
O'er whom thy fingers walk with gentle gait,
Making dead wood more blessed than living lips.
    Since saucy jacks[7] so happy are in this,
    Give them thy fingers, me thy lips to kiss.

129

Th' expense of spirit in a waste of shame
Is lust in action;[8] and till action, lust
Is perjured, murd'rous, bloody, full of blame,
Savage, extreme, rude,° cruel, not to trust;   *brutal*
5   Enjoyed no sooner but despisèd straight;°   *immediately*
Past reason hunted, and no sooner had,
Past reason hated as a swallowed bait
On purpose laid to make the taker mad:

---

7. Beautiful, equated with blond hair and coloring. "Old": former. "Black": dark hair and coloring, equated with ugliness.
8. Heir in line of succession.
9. Shrine. The next line suggests that natural (unpainted) beauty is now discredited.
1. I.e., nevertheless possess the appearance of beauty.
2. Keys of the spinet or virginal.
3. The harmony from the strings that overcomes my ear with delight.

4. The keys (actually, "jacks" are the plectra that pluck the strings when activated by the keys).
5. Their place in the order of things.
6. Physical location.
7. With a quibble on the sense "impertinent fellows."
8. The word order here is inverted and slightly obscures the meaning. Lust, when put into action, expends "spirit" (life, vitality; also semen) in a "waste" (desert; also with a pun on *waist*) of shame.

Mad in pursuit, and in possession so;
10 Had, having, and in quest to have, extreme;
A bliss in proof,[9] and proved, a very° woe;   *true*
Before, a joy proposed; behind, a dream.
    All this the world well knows; yet none knows well
    To shun the heaven that leads men to this hell.

130

My mistress' eyes are nothing like the sun;[1]
Coral is far more red than her lips' red;
If snow be white, why then her breasts are dun;
If hairs be wires, black wires grow on her head.
5 I have seen roses damasked,° red and white,   *dappled*
But no such roses see I in her cheeks;
And in some perfumes is there more delight
Than in the breath that from my mistress reeks.[2]
I love to hear her speak, yet well I know
10 That music hath a far more pleasing sound;
I grant I never saw a goddess go;°   *walk*
My mistress, when she walks, treads on the ground.
    And yet, by heaven, I think my love as rare°   *admirable; extraordinary*
    As any she belied° with false compare.   *misrepresented*

135

Whoever hath her wish, thou hast thy *Will*,[3]
And *Will* to boot, and *Will* in overplus;
More than enough am I that vex thee still,°   *always*
To thy sweet will making addition thus.
5 Wilt thou, whose will is large and spacious,
Not once vouchsafe° to hide my will in thine?   *consent*
Shall will in others seem right gracious,
And in° my will no fair acceptance shine?   *in the case of*
The sea, all water, yet receives rain still,
10 And in abundance addeth to his store,°   *plenty*
So thou being rich in *Will* add to thy *Will*
One will of mine to make thy large *Will* more.
    Let no unkind, no fair beseechers kill;[4]
    Think all but one, and me in that one *Will*.

138

When my love swears that she is made of truth,[5]
I do believe her, though I know she lies,[6]

---

9. A bliss during the experience.
1. An anti-Petrarchan sonnet. All of the details commonly attributed by other Elizabethan sonneteers to their ladies (e.g., in Spenser's *Amoretti* 64; see p. 488) are here denied to the poet's mistress.
2. Not with our pejorative sense, but simply "emanates."
3. (1) Wishes, (2) carnal desire, (3) the male and female sexual organs, (4) one or more lovers—evidently including Shakespeare—named Will. This is one of several sonnets punning on the word.
4. I.e., do not kill with unkindness any of your wooers.
5. (1) Is utterly honest, (2) is faithful.
6. With the obvious sexual pun (as also in lines 13–14).

That she might think me some untutored youth,
Unlearnèd in the world's false subtleties.
5 Thus vainly thinking that she thinks me young,
Although she knows my days are past the best,[7]
Simply° I credit her false-speaking tongue: *like a simpleton*
On both sides thus is simple truth suppressed.
But wherefore says she not she is unjust?°   *unfaithful*
10 And wherefore say not I that I am old?
Oh, love's best habit° is in seeming trust,   *clothing, guise*
And age in love loves not to have years told.°   *counted*
    Therefore I lie with her and she with me,
    And in our faults by lies we flattered be.

144

Two loves I have of comfort and despair,[8]
Which like two spirits do suggest me still:°   *tempt me constantly*
The better angel is a man right fair,
The worser spirit a woman colored ill.°   *dark*
5 To win me soon to hell, my female evil
Tempteth my better angel from my side,
And would corrupt my saint to be a devil,
Wooing his purity with her foul pride.[9]
And whether that my angel be turned fiend
10 Suspect I may, yet not directly tell;
But being both from° me, both to each° friend,   *away from / each other*
I guess one angel in another's hell.
    Yet this shall I ne'er know, but live in doubt,
    Till my bad angel fire my good one out.[1]

146

Poor soul, the center of my sinful earth,
Lord of[2] these rebel powers that thee array,[3]
Why dost thou pine within and suffer dearth,
Painting thy outward walls so costly gay?
5 Why so large cost, having so short a lease,
Dost thou upon thy fading mansion spend?
Shall worms, inheritors of this excess,
Eat up thy charge?[4] Is this thy body's end?°   *destiny; purpose*
Then, soul, live thou upon thy servant's loss,
10 And let that pine to aggravate thy store;[5]
Buy terms° divine in selling hours of dross;°   *long periods / rubbish*
Within be fed, without be rich no more.

---

7. Shakespeare was thirty-five or younger when he wrote this sonnet (it first appeared in *The Passionate Pilgrim*, 1599).
8. I have two beloveds, one bringing me comfort and the other despair.
9. (1) Vanity, (2) sexuality.
1. I.e., until she infects him with venereal disease.
2. "Lord of" is an emendation. The 1609 edition

repeats the last three words of line 1. Other suggestions are "Thrall to," "Starved by," "Pressed by," and leaving the repetition but dropping "that thee" in line 2.
3. The rebellious body that clothes you.
4. (1) Your expense, (2) the thing you were responsible for (i.e., the body).
5. Let "that" (i.e., the body) deteriorate to increase ("aggravate") the soul's riches ("thy store").

So shalt thou feed on death, that feeds on men,
And death once dead, there's no more dying then.

147

My love is as a fever, longing still°   *continually*
For that which longer nurseth[6] the disease,
Feeding on that which doth preserve the ill,°   *maintain the illness*
Th' uncertain sickly appetite[7] to please.
5 My reason, the physician to my love,
Angry that his prescriptions are not kept,
Hath left me, and I desperate now approve
Desire is death, which physic did except.[8]
Past cure I am, now reason is past care,[9]
10 And frantic mad with evermore unrest;
My thoughts and my discourse as madmen's are,
At random from the truth, vainly expressed:[1]
    For I have sworn thee fair, and thought thee bright,
    Who art as black as hell, as dark as night.

152

In loving thee thou know'st I am forsworn,[2]
But thou art twice forsworn to me love swearing:
In act thy bed-vow° broke, and new faith torn   *to husband (or lover)*
In vowing new hate after new love bearing.[3]
5 But why of two oaths' breach do I accuse thee
When I break twenty? I am perjured most,
For all my vows are oaths but to misuse° thee,   *deceive; misrepresent*
And all my honest faith in thee is lost.
For I have sworn deep oaths of thy deep kindness,
10 Oaths of thy love, thy truth, thy constancy,
And to enlighten thee gave eyes to blindness,[4]
Or made them swear against the thing they see.
    For I have sworn thee fair—more perjured eye°   *(punning on "I")*
    To swear against the truth so foul a lie.

1609

---

6. (1) Nourishes, (2) takes care of.
7. (1) Desire for food, (2) lust.
8. I.e., I learn by experience that desire, which rejected reason's medicine, is death.
9. I.e., medical care (of me). The line is a version of the proverb "past cure, past care."
1. Wide of the mark and senselessly uttered.

2. I.e., am breaking loving vows to another.
3. The object of the "new faith" followed by "new hate" could be either the speaker's young friend or the speaker himself.
4. And to make you fair (or give you insight), I looked blindly on your failings (or pretended to see what I couldn't).

Twelfth Night Women did not perform on the English public stage during Shakespeare's lifetime: all the great women's roles in Elizabethan and Jacobean plays, from Juliet and Lady Macbeth to the Duchess of Malfi, were written to be performed by trained adolescent boys. These boy actors were evidently extraordinarily skillful, and the audiences were sufficiently immersed in the conventions both of theater and of social life in general to accept gesture, makeup, and above all dress as a convincing representation of femininity. *Twelfth Night, or What You Will*, written for Shakespeare's all-male company, plays brilliantly with these conventions. The comedy depends on an actor's ability to transform himself, through costume, voice, and gesture, into a young noblewoman, Viola, who transforms herself, through costume, voice, and gesture, into a young serving man, Cesario. The play's delicious complications follow from the emotional tangles these transformations engender, unsettling fixed categories of sexual identity and social class and allowing characters to explore emotional territory that a culture officially hostile to same-sex desire and cross-class marriage would ordinarily have ruled out of bounds. In *Twelfth Night* conventional expectations repeatedly give way to a different mode of perceiving the world.

Shakespeare wrote *Twelfth Night* around 1601. He had already written such comedies as *A Midsummer Night's Dream*, *Much Ado About Nothing*, and *As You Like It*, with their playful, subtly ironic investigations of the ways in which heterosexual couples are produced out of the crosscurrents of male and female friendships; as interesting, perhaps, he had probably just recently completed *Hamlet*, with its unprecedented exploration of mourning, betrayal, antic humor, and tragic isolation. *Twelfth Night* would prove to be, in the view of many critics, both the most nearly perfect and in some sense the last of the great festive comedies. Shakespeare returned to comedy later in his career but always with more insistent overtones of bitterness, loss, and grief. There are dark notes in *Twelfth Night* as well—the countess Olivia is in mourning for her brother, Viola thinks that her brother too is dead, Antonio believes that he has been betrayed by the man he loves, Duke Orsino threatens to kill Cesario—but these notes are swept up in a giddy, carnivalesque dance of illusion, disguise, folly, and clowning.

The complex tonal shifts of Shakespeare's comedy are conveyed in part by the pervasive music and in part by the constant oscillation between blank verse and prose. Generally, the characters in the main, romantic plot speak in the more elevated, aristocratic, and dignified register of verse, while the comic subplot proceeds in prose. Yet these formal distinctions between serious and comic, high and low, are frequently undermined, as when the wronged steward Malvolio in his final speech addresses Olivia in dignified verse, or when the mercurial Viola shifts with the greatest ease between verse and prose.

The play's subtitle, *What You Will*, underscores the celebratory spirit associated with Twelfth Night, the Feast of the Epiphany (January 6), that in Elizabethan England marked the culminating night of the traditional Christmas revels. In the time-honored festivities associated with the midwinter season, a rigidly hierarchical social order that ordinarily demanded deference, sobriety, and strict obedience to authority temporarily gave way to raucous rituals of inversion: young boys were crowned for a day as bishops and carried through the streets in mock religious processions; abstemiousness was toppled by bouts of heavy drinking and feasting; and the spirit of parody, folly, and misrule reigned briefly in places normally reserved for stern-faced moralists and sober judges. The fact that these festivities were associated with Christian holidays—the Epiphany marked the visit of the Three Kings to Bethlehem to worship the Christ child—did not altogether obscure the continuities with pagan winter rituals such as the Roman Saturnalia, with its comparably explosive release from everyday discipline into a disorderly realm of belly laughter and belly cheer. Puritans emphasized these continuities in launching a fierce attack on the Elizabethan festive calendar and its whole ethos, just as they attacked the theater for what they saw as its links with paganism, idleness, and sexual license. Elizabethan and Jacobean authorities in the church and the state had their own concerns about idleness and subversion, but they generally protected and patronized both festive ritual and theater on the ground that these provided a valuable release from tensions that might otherwise prove dangerous. Sobriety, piety, and discipline were no doubt admirable virtues, but most human beings were not saints. "Dost thou think because thou art virtuous," the drunken Sir Toby asks the censorious Malvolio, "there shall be no more cakes and ale?" (2.3.106–07).

Fittingly, the earliest firm record of a performance of *Twelfth Night*, as noted in the diary of John Manningham, was "at our feast" in the Middle Temple (one of London's law schools) in February 1602. Manningham cannily noted the comedy's resemblance to Shakespeare's earlier play on twins, *The Comedy of Errors*, as well as to the Roman playwright Plautus's *Menaechmi* and to an early-sixteenth-century Italian comedy *Gl'Ingannati* (The Deceived). Shakespeare also drew on an English story, Barnabe Riche's tale "Apollonius and Silla" in *Riche His Farewell to the Military Profession* (1581), which was in turn based on French and Italian sources. There is, however, little precedent, in Riche or in any of the other known sources, for the aspect of *Twelfth Night* that Manningham found particularly memorable and that has continued to delight audiences: the gulling of Malvolio.

Malvolio (in Italian, "ill will") is explicitly linked to those among Shakespeare's contemporaries most hostile to the theater and to such holidays as Twelfth Night: "sometimes," says the Lady Olivia's gentlewoman Maria, "he is a kind of puritan" (2.3.129). Shakespeare does not hide the cruelty of the treatment to which Malvolio is subjected— "He hath been most notoriously abused" (5.1.374), says Olivia—nor does he shrink from showing the audience other disagreeable qualities in Malvolio's tormentors, Olivia's kinsman Sir Toby Belch and his companions. But while the close of the comedy seems to embrace these failings in a tolerant, amused aristocratic recognition of human folly, it can find no place for Malvolio's blend of puritanical moralizing and social climbing.

Robert Armin (from the title page of his comedy, *The History of the Two Maids of More-Clacke* [1609]) was the leading comic actor in Shakespeare's company after 1600. He played both Feste in *Twelfth Night* and the Fool in *King Lear*.

Malvolio is scapegoated for indulging in a fantasy that colors several of the key relationships in *Twelfth Night*: the fantasy of winning the favor, and ultimately the hand, of one of the noble and wealthy aristocrats who reign over the social world of the play. The beautiful heiress Olivia, mistress of a great house, is a glittering prize that lures not only Malvolio but also the foolish Sir Andrew and the elegant, imperious Duke Orsino. In falling in love with the duke's graceful messenger (and, as she thinks she has done, in marrying him), Olivia seems to have made precisely the kind of match that had fueled Malvolio's social-climbing imagination. As it turns out, the match is not between unequals: "Be not amazed," the duke tells her when she realizes that she has married someone she scarcely knows: "Right noble is his blood" (5.1.262). The social order then has not been overturned: as in a carnival, when the disguises are removed, the revelers resume their "proper," socially and sexually approved positions.

Yet there is something irreducibly odd about the marriages with which *Twelfth Night* ends. Sir Toby has married the lady's maid Maria as a reward for devising the plot against Malvolio. Olivia has entered into a "contract of eternal bond of love" (5.1.153) with someone whose actual identity is revealed to her only after the marriage is sealed. The strangeness of the bond between virtual strangers is matched by the strangeness of Orsino's instantaneous decision to marry Cesario—as soon as "he" can become Viola by changing into women's clothes. Shakespeare conspicuously chooses not to stage this return to conventionality.

Part of the quirky delight of the play's conclusion depends on the resilient hopefulness of its central character, Viola, a hopefulness that is linked to her improvisatory boldness, eloquent tongue, and keen wit. These qualities link her to the fool Feste, who does not have a major part in the comedy's plot but who occupies a place at its imaginative center. Viola seems to acknowledge this place in paying handsome tribute to Feste's intelligence: "This fellow is wise enough to play the fool, / And to do that well craves a kind of wit" (3.1.59–60). His wit often takes the form of a perverse literalism that slyly calls attention to the play's repeated confounding of such simple binaries as male and female, outside and inside, role and reality. Feste is irresponsible, vulnerable, and dependent, but he also understands, as he teasingly shows Olivia, that it is foolish to bewail forever a loss that cannot be recovered. And he understands that it is important to take such pleasures as life offers and not to wait: "In delay there lies no plenty," he sings, "Then come kiss me, sweet and twenty. / Youth's a stuff will not endure" (2.3.48–50). There is in this wonderful song, as in all of his jests, a current of sadness. Feste knows, as the refrain of the last of his songs puts it, that "the rain it raineth every day" (5.1.387). His counsel is for "present mirth" and "present laughter" (2.3.46). This is, of course, the advice of a fool. But do the Malvolios of the world have anything wiser to suggest?

Twelfth Night, or What You Will

THE PERSONS OF THE PLAY

ORSINO, duke of Illyria
VALENTINE ⎫
CURIO ⎭ attending on Orsino
FIRST OFFICER
SECOND OFFICER
VIOLA, a lady, later disguised as
 Cesario
A CAPTAIN
SEBASTIAN, Viola's twin brother
ANTONIO, another sea-captain
OLIVIA, a countess

MARIA, Olivia's waiting-gentlewoman
SIR TOBY Belch, Olivia's kinsman
SIR ANDREW Aguecheek, companion of
 Sir Toby
MALVOLIO, Olivia's steward
FABIAN, a member of Olivia's
 household
FESTE the clown, Olivia's jester
A PRIEST
A SERVANT of Olivia
Musicians, sailors, lords, attendants

1.1

Enter ORSINO, *Duke of Illyria,* CURIO, *and other lords, with musicians playing.*

ORSINO   If music be the food of love, play on.
 Give me excess of it, that, surfeiting,

1.1 Location: Illyria, Greek and Roman name for the eastern Adriatic coast; probably not suggesting a real country to Shakespeare's audience.

The appetite may sicken and so die.
That strain again! It had a dying fall.°   *cadence*
5 O, it came o'er my ear like the sweet sound
That breathes upon a bank of violets,
Stealing and giving odor. Enough; no more.
'Tis not so sweet now as it was before.
O spirit of love, how quick and fresh° art thou,   *lively and eager*
10 That, notwithstanding thy capacity,
Receiveth as the sea,° naught enters there,   *receives without limit*
Of what validity° and pitch° soe'er,   *value / height; excellence*
But falls into abatement° and low price   *lesser value*
Even in a minute. So full of shapes is fancy°   *love; desire*
15 That it alone is high fantastical.°   *uniquely imaginative*
CURIO   Will you go hunt, my lord?
ORSINO   What, Curio?
CURIO   The hart.°   *male deer*
ORSINO   Why, so I do, the noblest that I have.[1]
O, when mine eyes did see Olivia first,
Methought she purged the air of pestilence.[2]
20 That instant was I turned into a hart,
And my desires, like fell° and cruel hounds,   *savage*
E'er since pursue me.[3]

    Enter VALENTINE.

             How now, what news from her?
VALENTINE   So please my lord, I might° not be admitted,   *could*
But from her handmaid do return this answer:
25 The element itself, till seven years' heat,[4]
Shall not behold her face at ample° view,   *full*
But like a cloistress° she will veilèd walk,   *nun*
And water once a day her chamber round
With eye-offending brine°—all this to season   *stinging tears*
30 A brother's dead love,[5] which she would keep fresh
And lasting in her sad remembrance.
ORSINO   O, she that hath a heart of that fine° frame   *exquisitely made*
To pay this debt of love but to a brother,
How will she love when the rich golden shaft[6]
35 Hath killed the flock of all affections else°   *other emotions*
That live in her; when liver, brain, and heart,[7]
These sovereign thrones, are all supplied, and filled
Her sweet perfections[8] with one self° king!   *one and the same*
Away before me to sweet beds of flowers!
40 Love thoughts lie rich when canopied with bowers.

                    Exeunt.

---

1. Orsino plays on "hart/heart."
2. Plague and other illnesses were thought to be caused by bad air.
3. Alluding to the classical myth of Actaeon, who was turned into a stag and hunted by his own hounds for having seen the goddess Diana naked.
4. The sky itself for seven hot summers.

5. I.e., all this to preserve (by the salt of the tears) the love of a dead brother.
6. Of Cupid's golden-tipped arrow, which caused desire.
7. In Elizabethan psychology, the seats of passion, intellect, and feeling, respectively.
8. And her sweet perfections have been filled.

1.2

Enter VIOLA, A CAPTAIN, *and sailors.*

VIOLA[1] What country, friends, is this?

CAPTAIN   This is Illyria, lady.

VIOLA And what should I do in Illyria?
My brother he is in Elysium.[2]
Perchance° he is not drowned. What think you, sailors?   *perhaps*

5 CAPTAIN It is perchance° that you yourself were saved.   *by chance*

VIOLA O my poor brother! And so perchance may he be.

CAPTAIN True, madam. And to comfort you with chance,[3]
Assure yourself, after our ship did split,
When you and those poor number saved with you
10 Hung on our driving boat,[4] I saw your brother,
Most provident in peril, bind himself—
Courage and hope both teaching him the practice—
To a strong mast that lived° upon the sea,   *remained afloat*
Where, like Arion[5] on the dolphin's back,
15 I saw him hold acquaintance with the waves
So long as I could see.

VIOLA [*giving him money*] For saying so, there's gold.
Mine own escape unfoldeth to° my hope,   *encourages*
Whereto thy speech serves for authority,°   *support*
The like of him.[6] Know'st thou this country?

20 CAPTAIN Ay, madam, well, for I was bred and born
Not three hours' travel from this very place.

VIOLA Who governs here?

CAPTAIN A noble duke, in nature as in name.

VIOLA What is his name?

25 CAPTAIN Orsino.

VIOLA Orsino. I have heard my father name him.
He was a bachelor then.

CAPTAIN And so is now, or was so very late;°   *lately*
For but a month ago I went from hence,
30 And then 'twas fresh in murmur°—as, you know,   *newly rumored*
What great ones do the less will prattle of—
That he did seek the love of fair Olivia.

VIOLA What's she?

CAPTAIN A virtuous maid, the daughter of a count
35 That died some twelvemonth since, then leaving her
In the protection of his son, her brother,
Who shortly also died, for whose dear love,
They say, she hath abjured° the sight   *renounced*
And company of men.

1.2 Location: The coast of Illyria.
1. Viola is not named in the dialogue until
5.1.239.
2. The heaven of classical mythology.
3. With what may have happened.
4. The ship's boat. "Driving": being driven by the

wind.
5. A legendary Greek musician who, to save
himself from being murdered on a voyage,
jumped overboard and was carried to land by a
dolphin.
6. I.e., that he too has survived.

VIOLA   O, that I served that lady,
40   And might not be delivered° to the world   *revealed*
      Till I had made mine own occasion mellow,°   *ripe (to be revealed)*
      What my estate° is.   *social rank*
CAPTAIN   That were hard to compass,°   *achieve*
      Because she will admit no kind of suit,°   *petition*
      No, not the Duke's.
45 VIOLA   There is a fair behavior[7] in thee, captain,
      And though that nature with a beauteous wall
      Doth oft close in pollution, yet of thee
      I will believe thou hast a mind that suits
      With this thy fair and outward character.[8]
50   I prithee°—and I'll pay thee bounteously—   *pray thee*
      Conceal me what I am, and be my aid
      For such disguise as haply shall become
      The form° of my intent.[9] I'll serve this duke.   *shape*
      Thou shalt present me as an eunuch[1] to him.
55   It may be worth thy pains, for I can sing
      And speak to him in many sorts of music
      That will allow° me very worth his service.   *prove*
      What else may hap, to time I will commit.
      Only shape thou thy silence to my wit.°   *imagination; plan*
60 CAPTAIN   Be you his eunuch, and your mute[2] I'll be.
      When my tongue blabs, then let mine eyes not see.
    VIOLA   I thank thee. Lead me on.   *Exeunt.*

1.3

Enter SIR TOBY *[Belch] and* MARIA.
SIR TOBY   What a plague means my niece to take the death
      of her brother thus? I am sure care's an enemy to life.
MARIA   By my troth,° Sir Toby, you must come in earlier o'   *faith*
      nights. Your cousin,[1] my lady, takes great exceptions to
5   your ill hours.
SIR TOBY   Why, let her except before excepted![2]
MARIA   Ay, but you must confine yourself within the mod-
      est° limits of order.   *moderate*
SIR TOBY   Confine? I'll confine myself no finer[3] than I am.
10   These clothes are good enough to drink in, and so be
      these boots too. An° they be not, let them hang them-   *if*
      selves in their own straps!

---

7. Outward appearance; conduct.
8. Appearance (suggesting moral qualities).
9. That perhaps may be fitting to my purpose.
1. Castrati (hence, "eunuchs") were prized as male sopranos; the disguise would have explained Viola's feminine voice. Viola (or perhaps Shakespeare) seems to have changed plans: she presents herself instead as a young page.
2. In Turkish harems, eunuchs served as guards and were assisted by "mutes" (usually servants

whose tongues had been cut out).
1.3 Location: The Countess Olivia's house.
1. Term used generally of kinsfolk.
2. Playing on the legal jargon *exceptis excipiendis*, "with the previous stated exceptions." Sir Toby refuses to take Olivia's displeasure seriously.
3. Suggesting both "a refined manner of dress" and "narrowly" (referring to his girth).

MARIA That quaffing and drinking will undo you. I heard
my lady talk of it yesterday, and of a foolish knight that
15 you brought in one night here to be her wooer.

SIR TOBY Who, Sir Andrew Aguecheek?

MARIA Ay, he.

SIR TOBY He's as tall a man as any's[4] in Illyria.

MARIA What's that to th' purpose?

20 SIR TOBY Why, he has three thousand ducats a year!

MARIA Ay, but he'll have but a year in all these ducats.[5]
He's a very° fool and a prodigal.   *an absolute*

SIR TOBY Fie that you'll say so! He plays o' th' viol-de-
gamboys,[6] and speaks three or four languages word for
25 word without book,° and hath all the good gifts of nature.   *from memory*

MARIA He hath indeed, almost natural,[7] for besides that
he's a fool, he's a great quarreler, and but that he hath
the gift of a coward to allay the gust° he hath in quarrel-   *gusto*
ing, 'tis thought among the prudent he would quickly
30 have the gift of a grave.

SIR TOBY By this hand, they are scoundrels and substrac-
tors[8] that say so of him. Who are they?

MARIA They that add, moreover, he's drunk nightly in
your company.

35 SIR TOBY With drinking healths to my niece. I'll drink to
her as long as there is a passage in my throat and drink
in Illyria. He's a coward and a coistrel° that will not drink   *horse groom; lout*
to my niece till his brains turn o' th' toe like a parish top.[9]
What, wench! *Castiliano vulgo*,[1] for here comes Sir Andrew
40 Agueface.

          Enter SIR ANDREW [Aguecheek].

SIR ANDREW Sir Toby Belch! How now, Sir Toby Belch?

SIR TOBY Sweet Sir Andrew!

SIR ANDREW [*to* MARIA] Bless you, fair shrew.[2]

MARIA And you too, sir.

45 SIR TOBY Accost, Sir Andrew, accost![3]

SIR ANDREW What's that?

SIR TOBY My niece's chambermaid.[4]

SIR ANDREW Good Mistress Accost, I desire better
acquaintance.

50 MARIA My name is Mary, sir.

SIR ANDREW Good Mistress Mary Accost—

---

4. Any (man who) is. "Tall": brave; worthy. (Maria
takes it in the modern sense of height.)
5. I.e., he'll spend his fortune in a year.
6. A facetious corruption of "viola da gamba," a
bass viol held between the knees.
7. Idiots and fools were called "naturals."
8. Corruption of "detractors." (In reply, Maria
puns on "substract" as "subtract.")
9. Parishes kept large tops that were spun by
whipping them, for the parishioners' amusement

and exercise.
1. Variously interpreted, but may mean "Speak of
the devil," because Castilians were considered
devilish, and *vulgo* refers to the common tongue.
2. Sir Andrew possibly confuses "shrew" (ill-
tempered woman) with "mouse," an endearment.
3. Address (her); originally a naval term meaning "go alongside; greet."
4. Lady-in-waiting; not a menial servant, but a
gentlewoman in attendance on a great lady.

SIR TOBY   You mistake, knight. "Accost" is front° her, board   *confront*
her, woo her, assail[5] her.

SIR ANDREW   By my troth, I would not undertake[6] her in
this company.° Is that the meaning of "accost"?   *i.e., the audience*

MARIA   Fare you well, gentlemen. [*begins to exit*]

SIR TOBY   An thou let part so,[7] Sir Andrew, would thou
mightst never draw sword again.

SIR ANDREW   An you part so, mistress, I would I might
never draw sword again. Fair lady, do you think you have
fools in hand?°   *to deal with*

MARIA   Sir, I have not you by th' hand.

SIR ANDREW   Marry,[8] but you shall have, and here's my
hand.

MARIA [*taking his hand*]   Now, sir, thought is free.[9] I pray
you, bring your hand to th' butt'ry bar[1] and let it drink.

SIR ANDREW   Wherefore, sweetheart? What's your metaphor?

MARIA   It's dry,[2] sir.

SIR ANDREW   Why, I think so. I am not such an ass but I
can keep my hand dry.[3] But what's your jest?

MARIA   A dry jest,[4] sir.

SIR ANDREW   Are you full of them?

MARIA   Ay, sir, I have them at my fingers' ends.[5] Marry,
now I let go your hand, I am barren.°   *Exit*   *empty of jokes*

SIR TOBY   O knight, thou lack'st a cup of canary![6] When
did I see thee so put down?[7]

SIR ANDREW   Never in your life, I think, unless you see
canary put me down. Methinks sometimes I have no
more wit than a Christian[8] or an ordinary man has. But
I am a great eater of beef,[9] and I believe that does harm
to my wit.

SIR TOBY   No question.

SIR ANDREW   An I thought that, I'd forswear it. I'll ride
home tomorrow, Sir Toby.

SIR TOBY   *Pourquoi,*° my dear knight?   *why*

SIR ANDREW   What is "*pourquoi*"? Do, or not do? I would I
had bestowed that time in the tongues[1] that I have in
fencing, dancing, and bear-baiting. O, had I but followed
the arts!

SIR TOBY   Then hadst thou° had an excellent head of hair.   *you would have*

5. Greet (also nautical). "Board": speak to; tackle.
6. Take her on (with sexual implication).
7. If you let her go without protest or without bidding her farewell.
8. Indeed (originally, the name of the Virgin Mary used as an oath).
9. The customary retort to "Do you think I am a fool?"
1. Ledge on the half-door to a buttery or a wine cellar, on which drinks were served.
2. Thirsty; but a dry hand was also thought to be a sign of impotence.
3. Alluding to the proverb "Even fools have

enough wit to come in out of the rain."
4. A stupid joke (referring to Sir Andrew's stupidity); an ironic quip; a joke about dryness.
5. Always ready; or "by th' hand" (line 62).
6. A sweet wine, like sherry, originally from the Canary Islands.
7. Defeated in repartee; "put down" with drink.
8. i.e., an average man.
9. Contemporary medicine held that beef dulled the intellect ("wit").
1. Foreign languages; Sir Toby takes him to mean "curling tongs."

SIR ANDREW   Why, would that have mended° my hair?   *improved*

SIR TOBY   Past question, for thou seest it will not curl by
nature.[2]

95   SIR ANDREW   But it becomes me well enough, does't not?

SIR TOBY   Excellent! It hangs like flax on a distaff,[3] and I
hope to see a housewife[4] take thee between her legs and
spin it off.[5]

SIR ANDREW   Faith, I'll home tomorrow, Sir Toby. Your

100   niece will not be seen, or if she be, it's four to one she'll
none of me. The Count himself here hard by° woos her.   *nearby*

SIR TOBY   She'll none o' th' Count. She'll not match above
her degree,° neither in estate,[6] years, nor wit. I have heard   *social rank*
her swear't. Tut, there's life in't,[7] man.

105   SIR ANDREW   I'll stay a month longer. I am a fellow o' th'
strangest mind i' th' world. I delight in masques and revels sometimes altogether.

SIR TOBY   Art thou good at these kickshawses,[8] knight?

SIR ANDREW   As any man in Illyria, whatsoever he be,

110   under the degree of my betters; and yet I will not compare with an old man.[9]

SIR TOBY   What is thy excellence in a galliard,[1] knight?

SIR ANDREW   Faith, I can cut a caper.[2]

SIR TOBY   And I can cut the mutton to't.

115   SIR ANDREW   And I think I have the back-trick[3] simply as
strong as any man in Illyria.

SIR TOBY   Wherefore are these things hid? Wherefore have
these gifts a curtain[4] before 'em? Are they like to take
dust, like Mistress Mall's[5] picture? Why dost thou not go

120   to church in a galliard and come home in a coranto?[6]
My very walk should be a jig. I would not so much as
make water but in a cinquepace.[7] What dost thou mean?
Is it a world to hide virtues in? I did think, by the excellent constitution of thy leg, it was formed under the star

125   of a galliard.[8]

SIR ANDREW   Ay, 'tis strong, and it does indifferent° well in   *moderately*
a flame-colored stock.° Shall we set about some revels?   *stocking*

SIR TOBY   What shall we do else? Were we not born under
Taurus?[9]

---

2. To contrast with Sir Andrew's "arts" (line 90).
3. In spinning, flax would hang in long, thin, yel-
lowish strings on the "distaff," a pole held between
the knees.
4. Housewives spun flax; the pronunciation, "huswife," also suggests the meaning "prostitute."
5. Make him bald (as a result of venereal disease).
6. Status; possessions.
7. Proverbial: While there's life, there's hope.
8. Trifles; trivialities (from the French *quelque
chose*).
9. Expert (perhaps a backhanded compliment).
1. A lively, complex dance, including the caper.
2. Leap. (Sir Toby puns on the pickled flower buds
used in a sauce of mutton.)

3. Probably a dance movement, a kick of the foot
behind the body (also suggesting sexual prowess,
with later reference to "mutton" as "prostitute").
4. Used to protect paintings from dust.
5. Like "Moll[y]," "Mall" was a nickname for
"Mary."
6. An even more rapid dance than the galliard.
7. Galliard, or, more properly, the steps joining
the figures of the dance; punning on "sink," as in
"sewer."
8. Astrological influences favorable to dancing.
9. The astrological sign of the bull was usually
thought to govern the neck and throat (appropriate to heavy drinkers).

130   SIR ANDREW   Taurus? That's sides and heart.
     SIR TOBY   No, sir, it is legs and thighs. Let me see thee caper.
        [SIR ANDREW *dances*]
        Ha, higher! Ha, ha, excellent.   *Exeunt*

1.4

     Enter VALENTINE, *and* VIOLA *in man's attire [as Cesario]*
     VALENTINE   If the Duke continue these favors towards
     you, Cesario, you are like to be much advanced. He hath
     known you but three days, and already you are no
     stranger.

5   VIOLA   You either fear his humor° or my negligence, that   *moodiness*
     you call in question the continuance of his love. Is he
     inconstant, sir, in his favors?
     VALENTINE   No, believe me.
     VIOLA   I thank you. Here comes the Count.
        Enter ORSINO, CURIO, *and attendants*

10   ORSINO   Who saw Cesario, ho?
     VIOLA   On your attendance,° my lord, here.   *waiting at your service*
     ORSINO [*to* CURIO *and Attendants*]   Stand you a while
        aloof.° [*to* VIOLA] Cesario,   *aside*
        Thou know'st no less but all.° I have unclasped   *than everything*
        To thee the book even of my secret soul.

15   Therefore, good youth, address thy gait° unto her.   *go*
        Be not denied access, stand at her doors
        And tell them, there thy fixèd foot shall grow°   *take root*
        Till thou have audience.
     VIOLA   Sure, my noble lord,
        If she be so abandoned to her sorrow

20   As it is spoke, she never will admit me.
     ORSINO   Be clamorous and leap all civil bounds[1]
        Rather than make unprofited° return.   *unsuccessful*
     VIOLA   Say I do speak with her, my lord, what then?
     ORSINO   O, then unfold the passion of my love.

25   Surprise[2] her with discourse of my dear° faith.   *heartfelt*
        It shall become thee well to act my woes—
        She will attend° it better in thy youth   *pay attention to*
        Than in a nuncio's° of more grave aspect.°   *messenger's / appearance*
     VIOLA   I think not so, my lord.
     ORSINO   Dear lad, believe it;

30   For they shall yet° belie thy happy years°   *thus far / propitious youth*
        That say thou art a man. Diana's lip
        Is not more smooth and rubious,° thy small pipe°   *ruby red / voice*
        Is as the maiden's organ, shrill and sound,[3]
        And all is semblative° a woman's part.   *like*

35   I know thy constellation[4] is right apt

1.4 Location: Orsino's palace.
1. All constraints of polite behavior.
2. Capture by unexpected attack.

3. High-pitched and uncracked.
4. Nature and abilities (as supposedly determined by the stars).

For this affair. [*to* CURIO *and attendants*] Some four or
    five attend him,
All, if you will, for I myself am best
When least in company. [*to* VIOLA] Prosper well in this
And thou shalt live as freely as thy lord,
To call his fortunes thine.

40   VIOLA   I'll do my best
    To woo your lady. [*aside*] Yet a barful strife!⁵
    Whoe'er I woo, myself would be his wife.   *Exeunt.*

1.5

Enter MARIA *and* [FESTE,¹ *the*] *clown.*

MARIA   Nay, either tell me where thou hast been or I will
    not open my lips so wide as a bristle may enter in° way of   *by*
    thy excuse. My lady will hang thee for thy absence.

FESTE   Let her hang me. He that is well hanged in this
5   world needs to fear no colors.²

MARIA   Make that good.°   *explain that*

FESTE   He shall see none to fear.

MARIA   A good Lenten³ answer. I can tell thee where that
    saying was born, of "I fear no colors."

10   FESTE   Where, good Mistress Mary?

MARIA   In the wars;⁴ and that may you be bold to say in
    your foolery.

FESTE   Well, God give them wisdom that have it, and
    those that are fools, let them use their talents.⁵

15   MARIA   Yet you will be hanged for being so long absent, or
    to be turned away⁶—is not that as good as a hanging to
    you?

FESTE   Many a good hanging prevents a bad marriage,⁷
    and, for turning away, let summer bear it out.°   *make it endurable*

20   MARIA   You are resolute, then?

FESTE   Not so, neither, but I am resolved on two points.°   *matters; laces*

MARIA   That if one break, the other will hold, or, if both
    break, your gaskins° fall.   *wide breeches*

FESTE   Apt, in good faith, very apt. Well, go thy way. If Sir
25   Toby would leave drinking, thou wert as witty a piece of
    Eve's flesh⁸ as any in Illyria.

MARIA   Peace, you rogue. No more o' that. Here comes my
    lady. Make your excuse wisely, you were best.°   [*Exit.*]   *you had better*

---

5. An undertaking full of impediments.
1.5 Location: Olivia's house.
1. The name is used only once, at 2.4.11.
2. Proverbial for "fear nothing." "Colors": here,
worldly deceptions, with puns on "collars" as
"hangman's nooses" and "cholers" as "anger."
3. Thin or meager (like Lenten fare).
4. "Colors" in the saying originally referred to
military flags.
5. Alluding to the parable of the talents, Matthew
25:14–30. The comic implication is that a fool

should strive to increase his measure of folly.
Because "fool" and "fowl" had similar pronuncia-
tions, there may also be a play on "talents/talons."
6. Dismissed; also, perhaps, playing on turned off
as "hanged."
7. Proverbial. "Hanging": execution; sexual prowess.
8. Woman. Feste may imply both that Maria and
Toby would make a good match and that Maria is
as witty as Toby is sober.

Enter Lady OLIVIA *with* MALVOLIO [*and attendants*].

FESTE [*aside*] Wit,[9] an't° be thy will, put me into good   *if it*
30   fooling! Those wits that think they have thee do very oft
prove fools, and I that am sure I lack thee may pass for a
wise man. For what says Quinapalus?[1] "Better a witty
Fool than a foolish wit." God bless thee, lady.

OLIVIA [*to attendants*] Take the fool away.

35 FESTE Do you not hear, fellows? Take away the lady.

OLIVIA Go to, you're a dry[2] fool. I'll no more of you.
Besides, you grow dishonest.°   *unreliable*

FESTE Two faults, madonna,° that drink and good counsel   *my lady*
will amend. For give the dry fool drink, then is the fool
40   not dry. Bid the dishonest man mend° himself: if he   *reform*
mend, he is no longer dishonest; if he cannot, let the
botcher° mend him. Anything that's mended is but   *tailor; cobbler*
patched; virtue that transgresses is but patched with sin,
and sin that amends is but patched with virtue. If that
45   this simple syllogism will serve, so; if it will not, what
remedy? As there is no true cuckold but calamity, so
beauty's a flower.[3] The lady bade take away the fool.
Therefore, I say again, take her away.

OLIVIA Sir, I bade them take away you.

50 FESTE Misprision[4] in the highest degree! Lady, *cucullus*
non facit monachum.[5] That's as much to say as, I wear
not motley[6] in my brain. Good madonna, give me leave
to prove you a fool.

OLIVIA Can you do it?

55 FESTE Dexteriously,° good madonna.   *dexterously*

OLIVIA Make your proof.

FESTE I must catechize[7] you for it, madonna. Good my
mouse of virtue,° answer me.   *my good virtuous mouse*

OLIVIA Well, sir, for want of other idleness,° I'll bide° your   *pastime / await*
60   proof.

FESTE Good madonna, why mournest thou?

OLIVIA Good fool, for my brother's death.

FESTE I think his soul is in hell, madonna.

OLIVIA I know his soul is in heaven, fool.

65 FESTE The more fool, madonna, to mourn for your brother's soul, being in heaven. Take away the fool, gentlemen.

OLIVIA What think you of this fool, Malvolio? Doth he
not mend?[8]

---

9. Intelligence, which is often contrasted with will.
1. Feste frequently invents his own authorities.
2. Dull, but Feste interprets as "thirsty." "Go to": an expression of impatience.
3. In taking her vow (1.2.38–39), Olivia has wedded herself to calamity but must be unfaithful, or let pass her moment of beauty.

4. Misapprehension; wrongful arrest.
5. The cowl does not make the monk (a Latin proverb).
6. The multicolored costume of a fool.
7. Question (as in catechism, which tests the orthodoxy of belief).
8. Improve, but Malvolio takes "mend" to mean "grow more foolish."

70 MALVOLIO   Yes, and shall do till the pangs of death shake
him. Infirmity,° that decays the wise, doth ever make   *(old) age*
the better fool.⁹

FESTE   God send you, sir, a speedy infirmity, for the better
increasing your folly! Sir Toby will be sworn that I am no
75 fox, but he will not pass his word for twopence that you
are no fool.

OLIVIA   How say you to that, Malvolio?

MALVOLIO   I marvel your ladyship takes delight in such a
barren rascal. I saw him put down¹ the other day with an
80 ordinary fool that has no more brain than a stone. Look
you now, he's out of his guard° already. Unless you laugh   *defenseless*
and minister occasion² to him, he is gagged. I protest I
take these wise men that crow so at these set° kind of   *artificial*
fools no better than the fools' zanies.°   *"straight men"*

85 OLIVIA   O, you are sick of° self-love, Malvolio, and taste   *with*
with a distempered³ appetite. To be generous, guiltless,
and of free° disposition is to take those things for bird-   *magnanimous*
bolts⁴ that you deem cannon bullets. There is no slander
in an allowed° fool, though he do nothing but rail; nor no   *licensed*
90 railing in a known discreet man, though he do nothing
but reprove.

FESTE   Now Mercury indue thee with leasing,⁵ for thou
speakest well of fools.

Enter MARIA.

MARIA   Madam, there is at the gate a young gentleman
95 much desires to speak with you.

OLIVIA   From the Count Orsino, is it?

MARIA   I know not, madam. 'Tis a fair young man, and
well attended.

OLIVIA   Who of my people hold him in delay?

100 MARIA   Sir Toby, madam, your kinsman.

OLIVIA   Fetch him off, I pray you. He speaks nothing but
madman.° Fie on him! [MARIA *exits*.] Go you, Malvolio.   *madman's talk*
If it be a suit from the Count, I am sick, or not at home;
what you will, to dismiss it. [*Malvolio exits*.] Now you see,
105 sir, how your fooling grows old,° and people dislike it.   *stale*

FESTE   Thou hast spoke for us, madonna, as if thy eldest
son should be a fool, whose skull Jove cram with brains,
for—here he comes—one of thy kin has a most weak *pia
mater*.⁶

Enter SIR TOBY.

110 OLIVIA   By mine honor, half-drunk. What is he at the
gate, cousin?°   *kinsman*

SIR TOBY   A gentleman.

---

9. Make the fool more foolish.
1. Defeated in repartee.
2. And give opportunity.
3. Unbalanced; sick.

4. Blunt arrows for shooting birds.
5. May Mercury, the god of deception, endow
you with the talent of tactful lying.
6. Brain; or literally, the membrane enclosing it.

OLIVIA   A gentleman? What gentleman?

SIR TOBY   'Tis a gentleman here. [*He belches.*] A plague o'
115   these pickle herring!—How now, sot?°   *fool, drunkard*

FESTE   Good Sir Toby.

OLIVIA   Cousin, cousin, how have you come so early by
this lethargy?

SIR TOBY   Lechery? I defy lechery. There's one° at the gate.   *someone*
120   OLIVIA   Ay, marry, what is he?

SIR TOBY   Let him be the devil an° he will, I care not. Give   *if*
me faith,[7] say I. Well, it's all one.°   *Exit*   *it doesn't matter*

OLIVIA   What's a drunken man like, fool?

FESTE   Like a drowned man, a fool, and a madman. One
125   draught above heat[8] makes him a fool, the second mads
him, and a third drowns him.

OLIVIA   Go thou and seek the coroner and let him sit o'°   *hold an inquest for*
my coz,° for he's in the third degree of drink: he's   *cousin; uncle*
drowned. Go look after him.

130   FESTE   He is but mad yet, madonna, and the fool shall
look to the madman.   [*Exit.*]

Enter MALVOLIO.

MALVOLIO   Madam, yond young fellow swears he will
speak with you. I told him you were sick; he takes on
him to understand so much, and therefore[9] comes to
135   speak with you. I told him you were asleep; he seems to
have a foreknowledge of that too, and therefore comes
to speak with you. What is to be said to him, lady? He's
fortified against any denial.

OLIVIA   Tell him he shall not speak with me.

140   MALVOLIO   He's been told so, and he says he'll stand at
your door like a sheriff's post[1] and be the supporter to a
bench, but he'll speak with you.

OLIVIA   What kind o' man is he?

MALVOLIO   Why, of mankind.°   *like any other*

145   OLIVIA   What manner of man?

MALVOLIO   Of very ill manner. He'll speak with you, will
you or no.

OLIVIA   Of what personage° and years is he?   *appearance*

MALVOLIO   Not yet old enough for a man, nor young
150   enough for a boy—as a squash is before 'tis a peascod,
or a codling[2] when 'tis almost an apple. 'Tis with him in
standing water,[3] between boy and man. He is very well-
favored,° and he speaks very shrewishly.[4] One would   *handsome*
think his mother's milk were scarce out of him.

155   OLIVIA   Let him approach. Call in my gentlewoman.

MALVOLIO   Gentlewoman, my lady calls.   *Exit.*

---

7. To defy the devil by faith alone.
8. One drink ("draught") beyond the quantity
necessary to warm him.
9. For that very reason.
1. A decorative post set before a sheriff's door,

as a sign of authority.
2. An unripe apple. "Squash": an undeveloped
pea pod.
3. At the turn of the tide.
3. Sharply.

Enter MARIA.

OLIVIA Give me my veil. Come, throw it o'er my face.
We'll once more hear Orsino's embassy.

Enter VIOLA [*as Cesario*].

VIOLA The honorable lady of the house, which is she?

160 OLIVIA Speak to me. I shall answer for her. Your will?

VIOLA Most radiant, exquisite, and unmatchable beauty—
I pray you, tell me if this be the lady of the house, for I
never saw her. I would be loath to cast away° my speech,   *waste*
for, besides that it is excellently well penned, I have taken

165 great pains to con° it. Good beauties, let me sustain° no   *memorize / suffer*
scorn. I am very comptible,° even to the least sinister   *sensitive*
usage.[5]

OLIVIA Whence came you, sir?

VIOLA I can say little more than I have studied,[6] and that

170 question's out of my part. Good gentle one, give me
modest° assurance if you be the lady of the house, that   *adequate*
I may proceed in my speech.

OLIVIA Are you a comedian?°   *an actor*

VIOLA No, my profound heart.[7] And yet, by the very fangs

175 of malice, I swear I am not that° I play. Are you the lady   *what*
of the house?

OLIVIA If I do not usurp[8] myself, I am.

VIOLA Most certain, if you are she, you do usurp yourself,
for what is yours to bestow is not yours to reserve. But

180 this is from my commission.[9] I will on° with my speech in   *continue*
your praise and then show you the heart of my message.

OLIVIA Come to what is important in't, I forgive you° the   *excuse you from*
praise.

VIOLA Alas, I took great pains to study it, and 'tis poetical.

185 OLIVIA It is the more like to be feigned. I pray you, keep it
in. I heard you were saucy° at my gates, and allowed   *impertinent*
your approach rather to wonder at you than to hear you.
If you be not mad, be gone. If you have reason,° be brief.   *any sanity*
'Tis not that time of moon with me to make one in so

190 skipping a dialogue.[1]

MARIA Will you hoist sail, sir? Here lies your way.

VIOLA No, good swabber, I am to hull[2] here a little longer.
—Some mollification for your giant,[3] sweet lady. Tell me
your mind, I am a messenger.[4]

195 OLIVIA Sure you have some hideous matter to deliver,
when the courtesy of it is so fearful.[5] Speak your office.°   *business*

5. To the slightest discourteous treatment.
6. Learned by heart (a theatrical term).
7. My most wise lady; upon my soul.
8. Counterfeit; misappropriate.
9. Beyond my instructions.
1. I am not lunatic enough to take part in so
flighty a conversation. (Lunacy was thought to be
influenced by the phases of the moon.)

2. To lie unanchored with lowered sails.
3. Mythical giants guarded ladies; here, also
mocking Maria's diminutive size. "Some . . . for":
please pacify.
4. From Orsino; Olivia pretends she understands
her to mean a king's messenger, or a messenger-at-
arms, employed on important state affairs.
5. When the introduction of it is so fearsome.

VIOLA It alone concerns your ear. I bring no overture° of   *declaration*
war, no taxation of homage.[6] I hold the olive[7] in my hand.
My words are as full of peace as matter.°   *meaning*

200 OLIVIA Yet you began rudely. What are you? What would
you?

VIOLA The rudeness that hath appeared in me have I
learned from my entertainment.° What I am and what I   *reception*
would are as secret as maidenhead:° to your ears, divin-   *virginity*

205 ity; to any other's, profanation.

OLIVIA [*to* MARIA *and attendants*] Give us the place alone.
We will hear this divinity.° [MARIA *and attendants exit*.] *religious discourse*
Now, sir, what is your text?[8]

VIOLA Most sweet lady—

210 OLIVIA A comfortable° doctrine, and much may be said of   *comforting*
it. Where lies your text?

VIOLA In Orsino's bosom.

OLIVIA In his bosom? In what chapter of his bosom?

VIOLA To answer by the method,° in the first of his heart.   *in the same style*

215 OLIVIA O, I have read it; it is heresy. Have you no more to
say?

VIOLA Good madam, let me see your face.

OLIVIA Have you any commission from your lord to negoti-
ate with my face? You are now out of° your text. But we   *straying from*

220 will draw the curtain and show you the picture. [*She
removes her veil*.] Look you, sir, such a one I was this present.[9] Is't not well done?

VIOLA Excellently done, if God did all.[1]

OLIVIA 'Tis in grain,° sir; 'twill endure wind and weather.   *the dye is fast*

225 VIOLA 'Tis beauty truly blent,[2] whose red and white
Nature's own sweet and cunning° hand laid on.   *skillful*
Lady, you are the cruel'st she° alive   *woman*
If you will lead these graces to the grave
And leave the world no copy.[3]

230 OLIVIA O, sir, I will not be so hard-hearted! I will give
out divers schedules° of my beauty. It shall be invento-   *inventories*
ried and every particle and utensil labeled[4] to my will:
as, *item*, two lips, indifferent° red; *item*, two gray eyes,   *moderate*
with lids[5] to them; *item*, one neck, one chin, and so

235 forth. Were you sent hither to praise° me?   *appraise; flatter*

VIOLA I see you what you are. You are too proud.
But if° you were the devil, you are fair.   *even if*
My lord and master loves you. O, such love

6. Demand for dues paid to a superior.
7. Olive branch (as a symbol of peace).
8. Quotation (as a theme of a sermon, in keeping
with "divinity," "doctrine," "heresy," etc.).
9. Portraits usually gave the year of painting.
"This present" was a term used to date letters.
1. If it is natural (without the use of cosmetics).
2. Blended, or mixed (of paints). Shakespeare
uses the same metaphor in sonnet 20, lines 1–2.

As Cesario, Viola is playing with established conventions of poetic courtship.
3. Viola means "child"; Olivia takes her to mean
"list" or "inventory."
4. Every single part and article added as a codi-
cil (parodying the legal language of a last will
and testament).
5. Eyelids, but also punning on "pot lids" (punning on "utensil" as a household implement).

Could be but recompensed though[6] you were crowned
The nonpareil of beauty.°   *an unequaled beauty*

240 OLIVIA   How does he love me?

VIOLA   With adorations, fertile° tears,   *ever-flowing*
    With groans that thunder love, with sighs of fire.

OLIVIA   Your lord does know my mind. I cannot love him.
    Yet I suppose him virtuous, know him noble,
245   Of great estate,° of fresh and stainless youth;   *high status*
    In voices[7] well divulged,° free,° learned, and valiant,   *spoken of / generous*
    And in dimension and the shape of nature[8]
    A gracious person. But yet I cannot love him.
    He might have took his answer long ago.

250 VIOLA   If I did love you in° my master's flame,°   *with / passion*
    With such a suff'ring, such a deadly° life,   *deathlike*
    In your denial I would find no sense,
    I would not understand it.

OLIVIA   Why, what would you?

VIOLA   Make me a willow[9] cabin at your gate
255   And call upon my soul° within the house,   *i.e., Olivia*
    Write loyal cantons of contemnèd° love   *songs of rejected*
    And sing them loud even in the dead of night,
    Hallow[1] your name to the reverberate° hills   *echoing*
    And make the babbling gossip of the air[2]
260   Cry out "Olivia!" O, you should not rest
    Between the elements of air and earth
    But° you should pity me.   *unless*

OLIVIA   You might do much.
    What is your parentage?

265 VIOLA   Above my fortunes, yet my state° is well.   *social status*
    I am a gentleman.

OLIVIA   Get you to your lord.
    I cannot love him. Let him send no more—
    Unless perchance° you come to me again   *perhaps*
    To tell me how he takes it. Fare you well.
270   I thank you for your pains. Spend this for me.
       [*She offers money.*]

VIOLA   I am no fee'd post,° lady. Keep your purse.   *hired messenger*
    My master, not myself, lacks recompense.
    Love make his heart of flint that you shall love.[3]
    And let your fervor, like my master's, be
275   Placed in contempt. Farewell, fair cruelty.   *Exit.*

OLIVIA   "What is your parentage?"
    "Above my fortunes, yet my state is well.
    I am a gentleman." I'll be sworn thou art.
    Thy tongue, thy face, thy limbs, actions, and spirit

---

6. Would have to be requited even if.
7. In the general opinion.
8. "Dimension" and "shape of nature" are synonymous, meaning "bodily form."
9. Traditional symbol of rejected love.
1. Shout; or perhaps "hallow," as in "bless."

2. For the love of Narcissus, the nymph Echo wasted away to a mere voice, able to repeat only whatever she heard spoken.
3. May love make the heart of the man you love as hard as flint.

280 Do give thee fivefold blazon.[4] Not too fast! Soft,° soft—   *wait*
Unless the master were the man.[5] How now?
Even so quickly may one catch the plague?
Methinks I feel this youth's perfections
With an invisible and subtle stealth
285 To creep in at mine eyes. Well, let it be.—
What ho, Malvolio!
    Enter MALVOLIO.
MALVOLIO   Here, madam, at your service.
OLIVIA   Run after that same peevish messenger,
The County's° man. He left this ring behind him,   *Count's*
Would I° or not. Tell him I'll° none of it.   *whether I wished it / (have)*
290 Desire him not to flatter with° his lord,   *encourage*
Nor hold him up with hopes. I am not for him.
If that the youth will come this way tomorrow,
I'll give him reasons for't. Hie thee,° Malvolio.   *hurry*
MALVOLIO   Madam, I will.   *Exit.*
295 OLIVIA   I do I know not what, and fear to find
Mine eye too great a flatterer for my mind.[6]
Fate, show thy force. Ourselves we do not owe.°   *own*
What is decreed must be, and be this so.
    [*Exit at another door.*]

2.1

    Enter ANTONIO *and* SEBASTIAN.
ANTONIO   Will you stay no longer? Nor will° you not that I   *wish*
go with you?
SEBASTIAN   By your patience, no. My stars shine darkly[1]
over me. The malignancy of my fate[2] might perhaps
5 distemper° yours. Therefore I shall crave of you your   *infect*
leave[3] that I may bear my evils alone. It were° a bad rec-   *would be*
ompense for your love to lay any of them on you.
ANTONIO   Let me yet know of you whither you are bound.
SEBASTIAN   No, sooth,° sir. My determinate° voyage is   *truly / destined*
10 mere extravagancy.° But I perceive in you so excellent a   *idle wandering*
touch of modesty° that you will not extort from me what   *politeness*
I am willing to keep in. Therefore it charges me in manners[4] the rather to express° myself. You must know of me,   *reveal*
then, Antonio, my name is Sebastian, which I called
15 Roderigo. My father was that Sebastian of Messaline[5]
whom I know you have heard of. He left behind him
myself and a sister, both born in an° hour. If the heavens   *within the same*
had been pleased, would we had so ended! But you, sir,

4. Formal description of a gentleman's coat of arms.
5. If Orsino were Cesario ("man": servant).
6. I.e., my eye (through which love has entered my heart) has seduced my reason.
2.1 Location: Near the coast of Illyria.

1. Forebodingly; unfavorably.
2. Evil influence of the stars; "malignancy" also signifies a deadly disease.
3. Permission.
4. Therefore courtesy requires.
5. Possibly Messina, Sicily.

altered that, for some hour before you took me from the
20 breach° of the sea was my sister drowned.   *surf*
ANTONIO   Alas the day!
SEBASTIAN   A lady, sir, though it was said she much
resembled me, was yet of many accounted beautiful. But
though I could not with such estimable° wonder overfar   *appreciative*
25 believe that, yet thus far I will boldly publish° her: she   *proclaim*
bore a mind that envy° could not but call fair. She is   *malice*
drowned already, sir, with salt water, though I seem to
drown her remembrance again with more.
ANTONIO   Pardon me, sir, your bad entertainment.[6]
30 SEBASTIAN   O good Antonio, forgive me your trouble.
ANTONIO   If you will not murder me[7] for my love, let me
be your servant.
SEBASTIAN   If you will not undo what you have done—that
is, kill him whom you have recovered°—desire it not. Fare   *rescued*
35 ye well at once. My bosom is full of kindness,° and I am   *tender emotion*
yet° so near the manners of my mother[8] that, upon the   *still*
least occasion more, mine eyes will tell tales of me.° I am   *betray my feelings*
bound to the Count Orsino's court. Farewell.   *Exit.*
ANTONIO   The gentleness° of all the gods go with thee!   *favor*
40 I have many enemies in Orsino's court,
Else° would I very shortly see thee there.   *otherwise*
But come what may, I do adore thee so
That danger shall seem sport, and I will go.   *Exit.*

2.2

Enter VIOLA *and* MALVOLIO, *at several*° *doors.*   *separate*
MALVOLIO   Were not you even° now with the Countess   *just*
Olivia?
VIOLA   Even now, sir. On° a moderate pace I have since   *at*
arrived but hither.°   *come only this far*
5 MALVOLIO   She returns this ring to you, sir. You might
have saved me my pains to have taken° it away yourself.   *by taking*
She adds, moreover, that you should put your lord into a
desperate assurance° she will none of him.[1] And one thing   *hopeless certainty*
more, that you be never so hardy° to come again in his   *bold*
10 affairs, unless it be to report your lord's taking of this.[2]
Receive it so.
VIOLA   She took the ring of me.[3] I'll none of it.
MALVOLIO   Come, sir, you peevishly threw it to her, and
her will is it should be so returned.
        [He throws down the ring.]
15 If it be worth stooping for, there it lies, in your eye;° if   *sight*
not, be it his that finds it.   *Exit.*

---

6. Your poor reception; your inhospitality.
7. I.e., murder him by insisting that they part.
8. I.e., so near woman's readiness to weep.
2.2 Location: Between Olivia's house and Orsino's palace.

1. She will accept no part of his proposal.
2. Reception of this (rejection).
3. Viola pretends to believe Olivia's story. "Of":
from.

VIOLA I left no ring with her. What means this lady?
　　　[*She picks up the ring.*]
　　Fortune forbid my outside° have not charmed her! ——— appearance
　　She made good view of° me, indeed so much ——— looked carefully at
20　That sure methought her eyes had lost° her tongue, ——— made her lose
　　For she did speak in starts distractedly.
　　She loves me, sure! The cunning of her passion
　　Invites me in° this churlish messenger. ——— by means of
　　None of my lord's ring? Why, he sent her none!
25　I am the man.[4] If it be so, as 'tis,
　　Poor lady, she were better love a dream.
　　Disguise, I see thou art a wickedness
　　Wherein the pregnant enemy[5] does much.
　　How easy is it for the proper false[6]
30　In women's waxen hearts to set their forms![7]
　　Alas, our frailty is the cause, not we,
　　For such as we are made of, such we be.[8]
　　How will this fadge?° My master loves her dearly, ——— turn out
　　And I, poor monster,[9] fond° as much on him, ——— dote
35　And she, mistaken, seems to dote on me.
　　What will become of this? As I am man,
　　My state is desperate° for my master's love. ——— hopeless
　　As I am woman (now, alas the day!),
　　What thriftless° sighs shall poor Olivia breathe! ——— unprofitable
40　O Time, thou must untangle this, not I.
　　It is too hard a knot for me t' untie.　　　　　　[*Exit.*]

2.3

Enter SIR TOBY *and* SIR ANDREW.

SIR TOBY Approach, Sir Andrew. Not to be abed after
　midnight is to be up betimes,° and "*diliculo surgere*,"[1] ——— early
　thou knowest.
SIR ANDREW Nay, by my troth,° I know not. But I know to ——— faith
5　be up late is to be up late.
SIR TOBY A false conclusion. I hate it as an unfilled can.° ——— tankard
　To be up after midnight and to go to bed then, is early, so
　that to go to bed after midnight is to go to bed betimes.
　Does not our lives consist of the four elements?[2]
10　SIR ANDREW Faith, so they say, but I think it rather consists
　of eating and drinking.
SIR TOBY Thou'rt a scholar. Let us therefore eat and
　drink. Marian, I say, a stoup° of wine! ——— two-pint tankard
　　　Enter [FESTE, *the*] *clown.*
SIR ANDREW Here comes the fool, i' faith.

---

4. I.e., the man with whom she has fallen in
love.
5. The devil, teeming ("pregnant") with ideas.
6. Handsome, but deceitful (men).
7. To impress their images on women's affections (as a seal stamps its image in wax).
8. For being made of frail flesh, we are frail.

9. Because she is both man and woman.
2.3 Location: Olivia's house.
1. Part of a Latin proverb, meaning "to rise at
dawn (is most healthy)."
2. The four elements, thought to make up all
matter, were earth, air, fire, and water.

15 FESTE How now, my hearts? Did you never see the picture
of "We Three"?[3]
SIR TOBY Welcome, ass. Now let's have a catch.[4]
SIR ANDREW By my troth, the fool has an excellent breast.° *singing voice*
I had rather than forty shillings I had such a leg,° and so *(for dancing)*
20 sweet a breath to sing, as the fool has.—In sooth, thou
wast in very gracious fooling last night when thou spokest of Pigrogromitus, of the Vapians passing the equinoctial of Queubus.[5] 'Twas very good, i' faith. I sent thee
sixpence for thy leman.° Hadst it? *sweetheart*
25 FESTE I did impeticos thy gratillity,[6] for Malvolio's nose is
no whipstock, my lady has a white hand, and the Myrmidons are no bottle-ale houses.[7]
SIR ANDREW Excellent! Why, this is the best fooling, when
all is done. Now, a song.
30 SIR TOBY [*to* FESTE] Come on, there is sixpence for you.
Let's have a song.
SIR ANDREW [*to* FESTE] There's a testril[8] of me, too. If one
knight give a—[9]
FESTE Would you have a love song or a song of good life?
35 SIR TOBY A love song, a love song.
SIR ANDREW Ay, ay, I care not for good life.
FESTE *sings*
O mistress mine, where are you roaming?
O, stay and hear! Your truelove's coming,
That can sing both high and low.
40 Trip° no further, pretty sweeting. *go*
Journeys end in lovers meeting,
Every wise man's son doth know.[1]
SIR ANDREW Excellent good, i' faith.
SIR TOBY Good, good.
45 FESTE What is love? 'Tis not hereafter.
Present mirth hath present laughter.
What's to come is still° unsure. *always*
In delay there lies no plenty,
Then come kiss me, sweet and twenty.° *twenty-times sweet*
50 Youth's a stuff will not endure.
SIR ANDREW A mellifluous voice, as I am true knight.
SIR TOBY A contagious breath.[2]
SIR ANDREW Very sweet and contagious, i' faith.

---

3. A trick picture portraying two fools' or asses'
heads, the third being the viewer.
4. Round: a simple song for several voices.
5. "Pigrogromitus . . . Queubus": Feste's mock
learning. "Equinoctial": equator of the astronomical heavens.
6. Comic jargon for "impocket (or impetticoat)
your gratuity."
7. Perhaps it is the sheer inscrutability of Feste's
foolery that so impresses Sir Andrew (line 28).
"Whipstock": handle of a whip. "Myrmidons": in
the *Iliad*, Achilles's warriors. "Bottle-ale houses":
cheap taverns.
8. Sir Andrew's version of "tester" (sixpence).
9. In the First Folio, "give a" appears at the end
of a justified line; an omission is possible.
1. The words of the song are not certainly Shakespeare's; they fit the tune of an instrumental piece
printed in Thomas Morley's *First Book of Consort
Lessons* (1599). "Wise man's son": wise men were
thought to have foolish sons.
2. Catchy voice; with a play on "disease-causing
air."

SIR TOBY   To hear by the nose, it is dulcet in contagion.[3]
55   But shall we make the welkin° dance indeed? Shall we   sky
   rouse the night owl in a catch that will draw three souls
   out of one weaver?[4] Shall we do that?
SIR ANDREW   An° you love me, let's do't. I am dog° at a catch.   if / clever
FESTE   By'r Lady, sir, and some dogs will catch well.
60   SIR ANDREW   Most certain. Let our catch be "Thou Knave."
FESTE   "Hold thy peace, thou knave,"[5] knight? I shall be
   constrained in't to call thee "knave," knight.
SIR ANDREW   'Tis not the first time I have constrained one
   to call me "knave." Begin, Fool. It begins "Hold thy peace."
65   FESTE   I shall never begin if I hold my peace.
SIR ANDREW   Good, i' faith. Come, begin. [*They sing the catch.*]
   Enter MARIA.
MARIA   What a caterwauling do you keep here! If my lady
   have not called up her steward Malvolio and bid him turn
   you out of doors, never trust me.
70   SIR TOBY   My lady's a Cathayan,[6] we are politicians,° Mal-   schemers
   volio's a Peg-a'-Ramsey,[7] and [*sings*] "Three merry men be
   we."[8] Am not I consanguineous?[9] Am I not of her blood?
   Tillyvally!° "Lady"! [*sings*] "There dwelt a man in Baby-   fiddlesticks
   lon, lady, lady."[1]
75   FESTE   Beshrew° me, the knight's in admirable fooling.   curse
SIR ANDREW   Ay, he does well enough if he be disposed,
   and so do I, too. He does it with a better grace, but I do
   it more natural.[2]
SIR TOBY [*sings*]   "O' the twelfth day of December"[3]—
80   MARIA   For the love o' God, peace!
   Enter MALVOLIO.
MALVOLIO   My masters, are you mad? Or what are you?
   Have you no wit,° manners, nor honesty° but to gabble   sense / decency
   like tinkers at this time of night? Do ye make an alehouse
   of my lady's house, that you squeak out your coziers'°   cobblers'
85   catches without any mitigation or remorse[4] of voice? Is
   there no respect of place, persons, nor time in you?
SIR TOBY   We did keep time, sir, in our catches. Sneck up!°   go hang yourself
MALVOLIO   Sir Toby, I must be round° with you. My lady   plainspoken
   bade me tell you that, though she harbors you as her
90   kinsman, she's nothing allied to your disorders. If you
   can separate yourself and your misdemeanors, you are
   welcome to the house; if not, an° it would please you to   if
   take leave of her, she is very willing to bid you farewell.

3. If one could hear through the nose, the sound would be sweetly ("dulcet") infectious.
4. Weavers were traditionally addicted to psalm singing, so to move them with popular catches would be a great triumph. Music was said to be able to draw the soul from the body.
5. The words of the catch are "Hold thy peace, I prithee hold thy peace, thou knave." Each singer repeatedly calls the others knaves and tells them to stop singing.
6. Chinese; but also ethnocentric slang for "trickster" or "cheat."
7. Name of a dance and popular song; here, used contemptuously.
8. Refrain of a popular song.
9. A blood relative (of Olivia's).
1. The opening and refrain of a popular song.
2. Effortlessly; but, unconsciously playing on the sense of *natural* as "fool" or "idiot."
3. Snatch of a ballad; or possibly a drunken version of "twelfth day of Christmas," that is, Twelfth Night.
4. Without any abating or softening.

SIR TOBY [*sings*] "Farewell, dear heart, since I must needs
   be gone."[5]

95 MARIA Nay, good Sir Toby.

FESTE "His eyes do show his days are almost done."

MALVOLIO Is't even so?

SIR TOBY "But I will never die."

FESTE "Sir Toby, there you lie."

100 MALVOLIO This is much credit to you.

SIR TOBY "Shall I bid him go?"

FESTE "What an if° you do?"   *an if = if*

SIR TOBY "Shall I bid him go, and spare not?"

FESTE "O no, no, no, no, you dare not."

105 SIR TOBY Out o' tune, sir? Ye lie. Art any more than a
   steward? Dost thou think because thou art virtuous
   there shall be no more cakes and ale?[6]

FESTE Yes, by Saint Anne, and ginger[7] shall be hot i' th'
   mouth, too.

110 SIR TOBY Thou'rt i' th' right.—Go, sir, rub your chain
   with crumbs.[8]—A stoup of wine, Maria!

MALVOLIO Mistress Mary, if you prized my lady's favor at
   anything more than contempt, you would not give
   means for this uncivil rule.° She shall know of it, by this   *behavior*

115 hand.   *Exit.*[9]

MARIA Go shake your ears!°   *(like an ass)*

SIR ANDREW 'Twere as good a deed as to drink when a
   man's a-hungry, to challenge him the field° and then to   *to a duel*
   break promise with him and make a fool of him.

120 SIR TOBY Do't, knight. I'll write thee a challenge. Or I'll
   deliver thy indignation to him by word of mouth.

MARIA Sweet Sir Toby, be patient for tonight. Since the
   youth of the Count's was today with my lady, she is much
   out of quiet. For Monsieur Malvolio, let me alone with

125 him.° If I do not gull him into a nayword[1] and make him *leave him to me*
   a common recreation,° do not think I have wit enough to   *sport, jest*
   lie straight in my bed. I know I can do it.

SIR TOBY Possess° us, possess us, tell us something of him.   *inform*

MARIA Marry, sir, sometimes he is a kind of puritan.[2]

130 SIR ANDREW O, if I thought that, I'd beat him like a dog!

SIR TOBY What, for being a puritan? Thy exquisite° rea-   *ingenious*
   son, dear knight?

SIR ANDREW I have no exquisite reason for't, but I have
   reason good enough.

135 MARIA The devil a puritan that he is, or anything constantly but a time-pleaser;° an affectioned[3] ass that cons   *bootlicker*

---

5. Part of another song that Sir Toby and Feste
adapt for the occasion.
6. Traditionally associated with church festivals
and therefore disliked by Puritans.
7. Used to spice ale. Saint Anne was the mother
of the Virgin; the oath would be offensive to
Puritans, who attacked her cult.
8. Clean your steward's chain; mind your own

business.
9. Feste plays no further part in this scene. This
is the suggested exit for him too.
1. If I do not trick ("gull") him into a byword (for
"dupe").
2. Could mean "morally strict and censorious," as
well as "a follower of the Puritan religious faith."
3. Affected.

state without book and utters it by great swaths;[4] the best persuaded of himself,[5] so crammed, as he thinks, with excellencies, that it is his grounds of faith° that all that look on him love him. And on that vice in him will my revenge find notable cause to work.   *his creed*

SIR TOBY   What wilt thou do?

MARIA   I will drop in his way some obscure epistles of love, wherein by the color of his beard, the shape of his leg, the manner of his gait, the expressure° of his eye,   *expression* forehead, and complexion, he shall find himself most feelingly personated.° I can write very like my lady your   *represented* niece; on a forgotten° matter, we can hardly make dis-   *bygone* tinction of our hands.°   *handwriting*

SIR TOBY   Excellent! I smell a device.°   *plot, trick*

SIR ANDREW   I have't in my nose, too.

SIR TOBY   He shall think, by the letters that thou wilt drop, that they come from my niece, and that she's in love with him.

MARIA   My purpose is indeed a horse of that color.

SIR ANDREW   And your horse now would make him an ass.

MARIA   Ass° I doubt not.   *(punning on "as")*

SIR ANDREW   O, 'twill be admirable!

MARIA   Sport royal, I warrant you. I know my physic° will   *medicine* work with him. I will plant you two, and let the fool make a third, where he shall find the letter. Observe his construction° of it. For this night, to bed, and dream   *interpretation* on the event.° Farewell.   *Exit.*   *outcome*

SIR TOBY   Good night, Penthesilea.[6]

SIR ANDREW   Before me,[7] she's a good wench.

SIR TOBY   She's a beagle true bred, and one that adores me. What o' that?

SIR ANDREW   I was adored once, too.

SIR TOBY   Let's to bed, knight. Thou hadst need send for more money.

SIR ANDREW   If I cannot recover° your niece, I am a foul   *win* way out.°   *out of money*

SIR TOBY   Send for money, knight. If thou hast her not i' th' end, call me "Cut."[8]

SIR ANDREW   If I do not, never trust me, take it how you will.

SIR TOBY   Come, come, I'll go burn some sack.[9] 'Tis too late to go to bed now. Come, knight; come, knight.

                                                          Exeunt.

---

4. Memorizes dignified and high-flown language and utters it in great sweeps (like hay falling under a scythe).
5. Having the highest opinion of himself.
6. Queen of the Amazons (a joke about Maria's small size).
7. On my soul (a mild oath).
8. A dock-tailed horse; also, slang term for a gelding or for female genitals.
9. I'll go warm and spice some Spanish wine.

2.4

Enter ORSINO, VIOLA, CURIO, *and others.*

ORSINO   Give me some music. Now good morrow,° friends. *morning*
 Now good Cesario, but° that piece of song, *just*
 That old and antique° song we heard last night. *quaint*
 Methought it did relieve my passion° much, *suffering*
5 More than light airs and recollected° terms *studied; artificial*
 Of these most brisk and giddy-pacèd times.
 Come, but one verse.
CURIO   He is not here, so please your lordship, that should
 sing it.
10 ORSINO   Who was it?
CURIO   Feste the jester, my lord, a fool that the Lady Oliv-
 ia's father took much delight in. He is about the house.
ORSINO   Seek him out, and play the tune the while.

          [*Exit* CURIO.]

 Music plays.
 [*to* VIOLA] Come hither, boy. If ever thou shalt love,
15 In the sweet pangs of it remember me,
 For such as I am, all true lovers are,
 Unstaid° and skittish in all motions° else *unstable / emotions*
 Save° in the constant image of the creature *except*
 That is beloved. How dost thou like this tune?
20 VIOLA   It gives a very echo to the seat
 Where love is throned.[1]
ORSINO   Thou dost speak masterly.° *expertly*
 My life upon't, young though thou art, thine eye
 Hath stayed upon some favor° that it loves. *face*
 Hath it not, boy?
VIOLA   A little, by your favor.° *leave; face*
ORSINO   What kind of woman is't?
25 VIOLA   Of your complexion.
ORSINO   She is not worth thee, then. What years, i' faith?
VIOLA   About your years, my lord.
ORSINO   Too old, by heaven. Let still° the woman take *always*
 An elder than herself. So wears° she to him; *adapts*
30 So sways she level[2] in her husband's heart.
 For, boy, however we do praise ourselves,
 Our fancies° are more giddy and unfirm, *affections*
 More longing, wavering, sooner lost and worn,° *exhausted*
 Than women's are.
VIOLA   I think° it well, my lord. *believe*
35 ORSINO   Then let thy love be younger than thyself,
 Or thy affection cannot hold the bent.[3]
 For women are as roses, whose fair flower,
 Being once displayed,° doth fall that very hour. *opened*

2.4 Location: Orsino's palace.
1. I.e., it reflects back to the heart.
2. So does she balance (influence and affection).

3. Cannot remain at full stretch (like the taut-
ness of a bowstring).

VIOLA   And so they are. Alas, that they are so,
40   To die even° when they to perfection grow!   *just*
        Enter CURIO *and* [FESTE, *the*] *clown.*
ORSINO   O, fellow, come, the song we had last night.—
        Mark it, Cesario. It is old and plain;
        The spinsters° and the knitters in the sun   *spinners*
        And the free° maids that weave their thread with bones[4]   *carefree*
45   Do use to chant it. It is silly sooth,°   *simple truth*
        And dallies with° the innocence of love   *lingers lovingly on*
        Like the old age.°   *i.e., the Golden Age*
FESTE   Are you ready, sir?
ORSINO   Ay, prithee, sing.
        Music
50   FESTE [*sings*] Come away,° come away, death,   *come hither*
                And in sad cypress[5] let me be laid.
            Fly away, fly away, breath,
                I am slain by a fair cruel maid.
            My shroud of white, stuck all with yew,°   *yew sprigs*
55   O prepare it.
            My part of death, no one so true
                Did share it.[6]

            Not a flower, not a flower sweet
                On my black coffin let there be strewn;
60   Not a friend, not a friend greet
                My poor corpse, where my bones shall be thrown.
            A thousand thousand sighs to save,°   *prevent*
                Lay me, O, where
            Sad true lover never find my grave,
65   To weep there.
ORSINO [*giving money*]   There's for thy pains.
FESTE   No pains, sir. I take pleasure in singing, sir.
ORSINO   I'll pay thy pleasure, then.
FESTE   Truly, sir, and pleasure will be paid,° one time or   *paid for*
70   another.
ORSINO   Give me now leave° to leave° thee.   *permission / dismiss*
FESTE   Now the melancholy god[7] protect thee, and the
        tailor make thy doublet of changeable taffeta,[8] for thy
        mind is a very opal.[9] I would have men of such constancy
75   put to sea, that their business might be everything and
        their intent° everywhere, for that's it that always makes   *destination*
        a good voyage of nothing.[1] Farewell.   *Exit*
ORSINO   Let all the rest give place.°   *withdraw*
        [*Exeunt all but* ORSINO *and* VIOLA.]
                Once more, Cesario,

4. Bobbins made from bone, used to weave lace
(called "bone lace").
5. Cypress-wood coffin. Like yews, cypresses
were emblematic of mourning.
6. I.e., no one has died so true to love as I.
7. Saturn (thought to control the melancholic).
8. Shot silk, whose color changes with the angle

of vision. "Doublet": a close-fitting jacket.
9. An iridescent gemstone that changes color
depending on the angle from which it is seen.
1. I.e., this fickle lack of direction can make a
voyage in the notoriously changeful sea carefree
and consonant with one's desires.

Get thee to yond same sovereign° cruelty.   *supreme*
80   Tell her my love, more noble than the world,
Prizes not quantity of dirty lands.
The parts° that fortune hath bestowed upon her,   *possessions*
Tell her, I hold as giddily² as fortune.
But 'tis that miracle and queen of gems
85   That nature pranks° her in attracts my soul.   *adorns*
VIOLA But if she cannot love you, sir—
ORSINO I cannot be so answered.
VIOLA   Sooth,° but you must.   *in truth*
Say that some lady, as perhaps there is,
Hath for your love as great a pang of heart
90   As you have for Olivia. You cannot love her;
You tell her so. Must she not then be answered?
ORSINO There is no woman's sides
Can bide° the beating of so strong a passion   *withstand*
As love doth give my heart; no woman's heart
95   So big, to hold so much; they lack retention.°   *constancy*
Alas, their love may be called appetite,
No motion° of the liver, but the palate,³   *impulse*
That suffer surfeit, cloyment,° and revolt;°   *satiety / revulsion*
But mine is all as hungry as the sea,
100   And can digest as much. Make no compare
Between that love a woman can bear me
And that I owe° Olivia.   *have for*
VIOLA Ay, but I know—
ORSINO What dost thou know?
105   VIOLA Too well what love women to men may owe.
In faith, they are as true of heart as we.
My father had a daughter loved a man
As it might be, perhaps, were I a woman,
I should your lordship.
ORSINO   And what's her history?
110   VIOLA A blank, my lord. She never told her love,
But let concealment, like a worm i' th' bud,
Feed on her damask⁴ cheek. She pined in thought,
And with a green and yellow° melancholy   *pale and sallow*
She sat like Patience on a monument,⁵
115   Smiling at grief. Was not this love indeed?
We men may say more, swear more, but indeed
Our shows are more than will;⁶ for still° we prove   *always*
Much in our vows but little in our love.
ORSINO But died thy sister of her love, my boy?
120   VIOLA I am all the daughters of my father's house,
And all the brothers, too—and yet I know not.
Sir, shall I to this lady?

2. Lightly (fortune being fickle).
3. Appetite, like the palate, is easily sated and thus lacks the emotional depth and complexity of real love, whose seat is the liver.
4. Pink and white, like a damask rose.
5. A memorial statue symbolizing patience.
6. Our displays of love are greater than our actual feelings.

ORSINO   Ay, that's the theme.
To her in haste. Give her this jewel. Say
My love can give no place, bide no denay.[7]

Exeunt [severally.]

2.5

Enter SIR TOBY, SIR ANDREW, *and* FABIAN.

SIR TOBY   Come thy ways,° Signior Fabian.   *come along*

FABIAN   Nay, I'll come. If I lose a scruple° of this sport, let   *miss a scrap*
me be boiled to death with melancholy.[1]

SIR TOBY   Wouldst thou not be glad to have the niggardly°   *stingy*
5   rascally sheep-biter[2] come by some notable shame?

FABIAN   I would exult, man. You know he brought me out
o' favor with my lady about a bearbaiting[3] here.

SIR TOBY   To anger him, we'll have the bear again, and we
will fool° him black and blue, shall we not, Sir Andrew?   *mock*

10 SIR ANDREW   An° we do not, it is pity of our lives.   *if*

Enter MARIA [*with a letter*].

SIR TOBY   Here comes the little villain.—How now, my metal
of India?[4]

MARIA   Get ye all three into the boxtree.° Malvolio's com-   *hedge of boxwood*
ing down this walk. He has been yonder i' the sun prac-
15 ticing behavior to his own shadow this half hour. Observe
him, for the love of mockery, for I know this letter will
make a contemplative° idiot of him. Close,° in the name   *vacuous / hide*
of jesting! [*The men hide*.] Lie thou there, [*putting down
the letter*] for here comes the trout that must be caught
20 with tickling.[5]   *Exit.*

Enter MALVOLIO.

MALVOLIO   'Tis but fortune, all is fortune. Maria once told
me she° did affect° me, and I have heard herself come   *Olivia / care for*
thus near, that should she fancy,° it should be one of my   *fall in love*
complexion. Besides, she uses me with a more exalted
25 respect than anyone else that follows her. What should I
think on't?

SIR TOBY   Here's an overweening° rogue.   *presumptuous*

FABIAN   O, peace! Contemplation makes a rare turkey-
cock[6] of him. How he jets° under his advanced° plumes!   *struts / raised*

30 SIR ANDREW   'Slight,[7] I could so beat the rogue!

SIR TOBY   Peace, I say.

MALVOLIO   To be Count Malvolio!

SIR TOBY   Ah, rogue!

---

7. My love cannot be bated, nor tolerate refusal.
2.5 Location: Olivia's garden.
1. Melancholy was a cold humor. "Boiled" puns
on "bile," the surplus of which produced melancholy.
2. Literally, a dog that attacks sheep; here, a
malicious sneak.
3. Puritans disapproved of blood sports like

bearbaiting.
4. A woman worth her weight in gold.
5. Flattery; trout can supposedly be caught by
stroking them under the gills.
6. Proverbially proud; they display their feathers
like peacocks.
7. By God's light (an oath).

SIR ANDREW	Pistol° him, pistol him!	*shoot*
35	SIR TOBY	Peace, peace!	
MALVOLIO	There is example° for't. The Lady of the Strachy married the yeoman of the wardrobe.[8]	*precedent*
SIR ANDREW	Fie on him, Jezebel![9]	
FABIAN	O, peace, now he's deeply in. Look how imagin-	
40		ation blows him.°	*puffs him up*
MALVOLIO	Having been three months married to her, sit-	
	ting in my state°—	*chair of state*
SIR TOBY	O, for a stone-bow,[1] to hit him in the eye!	
MALVOLIO	Calling my officers about me, in my branched[2]	
45		velvet gown, having come from a daybed,° where I have	*couch*
	left Olivia sleeping—	
SIR TOBY	Fire and brimstone!	
FABIAN	O, peace, peace!	
MALVOLIO	And then to have the humor of state;[3] and	
50		after a demure travel of regard,[4] telling them I know my	
	place, as I would they should do theirs, to ask for my	
	kinsman Toby—	
SIR TOBY	Bolts and shackles!	
FABIAN	O, peace, peace, peace! Now, now.	
55	MALVOLIO	Seven of my people, with an obedient start,	
	make° out for him. I frown the while, and perchance wind	*go*
	up my watch, or play with my[5]—some rich jewel. Toby	
	approaches; curtsies° there to me—	*bows*
SIR TOBY	Shall this fellow live?	
60	FABIAN	Though our silence be drawn from us with cars,[6]	
	yet peace.	
MALVOLIO	I extend my hand to him thus, quenching my	
	familiar smile with an austere regard° of control—	*look*
SIR TOBY	And does not Toby take° you a blow o' the lips	*give*
65		then?	
MALVOLIO	Saying "Cousin Toby, my fortunes, having cast	
	me on your niece, give me this prerogative of speech"—	
SIR TOBY	What, what?	
MALVOLIO	"You must amend your drunkenness."	
70	SIR TOBY	Out, scab!	
FABIAN	Nay, patience, or we break the sinews of our plot.	
MALVOLIO	"Besides, you waste the treasure of your time	
	with a foolish knight"—	
SIR ANDREW	That's me, I warrant you.	
75 | MALVOLIO | "One Sir Andrew." | |

8. Perhaps an allusion to a noblewoman who had married her manservant, but there is no certain identification. "Yeoman of the wardrobe": keeper of clothes and linen.
9. Biblical allusion to the proud wife of Ahab, king of Israel.
1. Catapult, or crossbow for stones.
2. Embroidered with branch patterns. "Officers": household attendants.

3. To adopt the grand air of exalted greatness.
4. After casting my eyes gravely about the room.
5. Evidently touching his steward's chain. Malvolio momentarily forgets that he will have abandoned his chain. "My watch": watches were an expensive luxury at this time.
6. A prisoner might be tied to two carts or chariots ("cars") and pulled by horses in opposite directions to extort information.

SIR ANDREW   I knew 'twas I, for many do call me fool.

MALVOLIO [*seeing the letter*]   What employment° have we   business
here?

FABIAN   Now is the woodcock near the gin.[7]

80   SIR TOBY   O, peace, and the spirit of humors intimate[8]
reading aloud to him.

MALVOLIO [*taking up the letter*]   By my life, this is my lady's
hand. These be her very *c*'s, her *u*'s, and her *t*'s,[9] and thus
makes she her great *P*'s. It is in contempt of° question   beyond

85   her hand.

SIR ANDREW   Her *c*'s, her *u*'s, and her *t*'s? Why that?

MALVOLIO [*reads*]   "To the unknown beloved, this, and my
good wishes."—Her very phrases! By your leave, wax.[1]
Soft.° And the impressure her Lucrece,[2] with which she   wait

90   uses to seal°—'tis my lady! [*He opens the letter.*] To whom   habitually seals
should this be?

FABIAN   This wins him, liver[3] and all.

MALVOLIO [*reads*]   "Jove knows I love,
But who?

95   Lips, do not move;
No man must know."
"No man must know." What follows? The numbers altered.°   meter changed
"No man must know." If this should be thee, Malvolio!

SIR TOBY   Marry, hang thee, brock![4]

100   MALVOLIO [*reads*]   "I may command where I adore,
But silence, like a Lucrece knife,[5]
With bloodless stroke my heart doth gore;
M.O.A.I. doth sway my life."

FABIAN   A fustian° riddle!   bombastic

105   SIR TOBY   Excellent wench, say I.

MALVOLIO   "M.O.A.I. doth sway my life." Nay, but first let
me see, let me see, let me see.

FABIAN   What dish o' poison has she dressed° him!   prepared

SIR TOBY   And with what wing the staniel checks at it![6]

110   MALVOLIO   "I may command where I adore." Why, she may
command me; I serve her, she is my lady. Why, this is
evident to any formal capacity.[7] There is no obstruction
in this. And the end—what should that alphabetical pos-
ition° portend? If I could make that resemble something   arrangement

115   in me! Softly! "M.O.A.I."—

SIR TOBY   O, ay,[8] make up that.—He is now at a cold scent.

7. Snare. The woodcock is a proverbially foolish
bird.
8. And may a capricious impulse suggest.
9. Malvolio unwittingly spells out "cut," slang
for female genitals; the meaning is compounded
by "great *P*'s." In fact, these letters do not appear
on the outside of the letter.
1. He addresses himself to the sealing wax.
2. The figure of Lucrece, Roman model of chastity, is the device ("impressure") imprinted on the

seal.
3. Thought of as the seat of love.
4. Badger (proverbially stinking).
5. After being raped, Lucretia stabbed herself to
death.
6. And with what alacrity the sparrow hawk
goes after it.
7. Normal intelligence.
8. Playing on "O.I."

FABIAN Sowter will cry upon't for all this, though° it be as   *as though*
rank as a fox.[9]

MALVOLIO "M"—Malvolio. "M"—why, that begins my name!

120 FABIAN Did not I say he would work it out? The cur is
excellent at faults.[1]

MALVOLIO "M." But then there is no consonancy in the
sequel.[2] That suffers under probation.[3] "A" should follow,
but "O" does.

125 FABIAN And "O"[4] shall end, I hope.

SIR TOBY Ay, or I'll cudgel him and make him cry "O."

MALVOLIO And then "I" comes behind.

FABIAN Ay, an you had any eye behind you, you might
see more detraction° at your heels than fortunes before   *defamation*
130 you.

MALVOLIO "M.O.A.I." This simulation° is not as the former,   *disguise; riddle*
and yet to crush° this a little, it would bow° to me, for *force / yield; point*
every one of these letters are in my name. Soft, here fol-
lows prose. [*He reads.*] "If this fall into thy hand, revolve.°   *consider*
135 In my stars° I am above thee, but be not afraid of greatness.   *fortunes*
Some are born great, some achieve greatness, and some
have greatness thrust upon 'em. Thy fates open their
hands.° Let thy blood and spirit embrace them. And, to   *bestow gifts*
inure° thyself to what thou art like° to be, cast thy humble *accustom / likely*
140 slough[5] and appear fresh. Be opposite° with a kinsman,   *contrary*
surly with servants. Let thy tongue tang arguments of
state.[6] Put thyself into the trick of singularity.[7] She thus
advises thee that sighs for thee. Remember who commended thy yellow stockings and wished to see thee ever
145 cross-gartered.[8] I say, remember. Go to,[9] thou art made, if
thou desirest to be so. If not, let me see thee a steward still,
the fellow of servants, and not worthy to touch Fortune's
fingers. Farewell. She that would alter services[1] with thee.
The Fortunate-Unhappy."
150 Daylight and champaign discovers[2] not more! This is
open.° I will be proud, I will read politic° authors, I will   *clear / political*
baffle[3] Sir Toby, I will wash off gross acquaintance,[4] I will
be point-device the very man.[5] I do not now fool myself,
to let imagination jade° me; for every reason excites to   *trick*
155 this, that my lady loves me. She did commend my yellow

---

9. "Sowter" (the name of a hound), having lost
the scent, will start to bay loudly as he picks up
the new, rank (stinking) smell of the fox.
1. At picking up a scent after it is momentarily
lost. A "fault" is a "cold scent" (line 116).
2. There is no consistency in what follows.
3. That weakens upon being put to the test.
4. As in the hangman's noose; the last letter of
Malvolio's name; or "O" as a lamentation.
5. A snake's old skin, which peels away.
6. Let your tongue ring out arguments of statecraft or politics.
7. Cultivate eccentricity.

8. An antiquated way of adjusting a garter—
going once below the knee, crossing behind it,
and knotting above the knee at the side.
9. An emphatic expression, like "I tell you."
1. Change places (of servant and mistress or
master).
2. Open countryside reveals.
3. Term used to describe the formal unmaking
of a knight; hence "disgrace."
4. Cease knowing persons of humble station.
5. I will be in every detail the identical man
(described in the letter).

stockings of late, she did praise my leg being cross-
gartered, and in this she manifests herself to my love and,
with a kind of injunction, drives me to these habits° of her   *clothes*
liking. I thank my stars, I am happy. I will be strange,°   *aloof*
160 stout,° in yellow stockings, and cross-gartered, even with   *proud*
the swiftness of putting on. Jove and my stars be praised!
Here is yet a postscript. [*He reads.*] "Thou canst not
choose but know who I am. If thou entertainest° my love,   *accept*
let it appear in thy smiling; thy smiles become thee well.
165 Therefore in my presence still° smile, dear my sweet, I   *constantly*
prithee." Jove, I thank thee. I will smile, I will do everything that thou wilt have me.   *Exit.*

FABIAN   I will not give my part of this sport for a pension
of thousands to be paid from the Sophy.°   *shah of Persia*
170 SIR TOBY   I could marry this wench for this device.
SIR ANDREW   So could I, too.
SIR TOBY   And ask no other dowry with her but such
another jest.
SIR ANDREW   Nor I neither.
     Enter MARIA.
175 FABIAN   Here comes my noble gull-catcher.°   *trickster*
SIR TOBY   Wilt thou set thy foot o' my neck?
SIR ANDREW   Or o' mine either?
SIR TOBY   Shall I play° my freedom at tray-trip[6] and become   *wager*
thy bondslave?
180 SIR ANDREW   I' faith, or I either?
SIR TOBY   Why, thou hast put him in such a dream that
when the image° of it leaves him he must run mad.   *illusion*
MARIA   Nay, but say true, does it work upon him?
SIR TOBY   Like aqua vitae° with a midwife.   *spirits, liquor*
185 MARIA   If you will then see the fruits of the sport, mark
his first approach before my lady. He will come to her in
yellow stockings, and 'tis a color she abhors, and cross-
gartered, a fashion she detests; and he will smile upon
her, which will now be so unsuitable to her disposition,
190 being addicted to a melancholy as she is, that it cannot
but turn him into a notable contempt.[7] If you will see it,
follow me.
SIR TOBY   To the gates of Tartar,° thou most excellent dev-   *hell*
il of wit!
195 SIR ANDREW   I'll make one,° too.   *Exeunt.*   *go along*

---

6. A game of dice in which the winner throws a   7. A notorious object of contempt.
three ("tray" is from the Spanish *tres*).

3.1

Enter VIOLA *and* [FESTE, *the*] *clown* [, *with pipe and tabor*].[1]

VIOLA Save° thee, friend, and thy music. Dost thou live   *God save*
by[2] thy tabor?

FESTE No, sir, I live by° the church.   *near*

VIOLA Art thou a churchman?

5 FESTE No such matter, sir. I do live by the church, for I
do live at my house, and my house doth stand by the
church.

VIOLA So thou mayst say the king lies by[3] a beggar if a
beggar dwell near him, or the church stands° by thy tabor   *is maintained*
10 if thy tabor stand by the church.

FESTE You have said, sir. To see this age! A sentence° is   *saying*
but a chev'ril° glove to a good wit. How quickly the wrong   *kidskin*
side may be turned outward!

VIOLA Nay, that's certain. They that dally nicely° with   *play subtly*
15 words may quickly make them wanton.[4]

FESTE I would therefore my sister had had no name, sir.

VIOLA Why, man?

FESTE Why, sir, her name's a word, and to dally with that
word might make my sister wanton. But, indeed, words
20 are very rascals since bonds disgraced them.[5]

VIOLA Thy reason, man?

FESTE Troth, sir, I can yield you none without words, and
words are grown so false I am loath to prove reason with
them.

25 VIOLA I warrant thou art a merry fellow and carest for
nothing.

FESTE Not so, sir. I do care for something. But in my conscience, sir, I do not care for you. If that be to care for
nothing, sir, I would° it would make you invisible.   *wish*

30 VIOLA Art not thou the Lady Olivia's fool?

FESTE No indeed, sir. The Lady Olivia has no folly. She
will keep no fool, sir, till she be married, and fools are as
like husbands as pilchards[6] are to herrings: the husband's
the bigger. I am indeed not her fool but her corrupter of
35 words.

VIOLA I saw thee late° at the Count Orsino's.   *lately*

FESTE Foolery, sir, does walk about the orb[7] like the sun;
it shines everywhere. I would be sorry, sir, but the fool
should be as oft with your master as with my mistress.[8] I
40 think I saw your wisdom[9] there.

3.1 Location: Olivia's garden.
1. The dialogue demands only a tabor, but jesters commonly played a pipe with one hand while
tapping a tabor (small drum, hanging from the
neck) with the other.
2. Do you earn your keep with?
3. Lives near; punning on "goes to bed with."
4. Equivocal: Viola puns on the sense "unchaste."
5. Since legal contracts replaced a man's word of

honor. ("Bonds" plays on "sworn statements" and
"fetters," betokening criminality.)
6. Small fish similar to herring.
7. World; the sun was still believed to circle the
earth.
8. Unless ("but") Feste should visit his foolery
upon others, but also unless Orsino should be
called "fool" as often as Olivia.
9. A mocking title for Cesario.

VIOLA   Nay, an thou pass upon[1] me, I'll° no more with thee.   *I'll engage*
  Hold, there's expenses for thee. [*giving a coin*]

FESTE   Now Jove in his next commodity° of hair send thee   *shipment*
  a beard!

45 VIOLA   By my troth I'll tell thee, I am almost sick for one,[2]
  [*aside*] though I would not have it grow on *my* chin.—Is
  thy lady within?

FESTE   Would not a pair of these have bred,[3] sir?

VIOLA   Yes, being kept together and put to use.[4]

50 FESTE   I would play Lord Pandarus[5] of Phrygia, sir, to bring
  a Cressida to this Troilus.

VIOLA   I understand you, sir. 'Tis well begged. [*giving another coin*]

FESTE   The matter I hope is not great, sir, begging but a
55 beggar: Cressida was a beggar.[6] My lady is within, sir. I
  will conster° to them whence you come. Who you are and   *explain*
  what you would are out of my welkin—I might say "element," but the word is overworn.[7]   *Exit.*

VIOLA   This fellow is wise enough to play the fool,
60 And to do that well craves° a kind of wit.°   *requires / intelligence*
  He must observe their mood on whom he jests,
  The quality° of persons, and the time,°   *character; rank / occasion*
  And, like the haggard, check at every feather
  That comes before his eye.[8] This is a practice°   *skill*
65 As full of labor as a wise man's art,
  For folly that he wisely shows is fit,[9]
  But wise men, folly-fall'n,° quite taint[1] their wit.   *fallen into folly*
    Enter SIR TOBY *and* SIR ANDREW.

SIR TOBY   Save you,[2] gentleman.

VIOLA   And you, sir.

70 SIR ANDREW   *Dieu vous garde, monsieur.*[3]

VIOLA   *Et vous aussi. Votre serviteur!*[4]

SIR ANDREW   I hope, sir, you are, and I am yours.

SIR TOBY   Will you encounter[5] the house? My niece is
  desirous you should enter, if your trade be to her.

75 VIOLA   I am bound to° your niece, sir; I mean, she is the   *for*
  list° of my voyage.   *destination*

SIR TOBY   Taste° your legs, sir; put them to motion.   *try*

---

1. If you express an opinion of; if you joke about.
2. Almost eager for a beard; almost pining for a man (Orsino).
3. Would not a pair of coins such as these have multiplied (with possible pun on "be enough to buy bread").
4. Invested to produce interest.
5. Go-between or "pander," because Feste needs a "mate" for his coin(s). Shakespeare dramatizes the story in *Troilus and Cressida*.
6. In asking for the "mate" to his Troilus coin, Feste draws on a version of the story of Troilus and Cressida in which Cressida became a leprous beggar.

7. "Welkin" (sky or air) is synonymous with one meaning of "element," used in what Feste regards as the overworn phrase "out of my element."
8. I.e., as a wild hawk ("haggard") must be sensitive to its prey's disposition.
9. For folly that he skillfully displays is proper.
1. Discredit; spoil.
2. I.e., God save you.
3. God protect you, sir (French).
4. And you also, (I am) your servant. (Sir Andrew's awkward reply demonstrates that his French is limited.)
5. Pedantry for "enter" (Sir Toby mocks Viola's courtly language).

VIOLA My legs do better understand° me, sir, than I under-   *stand under*
stand what you mean by bidding me taste my legs.

80 SIR TOBY I mean, to go, sir, to enter.

VIOLA I will answer you with gait and entrance.
   Enter OLIVIA, *and* [MARIA, *her*] *gentlewoman.*
But we are prevented.° Most excellent accomplished lady,   *anticipated*
the heavens rain odors on you!

SIR ANDREW [*to* SIR TOBY] That youth's a rare° courtier.   *an excellent*
85 "Rain odors," well.°   *well put*

VIOLA My matter hath no voice,° lady, but to your own   *must not be spoken*
most pregnant° and vouchsafed° ear.   *receptive / proffered*

SIR ANDREW [*to* SIR TOBY] "Odors," "pregnant," and
"vouchsafed." I'll get 'em all three all ready.[6]

90 OLIVIA Let the garden door be shut, and leave me to my
hearing.   [*Exeunt* SIR TOBY, SIR ANDREW, *and* MARIA.]
Give me your hand, sir.

VIOLA My duty, madam, and most humble service.

OLIVIA What is your name?

95 VIOLA Cesario is your servant's name, fair princess.

OLIVIA My servant, sir? 'Twas never merry world[7]
Since lowly feigning° was called compliment.   *pretended humility*
You're servant to the Count Orsino, youth.

VIOLA And he is yours, and his must needs be yours.
100 Your servant's servant is *your* servant, madam.

OLIVIA For° him, I think not on him. For his thoughts,   *as for*
Would they were blanks rather than filled with me.

VIOLA Madam, I come to whet your gentle thoughts
On his behalf.

OLIVIA   O, by your leave,[8] I pray you.
105 I bade you never speak again of him;
But would you undertake another suit,
I had rather hear you to solicit that
Than music from the spheres.[9]

VIOLA   Dear lady—

OLIVIA Give me leave, beseech you. I did send,
110 After the last enchantment you did here,
A ring in chase of you. So did I abuse°   *deceive; dishonor*
Myself, my servant, and, I fear me, you.°   *and, as I fear, you*
Under your hard construction[1] must I sit,
To force° that on you in a shameful cunning   *for forcing*
115 Which you knew none of yours. What might you think?
Have you not set mine honor at the stake,
And baited it with all th' unmuzzled thoughts[2]
That tyrannous heart can think? To one of your receiving°   *perception*

6. I.e., to commit to memory for later use.
7. The proverbial "Things have never been the same."
8. Permit me to interrupt (polite expression).
9. Exquisite music thought to be made by the planets as they moved, but inaudible to mortal ears.
1. Your unfavorable interpretation (of my behavior).
2. As bears that were tied up at the stake and baited with dogs.

Enough is shown. A cypress,[3] not a bosom,
120 Hides my heart. So let me hear you speak.
VIOLA I pity you.
OLIVIA   That's a degree to° love.   *toward*
VIOLA No, not a grize,° for 'tis a vulgar proof°   *step / common experience*
That very oft we pity enemies.
OLIVIA Why then methinks 'tis time to smile again.[4]
125 O world, how apt° the poor are to be proud!   *ready*
If one should be a prey, how much the better
To fall before the lion than the wolf.[5]
        Clock strikes.
The clock upbraids° me with the waste of time.   *reproaches*
Be not afraid, good youth, I will not have you.
130 And yet when wit and youth is come to harvest,
Your wife is like to reap a proper° man.   *handsome; worthy*
There lies your way, due west.
VIOLA   Then westward ho![6]
Grace and good disposition° attend your ladyship.   *peace of mind*
You'll nothing, madam, to my lord by me?
135 OLIVIA Stay. I prithee, tell me what thou[7] think'st of me.
VIOLA That you do think you are not what you are.[8]
OLIVIA If I think so, I think the same of you.[9]
VIOLA Then think you right. I am not what I am.
OLIVIA I would you were as I would have you be.
140 VIOLA Would it be better, madam, than I am?
I wish it might, for now I am your fool.[1]
OLIVIA [aside] O, what a deal of scorn looks beautiful
In the contempt and anger of his lip!
A murd'rous guilt shows not itself more soon
145 Than love that would seem hid. Love's night is noon.[2]—
Cesario, by the roses of the spring,
By maidhood, honor, truth, and everything,
I love thee so, that, maugre° all thy pride,   *despite*
Nor° wit nor reason can my passion hide.   *neither*
150 Do not extort thy reasons from this clause,
For that° I woo, thou therefore hast no cause;[3]   *that because*
But rather reason thus with reason fetter:[4]
Love sought is good, but given unsought is better.
VIOLA By innocence I swear, and by my youth,
155 I have one heart, one bosom, and one truth,

---

3. Veil of transparent silken gauze; the cypress tree was also emblematic of mourning.
4. Time to discard love's melancholy.
5. I.e., if I had to fall prey to love, it would have been better to succumb to the noble Orsino than to the hardhearted Cesario.
6. Thames watermen's cry to attract London passengers for the court at Westminster.
7. Olivia changes from "you" to the familiar "thou."
8. That you think you are in love with a man, but you are mistaken.

9. Olivia may think that Cesario has suggested that she is mad; or she may mean to imply that she thinks that Cesario, despite his subordinate position, is noble.
1. You have made a fool of me.
2. Love, though attempting secrecy, still shines out as bright as day.
3. Do not take the position that just because I woo you, you are under no obligation to reciprocate.
4. But instead constrain your reasoning with this argument.

And that no woman has, nor never none
Shall mistress be of it, save I alone.
And so adieu, good madam. Nevermore
Will I my master's tears to you deplore.°   *lament*
160   OLIVIA   Yet come again, for thou perhaps mayst move
That heart, which now abhors, to like his love.
                                Exeunt [severally].

3.2

Enter SIR TOBY, SIR ANDREW, *and* FABIAN.

SIR ANDREW   No, faith, I'll not stay a jot longer.
SIR TOBY   Thy reason, dear venom,° give thy reason.   *venomous one*
FABIAN   You must needs yield your reason, Sir Andrew.
SIR ANDREW   Marry, I saw your niece do more favors to
5   the Count's servingman than ever she bestowed upon me.
    I saw't i' th' orchard.°   *garden*
SIR TOBY   Did she see thee the while,° old boy? Tell me that.   *meanwhile*
SIR ANDREW   As plain as I see you now.
FABIAN   This was a great argument° of love in her toward   *proof*
10   you.
SIR ANDREW   'Slight,° will you make an ass o' me?   *by God's light*
FABIAN   I will prove it legitimate, sir, upon the oaths of
    judgment and reason.
SIR TOBY   And they have been grand-jurymen[1] since before
15   Noah was a sailor.
FABIAN   She did show favor to the youth in your sight only
    to exasperate you, to awake your dormouse° valor, to put   *meek, timid*
    fire in your heart and brimstone in your liver. You should
    then have accosted her, and with some excellent jests,
20   fire-new from the mint,° you should have banged the   *newly minted*
    youth into dumbness. This was looked for at your hand,
    and this was balked.° The double gilt[2] of this opportunity   *neglected*
    you let time wash off, and you are now sailed into the
    north of my lady's opinion,[3] where you will hang like an
25   icicle on a Dutchman's[4] beard, unless you do redeem it
    by some laudable attempt either of valor or policy.°   *cunning*
SIR ANDREW   An't° be any way, it must be with valor, for   *if it*
    policy I hate. I had as lief° be a Brownist as a politician.[5]   *as soon*
SIR TOBY   Why then, build me thy fortunes upon the basis
30   of valor. Challenge me° the Count's youth to fight with   *for me*
    him. Hurt him in eleven places. My niece shall take note
    of it, and assure thyself, there is no love-broker in the
    world can more prevail in man's commendation with
    woman than report of valor.

3.2 Location: Olivia's house.
1. Grand-jurymen were supposed to be good judges of evidence.
2. Twice gilded and, as such, Sir Andrew's "golden opportunity" to prove both love and valor.

3. Into Olivia's cold disfavor.
4. Perhaps an allusion to William Barentz, who led an expedition to the Arctic in 1596–97.
5. Schemer. A Brownist was a member of the Puritan sect founded in 1581 by Robert Browne.

35 FABIAN There is no way but this, Sir Andrew.

SIR ANDREW Will either of you bear me a challenge to him?

SIR TOBY Go, write it in a martial hand. Be curst° and brief.   *sharp*
It is no matter how witty, so it be eloquent and full of
invention.[6] Taunt him with the license of ink.[7] If thou

40 "thou'st"[8] him some thrice, it shall not be amiss, and as
many lies[9] as will lie in thy sheet of paper, although the
sheet were big enough for the bed of Ware[1] in England,
set 'em down. Go, about it. Let there be gall[2] enough in
thy ink, though thou write with a goose-pen,[3] no matter.

45 About it.

SIR ANDREW Where shall I find you?

SIR TOBY We'll call thee at the cubiculo.° Go.   *little chamber*

Exit SIR ANDREW.

FABIAN This is a dear manikin° to you, Sir Toby.   *puppet*

SIR TOBY I have been dear° to him, lad, some two thousand   *costly*

50 strong, or so.

FABIAN We shall have a rare letter from him. But you'll not
deliver't?

SIR TOBY Never trust me, then. And by all means stir on
the youth to an answer. I think oxen and wainropes[4]

55 cannot hale° them together. For Andrew, if he were opened   *drag*
and you find so much blood in his liver[5] as will clog° the   *weigh down*
foot of a flea, I'll eat the rest of th' anatomy.°   *cadaver*

FABIAN And his opposite,° the youth, bears in his visage   *adversary*
no great presage° of cruelty.   *indication*

Enter MARIA.

60 SIR TOBY Look where the youngest wren of nine[6] comes.

MARIA If you desire the spleen,° and will laugh yourselves   *a laughing fit*
into stitches, follow me. Yond gull° Malvolio is turned hea-   *dupe*
then, a very renegado;[7] for there is no Christian that
means to be saved by believing rightly can ever believe

65 such impossible passages of grossness.[8] He's in yellow
stockings.

SIR TOBY And cross-gartered?

MARIA Most villainously,° like a pedant[9] that keeps a   *abominably*
school i' th' church.[1] I have dogged him like his murderer.

70 He does obey every point of the letter that I dropped to
betray him. He does smile his face into more lines than
is in the new map with the augmentation of the Indies.[2]

---

6. Imagination; untruth.
7. I.e., with the freedom taken in writing but not risked in conversation.
8. Call him "thou" (an insult, to a stranger).
9. Accusations of lying.
1. Famous Elizabethan bedstead, nearly eleven feet square, now in the Victoria and Albert Museum, London.
2. (1) Oak gall, an ingredient in ink; (2) bitterness or rancor.
3. Quill made of a goose feather. (The goose was proverbially cowardly and foolish.)
4. Wagon ropes pulled by oxen.

5. Supposed to be the source of blood, which engendered courage.
6. The smallest of small birds; the smallest wren in a family of nine.
7. Renegade (Spanish); a Christian converted to Islam.
8. Such patent absurdities (in the letter).
9. Teacher.
1. Because no schoolroom is available in a small rustic community.
2. Possibly refers to a map published in 1599 showing the East Indies more fully than in earlier maps and crisscrossed by many rhumb lines.

You have not seen such a thing as 'tis. I can hardly forbear
hurling things at him. I know my lady will strike him. If
75   she do, he'll smile and take't for a great favor.
SIR TOBY   Come, bring us, bring us where he is.   *Exeunt.*

3.3

Enter SEBASTIAN *and* ANTONIO.
SEBASTIAN   I would not by my will have troubled you,
  But, since you make your pleasure of your pains,
  I will no further chide you.
ANTONIO   I could not stay behind you. My desire,
5   More sharp than filèd steel, did spur me forth;
  And not all° love to see you—though so much   *only*
  As might have drawn one to a longer voyage—
  But jealousy° what might befall your travel,   *apprehension*
  Being skill-less in° these parts, which to a stranger,   *unfamiliar to*
10   Unguided and unfriended, often prove
  Rough and unhospitable. My willing love,
  The rather° by these arguments of fear,   *more willingly*
  Set forth in your pursuit.
SEBASTIAN   My kind Antonio,
  I can no other answer make but thanks,
15   And thanks, and ever oft° good turns   *very often*
  Are shuffled off° with such uncurrent[1] pay.   *shrugged off*
  But were my worth,° as is my conscience,° firm, *wealth / sense of indebtedness*
  You should find better dealing. What's to do?
  Shall we go see the relics° of this town?   *sights*
20 ANTONIO   Tomorrow, sir. Best first go see your lodging.
SEBASTIAN   I am not weary, and 'tis long to night.
  I pray you let us satisfy our eyes
  With the memorials and the things of fame
  That do renown this city.
ANTONIO   Would you'd pardon me.
25   I do not without danger walk these streets.
  Once in a sea fight 'gainst the Count his° galleys   *i.e., the Count's*
  I did some service, of such note indeed
  That were I ta'en° here it would scarce be answered.[2]   *captured*
SEBASTIAN   Belike° you slew great number of his people?   *perhaps*
30 ANTONIO   Th' offense is not of such a bloody nature,
  Albeit° the quality° of the time and quarrel   *although / circumstances*
  Might well have given us bloody argument.°   *cause for bloodshed*
  It might have since been answered in repaying
  What we took from them, which, for traffic's° sake,   *trade's*
35   Most of our city did. Only myself stood out,°   *i.e., made no reparation*
  For which if I be latchèd° in this place,   *caught*
  I shall pay dear.

3.3 Location: A street scene.
1. Out of currency; worthless.

2. It would be difficult for me to make reparation (and thus my life would be in danger).

SEBASTIAN   Do not then walk too open.

ANTONIO   It doth not fit me.° Hold, sir, here's my purse.   *serve me well*
     In the south suburbs at the Elephant°   *name of an inn*
40   Is best to lodge. I will bespeak our diet°   *order our meals*
     Whiles you beguile° the time and feed your knowledge   *pass*
     With viewing of the town. There shall you have me.

SEBASTIAN   Why I your purse?

ANTONIO   Haply° your eye shall light upon some toy°   *perhaps / trifle*
45   You have desire to purchase, and your store,°   *resources*
     I think, is not for idle markets,³ sir.

SEBASTIAN   I'll be your purse-bearer and leave you
     For an hour.

ANTONIO   To th' Elephant.

SEBASTIAN   I do remember.

                              Exeunt [severally].

                              3.4

          Enter OLIVIA *and* MARIA.

OLIVIA [*aside*]   I have sent after° him. He says he'll come.   *for*
     How shall I feast him? What bestow of° him?   *on*
     For youth is bought more oft than begged or borrowed.¹
     I speak too loud.—
5   [*to* MARIA] Where's Malvolio? He is sad° and civil°   *sober / respectful*
     And suits well for a servant with my fortunes.
     Where is Malvolio?

MARIA   He's coming, madam, but in very strange manner.
     He is sure possessed,° madam.   *(by the devil); insane*

10   OLIVIA   Why, what's the matter? Does he rave?

MARIA   No, madam, he does nothing but smile. Your lady-
     ship were best to have some guard about you if he come,
     for sure the man is tainted in's wits.

OLIVIA   Go call him hither.   [*Exit* MARIA.]
                    I am as mad as he,
15   If sad and merry madness equal be.
          *Enter [*MARIA *with*] MALVOLIO [*cross-gartered and*
          wearing yellow stockings].*
     How now, Malvolio?

MALVOLIO   Sweet lady, ho, ho!

OLIVIA   Smil'st thou? I sent for thee upon a sad occasion.°   *a serious matter*

MALVOLIO   Sad, lady? I could be sad. This does make some
20   obstruction in the blood,² this cross-gartering, but what
     of that? If it please the eye of one, it is with me as the
     very true sonnet° is: "Please one, and please all."³   *song*

OLIVIA   Why, how dost thou, man? What is the matter with
     thee?

---

3. Not large enough to spend on luxuries.
3.4 Location: The garden of Olivia's house.
1. Alluding to the proverb "Better to buy than to beg or borrow."

2. Restrict circulation.
3. If I please one, I please all I care to please (words of a popular bawdy ballad).

25 MALVOLIO Not black in my mind, though yellow[4] in my
legs. It did come to his hands, and commands shall be
executed. I think we do know the sweet Roman hand.°   *italic calligraphy*

OLIVIA Wilt thou go to bed,[5] Malvolio?

MALVOLIO [*kissing his hand*] To bed? "Ay, sweetheart,
30 and I'll come to thee."[6]

OLIVIA God comfort thee! Why dost thou smile so, and kiss
thy hand so oft?[7]

MARIA How do you, Malvolio?

MALVOLIO At your request? Yes, nightingales answer daws![8]

35 MARIA Why appear you with this ridiculous boldness
before my lady?

MALVOLIO "Be not afraid of greatness." 'Twas well writ.

OLIVIA What meanest thou by that, Malvolio?

MALVOLIO "Some are born great"—

40 OLIVIA Ha?

MALVOLIO "Some achieve greatness"—

OLIVIA What sayst thou?

MALVOLIO "And some have greatness thrust upon them."

OLIVIA Heaven restore thee!

45 MALVOLIO "Remember who commended thy yellow stockings"—

OLIVIA Thy yellow stockings?

MALVOLIO "And wished to see thee cross-gartered."

OLIVIA Cross-gartered?

50 MALVOLIO "Go to, thou art made, if thou desirest to be
so"—

OLIVIA Am I made?

MALVOLIO "If not, let me see thee a servant still."

OLIVIA Why, this is very midsummer° madness!   *the height of*

Enter a SERVANT.

55 SERVANT Madam, the young gentleman of the Count
Orsino's is returned. I could hardly entreat him back.
He attends your ladyship's pleasure.

OLIVIA I'll come to him.   [*Exit* SERVANT.]
Good Maria, let this fellow be looked to. Where's my
60 cousin Toby? Let some of my people have a special care
of him. I would not have him miscarry° for the half of my   *come to harm*
dowry.

[*Exeunt* OLIVIA *and* MARIA, *severally.*]

MALVOLIO O ho, do you come near° me now? No worse   *appreciate*
man than Sir Toby to look to me. This concurs directly
65 with the letter. She sends him on purpose that I may
appear stubborn to him, for she incites me to that in the

---

4. Black and yellow biles indicated choleric and
melancholic dispositions, respectively. "Black and
yellow" was the name of a popular song; to "wear
yellow hose" was to be jealous.
5. I.e., to cure his madness with sleep.

6. A line from a popular song.
7. I.e., why do you keep blowing me kisses?
8. Shall I deign to reply to you? Yes, because
even the nightingale sings in response to the
crowing of the jackdaw.

letter: "Cast thy humble slough," says she. "Be opposite with a kinsman, surly with servants; let thy tongue tang with arguments of state; put thyself into the trick of sin-
70 gularity," and consequently° sets down the manner how: *subsequently*
as, a sad face, a reverend carriage, a slow tongue, in the habit of some sir of note,° and so forth. I have limed[9] her,   *gentleman*
but it is Jove's doing, and Jove make me thankful! And when she went away now, "Let this fellow be looked to."
75 "Fellow."[1] Not "Malvolio," nor after my degree, but "fel-low." Why, everything adheres together, that no dram of a scruple, no scruple of a scruple,[2] no obstacle, no incred-ulous or unsafe circumstance[3]—what can be said? Nothing that can be can come between me and the full
80 prospect of my hopes. Well, Jove, not I, is the doer of this, and he is to be thanked.

    Enter SIR TOBY, FABIAN, *and* MARIA.

SIR TOBY   Which way is he, in the name of sanctity? If all the devils of hell be drawn in little,[4] and Legion[5] himself possessed him, yet I'll speak to him.

85 FABIAN   Here he is, here he is.—How is't with you, sir? How is't with you, man?

MALVOLIO   Go off, I discard you. Let me enjoy my private.°   *privacy*
Go off.

MARIA [*to* SIR TOBY]   Lo, how hollow° the fiend speaks   *resonantly*
90 within him! Did not I tell you? Sir Toby, my lady prays you to have a care of him.

MALVOLIO   Aha, does she so?

SIR TOBY   Go to, go to! Peace, peace. We must deal gently with him. Let me alone.°—How do you, Malvolio? How   *leave him to me*
95 is't with you? What, man, defy° the devil! Consider, he's   *renounce*
an enemy to mankind.

MALVOLIO   Do you know what you say?

MARIA   La° you, an° you speak ill of the devil, how he   *look / if*
takes it at heart! Pray God he be not bewitched!

100 FABIAN   Carry his water to th' wise woman.[6]

MARIA   Marry, and it shall be done tomorrow morning if I live. My lady would not lose him for more than I'll say.

MALVOLIO   How now, mistress?

MARIA   O Lord!

105 SIR TOBY   Prithee, hold thy peace. This is not the way. Do you not see you move° him? Let me alone with him.   *anger*

FABIAN   No way but gentleness, gently, gently. The fiend is rough° and will not be roughly used.   *violent*

---

9. Birds were caught by smearing sticky bird-lime on branches.
1. Malvolio takes the word to mean "companion."
2. Both phrases mean "no scrap of a doubt." "Dram": one-eighth of a fluid ounce. "Scruple": one-third of a dram.
3. Dubious or unreliable indication.
4. Be contracted into a small space (punning on

"painted in miniature").
5. Alluding to a scene of exorcism in Mark 5.8–9: "For he [Jesus] said unto him, Come out of the man, thou unclean spirit. And he asked him, What is thy name? And he answered saying, My name is Legion: for we are many."
6. Local healer, "good witch." "Water": urine (for medical diagnosis).

SIR TOBY Why, how now, my bawcock?[7] How dost thou,
chuck?[8]

MALVOLIO Sir!

SIR TOBY Ay, biddy,° come with me.—What, man, 'tis not   *hen*
for gravity to play at cherry-pit[9] with Satan. Hang him,
foul collier![1]

MARIA Get him to say his prayers, good Sir Toby; get him
to pray.

MALVOLIO My prayers, minx?°   *impertinent girl*

MARIA No, I warrant you, he will not hear of godliness.

MALVOLIO Go hang yourselves all! You are idle,° shallow   *foolish*
things. I am not of your element.° You shall know more   *social sphere*
hereafter.   *Exit.*

SIR TOBY Is't possible?

FABIAN If this were played upon a stage now, I could condemn it as an improbable fiction.

SIR TOBY His very genius° hath taken the infection of the   *spirit*
device,° man.   *trick*

MARIA Nay, pursue him now, lest the device take air and
taint.[2]

FABIAN Why, we shall make him mad indeed.

MARIA The house will be the quieter.

SIR TOBY Come, we'll have him in a dark room and bound.[3]
My niece is already in the belief that he's mad. We may
carry it thus,[4] for our pleasure and his penance, till our
very pastime, tired out of breath, prompt us to have mercy
on him, at which time we will bring the device to the bar[5]
and crown thee for a finder of madmen.[6] But see, but see!
        Enter SIR ANDREW.

FABIAN More matter for a May morning.[7]

SIR ANDREW [*presenting a paper*] Here's the challenge.
Read it. I warrant there's vinegar and pepper in't.

FABIAN Is't so saucy?

SIR ANDREW Ay, is't? I warrant him. Do but read.

SIR TOBY Give me. [*He reads.*] "Youth, whatsoever thou art,
thou art but a scurvy fellow."

FABIAN Good, and valiant.

SIR TOBY, "Wonder not, nor admire° not in thy mind, why   *marvel*
I do call thee so, for I will show thee no reason for't."

FABIAN A good note, that keeps you from the blow of the
law.[8]

---

7. Fine fellow (from the French *beau coq*, "fine
bird").
8. A term of endearment, perhaps from *chick*,
chicken.
9. A children's game in which cherry stones
were thrown into a hole. "For gravity": i.e., for a
man of dignity.
1. Dirty coalman (the devil was supposed to be
black).
2. Spoil (like leftover food) by exposure to air;

become known (and thus ruined).
3. Customary treatments for madness.
4. Continue the pretense.
5. Into the open court (to be judged).
6. I.e., one of a jury "finding," or declaring, a man
to be mad.
7. More pastime fit for a holiday.
8. That protects you from a charge of a breach of
peace.

SIR TOBY "Thou comest to the Lady Olivia, and in my sight
150 she uses thee kindly. But thou liest in thy throat;° that is   *deeply*
not the matter I challenge thee for."
FABIAN Very brief, and to exceeding good sense—
less.[9]
SIR TOBY "I will waylay thee going home, where if it be thy
155 chance to kill me"—
FABIAN Good.
SIR TOBY "Thou killest me like a rogue and a villain."
FABIAN Still you keep o' th' windy side[1] of the law. Good.
SIR TOBY "Fare thee well, and God have mercy upon one
160 of our souls. He may have mercy upon mine, but my hope
is better,[2] and so look to thyself. Thy friend, as thou
usest him, and thy sworn enemy,
                                    Andrew Aguecheek."
If this letter move° him not, his legs cannot. I'll give't him.   *provoke*
165 MARIA You may have very fit occasion for't. He is now in
some commerce° with my lady, and will by and by depart.   *conversation*
SIR TOBY Go, Sir Andrew. Scout me° for him at the corner   *look out*
of the orchard like a bum-baily.[3] So soon as ever thou
seest him, draw, and as thou drawest, swear horrible, for
170 it comes to pass oft that a terrible oath, with a swaggering
accent sharply twanged off, gives manhood more appro-
bation° than ever proof° itself would have earned him.   *credit / trial*
Away!
SIR ANDREW Nay, let me alone for swearing.[4]   *Exit.*
175 SIR TOBY Now will not I deliver his letter, for the behavior
of the young gentleman gives him out to be of good
capacity and breeding;[5] his employment between his
lord and my niece confirms no less. Therefore, this letter, being so excellently ignorant, will breed no terror in
180 the youth. He will find it comes from a clodpoll.° But,   *blockhead*
sir, I will deliver his challenge by word of mouth, set
upon Aguecheek a notable report of valor, and drive
the gentleman—as I know his youth will aptly receive
it[6]—into a most hideous opinion of his rage, skill, fury,
185 and impetuosity. This will so fright them both that they
will kill one another by the look, like cockatrices.[7]
        Enter OLIVIA *and* VIOLA
FABIAN Here he comes with your niece. Give them way°   *stand aside*
till he take leave, and presently after him.
SIR TOBY I will meditate the while upon some horrid mes-
190 sage for a challenge.
        [*Exeunt* SIR TOBY, FABIAN, *and* MARIA.]

---

9. The Folio's "sence-lesse" appears to use the
hyphen to signal an aside.
1. Downwind of the law—on the safe side of it.
2. Sir Andrew means he expects to survive, but
he ineptly implies that he expects to be damned.
3. Petty sheriff's officer employed to arrest debtors.

4. Have no doubts as to my swearing ability.
5. Upbringing. "Capacity": ability.
6. As I know his inexperience will readily believe
the report.
7. Basilisks; mythical creatures supposed to kill
at a glance.

OLIVIA I have said too much unto a heart of stone
And laid mine honor too unchary° on't.   *carelessly*
There's something in me that reproves my fault,
But such a headstrong potent fault it is
195   That it but mocks reproof.
VIOLA With the same 'havior that your passion bears[8]
Goes on my master's griefs.
OLIVIA Here, wear this jewel[9] for me. 'Tis my picture.
Refuse it not, it hath no tongue to vex you.
200   And I beseech you come again tomorrow.
What shall you ask of me that I'll deny,
That honor, saved, may upon asking give?[1]
VIOLA Nothing but this: your true love for my master.
OLIVIA How with mine honor may I give him that
Which I have given to you?
205   VIOLA   I will acquit you.[2]
OLIVIA Well, come again tomorrow. Fare thee well.
A fiend like thee might bear my soul to hell.   [*Exit.*]
          Enter [SIR] TOBY *and* FABIAN.
SIR TOBY Gentleman, God save thee.
VIOLA And you, sir.
210   SIR TOBY That defense thou hast, betake thee to't. Of what
nature the wrongs are thou hast done him, I know not,
but thy intercepter, full of despite,° bloody as the hunter,   *defiance*
attends° thee at the orchard end. Dismount thy tuck,[3] be   *awaits*
yare° in thy preparation, for thy assailant is quick, skillful,   *prompt*
215   and deadly.
VIOLA You mistake, sir, I am sure no man hath any quarrel
to me. My remembrance° is very free and clear from any   *memory*
image of offense done to any man.
SIR TOBY You'll find it otherwise, I assure you. Therefore,
220   if you hold your life at any price, betake you to your guard,
for your opposite° hath in him what youth, strength, skill,   *opponent*
and wrath can furnish man withal.
VIOLA I pray you, sir, what is he?
SIR TOBY He is knight dubbed with unhatched[4] rapier and
225   on carpet consideration,[5] but he is a devil in private
brawl. Souls and bodies hath he divorced three, and his
incensement° at this moment is so implacable that satis-   *anger*
faction can be none but by pangs of death and sepulcher.
"Hob, nob"[6] is his word;° "give't or take't."   *motto*
230   VIOLA I will return again into the house and desire some
conduct° of the lady. I am no fighter. I have heard of some   *escort*
kind of men that put quarrels purposely on others, to
taste° their valor. Belike this is a man of that quirk.   *test*

---

8. Behavior that characterizes your lovesickness.
9. Jeweled ornament, here a brooch or a locket
with Olivia's picture.
1. That honor may grant without compromising
itself.
2. I will release you from your promise.

3. Draw your rapier.
4. Unhacked, or undented, never used in battle.
5. A "carpet knight" obtained his title through
connections at court rather than valor on the
battlefield.
6. Have or have not ("all or nothing").

SIR TOBY   Sir, no. His indignation derives itself out of a very
competent° injury. Therefore get you on and give him his   *sufficient*
desire. Back you shall not to the house, unless you under-
take that° with me which with as much safety you might   *i.e., a duel*
answer him. Therefore on, or strip your sword stark
naked, for meddle° you must, that's certain, or forswear   *engage in a duel*
to wear iron about you.[7]

VIOLA   This is as uncivil as strange. I beseech you, do me
this courteous office, as to know of° the knight what my   *ascertain from*
offense to him is. It is something of my negligence, noth-
ing of my purpose.[8]

SIR TOBY   I will do so.—Signior Fabian, stay you by this
gentleman till my return.   *Exit.*

VIOLA   Pray you, sir, do you know of this matter?

FABIAN   I know the knight is incensed against you even to
a mortal arbitrement,° but nothing of the circumstance   *deadly duel*
more.

VIOLA   I beseech you, what manner of man is he?

FABIAN   Nothing of that wonderful promise, to read him by
his form,[9] as you are like to find him in the proof° of his   *experience*
valor. He is indeed, sir, the most skillful, bloody, and fatal
opposite° that you could possibly have found in any part   *opponent*
of Illyria. Will you° walk towards him, I will make your   *if you will*
peace with him if I can.

VIOLA   I shall be much bound to you for't. I am one that
had rather go with Sir Priest[1] than Sir Knight, I care not
who knows so much of my mettle.°   *Exeunt.*   *disposition*

Enter SIR TOBY *and* SIR ANDREW

SIR TOBY   Why, man, he's a very devil. I have not seen such
a virago.[2] I had a pass° with him, rapier, scabbard, and   *fencing bout*
all, and he gives me the stuck-in[3] with such a mortal
motion that it is inevitable; and on the answer,° he pays   *return hit*
you as surely as your feet hits the ground they step on.
They say he has been fencer to the Sophy.°   *shah of Persia*

SIR ANDREW   Pox on't! I'll not meddle with him.

SIR TOBY   Ay, but he will not now be pacified. Fabian can
scarce hold him yonder.

SIR ANDREW   Plague on't! An° I thought he had been vali-   *if*
ant and so cunning in fence, I'd have seen him damned
ere I'd have challenged him. Let him let the matter slip,
and I'll give him my horse, gray Capilet.

SIR TOBY   I'll make the motion.° Stand here, make a good   *offer*
show on't. This shall end without the perdition of souls.°   *loss of lives*
[*aside*] Marry, I'll ride your horse as well as I ride you.

Enter FABIAN *and* VIOLA.

---

7. Or forfeit your right to wear a sword.
8. I.e., any offense I committed was accidental,
not deliberate.
9. I.e., from his outward appearance, you cannot perceive him to be as remarkable.

1. Priests were often addressed as "sir."
2. Woman warrior (suggesting great ferocity with
a feminine appearance).
3. Thrust (from the Italian *stoccata*).

[*aside to* FABIAN] I have his horse to take up° the quarrel. I   settle
have persuaded him the youth's a devil.

FABIAN [*aside to* SIR TOBY]   He is as horribly conceited[4] of
280   him, and pants and looks pale as if a bear were at his heels.

SIR TOBY [*to* VIOLA]   There's no remedy, sir; he will fight
with you for's oath' sake. Marry, he hath better bethought
him of his quarrel, and he finds that now scarce to be
worth talking of. Therefore, draw for the supportance of
285   his vow. He protests he will not hurt you.

VIOLA [*aside*]   Pray God defend me. A little thing would
make me tell them how much I lack of a man.

FABIAN [*to* SIR ANDREW]   Give ground if you see him furious.

SIR TOBY   Come, Sir Andrew, there's no remedy. The
290   gentleman will, for his honor's sake, have one bout with
you. He cannot by the duello° avoid it. But he has prom-   code of dueling
ised me, as he is a gentleman and a soldier, he will not
hurt you. Come on, to't.

SIR ANDREW [*drawing his sword*]   Pray God he keep his
295   oath.

VIOLA [*drawing his sword*]   I do assure you, 'tis against my
will.

         Enter ANTONIO.

ANTONIO [*to* SIR ANDREW]   Put up your sword. If this
         young gentleman
Have done offense, I take the fault on me.
If you offend him, I for him defy you.

300   SIR TOBY   You, sir? Why, what are you?

ANTONIO [*drawing his sword*]   One, sir, that for his love dares
         yet do more
Than you have heard him brag to you he will.

SIR TOBY [*drawing his sword*]   Nay, if you be an undertaker,[5] I am for you.

         Enter OFFICERS.

305   FABIAN   O, good Sir Toby, hold. Here come the officers.

SIR TOBY [*to* ANTONIO]   I'll be with you anon.

VIOLA [*to* SIR ANDREW]   Pray, sir, put your sword up, if you
please.

SIR ANDREW   Marry, will I, sir. And for that° I promised you,   *as for that*
310   I'll be as good as my word. He° will bear you easily, and   *i.e., the horse*
reins well.

         [SIR ANDREW *and* VIOLA *put up their swords.*]

FIRST OFFICER   This is the man. Do thy office.

SECOND OFFICER   Antonio, I arrest thee at the suit of
Count Orsino.

315   ANTONIO   You do mistake me, sir.

FIRST OFFICER   No, sir, no jot. I know your favor° well,   *face*
Though now you have no sea-cap on your head.—
Take him away. He knows I know him well.

---

4. He has as terrifying an idea.
5. One who would take upon himself a task (here, a challenge).

ANTONIO   I must obey. [*to* VIOLA] This comes with seeking you.
320   But there's no remedy. I shall answer° it.   *answer for*
       What will you do, now my necessity
       Makes me to ask you for my purse? It grieves me
       Much more for what I cannot do for you
       Than what befalls myself. You stand amazed,
325   But be of comfort.
SECOND OFFICER   Come, sir, away.
ANTONIO [*to* VIOLA]   I must entreat of you some of that money.
VIOLA   What money, sir?
       For the fair kindness you have showed me here,
       And part° being prompted by your present trouble,   *in part*
330   Out of my lean and low ability
       I'll lend you something. My having is not much.
       I'll make division of my present° with you.   *ready money*
       Hold, there's half my coffer. [*offering him money*]
ANTONIO   Will you deny me now?
       Is't possible that my deserts to you
335   Can lack persuasion?[6] Do not tempt my misery,
       Lest that it make me so unsound° a man   *morally weak*
       As to upbraid you with those kindnesses
       That I have done for you.
VIOLA   I know of none,
       Nor know I you by voice or any feature.
340   I hate ingratitude more in a man
       Than lying, vainness, babbling drunkenness,
       Or any taint of vice whose strong corruption
       Inhabits our frail blood—
ANTONIO   O heavens themselves!
SECOND OFFICER   Come, sir, I pray you go.
345   ANTONIO   Let me speak a little. This youth that you see here
       I snatched one half out of the jaws of death,
       Relieved him with such sanctity° of love,   *great devotion*
       And to his image,[7] which methought did promise
       Most venerable worth,[8] did I devotion.
350   FIRST OFFICER   What's that to us? The time goes by. Away!
ANTONIO   But O, how vile an idol proves this god!
       Thou hast, Sebastian, done good feature° shame.   *physical beauty*
       In nature there's no blemish but the mind;
       None can be called deformed but the unkind.
355   Virtue is beauty, but the beauteous evil
       Are empty trunks o'er-flourished[9] by the devil.
FIRST OFFICER   The man grows mad. Away with him.—
       Come, come, sir.
ANTONIO   Lead me on.   *Exit [with* OFFICERS].
VIOLA [*aside*]   Methinks his words do from such passion fly

---

6. Is it possible my past kindness can fail to persuade you?
7. Appearance (with a play on "religious icon").
8. Was worthy of veneration.
9. Chests decorated with carving or painting;

beautified bodies.
1. I.e., believes I am Sebastian.
2. I.e., I do not entirely believe the passionate
hope (for my brother's rescue) that is arising in me.

360 That he believes himself;[1] so do not I.[2]
Prove true, imagination, O, prove true,
That I, dear brother, be now ta'en° for you!   *mistaken*

SIR TOBY Come hither, knight; come hither, Fabian. We'll
whisper o'er a couplet or two of most sage saws.°   *sayings, maxims*
[SIR TOBY, FABIAN, *and* SIR ANDREW *move aside.*]

365 VIOLA He named Sebastian. I my brother know
Yet living in my glass.° Even such and so   *mirror*
In favor° was my brother, and he went   *appearance*
Still° in this fashion, color, ornament,   *always*
For him I imitate. O, if it prove,°   *(true)*

370 Tempests are kind, and salt waves fresh in love! *Exit.*

SIR TOBY A very dishonest,° paltry boy, and more a coward   *dishonorable*
than a hare.[3] His dishonesty appears in leaving his
friend here in necessity, and denying him; and for his
coward-ship, ask Fabian.

375 FABIAN A coward, a most devout coward, religious in it.

SIR ANDREW 'Slid,° I'll after him again and beat him.   *by God's eyelid*

SIR TOBY Do, cuff him soundly, but never draw thy sword.

SIR ANDREW An I do not—   [*Exit.*]

FABIAN Come, let's see the event.°   *outcome*

380 SIR TOBY I dare lay any money 'twill be nothing yet.°   *after all*
     Exeunt.

4.1

Enter SEBASTIAN *and* [FESTE, *the*] *clown.*

FESTE Will you° make me believe that I am not sent for   *are you trying to*
you?

SEBASTIAN Go to, go to, thou art a foolish fellow.
Let me be clear° of thee.   *rid*

5 FESTE Well held out,° i' faith. No, I do not know you, nor   *kept up*
I am not sent to you by my lady to bid you come speak
with her, nor your name is not Master Cesario, nor this
is not my nose neither. Nothing that is so is so.

SEBASTIAN I prithee, vent° thy folly somewhere else.   *utter; excrete*

10 Thou know'st not me.

FESTE Vent my folly? He has heard that word of some great
man and now applies it to a fool. Vent my folly? I am
afraid this great lubber° the world will prove a cockney.[1]   *lout*
I prithee now, ungird thy strangeness[2] and tell me what

15 I shall vent to my lady. Shall I vent to her that thou art
coming?

SEBASTIAN I prithee, foolish Greek,° depart from me.   *buffoon*
There's money for thee. If you tarry longer,
I shall give worse payment.

20 FESTE By my troth, thou hast an open hand. These wise
men that give fools money get themselves a good report°—   *reputation*
after fourteen years' purchase.[3]

---

3. Proverbially cowardly.
4.1 Location: Near Olivia's house.
1. A pampered child.
2. I.e., stop pretending not to know me. (Feste

mocks Sebastian's affected language.)
3. I.e., at a high price. The purchase price of
land was normally twelve times its annual rent.

Enter SIR ANDREW, SIR TOBY, *and* FABIAN.

SIR ANDREW [*to* SEBASTIAN]   Now, sir, have I met you again?
[*striking him*] There's for you.

25 SEBASTIAN [*returning the blow*]   Why, there's for thee, and
there, and there.—Are all the people mad?

SIR TOBY   Hold, sir, or I'll throw your dagger o'er the house.

FESTE [*aside*]   This will I tell my lady straight.°   I would   straightaway
not be in some of your coats for twopence.   [*Exit.*]

30 SIR TOBY [*seizing Sebastian*]   Come on, sir, hold!

SIR ANDREW   Nay, let him alone. I'll go another way to work
with him. I'll have an action of battery[4] against him, if
there be any law in Illyria. Though I struck him first,
yet it's no matter for that.

35 SEBASTIAN [*to* SIR TOBY]   Let go thy hand!

SIR TOBY   Come, sir, I will not let you go. Come, my young
soldier, put up your iron. You are well fleshed.[5] Come on.

SEBASTIAN   I will be free from thee.
[*He pulls free and draws his sword.*]
                                        What wouldst thou now?
If thou dar'st tempt me further, draw thy sword.

40 SIR TOBY   What, what? Nay, then, I must have an ounce or
two of this malapert° blood from you.   impudent
[*He draws his sword.*]
                    Enter OLIVIA.

OLIVIA   Hold, Toby! On thy life I charge thee, hold!

SIR TOBY   Madam.

OLIVIA   Will it be ever thus? Ungracious wretch,
45 Fit for the mountains and the barbarous caves,
Where manners ne'er were preached! Out of my sight!—
Be not offended, dear Cesario.—
Rudesby,° be gone!   ruffian
                    [*Exeunt* SIR TOBY, SIR ANDREW, *and* FABIAN.]
                              I prithee, gentle friend,
Let thy fair wisdom, not thy passion, sway
50 In this uncivil and unjust extent°   assault
Against thy peace. Go with me to my house,
And hear thou there how many fruitless pranks
This ruffian hath botched up,° that thou thereby   clumsily contrived
Mayst smile at this. Thou shalt not choose but go.
55 Do not deny. Beshrew° his soul for me!   curse
He started one poor heart of mine, in thee.[6]

SEBASTIAN [*aside*]   What relish° is in this? How runs the   taste; meaning
stream?
Or° I am mad, or else this is a dream.   either
Let fancy still° my sense in Lethe[7] steep;   imagination ever
60 If it be thus to dream, still let me sleep!

---

4. Lawsuit for assault.
5. Experienced in combat. Hunting hounds were
said to be "fleshed" after being fed part of their
first kill.
6. By attacking Sebastian, Sir Toby frightened

Olivia, who has exchanged hearts with Sebastian. "Started": an allusion to hunting, creating a pun on "hart/heart."
7. A mythical river of the underworld, whose waters cause oblivion.

OLIVIA Nay, come, I prithee. Would thou'dst be ruled by me!
SEBASTIAN Madam, I will.
OLIVIA   O, say so, and so be!   *Exeunt.*

4.2

Enter MARIA *and* [FESTE, *the*] *clown.*

MARIA Nay, I prithee, put on this gown and this beard;
make him believe thou art Sir Topas[1] the curate. Do it
quickly. I'll call Sir Toby the whilst.°   [*Exit.*]   *in the meantime*
FESTE Well, I'll put it on, and I will dissemble[2] myself in't,
5   and I would I were the first that ever dissembled in such
a gown. [*He puts on gown and beard.*] I am not tall enough
to become the function well,[3] nor lean enough to be
thought a good student,[4] but to be said° an honest man   *reputed*
and a good housekeeper° goes as fairly as[5] to say a care-   *host*
10   ful man and a great scholar. The competitors° enter.   *associates*
            Enter SIR TOBY [*and* MARIA].
SIR TOBY Jove bless thee, Master Parson.
FESTE *Bonos dies,*[6] Sir Toby; for, as the old hermit of
Prague,[7] that never saw pen and ink, very wittily° said to   *intelligently*
a niece of King Gorboduc,[8] "That that is, is," so I, being
15   Master Parson, am Master Parson; for what is "that" but
"that" and "is" but "is"?
SIR TOBY To him, Sir Topas.
FESTE [*disguising his voice*] What ho, I say! Peace in this
prison!
20   SIR TOBY The knave counterfeits well. A good knave.
MALVOLIO *within.*
MALVOLIO Who calls there?
FESTE Sir Topas the curate, who comes to visit Malvolio
the lunatic.
MALVOLIO Sir Topas, Sir Topas, good Sir Topas, go to my
25   lady—
FESTE Out, hyperbolical fiend![9] How vexest thou this man!
Talkest thou nothing but of ladies?
SIR TOBY [*aside*] Well said, Master Parson.
MALVOLIO Sir Topas, never was man thus wronged. Good
30   Sir Topas, do not think I am mad. They have laid me here
in hideous darkness—
FESTE Fie, thou dishonest Satan! I call thee by the most
modest° terms, for I am one of those gentle ones that will   *mildest*
use the devil himself with courtesy. Sayst thou that
35   house° is dark?   *room*

4.2 Location: Olivia's house, where Malvolio
will be found (offstage) "in a dark room and
bound" (3.4.131).
1. The comical hero of Chaucer's *Tale of Sir
Thopas.* Also alluding to the topaz stone, which
was thought to have special curative qualities for
insanity.
2. Disguise; with subsequent play on "lie."
3. Grace the priestly office. "Tall": stout, rather
than of great height.
4. I.e., a student of divinity.
5. Sounds as well as.
6. Good day (false Latin).
7. Probably an invented authority.
8. Legendary British king.
9. Feste treats Malvolio as a man possessed by
vehement ("hyperbolical") evil spirits.

MALVOLIO As hell, Sir Topas.

FESTE Why, it hath bay windows transparent as barricadoes, and the clerestories[1] toward the south-north are as
lustrous as ebony;[2] and yet complainest thou of obstruc-
40   tion?

MALVOLIO I am not mad, Sir Topas. I say to you this house
is dark.

FESTE Madman, thou errest. I say there is no darkness but
ignorance, in which thou art more puzzled than the Egyp-
45   tians in their fog.[3]

MALVOLIO I say this house is as dark as ignorance, though
ignorance were as dark as hell. And I say there was never
man thus abused. I am no more mad than you are. Make
the trial of it in any constant question.°   *logical discussion*

50   FESTE What is the opinion of Pythagoras[4] concerning
wildfowl?

MALVOLIA That the soul of our grandam might haply°   *perhaps*
inhabit a bird.

FESTE What thinkest thou of his opinion?

55   MALVOLIO I think nobly of the soul, and no way approve
his opinion.

FESTE Fare thee well. Remain thou still in darkness. Thou
shalt hold th' opinion of Pythagoras ere I will allow of thy
wits,° and fear to kill a woodcock[5] lest thou dispossess   *certify your sanity*
60   the soul of thy grandam. Fare thee well.

MALVOLIO Sir Topas, Sir Topas!

SIR TOBY My most exquisite Sir Topas!

FESTE Nay, I am for all waters.[6]

MARIA Thou mightst have done this without thy beard and
65   gown. He sees thee not.

SIR TOBY To him in thine own voice, and bring me word
how thou findest him. I would we were well rid of this
knavery. If he may be conveniently delivered,° I would   *set free*
he were, for I am now so far in offense with my niece
70   that I cannot pursue with any safety this sport to the
upshot.° Come by and by to my chamber.   *conclusion*

                    [*Exeunt* SIR TOBY *and* MARIA.]

FESTE [*sings*][7] "Hey, Robin, jolly Robin,
                    Tell me how thy lady *does*."

MALVOLIO Fool!

75   FESTE [*sings*] "My lady is unkind, perdy."[8]

MALVOLIO Fool!

FESTE   "Alas, why is she so?"

---

1. Upper windows, usually in a church or great
hall. "Barricadoes": barricades (subsequent paradoxes are equivalent to "as clear as mud").
2. A dense and naturally dull black wood.
3. One of the plagues of Egypt was a "black darkness" lasting for three days (Exodus 10.21–23).
4. The ancient Greek philosopher held that the
same soul could successively inhabit different

creatures.
5. A traditionally stupid bird.
6. I am able to turn my hand to anything.
7. Feste's song, which makes Malvolio aware of
his presence, is traditional. There is a version by
Sir Thomas Wyatt.
8. A corruption of the French *pardieu*, "by God."

MALVOLIO Fool, I say!

FESTE   "She loves another"—Who calls, ha?

80 MALVOLIO Good fool, as ever thou wilt deserve well at my
hand, help me to a candle, and pen, ink, and paper. As
I am a gentleman, I will live to be thankful to thee for't.

FESTE Master Malvolio?

MALVOLIO Ay, good fool.

85 FESTE Alas, sir, how fell you besides° your five wits?[9]   *out of*

MALVOLIO Fool, there was never man so notoriously° *outrageously*
abused. I am as well in my wits, fool, as thou art.

FESTE But as well? Then you are mad indeed, if you be no
better in your wits than a fool.

90 MALVOLIO They have here propertied me,[1] keep me in
darkness, send ministers to me—asses!—and do all they
can to face me[2] out of my wits.

FESTE Advise you° what you say. The minister is here. *be careful*
[*as Sir Topas*] Malvolio, Malvolio, thy wits the heavens
95 restore. Endeavor thyself to sleep and leave thy vain
bibble-babble.

MALVOLIO Sir Topas!

FESTE [*as Sir Topas*] Maintain no words with him, good
fellow. [*as fool*] Who, I, sir? Not I, sir. God buy you,° good *God be with you*
100 Sir Topas. [*as Sir Topas*] Marry, amen. [*as fool*] I will, sir,
I will.

MALVOLIO Fool! Fool! Fool, I say!

FESTE Alas, sir, be patient. What say you, sir? I am shent° *scolded*
for speaking to you.

105 MALVOLIO Good fool, help me to some light and some
paper. I tell thee, I am as well in my wits as any man in
Illyria.

FESTE Welladay° that you were, sir! *alas*

MALVOLIO By this hand, I am. Good fool, some ink, paper,
110 and light; and convey what I will set down to my lady. It
shall advantage thee more than ever the bearing of letter
did.

FESTE I will help you to't. But tell me true, are you not
mad indeed, or do you but counterfeit?

115 MALVOLIO Believe me, I am not. I tell thee true.

FESTE Nay, I'll ne'er believe a madman till I see his brains.
I will fetch you light and paper and ink.

MALVOLIO Fool, I'll requite it in the highest degree. I
prithee, be gone.

120 FESTE [*sings*]   I am gone, sir,
         And anon, sir,
           I'll be with you again,
         In a trice,
         Like to the old Vice,[3]

---

9. Usually regarded as common sense, fantasy, memory, judgment, and imagination.
1. Treated me as a piece of property.

2. Brazenly construe me as.
3. A stock comic figure in the old morality plays; he often carried a wooden dagger.

125   Your need to sustain.
           Who with dagger of lath,
           In his rage and his wrath,
             Cries "aha!" to the devil;
           Like a mad lad,
130   "Pare thy nails, dad!
             Adieu, goodman[4] devil."   *Exit.*

4.3

Enter SEBASTIAN.

SEBASTIAN   This is the air; that is the glorious sun.
  This pearl she gave me, I do feel't and see't.
  And though 'tis wonder that enwraps me thus,
  Yet 'tis not madness. Where's Antonio, then?
5   I could not find him at the Elephant.
  Yet there he was;° and there I found this credit,°   *had been / report*
  That he did range the town to seek me out.
  His counsel now might do me golden service.
  For though my soul disputes well with my sense[1]
10   That this may be some error, but no madness,
  Yet doth this accident and flood of fortune
  So far exceed all instance,° all discourse,°   *precedent / reasoning*
  That I am ready to distrust mine eyes
  And wrangle with my reason that persuades me
15   To any other trust° but that I am mad—   *belief*
  Or else the lady's mad. Yet if 'twere so,
  She could not sway° her house, command her followers,   *rule*
  Take and give back affairs and their dispatch[2]
  With such a smooth, discreet, and stable bearing
20   As I perceive she does. There's something in't
  That is deceivable.° But here the lady comes.   *deceptive*

      Enter OLIVIA *and* PRIEST.

OLIVIA   Blame not this haste of mine. If you mean well,
  Now go with me and with this holy man
  Into the chantry by.° There, before him   *nearby chapel*
25   And underneath that consecrated roof,
  Plight me the full assurance of your faith,[3]
  That my most jealous and too doubtful soul
  May live at peace. He shall conceal it
  Whiles° you are willing it shall come to note,°   *until / be made public*
30   What° time we will our celebration keep   *at which*
  According to my birth.° What do you say?   *rank*
SEBASTIAN   I'll follow this good man and go with you
  And, having sworn truth, ever will be true.

---

4. Yeoman; a title given to one not of gentle birth, hence a parting insult to Malvolio.
4.3 Location: Near Olivia's house.
1. For though my reason and my sense both concur.
2. Undertake business, and ensure that it is carried out.
3. Enter into the solemn contract of betrothal.

OLIVIA   Then lead the way, good father, and heavens so shine
35   That they may fairly note⁴ this act of mine.   *Exeunt.*

5.1

Enter [FESTE, the] clown and FABIAN.

FABIAN   Now, as thou lovest me, let me see his letter.

FESTE   Good Master Fabian, grant me another request.

FABIAN   Anything.

FESTE   Do not desire to see this letter.

5 FABIAN   This is to give a dog and in recompense desire my
      dog again.¹

Enter ORSINO, VIOLA, CURIO, and lords.

ORSINO   Belong you to the Lady Olivia, friends?

FESTE   Ay, sir, we are some of her trappings.°   *ornaments*

ORSINO   I know thee well. How dost thou, my good fellow?

10 FESTE   Truly, sir, the better for my foes and the worse for
      my friends.

ORSINO   Just the contrary: the better for thy friends.

FESTE   No, sir, the worse.

ORSINO   How can that be?

15 FESTE   Marry, sir, they praise me and make an ass of me.
      Now my foes tell me plainly I am an ass; so that by my
      foes, sir, I profit in the knowledge of myself, and by my
      friends I am abused.° So that, conclusions to be as kisses,   *deceived*
      if your four negatives make your two affirmatives,² why
20   then the worse for my friends and the better for my foes.

ORSINO   Why, this is excellent.

FESTE   By my troth, sir, no—though it please you to be
      one of my friends.

ORSINO   [*giving a coin*] Thou shalt not be the worse for
25   me; there's gold.

FESTE   But° that it would be double-dealing,³ sir, I would   *except for the fact*
      you could make it another.

ORSINO   O, you give me ill counsel.

FESTE   Put your grace in your pocket,⁴ sir, for this once,
30   and let your flesh and blood obey it.⁵

ORSINO   Well, I will be so much a sinner to° be a double-   *as to*
      dealer. [*giving a coin*] There's another.

FESTE   *Primo, secundo, tertio*⁶ is a good play,° and the old   *game*
      saying is, the third pays for all.⁷ The triplex,° sir, is a   *triple time (music)*

---

4. Look favorably upon.
5.1 Location: Before Olivia's house.
1. Perhaps a reference to an anecdote, recorded in John Manningham's diary, in which Queen Elizabeth requested a dog, and the donor, when granted a wish in return, asked for the dog back.
2. As in grammar a double negative can make an affirmative (and therefore four negatives can make two affirmatives), so when a coy girl is asked for a kiss, her four refusals can be construed as "yes, yes."

3. (1) A duplicity; (2) a double donation.
4. Set aside (pocket up) your virtue; also (with a play on the customary form of address for a duke, "your grace"), reach into your pocket and grace me with another coin.
5. Let your normal human instincts (as opposed to grace) follow the "ill counsel" (line 28).
6. First, second, third (Latin); perhaps an allusion to a dice throw or a child's game.
7. Third time lucky (proverbial).

35   good tripping measure, or the bells of Saint Bennet,[8] sir,
        may put you in mind—one, two, three.
        ORSINO   You can fool no more money out of me at this
        throw.° If you will let your lady know I am here to speak   *throw of the dice*
        with her, and bring her along with you, it may awake my
40   bounty° further.   *generosity*
        FESTE   Marry, sir, lullaby to your bounty till I come again.
        I go, sir, but I would not have you to think that my desire
        of having is the sin of covetousness. But, as you say, sir, let
        your bounty take a nap. I will awake it anon.   *Exit.*
                Enter ANTONIO *and* OFFICERS.
45   VIOLA   Here comes the man, sir, that did rescue me.
        ORSINO   That face of his I do remember well.
        Yet when I saw it last, it was besmeared
        As black as Vulcan[9] in the smoke of war.
        A baubling° vessel was he captain of,   *trifling*
50   For shallow draft and bulk unprizable,[1]
        With which such scatheful° grapple did he make   *destructive*
        With the most noble bottom° of our fleet   *ship*
        That very envy° and the tongue of loss°   *even enmity / the losers*
        Cried fame and honor on him.—What's the matter?
55   FIRST OFFICER   Orsino, this is that Antonio
        That took the *Phoenix* and her freight from Candy,[2]
        And this is he that did the *Tiger* board
        When your young nephew Titus lost his leg.
        Here in the streets, desperate of shame and state,[3]
60   In private brabble° did we apprehend him.   *brawl*
        VIOLA   He did me kindness, sir, drew on my side,[4]
        But in conclusion put strange speech upon° me.   *spoke strangely to*
        I know not what 'twas but distraction.°   *if not insanity*
        ORSINO   Notable° pirate, thou salt-water thief,   *notorious*
65   What foolish boldness brought thee to their mercies
        Whom thou, in terms so bloody and so dear,°   *dire*
        Hast made thine enemies?
        ANTONIO   Orsino, noble sir,
        Be pleased that I shake off these names you give me.
        Antonio never yet was thief or pirate,
70   Though, I confess, on base° and ground enough,   *foundation*
        Orsino's enemy. A witchcraft drew me hither.
        That most ingrateful boy there by your side
        From the rude sea's enraged and foamy mouth
        Did I redeem; a wrack° past hope he was.   *castaway*
75   His life I gave him and did thereto add
        My love, without retention° or restraint,   *reservation*

---

8. A London church, across the Thames from the
Globe theater, was known as Saint Bennet Hithe.
9. Blacksmith god of the Romans.
1. Of no value because of its small size. "Draft":
water displaced by a vessel.

2. Candia, capital of Crete.
3. Recklessly oblivious of the danger to his honor
and his position (as a free man and public enemy).
4. Drew his sword in my defense.

All his in dedication. For his sake
Did I expose myself, pure° for his love,   *only*
Into the danger of this adverse° town;   *hostile*
80   Drew to defend him when he was beset;
Where, being apprehended, his false cunning—
Not meaning to partake with me in danger—
Taught him to face me out of his acquaintance[5]
And grew a twenty years' removèd thing
85   While one would wink;[6] denied me mine own purse,
Which I had recommended° to his use   *consigned*
Not half an hour before.
VIOLA   How can this be?
ORSINO [to Antonio]   When came he to this town?
90   ANTONIO   Today, my lord; and for three months before,
No int'rim, not a minute's vacancy,°   *interval*
Both day and night did we keep company.
      Enter OLIVIA *and attendants.*
ORSINO   Here comes the Countess. Now heaven walks on earth!—
But for thee, fellow: fellow, thy words are madness.
95   Three months this youth hath tended upon me—
But more of that anon. [to an OFFICER] Take him aside.
OLIVIA   What would my lord, but that he may not have,[7]
Wherein Olivia may seem serviceable?—
Cesario, you do not keep promise with me.
100   VIOLA   Madam?
ORSINO   Gracious Olivia—
OLIVIA   What do you say, Cesario?—Good my lord—
VIOLA   My lord would speak; my duty hushes me.
OLIVIA   If it be aught° to the old tune, my lord,   *anything*
105   It is as fat and fulsome° to mine ear   *gross and offensive*
As howling after music.
ORSINO   Still so cruel?
OLIVIA   Still so constant, lord.
ORSINO   What, to perverseness? You, uncivil lady,
110   To whose ingrate° and unauspicious° altars   *ungrateful / unfavorable*
My soul the faithful'st off'rings hath breathed out
That e'er devotion tendered—what shall I do?
OLIVIA   Even what it please my lord that shall become° him.   *be fitting for*
ORSINO   Why should I not, had I the heart to do it,
115   Like to th' Egyptian thief at point of death,
Kill what I love?[8]—a savage jealousy
That sometime savors nobly.° But hear me this: *of nobility*
Since you to non-regardance° cast my faith,   *oblivion*
And that I partly know the instrument

---

5. To brazenly deny my acquaintance.
6. I.e., in the wink of an eye, pretended we had been estranged for twenty years.
7. Except that which he may not have (my love).
8. In Heliodorus's *Ethiopica*, a Greek prose romance translated into English in 1569 and popular in Shakespeare's day, the Egyptian robber chief Thyamis tries to kill his captive Chariclea, whom he loves, when he is in danger from a rival band.

120 That screws° me from my true place in your favor,   *wrenches*
    Live you the marble-breasted tyrant still.
    But this your minion,° whom I know you love,   *darling*
    And whom, by heaven I swear, I tender° dearly,   *regard*
    Him will I tear out of that cruel eye
125 Where he sits crownèd in his master's spite—⁹
    Come, boy, with me. My thoughts are ripe in mischief.
    I'll sacrifice the lamb that I do love
    To spite a raven's heart within a dove.
VIOLA   And I, most jocund,° apt,° and willingly,   *cheerfully / ready*
130 To do you rest° a thousand deaths would die.   *give you relief*
OLIVIA   Where goes Cesario?
VIOLA   After him I love
    More than I love these eyes, more than my life,
    More by all mores¹ than e'er I shall love wife.
    If I do feign, you witnesses above,
135 Punish my life for tainting of my love.
OLIVIA   Ay me, detested! How am I beguiled!°   *deceived*
VIOLA   Who does beguile you? Who does do you wrong?
OLIVIA   Hast thou forgot thyself? Is it so long?
    Call forth the holy father.   [*Exit an attendant.*]
ORSINO [*to* VIOLA]   Come, away!
140 OLIVIA   Whither, my lord?—Cesario, husband, stay.
ORSINO   Husband?
OLIVIA   Ay, husband. Can he that deny?
ORSINO   Her husband, sirrah?²
VIOLA   No, my lord, not I.
OLIVIA   Alas, it is the baseness of thy fear
    That makes thee strangle thy propriety.³
145 Fear not, Cesario. Take thy fortunes up.
    Be that thou know'st thou art, and then thou art
    As great as that° thou fear'st.   *him whom*
            Enter PRIEST

                        O, welcome, father.
    Father, I charge thee by thy reverence
    Here to unfold—though lately we intended
150 To keep in darkness what occasion° now   *necessity*
    Reveals before 'tis ripe—what thou dost know
    Hath newly passed between this youth and me.
PRIEST   A contract of eternal bond of love,
    Confirmed by mutual joinder° of your hands,   *joining*
155 Attested by the holy close° of lips,   *meeting*
    Strengthened by interchangement of your rings,
    And all the ceremony of this compact
    Sealed in my function,⁴ by my testimony;
    Since when, my watch hath told me, toward my grave

9. To the mortification of his master.
1. More beyond all comparison.
2. Contemptuous form of address to an inferior.
3. That makes you deny your identity (as my husband).
4. Ratified by priestly authority.

160   I have traveled but two hours.

ORSINO [*to* VIOLA]   O thou dissembling cub! What wilt thou be
     When time hath sowed a grizzle on thy case?[5]
     Or will not else° thy craft° so quickly grow   *otherwise / craftiness*
     That thine own trip shall be thine overthrow?[6]

165   Farewell, and take her, but direct thy feet
     Where thou and I henceforth may never meet.

VIOLA   My lord, I do protest—

OLIVIA   O, do not swear.
     Hold little° faith, though thou hast too much fear.   *preserve some*
     Enter SIR ANDREW.

SIR ANDREW   For the love of God, a surgeon! Send one
170   presently° to Sir Toby.   *immediately*

OLIVIA   What's the matter?

SIR ANDREW   He's broke° my head across, and has given Sir   *cut*
     Toby a bloody coxcomb[7] too. For the love of God, your
     help! I had rather than forty pound I were at home.

175 OLIVIA   Who has done this, Sir Andrew?

SIR ANDREW   The Count's gentleman, one Cesario. We
     took him for a coward, but he's the very devil incardi-
     nate.[8]

ORSINO   My gentleman Cesario?

180 SIR ANDREW   'Od's lifelings,° here he is!—You broke my   *by God's little lives*
     head for nothing, and that that I did, I was set on to do't by
     Sir Toby.

VIOLA   Why do you speak to me? I never hurt you.
     You drew your sword upon me without cause,
185   But I bespake you fair[9] and hurt you not.

SIR ANDREW   If a bloody coxcomb be a hurt, you have
     hurt me. I think you set nothing by° a bloody coxcomb.   *think nothing of*
     Enter SIR TOBY *and* [FESTE, *the*] *clown.*
     Here comes Sir Toby halting.° You shall hear more. But   *limping*
     if° he had not been in drink, he would have tickled°   *if only / chastised*
190   you othergates° than he did.   *in other ways*

ORSINO   How now, gentleman? How is't with you?

SIR TOBY   That's all one.° He's hurt me, and there's th'   *no matter*
     end on't. [*to* FESTE] Sot,° didst see Dick Surgeon,   *fool; drunkard*
     sot?

195 FESTE   O, he's drunk, Sir Toby, an hour agone. His eyes
     were set[1] at eight i 'th' morning.

SIR TOBY   Then he's a rogue and a passy-measures pavan.[2]
     I hate a drunken rogue.

OLIVIA   Away with him! Who hath made this havoc with
200   them?

---

5. A gray hair ("grizzle") on your hide (sustaining the metaphor of "cub").
6. That your attempt to trip someone else will be
the cause of your downfall.
7. Head; also, a fool's cap, which resembles the
crest of a cock.
8. Sir Andrew's blunder for "incarnate" (in the

flesh).
9. But I spoke courteously to you.
1. Closed (as the sun sets).
2. A variety of the slow dance known as "pavane"
(from the Italian *passemezzo pavana*). Sir Toby
may think its swaying movements suggest drunkenness.

SIR ANDREW I'll help you, Sir Toby, because we'll be
    dressed³ together.
SIR TOBY Will *you* help?—an ass-head, and a coxcomb,° and   *fool*
    a knave, a thin-faced knave, a gull?°   *dupe*
205 OLIVIA Get him to bed, and let his hurt be looked to.
          [*Exeunt* SIR TOBY, SIR ANDREW, FESTE, *and* FABIAN.]
          Enter SEBASTIAN.
SEBASTIAN I am sorry, madam, I have hurt your kinsman,
    But, had it been the brother of my blood,
    I must have done no less with wit and safety.⁴
    You throw a strange regard upon me,° and by that   *regard me strangely*
210 I do perceive it hath offended you.
    Pardon me, sweet one, even for the vows
    We made each other but so late ago.
ORSINO One face, one voice, one habit, and two persons!
    A natural perspective,⁵ that is and is not!
215 SEBASTIAN Antonio, O, my dear Antonio!
    How have the hours racked and tortured me
    Since I have lost thee!
ANTONIO Sebastian are you?
SEBASTIAN Fear'st thou° that, Antonio?   *do you doubt*
220 ANTONIO How have you made division of yourself?
    An apple cleft in two is not more twin
    Than these two creatures. Which is Sebastian?
OLIVIA Most wonderful!°   *full of wonder*
SEBASTIAN [*looking at* VIOLA] Do I stand there? I never had a
    brother,
225 Nor can there be that deity° in my nature   *divine power*
    Of here and everywhere.° I had a sister,   *of omnipresence*
    Whom the blind waves and surges have devoured.
    Of charity,° what kin are you to me?   *please*
    What countryman? What name? What parentage?
230 VIOLA Of Messaline. Sebastian was my father.
    Such a Sebastian was my brother, too.
    So went he suited° to his watery tomb.   *in appearance; clad*
    If spirits can assume both form and suit,
    You come to fright us.
SEBASTIAN   A spirit I am indeed,
235 But am in that dimension grossly clad
    Which from the womb I did participate.⁶
    Were you a woman, as the rest goes even,°   *the rest suggests*
    I should my tears let fall upon your cheek
    And say "Thrice welcome, drownèd Viola."
240 VIOLA My father had a mole upon his brow.
SEBASTIAN And so had mine.
VIOLA And died that day when Viola from her birth

---

3. We'll have our wounds dressed.
4. With any sense of my welfare.
5. An optical illusion produced by nature (rather
than by a mirror).
6. I.e., I am clad, like all mortals, in the flesh in
which I was born.

Had numbered thirteen years.

SEBASTIAN   O, that record is lively[7] in my soul!

245   He finishèd indeed his mortal act

That day that made my sister thirteen years.

VIOLA   If nothing lets° to make us happy both   *hinders*

But this my masculine usurped attire,

Do not embrace me till each circumstance

250   Of place, time, fortune, do cohere and jump°   *agree*

That I am Viola; which to confirm,

I'll bring you to a captain in this town,

Where lie my maiden weeds;° by whose gentle help   *clothes*

I was preserved to serve this noble count.

255   All the occurrence of my fortune since

Hath been between this lady and this lord.

SEBASTIAN [*to* OLIVIA]   So comes it, lady, you have been mistook.

But nature to her bias drew in that.[8]

You would have been contracted° to a maid.   *betrothed*

260   Nor are you therein, by my life, deceived:

You are betrothed both to a maid and man.[9]

ORSINO [*to* OLIVIA]   Be not amazed; right noble is his blood.

If this be so, as yet the glass seems true,[1]

I shall have share in this most happy wrack.°—   *fortunate shipwreck*

265   Boy, thou hast said to me a thousand times

Thou never shouldst love woman like to me.

VIOLA   And all those sayings will I overswear°   *swear again*

And all those swearings keep as true in soul

As doth that orbèd continent[2] the fire

That severs day from night.

270   ORSINO   Give me thy hand,

And let me see thee in thy woman's weeds.

VIOLA   The captain that did bring me first on shore

Hath my maid's garments. He, upon some action,°   *legal charge*

Is now in durance° at Malvolio's suit,   *prison*

275   A gentleman and follower of my lady's.

OLIVIA   He shall enlarge° him. Fetch Malvolio hither.   *release*

And yet, alas, now I remember me,

They say, poor gentleman, he's much distract.°   *crazed*

    Enter [FESTE, *the*] *clown with a letter, and* FABIAN.

A most extracting° frenzy of mine own   *distracting*

280   From my remembrance clearly banished his.

How does he, sirrah?

FESTE   Truly, madam, he holds Beelzebub at the stave's

end[3] as well as a man in his case may do. He's here writ

a letter to you. I should have given't you today morning.

---

7. The memory of that is vivid.
8. But nature followed her inclination. (The image is from the game of bowls, which sometimes used a ball with an off-center weight that caused it to curve away from a straight course.)
9. I.e., a man who is a virgin.

1. The "natural perspective" (line 214) continues to seem real.
2. Referring to either the sun or the sphere within which the sun was thought to be fixed.
3. He holds the devil (who threatens to possess him) at a distance (proverbial).

285 But as a madman's epistles are no gospels,[4] so it skills°   *matters*
not much when they are delivered.

OLIVIA   Open't and read it.

FESTE   Look then to be well edified, when the fool deliv-
ers° the madman. [*He reads.*] "By the Lord, madam"—   *speaks the words of*

290 OLIVIA   How now, art thou mad?

FESTE   No, madam, I do but read madness. An your ladyship will have it as it ought to be, you must allow *vox.*[5]

OLIVIA   Prithee, read i' thy right wits.

FESTE   So I do, madonna. But to read his right wits[6] is

295 to read thus. Therefore, perpend,° my princess, and give   *pay attention*
ear.

OLIVIA [*giving letter to Fabian*]   Read it you, sirrah.

FABIAN   "By the Lord, madam, you wrong me, and the
world shall know it. Though you have put me into

300 darkness and given your drunken cousin rule over me, yet
have I the benefit of my senses as well as your Ladyship. I
have your own letter that induced me to the semblance°   *appearance*
I put on, with the which I doubt not but to do myself
much right or you much shame. Think of me as you

305 please. I leave my duty a little unthought of and speak
out of my injury.[7]

The madly-used Malvolio."

OLIVIA   Did he write this?

FESTE   Ay, madam.

310 ORSINO   This savors not much of distraction.°   *insanity*

OLIVIA   See him delivered,° Fabian. Bring him hither.   *released*

[Exit FABIAN.]

My lord, so please you, these things further thought on,
To think me as well a sister as a wife,[8]
One day shall crown th' alliance[9] on't, so please you,

315 Here at my house, and at my proper cost.°   *own expense*

ORSINO   Madam, I am most apt° t' embrace your offer.   *ready*
[*to* VIOLA] Your master quits° you; and for your service   *releases*
done him,
So much against the mettle° of your sex,   *disposition*
So far beneath your soft and tender breeding,

320 And since you called me "master" for so long,
Here is my hand. You shall from this time be
Your master's mistress.

OLIVIA [*to* VIOLA]

A sister! You are she.

Enter MALVOLIO [and FABIAN].

ORSINO   Is this the madman?

OLIVIA   Ay, my lord, this same.—

---

4. Gospel truths. "Epistles": letters (playing on
the sense of apostolic accounts of Christ in the
New Testament).
5. The appropriate voice (Latin).
6. To accurately represent his mental state.

7. I neglect the formality I owe you as your servant and speak as an injured person.
8. To think as well of me as a sister-in-law as you
would have thought of me as a wife.
9. The impending double-marriage ceremony.

How now, Malvolio?

MALVOLIO   Madam, you have done me wrong,
Notorious wrong.

325 OLIVIA   Have I, Malvolio? No.

MALVOLIA [*handing her a paper*]   Lady, you have. Pray
you peruse that letter.
You must not now deny it is your hand.°   *handwriting*
Write from° it if you can, in hand or phrase,   *differently from*
Or say 'tis not your seal, not your invention.°   *composition*
330 You can say none of this. Well, grant it then,
And tell me, in the modesty of honor,[1]
Why you have given me such clear lights° of favor?   *signs*
Bade me come smiling and cross-gartered to you,
To put on yellow stockings, and to frown
335 Upon Sir Toby and the lighter° people?   *lesser*
And, acting° this in an obedient hope,   *upon doing*
Why have you suffered° me to be imprisoned,   *allowed*
Kept in a dark house, visited by the priest,
And made the most notorious geck° and gull   *fool*
340 That e'er invention° played on? Tell me why.   *trickery*

OLIVIA   Alas, Malvolio, this is not my writing,
Though I confess much like the character.°   *handwriting*
But out of question, 'tis Maria's hand.
And now I do bethink me, it was she
345 First told me thou wast mad; then cam'st° in smiling,   *you came*
And in such forms which here were presupposed°   *previously suggested*
Upon thee in the letter. Prithee, be content.
This practice hath most shrewdly passed[2] upon thee.
But when we know the grounds and authors of it,
350 Thou shalt be both the plaintiff and the judge
Of thine own cause.

FABIAN   Good madam, hear me speak,
And let no quarrel nor no brawl to come
Taint the condition of this present hour,
Which I have wondered° at. In hope it shall not,   *marveled*
355 Most freely I confess myself and Toby
Set this device against Malvolio here,
Upon° some stubborn and uncourteous parts°   *because / behavior*
We had conceived against him.[3] Maria writ
The letter, at Sir Toby's great importance,°   *importunity, insistence*
360 In recompense whereof he hath married her.
How with a sportful° malice it was followed°   *playful / followed through*
May rather pluck on° laughter than revenge,   *incite*
If that the injuries be justly weighed
That have on both sides passed.

OLIVIA [*to* MALVOLIO]   Alas, poor fool, how have they
365 baffled° thee!   *disgraced*

---

1. Tell me with the propriety that becomes a noblewoman.

2. This trick has most mischievously played.
3. To which we took exception.

FESTE Why, "Some are born great, some achieve greatness, and some have greatness thrown upon them." I was
one, sir, in this interlude,° one Sir Topas, sir, but that's   *comedy*
all one. "By the Lord, fool, I am not mad"—but, do you
370 remember "Madam, why laugh you at such a barren rascal; an you smile not, he's gagged"? And thus the whirli-
gig° of time brings in his revenges.   *spinning top*
MALVOLIO I'll be revenged on the whole pack of you!
                                                      [*Exit.*]
OLIVIA He hath been most notoriously abused.
375 ORSINO Pursue him and entreat him to a peace.
                               [*Exit one or more.*]
He hath not told us of the captain yet.
When that is known, and golden time convents,°   *summons; is convenient*
A solemn combination shall be made
Of our dear souls. Meantime, sweet sister,
380 We will not part from hence.° Cesario, come—   *(Olivia's house)*
For so you shall be while you are a man.
But when in other habits° you are seen,   *attire*
Orsino's mistress, and his fancy's° queen.   *love's; imagination's*
                           Exeunt [*all but* FESTE].
FESTE *sings* When that I was and a little tiny boy,
385   With hey, ho, the wind and the rain,
    A foolish thing was but a toy,
      For the rain it raineth every day.

    But when I came to man's estate,
      With hey, ho, the wind and the rain,
390   'Gainst knaves and thieves men shut their gate,
      For the rain it raineth every day.

    But when I came, alas, to wive,
      With hey, ho, the wind and the rain,
    By swaggering° could I never thrive,   *bullying*
395   For the rain it raineth every day.

    But when I came unto my beds,
      With hey, ho, the wind and the rain,
    With tosspots° still had drunken heads,   *drunkards*
      For the rain it raineth every day.

400   A great while ago the world begun,
      With hey, ho, the wind and the rain,
    But that's all one, our play is done,
      And we'll strive to please you every day.
                                                 Exit.

ca. 1601   1623

Othello

Othello   *Othello* (1603–04), one of a succession of tragic masterpieces that Shakespeare wrote in the early years of the seventeenth century, is unrivaled in its excruciating intensity. With its almost clinical account of a malevolent assault on love and beauty, the play has for centuries aroused in audiences the paradoxical blend of pleasure and acute discomfort characteristic of great tragedy. The performance history of *Othello* includes anecdotes of spectators attempting to intervene by angrily denouncing the villain, shouting advice to the deceived hero, or even rushing onstage to save the doomed heroine. If such stories reveal a fundamental misunderstanding of the nature of theater, they also disclose Shakespeare's brilliant exploitation of the gap between the performers and the audience. We see what is happening; we understand where it is leading; we urgently want to prevent the catastrophe—but, as in a nightmare, we are powerless to do so. *Othello* is a prime instance of what a twentieth-century writer, Antonin Artaud, called "the theater of cruelty."

This cruelty is intensified by the fact that the plot of Shakespeare's tragedy is woven from some of the elements of the joyous comedies in which he had already distinguished himself. *Othello* begins with a miniature version of the traditional comedy of sexual fulfillment. Refusing to allow his daughter to elope with the man of her choosing, an angry father, well-born, wealthy, and powerful, lodges a formal complaint before the authorities. His daughter, he alleges, has been seduced by means of witchcraft; otherwise, she would never have been attracted to someone so far below her in social class and culture. At first the authorities—the senators of the Venetian Republic— seem inclined to agree, but after hearing testimony from the couple in question, Othello and Desdemona, they dismiss the father's complaint. The rigid hold of the older generation over the desires of the next is broken, paternal possessiveness is defeated, and romantic love triumphs over familial bonds. And lest this triumph should seem to threaten the social order, the romantic couple is legitimated by marriage, the newlywed husband makes clear his devotion to serving the state in its war against the Ottoman Turks, and the spouse who at first seemed socially unsuitable turns out to be the equal of his amorous conquest. "I fetch my life and being," Othello declares, "From men of royal siege" (1.2.21–22). All's well that ends well.

But, of course, it does not end well. Disturbing elements, also with roots in comedy, have already begun to surface in the first scenes. One of these is the familiar farce of January and May: the old man married to the much younger, lusty wife who is courted by handsome, unscrupulous suitors. Another is what we might call the comedy of fantastical passion: the person who awakens from the trance of love to find that the object of desire is in fact ridiculous. Still another is the braggart soldier, the preening, self-promoting hero who is revealed to be an empty shell. And yet another is the mocking of the alien, the collective ridiculing of an outsider who hopes to be accepted but whom the natives despise as outlandish, gullible, and grotesque.

There is one person who is particularly sensitive to all of these cruel comic undertones: Othello's devious, resentful third-in-command, Iago. Unable to derail Othello's elopement, Iago seizes on potentially destructive versions of Othello and Desdemona's story. Desdemona fell in love with Othello merely for his bragging, he tells the lovesick Roderigo, but she will soon realize her mistake and long for someone younger, more handsome, more appropriate. When Roderigo doubts that Desdemona can be so easily seduced—"I cannot believe that in her; she's full of most blessed condition"—Iago replies with the cynic's tough, deflating realism: "Blessed fig's-end! The wine she drinks is made of grapes" (2.1.246–49).

The problem for Iago, though, is that none of these conventional comic scenarios seems very promising. Desdemona shows no sign of restlessness with her choice, nor does she register any discomfort with the age difference between herself and her husband. Othello's martial heroism is the real thing, attested to by everyone and elegantly manifested in the serene self-confidence with which he greets the armed followers of his irate father-in-law: "Keep up your bright swords, for the dew will rust

"Men whose heads / Do grow beneath their shoulders" (*Othello* 1.3.143–44), in an engraving by Jodocus Hondius from a 1599 edition of Ralegh's *Discovery of Guiana*. These creatures, known as Blemmyes or Ewaipanoma, are reported as well in *Mandeville's Travels*.

them" (1.2.59). It is true that he initially allured Desdemona with exotic tales from what he calls "the story of my life" (1.3.128), but the bond between them is anything but superficial: consecrating her "soul and fortunes" to her husband, she declares that her "heart's subdued / Even to the very quality of my lord" (1.3.252, 248–49).

The strongest weapon in Iago's arsenal is racism, the contempt and revulsion with which many Europeans in the Middle Ages and the Renaissance routinely stigmatized dark skin and negroid features. This attitude, which is on display in several of the texts included in the "Wider World" section of this anthology, is also reflected in a document issued by Queen Elizabeth in 1601, complaining about the "great numbers of Negars and Blackamoors" who "are crept into this realm." Denouncing these unwelcome people as "infidels, having no understanding of Christ or his Gospel," the queen authorized their deportation (though it is not clear that any such expulsion was carried out). In the tragedy Shakespeare wrote only a few years after this order, his hero is a Moor, whether that refers to North Africa or to sub-Saharan Africa, and this identity is enough to trigger the vile abuse Iago and Roderigo shout in the darkness in the first moments of the play. Othello is an "old black ram," "a Barbary horse" (1.1.85, 108).

But even this weapon seems blunted. Othello is not a religious outsider, but a Christian. He is the valiant commander to whom the state of Venice turns when it needs to defend its strategic outpost Cyprus against the great Muslim enemy, the Turks. Racial slurs in this play are the hallmarks of viciousness, not the collective judgment of the community. As for Desdemona, her declaration that she "saw Othello's visage in his mind" (1.3.250) suggests, among other things, that the color of her husband's skin is not relevant to the great love that unites them.

How then does Iago do it? How does he succeed in undermining Othello's absolute faith in his wife and in shattering what seems an unshakable bond? Shakespeare depicts the destruction in one of the greatest scenes he ever wrote, a quiet conversation between the two men. The Turkish threat has vanished, blown away by a storm; Othello and Desdemona have been safely reunited in Cyprus; and though a drunken brawl in the night (cunningly instigated by Iago) has temporarily disgraced Othello's lieutenant Cassio, all the significant obstacles to harmony both public and private have been resolved. At this moment of almost perfect security, Iago injects the fatal poison of jealousy into Othello by little more than the intonation of the simple word "indeed" (3.3.101). Without leveling any direct accusation or offering a shred of evidence, with only a succession of apparently naive questions and broken phrases, Iago manages to insert himself into and remake—indeed, destroy—Othello's whole world.

Othello is not naive. He grasps that the verbal feints and dodges Iago is performing could "in a false disloyal knave" (3.3.124) be tricks designed to take in the gullible. But he knows Iago well, he thinks, and has confidence in his honesty. Tormented by the unbearable pain of aroused jealousy, Othello demands "ocular proof" (3.3.361) of Desdemona's adultery with Cassio. Iago, who has been promoted to lieutenant in Cassio's place, then embarks on a devious set of deceptions, centered on an embroidered handkerchief, a gift from Othello, that Desdemona has inadvertently mislaid. "Trifles light as air," Iago gleefully observes, "Are to the jealous confirmations strong / As proofs of holy writ" (3.3.323–25).

What is Iago's motive? Why should he want to destroy Othello, on whom his livelihood depends, and Desdemona, whom his own wife, Emilia, serves as lady's maid? Early in the play Iago presents himself as someone with an eye only for his own interests: "not I for love and duty, / But seeming so, for my peculiar end" (1.1.56–57). But it is difficult to make out how ruining his commander could help Iago. What is his peculiar—that is, personal—end?

As was his usual practice, Shakespeare did not make up the plot of his play from scratch but instead adapted it—in this case, from a short story by the sixteenth-century Italian writer Giraldi Cinthio. In Cinthio's account the villain's pathology is reasonably clear. Having fallen ardently in love with Desdemona, he tried to seduce her. When he did not succeed, the love he felt for the general's wife turned into violent loathing, and he set about to destroy her. Shakespeare discards this motivation. His villain does not dream of possessing Othello's wife, nor is she the particular object of his hatred. To be sure, there is a moment in which Iago seems to be heading in this direction—"Now I do love her too" (2.1.287), he declares in one of his sinister soliloquies—yet he immediately veers away from it toward a farrago of other explanations. Iago's repeated attempts to account for his obsessive, unappeasable hatred of Othello are famously unconvincing. Coleridge called them "the motive-hunting of motiveless malignity." Near the play's end, when he has come to understand that he has been duped into murdering his innocent, loving wife and that his life has been destroyed in the cruelest imaginable way, Othello asks why Iago "hath thus ensnared my soul and body?" Iago's spare, monosyllabic reply—his last utterance in the play—is a refusal to apologize or explain: "What you know, you know. / From this time forth I never will speak word" (5.2.307–09).

But why does Othello succumb? Why should a passion on which he has staked his whole being—"when I love thee not, / Chaos is come again" (3.3.91–92)—prove so fragile? Why should he doubt the faith of a woman so obviously single-minded in her devotion to him and so absolute in her love? The answer in part seems to lie in the terrible vulnerability of trust. As Iago coolly observes, Othello "[i]s of a constant, loving, noble nature" (2.1.285). That nature is bound up with his capacity to cherish his friends, rely on his subordinates, and above all, open his whole soul to his wife: "My life upon her faith!" (1.3.293). But such openness makes it possible for Iago to penetrate Othello's psychic defenses and refashion his perceptions.

Though Iago has a coarse and reductive account of human nature, he is a brilliant improviser, able to employ whatever comes to hand to shape illusions and to manipulate those around him like puppets in a theatrical performance of his making. He bustles about using people without a trace of moral restraint, shame, or decency, and he has the peculiar liberty of complete fraudulence: "I am not what I am" (1.1.62). In the end, he is exposed—by the wife whom he despises, abuses, and finally murders—but not before he has ruined whatever seemed most beautiful and precious in his world. Such is the power of cunning lies and twisted hatred over someone "that loved not wisely but too well" (5.2.349).

But perhaps this characterization of himself, offered by Othello just before his suicide, is not quite right, or at least not complete. Perhaps there is something disturbing in his love—some strain of anxiety about the future, about sexual pleasure, about his capacity for happiness—that Iago senses he can exploit. "If it were now to die," Othello has declared at the height of his joy,

> 'Twere now to be most happy; for I fear
> My soul hath her content so absolute
> That not another comfort like to this
> Succeeds in unknown fate. (2.1.187–91)

Desdemona attempts to offer reassurance—"The heavens forbid / But that our loves and comforts should increase / Even as our days do grow" (2.1.191–93)—but the malevolent worm of Iago's doubt is more powerful than her generous embrace. Or is it? Desdemona struggles in her last breath to commend herself to her "kind lord" (5.2.128), and Othello, desperately attempting to reestablish a moral order by executing himself, dies kissing the wife whose innocence he knows he has fatally wronged. Readers and audiences have, for more than four centuries, pondered how much these final gestures offer a glimpse of redemption through boundless love.

The Tragedy of Othello, the Moor of Venice[*]

The Names of the Actors[1]

OTHELLO, the Moor [and General of the Venetian forces]
BRABANTIO, father to Desdemona [and a Venetian Senator]
CASSIO, an honorable lieutenant [to Othello]
IAGO, a villain [and Othello's standard-bearer or ensign]
RODERIGO, a gulled° gentleman   deceived
DUKE of Venice
SENATORS
MONTANO, Governor of Cyprus
GENTLEMEN of Cyprus
LODOVICO and GRATIANO, two Noble Venetians [and kinsmen to Brabantio]
SAILORS
OFFICERS
CLOWN
DESDEMONA, wife to Othello
EMILIA, wife to Iago
BIANCA, a courtesan
MESSENGERS
MUSICIANS

Othello exists in two early texts, both of which have a claim to authority: a version published in the small, inexpensive quarto format in 1622 (Q) and a version published in the great First Folio of 1623 (F). There are many small and some substantial differences between them, including 160 lines that are found only in F. The text printed here is adapted from the Norton Critical Edition of *Othello*, edited by Edward Pechter. Like most modern editors of the play, Pechter bases his text on F, corrected by some readings from Q. Significant departures from Pechter's text have been footnoted.

1. The list of characters (with its misleading title) is reproduced from the First Folio, with some bracketed additions.

1.1

Enter RODERIGO *and* IAGO.[1]

RODERIGO Tush, never tell me![2] I take it much unkindly
　　That thou, Iago, who hast had my purse
　　As if the strings were thine, shouldst know of this.
IAGO 'Sblood,° but you'll not hear me! If ever I did dream　　*by Christ's blood*
　　Of such a matter, abhor me.
5　RODERIGO　　　　　　　　　　　Thou told'st me
　　Thou didst hold him in thy hate.
IAGO　　　　　　　　　　　Despise me
　　If I do not. Three great ones of the city,
　　In personal suit to make me his lieutenant,
　　Off-capped° to him; and by the faith of man　　*took off their caps*
10　I know my price; I am worth no worse a place.
　　But he, as loving his own pride and purposes,
　　Evades them with a bombast circumstance,[3]
　　Horribly stuffed with epithets of war,°　　*i.e., military jargon*
　　Non-suits° my mediators. For "Certes,"° says he,　　*denies / certainly*
15　"I have already chose my officer." And what was he?
　　Forsooth, a great arithmetician,[4]
　　One Michael Cassio, a Florentine,
　　A fellow almost damned in a fair wife,[5]
　　That° never set a squadron in the field,　　*who*
20　Nor the division° of a battle° knows　　*ordering / battalion*
　　More than a spinster°—unless the bookish theorick,°　　*housewife / learning*
　　Wherein the tonguèd consuls can propose[6]
　　As masterly as he. Mere prattle without practice
　　Is all his soldiership. But he, sir, had th'election
25　And I—of whom his eyes had seen the proof
　　At Rhodes, at Cyprus, and on other grounds,
　　Christened and heathen—must be beleed° and calmed[7]　　*without wind*
　　By debitor and creditor. This counter-caster,[8]
　　He in good time° must his lieutenant be,　　*indeed (scornful)*
30　And I—God bless the mark!° —his Moorship's ancient.[9]　　*God help us*
RODERIGO By heaven, I rather would have been his
　　hangman.
IAGO Why, there's no remedy. 'Tis the curse of service;
　　Preferment goes by letter and affection,[1]

1.1 Location: A street in Venice.
1. Iago's name may be related to that of Santiago Matamoros (Saint James the Moor-Slayer), the patron saint of Spain.
2. Expressive of annoyance, disbelief.
3. With an inflated circumlocution. "Bombast": cotton padding in clothes, a metaphor picked up by "stuffed" (line 13) and perhaps "Non-suits" (line 14).
4. Implying that Cassio's knowledge of war is purely theoretical.
5. Obscure. Cassio has not yet met Bianca and is unmarried (although in Shakespeare's source he is married). Perhaps Shakespeare's error, a reference to Cassio as a ladies' man, or an oblique anticipation of the main plot.

6. In which the glib senators can debate. In Q the senators are not "tonguèd" but "togaed," i.e., toga-wearing.
7. Becalmed.
8. Pejorative term for an accountant (Cassio), as is "debitor and creditor."
9. A variant form of ensign. Iago is something like a standard-bearer or third-in-command. He clearly ranks below "lieutenant" Cassio, the second-in-command. This reference to "his Moorship" is also the first indication about whom Iago has been complaining.
1. Promotion comes through connections and favoritism.

And not by old gradation,° where each second   *traditional seniority*
35 Stood heir to th'first. Now, sir, be judge yourself
Whether I in any just term am affined°   *am bound in any just way*
To love the Moor.[2]

RODERIGO   I would not follow him then.

IAGO O, sir, content you.°   *be content*
I follow him to serve my turn upon him.
40 We cannot all be masters, nor all masters
Cannot be truly followed. You shall mark
Many a duteous and knee-crooking knave
That, doting on his own obsequious bondage,
Wears out his time much like his master's ass,
For naught but provender;° and when he's old—   *animal feed*
45 cashiered.°   *fired*
Whip me° such honest knaves! Others there are   *the hell with*
Who, trimmed° in forms and visages of duty,   *outwardly decorated*
Keep yet their hearts attending on themselves
And, throwing but shows of service on their lords,
Do well thrive by them; and when they have lined their
50 coats,
Do themselves homage. These fellows have some soul,
And such a one do I profess myself. For, sir,
It is as sure as you are Roderigo,
Were I the Moor, I would not be Iago.
55 In following him, I follow but myself.
Heaven is my judge, not I for° love and duty,   *I am not driven by*
But seeming so, for my peculiar° end.   *personal*
For when my outward action doth demonstrate
The native act and figure[3] of my heart
60 In complement extern,° 'tis not long after   *outward appearance*
But I will wear my heart upon my sleeve
For daws° to peck at. I am not what I am.   *crowlike birds*

RODERIGO What a full fortune does the thick-lips owe°   *own*
If he can carry't thus!

IAGO   Call up her father,
65 Rouse him, make after him, poison his delight.
Proclaim him in the streets, incense her kinsmen,
And though he in a fertile climate dwell,
Plague him with flies. Though that his joy be joy,
Yet throw such chances of vexation on't,
70 As it may lose some color.

RODERIGO Here is her father's house. I'll call aloud.

IAGO Do, with like timorous accent° and dire yell   *frightening tone*

---

2. A Muslim of the mixed Berber and Arab people inhabiting northwest Africa. This term, like the comparison of Othello to a "Barbary horse" (an Arab, line 108), formerly led to the denial of Othello's blackness. But the passages describing Othello's appearance—"thick-lips," "black ram," "sooty bosom," "black Othello," "I am black," "black / As mine own face" (1.1.63, 1.1.85, 1.2.70, 2.3.29, 3.3.265, 3.3.388–89)—seem to have greater weight. In the Renaissance, "Moor" often meant sub-Saharan African.

3. The innate operation (or motivation) and shape (or nature).

As when, by night and negligence, the fire
Is spied in populous cities.

75 RODERIGO   What ho, Brabantio! Signor Brabantio, ho!

IAGO   Awake! What ho, Brabantio! Thieves, thieves!
Look to your house, your daughter, and your bags!
Thieves, thieves!

   [*Enter*] BRABANTIO *above at a window.*

BRABANTIO   What is the reason of this terrible summons?
80 What is the matter there?

RODERIGO   Signor, is all your family within?

IAGO   Are your doors locked?

BRABANTIO   Why? Wherefore ask you this?

IAGO   'Swounds,° sir, you're robbed! For shame, put on   *by Christ's wounds*
 your gown!
Your heart is burst, you have lost half your soul.
85 Even now, now, very now, an old black ram
Is tupping° your white ewe. Arise, arise!   *copulating with*
Awake the snorting° citizens with the bell,   *snoring*
Or else the devil will make a grandsire of you.
Arise, I say!

BRABANTIO   What, have you lost your wits?

90 RODERIGO   Most reverend signor, do you know my voice?

BRABANTIO   Not I; what are you?

RODERIGO   My name is Roderigo.

BRABANTIO   The worser welcome!
I have charged thee not to haunt about my doors;
In honest plainness thou hast heard me say
95 My daughter is not for thee. And now in madness,
Being full of supper and distemp'ring° draughts,   *destabilizing*
Upon malicious bravery,° dost thou come   *defiance*
To start° my quiet.   *upset*

RODERIGO   Sir, sir, sir—

BRABANTIO   But thou must needs be sure,
100 My spirits and my place° have in their power   *rank*
To make this bitter to thee.

RODERIGO   Patience, good sir.

BRABANTIO   What tell'st thou me of robbing? This is
 Venice;
My house is not a grange.°   *country house*

RODERIGO   Most grave Brabantio,
In simple and pure soul, I come to you.

105 IAGO   'Swounds, sir, you are one of those that will not
 serve God if the devil bid you. Because we come to do
 you service and you think we are ruffians, you'll have
 your daughter covered with a Barbary horse;[4] you'll
 have your nephews° neigh to you; you'll have coursers *grandsons*
110 for cousins and jennets for germans.[5]

---

4. Horse from northwest coastal Africa.
5. Close relatives. "Coursers": strong horses.

"Cousins": kinsmen. "Jennets": small Spanish
horses.

BRABANTIO   What profane wretch art thou?
IAGO   I am one, sir, that comes to tell you your daughter
    and the Moor are making the beast with two backs.°   *copulating*
BRABANTIO   Thou art a villain.
115 IAGO   You are a senator.
BRABANTIO   This thou shalt answer.° I know thee,   *account for*
    Roderigo.
RODERIGO   Sir, I will answer anything. But I beseech you,
    If't be your pleasure, and most wise consent—[6]
    As partly I find it is—that your fair daughter,
120 At this odd-even° and dull watch o'th' night,   *late (around midnight)*
    Transported with no worse nor better guard
    But with a knave of common° hire, a gondolier,   *public*
    To the gross clasps of a lascivious Moor—
    If this be known to you, and your allowance,°   *allowed by you*
125 We then have done you bold and saucy wrongs.
    But if you know not this, my manners tell me
    We have your wrong rebuke. Do not believe
    That from° the sense of all civility   *in opposition to*
    I thus would play and trifle with your reverence.
130 Your daughter, if you have not given her leave,
    I say again, hath made a gross revolt,
    Tying her duty, beauty, wit, and fortunes
    In an extravagant and wheeling stranger[7]
    Of here and everywhere. Straight° satisfy yourself.   *immediately*
135 If she be in her chamber or your house,
    Let loose on me the justice of the state
    For thus deluding you.
BRABANTIO   Strike on the tinder,° ho!   *a light*
    Give me a taper,° call up all my people!   *candle*
    This accident° is not unlike my dream;   *event*
140 Belief of it oppresses me already.
    Light, I say, light!   *Exit [above].*
IAGO   Farewell, for I must leave you.
    It seems not meet° nor wholesome to my place   *proper*
    To be producted°—as, if I stay, I shall—   *presented as witness*
    Against the Moor. For I do know the state,
145 However this may gall him with some check,°   *reprimand*
    Cannot with safety cast° him; for he's embarked°   *dismiss / committed*
    With such loud° reason to the Cyprus wars,   *urgent*
    Which even now stands in act,° that, for their souls,   *are taking place*
    Another of his fathom° they have none   *caliber*
150 To lead their business. In which regard,
    Though I do hate him as I do hell pains,
    Yet for necessity of present life
    I must show out a flag and sign of love,

6. Lines 118–34 do not appear in Q.
7. In a vagrant and vagabond foreigner.

Which is indeed but sign. That you shall surely find
    him,
155   Lead to the Sagittary[8] the raisèd search,°   *awakened searchers*
And there will I be with him. So farewell.   *Exit.*
    Enter [below] BRABANTIO *in his nightgown, with*
    servants and torches
BRABANTIO   It is too true an evil. Gone she is,
And what's to come of my despisèd time°   *lifetime*
Is naught but bitterness. Now, Roderigo,
160   Where didst thou see her?—O unhappy girl!—
With the Moor, say'st thou?—Who would be a father?—
How didst thou know 'twas she?—O, she deceives me
Past thought!—What said she to you?— [*to servants*] Get
    more tapers,
Raise all my kindred!   [*Exit one or more.*]
[*to* RODERIGO]   Are they married, think you?
165   RODERIGO   Truly, I think they are.
BRABANTIO   O heaven! How got she out? O treason of
    the blood!
Fathers, from hence trust not your daughters' minds
By what you see them act. Is there not charms°   *magic*
By which the property° of youth and maidhood°   *attribute / virginity*
170   May be abused? Have you not read, Roderigo,
Of some such thing?
RODERIGO   Yes, sir, I have indeed.
BRABANTIO [*to servants*]   Call up my brother.
[*to* RODERIGO]   O, would you had had her!
[*to servants*] Some one way, some another.
                     [*Exit one or more.*]
[*to* RODERIGO]   Do you know
Where we may apprehend her and the Moor?
175   RODERIGO   I think I can discover him, if you please
To get good guard and go along with me.
BRABANTIO   Pray you lead on. At every house I'll call;
I may command° at most.—Get weapons, ho!   *demand help*
And raise some special officers of night.—
180   On, good Roderigo; I will deserve° your pains.   *reward*
                       Exeunt.

1.2

    Enter OTHELLO, IAGO, [*and*] *attendants with torches.*
IAGO   Though in the trade of war I have slain men,
Yet do I hold it very stuff° o'th' conscience   *essence*
To do no contrived° murder. I lack iniquity,   *premeditated*

---

8. Perhaps indicating an inn named for the astrological sign Sagittarius, where Othello and Desdemona are staying. It may also suggest Othello himself, because Sagittarius is depicted as a centaur (a mythological being part man, part horse), and Iago has already likened Othello to a "Barbary horse."
1.2 Location: Another street in Venice, before Othello's lodgings.

Sometime, to do me service. Nine or ten times
5   I had thought t'have yerked him° here, under the ribs.   *stabbed (Roderigo)*
OTHELLO   'Tis better as it is.
IAGO   Nay, but he prated
And spoke such scurvy and provoking terms
Against your honor
That, with the little godliness I have,
10   I did full hard forbear him.[1] But I pray you, sir,
Are you fast° married? Be assured of this,   *legitimately*
That the magnifico° is much beloved,   *(Brabantio)*
And hath in his effect a voice potential°   *powerful*
As double as the duke's. He will divorce you,
15   Or put upon you what restraint or grievance
The law, with all his might to enforce it on,
Will give him cable.°   *scope*
OTHELLO   Let him do his spite.
My services, which I have done the signory,°   *Venetian government*
Shall out-tongue his complaints. 'Tis yet to know°—   *not publicly known*
20   Which, when I know that boasting is an honor,
I shall promulgate—I fetch my life and being
From men of royal siege;° and my demerits°   *rank / deserts*
May speak unbonneted[2] to as proud a fortune
As this that I have reached. For know, Iago,
25   But that I love the gentle Desdemona,
I would not my unhousèd° free condition   *unconfined*
Put into circumscription and confine
For the seas' worth. But look, what lights come yond?
        Enter CASSIO, *with officers and torches.*
IAGO   Those are the raisèd father and his friends.
You were best go in.
30   OTHELLO   Not I; I must be found.
My parts,° my title, and my perfect soul[3]   *qualities*
Shall manifest me rightly. Is it they?
IAGO   By Janus,° I think no.   *two-faced Roman god*
OTHELLO   The servants of the duke? And my lieutenant?
35   The goodness of the night upon you, friends.
What is the news?
CASSIO   The duke does greet you, general,
And he requires your haste-post-haste appearance
Even on the instant.
OTHELLO   What is the matter, think you?
CASSIO   Something from Cyprus, as I may divine.
40   It is a business of some heat.° The galleys   *urgency*
Have sent a dozen sequent° messengers   *successive*
This very night at one another's heels,
And many of the consuls, raised and met,
Are at the duke's already. You have been hotly called for;

1. I barely restrained myself from attacking him.   3. My clear conscience.
2. Without deference; modestly.

45 When, being not at your lodging to be found,
The senate hath sent about° three several quests   *out*
To search you out.
OTHELLO   'Tis well I am found by you.
I will but spend a word here in the house
And go with you.   [*Exit.*]
CASSIO   Ancient, what makes he here?
50 IAGO   Faith, he tonight hath boarded a land-carrack.[4]
If it prove lawful prize, he's made forever.
CASSIO   I do not understand.
IAGO   He's married.
CASSIO   To who?
IAGO   Marry,° to— [*Enter* OTHELLO.]   *by Mary (a mild oath)*
        Come, captain, will you go?
OTHELLO   Have with you.°   *let's go*
CASSIO   Here comes another troop to seek for you.
       Enter BRABANTIO [*and*] RODERIGO, *with officers and*
       torches.
55 IAGO   It is Brabantio; general, be advised,
He comes to bad intent.
OTHELLO   Holla, stand there!
RODERIGO   Signor, it is the Moor.
BRABANTIO   Down with him, thief!
       [*They draw on both sides.*]
IAGO   You, Roderigo? Come, sir, I am for you.
OTHELLO   Keep up° your bright swords, for the dew will   *put away*
    rust them.
60 Good signor, you shall more command with years
Than with your weapons.
BRABANTIO   O thou foul thief, where hast thou stowed
    my daughter?
Damned as thou art, thou hast enchanted her;
For I'll refer me to all things of sense,[5]
65 If she in chains of magic were not bound,
Whether a maid, so tender, fair, and happy,
So opposite to marriage that she shunned
The wealthy curlèd darlings of our nation,
Would ever have, t'incur a general mock,
70 Run from her guardage to the sooty bosom
Of such a thing as thou—to fear, not to delight.
Judge me the world if 'tis not gross in sense[6]
That thou hast practiced on her with foul charms,
Abused her delicate youth with drugs or minerals
75 That weakens motion.° I'll have't disputed on;[7]   *natural inclination*
'Tis probable and palpable to thinking.
I therefore apprehend and do attach° thee   *arrest*
For an abuser of the world, a practicer

---

4. A carrack is a large merchant ship.
5. For I'll ask, relying on common sense.
6. If it is not patently obvious. Lines 72–77 do

not appear in Q.
7. Argued by experts.

Of arts inhibited and out of warrant.°   *prohibited and illegal*
80   Lay hold upon him; if he do resist,
         Subdue him at his peril!
OTHELLO   Hold your hands,
         Both you of my inclining° and the rest.   *following*
         Were it my cue to fight, I should have known it
         Without a prompter. Where will you that I go
         To answer this your charge?
85   BRABANTIO   To prison, till fit time
         Of law and course of direct session
         Call thee to answer.
OTHELLO   What if I do obey?
         How may the duke be therewith satisfied,
         Whose messengers are here about my side
90   Upon some present business of the state
         To bring me to him?
OFFICER   'Tis true, most worthy signor.
         The duke's in council, and your noble self
         I am sure is sent for.
BRABANTIO   How? The duke in council?
         In this time of the night? Bring him away.°   *along*
95   Mine's not an idle cause. The duke himself,
         Or any of my brothers of the state,
         Cannot but feel this wrong as 'twere their own;
         For if such actions may have passage free,
         Bondslaves and pagans shall our statesmen be.
                                                  Exeunt.

                                    1.3

         Enter DUKE *and* SENATORS *set at a table, with lights
         and* OFFICERS.
DUKE   There's no composition in this news
         That gives them credit.[1]
FIRST SENATOR   Indeed, they are disproportioned;°   *inconsistent*
         My letters say a hundred and seven galleys.
DUKE   And mine a hundred forty.
SECOND SENATOR   And mine two hundred.
5   But though they jump not on a just account°—   *don't exactly agree*
         As in these cases where the aim reports
         'Tis oft with difference[2]—yet do they all confirm
         A Turkish fleet, and bearing up to Cyprus.
DUKE   Nay, it is possible enough to judgment;
10   I do not so secure me in the error
         But the main article I do approve
         In fearful sense.[3]

1.3 Location: A Venetian council room.
1. The reports lack the consistency that would
make them believable.
2. "Where . . . difference": where the reports are
estimates, there are often discrepancies among

them.
3. "I do not . . . sense": I am not so reassured by
the discrepancies as to dismiss the main
concern—the approach of a Turkish fleet.

SAILOR [*within*] What ho! what ho! what ho!
    Enter SAILOR.
OFFICER A messenger from the galleys.
DUKE   Now, what's the business?
SAILOR The Turkish preparation° makes for Rhodes.   *battle-ready fleet*
15   So was I bid report here to the state
    By Signor Angelo.[4]
DUKE How say you by this change?
FIRST SENATOR   This cannot be
    By no assay° of reason. 'Tis a pageant   *test*
    To keep us in false gaze. When we consider
20   Th' importancy of Cyprus to the Turk,
    And let ourselves again but understand
    That, as it more concerns the Turk than Rhodes,
    So may he with more facile question bear it,[5]
    For that it stands not in such warlike brace,
25   But altogether lacks th'abilities
    That Rhodes is dressed in—if we make thought of this,
    We must not think the Turk is so unskillful
    To leave that latest° which concerns him first,   *last*
    Neglecting an attempt of ease and gain
30   To wake and wage° a danger profitless.   *risk*
DUKE Nay, in all confidence, he's not for Rhodes.
OFFICER Here is more news.
    Enter a MESSENGER.
MESSENGER The Ottomites,° reverend and gracious,[6]   *Ottoman Turks*
    Steering with due course toward the isle of Rhodes,
35   Have there injointed them with an after° fleet.   *joined with another*
FIRST SENATOR Ay, so I thought. How many, as you guess?
MESSENGER Of thirty sail; and now they do re-stem°   *retrace*
    Their backward course, bearing with frank appearance
    Their purposes toward Cyprus. Signor Montano,
40   Your trusty and most valiant servitor,
    With his free duty recommends you thus,[7]
    And prays you to believe him.
DUKE 'Tis certain then for Cyprus.
    Marcus Luccicos[8]—is not he in town?
45 FIRST SENATOR He's now in Florence.
DUKE Write from us to him post-post-haste. Dispatch!
FIRST SENATOR Here comes Brabantio and the valiant
    Moor.
    Enter BRABANTIO, OTHELLO, CASSIO, IAGO, RODERIGO,
    and OFFICERS.
DUKE Valiant Othello, we must straight° employ you   *immediately*

---

4. Not mentioned elsewhere in the play, Angelus Sorianus was a Venetian sea captain who received the Venetian ambassador bearing from Constantinople the Turkish ultimatum to surrender Cyprus, shortly before its capture by the Turks in 1571.

5. So also can the Turkish fleet more easily win it.
6. Addressed to the senators.
7. With his freely given loyalty reports to you thus.
8. Not mentioned elsewhere in the play.

Against the general enemy° Ottoman.   (*of all Christendom*)
[*to* BRABANTIO] I did not see you; welcome, gentle°   *noble*
50   signor.
We lacked your counsel and your help tonight.
BRABANTIO   So did I yours. Good your grace, pardon me.
Neither my place° nor aught I heard of business   *official duty*
Hath raised me from my bed; nor doth the general care
55   Take hold on me. For my particular grief
Is of so floodgate and o'erbearing nature
That it engluts and swallows other sorrows,
And it is still itself.[9]
DUKE   Why, what's the matter?
BRABANTIO   My daughter, O my daughter!
SENATOR   Dead?
BRABANTIO   Ay, to me.
60   She is abused,° stol'n from me and corrupted   *deluded*
By spells and medicines bought of mountebanks;°   *quacks*
For nature so preposterously to err,
Being not deficient, blind, or lame of sense,
Sans° witchcraft could not.   *without*
65 DUKE   Whoe'er he be that in this foul proceeding
Hath thus beguiled your daughter of herself
And you of her, the bloody book of law
You shall yourself read in the bitter letter
After your own sense; yea, though our proper son
Stood in your action.[1]
70 BRABANTIO   Humbly I thank your grace.
Here is the man, this Moor, whom now it seems
Your special mandate for the state affairs
Hath hither brought.
ALL   We are very sorry for't.
DUKE [*to* OTHELLO]   What in your own part can you say
to this?
75 BRABANTIO   Nothing, but this is so.
OTHELLO   Most potent, grave, and reverend signors,
My very noble and approved good masters:
That I have ta'en away this old man's daughter
It is most true; true I have married her.
80   The very head and front° of my offending   *height and breadth*
Hath this extent, no more. Rude° am I in my speech,   *unpolished*
And little blessed with the soft phrase of peace;
For since these arms of mine had seven years' pith°   *strength*
Till now some nine moons wasted,° they have used   *nine months ago*
85   Their dearest° action in the tented field;   *most valued*
And little of this great world can I speak
More than pertains to feats of broils° and battle,   *combats*
And therefore little shall I grace my cause

---

9. That it (my grief) can incorporate other sorrows without being affected.

1. I.e., you yourself shall interpret the law as you
see fit, even if my own son was the one you accuse.

In speaking for myself. Yet, by your gracious patience,
90 I will a round° unvarnished tale deliver,   *plain*
Of my whole course of love: what drugs, what charms,
What conjuration and what mighty magic—
For such proceeding I am charged withal°—   *with*
I won his daughter.
BRABANTIO   A maiden never bold;
95 Of spirit so still and quiet that her motion
Blushed at herself² and she—in spite of nature,
Of years, of country, credit,° everything—   *reputation*
To fall in love with what she feared to look on?
It is a judgment maimed and most imperfect
100 That will confess perfection so could err
Against all rules of nature, and must° be driven   *(we therefore) must*
To find out practices of cunning hell
Why this should be. I therefore vouch again
That with some mixtures powerful o'er the blood,°   *passions*
105 Or with some dram conjured° to this effect,   *enchanted dose*
He wrought upon her.
DUKE   To vouch this is no proof,
Without more wider and more overt test
Than these thin habits and poor likelihoods
Of modern seeming do prefer against him.³
110 SENATOR But, Othello, speak;
Did you by indirect and forced courses°   *means*
Subdue and poison this young maid's affections?
Or came it by request and such fair question°   *conversation*
As soul to soul affordeth?
OTHELLO   I do beseech you
115 Send for the lady to the Sagittary,
And let her speak of me before her father.
If you do find me foul in her report,
The trust, the office I do hold of you,
Not only take away, but let your sentence
Even fall upon my life.
120 DUKE [to OFFICERS]   Fetch Desdemona hither.
OTHELLO Ancient, conduct them; you best know the
    place.
                Exit [IAGO and] two or three [attendants].
And till she come, as truly as to heaven
I do confess the vices of my blood,°   *sins of passion*
So justly to your grave ears I'll present
125 How I did thrive in this fair lady's love
And she in mine.
DUKE   Say it, Othello.
OTHELLO Her father loved me, oft invited me,

---

2. "Her . . . herself": she blushed at herself at
the slightest provocation.
3. "Without . . . him": without fuller and more
direct testimony than mere appearances and conjecture based on currently popular beliefs against
him.

Still° questioned me the story of my life   *constantly*
From year to year, the battles, sieges, fortunes
130   That I have past.
I ran it through, even from my boyish days
To th'very moment that he bade me tell it;
Wherein I spoke of most disastrous chances,°   *events*
Of moving accidents° by flood and field,   *events*
135   Of hair-breadth scapes i'th' imminent-deadly breach,[4]
Of being taken by the insolent foe
And sold to slavery, of my redemption thence
And portance° in my traveler's history;   *conduct*
Wherein of antars° vast and deserts idle,   *caves*
Rough quarries, rocks, and hills whose heads touch
140   heaven,
It was my hint° to speak—such was my process° —   *occasion / story*
And of the cannibals that each other eat,
The anthropophagi,[5] and men whose heads
Do grow beneath their shoulders. These things to hear
145   Would Desdemona seriously incline,
But still the house affairs would draw her thence,
Which ever as° she could with haste dispatch   *whenever*
She'd come again and with a greedy ear
Devour up my discourse; which I, observing,
150   Took once a pliant° hour and found good means   *convenient*
To draw from her a prayer of earnest heart
That I would all my pilgrimage dilate,°   *relate*
Whereof by parcels she had something heard,
But not intentively.° I did consent   *continuously*
155   And often did beguile her of her tears
When I did speak of some distressful stroke
That my youth suffered. My story being done,
She gave me for my pains a world of kisses;[6]
She swore in faith 'twas strange, 'twas passing° strange,   *exceptionally*
160   'Twas pitiful, 'twas wondrous pitiful.
She wished she had not heard it, yet she wished
That heaven had made her such a man.[7] She thanked me
And bade me, if I had a friend that loved her,
I should but teach him how to tell my story,
165   And that would woo her. Upon this hint I spake.
She loved me for the dangers I had past,
And I loved her that she did pity them.
This only is the witchcraft I have used.
Here comes the lady; let her witness it.
          Enter DESDEMONA, IAGO, [*and*] *attendants.*

4. In the immediately life-threatening gaps in a fortification.
5. Man-eaters. The term is from the ancient Roman writer Pliny the Elder. Shakespeare was also indebted to the travel literature of the Middle Ages (*The Travels of Sir John Mandeville*) and the Renaissance (Hakluyt's *Principal Navigations*, among others).
6. F reads "kisses," Q "sighs." It is hard to explain "kisses" as a textual error.
7. Made such a man for her; made her into such a man.

170 DUKE I think this tale would win my daughter too.
　　　Good Brabantio, take up this mangled matter at the
　　　　best.°　　　　　　　　　　　　　　　　　　　　*make the best of this*
　　　Men do their broken weapons rather use,
　　　Than their bare hands.
BRABANTIO　　　　　　　　I pray you hear her speak.
　　　If she confess that she was half the wooer,
175　　Destruction on my head if my bad blame
　　　Light on the man. Come hither, gentle mistress.
　　　Do you perceive in all this noble company
　　　Where most you owe obedience?
DESDEMONA　　　　　　　　My noble father,
　　　I do perceive here a divided duty.
180　　To you I am bound for life and education;
　　　My life and education both do learn° me　　　　　　*teach*
　　　How to respect you; you are the lord of duty;
　　　I am hitherto your daughter. But here's my husband;
　　　And so much duty as my mother showed
185　　To you, preferring you before her father,
　　　So much I challenge° that I may profess　　　　　　*assert*
　　　Due to the Moor my lord.
BRABANTIO　　　　　　　　God be with you; I have done.
　　　Please it° your grace, on to the state affairs;　　　*if it pleases*
　　　I had rather to adopt a child than get° it.　　　　*beget*
190　　Come hither, Moor.
　　　I here do give thee that° with all my heart　　　　*that which*
　　　Which, but° thou hast already, with all my heart　*except that*
　　　I would keep from thee. [*to* DESDEMONA] For your sake,
　　　　jewel,
　　　I am glad at soul I have no other child,
195　　For thy escape would teach me tyranny
　　　To hang clogs[8] on them. I have done, my lord.
DUKE Let me speak like yourself and lay a sentence°　*draw a moral*
　　　Which, as a grise° or step, may help these lovers　*step*
　　　Into your favor.
200　　When remedies are past, the griefs are ended
　　　By seeing the worst, which late on hopes depended.[9]
　　　To mourn a mischief that is past and gone
　　　Is the next way to draw new mischief on.
　　　What cannot be preserved, when fortune takes,
205　　Patience her injury a mockery makes.[1]
　　　The robbed that smiles steals something from the thief;
　　　He robs himself that spends a bootless° grief.　　　*pointless*
BRABANTIO So let the Turk of Cyprus us beguile:
　　　We lose it not, so long as we can smile.

8. Blocks of wood tied to criminals' legs to keep them from escaping.
9. By seeing those things come to pass that caused grief in anticipation. The duke paints the moral in rhyming couplets, to which Brabantio replies in kind.
1. Patience laughs at what cannot be helped (and thus reduces the "injury").

210 He bears the sentence° well that nothing bears   *saying; judgment*
    But the free comfort which from thence he hears.
    But he bears both the sentence and the sorrow
    That, to pay grief, must of poor patience borrow.
    These sentences, to sugar or to gall,°   *both sweet and bitter*
215 Being strong on both sides, are equivocal.
    But words are words; I never yet did hear
    That the bruised heart was piercèd[2] through the ear.
    I humbly beseech you proceed to th'affairs of state.
DUKE   The Turk with a most mighty preparation makes for
220   Cyprus. Othello, the fortitude of the place is best known
    to you; and though we have there a substitute of most
    allowed sufficiency,° yet opinion, a more sovereign mis-   *known ability*
    tress of effects, throws a more safer voice on you.[3] You
    must therefore be content to slubber° the gloss of your   *soil*
225   new fortunes with this more stubborn° and boisterous   *rougher*
    expedition.
OTHELLO   The tyrant custom, most grave senators,
    Hath made the flinty and steel couch of war
    My thrice-driven° bed of down. I do agnize°   *sifted / acknowledge*
230 A natural and prompt alacrity
    I find in hardness,° and do undertake   *hardship*
    This present wars against the Ottomites.
    Most humbly, therefore, bending to your state,°   *authority*
    I crave fit disposition for my wife,
235 Due reference of place, and exhibition,[4]
    With such accommodation and besort°   *suitable attendance*
    As levels with her breeding.
DUKE   Why, at her father's.
BRABANTIO   I will not have it so.
OTHELLO   Nor I.
DESDEMONA   Nor would I there reside,
240 To put my father in impatient thoughts
    By being in his eye. Most gracious duke,
    To my unfolding° lend your prosperous° ear,   *proposal / receptive*
    And let me find a charter° in your voice   *an authorization*
    T'assist my simpleness.
245 DUKE   What would you, Desdemona?
DESDEMONA   That I love the Moor to live with him,
    My downright violence and storm of fortunes[5]
    May trumpet to the world. My heart's subdued
    Even to the very quality[6] of my lord.
250 I saw Othello's visage in his mind,
    And to his honors and his valiant parts°   *qualities*
    Did I my soul and fortunes consecrate;

---

2. Surgically lanced (and presumably cured).
3. "Opinion . . . you": public opinion, which determines what gets done, finds greater security with you.
4. Proper accommodation and maintenance.

5. My outright defiance of custom.
6. Essential nature. In the Quarto, Desdemona says that her heart is subdued to Othello's "utmost pleasure."

So that, dear lords, if I be left behind,
A moth of peace, and he go to the war,
255 The rites° for why I love him are bereft me,   *(of love); (of war?)*
And I a heavy interim shall support
By his dear absence. Let me go with him.
OTHELLO [*to the* DUKE]   Let her have your voice.
Vouch with me, heaven, I therefor beg it not
260 To please the palate of my appetite,
Nor to comply with heat° (the young affects[7]   *sexual passion*
In me defunct) and proper° satisfaction,   *personal; fitting*
But to be free° and bounteous to her mind;   *liberal*
And heaven defend your good souls that you think
265 I will your serious and great business scant
When she is with me. No, when light-winged toys°   *diversions*
Of feathered Cupid seel° with wanton dullness   *blind*
My speculative and officed instruments,[8]
That my disports° corrupt and taint my business,   *sexual pleasures*
270 Let housewives make a skillet of my helm,
And all indign° and base adversities   *undignified*
Make head against my estimation.[9]
DUKE   Be it as you shall privately determine,
Either for her stay or going. Th'affair cries haste,
275 And speed must answer it.
SENATOR   You must away tonight.
DESDEMONA   Tonight, my lord?
DUKE   This night.[1]
OTHELLO   With all my heart.
DUKE   At nine i'th' morning here we'll meet again.
Othello, leave some officer behind,
280 And he shall our commission bring to you,
And such things else of quality and respect°   *weight and importance*
As doth import° you.   *concern*
OTHELLO   So please your grace, my ancient;
A man he is of honesty[2] and trust.
To his conveyance I assign my wife,
285 With what else needful your good grace shall think
To be sent after me.
DUKE   Let it be so.
Good night to every one. [*to* BRABANTIO] And, noble
   signor,
If virtue no delighted° beauty lack,   *delightful*
Your son-in-law is far more fair than black.
                              [*Exit* DUKE.]
290 SENATOR   Adieu, brave Moor; use Desdemona well.
BRABANTIO   Look to her,° Moor, if thou hast eyes to see: *watch her carefully*
   She has deceived her father, and may thee.

---

7. The youthful desires.
8. My duty-bound faculties of sense.
9. Raise an army against my good reputation.
1. This exchange between Desdemona and the
Duke is only in Q.
2. The first of many references to Iago's "honesty."

         Exeunt [BRABANTIO, CASSIO, SENATORS, *and* OFFICERS.]

OTHELLO   My life upon her faith!—Honest Iago,
My Desdemona must I leave to thee.
295   I prithee let thy wife attend on her,
And bring them after in the best advantage.[3]
Come, Desdemona; I have but an hour
Of love, of worldly matter and direction
To spend with thee. We must obey the time.

         Exeunt [OTHELLO *the*] *Moor and* DESDEMONA.

300 RODERIGO Iago?
IAGO What say'st thou, noble heart?
RODERIGO What will I do, think'st thou?
IAGO Why, go to bed and sleep.
RODERIGO I will incontinently° drown myself.   *immediately*
305 IAGO If thou dost, I shall never love thee after. Why, thou
silly gentleman?
RODERIGO It is silliness to live when to live is torment; and
then have we a prescription[4] to die when death is our
physician.
310 IAGO O villainous!° I have looked upon the world for four   *absurd*
times seven years, and since I could distinguish betwixt
a benefit and an injury, I never found man that knew how
to love himself. Ere I would say I would drown myself for
the love of a guinea-hen,° I would change my humanity   *woman*
315 with a baboon.
RODERIGO What should I do? I confess it is my shame to
be so fond, but it is not in my virtue° to amend it.   *native ability*
IAGO Virtue? A fig!° 'Tis in ourselves that we are thus or   *(an obscenity)*
thus. Our bodies are our gardens, to the which our wills
320 are gardeners. So that if we will plant nettles or sow lettuce, set hyssop° and weed up thyme, supply it with one   *mint herb*
gender° of herbs or distract it with many, either to have it   *kind*
sterile with idleness° or manured with industry, why, the   *noncultivation*
power and corrigible authority° of this lies in our wills. If   *ability to decide*
325 the balance of our lives had not one scale of reason to
poise° another of sensuality, the blood and baseness of   *counterweigh*
our natures would conduct us to most preposterous conclusions. But we have reason to cool our raging motions,°   *appetites*
our carnal stings or unbitted° lusts; whereof I take this   *unrestrained*
330 that you call love to be a sect or scion.°   *offshoot*
RODERIGO It cannot be.
IAGO It is merely a lust of the blood and a permission of
the will. Come, be a man! Drown thyself? Drown cats and
blind puppies. I have professed me thy friend, and I confess me knit to thy deserving with cables of perdurable°   *durable*
toughness. I could never better stead° thee than now.   *help*
Put money in thy purse. Follow thou the wars; defeat thy

---

3. And bring them along at the most favorable   4. Right; doctor's order.
moment.

favor with an usurped beard.[5] I say, put money in thy
purse. It cannot be long that Desdemona should continue her love to the Moor—put money in thy purse—
nor he his to her. It was a violent commencement[6] in
her, and thou shalt see an answerable sequestration[7]—
put but money in thy purse. These Moors are changeable in their wills—fill thy purse with money. The food
that to him now is as luscious as locusts[8] shall be to him
shortly as bitter as coloquintida.[9] She must change for
youth: when she is sated with his body, she will find
the error of her choice. Therefore, put money in thy
purse. If thou wilt needs° damn thyself, do it a more *if you must*
delicate way than drowning—make all the money thou
canst. If sanctimony° and a frail vow betwixt an erring[1] *holy rite*
barbarian and a super-subtle° Venetian be not too hard *highly sensitive*
for my wits and all the tribe of hell, thou shalt enjoy
her. Therefore make money. A pox of drowning thyself;
it is clean out of the way.° Seek thou rather to be hanged *of no use*
in compassing° thy joy than to be drowned and go with- *encompassing*
out her.

RODERIGO Wilt thou be fast° to my hopes, if I depend on *duty-bound*
the issue?° *outcome*

IAGO Thou art sure of me—go make money. I have told
thee often, and I retell thee again and again, I hate the
Moor. My cause is hearted;° thine hath no less reason. *heartfelt*
Let us be conjunctive° in our revenge against him. If thou *joined*
canst cuckold him, thou dost thyself a pleasure, me a
sport. There are many events in the womb of time which
will be delivered. Traverse,° go, provide thy money. We *go (to arms)*
will have more of this tomorrow. Adieu.

RODERIGO Where shall we meet i'th' morning?

IAGO At my lodging.

RODERIGO I'll be with thee betimes.° *early*

IAGO Go to, farewell. Do you hear, Roderigo?

RODERIGO I'll sell all my land.   *Exit.*

IAGO Thus do I ever make my fool my purse;
For I mine own gained knowledge should profane
If I would time expend with such a snipe° *fool*
But for my sport and profit. I hate the Moor,
And it is thought abroad° that 'twixt my sheets *rumored*
H'as done my office. I know not if't be true,
But I for mere suspicion in that kind
Will do° as if for surety. He holds° me well; *act / esteems*
The better shall my purpose work on him.
Cassio's a proper° man. Let me see now . . . *handsome*

---

5. Disguise your appearance with a fake beard.
6. An abruptly begun affair.
7. A correspondingly abrupt separation.
8. A sweet, exotic fruit, perhaps carob or honeysuckle.
9. Colocynth, a purgative—one of Iago's many
references to the digestive tract.
1. A wandering.

To get his place and to plume up° my will   *gratify*
In double knavery—how? how? Let's see . . .
385 After some time, to abuse Othello's ears
That he is too familiar with his wife.[2]
He hath a person and a smooth dispose°   *manner*
To be suspected, framed° to make women false.   *formed*
The Moor is of a free° and open nature   *liberal*
390 That thinks men honest that but seem to be so,
And will as tenderly° be led by th'nose   *easily*
As asses are. . . .
I have't! It is engendered! Hell and night
Must bring this monstrous birth to the world's light. *Exit.*

2.1

Enter MONTANO *and two* GENTLEMEN [*one above*].
MONTANO   What from the cape can you discern at sea?
FIRST GENTLEMAN   Nothing at all; it is a high-wrought
    flood.°   *very rough sea*
I cannot 'twixt the heaven and the main°   *sea*
Descry° a sail.   *discern*
5 MONTANO   Methinks the wind hath spoke aloud at land;
A fuller blast ne'er shook our battlements
If it hath ruffianed° so upon the sea,   *raged*
What ribs of oak, when mountains melt on them,
Can hold the mortise?[1] What shall we hear of this?
10 SECOND GENTLEMAN   A segregation° of the Turkish fleet: *separation*
For do but stand upon the foaming shore,
The chidden billow[2] seems to pelt the clouds;
The wind-shaked surge, with high and monstrous mane,
Seems to cast water on the burning Bear
15 And quench the guards of th'ever-fixèd pole.[3]
I never did like molestation view°   *see such a tumult*
On the enchafed° flood.   *raging*
MONTANO   If that the Turkish fleet
Be not ensheltered and embayed, they are drowned;
It is impossible to bear it out.
Enter a THIRD GENTLEMAN.
20 THIRD GENTLEMAN   News, lads! Our wars are done.
The desperate tempest hath so banged the Turks
That their designment° halts. A noble ship of Venice   *plan*
Hath seen a grievous wrack and sufferance°   *damage*
On most part of their fleet.
MONTANO   How? Is this true?

---

2. "He" is Cassio (as in line 387), but "his" refers
to Othello.
2.1 Location: A seaport in Cyprus; outdoors near
the harbor.
1. "What . . . mortise": what ship (with "ribs of
oak") can hold its joints ("mortise") together when
"mountains" of water pour on it?

2. The surging ocean, rebuked ("chidden") by the
wind (or repulsed by the land).
3. The "burning Bear" is the constellation Ursa
Minor; the "guards" are probably two stars in the
constellation that point in a line to the polestar,
also in Ursa Minor.

THIRD GENTLEMAN   The ship is here put in,
A Veronnesa.[4] Michael Cassio,
Lieutenant to the warlike Moor, Othello,
Is come on shore; the Moor himself at sea,
And is in full commission here for Cyprus.
MONTANO   I am glad on't—'tis a worthy governor.
THIRD GENTLEMAN   But this same Cassio, though he speak
     of comfort
Touching the Turkish loss, yet he looks sadly°   *seriously*
And prays the Moor be safe; for they were parted
With foul and violent tempest.
MONTANO   Pray heavens he be,
For I have served him, and the man commands
Like a full soldier. Let's to the seaside—ho!—
As well to see the vessel that's come in
As to throw out our eyes for brave Othello,
Even till we make the main and th'aerial blue
An indistinct regard.[5]
THIRD GENTLEMAN   Come, let's do so;
For every minute is expectancy
Of more arrivance.
          Enter CASSIO.
CASSIO   Thanks, you the valiant of the warlike isle,
That so approve the Moor! O, let the heavens
Give him defense against the elements,
For I have lost him on a dangerous sea.
MONTANO   Is he well shipped?
CASSIO   His bark is stoutly timbered, and his pilot
Of very expert and approved allowance;°   *known ability*
Therefore my hopes, not surfeited to death,°   *not excessive*
Stand in bold cure.°   *likely to be rewarded*
VOICES [*within*]   A sail! a sail! a sail!
CASSIO   What noise?
GENTLEMAN   The town is empty; on the brow o'th' sea
Stand ranks of people, and they cry "A sail!"
CASSIO   My hopes do shape him for° the governor.   *make it out to be*
     [*A shot.*]
SECOND GENTLEMAN   They do discharge their shot of
     courtesy—
Our friends, at least.
CASSIO   I pray you, sir, go forth
And give us truth who 'tis that is arrived.
SECOND GENTLEMAN   I shall.   *Exit.*
MONTANO   But, good lieutenant, is your general wived?
CASSIO   Most fortunately: he hath achieved a maid
That paragons° description and wild fame,   *stands above*

4. Meaning unclear: either a ship originally   5. "Even . . . regard": until we can't distinguish
from Verona, though now used by the Venetians;   sea from sky.
or perhaps a particular *kind* of ship.

One that excels the quirks of blazoning° pens,   *praise-giving*
And in th'essential vesture of creation
Does tire the engineer.[6]
    Enter SECOND GENTLEMAN.

65   How now? Who has put in?
SECOND GENTLEMAN   'Tis one Iago, ancient to the general.
CASSIO   He's had most favorable and happy speed:
    Tempests themselves, high seas, and howling winds,
    The guttered° rocks and congregated° sands,   *jagged / accumulated*
70   Traitors ensteeped° to enclog the guiltless keel,   *underwater*
    As having sense of beauty, do omit°   *forgo*
    Their mortal° natures, letting go safely by   *deadly*
    The divine Desdemona.
MONTANO   What is she?
CASSIO   She that I spake of, our great captain's captain,
75   Left in the conduct of the bold Iago,
    Whose footing here anticipates our thoughts
    A se'night's speed.[7] Great Jove, Othello guard,
    And swell his sail with thine own powerful breath,
    That he may bless this bay with his tall ship,
80   Make love's quick pants in Desdemona's arms,
    Give renewed fire to our extincted spirits,
    And bring all Cyprus comfort!
    Enter DESDEMONA, IAGO, RODERIGO, *and* EMILIA.
                    O, behold!
    The riches of the ship is come on shore.
    You men of Cyprus, let her have your knees.
85   Hail to thee, lady, and the grace of heaven
    Before, behind thee, and on every hand
    Enwheel thee round.
DESDEMONA   I thank you, valiant Cassio.
    What tidings can you tell me of my lord?
CASSIO   He is not yet arrived, nor know I aught
90   But that he's well and will be shortly here.
DESDEMONA   O, but I fear!—How lost you company?
CASSIO   The great contention of sea and skies
    Parted our fellowship.
VOICES *within*   A sail! a sail!
    [*A shot.*]
CASSIO   But hark—a sail.
GENTLEMAN   They give their greeting to the citadel;
    This likewise is a friend.
95 CASSIO   See for the news.
                   [*Exit* GENTLEMAN.]
    Good ancient, you are welcome. Welcome, mistress.
    [*Kisses* EMILIA.]

---

6. "In . . . engineer": whose natural beauty exhausts
the poet's capacity to invent praise.

7. Whose arrival predates our expectations by a
week.

Let it not gall your patience, good Iago,
That I extend my manners. 'Tis my breeding
That gives me this bold show of courtesy.

100 IAGO   Sir, would she give you so much of her lips
As of her tongue she oft bestows on me,
You would have enough.

DESDEMONA   Alas, she has no speech.[8]

IAGO   In faith, too much:
I find it still° when I have leave to sleep.   *always*

105 Marry, before your ladyship, I grant,
She puts her tongue a little in her heart[9]
And chides with thinking.

EMILIA   You have little cause to say so.

IAGO   Come on! come on! You are pictures[1] out of door,

110 Bells° in your parlors, wildcats in your kitchens,   *i.e., noisy*
Saints° in your injuries, devils being offended,   *i.e., martyrs*
Players in your huswifery, and huswives[2] in your beds.

DESDEMONA   O, fie upon thee, slanderer!

IAGO   Nay, it is true, or else I am a Turk:

115 You rise to play and go to bed to work.

EMILIA   You shall not write my praise.

IAGO   No, let me not.

DESDEMONA   What wouldst write of me, if thou shouldst
praise me?

IAGO   O, gentle lady, do not put me to't,
For I am nothing if not critical.

DESDEMONA   Come on, assay.° There's one gone to the   *essay, try*
120 harbor?

IAGO   Ay, madam.

DESDEMONA   I am not merry, but I do beguile°   *disguise*
The thing I am° by seeming otherwise.—   *(worried for Othello)*
Come, how wouldst thou praise me?

125 IAGO   I am about it, but indeed my invention
Comes from my pate as birdlime[3] does from frieze.°   *coarse wool cloth*
It plucks out brains and all. But my muse labors,°   *(in childbirth)*
And thus she is delivered:
"If she be fair and wise, fairness and wit,

130 The one's for use, the other useth it."[4]

DESDEMONA   Well praised! How if she be black and witty?

IAGO   "If she be black,[5] and thereto have a wit,
She'll find a white that shall her blackness fit."[6]

DESDEMONA   Worse and worse!

---

8. Perhaps both a defense of Emilia and a prod for her to speak.
9. She keeps her (critical) thoughts to herself.
1. Models of silent propriety. In this speech Iago shifts from Emilia to women generally.
2. Pronounced *hussies* and thus carrying opposed suggestions: wanton; businesslike, charily husbanding sexual favors (cf. line 115). "Players in

your huswifery": deceptive in managing household expenses.
3. Sticky substance used to trap small birds.
4. I.e., intelligence makes use of beauty.
5. Dark-haired or dark-complexioned.
6. With sexual double entendre. "White": fair-skinned person (with a pun on *wight*, "person").

135 EMILIA   How if fair and foolish?

IAGO   "She never yet was foolish that was fair,
   For even her folly° helped her to an heir."   *foolishness; lechery*

DESDEMONA   These are old fond° paradoxes, to make fools   *foolish*
   laugh i'th' alehouse. What miserable praise hast thou for
140   her that's foul° and foolish?   *ugly*

IAGO   "There's none so foul and foolish thereunto,°   *to boot*
   But does foul° pranks which fair and wise ones do."   *lascivious*

DESDEMONA   O, heavy ignorance! Thou praisest the worst
   best. But what praise couldst thou bestow on a deserv-
145   ing woman indeed? One that in the authority of her
   merit did justly put on the vouch[7] of very malice itself.

IAGO   "She that was ever fair, and never proud,
   Had tongue at will, and yet was never loud,
   Never lacked gold, and yet went never gay,°   *lavishly clothed*
150   Fled from her wish, and yet said "now I may";[8]
   She that, being angered, her revenge being nigh,
   Bade her wrong stay° and her displeasure fly;   *sense of injury end*
   She that in wisdom never was so frail
   To change the cod's head for the salmon's tail;[9]
155   She that could think, and ne'er disclose her mind,
   See suitors following, and not look behind:
   She was a wight (if ever such wights were) . . ."

DESDEMONA   To do what?

IAGO   "To suckle fools and chronicle small beer."[1]

160 DESDEMONA   O, most lame and impotent conclusion! Do
   not learn of him, Emilia, though he be thy husband.
   How say you, Cassio? Is he not a most profane and lib-
   eral° counselor?   *outspoken*

CASSIO   He speaks home, madam. You may relish him
165   more in° the soldier than in the scholar.   *as*

IAGO [*aside*]   He takes her by the palm. Ay, well said,°   *well done*
   whisper! With as little a web as this will I ensnare as
   great a fly as Cassio. Ay, smile upon her, do! I will gyve°   *shackle*
   thee in thine own courtship.°—You say true, 'tis so   *courtliness*
170   indeed.—If such tricks as these strip you out of your
   lieutenantry, it had been better you had not kissed your
   three fingers so oft,[2] which now again you are most apt
   to play the sir° in. Very good! well kissed and excellent   *gentleman*
   courtesy!—'Tis so indeed.—Yet again, your fingers to
175   your lips? Would they were clyster pipes° for your sake!   *enema tubes*
   Trumpets within
   The Moor! I know his trumpet.

CASSIO   'Tis truly so.

DESDEMONA   Let's meet him and receive him.

---

7. Compel the approval.
8. Voluntarily withstood temptation even when given the choice.
9. To make an unworthy exchange.

1. I.e., to breast-feed babies and keep track of trivial domestic goods.
2. It would have been better for you not to have blown her so many kisses.

CASSIO Lo, where he comes.
      Enter OTHELLO *and attendants.*
OTHELLO O, my fair warrior!
180 DESDEMONA   My dear Othello!
OTHELLO It gives me wonder great as my content
  To see you here before me. O! my soul's joy,
  If after every tempest come such calms,
  May the winds blow till they have wakened death,
185   And let the laboring bark° climb hills of seas   *small ship*
  Olympus-high,³ and duck again as low
  As hell's from heaven! If it were now to die,⁴
  'Twere now to be most happy; for I fear
  My soul hath her content so absolute
190   That not another comfort like to this
  Succeeds° in unknown fate.°   *will follow / future*
DESDEMONA   The heavens forbid
  But that our loves and comforts should increase
  Even as our days do grow.
OTHELLO   Amen to that, sweet powers!
  I cannot speak enough of this content;
195   It stops me here; it is too much of joy.
  And this, and this—   *They kiss.*
              the greatest discords be
  That e'er our hearts shall make!
IAGO [*aside*]   O, you are well tuned now;
  But I'll set down the pegs that make this music,⁵
  As honest as I am.
OTHELLO   Come, let us to the castle.
200   News, friends; our wars are done. The Turks are drowned.
  How does my old acquaintance of this isle?—
  Honey, you shall be well desired° in Cyprus;   *welcomed*
  I have found great love amongst them. O, my sweet,
  I prattle out of fashion, and I dote
205   In mine own comforts. I prithee, good Iago,
  Go to the bay and disembark my coffers.°   *trunks*
  Bring thou the master° to the citadel;   *captain*
  He is a good one, and his worthiness
  Does challenge° much respect. Come, Desdemona;   *deserve*
210   Once more well met at Cyprus.
        Exit OTHELLO *and* DESDEMONA [*and all but* IAGO *and*
        RODERIGO].
IAGO [*to a departing attendant*] Do thou meet me presently at the harbor. [*to* RODERIGO] Come hither. If thou
  be'st valiant—as they say base° men, being in love, have   *lowly born*
  then a nobility in their natures more than is native to
215   them—list° me. The lieutenant tonight watches on the   *listen to*

---

3. Mount Olympus, home of the Greek gods and
hence too high for mortals.
4. To perish, but also evoking the very common

sense "to have an orgasm."
5. I'll untune (by loosening) the "pegs" that hold
the strings of the musical instrument taut.

court of guard.[6] First I must tell thee this: Desdemona is
directly in love with him.

RODERIGO With him? Why, 'tis not possible.

IAGO Lay thy finger thus,° and let thy soul be instructed.   *be silent*
220 Mark me with what violence she first loved the Moor,
but° for bragging and telling her fantastical lies. To love   *only*
him still for prating, let not thy discreet heart think it.
Her eye must be fed. And what delight shall she have to
look on the devil? When the blood is made dull with the
225 act of sport, there should be—again to enflame it, and
to give satiety a fresh appetite—loveliness in favor,°   *looks*
sympathy in years, manners, and beauties, all which the
Moor is defective in. Now for want of these required
conveniences,° her delicate tenderness will find itself   *compatibilities*
230 abused,° begin to heave the gorge,[7] disrelish and abhor   *revolted*
the Moor. Very nature will instruct her in it and compel
her to some second choice. Now, sir, this granted—as it
is a most pregnant° and unforced position—who stands   *obvious; (sexual)*
so eminent in the degree of[8] this fortune as Cassio
235 does?—a knave very voluble,° no further conscionable[9]   *facile*
than in putting on the mere form of civil and humane
seeming for the better compass° of his salt[1] and most   *achievement*
hidden loose affection. Why none! why none! A slipper°   *slippery*
and subtle knave, a finder of occasion, that has an eye
240 can stamp and counterfeit advantages,[2] though true
advantage never present itself. A devilish knave! Besides,
the knave is handsome, young, and hath all those requi-
sites in him that folly° and green minds look after. A   *wantonness*
pestilent° complete knave! And the woman hath found   *damnably*
245 him already.

RODERIGO I cannot believe that in her; she's full of most
blessed condition.

IAGO Blessed fig's-end!° The wine she drinks is made of   *(obscene)*
grapes. If she had been blessed, she would never have
250 loved the Moor. Blessed pudding!° Didst thou not see   *sausage*
her paddle with the palm of his hand? Didst not mark
that?

RODERIGO Yes, that I did, but that was but courtesy.

IAGO Lechery, by this hand! an index and obscure° pro-   *encoded*
255 logue to the history° of lust and foul thoughts.[3] They   *story*
met so near with their lips that their breaths embraced
together. Villainous thoughts, Roderigo: when these
mutualities so marshal the way, hard at hand comes the
master and main exercise,[4] th'incorporate° conclusion.   *in the flesh*

6. I.e., Cassio is in charge of the watch at the
guardhouse.
7. Feel nausea.
8. As next in line for.
9. No more ethical.
1. Lewd.
2. Who can (like a counterfeiter) create his own

opportunities.
3. The analogy is to a dirty book. "Index": table
of contents.
4. When these intimacies have cleared the way,
the main event follows close behind. Here, the
analogy is to an official procession.

260 Pish! But, sir, be you ruled by me. I have brought you
from Venice. Watch you tonight. For the command, I'll
lay't upon you.[5] Cassio knows you not. I'll not be far from
you. Do you find some occasion to anger Cassio, either by
speaking too loud or tainting° his discipline, or from what   insulting
265 other course you please, which the time shall more favorably minister.°   provide
RODERIGO Well.
IAGO Sir, he's rash and very sudden in choler, and haply°   perhaps
may strike at you. Provoke him that he may; for even out
270 of that will I cause these of Cyprus to mutiny; whose
qualification shall come into no true taste again[6] but by
the displanting of Cassio. So shall you have a shorter
journey to your desires by the means I shall then have to
prefer° them, and the impediment most profitably   promote
275 removed without the which there were no expectation of
our prosperity.
RODERIGO I will do this if you can bring it to any opportunity.
IAGO I warrant thee. Meet me by and by at the citadel. I
280 must fetch his necessaries[7] ashore. Farewell.
RODERIGO Adieu.   *Exit.*
IAGO That Cassio loves her, I do well believ't;
That she loves him, 'tis apt and of great credit.°   likely and believable
The Moor, howbeit that I endure him not,
285 Is of a constant, loving, noble nature,
And I dare think he'll prove to Desdemona
A most dear° husband. Now I do love her too,   affectionate; costly
Not out of absolute lust (though peradventure
I stand accountant° for as great a sin),   accountable
290 But partly led to diet° my revenge,   feed
For that I do suspect the lusty Moor
Hath leaped into my seat°—the thought whereof   slept with my wife
Doth, like a poisonous mineral, gnaw my inwards,°   innards
And nothing can or shall content my soul
295 Till I am evened with him, wife for wife;
Or failing so, yet that I put the Moor
At least into a jealousy so strong
That judgment cannot cure; which thing to do,
If this poor trash of Venice, whom I trace
300 For his quick hunting, stand the putting on,[8]
I'll have our Michael Cassio on the hip,°   at my mercy
Abuse° him to the Moor in the rank garb°   slander / gross manner
(For I fear Cassio with my nightcap° too),   (as sexual rival)
Make the Moor thank me, love me, and reward me
305 For making him egregiously an ass

5. Stand watch tonight. I'll see that you receive
orders.
6. Who will not be adequately appeased.
7. Othello's possessions.

8. "If . . . on": if Roderigo, whom I follow (?), harness (?), is successfully set on the hunt when
incited.

And practicing upon° his peace and quiet   *undermining*
Even to madness. 'Tis here,° but yet confused;   *i.e., my plan is here*
Knavery's plain face is never seen till used.   *Exit.*

2.2

Enter OTHELLO'S HERALD *with a proclamation.*

HERALD [*reads*] "It is Othello's pleasure, our noble and
valiant general, that upon certain tidings now arrived
importing the mere perdition° of the Turkish fleet, every   *entire loss*
man put himself into triumph—some to dance, some to
5   make bonfires, each man to what sport and revels his
addition° leads him. For besides these beneficial news, it   *inclination*
is the celebration of his nuptial." So much was his pleasure should be proclaimed. All offices° are open, and   *storehouses*
there is full liberty of feasting from this present hour of
10   five till the bell have told eleven. Heaven bless the isle of
Cyprus and our noble general Othello!   *Exit.*

2.3

Enter OTHELLO, DESDEMONA, CASSIO, *and attendants.*

OTHELLO   Good Michael, look you to the guard tonight.
Let's teach ourselves that honorable stop,°   *self-restraint*
Not to outsport° discretion.   *pass the limits of*
CASSIO   Iago hath direction what to do;
5   But notwithstanding, with my personal eye
Will I look to't.
OTHELLO   Iago is most honest.
Michael, goodnight. Tomorrow with your earliest
Let me have speech with you.—Come, my dear love.
The purchase made, the fruits are to ensue,
10   That profit's yet to come 'tween me and you.[1]
Goodnight.
            Exit [OTHELLO, DESDEMONA, *and attendants*].
            Enter IAGO.
CASSIO   Welcome, Iago; we must to the watch.
IAGO   Not this hour, lieutenant; 'tis not yet ten o'th' clock.
Our general cast° us thus early for the love of his Desde-   *dismissed*
15   mona, who let us not therefore blame: he hath not yet
made wanton the night with her, and she is sport for
Jove.
CASSIO   She's a most exquisite lady.
IAGO   And, I'll warrant her, full of game.
20   CASSIO   Indeed, she's a most fresh and delicate creature.
IAGO   What an eye she has! Methinks it sounds a parley°   *(military) call*
to provocation.
CASSIO   An inviting eye; and yet, methinks, right modest.

2.2 Location: A street in Cyprus.   1. I.e., we haven't yet consummated our marriage.
2.3 Location: The citadel at Cyprus.

IAGO And when she speaks, is it not an alarum° to love?   *a call (to arms)*

25 CASSIO She is indeed perfection.

IAGO Well, happiness to their sheets! Come, lieutenant, I
have a stoup° of wine, and here without are a brace° of   *two quarts / pair*
Cyprus gallants that would fain have a measure² to the
health of black Othello.

30 CASSIO Not tonight, good Iago. I have very poor and
unhappy brains for drinking. I could well wish courtesy
would invent some other custom of entertainment.

IAGO O, they are our friends; but one cup; I'll drink for
you.

35 CASSIO I have drunk but one cup tonight, and that was
craftily qualified° too; and behold what innovation³ it   *well diluted*
makes here. I am unfortunate in the infirmity and dare
not task my weakness with any more.

IAGO What, man! 'Tis a night of revels—the gallants
40 desire it.

CASSIO Where are they?

IAGO Here at the door; I pray you call them in.

CASSIO I'll do't, but it dislikes me.°   *Exit.*   *I don't like it*

IAGO If I can fasten but one cup upon him
45 With that which he hath drunk tonight already,
He'll be as full of quarrel and offense
As my young mistress' dog. Now my sick fool, Roderigo,
Whom love hath turned almost the wrong side out,
To Desdemona hath tonight caroused
50 Potations pottle-deep; and he's to watch.⁴
Three else of Cyprus (noble swelling° spirits,   *proud*
That hold their honors in a wary distance,⁵
The very elements° of this warlike isle)   *typical residents*
Have I tonight flustered with flowing cups,
55 And they watch too. Now, 'mongst this flock of drunkards
Am I to put our Cassio in some action
That may offend the isle. But here they come.
    Enter CASSIO, MONTANO, *and* GENTLEMEN [*with wine*].
If consequence do but approve my dream,⁶
My boat sails freely, both with wind and stream.°   *current*

60 CASSIO 'Fore God, they have given me a rouse° already.   *full draft*

MONTANO Good faith, a little one; not past a pint, as I am
a soldier.

IAGO Some wine, ho!
    [*Sings*]
      And let me the cannikin° clink, clink,   *drinking vessel*
65   And let me the cannikin clink.
        A soldier's a man,
        O man's life's but a span,

---

2. Would like to drink.
3. Disorder.
4. "Caroused . . . watch": consumed drink to the
bottom of the tankard; and he's assigned guard
duty.
5. Who are touchy about their honor.
6. If events turn out as I hope.

Why then, let a soldier drink.
Some wine, boys!

70 CASSIO 'Fore God, an excellent song!

IAGO I learned it in England, where indeed they are most potent in potting.[7] Your Dane, your German, and your swag°-bellied Hollander—drink, ho!—are nothing to your English.

hanging

75 CASSIO Is your Englishman so exquisite in his drinking?

IAGO Why, he drinks you with facility your Dane dead drunk. He sweats not to overthrow your Almaine.° He gives your Hollander a vomit ere the next pottle° can be filled.

German

tankard

80 CASSIO To the health of our general!

MONTANO I am for it, lieutenant, and I'll do you justice.[8]

IAGO O sweet England!

[*Sings*]

King Stephen was and-a worthy peer,
    His breeches cost him but a crown;[9]

85 He held them sixpence all too dear,
    With that he called the tailor lown.°

lout

He was a wight of high renown,
    And thou art but of low degree;
'Tis pride° that pulls the country down,

ostentatious clothing

90   And take thy auld cloak about thee.
Some wine, ho!

CASSIO 'Fore God, this is a more exquisite song than the other.

IAGO Will you hear't again?

95 CASSIO No, for I hold him to be unworthy of his place that does those things. Well, God's above all, and there be souls must be saved, and there be souls must not be saved.[1]

IAGO It's true, good lieutenant.

100 CASSIO For mine own part—no offense to the general, nor any man of quality°—I hope to be saved.

rank

IAGO And so do I too, lieutenant.

CASSIO Ay; but by your leave, not before me. The lieutenant is to be saved before the ancient. Let's have no more

105 of this. Let's to our affairs. God forgive us our sins. Gentlemen, let's look to our business. Do not think, gentlemen, I am drunk. This is my ancient, this is my right hand, and this is my left. I am not drunk now. I can stand well enough, and I speak well enough.

110 GENTLEMAN Excellent well.

---

7. Most adept at drinking.
8. Match your drinking.
9. A coin (worth 60 pence).
1. Referring to the doctrine of predestination, the belief held by Calvinist Protestants that some souls are destined from all eternity to be saved and others to be damned.

CASSIO Why, very well then. You must not think, then,
    that I am drunk.   *Exit.*

MONTANO To th'platform, masters; come, let's set the
    watch.   *[Exeunt some* GENTLEMEN.*]*

115 IAGO *[to* MONTANO*]* You see this fellow that is gone before:
    He's a soldier fit to stand by Caesar
    And give direction. And do but see his vice:
    'Tis to his virtue a just equinox,°   *of equal size*
    The one as long as th'other. 'Tis pity of him;
120 I fear the trust Othello puts him in
    On some odd time of his infirmity
    Will shake this island.

MONTANO   But is he often thus?

IAGO 'Tis evermore his prologue to his sleep.
    He'll watch the horologe a double set[2]
    If drink rock not his cradle.

125 MONTANO   It were well
    The general were put in mind of it.
    Perhaps he sees it not, or his good nature
    Prizes the virtue that appears in Cassio
    And looks not on his evils. Is not this true?
          Enter RODERIGO.

130 IAGO *[aside]* How now, Roderigo?
    I pray you after the lieutenant—go!   *Exit* RODERIGO.

MONTANO And 'tis great pity that the noble Moor
    Should hazard such a place as his own second
    With one of an ingraft° infirmity.   *ingrained*
135 It were an honest action to say so
    To the Moor.

IAGO   Not I, for this fair island.
    I do love Cassio well and would do much
    To cure him of this evil.

VOICES *[within]* Help, help![3]
                 But hark, what noise?
      Enter CASSIO, *pursuing* RODERIGO.

140 CASSIO 'Swounds, you rogue! you rascal!

MONTANO What's the matter, lieutenant?

CASSIO A knave teach me my duty? I'll beat the knave
    into a twiggen° bottle.   *wicker-cased*

RODERIGO Beat me?

145 CASSIO Dost thou prate, rogue?   *[Attacks* RODERIGO.*]*

MONTANO Nay, good lieutenant! I pray you, sir, hold your
    hand.

CASSIO Let me go, sir, or I'll knock you o'er the mazzard.°   *head*

MONTANO Come, come; you're drunk!

150 CASSIO Drunk?   *[*CASSIO *and* MONTANO *fight.]*

---

2. He'll stay up twice around the clock.   3. The offstage shouts for help are only in Q.

IAGO [*aside to* RODERIGO]   Away, I say! Go out and cry a
mutiny.

[*Exit* RODERIGO.]

Nay, good lieutenant! God's will, gentlemen!
Help ho! Lieutenant! Sir—Montano—Sir!
155   Help, masters! Here's a goodly watch indeed!
  A bell rung.
Who's that which rings the bell? Diablo,° ho!   *the devil*
The town will rise. God's will, lieutenant, hold!
You'll be ashamed forever.

  Enter OTHELLO *and attendants.*

OTHELLO   What is the matter here?
160   MONTANO   'Swounds, I bleed still; I am hurt to th'death.
[*Attacks* CASSIO] He dies.
OTHELLO   Hold, for your lives!
IAGO   Hold, ho! Lieutenant—Sir—Montano—gentlemen!
Have you forgot all place of sense and duty?
165   Hold! The general speaks to you. Hold, for shame!
OTHELLO   Why, how now, ho? From whence ariseth this?
Are we turned Turks? and to ourselves do that
Which heaven hath forbid the Ottomites?°   *(by raising a storm)*
For Christian shame, put by this barbarous brawl!
170   He that stirs next, to carve for his own rage,°   *draw a sword in anger*
Holds his soul light; he dies upon his motion.
Silence that dreadful bell—it frights the isle
From her propriety. What is the matter, masters?
Honest Iago, that looks dead with grieving,
175   Speak. Who began this? On thy love, I charge thee.
IAGO   I do not know. Friends all, but now, even now,
In quarter° and in terms like bride and groom   *under control*
Divesting them° for bed; and then, but now,   *getting undressed*
As if some planet° had unwitted men,   *astrological influence*
180   Swords out and tilting one at other's breasts
In opposition bloody. I cannot speak
Any beginning to this peevish odds,°   *silly quarrel*
And would in action glorious I had lost
Those legs that brought me to a part of it.
185   OTHELLO   How comes it, Michael, you are thus forgot?
CASSIO   I pray you pardon me; I cannot speak.
OTHELLO   Worthy Montano, you were wont° to be civil;   *were accustomed*
The gravity and stillness of your youth
The world hath noted, and your name is great
190   In mouths of wisest censure.° What's the matter,   *judgment*
That you unlace your reputation thus
And spend your rich opinion° for the name   *reputation*
Of a night brawler? Give me answer to it.
MONTANO   Worthy Othello, I am hurt to danger.
195   Your officer, Iago, can inform you—
While I spare speech, which something now offends me[4]—

---

4. Somewhat now pains me.

Of all that I do know; nor know I aught
By me that's said or done amiss this night,
Unless self-charity° be sometimes a vice, · · · · · · · · · *care of oneself*
And to defend ourselves it be a sin
When violence assails us.

OTHELLO · · · · · · · · · · · · · · · · Now, by heaven,
My blood begins my safer guides to rule,
And passion, having my best judgment collied,° · · · · · · *darkened*
Assays° to lead the way. 'Swounds, if I stir · · · · · · · · *tries*
Or do but lift this arm, the best of you
Shall sink in my rebuke. Give me to know
How this foul rout began, who set it on;
And he that is approved° in this offense, · · · · · · · · · *proven guilty*
Though he had twinned with me, both at a birth,
Shall lose me. What! in a town of war,
Yet° wild, the people's hearts brimful of fear, · · · · · · · · *still*
To manage° private and domestic quarrel? · · · · · · · · · *carry on*
In night, and on the court and guard of safety?[5]
'Tis monstrous. Iago, who began't?

MONTANO   If partially affined,° or leagued in office, · · · *biased (for Cassio)*
Thou dost deliver more or less than truth,
Thou art no soldier.

IAGO · · · · · · · · · · · · · · · Touch me not so near.
I had rather have this tongue cut from my mouth
Than it should do offense to Michael Cassio;
Yet I persuade myself to speak the truth
Shall nothing wrong him. This it is, general:
Montano and myself being in speech,
There comes a fellow crying out for help,
And Cassio following him with determined sword
To execute upon° him. Sir, this gentleman · · · · · · · · · *to attack*
Steps in to Cassio and entreats his pause;
Myself the crying fellow did pursue,
Lest by his clamor—as it so fell out—
The town might fall in fright. He, swift of foot,
Outran my purpose; and I returned, the rather
For that I heard the clink and fall of swords
And Cassio high in oath, which till tonight
I ne'er might say before. When I came back—
For this was brief—I found them close together
At blow and thrust, even as again they were
When yourself did part them.
More of this matter cannot I report.
But men are men: the best sometimes forget.
Though Cassio did some little wrong to him,
As men in rage strike those that wish them best,
Yet surely Cassio, I believe, received
From him that fled some strange indignity

---

5. And at the place where safety and security are at stake (on the night watch).

Which patience could not pass.°   *let pass*
OTHELLO   I know, Iago,
Thy honesty and love doth mince° this matter,   *minimize*
245   Making it light to Cassio. Cassio, I love thee,
But never more be officer of mine.—
        Enter DESDEMONA, *attended.*
Look if my gentle love be not raised up!—
I'll make thee an example.
DESDEMONA   What is the matter, dear?
OTHELLO   All's well, sweeting;
250   Come away to bed. [*To* MONTANO] Sir, for your hurts
Myself will be your surgeon. Lead him off.
                    [*Exeunt attendants with* MONTANO.]
Iago, look with care about the town,
And silence those whom this vile brawl distracted.
Come, Desdemona; 'tis the soldier's life
255   To have their balmy slumbers waked with strife.
        Exeunt [OTHELLO *the*] *Moor,* DESDEMONA, *and attendants.*
IAGO   What, are you hurt, lieutenant?
CASSIO   Ay, past all surgery.
IAGO   Marry, God forbid!
CASSIO   Reputation, reputation, reputation! O, I have lost
260   my reputation! I have lost the immortal part of myself, and
what remains is bestial. My reputation, Iago, my reputation!
IAGO   As I am an honest man, I had thought you had
received some bodily wound; there is more sense in that
than in reputation. Reputation is an idle and most false
265   imposition,° oft got without merit and lost without   *artificial notion*
deserving. You have lost no reputation at all, unless you
repute yourself such a loser. What, man! there are more
ways to recover the general again. You are but now cast in
270   his mood, a punishment more in policy⁶ than in malice,
even so as one would beat his offenseless dog to affright
an imperious lion. Sue to° him again, and he's yours.   *petition*
CASSIO   I will rather sue to be despised than to deceive
so good a commander with so slight, so drunken, and so
275   indiscreet an officer. Drunk? And speak parrot?° And   *rant on*
squabble? Swagger? Swear? And discourse fustian° with   *nonsense*
one's own shadow? O, thou invisible spirit of wine! if
thou hast no name to be known by, let us call thee devil.
IAGO   What was he that you followed with your sword?
280   What had he done to you?
CASSIO   I know not.
IAGO   Is't possible?
CASSIO   I remember a mass of things, but nothing dis-
tinctly; a quarrel, but nothing wherefore.° O God! that   *but not why*
285   men should put an enemy in their mouths to steal away

---

6. "Cast . . . policy": dismissed in anger—a matter of policy (of public example).

their brains! that we should with joy, pleasance, revel, and applause transform ourselves into beasts!

IAGO   Why, but you are now well enough. How came you thus recovered?

290   CASSIO   It hath pleased the devil drunkenness to give place to the devil wrath; one unperfectness shows me another, to make me frankly despise myself.

IAGO   Come, you are too severe a moraler. As the time, the place, and the condition of this country stands, I
295   could heartily wish this had not befallen; but since it is as it is, mend it for your own good.

CASSIO   I will ask him for my place again. He shall tell me I am a drunkard. Had I as many mouths as Hydra,[7] such an answer would stop them all. To be now a sensible
300   man, by and by a fool, and presently a beast!—O, strange! Every inordinate cup is unblessed, and the ingredient is a devil.

IAGO   Come, come; good wine is a good familiar creature if it be well used. Exclaim no more against it. And, good
305   lieutenant, I think you think I love you.

CASSIO   I have well approved° it, sir—I drunk?   *tested*

IAGO   You or any man living may be drunk at a time, man. I tell you what you shall do. Our general's wife is now the general. I may say so in this respect, for that he
310   hath devoted and given up himself to the contemplation, mark, and devotement° of her parts[8] and graces. Confess   *observation* yourself freely to her; importune her help to put you in your place again. She is of so free,° so kind, so apt, so   *generous* blessed a disposition, she holds it a vice in her goodness
315   not to do more than she is requested. This broken joint between you and her husband entreat her to splinter,[9] and my fortunes against any lay° worth naming, this   *wager* crack of your love shall grow stronger than it was before.

CASSIO   You advise me well.
320   IAGO   I protest,° in the sincerity of love and honest kind-   *insist* ness.

CASSIO   I think it freely; and betimes° in the morning I   *early* will beseech the virtuous Desdemona to undertake for me. I am desperate of my fortunes if they check° me.   *stop*
325   IAGO   You are in the right. Good night, lieutenant; I must to the watch.

CASSIO   Good night, honest Iago.   *Exit* CASSIO.

IAGO   And what's he then that says I play the villain, When this advice is free I give and honest,
330   Probal° to thinking, and indeed the course   *wise* To win the Moor again? For 'tis most easy Th'inclining° Desdemona to subdue   *well-disposed*

---

7. A mythical serpent with many heads, who grew two more when one was cut off.
8. Qualities.
9. Heal with a splint.

In any honest suit: she's framed as fruitful°   *generous*
As the free elements; and then for her
335   To win the Moor, were't to renounce his baptism,
All seals and symbols of redeemèd sin,
His soul is so enfettered to her love
That she may make, unmake, do what she list,
Even as her appetite° shall play the god   *wishes*
340   With his weak function.° How am I then a villain   *faculties*
To counsel Cassio to this parallel° course   *suitable*
Directly to his good? Divinity° of hell!   *theology*
When devils will the blackest sins put on,
They do suggest at first with heavenly shows,
345   As I do now. For whiles this honest fool
Plies Desdemona to repair his fortune,
And she for him pleads strongly to the Moor,
I'll pour this pestilence into his ear:
That she repeals him° for her body's lust,   *appeals for him*
350   And by how much she strives to do him good
She shall undo her credit with the Moor.
So will I turn her virtue into pitch,[1]
And out of her own goodness make the net
That shall enmesh them all.
        Enter RODERIGO.
355   How now, Roderigo?
    RODERIGO   I do follow here in the chase, not like a hound
        that hunts, but one that fills up the cry.° My money is   *a pack follower*
        almost spent; I have been tonight exceedingly well cud-
        geled; and I think the issue will be I shall have so
360   much° experience for my pains, and so, with no money   *only this much*
        at all and a little more wit, return again to Venice.
    IAGO   How poor are they that have not patience!
        What wound did ever heal but by degrees?
        Thou know'st we work by wit and not by witchcraft,
365   And wit depends on dilatory° time.   *gradually unfolding*
        Does't not go well? Cassio hath beaten thee,
        And thou by that small hurt hath cashiered° Cassio.   *dismissed*
        Though other things grow fair against the sun,
        Yet fruits that blossom first will first be ripe.[2]
370   Content thyself awhile. By the Mass,° 'tis morning!   *(a mild oath)*
        Pleasure and action make the hours seem short.
        Retire thee; go where thou art billeted.
        Away! I say; thou shalt know more hereafter.
        Nay, get thee gone!   *Exit* RODERIGO.
                Two things are to be done:
375   My wife must move for Cassio to her mistress—
        I'll set her on—
        Myself a while to draw the Moor apart

---

1. Black, sticky substance used as a snare.   ing, your plan will be successful soonest because
2. I.e., although others may appear to be prosper-   it was set in motion first.

And bring him jump° when he may Cassio find   *exactly*
Soliciting his wife. Ay, that's the way!
380   Dull not device by coldness and delay.[3]   *Exit.*

3.1

Enter CASSIO, MUSICIANS, *and* CLOWN.

CASSIO   Masters, play here—I will content° your pains—   *reward*
Something that's brief; and bid "Good morrow, general."

CLOWN   Why, masters, have your instruments been in
Naples, that they speak i'th' nose thus?[1]

5   MUSICIAN   How, sir? how?

CLOWN   Are these, I pray you, wind instruments?[2]

MUSICIAN   Ay, marry, are they, sir.

CLOWN   O, thereby hangs a tail!

MUSICIAN   Whereby hangs a tale, sir?

10   CLOWN   Marry, sir, by many a wind instrument that I know.
But, masters, here's money for you; and the general so
likes your music that he desires you for love's sake to
make no more noise with it.

MUSICIAN   Well, sir, we will not.

15   CLOWN   If you have any music that may not° be heard, to't   *cannot*
again. But, as they say, to hear music the general does
not greatly care.

MUSICIAN   We have none such, sir.

CLOWN   Then put up your pipes in your bag, for I'll away.
20   Go! Vanish into air, away!   *Exeunt* MUSICIANS.

CASSIO   Dost thou hear, mine honest friend?

CLOWN   No, I hear not your honest friend: I hear you.

CASSIO   Prithee keep up thy quillets.[3] There's a poor piece
of gold for thee. If the gentlewoman that attends the
25   general be stirring, tell her there's one Cassio entreats
her a little favor of speech. Wilt thou do this?

CLOWN   She is stirring, sir. If she will stir hither, I shall
seem° to notify unto her.   *arrange*

CASSIO   Do, good my friend.   *Exit* CLOWN.

Enter IAGO   In happy time,° Iago.   *well met*

30   IAGO   You have not been abed then?

CASSIO   Why, no; the day had broke before we parted.
I have made bold, Iago, to send in to your wife.
My suit to her is that she will to virtuous Desdemona
Procure me some access.

IAGO   I'll send her to you presently;°   *immediately*
35   And I'll devise a mean to draw the Moor
Out of the way, that your converse and business

---

3. Don't let sluggishness and slowness to act
weaken the plot.
3.1 Location: Outside Othello and Desdemona's
room.
1. That they sound so nasal; perhaps a reference
to venereal disease, often associated with Naples,
or a phallic or anal joke.
2. The exchange that follows depends on the connections among wind instruments, flatulence, and
"tale/tail."
3. Pack up your puns.

May be more free.

CASSIO   I humbly thank you for't.   *Exit* [IAGO].
                              I never knew
A Florentine more kind and honest.

Enter EMILIA

40 EMILIA   Good morrow, good lieutenant. I am sorry
     For your displeasure, but all will sure° be well.   surely
     The general and his wife are talking of it,
     And she speaks for you stoutly. The Moor replies
     That he you hurt is of great fame in Cyprus
45   And great affinity,° and that in wholesome wisdom   well connected
     He might not but refuse you; but he protests he loves you
     And needs no other suitor but his likings
     To bring you in again.

CASSIO   Yet I beseech you,
     If you think fit, or that it may be done,
50   Give me advantage of some brief discourse
     With Desdemon alone.

EMILIA   Pray you come in.
     I will bestow you where you shall have time
     To speak your bosom° freely.   heart

CASSIO   I am much bound to you.
                              Exeunt.

3.2

Enter OTHELLO, IAGO, *and* GENTLEMEN

OTHELLO   These letters give, Iago, to the pilot,
     And by him do my duties° to the senate.   send my respects
     That done, I will be walking on the works;°   fortifications
     Repair° there to me.   come

IAGO   Well, my good lord; I'll do't.

5 OTHELLO   This fortification, gentlemen, shall we see't?

GENTLEMAN   We'll wait upon your lordship.   *Exeunt.*

3.3

Enter DESDEMONA, CASSIO, *and* EMILIA.

DESDEMONA   Be thou assured, good Cassio, I will do
     All my abilities in thy behalf.

EMILIA   Good madam, do. I warrant it grieves my husband
     As if the cause were his.

DESDEMONA   O, that's an honest fellow. Do not doubt,
5   Cassio,
     But I will have my lord and you again
     As friendly as you were.

CASSIO   Bounteous madam,
     Whatever shall become of Michael Cassio,
     He's never anything but your true servant.

3.2 Location: The citadel.
3.3 Location: The citadel's garden.

10 DESDEMONA I know't; I thank you. You do love my lord;
       You have known him long; and be you well assured
       He shall in strangeness stand no farther off
       Than in a politic distance.[1]
   CASSIO   Ay, but, lady,
       That policy may either last so long,
15   Or feed upon such nice and wat'rish diet,
       Or breed itself so out of circumstances,[2]
       That—I being absent, and my place supplied°—   *filled*
       My general will forget my love and service.
   DESDEMONA Do not doubt° that. Before Emilia here,   *fear*
20   I give thee warrant° of thy place. Assure thee,   *assurance*
       If I do vow a friendship, I'll perform it
       To the last article. My lord shall never rest:
       I'll watch him tame and talk him out of patience;[3]
       His bed shall seem a school, his board a shrift;°   *confessional*
25   I'll intermingle everything he does
       With Cassio's suit. Therefore be merry, Cassio,
       For thy solicitor° shall rather die   *advocate*
       Than give thy cause away.°   *up*
               Enter OTHELLO *and* IAGO.
   EMILIA Madam, here comes my lord.
30 CASSIO Madam, I'll take my leave.
   DESDEMONA Why, stay and hear me speak.
   CASSIO Madam, not now: I am very ill at ease,
       Unfit for mine own purposes.
   DESDEMONA Well, do your discretion.   *Exit* CASSIO.
   IAGO Ha! I like not that.
35 OTHELLO   What dost thou say?
   IAGO Nothing, my lord; or if . . . I know not what.
   OTHELLO Was not that Cassio parted from my wife?
   IAGO Cassio, my lord? No, sure, I cannot think it
       That he would steal away so guilty-like,
       Seeing your coming.
40 OTHELLO   I do believe 'twas he.
   DESDEMONA How now, my lord?
       I have been talking with a suitor here,
       A man that languishes in your displeasure.
   OTHELLO Who is't you mean?
45 DESDEMONA Why, your lieutenant, Cassio. Good my lord,
       If I have any grace or power to move you,
       His present reconciliation take;°   *accept him now*
       For if he be not one that truly loves you,
       That errs in ignorance and not in cunning,°   *not knowingly*
50   I have no judgment in an honest face.

1. He will distance himself from you only as
much as good diplomacy requires.
2. "Or feed . . . circumstances": or persist based
on such unimportant and poor justifications, or

continue by chance.
3. I'll keep him awake until he obeys me, and
talk to him beyond his endurance.

I prithee call him back.

OTHELLO   Went he hence now?

DESDEMONA   Yes, faith; so humbled
That he hath left part of his grief with me
To suffer with him. Good love, call him back.

55   OTHELLO   Not now, sweet Desdemon; some other time.

DESDEMONA   But shall't be shortly?

OTHELLO   The sooner, sweet, for you.

DESDEMONA   Shall't be tonight, at supper?

OTHELLO   No, not tonight.

DESDEMONA   Tomorrow dinner° then?   *midday meal*

OTHELLO   I shall not dine at home;
I meet the captains at the citadel.

60   DESDEMONA   Why then, tomorrow night, on Tuesday morn,
On Tuesday noon or night, on Wednesday morn.
I prithee name the time, but let it not
Exceed three days. In faith, he's penitent;
And yet his trespass, in our common reason°—   *normal judgment*

65   Save that, they say, the wars must make example
Out of her° best—is not almost a fault   *(war's)*
T'incur a private check.[4] When shall he come?
Tell me, Othello. I wonder in my soul
What you would ask me that I should deny,

70   Or stand so mamm'ring° on? What? Michael Cassio,   *hesitating*
That came a-wooing with you? and so many a time,
When I have spoke of you dispraisingly,
Hath ta'en your part—to have so much to do
To bring him in?° By'r Lady, I could do much[5]—   *into favor*

75   OTHELLO   Prithee, no more. Let him come when he will:
I will deny thee nothing.

DESDEMONA   Why, this is not a boon;
'Tis as I should entreat you wear your gloves,
Or feed on nourishing dishes, or keep you warm,
Or sue to you to do a peculiar° profit   *particular*

80   To your own person. Nay, when I have a suit
Wherein I mean to touch your love indeed,
It shall be full of poise° and difficult weight,   *balanced judgment*
And fearful to be granted.

OTHELLO   I will deny thee nothing.
Whereon I do beseech thee grant me this,

85   To leave me but a little to myself.

DESDEMONA   Shall I deny you? No. Farewell, my lord.

OTHELLO   Farewell, my Desdemona; I'll come to thee
straight.°   *immediately*

DESDEMONA   Emilia, come. [*to* OTHELLO] Be as your
fancies teach° you.   *as your whims lead*

---

4. Is barely worth even private criticism.
5. Do much to make you regret your reluctance (?).

Whate'er you be, I am obedient.

Exeunt DESDEMONA *and* EMILIA.

90 OTHELLO   Excellent wretch!° Perdition catch my soul   *(affectionate)*
But I do love thee! and when I love thee not,
Chaos is come again.

IAGO   My noble lord . . .

OTHELLO   What dost thou say, Iago?

IAGO   Did Michael Cassio, when you wooed my lady,
Know of your love?

95 OTHELLO   He did, from first to last.
Why dost thou ask?

IAGO   But for a satisfaction of my thought,
No further harm.

OTHELLO   Why of thy thought, Iago?

IAGO   I did not think he had been acquainted with her.

100 OTHELLO   O yes, and went between us very oft.

IAGO   Indeed?

OTHELLO   Indeed? Ay, indeed. Discern'st thou aught in that?
Is he not honest?

IAGO   Honest, my lord?

105 OTHELLO   Honest? Ay, honest.

IAGO   My lord, for aught I know.

OTHELLO   What dost thou think?

IAGO   Think, my lord?

OTHELLO   "Think, my lord?" By heaven, thou echo'st me
110 As if there were some monster in thy thought
Too hideous to be shown. Thou dost mean something:
I heard thee say even now thou lik'st not that,
When Cassio left my wife. What didst not like?
And when I told thee he was of my counsel,°   *in my confidence*
115 Of my whole course of wooing, thou cried'st "Indeed?"
And didst contract and purse thy brow together
As if thou then hadst shut up in thy brain
Some horrible conceit.° If thou dost love me,   *thought*
Show me thy thought.

IAGO   My lord, you know I love you.

120 OTHELLO   I think thou dost;
And for° I know thou'rt full of love and honesty,   *since*
And weigh'st thy words before thou giv'st them breath,
Therefore these stops° of thine fright me the more: *reluctances*
For such things in a false disloyal knave
125 Are tricks of custom;° but in a man that's just,   *habitual*
They're close dilations,[6] working from the heart
That passion cannot rule.°   *control*

IAGO   For Michael Cassio,
I dare be sworn I think that he is honest.

OTHELLO   I think so too.

---

6. I.e., involuntary revelations of interior, close-kept secrets.

IAGO   Men should be what they seem,
130   Or those that be not, would they might seem none.[7]
OTHELLO   Certain, men should be what they seem.
IAGO   Why then, I think Cassio's an honest man.
OTHELLO   Nay, yet there's more in this.
        I prithee speak to me as to thy thinkings,
135   As thou dost ruminate, and give thy worst of thoughts
        The worst of words.
IAGO   Good my lord, pardon me.
        Though I am bound to every act of duty,
        I am not bound to that all slaves are free to:[8]
        Utter my thoughts? Why, say they are vile and false—
140   As where's that palace whereinto foul things
        Sometimes intrude not? Who has that breast so pure
        But some uncleanly apprehensions
        Keep leets and law-days, and in sessions sit
        With meditations lawful?[9]
145   OTHELLO   Thou dost conspire against thy friend,° Iago,   (Othello)
        If thou but think'st him wronged and mak'st his ear
        A stranger to thy thoughts.
IAGO   I do beseech you,
        Though I perchance am vicious° in my guess   mistaken
        (As I confess it is my nature's plague
150   To spy into abuses, and oft my jealousy
        Shapes faults that are not), that your wisdom
        From one that so imperfectly conceits°   imagines
        Would take no notice, nor build yourself a trouble
        Out of his scattering° and unsure observance.   incoherent
155   It were not for your quiet, nor your good,
        Nor for my manhood, honesty, and wisdom,
        To let you know my thoughts.
OTHELLO   What dost thou mean?
IAGO   Good name in man and woman, dear my lord,
        Is the immediate jewel of their souls;
160   Who steals my purse steals trash: 'tis something, nothing;
        'Twas mine, 'tis his, and has been slave to thousands.
        But he that filches from me my good name
        Robs me of that which not enriches him
        And makes me poor indeed.
OTHELLO   By heaven, I'll know thy
                thoughts!
165   IAGO   You cannot, if my heart were in your hand,
        Nor shall not, whilst 'tis in my custody.
OTHELLO   Ha?
IAGO   O, beware, my lord, of jealousy!

7. "Or . . . none": if only those who are not what they seem didn't seem to be what they are not.
8. I.e., I am not obligated to reveal my inner thoughts, something about which even slaves have a choice.

9. "Uncleanly . . . lawful": illegitimate thoughts meet in court ("leets") from time to time (on "law-days") and debate (in court "sessions") with legitimate ones.

It is the green-eyed monster, which doth mock
The meat it feeds on.[1] That cuckold lives in bliss
170 Who, certain of his fate, loves not his wronger;[2]
But O, what damnèd minutes tells he o'er
Who dotes yet doubts, suspects yet strongly loves!

OTHELLO   O misery!

IAGO   Poor and content is rich, and rich enough,
175 But riches fineless° is as poor as winter   *boundless*
To him that ever fears he shall be poor.
Good God, the souls of all my tribe defend
From jealousy!

OTHELLO   Why, why is this?
Think'st thou I'd make a life of jealousy,
180 To follow still the changes of the moon°   *i.e., to renew endlessly*
With fresh suspicions? No! To be once in doubt
Is once to be resolved.° Exchange me for a goat   *to be finally settled*
When I shall turn the business of my soul
To such exsufflicate and blowed° surmises,   *inflated and blown up*
185 Matching thy inference. 'Tis not to make me jealous
To say my wife is fair, feeds well, loves company,
Is free of speech, sings, plays, and dances:
Where virtue is, these are more virtuous.
Nor from mine own weak merits will I draw
190 The smallest fear or doubt of her revolt,°   *or fear of her betrayal*
For she had eyes and chose me. No, Iago,
I'll see before I doubt; when I doubt, prove;
And on the proof there is no more but this:
Away at once with love or jealousy!

195 IAGO   I am glad of this; for now I shall have reason
To show the love and duty that I bear you
With franker spirit. Therefore, as I am bound,
Receive it from me. I speak not yet of proof.
Look to your wife; observe her well with Cassio;
200 Wear your eyes thus: not jealous, nor secure.
I would not have your free and noble nature
Out of self-bounty be abused.[3] Look to't.
I know our country disposition well:
In Venice they do let God see the pranks
They dare not show their husbands; their best
205   conscience
Is not to leave't undone, but keep't unknown.

OTHELLO   Dost thou say so?

IAGO   She did deceive her father, marrying you,
And when she seemed to shake, and fear your looks,
She loved them most.

OTHELLO   And so she did.

---

1. I.e., tortures, as it consumes, the heart of the jealous person.
2. Who, knowing it is his fate to be cuckolded, doesn't love his wife.
3. Be deceived on account of your own goodness.

210 IAGO   Why, go to° then.   *that's it*
    She that, so young, could give out such a seeming
    To seel her father's eyes up close as oak,[4]
    He thought 'twas witchcraft . . . ; but I am much to
       blame.
    I humbly do beseech you of your pardon
    For too much loving you.
215 OTHELLO   I am bound to thee forever.
IAGO   I see this hath a little dashed your spirits.
OTHELLO   Not a jot, not a jot.
IAGO   I'faith, I fear it has.
    I hope you will consider what is spoke
    Comes from my love. But I do see you're moved.
220 I am to pray you not to strain my speech
    To grosser issues° nor to larger reach   *greater conclusions*
    Than to suspicion.
OTHELLO   I will not.
IAGO   Should you do so, my lord,
    My speech should fall into such vile success
225 Which my thoughts aimed not. Cassio's my worthy
      friend—
    My lord, I see you're moved.
OTHELLO   No, not much moved;
    I do not think but Desdemona's honest.
IAGO   Long live she so! and long live you to think so!
OTHELLO   And yet how nature, erring from itself—
230 IAGO   Ay, there's the point! as to be bold with you,
    Not to affect° many proposed matches   *desire*
    Of her own clime, complexion, and degree,
    Whereto we see in all things nature tends—
    Foh! one may smell in such a will most rank,
235 Foul disproportions, thoughts unnatural.
    But, pardon me, I do not in position°   *argument*
    Distinctly speak of her, though I may fear
    Her will,° recoiling° to her better judgment,   *desire / submitting*
    May fall to match you with her country forms,[5]
    And happily° repent.   *perhaps*
240 OTHELLO   Farewell, farewell.
    If more thou dost perceive, let me know more.
    Set on thy wife to observe. Leave me, Iago.
IAGO [*going*]   My lord, I take my leave.
OTHELLO   Why did I marry? This honest creature,
      doubtless,
245 Sees and knows more, much more, than he unfolds.
IAGO [*returning*]   My lord, I would I might entreat your
      honor

---

4. Perhaps: to cover ("seel" means "to blind") her
father's eyes as tightly as oak (a fine-grained
wood).

5. May happen to compare you with Venetian
standards.

To scan this thing no farther; leave it to time.
Although 'tis fit that Cassio have his place
(For sure he fills it up with great ability),
250 Yet if you please to hold him off awhile,
You shall by that perceive him and his means.[6]
Note if your lady strain his entertainment°   *urge his reception*
With any strong or vehement importunity;
Much will be seen in that. In the meantime
255 Let me be thought too busy° in my fears   *meddlesome*
(As worthy cause I have to fear I am),
And hold her free,° I do beseech your honor.   *believe her innocent*
OTHELLO   Fear not my government.°   *self-conduct*
IAGO   I once more take my leave.   *Exit.*
260 OTHELLO   This fellow's of exceeding honesty,
And knows all qualities° with a learned spirit   *(human) types*
Of human dealings. If I do prove her haggard,°   *wild (from falconry)*
Though that her jesses were my dear heartstrings,
I'd whistle her off and let her down the wind
265 To prey at fortune.[7] Haply for° I am black,   *perhaps because*
And have not those soft parts of conversation°   *easy manners*
That chamberers° have, or for I am declined   *gallants*
Into the vale of years—yet that's not much—
She's gone, I am abused,° and my relief   *deceived*
270 Must be to loathe her. O curse of marriage!
That we can call these delicate creatures ours
And not their appetites! I had rather be a toad
And live upon the vapor of a dungeon
Than keep a corner in the thing I love
275 For others' uses. Yet 'tis the plague of great ones:
Prerogatived° are they less than the base;°   *privileged / lowborn*
'Tis destiny unshunnable, like death;
Even then this forkèd plague is fated to us
When we do quicken.[8]
          Enter DESDEMONA *and* EMILIA.
                    Look where she comes!
280 If she be false, O then heaven mocks itself;
I'll not believe't.
DESDEMONA   How now, my dear Othello?
Your dinner, and the generous° islanders   *noble*
By you invited, do attend° your presence.   *wait for*
OTHELLO   I am to blame.
DESDEMONA   Why do you speak so faintly?
285 Are you not well?
OTHELLO   I have a pain upon my forehead, here.°   *(from cuckold's horns)*

6. Method (for restoring himself to favor).
7. "Though . . . fortune": even if what tied her
("jesses" are leg straps put on a hawk) were my
own heartstrings, I'd set her loose downwind
forever to hunt on her own.
8. "Even . . . quicken": the "plague" of horns
(imagined to grow from the forehead of a cuckold)
is our fate as soon as we live.

DESDEMONA   Faith, that's with watching;° 'twill away   *from lack of sleep*
 again.
 Let me but bind it hard, within this hour
 It will be well.
OTHELLO   Your napkin° is too little;   *handkerchief*
      [*The handkerchief is dropped.*]
290 Let it alone. Come, I'll go in with you.
DESDEMONA   I am very sorry that you are not well.
      Exeunt OTHELLO *and* DESDEMONA.
EMILIA   I am glad I have found this napkin;
 This was her first remembrance° from the Moor.   *keepsake*
 My wayward husband hath a hundred times
295 Wooed me to steal it. But she so loves the token
 (For he conjured her° she should ever keep it)   *made her swear*
 That she reserves it evermore about her
 To kiss and talk to. I'll have the work ta'en out,°   *embroidery copied*
 And giv't Iago; what he will do with it
300 Heaven knows, not I:
 I nothing° but to please his fantasy.   *intend nothing*
  Enter IAGO.
IAGO   How now? What do you here alone?
EMILIA   Do not you chide; I have a thing for you.
IAGO   You have a thing for me? It is a common thing⁹—
305 EMILIA   Ha?
IAGO   To have a foolish wife.
EMILIA   O, is that all? What will you give me now
 For that same handkerchief?
IAGO   What handkerchief?
EMILIA   What handkerchief?
310 Why, that the Moor first gave to Desdemona,
 That which so often you did bid me steal.
IAGO   Hast stolen it from her?
EMILIA   No, faith; she let it drop by negligence,
 And to th'advantage° I, being here, took't up.   *taking the occasion*
 Look, here 'tis.
315 IAGO   A good wench! Give it me.
EMILIA   What will you do with't, that you have been so
 earnest
 To have me filch it?
IAGO [*taking it*] Why, what is that to you?
EMILIA   If it be not for some purpose of import,
 Giv't me again. Poor lady, she'll run mad
 When she shall lack it.
320 IAGO   Be not acknown on't;°   *don't let it be known*
 I have use for it. Go—leave me!   *Exit* EMILIA.
 I will in Cassio's lodging lose this napkin
 And let him find it. Trifles light as air

---

9. It is a vagina ("thing") available to all.

Are to the jealous confirmations strong
325   As proofs of holy writ. This may do something.
The Moor already changes with my poison:
Dangerous conceits° are in their natures poisons,   *ideas*
Which at the first are scarce found to distaste,
But with a little act° upon the blood   *effect*
Burn like the mines of sulphur.[1]
330   *Enter* OTHELLO.   I did say so—
Look where he comes! Not poppy nor mandragora[2]
Nor all the drowsy syrups of the world
Shall ever medicine thee to that sweet sleep
Which thou owedst° yesterday.   *owned*

OTHELLO   Ha! ha! false to me?
335 IAGO   Why, how now, general? No more of that!

OTHELLO   Avaunt! be gone! Thou hast set me on the rack.
I swear 'tis better to be much abused°   *mistreated; deceived*
Than but to know't a little.

IAGO   How now, my lord?

OTHELLO   What sense had I of her stol'n hours of lust?
340   I saw't not, thought it not; it harmed not me;
I slept the next night well, fed well, was free and merry;
I found not Cassio's kisses on her lips.
He that is robbed, not wanting° what is stol'n,   *missing*
Let him not know't, and he's not robbed at all.
345 IAGO   I am sorry to hear this.

OTHELLO   I had been happy if the general camp,
Pioneers° and all, had tasted her sweet body,   *manual laborers*
So° I had nothing known. O, now forever   *if*
Farewell the tranquil mind! farewell content!
350   Farewell the plumèd troops and the big wars
That makes ambition virtue! O, farewell!
Farewell the neighing steed and the shrill trump,°   *trumpet*
The spirit-stirring drum, th'ear-piercing fife,
The royal banner and all quality,°   *aspects*
355   Pride,° pomp, and circumstance° of glorious war!   *magnificence / ceremony*
And O you mortal engines° whose rude throats   *deadly cannons*
Th'immortal Jove's dread clamors° counterfeit,   *thunderclaps*
Farewell! Othello's occupation's gone!

IAGO   Is't possible, my lord?

OTHELLO [*grabs* IAGO *by the throat*]   Villain, be sure
360   thou prove my love a whore!
Be sure of it, give me the ocular proof,
Or by the worth of mine eternal soul,
Thou hadst been better have been born a dog
Than answer my waked wrath.

IAGO   Is't come to this?

---

1. Pliny the Elder (23/24–79 C.E.) describes two islands of sulfur between mainland Italy and Sicily that were rumored to be always on fire.

2. A sleep-inducing substance made from the mandrake root.

365 OTHELLO   Make me to see't, or at the least so prove it
      That the probation° bear no hinge nor loop   *proof*
      To hang a doubt on, or woe upon thy life!
   IAGO   My noble lord—
   OTHELLO   If thou dost slander her and torture me,
370   Never pray more; abandon all remorse;
      On horror's head horrors accumulate;
      Do deeds to make heaven weep, all earth amazed;
      For nothing canst thou to damnation add
      Greater than that.
   IAGO   O grace! O heaven forgive me!
375   Are you a man? Have you a soul? or sense?
      God buy you; take mine office.³ O wretched fool,°   *(to himself)*
      That lov'st to make thine honesty a vice!°   *fault*
      O monstrous world! Take note, take note, O world:
      To be direct and honest is not safe.
380   I thank you for this profit,° and from hence   *profitable lesson*
      I'll love no friend, sith° love breeds such offense.   *since*
   OTHELLO   Nay, stay; thou shouldst be honest.
   IAGO   I should be wise; for honesty's a fool
      And loses that° it works for.   *what*
   OTHELLO   By the world,⁴
385   I think my wife be honest, and think she is not;
      I think that thou art just, and think thou art not.
      I'll have some proof. My name, that was as fresh
      As Dian's⁵ visage, is now begrimed and black
      As mine own face. If there be cords or knives,
390   Poison, or fire, or suffocating streams,
      I'll not endure it. Would I were satisfied!
   IAGO   I see you are eaten up with passion;
      I do repent me that I put it to you.
      You would be satisfied?
   OTHELLO   Would? Nay, and I will.
395 IAGO   And may . . . but how? how satisfied, my lord?
      Would you, the supervisor,° grossly gape on?   *observer*
      Behold her topped?
   OTHELLO   Death and damnation! O!
   IAGO   It were a tedious° difficulty, I think,   *painful*
      To bring them to that prospect. Damn them then,
400   If ever mortal eyes do see them bolster°   *share a pillow*
      More° than their own.° What then? How then?   *other / own eyes*
      What shall I say? Where's satisfaction?
      It is impossible you should see this,
      Were they as prime° as goats, as hot as monkeys,   *lustful*
405   As salt as wolves in pride,⁶ and fools as gross

---

3. Good-bye, I resign my official position (ensign).
4. Othello's speech (lines 384–91) does not appear in Q.
5. Diana, goddess of chastity and of the (pale) moon. The Second Quarto (1630) replaces "My" (line 387) with "Her," a plausible but arguably less powerful reading that lacks textual authority.
6. As lecherous as wolves in heat.

As ignorance made drunk. But yet, I say,
If imputation and strong circumstances[7]
Which lead directly to the door of truth
Will give you satisfaction, you might have't.

410 OTHELLO   Give me a living° reason she's disloyal.   *sustainable; valid*
IAGO   I do not like the office.°   *task*
But sith I am entered in this cause so far,
Pricked to't° by foolish honesty and love,   *prodded on*
I will go on. I lay with Cassio lately,
415 And being troubled with a raging tooth,
I could not sleep. There are a kind of men
So loose of soul that in their sleeps will mutter
Their affairs; one of this kind is Cassio.
In sleep I heard him say "Sweet Desdemona,
420 Let us be wary, let us hide our loves!"
And then, sir, would he gripe° and wring my hand,   *grip*
Cry "O sweet creature!" then kiss me hard,
As if he plucked up kisses by the roots
That grew upon my lips, lay his leg o'er my thigh,
425 And sigh, and kiss, and then cry "Cursèd fate
That gave thee to the Moor!"
OTHELLO   O monstrous! monstrous!
IAGO   Nay, this was but his
dream.
OTHELLO   But this denoted a foregone conclusion;°   *an earlier event*
'Tis a shrewd doubt,° though it be but a dream.[8]   *reasonable fear*
430 IAGO   And this may help to thicken other proofs
That do demonstrate thinly.
OTHELLO   I'll tear her all to pieces!
IAGO   Nay, yet be wise; yet we see nothing done;
She may be honest yet. Tell me but this:
Have you not sometimes seen a handkerchief
435 Spotted with strawberries in your wife's hand?
OTHELLO   I gave her such a one; 'twas my first gift.
IAGO   I know not that; but such a handkerchief—
I am sure it was your wife's—did I today
See Cassio wipe his beard with.
OTHELLO   If it be that—
440 IAGO   If it be that, or any that was hers,
It speaks against her with the other proofs.
OTHELLO   O that the slave° had forty thousand lives!   *(Cassio)*
One is too poor, too weak for my revenge.
Now do I see 'tis true. Look here, Iago:
445 All my fond love thus do I blow to heaven.
'Tis gone.
Arise, black vengeance, from the hollow hell!

---

7. If inference and strong circumstantial evidence.
8. Q gives this line to Iago.

Yield up, O love, thy crown and hearted throne°   *rule of the heart*
To tyrannous hate! Swell, bosom, with thy fraught,°   *burden*
For 'tis of aspics'° tongues!   *poisonous snakes'*

450   IAGO   Yet be content.

OTHELLO   O, blood! blood! blood!

IAGO   Patience, I say; your mind may change.

OTHELLO   Never, Iago. Like to the Pontic Sea,°   *Black Sea*
Whose icy current and compulsive course

455   Ne'er keeps retiring ebb but keeps due on
To the Propontic and the Hellespont,[9]
Even so my bloody thoughts with violent pace
Shall ne'er look back, ne'er ebb to humble love,
Till that a capable° and wide revenge   *capacious*
Swallow them up.   OTHELLO *kneels.*

460   Now, by yond marble heaven,
In the due reverence of a sacred vow,
I here engage my words.

IAGO   Do not rise yet.   IAGO *kneels.*
Witness, you ever-burning lights above,
You elements that clip° us round about,   *embrace*

465   Witness that here Iago doth give up
The execution° of his wit, hands, heart,   *command*
To wronged Othello's service. Let him command,
And to obey shall be in me remorse,°   *pity (for Othello)*
What bloody business ever.°   [*They rise.*]   *soever*

OTHELLO   I greet thy love,

470   Not with vain thanks but with acceptance bounteous,
And will upon the instant put thee to't.°   *immediately test it*
Within these three days let me hear thee say
That Cassio's not alive.

IAGO   My friend is dead;
'Tis done at your request. But let her live.

OTHELLO   Damn her, lewd minx!° O, damn her! damn   *wanton*
475   her!
Come, go with me apart; I will withdraw
To furnish me with some swift means of death
For the fair devil. Now art thou my lieutenant.

IAGO   I am your own forever.   *Exeunt.*

3.4

Enter DESDEMONA, EMILIA, *and* CLOWN.

DESDEMONA   Do you know, sirrah,[1] where Lieutenant Cassio lies?

CLOWN   I dare not say he lies anywhere.

DESDEMONA   Why, man?

---

9. The Propontic was the body of water bounded by the straits of Bosphorus and the Dardanelles (Hellespont), the latter strait leading to the Aegean.
3.4 Location: Before the citadel.
1. A form of address to an inferior.

5 CLOWN   He's a soldier, and for me to say a soldier lies, 'tis
stabbing.

DESDEMONA   Go to; where lodges he?

CLOWN   To tell you where he lodges is to tell you where
I lie.

10 DESDEMONA   Can anything be made of this?

CLOWN   I know not where he lodges, and for me to devise
a lodging and say he lies here or he lies there were to lie in
mine own throat.°   *lie outrageously*

DESDEMONA   Can you inquire him out and be edified by
15 report?

CLOWN   I will catechize the world for him—that is, make
questions and by them answer.

DESDEMONA   Seek him, bid him come hither. Tell him I
have moved° my lord on his behalf and hope all will be   *petitioned*
20 well.

CLOWN   To do this is within the compass° of man's wit,   *scope*
and therefore I will attempt the doing it.   *Exit* CLOWN

DESDEMONA   Where should° I lose the handkerchief,   *did*
Emilia?

25 EMILIA   I know not, madam.

DESDEMONA   Believe me, I had rather have lost my purse
Full of crusadoes,° and but° my noble Moor   *gold coins / except that*
Is true of mind and made of no such baseness
As jealous creatures are, it were enough
To put him to ill-thinking.

30 EMILIA   Is he not jealous?

DESDEMONA   Who, he? I think the sun where he was born
Drew all such humors from him.²

Enter OTHELLO.

EMILIA   Look where he comes.

DESDEMONA [*aside*]   I will not leave him now till Cassio be
Called to him.—How is't with you, my lord?

35 OTHELLO   Well, my good lady. [*Aside*] O, hardness to dissemble!—
How do you, Desdemona?

DESDEMONA   Well, my good lord.

OTHELLO   Give me your hand. This hand is moist, my lady.

DESDEMONA   It hath felt no age nor known no sorrow.

OTHELLO   This argues fruitfulness and liberal heart.³
40 Hot, hot and moist. This hand of yours requires
A sequester from liberty: fasting and prayer,
Much castigation, exercise devout;
For here's a young and sweating devil here
That commonly rebels. 'Tis a good hand,
A frank° one.   *(sexually) open*

45 DESDEMONA   You may indeed say so,

2. As if the African sun dried up the bodily fluids ("humors") that produce jealousy.
3. This demonstrates fertility (perhaps, by impli-cation, lust) and a generous (hinting at "loose") heart. A moist hand was thought to be a sign of active desire.

For 'twas that hand that gave away my heart.
OTHELLO   A liberal hand. The hearts of old gave hands,
   But our new heraldry is hands, not hearts.[4]
DESDEMONA   I cannot speak of this. Come now, your promise.
50 OTHELLO   What promise, chuck?°   *woodchuck (affectionate)*
DESDEMONA   I have sent to bid Cassio come speak with you.
OTHELLO   I have a salt and sorry rheum° offends me;   *badly watering eyes*
   Lend me thy handkerchief.
DESDEMONA   Here, my lord.
OTHELLO   That which I gave you.
DESDEMONA   I have it not about me.
OTHELLO   Not?
DESDEMONA   No, faith, my lord.
OTHELLO   That's a fault. That
55   handkerchief
   Did an Egyptian to my mother give.
   She was a charmer° and could almost read   *sorceress*
   The thoughts of people. She told her, while she kept it,
   'Twould make her amiable° and subdue my father   *desirable*
60 Entirely to her love; but if she lost it
   Or made a gift of it, my father's eye
   Should hold her loathèd, and his spirits should hunt
   After new fancies. She, dying, gave it me,
   And bid me, when my fate would have me wived,
65 To give it her.° I did so; and—take heed on't!—   *to my wife*
   Make it a darling like your precious eye.
   To lose't or give't away were such perdition°   *loss; damnation*
   As nothing else could match.
DESDEMONA   Is't possible?
OTHELLO   'Tis true. There's magic in the web of it:
70 A sibyl° that had numbered in the world   *female prophet*
   The sun to course two hundred compasses,[5]
   In her prophetic fury° sewed the work;   *rapture*
   The worms were hallowed that did breed the silk,
   And it was dyed in mummy,[6] which the skillful
   Conserved of° maidens' hearts.   *preserved out of*
75 DESDEMONA   I'faith? Is't true?
OTHELLO   Most veritable; therefore look to't well.
DESDEMONA   Then would to God that I had never seen't!
OTHELLO   Ha? wherefore?
DESDEMONA   Why do you speak so startingly and rash?°   *fitfully and urgently*
80 OTHELLO   Is't lost? Is't gone? Speak, is't out o'th'way?
DESDEMONA   Heaven bless us!
OTHELLO   Say you?
DESDEMONA   It is not lost; but what an if° it were?   *an if = if*
OTHELLO   How?

---

4. I.e., these days the joining of hands doesn't   years old.
signify the joining of hearts.   6. Fluid drained from mummified bodies, sup-
5. "That . . . compasses": who was two hundred   posedly magical.

85 DESDEMONA   I say it is not lost.

OTHELLO   Fetch't, let me see't!

DESDEMONA   Why, so I can; but I will not now.
  This is a trick to put me from my suit.
  Pray you let Cassio be received again.

90 OTHELLO   Fetch me the handkerchief, my mind misgives—

DESDEMONA   Come, come!
  You'll never meet a more sufficient° man—   *complete*

OTHELLO   The handkerchief!

DESDEMONA   I pray, talk me of Cassio.

OTHELLO   The handkerchief!7

DESDEMONA   A man that all his time

95 Hath founded his good fortunes on your love,
  Shared dangers with you—

OTHELLO   The handkerchief!

DESDEMONA   I'faith, you are to blame.

OTHELLO   'Swounds!   *Exit* OTHELLO.

EMILIA   Is not this man jealous?

100 DESDEMONA   I ne'er saw this before.
  Sure, there's some wonder in this handkerchief;
  I am most unhappy in the loss of it.

EMILIA   'Tis not a year or two shows us a man.8
  They are all but° stomachs, and we all but food;   *nothing but*

105 They eat us hungerly, and when they are full
  They belch us.

              Enter IAGO *and* CASSIO.
                    Look you, Cassio and my husband.

IAGO   There is no other way; 'tis she must do't;
  And lo the happiness!9 go and importune her.

DESDEMONA   How now, good Cassio, what's the news
      with you?

110 CASSIO   Madam, my former suit. I do beseech you
  That by your virtuous means I may again
  Exist and be a member of his love
  Whom I, with all the office° of my heart,   *duty; loyal service*
  Entirely honor. I would not be delayed.

115 If my offense be of such mortal° kind   *deadly*
  That nor° my service past nor present sorrows   *neither*
  Nor purposed merit in futurity
  Can ransom me into his love again,
  But to know so° must be my benefit;   *even to know this*

120 So° shall I clothe me in a forced content   *if so*
  And shut° myself up in some other course   *give*
  To fortune's alms.

DESDEMONA   Alas, thrice-gentle Cassio,
  My advocation is not now in tune.1

---

7. Desdemona's "I pray, talk me of Cassio" and
Othello's "The handkerchief!" are only in Q.
8. I.e., it doesn't take long to see what a man is.

9. What a happy coincidence (seeing Desdemona).
1. My advocacy isn't working properly.

My lord is not my lord, nor should I know him,
125 Were he in favor° as in humor° altered.   *appearance / mood*
So help me every spirit sanctified
As I have spoken for you all my best
And stood within the blank² of his displeasure
For my free speech. You must awhile be patient.
130 What I can do I will, and more I will
Than for myself I dare. Let that suffice you.
IAGO   Is my lord angry?
EMILIA   He went hence but now,
And certainly in strange unquietness.
IAGO   Can he be angry? I have seen the cannon
135 When it hath blown his ranks into the air
And, like the devil, from his very arm
Puffed his own brother³—and is he angry?
Something of moment then. I will go meet him;
There's matter in't indeed if he be angry.
DESDEMONA   I prithee do so.   *Exit* [IAGO].
140   Something sure of state⁴—
Either from Venice, or some unhatched practice°   *unfinished plot*
Made demonstrable here in Cyprus to him—
Hath puddled his clear spirit; and in such cases
Men's natures wrangle with inferior things,
145 Though great ones are their object. 'Tis even so.
For let our finger ache, and it endues°   *induces*
Our other, healthful members even to a sense
Of pain. Nay, we must think men are not gods,
Nor of them look for such observancy°   *careful attention*
150 As fits the bridal.°—Beshrew me° much, Emilia.   *wedding / (mild curse)*
I was, unhandsome° warrior as I am,   *unskilled*
Arraigning his unkindness with my soul;
But now I find I had suborned the witness,
And he's indicted falsely.⁵
EMILIA   Pray heaven it be
155 State matters, as you think, and no conception
Nor no jealous toy° concerning you.   *whim*
DESDEMONA   Alas the day! I never gave him cause.
EMILIA   But jealous souls will not be answered so;
They are not ever jealous for the cause,
160 But jealous for they're jealous. It is a monster
Begot upon itself, born on itself.
DESDEMONA   Heaven keep the monster from Othello's
    mind!
EMILIA   Lady, amen!
DESDEMONA   I will go seek him; Cassio, walk here about.
165 If I do find him fit, I'll move your suit
And seek to effect it to my uttermost.

---

2. The "blank" was the white spot at the center
of a target.
3. Blew up his own brother (and Othello wasn't
angry even then).

4. Surely some official business.
5. Made the witness lie and so accused Othello
falsely.

CASSIO I humbly thank your ladyship.

Exeunt DESDEMONA *and* EMILIA.

Enter BIANCA.[6]

BIANCA Save you,° friend Cassio!   *God save you*

CASSIO   What make° you from   *brings*

home?

How is't with you, my most fair Bianca?

170   I'faith, sweet love, I was coming to your house.

BIANCA   And I was going to your lodging, Cassio.

What? keep a week away? seven days and nights?

Eightscore-cight hours? And lovers' absent hours

More tedious than the dial eightscore times!°[7]

O weary reckoning!°   *calculating*

175   CASSIO   Pardon me, Bianca;

I have this while with leaden thoughts been pressed,

But I shall in a more continuate° time   *opportune*

Strike off° this score of absence. Sweet Bianca,   *make up*

[*Gives her* DESDEMONA*'s handkerchief.*]

Take me this work out.°   *copy this embroidery*

BIANCA   O, Cassio! whence came this?

180   This is some token from a newer friend;

To the felt absence now I feel a cause.

Is't come to this? Well, well.

CASSIO   Go to,° woman!   *stop it*

Throw your vile guesses in the devil's teeth,

From whence you have them. You are jealous now

185   That this is from some mistress some remembrance;

No, by my faith, Bianca.

BIANCA   Why, whose is it?

CASSIO   I know not neither; I found it in my chamber.

I like the work well; ere it be demanded,°   *sought out*

As like° enough it will, I would have it copied.   *likely*

190   Take it and do't, and leave me for this time.

BIANCA   Leave you? Wherefore?

CASSIO   I do attend here on the general,

And think it no addition,° nor my wish,   *(to my cause)*

To have him see me womaned.

BIANCA   Why, I pray you?

CASSIO   Not that I love you not.

195   BIANCA   But that you do not love me.

I pray you bring me on the way a little,

And say if I shall see you soon at night.

CASSIO   'Tis but a little way that I can bring you,

For I attend here; but I'll see you soon.

200   BIANCA   'Tis very good—I must be circumstanced.[8]

Exeunt.

---

6. "Bianca" means "white" in Italian—an ironic reversal of conventional color imagery, given that Bianca is a "customer" (courtesan, 4.1.119).
7. "Lovers' . . . times": each hour lovers are parted is eightscore (160) times more tedious than normal clock time.
8. Content with what circumstances offer.

4.1

Enter OTHELLO *and* IAGO.

IAGO Will you think so?

OTHELLO   Think so, Iago?

IAGO   What,
  To kiss in private?

OTHELLO   An unauthorized kiss!

IAGO Or to be naked with her friend in bed
  An hour or more, not meaning any harm?

5 OTHELLO Naked in bed, Iago, and not mean harm?
  It is hypocrisy against the devil.[1]
  They that mean virtuously, and yet do so,
  The devil their virtue tempts, and they tempt heaven.[2]

IAGO If they do nothing, 'tis a venial slip;°   *an excusable sin*
10 But if I give my wife a handkerchief—

OTHELLO What then?

IAGO Why then, 'tis hers, my lord; and being hers,
  She may, I think, bestow't on any man.

OTHELLO She is protectress of her honor too;
15 May she give that?

IAGO Her honor is an essence that's not seen;
  They° have it very oft that have it not.   *they are reputed to*
  But for the handkerchief—

OTHELLO By heaven, I would most gladly have forgot it!
20 Thou said'st—O, it comes o'er my memory
  As doth the raven o'er the infectious° house,[3]   *plague-infested*
  Boding to all!—he had my handkerchief.

IAGO Ay, what of that?

OTHELLO   That's not so good now.

IAGO What if I had said I had seen him do you wrong?
25 Or heard him say—as knaves be such abroad[4]
  Who (having by their own importunate suit
  Or voluntary dotage° of some mistress   *doting*
  Convincèd or supplied° them) cannot choose   *seduced or satisfied*
  But they must blab—

OTHELLO   Hath he said anything?

30 IAGO He hath, my lord, but be you well assured,
  No more than he'll unswear.

OTHELLO   What hath he said?

IAGO Faith, that he did . . . I know not what he did.

OTHELLO What? What?

IAGO Lie . . .

OTHELLO   With her?

4.1 Location: Before the citadel.
1. I.e., by appearing to act sinfully while actually being good.
2. "They . . . heaven": those who mean well ("virtuously") but act in this lascivious fashion ("so") open themselves to temptation by the devil, and they tempt heaven (to give them over). "Thou shalt not tempt the Lord thy God" (Matthew 4.7).
3. The raven was thought to be an ill omen and a carrier of plague.
4. As such knaves do exist in the world.

	IAGO	With her, on her; what you will.	
35	OTHELLO	Lie with her? lie on her? We say lie on her when	

IAGO   With her, on her; what you will.

35 OTHELLO   Lie with her? lie on her? We say lie on her when
     they belie° her. Lie with her? 'Swounds, that's ful-   *slander*
     some.°—Handkerchief! confessions! handkerchief!—To[5]   *nauseating*
     confess, and be hanged for his labor. First to be hanged,
     and then to confess: I tremble at it. Nature would not
40   invest herself in such shadowing passion without some
     instruction.[6] It is not words that shakes me thus. Pish!
     Noses, ears, and lips! Is't possible? Confess? Handker-
     chief? O devil!   *Falls in a trance.*

IAGO   Work on;
45   My medicine works! Thus credulous fools are caught,
     And many worthy and chaste dames even thus,
     All guiltless, meet reproach.—What ho! my lord!
     My lord, I say! Othello!
         Enter CASSIO.
                  How now, Cassio?

CASSIO   What's the matter?

50 IAGO   My lord is fallen into an epilepsy.
     This is his second fit; he had one yesterday.

CASSIO   Rub him about the temples.

IAGO   No, forbear.
     The lethargy° must have his° quiet course;   *trance / its*
     If not, he foams at mouth and by and by
55   Breaks out to savage madness. Look, he stirs.
     Do you withdraw yourself a little while;
     He will recover straight.° When he is gone,   *immediately*
     I would on great occasion° speak with you.   *important matters*
                                   [Exit CASSIO.]
     How is it, general? Have you not hurt your head?[7]

OTHELLO   Dost thou mock me?

60 IAGO   I mock you not, by heaven.
     Would you would bear your fortune like a man!

OTHELLO   A hornèd man's a monster and a beast.

IAGO   There's many a beast then in a populous city,
     And many a civil° monster.   *city-dwelling*

OTHELLO   Did he confess it?

65 IAGO   Good sir, be a man:
     Think every bearded fellow that's but yoked
     May draw with you.[8] There's millions now alive
     That nightly lie in those unproper beds
     Which they dare swear peculiar.[9] Your case is better.
70   O, 'tis the spite of hell, the fiend's arch-mock,°   *devil's greatest mock*
     To lip° a wanton in a secure° couch   *kiss / an unsuspected*

---

5. The rest of the speech does not appear in Q.
6. "Nature . . . instruction": it isn't natural that I would feel such overwhelming ("shadowing") emotion (jealousy) unless there were some cause for it.
7. Othello takes this as suggesting that he has grown cuckold's horns.

8. Every married man ("yoked," like an ox, to his wife and hence to cuckoldry) labors ("draws") under the same fate.
9. Who lie in beds that don't belong entirely to them but that they would swear are exclusively their own.

And to suppose her chaste. No, let me know;
And knowing what I am,° I know what she shall be.   *(a cuckold)*

OTHELLO   O, thou art wise, 'tis certain.

IAGO   Stand you a while
     apart,

75   Confine yourself but in a patient list.°   *boundary*
Whilst you were here, o'er-whelmèd with your grief—
A passion most unsuiting such a man—
Cassio came hither. I shifted him away
And laid good 'scuses upon your ecstasy,°   *for your fit*

80   Bade him anon return and here speak with me,
The which he promised. Do but encave° yourself,   *hide*
And mark the fleers,° the gibes, and notable scorns   *sneers*
That dwell in every region of his face;
For I will make him tell the tale anew:

85   Where, how, how oft, how long ago, and when
He hath and is again to cope° your wife.   *copulate with*
I say, but mark his gesture. Marry, patience!
Or I shall say you're all in all in spleen,°   *completely impulsive*
And nothing of a man.

OTHELLO   Dost thou hear, Iago?

90   I will be found most cunning in my patience;
But—dost thou hear?—most bloody.

IAGO   That's not amiss,
But yèt keep time° in all. Will you withdraw?   *maintain control*
     [OTHELLO *withdraws.*]
Now will I question Cassio of Bianca,
A huswife° that by selling her desires   *hussy*

95   Buys herself bread and cloth. It is a creature
That dotes on Cassio—as 'tis the strumpet's plague
To beguile many and be beguiled by one.
He, when he hears of her, cannot restrain
From the excess of laughter. Here he comes.
     Enter CASSIO.

100   As he shall smile, Othello shall go mad;
And his unbookish° jealousy must conster°   *ignorant / construe*
Poor Cassio's smiles, gestures, and light behaviors
Quite in the wrong. How do you, lieutenant?

CASSIO   The worser that you give me the addition°   *title*

105   Whose want even kills me.

IAGO   Ply Desdemona well, and you are sure on't.
Now if this suit lay in Bianca's power,
How quickly should you speed!

CASSIO   Alas, poor caitiff!°   *wretch*

OTHELLO   Look how he laughs already!

110   IAGO   I never knew woman love man so.

CASSIO   Alas, poor rogue! I think, i'faith, she loves me.

OTHELLO   Now he denies it faintly and laughs it out.

IAGO   Do you hear, Cassio?

OTHELLO   Now he importunes him

To tell it o'er. Go to! well said, well said!
115 IAGO She gives it out that you shall marry her.
Do you intend it?
CASSIO Ha, ha, ha!
OTHELLO Do ye triumph, Roman?[1] do you triumph?
CASSIO I marry? What! a customer?° Prithee bear some   *courtesan*
120 charity to my wit;° do not think it so unwholesome. Ha, ha,   *sense*
ha!
OTHELLO So, so, so, so! they laugh that wins.
IAGO Faith, the cry goes that you marry her.
CASSIO Prithee say true.
125 IAGO I am a very villain else.°   *if it's not true*
OTHELLO Have you scored° me? Well.   *scored off*
CASSIO This is the monkey's own giving out.[2] She is persuaded I will marry her out of her own love and flattery,
not out of my promise.
130 OTHELLO Iago beckons me; now he begins the story.
[OTHELLO *draws closer.*]
CASSIO She was here even now; she haunts me in every
place. I was the other day talking on the sea-bank with
certain Venetians, and thither comes the bauble° and   *toy*
falls me thus about my neck—
135 OTHELLO Crying "O dear Cassio!" as it were: his gesture
imports° it.   *indicates*
CASSIO So hangs and lolls and weeps upon me, so shakes
and pulls me. Ha, ha, ha!
OTHELLO Now he tells how she plucked him to my cham-
140 ber. O, I see that nose of yours, but not that dog I shall
throw it to.[3]
CASSIO Well, I must leave her company.
IAGO Before me! look where she comes!
Enter BIANCA.
CASSIO 'Tis such another fitchew![4] marry, a perfumed one!
145 What do you mean by this haunting of me?
BIANCA Let the devil and his dam° haunt you! What did   *mother*
you mean by that same handkerchief you gave me even
now? I was a fine fool to take it. I must take out° the   *copy*
work? A likely piece of work,[5] that you should find it in
150 your chamber and know not who left it there! This is
some minx's token, and I must take out the work? There,
give it your hobby-horse!° Wheresoever you had it, I'll *mountable woman*
take out no work on't.
CASSIO How now, my sweet Bianca?
155 How now? how now?

1. Othello draws on associations either with Rome's imperial successes (and subsequent collapse) or with the Roman practice of holding celebratory processions (called triumphs) for military victors.
2. I.e., this is Bianca's own story.
3. I.e., I'm envisioning my revenge, but the time is not yet quite right.
4. Polecat, associated with prostitutes because of its bad smell and supposed lecherousness.
5. An implausible story.

OTHELLO   By heaven, that should° be my handkerchief!   *must*

BIANCA   If you'll come to supper tonight, you may; if you
   will not, come when you are next prepared for.[6]   *Exit.*

IAGO   After her, after her!

160   CASSIO   Faith, I must; she'll rail in the streets else.

IAGO   Will you sup there?

CASSIO   Faith, I intend so.

IAGO   Well, I may chance to see you, for I would very fain
   speak with you.

165   CASSIO   Prithee come, will you?

IAGO   Go to; say no more.   *Exit* CASSIO

OTHELLO [*comes forward*]   How shall I murder him, Iago?

IAGO   Did you perceive how he laughed at his vice?

OTHELLO   O Iago!

170   IAGO   And did you see the handkerchief?

OTHELLO   Was that mine?

IAGO   Yours, by this hand! and to see how he prizes the
   foolish woman, your wife! She gave it him, and he hath
   given it his whore.

175   OTHELLO   I would have him nine years a-killing![7]—A fine
   woman, a fair woman, a sweet woman!

IAGO   Nay, you must forget that.

OTHELLO   Ay, let her rot and perish and be damned
   tonight, for she shall not live! No, my heart is turned to

180   stone; I strike it, and it hurts my hand.—O, the world
   hath not a sweeter creature! She might lie by an emper-
   or's side and command him tasks.

IAGO   Nay, that's not your way.°   *(the way to think)*

OTHELLO   Hang her!—I do but say what she is: so delicate

185   with her needle; an admirable musician (O, she will sing
   the savageness out of a bear!); of so high and plenteous
   wit and invention!°   *imagination*

IAGO   She's the worse for all this.

OTHELLO   O, a thousand, a thousand times!—And then of

190   so gentle° a condition!   *highly born*

IAGO   Ay, too gentle.°   *generous (sexually)*

OTHELLO   Nay, that's certain.—But yet the pity of it, Iago!
   O Iago, the pity of it, Iago!

IAGO   If you are so fond° over her iniquity, give her patent°   *foolish / license*

195   to offend; for if it touch not you, it comes near nobody.

OTHELLO   I will chop her into messes!° Cuckold me!   *pieces of food*

IAGO   O, 'tis foul in her.

OTHELLO   With mine officer!

IAGO   That's fouler.

200   OTHELLO   Get me some poison, Iago, this night. I'll not
   expostulate with her, lest her body and beauty unprovide
   my mind° again. This night, Iago.   *weaken my resolve*

---

6. Come next time I prepare for you (never).   7. I would like to spend nine years killing him.

IAGO   Do it not with poison. Strangle her in her bed, even
    the bed she hath contaminated.

205 OTHELLO   Good, good! The justice of it pleases. Very
    good!

IAGO   And for Cassio, let me be his undertaker.° You shall   *murderer*
    hear more by midnight.

OTHELLO   Excellent good!
    A trumpet [within].

210 What trumpet is that same?

IAGO   I warrant something from Venice.
    Enter LODOVICO, DESDEMONA, *and attendants.*
    'Tis Lodovico; this comes from the duke.
    See, your wife's with him.

LODOVICO   God save you, worthy general.

215 OTHELLO   With all my heart,° sir.   *thank you*

LODOVICO   The duke and the senators of Venice greet you.
    [Gives him a letter.]

OTHELLO   I kiss the instrument° of their pleasures.°   *bearer / commands*
    [Opens the letter and reads.]

DESDEMONA   And what's the news, good cousin Lodovico?

IAGO   I am very glad to see you, signor.

220 Welcome to Cyprus.

LODOVICO   I thank you. How does Lieutenant Cassio?

IAGO   Lives, sir.

DESDEMONA   Cousin, there's fallen between him and my
    lord
    An unkind° breach; but you shall make all well.   *unnatural*

225 OTHELLO   Are you sure of that?

DESDEMONA   My lord?

OTHELLO *[reads]*   "This fail you not to do, as you will . . ."

LODOVICO   He did not call: he's busy in the paper.
    Is there division 'twixt my lord and Cassio?

230 DESDEMONA   A most unhappy one; I would do much
    T'atone° them, for the love I bear to Cassio.   *to reconcile*

OTHELLO   Fire and brimstone!

DESDEMONA   My lord?

OTHELLO   Are you wise?

DESDEMONA   What, is he angry?

LODOVICO   May be the letter moved him;
    For, as I think, they do command him home,
235   Deputing Cassio in his government.°   *official position*

DESDEMONA   By my troth, I am glad on't.

OTHELLO   Indeed!

DESDEMONA   My lord?

OTHELLO   I am glad to see you mad.[8]

DESDEMONA   Why, sweet Othello?

OTHELLO   Devil!   *[Strikes her.]*

---

8. Othello is pleased that Desdemona is rejoicing in Cassio's promotion and thus revealing their adulterous affair, which she would be "mad" to do in public and in front of him.

DESDEMONA   I have not deserved this.

240 LODOVICO   My lord, this would not be believed in Venice,
Though I should swear I saw't. 'Tis very much;°   *going too far*
Make her amends—she weeps.

OTHELLO   O devil, devil!
If that the earth could teem with° woman's tears,   *become pregnant by*
Each drop she falls would prove a crocodile.[9]
Out of my sight!

245 DESDEMONA   I will not stay to offend you.

LODOVICO   Truly obedient lady!
I do beseech your lordship call her back.

OTHELLO   Mistress!

DESDEMONA   My lord?

OTHELLO   What would you° with her, sir?   *do you wish*

250 LODOVICO   Who, I, my lord?

OTHELLO   Ay, you did wish that I would make her turn.°   *return*
Sir, she can turn, and turn,° and yet go on   *(sexually)*
And turn again. And she can weep, sir, weep.
And she's obedient; as you say, obedient,

255 Very obedient.—Proceed you in your tears.—
Concerning this, sir—O well-painted passion!—
I am commanded home.—Get you away!
I'll send for you anon.—Sir, I obey the mandate
And will return to Venice.—Hence, avaunt!°   *begone*

[*Exit* DESDEMONA.]

260 Cassio shall have my place. And, sir, tonight
I do entreat that we may sup together.
You are welcome, sir, to Cyprus.—Goats and monkeys![1]

Exit.

LODOVICO   Is this the noble Moor whom our full senate
Call all-in-all sufficient? Is this the nature

265 Whom passion could not shake? whose solid virtue
The shot of accident nor dart of chance
Could neither graze nor pierce?

IAGO   He is much changed.

LODOVICO   Are his wits safe? Is he not light of brain?

IAGO   He's that he is; I may not breathe my censure.

270 What he might be—if what he might he is not—
I would to heaven he were.

LODOVICO   What! Strike his wife?

IAGO   'Faith, that was not so well; yet would I knew
That stroke would prove the worst.

LODOVICO   Is it his use?°   *custom*
Or did the letters work upon his blood°   *passions*
And new create his fault?

275 IAGO   Alas, alas!

9. Each drop would cause the earth to conceive a   for their victims).
crocodile (crocodiles proverbially wept false tears   1. Symbols of lust.

It is not honesty in me to speak
What I have seen and known. You shall observe him,
And his own courses° will denote him so   *actions*
That I may save my speech. Do but go after
280   And mark how he continues.
LODOVICO   I am sorry that I am deceived in him.

                                         Exeunt.

4.2

Enter OTHELLO *and* EMILIA.

OTHELLO   You have seen nothing then?
EMILIA   Nor ever heard, nor ever did suspect.
OTHELLO   Yes, you have seen Cassio and she together.
EMILIA   But then I saw no harm, and then I heard
5   Each syllable that breath made up between them.
OTHELLO   What, did they never whisper?
EMILIA   Never, my lord.
OTHELLO   Nor send you out o'th' way?
EMILIA   Never.
OTHELLO   To fetch her fan, her gloves, her mask, nor nothing?
10   EMILIA   Never, my lord.
OTHELLO   That's strange.
EMILIA   I durst, my lord, to wager she is honest,
    Lay down my soul at stake. If you think other,
    Remove your thought; it doth abuse your bosom.
15   If any wretch have put this in your head,
    Let heaven requite it with the serpent's curse,[1]
    For if she be not honest, chaste, and true,
    There's no man happy. The purest of their wives
    Is foul as slander.
OTHELLO   Bid her come hither—go. *Exit* EMILIA.
20   She says enough; yet she's a simple bawd
    That cannot say as much.[2] This is a subtle whore:
    A closet lock and key° of villainous secrets;   *a hider*
    And yet she'll kneel and pray; I have seen her do't.
        Enter DESDEMONA *and* EMILIA.
DESDEMONA   My lord, what is your will?
OTHELLO   Pray you, chuck,
    come hither.
DESDEMONA   What is your pleasure?
25   OTHELLO   Let me see your eyes.
    Look in my face.
DESDEMONA   What horrible fancy's this?
OTHELLO [*to* EMILIA]   Some of your function,[3] mistress:
    Leave procreants° alone and shut the door;   *copulators*

4.2 Location: The citadel.
1. In Genesis, the curse that God laid on the serpent who deceived Eve.
2. Yet it would be a simpleminded go-between who couldn't say as much as she did.
3. Fulfill your bawd's function by guarding the door.

Cough or cry "hem" if anybody come.
30   Your mystery, your mystery!° Nay, dispatch! *Exit* EMILIA.   *profession*
DESDEMONA   Upon my knees, what doth your speech
        import?
      I understand a fury in your words,
      But not the words.
OTHELLO   Why? What art thou?
DESDEMONA   Your wife, my lord, your true and loyal wife.
35   OTHELLO   Come, swear it! damn thyself!
      Lest, being° like one of heaven, the devils themselves   *appearing*
      Should fear to seize thee. Therefore be double-damned:
      Swear thou art honest!
DESDEMONA   Heaven doth truly know it.
OTHELLO   Heaven truly knows that thou art false as hell.
DESDEMONA   To whom, my lord? With whom? How am I
40   false?
OTHELLO   Ah, Desdemon! away, away, away!
DESDEMONA   Alas the heavy day! Why do you weep?
      Am I the motive of these tears, my lord?
      If haply° you my father do suspect   *perhaps*
45   An instrument of this your calling back,
      Lay not your blame on me. If you have lost him,
      I have lost him too.
OTHELLO   Had it pleased heaven
      To try me with affliction, had they rained
      All kind of sores and shames on my bare head,
50   Steeped me in poverty to the very lips,
      Given to captivity me and my utmost hopes,
      I should have found in some place of my soul
      A drop of patience. But, alas, to make me
      The fixèd figure for the time of scorn
55   To point his slow and moving finger at!⁴
      Yet could I bear that too—well, very well;
      But there where I have garnered° up my heart,   *stored*
      Where either I must live or bear no life,
      The fountain from the which my current runs
60   Or else dries up; to be discarded thence,
      Or keep it as a cistern for foul toads
      To knot and gender⁵ in!—Turn thy complexion there,
      Patience,⁶ thou young and rose-lipped cherubin;
      Ay, here look grim as hell!
65   DESDEMONA   I hope my noble lord esteems me honest.
OTHELLO   O, ay, as summer flies are in the shambles,°   *slaughterhouse*
      That quicken even with blowing.⁷ O thou weed,
      Who art so lovely fair and smell'st so sweet

---

4. The designated object of scorn for this scornful time to point (as on a clock face) its slowly
moving hand at.
5. To couple and engender.
6. Change color at the thought of that, Patience.

7. Who come to life (or bring their offspring to
life and hence make the meat foul) as soon as the
eggs are deposited. The point seems to be the
speed of breeding, inferred from Desdemona's
supposed infidelity.

That the sense aches at thee,
70 Would thou hadst never been born!
DESDEMONA Alas, what ignorant sin have I committed?
OTHELLO Was this fair paper, this most goodly book,
Made to write "whore" upon? What committed?
Committed?[8] O, thou public commoner!°   *prostitute*
75 I should make very forges of my cheeks
That would to cinders burn up modesty
Did I but speak thy deeds. What committed?
Heaven stops the nose at it, and the moon winks;°   *closes its eyes*
The bawdy° wind that kisses all it meets   *promiscuous*
80 Is hushed within the hollow mine of earth°   *within a cave*
And will not hear't. What committed?
DESDEMONA By heaven, you do me wrong!
OTHELLO Are not you a strumpet?
DESDEMONA   No, as I am a Christian!
If to preserve this vessel for my lord
85 From any other foul unlawful touch
Be not to be a strumpet, I am none.
OTHELLO What, not a whore?
DESDEMONA   No, as I shall be saved!
OTHELLO Is't possible?
DESDEMONA O, heaven forgive us!
OTHELLO   I cry you mercy° then.   *I beg your pardon*
90 I took you for that cunning whore of Venice
That married with Othello.—You! Mistress!
That have the office opposite to Saint Peter
And keeps the gate of hell. You, you!
        Enter EMILIA.
                    Ay, you.
We have done our course;° [*giving her money*] there's   *business*
    money for your pains;
95 I pray you turn the key and keep our counsel.   *Exit.*
EMILIA Alas, what does this gentleman conceive?°   *believe*
How do you, madam? how do you, my good lady?
DESDEMONA Faith, half asleep.
EMILIA Good madam, what's the matter with my lord?
DESDEMONA With who?
100 EMILIA   Why, with my lord, madam.
DESDEMONA Who is thy lord?
EMILIA   He that is yours, sweet lady.
DESDEMONA I have none. Do not talk to me, Emilia;
I cannot weep, nor answers have I none
But what should go by water.° Prithee tonight   *appear in tears*
105 Lay on my bed my wedding sheets, remember;
And call thy husband hither.
EMILIA   Here's a change indeed!
                    Exit.

8. Lines 74–77 do not appear in Q.

DESDEMONA 'Tis meet° I should be used so, very meet.   *fitting*
How have I been behaved that he might stick
The small'st opinion on my least misuse?[9]
    Enter IAGO *and* EMILIA.

110 IAGO What is your pleasure, madam? How is't with you?

DESDEMONA I cannot tell. Those that do teach young babes
Do it with gentle means and easy tasks.
He might have chid me so; for in good faith
I am a child to chiding.

IAGO   What is the matter, lady?

115 EMILIA Alas, Iago, my lord hath so bewhored her,°   *called her a whore*
Thrown such despite° and heavy terms upon her,   *spite*
That true hearts cannot bear it.

DESDEMONA Am I that name, Iago?

IAGO   What name, fair lady?

DESDEMONA Such as she said my lord did say I was.

120 EMILIA He called her whore. A beggar in his drink
Could not have laid such terms upon his callet.°   *whore*

IAGO Why did he so?

DESDEMONA I do not know; I am sure I am none such.

IAGO Do not weep, do not weep. Alas the day!

125 EMILIA Hath she forsook so many noble matches,
Her father and her country and her friends,
To be called whore? Would it not make one weep?

DESDEMONA It is my wretched fortune.

IAGO   Beshrew° him for't!   *curse*
How comes this trick° upon him?   *behavior*

DESDEMONA   Nay, heaven doth know.

130 EMILIA I will be hanged if some eternal villain,
Some busy° and insinuating rogue,   *meddling*
Some cogging,° cozening° slave, to get some office,   *deceiving / cheating*
Have not devised this slander. I will be hanged else.

IAGO Fie! there is no such man; it is impossible.

135 DESDEMONA If any such there be, heaven pardon him.

EMILIA A halter° pardon him, and hell gnaw his bones!   *hangman's noose*
Why should he call her whore? Who keeps her company?
What place? what time? what form? what likelihood?
The Moor's abused by some most villainous knave,

140 Some base notorious knave, some scurvy fellow.
O heaven, that such companions thou'dst unfold,°   *reveal*
And put in every honest hand a whip
To lash the rascals naked through the world
Even from the east to th' west!

IAGO   Speak within door.°   *more softly*

145 EMILIA O, fie upon them! Some such squire° he was   *fellow*
That turned your wit the seamy side without°   *wrong side out*
And made you to suspect me with the Moor.

---

9. "That . . . misuse": that would cause him to suspect even slightly the least fault (?).

IAGO   You are a fool; go to.

DESDEMONA   O God,[1] Iago,

    What shall I do to win my lord again?

150   Good friend, go to him; for by this light of heaven,

    I know not how I lost him. Here I kneel:[2]

    If e'er my will did trespass 'gainst his love,

    Either in discourse of thought or actual deed,

    Or that mine eyes, mine ears, or any sense

155   Delighted them in any other form,[3]

    Or that I do not yet,° and ever did,   *still*

    And ever will (though he do shake me off

    To beggarly divorcement) love him dearly—

    Comfort forswear me!° Unkindness may do much,   *deny me divine solace*

160   And his unkindness may defeat my life,

    But never taint my love.   [*She rises.*]

                  I cannot say "whore."

    It does abhor[4] me now I speak the word.

    To do the act that might the addition° earn,   *label*

    Not the world's mass of vanity° could make me.   *all worldly splendor*

165   IAGO   I pray you be content; 'tis but his humor;°   *mood*

    The business of the state does him offense.

DESDEMONA   If 'twere no other—

IAGO   It is but so, I warrant.

    [*Trumpets within.*]

    Hark how these instruments summon to supper.

    The messengers of Venice stays the meat;°   *are waiting to eat*

170   Go in, and weep not; all things shall be well.

             Exeunt DESDEMONA *and* EMILIA.

      Enter RODERIGO.

    How now, Roderigo?

RODERIGO   I do not find that thou deal'st justly with me.

IAGO   What in the contrary?

RODERIGO   Every day thou doff'st me with some device,[5]

175   Iago, and rather, as it seems to me now, keep'st from me

    all conveniency° than suppliest me with the least advan-   *opportunity*

    tage of hope. I will indeed no longer endure it. Nor am I

    yet persuaded to put up in peace what already I have

    foolishly suffered.

180   IAGO   Will you hear me, Roderigo?

RODERIGO   Faith, I have heard too much; and your words

    and performances are no kin together.

IAGO   You charge me most unjustly.

RODERIGO   With naught but truth. I have wasted myself

185   out of my means. The jewels you have had from me to

    deliver Desdemona would half have corrupted a votarist.°   *nun*

---

1. The folio reads "Alas," in keeping with the censorship of oaths that led to many changes from the quarto text. Q's reading here, "O Good," is probably a misprint for "O God."
2. Lines 151–64 (beginning with "Here") do not appear in Q.
3. Took pleasure in anyone but him.
4. Fill me with abhorrence; make me abhorrent, with a pun on "ab-whore."
5. You put me off with some trick.

You have told me she hath received them, and returned
me expectations and comforts of sudden respect and
acquaintance, but I find none.

190 IAGO Well, go to, very well.

RODERIGO "Very well"! "go to"! I cannot go to,° man, nor   *succeed sexually*
'tis not very well. Nay, I think it is scurvy, and begin to
find myself fopped° in it.   *made a fool*

IAGO Very well.

195 RODERIGO I tell you 'tis not very well. I will make myself
known to Desdemona. If she will return me my jewels, I
will give over my suit and repent my unlawful solicitation. If not, assure yourself I will seek satisfaction of
you.

200 IAGO You have said° now.   *finished*

RODERIGO Ay, and said nothing but what I protest intend-
ment of doing.

IAGO Why, now I see there's mettle in thee, and even
from this instant do build on thee a better opinion than

205 ever before. Give me thy hand, Roderigo. Thou hast taken
against me a most just exception, but yet I protest I have
dealt most directly in thy affair.

RODERIGO It hath not appeared.

IAGO I grant indeed it hath not appeared, and your suspi-

210 cion is not without wit and judgment. But, Roderigo, if
thou hast that in thee indeed which I have greater reason to believe now than ever—I mean purpose, courage,
and valor—this night show it. If thou the next night following enjoy not Desdemona, take me from this world

215 with treachery and devise engines for° my life.   *plots against*

RODERIGO Well, what is it? Is it within reason and compass?°   *possibility*

IAGO Sir, there is especial commission come from Venice
to depute Cassio in Othello's place.

220 RODERIGO Is that true? Why, then Othello and Desdemona
return again to Venice.

IAGO O no; he goes into Mauritania[6] and taketh away
with him the fair Desdemona, unless his abode be lin-
gered here by some accident; wherein none can be so

225 determinate° as the removing of Cassio.   *effectual*

RODERIGO How do you mean "removing" him?

IAGO Why, by making him uncapable of Othello's place—
knocking out his brains.

RODERIGO And that you would have me to do.

230 IAGO Ay, if you dare do yourself a profit and a right. He
sups tonight with a harlotry, and thither will I go to him.
He knows not yet of his honorable fortune.° If you will   *his promotion*
watch his going thence, which I will fashion° to fall out   *arrange*

---

6. Country in the western Sahara.

between twelve and one, you may take him at your plea-
235 sure. I will be near to second your attempt, and he shall
fall between us. Come, stand not amazed at it, but go
along with me. I will show you such a necessity in his
death that you shall think yourself bound to put it on
him. It is now high suppertime, and the night grows to
240 waste. About it!

RODERIGO   I will hear further reason for this.

IAGO   And you shall be satisfied.   *Exeunt.*

4.3

Enter OTHELLO, LODOVICO, DESDEMONA, EMILIA, *and*
attendants.

LODOVICO   I do beseech you, sir, trouble yourself no
    further.

OTHELLO   O, pardon me; 'twill do me good to walk.

LODOVICO [*to* DESDEMONA]   Madam, good night. I humbly
    thank your ladyship.

DESDEMONA   Your honor is most welcome.

OTHELLO   Will you walk, sir?

5 O, Desdemona—

DESDEMONA   My lord?

OTHELLO   Get you to bed on th'instant. I will be returned
    forthwith. Dismiss your attendant there. Look't be done.

DESDEMONA   I will, my lord.

        Exeunt [OTHELLO *with* LODOVICO *and attendants*].

10 EMILIA   How goes it now? He looks gentler than he did.

DESDEMONA   He says he will return incontinent,°   *immediately*
    And hath commanded me to go to bed,
    And bid me to dismiss you.

EMILIA   Dismiss me?

DESDEMONA   It was his bidding; therefore, good Emilia,
15   Give me my nightly wearing, and adieu.
    We must not now displease him.

EMILIA   I would you had never seen him.

DESDEMONA   So would not I: my love doth so approve him
    That even his stubbornness, his checks, his frowns—
20   Prithee unpin¹ me—have grace and favor in them.

    [EMILIA *helps* DESDEMONA *undress*.]

EMILIA   I have laid those sheets you bade me on the bed.

DESDEMONA   All's one.° Good faith, how foolish are our   *it doesn't matter*
    minds!
    If I do die before thee, prithee shroud me
    In one of these same sheets.

EMILIA   Come, come—you talk.

25 DESDEMONA   My mother had a maid called Barbary;

4.3 Location: Scene continues.
1. To "unpin" a woman was to undo her dress, by the removal of pins.

She was in love, and he she loved proved mad
And did forsake her. She had a Song of "Willow"—
An old thing 'twas, but it expressed her fortune—
And she died singing it. That song tonight
30 Will not go from my mind; I² have much to do
But to³ go hang my head all at one side
And sing it, like poor Barbary. Prithee dispatch.°   *make haste*
EMILIA   Shall I go fetch your nightgown?
DESDEMONA   No. Unpin me here.
This Lodovico is a proper man.
35 EMILIA   A very handsome man.
DESDEMONA   He speaks well.
EMILIA   I know a lady in Venice would have walked barefoot
to Palestine for a touch of his nether° lip.   *lower*
DESDEMONA [*sings*]
The poor soul sat sighing by a sycamore tree,
40   Sing all a green willow;⁴
Her hand on her bosom, her head on her knee,
Sing willow, willow, willow.
The fresh streams ran by her and murmured her moans,
Sing willow, willow, willow;
45 Her salt tears fell from her and softened the stones,
Sing willow—
[*to* EMILIA] Lay by these.°   *put these things aside*
[*sings*]
willow, willow.
[*to* EMILIA] Prithee hie° thee—he'll come anon.°   *hurry / straightaway*
[*sings*]
50   Sing all a green willow must be my garland.
Let nobody blame him, his scorn I approve.
Nay, that's not next. Hark, who is't that knocks?
EMILIA   It's the wind.
DESDEMONA [*sings*]
I called my love false love, but what said he then?⁵
55   Sing willow, willow, willow;
If I court more women, you'll couch with more men.
[*to* EMILIA] So, get thee gone, good night. Mine eyes do
itch—
Doth that bode° weeping?   *foretell*
EMILIA   'Tis neither here nor there.
DESDEMONA   I have heard it said so. O, these men, these
men!⁶
60 Dost thou in conscience think—tell me, Emilia—
That there be women do abuse their husbands
In such gross kind?°   *fashion*
EMILIA   There be some such, no question.
DESDEMONA   Wouldst thou do such a deed for all the world?

2. Lines 30–52 ("I . . . next") do not appear in Q.   5. Lines 54–56 do not appear in Q.
3. I can barely bring myself not to.   6. Lines 59–62 do not appear in Q.
4. A conventional symbol of disappointed love.

EMILIA   Why, would not you?

DESDEMONA   No, by this heavenly light!

65 EMILIA   Nor I neither, by this heavenly light:
　　I might do't as well i'th' dark.

DESDEMONA   Wouldst thou do such a deed for all the
　　world?

EMILIA   The world's a huge thing: it is a great price for a
　　small vice.

DESDEMONA   In troth, I think thou wouldst not.

70 EMILIA   In troth, I think I should—and undo't when I had
　　done. Marry, I would not do such a thing for a joint
　　ring,[7] nor for measures of lawn,° nor for gowns, petti-　　　　　linen
　　coats, nor caps, nor any petty exhibition.° But for all the　　　gift
　　whole world—'Uds° pity! who would not make her hus-　　　God's
75　　band a cuckold to make him a monarch? I should venture
　　purgatory for't.

DESDEMONA   Beshrew me if I would do such a wrong for
　　the whole world!

EMILIA   Why, the wrong is but a wrong i'th' world; and
80　　having the world for your labor, 'tis a wrong in your own
　　world, and you might quickly make it right.

DESDEMONA   I do not think there is any such woman.

EMILIA   Yes, a dozen; and as many to'th' vantage as
　　would store the world they played for.[8]
85　　But I do think it is their husbands' faults[9]
　　If wives do fall. Say that they slack their duties°　　　　　marital duties
　　And pour our treasures into foreign laps;[1]
　　Or else break out in peevish jealousies,
　　Throwing restraint upon us; or say they strike us,
90　　Or scant our former having in despite.[2]
　　Why, we have galls;° and though we have some grace,[3]　　tempers
　　Yet have we some revenge. Let husbands know
　　Their wives have sense like them. They see, and smell,
　　And have their palates both for sweet and sour,
95　　As husbands have. What is it that they do
　　When they change us for others? Is it sport?
　　I think it is. And doth affection° breed it?　　　　　　　　lust
　　I think it doth. Is't frailty that thus errs?
　　It is so too. And have not we affections,
100　　Desires for sport, and frailty, as men have?
　　Then let them use us well; else let them know,
　　The ills we do, their ills instruct us so.

DESDEMONA   Good night, good night. God me such uses°　　habits
　　send,
　　Not to pick bad from bad, but by bad, mend![4]　　Exeunt.

---

7. A cheap ring in separable halves.
8. And as many more as it would take to popu-
late the world they gained by doing it.
9. Lines 85–102 do not appear in Q.
1. And give the semen that belongs to us to other

women.
2. Or reduce our allowances out of spite.
3. Capacity for goodness, forgiveness.
4. Not to take bad behavior as an example to be
followed, but to learn from it what to avoid.

5.1

Enter IAGO *and* RODERIGO.

IAGO   Here, stand behind this bulk,° straight¹ will he   *shop stall*
  come.
  Wear thy good rapier bare, and put it home.°   *drive it into him*
  Quick, quick, fear nothing! I'll be at thy elbow.
  It makes us or it mars us; think on that
5   And fix most firm thy resolution.
RODERIGO   Be near at hand; I may miscarry in't.
IAGO   Here, at thy hand. Be bold, and take thy stand.
     [*Stands aside.*]
RODERIGO   I have no great devotion to the deed,
  And yet he hath given me satisfying reasons;
10   'Tis but a man gone. Forth my sword: he dies!
IAGO   I have rubbed this young quat° almost to the sense,²   *pimple*
  And he grows angry. Now, whether he kill Cassio
  Or Cassio him, or each do kill the other,
  Every way makes my gain. Live Roderigo,°   *if Roderigo lives*
15   He calls me to a restitution large
  Of gold and jewels that I bobbed from him°   *defrauded him of*
  As gifts to Desdemona.
  It must not be. If Cassio do remain,
  He hath a daily beauty in his life
20   That makes me ugly; and besides, the Moor
  May unfold° me to him; there stand I in much peril.   *reveal*
  No, he must die. But so—I hear him coming.
     Enter CASSIO
RODERIGO   I know his gait; 'tis he. Villain, thou diest!
     [*Thrusts at* CASSIO.]
CASSIO   That thrust had been mine enemy indeed,
25   But that my coat is better° than thou know'st.   *thicker; more armored*
  I will make proof of° thine.   [*Wounds* RODERIGO.]   *test*
RODERIGO   O, I am slain!
     [IAGO *wounds* CASSIO *in the leg and exits.*]
CASSIO   I am maimed forever! Help, ho! murder! murder!
     Enter OTHELLO.
OTHELLO   The voice of Cassio. Iago keeps his word.
RODERIGO   O, villain that I am!
OTHELLO   It is even so.
30 CASSIO   O, help ho! light! a surgeon!
OTHELLO   'Tis he. O brave Iago, honest and just,
  That hast such noble sense of thy friend's wrong!
  Thou teachest me. Minion,° your dear lies dead,   *hussy (Desdemona)*
  And your unblest fate hies.° Strumpet, I come.   *damnation hurries on*
35   Forth of° my heart those charms, thine eyes, are blotted.   *out of*

5.1 Location: A street in Cyprus.   2. To the quick.
1. Right away.

Thy bed, lust-stained, shall with lust's blood be spotted.

Exit OTHELLO.

Enter LODOVICO *and* GRATIANO.

CASSIO What ho! no watch? no passage?° Murder, murder!   passerby

GRATIANO 'Tis some mischance; the voice is very direful.

CASSIO O help!

40 LODOVICO Hark!

RODERIGO O wretched villain!

LODOVICO Two or three groan. 'Tis heavy° night;   dark

These may be counterfeits; let's think't unsafe

To come into° the cry without more help.   go near

45 RODERIGO Nobody come? Then shall I bleed to death.

Enter IAGO *with a light.*

LODOVICO Hark.

GRATIANO Here's one comes in his shirt, with light and

weapons.

IAGO Who's there? Whose noise is this that cries on murder?

LODOVICO We do not know.

IAGO   Do not you hear a cry?

CASSIO Here, here! for heaven's sake, help me!

50 IAGO   What's the matter?

GRATIANO This is Othello's ancient, as I take it.

LODOVICO The same indeed, a very valiant fellow.

IAGO What are you here that cry so grievously?

CASSIO Iago? O, I am spoiled, undone by villains!

55 Give me some help.

IAGO O me, lieutenant! What villains have done this?

CASSIO I think that one of them is hereabout

And cannot make away.

IAGO   O treacherous villains!

[*to* LODOVICO *and* GRATIANO] What are you there? Come

in, and give some help.

60 RODERIGO O, help me there!

CASSIO That's one of them.

IAGO   O murd'rous slave! O villain!

[*Stabs* RODERIGO.]

RODERIGO O damned Iago! O inhuman dog!

IAGO Kill men i'th' dark?—Where be these bloody

thieves?—

How silent is this town!—Ho, murder, murder!—

[*to* LODOVICO *and* GRATIANO] What may you be? Are you

65 of good or evil?

LODOVICO As you shall prove us, praise us.

IAGO Signor Lodovico?

LODOVICO He, sir.

IAGO I cry you mercy. Here's Cassio hurt by villains.

70 GRATIANO Cassio?

IAGO How is't, brother?

CASSIO My leg is cut in two.

IAGO   Marry, heaven forbid!

Light, gentlemen. I'll bind it with my shirt.
    Enter BIANCA.
BIANCA   What is the matter, ho? Who is't that cried?
IAGO   Who is't that cried?
75 BIANCA   O, my dear Cassio!
   My sweet Cassio! O Cassio, Cassio, Cassio!
IAGO   O notable strumpet! Cassio, may you suspect
   Who they should be that have thus mangled you?
CASSIO   No.
GRATIANO   I am sorry to find you thus; I have been to
80   seek you.
IAGO   Lend me a garter.³ So . . . O for a chair°   *litter*
   To bear him easily hence!
BIANCA   Alas, he faints! O Cassio, Cassio, Cassio!
IAGO   Gentlemen all, I do suspect this trash
85   To be a party in this injury.—
   Patience awhile, good Cassio.—Come, come!
   Lend me a light. Know we this face or no?
   Alas! my friend and my dear countryman,
   Roderigo! No—yes, sure! O heaven, Roderigo!
GRATIANO   What, of Venice?
90 IAGO   Even he, sir. Did you know him?
GRATIANO   Know him? Ay.
IAGO   Signor Gratiano? I cry your gentle pardon.
   These bloody accidents must excuse my manners
   That so neglected you.
GRATIANO   I am glad to see you.
95 IAGO   How do you, Cassio? O, a chair, a chair!
GRATIANO   Roderigo?
IAGO   He, he, 'tis he. [*Enter attendants with a litter.*]
         O, that's well said, the chair.
   Some good man bear him carefully from hence;
   I'll fetch the general's surgeon.—For you, mistress,
100   Save you your labor.—He that lies slain here, Cassio,
   Was my dear friend. What malice was between you?
CASSIO   None in the world, nor do I know the man.
IAGO [*to* BIANCA]   What, look you pale? [*To attendants*] O,
   bear him out o'th'air.⁴
         [*Exeunt attendants with* CASSIO *in the*
              litter and with RODERIGO's *body.*]
   Stay you, good gentlemen.—Look you pale, mistress?—
105   Do you perceive the gastness° of her eye?—   *terror*
   Nay, if you stare, we shall hear more anon.—
   Behold her well; I pray you look upon her.
   Do you see, gentlemen? Nay, guiltiness will speak
   Though tongues were out of use.
       Enter EMILIA.

---

3. A band worn as a sash or belt. Iago wants to use one as a tourniquet.

4. Out of the open air (thought to be bad for wounds).

EMILIA Alas, what is the matter? what is the matter, hus-
110   band?
IAGO Cassio hath here been set on in the dark
    By Roderigo and fellows that are scaped.
    He's almost slain, and Roderigo quite dead.
EMILIA Alas, good gentleman! alas, good Cassio!
115 IAGO This is the fruits of whoring. Prithee, Emilia,
    Go know of Cassio where he supped tonight.—
    What, do you shake at that?
BIANCA He supped at my house, but I therefore shake not.
IAGO O did he so? I charge you go with me.
120 EMILIA O fie upon thee, strumpet!
BIANCA I am no strumpet, but of life as honest
    As you that thus abuse me.
EMILIA   As I? Fie upon thee!
IAGO Kind gentlemen, let's go see poor Cassio dressed.[5]—
    Come, mistress, you must tell's another tale.
125 Emilia, run you to the citadel
    And tell my lord and lady what hath happed.
                                    [*Exit* EMILIA.]
Will you go on afore?   *Exeunt* [*all but* IAGO].
            This is the night
That either makes me or fordoes° me quite.   [*Exit.*]   undoes

5.2

Enter OTHELLO *with a light,* DESDEMONA *in her bed* [*asleep*].
OTHELLO It is the cause,[1] it is the cause, my soul.
    Let me not name it to you, you chaste stars.
    It is the cause. Yet I'll not shed her blood,
    Nor scar that whiter skin of hers than snow,
5   And smooth as monumental alabaster.°   stone used in tombs
    Yet she must die, else she'll betray more men.
    Put out the light, and then put out the light.[2]
    If I quench thee, thou flaming minister,°   light that serves me
    I can again thy former light restore,
10   Should I repent me. But once put out thy light,
    Thou cunning'st pattern of excelling nature,[3]
    I know not where is that Promethean heat[4]
    That can thy light relume.° When I have plucked thy rose   relight
    I cannot give it vital growth again;
15   It needs must wither. I'll smell thee on the tree.
            [*He smells, then kisses her.*]
    O balmy breath, that dost almost persuade

5. I.e., see his wound dressed.
5.2 Location: Desdemona and Othello's bedroom.
1. I.e., Desdemona's infidelity is the "cause" of—
the thing that demands—justice, which Othello
sees himself as being required to execute.
2. This and the following lines compare the light
of Othello's lamp or torch to Desdemona's "light"
of life.
3. You most cleverly wrought example of nature's
surpassing work.
4. Life-giving fire. In Greek mythology, Prometheus stole fire from heaven to give it to
humankind; in a different tradition, he is credited
with animating humankind from clay.

Justice to break her sword! One more; one more.
   [*He kisses her.*]
Be thus when thou art dead, and I will kill thee
And love thee after. One more, and that's the last.
   He kisses her.
20 So sweet was ne'er so fatal. I must weep,
But they are cruel tears. This sorrow's heavenly:
It strikes where it doth love.[5] She wakes.

DESDEMONA Who's there? Othello?

OTHELLO   Ay, Desdemona.

DESDEMONA Will you come to bed, my lord?

OTHELLO Have you prayed tonight, Desdemon?

25 DESDEMONA   Ay, my lord.

OTHELLO If you bethink yourself of any crime
Unreconciled as yet to heaven and grace,
Solicit° for it straight.   *ask forgiveness*

DESDEMONA Alack, my lord, what may you mean by that?

30 OTHELLO Well, do it, and be brief; I will walk by.
I would not kill thy unpreparèd spirit.
No, heavens forfend! I would not kill thy soul.

DESDEMONA Talk you of killing?

OTHELLO   Ay, I do.

DESDEMONA   Then heaven
Have mercy on me!

OTHELLO   Amen, with all my heart!

35 DESDEMONA If you say so, I hope you will not kill me.

OTHELLO Humh.

DESDEMONA And yet I fear you, for you're fatal then
When your eyes roll so. Why I should fear, I know not,
Since guiltiness I know not; but yet I feel I fear.

OTHELLO Think on thy sins.

40 DESDEMONA   They are loves I bear to you.

OTHELLO Ay, and for that thou diest.

DESDEMONA That death's unnatural that kills for loving.
Alas, why gnaw you so your nether lip?
Some bloody passion shakes your very frame.

45 These are portents; but yet I hope, I hope,
They do not point on me.

OTHELLO   Peace, and be still.

DESDEMONA I will so. What's the matter?

OTHELLO   That handkerchief,
Which I so loved and gave thee, thou gav'st to Cassio.

DESDEMONA No, by my life and soul! Send for the man
50 And ask him.

OTHELLO Sweet soul, take heed; take heed of perjury;
Thou art on thy deathbed.

DESDEMONA Ay, but not yet to die.

---

5. See Hebrews 12.6: "For whom the Lord loveth, he chasteneth."

OTHELLO   Presently.°   *immediately*

Therefore confess thee freely of thy sin;

55   For to deny each article with oath

Cannot remove nor choke the strong conception

That I do groan withal.[6] Thou art to die.

DESDEMONA   Then Lord have mercy on me!

OTHELLO   I say amen.

DESDEMONA   And have you mercy too! I never did

60   Offend you in my life, never loved Cassio

But with such general warranty of heaven

As I might love. I never gave him token.

OTHELLO   By heaven, I saw my handkerchief in's hand!

O perjured woman! thou dost stone° my heart,   *harden*

65   And makes me call what I intend to do

A murder, which I thought a sacrifice.

I saw the handkerchief.

DESDEMONA   He found it then.

I never gave it him. Send for him hither.

Let him confess a truth.

OTHELLO   He hath confessed.

70 DESDEMONA   What, my lord?

OTHELLO   That he hath used thee.

DESDEMONA   How? unlawfully?

OTHELLO   Ay.

DESDEMONA   He will not say so.

OTHELLO   No, his mouth is stopped.

Honest Iago hath ta'en order for't.

DESDEMONA   O, my fear interprets! What, is he dead?

75 OTHELLO   Had all his hairs been lives, my great revenge

Had stomach for them all.

DESDEMONA [*weeping*]   Alas, he is betrayed and I undone!

OTHELLO   Out, strumpet! Weep'st thou for him to my
face?

DESDEMONA   O banish me, my lord, but kill me not!

80 OTHELLO [*attacking her*]   Down, strumpet!

DESDEMONA   Kill me tomorrow, let me live tonight!

OTHELLO   Nay, if you strive—

DESDEMONA   But half an hour!

OTHELLO   Being done, there is no
pause.[7]

DESDEMONA   But while I say one prayer!

OTHELLO   It is too late.

Smothers her.

85 DESDEMONA   O Lord, Lord, Lord!

EMILIA *calls within*   My lord, my lord! What ho! My lord,
my lord!

---

6. Cannot change the strong conviction I
have of your guilt (or the firm plan to kill you),
which makes me groan so. The metaphor is from
childbirth.
7. Now that I've started, there's no stopping.

OTHELLO   What noise is this? Not dead? not yet quite dead?
I that am cruel am yet merciful;
I would not have thee linger in thy pain.
90   So, so.
EMILIA *within* What ho? my lord, my lord!
OTHELLO   Who's there?
EMILIA [*within*] O good my lord, I would speak a word
    with you.
OTHELLO [*calling*] Yes.—'Tis Emilia.—[*calling*] By and
    by.°—She's dead.   *in a moment*
    'Tis like she comes to speak of Cassio's death.
95   The noise was high.° Ha, no more moving?   *commotion was loud*
    Still as the grave. Shall she come in? Were't good?
    I think she stirs again. No. What's best to do?
    If she come in, she'll sure speak to my wife.
    My wife, my wife! What wife? I have no wife.
100   O insupportable! O heavy hour!
    Methinks it should be now a huge eclipse
    Of sun and moon, and that th'affrighted globe
    Should yawn at alteration.[8]
EMILIA [*within*]   I do beseech you
    That I may speak with you. O good my lord!
105 OTHELLO   I had forgot thee. O, come in, Emilia.
    Soft,° by and by; let me the curtains draw.   *quiet*
    [*He closes the bed curtains.*]
    Where art thou? What's the matter with thee now?
    [*He unlocks the door.*] *Enter* EMILIA.
EMILIA   O my good lord, yonder's foul murders done!
OTHELLO   What? now?
110 EMILIA   But° now, my lord.   *just*
OTHELLO   It is the very error° of the moon;   *deviation*
    She comes more nearer earth than she was wont
    And makes men mad.
EMILIA   Cassio, my lord, hath killed
    A young Venetian called Roderigo.
115 OTHELLO   Roderigo killed? and Cassio killed?
EMILIA   No, Cassio is not killed.
OTHELLO   Not Cassio killed? Then murder's out of tune,
    And sweet revenge grows harsh.
DESDEMONA   O falsely, falsely murdered!
120 EMILIA   O Lord! what cry is that?
OTHELLO   That? What?
EMILIA   Out and alas! that was my lady's voice.
    [*She opens the bed curtains.*]
    Help, help ho, help! O, lady, speak again!
    Sweet Desdemona, O sweet mistress, speak!
125 DESDEMONA   A guiltless death I die.
EMILIA   O, who hath done this deed?

---

8. Should gape at the change. Earthquakes were associated with eclipses.

DESDEMONA Nobody. I myself. Farewell.
  Commend me to my kind lord. O, farewell!
    She dies.
OTHELLO Why, how should she be murdered?
EMILIA   Alas, who knows?

130 OTHELLO You heard her say herself it was not I.
EMILIA She said so; I must needs report the truth.
OTHELLO She's like a liar gone to burning hell!
  'Twas I that killed her!
EMILIA   O, the more angel she,
  And you the blacker devil!

135 OTHELLO She turned to folly,° and she was a whore.   *wantonness*
EMILIA Thou dost belie her, and thou art a devil.
OTHELLO She was false as water.
EMILIA   Thou art rash as fire to say
  That she was false. O, she was heavenly true!
OTHELLO Cassio did top her. Ask thy husband else.°   *if you doubt it*

140   O, I were damned beneath all depth in hell
  But that I did proceed upon just grounds
  To this extremity! Thy husband knew it all.
EMILIA My husband?
OTHELLO Thy husband.

145 EMILIA That she was false to wedlock?
OTHELLO Ay, with Cassio. Had she been true,
  If heaven would make me such another world
  Of one entire and perfect chrysolite,°   *topaz*
  I'd not have sold her for it.
EMILIA   My husband?

150 OTHELLO Ay, 'twas he that told me on her first.
  An honest man he is, and hates the slime
  That sticks on filthy deeds.
EMILIA   My husband?
OTHELLO What needs this iterance,° woman?   *repetition*
  I say, thy husband.

155 EMILIA O mistress, villainy hath made mocks with° love!⁹   *at*
  My husband say she was false?
OTHELLO   He, woman;
  I say, thy husband; dost understand the word?
  My friend, thy husband; honest, honest Iago.
EMILIA If he say so, may his pernicious soul

160   Rot half a grain a day! He lies to th'heart.
  She was too fond of her most filthy bargain.¹
OTHELLO Ha?
EMILIA Do thy worst.
  This deed of thine is no more worthy heaven
  Than thou wast worthy her.

165 OTHELLO   Peace, you were best!°   *it would be best for you*
EMILIA Thou hast not half that power to do me harm

---

9. Lines 155–58 do not appear in Q.
1. I.e., her marriage, or her husband.

As I have to be hurt. O gull,° O dolt!   *fool*
As ignorant as dirt! Thou hast done a deed—
   [He draws his sword.]
I care not for thy sword; I'll make thee known,
170   Though I lost twenty lives. Help, help, ho, help!
The Moor hath killed my mistress! Murder, murder!
   Enter MONTANO, GRATIANO, IAGO, *and others.*
MONTANO   What is the matter? How now, general?
EMILIA   O, are you come, Iago? You have done well,
That men must lay their murders on your neck.
175   GRATIANO   What is the matter?
EMILIA *[to* IAGO*]*   Disprove this villain, if thou be'st a man.
He says thou told'st him that his wife was false.
I know thou didst not; thou'rt not such a villain.
Speak, for my heart is full.
180   IAGO   I told him what I thought, and told no more
Than what he found himself was apt and true.
EMILIA   But did you ever tell him she was false?
IAGO   I did.
EMILIA   You told a lie, an odious damnèd lie!
185   Upon my soul, a lie! a wicked lie!
She false with Cassio? Did you say with Cassio?
IAGO   With Cassio, mistress! Go to, charm° your tongue!   *silence*
EMILIA   I will not charm my tongue; I am bound to speak:
My mistress here lies murdered in her bed—[2]
190   ALL   O heavens forfend!—
EMILIA *[to* IAGO*]*   And your reports have set the murder on.
OTHELLO   Nay, stare not, masters; it is true indeed.
GRATIANO   'Tis a strange truth.
MONTANO   O monstrous act!
195   EMILIA   Villainy, villainy, villainy!
I think upon't, I think I smell't. O villainy!
I thought so then.—I'll kill myself for grief!
O villainy! villainy!
IAGO   What, are you mad? I charge you get you home!
200   EMILIA   Good gentlemen, let me have leave to speak.
'Tis proper I obey him, but not now.
Perchance, Iago, I will ne'er go home.
OTHELLO   O! O! O!
   Falls on the bed.
EMILIA   Nay, lay thee down and roar,
205   For thou hast killed the sweetest innocent
That e'er did lift up eye.°   *(to heaven)*
OTHELLO *[rising]*   O, she was foul!
[to GRATIANO*]* I scarce did know you, uncle. There lies
   your niece,
Whose breath, indeed, these hands have newly stopped.
I know this act shows° horrible and grim.   *appears*

---

2. Lines 189–98 do not appear in Q.

210 GRATIANO Poor Desdemon, I am glad thy father's dead;   *marriage*
Thy match° was mortal to him, and pure grief
Shore his old thread in twain.³ Did he live now,
This sight would make him do a desperate turn;°   *act*
Yea, curse his better angel from his side
215 And fall to reprobance.⁴
OTHELLO 'Tis pitiful; but yet Iago knows
That she with Cassio hath the act of shame
A thousand times committed. Cassio confessed it,
And she did gratify his amorous works
220 With that recognizance° and pledge of love   *token*
Which I first gave her. I saw it in his hand;
It was a handkerchief, an antique token
My father gave my mother.
EMILIA O God! O heavenly God!
IAGO   'Swounds, hold your peace!
225 EMILIA 'Twill out, 'twill out! I peace?
No, I will speak as liberal as the north;⁵
Let heaven and men and devils, let them all,
All, all cry shame against me, yet I'll speak!
IAGO Be wise, and get you home.
    [IAGO *threatens* EMILIA *with his sword.*]
EMILIA   I will not!
230 GRATIANO Fie! Your sword upon a woman?
EMILIA O thou dull Moor, that handkerchief thou speak'st of
I found by fortune and did give my husband;
For often with a solemn earnestness—
More than indeed belonged to such a trifle—
He begged of me to steal't.
235 IAGO   Villainous whore!
EMILIA She give it Cassio? No, alas, I found it,
And I did giv't my husband.
IAGO   Filth, thou liest!
EMILIA By heaven, I do not! I do not, gentlemen.—
O murderous coxcomb!° What should such a fool   *fool*
Do with so good a wife?
240 OTHELLO   Are there no stones° in heaven   *thunderbolts*
But what serves for the thunder? Precious° villain!   *absolute*
    The Moor runs at IAGO. [MONTANO *disarms* OTHELLO.]
    IAGO [*stabs*] *his wife.*
GRATIANO The woman falls; sure he hath killed his wife.
EMILIA Ay, ay. O lay me by my mistress' side.   *Exit* IAGO.
GRATIANO He's gone, but his wife's killed.
245 MONTANO 'Tis a notorious villain. Take you this weapon,
Which I have here recovered from the Moor.
Come, guard the door without; let him not pass,
But kill him rather. I'll after that same villain,

3. Cut the thread of his life.
4. Suicide, the unforgivably sinful act of despair.
5. As freely as the north wind.

For 'tis a damnèd slave.
> *Exeunt* MONTANO, GRATIANO [*and all but* OTHELLO *and*
> EMILIA].

OTHELLO   I am not valiant neither,
250 But every puny whipster° gets my sword.   *insignificant person*
But why should honor outlive honesty?[6]
Let it go all.

EMILIA   What did thy song bode, lady?[7]
Hark, canst thou hear me? I will play the swan,
And die in music. [*Sings*] "Willow, willow, willow."
255 Moor, she was chaste. She loved thee, cruel Moor.
So come my soul to bliss as I speak true!
So speaking as I think, alas, I die.   *She dies.*

OTHELLO   I have another weapon in this chamber;
It was a sword of Spain, the ice-brook's temper.°   *tempered in icy water*
260 O, here it is.—Uncle, I must come forth.

GRATIANO [*within*]   If thou attempt it, it will cost thee dear;
Thou hast no weapon and perforce must suffer.

OTHELLO   Look in upon me then and speak with me,
Or, naked° as I am, I will assault thee.   *unarmed*
> [*Enter* GRATIANO.]

GRATIANO   What is the matter?

265 OTHELLO   Behold, I have a weapon;
A better never did itself sustain
Upon a soldier's thigh. I have seen the day
That with this little arm and this good sword
I have made my way through more impediments
270 Than twenty times your stop.° But O, vain boast!   *power to stop*
Who can control his fate? 'Tis not so now.
Be not afraid, though you do see me weaponed.[8]
Here is my journey's end, here is my butt°   *destination*
And very seamark° of my utmost sail.   *beacon*
275 Do you go back dismayed? 'Tis a lost° fear.   *an unnecessary*
Man but a rush° against Othello's breast   *aim even a reed*
And he retires.° Where should Othello go?   *falls back*
[*to* DESDEMONA] Now, how dost thou look now? O
    ill-starred wench,
Pale as thy smock. When we shall meet at count,°   *Judgment Day*
280 This look of thine will hurl my soul from heaven,
And fiends will snatch at it.
> [*He touches her.*]
                        Cold, cold, my girl?
Even like thy chastity. O cursèd, cursèd slave!
Whip me, ye devils,
From the possession of this heavenly sight!
285 Blow me about in winds, roast me in sulfur,

---

6. Why should military reputation outlive integrity?
7. Lines 252–54 ("What . . . willow.'") do not appear in Q.
8. Lines 272–78 do not appear in Q.

Wash me in steep-down gulfs of liquid fire!
O Desdemon! dead Desdemon; dead. O, O!

Enter LODOVICO, CASSIO *in a chair,* MONTANO, *and*
IAGO, *with* OFFICERS.

LODOVICO   Where is this rash and most unfortunate man?

OTHELLO   That's he that was Othello; here I am.

290   LODOVICO   Where is that viper? Bring the villain forth.

OTHELLO   I look down towards his feet,[9] but that's a fable;
    If that thou be'st a devil, I cannot kill thee.
      [*Wounds* IAGO.]

LODOVICO   Wrench his sword from him.

IAGO   I bleed, sir, but not killed.

OTHELLO   I am not sorry, neither; I'd have thee live,

295   For in my sense° 'tis happiness to die.   *state of feeling*

LODOVICO   O thou Othello, that was once so good,
    Fallen in the practice° of a cursèd slave,   *plot*
    What shall be said to thee?

OTHELLO   Why, anything:
    An honorable murderer, if you will;

300   For naught I did in hate, but all in honor.

LODOVICO   This wretch hath part confessed his villainy.
    Did you and he consent in Cassio's death?

OTHELLO   Ay.

CASSIO   Dear general, I never gave you cause.

305   OTHELLO   I do believe it, and I ask your pardon.
    Will you, I pray, demand° that demi-devil   *ask*
    Why he hath thus ensnared my soul and body?

IAGO   Demand me nothing. What you know, you know.
    From this time forth I never will speak word.

LODOVICO   What, not to pray?

310   GRATIANO   Torments° will ope your lips.   *tortures*

OTHELLO   Well, thou dost best.

LODOVICO   Sir, you shall understand what hath befall'n,
    Which, as I think, you know not. Here is a letter
    Found in the pocket of the slain Roderigo,

315   And here another. The one of them imports
    The death of Cassio, to be undertook
    By Roderigo.

OTHELLO   O villain!

CASSIO   Most heathenish and most gross!°   *monstrous*

LODOVICO   Now here's another discontented paper

320   Found in his pocket too; and this, it seems,
    Roderigo meant t'have sent this damnèd villain,
    But that, belike,° Iago in the interim   *most likely*
    Came in and satisfied him.

OTHELLO   O thou pernicious caitiff!°—   *wretch*
    How came you, Cassio, by that handkerchief

---

9. To look for the devil's cloven feet.

That was my wife's?

325   CASSIO   I found it in my chamber;
And he himself confessed it, but even now,
That there he dropped it for a special purpose
Which wrought to his desire.

OTHELLO   O fool, fool, fool!

CASSIO   There is besides in Roderigo's letter

330   How he upbraids Iago that he made him
Brave° me upon the watch, whereon it came   *defy*
That I was cast;° and even but now he spake,   *dismissed*
After long seeming dead, Iago hurt him,
Iago set him on.

LODOVICO [*to* OTHELLO]   You must forsake this room and
335   go with us.
Your power and your command is taken off,
And Cassio rules in Cyprus. For this slave,
If there be any cunning cruelty
That can torment him much and hold him° long,   *(alive)*
340   It shall be his. You shall close° prisoner rest   *tightly confined*
Till that the nature of your fault be known
To the Venetian state. [*to officers*] Come, bring away.

OTHELLO   Soft you;° a word or two before you go.   *wait*
I have done the state some service, and they know't;
345   No more of that. I pray you, in your letters,
When you shall these unlucky deeds relate,
Speak of me as I am. Nothing extenuate,
Nor set down aught in malice. Then must you speak
Of one that loved not wisely but too well;
350   Of one not easily jealous but, being wrought,
Perplexed in the extreme; of one whose hand,
Like the base Judean,¹ threw a pearl away
Richer than all his tribe, of one whose subdued° eyes,   *(by grief)*
Albeit unusèd to the melting mood,
355   Drops tears as fast as the Arabian trees
Their medicinable gum.° Set you down this;   *myrrh*
And say besides that in Aleppo once,
Where a malignant and a turbaned Turk
Beat a Venetian and traduced the state,
360   I took by th'throat the circumcisèd dog
And smote him—thus!
      He stabs himself.

LODOVICO   O bloody period!°   *conclusion*

GRATIANO   All that is spoke is marred.

OTHELLO [*to* DESDEMONA]   I kissed thee ere I killed thee.
No way but this,
Killing myself, to die upon a kiss.
      He [*kisses* DESDEMONA *and*] *dies.*

---

1. Probably alludes to Judas Iscariot, betrayer of Jesus. "Base Indian," in the quarto, suggests naive gullibility rather than malice.

365 CASSIO   This did I fear, but thought he had no weapon;
For he was great of heart.
LODOVICO [to IAGO]   O Spartan dog,[2]
More fell° than anguish, hunger, or the sea,   *cruel*
Look on the tragic loading of this bed:
This is thy work. The object poisons sight;
370 Let it be hid. Gratiano, keep the house
And seize upon the fortunes of the Moor,
For they succeed on you. [to CASSIO] To you, lord
governor,
Remains the censure° of this hellish villain;   *sentence*
The time, the place, the torture—O, enforce it!
375 Myself will straight aboard, and to the state
This heavy act with heavy heart relate.   *Exeunt.*

1603–04   1623

2. A bloodhound; hence a relentless, bloodthirsty man. Also the people of ancient Sparta were reputed
to be inhumane and unfeeling.

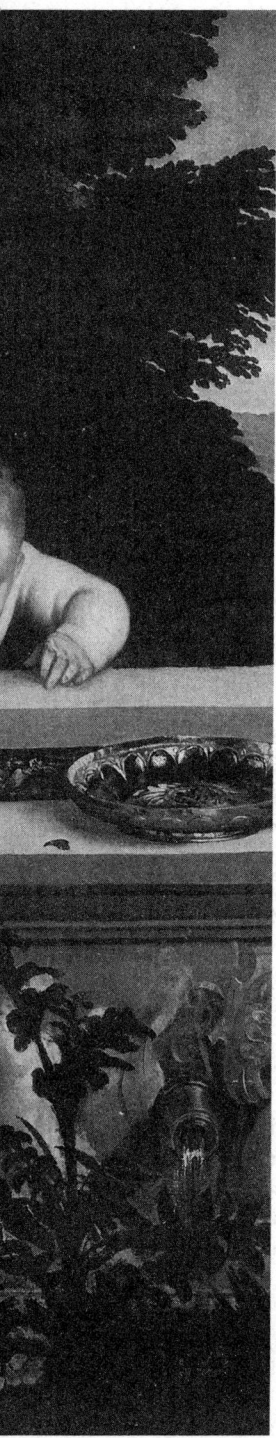

The Early Seventeenth Century 1603–1660

1603: Death of Elizabeth I; accession of James I, first Stuart king of England

1605: The Gunpowder Plot, a failed effort by Catholic extremists to blow up Parliament and the king

1607: Establishment of first permanent English colony in the New World at Jamestown, Virginia

1625: Death of James I; accession of Charles I

1642: Outbreak of civil war; theaters closed

1649: Execution of Charles I; beginning of Commonwealth and Protectorate, known inclusively as the Interregnum (1649–60)

1660: End of the Protectorate; restoration of Charles II

Queen Elizabeth died on March 24, 1603, after ruling England for more than four decades. The Virgin Queen had not, of course, produced a child to inherit her throne, but her kinsman, the thirty-six-year-old James Stuart, James VI of Scotland, succeeded her as James I without the violence that many had feared. Many welcomed the accession of a man in the prime of life, supposing that he would prove more decisive than his notoriously vacillating predecessor. Worries over the succession, which had plagued the reigns of the Tudor monarchs since Henry VIII, could finally subside: James already had several children with his queen, Anne of Denmark. Writers and scholars jubilantly noted that their new

Sacred and Profane Love (detail), ca. 1515, Titian. For more information about this image, see the color insert in this volume.

ruler had literary inclinations. He was the author of treatises on government and witchcraft, and some youthful efforts at poetry.

Nonetheless, there were grounds for disquiet. James had come to maturity in Scotland, in the seventeenth century a foreign land with a different church, different customs, and different institutions of government. Two of his books, *The True Law of Free Monarchies* (1598) and *Basilikon Doron* (1599), expounded authoritarian theories of kingship: James's views seemed incompatible with the English tradition of "mixed" government, in which power was shared by the monarch, the House of Lords, and the House of Commons. As Thomas Howard wrote in 1611, while Elizabeth "did talk of her subjects' love and good affection," James "talketh of his subjects' fear and subjection." James liked to imagine himself as a modern version of the wise, peace-loving Roman Augustus Caesar, who autocratically governed a vast empire. The Romans had deified their emperors, and while the Christian James could not expect the same, he insisted on his closeness to divinity. Kings, he believed, derived their powers from God rather than from the people. As God's specially chosen delegate, surely he deserved his subjects' reverent, unconditional obedience.

Yet unlike the charismatic Elizabeth, James was personally unprepossessing. One contemporary, Anthony Weldon, provides a barbed description: "His tongue too large for his mouth, which ever made him speak full in the mouth, and drink very uncomely as if eating his drink . . . he never washed his hands . . . his walk was ever circular, his fingers ever in that walk fiddling about his codpiece." Unsurprisingly, James did not always inspire in his subjects the deferential awe to which he thought himself entitled.

The relationship between the monarch and his people and the relationship between England and Scotland would be sources of friction throughout James's reign. James had hoped to unify his domains as a single nation, "the empire of Britain." But the two realms' legal and ecclesiastical systems proved difficult to reconcile, and the English Parliament, traditionally a sporadically convened advisory body to the monarch, offered robustly xenophobic opposition. The failure of unification was only one of several clashes with the English Parliament, especially with the House of Commons, which had authority over taxation. After James died in 1625 and his son, Charles I, succeeded him, tensions persisted and intensified. Charles, indeed, attempted to rule without summoning Parliament at all between 1629 and 1638. By 1642 England was up in arms, in a civil war between the king's forces and armies loyal to the House of Commons. The conflict ended with Charles's defeat and beheading in 1649.

Although in the early 1650s the monarchy as an institution seemed as dead as the man who had last worn the crown, an adequate replacement proved difficult to devise. Executive power devolved upon a "Lord Protector," Oliver Cromwell, former general of the parliamentary forces, who wielded power nearly as autocratically as Charles had done. Yet without an institutionally sanctioned method of transferring power upon Cromwell's death in 1658, the attempt to fashion a commonwealth without a hereditary monarch eventually failed. In 1660 Parliament invited the eldest son of the old king home from exile. He succeeded to the throne as King Charles II.

As James's accession marks the beginning of "the early seventeenth century," his grandson's marks the end. Literary periods often fail to correlate neatly with the reigns of monarchs, and the period 1603–60 can seem especially arbitrary. Many of the most important cultural trends in seventeenth-century Europe neither began nor ended in these years but were in the process of unfolding slowly, over several centuries. The Protestant Reformation of the sixteenth century was still ongoing in the seventeenth, and still producing turmoil. The printing press, invented in the fifteenth century, made books ever more widely available, contributing to an expansion of literacy and to a changed conception of authorship. Although the English economy remained primarily agrarian, its manufacturing and trade sectors were expanding rapidly. England was beginning to establish itself as a colonial power and as a leading maritime nation. From 1550 on, London grew explosively as a center of population, trade, and literary endeavor. All these developments got under way before James came to the throne, and many of them would continue after the 1714 death of James's great-granddaughter Queen Anne, the last of the Stuarts to reign in England.

From a literary point of view, 1603 can seem a particularly capricious dividing line because at the accession of James I so many writers happened to be in midcareer. The professional lives of William Shakespeare, Ben Jonson, John Donne, Francis Bacon, Walter Ralegh, and many less important writers—Thomas Dekker, George Chapman, Samuel Daniel, Michael Drayton, and Thomas Heywood, for instance—straddle the reigns of Elizabeth and James. The Restoration of Charles II, with which this section ends, is likewise a more significant political than literary milestone: John Milton completed *Paradise Lost* and wrote two other major poems in the 1660s. Nonetheless, recognizing the years 1603–60 as a period sharpens our awareness of some important political, intellectual, cultural, and stylistic currents that bear directly upon literary production. It helps focus attention too upon the seismic shift in national consciousness that, in 1649, could permit the formal trial, conviction, and execution of an anointed king at the hands of his former subjects.

STATE AND CHURCH, 1603–40

In James's reign, the most pressing difficulties were apparently financial, but money troubles were merely symptoms of deeper quandaries about the proper relationship between the king and the people. Compared to James's native Scotland, England seemed a prosperous nation, but James was less wealthy than he believed. Except in times of war, the Crown was supposed to fund the government not through regular taxation but through its own extensive land revenues and by exchanging Crown prerogatives, such as the collection of taxes on luxury imports, in return for money or services. Yet the Crown's independent income had declined throughout the sixteenth century as inflation eroded the value of land rents. Meanwhile, innovations in military technology and shipbuilding dramatically increased the expense of port security and other defenses, a traditional Crown responsibility. Elizabeth had responded to straitened finances with parsimony, transferring much of the expense of her court, for instance, onto wealthy subjects, whom she visited for extended periods on her summer "progresses." She kept a tight lid on honorific titles too, creating new knights or peers very rarely, even though the years of her reign saw considerable upward social mobility. In consequence, by 1603 there was considerable pent-up pressure both for "honors" and for more tangible rewards for government officials. As soon as James came to power, he was immediately besieged with supplicants.

James responded with what seemed to him appropriate royal munificence, knighting and ennobling many of his courtiers and endowing them with opulent gifts. His expenses were unavoidably higher than Elizabeth's, because he had to maintain not only his own household, but also separate establishments for his queen and for the heir apparent, Prince Henry. Yet he quickly became notorious for his financial heedlessness. Compared to Elizabeth's, his court was disorderly and wasteful, marked by hard drinking, gluttonous feasting, and a craze for hunting. "It is not possible for a king of England . . . to be rich or safe, but by frugality," warned James's lord treasurer, Robert Cecil, but James seemed unable to restrain himself. Soon he was deep in debt and unable to convince Parliament to bankroll him by raising taxes.

The king's financial difficulties set his authoritarian assertions about the monarch's supremacy at odds with Parliament's control over taxation. How were his prerogatives as a ruler to coexist with the rights of his subjects? Particularly disturbing to many was James's tendency to bestow high offices upon favorites apparently chosen for good looks rather than for good judgment. James's openly romantic attachment first to Robert Carr, earl of Somerset, and then to George Villiers, duke of Buckingham, gave rise to widespread rumors of homosexuality at court. The period had complex attitudes toward same-sex relationships; on the one hand, "sodomy" was a capital crime (though it was rarely prosecuted); on the other hand, passionately intense male friendship, sometimes suffused with eroticism, constituted an important cultural ideal. In James's case, at least, contemporaries considered his susceptibility to lovely, expensive youths more a political than a moral calamity. For his critics, it crystallized what was wrong with unlimited royal power: the ease with which a king could confuse his own whim with a divine mandate.

Despite James's ungainly demeanor, his frictions with Parliament, and his chronic problems of self-management, he was politically astute. Often, like Elizabeth, he succeeded not through decisiveness but through canny inaction. Cautious by temperament, he characterized himself as a peacemaker and, for many years, successfully kept England out of the religious wars raging on the Continent. His 1604 peace treaty with England's old enemy, Spain, made the Atlantic safe for English ships, a prerequisite for the colonization of the New World and for regular long-distance trading expeditions into the Mediterranean and down the African coast into the Indian Ocean. During James's reign the first permanent English settlements were established in North America, first at Jamestown, then in Bermuda, at Plymouth, and in the Caribbean. In 1611 the East India Company established England's first foothold in India. Even when expeditions ended disastrously, as did Henry Hudson's 1611 attempt to find the Northwest Passage and Walter Ralegh's 1617 expedition to Guiana, they often asserted territorial claims that England would exploit in later decades.

Although the Crown's deliberate attempts to manage the economy were often misguided, its frequent inattention or refusal to interfere had the unintentional effect of stimulating growth. Early seventeenth-century entrepreneurs undertook a wide variety of schemes for industrial or agricultural improvement. Some ventures were almost as loony as Sir Politic Would-be's ridiculous moneymaking notions in Ben Jonson's *Volpone* (1606), but others were serious, profitable enterprises. In the south, domestic industries began manufacturing goods like pins and light woolens that had previously been imported. In the north, newly developed coal mines provided fuel for England's growing cities. In the east, landowners drained wetlands, producing more arable land to feed England's rapidly growing population. These endeavors gave rise to a new respect for the practical arts, a faith in technology as a means of improving human life, and a conviction that the future might be better than the past: all important influences upon the scientific theories of Francis Bacon and his seventeenth-century followers. Economic growth in this period owed more to the initiative of individuals and small groups than to government policy, a factor that encouraged a reevaluation of the role of self-interest, the profit motive, and the role of business contracts in the betterment of the community. This reevaluation was a prerequisite for the secular, contractual political theories proposed by Thomas Hobbes and John Locke later in the seventeenth century.

On the vexations faced by the Church of England, James was likewise often most successful when he was least activist. Since religion cemented sociopolitical order, it seemed necessary to English rulers that all of their subjects belong to a single church. Yet how could they do so when the Reformation had discredited many familiar religious practices and had bred disagreement over many theological issues? Sixteenth- and seventeenth-century English people argued over many religious topics. How should public worship be conducted, and what sorts of qualifications should ministers possess? How should Scripture be understood? How should people pray? What did the sacrament of Communion mean? What happened to people's souls after they died? Elizabeth's government had needed to devise a common religious practice when actual consensus was impossible. Sensibly, it sought a middle ground between traditional and reformed views. Everyone was legally required to attend Church of England services, and the form of the services themselves was mandated in the Elizabethan Book of Common Prayer. The Book of Common Prayer deliberately avoided addressing abstruse theological controversies. The language of the English church service was carefully chosen to be open to several interpretations and acceptable to both Protestant- and Catholic-leaning subjects.

The Elizabethan compromise effectively tamed many of the Reformation's divisive energies and proved acceptable to the majority of Elizabeth's subjects. To staunch Catholics on one side and ardent Protestants on the other, however, the Elizabethan church seemed to have sacrificed truth to political expediency. Catholics wanted to return England to the Roman fold; while some of them were loyal subjects of the queen, others advocated invasion by a foreign Catholic power. Meanwhile the Puritans, as they were disparagingly called, pressed for more thoroughgoing reformation in doctrine, ritual, and church government, urging the elimination of "popish" elements from worship services and "idolatrous" religious images from churches. Some, the Presbyterians, wanted to separate lay and clerical power in the national church, so that church leaders would be appointed by other ministers, not by secular authorities. Others, the separatists, advocated abandoning a national church in favor of small congregations of the "elect."

The resistance of religious minorities to Elizabeth's established church opened them to state persecution. In the 1580s and 1590s, Catholic priests and the laypeople who harbored them were executed for treason, and radical Protestants for heresy. Both groups greeted James's accession enthusiastically; his mother had been the Catholic Mary, Queen of Scots, while his upbringing had been in the strict Reformed tradition of the Scottish Presbyterian Kirk.

James began his reign with a conference at Hampton Court, one of his palaces, at which advocates of a variety of religious views could openly debate them. Yet the Puritans failed to persuade him to make any substantive reforms. Practically speaking, the Puritan belief that congregations should choose their leaders diminished the monarch's power by stripping him of authority over ecclesiastical appointments. More generally, allowing people to choose their leaders in any sphere of life threatened to subvert the entire system of deference and hierarchy upon which the institution of monarchy itself seemed to rest. "No bishop, no king," James famously remarked.

Nor did Catholics fare well in the new reign. Initially inclined to lift Elizabeth's sanctions against them, James hesitated when he realized how entrenched was the opposition to toleration. Then, in 1605, a small group of disaffected Catholics packed a cellar adjacent to the Houses of Parliament with gunpowder, intending to detonate it on the day that the king formally opened Parliament, with Prince Henry, the Houses of Lords and Commons, and the leading justices in attendance. The conspirators were arrested before they could effect their plan. If the "Gunpowder Plot" had succeeded, it would have eliminated much of England's ruling class in a single tremendous explosion, leaving the land vulnerable to invasion by a foreign, Catholic power. Not surprisingly, the Gunpowder Plot dramatically heightened anti-Catholic paranoia in England, and its apparently miraculous revelation was widely seen as a sign of God's care for England's Protestant governors.

By and large, then, James's ecclesiastical policies continued along the lines laid down by Elizabeth. By appointing bishops of varying doctrinal views, he restrained any single faction from controlling church policy. The most important religious event of James's reign was a newly commissioned translation of the Bible. First published in 1611, it was a typically moderating document. A much more graceful rendering than its predecessor, the Geneva version produced by Puritan expatriates in the 1550s, the King James Bible immediately became the standard English Scripture. Its impressive rhythms and memorable phrasing would influence writers for centuries. On the one hand, the new translation contributed to the Protestant aim of making the Bible widely available to every reader in the vernacular. On the other hand, unlike the Geneva Bible, the King James Version translated controversial and ambiguous passages in ways that bolstered conservative preferences for a ceremonial church and for a hierarchically organized church government.

James's moderation was not universally popular. Some Protestants yearned for a more confrontational policy toward Catholic powers, particularly toward Spain, England's old enemy. In the first decade of James's reign, this party clustered around James's eldest son and heir apparent, Prince Henry,

The Execution of the Gunpowder Plot Conspirators. This engraving by the Dutch artist Crispijn van de Passe shows the execution of the Gunpowder Conspirators for treason in January 1606. The punishment for treason was deliberately "cruel and unusual": the traitor was sentenced to be dragged through town on a wicker hurdle "at horse's tail," hanged but cut down while still conscious, and then castrated, disemboweled, beheaded, and his body cut into four pieces and parboiled. Though the punishment was often commuted to simple beheading or hanging, in the case of the Gunpowder Conspirators it was carried out in its entirety. On the left, the condemned men are taken to the place of execution. In the middle, the heart of one of the conspirators is being torn out, to be thrown into the fire. On the right, the heads of the conspirators are mounted on poles for display.

who cultivated a militantly Protestant persona. When Henry died of typhoid fever in 1612, those who favored his policies were forced to seek avenues of power outside the royal court. By the 1620s, the House of Commons was developing a vigorous sense of its own independence, debating policy agendas often quite at odds with the Crown's and openly attempting to use its power to approve taxation as a means of exacting concessions from the king.

James's second son, Prince Charles, came to the throne upon James's death in 1625. Unlike his father, Charles was not a theorist of royal absolutism, but he acted on that principle with an inflexibility that his father had never been able to muster. By 1629 he had dissolved Parliament three times in frustration with its recalcitrance, and he then embarked upon more than a decade of "personal rule" without Parliament. Charles was more prudent in some respects than his father had been—he not only restrained the costs of his own court, but paid off his father's staggering debts by the early 1630s. Throughout his reign, he conscientiously applied himself to the business of government. Yet his refusal to involve powerful individuals and factions in the workings of the state inevitably alienated them, even while it cut him off dangerously from important channels of information about the reactions of his people. Money was a constant problem, too. Even a relatively frugal king required some funds for ambitious government initiatives; but without parliamentary approval, any taxes Charles imposed were widely perceived as illegal. As a result, even wise policies, such as Charles's effort to build up the English navy, spawned misgivings among many of his subjects.

Religious conflicts intensified. Charles's queen, the French princess Henrietta Maria, supported an entourage of Roman Catholic priests, protected English Catholics, and encouraged several noblewomen in her court to convert to the Catholic faith. While Charles remained a staunch member of the Church of England, he loved visual splendor and majestic ceremony in all aspects of life, spiritual and otherwise—proclivities that led his Puritan subjects to suspect him of popish sympathies. Charles's profound attachment to his wife, so different from James's neglect of Anne, only deepened their qualms. Like many fellow Puritans, Lucy Hutchinson blamed the entire debacle of Charles's reign on his wife's influence.

Charles's appointment of William Laud as archbishop of Canterbury, the ecclesiastical head of the English Church, further alienated Puritans. Laud subscribed to a theology that most Puritans rejected. As followers of the sixteenth-century reformer John Calvin, Puritans held that salvation depended upon faith in Christ, not "works." Works were meaningless because the deeds of sinful human beings could not be sanctified in the absence of faith; moreover, the Fall had so thoroughly corrupted human beings that they could not muster this faith without the help of God's grace. God chose (or refused) to extend grace to particular individuals on grounds that human beings were incapable of comprehending, and his decision had been made from eternity, before the individuals concerned were even born. In other words, Puritans believed, God predestined people to be saved or damned, and Christ's redemptive sacrifice was designed only for the saved group, the "elect." Laud, by contrast, advocated the Arminian doctrine that through Christ, God made redemption freely available to all human beings. Individuals could choose whether or not to respond to God's grace, and they could work actively toward their salvation by acts of charity, ritual devotion, and generosity to the church.

Although Laud's theology appears more generously inclusive than the Calvinist alternative, his ecclesiastical policies were uncompromising. Stripping many Puritan ministers of their posts, Laud aligned the doctrine and ceremonies of the English church with Roman Catholicism, which like Arminianism held works in high regard. In an ambitious project of church renovation, Laud installed religious paintings and images in churches; he thought they promoted reverence in worshippers, but the Puritans believed they encouraged idolatry. He rebuilt and resituated altars, making them more ornate and prominent: another change that dismayed Puritans, since it implied that the Eucharist rather than the sermon was the central element of a worship service. In the 1630s thousands of Puritans departed for the New England colonies, but many more remained at home, deeply discontented.

As the 1630s drew to a close, Archbishop Laud and Charles attempted to impose a version of the English liturgy and episcopal organization upon Presbyterian Scotland. Unlike his father, Charles had little acquaintance with his northern realm, and he drastically underestimated the difficulties involved. The Scots objected both on nationalist and on religious grounds, and they were not shy about expressing their objections: the bishop of Brechin, obliged to conduct divine service in the prescribed English style, mounted the pulpit armed with two pistols against his unruly congregation, while his wife, stationed on the floor below, backed him up with a blunderbuss. In the conflict that followed, the Bishops' Wars of 1639 and 1640, Charles's forces met with abject defeat. Exacerbating the situation, Laud was simultaneously insisting upon greater conformity within the English church. Riots in the London streets and the Scots' occupation of several northern English cities forced Charles to call the so-called Long Parliament, which would soon be managing a revolution.

LITERATURE AND CULTURE, 1603–40

Old Ideas and New

In the first part of the seventeenth century, exciting new scientific theories were in the air, but the older ways of thinking about the nature of things had not yet been superseded. Writers such as John Donne, Robert Burton, and Ben Jonson often invoked an inherited body of concepts even though they were aware that those concepts were being questioned or displaced. The Ptolemaic universe, with its fixed earth and circling sun, moon, planets, and stars, was a rich source of poetic imagery. So were the four elements—fire, earth, water, and air—that together were thought to comprise all matter, and the four bodily humors—choler, blood, phlegm, and black bile—which were supposed to determine a person's temperament and to cause physical and mental disease when out of balance. Late Elizabethans and Jacobeans (so called from *Jacobus*, Latin for James) considered themselves especially prone to melancholy, an ailment of scholars and thinkers stemming from an excess of black bile. Shakespeare's Hamlet is melancholic, as is Bosola in John Webster's *Duchess of Malfi* and Milton's title figure in "Il Pense-roso" ("the serious-minded one"). In his panoramic *Anatomy of Melancholy*, Burton argued that melancholy was universal.

Key concepts of the inherited system of knowledge were analogy and order. Donne was especially fond of drawing parallels between the macrocosm, or "big world," and the microcosm, or "little world," of the individual human being. Also widespread were versions of the "chain of being" that linked and ordered various kinds of beings in hierarchies. The order of nature, for instance, put God above angels, angels above human beings, human beings above animals, animals above plants, plants above rocks. The social order installed the king over his nobles, nobles over the gentry, gentry over yeo-men, yeomen over common laborers. The order of the family set husband above wife, parents above children, master and mistress above servants, the elderly above the young. Each level had its peculiar function, and each was connected to those above and beneath in a tight network of obligation and dependency. Items that occupied similar positions in different hierarchies were related by analogy: thus a monarch was like God, and he was also like a father, the head of the family, or like a lion, most majestic of beasts, or like the sun, the most excellent of heavenly bodies. A medieval or Renais-sance poet who calls a king a sun or a lion, then, imagines himself not to be forging a metaphor in his own creative imagination, but to be describing something like an obvious fact of nature. Many Jacobean tragedies depict the catastrophes that ensue when these hierarchies rupture and both the social order and the natural order disintegrate.

Yet this conceptual system was itself beginning to crumble. Francis Bacon advocated rooting out of the mind all the intellectual predilections that had made the old ideas so attractive: love of ingenious correlations, reverence for tradition, and a priori assumptions about what was possible in nature. Instead, he argued, groups of collaborators ought to design controlled exper-iments to find the truths of nature by empirical means. Even as Bacon was promoting his views in *The Advancement of Learning*, *Novum Organum*, and *The New Atlantis*, actual experiments and discoveries were calling the

The Great Chain of Being. This illustration of the "Great Chain of Being" shows the hierarchy of the universe according to Christian orthodoxy. God is at the top of the diagram surrounded by angels, with the blessed souls in heaven sitting on clouds just beneath; below them is the layer of humans, with Eve emerging from Adam's rib in the center; below that are layers of birds, fish, and beasts; below that is a layer of plants upon the earth. All these layers are connected by a chain running down the middle, imagined as connecting all of God's creation. At the bottom, detached from the Great Chain, are Satan and his rebel angels, who can be seen falling from heaven into hell in the right margin.

old verities into question. From the far-flung territories England was beginning to colonize or to trade with, collectors brought animal, plant, and ethnological novelties, many of which were hard to subsume under old categories of understanding. William Harvey's discovery that blood circulated in the body shook received views on the function of blood, casting doubt on the theory of the humors. Galileo's telescope provided evidence confirming Copernican astronomical theory, which dislodged the earth from its stable central position in the cosmos and, in defiance of all ordinary observation, set it whirling around the sun. Galileo found evidence as well of change in the heavens, which were supposed to be perfect and incorruptible above the level of the moon. Donne, like other writers of his age, responded with a mixture of excitement and anxiety to such novel ideas as these:

> And new philosophy calls all in doubt:
> The element of fire is quite put out;
> The sun is lost, and the earth, and no man's wit
> Can well direct him where to look for it.

Several decades later, however, Milton embraced the new science, proudly recalling a visit during his European tour to "the famous Galileo, grown old, a prisoner to the Inquisition for thinking in astronomy otherwise than the Franciscan and Dominican licensers thought." In *Paradise Lost*, he would make complex poetic use of the astronomical controversy, considering how, and how far, humans should pursue scientific knowledge.

Patrons, Printers, and Acting Companies

The social institutions, customs, and practices that had supported and regulated writers in Tudor times changed only gradually before 1640. As it had under Elizabeth, the church promoted writing of several kinds: devotional treatises; guides to meditation; controversial tracts; "cases of conscience," which work out difficult moral issues in complex situations; and especially sermons. Since everyone was required to attend church, everyone heard sermons at least once and often twice on Sunday, as well as on religious or national holidays. The essence of a sermon, Protestants agreed, was the careful exposition of Scripture, and its purpose was to instruct and to move. Yet styles varied; while some preachers, like Donne, strove to enthrall their congregations with all the resources of artful rhetoric, others, especially many Puritans, sought an undecorated style that would display God's word in its own splendor. Printing made it easy to circulate many copies of sermons, blurring the line between oral delivery and written text and enhancing the role of printers and booksellers in disseminating God's word.

Many writers of the period depended in one way or another upon literary patronage. A Jacobean or Caroline aristocrat, like his medieval forebears, was expected to reward dependents in return for services and homage. In the early seventeenth century, although commercial relationships were rapidly replacing feudal ones, patronage pervaded all walks of life: governing relationships between landlords and tenants, masters and servants, kings and courtiers. Writers were assimilated into this system partly because their works reflected well on the patron, and partly because their all-around intelligence made them useful members of a great man's household. Important patrons of the time included the royal family—especially Queen Anne, who sponsored the court masques, and Prince Henry—the members of the intermarried Sidney/Herbert family, and the Countess of Bedford, Queen Anne's confidante.

Because the patronage relationship often took the form of an exchange of favors rather than a simple financial transaction, its terms were variable and are difficult to recover with any precision at this historical remove. A poet might dedicate a poem or a work to a patron in the expectation of a simple cash payment. But a patron might provide a wide range of other benefits: a place to live; employment as a secretary, tutor, or household servant; or gifts of clothing (textiles were valuable commodities). Donne, for instance, received inexpensive lodging from the Drury family, for whom he wrote the *Anniversaries*; a suit of clerical attire from Lucy Russell, Countess of Bedford, when he took orders in the Church of England; and advancement in the church from King James. Ben Jonson lived for several years at the country estates of Lord Aubigny and of Robert Sidney, in whose honor he wrote "To Penshurst"; he received a regular salary from the king in return for writing court masques; and he served as chaperone to Sir Walter Ralegh's son on a Continental tour. Aemilia Lanyer apparently resided for some time in the household of Margaret Clifford, Countess of Cumberland. Andrew Marvell lived for two years with Thomas Fairfax, tutored his daughter, and wrote "Upon Appleton House" for him. All these quite different relationships and forms of remuneration fall under the rubric of patronage.

The patronage system required the poets involved to hone their skills at eulogizing their patrons. Jonson's epigrams and many of Lanyer's dedicatory poems evoke communities of virtuous poets and patrons joined by bonds of mutual respect and affection. Like the line between sycophantic flattery and truthful depiction, the line between patronage and friendship could be a thin one. Literary manuscripts circulated among circles of acquaintances and supporters, many of whom were, at least occasionally, writers as well as readers. Jonson esteemed Mary Wroth both as a fellow poet and as a member of the Sidney family to whom he owed so much. Donne became part of a coterie around Queen Anne's closest confidante, Lucy Russell, Countess of Bedford, who was also an important patron for Ben Jonson, Michael Drayton, and Samuel Daniel. The countess evidently wrote poems herself, although only one attributed to her has apparently survived.

Presenting a poem to a patron, or circulating it among the group of literary people who surrounded the patron, did not require printing it. In early-seventeenth-century England, the reading public for sophisticated literary works was tiny and concentrated in a few social settings: the royal court, the universities, and the Inns of Court or law schools. In these circumstances, manuscript circulation could be an effective way of reaching one's audience. So a great deal of writing remained in manuscript in early-seventeenth-century England. The collected works of many important writers of the period—most notably John Donne, George Herbert, William Shakespeare, and Andrew Marvell—appeared in print only posthumously, in editions produced by friends or admirers. Other writers, like Robert Herrick, collected and printed their own works long after they were written and (probably) circulated in manuscript. In consequence, it is often difficult to date accurately the composition of a seventeenth-century poem. In addition, when authors do not participate in the printing of their own works, editorial problems multiply—when, for instance, the printed version of a poem is inconsistent with a surviving manuscript copy.

Nonetheless, the printing of all kinds of literary works was becoming more common. Writers such as Francis Bacon or Robert Burton, who hoped to reach large numbers of readers with whom they were not acquainted, usually arranged for the printing of their texts soon after they were composed. The sense that the printing of lyric poetry, in particular, was a bit vulgar began to fade when the famous Ben Jonson collected his own works in a grand folio edition.

Until 1640 the Stuart kings kept in place the strict controls over print publication originally instituted by Henry VIII, in response to the ideological threat posed by the Reformation. King Henry had given the members of London's Stationer's Company a monopoly on all printing; in return for their privilege, they were supposed to submit texts to prepublication censorship. In the latter part of the sixteenth century, presses associated with the universities at Oxford and Cambridge would begin operation as well, but they were largely concerned with scholarly and theological books. As a result, with a few exceptions (such as George Herbert's *The Temple*, published by Cambridge University Press), almost all printed literary texts were produced in London. Most of them were sold there as well, in the booksellers' stalls set up outside St. Paul's Cathedral.

The licensing system located not only primary responsibility for a printed work but also its ownership, with the printer rather than with the author. Printers typically paid writers a onetime fee for the use of their work, but the payment was scanty, and the authors of popular texts realized no royalties from the many copies sold. As a result, no one could make a living as a writer in the early seventeenth century by producing best sellers. The first writer formally to arrange for royalties was apparently John Milton, who received five pounds up front for *Paradise Lost*, and another five pounds and two hundred copies at the end of each of the first three impressions. Still, legal ownership of and control over a printed work remained with the printer: authorial copyright would not become a reality until the early eighteenth century.

In monetary terms, a more promising outlet for writers was the commercial theater, which provided the first literary market in English history. Profitable and popular acting companies, established successfully in London in Elizabeth's time, continued to play a very important cultural role under James and Charles. Because the acting companies staged a large number of different plays and paid for them at a predictable, if not generous, rate, they enabled a few hardworking writers to support themselves as full-time professionals. One of them, Thomas Dekker, commented bemusedly on the novelty of being paid for the mere products of one's imagination: "the theater," he wrote, "is your poet's Royal Exchange upon which their muses—that are now turned to merchants—meeting, barter away that light commodity of words." In James's reign, Shakespeare was at the height of his powers: *Othello, King Lear, Macbeth, Antony and Cleopatra, The Winter's Tale, The Tempest*, and other major plays were first staged during these years. So were Jonson's major comedies: *Volpone, Epicene, The Alchemist*, and *Bartholomew Fair*. The most important new playwright was John Webster, whose dark tragedies *The White Devil* and *The Duchess of Malfi* combined gothic horror with stunningly beautiful poetry.

Just as printers were legally the owners of the texts they printed, so theater companies, not playwrights, were the owners of the texts they performed. Typically, companies guarded their scripts closely, permitting them to be printed only in times of financial distress or when they were so old that printing them seemed unlikely to reduce the paying audience. As a result, many Jacobean and Caroline plays are lost to us or available only in corrupt or posthumous versions. For contemporaries, though, a play was "published" not by being printed but by being performed. Aware of the dangerous potential of plays in arousing the sentiments of large crowds of onlookers, the Stuarts, like the Tudors before them, instituted tight controls over dramatic performances. Acting companies, like printers, were obliged to submit works to the censor before public presentation.

Authors, printers, and acting companies who flouted the censorships laws were subject to imprisonment, fines, or even bodily mutilation. Queen Elizabeth cut off the hand of a man who disagreed in print with her marriage plans, King Charles the ears of a man who inveighed against court masques. Jonson and his collaborators found themselves in prison for ridiculing King James's broad Scots accent in one of their comedies. The effects of censorship on writers' output were therefore far reaching across literary genres. Since overt criticism or satire of the great was so dangerous, political writing was apt to be oblique and allegorical. Writers often employed animal fables, tales of distant lands, or long-past historical events to comment upon contemporary issues.

While the commercial theaters were profitable businesses that made most of their money from paying audiences, several factors combined to bring writing for the theater closer to the Stuart court than it had been in Elizabeth's time. The Elizabethan theater companies had been officially associated with noblemen who guaranteed their legitimacy (in contrast to unsponsored traveling players, who were subject to punishment as vagrants). Early in his reign, James brought the major theater companies under royal auspices. Shakespeare's company, the most successful of the day, became the King's Men: it performed not only all of Shakespeare's plays but also *Volpone* and *The Duchess of Malfi*. Queen Anne, Prince Henry, Prince Charles, and Princess Elizabeth sponsored other companies of actors. Royal patronage, which brought with it tangible rewards and regular court performances, naturally encouraged the theater companies to pay more attention to courtly taste. Shakespeare's *Macbeth* put onstage Scots history and witches, two of James's own interests; in *King Lear*, the hero's disastrous division of his kingdom may reflect controversies over the proposed union of Scotland and England. In the first four decades of the seventeenth century, court-affiliated theater companies such as the King's Men increasingly cultivated audiences markedly more affluent than the audiences they had sought in the 1580s and 1590s, performing in intimate, expensive indoor theaters instead of, or as well as, in the cheap popular amphitheaters. *The Duchess of Malfi*, for instance, was probably written with the King's Men's indoor theater at Blackfriars in mind, because several scenes depend for their effect upon a control over lighting that is impossible outdoors. Partly because the commercial theaters seemed increasingly to cater to the affluent and courtly elements of society, they attracted the ire of the king's opponents when civil war broke out in the 1640s.

Jacobean Writers and Genres

The era saw important changes in poetic fashion. Some major Elizabethan genres fell out of favor—long allegorical or mythological narratives, sonnet sequences, and pastoral poems. The norm was coming to be short, concentrated, often witty poems. Poets and prose writers alike often preferred the jagged rhythms of colloquial speech to the elaborate ornamentation and near-musical orchestration of sound that many Elizabethans had sought. The major poets of these years, Jonson, Donne, and Herbert, led this shift and also promoted a variety of "new" genres: love elegy and satire after the classical models of Ovid and Horace, epigram, verse epistle, meditative religious lyric, and country-house poem. Although these poets differed enormously from one another, all three exercised a significant influence on the poets of the next generation.

A native Londoner, Jonson first distinguished himself as an acute observer of urban manners in a series of early, controversial satiric plays. Although he wrote two of his most moving poems to his dead children, Jonson focused rather rarely on the dynamics of the family relationships that so profoundly concerned his contemporary Shakespeare. When generational and dynastic matters do figure in his poetry, as they do at the end of "To Penshurst," they seem part of the agrarian, feudal order that Jonson may have romanticized but that he suspected was rapidly disappearing. By and large, Jonson interested himself in relationships that seemed to be negotiated by the participants, often in a bustling urban or courtly world in which blood kinship no longer decisively determined one's social place. Jonson's poems of praise celebrate and exemplify classical and humanist ideals of friendship: like-minded men and women elect to join in a community that fosters wisdom, generosity, civic responsibility, and mutual respect. In the plays and satiric poems, Jonson stages the violation of those values with such riotous comprehensiveness that the very survival of such ideals seem endangered: the plays swarm with voracious swindlers and their eager victims, social climbers both adroit and inept, and a dizzying assortment of morons and misfits. In many of Jonson's plays, rogues or wits collude to victimize others. These stormy, self-interested alliances, apparently so different from the virtuous friendships of the poems of praise, in fact resemble them in one respect: they are connections entered into by choice, not by law, inheritance, or custom.

Throughout his life, Jonson earned his living entirely from his writing, composing plays for the public theater while also attracting patronage as a poet and a writer of court masques. His acute awareness of his audience was partly, then, a sheerly practical matter. Yet Jonson's yearning for recognition ran far beyond any desire for material reward. A gifted poet, Jonson argued, was a society's proper judge and teacher, and he could be effective only if his audience understood and respected the poet's exalted role. Jonson set out unabashedly to create that audience and to monumentalize himself as a great English author. In 1616 he took the unusual step, for his time, of collecting his poems, plays, and masques in an elegant folio volume.

Jonson's influence upon the next generation of writers, and through them into the Restoration and the eighteenth century, was an effect both of his poetic mastery of his chosen modes and of his powerful personal example. Jonson mentored a group of younger poets, known as the Tribe, or Sons, of Ben, meeting regularly with some of them in the Apollo Room of the Devil Tavern in London. Many of the royalist, or Cavalier, poets—Robert Herrick, Thomas Carew, Richard Lovelace, Sir John Suckling, Edmund Waller, Henry Vaughan in his secular verse—proudly acknowledged their relationship to Jonson or gave some evidence of it in their verse. Most of them absorbed too Jonson's attitude toward print and in later decades supervised the publication of their own poems.

Donne, like Jonson, spent most of his life in or near London, often in the company of other writers and intellectuals—indeed, in the company of many of the same writers and intellectuals, since the two men were friends and shared some of the same patrons. Yet, unlike Jonson's, most of Donne's poetry concerns itself not with a crowded social panorama, but with a dyad—with the relationship between the speaker and one single other being, a woman or God—that in its intensity blots out the claims of lesser relationships. Love for Donne encompasses an astonishing range of emotional experiences: from the lusty impatience of "To His Mistress Going to Bed" to the cheerful promiscuity of "The Indifferent" and mysterious platonic telepathy of "Air and Angels"; from the vengeful wit of "The Apparition" to the postcoital tranquility of "The Good Morrow." While for Jonson the shared meal among friends often becomes an emblem of communion, for Donne sexual consummation has something of the same highly charged symbolic character, a moment in which the isolated individual can, however temporarily, escape the boundaries of selfhood in union with another:

> The phoenix riddle hath more wit
> By us: we two being one, are it.
> So, to one neutral thing both sexes fit.

In the religious poems, where Donne both yearns for a physical relationship with God and knows it is impossible, he does not abandon his characteristic bodily metaphors. The doctrine of the Incarnation—God's taking material form in the person of Jesus Christ—and the doctrine of the bodily resurrection of the dead at the Last Day are Christian teachings that fascinate Donne, to which he returns again and again in his poems, sermons, and devotional writings. While sexual and religious love had long shared a common vocabulary, Donne delights in making that overlap seem new and shocking. He likens conjoined lovers to saints; demands to be raped by God; speculates, after his wife's death, that God killed her because He was jealous of Donne's divided loyalty; imagines Christ encouraging his Bride, the church, to "open" herself to as many men as possible.

Throughout Donne's life, his faith, like his intellect, was anything but quiet. Born into a family of devout Roman Catholics just as the persecution of Catholics was intensifying in Elizabethan England, Donne eventually became a member of the Church of England. If "Satire 3" is any indication, the conversion was attended by profound doubts and existential crisis. Donne's restless mind can lead him in surprising and sometimes unorthodox directions. At the same time, overwhelmed with a sense of his own unworthiness, he courts God's punishment, demanding to be spat upon, flogged, burnt, broken down, in the expectation that suffering at God's hand will restore him to grace and favor.

In both style and content, Donne's poems were addressed to a select few rather than to the public at large. His style is demanding, characterized by learned terms, audaciously far-fetched analogies, and an intellectually sophisticated play of ironies. Even Donne's sermons, attended by large crowds, share the knotty difficulty of the poems, and something too of their quality of intimate address. Donne circulated his poems in manuscript and largely avoided print publication (most of his poems were printed after his death in 1631). By some critics Donne has been regarded as the founder of a Metaphysical school of poetry. We find echoes of Donne's style in many later poets: in Thomas Carew, who praised Donne as a "monarch of wit," George Herbert, Richard Crashaw, John Cleveland, Sir John Suckling, Abraham Cowley, and Andrew Marvell.

Herbert, the younger son of a wealthy, cultivated, and well-connected family, seemed destined in early adulthood for a brilliant career as a diplomat or government servant. Yet he turned his back on worldly greatness to be ordained a priest in the Church of England. Moreover, eschewing a highly visible career as an urban preacher, he spent the remaining years of his short life ministering to the tiny rural parish of Bemerton. Herbert's poetry is shot through with the difficulty and joy of this renunciation, with all it entailed for him. Literary ambition—pride in one's independent creativity—appears to Herbert a temptation that must be resisted, whether it takes the form of Jonson's openly competitive aspiration for literary preeminence or Donne's brilliantly ironic self-displaying performances. Instead, Herbert seeks other models for poetic agency: the secretary taking dictation from a master, the musician playing in harmonious consort with others, the member of a church congregation who speaks with and for a community.

Herbert destroyed his secular verse in English and he turned his volume of religious verse over to a friend only on his deathbed, desiring him to print it if he thought it would be useful to "some dejected poor soul," but otherwise to burn it. The 177 lyrics contained in that volume, *The Temple*, display a complex religious sensibility and great artistic subtlety in an amazing variety of stanza forms. Herbert was the major influence on the next generation of religious lyric poets and was explicitly recognized as such by Henry Vaughan and Richard Crashaw.

The Jacobean period saw the emergence of what would become a major prose genre, the familiar essay. The works of the French inventor of the form, Michel de Montaigne, appeared in English translation in 1603, influencing Shakespeare as well as such later writers as Sir Thomas Browne. Yet the first essays in English, the work of Francis Bacon, attorney general under Elizabeth and eventually lord chancellor under James, bear little resemblance to Montaigne's intimate, tentative, conversational pieces. Bacon's essays present pithy, sententious, sometimes provocative claims in a tone of cool objectivity, tempering moral counsel with an awareness of the importance of prudence and expediency in practical affairs. In *Novum Organum* Bacon adapts his deliberately discontinuous mode of exposition to outline a new scientific method, holding out the tantalizing prospect of eventual mastery over the natural world and boldly articulating the ways in which science might improve the human condition. In his fictional Utopia, described in *The New Atlantis*, Bacon imagines a society that realizes his dream of carefully orchestrated collaborative research, so different from the erratic, uncoordinated efforts of alchemists and amateurs in his own day. Bacon's philosophically revolutionary approach to the natural world profoundly impacted scientifically minded people over the next several generations. His writings influenced the materialist philosophy of his erstwhile secretary, Thomas Hobbes, encouraged Oliver Cromwell to attempt a large-scale overhaul of the university curriculum during the 1650s, and inspired the formation of the Royal Society, an organization of experimental scientists, after the Restoration.

The reigns of the first two Stuart kings mark the entry of Englishwomen, in some numbers, into authorship and publication. Most female writers of the period were from the nobility or gentry; all were much better educated than most women of the period, many of whom remained illiterate. In 1611 Aemilia Lanyer was the first Englishwoman to publish a substantial volume of original poems. It contained poetic dedications, a long poem on Christ's passion, and a country-house poem, all defending women's interests and importance. In 1613 Elizabeth Cary, Lady Falkland, was the first Englishwoman to publish a tragedy, *Mariam*, a closet drama that probes the situation of a queen subjected to her husband's domestic and political tyranny. In 1617 Rachel Speght, the first female polemicist who can be securely identified, published a defense of her sex in response to a notorious attack upon "Lewd, Idle, Froward and Unconstant Women"; she was also the author of a long dream-vision poem. Lady Mary Wroth, niece of Sir Philip Sidney and the Countess of Pembroke, wrote a long prose romance, *Urania* (1612), which presents a range of women's experiences as lovers, rulers, counselors, scholars, storytellers, poets, and seers. Her Petrarchan sonnet sequence *Pamphilia to Amphilanthus*, published with *Urania*, gives poetic voice to the female in love.

THE CAROLINE ERA, 1625–40

When King Charles came to the throne in 1625, "the fools and bawds, mimics and catamites of the former court grew out of fashion," as the Puritan Lucy Hutchinson recalled. The changed style of the court directly affected the arts and literature of the Caroline period (so called after *Carolus*, Latin for Charles). Charles and his queen, Henrietta Maria, were art collectors on a large scale and patrons of such painters as Peter Paul Rubens and Sir Anthony Van Dyke; the latter portrayed Charles as a heroic figure of knightly romance, mounted on a splendid stallion. The conjunction of chivalric virtue and divine beauty or love, symbolized in the union of the royal couple, was the dominant theme of Caroline court masques, which were even more extravagantly hyperbolic than their Jacobean predecessors. Even as Henrietta Maria encouraged an artistic and literary cult of platonic love, several courtier-poets, such as Carew and Suckling, wrote playful, sophisticated love lyrics that both alluded to this fashion and sometimes urged a more licentiously physical alternative.

The religious tensions between the Caroline court's Laudian church and the Puritan opposition produced something of a culture war. In 1633 Charles reissued the *Book of Sports*, originally published by his father in 1618, prescribing traditional holiday festivities and Sunday sports in every parish. Like his father, he saw these recreations as the rural, downscale equivalent of the court masque: harmless, healthy diversions for people who otherwise spent most of their waking hours hard at work. Puritans, however, regarded masques and rustic dances alike as occasions for sin, the

Maypole as a vestige of pagan phallus worship, and Sunday sports as a profanation of the Sabbath. In 1632 William Prynne staked out the most extreme Puritan position, publishing a tirade of over one thousand pages against stage plays, court masques, Maypoles, Laudian church rituals, stained-glass windows, mixed dancing, and other outrages, all of which he associated with licentiousness, effeminacy, and the seduction of popish idolatry. For this cultural critique, Prynne was stripped of his academic degrees, ejected from the legal profession, set in the pillory, sentenced to life imprisonment, and had his books burned and his ears cut off. The severity of the punishments indicates the perceived danger of the book and the inextricability of literary and cultural affairs from politics.

King Charles at Prayer. This frontispiece from *Eikon Basilike* represents the praying king as a Christlike martyr surrounded by allegorical representations of virtue under trial. The left background shows a rock besieged by waves in a storm, surmounted with a Latin caption reading "unmoved I triumph." The left foreground displays palm trees with weights hung to their branches, which was supposed to make them grow more vigorously; the Latin caption reads "Virtue grows under burdens." A shaft of light pierces the storm clouds to illuminate Charles's head, with the caption "More clear out of the shadows." Wearing his coronation robes, Charles is nonetheless shown turning away from this turmoil, having cast aside an earthly crown, labeled "Vanity," to grasp a crown of thorns, labeled "Grace." Set before him is a "treatise of Christ" and a Bible reading "In Your Words, My Hope." Charles is receiving a vision from heaven of the immortal crown, "blessed and eternal," with which his supporters believed God would reward him.

Milton's astonishingly virtuosic early poems also respond to the tensions of the 1630s. Milton repudiated both courtly aesthetics and Prynne's whole-sale prohibitions, developing reformed versions of pastoral, masque, and hymn. In "On the Morning of Christ's Nativity," the birth of Christ coincides with a casting out of idols and a flight of false gods, stanzas that suggest contemporary Puritan resistance to Archbishop Laud's policies. Milton's magnificent funeral elegy "Lycidas" firmly rejects the poetic career of the Cavalier poet, who disregards high artistic ambition to "sport with Amaryllis in the shade / Or with the tangles of Neaera's hair." The poem also vehemently denounces the establishment clergy, ignorant and greedy "blind mouths" who rob their flocks of spiritual nourishment.

THE REVOLUTIONARY ERA, 1640–60

Early in the morning on January 30, 1649, Charles Stuart, the dethroned king Charles I, set off across St. James Park for his execution, surrounded by a heavy guard. He wore two shirts because the weather was frigid, and he did not want to look as if he were shivering with fear to the thousands who had gathered to watch him be beheaded. The black-draped scaffold had been erected just outside James I's elegant Banqueting House, inside of which so many court masques, in earlier decades, had celebrated the might of the Stuart monarchs and assured them of their people's love and gratitude. To those who could not attend, newsbooks provided eyewitness accounts of the dramatic events of the execution, as they had of Charles's trial the week before. Andrew Marvell also memorably describes the execution scene in "An Horatian Ode."

The execution of Charles I was understood at the time, and is still seen by many historians today, as a watershed event in English history. How did it come to pass? Historians do not agree over what caused "the English revolution," or, as it is alternatively called, the English civil war. One group argues that long-term changes in English society and the English economy led to rising social tensions and eventually to violent conflict. New capitalist modes of production in agriculture, industry, and trade were often incompatible with older feudal norms. The gentry, an affluent, highly educated class below the nobility but above the artisans, mechanics, and yeomen, played an increasingly important part in national affairs, as did the rich merchants in London; but the traditional social hierarchies failed to grant them the economic, political, and religious freedoms they believed they deserved. Another group of historians, the "revisionists," emphasize instead short-term and avoidable causes of the war—unlucky chances, personal idiosyncrasies, and poor decisions made by a small group of individuals.

Whatever caused the outbreak of hostilities, there is no doubt that the twenty-year period between 1640 and 1660 saw the emergence of concepts central to bourgeois liberal thought for centuries to come: religious toleration, separation of church and state, freedom from press censorship, and popular sovereignty. These concepts developed out of bitter disputes centering on three fundamental questions: What is the ultimate source of political power? What kind of church government is laid down in Scripture, and therefore ought to be settled in England? What should be the relation between the church and the state? The theories that evolved in response to these questions contained the seeds of much that is familiar in modern thought, mixed with much that is forbiddingly alien. It is vital to recognize that the participants in the disputes were not haphazardly attempting to predict the shape of modern liberalism, but were responding powerfully to the most important problems of their day. The need to find right answers seemed particularly urgent for the Millenarians among them, who, interpreting the upheavals of the time through the lens of the apocalyptic Book of Revelation, believed that their day was very near to being the last day of all.

When the so-called Long Parliament convened in 1640, it did not plan to execute a monarch or even to start a war. It did, however, want to secure its rights in the face of King Charles's perceived absolutist tendencies. Refusing merely to approve taxes and go home, as Charles would have wished, Parliament insisted that it could remain in session until its members agreed to disband. Then it set about abolishing extralegal taxes and courts, reining in the bishops' powers, and arresting (and eventually trying and executing) the king's ministers, the earl of Strafford and Archbishop Laud. The collapse of effective royal government meant that the machinery of press censorship, which had been a Crown responsibility, no longer restrained the printing of explicit commentary on contemporary affairs of state. As Parliament debated, therefore, presses poured forth a flood of treatises arguing vociferously on all sides of the questions about church and state, creating a lively public forum for political discussion where none had existed before. The suspension of censorship permitted the development of weekly newsbooks that reported, and editorialized on, current domestic events from varying political and religious perspectives.

As the rift widened between Parliament and the king in 1641, Charles sought to arrest five members of Parliament for treason, and Londoners rose in arms against him. The king fled to York, while the queen escaped to the Continent. Negotiations for compromise broke down over the issues that would derail them at every future stage: control of the army and the church. On July 12, 1642, Parliament voted to raise an army, and on August 22 the king stood before a force of two thousand horse and foot at Nottingham, unfurled his royal standard, and summoned his liege men to his aid. Civil war had begun. Regions of the country, cities, towns, social classes, and even families found themselves painfully divided. The king set up court and an alternative parliament in Oxford, to which many in the House of Lords and some in the House of Commons transferred their allegiance.

In the First Civil War (1642–46), Parliament and the Presbyterian clergy that supported it had limited aims. They hoped to secure the rights of the House of Commons, to limit the king's power over the army and the church—but not to depose him—and to settle Presbyterianism as the national established church. As Puritan armies moved through the country, fighting at Edgehill, Marston Moor, Naseby, and elsewhere, they also undertook a crusade to stamp out idolatry in English churches, smashing religious images and stained-glass windows and lopping off the heads of statues as an earlier generation had done at the time of the English Reformation. Their ravages are still visible in English churches and cathedrals.

The Puritans were not, however, a homogeneous group, as the 1643 Toleration Controversy revealed. The Presbyterians wanted a national Presbyterian church, with dissenters punished and silenced as before. But Congregationalists, Independents, Baptists, and other separatists opposed a national church and pressed for some measure of toleration, for themselves at least. The religious radical Roger Williams, just returned from New England, argued that Christ mandated the complete separation of church and state and the civic toleration of all religions, even Roman Catholics, Jews, and Muslims. Yet to most people, the civil war itself seemed to confirm that people of different faiths could not coexist peacefully. Thus even as sects continued to proliferate—Seekers, Finders, Antinomians, Fifth Monarchists, Quakers, Muggletonians, Ranters—even the most broad-minded of the age often attempted to draw a line between what was acceptable and what was not. Predictably, their lines failed to coincide. In *Areopagitica* (1644), John Milton argues vigorously against press censorship and for toleration of most Protestants—but for him, Catholics are beyond the pale. Robert Herrick and Sir Thomas Browne regarded Catholic rites, and even some pagan ones, indulgently but could not stomach Puritan zeal.

In 1648, after a period of negotiation and a brief Second Civil War, the king's army was definitively defeated. His supporters were captured or fled into exile, losing position and property. Yet Charles, imprisoned on the Isle of Wight, remained a threat. He was a natural rallying point for those disillusioned by parliamentary rule—many people disliked Parliament's legal but heavy taxes even more than they had the king's illegal but lighter ones. Charles repeatedly attempted to escape and was accused of trying to open the realm to a foreign invasion. Some powerful leaders of the victorious New Model Army took drastic action. They expelled royalists and Presbyterians, who still wanted to come to an accommodation with the king, from the House of Commons and abolished the House of Lords. With consensus assured by the purgation of dissenting viewpoints, the army brought the king to trial for high treason in the Great Hall of Westminster.

After the king's execution, the Rump Parliament, the part of the House of Commons that had survived the purge, immediately established a new government "in the way of a republic, without king or House of Lords." The new state was extremely fragile. Royalists and Presbyterians fiercely resented their exclusion from power and pronounced the execution of the king a sacrilege. The Rump Parliament and the army were at odds, with the army rank and file arguing that voting rights ought not be restricted to men of property. The Levelers, led by John Lilburne, called for suffrage for all adult males. An associated but more radical group, called the Diggers or True Levelers, pushed for economic reforms to match the political ones. Their spokesman, Gerrard Winstanley, wrote eloquent manifestos developing a Christian communist program. Meanwhile, Millenarians and Fifth Monarchists wanted political power vested in the regenerate "saints" in preparation for the thousand-year reign of Christ on earth foretold in the biblical Book of Revelation. Quakers defied both state and church authority by refusing to take oaths and by preaching incendiary sermons in open marketplaces. Most alarming of all, out of proportion to their scant numbers, were the Ranters, who believed that because God dwelt in them none of their acts could be sinful. Notorious for sexual license and for public nudity, they got their name from their deliberate blaspheming and their penchant for rambling prophecy. In addition to internal disarray, the new state faced serious

Cromwell. This depiction of Oliver Cromwell, published in 1658, shows him in armor, surrounded by emblems symbolizing his military prowess, civic authority, piety, and divine favor.

external threats. After Charles I's execution, the Scots and the Irish—who had not been consulted about the trial—proclaimed his eldest son, Prince Charles, the new king. The prince, exiled on the Continent, was attempting to enlist the support of a major European power for an invasion.

The formidable Oliver Cromwell, now undisputed leader of the army, crushed external threats, suppressing rebellions in Ireland and Scotland. The Irish war was especially bloody, as Cromwell's army massacred the Catholic natives in a frenzy of religious hatred. When trade rivalries erupted with the Dutch over control of shipping lanes in the North Sea and the English Channel, the new republic was again victorious. Yet the domestic situation remained unstable. Given popular disaffection and the unresolved disputes between Parliament and the army, the republic's leaders dared not call new elections. In 1653 power effectively devolved upon Cromwell, who was sworn in as Lord Protector for life under England's first written constitution. Many property owners considered Cromwell the only hope for stability, while others, including Milton, saw him as a champion of religious liberty. Although persecution of Quakers and Ranters continued, Cromwell sometimes intervened to mitigate the lot of the Quakers. He also began a program to readmit Jews to England, partly in the interests of trade but also to open the way for their conversion, supposedly a precursor of the Last Day as prophesied in the Book of Revelation.

The problem of succession remained unresolved, however. When Oliver Cromwell died in 1658, his son, Richard, was appointed in his place, but he had inherited none of his father's leadership qualities. In 1660 General George Monck succeeded in calling elections for a new "full and free" parliament, open to supporters of the monarchy as well as of the republic. The new Parliament immediately recalled the exiled prince, officially proclaiming him King Charles II on May 8, 1660. The period that followed, therefore, is called the Restoration: it saw the restoration of the monarchy and with it the royal court, the established Church of England, and the professional theater.

Over the next few years, the new regime executed some of the regicides that had participated in Charles I's trial and execution and harshly repressed radical Protestants (the Baptist John Bunyan wrote *Pilgrim's Progress* in prison). Yet Charles II, who came to the throne at Parliament's invitation, could not lay claim to absolute power as his father had done. After his accession, Parliament retained its legislative supremacy and complete power over taxation and exercised some control over the king's choice of counselors. It assembled by its own authority, not by the king's mandate. During the Restoration years, the journalistic commentary and political debates that had first flourished in the 1640s remained forceful and open, and the first modern political parties developed out of what had been the royalist and republican factions in the civil war. In London and in other cities, the merchant classes, filled with dissenters, retained their powerful economic leverage. Although the English revolution was apparently dismantled in 1660, its long-term effects profoundly changed English institutions and English society.

LITERATURE AND CULTURE, 1640–60

The English civil war was disastrous for the English theater. One of Parliament's first acts after hostilities began in 1642 was to abolish public plays and sports, as "too commonly expressing lascivious mirth and levity." Some drama continued to be written and published, but performances were rare and would-be theatrical entrepreneurs had to exploit loopholes in the prohibitions by describing their works as "operas" or presenting their productions in semiprivate circumstances.

As the king's government collapsed, the patronage relationships centered upon the court likewise disintegrated. Many leading poets were staunch royalists, or Cavaliers, who suffered considerably in the war years. Robert Herrick lost his church employment; Richard Lovelace was imprisoned; Margaret Cavendish went into exile. With their usual networks of manuscript circulation disrupted, many royalist writers printed their verse. Volumes of poetry by Thomas Carew, John Denham, Richard Lovelace, and Robert Herrick appeared in the 1640s. Their poems, some dating from the

1620s or 1630s, celebrate the courtly ideal "of the good life: good food, plenty of wine, good verse, hospitality, and high-spirited loyalty, especially to the king." One characteristic genre is the elegant love lyric, often with a carpe diem theme. In Herrick's case especially, apparent ease and frivolity masks a frankly political subtext. The Puritans excoriated May Day celebrations, harvest-home festivities, and other time-honored holidays and "sports" as unscriptural, idolatrous, or frankly pagan. For Herrick, they sustained a community that strove neither for ascetic perfection nor for equality among social classes, but that knew the value of pleasure in cementing social harmony and that incorporated everyone—rich and poor, unlettered and learned—as the established church had traditionally tried to do.

During the 1640s and 1650s, as they faced defeat, the Cavaliers wrote movingly of the relationship between love and honor, of fidelity under duress, of like-minded friends sustaining one another in a hostile environment. They presented themselves as amateurs, writing verse in the midst of a life devoted to more important matters: war, love, the king's service, the endurance of loss. Rejecting the radical Protestant emphasis on the "inner light," which they considered merely a pretext for presumptuousness and violence, the Cavalier poets often cultivated a deliberately unidiosyncratic, even self-deprecating poetic persona. Thus the poems of Richard Lovelace memorably express sentiments that he represents not as the unique insights of an isolated genius, but as principles easily grasped by all honorable men. When in "The Vine" Herrick relates a wet dream, he laughs not only at himself but at those who mistake their own fantasies for divine inspiration.

During the 1650s, royalists wrote lyric poems in places far removed from the hostile centers of parliamentary power. In Wales, Henry Vaughan wrote religious verse expressing his intense longing for past eras of innocence and for the perfection of heaven or the millennium. Also in Wales, Katherine Philips wrote and circulated in manuscript poems that celebrate female friends in terms normally reserved for male friendships. The publication of her poems after the Restoration brought Philips some celebrity as "the Matchless Orinda." Richard Crashaw, an exile in Paris and Rome and a convert to Roman Catholicism, wrote lush religious poetry that attempted to reveal the spiritual by stimulating the senses. Margaret Cavendish, also in exile, with the queen in Paris, published two collections of lyrics when she returned to England in 1653; after the Restoration she published several dramas and a remarkable Utopian romance, *The Blazing World.*

Several prose works by royalist sympathizers have become classics in their respective genres. Thomas Hobbes, the most important English philosopher of the period, another exile in Paris, developed his materialist philosophy and psychology there and, in *Leviathan* (1651), his unflinching defense of absolute sovereignty based on a theory of social contract. Some royalist writing seems to have little to do with the contemporary scene, but in fact carries a political charge. In *Religio Medici* (1642–43), Sir Thomas Browne presents himself as a genial, speculative doctor who loves ritual and ceremony not for complicated theological reasons, but because they move him emotionally. While he can sympathize with all Christians, even Roman Catholics, and while he recognizes in himself many idiosyncratic views, he willingly submits his judgment to the Church of England, in sharp contrast to Puritans bent on ridding the church of its errors. Izaak Walton's treatise on fishing, *The Complete Angler* (1653), presents a dialogue between Walton's persona, Piscator the angler, and Venator the hunter. Piscator, speaking like many Cavalier poets for the values of warmheartedness, charity, and inclusiveness, converts the busy, warlike Venator, a figure for the Puritan, to the tranquil and contemplative pursuit of fishing.

The revolutionary era gave new impetus to women's writing. The circumstances of war placed women in novel, occasionally dangerous situations, giving them unusual events to describe and prompting self-discovery. The autobiographies of royalists Lady Anne Halkett and Margaret Cavendish, duchess of Newcastle, published after the Restoration, report their experiences and their sometimes daring activities during those trying days. Lucy Hutchinson's memoir of her husband, Colonel John Hutchinson, first published in 1806, narrates much of the history of the times from a republican point of view. Leveler women offered petitions and manifestos in support of their cause and of their imprisoned husbands. The widespread belief that the Holy Spirit was moving in unexpected ways encouraged a number of female prophets: Anna Trapnel, Mary Cary, and Lady Eleanor Davies. Their published prophecies often carried a strong political critique of Charles or of Cromwell. Quaker women came into their own as preachers and sometimes as writers of tracts, authorized by the Quaker belief in the spiritual equality of women and men and by the conviction that all persons should testify to whatever the inner light communicates to them. Many of their memoirs, such as Dorothy Waugh's "Relation," were originally published both to call attention to their sufferings and to inspire other Quakers to similar feats of moral fortitude.

While most writers during this period were royalists, two of the best, Andrew Marvell and John Milton, sided with the republic. Marvell wrote most of the poems for which he is still remembered while at Nunappleton in the early 1650s, tutoring the daughter of the retired parliamentary general Thomas Fairfax; in 1657 he joined his friend Milton in the office of Cromwell's Latin Secretariat. In Marvell's love poems and pastorals, older convictions about ordered harmony give way to wittily unresolved or unresolvable oppositions, some playful, some painful. Marvell's conflictual worldview seems unmistakably the product of the unsettled civil war decades. In his country-house poem "Upon Appleton House," even agricultural practices associated with regular changes of the season, like the flooding of fallow fields, become emblems of unpredictability, reversal, and category confusion. In other poems Marvell eschews an authoritative poetic persona in favor of speakers that seem limited or even a bit unbalanced: a mower who argues for the values of pastoral with disconcerting belligerence, a nymph who seems to exemplify virginal innocence but also immature self-absorption and possibly unconscious sexual perversity. Marvell's finest political poem, "An Horatian Ode upon Cromwell's Return from Ireland," celebrates Cromwell's providential victories even while inviting sympathy for the executed king and warning about the potential dangers of Cromwell's meteoric rise to power.

A promising, prolific young poet in the 1630s, Milton committed himself to the English republic as soon as the conflict between the king and Parliament began to take shape. His loyalty to the revolution remained unwavering despite his disillusion when it failed to realize his ideals: religious toleration for all Protestants and the free circulation of ideas without prior censorship. First as a self-appointed adviser to the state, then as its official defender, he addressed the great issues at stake in the 1640s and the 1650s. In a series of treatises he argued for church disestablishment and for the removal of bishops, for a republican government based on natural law and popular sovereignty, for the right of the people to dismiss from office and even execute their rulers, and, most controversial even to his usual allies, in favor of divorce on the grounds of incompatibility. Milton was a Puritan, but both his theological heterodoxies and his poetic vision mark him as a distinctly unusual one.

During his years as a political polemicist, Milton also wrote several sonnets, revising that small, love-centered genre to accommodate large private and public topics: a Catholic massacre of proto-Protestants in the foothills of Italy, the agonizing questions posed by his blindness, various threats to intellectual and religious liberty. In 1645 he published his collected English and Latin poems as a counterstatement to the royalist volumes of the 1640s. Yet his most ambitious poetry remained to be written. Milton probably wrote some part of *Paradise Lost* in the late 1650s and completed it after the Restoration, encompassing in it all he had thought, read, and experienced of tyranny, political controversy, evil, deception, love, and the need for companionship. This cosmic blank-verse epic assimilates and critiques the epic tradition and Milton's entire intellectual and literary heritage, classical and Christian. Yet it centers not on martial heroes but on a domestic couple who must discover how to live a good life day by day, in Eden and later in the fallen world, amid intense emotional pressures and the seductions of evil.

Seventeenth-century poetry, prose, and drama retains its hold on readers because so much of it is so very good, fusing intellectual power, emotional passion, and extraordinary linguistic artfulness. Poetry in this period ranges over an astonishing variety of topics and modes: highly erotic celebrations of sexual desire, passionate declarations of faith and doubt, lavishly embroidered paeans to friends and benefactors, tough-minded assessments of social and political institutions. English dramatists were at the height of their powers, situating characters of unprecedented complexity in plays sometimes remorselessly satiric, sometimes achingly moving. In these years English prose becomes a highly flexible instrument, suited to informal essays, scientific treatises, religious meditation, political polemic, biography and autobiography, and journalistic reportage. Literary forms evolve for the exquisitely modulated representation of the self: dramatic monologues, memoirs, spiritual autobiographies, sermons in which the preacher takes himself for an example. Finally, we have in Milton an epic poet who assumed the role of inspired prophet, envisioning a world created by God but shaped by human choice and imagination.

The Early Seventeenth Century

TEXTS	CONTEXTS
1603 James I, *Basilikon Doron* reissued	1603 Death of Elizabeth I; accession of James I. Plague
1604 William Shakespeare, *Othello*	
1605 Shakespeare, *King Lear*. Ben Jonson, *The Masque of Blackness*. Francis Bacon, *The Advancement of Learning*	1605 Gunpowder Plot, failed effort by Roman Catholic extremists to blow up Parliament
1606 Jonson, *Volpone*. Shakespeare, *Macbeth*	
	1607 Founding of Jamestown colony in Virginia
1609 Shakespeare, *Sonnets*	1609 Galileo begins observing the heavens with a telescope
1611 "King James" Bible (Authorized Version). Shakespeare, *The Tempest*. John Donne, *The First Anniversary*. Aemilia Lanyer, *Salve Deus Rex Judaeorum*	
1612 Donne, *The Second Anniversary*	1612 Death of Prince Henry
1613 Elizabeth Cary, *The Tragedy of Mariam*	
1614 John Webster, *The Duchess of Malfi*	
1616 Jonson, *Works*. James I, *Works*	1616 Death of Shakespeare
	1618 Beginning of the Thirty Years War
	1619 First African slaves in North America exchanged by Dutch frigate for food and supplies at Jamestown
1620 Bacon, *Novum Organum*	1620 Pilgrims land at Plymouth
1621 Mary Wroth, *The Countess of Montgomery's Urania* and *Pamphilia to Amphilanthus*. Robert Burton, *The Anatomy of Melancholy*	1621 Donne appointed dean of St. Paul's Cathedral
1623 Shakespeare, First Folio	
1625 Bacon, *Essays*	1625 Death of James I; accession of Charles I; Charles I marries Henrietta Maria
	1629 Charles I dissolves Parliament
1633 Donne, *Poems*. George Herbert, *The Temple*	1633 Galileo forced by the Inquisition to recant the Copernican theory
1637 John Milton, "Lycidas"	
1640 Thomas Carew, *Poems*	1640 Long Parliament called (1640–53). Archbishop Laud impeached
1642 Thomas Browne, *Religio Medici*. Milton, *The Reason of Church Government*	1642 First Civil War begins (1642–46). Parliament closes the theaters
1643 Milton, *The Doctrine and Discipline of Divorce*	1643 Accession of Louis XIV of France
1644 Milton, *Areopagitica*	

TEXTS	CONTEXTS
1645 Milton, *Poems*. Edmund Waller, *Poems*	**1645** Archbishop Laud executed. Royalists defeated at Naseby
1648 Robert Herrick, *Hesperides* and *Noble Numbers*	**1648** Second Civil War. "Pride's Purge" of Parliament
1649 Milton, *The Tenure of Kings and Magistrates* and *Eikonoklastes*	**1649** Trial and execution of Charles I. Republic declared. Milton becomes Latin Secretary (1649–59)
1650 Henry Vaughan, *Silex Scintillans* (Part II, 1655)	
1651 Thomas Hobbes, *Leviathan*. Andrew Marvell, "Upon Appleton House" (unpublished)	
	1652 Anglo-Dutch War (1652–54)
	1653 Cromwell made Lord Protector
	1658 Death of Cromwell; his son Richard made Protector
1660 Milton, *Ready and Easy Way to Establish a Free Commonwealth*	**1660** Restoration of Charles II to throne. Royal Society founded
	1662 Charles II marries Catherine of Braganza
	1665 The Great Plague
1666 Margaret Cavendish, *The Blazing World*	**1666** The Great Fire
1667 Milton, *Paradise Lost* (in ten books). Katherine Philips, *Collected Poems*. John Dryden, *Annus Mirabilis*	
1671 Milton, *Paradise Regained* and *Samson Agonistes*	
1674 Milton, *Paradise Lost* (in twelve books)	**1674** Death of Milton
1681 Marvell, *Poems*, published posthumously	

JOHN DONNE
1572–1631

Lovers' eyeballs threaded on a string. A god who assaults the human heart with a battering ram. A teardrop that encompasses and drowns the world. John Donne's poems abound with startling images. With his strange and playful intelligence, expressed in puns, paradoxes, and the elaborately sustained metaphors known as "conceits," Donne has enthralled and sometimes enraged readers from his day to our own. The tired clichés of love poetry—cheeks like roses, hearts pierced by the arrows of love—emerge reinvigorated and radically transformed, demanding from the reader an unprecedented level of mental alertness and engagement. Donne prided himself on his wit and displayed it not only in his conceits but in his grasp of learned discourses ranging from theology to alchemy, from cosmology to law. Yet for all their ostentatious intellectuality Donne's poems never give the impression of being academic exercises. Rather, they are intense dramatic monologues in which the speaker's ideas and feelings evolve from one line to the next. Donne's prosody is equally dramatic. His jagged rhythms capture the effect of speech (and elicited from his classically minded contemporary Ben Jonson the gruff observation that "Donne, for not keeping of accent deserved hanging").

Donne began life as an outsider, and in some respects remained one. He was born in London in 1572 into a devout Roman Catholic household. The family was prosperous, but, as the poet later remarked, none had suffered more heavily for its loyalty to the Catholic Church: "I have been ever kept awake in a meditation of martyrdom." Donne was distantly related to the great Catholic humanist and martyr Sir Thomas More. Two of Donne's uncles, Jesuit priests, were forced to flee the realm; Donne's brother Henry, arrested for harboring a priest, died in prison of the plague. As a Catholic in Protestant England, growing up in decades when anti-Roman feeling reached new heights, Donne could not expect any kind of public career, nor could he receive a university degree (he left Oxford without one and studied law for a time at the Inns of Court). What he could reasonably expect instead was prejudice, official harassment, and crippling financial penalties. He chose not to live under such conditions. At some point in the 1590s, having returned to London after travels abroad, and having devoted some years to studying theological issues, Donne converted to the English church.

The poems that belong with certainty to this period of his life—the five satires and most of the elegies—reveal a man both fascinated by and keenly critical of English society. Four of the satires treat commonplace Elizabethan topics—foppish and obsequious courtiers, bad poets, corrupt lawyers and a corrupt court—but are unique both in their visceral revulsion and in their intellectual excitement. Donne uses striking images of pestilence, vomit, excrement, and pox to create a unique satiric world, busy, vibrant, and corrupt, in which his dramatic speakers have only to step outside the door to be inundated by all the fools and knaves in Christendom. By contrast, the third satire treats the quest for true religion—the question that preoccupied him above all others in these years—in terms that are serious, passionately witty, and deeply felt. Donne argues that honest doubting search is better than the facile acceptance of any religious tradition, epitomizing that point brilliantly in the image of Truth on a craggy hill, very difficult to climb. Society's values are of no help whatsoever to the individual seeker—none will escape the final judgment by pleading that "A Harry, or a Martin taught [them] this." In the love elegies Donne seems intent on making up for his social powerlessness through witty representations of mastery in the bedroom and of adventurous travel. In "Elegy 16" he imagines his speaker embarking on a journey "O'er the white Alps" and with mingled tenderness and condescension argues down a naive mistress's proposal to accompany him. In "Elegy 19," his fondling of a naked lover becomes in a famous conceit the equivalent of exploration in America. Donne's interest in satire and elegy—classical Roman genres, which he helped introduce to English verse—is itself significant. He wrote in English, but he reached out to other traditions.

If Donne's conversion to the Church of England promised him security, social acceptance, and the possibility of a public career, that promise was soon to be cruelly withdrawn. In 1596–97 he participated in the earl of Essex's military expeditions against Catholic Spain in Cádiz and the Azores (the experience prompted two remarkable descriptive poems of life at sea, "The Storm" and "The Calm"), and upon his return he became secretary to Sir Thomas Egerton, Lord Keeper of the Great Seal. This appointment should have been the beginning of a successful public career. But his secret marriage in 1601 to Egerton's seventeen-year-old niece Ann More enraged Donne's employer and the bride's wealthy father; Donne was briefly imprisoned and dismissed from service. The poet was reduced to a retired country life beset by financial insecurity and a rapidly increasing family; Ann bore twelve children (not counting miscarriages) by the time she died at age thirty-three. At one point, Donne wrote despairingly that while the death of a child would mean one less mouth to feed, he could not afford the burial expenses. In this bleak period, he wrote but dared not publish *Biathanatos*, a defense of suicide.

As his family grew, Donne made every effort to reinstate himself in the favor of the great. To win the approval of James I, he penned *Pseudo-Martyr* (1610), defending the king's insistence that Catholics take the Oath of Allegiance. This set an irrevocable public stamp on his renunciation of Catholicism, and Donne followed up with a witty satire on the Jesuits, *Ignatius His Conclave* (1611). In the same period he was producing a steady stream of occasional poems for friends and patrons such as the earl of Somerset (the king's favorite), the Countess of Bedford, and Magdalen Herbert, and for small coteries of courtiers and ladies. Like most gentlemen of his era, Donne saw poetry as a polite accomplishment rather than as a trade or vocation, and in consequence he circulated his poems in manuscript but left most of them uncollected and unpublished. In 1611 and 1612, however, he published the first and second *Anniversaries* on the death of the daughter of his patron Sir Robert Drury.

For some years King James had urged an ecclesiastical career on Donne, denying him any other means of advancement. In 1615 Donne finally consented, overcoming his sense of unworthiness and the pull of other ambitions. He was ordained in the Church of England and entered upon a distinguished career as court preacher, reader in divinity at Lincoln's Inn, and dean of St. Paul's. Donne's metaphorical style, bold erudition, and dramatic wit established him as a great preacher in an age that appreciated learned sermons powerfully delivered. Some 160 of his sermons survive, preached to monarchs and courtiers, lawyers and London magistrates, city merchants and trading companies. As a distinguished clergyman in the Church of England, Donne had traveled an immense distance from the religion of his childhood and the adventurous life of his twenties. Yet in his sermons and late poems we find the same brilliant, idiosyncratic mind at work, refashioning his profane conceits to serve a new and higher purpose. In "Expostulation 19" he praises God as the greatest of literary stylists: "a figurative, a metaphorical God," imagining God as a conceit-maker like himself. In poems, meditations, and sermons, Donne came increasingly to be engaged in anxious contemplation of his own mortality. In "Hymn to God My God, in My Sickness," Donne imagines himself spread out on his deathbed like a map showing the route to the next world. Only a few days before his death he preached "Death's Duel," a terrifying analysis of all life as a decline toward death and dissolution, which contemporaries termed his own funeral sermon. In his final illness, according to his contemporary biographer Izaak Walton, Donne had a portrait made of himself in his shroud and meditated on it daily. Meditations upon skulls as emblems of mortality were common in the period, but nothing is more characteristic of Donne than to find a way to meditate on his own skull.

Given the shape of Donne's career, it is no surprise that his poems and prose works display an astonishing variety of attitudes, viewpoints, and feelings on the great subjects of love and religion. Yet this variety cannot be fully explained in biographical terms. The poet's own attempt to distinguish between Jack Donne, the young rake, and Dr. Donne, the grave and religious dean of St. Paul's, is (perhaps intentionally) misleading. We do not know the time and circumstances for most of Donne's verses, but it is clear that many of his finest religious poems predate his ordination, and it is possible that he continued to add to the love poems known as his "songs and sonnets" after he entered the church. Theological language abounds in his love poetry, and daringly erotic images in his religious verse.

Donne's "songs and sonnets" have been the cornerstone of his reputation almost since their publication in 1633. The title *Songs and Sonnets* associates them with the popular miscellanies of love poems and sonnet sequences in the Petrarchan tradition, but they directly challenge the popular Petrarchan sonnet sequences of the 1590s. The collection contains only one formal sonnet, the "songs" are not notably lyrical, and Donne draws upon and transforms a whole range of literary traditions concerned with love. Like Petrarch, Donne can present himself as the despairing lover of an unattainable lady ("The Funeral"). Like Ovid he can be lighthearted, witty, cynical, and frankly lustful ("The Flea," "The Indifferent"). Like the Neoplatonists, he espouses a theory of transcendent love, but he breaks from them with his insistence in many poems on the union of physical and spiritual love. What binds these poems together and grants them enduring power is their compelling immediacy. The speaker is always in the throes of intense emotion, and that emotion is not static but constantly shifting with the turns of the poet's thought. Donne seems supremely present in these poems, standing behind their various speakers. Where Petrarchan poets exhaustively catalogue their beloved's physical features (though in highly conventional terms), Donne's speakers tell us little or nothing about the loved woman, or about the male friends imagined as the audience for many poems. Donne's repeated insistence that the private world of lovers is superior to the wider public world, or that it somehow contains all of that world, is understandable in light of the many disappointments of his career. Yet this was also a poet who threw himself headlong into life, love, and sexuality, and later into the very visible role of court and city preacher.

Donne was long grouped with Herbert, Vaughan, Crashaw, Marvell, Traherne, and Cowley under the heading of "Metaphysical poets." The expression was first employed by critics like Samuel Johnson and William Hazlitt, who found the intricate conceits and self-conscious learning of these poets incompatible with poetic beauty and sincerity. Early in the twentieth century, T. S. Eliot sought to restore their reputation, attributing to them a unity of thought and feeling that had since their time been lost. There was, however, no formal "school" of Metaphysical poetry, and the characteristics ascribed to it by later critics pertain chiefly to Donne. Like Ben Jonson, John Donne immensely influenced the succeeding generation, but he remains a singularity.

The Sixteenth Century
(1485–1603)

St. George and the Dragon (London version), Paolo Uccello, ca. 1455–60

A depiction by the Florentine artist Uccello of the legend that was to inspire Edmund Spenser in Book 1 of *The Faerie Queene*. Already held on a leash by the elegant lady—as if the struggle's outcome were not in doubt—the dragon submits to the knight's lance (thrust through the nose in a gesture that better recalls the domestication of cattle than the thwarting of an enemy). The desolate cave is strangely conjoined with the formal garden and the lady's elegant court dress: the story is imagined as located at once in the wilderness and at the very center of civilization.

Thomas More, Hans Holbein, 1527

Painted on the eve of More's great conflict with Henry VIII over the validity of the king's marriage to Catherine of Aragon, Holbein's portrait emphasizes both the chancellor's importance and his strength of character. More wears the heavy gold chain and rich dress of high office, which he had satirized a decade earlier in *Utopia.* In all probability, if early biographies of More can be believed, he also wears a hair shirt under the velvet and fur, a hidden, painful reminder of the vulnerable flesh that he secretly mortified.

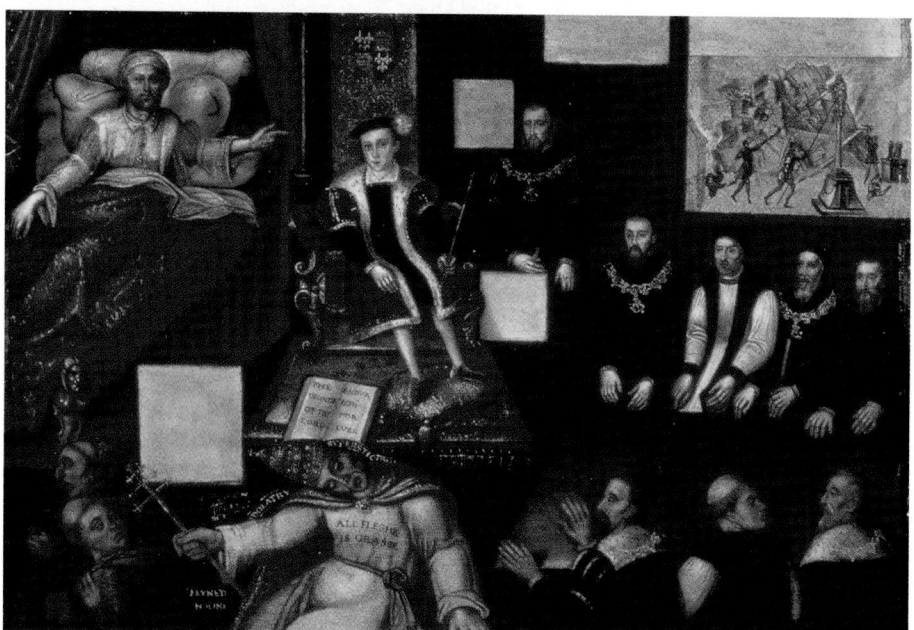

Edward VI and the Pope: An Allegory of the Reformation, English school, ca. 1568–71

The dying Henry VIII hands over the mandate for church reform to his young son and heir, Prince Edward. This is a polemical attempt to depict the religious revolution that had a deep impact on English society and literature. The open book, proclaiming the Protestant emphasis on the Word of God in vernacular translation, crushes the pope and the taglines of Catholic corruption that surround him. The Council of Regency (appointed to guide the king, who was only nine when he ascended the throne) is in attendance; to the left, two monks flee the pope's downfall. In the upper right, a painting (or view from the window?) heralds the collapse of the Old Church and the breaking of its "idols." Several places in the painting are intended for inscriptions, but for unknown reasons these were never completed.

The Wife and Daughter of a Chief,
John White, 1585

Accompanying Thomas Hariot's *Brief and True Report of the New-found Land of Virginia,* John White's watercolors chronicle Algonkian life as seen by the English voyagers. Here, a girl "of the age of 8 or 10 yeares" carries a European doll, dressed in full Elizabethan costume, that she has clearly been given as a gift by the strange visitors. The presentation of small gifts was a regular English practice, frequently alternating with murderous violence. White's drawing manages to convey both the exoticism and the dignity that Hariot and others perceived in the American natives.

Portrait of a Melancholy Young Man, Isaac Oliver, ca. 1590–95

Equally fashionable in attitude and dress, Oliver's young man displays the fascination of the English elite with the "melancholy humour." In addition to the sad expression, the black clothes and crossed arms are conventional markers of melancholy. Men in love, like Sidney's Astrophil (p. 586) and Duke Orsino in *Twelfth Night* (p. 741), found it particularly glamorous to parade their pensive dispositions. The romance of this "disease" figures in the couple just walking into the labyrinth-garden on the right.

Portrait of Abd al-Wahid bin Masoud bin Muhammad al-Annuri, artist unknown, 1600

In 1600 the forty-two-year-old al-Annuri arrived in London as the ambassador of the Moroccan ruler Mulay Ahmed al-Mansur with a proposal for a military alliance with England against Spain. The imposing appearance of the ambassador made a sensation in London and may have influenced Shakespeare's conception of what the Moor Othello looked like.

The Life and Death of Sir Henry Unton, anonymous, ca. 1597

A masque of musicians and dancers performs for a dinner party of Unton's friends. Theatrical life in this period, which often included music and dancing, was not restricted to the playhouse; it extended into other social settings, such as this one. Theater here is depicted as incidental entertainment: some guests turn their backs on the pageant; the actors are considerably smaller than their patrons, an index of relative social importance.

The "Chandos" Portrait of William Shakespeare, anonymous, date unknown

The formal portrait of the playwright that appears in the First Folio edition of his works depicts him stiffly posed in a brocade jacket and a heavily starched collar. Here, in a portrait named after its owner, the Duke of Chandos, Shakespeare is presented less formally and more as his friends and colleagues may have known him. The artist is unknown, but some speculate that it may have been Shakespeare's fellow actor Richard Burbage.

A Young Man, Nicholas Hilliard, ca. 1600

This tiny painting from a playing card approximately two inches square represents the "other side" of Elizabethan love poetry: passion replaces languor. The image of the lover tormented by the "fire" of his mistress's eyes or the hellish inner torment of desire was common. Though Sidney's Astrophil lives "in blackest winter night," he feels "the flames of hottest summer day" (p. 601), while even disillusioned lovers in Shakespeare's sonnets do not know how "To shun the heaven that leads men to this hell" (p. 736). The locket held by the young man presumably contains another miniature: a portrait of the beloved.

Elizabeth I in Procession, attributed to Robert Peake, ca. 1600

Carried on a litter like an image of the Virgin in the religious processions of previous centuries, the gorgeously arrayed Queen Elizabeth is shown here as a time-defying icon of purity and power. When the painting was executed, the queen was sixty-seven years old. Until the end of her life she continued her custom of going on "Progresses" through the realm: surrounded by her courtiers and ladies in waiting, she would venture forth to show herself to her people, many of whom nearly bankrupted themselves to entertain her in style.

Henry Wriothesley, Third Earl of Southampton, John de Critz, 1603

Henry Wriothesley, the third Earl of Southampton, was nearly executed for his part in the rebellion against Queen Elizabeth led by his friend the Earl of Essex in 1601. Though he was eventually pardoned, Southampton was imprisoned for two years in the Tower of London, where he is here depicted along with his favorite cat. Tradition has it that the cat found its way to him in prison and reached him by coming down the chimney. An early patron of Shakespeare, the wealthy earl may be the "Mr. W. H." (his initials reversed) to whom the first edition of the sonnets is dedicated (p. 723). On the eve of the Essex rebellion, Southampton seems to have instigated a performance of *Richard II* by Shakespeare's company to put the people of London in mind of deposition. The painting was clearly commissioned after his release, the date of which is painted on the tablet, along with the proud inscription "In Vinculis / Invictus" (Though in chains, unconquered).

The Early Seventeenth Century
(1603–1660)

The Expulsion from Paradise, Masaccio, ca. 1427–28

This striking fresco shows an agonized Adam and Eve being driven from Eden by a sword-wielding angel. Adam is so overcome he buries his face in his hands; Eve's face is a mask of despair. They do not touch: each seems imprisoned in his or her own pain. Milton's representation of the expulsion at the end of Book 12 of *Paradise Lost* is very different, and the comparison is instructive (see pp. 1725ff.).

The Three Graces (detail), *The Primavera*, Sandro Botticelli, ca. 1481

The Graces are a prominent allusive feature of seventeenth-century poetry and masques. At times they carry the allegorical significance suggested in Botticelli's portrayal of them as extensions of Venus, goddess of love and beauty, and as manifestations of the beauty, joy, and freshness of spring. Milton's "L'Allegro" (p. 1459) is couched as a literary hymn honoring Euphrosyne, the Grace who signifies youthful mirth; her sisters are Aglaia, splendor, and Thalia, abundance or pleasure. Their linked hands and postures are said to symbolize the giving and receiving of joy, bounty, and pleasure.

Sacred and Profane Love, Titian, ca. 1515

This image might almost serve as an emblem for the two kinds of love celebrated and often contrasted in seventeenth-century verse. In Titian's Neoplatonic program, the nude figure bearing the torch is the celestial Venus, the principle of universal and eternal beauty and love; the clothed figure is the earthly Venus, who creates the perishable images of beauty in humans, flowers and trees, gold and gems, and works of art. Cupid is placed between them but somewhat closer to the terrestrial Venus.

God Creating the Animals, Tintoretto, 1550–52

A remarkable rendering of the scene, with God the Father depicted as an immense figure, exuding power and energy, actively calling forth many varieties of animals. The conception invites comparison with Milton's rendering of the Genesis creation story in *Paradise Lost*, Book 7 (p. 1615).

John Donne, anonymous, ca. 1595

This portrait presents Donne in the guise of a melancholy lover fond of self-display; the signs are his broad-brimmed black hat, soulful eyes, sensual lips, delicate hands, and untied but expensive lace collar. Parts of Donne's *Songs and Sonnets* (pp. 923ff.) date from this period. Melancholy, supposedly caused by an excess of black bile and often associated with the scholarly and artistic temperament, was identified in Robert Burton's massive and very popular *Anatomy of Melancholy* as a well-nigh universal attribute of the period. It is the temperament of many literary characters, among them Hamlet, Duke Orsino (in *Twelfth Night*, p. 741), Jacques in *As You Like It*, and Milton's Il Penseroso (p. 1463).

Lady Sidney and Six of Her Children, Marcus Gheeraerts the Younger, ca. 1596

This portrait of Barbara (Gamage) Sidney, wife of Sir Robert Sidney of Penshurst, provides an insight into domestic relations in the period, as well as an illuminating comment on Ben Jonson's poem "To Penshurst" (p. 1096). Robert Sidney (brother of Sir Philip Sidney) is absent, serving as governor of the English stronghold in Flushing. Lady Sidney is portrayed as a fruitful, fostering mother. Her hands rest on her two sons—both still in skirts, though the heir wears a sword; the four daughters are arranged in two pairs, the elder of each pair imitating her mother's nurturing gesture. The eldest daughter will become Lady Mary Wroth, author of *Urania* and the sonnet sequence *Pamphilia to Amphilanthus* (pp. 1116ff.).

Lucy, Countess of Bedford, as a Masquer, attributed to John de Critz, ca. 1606

Lucy (Harrington) Russell, Countess of Bedford, prominent courtier, favorite of Queen Anne, patron of Donne and Jonson, and frequent planner of and participant in court masques, is shown in masquing costume for the wedding masque *Hymenaei*, by Ben Jonson and Inigo Jones. Jonson describes the masquing ladies as "attired richly and alike in the most celestial colors" associated with the rainbow, with elaborate headdresses and shoes, "all full of splendor, sovereignty, and riches." Their masque dances were "fully of subtlety and device."

The Garden of Eden with the Fall of Man, Jan Brueghel the Elder and Peter Paul Rubens, ca. 1615

Possibly foreshadowing Milton's portrayal of Eden in *Paradise Lost*, the painting presents an idyllic scene with cavorting animals in a lush landscape and a graceful human pair—perhaps just enjoying the garden's fruit, but at least intimating the moment of the Fall as a seductive Eve hands Adam an apple and a snake looks on. A favorite painter of Charles I, Rubens designed and painted for the king the splendid ceiling of Whitehall, portraying King James in apotheosis, as a supporter of wisdom, justice, concord, and peace.

Charles I on Horseback, Sir Anthony Van Dyck, 1637–38

One of Charles I's court painters, knighted and pensioned by the king, Van Dyck produced several portraits of the royal family and their circle at court. This magnificent equestrian portrait of the king in armor presents him as hero and warrior, in a pose that looks back to portraits and statues of Roman emperors on horseback. It was painted to be hung at the end of the Long Gallery in St. James Palace.

The Penitent Magdalen, Georges de La Tour, ca. 1638–43

This remarkable image of a young woman in meditative pose, her face lit by candlelight and her hand touching a skull, can serve as an emblem for the extensive meditative literature of the period—the poetry and prose of Donne, Herbert, Vaughan, and Traherne, among others—on such topics as sickness, human mortality, the transience of life and beauty, and the inevitability of death.

From Songs and Sonnets[1]

The Flea[2]

Mark but this flea, and mark in this,
How little that which thou deniest me is;
Me it sucked first, and now sucks thee,
And in this flea our two bloods mingled be;
5   Thou know'st that this cannot be said
A sin, or shame, or loss of maidenhead,°   *virginity*
   Yet this enjoys before it woo,
   And pampered° swells with one blood made of two,[3]   *overfed*
   And this, alas, is more than we would do.

10 Oh stay, three lives in one flea spare,
Where we almost, nay more than married are.
This flea is you and I, and this
Our marriage bed and marriage temple is;
Though parents grudge, and you, we are met,
15 And cloistered[4] in these living walls of jet.°   *black*
   Though use° make you apt to kill me,[5]   *habit*
   Let not to that, self-murder added be,
   And sacrilege, three sins in killing three.

   Cruel and sudden, hast thou since
20 Purpled thy nail in blood of innocence?
Wherein could this flea guilty be,
Except in that drop which it sucked from thee?
Yet thou triumph'st, and say'st that thou
Find'st not thy self nor me the weaker now;
25   'Tis true; then learn how false fears be:
   Just so much honor, when thou yield'st to me,
   Will waste, as this flea's death took life from thee.

1633

The Good-Morrow°   *morning greeting*

I wonder, by my troth,° what thou and I   *good faith*
Did, till we loved? Were we not weaned till then,

1. Donne's love poems were written over nearly two decades, beginning around 1595; they were not published in Donne's lifetime but circulated widely in manuscript. The title *Songs and Sonnets* was supplied in the second edition (1635), which grouped the poems by kind, but neither this arrangement nor the more haphazard organization of the first edition (1633) is Donne's own. In Donne's time the term "sonnet" often meant simply "love lyric," and in fact there is only one formal sonnet in this collection. For the poems we present we follow the 1635 edition, beginning with the extremely popular poem "The Flea."
2. This insect afforded a popular erotic theme for poets all over Europe, deriving from a pseudo-Ovidian medieval poem in which a lover envies the flea for the liberties it takes with his mistress's body.
3. The swelling suggests pregnancy.
4. As in a convent or monastery.
5. By denying me sexual gratification.

But sucked on country° pleasures, childishly?   *unsophisticated*
Or snorted° we in the seven sleepers' den?[1]   *snored*
5 'Twas so; but° this, all pleasures fancies be.   *except for*
If ever any beauty I did see,
Which I desired, and got, 'twas but a dream of thee.

And now good morrow to our waking souls,
Which watch not one another out of fear;
10 For love all love of other sights controls,
And makes one little room an everywhere.
Let sea-discoverers to new worlds have gone,
Let maps to others, worlds on worlds have shown:
Let us possess one world;[2] each hath one, and is one.

15 My face in thine eye, thine in mine appears,
And true plain hearts do in the faces rest;
Where can we find two better hemispheres,
Without sharp North, without declining West?
Whatever dies was not mixed equally;[3]
20 If our two loves be one, or thou and I
Love so alike that none do slacken, none can die.

1633

Song

Go and catch a falling star,
  Get with child a mandrake root,[1]
Tell me where all past years are,
  Or who cleft the Devil's foot,
5 Teach me to hear mermaids° singing,   *sirens*
Or to keep off envy's stinging,
    And find
    What wind
Serves to advance an honest mind.

10 If thou beest born to strange sights,
  Things invisible to see,
Ride ten thousand days and nights,
  Till age snow white hairs on thee,
Thou, when thou return'st, wilt tell me
15 All strange wonders that befell thee,
    And swear
    No where
Lives a woman true, and fair.

1. Cave in Ephesus where, according to legend, seven Christian youths hid from pagan persecutors and slept for 187 years.
2. "Our world" in many manuscripts.
3. Scholastic philosophy taught that when the elements were imperfectly mixed ("not mixed equally"), matter was mutable and mortal; conversely, when the elements were perfectly mixed, matter was immutable and hence immortal.
1. The mandrake root, or mandragora, is forked like the lower part of the human body. It was thought to shriek when pulled from the ground and to kill all humans who heard it; it was also (paradoxically) thought to help women conceive.

If thou find'st one, let me know,
20   Such a pilgrimage were sweet;
Yet do not, I would not go,
    Though at next door we might meet;
Though she were true when you met her,
And last till you write your letter,
25   Yet she
      Will be
False, ere I come, to two, or three.

1633

The Undertaking

I have done one braver° thing   *more glorious*
    Than all the Worthies[1] did,
And yet a braver thence doth spring,
    Which is, to keep that hid.

5   It were but madness now t' impart
    The skill of specular stone,[2]
When he which can have learned the art
    To cut it, can find none.

So, if I now should utter this,
10   Others (because no more
Such stuff to work upon, there is)
    Would love but as before.

But he who loveliness within
    Hath found, all outward loathes,
15   For he who color loves, and skin,
    Loves but their oldest clothes.

If, as I have, you also do
    Virtue attired in woman see,
And dare love that, and say so too,
20   And forget the He and She;

And if this love, though placèd so,
    From profane men you hide,
Which will no faith on this bestow,
    Or, if they do, deride;

1. According to medieval legend, the Nine Worthies, or supreme heroes of history, included three Jews (Joshua, David, Judas Maccabaeus), three pagans (Hector, Alexander, Julius Caesar), and three Christians (Arthur, Charlemagne, Godfrey of Boulogne).
2. A transparent or translucent material, reputed to have been used in antiquity for windows, but no longer known. Great skill was needed to cut it.

25   Then you have done a braver thing
      Than all the Worthies did;
   And a braver thence will spring,
      Which is, to keep that hid.

1633

The Sun Rising

      Busy old fool, unruly sun,
        Why dost thou thus
Through windows and through curtains call on us?
Must to thy motions lovers' seasons run?
5   Saucy pedantic wretch, go chide
      Late schoolboys and sour prentices,
   Go tell court huntsmen that the king will ride,[1]
   Call country ants to harvest offices;[2]
Love, all alike, no season knows nor clime,
10 Nor hours, days, months, which are the rags of time.

      Thy beams, so reverend and strong
        Why shouldst thou think?
I could eclipse and cloud them with a wink,
But that I would not lose her sight so long;
15   If her eyes have not blinded thine,
      Look, and tomorrow late, tell me,
   Whether both th' Indias of spice and mine[3]
   Be where thou leftst them, or lie here with me.
Ask for those kings whom thou saw'st yesterday,
20 And thou shalt hear, All here in one bed lay.

      She is all states,° and all princes I,   *nations*
        Nothing else is.
Princes do but play us; compared to this,
All honor's mimic, all wealth alchemy.
25   — Thou, sun, art half as happy as we,
      In that the world's contracted thus;
   Thine age asks ease, and since thy duties be
   To warm the world, that's done in warming us.
Shine here to us, and thou art everywhere;
30 This bed thy center is, these walls thy sphere.[4]

1633

---

1. King James was fond of hunting.
2. Autumn chores. "Country ants": farm drudges.
3. The India of "spice" is the East Indies; that of "mine" (gold), the West Indies.

4. According to the old Ptolemaic astronomy, the earth was the center of the sun's orbit, and the sun's motion was contained within its sphere.

The Indifferent

I can love both fair and brown,[1]
Her whom abundance melts, and her whom want betrays,
Her who loves loneness best, and her who masks and plays,
Her whom the country formed, and whom the town,
5 Her who believes, and her who tries,°   *tests*
Her who still° weeps with spongy eyes,   *always*
And her who is dry cork, and never cries;
I can love her, and her, and you, and you,
I can love any, so she be not true.

10 Will no other vice content you?
Will it not serve your turn to do as did your mothers?
Or have you all old vices spent, and now would find out others?
Or doth a fear that men are true torment you?
O we are not, be not you so;
15 Let me, and do you, twenty know.
Rob me, but bind me not, and let me go.
Must I, who came to travail thorough[2] you,
Grow your fixed subject, because you are true?

Venus heard me sigh this song,
20 And by love's sweetest part, variety, she swore,
She heard not this till now; and that it should be so no more.
She went, examined, and returned ere long,
And said, Alas, some two or three
Poor heretics in love there be,
25 Which think to 'stablish dangerous constancy.
But I have told them, Since you will be true,
You shall be true to them who are false to you.

1633

The Canonization[1]

For God's sake hold your tongue, and let me love,
    Or chide my palsy, or my gout,
My five gray hairs, or ruined fortune, flout,
    With wealth your state, your mind with arts improve,
5   Take you a course, get you a place,[2]
        Observe His Honor, or His Grace,[3]
Or the king's real, or his stampèd face[4]
        Contemplate; what you will, approve,°   *try, test*
        So you will let me love.

1. Both blonde and brunette.
2. Through. "Travail": grief.
1. The poem plays off against the Roman Catholic process of determining that certain persons are saints, proper objects of veneration and prayer.

2. An appointment, at court or elsewhere. "Take you a course": follow some career.
3. Pay court to some lord or bishop.
4. On coins; "real" (royal) refers also to a particular Spanish coin.

10   Alas, alas, who's injured by my love?
        What merchant's ships have my sighs drowned?
    Who says my tears have overflowed his ground?
        When did my colds a forward° spring remove?[5]   *early*
        When did the heats which my veins fill
15   Add one man to the plaguy bill?[6]
Soldiers find wars, and lawyers find out still
        Litigious men, which quarrels move,
        Though she and I do love.

    Call us what you will, we are made such by love;
20   Call her one, me another fly,
We're tapers too, and at our own cost die,[7]
        And we in us find the eagle and the dove.
        The phoenix riddle hath more wit
        By us: we two being one, are it.[8]
25   So, to one neutral thing both sexes fit.
        We die and rise the same, and prove
        Mysterious by this love.

    We can die by it, if not live by love,
        And if unfit for tombs and hearse
30   Our legend be, it will be fit for verse;
        And if no piece of chronicle° we prove,   *history*
        We'll build in sonnets pretty rooms;[9]
        As well a well-wrought urn becomes°   *befits*
The greatest ashes, as half-acre tombs,
35   And by these hymns,[1] all shall approve°   *confirm*
        Us canonized for love:

    And thus invoke us: You whom reverend love
        Made one another's hermitage;
You, to whom love was peace, that now is rage;
40   Who did the whole world's soul contract,[2] and drove
        Into the glasses of your eyes
        (So made such mirrors, and such spies,°   *spyglasses, telescopes*
That they did all to you epitomize)
        Countries, towns, courts:[3] Beg from above
45   A pattern of your love!

                                    1633

5. Petrarchan lovers traditionally sigh, weep, and are frozen because of their mistresses' neglect.
6. Deaths from the plague, which raged in summer, were recorded by parish in weekly lists.
7. Flies were emblems of transience and lustfulness; tapers (candles) attract flies to their death and also consume themselves. "Die" in the punning terminology of the period means to experience orgasm, and there was a superstition that intercourse shortened life.
8. The eagle signifies strength and vision; the dove, meekness and mercy. The phoenix was a mythic Arabian bird, only one of which existed at any one time. After living five hundred years, it was consumed by fire, then rose triumphantly from its ashes a new bird. Thus it was a symbol of immortality and sometimes associated with Christ. "Eagle" and "dove" are also alchemical terms for processes leading to the rise of "phoenix," a stage in the transmutation of metals to gold.
9. "Rooms" (punning on the Italian meaning of "stanza") will contain their exploits, as prose chronicle histories contain great deeds done in the world.
1. The lover's own poems.
2. An alternative meaning is "extract."
3. "Countries, towns, courts" are objects of the verb "drove." The notion is that eyes both see and reflect the outside world, and so can contain all of it.

Song

Sweetest love, I do not go,
　　For weariness of thee,
Nor in hope the world can show
　　A fitter love for me;
5　　　　But since that I
Must die at last, 'tis best,
To use myself in jest
　　Thus by feigned deaths° to die.　　　　　　*i.e., absences*

Yesternight the sun went hence
10　　And yet is here today,
He hath no desire nor sense,
　　Nor half so short a way:
　　　　Then fear not me,
But believe that I shall make
15 Speedier journeys, since I take
　　More wings and spurs than he.

O how feeble is man's power,
　　That if good fortune fall,°　　　　　　*happen*
Cannot add another hour,
20　　Nor a lost hour recall!
　　　　But come bad chance,
And we join to'it our strength,
And we teach it art and length,
　　Itself o'er us to'advance.

25 When thou sigh'st, thou sigh'st not wind,
　　But sigh'st my soul away,
When thou weep'st, unkindly¹ kind,
　　My life's blood doth decay.
　　　　It cannot be
30 That thou lov'st me, as thou say'st,
If in thine my life thou waste,
　　Thou art the best of me.

Let not thy divining° heart　　　　　　*prophetic*
　　Forethink me any ill,
35 Destiny may take thy part,
　　And may thy fears fulfill;
　　　　But think that we
Are but turned aside to sleep;
They who one another keep
40　　Alive, ne'er parted be.

1633

---

1. Also carries the meaning "unnaturally."

Air and Angels

Twice or thrice had I loved thee,
Before I knew thy face or name;
So in a voice, so in a shapeless flame,
Angels affect us oft, and worshipped be;
5   Still° when, to where thou wert, I came,   *always*
Some lovely glorious nothing[1] I did see.
    But since my soul, whose child love is,
Takes limbs of flesh, and else could nothing do,[2]
    More subtle° than the parent is   *rarefied*
10 Love must not be, but take a body too;
    And therefore what thou wert, and who,
        I bid love ask, and now
That it assume thy body I allow,
And fix itself in thy lip, eye, and brow.
15 Whilst thus to ballast love I thought,
And so more steadily to have gone,
With wares which would sink° admiration,   *overwhelm*
I saw I had love's pinnace° overfraught;°   *small boat / overloaded*
    Every thy hair for love to work upon
20 Is much too much, some fitter must be sought;
    For, nor in nothing, nor in things
Extreme and scatt'ring° bright, can love inhere.   *dazzling*
    Then as an angel, face and wings
Of air, not pure as it, yet pure doth wear,[3]
25   So thy love may be my love's sphere;[4]
        Just such disparity
As is 'twixt air and angels' purity,
'Twixt women's love and men's will ever be.

1633

Break of Day[1]

'Tis true, 'tis day; what though it be?
O wilt thou therefore rise from me?
Why should we rise because 'tis light?
Did we lie down because 'twas night?
5 Love, which in spite of darkness brought us hither,
Should in despite of light keep us together.

---

1. Spiritual beauty, the true object of love in
Neoplatonic philosophy.
2. My soul could not function unless it were in a
body.
3. It was commonly believed that angels, when
they appeared to humans, assumed a body of air
that, though pure, was less so than the angel's
spiritual essence.

4. Each sphere in the cosmos was thought to be
governed by an angel (an intelligence).
1. An aubade, or song of the lovers' parting at
dawn, this poem is unusual for Donne in having
a female speaker. The poem was given a musical
setting and published in 1622, in William Cork-
ine's *Second Book of Ayers*.

Light hath no tongue, but is all eye;
If it could speak as well as spy,
This were the worst that it could say,
10   That being well, I fain° would stay,   *gladly*
And that I loved my heart and honor so
That I would not from him, that had them, go.

Must business thee from hence remove?
O, that's the worst disease of love.
15   The poor, the foul, the false, love can
Admit, but not the busied man.
He which hath business, and makes love, doth do
Such wrong, as when a married man doth woo.

1622, 1633

A Valediction:[1] Of Weeping

Let me pour forth
My tears before thy face whilst I stay here,
For thy face coins them, and thy stamp° they bear,   *image*
And by this mintage they are something worth,
5   For thus they be
     Pregnant of thee;
Fruits of much grief they are, emblems° of more—   *symbols*
When a tear falls, that thou falls which it bore,
So thou and I are nothing then, when on a diverse° shore.   *different*

10   On a round ball
A workman that hath copies by can lay
An Europe, Afric, and an Asia,
And quickly make that, which was nothing, all;[2]
     So doth each tear
15   Which thee doth wear,[3]
A globe, yea world, by that impression grow,
Till thy tears mixed with mine do overflow
This world; by waters sent from thee, my heaven dissolvèd so.

     O more than moon,
20   Draw not up seas to drown me in thy sphere;[4]
Weep me not dead in thine arms, but forbear
To teach the sea what it may do too soon.
     Let not the wind
     Example find
25   To do me more harm than it purposeth;

1. A farewell poem, one of four so titled in the *Songs and Sonnets*. Another is "A Valediction: Forbidding Mourning," p. 935.
2. I.e., on a blank globe one can place maps of the continents and so convert "nothing" into the whole world ("all").
3. Which bears your image.
4. A star or planet with more power of attraction than the moon might not only affect tides but draw the very seas unto itself.

Since thou and I sigh one another's breath,
Whoe'er sighs most is cruelest, and hastes the other's death.

1633

Love's Alchemy

Some that have deeper digged love's mine than I,
Say where his centric° happiness doth lie: central
   I have loved, and got, and told,
But should I love, get, tell, till I were old,
5 I should not find that hidden mystery;
     O, 'tis imposture all:
And as no chemic° yet the elixir¹ got,   alchemist
   But glorifies his pregnant pot²
   If by the way to him befall
10 Some odoriferous thing, or medicinal;
   So lovers dream a rich and long delight,
   But get a winter-seeming summer's night.³

Our ease, our thrift, our honor, and our day,
Shall we for this vain bubble's shadow pay?
15   Ends love in this, that my man°   servant
Can be as happy as I can, if he can
Endure the short scorn of a bridegroom's play?
   That loving wretch that swears
'Tis not the bodies marry, but the minds,
20   Which he in her angelic finds,
    Would swear as justly that he hears,
In that day's rude hoarse minstrelsy, the spheres.⁴
   Hope not for mind in women; at their best
Sweetness and wit, they are but mummy, possessed.⁵

1633

A Nocturnal upon Saint Lucy's Day,
Being the Shortest Day¹

'Tis the year's midnight and it is the day's,
Lucy's, who scarce seven hours herself unmasks;

1. A magic medicine sought by alchemists and reputed to heal all ills.
2. A fertile (and womb-shaped) retort, calling up the common analogy between producing the elixir of life and human generation.
3. A night cold as in winter and short as in summer.
4. The perfect harmony of the planets, moving in concentric crystalline "spheres," is contrasted with the boisterous serenade of pots, pans, and trumpets performed on the wedding night.

5. The syntax of the last two lines is unclear, and they are punctuated differently in various copies. The 1633 edition reads: "at their best, / Sweetnesse, and wit they'are, but, *mummy*, possesst." Many modern editors punctuate as we do here. "Mummy" suggests a corpselike body, without mind or spirit.
1. The nocturne, or night office of the Roman Catholic Church, is a service held in the primitive church at midnight. St. Lucy's Day fell on December 13 according to the old calendar still in use in

The sun is spent, and now his flasks[2]
Send forth light squibs,° no constant rays.   *small fireworks*
5   The world's whole sap is sunk;
The general balm th' hydroptic[3] earth hath drunk,
Whither, as to the bed's feet, life is shrunk,
Dead and interred; yet all these seem to laugh,
Compared with me, who am their epitaph.

10   Study me, then, you who shall lovers be
At the next world, that is, at the next spring;
For I am every dead thing
In whom love wrought new alchemy.
For his art did express°   *extract*
15   A quintessence[4] even from nothingness,
From dull privations and lean emptiness.
He ruined me, and I am re-begot
Of absence, darkness, death: things which are not.

All others from all things draw all that's good,
20   Life, soul, form, spirit, whence they being have;
I, by love's limbeck,[5] am the grave
Of all that's nothing. Oft a flood
Have we two wept, and so
Drowned the whole world, us two; oft did we grow
25   To be two chaoses when we did show
Care to aught° else; and often absences   *anything*
Withdrew our souls, and made us carcasses.

But I am by her death (which word wrongs her)
Of the first nothing the elixir grown;[6]
30   Were I a man, that I were one
I needs must know; I should prefer,
If I were any beast,
Some ends, some means; yea plants, yea stones detest
And love.[7] All, all some properties invest.
35   If I an ordinary nothing were,
As shadow, a light and body must be here.

But I am none; nor will my sun renew.
You lovers, for whose sake the lesser sun
At this time to the Goat[8] is run
40   To fetch new lust and give it you,

England at the time, and its vigil (the previous day
and night) was the winter solstice, the shortest
day of the year. At this time of the year, the sun
rises after 8 A.M. in the latitude of London and
sets well before 4 P.M.
2. The stars are "flasks," thought to store up light
from the sun.
3. Dropsical, thus insatiably thirsty. "General
balm": the supposedly life-preserving essence of
all things.
4. The reputed fifth essence, a celestial element
beyond the mundane four elements (earth, water,

air, fire), thought to be latent in all things and
to be a universal cure. Alchemists sought to
extract it.
5. Alembic; a vessel used in distilling.
6. I.e., the quintessence of that absolute nothingness that existed before the creation.
7. Beasts have intentions; plants and even stones
(like lodestones) have attractions and antipathies.
8. The sign of Capricorn, which the sun enters
at the winter solstice; the goat is an emblem of
sexual vigor.

Enjoy your summer all.
Since she enjoys her long night's festival,
Let me prepare towards her, and let me call
This hour her vigil and her eve, since this
45   Both the year's and the day's deep midnight is.

1633

The Bait[1]

Come live with me and be my love,
And we will some new pleasures prove,°   *try*
Of golden sands and crystal brooks,
With silken lines and silver hooks.

5   There will the river whispering run,
Warmed by thine eyes more than the sun.
And there the enamored fish will stay,
Begging themselves they may betray.

When thou wilt swim in that live bath,
10   Each fish, which every channel hath,
Will amorously to thee swim,
Gladder to catch thee, than thou him.

If thou, to be so seen, beest loath,
By sun or moon, thou darkenest both;
15   And if myself have leave to see,
I need not their light, having thee.

Let others freeze with angling reeds,
And cut their legs with shells and weeds,
Or treacherously poor fish beset
20   With strangling snare or windowy net.

Let coarse bold hands from slimy nest
The bedded fish in banks outwrest,
Or curious traitors, sleave-silk flies,[2]
Bewitch poor fishes' wandering eyes.

25   For thee, thou need'st no such deceit,
For thou thyself art thine own bait;
That fish that is not catched thereby,
Alas, is wiser far than I.

1633

---

1. This poem is Donne's response to Marlowe's "Passionate Shepherd to His Love," p. 678. Another of the many responses was Ralegh's "The Nymph's Reply to the Shepherd," p. 527.
2. Flies (for fishing) made of unraveled silk. "Curious": exquisitely made.

The Apparition

When by thy scorn, O murderess, I am dead,
   And that thou thinkst thee free
   From all solicitation from me,
Then shall my ghost come to thy bed,
5 And thee, feigned vestal,[1] in worse arms shall see;
Then thy sick taper will begin to wink,°   *flicker*
And he whose thou art then, being tired before,
Will, if thou stir, or pinch to wake him, think
     Thou call'st for more,
10 And in false sleep will from thee shrink,
And then, poor aspen wretch,[2] neglected thou
Bathed in a cold quicksilver sweat[3] wilt lie
     A verier° ghost than I;   *truer*
What I will say, I will not tell thee now,
15 Lest that preserve thee; and since my love is spent,
I had rather thou shouldst painfully repent,
Than by my threatenings rest still innocent.

                                   1633

A Valediction: Forbidding Mourning[1]

As virtuous men pass mildly away,
   And whisper to their souls to go,
Whilst some of their sad friends do say
   The breath goes now, and some say, No;

5 So let us melt, and make no noise,
   No tear-floods, nor sigh-tempests move;
'Twere profanation° of our joys   *desecration*
   To tell the laity our love.

Moving of th' earth brings harms and fears,
10   Men reckon what it did and meant;
But trepidation of the spheres,
   Though greater far, is innocent.[2]

---

1. Virgins consecrated to the Roman goddess Vesta.
2. Aspen leaves flutter in the slightest breeze.
3. Sweating in terror; quicksilver (mercury) was a stock prescription for venereal disease, and sweating was part of the cure.
1. For "valediction" see p. 931, n. 1. Izaak Walton speculated that this poem was addressed to Donne's wife on the occasion of his trip to the Continent in 1611, but there is no proof of that.
2. Earthquakes cause damage and were thought to be portentous. "Trepidation" (in the Ptolemaic cosmology) is an oscillation of the ninth or crystalline sphere imparted to all the inner spheres. Though a much more violent motion than an earthquake, it is neither destructive nor sinister.

Dull sublunary³ lovers' love
    (Whose soul is sense) cannot admit
15 Absence, because it doth remove
    Those things which elemented° it.   *composed*

But we, by a love so much refined
    That ourselves know not what it is,
Inter-assurèd of the mind,
20   Care less, eyes, lips, and hands to miss.

Our two souls therefore, which are one,
    Though I must go, endure not yet
A breach, but an expansion,
    Like gold to airy thinness beat.

25 If they be two, they are two so
    As stiff twin compasses⁴ are two;
Thy soul, the fixed foot, makes no show
    To move, but doth, if th' other do.

And though it in the center sit,
30   Yet when the other far doth roam,
It leans and hearkens after it,
    And grows erect, as that comes home.

Such wilt thou be to me, who must,
    Like th' other foot, obliquely run;
35 Thy firmness makes my circle just,
    And makes me end where I begun.

                                                        1633

The Ecstasy¹

Where, like a pillow on a bed,
    A pregnant bank swelled up to rest
The violet's reclining head,
    Sat we two, one another's best.

5 Our hands were firmly cemented
    With a fast balm° which thence did spring,   *perspiration*
Our eye-beams² twisted, and did thread
    Our eyes upon one double string;

---

3. Beneath the moon, therefore earthly, sensual, and subject to change.
4. The two legs of a geometer's or draftsman's compass.
1. From *ekstasis* (Greek), a movement of the soul outside of the body.
2. Invisible shafts of light, thought of as going out of the eyes and thereby enabling one to see things.

So to intergraft our hands, as yet
10 Was all our means to make us one,
And pictures in our eyes[3] to get°   *beget*
Was all our propagation.

As 'twixt two equal armies Fate
Suspends uncertain victory,
15 Our souls (which to advance their state
Were gone out) hung 'twixt her and me;

And whilst our souls negotiate there,
We like sepulchral statues lay;
All day the same our postures were,
20 And we said nothing all the day.

If any, so by love refined
That he soul's language understood,
And by good love were grown all mind,
Within convenient distance stood,

25 He (though he knew not which soul spake,
Because both meant, both spake the same)
Might thence a new concoction[4] take,
And part far purer than he came.

This ecstasy doth unperplex,
30 We said, and tell us what we love;
We see by this it was not sex;
We see we saw not what did move;°   *motivate us*

But as all several° souls contain   *separate*
Mixture of things, they know not what,
35 Love these mixed souls doth mix again,
And makes both one, each this and that.

A single violet transplant,
The strength, the color, and the size
(All which before was poor and scant)
40 Redoubles still,° and multiplies.   *continually*

When love with one another so
Interinanimates two souls,
That abler soul, which thence doth flow,
Defects of loneliness controls.

45 We then, who are this new soul, know
Of what we are composed and made,
For th' atomies° of which we grow   *components*
Are souls, whom no change can invade.

___

3. Reflections of each in the other's eyes, often
called "making babies."

4. In the alchemical sense of sublimation or
purification.

But O alas, so long, so far
50   Our bodies why do we forbear?
They are ours, though they are not we; we are
      The intelligences, they the sphere.[5]

We owe them thanks because they thus
      Did us to us at first convey,
55   Yielded their forces, sense, to us,
      Nor are dross to us, but allay.[6]

On man heaven's influence works not so
      But that it first imprints the air:[7]
So soul into the soul may flow,
60   Though it to body first repair.°   go

As our blood labors to beget
      Spirits[8] as like souls as it can,
Because such fingers need° to knit   are needed
      That subtle knot which makes us man,

65   So must pure lovers' souls descend
      T' affections, and to faculties
Which sense may reach and apprehend;
      Else a great prince in prison lies.

To our bodies turn we then, that so
70   Weak men on love revealed may look;
Love's mysteries[9] in souls do grow,
      But yet the body is his book.

And if some lover, such as we,
      Have heard this dialogue of one,[1]
75   Let him still mark° us; he shall see   observe
      Small change when we are to bodies gone.

                                                                      1633

The Funeral

Whoever comes to shroud me, do not harm
      Nor question much
That subtle wreath of hair which crowns my arm;
The mystery, the sign you must not touch,

---

5. In Ptolemaic astronomy, each planet, set in a transparent "sphere" that revolved and so carried it around the earth, was inhabited by a controlling angelic "intelligence."
6. "Dross" is an impurity that weakens metal; "allay" (alloy) strengthens it.
7. Astrological influences were thought to work on people through the medium of the surrounding air.

8. Subtle substances thought to be produced by the blood to serve as intermediaries between body and soul.
9. The implied comparison is with God's mysteries, which are revealed and may be read in the book of Nature and the book of Scripture.
1. "Dialogue of one" because "both meant, both spake the same" (line 26).

5   For 'tis my outward soul,
  Viceroy to that, which then to heaven being gone,
    Will leave this to control,
  And keep these limbs, her[1] provinces, from dissolution.

  For if the sinewy thread[2] my brain lets fall
10   Through every part
  Can tie those parts and make me one of all,
  These hairs which upward grew, and strength and art
     Have from a better brain,
  Can better do it; except° she meant that I   *unless*
15   By this should know my pain,
  As prisoners then are manacled, when they're condemned to die.

  Whate'er she meant by it, bury it with me,
     For since I am
  Love's martyr, it might breed idolatry,
20 If into others' hands these relics[3] came:
     As 'twas humility
  To afford to it all that a soul can do,
    So 'tis some bravery,°   *defiance*
  That since you would save[4] none of me, I bury some of you.

              1633

The Blossom

   Little think'st thou, poor flower,
    Whom I have watched six or seven days,
  And seen thy birth, and seen what every hour
  Gave to thy growth, thee to this height to raise,
5 And now dost laugh and triumph on this bough,
     Little think'st thou
  That it will freeze anon, and that I shall
  Tomorrow find thee fall'n, or not at all.

   Little think'st thou, poor heart,
10   That labor'st yet to nestle thee,
  And think'st by hovering here to get a part
  In a forbidden or forbidding tree,[1]
  And hop'st her stiffness by long siege to bow,
     Little think'st thou
15 That thou tomorrow, ere that sun doth wake,
  Must with this sun and me a journey take.

---

1. The soul's, but also the mistress's (cf. "she," line 14).
2. The nervous system.
3. Body parts or other objects belonging to a saint, venerated by Roman Catholics.
4. All the early printed texts read "have" (which carries sexual connotations), while many manuscripts read "save."

1. The fruit of this tree is "forbidden" (presumably because the woman is married) or "forbidding" (because she is unwilling).

But thou, which lov'st to be
        Subtle to plague thyself, wilt say,
    Alas, if you must go, what's that to me?
20 Here lies my business, and here I will stay:
    You go to friends whose love and means present
                Various content°   *satisfactions*
    To your eyes, ears, and tongue, and every part.
    If then your body go, what need you a heart?

25   Well, then, stay here; but know,
        When thou hast stayed and done thy most,
    A naked thinking heart that makes no show
    Is to a woman but a kind of ghost.
    How shall she know my heart; or, having none,
30   Know thee for one?
    Practice may make her know some other part,
    But take my word, she doth not know a heart.

        Meet me at London, then,
        Twenty days hence, and thou shalt see
35 Me fresher and more fat° by being with men   *prosperous*
    Than if I had stayed still with her and thee.
    For God's sake, if you can, be you so too:
                I would give you
    There to another friend, whom we shall find
40 As glad to have my body as my mind.

                                                    1633

The Relic

    When my grave is broke up again
    Some second guest to entertain
    (For graves have learned that woman-head°   *female trait*
    To be to more than one a bed),[1]
5   And he that digs it spies
    A bracelet of bright hair about the bone,
        Will he not let us alone,
    And think that there a loving couple lies,
    Who thought that this device might be some way
10 To make their souls, at the last busy day,[2]
    Meet at this grave, and make a little stay?

        If this fall° in a time, or land,   *happen*
        Where mis-devotion[3] doth command,
        Then he that digs us up will bring
15   Us to the bishop and the king,

1. Graves were often used to inter successive corpses, the bones of previous occupants being deposited in charnel houses.
2. Judgment Day, when the bodies of the deceased are reunited with their souls (and the beloved comes to her lover's grave to reclaim her hair).
3. False devotion, superstition, i.e., Roman Catholicism.

To make us relics; then
Thou shalt be a Mary Magdalen, and I
   A something else thereby;
All women shall adore us, and some men;
20 And since at such times, miracles are sought,
I would have that age by this paper taught
What miracles we harmless lovers wrought.

   First, we loved well and faithfully,
   Yet knew not what we loved, nor why,
25   Difference of sex no more we knew,
   Than our guardian angels do;
     Coming and going, we
Perchance might kiss, but not between those meals;[4]
   Our hands ne'er touched the seals°   *sexual organs*
30 Which nature, injured by late law, sets free:[5]
These miracles we did: but now, alas,
All measure and all language I should pass,
Should I tell what a miracle she was.

                                                    1633

A Lecture upon the Shadow

   Stand still, and I will read to thee
   A lecture, Love, in love's philosophy.
     These three hours that we have spent
     Walking here, two shadows went
5 Along with us, which we ourselves produced;
But, now the sun is just above our head,
     We do those shadows tread
     And to brave° clearness all things are reduced.   *splendid*
So, whilst our infant loves did grow,
10 Disguises did and shadows flow
From us and our care;° but now, 'tis not so.   *caution*

   That love hath not attained the high'st degree
   Which is still diligent lest others see.

   Except° our loves at this noon stay,   *unless*
15 We shall new shadows make the other way.
     As the first were made to blind
     Others, these which come behind
Will work upon ourselves, and blind our eyes.
If our loves faint and westwardly decline,
20   To me thou falsely thine
     And I to thee mine actions shall disguise.
The morning shadows wear away,

4. The kisses of salutation and parting.
5. Human law forbids the free love permitted by nature. "Late": recent (comparatively speaking).

But these grow longer all the day,
But, oh, love's day is short if love decay.

25 Love is a growing or full constant light,
And his first minute after noon is night.

1635

Elegy[1] 16. On His Mistress

By our first strange and fatal° interview,   *fateful*
By all desires which thereof did ensue,
By our long starving hopes, by that remorse°   *pity*
Which my words' masculine persuasive force
5 Begot in thee, and by the memory
Of hurts which spies and rivals threatened me,
I calmly beg; but by thy father's wrath,
By all pains which want and divorcement hath,
I conjure thee; and all the oaths which I
10 And thou have sworn to seal joint constancy
Here I unswear and overswear them thus:
Thou shalt not love by ways so dangerous.
Temper, oh fair love, love's impetuous rage;
Be my true mistress still, not my feigned page.[2]
15 I'll go, and, by thy kind leave, leave behind
Thee, only worthy to nurse in my mind
Thirst to come back. Oh, if thou die before,
My soul from other lands to thee shall soar.
Thy (else almighty) beauty cannot move
20 Rage from the seas, nor thy love teach them love,
Nor tame wild Boreas' harshness.[3] Thou hast read
How roughly he in pieces shiverèd
Fair Orithea, whom he swore he loved.
Fall ill or good, 'tis madness to have proved°   *sought out*
25 Dangers unurged; feed on this flattery,
That absent lovers one in th' other be.
Dissemble nothing, not a boy, nor change
Thy body's habit,° nor mind's; be not strange   *clothing*
To thyself only; all will spy in thy face
30 A blushing womanly discovering grace.
Richly clothed apes are called apes, and as soon
Eclipsed as bright we call the moon the moon.
Men of France, changeable chameleons,
Spitals° of diseases, shops of fashions,   *hospitals*

---

1. In Latin poetry, an elegy is a discursive or reflective poem written in "elegiacs" (unrhymed couplets of alternating dactylic hexameters and pentameters). This meter was used for funeral laments and especially for love poetry. The most famous classical elegist was the Roman poet Ovid; his *Amores*, a collection of witty and sensual love poems, deeply influenced Donne's erotic poetry.

2. The speaker's mistress wanted to accompany him abroad, disguised as a page boy. Such escapades occasionally took place in real life; in 1605, Elizabeth Southwell, disguised as a page, went abroad with Sir Robert Dudley.

3. God of the north wind; in *Metamorphoses* 6 Ovid describes the wild force with which Boreas abducted Orithea.

35 Love's fuelers[4] and the rightest company
  Of players which upon the world's stage be,
  Will quickly know thee, and know thee; and alas![5]
  Th' indifferent° Italian, as we pass   *bisexual*
  His warm land, well content to think thee page,
40 Will hunt thee with such lust and hideous rage
  As Lot's fair guests were vexed.[6] But none of these
  Nor spongy, hydroptic[7] Dutch shall thee displease
  If thou stay here. O stay here, for, for thee,
  England is only a worthy gallery
45 To walk in expectation, till from thence
  Our greatest king call thee to his presence.[8]
  When I am gone, dream me some happiness,
  Nor let thy looks our long-hid love confess;
  Nor praise nor dispraise me, bless nor curse
50 Openly love's force, nor in bed fright thy nurse
  With midnight's startings, crying out "Oh, oh!
  Nurse, oh my love is slain, I saw him go
  O'er the white Alps alone; I saw him, I,
  Assailed, fight, taken, stabbed, bleed, fall, and die."
55 Augur me better chance, except dread Jove
  Think it enough for me t' have had thy love.

                 1635

Elegy 19. To His Mistress Going to Bed

  Come, Madam, come, all rest my powers defy,
  Until I labor, I in labor lie.[1]
  The foe ofttimes having the foe in sight,
  Is tired with standing though he never fight.
5 Off with that girdle,° like heaven's zone° glistering, *belt / zodiac*
  But a far fairer world encompassing.
  Unpin that spangled breastplate[2] which you wear
  That th' eyes of busy fools may be stopped there.
  Unlace yourself, for that harmonious chime
10 Tells me from you that now it is bed-time.
  Off with that happy busk,° which I envy,   *bodice*
  That still° can be and still can stand so nigh.   *always*
  Your gown going off, such beauteous state reveals
  As when from flowery meads th' hill's shadow steals.
15 Off with that wiry coronet and show
  The hairy diadem which on you doth grow;
  Now off with those shoes, and then safely tread

---

4. Providers of aphrodisiacs.
5. May pun on "a lass." "Know": in the sexual sense.
6. The inhabitants of Sodom tried to rape two angels who visited Lot in the guise of men to warn of the city's impending destruction (Genesis 19.1–11).
7. Dropsical, thus insatiably thirsty.

8. Throne rooms commonly had antechambers (galleries) where visitors waited until the monarch was ready to see them.
1. "Labor" in the dual sense of "get to work (sexually)" and "distress."
2. The stomacher, an ornamental, often jeweled, covering for the chest, worn under the lacing of the bodice.

In this love's hallowed temple, this soft bed.
In such white robes, heaven's angels used to be
20 Received by men; thou, angel, bring'st with thee
A heaven like Mahomet's paradise;[3] and though
Ill spirits walk in white, we easily know
By this these angels from an evil sprite,
Those set our hairs, but these our flesh upright.
25   License my roving hands, and let them go
Before, behind, between, above, below.
O my America! my new-found-land,
My kingdom, safeliest when with one man manned,
My mine of precious stones, my empery,°   *empire*
30 How blest am I in this discovering thee!
To enter in these bonds is to be free;
There where my hand is set, my seal shall be.[4]
   Full nakedness! All joys are due to thee.
As souls unbodied, bodies unclothed must be,
35 To taste whole joys. Gems which you women use
Are like Atalanta's balls,[5] cast in men's views,
That when a fool's eye lighteth on a gem,
His earthly soul may covet theirs, not them.
Like pictures, or like books' gay coverings, made
40 For laymen, are all women thus arrayed;
Themselves are mystic books, which only we
(Whom their imputed grace will dignify)
Must see revealed.[6] Then since that I may know,
As liberally as to a midwife show
45 Thyself: cast all, yea, this white linen hence,
Here is no penance, much less innocence.[7]
   To teach thee, I am naked first; why then
What need'st thou have more covering than a man?

1669

Satire 3   In satire the author holds a subject up to ridicule. Like his elegies, Donne's five verse satires were written in his twenties and are in the forefront of an effort in the 1590s (by Donne, Ben Jonson, Joseph Hall, and John Marston) to naturalize those classical forms in England. While elements of satire figure in many different kinds of literature, the great models for formal verse satire were the Roman poets Horace and Juvenal, the former for an urbanely witty style, the latter for an indignant or angry manner. While Donne's other satires call on these models, his third satire more nearly resembles those of a third Roman satirist, Persius, known

---

3. A place of sensual pleasure, thought to be populated by seductive houris for the delectation of the faithful.
4. The jokes mingle law with sex: where he has signed a document (placed his hand) he will now place his seal; and in the bonds of her arms he will find freedom.
5. Atalanta, running a race against her suitor Hippomenes, was beaten when he dropped golden apples ("balls") for her to pick up. Donne reverses the story.

6. By granting favors to their lovers, women impute to them grace that they don't deserve, as God, in Calvinist doctrine, imputes grace to undeserving sinners. Laymen can only look at the covers of mystic books (clothed women), but "we" elect can read them (see women naked).
7. Some manuscripts read: "There is no penance due to innocence." White garments would be appropriate either for the innocent virgin or for the sinner doing formal penance.

for an abstruse style and moralizing manner. This work is a strenuous discussion of an acute theological problem, for the age and for Donne himself: How may one discover the true Christian church among so many claimants to that role? At the time Donne wrote "Satire 3," he was in the process of leaving the Roman Catholic Church of his heritage for the Church of England.

Satire 3

Kind pity chokes my spleen;[1] brave° scorn forbids   *defiant*
Those tears to issue which swell my eyelids;
I must not laugh, nor weep° sins, and be wise: *lament*
Can railing then cure these worn maladies?
5 Is not our mistress, fair Religion,
As worthy of all our souls' devotion
As virtue was to the first blinded age?[2]
Are not heaven's joys as valiant to assuage
Lusts, as earth's honor was to them?° Alas,   *pagans*
10 As we do them in means, shall they surpass
Us in the end, and shall thy father's spirit
Meet blind philosophers in heaven, whose merit
Of strict life may be imputed faith,[3] and hear
Thee, whom he taught so easy ways and near
15 To follow, damned? O, if thou dar'st, fear this;
This fear great courage and high valor is.
Dar'st thou aid mutinous Dutch,[4] and dar'st thou lay
Thee in ships, wooden sepulchers, a prey
To leaders' rage, to storms, to shot, to dearth?°   *famine*
20 Dar'st thou dive seas and dungeons° of the earth?   *mines, caves*
Hast thou courageous fire to thaw the ice
Of frozen north discoveries?[5] And thrice
Colder than salamanders, like divine
Children in the oven,[6] fires of Spain and the line,
25 Whose countries limbecks to our bodies be,
Canst thou for gain bear?[7] And must every he
Which cries not "Goddess!" to thy mistress, draw,°   *fight a duel*
Or eat thy poisonous words? Courage of straw!
O desperate coward, wilt thou seem bold, and
30 To thy foes and His° (who made thee to stand   *God's*
Sentinel in his world's garrison) thus yield,
And for forbidden wars leave th' appointed field?[8]

---

1. The seat of bile, hence scorn and ridicule.
2. The age of paganism, blind to Christianity but capable of natural morality ("virtue").
3. Donne's formulation wittily turns on its head the key concept of Protestant theology—that salvation is to be achieved only by imputing Christ's merits to Christians through faith—by suggesting that virtuous pagans might be saved by imputing faith to them on the basis of their moral life.
4. English volunteers took frequent part with the Dutch in their wars against Spain. Donne himself had sailed in two raiding expeditions against the Spanish.

5. Many explorers tried to find a northwest passage to the Pacific.
6. In the biblical story (Daniel 3), Shadrach, Meshach, and Abednego were rescued from a fiery furnace. The salamander (a lizardlike creature) was thought to be so cold-blooded that it could live in fire.
7. The object of "bear" is "fires of Spain and the line"—inquisitorial and equatorial heats, which roast people as chemists heat materials in "limbecks" (alembics, or vessels for distilling).
8. Of moral struggle.

Know thy foes: The foul Devil (whom thou
Strivest to please) for hate, not love, would allow
35 Thee fain° his whole realm to be quit;° and as   *gladly / to satisfy you*
The world's all parts wither away and pass,[9]
So the world's self, thy other loved foe, is
In her decrepit wane, and thou, loving this,
Dost love a withered and worn strumpet; last,
40 Flesh (itself's death) and joys which flesh can taste
Thou lovest; and thy fair goodly soul, which doth
Give this flesh power to taste joy, thou dost loathe.
Seek true religion. O, where? Mirreus,[1]
Thinking her unhoused here, and fled from us,
45 Seeks her at Rome; there, because he doth know
That she was there a thousand years ago.
He loves her rags so, as we here obey
The statecloth[2] where the prince sat yesterday.
Crantz to such brave loves will not be enthralled,
50 But loves her only, who at Geneva is called
Religion—plain, simple, sullen, young,
Contemptuous, yet unhandsome; as among
Lecherous humors,° there is one that judges   *temperaments*
No wenches wholesome but coarse country drudges.
55 Graius stays still at home here, and because
Some preachers, vile ambitious bawds, and laws
Still new, like fashions, bid him think that she
Which dwells with us is only perfect, he
Embraceth her whom his godfathers will
60 Tender to him, being tender, as wards still
Take such wives as their guardians offer, or
Pay values.[3] Careless Phrygius doth abhor
All, because all cannot be good, as one
Knowing some women whores, dares marry none.
65 Graccus loves all as one, and thinks that so
As women do in divers countries go
In divers habits,° yet are still one kind,   *styles of clothing*
So doth, so is religion; and this blind-
ness too much light breeds;[4] but unmoved thou
70 Of force° must one, and forced but one allow;   *necessity*
And the right; ask thy father which is she,
Let him ask his; though truth and falsehood be
Near twins, yet truth a little elder is;
Be busy to seek her, believe me this,
75 He's not of none, nor worst, that seeks the best.[5]
To adore, or scorn an image, or protest,

---

9. The common belief that the world was growing old and becoming decrepit.
1. The satiric types in this passage represent
different creeds: "Mirreus" is a Roman Catholic;
"Crantz," an austere Calvinist Presbyterian of
Geneva; "Graius," a Church of England Erastian
who believes in any religion sponsored by the
state; "Phrygius," a skeptic; and "Graccus," a complete relativist.
2. The royal canopy, a symbol of kingly power.

3. If minors in care of a guardian (in wardship)
rejected the wives offered ("tendered") to them
they had to pay fines ("values").
4. I.e., Graccus considers the differences between
religions merely incidental, like women's clothes,
but his apparently tolerant, "enlightened" attitude
is itself a form of blindness.
5. The person who seeks the best church is neither an unbeliever nor the worst sort of believer.

May all be bad; doubt wisely; in strange way
To stand inquiring right, is not to stray;
To sleep, or run wrong, is. On a huge hill,
80 Cragged and steep, Truth stands, and he that will
Reach her, about must, and about must go,
And what the hill's suddenness resists, win so;
Yet strive so, that before age, death's twilight,
Thy soul rest, for none can work in that night.[6]
85 To will° implies delay, therefore now do. *intend a future act*
Hard deeds, the body's pains; hard knowledge too
The mind's endeavors reach,° and mysteries *achieve*
Are like the sun, dazzling, yet plain to all eyes.
Keep the truth which thou hast found; men do not stand
90 In so ill case here, that God hath with his hand
Signed kings' blank charters to kill whom they hate,
Nor are they vicars, but hangmen to fate.[7]
Fool and wretch, wilt thou let thy soul be tied
To man's laws, by which she shall not be tried
95 At the last day? O, will it then boot° thee *profit*
To say a Philip, or a Gregory,
A Harry, or a Martin taught thee this?[8]
Is not this excuse for mere° contraries *complete*
Equally strong? Cannot both sides say so?
100 That thou mayest rightly obey power, her bounds know;
Those passed, her nature and name is changed; to be
Then humble to her is idolatry.
As streams are, power is; those blest flowers that dwell
At the rough stream's calm head, thrive and prove well,
105 But having left their roots, and themselves given
To the stream's tyrannous rage, alas, are driven
Through mills, and rocks, and woods, and at last, almost
Consumed in going, in the sea are lost:
So perish souls, which more choose men's unjust
110 Power from God claimed, than God himself to trust.

1633

Sappho to Philaenis[1]

Where is that holy fire, which verse is said
To have? Is that enchanting force decayed?
Verse, that draws° Nature's works, from° Nature's law, *copies / according to*
Thee, her best work, to her work[2] cannot draw.

---

6. Echoes John 9.4, "the night cometh, when no man can work."
7. Kings are not God's vicars on earth, with license ("blank charters") to persecute or kill whomever they wish on grounds of religion.
8. "Philip" is Philip II of Spain, "Gregory" is Pope Gregory XIII or XIV, "Harry" is England's Henry VIII, and "Martin" is Martin Luther.
1. A heroic epistle, modeled on Ovid's *Heroi-* des, erotic poems set forth as letters between famous lovers and often with female speakers. Sappho was a famous woman poet of Lesbos (b. 612 B.C.E.). Her poems to her several female lovers made "lesbian" a term for same-sex love between women.
2. I.e., you are not drawn to sexual intimacy ("Nature's work") by poetry, which imitates nature's works.

5   Have my tears quenched my old poetic fire;
      Why quenched they not as well, that of desire?
Thoughts, my mind's creatures, often are with thee,
      But I, their maker, want their liberty.
Only thine image in my heart doth sit,
10   But that is wax, and fires environ it.
My fires have driven, thine have drawn it hence;
      And I am robbed of picture, heart, and sense.
Dwells with me still mine irksome memory,
      Which both to keep and lose, grieves equally.
15 That tells me how fair thou art: thou art so fair,
      As gods, when gods to thee I do compare,
Are graced thereby;[3] and to make blind men see,
      What things gods are, I say they are like to thee.
For, if we justly call each silly° man   *ordinary*
20   A little world,[4] what shall we call thee then?
Thou art not soft, and clear, and straight, and fair,
      As down, as stars, cedars, and lilies are,
But thy right hand, and cheek, and eye, only
      Are like thy other hand, and cheek, and eye.
25 Such was my Phao[5] awhile, but shall be never,
      As thou wast, art, and, oh, mayst thou be ever.
Here lovers swear in their idolatry,
      That I am such; but grief discolors me.
And yet I grieve the less, lest grief remove
30   My beauty, and make me unworthy of thy love.
Plays some soft boy with thee, oh there wants yet
      A mutual feeling which should sweeten it.
His chin, a thorny hairy unevenness
      Doth threaten, and some daily change possess.
35 Thy body is a natural paradise,
      In whose self, unmanured,° all pleasure lies,   *untilled, unfertilized*
Nor needs perfection,[6] why shouldst thou then
      Admit the tillage of a harsh rough man?
Men leave behind them that which their sin shows,
40   And are as thieves traced, which rob when it snows.
But of our dalliance no more signs there are,
      Than fishes leave in streams, or birds in air.
And between us all sweetness may be had;
      All, all that Nature yields, or Art can add.
45 My two lips, eyes, thighs, differ from thy two,
      But so, as thine from one another do;
And, oh, no more; the likeness being such,
      Why should they not alike in all parts touch?
Hand to strange hand, lip to lip none denies;
50   Why should they breast to breast, or thighs to thighs?
Likeness begets such strange self-flattery,

---

3. I.e., when I compare you to gods it is they who
are exalted by the comparison.
4. The traditional belief that man is a microcosm containing in himself everything that is in
the entire world, the macrocosm.

5. Sappho was said to have loved a handsome
youth named Phaon.
6. A woman was said to receive "perfection" only
when she married and had sex with her husband.

That touching myself, all seems done to thee.
Myself I embrace, and mine own hands I kiss,
And amorously thank myself for this.
55 Me, in my glass,° I call thee; but alas,   *mirror*
     When I would kiss, tears dim mine eyes, and glass.
O cure this loving madness, and restore
     Me to me; thee, my half,[7] my all, my more.
So may thy cheeks' red outwear scarlet dye,[8]
60   And their white, whiteness of the galaxy,°   *the Milky Way*
So may thy mighty, amazing beauty move
     Envy in all women, and in all men, love,
And so be change, and sickness, far from thee,
     As thou by coming near, keep'st them from me.

1633

An Anatomy of the World: The First Anniversary

An Anatomy of the World: The First Anniversary   Donne composed and published this poem in 1611 to mark the first anniversary of the death of Elizabeth Drury, fifteen-year-old daughter of his patron and friend Sir Robert Drury. On the actual occasion of her death he composed a "Funeral Elegy," and on the second anniversary he wrote a companion poem to this one, titled *The Progress of the Soul: The Second Anniversary*, publishing all three poems together in 1612. This is not a poem about personal grief: responding to criticism of his wildly hyperbolic praises of Elizabeth, Donne commented that he had never met the young woman but intended rather to describe "the idea of a woman, and not as she was." Nor is this merely a poem to please a patron, though Donne obviously hoped to do that. Rather, as the full title indicates, Donne took the occasion of Elizabeth's untimely death to analyze (the term "anatomy" evokes both a rigorous logical analysis and a medical dissection in an anatomy theater) the corruption, decay, and disintegration of the world in all its aspects, due ultimately to the Fall of humankind. Here, the death of the young virgin Elizabeth epitomizes that loss and all its dire effects; in *The Second Anniversary* her death figures the soul's progress to heavenly glory. The marginal glosses on the left-hand side are by Donne, added in 1612.

An Anatomy of the World: The First Anniversary

The entry into the work.   When that rich soul which to her heaven is gone,
     Whom all they celebrate who know they have one
     (For who is sure he hath a soul, unless
     It see, and judge, and follow worthiness,
     And by deeds praise it? He who doth not this,   5
     May lodge an inmate soul, but 'tis not his);
     When that queen ended here her progress time,[1]
     And, as to her standing house,[2] to heaven did climb,
     Where, loath to make the saints attend° her long,   *await*
     She's now a part both of the choir and song,   10

7. Some manuscripts read "heart."
8. Sappho promises that her verse will preserve her lover's beauty and its fame.
1. "That queen" is the soul of Elizabeth Drury, implicitly compared to Queen Elizabeth, who liked to go on "progresses," formal visits from one country house to another.
2. I.e., her royal palace or permanent residence.

This world in that great earthquake languishèd;
For in a common bath of tears it bled,
Which drew the strongest vital spirits[3] out:
But succored° then with a perplexèd doubt,   *comforted*
Whether the world did lose or gain in this   15
(Because since now no other way there is
But goodness to see her, whom all would see,
All must endeavor to be good as she),
This great consumption° to a fever turned,   *wasting disease*
And so the world had fits; it joyed, it mourned.   20
And as men think that agues physic are,[4]
And the ague being spent, give over care,
So thou, sick world, mistak'st thyself to be
Well, when, alas, thou art in a lethargy.°   *in a near-death coma*
Her death did wound and tame thee then, and then   25
Thou might'st have better spared the sun, or man;
That wound was deep, but 'tis more misery
That thou hast lost thy sense and memory.
'Twas heavy° then to hear thy voice of moan,   *sad, depressing*
But this is worse, that thou art speechless grown.   30
Thou hast forgot thy name thou hadst; thou wast
Nothing but she, and her thou hast o'erpast.°   *outlived*
For as a child kept from the font,° until   *baptismal font*
A prince, expected long, come to fulfill
The ceremonies, thou unnamed had'st laid,   35
Had not her coming, thee her palace made:[5]
Her name defined thee, gave thee form and frame,
And thou forget'st to celebrate thy name.
    Some months she hath been dead (but being dead,
Measures of times are all determinèd),°   *ceased*
But long she hath been away, long, long, yet none
Offers to tell us who it is that's gone.
But as in states doubtful of future heirs,
When sickness without remedy impairs
The present prince, they're loath it should be said   45
The prince doth languish, or the prince is dead:
So mankind, feeling now a general thaw,°   *melting, disintegration*
A strong example gone, equal to law,
The cèment which did faithfully compact
And glue all virtues, now resolved,° and slacked,   *dissolved*
Thought it some blasphemy to say she was dead,
Or that our weakness was discoverèd°   *disclosed*
In that confession; therefore spoke no more
Than tongues, the soul being gone, the loss deplore.
But though it be too late to succor thee,   55
Sick world, yea, dead, yea, putrefied, since she,
Thy intrinsic balm[6] and thy preservative,

3. "Vital spirits" of the blood were mysterious agents supposed to link soul with body.
4. "Ague" is chills and fever. "Physic": medicine. Some people think the fever stage of the disease is itself a cure.

5. The sick world is still being addressed; until it was made her palace, the world was a nameless nothing.
6. A medicine that preserved one in perfect health forever.

Can never be renewed, thou never live,
I (since no man can make thee live) will try
What we may gain by thy anatomy.[7]   60
Her death hath taught us dearly that thou art
Corrupt and mortal in thy purest part.
    Let no man say, the world itself being dead,
'Tis labor lost to have discoverèd
The world's infirmities, since there is none   65
Alive to study this dissection;

What life the world
hath still. For there's a kind of world remaining still,
Though she which did inanimate and fill
The world be gone, yet in this last long night,
Her ghost doth walk; that is, a glimmering light,   70
A faint weak love of virtue and of good
Reflects from her on them which understood
Her worth; and though she have shut in all day,
The twilight of her memory doth stay;
Which, from the carcass of the old world free,   75
Creates a new world; and new creatures be
Produced:[8] the matter and the stuff of this,
Her virtue, and the form our practice is;
And though to be thus elemented,° arm   *constituted*
These creatures, from home-born intrinsic harm   80
(For all assumed° unto this dignity   *raised*
So many weedless Paradises be,
Which of themselves produce no venomous sin,
Except some foreign serpent bring it in),
Yet, because outward storms the strongest break,   85
And strength itself by confidence grows weak,
This new world may be safer, being told

The sickness of the
world. The dangers and diseases of the old:
For with due temper men do then forgo
Or covet things, when they their true worth know.   90

Impossibility of
health.   There is no health; physicians say that we
At best enjoy but a neutrality.
And can there be worse sickness than to know
That we are never well, nor can be so?
We are born ruinous;° poor mothers cry   *falling into ruin*
That children come not right, nor orderly,
Except they headlong come and fall upon
An ominous precipitation.[9]
How witty's° ruin! How importunate   *ingenious is*
Upon mankind! It labored to frustrate   100
Even God's purpose; and made woman, sent
For man's relief, cause of his languishment.
They were to good ends, and they are so still,
But accessory, and principal in ill.[1]

---

7. I.e., by dissecting and analyzing the world's corpse.
8. The sun was thought to have power to breed new life out of carcasses and mud.
9. "We do not make account that a child comes right, except it come with the head forward, and

thereby prefigure that headlong falling into calamities which it must suffer after" (Donne, *Sermons*, ed. Potter and Simpson, 4.333).
1. Women are helpers in good but leaders in evil. "That first marriage" (line 105): Adam and Eve's.

For that first marriage was our funeral: 105
One woman at one blow then killed us all,
And singly, one by one, they kill us now.
We do delightfully ourselves allow
To that consumption; and profusely blind,
We kill ourselves to propagate our kind.[2]   110
    And yet we do not that; we are not men:
There is not now that mankind which was then

Shortness of life.

When as the sun and man did seem to strive
(Joint tenants[3] of the world) who should survive;
When stag and raven and the long-lived tree,   115
Compared with man, died in minority;[4]
When, if a slow-paced star had stolen away
From the observer's marking, he might stay
Two or three hundred years to see it again,
And then make up his observation plain;   120
When, as the age was long, the size was great;
Man's growth confessed and recompensed the meat;[5]
So spacious and large, that every soul
Did a fair kingdom and large realm control;
And when the very stature, thus erect,   125
Did that soul a good way towards heaven direct.
Where is this mankind now? Who lives to age
Fit to be made Methusalem his page?
Alas, we scarce live long enough to try
Whether a new-made clock run right, or lie.   130
Old grandsires talk of yesterday with sorrow,
And for our children we reserve tomorrow.
So short is life that every peasant strives,
In a torn house, or field, to have three lives.[6]
    And as in lasting, so in length is man   135

Smallness of stature.

Contracted to an inch, who was a span;[7]
For had a man at first in forests strayed,
Or shipwrecked in the sea, one would have laid
A wager that an elephant or whale
That met him would not hastily assail   140
A thing so equal to him: now, alas,
The fairies and the pygmies well may pass
As credible; mankind decays so soon,
We're scarce our fathers' shadows cast at noon.
Only death adds to our length:[8] nor are we grown   145
In stature to be men, till we are none.
But this were light,° did our less volume hold   *a trifle*
All the old text, or had we changed to gold

2. Popular superstition had it that every act of sex shortened one's life by a day.
3. Joint owners. The survivor would enjoy sole ownership.
4. Stags, ravens, and oak trees were thought to live particularly long, but compared with early humans, they died in youth.
5. Early humans were thought to have eaten better than modern humans, lived longer, and grown to greater stature. Methuselah ("Methusalem," below) is said to have lived 969 years (Genesis 5.27).
6. Leases of farmland were often made for "three lives," i.e., through the longest-lived of three designated persons.
7. I.e., the distance from the tip of the thumb to the tip of the little finger, about nine inches.
8. The corpse of a person was said to measure a little more than his or her height when alive.

Their silver; or disposed into less glass
Spirits of virtue,[9] which then scattered was.   150
But 'tis not so: we're not retired, but damped;[1]
And as our bodies, so our minds are cramped:
'Tis shrinking, not close weaving, that hath thus
In mind and body both bedwarfèd us.
We seem ambitious, God's whole work to undo;   155
Of nothing He made us, and we strive, too,
To bring ourselves to nothing back; and we
Do what we can to do it so soon as He.
With new diseases[2] on ourselves we war,
And with new physic,[3] a worse engine° far.   *contrivance*
     Thus man, this world's vice-emperor, in whom
All faculties, all graces are at home—
And if in other creatures they appear,
They're but man's ministers and legates there,
To work on their rebellions, and reduce   165
Them to civility, and to man's use—
This man, whom God did woo, and loath to attend°   *wait*
Till man came up, did down to man descend,
This man, so great, that all that is, is his,
Oh what a trifle, and poor thing he is!   170
If man were anything, he's nothing now:
Help, or at least some time to waste, allow°   *one might give*
To his other wants, yet when he did depart°   *part*
With her whom we lament, he lost his heart.
     She, of whom th' ancients seemed to prophesy   175
When they called virtues by the name of *she*;[4]
She in whom virtue was so much refined
That for allay° unto so pure a mind   *alloy*
She took the weaker sex, she that could drive
The poisonous tincture, and the stain of Eve,   180
Out of her thoughts and deeds, and purify
All, by a true religious alchemy;
She, she is dead; she's dead: when thou knowest this,
Thou knowest how poor a trifling thing man is.
And learn'st thus much by our anatomy,   185
The heart being perished, no part can be free.
And that except thou feed (not banquet[5]) on
The supernatural food, religion,
Thy better growth grows witherèd and scant;
Be more than man, or thou'rt less than an ant.   190
     Then, as mankind, so is the world's whole frame
Quite out of joint, almost created lame:
For, before God had made up all the rest,
Corruption entered and depraved the best.

9. I.e., distilled virtue, which would fit into a smaller bottle. "Virtue" includes the sense of "power" as well as that of "goodness."
1. I.e., not compressed but shrunk.
2. I.e., influenza, and especially syphilis.
3. New medications—said to be far worse than the diseases they ostensibly combated.
4. The virtues are all represented in Latin by feminine nouns and portrayed as female figures.
5. Taste, nibble. A banquet usually contained desserts and delicacies.

It seized the angels,[6] and then first of all 195
The world did in her cradle take a fall,
And turned her brains, and took a general maim,
Wronging each joint of th' universal frame.
The noblest part, man, felt it first; and then

Decay of nature in other parts.

Both beasts and plants, cursed in the curse of man.[7] 200
So did the world from the first hour decay,
That evening was beginning of the day,[8]
And now the springs and summers which we see
Like sons of women after fifty be.[9]
And new philosophy calls all in doubt: 205
The element of fire is quite put out;[1]
The sun is lost, and the earth, and no man's wit° *intellect*
Can well direct him where to look for it.
And freely men confess that this world's spent,° *exhausted*
When in the planets and the firmament° *sky*
They seek so many new;[2] they see that this
Is crumbled out again to his atomies.° *atoms*
'Tis all in pieces, all coherence gone;
All just supply, and all relation:
Prince, subject; father, son,[3] are things forgot, 215
For every man alone thinks he hath got
To be° a phoenix, and that there can be *has become*
None of that kind of which he is, but he.[4]
    This is the world's condition now, and now
She that should all parts to reunion bow, 220
She that had all magnetic force alone,
To draw and fasten sundered parts in one;
She whom wise nature had invented then
When she observed that every sort of men
Did in their voyage in this world's sea stray, 225
And needed a new compass for their way;
She that was best, and first original
Of all fair copies, and the general
Steward to Fate;[5] she whose rich eyes and breast
Gilt the West Indies, and perfumed the East;[6] 230
Whose having breathed in this world did bestow
Spice on those isles, and bade them still smell so,
And that rich Indie which doth gold inter
Is but as single money,° coined from her; *small change*
She to whom this world must itself refer 235

6. The angels who fell from heaven with Satan and became demons. As purely intellectual beings, angels are the world's "brains" (line 197).
7. For a similar account of the way humankind's fall corrupted the physical universe, see *Paradise Lost* 10.706ff.
8. The world's day began with the darkness of sin.
9. Women giving birth after the age of fifty were thought to produce feeble or defective children.
1. The Polish astronomer Copernicus in the 16th century and the Italian Galileo in the 17th argued a "new philosophy," that the sun, not the earth, was the center of the cosmos. This theory also

contradicted the notion that a realm of fire surrounded the earth beyond the air.
2. Galileo's first accounts of his telescope observations were published in 1610, intensifying speculations as to whether there were other inhabited worlds.
3. I.e., all traditional relationships.
4. Legend had it that there was only one phoenix on earth at any one time.
5. Fate or Providence disposes all things, but she was their "Steward," dispensing what has been decreed.
6. The West Indies were a source of gold, the East Indies a source of spices and perfumes.

As suburbs, or the microcosm of her,
She, she is dead; she's dead: when thou know'st this,
Thou know'st how lame a cripple this world is.
And learn'st thus much by our anatomy,
That this world's general sickness doth not lie   240
In any humor,[7] or one certain part;
But, as thou sawest it rotten at the heart,
Thou seest a hectic° fever hath got hold   *consumptive*
Of the whole substance, not to be controlled,
And that thou hast but one way not to admit   245
The world's infection, to be none of it.
For the world's subtlest immaterial parts
Feel this consuming wound, and age's darts.
For the world's beauty is decayed, or gone,

Deformity of parts.   Beauty, that's color and proportion.   250
We think the heavens enjoy their spherical
Their round proportion embracing all,[8]
But yet their various and perplexed° course,   *tangled, involuted*
Observed in divers ages doth enforce
Men to find out° so many eccentric parts,   *invent*
Such divers downright lines, such overthwarts,
As disproportion that pure form.[9] It tears
The firmament in eight and forty shires[1]
And in those constellations there arise
New stars, and old do vanish from our eyes,[2]   260
As though heaven suffered earthquakes, peace or war,
When new towns rise, and old demolished are.
They have impaled° within a zodiac[3]   *enclosed, imprisoned*
The freeborn sun, and keep twelve signs awake
To watch his steps, the Goat and Crab[4] control,   265
And fright him back, who else to either pole
(Did not those tropics fetter him) might run:
For his course is not round, nor can the sun
Perfect a circle, or maintain his way
One inch direct, but where he rose today   270
He comes no more,[5] but with a cozening° line,   *deceptive*
Steals by that point, and so is serpentine.

7. The four bodily "humors"—blood, phlegm, bile, choler—were thought to combine to make up a temperament; when they are out of balance a person is ill. So with the world.
8. The heavenly spheres' "course" was traditionally supposed to be "spherical," "round," but deviations and irregular motions ("eccentric parts," line 255) had long been recognized in the Ptolemaic system, and elliptical movements were posited by recent astronomers like Kepler.
9. Plato wrote that the heavenly bodies moved in perfect circles (a "pure form"). The "disproportion" of that form is marked in astronomical charts, with vertical ("downright") lines that crisscross horizontal lines ("overthwarts").
1. In the Ptolemaic system, the stars were divided into forty-eight constellations.
2. The traditional understanding was that the heavens are not subject to change. The modern astronomers Kepler and Brahe discovered "new stars," and Galileo's *Siderius Nuncius* (1610) revealed the discovery of four satellites of Jupiter and innumerable fixed stars. Other stars were observed to disappear.
3. A great circle of twelve star-groups (Aquarius, Pisces, Cancer, Capricorn, etc.) through which the sun passes in its supposed annual movement from west to east and north to south.
4. The Tropic of Capricorn (the "Goat") marks the sun's winter solstice and the Tropic of Cancer (the "Crab") its summer solstice, the points farthest north and south in its apparent annual journey.
5. The sun's path crosses the equator at a point slightly farther on each year, deviating from a circular path in a "serpentine" motion.

And seeming weary with his reeling thus,
He means to sleep, being now fall'n nearer us.[6]
So, of the stars which boast that they do run   275
In circle still, none ends where he begun.
All their proportion's lame, it sinks, it swells,
For of meridians, and parallels,[7]
Man hath weaved out a net, and this net thrown
Upon the heavens, and now they are his own.   280
Loth to go up the hill,[8] or labor thus
To go to heaven, we make heaven come to us.
We spur, we rein the stars, and to their race
They're diversely content t'obey our pace.
But keeps the earth her round proportion still?   285
Doth not a Tenerife,[9] or higher hill
Rise so high like a rock, that one might think
The floating moon would shipwreck there, and sink?
Seas are so deep, that whales being struck° today,   *harpooned*
Perchance tomorrow, scarce at middle way   290
Of their wished journey's end, the bottom, die.
And men, to sound depths, so much line untie
As one might think that there would rise
At end thereof, one of th'Antipodes.[1]
If under all, a vault infernal[2] be,   295
(Which sure is spacious,° except that we   *three syllables*
Invent another torment, that there must
Millions into a strait° hot room be thrust)   *narrow*
Then solidness, and roundness have no place.
Are these but warts, and pock-holes in the face   300
Of the earth? Think so. But yet confess, in this,
The world's proportion° disfigured is,   *four syllables*

Disorder in the world.   That those two legs whereon it doth rely,
Reward and punishment, are bent awry.°   *out of shape*
And oh! It can no more be questioned°   *three syllables*
That beauty's best, proportion, is dead,
Since even grief itself, which now alone
Is left us, is without proportion.
She by whose lines proportion should be
Examined, measure of all symmetry,   310
Whom had that Ancient[3] seen, who thought souls made
Of harmony, he would at next have said
That harmony was she, and thence infer
That souls were but resultances° from her   *emanations*
And did from her into our bodies go   315

---

6. Looking to the calculations of ancient astronomers, some Early Modern thinkers (e.g., Melancthon, Bodin, Hakewell) thought the sun was progressing closer to the earth.
7. Celestial longitude and latitude.
8. Commonplace symbol of the difficult path to heaven or to virtue.
9. The highest peak on the island of Tenerife in the Canary Islands, which rises sharply to around 12,000 feet, a standard reference in discussions of the earth's sphericity.
1. People on the other side of the world whose feet were supposedly planted opposite to ours. The belief was revived by Renaissance explorers.
2. Hell was traditionally located in the center of the earth; Dante imagined its several circles as crowded with the damned.
3. Probably Pythagoras, or Plato.

As to our eyes, the forms from objects flow.[4]
She, who if those great doctors truly said
That th'Ark to man's proportions was made,[5]
Had been a type for that, as that might be
A type of her in this, that contrary   320
Both elements and passions lived at peace
In her, who caused all civil wars to cease.
She, after whom, what form soe'er we see
Is discord, and rude incongruity.
She, she is dead, she's dead, when thou know'st this   325
Thou know'st how vile a monster this world is,
And learn'st thus much by our Anatomy,
That here is nothing to enamor thee;
And that, not only faults in inward parts,
Corruptions in our brains, or in our hearts,   330
Poisoning the fountains whence our actions spring
Endanger us, but that if everything
Be not done fitly and in proportion
To satisfy wise and good lookers on
(Since most men be such as most think they be)   335
They're loathsome too, by this deformity,
For good, and well,° must in our actions meet: *seemly, decorous*
Wicked is not much worse than indiscreet.
But beauty's other second element,
Color, and luster now, is as near spent   340
And had the world his just proportion,
Were it a ring still, yet the stone is gone.
As a compassionate turquoise which doth tell
By looking pale, the wearer is not well,[6]
As gold falls sick being stung with mercury[7]   345
All the world's parts of such complexion be.
When nature was most busy, the first week,[8]
Swaddling the newborn earth, God seemed to like
That she should sport herself sometimes, and play
To mingle, and vary colors every day.   350
And then, as though she could not make enow°   *enough*
Himself his various° rainbow did allow.   *multicolored*
Sight is the noblest sense of any one,
Yet sight hath only color to feed on,
And color is decayed: summer's robe grows   355
Dusky, and like an oft-dyed garment shows.
Our blushing red, which used in cheeks to spread,
Is inward sunk, and only our souls are red.[9]
Perchance the world might have recovered,

4. A theory ascribed to Aristotle held that objects emit rays that imprint the forms of those objects upon our eyes and mind.
5. Both Ambrose and Augustine held that Noah's Ark was built to the proportions of the human body, so "she" can be said to be a type of the Ark, and the Ark (in regard to the harmony of the animals it contained) a type of her.
6. Turquoise was believed to gain or lose luster reflecting the wearer's state of health.
7. An amalgam of gold and mercury is lighter in color, and of much less value, than pure gold.
8. The six days of creation described in Genesis 1, when the earth was clothed ("swaddled," like a newborn) with all forms of life.
9. Blushing red indicates innocence; souls are red with sin and guilt.

If she, whom we lament had not been dead.   360
But she, in whom all white, and red, and blue[1]
(Beauty's ingredients) voluntary grew,
As in an unvexed Paradise;° from whom   *unfallen Eden*
Did all things verdure,° and their luster come,   *grow green*
Whose composition was miraculous,   365
Being all color, all diaphanous
(For air and fire but thick gross bodies were,[2]
And liveliest stones but drowsy and pale to her,)
She, she is dead, she's dead: when thou know'st this,
Thou know'st how wan a ghost this our world is,   370
And learn'st thus much by our anatomy,
That it should more affright, than pleasure thee.
And that, since all fair color then did sink,
'Tis now but wicked vanity to think
To color vicious deeds with good pretence,   375
Or with bought colors to elude° men's sense,   *deceive*

Weakness in   Nor in ought more this world's decay appears,
the want of   Than that her influence the heav'n forbears,
correspondence of Or that the elements do not feel this.
heaven and earth. The father, or the mother, barren is.[3]   380
The clouds conceive not rain, or do not pour
In the due birth-time down their balmy[4] shower.
Th'air doth not motherly sit on the earth,
To hatch her seasons, and give all things birth,
Spring-times were common cradles, but are tombs,   385
And false conceptions° fill the general womb.   *abortions,*
Th'air shows such meteors,[5] as none can see,   *monsters*
Not only what they mean, but what they be.
Earth such new worms, as would have troubled much
Th'Egyptian mages to have made more such.[6]   390
What artist° now dares boast that he can bring   *alchemist or*
Heaven hither, or constellate[7] anything   *astrologer*
So as the influence of those stars may be
Imprisoned in an herb, or charm, or tree,
And do by touch all which those stars could do?   395
The art is lost, and correspondence[8] too.
For heaven gives little, and the earth takes less,
And man least knows their trade, and purposes.
If this commerce twixt heaven and earth were not
Embarred,° and all this traffic quite forgot,   *stopped, blocked*
She, for whose loss we have lamented thus,
Would work more fully and pow'rfully on us.
Since herbs and roots by dying, lose not all,

---

1. White symbolizes innocence, red, love, and blue, truth.
2. Air and fire were thought to be the lightest and purest of the four elements.
3. Either the stars and planets (the father) withhold their influence or the earth's elements (the mother) are not receptive, making for barrenness.
4. Balm was thought to preserve and heal.

5. Especially comets, thought to portend disaster.
6. Egyptian magicians ("mages") turned their rods into serpents ("worms"), Exodus 7.10–12.
7. Bring the stars together, or judge when their conjunction is favorable.
8. The close link between heaven and earth so that the powers of the various heavenly bodies are contained ("imprisoned") in particular herbs or stones, which can cure by "touch."

But they, yea ashes too, are medicinal,[9]
Death could not quench her virtue[1] so, but that   405
It would be (if not followed) wondered at:
And all the world would be one dying swan,[2]
To sing her funeral praise, and vanish then.
But as some serpents' poison hurteth not,
Except it be from the live serpent shot,[3]   410
So doth her virtue need her here, to fit
That unto us; she working more than it.
But she, in whom, to such maturity
Virtue was grown, past growth, that it must die,
She from whose influence all impressions came,   415
But, by receivers' impotencies, lame,
Who, though she could not transubstantiate°   *change the*
All states to gold, yet gilded every state,   *substance of*
So that some princes have some temperance,
Some counselors some purpose to advance   420
The common profit; and some people have
Some stay,° no more than kings should give, to crave; *restraint*
Some women have some taciturnity,
Some nunneries, some grains of chastity.
She, that thus much, and much more could do,   425
But that our age was iron, and rusty too,[4]
She, she is dead, she's dead: when thou know'st this
Thou know'st how dry a cinder this world is.
And learn'st thus much by our Anatomy,
That 'tis in vain to dew, or mollify°   *soften*
It with thy tears, or sweat, or blood: no thing
Is worth our travail, grief, or perishing,
But those rich joys, which did possess her heart,
Of which she's now partaker, and a part.

Conclusion.   But as in cutting up a man that's dead,   435
The body will not last out to have read
On every part, and therefore men direct
Their speech to parts that are of most effect;
So the world's carcass would not last, if I
Were punctual° in this Anatomy.   *detailed, point by point*
Nor smells it well to hearers, if one tell
Them their disease, who fain would think they're well.
Here therefore be the end: And, blessed maid,
Of whom is meant whatever hath been said,
Or shall be spoken well by any tongue,   445
Whose name refines coarse lines, and makes prose song,
Accept this tribute, and his first year's rent,
Who till his dark short taper's° end be spent,   *candle*

9. Healing power was thought to remain in certain dead herbs and roots, as well as in their ashes after burning.
1. Power, goodness.
2. Swans were believed to sing just once, before their deaths.
3. The allusion conflates the poison with which the first serpent (Satan) infected humankind, with the curative power against snakebite pos-

sessed by the serpent of brass that Moses raised up to cure the Israelites (Numbers 21.6–9)—identified by Christian biblical commentators as a type of Christ.
4. The present is the last of the legendary four ages—gold, silver, bronze, and iron—through which history was said to pass, each marking a decline.

As oft as thy feast° sees this widowed earth,   *saint's feastday*
Will yearly celebrate thy second birth,   450
That is, thy death. For though the soul of man
Be got when man is made, 'tis born but then
When man doth die. Our body's as the womb,
And as a midwife death directs it home.
And you her creatures, whom she works upon   455
And have your last, and best concoction°   *purification (in*
From her example, and her virtue, if you   *alchemy)*
In reverence to her, do think it due
That no one should her praises thus rehearse,
As matter fit for chronicle, not verse,[5]   460
Vouchsafe to call to mind, that God did make
A last, and lasting'st piece, a song.[6] He spake
To Moses, to deliver unto all
That song: because He knew they would let fall
The Law, the Prophets, and the History,[7]   465
But keep the song still in their memory.
Such an opinion (in due measure) made
Me this great office boldly to invade.
Nor could incomprehensibleness deter
Me from thus trying to imprison her.   470
Which when I saw that a strict grave could do,
I saw not why verse might not do so too.
Verse hath a middle nature: heaven keeps souls,
The grave keeps bodies, verse the fame enrolls.

1611

From Holy Sonnets[1]

1

Thou hast made me, and shall thy work decay?
Repair me now, for now mine end doth haste;
I run to death, and death meets me as fast,
And all my pleasures are like yesterday.
5 I dare not move my dim eyes any way,
Despair behind, and death before doth cast
Such terror, and my feeble flesh doth waste
By sin in it, which it towards hell doth weigh.°   *incline, weigh down*
Only thou art above, and when towards thee

---

5. "Chronicle" history is the appropriate genre for recording the great events of rulers and kingdoms; verse can treat themes of love and other private matters. Cf. Donne's The "Canonization," page 928, lines 31–34.
6. The Mosaic song in Deuteronomy 32.1–43 celebrating God's mercy to the Israelites, and threat of vengeance against them if they abandon him.
7. The books of the Hebrew Bible were often divided into these three categories.

1. Donne wrote a variety of religious poems (called "Divine Poems"), including a group of nineteen "holy sonnets" that reflect his interest in Jesuit and Protestant meditative procedures. He probably began writing them about 1609, a decade or so after leaving the Catholic Church. Our selections follow the traditional numbering established in Sir Herbert Grierson's influential edition, since for most of these sonnets we cannot tell when they were written or in what order they were intended to appear.

10   By thy leave I can look, I rise again;
But our old subtle foe so tempteth me
That not one hour myself I can sustain.
Thy grace may wing° me to prevent° his art,   *give wings to / forestall*
And thou like adamant° draw mine iron heart.   *magnetic lodestone*

1635

5

I am a little world[2] made cunningly
Of elements, and an angelic sprite;°   *spirit, soul*
But black sin hath betrayed to endless night
My world's both parts, and O, both parts must die.
5   You which beyond that heaven which was most high
Have found new spheres, and of new lands can write,[3]
Pour new seas in mine eyes, that so I might
Drown my world with my weeping earnestly,
Or wash it if it must be drowned no more.[4]
10   But O, it must be burnt! Alas, the fire
Of lust and envy have burnt it heretofore,
And made it fouler; let their flames retire,
And burn me, O Lord, with a fiery zeal
Of thee and thy house, which doth in eating heal.[5]

1635

7

At the round earth's imagined corners,[6] blow
Your trumpets, angels; and arise, arise
From death, you numberless infinities
Of souls, and to your scattered bodies go:
5   All whom the flood did, and fire[7] shall, o'erthrow,
All whom war, dearth,° age, agues,° tyrannies,   *famine / fevers*
Despair, law, chance hath slain, and you whose eyes
Shall behold God, and never taste death's woe.[8]
But let them sleep, Lord, and me mourn a space;
10   For, if above all these, my sins abound,
'Tis late to ask abundance of thy grace
When we are there. Here on this lowly ground,
Teach me how to repent; for that's as good
As if thou hadst sealed my pardon with thy blood.

1633

2. The traditional idea of the human being as microcosm (a "little world"), containing in miniature all the features of the macrocosm, or great world.
3. Astronomers, especially Galileo, and explorers.
4. God promised Noah (Genesis 9.11) never to flood the earth again.
5. See Psalm 69.9: "For the zeal of thine house hath eaten me up." These lines refer to three kinds of flame—those of the Last Judgment, those of lust and envy, and those of zeal, which alone save.
6. Cf. Revelation 7.1: "I saw four angels standing on the four corners of the earth."
7. Noah's flood, and the universal conflagration at the end of the world (Revelation 6.11).
8. Those who will be alive at the Second Coming (cf. Luke 9.27).

9

If poisonous minerals, and if that tree[9]
Whose fruit threw death on else-immortal us,
If lecherous goats, if serpents envious[1]
Cannot be damned, alas! why should I be?
5 Why should intent or reason, born in me,
Make sins, else equal, in me more heinous?
And, mercy being easy and glorious
To God, in his stern wrath why threatens he?
But who am I that dare dispute with thee
10 O God? Oh, of thine only worthy blood
And my tears, make a heavenly Lethean[2] flood,
And drown in it my sin's black memory.
That thou remember them some claim as debt;
I think it mercy if thou wilt forget.[3]

1633

10

Death, be not proud, though some have callèd thee
Mighty and dreadful, for thou art not so;
For those whom thou think'st thou dost overthrow
Die not, poor Death, nor yet canst thou kill me.
5 From rest and sleep, which but thy pictures be,
Much pleasure; then from thee much more must flow,
And soonest our best men with thee do go,
Rest of their bones, and soul's delivery.[4]
Thou art slave to fate, chance, kings, and desperate men,
10 And dost with poison, war, and sickness dwell,
And poppy° or charms can make us sleep as well   *opium*
And better than thy stroke; why swell'st° thou then?   *puff with pride*
One short sleep past, we wake eternally
And death shall be no more; Death, thou shalt die.[5]

1633

11

Spit in my face ye Jews, and pierce my side,
Buffet, and scoff,° scourge, and crucify me,   *scoff at*
For I have sinned, and sinned, and only he,
Who could do no iniquity, hath died:
5 But by my death cannot be satisfied°   *atoned for*

---

9. The Tree of Knowledge of Good and Evil, whose fruit was forbidden to Adam and Eve in Eden.
1. Traits commonly associated with these creatures.
2. In classical mythology, the waters of the river Lethe in the underworld caused total forgetfulness.

3. Cf. Jeremiah 31.34: "I will forgive their iniquity, and I will remember their sins no more."
4. I.e., to find rest for their bones and freedom ("delivery") for their souls.
5. Cf. 1 Corinthians 15.26: "The last enemy that shall be destroyed is death."

My sins, which pass the Jews' impiety:
They killed once an inglorious° man, but I   obscure
Crucify him daily,[6] being now glorified.
Oh let me then, his strange love still admire:°   wonder at
10   Kings pardon, but he bore our punishment.[7]
And Jacob came clothed in vile harsh attire
But to supplant, and with gainful intent:[8]
God clothed himself in vile man's flesh, that so
He might be weak enough to suffer woe.

1633

13

What if this present were the world's last night?
Mark in my heart, O soul, where thou dost dwell,
The picture of Christ crucified, and tell
Whether that countenance can thee affright.
5   Tears in his eyes quench the amazing light,
Blood fills his frowns, which from his pierced head fell;
And can that tongue adjudge thee unto hell
Which prayed forgiveness for his foes' fierce spite?
No, no; but as in my idolatry
10   I said to all my profane° mistresses,   secular
Beauty of pity, foulness only is
A sign of rigor:[9] so I say to thee,
To wicked spirits are horrid shapes assigned,
This beauteous form assures a piteous mind.

1633

14

Batter my heart, three-personed God; for you
As yet but knock, breathe, shine, and seek to mend;
That I may rise and stand, o'erthrow me, and bend
Your force to break, blow, burn, and make me new.
5   I, like an usurped town, to another due,
Labor to admit you, but O, to no end;
Reason, your viceroy[1] in me, me should defend,
But is captived, and proves weak or untrue.
Yet dearly I love you, and would be loved fain,°   gladly
10   But am betrothed[2] unto your enemy.
Divorce me, untie or break that knot again;

---

6. Cf. Hebrews 6.6: "they [sinners] crucify to themselves the Son of God afresh."
7. Kings may pardon crimes, but the King of Kings, Christ, bore the punishment due to our sins.
8. Jacob disguised himself in goatskins to gain from his blind father the blessing belonging to the firstborn son, his brother Esau (Genesis 27.1–36).

9. In Neoplatonic theory, beautiful features are the sign of a compassionate mind, while ugliness signifies the contrary.
1. The governor in your stead.
2. Humanity's relationship with God has been described in terms of marriage and adultery from the time of the Hebrew prophets.

Take me to you, imprison me, for I,
Except° you enthrall me, never shall be free,   *unless*
Nor ever chaste, except you ravish[3] me.

1633

17

Since she whom I loved hath paid her last debt[4]
To Nature, and to hers, and my good is dead,
And her soul early into heaven ravishèd,
Wholly on heavenly things my mind is set.
5   Here the admiring her my mind did whet
To seek thee, God; so streams do show the head;°   *source*
But though I have found thee, and thou my thirst hast fed,
A holy thirsty dropsy° melts me yet.   *immoderate thirst*
But why should I beg more love, whenas thou
10 Dost woo my soul, for hers offering all thine:
And dost not only fear lest I allow
My love to saints and angels, things divine,
But in thy tender jealousy dost doubt°   *fear*
Lest the world, flesh, yea, devil put thee out.

1899

18

Show me, dear Christ, thy spouse[5] so bright and clear.
What! is it she which on the other shore
Goes richly painted? or which, robbed and tore,
Laments and mourns in Germany and here?[6]
5   Sleeps she a thousand, then peeps up one year?
Is she self-truth, and errs? now new, now outwore?
Doth she, and did she, and shall she evermore
On one, on seven, or on no hill appear?[7]
Dwells she with us, or like adventuring knights
10 First travel we to seek, and then make love?
Betray, kind husband, thy spouse to our sights,
And let mine amorous soul court thy mild dove,
Who is most true and pleasing to thee then
When she is embraced and open to most men.[8]

1899

---

3. Rape, also overwhelm with wonder. "Enthrall": enslave, also enchant.
4. Donne's wife died in 1617 at the age of thirty-three, having just given birth to her twelfth child. This very personal sonnet and the following two survive in a single manuscript discovered only in 1892.
5. The church is commonly called the bride of Christ. Cf. Revelation 19.7–8: "The marriage of the Lamb is come, and his wife hath made herself ready. / And to her was granted that she should be arrayed in fine linen, clean and white."

6. I.e., the painted woman (the Church of Rome) or the ravished virgin (the Lutheran and Calvinist churches in Germany and England).
7. The church on one hill is probably Solomon's temple on Mount Moriah; that on seven hills is the Church of Rome; that on no hill is the Presbyterian church of Geneva.
8. The final lines wittily rework, with startling sexual associations, Song of Solomon 5.2: "Open to me, my sister, my love, my dove, my undefiled." That biblical book was often interpreted as the song of love between Christ and the church.

19

Oh, to vex me, contraries meet in one:
Inconstancy unnaturally hath begot
A constant habit; that when I would not
I change in vows, and in devotion.
5   As humorous° is my contrition   *subject to whim*
As my profane love, and as soon forgot:
As riddlingly distempered, cold and hot,[9]
As praying, as mute, as infinite, as none.
I durst not view heaven yesterday; and today
10   In prayers and flattering speeches I court God:
Tomorrow I quake with true fear of his rod.
So my devout fits come and go away
Like a fantastic ague:[1] save° that here   *except*
Those are my best days, when I shake with fear.

1899

Good Friday, 1613. Riding Westward

Let man's soul be a sphere, and then, in this,
The intelligence that moves, devotion is,[1]
And as the other spheres, by being grown
Subject to foreign motions, lose their own,
5   And being by others hurried every day,
Scarce in a year their natural form[2] obey;
Pleasure or business, so, our souls admit
For° their first mover, and are whirled by it.   *instead of*
Hence is 't, that I am carried towards the West
10   This day, when my soul's form bends towards the East.
There I should see a Sun[3] by rising, set,
And by that setting endless day beget:
But that Christ on this cross did rise and fall,
Sin had eternally benighted all.
15   Yet dare I almost be glad I do not see
That spectacle, of too much weight for me.
Who sees God's face, that is self-life, must die;[4]
What a death were it then to see God die?
It made his own lieutenant,° Nature, shrink;   *deputy*
20   It made his footstool crack, and the sun wink.[5]

9. Arising from the unbalanced humors, inexplicably changeable.
1. A fever, attended with paroxysms of hot and cold and trembling fits. "Fantastic": capricious, extravagant.
1. As angelic intelligences guide the celestial spheres, so devotion is or should be the guiding principle of the soul.
2. Their true moving principle or intelligence. The orbit of the celestial spheres was thought to be governed by an unmoving outermost sphere, the primum mobile, or first mover (line 8), but sometimes outside influences ("foreign motions,"

line 4) deflected the spheres from their correct orbits.
3. The "sun" / "Son" pun was an ancient one. Christ the Son of God "set" when he rose on the Cross, and that setting (death) gave rise to the Christian era and the promise of immortality.
4. God told Moses, "Thou canst not see my face, for there shall no man see me, and live" (Exodus 33.20).
5. An earthquake and eclipse supposedly accompanied the Crucifixion (Matthew 27.45, 51). Cf. Isaiah 66.1: "Thus saith the Lord, The heaven is my throne, and the earth is my footstool."

Could I behold those hands which span the poles,
And tune[6] all spheres at once, pierced with those holes?
Could I behold that endless height which is
Zenith to us, and t'our antipodes,[7]
25   Humbled below us? Or that blood which is
The seat° of all our souls, if not of his,   *dwelling place*
Make dirt of dust, or that flesh which was worn
By God for his apparel, ragg'd and torn?
If on these things I durst not look, durst I
30   Upon his miserable mother cast mine eye,
Who was God's partner here, and furnished thus
Half of that sacrifice which ransomed us?
Though these things, as I ride, be from° mine eye,   *away from*
They are present yet unto my memory,
35   For that looks towards them; and thou look'st towards me,
O Savior, as thou hang'st upon the tree.
I turn my back to thee but to receive
Corrections,[8] till thy mercies bid thee leave.°   *cease*
O think me worth thine anger; punish me;
40   Burn off my rusts and my deformity;
Restore thine image so much, by thy grace,
That thou may'st know me, and I'll turn my face.

                                                            1633

A Hymn to Christ, at the Author's Last Going into Germany[1]

In what torn ship soever I embark,
That ship shall be my emblem of thy ark;°   *Noah's ark*
What sea soever swallow me, that flood
Shall be to me an emblem of thy blood;
5   Though thou with clouds of anger do disguise
Thy face, yet through that mask I know those eyes,
    Which, though they turn away sometimes, they never will despise.

I sacrifice this island° unto thee,   *England*
And all whom I loved there, and who loved me;
10   When I have put our seas twixt them and me,
Put thou thy sea[2] betwixt my sins and thee.
As the tree's sap doth seek the root below
In winter, in my winter now I go
    Where none but thee, th' eternal root of true love, I may know.

15   Nor thou nor thy religion dost control°   *censure, restrain*
The amorousness of an harmonious soul,

---

6. Some manuscripts read "turn."
7. God is at once the highest point for us and for our "antipodes," those who live on the opposite side of the earth.
8. Suggests a flogging.
1. Donne went to Germany in 1619 as chaplain to the earl of Doncaster. The mission was a diplomatic one, to the king and queen of Bohemia, King James's son-in-law and daughter, who at that time were mainstays of the Protestant cause on the Continent.
2. Sea of Christ's blood.

But thou wouldst have that love thyself; as thou
Art jealous, Lord, so I am jealous now.
Thou lov'st not, till from loving more[3] thou free
20 My soul; whoever gives, takes liberty;
    Oh, if thou car'st not whom I love, alas, thou lov'st not me.

Seal then this bill of my divorce to all
On whom those fainter beams of love did fall;
Marry those loves which in youth scattered be
25 On fame, wit, hopes (false mistresses) to thee.
Churches are best for prayer that have least light:
To see God only, I go out of sight,
    And to 'scape stormy days, I choose an everlasting night.

1633

Hymn to God My God, in My Sickness[1]

Since I am coming to that holy room
    Where, with thy choir of saints for evermore,
I shall be made thy music; as I come
    I tune the instrument here at the door,
5   And what I must do then, think now before.[2]

Whilst my physicians by their love are grown
    Cosmographers, and I their map, who lie
Flat on this bed, that by them may be shown
    That this is my southwest discovery[3]
10   *Per fretum febris*,[4] by these straits to die,

I joy, that in these straits, I see my West;
    For, though their currents yield return to none,
What shall my West hurt me? As West and East
    In all flat maps (and I am one) are one,[5]
15   So death doth touch the resurrection.

Is the Pacific Sea my home? Or are
    The Eastern riches?° Is Jerusalem?   *Cathay, China*
Anyan,[6] and Magellan, and Gibraltar,
    All straits, and none but straits, are ways to them,
20   Whether where Japhet dwelt, or Cham, or Shem.[7]

3. From loving any other thing.
1. Though Izaak Walton, Donne's friend and biographer, assigns this poem to the last days of his life, it was probably written during another illness, in December 1623.
2. This and the previous poem are less hymns (songs of praise) than meditations preparing (tuning the instrument) for such hymns.
3. South is the region of heat, west the region of sunset and death.
4. Through the straits of fever, with a pun on straits as sufferings, rigors, and a geographical reference to the Strait of Magellan.
5. If a flat map is pasted on a round globe, west and east meet.
6. Anian, a strait on the west coast of America, shown on early maps as separating America from Asia.
7. The three sons of Noah by whom the world was repopulated after the Flood (Genesis 10). The descendants of Japhet were thought to inhabit Europe; those of Cham (Ham), Africa; and those of Shem, Asia.

We think that Paradise and Calvary,
   Christ's cross and Adam's tree, stood in one place;
Look, Lord and find both Adams[8] met in me;
   As the first Adam's sweat surrounds my face,
25   May the last Adam's blood my soul embrace.

So, in his purple wrapped,[9] receive me, Lord;
   By these his thorns° give me his other crown;   *crown of thorns*
And, as to others' souls I preached thy word,
   Be this my text, my sermon to mine own:
30   Therefore that he may raise the Lord throws down.

                1635

A Hymn to God the Father[1]

Wilt thou forgive that sin where I begun,
   Which is my sin, though it were done before?[2]
Wilt thou forgive that sin through which I run,
   And do run still, though still I do deplore?
5   When thou hast done,[3] thou hast not done,
      For I have more.

Wilt thou forgive that sin by which I have won
   Others to sin? and made my sin their door?
Wilt thou forgive that sin which I did shun
10   A year or two, but wallowed in a score?
     When thou hast done, thou hast not done,
      For I have more.

I have a sin of fear, that when I have spun
   My last thread, I shall perish on the shore;
15   Swear by thy self, that at my death thy Son
   Shall shine as he shines now and heretofore;
     And, having done that, thou hast done,
      I fear[4] no more.

                1633

---

8. Adam and Christ. Legend had it that Christ's cross was erected on the spot, or at least in the region, where the tree forbidden to Adam in Eden had stood.
9. In his blood, also in his kingly robes.
1. This hymn was used as a congregational hymn. Walton tells us that Donne wrote it during his illness of 1623, had it set to music, and was delighted to hear it performed (as it frequently was) by the choir of St. Paul's Cathedral.
2. I.e., he inherits the original sin of Adam and Eve.
3. In the refrains, Donne puns on his own name and may pun on his wife's maiden name, Ann More.
4. Some manuscripts read "have."

From Devotions upon Emergent Occasions[1]

Meditation 4

Medicusque vocatur.
The physician is sent for.[2]

It is too little to call man a little world; except God, man is a diminutive to nothing.[3] Man consists of more pieces, more parts, than the world; than the world doth, nay, than the world is. And if those pieces were extended and stretched out in man as they are in the world, man would be the giant and the world the dwarf; the world but the map, and the man the world. If all the veins in our bodies were extended to rivers, and all the sinews to veins of mines, and all the muscles that lie upon one another to hills, and all the bones to quarries of stones, and all the other pieces to the proportion of those which correspond to them in the world, the air would be too little for this orb of man to move in, the firmament would be but enough for this star. For as the whole world hath nothing to which something in man doth not answer,[4] so hath man many pieces of which the whole world hath no representation. Enlarge this meditation upon this great world, man, so far as to consider the immensity of the creatures this world produces. Our creatures are our thoughts, creatures that are born giants, that reach from east to west, from earth to heaven, that do not only bestride all the sea and land, but span the sun and firmament at once: my thoughts reach all, comprehend all.

Inexplicable mystery! I their creator am in a close prison, in a sick bed, anywhere, and any one of my creatures, my thoughts, is with the sun, and beyond the sun, overtakes the sun, and overgoes the sun in one pace, one step, everywhere. And then as the other world produces serpents and vipers, malignant and venomous creatures, and worms and caterpillars, that endeavor to devour that world which produces them, and monsters compiled and complicated[5] of divers parents and kinds, so this world, our selves, produces all these in us, in producing diseases and sicknesses of all those sorts; venomous and infectious diseases, feeding and consuming diseases, and manifold and entangled diseases made up of many several ones. And can the other world name so many venomous, so many consuming, so many monstrous creatures, as we can diseases of all these kinds? O miserable abundance, O beggarly riches! How much do we lack of having remedies for every disease, when as yet we have not names for them?

1. Donne's *Devotions* were composed in the aftermath of his serious illness in the winter of 1623, though Donne characteristically writes as if the events of the illness were happening as he describes them. The *Devotions* recount in twenty-three sections the stages ("emergent occasions") of the illness and recovery: the term associates the exercise with a popular kind of Protestant meditation on the occasions that daily life presents to us. Each section contains a "meditation upon our human condition," an "expostulation and debatement with God," and a prayer to God. The book was published almost immediately, offering its meditation on an intensely personal experience as exemplary for others.
2. Donne's Latin epigraphs are followed by his English translations, often quite free.
3. This meditation is based on the notion that each human being is a microcosm, a little world, analogous in every respect to the macrocosm, or great world. But in playing with this notion, Donne paradoxically reverses it.
4. Correspond.
5. Mixed.

But we have a Hercules against these giants, these monsters: that is the physician. He musters up all the forces of the other world to succor this, all nature to relieve man. We have the physician but we are not the physician. Here we shrink in our proportion, sink in our dignity in respect of very mean creatures who are physicians to themselves. The hart that is pursued and wounded, they say, knows an herb which, being eaten, throws off the arrow: a strange kind of vomit.[6] The dog that pursues it, though he be subject to sickness, even proverbially knows his grass that recovers him. And it may be true that the drugger is as near to man as to other creatures; it may be that obvious and present simples,[7] easy to be had, would cure him; but the apothecary is not so near him, nor the physician so near him, as they two are to other creatures.[8] Man hath not that innate instinct to apply these natural medicines to his present danger, as those inferior creatures have. He is not his own apothecary, his own physician, as they are. Call back therefore thy meditation again, and bring it down.[9] What's become of man's great extent and proportion, when himself shrinks himself and consumes himself to a handful of dust? What's become of his soaring thoughts, his compassing thoughts, when himself brings himself to the ignorance, to the thoughtlessness, of the grave? His diseases are his own, but the physician is not; he hath them at home, but he must send for the physician.

Meditation 17

Nunc lento sonitu dicunt, morieris.
Now this bell tolling softly for another, says to me,
Thou must die.

Perchance he for whom this bell[1] tolls may be so ill as that he knows not it tolls for him; and perchance I may think myself so much better than I am, as that they who are about me and see my state may have caused it to toll for me, and I know not that. The church is catholic, universal, so are all her actions; all that she does belongs to all. When she baptizes a child, that action concerns me; for that child is thereby connected to that head which is my head too, and ingrafted into that body[2] whereof I am a member. And when she buries a man, that action concerns me: all mankind is of one author and is one volume; when one man dies, one chapter is not torn out of the book, but translated[3] into a better language; and every chapter must be so translated. God employs several translators; some pieces are translated by age, some by sickness, some by war, some by justice; but God's hand is in every translation, and his hand shall bind up all our scattered leaves again for that library where every book shall lie open to one another. As therefore the bell that rings to a sermon calls not upon the preacher only, but upon the congregation to come, so this bell calls us all; but how much more me, who am brought so near the door by this sickness. There was a contention

---

6. Deer supposedly expelled arrows wounding them by eating the herb dittany.
7. Medicinal plants.
8. One who administers drugs might do this for man as well as for other creatures, but one who sells drugs ("the apothecary") and the physician

do not know how to prescribe for man as well as for other creatures.
9. I.e., apply it to the present situation.
1. The "passing bell" for the dying.
2. The church.
3. Punning on the literal sense, "carried across."

as far as a suit[4] (in which piety and dignity, religion and estimation,[5] were mingled) which of the religious orders should ring to prayers first in the morning; and it was determined that they should ring first that rose earliest. If we understand aright the dignity of this bell that tolls for our evening prayer, we would be glad to make it ours by rising early, in that application, that it might be ours as well as his whose indeed it is. The bell doth toll for him that thinks it doth; and though it intermit again, yet from that minute that that occasion wrought upon him, he is united to God. Who casts not up his eye to the sun when it rises? But who takes off his eye from a comet when that breaks out? Who bends not his ear to any bell which upon any occasion rings? But who can remove it from that bell which is passing a piece of himself out of this world? No man is an island, entire of itself; every man is a piece of the continent, a part of the main.[6] If a clod be washed away by the sea, Europe is the less, as well as if a promontory were, as well as if a manor of thy friend's or of thine own were. Any man's death diminishes me, because I am involved in mankind; and therefore never send to know for whom the bell tolls; it tolls for thee.[7] Neither can we call this a begging of misery or a borrowing of misery, as though we were not miserable enough of ourselves but must fetch in more from the next house, in taking upon us the misery of our neighbors. Truly it were an excusable covetousness if we did; for affliction is a treasure, and scarce any man hath enough of it. No man hath affliction enough that is not matured and ripened by it, and made fit for God by that affliction. If a man carry treasure in bullion, or in a wedge of gold, and have none coined into current moneys, his treasure will not defray[8] him as he travels. Tribulation is treasure in the nature of it, but it is not current money in the use of it, except we get nearer and nearer our home, heaven, by it. Another man may be sick too, and sick to death, and this affliction may lie in his bowels as gold in a mine and be of no use to him; but this bell that tells me of his affliction digs out and applies that gold to me, if by this consideration of another's danger I take mine own into contemplation and so secure myself by making my recourse to my God, who is our only security.

From *Expostulation 19*

[THE LANGUAGE OF GOD]

My God, my God, thou art a direct God, may I not say a literal God, a God that wouldst be understood literally and according to the plain sense of all that thou sayest. But thou art also (Lord, I intend it to thy glory, and let no profane misinterpreter abuse it to thy diminution), thou art a figurative, a metaphorical God too: a God in whose words there is such a height of figures, such voyages, such peregrinations to fetch remote and precious metaphors, such extensions, such spreadings, such curtains of allegories, such third heavens of hyperboles, so harmonious elocutions, so retired and so reserved expressions, so commanding persuasions, so persuading commandments, such sinews even in thy milk and such things in thy words, as

4. Controversy that went as far as a lawsuit.
5. Self-esteem.
6. Mainland.
7. This phrase gave Ernest Hemingway the title for his novel *For Whom the Bell Tolls*.
8. Meet his expenses.

all profane[9] authors seem of the seed of the serpent that creeps; thou art the dove that flies. Oh, what words but thine can express the inexpressible texture and composition of thy word; in which, to one man, that argument that binds his faith to believe that to be the word of God is the reverent simplicity of the word, and to another, the majesty of the word; and in which two men, equally pious, may meet, and one wonder that all should not understand it, and the other as much that any man should. So, Lord, thou givest us the same earth to labor on and to lie in; a house and a grave of the same earth; so, Lord, thou givest us the same word for our satisfaction and for our inquisition,[1] for our instruction and for our admiration too. For there are places that thy servants Jerome and Augustine would scarce believe (when they grew warm by mutual letters) of one another that they understood them, and yet both Jerome and Augustine call upon persons whom they knew to be far weaker than they thought one another (old women and young maids) to read thy Scriptures, without confining them to these or those places.[2]

Neither art thou thus a figurative, a metaphorical God, in thy word only, but in thy works too. The style of thy works, the phrase of thine actions, is metaphorical. The institution of thy whole worship in the old law was a continual allegory; types and figures[3] overspread all, and figures flowed into figures, and poured themselves out into further figures. Circumcision carried a figure of baptism,[4] and baptism carries a figure of that purity which we shall have in perfection in the New Jerusalem. Neither didst thou speak and work in this language only in the time of the prophets; but since thou spokest in thy son it is so too. How often, how much more often, doth thy son call himself a way and a light and a gate and a vine and bread than the son of God or of man? How much oftener doth he exhibit a metaphorical Christ than a real, a literal? This hath occasioned thine ancient servants, whose delight it was to write after thy copy,[5] to proceed the same way in their expositions of the Scriptures, and in their composing both of public liturgies and of private prayers to thee, to make their accesses to thee in such a kind of language as thou wast pleased to speak to them, in a figurative, in a metaphorical language; in which manner I am bold to call the comfort which I receive now in this sickness, in the indication of the concoction[6] and maturity thereof, in certain clouds[7] and residences[8] which the physicians observe, a discovering of land from sea after a long and tempestuous voyage. * * *

1623   1624

---

9. Secular.
1. Investigation.
2. Saints Jerome and Augustine did in fact differ over the proper way of interpreting the Bible, yet they both encouraged its use by the unlearned.
3. Anticipations or prefigurations, especially persons and events in the Hebrew Bible that were read as prefiguring Christ, or some aspect of the New Testament or of Christian practice. For a

beautiful poem exemplifying this process, see Herbert, "The Bunch of Grapes" (p. 1268).
4. Both circumcision and baptism are rites of admission to a religious community.
5. Text.
6. Ripening.
7. Cloudy urine.
8. Residues.

From Death's Duel[1]

[Donne's last sermon, on Psalm 68.20: "And unto God the Lord belong the issues[2] of Death"—i.e., from death.]

* * * First, then, we consider this *exitus mortis*, to be *liberatio à morte*, that with God, the Lord are the issues of death, and therefore in all our deaths, and the deadly calamities of this life, we may justly hope of a good issue from him; and all our periods and transitions in this life, are so many passages from death to death. Our very birth and entrance into this life is *exitus à morte*, an issue from death, for in our mother's womb we are dead so, as that we do not know we live, not so much as we do in our sleep, neither is there any grave so close, or so putrid a prison, as the womb would be unto us, if we stayed in it beyond our time, or died there before our time. In the grave the worms do not kill us, we breed and feed, and then kill the worms which we ourselves produced. In the womb the dead child kills the mother that conceived it, and is a murderer, nay a parricide, even after it is dead. And if we be not dead so in the womb, so as that being dead, we kill her that gave us our first life, our life of vegetation,[3] yet we are dead so, as David's idols are dead. In the womb we have eyes and see not, ears and hear not.[4] There in the womb we are fitted for works of darkness, all the while deprived of light: And there in the womb we are taught cruelty, by being fed with blood, and may be damned, though we be never born. * * *

But then this *exitus à morte* is but *introitus in mortem*, this issue, this deliverance from that death, the death of the womb, is an entrance, a delivering over to another death, the manifold deaths of this world. We have a winding-sheet[5] in our mother's womb, which grows with us from our conception, and we come into the world wound up in that winding-sheet, for we come to seek a grave. * * *

Now this which is so singularly peculiar to him [Christ], that his flesh should not see corruption, at his second coming, his coming to Judgment, shall extend to all then alive, their flesh shall not see corruption. . . . But for us that die now and sleep in the state of the dead, we must all pass this posthume death, this death after death, nay this death after burial, this dissolution after dissolution, this death of corruption and putrefaction, of vermiculation and incineration, of dissolution and dispersion in and from the grave. When those bodies that have been the children of royal parents, and the parents of royal children, must say with Job, to corruption, thou art my

---

1. The printed version of this sermon (1632) has the subtitle "A Consolation to the Soul, against the dying life, and living death of the body." Donne's friend and executor Henry King (later bishop of Chichester) supplied the further information that the sermon was delivered at Whitehall, before King Charles, that it was delivered only a few days before Donne's death, and that it was fitly styled "the author's own funeral sermon." Donne was a powerful and popular preacher, and this sermon was especially moving according to the testimony of many auditors, including Izaak Walton (see his account of Donne on his deathbed, pp. 976–80). Besides the personal drama of the preacher himself visibly ill and perhaps dying,

the audience must have responded to the almost unbearably graphic analysis of the forms of death and decay—a theme that often preoccupied Donne. As in his poems, the language is personal, rich in learning and curious lore, dazzling in verbal ingenuity and metaphor. As in the *Devotions*, the sentences are long, sinuous, and elaborate. Typically, he uses a number of Latin phrases, but almost always translates or paraphrases them immediately.
2. Passages out.
3. I.e., of growth.
4. Paraphrases Psalm 115.5–6.
5. The placenta.

father, and to the worm, thou art my mother and my sister.[6] Miserable riddle, when the same worm must be my mother, and my sister, and myself. Miserable incest, when I must be married to my mother and my sister, beget, and bear that worm which is all that miserable penury; when my mouth shall be filled with dust, and the worm shall feed, and feed sweetly upon me,[7] when the ambitious man shall have no satisfaction, if the poorest alive tread upon him, nor the poorest receive any contentment in being made equal to princes, for they shall be equal but in dust. One dies at his full strength, being wholly at ease and in quiet, and another dies in the bitterness of his soul, and never eats with pleasure, but they lie down alike in the dust, and the worm covers them.[8] The worm covers them in Job, and in Isaiah, it covers them and is spread under them, the worm is spread under thee, and the worm covers thee.[9] There's the mats and the carpets that lie under, and there's the state and the canopy,[1] that hangs over the greatest of the sons of men. Even those bodies that were the temple of the Holy Ghost, come to this dilapidation, to ruin, to rubbish, to dust: even the Israel of the Lord, and Jacob himself hath no other specification, no other denomination, but that *vermis Jacob*, thou worm of Jacob.[2] Truly the consideration of this posthume death, this death after burial, that after God (with whom are the issues of death) hath delivered me from the death of the womb, by bringing me into the world, and from the manifold deaths of the world, by laying me in the grave, I must die again in an incineration of this flesh, and in a dispersion of that dust. * * *

There we leave you in that blessed dependency, to hang upon him that hangs upon the Cross, there bathe in his tears, there suck at his wounds, and lie down in peace in his grave, till he vouchsafe you a resurrection, and an ascension into that Kingdom, which he hath purchased for you, with the inestimable price of his incorruptible blood. Amen.

1632

6. Paraphrases Job 17.14.
7. Echoes Job 24.20.
8. Echoes Job 21.23–26.
9. Echoes Isaiah 14.11.

1. Cloth of state, a canopy erected over a king's throne.
2. That epithet is used in Isaiah 41.14.

IZAAK WALTON
1593–1683

Walton's *Life of Donne*, first published in 1640 as a biographical introduction to Donne's collected sermons, was the most artistic and accurate English biography to date. Walton drew on his personal knowledge of and friendship with Donne in his later years, talked with others who knew him, and looked over his poems, letters, and papers; but he enlivens his narrative with anecdotes that are often questionably accurate, and he quotes conversations that he could not have heard. While Walton made an effort to research his facts, his is not a scholarly biography, written in accord with the canons of evidence that have evolved since Walton's time. Rather, it is shaped by the models of life-writing admired in the seventeenth century: Plutarch's *Lives of the Noble Grecians and Romans* portraying subjects as examples of virtue and vice; and hagiography or saints' lives, exemplified by Augustine's autobiographical *Confessions* (ca. 400) and by Foxe's *Book of Martyrs*. Walton explicitly reads Donne's life against that of St. Augustine: rakish in youth and saintly in age. The influence of hagiography is especially evident in the passage below, on Donne's remarkable preparations for death. It is no accident that this biography, published as religious tensions were growing acute and civil war loomed, represented Donne as a "saint" of Anglicanism. The other lives Walton wrote—of George Herbert, Richard Hooker, Henry Wotton, and Bishop Robert Sanderson—presented them as exemplary Anglican worthies to the triumphant Anglican church after the Restoration.

A prosperous merchant in the clothing trade, Walton lived for several years in the parish of St. Dunstans in the west, where Donne was vicar. He was a staunch royalist, credited with smuggling one of Prince Charles's jewels out of the country, but

Donne in His Shroud. Shortly before his death in 1631, Donne posed in the shroud in which he would be buried. The resulting painting, reproduced in the 1633 edition of Donne's collected poetry as the engraving shown here, served as a model for the stone effigy of Donne in St. Paul's Cathedral.

his life was otherwise unremarkable, save for his wildly popular book on fishing, *The Complete Angler* (1653). Written during the Cromwellian ascendancy, this series of dialogues between a fisherman and a hunter (and briefly a falconer) creates for Walton a fascinating surrogate self, Piscator, the angler. Setting the representative values of fishermen—moderation, peacefulness, generosity, thankfulness, contemplation—over against the contrasting values assigned to hunters and falconers, Walton makes "angling" stand in for the ceremonious, peaceful, ordered life of royalist Anglicans, now so violently disrupted. As a stylist Walton writes prose that is easy and colloquial but graceful and polished.

From The Life of Dr. John Donne[1]

[DONNE ON HIS DEATHBED]

It is observed that a desire of glory or commendation is rooted in the very nature of man; and that those of the severest and most mortified[2] lives, though they may become so humble as to banish self-flattery, and such weeds as naturally grow there; yet they have not been able to kill this desire of glory, but that like our radical heat,[3] it will both live and die with us; and many think it should do so; and we want not sacred examples to justify the desire of having our memory to outlive our lives; which I mention, because Dr. Donne, by the persuasion of Dr. Fox,[4] easily yielded at this very time to have a monument made for him; but Dr. Fox undertook not to persuade him how, or what monument it should be; that was left to Dr. Donne himself.

A monument being resolved upon, Dr. Donne sent for a carver to make for him in wood the figure of an urn, giving him directions for the compass and height of it; and to bring with it a board, of the just[5] height of his body. These being got, then without delay a choice painter was got to be in readiness to draw his picture, which was taken as followeth. Several charcoal fires being first made in his large study, he brought with him into that place his winding-sheet in his hand, and having put off all his clothes, had this sheet put on him, and so tied with knots at his head and feet, and his hands so placed, as dead bodies are usually fitted to be shrouded and put into their coffin or grave. Upon this urn he thus stood with his eyes shut and with so much of the sheet turned aside as might show his lean, pale, and deathlike face, which was purposely turned toward the east, from whence he expected the second coming of his and our savior Jesus. In this posture he was drawn at his just height; and when the picture was fully finished, he caused it to be set by his bedside, where it continued and became his hourly object till his death, and was then given to his dearest friend and executor Dr. Henry King,[6] then chief residentiary of St. Paul's, who caused him to be thus carved in one entire piece of white marble, as it now stands in that church;[7] and by Dr. Donne's own appointment, these words were to be affixed to it as his epitaph:

1. See Donne's sermon, "Death's Duel" (pp. 973–74), preached on February 25, 1631; he died on March 31 and was buried in St. Paul's on April 3.
2. Self-denying.
3. Bodily warmth.
4. His physician, Dr. Simeon Fox.

5. Exact.
6. Poet, canon ("residentiary") of St. Paul's, and later bishop of Chichester. "Object": of meditation.
7. The statue on Donne's tomb, executed by the well-known sculptor Nicholas Stone, survived the great fire and may still be seen in St. Paul's.

JOHANNES DONNE
Sac. Theol. Profess.

*Post varia studia quibus ab annis tenerrimis
fideliter, nec infeliciter incubuit,
instinctu et impulsu Sp. Sancti, monitu
et hortatu*

REGIS JACOBI, *ordines sacros
amplexus, anno sui Jesu, 1614, et suae aetatis 42,
decanatu huius ecclesiae indutus 27
Novembris, 1621,*

*exutus morte ultimo die Martii, 1631,
hic licet in occiduo cinere aspicit eum
cuius nomen est Oriens.*[8]

And now, having brought him through the many labyrinths and perplexities of a various life, even to the gates of death and the grave, my desire is he may rest till I have told my reader that I have seen many pictures of him in several habits and at several ages and in several postures; and I now mention this because I have seen one picture of him, drawn by a curious[9] hand, at his age of eighteen, with his sword and what other adornments might then suit with the present fashions of youth and the giddy gaieties of that age;[1] and his motto then was—

How much shall I be changed,
Before I am changed!

And if that young and his now dying picture were at this time set together, every beholder might say, "Lord! how much is Dr. Donne already changed, before he is changed!" And the view of them might give my reader occasion to ask himself with some amazement, "Lord! how much may I also, that am now in health, be changed before I am changed; before this vile, this changeable body shall put off mortality!" and therefore to prepare for it. But this is not writ so much for my reader's memento[2] as to tell him that Dr. Donne would often in his private discourses, and often publicly in his sermons, mention the many changes both of his body and mind; especially of his mind from a vertiginous giddiness; and would as often say, "his great and most blessed change was from a temporal to a spiritual employment"; in which he was so happy, that he accounted the former part of his life to be lost; and the beginning of it to be from his first entering into sacred orders and serving his most merciful God at his altar.

8. "John Donne, Professor of Sacred Theology. After various studies, which he plied from his tenderest youth faithfully and not unsuccessfully, moved by the instinct and impulse of the Holy Spirit and the admonition and encouragement of King James, he took holy orders in the year of his Jesus 1614 and the year of his age forty-two. On the 27th of November 1621, he was invested as dean of this church, and divested by death, the last day of March 1631. Here in the decline of ashes he looks to One whose name is the Rising Sun."

9. Skillful. "Habits": garbs.

1. The picture is reproduced as the frontispiece to the second edition (1635) of Donne's *Poems*. It bears the Spanish motto *Antes muerto que mudado* (Rather dead than changed, i.e., constant until death), which Walton mistranslates below.

2. Memento mori, remembrance of death.

Upon Monday after the drawing this picture, he took his last leave of his beloved study; and being sensible of his hourly decay, retired himself to his bedchamber; and that week sent at several[3] times for many of his most considerable friends, with whom he took a solemn and deliberate farewell, commending to their considerations some sentences useful for the regulation of their lives; and then dismissed them, as good Jacob did his sons, with a spiritual benediction. The Sunday following, he appointed his servants, that if there were any business yet undone that concerned him or themselves, it should be prepared against Saturday next; for after that day he would not mix his thoughts with anything that concerned this world; nor ever did; but, as Job, so he "waited for the appointed day of his dissolution."[4]

And now he was so happy as to have nothing to do but to die, to do which he stood in need of no longer time; for he had studied it long and to so happy a perfection that in a former sickness he called God to witness, "he was that minute ready to deliver his soul into his hands, if that minute God would determine his dissolution."[5] In that sickness he begged of God the constancy to be preserved in that estate forever; and his patient expectation to have his immortal soul disrobed from her garment of mortality makes me confident he now had a modest assurance that his prayers were then heard and his petition granted. He lay fifteen days earnestly expecting his hourly change; and in the last hour of his last day, as his body melted away and vapored into spirit, his soul having, I verily believe, some revelation of the beatifical vision, he said, "I were miserable if I might not die"; and after those words, closed many periods of his faint breath by saying often, "Thy kingdom come, thy will be done." His speech, which had long been his ready and faithful servant, left him not till the last minute of his life, and then forsook him, not to serve another master (for who speaks like him), but died before him; for that it was then become useless to him that now conversed with God on earth as angels are said to do in heaven, only by thoughts and looks. Being speechless, and seeing heaven by that illumination by which he saw it, he did, as St. Stephen, "look steadfastly into it, till he saw the Son of Man standing at the right hand of God his Father";[6] and being satisfied with this blessed sight, as his soul ascended and his last breath departed from him, he closed his own eyes; and then disposed his hands and body into such a posture as required not the least alteration by those that came to shroud him.

Thus variable, thus virtuous was the life; thus excellent, thus exemplary was the death of this memorable man.

He was buried in that place of St. Paul's Church which he had appointed for that use some years before his death; and by which he passed daily to pay his public devotions to almighty God (who was then served twice a day by a public form of prayer and praises in that place): but he was not buried privately, though he desired it; for, beside an unnumbered number of others, many persons of nobility, and of eminency for learning, who did love and honor him in his life, did show it at his death by a voluntary and sad attendance of his body to the grave, where nothing was so remarkable as a public sorrow.

To which place of his burial some mournful friends repaired, and, as Alexander the Great did to the grave of the famous Achilles,[7] so they strewed

3. Separate.
4. Job 14.14.
5. Walton paraphrases from Donne's *Devotions*

upon Emergent Occasions, Prayer 23.
6. Acts 7.55.
7. Plutarch, "Alexander," sec. 15.

his with an abundance of curious and costly flowers; which course they (who were never yet known) continued morning and evening for many days, not ceasing till the stones that were taken up in that church to give his body admission into the cold earth (now his bed of rest) were again by the mason's art so leveled and firmed as they had been formerly, and his place of burial undistinguishable to common view.

The next day after his burial, some unknown friend, some one of the many lovers and admirers of his virtue and learning, wrote this epitaph with a coal on the wall over his grave:

> Reader! I am to let thee know,
> Donne's body only lies below;
> For, could the grave his soul comprise,
> Earth would be richer than the skies!

Nor was this all the honor done to his reverend ashes; for, as there be some persons that will not receive a reward for that for which God accounts himself a debtor, persons that dare trust God with their charity and without a witness; so there was by some grateful unknown friend that thought Dr. Donne's memory ought to be perpetuated, an hundred marks sent to his two faithful friends and executors,[8] towards the making of his monument. It was not for many years known by whom; but after the death of Dr. Fox, it was known that it was he that sent it; and he lived to see as lively a representation of his dead friend as marble can express: a statue indeed so like Dr. Donne, that (as his friend Sir Henry Wotton hath expressed himself) "it seems to breathe faintly, and posterity shall look upon it as a kind of artificial miracle."

He was of stature moderately tall; of a straight and equally proportioned body, to which all his words and actions gave an unexpressible addition of comeliness.

The melancholy and pleasant humor were in him so contempered that each gave advantage to the other, and made his company one of the delights of mankind.

His fancy was unimitably high, equaled only by his great wit;[9] both being made useful by a commanding judgment.

His aspect was cheerful, and such as gave a silent testimony of a clear knowing soul, and of a conscience at peace with itself.

His melting eye showed that he had a soft heart, full of noble compassion; of too brave a soul to offer injuries and too much a Christian not to pardon them in others.

He did much contemplate (especially after he entered into his sacred calling) the mercies of almighty God, the immortality of the soul, and the joys of heaven; and would often say, in a kind of sacred ecstasy, "Blessed be God that he is God, only and divinely like himself."

He was by nature highly passionate, but more apt to reluct at[1] the excesses of it. A great lover of the offices of humanity, and of so merciful a spirit that he never beheld the miseries of mankind without pity and relief.

He was earnest and unwearied in the search of knowledge, with which his vigorous soul is now satisfied, and employed in a continual praise of that God

8. Henry King and Dr. John Monfort.
9. Mental acuity. "Fancy": imagination.

1. Struggle against.

that first breathed it into his active body: that body, which once was a temple of the Holy Ghost and is now become a small quantity of Christian dust:

But I shall see it reanimated.

Feb. 15, 1640

I.W.

1640, 1675

AEMILIA LANYER
1569–1645

A emilia Lanyer was the first Englishwoman to publish a substantial volume of original poems and the first to make an overt bid for patronage. She was daughter to an Italian family of court musicians who came to England in the reign of Henry VIII; they may have been Christianized Jews or, alternatively, Protestants forced to flee Catholic persecution in their native land. Some information about Lanyer's life has come down to us from the notebooks of the astrologer and fortune-teller Simon Forman, whom Lanyer consulted in 1597. Educated in the aristocratic household of the Countess of Kent, in her late teens and early twenties Lanyer was the mistress of Queen Elizabeth's lord chamberlain, Henry Carey, Lord Hunsdon. The wealthy Hunsdon, forty-five years her senior, was a notable patron of the arts— Shakespeare's company performed under his auspices in the 1590s—and he maintained his mistress in luxury. Yet when she became pregnant by Hunsdon at age twenty-three, she was married off to Alfonso Lanyer, one of another family of gentleman musicians attached to the courts of Elizabeth I and James I. Lanyer's fortunes declined after her marriage. Lanyer's poetry suggests that she resided for some time in the bookish and cultivated household of Margaret Clifford, Countess of Cumberland, and Margaret's young daughter Anne. Lanyer reports receiving their encouragement in learning, piety, and poetry, as well as, perhaps, some support in the unusual venture of offering her poems for publication. Yet her efforts to find some niche at the Jacobean court came to nothing.

Lanyer's single volume of poems, *Salve Deus Rex Judaeorum* (1611) has a decided feminist thrust. A series of dedicatory poems to former and would-be patronesses praises them as a community of contemporary good women. The title poem, a meditation on Christ's Passion that at times invites comparison with Donne and Crashaw, contrasts the good women in the Passion story with the weak, evil men portrayed there. It also incorporates a defense of Eve and all women. That defense and Lanyer's prose epistle, "To the Virtuous Reader," are spirited contributions to the so-called *querelle des femmes*, or "debate about women," a massive body of writings in several genres and languages: some examples include Chaucer's Wife of Bath's Prologue and Tale, Shakespeare's *Taming of the Shrew*, Joseph Swetnam's attack on "lewd, idle, froward and unconstant women," and Rachel Speght's reply. The final poem in Lanyer's volume, "The Description of Cookham," celebrates in elegiac mode the Crown estate occasionally occupied by the Countess of Cumberland, portraying it as an Edenic paradise of women, now lost. The poem may or may not have been written before Ben Jonson's "To Penshurst"—commonly thought to have inaugurated the "country-house" genre in English literature—but Lanyer's poem can claim priority in publication. The poems' different conceptions of the role of women in the ideal social order make an instructive comparison.

From Salve Deus Rex Judaeorum[1]

To the Doubtful Reader[2]

Gentle Reader, if thou desire to be resolved, why I give this title, *Salve Deus Rex Judaeorum*, know for certain, that it was delivered unto me in sleep many years before I had any intent to write in this manner, and was quite out of my memory, until I had written the Passion of Christ, when immediately it came into my remembrance, what I had dreamed long before. And thinking it a significant token[3] that I was appointed to perform this work, I gave the very same words I received in sleep as the fittest title I could devise for this book.

To the Queen's Most Excellent Majesty[4]

Renowned empress, and Great Britain's queen,
Most gracious mother of succeeding kings;
Vouchsafe° to view that which is seldom seen,   *be willing*
A woman's writing of divinest things:
5   Read it fair queen, though it defective be,
    Your excellence can grace both it and me.

*   *   *

Behold, great queen, fair Eve's apology,°   *defense*
Which I have writ in honor of your sex,
75   And do refer unto your majesty
To judge if it agree not with the text:[5]
    And if it do, why are poor women blamed,
    Or by more faulty men so much defamed.

*   *   *

My weak distempered brain and feeble spirits,
140   Which all unlearned have adventured, this
To write of Christ, and of his sacred merits,
Desiring that this book her° hands may kiss: *the queen's*
    And though I be unworthy of that grace,
    Yet let her blessed thoughts this book embrace.

---

1. "Hail God, King of the Jews," a variant of the inscription affixed to Christ's cross.
2. Lanyer placed this explanation at the end of her volume, not the beginning, as a further authorizing gesture. Invoking the familiar genre of the dream vision, she lays claim to poetic, even divine, inspiration. "Doubtful": doubting.
3. Sign.
4. The first of eight poems addressed to court ladies whom Lanyer sought to attract as patrons; such poems commonly preface literary works by male courtier-poets, though usually not in such numbers. These poems are followed by a prose address to her actual patron, the Countess of Cumberland, and then by the prose epistle included here, "To the Virtuous Reader." This first poem addresses Anne of Denmark, James I's queen, patron of writers such as Ben Jonson and Samuel Daniel, and mother of Prince Henry, Princess Elizabeth, and the future Charles I.
5. The biblical text (Genesis 1–3).

145   And pardon me, fair queen, though I presume
        To do that which so many better can;
        Not that I learning to myself assume,
        Or that I would compare with any man:
          But as they are scholars, and by art do write,
150   So Nature yields my soul a sad° delight.   *solemn, serious*

        And since all arts at first from Nature came,
        That goodly creature, mother of perfection
        Whom Jove's[6] almighty hand at first did frame,
        Taking both her and hers[7] in his protection:
155   Why should not she now grace my barren muse,
        And in a woman all defects excuse.

        So peerless princess humbly I desire,
        That your great wisdom would vouchsafe t'omit°   *overlook*
        All faults; and pardon if my spirits retire,
160   Leaving° to aim at what they cannot hit: *declining*
          To write your worth, which no pen can express,
          Were but t'eclipse your fame, and make it less.[8]

To the Virtuous Reader

Often have I heard, that it is the property of some women, not only to emulate the virtues and perfections of the rest, but also by all their powers of ill speaking, to eclipse the brightness of their deserved fame: now contrary to their custom, which men I hope unjustly lay to their charge, I have written this small volume, or little book, for the general use of all virtuous ladies and gentlewomen of this kingdom; and in commendation of some particular persons of our own sex, such as for the most part, are so well known to myself, and others, that I dare undertake Fame dares not to call any better. And this have I done, to make known to the world, that all women deserve not to be blamed though some forgetting they are women themselves, and in danger to be condemned by the words of their own mouths, fall into so great an error, as to speak unadvisedly against the rest of their sex; which if it be true, I am persuaded they can show their own imperfection in nothing more: and therefore could wish (for their own ease, modesties, and credit) they would refer such points of folly, to be practiced by evil-disposed men, who forgetting they were born of women, nourished of women, and that if it were not by the means of women, they would be quite extinguished out of the world, and a final end of them all, do like vipers deface the wombs wherein they were bred, only to give way and utterance to their want of discretion and goodness. Such as these, were they that dishonored Christ's apostles and prophets, putting them to shameful deaths. Therefore we are not to regard any imputations, that they undeservedly lay upon us, no otherwise than to make use of them to our own benefits, as spur to virtue, making us fly all occasions that

---

6. God as creator of Nature.
7. Nature and those (especially women) under Nature's protection.
8. As her poetry of praise cannot possibly do jus-

tice to the queen, she abandons an attempt that would obscure rather than promote the queen's fame.

may color their unjust speeches to pass current. Especially considering that they have tempted even the patience of God himself, who gave power to wise and virtuous women, to bring down their pride and arrogancy. As was cruel Cesarus by the discreet counsel of noble Deborah, judge and prophetess of Israel: and resolution of Jael wife of Heber the Kenite:[9] wicked Haman, by the divine prayers and prudent proceedings of beautiful Hester:[1] blasphemous Holofernes, by the invincible courage, rare wisdom, and confident carriage of Judith: and the unjust Judges, by the innocency of chaste Susanna:[2] with infinite others, which for brevity sake I will omit. As also in respect it pleased our lord and savior Jesus Christ, without the assistance of man, being free from original and all other sins, from the time of his conception, till the hour of his death, to be begotten of a woman, born of a woman, nourished of a woman, obedient to a woman; and that he healed women, pardoned women, comforted women: yea, even when he was in his greatest agony and bloody sweat, going to be crucified, and also in the last hour of his death, took care to dispose of a woman:[3] after his resurrection, appeared first to a woman, sent a woman[4] to declare his most glorious resurrection to the rest of his disciples. Many other examples I could allege of divers faithful and virtuous women, who have in all ages not only been confessors but also endured most cruel martyrdom for their faith in Jesus Christ. All which is sufficient to enforce all good Christians and honorable-minded men to speak reverently of our sex, and especially of all virtuous and good women. To the modest censures of both which, I refer these my imperfect endeavors, knowing that according to their own excellent dispositions they will rather cherish, nourish, and increase the least spark of virtue where they find it, by their favorable and best interpretations, than quench it by wrong constructions. To whom I wish all increase of virtue, and desire their best opinions.

Eve's Apology in Defense of Women[5]

Now Pontius Pilate is to judge the cause°   *case*
Of faultless Jesus, who before him stands,
Who neither hath offended prince, nor laws,
Although he now be brought in woeful bands.
5   O noble governor, make thou yet a pause,

9. Sisera (Canaanite leader, hence "Cesarus," i.e., "Caesar") was a Canaanite military commander (12th century B.C.E.) routed in battle by the Israelites under the leadership of the prophetess Deborah. Sisera was subsequently killed by the Kenite woman Jael, who enticed him to her tent and then drove a tent spike through his temples while he slept (Judges 4).
1. Esther (5th century B.C.E.), the Jewish wife of the Persian King Ahasuerus (Xerxes I), who by her wit and courage subverted the plot of the king's minister, Haman, to annihilate the Jews (Esther 1–7).
2. Jewish wife and example of chastity (6th century B.C.E.). She was falsely accused of adultery by two Jewish elders, in revenge for refusing their sexual advances, and condemned to death. The wise judge Daniel saved her by uncovering the elders' perjury (Apocrypha, Book of Susanna).

Judith in the 5th century B.C.E. delivered her Judean countrymen from the Assyrians by captivating their leader, Holofernes, with her charms and then decapitating him while he was drunk (Apocrypha, Book of Judith).
3. Christ asked his apostle John to care for his mother Mary (John 19.25–27). "Dispose of": provide for.
4. Mary Magdalen (John 20.1–18).
5. Lanyer supplies the title for this subsection of the *Salve Deus* on her title page. Eve is not, however, the speaker; rather, the narrator presents Eve's "Apology" (defense of her actions), which is also a defense of all women. She does so by means of an apostrophe (impassioned address) to Pilate, the Roman official who authorized the crucifixion of Jesus. Lanyer makes Pilate and Adam representatives of the male gender, whereas Eve and Pilate's wife represent womankind.

Do not in innocent blood inbrue° thy hands;   *stain*
But hear the words of thy most worthy wife,
Who sends to thee, to beg her Savior's life.[6]

Let barb'rous cruelty far depart from thee,
10   And in true justice take affliction's part;
Open thine eyes, that thou the truth may'st see.
Do not the thing that goes against thy heart,
Condemn not him that must thy Savior be;
But view his holy life, his good desert.
15   Let not us women glory in men's fall,[7]
Who had power given to overrule us all.

Till now your indiscretion sets us free.
And makes our former fault much less appear;
Our mother Eve, who tasted of the tree,
20   Giving to Adam what she held most dear,
Was simply good, and had no power to see;[8]
The after-coming harm did not appear:
The subtle serpent that our sex betrayed
Before our fall so sure a plot had laid.

25   That undiscerning ignorance perceived
No guile or craft that was by him intended;
For had she known of what we were bereaved,[9]
To his request she had not condescended.°   *consented*
But she, poor soul, by cunning was deceived;
30   No hurt therein her harmless heart intended:
For she alleged° God's word, which he° denies,   *asserted / serpent*
That they should die, but even as gods be wise.

But surely Adam cannot be excused;
Her fault though great, yet he was most to blame;
35   What weakness offered, strength might have refused,
Being lord of all, the greater was his shame.
Although the serpent's craft had her abused,
God's holy word ought all his actions frame,°   *determine*
For he was lord and king of all the earth,
40   Before poor Eve had either life or breath,

Who being framed° by God's eternal hand   *fashioned*
The perfectest man that ever breathed on earth;
And from God's mouth received that strait° command,   *strict*
The breach whereof he knew was present death;

---

6. Pilate's wife wrote her husband a letter urging Pilate to spare Jesus, about whom she had a warning dream (Matthew 27.19).
7. The fall of Adam, and the prospective fall of Pilate.
8. In Eden, Eve ate the forbidden fruit first, at the serpent's bidding. Genesis commentary usually emphasized Eve's full knowledge that God had forbidden them on pain of death and banishment from Eden to eat the fruit of the Tree of Knowledge of Good and Evil. Her action was usually ascribed to intemperance, pride, and ambition.
9. Deprived, specifically of eternal life. In Genesis 3, Eve was enticed by the serpent to eat the forbidden fruit; she in turn enticed her husband. God expelled them from Eden, condemning Adam to hard labor, Eve to pain in childbirth and subjection to her husband, and both to suffering and death.

45   Yea, having power to rule both sea and land,
     Yet with one apple won to lose that breath[1]
        Which God had breathed in his beauteous face,
        Bringing us all in danger and disgrace.

     And then to lay the fault on Patience' back,
50   That we (poor women) must endure it all.
     We know right well he did discretion lack,
     Being not persuaded thereunto at all.
     If Eve did err, it was for knowledge sake;
     The fruit being fair persuaded him to fall:
55   No subtle serpent's falsehood did betray him;
        If he would eat it, who had power to stay° him?   *prevent*

     Not Eve, whose fault was only too much love,
     Which made her give this present to her dear,
     That what she tasted he likewise might prove,°   *experience*
60   Whereby his knowledge might become more clear;
     He never sought her weakness to reprove
     With those sharp words which he of God did hear;
        Yet men will boast of knowledge, which he took
        From Eve's fair hand, as from a learned book.

65   If any evil did in her remain,
     Being made of him,[2] he was the ground of all.
     If one of many worlds[3] could lay a stain
     Upon our sex, and work so great a fall
     To wretched man by Satan's subtle train,[4]
70   What will so foul a fault amongst you all?
        Her weakness did the serpent's words obey,
        But you in malice God's dear Son betray,

     Whom, if unjustly you condemn to die,
     Her sin was small to what you do commit;
75   All mortal sins[5] that do for vengeance cry
     Are not to be compared unto it.
     If many worlds would altogether try
     By all their sins the wrath of God to get,
        This sin of yours surmounts them all as far
80   As doth the sun another little star.[6]

     Then let us have our liberty again,
     And challenge° to yourselves no sovereignty.   *claim*
     You came not in the world without our pain,
     Make that a bar against your cruelty;
85   Your fault being greater, why should you disdain
        Our being your equals, free from tyranny?

1. The breath of life, which would have been eternal.
2. Genesis 2.21–22 reports God's creation of Eve from Adam's rib.
3. May allude to the commonplace that man is a little world, applying it here to woman.
4. Tradition identifies Satan with the serpent, although that identification is not made in Genesis.
5. Sins punishable by damnation.
6. In the Ptolemaic system, the sun was larger than the other planets and the fixed stars.

If one weak woman simply did offend,
This sin of yours hath no excuse nor end,

To which, poor souls, we never gave consent.
90 Witness, thy wife, O Pilate, speaks for all,
Who did but dream, and yet a message sent
That thou shouldest have nothing to do at all
With that just man° which, if thy heart relent,   *Christ*
Why wilt thou be a reprobate° with Saul[7]   *damned*
95   To seek the death of him that is so good,
For thy soul's health to shed his dearest blood?

1611

The Description of Cookham[1]

Farewell, sweet Cookham, where I first obtained
Grace[2] from that grace where perfect grace remained;
And where the muses gave their full consent,
I should have power the virtuous to content;
5 Where princely palace willed me to indite,°   *write*
The sacred story of the soul's delight.[3]
Farewell, sweet place, where virtue then did rest,
And all delights did harbor in her breast;
Never shall my sad eyes again behold
10 Those pleasures which my thoughts did then unfold.
Yet you, great lady, mistress of that place,
From whose desires did spring this work of grace;
Vouchsafe° to think upon those pleasures past,   *be willing*
As fleeting worldly joys that could not last,
15 Or, as dim shadows of celestial pleasures,
Which are desired above all earthly treasures.
Oh how, methought, against° you thither came,   *in preparation for*
Each part did seem some new delight to frame!
The house received all ornaments to grace it,
20 And would endure no foulness to deface it.
And walks put on their summer liveries,[4]
And all things else did hold like similes:[5]
The trees with leaves, with fruits, with flowers clad,
Embraced each other, seeming to be glad,

7. King of Israel who sought the death of God's annointed prophet-king, David. The parallel is with Pilate, who sought Christ's death.
1. The poem was written in honor of Margaret Clifford, Countess of Cumberland, and celebrates a royal estate leased to her brother, at which the countess occasionally resided. The poem should be compared with Jonson's "To Penshurst" (pp. 1096–98). Lanyer's poem is based on a familiar classical topic, the "farewell to a place," which had its most famous development in Virgil's *Eclogue* 1. Lanyer makes extensive use of the common pastoral motif of nature's active sympathy with and response to human emotion—which

later came to be called the "pathetic fallacy."
2. Here, both God's grace and the favor of Her Grace, the Countess of Cumberland. Lanyer attributes both her religious conversion and her vocation as poet to a period of residence at Cookham in the countess's household. We do not know how long or under what circumstances Lanyer resided there.
3. Apparently a reference to the countess as her patron, commissioning her Passion poem.
4. Distinctive garments worn by persons in the service of great families, to indicate whose servants they were.
5. Behaved in similar fashion.

25   Turning themselves to beauteous canopies,
     To shade the bright sun from your brighter eyes;
     The crystal streams with silver spangles graced,
     While by the glorious sun they were embraced;
     The little birds in chirping notes did sing,
30   To entertain both you and that sweet spring.
     And Philomela[6] with her sundry lays,
     Both you and that delightful place did praise.
     Oh how me thought each plant, each flower, each tree
     Set forth their beauties then to welcome thee!
35   The very hills right humbly did descend,
     When you to tread on them did intend.
     And as you set your feet, they still did rise,
     Glad that they could receive so rich a prize.
     The gentle winds did take delight to be
40   Among those woods that were so graced by thee,
     And in sad murmur uttered pleasing sound,
     That pleasure in that place might more abound.
     The swelling banks delivered all their pride
     When such a phoenix[7] once they had espied.
45   Each arbor, bank, each seat, each stately tree,
     Thought themselves honored in supporting thee.
     The pretty birds would oft come to attend thee,
     Yet fly away for fear they should offend thee;
     The little creatures in the burrow by
50   Would come abroad to sport them in your eye,
     Yet fearful of the bow in your fair hand,
     Would run away when you did make a stand.
     Now let me come unto that stately tree,
     Wherein such goodly prospects you did see;
55   That oak that did in height his fellows pass,
     As much as lofty trees, low growing grass,
     Much like a comely cedar straight and tall,
     Whose beauteous stature far exceeded all.
     How often did you visit this fair tree,
60   Which seeming joyful in receiving thee,
     Would like a palm tree spread his arms abroad,
     Desirous that you there should make abode;
     Whose fair green leaves much like a comely veil,
     Defended Phoebus° when he would assail;   *resisted the sun*
65   Whose pleasing boughs did yield a cool fresh air,
     Joying° his happiness when you were there.   *enjoying*
     Where being seated, you might plainly see
     Hills, vales, and woods, as if on bended knee
     They had appeared, your honor to salute,
70   Or to prefer some strange unlooked-for suit;[8]

---

6. In myth, Philomela was raped by her brother-in-law Tereus, who also tore out her tongue; the gods transformed her into a nightingale. Here the bird's song is joyous but later mournful (line 189), associating her own woes with those of Cookham at the women's departure.

7. Mythical bird that lived alone of its kind for five hundred years, then was consumed in flame and reborn from its own ashes; metaphorically, a person of rare excellence. "All their pride": fish (cf. "To Penshurst," p. 1097, lines 31–36).

8. To urge some unexpected petition, as to a monarch.

All interlaced with brooks and crystal springs,
A prospect fit to please the eyes of kings.
And thirteen shires appeared all in your sight,
Europe could not afford much more delight.
75   What was there then but gave you all content,
While you the time in meditation spent
Of their Creator's power, which there you saw,
In all his creatures held a perfect law;
And in their beauties did you plain descry°   perceive
80   His beauty, wisdom, grace, love, majesty.
In these sweet woods how often did you walk,
With Christ and his apostles there to talk;
Placing his holy writ in some fair tree
To meditate what you therein did see.
85   With Moses you did mount his holy hill
To know his pleasure, and perform his will.[9]
With lowly David you did often sing
His holy hymns to heaven's eternal King.[1]
And in sweet music did your soul delight
90   To sound his praises, morning, noon, and night.
With blessed Joseph you did often feed
Your pined brethren, when they stood in need.[2]
And that sweet lady sprung from Clifford's race,
Of noble Bedford's blood, fair stem of grace,[3]
95   To honorable Dorset now espoused,[4]
In whose fair breast true virtue then was housed,
Oh what delight did my weak spirits find
In those pure parts° of her well framéd mind.   qualities
And yet it grieves me that I cannot be
100   Near unto her, whose virtues did agree
With those fair ornaments of outward beauty,
Which did enforce from all both love and duty.
Unconstant Fortune, thou art most to blame,
Who casts us down into so low a frame
105   Where our great friends we cannot daily see,
So great a difference is there in degree.[5]
Many are placéd in those orbs of state,
Parters[6] in honor, so ordained by Fate,
Nearer in show, yet farther off in love,
110   In which, the lowest always are above.[7]
But whither am I carried in conceit,°   thought, fancy

---

9. You sought out and followed God's law, like
Moses, who received the Ten Commandments
on Mount Sinai.
1. You often sang David's psalms.
2. Like Joseph, who fed the starving Israelites in
Egypt, you fed the hungry.
3. Main line of the family tree. Anne Clifford,
only surviving child of the seaman-adventurer
George Clifford, third earl of Cumberland, and
the countess, a Russell (of "Bedford's blood").
4. Anne Clifford was married to Richard Sackville, third earl of Dorset, on February 25, 1609;

the reference helps date Lanyer's poem.
5. These lines and lines 117–25 probably exag-
gerate Lanyer's former familiarity with Anne Clifford.
6. Separators, i.e., the various honorific ranks
("orbs of state") act to separate person from person.
7. An egalitarian sentiment playing on the Christian notion that in spiritual things—love and
charity—the poor and lowly surpass the great
ones.

My wit too weak to conster° of the great.   *construe*
Why not? Although we are but born of earth,
We may behold the heavens, despising death;
115 And loving heaven that is so far above,
May in the end vouchsafe us entire love.[8]
Therefore sweet memory do thou retain
Those pleasures past, which will not turn again:
Remember beauteous Dorset's[9] former sports,
120 So far from being touched by ill reports,
Wherein myself did always bear a part,
While reverend love presented my true heart.
Those recreations let me bear in mind,
Which her sweet youth and noble thoughts did find,
125 Whereof deprived, I evermore must grieve,
Hating blind Fortune, careless to relieve.
And you sweet Cookham, whom these ladies leave,
I now must tell the grief you did conceive
At their departure, when they went away,
130 How everything retained a sad dismay.
Nay long before, when once an inkling came,
Methought each thing did unto sorrow frame:
The trees that were so glorious in our view,
Forsook both flowers and fruit, when once they knew
135 Of your depart, their very leaves did wither,
Changing their colors as they grew together.
But when they saw this had no power to stay you,
They often wept, though, speechless, could not pray you,
Letting their tears in your fair bosoms fall,
140 As if they said, Why will ye leave us all?
This being vain, they cast their leaves away
Hoping that pity would have made you stay:
Their frozen tops, like age's hoary hairs,
Shows their disasters, languishing in fears.
145 A swarthy riveled rind° all over spread,   *bark*
Their dying bodies half alive, half dead.
But your occasions called you so away[1]
That nothing there had power to make you stay.
Yet did I see a noble grateful mind
150 Requiting each according to their kind,
Forgetting not to turn and take your leave
Of these sad creatures, powerless to receive
Your favor, when with grief you did depart,
Placing their former pleasures in your heart,
155 Giving great charge to noble memory
There to preserve their love continually.
But specially the love of that fair tree,
That first and last you did vouchsafe to see,
In which it pleased you oft to take the air

8. I.e., we (lowly) may also love God and enjoy God's love, and hence are equal to anyone.
9. As was common, Anne Clifford is here referred to by her husband's title.

1. After her husband's death (1605) Margaret Clifford chiefly resided in her dower properties in the north; Anne Clifford was married in 1609.

160 With noble Dorset, then a virgin fair,
  Where many a learned book was read and scanned,
  To this fair tree, taking me by the hand,
  You did repeat the pleasures which had passed,
  Seeming to grieve they could no longer last.
165 And with a chaste, yet loving kiss took leave,
  Of which sweet kiss I did it soon bereave,°   *soon take from it*
  Scorning a senseless creature should possess
  So rare a favor, so great happiness.
  No other kiss it could receive from me,
170 For fear to give back what it took of thee,
  So I ungrateful creature did deceive it
  Of that which you in love vouchsafed to leave it.
  And though it oft had given me much content,
  Yet this great wrong I never could repent;
175 But of the happiest made it most forlorn,
  To show that nothing's free from Fortune's scorn,
  While all the rest with this most beauteous tree
  Made their sad comfort sorrow's harmony.
  The flowers that on the banks and walks did grow,
180 Crept in the ground, the grass did weep for woe.
  The winds and waters seemed to chide together
  Because you went away they knew not whither;
  And those sweet brooks that ran so fair and clear,
  With grief and trouble wrinkled did appear.
185 Those pretty birds that wonted° were to sing,   *accustomed*
  Now neither sing, nor chirp, nor use their wing,
  But with their tender feet on some bare spray,
  Warble forth sorrow, and their own dismay.
  Fair Philomela leaves her mournful ditty,
190 Drowned in deep sleep, yet can procure no pity.
  Each arbor, bank, each seat, each stately tree
  Looks bare and desolate now for want of thee,
  Turning green tresses into frosty gray,
  While in cold grief they wither all away.
195 The sun grew weak, his beams no comfort gave,
  While all green things did make the earth their grave.
  Each briar, each bramble, when you went away
  Caught fast your clothes, thinking to make you stay;
  Delightful Echo wonted to reply
200 To our last words, did now for sorrow die;
  The house cast off each garment that might grace it,
  Putting on dust and cobwebs to deface it.
  All desolation then there did appear,
  When you were going whom they held so dear.
205 This last farewell to Cookham here I give,
  When I am dead thy name in this may live,
  Wherein I have performed her noble hest°   *commission*
  Whose virtues lodge in my unworthy breast,
  And ever shall, so long as life remains,
210 Tying my life to her by those rich chains.°   *her virtues*

1611

BEN JONSON
1572–1637

I n 1616 Ben Jonson published his *Works*, to the derision of those astounded to see mere plays and poems collected under the same title the king gave to his political treatises. Many of Jonson's contemporaries shied away from publication, either because, like Donne, they wrote for small coterie audiences or because, like Shakespeare, they wrote for theater companies that preferred not to let go of the scripts. Jonson knew and admired both Donne and Shakespeare and more than any Jacobean belonged to both of their very different worlds, but in publishing his *Works* he laid claim to higher literary status. He had risen from humble beginnings to become England's unofficial poet laureate, with a pension from the king and honorary degrees from both Oxford and Cambridge. If he was not the first professional author in England, he was the first to invest that role with dignity and respectability. His published *Works*, over which he labored with painstaking care, testify to an extraordinary feat of self-transformation.

Jonson's early life was tough and turbulent. The posthumous son of a London clergyman, he was educated at Westminster School under the great antiquarian scholar William Camden. There he developed his love of classical learning, but lacking the resources to continue his education, Jonson was forced to turn to his stepfather's trade of bricklaying, a life he "could not endure." He escaped by joining the English forces in Flanders, where, as he later boasted, he killed a man in single combat before the eyes of two armies. Back in London, his attempt to make a living as an actor and a playwright almost ended in early disaster. He was imprisoned in 1597 for collaborating with Thomas Nashe on the scandalous play *The Isle of Dogs* (now lost), and shortly after his release he killed one of his fellow actors in a duel. Jonson escaped the gallows by pleading benefit of clergy (a medieval privilege exempting felons who could read Latin from the death penalty). His learning had saved his life, but he emerged from captivity branded on the thumb, and with another mark against him as well. Under the influence of a priest imprisoned with him, he had converted to Catholicism. Jonson was now more than ever a marginal figure, distrusted by the society that he satirized brilliantly in his early plays.

Jonson's fortunes improved with the accession of James I, though not at once. In 1603 he was called before the Privy Council to answer charges of "popery and treason" found in his play *Sejanus*. Little more than a year later he was in jail again for his part in the play *Eastward Ho*, which openly mocked the king's Scots accent and propensity for selling knighthoods. Yet Jonson was now on the way to establishing himself at the new court. In 1605 he received the commission to organize the Twelfth Night entertainment, or masque; eventually he would produce twenty-four masques for the court, most of them in collaboration with the architect and scene designer Inigo Jones. In the same years that he was writing the masques, he produced his greatest works for the public theater. His first successful play, *Every Man in His Humor* (1598), had inaugurated the so-called comedy of humors, which ridicules the eccentricities of the characters, thought to be caused by physiological imbalance. He capitalized on this success with the comedies *Volpone* (1606), *Epicene* (1609), *The Alchemist* (1610), and *Bartholomew Fair* (1614). Jonson preserved the detached, satiric perspective of an outsider, but he was rising in society and making accommodations where necessary. In 1605, when suspicion fell upon him as a Catholic following the exposure of the Gunpowder Plot, he showed his loyalty

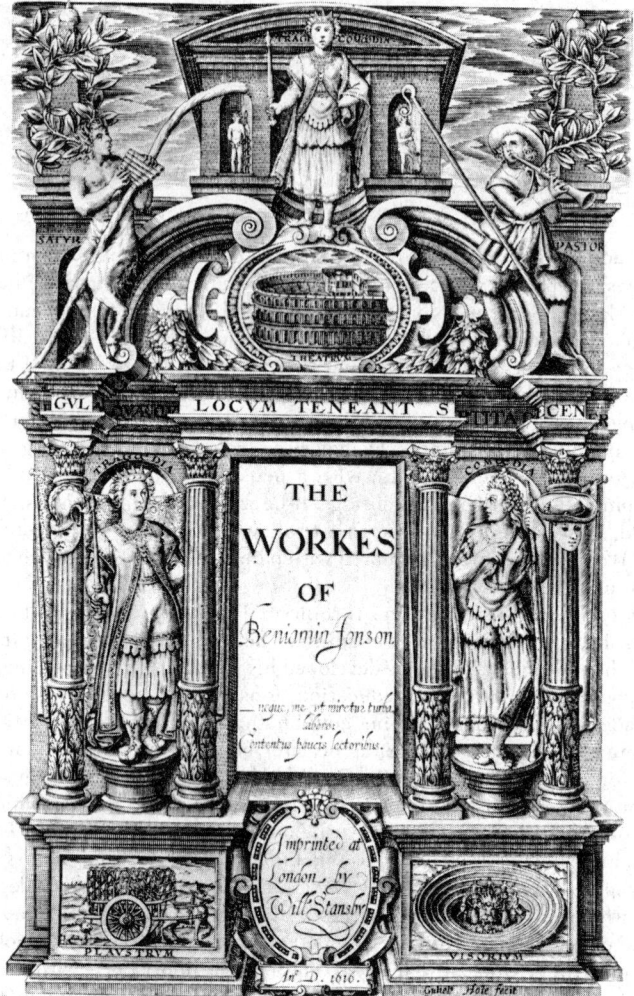

Jonson's 1616 *Works*. This title page makes a strong claim for the importance of Jonson's literary achievement and for the significance of English drama in general. The columned portico suggests Jonson's connection to the classical tradition, and the figures within it represent his mastery of various genres; they represent, clockwise from the top, Tragicomedy, Pastoral, Comedy, Tragedy, and Satire. Underneath Tragedy is a cart of the sort medieval traveling players would have used; underneath Comedy is an ancient Greek amphitheater. Centered just beneath Tragicomedy is a depiction of the English public theaters for which Jonson wrote many of his plays.

by agreeing to serve as a spy for the Privy Council. Five years later he would return to the Church of England.

Although he rose to a position of eminent respectability, Jonson retained a quarrelsome spirit all his life. Much of his best work emerged out of fierce tensions with collaborators and contemporaries. At the turn of the century he became embroiled in the so-called War of the Theaters, in which he satirized and was satirized by his fellow playwrights John Marston and Thomas Dekker. Later, his long partnership with Inigo Jones was marked by ever more bitter rivalry over the relative importance of words and scenery in the masques. Jonson also poured invective on the theater audiences when they failed, in his view, to appreciate his plays. The failure of his play *The New Inn* elicited his "Ode to Himself" (1629), a disgusted farewell to the "loathed stage." Yet even after a stroke in 1629 left him partially paralyzed and confined to his home, Jonson continued to write; and he was at work on a new play when he died in 1637.

In spite of his antagonistic nature, Jonson had a great capacity for friendship. His friends included Shakespeare, Donne, Francis Bacon, and John Selden. In later years he gathered about himself a group of admiring younger men known as the "Sons of Ben," among them Robert Herrick, Thomas Carew, and Sir John Suckling. He was a fascinating and inexhaustible conversationalist, as recorded by his friend William Drummond of Hawthornden, who carefully noted down Jonson's remarks on many subjects, ranging from his fellow poets to his sexual predilections. Jonson also moved easily among the great of the land. His patrons included Lady Mary Wroth and other members of the Sidney and Herbert families. In "To Penshurst," a celebration of Robert Sidney's country estate, Jonson offers an ideal image of a social order in which a virtuous patriarchal governor offers ready hospitality to guests of all stations, from poets to kings.

"To Penshurst," together with Aemilia Lanyer's "Description of Cookham," inaugurated the small genre of the "country-house poem" in England. Jonson tried his hand, usually with success, at a wide range of poetic genres, including epitaph and epigram, love and funeral elegy, verse satire and verse letter, song and ode. More often than not he looked back to classical precedents. From the Roman poets Horace and Martial he derived not only generic models but an ideal vision of the artist and society against which he measured himself and the court he served. In many poems he adopted the persona of a witty, keenly perceptive, and scrupulously honest judge of men and women. The classical values Jonson most admired are enumerated in "Inviting a Friend to Supper," which describes a dinner party characterized by moderation, civility, graciousness, and pleasure that delights without enslaving— all contrasting sharply with the excess and licentiousness that marked the banquets and entertainments of imperial Rome and Stuart England. Yet the poet who produced this image of moderation was a man of immense appetites, which found expression in his art as well as in his life. His best works seethe with an almost uncontrollable imaginative energy and lust for abundance. Even his profound classical learning manifests this impulse. The notes and references to learned authorities that spill across the margins of his *Works* can be seen as the literary equivalent of food and drink piled high on the poet's table. Years of hardship had taught Jonson to seek his feasts in his imagination, and he could make the most mundane object the basis for flights of high fancy. As he told Drummond, he once "consumed a whole night in lying looking to his great toe, about which he had seen Tartars and Turks, Romans and Carthaginians fight in his imagination." In Drummond's view, Jonson was "oppressed with fantasy." Perhaps it was so—but Jonson's capacity for fantasy also produced a wide variety of plays, masques, and poems, in styles ranging from witty comedy to delicate lyricism.

Volpone

This dark satire on human rapacity is set in Venice, but its true target is the city of London, or the city that, Jonson feared, London was about to become. It is a place devoted to commerce and mired in corruption, populated by greedy fools and conniving rascals. Like Shakespeare, Donne, and Thomas More before him, Jonson was deeply disturbed by the rise of a protocapitalist economic order

Fox Handling Masks. This woodcut from Andrea Alciato's *Emblemata* depicts the traditional association between foxes and deceptive human role-playing, a connection central to *Volpone*.

that seemed to emphasize competition and the acquisition of material goods over reciprocal goodwill and mutual obligation. On the other hand, Jonson was also fascinated by the entrepreneurial potential liberated by the new economic order. His protagonists, Volpone and Mosca, may be morally bankrupt, but they are also the most intelligent, adaptable characters in the play. Moreover, although Jonson was a strong advocate for the educational and morally improving potential of the theater—his theater in particular—the talents of his main characters are essentially those of theatrical performance and improvisation. In fact, as Jonson was well aware, he was himself deeply implicated in what he satirized. The low-born, unscrupulous, brilliantly inventive Mosca, a flattering aristocratic hanger-on who aspires to high status himself, at times seems to be the author's evil twin. Perhaps his very resemblances to Jonson required Jonson so energetically to repudiate his motives and punish his presumption at the end of the play.

Volpone combines elements from several sources. The classical satirist Lucian provided the theme of the rich old man playing with moneygrubbing scoundrels who hope to inherit his wealth. Roman comedy provided prototypes for some characters: the wily parasite, the unscrupulous lawyer, the avaricious dotard, the voluble woman. Some scenes, such as that in which Volpone disguised as a mountebank woos Celia at her window, are drawn from the Italian commedia dell'arte. Jonson draws as well upon ancient and medieval beast fables: stories about the crafty antihero Reynard the fox, as well as a fable about a fox that plays dead in order to catch greedy birds. But *Volpone* is much more than the sum of its borrowings. It is a work of enormous comic energy, full of black humor, which holds its loathsome characters up for appalled but gleeful inspection.

Volpone was first performed by the King's Men (Shakespeare's company) in the spring of 1606, at the Globe Theater. (See the illustration, in the appendices to this volume, of a contemporary popular theater constructed on similar lines.) The Globe seated some two thousand persons—aristocrats and prosperous citizens in the tiered galleries, lower-class "groundlings" in the pit in the front of the stage. The play was also performed to great applause before learned audiences at Oxford and Cambridge, to whom Jonson dedicated the printed edition of *Volpone*. It was first published in quarto form in 1607 and republished with a few changes in the 1616 *Works*, the basis for the present text.

Volpone

or

The Fox

THE PERSONS OF THE PLAY[1]

VOLPONE, *a magnifico*°	*Venetian nobleman*
MOSCA, *his parasite*°	*hanger-on*
NANO, *a dwarf*	
ANDROGYNO, *a hermaphrodite*	
CASTRONE, *an eunuch*	
VOLTORE, *an advocate*°	*lawyer*
CORBACCIO, *an old gentleman*	
BONARIO, *a young gentleman* [CORBACCIO's *son*]	
CORVINO, *a merchant*	
CELIA, *the merchant's wife*	
Servitore, a SERVANT [*to* CORVINO]	
[*Sir*] POLITIC *Would-be, a knight*	
Fine Madame [LADY] WOULD-BE, *the knight's wife*	
[*Two*] WOMEN [*servants to* LADY WOULD-BE]	
PEREGRINE, *a gentleman traveler*	
AVOCATORI,° *four magistrates*	*public prosecutors*
Notario [NOTARY], *the register*°	*court recorder*
COMMENDATORI,° *officers*	*court deputies*
[*Other court officials, litter-bearers*]	
Mercatori, three MERCHANTS	
Grege [*members of a* CROWD]	

SCENE. *Venice*

The Argument[1]

V olpone, childless, rich, feigns sick, despairs,°	*is despaired of*
O ffers his state° to hopes of several heirs,	*estate*
L ies languishing; his parasite receives	
P resents of all, assures, deludes, then weaves	
O ther cross-plots, which ope themselves,° are told.°	*unfold / exposed*
N ew tricks for safety are sought; they thrive—when, bold,	
E ach tempts th'other again, and all are sold.°	*betrayed*

Prologue

Now, luck yet send us, and a little wit
Will serve to make our play hit

The Persons of the Play
1. Many of the characters have allegorically apt names. "Volpone" is defined in John Florio's 1598 Italian-English dictionary as "an old fox . . . a sneaking, lurking, wily deceiver." "Mosca" means "fly." "Nano" means "dwarf." "Voltore" means "vulture." "Corbaccio" means "raven." "Bonario" is derived from *bono*, meaning "good." "Corvino" means "crow." "Celia" means "heaven." "Politic" means "worldly-wise" or "temporizing." "Peregrine" means "traveler" or "small hawk." In many performances the symbolism of the animal names is reinforced by costuming.
The Argument
1. Plot summary. Jonson imitates the acrostic "arguments" of the Latin playwright Plautus.

According to the palates of the season.°   *fashionable taste*
Here is rhyme not empty of reason.
5   This we were bid to credit° from our poet,   *asked to believe*
Whose true scope,° if you would know it,   *aim*
In all his poems still hath been this measure,
To mix profit with your pleasure;[1]
And not as some—whose throats their envy failing°—   *not fully expressing*
10   Cry hoarsely, "all he writes is railing,"°   *personal insult*
And when his plays come forth think they can flout them
With saying he was a year about them.[2]
To these there needs no lie° but this his creature,°   *denial / creation*
Which was, two months since, no feature;°   *nonexistent*
15   And, though he dares give them° five lives to mend it,   *his detractors*
'Tis known five weeks fully penned it
From his own hand, without a coadjutor,°   *collaborator*
Novice, journeyman,° or tutor.   *apprentice*
Yet thus much I can give you, as a token
20   Of his play's worth: no eggs are broken,
Nor quaking custards with fierce teeth affrighted,[3]
Wherewith your rout° are so delighted;   *mob*
Nor hales he in a gull,° old ends° reciting,   *fool / saws*
To stop gaps in his loose writing,
25   With such a deal of monstrous and forced action
As might make Bethlehem a faction.[4]
Nor made he his play for jests stol'n from each table,°   *plagiarized jokes*
But makes jests to fit his fable,
And so presents quick° comedy, refined   *lively*
30   As best critics have designed.
The laws of time, place, persons he observeth;[5]
From no needful rule he swerveth.
All gall and copperas[6] from his ink he draineth;
Only a little salt[7] remaineth
35   Wherewith he'll rub your cheeks, till, red with laughter,
They shall look fresh a week after.

Prologue
1. Rule, as laid down by Horace, that the poet ought to both please his audience and teach it something useful.
2. Thomas Dekker ridiculed the slow pace at which Jonson produced new work in *Satiromastix, or The Untrussing of the Humorous Poet* (1602), and John Marston did the same in *The Dutch Courtesan* (1605).
3. The satirist John Marston, in a line Jonson had previously ridiculed, boasted: "let custards [cowards] quake, my rage must freely run." Huge custards were a staple feature of city feasts.
4. As might win approval from lunatics (who inhabited Bethlehem hospital in London).
5. He observes the unities of time and place and the consistency of character.
6. Ferrous sulfate, like gall a corrosive substance used in ink.
7. A traditional metaphor for satiric wit.

Act 1

SCENE 1. VOLPONE's *house.*

[*Enter*] VOLPONE [*and*] MOSCA.[1]

VOLPONE   Good morning to the day, and, next, my gold!
Open the shrine that I may see my saint.
  [MOSCA *reveals the treasure.*][2]
Hail the world's soul,° and mine! More glad than is   *animating principle*
The teeming earth to see the longed-for sun
5 Peep through the horns of the celestial Ram[3]
Am I to view thy splendor darkening his,°   *outshining the sun's*
That, lying here amongst my other hoards,
Show'st like a flame by night, or like the day
Struck out of chaos, when all darkness fled
10 Unto the center.° O thou son of Sol[4]—   *center of the earth*
But brighter than thy father—let me kiss
With adoration thee and every relic
Of sacred treasure in this blessèd room.
Well did wise poets by thy glorious name
15 Title that age which they would have the best,[5]
Thou being the best of things, and far transcending
All style of joy in children, parents, friends,
Or any other waking dream on earth.
Thy looks when they to Venus did ascribe,
20 They should have giv'n her twenty thousand Cupids,[6]
Such are thy beauties and our loves.° Dear saint,   *our love of thee*
Riches, the dumb god, that giv'st all men tongues,
That canst do naught and yet mak'st men do all things,
The price of souls; even hell, with thee to boot,°   *in the bargain*
25 Is made worth heaven! Thou art virtue, fame,
Honor, and all things else. Who° can get thee,   *whoever*
He shall be noble, valiant, honest, wise—
MOSCA   And what he will, sir. Riches are in fortune
A greater good than wisdom is in nature.
30 VOLPONE   True, my belovèd Mosca. Yet I glory
More in the cunning purchase° of my wealth   *acquisition*
Than in the glad possession, since I gain
No common way. I use no trade, no venture;°   *risky commerce*
I wound no earth with plowshares; fat no beasts
35 To feed the shambles;° have no mills for iron,   *slaughterhouse*
Oil, corn, or men, to grind 'em into powder;

1.1
1. Alternatively, the play may begin with Volpone rising from his onstage bed.
2. The treasure is probably hidden behind a curtain in the alcove at the back of the stage.
3. Aries, the constellation ascendant in early spring.
4. Alchemists believed gold to have issued from the sun ("Sol"). Volpone blasphemously applies this metaphor to God's creation of the world in Genesis.
5. The mythical Golden Age (when, ironically, gold was not yet in use) was influentially described by Ovid in *The Metamorphoses.*
6. In Latin poetry, Venus was commonly described as *aurea,* meaning "golden." The throng of cupids Volpone imagines around her suggests gold's irresistible, and for him highly sexual, appeal.

I blow no subtle[7] glass; expose no ships
To threat'nings of the furrow-facèd sea;
I turn° no moneys in the public bank,   *exchange*
Nor usure° private—   *lend money at interest*

40 MOSCA   No, sir, nor devour
Soft prodigals. You shall ha' some will swallow
A melting° heir as glibly as your Dutch   *financially dwindling*
Will pills° of butter, and ne'er purge for't;[8]   *morsels*
Tear forth the fathers of poor families
45 Out of their beds and coffin them alive
In some kind, clasping° prison, where their bones *manacling*
May be forthcoming° when the flesh is rotten. *protruding; carted away*
But your sweet nature doth abhor these courses;
You loathe the widow's or the orphan's tears
50 Should wash your pavements, or their piteous cries
Ring in your roofs and beat the air for vengeance.
VOLPONE Right, Mosca, I do loathe it.
MOSCA   And besides, sir,
You are not like the thresher that doth stand
With a huge flail, watching a heap of corn,
55 And, hungry, dares not taste the smallest grain,
But feeds on mallows° and such bitter herbs; *unpalatable weeds*
Nor like the merchant who hath filled his vaults
With Romagnia and rich Candian wines,
Yet drinks the lees of Lombard's vinegar.[9]
60 You will not lie in straw whilst moths and worms
Feed on your sumptuous hangings° and soft beds. *bed curtains*
You know the use of riches, and dare give now
From that bright heap to me, your poor observer,° *follower*
Or to your dwarf, or your hermaphrodite,
65 Your eunuch, or what other household° trifle *menial*
Your pleasure allows maint'nance°— *you're pleased to support*
VOLPONE [*giving money*]   Hold thee, Mosca,
Take of my hand; thou strik'st on truth in all,
And they are envious term° thee parasite. *who term*
Call forth my dwarf, my eunuch, and my fool,
And let 'em make me sport.   [*Exit* MOSCA.]
70   What should I do
But cocker up my genius,° and live free *indulge my appetite*
To all delights my fortune calls me to?
I have no wife, no parent, child, ally
To give my substance to, but whom I make° *he whom I designate*
75 Must be my heir, and this makes men observe° me. *flatter*
This draws new clients° daily to my house, *petitioners*
Women and men of every sex and age,

7. (1) Delicate; (2) artful. (Venice was and is renowned for its art glass.)
8. Never use a remedy for gastric distress. (The Dutch were notoriously fond of butter.)
9. Romagnia and rich Candian wines are expensive wines from Greece and Crete. The lees of Lombard's vinegar are the dregs of cheap Italian wine.

That bring me presents, send me plate,° coin, jewels,   *gold or silver plate*
With hope that when I die—which they expect
80 Each greedy minute—it shall then return
Tenfold upon them; whilst some, covetous
Above the rest, seek to engross° me whole,   *swallow; monopolize*
And counterwork,° the one unto the other,   *compete; undermine*
Contend in gifts as they would seem in love;
85 All which I suffer, playing with their hopes,
And am content to coin 'em into profit,
And look upon their kindness and take more,
And look on that, still bearing them in hand,°   *leading them on*
Letting the cherry knock against their lips,
90 And draw it by their mouths and back again.[1]—
How now!

SCENE 2. *The scene continues.*

[*Enter*] MOSCA, NANO, ANDROGYNO, [*and*] CASTRONE.

NANO Now, room for fresh gamesters,° who do will   *entertainers*
    you to know
They do bring you neither play nor university show,[1]
And therefore do entreat you that whatsoever they rehearse
May not fare a whit the worse for the false pace of the verse.[2]
5 If you wonder at this, you will wonder more ere we pass,
For know here [*indicating* ANDROGYNO] is enclosed the soul
    of Pythagoras,[3]
That juggler° divine, as hereafter shall follow;   *trickster*
Which soul (fast and loose, sir) came first from Apollo,
And was breathed into Aethalides,[4] Mercurius his° son,   *Mercury's*
10 Where it had the gift to remember all that ever was done.
From thence it fled forth and made quick transmigration
To goldilocked Euphorbus,[5] who was killed in good fashion
At the siege of old Troy, by the cuckold of Sparta.[6]
Hermotimus[7] was next—I find it in my *charta*°—   *record*
15 To whom it did pass, where no sooner it was missing
But with one Pyrrhus of Delos° it learned to go   *another philosopher*
    a-fishing;
And thence did it enter the Sophist of Greece.°   *Pythagoras*
From Pythagore she went into a beautiful piece°   *slut*

1. In the game of chop-cherry, one player dangles a cherry in front of another, who tries to bite it.
1.2
1. University students performed classical plays or their imitations to hone their abilities in Latin oratory.
2. The four-stress meter of the skit Nano, Androgyno, and Castrone here perform was common in medieval drama but old-fashioned by Jonson's time.
3. Ancient Greek philosopher, mathematician, and music theorist who believed in the transmigration of souls and in the mystical properties of geometrical relationships (especially triangles [triangles = trigon]). His followers observed strict

dietary restrictions and took five-year vows of silence. His thigh was rumored to be made of gold. Jonson adapts much of the career of Pythagoras's soul from *The Dialogue of the Cobbler and the Cock*, by the Greek satirist Lucian.
4. The herald of the Greek Argonauts and son of the god Mercury, who inherited his father's divine gift of memory. Thus, unlike other souls, which forget their previous lives, Aethalides' soul can recall its transmigrations.
5. Trojan youth who injured Achilles' beloved friend, Patroclus, in the *Iliad*.
6. Menelaus, the Spartan king whose wife, Helen, was stolen by the Trojan prince Paris.
7. Greek philosopher of about 500 B.C.E.

Hight° Aspasia the meretrix;[8] and the next toss of her   *named*
20   Was again of a whore; she became a philosopher,
Crates the Cynic,[9] as itself doth relate it.
Since,° kings, knights, and beggars, knaves, lords, and fools   *since then*
   gat° it,   *received*
Besides ox and ass, camel, mule, goat, and brock,°   *badger*
In all which it hath spoke as in the cobbler's cock.[1]
25   But I come not here to discourse of that matter,
Or his one, two, or three, or his great oath, "By quater,"[2]
His musics, his trigon, his golden thigh,
Or his telling how elements° shift; but I   *earth, air, fire, water*
Would ask how of late thou hast suffered translation,°   *metamorphosis*
30   And shifted thy coat in these days of reformation?°   *religious change*

ANDROGYNO   Like one of the reformed, a fool,[3] as you see,
Counting all old doctrine heresy.

NANO   But not on thine own forbid meats hast thou ventured?

ANDROGYNO   On fish, when first a Carthusian I entered.[4]

35   NANO   Why, then thy dogmatical silence° hath left thee?   *vow of silence*

ANDROGYNO   Of that an obstreperous lawyer bereft me.

NANO   Oh, wonderful change! When Sir Lawyer forsook thee,
For Pythagore's sake, what body then took thee?

ANDROGYNO   A good dull mule.

NANO   And how, by that means,
40   Thou wert brought to allow of the eating of beans?

ANDROGYNO   Yes.

NANO   But from the mule into whom didst thou pass?

ANDROGYNO   Into a very strange beast, by some writers called
   an ass;
By others a precise, pure, illuminate brother[5]
45   Of those devour flesh and sometimes one another,°   *prey on each other*
And will drop forth a libel° or a sanctified lie   *polemic*
Betwixt every spoonful of a Nativity pie.[6]

NANO   Now quit thee, for heaven, of that profane nation,°   *sect*
And gently report thy next transmigration.

ANDROGYNO   To the same that I am.°   *what I am now*

50   NANO   A creature of delight?
And—what is more than a fool—an hermaphrodite?
Now pray thee, sweet soul, in all thy variation°   *of all your shapes*
Which body wouldst thou choose to take up thy station?

ANDROGYNO   Troth, this I am in, even here would I tarry.

55   NANO   'Cause here the delight of each sex thou canst vary?

---

8. Whore. Aspasia was the mistress of the Athenian statesman Pericles.
9. Student of Diogenes, founder of the Cynic philosophy.
1. The speaker in Lucian's dialogue (see p. 999, n. 3 above).
2. A quater is an equilateral triangle the sides of which are evenly divisible by four.
3. The "reformed" are Protestants in general, but more specifically the Puritan wing of the Church of England. Jonson was a Catholic when

he wrote *Volpone*.
4. Pythagoreans abstained from fish, but Carthusians, an order of Catholic monks, ate fish on fast days.
5. Puritan who claimed immediate, visionary knowledge of religious truth. Puritans did not observe the traditional fasting days (hence "devour flesh" in the following line).
6. Puritans substituted the term "Nativity" for "Christmas," to avoid reference to the Mass.

ANDROGYNO   Alas, those pleasures be stale and forsaken.
　No, 'tis your fool wherewith I am so taken,
　The only one creature that I can call blessèd,
　For all other forms I have proved° most distressèd.   *found to be*
60 NANO   Spoke true, as thou wert in Pythagoras still.
　This learnèd opinion we celebrate will,
　Fellow eunuch, as behooves us, with all our wit and art,
　To dignify that° whereof ourselves are so great and special a part.   *folly*
VOLPONE [*applauding*]   Now, very, very pretty! Mosca, this
　Was thy invention?
65 MOSCA   If it please my patron,
　Not else.
VOLPONE   It doth, good Mosca.
MOSCA   Then it was, sir.

SONG

NANO *and* CASTRONE [*sing*]
　　Fools, they are the only nation°   *group*
　　Worth men's envy or admiration,
　　Free from care or sorrow-taking,
70 　　Selves° and others merry making;   *themselves*
　　All they speak or do is sterling.
　　Your fool, he is your great man's dearling,
　　And your lady's sport and pleasure;
　　Tongue and bauble° are his treasure.   *fool's staff; penis*
75 　　E'en his face begetteth laughter,
　　And he speaks truth free from slaughter.°   *with impunity*
　　He's the grace of every feast,
　　And sometimes the chiefest guest,
　　Hath his trencher° and his stool,   *platter*
80 　　When wit waits upon the fool.
　　　Oh, who would not be
　　　He, he, he?   *One knocks without.*
VOLPONE   Who's that? Away!
　　　　　　　[*Exeunt* NANO *and* CASTRONE.]
　　　　　　　Look, Mosca.
MOSCA   Fool, begone!
　　　　　　　　[*Exit* ANDROGYNO.]
　'Tis Signor Voltore, the advocate;
　I know him by his knock.
85 VOLPONE   Fetch me my gown,
　My furs, and nightcaps; say my couch is changing,[7]
　And let him entertain himself awhile
　Without i'th'gallery.   [*Exit* MOSCA.]
　　　　　　Now, now, my clients
　Begin their visitation! Vulture, kite,
90 Raven, and gorcrow,° all my birds of prey   *carrion crow*
　That think me turning carcass, now they come.

---

7. My bedsheets are being changed.

I am not for 'em° yet.   *ready to die*
    [*Enter* MOSCA.]
              How now? The news?
MOSCA   A piece of plate,° sir.   *gold platter*
VOLPONE   Of what bigness?
MOSCA   Huge,
    Massy, and antique, with your name inscribed
    And arms° engraven.   *coat of arms*
95 VOLPONE   Good! And not a fox
    Stretched on the earth, with fine delusive sleights°   *deceptive tricks*
    Mocking a gaping crow?[8] Ha, Mosca?
MOSCA [*laughing*]   Sharp, sir.
VOLPONE   Give me my furs. Why dost thou laugh so, man?
MOSCA   I cannot choose, sir, when I apprehend
100 What thoughts he has, without,° now, as he walks: *outside*
    That this might be the last gift he should° give;   *would have to*
    That this would fetch you;° if you died today   *bring you around*
    And gave him all, what he should be tomorrow;
    What large return would come of all his ventures;
105 How he should worshipped be and reverenced;
    Ride with his furs and footcloths,[9] waited on
    By herds of fools and clients; have clear way
    Made for his mule, as lettered° as himself;   *educated*
    Be called the great and learnèd advocate;
110 And then concludes there's naught impossible.
VOLPONE   Yes, to be learnèd, Mosca.
MOSCA   Oh, no, rich
    Implies it.° Hood an ass with reverend purple,[1]   *wealth implies learning*
    So you can hide his two ambitious° ears,   *aspiring; upraised*
    And he shall pass for a cathedral doctor.°   *Doctor of Divinity*
115 VOLPONE   My caps, my caps, good Mosca. Fetch him in.
MOSCA   Stay, sir, your ointment for your eyes.
    [MOSCA *helps* VOLPONE *with his disguise.*]
VOLPONE   That's true.
    Dispatch, dispatch! I long to have possession
    Of my new present.
MOSCA   That, and thousands more
    I hope to see you lord of.
VOLPONE   Thanks, kind Mosca.
120 MOSCA   And that, when I am lost in blended dust,
    And hundred such as I am in succession—
VOLPONE   Nay, that were too much, Mosca.
MOSCA   —you shall live
    Still, to delude these harpies.[2]
VOLPONE   Loving Mosca!
    'Tis well. My pillow now, and let him enter.
                  [*Exit* MOSCA. VOLPONE *lies down.*]

8. In one of Aesop's *Fables*, the fox tricks the crow into dropping its cheese.
9. Ornamental cloths for the back of a horse.
1. Doctors of Divinity wore purple academic hoods.
2. Mythological ravenous monsters with women's heads and the bodies and claws of birds.

125 Now, my feigned cough, my phthisic,° and my gout, *consumption; asthma*
My apoplexy, palsy, and catarrhs,°   *mucus discharges*
Help with your forcèd functions this my posture,° *imposture*
Wherein this three year I have milked their hopes.
He comes, I hear him. [*Coughing*] Uh, uh, uh, uh! Oh—

SCENE 3. *The scene continues.*

[*Enter*] VOLTORE [*with a platter, ushered by*] MOSCA.
MOSCA [*to* VOLTORE] You still are what you were, sir.
  Only you,
Of all the rest, are he commands° his love; *the one who possesses*
And you do wisely to preserve it thus
With early visitation and kind notes°   *tokens*
5 Of your good meaning to° him, which, I know, *intentions toward*
Cannot but come most grateful. [*Loudly, to* VOLPONE]
  Patron, sir!
Here's Signor Voltore is come—
VOLPONE [*weakly*]   What say you?
MOSCA Sir, Signor Voltore is come this morning
  To visit you.
VOLPONE   I thank him.
MOSCA   And hath brought
10 A piece of antique plate bought of Saint Mark,[1]
With which he here presents you.
VOLPONE   He is welcome.
  Pray him to come more often.
MOSCA   Yes.
VOLTORE [*straining to hear*] What says he?
MOSCA He thanks you, and desires you see him often.
VOLPONE Mosca.
MOSCA   My patron?
VOLPONE [*groping*]   Bring him near. Where is he?
I long to feel his hand.
15 MOSCA [*guiding* VOLPONE'*s hands toward the platter*] The plate is here, sir.
VOLTORE How fare you, sir?
VOLPONE   I thank you, Signor Voltore.
  Where is the plate? Mine eyes are bad.
VOLTORE [*relinquishing the platter*] I'm sorry
  To see you still thus weak.
MOSCA [*aside*]   That he is not weaker.
VOLPONE You are too munificent.
VOLTORE   No, sir, would to heaven
20 I could as well give health to you as that plate.
VOLPONE You give, sir, what you can. I thank you. Your love
  Hath taste in° this, and shall not be unanswered. *is suggested by*
I pray you see me often.
VOLTORE   Yes, I shall, sir.

1.3
1. Goldsmiths kept shop in the square of St. Mark's Basilica.

VOLPONE Be not far from me.

MOSCA [*aside to* VOLTORE]   Do you observe that, sir?

25   VOLPONE Hearken unto me still. It will concern you.

MOSCA [*aside to* VOLTORE] You are a happy man, sir. Know your good.

VOLPONE I cannot now last long—

MOSCA (*aside to* VOLTORE)   You are his heir, sir.

VOLTORE (*aside to* MOSCA) Am I?

VOLPONE   I feel me going, uh, uh, uh, uh!

    I am sailing to my port, uh, uh, uh, uh!

30   And I am glad I am so near my haven.

        [*He pretends to lapse into unconsciousness.*]

MOSCA Alas, kind gentleman! Well, we must all go—

VOLTORE But Mosca—

MOSCA   Age will conquer.

VOLTORE   Pray thee, hear me.

    Am I inscribed his heir for certain?

MOSCA   Are you?

    I do beseech you, sir, you will vouchsafe

35   To write me i'your family.[2] All my hopes

    Depend upon Your Worship. I am lost

    Except° the rising sun do shine on me.   *unless*

VOLTORE It shall both shine and warm thee, Mosca.

MOSCA   Sir,

    I am a man that have not done your love

40   All the worst offices:° here I wear your keys,   *services*

    See all your coffers and your caskets locked,

    Keep the poor inventory of your jewels,

    Your plate, and moneys, am your steward, sir,

    Husband your goods here.

VOLTORE   But am I sole heir?

45   MOSCA Without a partner, sir, confirmed this morning;

    The wax° is warm yet, and the ink scarce dry   *of the seal*

    Upon the parchment.

VOLTORE   Happy, happy me!

    By what good chance, sweet Mosca?

MOSCA   Your desert, sir;

    I know no second cause.

VOLTORE   Thy modesty

50   Is loath to know it.° Well, we shall requite it.   *admit your role*

MOSCA He ever liked your course, sir; that first took him.

    I oft have heard him say how he admired

    Men of your large[3] profession, that could speak

    To every cause, and things mere contraries,°   *utterly contradictory*

55   Till they were hoarse again, yet all be law;

    That with most quick agility could turn

    And re-turn, make knots and undo them,

    Give forkèd° counsel, take provoking gold   *ambiguous*

---

2. Employ me in your household (after Volpone's death).

3. Expansive, liberal (with the suggestion of "unscrupulous").

On either hand, and put it up:[4] these men,
60 He knew, would thrive with their humility.°   *obsequiousness*
And for his part, he thought he should be blessed
To have his heir of such a suffering° spirit,   *long-suffering*
So wise, so grave, of so perplexed° a tongue,   *bewildering*
And loud withal,° that would not wag nor scarce   *besides*
65 Lie still without a fee, when every word
Your Worship but lets fall is a *cecchine!*°   *Another knocks.*   *gold coin*
Who's that? One knocks; I would not have you seen, sir.
And yet—pretend you came and went in haste;
I'll fashion an excuse. And, gentle sir,
70 When you do come to swim in golden lard,
Up to the arms in honey, that your chin
Is born up stiff with fatness of the flood,
Think on your vassal; but° remember me.   *only*
I ha' not been your worst of clients.
VOLTORE   Mosca—
75 MOSCA   When will you have your inventory brought, sir?
Or see a copy of the will? [*More knocking.*] Anon!°—   *Just a minute!*
I'll bring 'em to you, sir. Away, begone,
Put business i'your face.[5]   [*Exit* VOLTORE.]
VOLPONE   Excellent, Mosca!
Come hither, let me kiss thee.
MOSCA   Keep you still, sir.
Here is Corbaccio.
80 VOLPONE   Set the plate away.
The vulture's gone, and the old raven's come.

SCENE 4. *The scene continues.*

MOSCA [*to* VOLPONE]   Betake you to your silence and your sleep;
    [*He puts up the plate.*]
Stand there and multiply.°—Now shall we see   *beget more booty*
A wretch who is indeed more impotent
Than this° can feign to be, yet hopes to hop   *Volpone*
Over his grave.
    [*Enter*] CORBACCIO.
                  Signor Corbaccio!
5 You're very welcome, sir.
CORBACCIO   How does your patron?
MOSCA   Troth, as he did, sir: no amends.
CORBACCIO   What? Mends he?
MOSCA   No, sir, he is rather worse.
CORBACCIO   That's well. Where is he?
MOSCA   Upon his couch, sir, newly fall'n asleep.
CORBACCIO   Does he sleep well?
10 MOSCA   No wink, sir, all this night,

---

4. Take a bribe from each party to a suit and   5. Look as if you were here on business.
pocket it.

Nor yesterday, but slumbers.°   *dozes fitfully*
CORBACCIO   Good! He should take
Some counsel of physicians. I have brought him
An opiate here, from mine own doctor—
MOSCA He will not hear of drugs.
CORBACCIO   Why, I myself
15   Stood by while't was made, saw all th'ingredients,
And know it cannot but most gently work.
My life for his, 'tis but to make him sleep.
VOLPONE [*aside*] Ay, his last sleep, if he would take it.
MOSCA   Sir,
He has no faith in physic.°   *medicine*
CORBACCIO   'Say you? 'Say you?
20   MOSCA He has no faith in physic. He does think
Most of your doctors[1] are the greater danger
And worse disease t'escape. I often have
Heard him protest that your physician
Should never be his heir.
CORBACCIO   Not I his heir?
MOSCA Not your physician, sir.
25   CORBACCIO   Oh, no, no, no,
I do not mean it.
MOSCA   No, sir, nor their fees
He cannot brook.° He says they flay° a man   *tolerate / skin*
Before they kill him.
CORBACCIO   Right, I do conceive° you.   *understand*
MOSCA And then, they do it by experiment,[2]
30   For which the law not only doth absolve 'em,
But gives them great reward; and he is loath
To hire his death so.
CORBACCIO   It is true, they kill
With as much license as a judge.
MOSCA   Nay, more:
For he° but kills, sir, where the law condemns,   *the judge*
And these° can kill him,° too.   *the doctors / the judge*
35   CORBACCIO   Ay, or me
Or any man. How does his apoplex?°   *apoplexy, stroke*
Is that strong on him still?
MOSCA   Most violent.[3]
His speech is broken and his eyes are set,°   *fixed*
His face drawn longer than 'twas wont—
CORBACCIO   How? How?
Stronger than he was wont?
40   MOSCA   No, sir: his face
Drawn longer than 'twas wont.

1.4
1. Not Corbaccio's doctors, but doctors generally. (Also in line 23.)
2. By testing possible remedies on their patients.

3. In the following lines, Mosca attributes to
Volpone a wide variety of symptoms that were,
even occurring singly, considered sure signs of
impending death.

CORBACCIO   Oh, good.
MOSCA   His mouth
     Is ever gaping, and his eyelids hang.
CORBACCIO   Good.
MOSCA   A freezing numbness stiffens all his joints,
     And makes the color of his flesh like lead.
CORBACCIO   'Tis good.
MOSCA   His pulse beats slow and dull.
45   CORBACCIO   Good symptoms still.
MOSCA   And from his brain—
CORBACCIO   Ha? How? Not from his brain?
MOSCA   Yes, sir, and from his brain—
CORBACCIO   I conceive you, good.
MOSCA   —Flows a cold sweat with a continual rheum°   *mucus discharge*
     Forth the resolvèd° corners of his eyes.   *watery; limp*
50   CORBACCIO   Is't possible? Yet I am better, ha!
     How does he with the swimming of his head?
MOSCA   Oh, sir, 'tis past the scotomy;[4] he now
     Hath lost his feeling, and hath left to snort;°   *stopped snoring*
     You hardly can perceive him that he breathes.
55   CORBACCIO   Excellent, excellent. Sure I shall outlast him!
     This makes me young again a score of years.
MOSCA   I was a-coming for you, sir.
CORBACCIO   Has he made his will?
     What has he giv'n me?
MOSCA   No, sir.
CORBACCIO   Nothing? Ha?
MOSCA   He has not made his will, sir.
CORBACCIO   Oh, oh, oh.
60   What then did Voltore, the lawyer, here?
MOSCA   He smelt a carcass, sir, when he but heard
     My master was about his testament°—   *making his will*
     As I did urge him to it, for your good—
CORBACCIO   He came unto him, did he? I thought so.
65   MOSCA   Yes, and presented him this piece of plate.
CORBACCIO   To be his heir?
MOSCA   I do not know, sir.
CORBACCIO   True,
     I know it too.
MOSCA [*aside*]   By your own scale,° sir.   *scale of values*
CORBACCIO [*showing a bag of gold*]   Well,
     I shall prevent° him yet. See, Mosca, look,   *forestall*
     Here I have brought a bag of bright *cecchines*,
     Will quite weigh down his plate.
70   MOSCA   Yea, marry, sir!
     This is true physic, this your sacred medicine;
     No talk of opiates to° this great elixir.[5]   *compared to*

4. Dizziness, accompanied by partial blindness.   prolonging life indefinitely or changing base
5. In alchemy, a liquid thought to be capable of   metal into gold.

CORBACCIO 'Tis *aurum palpabile*, if not *potabile*.[6]

MOSCA It shall be ministered to him in his bowl?

CORBACCIO Ay, do, do, do.

75 MOSCA   Most blessed cordial!°   *heart medicine*
This will recover him.

CORBACCIO   Yes, do, do, do.

MOSCA I think it were not best, sir.

CORBACCIO   What?

MOSCA   To recover him.

CORBACCIO Oh, no, no, no; by no means.

MOSCA   Why, sir, this
Will work some strange effect, if he but feel it.

80 CORBACCIO 'Tis true, therefore forbear, I'll take my venture.°   *investment*
Give me 't again.   [*He snatches for the bag.*]

MOSCA [*keeping it out of his reach*]   At no hand.° Pardon me,   *By no means*
You shall not do yourself that wrong, sir. I
Will so advise you, you shall have it all.

CORBACCIO How?

MOSCA   All, sir, 'tis your right, your own; no man
85 Can claim a part. 'Tis yours without a rival,
Decreed by destiny.

CORBACCIO   How? How, good Mosca?

MOSCA I'll tell you, sir. This fit he shall recover—

CORBACCIO I do conceive you.

MOSCA   —and, on first advantage°   *opportunity*
Of his gained sense, will I re-importune him
90 Unto the making of his testament,
And show him this.

CORBACCIO   Good, good.

MOSCA   'Tis better yet,
If you will hear, sir.

CORBACCIO   Yes, with all my heart.

MOSCA Now, would I counsel you, make home with speed;
There frame a will, whereto you shall inscribe
My master your sole heir.

95 CORBACCIO   And disinherit
My son?

MOSCA   Oh, sir, the better, for that color°   *appearance, fiction*
Shall make it much more taking.°   *plausible; attractive*

CORBACCIO   Oh, but color?°   *it's only a ruse?*

MOSCA This will, sir, you shall send it unto me.
Now, when I come to enforce°—as I will do—   *urge*
100 Your cares, your watchings, and your many prayers,
Your more than many gifts, your this day's present,
And last produce your will, where—without thought
Or least regard unto your proper issue,°   *own offspring*
A son so brave° and highly meriting—   *splendid*

---

6. It is gold that can be felt, if not drunk (Latin). Dissolved gold was used as a medicine.

105   The stream of your diverted love hath thrown you
     Upon my master, and made him your heir,
     He cannot be so stupid or stone dead
     But out of conscience and mere gratitude—

CORBACCIO   He must pronounce me his?

MOSCA   'Tis true.

CORBACCIO   This plot
     Did I think on before.

110 MOSCA   I do believe it.

CORBACCIO   Do you not believe it?

MOSCA   Yes, sir.

CORBACCIO   Mine own project.

MOSCA   Which when he hath done, sir—

CORBACCIO   Published me his heir?

MOSCA   And you so certain to survive him—

CORBACCIO   Ay.

MOSCA   Being so lusty a man—

CORBACCIO   'Tis true.

MOSCA   Yes, sir—

115 CORBACCIO   I thought on that too. See how he° should be   *Mosca*
     The very organ to express my thoughts!

MOSCA   You have not only done yourself a good—

CORBACCIO   But multiplied it on my son?

MOSCA   'Tis right, sir.

CORBACCIO   Still my invention.

MOSCA   'Las, sir, heaven knows,
120   It hath been all my study, all my care,
     (I e'en grow gray withal) how to work things—

CORBACCIO   I do conceive, sweet Mosca.

MOSCA   You are he
     For whom I labor here.

CORBACCIO   Ay, do, do, do.
     I'll straight about it.   [CORBACCIO *starts to leave.*]

MOSCA   Rook go with you,[7] raven!

CORBACCIO   I know thee honest.

MOSCA   You do lie, sir—

125 CORBACCIO   And—

MOSCA   Your knowledge is no better than your ears, sir.

CORBACCIO   I do not doubt to be a father to thee.

MOSCA   Nor I to gull my brother of his blessing.[8]

CORBACCIO   I may ha' my youth restored to me, why not?

MOSCA   Your Worship is a precious ass—

130 CORBACCIO   What say'st thou?

MOSCA   I do desire Your Worship to make haste, sir.

---

7. May you be swindled ("rooked"). Playing on "rook" meaning "crow," "raven." This speech and Mosca's following lines, through line 130, could be considered asides since Corbaccio cannot hear them; but they need not be delivered sotto voce.
8. If Corbaccio were Mosca's father, then

Bonario would be his brother. A reference to Genesis 25, in which Jacob tricks his elder brother, Esau, into resigning his birthright, and Genesis 27, in which Jacob tricks their dying father, Isaac, into giving him the paternal blessing and property.

CORBACCIO 'Tis done, 'tis done, I go.   [*Exit*.]
VOLPONE [*leaping from the bed*]   Oh, I shall burst!
    Let out my sides,° let out my sides—   *loosen my clothes*
MOSCA   Contain
    Your flux of laughter, sir. You know this hope
135   Is such a bait it covers any hook.
VOLPONE Oh, but thy working and thy placing it!
    I cannot hold;° good rascal, let me kiss thee.   *contain my delight*
    I never knew thee in so rare a humor.°   *so excellently witty*
MOSCA Alas, sir, I but do as I am taught:
140   Follow your grave instructions, give 'em words,
    Pour oil into their ears,° and send them hence.   *flatter them*
VOLPONE 'Tis true, 'tis true. What a rare punishment
    Is avarice to itself!⁹
MOSCA   Ay, with our help, sir.
VOLPONE So many cares, so many maladies,
145   So many fears attending on old age,
    Yea, death so often called on,° as no wish   *invoked*
    Can be more frequent with 'em, their limbs faint,
    Their senses dull, their seeing, hearing, going,°   *ability to walk*
    All dead before them; yea, their very teeth,
150   Their instruments of eating, failing them—
    Yet this is reckoned life! Nay, here was one
    Is now gone home that wishes to live longer!
    Feels not his gout nor palsy, feigns himself
    Younger by scores of years, flatters his age
155   With confident belying it,¹ hopes he may
    With charms, like Aeson,² have his youth restored,
    And with these thoughts so battens,° as if fate   *gluts himself*
    Would be as easily cheated on as he,
    And all turns air!°   *Another knocks.*   *is illusory*
                      Who's that there, now? A third?
160 MOSCA Close,° to your couch again. I hear his voice.   *hide yourself*
    It is Corvino, our spruce° merchant.   *dapper*
VOLPONE [*lying down again*]   Dead.°   *I'll play dead*
MOSCA Another bout, sir, with your eyes.
    [*He applies ointment.*]
                              Who's there?

SCENE 5. *The scene continues.*

    [*Enter*] CORVINO.
    Signor Corvino! Come° most wished for! Oh,   *you come*
    How happy were you if you knew it now!
CORVINO Why? What? Wherein?
MOSCA   The tardy hour is come, sir.

---

9. Quoting the Stoic philosopher Seneca's *Moral
Epistles*, no. 115.
1. Deceives himself, and attempts to deceive
others, about his age by vigorously refusing to
admit the truth.
2. Father of the Greek hero Jason; his youth was
restored by Medea, his sorceress daughter-in-
law.

CORVINO   He is not dead?
MOSCA   Not dead, sir, but as good;
  He knows no man.
CORVINO   How shall I do, then?
5 MOSCA   Why, sir?
CORVINO   I have brought him here a pearl.
MOSCA   Perhaps he has
  So much remembrance left as to know you, sir;
  He still calls on you; nothing but your name
  Is in his mouth. Is your pearl orient,[1] sir?
10 CORVINO   Venice was never owner of the like.
VOLPONE [*weakly*]   Signor Corvino—
MOSCA   Hark.
VOLPONE   —Signor Corvino—
MOSCA   He calls you. Step and give it him.—He's here, sir,
  And he has brought you a rich pearl.
CORVINO [*to* VOLPONE]   How do you, sir?
  [*To* MOSCA] Tell him it doubles the twelfth carat.[2]
        [*He gives* VOLPONE *the pearl.*]
MOSCA [*to* CORVINO]   Sir,
15 He cannot understand. His hearing's gone;
  And yet it comforts him to see you—
CORVINO   Say
  I have a diamond for him too.
MOSCA   Best show't, sir.
  Put it into his hand; 'tis only there
  He apprehends; he has his feeling yet.
        [CORVINO *gives* VOLPONE *the diamond.*]
  See how he grasps it!
20 CORVINO   'Las, good gentleman!
  How pitiful the sight is!
MOSCA   Tut, forget, sir.
  The weeping of an heir should still° be laughter   *always*
  Under a visor.°   *mask*
CORVINO   Why, am I his heir?
MOSCA   Sir, I am sworn; I may not show the will
25 Till he be dead. But here has been Corbaccio,
  Here has been Voltore, here were others too,
  I cannot number 'em they were so many,
  All gaping here for legacies; but I,
  Taking the vantage° of his naming you—   *opportunity*
30 "Signor Corvino! Signor Corvino!"—took
  Paper and pen and ink, and there I asked him
  Whom he would have his heir? "Corvino." Who
  Should be executor? "Corvino." And
  To any question he was silent to,

1.5
1. Especially brilliant. (The most beautiful pearls came from the Indian Ocean.)
2. In the seventeenth century, a carat was between 1/144 and 1/150 of an ounce. A twenty-four-carat pearl was therefore very large, weighing roughly 1/6 of an ounce.

35   I still interpreted the nods he made
    Through weakness for consent, and sent home th'others,
    Nothing bequeathed them but to cry and curse.
CORVINO   Oh, my dear Mosca! [*They embrace.*] Does he not
    perceive us?
MOSCA   No more than a blind harper.[3] He knows no man,
40   No face of friend, nor name of any servant,
    Who 'twas that fed him last or gave him drink;
    Not those he hath begotten or brought up
    Can he remember.
CORVINO   Has he children?
MOSCA   Bastards,[4]
    Some dozen or more, that he begot on beggars,
45   Gypsies and Jews and blackmoors,° when he was drunk.   *black Africans*
    Knew you not that, sir? 'Tis the common fable.°   *rumor*
    The dwarf, the fool, the eunuch are all his;
    He's the true father of his family
    In all save° me, but he has given 'em nothing.   *except*
50 CORVINO   That's well, that's well. Art sure he does not
    hear us?
MOSCA   Sure, sir? Why, look you, credit your own sense.°   *believe your senses*
    [*Shouting at* VOLPONE] The pox° approach and add to   *syphilis*
    your diseases
    If it would send you hence the sooner, sir.
    For your incontinence, it hath deserved it
55   Throughly° and throughly, and the plague to boot.   *thoroughly*
    [*To* CORVINO] You may come near, sir. [*shouting at* VOLPONE *again*]
        Would you would once close
    Those filthy eyes of yours, that flow with slime
    Like two frog-pits,° and those same hanging cheeks,   *mud puddles*
    Covered with hide instead of skin—nay, help, sir—
60   That look like frozen dishclouts° set on end!   *dishrags*
CORVINO [*shouting at* VOLPONE]   Or like an old smoked wall on
    which the rain
    Ran down in streaks!
MOSCA   Excellent, sir! Speak out;
    You may be louder yet; a culverin°   *firearm*
    Dischargèd in his ear would hardly bore it.
65 CORVINO [*shouting*]   His nose is like a common sewer, still°   *continually*
    running.
MOSCA   'Tis good! And what his mouth?
CORVINO [*shouting*]   A very draught!°   *cesspool*
MOSCA   Oh, stop it up—
CORVINO   By no means.
MOSCA   Pray you let me.
    Faith, I could stifle him rarely with a pillow
    As well as any woman that should keep° him.   *take care of*
CORVINO   Do as you will, but I'll be gone.

3. Harp players were often blind.
4. By law, ordinarily barred from the line of inheritance.

70 MOSCA   Be so;
    It is your presence makes him last so long.
    CORVINO   I pray you, use no violence.
    MOSCA   No, sir? Why?
    Why should you be thus scrupulous? Pray you, sir.
    CORVINO   Nay, at your discretion.
    MOSCA   Well, good sir, begone.
75 CORVINO   I will not trouble him now to take my pearl?
    MOSCA   Pooh! Nor your diamond. What a needless care
    Is this afflicts you? Is not all here yours?
    Am not I here, whom you have made your creature?
    That owe my being to you?
    CORVINO   Grateful Mosca!
80 Thou art my friend, my fellow, my companion,
    My partner, and shalt share in all my fortunes.
    MOSCA   Excepting one.
    CORVINO   What's that?
    MOSCA   Your gallant° wife, sir.   *splendid*
                                     [*Exit* CORVINO.]
    Now is he gone. We had no other means
    To shoot him hence but this.
    VOLPONE   My divine Mosca!
    Thou hast today outgone thyself.   *Another knocks.*
85   Who's there?
    I will be troubled with no more. Prepare
    Me music, dances, banquets, all delights.
    The Turk[5] is not more sensual in his pleasures
    Than will Volpone.   [*Exit* MOSCA.]
                 Let me see, a pearl?
90 A diamond? Plate? *Cecchines?* Good morning's purchase.°   *haul*
    Why, this is better than rob churches, yet,
    Or fat by eating, once a month, a man.°   *i.e., taking monthly interest*
          [*Enter* MOSCA.]
    Who is't?
    MOSCA   The beauteous Lady Would-be, sir,
    Wife to the English knight, Sir Politic Would-be—
95 This is the style, sir, is directed me[6]—
    Hath sent to know how you have slept tonight,°   *last night*
    And if you would be visited.
    VOLPONE   Not now.
    Some three hours hence—
    MOSCA   I told the squire° so much.   *messenger*
    VOLPONE   When I am high with mirth and wine: then, then.
100 'Fore heaven, I wonder at the desperate° valor   *reckless*
    Of the bold English, that they dare let loose
    Their wives to all encounters![7]

---

5. Stereotyped as given to decadent luxuries.
6. This is the mode of address I've been told to use.
7. Married Englishwomen were reputed to enjoy more personal freedom than their southern European counterparts; Venetian wives in particular were much restricted, though Celia's situation is obviously extreme (see below, p. 1014, lines 118–26).

MOSCA   Sir, this knight
Had not his name for nothing. He is politic,°   *canny*
And knows, howe'er his wife affect strange° airs,   *foreign; bizarre*
105   She hath not yet the face[8] to be dishonest.°   *unchaste*
But had she Signor Corvino's wife's face—
VOLPONE   Has she so rare a face?
MOSCA   Oh, sir, the wonder,
The blazing star[9] of Italy! A wench
O'the first year!° A beauty ripe as harvest!   *unflawed and in her prime*
110   Whose skin is whiter than a swan, all over,
Than silver, snow, or lilies! A soft lip,
Would° tempt you to eternity of kissing!   *that would*
And flesh that melteth in the touch to blood![1]
Bright as your gold, and lovely as your gold!
VOLPONE   Why had not I known this before?
115 MOSCA   Alas, sir,
Myself but yesterday discovered it.
VOLPONE   How might I see her?
MOSCA   Oh, not possible.
She's kept as warily as is your gold:
Never does come abroad,° never takes air   *outside*
120   But at a window. All her looks are sweet
As the first° grapes or cherries, and are watched   *of the season*
As near° as they are.   *closely*
VOLPONE   I must see her—
MOSCA   Sir,
There is a guard of ten spies thick upon her—
All his whole household—each of which is set
125   Upon his fellow, and have all their charge
When he goes out; when he comes in, examined.[2]
VOLPONE   I will go see her, though but at her window.
MOSCA   In some disguise, then.
VOLPONE   That is true. I must
Maintain mine own shape still the same.[3] We'll think.

                                    [*Exeunt.*]

Act 2

SCENE 1. *Saint Mark's Square.*

[*Enter*] POLITIC WOULD-BE [*and*] PEREGRINE.

POLITIC   Sir, to a wise man all the world's his soil.[1]
It is not Italy, nor France, nor Europe
That must bound me if my fates call me forth.
Yet I protest it is no salt° desire   *inordinate*

---

8. (1) Beauty; (2) shamelessness.
9. Comet. (Rare and beautiful.)
1. (1) Blushes; (2) sexual responsiveness. (Mosca is evidently conjecturing here.)
2. Each member of the household spies on all the others; each gets his instructions when Corvino departs and is interrogated when he returns.
3. I must, in my own person, continue to pretend to be near death.
2.1
1. Proverbial, like most of Sir Pol's "original" advice. "Soil": native land.

5	Of seeing countries, shifting a religion,²
	Nor any disaffection to the state
	Where I was bred—and unto which I owe
	My dearest plots°—hath brought me out;° much less

projects / abroad

That idle, antique, stale, gray-headed project

10 Of knowing men's minds and manners with Ulysses;³

But a peculiar humor° of my wife's   *whim*

Laid for this height° of Venice, to observe,   *latitude*

To quote,° to learn the language, and so forth.—   *jot things down*

I hope you travel, sir, with license?⁴

PEREGRINE   Yes.

15 POLITIC   I dare the safelier converse. How long, sir,

Since you left England?

PEREGRINE   Seven weeks.

POLITIC   So lately!

You ha' not been with my Lord Ambassador?

PEREGRINE   Not yet, sir.

POLITIC   Pray you, what news, sir, vents our climate?⁵

I heard last night a most strange thing reported

20 By some of my lord's° followers, and I long   *the ambassador's*

To hear how't will be seconded.°   *confirmed*

PEREGRINE   What was't, sir?

POLITIC   Marry, sir, of a raven that should build°   *reportedly built*

In a ship royal of the King's.

PEREGRINE [*aside*]   This fellow,

Does he gull° me, trow?°—Or is gulled?—Your name, sir?   *trick / do you*

POLITIC   My name is Politic Would-be.   *suppose?*

25 PEREGRINE [*aside*]   Oh, that speaks° him.—   *characterizes*

A knight, sir?

POLITIC   A poor knight, sir.⁶

PEREGRINE   Your lady

Lies° here in Venice for intelligence°   *stays / news*

Of tires° and fashions and behavior   *apparel*

Among the courtesans?⁷ The fine Lady Would-be?

30 POLITIC   Yes, sir, the spider and the bee ofttimes

Suck from one flower.

PEREGRINE   Good Sir Politic,

I cry you mercy!° I have heard much of you.   *beg your pardon*

'Tis true, sir, of your raven.

POLITIC   On your knowledge?

PEREGRINE   Yes, and your lion's whelping in the Tower.⁸

POLITIC   Another whelp!

---

2. Throughout the 16th and 17th centuries, members of religious minorities throughout Europe sought refuge in lands more hospitable to their faiths.
3. The hero of the *Odyssey*, an archetype of the wise traveler.
4. A passport. (English people could not travel abroad without permission.)
5. Comes from our part of the world?

6. In the first decade of the 17th century, King James I raised badly needed money by selling knighthoods to many whose birth, attainments, or wealth would not have previously merited a title.
7. Venice was famous for its elegant prostitutes.
8. A lioness kept at the Tower of London gave birth in 1604 and 1605.

PEREGRINE   Another, sir.
35 POLITIC   Now, heaven!
What prodigies° be these? The fires at Berwick!   *strange occurrences*
And the new star![9] These things concurring,° strange!   *happening together*
And full of omen! Saw you those meteors?
PEREGRINE   I did, sir.
POLITIC   Fearful! Pray you sir, confirm me:
40 Were there three porpoises seen above the bridge,[1]
As they give out?°   *people report*
PEREGRINE   Six, and a sturgeon, sir.
POLITIC   I am astonished!
PEREGRINE   Nay, sir, be not so.
I'll tell you a greater prodigy than these—
POLITIC   What should these things portend!
PEREGRINE   The very day—
45 Let me be sure—that I put forth from London,
There was a whale discovered in the river
As high° as Woolwich,[2] that had waited there—   *far upstream*
Few know how many months—for the subversion
Of the Stode Fleet.[3]
POLITIC   Is't possible? Believe it,
50 'Twas either sent from Spain or the Archdukes.[4]
Spinola's[5] whale, upon my life, my credit!°   *honor*
Will they not leave these projects? Worthy sir,
Some other news.
PEREGRINE   Faith, Stone the fool is dead;
And they do lack a tavern-fool extremely.
POLITIC   Is Mas' Stone dead?[6]
55 PEREGRINE   He's dead, sir. Why, I hope
You thought him not immortal? [*aside*] Oh, this knight,
Were he well known, would be a precious thing
To fit our English stage. He that should write
But such a fellow should be thought to feign
Extremely, if not maliciously.
60 POLITIC   Stone dead!
PEREGRINE   Dead. Lord, how deeply, sir, you apprehend it!
He was no kinsman to you?
POLITIC   That° I know of.   *not that*
Well, that same fellow was an unknown fool.[7]

---

9. The fires at Berwick were aurora borealis visible above Berwick, Northumberland, in 1605, said to resemble battling armies. The new star, a supernova, was described by the astronomer Johannes Kepler in 1604.
1. A porpoise was found upstream of London Bridge in the Thames River the January before *Volpone* was first performed.
2. A town on the Thames, a bit to the east of London.
3. The English merchant adventurers' ships, which were harboring at Stade, in the mouth of the Elbe River.
4. The Archduke Albert of Austria and his wife,

Isabella, the Infanta of Spain, ruled the Netherlands in the name of Spain.
5. Ambrosio de Spinola was general of the Spanish army in the Netherlands.
6. "Mas'" means "master," a term of address for boys and fools. Stone, King James's outspoken court jester, was a well-known urban character. He was whipped the year before *Volpone*'s first performance for slandering the Lord Admiral. Politic is evidently unaware of the play on words in "Stone dead."
7. The person who said this was not commonly recognized as a spy; he used foolery as his cover.

PEREGRINE   And yet you knew him, it seems?

POLITIC   I did so. Sir,

65   I knew him one of the most dangerous heads
      Living within the state, and so I held° him.   *considered*

PEREGRINE   Indeed, sir?

POLITIC   While he lived, in action,°   *subversive activities*
      He has received weekly intelligence,
      Upon my knowledge, out of the Low Countries,

70   For all parts of the world, in cabbages,°   *a Dutch import*
      And those dispensed again to ambassadors
      In oranges, muskmelons, apricots,
      Lemons, pome-citrons,° and suchlike—sometimes   *grapefruitlike fruits*
      In Colchester oysters, and your Selsey cockles.[8]

PEREGRINE   You make me wonder!

75   POLITIC   Sir, upon my knowledge.
      Nay, I have observed him at your public ordinary°   *tavern*
      Take his advertisement° from a traveler—   *information*
      A concealed statesman—in a trencher° of meat,   *wooden plate*
      And instantly before the meal was done
      Convey an answer in a toothpick.[9]

80   PEREGRINE   Strange!
      How could this be, sir?

POLITIC   Why, the meat was cut
      So like his character,° and so laid as he   *code letters*
      Must easily read the cipher.

PEREGRINE   I have heard
      He could not read, sir.

POLITIC   So 'twas given out,

85   In polity,° by those that did employ him.   *craftily*
      But he could read, and had your languages,°   *knew foreign languages*
      And to't° as sound a noddle°—   *in addition / head*

PEREGRINE   I have heard, sir,
      That your baboons were spies, and that they were
      A kind of subtle nation near to China.

90   POLITIC   Ay, ay, your *Mamuluchi*.[1] Faith, they had
      Their hand in a French plot or two, but they
      Were so extremely given to women as
      They made discovery of° all. Yet I   *revealed*
      Had my advices° here, on Wednesday last,   *information*

95   From one of their own coat;° they were returned,   *kind*
      Made their relations,° as the fashion is,   *reports*
      And now stand fair° for fresh employment.   *ready*

PEREGRINE [*aside*]   Heart,
      This Sir Pol will be° ignorant of nothing.   *admit to being*
      [*To* POLITIC] It seems, sir, you know all?

POLITIC   Not all, sir. But

---

8. Expensive delicacies, unlikely tavern fare.
9. Presumably by inserting a tiny note into a
toothpick hollowed out for espionage use.

1. Mamluks, a class of warriors originally from
Asia Minor, who ruled Egypt from 1250 to 1517.

100   I have some general notions; I do love
    To note and to observe. Though I live out,°   *abroad*
    Free from the active torrent, yet I'd mark
    The currents and the passages of things
    For mine own private use, and know the ebbs
    And flows of state.
105 PEREGRINE   Believe it, sir, I hold
    Myself in no small tie unto my fortunes°   *much obliged to my luck*
    For casting me thus luckily upon you,
    Whose knowledge—if your bounty equal it—
    May do me great assistance in instruction
110   For my behavior and my bearing, which
    Is yet so rude and raw—
    POLITIC   Why, came you forth
    Empty of rules for travel?
    PEREGRINE   Faith, I had
    Some common ones from out that vulgar grammar,[2]
    Which he that cried° Italian to me taught me.   *taught orally*
115 POLITIC   Why, this it is that spoils all our brave bloods,°   *fine young men*
    Trusting our hopeful° gentry unto pedants,   *promising*
    Fellows of outside and mere bark.[3] You seem
    To be a gentleman of ingenuous race°—   *honorable family*
    I not profess it,° but my fate hath been   *don't declare it openly*
120   To be where I have been consulted with
    In this high kind,° touching some great men's sons,   *important matter*
    Persons of blood° and honor—   *noble birth*
    PEREGRINE   Who be these, sir?

SCENE 2. *The scene continues.*

    [*Enter*] MOSCA [*and*] NANO [*disguised as a mountebank's assistants*].
    MOSCA   Under that window, there't must be. The same.
               [MOSCA *and* NANO *set up a platform.*]
    POLITIC   Fellows to mount a bank!° Did your instructor   *platform*
    In the dear tongues[1] never discourse to you
    Of the Italian mountebanks?
    PEREGRINE   Yes, sir.
    POLITIC   Why,
    Here shall you see one.
5 PEREGRINE   They are quacksalvers,
    Fellows that live by venting° oils and drugs.   *selling*
    POLITIC   Was that the character he gave you of them?
    PEREGRINE   As I remember.
    POLITIC   Pity his ignorance.
    They are the only knowing men of Europe!
10   Great general scholars, excellent physicians,
    Most admired statesmen, professed favorites

---

2. Modern language textbook, which sometimes included travelers' tips.
3. Superficial accomplishments.

2.2
1. Italian was called the "cara lingua," a phrase Sir Pol translates.

And cabinet counselors° to the greatest princes!   *close advisers*
The only languaged° men of all the world!   *most eloquent*
PEREGRINE   And I have heard they are most lewd° impostors,   *ignorant*
15   Made all of terms° and shreds, no less beliers   *jargon*
Of great men's favors than their own vile med'cines,
Which they will utter° upon monstrous oaths,   *advertise for sale*
Selling that drug for twopence ere they part
Which they have valued at twelve crowns° before.   *silver or gold coins*
20   POLITIC   Sir, calumnies are answered best with silence.
Yourself shall judge. [*to* MOSCA *and* NANO] Who is it mounts, my friends?
MOSCA   Scoto of Mantua,[2] sir.
POLITIC   Is't he? [*to* PEREGRINE] Nay, then,
I'll proudly promise, sir, you shall behold
Another man than has been fancied° to you.   *presented in imagination*
25   I wonder yet that he should mount his bank
Here in this nook, that has been wont t'appear
In face of° the piazza! Here he comes.   *facing*
    [*Enter*] VOLPONE [*disguised as a mountebank, followed
    by*] *a crowd.*
VOLPONE [*to* NANO]   Mount, zany.°   *clown; performer*
    [VOLPONE *and* NANO *climb onto the platform.*]
CROWD   Follow, follow, follow, follow, follow!
30   POLITIC   See how the people follow him! He's a man
May write ten thousand crowns in bank here. Note,
Mark but his gesture. I do use° to observe   *make it my practice*
The state° he keeps, in getting up.   *stateliness*
PEREGRINE   'Tis worth it, sir.
VOLPONE   Most noble gentlemen and my worthy patrons, it
35   may seem strange that I, your Scoto Mantuano, who was
ever wont to fix my bank in face of the public piazza near
the shelter of the portico to the *procuratia*,[3] should now,
after eight months' absence from this illustrious city of
Venice, humbly retire myself into an obscure nook of the
40   piazza.
POLITIC [*to* PEREGRINE]   Did not I now object the same?°   *ask the same*
PEREGRINE   Peace, sir.   *question*
VOLPONE   Let me tell you: I am not, as your Lombard prov-
erb saith, cold on my feet,° or content to part with my com-   *in desperate*
modities at a cheaper rate than I accustomed; look not for   *straits*
45   it. Nor that the calumnious reports of that impudent detrac-
tor and shame to our profession (Alessandro Buttone,°   *a rival*
I mean) who gave out in public I was condemned a   *mountebank*
'*sforzato*° to the galleys for poisoning the Cardinal   *prisoner*
Bembo's—cook,[4] hath at all attached,° much less dejected   *stuck to*
50   me. No, no, worthy gentlemen. To tell you true, I cannot

---

2. An Italian juggler and magician who visited
England and performed before Elizabeth I in the
1570s.
3. Arcade on the north side of the Piazza di San
Marco.

4. Pietro Bembo (1470–1547) was a famous
humanist, featured as a speaker in Castiglione's
Courtier (1528). "Cook" is a teasing substitution
for "whore."

endure to see the rabble of these ground *ciarlitani*,[5] that
spread their cloaks on the pavement as if they meant to
do feats of activity° and then come in lamely with their   *acrobatics*
moldy tales out of Boccaccio, like stale Tabarine,[6] the
55   fabulist: some of them discoursing their travels and of
their tedious captivity in the Turks' galleys, when indeed,
were the truth known, they were the Christians' galleys,
where very temperately they ate bread and drunk water as
a wholesome penance, enjoined them by their confessors,
for base pilferies.
60 POLITIC [*to* PEREGRINE]   Note but his bearing and contempt
of these.
  VOLPONE   These turdy-facy-nasty-paty-lousy-fartical rogues,
with one poor groatsworth° of unprepared antimony,[7]   *fourpenceworth*
finely wrapped up in several *scartoccios*,° are able very well   *paper envelopes*
65   to kill their twenty a week, and play;° yet these meager   *as if a game*
starved spirits, who have half stopped the organs of their
minds with earthy oppilations,° want° not their favorers   *obstructions / lack*
among your shriveled, salad-eating artisans, who are over-
joyed that they may have their ha'p'orth° of physic; though   *halfpennyworth*
70   it purge 'em into another world, 't makes no matter.
  POLITIC   Excellent! Ha' you heard better language, sir?
  VOLPONE   Well, let 'em go.° And, gentlemen, honorable   *say no more*
gentlemen, know that for this time, our bank, being thus   *about them*
removed from the clamors of the *canaglia*,° shall be the   *mob*
75   scene of pleasure and delight. For I have nothing to sell,
little or nothing to sell.
  POLITIC   I told you, sir, his end.
  PEREGRINE   You did so, sir.
  VOLPONE   I protest, I and my six servants are not able to
make of this precious liquor so fast as it is fetched away
80   from my lodging by gentlemen of your city, strangers of the
terra firma,[8] worshipful merchants, ay, and senators too,
who ever since my arrival have detained me to their uses by
their splendidous liberalities. And worthily. For what avails
your rich man to have his magazines° stuffed with *mos-*   *storehouses*
85   *cadelli*,° or of° the purest grape, when his physicians pre-   *wine / wine of*
scribe him (on pain of death) to drink nothing but water
cocted° with anise seeds? Oh, health, health! The blessing   *boiled*
of the rich! The riches of the poor! Who can buy thee at
too dear a rate, since there is no enjoying this world with-
90   out thee? Be not then so sparing of your purses, honorable
gentlemen, as to abridge the natural course of life—
  PEREGRINE   You see his end?
  POLITIC   Ay, is't not good?

---

5. Charlatans too poor to afford a "bank," or
platform.
6. Boccaccio's *Decameron* is a storehouse of tales.
Tabarine was a member of an Italian comic troupe

that played in France and perhaps in England.
7. White metal used as an emetic and a poison.
8. Mainland territory of Venice.

VOLPONE   For when a humid flux° or catarrh, by the muta-   *runny discharge*
bility of air, falls from your head into an arm or shoulder
95   or any other part, take you a ducat or your *cecchine* of
gold and apply to the place affected; see what good effect
it can work. No, no, 'tis this blessed *unguento,*° this rare   *ointment*
extraction, that hath only power to disperse all malignant
humors that proceed either of hot, cold, moist, or windy
causes[9]—

PEREGRINE   I would he had put in "dry," too.

100   POLITIC   Pray you, observe.

VOLPONE   To fortify the most indigest and crude° stomach,   *upset*
ay, were it of one that, through extreme weakness, vomited blood, applying only a warm napkin to the place after
the unction and fricace;° for the *vertigine*° in the head   *massage /*
105   putting but a drop into your nostrils, likewise behind the   *dizziness*
ears, a most sovereign° and approved remedy; the *mal*   *potent*
caduco, cramps, convulsions, paralyses, epilepsies, *tremor*
cordia, retired nerves, ill vapors of the spleen, stoppings of
the liver, the stone, the strangury, *hernia ventosa, iliaca*
110   *passio*; stops a *dysenteria* immediately; easeth the torsion
of the small guts; and cures *melancholia hypochondriaca,*[1]
being taken and applied according to my printed receipt.°   *direction*
(*Pointing to his bill and his glass*°). For this is the physician,   *paper and flagon*
this the medicine; this counsels, this cures; this gives the
115   direction, this works the effect; and in sum, both together
may be termed an abstract of the theoric and practic in the
Aesculapian[2] art. 'Twill cost you eight crowns. And, Zan
Fritatta,[3] pray thee sing a verse extempore in honor of it.

POLITIC   How do you like him, sir?

PEREGRINE   Most strangely, I!

POLITIC   Is not his language rare?°   *unrivaled*

120   PEREGRINE   But° alchemy   *except for*
I never heard the like, or Broughton's books.[4]

SONG

NANO [*sings*]   Had old Hippocrates or Galen,[5]
That to their books put med'cines all in,
But known this secret, they had never
125   (Of which they will be guilty ever)
Been murderers of so much paper,°   *written so much*

---

9. Renaissance medicine was based on the theory
of the humors, four bodily fluids whose balance
within the body determined both physical and
mental health. Their qualities, in various combinations, were hot, cold, moist, and dry; hence Peregrine's comment in the next line.
1. Volpone's list of diseases includes *"mal caduco,"*
epilepsy; *"tremor cordia,"* palpitations; "retired
nerves," withered sinews; "ill vapors of the spleen,"
short temper; "stone," kidney stones; "strangury,"
painful urination; *"hernia ventosa,"* a hernia containing air; *"iliaca passio,"* intestinal cramps;
"dysenteria," diarrhea; "torsion of the small guts,"

spasmodic bowel pain; and *"melancholia hypo-*
chondriaca," depression.
2. Medical. Aesculapius was the classical god of
medicine.
3. Italian dialect for "Jack Omelet," the name of
the zany (see line 28), here referring to Nano.
4. Hugh Broughton was a Puritan rabbinical
scholar who wrote impenetrable treatises on
scriptural matters.
5. Greek physicians (ca. 460–377 B.C.E. and 129–
ca. 199 C.E., respectively) who developed the theory of humors.

Or wasted many a hurtless taper;°   *candle (working at night)*
No Indian drug had e'er been famed,
Tobacco, sassafras[6] not named,
130   Ne° yet of *guacum*[7] one small stick, sir,   *nor*
Nor Raymond Lully's great elixir.
Ne had been known the Danish Gonswart
Or Paracelsus with his long sword.[8]

PEREGRINE   All this yet will not do; eight crowns is high.

135 VOLPONE [*to* NANO]   No more.—Gentlemen, if I had but
time to discourse to you the miraculous effects of this my
oil, surnamed *oglio del Scoto*, with the countless catalogue
of those I have cured of th'aforesaid and many more diseases, the patents and privileges of all the princes and
140 commonwealths of Christendom, or but the depositions of
those that appeared on my part before the signory of the
Sanitá,[9] and most learned College of Physicians, where I
was authorized, upon notice taken of the admirable virtues
of my medicaments and mine own excellency in matter
145 of rare and unknown secrets, not only to disperse them
publicly in this famous city but in all the territories that
happily joy under the government of the most pious and
magnificent states of Italy. But may some other gallant fellow say, "Oh, there be divers that make profession° to have   *that claim*
150 as good and as experimented receipts as yours." Indeed,
very many have assayed like apes in imitation of that which
is really and essentially in me, to make of° this oil; bestowed   *some of*
great cost in furnaces, stills, alembics,[1] continual fires, and
preparation of the ingredients (as indeed there goes to it
155 six hundred several simples,° besides some quantity of   *different*
human fat for the conglutination,° which we buy of the   *ingredients / to*
anatomists); but, when these practitioners come to the last   *glue it together*
decoction,° blow, blow, puff, puff, and all flies *in fumo*.°   *boiling down /*
Ha, ha, ha! Poor wretches! I rather pity their folly and   *up in smoke*
160 indiscretion° than their loss of time and money; for those   *lack of*
may be recovered by industry, but to be a fool born is a   *discernment*
disease incurable. For myself, I always from my youth have
endeavored to get the rarest secrets and book° them, either   *record*
in exchange or for money; I spared nor° cost nor labor   *neither*
165 where anything was worthy to be learned. And, gentlemen,
honorable gentlemen, I will undertake, by virtue of chemi-
cal art, out of the honorable hat that covers your head to
extract the four elements—that is to say, the fire, air, water,
and earth—and return you your felt° without burn or stain.   *felt hat*
170 For, whilst others have been at the balloo° I have been at   *Venetian ball*
     game

---

6. New World plants, used medicinally.
7. The bark of a tropical tree, used medicinally.
8. Raymond Lully was a medieval astrologer
rumored to have discovered the elixir of life. "Danish Gonswart" has not been positively identified.

Paracelsus was an early 16th-century alchemist
who developed an alternative to Galenic medicine;
he carried his medicines in his sword pommel.
9. Venetian medical licensing board.
1. Vessels for purifying liquids.

my book, and am now past the craggy paths of study and
come to the flow'ry plains of honor and reputation.

POLITIC   I do assure you, sir, that is his aim.

VOLPONE   But to our price.

PEREGRINE   And that withal,° Sir Pol.   *as well*

175   VOLPONE   You all know, honorable gentlemen, I never valued this *ampulla*, or vial, at less than eight crowns, but for
this time I am content to be deprived of it for six; six crowns
is the price, and less, in courtesy, I know you cannot offer
me. Take it or leave it howsoever, both it and I am at your

180   service. I ask you not as the value of the thing, for then I
should demand° of you a thousand crowns; so the Cardi-   *ask*
nals Montalto, Fernese, the great Duke of Tuscany, my
gossip,° with divers other princes, have given me. But I   *buddy*
despise money. Only to show my affection to you, honor-

185   able gentlemen, and your illustrious state here, I have
neglected the messages of these princes, mine own offices,°   *duties*
framed° my journey hither only to present you with the   *devised*
fruits of my travels. [*to* NANO *and* MOSCA] Tune your voices
once more to the touch of your instruments, and give the

190   honorable assembly some delightful recreation.

PEREGRINE   What monstrous and most painful circum-
stance°   *beating around the bush*
Is here, to get some three or four *gazets!*°   *small Venetian coins*
Some threepence, i'th'whole, for that 'twill come to.

Song

[*During the song,* CELIA *appears at her window, above.*]

NANO [*sings*]°   You that would last long, list to my song,   *accompanied*

195   Make no more coil,° but buy of this oil.   *by Mosca / fuss*
Would you be ever fair and young?
Stout of teeth and strong of tongue?
Tart° of palate? Quick of ear?   *keen*
Sharp of sight? Of nostril clear?

200   Moist of hand[2] and light of foot?
Or (I will come nearer to't)°   *get to the point*
Would you live free from all diseases,
Do the act your mistress pleases,
Yet fright all aches° from your bones?   *venereal disease*

205   Here's a med'cine for the nones.°   *occasion*

VOLPONE   Well, I am in a humor at this time to make a present of the small quantity my coffer contains: to the rich in
courtesy, and to the poor for God's sake.° Wherefore, now   *charity*
mark; I asked you six crowns, and six crowns at other

210   times you have paid me. You shall not give me six crowns,
nor five, nor four, nor three, nor two, nor one, nor half a
ducat, no, nor a *moccenigo*.° Six—pence it will cost you, or   *worth ninepence*

2. Associated with youth and sexual vigor.

six hundred pound—expect no lower price, for by the
banner of my front,° I will not bate a *bagatine*,[3] that I will — *displayed on my "bank"*
215 have only a pledge of your loves, to carry something from
amongst you to show I am not contemned° by you. There- — *scorned*
fore now, toss your handkerchiefs cheerfully, cheerfully,
and be advertised° that the first heroic spirit that deigns to — *notified*
grace me with a handkerchief, I will give it a little remem-
220 brance of something beside, shall please° it better than if I — *which will please*
had presented it with a double *pistolet*.[4]

PEREGRINE Will you be that heroic spark,° Sir Pol? — *gallant*

CELIA *at the window throws down her handkerchief*
[with a coin tied inside it].

Oh, see! The window has prevented you.° — *beaten you to it*

VOLPONE Lady, I kiss your bounty, and, for this timely grace
225 you have done your poor Scoto of Mantua, I will return
you, over and above my oil, a secret of that high and inestimable nature shall° make you forever enamored on that — *which will*
minute wherein your eye first descended on so mean,° yet — *lowly*
not altogether to be despised, an object. Here is a powder
230 concealed in this paper of which, if I should speak to the
worth, nine thousand volumes were but as one page, that
page as a line, that line as a word—so short is this pilgrimage of man, which some call life, to° the expressing of it. — *compared to*
Would I reflect on the price, why, the whole world were but
235 as an empire, that empire as a province, that province as a
bank, that bank as a private purse, to the purchase of it. I
will only tell you it is the powder that made Venus a goddess, given her by Apollo,[5] that kept her perpetually young,
cleared her wrinkles, firmed her gums, filled° her skin, col- — *filled out*
240 ored her hair; from her derived to Helen, and at the sack
of Troy unfortunately lost; till now in this our age it was
as happily° recovered by a studious antiquary out of some — *fortunately*
ruins of Asia, who sent a moiety° of it to the court of — *part*
France (but much sophisticated)° wherewith the ladies — *adulterated*
245 there now color their hair. The rest, at this present, remains
with me, extracted to a quintessence,° so that wherever — *refined concentrate*
it but touches, in youth it perpetually preserves, in age
restores the complexion; seats your teeth, did° they dance — *even if*
like virginal jacks,[6] firm as a wall; makes them white as
250 ivory that were black as—

SCENE 3. *The scene continues.*

[*Enter*] CORVINO. *He beats away the mountebank, etc.*

CORVINO Spite o'the devil, and my shame! Come down here,
Come down! No house but mine to make your scene?° — *stage set*
Signor Flaminio, will you down, sir? Down!

---

3. I won't reduce the price by even a tiny coin.
4. Spanish gold coin worth about one English pound.
5. In his capacity as the god of health.

6. The virginal is a type of harpsichord; its "jacks" are quills that pluck strings when the keys are played, but the term was also sometimes used for the keys.

What, is my wife your Franciscina, sir?[1]
5 No windows on the whole piazza here
To make your properties° but mine? But mine?   *stage props*
Heart! Ere tomorrow I shall be new christened
And called the *pantalone di besogniosi*[2]
About the town.   [*Exeunt* VOLPONE, NANO, *and* MOSCA,
                    followed by CORVINO *and the crowd.*]
PEREGRINE   What should this mean, Sir Pol?
10 POLITIC   Some trick of state, believe it. I will home.
PEREGRINE   It may be some design on you.
POLITIC   I know not.
I'll stand upon my guard.
PEREGRINE   It is your best,° sir.   *best course of action*
POLITIC   This three weeks, all my advices, all my letters,
They have been intercepted,
PEREGRINE   Indeed, sir?
Best have a care.
POLITIC   Nay, so I will.   [*Exit.*]
15 PEREGRINE   This knight,
I may not lose him,° for my mirth, till night.   [*Exit.*] *I won't leave him*

SCENE 4. VOLPONE's *house.*

[*Enter*] VOLPONE [*and*] MOSCA.
VOLPONE   Oh, I am wounded!
MOSCA   Where, sir?
VOLPONE   Not without;°   *externally*
Those blows were nothing; I could bear them ever,
But angry Cupid, bolting° from her° eyes,   *shooting darts / Celia's*
Hath shot himself into me like a flame,
5 Where now he flings about his burning heat,
As in a furnace an ambitious° fire   *rising*
Whose vent is stopped. The fight is all within me.
I cannot live except thou help me, Mosca;
My liver[1] melts, and I, without the hope
10 Of some soft air from her refreshing breath,
Am but a heap of cinders.
MOSCA   'Las, good sir!
Would you had never seen her.
VOLPONE   Nay, would thou
Hadst never told me of her.
MOSCA   Sir, 'tis true;
I do confess I was unfortunate,
15 And you unhappy; but I'm bound in conscience

2.3
1. Corvino imagines the scene in terms of a stock episode from the Italian commedia dell'arte, in which the young lover, conventionally named Flaminio after the famous actor Flaminio Scala, seduces Franciscina, the easygoing serving wench. 2. The *pantalone* is another stock figure in the

commedia dell'arte, a decrepit old man suspicious of his desirable young wife. *Di besogniosi* is his jocular surname, meaning "descended from poor people."
2.4
1. Supposed to be the seat of lust.

No less than duty to effect my best
To your release of torment, and I will, sir.
VOLPONE Dear Mosca, shall I hope?
MOSCA   Sir, more than dear,
I will not bid you to despair of aught
Within a human compass.°   that's humanly possible
20 VOLPONE   Oh, there spoke
My better angel. Mosca, take my keys.
Gold, plate, and jewels, all's at thy devotion;°   disposal
Employ them how thou wilt; nay, coin me too,[2]
So° thou in this but crown my longings. Mosca?   provided that
MOSCA Use but your patience.
VOLPONE   So I have.[3]
25 MOSCA   I doubt not
To bring success to your desires.
VOLPONE   Nay, then,
I not repent me of my late disguise.
MOSCA If you can horn him,[4] sir, you need not.
VOLPONE   True;
Besides, I never meant him for my heir.
30 Is not the color o'my beard and eyebrows[5]
To make me known?
MOSCA   No jot.
VOLPONE   I did it well.
MOSCA So well, would I could follow you in mine
With half the happiness!° And yet I would   success
Escape your epilogue.°   the beating
VOLPONE   But were they gulled°   fooled
With a belief that I was Scoto?
35 MOSCA   Sir,
Scoto himself could hardly have distinguished!
I have not time to flatter you now. We'll part,
And, as I prosper, so applaud my art.   [Exeunt.]

SCENE 5. CORVINO'S house.

[Enter] CORVINO [and] CELIA.
CORVINO Death of mine honor, with the city's fool?
A juggling, tooth-drawing,[1] prating° mountebank?   chattering
And at a public window? Where, whilst he
With his strained action° and his dole of faces[2]   overacting
5 To his drug lecture draws your itching ears,
A crew of old, unmarried, noted lechers
Stood leering up like satyrs;° and you smile   lustful goat-men
Most graciously! And fan your favors forth

2. Use my coins as well. (But also with the implication "make coins out of me," i.e., "turn my body into money.")
3. Punning on the original meaning of "patience," "enduring blows."
4. Cuckold him. (The husbands of adulterous wives were traditionally supposed to sprout horns.)
5. Red, because he is a fox.
2.5
1. Mountebanks, like barbers, performed dental work.
2. Small repertory of facial expressions.

To give your hot spectators satisfaction!
10   What, was your mountebank their call? Their whistle?[3]
Or were you enamored on his copper rings?
His saffron jewel with the toadstone° in't?   *agatelike stone*
Or his embroidered suit with the cope-stitch,°   *gaudy needlework*
Made of a hearse-cloth? Or his old tilt-feather?[4]
15   Or his starched beard? Well! You shall have him, yes.
He shall come home and minister unto you
The fricace for the mother.[5] Or, let me see,
I think you'd rather mount?[6] Would you not mount?
Why, if you'll mount, you may; yes truly, you may—
20   And so you may be seen down to th'foot.
Get you a cittern, Lady Vanity,[7]
And be a dealer with the virtuous man;
Make one.[8] I'll but protest° myself a cuckold   *proclaim*
And save your dowry.[9] I am a Dutchman, I!
25   For if you thought me an Italian,
You would be damned ere you did this, you whore.[1]
Thou'dst tremble to imagine that the murder
Of father, mother, brother, all thy race,
Should follow as the subject of my justice!
CELIA   Good sir, have patience!
30   CORVINO [*drawing a weapon*]   What couldst thou propose
Less to thyself° than, in this heat of wrath   *as your punishment*
And stung with my dishonor, I should strike
This steel unto thee, with as many stabs
As thou wert gazed upon with goatish° eyes?   *lustful*
35   CELIA   Alas, sir, be appeased! I could not think
My being at the window should more now
Move your impatience than at other times.
CORVINO   No? Not to seek and entertain a parley°   *have a conversation*
With a known knave? Before a multitude?
40   You were an actor with your handkerchief!
Which he most sweetly kissed in the receipt,
And might, no doubt, return it with a letter,
And 'point the place where you might meet—your sister's,
Your mother's, or your aunt's might serve the turn.°   *occasion; sexual act*
45   CELIA   Why, dear sir, when do I make these excuses?
Or ever stir abroad but to the church?
And that, so seldom—
CORVINO   Well, it shall be less;
And thy restraint before was liberty

---

3. Used to lure trained falcons.
4. The feather from a tilting (jousting) helmet. A hearse-cloth is a heavy cloth for draping over a coffin.
5. Womb massage; with obvious sexual innuendo. "The mother" was a term for the uterus, but also for a variety of ailments, from cramps to depression, that were supposed to originate there.
6. (1) Climb up on the mountebank's stage yourself; (2) take the top sexual position.

7. Allegorical character of a morality play representing pride and worldly pleasure. A cittern is a guitarlike instrument that conventionally was played by whores.
8. Join up with him. (With sexual innuendo.)
9. The husbands of proven adultresses could divorce them and keep their dowry.
1. The Dutch were proverbially phlegmatic, in contrast to Italians, who were stereotypically impetuous and vengeful.

To what I now decree: and therefore, mark me.
50 [*Pointing to the window*] First, I will have this bawdy light dammed up,
And, till't be done, some two or three yards off
I'll chalk a line, o'er which if thou but chance
To set thy desp'rate foot, more hell, more horror,
More wild, remorseless rage shall seize on thee
55 Than on a conjurer that had heedless left
His circle's safety ere his devil was laid.[2]
Then here's a lock which I will hang upon thee.
    [*He shows a chastity belt.*]
And now I think on't, I will keep thee backwards;[3]
Thy lodging shall be backwards, thy walks backwards,
60 Thy prospect°—all be backwards; and no pleasure   *view (see n. 3)*
That thou shalt know but backwards. Nay, since you force
My honest nature, know it is your own
Being too open makes me use you thus,
Since you will not contain your subtle° nostrils   *delicate; crafty*
65 In a sweet° room, but they must snuff the air   *sweet-smelling*
Of rank and sweaty passengers°— *Knock within.*   *passersby*
                     One knocks.
Away, and be not seen, pain of thy life!
Not look toward the window. If thou dost—
                 [CELIA *begins to exit.*]
Nay stay, hear this—let me not prosper, whore,
70 But I will make thee an anatomy,[4]
Dissect thee mine own self, and read a lecture
Upon thee to the city, and in public.
Away!   [*Exit* CELIA.]
       Who's there?
     [*Enter*] *Servitore* [*a* SERVANT].
SERVANT   'Tis Signor Mosca, sir.

SCENE 6. *The scene continues.*

CORVINO   Let him come in.   [*Exit* SERVANT.]
              His master's dead! There's yet
Some good to help the bad.
     [*Enter*] MOSCA.
               My Mosca, welcome!
I guess your news.
MOSCA   I fear you cannot, sir.
CORVINO   Is't not his death?
MOSCA   Rather the contrary.
CORVINO   Not his recovery?
MOSCA   Yes, sir.
5 CORVINO   I am cursed,

2. Conjurers protected themselves from the devils who served them by staying inside a magical circle.
3. In the back part of the house, lacking a view out onto the piazza; but with the suggestion of anal intercourse, supposedly favored by Italians.
4. Use you for anatomical research. (In the early modern period, physicians obtained the bodies of executed criminals upon which to perform dissections, often before large crowds.)

I am bewitched! My crosses° meet to vex me!   *misfortunes*
How? How? How? How?

MOSCA   Why, sir, with Scoto's oil.
Corbaccio and Voltore brought of it
Whilst I was busy in an inner room—

10   CORVINO   Death! That damned mountebank! But for the law,
Now, I could kill the rascal. 'T cannot be
His oil should have that virtue. Ha' not I
Known him a common rogue, come fiddling in
To th'*osteria*° with a tumbling whore,   *tavern (Italian)*

15 And, when he has done all his forced tricks, been glad
Of a poor spoonful of dead wine with flies in't?
It cannot be. All his ingredients
Are a sheep's gall, a roasted bitch's marrow,
Some few sod° earwigs, pounded caterpillars,   *boiled*

20 A little capon's grease, and fasting spittle:[1]
I know 'em to a dram.°   *tiny amount*

MOSCA   I know not, sir,
But some on't there they poured into his ears,
Some in his nostrils, and recovered him,
Applying but the fricace.°   *massage*

CORVINO   Pox o'that fricace!

25 MOSCA   And since, to seem the more officious°   *zealous*
And flatt'ring of his health, there they have had—
At extreme fees—the College of Physicians
Consulting on him how they might restore him;
Where one would have a cataplasm[2] of spices,

30 Another a flayed ape clapped to his breast,
A third would ha' it a dog, a fourth an oil
With wildcats' skins. At last, they all resolved
That to preserve him was no other means
But some young woman must be straight sought out,

35 Lusty and full of juice, to sleep by him;
And to this service—most unhappily
And most unwillingly—am I now employed,
Which here I thought to preacquaint you with,
For your advice, since it concerns you most,

40 Because I would not do that thing might cross
Your ends,[3] on whom I have my whole dependence, sir.
Yet if I do it not, they may delate[4]
My slackness to my patron, work me out
Of his opinion;° and there all your hopes,   *favor*

45 Ventures, or whatsoever, are all frustrate.
I do but tell you, sir. Besides, they are all

2.6
1. Saliva of a fasting person. (Scoto cannot afford anything to eat.)
2. Poultice. (The substances described in the following lines were believed to work by absorbing the patient's infection, which bodes ill for the young woman prescribed for Volpone in lines 34–35.)
3. Do anything that might frustrate your purposes.
4. Report. (A legal term for making an accusation.)

Now striving who shall first present him. Therefore,
I could entreat you briefly, conclude somewhat;°   *decide something*
Prevent 'em if you can.

CORVINO   Death to my hopes!
50 This is my villainous fortune! Best to hire
Some common courtesan.

MOSCA   Ay, I thought on that, sir.
But they are all so subtle,° full of art,°   *cunning / deceit*
And age again° doting and flexible,   *old people moreover*
So as—I cannot tell—we may perchance
Light on a quean° may cheat us all.   *whore (who)*

55 CORVINO   'Tis true.

MOSCA No, no; it must be one that has no tricks, sir,
Some simple thing, a creature made unto° it;   *suited to; forced into*
Some wench you may command. Ha' you no kinswoman?
Godso°—think, think, think, think, think, think, think, sir.   *an oath*
60 One o'the doctors offered there his daughter.

CORVINO How!

MOSCA   Yes, Signor Lupo,° the physician.   *Wolf (Italian)*

CORVINO   His daughter?

MOSCA And a virgin, sir. Why, alas,
He knows the state of's body, what it is,
That naught can warm his blood, sir, but a fever,
65 Nor any incantation raise his spirit.°   *vigor; semen*
A long forgetfulness hath seized that part.°   *his penis*
Besides, sir, who shall know it? Some one or two—

CORVINO I pray thee give me leave.° [*He walks apart.*] If   *give me a minute*
any man
But I had had this luck—The thing in 'tself,
70 I know, is nothing.—Wherefore should not I
As well command my blood and my affections
As this dull doctor? In the point of honor
The cases are all one, of wife and daughter.

MOSCA [*aside*] I hear him coming.°   *coming around*

CORVINO [*aside*]   She shall do't. 'Tis done.
75 'Slight,° if this doctor, who is not engaged,   *by God's light (an oath)*
Unless 't be for his counsel (which is nothing),[5]
Offer his daughter, what should I, that am
So deeply in? I will prevent him. Wretch!
Covetous wretch!—Mosca, I have determined.

MOSCA How, sir?

80 CORVINO   We'll make all sure. The party you wot° of   *know*
Shall be mine own wife, Mosca.

MOSCA   Sir, the thing
(But that I would not seem to counsel you)
I should have motioned° to you at the first.   *proposed*
And, make your count,° you have cut all their throats.   *rest assured*

---

5. Who is not financially involved, except for whatever slight fee he could expect for his advice.

85 Why, 'tis directly taking a possession!⁶
  And in his next fit we may let him go.
  'Tis but to pull the pillow from his head
  And he is throttled; 't had been done before,
  But for your scrupulous doubts.
  CORVINO   Ay, a plague on't!
90 My conscience fools my wit.° Well, I'll be brief,   *common sense*
  And so be thou, lest they should be before us.
  Go home, prepare him, tell him with what zeal
  And willingness I do it; swear it was
  On the first hearing (as thou mayst do, truly)
  Mine own free motion.°   *initiative*
95 MOSCA   Sir, I warrant you,
  I'll so possess° him with it that the rest   *impress*
  Of his starved clients shall be banished all,
  And only you received. But come not, sir,
  Until I send, for I have something else
100 To ripen for your good; you must not know't.
  CORVINO But do not you forget to send, now.
  MOSCA   Fear not.
              [*Exit.*]

SCENE 7. *The scene continues.*

CORVINO Where are you, wife? My Celia? Wife?
  [*Enter*] CELIA [*weeping.*]
            What, blubbering?
  Come, dry those tears. I think thou thought'st me in earnest?
  Ha! By this light, I talked so but to try° thee.   *test*
  Methinks the lightness° of the occasion   *triviality*
5 Should ha' confirmed thee.¹ Come, I am not jealous.
  CELIA No?
  CORVINO Faith, I am not, I, nor never² was;
  It is a poor, unprofitable humor.
  Do not I know if women have a will
  They'll do 'gainst all the watches° o'the world? *despite the vigilance*
10 And that the fiercest spies are tamed with gold?
  Tut, I am confident in thee, thou shalt see't;
  And see, I'll give thee cause too, to believe it.
  Come, kiss me. Go and make thee ready straight
  In all thy best attire, thy choicest jewels;
15 Put 'em all on, and, with 'em thy best looks.
  We are invited to a solemn feast
  At old Volpone's, where it shall appear
  How far I am free from jealousy or fear. [*Exeunt.*]

---

6. A legal term for the heir's formal assumption of
inherited property.
2.7
1. Convinced you that I was not serious.

2. Double negatives are grammatical in Jacobean English.

Act 3

SCENE 1. *The piazza.*

[*Enter*] MOSCA.

MOSCA I fear I shall begin to grow in love
    With my dear self and my most prosp'rous parts,°   *talents*
    They do so spring and burgeon.° I can feel   *swell; thrive*
    A whimsy° i'my blood. I know not how,   *giddiness*
5   Success hath made me wanton. I could skip
    Out of my skin now like a subtle snake,
    I am so limber. Oh, your parasite
    Is a most precious thing, dropped from above,°   *sent from heaven*
    Not bred 'mongst clods and clodpolls here on earth.
10 I muse the mystery was not made a science,
    It is so liberally professed![1] Almost
    All the wise world is little else in nature
    But parasites or subparasites. And yet
    I mean not those that have your bare town-art,[2]
15 To know who's fit to feed 'em; have no house,
    No family, no care, and therefore mold
    Tales for men's ears,° to bait° that sense; or get   *tell juicy rumors / entice*
    Kitchen-invention, and some stale receipts°   *recipes*
    To please the belly and the groin;° nor those,   *as aphrodisiacs*
20 With their court-dog tricks, that can fawn and fleer,° *smile insincerely*
    Make their revenue out of legs and faces,
    Echo my lord, and lick away a moth;[3]
    But your fine, elegant rascal, that can rise
    And stoop almost together, like an arrow,
25 Shoot through the air as nimbly as a star,°   *meteor*
    Turn short as doth a swallow, and be here
    And there and here and yonder all at once,
    Present to any humor, all occasion,[4]
    And change a visor° swifter than a thought!   *mask; expression*
30 This is the creature had the art born with him,
    Toils not to learn it, but doth practice it
    Out of most excellent nature, and such sparks
    Are the true parasites, others but their zanies.°   *clownish imitators*

SCENE 2. *The scene continues.*

[*Enter*] BONARIO.

[*Aside*] Who's this? Bonario? Old Corbaccio's son?
The person I was bound° to seek.—Fair sir,   *on my way*
You are happ'ly met.

3.1
1. I wonder why the craft was not made a subject
for academic study, it is so frequently practiced!
(Punning on the "liberal professions.")
2. Crude skills of ingratiation, sufficient only
for getting free meals in taverns.

3. Make a living from bows and sycophantic
looks, repeat anything a nobleman says, and fawn
over him, fussing over every detail of his appearance.
4. Ready to respond to any mood or opportunity.

BONARIO   That cannot be by thee.

MOSCA   Why, sir?

BONARIO   Nay, pray thee know thy way and leave me.

5   I would be loath to interchange discourse

With such a mate° as thou art.   *fellow (contemptuous)*

MOSCA   Courteous sir,

Scorn not my poverty.

BONARIO   Not I, by heaven,

But thou shalt give me leave to hate thy baseness.

MOSCA   Baseness?

BONARIO   Ay. Answer me, is not thy sloth

10   Sufficient argument? Thy flattery?

Thy means of feeding?

MOSCA   Heaven, be good to me!

These imputations are too common, sir,

And eas'ly stuck on virtue when she's poor.

You are unequal° to me, and howe'er   *superior; unfair*

15   Your sentence° may be righteous, yet you are not,   *verdict*

That, ere you know me, thus proceed in censure.

Saint Mark bear witness 'gainst you, 'tis inhuman.   [*He weeps.*]

BONARIO [*aside*]   What? Does he weep? The sign is soft and good.

I do repent me that I was so harsh.

20   MOSCA   'Tis true that, swayed by strong necessity,

I am enforced to eat my careful bread

With too much obsequy;° 'tis true, beside,   *obsequiousness*

That I am fain° to spin mine own poor raiment   *obliged*

Out of my mere observance,° being not born   *deferential service*

25   To a free fortune. But that I have done

Base offices in rending friends asunder,

Dividing families, betraying counsels,

Whispering false lies, or mining° men with praises,   *undermining*

Trained° their credulity with perjuries,   *lured on*

30   Corrupted chastity, or am in love

With mine own tender ease, but would not rather

Prove° the most rugged and laborious course   *undergo*

That might redeem my present estimation,[1]

Let me here perish in all hope of goodness.

35   BONARIO [*aside*]   This cannot be a personated passion!—

I was to blame, so to mistake thy nature;

Pray thee forgive me, and speak out thy business.

MOSCA   Sir, it concerns you; and though I may seem

At first to make a main° offense in manners   *great*

40   And in my gratitude unto my master,

Yet for the pure love which I bear all right

And hatred of the wrong, I must reveal it.

This very hour your father is in purpose

To disinherit you—

BONARIO   How!

3.2

1. That might improve your current appraisal of me.

MOSCA   And thrust you forth

45   As a mere stranger to his blood. 'Tis true, sir.
The work no way engageth° me but as   *concerns*
I claim an interest in the general state
Of goodness and true virtue, which I hear
T'abound in you, and for which mere respect,°   *for which reason alone*
50   Without a second aim, sir, I have done it.
BONARIO   This tale hath lost thee much of the late° trust   *recent*
Thou hadst with me. It is impossible.
I know not how to lend it any thought°   *believe that*
My father should be so unnatural.
55 MOSCA   It is a confidence that well becomes
Your piety;° and formed, no doubt, it is   *filial loyalty*
From your own simple innocence, which makes
Your wrong more monstrous and abhorred. But, sir,
I now will tell you more. This very minute
60   It is or will be doing; and if you
Shall be but pleased to go with me, I'll bring you,
I dare not say where you shall see, but where
Your ear shall be a witness of the deed:
Hear yourself written bastard, and professed
The common issue of the earth.[2]
65 BONARIO   I'm mazed!
MOSCA   Sir, if I do it not, draw your just sword
And score your vengeance on my front° and face;   *brow*
Mark me your villain. You have too much wrong,
And I do suffer for you, sir. My heart
Weeps blood in anguish—
70 BONARIO   Lead. I follow thee. [*Exeunt.*]

SCENE 3. VOLPONE's *house.*

[*Enter*] VOLPONE, NANO, ANDROGYNO, [*and*] CASTRONE.
VOLPONE   Mosca stays long, methinks. Bring forth your sports
And help to make the wretched time more sweet.
NANO   Dwarf, fool, and eunuch, well met here we be.
A question it were now, whether° of us three,   *which*
5   Being all the known delicates° of a rich man,   *playthings*
In pleasing him, claim the precedency can?
CASTRONE   I claim for myself.
ANDROGYNO   And so doth the fool.
NANO   'Tis foolish indeed; let me set you both to school.
First, for your dwarf: he's little and witty,
10   And everything, as it is little, is pretty;
Else why do men say to a creature of my shape,
So soon as they see him, "It's a pretty little ape"?
And why a pretty ape? But for pleasing imitation
Of greater men's action in a ridiculous fashion.

---

2. A bastard was called *filius terrae,* "son of the earth."

15 Beside, this feat° body of mine doth not crave   *neat, trim*
    Half the meat, drink, and cloth one of your bulks will have.
    Admit your fool's face be the mother of laughter,
    Yet for his brain, it must always come after;°   *be lesser*
    And though that do feed him,° it's a pitiful case,[1]   *earns his keep*
20 His body is beholding° to such a bad face.   *One knocks.*   *beholden*
VOLPONE   Who's there? My couch. [*He lies down.*] Away,
        look, Nano, see!
    Give me my caps, first—go, inquire.
            [*Exeunt* NANO, ANDROGYNO, *and* CASTRONE.]
                                Now, Cupid
    Send° it be Mosca, and with fair return!°   *grant / good results*
            [*Enter* NANO.]
NANO   It is the beauteous Madam—
VOLPONE   Would-be—is it?
NANO   The same
25 VOLPONE   Now, torment on me! Squire her in,
    For she will enter or dwell here forever.
    Nay, quickly, that my fit were past!   [*Exit* NANO.]
                                I fear
    A second hell, too, that my loathing this
    Will quite expel my appetite to the other.°   *Celia*
30 Would she were taking, now, her tedious leave.
    Lord, how it threats me what I am to suffer!

                SCENE 4. *The scene continues.*

        [*Enter*] LADY [WOULD-BE *and*] NANO.
    LADY WOULD-BE [*to* NANO]   I thank you, good sir. Pray you signify
        Unto your patron I am here.[1] [*regarding herself in a mirror*] This
            band°   *ruff*
        Shows not my neck enough. I trouble you, sir.
        Let me request you, bid one of my women
        Come hither to me.   [*Exit* NANO.]
5   In good faith, I am dressed
        Most favorably today!° It is no matter;   *sarcastic*
        'Tis well enough.
                [*Enter* NANO *and* FIRST] WOMAN.
                        Look, see, these petulant things!°   *her women; her curls*
        How they have done this!
    VOLPONE [*aside*]   I do feel the fever
        Ent'ring in at mine ears. Oh, for a charm
        To fright it hence!
10 LADY WOULD-BE [*to* FIRST WOMAN]   Come nearer. Is this curl
        In his° right place? Or this? Why is this higher   *its*
        Than all the rest? You ha' not washed your eyes yet?

3.3
1. With a pun on "container."
3.4
1. Much of Lady Would-be's dialogue in the fol-   lowing scene is adapted from Libanius of Antioch's
    On Talkative Women.

Or do they not stand even° i'your head?   *level*
Where's your fellow? Call her.   [*Exit* FIRST WOMAN.]
NANO [*aside*]   Now Saint Mark
15   Deliver us! Anon she'll beat her women
Because her nose is red.
            [*Enter* FIRST *and* SECOND WOMEN.]
LADY WOULD-BE   I pray you, view
This tire,° forsooth. Are all things apt or no?   *headdress*
SECOND WOMAN   One hair a little here sticks out, forsooth.
LADY WOULD-BE   Does 't so, forsooth? [*to* FIRST WOMAN] And
        where was your dear sight
20   When it did so, forsooth? What now? Bird-eyed?°   *startled (?); asquint (?)*
[*to* SECOND WOMAN] And you, too? Pray you both approach
        and mend it.
                            [*They tend to her.*]
Now, by that light,° I muse you're not ashamed!   *i.e., by heaven*
I, that have preached these things so oft unto you,
Read you the principles, argued all the grounds,
25   Disputed every fitness, every grace,
Called you to counsel of so frequent dressings—
NANO (*aside*)   More carefully than of your fame° or honor.   *reputation*
LADY WOULD-BE   Made you acquainted what an ample dowry
The knowledge of these things would be unto you,
30   Able alone to get you noble husbands
At your return,° and you thus to neglect it?   *to England*
Besides, you seeing what a curious° nation   *fastidious*
Th'Italians are, what will they say of me?
"The English lady cannot dress herself."
35   Here's a fine imputation to our country!
Well, go your ways, and stay i'the next room.
This fucus° was too coarse, too; it's no matter.   *makeup*
[*to* NANO] Good sir, you'll give 'em entertainment?°   *look after them*
                    [*Exeunt* NANO *and* WOMEN.]
VOLPONE [*aside*]   The storm comes toward me.
LADY WOULD-BE [*approaching the bed*]   How does my Volp?
40   VOLPONE   Troubled with noise. I cannot sleep; I dreamt
That a strange Fury entered now my house,
And with the dreadful tempest of her breath
Did cleave my roof asunder.
LADY WOULD-BE   Believe me, and I
Had the most fearful dream, could I remember't—
45   VOLPONE [*aside*]   Out on° my fate! I ha' giv'n her the occasion   *curses on*
How to torment me: she will tell me hers.
LADY WOULD-BE   Methought the golden mediocrity,°   *golden mean*
Polite and delicate—
VOLPONE   Oh, if you do love me,
No more! I sweat and suffer at the mention
50   Of any dream. Feel how I tremble yet.
LADY WOULD-BE   Alas, good soul! The passion of the heart.°   *heartburn*
Seed pearl were good now, boiled with syrup of apples,

Tincture of gold and coral, citron pills,
Your elecampane° root, myrobalans²—   *perennial herb*

55 VOLPONE [*aside*]   Ay me, I have ta'en a grasshopper by the wing!
LADY WOULD-BE   Burnt silk and amber; you have muscadel
Good i'the house—
VOLPONE   You will not drink and part?
LADY WOULD-BE   No, fear not that. I doubt we shall not get
Some English saffron—half a dram would serve—
60 Your sixteen cloves, a little musk, dried mints,
Bugloss,° and barley-meal—   *an herb*
VOLPONE [*aside*]   She's in again.
Before I feigned diseases; now I have one.
LADY WOULD-BE   And these applied with a right scarlet cloth—
VOLPONE [*aside*]   Another flood of words! A very torrent!
LADY WOULD-BE   Shall I, sir, make you a poultice?
65 VOLPONE   No, no, no.
I'm very well; you need prescribe no more.
LADY WOULD-BE   I have a little studied physic, but now
I'm all for music, save i'the forenoons
An hour or two for painting. I would have
70 A lady indeed t' have all letters and arts,
Be able to discourse, to write, to paint,
But principal, as Plato holds,° your music   *in* The Republic
(And so does wise Pythagoras, I take it)
Is your true rapture, when there is concent°   *harmony*
75 In face, in voice, and clothes, and is indeed
Our sex's chiefest ornament.
VOLPONE   The poet°   *Sophocles, in* Ajax
As old in time as Plato, and as knowing,
Says that your highest female grace is silence.
LADY WOULD-BE   Which o' your poets? Petrarch? Or Tasso? Or Dante?
80 Guarini? Ariosto? Aretine?
Cieco di Hadria?³ I have read them all.
VOLPONE [*aside*]   Is everything a cause to my destruction?
LADY WOULD-BE [*searching her garments*]   I think I ha' two or three of 'em
about me.
VOLPONE [*aside*]   The sun, the sea will sooner both stand still
85 Than her eternal tongue! Nothing can scape it.
LADY WOULD-BE   Here's *Pastor Fido*⁴—
VOLPONE [*aside*]   Profess obstinate silence,
That's now my safest.
LADY WOULD-BE   All our English writers,
I mean such as are happy in th'Italian,
Will deign to steal out of this author mainly,
90 Almost as much as from Montaignié°   *French essayist*
He has so modern and facile° a vein,   *graceful*

2. Dried tropical fruits.
3. Lady Would-be juxtaposes major Italian writers with the minor di Hadria and the obscene Aretino (see p. 1038, n. 6).
4. A pastoral by Giovanni Guarini, translated into English in 1602.

Fitting the time, and catching the court ear.
Your Petrarch is more passionate, yet he,
In days of sonneting, trusted 'em with much.[5]

95 Dante is hard, and few can understand him.
But for a desperate° wit, there's Aretine!   outrageous
Only his pictures are a little obscene[6]—
You mark me not?

VOLPONE   Alas, my mind's perturbed.

LADY WOULD-BE   Why, in such cases we must cure ourselves,
Make use of our philosophy—

100 VOLPONE   Ay me!

LADY WOULD-BE   And, as we find our passions do rebel,
Encounter 'em with reason, or divert 'em
By giving scope unto some other humor
Of lesser danger—as in politic bodies°   political councils

105 There's nothing more doth overwhelm the judgment
And clouds the understanding than too much
Settling and fixing and (as 'twere) subsiding°   alchemical jargon
Upon one object. For the incorporating
Of these same outward things into that part

110 Which we call mental leaves some certain feces°   dregs
That stop the organs and, as Plato says,
Assassinates our knowledge.

VOLPONE [aside]   Now, the spirit
Of patience help me!

LADY WOULD-BE   Come, in faith, I must
Visit you more o'days and make you well.
Laugh and be lusty.°   merry

115 VOLPONE [aside]   My good angel save me!

LADY WOULD-BE   There was but one sole man in all the world
With whom I e'er could sympathize, and he
Would lie you° often three, four hours together   lie
To hear me speak, and be sometime so rapt

120 As he would answer me quite from the purpose,
Like you—and you are like him, just. I'll discourse—
An't° be but only, sir, to bring you asleep—   if it
How we did spend our time and loves together
For some six years.

VOLPONE   Oh, oh, oh, oh, oh, oh!

125 LADY WOULD-BE   For we were coaetani° and brought up—   the same age

VOLPONE [aside]   Some power, some fate, some fortune rescue me!

SCENE 5. *The scene continues.*

[Enter] MOSCA.

MOSCA   God save you, madam.

LADY WOULD-BE   Good sir.

---

5. When sonnet writing was popular, gave poets plenty to imitate.
6. The libertine poems of Aretine (Pietro Aret-ino 1492–1556) were published with pornographic illustrations by Giulio Romano.

VOLPONE [*aside to* MOSCA]   Mosca? Welcome,
 Welcome to my redemption.
MOSCA [*to* VOLPONE]   Why, sir?
VOLPONE [*aside to* MOSCA]   Oh,
 Rid me of this my torture quickly, there,
 My madam with the everlasting voice!
5 The bells in time of pestilence ne'er made
 Like noise, or were in that perpetual motion;[1]
 The cockpit° comes not near it. All my house   *cockfighting arena*
 But now steamed like a bath with her thick breath.
 A lawyer could not have been heard, nor scarce
10 Another woman, such a hail of words
 She has let fall. For hell's sake, rid her hence.
MOSCA [*aside to* VOLPONE] Has she presented?° *given a gift*
VOLPONE [*aside to* MOSCA]   Oh, I do not care.
 I'll take her absence upon any price,
 With any loss.
MOSCA   Madam—
LADY WOULD-BE I ha' brought your patron
 A toy,° a cap here, of mine own work— *trifle; embroidered piece*
15 MOSCA [*taking it from her*]   'Tis well.
 I had forgot to tell you, I saw your knight
 Where you'd little think it—
LADY WOULD-BE   Where?
MOSCA   Marry,
 Where yet, if you make haste, you may apprehend him,
 Rowing upon the water in a gondole
20 With the most cunning courtesan of Venice.
LADY WOULD-BE Is't true?
MOSCA   Pursue 'em, and believe your eyes.
 Leave me to make your gift. [*Exit* LADY WOULD-BE.]
      I knew 'twould take.° *do the trick*
 For lightly,° they that use themselves most license *commonly*
 Are still° most jealous.   *always*
VOLPONE   Mosca, hearty thanks
25 For thy quick fiction and delivery of me.
 Now, to my hopes, what say'st thou?
   [*Enter* LADY WOULD-BE.]
LADY WOULD-BE   But do you hear, sir?
VOLPONE [*aside*] Again! I fear a paroxysm.° *relapse*
LADY WOULD-BE   Which way
 Rowed they together?
MOSCA   Toward the Rialto.° *commercial district*
LADY WOULD-BE I pray you, lend me your dwarf.
MOSCA   I pray you, take him.
    [*Exit* LADY WOULD-BE.]

3.5
1. Church bells marked the deaths of parishioners; in times of plague they therefore rang almost constantly.

30　Your hopes, sir, are like happy blossoms: fair,
　　And promise timely fruit if you will stay
　　But the maturing. Keep you at your couch.
　　Corbaccio will arrive straight with the will;
　　When he is gone I'll tell you more.　　　　　　[*Exit.*]
VOLPONE　　　　　　　　　　　My blood,
35　My spirits are returned. I am alive;
　　And like your wanton° gamester at primero,[2]　　　　reckless; lustful
　　Whose thought had whispered to him, not go° less,　　don't gamble
　　Methinks I lie, and draw—for an encounter.[3]
　　　　[*He gets into bed and closes the bed curtains.*]

SCENE 6. *The scene continues.*

　　[*Enter*] MOSCA [*and*] BONARIO. [MOSCA *shows* BONARIO
　　to a hiding place.]
MOSCA　Sir, here concealed you may hear all. But pray you
　　Have patience, sir. [*One knocks.*] The same's your father knocks.
　　I am compelled to leave you.
BONARIO　　　　　　　　　Do so. Yet
　　Cannot my thought imagine this a truth.
　　　　[*He conceals himself.*]

SCENE 7. *The scene continues.*

　　[*Enter*] CORVINO [*and*] CELIA. MOSCA [*crosses the stage
　　to intercept them*].
MOSCA　Death on me! You are come too soon. What meant you?
　　Did not I say I would send?
CORVINO　　　　　　　　　Yes, but I feared
　　You might forget it, and then they prevent us.
MOSCA [*aside*]　Prevent? Did e'er man haste so for his horns?°　cuckold's horns
5　A courtier would not ply it so for a place.[1]
　　[*to* CORVINO] Well, now there's no helping it, stay here;
　　I'll presently return.　　[*He crosses the stage to* BONARIO.]
CORVINO　　　　　　　　　Where are you, Celia?
　　You know not wherefore I have brought you hither?
CELIA　Not well, except you told me.
CORVINO　　　　　　　　　Now I will.
　　Hark hither. [CORVINO *and* CELIA *talk apart.*]
10　MOSCA (*to* BONARIO)　Sir, your father hath sent word
　　It will be half an hour ere he come;
　　And therefore, if you please to walk the while
　　Into that gallery, at the upper end
　　There are some books to entertain the time;
15　And I'll take care no man shall come unto you, sir.
BONARIO　Yes, I will stay there. [*aside*] I do doubt this fellow.
　　　　[*He retires.*]

---

2. A card game.　　　　　　　　　　　3.7
3. (1) Winning play in primero; (2) sexual act.　　1. Work so hard for a position at court.

MOSCA   There, he is far enough; he can hear nothing.
And for° his father, I can keep him off.   *as for*
     [MOSCA *joins* VOLPONE *and opens his bed curtains.*]
CORVINO [*to* CELIA]   Nay, now, there is no starting back, and therefore
20   Resolve upon it; I have so decreed.
It must be done. Nor would I move't° afore,   *suggest it*
Because I would avoid all shifts° and tricks   *evasions*
That might deny me.
CELIA   Sir, let me beseech you,
Affect° not these strange trials. If you doubt   *undertake*
25   My chastity, why, lock me up forever;
Make me the heir of darkness. Let me live
Where I may please° your fears, if not your trust.   *satisfy*
CORVINO   Believe it, I have no such humor, I.
All that I speak, I mean; yet I am not mad,
30   Not horn-mad,° see you? Go to, show yourself   *crazy with jealousy*
Obedient, and a wife.
CELIA   O heaven!
CORVINO   I say it,
Do so.
CELIA   Was this the train?°   *scheme*
CORVINO   I have told you reasons:
What the physicians have set down; how much
It may concern me; what my engagements are;
35   My means, and the necessity of those means
For my recovery. Wherefore, if you be
Loyal and mine, be won, respect my venture.°   *support my endeavor*
CELIA   Before your honor?
CORVINO   Honor? Tut, a breath.
There's no such thing in nature; a mere term
40   Invented to awe fools. What is my gold
The worse for touching? Clothes for being looked on?
Why, this's no more. An old, decrepit wretch,
That has no sense,° no sinew; takes his meat   *sensory perception*
With others' fingers; only knows to gape
45   When you do scald his gums; a voice, a shadow.
And what can this man hurt you?
CELIA   Lord! What spirit
Is this hath entered him?
CORVINO   And for your fame,°   *reputation*
That's such a jig;° as if I would go tell it,   *joke*
Cry° it on the piazza! Who shall know it   *advertise*
50   But he that cannot speak it,° and this fellow°   *Volpone / Mosca*
Whose lips are i'my pocket, save yourself?
If you'll proclaim't, you may. I know no other
Should come to know it.
CELIA   Are heaven and saints then nothing?
Will they be blind or stupid?
CORVINO   How?°   *what's this?*
CELIA   Good sir,

55 Be jealous still, emulate them, and think
What hate they burn with toward every sin.
CORVINO   I grant you, if I thought it were a sin
I would not urge you. Should I offer this
To some young Frenchman, or hot Tuscan blood
60 That had read Aretine, conned° all his prints,   *learned by heart*
Knew every quirk within lust's labyrinth,
And were professed critic° in lechery,   *connoisseur*
And I would look upon him and applaud him,
This were a sin. But here 'tis contrary,
65 A pious work, mere charity, for physic,
And honest polity° to assure mine own.   *prudence*
CELIA   O heaven! Canst thou suffer such a change?
VOLPONE [*aside to* MOSCA]   Thou art mine honor, Mosca, and my pride,
My joy, my tickling, my delight! Go, bring 'em.
MOSCA [*to* CORVINO]   Please you draw near, sir.
70 CORVINO [*dragging* CELIA *toward* VOLPONE]   Come on, what—
You will not be rebellious? By that light—
MOSCA [*to* VOLPONE]   Sir, Signor Corvino here is come to see you.
VOLPONE   Oh!
MOSCA   And, hearing of the consultation had
So lately for your health, is come to offer,
Or rather, sir, to prostitute—
75 CORVINO   Thanks, sweet Mosca.
MOSCA   Freely, unasked or unentreated—
CORVINO   Well.
MOSCA   As the true, fervent instance of his love,
His own most fair and proper wife, the beauty
Only of price° in Venice—   *beyond comparison*
CORVINO   'Tis well urged.
80 MOSCA   To be your comfortress and to preserve you.
VOLPONE   Alas, I am past already! Pray you, thank him
For his good care and promptness. But for° that,   *as for*
'Tis a vain labor e'en to fight 'gainst heaven,
Applying fire to a stone (uh! uh! uh! uh!),
85 Making a dead leaf grow again. I take
His wishes gently, though; and you may tell him
What I have done for him. Marry, my state is hopeless!
Will him to pray for me, and t' use his fortune
With reverence when he comes to't.
MOSCA [*to* CORVINO]   Do you hear, sir?
Go to him with your wife.
90 CORVINO [*to* CELIA]   Heart of my father!°   *an oath*
Wilt thou persist thus? Come, I pray thee, come.
Thou see'st 'tis nothing. [*He threatens to strike her.*] Celia! By this hand,
I shall grow violent. Come, do't, I say.
CELIA   Sir, kill me, rather. I will take down poison,
Eat burning coals, do anything—
95 CORVINO   Be damned!
Heart! I will drag thee hence, home, by the hair,

Cry thee a strumpet through the streets, rip up
Thy mouth unto thine ears, and slit thy nose
Like a raw rochet!°—Do not tempt me. Come,   *a fish, the red gurnard*
100 Yield! I am loath—Death!° I will buy some slave   *God's death! (an oath)*
Whom I will kill,[2] and bind thee to him alive,
And at my window hang you forth, devising
Some monstrous crime, which I in capital letters
Will eat into thy flesh with *aquafortis*°   *nitric acid*
105 And burning cor'sives° on this stubborn breast.   *corrosives*
Now, by the blood thou hast incensed, I'll do't.
CELIA   Sir, what you please, you may; I am your martyr.
CORVINO   Be not thus obstinate. I ha' not deserved it.
Think who it is entreats you. Pray thee, sweet!
110 Good faith, thou shalt have jewels, gowns, attires,
What° thou wilt think and ask. Do but go kiss him.   *whatever*
Or touch him but. For my sake. At my suit.
This once. No? Not? I shall remember this.
Will you disgrace me thus? Do you thirst my undoing?
MOSCA   Nay, gentle lady, be advised.
115 CORVINO   No, no.
She has watched her time.[3] God's precious,[4] this is scurvy;
'Tis very scurvy, and you are—
MOSCA   Nay, good, sir.
CORVINO   An arrant locust,° by heaven, a locust. Whore,   *destroyer*
Crocodile,[5] that hast thy tears prepared,
Expecting° how thou'lt bid 'em flow!   *anticipating*
120 MOSCA   Nay, pray you, sir,
She will consider.
CELIA   Would my life would serve
To satisfy—
CORVINO   'Sdeath, if she would but speak to him
And save my reputation, 'twere somewhat—
But spitefully to effect my utter ruin!
125 MOSCA   Ay, now you've put your fortune in her hands.
Why, i'faith, it is her modesty; I must quit° her.   *absolve*
If you were absent she would be more coming,°   *compliant*
I know it, and dare undertake for her.
What woman can before her husband? Pray you,
Let us depart and leave her here.
130 CORVINO   Sweet Celia,
Thou mayst redeem all yet; I'll say no more.
If not, esteem yourself as lost.—Nay, stay there.
                  [*Exeunt* CORVINO *and* MOSCA.]
CELIA   O God and his good angels! Whither, whither
Is shame fled human breasts, that with such ease

---

2. In the following lines, Corvino elaborates
luridly upon the fate that the notorious rapist Tarquin promised the chaste Roman matron Lucretia if she did not capitulate; unlike Celia, Lucretia
yielded to threats.

3. Waited for her chance (to ruin me).
4. God's precious blood. (An oath.)
5. Which was supposed to weep while preying
upon its victims.

135 Men dare put off your° honors and their own?   *God's and the angels'*
Is that which ever was a cause of life°   *sex and wedlock*
Now placed beneath the basest circumstance,°   *lowest of concerns*
And modesty an exile made for money?
He [VOLPONE] *leaps off from his couch.*
VOLPONE   Ay, in Corvino, and such earth-fed minds
140 That never tasted the true heav'n of love.
Assure thee, Celia, he that would sell thee
Only for hope of gain, and that uncertain,
He would have sold his part of paradise
For ready money, had he met a copeman.°   *buyer*
145 Why art thou mazed to see me thus revived?
Rather applaud thy beauty's miracle;
'Tis thy great work, that hath, not now alone°   *not only just now*
But sundry times raised me in several shapes,
And but this morning like a mountebank
150 To see thee at thy window. Ay, before
I would have left my practice° for thy love,   *scheming*
In varying figures I would have contended
With the blue Proteus or the hornèd flood.[6]
Now art thou welcome.
CELIA   Sir!
VOLPONE   Nay, fly me not,
155 Nor let thy false imagination
That I was bedrid make thee think I am so.
Thou shalt not find it. I am now as fresh,
As hot, as high, and in as jovial plight°   *robust condition*
As when—in that so celebrated scene,
160 At recitation of our comedy
For entertainment of the great Valois[7]—
I acted young Antinoüs,[8] and attracted
The eyes and ears of all the ladies present,
T'admire each graceful gesture, note, and footing.°   *dance step*

SONG

165 [*He sings.*]   Come, my Celia, let us prove,[9]
While we can, the sports of love.
Time will not be ours forever;
He at length our good will sever.
Spend not then his gifts in vain.
170 Suns that set may rise again,
But if once we lose this light
'Tis with us perpetual night.
Why should we defer our joys?

---

6. Proteus is a shape-changing sea god with whom Menelaus wrestles in the *Odyssey*. The "hornèd flood" is the river god Achelous, defeated by Hercules despite changing into an ox.
7. Henry of Valois, Duke of Anjou, and later King Henry III of France (1574–89), was sumptuously entertained at Venice in 1574. His sexual taste for men was widely remarked.
8. The beautiful homosexual favorite of the Roman emperor Hadrian.
9. Try out. (The song is an adaptation of the Roman poet Catullus's fifth ode.)

Fame and rumor are but toys.°   *trifles*
175   Cannot we delude the eyes
Of a few poor household spies?
Or his° easier ears beguile,   *Corvino's*
Thus removèd by our wile?
'Tis no sin love's fruits to steal,
180   But the sweet thefts to reveal.
To be taken,° to be seen,   *caught*
These have crimes accounted been.
CELIA   Some serene° blast me, or dire lightning strike   *poisonous mist*
  This my offending face!
VOLPONE   Why droops my Celia?
185   Thou hast in place of a base husband found
A worthy lover. Use thy fortune well,
With secrecy and pleasure. See, behold
What thou art queen of, not in expectation,°   *merely in hope*
As I feed others, but possessed and crowned.
                 [*He reveals his treasures.*]
190   See here a rope of pearl, and each more orient°   *brilliant*
Than that the brave Egyptian queen caroused;[1]
Dissolve and drink 'em. See, a carbuncle[2]
May put out both the eyes of our Saint Mark;[3]
A diamond would have bought Lollia Paulina[4]
195   When she came in like starlight, hid with jewels
That were the spoils of provinces. Take these,
And wear, and lose 'em; yet remains an earring
To purchase them again, and this whole state.
A gem but worth a private patrimony
200   Is nothing; we will eat such at a meal.
The heads of parrots, tongues of nightingales,
The brains of peacocks and of ostriches
Shall be our food, and, could we get the phoenix,[5]
Though nature lost her kind,° she were our dish.   *it became extinct*
205 CELIA   Good sir, these things might move a mind affected
With such delights; but I, whose innocence
Is all I can think wealthy° or worth th'enjoying,   *valuable*
And which once lost, I have naught to lose beyond it,
Cannot be taken with these sensual baits.
If you have conscience—
210 VOLPONE   'Tis the beggar's virtue.
If thou hast wisdom, hear me, Celia.
Thy baths shall be the juice of July flowers,°   *clove pinks*
Spirit° of roses, and of violets,   *extract*
The milk of unicorns, and panthers' breath[6]

---

1. Cleopatra dissolved and drank a pearl during a banquet with her lover, Marc Antony. "Brave": magnificent.
2. Ruby, thought to emit light.
3. Patron saint of Venice, whose statue stood in the basilica.
4. Third wife of the Roman emperor Caligula.
5. Mythical bird, of which it was supposed that only one existed at a time; it died in flames and was reborn from its own ashes.
6. Panthers were believed to use their sweet-smelling breath to lure prey.

215   Gathered in bags, and mixed with Cretan wines.
    Our drink shall be preparèd gold and amber,
    Which we will take until my roof whirl round
    With the vertigo; and my dwarf shall dance,
    My eunuch sing, my fool make up the antic,[7]
220   Whilst we, in changèd shapes, act Ovid's tales:
    Thou like Europa now and I like Jove,
    Then I like Mars and thou like Erycine,[8]
    So of the rest, till we have quite run through
    And wearied all the fables of the gods.
225   Then will I have thee in more modern forms,
    Attirèd like some sprightly dame of France,
    Brave Tuscan lady, or proud Spanish beauty;
    Sometimes unto the Persian Sophy's° wife,   *Shah of Persia's*
    Or the Grand Signor's° mistress; and for change,   *Sultan of Turkey's*
230   To one of our most artful courtesans,
    Or some quick° Negro, or cold Russian.   *energetic*
    And I will meet thee in as many shapes,
    Where we may so transfuse° our wand'ring souls   *pour into each other*
    Out at our lips, and score up sums of pleasures,
235   [*He sings.*]   That the curious shall not know
                How to tell° them as they flow;   *count*
                And the envious, when they find
                What their number is, be pined.°   *tormented*
CELIA   If you have ears that will be pierced, or eyes
240   That can be opened, a heart may be touched,
    Or any part that yet sounds man[9] about you;
    If you have touch of holy saints or heaven,
    Do me the grace to let me scape. If not,
    Be bountiful and kill me. You do know
245   I am a creature hither ill betrayed
    By one whose shame I would forget it were.
    If you will deign me neither of these graces,
    Yet feed your wrath, sir, rather than your lust—
    It is a vice comes nearer manliness—
250   And punish that unhappy crime of nature
    Which you miscall my beauty. Flay my face
    Or poison it with ointments for seducing
    Your blood to this rebellion.° Rub these hands   *sexual mutiny*
    With what may cause an eating leprosy
255   E'en to my bones and marrow—anything
    That may disfavor me,° save in my honor—   *make me ugly*
    And I will kneel to you, pray for you, pay down
    A thousand hourly vows, sir, for your health,
    Report and think you virtuous—
VOLPONE   Think me cold,

---

7. Grotesque dance or pageant.
8. Ovid's *Metamorphoses* retells the pagan myths of transformation. Jove, king of the gods, became a bull to seduce the lovely Europa. The adulterous couple Mars, god of war, and Erycine (Venus), goddess of sexual love, were caught in a net by Vulcan, her husband.
9. That has a hint of manliness.

260　　　Frozen, and impotent, and so report me?
　　　That I had Nestor's[1] hernia, thou wouldst think.
　　　I do degenerate, and abuse my nation[2]
　　　To play with opportunity thus long.
　　　I should have done the act and then have parleyed.
　　　Yield, or I'll force thee.

CELIA　　　　　　　　　　O just God!

265　VOLPONE [*seizing* CELIA]　　　　In vain—
　　　　　He [BONARIO] *leaps out from where* MOSCA *had placed him.*

BONARIO　Forbear, foul ravisher, libidinous swine!
　　　Free the forced lady or thou diest, impostor.
　　　But that I am loath to snatch thy punishment
　　　Out of the hand of justice, thou shouldst yet
270　Be made the timely sacrifice of vengeance
　　　Before this altar and this dross,° thy idol.—　　　　　　　*the treasure*
　　　Lady, let's quit the place. It is the den
　　　Of villainy. Fear naught; you have a guard;
　　　And he° ere long shall meet his just reward.　　　　　　　*Volpone*
　　　　　　　　　[*Exeunt* BONARIO *and* CELIA.]

275　VOLPONE　Fall on me, roof, and bury me in ruin!
　　　Become my grave, that wert my shelter! Oh!
　　　I am unmasked, unspirited, undone,
　　　Betrayed to beggary, to infamy—

SCENE 8. *The scene continues.*

　　　　　[*Enter*] MOSCA [*bloody*].[1]

MOSCA　Where shall I run, most wretched shame of men,
　　　To beat out my unlucky brains?

VOLPONE　　　　　　　　　Here, here.
　　　What! Dost thou bleed?

MOSCA　　　　　　　　Oh, that his well-driv'n sword
　　　Had been so courteous to have cleft me down
5　　　Unto the navel, ere I lived to see
　　　My life, my hopes, my spirits, my patron, all
　　　Thus desperately engagèd° by my error!　　　　　　　*placed at risk*

VOLPONE　Woe on thy fortune!

MOSCA　　　　　　　　And my follies, sir.

VOLPONE　Th'hast made me miserable.

MOSCA　　　　　　　　　　And myself, sir.
10　Who would have thought he would have hearkened° so?　　　*eavesdropped*

VOLPONE　What shall we do?

MOSCA　　　　　　　　I know not. If my heart
　　　Could expiate the mischance, I'd pluck it out.
　　　Will you be pleased to hang me, or cut my throat?

---

1. Nestor was the oldest of the Greek leaders in the Trojan War.
2. I fall away from my ancestors' virtues and abuse the Italian reputation for virility.
3.8
1. Bonario apparently remembered Mosca's invi-

tation, in 3.2.66–68, to punish him if he turns out to be lying: "draw your just sword / And score your vengeance on my front and face; / Mark me your villain."

And I'll requite you, sir. Let's die like Romans,
Since we have lived like Grecians.[2]   *They knock without.*

15 VOLPONE   Hark, who's there?
I hear some footing: officers, the *Saffi*,°   *arresting officers*
Come to apprehend us! I do feel the brand
Hissing already at my forehead; now
Mine ears are boring.[3]

MOSCA   To your couch, sir; you
20 Make that place good, however.[4]   [VOLPONE *gets into bed*.]
                    Guilty men
Suspect° what they deserve still.°   [*He opens the door.*]   *dread / always*
                    Signor Corbaccio!

SCENE 9. *The scene continues.*

[*Enter*] CORBACCIO [*and converses with*] MOSCA; VOLTORE
[*enters unnoticed by them*].

CORBACCIO   Why, how now, Mosca!

MOSCA   Oh, undone, amazed, sir.
Your son—I know not by what accident—
Acquainted with your purpose to my patron
Touching° your will and making him your heir,   *concerning*
5 Entered our house with violence, his sword drawn,
Sought for you, called you wretch, unnatural,
Vowed he would kill you.

CORBACCIO   Me?

MOSCA   Yes, and my patron.

CORBACCIO   This act shall disinherit him indeed.
Here is the will.

MOSCA [*taking it from him*]   'Tis well, sir.

CORBACCIO   Right and well.
Be you as careful now for me.

10 MOSCA   My life, sir,
Is not more tendered;° I am only yours.   *cherished*

CORBACCIO   How does he? Will he die shortly, think'st thou?

MOSCA   I fear
He'll outlast May.

CORBACCIO   Today?

MOSCA   No, last out May, sir.

CORBACCIO   Couldst thou not gi' him a dram?°   *dose (of poison)*

MOSCA   Oh, by no means, sir.

CORBACCIO   Nay, I'll not bid you.

15 VOLTORE [*aside*]   This is a knave, I see.
[VOLTORE *comes forward to speak privately with* MOSCA.]

MOSCA [*aside*]   How, Signor Voltore! Did he hear me?

VOLTORE   Parasite!

MOSCA   Who's that? Oh, sir, most timely welcome—

---

2. Romans often committed suicide in adversity; Greeks were thought to be pleasure-loving.
3. Branding was a common criminal punishment; ear-boring is described as an Italian torture in

Thomas Nashe's *Unfortunate Traveler* (1594).
4. (1) Defend that place, whatever happens; (2) maintain your invalid's role at all costs, since that role suits you.

VOLTORE   Scarce°   *only just in time*
   To the discovery of your tricks, I fear.
   You are his only? And mine also? Are you not?
MOSCA   Who, I, sir? [*They speak out of* CORBACCIO'*s hearing.*]
20   VOLTORE   You, sir. What device° is this   *ruse*
   About a will?
MOSCA   A plot for you, sir.
VOLTORE   Come,
   Put not your foists° upon me. I shall scent 'em.   *tricks; stenches*
MOSCA   Did you not hear it?
VOLTORE   Yes, I hear Corbaccio
   Hath made your patron there his heir.
MOSCA   'Tis true,
25   By my device, drawn to it by my plot,
   With hope—
VOLTORE   Your patron should reciprocate?
   And you have promised?
MOSCA   For your good I did, sir.
   Nay, more, I told his son, brought, hid him here
   Where he might hear his father pass the deed,
30   Being persuaded to it by this thought, sir,
   That the unnaturalness, first, of the act,
   And then, his father's oft disclaiming in° him   *disowning*
   (Which I did mean t' help on) would sure enrage him
   To do some violence upon his parent,
35   On which the law should take sufficient hold,
   And you be stated° in a double hope.   *installed*
   Truth be my comfort and my conscience,
   My only aim was to dig you a fortune
   Out of these two old rotten sepulchres—
VOLTORE   I cry thee mercy, Mosca.
40   MOSCA   Worth your patience
   And your great merit, sir. And see the change!
VOLTORE   Why? What success?°   *outcome*
MOSCA   Most hapless!° You must help,   *unfortunate*
   sir.
   Whilst we expected th'old raven, in comes
   Corvino's wife, sent hither by her husband—
VOLTORE   What, with a present?
45   MOSCA   No, sir, on visitation—
   I'll tell you how, anon—and, staying long,
   The youth, he grows impatient, rushes forth,
   Seizeth the lady, wounds me, makes her swear—
   Or he would murder her, that was his vow—
50   T'affirm my patron to have done her rape,
   Which how unlike° it is, you see! And hence,   *unlikely*
   With that pretext, he's gone t'accuse his father,
   Defame my patron, defeat you—
VOLTORE   Where's her husband?
   Let him be sent for straight.

MOSCA   Sir, I'll go fetch him.
VOLTORE   Bring him to the *Scrutineo.*°   *Venetian law court*
55   MOSCA   Sir, I will.
VOLTORE   This must be stopped.
MOSCA   Oh, you do nobly, sir.
    Alas, 'twas labored all, sir, for your good;
    Nor was there want of counsel° in the plot.   *lack of wisdom*
    But fortune can at any time o'erthrow
60   The projects of a hundred learnèd clerks,° sir.   *scholars*
CORBACCIO [*striving to hear*]   What's that?
VOLTORE [*to* CORBACCIO]   Will't please you, sir, to go along?
                     [*Exeunt* CORBACCIO *and* VOLTORE.]
MOSCA   Patron, go in and pray for our success.
VOLPONE [*rising*]   Need makes devotion. Heaven your labor bless!

Act 4

SCENE 1. *The piazza.*

                 [*Enter*] POLITIC [*and*] PEREGRINE.
POLITIC   I told you, sir, it° was a plot. You see   *the mountebank episode*
    What observation is! You mentioned me
    For° some instructions; I will tell you, sir,   *as one who could give*
    Since we are met here, in this height° of Venice,   *latitude*
5   Some few particulars I have set down
    Only for this meridian, fit to be known
    Of your crude° traveler, and they are these.   *inexperienced*
    I will not touch, sir, at your phrase or clothes,
    For they are old.[1]
PEREGRINE   Sir, I have better.
POLITIC   Pardon,
    I meant as they are themes.°   *topics for advice*
10   PEREGRINE   Oh; sir, proceed.
    I'll slander° you no more of wit, good sir.   *accuse*
POLITIC   First, for your garb,[2] it must be grave and serious,
    Very reserved and locked;° not° tell a secret   *guarded / do not*
    On any terms, not to your father; scarce
15   A fable[3] but with caution. Make sure choice
    Both of your company and discourse. Beware
    You never speak a truth—
PEREGRINE   How!
POLITIC   Not to strangers,°   *foreigners*
    For those be they you must converse with most;
    Others° I would not know, sir, but at distance,   *fellow countrymen*
20   So as I still might be a saver[4] in 'em.

4.1
1. I will not discuss those familiar ("old") topics: the language one ought to use or the clothes one ought to wear. In the next line, in an attempt at a joke, Peregrine deliberately misconstrues "your . . . clothes" to refer to his own apparel, but Politic does not get it.

2. As for a traveler's bearing.
3. An apparently trivial story subject to political allegorization.
4. So that I might not be imposed upon. ("Be a saver" is a gambling term, meaning "to escape loss.")

You shall have tricks else passed upon you hourly.
And then, for your religion, profess none,
But wonder at the diversity of all,
And, for your part, protest, were there no other
25 But simply the laws o'th'land, you could content you.
Nick Machiavel and Monsieur Bodin both
Were of this mind.[5] Then must you learn the use
And handling of your silver fork° at meals,   *an Italian novelty*
The metal° of your glass—these are main matters   *composition*
30 With your Italian—and to know the hour
When you must eat your melons and your figs.
PEREGRINE   Is that a point of state,° too?   *statecraft*
POLITIC   Here it is.
For your Venetian, if he see a man
Preposterous in the least, he has° him straight;   *sees through*
35 He has, he strips° him. I'll acquaint you, sir.   *ridicules; defrauds*
I now have lived here—'tis some fourteen months;
Within the first week of my landing here,
All took me for a citizen of Venice,
I knew the forms so well—
PEREGRINE [*aside*]   And nothing else.
40 POLITIC   I had read Contarine,[6] took me a house,
Dealt with my Jews[7] to furnish it with movables°—   *household goods*
Well, if I could but find one man, one man
To mine own heart, whom I durst trust, I would—
PEREGRINE   What? What, sir?
POLITIC   Make him rich, make him a fortune.
45 He should not think° again. I would command it.   *have to think*
PEREGRINE   As how?
POLITIC   With certain projects° that I   *entrepreneurial schemes*
have—
Which I may not discover.°   *reveal*
PEREGRINE [*aside*]   If I had
But one° to wager with, I would lay odds, now,   *someone*
He tells me instantly.
POLITIC   One is—and that
50 I care not greatly who knows—to serve the state
Of Venice with red herrings for three years,
And at a certain rate, from Rotterdam,[8]
Where I have correspondence. [*He shows* PEREGRINE *a paper.*]
There's a letter
Sent me from one o'th'States,° and to that purpose;   *Dutch provinces*
55 He cannot write his name, but that's his mark.
PEREGRINE [*examining the paper*]   He is a chandler?[9]

5. Political theorists Niccolò Machiavelli (1469–1527) and Jean Bodin (1530–1596) argued that religious zeal was often politically inexpedient or divisive; as a result both were popularly thought to be atheists.
6. An English translation of Gasparo Contarini's important book, *The Commonwealth and Government of Venice*, was published in 1599.
7. The usual Jews. (In Venice Jews served as moneylenders and pawnbrokers.)
8. Venice, on the Adriatic Sea, had little need to import pickled fish from afar.
9. Candlemaker. (Evidently the paper is grease-stained.)

POLITIC   No, a cheesemonger.

There are some other° too, with whom I treat°   *others / deal*

About the same negotiation;

And I will undertake it, for 'tis thus

60   I'll do't with ease; I've cast it all.° Your hoy[1]   *figured it all out*

Carries but three men in her and a boy,

And she shall make me three returns° a year.   *round trips*

So if there come but one of three, I save;°   *break even*

If two, I can defalk.° But this is, now,   *pay off loans*

If my main project fail.

65 PEREGRINE   Then you have others?

POLITIC   I should be loath to draw° the subtle air   *breathe*

Of such a place without my thousand aims.

I'll not dissemble, sir: where'er I come,

I love to be considerative;° and 'tis true   *analytic*

70   I have at my free hours thought upon

Some certain goods° unto the state of Venice,   *benefits*

Which I do call my cautions,° and, sir, which   *precautions*

I mean, in hope of pension,° to propound   *financial reward*

To the Great Council, then unto the Forty,

75   So to the Ten.[2] My means° are made already—   *contacts*

PEREGRINE   By whom?

POLITIC   Sir, one that though his place b'obscure,

Yet he can sway and they will hear him. He's

A *commendatore*.

PEREGRINE   What, a common sergeant?

POLITIC   Sir, such as they are put it in their mouths

80   What they should say, sometimes, as well as greater.[3]

I think I have my notes to show you—

        [He searches in his garments.]

PEREGRINE   Good, sir.

POLITIC   But you shall swear unto me on your gentry°   *gentleman's honor*

Not to anticipate—

PEREGRINE   I, sir?

POLITIC   Nor reveal

A circumstance—My paper is not with me.

PEREGRINE   Oh, but you can remember, sir.

85 POLITIC   My first is

Concerning tinderboxes.° You must know   *for lighting fires*

No family is here without its box.

Now, sir, it being so portable a thing,

Put case° that you or I were ill affected°   *suppose / disposed*

90   Unto the state; sir, with it in our pockets

Might not I go into the Arsenale?[4]

Or you? Come out again? And none the wiser?

---

1. Small vessel, not suitable for long voyages. Sir Pol's scheme is thus obviously impractical.
2. The Great Council was a large legislative group made up of wealthy Venetians; the Councils of Forty were much smaller groups that oversaw judicial affairs; the Council of Ten consisted of the elected Doge and his cabinet.
3. Common men, as well as those of higher status, may sometimes make suggestions to the government.
4. Shipyard where Venice built and repaired its naval vessels.

PEREGRINE   Except yourself, sir.

POLITIC   Go to,° then. I therefore   *impatient expression*

   Advertise to° the state how fit it were   *warn*

95   That none but such as were known patriots,

   Sound lovers of their country, should be suffered

   T'enjoy them° in their houses, and even those   *tinderboxes*

   Sealed° at some office, and at such a bigness   *licensed; sealed shut*

   As might not lurk in pockets.

PEREGRINE   Admirable!

100   POLITIC   My next is, how t'inquire and be resolved°   *satisfied*

   By present° demonstration whether a ship   *immediate*

   Newly arrived from Syria, or from

   Any suspected part of all the Levant,°   *Middle East*

   Be guilty of the plague. And where they use°   *are accustomed*

105   To lie out° forty, fifty days sometimes   *at anchor*

   About the Lazaretto,[5] for their trial,

   I'll save that charge and loss unto the merchant,

   And in an hour clear the doubt.

PEREGRINE   Indeed, sir?

POLITIC   Or—I will lose my labor.

PEREGRINE   My faith, that's much.

110   POLITIC   Nay, sir, conceive° me. 'Twill cost me in onions[6]   *understand*

   Some thirty livres°—   *French coins*

PEREGRINE   Which is one pound sterling.

POLITIC   Beside my waterworks. For this I do, sir.

   First I bring in your ship° 'twixt two brick walls—   *a ship in question*

   But those the state shall venture.° On the one   *pay for*

115   I strain° me a fair tarpaulin, and in that   *stretch*

   I stick my onions cut in halves; the other

   Is full of loopholes out at which I thrust

   The noses of my bellows, and those bellows

   I keep with° waterworks in perpetual motion[7]—   *by means of*

120   Which is the easiest matter of a hundred.°   *as easy as can be*

   Now, sir, your onion, which doth naturally

   Attract th'infection, and your bellows, blowing

   The air upon him,° will show instantly   *it (the onion)*

   By his changed color if there be contagion,

125   Or else remain as fair as at the first.

   Now 'tis known, 'tis nothing.°   *there's nothing to it*

PEREGRINE   You are right, sir.

POLITIC   I would I had my note.

   [*He searches again in his garments.*]

PEREGRINE   Faith, so would I;

   But, you ha' done well for once, sir.

POLITIC   Were I false,°   *traitorous*

   Or would be made so, I could show you reasons

---

5. Quarantine hospital on an outlying island.
6. Onions were popularly supposed to absorb plague infection.
7. Perpetual-motion machines were popular attractions in early modern England, but Jonson regarded them contemptuously. Since Venice is in flat marshland, there are no waterfalls to harness there, as Sir Pol proposes.

130 How I could sell this state now to the Turk,[8]
Spite of their galleys° or their—   warships
PEREGRINE   Pray you, Sir Pol.
POLITIC I have 'em° not about me.   the notes
PEREGRINE   That I feared.
They are there, sir? [*He indicates a book* POLITIC *is holding.*]
POLITIC   No, this is my diary,
Wherein I note my actions of the day.[9]
135 PEREGRINE Pray you, let's see, sir. What is here? [*reading*]
"*Notandum,*°   be it noted
A rat had gnawn my spur leathers;° notwithstanding   laces
I put on new and did go forth, but first
I threw three beans over the threshold.° *Item,*   for good luck
I went and bought two toothpicks, whereof one
140 I burst immediately in a discourse
With a Dutch merchant, 'bout *ragion' del stato.*°   political expediency
From him I went, and paid a *moccinigo*°   small coin
For piecing° my silk stockings; by the way   mending
I cheapened sprats,[1] and at Saint Mark's I urined."
Faith, these are politic notes!
145 POLITIC   Sir, I do slip°   let pass
No action of my life thus but I quote° it.   without noting
PEREGRINE Believe me, it is wise!
POLITIC   Nay, sir, read forth.

SCENE 2. *The scene continues.*

[*Enter*] LADY [WOULD-BE], NANO, [*and the two*] WOMEN.
[*They do not see* POLITIC *and* PEREGRINE *at first.*]
LADY WOULD-BE Where should this loose knight be, trow?° do you suppose?
Sure he's housed.°   in a brothel
NANO Why, then he's fast.°   fast-moving; secure
LADY WOULD-BE   Ay, he plays both° with me.   both fast and loose
I pray you, stay. This heat will do more harm
To my complexion than his heart is worth.
5 I do not care to hinder, but to take° him.   catch
[*She rubs her cheeks.*]
How it° comes off!   the makeup
FIRST WOMAN [*pointing*] My master's yonder.
LADY WOULD-BE   Where?
FIRST WOMAN With a young gentleman.
LADY WOULD-BE   That same's the party,
In man's apparel![1] [*to* NANO] Pray you, sir, jog my knight.
I will be tender to his reputation,
However he demerit.°   deserves blame

---

8. The Ottoman Turks, southeast of Venice along the Adriatic Sea, were maritime and religious rivals and a long-standing military threat.
9. Many Renaissance travel writers recommended that travelers keep a written record of their journeys.
1. Bargained over some small fish.
4.2
1. Lady Would-be believes that Peregrine is the whore Mosca mentioned, in transvestite attire.

POLITIC [*seeing her*]   My lady!

10 PEREGRINE   Where?

POLITIC   'Tis she indeed, sir; you shall know her. She is,
　　Were she not mine,[2] a lady of that merit
　　For fashion and behavior; and for beauty
　　I durst compare—

PEREGRINE   It seems you are not jealous,
　　That dare commend her.

15 POLITIC   Nay, and for discourse—

PEREGRINE   Being your wife, she cannot miss° that.　　　　*lack (sarcastic)*

POLITIC [*introducing* PEREGRINE]   Madam,
　　Here is a gentleman; pray you use him fairly.
　　He seems a youth, but he is—

LADY WOULD-BE   None?

POLITIC   Yes, one
　　Has° put his face as soon° into the world—　　　　*who has / so young*

LADY WOULD-BE   You mean, as early? But today

20 POLITIC   How's this!

LADY WOULD-BE   Why, in this habit,° sir; you apprehend° me.　　　*apparel /*
　　Well, Master Would-be, this doth not become you;　　　*understand*
　　I had thought the odor, sir, of your good name
　　Had been more precious to you, that you would not

25 　　Have done this dire massacre on your honor—
　　One of your gravity and rank besides!
　　But knights, I see, care little for the oath
　　They make to ladies, chiefly their own ladies.

POLITIC   Now, by my spurs—the symbol of my knighthood—

30 PEREGRINE (*aside*)   Lord, how his brain is humbled[3] for an oath!

POLITIC   —I reach° you not.　　　　　　　　　*comprehend*

LADY WOULD-BE   Right, sir, your polity°　　　*cunning*
　　May bear° it through thus. [*to* PEREGRINE] Sir, a word with you.　　*bluff*
　　I would be loath to contest publicly
　　With any gentlewoman, or to seem

35 　　Froward° or violent; as *The Courtier*[4] says,　　　*bad-tempered*
　　It comes too near rusticity° in a lady,　　　　*ill breeding*
　　Which I would shun by all means. And however
　　I may deserve from Master Would-be, yet
　　T' have one fair gentlewoman° thus be made　　　*i.e., Peregrine*

40 　　Th'unkind instrument to wrong another,
　　And one she knows not, ay, and to persevere,
　　In my poor judgment is not warranted
　　From being a solecism° in our sex,　　　　*impropriety*
　　If not in manners.

PEREGRINE   How is this?

POLITIC   Sweet madam,
　　Come nearer to your aim.°　　　　　　　*speak more clearly*

---

2. Even though I, her husband, say so.
3. Literally, "brought down" to his feet—where
spurs, the appurtenances of a knight, are worn.

4. Baldassare Castiglione's famous handbook of
gentility.

45 LADY WOULD-BE   Marry, and will, sir.
　　　Since you provoke me with your impudence
　　　And laughter of your light land-siren[5] here,
　　　Your Sporus,[6] your hermaphrodite—
　PEREGRINE   What's here?
　　　Poetic fury and historic storms![7]
50 POLITIC   The gentleman, believe it, is of worth,
　　　And of our nation.
　LADY WOULD-BE   Ay, your Whitefriars° nation!　　　*London brothel district*
　　　Come, I blush for you, Master Would-be, I,
　　　And am ashamed you should ha' no more forehead°　　　*shame*
　　　Than thus to be the patron, or Saint George,[8]
55 　　To a lewd harlot, a base fricatrice,°　　　*whore*
　　　A female devil in a male outside.
　POLITIC [*to* PEREGRINE]   Nay,
　　　An° you be such a one, I must bid adieu　　　*If*
　　　To your delights. The case appears too liquid.[9]
　　　　　　[POLITIC *starts to leave.*]
　LADY WOULD-BE   Ay, you may carry't clear, with your state-
　　　face!°　　　*dignified expression*
60 　But for your carnival concupiscence,°　　　*lecherous strumpet*
　　　Who here is fled for liberty of conscience°　　　*licentious conduct*
　　　From furious persecution of the marshal,[1]
　　　Her will I disc'ple.°　　　*discipline*
　　　　　　[*Exit* POLITIC, LADY POLITIC *accosts* PEREGRINE.]
　PEREGRINE   This is fine, i'faith!
　　　And do you use this° often? Is this part　　　*act this way*
65 　Of your wit's exercise, 'gainst you have occasion?[2]
　　　Madam—
　LADY WOULD-BE   Go to,° sir.　　　*impatient expression*
　PEREGRINE   Do you hear me, lady?
　　　Why, if your knight have set you to beg shirts,[3]
　　　Or to invite me home, you might have done it
　　　A nearer° way by far.　　　*more direct*
　LADY WOULD-BE   This cannot work you
　　　Out of my snare.
70 PEREGRINE   Why, am I in it, then?
　　　Indeed, your husband told me you were fair,
　　　And so you are; only your nose inclines—
　　　That side that's next the sun—to the queen-apple.[4]
　LADY WOULD-BE   This cannot be endured by any patience.

---

5. The Sirens were mythical sea creatures who
lured sailors to their deaths by sitting on dangerous rocks and singing irresistibly. (Lady Would-
be refers to Peregrine.)
6. A eunuch whom the emperor Nero dressed in
drag and married.
7. Peregrine notes that even Lady Would-be's
tantrums include literary allusions.
8. Patron saint of England, often pictured rescuing a damsel from a dragon.
9. Obvious. (Sir Pol has become convinced that
his wife is right in believing that Peregrine is a

transvestite whore.)
1. Official charged with punishing prostitutes.
Lady Would-be thinks that Peregrine has dressed
as a man to flee prosecution.
2. To keep it ready for when it is really needed?
3. Peregrine pretends to believe that Lady
Would-be is tearing off his shirt in order to give
it to her husband. Probably she is just trying to
prevent his leaving.
4. A bright red apple. See 3.4.15–16, where we
learn that Lady Would-be is sensitive about her
red nose.

SCENE 3. *The scene continues.*

[*Enter*] MOSCA.

MOSCA   What's the matter, madam?

LADY WOULD-BE   If the Senate°   *Venetian government*
Right not my quest° in this, I will protest 'em   *petition*
To all the world no aristocracy.

MOSCA   What is the injury, lady?

LADY WOULD-BE   Why, the callet°   *prostitute*
5   You told me of, here I have ta'en disguised.

MOSCA   Who, this? What means Your Ladyship? The creature
I mentioned to you is apprehended now
Before the Senate. You shall see her—

LADY WOULD-BE   Where?

MOSCA   I'll bring you to her. This young gentleman,
10   I saw him land this morning at the port.

LADY WOULD-BE   Is't possible! How has my judgment wandered!
[*Releasing* PEREGRINE] Sir, I must, blushing, say to you I have erred,
And plead your pardon.

PEREGRINE   What, more changes yet?

LADY WOULD-BE   I hope you ha' not the malice to remember
15   A gentlewoman's passion. If you stay
In Venice here, please you to use me,¹ sir—

MOSCA   Will you go, madam?

LADY WOULD-BE   Pray you, sir, use me. In faith,
The more you see me, the more I shall conceive
You have forgot our quarrel.

[*Exeunt* MOSCA, LADY WOULD-BE, NANO, *and* WOMEN.]

PEREGRINE   This is rare!
20   Sir Politic Would-be? No, Sir Politic Bawd,
To bring me thus acquainted with his wife!
Well, wise Sir Pol, since you have practiced thus
Upon my freshmanship,² I'll try your salt-head,
What proof° it is against a counterplot.   [*Exit.*]   *how invulnerable*

SCENE 4. *The Scrutineo, or Court of Law, in the*
Doge's palace.

[*Enter*] VOLTORE, CORBACCIO, CORVINO, [*and*] MOSCA.

VOLTORE   Well, now you know the carriage° of the business,   *management*
Your constancy is all that is required
Unto the safety of it.

MOSCA   Is the lie
Safely conveyed° amongst us? Is that sure?   *agreed upon*
Knows every man his burden?°   *refrain, tune*

4.3
1. Make use of my services. (With a sexual innuendo continued in "The more you see me, the
more I shall conceive" [line 18], where "conceive"
means both "understand" and "conceive a child.")
2. Taken advantage of my inexperience. (Pere-

grine apparently believes that Sir Pol has deliberately involved him in a humiliating setup.
"Salt-head," following, plays on both "salt" meaning "seasoned," "old," and "salt" meaning "lecherous."

CORVINO   Yes.

5 MOSCA   Then shrink not.

CORVINO [*aside to* MOSCA]   But knows the advocate the truth?

MOSCA [*aside to* CORVINO]   Oh, sir,
 By no means. I devised a formal° tale   *elaborate*
 That salved your reputation. But be valiant, sir.

CORVINO   I fear no one but him,° that this his pleading   *Voltore*
 Should make him stand for a co-heir—

10 MOSCA   Co-halter!¹
 Hang him, we will but use his tongue, his noise,
 As we do Croaker's,° here.   *Corbaccio's*

CORVINO   Ay, what shall he do?

MOSCA   When we ha' done, you mean?

CORVINO   Yes.

MOSCA   Why, we'll think—
 Sell him for *mummia*;² he's half dust already.

15 ([*Aside*] *to* VOLTORE) Do not you smile to see this buffalo,³
 How he doth sport it with his head? [*to himself*] I should,
 If all were well and past. ([*aside*] *to* CORBACCIO) Sir, only you
 Are he that shall enjoy the crop° of all,   *harvest*
 And these not know for whom they toil.

CORBACCIO   Ay, peace!

20 MOSCA ([*aside*] *to* CORVINO)   But you shall eat it. [*To himself*]
     Much!° (*then to* VOLTORE *again*) Worshipful sir,   *Sure you will!*
 Mercury⁴ sit upon your thund'ring tongue,
 Or the French Hercules, and make your language
 As conquering as his club,⁵ to beat along,
 As with a tempest, flat, our adversaries!
 [*Aside to* CORVINO] But much more yours,° sir.   *your adversaries*

25 VOLTORE   Here they come. Ha' done.°   *shut up*

MOSCA   I have another witness° if you need, sir,   *Lady Would-be*
 I can produce.

VOLTORE   Who is it?

MOSCA   Sir, I have her.

SCENE 5. *The scene continues.*

 [*Enter*] *four* AVOCATORI, BONARIO, CELIA. *Notario*
 [NOTORY], COMMENDATORI° [*and other court officials*].   *law court deputies*

FIRST AVOCATORE   The like of this the Senate never heard of.

SECOND AVOCATORE   'Twill come most strange to them when we report it.

FOURTH AVOCATORE   The gentlewoman has been ever held
 Of unreprovèd name.

THIRD AVOCATORE   So, the young man.

5 FOURTH AVOCATORE   The more unnatural part that of his father.

4.4
1. Playing on "halter," a hangman's noose, to suggest that both Corbaccio and Voltore are being duped.
2. Powdered embalmed corpse, used medicinally.
3. Corvino, with his cuckold's horns.

4. May the god of rhetoric (and thieves).
5. After his tenth labor, according to some legendary accounts, Hercules, aged by now but powerfully eloquent, fathered the Celts in Gaul, or France. He was traditionally pictured with a club.

SECOND AVOCATORE   More of the husband.

FIRST AVOCATORE   I not know to give

His act a name, it is so monstrous!

FOURTH AVOCATORE   But the impostor,° he is a thing created   *Volpone*

T'exceed example!°   *precedent*

FIRST AVOCATORE   And all aftertimes!°   *later eras*

10   SECOND AVOCATORE   I never heard a true voluptuary

Described but him.

THIRD AVOCATORE   Appear yet those were cited?

NOTARY   All but the old magnifico, Volpone.

FIRST AVOCATORE   Why is not he here?

MOSCA   Please Your Fatherhoods,

Here is his advocate. Himself's so weak,

So feeble—

FOURTH AVOCATORE   What are you?

15   BONARIO   His parasite,

His knave, his pander! I beseech the court

He may be forced to come, that your grave eyes

May bear strong witness of his strange impostures.

VOLTORE   Upon my faith and credit with your virtues,

20   He is not able to endure the air.

SECOND AVOCATORE   Bring him, however.

THIRD AVOCATORE   We will see him.

FOURTH AVOCATORE   Fetch him.

                                        [*Exit officers.*]

VOLTORE   Your Fatherhoods' fit pleasures be obeyed,

But sure the sight will rather move your pities

Than indignation. May it please the court,

25   In the meantime he may be heard in me.

I know this place most void of prejudice,

And therefore crave it, since we have no reason

To fear our truth should hurt our cause.

THIRD AVOCATORE   Speak free.

VOLTORE   Then know, most honored fathers, I must now

30   Discover° to your strangely abusèd ears   *reveal*

The most prodigious and most frontless° piece   *shameless*

Of solid° impudence and treachery   *complete*

That ever vicious nature yet brought forth

To shame the state of Venice. [*indicating* CELIA] This lewd woman,

35   That wants° no artificial looks or tears   *who lacks*

To help the visor° she has now put on,   *(weeping) mask*

Hath long been known a close° adulteress   *secret; intimate*

To that lascivious youth there [*indicating* BONARIO]; not suspected,

I say, but known, and taken in the act

40   With him; and by this man, the easy° husband,   *lenient*

Pardoned; whose timeless° bounty makes him now   *unseasonable; endless*

Stand here, the most unhappy, innocent person

That ever man's own goodness made accused.[1]

4.5

1. That ever had his own goodness turned against him.

For these, not knowing how to owe° a gift   *acknowledge*
45 Of that dear grace but° with their shame, being placed   *other than*
So above all powers of their gratitude,[2]
Began to hate the benefit, and in place
Of thanks devise t'extirp° the memory   *to extirpate, wipe out*
Of such an act. Wherein I pray Your Fatherhoods
50 To observe the malice, yea, the rage of creatures
Discovered in their evils, and what heart°   *audacity*
Such take even from their crimes. But that anon
Will more appear. This gentleman, the father,
    [*indicating* CORBACCIO]
Hearing of this foul fact,° with many others   *deed*
55 Which daily struck at his too tender ears,
And grieved in nothing more than that he could not
Preserve himself a parent—his son's ills°   *evil deeds*
Growing to that strange flood—at last decreed
To disinherit him.
FIRST AVOCATORE   These be strange turns!
60 SECOND AVOCATORE   The young man's fame° was ever fair   *reputation*
    and honest.
VOLTORE   So much more full of danger is his vice,
That can beguile so under shade of virtue.
But, as I said, my honored sires, his father
Having this settled purpose, by what means
65 To him° betrayed we know not, and this day   *Bonario*
Appointed for the deed, that parricide—
I cannot style him better°—by confederacy   *give him a better name*
Preparing this his paramour to be there,
Entered Volpone's house—who was the man,
70 Your Fatherhoods must understand, designed
For the inheritance—there sought his father.
But with what purpose sought he him, my lords?
I tremble to pronounce it, that a son
Unto a father, and to such a father,
75 Should have so foul, felonious intent:
It was to murder him. When, being prevented
By his more happy° absence, what then did he?   *Corbaccio's fortunate*
Not check his wicked thoughts; no, now new deeds—
Mischief doth ever end where it begins[3]—
80 An act of horror, fathers! He dragged forth
The agèd gentleman, that had there lain bedrid
Three years and more, out of his innocent couch;
Naked upon the floor there left him; wounded
His servant in the face, and with this strumpet,
85 The stale° to his forged practice,° who was glad   *decoy / plot*
To be so active—I shall here desire
Your Fatherhoods to note but my collections°   *deductions*

---

2. Since the rare value of Corvino's forgiveness   3. Wickedness is always persistent.
was so far beyond their powers of gratitude.

As most remarkable—thought at once to stop
His father's ends,° discredit his free choice   *aims*
90   In the old gentleman,° redeem themselves   *Volpone*
By laying infamy upon this man°   *Corvino*
To whom with blushing they should owe their lives.
FIRST AVOCATORE What proofs have you of this?
BONARIO   Most honored fathers,
I humbly crave there be no credit given
To this man's mercenary tongue.
95   SECOND AVOCATORE   Forbear.
BONARIO His soul moves in his fee.
THIRD AVOCATORE   Oh, sir!
BONARIO   This fellow,
For six sols° more, would plead against his Maker.   *halfpennies*
FIRST AVOCATORE You do forget yourself.
VOLTORE   Nay, nay, grave fathers,
Let him have scope. Can any man imagine
100   That he will spare 's° accuser, that would not   *spare his*
Have spared his parent?
FIRST AVOCATORE   Well, produce your proofs.
CELIA I would I could forget I were a creature!°   *living being*
VOLTORE [*calling a witness*] Signor Corbaccio!
FOURTH AVOCATORE   What is he?
VOLTORE   The father.
SECOND AVOCATORE Has he had an oath?
NOTARY   Yes.
CORBACCIO   What must I do now?
NOTARY Your testimony's craved.
105   CORBACCIO [*mis-hearing*]   Speak to the knave?
I'll ha' my mouth first stopped with earth! My heart
Abhors his knowledge;° I disclaim in° him.   *knowing him / disavow*
FIRST AVOCATORE But for what cause?
CORBACCIO   The mere portent of nature.[4]
He is an utter stranger to my loins.
BONARIO Have they made you to this?
110   CORBACCIO   I will not hear thee,
Monster of men, swine, goat, wolf, parricide!
Speak not, thou viper.
BONARIO   Sir, I will sit down,
And rather wish my innocence should suffer
Than I resist the authority of a father.
VOLTORE [*calling a witness*] Signor Corvino!
SECOND AVOCATORE   This is strange!
115   FIRST AVOCATORE   Who's this?
NOTARY The husband.
FOURTH AVOCATORE Is he sworn?
NOTARY   He is.
THIRD AVOCATORE   Speak, then.

---

4. A completely monstrous birth. (A deformed child was often considered to be a portent, or evil omen.)

CORVINO   This woman, please Your Fatherhoods, is a whore
　　Of most hot exercise, more than a partridge,[5]
　　Upon record°—　　　　　　　　　　　　　　　　　as is well attested
FIRST AVOCATORE   No more.
CORVINO　　　　　　　　　　Neighs like a jennet.°　　　　　mare (in heat)
NOTARY   Preserve the honor of the court.

120　CORVINO　　　　　　　　　　　　　　　　I shall,
　　And modesty of your most reverend ears.
　　And yet I hope that I may say these eyes
　　Have seen her glued unto that piece of cedar,
　　That fine well-timbered gallant;[6] and that here

125　[Pointing to his forehead] The letters may be read, thorough the horn,[7]
　　That make the story perfect.°　　　　　　　　　　　complete
MOSCA [aside to CORVINO]　　Excellent, sir!
CORVINO [aside to MOSCA]   There is no shame in this, now, is there?
MOSCA [aside to CORVINO]　　　　　　　　　　　　None.
CORVINO [to the court]   Or if I said I hoped that she were
　　　　onward°　　　　　　　　　　　　　　　　well on her way
　　To her damnation, if there be a hell

130　Greater than whore and woman—a good Catholic
　　May make the doubt°—　　　　　　　　　　　may wonder
THIRD AVOCATORE　　　　His grief hath made him frantic.
FIRST AVOCATORE   Remove him hence.   She [CELIA] swoons.
SECOND AVOCATORE　　　　　　　　　Look to the woman!
CORVINO [taunting her]　　　　　　　　　　Rare!
　　Prettily feigned! Again!
FOURTH AVOCATORE　　Stand from about her.
FIRST AVOCATORE   Give her the air.
THIRD AVOCATORE [to MOSCA]　　What can you say?
MOSCA　　　　　　　　　　　　　My wound,

135　May't please Your Wisdoms, speaks for me, received
　　In aid of my good patron when he° missed　　　　Bonario
　　His sought-for father, when that well-taught dame
　　Had her cue given her to cry out a rape.
BONARIO   Oh, most laid° impudence! Fathers—　　premeditated
THIRD AVOCATORE　　　　　　　　Sir, be silent.

140　You had your hearing free,° so must they theirs.　uninterrupted
SECOND AVOCATORE   I do begin to doubt th'imposture here.
FOURTH AVOCATORE   This woman has too many moods.
VOLTORE　　　　　　　　　　　　Grave fathers,
　　She is a creature of a most professed
　　And prostituted lewdness.
CORVINO　　　　　　Most impetuous!
　　Unsatisfied,° grave fathers!　　　　　　　insatiable

145　VOLTORE　　　　　　　May her feignings

---

5. A bird capable of numerous consecutive sexual acts and so a byword for lechery.
6. Corvino sarcastically compliments Bonario as a strapping fellow to whom Celia no doubt wishes to cling. The cedars of the Middle East are tall and stately.
7. Children learned to read the alphabet from pages protected by transparent sheets of horn. (With an allusion to the cuckold's horn.)

Not take° Your Wisdoms! But° this day she baited   *take in / only*
A stranger, a grave knight, with her loose eyes
And more lascivious kisses. This man° saw 'em   *Mosca*
Together on the water in a gondola.

150 MOSCA   Here is the lady herself that saw 'em too,
Without;° who then had in the open streets   *waiting outside*
Pursued them, but for saving her knight's honor.

FIRST AVOCATORE   Produce that lady.

SECOND AVOCATORE   Let her come.

                 [*Exit* MOSCA.]

FOURTH AVOCATORE   These things,
They strike with wonder!

THIRD AVOCATORE   I am turned a stone!

SCENE 6. *The scene continues.*

[*Enter*] MOSCA [*and*] LADY [WOULD-BE].

MOSCA   Be resolute, madam.

LADY WOULD-BE   Ay, this same is she.
[*To* CELIA] Out, thou chameleon° harlot! Now thine   *deceitfully changeable*
eyes
Vie tears with the hyena.¹ Dar'st thou look
Upon my wrongèd face? [*to the* AVOCATORI] I cry° your pardons.   *beg*
5 I fear I have forgettingly transgressed
Against the dignity of the court—

SECOND AVOCATORE   No, madam.

LADY WOULD-BE   And been exorbitant°—   *excessive*

SECOND AVOCATORE   You have not, lady.

FOURTH AVOCATORE   These proofs are strong.

LADY WOULD-BE   Surely, I had no purpose
To scandalize your honors, or my sex's.

THIRD AVOCATORE   We do believe it.

10 LADY WOULD-BE   Surely, you may believe it.

SECOND AVOCATORE   Madam, we do.

LADY WOULD-BE   Indeed, you may. My breeding
Is not so coarse—

FOURTH AVOCATORE   We know it.

LADY WOULD-BE   —to offend
With pertinacy°—   *stubborn resolution*

THIRD AVOCATORE   Lady—

LADY WOULD-BE   —such a presence;
No, surely.

FIRST AVOCATORE   We well think it.

LADY WOULD-BE   You may think it.

FIRST AVOCATORE [*to the other* AVOCATORI]   Let her o'ercome.°   *have the last*
15 [*To* CELIA *and* BONARIO] What witnesses have you   *word*
To make good your report?

BONARIO   Our consciences.

4.6
1. A symbol of treachery, the hyena was supposed to be able to change its sex and the color of its eyes at will and to imitate human voices.

CELIA   And heaven, that never fails the innocent.

FOURTH AVOCATORE   These are no testimonies.

BONARIO   Not in your courts,
Where multitude and clamor overcomes.

FIRST AVOCATORE   Nay, then, you do wax insolent.

> VOLPONE *is brought in* [*on a litter*], *as impotent.*°   *disabled*
> [LADY WOULD-BE *embraces him.*]°   (*see* 5.2.97)

20   VOLTORE   Here, here
The testimony comes that will convince
And put to utter dumbness their bold tongues.
See here, grave fathers, here's the ravisher,
The rider on men's wives, the great impostor,
25   The grand voluptuary! Do you not think
These limbs should affect venery?[2] Or these eyes
Covet a concubine? Pray you, mark these hands:
Are they not fit to stroke a lady's breasts?
Perhaps he doth dissemble?

BONARIO   So he does.

VOLTORE   Would you ha' him tortured?

30   BONARIO   I would have him proved.[3]

VOLTORE   Best try him, then, with goads or burning irons;
Put him to the strappado.[4] I have heard
The rack[5] hath cured the gout; faith, give it him
And help him of a malady; be courteous.
35   I'll undertake, before these honored fathers,
He shall have yet as many left° diseases   *remaining*
As she has known adulterers, or thou strumpets.
O my most equal° hearers, if these deeds,   *impartial*
Acts of this bold and most exorbitant strain,
40   May pass with sufferance,° what one citizen   *be permitted*
But owes the forfeit of his life, yea, fame
To him that dares traduce him?[6] Which of you
Are safe, my honored fathers? I would ask,
With leave of Your grave Fatherhoods, if their plot
45   Have any face or color like to truth?
Or if unto the dullest nostril here
It smell not rank and most abhorrèd slander?
I crave your care of this good gentleman,
Whose life is much endangered by their fable;
50   And as for them, I will conclude with this:
That vicious persons, when they are hot, and fleshed[7]
In impious acts, their constancy° abounds.   *resoluteness*
Damned deeds are done with greatest confidence.

FIRST AVOCATORE   Take 'em to custody, and sever them.

---

2. Delight in sexual activity.
3. Tested for impotence, a regular court procedure in some divorce and rape cases. (Torture was another method sometimes used to extract confessions.)
4. Torture in which the victim's arms were tied behind his back; he was then hoisted up by the wrists and dropped.
5. Torture instrument that stretched the victim to the point of dislocating his joints.
6. What citizen is there whose life and reputation might not be forfeit to a slanderer?
7. Excited by the taste of blood, like hunting hounds.

55 SECOND AVOCATORE 'Tis pity two such prodigies° should live. *monsters*
                    [*Exeunt* CELIA *and* BONARIO, *guarded.*]
FIRST AVOCATORE Let the old gentleman be returned with care.
     I'm sorry our credulity wronged him.
                    [*Exeunt litter-bearers with* VOLPONE.]
FOURTH AVOCATORE These are two creatures!° *monsters*
THIRD AVOCATORE   I have an earthquake in me!
SECOND AVOCATORE Their shame, even in their cradles, fled their faces.
60 FOURTH AVOCATORE [*to* VOLTORE] You've done a worthy service to the
     state, sir,
     In their discovery.
FIRST AVOCATORE You shall hear ere night
     What punishment the court decrees upon 'em.
VOLTORE We thank Your Fatherhoods.
                    [*Exeunt* AVOCATORI, NOTARY, COMMENDATORI.]
     [*To* MOSCA]   How like you it?
MOSCA   Rare!
     I'd ha' your tongue, sir, tipped with gold for this;
65 I'd ha' you be the heir to the whole city;
     The earth I'd have want men ere you want living.° *lack income*
     They're bound to erect your statue in Saint Mark's.—
     Signor Corvino, I would have you go
     And show yourself,[8] that you have conquered.
CORVINO   Yes.
70 MOSCA [*aside to* CORVINO] It was much better that you should profess
     Yourself a cuckold thus, than that the other[9]
     Should have been proved.
CORVINO   Nay, I considered that.
     Now it is her fault.
MOSCA   Then it had been yours.
CORVINO True. I do doubt this advocate still.
MOSCA   I'faith,
75 You need not; I dare ease you of that care.
CORVINO I trust thee, Mosca.
MOSCA   As your own soul, sir.
                    [*Exit* CORVINO.]
CORBACCIO   Mosca!
MOSCA Now for your business, sir.
CORBACCIO   How? Ha' you business?
MOSCA Yes, yours, sir.
CORBACCIO   Oh, none else?
MOSCA   None else, not I.
CORBACCIO Be careful, then.
MOSCA   Rest you with both your eyes,° sir. *rest assured*
CORBACCIO Dispatch it.[1]
MOSCA   Instantly.
80 CORBACCIO   And look that all

---

8. Appear in public. (To indicate that he is not ashamed of having admitted to being a cuckold.)
9. The attempt to prostitute Celia to Volpone.

1. I.e., Hurry to make Volpone's will, since Corbaccio has already delivered on his half of the promise.

Whatever be put in: jewels, plate, moneys,
Household stuff, bedding, curtains.
MOSCA   Curtain rings, sir.
Only the advocate's fee must be deducted.
CORBACCIO   I'll pay him, now; you'll be too prodigal.
MOSCA   Sir, I must tender° it.   *present*
85   CORBACCIO   Two *cecchines* is well?
MOSCA   No, six, sir.
CORBACCIO   'Tis too much.
MOSCA   He talked a great while,
You must consider that, sir.
CORBACCIO [*giving money*]   Well, there's three—
MOSCA   I'll give it him.
CORBACCIO   Do so, and [*he tips* MOSCA] there's for thee.
                                    [*Exit* CORBACCIO.]
MOSCA [*aside*]   Bountiful bones! What horrid strange offense
90   Did he commit 'gainst nature in his youth
Worthy this age?² [*to* VOLTORE] You see, sir, how I work
Unto your ends; take you no notice.°   *leave it to me*
VOLTORE   No,
I'll leave you.
MOSCA   All is yours,   [*Exit* VOLTORE.]
                    [*aside*] the devil and all,
Good advocate! [*to* LADY WOULD-BE] Madam, I'll bring you home.
LADY WOULD-BE   No, I'll go see your patron.
95   MOSCA   That you shall not.
I'll tell you why. My purpose is to urge
My patron to reform° his will; and, for   *revise*
The zeal you've shown today, whereas before
You were but third or fourth, you shall be now
100   Put in the first, which would appear as begged
If you were present. Therefore—
LADY WOULD-BE   You shall sway me.
                                    [*Exeunt.*]

Act 5

SCENE 1. VOLPONE's *house.*

[*Enter*] VOLPONE [*attended*].
VOLPONE   Well, I am here, and all this brunt° is past.   *crisis*
I ne'er was in dislike with my disguise
Till this fled° moment; here 'twas good, in private,   *past*
But, in your public—*cavé*° whilst I breathe.   *watch out*
5   Fore God, my left leg 'gan to have the cramp,
And I apprehended straight° some power had struck me   *thought at once*
With a dead palsy.° Well, I must be merry   *paralysis*
And shake it off. A many of these fears
Would put me into some villainous disease,

2. To deserve this old age.

10 Should they come thick upon me. I'll prevent 'em.
Give me a bowl of lusty wine to fright
This humor from my heart.[1]—Hum, hum, hum!   *He drinks.*
'Tis almost gone already; I shall conquer,°   overcome my fears
Any device, now, of rare ingenious knavery,
15 That would possess me with a violent laughter,
Would make me up° again. So, so, so, so.   *Drinks again.*   restore me
This heat is life; 'tis blood by this time. [*calling*] Mosca!

SCENE 2. *The scene continues.*

[*Enter*] MOSCA.

MOSCA   How now, sir? Does the day look clear again?
Are we recovered and wrought out of error
Into our way, to see our path before us?
Is our trade free once more?
VOLPONE   Exquisite Mosca!
MOSCA   Was it not carried learnedly?
5 VOLPONE   And stoutly.°   resolutely
Good wits are greatest in extremities.
MOSCA   It were a folly beyond thought to trust
Any grand act unto a cowardly spirit.
You are not taken with it enough, methinks?
10 VOLPONE   Oh, more than if I had enjoyed the wench!
The pleasure of all womankind's not like it.
MOSCA   Why, now you speak, sir. We must here be fixed;
Here we must rest. This is our masterpiece.
We cannot think to go beyond this.
VOLPONE   True,
Th'hast played thy prize,[1] my precious Mosca.
15 MOSCA   Nay, sir,
To gull° the court—   hoodwink
VOLPONE   And quite divert the torrent
Upon the innocent.
MOSCA   Yes, and to make
So rare a music out of discords[2]—
VOLPONE   Right.
That yet to me's the strangest, how th'ast borne it!°   brought it off
20 That these,° being so divided 'mongst themselves,   these men
Should not scent° somewhat, or° in me or thee,   suspect / either
Or doubt their own side.°   position
MOSCA   True, they will not see't.
Too much light blinds 'em, I think. Each of 'em
Is so possessed and stuffed with his own hopes
25 That anything unto the contrary,
Never so true or never so apparent,

5.1
1. Wine was supposed to convert quickly to blood
(see line 17), thus giving courage to the drinker.
5.2
1. Professional fencers "played the prize," i.e.,
competed for purses and titles, in virtuoso displays of swordsmanship.
2. To bring harmony out of various discordant
elements was thought to be the highest achievement of art.

Never so palpable, they will resist it—
VOLPONE　Like a temptation of the devil.
MOSCA　　　　　　　　　　　　　Right, sir.
　Merchants may talk of trade, and your great signors

30　Of land that yields well; but if Italy
　Have any glebe° more fruitful than these fellows,　　　　　　　*soil*
　I am deceived. Did not your advocate rare?°　　　　　*do brilliantly*
VOLPONE　Oh!—"My most honored fathers, my grave fathers,
　Under correction of Your Fatherhoods,

35　What face of truth is here? If these strange deeds
　May pass, most honored fathers"—I had much ado
　To forbear laughing.
MOSCA　　　　　　　'T seemed to me you sweat,° sir.　*sweated (with fear)*
VOLPONE　In troth, I did a little.
MOSCA　　　　　　　　　　But confess, sir,
　Were you not daunted?
VOLPONE　　　　　　　In good faith, I was

40　A little in a mist,° but not dejected;°　　　*uncertain / overwhelmed*
　Never but still myself.
MOSCA　　　　　　I think° it, sir.　　　　　　　*believe*
　Now, so truth help me, I must needs say this, sir,
　And out of conscience for your advocate:
　He's taken pains, in faith, sir, and deserved,

45　In my poor judgment—I speak it under favor,°　　*with your permission*
　Not to contrary° you, sir—very richly—　　　　　　*contradict*
　Well—to be cozened.°　　　　　　　　　　　　*cheated*
VOLPONE　　　　　　Troth, and I think so too,
　By that° I heard him° in the latter end.　　　　　*what / him say*
MOSCA　Oh, but before, sir! Had you heard him first

50　Draw it to certain heads, then aggravate,[3]
　Then use his vehement figures°—I looked still　　*figures of speech*
　When he would shift[4] a shirt; and doing this
　Out of pure love, no hope of gain—
VOLPONE　　　　　　　　　　'Tis right.
　I cannot answer° him, Mosca, as I would,　　　　　　*repay*

55　Not yet; but for thy sake, at thy entreaty
　I will begin ev'n now to vex 'em all,
　This very instant.
MOSCA　　　　　Good, sir.
VOLPONE　　　　　　　Call the dwarf
　And eunuch forth.
MOSCA [*calling*]　　Castrone, Nano!
　　　[*Enter*] NANO [*and*] CASTRONE.
NANO　　　　　　　　　　　Here.
VOLPONE　Shall we have a jig, now?
MOSCA　　　　　　　What you please, sir.
VOLPONE [*to* CASTRONE *and* NANO]　　　　Go,

3. Arrange his material under various headings,　　4. Change (because his efforts made him sweat).
then bring charges.

60 Straight give out about the streets, you two,
That I am dead. Do it with constancy,°   *conviction*
Sadly, do you hear? Impute it to the grief
Of this late slander.   [*Exeunt* CASTRONE *and* NANO.]
MOSCA   What do you mean, sir?
VOLPONE   Oh,
I shall have instantly my vulture, crow,
65 Raven come flying hither on the news
To peck for carrion, my she-wolf° and all,   *Lady Would-be*
Greedy and full of expectation—
MOSCA   And then to have it ravished from their mouths?
VOLPONE   'Tis true. I will ha' thee put on a gown[5]
70 And take upon thee as° thou wert mine heir;   *act as though*
Show 'em a will. Open that chest and reach
Forth one of those that has the blanks.° I'll straight   *blank spaces*
Put in thy name.
MOSCA [*fetching a blank will*]   It will be rare, sir.
VOLPONE   Ay,
When they e'en gape, and find themselves deluded—
MOSCA   Yes.
75 VOLPONE   And thou use them scurvily. Dispatch,
Get on thy gown.
               [VOLPONE *signs the will* MOSCA *has given him.*
                    MOSCA *puts on a mourning garment.*]
MOSCA   But, what, sir, if they ask
After the body?
VOLPONE   Say it was corrupted.
MOSCA   I'll say it stunk, sir, and was fain° t'have it   *I was obliged*
Coffined up instantly and sent away.
80 VOLPONE   Anything; what thou wilt. Hold, here's my will.
Get thee a cap, a count-book, pen and ink,
Papers afore thee; sit as thou wert taking
An inventory of parcels.° I'll get up   *items*
Behind the curtain on a stool, and hearken;
85 Sometime peep over, see how they do look,
With what degrees their blood doth leave their faces.
Oh, 'twill afford me a rare meal of laughter!
MOSCA   Your advocate will turn stark dull° upon it.   *gloomy*
VOLPONE   It will take off his oratory's edge.
90 MOSCA   But your *clarissimo,*° old round-back, he   *aristocrat (Corbaccio)*
Will crump you° like a hog-louse with the touch.   *curl up on you*
VOLPONE   And what Corvino?
MOSCA   Oh, sir, look for him
Tomorrow morning with a rope and a dagger[6]
To visit all the streets; he must run mad.

---

5. This must be the long black gown ordinarily worn by chief mourners, not the *clarissimo's* (aristocrat's) garment, which Mosca dons later in the scene and which constitutes a different kind of insult to Voltore, Corbaccio, and Corvino.

6. Traditional equipment of suicidal madmen, borne by the allegorical figure of Despair in Spenser's *Faerie Queene* 1.9 and by the revenger Hieronimo in *The Spanish Tragedy.*

95 My lady, too, that came into the court
To bear false witness for Your Worship—
VOLPONE   Yes,
And kissed me 'fore the fathers, when my face
Flowed all with oils.°   (*see 4.6.20.1–2*)
MOSCA   And sweat, sir. Why, your gold
Is such another° med'cine, it dries up   *so effective a*
100 All those offensive savors! It transforms
The most deformèd, and restores 'em lovely,
As 'twere the strange poetical girdle.[7] Jove
Could not invent t'himself a shroud more subtle
To pass Acrisius' guards.[8] It is the thing
105 Makes all the world her grace, her youth, her beauty.
VOLPONE   I think she loves me.
MOSCA   Who? The lady, sir?
She's jealous of you.[9]
VOLPONE   Dost thou say so?
        [*Knocking offstage.*]
MOSCA   Hark,
There's some already.
VOLPONE   Look.
MOSCA [*peeping out the door*]   It is the vulture.
He has the quickest scent.
VOLPONE   I'll to my place,
Thou to thy posture.°   *pose*
MOSCA   I am set.
110 VOLPONE   But, Mosca,
Play the artificer° now; torture 'em rarely.   *artist*
        [VOLPONE *conceals himself.*]

SCENE 3. *The scene continues.*

        [*Enter*] VOLTORE.
VOLTORE   How now, my Mosca?
MOSCA [*pretending not to notice him, and reading from an
    inventory*]   "Turkey carpets,° nine"—   *Oriental rugs*
VOLTORE   Taking an inventory? That is well.
MOSCA   "Two suits of bedding, tissue"[1]—
VOLTORE   Where's the will?
Let me read that the while.°   *while you're busy*
        [*Enter*] CORBACCIO [*on a litter*].
CORBACCIO [*to the litter-beaters*]   So, set me down
And get you home.   [*Exeunt litter-bearers.*]
5 VOLTORE   Is he come now to trouble us?
MOSCA   "Of cloth-of-gold,[2] two more"—

7. The girdle of Venus, the goddess of love, made
its wearer irresistible.
8. King Acrisius shut his daughter Danaë in a
tower, but the god Jove came to her in a shower
of gold.
9. (1) Devoted to you; (2) covetous of your
wealth.

5.3
1. Sets of bedcovers and hangings, made of
cloth with gold or silver threads interwoven. The
fancy textiles Mosca mentions in this scene were
extremely expensive to produce in the days
before automation.
2. Cloth made of gold threads.

CORBACCIO   Is it done, Mosca?
MOSCA   "Of several velvets,° eight"—   *separate velvet hangings*
VOLTORE [*aside*]   I like his care.
CORBACCIO [*to* MOSCA]   Dost thou not hear?
        [*Enter*] CORVINO.
CORVINO   Ha! Is the hour come, Mosca?
        VOLPONE *peeps from behind a traverse.°*   *curtain*
VOLPONE [*aside*]   Ay, now they muster.°   *assemble*
CORVINO   What does the advocate here?
Or this Corbaccio?
CORBACCIO   What do these here?
        [*Enter*] LADY [WOULD-BE].
10   LADY WOULD-BE   Mosca,
Is his thread spun?³
MOSCA   "Eight chests of linen"—
VOLPONE [*aside*]   Oh,
My fine Dame Would-be, too!
CORVINO   Mosca, the will,
That I may show it these, and rid 'em hence.
MOSCA   "Six chests of diaper, four of damask"⁴—there.
        [*He gives them the will.*]
CORBACCIO   Is that the will?
MOSCA   "Down beds and bolsters"—
15   VOLPONE [*aside*]   Rare!
Be busy still. Now they begin to flutter;
They never think of me. Look, see, see, see!
How their swift eyes run over the long deed
Unto the name, and to the legacies,
What is bequeathed them there—
20   MOSCA   "Ten suits of hangings"°—   *tapestries*
VOLPONE [*aside*]   Ay, i' their garters,⁵ Mosca. Now their hopes
Are at the gasp.°   *last gasp*
VOLTORE   Mosca the heir!
CORBACCIO   What's that?
VOLPONE [*aside*]   My advocate is dumb. Look to my merchant;
He has heard of some strange storm, a ship is lost,
25   He faints. My lady will swoon. Old glazen-eyes,⁶
He hath not reached his despair yet.
CORBACCIO   All these
Are out of hope; I'm sure the man.
CORVINO   But, Mosca—
MOSCA   "Two cabinets"—
CORVINO   Is this in earnest?
MOSCA   "One
Of ebony"—

3. Is he dead? (In Greek mythology, the Fates
spin out the thread of a human being's life and
cut it at the time of death.)
4. Two kinds of costly textile with interwoven
motifs. Diaper was linen with a diamond pattern; damask could be linen or silk with floral or
other designs.
5. "Go hang yourself in your own garters" was a
common phrase of ridicule.
6. Corbaccio wears spectacles (see also line 63
below).

CORVINO   Or do you but delude me?

30 MOSCA "The other, mother-of-pearl"—I am very busy.
    Good faith, it is a fortune thrown upon me—
    "Item, one salt° of agate"—not my seeking.   *saltcellar*

LADY WOULD-BE Do you hear, sir?

MOSCA   "A perfumed box"—pray you, forbear;
    You see I am troubled°—"made of an onyx"—   *busy*

LADY WOULD-BE   How!

35 MOSCA Tomorrow or next day I shall be at leisure
    To talk with you all.

CORVINO   Is this my large hope's issue?°   *outcome*

LADY WOULD-BE Sir, I must have a fairer answer.

MOSCA   Madam!
    Marry, and shall: pray you, fairly° quit my house.   *positively*
    Nay, raise no tempest with your looks, but hark you,
40   Remember what Your Ladyship offered me°   *implicitly, sexual favors*
    To put you in° an heir; go to, think on't,   *your name in as*
    And what you said e'en your best madams did
    For maintenance,° and why not you? Enough.   *financial support*
    Go home and use the poor Sir Pol, your knight, well,
45   For fear I tell some riddles.° Go, be melancholic.   *secrets*
                 [*Exit* LADY WOULD-BE.]

VOLPONE [*aside*] Oh, my fine devil!

CORVINO   Mosca, pray you a word.

MOSCA Lord! Will not you take your dispatch hence yet?
    Methinks of all you should have been th'example.°   *led the way*
    Why should you stay here? With what thought? What promise?
50   Hear you, do not you know I know you an ass?
    And that you would most fain have been a wittol°   *willing cuckold*
    If fortune would have let you? That you are
    A declared cuckold, on good terms?° This pearl,   *in good standing*
    You'll say, was yours? Right. This diamond?
55   I'll not deny't, but thank you. Much here else?
    It may be so. Why, think that these good works
    May help to hide your bad. I'll not betray you.
    Although you be but extraordinary°   *in name only*
    And have it° only in title, it sufficeth.   *the name of cuckold*
60   Go home. Be melancholic too, or mad.   [*Exit* CORVINO.]

VOLPONE [*aside*] Rare, Mosca! How his villainy becomes him!

VOLTORE [*aside*] Certain he doth delude all these for me.

CORBACCIO [*finally making out the will*] Mosca the heir?

VOLPONE [*aside*]   Oh, his four eyes have found it!

CORBACCIO I'm cozened, cheated by a parasite-slave!
    Harlot,[7] th'ast gulled me.

65 MOSCA   Yes, sir. Stop your mouth,
    Or I shall draw the only tooth is left.
    Are not you he, that filthy covetous wretch
    With the three legs,° that here, in hope of prey,   *including his cane*

---

7. A word used of wicked men as well as women.

Have, any time this three year, snuffed about
70   With your most grov'ling nose, and would have hired
Me to the pois'ning of my patron? Sir?
Are not you he that have today in court
Professed the disinheriting of your son?
Perjured yourself? Go home, and die, and stink.
75   If you but croak a syllable, all comes out.
Away and call your porters. Go, go stink!   [*Exit* CORBACCIO.]
VOLPONE [*aside*]   Excellent varlet!°   *servant; rascal*
VOLTORE   Now, my faithful Mosca,
I find thy constancy—
MOSCA   Sir?
VOLTORE   Sincere.
MOSCA   "A table
Of porphyry"—I mar'l° you'll be thus troublesome.   *marvel*
VOLTORE   Nay, leave off now, they are gone.
80   MOSCA   Why, who are you?
What? Who did send for you? Oh, cry you mercy,°   *beg your pardon*
Reverend sir! Good faith, I am grieved for you,
That any chance of mine should thus defeat
Your—I must needs say—most deserving travails.
85   But I protest, sir, it was cast upon me,
And I could almost wish to be without it,
But that the will o'th'dead must be observed.
Marry, my joy is that you need it not;
You have a gift, sir—thank your education—
90   Will never let you want, while there are men
And malice to breed causes.° Would I had   *lawsuits*
But half the like, for all my fortune, sir!
If I have any suits—as I do hope,
Things being so easy and direct,[8] I shall not—
95   I will make bold with your obstreperous° aid,   *vociferous*
Conceive me, for your fee,[9] sir. In meantime
You, that have so much law, I know, ha' the conscience
Not to be covetous of what is mine.
Good sir, I thank you for my plate;° 'twill help   *(see 1.3.1–20)*
100   To set up a young man.° Good faith, you look   *set up my household*
As you were costive; best go home and purge, sir.
                              [*Exit* VOLTORE.]
VOLPONE [*coming from behind the traverse*]   Bid him eat
lettuce° well. My witty mischief,   *used as a laxative*
Let me embrace thee! [*He hugs* MOSCA.] Oh, that I could now
Transform thee to a Venus!° Mosca, go,   *for Volpone's sexual use*
105   Straight take my habit of *clarissimo*[1]
And walk the streets; be seen, torment 'em more.
We must pursue as well as plot. Who would

8. The situation being so straightforward.
9. It being understood that I will pay you, of course.
1. Aristocrat. (By obeying this order, Mosca vio-lates the sumptuary laws that restricted the wearing of distinctive high-status garments, such as the *clarissimo*'s robe, to persons of the appropriate rank.)

Have lost° this feast?   *missed*

MOSCA   I doubt° it will lose them.°   *fear / as dupes*

VOLPONE   Oh, my recovery shall recover all.[2]

110   That I could now but think on some disguise
To meet 'em in, and ask 'em questions.
How I would vex 'em still at every turn!

MOSCA   Sir, I can fit you.

VOLPONE   Canst thou?

MOSCA   Yes, I know
One o'the *commendatori*, sir, so like you,

115   Him will I straight make drunk, and bring you his habit.

VOLPONE   A rare disguise, and answering thy brain!°   *suiting your wit*
Oh, I will be a sharp disease unto 'em.

MOSCA   Sir, you must look for curses—

VOLPONE   Till they burst!
The fox fares ever best when he is curst.°   [*Exeunt.*]   *proverbial wisdom*

SCENE 4. *The* WOULD-BES' *house.*

[*Enter*] PEREGRINE [*in disguise, and*] *three* MERCATORI
[MERCHANTS].

PEREGRINE   Am I enough disguised?

FIRST MERCHANT   I warrant you.

PEREGRINE   All my ambition is to fright him only.

SECOND MERCHANT   If you could ship him away, 'twere excellent.

THIRD MERCHANT   To Zante, or to Aleppo?[1]

PEREGRINE   Yes, and ha' his

5   Adventures put i'th'book of voyages,[2]
And his gulled° story registered for truth?   *erroneous*
Well, gentlemen, when I am in awhile,
And that you think us warm in our discourse,
Know° your approaches.   *make*

FIRST MERCHANT   Trust it to our care.
[*Exeunt* MERCHANTS.]

[PEREGRINE *knocks. A*] WOMAN [*servant answers the
door*].

10   PEREGRINE   Save you, fair lady. Is Sir Pol within?

WOMAN   I do not know, sir.

PEREGRINE   Pray you, say unto him
Here is a merchant upon earnest business
Desires to speak with him.

WOMAN   I will see, sir.

PEREGRINE   Pray you.
[*Exit* WOMAN.]

I see the family is all female here.
[*Enter* WOMAN.]

2. Volpone believes that by "undoing" his death, he will be able to resuscitate his scam.
5.4
1. Zante is an island off Greece under Venetian control; Aleppo, a big trading center, is in Syria.

2. An enlarged edition of Richard Hakluyt's *Principal Navigations, Voyages, Traffics, and Discoveries of the English Nation* was published in 1598–1600.

15 WOMAN   He says, sir, he has weighty affairs of state
     That now require him whole;° some other time   *demand all his attention*
     You may possess° him.   *gain audience with*
   PEREGRINE   Pray you say again,
     If those require him whole, these will exact him°   *force him out*
     Whereof I bring him tidings.   [*Exit* WOMAN.]
                              What might be
20   His grave affair of state, now? How to make
     Bolognian sausages here in Venice, sparing
     One o'th'ingredients?
          [*Enter* WOMAN.]
   WOMAN   Sir, he says he knows
     By your word "tidings" that you are no statesman,[3]
     And therefore wills you stay.°   *wishes you to wait*
   PEREGRINE   Sweet, pray you return° him   *reply to*
25   I have not read so many proclamations
     And studied them for words as he has done,
     But—here he deigns to come.
          [*Enter*] POLITIC.
                              [*Exit* WOMAN.]
   POLITIC   Sir, I must crave
     Your courteous pardon. There hath chanced today
     Unkind disaster 'twixt my lady and me,
30   And I was penning my apology
     To give her satisfaction, as you came now.
   PEREGRINE   Sir, I am grieved I bring you worse disaster.
     The gentleman you met at th'port today,
     That told you he was newly arrived—
   POLITIC   Ay, was
     A fugitive punk?°   *prostitute*
35 PEREGRINE   No, sir, a spy set on you;
     And he has made relation to the Senate
     That you professed to him to have a plot
     To sell the state of Venice to the Turk.°   (*see 4.1.128–30*)
   POLITIC   Oh, me!
   PEREGRINE   For which warrants are signed by this time
40   To apprehend you, and to search your study
     For papers—
   POLITIC   Alas, sir, I have none but notes
     Drawn out of playbooks°—   *printed plays*
   PEREGRINE   All the better, sir.
   POLITIC   And some essays. What shall I do?
   PEREGRINE   Sir, best
     Convey yourself into a sugar-chest;
45   Or, if you could lie round, a frail were rare,[4]
     And I could send you aboard.
   POLITIC   Sir, I but talked so,

---

3. Government agent. (Sir Pol believes that a spy   4. If you could curl up, a fruit basket would be
would use the word "intelligence.")   excellent.

For discourse sake merely.°   *They knock without.*   *just to be conversing*
PEREGRINE   Hark, they are there!
POLITIC   I am a wretch, a wretch!
PEREGRINE   What will you do, sir?
   Ha' you ne'er a currant-butt° to leap into?   *casket for currants*
50   They'll put you to the rack; you must be sudden.
   POLITIC   Sir, I have an engine°—   *contrivance*
   THIRD MERCHANT [*without*]   Sir Politic Would-be!
   SECOND MERCHANT [*without*]   Where is he?
   POLITIC   That I have thought upon
      beforetime.
   PEREGRINE   What is it?
   POLITIC   I shall ne'er endure the torture!
      Marry, it is, sir, of a tortoiseshell, [*producing the shell*]
55   Fitted for these extremities. Pray you sir, help me.
      Here I have a place, sir, to put back my legs—
      Please you to lay it on, sir—with this cap
      And my black gloves. I'll lie, sir, like a tortoise
      Till they are gone.
   PEREGRINE [*laying the shell on* POLITIC's *back*]   And call you this an
      engine?
60   POLITIC   Mine own device—good sir, bid my wife's women
      To burn my papers.   [*Exit* PEREGRINE.]
            They [*the* MERCHANTS] *rush in.*
   FIRST MERCHANT   Where's he hid?
   THIRD MERCHANT   We must
      And will, sure, find him.
   SECOND MERCHANT   Which is his study?
            [*Enter* PEREGRINE.]
   FIRST MERCHANT   What
      Are you, sir?
   PEREGRINE   I'm a merchant, that came here
      To look upon this tortoise.
   THIRD MERCHANT   How?
   FIRST MERCHANT   Saint Mark!
      What beast is this?
   PEREGRINE   It is a fish.
65   SECOND MERCHANT [*to* POLITIC]   Come out here!
   PEREGRINE   Nay, you may strike him, sir, and tread upon him.
      He'll bear a cart.
   FIRST MERCHANT   What, to run over him?
   PEREGRINE   Yes.
   THIRD MERCHANT   Let's jump upon him.
   SECOND MERCHANT   Can he not go?°   *walk*
   PEREGRINE   He creeps, sir.
   FIRST MERCHANT [*poking* POLITIC]   Let's see him creep.
   PEREGRINE   No, good sir, you
      will hurt him.
70   SECOND MERCHANT   Heart! I'll see him creep, or prick his guts.
   THIRD MERCHANT [*to* POLITIC]   Come out here!

PEREGRINE   [*aside to* POLITIC]   Pray you, sir, creep a little.
   [POLITIC *creeps.*]
FIRST MERCHANT   Forth!
SECOND MERCHANT   Yet further.
PEREGRINE [*aside to* POLITIC]   Good sir, creep.
SECOND MERCHANT   We'll see his legs.
   They pull off the shell and discover° him.   expose
THIRD MERCHANT   Godso, he has garters!
FIRST MERCHANT   Ay, and gloves!
SECOND MERCHANT   Is this
   Your fearful tortoise?
PEREGRINE [*revealing himself*]   Now, Sir Pol, we are even.
75   For your next project I shall be prepared.
   I am sorry for the funeral of your notes, sir.
FIRST MERCHANT   'Twere a rare motion to be seen in Fleet Street!⁵
SECOND MERCHANT   Ay, i'the term.
FIRST MERCHANT   Or Smithfield, in the fair.⁶
THIRD MERCHANT   Methinks 'tis but a melancholic sight!
80 PEREGRINE   Farewell, most politic tortoise.
            [*Exeunt* PEREGRINE *and* MERCHANTS.]
     [*Enter* WOMAN.]
POLITIC   Where's my lady?
   Knows she of this?
WOMAN   I know not, sir.
POLITIC   Inquire.
            [*Exit* WOMAN.]
   Oh, I shall be the fable of all feasts,°   talk of the town
   The freight of the *gazetti*, ship boys' tale,⁷
   And, which is worst, even talk for ordinaries.°   taverns
   [*Enter* WOMAN.]
85 WOMAN   My lady's come most melancholic home,
   And says, sir, she will straight to sea for physic.
POLITIC   And I, to shun this place and clime forever,
   Creeping with house on back, and think it well
   To shrink my poor head in my politic shell.   [*Exeunt.*]

           SCENE 5. VOLPONE's *house.*

   [*Enter*] VOLPONE [*and*] MOSCA, *the first in the habit of a*
   commendatore, the other, of a clarissimo.°   (*see 5.3.104–15*)
VOLPONE   Am I then like him?
MOSCA   Oh, sir, you are he.
   No man can sever° you.   distinguish
VOLPONE   Good.
MOSCA   But what am I?
VOLPONE   'Fore heav'n, a brave° *clarissimo;* thou becom'st it!   splendid

---

5. Puppet shows, called "motions," were frequently performed on London's Fleet Street, adjacent to the Inns of Court, where attorneys were
trained and cases were argued during the three
law terms.

6. Smithfield, just northwest of London, was the
site every August of Bartholomew Fair; puppet
shows were a prime entertainment there.
7. Topic of the newspapers and the gossip of
boys serving on board ships.

Pity thou wert not born one.

MOSCA   If I hold

My made one, 'twill be well.

5   VOLPONE   I'll go and see

What news, first, at the court.

MOSCA   Do so.   [*Exit* VOLPONE.]

My fox

Is out on° his hole,[1] and ere he shall reenter   *of*

I'll make him languish in his borrowed case,°   *disguise*

Except he come to composition° with me.   *unless he makes a deal*

[*Calling*] Androgyno, Castrone, Nano!

[*Enter* ANDROGYNO, CASTRONE, *and* NANO.]

10   ALL   Here.

MOSCA   Go recreate yourselves abroad;° go sport.   *outside*

[*Exeunt* ANDROGYNO, CASTRONE, *and* NANO.]

So, now I have the keys, and am possessed.°   *in possession*

Since he will needs be dead afore his time,

I'll bury him or gain by him. I am his heir,

15   And so will keep me° till he share at least.   *remain*

To cozen him of all were but a cheat

Well placed; no man would construe it a sin.

Let his sport pay for't.° This is called the Fox Trap. [*Exit.*]   *for itself*

SCENE 6. *A street in Venice.*

[*Enter*] CORBACCIO [*and*] CORVINO.

CORBACCIO   They say the court is set.°   *in session*

CORVINO   We must maintain

Our first tale good, for both our reputations.

CORBACCIO   Why, mine's no tale; my son would there have killed me.

CORVINO   That's true; I had forgot. [*aside*] Mine is, I am sure.—

But for your will, sir.

5   CORBACCIO   Ay, I'll come upon him

For that hereafter, now his patron's dead.

[*Enter*] VOLPONE [*disguised*].

VOLPONE   Signor Corvino! And Corbaccio! Sir,

Much joy unto you.

CORVINO   Of what?

VOLPONE   The sudden good

Dropped down upon you—

CORBACCIO   Where?

VOLPONE   And none knows how—

From old Volpone, sir.

10   CORBACCIO   Out, arrant knave!

VOLPONE   Let not your too much wealth, sir, make you furious.°   *insane*

CORBACCIO   Away, thou varlet!

VOLPONE   Why, sir?

CORBACCIO   Dost thou mock me?

5.5

1. Alluding to the children's game, fox-in-the-hole.

VOLPONE   You mock the world, sir.[1] Did you not change° wills?   *exchange*
CORBACCIO   Out, harlot!
VOLPONE [*to* CORVINO]   Oh, belike you are the man,
15   Signor Corvino? Faith, you carry it° well;   *carry it off*
      You grow not mad withal. I love your spirit.
      You are not overleavened° with your fortune.   *too puffed up*
      You should ha' some would swell now like a wine-vat
      With such an autumn.° Did he gi' you all, sir?   *harvest*
CORBACCIO   Avoid,° you rascal!   *go away*
20 VOLPONE   Troth, your wife has shown
      Herself a very° woman. But you are well;   *typical*
      You need not care; you have a good estate
      To bear it out, sir, better by this chance—
      Except Corbaccio have a share?
CORBACCIO   Hence, varlet!
25 VOLPONE   You will not be aknown,[2] sir; why, 'tis wise.
      Thus do all gamesters at all games dissemble.
      No man will seem to win.°   *admit he's winning*
                    [*Exeunt* CORBACCIO *and* CORVINO.]
                    Here comes my vulture,
      Heaving his beak up i'the air and snuffing.

              SCENE 7. *The scene continues.*

          [*Enter*] VOLTORE.
VOLTORE [*to himself*]   Outstripped thus by a parasite? A slave
      Would run on errands, and make legs° for crumbs?   *curtsies*
      Well, what I'll do—
VOLPONE   The court stays for° Your Worship.   *awaits*
      I e'en rejoice, sir, at Your Worship's happiness,
5   And that it fell into so learnèd hands
      That understand the fingering[1]—
VOLTORE   What do you mean?
VOLPONE   I mean to be a suitor to Your Worship
      For the small tenement, out of reparations[2]—
      That at the end of your long row of houses
10   By the *piscaria*.° It was in Volpone's time,   *fish market*
      Your predecessor, ere he grew diseased,
      A handsome, pretty, customed° bawdy house   *much-patronized*
      As any was in Venice—none dispraised[3]—
      But fell with him; his body and that house
      Decayed together.
15 VOLTORE   Come, sir, leave your prating.°   *chattering*
VOLPONE   Why, if Your Worship give me but your hand,
      That I may ha' the refusal,° I have done.   *right of first refusal*

5.6
1. Volpone pretends to believe that Corbaccio is misleading people by refusing to admit to his good fortune.
2. You prefer not to be recognized (as heir).

5.7
1. That understand how to handle money.
2. For the rental house in bad repair.
3. Not to disparage the others.

'Tis a mere toy to you, sir, candle-rents,[4]
As Your learned Worship knows—
VOLTORE   What do I know?
20   VOLPONE   Marry, no end of your wealth, sir, God decrease[5] it.
VOLTORE   Mistaking knave! What, mock'st thou my misfortune?
VOLPONE   His° blessing on your heart, sir! Would 'twere more.   *God's*
                                          [*Exit* VOLTORE.]
    Now, to my first[6] again, at the next corner.

          SCENE 8. *The scene continues.*

    [*Enter*] CORBACCIO [*and*] CORVINO. [*Enter*] MOSCA,
       passant° [*over the stage in* clarissimo's *attire, and exit*].   *passing*
CORBACCIO   See, in our habit! See the impudent varlet!
CORVINO   That I could shoot mine eyes at him, like gunstones!°   *cannonballs*
VOLPONE   But, is this true, sir, of the parasite?
CORBACCIO   Again t'afflict us? Monster!
VOLPONE   In good faith, sir,
5   I'm heartily grieved a beard of your grave length°   *so wise an old man*
    Should be so overreached. I never brooked°   *could stand*
    That parasite's hair; methought his nose should cozen.°   *he had a cheating nose*
    There still° was somewhat in his look did promise.   *always*
    The bane° of a *clarissimo*.   *ruin*
CORBACCIO   Knave—
VOLPONE [*to* CORVINO]   Methinks
10   Yet you that are so traded° i'the world,   *experienced*
    A witty merchant, the fine bird Corvino,
    That have such moral emblems[1] on your name,
    Should not have sung your shame and dropped your cheese,
    To let the fox laugh at your emptiness.[2]
15   CORVINO   Sirrah, you think the privilege of the place,[3]
    And your red saucy cap, that seems to me
    Nailed to your jolt-head with those two *cecchines*,[4]
    Can warrant° your abuses. Come you hither.   *sanction*
    You shall perceive, sir, I dare beat you. Approach!
20   VOLPONE   No haste, sir, I do know your valor well,
    Since you durst publish° what you are, sir.   *make public*
          [VOLPONE *makes as if to leave.*]
CORVINO   Tarry!
    I'd speak with you.
VOLPONE   Sir, sir, another time—
CORVINO   Nay, now.
VOLPONE   Oh, God, sir! I were a wise man
    Would stand° the fury of a distracted cuckold.   *to withstand*
          MOSCA [*enters and*] *walks by 'em.*
CORBACCIO   What! Come again?

4. (1) Revenue from deteriorating property; (2)
"pin money," money for incidentals.
5. Instead of "increase".
6. The ones I was taunting earlier, Corvino and
Corbaccio.
5.8

1. Mottoes accompanying symbolic engravings.
2. As in Aesop's fable; see 1.2.95–97 and note.
3. Violence was forbidden near the court.
4. The *commendatore's* cap is decorated with
gold buttons.

25 VOLPONE [*aside to* MOSCA]   Upon 'em, Mosca; save me.
CORBACCIO   The air's infected where he breathes.
CORVINO   Let's fly him.
     [*Exeunt* CORVINO *and* CORBACCIO.]
VOLPONE   Excellent basilisk![5] Turn upon the vulture.

SCENE 9. *The scene continues.*

     [*Enter*] VOLTORE.
VOLTORE [*to Mosca*]   Well, flesh fly, it is summer with you now;
     Your winter will come on.
MOSCA   Good advocate,
     Pray thee not rail, nor threaten out of place° thus;   *unsuitably*
     Thou'lt make a solecism,° as madam says.   (*see 4.2.43*)
5   Get you a biggin[1] more; your brain breaks loose.
VOLTORE   Well, sir.   [*Exit* MOSCA.]
VOLPONE   Would you ha' me beat the insolent slave?
     Throw dirt upon his first good clothes?
VOLTORE   This same°   *the disguised Volpone*
     Is doubtless some familiar!°   *attendant devil*
VOLPONE   Sir, the court,
     In troth, stays for you. I am mad° a mule   *furious that*
10   That never read Justinian[2] should get up
     And ride an advocate. Had you no quirk°   *trick*
     To avoid gullage,° sir, by such a creature?   *deception*
     I hope you do but jest; he has not done't.
     This's but confederacy to blind the rest.°   *Corvino and Corbaccio*
     You are the heir?
15   VOLTORE   A strange, officious,
     Troublesome knave! Thou dost torment me.
VOLPONE   I know—
     It cannot be, sir, that you should be cozened;
     'Tis not within the wit of man to do it.
     You are so wise, so prudent, and 'tis fit
20   That wealth and wisdom still should go together.
                                                  [*Exeunt.*]

SCENE 10. *The law court.*

     [*Enter*] *four* AVOCATORI, NOTARIO [NOTARY], COMMEN-
     DATORI, BONARIO [*and*] CELIA [*under guard*], COR-
     BACCIO, [*and*] CORVINO.
FIRST AVOCATORE   Are all the parties here?
NOTARY   All but the advocate.
SECOND AVOCATORE   And here he comes.
FIRST AVOCATORE   Then bring 'em forth to sentence.
     [*Enter*] VOLTORE, [*and*] VOLPONE [*still disguised as a
     commendatore*].

---

5. A legendary monster whose breath and glance
were deadly.
5.9
1. A larger skullcap (worn by lawyers).

2. The Roman law, codified under Emperor Justinian and still influential on the Continent.
Lawyers traditionally rode mules to the courts;
here the image is comically inverted.

VOLTORE   O my most honored fathers, let your mercy
Once win upon° your justice, to forgive—   *prevail over*
I am distracted—
VOLPONE (*aside*)   What will he do now?
5 VOLTORE   Oh,
I know not which t'address myself to first,
Whether Your Fatherhoods or these innocents°—   *Celia and Bonario*
CORVINO [*aside*]   Will he betray himself?
VOLTORE   Whom equally
I have abused, out of most covetous ends—
CORVINO [*aside to* CORBACCIO]   The man is mad!
CORBACCIO   What's that?
10 CORVINO
                             He is possessed.
VOLTORE   For which, now struck in conscience, here I prostrate
Myself at your offended feet for pardon.
                         [*He throws himself down.*]
FIRST AND SECOND AVOCATORI   Arise!
CELIA   O heav'n, how just thou art!
VOLPONE [*aside*]   I'm caught
I' mine own noose—
CORVINO [*aside to* CORBACCIO]   Be constant, sir; naught now
Can help but impudence.   [VOLTORE *rises.*]
FIRST AVOCATORE [*to* VOLTORE]   Speak forward.°   *continue*
15 COMMENDATORI [*to the courtroom*]   Silence!
VOLTORE   It is not passion° in me, reverend fathers,   *madness*
But only conscience, conscience, my good sires,
That makes me now tell truth. That parasite,
That knave hath been the instrument of all.
SECOND AVOCATORE   Where is that knave? Fetch him.
VOLPONE [*as commendatore*]   I go. [*Exit.*]
20 CORVINO   Grave fathers,
This man's distracted; he confessed it now;°   *just now*
For, hoping to be old Volpone's heir,
Who now is dead—
THIRD AVOCATORE   How?
SECOND AVOCATORE   Is Volpone dead?
CORVINO   Dead since,° grave fathers—   *since his appearance here*
BONARIO   O sure vengeance!
FIRST AVOCATORE   Stay.
Then he was no deceiver?
25 VOLTORE   Oh, no, none.
The parasite, grave fathers.
CORVINO   He does speak
Out of mere envy, 'cause the servant's made
The thing he gaped° for. Please Your Fatherhoods,   *Voltore yearned*
This is the truth; though I'll not justify
30 The other,° but he may be somedeal° faulty.   *Mosca / somewhat*
VOLTORE   Ay, to your hopes as well as mine, Corvino;
But I'll use modesty.° Pleaseth Your Wisdoms   *self-control*

To view these certain notes, and but confer° them.   *compare*
As I hope favor, they shall speak clear truth.
    [*He gives documents to the* AVOCATORI.]
CORVINO   The devil has entered him!
35 BONARIO   Or bides in you.
FOURTH AVOCATORE   We have done ill, by a public officer
    To send for him, if he be heir.
SECOND AVOCATORE   For whom?
FOURTH AVOCATORE   Him that they call the parasite.
THIRD AVOCATORE   'Tis true;
    He is a man of great estate now left.°   *bequeathed to him*
40 FOURTH AVOCATORE [*to* NOTARY]   Go you and learn his name,
        and say the court
    Entreats his presence here but to the clearing
    Of some few doubts.   [*Exit* NOTARY.]
SECOND AVOCATORE   This same's a labyrinth!
FIRST AVOCATORE [*to* CORVINO]   Stand you unto° your first   *do you stand by*
    report?
CORVINO   My state,°   *estate*
    My life, my fame°—   *reputation*
BONARIO   Where is't?[1]
CORVINO   —are at the stake.
FIRST AVOCATORE [*to* CORBACCIO]   Is yours so too?
45 CORBACCIO   The advocate's a knave,
    And has a forkèd tongue—
SECOND AVOCATORE   Speak to the point.
CORBACCIO   So is the parasite, too.
FIRST AVOCATORE   This is confusion.
VOLTORE   I do beseech Your Fatherhoods, read but those.
CORVINO   And credit nothing the false spirit hath writ.
50   It cannot be but he is possessed, grave fathers.
    [*The* AVOCATORI *examine* VOLTORE's *papers.*]

SCENE 11. *A street.*[1]

    [*Enter*] VOLPONE [*on a separate part of the stage*].
VOLPONE   To make a snare for mine own neck! And run
    My head into it willfully! With laughter!
    When I had newly scaped, was free and clear!
    Out of mere wantonness!° Oh, the dull devil   *caprice*
5   Was in this brain of mine when I devised it,
    And Mosca gave it second. He must now
    Help to sear up° this vein, or we bleed dead.   *cauterize*
    [*Enter*] NANO, ANDROGYNO, [*and*] CASTRONE.
    How now, who let you loose? Whither go you now?
    What, to buy gingerbread? Or to drown kitlings?°   *kittens*

5.10
1. Implying that Corvino has nothing of worth
to lose.
5.11

1. The courtroom characters remain visible
onstage, perhaps in silent tableau, while Volpone
is understood to be outside.

10 NANO   Sir, Master Mosca called us out of doors,
    And bid us all go play, and took the keys.
ANDROGYNO   Yes.
VOLPONE   Did Master Mosca take the keys? Why, so!
    I am farther in.° These are my fine conceits!°   *in trouble / notions*
    I must be merry, with a mischief to me!
15   What a vile wretch was I, that could not bear
    My fortune soberly! I must ha' my crotchets°   *perverse whims*
    And my conundrums! Well, go you and seek him.
    His meaning may be truer than my fear.[2]
    Bid him he straight come to me, to the court.
20   Thither will I, and, if't be possible,
    Unscrew° my advocate upon° new hopes.   *dissuade / by means of*
    When I provoked him, then I lost myself.
                [*Exeunt* VOLPONE *and his entourage.*
               The AVOCATORI *and parties to the*
             courtroom proceedings remain onstage.]

SCENE 12. *The courtroom.*

FIRST AVOCATORE [*with* VOLTORE's *notes*]   These things can ne'er be
    reconciled. He here
  Professeth that the gentleman° was wronged,   *Bonario*
  And that the gentlewoman was brought thither,
    Forced by her husband, and there left.
VOLTORE   Most true.
CELIA   How ready is heav'n to those that pray!
5 FIRST AVOCATORE   But that
  Volpone would have ravished her, he holds
  Utterly false, knowing his impotence.
CORVINO   Grave fathers, he is possessed; again I say,
  Possessed. Nay, if there be possession
  And obsession, he has both.
10 THIRD AVOCATORE   Here comes our officer.
        [*Enter* VOLPONE, *still disguised.*]
VOLPONE   The parasite will straight be here, grave fathers.
FOURTH AVOCATORE   You might invent some other name, sir varlet.
THIRD AVOCATORE   Did not the notary meet him?
VOLPONE   Not that I know.
FOURTH AVOCATORE   His coming will clear all.
SECOND AVOCATORE   Yet it is misty.
VOLTORE   May't please Your Fatherhoods—
15 VOLPONE (*whispers* [*to*] *the advocate*)   Sir, the parasite
  Willed me to tell you that his master lives,
  That you are still the man, your hopes the same;
  And this was only a jest—
VOLTORE [*aside to* VOLPONE]   How?
VOLPONE [*aside to* VOLTORE]   Sir, to try
  If you were firm, and how you stood affected.°   *how loyal you were*

---

2. Mosca's intentions may be truer (more loyal) than my fear is true (accurate).

VOLTORE   Art sure he lives?

VOLPONE   Do I live,° sir?   *he's as alive as I am*

20 VOLTORE   Oh, me!
I was too violent.

VOLPONE   Sir, you may redeem it.
They said you were possessed; fall down, and seem so.
I'll help to make it good.   VOLTORE *falls.*
                    [*Aloud*] God bless the man!
[*Aside to* VOLTORE] Stop your wind hard, and swell.[1] [*Aloud*]
    See, see, see, see!

25 He vomits crooked pins! His eyes are set
Like a dead hare's hung in a poulter's[2] shop!
His mouth's running away!° [*to* CORVINO] Do you see,   *twitching*
    signor?   *spasmodically*
Now 'tis in his belly.

CORVINO   Ay, the devil!

VOLPONE   Now in his throat.

CORVINO   Ay, I perceive it plain.

30 VOLPONE   'Twill out, 'twill out! Stand clear. See where it flies,
In shape of a blue toad with a bat's wings!
[*To* CORBACCIO] Do not you see it, sir?

CORBACCIO   What? I think I do.

CORVINO   'Tis too manifest.

VOLPONE   Look! He comes t' himself!

VOLTORE   Where am I?

VOLPONE   Take good heart; the worst is past, sir.
You are dispossessed.

35 FIRST AVOCATORE   What accident° is this?   *unforeseen event*

SECOND AVOCATORE   Sudden, and full of wonder!

THIRD AVOCATORE   If he were
Possessed, as it appears, all this° is nothing.   *Voltore's written statement*

CORVINO   He has been often subject to these fits.

FIRST AVOCATORE   Show him that writing. [*To* VOLTORE] Do
    you know it, sir?

40 VOLPONE [*aside to* VOLTORE]   Deny it, sir; forswear it; know it not.

VOLTORE   Yes, I do know it well, it is my hand;
But all that it contains is false.

BONARIO   Oh, practice!°   *deception*

SECOND AVOCATORE   What maze is this!

FIRST AVOCATORE   Is he not guilty, then,
Whom you there name the parasite?

VOLTORE   Grave fathers,

45 No more than his good patron, old Volpone.

FOURTH AVOCATORE   Why, he is dead!

VOLTORE   Oh, no, my honored fathers.
He lives—

5.12
1. The details of Voltore's dispossession in the
following lines resemble the fake exorcisms
described in Samuel Harsnett's lively exposé, *A*

Discovery of the Fraudulent Practices of John Dar-
rell (1599). "Stop your wind": hold your breath.
2. Seller of poultry and small game.

FIRST AVOCATORE   How! Lives?

VOLTORE   Lives.

SECOND AVOCATORE   This is subtler yet!

THIRD AVOCATORE [*to* VOLTORE]   You said he was dead?

VOLTORE   Never.

THIRD AVOCATORE [*to* CORVINO]   You said so?

CORVINO   I heard so.

FOURTH AVOCATORE   Here comes the gentleman; make him way.
    [*Enter* MOSCA.]

50   THIRD AVOCATORE   A stool!

FOURTH AVOCATORE [*aside*]   A proper° man! And, were Volpone   *handsome*
   dead,
   A fit match for my daughter.

THIRD AVOCATORE   Give him way.

VOLPONE [*aside to* MOSCA]   Mosca, I was almost lost; the advocate
   Had betrayed all; but now it is recovered.

   All's o'the hinge° again. Say I am living.   *running smoothly*

55   MOSCA [*aloud*]   What busy° knave is this? Most reverend   *troublesome*
   fathers,
   I sooner had attended your grave pleasures,
   But that my order for the funeral
   Of my dear patron did require me—

VOLPONE (*aside*)   Mosca!

MOSCA   Whom I intend to bury like a gentleman.

VOLPONE [*aside*]   Ay, quick,° and cozen me of all.[3]   *alive*

60   SECOND AVOCATORE   Still stranger!
   More intricate!

FIRST AVOCATORE   And come about° again!   *reversing direction*

FOURTH AVOCATORE [*aside*]   It is a match; my daughter is bestowed.

MOSCA [*aside to* VOLPONE]   Will you gi' me half?

VOLPONE [*aside to* MOSCA]   First, I'll be hanged.

MOSCA [*aside to* VOLPONE]
                                               I know
   Your voice is good. Cry not so loud.

FIRST AVOCATORE   Demand°   *question*

65   The advocate. [*To* VOLTORE] Sir, did not you affirm
   Volpone was alive?

VOLPONE   Yes, and he is;
   This gent'man told me so. (*Aside to* MOSCA) Thou shalt have half.

MOSCA   Whose drunkard is this same? Speak, some that know him;
   I never saw his face. (*Aside to* VOLPONE) I cannot now
   Afford it you so cheap.

VOLPONE (*aside to* MOSCA)   No?

70   FIRST AVOCATORE [*to* VOLTORE]   What say you?

VOLTORE   The officer told me.

VOLPONE   I did, grave fathers,
   And will maintain he lives with mine own life,
   And that this creature° told me. (*aside*) I was born   *Mosca*

---

3. Volpone sees that Mosca's pious pretense of burying the "dead" Volpone will mean an end to all of
Volpone's hopes; he'll be cheated out of everything.

With all good stars my enemies.

MOSCA   Most grave fathers,

75   If such an insolence as this must pass°   *be permitted*
     Upon me, I am silent. 'Twas not this
     For which you sent, I hope.

SECOND AVOCATORE [*pointing to* VOLPONE]   Take him away.

VOLPONE (*aside to* MOSCA)   Mosca!

THIRD AVOCATORE   Let him be whipped.

VOLPONE (*aside to* MOSCA)   Wilt thou betray me?
     Cozen me?

THIRD AVOCATORE   And taught to bear himself
     Toward a person of his° rank.   *Mosca's*

80   FOURTH AVOCATORE   Away!
          [*Officers seize* VOLPONE.]

MOSCA   I humbly thank Your Fatherhoods.

VOLPONE   Soft, soft. [*Aside*] Whipped?
     And lose all that I have? If I confess,
     It cannot be much more.

FOURTH AVOCATORE [*to* MOSCA]   Sir, are you married?

VOLPONE [*aside*]   They'll be allied° anon; I must be resolute.   *linked by marriage*
     The fox shall here uncase.° *He puts off his disguise.*   *reveal himself*

MOSCA (*aside*)   Patron!

85   VOLPONE   Nay, now
     My ruins shall not come alone. Your match
     I'll hinder sure; my substance shall not glue you
     Nor screw you into a family.

MOSCA (*aside*)   Why, patron!

VOLPONE   I am Volpone, and [*pointing to* MOSCA] this is my knave;

90   [*Pointing to* VOLTORE] This his own knave; [*pointing to* CORBACCIO]
          this, avarice's fool;
     [*Pointing to* CORVINO] This, a chimera° of wittol,   *monstrous combination*
          fool, and knave;
     And, reverend fathers, since we all can hope
     Naught but a sentence, let's not now despair it.°   *be disappointed (ironic)*
     You hear me brief.°   *that's all I have to say*

CORVINO   May it please Your Fatherhoods—

COMMENDATORE[4]   Silence!

95   FIRST AVOCATORE   The knot is now undone by miracle!

SECOND AVOCATORE   Nothing can be more clear.

THIRD AVOCATORE   Or can more prove
     These innocent.

FIRST AVOCATORE   Give 'em their liberty.
          [BONARIO *and* CELIA *are released.*]

BONARIO   Heaven could not long let such gross crimes be hid.

SECOND AVOCATORE   If this be held the highway to get riches,
     May I be poor!

100 THIRD AVOCATORE   This's not the gain, but torment.

FIRST AVOCATORE   These possess wealth as sick men possess fevers,

---

4. Not Volpone, of course, but one of the genuine Commendatori. They are probably the officers who strip Mosca at line 103.

Which trulier may be said to possess them.

SECOND AVOCATORE Disrobe that parasite.

[MOSCA *is stripped of his* clarissimo's *robe*.]

CORVINO [*and*] **MOSCA**   Most honored fathers!

FIRST AVOCATORE Can you plead aught to stay the course of justice?
    If you can, speak.

CORVINO [*and*] **VOLTORE**   We beg favor—

105 **CELIA**   And mercy.

FIRST AVOCATORE [*to* CELIA] You hurt your innocence, suing°   *pleading*
    for the guilty.

    [*To the others*] Stand forth; and, first, the parasite. You appear
    T'have been the chiefest minister,° if not plotter,   *agent*
    In all these lewd° impostures, and now, lastly,   *vile, obscene*
110   Have with your impudence abused the court
    And habit° of a gentleman of Venice,   *garb*
    Being a fellow of no birth or blood;
    For which our sentence is, first thou be whipped,
    Then live perpetual prisoner in our galleys.

VOLPONE I thank you for him.

115 **MOSCA**   Bane to° thy wolfish nature!   *curses on*

FIRST AVOCATORE Deliver him to the *saffi*.° [MOSCA *is placed*   *bailiffs*
    under guard.] Thou, Volpone,
    By blood and rank a gentleman, canst not fall
    Under like censure;° but our judgment on thee   *the same sentence*
    Is that thy substance° all be straight confiscate   *wealth*
120   To the hospital of the *Incurabili*;[5]
    And since the most was gotten by imposture,
    By feigning lame, gout, palsy, and such diseases,
    Thou art to lie in prison, cramped with irons,
    Till thou be'st sick and lame indeed.—Remove him.

    [VOLPONE *is placed under guard*.]

125 **VOLPONE** This is called mortifying[6] of a fox.

FIRST AVOCATORE Thou, Voltore, to take away the scandal
    Thou hast giv'n all worthy men of thy profession,
    Art banished from their fellowship and our state.°   *Venice*

    [VOLTORE *is placed under guard*.]

    Corbaccio—bring him near.—We here possess
130   Thy son of all thy state,° and confine thee   *estate*
    To the monastery of San' Spirito,°   *the Holy Spirit*
    Where, since thou knew'st not how to live well here,
    Thou shalt be learned° to die well.   *taught*

CORBACCIO   Ha! What said he?

COMMENDATORE You shall know anon,° sir.   *soon enough*

    [CORBACCIO *is placed under guard*.]

FIRST AVOCATORE   Thou, Corvino, shalt
135   Be straight embarked from thine own house and rowed

---

5. The Hospital of the Incurables was founded in Venice in 1522 to care for people terminally ill with syphilis.
6. (1) Hanging of meat to make it tender; (2) disciplining spiritually; (3) killing. (Volpone's sentence is almost certain to bring about his death.)

Bound about Venice, through the Grand Canal,
Wearing a cap with fair° long ass's ears   *handsome; clearly visible*
Instead of horns, and so to mount, a paper
Pinned on thy breast, to the *berlino*[7]—

CORVINO   Yes,
140   And have mine eyes beat out with stinking fish,
Bruised fruit, and rotten eggs—'Tis well. I'm glad
I shall not see my shame yet.

FIRST AVOCATORE   And to expiate
Thy wrongs done to thy wife, thou art to send her
Home to her father with her dowry trebled.[8]
And these are all your judgments—

145 ALL   Honored fathers!

FIRST AVOCATORE   Which may not be revoked. Now you begin,
When crimes are done and past and to be punished,
To think what your crimes are.—Away with them!

     [MOSCA, VOLPONE, VOLTORE, CORBACCIO, *and* CORVINO
         retire to the back of the stage, guarded.][9]

Let all that see these vices thus rewarded
150 Take heart,° and love to study 'em. Mischiefs feed   *take them to heart*
Like beasts, till they be fat, and then they bleed.

                    [*The* AVOCATORI *step back.*]

     [VOLPONE *comes forward.*]

VOLPONE   The seasoning of a play is the applause
Now, though the fox be punished by the laws,
He yet doth hope there is no suff'ring due
155 Nor any fact° which he hath done 'gainst you.   *crime*
If there be, censure him; here he, doubtful,° stands.   *apprehensive*
If not, fare jovially, and clap your hands.   [*Exeunt.*]

performed 1606   *published* 1616

FROM EPIGRAMS[1]

To My Book

It will be looked for, book, when some but see
    Thy title, *Epigrams*, and named of me,

---

7. Pillory. Versions of such shaming punishments were commonly imposed for sexual and marital infractions. The offender typically had to wear a placard specifying his crimes; hence the paper pinned on Corvino's breast.

8. The judges grant Celia "separation from bed and board." Such legal separations could be permitted to the innocent party in a case of adultery or, as here, to a victim of gross spousal abuse. Because legal separation entailed the finding of serious fault, the guilty spouse could also, as here, be forced to pay financial damages. Legal separation did not bring with it, however, the right of remarriage for either party.

9. Alternatively, the prisoners, and later the Avocatori and the others, could exit, and Volpone could return to speak the epilogue. The advantage of the staging preferred here is that almost all the players are onstage to receive the audience's applause.

1. Epigrams are commonly thought of as brief, witty, incisive poems of personal invective, often with a surprise turn at the end. But Jonson uses the word in a more liberal sense. His "Epigrams," a separate section in his collected *Works* of 1616, include not only sharp, satiric poems but many complimentary ones to friends and patrons, as well as memorial epitaphs and a verse letter, "Inviting a Friend to Supper."

Thou should'st be bold, licentious, full of gall,
   Wormwood° and sulphur, sharp and toothed[2] withal,   *bitter-tasting plant*
5 Become a petulant thing, hurl ink and wit
   As madmen stones, not caring whom they hit.
Deceive their malice who could wish it so,
   And by thy wiser temper let men know
Thou art not covetous of least self-fame
10   Made from the hazard of another's shame[3]—
Much less with lewd, profane, and beastly phrase
   To catch the world's loose laughter or vain gaze.
He that departs° with his own honesty   *parts*
   For vulgar praise, doth it too dearly buy.

1616

On Something, That Walks Somewhere

At court I met it, in clothes brave° enough   *fine*
   To be a courtier, and looks grave enough
To seem a statesman: as I near it came,
   It made me a great face. I asked the name.
5 "A lord," it cried, "buried in flesh and blood,
   And such from whom let no man hope least good,
For I will do none; and as little ill,
   For I will dare none." Good lord, walk dead still.

1616

To William Camden[1]

Camden, most reverend head, to whom I owe
   All that I am in arts, all that I know
(How nothing's that!), to whom my country owes
   The great renown and name wherewith she goes;[2]
5 Than thee the age sees not that thing more grave,
   More high, more holy, that she more would crave.
What name, what skill, what faith hast thou in things!
   What sight in searching the most antique springs!
What weight and what authority in thy speech!
10   Man scarce can make that doubt, but[3] thou canst teach.
Pardon free truth and let thy modesty,
   Which conquers all, be once o'ercome by thee.

---

2. The distinction between toothed (biting) and toothless (general) satires was a commonplace.
3. Here, as often elsewhere, Jonson echoes the greatest Roman epigrammatist, Martial.
1. Camden, a distinguished scholar and antiquary, had been Jonson's teacher at Westminster School.
2. Camden's studies of his native land in *Britannia* (1586) and *Remains of a Greater Work Concerning Britain* (1605) ran to several editions and were translated abroad.
3. One hardly needs wonder whether.

Many of thine° this better could than I;   *your pupils*
    But for° their powers, accept my piety.   *in place of*

1616

On My First Daughter[1]

Here lies, to each her parents' ruth,°   *grief*
Mary, the daughter of their youth;
Yet all heaven's gifts being heaven's due,
It makes the father less to rue.°   *regret*
5 At six months' end she parted hence
With safety of her innocence;
Whose soul heaven's queen,° whose name she bears,   *Mary*
In comfort of her mother's tears,
Hath placed amongst her virgin-train:
10 Where, while that severed doth remain,
This grave partakes the fleshly birth;°   *the body*
Which cover lightly, gentle earth![2]

1616

To John Donne

Donne, the delight of Phoebus° and each Muse,   *god of poetry*
Who, to thy one, all other brains refuse;[1]
Whose every work, of thy most early wit,
Came forth example[2] and remains so yet;
5 Longer a-knowing than most wits do live,
And which no affection praise enough can give.
To it[3] thy language, letters, arts, best life,
Which might with half mankind maintain a strife.
All which I meant to praise, and yet I would,
10 But leave, because I cannot as I should.

1616

On Giles and Joan

Who says that Giles and Joan at discord be?
    Th' observing neighbors no such mood can see.
Indeed, poor Giles repents he married ever,
    But that his Joan doth too. And Giles would never
5 By his free will be in Joan's company;
    No more would Joan he should. Giles riseth early,

---

1. Probably written in the late 1590s, in Jonson's
Roman Catholic period (ca. 1598–1610).
2. A common sentiment in Latin epitaphs.
1. I.e., the muses shower their favors exclusively
on you.
2. A pattern for others to imitate.
3. In addition to your wit.

And having got him out of doors is glad;
    The like is Joan. But turning home is sad,
And so is Joan. Ofttimes, when Giles doth find
10   Harsh sights at home, Giles wisheth he were blind:
All this doth Joan. Or that his long-yearned[1] life
    Were quite outspun. The like wish hath his wife.
The children that he keeps Giles swears are none
    Of his begetting; and so swears his Joan.
15 In all affections° she concurreth still.   *desires*
    If now, with man and wife, to will and nill°   *not will*
The self-same things a note of concord be,
    I know no couple better can agree.

1616

On My First Son

Farewell, thou child of my right hand,[1] and joy;
My sin was too much hope of thee, loved boy.
Seven years thou wert lent to me, and I thee pay,
Exacted by thy fate, on the just day.
5   O could I lose all father now! For why
Will man lament the state he should envy,
To have so soon 'scaped world's and flesh's rage,
And, if no other misery, yet age?
Rest in soft peace, and asked, say, "Here doth lie
10 Ben Jonson his best piece of poetry."[2]
For whose sake henceforth all his vows be such
As what he loves may never like too much.[3]

1616

On Lucy, Countess of Bedford[1]

This morning, timely rapt with holy fire,
I thought to form unto my zealous muse,
What kind of creature I could most desire,
To honor, serve, and love; as poets use.[2]
5   I meant to make her fair, and free, and wise,
Of greatest blood, and yet more good than great;
I meant the day-star° should not brighter rise,   *the sun*

---

1. Spun from long skeins of yarn.
1. A literal translation of the Hebrew name "Benjamin," which implies the meaning "dexterous" or "fortunate." The boy was born in 1596 and died on his birthday in 1603.
2. Poet and father are both "makers," Jonson's favorite term for the poet.
3. The obscure grammar of the last lines allows for various readings; "like" may carry the sense of "please."

1. Lucy Russell, countess of Bedford, was a famous patroness of the age, to whom Jonson, Donne, and many other poets addressed poems of compliment.
2. This elegant epigram of praise plays off against the Pygmalion story, in which the sculptor molds a statue of his ideal woman and she then comes to life.

Nor lend like influence[3] from his lucent seat.
I meant she should be courteous, facile,° sweet,   *affable*
10   Hating that solemn vice of greatness, pride;
I meant each softest virtue, there should meet,
Fit in that softer bosom to reside.
Only a learnèd, and a manly soul
I purposed her; that should, with even powers,
15   The rock, the spindle, and the shears[4] control
Of destiny, and spin her own free hours.
Such when I meant to feign, and wished to see,
My muse bad,° *Bedford* write, and that was she.   *bade*

1616

To Lucy, Countess of Bedford, with Mr. Donne's Satires[1]

Lucy, you brightness[2] of our sphere, who are
Life of the Muses' day, their morning star!
If works, not th' authors, their own grace should look,°   *have regard to*
Whose poems would not wish to be your book?
5   But these, desired by you, the maker's ends
Crown with their own. Rare poems ask rare friends.
Yet satires, since the most of mankind be
Their unavoided° subject, fewest see: *inevitable*
For none e'er took that pleasure in sin's sense,°   *experience*
10   But, when they heard it taxed, took more offense.
They then that, living where the matter is bred,[3]
Dare for these poems yet both ask and read
And like them too, must needfully, though few,
Be of the best: and 'mongst those, best are you;
15   Lucy, you brightness of our sphere, who are
The Muses' evening, as their morning star.[4]

1616

To Sir Thomas Roe[1]

Thou hast begun well, Roe, which stand° well too,   *continue*
And I know nothing more thou hast to do.

---

3. Stars were supposed to emit an ethereal fluid, or "influence," that affected the affairs of mortals, for good or ill.
4. Emblems of the three Fates: Clotho spun the thread of life, Lachesis decided its length, and Atropos cut the thread to end life.
1. With this poem, Jonson offered a manuscript collection of Donne's satires (see pp. 944–47), such as commonly passed from hand to hand in court circles.

2. Lucy's name derives from the Latin *lux*, meaning "light."
3. I.e., at court.
4. The planet Venus is called Lucifer ("light-bearing") when it appears before sunrise, Hesperus when it appears after sunset.
1. Knighted in 1605, Roe was sent as ambassador to the Great Mogul in 1614. His collection of coins and of Greek and Oriental manuscripts is in the Bodleian Library.

He that is round° within himself, and straight,   *honest*
Need seek no other strength, no other height;
5   Fortune upon him breaks herself, if ill,
And what should hurt his virtue makes it still.°   *constant*
That thou at once, then, nobly may'st defend
With thine own course the judgment of thy friend,
Be always to thy gathered self the same,
10 And study conscience, more than thou wouldst fame.
Though both be good, the latter yet is worst,
And ever is ill got without the first.

1616

Inviting a Friend to Supper

Tonight, grave sir, both my poor house and I
Do equally desire your company:
Not that we think us worthy such a guest,
But that your worth will dignify our feast
5   With those that come; whose grace may make that seem
Something, which else could hope for no esteem.
It is the fair acceptance, sir, creates
The entertainment perfect: not the cates.°   *food*
Yet shall you have, to rectify your palate,
10   An olive, capers, or some better salad
Ushering the mutton; with a short-legged hen,
If we can get her, full of eggs, and then
Lemons and wine for sauce; to° these, a coney°   *besides / rabbit*
Is not to be despaired of for our money;
15 And though fowl now be scarce, yet there are clerks,°   *scholars*
The sky not falling, think we may have larks.
I'll tell you of more, and lie, so you will come:
Of partridge, pheasant, woodcock, of which some
May yet be there; and godwit if we can,
20   Knot, rail, and ruff, too.[1] Howsoe'er, my man°   *servant*
Shall read a piece of Virgil, Tacitus,
Livy, or of some better book to us,
Of which we'll speak our minds amidst our meat;°   *food (of any kind)*
And I'll profess° no verses to repeat: *promise*
25 To this,° if aught appear which I not know of,   *on this point*
That will the pastry, not my paper, show of.[2]
Digestive cheese and fruit there sure will be;
But that which most doth take my muse and me
Is a pure cup of rich canary wine,
30   Which is the Mermaid's now, but shall be mine;
Of which, had Horace or Anacreon[3] tasted,

1. All these are edible birds.
2. Paper-lined pans were used to keep pies from sticking; the writing sometimes rubbed off on the piecrust.
3. Horace and Anacreon (one in Latin, the other in Greek) wrote many poems in praise of wine. The Mermaid tavern was a favorite haunt of the poets; sweet wine from the Canary Islands was popular in England.

Their lives, as do their lines, till now had lasted.
    Tobacco, nectar, or the Thespian spring
    Are all but Luther's beer to this I sing.[4]
35 Of this we will sup free but moderately,
    And we will have no Pooly or Parrot[5] by;
    Nor shall our cups make any guilty men,
    But at our parting we will be as when
    We innocently met. No simple word
40 That shall be uttered at our mirthful board
    Shall make us sad next morning, or affright
    The liberty that we'll enjoy tonight.

1616

On Gut

Gut eats all day, and lechers all the night,
    So all his meat he tasteth over twice;
And striving so to double his delight,
    He makes himself a thoroughfare of vice.
5 Thus in his belly can he change a sin:
    Lust it comes out, that gluttony went in.

1616

Epitaph on S. P., a Child of Queen Elizabeth's Chapel[1]

Weep with me, all you that read
    This little story;
And know for whom a tear you shed,
    Death's self is sorry.
5 'Twas a child that so did thrive
    In grace and feature,
As Heaven and Nature seemed to strive
    Which owned the creature.
Years he numbered scarce thirteen
10   When Fates turned cruel,
Yet three filled zodiacs had he been
    The stage's jewel;[2]
And did act (what now we moan)
    Old men so duly,°   aptly
15 As, sooth,° the Parcae° thought him one,   in truth / Fates
    He played so truly.

4. Tobacco was an expensive New World novelty
in Jonson's time. Nectar is the drink of the gods.
The Thespian spring, on Mount Helicon, is a
legendary source of poetic inspiration. Compared with canary, these intoxicants are no better than inferior German beer.
5. Pooly and Parrot were government spies. As a

Roman Catholic, Jonson had reason to be wary
of undercover agents.
1. Salomon Pavy, a boy actor in the troupe
known as the Children of Queen Elizabeth's
Chapel, who had appeared in several of Jonson's
plays; he died in 1602.
2. He had been on the stage for three seasons.

So, by error, to his fate
    They all consented;
But, viewing him since (alas, too late),
20   They have repented,
And have sought (to give new birth)
    In baths[3] to steep him;
But, being so much too good for earth,
    Heaven vows to keep him.

1616

From The Forest[1]

To Penshurst[2]

Thou art not, Penshurst, built to envious show,
    Of touch[3] or marble; nor canst boast a row
Of polished pillars, or a roof of gold;
    Thou hast no lantern° whereof tales are told,   *cupola*
5 Or stair, or courts; but stand'st an ancient pile,°   *edifice*
    And, these grudged at,[4] art reverenced the while.
Thou joy'st in better marks, of soil, of air,
    Of wood, of water; therein thou art fair.
Thou hast thy walks for health, as well as sport;
10   Thy mount, to which the dryads° do resort,   *wood nymphs*
Where Pan and Bacchus their high feasts have made,
    Beneath the broad beech and the chestnut shade;
That taller tree, which of a nut was set
    At his great birth where all the Muses met.[5]
15 There in the writhèd bark are cut the names
    Of many a sylvan,° taken with his flames;   *countryman*
And thence the ruddy satyrs oft provoke
    The lighter fauns[6] to reach thy Lady's Oak.[7]
Thy copse° too, named of Gamage[8] thou hast there,   *little woods*
20   That never fails to serve thee seasoned deer
When thou wouldst feast or exercise thy friends.
    The lower land, that to the river bends,
Thy sheep, thy bullocks, kine,° and calves do feed;   *cattle*
    The middle grounds thy mares and horses breed.
25 Each bank doth yield thee conies;° and the tops,°   *rabbits / high ground*

---

3. Perhaps such magic baths as that of Medea, which restored Jason's father to his first youth (Ovid, *Metamorphoses* 7).
1. In the 1616 *Works*, Jonson grouped some of his nonepigrammatic poems under the heading "The Forest," a translation of the term *Sylvae,* meaning a poetic miscellany. "To Penshurst" and the two following poems are from that group.
2. Penshurst, in Kent, was the estate of Robert Sidney, Viscount Lisle (later, earl of Leicester), a younger brother of the poet Sir Philip Sidney. Along with Lanyer's "The Description of Cookham" (pp. 986–90), this poem inaugurated the small genre of English "country-house" poems, which includes Carew's "To Saxham" (pp. 1323–25) and Marvell's *Upon Appleton House* (pp. 1361–83).
3. Touchstone, an expensive black basalt.
4. More pretentious houses attract envy.
5. Sir Philip Sidney was born at Penshurst.
6. Satyrs and fauns were woodland spirits. Satyrs had the bodies of men and the legs (and horns) of goats. "Provoke": challenge to a race.
7. Named after a lady of the house who went into labor under its branches.
8. Lady Barbara (Gamage) Sidney, wife of Sir Robert.

Fertile of wood, Ashore and Sidney's copse,
　　To crown thy open table, doth provide
　　　The purpled pheasant with the speckled side;
　　The painted partridge lies in every field,
30　　　And for thy mess° is willing to be killed.　　　　　　　　　*table*
And if the high-swollen Medway[9] fail thy dish,
　　Thou hast thy ponds, that pay thee tribute fish:
　　　Fat agèd carps that run into thy net,
　　And pikes, now weary their own kind to eat,
35　As loath the second draft or cast to stay,
　　　Officiously° at first themselves betray;　　　　　　　　　*dutifully*
Bright eels that emulate them, and leap on land
　　Before the fisher, or into his hand.
　　Then hath thy orchard fruit, thy garden flowers,
40　　　Fresh as the air, and new as are the hours.
The early cherry, with the later plum,
　　Fig, grape, and quince, each in his time doth come;
　　　The blushing apricot and woolly peach
　　Hang on thy walls, that every child may reach.
45　And though thy walls be of the country stone,
　　　They're reared with no man's ruin, no man's groan;
There's none that dwell about them wish them down;
　　　But all come in, the farmer and the clown,°　　　　　　　*peasant*
And no one empty-handed, to salute
50　　Thy lord and lady, though they have no suit.°　　　*request to make*
Some bring a capon, some a rural cake,
　　Some nuts, some apples; some that think they make
　　　The better cheeses bring them, or else send
　　By their ripe daughters, whom they would commend
55　This way to husbands, and whose baskets bear
　　　An emblem of themselves in plum or pear.
But what can this (more than express their love)
　　Add to thy free provisions, far above
　　　The need of such? whose liberal board doth flow
60　　　With all that hospitality doth know;
Where comes no guest but is allowed to eat,
　　Without his fear, and of thy lord's own meat;°　　　　　　　*food*
　　　Where the same beer and bread, and selfsame wine,
　　That is his lordship's shall be also mine,[1]
65　And I not fain to sit (as some this day
　　　At great men's tables), and yet dine away.
Here no man tells° my cups; nor, standing by,　　　　　　　　*counts*
　　A waiter doth my gluttony envy,°　　　　　　　　　　　　　*resent*
　　　But gives me what I call, and lets me eat;
70　　He knows below° he shall find plenty of meat.　　*in the servants' quarters*
Thy tables hoard not up for the next day;
　　Nor, when I take my lodging, need I pray
　　　For fire, or lights, or livery;° all is there,　　　　　　　*provisions*
　　As if thou then wert mine, or I reigned here:

---

9. The local river.
1. Different courses might be served to different

guests, depending on their social status. The
lord would have the best food.

75　There's nothing I can wish, for which I stay.°   *wait*
　　　That found King James when, hunting late this way
　　With his brave son, the Prince,[2] they saw thy fires
　　　Shine bright on every hearth, as the desires
　　Of thy Penates° had been set on flame   *Roman household gods*
80　　To entertain them; or the country came
　　With all their zeal to warm their welcome here.
　　　What (great I will not say, but) sudden cheer
　　Didst thou then make 'em! And what praise was heaped
　　　On thy good lady then, who therein reaped
85　The just reward of her high housewifery;
　　　To have her linen, plate, and all things nigh,
　　When she was far; and not a room but dressed
　　　As if it had expected such a guest!
　　These, Penshurst, are thy praise, and yet not all.
90　　Thy lady's noble, fruitful, chaste withal.
　　His children thy great lord may call his own,
　　　A fortune in this age but rarely known.
　　They are, and have been, taught religion; thence
　　　Their gentler spirits have sucked innocence.
95　Each morn and even they are taught to pray,
　　　With the whole household, and may, every day,
　　Read in their virtuous parents' noble parts°   *attributes*
　　　The mysteries of manners,° arms, and arts.   *moral behavior*
　　Now, Penshurst, they that will proportion° thee   *compare*
100　　With other edifices, when they see
　　Those proud, ambitious heaps, and nothing else,
　　　May say, their lords have built, but thy lord dwells.

　　　　　　　　　　　　　　　　　　　　　　　　1616

Song: To Celia[1]

　　　　Drink to me only with thine eyes,
　　　　　And I will pledge with mine;
　　　　Or leave a kiss but in the cup,
　　　　　And I'll not look for wine.
5　　　The thirst that from the soul doth rise
　　　　　Doth ask a drink divine:
　　　　But might I of Jove's nectar sup,
　　　　　I would not change for thine.
　　　　I sent thee late a rosy wreath,
10　　　　Not so much honoring thee,
　　　　As giving it a hope that there
　　　　　It could not withered be.
　　　　But thou thereon didst only breathe,
　　　　　And sent'st it back to me;

---

2. Prince Henry, the heir apparent, who died in November 1612.

1. These famous lines translate a patchwork of five separate prose passages by Philostratus, a Greek sophist (3rd century c.e.). The music that has made it a barroom favorite is by an anonymous 18th-century composer.

15   Since when it grows and smells, I swear,
     Not of itself, but thee.

                          1616

To Heaven

Good and great God, can I not think of thee
  But it must straight° my melancholy be?   *immediately*
Is it interpreted in me disease
  That, laden with my sins, I seek for ease?
5 Oh, be thou witness, that the reins[1] dost know
  And hearts of all, if I be sad for show,
And judge me after, if I dare pretend
  To aught but grace, or aim at other end.
As thou art all, so be thou all to me,
10   First, midst, and last, converted° one and three, *interchanging*
My faith, my hope, my love; and in this state,
  My judge, my witness, and my advocate.
Where have I been this while exiled from thee,
  And whither rapt,° now thou but stoop'st to me?   *carried off*
15 Dwell, dwell here still:° Oh, being everywhere,   *always*
  How can I doubt to find thee ever here?
I know my state, both full of shame and scorn,
  Conceived in sin and unto labor born,
Standing with fear, and must with horror fall,
20   And destined unto judgment after all.
I feel my griefs too, and there scarce is ground
  Upon my flesh to inflict another wound.
Yet dare I not complain or wish for death
  With holy Paul,[2] lest it be thought the breath
25 Of discontent; or that these prayers be
  For weariness of life, not love of thee.

                          1616

From UNDERWOOD[1]

From A Celebration of Charis in Ten Lyric Pieces[2]

4. Her Triumph[3]

See the chariot at hand here of Love,
  Wherein my lady rideth!

1. Literally, kidneys, but also the seat of the affections, with a glance at Psalm 7.9: "the righteous God trieth the hearts and reins."
2. "Who shall deliver me from the body of this death?" (Romans 7.24).
1. Preparing a second edition of his *Works* (published posthumously in 1640–41), Jonson added a third section of poems, "Underwood," "out of the analogy they hold to *The Forest* in my former book."
2. The Greek word *charis*, from which Jonson's lady takes her name, means "grace" or "loveliness."
3. Following Petrarch, many Renaissance poets used the figure of the triumphal procession to celebrate a person or concept—time, chastity, fame, etc. Metrically, this poem is highly complex.

Each that draws is a swan or a dove,[4]
   And well the car Love guideth.
5 As she goes, all hearts do duty
      Unto her beauty;
And enamored do wish, so they might
      But enjoy such a sight,
That they still° were to run by her side,   *always*
10 Through swords, through seas, whither she would ride.

Do but look on her eyes, they do light
   All that Love's world compriseth!
Do but look on her hair, it is bright
   As Love's star° when it riseth!   *Venus, the morning star*
15 Do but mark,° her forehead's smoother   *observe*
      Than words that soothe her!
And from her archèd brows, such a grace
      Sheds itself through the face,
As alone there triumphs to the life
20 All the gain, all the good, of the elements' strife.[5]

Have you seen but a bright lily grow,
   Before rude hands have touched it?
Have you marked but the fall o' the snow,
   Before the soil hath smutched it?
25 Have you felt the wool o' the beaver,
      Or swan's down ever?
Or have smelt o' the bud o' the briar,
      Or the nard[6] i' the fire?
Or have tasted the bag o' the bee?
30 O so white! O so soft! O so sweet is she!

                    1640–41

A Sonnet, to the Noble Lady, the Lady Mary Wroth[1]

I that have been a lover, and could show it,
   Though not in these,° in rhymes not wholly dumb,   *in sonnets*
   Since I exscribe° your sonnets, am become   *copy out*
A better lover, and much better poet.
5 Nor is my muse, or I, ashamed to owe it
      To those true numerous graces; whereof some
      But charm the senses, others overcome
Both brains and hearts; and mine now best do know it:

---

4. Venus's birds.
5. The four elements—earth, water, air, fire—
were thought to be in perpetual conflict.
6. Spikenard, an aromatic ointment.
1. Mary Wroth, author of the sonnet sequence
Pamphilia to Amphilanthus (pp. 1116–21) and the
romance *The Countess of Montgomery's Urania*
(pp. 1112–16), was the daughter of Robert Sidney
and his wife, Barbara Gamage, of Penshurst, the

niece of Sir Philip Sidney and the countess of
Pembroke; she was the wife of Sir Robert Wroth,
whose country estate Jonson also praised in "The
Forest." The poem exhibits how poems were
exchanged within a coterie, though Jonson also
writes as a client to a patron. This is Jonson's only
sonnet, used here to pay tribute to Wroth's
sequence, and notably to its erotic power.

For in your verse all Cupid's armory,
10   His flames, his shafts, his quiver, and his bow,
     His very eyes are yours to overthrow.
But then his mother's° sweets you so apply,   *Venus's*
     Her joys, her smiles, her loves, as readers take
     For Venus' ceston,[2] every line you make.

1640–41

My Picture Left in Scotland[1]

I now think Love is rather deaf than blind,
     For else it could not be
          That she
Whom I adore so much should so slight me
5   And cast my love behind;
I'm sure my language to her was as sweet,
          And every close° did meet   *cadence*
          In sentence° of as subtle feet,°   *wise sayings / rhythm*
          As hath the youngest he
10   That sits in shadow of Apollo's tree.[2]

O, but my conscious fears
          That fly my thoughts between,
          Tell me that she hath seen
     My hundreds of gray hairs,
15   Told° seven and forty years,   *counted*
     Read so much waist[3] as she cannot embrace
     My mountain belly and my rocky face;
And all these through her eyes have stopped her ears.

1619   1640–41

The Ode on Cary and Morison   The ode, originally a classical form, is a lyric poem in an elevated style, celebrating a lofty theme, a noble personage, or a grand occasion. The Greek poet Pindar wrote many odes for winners of the Olympic games, known as Great Odes because of their exalted subject and style. Later, the Roman poet Horace wrote more restrained poems that came to be known as Lesser Odes. Jonson's Cary-Morison ode comes closer than any other in the language to the lofty style and manner of Pindar, while his "To Penshurst" is in the Horatian style, as is, later, Marvell's "Horatian Ode upon Cromwell's Return from Ireland."

    Pindar's odes were designed to be sung by a chorus and often followed a three-part scheme: the chorus moved in one direction while chanting the strophe, reversed direction for the antistrophe, and stood still for the epode. Jonson imitates

2. Venus's girdle or belt, which had aphrodisiacal powers; it aroused passion in all beholders.
1. After his walking tour of Scotland in 1618–19, Jonson sent a manuscript version of this poem to William Drummond, with whom he had stayed. The woman of the poem may or may not

be a real person.
2. Bay laurel, the tree associated with Apollo, god of poetry.
3. With a pun on "waste," meaning "untillable ground."

this pattern with his triple division of "turn," "counterturn," and "stand"—the terms more or less literally translated from the original Greek. His turns and counterturns rhyme in couplets, with line lengths varying in all stanzas according to a uniform scheme; the twelve-line stands follow a more complex but equally strict design. He imitates Pindar also in his moral generalizations and lofty but impersonal praise of the two noble friends. Later in the century, under the influence of Abraham Cowley and under a misapprehension about Pindar's style, odes became more extravagant, more vehement in tone, and more irregular in form.

To the Immortal Memory and Friendship of That Noble Pair, Sir Lucius Cary and Sir H. Morison[1]

The Turn

Brave infant of Saguntum,[2] clear°   *explain*
Thy coming forth in that great year
When the prodigious Hannibal did crown
His rage, with razing your immortal town.
5 Thou, looking then about
Ere thou wert half got out,
Wise child, didst hastily return
And mad'st thy mother's womb thine urn.°   *burial vessel*
How summed° a circle[3] didst thou leave mankind   *complete*
10 Of deepest lore, could we the center find!

The Counterturn

Did wiser nature draw thee back
From out the horror of that sack,
Where shame, faith, honor, and regard of right
Lay trampled on?—the deeds of death and night
15 Urged, hurried forth, and hurled
Upon th' affrighted world?
Sword, fire, and famine, with fell° fury met,   *fierce*
And all on utmost ruin set:
As, could they but life's miseries foresee,
20 No doubt all infants would return like thee.

The Stand

For what is life if measured by the space,
Not by the act?
Or maskèd man, if valued by his face,
Above his fact?°   *deeds*
25 Here's one outlived his peers

---

1. Henry Morison died in 1629 at the age of twenty. His good friend Lucius Cary (son of Elizabeth Cary, the author of *Mariam*) became the second Viscount Falkland. He was known for his learning, and he died fighting for King Charles in the first years of the civil war.

2. Pliny the Elder, a Roman writer, tells the story of an infant born while Sagunto, in Spain, was being assaulted by Hannibal; he dived back into his mother's womb (setting a record for brevity of life) and was buried there.
3. Emblem of perfection.

And told forth fourscore years:
He vexèd time, and busied the whole state,
Troubled both foes and friends,
But ever to no ends:
30   What did this stirrer but die late?[4]
How well at twenty had he fall'n or stood!
For three of his four score, he did no good.

The Turn

He[5] entered well, by virtuous parts,°   *qualities*
Got up and thrived with honest arts:
35   He purchased friends and fame and honors then,
And had his noble name advanced with men;
But, weary of that flight,
He stooped in all men's sight
To sordid flatteries, acts of strife,
40   And sunk in that dead sea of life
So deep, as he did then death's waters sup;
But that the cork of title buoyed him up.

The Counterturn

Alas, but Morison fell young;—
He never fell, thou fall'st,[6] my tongue.
45   He stood, a soldier, to the last right end,
A perfect patriot and a noble friend,
But most a virtuous son.
All offices° were done   *duties of life*
By him, so ample, full, and round
50   In weight, in measure, number, sound,
As, though his age imperfect might appear,
His life was of humanity the sphere.

The Stand

Go now, and tell out° days summed up with fears,   *count*
And make them years;
55   Produce thy mass of miseries on the stage
To swell thine age;
Repeat of things a throng,
To show thou hast been long,
Not lived; for life doth her great actions spell,°   *tell over*
60   By what was done and wrought
In season, and so brought
To light: her measures are, how well
Each syllab'e° answered, and was formed how fair;   *syllable*
These make the lines of life, and that's her air.[7]

4. Punning on "dilate," meaning "talk endlessly."
5. I.e., another man.
6. Slip, with a latent pun on Latin *fallo*, "to make a mistake."

7. Life is a poem set to music; life's "measures" are its metrical patterns as well as the standards by which it is judged.

The Turn

65 It is not growing like a tree
In bulk, doth make man better be,
Or standing long an oak, three hundred year,
To fall a log at last, dry, bald, and sere:°   *withered*
A lily of a day
70 Is fairer far in May,
Although it fall and die that night;
It was the plant and flower of light.
In small proportions we just beauties see,
And in short measures life may perfect be.

The Counterturn

75 Call, noble Lucius, then for wine,
And let thy looks with gladness shine:
Accept this garland,[8] plant it on thy head,
And think, nay, know, thy Morison's not dead.
He leaped the present age,
80 Possessed with holy rage,°   *inspiration*
To see that bright eternal day,
Of which we priests and poets say
Such truths as we expect for happy men,
And there he lives with memory: and Ben

The Stand

85 Jonson, who sung this of him ere he went
Himself to rest,
Or taste a part of that full joy he meant
To have expressed
In this bright asterism:°   *constellation*
90 Where it were friendship's schism
(Were not his Lucius long with us to tarry)
To separate these twi-
Lights, the Dioscuri,[9]
And keep the one half from his Harry.
95 But fate doth so alternate the design,
Whilst that in heaven, this light on earth must shine.

The Turn

And shine as you exalted are,
Two names of friendship, but one star,
Of hearts the union. And those not by chance
100 Made, or indentured,° or leased out t' advance   *contracted for*
The profits for a time.

---

8. Celebratory wreath; i.e., this poem.
9. The mythical Greek twins, Castor and Pollux, the Dioscuri, were said to have exchanged places regularly, after Castor's death, between earth and the underworld. They are the principal stars of the constellation Gemini (the twins).

No pleasures vain did chime
Of rhymes or riots at your feasts,
Orgies of drink, or feigned protests;
105 But simple love of greatness and of good
That knits brave minds and manners, more than blood.

The Counterturn

This made you first to know the why
You liked, then after to apply
That liking; and approach so one the tother,°   *other*
110 Till either grew a portion of the other;
Each stylèd° by his end,   *called*
The copy of his friend.
You lived to be the great surnames
And titles by which all made claims
115 Unto the virtue: nothing perfect done,
But as a Cary or a Morison.

The Stand

And such a force the fair example had,
As they that saw
The good and durst not practice it, were glad
120 That such a law
Was left yet to mankind;
Where they might read and find
Friendship in deed was written, not in words.
And with the heart, not pen,
125 Of two so early° men,   *youthful*
Whose lives[1] her rolls were, and records,
Who, ere the first down bloomèd on the chin
Had sowed these fruits, and got the harvest in.

1629   1640–41

Queen and Huntress[1]

Queen and huntress, chaste and fair,
Now the sun is laid to sleep,
Seated in thy silver chair,
State in wonted° manner keep;   *accustomed*
5 Hesperus entreats thy light,
Goddess excellently bright.

1. Some texts read "lines."
1. Also from *Cynthia's Revels* (4.3), this song is sung by Hesperus, the evening star, to Cynthia, or Diana, goddess of chastity and the moon—with whom Queen Elizabeth was constantly compared.

Earth, let not thy envious shade
Dare itself to interpose;[2]
Cynthia's shining orb was made
10   Heaven to clear, when day did close.
Bless us then with wishèd sight,
Goddess excellently bright.

Lay thy bow of pearl apart,
And thy crystal-shining quiver;
15   Give unto the flying hart
Space to breathe, how short soever.
Thou that mak'st a day of night,
Goddess excellently bright.

1600

To the Memory of My Beloved, The Author,
Mr. William Shakespeare, and What He Hath Left Us[1]

To draw no envy, Shakespeare, on thy name,
    Am I thus ample° to thy book and fame,   *copious*
While I confess thy writings to be such
    As neither man nor muse can praise too much.
5   'Tis true, and all men's suffrage.° But these ways   *admission*
    Were not the paths I meant unto thy praise;
For silliest° ignorance on these may light,   *simplest*
    Which, when it sounds at best, but echoes right;
Or blind affection, which doth ne'er advance
10   The truth, but gropes, and urgeth all by chance;
Or crafty malice might pretend this praise,
    And think to ruin where it seemed to raise.
These are as° some infamous bawd or whore   *as though*
    Should praise a matron. What could hurt her more?
15   But thou art proof against them, and, indeed,
    Above th' ill fortune of them, or the need.
I therefore will begin. Soul of the age!
    The applause! Delight! The wonder of our stage!
My Shakespeare, rise; I will not lodge thee by
20   Chaucer or Spenser, or bid Beaumont lie
A little further to make thee a room:[2]
    Thou art a monument without a tomb,
And art alive still while thy book doth live,
    And we have wits to read and praise to give.
25   That I not mix thee so, my brain excuses,
    I mean with great, but disproportioned° Muses;   *not comparable*
For, if I thought my judgment were of years,
    I should commit thee surely with thy peers,
And tell how far thou didst our Lyly outshine,

---

2. Eclipses were thought to portend evil.
1. This poem was prefixed to the first folio of
Shakespeare's plays (1623).

2. Chaucer, Spenser, and Francis Beaumont were
buried in Westminster Abbey; Shakespeare, in
Stratford.

30   Or sporting Kyd, or Marlowe's mighty line.[3]
And though thou hadst small Latin and less Greek,[4]
        From thence to honor thee I would not seek°   lack
For names, but call forth thund'ring Aeschylus,
        Euripides, and Sophocles to us,
35 Pacuvius, Accius, him of Cordova dead,[5]
        To life again, to hear thy buskin° tread   symbol of tragedy
And shake a stage; or, when thy socks° were on,   symbol of comedy
        Leave thee alone for the comparison
Of all that insolent Greece or haughty Rome
40   Sent forth, or since did from their ashes come.
Triumph, my Britain; thou hast one to show
        To whom all scenes° of Europe homage owe.   stages
He was not of an age, but for all time!
        And all the Muses still were in their prime
45 When like Apollo° he came forth to warm   god of poetry
        Our ears, or like a Mercury° to charm.   god of eloquence
Nature herself was proud of his designs,
        And joyed to wear the dressing of his lines,
Which were so richly spun, and woven so fit,
50   As, since, she will vouchsafe° no other wit: grant
The merry Greek, tart Aristophanes,
        Neat Terence, witty Plautus[6] now not please,
But antiquated and deserted lie,
        As they were not of Nature's family.
55 Yet must I not give nature all; thy art,
        My gentle Shakespeare, must enjoy a part.
For though the poet's matter° nature be,   subject matter
        His art doth give the fashion;° and that he   form, style
Who casts° to write a living line must sweat   undertakes
60   (Such as thine are) and strike the second heat
Upon the Muses' anvil; turn the same,
        And himself with it, that he thinks to frame,
Or for° the laurel he may gain a scorn;   instead of
        For a good poet's made as well as born,
65 And such wert thou. Look how the father's face
        Lives in his issue;° even so the race   offspring
Of Shakespeare's mind and manners brightly shines
        In his well-turnèd and true-filèd lines,
In each of which he seems to shake a lance,[7]
70   As brandished at the eyes of ignorance.
Sweet swan of Avon, what a sight it were
        To see thee in our waters yet appear,
And make those flights upon the banks of Thames
        That so did take Eliza and our James![8]

3. John Lyly, Thomas Kyd, and Christopher Marlowe were Elizabethan dramatists contemporary
or nearly contemporary with Shakespeare.
4. Shakespeare's Latin was pretty good, but Jonson is judging by the standard of his own remarkable scholarship.
5. Marcus Pacuvius, Lucius Accius (2nd century
B.C.E.), and "him of Cordova," Seneca the Younger

(1st century C.E.), were Latin tragedians. Seneca's
tragedies had a large influence on Elizabethan
revenge tragedy.
6. Aristophanes, an ancient Greek satirist and
writer of comedy; Terence and Plautus (2nd and
3rd centuries B.C.E.), Roman writers of comedy.
7. Pun on Shake-speare.
8. Queen Elizabeth and King James.

75 But stay; I see thee in the hemisphere
   Advanced and made a constellation there![9]
Shine forth, thou star of poets, and with rage
   Or influence[1] chide or cheer the drooping stage,
Which, since thy flight from hence, hath mourned like night,
80   And despairs day, but for thy volume's light.

1623

Ode to Himself[1]

Come, leave the loathèd stage,
   And the more loathsome age,
Where pride and impudence, in faction knit,
   Usurp the chair of wit,
5   Indicting and arraigning every day
      Something they call a play.
   Let their fastidious, vain
   Commission of the brain
Run on and rage, sweat, censure, and condemn:
10   They were not made for thee, less thou for them.

   Say that thou pour'st them wheat,
   And they will acorns eat;
'Twere simple° fury still thyself to waste   *foolish*
   On such as have no taste!
15   To offer them a surfeit of pure bread,
      Whose appetites are dead!
   No, give them grains their fill,
   Husks, draff to drink, and swill:[2]
If they love lees,° and leave the lusty wine,   *dregs*
20   Envy them not; their palate's with the swine.

   No doubt some moldy tale
   Like *Pericles*,[3] and stale
As the shrieve's° crusts, and nasty as his fish—   *sheriff's*
      Scraps, out of every dish
25   Thrown forth and raked into the common tub,[4]
      May keep up the play club:
   There, sweepings do as well
   As the best-ordered meal;
For who the relish of these guests will fit
30   Needs set them but the alms basket of wit.

---

9. Heroes and demigods were typically exalted after death to a place among the stars.
1. "Rage" and "influence" describe the supposed effects of the planets on earthly affairs. "Rage" also implies poetic inspiration.
1. The failure of Jonson's play *The New Inn* (1629) inspired this assault on criticism and the public taste. For Carew's affectionate, mocking rebuke, see pp. 1321–23.
2. All three items are food for pigs.
3. Shakespeare's play, at least in part (printed 1609).
4. The basket outside the jail to receive food for prisoners was called the sheriff's tub.

And much good do 't you then:
Brave plush and velvet men
Can feed on orts;° and, safe in your stage clothes,[5]   *scraps*
Dare quit,° upon your oaths,   *acquit*
35   The stagers and the stage-wrights[6] too, your peers,
Of larding your large ears
With their foul comic socks,°   *symbols of comedy*
Wrought upon twenty blocks;[7]
Which, if they're torn, and turned, and patched enough,
40   The gamesters° share your guilt,[8] and you their stuff.   *gamblers*

Leave things so prostitute
And take th' Alcaic lute;
Or thine own Horace, or Anacreon's lyre;
Warm thee by Pindar's fire:[9]
45   And though thy nerves° be shrunk, and blood be cold,   *sinews*
Ere years have made thee old,
Strike that disdainful heat
Throughout, to their defeat,
As curious fools, and envious of thy strain,
50   May, blushing, swear no palsy's in thy brain.[1]

But when they hear thee sing
The glories of thy king,
His zeal to God and his just awe o'er men,
They may, blood-shaken then,
55   Feel such a flesh-quake to possess their powers
As they shall cry, "Like ours,
In sound of peace or wars,
No harp e'er hit the stars
In tuning forth the acts of his sweet reign,
60   And raising Charles his chariot 'bove his Wain."[2]

1629   1631, 1640–41

---

5. Actors often wore on the stage clothes cast off by the gentry; these parasites wear clothes cast off by actors.
6. Playwrights. "Stagers": actors.
7. A pun: molds/blockheads.
8. A pun: guilt/gilt.
9. Alcaeus (ca. 600 B.C.E.), Horace, Anacreon, and Pindar were among the greatest lyric poets in ancient Greece and Rome.
1. By 1629 Jonson was partially paralyzed.
2. Jonson's poetry will elevate the chariot of Charles I (symbol of his royal power) above Charles's Wain (Wagon)—the seven bright stars of Ursa Major.

MARY WROTH
1587–1651?

Lady Mary Wroth was the most prolific, self-conscious, and impressive female author of the Jacobean era. Her published work (1621) includes two firsts for an Englishwoman: a 558-page romance, *The Countess of Montgomery's Urania*, which contains more than fifty poems, and appended to it a Petrarchan lyric sequence that had circulated some years in manuscript, 103 sonnets and elegant songs titled *Pamphilia to Amphilanthus*. Wroth left unpublished a long but unfinished continuation of the *Urania* and a pastoral drama, *Love's Victory*, also a first for an Englishwoman. Her achievement was fostered by her strong sense of identity as a Sidney, heir to the literary talent and cultural role of her famous uncle Sir Philip Sidney, her famous aunt Mary Sidney Herbert, countess of Pembroke, who may have served as mentor to her; and her father Robert Sidney, Viscount Lisle, author of a recently discovered sonnet sequence. But she used that heritage transgressively to replace heroes with heroines in genres employed by the male Sidney authors—notably Philip Sidney's *Astrophil and Stella* and *The Countess of Pembroke's Arcadia*—transforming their gender politics and exploring the poetics and situation of women writers.

As Robert Sidney's eldest daughter, she lived and was educated at Penshurst, the Sidney country house celebrated by Ben Jonson, and was often at her aunt's "little college" at Wilton. She was married (incompatibly) at age seventeen to Sir Robert Wroth of Durrance and Loughton Manor, whose office it was to facilitate the king's hunting; and she was patron to several poets, including Jonson. He celebrated her in two epigrams and in a verse letter honoring her husband, dedicated his great comedy *The Alchemist* to her, and claimed in his only sonnet (p. 1100–01) that the artistry and erotic power of her sonnets had made him a "better lover, and much better poet." After her husband's death she carried on a long-standing love affair with her married first cousin, William Herbert, earl of Pembroke, himself a poet, a powerful courtier, and a patron of the theater and of literature. That relationship produced two children and occasioned some scandal.

The significant names in the title of Wroth's Petrarchan sequence, *Pamphilia* ("all-loving") *to Amphilanthus* ("lover of two"), are from characters in her romance who at times shadow Wroth and her lover Pembroke. The Petrarchan lyric sequence had long served as the major genre for analyzing a male lover's passions, frustrations, and fantasies (and sometimes his career anxieties). So although the sonnet sequence was becoming passé by Wroth's time, it was an obvious choice for a woman poet undertaking the construction of subjectivity in a female lover-speaker. Wroth does not, however, simply reverse roles. Pamphilia addresses few sonnets to Amphilanthus and seldom assumes the Petrarchan lover's position of abject servitude to a cruel beloved. Instead, she proclaims subjection to Cupid, usually identified with the force of her own desire. This radical revision identifies female desire as the source and center of the love relationship and celebrates the woman lover-poet's movement from the bondage of chaotic passion to the freedom of self-chosen constancy.

Wroth's romance, *Urania*, breaks the romance convention of a plot centered on courtship, portraying instead married heroines and their love relationships, both inside and outside of marriage. It is in part an idealizing fantasy: the principal characters are queens, kings, and emperors, with the power and comparative freedom such positions allow. However, the landscape is not Arcadia or Fairyland but wartorn Europe and Asia. The romance fantasy, with Spenserian symbolic places and knights

Lady Mary Wroth, with archlute (artist unknown). The image represents Mary Wroth in a conventional pose and role, holding the archlute, which indicates that she has been educated in the graceful arts that an aristocratic woman was expected to know. But the massive archlute, emblem of song-making, also points to her Sidney heritage—as niece of the poets Sir Philip Sidney and the Countess of Pembroke, and as daughter of Sir Robert Sidney of Penshurst, also a poet—and to her own unconventional role as female poet.

fighting evil tyrants and monsters, only partially overlays a rigidly patriarchal Jacobean world rife with rape, incest, arranged or forced marriages, jealous husbands, tortured women, and endangered children. Those perils, affecting all women from shepherdesses to queens, are rendered in large part through the numerous stories interpolated in romance fashion within the principal plots. The male heroes are courageous fighters and attractive lovers, but all are flawed by inconstancy. For Wroth, true heroism consists of integrity in love despite social constraints and psychological pressures. A few women are heroic in this sense: Pamphilia, the good queen and pattern of constancy; Urania, the wise counselor who wins self-knowledge and makes wise choices in love; and Veralinda, who weds her true lover after great trials. Almost all Wroth's female characters define themselves through storytelling and making poems. The women compose twice as many of the poems as the men do. Pamphilia, Wroth's surrogate, is singled out as a poet by vocation, both by the number of her poems and by their recognized excellence.

Many contemporaries assumed that the *Urania* was a scandalous roman à clef, alluding not only to Sidney-Pembroke-Wroth affairs but to notable personages of the Jacobean court. A public outcry from one of them, Lord Edward Denny, elicited a spirited satiric response from Wroth. Although she suggested to the king's minister Buckingham that she withdraw the work from circulation, there is no evidence that she actually did so. The uproar, however, may have discouraged her from publishing part 2 of the romance and her pastoral drama.

From The Countess of Montgomery's Urania[1]

From *The First Book*

When the spring began to appear like the welcome messenger of summer, one sweet (and in that more sweet) morning, after Aurora[2] had called all careful eyes to attend the day, forth came the fair shepherdess Urania[3] (fair indeed; yet that far too mean a title for her, who for beauty deserved the highest style[4] could be given by best-knowing judgments). Into the mead[5] she came, where usually she drove her flocks to feed, whose leaping and wantonness showed they were proud of such a guide: but she, whose sad thoughts led her to another manner of spending her time, made her soon leave them, and follow her late-begun custom; which was (while they delighted themselves) to sit under some shade, bewailing her misfortune; while they fed, to feed upon her own sorrow and tears, which at this time she began again to summon, sitting down under the shade of a well-spread beech; the ground (then blest) and the tree, with full and fine-leaved branches, growing proud to bear and shadow such perfections. But she regarding nothing, in comparison of her woe, thus proceeded in her grief: "Alas Urania," said she (the true servant to misfortune), "of any misery that can befall woman, is not this the most and greatest which thou art fallen into? Can there be any near the unhappiness of being ignorant, and that in the highest kind, not being certain of mine own estate or birth? Why was I not still continued in the belief I was, as I appear, a shepherdess, and daughter to a shepherd? My ambition then went no higher than this estate, now flies it to a knowledge; then was I contented, now perplexed. O ignorance, can thy dullness yet procure so sharp a pain? and that such a thought as makes me now aspire unto knowledge? How did I joy in this poor life, being quiet! blessed in the love of those I took for parents, but now by them I know the contrary, and by that knowledge, now to know myself. Miserable Urania, worse art thou now than these thy lambs; for they know their dams, while thou dost live unknown of any." By this were others come into that mead with their flocks: but she, esteeming her sorrowing thoughts her best and choicest company, left that place, taking a little path which brought her to the further side of the plain, to the foot of the rocks, speaking as she went these lines, her eyes fixed upon the ground, her very soul turned into mourning.

> Unseen, unknown, I here alone complain
> To rocks, to hills, to meadows, and to springs,

---

1. Wroth's title echoes *The Countess of Pembroke's Arcadia*, the romance written by her uncle Sir Philip Sidney. The countess of Montgomery was Susan (Vere) Herbert, Wroth's close friend and the sister-in-law of her lover, William Herbert. The opening of the *Urania* is meant to be compared to (and contrasted with) the opening of the *Arcadia*, in which two shepherds lament the absence of their beloved, the mysterious shepherdess Urania.
2. The Greek goddess of the dawn.
3. The name has multiple associations: the Muse

of astronomy, the Muse of Christian poetry, a surname for Aphrodite (Venus) designating heavenly beauty. It was also an honorific commonly bestowed on Wroth's aunt, Mary Sidney, Countess of Pembroke. In Wroth's romance, Urania is a foundling adopted by shepherds but actually the daughter of the king of Naples: after losing one lover and gaining another, she marries, becomes a matriarch, and is throughout (as in this episode) a counselor of others.
4. Title.
5. Meadow.

Which can no help return to ease my pain,
    But back my sorrows the sad Echo[6] brings.
5 Thus still increasing are my woes to me,
    Doubly resounded by that moanful voice,
Which seems to second me in misery,
    And answer gives like friend of mine own choice.
Thus only she doth my companion prove,
10   The others silently do offer ease.
But those that grieve, a grieving note do love;
    Pleasures to dying eyes bring but disease:
And such am I, who daily ending live,
Wailing a state which can no comfort give.

In this passion she went on, till she came to the foot of a great rock, she thinking of nothing less than ease, sought how she might ascend it; hoping there to pass away her time more peaceably with loneliness, though not to find least respite from her sorrow, which so dearly she did value, as by no means she would impart it to any. The way was hard, though by some windings making the ascent pleasing. Having attained the top, she saw under some hollow trees the entry into the rock: she fearing nothing but the continuance of her ignorance, went in; where she found a pretty room, as if that stony place had yet in pity, given leave for such perfections to come into the heart as chiefest, and most beloved place, because most loving. The place was not unlike the ancient (or the descriptions of ancient) hermitages, instead of hangings, covered and lined with ivy, disdaining aught else should come there, that being in such perfection. This richness in Nature's plenty made her stay to behold it, and almost grudge the pleasant fullness of content that place might have, if sensible, while she must know to taste of torments. As she was thus in passion mixed with pain, throwing her eyes as wildly as timorous lovers do for fear of discovery, she perceived a little light, and such a one, as a chink doth oft discover to our sights. She curious to see what this was, with her delicate hands put the natural ornament aside, discerning a little door, which she putting from her, passed through it into another room, like the first in all proportion; but in the midst there was a square stone, like to a pretty table, and on it a wax candle burning; and by that a paper,[7] which had suffered itself patiently to receive the discovering of so much of it, as presented this sonnet (as it seemed newly written) to her sight.

Here all alone in silence might I mourn:
    But how can silence be where sorrows flow?
Sighs with complaints have poorer pains outworn;
    But broken hearts can only true grief show.
5 Drops of my dearest blood shall let Love know
    Such tears for her I shed, yet still do burn,
As no spring can quench least part of my woe,
    Till this live earth, again to earth do turn.
Hateful all thought of comfort is to me,

6. In classical mythology Echo was a wood nymph who pined away in unrequited love for the handsome Narcissus until only her voice remained (Ovid, *Metamorphoses* 3).
7. The episode alludes to an episode in Philip

Sidney's *Old Arcadia* in which one of the heroines, Cleophila, enters a darkened cave illuminated by a single candle and finds a poem on top of a stone table.

10 Despised day, let me still night possess;
Let me all torments feel in their excess,
And but this light allow my state to see.
Which still doth waste, and wasting as this light,
Are my sad days unto eternal night.

"Alas Urania!" sighed she. "How well do these words, this place, and all agree with thy fortune? Sure, poor soul, thou wert here appointed to spend thy days, and these rooms ordained to keep thy tortures in; none being assuredly so matchlessly unfortunate."

Turning from the table, she discerned in the room a bed of boughs, and on it a man lying, deprived of outward sense, as she thought, and of life, as she at first did fear, which struck her into a great amazement: yet having a brave spirit, though shadowed under a mean habit,[8] she stepped unto him, whom she found not dead, but laid upon his back, his head a little to her wards,[9] his arms folded on his breast, hair long, and beard disordered, manifesting all care;[1] but care itself had left him: curiousness thus far afforded him, as to be perfectly discerned the most exact piece of misery; apparel he had suitable to the habitation, which was a long gray[2] robe. This grieveful spectacle did much amaze the sweet and tender-hearted shepherdess; especially, when she perceived (as she might by the help of the candle) the tears which distilled from his eyes; who seeming the image of death, yet had this sign of worldly sorrow, the drops falling in that abundance, as if there were a kind strife among them, to rid their master first of that burdenous[3] carriage; or else meaning to make a flood, and so drown their woeful patient in his own sorrow, who yet lay still, but then fetching a deep groan from the profoundest part of his soul, he said:

"Miserable Perissus,[4] canst thou thus live, knowing she that gave thee life is gone? Gone, O me! and with her all my joy departed. Wilt thou (unblessed creature) lie here complaining for her death, and know she died for thee? Let truth and shame make thee do something worthy of such a love, ending thy days like thyself, and one fit to be her servant. But that I must not do: then thus remain and foster storms, still to torment thy wretched soul withal, since all are little, and too too little for such a loss. O dear Limena,[5] loving Limena, worthy Limena, and more rare, constant Limena: perfections delicately feigned to be in women were verified in thee, was such worthiness framed only to be wondered at by the best, but given as a prey to base and unworthy jealousy? When were all worthy parts joined in one, but in thee my best Limena? Yet all these grown subject to a creature ignorant of all but ill; like unto a fool, who in a dark cave, that hath but one way to get out, having a candle, but not the understanding what good it doth him, puts it out: this ignorant wretch not being able to comprehend thy virtues, did so by thee in thy murder, putting out the world's light, and men's admiration: Limena, Limena, O my Limena."

With that he fell from complaining into such a passion, as weeping and crying were never in so woeful a perfection, as now in him; which brought as deserved a compassion from the excellent shepherdess, who already had her

---

8. Lowly garment.
9. Toward her.
1. Trouble.
2. Gray is typically associated with mourning and

despair.
3. Burdensome.
4. Perissus: "Lost one."
5. Woman of home or threshold.

heart so tempered with grief, as that it was apt to take any impression that it would come to seal withal. Yet taking a brave courage to her, she stepped unto him, kneeling down by his side, and gently pulling him by the arm, she thus spoke.

"Sir," said she, "having heard some part of your sorrows, they have not only made me truly pity you, but wonder at you; since if you have lost so great a treasure, you should not lie thus leaving her and your love unrevenged, suffering her murderers to live, while you lie here complaining; and if such perfections be dead in her, why make you not the phoenix[6] of your deeds live again, as to new life raised out of the revenge you should take on them? Then were her end satisfied, and you deservedly accounted worthy of her favor, if she were so worthy as you say."

"If she were, O God," cried out Perissus, "what devilish spirit art thou, that thus dost come to torture me? But now I see you are a woman; and therefore not much to be marked, and less resisted: but if you know charity, I pray now practice it, and leave me who am afflicted sufficiently without your company; or if you will stay, discourse not to me."

"Neither of these will I do," said she.

"If you be then," said he, "some Fury[7] of purpose sent to vex me, use your force to the uttermost in martyring me; for never was there a fitter subject, then the heart of poor Perissus is."

"I am no Fury," replied the divine Urania, "nor hither come to trouble you, but by accident lighted on this place; my cruel hap being such, as only the like can give me content, while the solitariness of this like cave might give me quiet, though not ease. Seeking for such a one, I happened hither; and this is the true cause of my being here, though now I would use it to a better end if I might: Wherefore favor me with the knowledge of your grief; which heard, it may be I shall give you some counsel, and comfort in your sorrow."

"Cursed may I be," cried he, "if ever I take comfort, having such cause of mourning: but because you are, or seem to be afflicted, I will not refuse to satisfy your demand, but tell you the saddest story that ever was rehearsed by dying man to living woman, and such a one, as I fear will fasten too much sadness in you; yet should I deny it, I were to blame, being so well known to these senseless places; as were they sensible of sorrow, they would condole, or else amazed at such cruelty stand dumb as they do, to find that man should be so inhuman."

*　*　*

SONG[8]

Love what art thou? A vain thought
In our minds by fancy wrought.
Idle smiles did thee beget,
While fond wishes made the net
5　　Which so many fools have caught.

---

6. Mythical bird said to live five hundred years, then expire in flames, out of which a new phoenix arose. Only one phoenix existed at a time.
7. Goddess of vengeance.

8. This song, one of a group of eclogues that marks the conclusion of Book 1 of the *Urania*, is sung to a shepherdess by a shepherd, "being, as it seemed, fallen out with Love."

Love what art thou? Light and fair,
Fresh as morning, clear as th' air.
But too soon thy evening change
Makes thy worth with coldness range;
10   Still thy joy is mixed with care.

Love what art thou? A sweet flower
Once full blown,° dead in an hour.   *in full bloom*
Dust in wind as staid remains
As thy pleasure or our gains,
15   If thy humor° change, to lour.°   *whim / frown*

Love what art thou? Childish, vain,
Firm as bubbles made by rain,
Wantonness thy greatest pride.
These foul faults thy virtues hide—
20   But babes can no staidness gain.

Love what art thou? Causeless cursed,
Yet alas these not the worst:
Much more of thee may be said.
But thy law I once obeyed,
25   Therefore say no more at first.

                                                   1621

From Pamphilia to Amphilanthus[1]

1

When night's black mantle could most darkness prove,
    And sleep, death's image, did my senses hire
    From knowledge of myself, then thoughts did move
    Swifter than those most swiftness need require.
5 In sleep, a chariot drawn by winged desire
    I saw, where sat bright Venus, Queen of Love,
    And at her feet, her son,° still adding fire   *Cupid*
    To burning hearts, which she did hold above.
But one heart flaming more than all the rest
10   The goddess held, and put it to my breast.
    "Dear son, now shut,"[2] said she: "thus must we win."
He her obeyed, and martyred my poor heart.

---

1. Pamphilia ("all-loving") is the protagonist of the *Urania*. Her unfaithful beloved's name means "lover of two." These characters are first cousins, like Mary Wroth and William Herbert; their names adumbrate the main theme of both the romance and the appended sonnet sequence, constancy in the face of unfaithfulness.
    Pamphilia to Amphilanthus is broken into several separately numbered series (the first of which

includes forty-eight sonnets, with songs inserted after every sixth sonnet except the last). In Josephine A. Roberts's edition of Wroth's poetry, the poems are numbered consecutively throughout the work; we have adopted this convenient renumbering.
2. I.e., shut the burning heart into Pamphilia's breast.

I, waking, hoped as dreams it would depart:
Yet since, O me, a lover I have been.

16

Am I thus conquered? Have I lost the powers
  That to withstand, which joys to ruin me?[3]
Must I be still while it my strength devours,
  And captive leads me prisoner, bound, unfree?
5 Love first shall leave men's fancies to them free,[4]
  Desire shall quench Love's flames, spring hate sweet showers,
  Love shall loose all his darts, have sight, and see
  His shame, and wishings hinder happy hours.
Why should we not Love's purblind° charms resist?   *completely blind*
10 Must we be servile, doing what he list?°   *what pleases him*
No, seek some host to harbor thee: I fly
Thy babish tricks, and freedom do profess.
  But O my hurt makes my lost heart confess
  I love, and must: So farewell liberty.

25

Like to the Indians scorched with the sun,
  The sun which they do as their god adore,
  So am I used by Love, for evermore°   *the more*
  I worship him, less favors have I won.
5 Better are they who thus to blackness run,
  And so can only whiteness' want deplore:
  Than I, who pale and white am with grief's store,
  Nor can have hope, but to see hopes undone.
Besides their sacrifice received in sight
10 Of their chose Saint, mine hid as worthless rite,
Grant me to see where I my offerings give;
Then let me wear the mark of Cupid's might
  In heart, as they in skin of Phoebus° light,   *the sun god*
  Not ceasing offerings to Love while I live.

28

SONG[5]

Sweetest love, return again,
  Make not too long stay:
Killing mirth and forcing pain,
  Sorrow leading way.
5 Let us not thus parted be:
Love and absence ne'er agree.

---

3. I.e., have I lost the power to withstand love
("That"), which takes pleasure in ruining me?
4. I.e., this and the other impossibilities that follow will occur before I surrender to love.
5. The poem seems to revise one of Donne's songs:
"Sweetest love, I do not go," p. 929.

But since you must needs depart,
   And me hapless leave,
In your journey take my heart,
10   Which will not deceive.
Yours it is, to you it flies,
Joying in those lovèd eyes.

So in part we shall not part,
   Though we absent be:
15 Time, nor place, nor greatest smart
   Shall my bands make free.
Tied I am, yet think it gain:
In such knots I feel no pain.

But can I live, having lost
20   Chiefest part of me?
Heart is fled, and sight is crossed,
   These my fortunes be.
Yet dear heart go, soon return:
As good there as here to burn.

39

Take heed mine eyes, how you your looks do cast
   Lest they betray my heart's most secret thought,
   Be true unto yourselves, for nothing's bought
   More dear than doubt which brings a lover's fast.[6]
5 Catch you all watching eyes, ere they be past,
   Or take yours fixed where your best love hath sought
   The pride of your desires; let them be taught
   Their faults for shame, they could no truer last.
Then look, and look with joy for conquest won
10   Of those that searched your hurt in double kind;[7]
   So you kept safe, let them themselves look blind,
   Watch, gaze, and mark till they to madness run,
While you, mine eyes enjoy full sight of love
Contented that such happinesses move.

40

False hope which feeds but to destroy, and spill[8]
   What it first breeds; unnatural to the birth
   Of thine own womb; conceiving but to kill,
   And plenty gives to make the greater dearth,[9]
5 So tyrants do who falsely ruling earth
   Outwardly grace them,[1] and with profits fill,

---

6. Lack of nourishment for love, due to jealousy ("doubt").
7. Those who spy and pry with their two eyes, to discover my secret love.
8. Kill. The image is of miscarriage or infanticide.

9. Gives abundance only to make scarcity more painful afterward.
1. I.e., those whom they mean to destroy (see next line).

Advance those who appointed are to death,
To make their greater fall to please their will.
Thus shadow° they their wicked vile intent,   *conceal*
10   Coloring evil with a show of good
While in fair shows their malice so is spent;[2]
Hope kills the heart, and tyrants shed the blood.
For hope deluding brings us to the pride
Of our desires the farther down to slide.

64

Love like a juggler comes to play his prize,°   *perform skillfully*
And all minds draw his wonders to admire,
To see how cunningly he, wanting eyes,[3]
Can yet deceive the best sight of desire.
5   The wanton child how he can feign his fire
So prettily, as none sees his disguise!
How finely do his tricks; while we fools hire
The badge and office of his tyrannies.[4]
For in the end such juggling he doth make,
10   As he our hearts instead of eyes doth take;
For men can only by their sleights abuse
The sight with nimble and delightful skill;
But if he play, his gain is our lost will.
Yet child-like we cannot his sports refuse.

68

My pain, still smothered in my grievèd breast,
Seeks for some ease, yet cannot passage find
To be discharged of this unwelcome guest:
When most I strive, most fast his burdens bind,
5   Like to a ship on Goodwin's[5] cast by wind,
The more she strives, more deep in sand is pressed,
Till she be lost; so am I, in this kind,°   *manner*
Sunk, and devoured, and swallowed by unrest,
Lost, shipwrecked, spoiled, debarred of smallest hope,
10   Nothing of pleasure left; save thoughts have scope,
Which wander may. Go then, my thoughts, and cry
"Hope's perished, love tempest-beaten, joy lost:
Killing despair hath all these blessings crossed."
Yet faith still cries, "love will not falsify."

2. Expended, employed. "Shows": appearances.
3. Cupid, the god of Love, was represented as a blind child.
4. Seek, at our own cost, the external tokens and ceremonies of tyrannical Love.
5. Goodwin Sands, a line of shoals at the entrance to the Strait of Dover.

74

SONG

Love a child is ever crying,
    Please him, and he straight is flying;
    Give him, he the more is craving,
    Never satisfied with having.

5   His desires have no measure,
    Endless folly is his treasure;
    What he promiseth he breaketh:
    Trust not one word that he speaketh.

He vows nothing but false matter,
10   And to cozen° you he'll flatter.   *cheat*
    Let him gain the hand,° he'll leave you,   *the upper hand*
    And still glory to deceive you.

He will triumph in your wailing,
    And yet cause be of your failing:
15   These his virtues are, and slighter
    Are his gifts, his favors lighter.

Feathers are as firm in staying,
    Wolves no fiercer in their preying.
    As a child then leave him crying,
20   Nor seek him, so given to flying.

From *A Crown of Sonnets Dedicated to Love*[6]

77

In this strange labyrinth how shall I turn?
    Ways° are on all sides, while the way I miss: *paths*
    If to the right hand, there in love I burn;
    Let me go forward, therein danger is;
5   If to the left, suspicion hinders bliss,
    Let me° turn back, shame cries I ought return,   *if I*
    Nor faint though crosses[7] with my fortunes kiss;
    Stand still is harder, although sure to mourn.[8]
Then let me take the right- or left-hand way;
10   Go forward, or stand still, or back retire;

---

6. The "crown" is a difficult poetic form (originally Italian and usually known by its Italian name, *corona*) in which the last line of each poem serves as the first line of the next, until a circle is completed by the last line of the final poem, which is the same as the first line of the first one. The number of poems varies from seven to (as in Wroth's *corona*) fourteen.
    In contrast to the errant-child Cupid of the preceding part of the sequence, Love in this series is a mature and just monarch, whose true service ennobles lovers. The crown is in part a recantation of the harsh judgment of love earlier in the sequence. But Pamphilia relapses into melancholy afterward.
7. Troubles, adversity. "Faint": lose heart.
8. I.e., certain to make me mourn.

I must these doubts endure without allay°   *abatement*
Or help, but travail find for my best hire.[9]
Yet that which most my troubled sense doth move
Is to leave all, and take the thread of love.[1]

103

My muse now happy, lay thyself to rest,
    Sleep in the quiet of a faithful love,
    Write you no more, but let these fancies move
    Some other hearts, wake not to new unrest.
5   But if you study, be those thoughts addressed
    To truth, which shall eternal goodness prove;
    Enjoying of true joy, the most, and best,
    The endless gain which never will remove.
Leave the discourse of Venus and her son
10   To young beginners,[2] and their brains inspire
    With stories of great love, and from that fire
    Get heat to write the fortunes they have won.
And thus leave off, what's past shows you can love,
Now let your constancy your honor prove.[3]

1621

9. I.e., I find travail (with a pun on "travel," the spelling in the 1621 edition) is my only reward.
1. Ariadne gave Theseus a thread to follow so as to find his way out of the Labyrinth, after killing the Minotaur at its center.
2. In Neoplatonic love philosophy, "beginners" in love are attracted to physical beauty and sensory delights, while more advanced lovers love virtue and spiritual beauty. Writing love sonnets is traditionally the business of young lovers.
3. In a symbolic episode in the *Urania*, Pamphilia embodies the virtue of Constancy; she accepts the keys to the Throne of Love, "at which instant Constancy vanished as metamorphosing herself into her breast" (1.1.141).

JOHN WEBSTER
1580?–1625?

John Webster's fame rests on two remarkable tragedies, both set in Roman Catholic Italy and both evoking the common Jacobean stereotype of that land as a place of sophisticated corruption. Both have at their center bold heroines who choose for themselves in love and refuse to submit to male authority. *The White Devil*, first performed in 1608, is based on events that took place in Italy in 1581–85; in this play Vittoria Corombona defies a courtroom full of corrupt magistrates who convict her of adultery and murder. *The Duchess of Malfi*, first performed in 1614 and published in 1623, is based on an Italian novella. In this play, the spirited ruler of Malfi secretly marries her steward for love, defying her brothers, a duke and a cardinal, who demand that she remain a widow. Their dark motives include greed for her fortune, overweening pride in their noble blood, and incestuous desire. The play weds sublime poetry and gothic horror in the devious machinations set in motion against the duchess by her brothers' melancholy spy Bosola, in the macabre mental and physical torments to which they subject her, and in the final scenes in which the stage is littered with the slaughtered bodies of all the principal characters.

Webster was the son of a London tailor and a member of the Merchant Tailors' Company, but we know little else about him. He wrote a tragicomedy, *The Devil's Law Case* (1621), and collaborated on several plays with contemporary playwrights, among them Thomas Dekker in *Westward Ho* (1607) and John Marston in *The Malcontent* (1604). Of all the Stuart dramatists, Webster is the one who comes closest to Shakespeare in his power of tragic utterance and his flashes of poetic brilliance.

The Duchess of Malfi

DRAMATIS PERSONAE

FERDINAND, *Duke of Calabria*
THE CARDINAL, *his brother*
ANTONIO BOLOGNA, *steward of*
  the household to the DUCHESS
DELIO, *his friend*
DANIEL DE BOSOLA, *gentleman*
  of the horse to the DUCHESS
CASTRUCCIO, *an old lord*
MARQUIS OF PESCARA
COUNT MALATESTE
SILVIO, *a lord, of Milan*
RODERIGO ⎱ *gentlemen attending*
GRISOLAN ⎰ *on the* DUCHESS

DOCTOR
Several MADMEN, PILGRIMS,
  EXECUTIONERS, OFFICERS,
  ATTENDANTS &c.
THE DUCHESS OF MALFI, *sister*
  of FERDINAND *and the*
  CARDINAL
CARIOLA, *her woman*
JULIA, CASTRUCCIO'S *wife, and the*
  CARDINAL'S *mistress*
OLD LADY, LADIES, *and*
  CHILDREN

SCENE. *Amalfi, Rome, Loreto, and Milan*

Act 1

SCENE 1. *Amalfi; a hall in the* DUCHESS's *palace.*

[*Enter* ANTONIO *and* DELIO.]
DELIO   You are welcome to your country, dear Antonio;
  You have been long in France, and you return
  A very formal Frenchman in your habit.[1]
  How do you like the French court?
ANTONIO   I admire it:
5   In seeking to reduce both state and people
  To a fixed order, their judicious king
  Begins at home; quits° first his royal palace   *rids*
  Of flattering sycophants, of dissolute
  And infamous persons—which he sweetly terms

1.1
1. An absolute Frenchman in your dress.

10   His Master's masterpiece, the work of heaven[2]—
    Considering duly that a prince's court
    Is like a common fountain, whence should flow
    Pure silver drops in general, but if 't chance
    Some cursed example poison 't near the head,
15   Death and diseases through the whole land spread.
    And what is 't makes this blessed government
    But a most provident council, who dare freely
    Inform him the corruption of the times?
    Though some o' th' court hold it presumption
20   To instruct princes what they ought to do,
    It is a noble duty to inform them
    What they ought to foresee.—Here comes Bosola,
    The only court-gall;[3] yet I observe his railing
    Is not for simple love of piety.
25   Indeed, he rails at those things which he wants;
    Would be as lecherous, covetous, or proud,
    Bloody, or envious, as any man,
    If he had means to be so. Here's the cardinal.
        [*Enter the* CARDINAL *and* BOSOLA.]

30 BOSOLA   I do haunt you still.

CARDINAL   So.

BOSOLA   I have done you better service than to be slighted thus. Miserable age, where the only reward of doing well is the doing of it!

CARDINAL   You enforce your merit too much.

BOSOLA   I fell into the galleys[4] in your service; where, for two years
35   together, I wore two towels instead of a shirt, with a knot on the shoulder, after the fashion of a Roman mantle. Slighted thus? I will thrive some way. Blackbirds fatten best in hard weather; why not I in these dog days?[5]

CARDINAL   Would you could become honest!

BOSOLA   With all your divinity do but direct me the way to it. I have known
40   many travel far for it, and yet return as arrant knaves as they went forth, because they carried themselves always along with them. [*Exit* CARDINAL.] Are you gone? Some fellows, they say, are possessed with the devil, but this great fellow were able to possess the greatest devil, and make him worse.

45 ANTONIO   He hath denied thee some suit?

BOSOLA   He and his brother are like plum trees that grow crooked over standing pools;[6] they are rich and o'erladen with fruit, but none but crows, pies,[7] and caterpillars feed on them. Could I be one of their flattering panders, I would hang on their ears like a horse leech till I were
50   full and then drop off. I pray, leave me. Who would rely upon these miserable dependencies, in expectation to be advanced tomorrow? What creature ever fed worse than hoping Tantalus?[8] Nor ever died any

---

2. Alludes to Christ ridding the temple of money changers (John 2.13–22).
3. One who frets the court, but with the overtone of a disease, a blight.
4. Forced labor at the oar of a Mediterranean galley was the last penalty this side of torture and execution, and was likely to be a death sentence.

5. The hot, sultry season of midsummer.
6. Stagnant waters.
7. Magpies, birds of evil omen like blackbirds.
8. Tantalus, in classical mythology, was "tantalized" by the constant presence of delectable food and drink that, though he was desperate, he could never reach.

man more fearfully than he that hoped for a pardon. There are rewards
for hawks and dogs when they have done us service; but for a soldier
55   that hazards his limbs in a battle, nothing but a kind of geometry is his
last supportation.[9]
DELIO   Geometry?
BOSOLA   Aye, to hang in a fair pair of slings, take his latter swing in the
world upon an honorable pair of crutches, from hospital to hospital.[1]
60   Fare ye well, sir: and yet do not you scorn us; for places in the court are
but like beds in the hospital, where this man's head lies at that man's
foot, and so lower and lower.   [*Exit.*]
DELIO   I knew this fellow seven years[2] in the galleys
For a notorious murder; and 'twas thought
65   The cardinal suborned it. He was released
By the French general, Gaston de Foix,
When he recovered Naples.[3]
ANTONIO   'Tis great pity
He should be thus neglected; I have heard
He's very valiant. This foul melancholy
70   Will poison all his goodness; for, I'll tell you,
If too immoderate sleep be truly said
To be an inward rust unto the soul,
It then doth follow want of action
Breeds all black malcontents; and their close rearing,
75   Like moths in cloth, do hurt for want of wearing.[4]

SCENE 2. *The scene continues.*

[*Enter* CASTRUCCIO, SILVIO, RODERIGO, *and* GRISOLAN.]
DELIO   The presence° 'gins to fill: you promised me   *audience hall*
To make me the partaker of the natures
Of some of your great courtiers.
ANTONIO   The Lord Cardinal's,
And other strangers' that are now in court?
5   I shall. Here comes the great Calabrian duke.
[*Enter* FERDINAND *and* ATTENDANTS.]
FERDINAND   Who took the ring oftenest?[1]
SILVIO   Antonio Bologna, my lord.
FERDINAND   Our sister duchess' great master of her household? Give him
the jewel. When shall we leave this sportive action, and fall to action
10   indeed?
CASTRUCCIO   Methinks, my lord, you should not desire to go to war in person.
FERDINAND   Now for some gravity. Why, my lord?
CASTRUCCIO   It is fitting a soldier arise to be a prince, but not necessary a
prince descend to be a captain.

9. Support.
1. In the 17th century, a place of last resort for
the indigent dying.
2. In speaking to the cardinal himself (line 34),
Bosola had mentioned only two years.
3. Gaston de Foix, French commander, was active
in Italy during the early 1500s; hence, the time of
the tragedy is about a hundred years before Webster wrote. Ferdinand and the cardinal are Span-

iards established in Italy, like the infamous house
of Borgia.
4. I.e., enforced idleness breeds discontent, as
moths breed in unused clothing.
1.2
1. A common game around court, used in training for tournaments, involved catching a hanging
ring on the tip of a lance. But some of Webster's
audience would have caught a sexual analogy.

15 FERDINAND No?

CASTRUCCIO No, my lord, he were far better do it by a deputy.

FERDINAND Why should he not as well sleep or eat by a deputy? This might take idle, offensive, and base office from him, whereas the other deprives him of honor.

20 CASTRUCCIO Believe my experience, that realm is never long in quiet where the ruler is a soldier.

FERDINAND Thou told'st me thy wife could not endure fighting.

CASTRUCCIO True, my lord.

FERDINAND And of a jest she broke of a captain she met full of wounds. I
25 have forgot it.

CASTRUCCIO She told him, my lord, he was a pitiful fellow, to lie, like the children of Israel, all in tents.[2]

FERDINAND Why, there's a wit were able to undo all the chirurgeons[3] o' the city; for although gallants should quarrel and had drawn their weapons
30 and were ready to go to it, yet her persuasions would make them put up.

CASTRUCCIO That she would, my lord.

FERDINAND How do you like my Spanish gennet?[4]

RODERIGO He is all fire.

FERDINAND I am of Pliny's opinion, I think he was begot by the wind; he
35 runs as if he were ballassed[5] with quicksilver.

SILVIO True, my lord, he reels from the tilt often.[6]

RODERIGO and GRISOLAN Ha, ha, ha!

FERDINAND Why do you laugh? Methinks, you that are courtiers should be my touchwood, take fire when I give fire; that is, laugh but when I
40 laugh, were the subject never so witty.

CASTRUCCIO True, my lord, I myself have heard a very good jest, and have scorned to seem to have so silly a wit as to understand it.

FERDINAND But I can laugh at your fool, my lord.

CASTRUCCIO He cannot speak, you know, but he makes faces: my lady
45 cannot abide him.

FERDINAND No?

CASTRUCCIO Nor endure to be in merry company, for she says too much laughing and too much company fills her too full of the wrinkle.

FERDINAND I would, then, have a mathematical instrument made for her
50 face, that she might not laugh out of compass.[7] I shall shortly visit you at Milan, Lord Silvio.

SILVIO Your grace shall arrive most welcome.

FERDINAND You are a good horseman, Antonio. You have excellent riders in France. What do you think of good horsemanship?

55 ANTONIO Nobly, my lord: as out of the Grecian horse issued many famous princes,[8] so out of brave horsemanship arise the first sparks of growing resolution that raise the mind to noble action.

FERDINAND You have bespoke it worthily.

---

2. Lint bandages were called "tents."
3. Surgeons.
4. Sometimes "jennet": a small Spanish horse of Arabian stock.
5. Ballasted. Pliny in his *Natural History* tells about some Spanish horses generated by a swift wind (8.67).

6. Veers away from the target, undesirable in a warhorse.
7. Excessively; with a pun on the draftsman's compass.
8. The Trojan horse, in which the Greek warriors hid, to overrun Troy.

SILVIO   Your brother, the Lord Cardinal, and sister duchess.
  [*Reenter* CARDINAL, *with* DUCHESS, CARIOLA, *and* JULIA.]
CARDINAL   Are the galleys come about?
60 GRISOLAN   They are, my lord.
FERDINAND   Here's the Lord Silvio, is come to take his leave.
DELIO [*aside to* ANTONIO]   Now, sir, your promise. What's that Cardinal?
 I mean his temper? They say he's a brave fellow,
 Will play[9] his five thousand crowns at tennis, dance,
65 Court ladies, and one that hath fought single combats.
ANTONIO   Some such flashes superficially hang on him for form; but
 observe his inward character: he is a melancholy churchman; the spring
 in his face is nothing but the engendering of toads; where he is jealous of
 any man, he lays worse plots for them than ever was imposed on Hercu-
70 les,[1] for he strews in his way flatterers, panders, intelligencers,[2] atheists,
 and a thousand such political monsters. He should have been Pope; but
 instead of coming to it by the primitive decency of the church, he did
 bestow bribes so largely and so impudently as if he would have carried it
 away without heaven's knowledge. Some good he hath done—
75 DELIO   You have given too much of him. What's his brother?
ANTONIO   The duke there? A most perverse and turbulent nature.
 What appears in him mirth is merely outside;
 If he laugh heartily, it is to laugh
 All honesty out of fashion.
DELIO   Twins?
80 ANTONIO   In quality.
 He speaks with others' tongues, and hears men's suits
 With others' ears; will seem to sleep o' th' bench
 Only to entrap offenders in their answers;
 Dooms men to death by information;°   *testimony of spies*
 Rewards by hearsay.°   *random report*
85 DELIO   Then the law to him
 Is like a foul black cobweb to a spider:
 He makes of it his dwelling and a prison
 To entangle those shall feed him.
ANTONIO   Most true:
 He ne'er pays debts unless they be shrewd turns,°   *hurtful acts*
90 And those he will confess that he doth owe.
 Last, for his brother there, the Cardinal,
 They that do flatter him most say oracles
 Hang at his lips; and verily I believe them,
 For the devil speaks in them.
95 But for their sister, the right noble duchess,
 You never fixed your eye on three fair medals
 Cast in one figure, of so different temper.
 For her discourse, it is so full of rapture,
 You only will begin then to be sorry

---

9. Wager. "Brave": fine; ostentatious.
1. Hercules' uncle, King Eurystheus, sent him on
twelve suicide missions to get rid of him, but Her-

cules performed all these "labors" successfully.
2. Spies, "political" schemers.

100 When she doth end her speech, and wish, in wonder,
She held it less vainglory° to talk much,   *excessive pride*
Than your penance to hear her: whilst she speaks,
She throws upon a man so sweet a look,
That it were able to raise one to a galliard°   *gay and lively dance*
105 That lay in a dead palsy, and to dote
On that sweet countenance; but in that look
There speaketh so divine a continence
As cuts off all lascivious and vain hope.
Her days are practiced in such noble virtue
110 That sure her nights, nay, more, her very sleeps,
Are more in heaven than other ladies' shrifts.°   *confessions*
Let all sweet ladies break their flattering glasses,°   *mirrors*
And dress themselves in her.
DELIO   Fie, Antonio,
You play the wire-drawer[3] with her commendations.
115 ANTONIO   I'll case° the picture up only thus much;   *frame*
All her particular worth grows to this sum:
She stains° the time past, lights the time to come.   *darkens*
CARDINAL   You must attend my lady in the gallery,
Some half an hour hence.
ANTONIO   I shall.   [*Exeunt* ANTONIO *and* DELIO.]
FERDINAND   Sister, I have a suit to you.
120 DUCHESS   To me, sir?
FERDINAND   A gentleman here, Daniel de Bosola,
One that was in the galleys—
DUCHESS   Yes, I know him.
FERDINAND   A worthy fellow he is. Pray, let me entreat for
The provisorship of your horse.[4]
DUCHESS   Your knowledge of him
Commends him and prefers him.
125 FERDINAND   Call him hither.   [*Exit* ATTENDANT.]
We are now upon° parting. Good Lord Silvio,   *at the point of*
Do us commend to all our noble friends
At the leaguer.°   *camp*
SILVIO   Sir, I shall.
DUCHESS   You are for Milan?
SILVIO   I am.
DUCHESS   Bring the caroches. We'll bring you down to the haven.[5]
                    [*Exeunt all but* FERDINAND *and the* CARDINAL.]
130 CARDINAL   Be sure you entertain° that Bosola   *hire*
For your intelligence:° I would not be seen in 't;   *spy*
And therefore many times I have slighted him
When he did court our furtherance, as this morning.
FERDINAND   Antonio, the great master of her household,
Had been far fitter.
135 CARDINAL   You are deceived in him:

---

3. Draw out her praises excessively.
4. Let me beg (for him) the position of supervi-   sor of your horse.
5. Harbor. "Caroches": carriages.

His nature is too honest for such business.
He comes: I'll leave you.   [*Exit.*]
    [*Reenter* BOSOLA.]

BOSOLA   I was lured to you.
FERDINAND   My brother here the cardinal could never
  Abide you.
BOSOLA   Never since he was in my debt.

140 FERDINAND   Maybe some oblique character° in your face   *crooked feature*
  Made him suspect you.
BOSOLA   Doth he study physiognomy?
  There's no more credit to be given to th' face
  Than to a sick man's urine, which some call
  The physician's whore, because she cozens° him.   *tricks*
  He did suspect me wrongfully.

145 FERDINAND   For that
  You must give great men leave to take their times.
  Distrust doth cause us seldom be deceived:
  You see, the oft shaking of the cedar tree
  Fastens it more at root.
BOSOLA   Yet, take heed;

150 For to suspect a friend unworthily
  Instructs him the next° way to suspect you,   *nearest*
  And prompts him to deceive you.
FERDINAND [*giving him money*]   There's gold.
BOSOLA   So:
  What follows? Never rained such showers as these
  Without thunderbolts i' th' tail of them.

155 Whose throat must I cut?
FERDINAND   Your inclination to shed blood rides post°   *hurries*
  Before my occasion to use you. I give you that
  To live i' th' court here, and observe the duchess;
  To note all the particulars of her 'havior,

160 What suitors do solicit her for marriage,
  And whom she best affects. She's a young widow:
  I would not have her marry again.
BOSOLA   No, sir?
FERDINAND   Do not you ask the reason, but be satisfied
  I say I would not.
BOSOLA   It seems you would create me
  One of your familiars.°   *diabolical spirits*

165 FERDINAND   Familiar? What's that?
BOSOLA   Why, a very quaint invisible devil in flesh,
  An intelligencer.°   *spy*
FERDINAND   Such a kind of thriving thing
  I would wish thee, and ere long thou may'st arrive
  At a higher place by 't.
BOSOLA   Take your devils,

170 Which hell calls angels;[6] these cursed gifts would make

---

6. Gold coins, marked with the image of the archangel Michael.

You a corrupter, me an impudent traitor;
And should I take these, they'd take me to hell.
FERDINAND   Sir, I'll take nothing from you that I have given:
There is a place that I procured for you
175 This morning, the provisorship o' th' horse;
Have you heard on 't?
BOSOLA   No.
FERDINAND   'Tis yours. Is 't not worth thanks?
BOSOLA   I would have you curse yourself now, that your bounty,
Which makes men truly noble, e'er should make me
A villain. Oh, that to avoid ingratitude
180 For the good deed you have done me, I must do
All the ill man can invent! Thus the devil
Candies all sins o'er; and what heaven terms vile,
That names he complimental.°   gracious
FERDINAND   Be yourself;
Keep your old garb of melancholy; 'twill express
185 You envy those that stand above your reach,
Yet strive not to come near 'em: this will gain
Access to private lodgings, where yourself
May, like a politic dormouse—
BOSOLA   As I have seen some
Feed in a lord's dish, half asleep, not seeming
190 To listen to any talk; and yet these rogues
Have cut his throat in a dream. What's my place?
The provisorship o' th' horse? Say, then, my corruption
Grew out of horse dung. I am your creature.
FERDINAND   Away!
BOSOLA   Let good men, for good deeds, covet good fame,
195 Since place and riches oft are bribes of shame:
Sometimes the devil doth preach.   [*Exit.*]

SCENE 3. *The scene continues.*

[*Enter* DUCHESS, CARDINAL, *and* CARIOLA.]
CARDINAL   We are to part from you, and your own discretion
Must now be your director.
FERDINAND   You are a widow:
You know already what man is; and therefore
Let not youth, high promotion, eloquence—
5 CARDINAL   No, nor any thing without the addition, honor,
Sway your high blood.
FERDINAND   Marry! They are most luxurious°   lecherous
Will wed twice.
CARDINAL   Oh, fie!
FERDINAND   Their livers are more spotted
Than Laban's sheep.[1]

1.3
1. In Genesis 30.31–33, Laban promises to Jacob any speckled lambs born while Jacob is herding
Laban's sheep; the liver as seat of the passions was thought to be diseased when spotted.

DUCHESS   Diamonds are of most value,
  They say, that have passed through most jewelers' hands.
FERDINAND   Whores by that rule are precious.
10 DUCHESS   Will you hear me?
  I'll never marry.
CARDINAL   So most widows say;
  But commonly that motion° lasts no longer   *impulse*
  Than the turning of an hourglass; the funeral sermon
  And it end both together.
FERDINAND   Now hear me:
15 You live in a rank pasture, here, i' th' court;
  There is a kind of honeydew² that's deadly;
  'Twill poison your fame° look to 't; be not cunning;   *reputation*
  For they whose faces do belie their hearts
  Are witches ere they arrive at twenty years,
  Aye, and give the devil suck.
20 DUCHESS   This is terrible good counsel.
FERDINAND   Hypocrisy is woven of a fine small thread,
  Subtler than Vulcan's engine:³ yet, believe 't,
  Your darkest actions, nay, your privatest thoughts,
  Will come to light.
CARDINAL   You may flatter yourself,
25 And take your own choice; privately be married
  Under the eaves of night—
FERDINAND   Think 't the best voyage
  That e'er you made; like the irregular crab,
  Which, though 't goes backward, thinks that it goes right
  Because it goes its own way; but observe,
30 Such weddings may more properly be said
  To be executed than celebrated.
CARDINAL   The marriage night
  Is the entrance into some prison.
FERDINAND   And those joys,
  Those lustful pleasures, are like heavy sleeps
  Which do forerun man's mischief.
CARDINAL   Fare you well.
35 Wisdom begins at the end: remember it.   [*Exit.*]
DUCHESS   I think this speech between you both was studied,
  It came so roundly° off.   *glibly*
FERDINAND   You are my sister;
  This was my father's poniard,° do you see?   *dagger*
  I'd be loath to see 't look rusty, 'cause 'twas his.
40 I would have you to give o'er these chargeable° revels: *expensive*
  A visor⁴ and a mask are whispering rooms
  That were ne'er built for goodness—fare ye well—
  And women like that part which, like the lamprey,⁵

2. A sweet, sticky substance left on plants by aphids.
3. The net in which Vulcan, Venus's husband, caught her misbehaving with Mars.
4. A half-mask, worn by ladies at carnivals, theaters, and other dubious resorts.
5. Lamprey eels have a cartilaginous, not a bony, skeleton.

Hath never a bone in 't.
DUCHESS   Fie, sir!
FERDINAND   Nay,
45   I mean the tongue; variety of courtship.
      What cannot a neat knave with a smooth tale
      Make a woman believe? Farewell, lusty widow.   [*Exit.*]
DUCHESS   Shall this move me? If all my royal kindred
      Lay in my way unto this marriage,
50   I'd make them my low footsteps; and even now,
      Even in this hate, as men in some great battles,
      By apprehending danger, have achieved
      Almost impossible actions (I have heard soldiers say so),
      So I through frights and threatenings will assay°   *attempt*
55   This dangerous venture. Let old wives report
      I winked and chose a husband. Cariola,
      To thy known secrecy I have given up
      More than my life—my fame.
CARIOLA   Both shall be safe,
      For I'll conceal this secret from the world
60   As warily as those that trade in poison
      Keep poison from their children.
DUCHESS   Thy protestation
      Is ingenious° and hearty:° I believe it.   *ingenuous / sincere*
      Is Antonio come?
CARIOLA   He attends you.
DUCHESS   Good dear soul,
      Leave me, but place thyself behind the arras,[6]
65   Where thou mayst overhear us. Wish me good speed,
      For I am going into a wilderness
      Where I shall find nor path nor friendly clue
      To be my guide.   [CARIOLA *goes behind the arras.*]
            [*Enter* ANTONIO.]
                          I sent for you: sit down;
      Take pen and ink, and write. Are you ready?
ANTONIO   Yes.
DUCHESS   What did I say?
70   ANTONIO   That I should write somewhat.
DUCHESS   Oh, I remember:
      After these triumphs° and this large expense,   *tournaments*
      It's fit, like thrifty husbands,[7] we inquire
      What's laid up for tomorrow.
ANTONIO   So please your beauteous excellence.
75   DUCHESS   Beauteous?
      Indeed, I thank you: I look young for your sake;
      You have ta'en my cares upon you.
ANTONIO   I'll fetch your grace

---

6. Tapestries were often hung in Renaissance palaces to moderate the chill of the bare walls.
7. Though used here in its original sense of one who preserves and safeguards property, the word shows where the duchess's thoughts are tending.

The particulars of your revenue and expense.

DUCHESS Oh, you are an upright treasurer: but you mistook;

80   For when I said I meant to make inquiry
        What's laid up for tomorrow, I did mean
        What's laid up yonder for me.

ANTONIO   Where?

DUCHESS   In heaven.
        I am making my will (as 'tis fit princes should,
        In perfect memory), and I pray sir, tell me,

85   Were not one better make it smiling thus
        Than in deep groans and terrible ghastly looks,
        As if the gifts we parted with procured°   brought on
        That violent distraction?

ANTONIO   Oh, much better.

DUCHESS   If I had a husband now, this care were quit:

90   But I intend to make you overseer.
        What good deed shall we first remember? Say.

ANTONIO   Begin with that first good deed begun i' th' world
        After man's creation, the sacrament of marriage:
        I'd have you first provide for a good husband;
        Give him all.

DUCHESS   All?

95   ANTONIO   Yes, your excellent self.

DUCHESS   In a winding-sheet?

ANTONIO   In a couple.

DUCHESS   Saint Winfred, that were a strange will!⁸

ANTONIO   'Twere stranger if there were no will in you
        To marry again.

DUCHESS   What do you think of marriage?

100   ANTONIO   I take 't, as those that deny purgatory;
        It locally° contains or heaven or hell;   within itself
        There's no third place in 't.

DUCHESS   How do you affect it?°   feel about it

ANTONIO   My banishment,° feeding my melancholy,   solitary condition
        Would often reason thus—

DUCHESS   Pray, let's hear it.

105   ANTONIO   Say a man never marry, nor have children,
        What takes that from him? Only the bare name
        Of being a father, or the weak delight
        To see the little wanton ride a-cock-horse
        Upon a painted stick, or hear him chatter
        Like a taught starling.

110   DUCHESS   Fie, fie, what's all this?
        One of your eyes is bloodshot; use my ring to 't,
        They say 'tis very sovereign.⁹ 'Twas my wedding ring,
        And I did vow never to part with it

---

8. Saint Winifred, Welsh virgin and martyr, is an
odd saint for the Duchess of Malfi to swear on.
"In a couple": i.e., of sheets—but with a play on
"coupling."
9. Healing, but with an overtone implying royal
power.

But to my second husband.

ANTONIO   You have parted with it now.

DUCHESS   Yes, to help your eyesight.

ANTONIO   You have made me stark blind.

115   DUCHESS   How?

ANTONIO   There is a saucy and ambitious devil
     Is dancing in this circle.[1]

DUCHESS   Remove him.

ANTONIO   How?

DUCHESS   There needs small conjuration, when your finger
     May do it: thus; is it fit?   [*She puts the ring upon his finger; he kneels.*]

ANTONIO   What said you?

DUCHESS   Sir,

120   This goodly roof of yours[2] is too low built;
     I cannot stand upright in 't nor discourse,
     Without I raise it higher: raise yourself;
     Or, if you please, my hand to help you: so. [*Raises him.*]

ANTONIO   Ambition, madam, is a great man's madness,

125   That is not kept in chains and close-pent rooms,
     But in fair lightsome lodgings, and is girt
     With the wild noise of prattling visitants,
     Which makes it lunatic beyond all cure.
     Conceive not I am so stupid but I aim

130   Whereto your favors tend; but he's a fool
     That, being a-cold, would thrust his hands i' th' fire
     To warm them.

DUCHESS   So, now the ground's broke,
     You may discover what a wealthy mine
     I make you lord of.

ANTONIO   O my unworthiness!

135   DUCHESS   You were ill to sell° yourself: *evaluate*
     This darkening of your worth is not like that
     Which tradesmen use i' th' city; their false lights
     Are to rid bad wares off:[3] and I must tell you,
     If you will know where breathes a complete man

140   (I speak it without flattery), turn your eyes,
     And progress through yourself.

ANTONIO   Were there nor heaven
     Nor hell, I should be honest: I have long served virtue,
     And ne'er ta'en wages of her.

DUCHESS   Now she pays it.
     The misery of us that are born great!

145   We are forced to woo, because none dare woo us;
     And as a tyrant doubles° with his words   *speaks ambiguously*
     And fearfully equivocates, so we
     Are forced to express our violent passions

---

1. To conjure up a devil, the necromancer first draws a charmed circle on the ground—like the duchess's ring.

2. His head as he kneels.
3. Tradesmen in the city display their goods in a poor light so the defects won't be seen.

In riddles and in dreams, and leave the path
150 Of simple virtue, which was never made
To seem the thing it is not. Go, go brag
You have left me heartless;° mine is in your bosom: *without a heart*
I hope 'twill multiply love there. You do tremble:
Make not your heart so dead a piece of flesh,
155 To fear more than to love me. Sir, be confident:
What is 't distracts you? This is flesh and blood, sir;
'Tis not the figure cut in alabaster
Kneels at my husband's tomb. Awake, awake, man!
I do here put off all vain ceremony,
160 And only do appear to you a young widow
That claims you for her husband, and, like a widow,
I use but half a blush in 't.
ANTONIO   Truth speak for me,
I will remain the constant sanctuary
Of your good name.
DUCHESS   I thank you, gentle love:
165 And 'cause° you shall not come to me in debt,   *so that*
Being now my steward, here upon your lips
I sign your *Quietus est.*[4] This you should have begged now;
I have seen children oft eat sweetmeats thus,
As fearful to devour them too soon.
ANTONIO   But for your brothers?
170 DUCHESS   Do not think of them.
All discord without this circumference[5]
Is only to be pitied, and not feared;
Yet, should they know it, time will easily
Scatter the tempest.
ANTONIO   These words should be mine,
175 And all the parts you have spoke, if some part of it
Would not have savored flattery.
DUCHESS   Kneel.
                                  [CARIOLA *comes from behind the arras.*]
ANTONIO   Ha!
DUCHESS   Be not amazed; this woman's of my counsel:
I have heard lawyers say, a contract in a chamber
Per verba de presenti[6] is absolute marriage.   [*She and* ANTONIO *kneel.*]
180 Bless, heaven, this sacred gordian,° which let violence   *knot*
Never untwine!
ANTONIO   And may our sweet affections, like the spheres,
Be still° in motion!   *constantly*
DUCHESS   Quickening,° and make   *giving life*
The like soft music![7]
185 ANTONIO   That we may imitate the loving palms,

---

4. The legal formula for marking a bill "paid" or "acquitted."
5. Outside this room, or their embrace.
6. "By words in the present tense" (i.e., not a betrothal or promise for the future). In canon law,

the agreement of two parties to consider themselves married is valid with or without priest, ceremony, or witness.
7. Like the supposed music of the spheres.

Best emblem of a peaceful marriage, that ne'er
Bore fruit, divided!

DUCHESS   What can the church force more?

ANTONIO   That fortune may not know an accident,
Either of joy or sorrow, to divide
Our fixèd wishes!

190   DUCHESS   How can the church bind faster?°   *tighter*
We now are man and wife, and 'tis the church
That must but echo this. Maid, stand apart:[8]
I now am blind.

ANTONIO   What's your conceit° in this?   *idea*

DUCHESS   I would have you lead your fortune by the hand
195   Unto your marriage bed
(You speak in me this, for we now are one);
We'll only lie, and talk together, and plot
To appease my humorous° kindred; and if you please,   *choleric*
Like the old tale in *Alexander and Lodowick,*
200   Lay a naked sword between us, keep us chaste.[9]
Oh, let me shroud my blushes in your bosom,
Since 'tis the treasury of all my secrets!   [*Exeunt* DUCHESS *and* ANTONIO.]

CARIOLA   Whether the spirit of greatness or of woman
Reign most in her, I know not; but it shows
205   A fearful madness: I owe her much of pity.   [*Exit.*]

Act 2

SCENE 1. *The scene continues.*

[*Enter* BOSOLA *and* CASTRUCCIO.]

BOSOLA   You say you would fain be taken for an eminent courtier?

CASTRUCCIO   'Tis the very main of my ambition.

BOSOLA   Let me see: you have a reasonable good face for 't already, and
your nightcap expresses your ears sufficient largely. I would have you
5   learn to twirl the strings of your band[1] with a good grace, and in a set
speech, at th' end of every sentence, to hum three or four times, or blow
your nose till it smart again, to recover your memory. When you come to
be a president[2] in criminal causes, if you smile upon a prisoner, hang
him, but if you frown upon him and threaten him, let him be sure to
10   'scape the gallows.

CASTRUCCIO   I would be a very merry president.

BOSOLA   Do not sup o' nights; 'twill beget you an admirable wit.

CASTRUCCIO   Rather it would make me have a good stomach[3] to quarrel;
for they say, your roaring boys[4] eat meat seldom, and that makes them

---

8. The phrase is addressed to Cariola as the duchess shuts her eyes and rejects all support.
9. Alexander and Lodowick were look-alike friends in an old ballad. For purely virtuous reasons, one slept with the wife of the other, but with the precaution indicated.

2.1
1. The elaborate ruff of the day had strings attached to it.
2. Presiding magistrate.
3. Disposition.
4. London town bullies.

15   so valiant. But how shall I know whether the people take me for an emi-
          nent fellow?
      BOSOLA   I will teach a trick to know it: give out you lie a-dying, and if you
          hear the common people curse you, be sure you are taken for one of the
          prime nightcaps.[5]
          [*Enter an* OLD LADY.]
20   You come from painting now?
      OLD LADY   From what?
      BOSOLA   Why, from your scurvy face-physic. To behold thee not painted
          inclines somewhat near a miracle; these in thy face here were deep ruts
          and foul sloughs the last progress.[6] There was a lady in France that,
25   having had the smallpox, flayed the skin off her face to make it more
          level; and whereas before she looked like a nutmeg grater, after she
          resembled an abortive hedgehog.
      OLD LADY   Do you call this painting?
      BOSOLA   No, no, but you call it careening of an old morphewed lady, to
30   make her disembogue again: there's rough-cast phrase to your plastic.[7]
      OLD LADY   It seems you are well acquainted with my closet.
      BOSOLA   One would suspect it for a shop of witchcraft, to find in it the fat of
          serpents, spawn of snakes, Jews' spittle, and their young children's ordure;
          and all these for the face. I would sooner eat a dead pigeon taken from the
35   soles of the feet of one sick of the plague than kiss one of you fasting.[8]
          Here are two of you, whose sin of your youth is the very patrimony of the
          physician; makes him renew his footcloth with the spring, and change his
          high-prized courtesan with the fall of the leaf.[9] I do wonder you do not
          loathe yourselves. Observe my meditation now:
40   What thing is in this outward form of man
          To be beloved? We account it ominous,
          If nature do produce a colt, or lamb,
          A fawn, or goat, in any limb resembling
          A man, and fly from 't as a prodigy:°   *evil omen*
45   Man stands amazed to see his deformity
          In any other creature but himself.
          But in our own flesh, though we bear diseases
          Which have their true names only ta'en from beasts—
          As the most ulcerous wolf and swinish measle[1]—
50   Though we are eaten up of lice and worms,
          And though continually we bear about us
          A rotten and dead body, we delight
          To hide it in rich tissue: all our fear,
          Nay, all our terror, is lest our physician

---

5. Lawyers (who wore a white coif or skullcap;
cf. line 4, above).
6. A progress was a formal royal journey of state.
7. Scraping ("careening") of an old, scaly ("mor-
phewed") ship ("lady") to fit her for the ocean
("making her disembogue") again. All these metaphors are applied to the model ("plastic") of the
lady's condition as "rough-cast," a mixture of lime
and gravel, is troweled over a base.
8. Centuries of traditional invective about wom-
en's cosmetic practices lie behind this speech.

Freshly killed pigeons were applied to the feet of
plague victims to draw off the infection; fasting
was supposed to cause bad breath.
9. The physician grows rich on those who have
outworn their youth; every spring he buys a new
harness for his horse and every fall a new mistress
for himself.
1. "Wolf": cancer or lupus; "measle": an infection of swine, sometimes confused with human
measles.

55 Should put us in the ground to be made sweet—
Your wife's gone to Rome: you two couple, and get you
To the wells at Lucca to recover your aches.[2]

[Exeunt CASTRUCCIO *and* OLD LADY.]

I have other work on foot. I observe our duchess
Is sick a-days: she pukes, her stomach seethes,
60 The fins of her eyelids look most teeming blue,
She wanes i' th' cheek, and waxes fat i' th' flank,
And contrary to our Italian fashion,
Wears a loose-bodied gown: there's somewhat in 't.
I have a trick may chance discover it,
65 A pretty one; I have bought some apricots,
The first our spring yields.

[Enter ANTONIO *and* DELIO, *talking apart.]*

DELIO   And so long since married?
You amaze me.

ANTONIO   Let me seal your lips forever:
For, did I think that anything but th' air
Could carry these words from you, I should wish
70 You had no breath at all. *[turning to* BOSOLA]
Now, sir, in your contemplation? You are studying to become a great
wise fellow?

BOSOLA   Oh, sir, the opinion of wisdom is a foul tetter[3] that runs all over
a man's body. If simplicity[4] direct us to have no evil, it directs us to a
75 happy being, for the subtlest folly proceeds from the subtlest wisdom.
Let me be simply honest.

ANTONIO   I do understand your inside.

BOSOLA   Do you so?

ANTONIO   Because you would not seem to appear to th' world
Puffed up with your preferment, you continue
80 This out-of-fashion melancholy. Leave it, leave it.

BOSOLA   Give me leave to be honest in any phrase, in any compliment whatsoever. Shall I confess myself to you? I look no higher than I can reach:
they are the gods that must ride on winged horses. A lawyer's mule of a
slow pace will both suit my disposition and business; for, mark me, when a
85 man's mind rides faster than his horse can gallop, they quickly both tire.

ANTONIO   You would look up to heaven, but I think
The devil, that rules i' th' air, stands in your light.

BOSOLA   Oh, sir, you are lord of the ascendant,[5] chief man with the duchess;
a duke was your cousin-german removed.[6] Say you were lineally descended
90 from King Pepin,[7] or he himself, what of this? Search the heads of the
greatest rivers in the world, you shall find them but bubbles of water. Some
would think the souls of princes were brought forth by some more weighty
cause than those of meaner persons: they are deceived, there's the same
hand to them; the like passions sway them; the same reason that makes a

---

2. The wells at Lucca are the mineral springs at
nearby Montecatini, renowned as a place to "take
the cure." Aches are a symptom of syphilis.
3. Skin disease.
4. Foolishness.

5. In astrology, the predominating influence,
controlling destiny.
6. First cousin once removed.
7. Father of Charlemagne, hence source of a
great dynasty.

95　vicar go to law for a tithe-pig[8] and undo his neighbors, makes them spoil a
　　　whole province, and batter down goodly cities with the cannon.

　　　　　　[*Enter* DUCHESS *and* LADIES.]

　　DUCHESS　Your arm, Antonio; do I not grow fat?
　　　I am exceeding short-winded. Bosola,
　　　I would have you, sir, provide for me a litter,
100　Such a one as the Duchess of Florence rode in.
　　BOSOLA　The duchess used one when she was great with child.
　　DUCHESS　I think she did. Come hither, mend my ruff;
　　　Here, when? Thou art such a tedious° lady, and　　　　　*clumsy*
　　　Thy breath smells of lemon peels;[9] would thou hadst done;
105　Shall I swoon under thy fingers? I am
　　　So troubled with the mother![1]
　　BOSOLA [*aside*]　　　　　　　　I fear too much.
　　DUCHESS　I have heard you say that the French courtiers
　　　Wear their hats on 'fore the king.
　　ANTONIO　　　　　　　　　I have seen it.
　　DUCHESS　　　　　　　　　　　　In the presence?
　　ANTONIO　Yes.
110　DUCHESS　Why should not we bring up that fashion? 'Tis
　　　Ceremony more than duty that consists
　　　In the removing of a piece of felt.
　　　Be you the example to the rest o' th' court;
　　　Put on your hat first.
　　ANTONIO　　　　　　　You must pardon me.
115　I have seen, in colder countries than in France,
　　　Nobles stand bare to th' prince, and the distinction
　　　Methought showed reverently.
　　BOSOLA　I have a present for your grace.
　　DUCHESS　　　　　　　　　For me, sir?
　　BOSOLA　Apricots, madam.
　　DUCHESS　　　　　　　O, sir, where are they?
　　　I have heard of none to-year.
120　BOSOLA [*aside*]　　　　　　Good: her color rises.
　　DUCHESS　Indeed, I thank you: they are wondrous fair ones.
　　　What an unskillful fellow is our gardener!
　　　We shall have none this month.
　　BOSOLA　Will not your grace pare them?
125　DUCHESS　No. They taste of musk, methinks; indeed they do.
　　BOSOLA　I know not: yet I wish your grace had pared 'em.
　　DUCHESS　Why?
　　BOSOLA　　　　　I forgot to tell you, the knave gardener,
　　　Only to raise his profit by them the sooner,
　　　Did ripen them in horse dung.[2]
　　DUCHESS　　　　　　　O, you jest.
　　　You shall judge: pray taste one.

---

8. A parson was entitled to a tenth ("tithe") of his
parishioners' annual profit and was often paid in
crops or livestock, but was thought mean if he
sued for a petty sum.

9. Lemon peels, chewed to sweeten the breath.
1. Heartburn, but with a second meaning not
lost on Bosola.
2. Which grows warm as it decomposes.

130 ANTONIO   Indeed, madam,
    I do not love the fruit.
DUCHESS   Sir, you are loath
    To rob us of our dainties: 'tis a delicate fruit;
    They say they are restorative.
BOSOLA   'Tis a pretty art,
    This grafting.
DUCHESS   'Tis so; a bettering of nature.
135 BOSOLA   To make a pippin grow upon a crab,°   *crab apple*
    A damson on a blackthorn. [*aside*] How greedily she eats them!
    A whirlwind strike off these bawd farthingales!³
    For, but for that and the loose-bodied gown,
    I should have discovered apparently°   *certainly*
140   The young springal° cutting a caper in her belly.   *fellow*
DUCHESS   I thank you, Bosola. They were right good ones,
    If they do not make me sick.
ANTONIO   How now, madam?
DUCHESS   This green fruit and my stomach are not friends;
    How they swell me!
BOSOLA [*aside*]   Nay, you are too much swelled already.
DUCHESS   Oh, I am in an extreme cold sweat!
145 BOSOLA   I am very sorry.
DUCHESS   Lights to my chamber! O good Antonio,
    I fear I am undone!
DELIO   Lights there, lights!
        [*Exeunt* DUCHESS *and* LADIES. *Exit, on the other side,* BOSOLA.]
ANTONIO   O my most trusty Delio, we are lost!
    I fear she's fall'n in labor; and there's left
    No time for her remove.
150 DELIO   Have you prepared
    Those ladies to attend her? And procured
    That politic° safe conveyance for the midwife   *secret*
    Your duchess plotted?
ANTONIO   I have.
DELIO   Make use, then, of this forced occasion:
155   Give out that Bosola hath poisoned her
    With these apricots; that will give some color
    For her keeping close.
ANTONIO   Fie, fie, the physicians
    Will then flock to her.
DELIO   For that you may pretend
    She'll use some prepared antidote of her own,
160   Lest the physicians should re-poison her.
ANTONIO   I am lost in amazement:° I know not what   *confusion*
    to think on 't.   [*Exeunt.*]

---

3. Early hoopskirts, capable of concealing the figure.

SCENE 2. *The scene continues.*

[*Enter* BOSOLA.]

BOSOLA   So, so, there's no question but her tetchiness[1] and most vultur-
ous eating of the apricots are apparent signs of breeding.

[*Enter an* OLD LADY.]

Now?

OLD LADY   I am in haste, sir.

5   BOSOLA   There was a young waiting woman had a monstrous desire to see
the glasshouse[2]—

OLD LADY   Nay, pray let me go.

BOSOLA   And it was only to know what strange instrument it was should
swell up a glass to the fashion of a woman's belly.

10   OLD LADY   I will hear no more of the glasshouse. You are still[3] abusing
women!

BOSOLA   Who, I? No; only by the way now and then mention your frailties.
The orange tree bears ripe and green fruit and blossoms all together;
and some of you give entertainment for pure love, but more for more pre-
15   cious reward. The lusty spring smells well, but drooping autumn tastes
well. If we have the same golden showers that rained in the time of Jupiter the thunderer, you have the same Danaës still,[4] to hold up their laps
to receive them. Didst thou never study the mathematics?

OLD LADY   What's that, sir?

20   BOSOLA   Why, to know the trick how to make a many lines meet in one
center. Go, go, give your foster daughters good counsel: tell them that
the devil takes delight to hang at a woman's girdle, like a false rusty
watch, that she cannot discern how the time passes.   [*Exit* OLD LADY.]

[*Enter* ANTONIO, DELIO, RODERIGO, *and* GRISOLAN.]

ANTONIO   Shut up the courtgates.

RODERIGO   Why, sir? What's the danger?

25   ANTONIO   Shut up the posterns presently,[5] and call
All the officers o' th' court.

GRISOLAN   I shall instantly.   [*Exit.*]

ANTONIO   Who keeps the key o' th' park gate?

RODERIGO   Forobosco.

ANTONIO   Let him bring 't presently.

[*Reenter* GRISOLAN *with* SERVANTS.]

1 SERVANT   O, gentlemen o' the court, the foulest treason!

30   BOSOLA [*aside*]   If that these apricots should be poisoned now,
Without my knowledge!

1 SERVANT   There was taken even now
A Switzer° in the duchess' bedchamber—   *Swiss guard*

2 SERVANT   A Switzer?

1 SERVANT   With a pistol in his great codpiece.[6]

BOSOLA   Ha, ha, ha!

2.2
1. Irritability.
2. Where bottles were blown, near the theater in
Blackfriars.
3. Always.

4. Jupiter's success in wooing Danaë in a shower
of gold traditionally illustrated female venality.
5. At once. "Posterns": outer gates.
6. An outsize flap worn on the front of men's
trunk hose.

1 SERVANT   The codpiece was the case for 't.

2 SERVANT   There was

35   A cunning traitor: who would have searched his codpiece?

1 SERVANT   True, if he had kept out of the ladies' chambers.
      And all the molds of his buttons were leaden bullets.

2 SERVANT   O wicked cannibal!
      A firelock° in 's codpiece!   *pistol*

1 SERVANT   'Twas a French plot,
      Upon my life.

40   2 SERVANT   To see what the devil can do!

ANTONIO   Are all the officers here?

SERVANTS   We are.

ANTONIO   Gentlemen,
      We have lost much plate⁷ you know, and but this evening
      Jewels, to the value of four thousand ducats,
      Are missing in the duchess' cabinet.
      Are the gates shut?

SERVANT   Yes.

45   ANTONIO   'Tis the duchess' pleasure
      Each officer be locked into his chamber
      Till the sun-rising; and to send the keys
      Of all their chests and of their outward doors
      Into her bedchamber. She is very sick.

RODERIGO   At her pleasure.

50   ANTONIO   She entreats you take 't not ill:
      The innocent shall be the more approved by it.

BOSOLA   Gentlemen o' th' wood-yard, where's your Switzer now?

1 SERVANT   By this hand, 'twas credibly reported by one o' th' black guard.⁸
                          [*Exeunt all except* ANTONIO *and* DELIO.]

DELIO   How fares it with the duchess?

ANTONIO   She's exposed

55   Unto the worst of torture, pain, and fear.

DELIO   Speak to her all happy comfort.

ANTONIO   How I do play the fool with mine own danger!
      You are this night, dear friend, to post to Rome;
      My life lies in your service.

DELIO   Do not doubt me.

60   ANTONIO   Oh, 'tis far from me, and yet fear presents me
      Somewhat that looks like danger.

DELIO   Believe it,
      'Tis but the shadow of your fear, no more;
      How superstitiously we mind our evils!
      The throwing down salt, or crossing of a hare,

65   Bleeding at nose, the stumbling of a horse,
      Or singing of a cricket, are of power
      To daunt whole man° in us. Sir, fare you well: *all courage*
      I wish you all the joys of a blessed father:

7. Massive gold and silver dishes, a frequent form
of wealth in the days before banks.

8. Kitchen scullions. The "wood-yard" is a source
of firewood for kitchen and fireplaces.

And, for my faith, lay this unto your breast,
70   Old friends, like old swords, still are trusted best.   [*Exit.*]
      [*Enter* CARIOLA.]
   CARIOLA   Sir, you are the happy father of a son:
   Your wife commends him to you.
   ANTONIO   Blessed comfort!
   For heaven's sake tend her well: I'll presently
   Go set a figure for 's nativity.[9]   [*Exeunt.*]

SCENE 3. *The scene continues.*

      [*Enter* BOSOLA, *with a dark lantern.*]
   BOSOLA   Sure I did hear a woman shriek: list, ha!
   And the sound came, if I received it right,
   From the duchess' lodgings. There's some stratagem
   In the confining all our courtiers
5 To their several° wards: I must have part of it;   separate
   My intelligence will freeze else.[1] List, again!
   It may be 'twas the melancholy bird,
   Best friend of silence and of solitariness,
   The owl, that screamed so. Ha! Antonio?
      [*Enter* ANTONIO *with a candle, his sword drawn.*]
10 ANTONIO   I heard some noise. Who's there? What art thou? Speak.
   BOSOLA   Antonio? Put not your face nor body
   To such a forced expression of fear.
   I am Bosola, your friend.
   ANTONIO   Bosola!
   [*aside*] This mole does undermine me.—Heard you not
   A noise even now?
   BOSOLA   From whence?
15 ANTONIO   From the duchess' lodging.
   BOSOLA   Not I. Did you?
   ANTONIO   I did, or else I dreamed.
   BOSOLA   Let's walk towards it.
   ANTONIO   No, it may be 'twas
   But the rising of the wind.
   BOSOLA   Very likely.
   Methinks 'tis very cold, and yet you sweat:
   You look wildly.
20 ANTONIO   I have been setting a figure[2]
   For the duchess' jewels.
   BOSOLA   Ah, and how falls your question?
   Do you find it radical?°   significant
   ANTONIO   What's that to you?
   'Tis rather to be questioned what design,
   When all men were commanded to their lodgings,
   Makes you a nightwalker.

---

9. Cast his horoscope right away.
2.3
1. All my news will be cold otherwise.

2. Establishing the loss involved. But Bosola takes the expression astrologically, as if Antonio were casting a horoscope.

25 BOSOLA   In sooth, I'll tell you:
Now all the court's asleep, I thought the devil
Had least to do here; I came to say my prayers;
And if it do offend you I do so,
You are a fine courtier.
ANTONIO [*aside*]   This fellow will undo me.
30 You gave the duchess apricots today:
Pray heaven they were not poisoned!
BOSOLA   Poisoned? A Spanish fig[3]
For the imputation!
ANTONIO   Traitors are ever confident
Till they are discovered. There were jewels stolen, too;
In my conceit,° none are to be suspected   opinion
More than yourself.
35 BOSOLA   You are a false steward.
ANTONIO   Saucy slave, I'll pull thee up by the roots.
BOSOLA   May be the ruin will crush you to pieces.
ANTONIO   You are an impudent snake indeed, sir:
Are you scarce warm, and do you show your sting?
You libel well, sir.
40 BOSOLA   No, sir: copy it out,
And I will set my hand to 't.[4]
ANTONIO [*aside*]   My nose bleeds.
One that were superstitious would count
This ominous, when it merely comes by chance:
Two letters, that are wrought here for my name,[5]
45 Are drowned in blood!
Mere accident.—For you, sir, I'll take order
I' th' morn you shall be safe.° [*aside*] 'Tis that must color   under guard
Her lying-in.°—Sir, this door you pass not: giving birth
I do not hold it fit that you come near
50 The duchess' lodgings, till you have quit° yourself.   cleared
[*aside*] The great are like the base, nay, they are the same,
When they seek shameful ways to avoid shame.   [*Exit.*]
BOSOLA   Antonio hereabout did drop a paper:
Some of your help, false friend: [*opening his lantern*] Oh, here it is.
55 What's here? A child's nativity calculated?   [*reads*]
"The duchess was delivered of a son, 'tween the hours twelve and one
in the night, *Anno Dom.* 1504,"—that's this year—"*decimo nono
Decembris,*"[6]—that's this night—"taken according to the meridian of
Malfi"—that's our duchess: happy discovery! "The lord of the first house
60 being combust[7] in the ascendant, signifies short life; and Mars being in
a human sign, joined to the tail of the Dragon, in the eighth house, doth
threaten a violent death. *Caetera non scrutantur.*"[8]
Why, now 'tis most apparent: this precise° fellow   officious

---

3. An obscene gesture, which Bosola doubtless
makes onstage.
4. Bosola denies the charge, not by denying malignancy, but by offering to publish it.
5. Embroidered on the handkerchief.
6. December 19.

7. Burned up; i.e., the ruling planet is close to
the sun.
8. "The rest is not examined"—i.e., the horoscope
is incomplete. Mars and the Dragon are sinister
signs, even separately; fatal together.

Is the duchess' bawd:° I have it to my wish!   *procurer*
65   This is a parcel of intelligency
Our courtiers were cased up for: it needs must follow
That I must be committed on pretense
Of poisoning her; which I'll endure, and laugh at.
If one could find the father now! But that
70   Time will discover. Old Castruccio
I' th' morning posts to Rome: by him I'll send
A letter that shall make her brothers' galls
O'erflow their livers. This was a thrifty° way.   *shrewd*
Though lust do mask in ne'er so strange disguise,
75   She's oft found witty, but is never wise.   [*Exit.*]

SCENE 4. *The palace of the* CARDINAL *at Rome.*

[*Enter* CARDINAL *and* JULIA.]
CARDINAL   Sit. Thou art my best of wishes. Prithee, tell me
What trick didst thou invent to come to Rome
Without thy husband.
JULIA   Why, my lord, I told him
I came to visit an old anchorite°   *hermit*
Here for devotion.
5   CARDINAL   Thou are a witty false one—
I mean, to him.
JULIA   You have prevailed with me
Beyond my strongest thoughts! I would not now
Find you inconstant.
CARDINAL   Do not put thyself
To such a voluntary torture, which proceeds
Out of your own guilt.
JULIA   How, my lord?
10   CARDINAL   You fear
My constancy, because you have approved°   *experienced*
Those giddy and wild turnings in yourself.
JULIA   Did you e'er find them?
CARDINAL   Sooth, generally for women;
A man might strive to make glass malleable,
Ere he should make them fixed.
15   JULIA   So, my lord.
CARDINAL   We had need go borrow that fantastic glass
Invented by Galileo the Florentine[1]
To view another spacious world i' th' moon,
And look to find a constant woman there.
JULIA   This is very well, my lord.
20   CARDINAL   Why do you weep?
Are tears your justification? The selfsame tears
Will fall into your husband's bosom, lady,

2.4
1. In 1504, Galileo's telescope was more than one hundred years in the future, but the reference was topical for Webster's audience.

With a loud protestation that you love him
Above the world. Come, I'll love you wisely,
25 That's jealously, since I am very certain
You cannot make me cuckold.
JULIA   I'll go home
To my husband.
CARDINAL   You may thank me, lady,
I have taken you off your melancholy perch,
Bore you upon my fist, and showed you game,
30 And let you fly at it.[2] I pray thee, kiss me.
When thou wast with thy husband, thou wast watched
Like a tame elephant: still you are to thank me:
Thou hadst only kisses from him and high feeding;
But what delight was that? 'Twas just like one
35 That hath a little fingering on the lute,
Yet cannot tune it: still you are to thank me.
JULIA You told me of a piteous wound i' th' heart
And a sick liver, when you wooed me first,
And spake like one in physic.[3]   [A knock is heard.]
CARDINAL   Who's that?
40 Rest firm,° for my affection to thee,   be assured
Lightning moves slow to 't.°   by comparison
        [Enter SERVANT.]
SERVANT   Madam, a gentleman,
That's come post from Malfi, desires to see you.
CARDINAL Let him enter. I'll withdraw.   [Exit.]
SERVANT   He says
Your husband, old Castruccio, is come to Rome,
45 Most pitifully tired with riding post.[4]   [Exit.]
        [Enter DELIO.]
JULIA Signor Delio! [aside]—'tis one of my old suitors.
DELIO I was bold to come and see you.
JULIA   Sir, you are welcome.
DELIO Do you lie° here?   lodge
JULIA   Sure, your own experience
Will satisfy you no: our Roman prelates
Do not keep lodging for ladies.
50 DELIO   Very well.
I have brought you no commendations from your husband,
For I know none by him.
JULIA   I hear he's come to Rome.
DELIO I never knew man and beast, of a horse and a knight,
So weary of each other: if he had had a good back,
55 He would have undertook to have borne his horse,
His breech was so pitifully sore.
JULIA   Your laughter
Is my pity.

---

2. The cardinal speaks of himself as a falconer
training a bird (Julia).
3. Like a person under a doctor's care.

4. When riding post, one changed horses at regular intervals without stopping to rest oneself.

DELIO   Lady, I know not whether
You want money, but I have brought you some.
JULIA   From my husband?
DELIO   No, from mine own allowance.
60 JULIA   I must hear the condition, ere I be bound to take it.
DELIO   Look on 't, 'tis gold: hath it not a fine color?
JULIA   I have a bird more beautiful.
DELIO   Try the sound on 't.
JULIA   A lute string far exceeds it:
It hath no smell, like cassia or civet;
65   Nor is it physical,° though some fond° doctors   *medicinal / foolish*
Persuade us seethe 't in cullises:° I'll tell you,   *broth*
This is a creature bred by—
          [*Reenter* SERVANT.]
SERVANT   Your husband's come,
Hath delivered a letter to the Duke of Calabria
That, to my thinking, hath put him out of his wits.   [*Exit.*]
70 JULIA   Sir, you hear:
Pray, let me know your business and your suit
As briefly as can be.
DELIO   With good speed: I would wish you,
At such time as you are nonresident
With your husband, my mistress.
75 JULIA   Sir, I'll go ask my husband if I shall,
And straight return your answer.   [*Exit.*]
DELIO   Very fine!
Is this her wit, or honesty,° that speaks thus?   *chastity*
I heard one say the duke was highly moved
With a letter sent from Malfi. I do fear
80   Antonio is betrayed: how fearfully
Shows his ambition now! Unfortunate fortune!
They pass through whirlpools, and deep woes do shun,
Who the event weigh ere the action's done.[5]   [*Exit.*]

SCENE 5. *The scene continues.*

[*Enter* CARDINAL, *and* FERDINAND *with a letter.*]
FERDINAND   I have this night digged up a mandrake.[1]
CARDINAL   Say you?
FERDINAND   And I am grown mad with 't.
CARDINAL   What's the prodigy?°   *fearful wonder*
FERDINAND   Read there—a sister damned: she's loose i' th' hilts;[2]
Grown a notorious strumpet.
CARDINAL   Speak lower.
FERDINAND   Lower?
5   Rogues do not whisper 't now, but seek to publish 't
(As servants do the bounty of their lords)

---

5. I.e., who judge of actions before seeing their
final consequences.
2.5

1. A fabulous root, violently aphrodisiac but also
deadly poison. Both aspects apply to Ferdinand.
2. I.e., promiscuous.

Aloud; and with a covetous searching eye,
To mark who note them. O, confusion seize her!
She hath had most cunning bawds to serve her turn,
10 And more secure conveyances for lust
Than towns of garrison for service.°   *receiving supplies*

CARDINAL   Is 't possible?
Can this be certain?

FERDINAND   Rhubarb, oh, for rhubarb
To purge this choler![3] Here's the cursèd day
To prompt my memory, and here 't shall stick
15 Till of her bleeding heart I make a sponge
To wipe it out.

CARDINAL   Why do you make yourself
So wild a tempest?

FERDINAND   Would I could be one,
That I might toss her palace 'bout her ears,
Root up her goodly forests, blast her meads,°   *meadows*
20 And lay her general territory as waste
As she hath done her honors.

CARDINAL   Shall our blood,
The royal blood of Aragon and Castile,
Be thus attainted?

FERDINAND   Apply desperate physic:°   *medicine*
We must not now use balsamum,° but fire,°   *balm / cautery*
25 The smarting cupping glass[4] for that's the mean
To purge infected blood, such blood as hers.
There is a kind of pity in mine eye,
I'll give it to my handkercher; and now 'tis here,
I'll bequeath this to her bastard.

CARDINAL   What to do?

30 FERDINAND Why, to make soft lint for his mother's wounds,
When I have hewed her to pieces.

CARDINAL   Cursèd creature!
Unequal nature, to place women's hearts
So far upon the left side![5]

FERDINAND   Foolish men,
That e'er will trust their honor in a bark
35 Made of so slight weak bulrush as is woman,
Apt every minute to sink it!

CARDINAL Thus ignorance, when it hath purchased honor,
It cannot wield it.

FERDINAND   Methinks I see her laughing—
Excellent hyena! Talk to me somewhat, quickly,
40 Or my imagination will carry me
To see her in the shameful act of sin.

CARDINAL With whom?

FERDINAND Haply° with some strong-thighed bargeman,   *perhaps*

3. Rhubarb, as a laxative, was thought curative of the high pressures of hot rage.
4. By which people were bled.

5. The left is the sinister side, associated with bad luck, deceit, and passion.

Or one o' th' wood-yard that can quoit the sledge°   *throw the hammer*
45 Or toss the bar,[6] or else some lovely squire
That carries coal up to her privy lodgings.
CARDINAL You fly beyond your reason.
FERDINAND   Go to, mistress!
'Tis not your whore's milk that shall quench my wild fire,
But your whore's blood.
50 CARDINAL How idly shows this rage, which carries you,
As men conveyed by witches through the air,
On violent whirlwinds! This intemperate noise
Fitly resembles deaf men's shrill discourse,
Who talk aloud,° thinking all other men   *loudly*
To have their imperfection.
55 FERDINAND   Have not you
My palsy?
CARDINAL Yes, I can be angry, but
Without this rupture: there is not in nature
A thing that makes man so deformed, so beastly,
As doth intemperate anger. Chide yourself.
60 You have divers men who never yet expressed
Their strong desire of rest but by unrest,
By vexing of themselves. Come, put yourself
In tune.
FERDINAND So; I will only study to seem
The thing I am not. I could kill her now,
65 In you, or in myself; for I do think
It is some sin in us heaven doth revenge
By her.
CARDINAL Are you stark mad?
FERDINAND   I would have their bodies
Burnt in a coal pit with the ventage° stopped,   *chimney*
That their cursed smoke might not ascend to heaven;
70 Or dip the sheets they lie in in pitch or sulphur,
Wrap them in 't, and then light them like a match;
Or else to boil their bastard to a cullis,°   *broth*
And give 't his lecherous father to renew°   *repair*
The sin of his back.[7]
CARDINAL   I'll leave you.
FERDINAND   Nay, I have done.
75 I am confident, had I been damned in hell,
And should have heard of this, it would have put me
Into a cold sweat. In, in; I'll go sleep.
Till I know who leaps my sister, I'll not stir:
That known, I'll find scorpions to string my whips,[8]
80 And fix her in a general eclipse.   *[Exeunt.]*

---

6. Gross tests of strength.
7. As Atreus did to Thyestes in Greek legend.
"The sin of his back": sexual capacity.
8. Tipping the thongs of a whip with "scorpions"

(tips of jagged steel or lead that sting and bite the flesh) is an old metaphor for aggravated punishment.

Act 3

SCENE 1. *Amalfi.*

[*Enter* ANTONIO *and* DELIO.]

ANTONIO   Our noble friend, my most belovèd Delio!
Oh, you have been a stranger long at court;
Came you along with the Lord Ferdinand?

DELIO   I did, sir. And how fares your noble duchess?

5 ANTONIO   Right fortunately well: she's an excellent
Feeder of pedigrees; since you last saw her,
She hath had two children more, a son and daughter.

DELIO   Methinks 'twas yesterday: let me but wink,
And not behold your face, which to mine eye
10 Is somewhat leaner, verily I should dream
It were within this half-hour.

ANTONIO   You have not been in law, friend Delio,
Nor in prison, nor a suitor at the court,
Nor begged the reversion of some great man's place,
15 Nor troubled with an old wife, which doth make
Your time so insensibly° hasten.   *imperceptibly*

DELIO   Pray, sir, tell me,
Hath not this news arrived yet to the ear
Of the Lord Cardinal?

ANTONIO   I fear it hath:
The Lord Ferdinand, that's newly come to court,
Doth bear himself right dangerously.

20 DELIO   Pray, why?

ANTONIO   He is so quiet that he seems to sleep
The tempest out, as dormice do in winter.
Those houses that are haunted are most still
Till the devil be up.

DELIO   What say the common people?

25 ANTONIO   The common rabble do directly say
She is a strumpet.

DELIO   And your graver heads,
Which would be politic,° what censure° they?   *statesmanlike / opine*

ANTONIO   They do observe I grow to infinite purchase
The left-hand way,¹ and all suppose the duchess
30 Would amend it, if she could; for, say they,
Great princes, though they grudge their officers
Should have such large and unconfinèd means
To get wealth under them, will not complain,
Lest thereby they should make them odious
35 Unto the people; for other obligation
Of love or marriage between her and me
They never dream of.

3.1
1. I.e., they think I am getting rich dishonestly.

DELIO   The Lord Ferdinand
  Is going to bed.
      [*Enter* DUCHESS, FERDINAND, *and* BOSOLA.]
FERDINAND   I'll instantly to bed,
  For I am weary.—I am to bespeak
  A husband for you.
40 DUCHESS   For me, sir? Pray, who is 't?
FERDINAND   The great Count Malateste.
DUCHESS   Fie upon him!
  A count? He's a mere stick of sugar candy;
  You may look quite through him. When I choose
  A husband, I will marry for your honor.
45 FERDINAND   You shall do well in 't.—How is 't, worthy Antonio?
DUCHESS   But, sir, I am to have private conference with you
  About a scandalous report is spread
  Touching mine honor.
FERDINAND   Let me be ever deaf to 't:
  One of Pasquil's paper bullets,[2] court-calumny,
50   A pestilent air, which princes' palaces
  Are seldom purged of. Yet, say that it were true,
  I pour it in your bosom, my fixed love
  Would strongly excuse, extenuate, nay, deny
  Faults, were they apparent in you. Go, be safe
  In your own innocency.
55 DUCHESS [*aside*]   O blessèd comfort!
  This deadly air is purged.
      [*Exeunt* DUCHESS, ANTONIO, *and* DELIO.]
FERDINAND   Her guilt treads on
  Hot-burning coulters.[3] Now, Bosola,
  How thrives our intelligence?°   *detective work*
BOSOLA   Sir, uncertainly:
  'Tis rumored she hath had three bastards, but
  By whom, we may go read i' th' stars.
60 FERDINAND   Why, some
  Hold opinion all things are written there.
BOSOLA   Yes, if we could find spectacles to read them.
  I do suspect there hath been some sorcery
  Used on the duchess.
FERDINAND   Sorcery? To what purpose?
65 BOSOLA   To make her dote on some desertless fellow
  She shames to acknowledge.
FERDINAND   Can your faith give way
  To think there's power in potions or in charms,
  To make us love whether we will or no?
BOSOLA   Most certainly.
70 FERDINAND   Away! These are mere gulleries,° horrid things,   *deceits*

---

2. Anonymous satires were traditionally pasted on the statue of Pasquillo, or Pasquino, near Piazza Navona in Rome, and attributed to his authorship.

3. Medieval chastity inquests customarily required the questioned lady to walk barefoot over red-hot plowshares ("coulters").

Invented by some cheating mountebanks[4]
To abuse us. Do you think that herbs or charms
Can force the will? Some trials have been made
In this foolish practice, but the ingredients
75   Were lenitive° poisons, such as are of force   *slow-working*
To make the patient mad; and straight the witch
Swears by equivocation they are in love.
The witchcraft lies in her rank° blood. This night   *wanton*
I will force confession from her. You told me
80   You had got, within these two days, a false° key   *unauthorized*
Into her bedchamber.
BOSOLA   I have.
FERDINAND   As I would wish.
BOSOLA What do you intend to do?
FERDINAND   Can you guess?
BOSOLA   No.
FERDINAND Do not ask, then:
He that can compass° me, and know my drifts,°   *comprehend / purposes*
85   May say he hath put a girdle 'bout the world,
And sounded all her quicksands.
BOSOLA   I do not
Think so.
FERDINAND What do you think, then, pray?
BOSOLA   That you
Are your own chronicle too much, and grossly
Flatter yourself.
FERDINAND   Give me thy hand; I thank thee:
90   I ne'er gave pension but to flatterers,
Till I entertained° thee. Farewell.   *employed*
That friend a great man's ruin strongly checks,
Who rails into his belief all his defects.   [*Exeunt.*]

SCENE 2. *The bedchamber of the* DUCHESS.

[*Enter* DUCHESS, ANTONIO, *and* CARIOLA.]
DUCHESS Bring me the casket hither, and the glass.
You get no lodging here tonight, my lord.
ANTONIO Indeed, I must persuade one.
DUCHESS   Very good:
I hope in time 'twill grow into a custom,
5   That noblemen shall come with cap and knee
To purchase a night's lodging of their wives.
ANTONIO I must lie here.
DUCHESS   Must! You are a lord of misrule.[1]
ANTONIO Indeed, my rule is only in the night.
DUCHESS To what use will you put me?
ANTONIO   We'll sleep together.
10 DUCHESS Alas, what pleasure can two lovers find in sleep?

4. A mixture of street entertainer and patent
medicine salesman.

3.2
1. The mock-monarch of a carnival festival.

CARIOLA   My lord, I lie with her often, and I know
　　She'll much disquiet you.
ANTONIO　　　　　　　　　　See, you are complained of.
CARIOLA   For she's the sprawling'st bedfellow.
ANTONIO　　　　　　　　　　　　　　　I shall like her
　　The better for that.
CARIOLA　　　　　　　　Sir, shall I ask you a question?
ANTONIO   I pray thee, Cariola.
15　CARIOLA　　　　　　　　Wherefore still,° when you lie　　　*always*
　　with my lady,
　　Do you rise so early?
ANTONIO　　　　　　　　Laboring men
　　Count the clock oftenest, Cariola,
　　Are glad when their task's ended.
DUCHESS　　　　　　　　　　I'll stop your mouth.　[*Kisses him.*]
ANTONIO   Nay, that's but one; Venus had two soft doves
20　To draw her chariot; I must have another—　[*She kisses him again.*]
　　When wilt thou marry, Cariola?
CARIOLA　　　　　　　　　Never, my lord.
ANTONIO   Oh, fie upon this single life! Forgo it.
　　We read how Daphne, for her peevish flight,
　　Became a fruitless bay tree; Syrinx turned
25　To the pale empty reed; Anaxarete
　　Was frozen into marble: whereas those
　　Which married, or proved kind unto their friends,
　　Were by a gracious influence trans-shaped
　　Into the olive, pomegranate, mulberry,
30　Became flowers, precious stones, or eminent stars.[2]
CARIOLA   This is a vain poetry, but I pray you tell me,
　　If there were proposed me, wisdom, riches, and beauty,
　　In three several young men, which should I choose?
ANTONIO   'Tis a hard question: this was Paris' case,
35　And he was blind in 't, and there was great cause;
　　For how was 't possible he could judge right,
　　Having three amorous goddesses in view,
　　And they stark naked? 'Twas a motion[3]
　　Were able to benight the apprehension
40　Of the severest counselor of Europe.
　　Now I look on both your faces so well formed,
　　It puts me in mind of a question I would ask.
CARIOLA   What is 't?
ANTONIO　　　　　　　　I do wonder why hard-favored ladies,
　　For the most part, keep worse-favored waiting women
45　To attend them, and cannot endure fair ones.

---

2. The olive was created by Athena; the mulberry gained its color from the blood of Pyramus and Thisbe; the pomegranate seems to have no particular mythological origin. Most of the other stories of ladies being transformed for complying, or not complying, with the solicitations of a god are from Ovid's *Metamorphoses*.

3. Spectacle. Paris had to choose among Hera, Athena, and Aphrodite, goddesses of regal power, wisdom, and love; his selecting the third led to the Trojan War.

DUCHESS   Oh, that's soon answered.
　　Did you ever in your life know an ill painter
　　Desire to have his dwelling next door to the shop
　　Of an excellent picture-maker? 'Twould disgrace
50　His face-making, and undo him. I prithee,
　　When were we so merry?—My hair tangles.
ANTONIO   Pray thee, Cariola, let's steal forth the room,
　　And let her talk to herself: I have divers times
　　Served her the like, when she hath chafed extremely.
55　I love to see her angry. Softly, Cariola.   [*Exeunt* ANTONIO *and* CARIOLA.]
DUCHESS   Doth not the color of my hair 'gin to change?
　　When I wax gray, I shall have all the court
　　Powder their hair with arras,⁴ to be like me.
　　You have cause to love me; I entered you into my heart
60　Before you would vouchsafe to call for the keys.
　　　　[*Enter* FERDINAND *behind.*]
　　We shall one day have my brothers take you napping;
　　Methinks his presence, being now in court,
　　Should make you keep your own bed; but you'll say
　　Love mixed with fear is sweetest. I'll assure you,
65　You shall get no more children till my brothers
　　Consent to be your gossips.⁵ Have you lost your tongue?
　　　　　　　　　　　　[*She turns and sees* FERDINAND.]
　　'Tis welcome:
　　For know, whether I am doomed to live or die,
　　I can do both like a prince.
FERDINAND　　　　　　　　Die, then, quickly! [*Giving her a poniard.*⁶]
70　Virtue, where art thou hid? What hideous thing
　　Is it that doth eclipse thee?
DUCHESS　　　　　　　　Pray, sir, hear me.
FERDINAND   Or is it true thou art but a bare name,
　　And no essential° thing?　　　　　　　　　　　　　　　*actual*
DUCHESS　　　　　Sir—
FERDINAND　　　　　　　　Do not speak.
DUCHESS   No, sir: I will plant my soul in mine ears, to hear you.
75　FERDINAND   O most imperfect light of human reason,
　　That mak'st us so unhappy to foresee
　　What we can least prevent! Pursue thy wishes,
　　And glory in them: there's in shame no comfort
　　But to be past all bounds and sense of shame.
DUCHESS   I pray, sir, hear me. I am married.
80　FERDINAND　　　　　　　　　　　　So!
DUCHESS   Haply,° not to your liking: but for that,　　　　*perhaps*
　　Alas, your shears do come untimely now
　　To clip the bird's wings that's already flown!
　　Will you see my husband?

---

4. Orris root, used in powdered form to make　　5. Sponsors in baptism.
hair artificially gray.　　　　　　　　　　　　6. A knife.

FERDINAND   Yes, if I could change
  Eyes with a basilisk.[7]
85 DUCHESS   Sure, you came hither
  By his confederacy.
  FERDINAND   The howling of a wolf
  Is music to thee, screech owl: prithee, peace.
  Whate'er thou art that hast enjoyed my sister,
  For I am sure thou hear'st me, for thine own sake
90 Let me not know thee. I came hither prepared
  To work thy discovery; yet am now persuaded
  It would beget such violent effects
  As would damn us both. I would not for ten millions
  I had beheld thee: therefore use all means
95 I never may have knowledge of thy name;
  Enjoy thy lust still, and a wretched life,
  On that condition. And for thee, vile woman,
  If thou do wish thy lecher may grow old
  In thy embracements, I would have thee build
100 Such a room for him as our anchorites
  To holier use inhabit. Let not the sun
  Shine on him till he's dead; let dogs and monkeys
  Only converse with him, and such dumb things
  To whom nature denies use to sound his name;
105 Do not keep a paraquito,° lest she learn it;   *parrot*
  If thou do love him, cut out thine own tongue,
  Lest it bewray° him.   *betray*
  DUCHESS   Why might not I marry?
  I have not gone about in this to create
  Any new world or custom.
  FERDINAND   Thou art undone;
110 And thou hast ta'en that massy sheet of lead
  That hid thy husband's bones, and folded it
  About my heart.
  DUCHESS   Mine bleeds for 't.
  FERDINAND   Thine? Thy heart?
  What should I name 't unless a hollow bullet
  Filled with unquenchable wildfire?
  DUCHESS   You are in this
115 Too strict, and were you not my princely brother,
  I would say, too willful. My reputation
  Is safe.
  FERDINAND   Dost thou know what reputation is?
  I'll tell thee—to small purpose, since the instruction
  Comes now too late.
120 Upon a time, Reputation, Love, and Death
  Would travel o'er the world; and it was concluded
  That they should part, and take three several ways.
  Death told them, they should find him in great battles,

---

7. Monster that was fabled to kill with a glance.

Or cities plagued with plagues. Love gives them counsel
125 To inquire for him 'mongst unambitious shepherds,
Where dowries were not talked of, and sometimes
'Mongst quiet kindred that had nothing left
By their dead parents. "Stay," quoth Reputation,
"Do not forsake me; for it is my nature,
130 If once I part from any man I meet,
I am never found again." And so for you:
You have shook hands° with Reputation,   *parted*
And made him invisible. So, fare you well.
I will never see you more.
DUCHESS   Why should only I,
135 Of all the other princes of the world,
Be cased up, like a holy relic? I have youth
And a little beauty.
FERDINAND   So you have some virgins
That are witches. I will never see thee more.   [*Exit.*]
        [*Enter* ANTONIO *with a pistol, and* CARIOLA.]
DUCHESS   You saw this apparition?
ANTONIO   Yes. We are
140 Betrayed. How came he hither? I should turn
This to thee, for that.   [*Pointing the pistol at* CARIOLA.]
CARIOLA   Pray, sir, do; and when
That you have cleft my heart, you shall read there
Mine innocence.
DUCHESS   That gallery gave him entrance.
ANTONIO   I would this terrible thing would come again,
145 That, standing on my guard, I might relate
My warrantable⁸ love.   [*She shows the poniard.*]
                    Ha! What means this?
DUCHESS   He left this with me.
ANTONIO   And it seems did wish
You would use it on yourself.
DUCHESS   His action seemed
To intend so much.
ANTONIO   This hath a handle to 't
150 As well as a point: turn it towards him, and
So fasten the keen edge in his rank gall.   [*Knocking within.*]
How now! Who knocks? More earthquakes?
DUCHESS   I stand
As if a mine beneath my feet were ready
To be blown up.
CARIOLA   'Tis Bosola.
DUCHESS   Away!
155 O misery! Methinks unjust actions
Should wear these masks and curtains, and not we.
You must instantly part hence: I have fashioned it already.
                                [*Exit* ANTONIO.]

8. Legitimate, defensible.

[*Enter* BOSOLA.]

BOSOLA   The duke your brother is ta'en up in a whirlwind,
    Hath took horse, and 's rid post to Rome.

DUCHESS   So late?

160 BOSOLA   He told me, as he mounted into th' saddle,
    You were undone.

DUCHESS   Indeed, I am very near it.

BOSOLA   What's the matter?

DUCHESS   Antonio, the master of our household,
    Hath dealt so falsely with me in 's accounts:
165 My brother stood engaged with me for money
    Ta'en up of certain Neapolitan Jews,
    And Antonio lets the bonds be forfeit.⁹

BOSOLA   Strange!—[*aside*] This is cunning.

DUCHESS   And hereupon
    My brother's bills at Naples are protested
    Against.¹—Call up our officers.

170 BOSOLA   I shall.   [*Exit.*]

    [*Reenter* ANTONIO.]

DUCHESS   The place that you must fly to is Ancona:²
    Hire a house there; I'll send after you
    My treasure and my jewels. Our weak safety
    Runs upon enginous wheels: short syllables
175 Must stand for periods.³ I must now accuse you
    Of such a feignèd crime as Tasso calls
    Magnanima menzogna, a noble lie,
    'Cause it must shield our honors. Hark! They are coming.

    [*Reenter* BOSOLA *and* OFFICERS.]

ANTONIO   Will your grace hear me?

180 DUCHESS   I have got well by you; you have yielded me
    A million of loss: I am like to inherit
    The people's curses for your stewardship.
    You had the trick in audit time to be sick,
    Till I had signed your *quietus*;° and that cured you   *receipt*
185 Without help of a doctor.—Gentlemen,
    I would have this man be an example to you all;
    So shall you hold my favor; I pray, let him;°   *release him*
    For he's done that, alas, you would not think of,
    And, because I intend to be rid of him,
190 I mean not to publish. [*to* ANTONIO] Use your fortune elsewhere.

ANTONIO   I am strongly armed to brook my overthrow;
    As commonly men bear with a hard year,
    I will not blame the cause on 't; but do think
    The necessity of my malevolent star

---

9. I.e., my brother stood security for some money I
borrowed from Neapolitan moneylenders; now
Antonio has let them call on the duke for payment.
1. I.e., Duke Ferdinand's checks have bounced.
2. On the Adriatic coast of Italy, across the peninsula from Amalfi and well to the north.

3. Full sentences. "Enginous": delicately balanced, as in clockwork. The allusion to Tasso
(next line) is literally accurate (*Jerusalem Delivered* 2.22) but anachronistic, since Tasso's poem
was not published until 1574.

195　Procures this, not her humor. Oh, the inconstant
　　And rotten ground of service! You may see,
　　'Tis even like him that in a winter night
　　Takes a long slumber o'er a dying fire,
　　As loath to part from 't; yet parts thence as cold
200　As when he first sat down.

DUCHESS　　　　　　　　　　We do confiscate,
　　Towards the satisfying of your accounts,
　　All that you have.

ANTONIO　　　　　　　I am yours, and 'tis very fit
　　All mine should be so.

DUCHESS　　　　　　　So, sir, you have your pass.°　　　　　*passport*

ANTONIO　You may see, gentlemen, what 'tis to serve
205　A prince with body and soul.　　　　　　　[*Exit.*]

BOSOLA　Here's an example for extortion: what moisture is drawn out of the
　　sea, when foul weather comes, pours down, and runs into the sea again.

DUCHESS　I would know what are your opinions of this Antonio.

SECOND OFFICER　He could not abide to see a pig's head gaping: I thought
210　your grace would find him a Jew.[4]

THIRD OFFICER　I would you had been his officer, for your own sake.

FOURTH OFFICER　You would have had more money.

FIRST OFFICER　He stopped his ears with black wool, and to those came to
　　him for money said he was thick of hearing.

215　SECOND OFFICER　Some said he was an hermaphrodite, for he could not
　　abide a woman.

FOURTH OFFICER　How scurvy proud he would look when the treasury was
　　full! Well, let him go!

FIRST OFFICER　Yes, and the chippings of the buttery fly after him, to scour
220　his gold chain![5]

DUCHESS　Leave us. [*Exeunt* OFFICERS.] What do you think of these?

BOSOLA　That these are rogues that in 's prosperity, but to have waited on his
　　fortune, could have wished his dirty stirrup riveted through their noses,
　　and followed after 's mule, like a bear in a ring; would have prostituted their
225　daughters to his lust; made their firstborn intelligencers;[6] thought none
　　happy but such as were born under his blessed planet, and wore his livery:
　　and do these lice drop off now? Well, never look to have the like again:[7]
　　he hath left a sort of flattering rogues behind him; their doom must fol-
　　low. Princes pay flatterers in their own money: flatterers dissemble their
230　vices, and they dissemble their lies; that's justice. Alas, poor gentleman!

DUCHESS　Poor? He hath amply filled his coffers.

BOSOLA　Sure, he was too honest. Pluto, the god of riches, when he 's sent
　　by Jupiter to any man, he goes limping, to signify that wealth that comes
　　on God's name comes slowly; but when he's sent on the devil's errand, he
235　rides post and comes in by scuttles. Let me show you what a most unval-
　　ued[8] jewel you have in a wanton humor thrown away, to bless the man

4. Jews were identified by their antipathy to pork,
but the assumptions here are deliberately ridiculous.
5. A gold chain was the steward's traditional
badge of office. Bread crumbs (the "chippings of

the buttery") were used to polish gold and silver
plate.
6. Spies.
7. I.e., a servant as good as he was.
8. Invaluable. "By scuttles": in haste.

shall[9] find him. He was an excellent courtier and most faithful; a soldier that thought it as beastly to know his own value too little as devilish to acknowledge it too much. Both his virtue and form deserved a far better 240 fortune: his discourse rather delighted to judge itself than show itself; his breast was filled with all perfection, and yet it seemed a private whispering-room, it made so little noise of 't.

DUCHESS   But he was basely descended.

BOSOLA   Will you make yourself a mercenary herald, rather to examine 245 men's pedigrees than virtues? You shall want[1] him: for know, an honest statesman to a prince is like a cedar planted by a spring; the spring bathes the tree's root, the grateful tree rewards it with his shadow: you have not done so. I would sooner swim to the Bermoothes[2] on two politicians' rotten bladders, tied together with an intelligencer's heartstring, than depend 250 on so changeable a prince's favor. Fare thee well, Antonio! Since the malice of the world would needs down with thee, it cannot be said yet that any ill happened unto thee, considering thy fall was accompanied with virtue.

DUCHESS   Oh, you render me excellent music!

BOSOLA   Say you?

DUCHESS   This good one that you speak of is my husband.

255 BOSOLA   Do I not dream? Can this ambitious age
Have so much goodness in 't as to prefer
A man merely for worth, without these shadows
Of wealth and painted honors? Possible?

DUCHESS   I have had three children by him.

BOSOLA   Fortunate lady!

260 For you have made your private nuptial bed
The humble and fair seminary° of peace.   seedbed
No question but many an unbeneficed scholar[3]
Shall pray for you for this deed, and rejoice
That some preferment in the world can yet
265 Arise from merit. The virgins of your land
That have no dowries shall hope your example
Will raise them to rich husbands. Should you want
Soldiers, 'twould make the very Turks and Moors
Turn Christians, and serve you for this act.
270 Last, the neglected poets of your time,
In honor of this trophy of a man,
Raised by that curious° engine, your white hand,   exquisite
Shall thank you, in your grave, for 't; and make that
More reverend than all the cabinets
275 Of living princes.[4] For Antonio,
His fame shall likewise flow from many a pen,
When heralds shall want coats to sell to men.[5]

9. Who shall.
1. Miss.
2. The Bermudas, unknown at the time of the action, but very topical a hundred years later, when the play was written.
3. A scholar without an official appointment.

4. She will be more honored in her grave than living princes in their courts. "Cabinets": council chambers.
5. The Heralds' College (an English royal corporation) carried on a brisk trade in coats of arms.

DUCHESS As I taste comfort in this friendly speech,
 So would I find concealment.
280 BOSOLA Oh, the secret of my prince,
 Which I will wear on th' inside of my heart!
DUCHESS You shall take charge of all my coin and jewels,
 And follow him; for he retires himself
 To Ancona.
BOSOLA So.
DUCHESS Whither, within few days,
 I mean to follow thee.
285 BOSOLA Let me think:
 I would wish your grace to feign a pilgrimage
 To our Lady of Loreto,[6] scarce seven leagues
 From fair Ancona; so may you depart
 Your country with more honor, and your flight
290 Will seem a princely progress,° retaining   state journey
 Your usual train about you.
DUCHESS Sir, your direction
 Shall lead me by the hand.
CARIOLA In my opinion,
 She were better progress to the baths at Lucca,
 Or go visit the Spa in Germany;
295 For, if you will believe me, I do not like
 This jesting with religion, this feigned
 Pilgrimage.
DUCHESS Thou art a superstitious fool.
 Prepare us instantly for our departure.
 Past sorrows, let us moderately lament them;
300 For those to come, seek wisely to prevent them.
                    [Exit DUCHESS, with CARIOLA.]
BOSOLA A politician° is the devil's quilted anvil;   crafty intriguer
 He fashions all sins on him, and the blows
 Are never heard: he may work in a lady's chamber,
 As here for proof. What rests° but I reveal   remains
305 All to my lord? Oh, this base quality
 Of intelligencer! Why, every quality° i' th' world   profession
 Prefers° but gain or commendation: offers
 Now for this act I am certain to be raised,
 And men that paint weeds to the life are praised.   [Exit.]

                    SCENE 3. Rome.

     [Enter CARDINAL, FERDINAND, MALATESTE, PESCARA, SILVIO, DELIO.]
CARDINAL Must we turn soldier, then?
MALATESTE The Emperor,[1]
 Hearing your worth that way, ere you attained
 This reverend garment, joins you in commission

6. The shrine of the Virgin at Loreto was famous   3.3
throughout Europe.   1. The Spanish emperor, Charles V.

With the right fortunate soldier the Marquis of Pescara,
And the famous Lannoy.

5 CARDINAL   He that had the honor
Of taking the French king prisoner?[2]

MALATESTE   The same.
Here's a plot drawn for a new fortification
At Naples.   [*They talk apart.*]

FERDINAND   This great Count Malateste, I perceive,
Hath got employment?

DELIO   No employment, my lord;
10 A marginal note in the muster book, that he is
A voluntary lord.

FERDINAND   He's no soldier?

DELIO   He has worn gunpowder in 's hollow tooth for the toothache.[3]

SILVIO   He comes to the leaguer° with a full intent   siege
To eat fresh beef and garlic, means to stay
15 Till the scent be gone, and straight return to court.

DELIO   He hath read all the late service[4] as the city chronicle relates it,
and keeps two painters going, only to express battles in model.

SILVIO   Then he'll fight by the book.

DELIO   By the almanac, I think, to choose good days and shun the critical.
20 That's his mistress' scarf.

SILVIO   Yes, he protests he would do much for that taffeta.

DELIO   I think he would run away from a battle, to save it from taking[5]
prisoner.

SILVIO   He is horribly afraid gunpowder will spoil the perfume on 't.

25 DELIO   I saw a Dutchman break his pate once for calling him pot-gun;[6]
he made his head have a bore in 't like a musket.

SILVIO   I would he had made a touchhole to 't. He is indeed a guarded
sumpter cloth,[7] only for the remove of the court.

[*Enter* BOSOLA *and speaks to* FERDINAND *and the* CARDINAL.]

PESCARA   Bosola arrived? What should be the business?
30 Some falling out amongst the cardinals.
These factions amongst great men, they are like
Foxes; when their heads are divided,
They carry fire in their tails, and all the country
About them goes to wrack for 't.[8]

SILVIO   What's that Bosola?

35 DELIO   I knew him in Padua—a fantastical scholar, like such who study
to know how many knots were in Hercules' club, of what color Achilles'
beard was, or whether Hector were not troubled with the toothache.
He hath studied himself half blear-eyed to know the true symmetry of

---

2. Charles de Lannoy, Belgian by origin, did
indeed capture Francis I at Pavia in 1525, about
two decades after the date of the play's supposed
action. "Pescara": also a commander at Pavia.
3. Saltpeter was sometimes used to relieve a
toothache.
4. Recent military operations.
5. Being taken.

6. Popgun.
7. Decorated saddlecloth used only when the
court is changing its residence; i.e., he's only for
show. "Touchhole": where the match was applied
to set off a cannon.
8. Samson once tied some foxes together by the
tail and set them afire to burn down the fields of
the Philistines (Judges 15).

Caesar's nose by a shoeing-horn; and this he did to gain the name of a
40 speculative[9] man.
PESCARA Mark Prince Ferdinand:
A very salamander lives in 's eye,
To mock the eager violence of fire.[1]
SILVIO That Cardinal hath made more bad faces with his oppression
45 than ever Michelangelo[2] made good ones: he lifts up 's nose, like a foul
porpoise before a storm.
PESCARA The Lord Ferdinand laughs.
DELIO Like a deadly cannon that lightens ere it smokes.
PESCARA These are your true pangs of death,
50 The pangs of life, that struggle with great statesmen.
DELIO In such a deformed silence witches whisper
Their charms.
CARDINAL   Doth she make religion her riding hood
To keep her from the sun and tempest?
FERDINAND   That,
That damns her. Methinks her fault and beauty,
55 Blended together, show like leprosy,
The whiter, the fouler. I make it a question
Whether her beggarly brats were ever christened.
CARDINAL I will instantly solicit the state of Ancona
To have them banished.
FERDINAND   You are for Loreto?
60 I shall not be at your ceremony; fare you well.
Write to the Duke of Malfi, my young nephew
She had by her first husband, and acquaint him
With 's mother's honesty.
BOSOLA   I will.
FERDINAND   Antonio!
A slave that only smelled of ink and counters,
65 And never in 's life looked like a gentleman,
But in the audit time. Go, go presently,°   *at once*
Draw me out an hundred and fifty of our horse,°   *cavalry*
And meet me at the fort-bridge.[3]   [*Exeunt.*]

SCENE 4. *The shrine of Our Lady of Loreto.*

[*Enter* TWO PILGRIMS.]
FIRST PILGRIM I have not seen a goodlier shrine than this;
Yet I have visited many.
SECOND PILGRIM   The Cardinal of Aragon
Is this day to resign his cardinal's hat:
His sister duchess likewise is arrived
5 To pay her vow of pilgrimage. I expect

---

9. Profound, given to abstract thoughts. Intense
and especially fantastical scholarship was
thought to be a cause of melancholy—Bosola's
temperament—caused by an imbalance of black
bile.
1. The salamander was supposed to be so cold

and wet of constitution that it could live in fire.
2. Michelangelo Buonarroti (1475–1564), the
great Florentine painter and sculptor. Another
anachronism.
3. Drawbridge.

A noble ceremony.

FIRST PILGRIM   No question. They come.

[*Here the ceremony of the* CARDINAL'S *installment in the habit of a
soldier: performed in delivering up his cross, hat, robes, and ring
at the shrine, and investing him with sword, helmet, shield, and
spurs; then* ANTONIO, *the* DUCHESS, *and their children, having
presented themselves at the shrine, are, by a form of banishment in
dumb show expressed towards them by the* CARDINAL *and the state
of Ancona, banished: during all which ceremony, this ditty is sung,
to very solemn music, by divers churchmen.*][1]

Arms and honors deck thy story,
To thy fame's eternal glory!
Adverse fortune ever fly thee;

10   No disastrous fate come nigh thee!

I alone will sing thy praises,
Whom to honor virtue raises;
And thy study, that divine is,
Bent to martial discipline is.

15   Lay aside all those robes lie by thee;
Crown thy arts with arms, they'll beautify thee.

O worthy of worthiest name, adorned in this manner,
Lead bravely thy forces on under war's warlike banner!
Oh, mayst thou prove fortunate in all martial courses!

20   Guide thou still by skill in arts and forces!
Victory attend thee nigh, whilst fame sings loud thy powers;
Triumphant conquest crown thy head, and blessings pour down showers!

[*Exeunt all except the* TWO PILGRIMS.]

FIRST PILGRIM   Here's a strange turn of state! Who would have thought
So great a lady would have matched herself

25   Unto so mean a person? Yet the cardinal
Bears himself much too cruel.

SECOND PILGRIM   They are banished.

FIRST PILGRIM   But I would ask what power hath this state
Of Ancona to determine[2] of a free prince?

SECOND PILGRIM   They are a free state, sir, and her brother showed

30   How that the pope, fore-hearing of her looseness,
Hath seized into the protection of the church
The dukedom which she held as dowager.[3]

FIRST PILGRIM   But by what justice?

SECOND PILGRIM   Sure, I think by none,
Only her brother's instigation.

35   FIRST PILGRIM   What was it with such violence he took
Off from her finger?

SECOND PILGRIM   'Twas her wedding ring,

3.4
1. This song is not very suitable to the scene, and
Webster, in the edition of 1623, denied writing it.

2. Pass judgment on.
3. As widow to her first husband, the Duke of
Malfi.

Which he vowed shortly he would sacrifice
To his revenge.
FIRST PILGRIM   Alas, Antonio!
If that a man be thrust into a well,
40   No matter who sets hands to 't, his own weight
Will bring him sooner to th' bottom. Come, let's hence.
Fortune makes this conclusion general,
All things do help th' unhappy man to fall.   [*Exeunt.*]

SCENE 5. *Near Loreto.*

[*Enter* DUCHESS, ANTONIO, CHILDREN, CARIOLA, *and* SERVANTS.]
DUCHESS   Banished Ancona!
ANTONIO   Yes, you see what power
Lightens° in great men's breath.   *flashes out*
DUCHESS   Is all our train
Shrunk to this poor remainder?
ANTONIO   These poor men,
Which have got little in your service, vow
5   To take your fortune, but your wiser buntings,[1]
Now they are fledged, are gone.
DUCHESS   They have done wisely.
This puts me in mind of death: physicians thus,
With their hands full of money, use° to give o'er   *are accustomed*
Their patients.
ANTONIO   Right° the fashion of the world: *exactly*
10   From decayed fortunes every flatterer shrinks;
Men cease to build where the foundation sinks.
DUCHESS   I had a very strange dream tonight.°   *last night*
ANTONIO   What was 't?
DUCHESS   Methought I wore my coronet of state,
And on a sudden all the diamonds
Were changed to pearls.
15   ANTONIO   My interpretation
Is, you'll weep shortly, for to me the pearls
Do signify your tears.
DUCHESS   The birds that live
I' th' field on the wild benefit of nature
Live happier than we; for they may choose their mates,
20   And carol their sweet pleasures to the spring.
[*Enter* BOSOLA *with a letter.*]
BOSOLA   You are happily o'erta'en.
DUCHESS   From my brother?
BOSOLA   Yes, from the Lord Ferdinand your brother
All love and safety.
DUCHESS   Thou dost blanch° mischief,   *whitewash*
Wouldst make it white. See, see, like to calm weather
25   At sea before a tempest, false hearts speak fair

3.5
1. Migratory birds. "Take": accept.

To those they intend most mischief.
[*reads*] "Send Antonio to me; I want his head in a business."
A politic equivocation!
He doth not want your counsel, but your head;
30   That is, he cannot sleep till you be dead.
And here's another pitfall that's strewed o'er
With roses: mark it, 'tis a cunning one:
"I stand engaged for your husband for several debts at Naples: let not
that trouble him; I had rather have his heart than his money."
And I believe so too.
35 BOSOLA   What do you believe?
DUCHESS   That he so much distrusts my husband's love,
He will by no means believe his heart is with him
Until he see it: the devil is not cunning
Enough to circumvent us in riddles.
40 BOSOLA   Will you reject that noble and free league
Of amity and love which I present you?
DUCHESS   Their league is like that of some politic° kings,   *crafty*
Only to make themselves of strength and power
To be our after-ruin: tell them so.
BOSOLA   And what from you?
45 ANTONIO   Thus tell him: I will not come.
BOSOLA   And what of this? [*Pointing to the letter.*]
ANTONIO   My brothers have dispersed
Bloodhounds abroad; which till I hear are muzzled,
No truce, though hatched with ne'er such politic skill,
Is safe, that hangs upon our enemies' will.
I'll not come at° them.   *to*
50 BOSOLA   This proclaims your breeding:
Every small thing draws a base mind to fear,
As the adamant° draws iron. Fare you well, sir;   *lodestone*
You shall shortly hear from 's.   [*Exit.*]
DUCHESS   I suspect some ambush;
Therefore, by all my love I do conjure you
55   To take your eldest son, and fly towards Milan.
Let us not venture all this poor remainder
In one unlucky bottom.[2]
ANTONIO   You counsel safely.
Best of my life, farewell. Since we must part,
Heaven hath a hand in 't, but no otherwise
60   Than as some curious artist takes in sunder
A clock or watch, when it is out of frame,[3]
To bring 't in better order.
DUCHESS   I know not which is best,
To see you dead, or part with you. Farewell, boy:
65   Thou art happy that thou hast not understanding
To know thy misery; for all our wit

2. The metaphor is mercantile: let's not load all   3. Not working. "Curious artist": clever craftsman.
our cargo in one ship ("bottom").

And reading brings us to a truer sense
Of sorrow. In the eternal church,° sir,   *heavenly society*
I do hope we shall not part thus.
ANTONIO   Oh, be of comfort!
70   Make patience a noble fortitude,
And think not how unkindly we are used:
Man, like to cassia, is proved best being bruised.[4]
DUCHESS   Must I, like to a slave-born Russian,
Account it praise to suffer tyranny?
75   And yet, O heaven, thy heavy hand is in 't!
I have seen my little boy oft scourge his top,[5]
And compared myself to 't: naught made me e'er
Go right but heaven's scourge stick.
ANTONIO   Do not weep:
Heaven fashioned us of nothing, and we strive
80   To bring ourselves to nothing. Farewell, Cariola,
And thy sweet armful. If I do never see thee more,
Be a good mother to your little ones,
And save them from the tiger. Fare you well.
DUCHESS   Let me look upon you once more, for that speech
85   Came from a dying father. Your kiss is colder
Than that I have seen an holy anchorite°   *hermit*
Give to a dead man's skull.
ANTONIO   My heart is turned to a heavy lump of lead,
With which I sound[6] my danger. Fare you well.
                    [*Exeunt* ANTONIO *and his son.*]
90   DUCHESS   My laurel is all withered.
CARIOLA   Look, madam, what a troop of armèd men
Make toward us.
DUCHESS   Oh, they are very welcome:
When Fortune's wheel[7] is overcharged with princes,
The weight makes it move swift: I would have my ruin
Be sudden.
                    [*Enter* BOSOLA *vizarded,*° *with a guard.*]   *masked*
95   I am your adventure,[8] am I not?
BOSOLA   You are. You must see your husband no more.
DUCHESS   What devil art thou that counterfeits heaven's thunder?
BOSOLA   Is that terrible? I would have you tell me whether
Is that note worse that frights the silly birds
100   Out of the corn,° or that which doth allure them   *grain*
To the nets? You have hearkened to the last too much.
DUCHESS   Oh, misery! Like to a rusty o'ercharged cannon,
Shall I never fly in pieces?—Come, to what prison?
BOSOLA   To none.
DUCHESS   Whither, then?

---

4. Cinnamon bark ("cassia") is most aromatic
(virtuous) when pressed.
5. Children used to make tops spin by whipping
them.
6. Plumb the depths of.

7. The wheel of fortune is an ancient emblem of
mutability; people have their fixed positions on it
and rise or fall as it turns.
8. The object of your journey.

BOSOLA   To your palace.
DUCHESS   I have heard
105   That Charon's boat serves to convey all o'er
      The dismal lake,[9] but brings none back again.
BOSOLA   Your brothers mean you safety and pity.
DUCHESS   Pity!
      With such a pity men preserve alive
      Pheasants and quails, when they are not fat enough
110   To be eaten.
BOSOLA   These are your children?
DUCHESS   Yes.
BOSOLA   Can they prattle?
DUCHESS   No.
      But I intend, since they were born accursed,
      Curses shall be their first language.
BOSOLA   Fie, madam!
      Forget this base, low fellow—
DUCHESS   Were I a man,
115   I'd beat that counterfeit face° into thy other.   *mask*
BOSOLA   One of no birth.[1]
DUCHESS   Say that he was born mean,
      Man is most happy when 's own actions
      Be arguments and examples of his virtue.
BOSOLA   A barren, beggarly virtue!
120   DUCHESS   I prithee, who is greatest? Can you tell?
      Sad tales befit my woe: I'll tell you one.
      A salmon, as she swam unto the sea,
      Met with a dogfish, who encounters her
      With this rough language: "Why art thou so bold
125   To mix thyself with our high state of floods,
      Being no eminent courtier, but one
      That for the calmest and fresh time o' th' year
      Dost live in shallow rivers, rank'st thyself
      With silly° smelts and shrimps? And darest thou   *simple*
130   Pass by our dog-ship without reverence?"
      "Oh!" quoth the salmon, "sister, be at peace:
      Thank Jupiter we both have passed the net!
      Our value never can be truly known,
      Till in the fisher's basket we be shown:
135   I' th' market then my price may be the higher,
      Even when I am nearest to the cook and fire."
      So to great men the moral may be stretchèd:
      Men oft are valued high, when they're most wretched.
      But come, whither you please. I am armed 'gainst misery;
140   Bent to all sways of the oppressor's will:
      There's no deep valley but near some great hill.   [*Exeunt.*]

---

9. In classical mythology, Charon transports the   1. Of low rank by birth.
souls of the dead across the river Styx to Hades.

Act 4

SCENE 1. *Amalfi.*

[*Enter* FERDINAND *and* BOSOLA.]

FERDINAND   How doth our sister duchess bear herself
In her imprisonment?

BOSOLA   Nobly. I'll describe her.
She's sad as one long used to 't, and she seems
Rather to welcome the end of misery
5 Than shun it; a behavior so noble
As gives a majesty to adversity:
You may discern the shape of loveliness
More perfect in her tears than in her smiles;
She will muse four hours together; and her silence,
10 Methinks, expresseth more than if she spake.

FERDINAND   Her melancholy seems to be fortified
With a strange disdain.

BOSOLA   'Tis so; and this restraint,
Like English mastiffs that grow fierce with tying,
Makes her too passionately apprehend
Those pleasures she's kept from.

15 FERDINAND   Curse upon her!
I will no longer study in the book
Of another's heart. Inform her what I told you.   [*Exit.*]

    [*Enter* DUCHESS.]

BOSOLA   All comfort to your grace!

DUCHESS   I will have none.
Pray thee, why dost thou wrap thy poisoned pills
20 In gold and sugar?

BOSOLA   Your elder brother, the Lord Ferdinand,
Is come to visit you, and sends you word,
'Cause once he rashly made a solemn vow
Never to see you more, he comes i' th' night,
25 And prays you gently neither torch nor taper
Shine in your chamber. He will kiss your hand
And reconcile himself, but for his vow
He dares not see you.

DUCHESS   At his pleasure.
Take hence the lights: he's come.

    [*Enter* FERDINAND.]

FERDINAND   Where are you?

30 DUCHESS   Here, sir.

FERDINAND   This darkness suits you well.

DUCHESS   I would ask your pardon.

FERDINAND   You have it;
For I account it the honorabl'st revenge,
Where I may kill, to pardon. Where are your cubs?

DUCHESS   Whom?

35 FERDINAND   Call them your children;

For though our national law distinguish bastards
From true legitimate issue, compassionate nature
Makes them all equal.
DUCHESS   Do you visit me for this?
You violate a sacrament o' th' church
Shall make you howl in hell for 't.
40 FERDINAND   It had been well
Could you have lived thus always; for, indeed,
You were too much i' th' light[1]—but no more—
I come to seal my peace with you. Here's a hand
                [*Gives her a dead man's hand.*]
To which you have vowed much love; the ring upon 't
You gave.
45 DUCHESS   I affectionately kiss it.
FERDINAND   Pray, do, and bury the print of it in your heart.
I will leave this ring with you for a lovetoken,
And the hand as sure as the ring; and do not doubt
But you shall have the heart, too. When you need a friend,
50 Send it to him that owed° it; you shall see   owned
Whether he can aid you.
DUCHESS   You are very cold;
I fear you are not well after your travel.
Ha! Lights! Oh, horrible!
FERDINAND   Let her have lights enough.   [*Exit.*]
DUCHESS   What witchcraft doth he practice, that he hath left
55 A dead man's hand here?
         [*Here is discovered, behind a traverse,[2] the artificial figures of Antonio
         and his children, appearing as if they were dead.*]
BOSOLA   Look you, here's the piece from which 'twas ta'en.
He doth present you this sad spectacle,
That, now you know directly they are dead,
Hereafter you may wisely cease to grieve
60 For that which cannot be recovered.
DUCHESS   There is not between heaven and earth one wish
I stay for after this: it wastes[3] me more
Than were 't my picture, fashioned out of wax,
Stuck with a magical needle, and then buried
65 In some foul dunghill; and yond's an excellent property[4]
For a tyrant, which I would account mercy.
BOSOLA   What's that?
DUCHESS   If they would bind me to that lifeless trunk
And let me freeze to death.
BOSOLA   Come, you must live.
DUCHESS   That's the greatest torture souls feel in hell,
70 In hell: that they must live, and cannot die.
Portia,[5] I'll new-kindle thy coals again,

4.1
1. Punning on "light," wanton.
2. Curtain.
3. Consumes, as by secret disease; witches were supposed to be able to "waste" their enemies by

making wax images and tormenting them as indicated below.
4. Appropriate act.
5. Portia, the wife of Brutus, committed suicide by swallowing hot coals.

And revive the rare and almost dead example
Of a loving wife.
BOSOLA   Oh, fie! Despair? Remember
You are a Christian.
DUCHESS   The church enjoins fasting:
I'll starve myself to death.
75   BOSOLA   Leave this vain sorrow.
Things being at the worst begin to mend: the bee
When he hath shot his sting into your hand, may then
Play with your eyelid.
DUCHESS   Good comfortable fellow,
Persuade a wretch that's broke upon the wheel[6]
80   To have all his bones new set; entreat him live
To be executed again. Who must dispatch me?
I account this world a tedious theater,
For I do play a part in 't 'gainst my will.
BOSOLA   Come, be of comfort; I will save your life.
DUCHESS   Indeed,
85   I have not leisure to tend so small a business.
BOSOLA   Now, by my life, I pity you.
DUCHESS   Thou art a fool, then,
To waste thy pity on a thing so wretched
As cannot pity itself. I am full of daggers.
Puff, let me blow these vipers from me.
        [*Enter* SERVANT.]
What are you?
90   SERVANT   One that wishes you long life.
DUCHESS   I would thou wert hanged for the horrible curse
Thou hast given me. I shall shortly grow one
Of the miracles of pity. I'll go pray—
No, I'll go curse.
BOSOLA   Oh, fie!
DUCHESS   I could curse the stars—
95   BOSOLA   Oh, fearful!
DUCHESS   And those three smiling seasons of the year
Into a Russian winter,[7] nay, the world
To its first chaos.
BOSOLA   Look you, the stars shine still.
DUCHESS   Oh, but you must
100   Remember, my curse hath a great way to go.
Plagues, that make lanes through largest families,
Consume them!
BOSOLA   Fie, lady!
DUCHESS   Let them, like tyrants,
Never be remembered but for the ill they have done;
Let all the zealous prayers of mortified
Churchmen forget them!

6. Instrument of torture for stretching the body.
7. A Russian winter would last all year long.

105 BOSOLA   Oh, uncharitable!
DUCHESS   Let Heaven a little while cease crowning martyrs
 To punish them!
 Go, howl them this, and say, I long to bleed:
 It is some mercy when men kill with speed.
      [*Exeunt* DUCHESS *and* SERVANT.]
   [*Reenter* FERDINAND.]
110 FERDINAND   Excellent, as I would wish; she's plagued
 in art:°   *by a cunning device*
 These presentations are but framed in wax
 By the curious master in that quality,
 Vincentio Lauriola,[8] and she takes them
 For true substantial bodies.
BOSOLA   Why do you do this?
FERDINAND   To bring her to despair.
115 BOSOLA   'Faith, end here,
 And go no farther in your cruelty.
 Send her a penitential garment to put on
 Next to her delicate skin, and furnish her
 With beads and prayer books.
FERDINAND   Damn her! That body of hers,
120 While that my blood ran pure in 't, was more worth
 Than that which thou wouldst comfort, called a soul.
 I will send her masques of common courtesans,
 Have her meat° served up by bawds and ruffians, *food (of any kind)*
 And, 'cause she'll needs be mad, I am resolved
125 To remove forth the common hospital°   *asylum*
 All the mad-folk, and place them near her lodging;
 There let them practice together, sing and dance,
 And act their gambols to the full o' th' moon:
 If she can sleep the better for it, let her.
130 Your work is almost ended.
BOSOLA   Must I see her again?
FERDINAND   Yes.
BOSOLA   Never.
FERDINAND   You must.
BOSOLA   Never in mine own shape;
 That's forfeited by my intelligence°   *betrayal*
 And this last cruel lie. When you send me next,
 The business shall be comfort.
135 FERDINAND   Very likely.
 Thy pity is nothing of kin to thee.[9] Antonio
 Lurks about Milan: thou shalt shortly thither
 To feed a fire as great as my revenge,
 Which ne'er will slack till it have spent his fuel.
140 Intemperate agues[1] make physicians cruel. [*Exeunt.*]

---

8. The art of wax modeling was common enough,
but the name of the artist seems to be imaginary.

9. I.e., pity doesn't suit you very well.
1. Fevers that cannot be controlled.

SCENE 2

[*Enter* DUCHESS *and* CARIOLA.]

DUCHESS What hideous noise was that?

CARIOLA   'Tis the wild consort°   *band*
　Of madmen, lady, which your tyrant brother
　Hath placed about your lodging. This tyranny,
　I think, was never practiced till this hour.

5 DUCHESS Indeed, I thank him. Nothing but noise and folly
　Can keep me in my right wits, whereas reason
　And silence make me stark mad. Sit down;
　Discourse to me some dismal tragedy.

CARIOLA Oh, 'twill increase your melancholy.

DUCHESS   Thou art deceived:
10 　To hear of greater grief would lessen mine.
　This is a prison?

CARIOLA   Yes, but you shall live
　To shake this durance° off.   *imprisonment*

DUCHESS   Thou art a fool:
　The robin redbreast and the nightingale
　Never live long in cages.

CARIOLA   Pray, dry your eyes.
　What think you of, madam?

15 DUCHESS   Of nothing:
　When I muse thus, I sleep.

CARIOLA Like a madman, with your eyes open?

DUCHESS Dost thou think we shall know one another in th' other world?

CARIOLA Yes, out of question.

DUCHESS   Oh that it were possible we might
20 　But hold some two days' conference with the dead!
　From them I should learn somewhat, I am sure,
　I never shall know here. I'll tell thee a miracle;
　I am not mad yet, to my cause of sorrow:
　Th' heaven o'er my head seems made of molten brass,
25 　The earth of flaming sulphur, yet I am not mad.
　I am acquainted with sad misery
　As the tanned galley slave is with his oar;
　Necessity makes me suffer constantly,
　And custom makes it easy. Who do I look like now?

30 CARIOLA Like to your picture in the gallery,
　A deal of life in show, but none in practice;
　Or rather like some reverend monument
　Whose ruins are even pitied.

DUCHESS   Very proper.
　And Fortune seems only to have her eyesight
35 　To behold my tragedy.
　How now! What noise is that?

　　[*Enter* SERVANT.]

SERVANT   I am come to tell you
　Your brother hath intended you some sport.

A great physician, when the pope was sick
Of a deep melancholy, presented him
40　With several sorts of madmen, which wild object
Being full of change and sport, forced him to laugh,
And so the imposthume° broke. The selfsame cure　　　　　*abscess*
The duke intends on you.
DUCHESS　　　　　　　　Let them come in.
SERVANT　There's a mad lawyer; and a secular priest;[1]
45　A doctor that hath forfeited his wits
By jealousy; an astrologian
That in his works said such a day o' th' month
Should be the day of doom, and, failing of 't,
Ran mad; an English tailor crazed i' th' brain
50　With the study of new fashions; a gentleman-usher°　　　*doorkeeper*
Quite beside himself with care to keep in mind
The number of his lady's salutations
Or "How do you's" she employed him in each morning;
A farmer, too, an excellent knave in grain,
55　Mad 'cause he was hindered transportation:[2]
And let one broker that's mad loose to these,
You'd think the devil were among them.
DUCHESS　Sit, Cariola. Let them loose when you please,
For I am chained to endure all your tyranny.
　　　　[*Enter* MADMEN.]
　　　　[*Here by a* MADMAN *this song is sung to a dismal kind of music.*]

60　　　　Oh, let us howl some heavy note,
　　　　　Some deadly dogged howl,
　　　　Sounding as from the threatening throat
　　　　　Of beasts and fatal fowl!
　　　　As ravens, screech owls, bulls, and bears,
65　　　　　We'll bell° and bawl our parts,　　　　　*cry*
　　　　Till irksome noise have cloyed your ears
　　　　　And corrosived your hearts.
　　　　At last, whenas our choir wants breath,
　　　　　Our bodies being blest,
70　　　　We'll sing, like swans, to welcome death,
　　　　　And die in love and rest.

FIRST MADMAN　Doomsday not come yet? I'll draw it nearer by a perspective,[3]
or make a glass that shall set all the world on fire upon an instant. I cannot sleep; my pillow is stuffed with a litter of porcupines.
75　SECOND MADMAN　Hell is a mere glasshouse, where the devils are continually blowing up women's souls on hollow irons, and the fire never goes out.
THIRD MADMAN　I will lie with every woman in my parish the tenth night;
I will tithe them over like haycocks.[4]

4.2
1. One serving a parish, not a member of an order.
2. Forbidden to export.

3. Telescope.
4. As a priest takes his tenth ("tithe") of his parishioners' crops. "Haycocks": haystacks.

FOURTH MADMAN   Shall my pothecary outgo me because I am a cuckold? I
have found out his roguery; he makes alum of his wife's urine, and sells it
to puritans that have sore throats with overstraining.[5]

FIRST MADMAN   I have skill in heraldry.

SECOND MADMAN   Hast?

FIRST MADMAN   You do give for your crest a woodcock's[6] head with the
brains picked out on 't; you are a very ancient gentleman.

THIRD MADMAN   Greek is turned Turk: we are only to be saved by the Hel-
vetian translation.[7]

FIRST MADMAN   Come on, sir, I will lay the law to you.

SECOND MADMAN   Oh, rather lay a corrosive: the law will eat to the bone.

THIRD MADMAN   He that drinks but to satisfy nature is damned.

FOURTH MADMAN   If I had my glass[8] here, I would show a sight should
make all the women here call me mad doctor.

FIRST MADMAN   What's he? A rope maker?

SECOND MADMAN   No, no, no, a snuffling knave that, while he shows the
tombs, will have his hand in a wench's placket.

THIRD MADMAN   Woe to the caroche[9] that brought home my wife from the
masque at three o'clock in the morning! It had a large featherbed in it.

FOURTH MADMAN   I have pared the devil's nails forty times, roasted them
in raven's eggs, and cured agues with them.

THIRD MADMAN   Get me three hundred milchbats, to make possets[1] to procure sleep.

FOURTH MADMAN   All the college may throw their caps[2] at me: I have made
a soap boiler costive;[3] it was my masterpiece.

> [*Here the dance, consisting of eight* MADMEN, *with music answerable
> thereunto; after which* BOSOLA, *like an old man, enters.*]

DUCHESS   Is he mad too?

SERVANT   Pray, question him. I'll leave you.

>   [*Exeunt* SERVANT *and* MADMEN.]

BOSOLA   I am come to make thy tomb.

DUCHESS   Ha! My tomb?
Thou speak'st as if I lay upon my deathbed,
Gasping for breath. Dost thou perceive me sick?

BOSOLA   Yes, and the more dangerously, since thy sickness is insensible.[4]

DUCHESS   Thou art not mad, sure. Dost know me?

BOSOLA   Yes.

DUCHESS   Who am I?

BOSOLA   Thou art a box of worm-seed, at best but a salvatory of green
mummy. What's this flesh? A little crudded[5] milk, fantastical puff paste.
Our bodies are weaker than those paper prisons boys use to keep flies in,
more contemptible, since ours is to preserve earthworms. Didst thou ever
see a lark in a cage? Such is the soul in the body: this world is like her

---

5. In long prayers and sermons.
6. A proverbially stupid bird.
7. The Geneva Bible, a jibe at English Puritans
who used that translation.
8. Looking glass.
9. Carriage. "Placket": slit in a skirt.
1. Sedative drafts, here made of bat's milk.
2. Despair of emulating.

3. Constipated.
4. Imperceptible.
5. Curdled. "Worm-seed" is a matter whose ultimate end is the generation of worms. "A salvatory
of green mummy": the substance of mummified
bodies was considered medicinal. The living body
is a box ("salvatory") of such medicine, only not
yet ready for use.

little turf of grass, and the heaven o'er our heads, like her looking glass,
only gives us a miserable knowledge of the small compass of our prison.

DUCHESS   Am not I thy duchess?

120   BOSOLA   Thou art some great woman, sure, for riot[6] begins to sit on thy
forehead, clad in gray hairs, twenty years sooner than on a merry milkmaid's. Thou sleep'st worse than if a mouse should be forced to take up
her lodging in a cat's ear: a little infant that breeds its teeth,[7] should it
lie with thee, would cry out, as if thou wert the more unquiet bedfellow.

125   DUCHESS   I am Duchess of Malfi still.

BOSOLA   That makes thy sleep so broken:
Glories, like glowworms, afar off shine bright,
But, looked to near, have neither heat nor light.

DUCHESS   Thou art very plain.

130   BOSOLA   My trade is to flatter the dead, not the living; I am a tomb-maker.

DUCHESS   And thou com'st to make my tomb?

BOSOLA   Yes.

DUCHESS   Let me be a little merry. Of what stuff wilt thou make it?

BOSOLA   Nay, resolve° me first, of what fashion?   *inform*

135   DUCHESS   Why, do we grow fantastical in our deathbed? Do we affect
fashion in the grave?

BOSOLA   Most ambitiously. Princes' images on their tombs do not lie, as
they were wont, seeming to pray up to heaven, but with their hands
under their cheeks, as if they died of the toothache. They are not carved

140   with their eyes fixed upon the stars, but as their minds were wholly bent
upon the world, the selfsame way they seem to turn their faces.

DUCHESS   Let me know fully therefore the effect
Of this thy dismal preparation,
This talk fit for a charnel.[8]

BOSOLA   Now I shall.
[*Enter* EXECUTIONERS, *with a coffin, cords, and a bell.*]

145   Here is a present from your princely brothers;
And may it arrive welcome, for it brings
Last benefit, last sorrow.

DUCHESS   Let me see it:
I have so much obedience in my blood,
I wish it in their veins to do them good.

150   BOSOLA   This is your last presence chamber.[9]

CARIOLA   O my sweet lady!

DUCHESS   Peace, it affrights not me.

BOSOLA   I am the common bellman,
That usually° is sent to condemned persons   *by custom*
The night before they suffer.

DUCHESS   Even now thou said'st
Thou wast a tomb-maker.

155   BOSOLA   'Twas to bring you
By degrees to mortification.[1] Listen. [*rings the bell*]

---

6. Debauchery.
7. A teething infant.
8. A storage place for bones reserved from old

graves in the digging of new ones.
9. A noble person's reception room.
1. Repentance, also death and decomposition.

Hark, now everything is still
The screech owl and the whistler² shrill
Call upon our dame aloud,
160   And bid her quickly don her shroud!
Much you had of land and rent:
Your length in clay's now competent.°   *sufficient*
A long war disturbed your mind:
Here your perfect peace is signed.
165   Of what is 't fools make such vain keeping?
Sin their conception, their birth weeping,
Their life a general mist of error,
Their death a hideous storm of terror.
Strew your hair with powders sweet,
170   Don clean linen, bathe your feet,
And (the foul fiend more to check)
A crucifix let bless your neck:
'Tis now full tide 'tween night and day;
End your groan, and come away.

175 CARIOLA   Hence, villains, tyrants, murderers! Alas!
    What will you do with my lady? Call for help.
DUCHESS   To whom? To our next neighbors? They are mad-folks.
BOSOLA   Remove that noise.
DUCHESS   Farewell, Cariola.
    In my last will I have not much to give:
180   A many hungry guests have fed upon me;
    Thine will be a poor reversion.°   *inheritance*
CARIOLA   I will die with her.
DUCHESS   I pray thee, look thou giv'st my little boy
    Some syrup for his cold, and let the girl
    Say her prayers ere she sleep.   [CARIOLA *is forced out by the* EXECUTIONERS.]
                 Now what you please.
    What death?
185 BOSOLA   Strangling: here are your executioners.
DUCHESS   I forgive them:
    The apoplexy, catarrh, or cough o' th' lungs
    Would do as much as they do.
BOSOLA   Doth not death fright you?
DUCHESS   Who would be afraid on 't,
190   Knowing to meet such excellent company
    In th' other world?
BOSOLA   Yet, methinks,
    The manner of your death should much afflict you:
    This cord should terrify you.
DUCHESS   Not a whit.
    What would it pleasure me to have my throat cut
195   With diamonds? Or to be smothered
    With cassia?° Or to be shot to death with pearls?   *cinnamon*

---

2. A bird premonitory of death.

I know death hath ten thousand several doors
For men to take their exits, and 'tis found
They go on such strange geometrical hinges,
200   You may open them both ways.—Any way, for heaven sake,
So I were out of your whispering. Tell my brothers
That I perceive death, now I am well awake,
Best gift is they can give or I can take.
I would fain° put off my last woman's fault,   *gladly*
I'd not be tedious to you.
205 EXECUTIONER   We are ready.
DUCHESS   Dispose my breath how please you, but my body
Bestow upon my women, will you?
EXECUTIONER   Yes.
DUCHESS   Pull, and pull strongly, for your able strength
Must pull down heaven upon me—
210   Yet stay; heaven gates are not so high arched
As princes' palaces; they that enter there
Must go upon their knees. [*kneels*] Come, violent death.
Serve for mandragora³ to make me sleep!
Go tell my brothers, when I am laid out,
215   They then may feed in quiet.   [*They strangle her.*]
BOSOLA   Where's the waiting woman?
Fetch her. Some other strangle the children.
      [*Exeunt* EXECUTIONERS, *some of whom return with* CARIOLA.]
Look you, there sleeps your mistress.
CARIOLA   Oh, you are damned
Perpetually for this! My turn is next.
Is 't not so ordered?
220 BOSOLA   Yes, and I am glad
You are so well prepared for 't.
CARIOLA   You are deceived, sir,
I am not prepared for 't, I will not die;
I will first come to my answer,° and know   *judicial hearing*
How I have offended.
BOSOLA   Come, dispatch her.
225   You kept her counsel; now you shall keep ours.
CARIOLA   I will not die, I must not; I am contracted
To a young gentleman.
EXECUTIONER   Here's your wedding ring. [*showing the noose*]
CARIOLA   Let me but speak with the duke; I'll discover°   *reveal*
Treason to his person.
BOSOLA   Delays! Throttle her.
EXECUTIONER   She bites and scratches.
230 CARIOLA   If you kill me now,
I am damned; I have not been at confession
This two years.
BOSOLA [*to* EXECUTIONERS]   When!
CARIOLA   I am quick with child.

---

3. The word is used loosely for a stupefying drug.

BOSOLA   Why, then,
    Your credit's saved.[4]   [*They strangle* CARIOLA.]
                        Bear her into th' next room;
    Let this lie still.   [*Exeunt the* EXECUTIONERS *with the body of* CARIOLA.]
             [*Enter* FERDINAND.]
FERDINAND   Is she dead?
BOSOLA   She is what
235   You'd have her. But here begin your pity.   [*Shows the children strangled.*]
    Alas, how have these offended?
FERDINAND   The death
    Of young wolves is never to be pitied.
BOSOLA   Fix
    Your eye here.
FERDINAND   Constantly.
BOSOLA   Do you not weep?
    Other sins only speak; murder shrieks out:
240   The element of water moistens the earth,
    But blood flies upwards and bedews the heavens.
FERDINAND   Cover her face; mine eyes dazzle: she died young.
BOSOLA   I think not so; her infelicity°   *unhappiness*
    Seemed to have years too many.
FERDINAND   She and I were twins;
245   And should I die this instant, I had lived
    Her time to a minute.
BOSOLA   It seems she was born first:
    You have bloodily approved° the ancient truth,   *given proof of*
    That kindred commonly do worse agree
    Than remote strangers.
FERDINAND   Let me see her face again.
250   Why didst not thou pity her? What an excellent
    Honest man mightst thou have been,
    If thou hadst borne her to some sanctuary!
    Or, bold in a good cause, opposed thyself,
    With thy advancèd sword above thy head,
255   Between her innocence and my revenge!
    I bade thee, when I was distracted of my wits,
    Go kill my dearest friend, and thou hast done 't.
    For let me but examine well the cause:
    What was the meanness of her match to me?
260   Only I must confess I had a hope,
    Had she continued widow, to have gained
    An infinite mass of treasure by her death:
    And that was the main cause, her marriage,
    That drew a stream of gall quite through my heart.
265   For thee, as we observe in tragedies
    That a good actor many times is cursed
    For playing a villain's part, I hate thee for 't,
    And, for my sake, say thou hast done much ill well.

---

4. Your reputation will now be safe.

BOSOLA   Let me quicken your memory, for I perceive
270   You are falling into ingratitude: I challenge
The reward due to my service.
FERDINAND   I'll tell thee
What I'll give thee.
BOSOLA   Do.
FERDINAND   I'll give thee a pardon
For this murder.
BOSOLA   Ha!
FERDINAND   Yes, and 'tis
The largest bounty I can study to do thee.
275   By what authority didst thou execute
This bloody sentence?
BOSOLA   By yours.
FERDINAND   Mine! Was I her judge?
Did any ceremonial form of law
Doom her to not-being? Did a complete° jury   *qualified*
Deliver her conviction up i' th' court?
280   Where shalt thou find this judgment registered,
Unless in hell? See, like a bloody fool,
Thou'st forfeited thy life, and thou shalt die for 't.
BOSOLA   The office of justice is perverted quite
When one thief hangs another. Who shall dare
To reveal this?
285   FERDINAND   Oh, I'll tell thee;
The wolf shall find her grave, and scrape it up,
Not to devour the corpse, but to discover
The horrid murder.
BOSOLA   You, not I, shall quake for 't.
FERDINAND   Leave me.
BOSOLA   I will first receive my pension.
FERDINAND   You are a villain.
290   BOSOLA   When your ingratitude
Is judge, I am so.
FERDINAND   Oh, horror!
That not the fear of Him which binds the devils
Can prescribe man obedience!
Never look upon me more.
BOSOLA   Why, fare thee well.
295   Your brother and your self are worthy men:
You have a pair of hearts are rotten graves,
Rotten, and rotting others; and your vengeance,
Like two chained bullets, still° goes arm in arm.   *continually*
You may be brothers, for treason, like the plague,
300   Doth take much in a blood.[5] I stand like one
That long hath ta'en a sweet and golden dream.
I am angry with myself, now that I wake.

5. Treason and plague run in certain families.

FERDINAND   Get thee into some unknown part o' th' world,
       That I may never see thee.
BOSOLA   Let me know
305   Wherefore I should be thus neglected. Sir,
       I served your tyranny, and rather strove
       To satisfy yourself than all the world,
       And though I loathed the evil, yet I loved
       You that did counsel it; and rather sought
310   To appear a true servant than an honest man.
FERDINAND   I'll go hunt the badger by owl-light:
       'Tis a deed of darkness.   [Exit.]
BOSOLA   He's much distracted. Off, my painted honor!
       While with vain hopes our faculties we tire,
315   We seem to sweat in ice and freeze in fire.
       What would I do, were this to do again?
       I would not change my peace of conscience
       For all the wealth of Europe.—She stirs; here's life.
       Return, fair soul, from darkness, and lead mine
320   Out of this sensible° hell.—She's warm, she breathes.   living
       Upon thy pale lips I will melt my heart,
       To store them with fresh color.—Who's there!
       Some cordial° drink!—Alas! I dare not call: restorative
       So pity would destroy pity.—Her eye opes,
325   And heaven in it seems to ope, that late was shut,
       To take me up to mercy.
DUCHESS   Antonio!
BOSOLA   Yes, madam, he is living;
       The dead bodies you saw were but feigned statues:
       He's reconciled to your brothers: the pope hath wrought
       The atonement.°   reconciliation
330 DUCHESS   Mercy!   [She dies.]
BOSOLA   Oh, she's gone again! There the cords of life broke.
       Oh, sacred innocence, that sweetly sleeps
       On turtles'⁶ feathers, whilst a guilty conscience
       Is a black register wherein is writ
335   All our good deeds and bad, a perspective°   telescope
       That shows us hell! That we cannot be suffered°   allowed
       To do good when we have a mind to it!
       This is manly sorrow:
       These tears, I am very certain, never grew
340   In my mother's milk. My estate is sunk
       Below the degree of fear. Where were
       These penitent fountains while she was living?
       Oh, they were frozen up! Here is a sight
       As direful to my soul as is the sword
345   Unto a wretch hath slain his father. Come,
       I'll bear thee hence,

6. Turtledoves, emblems of a loving couple.

And execute thy last will; that's deliver
Thy body to the reverend dispose°   *disposition*
Of some good women: that the cruel tyrant
350   Shall not deny me. Then I'll post to Milan,
Where somewhat I will speedily enact
Worth my dejection.   [*Exit with the body.*]

Act 5

SCENE 1. *A public place in Milan.*

[*Enter* ANTONIO *and* DELIO.]
ANTONIO   What think you of my hope of reconcilement
To the Aragonian brethren?
DELIO   I misdoubt it;
For though they have sent their letters of safe conduct
For your repair° to Milan, they appear   *resort*
5   But nets to entrap you. The Marquis of Pescara,
Under whom you hold certain land in cheat,[1]
Much 'gainst his noble nature hath been moved
To seize those lands, and some of his dependents
Are at this instant making it their suit
10   To be invested in your revenues.[2]
I cannot think they mean well to your life
That do deprive you of your means of life,
Your living.
ANTONIO   You are still an heretic°   *skeptic*
To any safety I can shape myself.
15 DELIO   Here comes the marquis. I will make myself
Petitioner for some part of your land,
To know whither it is flying.
ANTONIO   I pray do.   [*Withdraws.*]
         [*Enter* PESCARA.]
DELIO   Sir, I have a suit to you.
PESCARA   To me?
DELIO   An easy one.
20   There is the citadel of Saint Bennet,
With some demesnes,[3] of late in the possession
Of Antonio Bologna; please you bestow them on me.
PESCARA   You are my friend, but this is such a suit,
Nor fit for me to give, nor you to take.
DELIO   No, sir?
25 PESCARA   I will give you ample reason for 't
Soon in private.—Here's the cardinal's mistress.
         [*Enter* JULIA.]
JULIA   My lord, I am grown your poor petitioner,
And should be an ill beggar, had I not

5.1   2. I.e., to be given your rents.
1. Escheat, i.e., subject to forfeiture under cer-   3. Associated estates. "Saint Bennet": St. Bene-
tain conditions.   dict.

A great man's letter here, the cardinal's,
To court you in my favor.   [*Gives a letter.*]

30 PESCARA   He entreats for you
The citadel of Saint Bennet, that belonged
To the banished Bologna.

JULIA   Yes.

PESCARA   I could not
Have thought of a friend I could rather pleasure with it;
'Tis yours.

JULIA   Sir, I thank you; and he shall know
35   How doubly I am engaged both in your gift,
And speediness of giving, which makes your grant
The greater.   [*Exit.*]

ANTONIO [*aside*]   How they fortify themselves
With my ruin!

DELIO   Sir, I am little bound to you.

PESCARA   Why?

DELIO   Because you denied this suit to me, and gave 't
To such a creature.

40 PESCARA   Do you know what it was?
It was Antonio's land, not forfeited
By course of law, but ravished from his throat
By the cardinal's entreaty. It were not fit
I should bestow so main° a piece of wrong   *egregious*
45   Upon my friend; 'tis a gratification
Only due to a strumpet, for it is injustice.
Shall I sprinkle the pure blood of innocents
To make those followers I call my friends
Look ruddier[4] upon me? I am glad
50   This land, ta'en from the owner by such wrong,
Returns again unto so foul an use
As salary for his lust. Learn, good Delio,
To ask noble things of me, and you shall find
I'll be a noble giver.

DELIO   You instruct me well.

55 ANTONIO [*aside*]   Why, here's a man now would fright impudence
From sauciest beggars.

PESCARA   Prince Ferdinand's come to Milan,
Sick, as they give out, of an apoplexy,°   *stroke*
But some say 'tis a frenzy.° I am going   *insanity*
To visit him.   [*Exit.*]

ANTONIO   'Tis a noble old fellow.

60 DELIO   What course do you mean to take, Antonio?

ANTONIO   This night I mean to venture all my fortune,
Which is no more than a poor lingering life,
To the cardinal's worst of malice. I have got
Private access to his chamber, and intend
65   To visit him about the mid of night,

4. More agreeably, literally with a healthier (ruddy) complexion.

As once his brother did our noble duchess.
It may be that the sudden apprehension
Of danger—for I'll go in mine own shape—
When he shall see it fraught with love and duty,
70   May draw the poison out of him, and work
A friendly reconcilement. If it fail,
Yet it shall rid me of this infamous calling,
For better fall once than be ever falling.
DELIO   I'll second you in all danger, and, howe'er,
75   My life keeps rank with yours.
ANTONIO   You are still my loved and best friend.   [*Exeunt.*]

SCENE 2. *The scene continues.*

[*Enter* PESCARA *and* DOCTOR.]
PESCARA   Now, doctor, may I visit your patient?
DOCTOR   If 't please your lordship: but he's instantly°   *very shortly*
To take the air here in the gallery
By my direction.
PESCARA   Pray thee, what's his disease?
5 DOCTOR   A very pestilent disease, my lord,
They call lycanthropia.
PESCARA   What's that?
I need a dictionary to 't.
DOCTOR   I'll tell you.
In those that are possessed with 't there o'erflows
Such melancholy humor, they imagine
10   Themselves to be transformèd into wolves;
Steal forth to churchyards in the dead of night,
And dig dead bodies up: as two nights since
One met the duke 'bout midnight in a lane
Behind Saint Mark's Church, with the leg of a man
15   Upon his shoulder; and he howled fearfully;
Said he was a wolf, only the difference
Was, a wolf's skin was hairy on the outside,
His on the inside; bade them take their swords,
Rip up his flesh, and try. Straight° I was sent for,   *immediately*
20   And, having ministered to him, found his grace
Very well recovered.
PESCARA   I'm glad on 't.
DOCTOR   Yet not without some fear
Of a relapse. If he grow to his fit again,
I'll go a nearer way to work with him
25   Than ever Paracelsus[1] dreamed of: if
They'll give me leave, I'll buffet his madness
Out of him. Stand aside; he comes.
[*Enter* FERDINAND, MALATESTE, CARDINAL, *and* BOSOLA *apart.*]
FERDINAND   Leave me.

5.2
1. The great Swiss alchemist, famous for his cures by sympathetic magic.

MALATESTE Why doth your lordship love this solitariness?

FERDINAND Eagles commonly fly alone: they are crows, daws, and star-
30 lings that flock together. Look, what's that follows me?

MALATESTE Nothing, my lord.

FERDINAND Yes.

MALATESTE 'Tis your shadow.

FERDINAND Stay it; let it not haunt me.

35 MALATESTE Impossible, if you move, and the sun shine.

FERDINAND I will throttle it. [*Throws himself on the ground.*]

MALATESTE O, my lord, you are angry with nothing.

FERDINAND You are a fool: how is 't possible I should catch my shadow,
unless I fall upon 't? When I go to hell, I mean to carry a bribe; for, look
40 you, good gifts evermore make way for the worst persons.

PESCARA Rise, good my lord.

FERDINAND I am studying the art of patience.

PESCARA 'Tis a noble virtue.

FERDINAND To drive six snails before me from this town to Moscow; nei-
45 ther use goad nor whip to them, but let them take their own time—the
patient'st man i' th' world match me for an experiment—and I'll crawl after
like a sheep-biter.[2]

CARDINAL Force him up.   [*They raise him.*]

FERDINAND Use me well, you were best. What I have done, I have done:
50 I'll confess nothing.

DOCTOR Now let me come to him. Are you mad, my lord? Are you out of
your princely wits?

FERDINAND What's he?

PESCARA Your doctor.

55 FERDINAND Let me have his beard sawed off, and his eyebrows filed more
civil.

DOCTOR I must do mad tricks with him, for that's the only way on 't.[3] I have
brought your grace a salamander's skin to keep you from sunburning.

FERDINAND I have cruel sore eyes.

60 DOCTOR The white of a cockatrix's[4] egg is present remedy.

FERDINAND Let it be a new-laid one, you were best. Hide me from him:
physicians are like kings—they brook no contradiction.

DOCTOR Now he begins to fear me: now let me alone with him.

CARDINAL How now? Put off your gown?

65 DOCTOR Let me have some forty urinals filled with rosewater: he and I'll
go pelt one another with them. Now he begins to fear me. Can you fetch
a frisk, sir?[5] Let him go, let him go, upon my peril: I find by his eye he
stands in awe of me; I'll make him as tame as a dormouse.

FERDINAND Can you fetch your frisks, sir? I will stamp him into a cullis,[6]
70 flay off his skin, to cover one of the anatomies[7] this rogue hath set i' th'
cold yonder in Barber-Surgeons' Hall. Hence, hence! You are all of you

---

2. A sheepdog.
3. I.e., to cure him.
4. A fabulous, and deadly poisonous, serpent,
supposed to be hatched of a cock's egg.
5. Cut a caper, dance a jig.

6. Broth.
7. Anatomical skeletons hung up in the surgeon's
college, which Ferdinand proposes to cover with
the doctor's flayed skin.

like beasts for sacrifice: there's nothing left of you but tongue and belly,
flattery and lechery.   [*Exit.*]
PESCARA   Doctor, he did not fear you thoroughly.
DOCTOR   True;
I was somewhat too forward.
75   BOSOLA [*aside*]   Mercy upon me,
What a fatal judgment hath fall'n upon this Ferdinand!
PESCARA   Knows your grace what accident hath brought
Unto the prince this strange distraction?
CARDINAL [*aside*]   I must feign somewhat.—Thus they say it grew:
80   You have heard it rumored, for these many years
None of our family dies but there is seen
The shape of an old woman, which is given
By tradition to us to have been murdered
By her nephews for her riches. Such a figure
85   One night, as the prince sat up late at 's book,
Appeared to him; when, crying out for help,
The gentlemen of 's chamber found his grace
All on a cold sweat, altered much in face
And language; since which apparition,
90   He hath grown worse and worse, and I much fear
He cannot live.
BOSOLA   Sir, I would speak with you.
PESCARA   We'll leave your grace,
Wishing to the sick prince, our noble lord,
All health of mind and body.
CARDINAL   You are most welcome.
      [*Exeunt* PESCARA, MALATESTE, *and* DOCTOR.]
95   Are you come? So. [*aside*] This fellow must not know
By any means I had intelligence°   *was accessory*
In our duchess' death; for, though I counseled it,
The full of all th' engagement seemed to grow
From Ferdinand.—Now, sir, how fares our sister?
100   I do not think but sorrow makes her look
Like to an oft-dyed garment: she shall now
Taste comfort from me. Why do you look so wildly?
Oh, the fortune of your master here the prince
Dejects you, but be you of happy comfort:
105   If you'll do one thing for me I'll entreat,
Though he had a cold tombstone o'er his bones,
I'll make you what you would be.
BOSOLA   Anything;
Give it me in a breath, and let me fly to 't:
They that think long, small expedition win,
110   For musing much o' th' end cannot begin.
      [*Enter* JULIA.]
JULIA   Sir, will you come in to supper?
CARDINAL   I am busy;
Leave me.
JULIA [*aside*]   What an excellent shape hath that fellow!   [*Exit.*]

CARDINAL   'Tis thus. Antonio lurks here in Milan:
    Inquire him out, and kill him. While he lives,
115   Our sister cannot marry, and I have thought
    Of an excellent match for her. Do this, and style me
    Thy advancement.[8]
BOSOLA   But by what means shall I find him out?
CARDINAL   There is a gentleman called Delio
    Here in the camp, that hath been long approved
120   His loyal friend. Set eye upon that fellow;
    Follow him to Mass; maybe Antonio,
    Although he do account religion
    But a school-name,° for fashion of the world   *an idle phrase*
    May accompany him; or else go inquire out
125   Delio's confessor, and see if you can bribe
    Him to reveal it. There are a thousand ways
    A man might find to trace him; as to know
    What fellows haunt the Jews for taking up
    Great sums of money, for sure he's in want;
130   Or else to go to th' picture-makers, and learn
    Who bought her picture lately. Some of these
    Haply may take.
BOSOLA   Well, I'll not freeze i' th' business:°   *delay*
    I would see that wretched thing, Antonio,
    Above all sights i' th' world.
CARDINAL   Do, and be happy.   [*Exit.*]
135 BOSOLA   This fellow doth breed basilisks in 's eyes,
    He's nothing else but murder; yet he seems
    Not to have notice of the duchess' death.
    'Tis his cunning: I must follow his example;
    There cannot be a surer way to trace
    Than that of an old fox.
        [*Reenter* JULIA, *with a pistol.*]
140 JULIA   So, sir, you are well met.
BOSOLA   How now?
JULIA   Nay, the doors are fast enough.
    Now, sir, I will make you confess your treachery.
BOSOLA   Treachery?
JULIA   Yes, confess to me
    Which of my women 'twas, you hired to put
    Love-powder into my drink?
145 BOSOLA   Love powder?
JULIA   Yes, when I was at Malfi.
    Why should I fall in love with such a face else?°   *otherwise*
    I have already suffered for thee so much pain,
    The only remedy to do me good
    Is to kill my longing.
150 BOSOLA   Sure, your pistol holds
    Nothing but perfumes or kissing-comfits.[9]

---

8. Call me your means of promotion.
9. Candies to sweeten the breath.

Excellent lady! You have a pretty way on 't
To discover° your longing. Come, come, I'll disarm you,   *reveal*
And arm you thus:[1] yet this is wondrous strange.
155 JULIA Compare thy form and my eyes together, you'll find
My love no such great miracle. Now you'll say
I am wanton: this nice° modesty in ladies   *fastidious*
Is but a troublesome familiar[2] that haunts them.
BOSOLA Know you me, I am a blunt soldier.
JULIA   The better:
160 Sure, there wants° fire where there are no lively sparks   *lacks*
Of roughness.
BOSOLA   And I want compliment.[3]
JULIA   Why, ignorance
In courtship cannot make you do amiss,
If you have a heart to do well.
BOSOLA   You are very fair.
JULIA Nay, if you lay beauty to my charge,
I must plead unguilty.
165 BOSOLA   Your bright eyes
Carry a quiver of darts in them, sharper
Than sunbeams.
JULIA   You will mar me with commendation,
Put yourself to the charge of courting me,
Whereas now I woo you.
170 BOSOLA [*aside*] I have it, I will work upon this creature.—
Let us grow most amorously familiar.
If the great cardinal now should see me thus,
Would he not count me a villain?
JULIA No, he might count me a wanton,
175 Not lay a scruple of offense on you;
For if I see and steal a diamond,
The fault is not i' th' stone, but in me the thief
That purloins it. I am sudden with you.
We that are great women of pleasure, use to cut off
180 These uncertain wishes and unquiet longings,
And in an instant join the sweet delight
And the pretty excuse together. Had you been i' th' street,
Under my chamber window, even there
I should have courted you.
BOSOLA   Oh, you are an excellent lady!
185 JULIA Bid me do somewhat for you presently°   *right away*
To express I love you.
BOSOLA   I will, and if you love me,
Fail not to effect it.
The cardinal is grown wondrous melancholy;

---

1. Disarm (by taking away her pistol); arm (by embracing her). 2. Attendant spirit or demon.
3. I don't have the gift of flattery.

Demand the cause, let him not put you off
190 With feigned excuse; discover the main ground on 't.
JULIA Why would you know this?
BOSOLA   I have depended on him,
And I hear he is fallen in some disgrace
With the emperor: if he be, like the mice
That forsake falling houses, I would shift
195 To other dependence.
JULIA You shall not need follow the wars;
I'll be your maintenance.
BOSOLA   And I your loyal servant;
But I cannot leave my calling.
JULIA   Not leave
An ungrateful general for the love of a sweet lady?
200 You are like some cannot sleep in featherbeds,
But must have blocks for their pillows.
BOSOLA   Will you do this?
JULIA Cunningly.
BOSOLA   Tomorrow I'll expect th' intelligence.
JULIA Tomorrow? Get you into my cabinet,°   *inner chamber*
You shall have it with you. Do not delay me,
205 No more than I do you. I am like one
That is condemned: I have my pardon promised,
But I would see it sealed. Go, get you in;
You shall see me wind my tongue about his heart
Like a skein of silk.   [*Exit* BOSOLA.]
      [*Reenter* CARDINAL.]
CARDINAL   Where are you?
      [*Enter* SERVANTS.]
SERVANTS   Here.
210 CARDINAL Let none, upon your lives,
Have conference with the Prince Ferdinand,
Unless I know it. [*aside*] In this distraction
He may reveal the murder.   [*Exeunt* SERVANTS.]
Yond's my lingering consumption:
215 I am weary of her, and by any means
Would be quit of.
JULIA   How now, my lord?
What ails you?
CARDINAL   Nothing.
JULIA   Oh, you are much altered:
Come, I must be your secretary,° and remove   *confidante*
This lead from off your bosom.⁴ What's the matter?
220 CARDINAL I may not tell you.
JULIA Are you so far in love with sorrow
You cannot part with part of it? Or think you
I cannot love your grace when you are sad

---

4. Secretaries opened letters addressed to their masters by removing the heavy lead seals.

As well as merry? Or do you suspect
225   I, that have been a secret to your heart
These many winters, cannot be the same
Unto your tongue?
CARDINAL   Satisfy thy longing—
The only way to make thee keep my counsel
Is not to tell thee.
230   JULIA   Tell your echo this,
Or flatterers, that like echoes still report
What they hear though most imperfect, and not me;
For if that you be true unto yourself,
I'll know.
CARDINAL   Will you rack° me?   *torture*
JULIA   No, judgment shall
Draw it from you: it is an equal fault,
235   To tell one's secrets unto all or none.
CARDINAL   The first argues folly.
JULIA   But the last, tyranny.
CARDINAL   Very well. Why, imagine I have committed
Some secret deed which I desire the world
May never hear of.
JULIA   Therefore may not I know it?
240   You have concealed for me as great a sin
As adultery. Sir, never was occasion
For perfect trial of my constancy
Till now: sir, I beseech you—
CARDINAL   You'll repent it.
JULIA   Never.
245   CARDINAL   It hurries thee to ruin: I'll not tell thee.
Be well advised, and think what danger 'tis
To receive a prince's secrets: they that do,
Had need have their breasts hooped with adamant°   *the hardest metal*
To contain them. I pray thee, yet be satisfied;
250   Examine thine own frailty; 'tis more easy
To tie knots than unloose them: 'tis a secret
That, like a lingering poison, may chance lie
Spread in thy veins, and kill thee seven year hence.
JULIA   Now you dally with me.
CARDINAL   No more; thou shalt know it.
255   By my appointment the great Duchess of Malfi
And two of her young children, four nights since,
Were strangled.
JULIA   O Heaven! Sir, what have you done?
CARDINAL   How now? How settles this? Think you your bosom
Will be a grave dark and obscure enough
For such a secret?
260   JULIA   You have undone yourself, sir.
CARDINAL   Why?
JULIA   It lies not in me to conceal it.
CARDINAL   No?

Come, I will swear you to 't upon this book.

JULIA   Most religiously.

CARDINAL   Kiss it.   [*She kisses the book.*]
                              Now you shall

Never utter it; thy curiosity
265   Hath undone thee: thou'rt poisoned with that book.
Because I knew thou couldst not keep my counsel,
I have bound thee to 't by death.
        [*Reenter* BOSOLA.]

BOSOLA   For pity sake,
Hold!

CARDINAL   Ha! Bosola?

JULIA   I forgive you
This equal piece of justice you have done;
270   For I betrayed your counsel to that fellow:
He overheard it; that was the cause I said
It lay not in me to conceal it.

BOSOLA   O foolish woman,
Couldst not thou have poisoned him?

JULIA   'Tis weakness,
Too much to think what should have been done. I go
I know not whither.   [*Dies.*]

275   CARDINAL   Wherefore com'st thou hither?

BOSOLA   That I might find a great man like yourself,
Not out of his wits as the Lord Ferdinand,
To remember my service.

CARDINAL   I'll have thee hewed in pieces.

BOSOLA   Make not yourself such a promise of that life
Which is not yours to dispose of.

280   CARDINAL   Who placed thee here?

BOSOLA   Her lust, as she intended.

CARDINAL   Very well.
Now you know me for your fellow murderer.

BOSOLA   And wherefore should you lay fair marble colors
Upon your rotten purposes to me?[5]
285   Unless you imitate some that do plot great treasons,
And when they have done, go hide themselves i' th' graves
Of those were actors in 't?

CARDINAL   No more; there is
A fortune attends thee.

BOSOLA   Shall I go sue to Fortune any longer?
'Tis the fool's pilgrimage.

290   CARDINAL   I have honors in store for thee.

BOSOLA   There are a many ways that conduct to seeming
Honor, and some of them very dirty ones.

CARDINAL   Throw to the devil
Thy melancholy; the fire burns well,
What need we keep a stirring of 't, and make

5. Plaster was often painted to look like marble.

295   A greater smother? Thou wilt kill Antonio?

BOSOLA   Yes.

CARDINAL   Take up that body.

BOSOLA   I think I shall
  Shortly grow the common bier for churchyards!

CARDINAL   I will allow thee some dozen of attendants
  To aid thee in the murder.

300 BOSOLA   Oh, by no means. Physicians that apply horse leeches to any rank
  swelling use to cut off their tails, that the blood may run through them
  the faster. Let me have no train[6] when I go to shed blood, lest it make me
  have a greater when I ride to the gallows.[7]

CARDINAL   Come to me after midnight, to help to remove that body to her

305   own lodging. I'll give out she died of the plague; 'twill breed the less
  inquiry after her death.

BOSOLA   Where's Castruccio her husband?

CARDINAL   He's rode to Naples to take possession of Antonio's citadel.

BOSOLA   Believe me, you have done a very happy turn.

310 CARDINAL   Fail not to come. There is the master key of our lodgings, and
  by that you may conceive what trust I plant in you.

BOSOLA   You shall find me ready.   [*Exit* CARDINAL.]
  Oh poor Antonio, though nothing be so needful
  To thy estate as pity, yet I find

315   Nothing so dangerous. I must look to my footing;
  In such slippery ice-pavements men had need
  To be frost-nailed well;[8] they may break their necks else;
  The precedent's here afore me. How this man
  Bears up in blood! Seems fearless! Why, 'tis well:

320   Security some men call the suburbs of hell,
  Only a dead° wall between. Well, good Antonio,   *bare*
  I'll seek thee out, and all my care shall be
  To put thee into safety from the reach
  Of these most cruel biters that have got

325   Some of thy blood already. It may be,
  I'll join with thee in a most just revenge:
  The weakest arm is strong enough that strikes
  With the sword of justice. Still methinks the duchess
  Haunts me. There, there, 'tis nothing but my melancholy.

330   O Penitence, let me truly taste thy cup,
  That throws men down only to raise them up!   [*Exit.*]

SCENE 3. *A fortification at Milan.*

[*Enter* ANTONIO *and* DELIO. *Echo from the* DUCHESS' *grave.*]

DELIO   Yond's the cardinal's window. This fortification
  Grew from the ruins of an ancient abbey;
  And to yond side o' th' river lies a wall,
  Piece of a cloister, which in my opinion

6. Followers.
7. Criminals, carted through the streets to be

hanged at Tyburn, were followed by crowds.
8. To wear hobnailed boots.

5   Gives the best echo that you ever heard,
       So hollow and so dismal, and withal°   *in addition*
       So plain in the distinction of our words,
       That many have supposed it is a spirit
       That answers.
ANTONIO   I do love these ancient ruins.
10   We never tread upon them but we set
       Our foot upon some reverend history:
       And, questionless, here in this open court,
       Which now lies naked to the injuries
       Of stormy weather, some men lie interred
15   Loved the church so well, and gave so largely to 't,
       They thought it should have canopied their bones
       Till doomsday; but all things have their end:
       Churches and cities, which have diseases like to men,
       Must have like death that we have.
ECHO   "Like death that we have."
DELIO   Now the echo hath caught you.
20 ANTONIO   It groaned, methought, and gave
       A very deadly accent.
ECHO   "Deadly accent."
DELIO   I told you 'twas a pretty one: you may make it
       A huntsman, or a falconer, a musician,
       Or a thing of sorrow.
ECHO   "A thing of sorrow."
ANTONIO   Aye, sure, that suits it best.
25 ECHO   "That suits it best."
ANTONIO   'Tis very like my wife's voice.
ECHO   "Aye, wife's voice."
DELIO   Come, let's walk further from 't. I would not have you
       Go to th' cardinal's tonight: do not.
ECHO   "Do not."
DELIO   Wisdom doth not more moderate wasting sorrow
30   Than time: take time for 't; be mindful of thy safety.
ECHO   "Be mindful of thy safety."
ANTONIO   Necessity compels me:
       Make° scrutiny throughout the passes   *if you make*
       Of your own life, you'll find it impossible
       To fly your fate.
ECHO   "Oh, fly your fate."
35 DELIO   Hark! The dead stones seem to have pity on you,
       And give you good counsel.
ANTONIO   Echo, I will not talk with thee,
       For thou art a dead thing.
ECHO   "Thou art a dead thing."
ANTONIO   My duchess is asleep now,
40   And her little ones, I hope sweetly: O heaven,
       Shall I never see her more?
ECHO   "Never see her more."
ANTONIO   I marked° not one repetition of the echo   *attended to*

But that, and on the sudden a clear light
Presented me a face folded in sorrow.

DELIO   Your fancy merely.

45 ANTONIO   Come, I'll be out of this ague,°   *fever*
For to live thus is not indeed to live;
It is a mockery and abuse of life.
I will not henceforth save myself by halves;
Lose all, or nothing.

DELIO   Your own virtue save you!

50 I'll fetch your eldest son, and second you°   *back you up*
It may be that the sight of his own blood
Spread in so sweet a figure° may beget   *face*
The more compassion.

ANTONIO   However, fare you well.
Though in our miseries Fortune have a part,
55 Yet in our noble sufferings she hath none:
Contempt of pain, that we may call our own.   [*Exeunt.*]

SCENE 4. *A room in the* CARDINAL's *palace.*

[*Enter* CARDINAL, PESCARA, MALATESTE, RODERIGO, *and* GRISOLAN.]

CARDINAL   You shall not watch tonight by the sick prince;
His grace is very well recovered.

MALATESTE   Good my lord, suffer° us.   *allow*

CARDINAL   Oh, by no means;
The noise and change of object in his eye
5 Doth more distract him. I pray, all to bed;
And though you hear him in his violent fit,
Do not rise, I entreat you.

PESCARA   So, sir; we shall not.

CARDINAL   Nay, I must have you promise upon your honors,
For I was enjoined to 't by himself; and he seemed
To urge it sensibly.°   *with strong feeling*

10 PESCARA   Let our honors bind
This trifle.

CARDINAL   Nor any of your followers.

MALATESTE   Neither.

CARDINAL   It may be, to make trial of your promise,
When he's asleep, myself will rise and feign
15 Some of his mad tricks, and cry out for help,
And feign myself in danger.

MALATESTE   If your throat were cutting,
I'd not come at you, now I have protested against it.

CARDINAL   Why, I thank you.   [*Withdraws.*]

GRISOLAN   'Twas a foul storm tonight.

RODERIGO   The Lord Ferdinand's chamber shook like an
osier.°   *a willow wand*

20 MALATESTE   'Twas nothing but pure kindness in the devil,
To rock his own child.   [*Exeunt all except the* CARDINAL.]

CARDINAL   The reason why I would not suffer° these   *allow*

About my brother is because at midnight
I may with better privacy convey
25 Julia's body to her own lodging. Oh, my conscience!
I would pray now, but the devil takes away my heart
For having any confidence in prayer.
About this hour I appointed Bosola
To fetch the body: when he hath served my turn,
30 He dies.   [Exit.]
          [Enter BOSOLA.]
BOSOLA   Ha! 'Twas the cardinal's voice; I heard him name
Bosola and my death. Listen! I hear
One's footing.
          [Enter FERDINAND.]
FERDINAND   Strangling is a very quiet death.
35 BOSOLA [aside]   Nay, then, I see I must stand upon my guard.
FERDINAND   What say to that? Whisper softly; do you agree to 't? So; it must
be done i' th' dark: the cardinal would not for a thousand pounds the doc-
tor should see it.   [Exit.]
BOSOLA   My death is plotted; here's the consequence of murder.
40 We value not desert nor Christian breath,
When we know black deeds must be cured with death.
          [Enter ANTONIO and SERVANT.]
SERVANT   Here stay, sir, and be confident, I pray:
I'll fetch you a dark lantern.   [Exit.]
ANTONIO   Could I take him at his prayers,
There were hope of pardon.
45 BOSOLA   Fall right, my sword!   [Stabs him.]
I'll not give thee so much leisure as to pray.
ANTONIO   Oh, I am gone! Thou hast ended a long suit[1]
In a minute.
BOSOLA   What art thou?
ANTONIO   A most wretched thing,
That only have thy benefit in death,
To appear myself.
          [Reenter SERVANT with a lantern.]
50 SERVANT   Where are you, sir?
ANTONIO   Very near my home. Bosola?
SERVANT   Oh, misfortune!
BOSOLA   Smother thy pity; thou art dead else.° Antonio?   otherwise
The man I would have saved 'bove mine own life!
We are merely the stars' tennis balls, struck and bandied
55 Which way please them.[2] O good Antonio,
I'll whisper one thing in thy dying ear
Shall make thy heart break quickly! Thy fair duchess
And two sweet children—
ANTONIO   Their very names
Kindle a little life in me.

5.4
1. Antonio thinks it is the cardinal, to whom he
came to address a plea ("suit"), who has stabbed
him.
2. The power of the stars over people's lives was
a Renaissance commonplace.

BOSOLA   Are murdered.

60 ANTONIO   Some men have wished to die
At the hearing of sad tidings; I am glad
That I shall do 't in sadness: I would not now
Wish my wounds balmed nor healed, for I have no use
To put my life to. In all our quest of greatness,
65 Like wanton boys, whose pastime is their care,
We follow after bubbles blown in th' air.
Pleasure of life, what is't? Only the good hours
Of an ague; merely a preparative to rest,
To endure vexation. I do not ask
70 The process° of my death; only commend me   reason, circumstances
To Delio.

BOSOLA   Break, heart!

ANTONIO   And let my son fly the courts of princes.   [*Dies.*]

BOSOLA   Thou seem'st to have loved Antonio?

SERVANT   I brought him hither
To have reconciled him to the cardinal.

75 BOSOLA   I do not ask thee that.
Take him up, if thou tender thine own life,
And bear him where the lady Julia
Was wont to lodge. Oh, my fate moves swift;
I have this cardinal in the forge already;
80 Now I'll bring him to th' hammer. Oh direful
    misprision!°   misunderstanding
I will not imitate things glorious,
No more than base; I'll be mine own example.
On, on, and look thou represent,° for silence,   imitate
The thing thou bear'st.[3]   [*Exeunt.*]

SCENE 5. *The scene continues.*

[*Enter* CARDINAL, *with a book.*]

CARDINAL   I am puzzled in a question about hell:
He says, in hell there's one material fire,
And yet it shall not burn all men alike.
Lay him by. How tedious is a guilty conscience!
5 When I look into the fish ponds in my garden,
Methinks I see a thing armed with a rake,
That seems to strike at me.
          [*Enter* BOSOLA, *and* SERVANT *bearing* ANTONIO's *body.*]
                              Now, art thou come?
Thou look'st ghastly:
There sits in thy face some great determination
Mixed with some fear.

10 BOSOLA   Thus it lightens° into action: ignites
I am come to kill thee.

CARDINAL   Ha! Help! Our guard!

BOSOLA   Thou art deceived; they are out of thy howling.

___

3. The corpse.

CARDINAL   Hold; and I will faithfully divide
　　Revenues with thee.
BOSOLA   Thy prayers and proffers
　　Are both unseasonable.
15 CARDINAL   Raise the watch!
　　We are betrayed!
BOSOLA   I have confined your flight:°   *cut off your escape*
　　I'll suffer your retreat to Julia's chamber,
　　But no further.
CARDINAL   Help! We are betrayed!
　　　　[*Enter, above,* PESCARA, MALATESTE, RODERIGO, *and* GRISOLAN.]
MALATESTE   Listen.
CARDINAL   My dukedom for rescue!
RODERIGO   Fie upon his counterfeiting!
MALATESTE   Why, 'tis not the cardinal.
20 RODERIGO   Yes, yes, 'tis he,
　　But I'll see him hanged ere I'll go down to him.
CARDINAL   Here's a plot upon me. I am assaulted! I am lost,
　　Unless some rescue.
GRISOLAN   He doth this pretty well,
　　But it will not serve to laugh me out of my honor.
CARDINAL   The sword's at my throat!
25 RODERIGO   You would not bawl so loud then.
MALATESTE   Come, come, let's go to bed. He told us thus much aforehand.
PESCARA   He wished you should not come at him; but, believe 't,
　　The accent of the voice sounds not in jest:
　　I'll down to him, howsoever, and with engines.°   *battering rams*
　　Force ope the doors.   [*Exit above.*]
30 RODERIGO   Let's follow him aloof,°   *at a distance*
　　And note how the cardinal will laugh at him.
　　　　[*Exeunt, above,* MALATESTE, RODERIGO, *and* GRISOLAN.]
BOSOLA   There's for you first,   [*He kills the* SERVANT.]
　　'Cause you shall not unbarricade the door
　　To let in rescue.
CARDINAL   What cause hast thou to pursue my life?
35 BOSOLA   Look there.
CARDINAL   Antonio?
BOSOLA   Slain by my hand unwittingly.
　　Pray, and be sudden: when thou killed'st thy sister,
　　Thou took'st from Justice her most equal balance,
　　And left her naught but her sword.
CARDINAL   Oh, mercy!
40 BOSOLA   Now it seems thy greatness was only outward;
　　For thou fall'st faster of thyself than calamity
　　Can drive thee. I'll not waste longer time: there!   [*Stabs him.*]
CARDINAL   Thou hast hurt me.
BOSOLA   Again!   [*Stabs him again.*]
CARDINAL   Shall I die like a leveret,[1]

5.5
1. A baby hare.

Without any resistance? Help, help, help!
45   I am slain!
      [*Enter* FERDINAND.]
  FERDINAND   Th' alarum? Give me a fresh horse;
  Rally the vaunt-guard, or the day is lost.
  Yield, yield! I give you the honor of arms,
  Shake my sword over you; will you yield?[2]
  CARDINAL   Help me; I am your brother!
50   FERDINAND   The devil!
  My brother fight upon the adverse party?
      [*He wounds the* CARDINAL *and, in the scuffle, gives* BOSOLA *his death
      wound.*]
  There flies your ransom.
  CARDINAL   O justice!
  I suffer now for what hath former° been: *earlier*
  Sorrow is held the eldest child of sin.
55   FERDINAND   Now you're brave fellows. Caesar's fortune was harder than
    Pompey's; Caesar died in the arms of prosperity, Pompey at the feet of
    disgrace. You both died in the field. The pain's nothing: pain many times
    is taken away with the apprehension of greater, as the toothache with the
    sight of a barber that comes to pull it out: there's philosophy for you.
60   BOSOLA   Now my revenge is perfect. Sink, thou main cause
                      [*He kills* FERDINAND.]
  Of my undoing! The last part of my life
  Hath done me best service.
  FERDINAND   Give me some wet hay; I am broken-winded.[3] I do account this
    world but a dog kennel: I will vault credit and affect high pleasures[4]
65   beyond death.
  BOSOLA   He seems to come to himself, now he's so near the bottom.
  FERDINAND   My sister, O my sister! There's the cause on 't.
  Whether we fall by ambition, blood, or lust,
  Like diamonds we are cut with our own dust.   [*Dies.*]
70   CARDINAL   Thou hast thy payment, too.
  BOSOLA   Yes, I hold my weary soul in my teeth.
  'Tis ready to part from me. I do glory
  That thou, which stood'st like a huge pyramid
  Begun upon a large and ample base,
75   Shalt end in a little point, a kind of nothing.
      [*Enter, below,* PESCARA, MALATESTE, RODERIGO, *and* GRISOLAN.]
  PESCARA   How now, my lord?
  MALATESTE   O sad disaster!
  RODERIGO   How comes this?
  BOSOLA   Revenge for the Duchess of Malfi murdered
  By th' Aragonian brethren; for Antonio
  Slain by this hand; for lustful Julia
80   Poisoned by this man; and lastly for myself,

---

2. Ferdinand thinks he's on the field of battle
and offering the "honor of arms" (liberal surrender terms) to his foes. "Vaunt-guard": vanguard.

3. Worn-out horses are said to be broken-winded.
4. Go beyond expectation and enjoy great pleasures.

That was an actor in the main of all,
Much 'gainst mine own good nature, yet i' th' end
Neglected.
PESCARA   How now, my lord?
CARDINAL   Look to my brother:
He gave us these large wounds as we were struggling
85   Here i' the rushes.[5] And now, I pray,
Let me be laid by and never thought of.   [*Dies.*]
PESCARA   How fatally, it seems, he did withstand
His own rescue!
MALATESTE   Thou wretched thing of blood,
How came Antonio by his death?
90   BOSOLA   In a mist: I know not how;
Such a mistake as I have often seen
In a play. Oh, I am gone!
We are only like dead walls or vaulted graves,
That, ruined, yield no echo. Fare you well.
95   It may be pain, but no harm to me to die
In so good a quarrel. Oh, this gloomy world,
In what a shadow or deep pit of darkness
Doth womanish and fearful mankind live!
Let worthy minds ne'er stagger in distrust
100   To suffer death or shame for what is just:
Mine is another voyage.   [*Dies.*]
PESCARA   The noble Delio, as I came to the palace,
Told me of Antonio's being here, and showed me
A pretty gentleman, his son and heir.
        [*Enter* DELIO *with* ANTONIO's SON.]
MALATESTE   O, sir, you come too late.
105   DELIO   I heard so, and
Was armed° for it ere I came. Let us make noble use   *prepared*
Of this great ruin, and join all our force
To establish this young hopeful° gentleman   *promising*
In 's mother's right. These wretched eminent things
110   Leave no more fame behind 'em, than should one
Fall in a frost, and leave his print in snow;
As soon as the sun shines, it ever melts
Both form and matter. I have ever thought
Nature doth nothing so great for great men
115   As when she's pleased to make them lords of truth:
Integrity of life is fame's best friend,
Which nobly, beyond death, shall crown the end.   [*Exeunt.*]

performed 1613   *published* 1623

5. Leafy plants, strewn over Elizabethan floors in lieu of carpets.

Gender Relations: Conflict and Counsel

What are women good for? By the English Renaissance, men had been debating this question for centuries. Seventeenth-century writing on the question of women's proper social place was an important topic in two quite different prose genres. On the one hand, rhetorically flashy polemics argued, often in a spirit of witty rhetorical gamesmanship, either that females were worthless or that they were superior to men. On the other hand, sober treatises of domestic management advised readers—generally presumptively male readers—how to choose a spouse and order a household. Of the selections here, Joseph Swetnam and Rachel Speght exemplify the first kind of writing, and William Gouge the second.

Joseph Swetnam (ca. 1570?–1621) published his *Arraignment of Lewd, Idle, Froward and Unconstant Women* in 1615, under the pseudonym Tom Tel-troth. Swetnam's rambling but lively attack on women cobbles together proverbs, rowdy jokes, and anecdotes, as well as often inexact or misattributed paraphrases of what various authorities had to say about women, evidently derived from anthologies and commonplace books. The latter were printed versions of the personal notebooks into which many readers were accustomed to copy, under various headings depending on interest and use, quotations and citations from their reading. *The Arraignment* touched off a pamphlet war between the years 1615 and 1620, including four reissues of Swetnam's book and at least eight rejoinders or related works. Two of the answers bear women's allegorical names, Esther Sowernam (a satiric play on Swe[e]tnam) and Constantia Munda ("steadfast world"); they may or may not have actually been written by women. Other works include a stage play, *Swetnam the Women-Hater Arraigned by Women* (1620), and two satires on cross-dressing (the satires are included in the NAEL Archive).

The first response to Swetnam, in 1617, and the only one of these tracts published under the author's own name, was *A Muzzle for Melastomus* (Black Mouth), by the nineteen-year-old Rachel Speght (ca. 1597–?). Speght was the first Englishwoman to claim the role of polemicist and critic of gender ideology. Her tract defending women was published by, and perhaps solicited by, Swetnam's bookseller, Thomas Archer. While *A Muzzle* employs the railing attacks and witty ripostes expected in such a controversy, in most of the treatise Speght undertakes a serious argument. Her strategy resembles Aemelia Lanyer's in *Salve Deus Rex Judaeorum* (pp. 981–86), reinterpreting controversial biblical texts to yield a more equitable concept of gender and challenging the stereotypes of female inferiority. Speght's father, a Calvinist clergyman and author himself, evidently provided her with some classical education—very rare for seventeenth-century women of any class. In her writings Rachel Speght displays a knowledge of Latin, some training in logic and rhetoric, and some familiarity with a range of learned authorities. In 1621 she published a long meditative poem, *Mortality's Memorandum*, which was occasioned by her mother's death. She prefaced it with an address to the reader reaffirming her authorship of *A Muzzle for Melastomus* and with a three-hundred-line autobiographical poem, "A Dream," available in the NAEL Archive, which vigorously defends the importance of education for women.

William Gouge (1575–1653) was a clergyman educated at King's College Cambridge, a prominent minister at St. Ann Blackfriars Church in London, and the father of thirteen children. His Puritan leanings occasionally led to friction with the authorities early in his career, but in the 1640s he was selected by Parliament to chair the committee that developed the Westminster Confession, a set of principles designed to reform the English church along Calvinist lines. The Protestant Reformation had altered attitudes toward marriage and family life; while the Catholic Church honored celibacy and enjoined it for clergy, Protestants centered godly life on a harmonious marriage and the upbringing of devout children according to principles laid out in the Bible. This conviction spawned advice literature on the right ordering of the household, much of it written by ministers. *Of Domestical Duties*, perhaps the most thorough and popular of these manuals, was first published in 1622; new editions appeared in 1626 and 1634. Gouge not only devotes chapters to the proper roles of husband and wife but also discusses the obligations of children, and the relations between masters and servants. (All but the humblest seventeenth-century households employed domestic help.) Gouge

Marriage. The Liturgy of Solemnizing Marriage from *The Book of Common Prayer* (1559) emphasized the purposes of marriage (with procreation primary), the indissolubility of marriage, and the biblical texts undergirding that definition of marriage. It also held up the ideal of mutual love and help, which is represented in this emblem from George Wither's *A Collection of Emblems* (1635). The Latin motto reads in English, "Hand Washes Hand."

exemplifies moderate Puritan opinion, emphasizing the importance of love between married partners and decrying the double sexual standard that tolerated adultery in the husband while condemning it in the wife. Yet Gouge is no feminist; he advocated a clear hierarchy in marriage, the husband firmly in charge and the wife embracing her submission willingly as her religious duty. The relation between a husband and wife, he argues, is analogous to the relationship between Christ and the church of which he is the head. It is interesting to compare Gouge's views to those of John Milton, another strongly Protestant writer, in *Paradise Lost*.

JOSEPH SWETNAM

From The Arraignment of Lewd, Idle, Froward[1] and Unconstant Women: Or the Vanity of Them, Choose You Whether

Neither to the best, nor yet to the worst;
but to the common sort of women.

Musing with myself being idle, and having little ease to pass the time withal, and I being in a great choler[2] against some women, I mean more than one, and so in the rough of my fury, taking my pen in hand to beguile the time withal. Indeed, I might have employed myself to better use, than in such an idle business.

* * *

To the Reader. Read it, if you please, and like as you list: neither to the wisest clerk,[3] nor yet to the starkest fool, but unto the ordinary sort of giddy-headed young men, I send this greeting.

If thou mean to see the bearbaiting[4] of women, then trudge to this bear garden apace, and get in betimes,[5] and view every room where thou mayest best sit, for thy own pleasure, profit, and heart's ease, and bear with my rudeness if I chance to offend thee. But before I do open this trunk full of torments against women, I think it were not amiss . . . to drive all the women out of my hearing, for doubt lest this little spark kindle into such a flame, and raise so many stinging hornets humming about my ears, that all the wit I have will not quench the one, nor quiet the other. For I fear me I have set down more than they will like of, and yet a great deal less than they deserve: and for better proof, I refer myself to the judgment of men which have more experience than myself. For I esteem little of the malice of women, for men will be persuaded by reason, but women must be answered with silence, for I know women will bark more at me than Cerberus the two-headed dog did at Hercules, when he came into Hell to fetch out the fair Proserpina.[6]

* * *

---

1. Unruly, stubbornly willful.
2. Anger. Choler was one of the four humors, this one supposedly the source of anger and irascibility.
3. Scholar; originally, a clergyman (cleric).
4. Popular sport in medieval and early modern England in which a bear, chained to a post by his neck or one leg, was attacked by several dogs. The Paris Garden in Southwark was the largest

and most popular bear garden in London.
5. In good time.
6. Swetnam has confused several classical myths. Cerberus, the monster guarding the entrance to Hades, was said to have three (not two) heads, and Mercury (Hermes), not Hercules, was sent by Jove to release Proserpina. But the twelfth labor of Hercules was to bring Cerberus from Hades to the upper world.

*Chapter I. This first chapter shows to what use women were made.
It also shows that most of them degenerate from the use they were framed
unto, by leading a proud, lazy, and idle life, to the great hindrance
of their poor husbands.*

Moses describes a woman thus: at the first beginning (says he) a woman was made to be a helper unto man,[7] and so they are indeed: for she helps to spend and consume that which man painfully gets. He also says that they were made of the rib of a man,[8] and that their froward nature shows; for a rib is a crooked thing, good for nothing else, and women are crooked by nature, for small occasion will cause them to be angry.

Again, in a manner, she was no sooner made, but straightway her mind was set upon mischief, for by her aspiring mind and wanton will she quickly procured man's fall, and therefore ever since they are and have been a woe unto man, and follow the line of their first leader.[9]

For I pray you let us consider the times past, with the time present. First, that of David and Solomon, if they had occasion so many hundred years ago to exclaim so bitterly against women, for the one of them said, that it was better to be a doorkeeper, and better dwell in a den among lions, than to be in the house with a froward and wicked woman. And the other said, that the climbing up of a sandy hill to an aged man was nothing so wearisome as to be troubled with a froward woman.[1] . . . If a woman hold an opinion, no man can draw her from it; tell her of her fault, she will not believe that she is in any fault; give her good counsel, but she will not take it. If you do but look after another woman, then she will be jealous, the more thou lovest her, the more she will disdain thee, and if thou threaten her, then she will be angry, flatter her, and then she will be proud, and if thou forbear her, it makes her bold, and if thou chasten her, then she will turn into a serpent. At a word, a woman will never forget an injury, nor give thanks for a good turn. What wise man then will exchange gold for dross, pleasure for pain, a quiet life, for wrangling brawls, from the which married men are never free.

❄   ❄   ❄

And what of all this? Why nothing, but to tell thee that a woman is better lost than found, better forsaken than taken. Saint Paul says, that they which marry, do well, but he also says, that they which marry not, do better,[2] and he no doubt was well advised what he spoke. Then, if thou be wise, keep thy head out of the halter and take heed before thou have cause to curse thy hard pennyworth,[3] or wish the priest speechless which knit the knot.

---

7. Genesis 2.18: "And the Lord God said, It is not good that the man should be alone; I will make him an help meet for him."
8. Genesis 2.21–22.
9. I.e., Eve.
1. Swetnam evidently relies on his imperfect memory or on careless notes. The comparisons he paraphrases are not from Solomon or David but from the biblical Apocrypha, attributed in the Book of Ecclesiasticus to Jesus Son of Sirach:

"I had rather dwell with a lion and a dragon, than to keep house with a wicked woman. . . . As the climbing up a sandy way is to the feet of the aged, so is a wife full of words to a quiet man."
2. 1 Corinthians 7.38: "So then he that giveth her [his virgin] in marriage doeth well; but he that giveth her not in marriage doeth better." Swetnam takes the quote out of context.
3. Something, in this case a wife, that is worth only a penny.

The philosophers which lived in the old time, their opinions were so hard of marriage that they never delighted therein, for one of them being asked why he married not? he answered, that it was too soon. And afterwards when he was old, he was asked the same question, and he said then that it was too late.

* * *

If thou marriest a woman of evil report, her discredits will be a spot in thy brow; thou canst not go in the street with her without mocks, nor among thy neighbors without frumps.[4] And commonly the fairest women are soonest enticed to yield unto vanity. He that has a fair wife and a whetstone, everyone will be whetting thereon.[5] And a castle is hard to keep when it is assaulted by many, and fair women are commonly caught at. He that marries a fair woman, everyone will wish his death to enjoy her. And if thou be never so rich, and yet but a clown[6] in condition, then will thy fair wife have her credit to please her fancy, for a diamond has not his grace but in gold, no more has a fair woman her full commendations but in the ornament of her bravery,[7] by which means there are divers women whose beauty has brought their husbands into great poverty and discredit by their pride and whoredom. A fair woman commonly will go like a peacock, and her husband must go like a woodcock.[8]

1615

4. Derisive jeers.
5. A whetstone is an abrasive stone for sharpening knives or other edged tools. The bawdy joke suggests that "everyone" will make use of both the stone and the fair wife.

6. A countryman, one who is uncouth or ill-bred.
7. Her rich and showy clothing and jewelry.
8. A common European migratory bird with mottled brown plumage; easily taken in a snare, it was associated with gullibility.

RACHEL SPEGHT

From A Muzzle for Melastomus[1]

Not unto the veriest idiot that ever set pen to paper, but to the cynical[2] baiter of women, or metamorphosed Misogunes,[3] Joseph Swetnam

From standing water, which soon putrifies, can no good fish be expected, for it produces no other creatures but those that are venomous or noisome, as snakes, and such like. Semblably,[4] no better stream can we look should issue from your idle corrupt brain than that whereto the rough of your fury (to use your own words) has moved you to open the sluice. In which excrement of your roving cognitions you have used such irregularities touching

1. Black mouth.
2. A play on the Latin *cynicus*, "canine," "doglike."
3. Hater of women (Greek, cf. Misogynist). Speght

identifies Swetnam as the author of the *Arraignment*, which he had signed Thomas Tel-troth.
4. Likewise.

concordance,[5] and observed so disordered a method, as I doubt not to tell you, that a very accidence scholar would have quite put you down[6] in both. You appear herein not unlike that painter who, seriously endeavoring to portray Cupid's bow, forgot the string.[7] For you, being greedy to botch up your mingle mangle invective against women, have not therein observed, in many places, so much as a grammar sense.[8] But the emptiest barrel makes the loudest sound, and so we will account of you.

Many propositions have you framed, which, as you think, make much against women, but if one would make a logical assumption, the conclusion would be flat against your own sex. Your dealing wants so much discretion that I doubt whether to bestow so good a name as the dunce upon you: but minority[9] bids me keep within my bounds. And therefore I only say unto you that your corrupt heart and railing tongue have made you a fit scribe for the Devil.

In that you have termed your virulent foam *The Bearbaiting of Women*, you have plainly displayed your own disposition to be cynical, in that there appears no other dog or bull to bait them, but yourself. Good had it been for you to have put on that muzzle which Saint James would have all Christians to wear: "Speak not evil one of another,"[1] and then you had not seemed so like the serpent Porphirus, as now you do; which, though full of deadly poison, yet being toothless, hurts none so much as himself.[2] For you having gone beyond the limits not of humanity alone but of Christianity, have done greater harm unto your own soul than unto women, as may plainly appear. First, in dishonoring of God by palpable blasphemy, wresting and perverting every place of Scripture that you have alleged, which by the testimony of Saint Peter, is to the destruction of them that do so.[3] Secondly, it appears by your disparaging of, and opprobrious speeches against, that excellent work of God's hands, which in his great love he perfected for the comfort of man. Thirdly, and lastly, by this your hodgepodge of heathenish sentences, similes, and examples, you have set forth yourself in your right colors unto the view of the world, and I doubt not but the judicious will account of you according to your demerit. As for the vulgar sort, which have no more learning than you have showed in your book, it is likely they will applaud you for your pains.

* * *

Of Woman's excellency, with the causes of her creation, and of the sympathy which ought to be in man and wife each toward other

* * *

True it is, as is already confessed, that women first sinned, yet find we no mention of spiritual nakedness till man had sinned. Then it is said, "Their

---

5. Agreement of the parts of a sentence, according to the rules of grammar.
6. Revealed your errors and thereby disgraced you. "Accidence scholar": a schoolboy learning his Latin grammar.
7. This may refer not to an actual image, but rather to the omission of what is crucially important.
8. See his first sentence for an example.

9. Her own youth (she is just nineteen years old).
1. James 4.11. This and later biblical texts, marked (M) in these notes, are identified in the margins of Speght's original text as evidence of scholarly accuracy.
2. This toothless but venomous serpent is discussed in the naturalist Topsell's volume *Serpents*, though not the quality of hurting only himself.
3. 2 Peter 3.16 (M).

eyes were opened,"[4] the eyes of their mind and conscience, and then perceived they themselves naked, that is, not only bereft of their integrity which they originally had, but felt the rebellion and disobedience of their members in the disordered motions of their now corrupt nature, which made them for shame to cover their nakedness. Then, and not before, it is said that they saw it, as if sin were imperfect, and unable to bring a deprivation of a blessing received, or death on all mankind, till man, in whom lay the active power of generation, had transgressed. The offense therefore of Adam and Eve is by Saint Augustine thus distinguished, "the man sinned against God and himself, the woman against God, herself, and her husband."[5] Yet in her giving of the fruit to eat she had no malicious intent toward him, but did therein show a desire to make her husband partaker of that happiness which she thought by their eating they should both have enjoyed. This her giving Adam of that sauce wherewith Satan had served her, whose sourness before he had eaten she did not perceive, was that which made her sin to exceed his. Wherefore, that she might not of him who ought to honor her be abhorred, the first promise that was made in Paradise God made to woman, that by her seed should the serpent's head be broken.[6] Whereupon Adam calls her *Hevah*, life,[7] that as the woman had been an occasion of sin, so should woman bring forth the Savior from sin, which was in the fullness of time accomplished . . . so that by Eve's blessed seed (as Saint Paul affirms) it is brought to pass, "that male and female are all one in Christ Jesus."[8]

* * *

The efficient cause of woman's creation was Jehovah the Eternal, the truth of which is manifest in Moses his narration of the six days works, where he says, "God created them male and female."[9] And David, exhorting all the earth to sing unto the Lord, meaning, by a metonymy,[1] earth, all creatures that live on the earth of which nation or sex soever, gives this reason, "For the Lord hath made us."[2] That work, then, cannot choose but be good, yea very good, which is wrought by so excellent a workman as the Lord, for he being a glorious creator, must needs effect a worthy creature. . . .

Secondly, the material cause, or matter whereof woman was made, was of a refined mold, if I may so speak. For man was created of the dust of the earth, but woman was made of a part of man, after that he was a living soul. Yet was she not produced from Adam's foot, to be his too low inferior, nor from his head to be his superior, but from his side, near his heart, to be his equal. That where he is lord she may be lady: and therefore said God concerning man and woman jointly, "Let them rule over the fish of the sea,

4. Genesis 3.7 (M).
5. This formula became a commonplace, perhaps derived (very loosely) from some phrases in St. Augustine's sermon "De Adam et Eva et Sancta Maria."
6. Genesis 3.15 (M).
7. Genesis 3.20 (M).
8. Galatians 3.28 (M).
9. Genesis 1.27 (M). Speght here begins her analysis of woman's creation according to Aristotle's four causes of the making of any object: the efficient cause is the agent who made it; the material cause is the matter of which it is made; the formal cause is the plan or design by which it is formed; the final cause is the purpose for which it is made.
1. A figure of speech in which a part or attribute of a thing is used for the whole.
2. Psalms 100.3 (M).

and over the fowls of the heaven, and over every beast that moves upon the earth."[3] By which words he makes their authority equal, and all creatures to be in subjection unto them both. . . .

Thirdly, the formal cause, fashion, and proportion of a woman was excellent. For she was neither like the beasts of the earth, fowls of the air, fishes of the sea, or any other inferior creature, but man was the only object which she did resemble. For as God gave man a lofty countenance, that he might look up toward heaven, so did he likewise give unto woman. And as the temperature[4] of man's body is excellent, so is woman's. . . . And (that more is) in the image of God were they both created; yea and to be brief, all the parts of their bodies, both external and internal, were correspondent and meet each for other.

Fourthly and lastly, the final cause or end, for which woman was made, was to glorify God, and to be a collateral companion for man to glorify God, in using her body and all the parts, powers, and faculties thereof, as instruments for his honor.

* * *

To the Reader[5]

Although (courteous reader) I am young in years and more defective in knowledge, that little smattering in learning which I have obtained being only the fruit of such vacant hours as I could spare from affairs befitting my sex, yet am I not altogether ignorant of that analogy which ought to be used in a literate responsory.[6] But the bearbaiting of women, unto which I have framed my apologetical[7] answer, being altogether without method, irregular, without grammatical concordance, and a promiscuous mingle mangle, it would admit no such order to be observed in the answering thereof, as a regular responsory requires. * * *

1617

3. Genesis 1.26 (M).
4. Mixture or composition of elements.
5. This preface introduces a brief satiric treatise appended to *A Muzzle*, titled "Certain *Quaeres* to the baiter of women, with confutation of some parts of his diabolical discipline."
6. Answer or reply.
7. Offering a defense or vindication.

WILLIAM GOUGE

From Of Domestical Duties

Of a wife's subjection in general

The first point to be handled in the treatise of wives' particular duties is the general matter of all under which all other particulars are comprised, for it hath as large an extent as that honor which is required in the first commandment being applied to wives. When first the Lord declared unto the woman[1] her duty, he set it down under this phrase: "Thy desire shall be subject to thine husband" (Genesis 3:16).

Objection. That was a punishment inflicted on her for her transgression?

Answer. And a law too, for trial of her obedience, which if it be not observed, her nature will be more depraved, and her fault more increased. Besides, we cannot but think that the woman was made before the Fall, that the man might rule over her. Upon this ground the Prophets and Apostles have oft urged the same. Sarah is commended for this, that she was subject to her husband (1 Peter 3:6).[2] Hereby the Holy Ghost would teach wives, that subjection ought to be as salt to season every duty which they perform to their husband. Their very opinion, affection, speech, action, and all that concerneth the husband, must savor of subjection. Contrary is the disposition of many wives, whom ambition hath tainted and corrupted within and without: they cannot endure to hear of subjection: they imagine that they are made slaves thereby. But I hope partly by that which hath been before delivered[3] concerning those common duties which man and wife do mutually owe each to other, and partly by the particulars which under this general are comprised, but most especially by the duties which the husband in particular oweth to his wife, it will evidently appear, that this subjection is no servitude. But were it more than it is, seeing God requireth subjection of a wife to her husband, the wife is bound to yield it. And good reason it is that she who first drew man into sin, should be now subject to him, lest by the like womanish weakness she fall again.

Of an husband's superiority over a wife, to be acknowledged by the wife

The subjection which is required of a wife to her husband implieth two things.

1. That she acknowledge her husband to be her superior.
2. That she respect him as her superior.

That acknowledgment of the husband's superiority is twofold,

1. General of any husband.
2. Particular of her own husband.

The general is the ground of the particular:[4] for till a wife be informed that an husband, by virtue of his place, is his wife's superior, she will not be persuaded that her own husband is above her, or hath any authority over her.

First therefore concerning the general, I will lay down some evident and undeniable proofs, to show that an husband is his wife's superior, and hath authority over her. The proofs are these following.

1. God of whom, the powers that be ordained, are (Romans 13:1), hath power to place his image in whom he will, and to whom God giveth superiority and authority, the same ought to be acknowledged to be due unto them. But God said of the man to the woman, he shall rule over thee (Genesis 3:16).

---

1. Eve, after the Fall in the Garden of Eden.
2. Sarah was the wife of the patriarch Abraham.
3. Earlier in Gouge's treatise.
4. Once the general premise (the superiority of all husbands) is established, the particular instance (the superiority of a woman's own husband) will follow logically from it.

2. Nature hath placed an eminency in the male over the female: so as where they are linked together in one yoke, it is given by nature that he should govern, she obey. This did the heathen by light of nature observe.

3. The titles and names, whereby an husband is set forth, do imply a superiority and authority in him, as "lord" (1 Peter 3:6), "master" (Esther), "guide" (Proverbs 2:17), "head" (1 Corinthians 2:3), "image and glory of God" (1 Corinthians 11:7).

4. The persons whom the husband by virtue of his place, and whom the wife by virtue of her place, represent, most evidently prove as much: for an husband representeth Christ, and a wife, the Church (Ephesians 5:23).

5. The circumstances noted by the Holy Ghost at the woman's creation imply no less, as that she was created after man, for man's good, and out of man's side (Genesis 2:18, etc.).

6. The very attire which nature and custom of all times and places have taught women to put on, comfirmeth the same: as long hair, veils, and other coverings over the head: this and the former argument doth the Apostle[5] himself use to this very purpose (1 Corinthians 11:7, etc.).

The point then being so clear, wives ought in conscience to acknowledge as much: namely that an husband hath superiority and authority over a wife. The acknowledgment hereof is a main and principal duty, and a ground of all other duties. Till a wife be fully instructed therein and truly persuaded thereof, no duty can be performed by her as it ought: for subjection hath relation to superiority and authority. The very notation of the word implieth as much. How then can subjection be yielded, if husbands be not acknowledged superiors? It may be forced, as one king conquered in battle by another, may be compelled to yield homage to the conqueror, but yet because he still thinketh with himself, that he is no whit inferior, he will hardly be brought willingly to yield a subject's duty to him, but rather expect a time when he may free himself and take revenge of the conqueror.

Of a fond conceit[6] that husband and wife are equal

Contrary to the forenamed subjection is the opinion of many wives, who think themselves every way as good as their husbands, and no way inferior to them.

The reason whereof seemeth to be that small inequality which is betwixt the husband and the wife: for of all degrees wherein there is any difference betwixt person and person, there is the least disparity betwixt man and wife. Though the man be as the head, yet is the woman as the heart, which is the most excellent part of the body next the head, far more excellent than any other member under the head, and almost equal to the head in many respects, and as necessary as the head. As an evidence, that a wife is to man as the heart to the head, she was at her first creation (Genesis 2:21) taken out of the side of man where his heart lieth; and though the woman was at first of the man (1 Corinthians 11:12) created out of his side, yet is the man also by the woman. Ever since the first creation man hath been born and brought forth out of the woman's womb: so as neither the man is without the woman, nor the woman without the man: yea, as the wife hath not power of his own

---

5. The Apostle Paul.   6. Foolish idea.

body, but he wife (1 Corinthians 7:4).[7] They are also heirs together of the grace of life (1 Peter 3:7). Besides, wives are mothers of the same children, whereof their husbands are fathers [for God said to both, multiply and increase (Genesis 1:28)] and mistresses of the same servants whereof they are masters [for Sarah is called mistress (Genesis 16:4)] and in many other respects there is common equity betwixt husbands and wives; whence many wives gather that in all things there ought to be a mutual equality.

But from some particulars to infer a general is a very weak argument.

1. Doth it follow, that because in many things there is a common equity betwixt judges of office, justices of peace, and constables of towns, that therefore there is in all things an equality betwixt them?

2. In many things there is not a common equity: for the husband may command his wife, but not she him.

3. Even in those things wherein there is a common equity, there is not an equality: for the husband hath ever even in all things a superiority: as if there be any difference even in the forenamed instances, the husband must have the stronger: as in giving the name of Rachel's youngest child, where the wife would have one name, the husband another, that name which the husband gave, stood (Genesis 35:18).

Though there seem to be never so little disparity, yet God having so expressly appointed subjection, it ought to be acknowledged: and though husband and wife may mutually serve one another through love: yet the Apostle suffereth not a woman to rule over a man. . . .

Of a wife's acknowledgment of her own husband's superiority

The truth and life of that general acknowledgment of husbands' honor, consisteth in the particular application thereof unto their own proper husbands.

The next duty therefore is, that wives acknowledge their own husbands, even those to whom by God's providence they are joined in marriage, to be worthy of an husband's honor, and to be their superior: thus much the Apostle intendeth by that particle of restraint (Ephesians 5:22,24) which he useth very often: so likewise doth St. Peter, exhorting wives to be in subjection to their own husbands (1 Peter 3:1,5): and hereunto restraining the commendation of the ancient good wives, that they were in subjection to their own husbands.

Objection. What if a man of mean place be married to a woman of eminent place, or a servant to be married to his mistress, or an aged woman to a youth, must such a wife acknowledge such an husband her superior?

Answer. Yea, verily: for in giving herself to be his wife, and taking him to be her husband, she advanceth him above herself, and subjecteth herself unto him. It meaneth nothing what either of them were before marriage: by virtue of that matrimonial bond the husband is made the head of his wife, though the husband were before marriage a very beggar, and of mean parentage, and the wife very wealthy and of a noble stock; or though he were her prentice, or bondslave; which also holdeth in the case betwixt an aged woman and a youth: for the Scripture hath made no exception in any of those cases.

---

7. The text seems corrupt at this point: Corinthians 1.7.4 reads in full: "The wife hath not power of her own body, but the husband: and likewise also the husband hath not power of his own body, but the wife."

2. *Objection.* But what if a man of lewd and beastly conditions, as a drunkard, a glutton, a profane swaggerer, an impious swearer, and blasphemer, be married to a wife, sober, religious matron, must she account him her superior, and worthy of an husband's honor?

Answer. Surely she must. For the evil quality and disposition of his heart and life, doth not deprive a man of that civil honor which God hath given unto him. Though an husband in regard of evil qualities may carry the image of the devil, yet in regard of his place and office he beareth the image of God: so do magistrates in the commonwealth, ministers in the church, parents and masters in the same family. Note for our present purpose, the exhortation of St. Peter to Christian wives which had infidel husbands, Be in subjection to them: let your conversation be in fear (1 Peter 3:1,2). If infidels carry not the devil's image, and are not, so long as they are infidels, vessels of Satan, who are? Yet wives must be subject to them, and fear them.

Of wives denying honor to their own husbands

Contrary thereunto is a very perverse disposition in some wives, who think they could better subject themselves to any husband, than their own. Though in general they acknowledge that an husband is his wife's superior, yet when the application cometh to themselves they fail, and cannot be brought to yield, that they are their husbands' inferiors. This is a vice worse than the former. For to acknowledge no husband to be superior over his wife, but to think man and wife in all things equal, may proceed from ignorance of mind, and error of judgment. But for a wife who knoweth and acknowledgeth the general, that an husband is above his wife, to imagine that she herself is not inferior to her husband, ariseth from monstrous self-conceit, and intolerable arrogancy, as if she herself were above her own sex, and more than a woman.

Contrary also is the practice of such women . . . as purposely marry a man so far lower than themselves, for this very end, that they may rule over their own husbands: and of others who being aged, for that end marry youths, if not very boys. A mind and practice very unseemly, and clean thwarting God's ordinance. But let them think of ruling what they list, the trust is, that they make themselves subjects both by God's law and man's: of which subjection such wives do oft feel the heaviest burden. Solomon noteth this to be one of the things for which the earth is disquieted, when a servant reigneth. Now when can a servant more domineer, than when he hath married his mistress? As for aged women who married youths, I may say, as in another case it was said, woe to thee, O wife whose husband is a child. Unmeet it is that an aged man should be married to a young maid, but much more unmeet for an aged woman to be married to a youth. . . .

Of a wife's obedience in general

Hitherto of a wife's reverence, it followeth to speak of her obedience: The first law that ever was given to woman since her fall, laid upon her this duty of obedience to her husband, in these words, "Thy desire shall be to thine husband, and he shall rule over thee" (Genesis 3:16). How can an husband rule over a wife, if she obey not him? The principal part of that *submission* which in this text (Ephesians 5:22), and in many other places is required of a wife, consisteth in obedience: and therefore it is expressly commended unto wives in the example of Sarah who obeyed Abraham (1 Peter 3:6). Thus by obedience doth the Church manifest her subjection to Christ.

The place wherein God hath set an husband; namely, to be an head (Ephesians 5:23); the authority which he hath given unto him, to be a Lord (1 Peter 3:6), do all require obedience of a wife. Is not obedience to be yielded to an head, lord, and master? Take away all authority from an husband, if ye exempt a wife from obedience.

Contrary is the stoutness of such wives as must have their own will, and do what they list, or else all shall be out of quiet. *Their* will must be done, *they* must rule and over-rule all, *they* must command not only children and servants, but husbands also, if at least the husband will be at peace. Look into families, observe the estate and condition of many of them, and then tell me if these things be not so. If an husband be a man of courage, and seek to stand upon his right, and maintain his authority by requiring obedience of his wife, strange it is to behold what an hurly burly she will make in the house: but if he be a milksop, and basely yield unto his wife, and suffer her to rule, then, it may be, there shall be some outward quiet. The ground hereof is an ambitious and proud humor in women, who must needs rule, or else they think themselves slaves. But let them think as they list: assuredly herein they thwart God's ordinance, pervert the order of nature, deface the image of Christ, overthrow the ground of all duty, hinder the good of the family, become an ill pattern to children and servants, lay themselves open to Satan, and incur many other mischiefs which cannot but follow upon the violating of this main duty of obedience, which if it be not performed, how can other duties be expected?

1622

Inquiry and Experience

The problem of knowledge—what we know, how we know, what areas most demand attention, what methods are useful in studying those areas—came to be of pressing concern to many seventeenth-century thinkers and writers. Throughout Europe, experimental scientists were producing treatises describing their discoveries—Galileo on astronomy, William Harvey on the circulation of the blood, William Gilbert on magnetism—challenging the received wisdom of the past. The emphasis in many of these works is on the writer's direct personal experience, imagined as more immediate and convincing than any secondhand account.

But what experiences were worth recording? For Francis Bacon, individual peculiarities, as well as some traits of the mind and senses shared by all human beings, skew scientific objectivity and interfere with the search for truth. According to Bacon, the investigator must become conscious of these mental impediments, or "idols," and purge his mind of them insofar as he can. In *The New Atlantis*, Bacon proposes collaborative research institutes, which by pooling and orchestrating scientific inquiry, multiply the profitability of any individual's explorations while simultaneously reducing the destructive effect of his quirks. In his essays, Bacon adopted the voice of accumulated public wisdom, writing from the perspective of a man of affairs eager to make his way in the murky world of Jacobean court culture. Bacon was not, however, himself a distinguished experimental scientist. William Harvey, a physician who discovers the circulation of the blood, is less concerned than Bacon with a theory of knowledge and more with the detailed, matter-of-fact descriptions of his actual experiments: he effectively practices what Bacon preaches.

While writers like Bacon and Harvey championed "objective," dispassionate scientific experimentation, other writers, such as Robert Burton and Sir Thomas Browne, find human idiosyncrasy a fascinating subject of inquiry in itself. Indeed, a new ideal of objectivity possibly allows human foibles to be delineated in sharper, because contrasting, relief. Burton writes about melancholy, a psychological condition he regards as simultaneously pathological and universal; Browne, examining himself, revels in his own lack of systematic rigor.

In these and other writings of the period we see English prose developing remarkable stylistic range: sometimes epigrammatic, sometimes homely and vulgar, sometimes witty and boldly imagistic, sometimes learnedly allusive, sometimes ornately Latinate. While sixteenth-century prose typically employs long sentences with complex patterns of subordination and parallelism, early seventeenth-century prose favors broken rhythms, irregular phrasing, and more loosely organized sentences. Both the self-conscious embrace of whimsy and the tone of objective reportage—the latter visible not only in scientific writing but also in early journalism—are key precursors to the rise of the novel.

SIR FRANCIS BACON

As a literary figure Sir Francis Bacon (1561–1626) played a central role in the development of the English essay and also inaugurated the genre of the scientific utopia in his *New Atlantis* (1627). But he was even more important to the intellectual and cultural history of the earlier seventeenth century for his treatises on reforming and promoting learning through experiment and induction. His life span closely overlapped that of Donne and Jonson, but unlike them he came from a noble family close to the centers of government and power. During Elizabeth's reign he studied law and entered Parliament. But it was under James I that his political fortunes took off: he was knighted in 1603, became attorney general in 1613, lord chancellor (the highest judicial post) and Baron Verulam in 1618, and Viscount St. Albans in 1621. That same year, however, he was convicted on twenty-three counts of corruption and accepting bribes and was fined, imprisoned, and forced from office. Bacon admitted the truth of the charges (though they were in part politically motivated), merely observing that everyone took bribes and that bribery never influenced his judgment. He later commented: "I was the justest judge that was in England these fifty years, but it was the justest censure in Parliament that was these 200 years."

As an essayist Bacon stands at almost the opposite pole from his great French predecessor Michel de Montaigne (1533–1592), who proposed to learn about humankind by an intensive analysis of his own sensations, emotions, attitudes, and ideas. Bacon's essays are instead on topics "Civil and Moral." Montaigne's are tentative in structure; witty, expansive, and reflective in style; intimate, candid, and affable in tone; and he speaks constantly in the first person. By contrast, Bacon adopts an aphoristic structure and a curt, often disjunctive style, as well as a tone of cool objectivity and weighty sententiousness; he seldom uses "I," but instead presents himself as a mouthpiece for society's accumulated practical wisdom. The ten short pieces of the first edition of his essays (1597) are little more than collections of maxims placed in sequence; the thirty-eight of the second edition (1612) are longer and looser; the fifty-eight of the final edition (1625) are still longer, are smoother in texture, use more figurative language, and are more unified. In that last edition, more than half of the essays deal with public life, and many of the others—even on such topics as truth, marriage, and love—are written from the vantage point of a man of affairs rather than that of a profound moralist. They evoke an atmosphere of expediency and self-interest but also voice precepts of moral wisdom and public virtue, offering a penetrating insight into the thinking of the Jacobean ruling class.

Early in his life Bacon declared, "I have taken all knowledge to be my province." Whereas Donne, in the *First Anniversary*, saw human history as a process of inevitable degeneration and decay, Bacon saw it as progressive and believed that his new "scientific" method would lead humankind to a better future. He attempted a survey of the entire field of learning in *The Advancement of Learning* (1605), analyzing the principal obstacles to that advancement (rhetoric prompting the study of words rather than things, medieval scholasticism that ignores nature and promotes a barren rationalism, and pseudosciences such as astrology and alchemy); then he set forth what remains to be investigated. His *Novum Organum* (1620), written in Latin, urged induction—combining empirical investigation with carefully limited and tested generalizations—as the right method of investigating nature: the title challenged Aristotle's *Organon*, still the basis of university education, with its heavy reliance on deduction. *Novum Organum* includes a trenchant analysis of four kinds of "Idols"—

psychological dispositions and intellectual habits that hold humankind back in its quest for truth. But despite his emphasis on experiment, Bacon generally ignored major scientific discoveries by Galileo, Harvey, Gilbert, and others; his true role was as a herald of the modern age. Despite his critique of rhetoric, he used the rich resources of figurative language—and of Utopian fiction in *The New Atlantis*—to urge a new faith in experiment and science. He segregated theology and science as "two truths," freeing science to go its own way unhampered by the old dogmas and unrestrained by the morality they supported. He is a primary creator of the myth of science as a pathway to Utopia; late in the century the Royal Society honored him as a prophet.

FROM ESSAYS[1]

Of Truth

"What is truth?" said jesting Pilate; and would not stay for an answer.[2] Certainly there be that delight in giddiness,[3] and count it a bondage to fix a belief; affecting free will in thinking, as well as in acting. And though the sects of philosophers of that kind be gone, yet there remain certain discoursing wits,[4] which are of the same veins, though there be not so much blood in them as was in those of the ancients. But it is not only the difficulty and labor which men take in finding out of truth; nor again, that when it is found, it imposeth upon[5] men's thoughts, that doth bring lies in favor; but a natural though corrupt love of the lie itself. One of the later school of the Grecians examineth the matter, and is at a stand[6] to think what should be in it, that men should love lies, where neither they make for pleasure, as with poets, nor for advantage, as with the merchant, but for the lie's sake. But I cannot tell: this same truth is a naked and open daylight, that doth not show the masques and mummeries and triumphs of the world half so stately and daintily as candlelights. Truth may perhaps come to the price of a pearl, that showeth best by day, but it will not rise to the price of a diamond or carbuncle,[7] that showeth best in varied lights. A mixture of a lie doth ever add pleasure. Doth any man doubt that if there were taken out of men's minds vain opinions, flattering hopes, false valuations, imaginations as one would, and the like, but it would leave the minds of a number of men poor shrunken things, full of melancholy and indisposition, and unpleasing to themselves? One of the fathers, in great severity, called poesy *vinum daemonum*,[8] because it filleth the imagination, and yet it is but with the shadow of a lie. But it is not the lie that passeth through the mind, but the lie that sinketh in, and settleth in it, that doth the hurt, such as we spake of before. But howsoever these things are thus in men's depraved judgments and affections, yet

---

1. Bacon's essays appeared in three editions, 1597 (10 essays), 1612 (38 essays), and 1625 (58 essays); we illustrate the considerable stylistic differences between the earliest and latest collections by presenting two versions of "Of Studies." Otherwise, all selections are from the 1625 collection, in which "Of Truth" stands first.
2. See John 18.38 for Pilate's idle query to Jesus.
3. Foolish changeability. "That": those who.

4. Discursive minds. "Philosophers of that kind": the Greek Skeptics, who taught the uncertainty of all things.
5. Restricts, controls.
6. I.e., is baffled.
7. Ruby.
8. "The wine of devils"; St. Augustine is probably being cited.

truth, which only doth judge itself, teacheth that the inquiry of truth, which is the lovemaking or wooing of it, the knowledge of truth, which is the presence of it, and the belief of truth, which is the enjoying of it, is the sovereign good of human nature. The first creature[9] of God, in the works of the days, was the light of the sense; the last was the light of reason; and his sabbath work ever since is the illumination of his Spirit. First he breathed light upon the face of the matter, or chaos; then he breathed light into the face of man; and still he breatheth and inspireth light into the face of his chosen. The poet that beautified the sect that was otherwise inferior to the rest[1] saith yet excellently well: "It is a pleasure to stand upon the shore, and to see ships tossed upon the sea; a pleasure to stand in the window of a castle, and to see a battle, and the adventures thereof below; but no pleasure is comparable to the standing upon the vantage ground of truth" (a hill not to be commanded,[2] and where the air is always clear and serene), "and to see the errors, and wanderings, and mists, and tempests, in the vale below": so always that this prospect[3] be with pity, and not with swelling or pride. Certainly, it is heaven upon earth to have a man's mind move in charity, rest in providence, and turn upon the poles of truth.

To pass from theological and philosophical truth to the truth of civil business, it will be acknowledged even by those that practice it not, that clear and round[4] dealing is the honor of man's nature, and that mixture of falsehood is like alloy in coin of gold and silver, which may make the metal work the better, but it embaseth[5] it. For these winding and crooked courses are the goings of the serpent; which goeth basely upon the belly, and not upon the feet. There is no vice that doth so cover a man with shame as to be found false and perfidious. And therefore Montaigne saith prettily, when he inquired the reason why the word of the lie should be such a disgrace, and such an odious charge, saith he, "If it be well weighed, to say that a man lieth is as much to say as that he is brave towards God and a coward towards men."[6] For a lie faces God, and shrinks from man. Surely the wickedness of falsehood and breach of faith cannot possibly be so highly expressed, as in that it shall be the last peal to call the judgments of God upon the generations of men, it being foretold that when Christ cometh, he shall not "find faith upon the earth."[7]

1625

Of Marriage and Single Life

He that hath wife and children hath given hostages to fortune; for they are impediments to great enterprises, either of virtue or mischief. Certainly the best works, and of greatest merit for the public, have proceeded from the unmarried or childless men, which both in affection and means have married

---

9. Creation.
1. Lucretius's *On the Nature of Things* expressed the Epicurean creed, which Bacon thought inferior because it emphasized pleasure.
2. Topped by anything higher.

3. I.e., provided always that this observation.
4. Upright.
5. Debases.
6. *Essays* 2.18.
7. Luke 18.8.

and endowed the public. Yet it were great reason that those that have children should have greatest care of future times, unto which they know they must transmit their dearest pledges. Some there are who, though they lead a single life, yet their thoughts do end with themselves, and account future times impertinences.[1] Nay, there are some other that account wife and children but as bills of charges. Nay more, there are some foolish rich covetous men that take a pride in having no children, because they may be thought so much the richer. For perhaps they have heard some talk, "Such an one is a great rich man," and another except to it, "Yea, but he hath a great charge of children"; as if it were an abatement to his riches. But the most ordinary cause of a single life is liberty, especially in certain self-pleasing and humorous[2] minds, which are so sensible of every restraint, as they will go near to think their girdles and garters to be bonds and shackles. Unmarried men are best friends, best masters, best servants, but not always best subjects, for they are light to run away, and almost all fugitives are of that condition. A single life doth well with churchmen, for charity will hardly water the ground where it must first fill a pool. It is indifferent for judges and magistrates, for if they be facile[3] and corrupt, you shall have a servant five times worse than a wife. For soldiers, I find the generals commonly in their hortatives[4] put men in mind of their wives and children; and I think the despising of marriage amongst the Turks maketh the vulgar soldier more base. Certainly wife and children are a kind of discipline of humanity; and single men, though they be many times more charitable, because their means are less exhaust,[5] yet, on the other side, they are more cruel and hardhearted (good to make severe inquisitors), because their tenderness is not so oft called upon. Grave natures, led by custom, and therefore constant, are commonly loving husbands, as was said of Ulysses, *Vetulam suam praetulit immortalitati.*[6] Chaste women are often proud and froward,[7] as presuming upon the merit of their chastity. It is one of the best bonds, both of chastity and obedience, in the wife if she think her husband wise, which she will never do if she find him jealous. Wives are young men's mistresses, companions for middle age, and old men's nurses; so as a man may have a quarrel[8] to marry when he will. But yet he was reputed one of the wise men that made answer to the question when a man should marry: "A young man not yet, an elder man not at all."[9] It is often seen that bad husbands have very good wives; whether it be that it raiseth the price of their husbands' kindness when it comes, or that the wives take a pride in their patience. But this never fails, if the bad husbands were of their own choosing, against their friends' consent; for then they will be sure to make good their own folly.

1612, 1625

---

1. Irrelevant concerns.
2. Unbalanced, whimsical.
3. Pliable.
4. Exhortations.
5. Exhausted.
6. "He preferred his old wife to immortality." Ulysses might have had immortality with the nymph Calypso but preferred to go back to Penelope.
7. Ill-tempered.
8. Pretext.
9. Thales (6th century B.C.E.), one of the Seven Sages of Greece.

Of Great Place

Men in great place are thrice servants: servants of the sovereign or state, servants of fame, and servants of business. So as they have no freedom, neither in their persons, nor in their actions, nor in their times. It is a strange desire, to seek power and to lose liberty, or to seek power over others and to lose power over a man's self. The rising unto place is laborious, and by pains men come to greater pains; and it is sometimes base, and by indignities men come to dignities. The standing is slippery, and the regress is either a downfall or at least an eclipse, which is a melancholy thing: *Cum non sis qui fueris, non esse cur velis vivere.*[1] Nay, retire men cannot when they would, neither will they when it were reason; but are impatient of privateness, even in age and sickness, which require the shadow;[2] like old townsmen, that will be still sitting at their street door, though thereby they offer age to scorn. Certainly great persons had need to borrow other men's opinions to think themselves happy; for if they judge by their own feeling, they cannot find it; but if they think with themselves what other men think of them, and that other men would fain be as they are, then they are happy, as it were by report; when perhaps they find the contrary within. For they are the first that find their own griefs, though they be the last that find their own faults. Certainly men in great fortunes are strangers to themselves, and while they are in the puzzle of business they have no time to tend their health, either of body or mind. *Illi mors gravis incubat, qui notus nimis omnibus, ignotus moritur sibi.*[3] In place there is license to do good and evil, whereof the latter is a curse; for in evil the best condition is not to will, the second not to can.[4] But power to do good is the true and lawful end of aspiring; for good thoughts (though God accept them) yet towards men are little better than good dreams, except they be put in act; and that cannot be without power and place, as the vantage and commanding ground. Merit and good works is the end of man's motion, and conscience[5] of the same is the accomplishment of man's rest; for if a man can be partaker of God's theater,[6] he shall likewise be partaker of God's rest. *Et conversus Deus, ut aspiceret opera quae fecerunt manus suae, vidit quod omnia essent bona nimis;*[7] and then the Sabbath.

In the discharge of thy place set before thee the best examples, for imitation is a globe[8] of precepts. And after a time set before thee thine own example; and examine thyself strictly, whether thou didst not best at first. Neglect not also the examples of those that have carried themselves ill in the same place; not to set off thyself by taxing[9] their memory, but to direct thyself what to avoid. Reform, therefore, without bravery, or scandal[1] of former times and persons; but yet set it down to thyself, as well to create good precedents as to follow them. Reduce things to the first institution,[2] and observe wherein and how they have degenerate; but yet ask counsel of both times; of

---

1. "When you aren't what you were, there's no reason to live" (Cicero, *Familiar Letters* 7.3).
2. "The shadow" of retirement, out of the glare of public life.
3. "Death lies heavily on him who, while too well known to everyone else, dies unknown to himself" (Seneca, *Thyestes*).
4. Be able.

5. Consciousness.
6. Actions in the world.
7. "And God saw every thing that he had made, and, behold, it was very good" (Genesis 1.31).
8. World.
9. Blaming.
1. Defaming. "Bravery": ostentation.
2. To their original form.

the ancient time what is best, and of the latter time what is fittest. Seek to make thy course regular, that men may know beforehand what they may expect; but be not too positive and peremptory, and express thyself well when thou digressest from thy rule. Preserve the right of thy place, but stir not questions of jurisdiction; and rather assume thy right in silence and *de facto*,[3] than voice it with claims and challenges. Preserve likewise the rights of inferior places, and think it more honor to direct in chief than to be busy in all. Embrace and invite helps and advices touching the execution of thy place, and do not drive away such as bring thee information as meddlers, but accept of them in good part. The vices of authority are chiefly four: delays, corruption, roughness, and facility.[4] For delays, give easy access, keep times appointed, go through with that which is in hand, and interlace not business[5] but of necessity. For corruption, do not only bind thine own hands or thy servants' hands from taking, but bind the hands of suitors also from offering. For integrity used doth the one; but integrity professed, and with a manifest detestation of bribery, doth the other. And avoid not only the fault, but the suspicion. Whosoever is found variable and changeth manifestly, without manifest cause, giveth suspicion of corruption. Therefore, always when thou changest thine opinion or course, profess it plainly and declare it, together with the reasons that move thee to change; and do not think to steal it.[6] A servant or a favorite, if he be inward,[7] and no other apparent cause of esteem, is commonly thought but a byway to close[8] corruption. For roughness, it is a needless cause of discontent; severity breedeth fear, but roughness breedeth hate. Even reproofs from authority ought to be grave, and not taunting. As for facility, it is worse than bribery; for bribes come but now and then, but if importunity or idle respects[9] lead a man, he shall never be without. As Solomon saith, "To respect persons is not good, for such a man will transgress for a piece of bread."[1]

It is most true that was anciently spoken, "A place showeth the man"; and it showeth some to the better and some to the worse. *Omnium consensu capax imperii, nisi imperasset,*[2] saith Tacitus of Galba; but of Vespasian he saith, *Solus imperantium Vespasianus mutatus in melius:*[3] though the one was meant of sufficiency, the other of manners and affection. It is an assured sign of a worthy and generous spirit, whom honor amends.[4] For honor is, or should be, the place of virtue; and as in nature things move violently to their place and calmly in their place, so virtue in ambition is violent, in authority settled and calm. All rising to great place is by a winding stair; and if there be factions, it is good to side a man's self[5] whilst he is in the rising, and to balance himself when he is placed. Use the memory of thy predecessor fairly and tenderly; for if thou dost not, it is a debt will sure be paid when thou art gone. If thou have colleagues, respect them, and rather call them when they look not for it, than exclude them when they have reason to look to be called. Be not too sensible[6]

---

3. Without debate, as a matter of course.
4. Docility, too great obligingness.
5. I.e., do not carry on different businesses at the same time.
6. Change your mind without its being noticed.
7. In his master's confidence.
8. Secret.
9. Irrelevant considerations.
1. Cf. Proverbs 28.21.

2. "Everyone would have thought him a good ruler, if he had not ruled."
3. "Of all the emperors, only Vespasian changed for the better."
4. I.e., whom promotion improves. "Sufficiency": abilities. "Affection": disposition.
5. For a man to take sides.
6. Sensitive.

or too remembering of thy place in conversation and private answers to suitors; but let it rather be said, "When he sits in place he is another man."

1612, 1625

Of Superstition[1]

It were better to have no opinion of God at all than such an opinion as is unworthy of him. For the one is unbelief, the other is contumely:[2] and certainly superstition is the reproach of the deity. Plutarch saith well to that purpose: "Surely" (saith he) "I had rather a great deal men should say there was no such man at all as Plutarch, than that they should say that there was one Plutarch that would eat his children as soon as they were born"—as the poets speak of Saturn.[3] And as the contumely is greater towards God, so the danger is greater towards men. Atheism leaves a man to sense, to philosophy, to natural piety, to laws, to reputation, all which may be guides to an outward moral virtue, though religion were not. But superstition dismounts all these, and erecteth an absolute monarchy in the minds of men. Therefore atheism did never perturb states, for it makes men wary of themselves as looking no further;[4] and we see the times inclined to atheism (as the time of Augustus Caesar) were civil times. But superstition hath been the confusion of many states, and bringeth in a new *primum mobile*, that ravisheth all the spheres of government.[5] The master of superstition is the people, and in all superstition wise men follow fools, and arguments are fitted to practice in a reversed order. It was gravely said by some of the prelates in the council of Trent, where the doctrine of the schoolmen bare great sway, *that the schoolmen were like astronomers, which did feign eccentrics and epicycles and such engines of orbs to save the phenomena, though they knew there were no such things;*[6] and in like manner that the schoolmen had framed a number of subtle and intricate axioms and theorems to save the practice of the church.

The causes of superstition are: pleasing and sensual rites and ceremonies; excess of outward and pharisaical holiness;[7] overgreat reverence of traditions, which cannot but load the church; the stratagems of prelates for their own ambition and lucre; the favoring too much of good intentions, which openeth the gate to conceits[8] and novelties; the taking an aim at divine matters by human, which cannot but breed mixture of imaginations; and lastly barbarous times, especially joined with calamities and disasters. Supersti-

1. Irrational religious practices founded on fear or ignorance.
2. Contempt.
3. Saturn (Cronos), god of time (among other things), was reputed to have eaten all his children, as time does. Many of the sentiments in Bacon's essay come from Plutarch's essay "On Superstition."
4. I.e., not looking beyond their own personal lifetimes. The rule of Augustus Caesar (following) was marked by general peace and civil quiet (i.e., civilized). In this period of Roman history, many members of the elite no longer believed in the pagan gods, though they participated in the

forms of state religion.
5. The prime mover (*primium mobile*) was supposed to control the motions of the other heavenly spheres; superstition is a second (and contrary) mover.
6. "Save the phenomena" means "explain appearances," as did the elaborate theories of pre-Copernican astronomers (epicycles, trepidation, and such concepts). So with the Scholastic philosophers ("schoolmen").
7. The Pharisees were the strict party among the Jews of Christ's time; they taught precise observance of the letter of Mosaic law.
8. Fancies.

tion without a veil is a deformed thing, for as it addeth deformity to an ape to be so like a man, so the similitude of superstition to religion makes it the more deformed. And as wholesome meat corrupteth to little worms, so good forms and orders corrupt into a number of petty observances. There is a superstition in avoiding superstition, when men think to do best if they go furthest from the superstition formerly received; therefore care would be had that (as it fareth in ill purgings) the good be not taken away with the bad, which commonly is done when the people is the reformer.[9]

1612, 1625

Of Plantations[1]

Plantations are amongst ancient, primitive, and heroical works. When the world was young it begat more children; but now it is old it begets fewer: for I may justly account new plantations to be the children of former kingdoms. I like a plantation in a pure soil; that is, where people are not displanted to the end to plant in others. For else it is rather an extirpation than a plantation. Planting of countries is like planting of woods; for you must make account to leese[2] almost twenty years profit, and expect your recompense in the end. For the principal thing that hath been the destruction of most plantations hath been the base and hasty drawing of profit in the first years. It is true, speedy profit is not to be neglected, as far as may stand[3] with the good of the plantation, but no further. It is a shameful and unblessed thing to take the scum of people, and wicked condemned men, to be the people with whom you plant; and not only so, but it spoileth the plantation, for they will ever live like rogues, and not fall to work, but be lazy, and do mischief, and spend victuals, and be quickly weary, and then certify over[4] to their country, to the discredit of the plantation. The people wherewith you plant ought to be gardeners, plowmen, laborers, smiths, carpenters, joiners,[5] fishermen, fowlers, with some few apothecaries, surgeons, cooks, and bakers.

In a country of plantation, first look about what kind of victual the country yields of itself to hand, as chestnuts, walnuts, pineapples, olives, dates, plums, cherries, wild honey, and the like, and make use of them. Then consider what victual or esculent[6] things there are which grow speedily and within the year, as parsnips, carrots, turnips, onions, radish, artichokes of

---

9. The final sentence is directed against Puritan reformers, who loathed ceremonies, traditions, liturgy, and images, which they considered "superstitions."
1. The planting of colonies had been a standard topic of political theory since Plato, with attention focused on such matters as the choice of site, the best mix of population, and the treatment of indigenous peoples. Sir Thomas More considered the matter in his *Utopia*, and it took on increased practical importance in the narratives of English explorers such as Sir Walter Ralegh, and especially in the early 17th century, with the establishment of the first permanent English settlements in the New World. Bacon's essay largely avoids the most acute moral issues English colonization was posing: English participation in the brutal African slave trade, and the stocking of "plantations" in Ireland with Scottish Presbyterian settlers (to supplement genocidal policies that were starving the indigenous Roman Catholics). These policies sowed the seeds of slavery in America and civil war in Ireland.
2. Lose.
3. Be consistent.
4. Report.
5. Workers in fine carpentry.
6. Edible.

Jerusalem,[7] maize, and the like. For wheat, barley, and oats, they ask[8] too much labor; but with peas and beans you may begin, both because they ask less labor and because they serve for meat[9] as well as for bread. And of rice likewise cometh a great increase, and it is a kind of meat. Above all, there ought to be brought store of biscuit, oatmeal, flour, meal, and the like in the beginning, till bread may be had. For beasts or birds, take chiefly such as are least subject to diseases, and multiply fastest, as swine, goats, cocks, hens, turkeys, geese, house doves, and the like. The victual in plantations ought to be expended almost as in a besieged town; that is, with certain[1] allowance. And let the main part of the ground employed to gardens or corn be to[2] a common stock, and to be laid in and stored up and then delivered out in proportion; besides some spots of ground that any particular person will manure[3] for his own private. Consider likewise what commodities the soil where the plantation is doth naturally yield, that they may some way help to defray the charge of the plantation (so it be not, as was said, to the untimely prejudice of the main business), as it hath fared with tobacco in Virginia. Wood commonly aboundeth but too much, and therefore timber is fit to be one. If there be iron ore and streams whereupon to set the mills, iron is a brave commodity, where wood aboundeth.[4] Making of bay-salt, if the climate be proper for it, would be put in experience.[5] Growing silk likewise, if any be, is a likely commodity. Pitch and tar, where store of firs and pines are, will not fail; so drugs and sweet woods, where they are, cannot but yield great profit. Soap ashes likewise, and other things that may be thought of. But moil[6] not too much underground, for the hope of mines is very uncertain, and useth to make the planters lazy in other things.

For government, let it be in the hands of one, assisted with some counsel; and let them have commission to exercise martial laws, with some limitation. And above all, let men make that profit of being in the wilderness, as they have God always, and his service, before their eyes. Let not the government of the plantation depend upon too many counselors and undertakers[7] in the country that planteth, but upon a temperate number; and let those be rather noblemen and gentlemen than merchants, for they look ever to the present gain. Let there be freedoms from custom[8] till the plantation be of strength; and not only freedom from custom, but freedom to carry their commodities where they may make their best of them, except there be some special cause of caution. Cram not in people by sending too fast, company after company, but rather harken how they waste,[9] and send supplies proportionably, but so as the number may live well in the plantation, and not by surcharge[1] be in penury.

It hath been a great endangering to the health of some plantations, that they have built along the sea and rivers, in marish[2] and unwholesome grounds.

---

7. Jerusalem artichokes, a species of sunflower having an edible root. "Jerusalem" is a mistranslation of the Italian word for sunflower, *girasole*.
8. Require. "For": as for.
9. I.e., as a main dish.
1. Fixed.
2. For. "Corn": grain.
3. Cultivate.
4. Waterpower and wood fires were required for getting iron out of ore. "Brave": excellent.
5. I.e., should be tried. "Bay-salt" is a coarse salt obtained by evaporating seawater. "Growing silk" (next sentence): vegetable silk.
6. Labor. "Soap ashes": ashes used for making soap.
7. Investors holding shares in the enterprise.
8. Customs duties.
9. I.e., observe at what rate the population declines.
1. I.e., by being overpopulated.
2. Marshy.

Therefore, though you begin there, to avoid carriage and other like discom-modities,[3] yet build still rather upwards from the streams than along. It con-cerneth likewise the health of the plantation that they have good store of salt with them, that they may use it in their victuals when it shall be neces-sary. If you plant where savages are, do not only entertain them with trifles and jingles, but use them justly and graciously, with sufficient guard nev-ertheless; and do not win their favor by helping them to invade their ene-mies, but for their defense it is not amiss. And send oft of them over to the country that plants, that they may see a better condition than their own, and commend it when they return. When the plantation grows to strength, then it is time to plant with women as well as with men, that the plantation may spread into generations and not be ever pieced from without. It is the sinfullest thing in the world to forsake or destitute a plantation once in forwardness; for besides the dishonor it is the guiltiness of blood of many commiserable[4] persons.

1625

Of Negotiating

It is generally better to deal by speech than by letter, and by the mediation of a third than by a man's self. Letters are good when a man would draw an answer by letter back again, or when it may serve for a man's justification afterwards to produce his own letter, or where it may be danger to be inter-rupted or heard by pieces. To deal in person is good when a man's face breed-eth regard, as commonly with inferiors, or in tender[1] cases, where a man's eye upon the countenance of him with whom he speaketh may give him a direction how far to go; and generally, where a man will reserve to himself liberty either to disavow or to expound. In choice of instruments, it is better to choose men of a plainer sort, that are like to do that that is committed to them, and to report back again faithfully the success,[2] than those that are cunning to contrive out of other men's business somewhat to grace them-selves, and will help the matter in report for satisfaction sake. Use also such persons as affect[3] the business wherein they are employed, for that quickeneth much; and such as are fit for the matter, as bold men for expostulation, fair-spoken men for persuasion, crafty men for inquiry and observation, froward and absurd men for business that doth not well bear out itself.[4] Use also such as have been lucky, and prevailed before in things wherein you have employed them; for that breeds confidence, and they will strive to maintain their pre-scription.[5] It is better to sound a person with whom one deals afar off, than to fall upon the point at first, except you mean to surprise him by some short question. It is better dealing with men in appetite,[6] than with those that are where they would be. If a man deal with another upon conditions, the start or

3. Disadvantages, inconveniences.
4. Worthy of compassion. "Destitute": abandon.
1. Delicate.
2. Result.
3. Like.

4. I.e., when your business is less than honest, use an ill-tempered or foolish person.
5. Keep up their reputation.
6. Who are hungry, i.e., ambitious men.

first performance is all, which a man cannot reasonably demand,[7] except either the nature of the thing be such which must go before, or else a man can persuade the other party that he shall still need him in some other thing, or else that he be counted the honester man. All practice is to discover or to work.[8] Men discover themselves in trust, in passion, at unawares, and of necessity, when they would have somewhat done and cannot find an apt pretext. If you would work any man, you must either know his nature and fashions, and so lead him; or his ends, and so persuade him; or his weakness and disadvantages, and so awe him; or those that have interest in him, and so govern him. In dealing with cunning persons, we must ever consider their ends, to interpret their speeches; and it is good to say little to them, and that which they least look for. In all negotiations of difficulty, a man may not look to sow and reap at once, but must prepare business, and so ripen it by degrees.

1597, 1625

Of Masques and Triumphs

These things are but toys to come amongst such serious observations; but yet, since princes will have such things, it is better they should be graced with elegancy, than daubed with cost. Dancing to song is a thing of great state and pleasure. I understand it that the song be in choir, placed aloft, and accompanied with some broken music,[1] and the ditty fitted to the device. Acting in song, especially in dialogues, hath an extreme good grace; I say acting, not dancing (for that is a mean and vulgar thing);[2] and the voices of the dialogue would be strong and manly (a bass and tenor, no treble), and the ditty high and tragical, not nice or dainty. Several choirs, placed one over against another, and taking the voices by catches anthem-wise, give great pleasure. Turning dances into figure[3] is a childish curiosity; and, generally, let it be noted, that those things which I here set down are such as to naturally take the sense, and not respect petty wonderments. It is true, the alterations of scenes, so it be quietly and without noise, are things of great beauty and pleasure for they feed and relieve the eye before it be full of the same object. Let the scenes abound with light, specially colored and varied; and let the masquers, or any other that are to come down from the scene,[4] have some motions upon the scene itself before their coming down; for it draws the eye strangely, and makes it with great pleasure to desire to see that it cannot perfectly discern. Let the songs be loud and cheerful, and not chirpings or pulings; let the music, likewise, be sharp and loud, and well placed. The colors that show best by candlelight[5] are

7. You cannot reasonably make special conditions favorable to you, except in the circumstances noted.

8. All sharp bargaining aims to find out what men are up to or to make use of them. "Discover" (next sentence): reveal.

1. Part-music, for different voices and different kinds of instruments.

2. Bacon's emphasis on dialogue and song (as opposed to dance) is in keeping with the increased emphasis on dialogue in later Jacobean and Car-oline masques; dance, however, remains at the center of both early and late masques.

3. Patterns with allegorical or numerological significance.

4. To unmask at the end and come onto the floor, so as to take part in the general dancing (the revels) with members of the court.

5. The Banqueting Hall at Whitehall, the site of many court masques, was lit only by candlelight; viewers complained that some masques were hard to see.

white, carnation, and a kind of seawater green; and oes or spangs,[6] as they are of no great cost, so they are of most glory. As for rich embroidery, it is lost and not discerned. Let the suits of the masquers be graceful, and such as become the person when the vizors are off; not after examples of known attires, Turks, soldiers, mariners, and the like. Let antimasques[7] not be long; they have been commonly of fools, satyrs, baboons, wild men, antics, beasts, sprites, witches, Ethiopes, pigmies, turquets,[8] nymphs, rustics, Cupids, statues moving, and the like. As for angels, it is not comical enough to put them in antimasques; and anything that is hideous, as devils, giants, is, on the other side, as unfit; but, chiefly, let the music of them be recreative, and with some strange changes. Some sweet odors suddenly coming forth, without any drops falling, are, in such a company as there is steam and heat, things of great pleasure and refreshment. Double masques, one of men, another of ladies, addeth state and variety; but all is nothing, except the room be kept clear and neat.

For jousts, and tourneys, and barriers,[9] the glories of them are chiefly in the chariots, wherein the challengers make their entry; especially if they be drawn with strange beasts, as lions, bears, camels, and the like; or in the devices of their entrance, or in the bravery of their liveries, or in the goodly furniture of their horses and armor. But enough of these toys.

1625

Of Studies

[1597 version][1]

Studies serve for pastimes, for ornaments, and for abilities. Their chief use for pastime is in privateness[2] and retiring; for ornament, is in discourse; and for ability, is in judgment. For expert men[3] can execute, but learned men are fittest to judge or censure. To spend too much time in them is sloth; to use them too much for ornament is affectation; to make judgment wholly by their rules is the humor[4] of a scholar. They perfect nature, and are perfected by experience. Crafty men contemn them, simple men admire them, wise men use them, for they teach not their own use; but that[5] is a wisdom without them, and above them, won by observation. Read not to contradict nor to believe, but to weigh and consider. Some books are to be tasted, others to be swallowed, and some few to be chewed and digested; that is, some books are to be read only in parts; others to be read but cursorily; and some few to be read wholly, and with diligence and attention.

6. Spangles shaped like the letter "O."
7. The antic dances (presented by professionals) that preceded the main masque dances and represented the vices, follies, or disorders that are to be dispelled with the arrival of the main masques (royal and noble personages).
8. Turkish dwarfs.
9. One form of masque was the "joust," "tourney" (tournament), or "barrier," which chiefly involved knights, who represented allegorical qualities, tilting lances against each other.
1. This version of the essay illustrates Bacon's early epigrammatic, aphoristic style, featuring balance, parallelism, disjunction between sentences, and a curtness that is occasionally cryptic. The 1625 version keeps some aphoristic elements unchanged but provides more connectives and transitions, resulting in a smoother, more flowing style.
2. Private life.
3. Men of experience.
4. Disposition, implying folly.
5. I.e., the knowledge of how to use them. "Without" (following): outside.

Reading maketh a full man, conference[6] a ready man, and writing an exact man. And therefore, if a man write little, he had need have a great memory; if he confer little, he had need have a present wit;[7] and if he read little, he had need have much cunning, to seem to know that[8] he doth not. Histories make men wise; poets, witty;[9] the mathematics, subtle; natural philosophy,[1] deep; moral,[2] grave; logic and rhetoric, able to contend.

Of Studies

[1625 version]

Studies serve for delight, for ornament, and for ability. Their chief use for delight is in privateness[1] and retiring; for ornament, is in discourse; and for ability, is in the judgment and disposition of business. For expert men[2] can execute, and perhaps judge of particulars, one by one; but the general counsels, and the plots and marshaling of affairs, come best from those that are learned. To spend too much time in studies is sloth; to use them too much for ornament is affectation; to make judgment wholly by their rules is the humor[3] of a scholar. They perfect nature, and are perfected by experience; for natural abilities are like natural plants, that need pruning by study; and studies themselves do give forth directions too much at large, except they be bounded in by experience. Crafty men contemn studies, simple men admire them, and wise men use them, for they teach not their own use; but that[4] is a wisdom without them, and above them, won by observation. Read not to contradict and confute, nor to believe and take for granted, nor to find talk and discourse, but to weigh and consider. Some books are to be tasted, others to be swallowed, and some few to be chewed and digested; that is, some books are to be read only in parts; others to be read, but not curiously;[5] and some few to be read wholly, and with diligence and attention. Some books also may be read by deputy and extracts made of them by others, but that would be only in the less important arguments and the meaner sort of books; else distilled books are like common distilled waters,[6] flashy things. Reading maketh a full man, conference[7] a ready man, and writing an exact man. And therefore, if a man write little, he had need have a great memory; if he confer little, he had need have a present wit;[8] and if he read little, he had need have much cunning, to seem to know that[9] he doth not. Histories make men wise; poets, witty;[1] the mathematics, subtle; natural philosophy,[2] deep; moral, grave; logic and rhetoric, able to contend. *Abeunt studia in mores.*[3] Nay, there is no stond or impediment in the wit but may be wrought out by fit studies, like as diseases of the body may have appropriate exercises. Bowling

6. Conversation.
7. Lively intelligence.
8. That which.
9. Clever.
1. Science.
2. Moral philosophy.
1. Private life.
2. Men of experience.
3. Folly.
4. I.e., the knowledge of how to use them. "Without" (following): outside.

5. Attentively.
6. Used as home remedies, without real value.
7. Conversation.
8. Lively intelligence.
9. That which.
1. Clever.
2. Science. "Moral" (following): i.e., moral philosophy.
3. "Studies culminate in manners" (Ovid, *Heroides*). "Stond" (following): stoppage.

is good for the stone and reins,[4] shooting for the lungs and breast, gentle walking for the stomach, riding for the head, and the like. So if a man's wit be wandering, let him study the mathematics; for in demonstrations, if his wit be called away never so little, he must begin again. If his wit be not apt to distinguish or find differences, let him study the schoolmen, for they are *cumini sectores*.[5] If he be not apt to beat over matters[6] and to call up one thing to prove and illustrate another, let him study the lawyer's cases. So every defect of the mind may have a special receipt.[7]

From The Advancement of Learning

[THE ABUSES OF LANGUAGE][1]

Martin Luther, conducted (no doubt) by an higher providence, but in discourse of reason finding what a province he had undertaken against the bishop of Rome[2] and the degenerate traditions of the church, and finding his own solitude being no ways aided by the opinions of his own time, was enforced to awake all antiquity and to call former times to his succor to make a party against the present time, so that the ancient authors both in divinity and in humanity which had long time slept in libraries began generally to be read and revolved.[3] This by consequence did draw on a necessity of a more exquisite travail in the languages original wherein those authors did write,[4] for the better understanding of those authors and the better advantage of pressing and applying their words. And thereof grew again a delight in their manner of style and phrase, and an admiration of that kind of writing, which was much furthered and precipitated by the enmity and opposition that the propounders of those (primitive but seeming new) opinions had against the schoolmen, who were generally of the contrary part, and whose writings were altogether in a differing style and form, taking liberty to coin and frame new terms of art to express their own sense and to avoid circuit of speech, without regard to the pureness, pleasantness, and (as I may call it) lawfulness of the phrase or word.[5] And again, because the greatest labor then was with the people (of whom the Pharisees were wont to say, *Execrabilis ista turba, quae non novit legem*[6]) for the winning and persuading of them there grew of necessity in chief price and request[7] eloquence and variety of discourse, as the fittest and forciblest access into the capacity of the

---

4. Gallstone and kidneys.
5. "Dividers of cuminseed," i.e., hairsplitters. "Schoolmen": Scholastic philosophers.
6. Discuss a subject thoroughly.
7. Cure, prescription.
1. Among the "three distempers of learning" that Bacon proposes to cure in this work, the most important involves "vain imaginations, vain altercations, and vain affectations"; to help explain these he offers a concise history of changes in the language of learned discourse since the Reformation.
2. The pope. "Province": task.
3. Considered. Luther (1483–1546) indeed looked back to the original languages of the Bible and to ancient authors in "divinity" (chiefly Augustine),

but he was not involved in the efforts of the humanists (including Erasmus and Sir Thomas More) to revive the classical languages and authors.
4. Classical Greek and Latin, and biblical Hebrew. "Exquisite travail": careful work.
5. The Scholastic philosophers ("schoolmen") used the living Latin of the Middle Ages, wrenching the language yet further from classical norms in applying it to subtle philosophical matters; the humanists denounced the Scholastics' Latin as barbarous and sought instead to imitate classical models, especially Cicero.
6. "This people who knoweth not the law are cursed" (John 7.49).
7. Worth and demand.

vulgar sort. So that these four causes concurring (the admiration of ancient authors, the hate of the schoolmen, the exact study of languages, and the efficacy of preaching) did bring in an affectionate study of eloquence and copy[8] of speech, which then began to flourish. This grew speedily to an excess, for men began to hunt more after words than matter, and more after the choiceness of the phrase, and the round and clean composition of the sentence, and the sweet falling of the clauses, and the varying and illustration of their works with tropes and figures[9] than after the weight of matter, worth of subject, soundness of argument, life of invention, or depth of judgment. Then grew the flowing and watery vein of Osorius, the Portugal bishop, to be in price. Then did Sturmius spend such infinite and curious pains upon Cicero the orator and Hermogenes the rhetorician, besides his own books of periods and imitation and the like.[1] Then did Carr of Cambridge and Ascham with their lectures and writings almost deify Cicero and Demosthenes, and allure all young men that were studious unto that delicate and polished kind of learning.[2] Then did Erasmus take occasion to make the scoffing echo, *Decem annos consumpsi in legendo Cicerone*, and the echo answered in Greek, *one, Asine*.[3] Then grew the learning of the schoolmen to be utterly despised as barbarous. In sum, the whole inclination and bent of those times was rather towards copy than weight.[4]

Here therefore is the first distemper of learning, when men study words and not matter, whereof though I have represented an example of late times, yet it hath been and will be *secundum maius et minus*[5] in all time. And how is it possible but this should have an operation to discredit learning, even with vulgar capacities, when they see learned men's works like the first letter of a patent or limned[6] book, which though it hath large flourishes, yet it is but a letter? It seems to me that Pygmalion's frenzy[7] is a good emblem or portraiture of this vanity, for words are but the images of matter, and except they have life of reason and invention, to fall in love with them is all one as to fall in love with a picture.

But yet notwithstanding, it is a thing not hastily to be condemned to clothe and adorn the obscurity even of philosophy itself with sensible and plausible elocution. For hereof we have great examples in Xenophon, Cicero, Seneca, Plutarch, and of Plato also in some degree; and hereof likewise there is great use, for surely to the severe inquisition of truth and the deep progress into philosophy it is some hindrance, because it is too early satisfactory to the mind of man, and quencheth the desire of further search before we come to a just period; but then if a man be to have any use of such knowledge in civil occasions of conference, counsel, persuasion, discourse, or the like, then shall he find it prepared to his hands in those authors which write

---

8. Copiousness. "Affectionate": affected.
9. Figurative language.
1. Jeronimo Osorio (1506–1580) wrote a history of Portuguese conquests in a flowing style that caused him to be known as the Portuguese Cicero. His contemporary, Johann Sturm, edited texts of Cicero and the Greek rhetorician Hermogenes; his "book of periods" was a rhetorical handbook.
2. Nicholas Carr was professor of Greek at Cambridge; Roger Ascham was tutor to Queen Elizabeth and author of *The Schoolmaster*. Both admired the rhetorical polish of the Roman orator

Cicero and the Greek orator Demosthenes.
3. "I spent ten years in reading Cicero." Echo answers, "Ass!" The joke is in the *Colloquies* of Erasmus.
4. Elegant phrasing rather than profundity.
5. More or less, depending on circumstances.
6. Illuminated, i.e., illustrated, as with elaborate initial capitals. Royal grants ("patents") were also engrossed with fancy initial letters.
7. Pygmalion's "frenzy" (delirium) was to fall in love with a statue he had carved of a beautiful woman.

in that manner. But the excess of this is so justly contemptible that as Hercules, when he saw the image of Adonis, Venus' minion, in a temple, said in disdain, *Nil sacri es*;[8] so there is none of Hercules' followers in learning, that is, the more severe and laborious sort of inquirers into truth,[9] but will despise those delicacies and affectations as indeed capable of no divineness.

1605

From Novum Organum[1]

19

There are and can be only two ways of searching into and discovering truth. The one flies from the senses and particulars to the most general axioms, and from these principles, the truth of which it takes for settled and immovable, proceeds to judgment and to the discovery of middle axioms.[2] And this way is now in fashion. The other derives from the senses and particulars, rising by a gradual and unbroken ascent, so that it arrives at the most general axioms last of all.[3] This is the true way, but as yet untried.

* * *

22

Both ways set out from the senses and particulars, and rest in the highest generalities, but the difference between them is infinite. For the one just glances at experiment and particulars in passing, the other dwells duly and orderly among them. The one, again, begins at once by establishing certain abstract and useless generalities, the other rises by gradual steps to that which is prior and better known in the order of nature.

* * *

38

The idols and false notions which are now in possession of the human understanding and have taken deep root therein, not only so beset men's minds that truth can hardly find entrance, but even after entrance is obtained, they will again in the very instauration[4] of the sciences meet and

8. "You're nothing holy." Adonis was the lover ("minion") of Venus, deified after his death while boar hunting.
9. Hercules early in life was offered a choice between a life of ignoble ease and sensory delights and one of strenuous virtue. He chose the latter, and so do his followers in learning.
1. *Novum Organum*, or "The New Instrument of Learning," was written not in English but in Latin, for an international scholarly audience. Nonetheless it requires our attention here, as it is the keystone of Bacon's vast project to reform the structure of human learning from the

ground up. His reform called for careful observation of all aspects of nature and controlled experiment, but the first part of the book analyzes the stumbling blocks in the way—among them, famously, the various "idols," or delusive images of truth that lead people away from the exact knowledge of science.
2. The deductive method, associated with Aristotle and the Scholastic philosophers.
3. The inductive method that Bacon here champions.
4. Renovation, renewal.

trouble us, unless men being forewarned of the danger fortify themselves as far as may be against their assaults.

* * *

41

The Idols of the Tribe have their foundation in human nature itself, and in the tribe or race of men. For it is a false assertion that the sense of man is the measure of things. On the contrary, all perceptions as well of the sense as of the mind are according to the measure of the individual and not according to the measure of the universe. And the human understanding is like a false mirror, which, receiving rays irregularly, distorts and discolors the nature of things by mingling its own nature with it.

42

The Idols of the Cave are the idols of the individual man. For everyone (besides the errors common to human nature in general) has a cave or den of his own, which refracts and discolors the light of nature, owing either to his own proper and peculiar nature, or to his education and conversation with others, or to the reading of books, and the authority of those whom he esteems and admires; or to the difference of impressions, accordingly as they take place in a mind preoccupied and predisposed or in a mind indifferent and settled, or the like. So that the spirit of man (according as it is meted out to different individuals) is in fact a thing variable and full of perturbation, and governed as it were by chance. Whence it was well observed by Heraclitus[5] that men look for sciences in their own lesser worlds, and not in the greater or common world.

43

There are also idols formed by the intercourse and association of men with each other, which I call Idols of the Marketplace, on account of the commerce and consort of men there. For it is by discourse that men associate, and words are imposed according to the apprehension of the vulgar. And therefore the fit and unfit choice of words wonderfully obstructs the understanding. Nor do the definitions or explanations wherewith in some things learned men are wont to guard and defend themselves, by any means set the matter right. But words plainly force and overrule the understanding, and throw all into confusion, and lead men away into numberless empty controversies and idle fancies.

44

Lastly, there are idols which have immigrated into men's minds from the various dogmas of philosophies, and also from wrong laws of demonstration.

---

5. Greek philosopher (ca. 513 B.C.E.) who considered knowledge to be based on perception by the senses and thought that everything was in flux.

These I call Idols of the Theater, because in my judgment all the received systems are but so many stage plays, representing worlds of their own creation after an unreal and scenic fashion. Nor is it only of the systems now in vogue or only of the ancient sects and philosophies that I speak; for many more plays of the same kind may yet be composed and in like artificial manner set forth, seeing that errors the most widely different have nevertheless causes for the most part alike. Neither again do I mean this only of entire systems, but also of the many principles and axioms in science, which by tradition, credulity, and negligence have come to be received.

* * *

59

But the Idols of the Marketplace are the most troublesome of all: idols which have crept into the understanding through the alliances of words and names. For men believe that their reason governs words; but it is also true that words react on the understanding; and this it is that has rendered philosophy and the sciences sophistical and inactive. Now words, being commonly framed and applied according to the capacity of the vulgar, follow those lines of division which are most obvious to the vulgar understanding. And whenever an understanding of greater acuteness or a more diligent observation would alter those lines to suit the true divisions of nature, words stand in the way and resist the change. Whence it comes to pass that the high and formal discussions of learned men end oftentimes in disputes about words and names; with which (according to the use[6] and wisdom of the mathematicians) it would be more prudent to begin, and so by means of definitions reduce them to order. Yet even definitions cannot cure this evil in dealing with natural and material things; since the definitions themselves consist of words, and those words beget others;[7] so that it is necessary to recur to individual instances, and those in due series and order; as I shall say presently when I come to the method and scheme for the formation of notions and axioms.

60

The idols imposed by words on the understanding are of two kinds. They are either names of things which do not exist (for as there are things left unnamed through lack of observation, so likewise are there names which result from fantastic suppositions and to which nothing in reality corresponds), or they are names of things which exist, but yet confused and ill-defined, and hastily and irregularly derived from realities. Of the former kind are Fortune, the Prime Mover, Planetary Orbits, Element of Fire, and like fictions which owe their origin to false and idle theories.[8] And this class

6. Custom.
7. Bacon's mistrust of words helped to prompt the Royal Society (founded in 1645) to cultivate a plain, stripped prose style for purposes of scientific communication.
8. The "Prime Mover" was a transparent sphere on the outside of the universe, supposed to move all the other spheres; the "Element of Fire" was an area of pure, invisible fire, supposed to exist above the atmosphere. By "Planetary Orbits" Bacon may be referring to the old notion of crystalline spheres in which the planets were supposed to be set. Obviously, these concepts could be based on no observation.

of idols is more easily expelled, because to get rid of them it is only necessary that all theories should be steadily rejected and dismissed as obsolete.[9]

But the other class, which springs out of a faulty and unskillful abstraction, is intricate and deeply rooted. Let us take for example such a word as *humid*; and see how far the several things which the word is used to signify agree with each other; and we shall find the word *humid* to be nothing else than a mark loosely and confusedly applied to denote a variety of actions which will not bear to be reduced to any constant meaning. For it both signifies that which easily spreads itself round any other body; and that which in itself is indeterminate and cannot solidize; and that which readily yields in every direction; and that which easily divides and scatters itself; and that which easily unites and collects itself; and that which readily flows and is put in motion; and that which readily clings to another body and wets it; and that which is easily reduced to a liquid, or being solid easily melts. Accordingly when you come to apply the word—if you take it in one sense, flame is humid; if in another, air is not humid; if in another, fine dust is humid; if in another, glass is humid. So that it is easy to see that the notion is taken by abstraction only from water and common and ordinary liquids, without any due verification.

There are however in words certain degrees of distortion and error. One of the least faulty kinds is that of names of substances, especially of lowest species and well-deduced (for the notion of *chalk* and of *mud* is good, of *earth* bad); a more faulty kind is that of actions, as *to generate, to corrupt, to alter*; the most faulty is of qualities (except such as are the immediate objects of the sense), as *heavy, light, rare, dense*, and the like. Yet in all these cases some notions are of necessity a little better than others, in proportion to the greater variety of subjects that fall within the range of the human sense.

* * *

62

Idols of the Theater, or of systems, are many, and there can be and perhaps will be yet many more. For were it not that now for many ages men's minds have been busied with religion and theology; and were it not that civil governments, especially monarchies, have been averse to such novelties, even in matters speculative, so that men labor therein to the peril and harming of their fortunes, not only unrewarded, but exposed also to contempt and envy; doubtless there would have arisen many other philosophical sects like to those which in great variety flourished once among the Greeks. For as on the phenomena of the heavens many hypotheses may be constructed, so likewise (and more also) many various dogmas may be set up and established on the phenomena of philosophy. And in the plays of this philosophical theater you may observe the same thing which is found in the theater of the poets, that stories invented for the stage are more compact and elegant, and more as one would wish them to be, than true stories out of history.

9. Bacon does not mean "theories" in the inclusive modern sense, but "abstractions loosely invoked to explain particular facts."

In general, however, there is taken for the material of philosophy either a great deal out of a few things, or a very little out of many things; so that on both sides philosophy is based on too narrow a foundation of experiment and natural history, and decides on the authority of too few cases. For the rational school of philosophers snatches from experience a variety of common instances, neither duly ascertained nor diligently examined and weighed, and leaves all the rest to meditation and agitation of wit.[1]

There is also another class of philosophers, who having bestowed much diligent and careful labor on a few experiments, have thence made bold to educe and construct systems; wresting all other facts in a strange fashion to conformity therewith.

And there is yet a third class, consisting of those who out of faith and veneration mix their philosophy with theology and traditions; among whom the vanity of some has gone so far aside as to seek the origin of sciences among spirits and genii. So that this parent stock of errors—this false philosophy—is of three kinds: the sophistical, the empirical, and the superstitious.

* * *

68

So much concerning the several classes of idols, and their equipage: all of which must be renounced and put away with a fixed and solemn determination, and the understanding thoroughly freed and cleansed; the entrance into the kingdom of man, founded on the sciences, being not much other than the entrance into the kingdom of heaven, whereinto none may enter except as a little child.

1620

From The New Atlantis[1]

[SOLOMON'S HOUSE]

We came at our day and hour, and I was chosen by my fellows for the private access.[2] We found him in a fair chamber, richly hanged, and carpeted under foot, without any degrees to the state.[3] He was set upon a low throne richly adorned, and a rich cloth of state over his head, of blue satin embroidered.

1. Bacon's enthusiasm for experiment at times led him to denigrate the value of reason, but what he chiefly opposes here is the excessive concern with logic he finds in the Scholastic philosophers.
1. Thomas More's *Utopia* (1516) set a fashion for accounts of imaginary communities with more or less ideal forms of government. Bacon's imaginary community has at its center an account of a research establishment, Solomon's House, that could exist in any society; indeed a version of it was established in England in 1662 as the Royal Society. Bacon's title alludes to the legendary island and ideal commonwealth in the Atlantic Ocean described by Plato in *Critias;* in the 17th century it was sometimes located in the New World. Bacon places his island, Bensalem, in the Pacific, roughly where the Solomon Islands had been discovered in 1568. After an imaginary journey the nameless narrator and his shipmates discover an island cut off from Hebrew and Greek civilization (though given a special revelation of Christianity) and thereby freed to focus on the development of science.
2. Audience with one of the scientific "Fathers" of Solomon's House.
3. Without stairs leading up to the dais.

He was alone, save that he had two pages of honor, on either hand one, finely attired in white. His undergarments were the like that we saw him wear in the chariot;[4] but instead of his gown, he had on him a mantle with a cape of the same fine black, fastened about him. When we came in, as we were taught, we bowed low at our first entrance, and when we were come near his chair, he stood up, holding forth his hand ungloved and in posture of blessing; and we every one of us stooped down, and kissed the hem of his tippet.[5] That done, the rest departed, and I remained. Then he warned the pages forth of the room, and caused me to sit down beside him, and spake to me thus in the Spanish tongue:

"God bless thee, my son; I will give thee the greatest jewel I have. For I will impart unto thee, for the love of God and men, a relation of the true state of Solomon's House. Son, to make you know the true state of Solomon's House, I will keep this order. First, I will set forth unto you the end of our foundation. Secondly, the preparations and instruments we have for our works. Thirdly, the several employments and functions whereto our fellows are assigned. And fourthly, the ordinances and rites which we observe.

"The end of our foundation is the knowledge of causes, and secret motions of things; and the enlarging of the bounds of human empire, to the effecting of all things possible.

"The preparations and instruments are these. We have large and deep caves of several depths: the deepest are sunk six hundred fathom; and some of them are digged and made under great hills and mountains; so that if you reckon together the depth of the hill and the depth of the cave, they are, some of them, above three miles deep. For we find that the depth of a hill, and the depth of a cave from the flat, is the same thing; both remote alike from the sun and heaven's beams, and from the open air. These caves we call the Lower Region, and we use them for all coagulations, indurations,[6] refrigerations, and conservations of bodies. We use them likewise for the imitation of natural mines, and the producing also of new artificial metals, by compositions and materials which we use, and lay there for many years. We use them also sometimes (which may seem strange) for curing of some diseases, and for prolongation of life in some hermits that choose to live there, well accommodated of[7] all things necessary, and indeed live very long; by whom also we learn many things.

"We have burials in several earths, where we put divers cements,[8] as the Chinese do their porcelain. But we have them in greater variety, and some of them more fine. We have also great variety of composts and soils, for the making of the earth fruitful.

"We have high towers, the highest about half a mile in height, and some of them likewise set upon high mountains, so that the vantage of the hill, with the tower, is in the highest of them three miles at least. And these places we call the Upper Region, accounting the air between the high places and the low as a Middle Region. We use these towers, according to their several heights and situations, for insolation,[9] refrigeration, conserva-

---

4. He had made a triumphal entry into the city the previous day, wearing an undergarment of white linen and a black robe.
5. Scarf.
6. Hardenings.
7. Provided with.
8. Clays and pottery mixtures.
9. Exposure to the sun.

tion, and for the view of divers meteors—as winds, rain, snow, hail; and some of the fiery meteors[1] also. And upon them, in some places, are dwellings of hermits, whom we visit sometimes, and instruct what to observe.

"We have great lakes, both salt and fresh, whereof we have use for the fish and fowl. We use them also for burials of some natural bodies, for we find a difference in things buried in earth, or in air below the earth, and things buried in water. We have also pools, of which some do strain fresh water out of salt, and others by art do turn fresh water into salt. We have also some rocks in the midst of the sea, and some bays upon the shore, for some works wherein is required the air and vapor of the sea. We have likewise violent streams and cataracts, which serve us for many motions; and likewise engines for multiplying and enforcing[2] of winds to set also on going divers motions.

"We have also a number of artificial wells and fountains, made in imitation of the natural sources and baths, as tincted upon[3] vitriol, sulphur, steel, brass, lead, niter, and other minerals; and again, we have little wells for infusions of many things, where the waters take the virtue[4] quicker and better than in vessels or basins. And amongst them we have a water which we call Water of Paradise, being by that we do to it, made very sovereign[5] for health and prolongation of life.

"We have also great and spacious houses, where we imitate and demonstrate meteors—as snow, hail, rain, some artificial rains of bodies and not of water, thunders, lightnings; also generations of bodies in air—as frogs, flies, and divers others.

"We have also certain chambers, which we call Chambers of Health, where we qualify[6] the air as we think good and proper for the cure of divers diseases and preservation of health.

"We have also fair and large baths, of several mixtures, for the cure of diseases and the restoring of man's body from arefaction;[7] and others for the confirming of it in strength of sinews, vital parts, and the very juice and substance of the body.

"We have also large and various orchards and gardens, wherein we do not so much respect beauty as variety of ground and soil, proper for divers trees and herbs, and some very spacious, where trees and berries are set, whereof we make divers kinds of drinks, besides the vineyards. In these we practice likewise all conclusions[8] of grafting and inoculating, as well of wild trees as fruit trees, which produceth many effects. And we make (by art) in the same orchards and gardens trees and flowers to come earlier or later than their seasons, and to come up and bear more speedily than by their natural course they do. We make them also by art greater much than their nature; and their fruit greater and sweeter, and of differing taste, smell, color, and figure, from their nature. And many of them we so order as they become of medicinal use.

"We have also means to make divers plants rise by mixtures of earths without seeds, and likewise to make divers new plants, differing from the vulgar,[9] and to make one tree or plant turn into another.

1. Anything that fell from the sky was, in Renaissance terminology, a meteor.
2. Reinforcing, strengthening.
3. Tinctured with.
4. Property (of the substances put into water).
5. Efficacious.
6. Modify.
7. Drying up.
8. Experiments.
9. Ordinary.

"We have also parks and enclosures of all sorts of beasts and birds; which we use not only for view or rareness, but likewise for dissections and trials,[1] that thereby we may take light what may be wrought upon the body of man. Wherein we find many strange effects: as continuing life in them, though divers parts, which you account vital, be perished and taken forth; resuscitating of some that seem dead in appearance; and the like. We try also all poisons and other medicines upon them, as well of chirurgery[2] as physic. By art likewise, we make them greater or taller than their kind is, and contrariwise dwarf them and stay their growth; we make them more fruitful and bearing than their kind is, and contrariwise barren and not generative. Also, we make them differ in color, shape, activity, many ways. We find means to make commixtures and copulations of different kinds, which have produced many new kinds,[3] and them not barren, as the general opinion is. We make a number of kinds of serpents, worms, fishes, flies, of putrefaction, whereof some are advanced (in effect) to be perfect creatures, like beasts or birds, and have sexes, and do propagate. Neither do we this by chance, but we know beforehand of what matter and commixture what kind of those creatures will arise.

"We have also particular pools where we make trials upon fishes, as we have said before of beasts and birds.

"We have also places for breed and generation of those kinds of worms and flies which are of special use; such as are with you your silkworms and bees."[4]

*   *   *

"For the several employments and offices of our fellows, we have twelve that sail into foreign countries under the names of other nations (for our own we conceal), who bring us the books and abstracts and patterns of experiments of all other parts. These we call Merchants of Light.

"We have three that collect the experiments which are in all books. These we call Depredators.

"We have three that collect the experiments of all mechanical arts, and also of liberal sciences, and also of practices which are not brought into arts. These we call Mystery-men.

"We have three that try new experiments, such as themselves think good. These we call Pioneers or Miners.

"We have three that draw the experiments of the former four into titles and tables, to give the better light for the drawing of observations and axioms out of them. These we call Compilers.

"We have three that bend themselves, looking into the experiments of their fellows, and cast about how to draw out of them things of use and practice for man's life and knowledge, as well for works as for plain demonstration of causes, means of natural divinations, and the easy and clear discovery of the virtues and parts of bodies. These we call Dowry-men or Benefactors.

---

1. Experiments.
2. Surgery.
3. Species. It was commonly supposed that all hybrids were sterile (see following).
4. The narrator continues to describe the various bakeries, vineyards, breweries, and kitchens operated by Solomon's House. He enumerates the medicines discovered there, as well as various experiments with heat. The researchers study light, sound, perfumes, mechanics, mathematics, and all ways of deceiving the senses.

"Then after divers meetings and consults of our whole number, to consider of the former labors and collections, we have three that take care out of them to direct new experiments, of a higher light, more penetrating into nature than the former. These we call Lamps.

"We have three others that do execute the experiments so directed, and report them. These we call Inoculators.

"Lastly, we have three that raise the former discoveries by experiments into greater observations, axioms, and aphorisms. These we call Interpreters of Nature.

"We have also, as you must think, novices and apprentices, that the succession of the former employed men do not fail; besides a great number of servants and attendants, men and women. And this we do also: we have consultations, which of the inventions and experiences which we have discovered shall be published, and which not; and take all an oath of secrecy for the concealing of those which we think fit to keep secret; though some of those we do reveal sometimes to the State, and some not.[5]

"For our ordinances and rites, we have two very long and fair galleries: in one of these we place patterns and samples of all manner of the more rare and excellent inventions; in the other we place the statues of all principal inventors. There we have the statue of your Columbus, that discovered the West Indies; also the inventor of ships; your monk that was the inventor of ordnance and of gunpowder;[6] the inventor of music; the inventor of letters; the inventor of printing; the inventor of observations of astronomy; the inventor of works in metal; the inventor of glass; the inventor of silk of the worm; the inventor of wine; the inventor of corn and bread; the inventor of sugars; and all these by more certain tradition than you have. Then we have divers inventors of our own, of excellent works, which since you have not seen, it were too long to make descriptions of them; and besides, in the right understanding of those descriptions you might easily err. For upon every invention of value we erect a statue to the inventor, and give him a liberal and honorable reward. These statues are some of brass, some of marble and touchstone,[7] some of cedar and other special woods gilt and adorned; some of iron, some of silver, some of gold.

"We have certain hymns and services, which we say daily, of laud and thanks to God for his marvelous works; and forms of prayer, imploring his aid and blessing for the illumination of our labors, and the turning of them into good and holy uses.

"Lastly, we have circuits or visits of divers principal cities of the kingdom; where, as it cometh to pass, we do publish such new profitable inventions as we think good. And we do also declare natural divinations of diseases, plagues, swarms of hurtful creatures, scarcity, tempests, earthquakes, great inundations, comets, temperature of the year, and divers other things; and we give counsel thereupon, what the people shall do for the prevention and remedy of them."

And when he had said this he stood up; and I, as I had been taught, kneeled down; and he laid his right hand upon my head, and said, "God bless thee,

---

5. Bacon allows his scientists considerable autonomy in relation to the state.
6. Tradition credited Roger Bacon, a 13th-century monk, with the discovery of gunpowder.
7. A hard basaltic-type rock.

my son, and God bless this relation which I have made. I give thee leave to publish it, for the good of other nations; for we here are in God's bosom, a land unknown." And so he left me; having assigned a value of about two thousand ducats for a bounty to me and my fellows. For they give great largesses, where they come, upon all occasions.

The rest was not perfected.

1627

WILLIAM HARVEY

William Harvey (1578–1657) received medical training at Cambridge University and then at the University of Padua, a leading center of anatomical research. Returning to England, he established a successful practice, serving as personal physician to King James and Charles as well as to many less exalted clients. After many years of investigation, in 1628 Harvey published a treatise arguing, against the authority of ancient writers, that blood circulated in the body, pumped by the heart. Because Harvey wished to engage a scientific readership not only in England but internationally, he published his treatise in Latin; the selection reproduced here comes from the first English translation, in 1653.

Direct observation of the circulation of the blood and of the heart in motion is challenging because, of course, in live bodies the process is concealed, and in dead ones it no longer occurs. Harvey's vivisection of animals—a skill he would have learned in Padua—allowed him to observe the movement of the heart and arteries in the time between the opening of an animal's body and its death. Without a microscope, Harvey could not directly observe the capillaries, but he experimented with tourniquets on his own and others' bodies, which allowed him correctly to hypothesize that tiny vessels must transfer blood from the arteries, which carried the blood away from the heart, to the veins, which returned blood to the heart.

The excerpt demonstrates Harvey's lucid, methodical presentation of his observations and hypotheses. His experiments on beating hearts led him to a conclusion directly opposite of the accepted view: while previous writers had believed that the pulse was the effect of the heart dilating, Harvey argues instead that the heart is actively at work, and producing a pulse, when it compresses itself and forces blood into the arteries.

While Harvey's friend and patient Francis Bacon influentially elaborated the theory of science, Harvey actually performed the kind of innovative experiment Bacon was recommending. Harvey's objective, scientific prose constituted a stylistic model different from the rhetorically embellished, self-consciously artful prose of such sixteenth-century writers as Philip Sidney, and different as well from the style of Robert Burton or Sir Thomas Browne, which draws attention to the individual personality of the writer. Harvey's writings, striving for objectivity and the recording of detailed empirical fact, strongly influenced the founders of the Royal Society in the later seventeenth century.

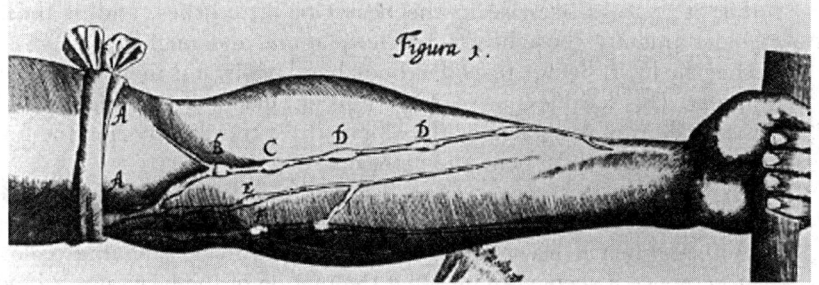

The Flow of Blood. This illustration from William Harvey's *On the Circulation of the Blood* (1628) depicts one of his experiments. Venal valves had already been discovered, but here Harvey shows that venal blood flows only toward the heart. He ligatured an arm to make obvious the veins and their valves, then pressed blood away from the heart and showed that the vein would remain empty because blocked by the valve.

The Anatomical Exercises of Dr. William Harvey Professor of Physic, and Physician to the King's Majesty, Concerning the Motion of the Heart and Blood. 1653

From *Chapter 2. What manner of motion the heart has in the dissection of living creatures*

First then in the hearts of all creatures, being dissected whilst they are yet alive, opening the crest, and cutting up the capsule which immediately environeth the heart, you may observe that the heart moves sometimes, sometimes rests: and that there is a time when it moves, and when it moves not.

This is more evident in the hearts of colder creatures, as the toads, serpents, frogs, house-snails, shrimps, crevises,[1] and all manner of little fishes. For it shews itself more manifestly in the hearts of hotter bodies, as of dogs, swine, if you observe attentively till the heart begin to die, and move faintly, and life is as it were departing from it. Then you may clearly and plainly see that the motions of it are more slow and seldom, and the restings of it of a longer continuance: and you may observe and distinguish more easily, what manner of motion it is, and which ways it is made; in the resting of it, as likewise in death, the heart is yielding, flagging weak, and lies as it were drooping.

At the motion, and whilst it is moving, three things are chiefly to be observed.

1. That the heart is erected, and that it raises itself upwards into a point, insomuch that it beats the breast at that time, so as the pulsation is felt outwardly.
2. That there is a contraction of it every way, especially of the sides of it, so that it appears lesser, longer, and contracted. The heart of an eel, taken out, and laid upon a trencher,[2] or upon one's hand, doth evidence

1. Crayfish.　　　　　　　　2. Plate.

this; it appears likewise in the hearts of little fishes, and of those colder animals whose hearts are sharp at top, and long.

3. That the heart being grasped in one's hand whilst it is in motion, feels harder. This hardness arises from tension, like as if one take hold of the tendons of one's arm by the elbow whilst they are moving the fingers, shall feel them bent and more resisting.

4. 'Tis moreover to be observed in fish, and colder animals which have blood, as serpents, frogs, at that time when the heart moves it becomes whitish, when it leaveth motion it appears full of sanguine[3] color. From hence it seemed to me, that the motion of the heart was a kind of tension in every part of it, according to the drawing and contraction of the fibers every way; because it appeared that in all its motions, it was erected, received vigor, grew lesser, and harder, and that the motion of it was like that of the muscles, where the contraction is made according to the drawing of the nervous parts, and fibers, for the muscles whilst they are in motion and in action, are invigorated and stretched, of soft become hard, they are uplifted and thickened; so likewise the heart.

From which observations with good reason we may gather that the heart at that time whilst it is in motion, suffers constriction, and is thickened in its outside, and so straitened in its ventricles, thrusting forth the blood contained within it: which from the fourth observation is evident because that in the tension it becomes white, having thrust out the blood contained within it, and presently after it in relaxation and rest, a purple and crimson color returns to the heart. But of this no man needs to make any further scruple, since upon the inflicting of a wound into the cavity of the ventricle, upon every motion and pulsation of the heart, in the very tension, you shall see the blood within contained to leap out.

So then these things happen at one and the same time: the tension of the heart, the erection of the point, and the beating (which is felt outwardly) by reason of its hitting against the breast, the incrassation[4] of the sides of it, and the forcible protrusion of the blood by constriction of the ventricles.

Hence the contrary of the commonly received opinion appears, which is, that the heart at that time when it beats against the breast, and the pulsation is outwardly felt, it is believed that the ventricles of the heart are dilated, and replete with blood, though you shall understand that it is otherwise, and that when the heart is contracted it is emptied. For that motion which is commonly thought the diastole[5] of the heart, is really the systole,[6] and so the proper motion of the heart is not a diastole but a systole, for the heart receives no vigor in the diastole, but in the systole, for then it is extended, moveth, and receiveth vigor.

---

3. Blood-red.
4. Compression.

5. Expansion.
6. Contraction.

ROBERT BURTON

Robert Burton's *Anatomy of Melancholy* assumes, unlike Bacon, that knowledge of psychology, not science, is humankind's greatest need. His enormous, baggy, delightful treatise analyzes in encyclopedic detail that ubiquitous Jacobean malady, melancholy, supposedly caused, according to contemporary humor theory, by an excess of black bile. It was responsible, according to Burton and others, for the wild passions and despair of lovers, the agonies and ecstasies of religious devotees, the frenzies of madmen, and the studious abstraction of scholars such as Shakespeare's Hamlet or Milton's Il Penseroso. But for Burton melancholy is more than a particular temperament or disease: it encompasses all the folly and madness intrinsic to the fallen human condition and so afflicts the whole world—necessarily including Burton himself.

Burton (1577–1640) was a scholar and cleric who lived in Christ Church College, Oxford, all his life: he never married, never traveled, never sought success in the world, but lived, as he says of himself in his preface, "a silent, sedentary, solitary, private life," researching his great book in the Bodleian Library and reading omnivorously in other topics. First published in 1621, the *Anatomy* went through five editions during the author's life, each one much augmented over the last. In his preface Burton creates a persona for himself, Democritus Junior, who proposes to complete the supposedly lost book on melancholy and madness by the Greek "laughing philosopher" Democritus. As Democritus Junior he promises not only to laugh but also to scoff, satirize, and lament.

The title term "anatomy" invites expectations of a clear, logical, ordered treatment of a medical subject after the manner of Vesalius, expectations also evoked by Donne in his *Anatomy of the World*. Burton's subtitle promises an analysis of "all the kinds, causes, symptoms, prognostics, and several cures" of melancholy, and a division into three parts—the Causes and Effects, the Cures, and the two principal kinds, Love Melancholy and Religious Melancholy—as well as various "sections, members, and subsections." But instead of such clarity and rigidity of structure, the categories collapse into each other. Since melancholy is universal, Burton finds warrant to be all-inclusive and digressive, to take us in picaresque disorder from one subject to the next, moving readily from the inner landscape to the world outside. The work contains a utopia, a treatise on climatology, and discourses on geography and meteorology, as well as case studies of various sufferers from melancholy: a man who thought he was glass; a man who thought he was butter; maids, nuns, and widows who suffer sexual deprivation; and so on. Also, Burton cites every authority who wrote about any aspect of melancholy, from classical times to his present, but in no special order and without privileging even citations from Scripture. Such randomness and their own contradictions undercut the authorities, collapsing them all into the idiosyncratic style of Burton/Democritus Junior. Burton's prose style of long, loose sentences, with their pell-mell momentum as of thoughts rushing beyond the author's control, suggests a disorderly world not at all amenable to Baconian logic and science. Burton concludes by offering the pragmatic advice "Be not idle" as the only remedy against melancholy. His book, were we to read it all, would keep us from idleness for a good long time.

From The Anatomy[1] of Melancholy

From *Love Melancholy*

PART 3, SECTION 2, MEMBER 1, SUBSECTION 2: HOW LOVE TYRANNIZETH OVER MEN. LOVE, OR HEROICAL MELANCHOLY, HIS DEFINITION, PART AFFECTED.

You have heard how this tyrant Love rageth with brute beasts and spirits; now let us consider what passions it causeth amongst men. *Improbe amor quid non mortalia pectora cogis,*[2] How it tickles the hearts of mortal men, *horresco referens,*[3] I am almost afraid to relate, amazed, and ashamed, it hath wrought such stupend and prodigious effects, such foul offences. Love indeed (I may not deny) first united provinces, built cities, and by a perpetual generation makes and preserves mankind, propagates the Church; but if it rage, it is no more love, but burning lust, a disease, frenzy, madness, hell. *Est orcus ille, vis est immedicabilis, est rabies insana,* 'tis no virtuous habit this, but a vehement perturbation of the mind, a monster of nature, wit, and art, as Alexis in Athenaeus[4] sets it out, *viriliter audax, muliebriter timidium, furore praeceps, labore infractum, mel felleum, blanda percussio,* etc. It subverts kingdoms, overthrows cities, towns, families, mars, corrupts, and makes a massacre of men; thunder and lightning, wars, fires, plagues, have not done that mischief to mankind, as this burning lust, this brutish passion. Let Sodom and Gomorrah, Troy (which Dares Phrygius and Dictys Cretensis will make good)[5] and I know not how many cities bear record,—*et fuit ante Helenam,*[6] etc., all succeeding ages will subscribe: Joanna of Naples in Italy, Fredegunde and Brunhalt in France,[7] all histories are full of these basilisks.[8] Besides those daily monomachies,[9] murders, effusion of blood, rapes, riot, and immoderate expense, to satisfy their lusts, beggary, shame, loss, torture, punishment, disgrace, loathsome diseases that proceed from thence, worse than calentures[1] and pestilent fevers, those often gouts, pox,

---

1. A logical dissection of a topic into its several parts, on an analogy with a medical anatomy. (See also Donne, *An Anatomy of the World,* pp. 949–60.) Burton's full title plays wittily with the term while pointing to the massive scope of his work: *The Anatomy of Melancholy. What it is, with all the kinds, causes, symptoms, prognostics, & several cures of it. In three Partitions, with their several sections, members, & subsections. Philosophically, medicinally, historically opened & cut up.*
2. Depraved love, to what do you not force mortal breasts?
3. Burton immediately translates the Latin into English ("I am almost afraid to relate") as is his habit throughout *The Anatomy of Melancholy.* The notes here will provide translations only when Burton does not.
4. Alexis is one of the interlocutors in Athenaeus's series of dialogues, *Deipnosophistae (The Banquet of the Learned)* written in the 3rd century C.E., which features dinner conversations on topics that include food, poetry, philology, and sexual mores; the English classicist Isaac Casaubon revived interest in the work by publishing his edition in 1612.
5. In Genesis 18–19, God annihilates the towns Sodom and Gomorrah with a rain of fire and brimstone to punish their sexual wickedness; the Greeks destroyed Troy after the Trojan prince Paris eloped with the beautiful Helen, wife of the Greek king Menelaus. Dares Phrygius and Dictys Cretensis were the supposed authors of eyewitness accounts of the Trojan War; the texts, actually dating from late antiquity, were available in Latin and thus became the basis for the medieval knowledge of the Troy legend, in an era when Greek was not widely known in Western Europe.
6. And these were before Helen.
7. Joanna of Naples, 1327–1381, conspired to assassinate her first husband; most of the plotters were ferociously executed, but Joanna was eventually acquitted and married three more times. Fredegund (died 59 C.E.) was a servant of the Frankish king Chilperic, who killed his wife and made Fredegund his consort. Brunhalt or Brunhilda (543–613 C.E.), the sister of Chilperic's wife and married to Chilperic's brother, encouraged her husband to go to war to avenge this murder; years of bloody conflict ensued.
8. Legendary serpent with poisonous breath and lethal gaze.
9. Single combats; duels.
1. Feverish delirium.

arthritis, palsies, cramps, sciatica, convulsions, aches, combustions, etc., which torment the body, that feral[2] melancholy which crucifies the soul in this life, and everlastingly torments in the world to come.

Notwithstanding they know these and many such miseries, threats, tortures, will surely come upon them, rewards, exhortations, *e contra*;[3] yet either out of their own weakness, a depraved nature, or love's tyranny, which so furiously rageth, they suffer themselves to be led like an ox to the slaughter: (*Facilis descensus Averni*) they go down headlong to their own perdition, they will commit folly with beasts, men "leaving the natural use of women," as Paul saith, "burned in lust one towards another, and man with man wrought filthiness."[4]

*   *   *[5]

I come at last to that heroical love which is proper to men and women, is a frequent cause of melancholy, and deserves much rather to be called burning lust, than by such an honorable title. There is an honest love, I confess, which is natural, *laqueus occultus captivans corda hominum, ut a mulieribus non possint separari*, "a secret snare to captivate the hearts of men," as Christopher Fonseca proves,[6] a strong allurement, of a most attractive, occult, adamantine property, and powerful virtue, and no man living can avoid it. *Et qui vim non sensit amoris, aut lapis est, aut bellua.* He is not a man but a block, a very stone, *aut Numen, aut Nebuchadnezzar*,[7] he hath a gourd for his head, a pepon[8] for his heart, that hath not felt the power of it, and a rare creature to be found, one in an age, *qui nunquam visae flagravit amore puellae*;[9] for *semel insanivimus omnes*, dote we either young or old, as he said,[1] and none are excepted but Minerva and the Muses: so Cupid in Lucian[2] complains to his mother Venus, that amongst all the rest his arrows could not pierce them. But this nuptial love is a common passion, an honest, for men to love in the way of marriage; *ut materia appetit formam, sic mulier virum*.[3] You know marriage is honorable, a blessed calling, appointed by God himself in Paradise; it breeds true peace, tranquility, content, and happiness, *qua nulla est aut fuit unquam sanctior conjunctio*, as Daphnaeus in Plutarch[4] could well prove, *et quae generi humano immortalitatem parat*,[5] when they live without jarring, scolding, lovingly as they should do.

> *Felices ter et amplius*
> *Quos irrupta tenet copula, nec ullis*
> *Divulsus querimoniis*
> *Suprema citius solvit amor die.*[6]

---

2. Deadly.
3. On the other hand.
4. In Romans 1.22–27, St. Paul writes that because of the pagans' idolatrous beliefs God "gave them up unto vile affections: for even their women did change the natural use into that which is against nature: And likewise also the men, leaving the natural use of the woman, burned in their lust one toward another."
5. In the omitted section, Burton provides, in Latin, a list of perverse loves as described by Ovid and other classical writers.
6. Quoting from the Spanish writer Christopher Fonseca's *Amphitheater of Love.*
7. "Either a god, or Nebuchadenezzar," i.e., an

extraordinary thing, quoting from the church father Tertullian's *Against Marcion*, book 4.
8. Pumpkin.
9. In whom the sight of a girl has never sparked love.
1. Chaucer.
2. Lucian, *Dialogue of the Gods* 19.
3. As matter seeks form, so a man seeks a woman.
4. Daphnaeus in Plutarch's *Dialogue on Love* argues for the sanctity of marital love, against Protogenes, who argues that true love is homosexual.
5. And which provides for the perpetuation of humankind.
6. Quoting Horace, *Odes* 1.13; the translation follows immediately.

> Thrice happy they, and more than that,
> Whom bond of love so firmly ties,
> That without brawls till death them part,
> 'Tis undissolv'd and never dies.

As Seneca lived with his Paulina, Abraham and Sarah, Orpheus and Eurydice, Arria and Poetus, Artemisia and Mausolus,[7] Rubenius Celer, that would needs have it engraven on his tomb, he had led his life with Ennea, his dear wife, forty-three years eight months, and never fell out. There is no pleasure in this world comparable to it, 'tis *summum mortalitatis bonum, hominum divumque voluptas, Alma Venus; latet enim in muliere aliquid majus potentiusque, omnibus aliis humanis voluptatibus,* as one holds, there's something in a woman beyond all human delight; a magnetic virtue, a charming quality, an occult and powerful motive. The husband rules her as head, but she again commands his heart, he is her servant, she is only joy and content: no happiness is like unto it, no love so great as this of man and wife, no such comfort as *placens uxor,* a sweet wife: *omnis amor magnus, sed aperto in conjuge major.*[8] When they love at last as fresh as they did at first, *charaque charo consenescit conjugi,*[9] as Homer brings Paris kissing Helen, after they had been married ten years, protesting withal that he loved her as dear as he did the first hour that he was betrothed.[1] And in their old age, when they make much of one another, saying, as he did to his wife in the poet,

> *Uxor vivamus quod viximus, et moriamur,*
> *Servantes nomen sumpsimus in thalamo;*
> *Nec ferat ulla dies ut commutemur in aevo,*
> *Quin tibi sim juvenis, tuque puella mihi.*[2]

> Dear wife, let's live in love, and die together,
> As hitherto we have in all good will:
> Let no day change or alter our affections.
> But let's be young to one another still.

Such should conjugal love be, still the same, and as they are one flesh, so should they be of one mind, as in an aristocratical government, one consent, Geyron-like,[3] *coalescere in unum,* have one heart in two bodies, will and nill the same. A good wife, according to Plutarch,[4] should be as a looking-glass to represent her husband's face and passion: if he be pleasant, she should be merry: if he laugh, she should smile: if he look sad, she should participate of his sorrow, and bear a part with him, and so should they continue in mutual love one towards another.

> *Et me ab amore tuo deducet nulla senectus,*
> *Sive ego Tythonus, sive ego Nestor ero.*[5]

> No age shall part my love from thee, sweet wife,
> Though I live Nestor or Tithonus' life.

7. Famously compatible couples from classical history, mythology, and the Bible.
8. Love is always great, but greatest in marriage.
9. Remaining dear to one another as they grow old together.
1. In *The Iliad*, book 3.
2. The opening lines of the Latin poet Ausonius's "Epigram 20."
3. In classical mythology, a monster with one head and three bodies.
4. In his *Advice to the Bride and Groom.*
5. From the Latin love poet Propertius, *Elegies,* book 2: 25.

And she again to him, as the bride saluted the bridegroom of old in Rome, *Ubi tu Caius, ego semper Caia,* be thou still Caius, I'll be Caia.[6]

'Tis a happy state this[7] indeed, when the fountain is blessed (saith Solomon, Proverbs v.18), "and he rejoiceth with the wife of his youth, and she is to him as the loving hind and pleasant roe,[8] and he delights in her continually." But this love of ours is immoderate, inordinate, and not to be comprehended in any bounds. It will not contain itself within the union of marriage or apply to one object, but is a wandering, extravagant, a domineering, a boundless, an irrefragable,[9] a destructive passion; sometimes this burning lust rageth after marriage, and then it is properly called jealousy; sometimes before, and then it is called heroical melancholy; it extends sometimes to corrivals, etc., begets rapes, incests, murders: *Marcus Antoninus compressit Faustinum sororem, Caracalla Juliam novercam, Nero matrem, Caligula sorores, Cinyras Myrrham filiam,*[1] etc. But it is confined within no terms of blood, years, sex, or whatsoever else. Some furiously rage before they come to discretion or age. Quartilla in Petronius[2] never remembered she was a maid; and the Wife of Bath in Chaucer cracks,

> Since I was twelve years old, believe,
> Husbands at kirk-door had I five.[3]

Aretine's Lucretia sold her maidenhead a thousand times before she was twenty-four years old, *plus millies vendideram virginitatem, etc., neque te celabo, non deerant qui ut integram ambirent.*[4] Rahab, that harlot, began to be a professed quean at ten years of age, and was but fifteen when she hid the spies, as Hugh Broughton proves, to whom Serrarius the Jesuit, *quaest.* 6 *in cap.* 2 Josue, subscribes. Generally women begin *pubescere* as they call it, or *catulire* as Julius Pollux cites, *lib. 2, cap. 3 Onomast.* out of Aristophanes, at fourteen years old, then they do offer themselves, and some plainly rage. Leo Afer[5] saith that in Africa a man shall scarce find a maid at fourteen years of age, they are so forward, and many amongst us after they come into the teens do not live without husbands, but linger.[6] What pranks in this kind the middle age have played is not to be recorded, *si mihi sint centum linguae, sint oraque centum,*[7] no tongue can sufficiently declare, every story is full of men and women's insatiable lust, Neros, Heliogabali, Bonosi,[8] etc. *Coelius Aufilenum, et Quintius Aufilenam depereunt,*[9] etc. They

6. The ancient Roman marriage vow included these words: "where you (the man, Caius) are, so I (the woman, Caia) will be likewise."
7. I.e., the state of matrimony.
8. The hind is a female and the roebuck ("roe") a male deer.
9. Not to be questioned.
1. "Marc Antony slept with his sister Faustina, Caracalla with his stepmother Julia, Nero with his mother, Caligula with his sisters, Cinyras with his daughter Myrrha."
2. A character in the *Satyricon* of Petronius Arbiter (1st century C.E.).
3. Burton cites from memory, and inaccurately.
4. "Nor will I conceal from you that there were those who sought her as though her virginity were intact." Burton gets this story from Kaspar Barth's Latin translation of a Spanish adaptation of Pietro Aretino's 1534 *Ragionamenti*, dialogues set in a brothel. The "quean" (whore)

Rahab (following) appears in Joshua 2. Hugh Broughton (below) was a biblical scholar of Burton's day.
5. Leo Afer, or Africanus, was a 16th-century Spanish Moor who wrote one of the first accounts of Africa. *Pubescere*: mature sexually. *Catulire*: desire a male. Julius Pollux compiled a dictionary (*Onomasticon*) that Burton cites frequently.
6. I.e., they waste away if they are not married.
7. "If I had a hundred tongues, a hundred mouths."
8. Nero and Heliogabalus were sexually depraved Roman emperors, their vices described in lurid detail by Roman historians and moralists. Bonosus, a 3rd-century C.E. Roman usurper, was merely a drunk, but his close associate Proculus boasted of having deflowered one hundred virgins in a single night.
9. "Coelius had an itch for Aufilenus, Quintius for Aufilena." From Catullus, the Roman erotic poet.

neigh after other men's wives (as Jeremy, *cap.* v.8 complaineth) like fed horses, or range like town bulls, *raptores virginum et viduarum,*[1] as many of our great ones do. Solomon's wisdom was extinguished in this fire of lust, Samson's strength enervated, piety in Lot's daughters quite forgot, gravity of priesthood in Eli's sons, reverend old age in the elders that would violate Susanna, filial duty in Absalom to his stepmother, brotherly love in Amnon towards his sister.[2] Human, divine laws, precepts, exhortations, fear of God and men, fair, foul means, fame, fortunes, shame, disgrace, honor cannot oppose, stave off, or withstand the fury of it, *omnia vincit amor,*[3] etc. No cord nor cable can so forcibly draw, or hold so fast, as love can do with a twined thread. The scorching beams under the equinoctial or extremity of cold within the circle Arctic, where the very seas are frozen, cold or torrid zone cannot avoid or expel this heat, fury, and rage of mortal men.

> *Quo fugis? ah, demens! nulla est fuga, tu licet usque*
> *Ad Tanaim fugias, usque sequetur amor.*[4]

Of women's unnatural, unsatiable lust, what country, what village doth not complain? Mother and daughter sometimes dote on the same man; father and son, master and servant on one woman.

> *Sed amor, sed ineffrenata libido,*
> *Quid castum in terris intentatumque reliquit?*[5]

What breach of vows and oaths, fury, dotage, madness might I reckon up! Yet this is more tolerable in youth, and such as are still in their hot blood; but for an old fool to dote, to see an old lecher, what more odious, what can be more absurd? And yet what so common? Who so furious? *Amare ea aetate si occeperint, multo insaniunt acrius.*[6] Some dote then more than ever they did in their youth. How many decrepit, hoary, harsh, writhen, bursten-bellied, crooked, toothless, bald, blear-eyed, impotent, rotten old men shall you see flickering still in every place? One gets him a young wife, another a courtesan, and when he can scarce lift his leg over a sill and hath one foot already in Charon's boat,[7] when he hath the trembling in his joints, the gout in his feet, a perpetual rheum in his head, a continuate cough, "his sight fails him, thick of hearing, his breath stinks,"[8] all his moisture is dried up and gone, may not spit from him, a very child again, that cannot dress himself or cut his own meat, yet he will be dreaming of and honing after wenches; what can be more unseemly? Worse it is in women than in men; when she is *aetate declivis, diu vidua, mater olim, parum decore matrimonium sequi videtur,* an old widow, a mother so long since (in Pliny's opinion),[9] she doth very unseemly

---

1. "Ravishers of maids and widows" (Jeremiah 5.8).
2. For these biblical stories see 1 Kings 11.3, Judges 16, Genesis 19.30–35, 1 Samuel 2.22, Daniel 13 (Apocrypha), 2 Samuel 16.22, 13.1–19.
3. "Love conquers all."
4. "Whither away? ah, madman! there is no escape. Flee to the remotest districts of the river Don, love will still follow." From Propertius, the Latin elegist.
5. "But love, unbridled passion, leaves nothing on earth untempted, nothing chaste." From Eurip-

ides, the Greek tragedian.
6. "When they start loving at that age, the madness takes them worse." From Plautus, the Roman comic dramatist.
7. Charon ferries the souls of the dead across the river Styx.
8. Quoted from Cyprian, 3rd-century bishop of Carthage.
9. Pliny, *Natural History* 8. The Latin is translated by Burton.

seek to marry; yet whilst she is so old, a crone, a beldam, she can neither see nor hear, go nor stand, a mere carcass, a witch, and scarce feel, she cater-wauls and must have a stallion, a champion, she must and will marry again, and betroth herself to some young man that hates to look on her but for her goods, abhors the sight of her, to the prejudice of her good name, her own undoing, grief of friends, and ruin of her children.

But to enlarge or illustrate this power and effects of love is to set a candle in the sun. It rageth with all sorts and conditions of men, yet is most evident among such as are young and lusty, in the flower of their years, nobly descended, high fed, such as live idly and at ease; and for that cause (which our divines call burning lust) this *ferinus insanus amor*, this mad and beastly passion, as I have said, is named by our physicians heroical love, and a more honorable title put upon it, *amor nobilis* as Savonarola[1] styles it, because noble men and women make a common practice of it and are so ordinarily affected with it. Avicenna,[2] *lib.* 3, *fen.* 1, *tract.* 4, *cap.* 23, calleth this passion *Ilishi* and defines it to be "a disease or melancholy vexation or anguish of mind, in which a man continually meditates of the beauty, gesture, manners of his mistress, and troubles himself about it"; "desiring" (as Savonarola adds) "with all intentions and eagerness of mind to compass or enjoy her; as commonly hunters trouble themselves about their sports, the covetous about their gold and goods, so is he tormented still about his mistress." Arnoldus Villa-novanus[3] in his book of heroical love defines it "a continual cogitation of that which he desires, with a confidence or hope of compassing it"; which definition his commentator cavils at. For continual cogitation is not the *genus* but a symptom of love; we continually think of that which we hate and abhor, as well as that which we love; and many things we covet and desire without all hope of attaining. Carolus à Lorme in his *Questions* makes a doubt *an amor sit morbus*, whether this heroical love be a disease: Julius Pollux, *Onomast.* lib. 6, *cap.* 44, determines it. They that are in love are likewise sick; *lascivus, salax, lasciviens, et qui in venerem furit, vere est aegrotus.*[4] Arnoldus will have it improperly so called, and a malady rather of the body than mind. Tully,[5] in his *Tusculans*, defines it a furious disease of the mind; Plato, madness itself; Ficinus, his commentator, *cap.* 12, a species of madness, "for many have run mad for women" (I Esdras iv.26); but Rhasis,[6] "a melancholy passion"; and most physicians make it a species or kind of melancholy (as will appear by the symptoms), and treat of it apart; whom I mean to imitate, and to discuss it in all his kinds, to examine his several causes, to show his symptoms, indications, prognostics, effects, that so it may be with more facility cured.

The part affected in the meantime, as Arnoldus supposeth, "is the former part of the head for want of moisture," which his commentator rejects. Langius, *Med. epist. lib.* 1, *cap.* 24, will have this passion sited in the liver, and to keep residence in the heart, "to proceed first from the eyes so carried

1. Not the Florentine reformer, but his grandfather Michele, a Paduan physician.
2. An encyclopedic Arabian physician of the 11th century.
3. Arnold of Villanova was a Spanish doctor, astrologer, and alchemist of the 13th and early 14th centuries.
4. "One who is lustful, lecherous, lascivious, and mad with desire is really sick."
5. I.e., Cicero.
6. Rhasis, or Rhazes, was an Arab physician of the 10th century.

by our spirits, and kindled with imagination in the liver and heart"; *cogit amare iecur,*[7] as the saying is. *Medium ferit per hepar,* as Cupid in Anacreon. For some such cause belike, Homer feigns Titius' liver (who was enamored of Latona) to be still gnawed by two vultures day and night in hell, "for that young men's bowels thus enamored are so continually tormented by love."[8] Gordonius, *cap.* 2, *part.* 2, "will have the testicles an immediate subject or cause, the liver an antecedent." Fracastorius agrees in this with Gordonius,[9] *inde primitus imaginatio venerea, erectio, etc.; titillatissimam partem vocat, ita ut nisi extruso semine gestiens voluptas non cessat, nec assidua veneris recordatio, addit Guastavinius, Comment.,* 4 *sect., prob.* 27 *Arist.*[1] But properly it is a passion of the brain, as all other melancholy, by reason of corrupt imagination, and so doth Jason Pratensis, cap. 19, *De morb. cerebri* (who writes copiously of this erotical love), place and reckon it amongst the affections of the brain. Melanchthon, *De anima,* confutes those that make the liver a part affected, and Guianerius, *tract.* 15, *cap.* 13 *et* 17, though many put all the affections in the heart, refers it to the brain. Ficinus, *cap.* 7, *In Convivium Platonis,* "will have the blood to be the part affected." Jo. Freitagius, *cap.* 14, *Noct. med.,* supposeth all four affected, heart, liver, brain, blood; but the major part concur upon the brain, 'tis *imaginatio laesa,*[2] and both imagination and reason are misaffected; because of his corrupt judgment and continual meditation of that which he desires, he may truly be said to be melancholy. If it be violent, or his disease inveterate, as I have determined in the precedent partitions, both imagination and reason are misaffected, first one, then the other.

1621, 1651

---

7. "The liver compels one to love"; and in the next phrase, "Love strikes through the liver." Anacreon was a Greek lyric poet.
8. *Odyssey* 11.
9. Gordonius, Guastavinius, Jason Pratensis, Guianerius, Freitagius, et al. (see following) are Renaissance physicians from the ragbag of Burton's encyclopedic reading. Two who stand out are Girolamo Fracastoro and Marsilio Ficino—the former a physician still remembered for his work on communicable diseases, the latter known mostly for his learned commentaries on the dialogues of Plato.
1. "Whence at first come erotic imaginings, erection, etc.; it so rouses the most excitable part, adds Guastavinius, that until emission takes place, the longing pleasure does not cease, nor the constant recollection of lovemaking."
2. A wounded imagination.

SIR THOMAS BROWNE

Sir Thomas Browne (1605–1682) presents his best-known work, *Religio Medici* (A Doctor's Religion), as "the true Anatomy of myself." This work is not, as we might expect from the title, a spiritual autobiography relating, like many in the period, an angst-filled story of conversion or an account of providential experiences. Nor does Browne report the facts of his life: that he was born into the family of a cloth merchant, attended Winchester School and Pembroke College, Oxford, studied at the best medical schools (Montpelier, Padua, Leiden), practiced medicine in Yorkshire and Norwich, married in 1641, and fathered twelve children. Instead, this work is an exercise in delighted self-analysis, outlining Browne's own sometimes eccentric views on a wide variety of topics pertaining to religious doctrine and practice. For this purpose Browne constructs an engaging persona: the genial, speculative doctor who finds nothing human foreign to him and so is the very personification of charity and inclusiveness: he can readily participate in the customs of others in food, drink, or religion (even in certain Roman Catholic practices) but yet value his own.

In this two-part treatise divided into short numbered paragraphs, Browne voices his fondness for Anglo-Catholic ritual but also his belief in Calvinist predestination; he denounces religious persecution but thinks many religious martyrs not particularly admirable; he believes in witches but is skeptical of latter-day miracles. His love of mystery and wonder (in sharp contrast to Bacon) leads him to revel in metaphor and take positive joy in accepting things contrary to reason: "I love to lose myself in a mystery, to pursue my reason to an O *altitudo!*" According to his preface, he wrote the work around 1636 for himself only and circulated it in manuscript to a few friends but then was forced by a pirated edition (1642) to print a correct version (1643). Yet his decision to publish just as the king and Parliament took to the battlefield in the civil war was hardly fortuitous, and the treatise has political resonance. Describing himself as one who sympathizes with and has himself held several erroneous or heretical views, Browne disparages dogmatism and holds up to gentle irony those who claim exclusive possession of the path to salvation. At the same time, he deplores schism and is ready to conform his mind to the teachings and practices of the Church of England. His self-analysis comments on the wider world of church and state, posing his example of tolerant inclusiveness against reforming Puritans eager to rid the church of its errors.

Browne was a favorite prose stylist of many later writers, among them Samuel Taylor Coleridge, Charles Lamb, Thomas De Quincey, and Herman Melville: polysyllabic and Latinate, his prose mixes wit and sumptuous rhetoric, often rising to a resonant poetry.

From Religio Medici[1]

From *Part 1*

1. For my religion, though there be several circumstances that might persuade the world I have none at all—as the general scandal of my profession,[2] the natural course of my studies, the indifferency[3] of my behavior and discourse in matters of religion, neither violently defending one, nor with that common ardor and contention opposing another—yet in despite hereof I dare without usurpation assume the honorable style of a Christian. Not that I merely owe this title to the font,[4] my education, or clime wherein I was born, as being bred up either to confirm those principles my parents instilled into my unwary understanding, or by a general consent proceed in the religion of my country; but having in my riper years and confirmed judgment seen and examined all, I find myself obliged by the principles of grace

---

1. The Religion of a Doctor. Browne avoids any conflict between science and religion by a forthright "fideism"—entirely separating reason from faith and thereby exempting faith from any critique by reason, or any support from it. This was also the stance of some contemporary Roman Catholic skeptics, notably Montaigne and Pierre Charron.
2. Doctors were popularly reputed to be irreligious or atheistic.
3. Impartiality.
4. The baptismal font.

and the law of mine own reason to embrace no other name but this. Neither doth herein my zeal so far make me forget the general charity I owe unto humanity, as rather to hate than pity Turks, infidels, and (what is worse) Jews;[5] rather contenting myself to enjoy that happy style than maligning those who refuse so glorious a title.

2. But because the name of a Christian is become too general to express our faith—there being a geography of religions as well as lands, and every clime distinguished not only by their laws and limits, but circumscribed by their doctrines and rules of faith—to be particular, I am of that reformed new-cast religion wherein I mislike nothing but the name;[6] of the same belief our Savior taught, the apostles disseminated, the Fathers authorized, and the martyrs confirmed; but by the sinister ends of princes, the ambition and avarice of prelates, and the fatal corruption of times, so decayed, impaired, and fallen from its native beauty that it required the careful and charitable hands of these times to restore it to its primitive integrity. Now the accidental occasion whereon, the slender means whereby, the low and abject condition of the person by whom so good a work was set on foot,[7] which in our adversaries beget contempt and scorn, fills me with wonder, and is the very same objection the insolent pagans first cast at Christ and his disciples.

3. Yet have I not so shaken hands with those desperate resolutions—who had rather venture at large their decayed bottom[8] than bring her in to be new trimmed in the dock, who had rather promiscuously retain all than abridge any, and obstinately be what they are than what they have been— as to stand in diameter[9] and sword's point with them. We have reformed from them, not against them; for, omitting those improperations and terms of scurrility betwixt us, which only difference[1] our affections and not our cause, there is between us one common name and appellation, one faith and necessary body of principles common to us both; and therefore I am not scrupulous to converse and live with them, to enter their churches in defect of ours, and either pray with them or for them. I could never perceive any rational consequence from those many texts which prohibit the children of Israel to pollute themselves with the temples of the heathens; we being all Christians, and not divided by such detested impieties as might profane our prayers or the place wherein we make them; or that a resolved conscience may not adore her Maker anywhere, especially in places devoted to his service; where, if their devotions offend him, mine may please him, if theirs profane it, mine may hallow it. Holy water and crucifix, dangerous to the common people, deceive not my judgment nor abuse my devotion at all. I am, I confess, naturally inclined to that which misguided zeal terms superstition.[2] My common conversation I do acknowledge austere, my behavior full of rigor, sometimes not without morosity; yet at my devotion I love to use the civility of my knee, my hat, and hand, with all those outward and sen-

---

5. Browne thought them worse because they had been given a better chance than the others to know and accept Christianity.
6. Protestantism, for its connotations of contentiousness.
7. Luther, who was a miner's son, began the Reformation.

8. The leaky ship of the Roman Catholic Church. "Shaken hands with": parted from.
9. In complete opposition.
1. Differentiate. "Improperations": reproaches.
2. He defines himself here and in the next few lines against Puritan iconoclasts who would uproot all such "superstitions."

sible motions which may express or promote my invisible devotion. I should violate my own arm rather than a church, nor willingly deface the memory of saint or martyr. At the sight of a cross or crucifix I can dispense with my hat, but scarce with the thought and memory of my Savior. I cannot laugh at, but rather pity, the fruitless journeys of pilgrims, or contemn the miserable condition of friars; for though misplaced in circumstance, there is somewhat in it of devotion. I could never hear the Ave-Maria bell without an elevation,[3] or think it a sufficient warrant, because they erred in one circumstance, for me to err in all—that is, in silence and dumb contempt. Whilst, therefore, they directed their devotions to her, I offered mine to God, and rectified the errors of their prayers by rightly ordering mine own. At a solemn procession I have wept abundantly while my consorts,[4] blind with opposition and prejudice, have fallen into an excess of scorn and laughter. There are questionless, both in Greek, Roman, and African churches, solemnities and ceremonies whereof the wiser zeals do make a Christian use; and stand condemned by us, not as evil in themselves, but as allurements and baits of superstition to those vulgar heads that look asquint on the face of truth, and those unstable judgments that cannot consist[5] in the narrow point and center of virtue without a reel or stagger to the circumference.

4. As there were many reformers, so likewise many reformations; every country proceeding in a particular way and method, according as their national interest together with their constitution and clime inclined them: some angrily and with extremity, others calmly and with mediocrity,[6] not rending but easily dividing the community, and leaving an honest possibility of a reconciliation; which, though peaceable spirits do desire, and may conceive that revolution of time and the mercies of God may effect, yet that judgment that shall consider the present antipathies between the two extremes, their contrarieties in condition, affection, and opinion, may with the same hopes expect an union in the poles of heaven.

5. But—to difference myself nearer, and draw into a lesser circle—there is no church whose every part so squares unto my conscience, whose articles, constitutions, and customs seem so consonant unto reason, and as it were framed to my particular devotion, as this whereof I hold my belief: the Church of England, to whose faith I am a sworn subject, and therefore in a double obligation subscribe unto her articles and endeavor to observe her constitutions. Whatsoever is beyond, as points indifferent, I observe according to the rules of my private reason or the humor and fashion of my devotion; neither believing this because Luther affirmed it nor disapproving that because Calvin hath disavouched it. I condemn not all things in the council of Trent nor approve all in the synod of Dort.[7] In brief, where the Scripture is silent, the church is my text; where that speaks, 'tis but my comment; where there is a joint silence of both, I borrow not the rules of my religion from Rome or Geneva,[8] but the dictates of my own reason. It is an unjust

---

3. Exaltation of mind. "Ave-Maria bell": Angelus, rung daily at 6:00 and 12:00, morning and night.
4. Companions.
5. Stand firm. "Asquint": cross-eyed.
6. Moderation. "Extremity": violence.
7. The Council of Trent (1545–63), in Italy,

defined Catholic dogma after the Reformation; the Council of Dort (1618–19), in Holland, defined Calvinist doctrine.
8. Rome was the center of Catholicism; Geneva was a Calvinist city-state.

scandal of our adversaries and a gross error in ourselves to compute the nativity of our religion from Henry the Eighth, who, though he rejected the Pope, refused not the faith of Rome, and effected no more than what his own predecessors desired and essayed in ages past, and was conceived the state of Venice would have attempted in our days.[9] It is as uncharitable a point in us to fall upon those popular scurrilities and opprobrious scoffs of the bishop of Rome, to whom as a temporal prince we owe the duty of good language. I confess there is cause of passion between us. By his sentence I stand excommunicated: "heretic" is the best language he affords me; yet can no ear witness I ever returned to him the name of "antichrist," "man of sin," or "whore of Babylon."[1] It is the method of charity to suffer without reaction. Those usual satires and invectives of the pulpit may perchance produce a good effect on the vulgar, whose ears are opener to rhetoric than logic; yet do they in no wise confirm the faith of wiser believers, who know that a good cause needs not to be patroned by a passion, but can sustain itself upon a temperate dispute.

6. I could never divide myself from any man upon the difference of an opinion, or be angry with his judgment for not agreeing with me in that from which perhaps within a few days I should dissent myself. I have no genius to disputes in religion, and have often thought it wisdom to decline them, especially upon a disadvantage, or when the cause of truth might suffer in the weakness of my patronage. Where we desire to be informed, 'tis good to contest with men above ourselves; but to confirm and establish our opinions, 'tis best to argue with judgments below our own, that the frequent spoils and victories over their reasons may settle in ourselves an esteem and confirmed opinion of our own. Every man is not a proper champion for truth, nor fit to take up the gauntlet in the cause of verity. Many, from the ignorance of these maxims and an inconsiderate zeal unto truth, have too rashly charged the troops of error, and remain as trophies unto the enemies of truth. A man may be in as just possession of truth as of a city, and yet be forced to surrender. 'Tis therefore far better to enjoy her with peace than to hazard her on a battle. If therefore there rise any doubts in my way, I do forget them or at least defer them till my better settled judgment and more manly reason be able to resolve them; for I perceive every man's own reason is his best Oedipus,[2] and will upon a reasonable truce find a way to loose those bonds wherewith the subtleties of error have enchained our more flexible and tender judgments. In philosophy, where truth seems double-faced, there is no man more paradoxical than myself, but in divinity I love to keep the road; and, though not in an implicit, yet an humble faith, follow the great wheel of the church, by which I move, not reserving any proper poles or motion from the epicycle of my own brain.[3] By this means I leave no gap for heresies, schisms, or errors, of which at present I hope I shall not injure truth to say I have no taint or tincture. I must confess my greener studies have been polluted with two or three—not any begotten in the latter centuries, but old and obsolete, such as could never have been revived but by such extravagant

9. Though he repudiated the pope, Henry VIII was for long an ambiguous Protestant. Venice was excommunicated in 1606 for challenging papal authority.
1. Stock terms of anti-Catholic abuse.
2. Solver of riddles, as Oedipus solved that of the Sphinx.

3. In Ptolemaic astronomy, an "epicycle" is a small circle centered on the largest circle of a planet's orbit, hypothesized to account for inexplicable variations in the planet's motion.

and irregular heads as mine. For indeed heresies perish not with their authors, but like the river Arethusa, though they lose their currents in one place, they rise up again in another.[4] One general council is not able to extirpate one singular heresy. It may be canceled for the present, but revolution of time and the like aspects from heaven will restore it, when it will flourish till it be condemned again; for as though there were a metempsychosis, and the soul of one man passed into another, opinions do find after certain revolutions men and minds like those that first begat them. To see ourselves again we need not look for Plato's year.[5] Every man is not only himself; there have been many Diogenes and as many Timons,[6] though but few of that name. Men are lived over again; the world is now as it was in ages past. There was none then but there hath been someone since that parallels him, and is as it were his revived self.

* * *

9. As for those wingy mysteries in divinity and airy subtleties in religion, which have unhinged the brains of better heads, they never stretched the *pia mater*[7] of mine. Methinks there be not impossibilities enough in religion for an active faith. The deepest mysteries ours contains have not only been illustrated but maintained by syllogism and the rule of reason. I love to lose myself in a mystery, to pursue my reason to an *O altitudo!*[8] 'Tis my solitary recreation to pose my apprehension with those involved enigmas and riddles of the Trinity, with Incarnation and Resurrection. I can answer all the objections of Satan and my rebellious reason with that odd resolution I learned of Tertullian, *Certum est quia impossibile est.*[9] I desire to exercise my faith in the difficultest points, for to credit ordinary and visible objects is not faith but persuasion. Some believe the better for seeing Christ his sepulcher, and when they have seen the Red Sea doubt not of the miracle. Now, contrarily, I bless myself and am thankful that I lived not in the days of miracles, that I never saw Christ nor his disciples. I would not have been one of those Israelites that passed the Red Sea, nor one of Christ's patients on whom he wrought his wonders: then had my faith been thrust upon me, nor should I enjoy that greater blessing pronounced to all that believe and saw not. 'Tis an easy and necessary belief to credit what our eye and sense hath examined. I believe he was dead, buried, and rose again; and desire to see him in his glory rather than to contemplate him in his cenotaph or sepulcher. Nor is this much to believe. As we have reason, we owe this faith unto history; they only had the advantage of a bold and noble faith who lived before his coming, who upon obscure prophecies and mystical types[1] could raise a belief and expect apparent impossibilities.

* * *

4. In myth, when the nymph Arethusa, in Greece, was pursued by the river god Alpheus, she dived into the sea and came up again in Sicily as a fountain.
5. Browne's note on this reads: "A revolution of certain thousand years, when all things should return unto their former estate."
6. Diogenes was a Cynic philosopher, Timon a noted misanthrope, both Greek.
7. A membrane covering the brain, often used to refer to the brain itself.
8. From Romans 11.33: "O the depth [Latin Vulgate, *altitudo*] of the riches both of the wisdom and knowledge of God! How unsearchable are his judgments, and his ways past finding out!" The Latin term can also mean "heights."
9. Tertullian commenting on the Resurrection: "It is certain because it is impossible."
1. Foreshadowings of Christ in the Old Testament.

15. * * * I could never content my contemplation with those general pieces of wonder, the flux and reflux of the sea, the increase of Nile, the conversion of the needle to the north; and have studied to match and parallel those in the more obvious and neglected pieces of nature, which without further travel I can do in the cosmography of myself. We carry with us the wonders we seek without us: there is all Africa and her prodigies[2] in us. We are that bold and adventurous piece of nature which he that studies wisely learns in a compendium what others labor at in a divided piece and endless volume.

16. Thus are there two books from whence I collect my divinity: besides that written one of God, another of his servant nature, that universal and public manuscript that lies expansed unto the eyes of all. Those that never saw him in the one have discovered him in the other. This was the scripture and theology of the heathens: the natural motion of the sun made them more admire him than its supernatural station[3] did the children of Israel; the ordinary effects of nature wrought more admiration in them than in the other all his miracles. Surely the heathens knew better how to join and read these mystical letters than we Christians, who cast a more careless eye on these common hieroglyphics, and disdain to suck divinity from the flowers of nature. Nor do I so forget God as to adore the name of nature; which I define not, with the schools, the principle of motion and rest, but that straight and regular line, that settled and constant course the wisdom of God hath ordained the actions of his creatures according to their several kinds. To make a revolution every day is the nature of the sun, because that necessary course which God hath ordained it, from which it cannot swerve but by a faculty[4] from that voice which first did give it motion. Now this course of nature God seldom alters or perverts, but like an excellent artist hath so contrived his work that with the selfsame instrument, without a new creation, he may effect his obscurest designs. Thus he sweetened the water with a wood;[5] preserved the creatures in the Ark, which the blast of his mouth might have as easily created: for God is like a skillful geometrician, who when more easily and with one stroke of his compass he might describe or divide a right line, had yet rather do this in a circle or longer way according to the constituted and forelaid principles of his art. Yet this rule of his he doth sometimes pervert, to acquaint the world with his prerogative, lest the arrogancy of our reason should question his power and conclude he could not. And thus I call the effects of nature the works of God, whose hand and instrument she only is; and therefore to ascribe his actions unto her is to devolve the honor of the principal agent upon the instrument: which if with reason we may do, then let our hammers rise up and boast they have built our houses, and our pens receive the honor of our writings. I hold there is a general beauty in the works of God, and therefore no deformity in any kind or species of creature whatsoever. I cannot tell by what logic we call a toad, a bear, or an elephant ugly; they being created in those outward shapes and figures which best express the actions of their inward forms, and having passed that general visitation of God, who saw

2. Marvels.
3. Standing still, as at the battle of Gibeon (Joshua 10.13).

4. Authority.
5. Exodus 15.25 tells how the Lord sweetened the bitter waters of Marah with a special tree.

that all that he had made was good[6]—that is, conformable to his will, which abhors deformity and is the rule of order and beauty. There is therefore no deformity but in monstrosity; wherein notwithstanding there is a kind of beauty, nature so ingeniously contriving the irregular parts as they become sometimes more remarkable than the principal fabric. To speak yet more narrowly, there was never anything ugly or misshapen but the chaos; wherein notwithstanding (to speak strictly) there was no deformity because no form, nor was it yet impregnate by the voice of God. Now, nature is not at variance with art nor art with nature, they both being the servants of his providence: art is the perfection of nature. Were the world now as it was the sixth day, there were yet a chaos: nature hath made one world and art another. In brief, all things are artificial, for nature is the art of God.

* * *

34. These[7] are certainly the magisterial and masterpieces of the Creator; the flower or (as we may say) the best part of nothing; actually existing what we are but in hopes and probability. We are only that amphibious piece between a corporal and spiritual essence; that middle form that links those two together, and makes good the method of God and nature, that jumps not from extremes but unites the incompatible distances by some middle and participating natures. That we are the breath and similitude of God it is indisputable and upon record of holy Scripture; but to call ourselves a microcosm or little world I thought it only a pleasant trope of rhetoric[8] till my nearer judgment and second thoughts told me there was a real truth therein. For first we are a rude mass and in the rank of creatures which only are and have a dull kind of being not yet privileged with life or preferred to sense or reason. Next we live the life of plants, the life of animals, the life of men, and at last the life of spirits; running on, in one mysterious nature, those five kinds of existences which comprehend the creatures not only of the world but of the universe. Thus is man that great and true amphibium whose nature is disposed to live not only like other creatures in divers elements but in divided and distinguished worlds. For though there be but one world to sense, there are two to reason; the one visible, the other invisible, whereof Moses seems to have left no description, and of the other[9] so obscurely that some parts thereof are yet in controversy: and truly for the first chapters of Genesis I must confess a great deal of obscurity. Though divines have, to the power of human reason, endeavored to make all go in a literal meaning, yet those allegorical interpretations are also probable, and perhaps the mystical method of Moses bred up in the hieroglyphical schools of the Egyptians.[1]

* * *

59. Again, I am confident and fully persuaded, yet dare not take my oath of my salvation. I am as it were sure, and do believe without all doubt, that there is such a city as Constantinople; yet for me to take my oath thereon were a kind of perjury, because I hold no infallible warrant from my own sense to

---

6. Genesis 1.31.
7. The angels.
8. Figure of speech.
9. The visible world. Moses was supposed to have been the author of Genesis.

1. Some Neoplatonists thought that Moses, reared among the Egyptians, understood their hieroglyphic symbolism and imitated it in his own writing.

confirm me in the certainty thereof. And truly, though many pretend an absolute certainty of their salvation, yet when an humble soul shall contemplate her own unworthiness she shall meet with many doubts and suddenly find how little we stand in need of the precept of St. Paul, *Work out your salvation with fear and trembling.*[2] That which is the cause of my election I hold to be the cause of my salvation, which was the mercy and beneplacit[3] of God before I was or the foundation of the world. *Before Abraham was, I am*, is the saying of Christ;[4] yet is it true in some sense if I say it of myself, for I was not only before myself but Adam, that is, in the idea of God and the decree of that synod held from all eternity. And in this sense, I say, the world was before the creation and at an end before it had a beginning; and thus was I dead before I was alive. Though my grave be England, my dying place was Paradise, and Eve miscarried of me before she conceived of Cain.

* * *

From *Part 2*

1. Now for that other virtue of charity,[5] without which faith is mere notion, and of no existence, I have ever endeavored to nourish the merciful disposition and humane inclination I borrowed from my parents, and regulate it to the written and prescribed laws of charity; and if I hold the true anatomy of myself,[6] I am delineated and naturally framed to such a piece of virtue. For I am of a constitution so general that it comforts and sympathizeth with all things; I have no antipathy, or rather idiosyncrasy, in diet, humor, air, anything. I wonder not at the French for their dishes of frogs, snails, and toadstools, nor at the Jews for locusts and grasshoppers; but being amongst them, make them my common viands, and I find they agree with my stomach as well as theirs. I could digest a salad gathered in a churchyard as well as in a garden. I cannot start at the presence of a serpent, scorpion, lizard, or salamander, at the sight of a toad or viper I find in me no desire to take up a stone to destroy them. I feel not in myself those common antipathies that I can discover in others: those national repugnances do not touch me, nor do I behold with prejudice the French, Italian, Spaniard, or Dutch; but where I find their actions in balance with my countrymen's, I honor, love and embrace them in the same degree. I was born in the eighth climate,[7] but seem for to be framed and constellated unto all. I am no plant that will not prosper out of a garden. All places, all airs make unto me one country; I am in England everywhere and under any meridian. I have been shipwrecked,[8] yet am not enemy with the sea or winds; I can study, play, or sleep in a tempest. In brief, I am averse from nothing; my conscience would give me the lie if I should say I absolutely detest or hate any essence but the devil, or so at least abhor anything but that we might come to composition.[9] If there be any among those common objects of hatred I do contemn and laugh at, it is that great enemy of reason, virtue,

2. Philippians 2.12. "Election" (following): chosen by God for salvation.
3. Good pleasure.
4. John 8.58.
5. Like many theological manuals, Browne's first book concerns faith, the second charity.
6. If I have properly analyzed myself. See Donne, *An Anatomy of the World* (pp. 949–60), and Burton, *The Anatomy of Melancholy* (pp. 1240–46), for the way this term is used. "Delineated" (following): designed.
7. In the eighth of the twenty-four regions between the equator and the poles.
8. Browne was shipwrecked returning to England from Ireland in 1630.
9. Reach an agreement.

and religion, the multitude—that numerous piece of monstrosity which, taken asunder, seem men and the reasonable creatures of God, but confused together make but one great beast, and a monstrosity more prodigious than Hydra.[1] It is no breach of charity to call these fools; it is the style all holy writers have afforded them, set down by Solomon in canonical Scripture[2] and a point of our faith to believe so. Neither in the name of multitude do I only include the base and minor sort of people; there is a rabble even amongst the gentry, a sort of plebeian heads whose fancy moves with the same wheel as these; men in the same level with mechanics, though their fortunes do somewhat gild their infirmities, and their purses compound for their follies.[3] But as in casting account, three or four men together come short in account of one man placed by himself below them, so neither are a troop of these ignorant dorados[4] of that true esteem and value as many a forlorn person whose condition doth place him below their feet. Let us speak like politicians, there is a nobility without heraldry, a natural dignity whereby one man is ranked with another, another filed before him, according to the quality of his desert, and preeminence of his good parts. Though the corruption of these times and the bias of present practice wheel another way, thus it was in the first and primitive commonwealths, and is yet in the integrity and cradle of well-ordered polities, till corruption getteth ground, ruder desires laboring after that which wiser considerations contemn, everyone having a liberty to amass and heap up riches, and they a license or faculty to do or purchase anything.

1642 (pirated)
1643 (authorized)

1. In Greek mythology, a nine-headed serpent that grew two heads for every one that was cut off.
2. E.g., Proverbs 1.7: "fools despise wisdom and instruction."
3. With the growing rebelliousness of the Puri-

tan merchants and even some of the aristocracy as his point of reference, Browne redefines the rabble in terms of attitude and moral worth, not class.
4. Wealthy persons.

GEORGE HERBERT
1593–1633

George Herbert's style in his volume of religious poetry, *The Temple*, is deceptively simple and graceful, especially compared to the learned, witty style of his friend John Donne. But it is also marked by self-irony, a remarkable intellectual and emotional range, and an artistry evident in the poems' tight construction, exact diction, perfect control of tone, and enormously varied stanzaic forms and rhythmic patterns. These poems reflect Herbert's struggle to define his relationship to God through biblical metaphors invested with the tensions of relationships familiar in his own society: king and subject, lord and courtier, master and servant, father and child, bridegroom and bride, friends of unequal status. None of Herbert's secular English poems survives, so his reputation rests on this single volume, published posthumously. *The Temple* contains a long prefatory poem, "The Church-Porch," and a long concluding poem, "Church Militant," which together enclose a collection of 177 short lyrics entitled *The Church*, among which are sonnets, songs, hymns, laments, meditative poems, dialogue poems, acrostic poems, emblematic poems, and more. Herbert's own description of the collection is apt: "a picture of the many spiritual conflicts that have passed between God and my soul." Izaak Walton reports that Herbert gave the manuscript to his friend Nicholas Farrar, head of a quasi-monastic community at Little Gidding, with instructions to publish it if he thought it would "turn to the advantage of any dejected poor soul" and otherwise to burn it. Fortunately, Farrar chose to publish, and *The Temple* became the major influence on the religious lyric poets of the Caroline age: Henry Vaughan, Richard Crashaw, Thomas Traherne, and even Edward Taylor, the American colonial poet.

The fifth son of an eminent Welsh family, Herbert (and his nine siblings) had an upbringing carefully monitored by his mother, Magdalen Herbert, patron and friend of Donne and several other scholars and poets. Herbert was educated at Westminster School and at Trinity College, Cambridge, where he subsequently held a fellowship and wrote Latin poetry: elegies on the death of Prince Henry (1612), witty epigrams, poems on Christ's Passion and death, and poems defending the rites of the English church. In 1620 he was appointed "public orator," the official spokesman and correspondent for the university. This was a step toward a career at court or in public service, as was his election as the member of Parliament from Montgomery in 1624. But that route was closed off by the death of influential patrons and the change of monarchs. Like Donne, Herbert hesitated for some years before being ordained, but in 1630 he took up pastoral duties in the small country parish at Bemerton in Wiltshire. Whereas Donne preached to monarchs and statesmen, Herbert ministered to a few cottagers, and none of his sermons survive. His small book on the duties of his new life, *A Priest to the Temple; or, The Country Parson*, testifies to the earnestness and joy, but also to the aristocratic uneasiness, with which he embraced that role. In chronic bad health, he lived only three more years—performing pastoral duties assiduously, writing and revising his poems, playing music, and listening to the organ and choir at nearby Salisbury Cathedral.

Herbert locates himself in the church through many poems that treat church liturgy, architecture, and art—e.g., "Church Monuments" and "The Windows"—but his primary emphasis is always on the soul's inner architecture. Unlike Donne, Herbert does not voice fears about his salvation or about his desperate sins; his anxieties center rather on his relationship with Christ, most often represented as that of friend with friend. Many poems register the speaker's distress over the vacillations and regressions in this relationship, over his lack of "fruition" in God's service, and over the instability of his own nature. In several dialogic poems the speaker's difficulties are alleviated by the voice of a divine friend heard within or recalled through a Scripture text (as

George Herbert. This engraving by Robert White was made from a portrait, now lost, painted during Herbert's lifetime and showing the poet in clerical garb. It was published in Isaak Walton's *Life of George Herbert* (1674).

in "The Collar"). In poem after poem he has to come to terms with the fact that his relationship with Christ is always radically unequal, that Christ must both initiate it and enable his own response. Herbert struggles constantly with the paradox that, as the works of a Christian poet, his poems ought to give fit praise to God but cannot possibly do so—an issue explored in "The Altar," the two "Jordan" poems, "Easter," "The Forerunners," and many more.

His recourse is to develop a biblical poetics that renounces conventional poetic styles—"fiction and false hair"—to depend instead on God's "art" wrought in his own soul and displayed in the language and symbolism of the Bible. He makes scant use of Donnean learned imagery, but his scriptural allusions carry profound significances. A biblical metaphor provides the unifying motif for the volume: the New Testament temple in the human heart (1 Corinthians 3.16). Another recurring biblical metaphor represents the Christian as plant or tree or flower in God's garden, needing pruning, rain, and nurture. Herbert was profoundly influenced by the genre of the emblem, which typically associated mysterious but meaningful pictures and mottoes with explanatory text. Shaped poems like "The Altar" or "Easter Wings" present image and picture at once; others, like "The Windows," resemble emblem commentary. Other poems allude to typological symbolism, which reads persons and events in the Old Testament as types or foreshadowings of Christ, the fulfillment or antitype. Often, as in "The Bunch of Grapes," Herbert locates both type and antitype in the speaker's soul.

FROM THE TEMPLE[1]

The Altar[2]

A broken A L T A R , Lord, thy servant rears,
Made of a heart, and cemented with tears:
　　Whose parts are as thy hand did frame;
　　No workman's tool hath touched the same.[3]
5　　　　　　　A H E A R T alone
　　　　　　　Is such a stone,
　　　　　　　As nothing but
　　　　　　　Thy power doth cut.
　　　　　　　Wherefore each part
10　　　　　　Of my hard heart
　　　　　　　Meets in this frame,
　　　　　　　To praise thy Name:
　　That, if I chance to hold my peace,
　　These stones to praise thee may not cease.[4]
15　Oh let thy blessed S A C R I F I C E be mine,
And　sanctify　this　A L T A R　to　be　thine.

1. The title of Herbert's volume sets his poems in relation to David's psalms for the Temple at Jerusalem; his are "psalms" for the New Testament temple in the heart. All of the following poems come from this volume, published in 1633.
2. A variety of emblem poem. Emblems customarily have three parts: a picture, a motto, and a poem. This kind collapses picture and poem into one, presenting the emblem image by its very shape. Shaped poems have been used by authors from Hellenistic times to Dylan Thomas.
3. A reference to Exodus 20.25, in which the Lord enjoins Moses to build an altar of uncut stones, not touched by any tool, and also to Psalm 51.17: "a broken and a contrite heart, O God, thou wilt not despise."
4. A reference to Luke 19.40: "I tell you that, if these should hold their peace, the stones would immediately cry out." Herbert's poems obtain much of their resonance from their biblical echoes.

Redemption[1]

Having been tenant long to a rich lord,
   Not thriving, I resolvèd to be bold,
And make a suit unto him, to afford
   A new small-rented lease, and cancel th' old.[2]

5 In heaven at his manor I him sought:
   They told me there that he was lately gone
About some land which he had dearly bought
   Long since on earth, to take possession.

I straight° returned, and knowing his great birth,   *at once*
10 Sought him accordingly in great resorts—
   In cities, theaters, gardens, parks, and courts:
At length I heard a ragged noise and mirth

Of thieves and murderers; there I him espied,
Who straight, "Your suit is granted," said, and died.

Easter[1]

Rise, heart, thy lord is risen. Sing his praise
       Without delays,
Who takes thee by the hand, that thou likewise
       With him may'st rise;
5 That, as his death calcinèd° thee to dust,   *burned to powder*
His life may make thee gold, and, much more, just.

Awake, my lute, and struggle for thy part
       With all thy art.
The cross taught all wood to resound his name
10   Who bore the same.
His stretchèd sinews taught all strings what key
Is best to celebrate this most high day.

Consort, both heart and lute, and twist[2] a song
       Pleasant and long;
15 Or, since all music is but three parts vied[3]
       And multiplied,
Oh let thy blessèd spirit bear a part,
And make up our defects with his sweet art.

---

1. Literally, "buying back." In this beautifully concise sonnet Herbert figures God as a landlord, himself as a discontented tenant.
2. I.e., to ask him for a new lease, with a smaller rent; the figure points to the New Testament supplanting the Old.

1. The first three stanzas work out the poetics of writing hymns; then comes the hymn itself.
2. Weave. "Consort": harmonize.
3. Increased by repetition. Harmony is based on the triad, the chord.

The Song

  I got me flowers to straw° thy way,[4]   *strew*
20 I got me boughs off many a tree;
  But thou wast up by break of day
  And brought'st thy sweets along with thee.

  The sun arising in the east,
  Though he give light and th' east perfume,
25 If they should offer to contest
  With thy arising, they presume.

  Can there be any day but this,
  Though many suns to shine endeavor?
  We count three hundred, but we miss:°   *misunderstand*
30 There is but one, and that one ever.

Easter Wings[1]

  Lord, who createdst man in wealth and store,° *abundance*
   Though foolishly he lost the same,
    Decaying more and more
     Till he became
5   Most poor:
      With thee
     O let me rise
    As larks, harmoniously,
   And sing this day thy victories:
10 Then shall the fall further the flight in me.[2]

  My tender age in sorrow did begin:
   And still with sicknesses and shame
    Thou didst so punish sin,
     That I became
15   Most thin.
      With thee
     Let me combine,
    And feel this day thy victory;
   For, if I imp[3] my wing on thine,
20 Affliction shall advance the flight in me.

4. Evokes the scene of Christ's entry into Jerusalem (Matthew 21.8).
1. Another emblem poem whose shape presents the emblem picture; the lines, increasing and decreasing, imitate flight, and also the spiritual experience of falling and rising. Early editions printed the poem with the lines running vertically, making the wing shape more apparent.
2. Refers to the "Fortunate Fall," which brought humankind so great a redeemer.
3. In falconry, to insert feathers in a bird's wing.

Affliction (1)[1]

When first thou didst entice to thee my heart,
    I thought the service brave:°   *splendid*
So many joys I writ down for my part,
    Besides what I might have
5 Out of my stock of natural delights,
Augmented with thy gracious benefits.

I lookèd on thy furniture so fine,
    And made it fine to me;
Thy glorious household stuff did me entwine,
10   And 'tice° me unto thee.   *entice*
Such stars I counted mine: both heaven and earth
Paid me my wages in a world of mirth.

What pleasures could I want,° whose king I served,   *lack*
    Where joys my fellows were?
15 Thus argued into hopes, my thoughts reserved
    No place for grief or fear;
Therefore my sudden soul caught at the place,
And made her youth and fierceness seek thy face.

At first thou gav'st me milk and sweetnesses;
20   I had my wish and way:
My days were strawed° with flowers and happiness;   *strewn*
    There was no month but May.
But with my years sorrow did twist and grow,
And made a party unawares° for woe.   *unwittingly*

25 My flesh began unto° my soul in pain,   *started complaining to*
    Sicknesses cleave° my bones;   *penetrate*
Consuming agues° dwell in every vein,   *fevers with convulsions*
    And tune my breath to groans.
Sorrow was all my soul; I scarce believed,
30 Till grief did tell me roundly, that I lived.

When I got health, thou took'st away my life,
    And more; for my friends die:
My mirth and edge was lost: a blunted knife
    Was of more use than I.
35 Thus thin and lean without a fence or friend,
I was blown through with every storm and wind.

Whereas my birth and spirit rather took
    The way that takes the town,
Thou didst betray me to a lingering book,
40   And wrap me in a gown.°   *priest's garb*

---

1. Herbert sometimes used the same title for several poems, thereby associating them; editors distinguish them by adding numbers.

I was entangled in the world of strife,
Before I had the power to change my life.

Yet, for I threatened oft the siege to raise,
      Not simpering all mine age,
45 Thou often didst with academic praise
      Melt and dissolve my rage.
I took thy sweetened pill, till I came where
I could not go away, nor persevere.

Yet lest perchance I should too happy be
50   In my unhappiness,
Turning my purge° to food, thou throwest me   *laxative*
      Into more sicknesses.
Thus doth thy power cross-bias me,° not making   *turn me from my aim*
Thine own gift good, yet me from my ways taking.

55 Now I am here, what thou wilt do with me
      None of my books will show:
I read, and sigh, and wish I were a tree,
      For sure then I should grow
To fruit or shade; at least, some bird would trust
60 Her household to me, and I should be just.

Yet, though thou troublest me, I must be meek;
      In weakness must be stout.
Well, I will change the service, and go seek
      Some other master out.
65 Ah, my dear God! though I am clean forgot,
Let me not love thee, if I love thee not.

Prayer (1)[1]

Prayer, the church's banquet; angels' age,
  God's breath in man returning to his birth;
The soul in paraphrase,[2] heart in pilgrimage;
  The Christian plummet,[3] sounding heaven and earth;

5 Engine against th' Almighty, sinner's tower,
  Reversèd thunder, Christ-side-piercing spear,
The six-days' world transposing[4] in an hour;
  A kind of tune which all things hear and fear:

Softness and peace and joy and love and bliss;
10   Exalted manna,[5] gladness of the best;

1. This extraordinary sonnet is a series of epithets without a main verb, defining prayer by metaphor.
2. Clarifying by expansion.
3. A weight used to measure ("sound") the depth of water.
4. A musical term indicating sounds produced at another pitch from the original.
5. The food God supplied to the Israelites in the wilderness.

Heaven in ordinary,[6] man well dressed,
The milky way, the bird of paradise,

Church bells beyond the stars heard, the soul's blood,
The land of spices; something understood.

Jordan (1)[1]

Who says that fictions only and false hair
Become a verse? Is there in truth no beauty?
Is all good structure in a winding stair?
May no lines pass, except they do their duty°   *pay reverence*
5   Not to a true, but painted chair?[2]

Is it no verse, except enchanted groves
And sudden arbors shadow coarse-spun lines?[3]
Must purling° streams refresh a lover's loves?   *rippling*
Must all be veiled,[4] while he that reads, divines,
10   Catching the sense at two removes?

Shepherds[5] are honest people: let them sing;
Riddle who list,° for me, and pull for prime:[6]   *wishes*
I envy no man's nightingale or spring;
Nor let them punish me with loss of rhyme,
15   Who plainly say, *My God, My King.*[7]

Church Monuments[1]

While that my soul repairs to her devotion,
Here I entomb my flesh, that it betimes°   *while time remains*
May take acquaintance of this heap of dust
To which the blast of death's incessant motion,
5   Fed with the exhalation of our crimes,
Drives all at last. Therefore I gladly trust

My body to this school, that it may learn
To spell his elements and find his birth
Written in dusty heraldry and lines°   *engraving, genealogy*

---

6. I.e., everyday heaven.
1. The river Jordan, which the Israelites crossed to enter the Promised Land, was also taken as a symbol for baptism.
2. It was the custom for men to bow before a throne, whether it was occupied or not (see Donne, "Satire 3," lines 47–48, p. 946), but to require bowing before a throne in a painting would be ridiculous.
3. "Sudden," i.e., that appear unexpectedly (an

artificial effect much sought after in landscape gardening). "Shadow": shade.
4. As in allegory.
5. Conventional pastoral poets.
6. To draw a lucky card in the game of primero. "For me": as far as I am concerned.
7. Echoes Psalm 145.1: "my God, O king."
1. The earlier, manuscript version of the poem does not divide it into stanzas.

10 Which dissolution sure doth best discern,
Comparing dust with dust and earth with earth.[2]
These laugh at jet and marble,[3] put for signs

To sever the good fellowship of dust
And spoil the meeting. What shall point out them[4]
15 When they shall bow and kneel and fall down flat
To kiss those heaps which now they have in trust?
Dear flesh, while I do pray, learn here thy stem
And true descent, that, when thou shalt grow fat

And wanton in thy cravings, thou mayest know
20 That flesh is but the glass° which holds the dust   *hourglass*
That measures all our time, which also shall
Be crumbled into dust. Mark here below
How tame these ashes are, how free from lust,
That thou mayest fit thyself against thy fall.

The Windows[1]

Lord, how can man preach thy eternal word?
  He is a brittle, crazy° glass,   *flawed, distorting*
Yet in thy temple thou dost him afford
  This glorious and transcendent place,
5   To be a window through thy grace.

But when thou dost anneal in glass[2] thy story,
  Making thy life to shine within
The holy preachers, then the light and glory
  More reverend grows, and more doth win,
10   Which else shows wat'rish, bleak, and thin.

Doctrine and life, colors and light, in one
  When they combine and mingle, bring
A strong regard and awe; but speech alone
  Doth vanish like a flaring thing,
15   And in the ear, not conscience, ring.

Denial

When my devotions could not pierce
    Thy silent ears,

---

2. Alludes to Genesis 3.19: "for dust thou art, and unto dust shalt thou return."
3. Jet (black basalt) and marble are used for tomb monuments. "These": i.e., dust and earth.
4. The inhabitants of the tombs.
1. From his little parish at Bemerton, Herbert used to walk twice a week across Salisbury Plain to the great cathedral, where he delighted not only in the music but in the stained-glass windows. This poem explores how the preacher himself may become such a window.
2. To burn colors into glass.

Then was my heart broken, as was my verse;
My breast was full of fears
5   And disorder;[1]

My bent thoughts, like a brittle bow,
Did fly asunder:
Each took his way; some would to pleasures go,
Some to the wars and thunder
10   Of alarms.

As good go anywhere, they say,
As to benumb
Both knees and heart in crying night and day,
Come, come, my God, O come!
15   But no hearing.

O that thou shouldst give dust a tongue
To cry to thee,
And then not hear it crying! All day long
My heart was in my knee,
20   But no hearing.

Therefore my soul lay out of sight,
Untuned, unstrung;
My feeble spirit, unable to look right,
Like a nipped° blossom, hung   *frostbitten*
25   Discontented.

O cheer and tune my heartless breast;
Defer no time,
That so thy favors granting my request,
They and my mind may chime,°   *ring together, agree*
30   And mend my rhyme.

Virtue

Sweet day, so cool, so calm, so bright,
The bridal of the earth and sky:
The dew shall weep thy fall tonight,
    For thou must die.

5   Sweet rose, whose hue, angry and brave,[1]
Bids the rash gazer wipe his eye:
Thy root is ever in its grave,
    And thou must die.

---

1. Unrhymed, as are the concluding lines of each stanza except the last.

1. Splendid. "Angry": having the hue of anger, red.

Sweet spring, full of sweet days and roses,
10   A box where sweets° compacted lie;   *perfumes*
My music shows ye have your closes,[2]
    And all must die.

Only a sweet and virtuous soul,
Like seasoned timber, never gives;
15   But though the whole world turn to coal,[3]
    Then chiefly lives.

Man

My God, I heard this day
That none doth build a stately habitation,
  But he that means to dwell therein.
  What house more stately hath there been,
5   Or can be, than is man? to[1] whose creation
    All things are in decay.

For man is every thing
And more; he is a tree, yet bears more[2] fruit;
  A beast, yet is or should be more;
10   Reason and speech we only bring.[3]
Parrots may thank us, if they are not mute:
    They go upon the score.[4]

Man is all symmetry,
Full of proportions, one limb to another,
15   And all to all the world besides;[5]
Each part may call the farthest, brother;
For head with foot hath private amity,
    And both with moons and tides.

Nothing hath got so far
20   But man hath caught and kept it as his prey.
His eyes dismount° the highest star: *bring down to earth*
He is in little all the sphere.°   *the universe*
Herbs gladly cure our flesh; because that they
    Find their acquaintance there.

25   For us the winds do blow,
The earth doth rest, heav'n move, and fountains flow;
  Nothing we see but means our good,

2. Concluding cadences in music. This poem has often been set to music.
3. Will be reduced to a cinder at the Last Judgment.
1. Compared to.
2. A textual variant is "no."
3. Man has a vegetable, an animal, and a spiritual nature; he is the only creature that speaks and reasons.
4. Parrots are indebted to us for speech.
5. The notion of man as microcosm, whose parts all correspond to features of the great world. Cf. Donne, *Holy Sonnet* 5, p. 961, and Browne, *Religio Medici*, p. 1247.

As our delight, or as our treasure.
The whole is either our cupboard of food,
30   Or cabinet of pleasure.

The stars have us to bed;
Night draws the curtain which the sun withdraws,
Music and light attend our head.
All things unto our flesh are kind°   akin
35   In their descent and being; to our mind
In their ascent and cause.

Each thing is full of duty.
Waters united are our navigation,
Distinguished,° our habitation;   separated
40   Below, our drink; above, our meat;[6]
Both are our cleanliness. Hath one such beauty?
Then how are all things neat!

More servants wait on man
Than he'll take notice of; in every path,
45   He treads down that[7] which doth befriend him,
When sickness makes him pale and wan.
O mighty love! Man is one world, and hath
Another to attend him.

Since then, my God, thou hast
50   So brave° a palace built, O, dwell in it,   splendid
That it may dwell with thee at last!
Till then, afford us so much wit,
That, as the world serves us, we may serve thee,
And both thy servants be.

Jordan (2)[1]

When first my lines of heavenly joys made mention,
Such was their luster, they did so excel,
That I sought out quaint words and trim invention;
My thoughts began to burnish,° sprout, and swell,   burgeon
5   Curling with metaphors a plain intention,
Decking the sense, as if it were to sell.°   for sale

Thousands of notions in my brain did run,
Offering their service, if I were not sped:°   supplied, satisfied
I often blotted what I had begun;
10   This was not quick° enough, and that was dead.   lively

---

6. Oceans are valuable for navigation; the earth
was created by dividing waters from waters (Genesis 1.6–7); on earth water is drink; from above it
provides rain to grow our food ("meat").

7. The herb that will cure him when he's sick.
1. Cf. "Jordan (1)" (p. 1262), and Sidney, *Astrophil
and Stella* 1 (p. 586).

Nothing could seem too rich to clothe the sun,
Much less those joys which trample on his head.[2]

As flames do work and wind when they ascend,
So did I weave myself into the sense;
15   But while I bustled, I might hear a friend
Whisper, "How wide[3] is all this long pretense!
There is in love a sweetness ready penned:
Copy out only that, and save expense."

Time

Meeting with Time, "Slack thing," said I,[1]
"Thy scythe is dull; whet it for shame."
"No marvel, sir," he did reply,
"If it at length deserve some blame;
5   But where one man would have me grind it,
Twenty for one too sharp do find it."

"Perhaps some such of old did pass,
Who above all things loved this life;
To whom thy scythe a hatchet was,
10   Which now is but a pruning knife.[2]
Christ's coming hath made man thy debtor,
Since by thy cutting he grows better.

"And in his blessing thou art blessed,
For where thou only wert before
15   An executioner at best,
Thou art a gardener now, and more,
An usher to convey our souls
Beyond the utmost stars and poles.

"And this is that makes life so long,
20   While it detains us from our God.
Ev'n pleasures here increase the wrong,
And length of days lengthens the rod.°   *used for blows*
Who wants° the place where God doth dwell   *lacks*
Partakes already half of hell.

25   "Of what strange length must that needs be,
Which ev'n eternity excludes!"—
Thus far Time heard me patiently,
Then chafing said, "This man deludes:
What do I here before his door?
30   He doth not crave less time, but more."

2. The "joys which trample on" the sun's head
are heavenly joys (line 1).
3. Irrelevant, wide of the mark.
1. Herbert's speaker reports his dialogue with
Time.
2. A hatchet kills; a pruning knife improves growing things.

The Bunch of Grapes[1]

Joy, I did lock thee up;° but some bad man   *hold you fast*
    Hath let thee out again,
And now methinks I am where I began
    Sev'n years ago: one vogue° and vein,   *tendency*
5   One air of thoughts usurps my brain.
I did towards Canaan draw, but now I am
Brought back to the Red Sea, the sea of shame.[2]

For as the Jews of old by God's command
    Traveled, and saw no town,
10 So now each Christian hath his journeys spanned;
    Their story pens and sets us down.[3]
    A single deed is small renown.
God's works are wide, and let in future times;
His ancient justice overflows our crimes.

15 Then have we too our guardian fires and clouds;
    Our Scripture-dew° drops fast;   *manna*
We have our sands and serpents, tents and shrouds;° *temporary shelters*
    Alas! our murmurings come not last.
    But where's the cluster? where's the taste
20 Of mine inheritance? Lord, if I must borrow,
Let me as well take up their joy as sorrow.

But can he want° the grape who hath the wine?   *lack*
    I have their fruit and more.
Blessèd be God, who prospered Noah's vine[4]
25   And made it bring forth grapes good store.
    But much more him I must adore
Who of the Law's sour juice[5] sweet wine did make,
Even God himself being pressèd for my sake.

The Pilgrimage

I traveled on, seeing the hill where lay
    My expectation.
A long it was and weary way.
    The gloomy cave of desperation

1. When the children of Israel almost lost hope in the wilderness, God inspired Moses to send forth scouts, who returned to report that Canaan was a land of milk and honey. They brought back a bunch of grapes so big they had to carry it between them on a pole (Numbers 13.23).
2. The Red Sea's color suggests blushing for shame. Because the Israelites complained about their long ordeal in the wilderness after leaving Egypt, God drove them back toward the Red Sea.
3. The wandering of the Israelites in the wilderness toward the land of Canaan was taken to be a type (prefiguration) of the Christian's trials on the path of salvation. "Spanned": measured out.
4. Noah's vine (Genesis 9) was taken as a type of the earth replenished by God after the Flood.
5. The severe rules of the Old Testament as contrasted with the sweeter and more liberal covenant of the New Testament, which Christ's crucifixion established.

⁵ I left on th' one, and on the other side
       The rock of pride.[1]

And so I came to fancy's meadow, strowed°   *strewn*
       With many a flower;
       Fain° would I here have made abode,   *gladly*
¹⁰   But I was quickened by my hour.[2]
So to care's copse° I came, and there got through   *thicket of trees*
       With much ado.

That led me to the wild of passion, which
       Some call the wold°—   *treeless plain, moor*
¹⁵   A wasted place but sometimes rich.
       Here I was robbed of all my gold
Save one good angel,[3] which a friend had tied
       Close to my side.

At length I got unto the gladsome hill
²⁰   Where lay my hope,
       Where lay my heart; and, climbing still,
       When I had gained the brow and top,
A lake of brackish waters on the ground
       Was all I found.

²⁵ With that abashed, and struck with many a sting
       Of swarming fears,
       I fell, and cried, "Alas, my king!
       Can both the way and end be tears?"
Yet taking heart I rose, and then perceived
³⁰   I was deceived:

My hill was further; so I flung away,
       Yet heard a cry,
       Just as I went: *None goes that way*
       And lives: "If that be all," said I,
³⁵ "After so foul a journey, death is fair,
       And but a chair."[4]

The Holdfast[1]

I threatened to observe the strict decree
       Of my dear God with all my power and might.
       But I was told by one, it could not be;
Yet I might trust in God to be my light.

---

1. The rock and cave allude to Scylla and Charybdis, perils faced by Odysseus and often allegorized. The spiritual pilgrimage through allegorical perils was a frequent literary motif: cf. Bunyan's *Pilgrim's Progress* and Vaughan's "Regeneration" (pp. 1278–80).
2. Short span of life.
3. A golden coin as well as (punningly) a guardian angel.

4. "Chair" implies rest and relaxation but also a conveyance (a sedan chair).
1. Alludes to Psalm 73.27 in the Book of Common Prayer: "It is good for me to hold me fast by God." The poem dramatizes the entire reliance on grace—and the abnegation of any human capacity to cooperate with it or claim any merit—that was a cornerstone of Calvinist theology.

5 Then will I trust, said I, in him alone.
  Nay, ev'n to trust in him, was also his;
  We must confess, that nothing is our own.
 Then I confess that he my succor is.

 But to have naught is ours, not to confess
10 That we have naught. I stood amazed at this,
  Much troubled, till I heard a friend express,
 That all things were more ours by being his.
  What Adam had, and forfeited for all,
  Christ keepeth now, who cannot fail or fall.

The Collar[1]

 I struck the board[2] and cried, "No more;
   I will abroad!
 What? Shall I ever sigh and pine?
My lines and life are free, free as the road,
5 Loose as the wind, as large as store.
   Shall I be still in suit?[3]
 Have I no harvest but a thorn
 To let me blood, and not restore
What I have lost with cordial° fruit?   *restorative to the heart*
10   Sure there was wine
  Before my sighs did dry it; there was corn°   *grain*
  Before my tears did drown it.
 Is the year only lost to me?
   Have I no bays[4] to crown it,
15 No flowers, no garlands gay? All blasted?
    All wasted?
 Not so, my heart; but there is fruit,
   And thou hast hands.
  Recover all thy sigh-blown age
20 On double pleasures: leave thy cold dispute
Of what is fit and not. Forsake thy cage,
   Thy rope of sands,
 Which petty thoughts have made, and made to thee
 Good cable,[5] to enforce and draw,
25   And be thy law,
 While thou didst wink and wouldst not see.
   Away! Take heed;
   I will abroad.

---

1. The emblematic title suggests a clerical collar that has become a slave's collar; also, punningly, the speaker's choler (anger) and, perhaps, the caller that he at last hears.
2. Table, with an allusion to the Communion table.
3. Always in attendance, waiting on someone for a favor.
4. The poet's laurel wreath, a symbol of recognized accomplishment.
5. Christian restrictions on behavior, which the "petty thoughts" of the docile believer have made into strong bonds.

Call in thy death's-head[6] there; tie up thy fears.
30   He that forbears
          To suit and serve his need,
          Deserves his load."
But as I raved and grew more fierce and wild
          At every word,
35   Methoughts I heard one calling, *Child!*[7]
          And I replied, *My Lord*.

The Pulley[1]

When God at first made man,
Having a glass of blessings standing by,
"Let us," said he, "pour on him all we can:
Let the world's riches, which dispersèd lie,
5   Contract into a span."

So strength first made a way;
Then beauty flowed, then wisdom, honor, pleasure.
When almost all was out, God made a stay,
Perceiving that, alone of all his treasure,
10   Rest° in the bottom lay.   *repose*

"For if I should," said He,
"Bestow this jewel also on my creature,
He would adore my gifts instead of me,
And rest in Nature, not the God of Nature;
15   So both should losers be.

"Yet let him keep the rest,[2]
But keep them with repining restlessness:
Let him be rich and weary, that at least,
If goodness lead him not, yet weariness
20   May toss him to my breast."

The Flower

How fresh, O Lord, how sweet and clean
Are thy returns! even as the flowers in spring,
     To which, besides their own demesne,°   *domain, demeanor*
The late-past frosts tributes of pleasure bring.

---

6. Skull, emblem of human mortality, and often used as an object for meditation.
7. The call "Child!" reminds the speaker of Paul's words (Romans 8.14–17) that Christians are not in "bondage again to fear" but are children of God, "and if children, then heirs."

1. The poem inverts the legend of Pandora's box, which released all manner of evils when opened but left Hope trapped inside.
2. "Rest" has two senses here: "remainder" and "repose."

5   Grief melts away
        Like snow in May,
      As if there were no such cold thing.

     Who would have thought my shriveled heart
    Could have recovered greenness? It was gone
10   Quite underground; as flowers depart
   To see their mother-root, when they have blown,°   *bloomed*
       Where they together
       All the hard weather,
    Dead to the world, keep house unknown.

15   These are thy wonders, Lord of power,
   Killing and quickening, bringing down to hell
    And up to heaven in an hour,
  Making a chiming of a passing-bell.[1]
       We say amiss
20   This or that is:
   Thy word is all, if we could spell.°   *read*

     O that I once past changing were,
   Fast in thy Paradise, where no flower can wither!
    Many a spring I shoot up fair,
25 Offering° at heaven, growing and groaning thither;   *aiming*
      Nor doth my flower
      Want a spring shower,°   *tears of contrition*
   My sins and I joining together.

     But while I grow in a straight line,
30 Still upwards bent,° as if heaven were mine own,   *directed*
    Thy anger comes, and I decline:
  What frost to that? What pole is not the zone
      Where all things burn,
      When thou dost turn,
35   And the least frown of thine is shown?[2]

     And now in age I bud again,
   After so many deaths I live and write;
    I once more smell the dew and rain,
  And relish versing. O my only light,
40   It cannot be
      That I am he
   On whom thy tempests fell all night.

     These are thy wonders, Lord of love,
   To make us see we are but flowers that glide;°   *slip silently away*
45   Which when we once can find and prove,°   *experience*

---

1. The "passing-bell," intended to mark the death of a parishioner, is tolled in a monotone; a "chiming" bell offers pleasant variety.

2. I.e., compared with God's wrath, what polar chill would not seem like the heat of the equator?

Thou hast a garden for us where to bide;
Who would be more,
Swelling through store,
Forfeit their Paradise by their pride.

The Forerunners

The harbingers are come: see, see their mark;
White is their color,[1] and behold my head.
But must they have my brain? Must they dispark°   *turn out*
Those sparkling notions which therein were bred?
5 Must dullness turn me to a clod?
Yet have they left me "Thou art still my God."[2]

Good men ye be to leave me my best room,
Even all my heart and what is lodgèd there:
I pass not,° I, what of the rest become,   *care not*
10 So "Thou art still my God" be out of fear.
  He will be pleasèd with that ditty;
And if I please Him, I write fine and witty.

Farewell, sweet phrases, lovely metaphors:
But will ye leave me thus? When ye before
15 Of stews° and brothels only knew the doors, *whorehouses*
Then did I wash you with my tears, and more,
  Brought you to church well-dressed and clad:
My God must have my best, even all I had.

Lovely enchanting language, sugarcane,
20 Honey of roses, whither wilt thou fly?
Hath some fond lover 'ticed° thee to thy bane?° *enticed / poison*
And wilt thou leave the church and love a sty?
  Fie! thou wilt soil thy 'broidered coat,
And hurt thyself and him that sings the note.

25 Let foolish lovers, if they will love dung,
With canvas, not with arras,° clothe their shame: *fine cloth*
Let Folly speak in her own native tongue.
True Beauty dwells on high; ours is a flame
  But borrowed thence to light us thither:
30 Beauty and beauteous words should go together.

Yet, if you go, I pass not;° take your way.   *I don't care*
For "Thou art still my God" is all that ye
Perhaps with more embellishment can say.

---

1. Harbingers rode ahead of a royal traveling party to requisition lodgings, marking the doors with chalk.

2. Echoes Psalm 31.14: "But I trusted in thee, O Lord: I said, Thou art my God."

Go, birds of spring; let winter have his fee;°   *due*
35   Let a bleak paleness chalk the door,
So all within be livelier than before.

Discipline

Throw away thy rod,
Throw away thy wrath:
       O my God,
Take the gentle path.

5   For my heart's desire
Unto thine is bent:
       I aspire
To a full consent.

Not a word or look
10   I affect° to own,   *wish, pretend*
       But by book,[1]
And thy book alone.

Though I fail, I weep:
Though I halt° in pace,   *limp*
15   Yet I creep
To the throne of grace.

Then let wrath remove;
Love will do the deed:
       For with love
20   Stony hearts will bleed.

Love is swift of foot;
Love's a man of war,[2]
       And can shoot,
And can hit from far.

25   Who can 'scape his bow?
That which wrought on thee,
       Brought thee low,
Needs must work on me.

Throw away thy rod;
30   Though man frailties hath,
       Thou art God:
Throw away thy wrath.

---

1. I.e., like an actor who follows his playbook.
2. The jubilant song sung by Moses in Exodus

15 calls the Lord "a man of war," but Herbert
also alludes to Cupid, another divine archer.

Death

Death, thou wast once an uncouth, hideous thing,
　　　　　Nothing but bones,
　　　The sad effect of sadder groans:
Thy mouth was open, but thou couldst not sing.

5　For we considered thee as at some six
　　　　　Or ten years hence,
　　　After the loss of life and sense,
Flesh being turned to dust and bones to sticks.

We looked on this side of thee, shooting short,
10　　　　　Where we did find
　　　The shells of fledge-souls left behind—
Dry dust, which sheds no tears, but may extort.[1]

But since our Savior's death did put some blood
　　　　　Into thy face,
15　　　Thou art grown fair and full of grace,
Much in request, much sought for as a good.

For we do now behold thee gay and glad
　　　　　As at doomsday,
　　　When souls shall wear their new array,
20　And all thy bones with beauty shall be clad.

Therefore we can go die as sleep, and trust
　　　　　Half that we have
　　　Unto an honest faithful grave,
Making our pillows either down or dust.

Love (3)

Love bade me welcome: yet my soul drew back,
　　　　　Guilty of dust and sin.
But quick-eyed Love, observing me grow slack°　　　　　*hesitant*
　　　　　From my first entrance in,
5　Drew nearer to me, sweetly questioning
　　　　　If I lacked anything.[1]

"A guest," I answered, "worthy to be here":
　　　　　Love said, "You shall be he."
"I, the unkind, ungrateful? Ah, my dear,

1. Souls that have left the body and gone to heaven are like fledgling chicks that have left the shell behind; that corpse ("dry dust") sheds no tears but may draw ("extort") tears from the sur-vivors.

1. The first question of tavern waiters to an entering customer would be "What d'ye lack?" (i.e., want).

10   I cannot look on thee."
Love took my hand, and smiling did reply,
      "Who made the eyes but I?"

"Truth, Lord; but I have marred them; let my shame
      Go where it doth deserve."
15   "And know you not," says Love, "who bore the blame?"
      "My dear, then I will serve."
"You must sit down," says Love, "and taste my meat."
      So I did sit and eat.[2]

2. In addition to the sacrament of Communion, the reference is especially to the banquet in heaven, when the Lord "shall gird himself, and make them to sit down to meat, and will come forth and serve them" (Luke 12.37).

HENRY VAUGHAN
1621–1695

Born to a family with deep roots in Wales, Henry Vaughan was educated at Oxford and the Inns of Court but returned to his native county of Breconshire at the outbreak of the civil war and spent the rest of his life there. He served as secretary to the Welsh circuit courts until 1645; briefly fought for King Charles at Chester, just over the border with England; and in his later years took up the practice of medicine without much formal study. In a volume of verse published in 1651, *Olor Iscanus* (The Swan of Usk), he drew attention to his heritage by terming himself "the Silurist": the Silures were an ancient tribe from southeast Wales. Some features of Vaughan's poetry derive from the rich Welsh-language poetic tradition: the frequency of assonance, consonance, and alliteration; the multiplication of comparisons and similes (*dyfalu*); and the sensitivity to nature, especially the countryside around the Usk River.

Some of Vaughan's poetry is secular—*Poems with the Tenth Satire of Juvenal, Englished* (1646), *Olor Iscanus* (1651), and a late-published collection of earlier verse, *Thalia Rediviva* (1678). Vaughan's modern reputation, though, rests almost entirely on his religious poetry. In 1650 Vaughan published his major collection of religious verse, *Silex Scintillans* (The Flashing Flint); it was republished in 1655 with a second book added. A conversion experience may have prompted Vaughan's turn to religious themes: the title of the book is explicated by the emblem of a flint-like heart struck by a bolt of lightning from the hand of God.

In the preface to *Silex Scintillans* Vaughan places himself among the many "pious converts" gained by George Herbert's holy life and verse. While his secular poetry recalls Ben Jonson's, the religious poetry overtly models itself on Herbert's. Some twenty-six poems appropriate their titles from *The Temple*, several owe their metrical form to Herbert, and many begin by quoting one of Herbert's lines (compare Vaughan's "Unprofitableness" with Herbert's "The Flower"). Yet no one with an ear for poetry will mistake Vaughan's long, loose poetic lines for Herbert's artful precision. Vaughan's religious sensibility too differs markedly from Herbert's. Unable to locate himself in a national Church of England, now dismantled by war, he wanders unaccompanied through a landscape at once biblical, emblematic, and contemporary, mourning lost innocence. One unifying motif of the poems in *Silex Scintillans* is pilgrimage, though the arrival at the destination is typically deferred. Vaughan seems unable to experience Christ as a friend or supporter in present trials, as Herbert so often does; instead, he longs for a full relationship with the divine yet to come, at the Last Day. Despite his restless solitude, however, Vaughan finds vestiges of the divine everywhere. "I saw eternity the other night," he begins his most famous poem, "The World," situating the "ring of pure and endless light" in a specific, quotidian moment of illumination. Eternity hovers tantalizingly over the human world of strife, pain, and exploitation, apparently entirely detached from that world but in fact accessible to God's elect, who soar from earthly shadows into the light. Vaughan's twin brother, Thomas, introduced him to Hermetic philosophy, an esoteric brand of Neoplatonism that found occult correspondences between the visible world of matter and the invisible world of spirits. The influence of this philosophical system, so congenial to Vaughan's sensibility, is most apparent in the poem "Cock Crowing."

FROM POEMS

A Song to Amoret[1]

If I were dead, and in my place,
    Some fresher youth designed,
To warm thee with new fires, and grace
    Those arms I left behind;

5 Were he as faithful as the sun,
    That's wedded to the sphere;[2]
His blood as chaste, and temperate run,
    As April's mildest tear;

Or were he rich, and with his heaps,
10   And spacious share of Earth,
Could make divine affection cheap,
    And court° his golden birth: *pay court to*

For all these arts I'ld not believe,
    (No though he should be thine)
15 The mighty amorist° could give   *lover*
    So rich a heart as mine.

Fortune and beauty thou mightst find,
    And greater men than I:
But my true resolvèd mind,
20   They never shall come nigh.

1. This poem comes from Vaughan's first collection, all on worldly themes and many on love. Amoret has sometimes been identified with Vaughan's first wife, but on no secure ground. Amoret (formed from *amor*, love) is a traditional name for a poet's beloved from classical literature; note Spenser's use of the name in *Faerie Queene* 3, and the variation on it in his sonnet sequence *Amoretti*.
2. In the Ptolemaic scheme, each of the planets (including the sun, which was regarded as a planet) occupied one of the spheres revolving around the earth.

For I not for an hour did love,
　Or for a day desire,
But with my soul had from above,
　This endless holy fire.

1646

FROM SILEX SCINTILLANS

Regeneration[1]

A ward, and still in bonds,[2] one day
　　I stole abroad;
It was high spring, and all the way
　　Primrosed[3] and hung with shade;
5　　Yet was it frost within,
　　　And surly winds
Blasted my infant buds, and sin
　　Like clouds eclipsed my mind.

Stormed thus, I straight perceived my spring
10　　　Mere stage and show,
My walk a monstrous, mountained thing,
　　Roughcast with rocks and snow;
　　　And as a pilgrim's eye,
　　　　Far from relief,
15　Measures the melancholy sky,
　　　Then drops and rains for grief,

So sighed I upwards still; at last
　　　'Twixt steps and falls
I reached the pinnacle, where placed
20　　I found a pair of scales;
　　　I took them up and laid
　　　　In th' one, late pains;
The other smoke and pleasures weighed,
　　But proved the heavier grains.[4]

25　With that, some cried, "Away!" Straight° I　　*immediately*
　　　Obeyed, and led
Full east, a fair, fresh field could spy;
　　Some called it Jacob's bed,[5]

1. The poem allegorizes in rather precise Calvinist terms the experience of God's grace calling the elect and distinguishing between the regenerate and the unregenerate.
2. He begins as one in the Pauline "spirit of bondage" to fear because of sin and as one still in his minority ("wardship") under the Old Testament law. This contrasts with the "spirit of adoption" whereby we are children of God: "And if children then heirs; heirs of God and joint-heirs with Christ" (Romans 8.14–17).

3. Alluding to the adage that the "primrose path" leads to perdition.
4. He climbs Mount Sinai (tries to live by the Old Testament law) but finds his sins and follies far outweigh that effort.
5. Jacob slept in an open field, where he had a vision of a ladder leading to heaven (Genesis 28.11–19); that place, Bethel, was taken as a type or figure for the church. Vaughan's poem "Jacobs Pillow, and Pillar" works out this allegory.

A virgin soil which no
30   Rude feet ere trod,
Where, since he stepped there, only go
        Prophets and friends of God.

Here I reposed; but scarce well set,
        A grove descried°   *perceived*
35 Of stately height, whose branches met
        And mixed on every side;
    I entered, and once in,
        Amazed to see 't,
Found all was changed, and a new spring[6]
40   Did all my senses greet.

The unthrift sun shot vital gold,
        A thousand pieces,
And heaven its azure did unfold,
        Checkered with snowy fleeces;
45 The air was all in spice,
        And every bush
A garland wore; thus fed my eyes,
        But all the ear lay hush.°   *quiet*

Only a little fountain[7] lent
50   Some use for ears,
And on the dumb shades language spent
        The music of her tears;
    I drew her near, and found
        The cistern full
55 Of divers stones, some bright and round,
        Others ill-shaped and dull.[8]

The first, pray mark, as quick as light
        Danced through the flood;
But the last, more heavy than the night,
60   Nailed to the center stood.
    I wondered much, but tired
        At last with thought,
My restless eye that still desired
        As strange an object brought:

65 It was a bank of flowers, where I descried,
        Though 'twas midday,
Some fast asleep, others broad-eyed
        And taking in the ray;
    Here musing long, I heard

6. Imagery in the following lines—spring, perfumes, flowers—alludes to the Song of Solomon in which the bride is traditionally allegorized as the church or the beloved soul.
7. In the Song of Solomon 4.15 the "fountain of waters, a well of living waters" was traditionally allegorized as Christ.
8. Alludes to 1 Peter 2.5, which refers to the faithful as "lively stones." The different sorts of stones and flowers here suggest the elect and the reprobate.

70   A rushing wind
   Which still increased, but whence it stirred
    Nowhere I could not find.

   I turned me round, and to each shade
    Dispatched an eye
75 To see if any leaf had made
    Least motion or reply;
   But while I listening sought
    My mind to ease
   By knowing where 'twas, or where not,
80 It whispered, "Where I please."⁹

   "Lord," then said I, "on me one breath,
   And let me die before my death!"

   "Arise O North, and come thou South wind,
   and blow upon my garden, that the spices
85 thereof may flow out."¹

                1650

The Retreat

   Happy those early days! when I
   Shined in my angel infancy.
   Before I understood this place
   Appointed for my second race,¹
5 Or taught my soul to fancy aught°   *anything*
   But a white, celestial thought;
   When yet I had not walked above
   A mile or two from my first love,
   And looking back, at that short space,
10 Could see a glimpse of His bright face;
   When on some gilded cloud or flower
   My gazing soul would dwell an hour,
   And in those weaker glories spy
   Some shadows of eternity;
15 Before I taught my tongue to wound
   My conscience with a sinful sound,
   Or had the black art to dispense
   A several° sin to every sense,   *different*
   But felt through all this fleshly dress
20 Bright shoots of everlastingness.

---

9. John 3.8: "The wind bloweth where it listeth, and thou hearest the sound thereof, but canst not tell whence it cometh, and whither it goeth, so is every one that is born of the Spirit."
1. Vaughan identifies this verse as Canticles (Song of Solomon) 5.17; it is properly 4.16.

1. The poem alludes throughout to the Platonic doctrine of preexistence, in conjunction with Christ's words (Mark 10.15): "Whosoever shall not receive the kingdom of God as a little child, he shall not enter therein." Comparisons are often made to Wordsworth's Immortality ode.

O, how I long to travel back,
And tread again that ancient track!
That I might once more reach that plain
Where first I left my glorious train,
25   From whence th' enlightened spirit sees
That shady city of palm trees.[2]
But, ah! my soul with too much stay°   *delay*
Is drunk, and staggers in the way.
Some men a forward motion love;
30   But I by backward steps would move,
And when this dust falls to the urn,
In that state I came, return.

1650

Silence, and Stealth of Days!

Silence, and stealth of days! 'tis now
    Since thou art gone[1]
Twelve hundred hours, and not a brow[2]
    But clouds hang on.
5   As he that in some cave's thick damp,
    Locked from the light,
Fixeth a solitary lamp
    To brave the night,
And walking from his sun, when past
10   That glimmering ray,
Cuts through the heavy mists in haste
    Back to his day,[3]
So o'er fled minutes I retreat
    Unto that hour
15   Which showed thee last, but did defeat
    Thy light and power;
I search and rack my soul to see
    Those beams again,
But nothing but the snuff[4] to me
20   Appeareth plain,
That dark and dead sleeps in its known
    And common urn;
But those[5] fled to their maker's throne,
    There shine and burn.
25   O could I track them! but souls must
    Track one the other,
And now the spirit, not the dust,

---

2. The New Jerusalem, the Heavenly City (for its identification with Jericho, the "city of Palm Trees," Deuteronomy 34.3).
1. As indicated in lines 27–28, the poem is on the loss of Vaughan's brother—not his twin brother, Thomas, the Hermetic philosopher, who did not die until 1666, but his younger brother, William, who died in July 1648.
2. Mountain ridge, or forehead.
3. The miner fixes his lamp halfway down the dark shaft, ventures a little beyond it, but then beats a hasty retreat.
4. The burned wick of the lamp or candle.
5. The reference is back to "beams."

                    Must be thy brother.
            Yet I have one pearl,[6] by whose light
  30   All things I see,
            And in the heart of earth and night,
                Find heaven and thee.

1648   1650

Corruption

        Sure it was so. Man in those early days
            Was not all stone and earth;
        He shined a little, and by those weak rays
            Had some glimpse of his birth.
  5   He saw heaven o'er his head, and knew from whence
            He came, condemnèd, hither;
        And, as first love draws strongest, so from hence
            His mind sure progressed thither.
        Things here were strange unto him: sweat and till,
  10   All was a thorn or weed:[1]
        Nor did those last, but (like himself) died still
            As soon as they did seed.
        They seemed to quarrel with him, for that act
            That felled him foiled them all:
  15   He drew the curse upon the world, and cracked
            The whole frame with his fall.[2]
        This made him long for home, as loath to stay
            With murmurers and foes;
        He sighed for Eden, and would often say,
  20   "Ah! what bright days were those!"
        Nor was heaven cold unto him; for each day
            The valley or the mountain
        Afforded visits, and still Paradise lay
            In some green shade or fountain.
  25   Angels lay lieger[3] here; each bush and cell,
            Each oak and highway knew them;
        Walk but the fields, or sit down at some well,
            And he was sure to view them.
        Almighty Love! where art thou now? Mad man
  30   Sits down and freezeth on;
        He raves, and swears to stir nor fire, nor fan,
            But bids the thread° be spun.   *thread of Fate*
        I see, thy curtains are close-drawn; thy bow[4]
            Looks dim, too, in the cloud;

---

6. Probably the Bible. The reference is to Matthew 13.45–46, to the merchant who sold all he had to buy a pearl of great price, there likened to the Kingdom of Heaven.
1. God's curse on Adam for eating the forbidden fruit included a curse on the earth: "Thorns also and thistles shall it bring forth to thee"

(Genesis 3.18).
2. Cf. Donne, *An Anatomy of the World*, lines 199–200 (p. 954).
3. As resident ambassadors (from heaven).
4. The rainbow, God's covenant with Noah after the Flood (Genesis 9.13).

35   Sin triumphs still, and man is sunk below
      The center, and his shroud.
  All's in deep sleep and night: thick darkness lies
      And hatcheth o'er thy people—
  But hark! what trumpet's that? what angel cries,
40   "Arise! thrust in thy sickle"?[5]

                         1650

Unprofitableness

How rich, O Lord! how fresh thy visits are![1]
'Twas but just now my bleak leaves hopeless hung,
      Sullied with dust and mud;
Each snarling blast shot through me, and did share°   *shear off*
5   Their youth and beauty; cold showers nipped and wrung
      Their spiciness and blood.
But since thou didst in one sweet glance survey
Their sad decays, I flourish, and once more
      Breathe all perfumes and spice;
10 I smell a dew like myrrh, and all the day
Wear in my bosom a full sun; such store
      Hath one beam from thy eyes.
But, ah, my God! what fruit hast thou of this?
What one poor leaf did ever I let[2] fall
15   To wait upon thy wreath?
Thus thou all day a thankless weed dost dress,
And when th' hast done, a stench or fog is all
      The odor I bequeath.

                         1650

The World

I saw eternity the other night,
Like a great ring of pure and endless light,
      All calm as it was bright;
And round beneath it, Time, in hours, days, years,
5   Driven by the spheres,[1]
Like a vast shadow moved, in which the world
      And all her train were hurled.
The doting lover in his quaintest° strain   *most ingenious*
      Did there complain;

5. Alludes to Revelation 14.15: "And another angel came out of the temple, crying with a loud voice to him that sat on the cloud, 'Thrust in thy sickle, and reap, for the harvest of the earth is now.'"

1. Cf. Herbert's "The Flower" (pp. 1271–73).
2. The original printed text reads "yet," emended here.
1. The concentric spheres of Ptolemaic astronomy.

10 Near him, his lute, his fancy, and his flights,° *caprices*
    Wit's sour delights,
With gloves and knots,° the silly snares of pleasure, *love knots*
    Yet his dear treasure,
All scattered lay, while he his eyes did pour
15   Upon a flower.

The darksome statesman hung with weights and woe
Like a thick midnight fog moved there so slow
    He did nor stay nor go;
Condemning thoughts, like sad eclipses, scowl
20   Upon his soul,
And clouds of crying witnesses[2] without
    Pursued him with one shout.
Yet digged the mole,[3] and, lest his ways be found,
    Worked underground,
25 Where he did clutch his prey. But one did see
    That policy:° *strategy*
Churches and altars fed him; perjuries
    Were gnats and flies;
It rained about him blood and tears; but he
30   Drank them as free.[4]

The fearful miser on a heap of rust
Sat pining all his life there, did scarce trust
    His own hands with the dust;
Yet would not place° one piece above, but lives *invest*
35   In fear of thieves.
Thousands there were as frantic as himself,
    And hugged each one his pelf:
The downright epicure placed heaven in sense,° *the senses*
    And scorned pretense;
40 While others, slipped into a wide excess,
    Said little less;
The weaker sort slight, trivial wares enslave,
    Who think them brave° *fine, showy*
And poor, despisèd Truth sat counting by° *recording*
45   Their victory.

Yet some, who all this while did weep and sing,
And sing and weep, soared up into the ring;
    But most would use no wing.
"O fools!" said I, "thus to prefer dark night
50   Before true light!
To live in grots and caves, and hate the day
    Because it shows the way,
The way which from this dead and dark abode
    Leads up to God,

---

2. In Hebrews 12, the "clouds of witnesses" testified to God's truth in past times. Here, these
champions of faith accuse one whose actions
deny God.
3. I.e., the "darksome statesman" (line 16).
4. I.e., as freely as they rained.

55 A way where you might tread the sun and be
     More bright than he!"
  But as I did their madness so discuss,
     One whispered thus:
  "This ring the bridegroom did for none provide,
60   But for his bride."[5]

John Chap. 2. ver. 16, 17

All that is in the world, the lust of the flesh, the
lust of the eyes, and the pride of life, is not of the
Father, but is of the world.
    And the world passeth away, and the lusts thereof,
but he that doth the will of God abideth forever.

1650

They Are All Gone into the World of Light!

They are all gone into the world of light!
  And I alone sit ling'ring here;
Their very memory is fair and bright,
  And my sad thoughts doth clear.

5 It glows and glitters in my cloudy breast
    Like stars upon some gloomy grove,
Or those faint beams in which this hill is dressed
    After the sun's remove.

I see them walking in an air of glory,
10   Whose light doth trample on my days;
My days, which are at best but dull and hoary,°   *gray with age*
    Mere glimmering and decays.

O holy hope, and high humility,
    High as the heavens above!
15 These are your walks, and you have showed them me
    To kindle my cold love.

Dear, beauteous death! the jewel of the just,
    Shining nowhere but in the dark;
What mysteries do lie beyond thy dust,
20   Could man outlook that mark!°   *boundary*

He that hath found some fledged bird's nest may know
    At first sight if the bird be flown;

---

5. Alludes to Revelation 19.7–9, the marriage of the Lamb and his Bride, allegorized as Christ and the church or Christ and the regenerate soul: "Blessed are they which are called unto the marriage supper of the Lamb."

But what fair well° or grove he sings in now,   *spring*
    That is to him unknown.

25 And yet, as angels in some brighter dreams
    Call to the soul when man doth sleep,
So some strange thoughts transcend our wonted° themes,   *accustomed*
    And into glory peep.

If a star were confined into a tomb,
30   Her captive flames must needs burn there;
But when the hand that locked her up gives room,
    She'll shine through all the sphere.

O Father of eternal life, and all
    Created glories under thee!
35 Resume thy spirit from this world of thrall°   *slavery*
    Into true liberty!

Either disperse these mists, which blot and fill
    My pèrspective[1] still as they pass,
Or else remove me hence unto that hill
40   Where I shall need no glass.

                                   1655

Cock-Crowing[1]

Father of lights! what sunny seed,[2]
What glance of day hast thou confined
Into this bird? To all the breed
This busy ray thou hast assigned;
5   Their magnetism works all night,
        And dreams of Paradise and light.

Their eyes watch for the morning hue,
Their little grain expelling night
So shines and sings, as if it knew
10 The path unto the house of light.
        It seems their candle, howe'r done,
        Was tinned° and lighted at the sun.   *kindled*

---

1. Literally, telescope, but more freely, distant vision.
1. The poem calls upon the Hermetic notion of sympathetic attraction between earthly and heavenly bodies, e.g., the cock whose crowing announces the sun's rising because it bears within itself a "seed" of the sun. Vaughan finds here an analogy for the attraction the soul has for its Maker.
2. The opening lines recall a passage from Henry's brother, the Hermetic philosopher Thomas Vaughan: "For she [the Anima or Soul] is guided in her operations by a spiritual metaphysical grain, a seed or glance of light . . . descending from the Father of lights." That term for God is from James 1.17. "Seed," "glance," "ray," and "grain" in line 8 are almost synonymous Hermetic terms for the bit of the sun implanted in the cock. "Magnetism" (line 5) refers to the attraction between the cock's "seed" and its source, the sun.

If such a tincture,[3] such a touch,
So firm a longing can impower,
15   Shall thy own image[4] think it much
To watch for thy appearing hour?
     If a mere blast so fill the sail,
     Shall not the breath of God[5] prevail?

O thou immortal light and heat!
20   Whose hand so shines through all this frame,°   *universe*
That by the beauty of the seat,
We plainly see, who made the same.
     Seeing thy seed abides in me,
     Dwell thou in it, and I in thee.

25   To sleep without thee, is to die;
Yea, 'tis a death partakes of hell:
For where thou dost not close the eye
It never opens, I can tell.
     In such a dark, Egyptian border,
30   The shades of death dwell and disorder.[6]

If joys, and hopes, and earnest throes,
And hearts, whose pulse beats still for light
Are given to birds; who, but thee, knows
A love-sick soul's exalted flight?
35   Can souls be tracked by any eye
     But his, who gave them wings to fly?

Only this veil[7] which thou hast broke,
And must be broken yet in me,
This veil, I say, is all the cloak
40   And cloud which shadows thee from me.
     This veil thy full-eyed love denies,
     And only gleams and fractions spies.

O take it off! Make no delay,
But brush me with thy light, that I
45   May shine unto a perfect day,
And warm me at thy glorious eye!
     O take it off! or till it flee,
     Though with no lily,[8] stay with me!

1655

---

3. Alchemical term for a spiritual principle whose quality may be infused into material things.
4. Alludes to Genesis 1.27: "So God created man in his own image."
5. Alludes to Genesis 2.7: "And the Lord God formed man of the dust of the ground, and breathed into his nostrils the breath of life; and man became a living soul."

6. Alludes to Exodus 10.21, Moses bringing down the plague of "darkness over the land of Egypt, even darkness which may be felt."
7. Echoes Hebrews 10.20: "By a new and living way, which he [Christ] hath consecrated for us, through the veil, that is to say, his flesh."
8. Echoes Song of Solomon 2.16: "My beloved is mine, and I am his: he feedeth among the lilies."

The Night

John 3.2[1]

Through that pure virgin-shrine,
That sacred veil drawn o'er thy glorious noon,
That men might look and live as glowworms shine
    And face the moon,
5   Wise Nicodemus saw such light
As made him know his God by night.

    Most blest believer he!
Who in that land of darkness and blind eyes
Thy long-expected healing wings[2] could see,
10   When thou didst rise,
And what can never more be done,
Did at midnight speak with the Sun!

    O who will tell me where
He found thee at that dead and silent hour?
15   What hallowed solitary ground did bear
    So rare a flower,
Within whose sacred leaves did lie
The fullness of the Deity?

    No mercy seat of gold,
20   No dead and dusty cherub nor carved stone,[3]
But his own living works did my Lord hold
    And lodge alone;
Where trees and herbs did watch and peep
And wonder while the Jews did sleep.

25   Dear night! this world's defeat,[4]
The stop to busy fools; care's check and curb;
The day of spirits; my soul's calm retreat
    Which none disturb!
Christ's progress and his prayer time;
30   The hours to which high heaven doth chime;

    God's silent, searching flight,
When my Lord's head is filled with dew, and all
His locks are wet with the clear drops of night;
    His still, soft call;[5]

1. John 3.1–2 describes how a Pharisee named Nicodemus came to Jesus by night and said, "Rabbi, we know that thou art a teacher come from God."
2. Echoes Malachi 4.2: "The Sun of righteousness [shall] arise with healing in his wings."
3. God commanded the Israelites to cover the Ark of the Covenant with "a mercy seat of pure gold . . . and . . . two cherubims of gold, of beaten work . . . in the two ends of the mercy seat" (Exo-

dus 25.17–18).
4. The style of this stanza and the next imitates Herbert's "Prayer (1)" (pp. 1261–62).
5. Echoes Song of Solomon 5.2: "I sleep, but my heart waketh: it is the voice of my beloved that knocketh, saying, Open to me, my sister, my love, my dove, my undefiled: for my head is filled with dew, and my locks with the drops of the night." For the allegory see "The World," n. 5 (p. 1285).

35   His knocking time; the soul's dumb watch,
    When spirits their fair kindred catch.

       Were all my loud, evil days
    Calm and unhaunted as is thy dark tent,
    Whose peace but by some angel's wing or voice
40   Is seldom rent,
    Then I in heaven all the long year
    Would keep, and never wander here.

       But living where the sun
    Doth all things wake, and where all mix and tire
45   Themselves and others, I consent and run
       To every mire,
    And by this world's ill-guiding light
    Err more than I can do by night.

       There is in God (some say)
50   A deep but dazzling darkness,[6] as men here
    Say it is late and dusky, because they
       See not all clear.
    Oh for that night, where I in him
    Might live invisible and dim!

            1655

The Waterfall[1]

With what deep murmurs through time's silent stealth
Doth thy transparent, cool, and watery wealth
      Here flowing fall,
      And chide, and call,
5 As if his liquid, loose retìnue stayed
Ling'ring, and were of this steep place afraid,
      The common pass
      Where, clear as glass,
      All must descend,
10   Not to an end,
But quickened by this steep and rocky grave,
Rise to a longer course more bright and brave.°   *resplendent*

Dear stream! dear bank! where often I
Have sat and pleased my pensive eye—
15 Why, since each drop of thy quick° store   *living*

---

6. Dionysius the Areopagite (ca. 5th century) deals with concepts of divine darkness, which the 14th-century philosopher Nicholas of Cusa later developed, referring to the "Darkness where truly dwells . . . the one who is beyond all" and "the superessential Darkness which is hidden by all the light that is in existing things."
1. The water, with its startling descent in a waterfall but ultimate circularity to its source, is for Vaughan an emblem of death and restoration of the soul to its source.

Runs thither whence it flowed before,
Should poor souls fear a shade or night,
Who came, sure, from a sea of light?
Or since those drops are all sent back
20   So sure to thee that none doth lack,
Why should frail flesh doubt any more
That what God takes he'll not restore?
O useful element and clear!
My sacred wash and cleanser here,
25   My first consigner° unto those   *in baptism*
Fountains of life where the Lamb goes![2]
What sublime truths and wholesome themes
Lodge in thy mystical deep streams!
Such as dull man can never find
30   Unless that Spirit lead his mind
Which first upon thy face did move
And hatched all with his quickening love.[3]
As this loud brook's incessant fall
In streaming rings restagnates° all   *makes still again*
35   Which reach by course the bank, and then
Are no more seen, just so pass men.
Oh my invisible estate,
My glorious liberty,[4] still late!
Thou art the channel my soul seeks,
40   Not this with cataracts and creeks.

                                                          1655

2. Echoes Revelation 7.17: "For the Lamb . . .
shall lead them unto living fountains of waters."
3. Alludes to Genesis 1.2: "And the Spirit of God
moved upon the face of the waters." The Latin
Vulgate version, *incubabant*, is closer to Vaughan's

"hatched" than to "moved."
4. Alludes to Romans 8.21, promising deliverance "from the bondage of corruption into the
glorious liberty of the children of God."

RICHARD CRASHAW
ca. 1613–1649

*S*teps to the Temple (1646, 1648), the name of Richard Crashaw's collection of
sacred poetry, clearly acknowledges George Herbert's primacy among devotional
poets. Yet Crashaw is hardly Herbert's slavish disciple. A Roman Catholic convert,
Crashaw was profoundly influenced by the Counter-Reformation, which reacted
against Protestant austerity by linking heightened spirituality to vivid bodily experiences. He is the only major English poet in the tradition of the Continental baroque,
a movement in literature and visual art that developed out of the Counter-Reformation.
Baroque style is exuberant, sensuous, and elaborately ornamented, and it deliberately
strains decorum, challenging formal restraints and generic limitations. Crashaw's
favorite subjects are typical of baroque art: the infant Jesus surrounded by angels and

cherubs; the crucified Savior, streaming blood; the sorrowful Virgin; the tearfully penitent Mary Magdalen; saintly martyrs wracked with ecstasy and pain. Although some have pronounced his images grotesque, Crashaw is alone among English poets in rendering the experience of rapture and religious ecstasy.

The son of a Puritan divine noted for hatred of popery, Crashaw was educated at Pembroke College, Cambridge, where he became an adherent of Laudian Anglicanism. In 1636 he was elected a fellow of Peterhouse, another Cambridge college. By 1639 he had become a priest of the Church of England, curate of Little St. Mary's, and a college lecturer. A contemporary wrote that his sermons "ravished more like poems," but apparently none survive. Crashaw called Peterhouse his "little contentful kingdom": his friends included the poet Abraham Cowley and George Herbert's literary executor Nicholas Ferrar, the founder of the Anglican monastic community Little Gidding. In 1643 the Puritans occupied Cambridge, violently disrupting Crashaw's life there. He fled to Paris and to the English court in exile, becoming a Roman Catholic in 1645. He was saved from destitution by obtaining various minor posts through the queen's influence, the last one at Loreto—thought to be Jesus's house at Nazareth, miraculously transported to Italy.

Crashaw's Latin epigrams, published as *Epigrammatum Sacrorum Liber* (1634), were much influenced by Jesuit epigram style and are among the best by an Englishman. In their Latin and later English versions, they are characterized by puns, paradoxes, and sometimes bizarre metaphors, as in the epigram on Luke 11. In 1646 Crashaw published, with the first version of *Steps to the Temple*, a book of secular poems, *The Delights of the Muses*, some of them in the restrained style of Ben Jonson. But the masterpiece of this book is "Music's Duel," a much-elaborated version of a poem by the Jesuit Famianus Strada about a contest between a nightingale and a lutenist, between melody and harmony. Crashaw imitates music by means of liquid vowels, gliding syntax, onomatopoeia, and the complex blending of sounds. Beyond that, he renders the ecstasy of the listening experience by collapsing one sense into another (synesthesia), creating an effect of continual metamorphosis.

Crashaw constantly revised his religious poems, usually making them longer. His posthumous volume, *Carmen Deo Nostro* (1652), includes emblems he may have executed himself, among them the padlocked heart prefixed to a poem urging the Countess of Denbigh to convert to Catholicism. Especially notable are the final versions of several hymns, ranging from the witty praise of St. Theresa in "The Flaming Heart" to the meltingly sweet "In the Holy Nativity."

FROM THE DELIGHTS OF THE MUSES

Music's Duel[1]

Now westward Sol° had spent the richest beams	*the sun*
Of noon's high glory, when hard by° the streams	*close to*
Of Tiber, on the scene of a green plat,	
Under protection of an oak, there sat	
5 A sweet lute's-master: in whose gentle airs	

---

1. Based on a much shorter Latin poem by the Jesuit Famianus Strada (1617), which also relates a contest between a nightingale and a lutenist, as a version of the contest between nature and art. Crashaw's poem also represents the contest of two kinds of music, melody (monody) and harmony (polyphony). The poem is especially remarkable for synesthesia, the blending of sensory images into one another, and sometimes the representation of one sense in the imagery of another.

He lost the day's heat, and his own hot cares.
   Close in the covert of the leaves there stood
A nightingale, come from the neighboring wood:
(The sweet inhabitant of each glad tree,
10 Their Muse, their Siren,[2] harmless Siren she)
There stood she listening, and did entertain
The music's soft report: and mold the same
In her own murmurs, that whatever mood
His curious° fingers lent, her voice made good: *skillful*
15 The man perceived his rival, and her art,
Disposed to give the light-foot lady sport
Awakes his lute, and 'gainst the fight to come
Informs it, in a sweet praeludium°   *prelude, introduction*
Of closer strains, and ere the war begin,
20 He lightly skirmishes on every string
Charged with a flying touch: and straightway she
Carves out her dainty voice as readily,
Into a thousand sweet distinguished tones,
And reckons up in soft divisions,°   *rapid melodic passages*
25 Quick volumes of wild notes; to let him know
By that shrill taste, she could do something too.
   His nimble hands instinct then taught each string
A cap'ring cheerfulness; and made them sing
To their own dance; now negligently rash
30 He throws his arm, and with a long drawn dash
Blends all together; then distinctly trips
From this to that; then quick returning skips
And snatches this again, and pauses there.
She measures every measure, everywhere
35 Meets art with art; sometimes as if in doubt
Not perfect yet, and fearing to be out°   *at a loss*
Trails her plain ditty[3] in one long-spun note
Through the sleek passage of her open throat:
A clear unwrinkled song, then doth she point it
40 With tender accents, and severely joint it
By short diminutives, that being reared
In controverting warbles evenly shared,
With her sweet self she wrangles; he amazed
That from so small a channel should be raised
45 The torrent of a voice, whose melody
Could melt into such sweet variety,
Strains higher yet; that tickled with rare art
The tattling° strings (each breathing in his part)   *prattling*
Most kindly do fall out;° the grumbling bass   *naturally quarrel*
50 In surly groans disdains the treble's grace.
The high-perched treble chirps at this, and chides,
Until his finger (moderator) hides
And closes the sweet quarrel, rousing all
Hoarse, shrill, at once; as when the trumpets call

---

2. The irresistible singing of sirens lures men to
their death.

3. Simple melody, without divisions.

55   Hot Mars to th'harvest of death's field, and woo
     Men's hearts into their hands; this lesson too
     She gives him back; her supple breast thrills out
     Sharp airs, and staggers in a warbling doubt
     Of dallying sweetness, hovers o'er her skill,
60   And folds in waved notes with a trembling bill,
     The pliant series of her slippery song.
     Then starts she suddenly into a throng
     Of short thick sobs, whose thundering volleys float,
     And roll themselves over her lubric° throat   *smooth*
65   In panting murmurs, stilled° out of her breast,   *distilled*
     That ever-bubbling spring; the sugared nest
     Of her delicious soul, that there does lie
     Bathing in streams of liquid melody;
     Music's best seed-plot, whence in ripened airs
70   A golden-headed harvest fairly rears
     His honey-dropping tops, plowed by her breath
     Which there reciprocally laboreth
     In that sweet soil. It seems a holy choir
     Founded to th'name of great Apollo's[4] lyre.
75   Whose silver roof rings with the sprightly notes
     Of sweet-lipped angel-imps, that swill their throats
     In cream of morning Helicon,[5] and then
     Prefer° soft anthems to the ears of men,   *offer*
     To woo them from their beds, still murmuring
80   That men can sleep while they their matins sing:
     (Most divine service) whose so early lay°   *song*
     Prevents° the eyelids of the blushing day.   *comes before*
     There might you hear her kindle her soft voice,
     In the close murmur of a sparkling noise,
85   And lay the groundwork of her hopeful song,
     Still keeping in the forward stream, so long
     Till a sweet whirlwind (striving to get out)
     Heaves her soft bosom, wanders round about,
     And makes a pretty earthquake in her breast,
90   Till the fledged notes at length forsake their nest;
     Fluttering in wanton shoals, and to the sky
     Winged with their own wild echoes prattling fly.
     She opes the floodgate, and lets loose a tide
     Of streaming sweetness, which in state doth ride
95   On the waved back of every swelling strain,
     Rising and falling in a pompous train.
     And while she thus discharges a shrill peal
     Of flashing airs, she qualifies° their zeal   *moderates*
     With the cool epode° of a graver note,   *lyric*
100   Thus high, thus low, as if her silver throat
     Would reach the brazen voice of war's hoarse bird;° *the raven*
     Her little soul is ravished: and so poured
     Into loose ecstasies, that she is placed

4. God of music and poetry, father of the Muses.
5. Mountain in Greece, home of the Muses; sometimes, the fountains there.

Above herself, music's enthusiast.[6]
105 Shame now and anger mixed a double stain
In the musician's face; yet once again,
Mistress, I come; now reach a strain, my lute,
Above her mock, or be forever mute.
Or tune a song of victory to me,
110 Or to thyself sing thine own obsequy;°   *funeral song*
So said, his hands sprightly as fire he flings,
And with a quavering coyness tastes the strings.
The sweet-lipped sisters° musically frighted,   *the Muses*
Singing their fears are fearfully delighted.
115 Trembling as when Apollo's golden hairs
Are fanned and frizzled, in the wanton airs
Of his own breath; which married to his lyre
Doth tune the spheres, and make heaven's self look higher.
From this to that, from that to this he flies,
120 Feels music's pulse in all her arteries,
Caught in a net which there Apollo spreads,
His fingers struggle with the vocal threads,
Following those little rills,[7] he sinks into
A Sea of Helicon;[8] his hand does go
125 Those parts of sweetness, which with nectar drop,
Softer than that which pants in Hebe's[9] cup.
The humorous° strings expound his learned touch   *capricious*
By various glosses; now they seem to grutch°   *grumble*
And murmur in a buzzing din, then jingle
130 In shrill tongued accents: striving to be single.
Every smooth turn, every delicious stroke
Gives life to some new grace; thus doth h'invoke
Sweetness by all her names; thus, bravely° thus   *splendidly*
(Fraught with a fury so harmonious)
135 The lute's light genius now does proudly rise,
Heaved on the surges of swollen rhapsodies.
Whose flourish, meteor-like, doth curl the air
With flash of high-borne fancies; here and there
Dancing in lofty measures, and anon
140 Creeps on the soft touch of a tender tone:
Whose trembling murmurs melting in wild airs
Runs to and fro, complaining his sweet cares
Because those precious mysteries that dwell,
In music's ravished soul he dare not tell,
145 But whisper to the world: thus do they vary
Each string his note, as if they meant to carry
Their master's blest soul (snatched out at his ears
By a strong ecstasy) through all the spheres
Of music's heaven; and seat it there on high
150 In th' empyreum° of pure harmony.   *highest heaven*
At length (after so long, so loud a strife

---

6. Literally, one inspired by a god.
7. Small streams; also, passages of liquid notes.
8. Resort of Apollo and the Muses.

9. Greek goddess of youth and cupbearer to the gods.

Of all the strings, still breathing the best life
Of blest variety attending on
His finger's fairest revolution
155   In many a sweet rise, many as sweet a fall)
A full-mouthed diapason[1] swallows all.
    This done, he lists what she would say to this,
And she although her breath's late exercise
Had dealt too roughly with her tender throat,
160   Yet summons all her sweet powers for a note
Alas! in vain! for while, sweet soul, she tries
To measure all those wild diversities
Of chatt'ring strings, by the small size of one
Poor simple voice, raised in a natural tone,
165   She fails, and failing grieves, and grieving dies.
She dies; and leaves her life the victor's prize,
Falling upon his lute; o fit to have
(That lived so sweetly) dead, so sweet a grave!

1646

FROM STEPS TO THE TEMPLE

To the Infant Martyrs[1]

Go, smiling souls, your new-built cages° break: *their bodies*
In heaven you'll learn to sing, ere here to speak.[2]
Nor let the milky fonts that bathe your thirst
      Be your delay;
5   The place that calls you hence is, at the worst,
      Milk all the way.[3]

1646

I Am the Door[1]

And now th' art set wide ope, the spear's sad art,
Lo! hath unlocked thee at the very heart;
    He to himself (I fear the worst)
      And his own hope
5   Hath shut these doors of heaven, that durst
      Thus set them ope.

1646

1. A grand burst of harmony.
1. This epigram and the three following were originally written in Latin in a volume of "Sacred Epigrams" and then rendered in English versions. Epigrams are brief, pithy, witty poems with, as was often said, "a sting in the tail." This poem addresses the Holy Innocents, the infants murdered by Herod in an effort to destroy the new-born Jesus, who was honored as King of the Jews by the Magi (Matthew 2.16–18).
2. Infant comes from the Latin *infans*, meaning "unable to speak."
3. The Milky Way will replace their mothers' milk.
1. "I am the door; by me if any man enter in, he shall be saved" (1 John 10.9).

On the Wounds of Our Crucified Lord

O these wakeful wounds of thine!
    Are they mouths? or are they eyes?
Be they mouths, or be they eyne,[1]
    Each bleeding part some one supplies.[2]

5 Lo! a mouth, whose full-bloomed lips
    At too dear a rate are roses.
Lo! a bloodshot eye! that weeps
    And many a cruel tear discloses.

O thou that on this foot hast laid
10   Many a kiss and many a tear,
Now thou shalt have all repaid,
    Whatsoe'er thy charges were.

This foot hath got a mouth and lips
    To pay the sweet sum of thy kisses;
15 To pay thy tears, an eye that weeps
    Instead of tears such gems as this is.

The difference only this appears
    (Nor can the change offend),
The debt is paid in ruby-tears
20   Which thou in pearls didst lend.

1646

Luke 11.[27][1]
Blessed be the paps which Thou hast sucked

Suppose he had been tabled at thy teats,
    Thy hunger feels not what he eats:
He'll have his teat e're long (a bloody one)[2]
    The Mother then must suck the Son.

1646

---

1. Eyes, an old plural form.
2. I.e., each wound of Christ is either an eye or a mouth.
1. The verse identifies the addressee: "And it came to pass, as he [Jesus] spake these things, a certain woman of the company lifted up her voice, and said unto him, 'Blessed is the womb that bare thee, and the paps which thou hast sucked.'"
2. The wound in Christ's side, making his breast (the fountain of all graces) bloody.

FROM CARMEN DEO NOSTRO

In the Holy Nativity of Our Lord God: A Hymn Sung as by the Shepherds[1]

CHORUS   Come we shepherds whose blest sight
        Hath met love's noon in nature's night;
           Come lift we up our loftier song,
        And wake the sun that lies too long.

5   To all our world of well-stol'n joy
           He° slept, and dreamt of no such thing,   *the sun*
        While we found out heaven's fairer eye,
           And kissed the cradle of our King.
        Tell him he rises now too late
10   To show us aught worth looking at.

        Tell him we now can show him more
           Than he e'er showed to mortal sight;
        Than he himself e'er saw before,
           Which to be seen needs not his light.
15   Tell him, Tityrus, where th' hast been;
        Tell him, Thyrsis,[2] what th' hast seen.

TITYRUS   Gloomy night embraced the place
           Where the noble infant lay.
        The babe looked up and showed his face:
20   In spite of darkness, it was day.
        It was thy day, sweet!° and did rise,   *sweet one*
        Not from the east, but from thine eyes.
          CHORUS   It was thy day, sweet, *etc.*

THYRSIS   Winter chid aloud, and sent
25   The angry north to wage his wars;
        The north forgot his fierce intent,
           And left perfumes instead of scars.
        By those sweet eyes' persuasive powers,
        Where he meant frost, he scattered flowers.
30   CHORUS   By those sweet eyes, *etc.*

BOTH   We saw thee in thy balmy° nest,   *eastern, perfumed*
           Young dawn of our eternal day!
        We saw thine eyes break from their east
           And chase the trembling shades away.
35   We saw thee; and we blessed the sight.
        We saw thee by thine own sweet light.

1. See Luke 2.8–20. The poem's form, the interweaving of chorus and alternating soloists, is structurally comparable to an oratorio, an Italian musical form that Crashaw may well have known from his sojourns on the Continent. Its form invites comparison with Dryden's "Alexander's Feast," and its subject with Milton's "On the Morning of Christ's Nativity" (pp. 1451–59). The last version of this poem (1652), printed here, differs considerably from the first version (1646). 2. Tityrus and Thyrsis are typical names for shepherds in classical pastoral poetry; Crashaw here identifies such pastoral figures with the biblical shepherds from the hillsides around Bethlehem.

TITYRUS Poor world (said I), what wilt thou do
   To entertain this starry stranger?
Is this the best thou canst bestow,
40   A cold, and not too cleanly, manger?
Contend, ye powers of heaven and earth,
To fit a bed for this huge birth.
  CHORUS Contend, ye powers, *etc.*

THYRSIS Proud world (said I), cease your contèst,
45   And let the Mighty Babe alone.
The phoenix builds the phoenix' nest;[3]
   Love's architecture is his own.
The Babe whose birth embraves° this morn *makes splendid*
Made his own bed ere he was born.
50   CHORUS The Babe whose, *etc.*

TITYRUS I saw the curl'd drops, soft and slow,
   Come hovering o'er the place's head,
Offering their whitest sheets of snow
   To furnish the fair Infant's bed:
55 Forbear (said I), be not too bold;
Your fleece is white, but 'tis too cold.
   CHORUS Forbear (said I), *etc.*

THYRSIS I saw the obsequious seraphims[4]
   Their rosy fleece of fire bestow,
60 For well they now can spare their wings
   Since heaven itself lies here below.
Well done (said I), but are you sure
Your down so warm will pass for pure?
   CHORUS Well done (said I), *etc.*

65 TITYRUS No, no; your King's not yet to seek
   Where to repose his royal head;
See, see; how soon his new-bloomed cheek
   Twixt mother's breasts is gone to bed.
Sweet choice (said we), no way but so
70 Not to lie cold, yet sleep in snow.
   CHORUS Sweet choice (said we), *etc.*

BOTH We saw thee in thy balmy nest,
   Bright dawn of our eternal day!
We saw thine eyes break from their east
75   And chase the trembling shades away.
We saw thee; and we blessed the sight.
We saw thee, by thine own sweet light.
   CHORUS We saw thee, *etc.*

3. The phoenix is the legendary bird of ancient Egypt, often taken as a symbol for Christ. Only one phoenix existed at any one time; after it had lived five hundred years, it was consumed in flame and a new phoenix rose from the ashes. Christ as Son of God took part in the making of the world long before his incarnation.
4. The highest order of angels, associated with fire because of their ardent love of God.

FULL CHORUS
Welcome, all wonders in one sight!
     Eternity shut in a span.
Summer in winter. Day in night.
     Heaven in earth, and God in man.
Great little one! whose all-embracing birth
Lifts earth to heaven, stoops heaven to earth.

Welcome! though not to gold nor silk,
     To more than Caesar's birthright is;
Two sister seas of virgin milk,
     With many a rarely tempered kiss
That breathes at once both maid° and mother,   *virgin*
Warms in the one, cools in the other.

Welcome! though not to those gay flies[5]
     Gilded i' th' beams of earthly kings—
Slippery souls in smiling eyes;
     But to poor shepherds, homespun things,
Whose wealth's their flock, whose wit to be
Well read in their simplicity.

Yet when young April's husband showers
     Shall bless the fruitful Maia's bed,[6]
We'll bring the firstborn of her flowers
     To kiss thy feet and crown thy head.
To thee, dread Lamb! whose love must keep
The shepherds more than they the sheep.

To Thee, meek Majesty! soft King
     Of simple graces and sweet loves,
Each of us his lamb will bring,
     Each his pair of silver doves,
Till burnt at last in fire of Thy fair eyes,
Ourselves become our own best sacrifice.

1646, 1652

---

5. Courtiers, stigmatized in three compressed lines as ephemeral, worldly, and hypocritical.
6. The showers of April make fruitful the bed of May (from Maia, identified with an ancient Italian goddess of the spring).

NON VI.[1]

'Tis not the work of force but skill
To find the way into man's will.
'Tis love alone can hearts unlock.
Who knows the WORD, *he needs not knock.*

T O   T H E
Noblest & best of Ladies, the
Countess of Denbigh.

Persuading her to Resolution in Religion, & to render herself without further delay into the Communion of the Catholic Church.[2]

What heaven-entreated heart is this,
Stands trembling at the gate of bliss,
Holds fast the door, yet dares not venture
Fairly to open it, and enter?
5   Whose definition is a doubt
'Twixt life and death, 'twixt in and out.
Say, lingering fair! why comes the birth
Of your brave soul so slowly forth?
Plead your pretenses (O you strong
10   In weakness!) why you choose so long
In labor of your self to lie,
Not daring quite to live nor die.
Ah, linger not, loved soul! A slow
And late consent was° a long no;   *would be*
15   Who grants at last, long time tried
And did his best to have denied.
What magic bolts, what mystic bars,
Maintain the will in these strange wars!

1. Not by force. Emblems were popular in Europe in the late Renaissance. Their elements were generally three: an image, an adage, and a poem explaining the relation of the other two. The image was often an enigma, with the poem often moralizing its various elements. Crashaw's poem to the countess of Denbigh takes its departure from an enigmatic image but, like the best emblem poems, goes far beyond it. The heart has a hinge on the right, to show that it can be opened, but is sealed on the left with a scroll or phylactery inscribed with letters standing for the Word, which alone enables one to open the heart. Crashaw is said to have engraved this image himself.

2. Susan, countess of Denbigh, was widowed in 1643, when her husband died fighting for the king. She went to Paris into exile with Queen Henrietta Maria in 1644 and, with some other ladies attached to the court of that Roman Catholic queen, was herself attracted to that religion. Crashaw himself was a new convert; here he engages in a poetic version of the pressure often exerted by Catholic priests and Anglican clergy on influential court ladies. As usual, he calls upon the imagery of erotic persuasion to urge her conversion.

What fatal° yet fantastic bands   *fateful*
20   Keep the free heart from its own hands!
So when the year takes cold, we see
Poor waters their own prisoners be;
Fettered and locked up fast they lie
In a sad self-captivity.
25   Th' astonished nymphs their flood's strange fate deplore,
To see themselves their own severer shore.
      Thou that alone canst thaw this cold,
And fetch the heart from its stronghold,
Almighty Love! end this long war,
30   And of a meteor make a star.³
O fix this fair indefinite;
And 'mongst thy shafts of sovereign° light   *supreme, effectual*
Choose out that sure decisive dart
Which has the key of this close heart,
35   Knows all the corners of 't, and can control
The self-shut cabinet of an unsearched soul.
O let it be at last love's hour!
Raise this tall trophy of thy power;
Come once the conquering way, not to confute,
40   But kill this rebel-word, *irresolute,*
That so, in spite of all this peevish strength
Of weakness, she may write, *resolved at length.*
      Unfold at length, unfold, fair flower,
And use the season of love's shower.
45   Meet his well-meaning wounds, wise heart,
And haste to drink the wholesome dart,
That healing shaft which heaven till now
Hath in love's quiver hid for you.
O dart of love! arrow of light!
50   O happy you, if it hit right;
It must not fall in vain, it must
Not mark the dry, regardless dust.
Fair one, it is your fate, and brings
Eternal worlds upon its wings.
55   Meet it with wide-spread arms, and see
Its seat your soul's just center be.
Disband dull fears; give faith the day.
To save your life, kill your delay.
It is love's siege, and sure to be
60   Your triumph, though his victory.
'Tis cowardice that keeps this field,
And want of courage not to yield.
Yield, then, O yield, that love may win
The fort at last, and let life in.
65   Yield quickly, lest perhaps you prove
Death's prey before the prize of love.
This fort of your fair self, if 't be not won,
He is repulsed indeed; but you are undone.

1652

3. Meteors were sublunary and therefore irregular and transient; stars, above the moon, were regular, fixed, and permanent.

The Flaming Heart   St. Teresa of Avila, a sixteenth-century Spanish mystic
and founder of an ascetic order of barefoot Carmelite nuns, was one of the great
figures of the Catholic Reformation. Her autobiography, popular throughout Europe
and translated into English in 1642 as *The Flaming Heart*, describes not only her
practical problems in establishing her order but also a series of ecstatic trances and
visitations that represent union with the divine in sensual, indeed erotic, imagery.
The Italian sculptor and architect Gianlorenzo Bernini portrayed a mystical experience described in the autobiography in a stunning baroque statue still in the church
of Santa Maria della Vittoria, in Rome. It shows the saint in an attitude of ecstatic,
swooning abandonment while a juvenile seraph stands over her, about to plunge a
golden arrow into her heart. Crashaw may or may not have seen this statue while
Bernini was at work on it (it was installed after Crashaw's death), but his poem
addresses a painter who produced a picture of this episode conceived much as
Bernini presented it.

THE

FLAMING HEART
UPON THE BOOK AND
Picture of the seraphical saint

TERESA,

(AS SHE IS USUALLY EX-
pressed with a SERAPHIM
beside her.)[1]

Well-meaning readers! you that come as friends,
And catch the precious name this piece pretends,°   *puts forward*
Make not too much haste to admire
That fair-cheeked fallacy of fire.
5   That is a seraphim, they say,
And this the great Teresia.
Readers, be ruled by me, and make
Here a well-placed and wise mistake:
You must transpose the picture quite
10   And spell° it wrong to read° it right;   *read / understand*
Read *him* for *her* and *her* for *him*,
And call the saint the seraphim.
   Painter, what didst thou understand,
To put her dart into his hand!
15   See, even the years and size of him
Shows this the mother seraphim.
This is the mistress-flame; and duteous he,
Her happy fireworks here comes down to see.
O most poor-spirited of men!
20   Had thy cold pencil kissed her pen[2]
Thou couldst not so unkindly err
To show us this faint shade for her.
Why, man, this speaks pure mortal frame,
And mocks with female frost love's manly flame.
25   One would suspect thou meant'st to paint
Some weak, inferior, woman saint.
But had thy pale-faced purple took
Fire from the burning cheeks of that bright book,
Thou wouldst on her have heaped up all
30   That could be found seraphical:

---

1. "Seraphim" is in fact the plural form of "seraph." This highest order of angels was thought to burn continuously in the fire of divine love.

2. I.e., if you had only been properly inspired by her book.

Whate'er this youth of fire wears fair,
Rosy fingers, radiant hair,
Glowing cheek and glistering wings,
All those fair and flagrant° things,   *burning*
35   But before all, that fiery dart
Had filled the hand of this great heart.
   Do then as equal right requires,
Since his the blushes be, and hers the fires,
Resume and rectify thy rude design,
40   Undress thy seraphim into mine.
Redeem this injury of thy art,
Give him the veil, give her the dart.
   Give him the veil, that he may cover
The red cheeks° of a rivaled lover,   *blushes*
45   Ashamed that our world now can show
Nests of new seraphims here below.[3]
   Give her the dart, for it is she
(Fair youth) shoots both thy shaft and thee.
Say, all ye wise and well-pierced hearts
50   That live and die amidst her darts,°   *i.e., her writings*
What is 't your tasteful spirits do prove°   *experience*
In that rare life of her and love?
Say and bear witness. Sends she not
A seraphim at every shot?
55   What magazines of immortal arms there shine!
Heaven's great artillery in each love-spun line.
Give then the dart to her who gives the flame,
Give him the veil who kindly takes the shame.
   But if it be the frequent fate
60   Of worst faults to be fortunate;
If all's prescription,[4] and proud wrong
Hearkens not to an humble song,
For all the gallantry of him,
Give me the suffering seraphim.[5]
65   His be the bravery° of all those bright things,   *splendor*
The glowing cheeks, the glistering wings,
The rosy hand, the radiant dart;
Leave her alone the Flaming Heart.
   Leave her that, and thou shalt leave her
70   Not one loose shaft, but love's whole quiver.
For in love's field was never found
A nobler weapon than a wound.
Love's passives are his activ'st part,
The wounded is the wounding heart.
75   O heart! the equal poise of love's both parts,
Big alike with wounds and darts,

---

3. Teresa burns on earth in love, as seraphim do
in heaven.
4. I.e., settled beforehand, by the decision of the

artist.
5. If Teresa can't be transformed into the angel,
Crashaw prefers her as the "suffering" lover.

Live in these conquering leaves,[6] live all the same;
And walk through all tongues one triumphant flame.
Live here, great heart; and love and die and kill,
80　And bleed and wound; and yield and conquer still.
Let this immortal life, where'er it comes,
Walk in a crowd of loves and martyrdoms.
Let mystic deaths wait on 't, and wise souls be
The love-slain witnesses of this life of thee.
85　O sweet incendiary! show here thy art,
Upon this carcass of a hard, cold heart;°　　　　　*Crashaw's heart*
Let all thy scattered shafts of light, that play
Among the leaves of thy large books of day,[7]
Combined against this breast, at once break in
90　And take away from me myself and sin!
This gracious robbery shall thy bounty be,
And my best fortunes such fair spoils of me.[8]
O thou undaunted daughter of desires!
By all thy dower of lights and fires;
95　By all the eagle in thee, all the dove;[9]
By all thy lives and deaths of love;
By thy large drafts of intellectual day,
And by thy thirsts of love more large than they;
By all thy brim-filled bowls of fierce desire,
100　By thy last morning's draft of liquid fire;
By the full kingdom of that final kiss
That seized thy parting soul, and sealed thee His;
By all the heavens thou hast in Him,
Fair sister of the seraphim,
105　By all of Him we have in thee,
Leave nothing of myself in me!
Let me so read thy life that I
Unto all life of mine may die!

1652

---

6. I.e., the leaves of St. Teresa's book.
7. Books filled with intellectual and spiritual light.
8. I.e., my best fortune will be to be despoiled in this way.

9. The eagle suggests wisdom and power, for its lofty flight and ability to look into the sun's eye; the dove suggests mercy and gentleness. Cf. Donne's "The Canonization," line 22 (pp. 927–28).

ROBERT HERRICK
1591–1674

Robert Herrick was the most devoted of the Sons of Ben, though his epigrams and lyrics (like Jonson's) also show the direct influence of classical poets: Horace, Anacreon, Catullus, Tibullus, Ovid, and Martial. Born in London the son of a goldsmith and apprenticed for some years in that craft, Herrick took B.A. and M.A. degrees at Cambridge and consorted in the early 1620s with Jonson and his "tribe," who met regularly at the Apollo Room. After his ordination in 1623, he apparently served as chaplain to various noblemen and in that role joined Buckingham's failed military expedition to rescue French Protestants at Rhé in 1627. In 1630 he was installed as the vicar of Dean Prior in Devonshire. Expelled as a royalist in 1647, he apparently lived in London until the Restoration, when he was reinstated at Dean Prior and remained there until his death.

Herrick's single volume of poems, *Hesperides* (1648), with its appended book of religious poems, *Noble Numbers*, contains over four hundred short poems. Many are love poems on the carpe diem theme—seize the day, time is fleeting, make love now; a famous example is the elegant song "To the Virgins, to Make Much of Time." But Herrick's range is much wider than is sometimes recognized. He moves from the pastoral to the cynical, from an almost rococo elegance to coarse, even vulgar, epigrams, and from the didactic to the dramatic. Also, he derives mythic energy and power from certain recurring motifs. One is metamorphosis, "times transshifting," the transience of all natural things. Another is celebration—festivals and feasts—evoking the social, ritualistic, and even anthropological signficances and energies contained in rural harvest festivals ("The Hock Cart") or the May Day rituals described in what is perhaps his finest poem, "Corinna's Going A-Maying." Yet another is the classical but also perennial ideal of the "good life," defined in his terms as "cleanly wantonness." For Herrick this involves love devoid of high passion (the several mistresses he addresses seem interchangeable and not very real); the pleasures of food, drink, and song; delight in the beauty of surfaces (as in "Upon Julia's Clothes"); and, finally, the creation of poetry as bulwark against the ravages of time.

Published just months before the execution of Charles I, these poems seem merely playful and charming, almost oblivious to the catastrophes of the war. But they are not. Poems celebrating rural feasts and festivals, ceremonial social occasions, and the rituals of good fellowship reinforce the conservative values of social stability, tradition, and order threatened by the Puritans. Several poems that draw upon the Celtic mythology of fairy folk make their feasts, temples, worship, and ceremonies stand in for the forbidden ceremonies of the Laudian church and a life governed by ritual. Still other poems, like "The Hock Cart" and "Corinna's Going A-Maying," celebrate the kind of rural festivals that were at the center of the culture wars between royalists and Puritans. Both James I and Charles I urged such activities in their *Book of Sports* as a means of reinforcing traditional institutions in the countryside and deflecting discontent, while Puritans vigorously opposed them as occasions for drunkenness and licentiousness.

From Hesperides[1]

The Argument[2] of His Book

I sing of brooks, of blossoms, birds, and bowers,
Of April, May, of June, and July flowers.
I sing of Maypoles, hock carts, wassails, wakes,[3]
Of bridegrooms, brides, and of their bridal cakes.
I write of youth, of love, and have access
By these to sing of cleanly wantonness.
I sing of dews, of rains, and, piece by piece,
Of balm, of oil, of spice, and ambergris.[4]
I sing of times trans-shifting,° and I write   *changing*
How roses first came red and lilies white.
I write of groves, of twilights, and I sing
The court of Mab and of the fairy king.[5]
I write of hell; I sing (and ever shall)
Of heaven, and hope to have it after all.

5

10

Upon the Loss of His Mistresses[1]

I have lost, and lately, these
Many dainty mistresses:
Stately Julia, prime of all;
Sappho next, a principal;
Smooth Anthea, for a skin
White and heaven-like crystalline;
Sweet Electra, and the choice
Myrrha, for the lute and voice;
Next Corinna for her wit
And the graceful use of it,
With Perilla; all are gone,
Only Herrick's left alone,
For to number sorrows by
Their departures hence, and die.

5

10

<hr>

1. In myth, the Hesperides, or Western Maidens, guarded an orchard and a garden, also called Hesperides, in which grew a tree bearing golden apples. Herrick's title suggests that his poems are golden apples from his residence in western Devonshire; the following poems are all from that volume published in 1648.
2. Subject matter, theme.
3. Festive, not funerary, occasions, to celebrate the dedication of a new church. "Hock carts" carried home the last load of the harvest, so they

were adorned and celebrated. "Wassails" were Twelfth Night celebrations.
4. A secretion of the sperm whale that is used in making perfume—hence it suggests something rare and delectable.
5. Mab was queen of the fairies and wife of their king, Oberon.
1. The ladies are imaginary, and their names are traditional in classical love poetry and pastoral poetry.

The Vine

I dreamed this mortal part of mine
Was metamorphosed to a vine,
Which, crawling one and every way,
Enthralled my dainty Lucia.[1]
5 Methought, her long small legs and thighs
I with my tendrils did surprise;
Her belly, buttocks, and her waist
By my soft nervelets were embraced.
About her head I writhing hung,
10 And with rich clusters (hid among
The leaves) her temples I behung,
So that my Lucia seemed to me
Young Bacchus ravished by his tree.°   *the grapevine*
My curls about her neck did crawl,
15 And arms and hands they did enthrall,
So that she could not freely stir
(All parts there made one prisoner).
But when I crept with leaves to hide
Those parts which maids keep unespied,
20 Such fleeting pleasures there I took
That with the fancy I awoke,
And found (ah me!) this flesh of mine
More like a stock° than like a vine.   *hard stalk*

Dreams

Here we are all, by day; by night, we're hurled
By dreams, each one into a several° world.   *separate*

Delight in Disorder[1]

A sweet disorder in the dress
Kindles in clothes a wantonness.
A lawn° about the shoulders thrown   *fine linen scarf*
Into a fine distractiòn;
5 An erring° lace, which here and there   *wandering*
Enthralls the crimson stomacher;[2]
A cuff neglectful, and thereby
Ribbons to flow confusedly;
A winning wave, deserving note,

---

1. For the sake of both rhyme and meter, the name of this lady is given three syllables here; in line 12 it has only two.
1. One of several poems in this period in which women's dress is a means by which to explore the relation of nature and art.
2. An ornamental covering of the chest, worn under the laces of the bodice.

10 In the tempestuous petticoat;
A careless shoestring, in whose tie
I see a wild civility:
Do more bewitch me than when art
Is too precise³ in every part.

His Farewell to Sack¹

Farewell, thou thing, time-past so known, so dear
To me as blood to life and spirit; near,
Nay, thou more near than kindred, friend, man, wife,
Male to the female, soul to body, life
5 To quick action, or the warm soft side
Of the resigning° yet resisting bride.   *yielding*
The kiss of virgins; first fruits of the bed;
Soft speech, smooth touch, the lips, the maidenhead;
These and a thousand sweets could never be
10 So near or dear as thou wast once to me.
O thou, the drink of gods and angels! Wine
That scatterest spirit and lust;° whose purest shine *pleasure*
More radiant than the summer's sunbeams shows,
Each way illustrious, brave;° and like to those   *splendid*
15 Comets we see by night, whose shagg'd² portents
Foretell the coming of some dire events,
Or° some full flame which with a pride aspires,   *or like to*
Throwing about his wild and active fires.
'Tis thou, above nectar, O divinest soul!
20 (Eternal in thyself) that canst control
That which subverts whole nature: grief and care,
Vexation of the mind, and damned despair.
'Tis thou alone who with thy mystic fan³
Work'st more than wisdom, art, or nature can
25 To rouse the sacred madness,⁴ and awake
The frost-bound blood and spirits, and to make
Them frantic with thy raptures, flashing through
The soul like lightning, and as active too.
'Tis not Apollo can, or those thrice three
30 Castalian sisters sing,⁵ if wanting° thee.   *lacking*
Horace, Anacreon both had lost their fame
Had'st thou not filled them with thy fire and flame.⁶
Phoebean splendor! and thou Thespian spring!⁷

---

3. "Precise" and "precision" were terms used satirically about Puritans. Herrick, in praising feminine disarray, is at one level praising the "sprezzatura," or careless grace, of Cavalier art.
1. Sherry wine, imported from Spain.
2. Hairy, referring to a comet's tail.
3. Instrument for winnowing grain; associated with Bacchus, god of wine.
4. Poetic inspiration or frenzy, often likened to intoxication.

5. Apollo, god of poetry, and the Nine Muses; the Castalian spring on Mount Parnassus was sacred to them.
6. Both Horace and Anacreon wrote about the pleasures of wine.
7. In addition to being an epithet of Apollo, *Phoebus* in Greek means bright, pure. The inhabitants of Thespiae, in Boeotia, worshipped the Muses and held an annual festival in their honor at the spring of Hippocrene, nearby.

Of which sweet swans must drink before they sing
35 Their true-paced numbers and their holy lays°   *songs*
Which makes them worthy cedar and the bays.[8]
But why? why longer do I gaze upon
Thee with the eye of admiration?
Since I must leave thee, and enforced must say
40 To all thy witching beauties, Go, away.
But if thy whimpering looks do ask me why,
Then know that nature bids thee go, not I.
'Tis her erroneous self has made a brain
Uncapable of such a sovereign
45 As is thy powerful self. Prithee not smile,
Or smile more inly, lest thy looks beguile
My vows denounced° in zeal, which thus much show thee,   *proclaimed*
That I have sworn but by thy looks to know thee.
Let others drink thee freely, and desire
50 Thee and their lips espoused, while I admire
And love thee but not taste thee. Let my muse
Fail of thy former helps, and only use
Her inadulterate strength. What's done by me
Hereafter shall smell of the lamp, not thee.[9]

Corinna's Going A-Maying

Get up! Get up for shame! The blooming morn
Upon her wings presents the god unshorn.[1]
   See how Aurora throws her fair
   Fresh-quilted colors through the air:[2]
5   Get up, sweet slug-a-bed, and see
   The dew bespangling herb and tree.
Each flower has wept and bowed toward the east
Above an hour since, yet you not dressed;
   Nay, not so much as out of bed?
10   When all the birds have matins° said,   *morning prayer*
   And sung their thankful hymns, 'tis sin,
   Nay, profanation° to keep in,   *impiety*
Whenas a thousand virgins on this day
Spring, sooner than the lark, to fetch in May.[3]

15 Rise, and put on your foliage, and be seen
To come forth, like the springtime, fresh and green,
   And sweet as Flora.[4] Take no care
   For jewels for your gown or hair;

---

8. Cedar oil was used to preserve papyrus; the poet's crown is woven of bay (i.e., laurel) leaves.
9. To "smell of the lamp" is a proverbial expression for a laborious and uninspired literary production.
1. Apollo, the sun god; sunbeams are seen as his flowing locks.

2. Aurora is goddess of the dawn.
3. On May Day morning, it was the custom to gather whitethorn blossoms and trim the house with them.
4. Flora, Italian goddess of flowers, had her festival in the spring.

Fear not; the leaves will strew
20   Gems in abundance upon you;
Besides, the childhood of the day has kept,
Against° you come, some orient pearls[5] unwept;   *until*
        Come and receive them while the light
        Hangs on the dew-locks of the night,
25   And Titan° on the eastern hill   *the sun*
        Retires himself, or else stands still
Till you come forth. Wash, dress, be brief in praying:
Few beads[6] are best when once we go a-Maying.

        Come, my Corinna, come; and, coming, mark
30   How each field turns° a street, each street a park   *turns into*
        Made green and trimmed with trees; see how
        Devotion gives each house a bough
        Or branch: each porch, each door ere this,
        An ark, a tabernacle is,[7]
35 Made up of whitethorn neatly interwove,
As if here were those cooler shades of love.
        Can such delights be in the street
        And open fields, and we not see 't?
        Come, we'll abroad; and let's obey
40   The proclamation[8] made for May,
And sin no more, as we have done, by staying;
But, my Corinna, come, let's go a-Maying.

        There's not a budding boy or girl this day
        But is got up and gone to bring in May;
45   A deal of youth, ere this, is come
        Back, and with whitethorn laden, home.
        Some have dispatched their cakes and cream
        Before that we have left to dream;
And some have wept, and wooed, and plighted troth,[9]
50 And chose their priest, ere we can cast off sloth.
        Many a green gown[1] has been given,
        Many a kiss, both odd and even;[2]
        Many a glance, too, has been sent
        From out the eye, love's firmament;°   *sky*
55 Many a jest told of the keys betraying
This night, and locks picked; yet we're not a-Maying.

        Come, let us go while we are in our prime,
        And take the harmless folly of the time.
        We shall grow old apace, and die
60   Before we know our liberty.

---

5. Pearls from the Orient were especially lustrous, like drops of dew.
6. Rosary beads of the "old" Catholic religion, but more generally, a casual term for prayers.
7. The doorways, ornamented with whitethorn, are like the Hebrew Ark of the Covenant or the sanctuary that housed it (Leviticus 23.40–42:

"Ye shall take you on the first day the boughs of goodly trees . . .").
8. Probably a reference to Charles I's "Declaration to his subjects concerning lawful sports."
9. Engaged themselves to marry.
1. Got by rolling in the grass.
2. Kisses are odd and even in kissing games.

Our life is short, and our days run
As fast away as does the sun;
And, as a vapor or a drop of rain,
Once lost, can ne'er be found again,
65   So when or you or I are made
A fable, song, or fleeting shade,
All love, all liking, all delight
Lies drowned with us in endless night.[3]
Then while time serves, and we are but decaying,
70   Come, my Corinna, come, let's go a-Maying.

To the Virgins, to Make Much of Time

Gather ye rosebuds while ye may,
  Old time is still° a-flying;[1]   *always*
And this same flower that smiles today,
  Tomorrow will be dying.

5   The glorious lamp of heaven, the sun,
  The higher he's a-getting,
The sooner will his race be run,
  And nearer he's to setting.

That age is best which is the first,
10   When youth and blood are warmer;
But being spent, the worse, and worst
  Times still succeed the former.

Then be not coy, but use your time,
  And while ye may, go marry;
15   For having lost but once your prime,
  You may forever tarry.

The Hock Cart,[1] or Harvest Home

to the Right Honorable Mildmay, Earl of Westmoreland

Come, sons of summer, by whose toil
We are the lords of wine and oil;[2]
By whose tough labors and rough hands
We rip up first, then reap our lands.

---

3. Some echoes of the apocryphal book Wisdom of Solomon 2.1–8: "For the ungodly said . . . the breath of our nostrils is as smoke, and a little spark . . . and our life shall pass away as the trace of a cloud. . . . Come on therefore . . . Let us crown ourselves with rose buds before they be withered." This carpe diem sentiment is a frequent theme in classical love poetry.
1. Translates the Latin *tempus fugit*.

1. The last cart carrying home the harvest; hence the occasion for a rural festival, traditional throughout Europe. Mildmay Fane, earl of Westmoreland (1628–1660), was one of Herrick's patrons.
2. Wine and oil are the yields of Mediterranean farming, connecting the English harvest festival to classical pastoral.

5   Crowned with the ears of corn,° now come   *grain*
And, to the pipe, sing harvest home.
Come forth, my lord, and see the cart
Dressed up with all the country art.
See here a maukin,° there a sheet,   *scarecrow*
10 As spotless pure as it is sweet,
The horses, mares, and frisking fillies
Clad all in linen, white as lilies,
The harvest swains° and wenches bound   *young men*
For joy to see the hock-cart crowned.
15   About the cart, hear how the rout
Of rural younglings raise the shout,
Pressing before, some coming after,
Those with a shout and these with laughter.
Some bless the cart, some kiss the sheaves,
20 Some prank° them up with oaken leaves;   *adorn*
Some cross the fill-horse,³ some with great
Devotion stroke the home-borne wheat;
While other rustics, less attent
To prayers than to merriment,
25 Run after with their breeches rent.
    Well, on, brave boys, to your lord's hearth,
Glittering with fire; where, for your mirth,
Ye shall see first the large and chief
Foundation of your feast, fat beef;
30 With upper stories, mutton, veal,
And bacon,° which makes full the meal,   *pork*
With several dishes standing by,
As here a custard, there a pie,
And here all-tempting frumenty.°   *pudding*
35 And for to make the merry cheer,
If smirking° wine be wanting° here,   *sparkling / lacking*
There's that which drowns all care, stout beer:
Which freely drink to your lord's health,
Then to the plow (the common-wealth),
40 Next to your flails, your fans,⁴ your vats,
Then to the maids with wheaten hats,
To the rough sickle and crook'd scythe,
Drink, frolic boys, till all be blithe.
    Feed, and grow fat; and, as ye eat,
45 Be mindful that the lab'ring neat,°   *cattle*
As you, may have their fill of meat.⁵
And know, besides, ye must revoke°   *call back*
The patient ox unto his yoke,
And all go back unto the plow
50 And harrow, though they're hanged up now.
And you must know, your lord's word's true,

3. The fill-horse is harnessed between the shafts of the cart. Crossing the horse and kissing the sheaves suggest the persistence of pre-Reformation rituals in the countryside.
4. "Flails" are threshing instruments; "fans" are used to winnow grain from chaff. The plow is the common source of everybody's wealth. In line with the anti-Puritan sentiments of the whole poem, the word "commonwealth," in this communal and earthy sense, invites a contrast with Puritan republican theories.
5. Food (grain or hay).

Feed him ye must whose food fills you,
And that this pleasure is like rain,
Not sent ye for to drown your pain
55   But for to make it spring again.[6]

How Roses Came Red[1]

Roses at first were white,
    Till they could not agree,
Whether my Sappho's breast,
    Or they more white should be.

5   But being vanquished quite,
    A blush their cheeks bespread;
Since which (believe the rest)
    The roses first came red.

Upon the Nipples of Julia's Breast

Have ye beheld (with much delight)
A red rose peeping through a white?
Or else a cherry (double graced)
Within a lily center-placed?
5   Or ever marked° the pretty beam   observed
A strawberry shows half drowned in cream?
Or seen rich rubies blushing through
A pure smooth pearl, and orient° too?   iridescent
So like to this, nay all the rest,
10 Is each neat niplet of her breast.

Upon Jack and Jill. Epigram[2]

When Jill complains to Jack for want of meat,
Jack kisses Jill, and bids her freely eat.
Jill says, Of what? Says Jack, On that sweet kiss,
Which full of nectar and ambrosia is,
5   The food of poets. So I thought, says Jill;
That makes them look so lank, so ghost-like still.
Let poets feed on air or what they will;
Let me feed full till that I fart, says Jill.

---

6. Spring is heralded by rain, but the lines also point to the continual renewal of the agricultural worker's pain and labor.
1. This poem and several others in the collec-
tion present minitransformations in witty allusion to Ovid's epiclike *Metamorphoses*.
2. Cf. Jonson, "On Giles and Joan," pp. 1091–92.

To Marigolds[3]

Give way, an° ye be ravished by the sun,   *if*
And hang the head whenas the act is done.
Spread as he spreads; wax less as he does wane,
And as he shuts, close up to maids° again.   *virgins*

His Prayer to Ben Jonson

When I a verse shall make,
Know I have prayed thee,
For old religion's sake,[4]
Saint Ben to aid me.

5 Make the way smooth for me
When I, thy Herrick,
Honoring thee, on my knee,
Offer my lyric.

Candles I'll give to thee
10 And a new altar;
And thou Saint Ben shalt be
Writ in my psalter.

The Bad Season Makes the Poet Sad[5]

Dull to myself and almost dead to these
My many fresh and fragrant mistresses,
Lost to all music now, since every thing
Puts on the semblance here of sorrowing.
5 Sick is the land to the heart, and doth endure
More dangerous faintings by her desperate cure.
But if that golden age would come again,
And Charles here rule as he before did reign,
If smooth and unperplexed the seasons were,
10 As when the sweet Maria livèd here,
I should delight to have my curls half drowned
In Tyrian dews,[6] and head with roses crowned,
And once more yet (ere I am laid out dead)
Knock at a star with my exalted head.[7]

3. The English pot marigold closes its flowers at dusk.
4. Herrick plays on the fact that Jonson was for a while a Catholic (of the "old religion"), as well as a saint in the mock religion of poetry.
5. The bad season is evidently political, not meteorological. Line 10 refers to Charles's queen, Henrietta Maria, so the poem must have been written after 1644, when she was forced to retire to France.
6. Perfume from Tyre was one of many Middle Eastern luxuries proverbial in Roman times.
7. The last line translates literally the last line of Horace's first ode, to his patron, Maecenas. Herrick hopes once more to have enlightened readers and an enlightened patron, so that he can feel something of Horace's exaltation.

The Night-Piece, to Julia

Her eyes the glowworm lend thee,
The shooting stars attend thee;
　　And the elves also,
　　Whose little eyes glow
5　Like the sparks of fire, befriend thee.

No Will-o'th'-Wisp mislight thee,[8]
Nor snake or slowworm° bite thee;　　　　　　　　*adder*
　　But on, on thy way,
　　Not making a stay,
10　Since ghost there's none to affright thee.

Let not the dark thee cumber;
What though the moon does slumber?
　　The stars of the night
　　Will lend thee their light
15　Like tapers clear without number.

Then, Julia, let me woo thee,
Thus, thus to come unto me:
　　And when I shall meet
　　Thy silv'ry feet,
20　My soul I'll pour into thee.

Upon His Verses

What offspring other men have got,
The how, where, when I question not.
These are the children I have left;
Adopted some, none got by theft.
5　But all are touched (like lawful plate)[9]
And no verse illegitimate.

His Return to London

From the dull confines of the drooping west,[1]
To see the day spring from the pregnant east,
Ravished in spirit, I come, nay more, I fly
To thee, blest place of my nativity!
5　Thus, thus with hallowed foot I touch the ground

8. Will-o'-the-wisp traditionally draws travelers astray with false lights.
9. A special variety of quartz, known as basanite, was used to test gold and silver objects; the color of the smear left on the touchstone revealed its purity.
1. Devonshire, where his parish, Dean Prior, was located.

With thousand blessings by thy fortune crowned.
O fruitful Genius![2] that bestowest here
An everlasting plenty, year by year.
O place! O people! Manners! framed to please
10   All nations, customs, kindreds, languages!
I am a free-born Roman;[3] suffer then
That I amongst you live a citizen.
London my home is, though by hard fate sent
Into a long and irksome banishment;
15   Yet since called back, henceforward let me be,
O native country, repossessed by thee!
For, rather than I'll to the west return,
I'll beg of thee first here to have mine urn.
Weak I am grown, and must in short time fall;
20   Give thou my sacred relics burial.

1647?

Upon Julia's Clothes

Whenas in silks my Julia goes,°   *walks*
Then, then, methinks, how sweetly flows
That liquefaction of her clothes.

Next, when I cast mine eyes and see
5   That brave° vibration each way free,   *splendid*
Oh, how that glittering taketh me!

Upon Prue, His Maid[4]

In this little urn is laid
Prudence Baldwin, once my maid,
From whose happy spark here let
Spring the purple violet.

To His Book's End[5]

To his book's end this last line he'd have placed:
Jocund° his muse was, but his life was chaste.   *merry, sprightly*

---

2. In classical Rome, the genius of a place was its guardian deity.
3. An ancient Roman born in the city was said to be "free of it," i.e., entitled to its special rights and privileges, including residence there.
4. This is an odd epitaph, since Prudence Baldwin died four years after Herrick.
5. The last poem of *Hesperides*.

From NOBLE NUMBERS

To His Conscience[1]

Can I not sin, but thou wilt be
My private protonotary?[2]
Can I not woo thee to pass by
A short and sweet iniquity?
5   I'll cast a mist and cloud upon
My delicate transgression
So utter dark as that no eye
Shall see the hugged° impiety.   *cherished*
Gifts blind the wise,[3] and bribes do please
10 And wind° all other witnesses: *pervert*
And wilt not thou with gold be tied
To lay thy pen and ink aside?
That in the mirk° and tongueless night   *black, murky*
Wanton I may, and thou not write?
15 It will not be; and therefore now
For times to come I'll make this vow,
From aberrations to live free,
So I'll not fear the Judge, or thee.

Another Grace for a Child

Here a little child I stand,
Heaving up my either hand;
Cold as paddocks° though they be,   *frogs*
Here I lift them up to thee,
5   For a benison° to fall   *blessing*
On our meat and on us all. *Amen.*

1. This and the following poem are from *Noble Numbers*, the collection of Herrick's religious poems that was bound together with *Hesperides*.

2. Chief recording clerk of a court.
3. Echoes Deuteronomy 16.19: "a gift doth blind the eyes of the wise."

THOMAS CAREW
1595–1640

Thomas Carew (pronounced *Carey*) is perhaps the Cavalier poet with the greatest range and complexity. He gained his B.A. at Merton College, Oxford, studied law (his father's profession), held several minor positions in the diplomatic and court bureaucracy, fought for his king in the ill-fated expedition against the Scots (the First Bishops' War, 1639), and died of syphilis. A brilliant, dissolute young man, he was a favorite with Charles I and Henrietta Maria.

His *Poems* (1640), published posthumously, are witty and often outrageous, but their emphasis on natural sensuality and the need for union between king and subjects encodes a serious critique of the Neoplatonic artifice of the Caroline court. Carew's spectacular court masque, *Coelum Britannicum*, performed at the Banqueting Hall at Whitehall on February 18, 1633, was based on a philosophical dialogue by Giordano Bruno. It combines a dramatization of serious social and political problems in the antimasque with wildly hyperbolic praise of the monarchs in the main masque. As a love poet Carew sometimes plays off Donnean situations and poems; elsewhere, as in "Ask me no more where Jove bestows," he imitates Jonson's most purely lyric vein. But his characteristic note is one of frank sexuality and emotional realism. "The Rapture," probably the most erotic poem of the era, describes the sexual act under the sustained metaphor of a voyage. He also wrote country-house poems that, unlike Jonson's "To Penshurst," describe Saxham and Wrest as places of refuge from the mounting dangers outside their gates. Carew's poems of literary criticism provide astute commentary on contemporary authors. "To Ben Jonson" evaluates Jonson with Jonsonian precision and judiciousness in weighing out praise and blame. His famous "Elegy" on Donne praises Donne's innovation, avoidance of classical tags, "giant fancy," and especially his tough masculinity of style, a feature Carew imitates in this poem's energetic runover couplets, quick changes of rhythms and images, and vigorous "strong lines."

An Elegy upon the Death of the Dean of Paul's, Dr. John Donne[1]

> Can we not force from widowed poetry,
> Now thou art dead, great Donne, one elegy
> To crown thy hearse? Why yet dare we not trust,
> Though with unkneaded dough-baked[2] prose, thy dust,
> 5 Such as the unscissored[3] churchman from the flower
> Of fading rhetoric, short-lived as his hour,
> Dry as the sand that measures it,[4] should lay
> Upon thy ashes on the funeral day?
> Have we no voice, no tune? Didst thou dispense°   *lay out, use up*
> 10 Through all our language both the words and sense?
> 'Tis a sad truth. The pulpit may her plain
> And sober Christian precepts still retain;
> Doctrines it may, and wholesome uses,° frame,   *customs*
> Grave homilies and lectures; but the flame
> 15 Of thy brave soul, that shot such heat and light
> As burnt our earth and made our darkness bright,
> Committed holy rapes upon our will,
> Did through the eye the melting heart distill,
> And the deep knowledge of dark truths so teach

---

1. First appearing with a number of other elegies in the 1633 edition of Donne's poems, then reprinted in 1640 with some changes, Carew's tribute is notable among 17th-century poems on poetry for its technical precision.

2. I.e., tedious and flat.
3. With uncut hair.
4. The hourglass was used by preachers to keep track of time.

20 As sense might judge what fancy could not reach,[5]
Must be desired° forever. So the fire   *missed*
That fills with spirit and heat the Delphic choir,[6]
Which, kindled first by thy Promethean[7] breath,
Glowed here a while, lies quenched now in thy death.
25 The Muses' garden, with pedantic weeds
O'erspread, was purged by thee; the lazy seeds
Of servile imitation thrown away,
And fresh invention planted; thou didst pay
The debts of our penurious bankrupt age—
30 Licentious thefts, that make poetic rage
A mimic fury, when our souls must be
Possessed or with Anacreon's ecstasy,
Or Pindar's,[8] not their own. The subtle cheat
Of sly exchanges, and the juggling feat
35 Of two-edged words,[9] or whatsoever wrong
By ours was done the Greek or Latin tongue,
Thou hast redeemed, and opened us a mine
Of rich and pregnant fancy, drawn a line
Of masculine expression, which had good
40 Old Orpheus[1] seen, or all the ancient brood
Our superstitious fools admire, and hold
Their lead more precious than thy burnished gold,
Thou hadst been their exchequer,° and no more   *treasury*
They in each other's dust had raked for ore.
45 Thou shalt yield no precedence but of time
And the blind fate of language, whose tuned chime°   *rhyme*
More charms the outward sense; yet thou mayest claim
From so great disadvantage greater fame,
Since to the awe of thy imperious wit
50 Our stubborn language bends, made only fit
With her tough thick-ribbed hoops to gird about
Thy giant fancy, which had proved too stout
For their soft melting phrases. As in time
They had the start, so did they cull the prime
55 Buds of invention many a hundred year,
And left the rifled fields, besides the fear
To touch their harvest; yet from those bare lands
Of what is purely thine, thy only hands
(And that thy smallest work) have gleanèd more
60 Than all those times and tongues could reap before.
    But thou art gone, and thy strict laws will be
Too hard for libertines in poetry.
They will repeal° the goodly exiled train   *recall from banishment*
Of gods and goddesses, which in thy just reign

---

5. I.e., so that things too abstract to be imagined might be made plain to sense.
6. The choir of poets, inspired by Apollo, whose oracle was at Delphi.
7. Prometheus stole fire from heaven to aid humankind.
8. Anacreon (6th and 5th centuries B.C.E.) and Pindar (first half of the 5th century B.C.E.) were famous Greek lyric poets.
9. "Sly exchanges": Carew seems to refer to the habit of using English words in their Latin senses. "Two-edged words" might be puns, but these were a favorite device of Donne's.
1. Ancient Greek poet and prophet, often used as the type of all poets.

65 Were banished nobler poems; now with these
The silenced tales o' th' *Metamorphoses*[2]
Shall stuff their lines and swell the windy page,
Till verse, refined by thee in this last age,
Turn ballad-rhyme, or those old idols be
70 Adored again with new apostasy.
    O pardon me, that break with untuned verse
The reverend silence that attends thy hearse,
Whose awful° solemn murmurs were to thee,   *awesome*
More than these faint lines, a loud elegy,
75 That did proclaim in a dumb eloquence
The death of all of the arts, whose influence,
Grown feeble, in these panting numbers° lies   *verses*
Gasping short-winded accents, and so dies:
So doth the swiftly turning wheel not stand
80 In th' instant we withdraw the moving hand,
But some small time maintain a faint weak course
By virtue of the first impulsive force;
And so whilst I cast on thy funeral pile
Thy crown of bays,° oh, let it crack awhile   *poet's laurel crown*
85 And spit disdain, till the devouring flashes
Suck all the moisture up; then turn to ashes.
    I will not draw the envy to engross
All thy perfections, or weep all our loss;
Those are too numerous for an elegy,
90 And this too great to be expressed by me.
Though every pen should take a distinct part,
Yet art thou theme enough to tire° all art.[3]   *exhaust*
Let others carve the rest; it shall suffice
I on thy tomb this epitaph incise:

95   *Here lies a king, that ruled as he thought fit*
   The universal monarchy of wit;
   Here lie two flamens,[4] *and both those the best:*
   Apollo's first, at last the true God's priest.

1633, 1640

To Ben Jonson

Upon occasion of his Ode of Defiance
annexed to his play of The New Inn[1]

'Tis true, dear Ben, thy just chastising hand
Hath fixed upon the sotted age a brand
To their swoll'n pride and empty scribbling due.

---

2. Ovid's tales in the *Metamorphoses* were a favorite stockpile of poetic properties for Renaissance poets, but Donne did not use them.
3. This line and the preceding one were omitted in the 1640 edition.
4. Priests of ancient Rome: Donne was first a priest of Apollo, the pagan god of poetry, and later a Christian priest.

1. Jonson's late play *The New Inn* was hissed from the stage in 1629 and published in 1631 with an angry "Ode to Himself" (pp. 1108–09) prefixed. Carew's remonstration must have been written shortly thereafter.

It can nor judge nor write; and yet 'tis true
5   Thy comic Muse from the exalted line
Touched by thy *Alchemist*[2] doth since decline
From that her zenith, and foretells a red
And blushing evening when she goes to bed—
Yet such as shall outshine the glimmering light
10   With which all stars shall gild the following night.
Nor think it much (since all thy eaglets may
Endure the sunny trial)[3] if we say,
This hath the stronger wing, or that doth shine
Tricked up in fairer plumes, since all are thine.
15   Who hath his flock of cackling geese compared
With thy tuned choir of swans? Or who hath dared
To call thy births deformed? But if thou bind
By city-custom, or by gavelkind,[4]
In equal shares thy love to all thy race,
20   We may distinguish of their sex and place:
Though one hand shape them and though one brain strike
Souls into all, they are not all alike.
Why should the follies then of this dull age
Draw from thy pen such an immodest rage
25   As seems to blast thy else-immortal bays,°   *poet's laurel crown*
When thine own tongue proclaims thy itch of praise?
Such thirst will argue drought. No, let be hurled
Upon thy works by the detracting world
What malice can suggest; let the rout° say   *rabble*
30   The running sands that, ere thou make a play,
Count the slow minutes might a Goodwin frame[5]
To swallow when th' hast done thy shipwrecked name.
Let them the dear° expense of oil upbraid,°   *extravagant / scold*
Sucked by thy watchful lamp that hath betrayed
35   To theft the blood of martyred authors, spilt
Into thy ink, while thou growest pale with guilt.[6]
Repine° not at the taper's thrifty waste,   *fret*
That sleeks thy terser poems; nor is haste
Praise, but excuse; and if thou overcome
40   A knotty writer, bring the booty home;
Nor think it theft if the rich spoils so torn
From conquered authors be as trophies worn.
Let others glut on the extorted praise
Of vulgar breath: trust thou to after days.
45   Thy labored works shall live when Time devours
Th' abortive offspring of their hasty hours.
Thou art not of their rank, the quarrel lies

---

2. Jonson's play (1610) about three confidence tricksters.
3. To make sure the young birds in his nest are genuine eaglets, the eagle is reputed to fly with them up toward the sun; true eagles will not be blinded by the rays.
4. "City-custom" (i.e., London City custom) and "gavelkind" (a system of land tenure once common in Kent) were two legal ways of dividing an estate equally among all the heirs—as opposed to the normal English rule of primogeniture (everything to the eldest son).
5. Goodwin Sands were shoals in the Strait of Dover, shifty and treacherous, on which many ships were lost. Jonson's slowness in composition was proverbial.
6. The other great charge against Jonson was that he copied or translated too liberally from other authors.

Within thine own verge[7]—then let this suffice,
The wiser world doth greater thee confess
50 Than all men else, than thy self only less.

ca. 1631   1640

A Song[1]

Ask me no more where Jove bestows,
When June is past, the fading rose;
For in your beauties orient° deep,   *lustrous*
These flowers, as in their causes, sleep.[2]

5 Ask me no more whither do stray
The golden atoms of the day;
For in pure love heaven did prepare
Those powders to enrich your hair.

Ask me no more whither doth haste
10 The nightingale when May is past;
For in your sweet dividing[3] throat
She winters, and keeps warm her note.

Ask me no more where those stars light,
That downwards fall in dead of night;
15 For in your eyes they sit, and there
Fixèd become, as in their sphere.

Ask me no more if east or west
The phoenix builds her spicy nest;[4]
For unto you at last she flies,
20 And in your fragrant bosom dies.

1640

To Saxham[1]

Though frost and snow locked from mine eyes
That beauty which without door lies,
Thy gardens, orchards, walks, that so

---

7. I.e., within your own territory, against yourself. Duels cannot properly take place between
two men of different rank, and as Jonson is out
of everyone else's class, he can fight only himself.
1. Widely popular and several times set to music,
this poem exists in different forms. Like Donne's
"Go and catch a falling star" (pp. 924–25), it is
built around a series of impossibilities.
2. Aristotelian philosophy suggested that objects
often lay latent in their causes. The lady is a

summation of last summer and cause of the next
one.
3. Warbling (from "division," or rapid melodic
passage).
4. The phoenix, a legendary bird, builds her nest
from spicy shrubs. She dies every five hundred
years and a new bird springs from her ashes.
1. Little Saxham, near Bury Saint Edmunds in
Suffolk, was the country residence of Sir John
Crofts, a friend of Carew's. Compare Jonson's
"To Penshurst" (pp. 1096–98).

I might not all thy pleasures know,
5   Yet, Saxham, thou within thy gate
   Art of thyself so delicate,
   So full of native sweets, that bless
   Thy roof with inward happiness,
   As neither from nor to thy store
10 Winter takes aught, or spring adds more.
   The cold and frozen air had starved°   *killed*
   Much poor, if not by thee preserved,
   Whose prayers have made thy table blest
   With plenty, far above the rest.
15 The season hardly did afford
   Coarse cates° unto thy neighbors' board,   *food*
   Yet thou hadst dainties, as the sky
   Had been thy only volary;°   *aviary*
   Or else the birds, fearing the snow
20 Might to another Deluge[2] grow,
   The pheasant, partridge, and the lark
   Flew to thy house, as to the Ark.
   The willing ox of himself came
   Home to the slaughter, with the lamb,
25 And every beast did thither bring
   Himself, to be an offering.
   The scaly herd more pleasure took
   Bathed in thy dish, than in the brook;
   Water, earth, air did all conspire
30 To pay their tributes to thy fire;
   Whose cherishing flames themselves divide
   Through every room, where they deride
   The night and cold abroad; whilst they,
   Like suns within, keep endless day.
35 Those cheerful beams send forth their light
   To all that wander in the night,
   And seem to beckon from aloof
   The weary pilgrim to thy roof,
   Where, if refreshed, he will away,
40 He's fairly welcome; or if stay,
   Far more; which he shall hearty find
   Both from the master and the hind.°   *servant*
   The stranger's welcome each man there
   Stamped on his cheerful brow doth wear,
45 Nor doth this welcome or his cheer
   Grow less 'cause he stays longer here;
   There's none observes, much less repines,
   How often this man sups or dines.
   Thou hast no porter at the door
50 T'examine or keep back the poor,
   Nor locks nor bolts: thy gates have been
   Made only to let strangers in;
   Untaught to shut, they do not fear

---

2. Noah's Flood (Genesis 7).

To stand wide open all the year,
55   Careless who enters, for they know
Thou never didst deserve a foe;
And as for thieves, thy bounty's such,
They cannot steal, thou giv'st so much.

A Rapture

I will enjoy thee now, my Celia, come
And fly with me to love's Elysium.[1]
The giant, Honor, that keeps cowards out,
Is but a masquer,° and the servile rout°   *actor / rabble*
5   Of baser subjects only bend in vain
To the vast idol, whilst the nobler train°   *procession*
Of valiant lovers daily sail between
The huge Colossus' legs,[2] and pass unseen
Unto the blissful shore. Be bold and wise,
10 And we shall enter; the grim Swiss[3] denies
Only tame fools a passage, that not know
He is but form and only frights in show
The duller eyes that look from far; draw near,
And thou shalt scorn what we were wont° to fear.   *used*
15 We shall see how the stalking pageant[4] goes
With borrowed legs, a heavy load to those
That made and bear him—not as we once thought
The seed of gods, but a weak model wrought
By greedy men, that seek to enclose the common,
20 And within private arms empale free woman.[5]
    Come then, and mounted on the wings of love,
We'll cut the flitting air and soar above
The monster's head, and in the noblest seats
Of those blessed shades, quench and renew our heats.
25 There shall the queens of love and innocence,
Beauty and nature banish all offense
From our close ivy twines, there I'll behold
Thy barèd snow and thy unbraided gold.
There my enfranchised hand on every side
30 Shall o'er thy naked polished ivory slide.
No curtain there, though of transparent lawn,°   *fine linen*
Shall be before thy virgin treasure drawn,
But the rich mine to the inquiring eye
Exposed, shall ready still° for mintage lie,   *always*

1. In classical mythology, the abode of the blessed spirits.
2. Tradition had it that the ancient Colossus of Rhodes bestrode the entrance to that harbor, so that ships entering or leaving passed between its legs.
3. The pope's Swiss Guard were renowned for their height.

4. Figure in a pageant, make-believe giant.
5. To "empale" is to surround with a fence, but the word has phallic overtones as well. The "enclosing" for landowners' private use of pastureland traditionally open to the whole community ("the commons") was a political issue in 17th-century England.

35　And we will coin young Cupids.[6] There a bed
　　Of roses and fresh myrtles shall be spread
　　Under the cooler shade of cypress groves;
　　Our pillows, of the down of Venus' doves,[7]
　　Whereon our panting limbs we'll gently lay
40　In the faint respites of our active play,
　　That so our slumbers may in dreams have leisure
　　To tell the nimble fancy our past pleasure,
　　And so our souls that cannot be embraced
　　Shall the embraces of our bodies taste.
45　Meanwhile the bubbling stream shall court the shore,
　　Th' enamored chirping wood-choir shall adore
　　In varied tunes the deity of love;
　　The gentle blasts of western winds shall move
　　The trembling leaves, and through their close boughs breathe
50　Still° music, while we rest ourselves beneath　　　　　　　　*soft*
　　Their dancing shade; till a soft murmur, sent
　　From souls entranced in amorous languishment
　　Rouse us, and shoot into our veins fresh fire
　　Till we in their sweet ecstasy expire.
55　　　Then, as the empty bee, that lately bore
　　Into the common treasure all her store,
　　Flies 'bout the painted field with nimble wing,
　　Deflowering the fresh virgins of the spring,
　　So will I rifle all the sweets that dwell
60　In my delicious paradise, and swell
　　My bag with honey, drawn forth by the power
　　Of fervent kisses from each spicy flower.
　　I'll seize the rosebuds in their perfumed bed,
　　The violet knots, like curious mazes spread
65　O'er all the garden, taste the ripened cherry,
　　The warm, firm apple, tipped with coral berry.
　　Then will I visit with a wandering kiss
　　The vale of lilies and the bower of bliss,
　　And where the beauteous region both divide
70　Into two milky ways, my lips shall slide
　　Down those smooth alleys, wearing as I go
　　A track° for lovers on the printed snow.　　　　　　　　　*path*
　　Thence climbing o'er the swelling Apennine,
　　Retire into thy grove of eglantine,°　　　　　　　　　*sweetbriar*
75　Where I will all those ravished sweets distill
　　Through love's alembic,[8] and with chemic skill
　　From the mixed mass one sovereign balm[9] derive,
　　Then bring that great elixir to thy hive.
　　　Now in more subtle wreaths I will entwine
80　My sinewy thighs, my legs and arms with thine;
　　Thou like a sea of milk shalt lie displayed,

---

6. Behind this metaphor of mine, mint, and coin
lies the ancient belief that in the creation of children woman contributes matter, and man, form
(*materia* and *forma*).
7. Venus rides in a chariot drawn by a yoke of
doves.

8. I.e., retort—a vessel used for distilling.
9. According to alchemical doctrine, skilled dis-
tillation could extract from common metals not
only the philosopher's stone but an ointment
("sovereign balm"), good to prevent as well as to
cure all diseases whatever.

Whilst I the smooth, calm ocèan invade
With such a tempest as when Jove of old
Fell down on Danaë in a storm of gold.[1]
85 Yet my tall pine shall in the Cyprian[2] strait
Ride safe at anchor and unlade her freight;
My rudder with thy bold hand like a tried
And skillful pilot thou shalt steer, and guide
My bark° into love's channel, where it shall   *vessel*
90 Dance as the bounding waves do rise or fall.
Then shall thy circling arms embrace and clip°   *clasp*
My naked body, and thy balmy lip
Bathe me in juice of kisses, whose perfume
Like a religious incense shall consume
95 And send up holy vapors to those powers
That bless our loves and crown our sportful hours,
That with such halcyon[3] calmness fix our souls
In steadfast peace, as no affright controls.°   *overpowers*
There no rude sounds shake us with sudden starts,
100 No jealous ears, when we unrip our hearts,
Suck our discourse in, no observing spies
This blush, that glance traduce;° no envious eyes   *slander*
Watch our close meetings, nor are we betrayed
To rivals by the bribèd chambermaid.
105 No wedlock bonds unwreathe our twisted loves,
We seek no midnight arbor, no dark groves
To hide our kisses; there the hated name
Of husband, wife, lust, modest, chaste, or shame
Are vain and empty words, whose very sound
110 Was never heard in the Elysian ground.
All things are lawful there that may delight
Nature or unrestrainèd appetite.
Like and enjoy, to will and act is one;
We only sin when love's rites are not done.
115   The Roman Lucrece there reads the divine
Lectures of love's great master, Aretine,
And knows as well as Laïs how to move
Her pliant body in the act of love.[4]
To quench the burning ravisher, she hurls
120 Her limbs into a thousand winding curls,
And studies artful postures, such as be
Carved on the bark of every neighboring tree
By learnèd hands, that so adorned the rind
Of those fair plants, which, as they lay entwined
125 Have fanned their glowing fires. The Grecian dame
That in her endless web toiled for a name
As fruitless as her work doth there display

1. Zeus (or Jove) wooed Danaë in a shower of gold, begetting Perseus.
2. Cyprus was reputed the birthplace of the goddess of love, Venus, sometimes called simply "the Cyprian." "Pine": mast, and by metonymy, ship.
3. While the halcyon (a legendary sea bird) nests on the waves, the ocean remains calm.

4. In Elysium, Lucrece (chastest of Roman matrons, who committed suicide to atone for the disgrace of her rape by Tarquin) reads Aretino (bawdiest of Italian pornographers) to provoke her attacker to new efforts. Laïs was a famous prostitute of Corinth.

Herself before the youth of Ithaca,
And th' amorous sport of gamesome nights prefer
130 Before dull dreams of the lost traveler.[5]
Daphne hath broke her bark, and that swift foot
Which th' angry gods had fastened with a root
To the fixed earth, doth now unfettered run
To meet th' embraces of the youthful sun.[6]
135 She hangs upon him like his Delphic lyre,[7]
Her kisses blow the old and breathe new fire;
Full of her god, she sings inspired lays,
Sweet odes of love, such as deserve the bays
Which she herself was.[8] Next her, Laura lies
140 In Petrarch's learnèd arms, drying those eyes
That did in such sweet smooth-paced numbers° flow,   *verses*
As made the world enamored of his woe.[9]
These and ten thousand beauties more, that died
Slave to the tyrant, now enlarged,[1] deride
145 His canceled laws, and for their time misspent
Pay into love's exchequer° double rent.   *treasury*
   Come then, my Celia, we'll no more forbear
To taste our joys, struck with a panic fear,
But will depose from his imperious sway
150 This proud usurper and walk free as they,
With necks unyoked; nor is it just that he
Should fetter your soft sex with chastity,
Which Nature made unapt for abstinence;
When yet this false impostor can dispense
155 With human justice and with sacred right,
And maugre° both their laws, command me fight   *in spite of*
With rivals or with emulous loves, that dare
Equal with thine their mistress' eyes or hair.
If thou complain of wrong, and call my sword
160 To carve out thy revenge, upon that word
He° bids me fight and kill, or else he brands   *i.e., Honor*
With marks of infamy my coward hands.
And yet religion bids from bloodshed fly,
And damns me for that act. Then tell me why
165 This goblin Honor which the world adores
Should make men atheists and not women whores.

1640

---

5. Penelope was the faithful wife of Odysseus
("the lost traveler"); during the twenty years
he was away (at Troy and on the way back), she
fended off her importunate suitors by weaving
an endless web—she unwove by night what she
wove by day—which she said she had to finish
before she could marry again. But in Elysium, she
welcomes "the youth of Ithaca" (the suitors) and
enjoys "gamesome nights" with them.
6. Closely pursued by Apollo, god of poetry and
the sun, Daphne cried out to her father, the river
god Peneus, who turned her into a laurel bush or
bay tree so that she could get away from Apollo.

7. The shrine of Apollo was at Delphi; he carries
a lyre as an emblem of poetic harmony.
8. The songs she sings deserve the laurel crown
of poetry—the laurel she had become.
9. Petrarch (1304–1374) wrote his celebrated
sonnet sequence to Laura, mourning his unsatisfied desire in the first part, and Laura's death
in the second.
1. The inhabitants of Elysium are liberated
("enlarged") from the prison of "the tyrant"
Honor, in which woman must be chaste and men
must fight duels.

RICHARD LOVELACE
1618–1657

The quintessential Cavalier, Richard Lovelace was described by a contemporary as "the most amiable and beautiful person that ever eye beheld." Born into a wealthy Kentish family, he was educated at Oxford and fought for Charles I in Scotland (in both expeditions, 1639 and 1640). He shared with his king a serious interest in art, especially the paintings of Rubens, Van Dyck, and Lely. He was imprisoned for a few months in 1642 for supporting the "Kentish Petition" that urged restoration of the king to his ancient rights; in "To Althea, from Prison," he finds freedom from external bondage in the Cavalier ideals of women, wine, and royalism. During 1643–46 he fought in Holland and France and in the king's armies in England and was wounded abroad. In a general roundup of known royalists in 1648 he was imprisoned for ten months, and while in prison prepared his poems for publication under the title *Lucasta* (1649). Besides witty and charming love songs, the volume includes the plaintive ballad about the conflict between love and honor, "To Lucasta, Going to the Wars," and also "The Grasshopper," a poem that presents the Cavalier ideal at its most attractive. Like that emblematic summer creature, the once-carefree Cavalier suffers in the Puritan "winter," but Lovelace finds in the fellowship of Cavalier friends a nobler version of the good life. After 1649 he endured years of poverty, largely dependent on the generosity of his friend and fellow royalist, Charles Cotton. His remaining poems appeared in 1659 as *Lucasta: Postume Poems*.

FROM LUCASTA

To Lucasta, Going to the Wars

Tell me not, sweet, I am unkind,
  That from the nunnery
Of thy chaste breast and quiet mind
  To war and arms I fly.

5 True, a new mistress now I chase,
  The first foe in the field;
And with a stronger faith embrace
  A sword, a horse, a shield.

Yet this inconstancy is such
10 As you too shall adore;
I could not love thee, dear, so much,
  Loved I not honor more.

1649

The Grasshopper[1]

To My Noble Friend, Mr. Charles Cotton

O thou that swing'st upon the waving hair
    Of some well-fillèd oaten beard,°   *head of grain*
Drunk every night with a delicious tear
    Dropped thee from heav'n, where now th' art reared,

5   The joys of earth and air are thine entire,
    That with thy feet and wings dost hop and fly;
And when thy poppy° works thou dost retire   *opiate*
    To thy carved acorn bed to lie.

Up with the day, the sun thou welcom'st then,
10   Sport'st in the gilt-plats° of his beams,   *golden fields*
And all these merry days mak'st merry men,
    Thyself, and melancholy streams.[2]

But ah, the sickle! golden ears are cropped,
    Ceres and Bacchus[3] bid goodnight;
15   Sharp frosty fingers all your flow'rs have topped,
    And what scythes spared, winds shave off quite.

Poor verdant fool! and now green ice! thy joys,
    Large and as lasting as thy perch of grass,
Bid us lay in 'gainst winter rain, and poise°   *counterbalance*
20   Their floods with an o'erflowing glass.

Thou best of men and friends! we will create
    A genuine summer in each other's breast;
And spite of this cold time and frozen fate
    Thaw us a warm seat to our rest.

25   Our sacred hearths shall burn eternally
    As vestal flames;[4] the North Wind, he
Shall strike his frost-stretched wings, dissolve, and fly
    This Etna in epitome.[5]

Dropping December shall come weeping in,
30   Bewail th' usurping of his reign;
But when in showers of old Greek we begin,
    Shall cry, he hath his crown again![6]

1. In *Aesop's Fables* the grasshopper lives in carefree idleness, in contrast with the industrious ant who lays up stores for the winter. The circumstances of the poem are those of the Interregnum, when a winter of Puritanism seemed, to royalists, to be settling over England and obliterating their mode of life. The grasshopper may also allude to the recently executed king, Charles I.
2. The three objects of "mak'st merry" are "men," "thyself," and "melancholy streams."
3. Goddess of grain and god of wine.
4. The Vestal Virgins, in Rome, were responsible for tending an eternal flame in the Temple of Vesta.
5. Boreas, the north wind, folding up ("striking") his wings, flees the heat of the volcano within Mount Etna, a figure for the fires of friendship.
6. Greek wine was favored in the classical world. "Crown" here has multiple associations: the crown worn by "King Christmas" at the festivities banned by Puritans; and the crown Cavaliers hoped would soon be restored to Charles II.

Night as clear Hesper° shall our tapers whip   *the evening star*
 From the light casements where we play,
35 And the dark hag[7] from her black mantle strip,
 And stick there everlasting day.

Thus richer than untempted kings are we,
 That asking nothing, nothing need:
Though lord of all that seas embrace, yet he
40 That wants° himself is poor indeed.   *lacks*

                1649

To Althea, from Prison

When Love with unconfinèd wings
 Hovers within my gates,
And my divine Althea brings
 To whisper at the grates;
5 When I lie tangled in her hair
 And fettered to her eye,
The gods[1] that wanton° in the air   *play*
 Know no such liberty.

When flowing cups run swiftly round,
10 With no allaying Thames,[2]
Our careless heads with roses bound,
 Our hearts with loyal flames;
When thirsty grief in wine we steep,
 When healths and drafts go free,
15 Fishes that tipple in the deep
 Know no such liberty.

When, like committed linnets,° I   *caged finches*
 With shriller throat shall sing
The sweetness, mercy, majesty,
20 And glories of my king;
When I shall voice aloud how good
 He is, how great should be,
Enlargèd winds, that curl the flood,
 Know no such liberty.

25 Stone walls do not a prison make,
 Nor iron bars a cage;
Minds innocent and quiet take
 That for an hermitage.
If I have freedom in my love,
30 And in my soul am free,

---

7. Hecate, a daughter of Night.
1. Some versions read "birds" instead of "gods."

2. No mixture of water (as from the river Thames) in the wine.

Angels alone, that soar above,
Enjoy such liberty.

1649

Love Made in the First Age.[1] To Chloris

In the nativity of time,
Chloris, it was not thought a crime
   In direct Hebrew for to woo.[2]
Now we make love as all on fire,
5 Ring retrograde[3] our loud desire,
   And court in English backward too.

Thrice happy was that golden age,
When compliment was construed rage,[4]
   And fine words in the center hid;
10 When cursèd *No* stained no maid's bliss,
And all discourse was summed in *Yes,*
   And naught forbade, but to forbid.

Love then unstinted, love did sip,
And cherries plucked fresh from the lip,
15   On cheeks and roses free he fed;
Lasses like autumn plums did drop,
And lads indifferently° did crop   *without preference*
   A flower and a maidenhead.

Then unconfinèd each did tipple
20 Wine from the bunch, milk from the nipple;
   Paps tractable as udders were;
Then equally the wholesome jellies
Were squeezed from olive trees and bellies,
   Nor suits of trespass did they fear.

25 A fragrant bank of strawberries,
Diapered° with violet's eyes,   *decorated, dappled*
   Was table, tablecloth, and fare;
No palace to the clouds did swell,
Each humble princess then did dwell
30   In the piazza[5] of her hair.

Both broken faith and th' cause of it,
All-damning gold, was damned to th' pit;

---

1. The Golden Age, described in Ovid's *Metamorphoses.*
2. Hebrew, supposed to be the original human language, is read from right to left; we have reversed this.
3. Backwards, in reverse. The term also has musical connotations, perhaps referring here to a pattern of bell ringing.
4. Passion. Compliments in the Golden Age were understood as ardent propositions.
5. Arcade, hence an artful structure.

Their troth, sealed with a clasp and kiss,
Lasted until that extreme day
35   In which they smiled their souls away,
And, in each other, breathed new bliss.

Because no fault, there was no tear;
No groan did grate the granting ear,
No false foul breath their del'cate smell:
40   No serpent kiss poisoned the taste,
Each touch was naturally chaste,
And their mere sense a miracle.

Naked as their own innocence,
And unembroidered from offense[6]
45   They went, above poor riches, gay;
On softer than the cygnet's° down,   *young swan*
In beds they tumbled of their own;
For each within the other lay.

Thus did they live; thus did they love,
50   Repeating only joys above;
And angels were, but with clothes on,
Which they would put off cheerfully,
To bathe them in the galaxy,°   *the Milky Way*
Then gird them with the heavenly zone.[7]

55   Now, Chloris, miserably crave°   *beg*
The offered bliss you would not have,
Which evermore I must deny,
Whilst ravished with these noble dreams
And crownèd with mine own soft beams,
60   Enjoying of my self I lie.

1659

---

6. I.e., not ornamented to hide an offense.   7. The zodiac of stars.

KATHERINE PHILIPS
1632–1664

T he best-known woman poet of her own and the next generation, Katherine
Philips was honored as "the Matchless Orinda," the classical name she chose
for herself in her poetic addresses to a coterie of chiefly female friends, especially
Mary Aubrey (M. A.) and Anne Owen (Lucasia). Sometimes reminiscent of Donne's
love lyrics and sometimes of the ancient Greek Sappho's erotic lyrics to women,

these poems develop an exalted ideal of female friendship as a Platonic union of souls. Born to a well-to-do Presbyterian family and educated at Mrs. Salmon's Presbyterian School, Philips was taken to Wales when her mother remarried. In 1648, at age seventeen, she was married to James Philips, a prominent member of Parliament. They lived together twelve years, chiefly in the small Welsh town of Cardigan, and had two children: Hector, whose death a few days after birth prompted one of her most moving poems, and Katherine, who lived to adulthood. A royalist despite her Puritan family connections, Philips forged connections with other displaced royalists. Her poems circulated in manuscript and elicited high praise from Vaughan in *Olor Iscanus*. They include elegies, epitaphs, poems at parting, and friendship poems to women and men, but also poetry on political themes: a denunciation of the regicide, "Upon the Double Murder of King Charles," and panegyrics on the restored Stuarts. After the Restoration, James Philips barely escaped execution as a regicide, had his estates confiscated, and lost his seat in Parliament, but Katherine became a favorite at court, promoted by her friend Sir Charles Cotterell ("Poliarchus"), who was master of ceremonies. In Ireland attempting (unsuccessfully) to redeem an investment, she translated Corneille's *Pompey* and her friend the Earl of Orrery produced and printed it in Dublin in 1663. The first edition of her poems, apparently pirated, appeared in 1664, the same year she died of smallpox. Her friend Cotterell brought out an authorized edition in 1667.

A Married State[1]

A married state affords but little ease
The best of husbands are so hard to please.
This in wives' careful° faces you may spell°   *full of cares / read*
Though they dissemble their misfortunes well.
5   A virgin state is crowned with much content;[2]
It's always happy as it's innocent.
No blustering husbands to create your fears;
No pangs of childbirth to extort your tears;
No children's cries for to offend your ears;
10 Few worldly crosses to distract your prayers:
Thus are you freed from all the cares that do
Attend on matrimony and a husband too.
Therefore Madam, be advised by me
Turn, turn apostate to love's levity,
15 Suppress wild nature if she dare rebel.
There's no such thing as leading apes in hell.[3]

ca. 1646   Ms; 1988

---

1. In a manuscript (Orielton MSS Box 24 at the National Library of Wales) this poem appears with another by Philips, addressed to Anne Barlow (whom she probably met in 1646); this one is probably also for Barlow. Both are signed by her maiden name, C. Fowler, so were evidently written before her marriage in 1648.
2. Praise of the single life is a common topic in women's poetry.
3. Proverbially, the fate of spinsters.

Upon the Double Murder of King Charles

In Answer to a Libelous Rhyme made by V. P.[1]

I think not on the state, nor am concerned
Which way soever that great helm[2] is turned,
But as that son whose father's danger nigh
Did force his native dumbness, and untie
5   His fettered organs: so here is a cause
That will excuse the breach of nature's laws.[3]
Silence were now a sin: nay passion now
Wise men themselves for merit would allow.[4]
What noble eye could see (and careless pass)
10 The dying lion kicked by every ass?
Hath Charles so broke God's laws, he must not have
A quiet crown, nor yet a quiet grave?
Tombs have been sanctuaries; thieves lie here
Secure from all their penalty and fear.
15 Great Charles his double misery was this,
Unfaithful friends, ignoble enemies;
Had any heathen been this prince's foe,
He would have wept to see him injured so.
His title was his crime, they'd reason good
20 To quarrel at the right they had withstood.
He broke God's laws, and therefore he must die,
And what shall then become of thee and I?
Slander must follow treason; but yet stay,
Take not our reason with our king away.
25 Though you have seized upon all our defense,
Yet do not sequester° our common sense.   confiscate
But I admire° not at this new supply: wonder
No bounds will hold those who at scepters fly.
Christ will be King, but I ne'er understood,
30 His subjects built his kingdom up with blood
(Except their own) or that he would dispense
With his commands, though for his own defense.
Oh! to what height of horror are they come
Who dare pull down a crown, tear up a tomb![5]

1649?   1664

---

1. The itinerant Welsh preacher Vavasour Powell was a Fifth Monarchist and an ardent republican who justified the regicide on the ground that Christ's second coming was imminent, when he would rule with his saints, putting down all earthly kings. His poem and Philips's answer were likely written shortly after Charles I's execution (January 30, 1649). Powell's poem has been published by Elizabeth H. Hageman in *English Manuscript Studies*.

2. Steering wheel for the "ships" of state.
3. Breaking the supposed law of nature that excludes women from speaking about public affairs.
4. Wise men, especially Stoic philosophers, normally counsel the firm control or elimination of passions.
5. Their slanders tear up Charles's tomb after his death.

Friendship's Mystery, To My Dearest *Lucasia*[1]

1

Come, my Lucasia, since we see
  That miracles men's faith do move,
By wonder and by prodigy
  To the dull angry world let's prove
5   There's a religion in our love.

2

For though we were designed t' agree,
  That fate no liberty destroys,
But our election is as free
  As angels, who with greedy choice
10   Are yet determined to their joys.[2]

3

Our hearts are doubled by the loss,
  Here mixture is addition grown;
We both diffuse,° and both engross:°   *spread out / collect*
  And we whose minds are so much one,
15   Never, yet ever are alone.

4

We court our own captivity
  Than thrones more great and innocent:
'Twere banishment to be set free,
  Since we wear fetters whose intent
20   Not bondage is, but ornament.

5

Divided joys are tedious found,
  And griefs united easier grow:
We are selves but by rebound,
  And all our titles shuffled so,
25   Both princes, and both subjects too.[3]

6

Our hearts are mutual victims laid,
  While they (such power in friendship lies)

---

1. This poem was first printed, with a musical setting by the royalist musician and composer Henry Lawes, as "Mutual Affection betweene *Orinda* and *Lucasia*" in Lawes's *The Second Book of Ayres* (1655); our text is from *Poems by the Most Deservedly Admired Mrs. Katherine Philips, the Matchless Orinda* (1667). Lucasia is Philips's name for her friend Anne Owen.
2. Angels, though created with free will, were thought to have become fixed in goodness when they turned toward God in the first moments after their creation.
3. Compare Donne, "The Sun Rising", line 21: "She is all states, and all princes, I" (p. 926).

Are altars, priests, and off'rings made:
  And each heart which thus kindly° dies,   *benevolently, naturally*
30 Grows deathless by the sacrifice.

1655, 1664

To Mrs. M. A.[1] at Parting

I have examined and do find,
  Of all that favor me
There's none I grieve to leave behind
  But only only thee.
5 To part with thee I needs must die,
Could parting separate thee and I.

But neither chance nor compliment
  Did element our love:
'Twas sacred sympathy was lent
10   Us from the choir above.
(That friendship fortune did create,
Still fears a wound from time or fate.)

Our changed and mingled souls are grown
  To such acquaintance now,
15 That if each would resume their own,
  Alas! we know not how.
We have each other so engrossed°   *absorbed*
That each is in the union lost.[2]

And thus we can no absence know,
20   Nor shall we be confined;
Our active souls will daily go
  To learn each other's mind.
Nay, should we never meet to sense,°   *physically*
Our souls would hold intelligence.°   *would still commune*

25 Inspirèd with a flame divine,
  I scorn to court a stay;[3]
For from that noble soul of thine
  I ne'er can be away.
But I shall weep when thou dost grieve;
30 Nor can I die whilst thou dost live.

By my own temper I shall guess
  At thy felicity,

1. M. A. was Mary Aubrey, the first and, until she married, the dearest member of Philips's "Society of Friendship." Orinda's valedictory poem to her—which Keats admired enough to copy it out in full in an early letter—recalls some of Donne's lyrics, especially "A Valediction: For- bidding Mourning" (pp. 935–36).
2. These lines play upon the Neoplatonic idea of friendship and spiritual love—two souls become one.
3. Postponement (of their parting).

And only like my happiness
    Because it pleaseth thee.
35 Our hearts at any time will tell
    If thou or I be sick or well.

All honor, sure, I must pretend,°   *aspire to*
    All that is good or great:
She that would be Rosania's[4] friend
40   Must be at least complete.
If I have any bravery,°   *splendor*
    'Tis cause I have so much of thee.

Thy leiger° soul in me shall lie,   *ambassadorial*
    And all thy thoughts reveal;
45 Then back again with mine shall fly,
    And thence to me shall steal.
Thus still to one another tend:
Such is the sacred name of friend.

Thus our twin souls in one shall grow,
50   And teach the world new love,
Redeem the age and sex, and show
    A flame fate dares not move:
And courting death to be our friend,
Our lives, together too, shall end.

55 A dew shall dwell upon our tomb
    Of such a quality
That fighting armies, thither come,
    Shall reconcilèd be.
We'll ask no epitaph, but say:
60 ORINDA and ROSANIA.

1664

On the Death of My First and Dearest Child, Hector Philips[1]

Twice forty months in wedlock[2] I did stay,
    Then had my vows crowned with a lovely boy.
And yet in forty days[3] he dropped away;
    O swift vicissitude of human joy!

5 I did but see him, and he disappeared,
    I did but touch the rosebud, and it fell;

---

4. The poetic name Philips gave to Mary Aubrey.
1. In Philips's manuscript the subtitle reads, "born the 23d of April, and died the 2d of May 1655. Set by Mr. Lawes." The musical setting has been published by Joan Applegate in *English*

Manuscript Studies.
2. Philips was married in August 1648.
3. The subtitle indicates that he lived barely ten days; the change here is clearly for the parallelism.

A sorrow unforeseen and scarcely feared,
    So ill can mortals their afflictions spell.°   *discern*

And now, sweet babe, what can my trembling heart
10   Suggest to right my doleful fate or thee?
Tears are my muse, and sorrow all my art,
    So piercing groans must be thy elegy.

Thus whilst no eye is witness of my moan,
    I grieve thy loss (ah, boy too dear to live!),
15   And let the unconcernèd world alone,
    Who neither will, nor can, refreshment give.

An off'ring too for thy sad tomb I have,
    Too just a tribute to thy early hearse.
Receive these gasping numbers to thy grave,
20   The last of thy unhappy mother's verse.[4]

1655   1667

4. This was not in fact Philips's last poem, but the sentiment is both true to human feeling and common in elegy. She had one other child, a year later—a daughter, Katherine, who survived her.

ANDREW MARVELL
1621–1678

Andrew Marvell's finest poems are second to none in this or any other period. He wrote less than Donne, Jonson, and Herbert did, but his range was in some ways greater, as he claimed both the private worlds of love and religion and the public worlds of political and satiric poetry and prose. His overriding concern with art, his elegant, well-crafted, limpid style, and the cool balance and reserve of some poems align him with Jonson. Yet his paradoxes and complexities of tone, his use of dramatic monologue, and his witty, dialectical arguments associate him with Donne. Above all, he is a supremely original poet, so complex and elusive that it is often hard to know what he really thought about the subjects he treated. Many of his poems were published posthumously in 1681, some thirty years after they were written, by a woman who claimed to be his widow but was probably his housekeeper. So their date and order of composition is often in doubt, as is his authorship of some anonymous works.

The son of a Church of England clergyman, Marvell grew up in Yorkshire, attended Trinity College, Cambridge (perhaps deriving the persistent strain of Neoplatonism in his poetry from the academics known as the Cambridge Platonists), ran off to London, and converted to Roman Catholicism until his father put an end to both ventures. He returned to Cambridge, took his degree in 1639, and stayed on as a scholar until his father's death in 1641. During the years of the civil wars (1642–48), he traveled in France, Italy, Holland, and Spain; much later he said of the Puritan "Good

Old Cause" that it was "too good to have been fought for." While his earliest poems associate him with royalists, those after 1649 celebrate the Commonwealth and Oliver Cromwell; although he is sometimes ambivalent, Marvell recognizes divine providence in the political changes. From 1650 to 1652 he lived at Nunappleton as tutor to the twelve-year-old daughter of Thomas Fairfax, who had given over his command of the parliamentary army to Cromwell because he was unwilling to invade Scotland. In these years of retirement and ease, Marvell probably wrote most of his love lyrics and pastorals as well as *Upon Appleton House*. Subsequently he was tutor to Cromwell's ward, William Dutton, and traveled with him on the Continent; in 1657 he joined the blind Milton, at Milton's request, in the post of Latin secretary to Cromwell's Council of State. Marvell accepted the Restoration but maintained his own independent vision and his abiding belief in religious toleration, a mixed state, and constitutional government. He helped his friend Milton avoid execution for his revolutionary polemics and helped negotiate Milton's release from a brief imprisonment. Elected a member of Parliament in 1659 from his hometown, Hull, in Yorkshire, he held that post until 1678, focusing his attention on the needs of his district; on two occasions he went on diplomatic missions—to Holland and Russia. His (necessarily anonymous) antiroyalist polemics of these years include several verse satires on Charles II and his ministers, as well as his best-known prose work, *The Rehearsal Transprosed* (1672–73), which defends Puritan dissenters and denounces censorship with verve and wit. He also wrote a brilliant poem of criticism and interpretation on Milton's *Paradise Lost* that was prefixed to the second edition (1674).

Many of Marvell's poems explore the human condition in terms of fundamental dichotomies that resist resolution. In religious or philosophical poems like "The Coronet" or "The Dialogue Between the Soul and Body," the conflict is between nature and grace, or body and soul, or poetic creation and sacrifice. In love poems such as "The Definition of Love" or "To His Coy Mistress," it is often between flesh and spirit, or physical sex and platonic love, or idealizing courtship and the ravages of time. In pastorals like the Mower poems and "The Garden," the opposition is between nature and art, or the fallen and the Edenic state, or violent passion and contentment. Marvell's most subtle and complex political poem, "An Horatian Ode upon Cromwell's Return from Ireland," sets stable traditional order and ancient right against providential revolutionary change, and the goods and costs of retirement and peace against those of action and war. *Upon Appleton House* also opposes the attractions of various kinds of retirement to the duties of action and reformation.

Marvell experimented with style and genre to striking effect. Many of his dramatic monologues are voiced by named, naive personas—the Mower, the Nymph—who stand at some remove from the author. "To His Coy Mistress," perhaps the best known of the century's carpe diem poems, is voiced by a witty and urbane speaker in balanced and artful couplets. But its rapid shifts from the world of fantasy to the charnel house of reality raise questions as to whether this is a clever seduction poem or a probing of existential angst, and whether Marvell intends to endorse or critique this speaker's view of passion and sex. In *Upon Appleton House* Marvell transforms the static, mythic features of Jonson's country-house poem "To Penshurst" to create a poem that incorporates history and the conflicts of contemporary society. It assimilates to the course of providential history the topographical features of the Fairfax estate, the Fairfax family myth of origin, the experiences of the poet-tutor on his progress around the estate, and the activities and projected future of the daughter of the house. In the poem's rich symbolism, biblical events—Eden, the first temptation, the Fall, the wilderness experience of the Israelites—find echoes in the experiences of the Fairfax family, the speaker, the history of the English Reformation, and the wanton destruction of the recent civil wars.

FROM Poems[1]

The Coronet[2]

When for the thorns with which I long, too long,
    With many a piercing wound,
    My Savior's head have crowned,
I seek with garlands to redress that wrong,
5   Through every garden, every mead,
I gather flowers (my fruits are only flowers),
    Dismantling all the fragrant towers°   *high headdress*
That once adorned my shepherdess's head:
And now, when I have summed up all my store,
10   Thinking (so I myself deceive)
    So rich a chaplet° thence to weave   *wreath*
As never yet the King of Glory wore,
    Alas! I find the serpent old,[3]
    That, twining° in his speckled breast,   *entwining*
15   About the flowers disguised does fold
    With wreaths of fame and interest.[4]
Ah, foolish man, that wouldst debase with them,
And mortal glory, heaven's diadem!
But thou who only couldst the serpent tame,
20   Either his slippery knots at once untie,
    And disentangle all his winding snare,
Or shatter too with him my curious frame,°   *elaborate construction*
    And let these wither, so that he may die,
    Though set with skill and chosen out with care;
25   That they, while thou on both their spoils dost tread,[5]
May crown thy feet, that could not crown thy head.

1650–52   1681

Bermudas[1]

    Where the remote Bermudas ride
    In th' ocean's bosom unespied,
    From a small boat that rowed along,
    The listening winds received this song:

5   "What should we do but sing His praise
    That led us through the wat'ry maze

1. Marvell's lyrics were published posthumously in 1681.
2. A floral wreath, also a garland of poems of praise.
3. Alludes to the serpent that tempted Eve (Genesis 3), traditionally understood to be an instrument for Satan.
4. Self-glorification, self-advancement.
5. See the curse on the serpent (Genesis 3.15), that the seed of Eve will bruise his head.

1. Otherwise known as the Summer Isles, the Bermudas were described in travel books like John Smith's *The General History of Virginia, New England, and the Summer Isles* (1624) as an Edenic paradise. The poem was probably written after 1653, when Marvell took up residence in the house of John Oxenbridge, who had twice visited the Bermudas.

Unto an isle so long unknown,
And yet far kinder than our own?
Where He the huge sea monsters wracks,[2]
10 That lift the deep upon their backs;
He lands us on a grassy stage,
Safe from the storms, and prelate's rage.[3]
He gave us this eternal spring
Which here enamels everything,
15 And sends the fowls to us in care,
On daily visits through the air;
He hangs in shades the orange bright,
Like golden lamps in a green night,
And does in the pomegranates close
20 Jewels more rich than Ormus[4] shows;
He makes the figs our mouths to meet,
And throws the melons at our feet;
But apples° plants of such a price,   *pineapples*
No tree could ever bear them twice;
25 With cedars, chosen by his hand
From Lebanon, he stores the land;
And makes the hollow seas that roar
Proclaim the ambergris[5] on shore;
He cast (of which we rather° boast)   *more properly*
30 The gospel's pearl upon our coast,
And in these rocks for us did frame
A temple, where to sound his name.
O let our voice his praise exalt
Till it arrive at heaven's vault,
35 Which, thence (perhaps) rebounding, may
Echo beyond the Mexique Bay."°   *Gulf of Mexico*

Thus sung they in the English boat
An holy and a cheerful note;
And all the way, to guide their chime,
40 With falling oars they kept the time.

ca. 1650–52   1681

A Dialogue Between the Soul and Body[1]

SOUL   O, who shall from this dungeon raise
A soul enslaved so many ways?[2]
With bolts of bones, that fettered stands

---

2. Probably an allusion to the event described in Edmund Waller's mock epic, a battle between the Bermudans and two stranded whales.
3. The Puritan settlers in Bermuda have escaped both the dangers of the sea voyage and religious persecution at home.
4. Hormuz, a pearl- and jewel-trading center in the Persian Gulf.

5. A substance found in sperm whales that was used in the manufacture of expensive perfume.
1. The poem derives from the medieval *debat* (debate) on this theme but alters the usual ending, which gives a clear victory to the soul.
2. The soul echoes Romans 7.24: "O wretched man that I am! who shall deliver me from the body of this death?"

In feet, and manacled in hands.
5 Here blinded with an eye, and there
Deaf with the drumming of an ear;
A soul hung up, as 'twere, in chains
Of nerves, and arteries, and veins;
Tortured, besides each other part,
10 In a vain head and double heart.

BODY   O, who shall me deliver whole
From bonds of this tyrannic soul?
Which, stretched upright, impales me so
That mine own precipice[3] I go;
15 And warms and moves this needless° frame   *without needs*
(A fever could but do the same),
And, wanting where° its spite to try,   *lacking an object*
Has made me live to let me die.
A body that could never rest
20 Since this ill spirit it possessed.

SOUL   What magic could me thus confine
Within another's grief to pine?
Where, whatsoever it complain,°   *suffer, complain of*
I feel, that cannot feel,[4] the pain;
25 And all my care itself employs,
That to preserve which me destroys;
Constrained not only to endure
Diseases, but, what's worse, the cure;
And, ready oft the port to gain,
30 Am shipwrecked into health again.

BODY   But physic° yet could never reach   *medicine*
The maladies thou me dost teach:
Whom first the cramp of hope does tear,
And then the palsy shakes of fear;
35 The pestilence of love does heat,
Or hatred's hidden ulcer eat;
Joy's cheerful madness does perplex,
Or sorrow's other madness vex;
Which knowledge forces me to know,
40 And memory will not forego.
What but a soul could have the wit
To build me up for sin so fit?
So architects do square and hew
Green trees that in the forest grew.

ca. 1650–52   1681

3. Having a soul allows humans to walk erect and so face the danger of falling.

4. The soul can sympathize ("feel") though it has no power of physical sensation.

The Nymph Complaining for the Death of Her Fawn[1]

The wanton troopers[2] riding by
Have shot my fawn, and it will die.
Ungentle men! They cannot thrive
To kill thee. Thou ne'er didst alive
5   Them any harm; alas, nor could
Thy death yet do them any good.
I'm sure I never wished them ill,
Nor do I for all this, nor will:
But if my simple prayers may yet
10   Prevail with heaven to forget
Thy murder, I will join my tears
Rather than fail. But, O my fears!
It cannot die so. Heaven's king
Keeps register of everything,
15   And nothing may we use in vain.
Even beasts must be with justice slain,
Else men are made their deodands.[3]
Though they should wash their guilty hands
In this warm lifeblood, which doth part
20   From thine, and wound me to the heart,
Yet could they not be clean; their stain
Is dyed in such a purple grain.
There is not such another in
The world to offer for their sin.
25   Unconstant Sylvio, when yet
I had not found him counterfeit,°   *false, deceitful*
One morning (I remember well),
Tied in this silver chain and bell,
Gave it to me; nay, and I know
30   What he said then, I'm sure I do.
Said he, Look how your huntsman here
Hath taught a fawn to hunt his dear.
But Sylvio soon had me beguiled;
This waxèd tame, while he grew wild,
35   And quite regardless of my smart,
Left me his fawn, but took his heart.[4]
     Thenceforth I set myself to play
My solitary time away
With this; and very well content
40   Could so mine idle life have spent.

1. The lament for the death of a pet is an ancient topic dating back to Catullus and Ovid; the closest analogue may be Virgil's story of Sylvia's deer killed wantonly by the Trojans (*Aeneid* 7.475ff). John Skelton has a mock-heroic poem on "Philip Sparrow." There are also echoes of the Song of Songs, which have prompted critical debate as to whether Marvell uses them with serious allegorical import or the nymph uses them quite inappropriately.

2. Soldiers of the invading Scots army were called "troopers" (ca. 1640), as were, sometimes, soldiers of Cromwell's New Model Army.

3. In English law, animals or objects forfeited to the Crown (literally, to God) because they were the immediate cause of a human being's death. The nymph applies the term to persons who cause the death of animals.

4. A pun: heart/hart (a deer); line 32 also puns on dear/deer.

For it was full of sport, and light
Of foot and heart, and did invite
Me to its game. It seemed to bless
Itself in me; how could I less
45 Than love it? O I cannot be
Unkind t' a beast that loveth me.
    Had it lived long, I do not know
Whether it too might have done so
As Sylvio did; his gifts might be
50 Perhaps as false or more than he.
But I am sure, for aught that I
Could in so short a time espy,
Thy love was far more better than
The love of false and cruel men.
55   With sweetest milk and sugar first
I it at mine own fingers nursed.
And as it grew, so every day
It waxed more sweet and white than they.
It had so sweet a breath! and oft
60 I blushed to see its foot more soft
And white—shall I say than my hand?—
Nay, any lady's of the land.
    It is a wondrous thing how fleet
'Twas on those little silver feet,
65 With what a pretty skipping grace
It oft would challenge me the race;
And when it had left me far away,
'Twould stay, and run again, and stay.
For it was nimbler much than hinds,[5]
70 And trod, as on the four winds.
    I have a garden of my own
But so with roses overgrown
And lilies that you would it guess
To be a little wilderness.
75 And all the springtime of the year
It only lovèd to be there.
Among the beds of lilies, I
Have sought it oft where it should lie,
Yet could not, till itself would rise,
80 Find it, although before mine eyes.
For in the flaxen lilies' shade
It like a bank of lilies laid.
Upon the roses it would feed,
Until its lips ev'n seemed to bleed;
85 And then to me 'twould boldly trip
And print those roses on my lip.
But all its chief delight was still
On roses thus itself to fill,
And its pure virgin limbs to fold
90 In whitest sheets of lilies cold.

5. I.e., full-grown deer.

Had it lived long, it would have been
Lilies without, roses within.
   O help! O help! I see it faint,
And die as calmly as a saint.
95 See how it weeps.[6] The tears do come
Sad, slowly dropping like a gum.
So weeps the wounded balsam, so
The holy frankincense doth flow.[7]
The brotherless Heliades
100 Melt in such amber tears as these.[8]
   I in a golden vial will
Keep these two crystal tears, and fill
It till it do o'erflow with mine,
Then place it in Diana's shrine.[9]
105   Now my sweet fawn is vanished to
Whither the swans and turtles° go,   *turtledoves*
In fair Elysium[1] to endure
With milk-white lambs and ermines pure.
O do not run too fast, for I
110 Will but bespeak° thy grave, and die.   *give orders for*
   First my unhappy statue shall
Be cut in marble, and withal,
Let it be weeping too; but there
Th' engraver sure his art may spare,
115 For I so truly thee bemoan
That I shall weep, though I be stone:[2]
Until my tears, still dropping, wear
My breast, themselves engraving there.
There at my feet shalt thou be laid,
120 Of purest alabaster made;
For I would have thine image be
White as I can, though not as thee.

ca. 1650–52   1681

To His Coy Mistress

   Had we but world enough, and time,
This coyness, lady, were no crime.
We would sit down, and think which way
To walk, and pass our long love's day.
5 Thou by the Indian Ganges' side
Shouldst rubies find; I by the tide

---

6. Deer were supposed to weep as they died.
7. Both balsam and frankincense are fragrant resins obtained a drop at a time from trees with holes bored in them.
8. The three daughters of the sun (Helios), grieving the death of their rash brother Phaëthon, were transformed to black poplar trees dropping "tears" of amber.
9. Diana was the goddess of chastity and woodland creatures; nymphs were her attendants.
1. The Elysian fields, a pagan version of heaven.
2. Niobe, lamenting the death of her many children, in whom she took inordinate pride, was turned to stone.

Of Humber would complain.[1] I would
Love you ten years before the Flood,
And you should, if you please, refuse
10 Till the conversion of the Jews.[2]
My vegetable love should grow
Vaster than empires, and more slow;
An hundred years should go to praise
Thine eyes, and on thy forehead gaze;
15 Two hundred to adore each breast,
But thirty thousand to the rest:
An age at least to every part,
And the last age should show your heart.
For, lady, you deserve this state,° *dignity*
20 Nor would I love at lower rate.
   But at my back I always hear
Time's wingèd chariot hurrying near;
And yonder all before us lie
Deserts of vast eternity.
25 Thy beauty shall no more be found,
Nor, in thy marble vault, shall sound
My echoing song; then worms shall try
That long-preserved virginity,
And your quaint[3] honor turn to dust,
30 And into ashes all my lust:
The grave's a fine and private place,
But none, I think, do there embrace.
   Now therefore, while the youthful hue
Sits on thy skin like morning dew,[4]
35 And while thy willing soul transpires
At every pore with instant fires,[5]
Now let us sport us while we may,
And now, like amorous birds of prey,
Rather at once our time devour
40 Than languish in his slow-chapped[6] power.
Let us roll all our strength and all
Our sweetness up into one ball,
And tear our pleasures with rough strife
Thorough° the iron gates of life:[7] *through*
45 Thus, though we cannot make our sun
Stand still, yet we will make him run.[8]

ca. 1650–52   1681

---

1. The exotic river Ganges in India is on one side of the world, the Humber flows past Marvell's city, Hull, on the opposite side. Complaints are poems of plaintive, unavailing love.

2. Popular belief had it that the Jews were to be converted just before the Last Judgment. The exaggerated offers in this stanza play off against conventional hyperbolic declarations of love in Petrarchan poetry.

3. "Quaint" puns on "out of date" and *queynte*, a term for the female genitals.

4. The text reads "glew," which could be correct, but "dew" is a common emendation.

5. Urgent, sudden enthusiasm. "Transpires": breathes forth.

6. Slowly devouring jaws.

7. One manuscript reads "grates," a somewhat different figure for the sexual act proposed.

8. The sun stood still for Joshua (Joshua 10.12) in his war against Gibeon; see the very different resolution in Donne's "The Sun Rising" (p. 926).

The Definition of Love

My Love is of a birth as rare
As 'tis, for object, strange and high;
It was begotten by Despair
Upon Impossibility.

5   Magnanimous Despair alone
Could show me so divine a thing,
Where feeble Hope could ne'er have flown
But vainly flapped its tinsel wing.

And yet I quickly might arrive
10 Where my extended soul is fixed;[1]
But Fate does iron wedges drive,
And always crowds itself betwixt.

For Fate with jealous eye does see
Two perfect loves, nor lets them close;°   *unite*
15 Their union would her ruin be,
And her tyrannic power depose.[2]

And therefore her decrees of steel
Us as the distant poles have placed
(Though Love's whole world on us doth wheel),[3]
20 Not by themselves to be embraced,

Unless the giddy heaven fall,
And earth some new convulsion tear,
And, us to join, the world should all
Be cramped into a planisphere.[4]

25 As lines, so loves oblique may well
Themselves in every angle greet;[5]
But ours, so truly parallel,
Though infinite, can never meet.

Therefore the Love which us doth bind,
30 But Fate so enviously debars,
Is the conjunction of the mind,
And opposition of the stars.[6]

ca. 1650–52   1681

1. The soul has extended itself from the speaker's body and fixed itself to his lover.
2. Two perfections, united, would not be subject to change and thereby to Fate.
3. Rotates as on its axis.
4. A two-dimensional map of the world; Marvell images a round globe collapsed into a flat pancake shape, top to bottom, which would bring the two poles together.
5. Oblique lines can touch in angles, as might "oblique" lovers that (in one meaning of the term) "deviate from right conduct or thought."
6. "Conjunction" is the coming together of two heavenly bodies in the same sign of the zodiac; "opposition" places them at diametrical opposites.

The Picture of Little T. C. in a Prospect of Flowers[1]

See with what simplicity
This nymph begins her golden days!
In the green grass she loves to lie,
And there with her fair aspect tames
5   The wilder flowers and gives them names,
But only with the roses plays,
      And them does tell
What color best becomes them and what smell.

Who can foretell for what high cause
10   This darling of the gods was born?
Yet this is she whose chaster laws
The wanton Love shall one day fear,
And under her command severe
See his bow broke and ensigns° torn.   *flags, pennants*
15   Happy who can
Appease this virtuous enemy of man!

O then let me in time compound°   *come to terms*
And parley with those conquering eyes
Ere they have tried their force to wound,
20   Ere with their glancing wheels they drive
In triumph over hearts that strive
And them that yield but more despise:
      Let me be laid
Where I may see thy glories from some shade.

25   Meantime, whilst every verdant thing
Itself does at thy beauty charm,
Reform the errors of the spring;
Make that the tulips may have share
Of sweetness, seeing they are fair;
30   And roses of their thorns disarm:
      But most procure
That violets may a longer age endure.

But O, young beauty of the woods,
Whom Nature courts with fruit and flowers,
35   Gather the flowers but spare the buds,
Lest Flora,[2] angry at thy crime
To kill her infants in their prime,
Do quickly make th' example yours;
      And ere we see,
40   Nip in the blossom all our hopes and thee.

ca. 1650–52   1681

1. The little girl, T. C., has not been identified with any certainty. "Prospect": landscape.

2. Roman goddess of flowers.

The Mower Against Gardens[1]

Luxurious° man, to bring his vice in use,[2]   *voluptuous*
    Did after him the world seduce,
And from the fields the flowers and plants allure,
    Where Nature was most plain and pure.
5 He first enclosed within the garden's square
    A dead and standing pool of air,
And a more luscious earth for them did knead,
    Which stupefied them while it fed.
The pink grew then as double as his mind;[3]
10   The nutriment did change the kind.
With strange perfumes he did the roses taint;
    And flowers themselves were taught to paint.
The tulip white did for complexion seek,
    And learned to interline its cheek;
15 Its onion root they then so high did hold,
    That one was for a meadow sold;[4]
Another world was searched through oceans new,
    To find the marvel of Peru;[5]
And yet these rarities might be allowed
20   To man, that sovereign thing and proud,
Had he not dealt between the bark and tree,[6]
    Forbidden mixtures there to see.
No plant now knew the stock from which it came;
    He grafts upon the wild the tame,
25 That the uncertain and adult'rate fruit
    Might put the palate in dispute.
His green seraglio[7] has its eunuchs too,
    Lest any tyrant him outdo;
And in the cherry he does Nature vex,
30   To procreate without a sex.[8]
'Tis all enforced, the fountain and the grot,°   *grotto*
    While the sweet fields do lie forgot,
Where willing Nature does to all dispense
    A wild and fragrant innocence;
35 And fauns and fairies do the meadows till
    More by their presence than their skill.
Their statues polished by some ancient hand
    May to adorn the gardens stand;

---

1. The four "Mower" poems are linked by their treatment of a distinctly unusual pastoral figure, a mower rather than a shepherd or goatherd, who provides a singular perspective on those familiar pastoral topics, nature versus art and nature's sympathy for man (the pathetic fallacy). As mower wielding a scythe, he evokes other figures (Time, Death).
2. Into common practice.
3. The double pink, or carnation, is a product of sophisticated ("double") minds.
4. A highly lucrative trade in Dutch tulip bulbs flourished during the 17th century.
5. *Mirabilis jalapa*, the four-o'clock, was an exotic, multicolored flower found originally in tropical America.
6. An adage for interfering between husband and wife, in reference, apparently, to grafting.
7. Enclosure, a harem in a sultan's palace.
8. Cherries were commonly propagated by grafting.

But, howsoe'er the figures do excel,
40   The gods themselves with us do dwell.

ca. 1650–52   1681

Damon the Mower

Hark how the mower Damon sung,
With love of Juliana stung![1]
While everything did seem to paint
The scene more fit for his complaint.[2]
5   Like her fair eyes the day was fair,
But scorching like his amorous care;
Sharp, like his scythe, his sorrow was,
And withered, like his hopes, the grass.

"Oh what unusual heats are here,
10 Which thus our sunburned meadows sear!
The grasshopper its pipe gives o'er,
And hamstringed° frogs can dance no more: *disabled*
But in the brook the green frog wades,
And grasshoppers seek out the shades.
15 Only the snake, that kept within,
Now glitters in its second skin.

"This heat the sun could never raise,
Nor Dog Star so inflame the days;[3]
It from an higher beauty grow'th,
20 Which burns the fields and mower both;
Which mads the dog, and makes the sun
Hotter than his own Phaëton.[4]
Not Jùly causeth these extremes,
But Juliana's scorching beams.

25 "Tell me where I may pass the fires
Of the hot day or hot desires,
To what cool cave shall I descend,
Or to what gelid° fountain bend?   *icy*
Alas! I look for ease in vain,
30 When remedies themselves complain:[5]
No moisture but my tears do rest,
No cold but in her icy breast.

1. Damon is a familiar classical name in pastoral; Juliana gets her name from July (lines 23–24).
2. The plaintive love song of an unrequited lover.
3. The Dog Star (Sirius in the constellation Canis Major) rises with the sun in late summer, producing the heats of "dog days."

4. Phaëthon, son of Helios, the sun god of Greek mythology; he tried to drive his father's chariot but let the horses run away and scorched the world.
5. I.e., fountain and cave themselves complain of unusual heat.

"How long wilt thou, fair shepherdess,
Esteem me and my presents less?
35 To thee the harmless snake I bring,
Disarmèd of its teeth and sting:
To thee chameleons, changing hue,
And oak leaves tipped with honeydew;
Yet thou, ungrateful, hast not sought
40 Nor what they are, nor who them brought.

"I am the mower Damon, known
Through all the meadows I have mown.
On me the morn her dew distills
Before her darling daffodils,
45 And if at noon my toil me heat,
The sun himself licks off my sweat;
While, going home, the evening sweet
In cowslip-water bathes my feet.

"What though the piping shepherd stock
50 The plains with an unnumbered flock?
This scythe of mine discovers° wide   *uncovers*
More ground than all his sheep do hide.
With this the golden fleece I shear
Of all these closes every year,[6]
55 And though in wool more poor than they,
Yet I am richer far in hay.

"Nor am I so deformed to sight
If in my scythe I lookèd right;
In which I see my picture done
60 As in a crescent moon the sun.
The deathless fairies take me oft
To lead them in their dances soft,
And when I tune myself to sing,
About me they contract their ring.[7]

65 "How happy might I still have mowed,
Had not Love here his thistles sowed!
But now I all the day complain,
Joining my labor to my pain;
And with my scythe cut down the grass,
70 Yet still my grief is where it was;
But when the iron blunter grows,
Sighing, I whet my scythe and woes."

While thus he threw his elbow round,
Depopulating all the ground,
75 And with his whistling scythe does cut
Each stroke between the earth and root,

6. Hay is the "wool" of the fields ("closes").
7. I.e., the "fairy ring," a discolored circle of grass popularly supposed to result from fairies dancing there.

The edgèd steel, by careless chance,
Did into his own ankle glance,
And there among the grass fell down[8]
80   By his own scythe the mower mown.

"Alas!" said he, "these hurts are slight
To those that die by Love's despite.
With shepherd's purse and clown's° all-heal[9]   *rustic's*
The blood I stanch and wound I seal.
85   Only for him no cure is found
Whom Juliana's eyes do wound.
'Tis Death alone that this must do;
For, Death, thou art a mower too."

ca. 1650–52   1681

The Mower to the Glowworms

Ye living lamps, by whose dear light
The nightingale does sit so late,
And studying all the summer night
Her matchless songs does meditate,

5   Ye country comets, that portend
No war nor prince's funeral,
Shining unto no higher end
Than to presage the grass's fall;

Ye glowworms, whose officious° flame   *helpful*
10   To wand'ring mowers shows the way,
That in the night have lost their aim,
And after foolish fires° do stray;   *will-o'-the-wisps*

Your courteous fires in vain you waste,
Since Juliana here is come,
15   For she my mind hath so displaced
That I shall never find my home.

ca. 1650–52   1681

The Mower's Song

My mind was once the true survey
Of all these meadows fresh and gay,
And in the greenness of the grass

---

8. Evokes the biblical phrase "All flesh is grass"
(Isaiah 40.6).

9. Folk names for popular remedies to heal
wounds, found in fields and hedges.

Did see its hopes[1] as in a glass;°   *mirror*
5   When Juliana came, and she,
What I do to the grass, does to my thoughts and me.[2]

But these, while I with sorrow pine,
Grew more luxuriant still and fine,
That not one blade of grass you spied
10   But had a flower on either side;
When Juliana came, and she,
What I do to the grass, does to my thoughts and me.

Unthankful meadows, could you so
A fellowship so true forego,
15   And in your gaudy May-games[3] meet,
While I lay trodden under feet?
When Juliana came, and she,
What I do to the grass, does to my thoughts and me.

But what you in compassion ought
20   Shall now by my revenge be wrought,
And flowers, and grass, and I, and all,
Will in one common ruin fall;
For Juliana comes, and she,
What I do to the grass, does to my thoughts and me.

25   And thus ye meadows, which have been
Companions of my thoughts more green,
Shall now the heraldry become
With which I shall adorn my tomb;
For Juliana comes, and she,
30   What I do to the grass, does to my thoughts and me.

ca. 1650–52   1681

The Garden

How vainly men themselves amaze°   *bewilder*
To win the palm, the oak, or bays,[1]
And their uncessant labors see
Crowned from some single herb or tree,
5   Whose short and narrow-vergèd° shade   *edged*
Does prudently their toils upbraid;°   *reprove*
While all flowers and all trees do close°   *unite, agree*
To weave the garlands of repose!

---

1. Green is the color of hope.
2. The alexandrine (twelve-syllable line) used here is the only example of a refrain in Marvell.
3. Festivals and merrymaking marked the first of May, May Day.

1. Honors, respectively, for military, civic, and poetic achievement.

Fair Quiet, have I found thee here,
10 And Innocence, thy sister dear?
Mistaken long, I sought you then
In busy companies of men.
Your sacred plants, if here below,°   *on earth*
Only among the plants will grow;
15 Society is all but rude,
To° this delicious solitude.   *compared to*

No white nor red[2] was ever seen
So amorous as this lovely green.
Fond lovers, cruel as their flame,
20 Cut in these trees their mistress' name:
Little, alas, they know or heed
How far these beauties hers exceed!
Fair trees, wheresoe'er your barks I wound,
No name shall but your own be found.[3]

25 When we have run our passion's heat,
Love hither makes his best retreat.
The gods, that mortal beauty chase,
Still° in a tree did end their race: *always*
Apollo hunted Daphne so,
30 Only that she might laurel grow;
And Pan did after Syrinx speed,
Not as a nymph, but for a reed.[4]

What wondrous life is this I lead!
Ripe apples drop about my head;
35 The luscious clusters of the vine
Upon my mouth do crush their wine;
The nectarine and curious° peach   *exquisite*
Into my hands themselves do reach;
Stumbling on melons[5] as I pass,
40 Ensnared with flowers, I fall on grass.

Meanwhile the mind, from pleasure less,
Withdraws into its happiness;
The mind, that ocean where each kind
Does straight° its own resemblance find;[6]   *immediately*
45 Yet it creates, transcending these,
Far other worlds and other seas,

---

2. Colors traditionally associated with female beauty.
3. Marvell proposes to carve in the bark of trees not "Sylvia" or "Laura," but "Beech" and "Oak."
4. Apollo, the god of poetry, chased Daphne until she turned into a laurel (the emblematic reward of poets); Pan pursued Syrinx until she became a reed, out of which he made panpipes. The gods'

motives were, of course, sexual, not horticultural.
5. "Melons," with etymological roots in the Greek word for "apple," may recall the apple over which all humankind stumbled.
6. As the ocean supposedly contained a counterpart of every creature on land, so the ocean of the mind holds the innate ideas of all things (in Neoplatonic philosophy).

Annihilating all that's made
To a green thought in a green shade.

Here at the fountain's sliding foot,
50 Or at some fruit tree's mossy root,
Casting the body's vest° aside,   *garment*
My soul into the boughs does glide:
There like a bird it sits and sings,
Then whets° and combs its silver wings,   *preens*
55 And, till prepared for longer flight,
Waves in its plumes the various light.[7]

Such was that happy garden-state,
While man there walked without a mate:
After a place so pure and sweet,
60 What other help could yet be meet![8]
But 'twas beyond a mortal's share
To wander solitary there:
Two paradises 'twere in one
To live in paradise alone.

65 How well the skillful gardener drew
Of flowers and herbs this dial new,[9]
Where from above the milder sun
Does through a fragrant zodiac run;
And as it works, th' industrious bee
70 Computes its time[1] as well as we!
How could such sweet and wholesome hours
Be reckoned but with herbs and flowers?

ca. 1650–52   1681

An Horatian Ode

Upon Cromwell's Return from Ireland[1]

The forward° youth that would appear   *eager, ambitious*
Must now forsake his Muses dear,
Nor in the shadows sing
His numbers languishing:

---

7. The multicolored light of this world, contrasted with the white radiance of eternity.
8. Genesis 2.18 recounts the Lord's decision to make a "help meet" for Adam, Eve.
9. The garden itself is laid out as a sundial.
1. With a pun on "thyme."
1. Oliver Cromwell, the general primarily responsible for Parliament's victory in the civil war, returned from conquering Ireland in May 1650, about eighteen months after the execution of

Charles I. The two events were persistently connected: Cromwell's success in Ireland was taken as a sign of God's favor to the new republican regime and to Cromwell as his chosen instrument. Pindaric odes (like Jonson's Cary-Morison ode, pp. 1101–05) are heroic and ecstatic; Horatian odes are poems of cool and balanced judgment, as this one is in its representations of Cromwell, Charles I, and the issues of power and providence.

The Execution of Charles I. A German print illustrates the beheading of Charles I before an enormous crowd, on a scaffold erected in front of the Banqueting House. At the top of the picture small portraits of General Fairfax and Cromwell, leaders of the Parliamentary forces, flank a portrait of King Charles, to whom an angel in the clouds is extending a heavenly crown. In the lower right corner, a woman faints.

5   'Tis time to leave the books in dust
And oil th' unusèd armor's rust,
      Removing from the wall
      The corselet° of the hall.[2]   *upper body armor*

So restless Cromwell could not cease
10   In the inglorious arts of peace,
      But through adventurous war
      Urgèd his active star;[3]

And, like the three-forked lightning, first
Breaking the clouds where it was nursed,
15   Did through his own side
      His fiery way divide:[4]

2. Here as elsewhere there are allusions to Lucan's *Pharsalia*, a poem of civil war whose sympathies are with Pompey, Cato, and the Roman Republic against Caesar and the empire. The poem's allusions to Caesar are most often to Charles I, but sometimes to Cromwell.
3. Normally the stars are thought to control men's fates, but Cromwell presses his own star forward.
4. The "three-forked lightning" identifies him with Zeus, suggesting the elemental force by which he surpassed all those in his own party ("side") of radical Independents; the imagery of giving birth to himself also suggests going Caesar (born by cesarean section) one better.

For 'tis all one to courage high,
The emulous, or enemy;
    And with such, to enclose
20   Is more than to oppose.

Then burning through the air he went,
And palaces and temples rent;
    And Caesar's head at last
    Did through his laurels blast.[5]

25 'Tis madness to resist or blame
The force of angry heaven's flame;
    And if we would speak true,
    Much to the man is due,

Who from his private gardens, where
30 He lived reservèd and austere
    (As if his highest plot
    To plant the bergamot),[6]

Could by industrious valor climb
To ruin the great work of time,
35   And cast the kingdom old
    Into another mold;

Though Justice against Fate complain,
And plead the ancient rights in vain:
    But those do hold or break,
40   As men are strong or weak.

Nature that hateth emptiness,
Allows of penetration less,[7]
    And therefore must make room
    Where greater spirits come.

45 What field of all the civil wars
Where his were not the deepest scars?
    And Hampton shows what part
    He had of wiser art;[8]

Where, twining subtle fears with hope,
50 He wove a net of such a scope
    That Charles himself might chase
    To Caresbrooke's narrow case,

5. Royal crowns were made of laurel because they were supposed to protect from lightning.
6. A pear-shaped orange (from the Turkish, "prince's pear").
7. Nature abhors a vacuum, but even more, the penetration of one body's space by another body.
8. Charles was confined at Hampton Court after his defeat, as Parliament attempted to negotiate terms for his restoration. Cromwell was rumored to have connived at his escape to Carisbrooke Castle, on the Isle of Wight, in order to convince Parliament that he could not be trusted and must be executed. Cromwell has shown himself master of the two "arts" of rule defined by Machiavelli, namely, force and craft.

That thence the royal actor[9] borne,
The tragic scaffold might adorn;
55   While round the armèd bands
     Did clap their bloody hands.

He nothing common did or mean
Upon that memorable scene,
     But with his keener eye
60   The ax's edge[1] did try;

Nor called the gods with vulgar spite
To vindicate his helpless right;
     But bowed his comely head
     Down, as upon a bed.

65 This was that memorable hour,
Which first assured the forcèd power;
     So when they did design
     The Capitol's first line,

A bleeding head where they begun
70 Did fright the architects to run;
     And yet in that the state
     Foresaw its happy fate.[2]

And now the Irish are ashamed
To see themselves in one year tamed;
75   So much one man can do,
     That does both act and know.

They can affirm his praises best,
And have, though overcome, confessed
     How good he is, how just,
80   And fit for highest trust.[3]

Nor yet grown stiffer with command,
But still in the republic's hand—
     How fit he is to sway,
     That can so well obey.[4]

9. The theater metaphors used for Charles are even more powerful because the "tragic scaffold" was erected outside Whitehall, where so many royal masques were produced. See a depiction of the king's execution on p. 1357.
1. A play on the Latin *acies*, which means the edge of a sword or ax, a keen glance, and the vanguard of a battle. Cf. the newsbook account of the king's execution, pp. 1388–91.
2. Livy and Pliny record that the workmen digging the foundations for a temple of Jupiter at Rome uncovered a bloody head which they were persuaded to take as an omen that Rome would be head (*caput*) of a great empire; the temple and the hill took the name Capitoline from that event.
3. Cromwell conducted a particularly brutal campaign in Ireland, and the Irish had no such testimonials for him; the lines are deeply equivocal.
4. The maxim about obedience fitting one to rule is a commonplace. The implications of "yet" and "still," along with the next stanza, suggest a Caesar figure who has not—but might—cross the Rubicon and defy the Republic, as Julius Caesar did.

85   He to the Commons' feet presents
        A kingdom for his first year's rents;
            And, what he may, forbears
            His fame to make it theirs;[5]

    And has his sword and spoils ungirt,
90   To lay them at the public's skirt:
            So, when the falcon high
            Falls heavy from the sky,

    She, having killed, no more does search,
    But on the next green bough to perch;
95   Where, when he first does lure,
           The falconer has her sure.

    What may not then our isle presume,
    While victory his crest does plume!
           What may not others fear,
100   If thus he crown each year!

    A Caesar he ere long to Gaul,
    To Italy an Hannibal,
           And to all states not free,
           Shall climactèric be.[6]

105   The Pict no shelter now shall find
    Within his parti-colored mind,
           But from this valor sad,°   *severe, solemn*
           Shrink underneath the plaid;[7]

    Happy if in the tufted brake
110   The English hunter him mistake,
           Nor lay his hounds in near
           The Caledonian° deer.   *Scottish*

    But thou, the war's and Fortune's son,
    March indefatigably on;
115   And for the last effect,
         Still keep thy sword erect;

    Besides the force it has to fright
    The spirits of the shady night,[8]

---

5. Thus far, Cromwell gives the Republic credit for his victories.

6. It was thought that Cromwell's military acumen might subdue France and Italy (which threatened to attack the new republic to restore Charles II), just as did Caesar and Hannibal of old. "Climacteric": a period of crucial, epochal change—here, the expectation that the example of a successful English republic would topple absolute monarchs abroad.

7. Early Scots were called Picts (from the Latin *pictus,* painted), because the warriors painted themselves many colors; contemporary Scots are "parti-colored" (divided into many factions) like a scotch plaid. Cromwell was about to go to subdue Scotland, which had declared for Charles II.

8. A sword carried with the blade upright evokes the classical tradition that underworld spirits (here, the slain king and his followers) are frightened off by raised weapons.

The same arts that did gain
A power must it maintain.[9]

120

1650

1650   1681

Upon Appleton House[1]

To My Lord Fairfax

1

Within this sober frame expect
Work of no foreign architect,
That unto caves the quarries drew,
And forests did to pastures hew;
5 Who of his great design in pain
Did for a model vault his brain,[2]
Whose columns should so high be raised
To arch the brows that on them gazed.

2

Why should of all things man unruled
10 Such unproportioned dwellings build?
The beasts are by their dens expressed,
And birds contrive an equal nest;[3]
The low-roofed tortoises do dwell
In cases fit of tortoiseshell:
15 No creature loves an empty space;
Their bodies measure out their place.

3

But he, superfluously spread,
Demands more room alive than dead;
And in his hollow palace goes
20 Where winds as he themselves may lose.
What need of all this marble crust

9. The maxim alludes to Machiavelli's advice that a kingdom won by force must for some time be maintained by force.
1. From 1651 to 1653, Marvell served as tutor to Mary Fairfax, daughter of Ann Vere and Thomas Fairfax, commander in chief of the parliamentary army throughout the civil wars. Fairfax opposed the regicide and in 1650 resigned his command rather than lead a preemptive strike against Scotland (which had declared for Charles II). Cromwell took over as Fairfax retired to his country estates in Yorkshire, especially Nunappleton, a comparatively simple brick structure on the site of a former Cistercian priory dissolved by Henry VIII along with all monasteries in 1542. The poem makes the house and its history figure the progress of the Reformation and the recent civil wars, played off against the Fall, the conflicts of the Israelites in the wilderness, and other biblical moments. The poem is structured as a journey around the estate, intersected by a long passage of family history. It was apparently written in the summer of 1651, when Mary Fairfax was twelve.
2. Did design in his brain the absurdly high vaulted ceilings of grand, magnificent houses built for showy display. This poem invites comparison and contrast with other country-house poems and the houses, estates, and society they describe: Jonson's "To Penshurst" (pp. 1096–98), Lanyer's "Description of Cookham" (pp. 986–90), and Carew's "To Saxham" (pp. 1323–25).
3. I.e., a nest proportioned to their size.

T' impark the wanton mote of dust,
That thinks by breadth the world t' unite
Though the first builders[4] failed in height?

4

25   But all things are composèd here
Like nature, orderly and near:
In which we the dimensions find
Of what more sober age and mind,
When larger sizèd men did stoop
30   To enter at a narrow loop;
As practicing, in doors so strait,
To strain themselves through heaven's gate.

5

And surely when the after age
Shall hither come in pilgrimage,
35   These sacred places to adore,
By Vere and Fairfax trod before,
Men will dispute how their extent
Within such dwarfish confines went;
And some will smile at this as well
40   As Romulus his bee-like cell.[5]

6

Humility alone designs
Those short but admirable lines,
By which, ungirt and unconstrained,
Things greater are in less contained.
45   Let other vainly strive t'immure
The circle in the quadrature![6]
These holy mathematics can
In ev'ry figure equal man.[7]

7

Yet thus the laden house does sweat,
50   And scarce endures the master great:
But where he comes the swelling hall
Stirs, and the square grows spherical;[8]
More by his magnitude distressed,
Than he is by its straitness pressed;
55   And too officiously° it slights   *overeagerly*
That in itself which him delights.

---

4. The proud builders of the Tower of Babel, who thought to make it reach to heaven (Genesis 11).
5. The thatched hut of the legendary founder of Rome.
6. To square the circle.
7. The circle symbolized perfection, the square variously virtue, justice, and prudence.
8. The square hall rises up into a domed cupola.

8

So honor better lowness bears,
Than that unwonted° greatness wears.   *unaccustomed*
Height with a certain grace does bend,
60   But low things clownishly° ascend.   *in rustic fashion*
And yet what needs there here excuse,
Where ev'ry thing does answer use?
Where neatness nothing can condemn,
Nor pride invent° what to contemn?   *find out*

9

65   A stately frontispiece of poor⁹
Adorns without the open door;
Nor less the rooms within commends
Daily new furniture of friends.
The house was built upon the place
70   Only as for a mark of grace;
And for an inn to entertain
Its lord a while, but not remain.¹

10

Him Bishops-Hill, or Denton may,
Or Bilbrough, better hold than they;
75   But Nature here hath been so free
As if she said, Leave this to me.
Art would more neatly° have defaced   *elegantly*
What she had laid so sweetly waste;
In fragrant gardens, shady woods,
80   Deep meadows, and transparent floods.

11

While with slow eyes we these survey,
And on each pleasant footstep stay,
We opportunely may relate
The progress of this house's fate.
85   A nunnery first gave it birth
For virgin buildings oft brought forth.
And all that neighbor-ruin shows
The quarries whence this dwelling rose.

12

Near to this gloomy cloister's gates
90   There dwelt the blooming virgin Thwaites²

---

9. Poor people awaiting Fairfax's alms.
1. The house is described as an inn, with an allusion to Hebrews 11.13–16 and the faithful who proclaim themselves "strangers and pilgrims on the earth" as they "desire a better country, that is, an heavenly."

2. In 1518 the heiress Isabel Thwaites was to marry Thomas Fairfax's ancestor, William, but was confined by her guardian, the prioress of Nunappleton; William obtained an order for her release and then seized her by force and married her.

Fair beyond measure, and an heir
Which might deformity make fair.
And oft she spent the summer suns
Discoursing with the subtle nuns.
95 Whence in these words one to her weaved
(As 'twere by chance) thoughts long conceived.

13

"Within this holy leisure we
Live innocently as you see.
These walls restrain the world without,
100 But hedge° our liberty about.   *defend*
These bars inclose that wider den
Of those wild creatures, callèd men;
The cloister outward shuts its gates,
And, from us, locks on them the grates.

14

105 "Here we, in shining armor white,°   *nun's habit*
Like virgin amazons do fight:
And our chaste lamps we hourly trim,
Lest the great bridegroom find them dim.[3]
Our orient° breaths perfumed are   *fresh*
110 With incense of incessant pray'r.
And holy water of our tears
Most strangely our complexion clears:

15

"Not tears of grief; but such as those
With which calm pleasure overflows;
115 Or pity, when we look on you
That live without this happy vow.
How should we grieve that must be seen
Each one a spouse, and each a queen;
And can in heaven hence behold
120 Our brighter robes and crowns of gold?

16

"When we have prayed all our beads,
Some one the holy legend° reads;   *a saint's life*
While all the rest with needles paint
The face and graces of the saint.
125 But what the linen can't receive
They in their lives do interweave.
This work the saints best represents;
That serves for altar's ornaments.

---

3. Matthew 25.1–13 contrasts the wise virgins who kept their lamps lit for the bridegroom (Christ) and
the foolish ones who did not and so were excluded from the marriage feast (heaven).

17

"But much it to our work would add
130 If here your hand, your face we had.
By it we would our Lady touch;[4]
Yet thus she you resembles much.
Some of your features, as we sewed,
Through every shrine should be bestowed:
135 And in one beauty we would take
Enough a thousand saints to make.

18

"And (for I dare not quench the fire
That me does for your good inspire)
'Twere sacrilege a man t' admit
140 To holy things, for heaven fit.
I see the angels in a crown
On you the lilies show'ring down;
And round about you glory breaks,
That something more than human speaks.

19

145 "All beauty, when at such a height,
Is so already consecrate.
Fairfax I know; and long ere this
Have marked the youth, and what he is.
But can he such a rival seem
150 For whom you heav'n should disesteem?
Ah, no! and 'twould more honor prove
He your devoto° were, than love.   devotee

20

"Here live beloved, and obeyed,
Each one your sister, each your maid.
155 And, if our rule seem strictly penned,
The rule itself to you shall bend.
Our abbess too, now far in age,
Doth your succession near presage.
How soft the yoke on us would lie,
160 Might such fair hands as yours it tie!

21

"Your voice, the sweetest of the choir,
Shall draw heav'n nearer, raise us higher:
And your example, if our head,
Will soon us to perfection lead.
165 Those virtues to us all so dear,

---

4. We could come close to representing the Virgin Mary in our designs with you as model.

Will straight° grow sanctity when here: *immediately*
And that, once sprung, increase so fast
Till miracles it work at last.

22

"Nor is our order yet so nice,°   *precise*
170   Delight to banish as a vice.
Here pleasure piety doth meet,
One perfecting the other sweet.
So through the mortal fruit we boil
The sugar's uncorrupting oil;
175   And that which perished while we pull,
Is thus preserved clear and full.

23

"For such indeed are all our arts;
Still handling nature's finest parts.
Flow'rs dress the altars; for the clothes,
180   The sea-born amber[5] we compose;
Balms for the grieved° we draw; and pastes   *injured*
We mold, as baits for curious tastes.
What need is here of man? unless
These as sweet sins we should confess.

24

185   "Each night among us to your side
Appoint a fresh and virgin bride;
Whom if our Lord at midnight find,
Yet neither should be left behind.
Where you may lie as chaste in bed,
190   As pearls together billeted,
All night embracing arm in arm,
Like crystal pure with cotton warm.

25

"But what is this to all the store
Of joys you see, and may make more!
195   Try but a while, if you be wise:
The trial neither costs, nor ties."
Now Fairfax seek her promised faith:°   *promise to wed*
Religion that dispensed hath;
Which she henceforward does begin:[6]
200   The nun's smooth tongue has sucked her in.

---

5. Ambergris from the sperm whale supplies the rich perfume for our altar cloths.

6. She now begins her "religious" life in the convent.

26

Oft, though he knew it was in vain,
Yet would he valiantly complain:
"Is this that sanctity so great,
An art by which you finelier cheat?
205 Hypocrite witches, hence avaunt,
Who though in prison yet enchant!
Death only can such thieves make fast,
As rob though in the dungeon cast.

27

"Were there but, when this house was made,
210 One stone that a just hand had laid,
It must have fall'n upon her head
Who first thee from thy faith misled.
And yet, how well soever meant,
With them 'twould soon grow fraudulent:
215 For like themselves they alter all,
And vice infects the very wall.

28

"But sure those buildings last not long,
Founded by folly, kept by wrong.
I know what fruit their gardens yield,
220 When they it think by night concealed.
Fly from their vices. 'Tis thy state,°   *estate*
Not thee, that they would consecrate.
Fly from their ruin. How I fear
Though guiltless lest thou perish there!"

29

225 What should he do? He would respect
Religion, but not right neglect;
For first religion taught him right,
And dazzled not but cleared his sight.
Sometimes resolved his sword he draws,
230 But reverenceth then the laws:
For justice still that courage led;
First from a judge, then soldier bred.[7]

30

Small honor would be in the storm.°   *storming the priory*
The court him grants the lawful form;
235 Which licensed either peace or force,
To hinder the unjust divorce.

7. His father was judge of the Common Pleas; his maternal grandfather was a heroic soldier.

Yet still the nuns his right debarred,
Standing upon their holy guard.
Ill-counseled women, do you know
240 Whom you resist, or what you do?

31

Is not this he whose offspring fierce
Shall fight through all the universe;
And with successive valor try
France, Poland, either Germany;
245 Till one, as long since prophesied,
His horse through conquered Britain ride?
Yet, against fate, his spouse they kept,
And the great race would intercept.[8]

32

Some to the breach against their foes
250 Their wooden saints in vain oppose.
Another bolder stands at push
With their old holy-water brush.
While the disjointed° abbess threads   *distracted*
The jingling chain-shot[9] of her beads.
255 But their loud'st cannon were their lungs;
And sharpest weapons were their tongues.

33

But, waving these aside like flies,
Young Fairfax through the wall does rise.
Then th' unfrequented vault appeared,
260 And superstitions vainly feared.
The relics false were set to view;
Only the jewels there were true—
But truly bright and holy Thwaites
That weeping at the altar waits.

34

265 But the glad youth away her bears
And to the nuns bequeaths her tears:
Who guiltily their prize bemoan,
Like gypsies that a child had stol'n.
Thenceforth (as when th' enchantment ends
270 The castle vanishes or rends)
The wasting cloister with the rest
Was in one instant dispossesed.[1]

---

8. Thomas Fairfax, son of William and Isabel
Thwaites, fought in Italy and Germany; his
descendants were also honored soldiers; the present Fairfax fulfilled the prophecy by his victories
in the Civil War.

9. Cannonballs linked in a chain and fired
together.
1. An allusion to Henry VIII's dissolution of the
monasteries.

35

At the demolishing, this seat
To Fairfax fell as by escheat.[2]
275 And what both nuns and founders willed
'Tis likely better thus fulfilled:
For if the virgin proved not theirs,
The cloister yet remained hers;
Though many a nun there made her vow,
280 'Twas no religious house till now.

36

From that blest bed the hero came,
Whom France and Poland yet does fame;
Who, when retired here to peace,
His warlike studies could not cease;
285 But laid these gardens out in sport
In the just figure of a fort;
And with five bastions it did fence,
As aiming one for ev'ry sense.[3]

37

When in the east the morning ray
290 Hangs out the colors of the day,
The bee through these known alleys hums,
Beating the dian° with its drums.   *reveille*
Then flow'rs their drowsy eyelids raise,
Their silken ensigns each displays,
295 And dries its pan[4] yet dank with dew,
And fills its flask° with odors new.   *powder flask*

38

These, as their governor goes by,
In fragrant volleys they let fly;
And to salute their governess
300 Again as great a charge they press:
None for the virgin nymph;[5] for she
Seems with the flow'rs a flow'r to be.
And think so still! though not compare[6]
With breath so sweet, or cheek so fair.

39

305 Well shot ye firemen!° Oh how sweet,   *shooters*
And round your equal fires do meet;

---

2. Legally, in the absence of an heir, the property reverted to him as lord of the manor; Henry
gave monastery lands to his nobles.
3. The garden's five (seeming) bulwarks or fortifications aim at the five senses.

4. In a musket, the hollow part of the lock that
receives the priming.
5. Mary Fairfax (Maria)—Marvell's pupil at Nunappleton.
6. The imperatives are addressed to the flowers.

Whose shrill report no ear can tell,
But echoes to the eye and smell.
See how the flow'rs, as at parade,
310 Under their colors stand displayed:
Each regiment in order grows,
That of the tulip, pink, and rose.

40

But when the vigilant patrol
Of stars walks round about the pole,
315 Their leaves, that to the stalks are curled,
Seem to their staves the ensigns furled.
Then in some flow'r's beloved hut
Each bee as sentinel is shut;
And sleeps so too: but, if once stirred,
320 She runs you through, nor asks the word.°   *password*

41

Oh thou,° that dear and happy isle   *England*
The garden of the world ere while,
Thou paradise of four[7] seas,
Which heaven planted us to please,
325 But, to exclude the world, did guard
With wat'ry if not flaming sword;[8]
What luckless apple did we taste,
To make us mortal, and thee waste?

42

Unhappy! shall we never more
330 That sweet militia restore,
When gardens only had their tow'rs,
And all the garrisons were flow'rs;
When roses only arms might bear,
And men did rosy garlands wear?
335 Tulips, in several colors barred,
Were then the Switzers[9] of our guard.

43

The gardener had the soldier's place,
And his more gentle forts did trace.
The nursery of all things green
340 Was then the only magazine.
The winter quarters were the stoves°   *hothouses*
Where he the tender plants removes.
But war all this doth overgrow;
We ordnance plant, and powder sow.

---

7. Pronounced with two syllables.
8. After the Fall, the garden in Eden was guarded by angels with flaming swords.

9. The papal Swiss guards wore multicolored uniforms.

44

345 And yet there walks one on the sod
Who, had it pleased him and God,
Might once have made our gardens spring
Fresh as his own and flourishing.
But he preferred to the Cinque Ports[1]
350 These five imaginary forts;
And, in those half-dry trenches, spanned°   *restrained*
Pow'r which the ocean might command.

45

For he did, with his utmost skill,
Ambition weed, but conscience till.
355 Conscience, that heaven-nursèd plant,
Which most our earthly gardens want.°   *lack, need*
A prickling leaf it bears, and such
As that which shrinks at every touch;
But flow'rs eternal, and divine,
360 That in the crowns of saints do shine.

46

The sight does from these bastions ply
Th' invisible artillery;
And at proud Cawood Castle[2] seems
To point the batt'ry of its beams,
365 As if it quarreled in° the seat   *found fault with*
Th' ambition of its prelate great;
But o'er the meads below it plays,
Or innocently seems to gaze.

47

And now to the abyss I pass
370 Of that unfathomable grass,
Where men like grasshoppers appear,
But grasshoppers are giants[3] there:
They, in their squeaking laugh, contemn
Us as we walk more low than them:
375 And, from the precipices tall
Of the green spires, to us do call.

48

To see men through this meadow dive,
We wonder how they rise alive;

1. The five ports on the southeast coast of England, of which Fairfax was warden for a time; the "imaginary forts" (next line) are the "five bastions" of line 287.
2. Seat of the archbishop of York, two miles from Appleton House.
3. Cf. Numbers 13.33: "And there we saw the giants . . . and we were in our own sight as grasshoppers, and so we were in their sight."

As, underwater, none does know
380 Whether he fall through it or go;°   *move forward*
But as the mariners that sound
And show upon their lead the ground,[4]
They bring up flow'rs so to be seen,
And prove they've at the bottom been.

49

385 No scene° that turns with engines strange   *stage set*
Does oft'ner than these meadows change:
For when the sun the grass hath vexed,
The tawny mowers enter next;
Who seem like Israelites to be
390 Walking on foot through a green sea.
To them the grassy deeps divide
And crowd a lane to either side.[5]

50

With whistling scythe and elbow strong,
These massacre the grass along:
395 While one, unknowing, carves the rail,[6]
Whose yet unfeathered quills her fail.
The edge all bloody from its breast
He draws, and does his stroke detest;
Fearing the flesh untimely mowed
400 To him a fate as black forebode.

51

But bloody Thestylis[7] that waits
To bring the mowing camp their cates,°   *food*
Greedy as kites° has trussed it up,   *birds of prey*
And forthwith means on it to sup;
405 When on another quick she lights,
And cries, he[8] called us Israelites;
But now, to make his saying true,
Rails rain for quails, for manna dew.[9]

52

Unhappy birds! what does it boot°   *avail*
410 To build below the grasses' root,
When lowness is unsafe as height,

---

4. Plumb the depths and show the nature of the ground below.
5. The mowers produce a lane in the grassy meadow, like that formed when the Red Sea parted to allow the Israelites passage.
6. The corncrake (land rail), a field bird.
7. The cook for the harvest workers, comically given the name of a classical shepherdess.
8. The author, at line 389. The Puritans constantly

compared themselves and their revolution to the Israelites battling enemies and wandering in the wilderness en route to Canaan, the Promised Land.
9. Exodus 13–15 describes the quails and manna (left after the dew evaporated) with which the Israelites were miraculously fed after crossing the Red Sea.

And chance o'ertakes what scapeth spite?
And now your orphan parents' call
Sounds your untimely funeral.
415　Death-trumpets creak in such a note,
And 'tis the sourdine[1] in their throat.

53

Or° sooner hatch or higher build: *either*
The mower now commands the field;
In whose new traverse° seemeth wrought   *track*
420　A camp of battle newly fought:
Where, as the meads with hay, the plain
Lies quilted o'er with bodies slain;
The women that with forks it fling,
Do represent the pillaging.

54

425　And now the careless victors play,
Dancing the triumphs of the hay;[2]
Where every mower's wholesome heat
Smells like an Alexander's sweat,[3]
Their females fragrant as the mead
430　Which they in fairy circles tread:
When at their dance's end they kiss,
Their new-made hay not sweeter is.

55

When after this 'tis piled in cocks,°   *haystacks*
Like a calm sea it shows the rocks:
435　We wond'ring in the river near
How boats among them safely steer.
Or, like the desert Memphis[4] sand,
Short pyramids of hay do stand.
And such the Roman camps do rise[5]
440　In hills for soldiers' obsequies.

56

This scene° again withdrawing brings   *stage set*
A new and empty face of things;
A leveled space, as smooth and plain,
As cloths for Lely[6] stretched to stain.
445　The world when first created sure
Was such a table rase[7] and pure;

---

1. A small pipe put into the mouth of a trumpet to produce a low sound.
2. A country dance (with a pun).
3. Plutarch wrote that Alexander the Great's sweat smelled sweet.
4. An ancient Egyptian city near the pyramids.

5. Hillocks that served as burial mounds; they were actually British in origin, not Roman.
6. Canvases for the Dutch portrait painter Sir Peter Lely, who came to England in 1643.
7. *Tabula rasa* (Latin): a clean or blank slate.

Or rather such is the toril
Ere the bulls enter at Madril.[8]

57

For to this naked equal flat,
450 Which Levellers[9] take pattern at,
The villagers in common° chase   *common pasture*
Their cattle, which it closer rase;°   *crops*
And what below the scythe increased°   *grew*
Is pinched yet nearer by the beast.
455 Such, in the painted world, appeared,
Davenant with th' universal herd.[1]

58

They seem within the polished grass
A landscape drawn in looking glass;
And shrunk in the huge pasture show
460 As spots, so shaped, on faces do.[2]
Such fleas, ere they approach the eye,
In multiplying° glasses lie.   *magnifying*
They feed so wide, so slowly move,
As constellations do above.

59

465 Then, to conclude these pleasant acts,
Denton sets ope' its cataracts;[3]
And makes the meadow truly be
(What it but seemed before) a sea.
For, jealous of its lord's long stay,
470 It tries t' invite him thus away.
The river in itself is drowned
And isles th' astonished cattle round.

60

Let others tell the paradox,
How eels now bellow in the ox;[4]
475 How horses at their tails do kick,
Turned as they hang to leeches quick;[5]
How boats can over bridges sail,
And fishes do the stables scale;

8. Madrid. "Toril": bull ring.
9. A radical faction, the Diggers or True Levellers, who sought social and economic equality. A group of Diggers began to put their tenets into practice by taking over and cultivating the land on St. George Hill, part of Fairfax's domain. See Gerrard Winstanley (pp. 1399–1405).
1. William Davenant, in his heroic poem *Gondibert* (2.6), describes a painting of creation, where on the sixth day "an universal herd" of animals appeared.
2. A landscape (or painted landscape) reflected in a mirror would be reduced in size.
3. Small waterfalls or dams. Denton, also a Fairfax estate (see line 73), was located on the Wharfe River, thirty miles from Nunappleton.
4. Because the ox swallowed them.
5. In popular superstition horse hairs in water became live leeches or eels.

How salmons trespassing are found,
480   And pikes are taken in the pound.°   *cattle pen*

61

But I, retiring from the flood,
Take sanctuary in the wood;
And, while it lasts, myself embark
In this yet green, yet growing ark;
485   Where the first carpenter[6] might best
Fit timber for his keel have pressed;°   *obtained*
And where all creatures might have shares,
Although in armies, not in pairs.

62

The double wood of ancient stocks
490   Linked in so thick an union locks,
It like two pedigrees[7] appears,
On one hand Fairfax, th' other Vere's:
Of whom though many fell in war,
Yet more to heaven shooting are:
495   And, as they nature's cradle decked,
Will in green age her hearse expect.

63

When first the eye this forest sees
It seems indeed as wood not trees;
As if their neighborhood° so old   *nearness*
500   To one great trunk them all did mold.
There the huge bulk takes place, as meant
To thrust up a fifth element;[8]
And stretches still so closely wedged
As if the night within were hedged.

64

505   Dark all without it knits; within
It opens passable and thin;
And in as loose an order grows
As the Corinthian porticoes.[9]
The arching boughs unite between
510   The columns of the temple green;
And underneath the winged choirs
Echo about their tuned fires.

---

6. Noah, who built an ark to escape a flood that would cover the earth (Genesis 6).
7. Genealogical trees, of the Fairfax and Vere families.
8. The so-called quintessence, beyond and superior to fire, air, water, and earth.
9. The most elaborate order of Greek columns.

65

The nightingale does here make choice
To sing the trials of her voice.
515 Low shrubs she sits in, and adorns
With music high the squatted thorns.
But highest oaks stoop down to hear,
And list'ning elders prick the ear.
The thorn, lest it should hurt her, draws
520 Within the skin its shrunken claws.

66

But I have for my music found
A sadder, yet more pleasing sound:
The stock doves,° whose fair necks are graced   *turtledoves*
With nuptial rings, their ensigns chaste;
525 Yet always, for some cause unknown,
Sad pair, unto the elms they moan.
O why should such a couple mourn,
That in so equal flames do burn!

67

Then as I careless on the bed
530 Of gelid strawberries do tread,
And through the hazels thick espy
The hatching throstle's shining eye,
The heron from the ash's top
The eldest of its young lets drop,
535 As if it stork-like[1] did pretend
That tribute to its lord to send.

68

But most the hewel's° wonders are,   *green woodpecker's*
Who here has the holtfelster's° care.   *woodcutter's*
He walks still upright from the root,
540 Meas'ring the timber with his foot;
And all the way, to keep it clean,
Doth from the bark the wood-moths glean.
He, with his beak, examines well
Which fit to stand and which to fell.

69

545 The good he numbers up, and hacks;
As if he marked them with the ax.
But where he, tinkling with his beak,

---

1. The stork upon leaving a nest was believed to leave behind one of its young as a tribute to the householder.

Does find the hollow oak[2] to speak,
That for his building he designs,
550 And through the tainted side he mines.
Who could have thought the tallest oak
Should fall by such a feeble stroke!

70

Nor would it, had the tree not fed
A traitor-worm, within it bred.
555 (As first our flesh corrupt within
Tempts impotent and bashful sin)
And yet that worm triumphs not long,
But serves to feed the hewel's young;
While the oak seems to fall content,
560 Viewing the treason's punishment.

71

Thus I, easy philosopher,
Among the birds and trees confer;
And little now to make me, wants°   *lacks*
Or° of the fowls, or of the plants.   *either*
565 Give me but wings as they, and I
Straight floating on the air shall fly:
Or turn me but, and you shall see
I was but an inverted tree.[3]

72

Already I begin to call
570 In their most learned original:
And where I language want, my signs
The bird upon the bough divines;
And more attentive there doth sit
Than if she were with lime[4] twigs knit.
575 No leaf does tremble in the wind
Which I returning cannot find.

73

Out of these scattered Sibyl's leaves
Strange prophecies my fancy weaves:[5]
And in one history consumes,
580 Like Mexique paintings, all the plumes.°   *feathers*
What Rome, Greece, Palestine, ere said
I in this light Mosaic[6] read.

2. The "royal" oak was traditionally an emblem of monarchy.
3. Originally classical, this is a widely used metaphor in the Renaissance.
4. Birdlime, a sticky substance smeared on twigs to trap birds.

5. The Cumaean Sibyl, in Virgil, committed her prophecies to leaves that Aeneas feared might be scattered (*Aeneid* 6.77).
6. The pattern formed by the trembling leaves; also the books of Moses, who was thought to have written the first five books of the Bible.

Thrice happy he who, not mistook,
Hath read in nature's mystic book.[7]

74

585 And see how chance's better wit
Could with a mask[8] my studies hit!
The oak-leaves me embroider all,
Between which caterpillars crawl;
And ivy, with familiar trails,
590 Me licks, and clasps, and curls, and hales.
Under this antic cope[9] I move
Like some great prelate of the grove.

75

Then, languishing with ease, I toss
On pallets swol'n of velvet moss;
595 While the wind, cooling through the boughs,
Flatters with air my panting brows.
Thanks for my rest, ye mossy banks,
And unto you, cool zephyrs,° thanks,   *gentle west winds*
Who, as my hair, my thoughts too shed,°   *part*
600 And winnow from the chaff my head.

76

How safe, methinks, and strong, behind
These trees have I encamped my mind;
Where beauty, aiming at the heart,
Bends in some tree its useless° dart;   *harmless*
605 And where the world no certain shot
Can make, or me it toucheth not.
But I on it securely play,
And gall its horsemen all the day.

77

Bind me ye woodbines in your twines,
610 Curl me about ye gadding vines,
And O so close your circles lace,
That I may never leave this place:
But, lest your fetters prove too weak,
Ere I your silken bondage break,
615 Do you, O brambles, chain me too,
And courteous briars, nail me through.[1]

7. The book of the creatures, or the book of God's
works.
8. Masque costume or disguise appropriate to
the speaker's studies.
9. Comic ecclesiastical vestment.
1. The imagery evokes imprisonment and crucifixion.

78

Here in the morning tie my chain,
Where the two woods have made a lane;
While, like a guard on either side,
620 The trees before their lord divide;
This, like a long and equal thread,
Betwixt two labyrinths does lead.
But, where the floods did lately drown,
There at the evening stake me down.

79

625 For now the waves are fall'n and dried,
And now the meadows fresher dyed;
Whose grass, with moister color dashed,
Seems as green silks but newly washed.
No serpent new nor crocodile
630 Remains behind our little Nile;[2]
Unless itself you will mistake,
Among these meads° the only snake.   *meadows*

80

See in what wanton harmless folds
It ev'rywhere the meadow holds;
635 And its yet muddy back doth lick,
Till as a crystal mirror slick;°   *smooth*
Where all things gaze themselves, and doubt
If they be in it or without.
And for his shade° which therein shines,   *shadow*
640 Narcissus-like, the sun too pines.[3]

81

Oh what a pleasure 'tis to hedge
My temples here with heavy sedge;
Abandoning my lazy side,
Stretched as a bank unto the tide;
645 Or to suspend my sliding foot
On th' osier's undermined root,
And in its branches tough to hang,
While at my lines the fishes twang!

82

But now away my hooks, my quills,°   *floats*
650 And angles, idle utensils.
The young Maria walks tonight:

2. Our river; serpents and crocodiles were thought
to be bred by spontaneous generation from the
mud of the Nile.

3. Narcissus lay beside water, staring at his
reflection, pining for himself.

Hide trifling youth thy pleasures slight.
'Twere shame that such judicious eyes
Should with such toys a man surprise;
655 She that already is the law
Of all her sex, her age's awe.

83

See how loose nature, in respect
To her, itself doth recollect;
And everything so whisht° and fine,   *hushed*
660 Starts forthwith to its bonne mine.°   *good appearance*
The sun himself, of her aware,
Seems to descend with greater care;
And lest she see him go to bed,
In blushing clouds conceals his head.

84

665 So when the shadows laid asleep
From underneath these banks do creep,
And on the river as it flows
With ebon shuts° begin to close;   *black shutters*
The modest halcyon⁴ comes in sight,
670 Flying betwixt the day and night;
And such an horror calm and dumb,
Admiring nature does benumb.

85

The viscous° air, wheresoe'r she fly,   *thick*
Follows and sucks her azure dye;
675 The jellying stream compacts° below,   *solidifies*
If it might fix her shadow so;
The stupid° fishes hang, as plain   *stupefied*
As flies in crystal overta'en;
And men the silent scene assist,°   *attend*
680 Charmed with the sapphire-wingèd mist.⁵

86

Maria such, and so° doth hush   *in like fashion*
The world, and through the ev'ning rush.
No newborn comet such a train
Draws through the sky, nor star new-slain.⁶
685 For straight those giddy rockets⁷ fail,
Which from the putrid earth exhale,
But by her flames, in heaven tried,
Nature is wholly vitrified.°   *turned to glass*

---

4. The kingfisher, who by nesting on the waves
was believed to bring absolute calm to the sea.
5. The bird in its flight.

6. Meteor, or shooting star.
7. Vapors exhaled from the earth.

87

'Tis she that to these gardens gave
690 That wondrous beauty which they have;
She straightness on the woods bestows;
To her the meadow sweetness owes;
Nothing could make the river be
So crystal-pure but only she;
695 She yet more pure, sweet, straight, and fair,
Than gardens, woods, meads, rivers are.

88

Therefore what first she on them spent,
They gratefully again present:
The meadow, carpets where to tread;
700 The garden, flow'rs to crown her head;
And for a glass, the limpid brook,
Where she may all her beauties look;
But, since she would not have them seen,
The wood about her draws a screen.

89

705 For she, to higher beauties raised,
Disdains to be for lesser praised.
She counts her beauty to converse
In all the languages as hers;
Nor yet in those herself employs
710 But for the wisdom, not the noise;
Nor yet that wisdom would affect,
But as 'tis heaven's dialect.

90

Blest nymph! that couldst so soon prevent
Those trains° by youth against thee meant: *artillery*
715 Tears (wat'ry shot that pierce the mind)
And sighs (love's cannon charged with wind)
True praise (that breaks through all defense)
And feigned complying innocence;
But knowing where this ambush lay,
720 She scaped the safe, but roughest way.

91

This 'tis to have been from the first
In a domestic heaven nursed,
Under the discipline severe
Of Fairfax, and the starry Vere;
725 Where not one object can come nigh
But pure, and spotless as the eye;

And goodness doth itself entail
On females, if there want a male.[8]

92

Go now fond° sex that on your face   *foolish*
730   Do all your useless study place,
Nor once at vice your brows dare knit
Lest the smooth forehead wrinkled sit;
Yet your own face shall at you grin,
Thorough° the black-bag° of your skin;   *through / mask*
735   When knowledge only could have filled
And virtue all those furrows tilled.

93

Hence she with graces more divine
Supplies beyond her sex the line;
And, like a sprig of mistletoe,
740   On the Fairfacian oak doth grow;
Whence, for some universal good,
The priest shall cut the sacred bud;[9]
While her glad parents most rejoice,
And make their destiny their choice.

94

745   Meantime ye fields, springs, bushes, flow'rs,
Where yet she leads her studious hours
(Till fate her worthily translates,
And find a Fairfax for our Thwaites),
Employ the means you have by her,
750   And in your kind yourselves prefer;[1]
That, as all virgins she precedes,
So you all woods, streams, gardens, meads.

95

For you Thessalian Tempe's[2] seat
Shall now be scorned as obsolete;
755   Aranjuez, as less, disdained;
The Bel-Retiro[3] as constrained;
But name not the Idalian grove,[4]
For 'twas the seat of wanton Love;
Much less the dead's Elysian Fields,[5]
760   Yet nor to them your beauty yields.

---

8. Maria was the only child and heir of the Fair-
faxes.
9. Maria is, of course, intended for marriage.
1. Make yourselves the best you can.
2. The Vale of Tempe, in Greece, was a kind of
paradise.

3. Spanish palaces.
4. A favorite haunt of Aphrodite (Venus), goddess of love, on Cyprus.
5. The pleasant habitation of the good in the
classical underworld.

96

'Tis not, what once it was, the world,
But a rude heap together hurled;
All negligently overthrown,
Gulfs, deserts, precipices, stone.
765 Your lesser world[6] contains the same,
But in more decent order tame;
You heaven's center, nature's lap,
And paradise's only map.

97

But now the salmon-fishers moist
770 Their leathern boats begin to hoist;
And, like antipodes in shoes,
Have shod their heads in their canoes.[7]
How tortoise-like, but not so slow,
These rational amphibii[8] go!
775 Let's in; for the dark hemisphere
Does now like one of them appear.

1651   1681

---

6. Appleton House.
7. The men who dwell at the "antipodes," on the other side of the world are sometimes said to wear their shoes on their heads; these English fishermen transport their leather boats on their heads.
8. As men, the fishermen are "rational"; and they live in two elements, land and water.

Crisis of Authority

M ost of the poets and prose writers who published in the "civil war decades," 1640 to 1660, registered in some way their responses to the conflicts swirling about them. The war and the issues over which it was fought shadow the poetry of Vaughan, Herrick, Lovelace, Suckling, and Marvell and the prose of Thomas Browne and Izaak Walton. Yet often such writers addressed the conflict only obliquely. When Marvell or Herrick celebrates peaceful gardens or fruitful countryside, when Vaughan envisions eternity as a "great ring of pure and endless light" suspended above all mortal turmoil, when Walton rhapsodizes about fishing, they create refuges of the imagination that might partially compensate for the trauma of war. Other writers confronted the issues of the age more straightforwardly. The readings included in this section sample this more explicitly political writing. They exemplify some of the genres encouraged by the new conditions in which literary materials could be written and circulated.

With the restoration of Charles II in 1660, many of the radical voices of the 1640s and 1650s were muted. Yet the war decades left a lasting imprint upon English literature. They established a tradition of overtly political, often ambitiously literary writing without which it is hard to imagine the works of such authors as Dryden, Swift, and Pope. They established prose as a dominant literary medium, especially for the description and analysis of everyday life. They initiated a tradition of apparently ordinary people bearing witness in writing to extraordinary events: a vital precedent for the rise of the novel.

This section presents examples of several kinds of writing that flourished during the Civil War and its immediate aftermath: the journalistic reporting of current events; political theory; and careful descriptions of contemporary history, personal experience, and individual character. These excerpts demonstrate a variety of ways in which writers might respond to the disturbing and exciting developments around them: by reporting the details of dramatic, unprecedented occurences; by analyzing the political and social problems posed by the conflict; by ruminating upon the character of great men; by seizing new opportunities for autobiographical reflection.

REPORTING THE NEWS

The following accounts of the king's trial and execution are excerpted from newsbooks, one of the most important new literary forms of the war years. In England the reportage of current events originated in the 1620s, when anxiety over the nation's entanglement in what would become the Thirty Years War on the Continent generated a demand for international news. In addition, in the 1620s and 1630s a few enterprising individuals provided "corantos," handwritten reports of court goings-on, to wealthy individuals in the provinces; these were technically considered private letters, although they sometimes circulated to several hundred paid subscribers. Yet even these modest ventures were always on legally shaky ground. The printing of domestic news, or commentary thereon, was strictly prohibited by Charles I, as it had been by his forebears.

In the early 1640s, censorship collapsed just when many people urgently wanted information about the momentous events transpiring in England, Scotland, and Ireland. The result was the explosive development of printed news. While in 1640 there were no newsbooks, by 1645 there were 755. Their format varied, but typically they were eight-page cheaply printed pamphlets, issued weekly. Most writers and compilers remained anonymous, though in some cases the identity of the authors was an open secret. Unlike the earlier corantos, the inexpensive newsbooks of the 1640s gave a broad spectrum of readers access to information about current events. Often, simultaneously, they propagandized on behalf of various parties to the developing conflict. The newsbooks thus encouraged an unprecedentedly wide and deep sense of civic involvement, and arguably also had the effect of hardening factional differences.

The newsbooks provided eyewitness, or what purported to be eyewitness, accounts of the king's trial and execution very shortly after they occurred. Both events were highly charged, with important and complex stakes on both sides. In the autumn of 1648, many in Parliament who had initially wanted to restrict the king's powers hesitated to remove him from the throne; they favored a negotiated end to hostilities. Yet the powerful leaders of the New Model Army, including Oliver Cromwell, were convinced that Charles was a threat to a reorganized commonwealth. Even if the king dealt with his opponents in good faith, which they doubted, he would be a constant rallying point for opposition to their policies. Conceivably, the war would never be over.

When Charles seemed to be planning to escape from his relatively light confinement on the Isle of Wight, the army council ordered him seized and brought to London, which the army occupied. Yet what were they to do with their captive? Simply to assassinate him would deprive his killers of any semblance of legitimacy. A formal trial, therefore, seemed necessary; but it was not easy to achieve. First, Parliament had to be purged of more than half its members, who disapproved of putting the king on trial. Once reconstituted so as to exclude opposition, Parliament then had to pass a law redefining treason as a crime against the state, not a crime against the king, of which the king himself could not logically have been guilty.

As in the case of most treason trials in the sixteenth and seventeenth centuries, a guilty verdict was a foregone conclusion. Yet the trial's value as propaganda was unpredictable. The judges and executioners pointedly assumed the regalia and symbolism of state power, and conducted both the trial and the execution with great punctiliousness, in order to bolster the impression of due process in the eyes of onlookers and newsbook readers. Charles's calmly defiant behavior, meanwhile, was not meant to secure his acquittal, which everyone knew would have been unforthcoming anyhow. Rather, he hoped to garner sympathy for his plight, to demonstrate publicly his unwavering adherence to his own principles, and to provoke prosecutors and judges into behaving like rabid zealots. Likewise, his conduct on the scaffold impressed even those who deplored his political position. While his judges and executioners strove to describe him as an overweening tyrant, Charles struggled to appear the heir to a Christian tradition of suffering innocence, a "martyr of the people." In 1660, as soon as the monarchy was restored, Charles I was canonized by the Church of England.

From The Moderate, No. 28

16–23 January 1649

At the high court of justice sitting in the Great Hall of Westminster, Sergeant Bradshaw President,[1] about 70 Members present. Oyez[2] made thrice, silence commanded. The president had the sword and mace carried before him, attended with Colonel Fox, and twenty other officers and gentlemen with partisans.[3] The act of the Commons in Parliament for trial of the king, read. After the court was called, and each member rising up as he was called. The king came into the court, his hat on, and the Commissioners with theirs on also; no congratulation or motion of hats at all.[4] The Sergeant ushered him in with the mace, Colonel Hacker[5] and about thirty officers and gentlemen more came as his guard; the president then spake in these words, viz.

"Charles Stuart, King of England, the Commons of England assembled in Parliament being sensible of the great calamities that have been brought upon this nation, of the innocent blood that hath been shed in this nation, which is referred[6] to you, as the author of it; and according to that duty which they owe to God, to the nation, and themselves, and according to that fundamental power and trust that is reposed in them by the people, have constituted this high court of justice before which you are now brought; and you are to hear the charge upon which the court will proceed."

Mr. Cook Solicitor General.[7] "My lord, in behalf of the Commons of England, and of all the people thereof, I do accuse Charles Stuart, here present, of high treason and high misdemeanors, and I do in the name of the Commons of England desire that the charge may be read unto him."

King. "Hold a little"—tapping the solicitor general twice on the shoulder with his cane, which drawing towards him again, the head thereon fell off, he stooping for it, put it presently[8] into his pocket. This is conceived will be very ominous.

Lord President. "Sir, the court commands the charge to be read; if you have any thing to say after, you may be heard."

The charge was read.

The king smiled often during the time, especially at those words therein, viz that Charles Stuart was a tyrant, traitor, murderer, and public enemy of the commonwealth.

---

1. John Bradshaw (1609–1659), chief justice of Cheshire and Wales, accepted the office of president after others declined. He lost this office after 1653, when he opposed Cromwell's consolidation of personal power. Bradshaw was posthumously convicted of treason at the Restoration in 1660; his body was exhumed and hanged in chains.
2. Hear ye (French).
3. John Fox (1610–1650) was commander of the Lord President's bodyguard, the members of which carried spears with a lobed base "partisan." The "sword and mace" symbolizes state power.

4. For either the king or the judges to doff their hats would be to acknowledge the others' superiority. "Congratulation": salutation.
5. Francis Hacker (1618–1660) commanded the soldiers who guarded the king, signed the king's death warrant, and supervised the guard on the scaffold. He was executed after the Restoration.
6. Attributed.
7. John Cook (1608–1660), a radical republican lawyer, acted as chief prosecutor. He was executed after the Restoration.
8. Immediately.

Lord President. "Sir, you have now heard your charge read, containing such matter as appears in it: you find that in the close of it, it is prayed to the court in the behalf of all the Commons of England, that you answer to your charge. The court expects your answer."

King. "I would know by what power I am called hither. I was not long ago in the Isle of Wight; how I came hither is a larger story then I think is fit at this time for me to speak of: But there I entered into a treaty with the two Houses of Parliament, with as much public faith as is possibly to be had of any people in the world. I treated there with a number of honorable lords and gentlemen, and treated honestly and uprightly. I cannot say but they did deal very nobly with me. We were upon conclusion of a treaty. Now I would know by what authority—I mean lawful; there are many unlawful authorities in the world, thieves and robbers by the highways—but I would know by what authority I was brought from thence, and carried from place to place; and when I know by what lawful authority, I shall answer.

"Remember, I am your king, your lawful king; and what sin you bring upon your heads, and the judgments of God upon this land, think well upon it; I say think well upon it before you go further, from one sin to a greater.[9] Therefore let me know by what lawful authority I am seated here, and I shall not be unwilling to answer. In the meantime, I shall not betray my trust. I have a trust committed to me by God, by old and lawful descent. I will not betray it, to answer to a new and unlawful authority. Therefore resolve me that, and you shall hear more of me."

Lord President. "If you had been pleased to have observed what was hinted to you by the court at our first coming hither, you would have known by what authority; which authority requires you in the name of the people of England, of which you are elected king, to answer them."

King. "No sir, I deny that."

Lord President. "If you acknowledge not the authority of the court, they must proceed."

King. "I do tell you so, England was never an elective kingdom, but an hereditary kingdom, for near a thousand years; therefore let me know by what authority I am called hither. I do stand more for the liberty of my people than any here that come to be my pretended judges; and therefore let me know by what lawful authority I am seated here, and I will answer it; otherwise I will not answer it."

Lord President told him he did interrogate the court, which beseemed not one in his condition, and it was known how he had managed his trust.

*　*　*

King. "I desire that you would give me, and all the world, satisfaction in this. For let me tell you, it is not a slight thing you are about. I am sworn to keep the peace by the duty I owe to God and my country; and I will do it to the last breath of my body: And therefore you shall do well to satisfy first God and then the country by what authority you do it; if by a reserved[1] authority, you cannot answer it. There is a God in heaven that will call you, and all that give you power, to an account. Satisfy me in that, and I will

---

9. From rebellion to regicide.　　　　1. Unexplained.

answer; otherwise, I betray my trust and the liberties of the people. And therefore think of that, and then I shall be willing. For I do vow, that it is as great a sin to withstand lawful authority, as it is to submit to a tyrannical or any otherways unlawful authority, And therefore satisfy me that, and you shall receive my answer."

Lord President. "The court expects a final answer. They are to adjourn till Monday. If you satisfy not yourself, though we tell you our authority, we are satisfied with our authority, and it is upon God's authority and the kingdom's; and that peace you speak of will be kept in the doing of justice; and that is our present work."

The court adjourned till Monday ten of clock to the Painted Chamber, and thence hither.

As the king went away, facing the court, the king said, "I fear not that," looking upon and meaning the sword.

Going down from the court, the people cried, "Justice, justice, justice!"

Jan. 21. The commissioners kept a fast this day in Whitehall. There preached before them Mr. Sprig, whose text was, "He that sheds blood, by man shall his blood be shed." Mr. Foxley's was "Judge not, lest you be judged." And Mr. Peters' was. "I will bind their kings in chains, and their nobles in fetters of iron."[2] The last sermon made amends for the two former.

1649

From A Perfect Diurnal of Some Passages in Parliament, No. 288

Tuesday, January 30

[THE EXECUTION OF CHARLES I]

This day the king was beheaded over against the Banqueting House by Whitehall.[1] The manner of execution and what passed before his death take thus.[2] He was brought from Saint James[3] about ten in the morning, walking on foot through the park with a regiment of foot for his guard, with colors flying, drums beating, his private guard of partisans,[4] with some of his gentlemen before, and some behind bareheaded, Dr. Juxon late Bishop of London[5] next behind him, and Colonel Tomlinson[6] (who had the charge of him) to the gallery in Whitehall, and so into the Cabinet Chamber where he used to lie, where he continued at his devotion, refusing to dine (having

2. The biblical texts are Genesis 9.6, Matthew 7.1, and Psalms 149.8. Hugh Peters (1598–1660), Independent preacher to Cromwell's New Model Army, passionately supported the king's execution. He was himself executed after the Restoration.
1. Whitehall Palace was the English monarch's principal residence from 1530 to 1698, when most of it was destroyed by fire. The Banqueting House, designed by Inigo Jones with ceilings painted by Peter Paul Rubens, was built for King James I in 1619–22 and was used to stage court masques. "Over against": just outside.
2. Accept the following account.

3. St. James Palace, near Whitehall.
4. Guards armed with partisans, spears with lobed points or halberds.
5. William Juxon (1582–1663), Charles I's personal chaplain, was bishop of London until 1649, when he was deprived of office. In the late 1630s he had also served as one of the king's financial advisers. After the Restoration he became archbishop of Canterbury.
6. Matthew Tomlinson commanded the guards assigned to Charles. He was tried after the Restoration but was spared because he had been courteous to the king.

before taken the sacrament) only about 12 at noon he drank a glass of claret wine, and eat a piece of bread. From thence he was accompanied by Dr. Juxon, Colonel Tomlinson, Colonel Hacker,[7] and the guards before mentioned through the Banqueting House adjoining to which the scaffold was erected between Whitehall Gate and the gate leading into the gallery from Saint James. The scaffold was hung round with black, and the floor covered with black, and the ax and block laid in the middle of the scaffold. There were divers companies of foot and horse on every side the scaffold, and the multitudes of people that came to be spectators very great. The king making a pass upon[8] the scaffold, looked very earnestly on the block, and asked Colonel Hacker if there were no higher; and then spake thus, directing his speech to the gentlemen upon the scaffold.

King. "I shall be very little heard of anybody here; I shall therefore speak a word unto you here. Indeed I could hold my peace[9] very well, if I did not think that holding my peace would make some men think that I did submit to the guilt as well as to the punishment. But I think it is my duty to God first, and to my country, for to clear myself both as an honest man, and a good king, and a good Christian. I shall begin first with my innocency. In troth I think it not very needful for me to insist long upon this, for all the world knows that I never did begin a war with the two Houses of Parliament, and I call God to witness, to whom I must shortly make an account, that I never did intend for to encroach upon their privileges; they began upon me. It is the militia they began upon;[1] they confessed that the militia was mine but they thought it fit to have it from me; and to be short, if anybody will look to the dates of commissions, theirs and mine, and likewise to the declarations,[2] will see clearly that they began these unhappy troubles, not I. So that as the guilt of these enormous crimes that are laid against me, I hope in God that God will clear me of it. I will not; I am in charity;[3] God forbid that I should lay it upon the two Houses of Parliament, there is no necessity of either.[4] I hope they are free of this guilt; for I do believe that ill instruments[5] between them and me has been the chief cause of all this bloodshed. So that by way of speaking, as I find myself clear of this, I hope and pray God that they may too. Yet for all this, God forbid that I should be so ill a Christian, as not to say that God's judgments are just upon me. Many times he does pay justice by an unjust sentence; that is ordinary. I only say this, that an unjust sentence (meaning Strafford)[6] that I suffered for to take effect, is punished now by an unjust sentence upon me. That is, so far I have said, to show you that I am an innocent man.

7. On Colonel Hacker, see p. 1386, note 5.
8. Traversing.
9. Remain silent. It was customary for condemned prisoners to address onlookers before their public executions. "You here": the small group standing on the scaffold, as distinguished from the large crowd watching the execution.
1. In 1642 Parliament's Militia Ordinance transferred local militias from the king's control to Parliament's. Despite its failure to secure Charles's assent to the measure, Parliament declared it legally binding.

2. "Commissions" and "declarations": warrants for enlisting troops and proclamations of war.
3. Practicing the charity that befits a Christian, I refuse to lay the blame for the war on my enemies.
4. Of blaming either side for the war.
5. Corrupt go-betweens.
6. In an attempt to appease his opponents in Parliament, Charles reluctantly consented to the execution of his adviser Thomas Wentworth, Earl of Strafford, for treason in 1641, despite lack of evidence that Strafford had committed any crime.

"Now for to show you that I am a good Christian, I hope there is" (pointing to Dr. Juxon) "a good man that will bear me witness that I have forgiven all the world, and those in particular that have been the chief causers of my death. Who they are, God knows; I do not desire to know. I pray God forgive them. But this is not all; my charity must go farther. I wish that they may repent, for indeed they have committed a great sin in that particular. I pray God with Saint Stephen that this be not laid to their charge;[7] nay, not only so, but that they may take the right way to the peace of the kingdom, for charity commands me not only to forgive particular men, but to endeavor to the last gasp the peace of the kingdom. Sirs, I do wish with all my soul, and I do hope there is some here will carry it further, that they may endeavor the peace of the kingdom.

"Now, sirs, I must show you both how you are out of the way, and will put you in a way.[8] First, you are out of the way, for certainly all the way[9] you ever have had yet as I could find by anything, is in the way of conquest. Certainly this is an ill way, for conquest, sir, in my opinion is never just, except there be a good just cause, either for matter of wrong or just title, and then if you go beyond it,[1] the first quarrel that you have to it, that makes it unjust at the end that was just at first. But if it be only matter of conquest, then it is a great robbery; as a pirate said to Alexander that he was a great robber, he was but a petty robber. And so, sir, I do think the way that you are in, is much out of the way. Now, sir, for to put you in the way, believe it you never do right, nor God will never prosper you,[2] until you give Him his due, the king his due (that is, my successors) and the people their due. I am as much for them[3] as any of you. You must give God his due by regulating rightly his Church, according to Scripture, which is now out of order. For to set you in a way particularly[4] now I cannot, but only this, a national synod freely called, freely debating among themselves, must settle this; when that every opinion is freely and clearly heard. For the king, indeed I will not—(Then turning to a gentleman that touched the ax, said, hurt not the ax that may hurt me.)—For the king, the laws of the land will clearly instruct you for that; therefore, because it concerns my own particular I only give you a touch of it.[5] For the people, and truly I desire their liberty and freedom, as much as anybody whomsoever; but I must tell you, that their liberty and their freedom consists in having of government, those laws by which their life and their goods may be most their own. It is not for having share in government, sir, that is nothing pertaining to them.[6] A subject and a sovereign are clean[7] different things; and therefore, until they do that, I mean, that you do put the people in that liberty as I say, certainly they will never enjoy themselves.[8] Sirs, it was for this[9] that now I am come here. If I would have given way to an arbitrary way, for to have all laws changed according to the power of the sword, I needed not to have come here; and

7. St. Stephen, the first Christian martyr, prayed that God not hold his persecutors responsible for their actions; recounted in Acts 7. "Particular" (previous line): regard.
8. Both show you how you are wrong and put you on a correct course.
9. All the rationale.
1. Beyond what is necessary to correct the wrong.

2. Allow you to flourish.
3. On the people's side.
4. In detail.
5. Because it concerns my own situation, I mention it only briefly.
6. Of their concern or responsibility.
7. Completely.
8. Be happy.
9. Because I upheld the liberty of the people.

therefore I tell you, and I pray God it be not laid to your charge, that I am the martyr of the people. In troth sirs, I shall not hold you much longer; for I will only say this to you, that in truth I could have desired some little time longer because that I would have put this that I have said in a little more order and a little better digested[1] than I have done; and therefore I hope you will excuse me. I have delivered[2] my conscience. I pray God that you do take those courses that are best for the good of the kingdom and your own salvations."

Dr. Juxon. "Will Your Majesty—though it may be very well known Your Majesty's affections to religion—yet it may be expected that you should say somewhat[3] for the world's satisfaction."

King. "I thank you very heartily, my lord, for that I had almost forgotten it. In troth, sirs, my conscience in religion I think is very well known to the world, and therefore I declare before you all that I die a Christian according to the profession of the Church of England as I found it left me by my father; and this honest man, I think, will witness it." Then turning to the officers said, "sirs, excuse me for this same.[4] I have a good cause, and I have a gracious God; I will say no more."

Then turning to Colonel Hacker, he said, "Take care that they do not put me to pain; and, sir, this, an it please you."[5] But then a gentleman coming near the ax, the king said, "Take heed of the ax, pray take heed of the ax." Then the king speaking to the executioner said, "I shall say but very short prayers, and then thrust out my hands."

Then the king called to Dr. Juxon for his nightcap, and having put it on he said to the executioner, "Does my hair trouble you?" Who desired him to put it all under his cap, which the king did accordingly, by the help of the executioner and the bishop. Then the king turning to Dr. Juxon said, "I have a good cause, and a gracious God on my side.

Dr. Juxon, "There is but one stage more. This stage is turbulent and troublesome; it is a short one: But you may consider it will soon carry you a very great way; it will carry you from earth to heaven, and there you shall find a great deal of cordial joy and comfort."

King. "I go from a corruptible to an incorruptible crown, where no disturbance can be."

Dr. Juxon. "You are exchanged from a temporal to an eternal crown, a good exchange."

Then the king took off his cloak and his George,[6] giving his George to Dr. Juxon, saying "Remember" (it is thought for the prince) and some other small ceremonies past. After which the king stooping down laid his neck upon the block, and after a very little pause stretching forth his hands, the executioner at one blow severed his head from his body. Then his body was put in a coffin covered with black velvet, and removed to his lodging chamber in Whitehall.

---

1. More methodically arranged.
2. Spoken
3. Something.
4. This religious profession. Charles did not accept the radical Protestantism espoused by many of his opponents.
5. As was customary, Charles tips Hacker, the person supervising the execution, in hopes of ensuring a quick death. "An": if.
6. A jeweled pendant representing St. George killing a dragon, worn by Knights of the Garter. The prince (following) is the king's eldest son, later King Charles II, who had escaped to exile in France.

POLITICAL WRITING

Not surprisingly, the tumult of civil war stimulated a good deal of thinking about the nature and ends of government. The four excerpts that follow give some idea of the arguments proposed by English political writers between 1630 and 1655.

Robert Filmer and Thomas Hobbes both favor an absolutist government that would concentrate power in the sovereign and deprive the people of any way to get rid of him. However, the two writers work from quite different premises. In *Patriarcha, or The Natural Power of Kings Defended Against the Unnatural Liberty of the People*, Filmer outlines a historical theory based on the authority of biblical patriarchs—Abraham, Isaac, and Jacob, for instance—over their families. God ratified kingly authority, Filmer argues, when he commanded the honoring of parents. Although many royalists retained a larger role for popular consent than Filmer did, Filmer's account of the king's fatherly care of his people, and the people's childlike incompetence to manage political affairs, was close to the Stuart kings' own view.

Unlike Filmer, Thomas Hobbes, a gifted mathematician, believed in working from clearly defined first principles to conclusions, grounding his political vision not on biblical history but upon a comprehensive philosophy of nature and of knowledge. He believed that human beings seek self-preservation as a primary goal, and power as a means to secure that goal; his politics spring directly from these premises. Since the best way to assure self-preservation, he argued, is to assent permanently to the creation of a strong authority, the founding political covenant cannot be revoked and rebellion against the sovereign is absurd. Hobbes's materialism and secularism—his virtual exclusion of God from politics—scandalized both the Puritans who opposed him, and many royalists as well.

The claims of royalists came under vigorous attack from the poet John Milton, who during the war years became one of the most effective polemicists for the parliamentary radicals. Milton wrote *The Tenure of Kings and Magistrates* in 1648, the days leading up to Charles's trial and execution, when many of those who had originally supported limiting the king's power shrank from actually beheading him. Milton decries this hesitation, seeing it as the effect of a misdirected awe for the privileges of monarchs. All political authorities, Milton argues, hold their power in trust from the people, and the people can revoke that trust whenever they choose.

Like Filmer, Milton bases his argument upon biblical history, but he cites very different passages. Filmer emphasizes the importance of fatherly authority in Genesis, which narrates the lives of Adam, Noah, Abraham, Isaac, Jacob, and Joseph. Milton acknowledges that the fall of Adam and Eve corrupted human nature so that individuals were henceforth unable to govern themselves properly without external discipline. Yet, he insists, since those charged with implementing that discipline are themselves sinners, they must be kept in check by laws and by strict limitations upon their authority. In Milton's account, problems with the exercise of authority became evident only gradually. Unlike Filmer, who assumes that the social arrangements described in Genesis are a pattern for modern political communities, Milton chooses his examples from later eras in Jewish history: for instance, the Book of Samuel, in which God disapproves of the Israelites' desire for a king.

For Filmer, Hobbes, and Milton, the central issue of the conflict between the king and Parliament is, who has ultimate authority, the king or the people? Gerrard Winstanley construes the problem differently, in primarily economic rather than political terms. Winstanley was a well-educated London linen draper who worked as a laborer in the countryside after suffering financial reverses during the war years. In his political writing, he concerns himself less with the way power is allocated than with the equitable distribution of wealth. The ownership of land is especially important to him, since it was the critical asset in a largely agrarian society. Members of the House of Commons, though they considered themselves the representatives of "the people," were actually fairly substantial property owners; indeed, those without land or income were not entitled to vote. In consequence, more than half the male population (and, of course, the entire female population) was denied the franchise. In *A New Year's Gift Sent to the Parliament and Army* (1650), Winstanley accuses Parliament of having merely transferred oppressive power from the king to itself, leaving most of England's population as impoverished and downtrodden as before.

Winstanley suggests a practical means to remedy his society's inequities: "the commons," undeveloped lands used for grazing, should be made available to poor people to farm communally. Since the commons, though traditionally used by all the residents on an estate, were legally the manorial landlord's private property, Winstanley's ideas were highly unpopular among landowners. Moreover, his proposal was not merely a theoretical recommendation. The year before he wrote *A New Year's Gift*, Winstanley and some of his followers, called Diggers, had settled on St. George's Hill in Surrey. They planted twelve acres of grain and built a number of makeshift houses before they were violently evicted.

Like Filmer and Milton, Winstanley turns to the Bible to justify his politics. And like them, he chooses passages that suit his argument. He reads contemporary history through the heady allegories of the Book of Revelation, as a confrontation between the powers of darkness and the powers of light. Jesus's concern for the poor and scorn for the rich loom large to him, and his social vision owes much to biblical accounts of early Christian communities, which held property in common and minimized class differences.

ROBERT FILMER

The eldest of eighteen children, Robert Filmer (1588–1653) attended Trinity College, Cambridge, and inherited his father's estate in Kent in 1629. When war broke out he was too old to participate as a soldier, but he was briefly imprisoned by Parliament as a known supporter of the king, and his property was seized and plundered. After his release, he published a number of treatises arguing for absolute monarchy, among them *The Anarchy of a Limited and Mixed Monarchy* (1648); *The Freeholder's Grand Inquest* (1648), which argued that Parliament could only meet at the will of the king; and a translation of excerpts from the works of the French absolutist Jean Bodin. However, Filmer's most important treatise, *Patriarcha*, was not among these publications. Scholars disagree about when it was written, but Filmer probably composed it in the early 1630s in the wake of Charles's conflicts with Parliament early in his reign. The treatise remained in manuscript until 1680. Printed during a heated debate between Tories (royalists) and Whigs (Parliamentarians) over the right of King Charles II's brother James to inherit the throne, *Patriarcha* was comprehensively savaged by John Locke in his *First Treatise of Government* (1690).

While Filmer's motive in writing *Patriarcha* was undoubtedly close-to-home disputes between the English king and his subjects, his explicit polemical target is not Charles's parliamentary opponents. Rather, Filmer argues against Continental political theorists such as the Jesuit Robert Cardinal Bellarmine, who had written a devastating critique of James I's treatises on monarchy earlier in the century. Bellarmine's aim had been to secure freedom of conscience and worship for Roman

Catholic subjects of a Protestant monarch, by arguing that the power of monarchs was constrained by their people. Charles's Puritan opponents would find many aspects of Bellarmine's line of reasoning irresistible. Since in the English-speaking tradition republican concepts eventually came to be strongly associated with Puritan dissent, it is worth remembering that for much of the sixteenth and early seventeenth centuries, it had been Protestants who advocated consolidating secular and spiritual power in the figure of a powerful king, and Catholics who had resisted that consolidation.

From Patriarcha, or The Natural Power of Kings Defended Against the Unnatural Liberty of the People

From Chapter 1: That the First Kings Were Fathers of Families

Since the time that school divinity[1] began to flourish there hath been a common opinion maintained, as well by divines as by divers other learned men, which affirms: "Mankind is naturally endowed and born with freedom from all subjection, and at liberty to choose what form of government it please, and that the power which any one man hath over others was at first bestowed according to the discretion of the multitude." This tenet was first hatched in the schools, and hath been fostered by all succeeding Papists for good divinity. The divines, also, of the reformed churches have entertained it, and the common people everywhere tenderly embrace it as being most plausible[2] to flesh and blood, for that it prodigally distributes a portion of liberty to the meanest of the multitude, who magnify liberty as if the height of human felicity were only to be found in it, never remembering that the desire of liberty was the first cause of the fall of Adam.

But howsoever this vulgar[3] opinion hath of late obtained a great reputation, yet it is not to be found in the ancient fathers and doctors of the primitive church. It contradicts the doctrine and history of the holy scriptures, the constant practice of all ancient monarchies, and the very principles of the law of nature. It is hard to say whether it be more erroneous in divinity or dangerous in policy.[4]

*   *   *

That the patriarchs[5] . . . were endowed with kingly power, their deeds do testify; for as Adam was lord of his children, so his children under him had a command and power over their own children, but still with subordination to the first parent, who is lord-paramount over his children's children to all generations, as being the grandfather of his people.

I see not then how the children of Adam, or of any man else, can be free from subjection to their parents. And this subjection of children being the fountain of all regal authority, by the ordination of God himself, it follows that civil power not only in general is by divine institution, but even the assignment of it specifically to the eldest parents, which quite takes away

1. Systematic theology, as undertaken by medieval philosophers in the universities ("schools").
2. Agreeable.
3. Commonly held.

4. The conduct of public affairs.
5. Forefathers of the Jews, including Adam, Noah, Abraham, Isaac, Jacob, and Jacob's twelve sons.

that new and common distinction which refers only power universal and absolute to God, but power respective[6] in regard of the special form of government to the choice of the people.

This lordship which Adam by command had over the whole world, and by right descending from him the patriarchs did enjoy, was as large and ample as the absolutest dominion of any monarch which hath been since the Creation. For dominion of life and death we find that Judah, the father, pronounced sentence of death against Thamar, his daughter-in-law, for playing the harlot. "Bring her forth," saith he, "that she may be burnt."[7] Touching war, we see that Abraham commanded an army of three hundred and eighteen soldiers of his own family. And Esau met his brother Jacob with four hundred men at arms. For matter of peace, Abraham made a league with Abimelech, and ratified the articles with an oath. These acts of judging in capital crimes, of making war, and concluding peace, are the chiefest marks of sovereignty that are found in any monarch.

* * *

It may seem absurd to maintain that kings now are the fathers of their people, since experience shows the contrary. It is true, all kings be not the natural parents of their subjects, yet they all either are, or are to be reputed, the next heirs to those first progenitors who were at first the natural parents of the whole people, and in their right succeed to the exercise of supreme jurisdiction; and such heirs are not only lords of their own children, but also of their brethren, and all others that were subject to their fathers. And therefore we find that God told Cain of his brother Abel, "His desires shall be subject unto thee, and thou shalt rule over him." Accordingly, when Jacob bought his brother's birthright, Isaac blessed him thus: "Be lord over thy brethren, and let the sons of thy mother bow before thee."[8]

As long as the first fathers of families lived, the name of patriarchs did aptly belong unto them; but after a few descents, when the true fatherhood itself was extinct, and only the right of the father descends to the true heir, then the title of prince or king was more significant to express the power of him who succeeds only to the right of that fatherhood which his ancestors did naturally enjoy. By this means it comes to pass that many a child, by succeeding a king, hath the right of a father over many a gray-headed multitude, and hath the title of *pater patriae.*[9]

To confirm this natural right of regal power, we find in the Decalogue[1] that the law which enjoins obedience to kings is delivered in the terms of "Honor thy father," as if all power were originally in the father. If obedience to parents be immediately due by a natural law, and subjection to princes but by the mediation of a human ordinance, what reason is there that the laws of nature should give place to the laws of men, as we see the power of the father over his child gives place and is subordinate to the power of the magistrate?

If we compare the natural rights of a father with those of a king, we find them all one, without any difference at all but only in the latitude or extent

6. Partial, limited.
7. Genesis 38.24. The examples following also come from Genesis, 14.14, 32.6, and 21.22–27.
8. The first reference is to Genesis 4.7, which Filmer reads tendentiously as establishing the elder brother Cain's authority over the younger Abel, and the second is to Genesis 27.29.
9. Father of his country.
1. Ten Commandments.

of them: as the father over one family, so the king, as father over many families, extends his care to preserve, feed, clothe, instruct, and defend the whole commonwealth. His war, his peace, his courts of justice, and all his acts of sovereignty, tend only to preserve and distribute to every subordinate and inferior father, and to their children, their rights and privileges, so that all the duties of a king are summed up in an universal fatherly care of his people.

1620s–40s   1680

JOHN MILTON[1]

From The Tenure[2] of Kings and Magistrates

If men within themselves would be governed by reason, and not generally give up their understanding to a double tyranny, of custom from without, and blind affections[3] within, they would discern better what it is to favor and uphold the tyrant of a nation. But being slaves within doors,[4] no wonder that they strive so much to have the public state conformably governed to the inward vicious rule by which they govern themselves. For indeed none can love freedom heartily but good men; the rest love not freedom but license; which never hath more scope or more indulgence than under tyrants. Hence it is that tyrants are not oft offended nor stand much in doubt of bad men, as being all naturally servile; but in whom[5] virtue and true worth most is eminent, them they fear in earnest as by right their masters; against them lies all their hatred and suspicion. Consequently neither do bad men hate tyrants, but have been always readiest with the falsified names of loyalty, and obedience, to color over their base compliances.[6] And although sometimes for shame, and when it comes to their own grievances, of purse especially, they would seem good patriots and side with the better cause, yet when others for the deliverance of their country, endued with fortitude and heroic virtue to fear nothing by the curse written against those "that do the work of the lord negligently,"[7] would go on to remove not only the calamities and thralldoms of a people but the roots and causes whence they spring, straight these men and sure helpers at need, as if they hated only the miseries but not the mischiefs,[8] after they have juggled and paltered[9] with the world, bandied and borne arms against their king, divested him, disanointed him, nay cursed him all over in their pulpits and their pamphlets, to the engaging of sincere and real men beyond what is possible or honest to retreat from, not only turn revolters from those

---

1. See headnote to Milton, pp. 1447–51.
2. Terms of holding office.
3. Impulses, passions.
4. I.e., within their own selves.
5. Those in whom.
6. Make their slavishness look good.

7. Milton apparently refers to Jeremiah 48.10: "Cursed be he that doeth the work of the Lord deceitfully, and cursed be he that keepeth back his sword from blood."
8. The suffering but not its causes.
9. Played fast and loose.

principles which only could at first move them, but lay the stain of disloyalty and worse on those proceedings which are the necessary consequences of their own former actions; nor disliked by themselves, were they managed to the entire advantages of their own faction; not considering the while that he toward whom they boasted their new fidelity counted them accessory;[1] and by those statutes and laws which they so impotently brandish against others would have doomed them to a traitor's death for what they have done already. 'Tis true, that most men are apt enough to civil wars and commotions as a novelty, and for a flash hot and active; but through sloth or inconstancy, and weakness of spirit either fainting ere their own pretences,[2] though never so just, be half attained, or through an inbred falsehood and wickedness, betray ofttimes to destruction with themselves men of noblest temper[3] joined with them for causes whereof they in their rash undertakings[4] were not capable.

*　*　*

No man who knows aught, can be so stupid to deny that all men naturally were born free, being the image and resemblance of God Himself, and were by privilege above all the creatures born to command and not to obey, and that they lived so. Till from the root of Adam's transgression,[5] falling among themselves to do wrong and violence, and foreseeing that such courses must needs tend to the destruction of them all, they agreed by common league to bind each other from mutual injury, and jointly to defend themselves against any that gave disturbance or opposition to such agreement. Hence came cities, towns, and commonwealths. And because no faith in all was found sufficiently binding,[6] they saw it needful to ordain some authority that might restrain by force and punishment what was violated against peace and common right. This authority and power of self-defense and preservation being originally and naturally in every one of them, and unitedly in them all, for ease, for order, and lest each man should be his own partial[7] judge, they communicated and derived[8] either to one, whom for the eminence of his wisdom and integrity they chose above the rest, or to more than one whom they thought of equal deserving: the first was called a king, the other magistrates. Not to be their lords and masters (though afterward those names in some places were given voluntarily to such as had been authors[9] of inestimable good to the people) but to be their deputies and commissioners, to execute, by virtue of their entrusted power, that justice which else every man by the bond of nature and of convenant must have executed for himself and for one another. And to him that shall consider well why among free persons, one man by civil right[1] should bear authority and jurisdiction over another, no other end or reason can be imaginable. These[2] for a while governed well, and with much equity decided all things at their own arbitrament:[3] till the temptation of such a power left absolute in their hands,

1. Guilty of being accessories to a crime.
2. Purposes.
3. Character.
4. Attempts, enterprises.
5. Adam's fall introduced sin and violence into human life.
6. Because merely trusting people to behave them-

selves did not suffice to control them.
7. Biased.
8. Delegated.
9. Doers.
1. Law.
2. Kings and magistrates.
3. Judgment.

perverted them at length to injustice and partiality. Then did they who now by trial[4] had found the danger and inconveniences of committing arbitrary power to any, invent laws either framed or consented to by all, that should confine and limit the authority of whom they chose to govern them: that so man,[5] of whose failing they had proof, might no more rule over them, but law and reason abstracted as much as might be from personal errors and frailties. While[6] as the magistrate was set above the people, so the law was set above the magistrate. When this would not serve, but that the law was either not executed or misapplied, they were constrained from that time, the only remedy left them, to put conditions[7] and take oaths from all kings and magistrates at their first installment to do impartial justice by law: who upon those terms and no other received allegiance from the people, that is to say, bond or covenant to obey them in execution of those laws which they the people had themselves made or assented to. And this ofttimes with express warning, that if the king or magistrate proved unfaithful to his trust, the people would be disengaged.[8] They added also counselors and parliaments, nor to be only at his beck,[9] but with him or without him, at set times, or at all times when any danger threatened to have care of the public safety.

* * *

It being thus manifest that the power of kings and magistrates is nothing else but what is only derivative, transferred and committed to them in trust from the people, to the common good of them all, in whom the power yet remains fundamentally, and cannot be taken from them without a violation of their natural birthright; and seeing that from hence Aristotle[1] and the best of political writers have defined a king, him who governs to the good and profit of his people and not for his own ends, it follows from necessary causes that the titles of sovereign lord, natural lord, and the like, are either arrogancies or flatteries, not admitted[2] by emperors and kings of best note, and disliked by the church both of Jews, Isaiah 26.13, and ancient Christians, as appears by Tertullian and others.[3] Although generally the people of Asia, and with them the Jews also, especially since the time they chose a king against the advice and counsel of God,[4] are noted by wise authors much inclinable to slavery.

Secondly, that to say, as is usual, the king hath as good right to his crown and dignity as any man to his inheritance, is to make the subject no better than the king's slave, his chattel or his possession that may be bought and sold. And doubtless if hereditary title were sufficiently inquired, the best foundation of it would be found either but in courtesy or convenience. But suppose it to be of right hereditary, what can be more just and legal, if a

---

4. Experience. "They": the people who had delegated power to the kings and magistrates.
5. An individual man.
6. Thus.
7. Specify restrictions on.
8. Freed from having to obey.
9. The king's command. Charles had claimed that Parliament could not assemble unless called into session by the king.
1. In *Nicomachean Ethics* 8.11.1.

2. Permitted.
3. Isaiah 26.13: "O Lord our God, other lords beside thee have had dominion over us; but by thee only will we make mention of thy name." The Church Father Tertullian wrote against earthly monarchs in *On the Crown*.
4. The Israelites, traditionally governed by judges, demanded a king despite God's warning against monarchy, as conveyed by the prophet Samuel (1 Samuel 8).

subject for certain crimes be to forfeit by law from himself, and posterity, all his inheritance to the king,[5] than that a king for crimes proportional should forfeit all his title and inheritance to the people: unless the people must be thought created all for him, he not for them, and they all in one body inferior to him single, which were a kind of treason against the dignity of mankind to affirm.

Thirdly it follows that to say kings are accountable to none but God is the overturning of all law and government. For if they may refuse to give account, then all covenants made with them at coronation, all oaths are in vain and mere mockeries, all laws which they swear to keep made to no purpose; for if the king fear not God—as how many of them do not?—we hold then our lives and estates by the tenure of his mere grace and mercy, as from a God, not a mortal magistrate, a position that none but court parasites or men besotted would maintain.

* * *

It follows lastly, that since the king or magistrate holds his authority of the people, both originally and naturally for their good in the first place, and not his own, then may the people as oft as they shall judge it for the best, either choose him or reject him, retain him or depose him though no tyrant, merely by the liberty and right of freeborn men to be governed as seems to them best.

1649

5. Convicted felons forfeited their property to the king.

GERRARD WINSTANLEY

The demand for democratic elections by a political faction called the Levelers raised the fear in Cromwell and his conservative associates that, with unpropertied voters outnumbering the propertied by five to one, they might divide or even abolish private property. That was in fact the program of a small group calling themselves True Levelers or, later, Diggers, who were a group of Christian communists. Their leader was Gerrard Winstanley (1609–1676?), a failed businessman and subsequently a hired laborer, who began to publish tracts in 1648, became notorious in 1649 with the attempted enactment of the Diggers' program, and lapsed back into obscurity after his last published work in 1652.

In the spring of 1649, the Diggers began to put their ideals into practice, digging up the wasteland of St. George's Hill in Surrey and preparing it for crops. Though this land was not enclosed, all over England landowners claimed property rights in such common land, and the Diggers' gesture of cultivation here and in a few other Digger communities made a threatening counterclaim on behalf of the poor and propertyless. Their aim was at one level practical: at least one-third of England, they claimed, was barren waste, and if properly cultivated could vastly increase the food supply, to the great benefit of the poor. At another level their aim was ideological, a fundamental challenge to the concept of private ownership of land, as the tract excerpted here argues—at least in regard to the common land. The army and the civil authorities were not very hard on the Diggers, but the local landholders were, beating them up, expelling them, and destroying their several settlements. But their often-eloquent tracts survived to inspire later communes.

From A New Year's Gift[1] Sent to the Parliament and Army

Gentlemen of the Parliament and army: you and the common people have assisted each other to cast out the head of oppression which was kingly power seated in one man's hand, and that work is now done; and till that work was done you called upon the people to assist you to deliver this distressed, bleeding, dying nation out of bondage; and the people came and failed you not, counting neither purse nor blood too dear to part with to effect this work.

The Parliament after this have made an act to cast out kingly power, and to make England a free commonwealth. These acts the people are much rejoiced with, as being words forerunning their freedom, and they wait for their accomplishment that their joy may be full; for as words without action are a cheat and kills the comfort of a righteous spirit, so words performed in action does comfort and nourish the life thereof.

Now, sirs, wheresoever we spy out kingly power, no man I hope shall be troubled to declare it, nor afraid to cast it out, having both act of Parliament, the soldiers' oath, and the common people's consent on his side; for kingly power is like a great spread tree, if you lop the head or top bough, and let the other branches and root stand, it will grow again and recover fresher strength.

If any ask me what kingly power is, I answer, there is a twofold kingly power. The one is the kingly power of righteousness, and this is the power of almighty God, ruling the whole creation in peace and keeping it together. And this is the power of universal love, leading people into all truth, teaching everyone to do as he would be done unto: now once more striving with flesh and blood, shaking down everything that cannot stand, and bringing everyone into the unity of himself, the one spirit of love and righteousness, and so will work a thorough restoration. But this kingly power is above all and will tread all covetousness, pride, envy, and self-love, and all other enemies whatsoever, under his feet, and take the kingdom and government of the creation out of the hand of self-seeking and self-honoring flesh,[2] and rule the alone king of righteousness in the earth; and this indeed is Christ himself, who will cast out the curse.[3] But this is not that kingly power intended by that act of Parliament to be cast out, but pretended to be set up, though this kingly power be much fought against both by Parliament, army, clergy, and people; but when they are made to see him, then they shall mourn because they have persecuted him.[4]

1. In 17th-century England, gifts were customarily exchanged on New Year's Day, not at Christmas.
2. "Flesh" is imagined as everything mortal and fallible, that which rebels against divine righteousness.
3. The curse upon mankind that was the punishment of Adam's fall.
4. I.e., Parliament and the army do not expressly intend to cast out God's kingly power, but rather they act as if they are conforming to God's teachings, and yet often they resist God until they are brought to recognize him.

But the other kingly power is the power of unrighteousness, which indeed is the devil. And O, that there were such a heart in Parliament and army as to perform your own act.[5] Then people would never complain of you for breach of covenant, for your covetousness, pride, and too much self-seeking that is in you. And you on the other side would never have cause to complain of the people's murmurings against you. Truly this jarring that is between you and the people is the kingly power; yea that very kingly power which you have made an act to cast out. Therefore see it be fulfilled on your part; for the kingly power of righteousness expects it, or else he will cast you out for hypocrites and unsavory salt;[6] for he looks upon all your actions, and truly there is abundance of rust about your actings, which makes them that they do not shine bright.

This kingly power is covetousness in his branches,[7] or the power of self-love ruling in one or in many men over others and enslaving those who in the creation are their equals; nay, who are in the strictness of equity rather their masters. And this kingly power is usually set in the chair of government under the name of prerogative[8] when he rules in one over other: and under the name of state privilege of Parliament when he rules in many over others: and this kingly power is always raised up and established by the sword, and therefore he is called the murderer, or the great red dragon which fights against Michael,[9] for he enslaves the weakness of the people under him, denying an equal freedom in the earth to everyone, which the law of righteousness gave every man in his creation. This I say is kingly power under darkness; and as he rules in men, so he makes men jar one against another, and is the cause of all wars and complainings. He is known by his outward actions, and his action at this very day fills all places; for this power of darkness rules, and would rule, and is that only enemy that fights against creation and national freedom. And this kingly power is he which you have made an act of Parliament to cast out. And now, you rulers of England, play the men and be valiant for the truth, which is Christ: for assure yourselves God will not be mocked, nor the devil will not be mocked. For first you say and profess you own[1] the scriptures of prophets and apostles, and God looks that you should perform that word in action. Secondly you have declared against the devil, and if you do not now go through with your work but slack your hand by hypocritical self-love, and so suffer this dark kingly power to rise higher and rule, you shall find he will maul both you and yours to purpose.[2]

*   *   *

In the time of the kings, who came in as conquerors and ruled by the power of the sword, not only the common land but the enclosures[3] also were

---

5. Enforce the act already passed by Parliament.
6. Matthew 5.13: "Ye are the salt of the earth: but if the salt have lost his savour, wherewith shall it be salted? it is thenceforth good for nothing, but to be cast out, and to be trodden under foot of men."
7. I.e., covetousness is one manifestation of unrighteous kingly power.
8. The monarch's special powers.
9. Revelation 12.3–9: "And there appeared another wonder in heaven; and behold a great red dragon, having seven heads and ten horns, and seven

crowns upon his heads. . . . And there was war in heaven: Michael and his angels fought against the dragon; and the dragon fought and his angels, / and prevailed not; neither was their place found any more in heaven. / And the great dragon was cast out, that old serpent, called the Devil, and Satan, which deceiveth the whole world."
1. Acknowledge.
2. Thoroughly.
3. Privately held land.

captivated under the will of those kings, till now of late that our later kings granted more freedom to the gentry than they had presently after the Conquest:[4] yet under bondage still. For what are prisons, whips, and gallows in the times of peace but the laws and power of the sword, forcing and compelling obedience, and so enslaving as if the sword raged in the open field? England was in such a slavery under the kingly power that both gentry and commonalty[5] groaned under bondage; and to ease themselves, they endeavored to call a parliament, that by their counsels and decrees they might find some freedom.

But Charles the then king perceiving that the freedom they strove for would derogate from his prerogative tyranny,[6] thereupon he goes into the north to raise a war against the Parliament; and took William the Conqueror's sword into his hand again, thereby to keep under the former conquered English, and to uphold his kingly power of self-will and prerogative, which was the power got by former conquests; that is, to rule over the lives and estates of all men at his will, and so to make us pure slaves and vassals.

Well, this Parliament, that did consist of the chief lords, lords of manors, and gentry, and they seeing that the king, by raising an army, did thereby declare his intent to enslave all sorts to him by the sword; and being in distress and in a low ebb, they call upon the common people to bring in their plate, monies, taxes, free-quarter, excise,[7] and to adventure their lives with them, and they would endeavor to recover England from that Norman yoke and make us a free people. And the common people assent hereunto, and call this the Parliament's cause, and own it and adventure person and purse to preserve it; and by the joint assistance of Parliament and people the king was beaten in the field, his head taken off, and his kingly power voted down. And we the commons thereby virtually have recovered ourselves from the Norman conquest; we want nothing but possession of the spoil,[8] which is a free use of the land for our livelihood.

And from hence we the common people, or younger brothers,[9] plead our property in the common land as truly our own by virtue of this victory over the king, as our elder brothers can plead property in their enclosures; and that for three reasons in England's law.

First, by a lawful purchase or contract between the Parliament and us; for they were our landlords and lords of manors, that held the freedom of the commons from us[1] while the king was in his power; for they held title thereunto from him,[2] he being the head and they branches of the kingly power that enslaved the people by that ancient conqueror's sword, that was the ruling power. For they said, "Come and help us against the king that enslaves us, that we may be delivered from his tyranny, and we will make you a free people."

---

4. The conquest of England by the Norman William the Conqueror in 1066. Winstanley argued that the oppression of the poor and the landless was a consequence of nearly six centuries of occupation of England by a foreign power.
5. Common people.
6. Absolute rule.
7. A tax on domestically manufactured goods, first imposed by Parliament in 1643 to finance the war against the king. "Plate": silver plate. "Free-

quarter": free room and board for soldiers, or its monetary equivalent imposed as a tax.
8. Reward of victory.
9. Estates commonly passed to the eldest brother, leaving the younger brothers landless.
1. Kept the right to use the common lands from us, the common people.
2. Under the feudal system, the great lords held their lands on grant from the king, in return for their allegiance.

Now they cannot make us free unless they deliver us from the bondage[3] which they themselves held us under; and that is, they held the freedom of the earth from us: for we in part with them have delivered ourselves from the king. Now we claim freedom from that bondage you have and yet do hold us under, by the bargain and contract between Parliament and us, who, I say, did consist of lords of manors and landlords, whereof Mr. Drake,[4] who hath arrested me for digging upon the common, was one at that time. Therefore by the law of bargain and sale we claim of them our freedom, to live comfortably with them in this land of our nativity; and this we cannot do so long as we lie under poverty, and must not be suffered to plant the commons and wasteland for our livelihood. For take away the land from any people, and those people are in a way of continual dearth and misery; and better not to have had a body, than not to have food and raiment for it. But, I say, they have sold us our freedom in the common, and have been largely paid for it; for by means of our bloods and money they sit in peace: for if the king had prevailed, they had lost all, and been in slavery to the meanest cavalier, if the king would.[5] Therefore we the commons say, give us our bargain: if you deny us our bargain, you deny God, Christ, and scriptures; and all your profession[6] then is and hath been hypocrisy.

Secondly, the commons and crown land is our property by equal conquest over the kingly power: for the Parliament did never stir up the people by promises and covenant to assist them to cast out the king and to establish them in the king's place and prerogative power. No, but all their declarations were for the safety and peace of the whole nation.

Therefore the common people being part of the nation, and especially they that bore the greatest heat of the day in casting out the oppressor; and the nation cannot be in peace so long as the poor oppressed are in wants and the land is entangled and held from them by bondage.

But the victory being obtained over the king, the spoil, which is properly the land, ought in equity to be divided now between the two parties, that is Parliament and common people. The Parliament, consisting of lords of manors and gentry, ought to have their enclosure lands free to them without molestation. . . . And the common people, consisting of soldiers and such as paid taxes and free-quarter, ought to have the freedom of all waste and common land and crown land equally among them. The soldiery ought not in equity to have all, nor the other people that paid them to have all; but the spoil ought to be divided between them that stayed at home and them that went to war; for the victory is for the whole nation.

And as the Parliament declared they did all for the nation, and not for themselves only; so we plead with the army, they did not fight for themselves, but for the freedom of the nation: and I say, we have bought our freedom of them likewise by taxes and free-quarter. Therefore we claim an equal freedom with them in this conquest over the king.

---

3. Technically bondage refers to the services and goods legally required by feudal landowners of their tenants.
4. Sir Francis Drake, a member of Parliament who owned St. George's Hill, on which Winstanley and his followers had established a commune. At first sympathetic to the Diggers, Drake eventually took legal action to have them evicted.
5. To the lowest soldier of the king, if the king so commanded.
6. Statement of principles.

Thirdly, we claim an equal portion in the victory over the king by virtue of the two acts of Parliament: the one to make England a free commonwealth, the other to take away kingly power. Now the kingly power, you have heard, is a power that rules by the sword in covetousness and self, giving the earth to some and denying it to others: and this kingly power was not in the hand of the king alone, but lords, and lords of manors, and corrupt judges and lawyers especially held it up likewise. For he was the head and they, with the tithing priests,[7] are the branches of that tyrannical kingly power; and all the several limbs and members must be cast out before kingly power can be pulled up root and branch. Mistake me not, I do not say, cast out the persons of men. No, I do not desire their fingers to ache;[8] but I say, cast out their power whereby they hold the people in bondage, as the king held them in bondage. And I say, it is our own freedom we claim, both by bargain and by equality in the conquest; as well as by the law of righteous creation which gives the earth to all equally.

And the power of lords of manors lies in this: they deny the common people the use and free benefit of the earth, unless they give them leave and pay them for it, either in rent, in fines, in homages or heriots.[9] Surely the earth was never made by God that the younger brother should not live in the earth unless he would work for and pay his elder brother rent for the earth. No, this slavery came in by conquest, and it is part of the kingly power; and England cannot be a free commonwealth till this bondage be taken away. You have taken away the king; you have taken away the House of Lords. Now step two steps further, and take away the power of lords of manors and of tithing priests, and the intolerable oppressions of judges by whom laws are corrupted; and your work will be honorable.

Fourthly, if this freedom be denied the common people, to enjoy the common land; then Parliament, army, and judges will deny equity and reason, whereupon the laws of a well-governed commonwealth ought to be built. And if this equity be denied, then there can be no law but club law[1] among the people: and if the sword must reign, then every party will be striving to bear the sword; and then farewell peace; nay, farewell religion and gospel, unless it be made use of to entrap one another, as we plainly see some priests and others make it a cloak for their knavery. If I adventure my life and fruit of my labor equal with you, and obtain what we strive for; it is both equity and reason that I should equally divide the spoil with you, and not you to have all and I none. And if you deny us this, you take away our property from us, our monies and blood, and give us nothing for it.

Therefore, I say, the common land is my own land, equal with my fellow-commoners, and our true property, by the law of creation. It is everyone's, but not one single one's. . . . True religion and undefiled is this, to make restitution of the earth, which hath been taken and held from the common people by the power of conquests formerly, and so set the oppressed free. Do not

---

7. Priests of the Church of England were legally entitled to a tenth, or "tithe," of the goods of every parishioner; those people who wished to separate from the established church fiercely resented the involuntary nature of the tithe.

8. Wish the least physical harm to them.
9. Fees or goods paid by tenants to landlords in addition to rent.
1. That is, might makes right.

all strive to enjoy the land? The gentry strive for land, the clergy strive for land, the common people strive for land; and buying and selling is an art whereby people endeavor to cheat one another of the land. Now if any can prove from the law of righteousness that the land was made peculiar to him and his successively,[2] shutting others out, he shall enjoy it freely for my part. But I affirm it was made for all; and true religion is to let everyone enjoy it. Therefore, you rulers of England, make restitution of the lands which the kingly power holds from us: set the oppressed free, and come in and honor Christ, who is the restoring power, and you shall find rest.

1650

2. By inheritance.

THOMAS HOBBES

The English civil war and its aftermath raised fundamental questions about the nature and legitimacy of state power. In 1651 Thomas Hobbes (1588–1679) attempted to answer those questions in his ambitious masterwork of political philosophy, *Leviathan*. He grounded his political vision upon a comprehensive philosophy of nature and knowledge. Hobbes held that everything in the universe is composed only of matter; spirit does not exist. All knowledge is gained through sensory impressions, which are nothing but matter in motion. What we call the self is, for Hobbes, simply a tissue of sensory impressions—clear and immediate in the presence of the objects that evoke them, vague and less vivid in their absence. As a result, an iron determinism of cause and effect governs everything in the universe, including human action.

Because, Hobbes argues, all humans are roughly equal mentally and physically, they possess equal hopes of attaining goods, as well as equal fears of danger from others. In the state of nature, prior to the foundation of some sovereign power to keep them in awe, everyone is continually at war with everyone else, and life, in Hobbes's memorable phrase, is "solitary, poor, nasty, brutish, and short." To escape this ghastly strife, humans covenant with one another to establish a sovereign government over all of them. That sovereign power—which need not be a king but is always indivisible—incorporates the wills and individuality of them all, so that the people no longer have rights or liberties apart from the sovereign's will. The sovereign's dominion over his subjects extends to the right to pronounce on all matters of religion.

While other versions of covenant theory, for instance Milton's *Tenure of Kings and Magistrates*, insisted that the power transferred by the people to the sovereign could be limited or revoked, in Hobbes's system, the founding political covenant must be a permanent one, since no tyranny can be so evil as the state of war that the sovereign power prevents. Yet if the sovereign power should be overthrown, the individual ruler has no further claim, and the people, for their safety, must accept the new sovereign unconditionally. Hobbes was generally associated with the royalist cause, as a tutor to the Cavendish family and as an exile in Paris from 1640 to 1651, where he tutored the future Charles II. Yet his argument made no distinction between a legitimate monarch and a successful usurper, like Oliver Cromwell. Moreover, Hobbes's philosophical materialism led many to suspect him of atheism;

after the Restoration, the publication of many of his books, including a history of the civil war entitled *Behemoth*, was prohibited for a number of years. Undeterred, Hobbes continued to write on a variety of psychological, political, and mathematical topics, completing a translation of Homer's *Iliad* and *Odyssey* at the age of eighty-six.

Hobbes's political theory did not fit easily into the established patterns of English thought partly because his perspective was unusually cosmopolitan. Educated at Oxford as a classicist, Hobbes traveled widely in Europe between 1610 and 1660 as a companion and tutor of noblemen, often remaining abroad for years at a time. During these lengthy sojourns he became acquainted with many of the leading intellectuals and scientists on the Continent, including Galileo, Descartes, and the prominent French mathematician Pierre Gassendi, who argued that the universe was governed entirely by mechanical principles. The most important political philosophers for Hobbes were also Continental figures: the Italian Niccolò Machiavelli, who saw human beings as naturally competitive and power hungry, and Jean Bodin, a French theorist of indivisible, absolute monarchy. One English writer who did influence Hobbes profoundly was Francis Bacon, whose amanuensis Hobbes had been in Bacon's last years. Ironically, Hobbes was not invited to join the Royal Society, established after the Restoration on Baconian principles, because his religious views were suspect and because he had quarreled with several of the society's founders. Yet Hobbes is truly Bacon's heir, sharing Bacon's utter lack of sentimentality and a memorably astringent prose style.

From Leviathan[1]

From *The Introduction*

[THE ARTIFICIAL MAN]

Nature (the art whereby God hath made and governs the world) is by the art of man, as in many other things, so in this also imitated, that it can make an artificial[2] animal. For seeing life is but a motion of limbs, the beginning whereof is in some principal part within, why may we not say that all automata (engines that move themselves by springs and wheels as doth a watch) have an artificial life?[3] For what is the heart but a spring; and the nerves but so many strings; and the joints but so many wheels, giving motion to the whole body such as was intended by the artificer? Art goes yet further, imitating that rational and most excellent work of nature, man. For by art is created that great Leviathan called a Commonwealth or State (in Latin, *Civitas*), which is but an artificial man, though of greater stature and strength than the natural, for whose protection and defense it was intended; and in which the sovereignty is an artificial soul, as giving life and motion to the whole body; the magistrates and other officers of judicature and execution, artificial joints; reward and punishment (by which, fastened to the seat of the sovereignty, every joint and member is moved to perform his duty) are the nerves, that do the same in the body natural; the wealth and riches

---

1. The title refers to the primordial sea creature Leviathan, described in Job 41 as the prime evidence of and analogue to God's power, beyond all human measure and comprehension. Hobbes takes him as figure for the sovereign power in the state. Leviathan was also sometimes taken as a figure for Satan, on the basis of Job 41.34: "he is a king over all the children of pride."
2. Made by art.
3. Hobbes's definition of life as motion collapses the distinction between the life of humans and the life of machines or institutions.

of all the particular members are the strength; *salus populi* (the people's safety) its business; counselors, by whom all things needful for it to know are suggested unto it, are the memory; equity and laws an artificial reason and will; concord, health; sedition, sickness; and civil war, death. Lastly, the pacts and covenants by which the parts of this body politic were at first made, set together, and united, resemble that *Fiat* or the "let us make man," pronounced by God in the creation.[4]

* * *

From *Part 1. Of Man*

CHAPTER 1. OF SENSE

Concerning the thoughts of man, I will consider them first singly and afterwards in train or dependence upon one another. Singly, they are every one a representation or appearance of some quality or other accident of a body without us, which is commonly called an object. Which object worketh on the eyes, ears, and other parts of man's body, and by diversity of working produceth diversity of appearances.

The original of them all is that which we call sense. (For there is no conception in a man's mind which hath not at first, totally or by parts, been begotten upon the organs of sense.)[5] The rest are derived from that original.

To know the natural cause of sense is not very necessary to the business now in hand, and I have elsewhere written of the same at large. Nevertheless, to fill each part of my present method, I will briefly deliver the same in this place.

The cause of sense is the external body or object which presseth the organ proper to each sense, either immediately as in the taste and touch, or mediately, as in seeing, hearing, and smelling; which pressure, by the mediation of nerves and other strings and membranes of the body continued inwards to the brain and heart, causeth there a resistance or counterpressure or endeavor of the heart to deliver itself;[6] which endeavor, because outward, seemeth to be some matter without. And this seeming or fancy is that which men call sense; and consisteth, as to the eye, in a light or color figured; to the ear, in a sound; to the nostril in an odor; to the tongue and palate in a savor; and to the rest of the body in heat, cold, hardness, softness, and such other qualities as we discern by feeling. All which qualities called "sensible"[7] are, in the object that causeth them, but so many several motions of the matter by which it presseth our organs diversely. Neither, in us that are pressed, are they anything else but diverse motions; for motion produceth nothing but motion. But their appearance to us is fancy, the same waking, that dreaming. And as pressing, rubbing, or striking the eye makes us fancy a light; and pressing the ear produceth a din; so do the bodies also we see or hear produce the same by their strong though unobserved actions. For if those colors and sounds were in the bodies or objects that cause them, they

4. Genesis 1.26.
5. This view of the mind as a blank sheet written on by physical experience will influence the philosophy of John Locke and David Hume.
6. Hobbes's physiology of sense is, in keeping with his premises, strictly mechanical.
7. I.e., accessible through the senses.

Leviathan. Abraham Bosse's frontispiece for *Leviathan* was based on a sketch by Hobbes. The "Leviathan" or commonwealth is shown as a gigantic human figure holding a scepter and a sword; the figure is made up of many tiny individual humans who have joined together in the social contract. Hobbes's royalist sympathies are betrayed in the figure's face, which is that of King Charles. The small pictures in the lower part of the engraving display the various attributes of civil power on the left, and ecclesiastical power on the right.

could not be severed from them, as by glasses[8] and in echoes by reflection we see they are; where we know the thing we see is in one place, the appearance in another. And though at some certain distance the real and very object seem invested with the fancy it begets in us, yet still the object is one thing, the image or fancy is another. So that sense in all cases is nothing

8. Mirrors.

else but original fancy, caused (as I have said) by the pressure, that is by the motion, of external things upon our eyes, ears, and other organs thereunto ordained.

But the philosophy schools[9] through all the universities of Christendom, grounded upon certain texts of Aristotle, teach another doctrine, and say for the cause of vision, that the thing seen sendeth forth on every side a visible species—in English, a visible show, apparition, or aspect, or a being seen—the receiving whereof into the eye is seeing. And for the cause of hearing, that the thing heard sendeth forth an audible species, that is an audible aspect or audible being seen, which entering at the ear maketh hearing. Nay for the cause of understanding also they say the thing understood sendeth forth intelligible species, that is an intelligible being seen, which coming into the understanding makes us understand. I say not this as disapproving the use of universities, but because I am to speak hereafter of their office in a commonwealth, I must let you see on all occasions by the way what things would be amended in them; amongst which the frequency of insignificant speech[1] is one.

* * *

CHAPTER 13. OF THE NATURAL CONDITION OF MANKIND AS CONCERNING THEIR FELICITY AND MISERY

Nature hath made men so equal in the faculties of body and mind as that, though there be found one man sometimes manifestly stronger in body or of quicker mind than another, yet when all is reckoned together, the difference between man and man is not so considerable as that one man can thereupon claim to himself any benefit, to which another may not pretend as well as he. For as to the strength of body, the weakest has strength enough to kill the strongest, either by secret machination, or by confederacy[2] with others that are in the same danger with himself.

And as to the faculties of the mind—setting aside the arts grounded upon words, and especially that skill of proceeding upon general and infallible rules, called science; which very few have, and but in few things; as being not a native faculty, born with us; nor attained, as prudence, while we look after somewhat else—I find yet a greater equality amongst men than that of strength. For prudence is but experience, which equal time equally bestows on all men, in those things they equally apply themselves unto. That which may perhaps make such equality incredible is but a vain conceit of one's own wisdom, which almost all men think they have in a greater degree than the vulgar—that is, than all men but themselves and a few others, whom by fame, or for concurring with themselves, they approve. For such is the nature of men, that howsoever they may acknowledge many others to be more witty, or more eloquent, or more learned, yet they will hardly believe there be many so wise as themselves; for they see their own wit at hand, and other men's at a distance. But this proveth rather that men are in that point equal, than unequal. For there is not ordinarily a greater

9. Led by the Scholastic philosophers (school-men).
1. Unmeaningful speech. Cf. Bacon's critique of

the idols of the marketplace and the theater in *Novum Organum* 43–44 and 59–62.
2. Alliance.

sign of the equal distribution of anything than that every man is contented with his share.

From this equality of ability ariseth equality of hope in the attaining of our ends. And therefore if any two men desire the same thing, which nevertheless they cannot both enjoy, they become enemies; and in the way to their end (which is principally their own conservation, and sometimes their delectation[3] only) endeavor to destroy or subdue one another. And from hence it comes to pass, that where an invader hath no more to fear than another man's single power, if one plant, sow, build, or possess a convenient seat, others may probably be expected to come prepared with forces united, to dispossess and deprive him, not only of the fruit of his labor, but also of his life or liberty. And the invader again is in the like danger of another.

And from this diffidence[4] of one another, there is no way for any man to secure himself so reasonable as anticipation; that is, by force or wiles to master the persons of all men he can, so long, till he see no other power great enough to endanger him; and this is no more than his own conservation requireth, and is generally allowed. Also because there be some, that taking pleasure in contemplating their own power in the acts of conquest, which they pursue farther than their security requires; if others that otherwise would be glad to be at ease within modest bounds, should not by invasion increase their power, they would not be able long time, by standing only on their defense, to subsist. And by consequence, such augmentation of dominion over men being necessary to a man's conservation, it ought to be allowed him.

Again, men have no pleasure, but on the contrary a great deal of grief, in keeping company, where there is no power able to overawe them all. For every man looketh that his companion should value him at the same rate he sets upon himself; and upon all signs of contempt, or undervaluing, naturally endeavors, as far as he dares (which amongst them that have no common power to keep them in quiet, is far enough to make them destroy each other), to extort a greater value from his contemners[5] by damage, and from others by the example.

So that in the nature of man, we find three principal causes of quarrel. First, competition; secondly, diffidence; thirdly, glory.

The first maketh men invade for gain; the second, for safety; and the third, for reputation. The first use violence to make themselves masters of other men's persons, wives, children, and cattle; the second, to defend them; the third, for trifles, as a word, a smile, a different opinion, and any other sign of undervalue, either direct in their persons, or by reflection in their kindred, their friends, their nation, their profession, or their name.

Hereby it is manifest that during the time men live without a common power to keep them all in awe, they are in that condition which is called war; and such a war as is of every man against every man. For war consisteth not in battle only, or the act of fighting, but in a tract of time wherein the will to contend by battle is sufficiently known; and therefore the notion of time is to be considered in the nature of war, as it is in the nature of weather. For as the nature of foul weather lieth not in a shower or two of rain, but in an

---

3. Pleasure.
4. Lack of faith, mistrust.

5. Scorners.

inclination thereto of many days together; so the nature of war consisteth not in actual fighting, but in the known disposition thereto, during all the time there is no assurance to the contrary. All other time is peace.

Whatsoever therefore is consequent to a time of war, where every man is enemy to every man, the same is consequent to the time wherein men live without other security than what their own strength and their own invention shall furnish them withal. In such condition there is no place for industry, because the fruit thereof is uncertain, and consequently no culture of the earth; no navigation, nor use of the commodities that may be imported by sea; no commodious building; no instruments of moving, and removing, such things as require much force; no knowledge of the face of the earth; no account of time; no arts; no letters; no society; and, which is worst of all, continual fear, and danger of violent death; and the life of man, solitary, poor, nasty, brutish, and short.

It may seem strange to some man that has not well weighed these things, that nature should thus dissociate and render men apt to invade and destroy one another; and he may therefore, not trusting to this inference, made from the passions, desire perhaps to have the same confirmed by experience. Let him therefore consider with himself, when taking a journey, he arms himself and seeks to go well accompanied; when going to sleep, he locks his doors; when even in his house he locks his chests; and this when he knows there be laws, and public officers, armed, to revenge all injuries shall be done him; what opinion he has of his fellow subjects, when he rides armed; of his fellow citizens, when he locks his doors; and of his children and servants, when he locks his chests. Does he not there as much accuse mankind by his actions, as I do by my words? But neither of us accuse man's nature in it. The desires and other passions of man are in themselves no sin. No more are the actions that proceed from those passions, till they know a law that forbids them, which, till laws be made, they cannot know; nor can any law be made, till they have agreed upon the person that shall make it.

It may peradventure be thought there was never such a time nor condition of war as this; and I believe it was never generally so, over all the world; but there are many places where they live so now. For the savage people in many places of America, except the government of small families, the concord whereof dependeth on natural lust, have no government at all and live at this day in that brutish manner as I said before. Howsoever, it may be perceived what manner of life there would be, where there were no common power to fear, by the manner of life which men that have formerly lived under a peaceful government use to degenerate into in a civil war.[6]

But though there had never been any time wherein particular men were in a condition of war one against another, yet in all times, kings and persons of sovereign authority, because of their independency, are in continual jealousies, and in the state and posture of gladiators; having their weapons pointing, and their eyes fixed on one another; that is, their forts, garrisons, and guns upon the frontiers of their kingdoms, and continual spies upon their neighbors, which is a posture of war. But because they uphold thereby

6. Hobbes is thinking of the recent civil wars in England, and perhaps also of the Greek civil wars described by Thucydides (whom he translated).

the industry of their subjects, there does not follow from it that misery which accompanies the liberty of particular men.

To this war of every man against every man, this also is consequent: that nothing can be unjust. The notions of right and wrong, justice and injustice, have there no place. Where there is no common power, there is no law; where no law, no injustice. Force and fraud are in war the two cardinal virtues. Justice and injustice are none of the faculties neither of the body nor mind. If they were, they might be in a man that were alone in the world, as well as his senses and passions. They are qualities that relate to men in society, not in solitude. It is consequent also to the same condition that there be no propriety,[7] no dominion, no *mine* and *thine* distinct; but only that to be every man's, that he can get; and for so long as he can keep it. And thus much for the ill condition which man by mere nature is actually placed in; though with a possibility to come out of it, consisting partly in the passions, partly in his reason.

The passions that incline men to peace are fear of death, desire of such things as are necessary to commodious living, and a hope by their industry to obtain them. And reason suggesteth convenient articles of peace, upon which men may be drawn to agreement. These articles are they which otherwise are called the Laws of Nature, whereof I shall speak more particularly in the two following chapters.

FROM CHAPTER 14. OF THE FIRST AND SECOND NATURAL LAWS

The Right of Nature, which writers commonly call *ius naturale*, is the liberty each man hath to use his own power as he will himself for the preservation of his own nature, that is to say, of his own life; and consequently of doing anything which in his own judgment and reason he shall conceive to be the aptest means thereunto.

By Liberty is understood, according to the proper signification of the word, the absence of external impediments, which impediments may oft take away part of a man's power to do what he would, but cannot hinder him from using the power left him according as his judgment and reason shall dictate to him.

A Law of Nature (*lex naturalis*) is a precept or general rule found out by reason, by which a man is forbidden to do that which is destructive of his life or taketh away the means of preserving the same; and to omit that by which he thinketh it may be best preserved. For though they that speak of this subject use to confound[8] *Ius* and *Lex*, *Right* and *Law*, yet they ought to be distinguished, because Right consisteth in liberty to do or to forbear, whereas Law determineth and bindeth to one of them: so that Law and Right differ as much as obligation and liberty, which in one and the same matter are inconsistent.

And because the condition of man (as hath been declared in the precedent chapter) is a condition of war of every one against every one, in which case every one is governed by his own reason, and there is nothing he can make use of that may not be a help unto him in preserving his life against his enemies: it followeth that in such a condition every man has a right to

7. Property.   8. Confuse.

every thing, even to one another's body. And therefore as long as this natural right of every man to every thing endureth, there can be no security to any man (how strong or wise soever he be) of living out the time which nature ordinarily alloweth men to live. And consequently it is a precept or general rule of reason, *That every man ought to endeavor peace, as far as he has hope of obtaining it; and when he cannot obtain it, that he may seek and use all helps and advantages of war.* The first branch of which rule containeth the first and fundamental law of nature, which is *to seek peace and follow it.* The second, the sum of the right of nature, which is, *by all means we can to defend ourselves.*

From this fundamental law of nature, by which men are commanded to endeavor peace, is derived this second law: *That a man be willing, when others are so too, as far-forth as*[9] *for peace and defense of himself he shall think it necessary, to lay down this right to all things, and be contented with so much liberty against other men as he would allow other men against himself.* For as long as any man holdeth this right of doing anything he liketh, so long are all men in the condition of war. But if other men will not lay down their right, as well as he, then there is no reason for anyone to divest himself of his. For that were to expose himself to prey (which no man is bound to) rather than to dispose himself to peace. This is that law of the Gospel: *Whatsoever you require that others should do to you, that do ye to them.*[1]

* * *

FROM CHAPTER 15. OF OTHER LAWS OF NATURE

From that law of nature by which we are obliged to transfer to another such rights as, being retained, hinder the peace of mankind, there followeth a third, which is this: *That men perform their covenants made:*[2] without which, covenants are in vain, and but empty words; and, the right of all men to all things remaining, we are still in the condition of war.

And in this law of nature consisteth the fountain and original of Justice. For where no covenant hath preceded, there hath no right been transferred, and every man has right to every thing; and consequently no action can be unjust. But when a covenant is made, then to break it is unjust; and the definition of injustice is no other than *the not performance of covenant.* And whatsoever is not unjust is just. * * *

For the question is not of promises mutual where there is no security of performance on either side, as when there is no civil power erected over the parties promising; for such promises are no covenants. But either where one of the parties has performed already, or where there is a power to make him perform: there is the question whether it be against reason, that is against the benefit of the other, to perform or not. And I say it is not against reason.[3] For the manifestation whereof, we are to consider: first, that when a man doth a thing which (notwithstanding anything can be foreseen and

9. Insofar as.
1. The Golden Rule: Matthew 7.12, Luke 6.31.
2. Though the terms are general, Hobbes refers in this chapter especially to the covenants men make with each other when they transfer power

to the sovereign. Milton makes very different use of covenant theory to justify the rebellion and regicide in *The Tenure of Kings and Magistrates.*
3. I.e., to perform the promise.

reckoned on) tendeth to his own destruction, howsoever[4] some accident, which he could not expect, arriving may turn it to his benefit; yet such events do not make it reasonably or wisely done. Secondly, that in a condition of war, wherein every man to every man, for want of a common power to keep them all in awe, is an enemy, there is no man can hope by his own strength or wit to defend himself from destruction without the help of confederates; where everyone expects the same defense by the confederation that anyone else does. And therefore he which declares he thinks it reason to deceive those that help him can in reason expect no other means of safety than what can be had from his own single power. He therefore that breaketh his covenant, and consequently declareth that he thinks he may with reason do so, cannot be received into any society that unite themselves for peace and defense, but by the error of them that receive him; nor when he is received be retained in it without seeing the danger of their error; which errors a man cannot reasonably reckon upon as the means of his security. And therefore if he be left or cast out of society, he perisheth; and if he live in society, it is by the errors of other men, which he could not foresee nor reckon upon; and consequently against the reason of his preservation; and so as all men that contribute not to his destruction forbear him only out of ignorance of what is good for themselves.

As for the instance of gaining the secure and perpetual felicity of heaven by any way, it is frivolous: there being but one way imaginable, and that is not breaking, but keeping of covenant.

And for the other instance of attaining sovereignty by rebellion, it is manifest that though the event follow, yet because it cannot reasonably be expected, but rather the contrary; and because by gaining it so others are taught to gain the same in like manner, the attempt thereof is against reason. Justice therefore, that is to say, keeping of covenant, is a rule of reason, by which we are forbidden to do anything destructive to our life, and consequently a law of nature.

* * *

From *Part 2: Of Commonwealth*

CHAPTER 17. OF THE CAUSES, GENERATION, AND DEFINITION OF A COMMONWEALTH

The final cause, end, or design of men, who naturally love liberty and dominion over others, in the introduction of that restraint upon themselves in which we see them live in commonwealths, is the foresight of their own preservation and of a more contented life thereby—that is to say, of getting themselves out from their miserable condition of war which is necessarily consequent, as has been shown (Chapter 13), to the natural passions of men when there is no visible power to keep them in awe and tie them by fear of punishment to the performance of their convenants and observation of those laws of nature set down in the fourteenth and fifteenth chapters.

4. Even though.

For the laws of nature—as justice, equity, modesty, mercy, and, in sum, doing to others as we would be done to—of themselves, without the terror of some power to cause them to be observed, are contrary to our natural passions, that carry us to partiality,[5] pride, revenge, and the like. And covenants without the sword are but words, and of no strength to secure a man at all. Therefore, notwithstanding the laws of nature (which everyone has then kept when he had the will to keep them, when he can do it safely), if there be no power erected, or not great enough for our security, every man will—and may lawfully—rely on his own strength and art for caution[6] against all other men. And in all places where men have lived by small families, to rob and spoil one another has been a trade, and so far from being reputed against the law of nature that the greater spoils they gained, the greater was their honor; and men observed no other laws therein but the laws of honor—that is to abstain from cruelty, leaving to men their lives and instruments of husbandry. And as small families did then, so now do cities and kingdoms, which are but greater families, for their own security enlarge their dominions upon all pretenses of danger and fear of invasion or assistance that may be given to invaders, and endeavor as much as they can to subdue or weaken their neighbors by open force and secret arts, for want of other caution, justly; and are remembered for it in after ages with honor.

Nor is it the joining together of a small number of men that gives them this security, because in small numbers small additions on the one side or the other make the advantage of strength so great as is sufficient to carry the victory, and therefore gives encouragement to an invasion. The multitude sufficient to confide in for our security is not determined by any certain number but by comparison with the enemy we fear, and is then sufficient when the odds of the enemy is not of so visible and conspicuous moment to determine the event[7] of war as to move him to attempt.

And be there never so great a multitude, yet if their actions be directed according to their particular judgments and particular appetites, they can expect thereby no defense nor protection, neither against a common enemy nor against the injuries of one another. For being distracted in opinion[8] concerning the best use and application of their strength, they do not help but hinder one another, and reduce their strength by mutual opposition to nothing; whereby they are easily not only subdued by a very few that agree together, but also, when there is no common enemy, they make war upon each other for their particular interest. For if we could suppose a great multitude of men to consent in the observation of justice and other laws of nature without a common power to keep them all in awe, we might as well suppose all mankind to do the same, then there neither would be, nor need to be, any civil government or commonwealth at all, because there would be peace without subjection.

Nor is it enough for the security which men desire should last all the time of their life that they be governed and directed by one judgment for a limited time, as in one battle or one war. For though they obtain a victory by their unanimous endeavor against a foreign enemy, yet afterwards, when either

---

5. Favoritism, to oneself or another.
6. Precaution, defense.

7. Outcome.
8. I.e., by opinions.

they have no common enemy or he that by one part is held for an enemy is by another part held for a friend, they must needs, by the difference of their interests, dissolve and fall again into a war among themselves.

It is true that certain living creatures, as bees and ants, live sociably one with another—which are therefore by Aristotle numbered among political creatures—and have no other direction than their particular judgments and appetites, nor speech whereby one of them can signify to another what he thinks expedient for the common benefit; and therefore some man may perhaps desire to know why mankind cannot do the same. To which I answer:

First, that men are continually in competition for honor and dignity, which these creatures are not; and consequently among men there arises on that ground envy and hatred and finally war, but among these not so.

Secondly, that among these creatures the common good differs not from the private; and being by nature inclined to their private, they procure thereby the common benefit. But man, whose joy consists in comparing himself with other men, can relish nothing but what is eminent.

Thirdly, that these creatures—having not, as man, the use of reason—do not see nor think they see any fault in the administration of their common business; whereas among men there are very many that think themselves wiser and abler to govern the public better than the rest, and these strive to reform and innovate, one this way, another that way, and thereby bring it into distraction and civil war.

Fourthly, that these creatures, though they have some use of voice in making known to one another their desires and other affections, yet they want that art of words by which some men can represent to others that which is good in the likeness of evil, and evil in the likeness of good, and augment or diminish this apparent greatness of good and evil, discontenting men and troubling their peace at their pleasure.

Fifthly, irrational creatures cannot distinguish between injury and damage, and therefore, as long as they be at ease, they are not offended with their fellows; whereas man is then most troublesome when he is most at ease, for then it is that he loves to show his wisdom and control the actions of them that govern the commonwealth.

Lastly, the agreement of these creatures is natural, that of men is by covenant only, which is artificial, and therefore it is no wonder if there be somewhat else required besides covenant to make their agreement constant and lasting, which is a common power to keep them in awe and to direct their actions to the common benefit.

The only way to erect such a common power as may be able to defend them from the invasion of foreigners and the injuries of one another, and thereby to secure them in such sort as that by their own industry and by the fruits of the earth they may nourish themselves and live contentedly, is to confer all their power and strength upon one man, or upon one assembly of men that may reduce all their wills, by plurality of voices, into one will, which is as much as to say, to appoint one man or assembly of men to bear their person, and everyone to own and acknowledge himself to be the author of whatsoever he that so bears their person shall act or cause to be acted in those things which concern the common peace and safety, and therein to submit their wills everyone to his will, and their judgments to his judgment. This is more than consent or concord; it is a real unity of them all in one and the same person, made by covenant of every man with every man, in such manner as if every man should say to every man, "I authorize and give up my right of governing myself to this man, or to this assembly of men, on the condition that you give up your right to him and authorize all his actions in like manner." This done, the multitude so united in one person is called a commonwealth, in Latin *civitas*. This is the generation of that great Leviathan (or rather, to speak more reverently, of that mortal god) to whom we owe, under the immortal God, our peace and defense. For by this authority, given him by every particular man in the commonwealth, he has the use of so much power and strength conferred on him that, by terror thereof, he is enabled to form the wills of them all to peace at home and mutual aid against their enemies abroad. And in him consists the essence of the commonwealth, which, to define it, is one person, of whose acts a great multitude, by mutual covenants one with another, have made themselves everyone the author, to the end he may use the strength and means of them all as he shall think expedient for their peace and common defense. And he that carries this person is called sovereign and said to have sovereign power; and everyone besides, his subject.

1651

WRITING THE SELF

The seventeenth century saw an explosion of interest in the intimate texture of day-to-day experience, in the sometimes surprising twists and turns of individual lives, in the relationship between character and destiny. Of course, such concerns were not entirely new: Chaucer's *Canterbury Tales* had dwelt lovingly upon the quirky diversity of its pilgrims. Some seventeenth-century writers looked back as well to classical or foreign precedents: the *Lives* of the late-classical biographer Plutarch, with their marvelously revelatory anecdotes and shrewd assessments of human moral complexity, the essays of the French Michel de Montaigne, who described his own opinions and experiences in frank detail. Both Plutarch and Montaigne profoundly influenced William Shakespeare, whose unparalleled gift for delineating character has led one recent critic to credit him with having "invented the human." Other writers, particularly religious ones, owed much to the medieval tradition of hagiography, or the narrating of the lives of saints and martyrs as models for the faithful to admire and imitate. Izaak Walton, in biographies of John Donne, George Herbert, and other worthies that draw upon his personal experience with them as well as upon his research, was one practitioner in a Protestant hagiographic tradition (pp. 976–80). Other Protestants directed their gaze inward, convinced of the importance of spiritual self-scrutiny ummediated by ritual or clergyman. Many Puritans kept spiritual accountings in writing—part diaries, part prayers—that effectively substituted for the Catholic practice of oral confession to a priest.

During the civil war and its aftermath, interest in "writing the self" only intensified. For the autobiographically inclined, the physical and ideological turmoil of the midcentury could intensify a sense of the individual's isolation and uniqueness, forcing (or permitting) him to experience a range of events for which his upbringing could not have prepared him. Those who reflected upon the history of the period, as Lucy Hutchinson and Edward Hyde did, were often enthralled by the clash of strong personalities as well as the struggle between political principles, social trends, or cultural movements. Both Hutchinson and Hyde, from their different ends of the political spectrum, saw Cromwell and Charles I as locked in a fateful rivalry, each leader a complex mixture of personal strengths and failings.

The prominence of women writers in this section is no accident. Even though women were excluded from formal political participation, the war contributed to the development of their political interests and consciousness, and sometimes allowed them to play important informal or improvised roles in momentous events. The resourceful, adventurous Anne Halkett obviously relished her daring contribution to the rescue of the Duke of York. Some women writers explicitly eschewed a feminist agenda: Lucy Hutchinson's trenchant historical analysis coexists with thoroughly traditional beliefs about the proper submission of wife to husband and about the danger of women with political ambition, notably Charles I's queen. She excuses her own writing, to others and perhaps also to herself, by casting her work as a tribute to her beloved husband. In other cases, a challenge to political authority is inextricable from an assault on male privilege. Dorothy Waugh, a Quaker, refused like others of her faith to defer to political or religious authorities and insisted on the spiritual equality between women and men. Waugh suffered as much on account of her sex as on account of her religion, for she describes how the mayor of Carlisle is outraged not only by her unauthorized preaching but by the fact that the preacher is female. She is punished by being forced to wear a "scold's bridle," a traditional humiliation meted out to outspoken, argumentative women who refused to obey their husbands.

LUCY HUTCHINSON

Lucy Hutchinson, née Apsley (1620–1681), whose life centered in the North Country city of Nottingham, was a staunch republican, memoirist, poet, translator of Lucretius, and biographer and historian of the revolutionary period. In a fragmentary autobiography, she relates that she could read English perfectly by the age of four, and that "having a great memory, I was carried to sermons, and while I was very young could remember and repeat them . . . exactly." Her parents allowed her to receive at home as good an education as her brothers got at school She reports that her future husband learned of her existence by noticing some of her Latin books. She was married at eighteen to John Hutchinson, a man of unyielding conviction and courage: he fought in the Puritan armies, served as governor of Nottingham Castle, sat in the Long Parliament, voted for the execution of Charles I, supported the republican commonwealth (1649–53), but withdrew support from Cromwell when he overrode and dismissed parliaments. Hutchinson was arrested after the Restoration and died in prison in 1664. After his death his wife of twenty-six years wrote *Memoirs of the Life of Colonel John Hutchinson*, purportedly to preserve his memory for her children. But within that eyewitness account of the remarkable period they had lived through, she enfolded a broad history of and commentary upon the Puritan movement and the revolution. Almost certainly she hoped for a broader audience of nonconformists and republicans who might someday revive the "Good Old Cause," though because of its politics this work was not published until 1806. Also unpublished in her lifetime were several elegiac and satiric poems, as well as most of a long but unfinished epic poem, *Order and Disorder*, which treats biblical history from the Creation to the story of Jacob in twenty cantos, the first five of which were published in 1679. Much of the poem is indebted to *Paradise Lost*.

From Memoirs of the Life of Colonel John Hutchinson

[CHARLES I AND HENRIETTA MARIA]

The face of the court was much changed in the change of the king; for King Charles was temperate, chaste, and serious, so that the fools and bawds, mimics and catamites[1] of the former court grew out of fashion; and the nobility and courtiers, who did not quite abandon their debaucheries, yet so reverenced the king as to retire into corners to practice them. Men of learning and ingenuity in all arts were in esteem, and received encouragement from the king, who was a most excellent judge and great lover of paintings, carvings, gravings,[2] and many other ingenuities, less offensive than the bawdry and profane abusive[3] wit which was the only exercise of the other court. But, as in the primitive times,[4] it is observed that the best emperors were some of them stirred up by Satan to be the bitterest persecutors of the church, so this king was a worse encroacher upon the civil and spiritual liberties of his people by far than his father. He married a papist,[5] a French lady of a haughty spirit, and a great wit and beauty, to whom he became a most uxorious husband. By this means the court was replenished with papists, and many who hoped to advance themselves by the change, turned to that religion. All the papists in the kingdom were favored, and, by the king's example, matched into the best families. The puritans were more than ever discountenanced[6] and persecuted, insomuch that many of them chose to abandon their native country and leave their dearest relations, to retire into any foreign soil or plantation[7] where they might amidst all outward inconveniences enjoy the free exercise of God's worship. Such as could not flee were tormented in the bishops' court,[8] fined, whipped, pilloried, imprisoned, and suffered to enjoy no rest, so that death was better than life to them; and notwithstanding their patient sufferance of all these things, yet was not the king satisfied till the whole land was reduced to perfect slavery. The example of the French king[9] was propounded to him, and he thought himself no monarch so long as his will was confined to the bounds of any law; but knowing that the people of England were not pliable to an arbitrary rule, he plotted to subdue them to his yoke by a foreign force;[1] and till he could effect it made no conscience of granting anything

1. Clowns and homosexuals.
2. Engravings.
3. Satiric.
4. Early Christian period.
5. Roman Catholic.
6. Thwarted, out of favor.
7. Colony, such as the Massachusetts Bay Colony, founded in 1630. "Inconveniences" (following): misfortunes.

8. Courts administered by the Church of England tried and punished those who refused to attend church services, frequented alternative religious gatherings, or disputed church doctrines or policies.
9. The French king reigned without a parliament.
1. Puritans suspected that Charles planned to invite Catholic forces to invade his realm in order to consolidate his own power.

to the people, which he resolved should not oblige him longer than it served his turn; for he was a prince that had nothing of faith or truth, justice or generosity in him. He was the most obstinate person in his self-will that ever was, and so bent upon being an absolute, uncontrollable sovereign that he was resolved either to be such a king or none. His firm adherence to prelacy[2] was not for conscience of one religion more than another, for it was his principle that an honest man might be saved in any profession; but he had a mistaken principle that kingly government in the state could not stand without episcopal government in the church; and therefore, as the bishops flattered him with preaching up his prerogative,[3] and inveighing against the puritans as factious and disloyal, so he protected them in their pomp and pride and insolent practices against all the godly and sober people of the land.

*   *   *

But above all these the king had another instigator of his own violent purpose, more powerful than all the rest; and that was the queen, who, grown out of her childhood, began to turn her mind from those vain extravagancies she lived in at first to that which did less become her, and was more fatal to the kingdom; which is never in any place happy where the hands which were made only for distaffs affect[4] the management of scepters. If any one object the fresh example of Queen Elizabeth, let them remember that the felicity of her reign was the effect of her submission to her masculine and wise counselors; but wherever male princes are so effeminate as to suffer women of foreign birth and different religions to intermeddle with the affairs of state, it is always found to produce sad desolations; and it hath been observed that a French queen never brought any happiness to England. Some kind of fatality[5] too the English imagined to be in her name of Marie, which, it is said, the king rather chose to have her called by than her other, Henrietta, because the land should find a blessing in that name which had been more unfortunate;[6] but it was not in his power, though a great prince, to control destiny. This lady being by her priests affected with the meritoriousness of advancing her own religion, whose principle it is to subvert all other, applied that way her great wit and parts,[7] and the power her haughty spirit kept over her husband, who was enslaved in his affection only to her, though she had no more passion for him than what served to promote her design. Those brought her into a very good correspondence with the archbishop[8] and his prelatical crew, both joining in the cruel design of rooting the godly out of the land. . . . But how much soever their designs were framed in the dark, God revealed them to his servants, and most miraculously ordered providences for their preservation.

1806

---

2. Rule of the church by bishops.
3. Kingly powers.
4. Aspire to. "Distaff": spinning staff, emblem of female household management.
5. Fatefulness.
6. "Bloody Mary" Tudor, queen of England from 1553 to 1558, reintroduced Roman Catholicism to England and burned many Protestants for heresy; the Scottish Mary, Queen of Scots, also

Catholic, was executed in 1587 for plotting to assassinate Elizabeth I.
7. Abilities.
8. William Laud, archbishop of Canterbury, favored a highly ritualized form of worship that Puritans considered tantamount to Roman Catholicism. He was executed by the Parliamentarians in 1645.

EDWARD HYDE, EARL OF CLARENDON

E dward Hyde (1609–1674) was educated at Oxford and during the 1630s practiced law. From about 1641 onward, he was among the chief supporters and
advisers of Charles I; he went into exile with the boy who was to become Charles II
and was privy to the various plots and plans of the royalists to restore him to power.
After the Restoration he became lord chancellor and prime minister to Charles II,
and he was instrumental in enacting the so-called Clarendon Code, a series of
harsh laws against all nonconformists to the reestablished Church of England. He
was impeached in 1667, owing partly to England's ill success in the Dutch War, and
spent the last seven years of his life in France.

Clarendon wrote part of his great *History of the Rebellion* amid the events it
describes. For the Muse of History such a short view can be a mixed blessing. But
Clarendon's learning—legal, classical, and historical—and the formality of his
method save him from many of the failings of partisanship. He wrote with dignity
and for posterity. His *History*, which first appeared in print thirty years after his
death, was remarkable not only for the largeness of its canvas but also for the force
and coherence of the conservative social philosophy informing it. As a historian and
rhetorician, Clarendon invites comparison with his classical models, Thucydides and
Tacitus. As an evaluator of character, he invites comparison with Plutarch, whose
judiciousness he shares.

From The History of the Rebellion

[THE CHARACTER OF OLIVER CROMWELL][1]

About the middle of August he was seized on by a common tertian ague,[2]
from which he believed a little ease and divertissement at Hampton Court[3]
would have freed him; but the fits grew stronger and his spirits much
abated, so that he returned again to Whitehall,[4] when his physicians began
to think him in danger, though the preachers who prayed always about him
and told God Almighty what great things he had done for Him, and how
much more need He had still of his service, declared as from God that he
should recover, and he himself did not think he should die, till even the time
that his spirits failed him, and then declared to them that he did appoint his
son to succeed him, his eldest son Richard. And so expired upon the third
day of September (a day he thought always very propitious to him, and on
which he had triumphed for several victories),[5] 1658, a day very memorable

---

1. After the manner of ancient historians, Clarendon describes the last days, sickness, and
death of Cromwell, then summarizes his character. The Protector, who had been depressed for
some time by the death of a favorite daughter,
first grew ill in the summer of 1658.
2. An acute fever, with paroxysms recurring every
third day.

3. Hampton Court, built by Cardinal Wolsey
and ceded by him to Henry VIII, is a splendid old
palace up the Thames from London. "Divertissement": diversion.
4. Whitehall, in London, was the traditional
residence of the head of state.
5. Dunbar and Worcester were important battles that Cromwell had won on September 3.

for the greatest storm of wind that had been ever known for some hours before and after his death, which overthrew trees, houses, and made great wrecks at sea, and was so universal that there were terrible effects of it both in France and Flanders, where all people trembled at it, besides the wrecks all along the coast, many boats having been cast away in the very rivers; and within few days after, that circumstance of his death that accompanied that storm was known.

He was one of those men *quos vituperare ne inimici quidem possunt, nisi ut simul laudent,*[6] for he could never have done half that mischief without great parts of courage and industry and judgment, and he must have had a wonderful understanding in the natures and humors of men, and as great a dexterity in the applying them, who from a private and obscure birth (though of a good family), without interest of estate, alliance, or friendships, could raise himself to such a height, and compound and knead such opposite and contradictory tempers, humors, and interests into a consistence that contributed to his designs and to their own destruction, whilst himself grew insensibly powerful enough to cut off those by whom he had climbed, in the instant that they projected to demolish their own building.[7] What Velleius Paterculus said of Cinna may very justly be said of him, *Ausum eum quae nemo auderet bonus, perfecisse quae a nullo nisi fortissimo perfici possunt.*[8] Without doubt no man with more wickedness ever attempted anything, or brought to pass what he desired more wickedly, more in the face and contempt of religion and moral honesty; yet wickedness as great as his could never have accomplished those trophies without the assistance of a great spirit, an admirable circumspection and sagacity, and a most magnanimous resolution. When he appeared first in the Parliament he seemed to have a person in no degree gracious, no ornament of discourse, none of those talents which use to reconcile the affections of the standers-by; yet as he grew into place and authority, his parts[9] seemed to be renewed, as if he had concealed faculties till he had occasion to use them, and when he was to act the part of a great man, he did it without any indecency[1] through the want of custom.

After he was confirmed and invested Protector by the Humble Petition and Advice,[2] he consulted with very few upon any action of importance, nor communicated any enterprise he resolved upon with more than those who were to have principal parts in the execution of it, nor to them sooner than was absolutely necessary. What he once resolved, in which he was not rash, he would not be dissuaded from, nor endure any contradiction of his power and authority, but extorted obedience from them who were not willing to yield it.

6. "Whom not even his enemies could curse without praising him." The source of the phrase is unknown.

7. Clarendon's judgment can be compared with that of Marvell in "An Horatian Ode" (pp. 1356–61). "Insensibly": imperceptibly.

8. "He dared undertake what no good man would have tried and triumphed where only the strongest of men could have succeeded." Velleius Paterculus (died 30 C.E.) wrote a concise *History of Rome*; the quotation is from 2.24.

9. Personal qualities.

1. Indecorum.

2. In December 1653, Cromwell was invested as Protector under a written constitution called the Instrument of Government. In 1657 another constitution, the Humble Petition and Advice, invested him with quasi-monarchical powers and restored the House of Lords.

When he had laid some very extraordinary tax upon the city, one Cony, an eminent fanatic,[3] and one who had heretofore served him very notably, positively refused to pay his part and loudly dissuaded others from submitting to it, as an imposition notoriously against the law and the property of the subject, which all honest men were bound to defend. Cromwell sent for him and cajoled him with the memory of the old kindness and friendship that had been between them, and that of all men he did not expect this opposition from him in a matter that was so necessary for the good of the commonwealth. But it was always his fortune to meet with the most rude and obstinate behavior from those who had formerly been absolutely governed by him, and they commonly put him in mind of some expressions and sayings of his own in cases of the like nature. So this man remembered[4] him how great an enemy he had expressed himself to such grievances, and declared that all who submitted to them and paid illegal taxes were more to blame, and greater enemies to their country, than they who imposed them; and that the tyranny of princes could never be grievous but by the tameness and stupidity of the people.

When Cromwell saw that he could not convert him, he told him that he had a will as stubborn as his, and he would try which of them two should be master, and thereupon with some terms of reproach and contempt he committed the man to prison—whose courage was nothing abated by it, but as soon as the term came, he brought his *habeas corpus*[5] in the King's Bench, which they then called the Upper Bench. Maynard, who was of counsel with the prisoner, demanded his liberty with great confidence, both upon the illegality of the commitment and the illegality of the imposition,[6] as being laid without any lawful authority. The judges could not maintain or defend either, but enough declared what their sentence would be, and therefore the Protector's attorney required a further day to answer what had been urged. Before that day, Maynard was committed to the Tower for presuming to question or make doubt of his authority, and the judges were sent for and severely reprehended for suffering that license; and when they with all humility mentioned the law, and Magna Carta, Cromwell told them their Magna Carta should not control his actions, which he knew were for the safety of the commonwealth. He asked them who made them judges; whether they had any authority to sit there but what he gave them, and that if his authority were at an end, they knew well enough what would become of themselves. And therefore advised them to be more tender of that which could only preserve them, and so dismissed them with caution that they should not suffer the lawyers to prate what it would not become them to hear.

Thus he subdued a spirit that had been often troublesome to the most sovereign power, and made Westminster Hall[7] as obedient and subservient to his commands as any of the rest of his quarters. In all other matters which did not concern the life of his jurisdiction, he seemed to have great

---

3. In Clarendon's vocabulary, a radical Puritan. "The city": the City of London.
4. Reminded.
5. Writ to release a prisoner.
6. I.e., the original tax.

7. The center of the law courts and legal profession. Clarendon never tells us what happened to poor George Cony; the lawyer and judges made their submission and got off, but the fate of the plaintiff remains obscure.

reverence for the law, and rarely interposed between party and party; and as he proceeded with this kind of indignation and haughtiness with those who were refractory and dared to contend with his greatness, so towards those who complied with his good pleasure and courted his protection he used a wonderful civility, generosity, and bounty.

To reduce three nations which perfectly hated him to an entire obedience to all his dictates, to awe and govern those nations by an army that was indevoted to him and wished his ruin, was an instance of a very prodigious address;[8] but his greatness at home was but a shadow of the glory he had abroad. It was hard to discover which feared him most, France, Spain, or the Low Countries, where his friendship was current at the value he put upon it; and as they did all sacrifice their honor and their interest to his pleasure, so there is nothing he could have demanded that either of them would have denied him.

※ ※ ※

He was not a man of blood, and totally declined Machiavel's method, which prescribes upon any alteration of a government, as a thing absolutely necessary, to cut off all the heads of those, and extirpate their families, who are friends to the old;[9] and it was confidently reported in the Council of Officers, it was more than once proposed that there might be a general massacre of all the royal party as the only expedient to secure the government, but Cromwell would never consent to it, it may be out of too much contempt of his enemies. In a word, as he had all the wickednesses against which damnation is denounced and for which hellfire is prepared, so he had some virtues which have caused the memory of some men in all ages to be celebrated, and he will be looked upon by posterity as a brave, bad man.

1702–4

8. Skill. "Indevoted": Clarendon's word, carefully coined to express the far from unanimous feelings of the army.
9. See *The Prince*, chapters 3 and 7.

LADY ANNE HALKETT

L ady Anne Halkett, née Anne Murray (1622–1699), was born into a family of the royal household; her father was a tutor to Prince Charles, later Charles I. Her allegiance to the royalist cause was an attachment by comparison with which her several love affairs were mere incidents. Halkett was a tough and active partisan who, more directly than most women of her day, engaged in the intrigues of the civil wars. With one of her particular admirers, Colonel Bamfield, she assisted the young Duke of York (future King James II of England) in making his escape from parliamentary custody. Her account of this adventure appeared in her memoirs, published many years later. We pick up the story in April 1648 with the question of Colonel Bamfield's intentions.

From The Memoirs

[SPRINGING THE DUKE]

This gentleman came to see me sometimes in the company of ladies who had been my mother's neighbors in St. Martin's Lane, and sometimes alone, but whenever he came his discourse was serious, handsome, and tending to impress the advantages of piety, loyalty, and virtue; and these subjects were so agreeable to my own inclination that I could not but give them a good reception, especially from one that seemed to be so much an owner of them himself. After I had been used to freedom of discourse with him, I told him I approved much of his advice to others, but I thought his own practice contradicted much of his profession, for one of his acquaintance had told me he had not seen his wife in a twelvemonth, and it was impossible in my opinion for a good man to be an ill husband; and therefore he must defend himself from one before I could believe the other of him. He said it was not necessary to give everyone that might condemn him the reason of his being so long from her, yet to satisfy me he would tell me the truth, which was that, he being engaged in the king's service,[1] he was obliged to be at London where it was not convenient for her to be with him, his stay in any place being uncertain; besides, she lived amongst her friends who, though they were kind to her, yet were not so to him, for most of that country had declared for the Parliament and were enemies to all that had or did serve the king, and therefore his wife, he was sure, would not condemn him for what he did by her own consent. This seeming reasonable, I did insist no more upon that subject.

At this time he had frequent letters from the king, who employed him in several affairs, but that of the greatest concern which he was employed in was to contrive the Duke of York's escape out of St. James[2] (where His Highness and the Duke of Gloucester and the Princess Elizabeth lived under the care of the Earl of Northumberland and his lady). The difficulties of it was represented by Colonel Bamfield; but His Majesty still pressed it, and I remember this expression was in one of the letters: "I believe it will be difficult, and if he miscarry in the attempt, it will be the greatest affliction that can arrive to me; but I look upon James's escape as Charles's preservation,[3] and nothing can content me more; therefore be careful what you do."

This letter, amongst others, he showed me, and where the king approved of his choice of me to entrust with it, for to get the duke's clothes made and to dress him in his disguise. So now all Colonel Bamfield's business and care was how to manage this business of so important concern, which could not be performed without several persons' concurrence in it, for he being generally known as one whose stay at London was in order to serve the king, few of those who were entrusted by the Parliament in public concerns durst own converse or hardly civility to him, lest they should have been suspect

---

1. The service of Charles I, then a close prisoner of the parliamentary army under Cromwell. In less than a year he would be executed.
2. St. James's Palace, the royal residence. The two named below were other children of Charles I.
3. Charles I must have feared the capture or assassination of the heir apparent, Prince Charles, then in France with his mother, Queen Henrietta Maria. If the younger son, James, were alive and at liberty, there would be no point in such an attempt to cut off the succession.

by their party, which made it difficult for him to get access to the duke. But, to be short, having communicated the design to a gentleman attending His Highness who was full of honor and fidelity, by his means he had private access to the duke, to whom he presented the king's letter and order to His Highness for consenting to act what Colonel Bamfield should contrive for his escape, which was so cheerfully entertained and so readily obeyed, that being once designed there was nothing more to do than to prepare all things for the execution. I had desired him to take a ribbon with him and bring me the bigness of the duke's waist and his length, to have clothes made fit for him. In the meantime, Colonel Bamfield was to provide money for all necessary expense, which was furnished by an honest citizen. When I gave the measure to my tailor to inquire how much mohair would serve to make a petticoat and waistcoat to a young gentlewoman of that bigness and stature, he considered it a long time, and said he had made many gowns and suits, but he had never made any to such a person in his life. I thought he was in the right; but his meaning was he had never seen any woman of so low a stature have so big a waist. However, he made it as exactly fit as if he had taken the measure himself. It was a mixed mohair of a light hair color and black, and the under-petticoat was scarlet.

All things being now ready, upon the 20th of April 1648 in the evening was the time resolved for the duke's escape. And in order to that, it was designed for a week before every night as soon as the duke had supped he and those servants that attended His Highness (till the Earl of Northumberland and the rest of the house had supped) went to a play called *hide and seek*,[4] and sometimes he would hide himself so well that in half an hour's time they could not find him. His Highness had so used them to this that when he went really away they thought he was but at the usual sport. A little before the duke went to supper that night, he called for the gardener, who only had a treble key besides that which the duke had, and bid him give him that key till his own was mended, which he did. And after His Highness had supped, he immediately called to go to the play, and went down the privy stairs into the garden, and opened the gate that goes into the park, treble locking all the doors behind him. And at the garden gate Colonel Bamfield waited for His Highness, and putting on a cloak and periwig, hurried him away to the park gate, where a coach waited that carried them to the waterside, and, taking the boat that was appointed for that service, they rowed to the stairs next the bridge, where I and Miriam[5] waited in a private house hard by that Colonel Bamfield had prepared for dressing His Highness, where all things were in a readiness. But I had many fears, for Colonel Bamfield had desired me, if they came not there precisely by ten o'clock, to shift for myself, for then I might conclude they were discovered, and so my stay there could do no good but prejudice myself. Yet this did not make me leave the house though ten o'clock did strike, and he that was entrusted often went to the landing place and saw no boat coming was much discouraged, and asked me what I would do. I told him I came there with a resolution to serve His Highness, and I was fully determined not to leave that place till I was out of hopes of doing what I came there for, and would take my hazard. He left me to go

4. As a boy of fourteen, James could play such a game without arousing suspicion and could be dis- guised without much difficulty in women's clothes.
5. Anne Murray's personal maidservant.

again to the waterside, and while I was fortifying myself against what might arrive to me, I heard a great noise of many as I thought coming upstairs, which I expected to be soldiers to take me, but it was a pleasing disappointment, for the first that came in was the duke, who with much joy I took in my arms and gave God thanks for his safe arrival. His Highness called "Quickly, quickly, dress me!"; and, putting off his clothes, I dressed him in the women's habit that was prepared, which fitted His Highness very well, and was very pretty in it.

After he had eaten something I made ready while I was idle, lest His Highness should be hungry, and having sent for a Wood Street cake (which I knew he loved) to take in the barge, with as much haste as could be His Highness went cross the bridge to the stairs where the barge lay, Colonel Bamfield leading him; and immediately the boatmen plied the oar so well that they were soon out of sight, having both wind and tide with them. But I afterwards heard the wind changed, and was so contrary that Colonel Bamfield told me he was terribly afraid they should have been blown back again. And the duke said, "Do anything with me rather than let me go back again," which put Colonel Bamfield to seek help where it was only to be had, and, after he had most fervently supplicated assistance from God, presently the wind blew fair, and they came safely to their intended landing place. But I heard there was some difficulty before they got to the ship at Gravesend, which had like to have discovered them had not Colonel Washington's lady[6] assisted them.

After the duke's barge was out of sight of the bridge, I and Miriam went where I appointed the coach to stay for me, and made drive as fast as the coachman could to my brother's house, where I stayed. I met none in the way that gave me any apprehension that the design was discovered, nor was it noised abroad till the next day, for (as I related before) the duke having used to play at hide and seek, and to conceal himself a long time, when they missed him at the same play, thought he would have discovered himself as formerly when they had given over seeking him. But a much longer time being passed than usually was spent in that divertisement, some began to apprehend that His Highness was gone in earnest past their finding, which made the Earl of Northumberland (to whose care he was committed), after strict search made in the house of St. James and all thereabouts to no purpose, to send and acquaint the Speaker of the House of Commons that the duke was gone, but how or by what means he knew not, but desired that there might be orders sent to the Cinque Ports[7] for stopping all ships going out till the passengers were examined and search made in all suspected places where His Highness might be concealed.

Though this was gone about with all the vigilancy imaginable, yet it pleased God to disappoint them of their intention by so infatuating those several persons who were employed for writing orders that none of them were able to write one right, but ten or twelve of them were cast by before one was according to their mind. This account I had from Mr. N. who was mace-bearer to the Speaker all that time and a witness of it. This disorder of the clerks

---

6. Most likely, the wife of Colonel Henry Washington, a royalist soldier (and distant relative of George Washington).
7. A group of channel ports, originally five in number (*cinque* is French for "five"); most English shipping to or from the Continent passed through them.

contributed much to the duke's safety, for he was at sea before any of the orders came to the ports, and so was free from what was designed if they had taken His Highness. Though several were suspected for being accessory to the escape, yet they could not charge any with it but the person who went away, and he being out of their reach, they took no notice as either to examine or imprison others.[8]

1778

8. Despite this romantic beginning to their friendship, Colonel Bamfield and Murray never did get together, because Bamfield's estranged wife was still living. In 1656 Murray married Sir James Halkett.

DOROTHY WAUGH

Around 1647, a group of disciples began forming around the charismatic itinerant preacher George Fox. Like many religious radicals of the period, Fox taught the importance of relying upon the Inner Light—one's own conscience as guided by the Holy Spirit—in preference to human law or holy writ. Fox believed that the days of prophecy and revelation had not ended in biblical times but were ongoing, so that the teachings of Scripture were open to revision. Moreover, sacred illumination was available to all sincere believers regardless of sex, education, or social rank. Fox's followers were derisively called "Quakers" because, in the grip of a visitation by the Holy Spirit, they would suffer paroxysms similar to epileptic convulsions.

Because Quakers believed all human beings to be spiritually equal, they refused to perform the acts of deference that permeated social life in seventeenth-century England—bowing before and doffing the hat to superiors or addressing them with the honorific "you" rather than the familiar "thou." They felt called upon to testify to their beliefs wherever, and whenever, the Inner Light prompted, answering back to ministers in the pulpit, inveighing against what they considered social injustices, and sermonizing without a license in public places. Often, their outspokenness enraged secular and ecclesiastical authorities.

Dorothy Waugh (ca. 1636–?) worked as a maidservant in Preston Patrick, in northwest England, a hotbed of Quaker activity. She probably became one of Fox's followers in the early 1650s, when she was still a teenager. Like Fox and a number of other missionary spirits, sometimes called "the Valiant Sixty," she traveled through England on foot, spreading the Quaker message to all who would listen. In 1656, aged about twenty, she was one of the Friends who arrived in Boston, Massachusetts, aboard the *Speedwell*: the party was imprisoned for ten days by the staunch Puritan governor John Endicott, and then forced to return to England. Undaunted, Waugh embarked for the colonies again, with another small group of missionary Quakers, the following year, this time landing in New Amsterdam (modern New York). They were no more welcome here than they had been in Boston. After a brief imprisonment, they were shipped in shackles to the colony of Rhode Island, where complete religious toleration was the rule. In the late 1650s, probably between voyages to the New World, Waugh married William Lotherington of Yorkshire, but nothing is known about her later life or the circumstances of her death. Other Quakers traveled even farther than Waugh on missionary expeditions; one woman made it as far as the Ottoman Empire and gave a sermon before the Grand Turk; when she failed to convert him, she walked back home to England.

Waugh's account of her treatment in Carlisle was published in *The Lamb's Defence Against Lies*, a collection in which various Quakers testified to their maltreatment by secular and religious authorities. Although the Friends were pacifists who refused to retaliate physically or verbally against their persecutors, they were fully aware of the propaganda value of unmerited suffering—indeed, their enemies believed that they deliberately courted abuse as a publicity stunt. More probably, their bad reception only reinforced their conviction that they constituted a tiny remnant of holiness, bravely resisting the overwhelming powers of worldliness and evil. The Quakers' published accounts of their victimization, typically reported in understated, factual, but gruesome detail, owed much to the sixteenth-century writer John Foxe's influential tales of Protestant martyrdom under the Catholic queen "Bloody Mary" Tudor. In the years between 1650 and 1700, numerous male and female Friends published memoirs of their arduous lives, producing some of the first printed autobiographical writing in English by women and by people of humble status.

A Relation Concerning Dorothy Waugh's Cruel Usage by the Mayor of Carlisle

Upon a seventh day about the time called Michaelmas in the year of the world's account 1655[1] I was moved of the Lord to go into the market of Carlisle, to speak against all deceit and ungodly practices, and the mayor's officer came and violently haled me off the cross[2] and put me in prison, not having anything to lay to my charge. And presently the mayor came up where I was, and asked me from whence I came; and I said, "Out of Egypt,[3] where thou lodgest." But after these words, he was so violent and full of passion he scarce asked me any more questions, but called to one of his followers to bring the bridle[4] as he called it to put upon me, and was to be on three hours. And that which they called so was like a steel cap and my hat being violently plucked off which was pinned to my head whereby they tore my clothes to put on their bridle as they called it, which was a stone weight of iron by the relation of their own generation,[5] and three bars of iron to come over my face, and a piece of it was put in my mouth, which was so unreasonable big a thing for that place as cannot be well related, which was locked to my head. And so I stood their time with my hands bound behind me, with the stone weight of iron upon my head and the bit in my mouth to keep me from speaking. And the mayor said he would make me an example to all that should ever come in that name.[6] And the people to see me so violently abused were broken into tears, but he cried out on them and said, "For foolish pity, one may spoil a whole city." And the man that kept the prison door demanded two pence of everyone that came to see me while

---

1. Quakers saw themselves as separated from "the world" and its conventional means of marking dates, particularly objecting to terms left over from medieval Catholicism, like "Michaelmas," or the Mass of the Archangel Michael, celebrated on September 29. "Seventh day": Sabbath.
2. A large stone cross marked the main intersection of most English towns; public speakers could mount the steps in order to be heard better.

3. In the Bible, the place where God's chosen people were enslaved and where most of the population worshipped false gods.
4. An instrument of torture and humiliation, typically used to punish women who "scolded" their husbands or neighbors in public.
5. By their own report. A stone is fourteen pounds.
6. As professed Friends, or Quakers.

their bridle remained upon me. Afterwards it was taken off and they kept me in prison for a little season, and after a while the mayor came again and caused it to be put on again, and sent me out of the city with it on, and gave me very vile and unsavory words, which were not fit to proceed out of any man's mouth, and charged the officer to whip me out of the town, from constable to constable to send me till I came to my own home, whenas[7] they had not anything to lay to my charge.

1656

7. Inasmuch as.

THOMAS TRAHERNE
1637–1674

Thomas Traherne's most remarkable works—his stanzaic poems, free verse *Thanksgivings*, and the brilliant prose meditative sequence *Centuries of Meditations*—were lost for over two centuries. With them was lost a unique religious and aesthetic sensibility that conceives of heavenly felicity as a state that can be enjoyed in this world by recovering the perspective of lost childhood innocence. In 1673 Traherne published a polemic against Roman Catholics (*Roman Forgeries*), and some works of moral philosophy, meditation, and devotion received posthumous publication over the next several years. But his poems and the *Centuries* were discovered in manuscript only in 1896–97, and at first his poems were attributed to Henry Vaughan. Little is known of Traherne's life. The son of a Herefordshire shoemaker, he received a degree from Brasenose College, Oxford; took orders and became rector of Credenhill in Herefordshire in 1661; became chaplain about 1660 to Sir Orlando Bridgeman, Lord Keeper of the Great Seal; and spent his last years in and near London. The *Centuries* consists of four books of one hundred items each and a fifth unfinished. They contain prose meditations (which are often ecstatic prose poems) and some interpolated poems; the work was addressed to Traherne's good friend Mrs. Susanna Hopton, to help her attain "felicity." The poems render moments of spiritual experience: the speaker's enjoyment of a wondrous heavenly felicity in childhood, his painful loss of it in maturity, and his successful efforts to recover that heavenly perspective.

From Centuries of Meditation

From *The Third Century*

3

The corn was orient and immortal wheat, which never should be reaped, nor was ever sown. I thought it had stood from everlasting to everlasting. The dust and stones of the street were as precious as gold: the gates were at first the end of the world. The green trees when I saw them first through one of the gates transported and ravished me; their sweetness and unusual beauty made my heart to leap, and almost mad with ecstasy, they were such strange and wonderful things. The men! O what venerable and reverend creatures did the aged seem! Immortal cherubims! And young men glittering and sparkling angels, and maids strange seraphic pieces of life and beauty! Boys and girls tumbling in the street, and playing, were moving jewels. I knew not that they were born or should die; but all things abided eternally as they were in their proper places. Eternity was manifest in the light of the day, and something infinite behind everything appeared, which talked with my expectation and moved my desire. The city seemed to stand in Eden, or to be built in Heaven. The streets were mine, the temple was mine, the people were mine, their clothes and gold and silver were mine, as much as their sparkling eyes, fair skins, and ruddy faces. The skies were mine, and so were the sun and moon and stars, and all the world was mine; and I the only spectator and enjoyer of it. I knew no churlish proprieties,[1] nor bounds, nor divisions: but all proprieties and divisions were mine: all treasures and the possessors of them. So that with much ado I was corrupted, and made to learn the dirty devices of this world, which now I unlearn, and become, as it were, a little child again that I may enter into the Kingdom of God.

1908

Wonder

How like an angel came I down!
 How bright are all things here!
When first among his works I did appear,
 O how their glory me did crown!
5 The world resembled his eternity,
  In which my soul did walk,
 And everything that I did see
  Did with me talk.

The skies in their magnificence,
10 The lively, lovely air;
O how divine, how soft, how sweet, how fair!
 The stars did entertain my sense,[1]
And all the works of God so bright and pure,
  So rich and great did seem,
15 As if they ever must endure,
  In my esteem.

A native health and innocence
  Within my bones did grow,
And while my God did all his glories show,
20 I felt a vigor in my sense

---

1. Private property rights.　　　　　1. Sight.

That was all Spirit. I within did flow
With seas of life like wine;
I nothing in the world did know
But 'twas divine.

25   Harsh ragged objects were concealed,
Oppression's tears and cries,
Sins, griefs, complaints, dissensions, weeping eyes,
Were hid; and only things revealed
Which heavenly spirits and the angels prize.
30   The state of innocence
And bliss, not trades and poverties,
Did fill my sense.

The streets were paved with golden stones,
The boys and girls were mine,
35   O how did all their lovely faces shine!
The sons of men were holy ones.
Joy, beauty, welfare did appear to me
And everything which here I found
While like an angel I did see,
40   Adorned the ground.

Rich diamond and pearl and gold
In every place was seen;
Rare splendors, yellow, blue, red, white, and green,
Mine eyes did everywhere behold.
45 Great wonders clothed with glory did appear,
Amazement was my bliss.
That and my wealth was everywhere:
No joy to this!°   *compared to this*

Cursed and devised proprieties,[2]
50   With envy, avarice,
And fraud, those fiends that spoil even paradise,
Fled from the splendor of mine eyes.
And so did hedges, ditches, limits, bounds:
I dreamed not aught of those,
55 But wandered over all men's grounds,
And found repose.

Proprieties themselves were mine,
And hedges ornaments;
Walls, boxes, coffers, and their rich contents
60   Did not divide my joys, but shine.
Clothes, ribbons, jewels, laces, I esteemed
My joys by others worn;
For me they all to wear them seemed
When I was born.

1903

2. Private property rights.

On Leaping over the Moon

I saw new worlds beneath the water lie,
  New people, and another sky
    And sun, which seen by day
    Might things more clear display.
5   Just such another[1]
      Of late my brother[2]
Did in his travel see, and saw by night,
  A much more strange and wondrous sight;
Nor could the world exhibit such another
10   So great a sight, but in a brother.

Adventure strange! no such in story we
  New or old, true or feignèd see.
    On earth he seemed to move,
    Yet heaven went above;[3]
15   Up in the skies
      His body flies,
In open, visible, yet magic sort:
  As he along the way did sport,
Like Icarus[4] over the flood he soars
20   Without the help of wings or oars.

As he went tripping o'er the king's highway,
  A little pearly river lay
    O'er which, without a wing
    Or oar, he dared to swim,
25   Swim through the air
      On body fair;
He would not use nor trust Icarian wings[5]
  Lest they should prove deceitful things;
For had he fallen, it had been wondrous high,
30   Not from, but from above, the sky.

He might have dropped through that thin element
  Into a fathomless descent
    Unto the nether sky
    That did beneath him lie
35   And there might tell
      What wonders dwell
On earth above. Yet bold he briskly runs,
  And soon the danger overcomes,
Who, as he leapt, with joy related soon
40   How happy he o'erleaped the moon.

---

1. Another world.
2. Traherne's brother Philip.
3. I.e., yet went above the heavens.
4. Icarus soared on waxen wings.
5. Icarus's wings melted in the sun, and he fell into the sea.

What wondrous things upon the earth are done
   Beneath and yet above the sun!
     Deeds all appear again
     In higher spheres; remain
45   In clouds as yet:
      But there they get
Another light, and in another way
   Themselves to us above display.
The skies themselves this earthly globe surround;
50   We're even here within them found.

On heavenly ground within the skies we walk,
   And in this middle center talk:
     Did we but wisely move
     On earth in heaven above,
55   We then should be
      Exalted high
Above the sky: from whence whoever falls,
   Through a long dismal precipice,°   *headlong fall*
Sinks to the deep abyss where Satan crawls,
60   Where horrid death and dèspair lies.

As much as others thought themselves to lie
   Beneath the moon, so much more high
     Himself he thought to fly
     Above the starry sky,
65   As that he spied
      Below the tide.
Thus did he yield me in the shady night
   A wondrous and instructive light,
Which taught me that under our feet there is,
70   As o'er our heads, a place of bliss.

                           1910

MARGARET CAVENDISH
1623–1673

Margaret (Lucas) Cavendish, duchess of Newcastle, wrote and published numerous works during the Interregnum and Restoration era, in a great variety of genres: poetry (*Poems and Fancies*, 1653), essays (*Philosophical Fancies*, 1653; *The World's Olio*, 1655), short fiction (*Nature's Pictures*, 1656), autobiography (*A True Relation of My Birth, Breeding, and Life*, 1656), Utopian romance (*The Blazing World*, 1666), scientific essays chiefly critical of the new science, letters, a biography of her husband (*The Life of . . . William Cavendish*, 1667), and some eighteen plays, of which one, *The Forced Marriage*, was produced in 1670. Most were published in lavish editions at the Newcastles' own expense. At the time they elicited more derision than praise: for a woman, especially an aristocratic woman, to publish works dealing so intimately with her desires, opinions, personal circumstances, and aspirations to fame and authorship seemed to many disgraceful. Samuel Pepys concluded, after reading her life of her husband the duke, that she was "a mad, conceited, ridiculous woman, and he an ass to suffer [her] to write what she writes to him and of him." Her fantastic dress and sometimes idiosyncratic behavior abetted that characterization: she took pride in "singularity" and even paid a visit to the all-male Royal Society. But the philosopher Thomas Hobbes thought well of her, and her rediscoverers in recent decades have praised her works and her self-construction as a female author.

Cavendish's autobiography analyzes her responses to the circumstances of her life. Born into a wealthy royalist family that encouraged her disposition to read and write, she became maid of honor to Queen Henrietta Maria, whom she followed into exile in Paris. There she married, in 1645, the widowed William Cavendish, thirty years her senior, who was one of Charles I's generals and later Duke of Newcastle. Exiled for fifteen years on the Continent, where (his estates having been sequestered) they ran up exorbitant debts, they were restored to status and fortune after the Restoration. The duke, who was himself a poet, playwright, and philosopher, supported and promoted Margaret's literary endeavors, for which she was profoundly grateful. In polemical prefaces to her several works, she develops a fragmentary poetics, trenchantly defends her right to publish and to participate in contemporary intellectual exchange, defends women's rational powers, and decries their educational disadvantages and exclusion from the public domain.

From Poems and Fancies

The Poetess's Hasty Resolution

Reading my verses, I liked them so well,
Self-love did make my judgment to rebel.
Thinking them so good, I thought more to write;
Considering not how others would them like.
5   I writ so fast, I thought, if I lived long,
A pyramid of fame[1] to build thereon.
Reason observing which way I was bent,
Did stay my hand, and asked me what I meant;
Will you, said she, thus waste your time in vain,
10 On that which in the world small praise shall gain?
For shame, leave off, said she, the printer spare,
He'll lose by your ill poetry, I fear.
Besides the world hath already such a weight
Of useless books, as it is overfraught.[2]
15 Then pity take, do the world a good turn,
And all you write cast in the fire, and burn.
Angry I was, and Reason struck away,
When I did hear, what she to me did say.

---

1. A poetic monument.
2. Like a ship with too heavy a cargo, in danger of sinking.

Then all in haste I to the press it sent,
20 Fearing persuasion might my book prevent.
But now 'tis done, with grief repent do I,
Hang down my head with shame, blush, sigh, and cry.
Take pity, and my drooping spirits raise,
Wipe off my tears with handkerchiefs of praise.

1653

The Hunting of the Hare

Betwixt two ridges of plowed land lay Wat,[1]
Pressing his body close to earth lay squat.
His nose upon his two forefeet close lies,
Glazing obliquely with his great gray eyes.
5 His head he always sets against the wind,
If turn his tail, his hairs blow up behind:
Which he too cold will grow, but he is wise,
And keeps his coat still° down, so warm he lies.   constantly
Then resting all the day, till, sun doth set,
10 Then riseth up, his relief for to get.
Walking about until the sun doth rise,
Then back returns, down in his form° he lies.   nest
At last, poor Wat was found, as he there lay,
By huntsmen, with their dogs which came that way.
15 Seeing, gets up, and fast begins to run,
Hoping some ways the cruel dogs to shun.
But they by nature have so quick a scent,
That by their nose they trace what way he went.
And with their deep, wide mouths set forth a cry,
20 Which answered was by echoes in the sky.
Then Wat was struck with terror, and with fear,
Thinks every shadow still the dogs they were.
And running out some distance from the noise,
To hide himself, his thoughts he new employs.
25 Under a clod of earth in sand pit wide,
Poor Wat sat close, hoping himself to hide.
There long he had not sat, but straight° his ears   immediately
The winding° horns and crying dogs he hears: blowing
Staring with fear, up leaps, then doth he run,
30 And with such speed, the ground scarce treads upon.
Into a great thick wood he straightway gets.
Where underneath a broken bough he sits.
At every leaf that with the wind did shake,
Did bring such terror, made his heart to ache.
35 That place he left, to champaign° plains he went,   open
Winding about, for to deceive their scent.
And while they snuffling were, to find his track,

1. Conventional name for a hare.

Poor Wat, being weary, his swift pace did slack.
On his two hinder legs for ease did sit,
His forefeet rubbed his face from dust, and sweat.
Licking his feet, he wiped his ears so clean,
That none could tell that Wat had hunted been.
But casting round about his fair great eyes,
The hounds in full career he near him spies:
To Wat it was so terrible a sight,
Fear gave him wings, and made his body light.
Though weary was before, by running long,
Yet now his breath he never felt more strong.
Like those that dying are, think health returns,
When 'tis but a faint blast, which life out burns.
For spirits seek to guard the heart about,
Striving with death, but death doth quench them out.
Thus they so fast came on, with such loud cries,
That he no hopes hath left, nor help espies.
With that the winds did pity poor Wat's case,
And with their breath the scent blew from the place.
Then every nose is busily employed,
And every nostril is set open wide,
And every head doth seek a several° way,   *different*
To find what grass, or track, the scent on lay.
Thus quick industry° that is not slack,   *clever work*
Is like to witchery,° brings lost things back.   *witchcraft*
For though the wind had tied the scent up close,
A busy dog thrust in his snuffling nose
And drew it out, with it did foremost run,
Then horns blew loud, for th'rest to follow on.
The great slow hounds, their throats did set a bass,
The fleet swift hounds, as tenors next in place,
The little beagles they a treble sing,
And through the air their voices round did ring.
Which made a consort, as they ran along;
If they but words could speak, might sing a song.
The horns kept time, the hunters shout for joy,
And valiant seem, poor Wat for to destroy:
Spurring their horses to a full career,
Swim rivers deep, leap ditches without fear;
Endanger life and limbs so fast will ride,
Only to see how patiently Wat died.
At last,[2] the dogs so near his heels did get,
That they their sharp teeth in his breech did set;
Then tumbling down, did fall with weeping eyes,
Gives up his ghost, and thus poor Wat he dies.
Men whooping loud, such acclamations make,
As if the Devil they did prisoner take.
When they do but a shiftless° creature kill;   *helpless*
To hunt, there needs no valiant soldier's skill.
But man doth think that exercise and toil,

---

2. From the 1664 edition; 1653 has "For why."

To keep their health, is best, which makes most spoil.
Thinking that food and nourishment so good,
90 And appetite, that feeds on flesh and blood.
When they do lions, wolves, bears, tigers see,
To kill poor sheep, straight say, they cruel be,
But for themselves all creatures think too few
For luxury, wish God would make them new.
95 As if that God made creatures for man's meat,
To give them life and sense, for man to eat;
Or else for sport, or recreation's sake,
Destroy those lives that God saw good to make:
Making their stomachs, graves, which full they fill
100 With murdered bodies that in sport they kill.
Yet man doth think himself so gentle, mild,
When he of creatures is most cruel wild.
And is so proud, thinks only he shall live,
That God a godlike nature did him give.
105 And that all creatures for his sake alone
Was made for him, to tyrannize upon.

1653, 1664

From A True Relation of My Birth, Breeding, and Life[1]

As for my breeding, it was according to my birth and the nature of my sex, for my birth was not lost in my breeding; for as my sisters had been bred, so was I in plenty, or rather with superfluity. . . .'Tis true my mother might have increased her daughters' portions by a thrifty sparing, yet she chose to bestow it on our breeding, honest pleasures, and harmless delight, out of an opinion that if she bred us with needy necessity it might chance to create in us shark-ing[2] qualities, mean thoughts, and base actions, which she knew my father as well as herself did abhor. Likewise we were bred tenderly, for my mother naturally did strive to please and delight her children, not to cross or torment them, terrifying them with threats or lashing them with slavish whips. But instead of threats, reason was used to persuade us, and instead of lashes, the deformities of vices was discovered,[3] and the graces and virtues were presented unto us.

* * *

After the Queen went from Oxford, and so out of England, I was parted from them.[4] For when the Queen was in Oxford I had a great desire to be one of her maids of honor. . . . And though I might have learned more wit,

----

1. Cavendish's autobiography is a concise account, factual and at times self-reflective, of her early life. It comprises the final section of *Nature's Pictures* (1656), a collection of her fiction written during the Newcastles' exile in Antwerp during the Cromwell regime. "Breeding": upbringing.
2. Greedy.
3. Shown.

4. Her mother and family; her father had died when she was two years old. In 1643 Charles I moved his family and court to Oxford, where Margaret became maid of honor to Queen Henrietta Maria; in 1644 the queen fled with some supporters, Margaret among them, to her native Paris, to urge support for the royalist cause.

and advanced my understanding by living in a court, yet being dull, fearful, and bashful, I neither heeded what was said or practiced, but just what belonged to my loyal duty and my own honest reputation. And indeed I was so afraid to dishonor my friends and family by my indiscreet actions that I rather chose to be accounted a fool than to be thought rude or wanton. In truth my bashfulness and fears made me repent my going from home to see the world abroad. . . .

So I continued almost two years, until such time as I was married from thence. For my Lord the Marquis of Newcastle did approve of those bashful fears which many condemned, and would choose such a wife as he might bring to his own humors,[5] and not such an one as was wedded to self-conceit, or one that had been tempered to the humors of another, for which he wooed me for his wife. And though I did dread marriage, and shunned men's companies as much as I could, yet I could not nor had not the power to refuse him, by reason my affections were fixed on him, and he was the only person I ever was in love with. Neither was I ashamed to own it, but gloried therein, for it was not amorous love. I never was infected therewith—it is a disease, or a passion, or both, I know by relation, not by experience. Neither could title, wealth, power, or person entice me to love. But my love was honest and honorable, being placed upon merit; which affection joyed at the fame of his worth, pleased with delight in his wit, proud of the respects he used to me, and triumphing in the affections he professed for me. . . . And though my lord hath lost his estate, and banished out of his country for his loyalty to his king and country, yet neither despised poverty nor pinching necessity could make him break the bonds of friendship, or weaken his loyal duty to his king or country.

* * *

When I am writing any sad feigned stories or serious humors or melancholy passions, I am forced many times to express them with the tongue before I can write them with the pen, by reason those thoughts that are sad, serious, and melancholy are apt to contract and to draw back too much, which oppression doth as it were overpower or smother the conception in the brain. But when some of those thoughts are sent out in words, they give the rest more liberty to place themselves in a more methodical order, marching more regularly with my pen on the ground of white paper. But my letters seem rather as a ragged rout, than a well-armed body, for the brain being quicker in creating than the hand in writing, or the memory in retaining, many fancies are lost by reason they ofttimes outrun the pen. Where I, to keep speed in the race, write so fast as I stay not so long as to write my letters plain, insomuch as some have taken my handwriting for some strange character.[6] . . . My only trouble is lest my brain should grow barren, or that the root of my fancies should become insipid, withering into a dull stupidity, for want of maturing subjects to write on.

* * *

5. Disposition. William Cavendish (1593–1676), a general in the king's army, fled to the Continent in 1644. Margaret was his second wife, whom he married in 1645 in Paris.
6. Alphabet.

Since I have writ in general thus far of my life, I think it fit, I should speak something of my humor, particular practice, and disposition. As for my humor, I was from my childhood given to contemplation, being more taken or delighted with thoughts than in conversation with a society, in so much as I would walk two or three hours, and never rest, in a musing, considering, contemplating manner, reasoning with myself of everything my senses did present. . . . Likewise I had a natural stupidity towards the learning of any other language than my native tongue, for I could sooner and with more facility understand the sense than remember the words, and for want of such memory makes me so unlearned in foreign languages as I am: as for my practice,[7] I was never very active, by reason I was given so much to contemplation. . . . As for my study of books it was little, yet I chose rather to read, than to employ my time in any other work, or practice, and when I read what I understood not, I would ask my brother, the lord Lucas, he being learned, the sense of meaning thereof; but my serious study could not be much, by reason I took great delight in attiring, fine dressing, and fashions, especially such fashions as I did invent myself, not taking that pleasure in such fashions as was invented by others: also I did dislike any should follow my fashions, for I always took delight in a singularity, even in the accoutrements of habits, but whatsoever I was addicted to, either in fashion of clothes, contemplations of thoughts, actions of life, they were lawful, honorable, and modest, of which I can avouch to the world with a great confidence, because it is a pure truth.

*   *   *

I am a great emulator; for though I wish none worse than they are, yet it is lawful for me to wish myself the best, and to do my honest endeavor thereunto; for I think it no crime to wish myself the exactest[8] of Nature's works, my thread of life the longest, my chain of destiny the strongest, my mind the peaceablest, my life the pleasantest, my death the easiest, and the greatest saint in heaven. Also to do my endeavor, so far as honor and honesty doth allow of, to be the highest on fortune's wheel, and to hold the wheel from turning if I can; and if it be commendable to wish another's good, it were a sin not to wish my own; for as envy is a vice, so emulation is a virtue, but emulation is in the way to ambition, or indeed it is a noble ambition. But I fear my ambition inclines to vainglory, for I am very ambitious; yet 'tis neither for beauty, wit, titles, wealth, or power, but as they are steps to raise me to fame's tower, which is to live by remembrance on after-ages. . . . But I hope my readers will not think me vain for writing my life, since there have been many that have done the like, as Caesar, Ovid,[9] and many more, both men and women, and I know no reason I may not do it as well as they: but I verily believe some censuring readers will scornfully say, Why hath this lady writ her own life? since none cares to know whose daughter she was, or whose wife she is, or how she was bred, or what fortunes she had, or how she lived, or what humor or disposition she was of? I answer that it is true, that

---

7. Refers, probably, to practicing a musical instrument, music being an accomplishment cultivated by highborn young ladies.
8. Most perfect.

9. Julius Caesar wrote an account of his military campaigns (*Commentaries*); the Roman poet Ovid wrote poems ostensibly about his own life and loves.

'tis to no purpose to the readers, but it is to the authoress, because I write it for my own sake, not theirs; neither did I intend this piece for to delight, but to divulge; not to please the fancy but to tell the truth, lest after-ages should mistake, in not knowing I was daughter to one Master Lucas[1] of St. Johns, near Colchester, in Essex, second wife to the Lord Marquis of Newcastle; for my lord having had two wives, I might easily have been mistaken, especially if I should die and my lord marry again.

1656

The Blazing World

Part romance, part utopia, and part science fiction, *The Blazing World* is also an idealized version of Cavendish's own fantasies in that it portrays the effortless rise of a woman to absolute power. It begins in the vein of romance: a young woman is abducted and miraculously saved as a tempest carries the abductors' boat to the North Pole and on to another universe, the Blazing World, whose emperor promptly marries her and turns over the entire government of the realm to her. It takes on a utopian character, as the new empress learns from the fantastically diverse inhabitants about their numerous scientific experiments and about the royalist politics and religious uniformity of the place. The empress then brings Margaret Cavendish to be her scribe and returns with Margaret (in the state of disembodied spirits and Platonic friends) to visit and learn about Margaret's world; she also puts down a rebellion at home and subjects other nations to her beneficent rule. Cavendish's preface makes a bold claim for authorial self-sufficiency, equating her creation of and rule over her textual world with the conquering and ruling of empires by Caesar and Alexander. She emphasizes the satisfactions of authorship, but in doing so she also underscores the social and political restrictions on women that have confined her sphere of action to an imagined world.

The Description of a New World, Called The Blazing World[1]

To the Reader

* * *This is the reason, why I added this piece of fancy to my philosophical observations, and joined them as two worlds at the ends of their poles; both for my own sake, to divert my studious thoughts, which I employed in the contemplation thereof, and to delight the reader with variety, which is always pleasing. But lest my fancy should stray too much, I chose such a fiction as would be agreeable to the subject treated of in the former parts; it is a description of a new world, not such as Lucian's or the French-man's world in the moon;[2] but a world of my own creating, which I call the Blazing World: the first part whereof is romancical, the second philosophical, and the third is merely fancy, or (as I may call it) fantastical, which if it add

---

1. Thomas Lucas (ca. 1573–1625), a gentleman of large fortune and estates. Margaret describes him as "not a peer of the realm, yet there were few peers who had much greater estates, or lived more noble therewith."
1. *The Blazing World* was published in 1666 and 1668, together with Newcastle's *Observations upon Experimental Philosophy*, a critique of the

new science emphasizing the limitations of experiment founded on human perception and such instruments as the microscope and the telescope.
2. Cyrano de Bergerac (1619–1655), author of *Histoire comique des états et empires de la lune* (1656). The Greek satirist Lucian of Samosata (125–200? C.E.) wrote dialogues about an imaginary voyage, translated in 1634.

any satisfaction to you, I shall account myself a happy creatoress; if not, I must be content to live a melancholy life in my own world; I cannot call it a poor world, if poverty be only want of gold, silver, and jewels; for there is more gold in it than all the chemists ever did, and (as I verily believe) will ever be able to make. As for the rocks of diamonds, I wish with all my soul they might be shared amongst my noble female friends, and upon that condition, I would willingly quit my part; and of the gold I should only desire so much as might suffice to repair my noble lord and husband's losses:[3] for I am not covetous, but as ambitious as ever any of my sex was, is, or can be; which makes, that though I cannot be Henry the Fifth, or Charles the Second, yet I endeavor to be Margaret the First; and although I have neither power, time nor occasion to conquer the world as Alexander and Caesar did; yet rather than not to be mistress of one, since fortune and the fates would give me none, I have made a world of my own: for which nobody, I hope, will blame me, since it is in everyone's power to do the like.

———————

* * *No sooner was the lady brought before the emperor, but he conceived her to be some goddess, and offered to worship her; which she refused, telling him, (for by that time she had pretty well learned their language) that although she came out of another world, yet was she but a mortal; at which the emperor rejoicing, made her his wife, and gave her an absolute power to rule and govern all that world as she pleased. But her subjects, who could hardly be persuaded to believe her mortal, tendered her all the veneration and worship due to a deity. . . .

Their priests and governors were princes of the imperial blood, and made eunuchs for that purpose; and as for the ordinary sort of men in that part of the world where the emperor resided, they were of several complexions; not white, black, tawny, olive or ash-colored; but some appeared of an azure, some of a deep purple, some of a grass-green, some of a scarlet, some of an orange color, etc. Which colors and complexions, whether they were made by the bare reflection of light, without the assistance of small particles, or by the help of well-ranged and ordered atoms; or by a continual agitation of little globules; or by some pressing and reacting motion, I am not able to determine. The rest of the inhabitants of that world, were men of several different sorts, shapes, figures, dispositions, and humors, as I have already made mention heretofore; some were bear-men, some worm-men, some fish- or mear-men,[4] otherwise called sirens; some bird-men, some fly-men, some ant-men, some geese-men, some spider-men, some lice-men, some fox-men, some ape-men, some jackdaw-men, some magpie-men, some parrot-men, some satyrs, some giants, and many more, which I cannot all remember; and of these several sorts of men, each followed such a profession as was most proper for the nature of their species, which the empress encouraged them in, especially those that had applied themselves to the study of several arts and sciences; for they were as ingenious and witty in the invention of profitable

———

3. Cavendish's husband, William, was formally banished from England and his estates confiscated in 1649; they were all restored after the Restoration. During his banishment Margaret estimated that he suffered financial losses of around £940,000.

4. Mermen, the male counterparts of mermaids.

and useful arts, as we are in our world, nay, more; and to that end she erected schools, and founded several societies. The bear-men were to be her experimental philosophers, the bird-men her astronomers, the fly-, worm-, and fish-men her natural philosophers, the ape-men her chemists, the satyrs her Galenic physicians, the fox-men her politicians, the spider- and lice-men her mathematicians, the jackdaw-, magpie-, and parrot-men her orators and logicians, the giants her architects, etc. But before all things, she having got a sovereign power from the emperor over all the world, desired to be informed both of the manner of their religion and government, and to that end she called the priests and statesmen, to give her an account of either. Of the statesmen she inquired, first, why they had so few laws? To which they answered, that many laws made many divisions, which most commonly did breed factions, and at last break out into open wars. Next, she asked, why they preferred the monarchical form of government before any other? They answered, that as it was natural for one body to have but one head, so it was also natural for a politic body to have but one governor; and that a commonwealth, which had many governors, was like a monster with many heads: besides, said they, a monarchy is a divine form of government, and agrees most with our religion; for as there is but one God, whom we all unanimously worship and adore with one faith, so we are resolved to have but one emperor, to whom we all submit with one obedience.

Then the empress seeing that the several sorts of her subjects had each their churches apart, asked the priests whether they were of several religions? They answered Her Majesty, that there was no more but one religion in all that world, nor no diversity of opinions in that same religion; for though there were several sorts of men, yet had they all but one opinion concerning the worship and adoration of God. The empress asked them, whether they were Jews, Turks, or Christians? We do not know, said they, what religions those are; but we do all unanimously acknowledge, worship, and adore the only, omnipotent, and eternal God, with all reverence, submission, and duty. Again, the empress inquired, whether they had several forms of worship? They answered, no: for our devotion and worship consists only in prayers, which we frame according to our several necessities, in petitions, humiliations, thanksgiving, etc. Truly, replied the empress, I thought you had been either Jews, or Turks, because I never perceived any women in your congregations; but what is the reason, you bar them from your religious assemblies? It is not fit, said they, that men and women should be promiscuously together in time of religious worship; for their company hinders devotion, and makes many, instead of praying to God, direct their devotion to their mistresses. But, asked the empress, have they no congregation of their own, to perform the duties of divine worship, as well as men? No, answered they: but they stay at home, and say their prayers by themselves in their closets.[5] Then the empress desired to know the reason why the priests and governors of their world were made eunuchs? They answered, to keep them from marriage: for women and children most commonly make disturbance both in church and state. But, said she, women and children have no employment in church or state. 'Tis true, answered they; but although they are not admitted to public

5. Private chambers.

employments, yet are they so prevalent[6] with their husbands and parents, that many times by their importunate persuasions, they cause as much, nay, more mischief secretly, than if they had the management of public affairs.

* * *

[THE EMPRESS BRINGS THE DUCHESS OF NEWCASTLE TO THE BLAZING WORLD]

After some time, when the spirits had refreshed themselves in their own vehicles, they sent one of their nimblest spirits, to ask the empress, whether she would have a scribe.* * * Then the spirit asked her, whether she would have the soul of a living or a dead man? Why, said the empress, can the soul quit a living body, and wander or travel abroad? Yes, answered he, for according to Plato's doctrine, there is a conversation of souls, and the souls of lovers live in the bodies of their beloved. Then I will have, answered she, the soul of some ancient famous writer, either of Aristotle, Pythagoras, Plato, Epicurus,[7] or the like. The spirit said, that those famous men were very learned, subtle, and ingenious writers, but they were so wedded to their own opinions, that they would never have the patience to be scribes. Then, said she, I'll have the soul of one of the most famous modern writers, as either of Galileo, Gassendus, Descartes, Helmont, Hobbes, H. More,[8] etc. The spirit answered, that they were fine ingenious writers, but yet so self-conceited, that they would scorn to be scribes to a woman. But, said he, there's a lady, the Duchess of Newcastle, which although she is not one of the most learned, eloquent, witty, and ingenious, yet is she a plain and rational writer, for the principle of her writings, is sense and reason, and she will without question, be ready to do you all the service she can. This lady then, said the empress, will I choose for my scribe, neither will the emperor have reason to be jealous, she being one of my own sex. In truth, said the spirit, husbands have reason to be jealous of platonic lovers, for they are very dangerous, as being not only very intimate and close, but subtle and insinuating. You say well, replied the empress; wherefore I pray send me the Duchess of Newcastle's soul; which the spirit did; and after she came to wait on the empress, at her first arrival the empress embraced and saluted her with a spiritual kiss.

* * *

[THE DUCHESS WANTS A WORLD TO RULE]

Well, said the duchess, setting aside this dispute, my ambition is, that I would fain be as you are, that is, an empress of a world, and I shall never be at quiet until I be one. I love you so well, replied the empress, that I wish

6. I.e., they prevail so much.
7. Classical philosophers and founders, respectively, of schools of philosophy: the Peripatetics, the Pythagoreans, the Academics, the Epicureans.
8. Galileo Galilei (1564–1642), Italian astronomer and defender of the Copernican system; Pierre Gassendi (1592–1655), proponent of a mechanistic theory of matter; René Descartes (1596–1650),

French mathematician and philosopher who had a major influence on the new science; Jan Baptista van Helmont (1579–1644), Flemish chemist; Thomas Hobbes, English mechanistic philosopher and political scientist, author of *Leviathan*; Henry More (1614–1687), one of the antimaterialist Cambridge Platonists.

with all my soul, you had the fruition of your ambitious desire, and I shall not fail to give you my best advice how to accomplish it; the best informers are the immaterial spirits, and they'll soon tell you, whether it be possible to obtain your wish. But, said the duchess, I have little acquaintance with them, for I never knew any before the time you sent for me. They know you, replied the empress; for they told me of you, and were the means and instrument of your coming hither: wherefore I'll confer with them, and inquire whether there be not another world, whereof you may be empress as well as I am of this. No sooner had the empress said this, but some immaterial spirits came to visit her, of whom she inquired, whether there were but three worlds in all, to wit, the Blazing World where she was in, the world which she came from, and the world where the duchess lived? The spirits answered, that there were more numerous worlds than the stars which appeared in these three mentioned worlds. Then the empress asked, whether it was not possible, that her dearest friend the Duchess of Newcastle, might be empress of one of them.[9] Although there be numerous, nay, infinite worlds, answered the spirits, yet none is without government. But is none of these worlds so weak, said she, that it may be surprised or conquered? The spirits answered, that Lucian's world of lights, had been for some time in a snuff,[1] but of late years one Helmont had got it, who since he was emperor of it, had so strengthened the immortal parts thereof with mortal outworks, as it was for the present impregnable. Said the empress, if there be such an infinite number of worlds, I am sure, not only my friend, the duchess, but any other might obtain one. Yes, answered the spirits, if those worlds were uninhabited; but they are as populous as this, your majesty governs. Why, said the empress, it is not impossible to conquer a world. No, answered the spirits, but, for the most part, conquerors seldom enjoy their conquest, for they being more feared than loved, most commonly come to an untimely end. If you will but direct me, said the duchess to the spirits, which world is easiest to be conquered, her Majesty will assist me with means, and I will trust to fate and fortune; for I had rather die in the adventure of noble achievements, than live in obscure and sluggish security; since by the one, I may live in a glorious fame, and by the other I am buried in oblivion. The spirits answered, that the lives of fame were like other lives; for some lasted long, and some died soon. 'Tis true, said the duchess; but yet the shortest-lived fame lasts longer than the longest life of man. But, replied the spirits, if occasion does not serve you, you must content yourself to live without such achievements that may gain you a fame: but we wonder, proceeded the spirits, that you desire to be empress of a terrestrial world, whenas you can create yourself a celestial world if you please. What, said the empress, can any mortal be a creator? Yes, answered the spirits; for every human creature can create an immaterial world fully inhabited by immaterial creatures, and populous of immaterial subjects, such as we are, and all this within the compass of the head or skull; nay, not only so, but he may create a world of what fashion and government he will, and give the creatures thereof such motions, figures, forms, colors, perceptions, etc. as he pleases, and make whirlpools, lights, pressures, and reactions, etc.

9. Speculation about multiple inhabited worlds was an occasional topic in texts on the new astronomy. Milton's Raphael introduces the idea to Adam (*Paradise Lost* 8.140–58).
1. On the point of extinction.

as he thinks best; nay, he may make a world full of veins, muscles, and nerves, and all these to move by one jolt or stroke: also he may alter that world as often as he pleases, or change it from a natural world, to an artificial; he may make a world of ideas, a world of atoms, a world of lights, or whatsoever his fancy leads him to. And since it is in your power to create such a world, what need you to venture life, reputation and tranquility, to conquer a gross mate- rial world? . . . You have converted me, said the duchess to the spirits, from my ambitious desire; wherefore I'll take your advice, reject and despise all the worlds without me, and create a world of my own.

* * *

The Epilogue to the Reader

By this poetical description, you may perceive, that my ambition is not only to be empress, but authoress of a whole world; and that the worlds I have made, both the Blazing and the other Philosophical World, mentioned in the first part of this description, are framed and composed of the most pure, that is, the rational parts of matter, which are the parts of my mind; which creation was more easily and suddenly effected, than the conquests of the two famous monarchs of the world, Alexander and Caesar:[2] neither have I made such disturbances, and caused so many dissolutions of particulars, otherwise named deaths, as they did; for I have destroyed but some few men in a little boat, which died through the extremity of cold, and that by the hand of justice, which was necessitated to punish their crime of stealing away a young and beauteous lady.[3] And in the formation of those worlds, I take more delight and glory, than ever Alexander or Caesar did in conquering this terrestrial world; and though I have made my Blazing World, a peaceable world, allowing it but one religion, one language, and one government; yet could I make another world, as full of factions, divisions, and wars, as this is of peace and tranquility; and the rational figures of my mind might express as much courage to fight, as Hector and Achilles had; and be as wise as Nestor, as eloquent as Ulysses, and as beautiful as Helen.[4] But I esteeming peace before war, wit before policy,[5] honesty before beauty; instead of the figures of Alexander, Caesar, Hector, Achilles, Nestor, Ulysses, Helen, etc. chose rather the figure of honest Margaret Newcastle, which now I would not change for all this terrestrial world; and if any should like the world I have made, and be willing to be my subjects, they may imagine themselves such, and they are such, I mean, in their minds, fancies, or imaginations; but if they cannot endure to be subjects, they may create worlds of their own, and govern themselves as they please: but yet let them have a care, not to prove unjust usurpers, and to rob me of mine; for concerning the Philosophical World, I am empress of it myself; and

2. Alexander the Great and Julius Caesar were both famed as conquerors of much of the world known to them.

3. A reference to the romancelike incident with which *The Blazing World* begins, the abduction of a young woman by a party of adventurers whose boat is blown in a tempest to the North Pole, where they perish (except for the woman, who enters into the Blazing World).

4. Hector the Trojan and Achilles the Greek are the principal heroes of Homer's *Iliad*; Nestor, wise adviser to the Greeks; Ulysses, hero of Homer's *Odyssey*, Helen, the one whose beauty caused the Trojan War, as it prompted the Trojan Paris to steal her away from her Greek husband, Menelaus.

5. Intelligence before cunning.

as for the Blazing World, it having an empress already, who rules it with great wisdom and conduct, which empress is my dear platonic friend; I shall never prove so unjust, treacherous, and unworthy to her, as to disturb her government, much less to depose her from her imperial throne, for the sake of any other; but rather choose to create another world for another friend.

1666, 1668

JOHN MILTON
1608–1674

As a young man, John Milton proclaimed himself the future author of a great English epic. He promised a poem devoted to the glory of the nation, centering on the deeds of King Arthur or some other ancient hero. When Milton finally published his epic thirty years later, readers found instead a poem about the Fall of Satan and humankind, set in Heaven, Hell, and the Garden of Eden, in which traditional heroism is denigrated and England not once mentioned. What lay between the youthful promise and the eventual fulfillment was a career marked by private tragedy and public controversy.

In his poems and prose tracts Milton often alludes to crises in his own life: his choice of a vocation, the early death of friends, painful disappointment in marriage, and the catastrophe of blindness. At the same time, no other major English poet has been so deeply involved in the great questions and political crises of his times. His works reflect upon and help develop some basic Western concepts that were taking modern form in his lifetime: companionate marriage, the new science, freedom of the press, religious liberty and toleration, republicanism, and more. It is scarcely possible to treat Milton's career separately from the history of England in his lifetime, not only because he was an active participant in affairs of church and state, but also because when he signed himself, as he often did, "John Milton, Englishman," he was presenting himself as England's prophetic bard. He considered himself the spokesman for the nation as a whole even when he found himself in a minority of one.

No English poet before Milton fashioned himself quite so self-consciously as an author. The young Milton deliberately set out to follow the steps of the ideal poetic

Milton.

career—beginning with pastoral (the mode of several of his early poems) and ending with epic. His models for this progression were Virgil and Spenser: he called the latter "a better teacher than Scotus or Aquinas." In his systematic approach to his vocation he stood at the opposite end of the spectrum from such Cavalier contemporaries as Richard Lovelace, who turned to verse with an air of studied carelessness. Milton resembles Spenser especially in his constant use of myth and archetype and also in his readiness to juxtapose biblical and classical stories. He is everywhere concerned with the conventions of genre, yet he infused every genre he used with new energy, transforming it for later practitioners. The Western literary and intellectual heritage impinged on his writing as immediately and directly as the circumstances of his own life, but he continually reconceived the ideas, literary forms, and values of this heritage to make them relevant to himself and to his age.

Milton's family was bourgeois, cultured, and staunchly Protestant. His father was a scrivener—a combination solicitor, investment adviser, and moneylender—as well as an amateur composer with some reputation in musical circles. Milton had a younger brother, Christopher, who practiced law, and an elder sister, Anne. At age seventeen he wrote a funeral elegy for the death of Anne's infant daughter and later educated her two sons, Edward and John (Edward wrote his biography). Milton had private tutors at home and also attended one of the finest schools in the land, St. Paul's. At school he began a close friendship with Charles Diodati, with whom he exchanged Latin poems and letters over several years, and for whose death in 1638 he wrote a moving Latin elegy. Milton's excellent early education gave him special facility in languages (Latin, Greek, Hebrew and its dialects, Italian, and French; later he learned Spanish and Dutch).

In 1625 Milton entered Christ's College, Cambridge. He was briefly suspended during his freshman year over some dispute with his tutor, but he graduated in 1629 and was made Master of Arts three years later. As his surviving student orations indicate, he was profoundly disappointed in his university education, reviling the scholastic logic and Latin rhetorical exercises that still formed its core as "futile and barren controversies and wordy disputes" that "stupefy and benumb the mind." He went to university with the serious intention of taking orders in the Church of England—the obvious vocation for a young man of his scholarly and religious bent— but became increasingly disenchanted with the lack of reformation in the church under Archbishop William Laud, and in the hindsight of 1642 he proclaimed himself "church-outed by the prelates." No doubt his change of direction was also linked to the fastidious contempt he expressed for the ignorant and clownish clergymen-in-the-making who were his fellow students at Cambridge: "They thought themselves gallant men, and I thought them fools." Those students retaliated by dubbing Milton "the Lady of Christ's College."

Above all, Milton came to believe more and more strongly that he was destined to serve his language, his country, and his God as a poet. He began by writing occasional poetry in Latin, the usual language for collegiate poets and for poets who sought a European audience. Milton wrote some of the century's best Latin poems, but as early as 1628 he announced to a university audience his determination to glorify England and the English language in poetry. In his first major English poem (at age twenty-one), the hymn "On the Morning of Christ's Nativity," Milton already portrayed himself as a prophetic bard. This poem is very different from Richard Crashaw's Nativity hymn, with its Spenserian echoes, its allusion to Roman Catholic and Laudian "idolatry" in the long passage on the expulsion of the pagan gods, and its stunning moves from the Creation to Doomsday, from the manger at Bethlehem to the cosmos, and from the shepherd's chatter to the music of the spheres. Two or three years later, probably, Milton wrote the companion poems "L'Allegro" and "Il Penseroso," achieving a stylistic tour de force by creating from the same meter (octosyllabic couplets) entirely different sound qualities, rhythmic effects, and moods. These poems celebrate, respectively, Mirth and Melancholy, defining them by their ancestry, lifestyles, associates, landscapes, activities, music, and literature. In 1634, at the invitation of his musician friend Henry Lawes, he wrote the masque called *Comus*, in which the villain is portrayed as a refined, seductive, and dissolute Cavalier. *Comus* challenges the absolutist politics of previous court masques by locating true virtue and good pleasure in the households of the country aristocracy rather than at court.

After university, as part of his preparation for a poetic career, Milton undertook a six-year program of self-directed reading in ancient and modern theology, philosophy, history, science, politics, and literature. He was profoundly grateful to his father for sparing him the grubby business of making money and for financing these years of private study, followed by a fifteen-month "grand tour" of France, Italy, and Switzerland. In 1638 Milton contributed the pastoral elegy "Lycidas" to a Cambridge volume lamenting the untimely death of a college contemporary. This greatest of English funeral elegies explores Milton's deep anxieties about poetry as a vocation, confronts the terrors of mortality in language of astonishing resonance and power, and incorporates a furious apocalyptic diatribe on the corrupt Church of England clergy. Nonetheless, while he was in Italy he exchanged verses and learned compliments with various Catholic intellectuals and men of letters, some of whom became his friends. Milton could always maintain friendships and family relationships across ideological divides. In 1645 his English and Latin poems were published together in a two-part volume, *Poems of Mr. John Milton*.

Upon his return to England, Milton opened a school and was soon involved in Presbyterian efforts to depose the bishops and reform church liturgy, writing five "antiprelatical tracts" denouncing and satirizing bishops. These were the first in a series of political interventions Milton produced over the next twenty years, characterized by remarkable courage and independence of thought. He wrote successively on church government, divorce, education, freedom of the press, regicide, and republicanism. From the outbreak of the Civil War in 1642 until his death, Milton allied himself with the Puritan cause, but his religious opinions developed throughout his life, from relative orthodoxy in his youth to ever more heretical positions in his later years. And while his family belonged to the class that benefited most directly from Europe's first bourgeois revolution, his brother, Christopher, fought on the royalist side. The Milton brothers, like most of their contemporaries, did not see these wars as a confrontation of class interests, but as a conflict between radically differing theories of government and, above all, religion.

Some of Milton's treatises were prompted by personal concerns. He interrupted his polemical tract, *The Reason of Church Government Urged Against Prelaty* (1642), to devote several pages to a discussion of his poetic vocation and the great works he hoped to produce in the future. His tracts about divorce, which can hardly have seemed the most pressing of issues in the strife-torn years 1643–45, were motivated by his own disastrous marriage. Aged thirty-three, inexperienced with women, and idealistic about marriage as in essence a union of minds and spirits, he married a young woman of seventeen, Mary Powell, who returned to her royalist family just a few months after the wedding. In response, Milton wrote several tracts vigorously advocating divorce on the grounds of incompatibility and with the right to remarry—a position almost unheard of at the time and one that required a boldly antiliteral reading of the Gospels. The fact that these tracts could not be licensed and were roundly denounced in Parliament, from pulpits, and in print prompted him to write *Areopagitica* (1644), an impassioned defense of a free press and the free commerce in ideas against a Parliament determined to restore effective censorship. He saw these personal issues—reformed poetry, domestic liberty achieved through needful divorce, and a free press—as vital to the creation of a reformed English culture.

In 1649, just after Charles I was executed, Milton published *The Tenure of Kings and Magistrates* (see pp. 1396–99). This treatise defends the revolution and the regicide and develops a "contract theory" of government based on the inalienable sovereignty of the people—a version of contract very different from that of Thomas Hobbes. Milton was appointed Latin Secretary to the Commonwealth government (1649–53) and to Oliver Cromwell's Protectorate (1654–58), which meant that he wrote the official letters—mostly in Latin—to foreign governments and heads of state. He also wrote polemical defenses of the new government: *Eikonoklastes* (1649), to counter the powerful emotional effect of *Eikon Basilike*, supposedly written by the king just before his death, and two Latin *Defenses* upholding the regicide and the new republic to European audiences.

During these years Milton suffered a series of agonizing tragedies. Mary Powell returned to him in 1645 but died in childbirth in 1652, leaving four children; the only son, John, died a few months later. That same year Milton became totally blind; he thought his boyhood habit of reading until midnight had weakened his eyesight and that writing his first *Defense* to answer the famous French scholar Claudius Salmasius had destroyed it. Milton married again in 1656, apparently happily, but his new wife, Katherine Woodcock, was dead two years later, along with their infant daughter. Katherine is probably the subject of his sonnet "Methought I Saw My Late Espoused Saint," a moving dream vision poignant with the sense of loss—both of sight and of love. Milton had little time for poetry in these years, but his few sonnets revolutionized the genre. He used the small sonnet form, hitherto confined mainly to matters of love, for new and grand subjects: praises of Cromwell and other statesmen mixed with admonition and political advice; a prophetic denunciation calling down God's vengeance for Protestants massacred in Piedmont; and an emotion-filled account of his continuing struggle to come to terms with his blindness as part of God's providence.

Cromwell's death in 1658 led to mounting political chaos, and soon the restoration of the Stuart monarchy seemed inevitable. Milton held out against that tide. His several tracts of 1659–60 developed radical arguments for broad toleration, church disestablishment, and republican government. And just as he was among the first to attack the power of the bishops, so he was virtually the last defender of the "Good Old Cause" of the Revolution; the second edition of his *Ready and Easy Way to Establish a Free Commonwealth* appeared in late April 1660, scarcely two weeks before the monarchy was restored. For several months after that event, Milton was in hiding, his life in danger. Friends, especially the poet Andrew Marvell, managed to secure his pardon and later his release from a brief imprisonment. He lived out his last years in reduced circumstances, plagued by ever more serious attacks of gout but grateful for the domestic comforts provided by his third wife, Elizabeth Minshull, whom he married in 1663 and who survived him.

In such conditions, dismayed by the defeat of his political and religious cause, totally blind and often ill, threatened by the horrific plague of 1665 and the great fire of 1666, and entirely dependent on amanuenses and friends to transcribe his dictation, he completed his great epic poem. *Paradise Lost* (1667/74) radically reconceives the epic genre and epic heroism, choosing as protagonists a domestic couple rather than martial heroes and degrading the military glory celebrated in epic tradition in favor of "the better fortitude / Of patience and heroic martyrdom." It offers a sweeping imaginative vision of Hell, Chaos, and Heaven; prelapsarian life in Eden; the power of the devil's political rhetoric; the psychology of Satan, Adam, and Eve; and the high drama of the Fall and its aftermath.

In his final years, Milton published works on grammar and logic chiefly written during his days as a schoolmaster, a history of Britain (1670) from the earliest times to the Norman Conquest, and a treatise urging toleration for Puritan dissenters (1673). He also continued work on his *Christian Doctrine*, a Latin treatise that reveals how far he had moved from the orthodoxies of his day. The work denies the Trinity (making the Son and the Holy Spirit much inferior to God the Father), insists upon free will against Calvinist predestination, and privileges the inspiration of the Spirit even above the Scriptures and the Ten Commandments. Such heterodox positions could not be made public in Milton's lifetime, and *Christian Doctrine* was lost to view for over 150 years.

In 1671 Milton published two poems that reflected the harsh repression all Puritan dissenters faced after the Restoration. *Paradise Regained*, a brief epic in four books, treats Jesus's Temptation in the Wilderness as an intellectual struggle through which the hero comes to understand both himself and his mission. He defeats Satan by renouncing the whole panoply of faulty versions of the good life and of God's kingdom. *Samson Agonistes*, a classical tragedy, is the more harrowing for the resemblances between its tragic hero and its author. The deeply flawed, pain-wracked, blind, and defeated Samson struggles, in dialogues with his visitors, to gain self-knowledge, discovering at last a desperate way to triumph over his captors and offer his people a chance to regain their freedom. In these last poems Milton sought to educate his readers in moral and political wisdom and virtue. Only through such inner transformation, Milton now firmly believed, would men and women come to value— and so perhaps reclaim—the intellectual, religious, and political freedom he so vigorously promoted in his prose and poetry.

From Poems

On the Morning of Christ's Nativity[1]

1

This is the month, and this the happy morn
Wherein the son of Heaven's eternal King,
Of wedded maid and virgin mother born,
Our great redemption from above did bring;
5   For so the holy sages once did sing,
     That he our deadly forfeit[2] should release,
And with his Father work us a perpetual peace.

2

That glorious form, that light unsufferable,°   *unable to be endured*
And that far-beaming blaze of majesty
10 Wherewith he wont° at Heaven's high council-table   *was accustomed*
To sit the midst of Trinal Unity,[3]

---

1. This ode was written on Christmas 1629, a few weeks after Milton's twenty-first birthday. He placed it first in the 1645 edition of his poems, claiming in it his vocation as inspired poet. The poem often looks back to Spenser: the first four stanzas are an adaptation of the Spenserian stanza; there are several Spenserian archaisms (y- prefixes) and some Spenser-like onamatopoeia (lines 156, 172). Comparison with Crashaw's Nativity poem (pp. 1297–99) will highlight some important differences between Roman Catholic and Puritan aesthetics in this period.
2. The sentence of death consequent on the Fall. "Holy sages": for example, the prophet Isaiah (chaps. 9 and 40) and Job (chap. 19) were thought to have foretold Christ as Messiah.
3. The Trinity: Father, Son (incarnate in Christ), and Holy Ghost.

He laid aside; and here with us to be,
    Forsook the courts of everlasting day,
And chose with us a darksome house of mortal clay.

3

15 Say, heavenly Muse, shall not thy sacred vein
Afford a present to the infant God?
Hast thou no verse, no hymn, or solemn strain,
To welcome him to this his new abode,
Now while the heaven by the sun's team untrod[4]
20   Hath took no print of the approaching light,
And all the spangled host° keep watch in squadrons bright?   *angels*

4

See how from far upon the eastern road
The star-led wizards[5] haste with odors sweet:
O run, prevent° them with thy humble ode,   *anticipate*
25 And lay it lowly at his blessèd feet;
Have thou the honor first thy Lord to greet,
    And join thy voice unto the angel choir,
From out His secret altar touched with hallowed fire.[6]

The Hymn

1

It was the winter wild
30 While the Heaven-born child
    All meanly wrapped in the rude manger lies;
Nature in awe to him
Had doffed her gaudy trim[7]
    With her great Master so to sympathize;
35 It was no season then for her
To wanton with the sun, her lusty paramour.

2

Only with speeches fair
She woos the gentle air
    To hide her guilty front° with innocent snow,   *brow*
40 And on her naked shame,
Pollute with sinful blame,
    The saintly veil of maiden white to throw,[8]

---

4. In classical myth, the sun (Phoebus Apollo) drove across heaven in a chariot drawn by horses.
5. The Magi who followed the star of Bethlehem to find and adore the infant Christ.
6. Isaiah's lips were touched by a burning coal from the altar, purifying him and confirming him as a prophet (Isaiah 6.7).
7. Put off her garments of leaves and flowers.
8. Nature fell also with the Fall, so she is a harlot (line 36), not a pure maiden, despite her white garment of snow.

Confounded that her Maker's eyes
Should look so near upon her foul deformities.

3

45   But he her fears to cease
Sent down the meek-eyed Peace;
    She, crowned with olive green, came softly sliding
Down through the turning sphere,[9]
His ready harbinger,°   *forerunner*
50   With turtle[1] wing the amorous clouds dividing,
And waving wide her myrtle wand,
She strikes a universal peace through sea and land.

4

No war or battle's sound
Was heard the world around;[2]
55   The idle spear and shield were high up-hung;
The hookèd chariot[3] stood
Unstained with hostile blood,
    The trumpet spake not to the armèd throng,
And kings sat still with awful° eye,   *filled with awe*
60   As if they surely knew their sovereign Lord was by.

5

But peaceful was the night
Wherein the Prince of Light
    His reign of peace upon the earth began:
The winds, with wonder whist,°   *hushed*
65   Smoothly the waters kissed,
    Whispering new joys to the mild oceàn,
Who now hath quite forgot to rave,
While birds of calm[4] sit brooding on the charmèd wave.

6

The stars with deep amaze
70   Stand fixed in steadfast gaze,
    Bending one way their precious influence,
And will not take their flight
For all the morning light,
    Or Lucifer[5] that often warned them thence;
75   But in their glimmering orbs did glow
Until their Lord himself bespake,° and bid them go.   *spoke out*

9. The Ptolemaic spheres, revolving around the earth.
1. Like a turtledove, which, like the myrtle (next line), is an emblem of Venus (Love), as the olive crown is of peace.
2. Around the time of Christ's birth, the "Peace of Augustus" held, during which no major wars disturbed the Roman Empire; that peace was sometimes attributed to Christ.
3. War chariots were built with scythelike hooks on the axles, to wound and kill.
4. Kingfishers (halcyons) were thought to calm the seas during the time they nested on its waves.
5. Not Satan but the morning star, Venus.

7

And though the shady gloom
Had given day her room,
   The sun himself withheld his wonted speed,
80 And hid his head for shame
As° his inferior flame   *as if*
   The new-enlightened world no more should need;
He saw a greater Sun[6] appear
Than his bright throne or burning axletree° could bear.   *chariot axle*

8

85 The shepherds on the lawn
Or ere the point of° dawn   *just before*
   Sat simply chatting in a rustic row;
Full little thought they than°   *then*
That the mighty Pan[7]
90   Was kindly[8] come to live with them below;
Perhaps their loves or else their sheep
Was all that did their silly° thoughts so busy keep.   *simple, humble*

9

When such music sweet
Their hearts and ears did greet
95   As never was by mortal finger struck,
Divinely warbled voice
Answering the stringèd noise,
   As all their souls in blissful rapture took;
The air, such pleasure loath to lose,
100 With thousand echoes still prolongs each heavenly close.°   *cadence*

10

Nature that heard such sound
Beneath the hollow round
   Of Cynthia's seat,[9] the airy region thrilling,°   *piercing, delighting*
Now was almost won
105 To think her part was done,
   And that her reign had here its last fulfilling;
She knew such harmony alone
Could hold all heaven and earth in happier uniòn.

11

At last surrounds their sight
110 A globe of circular light

---

6. The familiar Son/sun pun.
7. Pan, patron of shepherds, is a merry, goat-footed god, but he was often conceived in more exalted terms and identified with Christ, because his name in Greek means "all."
8. By nature; also, benevolently.

9. Cynthia is the moon. Nature rules below the moon (the region of the four elements and subject to decay). The unchanging, perfect region above the moon is normally the only place one could hear either angels' hymnody or the music of the spheres.

That with long beams the shamefaced night arrayed;°   *adorned with rays*
The helmèd cherubim
And sworded seraphim[1]
Are seen in glittering ranks with wings displayed,
115   Harping in loud and solemn choir
With unexpressive° notes to Heaven's newborn heir.   *inexpressible*

12

Such music (as 'tis said)
Before was never made,
    But when of old the sons of morning sung,[2]
120   While the Creator great
His constellations set,
    And the well-balanced world on hinges° hung,   *the two poles*
And cast the dark foundations deep,
And bid the welt'ring waves their oozy channel keep.

13

125   Ring out, ye crystal spheres,
Once bless our human ears
    (If ye have power to touch our senses so),
And let your silver chime
Move in melodious time,
130   And let the bass of Heaven's deep organ blow;
And with your ninefold harmony[3]
Make up full consort to th' angelic symphony.

14

For if such holy song
Enwrap our fancy long,
135   Time will run back and fetch the age of gold;[4]
And speckled vanity
Will sicken soon and die,
    And leprous sin will melt from earthly mold,
And Hell itself will pass away,
140   And leave her dolorous mansions to the peering day.

15

Yea, Truth and Justice then
Will down return to men,
    Th' enameled arras° of the rainbow wearing,   *brightly colored fabric*

1. Seraphim and cherubim are the highest of the traditional nine orders of angels; they are often portrayed in martial attire.
2. Job 38.4–7: "Where wast thou when I laid the foundations of the earth? . . . / When the morning stars sang together and all the sons of God shouted for joy?"
3. In Pythagorean theory, each of the nine moving spheres sounds a distinctive note (the tenth, the primum mobile, does not move). It was supposed that, after the Fall, this harmonious music of the spheres could not be heard on earth. Earth would be the "bass" of the cosmic organ, sounding under that planetary harmony.
4. The first age, of human innocence, classical mythology's equivalent to the Garden of Eden.

And Mercy set between,[5]
145   Throned in celestial sheen,
       With radiant feet the tissued[6] clouds down steering;
    And Heaven, as at some festival,
    Will open wide the gates of her high palace hall.

16

    But wisest Fate says no,
150   This must not yet be so;
       The Babe lies yet in smiling infancy[7]
    That on the bitter cross
    Must redeem our loss,
       So both himself and us to glorify;
155   Yet first to those ychained[8] in sleep
    The wakeful trump of doom must thunder through the deep,

17

    With such a horrid clang
    As on Mount Sinai rang
       While the red fire and smoldering clouds outbrake;
160   The agèd earth, aghast
    With terror of that blast,
       Shall from the surface to the center shake,
    When at the world's last sessiòn,
    The dreadful Judge in middle air shall spread His throne.[9]

18

165   And then at last our bliss
    Full and perfect is,
       But now begins; for from this happy day
    Th' old dragon under ground,[1]
    In straiter limits bound,
170   Not half so far casts his usurpèd sway,
    And wroth to see his kingdom fail,
    Swinges° the scaly horror of his folded tail.   *lashes*

19

    The oracles are dumb;[2]
    No voice or hideous hum
175   Runs through the archèd roof in words deceiving.

5. This allegorical scene, suggesting a masque descent, alludes to Psalm 85.10, part of the liturgy for Christmas: "Mercy and truth are met together; righteousness and peace have kissed each other." Peace, in the poem, has already descended (lines 45–52). The lines also evoke the flight of Astraea, the classical goddess of justice, at the end of the Golden Age, and her return with its restoration, celebrated by Virgil in his fourth eclogue, applied by him to the birth of Pollio but by Christians to Christ.
6. Cloth woven with silver and gold.

7. The Latin word, *infans*, means, literally, "non-speaking."
8. One of Spenser's archaic *y*- prefixes.
9. Moses received the Ten Commandments amid thunder and lightning atop Mount Sinai (Exodus 19); the Last Judgment will take place amid similar uproar. "Session": court proceeding.
1. The devil (Revelation 20.2).
2. An ancient tradition held that pagan oracles ceased with the coming of Christ; another identified the pagan gods with the fallen angels.

Apollo from his shrine
Can no more divine,
   With hollow shriek the steep of Delphos leaving.[3]
No nightly trance or breathèd spell
180 Inspires the pale-eyed priest from the prophetic cell.

20

The lonely mountains o'er
And the resounding shore
   A voice of weeping heard and loud lament;
From haunted spring and dale
185 Edged with the poplar pale,
   The parting genius[4] is with sighing sent;
With flower-in-woven tresses torn
The nymphs in twilight shade of tangled thickets mourn.

21

In consecrated earth
190 And on the holy hearth,
   The lars and lemures[5] moan with midnight plaint;
In urns and altars round
A drear and dying sound
   Affrights the flamens[6] at their service quaint;
195 And the chill marble seems to sweat,
While each peculiar power forgoes his wonted seat.

22

Peor and Baalim[7]
Forsake their temples dim,
   With that twice-battered god of Palestine,[8]
200 And moonèd Ashtaroth,[9]
Heaven's queen and mother both,
   Now sits not girt with tapers' holy shine;
The Libyc Hammon[1] shrinks° his horn;   *draws in*
In vain the Tyrian maids their wounded Thammuz mourn.[2]

23

205 And sullen Moloch,[3] fled,
Hath left in shadows dread
   His burning idol all of blackest hue;

3. Apollo's main shrine was at Delphi, on the slopes of Mount Parnassus.
4. A local deity guarding a particular place.
5. Spirits of the dead. "Lars": household gods.
6. Roman priests.
7. Other manifestations of Baal, a Canaanite sun god.
8. Dagon, the Philistine god whose image at Ashdod was twice thrown down when the Ark of the Covenant was placed beside it (1 Samuel 5.2–4).
9. Ashtaroth, also known as Astarte, was a Phoe-

nician fertility goddess identified with the moon.
1. Hammon, also Ammon, an Egyptian and Libyan god, depicted as a ram.
2. Thammuz, lover of Ashtaroth, was killed by a boar and lamented by the Phoenician women; he was taken into the Greek pantheon as Adonis.
3. Moloch was a Phoenician fire god, a brazen idol with a human body and a calf's, head; the statue ("his burning idol," line 207) was heated flaming hot and children were thrown into its embrace, with cymbals drowning out their cries (2 Kings 22.10).

In vain with cymbals' ring
They call the grisly king
In dismal dance about the furnace blue;
The brutish gods of Nile as fast,[4]
Isis and Orus and the dog Anubis haste.

24

Nor is Osiris seen
In Memphian grove or green,
Trampling the unshowered° grass with lowings loud,   *rainless*
Nor can he be at rest
Within his sacred chest;
Naught but profoundest Hell can be his shroud.
In vain with timbrelled anthems dark
The sable-stolèd sorcerers bear his worshipped ark.[5]

25

He feels from Judah's land
The dreaded Infant's hand,
The rays of Bethlehem blind his dusky eyne;°   *eyes*
Nor all the gods beside
Longer dare abide,
Not Typhon huge, ending in snaky twine;
Our Babe, to show his godhead true,
Can in his swaddling bands control the damnèd crew.[6]

26

So when the sun in bed,
Curtained with cloudy red,
Pillows his chin upon an orient° wave,   *eastern, bright*
The flocking shadows pale
Troop to th' infernal jail;
Each fettered ghost slips to his several° grave;   *separate*
And the yellow-skirted fays
Fly after the night-steeds, leaving their moon-loved maze.[7]

27

But see! the Virgin blessed
Hath laid her Babe to rest.
Time is our tedious song should here have ending.
Heaven's youngest-teemèd° star   *latest born*
Hath fixed her polished car,°   *gleaming chariot*

---

4. Egyptian gods had some features of animals: Isis (next line) was represented with cow's horns, Orus, or Horus, with a hawk's head; Osiris (lines 213–15) sometimes had the shape of a bull.
5. Osiris's image was carried from temple to temple in a wooden chest, and his priests accompanied it with tambourines ("timbrels").
6. Typhon was a hundred-headed monster who was a serpent below the waist, a figure for the devil. The infant Christ controlling him calls up (as a foreshadowing) the story of the infant Hercules strangling two giant serpents in his cradle.
7. Fairy rings. "Night-steeds": horses drawing Night's chariot.

Her sleeping Lord with handmaid lamp attending:
And all about the courtly stable
Bright-harnessed° angels sit in order serviceàble.   *bright-armored*

1629   1645

On Shakespeare[1]

   What needs my Shakespeare for his honored bones
   The labor of an age in pilèd stones,
   Or that his hallowed relics should be hid
   Under a star-ypointing[2] pyramid?
5 Dear son of memory,[3] great heir of fame,
   What° need'st thou such weak witness of thy name?   *why*
   Thou in our wonder and astonishment
   Hast built thyself a livelong° monument.   *enduring*
   For whilst to th' shame of slow-endeavoring art
10 Thy easy numbers° flow, and that each heart   *verses*
   Hath from the leaves of thy unvalued° book   *invaluable*
   Those Delphic[4] lines with deep impression took,
   Then thou, our fancy of itself bereaving,
   Dost make us marble with too much conceiving;[5]
15 And so sepùlchered in such pomp dost lie,
   That kings for such a tomb would wish to die.

1630   1632

L'Allegro[1]

   Hence loathèd Melancholy,[2]
      Of Cerberus[3] and blackest midnight born,
   In Stygian[4] cave forlorn
      'Mongst horrid shapes, and shrieks, and sights unholy,
5 Find out some uncouth° cell,   *desolate*

---

1. This tribute, Milton's first published poem, appeared in the Second Folio of Shakespeare's plays (1632).
2. A Spenserian archaism.
3. As "son of memory" Shakespeare is a brother of the Muses, who are the daughters of Mnemosyne (Memory).
4. Apollo, god of poetry, had his oracle at Delphi.
5. Shakespeare's mesmerized readers are themselves his ("marble") monument.
1. The companion poems "L'Allegro" and "Il Penseroso" are both written in tetrameter couplets, except for the first ten lines, but Milton's virtuosity produces entirely different tempos and sound qualities in the two poems. The Italian titles name, respectively, the cheerful, mirthful man and the melancholy, contemplative man.

The poems are carefully balanced and their different values celebrated, though "Il Penseroso's" greater length and final coda may intimate that life's superiority. Mirth, the presiding deity of "L'Allegro," is described in terms that evoke Botticelli's presentation of the Grace Euphrosyne (youthful mirth) and her sisters in his *Primavera*.
2. The black melancholy recognized and here exorcized by Mirth's man is a disease leading to madness. "Il Penseroso" celebrates "white" melancholy as the temperament of the scholarly, contemplative man, represented in Dürer's famous engraving *Melancholy*. Burton's *Anatomy of Melancholy* (excerpt on pp. 1240–46) treats the entire range of possibilities.
3. The three-headed hellhound of classical mythology.
4. Near the river Styx, in the underworld.

Where brooding Darkness spreads his jealous wings,
And the night raven sings;
   There under ebon shades and low-browed rocks,
As ragged as thy locks,
10   In dark Cimmerian⁵ desert ever dwell.
But come thou goddess fair and free,
In heaven yclept Euphrosyne,⁶
And by men, heart-easing Mirth,
Whom lovely Venus at a birth
15 With two sister Graces more
To ivy-crownèd Bacchus bore;
Or whether (as some sager sing)
The frolic wind that breathes the spring,
Zephyr with Aurora playing,
20 As he met her once a-Maying,
There on beds of violets blue,
And fresh-blown° roses washed in dew,   *newly opened*
Filled her with thee a daughter fair,
So buxom,° blithe, and debonair.   *lively*
25 Haste thee nymph, and bring with thee
Jest and youthful Jollity,
Quips° and Cranks,° and wanton Wiles,   *witty sayings / jokes*
Nods, and Becks,° and wreathèd Smiles,   *beckonings*
Such as hang on Hebe's⁷ cheek,
30 And love to live in dimple sleek;
Sport that wrinkled Care derides,
And Laughter holding both his sides.
Come, and trip it° as ye go   *dance*
On the light fantastic toe,
35 And in thy right hand lead with thee
The mountain nymph, sweet Liberty;
And if I give thee honor due,
Mirth, admit me of thy crew
To live with her and live with thee,
40 In unreprovèd° pleasures free;   *irreproachable*
To hear the lark begin his flight,
And, singing, startle the dull night,
From his watch tower in the skies,
Till the dappled dawn doth rise;
45 Then to come in spite of° sorrow,   *in defiance of*
And at my window bid good morrow,
Through the sweetbriar or the vine,
Or the twisted eglantine.
While the cock with lively din
50 Scatters the rear of darkness thin,

---

5. Homer's Cimmereans (*Odyssey* 11.13–19) live
on the outer edge of the world, in perpetual
darkness.
6. The three Graces—Euphrosyne (four syllables) figuring Youthful Mirth; Aglaia, Brilliance;
and Thalia, Bloom—were commonly taken to be
offspring of Venus (Love and Beauty) and Bacchus (god of wine). Milton proceeds, however, to
devise another, more innocent parentage for
Euphrosyne (ascribing it to "some sager," lines
17–24): Zephyr, the West Wind, and Aurora,
goddess of the Dawn.
7. Goddess of youth and cupbearer to the gods.

And to the stack or the barn door,
Stoutly struts his dames before;
Oft listening how the hounds and horn
Cheerly rouse the slumbering morn,
55 From the side of some hoar° hill,   *ancient*
Through the high wood echoing shrill.
Sometime walking not unseen
By hedgerow elms, on hillocks green,
Right against the eastern gate,
60 Where the great sun begins his state,[8]
Robed in flames and amber light,
The clouds in thousand liveries dight;°   *dressed*
While the plowman near at hand
Whistles o'er the furrowed land,
65 And the milkmaid singeth blithe,
And the mower whets his scythe,
And every shepherd tells his tale
Under the hawthorn in the dale.
Straight° mine eye hath caught new pleasures   *immediately*
70 Whilst the landscape round it measures,
Russet lawns and fallows° gray,   *plowed land*
Where the nibbling flocks do stray,
Mountains on whose barren breast
The laboring clouds do often rest;
75 Meadows trim with daisies pied,°   *multicolored*
Shallow brooks, and rivers wide.
Towers and battlements it sees
Bosomed high in tufted trees,
Where perhaps some beauty lies,
80 The cynosure[9] of neighboring eyes.
Hard by, a cottage chimney smokes
From betwixt two agèd oaks,
Where Corydon and Thyrsis met
Are at their savory dinner set
85 Of herbs and other country messes,
Which the neat-handed° Phyllis dresses;   *dexterous*
And then in haste her bower she leaves,
With Thestylis[1] to bind the sheaves;
Or if the earlier season lead
90 To the tanned° haycock in the mead.   *sun-dried*
Sometimes with secure° delight   *careless*
The upland hamlets will invite,
When the merry bells ring round
And the jocund rebecks[2] sound
95 To many a youth and many a maid,
Dancing in the checkered shade;
And young and old come forth to play

8. Stately procession, as by a monarch.
9. Literally, the bright polestar, or North Star, by which mariners steer; here, a splendid object, much gazed at.
1. Milton uses traditional names from classical

pastoral—Corydon, Thyrsis, Phyllis, Thestylis—for his rustic English shepherds.
2. A small three-stringed fiddle. "Jocund": merry, sprightly.

On a sunshine holiday,
Till the livelong daylight fail;
100 Then to the spicy nut-brown ale,
With stories told of many a feat,
How fairy Mab the junkets³ eat;
She was pinched and pulled, she said,
And he, by friar's lantern led,
105 Tells how the drudging goblin⁴ sweat
To earn his cream bowl duly set,
When in one night, ere glimpse of morn,
His shadowy flail hath threshed the corn
That ten day laborers could not end;
110 Then lies him down the lubber fiend,⁵
And stretched out all the chimney's° length,   *fireplace's*
Basks at the fire his hairy strength;
And crop-full° out of doors he flings   *satiated*
Ere the first cock his matin rings.
115 Thus done the tales, to bed they creep,
By whispering winds soon lulled asleep.
Towered cities please us then,
And the busy hum of men,
Where throngs of knights and barons bold
120 In weeds of peace high triumphs⁶ hold,
With store of ladies, whose bright eyes
Rain influence,⁷ and judge the prize
Of wit or arms, while both contend
To win her grace, whom all commend.
125 There let Hymen⁸ oft appear
In saffron robe, with taper clear,
And pomp and feast and revelry,
With masque and antique° pageantry;   *ancient, also antic*
Such sights as youthful poets dream
130 On summer eves by haunted stream.
Then to the well-trod stage anon,
If Jonson's learned sock be on,
Or sweetest Shakespeare, fancy's child,
Warble his native woodnotes wild.⁹
135 And ever against eating cares;¹
Lap me in soft Lydian airs,²
Married to immortal verse
Such as the meeting soul may pierce

3. Sweetmeats, especially with cream. Queen Mab is the fairy queen, consort of Oberon. "She" and "he" in the next two lines are country folk telling of their experiences with fairies.
4. Robin Goodfellow, alias Puck, Pook, or Hobgoblin. "Friar's lantern": will-o'-the-wisp.
5. Puck, here identified with the folktale goblin, Lob-lie-by-the-fire. Robin traditionally did all manner of drudging work for people, to be rewarded with a bowl of cream.
6. Pageants. "Weeds of peace": courtly raiment.
7. The ladies' eyes are stars and so have astrological influence over the men.
8. Roman god of marriage. An orange-yellow ("saffron") robe and a torch are his attributes.
9. It was conventional to contrast Jonson as a "learned" poet and Shakespeare as a "natural" one, but L'Allegro's views and choices of literature also suits with his nature. "Sock": the comedian's low-heeled slipper, contrasted with the tragedian's buskin, a high-heeled boot.
1. "Eating cares" (Horace, Odes 2.11.18) is one of many classical echoes in the poem.
2. Plato considered "Lydian airs" to be enervating, soft, and sensual; he preferred the solemn Doric mode. Some others thought Lydian airs relaxing and delightful.

In notes with many a winding bout°   *circuit*
140　Of linkèd sweetness long drawn out,
With wanton heed and giddy cunning,
The melting voice through mazes running,
Untwisting all the chains that tie
The hidden soul of harmony;
145　That Orpheus' self may heave his head
From golden slumber on a bed
Of heaped Elysian flowers, and hear
Such strains as would have won the ear
Of Pluto, to have quite set free
150　His half-regained Eurydice.[3]
These delights if thou canst give,
Mirth, with thee I mean to live.[4]

ca. 1631   1645

Il Penseroso[1]

Hence vain deluding joys,[2]
　The brood of Folly without father bred,
How little you bestead,°   *avail*
　Or fill the fixèd mind with all your toys°   *trifles*
5　Dwell in some idle brain,
　And fancies fond° with gaudy shapes possess,   *foolish*
As thick and numberless
　As the gay motes that people the sunbeams,
Or likest hovering dreams,
10　The fickle pensioners of Morpheus'[3] train.
But hail thou Goddess sage and holy,
Hail, divinest Melancholy,
Whose saintly visage is too bright
To hit° the sense of human sight,   *suit*
15　And therefore to our weaker view
O'erlaid with black, staid wisdom's hue;[4]
Black, but such as in esteem,
Prince Memnon's sister[5] might beseem,
Or that starred Ethiope queen[6] that strove

3. Orpheus's music so moved Pluto that he agreed to release Orpheus's dead wife Eurydice (four syllables, accent on the second) from the underworld (Elysium), but he violated the condition set—that he not look back at her—and so lost her again. Milton often uses Orpheus as a figure for the poet.
4. The final lines echo Marlowe's "The Passionate Shepherd to His Love" (p. 678): "If these delights thy mind may move, / Then live with me and be my love."
1. Il Penseroso whose name is Italian for "the thoughtful one," celebrates a melancholy that does not produce madness but the scholarly temperament, ruled by Saturn. For "L'Allegro" see 2nd n. 2 on p. 1459.

2. In "Il Penseroso," Mirth is not the innocent joys of "L'Allegro," but "vain deluding joys."
3. Morpheus is the god of sleep. "Pensioners": followers.
4. The melancholy humor, caused by black bile, was thought to make the face dark or saturnine—from the ancient god Saturn, allegorized in Neoplatonic philosophy as "the collective angelic mind."
5. Memnon, in *Odyssey* 11, was a handsome Ethiopian prince; his sister Himera's beauty was mentioned by later commentators. Cf. Song of Solomon 1.5, "I am black but comely."
6. Cassiopeia was turned into a constellation ("starred") for bragging that she was more beautiful than the sea nymphs.

20   To set her beauty's praise above
        The sea nymphs, and their powers offended.
        Yet thou art higher far descended;
        Thee bright-haired Vesta long of yore
        To solitary Saturn bore;[7]
25   His daughter she (in Saturn's reign
        Such mixture was not held a stain).
        Oft in glimmering bowers and glades
        He met her, and in secret shades
        Of woody Ida's inmost grove,
30   While yet there was no fear of Jove.
        Come pensive nun, devout and pure,
        Sober, steadfast, and demure,
        All in a robe of darkest grain,°   *color*
        Flowing with majestic train,
35   And sable stole[8] of cypress lawn
        Over thy decent° shoulders drawn.   *comely, modestly covered*
        Come, but keep thy wonted° state,°   *usual / dignity*
        With even step and musing gait,
        And looks commercing with the skies,
40   Thy rapt soul sitting in thine eyes:
        There held in holy passion still,
        Forget thyself to marble,[9] till
        With a sad° leaden downward cast°   *grave, dignified / glance*
        Thou fix them on the earth as fast.
45   And join with thee calm Peace and Quiet,
        Spare Fast, that oft with gods doth diet,
        And hears the Muses in a ring
        Aye° round about Jove's altar sing.   *continually*
        And add to these retired Leisure,
50   That in trim gardens takes his pleasure;
        But first, and chiefest, with thee bring
        Him that yon soars on golden wing,
        Guiding the fiery-wheelèd throne,
        The cherub Contemplatìon;[1]
55   And the mute Silence hist° along,   *summon*
        'Less Philomel[2] will deign a song,
        In her sweetest, saddest plight,°   *mood*
        Smoothing the rugged brow of night,
        While Cynthia[3] checks her dragon yoke
60   Gently o'er th' accustomed oak;
        Sweet bird that shunn'st the noise of folly,

7. Vesta, daughter of Saturn, was goddess of the household and a virgin, as were her priestesses. Milton invented the story of her sexual congress with Saturn on Mount Ida, resulting in Melancholy's birth. Saturn ruled the gods and the world during the Golden Age, which ended when he was murdered by his son Jove.
8. A delicate black cloth.
9. Still as a statue.
1. The special function of cherubim is contemplation of God; Milton alludes also (line 53) to their identification with the wheels of the mystical chariot/throne of God described by Ezekiel (Ezekiel 10).
2. The nightingale (the bird into which Philomela was transformed after her rape by her brother-in-law Tereus) traditionally sings a mournful song. "'Less": unless.
3. Goddess of the moon, also associated with Hecate, goddess of the underworld, who drives a pair of sleepless dragons.

Most musical, most melancholy!
Thee chantress oft the woods among
I woo to hear thy evensong;[4]
65 And missing thee, I walk unseen
On the dry smooth-shaven green,
To behold the wandering moon,
Riding near her highest noon,
Like one that had been led astray
70 Through the heaven's wide pathless way;
And oft as if her head she bowed,
Stooping through a fleecy cloud.
Oft on a plat° of rising ground,   *plot, open field*
I hear the far-off curfew sound
75 Over some wide-watered shore,
Swinging slow with sullen° roar;   *deep, mournful*
Or if the air will not permit,
Some still removèd place will fit,
Where glowing embers through the room
80 Teach light to counterfeit a gloom,
Far from all resort of mirth,
Save the cricket on the hearth,
Or the bellman's[5] drowsy charm,
To bless the doors from nightly harm;
85 Or let my lamp at midnight hour
Be seen in some high lonely tower,
Where I may oft outwatch the Bear,[6]
With thrice-great Hermes, or unsphere
The spirit of Plato[7] to unfold
90 What words or what vast regions hold
The immortal mind that hath forsook
Her mansion in this fleshly nook;
And of those demons[8] that are found
In fire, air, flood, or underground,
95 Whose power hath a true consent°   *agreement*
With planet, or with element.
Sometime let gorgeous Tragedy
In sceptered pall[9] come sweeping by,
Presenting Thebes, or Pelops' line,
100 Or the tale of Troy divine,[1]
Or what (though rare) of later age
Ennobled hath the buskined[2] stage.

---

4. The evening liturgy traditionally sung by cloistered monks and nuns ("chantress" evokes such a
singer); "L'Allegro's" cock, by contrast, calls hearers to the morning liturgy, "matins" (line 114).
5. Night watchman who rang a bell to mark the
hours.
6. The Great Bear constellation never sets in
northern skies.
7. Various esoteric books (actually written in the
3rd and 4th centuries) were attributed to an
ancient Egyptian, Hermes Trismegistus ("thrice
great"). Neoplatonists made him the father of all
knowledge; later he became a patron of magi-

cians and alchemists. To "unsphere" Plato is to
bring him magically back to earth from whatever
sphere he now inhabits—in practical terms, by
reading his books.
8. Demons (daemons), halfway between gods
and men, preside over the four elements.
9. Royal robe, worn by tragic actors.
1. Tragedies about Thebes include Sophocles'
Oedipus cycle, those about the line of Pelops,
Aeschylus's *Oresteia*, and those about Troy,
Euripedes' *Trojan Women*.
2. The buskin (high boot) of tragedy, contrasted
with the "sock" of comedy ("L'Allegro," line 132).

But, O sad virgin, that thy power
Might raise Musaeus[3] from his bower,
105   Or bid the soul of Orpheus[4] sing
Such notes as, warbled to the string,
Drew iron tears down Pluto's cheek,
And made Hell grant what love did seek.
Or call up him[5] that left half told
110   The story of Cambuscan bold,
Of Camball and of Algarsife,
And who had Canacee to wife,
That owned the virtuous° ring and glass,   *having magical*
And of the wondrous horse of brass,   *powers*
115   On which the Tartar king did ride;
And if aught° else great bards beside   *anything*
In sage and solemn tunes have sung,
Of tourneys and of trophies hung,
Of forests and enchantments drear,
120   Where more is meant than meets the ear.[6]
Thus, Night, oft see me in thy pale career,
Till civil-suited Morn appear,
Not tricked and frounced as she was wont
With the Attic boy to hunt,[7]
125   But kerchiefed in a comely cloud,
While rocking winds are piping loud,
Or ushered with a shower still,°   *gentle*
When the gust hath blown his fill,
Ending on the rustling leaves,
130   With minute drops from off the eaves.
And when the sun begins to fling
His flaring beams, me, Goddess, bring
To archèd walks of twilight groves,
And shadows brown that Sylvan[8] loves
135   Of pine or monumental oak,
Where the rude ax with heavèd stroke
Was never heard the nymphs to daunt,
Or fright them from their hallowed haunt.
There in close covert° by some brook,   *hidden place*
140   Where no profaner eye may look,
Hide me from day's garish eye,
While the bee with honeyed thigh,
That at her flowery work doth sing,
And the waters murmuring
145   With such consort° as they keep,   *musical harmony*
Entice the dewy-feathered sleep;
And let some strange mysterious dream
Wave at his wings in airy stream

---

3. Mythical poet-priest of the pre-Homeric age,
supposedly a son or pupil of Orpheus.
4. For the story of Orpheus, see "L'Allegro," line
145, and n. 3 (on line 150).
5. Chaucer, whose Squire's Tale is unfinished.
6. A capsule definition of allegory.

7. The now soberly dressed Aurora, goddess of
the dawn, once fell in love with Cephalus ("the
Attic boy") and hunted with him. "Tricked and
frounced": adorned and with frizzled hair.
8. Roman god of woodlands.

Of lively portraiture displayed
150 Softly on my eyelids laid.
And as I wake, sweet music breathe
Above, about, or underneath,
Sent by some spirit to mortals good,
Or th' unseen genius° of the wood.   *guardian deity*
155 But let my due feet never fail
To walk the studious cloister's pale,°   *enclosure*
And love the high embowèd roof,
With antic pillars massy proof,[9]
And storied windows richly dight,[1]
160 Casting a dim religious light.
There let the pealing organ blow
To the full-voiced choir below,
In service high and anthems clear,
As may with sweetness, through mine ear,
165 Dissolve me into ecstasies,
And bring all heaven before mine eyes.
And may at last my weary age
Find out the peaceful hermitage,
The hairy gown and mossy cell,
170 Where I may sit and rightly spell°   *study*
Of every star that heaven doth shew,
And every herb that sips the dew,
Till old experience do attain
To something like prophetic strain.
175 These pleasures, Melancholy, give,[2]
And I with thee will choose to live.

ca. 1631   1645

Lycidas

Milton wrote this pastoral elegy for a volume of Latin, Greek, and English poems, *Justa Edouardo King Naufrago* (1638), commemorating the death by shipwreck of his college classmate Edward King, three years younger than himself. King was not a close friend, but Milton's deepest emotions, anxieties, and fears are engaged here because, as poet and minister, King could serve Milton as a kind of alter ego. Still engaged in preparing himself, at the age of twenty-nine, for his projected poetic career, Milton was forced to recognize the uncertainty of all human endeavors. King's death posed the problem of mortality in its most agonizing form: the death of the young, the unfulfilled, the good seems to deny all meaning to life, to demonstrate the uselessness of exceptional talent, lofty ambition, and noble ideals of service to God.

While the poem expresses Milton's anxieties, it also serves as an announcement of his grand ambitions. Like Edmund Spenser, Milton saw mastery of the pastoral mode as the first step in a great poetic career. In "Lycidas" that mastery is complete. In the tradition that Milton received from classical and Renaissance predecessors,

---

9. Massive and strong. "Antic": covered with quaint or grotesque carvings, also antique.
1. Dressed. "Storied windows": stained-glass windows depicting biblical stories.

2. Compare "L'Allegro," lines 151–52 (p. 1463), and the final lines of Marlowe's "Passionate Shepherd" (p. 678).

including Theocritus, Virgil, Petrarch, and Spenser, the pastoral landscape was invested with profound significances that had little indeed to do with the hard life of agricultural labor. In lines 25–36, Milton evokes the conventional pastoral topic of carefree shepherds who engage in singing contests, watch contentedly over their grazing sheep, fall in love, and write poetry, offering an image of human life in harmony with nature and the seasonal processes of fruition and mellowing before the winter of death. That classical image of the shepherd as poet is mingled with the Christian understanding of the shepherd as pastor (Christ is the Good Shepherd), and sometimes as the prophet called to his mission from the fields, like David or Isaiah. Milton calls on all these associations, along with other motifs specific to pastoral funeral elegy: the recollection of past friendship, a questioning of destiny for cutting short this life, a procession of mourners (often mythological figures), and a "flower passage" in which nature pays tribute to the dead shepherd.

"Lycidas" uses but continually tests and challenges the assumptions and conventions of pastoral elegy, making for profound tensions and clashes of tone. The pastoral "oaten flute" is interrupted by divine pronouncements and bitter invective; nature seems rife with examples of meaningless waste and early death; the "blind Fury" often cuts off the poet's "thin-spun life" before he can win fame; good pastors die young while corrupt "Blind mouths" remain; and Nature cannot even pay her tribute of flowers to Lycidas's funeral bier since he welters in the deep, his bones hurled to the "bottom of the monstrous world." In response to these fierce challenges come pronouncements by Apollo and St. Peter, and images of protection and resurrection in nature and myth, culminating in a new vision of pastoral: in heaven Lycidas enjoys a perfected pastoral existence, and in the coda the consoled shepherd arises and carries his song to "pastures new." Milton's questioning leads to a final reassertion of confidence in his calling as national poet. Moreover, in the headnote added in the 1645 volume of his *Poems*, he lays claim to prophetic authority, for the Church of England clergy he denounced as corrupt in 1638 had mostly been expelled from their livings by Puritan reformers in 1645.

Lycidas

In this monody[1] the author bewails a learned friend, unfortunately drowned in his passage from Chester on the Irish seas, 1637. And by occasion foretells the ruin of our corrupted clergy, then in their height.

Yet once more, O ye laurels, and once more
Ye myrtles brown, with ivy never sere,[2]
I come to pluck your berries harsh and crude,°   *unripe*
And with forced fingers rude,°   *unskilled*
5   Shatter your leaves before the mellowing year.
Bitter constraint, and sad occasion dear,°   *heartfelt, also dire*
Compels me to disturb your season due;
For Lycidas is dead, dead ere his prime,[3]
Young Lycidas, and hath not left his peer.

---

1. A dirge sung by a single voice, though this one incorporates several other voices. Milton added this headnote in the edition of 1645; it identifies Milton as a prophet in the passage denouncing the clergy in this 1638 poem (lines 112–31) and invites the reader to remember Milton's 1641–42 polemics against the English bishops and church government (now dismantled).

2. "Laurels," associated with Apollo and poetry; "myrtle," associated with Venus and love; "ivy," associated with Bacchus and frenzy (also learning). All three are evergreens ("never sere") linked to poetic inspiration.

3. King was twenty-five.

10   Who would not sing for Lycidas? He knew
     Himself to sing, and build the lofty rhyme.[4]
     He must not float upon his watery bier
     Unwept, and welter° to the parching wind,   *be tossed about*
     Without the meed° of some melodious tear.°   *reward / elegy*
15   Begin then, sisters of the sacred well[5]
     That from beneath the seat of Jove doth spring,
     Begin, and somewhat loudly sweep the string.
     Hence with denial vain, and coy excuse;
     So may some gentle muse[6]
20   With lucky words favor my destined urn,
     And as he passes turn,
     And bid fair peace be to my sable shroud.
     For we were nursed upon the selfsame hill,
     Fed the same flock, by fountain, shade, and rill.
25   Together both, ere the high lawns° appeared   *upland pastures*
     Under the opening eyelids of the morn,
     We drove afield, and both together heard
     What time the grayfly winds her sultry horn,[7]
     Battening° our flocks with the fresh dews of night,   *feeding fat*
30   Oft till the star that rose at evening bright[8]
     Toward heaven's descent had sloped his westering wheel.
     Meanwhile the rural ditties were not mute,
     Tempered to th' oaten flute,[9]
     Rough satyrs danced, and fauns with cloven heel
35   From the glad sound would not be absent long,
     And old Damoetas[1] loved to hear our song.
         But O the heavy change, now thou art gone,
     Now thou art gone, and never must return!
     Thee, shepherd, thee the woods and desert caves,
40   With wild thyme and the gadding° vine o'ergrown,   *wandering*
     And all their echoes mourn.
     The willows and the hazel copses° green   *thickets of trees*
     Shall now no more be seen,
     Fanning their joyous leaves to thy soft lays.
45   As killing as the canker° to the rose,   *cankerworm*
     Or taint-worm[2] to the weanling herds that graze,
     Or frost to flowers that their gay wardrobe wear
     When first the white-thorn blows;[3]
     Such, Lycidas, thy loss to shepherd's ear.
50   Where were ye, nymphs,[4] when the remorseless deep
     Closed o'er the head of your loved Lycidas?
     For neither were ye playing on the steep

4. King had written several poems of compliment in the patronage mode, chiefly on members
of the royal family.
5. The nine (sister) Muses called (probably) from
the fountain Aganippe, near Mount Helicon.
6. Here, some kindly poet.
7. I.e., heard the grayfly when she buzzes.
8. Hesperus, the evening star.
9. Panpipes, played traditionally by shepherds in
pastoral.

1. A type name from pastoral poetry, possibly
referring to some particular tutor at Cambridge.
"Satyrs": goat-legged woodland creatures, Pan's
boisterous attendants.
2. Internal parasite fatal to newly weaned
lambs.
3. Hawthorn blooms.
4. Nature deities.

Where your old bards, the famous Druids,[5] lie,
Nor on the shaggy top of Mona high,
55 Nor yet where Deva spreads her wizard stream:[6]
Ay me! I fondly dream—
Had ye been there—for what could that have done?
What could the Muse[7] herself that Orpheus bore,
The Muse herself, for her enchanting[8] son
60 Whom universal Nature did lament,
When by the rout that made the hideous roar
His gory visage down the stream was sent,
Down the swift Hebrus to the Lesbian shore?[9]
Alas! What boots° it with incessant care   *profits*
65 To tend the homely slighted shepherd's trade,
And strictly meditate the thankless muse?[1]
Were it not better done as others use,
To sport with Amaryllis in the shade,
Or with the tangles of Neaera's hair?[2]
70 Fame is the spur that the clear spirit doth raise
(That last infirmity of noble mind)
To scorn delights, and live laborious days;
But the fair guerdon° when we hope to find,   *reward*
And think to burst out into sudden blaze,
75 Comes the blind Fury[3] with th' abhorrèd shears,
And slits the thin-spun life. "But not the praise,"
Phoebus replied, and touched my trembling ears;[4]
"Fame is no plant that grows on mortal soil,
Nor in the glistering foil[5]
80 Set off to th' world, nor in broad rumor lies,
But lives and spreads aloft by those pure eyes,
And perfect witness of all-judging Jove;
As he pronounces lastly on each deed,
Of so much fame in heaven expect thy meed."°   *reward*
85   O fountain Arethuse, and thou honored flood,
Smooth-sliding Mincius, crowned with vocal reeds,
That strain I heard was of a higher mood.[6]
But now my oat° proceeds,   *pastoral flute*

---

5. Priestly poet-kings of Celtic Britain, who worshipped the forces of nature. They are buried on the mountain ("steep") Kerig-y-Druidion in Wales.
6. Mona is the island of Anglesey. Deva, the river Dee in Cheshire, was magic ("wizard") because its shifting stream foretold prosperity or dearth for the land. All these places are in the West Country, near where King drowned.
7. Calliope, Muse of epic poetry, was the mother of Orpheus.
8. Implies both song and magic; the root word survives in "incantation."
9. Orpheus's song was drowned out by the screams of a mob ("rout") of Thracian women, the Bacchantes, who then were able to tear him to pieces and throw his gory head into the river Hebrus, which carried it—still singing—to the island of Lesbos, bringing that island the gift of poetry.

1. I.e., study to write poetry (a Virgilian phrase).
2. "Amaryllis" and "Neaera" (*Nee-eye-ra*), conventional names for pretty shepherdesses wooed in song by pastoral shepherds.
3. Atropos, one of the three Fates, whose scissors cuts the thread of human life after her sisters spin and measure it. Milton makes her a savage, and blind, Fury.
4. Phoebus Apollo, god of poetic inspiration. In *Eclogue* 6.3–4 he plucked Virgil's ears, warning him against impatient ambition.
5. Flashy, glittering metal foil, set under a gem to enhance its brilliance.
6. Arethusa was a fountain in Sicily associated with Greek pastoral poetry (Theocritus), Mincius a river in Lombardy associated with Latin pastoral (Virgil); Milton invokes them as a return to the pastoral after the "higher mood" of Apollo's speech.

And listens to the herald of the sea[7]
90 That came in Neptune's plea.
    He asked the waves, and asked the felon° winds,   *savage*
    "What hard mishap hath doomed this gentle swain?"°   *shepherd*
    And questioned every gust of rugged° wings   *stormy*
    That blows from off each beakèd promontory;
95 They knew not of his story,
    And sage Hippotades[8] their answer brings,
    That not a blast was from his dungeon strayed;
    The air was calm, and on the level brine,
    Sleek Panope[9] with all her sisters played.
100 It was that fatal and perfidious bark,
    Built in th' eclipse,[1] and rigged with curses dark,
    That sunk so low that sacred head of thine.
        Next Camus,[2] reverend sire, went footing slow,
    His mantle hairy, and his bonnet sedge,°   *formed of reeds*
105 Inwrought with figures dim, and on the edge
    Like to that sanguine flower inscribed with woe.[3]
    "Ah! who hath reft," quoth he, "my dearest pledge?"
    Last came and last did go
    The pilot of the Galilean lake;[4]
110 Two massy keys he bore of metals twain
    (The golden opes, the iron shuts amain).°   *forever*
    He shook his mitered locks, and stern bespake:
    "How well could I have spared for° thee, young swain,   *in place of*
    Enow° of such as for their bellies' sake   *enough (plural)*
115 Creep and intrude and climb into the fold![5]
    Of other care they little reckoning make,
    Than how to scramble at the shearers' feast,[6]
    And shove away the worthy bidden guest.
    Blind mouths![7] that scarce themselves know how to hold
120 A sheep-hook, or have learned aught else the least
    That to the faithful herdsman's art belongs!
    What recks it them? What need they? They are sped;[8]
    And when they list,° their lean° and flashy songs   *choose / meager*
    Grate on their scrannel° pipes of wretched straw.   *harsh, thin*

---

7. Triton, who comes gathering evidence about the accident for Neptune's court.
8. Aeolus, god of winds.
9. The chief Nereid, or sea nymph.
1. Eclipses were taken as evil omens.
2. God of the river Cam, representing Cambridge University.
3. Like the AI AI cry of grief supposedly found on the hyacinth, a "sanguine flower" sprung from the blood of the youth Hyacinthus, beloved of Apollo and accidentally killed by him.
4. St. Peter, originally a fisherman on the sea of Galilee, was Christ's chief apostle; his keys open and shut the gates of heaven. He wears a bishop's miter (line 112): Milton in his "antiprelatical tracts" allows for a special role for apostles but denies any distinction in office between bishops and ministers in the later church.

5. Cf. John 10.1: "He that entereth not by the door into the sheepfold, but climbeth up some other way, the same is a thief and a robber."
6. Festive suppers for the sheepshearers (hence, the material rewards of their ministry). "Worthy bidden guest" (next line): cf. Matthew 22.8, the parable of the marriage feast, "they which were bidden were not worthy."
7. Collapsing blindness with greed, this audacious metaphor accuses churchmen of shirking oversight (*episcopus*, bishop, means "supervision") and of glutting themselves, although pastors ought to feed their flocks. "Sheep-hook" (next line): the bishop's staff is in the form of a shepherd's crook.
8. Provided for. "What recks it them?": what do they care?

125　The hungry sheep look up, and are not fed,
　　　But swol'n with wind, and the rank mist they draw,° 　　*inhale*
　　　Rot inwardly,[9] and foul contagion spread,
　　　Besides what the grim wolf with privy paw[1]
　　　Daily devours apace, and nothing said.
130　But that two-handed engine at the door[2]
　　　Stands ready to smite once, and smite no more."
　　　　　Return, Alpheus,[3] the dread voice is past,
　　　That shrunk thy streams; return, Sicilian muse,
　　　And call the vales, and bid them hither cast
135　Their bells and flowerets of a thousand hues.[4]
　　　Ye valleys low where the mild whispers use,° 　　*frequent*
　　　Of shades and wanton winds, and gushing brooks,
　　　On whose fresh lap the swart star[5] sparely looks,
　　　Throw hither all your quaint enameled eyes,[6]
140　That on the green turf suck the honeyed showers,
　　　And purple all the ground with vernal flowers.
　　　Bring the rathe° primrose that forsaken dies, 　　*early*
　　　The tufted crow-toe, and pale jessamine,[7]
　　　The white pink, and the pansy freaked° with jet, 　　*flecked*
145　The glowing violet,
　　　The musk rose, and the well-attired woodbine,
　　　With cowslips wan° that hang the pensive head, 　　*pale*
　　　And every flower that sad embroidery wears:
　　　Bid amaranthus[8] all his beauty shed,
150　And daffadillies fill their cups with tears,
　　　To strew the laureate hearse° where Lycid lies. 　　*laurel-decked bier*
　　　For so to interpose a little ease,
　　　Let our frail thoughts dally with false surmise.[9]
　　　Ay me! whilst thee the shores and sounding seas
155　Wash far away, where'er thy bones are hurled,
　　　Whether beyond the stormy Hebrides,[1]
　　　Where thou perhaps under the whelming° tide 　　*engulfing*
　　　Visit'st the bottom of the monstrous world;
　　　Or whether thou, to our moist vows denied,
160　Sleep'st by the fable of Bellerus old,[2]
　　　Where the great vision of the guarded mount

9. Sheep rot is used as an allegory of church corruption by both Petrarch and Dante.
1. I.e., Roman Catholicism, whole agents operated in secret ("privy"). Conversions in the court of the Roman Catholic queen Henrietta Maria were notorious.
2. A celebrated crux, variously explained as the two houses of Parliament, St. Peter's keys, the two-edged sword of the Book of Revelation, a sword wielded by two hands, and by other guesses; what is clear is the denunciation of impending, apocalyptic vengeance. In Matthew 24.33 the Last Judgment is said to be "even at the doors."
3. A river in Arcadia, fabled to pass unmixed through the sea before mixing its waters with the "fountain Arethuse" in Sicily, again reviving the pastoral mode after the fierce denunciation of Peter (see lines 85–87).

4. A catalogue of flowers was a common pastoral topic. "Bells": bell-shaped flowers.
5. The Dog Star, Sirius, associated with the heats of late summer.
6. Flowers curiously patterned and adorned with many colors.
7. White jasmine. "Tufted crow-toe": hyacinth or buttercup, growing in clusters. "Woodbine" (line 146): honeysuckle.
8. In Greek, "unfading," a legendary flower of immortality, one that never fades.
9. False, because Lycidas's body is not here to receive floral and poetic tributes.
1. Islands off the coast of Scotland, the northern terminus of the Irish Sea.
2. A fabulous giant invented by Milton as the origin of the Latin name for Land's End in Cornwall, *Bellerium*. "Monstrous world" (line 158): filled with monsters, also, immense.

Looks toward Namancos and Bayona's hold;[3]
Look homeward angel now, and melt with ruth:°   *pity*
And, O ye dolphins,[4] waft the hapless youth.
165   Weep no more, woeful shepherds, weep no more,
For Lycidas your sorrow is not dead,
Sunk though he be beneath the wat'ry floor;
So sinks the daystar° in the ocean bed,   *the sun*
And yet anon repairs his drooping head,
170   And tricks° his beams, and with new-spangled ore   *adorns, trims*
Flames in the forehead of the morning sky:
So Lycidas sunk low, but mounted high,
Through the dear might of him that walked the waves,[5]
Where, other groves and other streams along,[6]
175   With nectar pure his oozy° locks he laves,   *moist*
And hears the unexpressive nuptial song,[7]
In the blest kingdoms meek of joy and love.
There entertain him all the saints above,
In solemn troops and sweet societies
180   That sing, and singing in their glory move,
And wipe the tears forever from his eyes.
Now, Lycidas, the shepherds weep no more;
Henceforth thou art the Genius[8] of the shore,
In thy large recompense, and shalt be good
185   To all that wander in that perilous flood.
        Thus sang the uncouth swain[9] to th' oaks and rills,
While the still morn went out with sandals gray;
He touched the tender stops of various quills,[1]
With eager thought warbling his Doric[2] lay:
190   And now the sun had stretched out all the hills,
And now was dropped into the western bay;
At last he rose, and twitched his mantle blue:[3]
Tomorrow to fresh woods, and pastures new.

November 1637   1638

---

3. "The guarded mount" is St. Michael's Mount in Cornwall, where the archangel was said to have appeared to fishermen in 495, and from which he is envisioned as looking over the Atlantic toward a region and fortress ("Bayona's hold") in northern Spain, thereby guarding Protestant England against the continuing Roman Catholic threat.
4. Dolphins brought the Greek poet Arion safely ashore, for love of his verse, and also performed other sea rescues.
5. Christ, who rescued Peter when he tried and failed to walk on the Sea of Galilee (Matthew 14.25–31).

6. See Revelation 22.1–2, on the "pure river of water of life," and the "tree of life, which bare twelve manner of fruits."
7. Inexpressible hymn of joy sung at "the marriage supper of the Lamb" (Revelation 19).
8. Local guardian spirit.
9. Another voice now seems to take over from the previously heard voice of the "uncouth swain" (unknown, unskilled shepherd).
1. The oaten stalks of panpipes.
2. Rustic, the dialect of Theocritus and other famous Greek pastoral poets.
3. The color of hope. "Twitched": pulled up around his shoulders.

From The Reason of Church Government Urged Against Prelaty[1]

[PLANS AND PROJECTS]

* * * Concerning therefore this wayward subject against prelaty,[2] the touching whereof is so distasteful and disquietous[3] to a number of men, as by what hath been said I may deserve of charitable readers to be credited that neither envy nor gall hath entered me upon this controversy, but the enforcement of conscience only and a preventive fear lest the omitting of this duty should be against me when I would store up to myself the good provision of peaceful hours; so lest it should be still imputed to me, as I have found it hath been, that some self-pleasing humor of vainglory hath incited me to contest with men of high estimation, now while green years are upon my head;[4] from this needless surmisal I shall hope to dissuade the intelligent and equal auditor, if I can but say successfully that which in this exigent[5] behooves me; although I would be heard only, if it might be, by the elegant and learned reader, to whom principally for a while I shall beg leave I may address myself. To him it will be no new thing though I tell him that if I hunted after praise by the ostentation of wit and learning, I should not write thus out of mine own season when I have neither yet completed to my mind the full circle of my private studies,[6] although I complain not of any insufficiency to the matter in hand; or, were I ready to my wishes, it were a folly to commit anything elaborately composed to the careless and interrupted listening of these tumultuous times. Next, if I were wise only to mine own ends, I would certainly take such a subject as of itself might catch applause, whereas this hath all the disadvantages on the contrary, and such a subject as the publishing whereof might be delayed at pleasure, and time enough to pencil it over with all the curious touches of art, even to the perfection of a faultless picture; whenas in this argument the not deferring is of great moment to the good speeding,[7] that if solidity have leisure to do her office, art cannot have much. Lastly, I should not choose this manner of writing, wherein knowing myself inferior to myself, led by the genial power of nature[8] to another task, I have the use, as I may account it, but of my left hand. And though I shall be foolish in saying more to this purpose, yet, since it will be such a folly as wisest men going about to commit have only confessed and so

---

1. This was the fourth of five tracts Milton published attacking the bishops, liturgy, and church government of the Church of England, in support of Presbyterian reform, though these tracts also show signs of the more radical positions he will soon adopt. This 1642 treatise is the first one to carry his name, so the autobiographical passage is in part to introduce himself to the reader and explain why, though a layman and a young man, he feels himself called, and well prepared, to write on theology and ecclesiastical order. Beyond that rhetorical purpose, this is also the fullest account Milton ever set forth of his poetics: his sense of the poet's calling, of the nature and multiple uses of poetry, and of the several genres he already has employed or hopes to attempt. It also registers his inner conflict between duty (to serve God and his church with his learning) and desire (to write poetry).

2. Government by prelates (bishops). "Wayward": untoward, unpromising.

3. Distressing.

4. Milton's opponents, Bishops Joseph Hall, James Ussher, and Lancelot Andrewes, were famous, and he was still almost unknown, at age thirty-four.

5. Urgent occasion. "Equal": impartial.

6. After taking his B.A. and M.A. degrees from Cambridge, Milton spent nearly six more years in private study at home; he was still continuing that program of reading.

7. Prompt publication is essential in polemic, so substance rather than art must be the priority. "Office": duty.

8. Intellectual gifts or natural disposition.

committed, I may trust with more reason, because with more folly, to have courteous pardon. For although a poet, soaring in the high region of his fancies with his garland and singing robes about him, might without apology speak more of himself than I mean to do, yet for me sitting here below in the cool element of prose, a mortal thing among many readers of no empyreal conceit,[9] to venture and divulge unusual things of myself, I shall petition to the gentler sort, it may not be envy[1] to me.

I must say, therefore, that after I had from my first years by the ceaseless diligence and care of my father (whom God recompense) been exercised to the tongues and some sciences, as my age would suffer,[2] by sundry masters and teachers both at home and at the schools, it was found that whether aught was imposed me by them that had the overlooking, or betaken to of mine own choice in English or other tongue, prosing or versing (but chiefly this latter), the style, by certain vital signs it had, was likely to live. But much latelier in the private academies of Italy,[3] whither I was favored to resort—perceiving that some trifles which I had in memory, composed at under twenty or thereabout (for the manner is that everyone must give some proof of his wit[4] and reading there) met with acceptance above what was looked for, and other things which I had shifted in scarcity of books and conveniences to patch up amongst them, were received with written encomiums,[5] which the Italian is not forward to bestow on men of this side the Alps—I began thus far to assent both to them and divers of my friends here at home, and not less to an inward prompting which now grew daily upon me, that by labor and intent study (which I take to be my portion in this life) joined with the strong propensity of nature, I might perhaps leave something so written to aftertimes, as they should not willingly let it die. These thoughts at once possessed me, and these other: that if I were certain to write as men buy leases, for three lives and downward,[6] there ought no regard be sooner had than to God's glory by the honor and instruction of my country. For which cause, and not only for that I knew it would be hard to arrive at the second rank among the Latins, I applied myself to that resolution which Ariosto followed against the persuasions of Bembo,[7] to fix all the industry and art I could unite to the adorning of my native tongue; not to make verbal curiosities the end—that were a toilsome vanity—but to be an interpreter and relater of the best and sagest things among mine own citizens throughout this island in the mother dialect. That what the greatest and choicest wits of Athens, Rome, or modern Italy, and those Hebrews of old did for their country, I, in my proportion, with this over and above of being a Christian,[8] might do for mine; not caring to be once named abroad, though perhaps I could attain to that, but content with these British islands as my world; whose fortune hath hitherto been that if the Athenians, as

---

9. Without sublime and elevated conceits.
1. Cause for odium or disrespect.
2. Admit. "Tongues": foreign languages. In *Ad Patrem* Milton says that as a boy he learned Latin, Greek, French, Italian, and Hebrew.
3. When on the grand tour of the Continent (1638–39) Milton enjoyed attending academies in Rome and especially Florence, which were centers for literary, scientific, and social exchange.
4. Ingenuity; creative powers; Milton read some of his Latin poems to the academies.

5. Praises. Milton published five of these encomiums, four in Latin, one in Italian, as prefatory material to the Latin part of his 1645 *Poems*.
6. Leases were often drawn for a tenancy to run through the longest-lived of three named persons.
7. Rejecting Cardinal Bembo's advice, Ariosto said he would rather be first among the Italian poets than second among those writing Latin.
8. The advantage would be in having "true" subjects to write about.

some say, made their small deeds great and renowned by their eloquent writers, England hath had her noble achievements made small by the unskillful handling of monks and mechanics.

Time serves not now, and perhaps I might seem too profuse to give any certain account of what the mind at home in the spacious circuits of her musing hath liberty to propose to herself, though of highest hope and hardest attempting: whether that epic form whereof the two poems of Homer and those other two of Virgil and Tasso are a diffuse, and the book of Job a brief, model;[9] or whether the rules of Aristotle herein are strictly to be kept, or nature to be followed,[1] which in them that know art and use judgment is no transgression but an enriching of art; and lastly, what king or knight before the conquest[2] might be chosen in whom to lay the pattern of a Christian hero. And as Tasso gave to a prince of Italy his choice whether he would command him to write of Godfrey's expedition against the infidels, or Belisarius against the Goths, or Charlemagne against the Lombards;[3] if to the instinct of nature and the emboldening of art aught may be trusted, and that there be nothing adverse in our climate[4] or the fate of this age, it haply would be no rashness from an equal diligence and inclination to present the like offer in our own ancient stories; or whether those dramatic constitutions[5] wherein Sophocles and Euripides reign shall be found more doctrinal and exemplary to a nation. The Scripture also affords us a divine pastoral drama in the Song of Solomon, consisting of two persons and a double chorus, as Origen rightly judges. And the Apocalypse of St. John is the majestic image of a high and stately tragedy, shutting up and intermingling her solemn scenes and acts with a sevenfold chorus of hallelujahs and harping symphonies; and this my opinion the grave authority of Paraeus, commenting that book, is sufficient to confirm.[6] Or if occasion shall lead to imitate those magnific odes and hymns wherein Pindarus and Callimachus[7] are in most things worthy, some others in their frame judicious, in their matter most an end[8] faulty. But those frequent songs throughout the law and prophets beyond all these, not in their divine argument alone, but in the very critical art of composition, may be easily made appear over all the kinds of lyric poesy to be incomparable.[9] These abilities, wheresoever they be found, are the inspired gift of God rarely bestowed, but yet to some

9. The great models for the "diffuse" or long, epic were Homer's *Iliad* and *Odyssey*, Virgil's *Aeneid*, and Torquato Tasso's *Gerusalemme liberata*; there was also a long tradition of reading the Book of Job as a "brief" epic, a moral conflict between Job and Satan. Milton's brief epic, *Paradise Regained* (1671), makes some use of that model. For all the genres he discusses, Milton cites both classical and biblical models.

1. One contemporary debate concerned whether the Aristotelian rule of beginning in medias res was to be followed, or Ariosto's "natural" method of beginning at the beginning of the story.

2. At first Milton considered as potential epic subjects King Arthur, who fought against invading Saxons, and King Alfred, who warred with invading Danes; he excluded those after the Norman Conquest.

3. Tasso offered this choice to his patron, Alfonso II d'Este, Duke of Ferrara.

4. Milton often speculated that the cold climate

of England might not be conducive to poetry, as the warmer climate of Italy and Greece had been.

5. Plays.

6. Sophocles and Euripides are supreme examples of Greek tragedy; the Scripture models for drama are the Song of Solomon as a "divine pastoral drama" (Milton cites Origen, an Alexandrine Father of the 3rd century), and the Book of Revelation as a "high and stately tragedy" (he cites David Paraeus, a German theologian of the 16th and 17th centuries).

7. Pindar, a 5th century B.C.E. Greek poet, wrote numerous odes especially on winners of the Olympic games; Callimachus, a 3rd century B.C.E. Alexandrine Greek, wrote elegant elegiac verse on the origin of various myths and rituals.

8. Almost entirely.

9. He thinks especially of the Psalms, often compared to classical lyric.

(though most abuse) in every nation; and are of power beside the office of a pulpit to inbreed and cherish in a great people the seeds of virtue and public civility, to allay the perturbations of the mind and set the affections in right tune, to celebrate in glorious and lofty hymns the throne and equipage of God's almightiness, and what he works and what he suffers to be wrought with high providence in his church, to sing the victorious agonies of martyrs and saints, the deeds and triumphs of just and pious nations doing valiantly through faith against the enemies of Christ, to deplore the general relapses of kingdoms and states from justice and God's true worship. Lastly, whatsoever in religion is holy and sublime, in virtue amiable or grave, whatsoever hath passion or admiration in all the changes of that which is called fortune from without or the wily subtleties and refluxes of man's thoughts from within, all these things with a solid and treatable smoothness to paint out and describe.[1] Teaching over the whole book of sanctity and virtue through all the instances of example, with such delight to those especially of soft and delicious temper,[2] who will not so much as look upon truth herself unless they see her elegantly dressed, that whereas the paths of honesty and good life appear now rugged and difficult, though they be indeed easy and pleasant, they would then appear to all men both easy and pleasant, though they were rugged and difficult indeed. And what a benefit this would be to our youth and gentry may be soon guessed by what we know of the corruption and bane which they suck in daily from the writings and interludes of libidinous and ignorant poetasters,[3] who, having scarce ever heard of that which is the main consistence of a true poem, the choice of such persons as they ought to introduce, and what is moral and decent to each one, do for the most part lap up[4] vicious principles in sweet pills to be swallowed down, and make the taste of virtuous documents harsh and sour.

But because the spirit of man cannot demean[5] itself lively in this body without some recreating intermission of labor and serious things, it were happy for the commonwealth if our magistrates, as in those famous governments of old, would take into their care, not only the deciding of our contentious law cases and brawls, but the managing of our public sports and festival pastimes, that they might be, not such as were authorized a while since,[6] the provocations of drunkenness and lust, but such as may inure and harden our bodies by martial exercises to all warlike skill and performance, and may civilize, adorn, and make discreet our minds by the learned and affable meeting of frequent academies, and the procurement of wise and artful recitations sweetened with eloquent and graceful enticements to the love and practice of justice, temperance, and fortitude, instructing and bettering the nation at all opportunities, that the call of wisdom and virtue may be heard everywhere, as Solomon saith: "She crieth without, she uttereth her voice in the streets, in the top of high places, in the chief concourse, and

---

1. See the wide range of kinds and subjects and functions suggested for the serious national poet.
2. Temperament. Milton here paraphrases Horace's formula echoed by Sidney and Jonson, that poetry both teaches and delights, and that it encourages virtuous endeavor.
3. Some of the pseudo-poets of the Cavalier court who wrote on lascivious topics.
4. Roll up.
5. Comport.
6. Charles I's republication (1633) of James I's *Book of Sports*, encouraging sports, dancing, and rural festivals on Sundays—anathema to Puritans.

in the openings of the gates."[7] Whether this may not be, not only in pulpits, but after another persuasive method,[8] at set and solemn panegyries, in theaters, porches,[9] or what other place or way may win most upon the people to receive at once both recreation and instruction, let them in authority consult.

The thing which I had to say, and those intentions which have lived within me ever since I could conceive myself anything worth to my country, I return to crave excuse that urgent reason hath plucked from me by an abortive and foredated discovery.[1] And the accomplishment of them lies not but in a power above man's to promise; but that none hath by more studious ways endeavored, and with more unwearied spirit that none shall, that I dare almost aver of myself as far as life and free leisure will extend; and that the land had once enfranchised herself from this impertinent[2] yoke of prelaty, under whose inquisitorious and tyrannical duncery no free and splendid wit can flourish. Neither do I think it shame to covenant with any knowing reader that for some few years yet I may go on trust with him toward the payment of what I am now indebted, as being a work not to be raised from the heat of youth or the vapors of wine, like that which flows at waste from the pen of some vulgar amorist or the trencher fury of a rhyming parasite, nor to be obtained by the invocation of Dame Memory and her siren daughters,[3] but by devout prayer to that Eternal Spirit who can enrich with all utterance and knowledge, and sends out his seraphim with the hallowed fire of his altar to touch and purify the lips of whom he pleases.[4] To this must be added industrious and select reading, steady observation, insight into all seemly and generous arts and affairs; till which in some measure be compassed, at mine own peril and cost I refuse not to sustain this expectation.* * * But were it the meanest under-service, if God by his secretary conscience enjoin it, it were sad for me if I should draw back; for me especially, now when all men offer their aid to help ease and lighten the difficult labors of the church, to whose service by the intentions of my parents and friends I was destined of a child, and in mine own resolutions: till coming to some maturity of years and perceiving what tyranny had invaded the church, that he who would take orders must subscribe slave and take an oath withal,[5] which, unless he took with a conscience that would retch, he must either straight perjure or split his faith; I thought it better to prefer a blameless silence before the sacred office of speaking, bought and begun with servitude and forswearing. Howsoever, thus church-outed by the prelates,

---

7. The phrases are from Proverbs 1.20–21 and 8.2–3. Milton would not ban recreation or festival pastimes but reform them: his models are the lofty encomiastic poems and recitations Plato would admit into his *Republic*, the literary and social exchanges of the Italian academies, and martial exercises (to prepare the citizenry for war, now imminent).
8. I.e., poetry.
9. Porticos. "Panegyries": solemn public meetings.
1. I.e., I have been forced to write for my country's sake and to reveal my poetic plans before I was ready to do either.
2. Unsuitable, absurd.
3. True poetry comes, not from youth, wine, a

full plate, or even Memory (and her daughters the Muses): tradition alone does not make a poet.
4. The coal from the altar that purifies the prophet's lips (Isaiah 6.6–7): the passage makes poetry first and foremost the product of inspiration, but Milton also insists on his need to attain well-nigh universal knowledge and experience.
5. Milton was not willing to subscribe the oath affirming that the Book of Common Prayer and the present government of the church by bishops were according to the word of God; still less was he willing to subscribe the notorious "etcetera" oath required in 1640, that the minister would never seek to alter the government of the church "by archbishops, bishops, deacons, and archdeacons, etc."

hence may appear the right I have to meddle in these matters, as before the necessity and constraint appeared.

1642

Areopagitica   This passionate, trenchant defense of intellectual liberty has had a powerful influence on the evolving liberal conception of freedom of speech, press, and thought. Milton's specific target is the Press Ordinance of June 14, 1643, Parliament's attempt to crack down on the flood of pamphlets (including Milton's own controversial treatises on divorce) that poured forth both from legal and from underground presses as the Civil War raged. Like Tudor and Stuart censorship laws, Parliament's ordinance demanded that works be registered with the stationers and licensed by the censors before publication, and that both author and publisher be identified, on pain of fines and imprisonment for both. Milton vigorously protests the prepublication licensing of books, arguing that such measures have only been used by, and are only fit for, degenerate cultures. In the regenerate English nation, now "rousing herself like a strong man after sleep," men and women must be allowed to develop in virtue by participating in the clash and conflict of ideas. Truth will always overcome falsehood in reasoned debate. Thus, in opposition to the Presbyterians then in power, Milton defends widespread religious toleration, though with restrictions on Roman Catholicism, which, like most of his Protestant contemporaries, he viewed as a political threat and a tyranny binding individual conscience to the pope.

The title associates the tract with the speech of the Greek orator Isocrates to the Areopagus, the Council of the Wise in Athens. Learned readers would have recognized the irony of this. While Isocrates instructed the council to reform Athens by careful supervision of the private lives of citizens, Milton argues that only liberty and removal of censorship can advance reformation. This association explains the oratorical tone of the tract, which was, in fact, subtitled "A Speech." In this most literary of his tracts, Milton's style is elevated, eloquent, dense with poetic figures, and ranges in tone from satire and ridicule to urgent pleading and florid praise. His arguments and principles are often couched in striking images and phrases. One example is his passionate testimony to the potency and inestimable value of books: "As good almost kill a man as kill a good book . . ." Most memorable is his ringing credo that echoes down the centuries to protest every new tyranny: "Give me the liberty to know, to utter, and to argue freely according to conscience, above all liberties."

From Areopagitica

I deny not, but that it is of greatest concernment in the church and commonwealth, to have a vigilant eye how books demean[1] themselves as well as men; and thereafter to confine, imprison, and do sharpest justice on them as malefactors:[2] For books are not absolutely dead things, but do contain a potency of life in them to be as active as that soul was whose progeny they are; nay they do preserve as in a vial the purest efficacy and extraction of that living intellect that bred them. I know they are as lively, and as vigorously

---

1. Behave.
2. Milton allows that books may be called to account after publication, if they are proved to

contain libels or other manifest crimes (he leaves this quite vague).

productive, as those fabulous dragon's teeth; and being sown up and down, may chance to spring up armed men.[3] And yet on the other hand unless wariness be used, as good almost kill a man as kill a good book; who kills a man kills a reasonable creature, God's image; but he who destroys a good book, kills reason itself, kills the image of God, as it were in the eye. Many a man lives a burden to the earth; but a good book is the precious lifeblood of a master spirit, embalmed and treasured up on purpose to a life beyond life. 'Tis true, no age can restore a life, whereof perhaps there is no great loss; and revolutions of ages do not oft recover the loss of a rejected truth, for the want of which whole nations fare the worse. We should be wary therefore what persecution we raise against the living labors of public men, how we spill that seasoned life of man preserved and stored up in books; since we see a kind of massacre, whereof the execution ends not in the slaying of an elemental life, but strikes at that ethereal and fifth essence,[4] the breath of reason itself, slays an immortality rather than a life. But lest I should be condemned of introducing licence, while I oppose licensing, I refuse not the pains to be so much historical, as will serve to show what hath been done by ancient and famous commonwealths, against this disorder, till the very time that this project of licensing crept out of the Inquisition,[5] was catched up by our prelates, and hath caught some of our presbyters.[6] * * *

* * *Good and evil we know in the field of this world grow up together almost inseparably; and the knowledge of good is so involved and interwoven with the knowledge of evil, and in so many cunning resemblances hardly to be discerned, that those confused seeds which were imposed on Psyche as an incessant labor to cull out and sort asunder were not more intermixed.[7] It was from out the rind of one apple tasted, that the knowledge of good and evil, as two twins cleaving together, leaped forth into the world. And perhaps this is that doom which Adam fell into of knowing good and evil, that is to say of knowing good by evil.

As therefore the state of man now is, what wisdom can there be to choose, what continence to forbear, without the knowledge of evil? He that can apprehend and consider vice with all her baits and seeming pleasures, and yet abstain, and yet distinguish, and yet prefer that which is truly better, he is the true wayfaring[8] Christian. I cannot praise a fugitive and cloistered virtue, unexercised and unbreathed,[9] that never sallies out and sees her adversary, but slinks out of the race where that immortal garland is to be run for, not without dust and heat. Assuredly we bring not innocence into the world, we bring impurity much rather; that which purifies us is trial,

3. After Cadmus killed a dragon on his way to founding Thebes, on a god's advice he sowed the dragon's teeth, which sprang up as an army, the belligerent forefathers of Sparta.
4. Quintessence, a pure, mystical substance above the four elements (fire, air, water, earth).
5. The Roman Catholic institution for suppressing heresy, especially strong in Spain.
6. The Presbyterians, powerful in the Parliament, were striving to establish theirs as the national church and suppress others. Milton, who began by supporting them in *The Reason of Church Government* and his other antiprelatical tracts (1641–42), now rejects them, in large part because they seek to supplant one repressive

church with another.
7. Angry at her son Cupid's love for Psyche, Venus set the girl many trials, among them to sort out a vast mound of mixed seeds, but the ants took pity on her and did the work.
8. The printed text reads "wayfaring," calling up the image of the Christian pilgrim; several presentation copies correct it (by hand) to "warfaring," calling up the image of the Christian warrior. Both suit the passage.
9. Not forced by exertion to breathe hard. "Immortal garland" (next line): the prize for the winner of a race, as figure for the "crown of life" promised to those who endure temptation (James 1.12).

and trial is by what is contrary. That virtue therefore which is but a young-ling in the contemplation of evil, and knows not the utmost that vice prom-ises to her followers, and rejects it, is but a blank virtue, not a pure; her whiteness is but an excremental[1] whiteness; which was the reason why our sage and serious poet Spenser (whom I dare be known to think a better teacher than Scotus or Aquinas), describing true temperance under the per-son of Guyon, brings him in with his Palmer through the Cave of Mammon and the Bower of Earthly Bliss,[2] that he might see and know, and yet abstain.

Since therefore the knowledge and survey of vice is in this world so nec-essary to the constituting of human virtue, and the scanning of error to the confirmation of truth, how can we more safely, and with less danger, scout into the regions of sin and falsity than by reading all manner of tractates and hearing all manner of reason? And this is the benefit which may be had of books promiscuously read.

But of the harm that may result hence, three kinds are usually reckoned. First is feared the infection that may spread; but then all human learning and controversy in religious points must remove out of the world, yea, the Bible itself; for that ofttimes relates blasphemy not nicely,[3] it describes the carnal sense of wicked men not unelegantly, it brings in holiest men passion-ately murmuring against providence through all the arguments of Epicu-rus;[4] in other great disputes it answers dubiously and darkly to the common reader.[5]

* * *

To sequester out of the world into Atlantic and Utopian politics,[6] which never can be drawn into use, will not mend our condition, but to ordain wisely as in this world of evil, in the midst whereof God hath placed us unavoidably. . . . Impunity and remissness, for certain, are the bane of a commonwealth; but here the great art lies, to discern in what the law is to bid restraint and punishment, and in what things persuasion only is to work. If every action which is good or evil in man at ripe years were to be under pittance[7] and prescription and compulsion, what were virtue but a name, what praise could be then due to well-doing, what gramercy[8] to be sober, just, or conti-nent?

Many there be that complain of divine providence for suffering Adam to transgress; foolish tongues! When God gave him reason, he gave him free-dom to choose, for reason is but choosing; he had been else a mere artificial Adam, such an Adam as he is in the motions.[9] We ourselves esteem not of that obedience, or love, or gift, which is of force: God therefore left him

---

1. Exterior only.
2. John Duns Scotus and Thomas Aquinas, major Scholastic theologians. Guyon (follow-ing), the hero of Book 2 of the *Faerie Queene*, passes through the Cave of Mammon (symbolic of all worldly goods and honors) without his Palmer-guide, but that figure does accompany him through the Bower of Bliss.
3. Daintily.
4. Greek philosopher (342–270 B.C.E.) who taught that happiness is the greatest good, and that virtue should be practiced because it brings happiness; some of his followers equated happi-

ness with sensual enjoyment. Milton may be thinking of the biblical book of Ecclesiastes.
5. Milton goes on to argue that a fool can find material for folly in the best books, and a wise person material for wisdom in the worst. Also, one cannot remove evil by censoring books with-out also censoring ballads, fiddlers, clothing, conversation, and all social life.
6. Milton alludes to More's *Utopia* and Bacon's *New Atlantis*.
7. Rationing.
8. Reward, thanks.
9. Puppet shows.

free, set before him a provoking object, ever almost in his eyes; herein consisted his merit, herein the right of his reward, the praise of his abstinence.[1] Wherefore did he create passions within us, pleasures round about us, but that these rightly tempered are the very ingredients of virtue? They are not skillful considerers of human things, who imagine to remove sin by removing the matter of sin; for, besides that it is a huge heap increasing under the very act of diminishing, though some part of it may for a time be withdrawn from some persons, it cannot from all, in such a universal thing as books are; and when this is done, yet the sin remains entire. Though ye take from a covetous man all his treasure, he has yet one jewel left: ye cannot bereave him of his covetousness. Banish all objects of lust, shut up all youth into the severest discipline that can be exercised in any hermitage, ye cannot make them chaste that came not thither so: such great care and wisdom is required to the right managing of this point.

Suppose we could expel sin by this means; look how much we thus expel of sin, so much we expel of virtue: for the matter of them both is the same; remove that, and ye remove them both alike. This justifies the high providence of God, who, though he commands us temperance, justice, continence, yet pours out before us, even to a profuseness, all desirable things, and gives us minds that can wander beyond all limit and satiety. Why should we then affect a rigor contrary to the manner of God and of nature, by abridging or scanting those means, which books freely permitted are, both to the trial of virtue and the exercise of truth? It would be better done to learn that the law must needs be frivolous which goes to restrain things uncertainly and yet equally working to good and to evil. And were I the chooser, a dram of well-doing should be preferred before many times as much the forcible hindrance of evil-doing. For God sure esteems the growth and completing of one virtuous person more than the restraint of ten vicious.

* * *

What advantage is it to be a man over it is to be a boy at school, if we have only scaped the ferula to come under the fescue of an *imprimatur*;[2] if serious and elaborate writings, as if they were no more than the theme of a grammarlad under his pedagogue, must not be uttered without the cursory eyes of a temporizing and extemporizing licenser?[3] He who is not trusted with his own actions, his drift not being known to be evil, and standing to the hazard of law and penalty, has no great argument to think himself reputed, in the commonwealth wherein he was born, for other than a fool or a foreigner.

When a man writes to the world, he summons up all his reason and deliberation to assist him; he searches, meditates, is industrious, and likely consults and confers with his judicious friends, after all which done he takes himself to be informed in what he writes, as well as any that writ before him. If in this the most consummate act of his fidelity and ripeness, no years, no industry, no former proof of his abilities can bring him to that state

---

1. Compare Milton's representation of Adam and Eve in Eden in *Paradise Lost*.
2. "Ferula": a schoolmaster's rod; "fescue": a pointer, "imprimatur": "it may be printed" (Latin), appears on the title page of books approved by the Roman Catholic censors. Milton's keen sense of the affront to scholars and scholarship, and to himself, is evident in this passage.
3. He temporizes in following the times, and acts by whim (extemporizes).

of maturity as not to be still mistrusted and suspected (unless he carry all his considerate diligence, all his midnight watchings, and expense of Palladian[4] oil, to the hasty view of an unleisured licenser, perhaps much his younger, perhaps far his inferior in judgment, perhaps one who never knew the labor of book-writing), and if he be not repulsed, or slighted, must appear in print like a puny[5] with his guardian, and his censor's hand on the back of his title to be his bail and surety that he is no idiot, or seducer; it cannot be but a dishonor and derogation to the author, to the book, to the privilege and dignity of learning.* * *

And how can a man teach with authority, which is the life of teaching, how can he be a doctor[6] in his book as he ought to be, or else had better be silent, whenas all he teaches, all he delivers, is but under the tuition, under the correction of his patriarchal[7] licenser to blot or alter what precisely accords not with the hide-bound humor which he calls his judgment? When every acute reader upon the first sight of a pedantic license, will be ready with these like words to ding the book a quoit's[8] distance from him: "I hate a pupil teacher, I endure not an instructor that comes to me under the wardship of an overseeing fist. I know nothing of the licenser, but that I have his own hand here for his arrogance; who shall warrant me his judgment?"

"The state, sir," replies the stationer,[9] but has a quick return: "The state shall be my governors, but not my critics; they may be mistaken in the choice of a licenser, as easily as this licenser may be mistaken in an author."

*   *   *

Well knows he who uses to consider, that our faith and knowledge thrives by exercise, as well as our limbs and complexion.[1] Truth is compared in Scripture to a streaming fountain;[2] if her waters flow not in a perpetual progression, they sicken into a muddy pool of conformity and tradition. A man may be a heretic in the truth; and if he believe things only because his pastor says so, or the Assembly[3] so determines, without knowing other reason, though his belief be true, yet the very truth he holds becomes his heresy.

*   *   *

Truth indeed came once into the world with her Divine Master, and was a perfect shape most glorious to look on: but when he ascended, and his apostles after him were laid asleep, then straight arose a wicked race of deceivers, who, as that story goes of the Egyptian Typhon with his conspirators, how they dealt with the good Osiris,[4] took the virgin Truth, hewed her lovely form into a thousand pieces, and scattered them to the four winds. From that time ever since, the sad friends of Truth, such as durst appear, imitating the careful search that Isis made for the mangled body of Osiris, went

4. Pertaining to Pallas Athena, goddess of wisdom.
5. A minor, hence, young, unseasoned.
6. Teacher.
7. Taking on the role of a father; also, standing in for ecclesiastical patriarchs or prelates (like Archbishop Laud).
8. A flat disc of stone or metal, thrown as an exercise of strength or skill.
9. Printer, who was responsible for submitting books before publication to the "licenser" (censor).
1. Constitution, the proper mingling of qualities in the body.
2. In Psalm 85.11.
3. The Westminster Assembly, convened by Parliament in 1643 to reorganize the English church along Presbyterian lines.
4. Plutarch tells, in "Isis and Osiris," of Typhon's scattering the fragments of his brother Osiris and of Isis's efforts to recover them.

up and down gathering up limb by limb, still as they could find them. We have not yet found them all, Lords and Commons, nor ever shall do, till her Master's second coming; he shall bring together every joint and member, and shall mold them into an immortal feature of loveliness and perfection. Suffer not these licensing prohibitions to stand at every place of opportunity, forbidding and disturbing them that continue seeking, that continue to do our obsequies[5] to the torn body of our martyred saint.

We boast our light; but if we look not wisely on the sun itself, it smites us into darkness. Who can discern those planets that are oft combust,[6] and those stars of brightest magnitude that rise and set with the sun, until the opposite motion of their orbs bring them to such a place in the firmament where they may be seen evening or morning? The light which we have gained was given us, not to be ever staring on, but by it to discover onward things more remote from our knowledge. It is not the unfrocking of a priest, the unmitering of a bishop, and the removing him from off the Presbyterian shoulders, that will make us a happy nation. No, if other things as great in the church, and in the rule of life both economical and political, be not looked into and reformed, we have looked so long upon the blaze that Zwinglius and Calvin[7] hath beaconed up to us, that we are stark blind.

There be who perpetually complain of schisms and sects, and make it such a calamity that any man dissents from their maxims. 'Tis their own pride and ignorance which causes the disturbing, who neither will hear with meekness, nor can convince; yet all must be suppressed which is not found in their syntagma.[8] They are the troublers, they are the dividers of unity, who neglect and permit not others to unite those dissevered pieces which are yet wanting to the body of Truth. To be still searching what we know not by what we know, still closing up truth to truth as we find it (for all her body is homogeneal and proportional), this is the golden rule in theology as well as in arithmetic, and makes up the best harmony in a church; not the forced and outward union of cold and neutral and inwardly divided minds.

Lords and Commons of England, consider what nation it is whereof ye are, and whereof ye are the governors: a nation not slow and dull, but of a quick, ingenious, and piercing spirit, acute to invent, subtle and sinewy to discourse, not beneath the reach of any point the highest that human capacity can soar to. Therefore the studies of learning in her deepest sciences have been so ancient and so eminent among us, that writers of good antiquity and ablest judgment have been persuaded that even the school of Pythagoras and the Persian wisdom took beginning from the old philosophy of this island.[9] And that wise and civil Roman, Julius Agricola,[1] who governed once here for Caesar, preferred the natural wits of Britain before the labored studies of the French. Nor is it for nothing that the grave and

---

5. Funeral or commemorative rites.
6. Burned up; in astrology, so close to the sun as not to be visible.
7. Zwingli and Calvin, famous Protestant reformers, were mainstays of the Presbyterian cause. "Economical": domestic.
8. Compilations of beliefs, creeds.
9. Some speculation existed as to whether the Pythagorean notion of the transmigration of souls might trace back to the Druids, but the

notion was mostly denied.
1. The "civil" (cultured, civilized) Agricola's opinion of the British intellect is found in Tacitus's *Life of Agricola*. Transylvania (following; now Romania) was an independent Protestant country whose citizens sometimes came to England to study. "Hercynian wilderness": Roman name for a forested and mountainous region of Germany.

frugal Transylvanian[2] sends out yearly from as far as the mountainous borders of Russia, and beyond the Hercynian wilderness, not their youth, but their staid men, to learn our language and our theologic arts.

Yet that which is above all this, the favor and the love of heaven we have great argument to think in a peculiar manner propitious and propending[3] towards us. Why else was this nation chosen before any other, that out of her, as out of Zion,[4] should be proclaimed and sounded forth the first tidings and trumpet of Reformation to all Europe? And had it not been the obstinate perverseness of our prelates against the divine and admirable spirit of Wycliffe to suppress him as a schismatic and innovator, perhaps neither the Bohemian Huss and Jerome,[5] no, nor the name of Luther or of Calvin, had been ever known: the glory of reforming all our neighbors had been completely ours. But now, as our obdurate clergy have with violence demeaned the matter, we are become hitherto the latest and the backwardest scholars of whom[6] God offered to have made us the teachers.

Now once again by all concurrence of signs, and by the general instinct of holy and devout men, as they daily and solemnly express their thoughts, God is decreeing to begin some new and great period in his church, even to the reforming of Reformation itself; what does he then but reveal himself to his servants, and as his manner is, first to his Englishmen? I say, as his manner is, first to us, though we mark not the method of his counsels, and are unworthy. Behold now this vast city: a city of refuge,[7] the mansion house of liberty, encompassed and surrounded with his protection; the shop of war hath not there more anvils and hammers waking, to fashion out the plates[8] and instruments of armed justice in defense of beleaguered truth, than there be pens and heads there, sitting by their studious lamps, musing, searching, revolving new notions and ideas wherewith to present, as with their homage and their fealty, the approaching Reformation: others as fast reading, trying all things, assenting to the force of reason and convincement.

What could a man require more from a nation so pliant and so prone to seek after knowledge? What wants there to such a towardly and pregnant[9] soil, but wise and faithful laborers, to make a knowing people, a nation of prophets,[1] of sages, and of worthies? We reckon more than five months yet to harvest; there need not be five weeks; had we but eyes to lift up, the fields are white already.[2] Where there is much desire to learn, there of necessity will be much arguing, much writing, many opinions; for opinion in good men is but knowledge in the making. Under these fantastic terrors of sect and schism we wrong the earnest and zealous thirst after knowledge and understanding which God hath stirred up in this city.

2. The Protestant princes of Transylvania encouraged their theologians and humanist scholars to study at English universities.
3. Inclining, favorable. "Argument": reason.
4. Mount Zion, in Jerusalem, the site of the Temple.
5. John Wycliffe was a 14th-century English reformer and translator of the Bible, whose books were forbidden by Pope Alexander V in 1409. John Huss spread Wycliffe's doctrines on the Continent; he was burned at the stake in 1415, as was (the next year) his follower Jerome of Prague.
6. Of those whom. "Demeaned": conducted,

degraded.
7. Numbers 35 instructs the Jews to establish "cities of refuge" where those accused of crimes will be protected from "revengers of blood."
8. Plate mail, for armor.
9. Favorable and fertile.
1. In Numbers 11.29 Moses reproaches Joshua, who complained of the presence of other prophets: "Enviest thou for my sake? Would God that all the Lord's people were prophets."
2. Milton is paraphrasing Christ's words to his disciples (John 4.35): "Lift up your eyes, and look on the fields: for they are white already to harvest."

What some lament of, we rather should rejoice at, should rather praise this pious forwardness among men, to reassume the ill-deputed care of their religion into their own hands again. A little generous prudence, a little forbearance of one another, and some grain of charity might win all these diligences to join, and unite into one general and brotherly search after truth; could we but forgo this prelatical tradition of crowding free consciences and Christian liberties into canons and precepts of men. I doubt not, if some great and worthy stranger should come among us, wise to discern the mold and temper of a people, and how to govern it, observing the high hopes and aims, the diligent alacrity of our extended thoughts and reasonings in the pursuance of truth and freedom, but that he would cry out as Pyrrhus did, admiring the Roman docility and courage: "If such were my Epirots, I would not despair the greatest design that could be attempted, to make a church or kingdom happy."[3] Yet these are the men cried out against for schismatics and sectaries;[4] as if, while the temple of the Lord was building, some cutting, some squaring the marble, others hewing the cedars, there should be a sort of irrational men, who could not consider there must be many schisms and many dissections[5] made in the quarry and in the timber, ere the house of God can be built. And when every stone is laid artfully together, it cannot be united into a continuity, it can but be contiguous in this world; neither can every piece of the building be of one form; nay rather the perfection consists in this, that out of many moderate varieties and brotherly dissimilitudes that are not vastly disproportional, arises the goodly and the graceful symmetry that commends the whole pile and structure. Let us therefore be more considerate builders, more wise in spiritual architecture, when great reformation is expected. For now the time seems come, wherein Moses the great prophet may sit in heaven rejoicing to see that memorable and glorious wish of his fulfilled, when not only our seventy elders, but all the Lord's people, are become prophets.[6]

* * *

Methinks I see in my mind a noble and puissant nation rousing herself like a strong man after sleep, and shaking her invincible locks:[7] methinks I see her as an eagle mewing her mighty youth, and kindling her undazzled eyes at the full midday beam;[8] purging and unsealing her long-abused sight at the fountain itself of heavenly radiance; while the whole noise of timorous and flocking birds, with those also that love the twilight, flutter about, amazed at what she means, and in their envious gabble would prognosticate[9] a year of sects and schisms.

What should ye do then, should ye suppress all this flowery crop of knowledge and new light sprung up and yet springing daily in this city? Should ye

---

3. Though King Pyrrhus of Epirus beat the Roman armies at Heraclea in 280 B.C.E., he was much impressed by their discipline.
4. "Schismatics": those who cut up or divide the church; "sectaries": members of Protestant communions outside the national church.
5. Milton is playing on the literal meaning of "schism," cutting up or dividing.
6. Again alluding to Numbers 11.29, Milton equates the English assembly of clergy to set doc-

trine and church order (the Westminster Assembly) with the Jewish Sanhedrin of seventy elders.
7. The allusion is to Samson, whose uncut hair made him invincible, when he frustrated the first three attempts of Delilah and the Philistines to subdue him in sleep (Judges 16.6–14).
8. Eagles were thought to be able to look directly at the sun. "Mewing": molting, when the eagle sheds it feathers and thereby renews its coat.
9. Predict.

set an oligarchy of twenty engrossers[1] over it, to bring a famine upon our minds again, when we shall know nothing but what is measured to us by their bushel? Believe it, Lords and Commons, they who counsel ye to such a suppressing do as good as bid ye suppress yourselves; and I will soon show how.[2]

* * *

And now the time in special is by privilege to write and speak what may help to the further discussing of matters in agitation. The temple of Janus with his two controversial faces might now not unsignificantly be set open.[3] And though all the winds of doctrine were let loose to play upon the earth, so Truth be in the field, we do injuriously by licensing and prohibiting to misdoubt her strength. Let her and Falsehood grapple; who ever knew Truth put to the worse in a free and open encounter? Her[4] confuting is the best and surest suppressing. He who hears what praying there is for light and clearer knowledge to be sent down among us would think of other matters to be constituted beyond the discipline of Geneva framed and fabriced already to our hands.[5]

Yet when the new light which we beg for shines in upon us, there be who envy and oppose if it come not first in at their casements. What a collusion is this, whenas we are exhorted by the wise man to use diligence, to seek for wisdom as for hidden treasures early and late,[6] that another order shall enjoin us to know nothing but by statute. When a man hath been laboring the hardest labor in the deep mines of knowledge, hath furnished out his findings in all their equipage, drawn forth his reasons as it were a battle[7] ranged, scattered and defeated all objections in his way, calls out his adversary into the plain, offers him the advantage of wind and sun if he please, only that he may try the matter by dint of argument; for his opponents then to skulk, to lay ambushments, to keep a narrow bridge of licensing where the challenger should pass, though it be valor enough in soldiership, is but weakness and cowardice in the wars of Truth.

For who knows not that Truth is strong, next to the Almighty? She needs no policies nor stratagems nor licensings to make her victorious—those are the shifts and the defenses that error uses against her power. Give her but room, and do not bind her when she sleeps, for then she speaks not true, as the old Proteus[8] did, who spake oracles only when he was caught and bound, but then rather she turns herself into all shapes except her own, and perhaps tunes her voice according to the time, as Micaiah did before Ahab,[9] until she be adjured into her own likeness.

---

1. Engrossers, much hated in the English countryside, bought up great quantities of grain and held it for times of famine, selling it at high prices; Milton equates them with the twenty authorized printers, the stationers.
2. Milton goes on to argue that Parliament, by its own liberalizing reforms to date, has created the vigorous and inquiring minds it now seeks to suppress.
3. Janus, as god of beginnings and endings, had two faces looking in opposite directions; a door dedicated to him in Rome was kept open in time of war, closed in time of peace.
4. I.e., Falsehood's.

5. Milton was already disenchanted with Genevan "Discipline" (Presbyterian church government) and within a year or so would be writing "New *presbyter* is but old *priest*, writ large." "Fabriced": fabricated.
6. Solomon's advice in Proverbs 8.11.
7. Line of battle. Wind and sun (below) were significant advantages in a fight with swords.
8. The sea god who could change shape at will, to avoid capture (*Odyssey* 4).
9. Micaiah, a prophet of God, tried for a time to disguise an unpleasant prophecy from King Ahab but then spoke truth when adjured to do so (1 Kings 22.10–28).

Yet it is not impossible that she may have more shapes than one. What else is all that rank of things indifferent, wherein Truth may be on this side or on the other without being unlike herself? What but a vain shadow else is the abolition of those ordinances, that handwriting nailed to the cross?[1] What great purchase is this Christian liberty which Paul so often boasts of? His doctrine is that he who eats or eats not, regards a day or regards it not, may do either to the Lord.[2] How many other things might be tolerated in peace and left to conscience, had we but charity, and were it not the chief stronghold of our hypocrisy to be ever judging one another? I fear yet this iron yoke of outward conformity hath left a slavish print upon our necks; the ghost of a linen decency[3] yet haunts us. We stumble and are impatient at the least dividing of one visible congregation from another, though it be not in fundamentals; and through our forwardness to suppress and our backwardness to recover any enthralled piece of truth out of the grip of custom, we care not[4] to keep truth separated from truth, which is the fiercest rent and disunion of all. We do not see that while we still affect by all means a rigid and external formality, we may as soon fall again into a gross conforming stupidity, a stark and dead congealment of "wood and hay and stubble,"[5] forced and frozen together, which is more to the sudden degenerating of a church than many subdichotomies of petty schisms.

Not that I can think well of every light separation, or that all in a church is to be expected "gold and silver and precious stones." It is not possible for man to sever the wheat from the tares, the good fish from the other fry; that must be the angels' ministry at the end of mortal things.[6] Yet if all cannot be of one mind—as who looks they should be?—this doubtless is more wholesome, more prudent, and more Christian, that many be tolerated rather than all compelled. I mean not tolerated popery and open superstition, which, as it extirpates all religions and civil supremacies, so itself should be extirpate, provided first that all charitable and compassionate means be used to win and regain the weak and the misled; that also which is impious or evil absolutely, either against faith or manners,[7] no law can possibly permit that intends not to unlaw itself; but those neighboring differences or rather indifferences are what I speak of, whether in some point of doctrine or of discipline, which though they may be many yet need not interrupt "the unity of spirit," if we could but find among us the "bond of peace."[8]

In the meanwhile, if anyone would write and bring his helpful hand to the slow-moving reformation which we labor under, if truth have spoken to him before others, or but seemed at least to speak, who hath so bejesuited[9] us that we should trouble that man with asking license to do so worthy a deed? And not consider this, that if it come to prohibiting, there is not aught more likely to be prohibited than truth itself; whose first appearance to our

---

1. The locution, from Colossians 2.14, implies that the Crucifixion canceled all the rules and penalties of the Mosaic law. Paul's doctrine of Christian liberty (below) is expressed in Galatians 5 and elsewhere.
2. In the Lord's service.
3. White bands around the necks of clergymen are made emblems of formal piety.
4. Scruple not.

5. The contrast between "wood and hay and stubble" and "gold and silver and precious stones" (next paragraph) is from 1 Corinthians 3.12.
6. In Matthew 13.24–30, 36–43, Christ in a parable tells his disciples to let the wheat and tares (weeds) grow up together till harvest time.
7. Morals.
8. The quoted phrases are from Ephesians 4.3.
9. Imposed on us Jesuit ideas (of censorship).

eyes bleared and dimmed with prejudice and custom is more unsightly and unplausible than many errors, even as the person is of many a great man slight and contemptible to see to. And what do they tell us vainly of new opinions, when this very opinion of theirs, that none must be heard but whom they like, is the worst and newest opinion of all others, and is the chief cause why sects and schisms do so much abound, and true knowledge is kept at distance from us; besides yet a greater danger which is in it. For when God shakes a kingdom[1] with strong and healthful commotions to a general reforming, it is not untrue that many sectaries and false teachers are then busiest in seducing; but yet more true it is that God then raises to his own work men of rare abilities and more than common industry, not only to look back and revise what hath been taught heretofore, but to gain further and go on some new enlightened steps in the discovery of truth.

1644

Sonnets Milton wrote twenty-four sonnets between 1630 and 1658. Five in Italian constitute a mini-Petrarchan sequence on a perhaps imaginary Italian lady. The rest, in English, are individual poems on a wide variety of topics and occasions, though not on the usual sonnet topics (love, as in the sequences of Sidney, Spenser, and Shakespeare, or religious devotion, as in that of Donne). Milton writes sometimes about personal crises (his blindness, the death of his wife), sometimes about political issues or personages (Cromwell, the persecuting Parliament), sometimes about friends and friendship (Cyriack Skinner, Lady Margaret Ley), sometimes about historical events (a threatened royalist attack on London, the massacre of Protestants in Piedmont). His tone ranges from Jonsonian urbanity to prophetic denunciation. The form of the sonnets is Petrarchan (see "Poetic Forms and Literary Terminology," in the appendices to this volume), but in the later sonnets especially (e.g., the Blindness and Piedmont sonnets) the sense runs on from line to line, overriding the expected end-stopped lines and the octave/sestet shift. There is some precedent for this in the Italian sonneteer Giovanni della Casa, but not for the powerful tension Milton creates as meaning and emotion strive within and against the formal metrics of the Petrarchan sonnet. Milton's new ways with the sonnet had a profound and acknowledged influence on the Romantic poets, especially Wordsworth and Shelley.

How Soon Hath Time

> How soon hath Time, the subtle thief of youth,
>   Stol'n on his wing my three and twentieth year!
>   My hasting days fly on with full career,
>   But my late spring no bud or blossom shew'th.
> 5 Perhaps my semblance might deceive[1] the truth,

---

1. Milton alludes to Haggai 2.7: "I will shake all nations, and the desire of all nations shall come, and I will fill this house with glory, saith the Lord of hosts."

1. Misrepresent. "Semblance": appearance.

That I to manhood am arrived so near,
And inward ripeness doth much less appear,
That some more timely-happy spirits endu'th.°   *endows*
Yet be it less or more, or soon or slow,
It shall be still in strictest measure even[2]
To that same lot, however mean or high,
Toward which Time leads me, and the will of Heaven;
All is, if I have grace to use it so,
As ever in my great Taskmaster's eye.[3]

1632?   1645

On the New Forcers of Conscience under the Long Parliament[1]

Because you have thrown off your prelate lord,[2]
And with stiff vows renounced his liturgy,
To seize the widowed whore Plurality[3]
From them whose sin ye envied, not abhorred,
Dare ye for this adjure° the civil sword[4]   *invoke*
To force our consciences that Christ set free,
And ride us with a classic hierarchy[5]
Taught ye by mere A. S. and Rutherford?[6]
Men whose life, learning, faith, and pure intent
Would have been held in high esteem with Paul
Must now be named and printed heretics
By shallow Edwards and Scotch what-d'ye-call:[7]
But we do hope to find out all your tricks,
Your plots and packing° worse than those of Trent,[8]   *fraudulent*
That so the Parliament[9]   *dealings*

5

10

15

2. Equal, adequate. "It": Milton's inner growth. "Even / To that same lot": conformed to my appointed destiny.
3. The final lines allow for various readings. "Taskmaster" identifies God with the parable (Matthew 20.1–16) in which a vineyard keeper takes on workers throughout the day, paying the same wages to those hired at the first and at the eleventh hour.
1. The sonnet targets the Presbyterians, whom Milton in *The Reason of Church Government* (pp. 1474–79) and other antiprelatical tracts of 1641–42 had supported against the bishops. Now that they have overthrown the bishops and dominate the Long Parliament, they seek to become the national church, repressing all others. This *sonetto cauduto*, or "tailed sonnet" (an Italian form) has the usual fourteen lines followed by two "tails" of three lines each.
2. Bishops and the ecclesiastical church structure.
3. The practice of holding several benefices at once; she is a "widowed whore" because her earlier lovers, the Anglican clergy, can no longer possess her.

4. State authority.
5. The Presbyterian church order comprised of synods and classes as governing boards and disciplinary courts.
6. Adam Stuart and Samuel Rutherford, Scottish Presbyterian pamphleteers who urged the establishment of an English national Presbyterian church on the Scottish model.
7. Thomas Edwards analyzed hundreds of so-called heresies in a book picturesquely titled *Gangraena* (1645, 1646). It even identifies Milton as the founder of a sect of Divorcers, promoting "divorce at pleasure." "Scotch what-d'ye-call" may refer to another Scots cleric, Robert Baillie, or may simply be a sneer at the unpronounceability of Scottish names.
8. The Council of Trent, held by the Roman Church to deal with the Protestant Reformation, was notorious as a scene of political jockeying.
9. In the previous few months Independents and more secular-minded republicans had gained some strength in the Parliament, so Milton could hope they might weigh in against Presbyterian repression.

Mother with infant down the rocks. Their moans
The vales redoubled to the hills, and they
10   To heaven. Their martyred blood and ashes sow
O'er all th' Italian fields, where still doth sway
The triple tyrant:[5] that from these may grow
A hundredfold, who having learnt thy way
Early may fly the Babylonian woe.[6]

1655   1673

Methought I Saw My Late Espousèd Saint[1]

Methought I saw my late espousèd saint
Brought to me like Alcestis[2] from the grave,
Whom Jove's great son to her glad husband gave,
Rescued from death by force though pale and faint.
5   Mine, as whom[3] washed from spot of childbed taint,
Purification in the old law did save,[4]
And such, as yet once more I trust to have
Full sight of her in heaven without restraint,
Came vested all in white, pure as her mind.
10   Her face was veiled, yet to my fancied sight[5]
Love, sweetness, goodness, in her person shined
So clear, as in no face with more delight.
But O, as to embrace me she inclined,
I waked, she fled, and day brought back my night.

1658   1673

Paradise Lost   The setting of Milton's great epic encompasses Heaven, Hell, primordial Chaos, and the planet earth. It features battles among immortal spirits, voyages through space, and lakes of fire. Yet its protagonists are a married couple living in a garden, and its climax consists in the eating of a piece of fruit. *Paradise Lost* is ultimately about the human condition, the Fall that caused "all our woe," and the promise and means of restoration. It is also about knowing and choosing, about free will. In the opening passages of Books 1, 3, 7, and 9, Milton highlights

5. The pope, wearing his tiara with three crowns. The passage alludes to Tertullian's maxim that "the blood of the martyrs is the seed of the church"; also to the parable of the sower (Matthew 13.3), some of whose seed brought forth fruit "an hundredfold" (see next line); and also to Cadmus, who sowed dragon's teeth that sprang forth armed men.

6. Protestants often identified the Roman Church with the whore of Babylon (Revelation 17–18).

1. There is some debate as to whether this poem refers to Milton's first wife, Mary Powell, who died in May 1652, three days after giving birth to her third daughter, or his second wife, Katherine Woodcock, who died in February 1658, after giving birth (in October 1657) to a daughter. The

text can support either, but the latter seems more likely. The sonnet is couched as a dream vision.

2. In Euripides' *Alcestis*, Alcestis, wife of Admetus, is rescued from the underworld by Hercules ("Jove's great son," next line) and restored, veiled, to Admetus; he is overjoyed when he lifts the veil, but she must remain silent until she is ritually cleansed.

3. As one whom.

4. The Mosaic Law (Leviticus 12.2–8) prescribed periods for the purification of women after childbirth (eighty days for a daughter).

5. She is veiled like Alcestis, and Milton's sight of her is only "fancied"; he never saw the face of his second wife, Katherine, because of his blindness.

the choices and difficulties he faced in creating his poem. His central characters—Satan, Beelzebub, Abdiel, Adam, and Eve—are confronted with hard choices under the pressure of powerful desires and sometimes devious temptations. Milton's readers, too, are continually challenged to choose and to reconsider their most basic assumptions about freedom, heroism, work, pleasure, language, nature, and love. The great themes of *Paradise Lost* are intimately linked to the political questions at stake in the English Revolution and the Restoration, but the connection is by no means straightforward. This is a poem in which Satan leads a revolution against an absolute monarch and in which questions of tyranny, servitude, and liberty are debated in a parliament in Hell. Milton's readers are hereby challenged to rethink these topics and, like Abdiel debating with Satan in Books 5 and 6, to make crucial distinctions between God as monarch and earthly kings.

In Milton's time, the conventions of epic poetry followed a familiar recipe. The action was to begin *in medias res* (in the middle of things), following the poet's statement of his theme and invocation of his Muse. The reader could expect grand battles and love affairs, supernatural intervention, a descent into the underworld, catalogues of warriors, and epic similes. Milton had absorbed the epic tradition in its entirety, and his poem abounds with echoes of Homer and Virgil, the fifteenth-century Italians Tasso and Ariosto, and the English Spenser. But in *Paradise Lost* he at once heightens epic conventions and values and utterly transforms them. This is the epic to end all epics. Milton gives us the first and greatest of all wars (between God and Satan) and the first and greatest of love affairs (between Adam and Eve). His theme is the destiny of the entire human race, caught up in the temptation and Fall of our first "grand parents."

Milton challenges his readers in *Paradise Lost*, at once fulfilling and defying all of our expectations. Nothing in the epic tradition or in biblical interpretation can prepare us for the Satan who hurtles into view in Book 1, with his awesome energy and defiance, incredible fortitude, and, above all, magnificent rhetoric. For some readers, including Blake and Shelley, Satan is the true hero of the poem. But Milton is engaged in a radical reevaluation of epic values, and Satan's version of heroism must be contrasted with those of the loyal Abdiel and the Son of God. Moreover, the poem's truly epic action takes place not on the battlefield but in the moral and domestic arena. Milton's Adam and Eve are not conventional epic heroes, but neither are they the conventional Adam and Eve. Their state of innocence is not childlike, tranquil, and free of sexual desire. Instead, the first couple enjoy sex, experience tension and passion, make mistakes of judgment, and grow in knowledge. Their task is to prune what is unruly in their own natures as they prune the vegetation in their garden, for both have the capacity to grow wild. Their relationship exhibits gender hierarchy, but Milton's early readers may have been surprised by the fullness and complexity of Eve's character and the centrality of her role, not only in the Fall but in the promised restoration.

We expect in epics a grand style, and Milton's style engulfs us from the outset with its energy and power, as those rushing, enjambed, blank-verse lines propel us along with only a few pauses for line endings or grammar (there is only one full stop in the first twenty-six lines). The elevated diction and complex syntax, the sonorities and patternings make a magnificent music. But that music is an entire orchestra of tones, including the high political rhetoric of Satan in Books 1 and 2, the evocative sensuousness of the descriptions of Eden, the delicacy of Eve's love lyric to Adam in Book 4, the relatively plain speech of God in Book 3, and the speech rhythms of Adam and Eve's marital quarrel in Book 9. This majestic achievement depends on the poet's rejection of heroic couplets, the norm for epic and tragedy in the Restoration, vigorously defended by Dryden but denounced by Milton in his note on "The Verse." The choice of verse form was, like so many other things in Milton's life, in part a question of politics. Milton's terms associate the "troublesome and modern bondage of rhyming" with Restoration monarchy and the repression of dissidents and present his use of unrhymed blank verse as a recovery of "ancient liberty."

The first edition (1667) presented *Paradise Lost* in ten books; the second (1674) recast it into twelve books, after the Virgilian model, splitting the original Books 7 and 10. We present the twelve-book epic in its entirety, to allow readers to experience the impact of the whole.

PARADISE LOST

SECOND EDITION (1674)

The Verse

The measure is English heroic verse without rhyme, as that of Homer in Greek and of Virgil in Latin; rhyme being no necessary adjunct or true ornament of poem or good verse, in longer works especially, but the invention of a barbarous age, to set off wretched matter[1] and lame meter; graced indeed since by the use of some famous modern poets,[2] carried away by custom, but much to their own vexation, hindrance, and constraint to express many things otherwise, and for the most part worse than else they would have expressed them. Not without cause therefore some both Italian[3] and Spanish poets of prime note have rejected rhyme both in longer and shorter works, as have also long since our best English tragedies, as a thing of itself, to all judicious ears, trivial and of no true musical delight; which consists only in apt numbers,[4] fit quantity of syllables, and the sense variously drawn out from one verse into another, not in the jingling sound of like endings, a fault avoided by the learned ancients both in poetry and all good oratory. This neglect then of rhyme so little is to be taken for a defect, though it may seem so perhaps to vulgar readers, that it rather is to be esteemed an example set, the first in English, of ancient liberty recovered to heroic poem from the troublesome and modern bondage of rhyming.

Book 1

The Argument[1]

This first book proposes, first in brief, the whole subject, man's disobedience, and the loss thereupon of Paradise wherein he was placed: then touches the prime cause of his fall, the Serpent, or rather Satan in the Serpent; who revolting from God, and drawing to his side many legions of angels, was by the command of God driven out of Heaven with all his crew

1. Perhaps the bawdy content of the Latin songs composed by goliardic poets of the Middle Ages; they learned rhyme from medieval hymns.
2. Notably, Dryden. See his *Essay of Dramatic Poesy*.
3. Trissino and Tasso.
4. Appropriate rhythm.

1. *Paradise Lost* appeared originally without any sort of prose aid to the reader, but the printer asked Milton for some "Arguments," or summary explanations of the action in the various books, and these were prefixed to later issues of the poem.

into the great deep. Which action passed over, the poem hastes into the midst of things,[2] presenting Satan with his angels now fallen into Hell, described here, not in the center[3] (for Heaven and Earth may be supposed as yet not made, certainly not yet accursed) but in a place of utter darkness, fitliest called Chaos: here Satan with his angels lying on the burning lake, thunderstruck and astonished, after a certain space recovers, as from confusion, calls up him who next in order and dignity lay by him; they confer of their miserable fall. Satan awakens all his legions, who lay till then in the same manner confounded; they rise, their numbers, array of battle, their chief leaders named, according to the idols known afterwards in Canaan and the countries adjoining. To these Satan directs his speech, comforts them with hope yet of regaining Heaven, but tells them lastly of a new world and new kind of creature to be created, according to an ancient prophecy or report in Heaven; for that angels were long before this visible creation, was the opinion of many ancient Fathers.[4] To find out the truth of this prophecy, and what to determine[5] thereon he refers to a full council. What his associates thence attempt. Pandemonium the palace of Satan rises, suddenly built out of the deep: the infernal peers there sit in council.

	Of man's first disobedience, and the fruit[1]	
	Of that forbidden tree, whose mortal° taste	*deadly*
	Brought death into the world, and all our woe,	
	With loss of Eden, till one greater Man[2]	
5	Restore us, and regain the blissful seat,	
	Sing Heav'nly Muse,[3] that on the secret top	
	Of Oreb, or of Sinai, didst inspire	
	That shepherd, who first taught the chosen seed,	
	In the beginning how the heav'ns and earth	
10	Rose out of Chaos: or if Sion hill[4]	
	Delight thee more, and Siloa's brook that flowed	
	Fast by the oracle of God; I thence	
	Invoke thy aid to my advent'rous song,	
	That with no middle flight intends to soar	
15	Above th' Aonian mount,[5] while it pursues	
	Things unattempted yet in prose or rhyme.[6]	
	And chiefly thou O Spirit,[7] that dost prefer	
	Before all temples th' upright heart and pure,	
	Instruct me, for thou know'st; thou from the first	
20	Wast present, and with mighty wings outspread	

2. According to Horace, the epic poet should begin "in medias res."
3. I.e., of the earth.
4. Church Fathers, the Christian writers of the first centuries.
5. I.e., what action to take.
1. Eve's apple, and all the consequences of eating it. This first proem (lines 1–26) combines the epic statement of theme and invocation.
2. Christ, the second Adam.
3. In Greek mythology, Urania, Muse of astronomy; here, however, by the references to Oreb (Horeb) and Sinai (following), identified with the Muse who inspired Moses ("that shepherd")

to write Genesis and the other four books of the Pentateuch for the instruction of the Jews ("the chosen seed").
4. Mount Zion: the site of Solomon's Temple. "Siloa's brook" (next line): a spring near the Temple where Christ cured a blind man.
5. Helicon, home of the classical Muses. Milton will attempt to surpass Homer and Virgil.
6. Paradoxically, Milton vaunts his originality in a translated line from Ariosto's *Orlando Furioso* 1.2. The allusion also challenges the romantic epic in Ariosto's tradition.
7. Here identified with God's creating power.

Dove-like sat'st brooding[8] on the vast abyss
And mad'st it pregnant: what in me is dark
Illumine, what is low raise and support;
That to the height of this great argument°   *subject, theme*
25 I may assert Eternal Providence,
And justify° the ways of God to men.   *show the justice of*
     Say first, for Heav'n hides nothing from thy view
Nor the deep tract of Hell, say first what cause[9]
Moved our grand parents in that happy state,
30 Favored of Heav'n so highly, to fall off
From their Creator, and transgress his will
For° one restraint, lords of the world besides?°   *because of / otherwise*
Who first seduced them to that foul revolt?
Th' infernal Serpent; he it was, whose guile
35 Stirred up with envy and revenge, deceived
The mother of mankind, what time° his pride   *when*
Had cast him out from Heav'n, with all his host
Of rebel angels, by whose aid aspiring
To set himself in glory above his peers,°   *equals*
40 He trusted to have equaled the Most High,
If he opposed; and with ambitious aim
Against the throne and monarchy of God
Raised impious war in Heav'n and battle proud
With vain attempt. Him the Almighty Power
45 Hurled headlong flaming from th' ethereal sky
With hideous ruin and combustion down
To bottomless perdition, there to dwell
In adamantine[1] chains and penal fire,
Who durst defy th' Omnipotent to arms.
50 Nine times the space[2] that measures day and night
To mortal men, he with his horrid crew
Lay vanquished, rolling in the fiery gulf
Confounded though immortal: but his doom
Reserved him to more wrath; for now the thought
55 Both of lost happiness and lasting pain
Torments him; round he throws his baleful° eyes   *malignant*
That witnessed huge affliction and dismay
Mixed with obdúrate pride and steadfast hate:
At once as far as angels' ken° he views   *range of sight*
60 The dismal situation waste and wild,
A dungeon horrible, on all sides round
As one great furnace flamed, yet from those flames
No light, but rather darkness visible
Served only to discover sights of woe,
65 Regions of sorrow, doleful shades, where peace

---

8. A composite of phrases and ideas from Genesis 1.2 ("And the earth was without form, and void, and darkness was upon the face of the deep. And the Spirit of God moved upon the face of the waters"). Only a small number of Milton's many allusions to the Bible (in many versions) can be indicated in the notes. Milton's brooding dove image comes from the Latin (Tremellius) Bible version, *incubabat*, "incubated."
9. An opening question like this is an epic convention.
1. A mythical substance of great hardness.
2. Extent of time.

And rest can never dwell, hope never comes
That comes to all;[3] but torture without end
Still urges,° and a fiery deluge, fed   *always provokes*
With ever-burning sulphur unconsumed:
70 Such place Eternal Justice had prepared
For those rebellious, here their prison ordained
In utter darkness, and their portion set
As far removed from God and light of Heav'n
As from the center thrice to th' utmost pole.[4]
75 O how unlike the place from whence they fell!
There the companions of his fall, o'erwhelmed
With floods and whirlwinds of tempestuous fire,
He soon discerns, and welt'ring° by his side   *rolling in the waves*
One next himself in power, and next in crime,
80 Long after known in Palestine, and named
Beëlzebub.[5] To whom th' Arch-Enemy,
And thence in Heav'n called Satan,[6] with bold words
Breaking the horrid silence thus began.
    "If thou beest he; but O how fall'n![7] how changed
85 From him, who in the happy realms of light
Clothed with transcendent brightness didst outshine
Myriads though bright: if he whom mutual league,
United thoughts and counsels, equal hope
And hazard in the glorious enterprise,
90 Joined with me once, now misery hath joined
In equal ruin: into what pit thou seest
From what height fall'n, so much the stronger proved
He with his thunder:° and till then who knew   *thunderbolt*
The force of those dire arms? Yet not for those,
95 Nor what the potent victor in his rage
Can else inflict, do I repent or change,
Though changed in outward luster, that fixed mind
And high disdain, from sense of injured merit,
That with the mightiest raised me to contend,
100 And to the fierce contention brought along
Innumerable force of spirits armed
That durst dislike his reign, and me preferring,
His utmost power with adverse power opposed
In dubious° battle on the plains of Heav'n,   *of uncertain outcome*
105 And shook his throne. What though the field be lost?
All is not lost; the unconquerable will,
And study° of revenge, immortal hate,   *intense consideration*

3. The phrase alludes to Dante ("All hope abandon, ye who enter here").
4. Milton makes use of various images of the cosmos in *Paradise Lost*: (1) the earth is the center of the (Ptolemaic) cosmos of ten concentric spheres; (2) the earth and the whole cosmos are an appendage hanging from Heaven by a golden chain; (3) the cosmos seems Copernican from the angels' perspective (see Book 8). Here, the fall from Heaven to Hell is described as thrice as far as the distance from the center (earth) to the outermost sphere.

5. A Phoenician deity, or Baal (the name means "Lord of Flies"). He is called the prince of devils in Matthew 12.24. As with the other fallen angels, his angelic name has been obliterated, and he is now called by the name he will bear as a pagan deity. That literary strategy evokes all the evil associations attaching to those names in human history.
6. In Hebrew the name means "adversary."
7. Alludes to Isaiah 14.12: "How art thou fallen from heaven, O Lucifer, Son of the morning."

And courage never to submit or yield:
And what is else not to be overcome?[8]
110　That glory never shall his wrath or might
Extort from me. To bow and sue for grace
With suppliant knee, and deify his power
Who from the terror of this arm so late
Doubted° his empire, that were low indeed,   *feared for*
115　That were an ignominy and shame beneath
This downfall; since by fate the strength of gods[9]
And this empyreal substance cannot fail,°   *cease to exist*
Since through experience of this great event
In arms not worse, in foresight much advanced,
120　We may with more successful hope resolve
To wage by force or guile eternal war
Irreconcilable, to our grand foe,
Who now triúmphs, and in th' excess of joy
Sole reigning holds the tyranny of Heav'n."
125　　So spake th' apostate angel, though in pain,
Vaunting aloud, but racked with deep despair:
And him thus answered soon his bold compeer.°   *comrade*
　　"O Prince, O Chief of many thronéd Powers,
That led th' embattled Seraphim[1] to war
130　Under thy conduct, and in dreadful deeds
Fearless, endangered Heav'ns perpetual King;
And put to proof his high supremacy,
Whether upheld by strength, or chance, or fate;
Too well I see and rue the dire event,°   *outcome*
135　That with sad overthrow and foul defeat
Hath lost us Heav'n, and all this mighty host
In horrible destruction laid thus low,
As far as gods and heav'nly essences
Can perish: for the mind and spirit remains
140　Invincible, and vigor soon returns,
Though all our glory extinct, and happy state
Here swallowed up in endless misery.
But what if he our conqueror (whom I now
Of force° believe almighty, since no less   *necessarily*
145　Than such could have o'erpow'red such force as ours)
Have left us this our spirit and strength entire
Strongly to suffer and support our pains,
That we may so suffice° his vengeful ire,   *satisfy*
Or do him mightier service as his thralls
150　By right of war, whate'er his business be
Here in the heart of Hell to work in fire,
Or do his errands in the gloomy deep;
What can it then avail though yet we feel

---

8. I.e., what else does it mean not to be overcome?
9. A term commonly used in the poem for angels. But to Satan and his followers it means more, as Satan claims the position of a god, subject to fate but nothing else. Their substance is "empyreal" (next line), of the empyrean.

1. According to tradition, there were nine orders of angels, arranged hierarchically—seraphim, cherubim, thrones, dominions, virtues, powers, principalities, archangels, and angels. The poem makes use of some of these titles but does not keep this hierarchy.

Strength undiminished, or eternal being
155 To undergo eternal punishment?"
Whereto with speedy words th' Arch-Fiend replied.
    "Fall'n Cherub, to be weak is miserable
Doing or suffering: but of this be sure,
To do aught° good never will be our task,   *anything*
160 But ever to do ill our sole delight,
As being the contrary to his high will
Whom we resist. If then his providence
Out of our evil seek to bring forth good,
Our labor must be to pervert that end,
165 And out of good still to find means of evil;
Which ofttimes may succeed, so as perhaps
Shall grieve him, if I fail° not, and disturb   *err*
His inmost counsels from their destined aim.
But see the angry victor hath recalled
170 His ministers of vengeance and pursuit
Back to the gates of Heav'n: the sulphurous hail
Shot after us in storm, o'erblown hath laid°   *calmed*
The fiery surge, that from the precipice
Of Heav'n received us falling, and the thunder,
175 Winged with red lightning and impetuous rage,
Perhaps hath spent his shafts, and ceases now
To bellow through the vast and boundless deep.
Let us not slip° th' occasion, whether scorn,   *let slip*
Or satiate fury yield it from our foe.
180 Seest thou yon dreary plain, forlorn and wild,
The seat of desolation, void of light,
Save what the glimmering of these livid° flames   *bluish*
Casts pale and dreadful? Thither let us tend
From off the tossing of these fiery waves,
185 There rest, if any rest can harbor there,
And reassembling our afflicted powers,°   *armies*
Consult how we may henceforth most offend°   *harm, vex*
Our enemy, our own loss how repair,
How overcome this dire calamity,
190 What reinforcement we may gain from hope,
If not what resolution from despair."[2]
    Thus Satan talking to his nearest mate
With head uplift above the wave, and eyes
That sparkling blazed, his other parts besides
195 Prone on the flood, extended long and large
Lay floating many a rood,[3] in bulk as huge
As whom° the fables name of monstrous size,   *as those whom*
Titanian, or Earth-born, that warred on Jove,
Briareos or Typhon,[4] whom the den

---

2. Five of the last nine lines of Satan's speech rhyme.
3. An old unit of measure, between six and eight yards.
4. Both the Titans, led by Briareos (said to have had a hundred hands), and the earth-born Giants, represented by Typhon (who lived in Cilicea near Tarsus and was said to have had a hundred heads), fought with Jove. They were punished by being thrown into the underworld. Christian mythographers found in these stories an analogy to Satan's revolt and punishment.

200 By ancient Tarsus held, or that sea-beast
Leviathan,[5] which God of all his works
Created hugest that swim th' ocean stream:
Him haply° slumb'ring on the Norway foam   *perhaps*
The pilot of some small night-foundered° skiff,   *overcome by night*
205 Deeming some island, oft, as seamen tell,[6]
With fixèd anchor in his scaly rind
Moors by his side under the lee,° while night   *out of the wind*
Invests° the sea, and wishèd morn delays: *covers*
So stretched out huge in length the Arch-Fiend lay
210 Chained on the burning lake, nor ever thence
Had ris'n or heaved his head, but that the will
And high permission of all-ruling Heaven
Left him at large to his own dark designs,
That with reiterated crimes he might
215 Heap on himself damnation, while he sought
Evil to others, and enraged might see
How all his malice served but to bring forth
Infinite goodness, grace, and mercy shown
On man by him seduced, but on himself
220 Treble confusion, wrath, and vengeance poured.
Forthwith upright he rears from off the pool
His mighty stature; on each hand the flames
Driv'n backward slope their pointing spires,° and rolled *points of flames*
In billows, leave i' th' midst a horrid° vale.   *dreadful, bristling*
225 Then with expanded wings he steers his flight
Aloft, incumbent on° the dusky air   *resting on*
That felt unusual weight, till on dry land
He lights,° if it were land that ever burned   *alights*
With solid, as the lake with liquid fire,
230 And such appeared in hue; as when the force
Of subterranean wind transports a hill
Torn from Pelorus, or the shattered side
Of thund'ring Etna,[7] whose combustible
And fueled entrails thence conceiving fire,
235 Sublimed° with mineral fury, aid the winds,   *vaporized*
And leave a singèd bottom all involved°   *enveloped*
With stench and smoke: such resting found the sole
Of unblest feet. Him followed his next mate,
Both glorying to have scaped the Stygian° flood   *Styxlike, hellish*
240 As gods, and by their own recovered strength,
Not by the sufferance° of supernal power.   *permission*
   "Is this the region, this the soil, the clime,"
Said then the lost Archangel, "this the seat°   *estate*
That we must change for Heav'n, this mournful gloom
245 For that celestial light? Be it so, since he
Who now is sov'reign can dispose and bid

---

5. The whale, often identified with the great sea
monster and enemy of the Lord in Isaiah 17.1
and the crocodile-like dragon of Job 41. Both
were also identified with Satan.
6. The story of the deceived sailor and the illu-
sory island was a commonplace, but the reference to Norway suggests a 16th-century version
by Olaus Magnus, a Swedish historian.
7. Pelorus and Etna are volcanic mountains in
Sicily.

What shall be right: farthest from him is best
Whom reason hath equaled, force hath made supreme
Above his equals. Farewell happy fields
250 Where joy forever dwells: Hail horrors, hail
Infernal world, and thou profoundest Hell
Receive thy new possessor: one who brings
A mind not to be changed by place or time.
The mind is its own place, and in itself
255 Can make a Heav'n of Hell, a Hell of Heav'n.[8]
What matter where, if I be still the same,
And what I should be, all but less than° he   barely less than
Whom thunder hath made greater? Here at least
We shall be free; th' Almighty hath not built
260 Here for his envy,[9] will not drive us hence:
Here we may reign secure, and in my choice
To reign is worth ambition though in Hell:
Better to reign in Hell, than serve in Heav'n.[1]
But wherefore let we then our faithful friends,
265 Th' associates and copartners of our loss
Lie thus astonished° on th' oblivious pool,[2]   stunned
And call them not to share with us their part
In this unhappy mansion, or once more
With rallied arms to try what may be yet
270 Regained in Heav'n, or what more lost in Hell?"
        So Satan spake, and him Beëlzebub
Thus answered. "Leader of those armies bright,
Which but th' Omnipotent none could have foiled,
If once they hear that voice, their liveliest pledge
275 Of hope in fears and dangers, heard so oft
In worst extremes, and on the perilous edge°   front lines
Of battle when it raged, in all assaults
Their surest signal, they will soon resume
New courage and revive, though now they lie
280 Groveling and prostrate on yon lake of fire,
As we erewhile, astounded and amazed,
No wonder, fall'n such a pernicious highth."
        He scarce had ceased when the superior Fiend
Was moving toward the shore; his ponderous shield
285 Ethereal temper,[3] massy, large and round,
Behind him cast; the broad circumference
Hung on his shoulders like the moon, whose orb
Through optic glass the Tuscan artist views[4]
At evening from the top of Fesole,
290 Or in Valdarno, to descry new lands,
Rivers or mountains in her spotty globe.

---

8. Compare Satan's soliloquy, 4.32–113.
9. I.e., because he desires this place.
1. An ironic echo of *Odyssey* 11.489–91, where
the shade of Achilles tells Odysseus that it is better to be a farmhand on earth than king among
the dead.
2. The epithet "oblivious" is transferred from
the fallen angels to the pool into which they have

fallen.
3. I.e., tempered in celestial fire.
4. Galileo, who looked through a telescope
("optic glass") from the hill town of Fiesole, outside Florence, in the valley of the Arno River
("Valdarno," val d'Arno, line 290). In 1610 he
published a book describing the mountains on
the moon.

His spear, to equal which the tallest pine
Hewn on Norwegian hills, to be the mast
Of some great ammiral,° were but a wand   *admiral's ship*
295 He walked with to support uneasy steps
Over the burning marl,° not like those steps   *soil*
On heaven's azure; and the torrid clime
Smote on him sore besides, vaulted with fire;
Nathless° he so endured, till on the beach   *nevertheless*
300 Of that inflamed° sea, he stood and called   *flaming*
His legions, angel forms, who lay entranced
Thick as autumnal leaves that strow the brooks
In Vallombrosa,⁵ where th' Etrurian shades
High overarched embow'r;° or scattered sedge°   *form bowers / seaweed*
305 Afloat, when with fierce winds Orion armed
Hath vexed the Red Sea coast,⁶ whose waves o'erthrew
Busiris⁷ and his Memphian chivalry,
While with perfidious hatred they pursued
The sojourners of Goshen, who beheld
310 From the safe shore their floating carcasses
And broken chariot wheels; so thick bestrown
Abject and lost lay these, covering the flood,
Under amazement of their hideous change.
He called so loud, that all the hollow deep
315 Of Hell resounded. "Princes, Potentates,
Warriors, the flow'r of Heav'n, once yours, now lost,
If such astonishment as this can seize
Eternal Spirits: or have ye chos'n this place
After the toil of battle to repose
320 Your wearied virtue,° for the ease you find   *strength, valor*
To slumber here, as in the vales of Heav'n?
Or in this abject posture have ye sworn
To adore the conqueror? who now beholds
Cherub and Seraph rolling in the flood
325 With scattered arms and ensigns,° till anon   *battle flags*
His swift pursuers from Heav'n gates discern
Th' advantage, and descending tread us down
Thus drooping, or with linkèd thunderbolts
Transfix us to the bottom of this gulf.
330 Awake, arise, or be forever fall'n."
       They heard, and were abashed, and up they sprung
Upon the wing, as when men wont° to watch   *accustomed*
On duty, sleeping found by whom they dread,
Rouse and bestir themselves ere well awake.
335 Nor did they not perceive the evil plight
In which they were, or the fierce pains not feel;⁸

---

5. The name means "shady valley" and refers to a region high in the Apennines, about twenty miles from Florence, in Tuscany ("Etruria"). Similes comparing the numberless dead to falling leaves are frequent in epic (e.g., *Aeneid* 6.309–10).
6. Orion is a constellation whose rising near sunset in late summer and autumn was associated with storms in the Red Sea.

7. Mythical Egyptian pharaoh, whom Milton associates with the pharaoh of Exodus 14, who pursued the Israelites ("sojourners of Goshen," line 309) into the Red Sea, which God parted for them. His "chivalry" (following) are horsemen from Memphis.
8. The double negatives make a positive: they did perceive both plight and pain.

Yet to their general's voice they soon obeyed
Innumerable. As when the potent rod
Of Amram's son[9] in Egypt's evil day
340 Waved round the coast, up called a pitchy cloud
Of locusts, warping° on the eastern wind,   *swarming*
That o'er the realm of impious Pharaoh hung
Like night, and darkened all the land of Nile:
So numberless were those bad angels seen
345 Hovering on wing under the cope° of Hell   *roof*
'Twixt upper, nether, and surrounding fires;
Till, as a signal giv'n, th' uplifted spear
Of their great Sultan[1] waving to direct
Their course, in even balance down they light
350 On the firm brimstone, and fill all the plain;
A multitude, like which the populous north
Poured never from her frozen loins, to pass
Rhene or the Danaw, when her barbarous sons
Came like a deluge on the south, and spread
355 Beneath Gibraltar to the Libyan sands.[2]
Forthwith from every squadron and each band
The heads and leaders thither haste where stood
Their great commander; godlike shapes and forms
Excelling human, princely dignities,
360 And powers that erst° in Heaven sat on thrones;   *formerly*
Though of their names in heav'nly records now
Be no memorial, blotted out and razed°   *erased*
By their rebellion, from the Books of Life.
Nor had they yet among the sons of Eve
365 Got them new names, till wand'ring o'er the earth,
Through God's high sufferance for the trial of man,
By falsities and lies the greatest part
Of mankind they corrupted to forsake
God their Creator, and th' invisible
370 Glory of him that made them, to transform
Oft to the image of a brute, adorned
With gay religions° full of pomp and gold,   *showy rites*
And devils to adore for deities:
Then were they known to men by various names,
375 And various idols through the heathen world.
    Say, Muse, their names then known, who first, who last,[3]
Roused from the slumber on that fiery couch,
At their great emperor's call, as next in worth
Came singly° where he stood on the bare strand,   *one at a time*
380 While the promiscuous° crowd stood yet aloof.   *mixed*
    The chief were those who from the pit of Hell
Roaming to seek their prey on earth, durst fix

---

9. Moses, who drew down a plague of locusts on
Egypt (Exodus 10.12–15).
1. A first use of this description of Satan as an
Oriental despot.
2. The barbarian invasions of Rome began with

crossings of the Rhine ("Rhene") and Danube
("Danaw") rivers and spread across Spain, via
Gibraltar, to North Africa.
3. The catalogue of gods here is an epic convention; Homer catalogues ships; Virgil, warriors.

Their seats long after next the seat of God,[4]
Their altars by his altar, gods adored
385 Among the nations round, and durst abide
Jehovah thund'ring out of Zion, throned
Between the Cherubim;[5] yea, often placed
Within his sanctuary itself their shrines,
Abomination; and with cursèd things
390 His holy rites, and solemn feasts profaned,
And with their darkness durst affront his light.
First Moloch,[6] horrid king besmeared with blood
Of human sacrifice, and parents' tears,
Though for the noise of drums and timbrels° loud   *tambourines*
395 Their children's cries unheard, that passed through fire
To his grim idol. Him the Ammonite[7]
Worshipped in Rabba and her wat'ry plain,
In Argob and in Basan, to the stream
Of utmost Arnon. Nor content with such
400 Audacious neighborhood, the wisest heart
Of Solomon he led by fraud to build
His temple right against the temple of God
On that opprobrious hill, and made his grove
The pleasant valley of Hinnom, Tophet thence
405 And black Gehenna called, the type of Hell.[8]
Next Chemos,[9] th' obscene dread of Moab's sons,
From Aroer to Nebo, and the wild
Of southmost Abarim; in Hesebon
And Horanaim, Seon's realm, beyond
410 The flow'ry dale of Sibma clad with vines,
And Elealè to th' Asphaltic Pool.[1]
Peor[2] his other name, when he enticed
Israel in Sittim on their march from Nile
To do him wanton rites, which cost them woe.
415 Yet thence his lustful orgies he enlarged
Even to that hill of scandal,[3] by the grove
Of Moloch homicide, lust hard by° hate;   *close by*
Till good Josiah drove them thence to Hell.
With these came they, who from the bord'ring flood
420 Of old Euphrates to the brook that parts

---

4. The first group of devils come from the Middle East, close neighbors of Jehovah "throned" in his sanctuary in Jerusalem.
5. Golden cherubim adorned opposite ends of the gold cover on the Ark of the Covenant.
6. Moloch was a sun god, sometimes represented as a roaring bull or with a calf's head, within whose brazen image living children were supposedly burned as sacrifices.
7. The Ammonites lived east of the Jordan River. "Rabba" (next line) is modern Amman, in Jordan; "Argob," "Basan," "utmost Arnon" (lines 398–99) are lands east of the Dead Sea.
8. The rites of Moloch on "that opprobrious hill" (the Mount of Olives), just opposite the Jewish temple, and in the valley of Hinnom so polluted those places that they were turned into the refuse dump of Jerusalem. Under the name "Tophet" and "Gehenna," Hinnom became a type of Hell.
9. Chemos, or Chemosh, associated with Moloch in 1 Kings 11.7, was the god of the Moabites, whose lands (many drawn from Isaiah 15–16) are mentioned in the following lines.
1. The Dead Sea.
2. The story of Peor seducing the Israelites in Sittim is told in Numbers 25.
3. The Mount of Olives, where Solomon built temples for Chemos and Moloch (1 Kings 11.7); epithets were commonly attached to the names of gods, as in the next line, Moloch "homicide." Josiah (following line) destroyed pagan idols in Jerusalem and other cities (2 Chronicles 34).

Egypt from Syrian ground,[4] had general names
Of Baalim and Ashtaroth, those male,
These feminine.[5] For Spirits when they please
Can either sex assume, or both; so soft
425   And uncompounded is their essence pure,
Not tied or manacled with joint or limb,
Nor founded on the brittle strength of bones,
Like cumbrous flesh; but in what shape they choose
Dilated or condensed, bright or obscure,
430   Can execute their airy purposes,
And works of love or enmity fulfill.
For those the race of Israel oft forsook
Their Living Strength, and unfrequented left
His righteous altar, bowing lowly down
435   To bestial gods; for which their heads as low
Bowed down in battle, sunk before the spear
Of despicable foes. With these in troop
Came Astoreth, whom the Phoenicians called
Astartè, queen of Heav'n, with crescent horns;
440   To whose bright image nightly by the moon
Sidonian virgins[6] paid their vows and songs,
In Sion also not unsung, where stood
Her temple on th' offensive mountain,[7] built
By that uxorious king, whose heart though large,
445   Beguiled by fair idolatresses, fell
To idols foul. Thammuz[8] came next behind,
Whose annual wound in Lebanon allured
The Syrian damsels to lament his fate
In amorous ditties all a summer's day,
450   While smooth Adonis[9] from his native work
Ran purple to the sea, supposed with blood
Of Thammuz yearly wounded: the love-tale
Infected Sion's daughters with like heat,
Whose wanton passions in the sacred porch
455   Ezekiel[1] saw, when by the vision led
His eye surveyed the dark idolatries
Of alienated Judah. Next came one
Who mourned in earnest, when the captive ark
Maimed his brute image, head and hands lopped off
460   In his own temple, on the grunsel edge,[2]
Where he fell flat, and shamed his worshippers:

4. Palestine lies between the Euphrates and "the brook Besor" (1 Samuel 30.10).
5. Plural forms, masculine and feminine, respectively, denoting aspects of the sun god Baal and the moon goddess Astarte (called "Astoreth" in line 438, below).
6. Sidon and Tyre were the chief cities of Phoenicia.
7. The Mount of Olives again. "That uxorious king" (next line) is Solomon, who "loved many strange women" (2 Kings 11.1–8).
8. A Syrian god, supposedly killed by a boar in Lebanon; his Greek form was Adonis, beloved of

Aphrodite and god of the solar year. Annual festivals mourned his death and celebrated his revival as signifying the death and rebirth of vegetation.
9. Here, the Lebanese river named for the deity because every spring it turned bloodred from sedimentary mud.
1. The prophet complained that Jewish women were worshipping Thammuz (Ezekiel 8.14).
2. When the Philistines stole the ark of God, they placed it in the temple of their sea god, Dagon, but in the morning the mutilated statue of Dagon was found on the threshhold ("grunsel edge") (1 Samuel 5.1–5).

Dagon his name, sea monster, upward man
And downward fish: yet had his temple high
Reared in Azotus, dreaded through the coast
465 Of Palestine, in Gath and Ascalon
And Accaron and Gaza's[3] frontier bounds.
Him followed Rimmon,[4] whose delightful seat
Was fair Damascus, on the fertile banks
Of Abbana and Pharphar, lucid streams.
470 He also against the house of God was bold:
A leper once he lost and gained a king,
Ahaz his sottish conqueror, whom he drew
God's altar to disparage and displace
For one of Syrian mode,[5] whereon to burn
475 His odious off'rings, and adore the gods
Whom he had vanquished. After these appeared
A crew who under names of old renown,
Osiris, Isis, Orus[6] and their train
With monstrous shapes and sorceries abused
480 Fanatic Egypt and her priests, to seek
Their wand'ring gods disguised in brutish forms
Rather than human. Nor did Israel scape
Th' infection when their borrowed gold composed
The calf in Oreb:[7] and the rebel king
485 Doubled that sin in Bethel and in Dan,
Lik'ning his Maker to the grazèd ox,[8]
Jehovah, who in one night when he passed
From Egypt marching, equaled° with one stroke   *leveled*
Both her firstborn and all her bleating gods.[9]
490 Belial came last,[1] than whom a spirit more lewd
Fell not from Heaven, or more gross to love
Vice for itself: to him no temple stood
Or altar smoked; yet who more oft than he
In temples and at altars, when the priest
495 Turns atheist, as did Eli's sons,[2] who filled
With lust and violence the house of God.
In courts and palaces he also reigns
And in luxurious cities, where the noise
Of riot ascends above their loftiest tow'rs,
500 And injury and outrage: and when night

---

3. The five chief cities of the Philistines, sites of Dagon's worship.
4. A Phoenician god whose temple was in Damascus.
5. A Syrian general, Naaman, was cured of leprosy and converted from worship of Rimmon by the waters of the Jordan (2 Kings 5), while King Ahaz, an Israelite monarch who conquered Damascus, was converted there to Rimmon's worship.
6. The second group of devils includes the Egyptian gods driven from Heaven by the revolt of the giants (Ovid, *Metamorphoses* 5) and forced to wander in "monstrous" (next line) animal disguises.
7. In the wilderness of Egypt, while Moses was receiving the Law, Aaron made a golden calf,

thought to be an idol of the Egyptian god Apis and made of ornaments brought out of Egypt (Exodus 32).
8. Jeroboam, "the rebel king" who led the ten tribes of Israel in revolt against Solomon's son, Rehoboam; he doubled Aaron's sin by making two golden calves (1 Kings 12.25–30).
9. Jehovah smote the firstborn of all Egyptian families as well as their gods (Exodus 12.12).
1. Belial was never worshipped as a god; his name means "wickedness," but its use in phrases like "sons of Belial" encouraged personification.
2. Priests who were termed "sons of Belial" because they seized for themselves offerings made to God and lay with women who assembled at the door of the tarbernacle (1 Samuel 2.12–22).

Darkens the streets, then wander forth the sons
Of Belial, flown° with insolence and wine.³   *flushed*
Witness the streets of Sodom, and that night
In Gibeah, when the hospitable door
505   Exposed a matron to avoid worse rape.⁴
        These were the prime in order and in might;
The rest were long to tell, though far renowned,
Th' Ionian gods, of Javan's issue held
Gods, yet confessed later than Heav'n and Earth
510   Their boasted parents;⁵ Titan Heav'n's firstborn
With his enormous brood, and birthright seized
By younger Saturn, he from mightier Jove,
His own and Rhea's son, like measure found;
So Jove usurping reigned:⁶ these first in Crete
515   And Ida known, thence on the snowy top
Of cold Olympus ruled the middle air
Their highest heav'n; or on the Delphian cliff,
Or in Dodona, and through all the bounds
Of Doric land;⁷ or who with Saturn old
520   Fled over Adria to th' Hesperian fields,
And o'er the Celtic roamed the utmost isles.⁸
        All these and more came flocking; but with looks
Downcast and damp,° yet such wherein appeared   *depressed, dazed*
Obscure some glimpse of joy, to have found their chief
525   Not in despair, to have found themselves not lost
In loss itself; which on his count'nance cast
Like doubtful hue:⁹ but he his wonted° pride   *accustomed*
Soon recollecting, with high words, that bore
Semblance of worth, not substance, gently raised
530   Their fainting courage, and dispelled their fears.
Then straight° commands that at the warlike sound   *immediately*
Of trumpets loud and clarions be upreared
His mighty standard; that proud honor claimed
Azazel¹ as his right, a Cherub tall:
535   Who forthwith from the glittering staff unfurled
Th' imperial ensign, which full high advanced
Shone like a meteor streaming to the wind
With gems and golden luster rich emblazed,
Seraphic arms and trophies:² all the while

---

3. This passage, with its present-tense verbs, invites application to current examples—at court and in Restoration London.

4. Lot begged the Sodomites to rape his daughters rather than his (male) angel guests (Genesis 19); in Gibeah a Levite avoided "worse" (homosexual) rape by surrendering his concubine to riotous "sons of Belial" (Judges 19.21–30).

5. The Ionian Greeks ("Javan's issue," i.e., of the line of Javan, grandson of Noah) regarded the Titans as gods; their supposed parents were Heaven (Uranus) and Earth (Gaia).

6. The Titan Cronos, or Saturn, deposed his father, married his sister Rhea, and ruled until he was deposed by his son, Zeus (Jove), who had been reared in secret on Mount Ida in Crete.

7. Zeus and the other Olympian gods had their seat on Mount Olympus, in "middle air"; they were worshipped in Delphi, Dodona, and throughout Greece ("Doric lands").

8. Saturn, after his downfall, fled over "Adria" (the Adriatic Sea) to the "Hesperian fields" (Italy), crossed the "Celtic" fields of France, and thence to Britain, the "utmost isles."

9. Satan's face reflected the same mixed emotions.

1. Traditionally, one of the four standard-bearers in Satan's army. "Clarions" (line 532): small, shrill trumpets.

2. Their flags bear the heraldic arms of the various orders of angels and memorials of their battles.

540   Sonorous metal° blowing martial sounds: *trumpets*
       At which the universal host upsent
       A shout that tore Hell's concave,° and beyond   *vault*
       Frighted the reign of Chaos and old Night.[3]
       All in a moment through the gloom were seen
545   Ten thousand banners rise into the air
       With orient° colors waving: with them rose   *lustrous*
       A forest huge of spears: and thronging helms
       Appeared, and serried° shields in thick array   *pushed close together*
       Of depth immeasurable: anon they move
550   In perfect phalanx to the Dorian[4] mood
       Of flutes and soft recorders; such as raised
       To highth of noblest temper heroes old
       Arming to battle, and instead of rage
       Deliberate valor breathed, firm and unmoved
555   With dread of death to flight or foul retreat,
       Nor wanting power to mitigate and swage°   *assuage*
       With solemn touches, troubled thoughts, and chase
       Anguish and doubt and fear and sorrow and pain
       From mortal or immortal minds. Thus they
560   Breathing united force with fixèd thought
       Moved on in silence to soft pipes that charmed
       Their painful steps o'er the burnt soil; and now
       Advanced in view they stand, a horrid° front   *bristling with spears*
       Of dreadful length and dazzling arms, in guise
565   Of warriors old with ordered spear and shield,
       Awaiting what command their mighty chief
       Had to impose. He through the armèd files
       Darts his experienced eye, and soon traverse°   *across*
       The whole battalion views, their order due,
570   Their visages and stature as of gods,
       Their number last he sums. And now his heart
       Distends with pride, and hard'ning in his strength
       Glories: for never since created man[5]
       Met such embodied force, as named° with these   *composed*
575   Could merit more than that small infantry
       Warred on by cranes:[6] though all the giant brood
       Of Phlegra with th' heroic race were joined
       That fought at Thebes and Ilium,[7] on each side
       Mixed with auxiliar° gods; and what resounds   *allied*
580   In fable or romance of Uther's son
       Begirt with British and Armoric knights;
       And all who since, baptized or infidel
       Jousted in Aspramont or Montalban,
       Damasco, or Morocco, or Trebisond,

---

3. In *Paradise Lost* 2.894–909, 959–70 Chaos and Night rule the region of unformed matter between Heaven and earth.
4. Severe, martial music used by the Spartans marching to battle. "Phalanx": battle formation.
5. I.e., since the creation of man.
6. Pygmies (little people, with a pun, in "infantry" on "infants") had periodic fights with the cranes, in Pliny's account. Compared with Satan's forces, all other armies are puny.
7. In Greek mythology, the Giants fought the gods at Phlegra in Macedonia; in Roman myth, it was at Phlegra in Italy. Satan's forces surpass them, even if joined with the Seven who fought against Thebes and the whole Greek host that besieged Troy ("Ilium").

585 Or whom Biserta sent from Afric shore
When Charlemagne with all his peerage fell
By Fontarabia.[8] Thus far these beyond
Compare of mortal prowess, yet observed°   *obeyed*
Their dread commander: he above the rest
590 In shape and gesture proudly eminent
Stood like a tow'r; his form had yet not lost
All her[9] original brightness, nor appeared
Less than Archangel ruined, and th' excess
Of glory obscured: as when the sun new-ris'n
595 Looks through the horizontal° misty air   *on the horizon*
Shorn of his beams, or from behind the moon
In dim eclipse disastrous° twilight sheds   *ill-starred*
On half the nations, and with fear of change
Perplexes monarchs. Darkened so, yet shone
600 Above them all th' Archangel: but his face
Deep scars of thunder had intrenched,° and care   *furrowed*
Sat on his faded cheek, but under brows
Of dauntless courage, and considerate° pride   *conscious, deliberate*
Waiting revenge: cruel his eye, but cast
605 Signs of remorse and passion° to behold   *compassion, pain*
The fellows of his crime, the followers rather
(Far other once beheld in bliss) condemned
Forever now to have their lot in pain,
Millions of Spirits for his fault amerced°   *deprived*
610 Of Heav'n, and from eternal splendors flung
For his revolt, yet faithful how they stood,
Their glory withered: as when Heaven's fire
Hath scathed° the forest oaks, or mountain pines,   *damaged*
With singèd top their stately growth though bare
615 Stands on the blasted heath. He now prepared
To speak; whereat their doubled ranks they bend
From wing to wing, and half enclose him round
With all his peers: attention held them mute.
Thrice he essayed,° and thrice, in spite of scorn,   *attempted*
620 Tears such as angels weep burst forth: at last
Words interwove with sighs found out their way.
    "O myriads of immortal Spirits, O Powers
Matchless, but with th' Almighty, and that strife
Was not inglorious, though th' event° was dire,   *outcome*
625 As this place testifies, and this dire change
Hateful to utter: but what power of mind
Foreseeing or presaging, from the depth
Of knowledge past or present, could have feared,
How such united force of gods, how such
630 As stood like these, could ever know repulse?
For who can yet believe, though after loss,

8. Satan's forces also surpass the "British and Armoric" (from Brittany) knights who fought with King Arthur ("Uther's son") and all the romance knights who fought at the famous named sites in the following lines. Roncesvalles, near Fontara-

bia, was the place where Charlemagne's "peerage," including his best knight, Roland, were defeated in battle (though not Charlemagne himself).
9. *Forma* in Latin is feminine.

That all these puissant° legions, whose exile   *potent, powerful*
Hath emptied Heav'n, shall fail to reascend
Self-raised, and repossess their native seat?
635 For me, be witness all the host of Heav'n,
If counsels different,° or danger shunned   *contradictory*
By me, have lost our hopes. But he who reigns
Monarch in Heav'n, till then as one secure
Sat on his throne, upheld by old repute,
640 Consent or custom, and his regal state
Put forth at full, but still° his strength concealed,   *always*
Which tempted our attempt, and wrought our fall.
Henceforth his might we know, and know our own
So as not either to provoke, or dread
645 New war, provoked; our better part remains
To work in close design, by fraud or guile
What force effected not: that he no less
At length from us may find, who overcomes
By force, hath overcome but half his foe.
650 Space may produce new worlds; whereof so rife°   *common*
There went a fame° in Heav'n that he ere long   *rumor*
Intended to create, and therein plant
A generation, whom his choice regard
Should favor equal to the sons of Heaven:
655 Thither, if but to pry, shall be perhaps
Our first eruption,° thither or elsewhere: *breaking out*
For this infernal pit shall never hold
Celestial Spirits in bondage, not th' abyss
Long under darkness cover. But these thoughts
660 Full counsel must mature: peace is despaired,
For who can think submission? War then, war
Open or understood° must be resolved."   *covert*
    He spake: and to confirm his words, out flew
Millions of flaming swords, drawn from the thighs
665 Of mighty Cherubim; the sudden blaze
Far round illumined Hell: highly they raged
Against the Highest, and fierce with graspèd arms
Clashed on their sounding shields the din of war,[1]
Hurling defiance toward the vault of Heav'n.
670   There stood a hill not far whose grisly top
Belched fire and rolling smoke; the rest entire
Shone with a glossy scurf,° undoubted sign   *crust*
That in his womb was hid metallic ore,
The work of sulphur.[2] Thither winged with speed
675 A numerous brígade hastened. As when bands
Of pioneers° with spade and pickax armed   *military engineers*
Forerun the royal camp, to trench a field,
Or cast a rampart. Mammon[3] led them on,

---

1. Like Roman legionnaires, the fallen angels
applaud by beating swords on shields.
2. Sulfur and mercury were considered the basic
substances of all metals.
3. "Mammon," an abstract word for riches, came
to be personified and associated with the god of
wealth, Plutus, and so with Pluto, god of the
underworld. Cf. Matthew 6.24: "Ye cannot serve
God and mammon."

Mammon, the least erected Spirit that fell
680 From Heav'n, for ev'n in Heav'n his looks and thoughts
Were always downward bent, admiring more
The riches of Heav'n's pavement, trodden gold,
Than aught divine or holy else enjoyed
In vision beatific: by him first
685 Men also, and by his suggestion taught,
Ransacked the center, and with impious hands
Rifled the bowels of their mother earth
For treasures better hid. Soon had his crew
Opened into the hill a spacious wound
690 And digged out ribs of gold. Let none admire°   wonder
That riches grow in Hell; that soil may best
Deserve the precious bane.° And here let those   poison
Who boast in mortal things, and wond'ring tell
Of Babel, and the works of Memphian kings,[4]
695 Learn how their greatest monuments of fame,
And strength and art are easily outdone
By Spirits reprobate, and in an hour
What in an age they with incessant toil
And hands innumerable scarce perform.
700 Nigh on the plain in many cells prepared,
That underneath had veins of liquid fire
Sluiced from the lake, a second multitude
With wondrous art founded° the massy ore,   melted
Severing° each kind, and scummed the bullion dross:°   separating / boiling dregs
705 A third as soon had formed within the ground
A various mold, and from the boiling cells
By strange conveyance filled each hollow nook,
As in an organ from one blast of wind
To many a row of pipes the soundboard breathes.
710 Anon out of the earth a fabric huge
Rose like an exhalation, with the sound
Of dulcet symphonies and voices sweet,
Built like a temple,[5] where pilasters° round   columns set in a wall
Were set, and Doric pillars[6] overlaid
715 With golden architrave; nor did there want
Cornice or frieze, with bossy° sculptures grav'n;   embossed
The roof was fretted° gold. Not Babylon,   richly ornamented
Nor great Alcairo such magnificence
Equaled in all their glories, to enshrine
720 Belus or Serapis[7] their gods, or seat
Their kings, when Egypt with Assyria strove
In wealth and luxury. Th' ascending pile
Stood fixed° her stately height, and straight° the doors   complete / at once
Opening their brazen folds discover° wide   reveal

4. The Tower of Babel and the pyramids of Egypt.
5. After melting the gold with fire from the lake
and pouring it into molds, the devils cause their
building to rise as by magic, to the sounds of marvelous music.
6. Doric pillars are severe and plain. The devils'
palace combines classical architectural features

with elaborate ornamentation, suggesting, perhaps, St. Peter's in Rome.
7. At Babylon, in Assyria, there were temples
to "Belus" or Baal; at Alcairo (modern Cairo,
ancient Memphis), in Egypt, they were to Osiris
("Serapis").

725 Within, her ample spaces, o'er the smooth
And level pavement: from the archèd roof
Pendent by subtle magic many a row
Of starry lamps and blazing cressets[8] fed
With naphtha and asphaltus yielded light
730 As from a sky. The hasty multitude
Admiring entered, and the work some praise
And some the architect: his hand was known
In Heav'n by many a towered structure high,
Where sceptered angels held their residence,
735 And sat as princes, whom the Súpreme King
Exalted to such power, and gave to rule,
Each in his hierarchy, the orders bright.
Nor was his name unheard or unadored
In ancient Greece and in Ausonian land
740 Men called him Mulciber[9] and how he fell
From Heav'n, they fabled, thrown by angry Jove
Sheer o'er the crystal battlements: from morn
To noon he fell, from noon to dewy eve,
A summer's day; and with the setting sun
745 Dropped from the zenith like a falling star,
On Lemnos th' Aégean isle: thus they relate,
Erring; for he with this rebellious rout
Fell long before; nor aught availed him now
To have built in Heav'n high tow'rs; nor did he scape
750 By all his engines, but was headlong sent
With his industrious crew to build in Hell.
    Meanwhile the wingèd heralds by command
Of sov'reign power, with awful ceremony
And trumpet's sound throughout the host proclaim
755 A solemn council forthwith to be held
At Pandemonium,[1] the high capitol
Of Satan and his peers:° their summons called   *nobles*
From every band and squarèd regiment
By place° or choice° the worthiest; they anon   *rank / election*
760 With hundreds and with thousands trooping came
Attended: all access was thronged, the gates
And porches wide, but chief the spacious hall
(Though like a covered field, where champions bold
Wont ride in armed, and at the soldan's° chair   *sultan's*
765 Defied the best of paynim° chivalry   *pagan*
To mortal combat or career with lance)
Thick swarmed, both on the ground and in the air,
Brushed with the hiss of rustling wings. As bees
In springtime, when the sun with Taurus rides,[2]
770 Pour forth their populous youth about the hive
In clusters; they among fresh dews and flowers

8. Basketlike lamps, hung from the ceiling.
9. Hephaestus, or Vulcan, was sometimes known in "Ausonian land" (Italy) as "Mulciber." The story of Jove's tossing him out of Heaven (see following lines) is told in Book 1 of the *Iliad*.

1. "Pandemonium" (a Miltonic coinage) means literally "all demons," an inversion of "pantheon," "all gods."
2. The sun is in the zodiacal sign of Taurus from about April 19 to May 20.

Fly to and fro, or on the smoothèd plank,
The suburb of their straw-built citadel,
New rubbed with balm, expatiate and confer[3]
775   Their state affairs. So thick the aery crowd
Swarmed and were straitened; till the signal giv'n,
Behold a wonder! They but now who seemed
In bigness to surpass Earth's giant sons
Now less than smallest dwarfs, in narrow room
780   Throng numberless, like that Pygmean race
Beyond the Indian mount,[4] or fairy elves,
Whose midnight revels, by a forest side
Or fountain some belated peasant sees,
Or dreams he sees, while overhead the moon
785   Sits arbitress,° and nearer to the earth   *witness*
Wheels her pale course: they on their mirth and dance
Intent, with jocund° music charm his ear;[5]   *merry*
At once with joy and fear his heart rebounds.
Thus incorporeal Spirits to smallest forms
790   Reduced their shapes immense, and were at large,
Though without number still amidst the hall
Of that infernal court. But far within
And in their own dimensions like themselves
The great Seraphic Lords and Cherubim
795   In close recess and secret conclave sat,
A thousand demigods on golden seats,
Frequent and full.[6] After short silence then
And summons read, the great consult[7] began.

Book 2

The Argument

The consultation begun, Satan debates whether another battle be to be hazarded for the recovery of heaven: some advise it, others dissuade: a third proposal is preferred, mentioned before by Satan, to search the truth of that prophecy or tradition in heaven concerning another world, and another kind of creature equal or not much inferior to themselves, about this time to be created: their doubt who shall be sent on this difficult search; Satan their chief undertakes alone the voyage, is honored and applauded. The council thus ended, the rest betake them several ways and to several employments, as their inclinations lead them, to entertain the time till Satan return. He passes on his journey to hell gates, finds them shut, and who sat there to guard them, by whom at length they are opened, and discover to him the great gulf between hell and heaven; with what difficulty he passes through, directed by Chaos, the power of that place, to the sight of this new world which he sought.

---

3. Spread out and discuss. Bee similes were common in epic from Homer on; also, the bees' (royalist) society was often cited in political argument. The simile prepares for the sudden contraction of the devils, who can shrink or dilate at will.

4. The pygmies were supposed to live beyond the Himalayas.
5. The belated peasant's.
6. Crowded together, and in full complement.
7. Consultation, often secret and seditious.

High on a throne of royal state, which far
Outshone the wealth of Ormus and of Ind,[1]
Or where the gorgeous East with richest hand
Show'rs on her kings barbaric pearl and gold,
5 Satan exalted sat, by merit raised
To that bad eminence; and from despair
Thus high uplifted beyond hope, aspires
Beyond thus high, insatiate to pursue
Vain war with Heav'n, and by success° untaught   *the outcome*
10 His proud imaginations° thus displayed.   *schemes*
　　"Powers and Dominions,[2] deities of Heaven,
For since no deep within her gulf can hold
Immortal vigor, though oppressed and fall'n,
I give not Heav'n for lost. From this descent
15 Celestial Virtues rising, will appear
More glorious and more dread than from no fall,
And trust themselves to fear no second fate.
Me though just right, and the fixed laws of Heav'n
Did first create your leader, next, free choice,
20 With what besides, in counsel or in fight,
Hath been achieved of merit, yet this loss
Thus far at least recovered, hath much more
Established in a safe unenvied throne
Yielded with full consent. The happier state
25 In Heav'n, which follows dignity, might draw
Envy from each inferior; but who here
Will envy whom the highest place exposes
Foremost to stand against the Thunderer's aim
Your bulwark, and condemns to greatest share
30 Of endless pain? Where there is then no good
For which to strive, no strife can grow up there
From faction; for none sure will claim in Hell
Precédence, none, whose portion is so small
Of present pain, that with ambitious mind
35 Will covet more. With this advantage then
To union, and firm faith, and firm accord,
More than can be in Heav'n, we now return
To claim our just inheritance of old,
Surer to prosper than prosperity
40 Could have assured us;[3] and by what best way,
Whether of open war or covert guile,[4]
We now debate; who can advise, may speak."
　　He ceased, and next him Moloch, sceptered king
Stood up, the strongest and the fiercest Spirit
45 That fought in Heav'n; now fiercer by despair:
His trust was with th' Eternal to be deemed
Equal in strength, and rather than be less

1. India. "Ormus": an island in the Persian Gulf,
modern Hormuz, famous for pearls.
2. Angelic orders.
3. Note the play on "surer," "prosper," "prosperity," "assured," a favorite device of Milton's.

4. A typical epic convention (in Homer, Virgil,
Tasso, and elsewhere) involved councils debating
war or peace, with spokesmen on each side. Satan
offers only the option of war, open or covert.

Cared not to be at all; with that care lost
Went all his fear: of God, or Hell, or worse
50 He recked° not, and these words thereafter spake.   *cared*
    "My sentence° is for open war: of wiles,   *judgment*
More unexpért,° I boast not: them let those   *less experienced*
Contrive who need, or when they need, not now.
For while they sit contriving, shall the rest,
55 Millions that stand in arms, and longing wait
The signal to ascend, sit lingering here
Heav'n's fugitives, and for their dwelling place
Accept this dark opprobrious den of shame,
The prison of his tyranny who reigns
60 By our delay? No, let us rather choose
Armed with Hell flames and fury all at once
O'er Heav'n's high tow'rs to force resistless way,
Turning our tortures into horrid° arms   *bristling, horrifying*
Against the Torturer; when to meet the noise
65 Of his almighty engine° he shall hear   *the thunderbolt*
Infernal thunder, and for lightning see
Black fire and horror shot with equal rage
Among his angels; and his throne itself
Mixed with Tartarean⁵ sulfur, and strange fire,
70 His own invented torments. But perhaps
The way seems difficult and steep to scale
With upright wing against a higher foe.
Let such bethink them, if the sleepy drench°   *large draught*
Of that forgetful° lake benumb not still,   *causing oblivion*
75 That in our proper° motion we ascend   *natural to us*
Up to our native seat: descent and fall
To us is adverse. Who but felt of late
When the fierce foe hung on our broken rear
Insulting,⁶ and pursued us through the deep,
80 With what compulsion and laborious flight
We sunk thus low? Th' ascent is easy then;
Th' event° is feared; should we again provoke   *outcome*
Our stronger, some worse way his wrath may find
To our destruction: if there be in Hell
85 Fear to be worse destroyed: what can be worse
Than to dwell here, driven out from bliss, condemned
In this abhorrèd deep to utter woe;
Where pain of unextinguishable fire
Must exercise° us without hope of end   *vex, afflict*
90 The vassals⁷ of his anger, when the scourge
Inexorably, and the torturing hour
Calls us to penance? More destroyed than thus
We should be quite abolished and expire.
What fear we then? What° doubt we to incense   *why*
95 His utmost ire? which to the height enraged,
Will either quite consume us, and reduce

---

5. Tartarus is a classical name for hell.
6. With the Latin sense of stamping on; also, triumphantly scorning.

7. Servants, but perhaps also vessels. See Romans
9.22: "vessels of wrath fitted to destruction."

To nothing this essential,° happier far   *essence*
Than miserable to have eternal being:
Or if our substance be indeed divine,
100 And cannot cease to be, we are at worst
On this side nothing;[8] and by proof we feel
Our power sufficient to disturb his Heav'n,
And with perpetual inroads to alarm,
Though inaccessible, his fatal[9] throne:
105 Which if not victory is yet revenge."
    He ended frowning, and his look, denounced°   *portended*
Desperate revenge, and battle dangerous
To less than gods. On th' other side up rose
Belial, in act more graceful and humane;°   *civil, polite*
110 A fairer person lost not Heav'n; he seemed
For dignity composed and high exploit:
But all was false and hollow; though his tongue
Dropped manna, and could make the worse appear
The better reason,[1] to perplex and dash°   *confuse*
115 Maturest counsels: for his thoughts were low;
To vice industrious, but to nobler deeds
Timorous and slothful: yet he pleased the ear,
And with persuasive accent thus began.
    "I should be much for open war, O Peers,
120 As not behind in hate; if what was urged
Main reason to persuade immediate war,
Did not dissuade me most, and seem to cast
Ominous conjecture on the whole success:
When he who most excels in fact° of arms,   *feat*
125 In what he counsels and in what excels
Mistrustful, grounds his courage on despair
And utter dissolution, as the scope
Of all his aim, after some dire revenge.
First, what revenge? The tow'rs of Heav'n are filled
130 With armèd watch, that render all access
Impregnable; oft on the bordering deep
Encamp their legions, or with óbscure wing
Scout far and wide into the realm of Night,
Scorning surprise. Or could we break our way
135 By force, and at our heels all Hell should rise
With blackest insurrection, to confound
Heav'n's purest light, yet our great enemy
All incorruptible would on his throne
Sit unpolluted, and th' ethereal mold[2]
140 Incapable of stain would soon expel
Her mischief, and purge off the baser fire
Victorious. Thus repulsed, our final hope
Is flat despair: we must exasperate

---

8. I.e., we cannot be worse off than we are now, and still live.
9. Established by Fate; also, deadly.
1. The Sophists, mercenary teachers of rhetoric in ancient Greece, were denounced by Plato for making "the worse appear / The better reason."

"His tongue / Dropped manna": his honeyed words seemed like the manna supplied to the Israelites in the desert.
2. Heavenly substance, derived from "ether," the fifth and purest element, thought to be incorruptible.

Th' almighty victor to spend all his rage,
145 And that must end us, that must be our cure,
To be no more; sad cure; for who would lose,
Though full of pain, this intellectual being,
Those thoughts that wander through eternity,
To perish rather, swallowed up and lost
150 In the wide womb of uncreated night,
Devoid of sense and motion? And who knows,
Let this be good, whether our angry foe
Can give it, or will ever? How he can
Is doubtful; that he never will is sure.
155 Will he, so wise, let loose at once his ire,
Belike° through impotence, or unaware,   *perhaps*
To give his enemies their wish, and end
Them in his anger, whom his anger saves
To punish endless? 'Wherefore cease we then?'
160 Say they who counsel war, 'We are decreed,
Reserved and destined to eternal woe;
Whatever doing, what can we suffer more,
What can we suffer worse?' Is this then worst,
Thus sitting, thus consulting, thus in arms?
165 What when we fled amain,° pursued and strook°   *headlong / struck*
With Heav'n's afflicting thunder, and besought
The deep to shelter us? This Hell then seemed
A refuge from those wounds. Or when we lay
Chained on the burning lake? That sure was worse.
170 What if the breath that kindled those grim fires
Awaked should blow them into sevenfold rage
And plunge us in the flames? Or from above
Should intermitted° vengeance arm again   *suspended*
His red right hand to plague us? What if all
175 Her° stores were opened, and this firmament°   *Hell's / sky*
Of Hell should spout her cataracts° of fire,   *cascades*
Impendent[3] horrors, threat'ning hideous fall
One day upon our heads; while we perhaps
Designing or exhorting glorious war,
180 Caught in a fiery tempest shall be hurled
Each on his rock transfixed, the sport and prey
Of racking whirlwinds, or forever sunk
Under yon boiling ocean, wrapped in chains;
There to converse with everlasting groans,
185 Unrespited, unpitied, unreprieved,
Ages of hopeless end; this would be worse.
War therefore, open or concealed, alike
My voice dissuades; for what can force or guile[4]
With him, or who deceive his mind, whose eye
190 Views all things at one view? He from Heav'n's high
All these our motions° vain, sees and derides;   *proposals*
Not more almighty to resist our might

---

3. In the Latin sense, hanging down, threatening.

4. The verb "accomplish" or "achieve" is understood.

Than wise to frustrate all our plots and wiles.
Shall we then live thus vile, the race of Heav'n
195 Thus trampled, thus expelled to suffer here
Chains and these torments? Better these than worse
By my advice; since fate inevitable
Subdues us, and omnipotent decree,
The victor's will. To suffer, as to do,
200 Our strength is equal, nor the law unjust
That so ordains: this was at first resolved,
If we were wise, against so great a foe
Contending, and so doubtful what might fall.
I laugh, when those who at the spear are bold
205 And vent'rous, if that fail them, shrink and fear
What yet they know must follow, to endure
Exile, or ignominy, or bonds, or pain,
The sentence of their conqueror: This is now
Our doom; which if we can sustain and bear,
210 Our Súpreme Foe in time may much remit
His anger, and perhaps thus far removed
Not mind us not offending, satisfied
With what is punished; whence these raging fires
Will slacken, if his breath stir not their flames.
215 Our purer essence then will overcome
Their noxious vapor, or inured° not feel,   *accustomed*
Or changed at length, and to the place conformed
In temper and in nature, will receive
Familiar the fierce heat, and void of pain;
220 This horror will grow mild, this darkness light,
Besides what hope the never-ending flight
Of future days may bring, what chance, what change
Worth waiting, since our present lot appears
For happy though but ill, for ill not worst,[5]
225 If we procure not to ourselves more woe."
    Thus Belial, with words clothed in reason's garb,
Counseled ignoble ease and peaceful sloth,
Not peace: and after him thus Mammon spake.
    "Either to disenthrone the King of Heav'n
230 We war, if war be best, or to regain
Our own right lost: him to unthrone we then
May hope when everlasting Fate shall yield
To fickle Chance, and Chaos judge the strife:
The former vain to hope argues° as vain   *proves*
235 The latter: for what place can be for us
Within Heav'n's bound, unless Heav'n's Lord supreme
We overpower? Suppose he should relent
And publish grace to all, on promise made
Of new subjection; with what eyes could we
240 Stand in his presence humble, and receive
Strict laws imposed, to celebrate his throne
With warbled hymns, and to his Godhead sing

5. I.e., from the point of view of happiness, the devils are in an ill state, but it could be worse.

Forced hallelujahs; while he lordly sits
Our envied Sov'reign, and his altar breathes
245 Ambrosial° odors and ambrosial flowers,   *fragrant, immortal*
Our servile offerings. This must be our task
In Heav'n, this our delight; how wearisome
Eternity so spent in worship paid
To whom we hate. Let us not then pursue
250 By force impossible, by leave obtained
Unácceptable, though in Heav'n, our state
Of splendid vassalage,° but rather seek   *servitude*
Our own good from ourselves, and from our own
Live to ourselves, though in this vast recess,
255 Free, and to none accountable, preferring
Hard liberty before the easy yoke
Of servile pomp. Our greatness will appear
Then most conspicuous, when great things of small,
Useful of hurtful, prosperous of adverse
260 We can create, and in what place soe'er
Thrive under evil, and work ease out of pain
Through labor and endurance. This deep world
Of darkness do we dread? How oft amidst
Thick clouds and dark doth Heav'n's all-ruling Sire
265 Choose to reside, his glory unobscured,
And with the majesty of darkness round
Covers his throne; from whence deep thunders roar
Must'ring their rage, and Heav'n resembles Hell?
As he our darkness, cannot we his light
270 Imitate when we please? This desert soil
Wants° not her hidden luster, gems and gold;   *lacks*
Nor want we skill or art, from whence to raise
Magnificence; and what can Heav'n show more?
Our torments also may in length of time
275 Become our elements, these piercing fires
As soft as now severe, our temper° changed   *constitution*
Into their temper; which must needs remove
The sensible of pain.[6] All things invite
To peaceful counsels, and the settled state
280 Of order, how in safety best we may
Compose° our present evils, with regard   *come to terms with*
Of what we are and where, dismissing quite
All thoughts of war: ye have what I advise."
    He scarce had finished, when such murmur filled
285 Th' assembly, as when hollow rocks retain
The sound of blust'ring winds, which all night long
Had roused the sea, now with hoarse cadence lull
Seafaring men o'erwatched,° whose bark by chance   *worn out from watching*
Or pinnace° anchors in a craggy bay   *boat*
290 After the tempest: such applause was heard
As Mammon ended, and his sentence pleased,
Advising peace: for such another field°   *battlefield*

6. Pain felt by the senses.

They dreaded worse than Hell: so much the fear
Of thunder and the sword of Michaël[7]
295 Wrought still within them; and no less desire
To found this nether empire, which might rise
By policy,° and long process of time, statecraft
In emulation opposite to Heav'n.
Which then Beëlzebub perceived, than whom,
300 Satan except, none higher sat, with grave
Aspect he rose, and in his rising seemed
A pillar of state; deep on his front° engraven brow
Deliberation sat and public care;
And princely counsel in his face yet shone,
305 Majestic though in ruin: sage he stood
With Atlantean[8] shoulders fit to bear
The weight of mightiest monarchies; his look
Drew audience and attention still as night
Or summer's noontide air, while thus he spake.
310 "Thrones and imperial Powers, offspring of Heav'n
Ethereal Virtues; or these titles[9] now
Must we renounce, and changing style° be called title
Princes of Hell? for so the popular vote
Inclines, here to continue, and build up here
315 A growing empire. Doubtless! while we dream,
And know not that the King of Heav'n hath doomed
This place our dungeon, not our safe retreat
Beyond his potent arm, to live exempt
From Heav'n's high jurisdiction, in new league
320 Banded against his throne, but to remain
In strictest bondage, though thus far removed,
Under th' inevitable curb, reserved
His captive multitude: for he, be sure,
In height or depth, still first and last will reign
325 Sole King, and of his kingdom lose no part
By our revolt, but over Hell extend
His empire, and with iron scepter rule
Us here, as with his golden those in Heav'n.
What° sit we then projecting peace and war? why
330 War hath determined us,[1] and foiled with loss
Irreparable; terms of peace yet none
Vouchsafed° or sought; for what peace will be giv'n granted
To us enslaved, but custody severe,
And stripes, and arbitrary punishment
335 Inflicted? And what peace can we return,
But, to our power,[2] hostility and hate,
Untamed reluctance,° and revenge though slow, resistance
Yet ever plotting how the conqueror least
May reap his conquest, and may least rejoice
340 In doing what we most in suffering feel?

7. The warrior angel, chief of the angelic armies.
8. Worthy of Atlas, the Titan who as a punishment for rebellion was condemned to hold up the heavens on his shoulders.
9. The official titles of angelic orders.
1. I.e., war has decided the question for us, but also limited us.
2. I.e., to the best of our power.

Nor will occasion want,° nor shall we need   *be lacking*
With dangerous expedition to invade
Heav'n, whose high walls fear no assault or siege,
Or ambush from the deep. What if we find
345   Some easier enterprise? There is a place
(If ancient and prophetic fame° in Heav'n   *rumor*
Err not) another world, the happy seat
Of some new race called Man, about this time
To be created like to us, though less
350   In power and excellence, but favored more
Of him who rules above; so was his will
Pronounced among the gods, and by an oath,
That shook Heav'n's whole circumference, confirmed.
Thither let us bend all our thoughts, to learn
355   What creatures there inhabit, of what mold,
Or substance, how endued,° and what their power,   *endowed*
And where their weakness, how attempted° best,   *attacked, tempted*
By force or subtlety. Though Heav'n be shut,
And Heav'n's high arbitrator sit secure
360   In his own strength, this place may lie exposed,
The utmost border of his kingdom, left
To their defense who hold it:[3] here perhaps
Some advantageous act may be achieved
By sudden onset, either with hellfire
365   To waste° his whole creation, or possess   *lay waste*
All as our own, and drive as we were driven,
The puny habitants, or if not drive,
Seduce them to our party, that their God
May prove their foe, and with repenting hand
370   Abolish his own works.[4] This would surpass
Common revenge, and interrupt his joy
In our confusion, and our joy upraise
In his disturbance; when his darling sons
Hurled headlong to partake with us, shall curse
375   Their frail original,° and faded bliss,   *originator, parent*
Faded so soon. Advise° if this be worth   *consider*
Attempting, or to sit in darkness here
Hatching vain empires." Thus Beëlzebub
Pleaded his devilish counsel, first devised
380   By Satan, and in part proposed: for whence,
But from the author of all ill could spring
So deep a malice, to confound° the race   *ruin*
Of mankind in one root,[5] and earth with Hell
To mingle and involve, done all to spite
385   The great Creator? But their spite still serves
His glory to augment. The bold design
Pleased highly those infernal States,° and joy   *nobles*
Sparkled in all their eyes; with full assent
They vote: whereat his speech he thus renews.

---

3. To be defended by the occupants.
4. Cf. Genesis 6.7: "And the Lord said, 'I will destroy man [and all other creatures]; for it repen- teth me that I have made them.'"
5. Adam, the first man, is the "root" of the human race.

390   "Well have ye judged, well ended long debate,
     Synod of gods, and like to what ye are,
     Great things resolved, which from the lowest deep
     Will once more lift us up, in spite of fate,
     Nearer our ancient seat; perhaps in view
395   Of those bright confines, whence with neighboring arms
     And opportune excursion we may chance
     Reenter Heav'n; or else in some mild zone
     Dwell not unvisited of Heav'n's fair light
     Secure, and at the bright'ning orient° beam   *lustrous*
400   Purge off this gloom; the soft delicious air,
     To heal the scar of these corrosive fires
     Shall breathe her balm. But first whom shall we send
     In search of this new world, whom shall we find
     Sufficient? Who shall tempt° with wand'ring feet   *attempt, venture*
405   The dark unbottomed infinite abyss
     And through the palpable obscure[6] find out
     His uncouth° way, or spread his aery flight   *unknown*
     Upborne with indefatigable wings
     Over the vast abrupt,[7] ere he arrive
410   The happy isle? What strength, what art can then
     Suffice, or what evasion bear him safe
     Through the strict senteries° and stations thick   *sentries*
     Of angels watching round? Here he had need
     All circumspection, and we now no less
415   Choice° in our suffrage; for on whom we send,   *discrimination*
     The weight of all and our last hope relies."
      This said, he sat; and expectation held
     His look suspense,[8] awaiting who appeared
     To second, or oppose, or undertake
420   The perilous attempt: but all sat mute,
     Pondering the danger with deep thoughts; and each
     In other's count'nance read his own dismay
     Astonished. None among the choice and prime
     Of those Heav'n-warring champions could be found
425   So hardy as to proffer or accept
     Alone the dreadful voyage; till at last
     Satan, whom now transcendent glory raised
     Above his fellows, with monarchal pride
     Conscious of highest worth, unmoved thus spake.
430   "O progeny of Heav'n, empyreal Thrones,
     With reason hath deep silence and demur°   *hesitation*
     Seized us, though undismayed: long is the way
     And hard, that out of Hell leads up to light;
     Our prison strong, this huge convex of fire,
435   Outrageous to devour, immures us round
     Ninefold,[9] and gates of burning adamant
     Barred over us prohibit all egress.

---

6. Darkness so thick it can be felt (cf. Exodus 10.21).
7. Chaos, a striking example of sound imitating sense.
8. I.e., he sat waiting in suspense.
9. Hell's fiery walls and gates have nine thicknesses (see lines 645ff.). "Adamant" (following): a fabulously hard metal.

These passed, if any pass, the void profound
Of unessential Night receives him next

440   Wide gaping, and with utter loss of being
Threatens him, plunged in that abortive gulf.[1]
If thence he scape into whatever world,
Or unknown region, what remains him less°   *awaits him except*
Than unknown dangers and as hard escape?

445   But I should ill become this throne, O Peers,
And this imperial sov'reignty, adorned
With splendor, armed with power, if aught proposed
And judged of public moment,° in the shape   *importance*
Of difficulty or danger could deter

450   Me from attempting. Wherefore do I assume
These royalties, and not refuse to reign,
Refusing° to accept as great a share   *if I refuse*
Of hazard as of honor, due alike
To him who reigns, and so much to him due

455   Of hazard more, as he above the rest
High honored sits? Go therefore mighty Powers,
Terror of Heav'n, though fall'n; intend° at home,   *consider*
While here shall be our home, what best may ease
The present misery, and render Hell

460   More tolerable; if there be cure or charm
To respite or deceive, or slack the pain
Of this ill mansion: intermit no watch
Against a wakeful foe, while I abroad
Through all the coasts° of dark destruction seek   *districts*

465   Deliverance for us all: this enterprise
None shall partake with me." Thus saying rose
The monarch, and prevented° all reply,   *forestalled*
Prudent, lest from his resolution raised°   *roused*
Others among the chief might offer now

470   (Certain to be refused) what erst° they feared;   *formerly*
And so refused might in opinion stand
His rivals, winning cheap the high repute
Which he through hazard huge must earn. But they
Dreaded not more th' adventure than his voice

475   Forbidding; and at once with him they rose;
Their rising all at once was as the sound
Of thunder heard remote. Towards him they bend
With awful° reverence prone; and as a god   *full of awe*
Extol him equal to the Highest in Heav'n:

480   Nor failed they to express how much they praised,
That for the general safety he despised
His own: for neither do the Spirits damned
Lose all their virtue; lest bad men should boast
Their specious° deeds on earth, which glory excites,   *pretending to worth*

485   Or close° ambition varnished o'er with zeal.   *secret*
    Thus they their doubtful consultations dark

---

1. Chaos is a womb in which all potential forms fragment (see lines 895ff.) "Unessential" (line 439): i.e., having no real essence.

Ended rejoicing in their matchless chief:
As when from mountaintops the dusky clouds
Ascending, while the north wind sleeps, o'erspread
490 Heav'n's cheerful face, the louring element°   *threatening sky*
Scowls o'er the darkened landscape snow, or show'r;
If chance the radiant sun with farewell sweet
Extend his evening beam, the fields revive,
The birds their notes renew, and bleating herds
495 Attest their joy, that hill and valley rings.
O shame to men! Devil with devil damned
Firm concord holds, men only disagree
Of creatures rational, though under hope
Of heavenly grace: and God proclaiming peace,
500 Yet live in hatred, enmity, and strife
Among themselves, and levy cruel wars,
Wasting the earth, each other to destroy:
As if (which might induce us to accord)
Man had not hellish foes enow° besides,   *enough*
505 That day and night for his destruction wait.
     The Stygian° council thus dissolved; and forth   *Styx-like, hellish*
In order came the grand infernal peers:
Midst came their mighty paramount,° and seemed   *supreme ruler*
Alone th' antagonist of Heav'n, nor less
510 Than Hell's dread emperor with pomp supreme,
And godlike imitated state; him round
A globe° of fiery Seraphim enclosed   *band, circle*
With bright emblazonry and horrent² arms.
Then of their session ended they bid cry
515 With trumpet's regal sound the great result:
Toward the four winds four speedy Cherubim
Put to their mouths the sounding alchemy³
By herald's voice explained; the hollow abyss
Heard far and wide, and all the host of Hell
520 With deaf'ning shout, returned them loud acclaim.
Thence more at ease their minds and somewhat raised
By false presumptuous hope, the rangèd° powers   *arrayed in ranks*
Disband, and wand'ring, each his several way
Pursues, as inclination or sad choice
525 Leads him perplexed, where he may likeliest find
Truce to his restless thoughts, and entertain
The irksome hours, till his great chief return.
Part on the plain, or in the air sublime°   *aloft*
Upon the wing, or in swift race contend,
530 As at th' Olympian games or Pythian fields;⁴
Part curb their fiery steeds, or shun the goal⁵
With rapid wheels, or fronted° brigades form.   *confronting*
As when to warn proud cities war appears
Waged in the troubled sky, and armies rush

2. Bristling. "Emblazonry": decorated shields.
3. Trumpets (made of the goldlike alloy brass).
4. The Olympic games were held at Olympia,
the Pythian games at Delphi. Games celebrating

a (usually dead) hero are an epic convention.
5. To drive a chariot as close as possible around
a column without hitting it.

535 To battle in the clouds,[6] before each van°   *vanguard*
      Prick° forth the aery knights, and couch their spears   *spur*
      Till thickest legions close; with feats of arms
      From either end of Heav'n the welkin° burns.   *sky*
      Others with vast Typhoean[7] rage more fell°   *fierce*
540 Rend up both rocks and hills, and ride the air
      In whirlwind; Hell scarce holds the wild uproar.
      As when Alcides from Oechalia crowned
      With conquest, felt th' envenomed robe, and tore
      Through pain up by the roots Thessalian pines,
545 And Lichas from the top of Oeta threw
      Into th' Euboic sea.[8] Others more mild,
      Retreated in a silent valley, sing
      With notes angelical to many a harp
      Their own heroic deeds and hapless fall
550 By doom of battle; and complain that fate
      Free virtue should enthrall to force or chance.
      Their song was partial,° but the harmony   *prejudiced*
      (What could it less when Spirits immortal sing?)
      Suspended° Hell, and took with ravishment   *held in suspense*
555 The thronging audience. In discourse more sweet
      (For eloquence the soul, song charms the sense)
      Others apart sat on a hill retired,
      In thoughts more elevate, and reasoned high
      Of providence, foreknowledge, will, and fate,
560 Fixed fate, free will, foreknowledge absolute,
      And found no end, in wand'ring mazes lost.
      Of good and evil much they argued then,
      Of happiness and final misery,
      Passion and apathy,[9] and glory and shame,
565 Vain wisdom all, and false philosophy:
      Yet with a pleasing sorcery could charm
      Pain for a while or anguish, and excite
      Fallacious hope, or arm th' obdurèd° breast   *hardened*
      With stubborn patience as with triple steel.
570 Another part in squadrons and gross° bands,   *solid, dense*
      On bold adventure to discover wide
      That dismal world, if any clime perhaps
      Might yield them easier habitation, bend
      Four ways their flying march, along the banks
575 Of four infernal rivers that disgorge
      Into the burning lake their baleful streams:[1]
      Abhorrèd Styx the flood of deadly hate,
      Sad Acheron of sorrow, black and deep;
      Cocytus, named of lamentation loud

6. The appearance of warfare in the skies, reported before several notable battles, portends trouble on earth.

7. Like that of Typhon, the hundred-headed Titan (see 1.199).

8. Wearing a poisoned robe given him in a deception, Hercules ("Alcides") in his dying agonies threw his beloved companion Lichas, along with a good part of Mount Oeta, into the Euboean Sea, near Thermopylae.

9. The Stoic goal of freedom from passion.

1. These four rivers are traditional in hellish geography. Milton distinguishes them by the original meanings of their Greek names: Styx means "hateful," Acheron "woeful," etc. Lethe is "far off" and quite different from the others, oblivion being a desired state in Hell.

580 Heard on the rueful stream; fierce Phlegethon
Whose waves of torrent fire inflame with rage.
Far off from these a slow and silent stream,
Lethe the river of oblivion rolls
Her wat'ry labyrinth, whereof who drinks,
585 Forthwith his former state and being forgets,
Forgets both joy and grief, pleasure and pain.
Beyond this flood a frozen continent
Lies dark and wild, beat with perpetual storms
Of whirlwind and dire hail, which on firm land
590 Thaws not, but gathers heap,[2] and ruin seems
Of ancient pile; all else deep snow and ice,
A gulf profound as that Serbonian bog[3]
Betwixt Damiata and Mount Casius old,
Where armies whole have sunk: the parching air
595 Burns frore,° and cold performs th' effect of fire.   *frozen*
Thither by harpy-footed[4] Furies haled,°   *driven*
At certain revolutions° all the damned   *recurring times*
Are brought: and feel by turns the bitter change
Of fierce extremes, extremes by change more fierce,
600 From beds of raging fire to starve° in ice   *make numb*
Their soft ethereal warmth, and there to pine
Immovable, infixed, and frozen round,
Periods of time; thence hurried back to fire.
They ferry over this Lethean sound
605 Both to and fro, their sorrow to augment,
And wish and struggle, as they pass, to reach
The tempting stream, with one small drop to lose
In sweet forgetfulness all pain and woe,
All in one moment, and so near the brink;
610 But fate withstands, and to oppose th' attempt
Medusa[5] with Gorgonian terror guards
The ford, and of itself the water flies
All taste of living wight,° as once it fled   *creature*
The lip of Tantalus.[6] Thus roving on
615 In cónfused march forlorn, th' advent'rous bands
With shudd'ring horror pale, and eyes aghast
Viewed first their lamentable lot, and found
No rest: through many a dark and dreary vale
They passed, and many a region dolorous,
620 O'er many a frozen, many a fiery alp,°   *volcano*
Rocks, caves, lakes, fens, bogs, dens, and shades of death,
A universe of death, which God by curse
Created evil, for evil only good,
Where all life dies, death lives, and nature breeds,
625 Perverse, all monstrous, all prodigious things,

---

2. In a heap, resembling the ruin of an old building ("ancient pile," next line).
3. Lake Serbonis, once famous for its quicksands, lies near the city of Damietta ("Damiata," next line), just east of the Nile.
4. Taloned. In Greek mythology the Harpies (monsters with women's faces) carried off individuals to the Furies, who avenged crimes.
5. One of the three Gorgons, women with snaky hair, scaly bodies, and boar's tusks, the sight of whose faces changed men to stone.
6. Tantalus, afflicted with a raging thirst, stood in the middle of a lake, the water of which always receded when he tried to drink (hence, "tantalize").

Abominable, inutterable, and worse
Than fables yet have feigned, or fear conceived,
Gorgons and Hydras, and Chimeras[7] dire.
    Meanwhile the Adversary[8] of God and man,
630 Satan, with thoughts inflamed of highest design,
Puts on swift wings,° and towards the gates of Hell   *flies swiftly*
Explores his solitary flight; sometimes
He scours the right-hand coast, sometimes the left,
Now shaves with level wing the deep, then soars
635 Up to the fiery concave° tow'ring high.   *vault*
As when far off at sea a fleet descried
Hangs on the clouds, by equinoctial° winds   *from the equator*
Close sailing from Bengala,° or the isles   *Bengal*
Of Ternate and Tidore,[9] whence merchants bring
640 Their spicy drugs: they on the trading flood
Through the wide Ethiopian to the Cape
Ply stemming nightly toward the pole:[1] so seemed
Far off the flying Fiend. At last appear
Hell bounds high reaching to the horrid roof,
645 And thrice threefold the gates; three folds were brass,
Three iron, three of adamantine rock,
Impenetrable, impaled with circling fire,
Yet unconsumed. Before the gates there sat
On either side a formidable shape;[2]
650 The one seemed woman to the waist, and fair,
But ended foul in many a scaly fold
Voluminous and vast, a serpent armed
With mortal sting: about her middle round
A cry° of hellhounds never ceasing barked   *pack*
655 With wide Cerberean[3] mouths full loud, and rung
A hideous peal: yet, when they list,° would creep,   *wish*
If aught disturbed their noise, into her womb,
And kennel there, yet there still barked and howled,
Within unseen. Far less abhorred than these
660 Vexed Scylla[4] bathing in the sea that parts
Calabria from the hoarse Trinacrian shore:
Nor uglier follow the night-hag,[5] when called
In secret, riding through the air she comes
Lured with the smell of infant blood, to dance
665 With Lapland witches, while the laboring° moon   *troubled*
Eclipses at their charms.° The other shape,   *magic*

---

7. The Hydra was a serpent whose multiple heads grew back when severed; the Chimera was a fire-breathing creature, part lion, part dragon, part goat.

8. *Satan* in Hebrew means "adversary."

9. Two of the Moluccas, or Spice Islands, modern Indonesia.

1. The South Pole. "Ethiopian": the Indian Ocean. "The Cape" is the Cape of Good Hope.

2. The allegorical figures of Sin and Death are founded on James 1.15: "Then when lust hath conceived, it bringeth forth sin: and sin, when it is finished, bringeth forth death." But the incestuous relations of Sin and Death are Milton's own invention. Physically, Sin is modeled on Virgil's or Ovid's Scylla, with some touches adopted from Spenser's Error. Death is a traditional figure, vague and vast.

3. Like Cerberus, the multiheaded hound of Hell.

4. Circe, out of jealousy, threw poison into the water where Scylla bathed, in the straits between Calabria and Sicily ("Trinacria," next line); the poison caused Scylla to develop a ring of barking, snapping dogs around her waist.

5. Hecate (three syllables), goddess of sorcery. She attends orgies of witches in Lapland (line 665, famous for witchcraft), drawn by the blood of babies sacrificed for the occasion.

If shape it might be called that shape had none
Distinguishable in member, joint, or limb,
Or substance might be called that shadow seemed,
670 For each seemed either; black it stood as night,
Fierce as ten Furies, terrible as hell,
And shook a dreadful dart; what seemed his head
The likeness of a kingly crown had on.
Satan was now at hand, and from his seat
675 The monster moving onward came as fast
With horrid strides. Hell trembled as he strode.
Th' undaunted Fiend what this might be admired,°   *wondered*
Admired, not feared; God and his Son except,
Created thing naught valued he nor shunned;
680 And with disdainful look thus first began.
   "Whence and what art thou, execrable shape,
That dar'st, though grim and terrible, advance
Thy miscreated front° athwart my way   *misshapen face*
To yonder gates? Through them I mean to pass,
685 That be assured, without leave asked of thee:
Retire, or taste° thy folly, and learn by proof,   *experience*
Hell-born, not to contend with Spirits of Heav'n."
   To whom the goblin full of wrath replied:
"Art thou that traitor angel, art thou he,
690 Who first broke peace in Heav'n and faith, till then
Unbroken, and in proud rebellious arms
Drew after him the third part of Heav'n's sons
Conjured° against the Highest, for which both thou   *sworn together*
And they outcast from God, are here condemned
695 To waste eternal days in woe and pain?
And reckon'st thou thyself with Spirits of Heav'n,
Hell-doomed, and breath'st defiance here and scorn,
Where I reign king, and to enrage thee more,
Thy king and lord? Back to thy punishment,
700 False fugitive, and to thy speed add wings,
Lest with a whip of scorpions I pursue
Thy ling'ring, or with one stroke of this dart
Strange horror seize thee, and pangs unfelt before."
   So spake the grisly terror, and in shape,
705 So speaking and so threat'ning, grew tenfold
More dreadful and deform: on th' other side
Incensed with indignation Satan stood
Unterrified, and like a comet burned
That fires the length of Ophiuchus[6] huge
710 In th' arctic sky, and from his horrid° hair   *bristling*
Shakes pestilence and war. Each at the head
Leveled his deadly aim; their fatal hands
No second stroke intend, and such a frown
Each cast at th' other, as when, two black clouds
715 With Heav'n's artillery fraught,[7] come rattling on

---

6. A vast northern constellation, "the Serpent   7. Loaded with thunderbolts.
Bearer."

Over the Caspian,[8] then stand front to front
Hov'ring a space, till winds the signal blow
To join their dark encounter in mid-air:
So frowned the mighty combatants, that Hell
720 Grew darker at their frown, so matched they stood;
For never but once more was either like
To meet so great a foe.[9] And now great deeds
Had been achieved, whereof all Hell had rung,
Had not the snaky sorceress that sat
725 Fast by Hell gate, and kept the fatal key,
Ris'n, and with hideous outcry rushed between.
　　"O father, what intends thy hand," she cried,
"Against thy only son?[1] What fury O son,
Possesses thee to bend that mortal dart
730 Against thy father's head? And know'st for whom;
For him who sits above and laughs the while
At thee ordained his drudge, to execute
Whate'er his wrath, which he calls justice, bids,
His wrath which one day will destroy ye both."
735 　　She spake, and at her words the hellish pest
Forbore, then these to her Satan returned.
　　"So strange thy outcry, and thy words so strange
Thou interposest, that my sudden hand
Prevented° spares to tell thee yet by deeds　　　　　　　　*forestalled*
740 What it intends; till first I know of thee,
What thing thou art, thus double-formed, and why
In this infernal vale first met thou call'st
Me father, and that phantasm call'st my son?
I know thee not, nor ever saw till now
745 Sight more detestable than him and thee."
　　T' whom thus the portress of Hell gate replied:
"Hast thou forgot me then, and do I seem
Now in thine eye so foul, once deemed so fair
In Heav'n, when at th' assembly, and in sight
750 Of all the Seraphim with thee combined
In bold conspiracy against Heav'n's King,
All on a sudden miserable pain
Surprised thee, dim thine eyes, and dizzy swum
In darkness, while thy head flames thick and fast
755 Threw forth, till on the left side op'ning wide,
Likest to thee in shape and count'nance bright,
Then shining heav'nly fair, a goddess armed
Out of thy head I sprung:[2] amazement seized
All th' host of Heav'n; back they recoiled afraid
760 At first, and called me Sin, and for a sign
Portentous held me; but familiar grown,
I pleased, and with attractive graces won
The most averse, thee chiefly, who full oft

8. The Caspian is a particularly stormy area.
9. I.e., the Son of God.
1. Sin, Death, and Satan, in their various inter-
relations, parody obscenely the relations between
God and the Son, Adam and Eve.
2. As Athena sprang full grown from the head
of Zeus.

Thyself in me thy perfect image viewing
765 Becam'st enamored, and such joy thou took'st
With me in secret, that my womb conceived
A growing burden. Meanwhile war arose,
And fields were fought in Heav'n; wherein remained
(For what could else) to our almighty foe
770 Clear victory, to our part loss and rout
Through all the empyrean: down they fell
Driv'n headlong from the pitch° of Heaven, down   *summit*
Into this deep, and in the general fall
I also; at which time this powerful key
775 Into my hand was giv'n, with charge to keep
These gates forever shut, which none can pass
Without my op'ning. Pensive here I sat
Alone, but long I sat not, till my womb
Pregnant by thee, and now excessive grown
780 Prodigious motion felt and rueful throes.
At last this odious offspring whom thou seest
Thine own begotten, breaking violent way
Tore through my entrails, that with fear and pain
Distorted, all my nether shape thus grew
785 Transformed: but he my inbred enemy
Forth issued, brandishing his fatal dart
Made to destroy: I fled, and cried out 'Death';
Hell trembled at the hideous name, and sighed
From all her caves, and back resounded 'Death.'
790 I fled, but he pursued (though more, it seems,
Inflamed with lust than rage) and swifter far,
Me overtook his mother all dismayed,
And in embraces forcible and foul
Engend'ring with me, of that rape begot
795 These yelling monsters that with ceaseless cry
Surround me, as thou saw'st, hourly conceived
And hourly born, with sorrow infinite
To me, for when they list,° into the womb   *wish*
That bred them they return, and howl and gnaw
800 My bowels, their repast; then bursting forth
Afresh with conscious terrors vex me round,
That rest or intermission none I find.
Before mine eyes in opposition sits
Grim Death my son and foe, who sets them on,
805 And me his parent would full soon devour
For want of other prey, but that he knows
His end with mine involved; and knows that I
Should prove a bitter morsel, and his bane,°   *poison*
Whenever that shall be; so fate pronounced.
810 But thou O father, I forewarn thee, shun
His deadly arrow; neither vainly hope
To be invulnerable in those bright arms,
Though tempered heav'nly, for that mortal dint,°   *blow*
Save he who reigns above, none can resist."
815   She finished, and the subtle Fiend his lore°   *lesson*

Soon learned, now milder, and thus answered smooth.
"Dear daughter, since thou claim'st me for thy sire,
And my fair son here show'st me, the dear pledge
Of dalliance had with thee in Heav'n, and joys
820 Then sweet, now sad to mention, through dire change
Befall'n us unforeseen, unthought of, know
I come no enemy, but to set free
From out this dark and dismal house of pain,
Both him and thee, and all the heav'nly host
825 Of Spirits that in our just pretenses° armed   *claims*
Fell with us from on high: from them I go
This uncouth errand³ sole, and one for all
Myself expose, with lonely steps to tread
Th' unfounded° deep, and through the void immense   *bottomless*
830 To search with wand'ring quest a place foretold
Should be, and, by concurring signs, ere now
Created vast and round, a place of bliss
In the purlieus° of Heav'n, and therein placed   *outskirts*
A race of upstart creatures, to supply
835 Perhaps our vacant room, though more removed,
Lest Heav'n surcharged° with potent multitude   *overcrowded*
Might hap to move new broils:° be this or aught   *controversies*
Than this more secret now designed, I haste
To know, and this once known, shall soon return,
840 And bring ye to the place where thou and Death
Shall dwell at ease, and up and down unseen
Wing silently the buxom° air, embalmed°   *yielding / made fragrant*
With odors; there ye shall be fed and filled
Immeasurably, all things shall be your prey."
845 He ceased, for both seemed highly pleased, and Death
Grinned horrible a ghastly smile, to hear
His famine° should be filled, and blessed his maw°   *ravenous hunger / belly*
Destined to that good hour: no less rejoiced
His mother bad, and thus bespake her sire.
850   "The key of this infernal pit by due,
And by command of Heav'n's all-powerful King
I keep, by him forbidden to unlock
These adamantine gates; against all force
Death ready stands to interpose his dart,
855 Fearless to be o'ermatched by living might.
But what owe I to his commands above
Who hates me, and hath hither thrust me down
Into this gloom of Tartarus profound,
To sit in hateful office here confined,
860 Inhabitant of Heav'n, and heav'nly-born,
Here in perpetual agony and pain,
With terrors and with clamors compassed round
Of mine own brood, that on my bowels feed?
Thou art my father, thou my author, thou
865 My being gav'st me; whom should I obey

3. Unknown journey—a parody of Christ's errand on earth (3.236–65).

But thee, whom follow? Thou wilt bring me soon
To that new world of light and bliss, among
The gods who live at ease, where I shall reign
At thy right hand voluptuous,[4] as beseems
870 Thy daughter and thy darling, without end."
 Thus saying, from her side the fatal key,
Sad instrument of all our woe, she took;
And towards the gate rolling her bestial train,[5]
Forthwith the huge portcullis high up drew,
875 Which but herself not all the Stygian powers°   armies of Hell
Could once have moved; then in the keyhole turns
Th' intricate wards, and every bolt and bar
Of massy iron or solid rock with ease
Unfastens: on a sudden open fly
880 With impetuous recoil and jarring sound
Th' infernal doors, and on their hinges grate
Harsh thunder, that the lowest bottom shook
Of Erebus.° She opened, but to shut   Hell
Excelled° her power; the gates wide open stood,   exceeded
885 That with extended wings a bannered host
Under spread ensigns° marching might pass through   flags, standards
With horse and chariots ranked in loose array;
So wide they stood, and like a furnace mouth
Cast forth redounding° smoke and ruddy flame.   billowing
890 Before their eyes in sudden view appear
The secrets of the hoary° deep, a dark   ancient
Illimitable° ocean without bound,   without limit
Without dimension, where length, breadth, and height,
And time and place are lost; where eldest Night
895 And Chaos, ancestors of Nature, hold
Eternal anarchy, amidst the noise
Of endless wars, and by confusion stand.
For Hot, Cold, Moist, and Dry, four champions fierce
Strive here for mastery, and to battle bring
900 Their embryon atoms;[6] they around the flag
Of each his faction, in their several clans,
Light-armed or heavy, sharp, smooth, swift or slow,
Swarm populous, unnumbered as the sands
Of Barca or Cyrene's torrid soil,[7]
905 Levied to side with warring winds, and poise[8]
Their lighter wings. To whom these most adhere,
He rules a moment; Chaos[9] umpire sits,
And by decision more embroils the fray
By which he reigns: next him high arbiter
910 Chance governs all. Into this wild abyss,

4. As the Son sits at God's right hand, Sin will at
Satan's, a blasphemous parody of the Apostles'
Creed and of *Paradise Lost* 3.250–80.
5. I.e. propelling her yelping offspring.
6. These subatomic qualities combine together in
nature to form the four elements, fire, earth, water,
and air, but they struggle endlessly in Chaos, where
the atoms of these elements remain undeveloped

(in "embryo").
7. Cities built on the shifting sands of North
Africa.
8. Give weight to. "Levied": both enlisted and
raised up.
9. Chaos is both the place where confusion reigns
and personified confusion itself.

The womb of Nature and perhaps her grave,
Of neither sea, nor shore, nor air, nor fire,
But all these in their pregnant causes° mixed   *seeds*
Confus'dly, and which thus must ever fight,
915 Unless th' Almighty Maker them ordain
His dark materials to create more worlds,
Into this wild abyss the wary Fiend
Stood on the brink of Hell and looked a while,
Pondering his voyage; for no narrow frith°   *channel, firth*
920 He had to cross. Nor was his ear less pealed°   *dinned*
With noises loud and ruinous (to compare
Great things with small) than when Bellona[1] storms,
With all her battering engines bent to raze
Some capital city; or less than if this frame°   *structure*
925 Of Heav'n were falling, and these elements
In mutiny had from her axle torn
The steadfast earth. At last his sail-broad vans°   *wings*
He spreads for flight, and in the surging smoke
Uplifted spurns the ground, thence many a league
930 As in a cloudy chair ascending rides
Audacious, but that seat soon failing, meets
A vast vacuity: all unawares
Flutt'ring his pennons[2] vain plumb down he drops
Ten thousand fathom deep, and to this hour
935 Down had been falling, had not by ill chance
The strong rebuff° of some tumultuous cloud   *counterblast*
Instinct° with fire and niter° hurried him   *filled / saltpeter*
As many miles aloft: that fury stayed,
Quenched in a boggy Syrtis,[3] neither sea,
940 Nor good dry land: nigh foundered° on he fares,   *drowned*
Treading the crude consistence, half on foot,
Half flying; behoves° him now both oar and sail.   *befits*
As when a griffin through the wilderness
With wingèd course o'er hill or moory° dale,   *marshy*
945 Pursues the Arimaspian, who by stealth
Had from his wakeful custody purloined
The guarded gold:[4] so eagerly the Fiend
O'er bog or steep, through strait, rough, dense, or rare,
With head, hands, wings, or feet pursues his way,
950 And swims or sinks, or wades, or creeps, or flies:
At length a universal hubbub wild
Of stunning sounds and voices all confused
Borne through the hollow dark assaults his ear
With loudest vehemence: thither he plies,
955 Undaunted to meet there whatever Power
Or Spirit of the nethermost abyss
Might in that noise reside, of whom to ask

---

1. Goddess of war.
2. Useless wings ("pinions").
3. Quicksand in North African gulfs, famous for their shifting sandbars.

4. Griffins, mythical creatures, half-eagle, half-lion, hoarded gold that was stolen from them by the one-eyed Arimaspians.

Which way the nearest coast of darkness lies
Bordering on light; when straight behold the throne
960 Of Chaos, and his dark pavilion spread
Wide on the wasteful deep; with him enthroned
Sat sable-vested Night, eldest of things,
The consort of his reign; and by them stood
Orcus and Ades,[5] and the dreaded name
965 Of Demogorgon,[6] Rumor next and Chance,
And Tumult and Confusion all embroiled,
And Discord with a thousand various mouths.
  T' whom Satan turning boldly, thus. "Ye Powers
And Spirits of this nethermost abyss,
970 Chaos and ancient Night, I come no spy,
With purpose to explore or to disturb
The secrets of your realm, but by constraint
Wand'ring this darksome desert, as my way
Lies through your spacious empire up to light,
975 Alone, and without guide, half lost, I seek
What readiest path leads where your gloomy bounds
Confine with° Heav'n; or if some other place   *border on*
From your dominion won, th' Ethereal King
Possesses lately, thither to arrive
980 I travel this profound;° direct my course;   *deep pit*
Directed, no mean recompense it brings
To your behoof,° if I that region lost,   *on your behalf*
All usurpation thence expelled, reduce
To her original darkness and your sway
985 (Which is my present journey)[7] and once more
Erect the standard there of ancient Night;
Yours be th' advantage all, mine the revenge."
  Thus Satan; and him thus the anarch[8] old
With falt'ring speech and visage incomposed°   *disordered*
990 Answered. "I know thee, stranger, who thou art,
That mighty leading angel, who of late
Made head against Heav'n's King, though overthrown.
I saw and heard, for such a numerous host
Fled not in silence through the frighted deep
995 With ruin upon ruin, rout on rout,
Confusion worse confounded; and Heav'n gates
Poured out by millions her victorious bands
Pursuing. I upon my frontiers here
Keep residence; if all I can will serve,
1000 That little which is left so to defend,
Encroached on still° through our intestine broils°   *constantly / civil wars*
Weak'ning the scepter of old Night: first Hell
Your dungeon stretching far and wide beneath;
Now lately heaven and earth,[9] another world

---

5. Latin and Greek names of Pluto, god of Hell.
6. A mysterious deity associated with Fate; Milton elsewhere identifies him with Chaos.
7. The purpose of my present journey.

8. Chaos is not monarch of his realm but, appropriately, "anarch," nonruler.
9. The cosmos, with its own "heaven" (not the empyrean, the Heaven of God and the angels).

1005   Hung o'er my realm, linked in a golden chain
     To that side Heav'n from whence your legions fell:
     If that way be your walk, you have not far;
     So much the nearer danger; go and speed;
     Havoc and spoil and ruin are my gain."
1010   He ceased; and Satan stayed not to reply,
     But glad that now his sea should find a shore,
     With fresh alacrity and force renewed
     Springs upward like a pyramid of fire
     Into the wild expanse, and through the shock
1015   Of fighting elements, on all sides round
     Environed wins his way; harder beset
     And more endangered, than when Argo passed
     Through Bosporus betwixt the justling rocks:[1]
     Or when Ulysses on the larboard shunned
1020   Charybdis, and by th' other whirlpool steered.[2]
     So he with difficulty and labor hard
     Moved on, with difficulty and labor he;
     But he once passed, soon after when man fell,
     Strange alteration! Sin and Death amain°   *at full speed*
1025   Following his track, such was the will of Heav'n,
     Paved after him a broad and beaten way
     Over the dark abyss, whose boiling gulf
     Tamely endured a bridge of wondrous length
     From Hell continued reaching th' utmost orb[3]
1030   Of this frail world; by which the Spirits perverse
     With easy intercourse pass to and fro
     To tempt or punish mortals, except whom
     God and good angels guard by special grace.
     But now at last the sacred influence
1035   Of light appears, and from the walls of Heav'n
     Shoots far into the bosom of dim Night
     A glimmering dawn; here Nature first begins
     Her farthest verge,° and Chaos to retire   *threshold*
     As from her outmost works a broken foe
1040   With tumult less and with less hostile din,
     That° Satan with less toil, and now with ease   *so that*
     Wafts on the calmer wave by dubious light
     And like a weather-beaten vessel holds°   *makes for*
     Gladly the port, though shrouds and tackle torn;
1045   Or in the emptier waste, resembling air
     Weighs° his spread wings, at leisure to behold   *balances*
     Far off th' empyreal Heav'n, extended wide
     In circuit, undetermined square or round,
     With opal tow'rs and battlements adorned
1050   Of living sapphire, once his native seat;
     And fast by hanging in a golden chain

1. Jason and his fifty Argonauts, sailing through the Bosporus to the Black Sea in pursuit of the Golden Fleece, had to pass through the Symplegades, or clashing rocks.
2. Homer's Ulysses, sailing where Italy almost touches Sicily, had to pass between Charybdis, a whirlpool, and Scylla, a monster who devoured six of his men (not another whirlpool, as used here).
3. The bridge ends on the outermost sphere of the ten concentric spheres making up the universe.

This pendent world,° in bigness as a star   *universe*
Of smallest magnitude close by the moon.
Thither full fraught with mischievous revenge,
1055   Accursed, and in a cursèd hour, he hies.

Book 3

The Argument

God sitting on his throne sees Satan flying towards this world, then newly
created; shows him to the Son who sat at his right hand; foretells the success
of Satan in perverting mankind; clears his own justice and wisdom from all
imputation, having created man free and able enough to have withstood his
tempter; yet declares his purpose of grace towards him, in regard he fell not
of his own malice, as did Satan, but by him seduced. The Son of God renders
praises to his Father for the manifestation of his gracious purpose towards
man; but God again declares, that grace cannot be extended towards man
without the satisfaction of divine justice; man hath offended the majesty of
God by aspiring to Godhead, and therefore with all his progeny devoted to
death must die, unless someone can be found sufficient to answer for his
offense, and undergo his punishment. The Son of God freely offers himself a
ransom for man: the Father accepts him, ordains his incarnation, pronounces
his exaltation about all names in heaven and earth; commands all the angels
to adore him; they obey, and hymning to their harps in full choir, celebrate the
Father and the Son. Meanwhile Satan alights upon the bare convex of this
world's outermost orb; where wandering he first finds a place since called the
Limbo of Vanity; what persons and things fly up thither; thence comes to the
gate of heaven, described ascending by stairs, and the waters above the firmament that flow about it: his passage thence to the orb of the sun; he finds there
Uriel the regent of that orb, but first changes himself into the shape of a
meaner angel; and pretending a zealous desire to behold the new creation
and man whom God had placed there, inquires of him the place of his habitation, and is directed; alights first on Mount Niphates.

Hail holy Light, offspring of Heav'n firstborn,
Or of th' Eternal coeternal beam
May I express thee unblamed?[1] Since God is light,
And never but in unapproachèd light
5   Dwelt from eternity, dwelt then in thee,
Bright effluence of bright essence increate.°   *uncreated, eternal*
Or hear'st thou rather[2] pure ethereal stream,
Whose fountain who shall tell? Before the sun,
Before the heavens thou wert, and at the voice
10   Of God, as with a mantle, didst invest°   *cover*
The rising world of waters dark and deep,
Won from the void and formless infinite.

---

1. This second proem or invocation (3.1–55) is a
hymn to Light, addressed either as the first creature of God or as coeternal with God, with allusion to 1 John 1.5, "God is Light, and in him is
no darkness at all."
2. I.e., would you rather be called (a Latinism).

Thee I revisit now with bolder wing,
Escaped the Stygian pool, though long detained
15 In that obscure sojourn, while in my flight
Through utter and through middle darkness³ borne
With other notes than to th' Orphéan lyre⁴
I sung of Chaos and eternal Night,
Taught by the Heav'nly Muse⁵ to venture down
20 The dark descent, and up to reascend,
Though hard and rare: thee I revisit safe,
And feel thy sov'reign vital lamp; but thou
Revisit'st not these eyes, that roll in vain
To find thy piercing ray, and find no dawn;
25 So thick a drop serene hath quenched their orbs,
Or dim suffusion⁶ veiled. Yet not the more
Cease I to wander where the Muses haunt
Clear spring, or shady grove, or sunny hill,
Smit with the love of sacred song; but chief
30 Thee Sion⁷ and the flow'ry brooks beneath
That wash thy hallowed feet, and warbling flow,
Nightly I visit: nor sometimes forget°   *always remember*
Those other two equaled with me in fate,⁸
So were I equaled with them in renown,
35 Blind Thamyris and blind Maeonides,
And Tiresias and Phineus prophets old,⁹
Then feed on thoughts, that voluntary move
Harmonious numbers;° as the wakeful bird°   *verses / nightingale*
Sings darkling,° and in shadiest covert hid   *in the dark*
40 Tunes her nocturnal note. Thus with the year
Seasons return, but not to me returns
Day, or the sweet approach of ev'n or morn,
Or sight of vernal bloom, or summer's rose,
Or flocks, or herds, or human face divine;
45 But cloud instead, and ever-during° dark   *everlasting*
Surrounds me, from the cheerful ways of men
Cut off, and for the book of knowledge° fair   *Book of Nature*
Presented with a universal blank
Of nature's works to me expunged and razed,°   *erased*
50 And wisdom at one entrance quite shut out.
So much the rather thou celestial Light
Shine inward, and the mind through all her powers
Irradiate, there plant eyes, all mist from thence
Purge and disperse, that I may see and tell
55 Of things invisible to mortal sight.
    Now had the Almighty Father from above,
From the pure empyrean° where he sits   *Heaven*

3. Hell is "utter" (i.e., outer) darkness; Chaos is middle darkness.
4. One of the so-called Orphic hymns is "To Night," and Orpheus himself visited the underworld. But Milton's song, Christian and epic, is of a different kind.
5. Urania (though not named until 7.1).
6. Cataract—*suffusio nigra.* "Drop serene": *gutta serena,* the medical term for Milton's kind of blindness.
7. The mountain of scriptural inspiration, with its brooks Siloa and Kidron.
8. I.e., blind like me.
9. Thamyris was a blind Thracian poet who lived before Homer; "Maeonides" is an epithet of Homer; Tiresias was the blind prophet of Thebes; Phineus was a blind king and seer (*Aeneid* 3).

High throned above all height, bent down his eye,
His own works and their works at once to view:
60 Above him all the sanctities° of Heaven   *angels*
Stood thick as stars, and from his sight received
Beatitude past utterance; on his right
The radiant image of his glory sat,
His only Son; on earth he first beheld
65 Our two first parents, yet the only two
Of mankind, in the happy garden placed,
Reaping immortal fruits of joy and love,
Uninterrupted joy, unrivaled love
In blissful solitude; he then surveyed
70 Hell and the gulf between, and Satan there
Coasting the wall of Heav'n on this side Night
In the dun° air sublime,° and ready now   *dusky / aloft*
To stoop° with wearied wings, and willing feet *swoop down*
On the bare outside of this world,° that seemed *universe*
75 Firm land embosomed without firmament,°   *atmosphere*
Uncertain which, in ocean or in air.
Him God beholding from his prospect high,
Wherein past, present, future he beholds,
Thus to his only Son foreseeing spake.
80 "Only begotten Son, seest thou what rage
Transports our Adversary, whom no bounds
Prescribed, no bars of Hell, nor all the chains
Heaped on him there, nor yet the main° abyss   *vast*
Wide interrupt[1] can hold; so bent he seems
85 On desperate revenge, that shall redound°   *flow back*
Upon his own rebellious head. And now
Through all restraint broke loose he wings his way
Not far off Heav'n, in the precincts of light,
Directly towards the new-created world,
90 And man there placed, with purpose to essay°   *try*
If him by force he can destroy, or worse,
By some false guile pervert; and shall pervert;
For man will hearken to his glozing° lies,   *flattering*
And easily transgress the sole command,
95 Sole pledge of his obedience: so will fall
He and his faithless progeny: whose fault?
Whose but his own? Ingrate, he had of me
All he could have; I made him just and right,
Sufficient to have stood, though free to fall.
100 Such I created all th' ethereal Powers
And Spirits, both them who stood and them who failed;
Freely they stood who stood, and fell who fell.
Not free, what proof could they have giv'n sincere
Of true allegiance, constant faith or love,
105 Where only what they needs must do, appeared,
Not what they would? What praise could they receive?
What pleasure I from such obedience paid,

1. Forming a wide breach between Heaven and Hell.

When will and reason (reason also is choice)
Useless and vain, of freedom both despoiled,
110 Made passive both, had served necessity,
Not me. They therefore as to right belonged,
So were created, nor can justly accuse
Their Maker, or their making, or their fate,
As if predestination overruled
115 Their will, disposed by absolute decree
Or high foreknowledge; they themselves decreed
Their own revolt, not I: if I foreknew,
Foreknowledge had no influence on their fault,
Which had no less proved certain unforeknown.[2]
120 So without least impulse or shadow of fate,
Or aught by me immutably foreseen,
They trespass, authors to themselves in all
Both what they judge and what they choose; for so
I formed them free, and free they must remain,
125 Till they enthrall themselves: I else must change
Their nature, and revoke the high decree
Unchangeable, eternal, which ordained
Their freedom, they themselves ordained their fall.
The first sort[3] by their own suggestion fell,
130 Self-tempted, self-depraved: man falls deceived
By the other first: man therefore shall find grace,
The other none: in mercy and justice both,
Through Heav'n and earth, so shall my glory excel,
But mercy first and last shall brightest shine."
135   Thus while God spake, ambrosial° fragrance filled   *fragrant, immortal*
All Heav'n, and in the blessèd Spirits elect°   *unfallen*
Sense of new joy ineffable° diffused: *inexpressible*
Beyond compare the Son of God was seen
Most glorious, in him all his Father shone
140 Substantially expressed, and in his face
Divine compassion visibly appeared,
Love without end, and without measure grace,
Which uttering thus he to his Father spake.
    "O Father, gracious was that word which closed
145 Thy sov'reign sentence, that man should find grace;
For which both Heav'n and earth shall high extol
Thy praises, with th' innumerable sound
Of hymns and sacred songs, wherewith thy throne
Encompassed shall resound thee ever blessed.
150 For should man finally be lost, should man
Thy creature late so loved, thy youngest son
Fall circumvented thus by fraud, though joined
With his own folly? That be from thee far,
That far be from thee, Father, who art judge
155 Of all things made, and judgest only right.[4]

---

2. I.e., if I had not foreknown it.
3. Satan and his crew.
4. The Son echoes (or rather foreshadows) Abraham pleading with the Lord to spare Sodom: "That be far from thee to do after this manner, to slay the righteous with the wicked . . . that be far from thee: Shall not the Judge of all the earth do right?" (Genesis 18.25).

Or shall the Adversary thus obtain
His end, and frustrate thine, shall he fulfill
His malice, and thy goodness bring to naught,
Or proud return though to his heavier doom,
160 Yet with revenge accomplished, and to Hell
Draw after him the whole race of mankind,
By him corrupted? Or wilt thou thyself
Abolish thy creation, and unmake,
For him, what for thy glory thou hast made?
165 So should thy goodness and thy greatness both
Be questioned and blasphemed° without defense."   *profaned*
    To whom the great Creator thus replied.
"O Son, in whom my soul hath chief delight,
Son of my bosom, Son who art alone
170 My Word, my wisdom, and effectual might,[5]
All hast thou spoken as my thoughts are, all
As my eternal purpose hath decreed:
Man shall not quite be lost, but saved who will,
Yet not of will in him, but grace in me
175 Freely vouchsafed;° once more I will renew   *bestowed*
His lapsèd powers, though forfeit and enthralled
By sin to foul exorbitant desires;
Upheld by me, yet once more he shall stand
On even ground against his mortal foe,
180 By me upheld, that he may know how frail
His fall'n condition is, and to me owe
All his deliv'rance, and to none but me.
Some I have chosen of peculiar grace
Elect above the rest;[6] so is my will:
185 The rest shall hear me call, and oft be warned°   *warned about*
Their sinful state, and to appease betimes
Th' incensèd Deity, while offered grace
Invites; for I will clear their senses dark,
What may suffice, and soften stony hearts
190 To pray, repent, and bring obedience due.
To prayer, repentance, and obedience due,
Though but endeavored with sincere intent,
Mine ear shall not be slow, mine eye not shut.
And I will place within them as a guide
195 My umpire conscience, whom if they will hear,
Light after light well used they shall attain,[7]
And to the end persisting, safe arrive.
This my long sufferance and my day of grace
They who neglect and scorn, shall never taste;
200 But hard be hardened, blind be blinded more,
That they may stumble on, and deeper fall;
And none but such from mercy I exclude.

---

5. God's speech is rhythmic and sometimes rhymed.
6. In this speech, Milton's God rejects the Calvinist doctrine that he had from the beginning predestined the damnation or salvation of each individual soul; he claims rather that grace sufficient for salvation is offered to all, enabling everyone, if they choose to do so, to believe and persevere. He does, however, assert his right to give special grace to some.
7. By using the light of conscience well they will gain more light.

But yet all is not done; man disobeying,
Disloyal breaks his fealty, and sins
205 Against the high supremacy of Heav'n,
Affecting° Godhead, and so losing all,   *aspiring to*
To expiate his treason hath naught left,
But to destruction sacred and devote,°   *consecrated*
He with his whole posterity must die,
210 Die he or justice must; unless for him
Some other able, and as willing, pay
The rigid satisfaction, death for death.
Say heav'nly Powers, where shall we find such love,
Which of ye will be mortal to redeem
215 Man's mortal crime,[8] and just th' unjust to save,
Dwells in all Heaven charity so dear?"
     He asked, but all the heav'nly choir stood mute,[9]
And silence was in Heav'n; on man's behalf
Patron or intercessor none appeared,
220 Much less that durst upon his own head draw
The deadly forfeiture, and ransom set.
And now without redemption all mankind
Must have been lost, adjudged to death and Hell
By doom severe, had not the Son of God,
225 In whom the fullness dwells of love divine,
His dearest mediation° thus renewed.   *intercession*
     "Father, thy word is passed, man shall find grace;
And shall grace not find means, that finds her way,
The speediest of thy wingèd messengers,
230 To visit all thy creatures, and to all
Comes unprevented,° unimplored, unsought,   *unanticipated*
Happy for man, so coming; he her aid
Can never seek, once dead in sins and lost;
Atonement for himself or offering meet,°   *fitting*
235 Indebted and undone, hath none to bring:
Behold me then, me for him, life for life
I offer, on me let thine anger fall;
Account me man; I for his sake will leave
Thy bosom, and this glory next to thee
240 Freely put off, and for him lastly die
Well pleased, on me let Death wreak all his rage;
Under his gloomy power I shall not long
Lie vanquished; thou hast giv'n me to possess
Life in myself forever, by thee I live,
245 Though now to Death I yield, and am his due
All that of me can die, yet that debt paid,
Thou wilt not leave me in the loathsome grave
His prey, nor suffer my unspotted soul
Forever with corruption there to dwell;
250 But I shall rise victorious, and subdue
My vanquisher, spoiled of his vaunted spoil;

8. "Mortal" means "human" in line 214, but   9. Compare the devils in the Great Consult,
"deadly" in line 215.   2.420–26.

Death his death's wound shall then receive, and stoop
Inglorious, of his mortal sting disarmed.
I through the ample air in triumph high
255 Shall lead Hell captive maugre° Hell, and show   *in spite of*
The powers of darkness bound. Thou at the sight
Pleased, out of Heaven shalt look down and smile,
While by thee raised I ruin¹ all my foes,
Death last, and with his carcass glut the grave:
260 Then with the multitude of my redeemed
Shall enter Heaven long absent, and return,
Father, to see thy face, wherein no cloud
Of anger shall remain, but peace assured,
And reconcilement; wrath shall be no more
265 Thenceforth, but in thy presence joy entire."
     His words here ended, but his meek aspéct
Silent yet spake, and breathed immortal love
To mortal men, above which only shone
Filial obedience: as a sacrifice
270 Glad to be offered, he attends the will
Of his great Father. Admiration° seized   *wonder*
All Heav'n, what this might mean, and whither tend
Wond'ring; but soon th' Almighty thus replied:
     "O thou in Heav'n and earth the only peace
275 Found out for mankind under wrath, O thou
My sole complacence!° well thou know'st how dear   *pleasure, delight*
To me are all my works, nor man the least
Though last created, that for him I spare
Thee from my bosom and right hand, to save,
280 By losing thee a while, the whole race lost.
Thou therefore whom² thou only canst redeem,
Their nature also to thy nature join;
And be thyself man among men on earth,
Made flesh, when time shall be, of virgin seed,
285 By wondrous birth: be thou in Adam's room
The head of all mankind, though Adam's son.³
As in him perish all men, so in thee
As from a second root shall be restored,
As many as are restored, without thee none.
290 His crime makes guilty all his sons; thy merit
Imputed shall absolve them who renounce
Their own both righteous and unrighteous deeds,
And live in thee transplanted, and from thee
Receive new life.⁴ So man, as is most just,
295 Shall satisfy for man, be judged and die,
And dying rise, and rising with him raise
His brethren, ransomed with his own dear life.

---

1. In the Latin sense, throw down.
2. The antecedent of "whom" is, loosely construed, the "their nature" that follows it.
3. The Son of God, who long antedates the creation of Adam and who is actually the first created
being (3.383), is later incarnated in Jesus Christ;
he is called Second Adam and Son of Man by rea-

son of his descent from the first man, Adam. Cf.
1 Corinthians 15.22: "For as in Adam all die,
even so in Christ shall all be made alive."
4. The merit of Christ attributed vicariously
("imputed") to human beings frees from original
sin those who renounce their own deeds, good
and bad, and hope to be saved by faith.

So heav'nly love shall outdo hellish hate,
Giving to death, and dying to redeem,
300 So dearly to redeem what hellish hate
So easily destroyed, and still destroys
In those who, when they may, accept not grace.
Nor shalt thou by descending to assume
Man's nature, lessen or degrade thine own.
305 Because thou hast, though throned in highest bliss
Equal to God, and equally enjoying
Godlike fruition,° quitted all to save   *pleasurable possession*
A world from utter loss, and hast been found
By merit more than birthright Son of God,[5]
310 Found worthiest to be so by being good,
Far more than great or high; because in thee
Love hath abounded more than glory abounds.
Therefore thy humiliation shall exalt
With thee thy manhood also to this throne;
315 Here shalt thou sit incarnate, here shalt reign
Both God and man, Son both of God and man,
Anointed[6] universal King; all power
I give thee, reign forever, and assume
Thy merits; under thee as Head Supreme
320 Thrones, Princedoms, Powers, Dominions[7] I reduce:
All knees to thee shall bow, of them that bide
In Heaven, or earth, or under earth in Hell;
When thou attended gloriously from Heav'n
Shalt in the sky appear, and from thee send
325 The summoning Archangels to proclaim
Thy dread tribunal: forthwith from all winds°   *directions*
The living, and forthwith the cited° dead   *summoned*
Of all past ages to the general doom°   *judgment*
Shall hasten, such a peal shall rouse their sleep.
330 Then all thy saints assembled, thou shalt judge
Bad men and angels, they arraigned° shall sink   *accursed*
Beneath thy sentence; Hell, her numbers full,
Thenceforth shall be forever shut. Meanwhile
The world shall burn, and from her ashes spring
335 New heav'n° and earth, wherein the just shall dwell,[8]   *sky, cosmos*
And after all their tribulations long
See golden days, fruitful of golden deeds,
With joy and love triumphing, and fair truth.
Then thou thy regal scepter shalt lay by,
340 For regal scepter then no more shall need,°   *be needed*
God shall be all in all. But all ye gods,°   *angels*
Adore him, who to compass all this dies,
Adore the Son, and honor him as me."
No sooner had th' Almighty ceased, but all

---

5. A heterodox doctrine, that Christ was Son of
God by merit. Compare with Satan (2.5).
6. In Hebrew "Messiah" means "the anointed
one."
7. Orders of angels.

8. Milton's description of the Last Judgment
draws on several biblical texts, including Matthew
24.30–31 and 25.31–32; the account of the burning and re-creation of the heavens and earth is
from 2 Peter 3.12–13.

345 The multitude of angels with a shout
Loud as from numbers without number, sweet
As from blest voices, uttering joy, Heav'n rung[9]
With jubilee, and loud hosannas filled
Th' eternal regions: lowly reverent
350 Towards either throne[1] they bow, and to the ground
With solemn adoration down they cast
Their crowns inwove with amarant[2] and gold,
Immortal amarant, a flow'r which once
In Paradise, fast by the Tree of Life
355 Began to bloom, but soon for man's offense
To Heav'n removed where first it grew, there grows,
And flow'rs aloft shading the Fount of Life,
And where the river of bliss through midst of Heav'n
Rolls o'er Elysian[3] flow'rs her amber stream;
360 With these that never fade the Spirits elect
Bind their resplendent locks inwreathed with beams,
Now in loose garlands thick thrown off, the bright
Pavement that like a sea of jasper shone
Impurpled with celestial roses smiled.
365 Then crowned again their golden harps they took,
Harps ever tuned, that glittering by their side
Like quivers hung, and with preamble sweet
Of charming symphony they introduce
Their sacred song, and waken raptures high;
370 No voice exempt,° no voice but well could join   excluded
Melodious part, such concord is in Heav'n.
   Thee Father first they sung omnipotent,
Immutable, immortal, infinite,
Eternal King; thee Author of all being,
375 Fountain of light, thyself invisible
Amidst the glorious brightness where thou sitt'st
Throned inaccessible, but° when thou shad'st   except
The full blaze of thy beams, and through a cloud
Drawn round about thee like a radiant shrine,[4]
380 Dark with excessive bright thy skirts appear,
Yet dazzle Heav'n, that brightest Seraphim
Approach not, but with both wings veil their eyes.
Thee next they sang of all creation first,[5]
Begotten Son, Divine Similitude,
385 In whose conspicuous count'nance, without cloud
Made visible, th' Almighty Father shines,
Whom else no creature can behold;[6] on thee
Impressed th' effulgence of his glory abides,
Transfused on thee his ample spirit rests.
390 He Heav'n of heavens and all the Powers therein

---

9. "Multitude" (line 345) is the subject of the sentence, "rung" the verb, and "Heav'n" the object.
1. Thrones of God and the Son.
2. In Greek, "unfading," a legendary immortal flower.
3. Milton draws freely, for his Christian Heaven, on descriptions of the classical paradisal place,
the Elysian Fields.
4. The turn from theological debate to images that evoke a more mystical aspect of God.
5. The Son is not eternal, as in Trinitarian doctrine, but rather, God's first creation.
6. If it were not for the Son who is God's image, no creature could see God.

By thee created, and by thee threw down
Th' aspiring Dominations.[7] Thou that day
Thy Father's dreadful thunder didst not spare,
Nor stop thy flaming chariot wheels, that shook
395 Heav'n's everlasting frame, while o'er the necks
Thou drov'st of warring angels disarrayed.
Back from pursuit thy Powers° with loud acclaim   *angels*
Thee only extolled, Son of thy Father's might,
To execute fierce vengeance on his foes,
400 Not so on man; him through their malice fall'n,
Father of mercy and grace, thou didst not doom
So strictly, but much more to pity incline:
No sooner did thy dear and only Son
Perceive thee purposed not to doom° frail man   *judge*
405 So strictly, but much more to pity inclined,
He to appease thy wrath, and end the strife
Of mercy and justice in thy face discerned,
Regardless of the bliss wherein he sat
Second to thee, offered himself to die
410 For man's offense. O unexampled love,
Love nowhere to be found less than divine!
Hail Son of God, Savior of men, thy name
Shall be the copious matter of my[8] song
Henceforth, and never shall my harp thy praise
415 Forget, nor from thy Father's praise disjoin.
  Thus they in Heav'n, above the starry sphere,
Their happy hours in joy and hymning spent.
Meanwhile upon the firm opacous° globe   *opaque*
Of this round world, whose first convex divides
420 The luminous inferior orbs, enclosed
From Chaos and th' inroad of Darkness old,
Satan alighted walks:[9] a globe far off
It seemed, now seems a boundless continent
Dark, waste, and wild, under the frown of Night
425 Starless exposed, and ever-threatening storms
Of Chaos blust'ring round, inclement sky;
Save on that side which from the wall of Heav'n
Though distant far some small reflection gains
Of glimmering air less vexed with tempest loud:
430 Here walked the Fiend at large in spacious field.
As when a vulture on Imaus bred,
Whose snowy ridge the roving Tartar bounds,[1]
Dislodging from a region scarce of prey
To gorge the flesh of lambs or yeanling° kids   *newborn*
435 On hills where flocks are fed, flies toward the springs
Of Ganges or Hydaspes, Indian streams;[2]

7. The rebel angels.
8. Either Milton here quotes the angels singing as a single chorus, or he associates himself with their song, or both.
9. Satan is on the outermost of the ten concentric spheres that make up the cosmos.
1. Imaus, a ridge of mountains beyond the mod-

ern Himalayas, runs north through Asia from modern Afghanistan to the Arctic Circle.
2. Both the Ganges and the Hydaspes (a tributary of the Indus) rise from the mountains of northern India. Sericana (line 438) is a region in northwest China.

But in his way lights on the barren plains
Of Sericana, where Chineses drive
With sails and wind their cany wagons light:
440 So on this windy sea of land, the Fiend
Walked up and down alone bent on his prey,
Alone, for other creature in this place
Living or lifeless to be found was none,
None yet, but store hereafter from the earth
445 Up hither like aërial vapors flew
Of all things transitory and vain, when sin
With vanity had filled the works of men:
Both all things vain, and all who in vain things
Built their fond° hopes of glory or lasting fame,   *foolish*
450 Or happiness in this or th' other life;
All who have their reward on earth, the fruits
Of painful superstition and blind zeal,
Naught seeking but the praise of men, here find
Fit retribution, empty as their deeds;
455 All th' unaccomplished° works of nature's hand,   *imperfect*
Abortive, monstrous, or unkindly° mixed,   *unnaturally*
Dissolved on earth, fleet° hither, and in vain,   *float*
Till final dissolution, wander here,
Not in the neighboring moon, as some[3] have dreamed;
460 Those argent° fields more likely habitants,   *silver*
Translated saints,[4] or middle Spirits hold
Betwixt th' angelical and human kind:
Hither of ill-joined sons and daughters born
First from the ancient world those giants came
465 With many a vain exploit, though then renowned:[5]
The builders next of Babel on the plain
Of Sennaär,[6] and still with vain design
New Babels, had they wherewithal, would build:
Others came single; he who to be deemed
470 A god, leaped fondly° into Etna flames,   *foolishly*
Empedocles, and he who to enjoy
Plato's Elysium, leaped into the sea,
Cleombrotus, and many more too long,[7]
Embryos and idiots, eremites° and friars   *hermits*
475 White, black, and gray, with all their trumpery.[8]
Here pilgrims roam, that strayed so far to seek
In Golgotha[9] him dead, who lives in Heav'n;
And they who to be sure of paradise
Dying put on the weeds° of Dominic,   *garments*

---

3. Milton's Paradise of Fools (named in line 496) was inspired by Ariosto's Limbo of Vanity in *Orlando Furioso* (Book 34, lines 73ff.); Milton's region is reserved for deluded victims of misplaced devotion, chiefly Roman Catholics.
4. Holy men like Enoch and Elijah, transported to Heaven while yet alive. (Genesis 5.24; 2 Kings 2.11–12).
5. Giants, born of unnatural marriages between the "sons of God" and the daughters of men (Genesis 6.4), are creatures unkindly mixed.

6. Shinar, the plain of Babel (Genesis 11.2–9); the Tower of Babel is an emblem of human pride and folly.
7. I.e., it would take too long to name them. Both Empedocles and Cleombrotus foolishly carried piety to the point of suicide.
8. Religious paraphernalia. The white friars are Carmelites; the black, Dominicans; and the gray, Franciscans.
9. Place where Christ was crucified.

480   Or in Franciscan think to pass disguised;[1]
       They pass the planets seven, and pass the fixed,
       And that crystalline sphere whose balance weighs
       The trepidation talked, and that first moved;[2]
       And now Saint Peter at Heav'n's wicket seems
485   To wait them with his keys, and now at foot
       Of Heav'n's ascent they lift their feet, when lo
       A violent crosswind from either coast
       Blows them transverse ten thousand leagues awry
       Into the devious° air. Then might ye see   *erratic*
490   Cowls, hoods, and habits[3] with their wearers tossed
       And fluttered into rags; then relics, beads,
       Indulgences, dispenses, pardons, bulls,
       The sport of winds: all these upwhirled aloft
       Fly o'er the backside° of the world far off   *rump*
495   Into a limbo large and broad, since called
       The Paradise of Fools, to few unknown
       Long after, now unpeopled, and untrod;
       All this dark globe the Fiend found as he passed,
       And long he wandered, till at last a gleam
500   Of dawning light turned thitherward in haste
       His traveled° steps; far distant he descries   *travel-weary*
       Ascending by degrees° magnificent   *steps*
       Up to the wall of Heaven a structure high,
       At top whereof, but far more rich appeared
505   The work as of a kingly palace gate
       With frontispiece° of diamond and gold   *pediment*
       Embellished; thick with sparkling orient° gems   *lustrous*
       The portal shone, inimitable on earth,
       By model, or by shading pencil drawn.
510   The stairs were such as whereon Jacob saw
       Angels ascending and descending, bands
       Of guardians bright, when he from Esau fled
       To Padan-Aram in the field of Luz,
       Dreaming by night under the open sky,
515   And waking cried, "This is the gate of Heav'n."[4]
       Each stair mysteriously was meant, nor stood
       There always, but drawn up to Heav'n sometimes
       Viewless,° and underneath a bright sea flowed   *invisible*
       Of jasper, or of liquid pearl, whereon
520   Who after came from earth, sailing arrived,
       Wafted by angels, or flew o'er the lake
       Rapt in a chariot drawn by fiery steeds.[5]
       The stairs were then let down, whether to dare
       The Fiend by easy ascent, or aggravate

1. Some try to trick God into granting them salvation by wearing on their deathbeds the garb of various religious orders.
2. Milton follows their souls through the spheres of the moon and sun, the five then-known planets, the fixed stars, and the sphere responsible for the "trepidation" (a periodic corrective shudder of the cosmos), up to the primum mobile, or prime mover. The next step seems to be the empyreal Heaven.
3. The dress of religious orders, together with (next lines) saints' relics, rosary beads, various kinds of pardon for sins, and papal decrees ("bulls").
4. The story of Jacob's vision is summarized from Genesis 28.1–19; the stairs of the ladder (next line) allegorically ("mysteriously") represent stages of spiritual growth.
5. Elijah was wafted to heaven in a chariot.

525 His sad exclusion from the doors of bliss.
Direct against which opened from beneath,
Just o'er the blissful seat of Paradise,
A passage down to th' earth, a passage wide,[6]
Wider by far than that of aftertimes
530 Over Mount Zion, and, though that were large,
Over the Promised Land to God so dear,
By which, to visit oft those happy tribes,
On high behests his angels to and fro
Passed frequent, and his eye with choice° regard   *discriminating*
535 From Paneas the fount of Jordan's flood
To Beërsaba, where the Holy Land
Borders on Egypt and the Arabian shore;[7]
So wide the op'ning seemed, where bounds were set
To darkness, such as bound the ocean wave.
540 Satan from hence now on the lower stair
That scaled by steps of gold to Heaven gate
Looks down with wonder at the sudden view
Of all this world at once. As when a scout
Through dark and desert ways with peril gone
545 All night; at last by break of cheerful dawn
Obtains° the brow of some high-climbing hill,   *gains*
Which to his eye discovers unaware
The goodly prospect of some foreign land
First seen, or some renowned metropolis
550 With glistering spires and pinnacles adorned,
Which now the rising sun gilds with his beams.
Such wonder seized, though after Heaven seen,
The Spirit malign, but much more envy seized
At sight of all this world beheld so fair.
555 Round he surveys, and well might, where he stood
So high above the circling canopy
Of night's extended shade; from eastern point
Of Libra to the fleecy star that bears
Andromeda far off Atlantic seas[8]
560 Beyond th' horizon; then from pole to pole
He views in breadth, and without longer pause
Down right into the world's first region throws
His flight precipitant, and winds with ease
Through the pure marble° air his oblique way   *sparkling*
565 Amongst innumerable stars, that shone
Stars distant, but nigh hand seemed other worlds,
Or other worlds they seemed, or happy isles,
Like those Hesperian gardens famed of old,
Fortunate fields, and groves and flow'ry vales,[9]
570 Thrice happy isles, but who dwelt happy there
He stayed not to inquire: above them all

6. A passage through the crystalline spheres, otherwise impenetrable.
7. From Paneas (or Dan) in northern Palestine to Beersaba, or Beersheba, near the Egyptian border—the entire land of Israel.
8. In the zodiac, Libra is diametrically oppo-site Aries, or the Ram ("the fleecy star"), which seems to carry the constellation Andromeda on its back.
9. The gardens of the Hesperides and the "fortu-nate isles" of Greek mythology, classical versions of paradise, lay far out in the Atlantic.

The golden sun in splendor likest Heaven
Allured his eye: thither his course he bends
Through the calm firmament;° but up or down   *sky*
575 By center, or eccentric, hard to tell,
Or longitude,[1] where the great luminary
Aloof the vulgar constellations thick,
That from his lordly eye keep distance due,
Dispenses light from far; they as they move
580 Their starry dance in numbers that compute
Days, months, and years, towards his all-cheering lamp
Turn swift their various motions, or are turned
By his magnetic beam, that gently warms
The universe, and to each inward part
585 With gentle penetration, though unseen,
Shoots invisible virtue° even to the deep: *influence, strength*
So wondrously was set his station bright.
    There lands the Fiend, a spot like which perhaps
Astronomer in the sun's lucent orb
590 Through his glazed optic tube yet never saw.[2]
The place he found beyond expression bright,
Compared with aught on earth, metal or stone;
Not all parts like, but all alike informed
With radiant light, as glowing iron with fire;
595 If metal, part seemed gold, part silver clear;
If stone, carbuncle most or chrysolite,[3]
Ruby or topaz, to the twelve that shone
In Aaron's breastplate,[4] and a stone besides
Imagined rather oft than elsewhere seen,[5]
600 That stone, or like to that which here below
Philosophers in vain so long have sought,[6]
In vain, though by their powerful art they bind
Volátile Hermes, and call up unbound
In various shapes old Proteus from the sea,
605 Drained through a limbec to his native form.[7]
What wonder then if fields and regions here
Breathe forth elixir pure,[8] and rivers run
Potable° gold, when with one virtuous° touch   *drinkable / powerful*
Th' arch-chemic° sun so far from us remote   *chief alchemist*
610 Produces with terrestrial humor° mixed   *earth's moisture*
Here in the dark so many precious things
Of color glorious and effect so rare?
Here matter new to gaze the Devil met
Undazzled, far and wide his eye commands,

---

1. The passage leaves open whether the sun or the earth is at the center of the cosmos.
2. Galileo first observed sunspots through his telescope in 1609.
3. Any green stone. "Carbuncle": any red stone.
4. In Exodus 28.15–20, Aaron's "breastplate" is described as decorated with twelve different gems, of which Milton lists the first four.
5. I.e., elsewhere imagined more often than seen.
6. Alchemists had identified the "philosophers" store with the *urim* on Aaron's breastplate (Exo-

dus 28.30); that stone reputedly could heal all diseases, restore paradise, and transmute base metals to gold.
7. "Hermes": the winged god and the element mercury, which evaporated readily ("volatile"). "Proteus": the shape-shifting sea god, a symbol of matter. Alchemists would "bind" (solidify) mercury and dissolve or refine matter to its "native form" in a vessel (alembic, "limbec").
8. The liquid form of the philosopher's stone. "Here": in the sun.

615 For sight no obstacle found here, nor shade,
But all sunshine, as when his beams at noon
Culminate from th' equator, as they now
Shot upward still direct, whence no way round
Shadow from body opaque can fall,[9] and the air,
620 Nowhere so clear, sharpened his visual ray
To objects distant far,[1] whereby he soon
Saw within ken° a glorious angel stand,   *range of vision*
The same whom John saw also in the sun:[2]
His back was turned, but not his brightness hid;
625 Of beaming sunny rays, a golden tiar°   *tiara, crown*
Circled his head, nor less his locks behind
Illustrious° on his shoulders fledge° with wings   *lustrous / feathered*
Lay waving round; on some great charge employed
He seemed, or fixed in cogitation deep.
630 Glad was the Spirit impure; as now in hope
To find who might direct his wand'ring flight
To Paradise the happy seat of man,
His journey's end and our beginning woe.
But first he casts° to change his proper shape,   *contrives*
635 Which else might work him danger or delay:
And now a stripling Cherub he appears,
Not of the prime,[3] yet such as in his face
Youth smiled celestial, and to every limb
Suitable grace diffused, so well he feigned;
640 Under a coronet his flowing hair
In curls on either cheek played, wings he wore
Of many a colored plume sprinkled with gold,
His habit fit for speed succinct,° and held   *close-fitting*
Before his decent° steps a silver wand.   *comely*
645 He drew not nigh unheard; the angel bright,
Ere he drew nigh, his radiant visage turned,
Admonished by his ear, and straight° was known   *immediately*
Th' Archangel Uriel, one of the sev'n
Who in God's presence, nearest to his throne[4]
650 Stand ready at command, and are his eyes
That run through all the heav'ns, or down to th' earth
Bear his swift errands over moist and dry,
O'er sea and land: him Satan thus accosts:
    "Uriel, for thou of those sev'n Spirits that stand
655 In sight of God's high throne, gloriously bright,
The first art wont° his great authentic° will   *used / authoritative*
Interpreter through highest Heav'n to bring,
Where all his sons thy embassy attend;
And here art likeliest by supreme decree
660 Like honor to obtain, and as his eye

9. Before the Fall (and the consequent tipping of the earth's axis) the sun at noon, on the equator, never cast a shadow. "Culminate": reach their zenith.
1. The eye was thought to emit a beam into the object perceived.
2. "I saw an angel standing in the sun" (Reve-

lation 19.17).
3. Not yet in the prime of life.
4. Uriel—in Hebrew, "light" (or "fire") of God—is the angel named first (in 2 Esdras 4.1–5, *apocrypha*) among the seven angels who stood before God's throne.

To visit oft this new creation round;
Unspeakable desire to see, and know
All these his wondrous works, but chiefly man,
His chief delight and favor,° him for whom   *favorite*
665   All these his works so wondrous he ordained,
Hath brought me from the choirs of Cherubim
Alone thus wand'ring. Brightest Seraph tell
In which of all these shining orbs hath man
His fixèd seat, or fixèd seat hath none,
670   But all these shining orbs his choice to dwell;
That I may find him, and with secret gaze,
Or open admiration him behold
On whom the great Creator hath bestowed
Worlds, and on whom hath all these graces poured;
675   That both in him and all things, as is meet,°   *fitting*
The Universal Maker we may praise;
Who justly hath driv'n out his rebel foes
To deepest Hell, and to repair that loss
Created this new happy race of men
680   To serve him better: wise are all his ways."
         So spake the false dissembler unperceived;
For neither man nor angel can discern
Hypocrisy, the only evil that walks
Invisible, except to God alone,
685   By his permissive will, through Heav'n and earth:
And oft though wisdom wake, suspicion sleeps
At wisdom's gate, and to simplicity
Resigns her charge, while goodness thinks no ill
Where no ill seems: which now for once beguiled
690   Uriel, though regent of the sun, and held
The sharpest-sighted Spirit of all in Heav'n;
Who to the fraudulent impostor foul
In his uprightness answer thus returned:
         "Fair angel, thy desire which tends° to know   *inclines*
695   The works of God, thereby to glorify
The great Work-Master, leads to no excess
That reaches blame, but rather merits praise
The more it seems excess, that led thee hither
From thy empyreal mansion thus alone,
700   To witness with thine eyes what some perhaps
Contented with report hear only in Heav'n:
For wonderful indeed are all his works,
Pleasant to know, and worthiest to be all
Had in remembrance always with delight;
705   But what created mind can comprehend
Their number, or the wisdom infinite
That brought them forth, but hid their causes deep.
I saw when at his word the formless mass,
This world's material mold,° came to a heap: *substance*
710   Confusion heard his voice, and wild uproar
Stood ruled, stood vast infinitude confined;
Till at his second bidding darkness fled,

Light shone, and order from disorder sprung:
Swift to their several quarters hasted then
715 The cumbrous elements, earth, flood, air, fire,
And this ethereal quíntessence[5] of Heav'n
Flew upward, spirited with various forms,
That rolled orbicular,[6] and turned to stars
Numberless, as thou seest, and how they move;
720 Each had his place appointed, each his course,
The rest in circuit walls this universe.
Look downward on that globe whose hither side
With light from hence, though but reflected, shines;
That place is earth the seat of man, that light
725 His day, which else as th' other hemisphere
Night would invade, but there the neighboring moon
(So call that opposite fair star) her aid
Timely interposes, and her monthly round
Still ending, still renewing through mid-Heav'n,
730 With borrowed light her countenance triform[7]
Hence[8] fills and empties to enlighten th' earth,
And in her pale dominion checks the night.
That spot to which I point is Paradise,
Adam's abode, those lofty shades his bow'r.
735 Thy way thou canst not miss, me mine requires."
    Thus said, he turned, and Satan bowing low,
As to superior Spirits is wont in Heav'n,
Where honor due and reverence none neglects,
Took leave, and toward the coast of earth beneath,
740 Down from th' ecliptic,° sped with hoped success,   *the sun's orbit*
Throws his steep flight in many an airy wheel,
Nor stayed, till on Niphates' top[9] he lights.

Book 4

The Argument

Satan now in prospect of Eden, and nigh the place where he must now attempt the bold enterprise which he undertook alone against God and man, falls into many doubts with himself, and many passions, fear, envy, and despair; but at length confirms himself in evil, journeys on to Paradise, whose outward prospect and situation is described, overleaps the bounds, sits in the shape of a cormorant on the Tree of Life, as highest in the Garden to look about him. The Garden described; Satan's first sight of Adam and Eve; his wonder at their excellent form and happy state, but with resolution to work their fall; overhears their discourse, thence gathers that the Tree of Knowledge was forbidden them to eat of, under penalty of death; and thereon intends to found his temptation, by seducing them to transgress: then leaves

---

5. The fifth element, of which the incorruptible heavenly bodies were made.
6. The spherical shape of the stars and their orbits. "Spirited with various forms": presided over or inhabited by various angelic spirits or intel-

ligences (Plato, *Timaeus* 41E).
7. The moon was said to have a triple nature: Luna in Heaven, Diana on earth, and Hecate in Hell.
8. From here (the sun).
9. A mountain in Assyria.

them a while, to know further of their state by some other means. Meanwhile Uriel descending on a sunbeam warns Gabriel, who had in charge the gate of Paradise, that some evil Spirit had escaped the deep, and passed at noon by his sphere in the shape of a good angel down to Paradise, discovered after by his furious gestures in the mount. Gabriel promises to find him ere morning. Night coming on, Adam and Eve discourse of going to their rest: their bower described; their evening worship. Gabriel drawing forth his bands of nightwatch to walk the round of Paradise, appoints two strong angels to Adam's bower, lest the evil Spirit should be there doing some harm to Adam or Eve sleeping; there they find him at the ear of Eve, tempting her in a dream, and bring him, though unwilling, to Gabriel; by whom questioned, he scornfully answers, prepares resistance, but hindered by a sign from heaven, flies out of Paradise.

O for that warning voice, which he who saw
Th' Apocalypse, heard cry in Heaven aloud,
Then when the Dragon, put to second rout,
Came furious down to be revenged on men,
5   "Woe to the inhabitants on earth!"[1] that now,
While time was, our first parents had been warned
The coming of their secret foe, and scaped
Haply° so scaped his mortal° snare; for now   *perhaps / deadly*
Satan, now first inflamed with rage, came down,
10 The tempter ere° th' accuser of mankind,   *before being*
To wreak° on innocent frail man his loss   *avenge*
Of that first battle, and his flight to Hell:
Yet not rejoicing in his speed, though bold,
Far off and fearless, nor with cause to boast,
15 Begins his dire attempt, which nigh the birth
Now rolling, boils in his tumultuous breast,
And like a devilish engine back recoils
Upon himself; horror and doubt distract
His troubled thoughts, and from the bottom stir
20 The Hell within him, for within him Hell
He brings, and round about him, nor from Hell
One step no more than from himself can fly
By change of place: now conscience wakes despair
That slumbered, wakes the bitter memory
25 Of what he was, what is, and what must be
Worse; of worse deeds worse sufferings must ensue.
Sometimes towards Eden which now in his view
Lay pleasant, his grieved look he fixes sad,
Sometimes towards Heav'n and the full-blazing sun,
30 Which now sat high in his meridian tow'r:[2]
Then much revolving,° thus in sighs began.   *pondering*
   "O thou that with surpassing glory crowned,[3]
Look'st from thy sole dominion like the god

---

1. John of Patmos, in Revelation 12.3–12, hears such a cry during a second war in Heaven, between the Dragon and the angels.
2. At midday, the height of noon.

3. Milton's nephew, Edward Phillips, said that this soliloquy was written "several years before the poem was begun," and was intended to begin a drama on the topic, *Adam Unparadised*.

Of this new world: at whose sight all the stars
35 Hide their diminished heads; to thee I call,
But with no friendly voice, and add thy name
O sun, to tell thee how I hate thy beams
That bring to my remembrance from what state
I fell, how glorious once above thy sphere;
40 Till pride and worse ambition threw me down
Warring in Heav'n against Heav'n's matchless King:
Ah wherefore! he deserved no such return
From me, whom he created what I was
In that bright eminence, and with his good
45 Upbraided⁴ none, nor was his service hard.
What could be less than to afford him praise,
The easiest recompense, and pay him thanks,
How due! yet all his good proved ill in me,
And wrought but malice; lifted up so high
50 I 'sdained° subjection, and thought one step higher   *disdained*
Would set me highest, and in a moment quit°   *pay*
The debt immense of endless gratitude,
So burthensome still° paying, still to owe;   *always*
Forgetful what from him I still received,
55 And understood not that a grateful mind
By owing owes not, but still pays, at once
Indebted and discharged; what burden then?
O had his powerful destiny ordained
Me some inferior angel, I had stood
60 Then happy; no unbounded hope had raised
Ambition. Yet why not? some other Power°   *angel*
As great might have aspired, and me though mean
Drawn to his part; but other Powers as great
Fell not, but stand unshaken, from within
65 Or from without, to all temptations armed.
Hadst thou⁵ the same free will and power to stand?
Thou hadst: whom hast thou then or what to accuse,
But Heav'n's free love dealt equally to all?
Be then his love accursed, since love or hate,
70 To me alike, it deals eternal woe.
Nay cursed be thou; since against his thy will
Chose freely what it now so justly rues.
Me miserable!⁶ which way shall I fly
Infinite wrath, and infinite despair?
75 Which way I fly is Hell; myself am Hell;⁷
And in the lowest deep a lower deep
Still threat'ning to devour me opens wide,
To which the Hell I suffer seems a Heav'n.
O then at last relent! is there no place
80 Left for repentance, none for pardon left?
None left but by submission; and that word

---

4. Reproached (James 1.5).
5. Compare Satan's address to himself here with Adam's soliloquy in parallel circumstances (10.758ff.).
6. A Latinism, *me miserum!*
7. Compare Satan's earlier claim that "the mind is its own place" (1.254).

Disdain forbids me, and my dread of shame
Among the Spirits beneath, whom I seduced
With other promises and other vaunts
85   Than to submit, boasting I could subdue
Th' Omnipotent. Ay me, they little know
How dearly I abide° that boast so vain,   *pay the penalty far*
Under what torments inwardly I groan:
While they adore me on the throne of Hell,
90   With diadem and scepter high advanced
The lower still I fall, only supreme
In misery; such joy ambition finds.
But say I could repent and could obtain
By act of grace⁸ my former state; how soon
95   Would heighth recall high thoughts, how soon unsay
What feigned submission swore: ease would recant
Vows made in pain, as violent° and void.   *forced*
For never can true reconcilement grow
Where wounds of deadly hate have pierced so deep:
100 Which would but lead me to a worse relapse,
And heavier fall: so should I purchase dear
Short intermission bought with double smart.
This knows my punisher; therefore as far
From granting he, as I from begging peace:
105 All hope excluded thus, behold instead
Of us outcast, exiled, his new delight,
Mankind created, and for him this world.
So farewell hope, and with hope farewell fear,
Farewell remorse: all good to me is lost;
110 Evil be thou my good; by thee at least
Divided empire with Heav'n's King I hold
By thee, and more than half perhaps will reign;
As man ere long, and this new world shall know."
     Thus while he spake, each passion dimmed his face
115 Thrice changed with pale,° ire, envy, and despair,   *pallor*
Which marred his borrowed visage, and betrayed
Him counterfeit, if any eye beheld.
For heav'nly minds from such distempers foul
Are ever clear. Whereof he soon aware,
120 Each perturbation smoothed with outward calm,
Artificer of fraud; and was the first
That practiced falsehood under saintly show,
Deep malice to conceal, couched° with revenge: *hidden*
Yet not enough had practiced to deceive
125 Uriel once warned; whose eye pursued him down
The way he went, and on th' Assyrian mount°   *Niphates*
Saw him disfigured, more than could befall
Spirit of happy sort: his gestures fierce
He marked and mad demeanor, then alone,
130 As he supposed, all unobserved, unseen.
     So on he fares, and to the border comes

8. The technical term for a formal pardon.

Of Eden, where delicious Paradise,[9]
Now nearer, crowns with her enclosure green,
As with a rural mound the champaign head°   *open summit*
135 Of a steep wilderness, whose hairy sides
With thicket overgrown, grotesque[1] and wild,
Access denied; and overhead up grew
Insuperable heighth of loftiest shade,
Cedar, and pine, and fir, and branching palm,
140 A sylvan scene, and as the ranks ascend
Shade above shade, a woody theater[2]
Of stateliest view. Yet higher than their tops
The verdurous wall of Paradise up sprung:
Which to our general sire gave prospect large
145 Into his nether empire neighboring round.
And higher than that wall a circling row
Of goodliest trees loaden with fairest fruit,
Blossoms and fruits at once of golden hue
Appeared, with gay enameled° colors mixed: *bright*
150 On which the sun more glad impressed his beams
Than in fair evening cloud, or humid bow,°   *rainbow*
When God hath show'red the earth; so lovely seemed
That landscape: and of pure now purer air[3]
Meets his approach, and to the heart inspires°   *infuses*
155 Vernal delight and joy, able to drive°   *drive out*
All sadness but despair: now gentle gales
Fanning their odoriferous° wings dispense   *fragrance-bearing*
Native perfumes, and whisper whence they stole
Those balmy spoils. As when to them who sail
160 Beyond the Cape of Hope,° and now are past   *Cape of Good Hope*
Mozambic, off at sea northeast winds blow
Sabean odors from the spicy shore
Of Araby the Blest,[4] with such delay
Well pleased they slack their course, and many a league
165 Cheered with the grateful° smell old Ocean smiles.   *pleasing*
So entertained those odorous sweets the Fiend
Who came their bane,° though with them better pleased   *poison*
Than Asmodeus with the fishy fume,
That drove him, though enamored, from the spouse
170 Of Tobit's son, and with a vengeance sent
From Media post to Egypt, there fast bound.[5]
     Now to th'ascent of that steep savage° hill   *wooded, wild*
Satan had journeyed on, pensive and slow;
But further way found none, so thick entwined,
175 As one continued brake,° the undergrowth   *thicket*

9. Paradise is a delightful ("delicious") garden
on top of a steep hill situated in the east of the
land of Eden.
1. Characterized by interwoven, tangled vines and
branches.
2. As if in a Greek amphitheater, the trees are set
row on row.
3. The air becomes still purer.
4. *Arabia Felix* (modern Yemen). "Sabean": the

biblical Sheba.
5. The Apocryphal book of Tobit tells of Tobias,
Tobit's son, who married Sara and avoided the
fate of her previous seven husbands (killed on
their wedding night by the demon Asmodeus) by
following the instructions of the angel Raphael
and making a fishy smell to drive him off; Asmodeus then fled to Egypt, where Raphael bound
him.

Of shrubs and tangling bushes had perplexed
All path of man or beast that passed that way:
One gate there only was, and that looked east
On th' other side: which when th' arch-felon saw
180 Due entrance he disdained, and in contempt,
At one slight bound high overleaped all bound
Of hill or highest wall, and sheer within
Lights on his feet. As when a prowling wolf,
Whom hunger drives to seek new haunt for prey,
185 Watching where shepherds pen their flocks at eve
In hurdled cotes° amid the field secure,   *pens of woven reeds*
Leaps o'er the fence with ease into the fold:
Or as a thief bent to unhoard the cash
Of some rich burgher, whose substantial doors,
190 Cross-barred and bolted fast, fear no assault,
In at the window climbs, or o'er the tiles;
So clomb° this first grand thief into God's fold: *climbed*
So since into his church lewd hirelings[6] climb.
Thence up he flew, and on the Tree of Life,
195 The middle tree and highest there that grew,
Sat like a cormorant;[7] yet not true life
Thereby regained, but sat devising death
To them who lived; nor on the virtue° thought   *power*
Of that life-giving plant, but only used
200 For prospect,° what well used had been the pledge   *as a lookout*
Of immortality. So little knows
Any, but God alone, to value right
The good before him, but perverts best things
To worst abuse, or to their meanest use.
205   Beneath him with new wonder now he views
To all delight of human sense exposed
In narrow room nature's whole wealth, yea more,
A heav'n on earth: for blissful Paradise
Of God the garden was, by him in the east
210 Of Eden planted; Eden stretched her line
From Auran eastward to the royal tow'rs
Of great Seleucia, built by Grecian kings,
Or where the sons of Eden long before
Dwelt in Telassar:[8] in this pleasant soil
215 His far more pleasant garden God ordained;
Out of the fertile ground he caused to grow
All trees of noblest kind for sight, smell, taste;
And all amid them stood the Tree of Life,
High eminent, blooming ambrosial° fruit   *divinely fragrant*
220 Of vegetable gold; and next to life
Our death the Tree of Knowledge grew fast by,
Knowledge of good bought dear by knowing ill.

6. Base men interested only in money; Milton would have clergymen not paid by required tithes or by the state, to ensure their purity of motive.
7. A sea bird, noted for gluttony.
8. Auran is the province of Hauran on the eastern border of Israel. Selucia, a powerful city on the Tigris, near modern Baghdad, was founded by one of Alexander's generals ("built by Grecian kings"). Telassar is another Near Eastern kingdom.

Southward through Eden went a river large,[9]
Nor changed his course, but through the shaggy hill
225 Passed underneath engulfed, for God had thrown
That mountain as his garden mold° high raised   *rich earth*
Upon the rapid current, which through veins
Of porous earth with kindly° thirst up drawn,   *natural*
Rose a fresh fountain, and with many a rill
230 Watered the garden; thence united fell
Down the steep glade, and met the nether flood,
Which from his darksome passage now appears,
And now divided into four main streams,
Runs diverse, wand'ring many a famous realm
235 And country whereof here needs no account,
But rather to tell how, if art could tell,
How from that sapphire fount the crispèd° brooks,   *wavy, rippling*
Rolling on orient pearl and sands of gold,
With mazy error[1] under pendent shades
240 Ran nectar, visiting each plant, and fed
Flow'rs worthy of Paradise which not nice° art   *fastidious*
In beds and curious knots, but nature boon°   *bounteous*
Poured forth profuse on hill and dale and plain,
Both where the morning sun first warmly smote
245 The open field, and where the unpierced shade
Embrowned° the noontide bow'rs. Thus was this place,   *darkened*
A happy rural seat of various view,[2]
Groves whose rich trees wept odorous gums and balm,
Others whose fruit burnished with golden rind
250 Hung amiable,° Hesperian fables true,[3]   *lovely*
If true, here only, and of delicious taste:
Betwixt them lawns, or level downs,° and flocks   *uplands*
Grazing the tender herb, were interposed,
Or palmy hillock, or the flow'ry lap
255 Of some irriguous° valley spread her store,   *well-watered*
Flow'rs of all hue, and without thorn the rose:
Another side, umbrageous° grots and caves   *shady*
Of cool recess, o'er which the mantling° vine   *enveloping*
Lays forth her purple grape, and gently creeps
260 Luxuriant; meanwhile murmuring waters fall
Down the slope hills, dispersed, or in a lake,
That to the fringèd bank with myrtle crowned,
Her crystal mirror holds, unite their streams.
The birds their choir apply; airs,[4] vernal airs,
265 Breathing the smell of field and grove, attune
The trembling leaves, while universal Pan[5]
Knit° with the Graces and the Hours in dance   *clasping hands*
Led on th' eternal spring. Not that fair field

9. The Tigris (identified at 9.71) flowed under the hill.
1. From Latin *errare*, wandering.
2. Like a country estate, with a variety of prospects.
3. These were real golden apples, by contrast to those feigned golden apples of the Hesperides, fabled paradisal islands in the Western Ocean.
4. Both breezes and melodies. "Their choir apply": practice their songs.
5. The god of all nature—*pan* in Greek means "all."

Of Enna, where Proserpine gathering flow'rs
270 Herself a fairer flow'r by gloomy Dis
Was gathered, which cost Ceres all that pain
To seek her through the world; nor that sweet grove
Of Daphne by Orontes, and th' inspired
Castalian spring, might with this Paradise
275 Of Eden strive;[6] nor that Nyseian isle
Girt with the river Triton, where old Cham,
Whom Gentiles Ammon call and Libyan Jove,
Hid Amalthea and her florid° son   wine-flushed
Young Bacchus from his stepdame Rhea's eye;[7]
280 Nor where Abassin kings their issue guard,
Mount Amara,[8] though this by some supposed
True Paradise under the Ethiop line°   equator
By Nilus'° head, enclosed with shining rock,   Nile's
A whole day's journey high, but wide remote
285 From this Assyrian garden,° where the Fiend   Eden
Saw undelighted all delight, all kind
Of living creatures new to sight and strange:
    Two of far nobler shape erect and tall,
Godlike erect, with native honor clad
290 In naked majesty seemed lords of all,
And worthy seemed, for in their looks divine
The image of their glorious Maker shone,
Truth, wisdom, sanctitude severe and pure,
Severe but in true filial freedom placed;
295 Whence true authority in men;[9] though both
Not equal, as their sex not equal seemed;
For contemplation he and valor formed,
For softness she and sweet attractive grace,
He for God only, she for God in him:[1]
300 His fair large front° and eye sublime declared   forehead
Absolute rule; and hyacinthine[2] locks
Round from his parted forelock manly hung
Clust'ring, but not beneath his shoulders broad:
She as a veil down to the slender waist
305 Her unadorned golden tresses wore
Disheveled, but in wanton° ringlets waved   unrestrained
As the vine curls her tendrils,[3] which implied
Subjection, but required° with gentle sway,°   requested / persuasion
And by her yielded, by him best received,
310 Yielded with coy° submission, modest pride,   shyly reserved

6. Milton compares Paradise with famous beauty spots of antiquity. Enna in Sicily was a lovely meadow from which Proserpine was kidnapped by "gloomy Dis" (i.e., Pluto); her mother Ceres sought her throughout the world. The grove of Daphne, near Antioch and the Orontes River in the Near East, had a spring called "Castalia" after the Muses' fountain near Parnassus.
7. The isle of Nysa in the river Triton in Tunisia was where Ammon (an Egyptian god, identified with Cham, or Ham, the son of Noah) hid Bacchus, his child by Amalthea (who later became the god of wine), away from the eyes of his wife Rhea.

8. Atop Mount Amara, the "Abassin" (Abyssinian) king had a splendid palace in a paradisal garden.
9. This phrase underscores Milton's idea that true freedom involves obedience to natural superiors (i.e., God).
1. The phrase has as its context 1 Corinthians 11.3: "The head of every man is Christ; and the head of the woman is the man."
2. A classical metaphor for hair curled in the form of hyacinth petals, and perhaps also implying dark or flowing.
3. Eve's hair is curly, abundant, not subjected to rigid control, like the vegetation in Paradise.

And sweet reluctant amorous delay.
Nor those mysterious parts were then concealed,
Then was not guilty shame, dishonest° shame   *unchaste*
Of nature's works, honor dishonorable,
315 Sin-bred, how have ye troubled all mankind
With shows instead, mere shows of seeming pure,
And banished from man's life his happiest life,
Simplicity and spotless innocence.
So passed they naked on, nor shunned the sight
320 Of God or angel, for they thought no ill:
So hand in hand they passed, the loveliest pair
That ever since in love's embraces met,
Adam the goodliest man of men since born
His sons, the fairest of her daughters Eve.
325 Under a tuft of shade that on a green
Stood whispering soft, by a fresh fountain side
They sat them down, and after no more toil
Of their sweet gard'ning labor than sufficed
To recommend cool Zephyr,[4] and made ease
330 More easy, wholesome thirst and appetite
More grateful, to their supper fruits they fell,
Nectarine° fruits which the compliant boughs   *sweet as nectar*
Yielded them, sidelong as they sat recline
On the soft downy bank damasked with flow'rs:
335 The savory pulp they chew, and in the rind
Still as they thirsted scoop the brimming stream;
Nor gentle purpose,° nor endearing smiles   *conversation*
Wanted,° nor youthful dalliance as beseems   *lacked*
Fair couple, linked in happy nuptial league,
340 Alone as they. About them frisking played
All beasts of th' earth, since wild, and of all chase°   *game animals*
In wood or wilderness, forest or den;
Sporting the lion ramped,° and in his paw   *stood on hind legs*
Dandled the kid; bears, tigers, ounces,° pards°   *lynxes / leopards*
345 Gamboled before them; th' unwieldy elephant
To make them mirth used all his might, and wreathed
His lithe proboscis;° close the serpent sly   *trunk*
Insinuating,° wove with Gordian twine   *writhing, twisting*
His braided train,[5] and of his fatal guile
350 Gave proof unheeded; others on the grass
Couched, and now filled with pasture gazing sat,
Or bedward ruminating:° for the sun   *chewing the cud*
Declined was hasting now with prone° career   *sinking*
To th' Ocean Isles,° and in th' ascending scale   *the Azores*
355 Of Heav'n the stars that usher evening rose:
When Satan still in gaze, as first he stood,
Scarce thus at length failed speech recovered sad.
    "O Hell! what do mine eyes with grief behold,
Into our room of bliss thus high advanced

---

4. I.e., to make a cool breeze welcome.
5. Checkered body. "Gordian twine": cords as
convoluted as the Gordian knot that Alexander the Great had to cut with his sword.

360 Creatures of other mold, earth-born perhaps,
Not Spirits, yet to heav'nly Spirits bright
Little inferior; whom my thoughts pursue
With wonder, and could love, so lively shines
In them divine resemblance, and such grace
365 The hand that formed them on their shape hath poured.
Ah gentle pair, ye little think how nigh
Your change approaches, when all these delights
Will vanish and deliver ye to woe,
More woe, the more your taste is now of joy;
370 Happy, but for so happy° ill secured   *such happiness*
Long to continue, and this high seat your heav'n
Ill fenced for Heav'n to keep out such a foe
As now is entered; yet no purposed foe
To you whom I could pity thus forlorn
375 Though I unpitied: league with you I seek,
And mutual amity so strait,° so close,   *intimate*
That I with you must dwell, or you with me
Henceforth; my dwelling haply° may not please   *perhaps*
Like this fair Paradise, your sense, yet such
380 Accept your Maker's work; he gave it me,
Which I as freely give; Hell shall unfold,
To entertain you two, her widest gates,
And send forth all her kings; there will be room,
Not like these narrow limits, to receive
385 Your numerous offspring; if no better place,
Thank him who puts me loath to this revenge
On you who wrong me not for° him who wronged.   *in place of*
And should I at your harmless innocence
Melt, as I do, yet public reason just,
390 Honor and empire with revenge enlarged
By conquering this new world, compels me now
To do what else though damned I should abhor."6
    So spake the Fiend, and with necessity,
The tyrant's plea, excused his devilish deeds.
395 Then from his lofty stand on that high tree
Down he alights among the sportful herd
Of those four-footed kinds, himself now one,
Now other, as their shape served best his end
Nearer to view his prey, and unespied
400 To mark what of their state he more might learn
By word or action marked: about them round
A lion now he stalks with fiery glare,
Then as a tiger, who by chance hath spied
In some purlieu° two gentle fawns at play,   *outskirts of a forest*
405 Straight° couches close, then rising changes oft   *at once*
His couchant watch, as one who chose his ground
Whence rushing he might surest seize them both
Gripped in each paw: when Adam first of men
To first of women Eve thus moving speech

6. Satan's excuse—reason of state, public interest, empire, etc.—is called "the tyrant's plea" in line 394.

410 Turned him all ear to hear new utterance flow:
   "Sole partner and sole° part of all these joys,   *chief*
Dearer thyself than all; needs must the Power
That made us, and for us this ample world
Be infinitely good, and of his good
415 As liberal and free as infinite,
That raised us from the dust and placed us here
In all this happiness, who at his hand
Have nothing merited, nor can perform
Aught whereof he hath need, he who requires
420 From us no other service than to keep
This one, this easy charge, of all the trees
In Paradise that bear delicious fruit
So various, not to taste that only Tree
Of Knowledge, planted by the Tree of Life,
425 So near grows death to life, whate'er death is,
Some dreadful thing no doubt; for well thou know'st
God hath pronounced it death to taste that Tree,
The only sign of our obedience left
Among so many signs of power and rule
430 Conferred upon us, and dominion giv'n
Over all other creatures that possess
Earth, air, and sea. Then let us not think hard
One easy prohibition, who enjoy
Free leave so large to all things else, and choice
435 Unlimited of manifold delights:
But let us ever praise him, and extol
His bounty, following our delightful task
To prune these growing plants, and tend these flow'rs,
Which were it toilsome, yet with thee were sweet."
440   To whom thus Eve replied. "O thou for whom
And from whom I was formed flesh of thy flesh,
And without whom am to no end, my guide
And head, what thou hast said is just and right.
For we to him indeed all praises owe,
445 And daily thanks, I chiefly who enjoy
So far the happier lot, enjoying thee
Preeminent by so much odds,° while thou   *advantage*
Like consort to thyself canst nowhere find.
That day I oft remember, when from sleep
450 I first awaked, and found myself reposed°   *resting*
Under a shade on flowers, much wond'ring where
And what I was, whence thither brought, and how.
Not distant far from thence a murmuring sound
Of waters issued from a cave and spread
455 Into a liquid plain, then stood unmoved
Pure as th' expanse of Heav'n; I thither went
With unexperienced thought, and laid me down
On the green bank, to look into the clear
Smooth lake, that to me seemed another sky.
460 As I bent down to look, just opposite,
A shape within the wat'ry gleam appeared

Bending to look on me, I started back,
It started back, but pleased I soon returned,
Pleased it returned as soon with answering looks
465 Of sympathy and love; there I had fixed
Mine eyes till now, and pined with vain° desire,[7]   *futile*
Had not a voice thus warned me, 'What thou seest,
What there thou seest fair creature is thyself,
With thee it came and goes: but follow me,
470 And I will bring thee where no shadow stays°   *hinders*
Thy coming, and thy soft embraces, he
Whose image thou art, him thou shalt enjoy
Inseparably thine, to him shalt bear
Multitudes like thyself, and thence be called
475 Mother of human race': what could I do,
But follow straight° invisibly thus led?   *at once*
Till I espied thee, fair indeed and tall,
Under a platan,° yet methought less fair,   *plane tree*
Less winning soft, less amiably mild,
480 Than that smooth wat'ry image; back I turned,
Thou following cried'st aloud, 'Return fair Eve,
Whom fli'st thou? Whom thou fli'st, of him thou art,
His flesh, his bone; to give thee being I lent
Out of my side to thee, nearest my heart
485 Substantial life, to have thee by my side
Henceforth an individual° solace dear;   *inseparable, distinct*
Part of my soul I seek thee, and thee claim
My other half': with that thy gentle hand
Seized mine, I yielded, and from that time see
490 How beauty is excelled by manly grace
And wisdom, which alone is truly fair."
    So spake our general mother, and with eyes
Of conjugal attraction unreproved,
And meek surrender, half embracing leaned
495 On our first father, half her swelling breast
Naked met his under the flowing gold
Of her loose tresses hid: he in delight
Both of her beauty and submissive charms
Smiled with superior love, as Jupiter
500 On Juno smiles, when he impregns° the clouds   *impregnates*
That shed May flowers; and pressed her matron lip
With kisses pure: aside the Devil turned
For envy, yet with jealous leer malign
Eyed them askance, and to himself thus plained.°   *complained*
505   "Sight hateful, sight tormenting! thus these two
Imparadised in one another's arms
The happier Eden, shall enjoy their fill
Of bliss on bliss, while I to Hell am thrust,
Where neither joy nor love, but fierce desire,
510 Among our other torments not the least,

---

7. Eve's experience reprises (but with significant differences) the story of Narcissus, who fell in love
with his own reflection and was transformed into a flower.

Still° unfulfilled with pain of longing pines;   *always*
Yet let me not forget what I have gained
From their own mouths; all is not theirs it seems:
One fatal tree there stands of Knowledge called,
515 Forbidden them to taste: knowledge forbidden?
Suspicious, reasonless. Why should their Lord
Envy° them that? Can it be sin to know,   *begrudge*
Can it be death? And do they only stand
By ignorance, is that their happy state,
520 The proof of their obedience and their faith?
O fair foundation laid whereon to build
Their ruin! Hence I will excite their minds
With more desire to know, and to reject
Envious commands, invented with design
525 To keep them low whom knowledge might exalt
Equal with gods; aspiring to be such,
They taste and die: what likelier can ensue?
But first with narrow search I must walk round
This garden, and no corner leave unspied;
530 A chance, but chance[8] may lead where I may meet
Some wand'ring Spirit of Heav'n, by fountain side,
Or in thick shade retired, from him to draw
What further would be learnt. Live while ye may,
Yet happy pair; enjoy, till I return,
535 Short pleasures, for long woes are to succeed."
    So saying, his proud step he scornful turned,
But with sly circumspection, and began
Through wood, through waste, o'er hill, o'er dale his roam.°   *act of wandering*
Meanwhile in utmost longitude, where heav'n°   *the sky*
540 With earth and ocean meets, the setting sun
Slowly descended, and with right aspéct
Against the eastern gate of Paradise
Leveled his evening rays.[9] It was a rock
Of alabaster,[1] piled up to the clouds,
545 Conspicuous far, winding with one ascent
Accessible from earth, one entrance high;
The rest was craggy cliff, that overhung
Still as it rose, impossible to climb.
Betwixt these rocky pillars Gabriel[2] sat
550 Chief of th' angelic guards, awaiting night;
About him exercised heroic games
Th' unarmèd youth of Heav'n, but nigh at hand
Celestial armory, shields, helms, and spears
Hung high with diamond flaming, and with gold.
555 Thither came Uriel, gliding through the even
On a sunbeam, swift as a shooting star
In autumn thwarts° the night, when vapors fired   *passes across*
Impress the air, and shows the mariner
From what point of his compass to beware

8. An opportunity, even if only by luck.
9. Setting in the west, the sun struck the eastern
gate from the inside, at a ninety-degree angle.

1. White, translucent marble veined with colors.
2. In Hebrew, "strength of God." A tradition (cf. 1
Enoch 20.7) gave Gabriel charge of Paradise.

560 Impetuous winds:³ he thus began in haste.
　　"Gabriel, to thee thy course by lot hath giv'n
Charge and strict watch that to this happy place
No evil thing approach or enter in;
This day at height of noon came to my sphere
565 A Spirit, zealous, as he seemed, to know
More of th' Almighty's works, and chiefly man
God's latest image: I described° his way　　　　　　*descried, observed*
Bent all on speed, and marked his airy gait;°　　　　　　*path*
But in the mount that lies from Eden north,
570 Where he first lighted, soon discerned his looks
Alien from Heav'n, with passions foul obscured:
Mine eye pursued him still, but under shade°　　　　　　*trees*
Lost sight of him; one of the banished crew
I fear, hath ventured from the deep, to raise
575 New troubles; him thy care must be to find."
　　To whom the winged warrior thus returned:
"Uriel, no wonder if thy perfect sight,
Amid the sun's bright circle where thou sitt'st,
See far and wide. In at this gate none pass
580 The vigilance here placed, but such as come
Well known from Heav'n; and since meridian hour°　　　　　　*noon*
No creature thence: if Spirit of other sort,
So minded, have o'erleaped these earthy bounds
On purpose, hard thou know'st it to exclude
585 Spiritual substance with corporeal bar.
But if within the circuit of these walks,
In whatsoever shape he lurk, of whom
Thou tell'st, by morrow dawning I shall know."
　　So promised he, and Uriel to his charge
590 Returned on that bright beam, whose point now raised
Bore him slope downward to the sun now fall'n
Beneath th' Azorès; whether the prime orb,
Incredible how swift, had thither rolled
Diurnal,° or this less volúble° earth　　　　　　*daily / swift-turning*
595 By shorter flight to th' east,⁴ had left him there
Arraying with reflected purple and gold
The clouds that on his western throne attend.
Now came still evening on, and twilight gray
Had in her sober livery all things clad;
600 Silence accompanied, for beast and bird,
They to their grassy couch, these to their nests
Were slunk, all but the wakeful nightingale;
She all night long her amorous descant° sung;　　　　　　*melody*
Silence was pleased: now glowed the firmament
605 With living sapphires: Hesperus⁵ that led
The starry host, rode brightest, till the moon
Rising in clouded majesty, at length

---

3. Shooting stars were thought to indicate by the direction of their fall the source of oncoming storms. "Vapors fired": heat lightning.
4. Here and elsewhere Milton leaves open the question of whether the sun moves around the earth, or vice versa.
5. Called Venus when it appears in the evening sky.

Apparent° queen unveiled her peerless light,   *clearly seen*
And o'er the dark her silver mantle threw.
610   When Adam thus to Eve: "Fair consort, th' hour
Of night, and all things now retired to rest
Mind us of like repose, since God hath set
Labor and rest, as day and night to men
Successive, and the timely dew of sleep
615   Now falling with soft slumbrous weight inclines
Our eyelids; other creatures all day long
Rove idle unemployed, and less need rest;
Man hath his daily work of body or mind
Appointed, which declares his dignity,
620   And the regard of Heav'n on all his ways;
While other animals unactive range,
And of their doings God takes no account.
Tomorrow ere fresh morning streak the east
With first approach of light, we must be ris'n,
625   And at our pleasant labor, to reform
Yon flow'ry arbors, yonder alleys green,
Our walk at noon, with branches overgrown,
That mock our scant manuring,° and require   *cultivating*
More hands than ours to lop their wanton° growth: *luxuriant*
630   Those blossoms also, and those dropping gums,
That lie bestrown unsightly and unsmooth,
Ask riddance,° if we mean to tread with ease;   *need to be cleared*
Meanwhile, as nature wills, night bids us rest."
        To whom thus Eve with perfect beauty adorned.
635   "My author and disposer, what thou bidd'st
Unargued I obey; so God ordains,
God is thy law, thou mine: to know no more
Is woman's happiest knowledge and her praise.
With thee conversing I forget all time.
640   All seasons° and their change, all please alike.   *times of day*
Sweet⁶ is the breath of morn, her rising sweet,
With charm⁷ of earliest birds; pleasant the sun
When first on this delightful land he spreads
His orient° beams, on herb, tree, fruit, and flow'r,   *lustrious, eastern*
645   Glist'ring with dew; fragrant the fertile earth
After soft showers; and sweet the coming on
Of grateful evening mild, then silent night
With this her solemn bird° and this fair moon,   *the nightingale*
And these the gems of heav'n, her starry train:
650   But neither breath of morn when she ascends
With charm of earliest birds, nor rising sun
On this delightful land, nor herb, fruit, flow'r,
Glist'ring with dew, nor fragrance after showers,
Nor grateful evening mild, nor silent night
655   With this her solemn bird, nor walk by moon,
Or glittering starlight without thee is sweet.

6. With this embedded lyric, beginning here,   rhetorical figures of circularity and repetition.
Eve displays her literary talents in an elegant   7. Blended singing of many birds.
love song, sonnetlike and replete with striking

But wherefore all night long shine these, for whom
This glorious sight, when sleep hath shut all eyes?"
   To whom our general ancestor replied.
660 "Daughter of God and man, accomplished[8] Eve,
Those have their course to finish, round the earth,
By morrow evening, and from land to land
In order, though to nations yet unborn,
Minist'ring light prepared, they set and rise;
665 Lest total darkness should by night regain
Her old possession, and extinguish life
In nature and all things, which these soft° fires   *agreeable*
Not only enlighten, but with kindly° heat   *natural, benevolent*
Of various influence foment° and warm,   *foster*
670 Temper or nourish, or in part shed down
Their stellar virtue on all kinds that grow
On earth, made hereby apter to receive
Perfection from the sun's more potent ray.[9]
These then, though unbeheld in deep of night,
675 Shine not in vain, nor think, though men were none,
That heav'n would want° spectators, God want praise;   *lack*
Millions of spiritual creatures walk the earth
Unseen, both when we wake, and when we sleep:
All these with ceaseless praise his works behold
680 Both day and night: how often from the steep
Of echoing hill or thicket have we heard
Celestial voices to the midnight air,
Sole, or responsive each to other's note
Singing their great Creator: oft in bands
685 While they keep watch, or nightly rounding walk,
With heav'nly touch of instrumental sounds
In full harmonic number joined, their songs
Divide[1] the night, and lift our thoughts to Heaven."
   Thus talking hand in hand alone they passed
690 On to their blissful bower; it was a place
Chos'n by the sov'reign Planter, when he framed°   *fashioned*
All things to man's delightful use; the roof
Of thickest covert was inwoven shade
Laurel and myrtle, and what higher grew
695 Of firm and fragrant leaf; on either side
Acanthus, and each odorous bushy shrub
Fenced up the verdant wall; each beauteous flow'r,
Iris all hues, roses, and jessamine°   *jasmine*
Reared high their flourished° heads between, and wrought   *flowering*
700 Mosaic; underfoot the violet,
Crocus, and hyacinth with rich inlay
Broidered the ground, more colored than with stone
Of costliest emblem:° other creature here   *inlaid work*
Beast, bird, insect, or worm durst enter none,

---

8. Having many talents and achievements; perfect, complete.
9. The stars were thought to have their own occult influence, and also to moderate that of the sun.
1. Mark the watches of the night; also, perform musical "divisions," elaborate melodic passages.

705 Such was their awe of man. In shadier bower
     More sacred and sequestered,° though but feigned,   *secluded*
     Pan or Silvanus never slept, nor nymph,
     Nor Faunus[2] haunted. Here in close recess
     With flowers, garlands, and sweet-smelling herbs
710 Espousèd Eve decked first her nuptial bed,
     And heav'nly choirs the hymenean° sung,   *wedding song*
     What day the genial[3] angel to our sire
     Brought her in naked beauty more adorned,
     More lovely than Pandora, whom the gods
715 Endowed with all their gifts, and O too like
     In sad event,° when to the unwiser son   *outcome*
     Of Japhet brought by Hermes, she ensnared
     Mankind with her fair looks, to be avenged
     On him who had stole Jove's authentic fire.[4]
720   Thus at their shady lodge arrived, both stood,
     Both turned, and under open sky adored
     The God that made both sky, air, earth, and heav'n
     Which they beheld, the moon's resplendent globe
     And starry pole:° "Thou also mad'st the night,   *sky*
725 Maker Omnipotent, and thou the day,
     Which we in our appointed work employed
     Have finished happy in our mutual help
     And mutual love, the crown of all our bliss
     Ordained by thee, and this delicious place
730 For us too large, where thy abundance wants
     Partakers, and uncropped falls to the ground.
     But thou hast promised from us two a race
     To fill the earth, who shall with us extol
     Thy goodness infinite, both when we wake,
735 And when we seek, as now, thy gift of sleep."
         This said unanimous, and other rites
     Observing none, but adoration pure
     Which God likes best,[5] into their inmost bow'r
     Handed° they went; and eased° the putting off   *hand in hand / spared*
740 These troublesome disguises which we wear,
     Straight side by side were laid, nor turned I ween°   *surmise*
     Adam from his fair spouse, nor Eve the rites
     Mysterious[6] of connubial love refused:
     Whatever hypocrites austerely talk
745 Of purity and place and innocence,
     Defaming as impure what God declares
     Pure, and commands to some, leaves free to all.

---

2. Forest and field divinities of classical mythology.
3. Presiding over marriage and generation.
4. Pandora (the name means "all gifts") was an artificial woman, molded of clay, bestowed by the gods on Epimetheus, brother of Prometheus (who angered Jove by stealing fire from heaven). She brought a box that foolish Epimetheus opened, releasing all the ills of the human race, leaving only hope inside. The brothers were sons of Iapetos, whom Milton identifies with Japhet,

Noah's third son. The Eve-Pandora parallel was often noted.
5. Like many Puritans, Milton objected to set forms of prayer, so Adam and Eve pray spontaneously (therefore sincerely), but also, paradoxically, together. Their prayer develops variations on Psalm 104.20–24.
6. Ephesians 5.32 calls the union of man and woman a "mystery" paralleling that of Christ and the church.

Our Maker bids increase,[7] who bids abstain
But our destroyer, foe to God and man?
750 Hail wedded Love, mysterious law, true source
Of human offspring, sole propriety°   *private property*
In Paradise of all things common else.
By thee adulterous lust was driv'n from men
Among the bestial herds to range, by thee
755 Founded in reason, loyal, just, and pure,
Relations dear, and all the charities°   *loves*
Of father, son, and brother first were known.
Far be it, that I should write thee sin or blame,
Or think thee unbefitting holiest place,
760 Perpetual fountain of domestic sweets,
Whose bed is undefiled and chaste pronounced,
Present, or past, as saints and patriarchs used.[8]
Here Love his golden shafts employs,[9] here lights
His constant lamp, and waves his purple wings,
765 Reigns here and revels; not in the bought smile
Of harlots, loveless, joyless, unendeared,
Casual fruition, nor in court amours,
Mixed dance, or wanton masque, or midnight ball,
Or serenade, which the starved° lover sings   *deprived*
770 To his proud fair, best quitted with disdain.
These lulled by nightingales embracing slept,
And on their naked limbs the flow'ry roof
Show'red roses, which the morn repaired.° Sleep on,   *replaced*
Blest pair; and O yet happiest if ye seek
775 No happier state, and know to know no more.[1]
     Now had night measured with her shadowy cone
Halfway up hill this vast sublunar vault,[2]
And from their ivory port the Cherubim
Forth issuing at th' accustomed hour stood armed
780 To their night watches in warlike parade,
When Gabriel to his next in power thus spake:
     "Uzziel,[3] half these draw off, and coast° the south   *skirt*
With strictest watch; these other wheel[4] the north,
Our circuit meets full west." As flame they part
785 Half wheeling to the shield, half to the spear.
From these, two strong and subtle Spirits he called
That near him stood, and gave them thus in charge:
     "Ithuriel and Zephon,[5] with winged speed
Search through this garden, leave unsearched no nook,
790 But chiefly where those two fair creatures lodge,
Now laid perhaps asleep secure of° harm.   *from*

---

7. Genesis 1.28: "Be fruitful and multiply, and replenish the earth."
8. Throughout history ("present or past"), Old and New Testament worthies have "used" matrimony as a noble estate.
9. The "golden shafts" (arrows) of Cupid produce true love, his lead-tipped arrows, hate.
1. Know enough to be content with what you know.

2. The conical shadow cast by the earth has moved halfway up to its zenith, so it is 9 P.M., the end of the first three-hour watch.
3. Hebrew, "my strength is God."
4. "Wheel": turn to (military term); "shield" (line 785) is left, "spear" is right.
5. Hebrew, "a looking out." "Ithuriel": Hebrew, "discovery of God."

This evening from the sun's decline arrived
Who° tells of some infernal Spirit seen   *one who*
Hitherward bent; who could have thought? escaped
795   The bars of Hell, on errand bad no doubt:
Such where ye find, seize fast, and hither bring."
        So saying, on he led his radiant files,
Dazzling the moon; these to the bower direct
In search of whom they sought: him there they found
800   Squat like a toad, close at the ear of Eve;
Assaying° by his devilish art to reach   *attempting*
The organs of her fancy,[6] and with them forge
Illusions as he list,° phantasms and dreams;   *pleased*
Or if, inspiring° venom, he might taint   *breathing*
805   Th' animal spirits that from pure blood arise
Like gentle breaths from rivers pure, thence raise
At least distempered,° discontented thoughts,   *disordered*
Vain hopes, vain aims, inordinate desires
Blown up with high conceits° engend'ring pride.   *notions*
810   Him thus intent Ithuriel with his spear
Touched lightly; for no falsehood can endure
Touch of celestial temper,[7] but returns
Of force to its own likeness: up he starts
Discovered and surprised. As when a spark
815   Lights on a heap of nitrous powder,[8] laid
Fit for the tun some magazine to store
Against a rumored war, the smutty° grain   *black*
With sudden blaze diffused, inflames the air:
So started up in his own shape the Fiend.
820   Back stepped those two fair angels half amazed
So sudden to behold the grisly king;
Yet thus, unmoved with fear, accost him soon:
        "Which of those rebel Spirits adjudged to Hell
Com'st thou, escaped thy prison; and transformed,
825   Why sat'st thou like an enemy in wait
Here watching at the head of these that sleep?"
        "Know ye not then," said Satan, filled with scorn,
"Know ye not me? Ye knew me once no mate
For you, there sitting where ye durst not soar;
830   Not to know me argues° yourselves unknown,   *proves*
The lowest of your throng; or if ye know,
Why ask ye, and superfluous begin
Your message, like to end as much in vain?"
        To whom thus Zephon, answering scorn with scorn:
835   "Think not, revolted Spirit, thy shape the same,
Or undiminished brightness, to be known
As when thou stood'st in Heav'n upright and pure;
That glory then, when thou no more wast good,
Departed from thee, and thou resembl'st now

---

6. The faculty of forming mental images.
7. Anything, like the spear, made ("tempered")
in Heaven.
8. Alights or kindles ("lights") gunpowder ("nitrous

powder"), ready (next lines) to be stored in some
barrel ("tun") laid up in some storehouse ("magazine"), in preparation for ("against") rumors of war.

840 Thy sin and place of doom obscure° and foul.   *dark*
But come, for thou, be sure, shalt give account
To him who sent us, whose charge is to keep
This place inviolable, and these from harm."
     So spake the Cherub, and his grave rebuke
845 Severe in youthful beauty, added grace
Invincible: abashed the Devil stood,
And felt how awful° goodness is, and saw   *awe-inspiring*
Virtue in her shape how lovely, saw, and pined°   *mourned*
His loss; but chiefly to find here observed
850 His luster visibly impaired; yet seemed
Undaunted. "If I must contend," said he,
"Best with the best, the sender not the sent,
Or all at once; more glory will be won,
Or less be lost." "Thy fear," said Zephon bold,
855 "Will save us trial what the least can do
Single° against thee wicked, and thence weak."   *in single combat*
     The Fiend replied not, overcome with rage;
But like a proud steed reined, went haughty on,
Champing his iron curb: to strive or fly
860 He held it vain; awe from above had quelled
His heart, not else dismayed. Now drew they nigh
The western point, where those half-rounding guards
Just met, and closing stood in squadron joined
Awaiting next command. To whom their chief
865 Gabriel from the front thus called aloud:
     "O friends, I hear the tread of nimble feet
Hasting this way, and now by glimpse discern
Ithuriel and Zephon through the shade,°   *trees*
And with them comes a third of regal port,°   *bearing*
870 But faded splendor wan;° who by his gait   *faint, dark*
And fierce demeanor seems the Prince of Hell,
Not likely to part hence without contést;
Stand firm, for in his look defiance lours."°   *frowns*
     He scarce had ended, when those two approached
875 And brief related whom they brought, where found,
How busied, in what form and posture couched.
     To whom with stern regard thus Gabriel spake:
"Why hast thou, Satan, broke the bounds prescribed
To thy transgressions, and disturbed the charge°   *responsibility*
880 Of others, who approve not to transgress
By thy example, but have power and right
To question thy bold entrance on this place;
Employed it seems to violate sleep, and those
Whose dwelling God hath planted here in bliss?"
885 To whom thus Satan, with contemptuous brow:
"Gabriel, thou hadst in Heav'n th' esteem° of wise,   *reputation of being*
And such I held thee; but this question asked
Puts me in doubt. Lives there who loves his pain?
Who would not, finding way, break loose from Hell,
890 Though thither doomed? Thou wouldst thyself, no doubt,
And boldly venture to whatever place

Farthest from pain, where thou mightst hope to change°   *exchange*
Torment with ease, and soonest recompense
Dole° with delight, which in this place I sought;   *pain, grief*
895 To thee no reason, who know'st only good,
But evil hast not tried: and wilt object[9]
His will who bound us? Let him surer bar
His iron gates, if he intends our stay
In that dark durance:° thus much what was asked.[1]   *confinement*
900 The rest is true, they found me where they say;
But that implies not violence or harm."
    Thus he in scorn. The warlike angel moved,
Disdainfully half smiling thus replied:
"O loss of one in Heav'n to judge of wise,
905 Since Satan fell, whom folly overthrew,[2]
And now returns him from his prison scaped,
Gravely in doubt whether to hold them wise
Or not, who ask what boldness brought him hither
Unlicensed from his bounds in Hell prescribed;
910 So wise he judges it to fly from pain
However,° and to scape his punishment.   *howsoever*
So judge thou still, presumptuous, till the wrath,
Which thou incurr'st by flying, meet thy flight
Sevenfold, and scourge that wisdom back to Hell,
915 Which taught thee yet no better, that no pain
Can equal anger infinite provoked.
But wherefore thou alone? Wherefore with thee
Came not all Hell broke loose? Is pain to them
Less pain, less to be fled, or thou than they
920 Less hardy to endure? Courageous chief,
The first in flight from pain, hadst thou alleged
To thy deserted host this cause of flight,
Thou surely hadst not come sole fugitive."
    To which the Fiend thus answered frowning stern:
925 "Not that I less endure, or shrink from pain,
Insulting angel, well thou know'st I stood°   *withstood*
Thy fiercest, when in battle to thy aid
The blasting volleyed thunder made all speed
And seconded thy else not dreaded spear.
930 But still thy words at random, as before,
Argue thy inexperience what behoves
From° hard assays° and ill successes past   *after / attempts*
A faithful leader, not to hazard all
Through ways of danger by himself untried.
935 I therefore, I alone first undertook
To wing the desolate abyss, and spy
This new-created world, whereof in Hell
Fame° is not silent, here in hope to find   *rumor*
Better abode, and my afflicted powers°   *downcast armies*

9. Put forward as an objection.
1. I.e., thus much (answers) what was asked.
2. Irony: "O what a loss to Heaven to lose such a

judge of wisdom as Satan, whose folly led to his fall."

940 To settle here on earth, or in midair;[3]
Though for possession put° to try once more   *forced*
What thou and thy gay° legions dare against;   *showy*
Whose easier business were to serve their Lord
High up in Heav'n, with songs to hymn his throne,
945 And practiced distances to cringe, not fight."[4]
        To whom the warrior angel soon replied:
"To say and straight unsay, pretending first
Wise to fly pain, professing next the spy,
Argues no leader, but a liar traced,°   *found out*
950 Satan, and couldst thou faithful add? O name,
O sacred name of faithfulness profaned!
Faithful to whom? To thy rebellious crew?
Army of fiends, fit body to fit head;
Was this your discipline and faith engaged,
955 Your military obedience, to dissolve
Allegiance to th' acknowledged Power Supreme?
And thou sly hypocrite, who now wouldst seem
Patron of liberty, who more than thou
Once fawned, and cringed, and servilely adored
960 Heav'n's awful Monarch?[5] Wherefore but in hope
To dispossess him, and thyself to reign?
But mark what I areed° thee now, avaunt;°   *advise / be gone*
Fly thither whence thou fledd'st: if from this hour
Within these hallowed limits thou appear,
965 Back to th' infernal pit I drag thee chained,
And seal thee so, as henceforth not to scorn
The facile° gates of Hell too slightly barred."   *easily moved*
        So threatened he, but Satan to no threats
Gave heed, but waxing° more in rage replied: *growing*
970   "Then when I am thy captive talk of chains,
Proud limitary[6] Cherub, but ere then
Far heavier load thyself expect to feel
From my prevailing arm, though Heaven's King
Ride on thy wings, and thou with thy compeers,
975 Used to the yoke, draw'st his triumphant wheels
In progress through the road of heav'n star-paved."
        While thus he spake, th' angelic squadron bright
Turned fiery red, sharp'ning in moonèd horns[7]
Their phalanx, and began to hem him round
980 With ported[8] spears, as thick as when a field
Of Ceres[9] ripe for harvest waving bends
Her bearded grove of ears, which way the wind
Sways them; the careful plowman doubting stands
Lest on the threshing floor his hopeful sheaves

---

3. Satan will become "prince of the power of the air" (Ephesians 2.2).
4. Satan contemptuously parallels the angels' courtly deference ("distances") before God's throne and keeping a safe distance from battle. "Cringe": bow or kneel in fear or servility.
5. See 5.617 for Satan's "servile" adoration on the day of the Son's exaltation, when he "seemed well pleased" but was not.
6. Frontier guard, also, one of limited authority.
7. A crescent-shaped military formation.
8. Held slantwise in front.
9. Roman goddess of grain; here, the grain itself. A Homeric simile compares an excited army to windswept corn (*Iliad* 2.147–50).

985   Prove chaff. On th' other side Satan alarmed°   *called to arms*
        Collecting all his might dilated stood,
        Like Tenerife or Atlas[1] unremoved:°   *unremovable*
        His stature reached the sky, and on his crest
        Sat Horror plumed; nor wanted in his grasp
990   What seemed both spear and shield: now dreadful deeds
        Might have ensued, nor only Paradise
        In this commotion, but the starry cope°   *vault*
        Of Heav'n perhaps, or all the elements
        At least had gone to wrack, disturbed and torn
995   With violence of this conflict, had not soon
        Th' Eternal to prevent such horrid fray
        Hung forth in Heav'n his golden scales, yet seen
        Betwixt Astraea and the Scorpion sign,[2]
        Wherein all things created first he weighed,
1000 The pendulous round earth with balanced air
        In counterpoise, now ponders all events,
        Battles and realms: in these he put two weights
        The sequel each of parting and of fight;[3]
        The latter quick up flew, and kicked the beam;
1005 Which Gabriel spying, thus bespake the Fiend:
          "Satan, I know thy strength, and thou know'st mine,
        Neither our own but giv'n; what folly then
        To boast what arms can do, since thine no more
        Than Heav'n permits, nor mine, though doubled now
1010 To trample thee as mire: for proof look up,
        And read thy lot in yon celestial sign
        Where thou art weighed, and shown how light, how weak,[4]
        If thou resist." The Fiend looked up and knew
        His mounted scale aloft: nor more; but fled
1015 Murmuring, and with him fled the shades of night.

Book 5

The Argument

Morning approached, Eve relates to Adam her troublesome dream; he likes it not, yet comforts her: they come forth to their day labors: their morning hymn at the door of their bower. God to render man inexcusable sends Raphael to admonish him of his obedience, of his free estate, of his enemy near at hand; who he is, and why his enemy, and whatever else may avail Adam to know. Raphael comes down to Paradise, his appearance described, his coming discerned by Adam afar off sitting at the door of his bower; he goes out to meet him, brings him to his lodge, entertains him with the choicest fruits of

---

1. A mountain in Morocco. "Tenerife": a mountain in the Canary Islands.
2. The zodiac sign Libra, represented by a pair of scales, is between Virgo (identified with Astraea, goddess of Justice, who fled the earth at the end of the Golden Age) and Scorpio.
3. In several classical epic similes the fates of

opposing heroes are weighed in scales by the gods, but here God "ponders" (weighs the consequences of) all events, including parting or fighting. Battle, desired by Satan, proves lighter ("kicked the beam," line 1004).
4. Cf. Daniel 5.27: "Thou art weighed in the balances, and art found wanting."

Paradise got together by Eve; their discourse at table: Raphael performs his
message, minds Adam of his state and of his enemy; relates at Adam's request
who that enemy is, and how he came to be so, beginning from his first revolt
in heaven, and the occasion thereof; how he drew his legions after him to the
parts of the north, and there incited them to rebel with him, persuading all
but only Abdiel a Seraph, who in argument dissuades and opposes him, then
forsakes him.

Now Morn her rosy steps in th' eastern clime
Advancing, sowed the earth with orient pearl,°   *sparkling dew*
When Adam waked, so customed, for his sleep
Was aery light, from pure digestion bred,
5   And temperate vapors bland,° which th' only sound   *gentle, balmy*
Of leaves and fuming rills, Aurora's fan,[1]
Lightly dispersed, and the shrill matin° song   *morning*
Of birds on every bough; so much the more
His wonder was to find unwakened Eve
10   With tresses discomposed, and glowing cheek,
As through unquiet rest: he on his side
Leaning half-raised, with looks of cordial° love   *heartfelt*
Hung over her enamored, and beheld
Beauty, which whether waking or asleep,
15   Shot forth peculiar° graces; then with voice   *its own*
Mild, as when Zephyrus on Flora[2] breathes,
Her hand soft touching, whispered thus: "Awake
My fairest, my espoused, my latest found,
Heav'n's last best gift, my ever new delight,
20   Awake, the morning shines, and the fresh field
Calls us, we lose the prime, to mark how spring
Our tended plants, how blows° the citron grove,   *blooms*
What drops the myrrh, and what the balmy reed,°   *balsam*
How nature paints her colors, how the bee
25   Sits on the bloom extracting liquid sweet."[3]
     Such whispering waked her, but with startled eye
On Adam, whom embracing, thus she spake:
     "O sole in whom my thoughts find all repose,
My glory, my perfection, glad I see
30   Thy face, and morn returned, for I this night,
Such night till this I never passed, have dreamed,
If dreamed, not as I oft am wont,° of thee,   *accustomed*
Works of day past, or morrow's next design,
But of offense and trouble, which my mind
35   Knew never till this irksome night. Methought
Close at mine ear one called me forth to walk
With gentle voice, I thought it thine; it said,
'Why sleep'st thou Eve? Now is the pleasant time,

1. Rustling leaves and streams ("rills") stirred by
Aurora, goddess of the dawn.
2. Zephyrus is god of the gentle west wind, Flora
goddess of flowers.
3. Adam sings a morning love song (*aubade*) to
Eve, which works variations on Song of Solomon

2.10–12: "Rise up, my love, my fair one, and come
away. . . . The flowers appear on the earth; the
time of the singing of birds is come." Compare
Satan's serenade (5.38–47), a parody of Adam's
aubade and the Song of Solomon. "Prime" (line
21): first hour of the day.

The cool, the silent, save where silence yields
40 To the night-warbling bird, that now awake
Tunes sweetest his love-labored song; now reigns
Full-orbed the moon, and with more pleasing light
Shadowy sets off the face of things, in vain,
If none regard; heav'n wakes with all his eyes,°   *stars*
45 Whom to behold but thee, nature's desire,
In whose sight all things joy, with ravishment
Attracted by thy beauty still° to gaze.'   *continually*
I rose as at thy call, but found thee not;
To find thee I directed then my walk;
50 And on, me thought, alone I passed through ways
That brought me on a sudden to the tree
Of interdicted knowledge: fair it seemed,
Much fairer to my fancy than by day:
And as I wond'ring looked, beside it stood
55 One shaped and winged like one of those from Heav'n
By us oft seen; his dewy locks distilled
Ambrosia;° on that tree he also gazed;   *heavenly fragrance*
And 'O fair plant,' said he, 'with fruit surcharged,°   *overburdened*
Deigns none to ease thy load and taste thy sweet,
60 Nor god,° nor man? Is knowledge so despised?   *angel*
Or envy, or what reserve forbids to taste?[4]
Forbid who will, none shall from me withhold
Longer thy offered good, why else set here?'
This said he paused not, but with vent'rous arm
65 He plucked, he tasted; me damp horror chilled
At such bold words vouched with° a deed so bold: *backed by*
But he thus overjoyed, 'O fruit divine,
Sweet of thyself, but much more sweet thus cropped,
Forbidden here, it seems, as only fit
70 For gods, yet able to make gods of men:
And why not gods of men, since good, the more
Communicated, more abundant grows,
The author not impaired,° but honored more?   *injured, diminished*
Here, happy creature, fair angelic Eve,
75 Partake thou also; happy though thou art,
Happier thou may'st be, worthier canst not be:
Taste this, and be henceforth among the gods
Thyself a goddess, not to earth confined,
But sometimes in the air, as we, sometimes
80 Ascend to Heav'n, by merit thine, and see
What life the gods live there, and such live thou.'
So saying, he drew nigh, and to me held,
Even to my mouth of that same fruit held part
Which he had plucked; the pleasant savory smell
85 So quickened appetite, that I, methought,
Could not but taste. Forthwith up to the clouds
With him I flew, and underneath beheld
The earth outstretched immense, a prospect wide

---

4. I.e., does envy or some other barrier ("reserve") forbid your being tasted?

And various: wond'ring at my flight and change
90 To this high exaltation: suddenly
My guide was gone, and I, methought, sunk down,
And fell asleep; but O how glad I waked
To find this but a dream!" Thus Eve her night
Related, and thus Adam answered sad.°   *gravely, soberly*
95   "Best image of myself and dearer half,
The trouble of thy thoughts this night in sleep
Affects me equally; nor can I like
This uncouth° dream, of evil sprung I fear;   *strange, unpleasant*
Yet evil whence? In thee can harbor none,
100 Created pure. But know that in the soul
Are many lesser faculties[5] that serve
Reason as chief; among these fancy next
Her office holds; of all external things,
Which the five watchful senses represent,
105 She forms imaginations,° aery shapes,   *images*
Which reason joining or disjoining, frames
All what we affirm or what deny, and call
Our knowledge or opinion; then retires
Into her private cell when nature rests.
110 Oft in her absence mimic fancy wakes
To imitate her; but misjoining shapes,
Wild work produces oft, and most in dreams,
Ill matching words and deeds long past or late.
Some such resemblances methinks I find
115 Of our last evening's talk in this thy dream,[6]
But with addition strange; yet be not sad.
Evil into the mind of god[7] or man
May come and go, so unapproved,[8] and leave
No spot or blame behind: which gives me hope
120 That what in sleep thou didst abhor to dream,
Waking thou never wilt consent to do.
Be not disheartened then, nor cloud those looks
That wont to be° more cheerful and serene   *usually are*
Than when fair morning first smiles on the world,
125 And let us to our fresh employments rise
Among the groves, the fountains, and the flow'rs
That open now their choicest bosomed smells
Reserved from night, and kept for thee in store."
    So cheered he his fair spouse, and she was cheered,
130 But silently a gentle tear let fall
From either eye, and wiped them with her hair;
Two other precious drops that ready stood,
Each in their crystal sluice, he ere they fell
Kissed as the gracious signs of sweet remorse

---

5. Adam's explanation of the dream (lines 100–
116) summarizes the orthodox faculty psychology
and dream theory of Milton's time—one among
many kinds of knowledge with which unfallen
man was endowed.
6. Adam recalls his own words in 4.411–39.

7. Probably "angel" as elsewhere, but perhaps God,
whose omniscience must encompass knowledge
of evil as well as good.
8. If not willed (approved of) or not acted on
(put to the proof).

135 And pious awe, that feared to have offended.
        So all was cleared, and to the field they haste.
      But first from under shady arborous° roof,   *consisting of trees*
      Soon as they forth were come to open sight
      Of day-spring,° and the sun, who scarce up risen   *daybreak*
140 With wheels yet hov'ring o'er the ocean brim,
      Shot parallel to the earth his dewy ray,
      Discovering in wide landscape all the east
      Of Paradise and Eden's happy plains,
      Lowly they bowed adoring, and began
145 Their orisons,° each morning duly paid   *prayers*
      In various style, for neither various style
      Nor holy rapture° wanted they to praise   *ecstasy*
      Their Maker, in fit strains pronounced or sung
      Unmeditated,⁹ such prompt eloquence
150 Flowed from their lips, in prose or numerous° verse,   *rhythmic*
      More tuneable° than needed lute or harp   *melodious*
      To add more sweetness, and they thus began:
        "These are thy glorious works, Parent of good,¹
      Almighty, thine this universal frame,
155 Thus wondrous fair; thyself how wondrous then!
      Unspeakable, who sitt'st above these heavens,
      To us invisible or dimly seen
      In these thy lowest works, yet these declare
      Thy goodness beyond thought, and power divine:
160 Speak ye who best can tell, ye sons of light,
      Angels, for ye behold him, and with songs
      And choral symphonies,° day without night,   *music in parts*
      Circle his throne rejoicing, ye in Heav'n,
      On earth join all ye creatures to extol
165 Him first, him last, him midst, and without end.
      Fairest of stars,² last in the train° of night,   *procession*
      If better thou belong not to the dawn,
      Sure pledge of day, that crown'st the smiling morn
      With thy bright circlet, praise him in thy sphere
170 While day arises, that sweet hour of prime.
      Thou sun, of this great world both eye and soul,
      Acknowledge him thy greater, sound his praise
      In thy eternal course, both when thou climb'st,
      And when high noon hast gained, and when thou fall'st.
175 Moon, that now meet'st the orient sun, now fli'st
      With the fixed stars, fixed in their orb that flies,
      And ye five other wand'ring fires that move
      In mystic dance not without song,³ resound
      His praise, who out of darkness called up light.
180 Air, and ye elements the eldest birth

9. In a variety of styles or forms of speech and song, which harmonize together but are at the same time impromptu, spontaneous, and ecstatic.
1. Their morning hymn works variations on Psalms 148, 104, and 19, as well as the canticle "Benedicite."

2. Venus, the morning star and (as Hesperus) the evening star.
3. The planets, unlike the fixed stars, change their relative positions; their motion produces the music of the spheres, audible to unfallen humans.

Of nature's womb, that in quaternion⁴ run
Perpetual circle, multiform, and mix
And nourish all things, let your ceaseless change
Vary to our great Maker still° new praise.   *continually*
185 Ye mists and exhalations that now rise
From hill or steaming lake, dusky or gray,
Till the sun paint your fleecy skirts with gold,
In honor to the world's great Author rise,
Whether to deck with clouds the uncolored sky,
190 Or wet the thirsty earth with falling showers,
Rising or falling still advance his praise.
His praise ye winds, that from four quarters blow,
Breathe soft or loud; and wave your tops, ye pines,
With every plant, in sign of worship wave.
195 Fountains and ye, that warble, as ye flow,
Melodious murmurs, warbling tune his praise.
Join voices all ye living souls: ye birds,
That singing up to heaven gate ascend,
Bear on your wings and in your notes his praise.
200 Ye that in waters glide, and ye that walk
The earth, and stately tread, or lowly creep;
Witness if I be silent, morn or even,
To hill, or valley, fountain, or fresh shade
Made vocal by my song, and taught his praise.
205 Hail universal Lord, be bounteous still°   *always*
To give us only good; and if the night
Have gathered aught of evil or concealed,
Disperse it, as now light dispels the dark."
So prayed they innocent, and to their thoughts
210 Firm peace recovered soon and wonted calm.
On to their morning's rural work they haste
Among sweet dews and flow'rs; where any row
Of fruit trees over-woody° reached too far   *too bushy*
Their pampered boughs, and needed hands to check
215 Fruitless embraces: or they led the vine
To wed her elm;⁵ she spoused about him twines
Her marriageable arms, and with her brings
Her dow'r th' adopted clusters, to adorn
His barren leaves. Them thus employed beheld
220 With pity Heav'n's high King, and to him called
Raphael, the sociable Spirit, that deigned
To travel with Tobias, and secured
His marriage with the seven-times-wedded maid.⁶
"Raphael," said he, "thou hear'st what stir on earth
225 Satan from Hell scaped through the darksome gulf
Hath raised in Paradise, and how disturbed
This night the human pair, how he designs

---

4. The fourfold changing relationship of the four elements.
5. A familiar emblem of matrimony, the elm symbolizing masculine strength, and the vine, feminine fruitfulness, softness, and sweetness; note,
however, the matriarchal implications of "adopted clusters" (line 218).
6. Raphael (in Hebrew, "health of God") was the adviser of Tobias in winning his wife (see 4.168–71 and note).

In them at once to ruin all mankind.
Go therefore, half this day as friend with friend
230   Converse with Adam, in what bow'r or shade
Thou find'st him from the heat of noon retired,
To respite his day labor with repast,
Or with repose; and such discourse bring on,
As may advise him of his happy state,
235   Happiness in his power left free to will,
Left to his own free will, his will though free,
Yet mutable; whence warn him to beware
He swerve not too secure:° tell him withal   *overconfident*
His danger, and from whom, what enemy
240   Late fall'n himself from Heav'n, is plotting now
The fall of others from like state of bliss;
By violence, no, for that shall be withstood,
But by deceit and lies; this let him know,
Lest wilfully transgressing he pretend°   *plead*
245   Surprisal, unadmonished, unforewarned."
    So spake th' Eternal Father, and fulfilled
All justice: nor delayed the wingèd saint°   *angel*
After his charge received; but from among
Thousand celestial ardors,[7] where he stood
250   Veiled with his gorgeous wings, up springing light
Flew through the midst of Heav'n; th' angelic choirs
On each hand parting, to his speed gave way
Through all th' empyreal road; till at the gate
Of Heav'n arrived, the gate self-opened wide
255   On golden hinges turning, as by work°   *mechanism*
Divine the sov'reign Architect had framed.
From hence, no cloud, or, to obstruct his sight,
Star interposed, however small he sees,
Not unconform to other shining globes,
260   Earth and the gard'n of God, with cedars crowned
Above all hills. As when by night the glass°   *telescope*
Of Galileo, less assured, observes
Imagined lands and regions in the moon:
Or pilot from amidst the Cyclades
265   Delos or Samos first appearing kens°   *discerns*
A cloudy spot.[8] Down thither prone° in flight   *bent forward*
He speeds, and through the vast ethereal sky
Sails between worlds and worlds, with steady wing
Now on the polar wings, then with quick fan
270   Winnows the buxom air; till within soar
Of tow'ring eagles,[9] to all the fowls he seems
A phoenix, gazed by all, as that sole bird
When to enshrine his relics in the sun's

---

7. Bright spirits burning in love; the Hebrew *seraph* means "to burn."
8. The Cyclades are a circular group of islands in the south Aegean Sea; the two islands seen as "spots" from within the archipelago are Delos (the traditional center but famous for having floated adrift) and Samos (outside the group).
9. Raphael sails with steady wing, turns at the pole, beats ("fans") with his wings the yielding ("buxom") air, and then comes within range of the eagle's soaring flight.

Bright temple, to Egyptian Thebes he flies.[1]
275 At once on th' eastern cliff of Paradise
He lights, and to his proper shape returns
A Seraph winged; six wings he wore, to shade
His lineaments° divine; the pair that clad   *parts of the body*
Each shoulder broad, came mantling° o'er his breast   *draping*
280 With regal ornament; the middle pair
Girt like a starry zone° his waist, and round   *belt*
Skirted his loins and thighs with downy gold
And colors dipped in Heav'n; the third his feet
Shadowed from either heel with feathered mail[2]
285 Sky-tinctured grain.° Like Maia's son[3] he stood,   *dye*
And shook his plumes, that heav'nly fragrance filled
The circuit wide. Straight° knew him all the bands   *at once*
Of angels under watch; and to his state,°   *rank*
And to his message° high in honor rise;   *mission*
290 For on some message high they guessed him bound.
Their glittering tents he passed, and now is come
Into the blissful field; through groves of myrrh,
And flow'ring odors, cassia, nard, and balm;[4]
A wilderness of sweets; for nature here
295 Wantoned° as in her prime, and played° at will   *reveled / acted out*
Her virgin fancies, pouring forth more sweet,
Wild above rule or art; enormous° bliss.   *immense, beyond rule*
Him through the spicy forest onward come
Adam discerned, as in the door he sat[5]
300 Of his cool bow'r, while now the mounted sun
Shot down direct his fervid rays, to warm
Earth's inmost womb, more warmth than Adam needs;
And Eve within, due° at her hour prepared   *fittingly*
For dinner savory fruits, of taste to please
305 True appetite and not disrelish thirst,
Of nectarous drafts between, from milky stream,
Berry or grape: to whom thus Adam called:
    "Haste hither Eve, and worth thy sight behold
Eastward among those trees, what glorious shape
310 Comes this way moving; seems another morn
Ris'n on mid-noon; some great behest from Heav'n
To us perhaps he brings, and will vouchsafe
This day to be our guest. But go with speed,
And what thy stores contain, bring forth and pour
315 Abundance, fit to honor and receive
Our heav'nly stranger; well we may afford
Our givers their own gifts, and large bestow
From large bestowed, where nature multiplies
Her fertile growth, and by disburd'ning grows

---

1. The phoenix was a mythical, unique ("sole") bird that lived five hundred years, was consumed by fire, and was reborn from the ashes, which it then carried to the temple of the sun at Heliopolis in Egypt.
2. Plumage suggesting scale armor.
3. Mercury, messenger of the gods.

4. "Odors": aromatic substances; "cassia": cinnamon; "nard": spikenard; "balm": balsam—all were used to make perfumed ointments.
5. Raphael's visit to Adam is modeled on Abraham's entertainment of three angels (Genesis 18.1–16).

320 More fruitful, which instructs us not to spare."
　　To whom thus Eve: "Adam, earth's hallowed mold,[6]
Of God inspired, small store will serve, where store,[7]
All seasons, ripe for use hangs on the stalk;
Save what by frugal storing firmness gains
325 To nourish, and superfluous moist consumes:
But I will haste and from each bough and brake
Each plant and juiciest gourd will pluck such choice
To entertain our angel guest, as he
Beholding shall confess that here on earth
330 God hath dispensed his bounties as in Heav'n."
　　So saying, with dispatchful looks in haste
She turns, on hospitable thoughts intent
What choice to choose for delicacy best,
What order, so contrived as not to mix
335 Tastes, not well joined, inelegant, but bring
Taste after taste upheld° with kindliest° change,　　　*maintained / most natural*
Bestirs her then, and from each tender stalk
Whatever earth all-bearing mother yields
In India east or west, or middle shore
340 In Pontus or the Punic coast,[8] or where
Alcinous reigned, fruit of all kinds, in coat,
Rough, or smooth-rined, or bearded husk, or shell
She gathers, tribute large, and on the board
Heaps with unsparing hand; for drink the grape
345 She crushes, inoffensive must, and meaths[9]　　　
From many a berry, and from sweet kernels pressed
She tempers° dulcet creams, nor these to hold　　　*blends*
Wants° her fit vessels pure, then strews the ground　　　*lacks*
With rose and odors from the shrub unfumed.[1]
350 Meanwhile our primitive° great sire, to meet　　　*original*
His godlike guest, walks forth, without more train°　　　*attendants*
Accompanied than with his own complete
Perfections, in himself was all his state,°　　　*dignity, authority*
More solemn° than the tedious pomp that waits　　　*awe-inspiring*
355 On princes, when their rich retínue long
Of horses led, and grooms besmeared with gold
Dazzles the crowd, and sets them all agape.
Nearer his presence Adam though not awed,
Yet with submiss approach and reverence meek,
360 As to a superior nature, bowing low,
　　Thus said: "Native of Heav'n, for other place:
None can than Heav'n such glorious shape contain;
Since by descending from the thrones above,
Those happy places thou hast deigned° a while　　　*condescended*
365 To want,° and honor these, vouchsafe with us　　　*be parted from*

---

6. Revered shape of earth's substance. The name "Adam" signifies red earth.
7. A great quantity. "Small store": few stored foods.
8. The "middle shore" includes Pontus, the south coast of the Black Sea, famous for nuts and fruits, and the "Punic" (Carthaginian) coast of North Africa on the Mediterranean, famous for figs; the gardens of Alcinous (next line) are described in the *Odyssey* 7.113–21 as perpetually fruitful.
9. Meads, drinks sweetened with honey. "Must": unfermented fruit juice.
1. Naturally scented, not burned for incense.

Two only, who yet by sov'reign gift possess
This spacious ground, in yonder shady bow'r
To rest, and what the garden choicest bears
To sit and taste, till this meridian° heat   *noontime*
370 Be over, and the sun more cool decline."
    Whom thus the angelic Virtue[2] answered mild:
"Adam, I therefore came, nor art thou such
Created, or such place hast here to dwell,
As may not oft invite, though Spirits of Heav'n
375 To visit thee; lead on then where thy bow'r
O'ershades; for these mid-hours, till evening rise
I have at will." So to the sylvan lodge
They came, that like Pomona's[3] arbor smiled
With flow'rets decked° and fragrant smells; but Eve   *covered*
380 Undecked, save with herself more lovely fair
Than wood nymph, or the fairest goddess feigned
Of three that in Mount Ida naked strove,[4]
Stood to entertain her guest from Heav'n; no veil
She needed, virtue-proof,° no thought infirm   *armored in virtue*
385 Altered her cheek. On whom the Angel "Hail"
Bestowed, the holy salutation used
Long after to blest Mary, second Eve.[5]
    "Hail mother of mankind, whose fruitful womb
Shall fill the world more numerous with thy sons
390 Than with these various fruits the trees of God
Have heaped this table." Raised of grassy turf
Their table was, and mossy seats had round,
And on her ample square from side to side
All autumn piled, though spring and autumn here
395 Danced hand in hand. A while discourse they hold;
No fear lest dinner cool; when thus began
Our author:° "Heav'nly stranger, please to taste   *forefather*
These bounties which our Nourisher, from whom
All perfect good unmeasured out, descends,
400 To us for food and for delight hath caused
The earth to yield; unsavory food perhaps
To spiritual natures; only this I know,
That one Celestial Father gives to all."
    To whom the angel: "Therefore what he gives
405 (Whose praise be ever sung) to man in part
Spiritual, may of° purest Spirits be found   *by*
No ingrateful food: and food alike those pure
Intelligential substances require[6]

---

2. Milton uses these angelic titles freely, in the Protestant manner, not as designations of the nine traditional orders (Raphael was called "Seraph" at line 277).
3. The Roman goddess of fruit trees.
4. On Mount Ida, Venus, Juno, and Minerva "strove" naked for the title of the most beautiful; Paris awarded the prize (the apple of discord) to Venus, which led to the rape of Helen and the Trojan War.
5. Cf. the angel's words to Mary announcing that she would bear a son, Jesus (Luke 1.28): "Hail, thou that art highly favored, the Lord is with thee: blessed art thou among women."
6. Milton's angels ("intelligential substances") require real food, even as "rational" men do (see below, lines 430–38). As a monist (believer that all creation is of one matter), Milton denied the more common (dualistic) idea that angels are pure spirit, holding instead that they are of a very highly refined material substance.

As doth your rational; and both contain
410 Within them every lower faculty
Of sense, whereby they hear, see, smell, touch, taste,
Tasting concoct, digest, assimilate,[7]
And corporeal to incorporeal turn.
For know, whatever was created, needs
415 To be sustained and fed; of elements
The grosser feeds the purer, earth the sea,
Earth and the sea feed air, the air those fires
Ethereal, and as lowest first the moon;
Whence in her visage round those spots, unpurged
420 Vapors not yet into her substance turned.[8]
Nor doth the moon no nourishment exhale
From her moist continent to higher orbs.[9]
The sun that light imparts to all, receives
From all his alimental° recompense   *nourishing*
425 In humid exhalations, and at even
Sups with the ocean:[1] though in Heav'n the trees
Of life ambrosial° fruitage bear, and vines   *divinely fragrant*
Yield nectar,[2] though from off the boughs each morn
We brush mellifluous° dews, and find the ground   *honey-flowing*
430 Covered with pearly grain; yet God hath here
Varied his bounty so with new delights,
As may compare with Heaven; and to taste
Think not I shall be nice."° So down they sat,   *fastidious, finicky*
And to their viands fell, nor seemingly°   *in show*
435 The angel, nor in mist, the common gloss°   *explanation*
Of theologians, but with keen dispatch
Of real hunger, and concoctive° heat   *digestive*
To transubstantiate;[3] what redounds, transpires
Through Spirits with ease; nor wonder, if by fire
440 Of sooty coal the empiric° alchemist   *experimental*
Can turn, or holds it possible to turn
Metals of drossiest ore to perfect gold
As from the mine. Meanwhile at table Eve
Ministered naked, and their flowing cups
445 With pleasant liquors crowned.° O innocence   *filled to the brim*
Deserving Paradise! if ever, then,
Then had the Sons of God excuse t' have been
Enamored at that sight,[4] but in those hearts
Love unlibidinous° reigned, nor jealousy   *without lust*

7. Three stages in digestion.
8. Here Raphael describes lunar spots as still-undigested vapors (in keeping with his exposition of the universal need of nourishment); in 1.287–91 he referred to moon spots in Galileo's terms, as landscape features.
9. A double negative: the moon does exhale such nourishment to other planets.
1. Milton explains evaporation as the sun dining off moisture exhaled from the oceans.
2. Ambrosia is the food and nectar the drink of the classical gods; Milton adds "pearly grain" (line 430), like the manna showered on the Israelites in the desert (Exodus 16.14–15).

3. In common theological use, transubstantiation is the Roman Catholic doctrine that the bread and wine of the Eucharist become the body and blood of Christ. Milton vigorously denied that doctrine, but he describes the angels' transforming of earthly food into their more highly refined spiritual substance as a true transubstantiation. The excess ("what redounds") is exhaled ("transpires") through angelic pores.
4. Genesis 6.2 tells of the marriage of "the daughters of men" with "the sons of God," usually identified as sons of Seth, but a patristic tradition (alluded to here) identifies them as angels.

450 Was understood, the injured lover's hell.
　　Thus when with meats and drinks they had sufficed,
Not burdened nature, sudden mind arose
In Adam, not to let th' occasion pass
Given him by this great conference to know
455 Of things above his world, and of their being
Who dwell in Heav'n, whose excellence he saw
Transcend his own so far, whose radiant forms
Divine effulgence,° whose high power so far　　　　　　　　　*shining forth*
Exceeded human, and his wary speech
460 Thus to th' empyreal minister he framed:
　　"Inhabitant with God, now know I well
Thy favor, in this honor done to man,
Under whose lowly roof thou hast vouchsafed
To enter and these earthly fruits to taste,
465 Food not of angels, yet accepted so,
As that more willingly thou couldst not seem
At Heav'n's high feasts t' have fed: yet what compare?"
　　To whom the wingèd hierarch° replied:　　　　　　　　　*authority*
"O Adam, one Almighty is, from whom
470 All things proceed, and up to him return,
If not depraved from good, created all
Such to perfection, one first matter all,[5]
Endued with various forms, various degrees
Of substance, and in things that live, of life;
475 But more refined, more spiritous, and pure,
As nearer to him placed or nearer tending
Each in their several active spheres assigned,
Till body up to spirit work, in bounds
Proportioned to each kind.[6] So from the root
480 Springs lighter the green stalk, from thence the leaves
More airy, last the bright consummate flow'r
Spirits odorous breathes:[7] flow'rs and their fruit
Man's nourishment, by gradual scale sublimed°　　　　　　　　*purified*
To vital spirits aspire, to animal,
485 To intellectual, give both life and sense,
Fancy° and understanding, whence the soul　　　　　　　　*imagination*
Reason receives, and reason is her being,
Discursive, or intuitive;[8] discourse

5. Milton held that the universe was created out of Chaos, not out of nothing: the primal matter of Chaos had its origin in God, who subsequently created all things from that matter (see 7.168–73, 210–42). This materialist "monism" denies sharp distinctions between angels and men, spirit and matter: all beings are of one substance, of varying degrees of refinement and life.
6. Milton's version of the chain of being qualifies natural hierarchy by allowing for movement up or down; beings may become increasingly spiritual ("more spiritous") or increasingly gross (as the rebel angels do), depending on their moral choices—"nearer tending."
7. The plant figure—root, stalk, leaves, flowers, and fruit—provides an illustration of the dyna-

mism of being in the universe and further explains why Raphael can eat the fruit. Such food is then transformed (next lines) into various orders of "spirits"—"vital," "animal," and "intellectual" (fluids in the blood that sustain life, sensation, motion, and finally intellect and its functions, "fancy," "understanding," and "reason"), indicating that the soul is also material.
8. Traditionally, on the dualist assumption that angels are pure spirit and humans a combination of matter and spirit, angelic intuition (immediate apprehension of truth) was absolutely distinguished from human "discourse" of reason (arguing from premises to conclusions). Milton, denying that assumption, makes the distinction only relative, a matter of "degree" (line 490).

Is oftest yours, the latter most is ours,
490   Differing but in degree, of kind the same.
Wonder not then, what God for you saw good
If I refuse not, but convert, as you,
To proper° substance; time may come when men   *our own*
With angels may participate, and find
495   No inconvenient diet, nor too light fare:
And from these corporal nutriments perhaps
Your bodies may at last turn all to spirit,
Improved by tract° of time, and winged ascend   *passage*
Ethereal as we, or may at choice
500   Here or in heav'nly paradises dwell;
If ye be found obedient, and retain
Unalterably firm his love entire
Whose progeny you are. Meanwhile enjoy
Your fill what happiness this happy state
505   Can comprehend, incapable° of more."   *unable to contain*
      To whom the patriarch of mankind replied:
"O favorable Spirit, propitious guest,
Well hast thou taught the way that might direct
Our knowledge, and the scale of nature set
510   From center to circumference, whereon
In contemplation of created things
By steps we may ascend to God. But say,
What meant that caution joined, 'If ye be found
Obedient'? Can we want° obedience then   *lack*
515   To him, or possibly his love desert
Who formed us from the dust, and placed us here
Full to the utmost measure of what bliss
Human desires can seek or apprehend?"
      To whom the angel: "Son of Heav'n and earth,
520   Attend: that thou art happy, owe° to God;   *attribute*
That thou continu'st such, owe to thyself,
That is, to thy obedience; therein stand.
This was that caution giv'n thee; be advised.
God made thee perfect, not immutable;°   *unchangeable*
525   And good he made thee, but to persevere
He left it in thy power, ordained thy will
By nature free, not overruled by fate
Inextricable, or strict necessity,
Our voluntary service he requires,
530   Not our necessitated, such with him
Finds no acceptance, nor can find, for how
Can hearts, not free, be tried whether they serve
Willing or no, who will but what they must
By destiny, and can no other choose?
535   Myself and all th' angelic host that stand
In sight of God enthroned, our happy state
Hold, as you yours, while our obedience holds;
On other surety° none; freely we serve,   *guarantee*
Because we freely love, as in our will
540   To love or not; in this we stand or fall:

And some are fall'n, to disobedience fall'n,
And so from Heav'n to deepest Hell; O fall
From what high state of bliss into what woe!"
    To whom our great progenitor: "Thy words
545 Attentive, and with more delighted ear,
Divine instructor, I have heard, than when
Cherubic songs° by night from neighboring hills   *songs of Cherubim*
Aerial music send: nor knew I not[9]
To be both will and deed created free;
550 Yet that we never shall forget to love
Our Maker, and obey him whose command
Single, is yet° so just, my constant thoughts   *also*
Assured me, and still assure: though what thou tell'st
Hath passed in Heav'n, some doubt within me move,
555 But more desire to hear, if thou consent,
The full relation, which must needs be strange,
Worthy of sacred silence to be heard;
And we have yet large° day, for scarce the sun   *ample*
Hath finished half his journey, and scarce begins
560 His other half in the great zone of Heav'n."
    Thus Adam made request, and Raphael
After short pause assenting, thus began:
    "High matter[1] thou enjoin'st me, O prime of men,
Sad task and hard, for how shall I relate
565 To human sense th' invisible exploits
Of warring Spirits; how without remorse
The ruin of so many glorious once
And perfect while they stood; how last unfold
The secrets of another world, perhaps
570 Not lawful to reveal? Yet for thy good
This is dispensed, and what surmounts the reach
Of human sense, I shall delineate so,
By lik'ning spiritual to corporal forms,
As may express them best, though what if earth
575 Be but the shadow of Heav'n, and things therein
Each to other like, more than on earth is thought?
    "As yet this world was not, and Chaos wild
Reigned where these heav'ns now roll, where earth now rests
Upon her center poised, when on a day
580 (For time, though in eternity, applied
To motion, measures all things durable
By present, past, and future)[2] on such day
As Heav'n's great year[3] brings forth, th' empyreal host
Of angels by imperial summons called,
585 Innumerable before th' Almighty's throne
Forthwith from all the ends of Heav'n appeared

---

9. A double negative; i.e., "I did know."
1. Raphael's account of the war in Heaven is an epic device, a narrative of past action; it is also a mini-epic itself, with traditional battles, challenges, and single combats. As an "epic" poet treating sacred matter, Raphael confronts a narrative challenge similar to Milton's own.

2. Countering a long philosophical tradition, Milton asserts the existence of time in Heaven, before the creation of the universe.
3. Plato and others defined the "great year" as the cycle completed when all the heavenly bodies simultaneously return to the positions they held at the cycle's beginning.

Under their hierarchs° in orders bright.   *leaders*
Ten thousand thousand ensigns high advanced,
Standards, and gonfalons° twixt van and rear   *banners*
590 Stream in the air, and for distinction serve
Of hierarchies, of orders, and degrees;
Or in their glittering tissues° bear emblazed   *cloth*
Holy memorials, acts of zeal and love
Recorded eminent. Thus when in orbs
595 Of circuit° inexpressible they stood,   *circumference*
Orb within orb, the Father Infinite,
By whom in bliss embosomed sat the Son,
Amidst as from a flaming mount, whose top
Brightness had made invisible, thus spake:
600   "'Hear all ye angels, progeny of Light,
Thrones, Dominations, Princedoms, Virtues, Powers,
Hear my decree, which unrevoked shall stand.
This day I have begot whom I declare
My only Son, and on this holy hill
605 Him have anointed,[4] whom ye now behold
At my right hand; your head I him appoint;
And by myself have sworn to him shall bow
All knees in Heav'n, and shall confess him Lord:
Under his great vicegerent[5] reign abide
610 United as one individual° soul   *indivisible*
Forever happy: him who° disobeys   *whoever*
Me disobeys, breaks union, and that day
Cast out from God and blessèd vision, falls
Into utter° darkness, deep engulfed, his place   *outer, total*
615 Ordained without redemption, without end.'
      "So spake th' Omnipotent, and with his words
All seemed well pleased, all seemed, but were not all.
That day, as other solemn° days, they spent   *ceremonial*
In song and dance about the sacred hill,
620 Mystical dance, which yonder starry sphere
Of planets and of fixed° in all her wheels   *fixed stars*
Resembles nearest, mazes intricate,
Eccentric,° intervolved,° yet regular   *off center / intertwined*
Then most, when most irregular they seem:
625 And in their motions harmony divine
So smooths her charming tones,[6] that God's own ear
Listens delighted. Evening now approached
(For we have also our evening and our morn,
We ours for change delectable, not need)
630 Forthwith from dance to sweet repast they turn
Desirous; all in circles as they stood,
Tables are set, and on a sudden piled

---

4. Cf. Psalm 2.7: "I will declare the decree: . . .
Thou art my Son; this day have I begotten
thee." The episode refers to the exaltation of
the Son as King, not his actual begetting, since
he is elsewhere described as "of all creation
first" (3.383) and as God's agent in creating the

angels and everything else.
5. Vice-regent, one appointed by the supreme
ruler (here, God) to wield his authority.
6. The movements of the angels in their dance
produce harmony, like those of the planets in the
Pythagorean theory of the music of the spheres.

With angels' food, and rubied nectar flows
In pearl, in diamond, and massy gold,
635 Fruit of delicious vines, the growth of Heav'n.
On flow'rs reposed, and with fresh flow'rets crowned,
They eat, they drink, and in communion sweet
Quaff immortality and joy, secure
Of surfeit where full measure only bounds
640 Excess, before th' all-bounteous King, who show'red
With copious hand, rejoicing in their joy.
Now when ambrosial° night with clouds exhaled   *fragrant*
From that high mount of God, whence light and shade
Spring both, the face of brightest Heav'n had changed
645 To grateful° twilight (for night comes not there   *pleasing*
In darker veil) and roseate° dews disposed   *rose-scented*
All but the unsleeping eyes of God to rest,
Wide over all the plain, and wider far
Than all this globous earth in plain outspread,
650 (Such are the courts of God) th' angelic throng
Dispersed in bands and files their camp extend
By living streams among the trees of life,
Pavilions numberless, and sudden reared,
Celestial tabernacles, where they slept
655 Fanned with cool winds, save those who in their course
Melodious hymns about the sov'reign throne
Alternate all night long: but not so waked
Satan, so call him now, his former name
Is heard no more in Heav'n; he of the first,
660 If not the first Archangel, great in power,
In favor and preeminence, yet fraught
With envy against the Son of God, that day
Honored by his great Father, and proclaimed
Messiah[7] King anointed, could not bear
665 Through pride that sight, and thought himself impaired.
Deep malice thence conceiving and disdain,
Soon as midnight brought on the dusky hour
Friendliest to sleep and silence, he resolved
With all his legions to dislodge,° and leave   *leave camp*
670 Unworshipped, unobeyed the throne supreme
Contemptuous, and his next subordinate[8]
Awak'ning, thus to him in secret spake:
    "'Sleep'st thou companion dear, what sleep can close
Thy eyelids? and remember'st what decree
675 Of yesterday, so late hath passed the lips
Of Heav'n's Almighty. Thou to me thy thoughts
Wast wont,° I mine to thee was wont to impart;   *in the habit of*
Both waking we were one; how then can now
Thy sleep dissent? New laws thou seest imposed;
680 New laws from him who reigns, new minds° may raise   *purposes*
In us who serve, new counsels, to debate

---

7. Hebrew, "anointed."
8. His original name in Heaven is lost (1.356–63), but he will come to be known as Beelzebub.

What doubtful may ensue, more in this place
To utter is not safe. Assemble thou
Of all those myriads which we lead the chief;
685 Tell them that by command, ere yet dim night
Her shadowy cloud withdraws, I am to haste,
And all who under me their banners wave,
Homeward with flying march where we possess
The quarters of the north, there to prepare
690 Fit entertainment to receive our King
The great Messiah, and his new commands,
Who speedily through all the hierarchies
Intends to pass triumphant, and give laws.'
　　"So spake the false Archangel, and infused
695 Bad influence into th' unwary breast
Of his associate; he together calls,
Or several one by one, the regent powers,
Under him regent, tells, as he was taught,
That the Most High commanding, now ere night,
700 Now ere dim night had disencumbered Heav'n,
The great hierarchal standard was to move;
Tells the suggested° cause, and casts between　　　　*insinuated*
Ambitious words and jealousies, to sound°　　　　*make trials of*
Or taint integrity; but all obeyed
705 The wonted signal, and superior voice
Of their great potentate° for great indeed　　　　*ruler*
His name, and high was his degree in Heav'n;
His count'nance as the morning star that guides
The starry flock, allured them, and with lies
710 Drew after him the third part of Heav'n's host:
Meanwhile, th' Eternal Eye, whose sight discerns
Abstrusest° thoughts, from forth his holy mount　　　　*most secret*
And from within the golden lamps that burn
Nightly before him, saw without their light
715 Rebellion rising, saw in whom, how spread
Among the sons of morn, what multitudes
Were banded to oppose his high decree;
And smiling to his only Son thus said:
　　"'Son, thou in whom my glory I behold
720 In full resplendence, heir of all my might,
Nearly it now concerns us to be sure
Of our omnipotence, and with what arms
We mean to hold what anciently we claim
Of deity or empire, such a foe
725 Is rising, who intends to erect his throne
Equal to ours, throughout the spacious north;
Nor so content, hath in his thought to try
In battle, what our power is, or our right.
Let us advise, and to this hazard draw
730 With speed what force is left, and all employ
In our defense, lest unawares we lose
This our high place, our sanctuary, our hill.'
　　"To whom the Son with calm aspect and clear

Lightning divine, ineffable, serene,
735 Made answer: 'Mighty Father, thou thy foes
Justly hast in derision, and secure
Laugh'st at their vain designs and tumults vain,[9]
Matter to me of glory, whom their hate
Illustrates,° when they see all regal power   *makes illustrious*
740 Giv'n me to quell their pride, and in event°   *in the outcome*
Know whether I be dextrous to subdue
Thy rebels, or be found the worst in Heav'n.'
 "So spake the Son, but Satan with his powers°   *armies*
Far was advanced on wingèd speed, an host
745 Innumerable as the stars of night,
Or stars of morning, dewdrops, which the sun
Impearls on every leaf and every flower.
Regions they passed, the mighty regencies°   *dominions*
Of Seraphim and Potentates and Thrones
750 In their triple degrees, regions to° which   *compared to*
All thy dominion, Adam, is no more
Than what this garden is to all the earth,
And all the sea, from one entire globose°   *globe*
Stretched into longitude° which having passed   *spread out flat*
755 At length into the limits° of the north   *regions*
They came, and Satan to his royal seat
High on a hill, far blazing, as a mount
Raised on a mount, with pyramids and tow'rs
From diamond quarries hewn, and rocks of gold,
760 The palace of great Lucifer (so call
That structure in the dialect of men
Interpreted) which not long after, he
Affecting° all equality with God,   *arrogating*
In imitation of that mount whereon
765 Messiah was declared in sight of Heav'n,
The Mountain of the Congregation called;
For thither he assembled all his train,
Pretending so commanded to consult
About the great reception of their King,
770 Thither to come, and with calumnious art
Of counterfeited truth thus held their ears:
 "'Thrones, Dominations, Princedoms, Virtues, Powers,
If these magnific titles yet remain
Not merely titular, since by decree
775 Another now hath to himself engrossed°   *monopolized*
All power, and us eclipsed under the name
Of King anointed, for whom all this haste
Of midnight march, and hurried meeting here,
This only to consult how we may best
780 With what may be devised of honors new
Receive him coming to receive from us
Knee-tribute yet unpaid, prostration vile,
Too much to one, but double how endured,

---

9. Cf. Psalm 2.4: "He that sitteth in the heavens shall laugh: the Lord shall have them in derision."

To one and to his image now proclaimed?
785   But what if better counsels might erect
Our minds and teach us to cast off this yoke?
Will ye submit your necks, and choose to bend
The supple knee? Ye will not, if I trust
To know ye right, or if ye know yourselves
790   Natives and sons of Heav'n possessed before
By none, and if not equal all, yet free,
Equally free; for orders and degrees
Jar not with liberty, but well consist.
Who can in reason then or right assume
795   Monarchy over such as live by right
His equals,[1] if in power and splendor less,
In freedom equal? or can introduce
Law and edíct on us, who without law
Err not, much less for this to be our Lord,
800   And look for adoration to th' abuse
Of those imperial titles which assert
Our being ordained to govern, not to serve?'
      "Thus far his bold discourse without control°   *hindrance*
Had audience, when among the Seraphim
805   Abdiel,[2] than whom none with more zeal adored
The Deity, and divine commands obeyed,
Stood up, and in a flame of zeal severe
The current of his fury thus opposed:
      "'O argument blasphémous, false and proud!
810   Words which no ear ever to hear in Heav'n
Expected, least of all from thee, ingrate,
In place thyself so high above thy peers.
Canst thou with impious obloquy condemn
The just decree of God, pronounced and sworn,
815   That to his only Son by right endued
With regal scepter, every soul in Heav'n
Shall bend the knee, and in that honor due
Confess him rightful King? Unjust thou says't,
Flatly unjust, to bind with laws the free,
820   And equal over equals to let reign,
One over all with unsucceeded° power.   *without successor*
Shalt thou give law to God, shalt thou dispute
With him the points of liberty, who made
Thee what thou art, and formed the pow'rs of Heav'n
825   Such as he pleased, and circumscribed their being?
Yet by experience taught we know how good,
And of our good, and of our dignity
How provident he is, how far from thought
To make us less, bent rather to exalt
830   Our happy state under one head more near
United. But to grant it thee unjust,

1. Satan here paraphrases the republican theory against earthly monarchy like that urged by Milton in his *Tenure of Kings and Magistrates* (1649); see pp. 1396–99. Abdiel, however, insists (lines 809–41) that the argument from equality cannot pertain to God and the angels.
2. Hebrew, "servant of God."

That equal over equals monarch reign:
Thyself though great and glorious dost thou count,
Or all angelic nature joined in one,
835 Equal to him begotten Son, by whom
As by his Word the mighty Father made
All things, ev'n thee, and all the Spirits of Heav'n
By him created in their bright° degrees,   *illustrious*
Crowned them with glory, and to their glory named
840 Thrones, Dominations, Princedoms, Virtues, Powers,
Essential Powers, nor by his reign obscured,
But more illustrious made, since he the head
One of our number thus reduced becomes,[3]
His laws our laws, all honor to him done
845 Returns our own. Cease then this impious rage,
And tempt not these; but hasten to appease
Th' incensèd Father and th' incensèd Son,
While pardon may be found in time besought.'
    "So spake the fervent angel, but his zeal
850 None seconded, as out of season judged,
Or singular and rash, whereat rejoiced
Th' Apostate,° and more haughty thus replied.   *religious renegade*
'That we were formed then say'st thou? and the work
Of secondary hands, by task transferred
855 From Father to his Son? Strange point and new!
Doctrine which we would know whence learnt: who saw
When this creation was? Remember'st thou
Thy making, while the Maker gave thee being?
We know no time when we were not as now;
860 Know none before us, self-begot, self-raised,
By our own quick'ning power, when fatal course°   *the course of fate*
Had circled his full orb, the birth mature
Of this our native Heav'n, ethereal sons.[4]
Our puissance° is our own, our own right hand   *power*
865 Shall teach us highest deeds, by proof to try
Who is our equal: then thou shalt behold
Whether by supplication we intend
Address, and to begirt th' Almighty throne
Beseeching or besieging. This report,
870 These tidings carry to th' anointed King;
And fly, ere evil intercept thy flight.'
    "He said, and as the sound of waters deep
Hoarse murmur echoed to his words applause
Through the infinite host, nor less for that
875 The flaming Seraph fearless, though alone
Encompassed round with foes, thus answered bold:
    "'O alienate from God, O Spirit accurst,
Forsaken of all good; I see thy fall
Determined, and thy hapless crew involved

---

3. Abdiel suggests that the Son's appointment as
the angels' king is something like an "incarnation" for them.
4. Satan's (illogical) argument is that since the

angels cannot remember their creation, they created themselves. Cf. Adam's comment on his recollection of origins (8.250–51, 270–79).

880 In this perfidious fraud, contagion spread
Both of thy crime and punishment: henceforth
No more be troubled how to quit the yoke
Of God's Messiah; those indulgent laws
Will not be now vouchsafed, other decrees
885 Against thee are gone forth without recall;
That golden scepter which thou didst reject
Is now an iron rod to bruise and break
Thy disobedience. Well thou didst advise,
Yet not for thy advice or threats I fly
890 These wicked tents devoted,° lest the wrath   *doomed*
Impendent,° raging into sudden flame   *impending*
Distinguish not: for soon expect to feel
His thunder on thy head, devouring fire.
Then who created thee lamenting learn,
895 When who can uncreate thee thou shalt know.'
    "So spake the Seraph Abdiel faithful found,
Among the faithless, faithful only he;
Among innumerable false, unmoved,
Unshaken, unseduced, unterrified
900 His loyalty he kept, his love, his zeal;
Nor number, nor example with him wrought
To swerve from truth, or change his constant mind
Though single. From amidst them forth he passed,
Long way through hostile scorn, which he sustained
905 Superior, nor of violence feared aught;°   *anything*
And with retorted scorn his back he turned
On those proud tow'rs to swift destruction doomed."

Book 6

The Argument

Raphael continues to relate how Michael and Gabriel were sent forth to battle against Satan and his angels. The first fight described: Satan and his powers retire under night: he calls a council, invents devilish engines, which in the second day's fight put Michael and his angels to some disorder; but they at length pulling up mountains overwhelmed both the force and machines of Satan: yet the tumult not so ending, God on the third day sends Messiah his Son, for whom he had reserved the glory of that victory: he in the power of his Father coming to the place, and causing all his legions to stand still on either side, with his chariot and thunder driving into the midst of his enemies, pursues them unable to resist towards the wall of heaven; which opening, they leap down with horror and confusion into the place of punishment prepared for them in the deep: Messiah returns with triumph to this Father.

All night the dreadless angel[1] unpursued
Through Heav'n's wide champaign° held his way, till Morn,   *plain*
Waked by the circling Hours,[2] with rosy hand

1. I.e., Abdiel.
2. Daughters of Jove, who control the seasons   and guard the gates of Heaven. "Morn": Aurora, goddess of dawn.

Unbarred the gates of light. There is a cave
5   Within the mount of God, fast° by his throne,   *close*
Where light and darkness in perpetual round
Lodge and dislodge by turns, which makes through Heav'n
Grateful vicissitude,° like day and night;   *delightful change*
Light issues forth, and at the other door
10   Obsequious° darkness enters, till her hour   *compliant*
To veil the Heav'n, though darkness there might well
Seem twilight here; and now went forth the Morn
Such as in highest Heav'n, arrayed in gold
Empyreal;° from before her vanished night,   *heavenly*
15   Shot through with orient beams: when all the plain
Covered with thick embattled° squadrons bright,   *in battle array*
Chariots and flaming arms, and fiery steeds
Reflecting blaze on blaze, first met his view:
War he perceived, war in procinct,° and found   *preparation*
20   Already known what he for news had thought
To have reported: gladly then he mixed
Among those friendly Powers who him received
With joy and acclamations loud, that one
That of so many myriads fall'n, yet one
25   Returned not lost: on to the sacred hill
They led him high applauded, and present
Before the seat supreme; from whence a voice:
From midst a golden cloud thus mild was heard.
"'Servant of God,[3] well done, well hast thou fought
30   The better fight, who single hast maintained
Against revolted multitudes the cause
Of truth, in word mightier than they in arms;
And for the testimony of truth hast borne
Universal reproach, far worse to bear
35   Than violence: for this was all thy care
To stand approved in sight of God, though worlds
Judged thee perverse: the easier conquest now
Remains thee, aided by this host of friends,
Back on thy foes more glorious to return
40   Than scorned thou didst depart, and to subdue
By force, who reason for their law refuse,
Right reason° for their law, and for their King   *upright, true reason*
Messiah, who by right of merit reigns.
Go Michael of celestial armies prince,
45   And thou in military prowess next
Gabriel, lead forth to battle these my sons°   *angels*
Invincible, lead forth my armèd saints
By thousands and by millions ranged for fight;
Equal in number to that godless crew
50   Rebellious,[4] them with fire and hostile arms
Fearless assault, and to the brow of Heav'n

---

3. The literal meaning (Hebrew) of the name Abdiel.
4. God sends out only an equal force to match the one-third of the angelic host that rebelled, not the two-thirds that remained loyal.

Pursuing drive them out from God and bliss,
Into their place of punishment, the gulf
Of Tartarus,° which ready opens wide   Hell
55 His fiery chaos to receive their fall.'
      "So spake the Sovereign Voice, and clouds began
To darken all the hill, and smoke to roll
In dusky wreaths reluctant° flames, the sign   writhing
Of wrath awaked: nor with less dread the loud
60 Ethereal trumpet from on high gan° blow: began to
At which command the powers militant,
That stood for Heav'n, in mighty quadrate⁵ joined
Of union irresistible, moved on
In silence their bright legions, to the sound
65 Of instrumental harmony that breathed
Heroic ardor to advent'rous deeds
Under their godlike leaders, in the cause
Of God and his Messiah. On they move
Indissolubly firm; nor obvious° hill,   standing in the way
70 Nor strait'ning vale,⁶ nor wood, nor stream divides
Their perfect ranks; for high above the ground
Their march was, and the passive air upbore
Their nimble tread; as when the total kind
Of birds in orderly array on wing
75 Came summoned over Eden to receive
Their names of thee; so over many a tract
Of Heav'n they marched, and many a province wide
Tenfold the length of this terrene:° at last   earth, terrain
Far in th' horizon to the north appeared
80 From skirt to skirt a fiery region, stretched
In battailous° aspéct, and nearer view   warlike
Bristled with upright beams° innumerable   shafts
Of rigid spears, and helmets thronged, and shields
Various, with boastful argument° portrayed,   heraldic devices
85 The banded powers of Satan hasting on
With furious expedition;° for they weened°   speed / thought
That selfsame day by fight, or by surprise
To win the mount of God, and on his throne
To set the envier of his state, the proud
90 Aspirer, but their thoughts proved fond° and vain   foolish
In the mid-way: though strange to us it seemed
At first, that angel should with angel war,
And in fierce hosting⁷ meet, who wont° to meet   were accustomed
So oft in festivals of joy and love
95 Unanimous, as sons of one great Sire
Hymning th' Eternal Father: but the shout
Of battle now began, and rushing sound
Of onset ended soon each milder thought.
High in the midst exalted as a god
100 Th' Apostate in his sun-bright chariot sat

5. A square military formation.   march in a file.
6. A narrow valley would force other armies to   7. Hostile encounter.

Idol of majesty divine, enclosed
With flaming Cherubim, and golden shields;
Then lighted from his gorgeous throne, for now
'Twixt host° and host but narrow space was left,   *army*
105 A dreadful interval, and front to front°   *face to face*
Presented stood in terrible array
Of hideous length: before the cloudy van,°   *frowning vanguard*
On the rough edge of battle° ere it joined,   *front line*
Satan with vast and haughty strides advanced,
110 Came tow'ring, armed in adamant and gold;
Abdiel that sight endured not, where he stood
Among the mightiest, bent on highest deeds,
And thus his own undaunted heart explores:
    "'O Heav'n! that such resemblance of the Highest
115 Should yet remain, where faith and realty°   *sincerity*
Remain not; wherefore should not strength and might
There fail where virtue fails, or weakest prove
Where boldest; though to sight° unconquerable?   *seemingly*
His puissance,° trusting in th' Almighty's aid,   *power*
120 I mean to try, whose reason I have tried°   *proved by trial*
Unsound and false; nor is it aught but just,
That he who in debate of truth hath won,
Should win in arms, in both disputes alike
Victor; though brutish that contést and foul,
125 When reason hath to deal with force, yet so
Most reason is that reason overcome.'
    "So pondering, and from his armèd peers
Forth stepping opposite, halfway he met
His daring foe, at this prevention° more   *obstruction*
130 Incensed, and thus securely° him defied: *confidently*
    "'Proud, art thou met? Thy hope was to have reached
The height of thy aspiring unopposed,
The throne of God unguarded, and his side
Abandoned at the terror of thy power
135 Or potent tongue; fool, not to think how vain
Against the Omnipotent to rise in arms;
Who out of smallest things could without end
Have raised incessant armies to defeat
Thy folly; or with solitary hand
140 Reaching beyond all limit at one blow
Unaided could have finished thee, and whelmed
Thy legions under darkness; but thou seest
All are not of thy train; there be° who faith   *there are those*
Prefer, and piety° to God, though then   *devotion*
145 To thee not visible, when I alone
Seemed in thy world erroneous to dissent
From all: my sect[8] thou seest, now learn too late

---

8. The term carries political resonance, since the national English church, Anglican or (during the revolution) Presbyterian, sought to suppress and persecute the sects who separated from it (Baptists, Quakers, Socinians, and others), often denouncing them as heretics. Satan claims that a "synod" (line 156, term for a Presbyterian assembly) has proclaimed the truth of the rebel angels' case; Abdiel insists that truth may rather reside (as here) with a single "dissenter" or a sect of a few.

How few sometimes may know, when thousand err.'
      "Whom the grand Foe with scornful eye askance
150 Thus answered. 'Ill for thee, but in wished hour
Of my revenge, first sought for thou return'st
From flight, seditious angel, to receive
Thy merited reward, the first assay
Of this right hand provoked, since first that tongue
155 Inspired with contradiction durst oppose
A third part of the gods, in synod met
Their deities to assert, who while they feel
Vigor divine within them, can allow
Omnipotence to none. But well thou com'st
160 Before thy fellows, ambitious to win
From me some plume, that thy success⁹ may show
Destruction to the rest: this pause between
(Unanswered lest thou boast)¹ to let thee know;
At first I thought that liberty and Heav'n
165 To heav'nly souls had been all one;° but now   *one and the same*
I see that most through sloth had rather serve,
Minist'ring Spirits, trained up in feast and song;
Such hast thou armed, the minstrelsy² of Heav'n,
Servility° with freedom to contend,   *bondage, obsequiousness*
170 As both their deeds compared this day shall prove.'
      "To whom in brief thus Abdiel stern replied:
'Apostate, still thou err'st, nor end wilt find
Of erring, from the path of truth remote:
Unjustly thou deprav'st° it with the name   *vilify*
175 Of servitude to serve whom God ordains,
Or nature; God and nature bid the same,
When he who rules is worthiest, and excels
Them whom he governs. This is servitude,
To serve th' unwise, or him who hath rebelled
180 Against his worthier, as thine now serve thee,
Thyself not free, but to thyself enthralled;³
Yet lewdly° dar'st our minist'ring upbraid.   *ignorantly, basely*
Reign thou in Hell thy kingdom, let me serve
In Heav'n God ever blest, and his divine
185 Behests obey, worthiest to be obeyed;
Yet chains in Hell, not realms expect: meanwhile
From me returned, as erst° thou saidst, from flight,   *formerly*
This greeting on thy impious crest receive.'
      "So saying, a noble stroke he lifted high,
190 Which hung not, but so swift with tempest fell
On the proud crest of Satan, that no sight,
Nor motion of swift thought, less could his shield
Such ruin intercept: ten paces huge
He back recoiled; the tenth on bended knee

---

9. The outcome of your action. "Plume": token
of victory.
1. I.e., lest thou boast that I did not answer your
argument.
2. Satan's contemptuous pun links together the
loyal angels' service ("Minist'ring," line 167) with
their song, likened to the street songs of minstrels.
3. Abdiel cites the "natural law" principle that
rule rightly belongs to the best or worthiest, and
that tyrants are enslaved to their own passions.

195　His massy spear upstayed; as if on earth
　　Winds under ground or waters forcing way
　　Sidelong, had pushed a mountain from his seat
　　Half sunk with all his pines. Amazement seized
　　The rebel Thrones,⁴ but greater rage to see
200　Thus foiled their mightiest: ours joy filled, and shout,
　　Presage of victory and fierce desire
　　Of battle: whereat Michaël bid sound
　　Th' Archangel trumpet; through the vast of Heav'n
　　It sounded, and the faithful armies rung
205　Hosanna to the Highest: nor stood at gaze
　　The adverse legions, nor less hideous joined
　　The horrid shock: now storming fury rose,
　　And clamor such as heard in Heav'n till now
　　Was never, arms on armor clashing brayed⁵
210　Horrible discord, and the madding° wheels　　　　　　　　_whirling madly_
　　Of brazen chariots raged; dire was the noise
　　Of conflict; overhead the dismal° hiss　　　　　　　　　_dreadful_
　　Of fiery darts in flaming volleys flew,
　　And flying vaulted either host with fire.
215　So under fiery cope° together rushed　　　　　　　　　　_sky_
　　Both battles main,⁶ with ruinous assault
　　And inextinguishable rage; all Heav'n
　　Resounded, and had earth been then, all earth
　　Had to her center shook. What wonder? when
220　Millions of fierce encount'ring angels fought
　　On either side, the least of whom could wield
　　These elements,⁷ and arm him with the force
　　Of all their regions: how much more of power
　　Army against army numberless to raise
225　Dreadful combustion° warring, and disturb,　　　　　　_tumult_
　　Though not destroy, their happy native seat;
　　Had not th' Eternal King Omnipotent
　　From his stronghold of Heav'n high overruled
　　And limited their might; though numbered such
230　As each divided legion might have seemed
　　A numerous host, in strength each armèd hand
　　A legion; led in fight, yet leader seemed
　　Each warrior single as in chief,⁸ expert
　　When to advance, or stand, or turn the sway°　　　　　　_force_
235　Of battle, open when, and when to close
　　The ridges° of grim war; no thought of flight,　　　　　_ranks_
　　None of retreat, no unbecoming deed
　　That argued fear; each on himself relied,
　　As° only in his arm the moment⁹ lay　　　　　　　　　　_as if_
240　Of victory; deeds of eternal fame

4. Here as elsewhere Milton uses the name of one angelic order to stand for all. But the choice of "Thrones" here carries political resonance, linking monarchs with rebels against God's kingdom.
5. Made a harsh, jarring sound.
6. The principal body of an army, as opposed to the van, rear, and wing.
7. The four elements—fire, air, water, earth—that constitute the several "regions" (next line) of planet earth.
8. I.e., the angelic legions had leaders, yet each single warrior seemed like such a leader.
9. Weight that will tip the scales.

Were done, but infinite: for wide was spread
That war and various; sometimes on firm ground
A standing fight, then soaring on main° wing   *strong, powerful*
Tormented° all the air; all air seemed then   *agitated*
245 Conflicting fire: long time in even scale
The battle hung; till Satan, who that day
Prodigious power had shown, and met in arms
No equal, ranging through the dire attack
Of fighting Seraphim confused, at length
250 Saw where the sword of Michael smote, and felled
Squadrons at once; with huge two-handed sway
Brandished aloft the horrid edge came down
Wide-wasting; such destruction to withstand
He hasted, and opposed the rocky orb
255 Of tenfold adamant, his ample shield[1]
A vast circumference: at his approach
The great Archangel from his warlike toil
Surceased, and glad as hoping here to end
Intestine war° in Heav'n, the Arch-Foe subdued   *civil war*
260 Or captive dragged in chains, with hostile frown
And visage all inflamed first thus began:
  "'Author of evil, unknown till thy revolt,
Unnamed in Heav'n, now plenteous, as thou seest
These acts of hateful strife, hateful to all,
265 Though heaviest by just measure on thyself
And thy adherents: how hast thou disturbed
Heav'n's blessèd peace, and into nature brought
Misery, uncreated till the crime
Of thy rebellion! how hast thou instilled
270 Thy malice into thousands, once upright
And faithful, now proved false! But think not here
To trouble holy rest; Heav'n casts thee out
From all her confines. Heav'n the seat of bliss
Brooks° not the works of violence and war.   *endures*
275 Hence then, and evil go with thee along
Thy offspring, to the place of evil, Hell,
Thou and thy wicked crew; there mingle° broils,   *concoct*
Ere this avenging sword begin thy doom,
Or some more sudden vengeance winged from God
280 Precipitate thee with augmented pain.'
  "So spake the Prince of Angels; to whom thus
The Adversary: 'Nor think thou with wind
Of airy threats to awe whom yet with deeds
Thou canst not. Hast thou turned the least of these
285 To flight, or if to fall, but that they rise
Unvanquished, easier to transact with me
That thou shouldst hope, imperious, and with threats
To chase me hence?[2] Err not that so shall end

---

1. Satan's shield is a rocklike ("rocky") circle, made of impenetrable "adamant" (probably diamond), ten layers thick.
2. I.e., Have you made even the least of my follow-ers flee, or seen them fall and fail to rise, that you would hope "imperiously" to deal ("transact") oth-erwise with me, driving me off by mere threats? "Err not" (following): don't falsely suppose.

The strife which thou call'st evil, but we style
290 The strife of glory: which we mean to win,
Or turn this Heav'n itself into the Hell
Thou fablest, here however to dwell free,
If not to reign: meanwhile thy utmost force,
And join him named Almighty to thy aid,
295 I fly not, but have sought thee far and nigh.'
　　"They ended parle,° and both addressed° for fight　　　*parley / prepared*
Unspeakable; for who, though with the tongue
Of angels, can relate, or to what things
Liken on earth conspicuous, that may lift
300 Human imagination to such height
Of godlike power: for likest gods they seemed,
Stood they or moved, in stature, motion, arms
Fit to decide the empire of great Heav'n.
Now waved their fiery swords, and in the air
305 Made horrid circles; two broad suns their shields
Blazed opposite, while Expectation stood[3]
In horror; from each hand with speed retired
Where erst° was thickest fight, th' angelic throng,　　　*ever*
And left large field, unsafe within the wind
310 Of such commotion, such as to set forth
Great things by small, if nature's concord broke,
Among the constellations war were sprung,
Two planets rushing from aspéct malign
Of fiercest opposition in midsky,
315 Should combat, and their jarring spheres confound.[4]
Together both with next to almighty arm,
Uplifted imminent one stroke they aimed
That might determine,° and not need repeat,°　　　*end / repetition*
As not of power,[5] at once; nor odds° appeared　　　*inequality*
320 In might or swift prevention;° but the sword　　　*anticipation*
Of Michael from the armory of God
Was giv'n him tempered so, that neither keen
Nor solid might resist that edge: it met
The sword of Satan with steep force to smite
325 Descending, and in half cut sheer, nor stayed,
But with swift wheel reverse, deep ent'ring shared°　　　*cut off*
All his right side; then Satan first knew pain,
And writhed him to and fro convolved;° so sore　　　*contorted*
The griding° sword with discontinuous° wound　　　*keenly cutting / gaping*
330 Passed through him, but th' ethereal substance closed
Not long divisible, and from the gash
A stream of nectarous humor issuing flowed
Sanguine,° such as celestial Spirits may bleed,　　　*blood-red*
And all his armor stained erewhile so bright.
335 Forthwith on all sides to his aid was run

3. Personifying the angels' apprehension.
4. An epic simile comparing the clash of these armies ("great things") with war among the planets, in which two planets clashing together from diametrically opposed positions ("aspect malign"), would cast the planetary system and its music ("jarring spheres") into confusion ("confound").
5. I.e., because they would not have power to repeat the blow.

By angels many and strong, who interposed
Defense, while others bore him on their shields
Back to his chariot, where it stood retired
From off the files of war; there they him laid
340 Gnashing for anguish and despite and shame
To find himself not matchless, and his pride
Humbled by such rebuke, so far beneath
His confidence to equal God in power.
Yet soon he healed; for Spirits that live throughout
345 Vital in every part, not as frail man
In entrails, heart or head, liver or reins,°   *kidneys*
Cannot but by annihilating die;
Nor in their liquid texture mortal wound
Receive, no more than can the fluid air:
350 All heart they live, all head, all eye, all ear,
All intellect, all sense, and as they please,
They limb themselves,[6] and color, shape, or size
Assume, as likes° them best, condense or rare.   *pleases*
    "Meanwhile in other parts like deeds deserved
355 Memorial, where the might of Gabriel fought,
And with fierce ensigns pierced the deep array
Of Moloch furious king,[7] who him defied,
And at his chariot wheels to drag him bound
Threatened, nor from the Holy One of Heav'n
360 Refrained his tongue blasphémous; but anon
Down clov'n to the waist, with shattered arms
And uncouth° pain fled bellowing. On each wing   *unfamiliar*
Uriel and Raphael his vaunting foe,
Though huge, and in a rock of diamond armed,
365 Vanquished Adramelech, and Asmadai,[8]
Two potent Thrones, that to be less than gods
Disdained, but meaner thoughts learned in their flight,
Mangled with ghastly wounds through plate and mail.
Nor stood unmindful Abdiel to annoy°   *injure*
370 The atheist° crew, but with redoubled blow   *impious*
Ariel and Arioch, and the violence
Of Ramiel[9] scorched and blasted overthrew.
I might relate of thousands, and their names
Eternize here on earth; but those elect
375 Angels contented with their fame in Heav'n
Seek not the praise of men: the other sort
In might though wondrous and in acts of war,
Nor of renown less eager, yet by doom
Canceled from Heav'n and sacred memory,
380 Nameless in dark oblivion let them dwell.
For strength from truth divided and from just,
Illaudable,° naught merits but dispraise   *unworthy of praise*

---

6. I.e., provide themselves with limbs. "Condense
or rare" (line 353): dense or airy.
7. With his companies ("ensigns") he pierced
Moloch's troops in their dense formation ("deep
array").

8. Asmodeus, a Persian god (cf. 4.167–71).
"Adramelech": "king of fire," a god worshipped at
Samaria with human sacrifice.
9. "Ariel": "lion of God." "Arioch": "lionlike."
"Ramiel": "thunder of God."

And ignominy, yet to glory aspires
Vainglorious, and through infamy seeks fame:
385 Therefore eternal silence be their doom.
    "And now their mightiest quelled, the battle swerved,[1]
With many an inroad gored; deformèd rout
Entered, and foul disorder; all the ground
With shivered armor strown, and on a heap
390 Chariot and charioteer lay overturned
And fiery foaming steeds; what° stood, recoiled   *those who*
O'erwearied, through the faint Satanic host
Defensive scarce,[2] or with pale fear surprised,°   *seized unexpectedly*
Then first with fear surprised and sense of pain
395 Fled ignominious, to such evil brought
By sin of disobedience, till that hour
Not liable to fear or flight or pain.
Far otherwise th' inviolable saints
In cubic phalanx° firm advanced entire,   *formation*
400 Invulnerable, impenetrably armed:
Such high advantages their innocence
Gave them above their foes, not to have sinned,
Not to have disobeyed; in fight they stood
Unwearied, unobnoxious° to be pained   *not liable*
405 By wound, though from their place by violence moved.
    "Now night her course began, and over Heav'n
Inducing darkness, grateful truce imposed,
And silence on the odious din of war:
Under her cloudy covert both retired,
410 Victor and vanquished: on the foughten field
Michaël and his angels prevalent°   *victorious*
Encamping, placed in guard their watches round,
Cherubic waving fires: on th' other part
Satan with his rebellious disappeared,
415 Far in the dark dislodged,° and void of rest,   *shifted quarters*
His potentates to council called by night;
And in the midst thus undismayed began:
    "'O now in danger tried, now known in arms
Not to be overpowered, companions dear,
420 Found worthy not of liberty alone,
Too mean pretense,° but what we more affect,[3]   *low aim*
Honor, dominion, glory, and renown,
Who have sustained one day in doubtful° fight,   *indecisive*
(And if one day, why not eternal days?)
425 What Heaven's Lord had powerfullest to send
Against us from about his throne, and judged
Sufficient to subdue us to his will,
But proves not so: then fallible, it seems,
Of future° we may deem him, though till now   *in the future*
430 Omniscient thought. True is, less firmly armed,
Some disadvantage we endured and pain,

1. I.e., the army gave way.   3. Aspire to.
2. Scarcely defending themselves.

Till now not known, but known as soon contemned,[4]
Since now we find this our empyreal form
Incapable of mortal injury
435   Imperishable, and though pierced with wound,
Soon closing, and by native vigor healed.
Of evil then so small as easy think
The remedy; perhaps more valid° arms,   *powerful*
Weapons more violent, when next we meet,
440   May serve to better us, and worse° our foes,   *injure*
Or equal what between us made the odds,
In nature none: if other hidden cause
Left them superior, while we can preserve
Unhurt our minds, and understanding sound,
445   Due search and consultation will disclose.'
    "He sat; and in th' assembly next upstood
Nisroch,[5] of Principalities the prime;
As one he stood escaped from cruel fight,
Sore toiled, his riven arms to havoc hewn,°   *cut to pieces*
450   And cloudy in aspéct thus answering spake:
'Deliverer from new lords, leader to free
Enjoyment of our right as gods; yet hard
For gods, and too unequal work we find
Against unequal arms to fight in pain,
455   Against unpained, impassive;[6] from which evil
Ruin must needs ensue; for what avails
Valor or strength, though matchless, quelled with pain
Which all subdues, and makes remiss° the hands   *slack, weak*
Of mightiest. Sense of pleasure we may well
460   Spare out of life perhaps, and not repine,
But live content, which is the calmest life:
But pain is perfect misery, the worst
Of evils, and excessive, overturns
All patience. He who therefore can invent
465   With what more forcible we may offend°   *attack*
Our yet unwounded enemies, or arm
Ourselves with like defense, to me° deserves   *in my opinion*
No less than for deliverance what we owe.'[7]
    "Whereto with look composed Satan replied.
470   'Not uninvented that, which thou aright
Believ'st so main° to our success, I bring;   *essential*
Which of us who beholds the bright surfáce
Of this ethereous mold° whereon we stand,   *ethereal matter*
This continent of spacious Heav'n, adorned
475   With plant, fruit, flow'r ambrosial, gems and gold,
Whose eye so superfically surveys
These things, as not to mind° from whence they grow   *consider*
Deep underground, materials dark and crude,
Of spiritous and fiery spume,° till touched   *frothy matter*
480   With Heav'n's ray, and tempered they shoot forth

---

4. No sooner known than despised.   6. Not liable to suffering.
5. An Assyrian god; the Hebrew name was said   7. I.e., we would owe such a one our deliverance.
to mean flight or luxurious temptation.

So beauteous, op'ning to the ambient° light. *enveloping*
These in their dark nativity the deep
Shall yield us, pregnant with infernal° flame, *from underground*
Which into hollow engines° long and round *cannon*
485 Thick-rammed, at th' other bore[8] with touch of fire
Dilated and infuriate° shall send forth *raging*
From far with thund'ring noise among our foes
Such implements of mischief as shall dash
To pieces, and o'erwhelm whatever stands
490 Adverse, that they shall fear we have disarmed
The Thunderer of his only° dreaded bolt. *unique*
Nor long shall be our labor, yet ere dawn,
Effect shall end our wish. Meanwhile revive;
Abandon fear; to strength and counsel joined
495 Think nothing hard, much less to be despaired.'
    He ended, and his words their drooping cheer° *spirits*
Enlightened, and their languished hope revived.
Th' invention all admired,° and each, how he *marveled at*
To be th' inventor missed, so easy it seemed
500 Once found, which yet unfound most would have thought
Impossible: yet haply° of thy race *possibly*
In future days, if malice should abound,
Someone intent on mischief, or inspired
With dev'lish machination might devise
505 Like instrument to plague the sons of men
For sin, on war and mutual slaughter bent.
Forthwith from council to the work they flew,
None arguing stood, innumerable hands
Were ready, in a moment up they turned
510 Wide the celestial soil, and saw beneath
Th' originals° of nature in their crude *original elements*
Conception; sulphurous and nitrous foam[9]
They found, they mingled, and with subtle art,
Concocted° and adjusted° they reduced *heated / dried*
515 To blackest grain, and into store conveyed:
Part hidden veins digged up (nor hath this earth
Entrails unlike) of mineral and stone,
Whereof to found° their engines and their balls *cast*
Of missive° ruin; part incentive° reed *missile / kindling*
520 Provide, pernicious° with one touch to fire. *quick, destructive*
So all ere day-spring,° under conscious[1] night *dawn*
Secret they finished, and in order set,
With silent circumspection unespied.
Now when fair morn orient in Heav'n appeared
525 Up rose the victor angels, and to arms
The matin° trumpet sung: in arms they stood *morning*
Of golden panoply, refulgent° host, *shining*
Soon banded; others from the dawning hills
Looked round, and scouts each coast light-armèd scour,

---

8. The touchhole into which fine powder was poured to serve as fuse for the charge. "Thick": compactly.

9. Saltpeter ("nitrous foam") and sulphur are the ingredients of gunpowder.
1. Aware, as an accessory to a crime.

530 Each quarter, to descry the distant foe,
Where lodged, or whither fled, or if for fight,
In motion or in alt:° him soon they met   *halt*
Under spread ensigns moving nigh, in slow
But firm battalion; back with speediest sail
535 Zophiel,[2] of Cherubim the swiftest wing,
Came flying, and in mid-air aloud thus cried:
   "'Arm, warriors, arm for fight, the foe at hand,
Whom fled we thought, will save us long pursuit
This day, fear not his flight; so thick a cloud
540 He comes, and settled in his face I see
Sad° resolution and secure:° let each   *sober / confident*
His adamantine° coat gird well, and each   *of hardest metal*
Fit well his helm, gripe fast his orbèd shield,
Borne ev'n° or high, for this day will pour down,   *straight out*
545 If I conjecture° aught, no drizzling shower,   *interpret signs*
But rattling storm of arrows barbed with fire.'
So warned he them aware themselves, and soon
In order, quit of all impediment;°   *hindrance*
Instant without disturb° they took alarm,   *disorder*
550 And onward move embattled;° when behold   *in battle order*
Not distant far the heavy pace the foe
Approaching gross° and huge; in hollow cube   *compact*
Training° his devilish enginry, impaled°   *hauling / fenced in*
On every side with shadowing squadrons deep,
555 To hide the fraud. At interview° both stood   *at mutual view*
A while, but suddenly at head appeared
Satan: and thus was heard commanding loud:
   "'Vanguard, to right and left the front unfold;
That all may see who hate us, how we seek
560 Peace and composure,° and with open breast   *agreement*
Stand ready to receive them, if they like
Our overture,[3] and turn not back perverse;
But that I doubt, however witness Heaven,
Heav'n witness thou anon, while we discharge
565 Freely our part: ye who appointed stand
Do as you have in charge, and briefly touch
What we propound, and loud that all may hear.'
   "So scoffing in ambiguous words, he scarce
Had ended; when to right and left the front
570 Divided, and to either flank retired.
Which to our eyes discovered new and strange,
A triple-mounted° row of pillars laid   *in three rows*
On wheels (for like to pillars most they seemed
Or hollowed bodies made of oak or fir
575 With branches lopped, in wood or mountain felled)
Brass, iron, stony mold,° had not their mouths   *matter*
With hideous orifice gaped on us wide,

2. Hebrew, "spy of God."
3. A pun on "offer to negotiate" and "opening" (aperture), the hole or muzzle of the cannon. The passage is full of puns: e.g., "perverse" (line 562, peevish, turned the wrong way), "discharge" (line 564), "charge," "touch," "propound," "loud" (lines 566–67), "hollow" (line 578).

Portending hollow truce; at each behind
A Seraph stood, and in his hand a reed
580 Stood waving tipped with fire; while we suspense,°   *in suspense*
Collected stood within our thoughts amused,°   *puzzled*
Not long, for sudden all at once their reeds
Put forth, and to a narrow vent applied
With nicest° touch. Immediate in a flame,   *most exact*
585 But soon obscured with smoke, all Heav'n appeared,
From those deep-throated engines belched,[4] whose roar
Emboweled° with outrageous noise the air,   *disemboweled*
And all her entrails tore, disgorging foul
Their devilish glut, chained[5] thunderbolts and hail
590 Of iron globes, which on the victor host
Leveled, with such impetuous fury smote,
That whom they hit, none on their feet might stand,
Though standing else as rocks, but down they fell
By thousands, Angel on Archangel rolled,
595 The sooner for their arms; unarmed they might
Have easily as Spirits evaded swift
By quick contraction or remove; but now
Foul dissipation° followed and forced rout;   *dispersal*
Nor served it to relax their serried files.[6]
600 What should they do? If on they rushed, repulse
Repeated, and indecent° overthrow   *shameful*
Doubled, would render them yet more despised,
And to their foes a laughter; for in view
Stood ranked of Seraphim another row
605 In posture to displode° their second dire°   *explode / volley*
Of thunder: back defeated to return
They worse abhorred. Satan beheld their plight,
And to his mates thus in derision called:
"'O friends, why come not on these victors proud?
610 Erewhile they fierce were coming, and when we,
To entertain them fair with open front°   *candid face*
And breast,° (what could we more?) propounded[7] terms   *heart*
Of composition, straight they changed their minds,
Flew off, and into strange vagaries° fell,   *eccentric motions*
615 As they would dance, yet for a dance they seemed
Somewhat extravagant and wild, perhaps
For joy of offering peace: but I suppose
If our proposals once again were heard
We should compel them to a quick result.'
620   "To whom thus Belial in like gamesome mood:
'Leader, the terms we sent were terms of weight,
Of hard contents, and full of force urged home,
Such as we might perceive amused them[8] all,

---

4. See the sustained debased imagery relating to bodily functions, e.g., "belched," "emboweled," "entrails."
5. Chainshot, which was linked cannonballs.
6. I.e., nor did it do any good ("served it") to loosen up ("relax") their rows pressed close together ("serried files").

7. More puns, on "propounded," "terms of composition," "flew off."
8. A pun on "held their attention" and "bewildered them." Belial also puns on (among other terms) "stumbled" ("nonplussed" and "tripped up") and "understand" ("comprehend" and "prop up").

And stumbled many: who receives them right,
625 Had need from head to foot well understand;
Not understood, this gift they have besides,
They show us when our foes walk not upright."
    "So they among themselves in pleasant° vein   *jesting*
Stood scoffing, heightened in their thoughts beyond
630 All doubt of victory, Eternal Might
To match with their inventions they presumed
So easy, and of his thunder made a scorn,
And all his host derided, while they° stood   *the good angels*
A while in trouble; but they stood not long,
635 Rage prompted them at length, and found them arms
Against such hellish mischief fit to oppose.
Forthwith (behold the excellence, the power,
Which God hath in his mighty angels placed)
Their arms away they threw, and to the hills
640 (For earth hath this variety from Heav'n
Of pleasure situate in hill and dale)
Light as the lightning glimpse they ran, they flew,
From their foundations loos'ning to and fro
They plucked the seated hills with all their load,[9]
645 Rocks, waters, woods, and by the shaggy tops
Uplifting bore them in their hands: amaze,°   *astonishment, panic*
Be sure, and terror seized the rebel host,
When coming towards them so dread they saw
The bottom of the mountains upward turned,
650 Till on those cursèd engines' triple-row
They saw them whelmed, and all their confidence
Under the weight of mountains buried deep,
Themselves invaded° next, and on their heads   *attacked*
Main° promontories flung, which in the air   *great, solid*
655 Came shadowing, and oppressed° whole legions armed.   *pressed down*
Their armor helped their harm, crushed in and bruised
Into their substance pent,° which wrought them pain   *closely confined*
Implacable, and many a dolorous groan,
Long struggling undernearth, ere they could wind
660 Out of such prison, though Spirits of purest light,
Purest at first, now gross by sinning grown.
The rest in imitation to like arms
Betook them, and the neighboring hills uptore;
So hills amid the air encountered hills
665 Hurled to and fro with jaculation° dire,   *hurling*
That underground they fought in dismal shade;
Infernal noise; war seemed a civil° game   *humane, refined*
To° this uproar; horrid confusion heaped   *compared to*
Upon confusion rose: and now all Heav'n
670 Had gone to wrack, with ruin overspread,
Had not th' Almighty Father where he sits
Shrined in his sanctuary of Heav'n secure,

9. The hurling of hills as missiles is taken from the war between the Olympian gods and the Giants, in Hesiod's *Theogony*.

Consulting° on the sum of things, foreseen   *considering*
This tumult, and permitted all, advised:°   *deliberately*
675 That his great purpose he might so fulfill,
To honor his anointed Son avenged
Upon his enemies, and to declare
All power on him transferred: whence to his Son
Th' assessor[1] of his throne he thus began:
680   "'Effulgence° of my glory, Son beloved,   *radiance*
Son in whose face invisible is beheld
Visibly,[2] what by Deity I am,
And in whose hand what by decree I do,
Second Omnipotence,[3] two days are passed,
685 Two days, as we compute the days of Heav'n,
Since Michael and his powers went forth to tame
These disobedient; sore hath been their fight,
As likeliest was, when two such foes met armed;
For to themselves I left them, and thou know'st,
690 Equal in their creation they were formed,
Save what sin hath impaired, which yet hath wrought
Insensibly,° for I suspend their doom;   *imperceptively*
Whence in perpetual fight they needs must last
Endless, and no solution will be found:
695 War wearied hath performed what war can do,
And to disordered rage let loose the reins,
With mountains as with weapons armed, which makes
Wild work in Heav'n, and dangerous to the main.°   *whole continent*
Two days are therefore passed, the third is thine;
700 For thee I have ordained it, and thus far
Have suffered,° that the glory may be thine   *permitted*
Of ending this great war, since none but thou
Can end it. Into thee such virtue and grace
Immense I have transfused, that all may know
705 In Heav'n and Hell thy power above compare,
And this perverse commotion governed thus,
To manifest thee worthiest to be heir
Of all things, to be heir and to be King
By sacred unction,° thy deservèd right.   *anointing*
710 Go then thou mightiest in thy Father's might,
Ascend my chariot, guide the rapid wheels
That shake Heav'n's basis, bring forth all my war,°   *instruments of war*
My bow and thunder, my almighty arms
Gird on, and sword upon thy puissant thigh;
715 Pursue these sons of darkness, drive them out
From all Heav'n's bounds into the utter° deep: *outer*
There let them learn, as likes them, to despise
God and Messiah his anointed[4] King.'
   "He said, and on his Son with rays direct

1. One who sits beside, an associate.
2. Cf. Colossians 1.15: "Who is the image of the invisible God."
3. Two omnipotences are a logical impossibility; the phrase underscores Milton's view that the Son receives all power from the Father. Cf. John

5.19, "The Son can do nothing of himself, but what he seeth the Father do," which Milton cites in *Christian Doctrine* 1.5 to argue that the Son derives all power from the Father.
4. The literal meaning of "messiah."

720 Shone full, he all his Father full expressed
Ineffably° into his face received,   *inexpressibly*
And thus the Filial Godhead answering spake:
"'O Father, O Supreme of heav'nly Thrones,
First, highest, holiest, best, thou always seek'st
725 To glorify thy Son, I always thee,
As is most just; this I my glory account,
My exaltation, and my whole delight,
That thou in me well pleased, declar'st thy will
Fulfilled, which to fulfill is all my bliss.
730 Scepter and power, thy giving, I assume,
And gladlier shall resign, when in the end
Thou shalt be all in all, and I in thee
Forever, and in me all whom thou lov'st:
But whom thou hat'st, I hate, and can put on
735 Thy terrors, as I put thy mildness on,
Image of thee in all things; and shall soon,
Armed with thy might, rid Heav'n of these rebelled,
To their prepared ill mansion driven down
To chains of darkness, and th' undying worm,
740 That from thy just obedience could revolt,
Whom to obey is happiness entire.
Then shall thy saints unmixed, and from th' impure
Far separate, circling thy holy mount
Unfeignèd hallelujahs to thee sing,
745 Hymns of high praise, and I among them chief.'
So said, he o'er his scepter bowing, rose
From the right hand of Glory where he sat,
And the third sacred morn began to shine
Dawning through Heav'n: forth rushed with whirlwind sound
750 The chariot of Paternal Deity,
Flashing thick flames, wheel within wheel undrawn,
Itself instinct with° spirit, but convoyed   *animated by*
By four Cherubic shapes, four faces each[5]
Had wondrous, as with stars their bodies all
755 And wings were set with eyes, with eyes the wheels
Of beryl, and careering fires between;[6]
Over their heads a crystal firmament,
Whereon a sapphire throne, inlaid with pure
Amber, and colors of the show'ry arch.°   *rainbow*
760 He in celestial panoply all armed
Of radiant urim,[7] work divinely wrought,
Ascended, at his right hand Victory
Sat eagle-winged, beside him hung his bow
And quiver with three-bolted thunder stored,[8]
765 And from about him fierce effusion° rolled   *copious emission*

5. The Son's living chariot, with its four-faced Cherubim—the faces being man, lion, ox, and eagle—is taken from Ezekiel 1 (especially 1.10) and 10.
6. Cf. Ezekiel 10.12: "And their whole body, and their backs, and their hands, and their wings, and the wheels, were full of eyes round about, even the wheels that they four had."
7. Gems worn by Aaron in his "breastplate of judgment" (Exodus 28.30).
8. Jove's bird was the eagle; his weapon was the thunderbolt.

Of smoke and bickering° flame, and sparkles dire;   *flickering*
Attended with ten thousand thousand saints,
He onward came, far off his coming shone,
And twenty thousand[9] (I their number heard)
770 Chariots of God, half on each hand were seen:
He on the wings of Cherub rode sublime°   *lifted up*
On the crystálline sky, in sapphire throned,
Illustrious° far and wide, but by his own   *shining*
First seen: them unexpected joy surprised,
775 When the great ensign of Messiah blazed
Aloft by angels borne, his sign in Heav'n:
Under whose conduct Michael soon reduced°   *led back*
His army, circumfused° on either wing,   *spread around*
Under their Head embodied all in one.
780 Before him Power Divine his way prepared;
At his command the uprooted hills retired
Each to his place, they heard his voice and went
Obsequious,° Heav'n his wonted face renewed,   *dutiful*
And with fresh flow'rets hill and valley smiled.
785 This saw his hapless foes but stood obdured,°   *hardened*
And to rebellious fight rallied their powers
Insensate, hope conceiving from despair.
In heav'nly Spirits could such perverseness dwell?
But to convince the proud what signs avail,
790 Or wonders move th' obdúrate to relent?
They hardened more by what might most reclaim,
Grieving° to see his glory, at the sight   *aggrieved*
Took envy, and aspiring to his height,
Stood re-embattled[1] fierce, by force or fraud
795 Weening° to prosper, and at length prevail   *thinking*
Against God and Messiah, or to fall
In universal ruin last, and now
To final battle drew; disdaining flight,
Or faint retreat; when the great Son of God
800 To all his host on either hand thus spake:
   "'Stand still in bright array ye saints, here stand
Ye angels armed, this day from battle rest;[2]
Faithful hath been your warfare, and of God
Accepted, fearless in his righteous cause,
805 And as ye have received, so have ye done
Invincibly; but of this cursed crew
The punishment to other hand belongs,
Vengeance is his,[3] or whose he sole appoints;
Number to this day's work is not ordained
810 Nor multitude, stand only and behold
God's indignation on these godless poured
By me, not you but me they have despised,

---

9. Cf. Psalm 68.17: "The chariots of God are twenty thousand, even thousands of angels: the Lord is among them."
1. Drawn up again in battle formation.
2. Echoes Moses's words when God destroyed the Egyptians in the Red Sea (Exodus 14.13): "Fear ye not, stand still, and see the salvation of the Lord, which he will shew to you to day."
3. Cf. Romans 12.19: "Vengeance is mine; I will repay, saith the Lord."

Yet envied; against me is all their rage,
Because the Father, t' whom in Heav'n supreme
815 Kingdom and power and glory appertains,
Hath honored me according to his will.
Therefore to me their doom he hath assigned;
That they may have their wish, to try with me
In battle which the stronger proves, they all,
820 Or I alone against them, since by strength
They measure all, of other excellence
Not emulous,° nor care who them excels;   *desirous of rivaling*
Nor other strife with them do I vouchsafe.'°   *grant*
　　"So spake the Son, and into terror changed
825 His count'nance too severe to be beheld
And full of wrath bent on his enemies.
At once the Four[4] spread out their starry wings
With dreadful shade contiguous, and the orbs
Of his fierce chariot rolled, as with the sound
830 Of torrent floods, or of a numerous host.
He on his impious foes right onward drove,
Gloomy as night; under his burning wheels
The steadfast empyrean shook throughout,
All but the throne itself of God. Full soon
835 Among them he arrived; in his right hand
Grasping ten thousand thunders, which he sent
Before him, such as in their souls infixed
Plagues; they astonished° all resistance lost,   *struck with fear*
All courage; down their idle weapons dropped;
840 O'er shields and helms, and helmèd heads he rode
Of Thrones and mighty Seraphim prostráte,
That wished the mountains now might be again
Thrown on them as a shelter from his ire.
Nor less on either side tempestuous fell
845 His arrows, from the fourfold-visaged Four,
Distinct° with eyes, and from the living wheels,   *adorned*
Distinct alike with multitude of eyes;
One spirit in them ruled, and every eye
Glared lightning, and shot forth pernicious° fire   *deadly*
850 Among th' accursed, that withered all their strength,
And of their wonted° vigor left them drained,   *accustomed*
Exhausted, spiritless, afflicted, fall'n.
Yet half his strength he put not forth, but checked
His thunder in mid-volley, for he meant
855 Not to destroy, but root them out of Heav'n:
The overthrown he raised, and as a herd
Of goats or timorous flock together thronged
Drove them before him thunderstruck, pursued
With terrors and with furies to the bounds
860 And crystal wall of Heav'n, which op'ning wide,
Rolled inward, and a spacious gap disclosed
Into the wasteful° deep; the monstrous sight   *desolate*

---

4. The four "Cherubic shapes" of line 753.

Strook them with horror backward, but far worse
Urged them behind; headlong themselves they threw
865   Down from the verge of Heav'n, eternal wrath
Burnt after them to the bottomless pit.
      "Hell heard th' unsufferable noise, Hell saw
Heav'n ruining° from Heav'n, and would have fled   *falling headlong*
Affrighted; but strict fate had cast too deep
870   Her dark foundations, and too fast had bound.
Nine days they fell; confounded Chaos roared,
And felt tenfold confusion in their fall
Through his wild anarchy, so huge a rout°   *defeated army*
Encumbered° him with ruin: Hell at last   *burdened*
875   Yawning received them whole, and on them closed,
Hell their fit habitation fraught with fire
Unquenchable, the house of woe and pain.
Disburdened Heav'n rejoiced, and soon repaired
Her mural° breach, returning whence it rolled.   *in the wall*
880   Sole victor from th' expulsion of his foes
Messiah his triumphal chariot turned:
To meet him all his saints, who silent stood
Eyewitnesses of his almighty acts,
With jubilee° advanced; and as they went,   *joyful shouts*
885   Shaded with branching palm, each order bright
Sung triumph, and him sung victorious King,
Son, Heir, and Lord, to him dominion giv'n,
Worthiest to reign: he celebrated rode
Triumphant through mid-Heav'n, into the courts
890   And temple of his mighty Father throned
On high: who into glory him received,
Where now he sits at the right hand of bliss.
      "Thus measuring things in Heav'n by things on earth
At thy request, and that thou may'st beware
895   By what is past, to thee I have revealed
What might have else to human race been hid;
The discord which befell, and war in Heav'n
Among th' angelic powers,° and the deep fall   *armies*
Of those too high aspiring, who rebelled
900   With Satan, he who envies now thy state,
Who now is plotting how he may seduce
Thee also from obedience, that with him
Bereaved of happiness thou may'st partake
His punishment, eternal misery;
905   Which would be all his solace and revenge,
As a despite° done against the Most High,   *malicious act*
Thee once to gain companion of his woe.
But listen not to his temptations, warn
Thy weaker;[5] let it profit thee to have heard
910   By terrible example the reward
Of disobedience; firm they might have stood,
Yet fell; remember, and fear to transgress."

---

5. Eve, who is, however, present for this story.

Book 7

The Argument

Raphael at the request of Adam relates how and wherefore this world was first created; that God, after the expelling of Satan and his angels out of heaven, declared his pleasure to create another world and other creatures to dwell therein; sends his Son with glory and attendance of angels to perform the work of creation in six days: the angels celebrate with hymns the performance thereof, and his reascension into heaven.

Descend from Heav'n Urania,[1] by that name
If rightly thou art called, whose voice divine
Following, above th' Olympian hill I soar,
Above the flight of Pegasean wing.[2]
5   The meaning, not the name I call: for thou
Nor of the muses nine, nor on the top
Of old Olympus dwell'st, but heav'nly born
Before the hills appeared, or fountain flowed,
Thou with eternal Wisdom[3] didst converse,°   *associate*
10 Wisdom thy sister, and with her didst play
In presence of th' Almighty Father, pleased
With thy celestial song. Up led by thee
Into the Heav'n of Heav'ns I have presumed,
An earthly guest, and drawn empyreal air,
15 Thy temp'ring;° with like safety guided down   *made suitable by thee*
Return me to my native element:
Lest from this flying steed unreined (as once
Bellerophon,[4] though from a lower clime)°   *region*
Dismounted, on th' Aleian field I fall
20 Erroneous° there to wander and forlorn.   *straying*
Half yet remains unsung, but narrower bound
Within the visible diurnal sphere;[5]
Standing on earth, not rapt° above the pole,   *transported, enraptured*
More safe I sing with mortal voice, unchanged
25 To hoarse or mute, though fall'n on evil days,
On evil days though fall'n, and evil tongues;
In darkness, and with dangers compassed round,[6]
And solitude; yet not alone, while thou

1. Urania, the Greek Muse of astronomy, had been made into the Muse of Christian poetry by du Bartas and other religious poets. Milton, however, constructs another derivation for her (line 5ff.). Milton begins Book 7 with a third proem (lines 1–39).
2. Pegasus, the flying horse of inspired poetry, suggests (in connection with Bellerophon, line 18) Milton's sense of perilous audacity in writing this poem.
3. In Proverbs 8.24–31 Wisdom tells of her activities before the Creation: "Then I was by him [God], as one brought up with him: and I was daily his delight, rejoicing always before him." Milton describes "eternal Wisdom" as a daughter of God (personification of his wisdom) and devises a

myth in which the Muse of divine poetry ("celestial song," line 12) is Wisdom's "sister"—also, thereby, originating from God.
4. Bellerophon incurred the gods' anger when he tried to fly to heaven upon Pegasus; Zeus sent an insect to sting the horse, and Bellerophon fell down to the "Aleian field" (plain of error), where he wandered alone and blind until his death.
5. The universe, which appears to rotate daily.
6. After the Restoration of Charles II (May 1660) and until the passage of the Act of Oblivion (August 1660), Milton was in danger of death and dismemberment (like Orpheus, lines 34–35); several of his republican colleagues were hanged, disembowelled, and quartered for their part in the revolution and regicide.

Visit'st my slumbers nightly, or when morn
30 Purples the east: still govern thou my song,
Urania, and fit audience find, though few.
But drive far off the barbarous dissonance
Of Bacchus and his revelers, the race
Of that wild rout that tore the Thracian bard
35 In Rhodope, where woods and rocks had ears
To rapture, till the savage clamor drowned
Both harp and voice;[7] nor could the Muse defend
Her son.[8] So fail not thou, who thee implores:
For thou art heav'nly, she an empty dream.
40   Say goddess, what ensued when Raphael,
The affable Archangel, had forewarned
Adam by dire example to beware
Apostasy, by what befell in Heaven
To those apostates, lest the like befall
45 In Paradise to Adam or his race,
Charged not to touch the interdicted tree,
If they transgress, and slight that sole command,
So easily obeyed amid the choice
Of all tastes else° to please their appetite,   *besides*
50 Though wand'ring. He with his consorted° Eve   *wedded*
The story heard attentive, and was filled
With admiration,° and deep muse to hear   *amazement*
Of things so high and strange, things to their thought
So unimaginable as hate in Heav'n,
55 And war so near the peace of God in bliss
With such confusion: but the evil soon
Driv'n back redounded° as a flood on those   *flowed back*
From whom it sprung, impossible to mix
With blessedness. Whence Adam soon repealed°   *abandoned*
60 The doubts that in his heart arose: and now
Led on, yet sinless, with desire to know
What nearer might concern him, how this world
Of Heav'n and earth conspicuous° first began,   *visible*
When, and whereof created, for what cause,
65 What within Eden or without was done
Before his memory, as one whose drouth°   *thirst*
Yet scarce allayed still eyes the current° stream,   *flowing*
Whose liquid murmur heard new thirst excites,
Proceeded thus to ask his heav'nly guest:
70   "Great things, and full of wonder in our ears,
Far differing from this world, thou hast revealed
Divine interpreter, by favor sent
Down from the empyrean to forewarn
Us timely of what might else° have been our loss,   *otherwise*

---

7. The music of the "Thracian bard" Orpheus, type of the poet, charmed even "woods and rocks," but his song was drowned out by the Bacchantes, a "wild rout" of screaming women who murdered and dismembered him and threw his body parts into the Hebrus River, which rises in the "Rhodope" mountains. Milton fears that a similar "barbarous dissonance" unleashed by the Restoration will drown out his voice and threaten his life.

8. Orpheus's mother is Calliope, Muse of epic poetry.

75   Unknown, which human knowledge could not reach:
For which to the Infinitely Good we owe
Immortal thanks, and his admonishment
Receive with solemn purpose to observe
Immutably his sov'reign will, the end°   *purpose*
80   Of what we are. But since thou hast vouchsafed
Gently for our instruction to impart
Things above earthly thought, which yet concerned
Our knowing, as to Highest Wisdom seemed,
Deign to descend now lower, and relate
85   What may no less perhaps avail us known,
How first began this Heav'n which we behold
Distant so high, with moving fires adorned
Innumerable, and this which yields or fills
All space, the ambient° air wide interfused   *yielding*
90   Embracing round this florid° earth, what cause   *flowery*
Moved the Creator in his holy rest
Through all eternity so late to build
In Chaos,[9] and the work begun, how soon
Absolved,° if unforbid thou may'st unfold   *finished*
95   What we, not to explore the secrets ask
Of his eternal empire, but the more
To magnify° his works, the more we know.   *glorify*
And the great light of day yet wants to run
Much of his race though steep, suspense° in Heav'n   *attentive, suspended*
100   Held by thy voice, thy potent voice he hears,
And longer will delay to hear thee tell
His generation,° and the rising birth   *creation*
Of nature from the unapparent[1] deep:
Or if the star of evening and the moon
105   Haste to thy audience, night with her will bring
Silence, and sleep list'ning to thee will watch,°   *stay awake*
Or we can bid his absence, till thy song
End, and dismiss thee ere the morning shine."
    Thus Adam his illustrious guest besought:
110   And thus the godlike angel answered mild:
"This also thy request with caution asked
Obtain: though to recount almighty works
What words or tongue of Seraph can suffice,
Or heart of man suffice to comprehend?
115   Yet what thou canst attain, which best may serve
To glorify the Maker, and infer°   *make, render*
Thee also happier, shall not be withheld
Thy hearing, such commission from above
I have received, to answer thy desire
120   Of knowledge within bounds; beyond abstain
To ask, nor let thine own inventions° hope   *speculations*
Things not revealed, which th' invisible King,

9. Adam's question about God's actions before the Creation was often cited as an example of presumptuous and dangerous speculation, especially when, as here, it implies mutability in God. But in Milton's Eden, error that is not deliberate is not sinful.

1. Invisible, because dark and without form.

Only omniscient, hath suppressed in night,
To none communicable in earth or Heaven:
125 Enough is left besides to search and know.
But knowledge is as food, and needs no less
Her temperance over appetite, to know
In measure what the mind may well contain,
Oppresses else with surfeit, and soon turns
130 Wisdom to folly, as nourishment to wind.
   "Know then, that after Lucifer from Heav'n
(So call him, brighter once amidst the host
Of angels, than that star the stars among)[2]
Fell with his flaming legions through the deep
135 Into his place, and the great Son returned
Victorious with his saints, th' Omnipotent
Eternal Father from his throne beheld
Their multitude, and to his Son thus spake:
   "'At least our envious foe hath failed, who thought
140 All like himself rebellious, by whose aid
This inaccessible high strength, the seat
Of Deity supreme, us dispossessed,[3]
He trusted to have seized, and into fraud°   deception, error
Drew many, whom their place knows here no more;
145 Yet far the greater part have kept, I see,
Their station, Heav'n yet populous retains
Number sufficient to possess her realms
Though wide, and this high temple to frequent
With ministeries due and solemn rites:
150 But lest his heart exalt him in the harm
Already done, to have dispeopled Heav'n,
My damage fondly° deemed, I can repair   foolishly
That detriment, if such it be to lose
Self-lost, and in a moment will create
155 Another world, out of one man a race
Of men innumerable, there to dwell,
Not here, till by degrees of merit raised
They open to themselves at length the way
Up hither, under long obedience tried,
160 And earth be changed to Heav'n and Heav'n to earth,
One kingdom, joy and union without end.
Meanwhile inhabit lax,° ye Powers of Heav'n;   spread out
And thou my Word, begotten Son, by thee
This I perform, speak thou, and be it done:[4]
165 My overshadowing Spirit and might with thee
I send along, ride forth, and bid the deep
Within appointed bounds be heav'n and earth,
Boundless the deep, because I am who fill
Infinitude, nor vacuous the space.
170 Though I uncircumscribed myself retire,

2. I.e., Lucifer (Satan) was once brighter among   3. I.e., once he had dispossessed us.
the angels than the star bearing his name is among   4. God identifies himself as Creator, the Son as
the stars.   his agent to speak his creating Word.

And put not forth my goodness, which is free
To act or not,[5] necessity and chance
Approach not me, and what I will is fate.'
   "So spake th' Almighty and to what he spake
175 His Word, the Filial Godhead, gave effect.
Immediate are the acts of God, more swift
Than time or motion, but to human ears
Cannot without process of speech be told,
So told as earthly notion° can receive.[6]   *human understanding*
180 Great triumph and rejoicing was in Heav'n
When such was heard declared the Almighty's will;
'Glory' they sung to the Most High, 'good will
To future men, and in their dwellings peace:
Glory to him whose just avenging ire
185 Had driven out th' ungodly from his sight
And th' habitations of the just; to him
Glory and praise, whose wisdom had ordained
Good out of evil to create, instead
Of Spirits malign a better race to bring
190 Into their vacant room, and thence diffuse
His good to worlds and ages infinite.'
So sang the hierarchies: meanwhile the Son
On his great expedition now appeared,
Girt with omnipotence, with radiance crowned
195 Of majesty divine, sapience° and love   *wisdom*
Immense, and all his Father in him shone.
About his chariot numberless were poured
Cherub and Seraph, Potentates and Thrones,
And Virtues, winged Spirits, and chariots winged,
200 From the armory of God, where stand of old
Myriads between two brazen mountains lodged
Against° a solemn day, harnessed at hand,   *in preparation for*
Celestial equipage; and now came forth
Spontaneous, for within them spirit lived,
205 Attendant on their Lord: Heav'n opened wide
Her ever-during° gates, harmonious sound   *lasting*
On golden hinges moving, to let forth
The King of Glory[7] in his powerful Word
And Spirit coming to create new worlds.
210 On heav'nly ground they stood, and from the shore
They viewed the vast immeasurable abyss
Outrageous° as a sea, dark, wasteful, wild,   *enormous, violent*
Up from the bottom turned by furious winds
And surging waves, as mountains to assault
215 Heav'n's height, and with the center mix the pole.
   "'Silence, ye troubled waves, and thou deep, peace,'

---

5. Milton's God creates out of Chaos, not out of nothing; the matter of Chaos emanated from God, and Chaos is therefore "infinite" because God fills it even while he withholds his "goodness" (creating power) from it. Neither necessity nor chance affect in any way God's freely willed creative act.
6. Raphael explains the principle of accommoda-
tion, whereby God's acts are said to be translated into terms humans can understand: here, a six-day creation. This principle allows for an escape from biblical literalism.
7. Cf. Psalm 24.9: "Lift up your heads, O ye gates; even lift them up, ye everlasting doors; and the King of glory shall come in."

Said then th' Omnific° Word, 'your discord end':   *all-creating*
   "Nor stayed, but on the wings of Cherubim
Uplifted, in paternal glory rode
220 Far into Chaos, and the world unborn;
For Chaos heard his voice: him all his train
Followed in bright procession to behold
Creation, and the wonders of his might.
Then stayed the fervid° wheels, and in his hand   *burning*
225 He took the golden compasses, prepared
In God's eternal store, to circumscribe
This universe, and all created things:
One foot he centered, and the other turned
Round through the vast profundity obscure,
230 And said, 'Thus far extend, thus far thy bounds,
This be thy just° circumference O world.'   *exact*
Thus God the heav'n° created, thus the earth,   *the sky*
Matter unformed and void: darkness profound
Covered th' abyss: but on the wat'ry calm
235 His brooding wings the Spirit of God outspread,
And vital virtue° infused, and vital warmth   *power*
Throughout the fluid mass, but downward purged
The black tartareous cold infernal dregs[8]
Adverse to life: then founded, then conglobed
240 Like things to like, the rest to several place
Disparted, and between spun out the air,
And earth self-balanced on her center hung.
   "'Let there be light,' said God,[9] and forthwith light
Ethereal, first of things, quintessence[1] pure
245 Sprung from the deep, and from her native east
To journey through the airy gloom began,
Sphered in a radiant cloud, for yet the sun
Was not; she in a cloudy tabernacle
Sojourned the while. God saw the light was good;
250 And light from darkness by the hemisphere
Divided: light the day, and darkness night
He named. Thus was the first day ev'n and morn:[2]
Nor passed uncelebrated, nor unsung
By the celestial choirs, when orient light
255 Exhaling° first from darkness they beheld;   *rising as vapor*
Birthday of heav'n° and earth; with joy and shout   *the sky*
The hollow universal orb they filled,
And touched their golden harps, and hymning praised
God and his works, Creator him they sung,
260 Both when first evening was, and when first morn.
   "Again, God said, 'Let there be firmament
Amid the waters, and let it divide

---

8. Crusty, gritty stuff left over from the elements infused with life that make up the universe; it is associated with Hell ("infernal," "tartarous") and presumably used in its composition.
9. God's creating words, here and later, are quoted from Genesis 1–2, but Milton freely elaborates the creatures' responses to those words.
1. Ether was thought to be a fifth element or "quintessence," the substance of the celestial bodies above the moon.
2. One twenty-four-hour period measured in the Hebrew manner from sundown to sundown.

The waters from the waters': and God made
The firmament, expanse of liquid,° pure,   *clear, bright*
265 Transparent, elemental air diffused
In circuit to the uttermost convex°   *vault*
Of this great round:° partition firm and sure,   *universe*
The waters underneath from those above
Dividing: for as earth, so he the world
270 Built on circumfluous° waters calm, in wide   *flowing around*
Crystálline ocean, and the loud misrule
Of Chaos far removed, lest fierce extremes
Contiguous might distemper the whole frame:[3]
And heav'n° he named the firmament: so ev'n   *the sky*
275 And morning chorus sung the second day.
    "The earth was formed, but in the womb as yet
Of waters, embryon[4] immature involved°   *enfolded*
Appeared not: over all the face of earth
Main° ocean flowed, not idle, but with warm   *of great expanse*
280 Prolific humor° soft'ning all her globe,   *generative moisture*
Fermented the great mother to conceive,
Satiate with genial° moisture, when God said,   *generative*
'Be gathered now ye waters under heav'n
Into one place, and let dry land appear.'
285 Immediately the mountains huge appear
Emergent, and their broad bare backs upheave
Into the clouds, their tops ascend the sky:
So high as heaved the tumid° hills, so low   *swollen*
Down sunk a hollow bottom broad and deep,
290 Capacious bed of waters: thither they
Hasted with glad precipitance,° uprolled   *headlong fall*
As drops on dust conglobing from the dry;
Part rise in crystal wall, or ridge direct°   *surge forward*
For haste; such flight the great command impressed
295 On the swift floods: as armies at the call
Of trumpet (for of armies thou hast heard)
Troop to their standard, so the wat'ry throng,
Wave rolling after wave, where way they found,
If steep, with torrent rapture,° if through plain,   *force*
300 Soft-ebbing; nor withstood them rock or hill,
But they, or° underground, or circuit wide   *whether*
With serpent error° wand'ring, found their way,   *winding course*
And on the washy ooze deep channels wore;
Easy, ere God had bid the ground be dry,
305 All but within those banks, where rivers now
Stream, and perpetual draw their humid train.°   *following*
The dry land, earth, and the great receptacle
Of congregated waters he called seas:
And saw that it was good, and said, 'Let th' earth
310 Put forth the verdant grass, herb yielding seed,
And fruit tree yielding fruit after her kind;

---

3. Disturb the order and mixture of the elements and the created "frame" of the universe.
4. The earth is at first the "embryo" enveloped in a "womb of waters" and is then herself the "great mother" (line 281), made ready ("fermented") to conceive and bear every other being.

Whose seed is in herself upon the earth.'
He scarce had said, when the bare earth, till then
Desert and bare, unsightly, unadorned,
315 Brought forth the tender grass, whose verdure clad
Her universal face with pleasant green,
Then herbs of every leaf, that sudden flow'red
Op'ning their various colors, and made gay
Her bosom smelling sweet: and these scarce blown,°   *blossomed*
320 Forth flourished thick the clust'ring vine, forth crept
The swelling gourd, up stood the corny° reed   *hard as horn*
Embattled in her field: add the humble° shrub,   *low-growing*
And bush with frizzled hair implicit:° last   *tangled*
Rose as in dance the stately trees, and spread
325 Their branches hung with copious fruit; or gemmed°   *put forth buds*
Their blossoms: with high woods the hills were crowned,
With tufts the valleys and each fountain side,
With borders long the rivers. That earth now
Seemed like to Heav'n, a seat where gods might dwell,
330 Or wander with delight, and love to haunt
Her sacred shades: though God had yet not rained
Upon the earth, and man to till the ground
None was, but from the earth a dewy mist
Went up and watered all the ground, and each
335 Plant of the field, which ere it was in the earth
God made, and every herb, before it grew
On the green stem; God saw that it was good:
So ev'n and morn recorded the third day.
    "Again th' Almighty spake: 'Let there be lights
340 High in th' expanse of heaven° to divide   *the sky*
The day from night; and let them be for signs,
For seasons, and for days, and circling years,
And let them be for lights as I ordain
Their office° in the firmament of heav'n   *function*
345 To give light on the earth'; and it was so.
And God made two great lights, great for their use
To man, the greater to have rule by day,
The less by night altern:° and made the stars,   *in turns*
And set them in the firmament of heav'n
350 To illuminate the earth, and rule the day
In their vicissitude,° and rule the night,   *regular alternation*
And light from darkness to divide. God saw,
Surveying his great work, that it was good:
For of celestial bodies first the sun
355 A mighty sphere he framed, unlightsome first,
Though of ethereal mold:° then formed the moon   *fashioned from ether*
Globose, and every magnitude of stars,
And sowed with stars the heav'n thick as a field:
Of light by far the greater part he took,
360 Transplanted from her cloudy shrine,[5] and placed
In the sun's orb, made porous to receive

5. The "cloudy tabernacle" of line 248.

And drink the liquid light, firm to retain
Her gathered beams, great palace now of light.
Hither as to their fountain other stars
365 Repairing,° in their golden urns draw light,   resorting
And hence the morning planet gilds her horns;[6]
By tincture° or reflection they augment   absorption
Their small peculiar,° though from human sight   own small light
So far remote, with dimunition seen.
370 First in his east the glorious lamp was seen,
Regent of day, and all th' horizon round
Invested with bright rays, jocund° to run   merry
His longitude° through heav'n's high road: the gray   distance
Dawn, and the Pleiades[7] before him danced
375 Shedding sweet influence: less bright the moon,
But opposite in leveled west was set
His mirror, with full face borrowing her light
From him, for other light she needed none
In that aspect,° and still that distance keeps   when full
380 Till night, then in the east her turn she shines,
Revolved on heav'n's great axle, and her reign
With thousand lesser lights dividual° holds,   divided
With thousand thousand stars, that then appeared
Spangling the hemisphere: then first adorned
385 With their bright luminaries that set and rose,
Glad° evening and glad morn crowned the fourth day.   bright, gay
        And God said, 'Let the waters generate
Reptile° with spawn abundant, living soul: creeping animals
And let fowl fly above the earth, with wings
390 Displayed° on the op'n firmament of heav'n.'   spread out
And God created the great whales, and each
Soul living, each that crept, which plenteously
The waters generated by their kinds,
And every bird of wing after his kind;
395 And saw that it was good, and blessed them, saying,
'Be fruitful, multiply, and in the seas
And lakes and running streams the waters fill;
And let the fowl be multiplied on the earth.'
Forthwith the sounds and seas, each creek and bay
400 With fry° innumerable swarm, and shoals   young fish
Of fish that with their fins and shining scales
Glide under the green wave, in sculls that oft
Bank the mid-sea:[8] part single or with mate
Graze the seaweed their pasture, and through groves
405 Of coral stray, or sporting with quick glance
Show to the sun their waved° coats dropped° with gold,   striped / flecked
Or in their pearly shells at ease, attend°   watch for
Moist nutriment, or under rocks their food

---

6. Venus, which Galileo's telescope found to be
crescent-shaped in her first quarter.
7. A cluster of seven stars in the constellation
Taurus. They appear at dawn ahead of the sun.
See Job 38.31.

8. The fishes' darting motions resemble boats
oared now on one side, now on the other ("sculls"),
as they turn they seem to form banks within
the sea.

In jointed armor watch: on smooth the seal,
410 And bended[9] dolphins play: part huge of bulk
Wallowing unwieldy, enormous in their gait
Tempest° the ocean: there leviathan[1]   *stir up*
Hugest of living creatures, on the deep
Stretched like a promontory sleeps or swims,
415 And seems a moving land, and at his gills
Draws in, and at his trunk spouts out a sea.
Meanwhile the tepid caves, and fens and shores
Their brood as numerous hatch, from th' egg that soon
Bursting with kindly° rupture forth disclosed   *natural*
420 Their callow° young, but feathered soon and fledge   *without feathers*
They summed their pens,[2] and soaring th' air sublime
With clang° despised the ground, under a cloud   *harsh cry*
In prospect;[3] there the eagle and the stork
On cliffs and cedar tops their eyries build:
425 Part loosely° wing the region,° part more wise   *separately / sky*
In common, ranged in figure wedge their way,[4]
Intelligent° of seasons, and set forth   *understanding*
Their aery caravan high over seas
Flying, and over lands with mutual wing
430 Easing their flight;[5] so steers the prudent crane
Her annual voyage, borne on winds; the air
Floats,° as they pass, fanned with unnumbered plumes: *undulates*
From branch to branch the smaller birds with song
Solaced the woods, and spread their painted wings
435 Till ev'n, nor then the solemn nightingale
Ceased warbling, but all night tuned her soft lays:°   *songs*
Others on silver lakes and rivers bathed
Their downy breast; the swan, with archèd neck
Between her white wings mantling proudly, rows
440 Her state with oary feet:[6] yet oft they quit
The dank,° and rising on stiff pennons, tow'r°   *pool / soar into*
The mid-aerial sky: others on ground
Walked firm; the crested cock whose clarion sounds
The silent hours, and th' other° whose gay train   *the peacock*
445 Adorns him, colored with the florid hue
Of rainbows and starry eyes. The waters thus
With fish replenished,° and the air with fowl,   *fully supplied*
Evening and morn solemnized the fifth day.
    "The sixth, and of creation last arose
450 With evening harps and matin,° when God said,   *morning*
'Let th' earth bring forth soul living in her kind,
Cattle and creeping things, and beast of the earth,
Each in their kind.' The earth obeyed, and straight
Op'ning her fertile womb teemed° at a birth   *brought forth*

---

9. Curved in leaping. "Smooth": a stretch of calm
water.
1. The great whale (see 1.200–208).
2. Brought their feathers to full growth.
3. The ground seems covered by a cloud of birds.
4. Fly in a wedge formation.

5. Birds were thought to support each other
with their wings when they flew in formation.
6. The swan's outstretched ("mantling") wings
form a mantle, and it seems like a monarch on a
royal barge rowed by its own "oary" feet.

455 Innumerous living creatures, perfect forms,
Limbed and full grown: out of the ground up rose
As from his lair the wild beast where he wons°   dwells
In forest wild, in thicket, brake, or den;
Among the trees in pairs they rose, they walked:
460 The cattle in the fields and meadows green:
Those rare and solitary, these⁷ in flocks
Pasturing at once,° and in broad herds upsprung.   immediately
The grassy clods° now calved, now half appeared   mounds of earth
The tawny lion, pawing to get free
465 His hinder parts, then springs as broke from bonds,
And rampant shakes his brinded° mane; the ounce,°   streaked / lynx
The libbard,° and the tiger, as the mole   leopard
Rising, the crumbled earth above them threw
In hillocks; the swift stag from underground
470 Bore up his branching head: scarce from his mold
Behemoth⁸ biggest born of earth upheaved
His vastness: fleeced the flocks and bleating rose,
As plants: ambiguous between sea and land
The river-horse⁹ and scaly crocodile.
475 At once came forth whatever creeps the ground,
Insect or worm;¹ those waved their limber fans
For wings, and smallest lineaments exact
In all the liveries decked of summer's pride
With spots of gold and purple, azure and green:
480 These as a line their long dimension drew,
Streaking the ground with sinuous trace; not all
Minims° of nature; some of serpent kind   smallest animals
Wondrous in length and corpulence involved°   coiled
Their snaky folds, and added wings. First crept
485 The parsimonious emmet,° provident   thrifty ant
Of future, in small room large heart° enclosed,   great wisdom
Pattern of just equality perhaps
Hereafter, joined in her popular tribes
Of commonalty:² swarming next appeared
490 The female bee that feeds her husband drone
Deliciously, and builds her waxen cells
With honey stored: the rest are numberless,
And thou their natures know'st, and gav'st them names,³
Needless to thee repeated; nor unknown
495 The serpent subtlest beast of all the field,
Of huge extent sometimes, with brazen eyes
And hairy mane⁴ terrific,° though to thee   terrifying
Not noxious, but obedient at thy call.

---

7. "These" are the domestic cattle who come forth in "flocks" and "herds" in pastures; "those" are the wild beasts who come forth "in pairs" (line 459), and spread out ("rare") at wide intervals.
8. A huge biblical beast (Job 40.15), often identified with the elephant.
9. Translates the Greek name "hippopotamus."
1. Any creeping creature, including serpents.
2. The ant will become the symbol of a frugal and self-governing republic ("pattern of just equality")

with the "popular" (populous, plebian) tribes of common people ("commonalty") joined in rule (lines 486–89); Milton made it such a symbol in his prose tract *The Ready and Easy Way*. Bees here (lines 489–93) suggest delightful ease but are not yet (as in 1.768–75) a symbol of monarchy and associated with Hell.
3. See 8.342–54, and Genesis 2.19–20.
4. Sea serpents were so described in *Aeneid* 2.203–7.

Now heav'n in all her glory shone, and rolled
500 Her motions, as the great First Mover's hand
First wheeled their course; earth in her rich attire
Consummate° lovely smiled; air, water, earth,   complete, perfect
By fowl, fish, beast, was flown, was swum, was walked
Frequent;° and of the sixth day yet remained;   in throngs
505 There wanted yet the master work, the end°   purpose
Of all yet done; a creature who not prone
And brute as other creatures, but endued
With sanctity of reason, might erect
His stature,[5] and upright with front° serene   brow, face
510 Govern the rest, self-knowing, and from thence
Magnanimous to correspond[6] with Heav'n,
But grateful to acknowledge whence his good
Descends, thither with heart and voice and eyes
Directed in devotion, to adore
515 And worship God supreme, who made him chief
Of all his works: therefore th' Omnipotent
Eternal Father (for where is not he
Present) thus to his Son audibly spake:
    "'Let us make now man in our image, man
520 In our similitude, and let them rule
Over the fish and fowl of sea and air,
Beast of the field, and over all the earth,
And every creeping thing that creeps the ground.'
This said, he formed thee, Adam, thee O man
525 Dust of the ground, and in thy nostrils breathed
The breath of life; in his own image he
Created thee, in the image of God
Express,° and thou becam'st a living soul.   exact, manifest
Male he created thee, but thy consort
530 Female for race; then blessed mankind, and said,
'Be fruitful, multiply, and fill the earth,
Subdue it, and throughout dominion hold
Over fish of the sea, and fowl of the air,
And every living thing that moves on the earth.'
535 Wherever thus created, for no place
Is yet distinct by name, thence,° as thou know'st   from there
He brought thee into this delicious° grove,   delightful
This garden, planted with the trees of God,
Delectable both to behold and taste;
540 And freely all their pleasant fruit for food
Gave thee, all sorts are here that all th' earth yields,
Variety without end; but of the tree
Which tasted works knowledge of good and evil,
Thou may'st not; in the day thou eat'st, thou di'st;
545 Death is the penalty imposed, beware,
And govern well thy appetite, lest Sin
Surprise thee, and her black attendant Death.

---

5. Both "stand erect" and "elevate his condi-   that he was created for Heaven.
tion": his erect stance was understood to signify   6. Both "be in harmony" and "communicate."

Here finished he, and all that he had made
Viewed, and behold all was entirely good;
550　So ev'n and morn accomplished the sixth day:
Yet not till the Creator from his work
Desisting, though unwearied, up returned
Up to the Heav'n of Heav'ns his high abode,
Thence to behold his new-created world
555　Th' addition of his empire, how it showed
In prospect from his throne, how good, how fair,
Answering his great Idea.[7] Up he rode
Followed with acclamation and the sound
Symphonious of ten thousand harps that tuned°　　　　*performed*
560　Angelic harmonies: the earth, the air
Resounded (thou remember'st, for thou heard'st),
The heav'ns and all the constellations rung,
The planets in their stations list'ning stood,
While the bright pomp° ascended jubilant.　　　　*triumphal procession*
565　　"'Open, ye everlasting gates,' they sung,
'Open, ye Heav'ns, your living doors; let in
The great Creator from his work returned
Magnificent,[8] his six days' work, a world;
Open, and henceforth oft; for God will deign
570　To visit oft the dwellings of just men
Delighted, and with frequent intercourse
Thither will send his wingèd messengers
On errands of supernal° grace.' So sung　　　　*heavenly*
The glorious train ascending: he through Heav'n,
575　That opened wide her blazing° portals, led　　　　*radiant*
To God's eternal house direct the way,
A broad and ample road, whose dust is gold
And pavement stars, as stars to thee appear,
Seen in the galaxy, that Milky Way
580　Which nightly as a circling zone° thou seest　　　　*belt*
Powdered with stars. And now on earth the seventh
Evening arose in Eden, for the sun
Was set, and twilight from the east came on,
Forerunning night; when at the holy mount
585　Of Heav'n's high-seated top, th' imperial throne
Of Godhead, fixed forever firm and sure,
The Filial Power arrived, and sat him down
With his great Father, for he[9] also went
Invisible, yet stayed (such privilege
590　Hath Omnipresence) and the work ordained,°　　　　*ordered, enacted*
Author and end of all things, and from work
Now resting, blessed and hallowed the sev'nth day,
As resting on that day from all his work,
But not in silence holy kept; the harp
595　Had work and rested not, the solemn pipe,

---

7. Eternal archetype or pattern, as in Plato: concept in the mind of God.
8. Cf. Psalm 24.7: "Lift up your heads, O ye gates; and be ye lift up, ye everlasting doors; and the King of glory shall come in."
9. The Father.

And dulcimer, all organs° of sweet stop,   *wind instruments*
All sounds on fret[1] by string or golden wire
Tempered° soft tunings, intermixed with voice   *brought into harmony*
Choral° or unison: of incense clouds   *in parts*
600 Fuming from golden censers hid the mount.
    "Creation and the six days' acts they sung:
'Great are thy works, Jehovah, infinite
Thy power; what thought can measure thee or tongue
Relate thee; greater now in thy return
605 Than from the giant[2] angels; thee that day
Thy thunders magnified; but to create
Is greater than created to destroy.
Who can impair thee, Mighty King, or bound
Thy empire? Easily the proud attempt
610 Of Spirits apostate and their counsels vain
Thou hast repelled, while impiously they thought
Thee to diminish, and from thee withdraw
The number of thy worshippers. Who seeks
To lessen thee, against his purpose serves
615 To manifest the more thy might: his evil
Thou usest, and from thence creat'st more good.
Witness this new-made world, another heav'n
From Heaven gate not far, founded in view
On the clear hyaline,[3] the glassy sea;
620 Of amplitude almost immense,° with stars   *immeasurable*
Numerous, and every star perhaps a world
Of destined habitation; but thou know'st
Their seasons: among these the seat of men,
Earth with her nether ocean circumfused,°   *surrounded, bathed*
625 Their pleasant dwellingplace. Thrice happy men,
And sons of men, whom God hath thus advanced,
Created in his image, there to dwell
And worship him, and in reward to rule
Over his works, on earth, in sea, or air,
630 And multiply a race of worshippers
Holy and just: thrice happy if they know
Their happiness, and persevere upright.'
    "So sung they, and the empyrean rung,
With hallelujahs:[4] thus was Sabbath kept.
635 And thy request think now fulfilled, that asked
How first this world and face of things began,
And what before thy memory was done
From the beginning, that posterity
Informed by thee might know; if else thou seek'st
640 Aught, not surpassing human measure, say."

---

1. Bar on the fingerboard of a stringed instrument. "Dulcimer": the Hebrew bagpipe (Daniel 3.5).
2. The allusion implies that the myth of the Giants' revolt against Jove is a classical type or version of the angels' rebellion.
3. From the Greek word for glass (Revelation 4.6), the waters above the firmament as contrasted with the "nether ocean" (line 624), the earth's seas.
4. Hebrew, "praise the Lord."

Book 8

The Argument

Adam inquires concerning celestial motions, is doubtfully answered, and exhorted to search rather things more worthy of knowledge: Adam assents, and still desirous to detain Raphael, relates to him what he remembered since his own creation, his placing in Paradise, his talk with God concerning solitude and fit society, his first meeting and nuptials with Eve, his discourse with the angel thereupon; who after admonitions repeated departs.

The angel ended, and in Adam's ear
So charming° left his voice, that he a while   *spell-binding*
Thought him still speaking, still stood fixed to hear;
Then as new-waked thus gratefully replied:[1]
5   "What thanks sufficient, or what recompense
Equal have I to render thee, divine
Historian, who thus largely hast allayed
The thirst I had of knowledge, and vouchsafed
This friendly condescension to relate
10 Things else by me unsearchable, now heard
With wonder, but delight, and, as is due,
With glory attributed to the high
Creator; something yet of doubt remains,
Which only thy solution° can resolve.   *explanation*
15 When I behold this goodly frame,° this world   *the universe*
Of heav'n and earth consisting, and compute
Their magnitudes, this earth a spot, a grain,
An atom, with the firmament compared
And all her numbered° stars, that seem to roll   *numerous*
20 Spaces incomprehensible (for such
Their distance argues and their swift return
Diurnal)° merely to officiate° light   *daily / supply*
Round this opacous° earth, this punctual° spot, *dark / pointlike*
One day and night; in all their vast survey
25 Useless besides; reasoning I oft admire,°   *wonder*
How Nature wise and frugal could commit
Such disproportions, with superfluous hand
So many nobler bodies to create,
Greater so manifold,° to this one use,   *so much greater*
30 For aught appears,° and on their orbs impose *as it seems*
Such restless revolution day by day
Repeated, while the sedentary° earth,   *motionless*
That better might with far less compass° move, *circular course*
Served by more noble than herself, attains
35 Her end without least motion, and receives,
As tribute such a sumless° journey brought *incalculable*
Of incorporeal° speed, her warmth and light; *like that of spirits*

---

1. When Milton divided Book 7 of the ten-book version of 1667 into the present Books 7 and 8, he replaced a line reading "To whom thus Adam gratefully replied" with these introductory lines.

Speed, to describe whose swiftness number fails."
    So spake our sire, and by his count'nance seemed
40   Ent'ring on studious thoughts abstruse, which Eve
Perceiving where she sat retired in sight,
With lowliness majestic from her seat,
And grace that won who saw to wish her stay,
Rose, and went forth among her fruits and flow'rs,
45   To visit° how they prospered, bud and bloom,   *see*
Her nursery;[2] they at her coming sprung
And touched by her fair tendance gladlier grew.
Yet went she not as not with such discourse
Delighted, or not capable her ear
50   Of what was high: such pleasure she reserved,
Adam relating, she sole auditress;
Her husband the relater she preferred
Before the angel, and of him to ask
Chose rather;[3] he, she knew, would intermix
55   Grateful° digressions, and solve high dispute   *gratifying*
With conjugal caresses, from his lip
Not words alone pleased her. O when meet now
Such pairs, in love and mutual honor joined?
With goddess-like demeanor forth she went;
60   Not unattended, for on her as queen
A pomp° of winning Graces[4] waited still,   *procession*
And from about her shot darts of desire
Into all eyes to wish her still in sight.
And Raphael now to Adam's doubt proposed
65   Benevolent and facile° thus replied.   *easy, affable*
    "To ask or search I blame thee not, for heav'n
Is as the book of God before thee set,
Wherein to read his wondrous works, and learn
His seasons, hours, or days, or months, or years:
70   This to attain, whether heav'n move or earth,
Imports not, if thou reckon right; the rest[5]
From man or angel the great Architect
Did wisely to conceal, and not divulge
His secrets to be scanned° by them who ought   *judged critically*
75   Rather admire;° or if they list to try   *marvel*
Conjecture, he his fabric° of the heav'ns   *design*
Hath left to their disputes, perhaps to move
His laughter at their quaint opinions wide°   *wide of the mark*
Hereafter, when they come to model heav'n
80   And calculate the stars, how they will wield
The mighty frame, how build, unbuild, contrive
To save appearances,[6] how gird the sphere
With centric and eccentric scribbled o'er,

2. Her garden, where she "nurses" her flowers and plants.
3. The emphasis on choice suggests that Eve is not bound in Eden by the Pauline directive (1 Corinthians 14.34–35) that women refrain from speaking in church and instead learn at home from their husbands, but she voluntarily and for her own pleasure observes this hierarchical decorum.
4. The Graces attended on Venus.
5. Presumably, God's ways with other worlds and other creatures inhabiting them (if any).
6. To find ways of explaining discrepancies between their hypotheses and observed facts.

Cycle and epicycle,[7] orb in orb:
85 Already by thy reasoning this I guess,
Who art to lead thy offspring, and supposest
That bodies bright and greater should not serve
The less not bright, nor heav'n such journeys run,
Earth sitting still, when she alone receives
90 The benefit: consider first, that great
Or bright infers° not excellence: the earth   *implies*
Though, in comparison of heav'n, so small,
Nor glistering, may of solid good contain
More plenty than the sun that barren shines,
95 Whose virtue on itself works no effect,
But in the fruitful earth; there first received
His beams, unactive° else, their vigor find.   *ineffective*
Yet not to earth are those bright luminaries
Officious,° but to thee earth's habitant.   *attentive, dutiful*
100 And for the heav'n's wide circuit, let it speak
The Maker's high magnificence, who built
So spacious, and his line stretched out so far;
That man may know he dwells not in his own;
An edifice too large for him to fill,
105 Lodged in a small partition, and the rest
Ordained for uses to his Lord best known.
The swiftness of those circles° áttribute,   *orbits*
Though numberless,° to his omnipotence,   *innumerable*
That to corporeal substances could add
110 Speed almost spiritual;° me thou think'st not slow,   *that of angels*
Who since the morning hour set out from Heav'n
Where God resides, and ere midday arrived
In Eden, distance inexpressible
By numbers that have name. But this I urge,
115 Admitting motion in the heav'ns, to show
Invalid that which thee to doubt it moved;
Not that I so affirm, though so it seem
To thee who hast thy dwelling here on earth.[8]
God to remove his ways from human sense,
120 Placed heav'n from earth so far, that earthly sight,
If it presume, might err in things too high,
And no advantage gain. What if the sun
Be center to the world, and other stars
By his attractive virtue° and their own   *magnetism*
125 Incited, dance about him various rounds?°   *circles*
Their wand'ring course now high, now low, then hid,
Progressive, retrograde,° or standing still,   *backward*

---

7. In the Ptolemaic system, observed irregularities in the motion of heavenly bodies were first explained by hypothesizing eccentric orbits, then by adding epicycles, which were smaller orbits whose centers ride on the circumference of the main eccentric circles and carry the planets. The Copernican system also had some recourse to epicycles.
8. Raphael declines to "reveal" astronomical truth to Adam, leaving that matter open to human scientific speculation. He suggests here that Adam's Ptolemaic assumptions result from his earth-bound perspective, and he implies that angels see the universe in different terms. In the following lines (122–58) he sets forth advanced scientific notions Adam had not imagined: not only Copernican astronomy but multiple universes and other inhabited planets.

In six thou seest,[9] and what if sev'nth to these
The planet earth, so steadfast though she seem,
130 Insensibly three different motions move?[1]
Which else to several spheres thou must ascribe,
Moved contrary with thwart obliquities,[2]
Or save the sun his labor, and that swift
Nocturnal and diurnal rhomb[3] supposed,
135 Invisible else above all stars, the wheel
Of day and night; which needs not thy belief,
If earth industrious of herself fetch day
Traveling east, and with her part averse
From the sun's beam meet night, her other part
140 Still luminous by his ray. What if that light
Sent from her through the wide transpicuous° air,   *transparent*
To the terrestrial moon be as a star
Enlight'ning her by day, as she by night
This earth? Reciprocal, if land be there,
145 Fields and inhabitants: her spots thou seest
As clouds, and clouds may rain, and rain produce
Fruits in her softened soil, for some to eat
Allotted there; and other suns perhaps
With their attendant moons thou wilt descry
150 Communicating male° and female° light,   *original / reflected*
Which two great sexes animate° the world,   *endow with life*
Stored in each orb perhaps with some that live.
For such vast room in nature unpossessed
By living soul, desert and desolate,
155 Only to shine, yet scarce to cóntribute
Each orb a glimpse of light, conveyed so far
Down to this habitable,° which returns   *inhabited place*
Light back to them, is obvious to dispute.°   *open to dispute*
But whether thus these things, or whether not,
160 Whether the sun predominant in heav'n
Rise on the earth, or earth rise on the sun,
He from the east his flaming road begin,
Or she from west her silent course advance
With inoffensive° pace that spinning sleeps   *unobstructed, harmless*
165 On her soft axle, while she paces ev'n,
And bears thee soft with the smooth air along,
Solicit° not thy thoughts with matters hid,   *disturb*
Leave them to God above, him serve and fear;
Of other creatures, as him pleases best,
170 Wherever placed, let him dispose: joy thou
In what he gives to thee, this Paradise
And thy fair Eve; heav'n is for thee too high
To know what passes there; be lowly wise:

9. Mercury, Venus, Mars, Jupiter, Saturn, and the moon. In the Ptolemaic system, the "seventh" is the sun; in the Copernican, earth.
1. Copernicus described the three motions as daily, annual, and "motion in declination" whereby the earth's axis swerved so as always to point in the same direction.

2. Oblique paths that cross each other.
3. Wheel, that is, the primum mobile, which (if we accept the Ptolemaic system and "save the sun his labor") revolves around the universe every twenty-four hours, carrying the planets and their spheres with it.

Think only what concerns thee and thy being;
175 Dream not of other worlds, what creatures there
Live, in what state, condition, or degree,
Contented that thus far hath been revealed
Not of earth only but of highest Heav'n."
    To whom thus Adam cleared of doubt, replied:
180 "How fully hast thou satisfied me, pure
Intelligence° of Heav'n, angel serene,   *spirit*
And freed from intricacies, taught to live
The easiest way, nor with perplexing thoughts
To interrupt the sweet of life, from which
185 God hath bid dwell far off all anxious cares,
And not molest us, unless we ourselves
Seek them with wand'ring thoughts, and notions vain.
But apt the mind or fancy is to rove
Unchecked, and of her roving is no end;
190 Till warned, or by experience taught, she learn,
That not to know at large of things remote
From use, obscure and subtle, but to know
That which before us lies in daily life,
Is the prime wisdom; what is more, is fume,°   *vapor*
195 Or emptiness, or fond impertinence,°   *foolish irrelevance*
And renders us in things that most concern
Unpracticed, unprepared, and still to seek.°   *always searching*
Therefore from this high pitch let us descend
A lower flight, and speak of things at hand
200 Useful, whence haply° mention may arise   *perhaps*
Of something not unseasonable to ask
By sufferance,° and thy wonted° favor deigned.   *permission / usual*
Thee I have heard relating what was done
Ere my remembrance: now hear me relate
205 My story, which perhaps thou hast not heard;
And day is yet not spent; till then thou seest
How subtly to detain thee I devise,
Inviting thee to hear while I relate,
Fond,° were it not in hope of thy reply: *foolish*
210 For while I sit with thee, I seem in Heav'n,
And sweeter thy discourse is to my ear
Than fruits of palm tree pleasantest to thirst
And hunger both, from labor, at the hour
Of sweet repast; they satiate, and soon fill,
215 Though pleasant, but thy words with grace divine
Imbued, bring to their sweetness no satiety."
    To whom thus Raphael answered heav'nly meek:
"Nor are thy lips ungraceful, sire of men,
Nor tongue ineloquent; for God on thee
220 Abundantly his gifts hath also poured
Inward and outward both, his image fair:
Speaking or mute all comeliness and grace
Attends thee, and each word, each motion forms.
Nor less think we in Heav'n of thee on earth
225 Than of our fellow-servant, and inquire

Gladly into the ways of God with man:
For God we see hath honored thee, and set
On man his equal love: say therefore on;
For I that day was absent, as befell,
230 Bound on a voyage uncouth° and obscure,   *strange*
Far on excursion toward the gates of Hell;
Squared in full legion (such command we had)
To see that none thence issued forth a spy,
Or enemy, while God was in his work,
235 Lest he incensed at such eruption bold,
Destruction with creation might have mixed.
Not that they durst without his leave attempt,
But us he sends upon his high behests
For state,° as sov'reign King, and to inure°   *ceremony / strengthen*
240 Our prompt obedience. Fast we found, fast shut
The dismal gates, and barricadoed strong;
But long ere our approaching heard within
Noise, other than the sound of dance or song,
Torment, and loud lament, and furious rage.
245 Glad we returned up to the coasts of light
Ere Sabbath evening: so we had in charge.
But thy relation now; for I attend,
Pleased with thy words no less than thou with mine."
        So spake the godlike Power, and thus our sire:
250 "For man to tell how human life began
Is hard; for who himself beginning knew?[4]
Desire with thee still longer to converse
Induced me. As new-waked from soundest sleep
Soft on the flow'ry herb I found me laid
255 In balmy sweat, which with his beams the sun
Soon dried, and on the reeking° moisture fed.   *steaming*
Straight toward heav'n my wond'ring eyes I turned,
And gazed a while the ample sky, till raised
By quick instinctive motion up I sprung
260 As thitherward endeavoring, and upright
Stood on my feet; about me round I saw
Hill, dale, and shady woods, and sunny plains,
And liquid lapse° of murmuring streams; by these,   *flow*
Creatures that lived, and moved, and walked, or flew,
265 Birds on the branches warbling; all things smiled,
With fragrance and with joy my heart o'erflowed.
Myself I then perused, and limb by limb
Surveyed, and sometimes went,° and sometimes ran   *walked*
With supple joints, as lively vigor led:
270 But who I was, or where, or from what cause,
Knew not; to speak I tried, and forthwith spake,
My tongue obeyed and readily could name
Whate'er I saw.[5] 'Thou sun,' said I, 'fair light,

---

4. Compare Satan's inability to remember his origins (5.856–63), from which he infers self-creation,
whereas Adam infers a Maker (line 278).

5. Adam's ability to name the creatures was said
to signify his intuitive understanding of their
natures.

And thou enlightened earth, so fresh and gay,
275   Ye hills and dales, ye rivers, woods, and plains,
And ye that live and move, fair creatures, tell,
Tell, if ye saw, how came I thus, how here?
Not of myself; by some great Maker then,
In goodness and in power preeminent;
280   Tell me, how may I know him, how adore,
From whom I have that thus I move and live,
And feel that I am happier than I know.'
While thus I called, and strayed I knew not whither,
From where I first drew air, and first beheld
285   This happy light, when answer none returned,
On a green shady bank profuse of flow'rs
Pensive I sat me down; there gentle sleep
First found me, and with soft oppression seized
My drowsèd sense, untroubled, though I thought
290   I then was passing to my former state
Insensible, and forthwith to dissolve:
When suddenly stood at my head a dream,
Whose inward apparition gently moved
My fancy to believe I yet had being,
295   And lived: one came, methought, of shape divine,
And said, 'Thy mansion° wants° thee, Adam, rise,   *habitation / lacks*
First man, of men innumerable ordained
First father, called by thee I come thy guide
To the garden of bliss, thy seat° prepared.'   *residence*
300   So saying, by the hand he took me raised,
And over fields and waters, as in air
Smooth sliding without step, last led me up
A woody mountain whose high top was plain,
A circuit wide, enclosed, with goodliest trees
305   Planted, with walks, and bowers, that what I saw
Of earth before scarce pleasant seemed. Each tree
Load'n with fairest fruit, that hung to the eye
Tempting, stirred in me sudden appetite
To pluck and eat; whereat I waked, and found
310   Before mine eyes all real, as the dream
Had lively° shadowed: here had new begun   *vividly*
My wand'ring, had not he who was my guide
Up hither, from among the trees appeared,
Presence Divine. Rejoicing, but with awe
315   In adoration at his feet I fell
Submiss:° he reared me, and 'Whom thou sought'st I am,'   *submissive*
Said mildly, 'Author of all this thou seest
Above, or round about thee or beneath.
This Paradise I give thee, count it thine
320   To till and keep,° and of the fruit to eat: *care for*
Of every tree that in the garden grows
Eat freely with glad heart; fear here no dearth:
But of the tree whose operation° brings   *action*
Knowledge of good and ill, which I have set
325   The pledge of thy obedience and thy faith,

Amid the garden by the Tree of Life,
Remember what I warn thee, shun to taste,
And shun the bitter consequence: for know,
The day thou eat'st thereof, my sole command
330 Transgressed, inevitably thou shalt die;
From that day mortal, and this happy state
Shalt lose, expelled from hence into a world
Of woe and sorrow.'⁶ Sternly he pronounced
The rigid interdiction,° which resounds   *prohibition*
335 Yet dreadful in mine ear, though in my choice
Not to incur; but soon his clear aspéct°   *untroubled expression*
Returned and gracious purpose° thus renewed: *speech*
'Not only these fair bounds, but all the earth
To thee and to thy race I give; as lords
340 Possess it, and all things that therein live,
Or live in sea, or air, beast, fish, and fowl.
In sign whereof each bird and beast behold
After their kinds; I bring them to receive
From thee their names, and pay thee fealty
345 With low subjection; understand the same
Of fish within their wat'ry residence,
Not hither summoned, since they cannot change
Their element to draw the thinner air.'
As thus he spake, each bird and beast behold
350 Approaching two and two, these° cow'ring low   *the beasts*
With blandishment,° each bird stooped on his wing.   *flattering gesture*
I named them, as they passed, and understood
Their nature, with such knowledge God endued
My sudden apprehension:⁷ but in these
355 I found not what methought I wanted still;
And to the heav'nly Vision thus presumed:
    "'O by what name, for thou above all these,
Above mankind, or aught than mankind higher,
Surpassest far my naming,⁸ how may I
360 Adore thee, Author of this universe,
And all this good to man, for whose well-being
So amply, and with hands so liberal
Thou hast provided all things: but with me
I see not who partakes. In solitude
365 What happiness, who can enjoy alone,
Or all enjoying, what contentment find?'
Thus I presumptuous; and the Vision bright,
As with a smile more brightened, thus replied:
    "'What call'st thou solitude? Is not the earth
370 With various living creatures, and the air
Replenished,° and all these at thy command   *fully stocked*
To come and play before thee? Know'st thou not

---

6. Compare God's commands to Adam (Genesis 1.28–30, 2.16–17) with Milton's elaboration here.
7. Adam had already begun naming the sun and features of the earth (lines 272–74), but here he names (and thereby shows he understands) all living creatures.

8. Adam reasons, as the Scholastics did, from the creatures to the fact of a Creator, but he cannot name (and so indicates that he cannot understand) God, except as God reveals himself.

Their language and their ways? They also know,°   *have understanding*
And reason not contemptibly; with these
375 Find pastime, and bear rule; thy realm is large.'
So spake the Universal Lord, and seemed
So ordering. I with leave of speech implored,
And humble deprecation thus replied:
    "'Let not my words offend thee, Heav'nly Power,
380 My Maker, be propitious while I speak.
Hast thou not made me here thy substitute,
And these inferior far beneath me set?
Among unequals what society
Can sort,° what harmony or true delight?   *agree*
385 Which must be mutual, in proportion due
Giv'n and received; but in disparity
The one intense, the other still remiss
Cannot well suit with either,[9] but soon prove
Tedious alike. Of fellowship I speak
390 Such as I seek, fit to participate°   *partake of*
All rational delight, wherein the brute
Cannot be human consort; they rejoice
Each with their kind, lion with lioness;
So fitly them in pairs thou hast combined;
395 Much less can bird with beast, or fish with fowl
So well converse, nor with the ox the ape;
Worse then can man with beast, and least of all.'
    "Whereto th' Almighty answered, not displeased:
'A nice° and subtle happiness I see   *fastidious*
400 Thou to thyself proposest, in the choice
Of thy associates, Adam, and wilt taste
No pleasure, though in pleasure, solitary.
What think'st thou then of me, and this my state?
Seem I to thee sufficiently possessed
405 Of happiness, or not? who am alone
From all eternity, for none I know
Second to me or like, equal much less.
How have I then with whom to hold converse
Save with the creatures which I made, and those
410 To me inferior, infinite descents
Beneath what other creatures are to thee?'
    "He ceased, I lowly answered: 'To attain
The height and depth of thy eternal ways
All human thoughts come short, Supreme of things;
415 Thou in thyself art perfect, and in thee
Is no deficience found; not so is man,
But in degree, the cause of his desire
By conversation with his like to help,
Or solace his defects.[1] No need that thou

---

9. As with poorly matched musical instruments, Adam's string is too taut ("intense") and the animals' is too slack ("remiss") to be in harmony ("suit").

1. God is absolutely perfect, man only relatively so ("in degree"), and thereby needs companionship with a fit mate to assuage ("solace") the "defects" arising from solitude.

420 Shouldst propagate, already infinite;
And through all numbers absolute, though One;
But man by number is to manifest
His single imperfection, and beget
Like of his like, his image multiplied,
425 In unity defective,[2] which requires
Collateral° love, and dearest amity.   *mutual*
Thou in thy secrecy° although alone,   *seclusion*
Best with thyself accompanied, seek'st not
Social communication, yet so pleased,
430 Canst raise thy creature to what height thou wilt
Of union or communion, deified;
I by conversing cannot these erect
From prone, nor in their ways complacence° find.'   *satisfaction*
Thus I emboldened spake, and freedom used
435 Permissive,° and acceptance found, which gained   *permitted*
This answer from the gracious Voice Divine:
    "'Thus far to try thee, Adam, I was pleased,
And find thee knowing not of beasts alone,
Which thou hast rightly named, but of thyself,
440 Expressing well the spirit within thee free,
My image, not imparted to the brute,
Whose fellowship therefore unmeet° for thee   *unsuitable*
Good reason was thou freely shouldst dislike,
And be so minded still. I, ere thou spak'st,
445 Knew it not good for man to be alone,
And no such company as then thou saw'st
Intended thee, for trial only brought,
To see how thou couldst judge of fit and meet:
What next I bring shall please thee, be assured,
450 Thy likeness, thy fit help, thy other self,
Thy wish, exactly to thy heart's desire.'[3]
    "He ended, or I heard no more, for now
My earthly by his heav'nly overpowered,
Which it had long stood under,° strained to the height   *been exposed to*
455 In that celestial colloquy sublime,
As with an object that excels° the sense,   *exceeds*
Dazzled and spent, sunk down, and sought repair
Of sleep, which instantly fell on me, called
By nature as in aid, and closed mine eyes.
460 Mine eyes he closed, but open left the cell
Of fancy° my internal sight, by which   *imagination*
Abstract° as in a trance methought I saw,   *withdrawn*
Though sleeping, where I lay, and saw the shape
Still glorious before whom awake I stood;
465 Who stooping opened my left side, and took
From thence a rib, with cordial° spirits warm,   *from the heart*

---

2. God, "though One," (line 421), contains all numbers, but man has to remedy the "imperfection" of being single (line 423) by procreating and thereby multiplying his single and thereby "defective" image (line 425).

3. Compare the account in Genesis 2.18 with Milton's elaboration.

And lifeblood streaming fresh; wide was the wound,
But suddenly with flesh filled up and healed:
The rib he formed and fashioned with his hands;
470 Under his forming hands a creature grew,
Manlike, but different sex, so lovely fair
That what seemed fair in all the world seemed now
Mean, or in her summed up, in her contained
And in her looks, which from that time infused
475 Sweetness into my heart, unfelt before,
And into all things from her air° inspired   *mien, look*
The spirit of love and amorous delight.
She disappeared, and left me dark, I waked
To find her, or forever to deplore
480 Her loss, and other pleasures all abjure:
When out of hope, behold her, not far off,
Such as I saw her in my dream, adorned
With what all earth or heaven could bestow
To make her amiable:° on she came,   *lovely*
485 Led by her heav'nly Maker, though unseen,[4]
And guided by his voice, nor uninformed
Of nuptial sanctity and marriage rites:
Grace was in all her steps, Heav'n in her eye,
In every gesture dignity and love.
490 I overjoyed could not forbear aloud:
    "'This turn hath made amends; thou hast fulfilled
Thy words, Creator bounteous and benign,
Giver of all things fair, but fairest this
Of all thy gifts, nor enviest.° I now see   *given reluctantly*
495 Bone of my bone, flesh of my flesh, my self
Before me; woman is her name, of man
Extracted; for this cause he shall forgo
Father and mother, and to his wife adhere;
And they shall be one flesh, one heart, one soul.'[5]
500   "She heard me thus, and though divinely brought,
Yet innocence and virgin modesty,
Her virtue and the conscience° of her worth   *consciousness*
That would be wooed, and not unsought be won,
Not obvious,° not obtrusive,° but retired,   *bold / forward*
505 The more desirable, or to say all,
Nature herself, though pure of sinful thought,
Wrought in her so that, seeing me, she turned;
I followed her, she what was honor knew,
And with obsequious° majesty approved   *compliant*
510 My pleaded reason. To the nuptial bow'r
I led her blushing like the morn: all heav'n,
And happy constellations on that hour
Shed their selectest influence; the earth
Gave sign of gratulation,° and each hill;   *rejoicing, congratulation*

4. Compare Eve's version of these events (4.440–91).
5. Compare the account in Genesis 2.23–24.

515 Joyous the birds; fresh gales and gentle airs[6]
Whispered it to the woods, and from their wings
Flung rose, flung odors from the spicy shrub,
Disporting,° till the amorous bird of night°   *frolicking / nightingale*
Sung spousal, and bid haste the evening star°   *Venus*
520 On his hill top, to light the bridal lamp.
     Thus I have told thee all my state, and brought
My story to the sum of earthly bliss
Which I enjoy, and must confess to find
In all things else delight indeed, but such
525 As used or not, works in the mind no change,
Nor vehement desire, these delicacies
I mean of taste, sight, smell, herbs, fruits, and flow'rs,
Walks, and the melody of birds; but here
Far otherwise, transported° I behold,   *enraptured*
530 Transported touch; here passion first I felt,
Commotion° strange, in all enjoyments else   *mental agitation*
Superior and unmoved, here only weak
Against the charm of beauty's powerful glance.
Or° nature failed in me, and left some part   *either*
535 Not proof enough such object to sustain,°   *withstand*
Or from my side subducting,° took perhaps   *subtracting*
More than enough; at least on her bestowed
Too much of ornament, in outward show
Elaborate, of inward less exact.
540 For well I understand in the prime end
Of nature her th' inferior, in the mind
And inward faculties, which most excel,
In outward also her resembling less
His image who made both, and less expressing
545 The character of that dominion giv'n
O'er other creatures; yet when I approach
Her loveliness, so absolute° she seems   *perfect, independent*
And in herself complete, so well to know
Her own, that what she wills to do or say,
550 Seems wisest, virtuousest, discreetest, best;
All higher knowledge in her presence falls
Degraded, wisdom in discourse with her
Loses discount'nanced,° and like folly shows;   *disconcerted, abashed*
Authority and reason on her wait,
555 As one intended first, not after made
Occasionally;° and to consúmmate all,   *incidentally*
Greatness of mind and nobleness their seat
Build in her loveliest, and create an awe
About her, as a guard angelic placed."
560 To whom the angel with contracted brow:
     "Accuse not nature, she hath done her part;
Do thou but thine, and be not diffident°   *mistrustful*
Of wisdom, she deserts thee not, if thou

6. Both breezes and melodies. "Gales": winds.

Dismiss not her, when most thou need'st her nigh,
565 By áttributing overmuch to things
Less excellent, as thou thyself perceiv'st.
For what admir'st thou, what transports thee so,
An outside? Fair no doubt, and worthy well
Thy cherishing, thy honoring, and thy love,
570 Not thy subjection: weigh with her thyself;
Then value: ofttimes nothing profits more
Than self-esteem, grounded on just and right
Well managed; of that skill the more thou know'st,
The more she will acknowledge thee her head,[7]
575 And to realities yield all her shows:
Made so adorn for thy delight the more,
So awful,° that with honor thou may'st love   *awe-inspiring*
Thy mate, who sees when thou art seen least wise.
But if the sense of touch whereby mankind
580 Is propagated seem such dear delight
Beyond all other, think the same vouchsafed
To cattle and each beast; which would not be
To them made common and divulged,° if aught   *imparted generally*
Therein enjoyed were worthy to subdue
585 The soul of man, or passion in him move.
What higher in her society thou find'st
Attractive, human, rational, love still;
In loving thou dost well, in passion not,
Wherein true love consists not; love refines
590 The thoughts, and heart enlarges, hath his seat
In reason, and is judicious, is the scale[8]
By which to heav'nly love thou may'st ascend,
Not sunk in carnal pleasure, for which cause
Among the beasts no mate for thee was found."
595   To whom thus half abashed Adam replied.
"Neither her outside formed so fair, nor aught
In procreation common to all kinds
(Though higher of the genial[9] bed by far,
And with mysterious reverence I deem)
600 So much delights me, as those graceful acts,
Those thousand decencies° that daily flow   *fitting acts*
From all her words and actions, mixed with love
And sweet compliance, which declare unfeigned
Union of mind, or in us both one soul;
605 Harmony to behold in wedded pair
More grateful than harmonious sound to the ear.
Yet these subject not; I to thee disclose
What inward thence I feel, not therefore foiled,°   *overcome*

---

7. See 1 Corinthians 11.3: "the head of every man is Christ; and the head of the woman is the man; and the head of Christ is God."
8. The ladder of love, a Neoplatonic concept for the movement from sensual love to higher forms, and ultimately to love of God.

9. Both "nuptial" and "generative." Adam takes respectful issue with the apparent denigration of human sex in Raphael's account of the Neoplatonic ladder, which prompts his question about angelic sex (lines 615–17).

Who meet with various objects, from the sense
610 Variously representing;[1] yet still free
Approve the best, and follow what I approve.
To love thou blam'st me not, for love thou say'st
Leads up to Heav'n, is both the way and guide;
Bear with me then, if lawful what I ask;
615 Love not the heav'nly Spirits, and how their love
Express they, by looks only, or do they mix
Irradiance, virtual or immediate° touch?"   *actual*
   To whom the angel with a smile that glowed
Celestial rosy red, love's proper hue,[2]
620 Answered. "Let it suffice thee that thou know'st
Us happy, and without love no happiness.
Whatever pure thou in the body enjoy'st
(And pure thou wert created) we enjoy
In eminence,° and obstacle find none   *higher degree*
625 Of membrane, joint, or limb, exclusive bars:
Easier than air with air, if Spirits embrace,
Total they mix, union of pure with pure
Desiring; nor restrained conveyance need
As flesh to mix with flesh, or soul with soul.
630 But I can now no more; the parting sun
Beyond the earth's green cape and verdant isles
Hesperian sets,[3] my signal to depart.
Be strong, live happy, and love, but first of all
Him whom to love is to obey, and keep
635 His great command; take heed lest passion sway
Thy judgment to do aught, which else free will
Would not admit;° thine and of all thy sons   *permit*
The weal or woe in thee is placed; beware.
I in thy persevering shall rejoice,
640 And all the blest: stand fast; to stand or fall
Free in thine own arbitrament° it lies.   *determination*
Perfect within, no outward aid require;°   *depend on*
And all temptation to transgress repel."
   So saying, he arose; whom Adam thus
645 Followed with benediction. "Since to part,
Go heavenly guest, ethereal messenger,
Sent from whose sov'reign goodness I adore.
Gentle to me and affable hath been
Thy condescension, and shall be honored ever
650 With grateful memory: thou to mankind
Be good and friendly still,° and oft return."   *always*
   So parted they, the angel up to Heav'n
From the thick shade, and Adam to his bow'r.

---

1. I.e., various objects, variously represented to me by my senses.

2. This is not likely to be an embarrassed blush: red is the color traditionally associated with Seraphim, who burn with ardor. Raphael's smile also glows with friendship for Adam and appre-ciation of his perceptive inference about angelic love.

3. Cape Verde, near Dakar, and the islands off that coast are the westernmost ("Hesperian") points of Africa.

Book 9

The Argument

Satan having compassed the earth, with meditated guile returns as a mist by night into Paradise, enters into the serpent sleeping. Adam and Eve in the morning go forth to their labors, which Eve proposes to divide in several places, each laboring apart: Adam consents not, alleging the danger, lest that enemy, of whom they were forewarned, should attempt her found alone: Eve loath to be thought not circumspect or firm enough, urges her going apart, the rather desirous to make trial of her strength; Adam at last yields: the Serpent finds her alone; his subtle approach, first gazing, then speaking, with much flattery extolling Eve above all other creatures. Eve wondering to hear the Serpent speak, asks how he attained to human speech and such understanding not till now; the Serpent answers, that by tasting of a certain tree in the garden he attained both to speech and reason, till then void of both: Eve requires him to bring her to that tree, and finds it to be the Tree of Knowledge forbidden: the Serpent now grown bolder, with many wiles and arguments induces her at length to eat; she pleased with the taste deliberates a while whether to impart thereof to Adam or not, at last brings him of the fruit, relates what persuaded her to eat thereof: Adam at first amazed, but perceiving her lost, resolves through vehemence of love to perish with her; and extenuating the trepass, eats also of the fruit: the effects thereof in them both; they seek to cover their nakedness; then fall to variance and accusation of one another.

	No more of talk where God or angel guest	
	With man, as with his friend, familiar used	
	To sit indulgent, and with him partake	
	Rural repast, permitting him the while	
5	Venial° discourse unblamed: I now must change	*permissible*
	Those notes to tragic; foul distrust, and breach	
	Disloyal on the part of man, revolt,	
	And disobedience: on the part of Heav'n	
	Now alienated, distance and distaste,°	*aversion*
10	Anger and just rebuke, and judgment giv'n,	
	That brought into this world a world of woe,	
	Sin and her shadow Death, and misery	
	Death's harbinger:° sad task, yet argument°	*forerunner / subject*
	Not less but more heroic than the wrath	
15	Of stern Achilles on his foe pursued	
	Thrice fugitive about Troy wall; or rage	
	Of Turnus for Lavinia disespoused,	
	Or Neptune's ire or Juno's, that so long	
	Perplexed the Greek and Cytherea's son;[1]	

---

1. In this fourth proem (lines 1–47), after signaling his change from pastoral to tragic mode (lines 1–6), Milton emphasizes tragic elements in several classical epics: Achilles pursuing Hector three times around the wall of Troy before killing him (*Iliad* 22); Turnus fighting Aeneas over the loss of his betrothed Lavinia, and then killed by Aeneas; Odysseus ("the Greek") and Aeneas ("Cytherea's son," i.e., Venus's son) tormented ("perplexed") by Neptune (Poseidon) and Juno, respectively.

20 If answerable° style I can obtain   *fitting*
 Of my celestial patroness, who deigns
 Her nightly visitation unimplored,[2]
 And dictates to me slumb'ring, or inspires
 Easy my unpremeditated verse:
25 Since first this subject for heroic song
 Pleased me long choosing, and beginning late;
 Not sedulous° by nature to indite   *eager*
 Wars, hitherto the only argument°   *subject*
 Heroic deemed, chief mastery to dissect
30 With long and tedious havoc fabled knights
 In battles feigned; the better fortitude
 Of patience and heroic martyrdom
 Unsung; or to describe races and games,
 Or tilting furniture, emblazoned shields,
35 Impresses quaint, caparisons and steeds;
 Bases[3] and tinsel trappings, gorgeous knights
 At joust and tournament; then marshaled feast
 Served up in hall with sewers,° and seneschals;° *waiters / stewards*
 The skill of artifice° or office mean,   *mechanic art*
40 Not that which justly gives heroic name
 To person or to poem. Me of these
 Nor skilled nor studious, higher argument
 Remains,[4] sufficient of itself to raise
 That name, unless an age too late, or cold
45 Climate, or years damp my intended wing
 Depressed, and much they may, if all be mine,
 Not hers who brings it nightly to my ear.
  The sun was sunk, and after him the star
 Of Hesperus,[5] whose office is to bring
50 Twilight upon the earth, short arbiter
 'Twixt day and night, and now from end to end
 Night's hemisphere had veiled the horizon round:
 When Satan who late° fled[6] before the threats *recently*
 Of Gabriel out of Eden, now improved°   *increased*
55 In meditated fraud and malice, bent
 On man's destruction, maugre what might hap
 Of heavier on himself,[7] fearless returned.
 By night he fled, and at midnight returned
 From compassing the earth, cautious of day,
60 Since Uriel regent of the sun descried
 His entrance, and forewarned the Cherubim
 That kept their watch; thence full of anguish driv'n,

---

2. Milton does not here invoke the Muse but testifies to her customary nightly visits. Milton's nephew reports that he often awoke in the morning with lines of poetry fully formed in his head, ready to dictate them to a scribe.

3. Cloth coverings for horses; "tilting furniture": equipment for jousting; "impresses quaint": cunningly designed heraldic devices on shields; "caparisons": ornamental trappings or armor for horses. After rejecting the classical epic subjects, Milton here rejects the familiar topics of romance.

4. For a heroic poem. He proceeds to recap worries he has voiced before: that the times might not be receptive to such poems ("age too late"), that the "cold Climate" of England or his own advanced age might "damp" (benumb, dampen) his "intended wing / Depressed" (poetic flights held down, kept from soaring).

5. Venus, the evening star.

6. At the end of Book 4.

7. I.e., despite ("maugre") what might result in heavier punishments for himself.

The space of seven continued nights he rode
With darkness, thrice the equinoctial line°   *equator*
65 He circled, four times crossed the car of Night
From pole to pole, traversing each colure;[8]
On the eighth returned, and on the coast averse°   *turned away*
From entrance on Cherubic watch, by stealth
Found unsuspected way. There was a place,
70 Now not, though sin, not time, first wrought the change,
Where Tigris at the foot of Paradise
Into a gulf shot underground, till part
Rose up a fountain by the Tree of Life;
In with the river sunk, and with it rose
75 Satan involved° in rising mist, then sought   *enveloped*
Where to lie hid. Sea he had searched and land
From Eden over Pontus,[9] and the pool
Maeotis, up beyond the river Ob;
Downward as far Antarctic; and in length
80 West from Orontes to the ocean barred
At Darien, thence to the land where flows
Ganges and Indus: thus the orb he roamed
With narrow° search; and with inspection deep   *strict*
Considered every creature, which of all
85 Most opportune might serve his wiles, and found
The serpent subtlest beast of all the field.[1]
Him after long debate, irresolute°   *undecided*
Of° thoughts revolved, his final sentence° chose   *among / decision*
Fit vessel, fittest imp° of fraud, in whom   *offshoot*
90 To enter, and his dark suggestions hide
From sharpest sight: for in the wily snake,
Whatever sleights° none would suspicious mark,   *artifices*
As from his wit and native subtlety
Proceeding, which in other beasts observed
95 Doubt° might beget of diabolic pow'r   *suspicion*
Active within beyond the sense of brute.
Thus he resolved, but first from inward grief
His bursting passion into plaints thus poured:
    "O earth, how like to Heav'n, if not preferred
100 More justly, seat worthier of gods, as built
With second thoughts, reforming what was old!
For what God after better worse would build?
Terrestrial heav'n, danced round by other heav'ns
That shine, yet bear their bright officious° lamps,   *dutiful*
105 Light above light, for thee alone, as seems,[2]
In thee concent'ring all their precious beams

8. The colures are two great circles that intersect at right angles at the poles. By circling the globe from east to west at the equator and then over the north and south poles, Satan can remain in darkness, keeping the earth between himself and the sun. "Car of Night" (line 65): the earth's shadow, imagined as the chariot of the goddess Night.
9. The Black Sea. Satan's journey (lines 77–82) takes him from there to the Sea of Azov in Russia ("Maeotis"), beyond the river "Ob" in Siberia, which flows into the Arctic Ocean, then south to Antarctica; thence west from "Orontes" (a river in Syria) across the Atlantic to "Darien" (the Isthmus of Panama), then across the Pacific and Asia to India where the "Ganges" and "Indus" rivers flow.
1. The serpent is so described in Genesis 3.1.
2. Like Adam (8.15ff.) and Eve (4.657–58) but not Raphael (8.114–78), Satan assumes a Ptolemaic universe centered on the earth and humankind.

Of sacred influence: as God in Heav'n
Is center, yet extends to all, so thou
Centring receiv'st from all those orbs; in thee,
110 Not in themselves, all their known virtue appears
Productive in herb, plant, and nobler birth
Of creatures animate with gradual life
Of growth, sense, reason,³ all summed up in man.
With what delight could I have walked thee round,
115 If I could joy in aught, sweet interchange
Of hill and valley, rivers, woods and plains,
Now land, now sea, and shores with forest crowned,
Rocks, dens, and caves; but I in none of these
Find place or refuge; and the more I see
120 Pleasures about me, so much more I feel
Torment within me, as from the hateful siege°   conflict
Of contraries; all good to me becomes
Bane,° and in Heav'n much worse would be my state.   poison
But neither here seek I, no nor in Heav'n
125 To dwell, unless by mastering Heav'n's Supreme;
Nor hope to be myself less miserable
By what I seek, but others to make such
As I, though thereby worse to me redound:
For only in destroying I find ease
130 To my relentless thoughts; and him⁴ destroyed,
Or won to what may work his utter loss,
For whom all this was made, all this will soon
Follow, as to him linked in weal or woe:
In woe then; that destruction wide may range:
135 To me shall be the glory sole among
The infernal Powers, in one day to have marred
What he Almighty styled,° six nights and days   called
Continued making, and who knows how long
Before had been contriving, though perhaps
140 Not longer than since I in one night freed
From servitude inglorious well-nigh half
Th' angelic name, and thinner left the throng
Of his adorers. He to be avenged,
And to repair his numbers thus impaired,
145 Whether such virtue° spent of old now failed   power
More angels to create, if they at least
Are his created, or to spite us more,
Determined to advance into our room
A creature formed of earth, and him endow,
150 Exalted from so base original,°   origin
With Heav'nly spoils, our spoils: what he decreed
He effected; man he made, and for him built
Magnificent this world, and earth his seat,
Him lord pronounced, and, O indignity!
155 Subjected to his service angel wings,

---

3. Graduated in steps ("gradual," 112) from vegetable to animal to rational forms (souls); cf. 5.469–90.
4. Adam. "This" (line 132): the universe.

And flaming ministers to watch and tend
Their earthy charge: of these the vigilance
I dread, and to elude, thus wrapped in mist
Of midnight vapor glide obscure, and pry
160   In every bush and brake, where hap° may find   *luck*
The serpent sleeping, in whose mazy folds
To hide me, and the dark intent I bring.
O foul descent! that I who erst contended
With gods to sit the highest, am now constrained
165   Into a beast, and mixed with bestial slime,
This essence to incarnate and imbrute,[5]
That to the height of deity aspired;
But what will not ambition and revenge
Descend to? Who aspires must down as low
170   As high he soared, obnoxious° first or last   *exposed*
To basest things. Revenge, at first though sweet,
Bitter ere long back on itself recoils;
Let it; I reck° not, so it light well aimed,   *care*
Since higher I fall short, on him who next
175   Provokes my envy, this new favorite
Of Heav'n, this man of clay, son of despite,
Whom us the more to spite his Maker raised
From dust: spite then with spite is best repaid."
    So saying, through each thicket dank or dry,
180   Like a black mist low creeping, he held on
His midnight search, where soonest he might find
The serpent: him fast sleeping soon he found
In labyrinth of many a round self-rolled,
His head the midst, well stored with subtle wiles:
185   Not yet in horrid shade or dismal den,
Nor nocent° yet, but on the grassy herb   *harmful, guilty*
Fearless unfeared he slept: in at his mouth
The Devil entered, and his brutal° sense,   *animal*
In heart or head, possessing soon inspired
190   With act intelligential: but his sleep
Disturbed not, waiting close° th' approach of morn.   *hidden*
Now whenas sacred light began to dawn
In Eden on the humid flow'rs, that breathed
Their morning incense, when all things that breathe,
195   From th' earth's great altar send up silent praise
To the Creator, and his nostrils fill
With grateful° smell, forth came the human pair   *pleasing*
And joined their vocal worship to the choir
Of creatures wanting° voice; that done, partake   *lacking*
200   The season, prime° for sweetest scents and airs: *best*
Then cómmune how that day they best may ply
Their growing work; for much their work outgrew
The hands' dispatch of two gard'ning so wide.
And Eve first to her husband thus began:

5. Satan "imbruting" himself in a snake parodies, grotesquely, the Son's incarnation in human form, as Christ.

205   "Adam, well may we labor still° to dress   *continually*
     This garden, still to tend plant, herb, and flow'r,
     Our pleasant task enjoined, but till more hands
     Aid us, the work under our labor grows,
     Luxurious° by restraint; what we by day   *luxuriant*
210   Lop overgrown, or prune, or prop, or bind,
     One night or two with wanton° growth derides,   *unrestrained*
     Tending to wild. Thou therefore now advise
     Or hear what to my mind first thoughts present,
     Let us divide our labors, thou where choice
215   Leads thee, or where most needs, whether to wind
     The woodbine round this arbor, or direct
     The clasping ivy where to climb, while I
     In yonder spring° of roses intermixed   *growth*
     With myrtle, find what to redress° till noon: *set upright*
220   For while so near each other thus all day
     Our task we choose, what wonder if so near
     Looks intervene and smiles, or object new
     Casual discourse draw on, which intermits°   *interrupts*
     Our day's work brought to little, though begun
225   Early, and th' hour of supper comes unearned."
       To whom mild answer Adam thus returned:
     "Sole Eve, associate sole,[6] to me beyond
     Compare above all living creatures dear,
     Well hast thou motioned,° well thy thoughts employed   *proposed*
230   How we might best fulfill the work which here
     God hath assigned us, nor of me shalt pass
     Unpraised: for nothing lovelier can be found
     In woman, than to study household good,
     And good works in her husband to promote.[7]
235   Yet not so strictly hath our Lord imposed
     Labor, as to debar us when we need
     Refreshment, whether food, or talk between,
     Food of the mind, or this sweet intercourse
     Of looks and smiles, for smiles from reason flow,
240   To brute denied, and are of love the food,
     Love not the lowest end of human life.
     For not to irksome toil, but to delight
     He made us, and delight to reason joined.
     These paths and bowers doubt not but our joint hands
245   Will keep from wilderness with ease, as wide
     As we need walk, till younger hands ere long
     Assist us: but if much convérse perhaps
     Thee satiate, to short absence I could yield.
     For solitude sometimes is best society,
250   And short retirement urges sweet return.
     But other doubt possesses me, lest harm
     Befall thee severed from me; for thou know'st
     What hath been warned us, what malicious foe

---

6. Adam puns on "sole" as "unrivaled" and "only" (cf. 4.411).
7. Adam's compliments resemble the praises of a good wife in Proverbs 31.

Envying our happiness, and of his own
255   Despairing, seeks to work us woe and shame
By sly assault; and somewhere nigh at hand
Watches, no doubt, with greedy hope to find
His wish and best advantage, us asunder,
Hopeless to circumvent us joined, where each
260   To other speedy aid might lend at need;
Whether his first design be to withdraw
Our fealty° from God, or to disturb   *allegiance*
Conjugal love, than which perhaps no bliss
Enjoyed by us excites his envy more;
265   Or° this, or worse, leave not the faithful side   *whether*
That gave thee being, still shades thee and protects.
The wife, where danger or dishonor lurks,
Safest and seemliest by her husband stays,
Who guards her, or with her the worst endures."
270   To whom the virgin[8] majesty of Eve,
As one who loves, and some unkindness meets,
With sweet austere composure thus replied.
    "Offspring of Heav'n and earth, and all earth's lord,
That such an enemy we have, who seeks
275   Our ruin, both by thee informed I learn,
And from the parting angel overheard
As in a shady nook I stood behind,
Just then returned at shut of evening flow'rs.[9]
But that thou shouldst my firmness therefore doubt
280   To God or thee, because we have a foe
May tempt it, I expected not to hear.
His violence thou fear'st not, being such,
As we, not capable of death or pain,
Can either not receive, or can repel.
285   His fraud is then thy fear, which plain infers
Thy equal fear that my firm faith and love
Can by his fraud be shaken or seduced;
Thoughts, which how found they harbor in thy breast,
Adam, misthought of° her to thee so dear?"   *misapplied to*
290   To whom with healing words Adam replied.
"Daughter of God and man, immortal Eve,
For such thou art, from sin and blame entire:°   *untouched*
Not diffident° of thee do I dissuade   *distrustful*
Thy absence from my sight, but to avoid
295   Th' attempt itself, intended by our foe.
For he who tempts, though in vain, at least asperses°   *bespatters*
The tempted with dishonor foul, supposed
Not incorruptible of faith, not proof
Against temptation: thou thyself with scorn
300   And anger wouldst resent the offered wrong,

---

8. The term here means unspotted or peerless;
Milton has insisted at the end of Books 4 and 8
that Adam and Eve have sex.
9. Somewhat confusing, since Eve heard the full
story of the war in Heaven and Raphael's earlier

warnings; Raphael's parting words (8.630–43)
overheard by Eve do not specifically mention
Satan but warn Adam to resist his passion for
Eve. He does, however, reiterate the charge to
obey the "great command" and repel temptation.

Though ineffectual found; misdeem not then,
If such affront I labor to avert
From thee alone, which on us both at once
The enemy, though bold, will hardly dare,
305   Or daring, first on me th' assault shall light.
Nor thou his malice and false guile contemn;°   *despise*
Subtle he needs must be, who could seduce
Angels, nor think superfluous others' aid.
I from the influence of thy looks receive
310   Access° in every virtue, in thy sight   *increase*
More wise, more watchful, stronger, if need were
Of outward strength; while shame, thou looking on,
Shame to be overcome or overreached°   *outwitted*
Would utmost vigor raise, and raised unite.
315   Why shouldst not thou like sense within thee feel
When I am present, and thy trial choose
With me, best witness of thy virtue tried."
      So spake domestic Adam in his care
And matrimonial love; but Eve, who thought
320   Less° attribúted to her faith sincere,   *too little*
Thus her reply with accent sweet renewed.
      "If this be our condition, thus to dwell
In narrow circuit straitened° by a foe,   *confined*
Subtle or violent, we not endued
325   Single with like defense, wherever met,
How are we happy, still° in fear of harm?   *always*
But harm precedes not sin: only our foe
Tempting affronts us with his foul esteem
Of our integrity: his foul esteem
330   Sticks no dishonor on our front,° but turns   *forehead*
Foul on himself; then wherefore shunned or feared
By us? who rather double honor gain
From his surmise proved false, find peace within,
Favor from Heav'n, our witness from th' event.°   *outcome*
335   And what is faith, love, virtue unassayed
Alone, without exterior help sustained?[1]
Let us not then suspect our happy state
Left so imperfect by the Maker wise,
As not secure to single° or combined.   *one alone*
340   Frail is our happiness, if this be so,
And Eden were no Eden thus exposed."
      To whom thus Adam fervently replied.
"O woman, best are all things as the will
Of God ordained them, his creating hand
345   Nothing imperfect or deficient left
Of all that he created, much less man,
Or aught that might his happy state secure,
Secure from outward force; within himself
The danger lies, yet lies within his power:

---

1. Compare and contrast *Areopagitica*, pp. 1479–89.

350 Against his will he can receive no harm.
But God left free the will, for what obeys
Reason, is free, and reason he made right,[2]
But bid her well beware, and still erect,°   *ever-alert*
Lest by some fair appearing good surprised
355 She dictate false, and misinform the will
To do what God expressly hath forbid.
Not then mistrust, but tender love enjoins,
That I should mind° thee oft, and mind thou me.   *remind, pay heed to*
Firm we subsist,° yet possible to swerve,   *stand, exist*
360 Since reason not impossibly may meet
Some specious° object by the foe suborned,   *deceptively attractive*
And fall into deception unaware,
Not keeping strictest watch, as she was warned.
Seek not temptation then, which to avoid
365 Were better, and most likely if from me
Thou sever not: trial will come unsought.
Wouldst thou approve° thy constancy, approve   *prove*
First thy obedience; th' other who can know,
Not seeing thee attempted, who attest?
370 But if thou think, trial unsought may find
Us both securer° than thus warned thou seem'st,   *overconfident*
Go; for thy stay, not free, absents thee more;
Go in thy native innocence, rely
On what thou hast of virtue, summon all,
375 For God towards thee hath done his part, do thine."
    So spake the patriarch of mankind, but Eve
Persisted, yet submiss, though last, replied:
    "With thy permission then, and thus forewarned
Chiefly by what thy own last reasoning words
380 Touched only, that our trial, when least sought,
May find us both perhaps far less prepared,
The willinger I go, nor much expect
A foe so proud will first the weaker seek;
So bent, the more shall shame him his repulse."
385 Thus saying, from her husband's hand her hand
Soft she withdrew, and like a wood nymph light[3]
Oread or Dryad, or of Delia's train,
Betook her to the groves, but Delia's self
In gait surpassed and goddess-like deport,°   *bearing*
390 Though not as she with bow and quiver armed,
But with such gardening tools as art yet rude,
Guiltless of fire[4] had formed, or angels brought.
To Pales, or Pomona, thus adorned,
Likest she seemed Pomona when she fled

2. Right reason, a classical concept accommodated to Christian thought, is the God-given
power to apprehend truth and moral law.
3. Light-footed, with overtones of "fickle" or "frivolous." "Oread" (next line): a mountain nymph.
"Dryad": a wood nymph. "Delia": Diana, born on

the isle of Delos, hunted with a "train" of
nymphs.
4. Having no experience of fire, not needed in
Paradise. Milton may be alluding to the guilt of
Prometheus, who stole fire from heaven.

395　Vertumnus, or to Ceres in her prime,
　　　Yet virgin of Proserpina from Jove.[5]
　　　Her long with ardent look his eye pursued
　　　Delighted, but desiring more her stay.
　　　Oft he to her his charge of quick return
400　Repeated, she to him as oft engaged
　　　To be returned by noon amid the bow'r,
　　　And all things in best order to invite
　　　Noontide repast, or afternoon's repose.
　　　O much deceived, much failing,° hapless° Eve,　　　　*erring / unlucky*
405　Of thy presumed return! event° perverse!　　　　　　　*outcome*
　　　Thou never from that hour in Paradise
　　　Found'st either sweet repast, or sound repose;
　　　Such ambush hid among sweet flow'rs and shades
　　　Waited with hellish rancor imminent
410　To intercept thy way, or send thee back
　　　Despoiled of innocence, of faith, of bliss.
　　　For now, and since first break of dawn the Fiend,
　　　Mere serpent in appearance, forth was come,
　　　And on his quest, where likeliest he might find
415　The only two of mankind, but in them
　　　The whole included race, his purposed prey.
　　　In bow'r and field he sought, where any tuft
　　　Of grove or garden plot more pleasant lay,
　　　Their tendance or plantation for delight,[6]
420　By fountain or by shady rivulet
　　　He sought them both, but wished his hap° might find　　　*luck*
　　　Eve separate; he wished, but not with hope
　　　Of what so seldom chanced, when to his wish,
　　　Beyond his hope, Eve separate he spies,
425　Veiled in a cloud of fragrance, where she stood,
　　　Half spied, so thick the roses bushing round
　　　About her glowed, oft stooping to support
　　　Each flow'r of slender stalk, whose head though gay
　　　Carnation, purple, azure, or specked with gold,
430　Hung drooping unsustained, them she upstays
　　　Gently with myrtle band, mindless° the while,　　　　*heedless*
　　　Herself, though fairest unsupported flow'r
　　　From her best prop so far, and storm so nigh.[7]
　　　Nearer he drew, and many a walk traversed
435　Of stateliest covert, cedar, pine, or palm,
　　　Then voluble° and bold, now hid, now seen　　　　　*undulating*
　　　Among thick-woven arborets° and flow'rs　　　　　*small trees*
　　　Embordered on each bank, the hand° of Eve:　　　　*handiwork*
　　　Spot more delicious than those gardens feigned
440　Or° of revived Adonis, or renowned　　　　　　　*either*

5. These goddesses, like Eve, are associated with agriculture (lines 393–96)—Pales, with flocks and pastures; Pomona, with fruit trees; Ceres, with harvests—and the latter two foreshadow Eve's situation. Pomona was chased by the wood god "Vertumnus" in many guises before surrendering to him; Ceres was impregnated by Jove with Proserpina—later carried off to Hades by Pluto.
6. I.e., which they had cultivated or planted for their pleasure.
7. The conceit of the flower-gatherer who is herself gathered evokes the story of Proserpina, to whom it was applied in 4.269–71.

"Wonder not, sovereign mistress, if perhaps
Thou canst, who art sole wonder, much less arm
Thy looks, the heav'n of mildness, with disdain,
535 Displeased that I approach thee thus, and gaze
Insatiate, I thus single, nor have feared
Thy awful° brow, more awful thus retired.   *awe-inspiring*
Fairest resemblance of thy Maker fair,
Thee all things living gaze on, all things thine
540 By gift, and thy celestial beauty adore
With ravishment beheld, there best beheld
Where universally admired; but here
In this enclosure wild, these beasts among,
Beholders rude, and shallow to discern
545 Half what in thee is fair, one man except,
Who sees thee? (and what is one?) who shouldst be seen
A goddess among gods, adored and served
By angels numberless, thy daily train."6
   So glozed° the Tempter, and his proem° tuned;   *flattered / prelude*
550 Into the heart of Eve his words made way,
Though at the voice much marveling; at length
Not unamazed she thus in answer spake.
"What may this mean? Language of man pronounced
By tongue of brute, and human sense expressed?
555 The first at least of these I thought denied
To beasts, whom God on their creation day
Created mute to all articulate sound;
The latter I demur,° for in their looks   *hesitate about*
Much reason, and in their actions oft appears.
560 Thee, Serpent, subtlest beast of all the field
I knew, but not with human voice endued;°   *endowed*
Redouble then this miracle, and say,
How cam'st thou speakable° of mute, and how   *able to speak*
To me so friendly grown above the rest
565 Of brutal kind, that daily are in sight?
Say, for such wonder claims attention due."
   To whom the guileful Tempter thus replied:
"Empress of this fair world, resplendent Eve,
Easy to me it is to tell thee all
570 What thou command'st, and right thou shouldst be obeyed:
I was at first as other beasts that graze
The trodden herb, of abject thoughts and low,
As was my food, nor aught but food discerned
Or sex, and apprehended nothing high:
575 Till on a day roving the field, I chanced
A goodly tree far distant to behold
Loaden with fruit of fairest colors mixed,
Ruddy and gold: I nearer drew to gaze;
When from the boughs a savory odor blown,
580 Grateful to appetite, more pleased my sense
Than smell of sweetest fennel, or the teats

---

6. Satan's entire speech is couched in the extravagant praises of the Petrarchan love convention.

Of ewe or goat dropping with milk at ev'n,[7]
Unsucked of lamb or kid, that tend their play.
To satisfy the sharp desire I had
585 Of tasting those fair apples, I resolved
Not to defer;° hunger and thirst at once,   *delay*
Powerful persuaders, quickened at the scent
Of that alluring fruit, urged me so keen.
About the mossy trunk I wound me soon,
590 For high from ground the branches would require
Thy utmost reach or Adam's: round the tree
All other beasts that saw, with like desire
Longing and envying stood, but could not reach.
Amid the tree now got, where plenty hung
595 Tempting so nigh, to pluck and eat my fill
I spared° not, for such pleasure till that hour   *refrained*
At feed or fountain never had I found.
Sated at length, ere long I might perceive
Strange alteration in me, to degree
600 Of reason in my inward powers, and speech
Wanted° not long, though to this shape retained.[8]   *lacked*
Thenceforth to speculations high or deep
I turned my thoughts, and with capacious mind
Considered all things visible in Heav'n,
605 Or earth, or middle,° all things fair and good;   *regions between*
But all that fair and good in thy divine
Semblance, and in thy beauty's heav'nly ray
United I beheld; no fair° to thine   *beauty*
Equivalent or second, which compelled
610 Me thus, though importune° perhaps, to come   *inopportunely*
And gaze, and worship thee of right declared
Sov'reign of creatures, universal dame."[9]
    So talked the spirited[1] sly snake; and Eve
Yet more amazed unwary thus replied:
615   "Serpent, thy overpraising leaves in doubt
The virtue° of that fruit, in thee first proved: *power*
But say, where grows the tree, from hence how far?
For many are the trees of God that grow
In Paradise, and various, yet unknown
620 To us, in such abundance lies our choice,
As leaves a greater store of fruit untouched,
Still hanging incorruptible, till men
Grow up to their provision,[2] and more hands
Help to disburden nature of her birth."
625   To whom the wily adder, blithe and glad:

---

7. According to Pliny, serpents ate fennel to aid in shedding their skins and to sharpen their eyesight; folklore had it that they drank the milk of sheep and goats.
8. There is no precedent in Genesis or the interpretative tradition for Satan's powerfully persuasive argument by analogy based on the snake's supposed experience of attaining to reason and speech by eating the forbidden fruit.
9. Satan continues his Petrarchan language of courtship.
1. Both inspired by and possessed by an evil spirit, Satan.
2. I.e., until the numbers of the human race are such as to consume the food God has provided.

"Empress, the way is ready, and not long,
Beyond a row of myrtles, on a flat,
Fast by° a fountain, one small thicket past   *close by*
Of blowing myrrh and balm;³ if thou accept
630   My conduct,° I can bring thee thither soon."   *guidance*
        "Lead then," said Eve. He leading swiftly rolled
In tangles, and made intricate seem straight,
To mischief swift. Hope elevates, and joy
Brightens his crest, as when a wand'ring fire,°   *will-o'-the-wisp*
635   Compact° of unctuous° vapor, which the night   *composed / oily*
Condenses, and the cold environs round,
Kindled through agitation to a flame,
Which oft, they say, some evil spirit attends,
Hovering and blazing with delusive light,
640   Misleads th' amazed° night-wanderer from his way   *bewildered*
To bogs and mires, and oft through pond or pool,
There swallowed up and lost, from succor far.
So glistered the dire snake, and into fraud
Led Eve our credulous mother, to the tree
645   Of prohibition, root of all our woe;
Which when she saw, thus to her guide she spake:
        "Serpent, we might have spared our coming hither,
Fruitless to me, though fruit be here to excess,
The credit of whose virtue° rest with thee,   *power*
650   Wondrous indeed, if cause of such effects.
But of this tree we may not taste nor touch;
God so commanded, and left that command
Sole daughter of his voice;⁴ the rest, we live
Law to ourselves, our reason is our law."
655   To whom the Tempter guilefully replied:
"Indeed? hath God then said that of the fruit
Of all these garden trees ye shall not eat,
Yet lords declared of all in earth or air?"
        To whom thus Eve yet sinless: "Of the fruit
660   Of each tree in the garden we may eat,
But of the fruit of this fair tree amidst
The garden, God hath said, 'Ye shall not eat
Thereof, nor shall ye touch it, lest ye die.'"⁵
        She scarce had said, though brief, when now more bold
665   The Tempter, but with show of zeal and love
To man, and indignation at his wrong,
New part puts on, and as to passion moved,
Fluctuates disturbed, yet comely, and in act
Raised,⁶ as of some great matter to begin.
670   As when of old some orator renowned

---

3. Blooming trees that exude the aromatic gums
myrrh and balm (balsam).
4. God's only direct commandment (in Hebrew,
Bath Kol, "daughter of a voice" from heaven).
Otherwise (see following), they follow the moral
law of nature, known to them perfectly by their
unfallen reason, "our reason is our law."

5. Eve's formulation indicates her "sufficient"
understanding of the prohibition and the conditions of life in Eden. See 3.98–101.
6. Drawn up to full dignity. Satan as the snake
takes on the role of a Greek or Roman orator
defending liberty (lines 670–72), a Demosthenes
or a Cicero.

In Athens or free Rome, where eloquence
Flourished, since mute, to some great cause addressed,
Stood in himself collected, while each part,
Motion, each act won audience ere the tongue,°   *before speaking*
675 Sometimes in height began, as no delay
Of preface brooking[7] through his zeal of right.
So standing, moving, or to high upgrown
The Tempter all impassioned thus began:
    "O sacred, wise, and wisdom-giving plant,
680 Mother of science,° now I feel thy power   *knowledge*
Within me clear, not only to discern
Things in their causes, but to trace the ways
Of highest agents, deemed however wise.
Queen of this universe, do not believe
685 Those rigid threats of death; ye shall not die:
How should ye? By the fruit? It gives you life
To knowledge.[8] By the Threat'ner? Look on me,
Me who have touched and tasted, yet both live,
And life more perfect have attained than fate
690 Meant me, by vent'ring higher than my lot.
Shall that be shut to man, which to the beast
Is open? Or will God incense his ire
For such a petty trespass, and not praise
Rather your dauntless virtue,° whom the pain   *courage*
695 Of death denounced,° whatever thing death be,   *threatened*
Deterred not from achieving what might lead
To happier life, knowledge of good and evil;
Of good, how just?[9] Of evil, if what is evil
Be real, why not known, since easier shunned?
700 God therefore cannot hurt ye, and be just;
Not just, not God; not feared then,[1] nor obeyed:
Your fear itself of death removes the fear.
Why then was this forbid? Why but to awe,
Why but to keep ye low and ignorant,
705 His worshippers; he knows that in the day
Ye eat thereof, your eyes that seem so clear,
Yet are but dim, shall perfectly be then
Opened and cleared, and ye shall be as gods,[2]
Knowing both good and evil as they know.
710 That ye should be as gods, since I as man,
Internal man, is but proportion meet,
I of brute human, ye of human gods.[3]
So ye shall die perhaps, by putting off
Human, to put on gods, death to be wished,
715 Though threatened, which no worse than this can bring.

---

7. Bursting into the middle of his speech without a preface, and "upgrown" to the impassioned
high style ("high") at once (lines 675–78).
8. I.e., life as well as knowledge, and a better life
enhanced by knowledge, which Satan in the
snake presents as a magical property of the tree.
9. I.e., how can it be just to forbid the knowledge
of good?

1. Satan's sophism invites atheism: if God forbids knowledge of good and evil he is not just,
therefore not God, therefore his threat of death
need not be feared.
2. Hereafter, Satan speaks of "gods," not God.
3. Satan invites the aspiration to divinity, based
on analogy to the supposed experience of the
snake.

And what are gods that man may not become
As they, participating° godlike food?   *partaking of*
The gods are first, and that advantage use
On our belief, that all from them proceeds;
720 I question it, for this fair earth I see,
Warmed by the sun, producing every kind,
Them nothing: if they all° things, who enclosed   *produce all*
Knowledge of good and evil in this tree,
That whoso eats thereof, forthwith attains
725 Wisdom without their leave? And wherein lies
Th' offense, that man should thus attain to know?
What can your knowledge hurt him, or this tree
Impart against his will if all be his?
Or is it envy, and can envy dwell
730 In heav'nly breasts? These, these and many more
Causes import° your need of this fair fruit.   *prove*
Goddess humane,⁴ reach then, and freely taste."
     He ended, and his words replete with guile
Into her heart too easy entrance won:
735 Fixed on the fruit she gazed, which to behold
Might tempt alone, and in her ears the sound
Yet rung of his persuasive words, impregned°   *impregnated*
With reason, to her seeming, and with truth;
Meanwhile the hour of noon drew on, and waked
740 An eager appetite, raised by the smell
So savory of that fruit, which with desire,
Inclinable now grown to touch or taste,
Solicited her longing eye; yet first
Pausing a while, thus to herself she mused:
745 "Great are thy virtues,° doubtless, best of fruits,   *powers*
Though kept from man, and worthy to be admired,
Whose taste, too long forborne, at first assay°   *try*
Gave elocution to the mute, and taught
The tongue not made for speech to speak thy praise:
750 Thy praise he also who forbids thy use,
Conceals not from us, naming thee the Tree
Of Knowledge, knowledge both of good and evil;
Forbids us then to taste, but his forbidding
Commends thee more, while it infers° the good   *implies*
755 By thee communicated, and our want:°   *lack*
For good unknown, sure is not had, or had
And yet unknown, is as not had at all.
In plain° then, what forbids he but to know,   *in plain words*
Forbids us good, forbids us to be wise?
760 Such prohibitions bind not. But if death
Bind us with after-bands,° what profits then   *later bonds*
Our inward freedom? In the day we eat
Of this fair fruit, our doom is, we shall die.
How dies the serpent? He hath eat'n and lives,
765 And knows, and speaks, and reasons, and discerns,

---

4. Both "human" and "gracious" or "kindly."

Irrational till then. For us alone
Was death invented? Or to us denied
This intellectual food, for beasts reserved?
For beasts it seems: yet that one beast which first
770 Hath tasted, envies° not, but brings with joy   *begrudges*
The good befall'n him, author unsuspect,[5]
Friendly to man, far from deceit or guile.
What fear I then, rather what know to fear
Under this ignorance of good and evil,
775 Of God or death, of law or penalty?
Here grows the cure of all, this fruit divine,
Fair to the eye, inviting to the taste,
Of virtue° to make wise: what hinders then   *power*
To reach, and feed at once both body and mind?"
780 So saying, her rash hand in evil hour
Forth reaching to the fruit, she plucked, she eat.[6]
Earth felt the wound, and nature from her seat
Sighing through all her works gave signs of woe,
That all was lost. Back to the thicket slunk
785 The guilty serpent, and well might, for Eve
Intent now wholly on her taste, naught else
Regarded, such delight till then, as seemed,
In fruit she never tasted, whether true
Or fancied so, through expectation high
790 Of knowledge, nor was godhead from her thought.
Greedily she engorged without restraint,
And knew not eating death:[7] satiate at length,
And heightened as with wine, jocund° and boon,°   *merry / jolly*
Thus to herself she pleasingly began:
795 "O sov'reign, virtuous, precious of all trees
In Paradise, of operation blest
To sapience, hitherto obscured, infamed,[8]
And thy fair fruit let hang, as to no end
Created; but henceforth my early care,
800 Not without song, each morning, and due praise
Shall tend thee, and the fertile burden ease
Of thy full branches offered free to all;
Till dieted by thee I grow mature
In knowledge, as the gods who all things know;
805 Though others envy what they cannot give;
For had the gift been theirs,[9] it had not here
Thus grown. Experience, next to thee I owe,
Best guide; not following thee, I had remained
In ignorance, thou open'st wisdom's way,
810 And giv'st accéss, though secret° she retire.   *hidden*
And I perhaps am secret;° Heav'n is high,   *unseen*
High and remote to see from thence distinct

5. An authority or informant beyond suspicion.
6. Ate: an accepted past tense, pronounced *et*.
7. I.e., she is eating death and doesn't know it, or experience it yet, but also, punning, death is eating her too.

8. Slandered. "Sapience": both knowledge and tasting (Latin *sapere*).
9. Like Satan, Eve now conflates gods and God, ascribing envy but also lack of power to "them."

Each thing on earth; and other care perhaps
May have diverted from continual watch
815 Our great Forbidder, safe with all his spies
About him. But to Adam in what sort°   *guise*
Shall I appear? Shall I to him make known
As yet my change, and give him to partake
Full happiness with me, or rather not,
820 But keep the odds° of knowledge in my power   *advantage*
Without copartner? so to add what wants°   *lacks*
In female sex, the more to draw his love,
And render me more equal, and perhaps,
A thing not undesirable, sometime
825 Superior; for inferior who is free?[1]
This may be well: but what if God have seen,
And death ensue? Then I shall be no more,
And Adam wedded to another Eve,
Shall live with her enjoying, I extinct;
830 A death to think. Confirmed then I resolve,
Adam shall share with me in bliss or woe:
So dear I love him, that with him all deaths
I could endure, without him live no life."
        So saying, from the tree her step she turned,
835 But first low reverence done, as to the power
That dwelt within,[2] whose presence had infused
Into the plant sciential° sap, derived   *knowledge-producing*
From nectar, drink of gods. Adam the while
Waiting desirous her return, had wove
840 Of choicest flow'rs a garland to adorn
Her tresses, and her rural labors crown,
As reapers oft are wont° their harvest queen.   *accustomed*
Great joy he promised to his thoughts, and new
Solace in her return, so long delayed;
845 Yet oft his heart, divine of° something ill,   *foreboding*
Misgave him; he the falt'ring measure° felt;   *heartbeat*
And forth to meet her went, the way she took
That morn when first they parted; by the Tree
Of Knowledge he must pass; there he her met,
850 Scarce from the tree returning; in her hand
A bough of fairest fruit that downy smiled,
New gathered, and ambrosial° smell diffused.   *fragrant*
To him she hasted, in her face excuse
Came prologue,[3] and apology to prompt,
855 Which with bland° words at will she thus addressed. *mild, coaxing*
        "Hast thou not wondered, Adam, at my stay?
Thee I have missed, and thought it long, deprived
Thy presence, agony of love till now
Not felt, nor shall be twice, for never more
860 Mean I to try, what rash untried I sought,

---

1. Cf. Satan, 1.248–63, 5.790–97.
2. Eve ends with idolatry, worship of the tree.
3. I.e., excuse came like the prologue in a play,
and apology (justification, self-defense) served
as prompter.

The pain of absence from thy sight. But strange
Hath been the cause, and wonderful to hear:
This tree is not as we are told, a tree
Of danger tasted,° nor to evil unknown   *if tasted*
865 Op'ning the way, but of divine effect
Το open eyes, and make them gods who taste;
And hath been tasted such: the serpent wise,
Or° not restrained as we, or not obeying,   *either*
Hath eaten of the fruit, and is become,
870 Not dead, as we are threatened, but thenceforth
Endued with human voice and human sense,
Reasoning to admiration,° and with me   *wonderfully well*
Persuasively° hath so prevailed, that I   *by persuasion*
Have also tasted, and have also found
875 Th' effects to correspond, opener mine eyes,
Dim erst,° dilated spirits, ampler heart,   *before*
And growing up to godhead; which for thee
Chiefly I sought, without thee can despise.
For bliss, as thou hast part, to me is bliss,
880 Tedious, unshared with thee, and odious soon.
Thou therefore also taste, that equal lot
May join us, equal joy, as equal love;
Lest thou not tasting, different degree°   *rank*
Disjoin us, and I then too late renounce
885 Deity for thee, when fate will not permit."⁴
     Thus Eve with count'nance blithe her story told;
But in her cheek distemper⁵ flushing glowed.
On th' other side, Adam, soon as he heard
The fatal trespass done by Eve, amazed,°   *stunned*
890 Astonied° stood and blank, while horror chill   *petrified*
Ran through his veins, and all his joints relaxed;
From his slack hand the garland wreathed for Eve
Down dropped, and all the faded roses shed:
Speechless he stood and pale, till thus at length
895 First to himself he inward silence broke:
     "O fairest of creation, last and best
Of all God's works, creature in whom excelled
Whatever can to sight or thought be formed,
Holy, divine, good, amiable, or sweet!
900 How art thou lost, how on a sudden lost,
Defaced, deflow'red, and now to death devote?°   *doomed*
Rather how hast thou yielded to transgress
The strict forbiddance, how to violate
The sacred° fruit forbidd'n! Some cursèd fraud   *consecrated*
905 Of enemy hath beguiled thee, yet unknown,
And me with thee hath ruined, for with thee
Certain my resolution is to die;
How can I live without thee, how forgo
Thy sweet converse and love so dearly joined,

---

4. Compare Eve in soliloquy, lines 817–33.
5. I.e., disorder arising from disturbance of the balance of humors in the body, intoxication.

910 To live again in these wild woods forlorn?
Should God create another Eve, and I
Another rib afford, yet loss of thee
Would never from my heart; no no, I feel
The link of nature draw me: flesh of flesh,
915 Bone of my bone thou art,[6] and from thy state
Mine never shall be parted, bliss or woe."
    So having said, as one from sad dismay
Recomforted, and after thoughts disturbed
Submitting to what seemed remédiless,
920 Thus in calm mood his words to Eve he turned:
    "Bold deed thou hast presumed, advent'rous Eve,
And peril great provoked, who thus hast dared
Had it been only coveting to eye
That sacred fruit, sacred° to abstinence,   *set apart*
925 Much more to taste it under ban to touch.
But past who can recall, or done undo?
Not God omnipotent, nor fate; yet so
Perhaps thou shalt not die, perhaps the fact°   *deed*
Is not so heinous now, foretasted fruit,
930 Profaned first by the serpent, by him first
Made common and unhallowed ere our taste;
Nor yet on him found deadly, he yet lives,
Lives, as thou saidst, and gains to live as man
Higher degree of life, inducement strong
935 To us, as likely tasting to attain
Proportional ascent, which cannot be
But to be gods, or angels demigods.
Nor can I think that God, Creator wise,
Though threat'ning, will in earnest so destroy
940 Us his prime creatures, dignified so high,
Set over all his works, which in our fall,
For us created, needs with us must fail,
Dependent made; so God shall uncreate,
Be frustrate, do, undo, and labor lose,
945 Not well conceived of God, who though his power
Creation could repeat, yet would be loath
Us to abolish, lest the Adversary°   *Satan*
Triumph and say; 'Fickle their state whom God
Most favors, who can please him long? Me first
950 He ruined, now mankind; whom will he next?'
Matter of scorn, not to be given the Foe.
However I with thee have fixed my lot,
Certain° to undergo like doom; if death   *resolved*
Consort° with thee, death is to me as life;   *associate*
955 So forcible within my heart I feel
The bond of nature draw me to my own,
My own in thee, for what thou art is mine;
Our state cannot be severed, we are one,
One flesh; to lose thee were to lose myself."

6. Adam echoes Genesis 2.23–24.

960   So Adam, and thus Eve to him replied:
       "O glorious trial of exceeding[7] love,
       Illustrious evidence, example high!
       Engaging me to emulate, but short
       Of thy perfection, how shall I attain,
965   Adam, from whose dear side I boast me sprung,
       And gladly of our union hear thee speak,
       One heart, one soul in both; whereof good proof
       This day affords, declaring thee resolved,
       Rather than death or aught° than death more dread   *anything other*
970   Shall separate us, linked in love so dear,
       To undergo with me one guilt, one crime,
       If any be, of tasting this fair fruit,
       Whose virtue,° for of good still good proceeds,   *power*
       Direct, or by occasion° hath presented   *indirectly*
975   This happy trial of thy love, which else
       So eminently never had been known.
       Were it° I thought death menaced would ensue°   *if / result from*
       This my attempt, I would sustain alone
       The worst, and not persuade thee, rather die
980   Deserted, than oblige° thee with a fact°   *bind / deed*
       Pernicious to thy peace, chiefly assured
       Remarkably so late of thy so true,
       So faithful love unequaled;[8] but I feel
       Far otherwise th' event,° not death, but life   *result*
985   Augmented, opened eyes, new hopes, new joys,
       Taste so divine, that what of sweet before
       Hath touched my sense, flat seems to this, and harsh.
       On my experience, Adam, freely taste,
       And fear of death deliver to the winds."
990   So saying, she embraced him, and for joy
       Tenderly wept, much won that he his love
       Had so ennobled, as of choice to incur
       Divine displeasure for her sake, or death.
       In recompense (for such compliance bad
995   Such recompense best merits) from the bough
       She gave him of that fair enticing fruit
       With liberal hand: he scrupled not to eat
       Against his better knowledge, not deceived,[9]
       But fondly° overcome with female charm.   *foolishly*
1000   Earth trembled from her entrails, as again
       In pangs, and nature gave a second groan;
       Sky loured, and muttering thunder, some sad drops
       Wept at completing of the mortal sin
       Original;[1] while Adam took no thought,
1005   Eating his fill, nor Eve to iterate°   *repeat*

7. The word, which Eve intends as praise, carries the implication of "excessive."
8. I.e., since I have so recently been assured of
your unparalleled love.
9. Cf. 1 Timothy 2.14: "And Adam was not
deceived, but the woman being deceived was in

the transgression."
1. The theological doctrine that all Adam's
descendants are stained by Adam's sin and are
thereby subject to physical death and (unless
saved by grace) to damnation.

Her former trespass feared, the more to soothe
Him with her loved society, that now
As with new wine intoxicated both
They swim in mirth, and fancy that they feel
1010 Divinity within them breeding wings
Wherewith to scorn the earth: but that false fruit
Far other operation first displayed,
Carnal desire inflaming, he on Eve
Began to cast lascivious eyes, she him
1015 As wantonly repaid; in lust they burn:
Till Adam thus 'gan Eve to dalliance move:
  "Eve, now I see thou art exact of taste,
And elegant, of sapience[2] no small part,
Since to each meaning savor we apply,
1020 And palate call judicious; I the praise
Yield thee, so well this day thou hast purveyed.°   *provided*
Much pleasure we have lost, while we abstained
From this delightful fruit, nor known till now
True relish, tasting; if such pleasure be
1025 In things to us forbidden, it might be wished,
For this one tree had been forbidden ten.
But come, so well refreshed, now let us play,
As meet° is, after such delicious fare;   *appropriate*
For never did thy beauty since the day
1030 I saw thee first and wedded thee, adorned
With all perfections, so inflame my sense
With ardor to enjoy thee, fairer now
Than ever, bounty of this virtuous tree."
  So said he, and forbore not glance or toy°   *caress*
1035 Of amorous intent, well understood
Of° Eve, whose eye darted contagious fire.   *by*
Her hand he seized, and to a shady bank,
Thick overhead with verdant roof embow'red
He led her nothing loath; flow'rs were the couch,
1040 Pansies, and violets, and asphodel,
And hyacinth, earth's freshest softest lap.
There they their fill of love and love's disport
Took largely, of their mutual guilt the seal,
The solace of their sin, till dewy sleep
1045 Oppressed them, wearied with their amorous play.
Soon as the force of that fallacious fruit,
That with exhilarating vapor bland°   *pleasing*
About their spirits had played, and inmost powers
Made err, was now exhaled, and grosser sleep
1050 Bred of unkindly fumes,° with conscious dreams   *unnatural vapors*
Encumbered,° now had left them, up they rose   *oppressed*
As from unrest, and each the other viewing,
Soon found their eyes how opened, and their minds
How darkened; innocence, that as a veil

2. Adam commends Eve for her fine ("exact") and discriminating ("elegant") taste, as a part of "sapience," which means both "taste" and "wisdom."

1055 Had shadowed them from knowing ill, was gone,
Just confidence, and native righteousness,
And honor from about them, naked left
To guilty shame: he° covered, but his robe   *shame*
Uncovered more. So rose the Danite strong
1060 Hercúlean Samson from the harlot-lap
Of Philistéan Dálilah, and waked
Shorn of his strength,³ they destitute and bare
Of all their virtue: silent, and in face
Confounded long they sat, as strucken mute,
1065 Till Adam, though not less than Eve abashed,
At length gave utterance to these words constrained:°   *forced*
"O Eve, in evil⁴ hour thou didst give ear
To that false worm, of whomsoever taught
To counterfeit man's voice, true in our fall,
1070 False in our promised rising; since our eyes
Opened we find indeed, and find we know
Both good and evil, good lost and evil got,⁵
Bad fruit of knowledge, if this be to know,
Which leaves us naked thus, of honor void,
1075 Of innocence, of faith, of purity,
Our wonted° ornaments now soiled and stained,   *accustomed*
And in our faces evident the signs
Of foul concupiscence;⁶ whence evil store;
Even shame, the last of evils; of the first
1080 Be sure then. How shall I behold the face
Henceforth of God or angel, erst with joy
And rapture so oft beheld? Those heav'nly shapes
Will dazzle now this earthly, with their blaze
Insufferably bright. O might I here
1085 In solitude live savage, in some glade
Obscured, where highest woods impenetrable
To star or sunlight, spread their umbrage° broad,   *shadow, foliage*
And brown as evening: cover me ye pines,
Ye cedars, with innumerable boughs
1090 Hide me, where I may never see them more.
But let us now, as in bad plight, devise
What best may for the present serve to hide
The parts of each from other, that seem most
To shame obnoxious,° and unseemliest seen,   *exposed*
1095 Some tree whose broad smooth leaves together sewed,
And girded on our loins, may cover round
Those middle parts, that this newcomer, shame,
There sit not, and reproach us as unclean."
    So counseled he, and both together went

---

3. Samson, of the tribe of Dan, told the "harlot"
Philistine Delilah that the secret of his strength
(like that of Hercules) lay in his hair; she sheared
it off while he slept, and when he awoke he was
easily captured and blinded by his enemies.
4. Adam's bitter pun—Eve, evil—repudiates the
actual etymology of Eve, "life," which Adam will
later reaffirm (11.159–61).

5. Milton, like most commentators, derives the
tree's name from the event (4.222, 11.84–89).
6. The theological term for the unruly human
passions and desires seen as one effect of the
Fall, a sign of abundance ("store") of evils. If
"shame" (see following lines) is the "last" evil, the
"first" is probably the guiltiness that produces it,
according to Milton's *Christian Doctrine* (1.12).

1100   Into the thickest wood, there soon they chose
      The fig tree,[7] not that kind for fruit renowned,
      But such as at this day to Indians known
      In Malabar or Deccan spreads her arms
      Branching so broad and long, that in the ground
1105   The bended twigs take root, and daughters grow
      About the mother tree, a pillared shade
      High overarched, and echoing walks between;
      There oft the Indian herdsman shunning heat
      Shelters in cool, and tends his pasturing herds
1110   At loopholes cut through thickest shade: those leaves
      They gathered, broad as Amazonian targe,°   *shields*
      And with what skill they had, together sewed,
      To gird their waist, vain covering if to hide
      Their guilt and dreaded shame. O how unlike
1115   To that first naked glory. Such of late
      Columbus found th' American so girt
      With feathered cincture,° naked else and wild,   *belt*
      Among the trees on isles and woody shores.
      Thus fenced, and as they thought, their shame in part
1120   Covered, but not at rest or ease of mind,
      They sat them down to weep, nor only tears
      Rained at their eyes, but high winds worse within
      Began to rise, high passions, anger, hate,
      Mistrust, suspicion, discord, and shook sore
1125   Their inward state of mind, calm region once
      And full of peace, now tossed and turbulent:
      For understanding ruled not, and the will
      Heard not her lore, both in subjection now
      To sensual appetite, who from beneath
1130   Usurping over sov'reign reason claimed
      Superior sway: from thus distempered breast,[8]
      Adam, estranged° in look and altered style,   *unlike himself*
      Speech intermitted° thus to Eve renewed: *interrupted*
         "Would thou hadst hearkened to my words, and stayed
1135   With me, as I besought thee, when that strange
      Desire of wand'ring this unhappy morn,
      I know not whence possessed thee; we had then
      Remained still happy, not as now, despoiled
      Of all our good, shamed, naked, miserable.
1140   Let none henceforth seek needless cause to approve°   *prove*
      The faith they owe; when earnestly they seek
      Such proof, conclude, they then begin to fail."
        To whom soon moved with touch of blame thus Eve:
      "What words have passed thy lips, Adam severe,
1145   Imput'st thou that to my default, or will
      Of wand'ring, as thou call'st it, which who knows
      But might as ill have happened thou being by,

---

7. The banyan, or Indian fig, has small leaves, but the account Milton draws on from Gerard's *Herbal* (1597) contains the details of lines 1104–11; Malabar and Deccan (line 1103) are in southern India.
8. The immediate psychological effects of the Fall are evident in the subjection of reason to the lower faculties of sensual appetite.

Or to thyself perhaps: hadst thou been there,
Or here th' attempt, thou couldst not have discerned
1150 Fraud in the serpent, speaking as he spake;
No ground of enmity between us known,
Why he should mean me ill, or seek to harm.
Was I to have never parted from thy side?
As good have grown there still a lifeless rib.
1155 Being as I am, why didst not thou the head
Command me absolutely not to go,
Going into such danger as thou saidst?
Too facile° then thou didst not much gainsay,°   *easy, mild / oppose*
Nay didst permit, approve, and fair dismiss.
1160 Hadst thou been firm and fixed in thy dissent,
Neither had I transgressed, nor thou with me."
   To whom then first incensed Adam replied.
"Is this the love, is this the recompense
Of mine to thee, ingrateful Eve, expressed°   *demonstrated*
1165 Immutable when thou wert lost, not I,
Who might have lived and joyed immortal bliss,
Yet willingly chose rather death with thee:
And am I now upbraided, as the cause
Of thy transgressing? not enough severe,
1170 It seems, in thy restraint: what could I more?
I warned thee, I admonished thee, foretold
The danger, and the lurking enemy
That lay in wait; beyond this had been force,
And force upon free will hath here no place.
1175 But confidence then bore thee on, secure°   *self-assured*
Either to meet no danger, or to find
Matter of glorious trial; and perhaps
I also erred in overmuch admiring
What seemed in thee so perfect, that I thought
1180 No evil durst attempt thee, but I rue
That error now, which is become my crime,
And thou th' accuser. Thus it shall befall
Him who to worth in women overtrusting
Lets her will rule; restraint she will not brook,°   *accept*
1185 And left to herself, if evil thence ensue,
She first his weak indulgence will accuse."
   Thus they in mutual accusation spent
The fruitless hours, but neither self-condemning,
And of their vain contést appeared no end.

Book 10

The Argument

Man's transgression known, the guardian angels forsake Paradise, and return
up to heaven to approve their vigilance, and are approved, God declaring that
the entrance of Satan could not be by them prevented. He sends his Son to
judge the transgressors, who descends and gives sentence accordingly; then

in pity clothes them both, and reascends. Sin and Death, sitting till then at the gates of hell, by wondrous sympathy feeling the success of Satan in this new world, and the sin by man there committed, resolve to sit no longer confined in hell, but to follow Satan their sire up to the place of man: to make the way easier from hell to this world to and fro, they pave a broad highway or bridge over chaos, according to the track that Satan first made; then preparing for earth, they meet him proud of his success returning to hell; their mutual gratulation. Satan arrives at Pandemonium, in full assembly relates with boasting his success against man; instead of applause is entertained with a general hiss by all his audience, transformed with himself also suddenly into serpents, according to his doom given in Paradise; then deluded with a show of the Forbidden Tree springing up before them, they greedily reaching to take of the fruit, chew dust and bitter ashes. The proceedings of Sin and Death; God foretells the final victory of his Son over them, and the renewing of all things; but for the present commands his angels to make several alterations in the heavens and elements. Adam more and more perceiving his fallen condition, heavily bewails, rejects the condolement of Eve; she persists and at length appeases him: then to evade the curse likely to fall on their offspring, proposes to Adam violent ways which he approves not, but conceiving better hope, puts her in mind of the late promise made them, that her seed should be revenged on the Serpent, and exhorts her with him to seek peace of the offended Deity, by repentance and supplication.

Meanwhile the heinous and despiteful act
Of Satan done in Paradise, and how
He in the serpent had perverted Eve,
Her husband she, to taste the fatal fruit,
5   Was known in Heav'n; for what can scape the eye
Of God all-seeing, or deceive his heart
Omniscient, who in all things wise and just,
Hindered not Satan to attempt the mind
Of man, with strength entire, and free will armed,
10 Complete° to have discovered and repulsed   *fully equipped*
Whatever wiles of foe or seeming friend.
For still they knew, and ought to have still° remembered   *always*
The high injunction not to taste that fruit,
Whoever tempted; which they not obeying,
15 Incurred, what could they less, the penalty,
And manifold in sin, deserved to fall.
Up into Heav'n from Paradise in haste
Th' angelic guards ascended, mute and sad
For man, for of his state by this° they knew,   *this time*
20 Much wond'ring how the subtle Fiend had stol'n
Entrance unseen. Soon as th' unwelcome news
From earth arrived at Heaven gate, displeased
All were who heard, dim sadness did not spare
That time celestial visages, yet mixed
25 With pity, violated not their bliss.
About the new-arrived, in multitudes
Th' ethereal people ran, to hear and know
How all befell: they towards the throne supreme

Accountable made haste to make appear
30 With righteous plea, their utmost vigilance,
And easily approved;[1] when the Most High
Eternal Father from his secret cloud,
Amidst in thunder uttered thus his voice:
    "Assembled Angels, and ye Powers returned
35 From unsuccessful charge, be not dismayed,
Nor troubled at these tidings from the earth,
Which your sincerest care could not prevent,
Foretold so lately what would come to pass,
When first this tempter crossed the gulf from Hell.
40 I told ye then he should prevail and speed°   *succeed*
On his bad errand, man should be seduced
And flattered out of all, believing lies
Against his Maker; no decree of mine
Concurring to necessitate his fall, -
45 Or touch with lightest moment[2] of impulse
His free will, to her own inclining left
In even scale. But fall'n he is, and now
What rests,° but that the mortal sentence pass   *remains*
On his transgression, death denounced° that day,   *decreed*
50 Which he presumes already vain and void,
Because not yet inflicted, as he feared,
By some immediate stroke; but soon shall find
Forbearance no acquittance ere day end.[3]
Justice shall not return as bounty scorned.
55 But whom send I to judge them? Whom but thee
Vicegerent Son, to thee I have transferred
All judgment, whether in Heav'n, or earth, or Hell.[4]
Easy it may be seen that I intend
Mercy colleague with justice, sending thee
60 Man's friend, his mediator, his designed
Both ransom and redeemer voluntary,
And destined man himself to judge man fall'n."
    So spake the Father, and unfolding bright
Toward the right hand his glory, on the Son
65 Blazed forth unclouded deity; he full
Resplendent all his Father manifest
Expressed, and thus divinely answered mild:
    "Father Eternal, thine is to decree,
Mine both in Heav'n and earth to do thy will
70 Supreme, that thou in me thy Son beloved
May'st ever rest well pleased. I go to judge
On earth these thy transgressors; but thou know'st,
Whoever judged, the worst on me must light,
When time shall be, for so I undertook
75 Before thee; and not repenting, this obtain

1. The angels, "accountable" for guarding Eden, rush to God's throne to explain that they had exercised "utmost vigilance"; their plea is readily accepted ("easily approved").
2. The smallest weight that would tip the scales.
3. A proverb: "Abstinence from enforcing a debt is not release from it." Next line: My justice must not be scorned as my generosity has been.
4. Cf. John 5.22: "For the Father judgeth no man, but hath committed all judgment unto the Son."

Of right, that I may mitigate their doom
On me derived,° yet I shall temper so   *diverted*
Justice with mercy, as may illustrate most°   *best show*
Them fully satisfied, and thee appease.
80 Attendance none shall need, nor train,° where none   *attendants*
Are to behold the judgment, but the judged,
Those two; the third best absent is condemned,
Convict° by flight, and rebel to all law: *proved guilty*
Conviction to the serpent none belongs."
85   Thus saying, from his radiant seat he rose
Of high collateral° glory: him Thrones and Powers,   *placed side by side*
Princedoms, and Dominations ministrant
Accompanied to Heaven gate, from whence
Eden and all the coast° in prospect lay.   *region*
90 Down he descended straight; the speed of gods
Time counts not,[5] though with swiftest minutes winged.
Now was the sun in western cadence° low   *falling*
From noon, and gentle airs due at their hour
To fan the earth now waked, and usher in
95 The evening cool, when he from wrath more cool
Came the mild Judge and Intercessor both
To sentence man: the voice of God they heard
Now walking in the garden, by soft winds
Brought to their ears, while day declined; they heard,
100 And from his presence hid themselves among
The thickest trees, both man and wife, till God
Approaching, thus to Adam called aloud.
    "Where art thou Adam, wont° with joy to meet   *used before*
My coming seen far off? I miss thee here,
105 Not pleased, thus entertained with solitude,
Where obvious duty erewhile appeared unsought:
Or come I less conspicuous, or what change
Absents thee, or what chance detains? Come forth."
He came, and with him Eve, more loath, though first
110 To offend, discount'nanced both, and discomposed;
Love was not in their looks, either to God
Or to each other, but apparent° guilt,   *easily seen*
And shame, and perturbation, and despair,
Anger, and obstinacy, and hate, and guile.
115 Whence Adam falt'ring long, thus answered brief:
    "I heard thee in the garden, and of thy voice
Afraid, being naked, hid myself." To whom
The gracious Judge without revile° replied: *abuse*
    "My voice thou oft hast heard, and hast not feared,
120 But still° rejoiced, how is it now become   *always*
So dreadful to thee? That thou art naked, who
Hath told thee? Hast thou eaten of the tree
Whereof I gave thee charge thou shouldst not eat?"
    To whom thus Adam sore beset replied.

---

5. The Son's descent is immediate; Raphael had taken much of the morning to travel from Heaven to earth (8.110–14).

125 "O Heav'n! in evil strait this day I stand
Before my Judge, either to undergo
Myself the total crime, or to accuse
My other self, the partner of my life;
Whose failing, while her faith to me remains,
130 I should conceal, and not expose to blame
By my complaint; but strict necessity
Subdues me, and calamitous constraint,
Lest on my head both sin and punishment,
However insupportable, be all
135 Devolved;° though should I hold my peace, yet thou   *fallen on*
Wouldst easily detect what I conceal.
This woman whom thou mad'st to be my help,
And gav'st me as thy perfect gift, so good,
So fit, so acceptáble, so divine,
140 That from her hand I could suspect no ill,
And what she did, whatever in itself,
Her doing seemed to justify the deed;
She gave me of the tree, and I did eat."[6]
    To whom the Sov'reign Presence thus replied.
145 "Was she thy God, that her thou didst obey
Before his voice, or was she made thy guide,
Superior, or but equal, that to her
Thou didst resign thy manhood, and the place
Wherein God set thee above her made of thee,
150 And for thee,[7] whose perfection far excelled
Hers in all real dignity: adorned
She was indeed, and lovely to attract
Thy love, not thy subjection, and her gifts
Were such as under government well seemed,
155 Unseemly to bear rule, which was thy part
And person,[8] hadst thou known thyself aright."
    So having said, he thus to Eve in few°   *few words*
"Say woman, what is this which thou hast done?"
    To whom sad Eve with shame nigh overwhelmed,
160 Confessing soon, yet not before her Judge
Bold or loquacious, thus abashed replied:
"The serpent me beguiled and I did eat."
    Which when the Lord God heard, without delay
To judgment he proceeded on th' accused
165 Serpent though brute, unable to transfer
The guilt on him who made him instrument
Of mischief, and polluted from the end°   *purpose*
Of his creation; justly then accursed,
As vitiated in nature:[9] more to know

---

6. Compare Adam's speech in Genesis 3.12, and the elements Milton adds of complaint, veiled accusation of God, and self-exculpation; also compare Eve's answer in Genesis 3.13 and in lines 159–62 below.
7. Cf. 1 Corinthians 11.8–9: "For the man is not of the woman; but the woman of the man. / Neither was the man created for the woman; but the

woman for the man."
8. Role and character (persona), as in a drama.
9. The serpent was "unable to transfer" (line 165) his own guilt in being "polluted" from his proper end and nature onto Satan, who made him "instrument," so he was "justly . . . accursed," but the terms of that judgment have a "mysterious" (line 173) or hidden meaning that applies to Satan.

170 Concerned not man (since he no further knew)
Nor altered his offense; yet God at last
To Satan first in sin his doom applied,
Though in mysterious terms, judged as then best:
And on the serpent thus his curse let fall.
175 "Because thou hast done this, thou art accursed
Above all cattle, each beast of the field;
Upon thy belly groveling thou shalt go,
And dust shalt eat all the days of thy life.
Between thee and the woman I will put
180 Enmity, and between thine and her Seed;
Her Seed shall bruise thy head, thou bruise his heel."[1]
So spake this oracle, then verified
When Jesus son of Mary second Eve,
Saw Satan fall like lightning down from Heav'n,[2]
185 Prince of the air; then rising from his grave
Spoiled Principalities and Powers, triumphed
In open show, and with ascension bright
Captivity led captive through the air,
The realm itself of Satan long usurped,
190 Whom he shall tread at last under our feet;
Ev'n he who now foretold his fatal bruise,
And to the woman thus his sentence turned.
"Thy sorrow I will greatly multiply
By thy conception; children thou shalt bring
195 In sorrow forth, and to thy husband's will
Thine shall submit, he over thee shall rule."
On Adam last thus judgment he pronounced.
"Because thou hast hearkened to the voice of thy wife,
And eaten of the tree concerning which
200 I charged thee, saying: Thou shalt not eat thereof,
Cursed is the ground for thy sake, thou in sorrow
Shalt eat thereof all the days of thy life;
Thorns also and thistles it shall bring thee forth
Unbid, and thou shalt eat th' herb of the field,
205 In the sweat of thy face shalt thou eat bread,
Till thou return unto the ground, for thou
Out of the ground wast taken: know thy birth,
For dust thou art, and shalt to dust return."
So judged he man, both judge and savior sent,
210 And th' instant stroke of death denounced° that day   *announced*
Removed far off; then pitying how they stood
Before him naked to the air, that now
Must suffer change, disdained not to begin
Thenceforth the form of servant to assume,
215 As when he washed his servants' feet,[3] so now

---

1. This is the so-called protoevangelion or judgment of the Serpent (Satan) that contains at the same time the promise of the Redeemer ("her Seed"); Adam and Eve are led to understand it by degrees.
2. Cf. Christ's comment to his disciples (Luke 10.18: "I beheld Satan as lightning fall from heaven"), and also Colossians 2.15 and Ephesians 4.8, to the following lines, 185–88.
3. Cf. Philippians 2.7: "[Christ] took upon him the form of a servant"; John 13.5: "he poureth water into a basin, and began to wash the disciples' feet."

As father of his family he clad
Their nakedness with skins of beasts, or° slain,   *either*
Or as the snake with youthful coat repaid;
And thought not much° to clothe his enemies: *too much*
220 Nor he their outward only with the skins
Of beasts, but inward nakedness, much more
Opprobrious, with his robe of righteousness,
Arraying covered from his Father's sight.
To him with swift ascent he up returned,
225 Into his blissful bosom reassumed
In glory as of old, to him appeased
All, though all-knowing, what had passed with man
Recounted, mixing intercession sweet.
Meanwhile ere thus was sinned and judged on earth,
230 Within the gates of Hell sat Sin and Death,
In counterview within the gates, that now
Stood open wide, belching outrageous° flame   *unrestrained*
Far into Chaos, since the Fiend passed through,
Sin opening, who thus now to Death began:
235   "O son, why sit we here each other viewing
Idly, while Satan our great author° thrives   *father*
In other worlds, and happier seat provides
For us his offspring dear? It cannot be,
But that success attends him; if mishap,
240 Ere this he had returned, with fury driv'n
By his avengers, since no place like° this   *as well as*
Can fit his punishment, or their revenge.
Methinks I feel new strength within me rise,
Wings growing, and dominion giv'n me large
245 Beyond this deep; whatever draws me on,
Or sympathy, or some connatural force
Powerful at greatest distance to unite
With secret amity things of like kind
By secretest conveyance.⁴ Thou my shade
250 Inseparable must with me along:
For Death from Sin no power can separate.
But lest the difficulty of passing back
Stay his return perhaps over this gulf
Impassable, impervious,° let us try   *impenetrable*
255 Advent'rous work, yet to thy power and mine
Not unagreeable, to found° a path   *establish*
Over this main from Hell to that new world
Where Satan now prevails, a monument
Of merit high to all th' infernal host,
260 Easing their passage hence, for intercourse,°   *passing back and forth*
Or transmigration,° as their lot shall lead.   *emigration*
Nor can I miss the way, so strongly drawn
By this new-felt attraction and instínct."
  Whom thus the meager° shadow answered soon: *emaciated*

---

4. Sin feels an attraction ("sympathy") drawing two things together, or an innate ("connatural") force, linking her to Satan.

265 "Go whither fate and inclination strong
Leads thee, I shall not lag behind, nor err
The way, thou leading, such a scent I draw
Of carnage, prey innumerable, and taste
The savor of death from all things there that live:
270 Nor shall I to the work thou enterprisest
Be wanting, but afford thee equal aid."
      So saying, with delight he snuffed the smell
Of mortal change on earth. As when a flock
Of ravenous fowl, though many a league remote,
275 Against° the day of battle, to a field,   *anticipating*
Where armies lie encamped, come flying, lured
With scent of living carcasses designed°   *marked out*
For death, the following day, in bloody fight.
So scented the grim feature,° and upturned   *form, shape*
280 His nostril wide into the murky air,
Sagacious° of his quarry from so far.   *keenly smelling, wise*
Then both from out Hell gates into the waste
Wide anarchy of Chaos damp and dark
Flew diverse,° and with power (their power was great)   *in different directions*
285 Hovering upon the water, what they met
Solid or slimy, as in raging sea
Tossed up and down, together crowded drive
From each side shoaling° towards the mouth of Hell.   *assembling*
As when two polar winds blowing adverse
290 Upon the Cronian Sea,⁵ together drive
Mountains of ice, that stop th' imagined way
Beyond Petsora eastward, to the rich
Cathaian coast. The aggregated soil
Death with his mace petrific,⁶ cold and dry,
295 As with a trident smote, and fixed as firm
As Delos floating once; the rest his look
Bound with Gorgonian rigor not to move,⁷
And with asphaltic slime;° broad as the gate,   *pitch*
Deep to the roots of Hell the gathered beach
300 They fastened, and the mole° immense wrought on   *pier*
Over the foaming deep high-arched, a bridge
Of length prodigious joining to the wall°   *outer shell*
Immovable of this now fenceless world
Forfeit to Death; from hence a passage broad,
305 Smooth, easy, inoffensive° down to Hell.   *free from obstacle*
So, if great things to small may be compared,
Xerxes,⁸ the liberty of Greece to yoke,
From Susa his Memnonian palace high

---

5. The Arctic Ocean; the "imagined way" (lines
291–93) is the Northeast Passage to North
China ("Cathay") from Pechora ("Petsora"), a
river in Siberia, which Henry Hudson could
only imagine (in 1608) because it was blocked
with ice.
6. Turning things to stone.
7. Anything the Gorgon Medusa looked upon
turned to stone. Death's materials are the "cold

and dry" elements; his mace is associated with
Neptune's "trident," which was said to have
"fixed" the floating Greek island of Delos.
8. The Persian king Xerxes ordered the sea
whipped when it destroyed the bridge of ships he
built over the Hellespont (linking Europe and
Asia) so as to invade Greece. "Susa" (next line):
Xerxes' winter residence, founded by the mythical prince Memnon.

Came to the sea, and over Hellespont
310　Bridging his way, Europe with Asia joined,
　　And scourged with many a stroke th' indignant waves.
　　Now had they brought the work by wondrous art
　　Pontifical,[9] a ridge of pendent rock
　　Over the vexed° abyss, following the track　　　　　　　　　　　*stormy*
315　Of Satan, to the selfsame place where he
　　First lighted from his wing, and landed safe
　　From out of Chaos to the outside bare
　　Of this round world: with pins of adamant
　　And chains they made all fast, too fast they made
320　And durable; and now in little space
　　The confines° met of empyrean Heav'n　　　　　　　　　　　*boundaries*
　　And of this world, and on the left hand Hell
　　With long reach interposed; three sev'ral ways
　　In sight, to each of these three places led.[1]
325　And now their way to earth they had descried,°　　　　　　　*perceived*
　　To Paradise first tending, when behold
　　Satan in likeness of an angel bright
　　Betwixt the Centaur and the Scorpion[2] steering
　　His zenith, while the sun in Aries rose:
330　Disguised he came, but those his children dear
　　Their parent soon discerned, though in disguise.
　　He, after Eve seduced, unminded° slunk　　　　　　　　　　*unnoticed*
　　Into the wood fast by, and changing shape
　　To observe the sequel, saw his guileful act
335　By Eve, though all unweeting,° seconded　　　　　　　　　　*unaware*
　　Upon her husband, saw their shame that sought
　　Vain covertures;° but when he saw descend　　　　　　　　　*garments*
　　The Son of God to judge them, terrified
　　He fled, not hoping to escape, but shun
340　The present, fearing guilty what his wrath
　　Might suddenly inflict; that past, returned
　　By night, and list'ning where the hapless pair
　　Sat in their sad discourse, and various plaint,
　　Thence gathered his own doom, which understood
345　Not instant, but of future time.[3] With joy
　　And tidings fraught, to Hell he now returned,
　　And at the brink of Chaos, near the foot
　　Of this new wondrous pontifice,° unhoped　　　　　　　　　*bridge*
　　Met who to meet him came, his offspring dear.
350　Great joy was at their meeting, and at sight
　　Of that stupendous bridge his joy increased.
　　Long he admiring stood, till Sin, his fair
　　Enchanting daughter, thus the silence broken:
　　　"O parent, these are thy magnific deeds,

---

9. Bridge-building, with a pun on "papal" (the pope had the title "pontifex maximus").
1. The golden staircase or chain linking the universe to Heaven, the new bridge linking it to Hell, and the passage through the spheres down to earth.
2. Satan steered between Sagittarius ("the Centaur") and Scorpio, thereby passing through Anguis, the constellation of the Serpent.
3. This evidently refers to the plaints and discourse of Adam and Eve (lines 720–1104 below), which therefore precede Satan's return to Hell (lines 345–609).

355 Thy trophies,⁴ which thou view'st as not thine own,
Thou art their author and prime architect:
For I no sooner in my heart divined,
My heart, which by a secret harmony
Still moves with thine, joined in connection sweet,
360 That thou on earth hadst prospered, which thy looks
Now also evidence, but straight° I felt   *at once*
Though distant from thee worlds between, yet felt
That I must after thee with this thy son;
Such fatal consequence⁵ unites us three:
365 Hell could no longer hold us in her bounds,
Nor this unvoyageable gulf obscure
Detain from following thy illustrious track.
Thou hast achieved our liberty, confined
Within Hell gates till now, thou us empow'red
370 To fortify thus far, and overlay
With this portentous° bridge the dark abyss.   *marvelous, ominous*
Thine now is all this world, thy virtue° hath won   *power, courage*
What thy hands builded not, thy wisdom gained
With odds° what war hath lost, and fully avenged   *advantage*
375 Our foil in Heav'n; here thou shalt monarch reign,
There didst not; there let him still victor sway,
As battle hath adjudged, from this new world
Retiring, by his own doom alienated,
And henceforth monarchy with thee divide
380 Of all things parted by th' empyreal bounds,
His quadrature, from thy orbicular world,⁶
Or try° thee now more dangerous to his throne."   *discover by experience*
    Whom thus the Prince of Darkness answered glad:
"Fair daughter, and thou son and grandchild both,
385 High proof ye now have giv'n to be the race
Of Satan (for I glory in the name,
Antagonist⁷ of Heav'n's Almighty King)
Amply have merited of me, of all
Th' infernal empire, that so near Heav'n's door
390 Triumphal with triumphal act⁸ have met,
Mine with this glorious work, and made one realm
Hell and this world, one realm, one continent
Of easy thoroughfare. Therefore while I
Descend through darkness, on your road with ease
395 To my associate powers, them to acquaint
With these successes, and with them rejoice,
You two this way, among those numerous orbs
All yours, right down to Paradise descend;

---

4. Objects or persons captured in battle were displayed in the Triumphs accorded Roman generals and emperors who had won a great military victory; the term casts Satan's conquests in Eden in such terms.
5. Connection of cause and effect.
6. Revelation 21.16 describes the City of God as "foursquare, and the length is as large as the breadth"; Satan's new conquest, earth, is an orb.

Sin may imply its superiority (being a sphere).
7. The name "Satan" means "adversary" or "antagonist."
8. The repeated word emphasizes that Satan is enacting a Triumph, passing over a triumphal bridge rather than through triumphal arches; the scene would likely evoke the "Roman" Triumph and triumphal arches celebrating the Restoration of Charles II.

There dwell and reign in bliss, thence on the earth
400 Dominion exercise and in the air,
Chiefly on man, sole lord of all declared,
Him first make sure your thrall,° and lastly kill.   *slave*
My substitutes I send ye, and create
Plenipotent° on earth, of matchless might   *with full power*
405 Issuing from me: on your joint vigor now
My hold of this new kingdom all depends,
Through Sin to Death exposed by my exploit.
If your joint power prevail, th' affairs of Hell
No detriment need fear, go and be strong."
410   So saying he dismissed them, they with speed
Their course through thickest constellations held
Spreading their bane;° the blasted° stars looked wan,   *poison / ruined*
And planets, planet-strook,⁹ real eclipse
Then suffered. Th' other way Satan went down
415 The causey° to Hell gate; on either side   *causeway*
Disparted Chaos over-built exclaimed,
And with rebounding surge the bars assailed,
That scorned his indignation.¹ Through the gate,
Wide open and unguarded, Satan passed,
420 And all about found desolate; for those²
Appointed to sit there, had left their charge,
Flown to the upper world; the rest were all
Far to the inland retired, about the walls
Of Pandemonium, city and proud seat
425 Of Lucifer, so by allusion° called,   *metaphor*
Of that bright star to Satan paragoned.³
There kept their watch the legions, while the grand⁴
In council sat, solicitous° what chance   *anxious*
Might intercept their emperor sent, so he
430 Departing gave command, and they observed.
As when the Tartar from his Russian foe
By Astracan over the snowy plains
Retires, or Bactrian Sophi from the horns
Of Turkish crescent, leaves all waste beyond
435 The realm of Aladule, in his retreat
To Tauris or Casbeen:⁵ so these the late
Heav'n-banished host, left desert utmost Hell
Many a dark league, reduced° in careful watch   *drawn together*
Round their metropolis, and now expecting
440 Each hour their great adventurer from the search
Of foreign worlds: he through the midst unmarked,°   *unnoticed*

9. Suffering not merely a temporary eclipse but a real loss of light, as from the malign influence of an adverse planet.
1. Chaos is the instinctive enemy of all order, so hostile to the bridge built over it.
2. Sin and Death.
3. Satan before his fall was Lucifer, the Light-bringer, and the morning star is named Lucifer because it is compared ("paragoned") to him.
4. The "grand infernal peers" who govern (cf. 2.507).

5. The simile, begun in line 431, compares the fallen angels, withdrawn from other regions of Hell to guard their metropolis, to Tartars retiring before attacking Russians and Persians retreating before the attacking Turks. "Astracan": a region west of the Caspian Sea inhabited by Russia and defended against Turks and Tartars; "Aladule": the region of Armenia, from which the last Persian ruler, called Anadule, a "Bactrian Sophi" (Persian shah), was forced to retreat from the Turks, to Tabriz ("Tauris") and Kazvin ("Casbeen").

In show plebeian angel militant
Of lowest order, passed; and from the door
Of that Plutonian[6] hall, invisible
445 Ascended his high throne, which under state°   *canopy*
Of richest texture spread, at th' upper end
Was placed in regal luster. Down a while
He sat, and round about him saw unseen:
At last as from a cloud his fulgent head
450 And shape star-bright appeared, or brighter, clad
With what permissive° glory since his fall   *permitted*
Was left him, or false glitter: all amazed
At that so sudden blaze the Stygian[7] throng
Bent their aspéct, and whom they wished beheld,
455 Their mighty chief returned: loud was th' acclaim:
Forth rushed in haste the great consulting peers,
Raised from their dark divan,[8] and with like joy
Congratulant approached him, who with hand
Silence, and with these words attention won:
460   "Thrones, Dominations, Princedoms, Virtues, Powers,
For in possession such, not only of right,
I call ye[9] and declare ye now, returned
Successful beyond hope, to lead ye forth
Triumphant out of this infernal pit
465 Abominable, accurst, the house of woe,
And dungeon of our tyrant: now possess,
As lords, a spacious world, to our native Heaven
Little inferior, by my adventure hard
With peril great achieved. Long were to tell
470 What I have done, what suffered, with what pain
Voyaged th' unreal,° vast, unbounded deep   *unformed*
Of horrible confusion, over which
By Sin and Death a broad way now is paved
To expedite your glorious march; but I
475 Toiled out my uncouth° passage, forced to ride   *strange*
Th' untractable abyss, plunged in the womb
Of unoriginal[1] Night and Chaos wild,
That jealous of their secrets fiercely opposed
My journey strange, with clamorous uproar
480 Protesting Fate[2] supreme; thence how I found
The new-created world, which fame in Heav'n
Long had foretold, a fabric wonderful
Of absolute perfection, therein man
Placed in a paradise, by our exile
485 Made happy: him by fraud I have seduced
From his Creator, and the more to increase
Your wonder, with an apple. He thereat
Offended, worth your laughter, hath giv'n up
Both his beloved man and all his world,

---

6. Pertaining to Pluto, ruler of the classical underworld.
7. Of the river Styx in Hades, the river of hate.
8. The Turkish Council of State.

9. I.e., you now have these titles not only by right but by possession (from the conquest on earth).
1. Having no origin, uncreated.
2. Protesting both to and against Fate.

490 To Sin and Death a prey, and so to us,
Without our hazard, labor, or alarm,
To range in, and to dwell, and over man
To rule, as over all he should have ruled.
True is, me also he hath judged, or rather
495 Me not, but the brute serpent in whose shape
Man I deceived; that which to me belongs,
Is enmity, which he will put between
Me and mankind; I am to bruise his heel;
His seed, when is not set, shall bruise my head:
500 A world who would not purchase with a bruise,
Or much more grievous pain? Ye have th' account
Of my performance: what remains, ye gods,
But up and enter now into full bliss."[3]
    So having said, a while he stood, expecting
505 Their universal shout and high applause
To fill his ear, when contrary he hears
On all sides, from innumerable tongues
A dismal universal hiss, the sound
Of public scorn; he wondered, but not long
510 Had leisure, wond'ring at himself now more;
His visage drawn he felt to sharp and spare,
His arms clung to his ribs, his legs entwining
Each other, till supplanted° down he fell   *tripped up*
A monstrous serpent on his belly prone,
515 Reluctant,° but in vain, a greater power   *struggling*
Now ruled him, punished in the shape he sinned,
According to his doom: he would have spoke,
But hiss for hiss returned with forkèd tongue
To forkèd tongue, for now were all transformed
520 Alike, to serpents[4] all as accessories
To his bold riot:° dreadful was the din   *revolt*
Of hissing through the hall, thick swarming now
With complicated° monsters, head and tail,   *tangled*
Scorpion and asp, and amphisbaena dire,
525 Cerastes horned, hydrus, and ellops drear,
And dipsas[5] (not so thick swarmed once the soil
Bedropped with blood of Gorgon, or the isle
Ophiusa)[6] but still greatest he the midst,
Now dragon grown, larger than whom the sun
530 Engendered in the Pythian vale on slime,
Huge Python,[7] and his power no less he seemed
Above the rest still to retain; they all

---

3. Ironically, the final word of Satan's proud, triumphal speech rhymes with and so prepares for the "hiss" (line 508) that will soon greet him, as his would-be triumph is turned by God to abject humiliation.
4. The scene recalls Dante's vivid description of the thieves metamorphosed to snakes in *Inferno* 24–25.
5. The "scorpion" has a venomous sting at the tip of the tail; "asp" is a small Egyptian viper; "amphisbaena" supposedly had a head at each end; "Cerastes" is an asp with horny projections over each eye; "hydrus" and "ellops" were mythical water snakes; "dipsas" was a mythical snake whose bite caused raging thirst.
6. Drops of blood from the Gorgon Medusa's severed head turned into snakes; "Ophiusa" in Greek means "isle of snakes."
7. A gigantic serpent engendered from the slime left by Deucalion's flood; Apollo slew him and appropriated the "Pythian" vale and shrine at Delphi.

Him followed issuing forth to th' open field,
Where all yet left of that revolted rout
535 Heav'n-fall'n, in station stood or just array,[8]
Sublime° with expectation when to see   *raised up*
In triumph issuing forth their glorious chief;
They saw, but other sight instead, a crowd
Of ugly serpents; horror on them fell,
540 And horrid sympathy; for what they saw,
They felt themselves now changing; down their arms,
Down fell both spear and shield, down they as fast,
And the dire hiss renewed, and the dire form
Catched by contagion, like in punishment,
545 As in their crime. Thus was th' applause they meant,
Turned to exploding hiss, triumph to shame
Cast on themselves from their own mouths. There stood
A grove hard by, sprung up with this their change,
His will who reigns above, to aggravate
550 Their penance,° laden with fair fruit, like that   *punishment*
Which grew in Paradise, the bait of Eve
Used by the Tempter: on that prospect strange
Their earnest eyes they fixed, imagining
For one forbidden tree a multitude
555 Now ris'n, to work them further woe or shame;
Yet parched with scalding thirst and hunger fierce,
Though to delude them sent, could not abstain,
But on they rolled in heaps, and up the trees
Climbing, sat thicker than the snaky locks
560 That curled Megaera:[9] greedily they plucked
The fruitage fair to sight, like that which grew
Near that bituminous lake where Sodom flamed;[1]
This more delusive, not the touch, but taste
Deceived; they fondly° thinking to allay   *foolishly*
565 Their appetite with gust,° instead of fruit   *relish*
Chewed bitter ashes, which th' offended taste
With spattering noise rejected: oft they assayed,°   *attempted*
Hunger and thirst constraining, drugged as oft,
With hatefulest disrelish writhed their jaws
570 With soot and cinders filled; so oft they fell
Into the same illusion, not as man
Whom they triumphed once lapsed.[2] Thus were they plagued
And worn with famine, long and ceaseless hiss,
Till their lost shape, permitted, they resumed,[3]
575 Yearly enjoined, some say, to undergo
This annual humbling certain numbered days,
To dash their pride, and joy for man seduced.
However some tradition they dispersed
Among the heathen of their purchase° got,   *plunder*

8. I.e., at their posts or on parade.
9. One of three Furies with snaky hair.
1. Sodom apples reputedly grew on the spot where
the accursed city once stood, now the Dead Sea
("that bituminous lake"); the apples look good but
dissolve into ashes when eaten.

2. Unlike man who fell once, they try to eat the
dissolving apples over and over again.
3. God permitted them to regain their "lost shape"
as fallen angels; but they are undergoing a slower,
natural metamorphosis into grosser substance by
their continuing commitment to and choice of evil.

580　And fabled how the serpent, whom they called
　　　Ophion with Eurynome, the wide-
　　　Encroaching Eve perhaps, had first the rule
　　　Of high Olympus, thence by Saturn driv'n
　　　And Ops, ere yet Dictaean Jove was born.[4]
585　Meanwhile in Paradise the hellish pair
　　　Too soon arrived, Sin there in power before,
　　　Once actual, now in body, and to dwell
　　　Habitual habitant;[5] behind her Death
　　　Close following pace for pace, not mounted yet
590　On his pale horse:[6] to whom Sin thus began:
　　　　　"Second of Satan sprung, all-conquering Death,
　　　What think'st thou of our empire now, though earned
　　　With travail° difficult, not better far　　　　　　　　　　　　*labor*
　　　Than still at Hell's dark threshold to have sat watch,
595　Unnamed, undreaded, and thyself half-starved?"
　　　　　Whom thus the Sin-born monster answered soon:
　　　"To me, who with eternal famine pine,
　　　Alike is Hell, or Paradise, or Heaven,
　　　There best, where most with ravin° I may meet;　　　　　　　*prey*
600　Which here, though plenteous, all too little seems
　　　To stuff this maw, this vast unhidebound corpse."[7]
　　　　　To whom th' incestuous mother thus replied:
　　　"Thou therefore on these herbs, and fruits, and flow'rs
　　　Feed first, on each beast next, and fish, and fowl,
605　No homely morsels, and whatever thing
　　　Thy scythe of Time mows down, devour unspared,
　　　Till I in man residing through the race,
　　　His thoughts, his looks, words, actions all infect,
　　　And season him thy last and sweetest prey."
610　　　This said, they both betook them several ways,
　　　Both to destroy, or unimmortal make
　　　All kinds, and for destruction to mature
　　　Sooner or later; which th' Almighty seeing,
　　　From his transcendent seat the saints among,
615　To those bright orders uttered thus his voice:
　　　　　"See with what heat these dogs of Hell advance
　　　To waste and havoc° yonder world, which I　　　　　　　　*plunder*
　　　So fair and good created, and had still
　　　Kept in that state, had not the folly of man
620　Let in these wasteful furies, who impute
　　　Folly to me, so doth the Prince of Hell
　　　And his adherents, that with so much ease
　　　I suffer them to enter and possess
　　　A place so heav'nly, and conniving seem

---

4. The Titan Ophion (whose name means "snake") and his wife Eurynome ("the wide-reacher") ruled Olympus until driven away by "Saturn" and his wife Ops, who were in turn overthrown by Jove, who lived on the mountain Dicte. Milton suggests that these may represent versions of the story transmitted by the fallen angels to the pagans (lines 578–79).

5. Sin was present in Eden in the actual sins committed by Adam and Eve; now she will dwell there in her own body and in all other bodies.
6. Cf. Revelation 6.8: "behold a pale horse: and his name that sat on him was Death, and Hell followed with him."
7. Its hide does not cling close to its bones: Death's hunger is such that it can never fill its skin.

625 To gratify my scornful enemies,
That laugh, as if transported with some fit
Of passion, I to them had quitted all,°   *handed everything over*
At random yielded up to their misrule;
And know not that I called and drew them thither
630 My hellhounds, to lick up the draff° and filth   *dregs*
Which man's polluting sin with taint hath shed
On what was pure, till crammed and gorged, nigh burst
With sucked and glutted offal, at one sling
Of thy victorious arm, well-pleasing Son,
635 Both Sin, and Death, and yawning grave at last
Through Chaos hurled, obstruct the mouth of Hell
Forever, and seal up his ravenous jaws.
Then Heav'n and earth renewed shall be made pure
To sanctity that shall receive no stain:
640 Till then the curse pronounced on both precedes."°   *takes precedence*
    He ended, and the heav'nly audience loud
Sung hallelujah, as the sound of seas,
Through multitude that sung: "Just are thy ways,
Righteous are thy decrees on all thy works;
645 Who can extenuate° thee? Next, to the Son,   *disparage*
Destined restorer of mankind, by whom
New heav'n and earth shall to the ages rise,
Or down from Heav'n descend." Such was their song,
While the Creator calling forth by name
650 His mighty angels gave them several charge,
As sorted° best with present things. The sun   *suited*
Had first his precept so to move, so shine,
As might affect the earth with cold and heat
Scarce tolerable, and from the north to call
655 Decrepit winter, from the south to bring
Solstitial summer's heat. To the blank° moon   *white, pale*
Her office they prescribed, to th' other five
Their planetary motions and aspécts[8]
In sextile, square, and trine, and opposite,
660 Of noxious efficacy, and when to join
In synod° unbenign, and taught the fixed°   *conjunction / fixed stars*
Their influence malignant when to show'r,
Which of them rising with the sun, or falling,
Should prove tempestuous:° to the winds they set   *productive of storms*
665 Their corners, when with bluster to confound
Sea, air, and shore, the thunder when to roll
With terror through the dark aerial hall.
Some say[9] he bid his angels turn askance
The poles of earth twice ten degrees and more
670 From the sun's axle; they with labor pushed
Oblique the centric globe:° some say the sun   *the earth*

8. Astrological positions. The next line names positions of 60, 90, 120, and 180 degrees, respectively.
9. The poem offers both a Ptolemaic and a Copernican explanation of the shifts made in the cosmic order so as to change the prelapsarian eternal spring. The Copernican explanation (offered first) proposes that the earth's axis is now tilted (lines 668–71); the Ptolemaic explanation is that the plane of the sun's orbit is tilted (lines 671–78).

Was bid turn reins from th' equinoctial road°   *the equator*
Like distant breadth to Taurus[1] with the sev'n
Atlantic Sisters, and the Spartan Twins
675   Up to the Tropic Crab; thence down amain°   *at full speed*
By Leo and the Virgin and the Scales,
As deep as Capricorn, to bring in change
Of seasons to each clime; else° had the spring   *otherwise*
Perpetual smiled on earth with vernant° flow'rs,   *spring*
680   Equal in days and nights, except to those
Beyond the polar circles; to them day
Had unbenighted° shone, while the low sun   *without any night*
To recompense his distance, in their sight
Had rounded still° th' horizon, and not known   *always*
685   Or° east or west, which had forbid the snow   *either*
From cold Estotiland, and south as far
Beneath Magellan.[2] At that tasted fruit
The sun, as from Thyestean banquet, turned
His course intended;[3] else how had the world
690   Inhabited, though sinless, more than now,
Avoided pinching cold and scorching heat?
These changes in the heav'ns, though slow, produced
Like change on sea and land, sideral blast,[4]
Vapor, and mist, and exhalation hot,
695   Corrupt and pestilent: now from the north
Of Norumbega, and the Samoed shore
Bursting their brazen dungeon, armed with ice
And snow and hail and stormy gust and flaw,°   *squall*
Boreas and Caecias and Argestes loud
700   And Thrascias rend the woods and seas upturn;
With adverse blast upturns them from the south
Notus and Afer black with thund'rous clouds
From Serraliona,[5] thwart of these as fierce
Forth rush the Levant and the ponent° winds   *opposing*
705   Eurus and Zephyr with their lateral noise,
Sirocco and Libecchio.[6] Thus began
Outrage from lifeless things; but Discord first
Daughter of Sin, among th' irrational,
Death introduced through fierce antipathy:[7]
710   Beast now with beast gan war, and fowl with fowl,
And fish with fish; to graze the herb° all leaving,   *grass*
Devour'd each other; nor stood much in awe

---

1. Lines 673–78 trace the sun's apparent (Ptolemaic) journey from Aries through Taurus and the rest of the zodiac over the course of the year.
2. The region of the Straits of Magellan, at the tip of South America. "Estotiland" (line 686): northern Labrador.
3. As a revenge, Atreus killed one of the sons of his brother Thyestes and served him in a banquet to that brother; the sun changed course to avoid the sight.
4. Malevolent stellar influences. "Norumbega" (line 696): northern New England and maritime Canada; "Samoed" Shore: northeastern Siberia.
5. Winds (701–6) from the south ("Notus," "Afer")

come from Sierra Leone ("Serraliona") on the west coast of Africa; "Boreas," "Caecias," "Argestes," and "Thrascias" are all winds that blow from the north, northeast, and northwest, bursting from the cave ("brazen dungeon") in which Aeolus imprisoned the winds (lines 695–700).
6. Crossing the north and south winds ("thwart," line 703) are the "Levant" (from the east) and "Eurus" (east southeast), from the west "Zephyr," the west wind; "Sirocco" and "Libecchio" come from the southeast and southwest, respectively.
7. Discord (personified as daughter of Sin) introduced Death among the animals ("th' irrational") by stirring up "antipathy" among them.

Of man, but fled him, or with count'nance grim
Glared on him passing: these were from without
715 The growing miseries, which Adam saw
Already in part, though hid in gloomiest shade,
To sorrow abandoned, but worse felt within,
And in a troubled sea of passion tossed,
Thus to disburden sought with sad complaint:
720   "O miserable of happy![8] Is this the end
Of this new glorious world, and me so late
The glory of that glory, who now become
Accurst of blessèd, hide me from the face
Of God, whom to behold was then my height
725 Of happiness: yet well, if here would end
The misery, I deserved it, and would bear
My own deservings; but this will not serve;
All that I eat or drink, or shall beget,
Is propagated[9] curse. O voice once heard
730 Delightfully, 'Increase and multiply,'
Now death to hear! For what can I increase
Or multiply, but curses on my head?
Who of all ages to succeed, but feeling
The evil on him brought by me, will curse
735 My head: 'Ill fare our ancestor impure,
For this we may thank Adam'; but his thanks
Shall be the execration; so besides
Mine own that bide upon me, all from me
Shall with a fierce reflux on me redound,
740 On me as on their natural center light
Heavy, though in their place.[1] O fleeting joys
Of Paradise, dear bought with lasting woes!
Did I request thee, Maker, from my clay
To mold me man, did I solicit thee
745 From darkness to promote me, or here place
In this delicious garden? As my will
Concurred not to my being, it were but right
And equal° to reduce me to my dust,   *just*
Desirous to resign, and render back
750 All I received, unable to perform
Thy terms too hard, by which I was to hold
The good I sought not. To the loss of that,
Sufficient penalty, why hast thou added
The sense of endless woes? Inexplicable
755 Thy justice seems; yet to say truth, too late
I thus contest; then should have been refused
Those terms whatever, when they were proposed:
Thou[2] didst accept them; wilt thou enjoy the good,

8. Adam's complaint begins with the classical formula for a tragic fall, or *peripeteia*, the change from happiness to misery.
9. Handed down from one generation to the next.
1. I.e., Adam's "own" curse will remain ("bide") with him, and the curse ("execration") of "all" who descend from him will "redound" on him as to their "natural center"; objects so placed ("in their place") were thought to be weightless ("light"), but these curses will be "heavy."
2. Adam turns from addressing God to address himself.

Then cavil° the conditions? And though God   *object frivolously to*
760 Made thee without thy leave, what if thy son
    Prove disobedient, and reproved, retort,
    'Wherefore didst thou beget me? I sought it not':
    Wouldst thou admit for his contempt of thee
    That proud excuse? Yet him not thy election,°   *choice*
765 But natural necessity begot.
    God made thee of choice his own, and of his own
    To serve him, thy reward was of his grace,
    Thy punishment then justly is at his will.
    Be it so, for I submit, his doom is fair,
770 That dust I am, and shall to dust return:
    O welcome hour whenever! Why delays
    His hand to execute what his decree
    Fixed on this day? Why do I overlive,
    Why am I mocked with death, and lengthened out
775 To deathless pain? How gladly would I meet
    Mortality my sentence, and be earth
    Insensible, how glad would lay me down
    As in my mother's lap! There I should rest
    And sleep secure; his dreadful voice no more
780 Would thunder in my ears, no fear of worse
    To me and to my offspring would torment me
    With cruel expectation. Yet one doubt
    Pursues me still, lest all I° cannot die,   *all of me*
    Lest that pure breath of life, the spirit of man
785 Which God inspired, cannot together perish
    With this corporeal clod; then in the grave,
    Or in some other dismal place, who knows
    But I shall die a living death? O thought
    Horrid, if true! Yet why? It was but breath
790 Of life that sinned; what dies but what had life
    And sin? The body properly hath neither.
    All of me then shall die:[3] let this appease
    The doubt, since human reach no further knows.
    For though the Lord of all be infinite,
795 Is his wrath also? Be it, man is not so,
    But mortal doomed. How can he exercise
    Wrath without end on man whom death must end?
    Can he make deathless death? That were to make
    Strange contradiction, which to God himself
800 Impossible is held, as argument
    Of weakness, not of power. Will he draw out,
    For anger's sake, finite to infinite
    In punished man, to satisfy his rigor
    Satisfied never; that were to extend
805 His sentence beyond dust and nature's law,
    By which all causes else according still

3. After debating the matter, Adam concludes that the soul dies with the body; Milton in his *Christian Doctrine* worked out this "mortalist" doctrine, with its corollary, that both soul and body rise at the Last Judgment.

To the reception of their matter act,
Not to th' extent of their own sphere.[4] But say
That death be not one stroke, as I supposed,
810 Bereaving° sense, but endless misery   *taking away*
From this day onward, which I feel begun
Both in me, and without° me, and so last   *outside of*
To perpetuity; ay me, that fear
Comes thund'ring back with dreadful revolution°   *return*
815 On my defenseless head; both Death and I
Am found eternal, and incorporate° both,   *made one body*
Nor I on my part single, in me all
Posterity stands cursed: fair patrimony
That I must leave ye, sons; O were I able
820 To waste it all myself, and leave ye none!
So disinherited how would ye bless
Me now your curse! Ah, why should all mankind
For one man's fault thus guiltless be condemned,
If guiltless? But from me what can proceed,
825 But all corrupt, both mind and will depraved,
Not to do° only, but to will the same   *act*
With me? How can they then acquitted stand
In sight of God? Him after all disputes
Forced I absolve: all my evasions vain
830 And reasonings, though through mazes, lead me still
But to my own conviction: first and last
On me, me only, as the source and spring
Of all corruption, all the blame lights due;
So might the wrath.[5] Fond° wish! Couldst thou support   *foolish*
835 That burden heavier than the earth to bear,
Than all the world much heavier, though divided
With that bad woman? Thus what thou desir'st,
And what thou fear'st, alike destroys all hope
Of refuge, and concludes thee miserable
840 Beyond all past example and future,
To Satan only like both crime and doom.
O conscience, into what abyss of fears
And horrors hast thou driv'n me; out of which
I find no way, from deep to deeper plunged!"
845   Thus Adam to himself lamented loud
Through the still night, not now, as ere man fell,
Wholesome and cool, and mild, but with black air
Accompanied, with damps° and dreadful gloom,   *noxious vapors*
Which to his evil conscience represented
850 All things with double terror: on the ground
Outstretched he lay, on the cold ground, and oft
Cursed his creation, Death as oft accused
Of tardy execution, since denounced°   *pronounced*
The day of his offense: "Why comes not Death,"

---

4. Adam convinces himself that "finite" matter (line 802) cannot suffer "infinite" punishment by an axiom of traditional philosophy, that by "nature's law" (line 805) the actions of agents are limited by the nature of the object they act upon.
5. Cf. the Son's offer to accept all humankind's guilt (3.236–41), and Eve's similar offer (10.933–36).

855   Said he, "with one thrice-acceptáble stroke
    To end me? Shall Truth fail to keep her word,
    Justice divine not hasten to be just?
    But Death comes not at call, Justice divine
    Mends not her slowest pace for prayers or cries.
860   O woods, O fountains, hillocks, dales, and bow'rs,
    With other echo late I taught your shades
    To answer, and resound far other song."[6]
    Whom thus afflicted when sad Eve beheld,
    Desolate where she sat, approaching nigh,
865   Soft words to his fierce passion she assayed;°   *attempted*
    But her with stern regard he thus repelled:
      "Out of my sight, thou serpent,[7] that name best
    Befits thee with him leagued, thyself as false
    And hateful; nothing wants,° but that thy shape,   *is lacking*
870   Like his, and color serpentine may show
    Thy inward fraud, to warn all creatures from thee
    Henceforth; lest that too heav'nly form, pretended[8]
    To hellish falsehood, snare them. But° for thee   *except*
    I had persisted happy, had not thy pride
875   And wand'ring vanity, when least was safe,
    Rejected my forewarning, and disdained
    Not to be trusted, longing to be seen
    Though by the Devil himself, him overweening°   *overconfident*
    To overreach, but with the serpent meeting
880   Fooled and beguiled, by him thou, I by thee,
    To trust thee from my side, imagined wise,
    Constant, mature, proof against all assaults,
    And understood not all was but a show
    Rather than solid virtue, all but a rib
885   Crooked by nature, bent, as now appears,
    More to the part siníster° from me drawn,   *the left side*
    Well if thrown out, as supernumerary
    To my just number found.[9] O why did God,
    Creator wise, that peopled highest heav'n
890   With Spirits masculine,[1] create at last
    This novelty on earth, this fair defect
    Of nature,[2] and not fill the world at once
    With men as angels without feminine,
    Or find some other way to generate
895   Mankind? This mischief had not then befall'n,
    And more that shall befall, innumerable
    Disturbances on earth through female snares,
    And strait conjunction[3] with this sex: for either
    He never shall find out fit mate, but such

---

6. Cf. their morning hymn (5.153–208).
7. Adam's bitter, misogynistic outcry begins with reference to the patristic notion that the name Eve, aspirated, means "serpent."
8. Held in front, as a cover or mask.
9. It was supposed that Adam had thirteen ribs on the left side, so he could spare one for the creation of Eve and still retain the proper ("just")

number, twelve.
1. The Miltonic bard indicated that angels can assume at will "either sex . . . or both" (1.424).
2. Aristotle had claimed that the female is a defective male.
3. Close, hard-pressing, binding union: Adam then projects the problems of future marriages.

900 As some misfortune brings him, or mistake,
Or whom he wishes most shall seldom gain
Through her perverseness, but shall see her gained
By a far worse, or if she love, withheld
By parents, or his happiest choice too late
905 Shall meet, already linked and wedlock-bound
To a fell° adversary, his hate or shame: *bitter*
Which infinite calamity shall cause
To human life, and household peace confound."
    He added not, and from her turned, but Eve
910 Not so repulsed, with tears that ceased not flowing,
And tresses all disordered, at his feet
Fell humble, and embracing them, besought
His peace, and thus proceeded in her plaint:
    "Forsake me not thus, Adam, witness Heav'n
915 What love sincere, and reverence in my heart
I bear thee, and unweeting° have offended,   *unintentionally*
Unhappily deceived; thy suppliant
I beg, and clasp thy knees;⁴ bereave me not,
Whereon I live, thy gentle looks, thy aid,
920 Thy counsel in this uttermost distress,
My only strength and stay: forlorn of thee,
Whither shall I betake me, where subsist?
While yet we live, scarce one short hour perhaps,
Between us two let there be peace, both joining,
925 As joined in injuries, one enmity
Against a foe by doom express° assigned us,   *explicit judgment*
That cruel serpent: on me exercise not
Thy hatred for this misery befall'n,
On me already lost, me than thyself
930 More miserable; both have sinned, but thou
Against God only, I against God and thee,
And to the place of judgment will return,
There with my cries importune Heaven, that all
The sentence from thy head removed may light
935 On me, sole cause to thee of all this woe,
Me me only just object of his ire."⁵
    She ended weeping, and her lowly plight,°   *posture*
Immovable till peace obtained from fault
Acknowledged and deplored, in Adam wrought
940 Commiseration; soon his heart relented
Towards her, his life so late and sole delight,
Now at his feet submissive in distress,
Creature so fair his reconcilement seeking,
His counsel whom she had displeased, his aid;
945 As one disarmed, his anger all he lost,
And thus with peaceful words upraised her soon:
    "Unwary, and too desirous, as before,
So now of what thou know'st not, who desir'st

---

4. Eve assumes the posture of the classical suppliant, clasping the knees of the one she begs from.

5. Eve also echoes the Son's offer (3.236–41).
Cf. Adam's cry (10.832–34).

The punishment all on thyself; alas!
950 Bear thine own first, ill able to sustain
His full wrath whose thou feel'st as yet least part,
And my displeasure bear'st so ill.[6] If prayers
Could alter high decrees, I to that place
Would speed before thee, and be louder heard,
955 That on my head all might be visited,
Thy frailty and infirmer sex forgiv'n,
To me committed and by me exposed.
But rise, let us no more contend, nor blame
Each other, blamed enough elsewhere, but strive
960 In offices of love, how we may light'n
Each other's burden in our share of woe;
Since this day's death denounced, if aught I see,
Will prove no sudden, but a slow-paced evil,
A long day's dying to augment our pain,
965 And to our seed (O hapless seed!) derived."°   *passed on*
    To whom thus Eve, recovering heart, replied:
"Adam, by sad experiment I know
How little weight my words with thee can find,
Found so erroneous, thence by just event°   *consequence*
970 Found so unfortunate; nevertheless,
Restored by thee, vile as I am, to place
Of new acceptance, hopeful to regain
Thy love, the sole contentment of my heart
Living or dying, from thee I will not hide
975 What thoughts in my unquiet breast are ris'n,
Tending to some relief of our extremes,
Or end, though sharp and sad, yet tolerable,
As in our evils, and of easier choice.
If care of our descent perplex us most,[7]
980 Which must be born to certain woe, devoured
By Death at last, and miserable it is
To be to others cause of misery,
Our own begotten, and of our loins to bring
Into this cursèd world a woeful race,
985 That after wretched life must be at last
Food for so foul a monster, in thy power
It lies, yet ere conception to prevent
The race unblest, to being yet unbegot.
Childless thou art, childless remain; so Death
990 Shall be deceived° his glut, and with us two   *cheated of*
Be forced to satisfy his rav'nous maw.
But if thou judge it hard and difficult,
Conversing, looking, loving, to abstain
From love's due rites, nuptial embraces sweet,
995 And with desire to languish without hope,
Before the present object[8] languishing

6. I.e., you could hardly bear God's "full wrath" since you are so distraught when you feel only the smallest part of it, and you can "ill" bear my displeasure.

7. I.e., if concern for our descendants most torment ("perplex") us.
8. I.e., Eve herself, who then projects her own frustrated desire if they were to forgo sex.

With like desire, which would be misery
And torment less than none of what we dread,
Then both ourselves and seed at once to free
1000 From what we fear for both, let us make short,°   *lose no time*
Let us seek Death, or he not found, supply
With our own hands his office on ourselves;
Why stand we longer shivering under fears,
That show no end but death, and have the power,
1005 Of many ways to die the shortest choosing,
Destruction with destruction to destroy."
    She ended here, or vehement despair
Broke off the rest; so much of death her thoughts
Had entertained, as dyed her cheeks with pale.
1010 But Adam with such counsel nothing swayed,
To better hopes his more attentive mind
Laboring had raised, and thus to Eve replied.
    "Eve thy contempt of life and pleasure seems
To argue in thee something more sublime
1015 And excellent than what thy mind contemns;°   *despises*
But self-destruction therefore sought, refutes
That excellence thought in thee, and implies,
Not thy contempt, but anguish and regret
For loss of life and pleasure overloved.
1020 Or if thou covet death, as utmost end
Of misery, so thinking to evade
The penalty pronounced, doubt not but God
Hath wiselier armed his vengeful ire than so
To be forestalled; much more I fear lest death
1025 So snatched will not exempt us from the pain
We are by doom to pay: rather such acts
Of contumácy° will provoke the Highest   *contempt*
To make death in us live. Then let us seek
Some safer resolution, which methinks
1030 I have in view, calling to mind with heed
Part of our sentence, that thy seed shall bruise
The serpent's head; piteous amends, unless
Be meant, whom I conjecture, our grand foe
Satan, who in the serpent hath contrived
1035 Against us this deceit: to crush his head
Would be revenge indeed; which will be lost
By death brought on ourselves, or childless days
Resolved, as thou proposest; so our foe
Shall scape his punishment ordained, and we
1040 Instead shall double ours upon our heads.
No more be mentioned then of violence
Against ourselves, and willful barrenness,
That cuts us off from hope, and savors only
Rancor and pride, impatience and despite,
1045 Reluctance° against God and his just yoke   *resistance*
Laid on our necks. Remember with what mild
And gracious temper he both heard and judged
Without wrath or reviling; we expected

Immediate dissolution, which we thought
1050 Was meant by death that day, when lo, to thee
Pains only in childbearing were foretold,
And bringing forth, soon recompensed with joy,
Fruit of thy womb:[9] on me the curse aslope
Glanced on the ground,[1] with labor I must earn
1055 My bread; what harm? Idleness had been worse;
My labor will sustain me; and lest cold
Or heat should injure us, his timely care
Hath unbesought provided, and his hands
Clothed us unworthy, pitying while he judged;
1060 How much more, if we pray him, will his ear
Be open, and his heart to pity incline,
And teach us further by what means to shun
Th' inclement seasons, rain, ice, hail, and snow,
Which now the sky with various face begins
1065 To show us in this mountain, while the winds
Blow moist and keen, shattering° the graceful locks   *scattering*
Of these fair spreading trees; which bids us seek
Some better shroud,° some better warmth to cherish   *shelter*
Our limbs benumbed, ere this diurnal star°   *the sun*
1070 Leave cold the night, how we his gathered beams
Reflected, may with matter sere° foment,   *dry*
Or by collision of two bodies grind
The air attrite to fire,[2] as late the clouds
Justling or pushed with winds rude in their shock
1075 Tine° the slant lightning, whose thwart° flame driv'n down   *ignite / slanting*
Kindles the gummy bark of fir or pine,
And sends a comfortable heat from far,
Which might supply° the sun: such fire to use,   *take the place of*
And what may else be remedy or cure
1080 To evils which our own misdeeds have wrought,
He will instruct us praying, and of grace
Beseeching him, so as we need not fear
To pass commodiously this life, sustained
By him with many comforts, till we end
1085 In dust, our final rest and native home.
What better can we do, than to the place
Repairing where he judged us, prostrate fall
Before him reverent, and there confess
Humbly our faults, and pardon beg, with tears
1090 Watering the ground, and with our sighs the air
Frequenting,° sent from hearts contrite, in sign   *filling*
Of sorrow unfeigned, and humiliation meek.
Undoubtedly he will relent and turn
From his displeasure; in whose look serene,
1095 When angry most he seemed and most severe,

9. Adam's prophetic echo of Elizabeth's address to Mary, mother of Jesus (Luke 1.41–42), "blessed is the fruit of thy womb," lays the ground for their fuller understanding of the promise about the "seed" of the woman.
1. I.e., the curse, like a spear that almost missed its target, glanced aside and hit the ground.
2. Adam projects the invention of fire: they might, by striking two bodies together, rub ("attrite") the air into fire by friction; or else (lines 1070–71) focus reflected sunbeams (through some equivalent of glass) on dry ("sere") matter.

What else but favor, grace, and mercy shone?"
    So spake our father penitent, nor Eve
Felt less remorse: they forthwith to the place
Repairing where he judged them prostrate fell
1100 Before him reverent, and both confessed
Humbly their faults, and pardon begged, with tears
Watering the ground, and with their sighs the air
Frequenting, sent from hearts contrite, in sign
Of sorrow unfeigned, and humiliation meek.[3]

Book 11

The Argument

The Son of God presents to his Father the prayers of our first parents now repenting, and intercedes for them: God accepts them, but declares that they must no longer abide in Paradise; sends Michael with a band of Cherubim to dispossess them; but first to reveal to Adam future things: Michael's coming down. Adam shows to Eve certain ominous signs; he discerns Michael's approach, goes out to meet him: the angel denounces their departure. Eve's lamentation. Adam pleads, but submits: the angel leads him up to a high hill, sets before him in vision what shall happen till the Flood.

Thus they in lowliest plight repentant stood[1]
Praying, for from the mercy-seat above
Prevenient grace[2] descending had removed
The stony from their hearts, and made new flesh
5 Regenerate grow instead, that sighs now breathed
Unutterable, which the spirit of prayer
Inspired, and winged for Heav'n with speedier flight
Than loudest oratory: yet their port
Not of mean suitors, nor important less
10 Seemed their petition, than when th' ancient pair
In fables old, less ancient yet than these,
Deucalion and chaste Pyrrha to restore
The race of mankind drowned, before the shrine
Of Themis stood devout.[3] To Heav'n their prayers
15 Flew up, nor missed the way, by envious winds
Blown vagabond or frustrate:[4] in they passed
Dimensionless through heav'nly doors; then clad
With incense, where the golden altar fumed,
By their great Intercessor, came in sight

3. The final six lines repeat, almost word for word, lines 1086–92, as the poet describes Adam's proposed gesture of repentance carried out in every detail.
1. "Stood" may mean "remained," or that, after prostrating themselves (10.1099) they prayed standing upright; their demeanor ("port") was "Not of mean suitors" (11.8–9), and they had stood to pray before (4.720).
2. Grace given before the human will can turn

from sin, enabling it to do so.
3. In Greek myth, when Deucalion and his wife Pyrrha (like Noah's family) alone survived a universal flood, they sought direction from Themis, goddess of justice; she told them to throw stones behind them, which became men and women.
4. I.e., their prayers were not scattered ("blown vagabond") by spiteful ("envious") winds, or prevented ("frustrate") from reaching their goal. "Dimensionless": without physical extension.

20 Before the Father's throne: them the glad° Son   *pleased*
  Presenting, thus to intercede began:
    "See Father, what firstfruits on earth are sprung
  From thy implanted grace in man, these sighs
  And prayers, which in this golden censer, mixed
25 With incense, I thy priest before thee bring,
  Fruits of more pleasing savor from thy seed
  Sown with contrition in his heart, than those
  Which his own hand manuring° all the trees   *cultivating*
  Of Paradise could have produced, ere fall'n
30 From innocence. Now therefore bend thine ear
  To supplication, hear his sighs though mute;
  Unskillful with what words to pray, let me
  Interpret for him, me his advocate
  And propitiation, all his works on me
35 Good or not good ingraft,[5] my merit those
  Shall perfect, and for these my death shall pay.
  Accept me, and in me from these receive
  The smell of peace toward mankind, let him live
  Before thee reconciled, at least his days
40 Numbered, though sad, till death, his doom (which I
  To mitigate thus plead, not to reverse)
  To better life shall yield him, where with me
  All my redeemed may dwell in joy and bliss,
  Made one with me as I with thee am one."
45   To whom the Father, without cloud, serene:
  "All thy request for man, accepted Son,
  Obtain, all thy request was my decree:
  But longer in that Paradise to dwell,
  The law I gave to nature him forbids:
50 Those pure immortal elements that know
  No gross, no unharmonious mixture foul,
  Eject him tainted now, and purge him off
  As a distemper, gross to air as gross,
  And mortal food,[6] as may dispose him best
55 For dissolution° wrought by sin, that first   *death*
  Distempered all things, and of incorrupt
  Corrupted. I at first with two fair gifts
  Created him endowed, with happiness
  And immortality: that fondly° lost,   *foolishly*
60 This other served but to eternize woe;
  Till I provided death; so death becomes
  His final remedy, and after life
  Tried in sharp tribulation, and refined
  By faith and faithful works, to second life,
65 Waked in the renovation[7] of the just,

---

5. The theological term for Christ's standing in the place of humankind, taking onto himself all their deeds, perfecting the good by his merit, and, by his death, "paying" (see next line) the debt due God's justice for their evil deeds.
6. The pure elements of the Garden of Eden will themselves "purge" Adam and Eve as an impurity or disorder ("distemper"), ejecting them to a place where the air and food are more gross, like themselves.
7. The resurrection and renewal of body and soul on the Last Day.

Resigns him up with Heav'n and earth renewed.
But let us call to synod° all the blest   *assembly*
Through Heav'n's wide bounds; from them I will not hide
My judgments, how with mankind I proceed,
70   As how with peccant° angels late they saw;   *sinning*
And in their state, though firm, stood more confirmed."
        He ended, and the Son gave signal high
To the bright minister that watched, he blew
His trumpet, heard in Oreb[8] since perhaps
75   When God descended, and perhaps once more
To sound at general doom. Th' angelic blast
Filled all the regions: from their blissful bow'rs
Of amarantine° shade, fountain or spring,   *unfading*
By the waters of life, where'er they sat
80   In fellowships of joy, the sons of light
Hasted, resorting to the summons high,
And took their seats; till from his throne supreme
Th' Almighty thus pronounced his sov'reign will:
        "O sons, like one of us man is become
85   To know both good and evil, since his taste
Of that defended° fruit; but let him boast   *forbidden*
His knowledge of good lost, and evil got,
Happier, had it sufficed him to have known
Good by itself, and evil not at all.
90   He sorrows now, repents, and prays contrite,
My motions° in him; longer than they move,   *promptings*
His heart I know, how variable and vain
Self-left.[9] Lest therefore his now bolder hand
Reach also of the Tree of Life, and eat,
95   And live forever, dream at least to live
Forever,[1] to remove him I decree,
And send him from the garden forth to till
The ground whence he was taken, fitter soil.
        "Michael, this my behest have thou in charge,
100 Take to thee from among the Cherubim
Thy choice of flaming warriors, lest the Fiend
Or° in behalf of man, or to invade   *either*
Vacant possession some new trouble raise:
Haste thee, and from the Paradise of God
105 Without remorse° drive out the sinful pair,   *pity*
From hallowed ground th' unholy, and denounce
To them and to their progeny from thence
Perpetual banishment. Yet lest they faint°   *lose courage*
At the sad sentence rigorously urged,
110 For I behold them softened and with tears
Bewailing their excess,° all terror hide.   *violation of law*

8. Where God delivered the Ten Commandments to the sound of a trumpet (Exodus 19.19);
it will sound again at the Last Judgment ("general doom," line 76).
9. Left to itself, without my continual promptings ("motions," line 91), I know his heart to be

"variable and vain."
1. Milton adds the phrase "dream at least to live
forever" to suggest that parts of God's speech
(especially lines 84–85 and 93–95, closely
quoted from Genesis 3.22) are ironic.

If patiently thy bidding they obey,
Dismiss them not disconsolate; reveal
To Adam what shall come in future days,
As I shall thee enlighten,[2] intermix
My cov'nant in the woman's seed renewed;
So send them forth, though sorrowing, yet in peace:
And on the east side of the garden place,
Where entrance up from Eden easiest climbs,
Cherubic watch, and of a sword the flame
Wide-waving, all approach far off to fright,
And guard all passage to the Tree of Life:[3]
Lest Paradise a receptácle prove
To spirits foul, and all my trees their prey,
With whose stol'n fruit man once more to delude."
   He ceased; and th' archangelic power prepared
For swift descent, with him the cohort bright
Of watchful Cherubim; four faces each[4]
Had, like a double Janus, all their shape
Spangled with eyes more numerous than those
Of Argus, and more wakeful than to drowse,
Charmed with Arcadian pipe, the pastoral reed
Of Hermes, or his opiate rod. Meanwhile
To resalute the world with sacred light
Leucóthea[5] waked, and with fresh dews embalmed
The earth, when Adam and first matron Eve
Had ended now their orisons, and found
Strength added from above, new hope to spring
Out of despair, joy, but with fear yet linked;
Which thus to Eve his welcome words renewed:
   "Eve, easily may faith admit, that all
The good which we enjoy, from Heav'n descends;
But that from us aught should ascend to Heav'n
So prevalent° as to concern the mind   *influential*
Of God high-blest, or to incline his will,
Hard to belief may seem; yet this will prayer,
Or one short sigh of human breath, upborne
Ev'n to the seat of God. For since I sought
By prayer th' offended Deity to appease,
Kneeled and before him humbled all my heart,
Methought I saw him placable and mild,
Bending his ear; persuasion in me grew
That I was heard with favor; peace returned
Home to my breast, and to my memory

Line numbers: 115, 120, 125, 130, 135, 140, 145, 150

---

2. God, it seems, has to "enlighten" Michael with knowledge of humankind's future at the same time Michael presents that future to Adam (cf. 12.128); Michael is told to "intermix" in his account God's "cov'nant in the woman's seed" (lines 115–16), the "mysterious" promise of the redeemer hinted when the Son pronounced judgment on the serpent (10.179–81).
3. Cf. Genesis 3.24: "he placed at the east of the garden of Eden Cherubims, and a flaming sword which turned every way, to keep the way of the tree of life."
4. Ezekiel 1.6 Janus (line 129), the Roman god of doorways, had two faces; in one version he had four, corresponding to the four seasons and the four quarters of the earth. Argus (line 131), a giant with one hundred eyes, was set by Juno to watch Jove's mistress Io, but Hermes (Mercury) put all of his eyes to sleep with his music ("pipe") and his sleep-producing caduceus ("opiate rod").
5. Roman goddess of the dawn.

155   His promise, that thy seed shall bruise our foe;
     Which then not minded in dismay, yet now
     Assures me that the bitterness of death
     Is past, and we shall live. Whence hail to thee,
     Eve rightly called, mother of all mankind,
160   Mother of all things living, since by thee
     Man is to live, and all things live for man."[6]
       To whom thus Eve with sad demeanor meek:
     "Ill-worthy I such title should belong
     To me transgressor, who for thee ordained
165   A help, became thy snare; to me reproach
     Rather belongs, distrust and all dispraise:
     But infinite in pardon was my Judge,
     That I who first brought death on all, am graced
     The source of life; next favorable thou,
170   Who highly thus to entitle me vouchsaf'st,
     Far other name deserving. But the field
     To labor calls us now with sweat imposed,
     Though after sleepless night; for see the morn,
     All unconcerned with our unrest, begins
175   Her rosy progress smiling; let us forth,
     I never from thy side henceforth to stray,
     Where'er our day's work lies, though now enjoined
     Laborious, till day droop; while here we dwell,
     What can be toilsome in these pleasant walks?
180   Here let us live, though in fall'n state, content."
       So spake, so wished much-humbled Eve, but fate
     Subscribed not; nature first gave signs,° impressed   *omens*
     On bird, beast, air, air suddenly eclipsed°   *darkened*
     After short blush of morn; nigh in her sight
185   The bird of Jove, stooped from his airy tow'r,[7]
     Two birds of gayest plume before him drove:
     Down from a hill the beast that reigns in woods,[8]
     First hunter then, pursued a gentle brace,°   *pair*
     Goodliest of all the forest, hart and hind;
190   Direct to th' eastern gate was bent their flight.
     Adam observed, and with his eye the chase
     Pursuing, not unmoved to Eve thus spake:
       "O Eve, some further change awaits us nigh,
     Which Heaven by these mute signs in nature shows
195   Forerunners of his purpose, or to warn
     Us haply too secure° of our discharge   *overconfident*
     From penalty, because from death released
     Some days; how long, and what till then our life,
     Who knows, or more than this, that we are dust,
200   And thither must return and be no more.
     Why else this double object in our sight
     Of flight pursued in th' air and o'er the ground

---

6. The name Eve is cognate with the Hebrew word meaning "life." In Genesis 3.20 Adam names his wife Eve only after the Fall; Milton's Adam has named her before (4.481) and now affirms that that name is right.
7. The eagle swooped ("stooped") from his soaring flight ("tow'r").
8. The lion.

One way the selfsame hour? Why in the east
Darkness ere day's mid-course, and morning light
205 More orient° in yon western cloud that draws   *bright*
O'er the blue firmament a radiant white,
And slow descends, with something heav'nly fraught."°   *laden*
   He erred not, for by this° the heav'nly bands   *by this time*
Down from a sky of jasper lighted° now   *alighted, shone*
210 In Paradise, and on a hill made alt,°   *halt*
A glorious apparition, had not doubt
And carnal fear that day dimmed Adam's eye.
Not that more glorious, when the angels met
Jacob in Mahanaim,[9] where he saw
215 The field pavilioned with his guardians bright;
Nor that which on the flaming mount appeared
In Dothan, covered with a camp of fire,
Against the Syrian king, who to surprise
One man, assassin-like had levied war,
220 War unproclaimed.[1] The princely hierarch[2]
In their bright stand, there left his powers to seize
Possession of the garden; he alone,
To find where Adam sheltered, took his way,
Not unperceived of Adam, who to Eve,
225 While the great visitant approached, thus spake:
   "Eve, now expect great tidings, which perhaps
Of us will soon determine,° or impose   *make an end*
New laws to be observed; for I descry
From yonder blazing cloud that veils the hill
230 One of the heav'nly host, and by his gait
None of the meanest, some great potentate
Or of the Thrones above, such majesty
Invests him coming; yet not terrible,
That I should fear, nor sociably mild,
235 As Raphael, that I should much confide,
But solemn and sublime, whom not to offend,
With reverence I must meet, and thou retire."
He ended; and th' Archangel soon drew nigh,
Not in his shape celestial, but as man
240 Clad to meet man; over his lucid arms
A military vest of purple flowed
Livelier than Meliboean, or the grain
Of Sarra,[3] worn by kings and heroes old
In time of truce; Iris[4] had dipped the woof;
245 His starry helm unbuckled showed him prime
In manhood where youth ended; by his side
As in a glistering zodiac° hung the sword,   *belt*
Satan's dire dread, and in his hand the spear.

---

9. Jacob gave that name, meaning "armies" or "camps" ("field pavilioned," line 215), to a place where he saw an army of angels (Genesis 32.2).
1. The Syrian king levied war against "Dothan" (line 217) in order to capture Elisha the prophet ("One man," line 219), but the Lord saved Elisha by sending "horses and chariots of fire"

(2 Kings 6.8ff.).
2. Michael, who left his angelic forces ("powers") in their formation ("stand") to take possession of the garden (lines 221–22).
3. Both Meliboea and Tyre ("Sarra") in Thessaly were famous for purple dye.
4. Goddess of the rainbow.

Adam bowed low, he kingly from his state°   *stately bearing*
250   Inclined not, but his coming thus declared:
     "Adam, Heav'n's high behest no preface needs:
     Sufficient that thy prayers are heard, and Death,
     Then due by sentence when thou didst transgress,
     Defeated° of his seizure° many days   *cheated / possession*
255   Giv'n thee of grace, wherein thou may'st repent,
     And one bad act with many deeds well done
     May'st cover: well may then thy Lord appeased
     Redeem thee quite from Death's rapacious claim;
     But longer in this Paradise to dwell
260   Permits not; to remove thee I am come,
     And send thee from the garden forth to till
     The ground whence thou wast taken, fitter soil."
       He added not, for Adam at the news
     Heart-strook with chilling gripe° of sorrow stood,   *spasm*
265   That all his senses bound; Eve, who unseen
     Yet all had heard, with audible lament
     Discovered° soon the place of her retire: *revealed*
       "O unexpected stroke, worse than of Death!
     Must I thus leave thee Paradise? thus leave
270   Thee native soil,[5] these happy walks and shades,
     Fit haunt of gods? where I had hope to spend,
     Quiet though sad, the respite° of that day   *delay*
     That must be mortal to us both. O flow'rs,
     That never will in other climate grow,
275   My early visitation, and my last
     At ev'n which I bred up with tender hand
     From the first op'ning bud, and gave ye names,[6]
     Who now shall rear ye to the sun, or rank
     Your tribes,° and water from th' ambrosial° fount?   *species / fragrant*
280   Thee lastly nuptial bower, by me adorned
     With what to sight or smell was sweet; from thee
     How shall I part, and whither wander down
     Into a lower world, to° this obscure   *compared to*
     And wild, how shall we breathe in other air
285   Less pure, accustomed to immortal fruits?"
      Whom thus the angel interrupted mild:
     "Lament not Eve, but patiently resign
     What justly thou hast lost; nor set thy heart,
     Thus overfond, on that which is not thine;
290   Thy going is not lonely, with thee goes
     Thy husband, him to follow thou art bound;
     Where he abides, think there thy native soil."
      Adam by this from the cold sudden damp°   *dejection*
     Recovering, and his scattered spirits returned,
295   To Michael thus his humble words addressed:
      "Celestial, whether among the Thrones, or named

5. Unlike Adam, Eve was created in the Paradise of Eden.
6. Departing from Genesis 2.19–20, in which Adam alone gives names, Milton has Eve name the flowers, an action that signifies (like Adam's naming of the beasts, 8.352–54) intuitive knowledge of their nature.

Of them the highest, for such of shape may seem
Prince above princes, gently hast thou told
Thy message, which might else in telling wound,
300 And in performing end us; what besides
Of sorrow and dejection and despair
Our frailty can sustain, thy tidings bring,
Departure from this happy place, our sweet
Recess, and only consolation left
305 Familiar to our eyes, all places else
Inhospitable appear and desolate,
Nor knowing us nor known: and if by prayer
Incessant I could hope to change the will
Of him who all things can,° I would not cease   knows, can do
310 To weary him with my assiduous cries:
But prayer against his absolute decree
No more avails than breath against the wind,
Blown stifling back on him that breathes it forth:
Therefore to his great bidding I submit.
315 This most afflicts me, that departing hence,
As from his face I shall be hid, deprived
His blessed count'nance; here I could frequent,
With worship, place by place where he vouchsafed
Presence Divine, and to my sons relate:
320 'On this mount he appeared, under this tree
Stood visible, among these pines his voice
I heard, here with him at this fountain talked:'
So many grateful altars I would rear
Of grassy turf, and pile up every stone
325 Of luster from the brook, in memory,
Or monument to ages, and thereon
Offer sweet-smelling gums and fruits and flow'rs:
In yonder nether world where shall I seek
His bright appearances, or footstep trace?
330 For though I fled him angry, yet recalled
To life prolonged and promised race,[7] I now
Gladly behold though but his utmost skirts
Of glory, and far off his steps adore."
       To whom thus Michael with regard benign:
335 "Adam, thou know'st Heav'n his, and all the earth,
Not this rock only; his omnipresence fills
Land, sea, and air, and every kind that lives,
Fomented° by his virtual° power and warmed: nurtured / potent
All th' earth he gave thee to possess and rule,
340 No despicable gift; surmise not then
His presence to these narrow bounds confined
Of Paradise or Eden: this had been
Perhaps thy capital seat, from whence had spread
All generations, and had hither come
345 From all the ends of th' earth, to celebrate

7. His descendants, from whom will spring the "promised Seed." See 10.180–81 and n. 1, and 12.623.

And reverence thee their great progenitor.
But this preeminence thou hast lost, brought down
To dwell on even ground now with thy sons:
Yet doubt not but in valley and in plain
350   God is as here, and will be found alike
Present, and of his presence many a sign
Still following thee, still compassing thee round
With goodness and paternal love, his face
Express, and of his steps the track divine.
355   Which that thou may'st believe, and be confirmed,
Ere thou from hence depart, know I am sent
To show thee what shall come in future days
To thee and to thy offspring,[8] good with bad
Expect to hear, supernal° grace contending   *heavenly*
360   With sinfulness of men; thereby to learn
True patience, and to temper joy with fear
And pious sorrow, equally inured°   *tempered*
By moderation either state to bare,
Prosperous or adverse: so shalt thou lead
365   Safest thy life, and best prepared endure
Thy mortal passage when it comes. Ascend
This hill; let Eve (for I have drenched her eyes)[9]
Here sleep below while thou to foresight wak'st,
As once thou slept'st while she to life was formed."
370   To whom thus Adam gratefully replied:
"Ascend, I follow thee, safe guide, the path
Thou lead'st me, and to the hand of Heav'n submit,
However chast'ning, to the evil turn
My obvious° breast, arming to overcome   *exposed*
375   By suffering, and earn rest from labor won,
If so I may attain." So both ascend
In the visions of God: it was a hill
Of Paradise the highest, from whose top
The hemisphere of earth in clearest ken°   *view*
380   Stretched out to amplest reach of prospect lay.
Not higher that hill nor wider looking round,
Whereon for different cause the Tempter set
Our second Adam in the wilderness,
To show him all earth's kingdoms and their glory.[1]
385   His eye might there command wherever stood
City of old or modern fame, the seat
Of mightiest empire, from the destined walls
Of Cambalu, seat of Cathaian Can,
And Samarkand by Oxus, Temir's throne,
390   To Paquin of Sinaean kings, and thence
To Agra and Lahore of Great Mogul

8. Prophetic visions are a common feature in epic, e.g., Aeneas's vision of his descendants culminating in the Roman Empire (Virgil, *Aeneid* 6.754–854).
9. Put a soporific liquid ("drench") in her eyes.
1. When Satan tempted Christ (the subject of Milton's "brief epic" *Paradise Regained*), he took him up to "an exceeding high mountain" and showed him "all the kingdoms of the world, and the glory of them" (Matthew 4.8). The passage that follows details the places "he" (Christ and/or Adam) might see (lines 386–411).

Down to the golden Chersonese,[2] or where
The Persian in Ecbatan sat, or since
In Hispahan, or where the Russian czar
395   In Moscow, or the sultan in Bizance,
Turkéstan-born;[3] nor could his eye not ken°   *view*
Th' empire of Negus to his utmost port
Ercoco and the less maritime kings
Mombaza, and Quiloa, and Melind,
400   And Sofala thought Ophir, to the realm
Of Congo, and Angola farthest south;[4]
Or thence from Niger flood to Atlas mount
The kingdoms of Almansor, Fez and Sus,
Morocco and Algiers, and Tremisen;[5]
405   On Europe thence, and where Rome was to sway
The world: in spirit perhaps he also saw
Rich Mexico the seat of Motezume,
And Cuzco in Peru, the richer seat
Of Atabalipa, and yet unspoiled
410   Guiana, whose great city Geryon's sons
Call El Dorado:[6] but to nobler sights
Michael from Adam's eyes the film removed
Which that false fruit that promised clearer sight
Had bred; then purged with euphrasy and rue[7]
415   The visual nerve, for he had much to see;
And from the well of life three drops instilled.
So deep the power of these ingredients pierced,
Ev'n to the inmost seat of mental sight,
That Adam now enforced to close his eyes,
420   Sunk down and all his spirits became entranced:
But him the gentle angel by the hand
Soon raised, and his attention thus recalled:
    "Adam, now ope thine eyes, and first behold
Th' effects which thy original crime hath wrought
425   In some to spring from thee, who never touched

---

2. His first views are of "destined" (yet to come) great kingdoms in Asia: "Cambalu," capital of "Cathay," the region of North China ruled by such khans as Genghis and Kublai; "Samarkand," ruled by Tamburlaine ("Temir"), near the "Oxus" river near modern Uzbekistan; Beijing ("Paquin," Peking), ruled by Chinese ("Sinaean") kings; "Agra" and "Lahore," capitals in northern India ruled by the "Great Mogul"; "golden Chersonese," an area sometimes identified with the Malay Peninsula.

3. Next, Persian and Turkish kingdoms. From Persia (Iran): Ecbatana ("Ecbatan"), a summer residence of Persian kings, and the 16th-century Persian capital Isfahan ("Hispahan"); and Byzantium ("Bizance," Constantinople, Istanbul), capital of the Ottoman Empire after falling to the Turks in 1453.

4. From Africa: Abyssinia (empire of King "Negus"); Arkiko ("Ercoco") in Ethiopia, a Red Sea port; Mombasa ("Mombaza") and Malindi ("Melind") in Kenya; Kilwa ("Quiloa") in Tanzania; "Sofala," sometimes identified with the biblical "Ophir" from which Solomon took gold for his

Temple (1 Kings 9.28); and "Congo" and "Angola" on the west coast.

5. In North Africa: the kingdoms of "Almansor" (the name shared by various Muslim rulers, here referring probably to Abu-Amir al Ma-Ma'afiri, caliph of Cordova) reached from the "Niger" River in northern Morocco to the "Atlas" Mountains in Algeria, taking in Morocco (and its capital, "Fez"), Tunis ("Sus"), and part of Algeria called Tiemecen ("Tremisen").

6. Because they lay on the other side of the spherical earth, Christ and/or Adam could only see places in the New World "in spirit" (line 406): Mexico, the seat of Montezuma ("Motezume"), the last Aztec emperor; "Cuzco in Peru," seat of Atahualpa ("Atabalipa"), the last Incan emperor (murdered by Pizarro); and "Guiana" (a region including Surinam, Guyana, and parts of Venezuela and Brazil). Unlike Mexico and Peru it was "yet unspoiled" by the Spaniards (sons of the evil monster "Geryon," in Spenser an allegory of the great power and oppression of Spain), though they identified its chief city, Manoa, with the fabled city of gold, "El Dorado."

7. Both herbs were thought to sharpen eyesight.

Th' excepted° tree, nor with the snake conspired,   *forbidden*
Nor sinned thy sin, yet from that sin derive
Corruption to bring forth more violent deeds."
　　His eyes he opened, and beheld a field,
430　Part arable and tilth,° whereon were sheaves   *cultivated*
New-reaped, the other part sheep-walks and folds;
I' th' midst an altar as the landmark° stood   *boundary marker*
Rustic, of grassy sord;° thither anon   *turf*
A sweaty reaper from his tillage brought
435　Firstfruits, the green ear, and the yellow sheaf,
Unculled,° as came to hand; a shepherd next   *picked at random*
More meek came with the firstlings of his flock
Choicest and best; then sacrificing, laid
The inwards and their fat, with incense strewed,
440　On the cleft wood, and all due rites performed.
His off'ring soon propitious fire from Heav'n
Consumed with nimble glance, and grateful steam;
The other's not, for his was not sincere;[8]
Whereat he inly raged, and as they talked,
445　Smote him into the midriff with a stone
That beat out life; he fell, and deadly pale
Groaned out his soul with gushing blood effused.
Much at that sight was Adam in his heart
Dismayed, and thus in haste to th' angel cried:
450　　"O teacher, some great mischief hath befall'n
To that meek man, who well had sacrificed;
Is piety thus and pure devotion paid?"
　　T' whom Michael thus, he also moved, replied:
"These two are brethren, Adam, and to come
455　Out of thy loins;[9] th' unjust the just hath slain,
For envy that his brother's offering found
From Heav'n acceptance; but the bloody fact°   *crime*
Will be avenged, and th' other's faith approved
Lose no reward, though here thou see him die,
460　Rolling in dust and gore." To which our sire:
　　"Alas, both for the deed and for the cause!
But have I now seen death? Is this the way
I must return to native dust? O sight
Of terror, foul and ugly to behold,
465　Horrid to think, how horrible to feel!"
　　To whom thus Michaël: "Death thou hast seen
In his first shape on man; but many shapes
Of Death, and many are the ways that lead
To his grim cave, all dismal; yet to sense
470　More terrible at th' entrance than within.
Some, as thou saw'st, by violent stroke shall die,
By fire, flood, famine; by intemperance more
In meats and drinks, which on the earth shall bring
Diseases dire, of which a monstrous crew

---

8. Milton's version of the Cain and Abel story
(Genesis 4.1–16) provides a clear reason for
God's rejection of Cain's sacrifice.

9. Adam has to be told that these are his own
sons, not simply descendants.

475　Before thee shall appear; that thou may'st know
　　What misery th' inabstinence of Eve
　　Shall bring on men." Immediately a place[1]
　　Before his eyes appeared, sad,° noisome, dark,　　　　　　　　　*lamentable*
　　A lazar-house it seemed, wherein were laid
480　Numbers of all diseased, all maladies
　　Of ghastly spasm, or racking torture, qualms
　　Of heartsick agony, all feverous kinds,
　　Convulsions, epilepsies, fierce catarrhs,
　　Intestine stone and ulcer, colic pangs,
485　Demoniac frenzy, moping melancholy
　　And moonstruck madness,° pining atrophy,　　　　　　　　　*lunacy*
　　Marasmus, and wide-wasting pestilence,[2]
　　Dropsies, and asthmas, and joint-racking rheums.
　　Dire was the tossing, deep the groans, Despair
490　Tended the sick busiest from couch to couch;
　　And over them triumphant Death his dart
　　Shook, but delayed to strike, though oft invoked
　　With vows, as their chief good, and final hope.
　　Sight so deform what heart of rock could long
495　Dry-eyed behold? Adam could not, but wept,
　　Though not of woman born; compassion quelled
　　His best of man,° and gave him up to tears　　　　　*manliness, courage*
　　A space, till firmer thoughts restrained excess,
　　And scarce recovering words his plaint renewed:
500　　"O miserable mankind, to what fall
　　Degraded, to what wretched state reserved!
　　Better end here unborn. Why is life giv'n
　　To be thus wrested from us? Rather why
　　Obtruded on us thus? who if we knew
505　What we receive, would either not accept
　　Life offered, or soon beg to lay it down,
　　Glad to be so dismissed in peace. Can thus
　　Th' image of God in man created once
　　So goodly and erect, though faulty since,
510　To such unsightly sufferings be debased
　　Under inhuman pains? Why should not man,
　　Retaining still divine similitude
　　In part, from such deformities be free,
　　And for his Maker's image sake exempt?"
515　　"Their Maker's image," answered Michael, "then
　　Forsook them, when themselves they vilified°　　　　　　　*debased*
　　To serve ungoverned appetite, and took°　　　　　　　　　*took away*
　　His image whom they served, a brutish vice,
　　Inductive° mainly to° the sin of Eve.　　　　　　　　*produced / from*
520　Therefore so abject is their punishment,
　　Disfiguring not God's likeness, but their own,
　　Or if his likeness, by themselves defaced
　　While they pervert pure nature's healthful rules

---

1. This is the only nonbiblical sight shown to　　syphilis.
Adam, a "lazar-house" (line 479)—a hospital　　2. The plague. "Marasmus": a wasting disease of
for leprosy and infectious diseases, especially　　the body.

To loathsome sickness, worthily,° since they   *deservedly*
525   God's image did not reverence in themselves."
     "I yield it just," said Adam, "and submit.
But is there yet no other way, besides
These painful passages, how we may come
To death, and mix with our connatural dust?"
530   "There is," said Michael, "if thou well observe
The rule of not too much, by temperance taught
In what thou eat'st and drink'st, seeking from thence
Due nourishment, not gluttonous delight,
Till many years over thy head return:
535   So may'st thou live, till like ripe fruit thou drop
Into thy mother's[3] lap, or be with ease
Gathered, not harshly plucked, for death mature:
This is old age; but then thou must outlive
Thy youth, thy strength, thy beauty, which will change
540   To withered weak and gray; thy senses then
Obtuse, all taste of pleasure must forgo,
To what thou hast, and for the air of youth
Hopeful and cheerful, in thy blood will reign
A melancholy damp° of cold and dry   *depression of spirits*
545   To weigh thy spirits down, and last consume
The balm° of life." To whom our ancestor: *preservative essence*
     "Henceforth I fly not death, nor would prolong
Life much, bent rather how I may be quit
Fairest and easiest of this cumbrous charge,
550   Which I must keep till my appointed day
Of rend'ring up, and patiently attend°   *await*
My dissolution." Michaël replied:
     "Nor love thy life, nor hate; but what thou liv'st
Live well, how long or short permit to Heav'n:
555   And now prepare thee for another sight."
     He looked and saw a spacious plain,[4] whereon
Were tents of various hue; by some were herds
Of cattle grazing: others, whence the sound
Of instruments that made melodious chime
560   Was heard, of harp and organ; and who moved
Their stops and chords was seen: his volant touch
Instinct through all proportions low and high
Fled and pursued transverse the resonant fugue.[5]
In other part stood one[6] who at the forge
565   Laboring, two massy clods of iron and brass
Had melted (whether found where casual° fire   *accidental*
Had wasted woods on mountain or in vale,
Down to the veins of earth, thence gliding hot
To some cave's mouth, or whether washed by stream
570   From underground) the liquid ore he drained

---

3. "Mother" earth.
4. Adam's third vision is based on Genesis 4.19–22; "tents" (next line) identifies these as the descendants of Cain, described as "such as dwell in tents."
5. Genesis 4.21 describes Cain's descendant Jubal as "father of all such as handle the harp

and organ." "Volant": nimble; "instinct": instinctive; "proportions": ratios of pitches; "fugue": musical form in which one statement of the theme seems to chase another.
6. Tubal-cain, "instructor of every artificer in brass and iron" (Genesis 4.22).

Into fit molds prepared; from which he formed
First his own tools; then, what might else be wrought
Fusile° or grav'n in metal. After these,   cast
But on the hither side a different sort[7]
575 From the high neighboring hills, which was their seat,
Down to the plain descended: by their guise
Just men they seemed, and all their study bent
To worship God aright, and know his works
Not hid,[8] nor those things last which might preserve
580 Freedom and peace to men: they on the plain
Long had not walked, when from the tents behold
A bevy of fair women, richly gay
In gems and wanton dress; to the harp they sung
Soft amorous ditties, and in dance came on:
585 The men though grave, eyed them, and let their eyes
Rove without rein, till in the amorous net
Fast caught, they liked, and each his liking chose;
And now of love they treat till th' evening star[9]
Love's harbinger appeared; then all in heat
590 They light the nuptial torch, and bid invoke
Hymen,[1] then first to marriage rites invoked;
With feast and music all the tents resound.
Such happy interview and fair event°   outcome
Of love and youth not lost, songs, garlands, flow'rs,
595 And charming symphonies attached° the heart   seized
Of Adam, soon° inclined to admit delight,   easily
The bent of nature; which he thus expressed:
    "True opener of mine eyes, prime angel blest,
Much better seems this vision, and more hope
600 Of peaceful days portends, than those two past;
Those were of hate and death, or pain much worse,
Here nature seems fulfilled in all her ends."
    To whom thus Michael: "Judge not what is best
By pleasure, though to nature seeming meet,°   appropriate
605 Created, as thou art, to nobler end
Holy and pure, conformity divine.
Those tents thou saw'st so pleasant, were the tents
Of wickedness, wherein shall dwell his race
Who slew his brother; studious they appear
610 Of arts that polish life, inventors rare,
Unmindful of their Maker, though his spirit
Taught them, but they his gifts acknowledged none.
Yet they a beauteous offspring shall beget;
For that fair female troop thou saw'st, that seemed
615 Of goddesses, so blithe, so smooth, so gay,
Yet empty of all good wherein consists
Woman's domestic honor and chief praise;
Bred only and completed° to the taste   accomplished

---

7. The descendants of Seth, Adam's third son
(Genesis 5.3); "hither side": away from the "east"
(Genesis 4.16), where Cain's sons lived.
8. They studied God's visible works, not the

"matters hid" that Raphael had warned Adam
against.
9. Venus.
1. God of marriage.

Of lustful appetence,° to sing, to dance,   *desire*
620 To dress, and troll° the tongue, and roll the eye.   *move*
To these that sober race of men, whose lives
Religious titled them the sons of God,[2]
Shall yield up all their virtue, all their fame
Ignobly, to the trains° and to the smiles   *wiles, snares*
625 Of these fair atheists, and now swim in joy,
(Erelong to swim at large) and laugh; for which
The world erelong a world of tears must weep."
  To whom thus Adam of short joy bereft:
"O pity and shame, that they who to live well
630 Entered so fair, should turn aside to tread
Paths indirect, or in the mid-way faint!
But still I see the tenor of man's woe
Holds on the same, from woman to begin."
  "From man's effeminate slackness it begins,"
635 Said th' angel, "who should better hold his place
By wisdom, and superior gifts received.
But now prepare thee for another scene."
  He looked and saw wide territory spread
Before him, towns, and rural works between,
640 Cities of men with lofty gates and tow'rs,
Concourse° in arms, fierce faces threat'ning war, *encounters*
Giants[3] of mighty bone, and bold emprise;° *chivalric adventure*
Part wield their arms, part curb the foaming steed,
Single or in array of battle ranged°   *drawn up in ranks*
645 Both horse and foot, nor idly must'ring stood;
One way a band select from forage drives
A herd of beeves, fair oxen and fair kine
From a fat meadow ground; or fleecy flock,
Ewes and their bleating lambs over the plain,
650 Their booty; scarce with life the shepherds fly,
But call in aid, which makes a bloody fray;
With cruel tournament the squadrons join;
Where cattle pastured late, now scattered lies
With carcasses and arms th' ensanguined° field *blood-stained*
655 Deserted: others to a city strong
Lay siege, encamped; by battery, scale, and mine,[4]
Assaulting; others from the wall defend
With dart and jav'lin, stones and sulphurous fire;
On each hand slaughter and gigantic deeds.
660 In other part the sceptered heralds call
To council in the city gates: anon
Gray-headed men and grave, with warriors mixed,
Assemble, and harangues are heard, but soon
In factious opposition, till at last

---

2. Like many exegetes, Milton identifies the "sons of God" as the descendants of Seth, and the "daughters of men" whom they wed (Genesis 6.2) as the descendants of Cain.
3. Adam's fourth vision, based on Genesis 6.4, is of the "Giant" offspring of the previous mar-

riages (identified at lines 683–84); Milton makes them exemplify false heroism and false glory sought through military might and conquest (lines 689–99).
4. I.e., by battering, scaling, and tunneling under the walls.

665 Of middle age one⁵ rising, eminent
In wise deport, spake much of right and wrong,
Of justice, of religion, truth and peace,
And judgment from above: him old and young
Exploded,° and had seized with violent hands,   *mocked*
670 Had not a cloud descending snatched him thence
Unseen amid the throng: so violence
Proceeded, and oppression, and sword-law
Through all the plain, and refuge none was found.
Adam was all in tears, and to his guide
675 Lamenting turned full sad; "O what are these,
Death's ministers, not men, who thus deal death
Inhumanly to men, and multiply
Ten-thousandfold the sin of him who slew
His brother; for of whom such massacre
680 Make they but of their brethren, men of men?
But who was that just man, whom had not Heav'n
Rescued, had in his righteousness been lost?"
    To whom thus Michael: "These are the product
Of those ill-mated marriages thou saw'st:
685 Where good with bad were matched, who of themselves
Abhor to join; and by imprudence mixed,
Produce prodigious births of body or mind.
Such were these giants, men of high renown;
For in those days might only shall be admired,
690 And valor and heroic virtue called;
To overcome in battle, and subdue
Nations, and bring home spoils with infinite
Manslaughter, shall be held the highest pitch
Of human glory, and for glory done
695 Of triumph, to be styled great conquerors,
Patrons of mankind, gods, and sons of gods,
Destroyers rightlier called and plagues of men.
Thus fame shall be achieved, renown on earth,
And what most merits fame in silence hid.
700 But he the sev'nth from thee,⁶ whom thou beheld'st
The only righteous in a world perverse,
And therefore hated, therefore so beset
With foes for daring single to be just,
And utter odious truth, that God would come
705 To judge them with his saints: him the Most High
Rapt in a balmy cloud with winged steeds
Did, as thou saw'st, receive, to walk with God
High in salvation and the climes of bliss,
Exempt from death; to show thee what reward
710 Awaits the good, the rest what punishment;
Which now direct thine eyes and soon behold."

---

5. Enoch, who "walked with God: and he was
not; for God took him" (Genesis 5.24); Milton
elaborates on the story.
6. Here Enoch is more precisely identified by
generation, but neither he nor the other biblical

personages in these pageants are named. Apparently, Michael and Adam together see the pageants, and Michael (by God's illumination) can
interpret them rightly, but neither of the two
knows the names these persons will later bear.

He looked, and saw the face of things quite changed;
The brazen throat of war had ceased to roar,
All now was turned to jollity and game,
715 To luxury° and riot,° feast and dance,   *lust / debauchery*
Marrying or prostituting, as befell,
Rape or adultery, where passing fair°   *surpassing beauty*
Allured them; thence from cups to civil broils.
At length a reverend sire[7] among them came,
720 And of their doings great dislike declared,
And testified against their ways; he oft
Frequented their assemblies, whereso met,
Triumphs or festivals, and to them preached
Conversion and repentance, as to souls
725 In prison under judgments imminent:
But all in vain: which when he saw, he ceased
Contending, and removed his tents far off;
Then from the mountain hewing timber tall,
Began to build a vessel of huge bulk,
730 Measured by cubit, length, and breadth, and height,
Smeared round with pitch, and in the side a door
Contrived, and of provisions laid in large
For man and beast: when lo a wonder strange!
Of every beast, and bird, and insect small
735 Came sevens and pairs, and entered in, as taught
Their order: last the sire and his three sons
With their four wives; and God made fast the door.
Meanwhile the south wind rose, and with black wings
Wide hovering, all the clouds together drove
740 From under heav'n; the hills to their supply°   *assistance*
Vapor, and exhalation dusk° and moist,   *dark mist*
Sent up amain;° and now the thickened sky   *with main force*
Like a dark ceiling stood; down rushed the rain
Impetuous, and continued till the earth
745 No more was seen; the floating vessel swum
Uplifted; and secure with beakèd prow
Rode tilting o'er the waves, all dwellings else
Flood overwhelmed, and them with all their pomp
Deep underwater rolled; sea covered sea,
750 Sea without shore;[8] and in their palaces
Where luxury late reigned, sea monsters whelped
And stabled; of mankind, so numerous late,
All left, in one small bottom° swum embarked.   *boat*
How didst thou grieve then, Adam, to behold
755 The end of all thy offspring, end so sad,
Depopulation; thee another flood,
Of tears and sorrow a flood thee also drowned,
And sunk thee as thy sons; till gently reared
By th' angel, on thy feet thou stood'st at last,
760 Though comfortless, as when a father mourns

7. Noah. Milton's account is based on Genesis 6–9.
8. The "sea without shore" and some other features of this description are taken from Ovid's account of Deucalion's Flood (*Metamorphoses* 1.292–300, Sandys translation).

His children, all in view destroyed at once;
And scarce to th' angel utter'dst thus thy plaint:
  "O visions ill foreseen! Better had I
Lived ignorant of future, so had borne
765   My part of evil only, each day's lot
Enough to bear; those now, that were dispensed
The burd'n of many ages, on me light
At once, by my foreknowledge[9] gaining birth
Abortive, to torment me ere their being,
770   With thought that they must be. Let no man seek
Henceforth to be foretold what shall befall
Him or his children, evil he may be sure,
Which neither his foreknowing can prevent,
And he the future evil shall no less
775   In apprehension than in substance feel
Grievous to bear: but that care now is past,
Man is not whom to warn:[1] those few escaped
Famine and anguish will at last consume
Wand'ring that wat'ry desert: I had hope
780   When violence was ceased, and war on earth,
All would have then gone well, peace would have crowned
With length of happy days the race of man;
But I was far deceived; for now I see
Peace to corrupt no less than war to waste.
785   How comes it thus? Unfold, celestial guide,
And whether here the race of man will end."
   To whom thus Michael: "Those whom last thou saw'st
In triumph and luxurious wealth, are they
First seen in acts of prowess eminent
790   And great exploits, but of true virtue void;
Who having spilt much blood, and done much waste
Subduing nations, and achieved thereby
Fame in the world, high titles, and rich prey,
Shall change their course to pleasure, ease, and sloth,
795   Surfeit, and lust, till wantonness and pride
Raise out of friendship hostile deeds in peace.
The conquered also, and enslaved by war
Shall with their freedom lost all virtue lose
And fear of God, from whom their piety feigned
800   In sharp contést of battle found no aid
Against invaders; therefore cooled in zeal
Thenceforth shall practice how to live secure,
Worldly or dissolute, on what their lords
Shall leave them to enjoy, for th' earth shall bear
805   More than enough, that temperance may be tried:
So all shall turn degenerate, all depraved,
Justice and temperance, truth and faith forgot;[2]

---

9. The term suggests that Adam is experiencing something akin to God's foreknowledge, which the poem insists is not predestination. Adam knows what is to happen but can neither cause it nor prevent it.

1. I.e., there is no man to warn, all will die.
2. This passage (lines 797–807) may also allude to the backsliding Puritans who betrayed the Commonwealth in 1660 and have now taken on the vices of the restored royalists.

One man except, the only son of light
In a dark age, against example good,

810 Against allurement, custom, and a world
Offended;° fearless of reproach and scorn,   *hostile*
Or violence, he of their wicked ways
Shall them admonish, and before them set
The paths of righteousness, how much more safe,

815 And full of peace, denouncing° wrath to come   *proclaiming*
On their impenitence; and shall return
Of them derided, but of God observed
The one just man alive; by his command
Shall build a wondrous ark, as thou beheld'st,

820 To save himself and household from amidst
A world devote° to universal wrack.   *doomed*
No sooner he with them of man and beast
Select for life shall in the ark be lodged,
And sheltered round, but all the cataracts°   *floodgates*

825 Of heav'n set open on the earth shall pour
Rain day and night, all fountains of the deep
Broke up, shall heave the ocean to usurp
Beyond all bounds, till inundation rise
Above the highest hills: then shall this mount

830 Of Paradise by might of waves be moved
Out of his place, pushed by the hornèd flood,[3]
With all his verdure spoiled, and trees adrift
Down the great river to the op'ning gulf,[4]
And there take root an island salt and bare,

835 The haunt of seals and ores,° and sea mews'° clang.   *sea monsters / seagulls*
To teach thee that God áttributes to place
No sanctity, if none be thither brought
By men who there frequent, or therein dwell.
And now what further shall ensue, behold."

840 He looked, and saw the ark hull° on the flood,   *drift*
Which now abated, for the clouds were fled,
Driv'n by a keen north wind, that blowing dry
Wrinkled the face of deluge, as decayed;
And the clear sun on his wide wat'ry glass

845 Gazed hot, and of the fresh wave largely drew,
As after thirst, which made their flowing shrink
From standing lake to tripping° ebb, that stole   *running*
With soft foot towards the deep, who now had stopped
His sluices, as the heav'n his windows shut.

850 The ark no more now floats, but seems on ground
Fast on the top of some high mountain fixed.[5]
And now the tops of hills as rocks appear;
With clamor thence the rapid currents drive
Towards the retreating sea their furious tide.

855 Forthwith from out the ark a raven flies,
And after him, the surer messenger,

---

3. Classical river gods were often depicted as horned.

4. I.e., down the Euphrates to the Persian Gulf.

5. Mount Ararat (Genesis 8.4).

A dove sent forth once and again to spy
Green tree or ground whereon his foot may light;
The second time returning, in his bill
860 An olive leaf he brings, pacific sign:
Anon dry ground appears, and from his ark
The ancient sire descends with all his train;
Then with uplifted hands, and eyes devout,
Grateful to Heav'n, over his head beholds
865 A dewy cloud, and in the cloud a bow
Conspicuous with three listed colors gay,[6]
Betok'ning peace from God, and covenant new.
Whereat the heart of Adam erst so sad
Greatly rejoiced, and thus his joy broke forth:
870 "O thou who future things canst represent
As present, heav'nly instructor, I revive
At this last sight, assured that man shall live
With all the creatures, and their seed preserve.
Far less I now lament for one whole world
875 Of wicked sons destroyed, than I rejoice
For one man found so perfect and so just,
That God vouchsafes to raise another world
From him, and all his anger to forget.[7]
But say, what mean those colored streaks in heav'n,
880 Distended° as the brow of God appeased,   spread out
Or serve they as a flow'ry verge to bind
The fluid skirts of that same wat'ry cloud,
Lest it again dissolve and show'r the earth?"
To whom th' Archangel: "Dextrously thou aim'st;
885 So willingly doth God remit his ire,
Though late repenting him of man depraved,
Grieved at his heart, when looking down he saw
The whole earth filled with violence, and all flesh
Corrupting each their way; yet those removed,
890 Such grace shall one just man find in his sight,
That he relents, not to blot out mankind,
And makes a cov'nant[8] never to destroy
The earth again by flood, nor let the sea
Surpass his bounds, nor rain to drown the world
895 With man therein or beast; but when he brings
Over the earth a cloud, will therein set
His triple-colored bow, whereon to look
And call to mind his cov'nant: day and night,
Seed-time and harvest, heat and hoary frost
900 Shall hold their course, till fire purge all things new,
Both heav'n and earth, wherein the just shall dwell."[9]

---

6. The primary colors, red, yellow, and blue.
7. The language invites recognition of Noah as a type (foreshadowing) of Christ, the one "perfect" and "just" who will cause God to forget his anger.
8. The language of covenant makes this promise—that God will not again destroy the

earth by flood—a type of the "covenant of grace" through which God will save humankind.
9. The restoration of the orderly processes of nature after the Flood is identified as a type (foreshadowing) of the final renewal of all things after the final conflagration at the Last Judgment.

Book 12

The Arguments

The angel Michael continues from the Flood to relate what shall succeed;
then, in the mention of Abraham, comes by degrees to explain, who that Seed
of the Woman shall be, which was promised Adam and Eve in the Fall; his
incarnation, death, resurrection, and ascension; the state of the church till his
second coming. Adam greatly satisfied and recomforted by these relations and
promises descends the hill with Michael; wakens Eve, who all this while had
slept, but with gentle dreams composed to quietness of mind and submission.
Michael in either hand leads them out of Paradise, the fiery sword waving
behind them, and the Cherubim taking their stations to guard the place.

	As one who in his journey bates° at noon,	*stops for refreshment*
	Though bent on speed, so here the Archangel paused	
	Betwixt the world destroyed and world restored,	
	If Adam aught perhaps might interpose;	
5	Then with transition sweet new speech resumes:[1]	
	"Thus thou hast seen one world begin and end;	
	And man as from a second stock proceed.	
	Much thou hast yet to see, but I perceive	
	Thy mortal sight to fail; objects divine	
10	Must needs impair and weary human sense:	
	Henceforth what is to come I will relate,[2]	
	Thou therefore give due audience, and attend.	
	This second source of men, while yet but few,	
	And while the dread of judgment past remains	
15	Fresh in their minds, fearing the Deity,	
	With some regard to what is just and right	
	Shall lead their lives, and multiply apace,	
	Laboring the soil, and reaping plenteous crop,	
	Corn, wine, and oil; and from the herd or flock,	
20	Oft sacrificing bullock, lamb, or kid,	
	With large wine-offerings poured, and sacred feast,	
	Shall spend their days in joy unblamed, and dwell	
	Long time in peace by families and tribes	
	Under paternal rule; till one[3] shall rise	
25	Of proud ambitious heart, who not content	
	With fair equality, fraternal state,	
	Will arrogate dominion undeserved	
	Over his brethren, and quite dispossess	
	Concord and law of nature from the earth;	
30	Hunting (and men not beasts shall be his game)	
	With war and hostile snare such as refuse	
	Subjection to his empire tyrannous:	
	A mighty hunter thence he shall be styled°	*called*

---

1. The first five lines were added when Book 10 of the 1667 edition was divided to make Books 11 and 12 of the 1674 edition.
2. Adam no longer sees visions or pageants, as before, but simply listens to Michael's narration.
3. Nimrod (Genesis 10.8–10) is described as the first king, in terms that equate kingship itself with tyranny (lines 25–29).

Before the Lord, as in despite of Heav'n,
35　Or from Heav'n claiming second sov'reignty;[4]
And from rebellion shall derive his name,
Though of rebellion others he accuse.
He with a crew, whom like ambition joins
With him or under him to tyrannize,
40　Marching from Eden towards the west, shall find
The plain, wherein a black bituminous gurge°　　　　　　　*whirlpool*
Boils out from underground, the mouth of Hell;
Of brick, and of that stuff they cast° to build　　　　　　　*set about*
A city and tow'r,[5] whose top may reach to Heav'n;
45　And get themselves a name, lest far dispersed
In foreign lands their memory be lost,
Regardless whether good or evil fame.
But God who oft descends to visit men
Unseen, and through their habitations walks
50　To mark their doings, them beholding soon,
Comes down to see their city, ere the tower
Obstruct Heav'n tow'rs, and in derision sets
Upon their tongues a various° spirit to raze　　　　　　　*divisive*
Quite out their native language, and instead
55　To sow a jangling noise of words unknown:
Forthwith a hideous gabble[6] rises loud
Among the builders; each to other calls
Not understood, till hoarse, and all in rage,
As mocked they storm; great laughter was in Heav'n
60　And looking down, to see the hubbub strange
And hear the din; thus was the building left
Ridiculous, and the work Confusion[7] named."
　　Whereto thus Adam fatherly displeased:
"O execrable son so to aspire
65　Above his brethren, to himself assuming
Authority usurped, from God not giv'n:
He gave us only over beast, fish, fowl
Dominion absolute; that right we hold
By his donation; but man over men
70　He made not lord; such title to himself
Reserving, human left from human free.[8]
But this usurper his encroachment proud
Stays not on man; to God his tower intends
Siege and defiance: wretched man! What food
75　Will he convey up thither to sustain
Himself and his rash army, where thin air
Above the clouds will pine° his entrails gross,　　　　　　　*waste away*

4. Milton offers two explanations of the biblical phrase "Before the Lord": either he openly defied God ("despite") or he claimed divine right ("second sov'reignty") like the Stuart kings. Drawing on the (false) etymology linking the name Nimrod with the Hebrew word meaning "to rebel," Milton implies that the paradox developed in the next two lines (that he accuses others of rebellion but is himself a rebel against God) extends to other kings, especially Charles I, who accused his opponents in the civil war of rebellion.
5. Babylon is the city, Babel the tower.
6. Genesis 11.1–9 recounts the building of the Tower of Babel reaching to Heaven; God punished this presumption by confounding the builders' original language into multiple languages.
7. "Confusion" was taken to be the meaning of "Babel."
8. Adam states the assumption Milton often invokes to support republicanism.

And famish him of breath, if not of bread?"
    To whom thus Michael: "Justly thou abhorr'st
80 That son, who on the quiet state of men
Such trouble brought, affecting° to subdue   *aspiring*
Rational liberty; yet know withal,
Since thy original lapse, true liberty
Is lost, which always with right reason dwells
85 Twinned, and from her hath no dividual° being:[9]   *separate*
Reason in man obscured, or not obeyed,
Immediately inordinate desires
And upstart passions catch the government
From reason, and to servitude reduce
90 Man till then free. Therefore since he permits
Within himself unworthy powers to reign
Over free reason, God in judgment just
Subjects him from without to violent lords;
Who oft as undeservedly enthrall
95 His outward freedom: tyranny must be,
Though to the tyrant thereby no excuse.
Yet sometimes nations will decline so low
From virtue, which is reason, that no wrong,
But justice, and some fatal curse annexed
100 Deprives them of their outward liberty,
Their inward lost: witness th' irreverent son[1]
Of him who built the ark, who for the shame
Done to his father, heard this heavy curse,
'Servant of servants,' on his vicious race.[2]
105 Thus will this latter, as the former world,
Still tend from bad to worse, till God at last
Wearied with their iniquities, withdraw
His presence from among them, and avert
His holy eyes; resolving from thenceforth
110 To leave them to their own polluted ways;
And one peculiar° nation to select   *special*
From all the rest, of whom to be invoked,
A nation from one faithful man[3] to spring:
Him on this side Euphrates yet residing,
115 Bred up in idol-worship; O that men
(Canst thou believe?) should be so stupid grown,
While yet the patriarch[4] lived, who scaped the Flood,
As to forsake the living God, and fall
To worship their own work in wood and stone

9. As Milton (following classical theorists) often did, and as Abdiel did earlier (6.178–81), Michael links political to psychological servitude, and political liberty to inner freedom, i.e., the exercise of "right reason" and the control of passion. Loss of liberty is often (though not always) God's just punishment for national decline (lines 81–100). The long passage alludes to the "baseness" of the English in restoring monarchy in 1660.
1. Ham, son of Noah, who looked on the nakedness of his father and brought down the curse that his descendants would be "servant of servants" to their brethren (Genesis 9.22–25).
2. Tribe. "Race" did not then bear its modern sense, so Milton is probably thinking of the Canaanites (descendants of Ham's son Canaan), rather than black Africans; blacks were, however, classed among Ham's descendants, and this biblical text was often used to justify slavery.
3. Abraham, whose name means "father of many nations"; the passage is based on Genesis 11.27 to 25.10.
4. Noah, who lived for 350 years after the Flood.

120   For gods! Yet him God the Most High vouchsafes
     To call by vision from his father's house,
     His kindred and false gods, into a land
     Which he will show him, and from him will raise
     A mighty nation, and upon him show'r
125   His benediction so, that in his seed
     All nations shall be blest; he straight° obeys,   *immediately*
     Not knowing to what land, yet firm believes:
     I see him, but thou canst not,[5] with what faith
     He leaves his gods, his friends, and native soil
130   Ur[6] of Chaldaea, passing now the ford
     To Haran, after him a cumbrous train
     Of herds and flocks, and numerous servitude;°   *servants and slaves*
     Not wand'ring poor, but trusting all his wealth
     With God, who called him, in a land unknown.
135   Canaan he now attains, I see his tents
     Pitched about Sechem, and the neighboring plain
     Of Moreh; there by promise he receives
     Gift to his progeny of all that land;
     From Hamath northward to the desert south
140   (Things by their names I call, though yet unnamed)
     From Hermon east to the great western sea,[7]
     Mount Hermon, yonder sea, each place behold
     In prospect, as I point them; on the shore
     Mount Carmel; here the double-founted stream
145   Jordan, true limit eastward; but his sons
     Shall dwell to Senir, that long ridge of hills.[8]
     This ponder, that all nations of the earth
     Shall in his seed be blessed; by that Seed
     Is meant thy great Deliverer,[9] who shall bruise
150   The Serpent's head; whereof to thee anon
     Plainlier shall be revealed. This patriarch blest,
     Whom 'faithful Abraham'[1] due time shall call,
     A son, and of his son a grandchild leaves,
     Like him in faith, in wisdom, and renown;
155   The grandchild with twelve sons increased, departs
     From Canaan, to a land hereafter called
     Egypt, divided by the river Nile;
     See where it flows,[2] disgorging at seven mouths
     Into the sea: to sojourn in that land

---

5. Michael evidently continues to see the stories he recounts as visionary scenes or pageants; Adam must accept the story of Abraham "by faith," analogous to the faith Abraham himself displays.
6. Ur was on one bank of the Euphrates, Haran (line 131) on the other, to the northwest.
7. The Promised Land was bounded on the north by Hamath, a city on the Orontes River in west Syria; on the south by the wilderness "desert" of Zin; on the east by Mount Hermon; and on the west by the Mediterranean, the "great western sea."
8. "Mount Carmel": a mountain range near Haifa, on the Mediterranean coast of Israel;

"Jordan": the river thought incorrectly to have two sources ("double-founted"), the Jor and the Dan; "Senir": a peak of Mount Hermon.
9. Michael interprets the promise to Abraham (Genesis 17.5, "a father of many nations have I made thee") typologically, as to be fulfilled in Christ, the "Woman's Seed." See 10.180–81 and note 1, and 12.322–28, 12.600–601, 12.623.
1. Echoes Galatians 3.9: "So then they which be of faith are blessed with faithful Abraham." His son (line 153) is Isaac, and his grandson, Jacob.
2. Adam can see geographical features from his mountaintop, though not the scenes Michael sees and describes.

160 He comes invited by a younger son[3]
In time of dearth,° a son whose worthy deeds   *famine*
Raise him to be the second in that realm
Of Pharaoh: there he dies, and leaves his race
Growing into a nation, and now grown
165 Suspected to° a sequent° king, who seeks   *by / successive*
To stop their overgrowth, as inmate° guests   *foreign*
Too numerous; whence of guests he makes them slaves
Inhospitably, and kills their infant males:
Till by two brethren (those two brethren call
170 Moses and Aaron) sent from God to claim
His people from enthrallment, they return
With glory and spoil back to their promised land.[4]
But first the lawless tyrant, who denies°   *refuses*
To know their God, or message to regard,
175 Must be compelled by signs and judgments dire;[5]
To blood unshed the rivers must be turned,
Frogs, lice, and flies must all his palace fill
With loathed intrusion, and fill all the land;
His cattle must of rot and murrain° die,   *cattle plague*
180 Botches and blains must all his flesh emboss,[6]
And all his people; thunder mixed with hail,
Hail mixed with fire must rend th' Egyptian sky
And wheel on th' earth, devouring where it rolls;
What it devours not, herb, or fruit, or grain,
185 A darksome cloud of locusts swarming down
Must eat, and on the ground leave nothing green:
Darkness must overshadow all his bounds,
Palpable darkness, and blot out three days;
Last with one midnight stroke all the firstborn
190 Of Egypt must lie dead. Thus with ten wounds°   *plagues*
The river-dragon[7] tamed at length submits
To let his sojourners depart, and oft
Humbles his stubborn heart, but still as ice
More hardened after thaw, till in his rage
195 Pursuing whom he late dismissed, the sea
Swallows him with his host, but them lets pass
As on dry land between two crystal walls,
Awed by the rod of Moses so to stand
Divided, till his rescued gain their shore:[8]
200 Such wondrous power God to his saint will lend,
Though present in his angel, who shall go
Before them in a cloud, and pillar of fire,

3. Joseph, the next youngest of Jacob's twelve sons, invited the Israelites to Egypt to escape famine, but they were subsequently made slaves (Genesis 21–50).
4. The story of Moses and Aaron leading the Israelites from captivity to the Promised Land is told in Exodus and Deuteronomy.
5. The ten plagues, recounted in lines 176–90.
6. "Botches": boils; "blains": blisters; "emboss": cover as with studs.
7. The Egyptian pharaoh is termed "the great dragon that lieth in the midst of his rivers" (Ezekiel 29.3).
8. The Red Sea was parted by the rod of Moses; the Israelites passed through, but Pharaoh's pursuing forces drowned as the water rushed back (Exodus 13.17–22 and 14.5–31).

By day a cloud, by night a pillar of fire,
To guide them in their journey,[9] and remove
205 Behind them, while th' obdúrate king pursues:
All night he will pursue, but his approach
Darkness defends° between till morning watch;   *prevents*
Then through the fiery pillar and the cloud
God looking forth will trouble all his host
210 And craze° their chariot wheels: when by command   *shatter*
Moses once more his potent rod extends
Over the sea; the sea his rod obeys;
On their embattled ranks the waves return,
And overwhelm their war:° the race elect   *armies*
215 Safe towards Canaan from the shore advance
Through the wild desert, not the readiest way,
Lest ent'ring on the Canaanite alarmed°   *prepared to fight*
War terrify them inexpert, and fear
Return them back to Egypt, choosing rather
220 Inglorious life with servitude; for life
To noble and ignoble is more sweet
Untrained in arms, where rashness leads not on.[1]
This also shall they gain by their delay
In the wide wilderness, there they shall found
225 Their government, and their great senate[2] choose
Through the twelve tribes, to rule by laws ordained:
God from the mount of Sinai, whose gray top
Shall tremble, he descending, will himself
In thunder, lightning, and loud trumpet's sound
230 Ordain them laws; part such as appertain
To civil justice, part religious rites
Of sacrifice,[3] informing them, by types
And shadows, of that destined Seed to bruise
The Serpent, by what means he shall achieve
235 Mankind's deliverance.[4] But the voice of God
To mortal ear is dreadful; they beseech
That Moses might report to them his will,
And terror cease; he grants what they besought
Instructed that to God is no access
240 Without mediator, whose high office now
Moses in figure[5] bears, to introduce
One greater, of whose day he shall foretell,
And all the prophets in their age the times
Of great Messiah shall sing. Thus laws and rites
245 Established, such delight hath God in men

---

9. Milton repeats here a view developed in his *Christian Doctrine*, that God was "present in his angel," not in his own person, in the cloud and pillar of fire that led the Israelites on their journey (Exodus 13.21–22).

1. I.e., unless prompted by "rashness," those "untrained in arms" will choose servitude rather than battle.

2. The "Seventy Elders" of the Sanhedrin, whom Milton cites as a model for republican government in his *Ready and Easy Way.*

3. God delivered ceremonial, civil, and moral/religious laws (the Ten Commandments) to Moses on Mount Sinai, with thunder and lightning (lines 227–32; Exodus 19–31).

4. The principle of typology, whereby persons and events in the Old Testament are seen to prefigure Christ or matters pertaining to his life or the Christian church.

5. Moses is a type of Christ in his role as mediator between the people and God.

Obedient to his will, that he vouchsafes
Among them to set up his tabernacle,
The Holy One with mortal men to dwell:
By his prescript a sanctuary is framed
250 Of cedar, overlaid with gold, therein
An ark, and in the ark his testimony,
The records of his cov'nant, over these
A mercy-seat of gold between the wings
Of two bright Cherubim, before him burn
255 Seven lamps as in a zodiac° representing   *like the planets*
The heav'nly fires; over the tent a cloud
Shall rest by day, a fiery gleam by night,
Save when they journey, and at length they come,
Conducted by his angel to the land
260 Promised to Abraham and his seed: the rest
Were long to tell, how many battles fought,
How many kings destroyed, and kingdoms won,
Or how the sun shall in mid-heav'n stand still
A day entire, and night's due course adjourn,
265 Man's voice commanding, 'Sun in Gibeon stand,
And thou moon in the vale of Aialon,
Till Israel overcome';[6] so call the third
From Abraham, son of Isaac, and from him
His whole descent,[7] who thus shall Canaan win."
270   Here Adam interposed: "O sent from Heav'n,
Enlight'ner of my darkness, gracious things
Thou hast revealed, those chiefly which concern
Just Abraham and his seed: now first I find
Mine eyes true op'ning, and my heart much eased,
275 Erewhile perplexed with thoughts what would become
Of me and all mankind; but now I see
His day, in whom all nations shall be blest,[8]
Favor unmerited by me, who sought
Forbidden knowledge by forbidden means.
280 This yet I apprehend not, why to those
Among whom God will deign to dwell on earth
So many and so various laws are giv'n;
So many laws argue so many sins
Among them; how can God with such reside?"
285   To whom thus Michael: "Doubt not but that sin
Will reign among them, as of thee begot;
And therefore was law given them to evince°   *make evident*
Their natural pravity,° by stirring up   *original sin*
Sin against law to fight; that when they see
290 Law can discover sin, but not remove,
Save by those shadowy expiations weak,
The blood of bulls and goats, they may conclude

---

6. The story of Joshua, at whose bidding the sun
stood still in Gibeon, and the moon in Ajalon (both
a few miles north of Jerusalem), until Israel won its
battle against the Amorites (Joshua 10.12–23).
7. Isaac's son Jacob was named Israel, and his

descendants after him (Genesis 33.28).
8. Adam supposes that the promise made to him
is fulfilled in the covenant with Abraham; he has
yet to understand that in this Abraham is a type
of Christ.

Some blood more precious must be paid for man,
Just for unjust, that in such righteousness
295 To them by faith imputed, they may find
Justification towards God, and peace
Of conscience,[9] which the law by ceremonies
Cannot appease, nor man the moral part
Perform, and not performing cannot live.[1]
300 So law appears imperfect, and but giv'n
With purpose to resign° them in full time   *yield*
Up to a better cov'nant, disciplined
From shadowy types to truth, from flesh to spirit,
From imposition of strict laws, to free
305 Acceptance of large grace, from servile fear
To filial, works of law to works of faith.[2]
And therefore shall not Moses, though of God
Highly beloved, being but the minister
Of law, his people into Canaan lead;
310 But Joshua whom the Gentiles Jesus call,[3]
His name and office bearing, who shall quell
The adversary Serpent, and bring back
Through the world's wilderness long-wandered man
Safe to eternal paradise of rest.
315 Meanwhile they in their earthly Canaan placed
Long time shall dwell and prosper, but when sins
National interrupt their public peace,
Provoking God to raise them enemies:
From whom as oft he saves them penitent°   *when penitent*
320 By judges first, then under kings; of whom
The second, both for piety renowned
And puissant° deeds, a promise shall receive   *mighty*
Irrevocable, that his regal throne
Forever shall endure;[4] the like shall sing
325 All prophecy, that of the royal stock
Of David (so I name this king) shall rise
A son, the Woman's Seed to thee foretold,[5]
Foretold to Abraham, as in whom shall trust
All nations, and to kings foretold, of kings
330 The last, for of his reign shall be no end.
But first a long succession must ensue,
And his next son for wealth and wisdom famed,
The clouded ark of God till then in tents
Wand'ring, shall in a glorious temple enshrine.[6]

---

9. The ceremonial sacrifices of "bulls and goats" under the Law are types, "shadowy expiations," pointing to Christ's efficacious sacrifice that alone can win "Justification" for humankind, by Christ's merits being "imputed" (attributed vicariously) to them through faith (lines 290–96).
1. The theological doctrine that the Law is intended to lead humans to the "better cov'nant" (line 302) of grace, by demonstrating that fallen men cannot fulfill the commandments of the Law or appease God through ceremonial sacrifices (lines 297–302).

2. A more complete explanation of the principle of typology.
3. "Jesus" is the Greek equivalent of the Hebrew "Joshua," who, rather than Moses, led the children of Israel into the Promised Land of Canaan, being in this a type of Christ.
4. The history summarized in lines 315–30 is recounted in Judges, Samuel, and Kings.
5. The Messiah was prophesied to come of David's line, and Jesus was referred to as the "Son of David."
6. Solomon, son of David, built a "glorious temple" to house the Ark of the Covenant.

335 Such follow him, as shall be registered
    Part good, part bad, of bad the longer scroll,
    Whose foul idolatries and other faults
    Heaped° to the popular sum, will so incense   *added*
    God, as to leave them, and expose their land,
340 Their city, his temple, and his holy ark
    With all his sacred things, a scorn and prey
    To that proud city, whose high walls thou saw'st
    Left in confusion, Babylon thence called.
    There in captivity he lets them dwell
345 The space of seventy years,[7] then brings them back,
    Rememb'ring mercy, and his cov'nant sworn
    To David, stablished as the days of Heav'n.
    Returned from Babylon by leave of kings[8]
    Their lords, whom God disposed,° the house of God   *made well-disposed*
350 They first re-edify, and for a while
    In mean estate live moderate, till grown
    In wealth and multitude, factious they grow;
    But first among the priests dissension springs,
    Men who attend the altar, and should most
355 Endeavor peace: their strife pollution brings
    Upon the Temple itself: at last they seize
    The scepter, and regard not David's sons,°   *descendants*
    Then lose it to a stranger,[9] that the true
    Anointed King Messiah might be born
360 Barred of his right; yet at his birth a star
    Unseen before in heav'n proclaims him come,
    And guides the eastern sages,° who inquire   *the Magi*
    His place, to offer incense, myrrh, and gold;
    His place of birth a solemn° angel tells   *awe-inspiring*
365 To simple shepherds, keeping watch by night;
    They gladly thither haste, and by a choir
    Of squadroned angels hear his carol sung.
    A virgin is his mother, but his sire
    The Power of the Most High; he shall ascend
370 The throne hereditary, and bound his reign
    With earth's wide bounds, his glory with the heav'ns."
       He ceased, discerning Adam with such joy
    Surcharged,° as had like grief been dewed in tears,   *overwhelmed*
    Without the vent of words, which these he breathed:
375   "O prophet of glad tidings, finisher
    Of utmost hope! now clear I understand
    What oft my steadiest thoughts have searched in vain,
    Why our great expectation should be called
    The Seed of Woman: Virgin Mother, hail,

---

7. The seventy-year Babylonian Captivity of the Jews and destruction of the Temple (6th century B.C.E.).
8. The Persian kings Cyrus the Great, Darius, and Artaxerxes allowed the Jews to return from Babylon and rebuild the Temple.
9. Antiochus, father of Herod the Great (who ruled at the time of Christ's birth), was made gov-ernor of Jerusalem in 61 B.C.E. by the Romans, and procurator of Judaea in 47 B.C.E. Prior to this (lines 353–57), strife among the priests allowed the Seleucid king Antiochus IV to sack Jerusalem and pollute the Temple; then one of the Macca-bees seized the throne, disregarding the claims of David's dynasty.

380 High in the love of Heav'n, yet from my loins
Thou shalt proceed, and from thy womb the Son
Of God Most High; so God with man unites.
Needs must the Serpent now his capital° bruise   *on the head, fatal*
Expect with mortal pain: say where and when
385 Their fight, what stroke shall bruise the victor's heel."
    To whom thus Michael: "Dream not of their fight,
As of a duel, or the local wounds
Of head or heel: not therefore joins the Son
Manhood to Godhead, with more strength to foil
390 Thy enemy; nor so is overcome
Satan, whose fall from Heav'n, a deadlier bruise,
Disabled not to give thee thy death's wound:
Which he who comes thy Savior, shall recure,°   *heal*
Not by destroying Satan, but his works
395 In thee and in thy seed: nor can this be,
But by fulfilling that which thou didst want,°   *lack*
Obedience to the law of God, imposed
On penalty of death, and suffering death,
The penalty to thy transgression due,
400 And due to theirs which out of thine will grow:
So only can high justice rest apaid.°   *satisfied*
The law of God exact he shall fulfill
Both by obedience and by love, though love
Alone fulfill the law; thy punishment
405 He shall endure by coming in the flesh
To a reproachful life and cursèd death,
Proclaiming life to all who shall believe
In his redemption, and that his obedience
Imputed becomes theirs by faith, his merits
410 To save them, not their own, though legal works.[1]
For this he shall live hated, be blasphemed,
Seized on by force, judged, and to death condemned
A shameful and accursed, nailed to the cross
By his own nation, slain for bringing life;
415 But to the cross he nails thy enemies,
The law that is against thee, and the sins
Of all mankind, with him there crucified,
Never to hurt them more who rightly trust
In this his satisfaction; so he dies,
420 But soon revives, Death over him no power
Shall long usurp; ere the third dawning light
Return, the stars of morn shall see him rise
Out of his grave, fresh as the dawning light,
Thy ransom paid, which man from Death redeems,
425 His death for man, as many as offered life
Neglect not,[2] and the benefit embrace
By faith not void of works: this Godlike act

---

1. Michael restates the theological doctrine that humans can be saved only by Christ's merits attributed to them vicariously ("imputed"), not by their own good works performed according to God's law ("legal").
2. I.e., for as many as accept ("neglect not") his offer of life.

Annuls thy doom, the death thou shouldst have died,
In sin forever lost from life; this act
430 Shall bruise the head of Satan, crush his strength
Defeating Sin and Death, his two main arms,
And fix far deeper in his head their stings
Than temporal death shall bruise the victor's heel,
Or theirs whom he redeems, a death like sleep,
435 A gentle wafting to immortal life.
Nor after resurrection shall he stay
Longer on earth than certain times to appear
To his disciples, men who in his life
Still followed him; to them shall leave in charge
440 To teach all nations what of him they learned
And his salvation, them who shall believe
Baptizing in the profluent° stream, the sign   *flowing*
Of washing them from guilt of sin to life
Pure, and in mind prepared, if so befall,
445 For death, like that which the Redeemer died.
All nations they shall teach; for from that day
Not only to the sons of Abraham's loins
Salvation shall be preached, but to the sons
Of Abraham's faith wherever through the world;
450 So in his seed all nations shall be blest.[3]
Then to the Heav'n of Heav'ns he shall ascend
With victory, triumphing through the air
Over his foes and thine; there shall surprise
The Serpent, prince of air, and drag in chains
455 Through all his realm, and there confounded leave;
Then enter into glory, and resume
His seat at God's right hand, exalted high
Above all names in Heav'n; and thence shall come,
When this world's dissolution shall be ripe
460 With glory and power to judge both quick° and dead,   *living*
To judge th' unfaithful dead, but to reward
His faithful, and receive them into bliss,
Whether in Heav'n or earth, for then the earth
Shall all be paradise, far happier place
465 Than this of Eden, and far happier days."
      So spake th' Archangel Michaël, then paused,
As at the world's great period;° and our sire   *consummation*
Replete with joy and wonder thus replied:
      "O goodness infinite, goodness immense!
470 That all this good of evil shall produce,
And evil turn to good; more wonderful
Than that which by creation first brought forth
Light out of darkness! Full of doubt I stand,
Whether I should repent me now of sin
475 By me done and occasioned, or rejoice
Much more, that much more good thereof shall spring,
To God more glory, more good will to men

---

3. Michael spells out the application to Christ of the promise offered typologically to Abraham's seed.

From God, and over wrath grace shall abound.[4]
But say, if our Deliverer up to Heav'n
480 Must reascend, what will betide the few
His faithful, left among th' unfaithful herd,
The enemies of truth; who then shall guide
His people, who defend? Will they not deal
Worse with his followers than with him they dealt?"
485   "Be sure they will," said th' angel; "but from Heav'n
He to his own a Comforter will send,[5]
The promise of the Father, who shall dwell
His Spirit within them, and the law of faith
Working through love, upon their hearts shall write,
490 To guide them in all truth, and also arm
With spiritual armor, able to resist
Satan's assaults, and quench his fiery darts,[6]
What° man can do against them, not afraid,   *as much as*
Though to the death, against such cruelties
495 With inward consolations recompensed,
And oft supported so as shall amaze
Their proudest persecutors: for the Spirit
Poured first on his apostles, whom he sends
To evangelize the nations, then on all
500 Baptized, shall them with wondrous gifts endue°   *endow*
To speak all tongues, and do all miracles,
As did their Lord before them. Thus they win
Great numbers of each nation to receive
With joy the tidings brought from Heav'n: at length
505 Their ministry performed, and race well run,
Their doctrine and their story written left,[7]
They die; but in their room, as they forewarn,
Wolves shall succeed for teachers, grievous wolves,
Who all the sacred mysteries of Heav'n
510 To their own vile advantages shall turn
Of lucre° and ambition, and the truth   *wealth*
With superstitions and traditions taint,[8]
Left only in those written records pure,
Though not but by the Spirit understood.
515 Then shall they seek to avail themselves of names,°   *honors*
Places° and titles, and with these to join   *offices*
Secular power, though feigning still to act
By spiritual, to themselves appropriating

---

4. These lines do not formulate the medieval idea of the *felix culpa*—that the Fall was fortunate in bringing humans greater happiness than they would otherwise have enjoyed—only that the Fall has provided God an occasion to bring still greater good out of evil. The poem makes clear that Adam and Eve would have grown in perfection and advanced to Heaven had they not sinned.
5. The Holy Spirit, who for Milton is much subordinate to both Father and Son.
6. Cf. Ephesians 6.11–16: "Put on the whole armor of God, that ye may be able to stand against the wiles of the devil. . . . Above all, tak-

ing the shield of faith, wherewith ye shall be able to quench all the fiery darts of the wicked." The subsequent history (lines 493–507) is that of the early Christian church in apostolic times.
7. I.e., in the Gospels and Epistles.
8. The history summarized in lines 508–40 is of the corruption of the Christian church by superstitions, traditions, and persecutions of conscience in patristic times under the popes and the Christian emperors, but also extending to the Last Day. The terms point especially to what Milton saw as the revival of "popish" superstitions in the English church of the Restoration and to the fierce persecution of dissenters.

The Spirit of God, promised alike and giv'n
520 To all believers; and from that pretense,
Spiritual laws by carnal° power shall force   *fleshly, worldly*
On every conscience;⁹ laws which none shall find
Left them enrolled, or what the Spirit within
Shall on the heart engrave.¹ What will they then
525 But force the Spirit of Grace itself, and bind
His consort Liberty; what, but unbuild
His living temples,² built by faith to stand,
Their own faith not another's: for on earth
Who against faith and conscience can be heard
530 Infallible?³ Yet many will presume:
Whence heavy persecution shall arise
On all who in the worship persevere
Of Spirit and Truth; the rest, far greater part,
Will deem in outward rites and specious forms
535 Religion satisfied; Truth shall retire
Bestuck with sland'rous darts, and works of faith
Rarely be found: so shall the world go on,
To good malignant, to bad men benign,
Under her own weight groaning, till the day
540 Appear of respiration° to the just,   *respite*
And vengeance to the wicked, at return
Of him so lately promised to thy aid,
The Woman's Seed,⁴ obscurely then foretold,
Now amplier known thy Savior and thy Lord,
545 Last in the clouds from Heav'n to be revealed
In glory of the Father, to dissolve
Satan with his perverted world, then raise
From the conflagrant mass,° purged and refined,   *the burning world*
New heav'ns, new earth, ages of endless date
550 Founded in righteousness and peace of love,
To bring forth fruits joy and eternal bliss."
        He ended; and thus Adam last replied:
"How soon hath thy prediction, seer blest,
Measured this transient world, the race of time,
555 Till time stand fixed: beyond is all abyss,
Eternity, whose end no eye can reach.
Greatly instructed I shall hence depart,
Greatly in peace of thought, and have my fill
Of knowledge, what° this vessel can contain;   *as much as*
560 Beyond which was my folly to aspire.
Henceforth I learn, that to obey is best,

9. These lines affirm the Protestant principle of every Christian's right to interpret Scripture according to the "inner light" of the Spirit, and denounce (as Milton consistently did in his tracts) the use of civil ("carnal") power to enforce orthodoxy.
1. I.e., there is nothing in Scripture or in the Spirit's inner teaching that sanctions persecution for conscience.
2. Cf. 1 Corinthians 3.16: "Know ye not that ye are the temple of God?" "His consort Liberty":

Milton typically insists that Christ's gospel and the Spirit of God teach liberty, religious and civil, alluding as here to 2 Corinthians 3.17: "where the Spirit of the Lord is, there is liberty."
3. An attack on papal claims to infallibility, asserted though not yet proclaimed as doctrine.
4. Michael's story ends with the full explication of the promised "Woman's Seed" as Christ, and with the renewal of all things after the Last Judgment (lines 545–51).

And love with fear the only God, to walk
As in his presence, ever to observe
His providence, and on him sole depend,
565   Merciful over all his works, with good
Still overcoming evil, and by small
Accomplishing great things, by things deemed weak
Subverting worldly strong, and worldly wise
By simply meek; that suffering for truth's sake
570   Is fortitude to highest victory,
And to the faithful death the gate of life;
Taught this by his example whom I now
Acknowledge my Redeemer ever blest."
    To whom thus also th' angel last replied:
575   "This having learnt, thou hast attained the sum
Of wisdom; hope no higher, though all the stars
Thou knew'st by name,[5] and all th' ethereal powers,
All secrets of the deep, all nature's works,
Or works of God in heav'n, air, earth, or sea,
580   And all the riches of this world enjoy'dst,
And all the rule, one empire; only add
Deeds to thy knowledge answerable,° add faith,   *corresponding*
Add virtue, patience, temperance, add love,
By name to come called charity, the soul
585   Of all the rest: then wilt thou not be loath
To leave this Paradise, but shalt possess
A paradise within thee, happier far.
Let us descend now therefore from this top
Of speculation;° for the hour precise   *hill of speculation*
590   Exacts° our parting hence; and see the guards,   *requires*
By me encamped on yonder hill, expect
Their motion,° at whose front a flaming sword,   *await their orders*
In signal of remove, waves fiercely round;
We may no longer stay: go, waken Eve;
595   Her also I with gentle dreams have calmed
Portending good, and all her spirits composed
To meek submission: thou at season fit
Let her with thee partake what thou hast heard,
Chiefly what may concern her faith to know,
600   The great deliverance by her seed to come
(For by the Woman's Seed) on all mankind.
That ye may live, which will be many days,
Both in one faith unanimous though sad,
With cause for evils past, yet much more cheered
605   With meditation on the happy end."
    He ended, and they both descend the hill;
Descended, Adam to the bow'r where Eve
Lay sleeping ran before, but found her waked;
And thus with words not sad she him received:
610   "Whence thou return'st, and whither went'st, I know;

---

5. Michael glances back at Raphael's warning in Book 8 that Adam should concern himself first with matters pertaining to his own life and world, rather than speculating overmuch about the cosmos.

For God is also in sleep, and dreams advise,[6]
Which he hath sent propitious, some great good
Presaging, since with sorrow and heart's distress
Wearied I fell asleep: but now lead on;
615 In me is no delay; with thee to go,
Is to stay here; without thee here to stay,
Is to go hence unwilling; thou to me
Art all things under heav'n, all places thou,[7]
Who for my willful crime art banished hence.
620 This further consolation yet secure
I carry hence; though all by me is lost,
Such favor I unworthy am vouchsafed,
By me the promised Seed shall all restore."
     So spake our mother Eve, and Adam heard
625 Well pleased, but answered not; for now too nigh
Th' Archangel stood, and from the other hill
To their fixed station, all in bright array
The Cherubim descended; on the ground
Gliding metéorous,° as evening mist   *like a meteor*
630 Ris'n from a river o'er the marish° glides,   *marsh*
And gathers ground fast at the laborer's heel
Homeward returning. High in front advanced,
The brandished sword of God before them blazed
Fierce as a comet; which with torrid heat,
635 And vapor° as the Libyan air adust,°   *smoke / parched*
Began to parch that temperate clime; whereat
In either hand the hast'ning angel caught
Our ling'ring parents, and to th' eastern gate
Led them direct, and down the cliff as fast
640 To the subjected° plain; then disappeared.   *low-lying*
They looking back, all th' eastern side beheld
Of Paradise, so late their happy seat,°   *estate*
Waved over by that flaming brand,° the gate   *sword*
With dreadful faces thronged and fiery arms:
645 Some natural tears they dropped, but wiped them soon;
The world was all before them, where to choose
Their place of rest, and Providence their guide:
They hand in hand with wand'ring steps and slow,
Through Eden took their solitary way.

1674

---

6. The lines suggest that Eve's dream has provided her a parallel (if lesser) prophecy to Adam's
visions and instruction. Cf. Numbers 12.6: "If
there be a prophet among you, I the Lord will
make myself known unto him in a vision, and
will speak unto him in a dream."
7. Eve's lines—the final speech in the poem—
recall her prelapsarian love song to Adam
(4.641ff.) and Ruth's promise to accompany her
mother-in-law, Naomi (Ruth 1.16).

Samson Agonistes A violent and promiscuous strongman given to playing brutal practical jokes on his enemies, Samson may not seem a compelling tragic hero. Yet Milton's interest in his story, told in the biblical Book of Judges, was long-standing. In a notebook he kept in the 1640s, he sketched out ideas for a Samson play that he seems not to have immediately pursued. Although its date of composition is uncertain, *Samson Agonistes* was not published until 1671, when it was included in a volume with Milton's "brief epic," *Paradise Regained*. The story of Samson as Milton tells it, blinded and imprisoned by his enemies but still endowed with astounding god-given faculties, may have had a special pertinence for the author in the period after 1660. In these years, the aging, blind poet saw his revolutionary political dreams definitively crushed, but also at last finished the great series of poems he had felt called to write all his life.

The name of the tragedy, combining the Hebrew name Samson with the Greek word *agonistes,* meaning "one who struggles," announces that like much of Milton's work it will combine biblical stories and classical literary techniques. *Samson Agonistes* is a "closet drama," designed for reading rather than for stage performance. Like Greek drama but unlike the tragedies performed in Milton's time, it observes the unity of time and place, eschews violence on the imagined stage, and employs a Chorus to comment on the hero and his situation. The play is structured as a series of encounters: with the Chorus; with Samson's father, Manoa; with Samson's wife, Dalila; and with a blustering challenger, Harapha. Over the course of these encounters, Samson must come to terms with his own apparently disastrous choices and with the treachery of those he had trusted. Because of his extraordinary gifts, some of the rules that normally govern human behavior do not apply to him, but he must then consider how to act properly in the absence of such rules. His struggle to understand his situation is mirrored in the reader's interpretive dilemmas. Throughout the tragedy, especially at its cataclysmic end, we must ask to what extent Samson's failures and suffering in fact continue to serve the inscrutable design of Providence.

Samson Agonistes

A DRAMATIC POEM

Of That Sort of Dramatic Poem Which Is Called Tragedy

Tragedy, as it was anciently composed, hath been ever held the gravest, moralest, and most profitable of all other poems: therefore said by Aristotle to be of power, by raising pity and fear, or terror, to purge the mind of those and suchlike passions, that is, to temper and reduce them to just measure with a kind of delight, stirred up by reading or seeing those passions well imitated.[1] Nor is Nature wanting in her own effects to make good his assertion; for so, in physic, things of melancholic hue and quality are used against melancholy, sour against sour, salt to remove salt humors.[2] Hence philosophers and other gravest writers, as Cicero, Plutarch, and others, frequently cite out of tragic poets, both to adorn and illustrate their discourse. The Apostle Paul himself thought it not unworthy to insert a verse of Euripides into the text of Holy Scripture, 1 Cor. 15.33; and Paraeus, commenting on the Revelation, divides the whole book, as a tragedy, into acts, distinguished each by a chorus of heavenly harpings and song between.[3] Heretofore men in highest dignity have

1. Milton is paraphrasing Aristotle's *Poetics* 6.
2. Italian Renaissance critics had applied notions of homeopathic medicine (like cures like) to tragedy; the idea is not Aristotelean. "Physic": medicine.
3. David Paraeus (1548–1622) was a German Calvinist who wrote biblical commentaries.

labored not a little to be thought able to compose a tragedy. Of that honor Dionysius the elder was no less ambitious, than before of his attaining to the tyranny.[4] Augustus Caesar also had begun his *Ajax*, but unable to please his own judgment with what he had begun, left it unfinished. Seneca the philosopher is by some thought the author of those tragedies (at least the best of them) that go under that name. Gregory Nazianzen, a Father of the Church, thought it not unbeseeming the sanctity of his person to write a tragedy, which he entitled *Christ Suffering*.[5] This is mentioned to vindicate tragedy from the small esteem, or rather infamy, which in the account of many it undergoes at this day, with other common interludes[6]—happening through the poet's error of intermixing comic stuff with tragic sadness and gravity, or introducing trivial and vulgar persons, which by all judicious hath been counted absurd, and brought in without discretion, corruptly to gratify the people. And, though ancient tragedy use no prologue,[7] yet using sometimes, in case of self-defense or explanation, that which Martial calls an epistle;[8] in behalf of this tragedy, coming forth after the ancient manner, much different from what among us passes for best, thus much beforehand may be epistled: that chorus is here introduced after the Greek manner, not ancient only, but modern, and still in use among the Italians.[9] In the modeling therefore of this poem, with good reason, the ancients and Italians are rather followed, as of much more authority and fame. The measure of verse used in the chorus is of all sorts, called by the Greeks *monostrophic*,[1] or rather *apolelymenon*,[2] without regard had to strophe, antistrophe, or epode, which were a kind of stanzas framed only for the music, then used with the chorus that sung; not essential to the poem, and therefore not material; or, being divided into stanzas or pauses, they may be called *alloeostropha*.[3] Division into act and scene, referring chiefly to the stage (to which this work never was intended), is here omitted.[4] It suffices if the whole drama be found not produced[5] beyond the fifth act.

Of the style and uniformity, and that commonly called the plot, whether intricate or explicit—which is nothing indeed but such economy, or disposition of the fable, as may stand best with verisimilitude and decorum[6]—they only will best judge who are not unacquainted with Aeschylus, Sophocles, and Euripides, the three tragic poets unequaled yet by any, and the best rule to all who endeavor to write tragedy. The circumscription of time wherein the whole drama begins and ends is, according to ancient rule and best example, within the space of twenty-four hours.[7]

4. Dionysius (4th century B.C.E.) won a prize at Athens for tragedy, after becoming tyrant of Syracuse.

5. Seneca the philosopher was indeed the author of tragedies; but Gregory Nazianzen, a Greek ecclesiastic of the 4th century, did not write the tragedy *Christ Suffering*, which scholarly opinion of Milton's day attributed to him.

6. Stage plays.

7. Prologues and epilogues were frequent on the Restoration stage; Milton sets himself apart from contemporary styles.

8. Martial, the Roman epigrammatist of the 1st century C.E., prefixed an epistle to his book of epigrams.

9. For example, Tasso's tragedy *Re Torrismondo* was modeled closely on classical examples.

1. Not divided into strophe, antistrophe, and epode.

2. Free from stanzaic patterns altogether.

3. With various forms of strophe, irregular.

4. It is not hard to divide Milton's drama into the customary five acts, each ending with a chorus: act 1 (Samson and Chorus), lines 1–325; 2 (Samson and Manoa), 326–709; 3 (Samson and Dalila), 710–1060; 4 (Samson and Harapha), 1061–1296; 5 (Catastrophe), 1297–the end.

5. Drawn out.

6. "Decorum," for a Renaissance writer, is not simply solemn or sedate behavior but the use of appropriate and suitable style, depending on speaker, subject, setting, genre, and so on. "Intricate or explicit": complex or simple.

7. The so-called unity of time, limiting dramatic action to twenty-four hours, was derived from Aristotle's *Poetics* by the Renaissance critic Castelvetro.

The Argument

Samson, made captive, blind, and now in the prison at Gaza,[8] there to labor as in a common workhouse, on a festival day, in the general cessation from labor, comes forth into the open air, to a place nigh, somewhat retired, there to sit a while and bemoan his condition. Where he happens at length to be visited by certain friends and equals[9] of his tribe, which make the chorus, who seek to comfort him what they can; then by his old father, Manoa, who endeavors the like, and withal tells him his purpose to procure his liberty by ransom; lastly, that this feast was proclaimed by the Philistines as a day of thanksgiving for their deliverance from the hands of Samson—which yet more troubles him. Manoa then departs to prosecute his endeavor with the Philistian lords for Samson's redemption; who in the meanwhile is visited by other persons, and, lastly, by a public officer to require his coming to the feast before the lords and people, to play or show his strength in their presence. He at first refuses, dismissing the public officer with absolute denial to come; at length persuaded inwardly that this was from God, he yields to go along with him, who came now the second time with great threatenings to fetch him. The chorus yet remaining on the place, Manoa returns full of joyful hope to procure ere long his son's deliverance: in the midst of which discourse an Hebrew comes in haste, confusedly at first, and afterward more distinctly, relating the catastrophe—what Samson had done to the Philistines, and by accident to himself; wherewith the tragedy ends.

THE PERSONS

SAMSON	DALILA, his wife	MESSENGER
MANOA, the father of	HARAPHA of Gath	CHORUS of Danites[1]
Samson	PUBLIC OFFICER	

The Scene, before the Prison in Gaza.

SAMSON   A little onward lend thy guiding hand
    To these dark steps, a little further on;
    For yonder bank hath choice of sun or shade.
    There I am wont to sit, when any chance
5   Relieves me from my task of servile toil,
    Daily in the common prison else enjoined me,[2]
    Where I, a prisoner chained, scarce freely draw
    The air, imprisoned also, close and damp,
    Unwholesome draught. But here I feel amends—
10   The breath of heaven fresh blowing, pure and sweet,
    With day-spring° born; here leave me to respire.   *break of day*
    This day a solemn feast the people hold

---

8. The Philistines, warlike and commercial, lived in southwest Palestine (the southern coast of modern Israel between, approximately, Tel Aviv and Gaza) in five cities named Ashdod, Eshkol, Gaza, Gath, and Ashkalon. They were a wholly urban people as compared to the largely rural Israelites.

9. People of about the same age.

1. Hebrews of the tribe of Dan, Samson's tribe. When the land of Canaan was divided among the twelve tribes, the Danites received the southern portion, adjacent to the Philistines.

2. The metrical pattern of this line, with its many unaccented syllables and careful placement of the strong word "else," merits careful study. Similar bold effects are found throughout.

To Dagon[3] their sea-idol, and forbid
Laborious works. Unwillingly this rest
15 Their superstition yields me; hence, with leave
Retiring from the popular noise, I seek
This unfrequented place, to find some ease—
Ease to the body some, none to the mind
From restless thoughts, that like a deadly swarm
20 O hornets armed, no sooner found alone
But rush upon me thronging, and present
Times past, what once I was, and what am now.
O, wherefore was my birth from Heaven foretold
Twice by an angel,[4] who at last, in sight
25 Of both my parents, all in flames ascended
From off the altar where an offering burned,
As in a fiery column charioting
His godlike presence, and from some great act
Or benefit revealed to Abraham's race?
30 Why was my breeding ordered and prescribed
As of a person separate to God,
Designed for great exploits,[5] if I must die
Betrayed, captived, and both my eyes put out,
Made of my enemies the scorn and gaze,
35 To grind in brazen fetters under task
With this heaven-gifted strength? O glorious strength,
Put to the labor of a beast, debased
Lower than bondslave! Promise was that I
Should Israel from Philistian yoke deliver;
40 Ask for this great deliverer now, and find him
Eyeless in Gaza at the mill with slaves,
Himself in bonds under Philistian yoke.
Yet stay; let me not rashly call in doubt
Divine prediction. What if all foretold
45 Had been fulfilled but through mine own default?
Whom have I to complain of but myself,
Who this high gift of strength committed to me,
In what part lodged, how easily bereft me,
Under the seal of silence could not keep,[6]
50 But weakly to a woman must reveal it,
O'ercome with importunity and tears?
O impotence of mind in body strong!
But what is strength without a double share
Of wisdom? Vast, unwieldy, burdensome,
55 Proudly secure,[7] yet liable to fall
By weakest subtleties; not made to rule,
But to subserve where wisdom bears command.

3. Dagon's name comes from *dag*, "fish," and he seems to have had a fishy shape. His would thus be a marine cult to correspond with that of the many Baals, or land gods, of the Philistines (see *Paradise Lost* 1.457–66).
4. Before Samson was born, an angel foretold that he would begin the delivery of Israel from the Philistines (Judges 13.5).
5. Samson was a Nazarite, a member of an ascetic group dedicated to the service of God (see Numbers 6).
6. I.e., who could not keep silent about the high gift of strength committed to me, or about where it was located, or about how easily it could be taken from me.
7. Confident, free from care (Latin *securus*).

God, when he gave me strength, to show withal
How slight the gift was, hung it in my hair.
60 But peace! I must not quarrel with the will
Of highest dispensation,° which herein   *providence*
Haply had ends above my reach to know.
Suffices that to me strength is my bane,
And proves the source of all my miseries,
65 So many, and so huge, that each apart
Would ask a life to wail. But, chief of all,
O loss of sight, of thee I most complain!
Blind among enemies! O worse than chains,
Dungeon, or beggary, or decrepit age!
70 Light, the prime work of God,[8] to me is extinct,
And all her various objects of delight
Annulled, which might in part my grief have eased.
Inferior to the vilest now become
Of man or worm, the vilest here excel me:
75 They creep, yet see; I, dark in light, exposed
To daily fraud, contempt, abuse, and wrong,
Within doors or without, still as a fool,
In power of others, never in my own—
Scarce half I seem to live, dead more than half.
80 O dark, dark, dark, amid the blaze of noon,
Irrecoverably dark, total eclipse
Without all hope of day!
O first-created beam, and thou great Word,
"Let there be light, and light was over all,"
85 Why am I thus bereaved thy prime decree?[9]
The sun to me is dark
And silent° as the moon,   *unperceived*
When she deserts the night,
Hid in her vacant interlunar cave.[1]
90 Since light so necessary is to life,
And almost life itself, if it be true
That light is in the soul,
She all in every part,[2] why was the sight
To such a tender ball as th' eye confined,
95 So obvious° and so easy to be quenched,   *exposed*
And not, as feeling, through all parts diffused,
That she might look at will through every pore?
Then had I not been thus exiled from light,
As in the land of darkness, yet in light,
100 To live a life half dead, a living death,
And buried; but, O yet more miserable!
Myself my sepulcher, a moving grave;
Buried, yet not exempt

8. God's first ("prime") act in creating the world
was to say "Let there be light" (Genesis 1.3), a
phrase Milton paraphrases below.
9. I.e., why am I thus deprived of the first-
created (and most important) thing?
1. Ancient astronomers posited that during its

dark ("interlunar") phase, the moon hid in a
cave. "Vacant": i.e., where the moon is at ease
(Latin *vacare*, whence modern "vacation").
2. A famous formula of Plotinus (*Enneads* 4.2.1)
describes the soul as "all in all and all in every
part."

By privilege of death and burial
105 From worst of other evils, pains, and wrongs;
But made hereby obnoxious° more   *vulnerable*
To all the miseries of life,
Life in captivity
Among inhuman foes.
110 But who are these? for with joint pace I hear
The tread of many feet steering this way;
Perhaps my enemies, who come to stare
At my affliction, and perhaps to insult,
Their daily practice to afflict me more.
115 CHORUS   This, this is he; softly a while;
Let us not break in upon him.
O change beyond report, thought, or belief!
See how he lies at random, carelessly diffused,[3]
With languished head unpropped,
120 As one past hope, abandoned,
And by himself given over,
In slavish habit, ill-fitted weeds°   *rags*
O'er-worn and soiled.
Or do my eyes misrepresent? Can this be he,
125 That heroic, that renowned,
Irresistible Samson? whom, unarmed,
No strength of man, or fiercest wild beast, could withstand:[4]
Who tore the lion as the lion tears the kid;
Ran on embattled armies clad in iron,
130 And, weaponless himself,
Made arms ridiculous, useless the forgery[5]
Of brazen shield and spear, the hammered cuirass,
Chalybean-tempered steel, and frock of mail
Adamantean proof;[6]
135 But safest he who stood aloof,
When insupportably° his foot advanced,   *irresistably*
In scorn of their proud arms and warlike tools,
Spurned them to death by troops. The bold Ascalonite
Fled from his lion ramp;[7] old warriors turned
140 Their plated backs under his heel,
Or groveling soiled their crested helmets in the dust.
Then with what trivial weapon came to hand,
The jaw of a dead ass, his sword of bone,
A thousand foreskins fell, the flower of Palestine,
145 In Ramath-lechi, famous to this day;
Then by main force pulled up, and on his shoulders bore,
The gates of Azza,[8] post and massy bar,

3. Literally, "poured forth," sprawled.
4. Judges 14.5–6 tells the story of Samson ripping apart a lion with his bare hands.
5. Weapons of forged steel, but also fraudulent, exterior protections.
6. Hard as adamant, i.e., diamond. The Chalybes lived on the Black Sea and were famous ironworkers.
7. A lion in the act of attacking its prey, rampant. "Ascalonite": a man from Ascalon, or Ashkalon, one of the five great Philistine cities.
8. On one occasion Samson killed a thousand Philistines (i.e., "foreskins," uncircumcised warriors), using the jawbone of an ass (Judges 15.15–17). Judges 16.3 tells how Samson, to escape his enemies, picked up and carried off the gates of Gaza (Azza).

Up to the hill by Hebron, seat of giants old,
No journey of a Sabbath day, and loaded so,
150 Like whom the Gentiles feign to bear up heaven.[9]
Which shall I first bewail,
Thy bondage or lost sight,
Prison within prison
Inseparably dark?
155 Thou art become (O worst imprisonment!)
The dungeon of thyself; thy soul
(Which men enjoying sight oft without cause complain)
Imprisoned now indeed,
In real darkness of the body dwells,
160 Shut up from outward light
To incorporate with gloomy night;
For inward light, alas!
Puts forth no visual beam.[1]
O mirror of our fickle state,
165 Since man on earth unparalleled![2]
The rarer thy example stands,
By how much from the top of wondrous glory,
Strongest of mortal men,
To lowest pitch of abject fortune thou art fallen!
170 For him I reckon not in high estate
Whom long descent of birth,
Or the sphere of fortune,[3] raises;
But thee, whose strength, while virtue was her mate,
Might have subdued the Earth,
175 Universally crowned with highest praises.
SAMSON   I hear the sound of words; their sense the air
Dissolves unjointed ere it reach my ear.
CHORUS   He speaks: let us draw nigh. Matchless in might,
The glory late of Israel, now the grief!
180 We come, thy friends and neighbors not unknown,
From Eshtaol and Zora's fruitful vale,
To visit or bewail thee; or, if better,
Counsel or consolation we may bring,
Slave to thy sores: apt words have power to swage°   assuage
185 The tumors of a troubled mind,
And are as balm to festered wounds.
SAMSON   Your coming, friends, revives me; for I learn
Now of my own experience, not by talk,
How counterfeit a coin they are who "friends"
190 Bear in their superscription (of the most
I would be understood). In prosperous days
They swarm, but in adverse withdraw their head,

9. In Greek (or, as Milton calls it, Gentile) mythology, Atlas supports the heavens. From Gaza to Hebron would be about forty miles—no journey for the day of rest.
1. Renaissance physiologists believed that the eye saw by sending forth a "visual beam," which it directed at various objects.
2. I.e., no such example (has been seen) since

man (was) on earth. "Fickle": changeable.
3. "Sphere": wheel. Fortune was described as possessing a wheel that, merely by rotating, automatically interchanged the highest and lowest social positions. Milton's definition of "high estate" is interior and spiritual; he has no interest in the old "Fall of Princes" theme. In fact, the play exactly reverses that theme.

Not to be found, though sought. Ye see, O friends,
How many evils have enclosed me round;
195 Yet that which was the worst now least afflicts me,
Blindness; for, had I sight, confused with shame,
How could I once look up, or heave° the head,   *lift*
Who like a foolish pilot have shipwrecked
My vessel trusted to me from above,
200 Gloriously rigged, and for a word, a tear,
Fool! have divulged the secret gift of God
To a deceitful woman? Tell me, friends,
Am I not sung and proverbed for a fool
In every street? Do they not say, "How well
205 Are come upon him his deserts"? Yet why?
Immeasurable strength they might behold
In me; of wisdom nothing more than mean.°   *average*
This with the other should at least have paired;°   *been equal*
These two, proportioned ill, drove me transverse.°   *off course*
210 CHORUS   Tax not divine disposal. Wisest men
Have erred, and by bad women been deceived;
And shall again, pretend they ne'er so wise.[4]
Deject not then so overmuch thyself,
Who hast of sorrow thy full load besides.
215 Yet, truth to say, I oft have heard men wonder
Why thou should'st wed Philistian women rather
Than of thine own tribe fairer, or as fair,
At least of thy own nation, and as noble.
SAMSON   The first I saw at Timna, and she pleased
220 Me, not my parents, that I sought to wed
The daughter of an infidel.[5] They knew not
That what I motioned° was of God; I knew   *intended*
From intimate impulse, and therefore urged
The marriage on, that, by occasion hence,[6]
225 I might begin Israel's deliverance,
The work to which I was divinely called.
She proving false, the next I took to wife
(O that I never had! fond wish too late!)
Was in the vale of Sorec, Dàlila,[7]
230 That specious monster, my accomplished snare.
I thought it lawful from my former act,
And the same end, still watching to oppress
Israel's oppressors. Of what now I suffer
She was not the prime cause, but I myself,
235 Who, vanquished with a peal of words (O weakness!),
Gave up my fort of silence to a woman.
CHORUS   In seeking just occasion to provoke
The Philistine, thy country's enemy,
Thou never wast remiss, I bear thee witness;
240 Yet Israel still serves with all his sons.[8]

4. I.e., however much they profess to be wise.
5. Judges 14.1–4 tells the story of Samson's first decision to marry outside his own tribe and nation.
6. I.e., so that it might provide an occasion for me to begin Israel's deliverance.
7. Judges 16.4 describes this wedding.
8. I.e., Israel and the children of Israel are still in servitude.

SAMSON   That fault I take not on me, but transfer
     On Israel's governors and heads of tribes,
     Who, seeing those great acts which God had done
     Singly by me against their conquerors,
245   Acknowledged not, or not at all considered
     Deliverance offered. I, on th' other side,
     Used no ambition to commend my deeds;[9]
     The deeds themselves, though mute, spoke loud the doer.
     But they persisted deaf, and would not seem
250   To count them things worth notice, till at length
     Their lords, the Philistines, with gathered powers,
     Entered Judea seeking me, who then
     Safe to the rock of Etham was retired,
     Not flying, but forecasting in what place
255   To set upon them, what advantaged best.
     Meanwhile the men of Judah, to prevent
     The harass of their land, beset me round;
     I willingly on some conditions came
     Into their hands, and they as gladly yield me
260   To the uncircumcised[1] a welcome prey,
     Bound with two cords. But cords to me were threads
     Touched with the flame: on their whole host I flew
     Unarmed, and with a trivial weapon felled
     Their choicest youth; they only lived who fled.[2]
265   Had Judah that day joined, or one whole tribe,
     They had by this° possessed the towers of Gath,   *by this time*
     And lorded over them whom now they serve.
     But what more oft, in nations grown corrupt,
     And by their vices brought to servitude,
270   Than to love bondage more than liberty,
     Bondage with ease than strenuous liberty,[3]
     And to despise, or envy, or suspect,
     Whom God hath of his special favor raised
     As their deliverer? If he aught begin,
275   How frequent to desert him, and at last
     To heap ingratitude on worthiest deeds!
CHORUS   Thy words to my remembrance bring
     How Succoth and the fort of Penuel
     Their great deliverer contemned,
280   The matchless Gideon, in pursuit
     Of Madian and her vanquished kings;[4]
     And how ingrateful Ephraim
     Had dealt with Jephtha, who by argument,
     Not worse than by his shield and spear,
285   Defended Israel from the Ammonite,
     Had not his prowess quelled their pride
     In that sore battle when so many died

---

9. I.e., sought for no testimonials to my actions.
1. Foreigners, the people outside the covenant of Abraham.
2. Judges 15.8–17 tells the tale of Samson's single-handed victory, using a "trivial weapon," the jawbone of an ass.

3. Milton appears to have in mind not only early Israel but also contemporary England.
4. Judges 8: Succoth and Penuel refused aid to Gideon when he was pursuing the common foe, and he punished them.

Without reprieve, adjudged to death
For want of well pronouncing *Shibboleth*.[5]
290　SAMSON　Of such examples add me to the roll.
Me easily indeed mine° may neglect,　　　　　　　　　　*my people*
But God's proposed deliverance not so.
　　CHORUS　Just are the ways of God,
And justifiable to men,
295　Unless there be who think not God at all.
If any be, they walk obscure;
For of such doctrine never was there school,
But the heart of the fool,
And no man therein doctor but himself.[6]
300　　　Yet more there be who doubt his ways not just,
As to his own edicts found contradicting;
Then give the reins to wandering thought,
Regardless of his glory's diminution,
Till, by their own perplexities involved,
305　They ravel[7] more, still less resolved,
But never find self-satisfying solution.
As if they would confine th' Interminable,°　　　　　　　*Infinite*
And tie him to his own prescript,
Who made our laws to bind us, not himself,
310　And hath full right to exempt
Whomso it pleases him by choice
From national obstriction,[8] without taint
Of sin, or legal debt;
For with his own laws he can best dispense.
315　　　He would not else, who never wanted means,
Nor in respect of the enemy just cause
To set his people free,
Have prompted this heroic Nazarite,
Against his vow of strictest purity,
320　　　To seek in marriage that fallacious bride,
Unclean, unchaste.
　　　　Down, Reason, then; at least, vain reasonings down;
Though Reason here aver
That moral verdict quits her of unclean:
325　Unchaste was subsequent; her stain, not his.[9]
　　　　But see! here comes thy reverend sire,
With careful step, locks white as down,[1]
Old Manoa: advise[2]
Forthwith how thou ought'st to receive him.
330　SAMSON　Ay me! another inward grief, awaked
　　With mention of that name, renews th' assault.
　　MANOA　Brethren and men of Dan (for such ye seem,

---

5. See Judges 11 and 12.
6. Psalm 14 deals with the fool who says in his heart there is no God. "Doctor": teacher.
7. Become entangled.
8. Obligation, i.e., the law against marrying Gentiles (Deuteronomy 7.3). The chorus here accepts Samson's argument that God had prompted him inexplicably to marry the woman of Timna.

9. The Chorus, having accused the woman of Timna of being unclean (i.e., Gentile and taboo) and unchaste, now admits that since Samson married her at God's instigation she was not unclean to him and that she was unchaste only after Samson left her. Reason is therefore puzzled.
1. Swan's down. "Careful": full of care.
2. Reflect, consider inwardly.

Though in this uncouth° place), if old respect,   *unfamiliar*
As I suppose, towards your once gloried friend,
335   My son, now captive, hither hath informed°   *directed*
Your younger feet, while mine, cast back with age,
Came lagging after, say if he be here.
    CHORUS   As signal° now in low dejected state   *notable*
As erst in highest, behold him where he lies.
340   MANOA   O miserable change! Is this the man,
That invincible Samson, far renowned,
The dread of Israel's foes, who with a strength
Equivalent to angels' walked their streets,
None offering fight; who, single combatant,
345   Dueled their armies ranked in proud array,
Himself an army—now unequal match
To save himself against a coward armed
At one spear's length? O ever-failing trust
In mortal strength! and, oh, what not in man
350   Deceivable and vain?³ Nay, what thing good
Prayed for, but often proves our woe, our bane?
I prayed for children, and thought barrenness
In wedlock a reproach; I gained a son,
And such a son as all men hailed me happy:
355   Who would be now a father in my stead?
O wherefore did God grant me my request,
And as a blessing with such pomp adorned?
Why are his gifts desirable, to tempt
Our earnest prayers, then, given with solemn hand
360   As graces, draw a scorpion's tail behind?
For this did the angel twice descend?⁴ for this
Ordained thy nurture holy, as of a plant
Select and sacred? glorious for a while,
The miracle of men; then in an hour
365   Ensnared, assaulted, overcome, led bound,
Thy foes' derision, captive, poor and blind,
Into a dungeon thrust, to work with slaves!
Alas! methinks whom God hath chosen once
To worthiest deeds, if he through frailty err,
370   He should not so o'erwhelm, and as a thrall
Subject him to so foul indignities,
Be it but for honor's sake of former deeds.
    SAMSON   Appoint not heavenly disposition,⁵ father.
Nothing of all these evils hath befallen me
375   But justly; I myself have brought them on;
Sole author I, sole cause.⁶ If aught seem vile,
As vile hath been my folly, who have profaned
The mystery of God, given me under pledge

---

3. I.e., what is there in man that is not deceivable and vain?

4. The angel who announced Samson's birth was sent a second time, in answer to Manoa's request, to give instructions concerning his education and training.

5. I.e., do not presume to control heaven's decisions.

6. Like Adam, in *Paradise Lost* 10, Samson proves his own resurgent virtue by accepting responsibility for his own faults.

Of vow, and have betrayed it to a woman,
380 A Canaanite, my faithless enemy.
This well I knew, nor was at all surprised,
But warned by oft experience. Did not she
Of Timna first betray me, and reveal
The secret wrested from me in her height
385 Of nuptial love professed, carrying it straight
To them who had corrupted her, my spies
And rivals?[7] In this other was there found
More faith, who, also in her prime of love,
Spousal embraces, vitiated with gold,
390 Though offered only, by the scent conceived
Her spurious first-born, treason against me?[8]
Thrice she essayed, with flattering prayers and sighs,
And amorous reproaches, to win from me
My capital secret,[9] in what part my strength
395 Lay stored, in what part summed, that she might know;
Thrice I deluded her, and turned to sport
Her importunity, each time perceiving
How openly and with what impudence
She purposed to betray me, and (which was worse
400 Than undissembled hate) with what contempt
She sought to make me traitor to myself.[1]
Yet the fourth time, when, mustering all her wiles,
With blandished parleys, feminine assaults,
Tongue-batteries, she surceased° not day nor night   *forebore*
405 To storm me, over-watched and wearied out,
At times when men seek most repose and rest,
I yielded, and unlocked her all my heart,
Who, with a grain of manhood well resolved,
Might easily have shook off all her snares;
410 But foul effeminacy[2] held me yoked
Her bondslave. O indignity, O blot
To honor and religion! servile mind
Rewarded well with servile punishment!
The base degree to which I now am fallen,
415 These rags, this grinding, is not yet so base
As was my former servitude, ignoble,
Unmanly, ignominious, infamous,
True slavery; and that blindness worse than this,
That saw not how degenerately I served.
420 MANOA   I cannot praise thy marriage-choices, son,
Rather approved them not; but thou didst plead
Divine impulsion[3] prompting how thou might'st

---

7. Samson's first wife, the woman of Timna, revealed Samson's riddle to his enemies (Judges 14.8–19).
8. At the mere scent of gold, Dalila conceived a bastard ("spurious") offspring for Samson—treason.
9. The secret Dalila learned was of capital importance; also, it involved the hair on Sam-

son's head (Latin *caput*).
1. Judges 16.5–20.
2. Uxoriousness, overfondness, the fault of Adam.
3. Samson's repeated reliance on extraordinary divine inspiration aligns him, for Milton, with the godly party of the 17th century—as against worldlings who doubted or disliked the idea of recurring divine intervention.

Find some occasion to infest our foes.
I state not[4] that; this I am sure, our foes
425 Found soon occasion thereby to make thee
Their captive, and their triumph; thou the sooner
Temptation found'st, or over-potent charms,
To violate the sacred trust of silence
Deposited within thee; which to have kept
430 Tacit° was in thy power. True; and thou bear'st   silent
Enough, and more, the burden of that fault;
Bitterly hast thou paid, and still art paying,
That rigid score.° A worse thing yet remains: debt
This day the Philistines a popular feast
435 Here celebrate in Gaza, and proclaim
Great pomp and sacrifice and praises loud,
To Dagon, as their god who hath delivered
Thee, Samson, bound and blind, into their hands,
Them out of thine, who slew'st them many a slain.
440 So Dagon shall be magnified,[5] and God,
Besides whom is no god, compared with idols,
Disglorified, blasphemed, and had in scorn
By th' idolatrous rout amidst their wine;
Which to have come to pass by means of thee,
445 Samson, of all thy sufferings think the heaviest,
Of all reproach the most with shame that ever
Could have befallen thee and thy father's house.
SAMSON   Father, I do acknowledge and confess
That I this honor, I this pomp, have brought
450 To Dagon, and advanced his praises high
Among the heathen round; to God have brought
Dishonor, obloquy, and oped the mouths
Of idolists and atheists; have brought scandal
To Israel, diffidence° of God, and doubt   mistrust
455 In feeble hearts, propense° enough before   inclined
To waver, or fall off and join with idols:
Which is my chief affliction, shame and sorrow,
The anguish of my soul, that suffers not
Mine eye to harbor sleep, or thoughts to rest.
460 This only hope relieves me, that the strife
With me hath end. All the contèst is now
'Twixt God and Dagon. Dagon hath presumed,
Me overthrown, to enter lists[6] with God,
His deity comparing and preferring
465 Before the God of Abraham. He, be sure,
Will not connive° or linger, thus provoked,   hesitate
But will arise, and his great name assert.
Dagan must stoop, and shall ere long receive
Such a discomfit as shall quite despoil him
470 Of all these boasted trophies won on me,
And with confusion blank[7] his worshipers.

4. Offer no opinion on. "Infest": attack.
5. Glorified. "Who slew'st them many a slain":
i.e., who slew many a one of them.

6. Jousting courts, as in medieval tourneys.
7. Confound, turn pale.

MANOA   With cause this hope relieves thee; and these words
I as a prophecy receive; for God
(Nothing more certain) will not long defer
475   To vindicate the glory of his name
Against all competition, nor will long
Endure it doubtful whether God be Lord,
Or Dagon. But for thee what shall be done?
Thou must not in the meanwhile, here forgot,
480   Lie in this miserable loathsome plight
Neglected. I already have made way
To some Philistian lords, with whom to treat
About thy ransom. Well they may by this°   *by this time*
Have satisfied their utmost of revenge
485   By pains and slaveries, worse than death, inflicted
On thee, who now no more canst do them harm.
SAMSON   Spare that proposal, father; spare the trouble
Of that solicitation. Let me here,
As I deserve, pay on my punishment,
490   And expiate, if possible, my crime,
Shameful garrulity. To have revealed
Secrets of men, the secrets of a friend,
How heinous had the fact been, how deserving
Contempt and scorn of all; to be excluded
495   All friendship, and avoided as a blab,
The mark of fool set on his front!° But I   *forehead*
God's counsel have not kept, his holy secret
Presumptuously have published, impiously,
Weakly at least and shamefully: a sin
500   That Gentiles in their parables condemn
To their abyss and horrid pains confined.[8]
MANOA   Be penitent, and for thy fault contrite,
But act not in thy own affliction, son.
Repent the sin, but if the punishment
505   Thou canst avoid, self-preservation bids;
Or th' execution leave to high disposal,
And let another hand, not thine, exact
Thy penal forfeit from thyself. Perhaps
God will relent, and quit° thee of all his debt;   *free*
510   Who ever more approves and more accepts
(Best pleased with humble and filial submission)
Him who, imploring mercy, sues for life,
Than who, self-rigorous, chooses death as due;[9]
Which argues over-just, and self-displeased
515   For self-offense more than for God offended.
Reject not, then, what offered means who knows
But God hath set before us to return thee
Home to thy country and his sacred house,
Where thou may'st bring thy offerings, to avert
520   His further ire, with prayers and vows renewed.

8. In classical legend, Tantalus was confined to hell and torment because he betrayed the secrets of the gods, and Prometheus was savagely pun-ished for giving humanity the secret of fire.
9. This is similar to Adam's argument against suicide in *Paradise Lost* 10.1013–19.

SAMSON   His pardon I implore; but, as for life,
To what end should I seek it? When in strength
All mortals I excelled, and great in hopes,
With youthful courage, and magnanimous thoughts
525   Of birth from Heaven foretold and high exploits,
Full of divine instinct, after some proof
Of acts indeed heroic, far beyond
The sons of Anak, famous now and blazed,[1]
Fearless of danger, like a petty god
530   I walked about, admired of all, and dreaded
On hostile ground, none daring my affront—
Then, swoll'n with pride, into the snare I fell
Of fair fallacious looks, venereal trains,°   *sexual lures*
Softened with pleasure and voluptuous life;
535   At length to lay my head and hallowed pledge
Of all my strength in the lascivious lap
Of a deceitful concubine, who shore me,
Like a tame wether,° all my precious fleece,   *castrated sheep*
Then turned me out ridiculous, despoiled,
540   Shaven, and disarmed among my enemies.
CHORUS   Desire of wine and all delicious drinks,
Which many a famous warrior overturns,
Thou could'st repress; nor did the dancing ruby,
Sparkling out-poured, the flavor or the smell,
545   Or taste, that cheers the heart of gods and men,
Allure thee from the cool crystàlline stream.
SAMSON   Wherever fountain or fresh current flowed
Against the eastern ray, translucent pure
With touch ethereal of Heaven's fiery rod,[2]
550   I drank, from the clear milky juice allaying
Thirst, and refreshed; nor envied them the grape
Whose heads that turbulent liquor fills with fumes.
CHORUS   O madness! to think use of strongest wines
And strongest drinks our chief support of health,
555   When God with these forbidden made choice to rear
His mighty champion, strong above compare,
Whose drink was only from the liquid brook![3]
SAMSON   But what availed this temperance, not complete
Against another object more enticing?
560   What boots it at one gate to make defense,
And at another to let in the foe,
Effeminately vanquished? by which means,
Now blind, disheartened, shamed, dishonored, quelled,
To what can I be useful? wherein serve
565   My nation, and the work from Heaven imposed?
But to sit idle on the household hearth,
A burdenous drone; to visitants a gaze,°   *spectacle*

---

1. Emblazoned, glorified. "Sons of Anak": giants, described in Numbers 13.
2. The rays of the sun. Samson is saying that wherever water was purest and cleanest, he drank of it—never of wine. "Rod" intimates a parallel with Moses, who like Samson brought forth a spring in the middle of the desert.
3. Samson's calling as a Nazarite forbade him the use of wine.

Or pitied object; these redundant locks,
Robustious[4] to no purpose, clustering down,
570 Vain monument of strength; till length of years
And sedentary numbness craze° my limbs   *weaken, twist*
To a contemptible old age obscure.
Here rather let me drudge, and earn my bread,
Till vermin, or the draff[5] of servile food,
575 Consume me, and oft-invocated death
Hasten the welcome end of all my pains.
MANOA   Wilt thou then serve the Philistines with that gift
Which was expressly given thee to annoy them?
Better at home lie bed-rid, not only idle,
580 Inglorious, unemployed, with age outworn.
But God, who caused a fountain at thy prayer
From the dry ground to spring, thy thirst to allay
After the brunt of battle,[6] can as easy
Cause light again within thy eyes to spring,
585 Wherewith to serve him better than thou hast.
And I persuade me so. Why else this strength
Miraculous yet remaining in those locks?
His might continues in thee not for naught,
Nor shall his wondrous gifts be frustrate thus.
590 SAMSON   All otherwise to me my thoughts portend,
That these dark orbs no more shall treat with light,
Nor th' other light of life continue long,
But yield to double darkness nigh at hand;
So much I feel my genial spirits° droop,   *life forces*
595 My hopes all flat. Nature within me seems
In all her functions weary of herself;
My race of glory run, and race of shame,
And I shall shortly be with them that rest.
MANOA   Believe not these suggestions, which proceed
600 From anguish of the mind, and humors black
That mingle with thy fancy.[7] I, however,
Must not omit a father's timely care
To prosecute the means of thy deliverance
By ransom or how else: meanwhile be calm,
605 And healing words from these thy friends admit.
SAMSON   O that torment should not be confined
To the body's wounds and sores,
With maladies innumerable
In heart, head, breast, and reins,°   *kidneys*
610 But must secret passage find
To th' inmost mind,
There exercise all his fierce accidents,[8]
And on her purest spirits prey,

4. Strong. "Redundant": in its Latin sense, "flowing"; in the English sense, "unnecessary" or "unemployed."
5. Garbage given to slaves as food.
6. The story of how Samson, with divine aid, created a spring in the desert after the battle

with the ass's jawbone is told in Judges 15.18–19.
7. Black bile, the melancholy humor, was supposed to have ill effects on the imagination.
8. I.e., there put into effect all the fierce qualities (of torment).

As on entrails, joints, and limbs,
615   With answerable pains, but more intense,
Though void of corporal sense!
     My griefs not only pain me
As a lingering disease,
But, finding no redress, ferment and rage;
620   Nor less than wounds immedicable
Rankle, and fester, and gangrene,
To black mortification.⁹
Thoughts, my tormentors, armed with daily stings,
Mangle my apprehensive tenderest parts,
625   Exasperate, exulcerate, and raise
Dire inflammation which no cooling herb
Or med'cinal liquor can assuage,
Nor breath of vernal air from snowy alp.
Sleep hath forsook and given me o'er
630   To death's benumbing opium as my only cure;
Thence faintings, swoonings of despair,
And sense of Heaven's desertion.¹
     I was his nursling once and choice delight,
His destined from the womb,
635   Promised by heavenly message° twice descending.   *messenger*
Under his special eye
Abstemious I grew up and thrived amain;
He led me on to mightiest deeds,
Above the here° of mortal arm,   *sinew, strength*
640   Against the uncircumcised, our enemies:
But now hath cast me off as never known,
And to those cruel enemies,
Whom I by his appointment had provoked,
Left me all helpless with th' irreparable loss
645   Of sight, reserved alive to be repeated°   *continually*
The subject of their cruelty or scorn.
Nor am I in the list of them that hope;
Hopeless are all my evils, all remèdiless.
This one prayer yet remains, might I be heard,
650   No long petition—speedy death,
The close of all my miseries, and the balm.
CHORUS   Many are the sayings of the wise,
In ancient and in modern books enrolled,
Extolling patience as the truest fortitude,
655   And to the bearing well of all calamities,
All chances incident to man's frail life;
Consolatories writ
With studied argument, and much persuasion sought,
Lenient² of grief and anxious thought.
660   But with th' afflicted in his pangs their sound
Little prevails, or rather seems a tune

---

9. A medical term for decay.
1. Samson comes close here to suggesting that religious despair is the symptom of a physical

condition.
2. Soothing (from Latin *leniens*).

Harsh, and of dissonant mood[3] from his complaint,
Unless he feel within
Some source of consolation from above,
665 Secret refreshings that repair his strength
And fainting spirits uphold.[4]
    God of our fathers! what is man,
That thou towards him with hand so various—
Or might I say contrarious?—
670 Temper'st thy providence through his short course:
Not evenly, as thou rul'st
The angelic orders, and inferior creatures mute,
Irrational and brute.[5]
Nor do I name of men the common rout,
675 That, wandering loose about,
Grow up and perish as the summer fly,
Heads without name, no more remembered;
But such as thou hast solemnly elected,
With gifts and graces eminently adorned,
680 To some great work, thy glory,
And people's safety, which in part they effect.
Yet toward these, thus dignified, thou oft,
Amidst their height of noon,
Changest thy countenance and thy hand, with no regard
685 Of highest favors past
From thee on them, or them to thee of service.[6]
    Nor only dost degrade them, or remit
To life obscured, which were a fair dismission,
But throw'st them lower than thou didst exalt them high,
690 Unseemly falls in human eye,
Too grievous for the trespass or omission;
Oft leav'st them to the hostile sword
Of heathen and profane, their carcasses
To dogs and fowls a prey, or else captived,
695 Or to the unjust tribunals, under change of times,
And condemnation of the ingrateful multitude.[7]
If these they 'scape, perhaps in poverty
With sickness and disease thou bow'st them down,
Painful diseases and deformed,
700 In crude[8] old age;
Though not disordinate, yet causeless suffering
The punishment of dissolute days. In fine,[9]
Just or unjust alike seem miserable,
For oft alike both come to evil end.
705   So deal not with this once thy glorious champion,

3. The musical mode, or psychological mood, of the comforter jars on that of the sufferer.
4. Cf. Job's answers to his comforters, especially in chapter 14.
5. The Chorus feels that the beings above and below man on the Great Chain of Being (the nine orders of angels above, the mute beasts below) are ruled by a less capricious code than is man.
6. Manoa has already voiced this plaint (lines 368–72).

7. After the Restoration, many Puritan leaders were executed, jailed, or exiled; even the corpses of some were exhumed, beheaded, and publicly exhibited.
8. Literally, "raw," but figuratively, "premature."
9. In short. "Though not disordinate": i.e., though they have not been dissipated. Milton resented having the gout, supposed to be a disease of the rich.

The image of thy strength, and mighty minister.[1]
What do I beg? how hast thou dealt already!
Behold him in this state calamitous, and turn
His labors, for thou canst, to peaceful end.

710   But who is this? what thing of sea or land—
Female of sex it seems—
That, so bedecked, ornate, and gay,
Comes this way sailing
Like a stately ship

715   Of Tarsus, bound for th' isles
Of Javan or Gadire,[2]
With all her bravery on, and tackle trim,
Sails filled, and streamers waving,
Courted by all the winds that hold them play;

720   An amber° scent of odorous perfume   *ambergris*
Her harbinger, a damsel train behind?
Some rich Philistian matron she may seem;
And now, at nearer view, no other certain
Than Dàlila thy wife.

725   SAMSON   My wife! my traitress! let her not come near me.
CHORUS   Yet on she moves; now stands and eyes thee fixed,
About t' have spoke; but now, with head declined
Like a fair flower surcharged with dew, she weeps,
And words addressed seem into tears dissolved,

730   Wetting the borders of her silken veil.
But now again she makes address to speak.
DALILA   With doubtful feet and wavering resolution
I came, still dreading thy displeasure, Samson;
Which to have merited, without excuse,

735   I cannot but acknowledge. Yet if tears
May expiate (though the fact more evil drew
In the perverse event than I foresaw),[3]
My penance hath not slackened, though my pardon
No way assured. But conjugal affection,

740   Prevailing over fear and timorous doubt,
Hath led me on, desirous to behold
Once more thy face, and know of thy estate,°   *condition*
If aught in my ability may serve
To lighten what thou suffer'st, and appease

745   Thy mind with what amends is in my power—
Though late, yet in some part to recompense
My rash but more unfortunate misdeed.
SAMSON.   Out, out, hyena![4] These are thy wonted arts,
And arts of every woman false like thee,

750   To break all faith, all vows, deceive, betray;

---

1. Agent, but with a religious connotation as well.
2. Tarsus (the birthplace of St. Paul) is a trading city in modern Turkey. The isles of Javan are the isles of Greece, supposed to be populated by descendants of Javan, son of Noah's son Japhet. Gadire is modern Cádiz in Spain. "Ships of Tarshish" is a common Old Testament emblem of pride and worldliness (e.g., Isaiah 23, Psalm 48).
3. I.e., my action turned out worse than intended.
4. Apart from being an animal believed to be of unpleasant habits and appearance, the hyena was a traditional beast of hypocrisy, supposed to entice men to destruction by its power of imitating the human voice.

Then, as repentant, to submit, beseech,
And reconcilement move with feigned remorse,
Confess, and promise wonders in her change,
Not truly penitent, but chief to try
755 Her husband, how far urged his patience bears,
His virtue or weakness which way to assail:
Then, with more cautious and instructed skill,
Again transgresses, and again submits;
That wisest and best men, full oft beguiled,
760 With goodness principled not to reject
The penitent, but ever to forgive,
Are drawn to wear out miserable days,
Entangled with a poisonous bosom-snake,
If not by quick destruction soon cut off,
765 As I by thee, to ages an example.
DALILA. Yet hear me, Samson; not that I endeavor
To lessen or extenuate my offense,
But that, on th' other side, if it be weighed
By itself, with aggravations not surcharged,
770 Or else with just allowance counterpoised,
I may, if possible, thy pardon find
The easier towards me, or thy hatred less.
First granting, as I do, it was a weakness
In me, but incident to all our sex,
775 Curiosity, inquisitive, importùne
Of secrets, then with like infirmity
To publish them, both common female faults;
Was it not weakness also to make known,
For importunity, that is for naught,
780 Wherein consisted all thy strength and safety?
To what I did thou show'dst me first the way.
But I to enemies revealed, and should not!
Nor should'st thou have trusted that to woman's frailty:[5]
Ere I to thee, thou to thyself wast cruel.
785 Let weakness then with weakness come to parle,°   parley, agreement
So near related, or the same of kind;
Thine forgive mine, that men may censure thine
The gentler, if severely thou exact not
More strength from me than in thyself was found.
790 And what if love, which thou interpret'st hate,
The jealousy of love, powerful of sway
In human hearts, nor less in mine towards thee,
Caused what I did? I saw thee mutable
Of fancy; feared lest one day thou would'st leave me,
795 As her at Timna; sought by all means therefore
How to endear, and hold thee to me firmest:
No better way I saw than by importuning
To learn thy secrets, get into my power

5. Like Eve, who wore down Adam with her insistance, then blamed him for giving in (*Paradise Lost* 9.1155–61), Dalila blames Samson for doing what she herself had demanded. Underlying the scene as a whole are the ancient stereotypes and accusations of traditional antifeminism.

Thy key of strength and safety. Thou wilt say,
800   "Why, then, revealed?" I was assured by those
Who tempted me that nothing was designed
Against thee but safe custody and hold.
That made for me; I knew that liberty
Would draw thee forth to perilous enterprises,
805   While I at home sat full of cares and fears,
Wailing thy absence in my widowed bed;
Here I should still enjoy thee, day and night,
Mine and love's prisoner, not the Philistines',
Whole to myself, unhazarded abroad,
810   Fearless at home of partners in my love.
These reasons in love's law have passed for good,
Though fond° and reasonless to some perhaps;   *foolish*
And love hath oft, well meaning, wrought much woe,
Yet always pity or pardon hath obtained.
815   Be not unlike all others, not austere
As thou art strong, inflexible as steel.
If thou in strength all mortals dost exceed,
In uncompassionate anger do not so.
SAMSON   How cunningly the sorceress displays
820   Her own transgressions, to upbraid me mine!
That malice, not repentance, brought thee hither,
By this appears. I gave, thou say'st, th' example,
I led the way—bitter reproach, but true;
I to myself was false ere thou to me.
825   Such pardon, therefore, as I give my folly
Take to thy wicked deed; which when thou seest
Impartial, self-severe, inexorable,
Thou wilt renounce thy seeking, and much rather
Confess it feigned. Weakness is thy excuse,
830   And I believe it, weakness to resist
Philistian gold. If weakness may excuse,
What murderer, what traitor, parricide,
Incestuous, sacrilegious, but may plead it?
All wickedness is weakness; that plea, therefore,
835   With God or man will gain thee no remission.
But love constrained thee? Call it furious rage
To satisfy thy lust. Love seeks to have love;
My love how could'st thou hope, who took'st the way
To raise in me inexpiable° hate,   *inextinguishable*
840   Knowing, as needs I must, by thee betrayed?
In vain thou striv'st to cover shame with shame,
Or by evasions thy crime uncover'st more.
DALILA   Since thou determin'st weakness for no plea
In man or woman, though to thy own condemning,
845   Hear what assaults I had, what snares besides,
What sieges girt me round, ere I consented;
Which might have awed the best-resolved of men,
The constantest, to have yielded without blame.
It was not gold, as to my charge thou lay'st,

850   That wrought with me.[6] Thou know'st the magistrates
    And princes of my country came in person,
    Solicited, commanded, threatened, urged,
    Adjured by all the bonds of civil duty
    And of religion—pressed how just it was,
855   How honorable, how glorious, to entrap
    A common enemy, who had destroyed
    Such numbers of our nation: and the priest
    Was not behind, but ever at my ear,
    Preaching how meritorious with the gods
860   It would be to ensnare an irreligious
    Dishonorer of Dagon. What had I
    To oppose against such powerful arguments?
    Only my love of thee held long debate,
    And combated in silence all these reasons
865   With hard contèst. At length, that grounded maxim,
    So rife and celebrated in the mouths
    Of wisest men, that to the public good
    Private respects must yield,[7] with grave authority
    Took full possession of me, and prevailed;
870   Virtue, as I thought, truth, duty, so enjoining.
    SAMSON   I thought where all thy circling wiles would end,
    In feigned religion, smooth hypocrisy!
    But had thy love, still odiously pretended,
    Been, as it ought, sincere, it would have taught thee
875   Far other reasonings, brought forth other deeds.
    I before all the daughters of my tribe
    And of my nation chose thee from among
    My enemies, loved thee, as too well thou knew'st;
    Too well; unbosomed all my secrets to thee,
880   Not out of levity, but overpowered
    By thy request, who could deny thee nothing;
    Yet now am judged an enemy. Why then
    Didst thou at first receive me for thy husband,
    Then, as since then, thy country's foe professed?
885   Being once a wife, for me thou wast to leave
    Parents and country; nor was I their subject,
    Nor under their protection, but my own;
    Thou mine, not theirs.[8] If aught against my life
    Thy country sought of thee, it sought unjustly,
890   Against the law of nature, law of nations;
    No more thy country, but an impious crew
    Of men conspiring to uphold their state
    By worse than hostile deeds, violating the ends
    For which our country is a name so dear;
895   Not therefore to be obeyed. But zeal moved thee;
    To please thy gods thou didst it! Gods unable

---

6. Judges 16 is explicit that Dalila betrayed Samson for money—eleven hundred pieces of silver offered her by each one of the Philistine lords.

7. Reason of state, political "necessity," was in Milton's eyes the worst of all possible motives for an action (cf. *Paradise Lost* 4.393–94).

8. I.e., you were under my protection, not theirs.

To acquit themselves and prosecute their foes
But by ungodly deeds, the contradiction
Of their own deity, gods cannot be;
900   Less therefore to be pleased, obeyed, or feared.
These false pretexts and varnished colors failing,
Bare in thy guilt, how foul must thou appear!
DALILA   In argument with men a woman ever
Goes by the worse,[9] whatever be her cause.
905   SAMSON   For want of words, no doubt, or lack of breath!
Witness when I was worried with thy peals.
DALILA   I was a fool, too rash, and quite mistaken
In what I thought would have succeeded best.
Let me obtain forgiveness of thee, Samson;
910   Afford me place to show what recompense
Towards thee I intend for what I have misdone,
Misguided. Only what remains past cure
Bear not too sensibly,[1] nor still insist
To afflict thyself in vain. Though sight be lost,
915   Life yet hath many solaces, enjoyed
Where other senses want not their delights
At home, in leisure and domestic ease,
Exempt from many a care and chance to which
Eyesight exposes, daily, men abroad.
920   I to the lords will intercede, not doubting
Their favorable ear, that I may fetch thee
From forth this loathsome prison-house, to abide
With me, where my redoubled love and care,
With nursing diligence, to me glad office,
925   May ever tend about thee to old age,
With all things grateful cheered, and so supplied
That what by me thou hast lost thou least shalt miss.
SAMSON   No, no; of my condition take no care;
It fits not; thou and I long since are twain;
930   Nor think me so unwary or accursed[2]
To bring my feet again into the snare
Where once I have been caught. I know thy trains,
Though dearly to my cost, thy gins, and toils.[3]
Thy fair enchanted cup, and warbling charms,
935   No more on me have power; their force is nulled;
So much of adder's wisdom I have learnt,
To fence my ear against thy sorceries.[4]
If in my flower of youth and strength, when all men
Loved, honored, feared me, thou alone could hate me,
940   Thy husband, slight me, sell me, and forgo me,
How would'st thou use me now, blind, and thereby
Deceivable, in most things as a child,
Helpless, thence easily contemned and scorned,

9. Comes off second best.
1. With too great sensitivity.
2. I.e., so neglectful or bewitched.
3. Nets. "Trains": tricks. "Gins": snares. The traditional images for female wiles are heightened by

reference to an enchanting cup and warbled charms reminiscent of Homer's Circe (*Odyssey* 10).
4. Psalms 58.4–5 describes the "deaf adder that stoppeth her ear; which will not hearken to the voice of charmers, charming never so wisely."

And last neglected! How would'st thou insult,
945   When I must live uxorious to thy will
In perfect thraldom! how again betray me,
Bearing my words and doings to the lords
To gloss upon, and, censuring, frown or smile![5]
This jail I count the house of liberty
950   To thine,[6] whose doors my feet shall never enter.
DALILA   Let me approach at least, and touch thy hand.
SAMSON   Not for thy life, lest fierce remembrance wake
My sudden rage to tear thee joint by joint.[7]
At distance I forgive thee, go with that;
955   Bewail thy falsehood, and the pious works
It hath brought forth to make thee memorable
Among illustrious women, faithful wives;
Cherish thy hastened widowhood with the gold
Of matrimonial treason: so farewell.
960 DALILA   I see thou art implacable, more deaf
To prayers than winds and seas. Yet winds to seas
Are reconciled at length, and sea to shore:
Thy anger, unappeasable, still rages,
Eternal tempest never to be calmed.
965   Why do I humble thus myself, and, suing
For peace, reap nothing but repulse and hate,
Bid go with evil omen,[8] and the brand
Of infamy upon my name denounced?
To mix with thy concernments I desist
970   Henceforth, nor too much disapprove my own.
Fame, if not double-faced, is double-mouthed,
And with contràry blast proclaims most deeds;[9]
On both his wings, one black, th' other white,
Bears greatest names in his wild airy flight.
975   My name, perhaps, among the circumcised
In Dan, in Judah, and the bordering tribes,
To all posterity may stand defamed,
With malediction mentioned, and the blot
Of falsehood most unconjugal traduced.
980   But in my country, where I most desire,
In Ekron, Gaza, Asdod, and in Gath,
I shall be named among the famousest
Of women, sung at solemn festivals,
Living and dead recorded, who to save
985   Her country from a fierce destroyer chose
Above the faith of wedlock bands; my tomb
With odors° visited and annual flowers;   *perfumes*
Not less renowned than in Mount Ephraim
Jael, who, with inhospitable guile,

---

5. Milton's hatred of censorship and managed
liberty is apparent. "Gloss": comment.
6. Compared to thine.
7. What Samson might remember, at the touch
of Dalila, would lead him to tear her to pieces.
8. I.e., dismissed with predictions of ill fame.

9. The figure of Fame, in Milton's youthful poem
"On the Fifth of November," does indeed have a
double tongue, one for truth and one for lies.
Fame or Rumor was a favorite grotesque allegorical figure in classical poets like Ovid (*Metamorphoses* 12.43ff.) and Virgil (*Aeneid* 4.173ff.).

990   Smote Sisera sleeping, through the temples nailed.[1]
         Nor shall I count it heinous to enjoy
         The public marks of honor and reward
         Conferred upon me for the piety
         Which to my country I was judged to have shown.
995   At this whoever envies or repines,
         I leave him to his lot, and like my own.
       CHORUS   She's gone, a manifest serpent by her sting
         Discovered in the end, till now concealed.
       SAMSON   So let her go. God sent her to debase me,
1000   And aggravate my folly, who committed
         To such a viper his most sacred trust
         Of secrecy, my safety, and my life.
       CHORUS   Yet beauty, though injurious, hath strange power,
         After offense returning, to regain
1005   Love once possessed, nor can be easily
         Repulsed, without much inward passion° felt,   *suffering*
         And secret sting of amorous remorse.
       SAMSON   Love-quarrels oft in pleasing concord end;
         Not wedlock-treachery, endangering life.
1010   CHORUS   It is not virtue, wisdom, valor, wit,
         Strength, comeliness of shape, or amplest merit
         That woman's love can win, or long inherit;°   *possess*
         But what it is, hard is to say,
         Harder to hit,
1015   Which way soever men refer it
         (Much like thy riddle, Samson),[2] in one day
         Or seven though one should musing sit.
         If any of these, or all, the Timnian bride
         Had not so soon preferred
1020   Thy paranymph, worthless to thee compared,
         Successor in thy bed,[3]
         Nor both so loosely disallied
         Their nuptials,[4] nor this last so treacherously
         Had shorn the fatal harvest of thy head.
1025   Is it for that° such outward ornament   *because*
         Was lavished on their sex, that inward gifts
         Were left for haste unfinished, judgment scant,
         Capacity not raised to apprehend
         Or value what is best
1030   In choice, but oftest to affect° the wrong?   *desire*
         Or was too much of self-love mixed,
         Of constancy no root infixed,
         That either they love nothing, or not long?
         Whate'er it be, to wisest men and best,
1035   Seeming at first all heavenly under virgin veil,

---

1. Jael lured Sisera, who saw in her the wife of
his ally and friend, into a tent and there drove a
large nail into his head (Judges 4.17–21).
2. Samson's riddle is set forth and answered in
Judges 14.14, 18.
3. I.e., if any of these (virtue, etc., lines 1010–

11) sufficed, Samson's first wife ("the Timnian
bride") would not have preferred to marry his
"paranymph" (best man) (see Judges 14).
4. I.e., nor would both your wives have been so
careless about their marriage vows.

Soft, modest, meek, demure,
Once joined, the contrary she proves, a thorn
Intestine,[5] far within defensive arms
A cleaving[6] mischief, in his way to virtue
1040   Adverse and turbulent; or by her charms
Draws him awry, enslaved
With dotage, and his sense depraved
To folly and shameful deeds, which ruin ends.
What pilot so expert but needs must wreck,
1045   Embarked with such a steers-mate at the helm?
    Favored of Heaven who finds
One virtuous, rarely found,
That in domestic good combines:
Happy that house! his way to peace is smooth:
1050   But virtue which breaks through all opposition,
And all temptation can remove,
Most shines and most is acceptable above.
    Therefore God's universal law
Gave to the man despotic power
1055   Over his female in due awe,
Nor from that right to part an hour,
Smile she or lour:
So shall he least confusion draw
On his whole life, not swayed
1060   By female usurpation, nor dismayed.
    But had we best retire? I see a storm.
SAMSON   Fair days have oft contracted[7] wind and rain.
CHORUS   But this another kind of tempest brings.
SAMSON   Be less abstruse; my riddling days are past.
1065   CHORUS   Look now for no enchanting voice, nor fear
The bait of honeyed words; a rougher tongue
Draws hitherward, I know him by his stride,
The giant Harapha[8] of Gath, his look
Haughty, as is his pile[9] high-built and proud.
1070   Comes he in peace? What wind hath blown him hither
I less conjecture than when first I saw
The sumptuous Dalila floating this way:[1]
His habit carries peace, his brow defiance.
SAMSON   Or peace or not, alike to me he comes.
1075   CHORUS   His fraught[2] we soon shall know: he now arrives.
HARAPHA   I come not, Samson, to condole thy chance,
As these[3] perhaps, yet wish it had not been,
Though for no friendly intent. I am of Gath;
Men call me Harapha, of stock renowned

---

5. An inward thorn, a viper in the bosom.
6. Clinging; a traditional emblem of marriage was the elm and the vine.
7. Drawn after them.
8. Harapha does not appear in the story told in the Book of Judges; Milton invented him with the help of some hints from the image of Goliath in 1 Samuel 17 and some other giants in 2 Samuel 21. *Rapha* means "giant" in Hebrew.

9. Body; with the suggestion that he is as tall as a tower.
1. That the various visitors of Samson are blown hither and yon by the winds of occasion serves to emphasize the deep steadiness of Samson's final resolution. "Habit" (next line): garb. (He's not dressed for fighting.)
2. Freight, i.e., business.
3. The chorus of Danites.

1080 As Og, or Anak, and the Emims old
That Kiriathaim held.[4] Thou know'st me now,
If thou at all art known.[5] Much I have heard
Of thy prodigious might and feats performed,
Incredible to me, in this displeased,
1085 That I was never present on the place
Of those encounters, where we might have tried
Each other's force in camp or listed field;[6]
And now am come to see of whom such noise
Hath walked about, and each limb to survey,
1090 If thy appearance answer loud report.
SAMSON   The way to know were not to see, but taste.°   make trial
HARAPHA   Dost thou already single me? I thought
Gyves[7] and the mill had tamed thee. O that fortune
Had brought me to the field where thou art famed
1095 To have wrought such wonders with an ass's jaw!
I should have forced thee soon wish[8] other arms,
Or left thy carcass where the ass lay thrown;
So had the glory of prowess been recovered
To Palestine, won by a Philistine
1100 From the unforeskinned race, of whom thou bear'st
The highest name for valiant acts. That honor,
Certain to have won by mortal duel from thee,
I lose, prevented by thy eyes put out.
SAMSON   Boast not of what thou would'st have done, but do
1105 What then thou would'st; thou seest it in thy hand.
HARAPHA   To combat with a blind man I disdain,
And thou hast need much washing to be touched.
SAMSON   Such usage as your honorable lords
Afford me, assassinated[9] and betrayed;
1110 Who durst not with their whole united powers
In fight withstand me single and unarmed,
Nor in the house with chamber ambushes[1]
Close-banded durst attack me, no, not sleeping,
Till they had hired a woman with their gold,
1115 Breaking her marriage-faith, to circumvent me.
Therefore, without feigned shifts, let be assigned
Some narrow place enclosed, where sight may give thee,
Or rather flight, no great advantage on me;
Then put on all thy gorgeous arms, thy helmet
1120 And brigandine of brass, thy broad habergeon,
Vant-brace and greaves and gauntlet; add thy spear,

4. Og was a giant king of Bashan in Deuteronomy
3.11; Anak and his sons were giants in Numbers
13.33; the Emims were giants in Deuteronomy
2.10–11 and Genesis 14.5.
5. I.e., you know me now if you know anything;
but also, "if you are anyone worth knowing." Cf.
Satan's brag to Zephon and Ithuriel: "Not to
know me argues yourselves unknown" (*Paradise
Lost* 4.830).
6. Lists, tourney ground. "Camp": field of battle

(from Latin *campus*).
7. Chains. "Single": challenge.
8. In the 18th century, editors changed "wish" to
"with," easing the grammar at the expense of the
sense.
9. Treacherously assailed.
1. Samson refers to the four occasions on which
Philistines hid in his bedroom while Dalila tried
unsuccessfully to betray him to them.

A weaver's beam,[2] and seven-times-folded shield:
I only with an oaken staff will meet thee,
And raise such outcries on thy clattered iron,
1125 Which long shall not withhold me from thy head,
That in a little time, while breath remains thee,
Thou oft shalt wish thyself at Gath, to boast
Again in safety what thou would'st have done
To Samson, but shalt never see Gath more.
1130 HARAPHA   Thou durst not thus disparage glorious arms,
Which greatest heroes have in battle worn,
Their ornament and safety, had not spells
And black enchantments, some magician's art,
Armed thee or charmed thee strong, which thou from Heaven
1135 Feign'dst at thy birth was given thee in thy hair,
Where strength can least abide, though all thy hairs
Were bristles ranged like those that ridge the back
Of chafed wild boars or ruffled porcupines.
SAMSON   I know no spells, use no forbidden arts;
1140 My trust is in the Living God, who gave me
At my nativity this strength, diffused
No less through all my sinews, joints, and bones,
Than thine, while I preserved these locks unshorn,
The pledge of my unviolated vow.
1145 For proof hereof, if Dagon be thy god,
Go to his temple, invocate his aid
With solemnest devotion, spread before him
How highly it concerns his glory now
To frustrate and dissolve these magic spells,
1150 Which I to be the power of Israel's God
Avow, and challenge Dagon to the test,
Offering to combat thee, his champion bold,
With th' utmost of his godhead seconded:
Then thou shalt see, or rather to thy sorrow
1155 Soon feel, whose God is strongest, thine or mine.
HARAPHA   Presume not on thy God. Whate'er he be,
Thee he regards not, owns not, hath cut off
Quite from his people, and delivered up
Into thy enemies' hand; permitted them
1160 To put out both thine eyes, and fettered send thee
Into the common prison, there to grind
Among the slaves and asses, thy comràdes,
As good for nothing else, no better service
With those thy boisterous locks; no worthy match
1165 For valor to assail, nor by the sword
Of noble warrior, so to stain his honor,
But by the barber's razor best subdued.
SAMSON   All these indignities, for such they are

2. "Brigandine": a padded chest-protector, covered with iron scales or rings. "Habergeon": a coat of mail, a hauberk. "Vant-brace": a steel cuff for the forearm. Greaves protect the shins and thighs, and gauntlets the hands. A weaver's beam, emblem of weightiness, is used to keep threads hanging tautly in a loom. All these military details are from the description of Goliath, 1 Samuel 17.4–7.

From thine,° these evils I deserve and more,   *thy people*
1170   Acknowledge them from God inflicted on me
Justly, yet despair not of his final pardon,
Whose ear is ever open, and his eye
Gracious to readmit the suppliant;
In confidence whereof I once again
1175   Defy thee to the trial of mortal fight,
By combat to decide whose god is God,
Thine, or whom I with Israel's sons adore.
HARAPHA   Fair honor that thou dost thy God, in trusting
He will accept thee to defend his cause,
1180   A murderer, a revolter, and a robber!
SAMSON   Tongue-doughty giant, how dost thou prove me these?
HARAPHA   Is not thy nation subject to our lords?
Their magistrates confessed it when they took thee
As a league-breaker, and delivered bound
1185   Into our hands; for hadst thou not committed
Notorious murder on those thirty men[3]
At Ascalon, who never did thee harm,
Then, like a robber, stripp'dst them of their robes?
The Philistines, when thou hadst broke the league,
1190   Went up with armèd powers thee only seeking,
To others did no violence nor spoil.
SAMSON   Among the daughters of the Philistines
I chose a wife, which argued me no foe,
And in your city held my nuptial feast;
1195   But your ill-meaning politician lords,
Under pretense of bridal friends and guests,
Appointed to await me thirty spies,
Who, threatening cruel death, constrained the bride
To wring from me, and tell to them, my secret,
1200   That solved the riddle which I had proposed.
When I perceived all set on enmity,
As on my enemies, wherever chanced,
I used hostility, and took their spoil,
To pay my underminers in their coin.
1205   My nation was subjected to your lords![4]
It was the force of conquest; force with force
Is well ejected when the conquered can.
But I, a private person, whom my country
As a league-breaker gave up bound, presumed
1210   Single rebellion, and did hostile acts!
I was no private,[5] but a person raised,
With strength sufficient, and command from Heaven,
To free my country. If their servile minds
Me, their deliverer sent, would not receive,
1215   But to their masters gave me up for naught,

3. Judges 14.8–20 and 15.9–15 describe the episode. When he came to Timna to be married, Samson proposed a riddle and a bet to the marriage guests; they convinced his intended bride to reveal the riddle, and in revenge, he killed thirty of their people and left the lady to the "paranymph," or best man. Old Testament Samson is indeed a rude and savage figure; Milton, with characteristic confidence, undertakes his legal defense in everything.
4. I.e., you argue that my nation was subjected to your lords.
5. I.e., lawless individual.

Th' unworthier they; whence to this day they serve.
I was to do my part from Heaven assigned,
And had performed it if my known offense
Had not disabled me, not all your force.
1220 These shifts refuted, answer thy appellant,[6]
Though by his blindness maimed for high attempts,
Who now defies thee thrice to single fight,
As a petty enterprise of small enforce.°   *difficulty*
HARAPHA   With thee, a man condemned, a slave enrolled,
1225 Due by the law to capital punishment?
To fight with thee no man of arms will deign.
SAMSON   Cam'st thou for this, vain boaster, to survey me,
To descant on my strength, and give thy verdict?
Come nearer; part not hence so slight informed;
1230 But take good heed my hand survey not thee.
HARAPHA   O Baal-zebub![7] can my ears unused
Hear these dishonors, and not render death?
SAMSON   No man withholds thee; nothing from thy hand
Fear I incurable; bring up thy van;[8]
1235 My heels are fettered, but my fist is free.
HARAPHA   This insolence other kind of answer fits.
SAMSON   Go, baffled coward, lest I run upon thee,
Though in these chains, bulk without spirit vast,
And with one buffet lay thy structure low,
1240 Or swing thee in the air, then dash thee down,
To the hazard of thy brains and shattered sides.
HARAPHA   By Astaroth,[9] ere long thou shalt lament
These braveries,° in irons loaden on thee.   *boasts*
CHORUS   His giantship is gone somewhat crestfallen,
1245 Stalking with less unconscionable° strides,   *excessive*
And lower looks, but in a sultry chafe.
SAMSON   I dread him not, nor all his giant brood,
Though fame divulge him father of five sons,
All of gigantic size, Goliath chief.[1]
1250 CHORUS   He will directly to the lords, I fear,
And with malicious counsel stir them up
Some way or other yet further to afflict thee.
SAMSON   He must allege some cause, and offered fight
Will not dare mention, lest a question rise
1255 Whether he durst accept the offer or not;
And that he durst not plain enough appeared.
Much more affliction than already felt
They cannot well impose, nor I sustain,
If they intend advantage of my labors,
1260 The work of many hands, which earns my keeping,
With no small profit daily to my owners.

6. I.e., now that we've disposed of these dodges, answer your challenger. "Apellant": literally, caller, one who calls you out.
7. Baal-zebub is Beëlzebub, god of the flies.
8. The vanguard of an army was, naturally, the first group engaged. Samson invites Harapha to start the fight.

9. Moon goddess of the Philistines, consort of Dagon (see *Paradise Lost* 1.437–46).
1. 2 Samuel 21 describes four giants "born to the giant in Gath" and brothers of Goliath, slain by David's men; Milton makes the identification with Harapha on his own.

But come what will; my deadliest foe will prove
My speediest friend, by death to rid me hence;
The worst that he can give, to me the best.
1265 Yet so it may fall out, because their end
Is hate, not help to me, it may with mine
Draw their own ruin who attempt the deed.
CHORUS   O how comely it is, and how reviving
To the spirits of just men long oppressed,
1270 When God into the hands of their deliverer
Puts invincible might
To quell the mighty of the earth, th' oppressor,
The brute and boisterous force of violent men,
Hardy and industrious to support
1275 Tyrannic power, but raging to pursue
The righteous, and all such as honor truth!
He all their ammunition
And feats of war defeats,[2]
With plain heroic magnitude of mind
1280 And celestial vigor armed;
Their armories and magazines[3] contemns,   haste
Renders them useless, while
With wingèd expedition°
Swift as the lightning glance he executes
1285 His errand on the wicked, who, surprised,
Lose their defense, distracted and amazed.
But patience is more oft the exercise
Of saints, the trial of their fortitude,
Making them each his own deliverer,
1290 And victor over all
That tyranny or fortune can inflict.
Either of these is in thy lot,°   fate
Samson, with might endued
Above the sons of men; but sight bereaved
1295 May chance to number thee with those
Whom patience finally must crown.[4]
     This idol's day hath been to thee no day of rest,
Laboring thy mind
More than the working day thy hands.
1300 And yet, perhaps, more trouble is behind;
For I descry this way
Some other tending; in his hand
A scepter or quaint° staff he bears,   ornamented
Comes on amain, speed in his look.
1305 By his habit I discern him now
A public officer, and now at hand.
His message will be short and voluble.°   to the point
OFFICER   Hebrews, the prisoner Samson here I seek.
CHORUS   His manacles remark° him; there he sits.   distinguish

2. A touch of Miltonic punning.
3. Storerooms, hence the contents, military stores.
4. The Christian tragedy, like the Christian epic, must center ultimately on an act of passive, not active, fortitude. It is the special achievement of Samson to combine in a single dramatic action both qualities.

1310 OFFICER Samson, to thee our lords thus bid me say:
         This day to Dagon is a solemn feast,
         With sacrifices, triumph, pomp, and games;
         Thy strength they know surpassing human rate,
         And now some public proof thereof require
1315   To honor this great feast, and great assembly.
         Rise, therefore, with all speed, and come along,
         Where I will see thee heartened and fresh clad,
         To appear as fits before th' illustrious lords.
       SAMSON Thou know'st I am an Hebrew; therefore tell them
1320   Our Law forbids at their religious rites
         My presence; for that cause I cannot come.
       OFFICER This answer, be assured, will not content them.
       SAMSON Have they not sword-players, and every sort
         Of gymnic artists, wrestlers, riders, runners,
1325   Jugglers and dancers, antics, mummers,⁵ mimics,
         But they must pick me out, with shackles tired,
         And over-labored at their public mill,
         To make them sport with blind activity?
         Do they not seek occasion of new quarrels,
1330   On my refusal, to distress me more,
         Or make a game of my calamities?
         Return the way thou cam'st; I will not come.
       OFFICER Regard thyself; this will offend them highly.
       SAMSON Myself? my conscience, and internal peace.
1335   Can they think me so broken, so debased
         With corporal servitude, that my mind ever
         Will condescend to such absurd commands?
         Although their drudge, to be their fool or jester,
         And in my midst of sorrow and heart-grief
1340   To show them feats, and play before their god,
         The worst of all indignities, yet on me
         Joined° with supreme contempt! I will not come.   *enjoined, ordered*
       OFFICER My message was imposed on me with speed,
         Brooks no delay: is this thy resolution?
1345   SAMSON So take it with what speed thy message needs.
       OFFICER I am sorry what this stoutness° will produce.   *defiance*
       SAMSON Perhaps thou shalt have cause to sorrow indeed.
       CHORUS Consider, Samson; matters now are strained
         Up to the height, whether to hold or break.
1350   He's gone, and who knows how he may report
         Thy words by adding fuel to the flame?
         Expect another message, more imperious,
         More lordly thundering than thou well wilt bear.
       SAMSON Shall I abuse this consecrated gift
1355   Of strength, again returning with my hair
         After my great transgression, so requite
         Favor renewed, and add a greater sin
         By prostituting holy things to idols,
         A Nazarite in place abominable

---

5. Actors. "Gymnic artists": gymnasts. "Antics": clowns.

1360   Vaunting my strength in honor to their Dagon?
    Besides how vile, contemptible, ridiculous,
    What act more execrably unclean,° profane?   *taboo*
  CHORUS   Yet with this strength thou serv'st the Philistines,
    Idolatrous, uncircumcised, unclean.
1365   SAMSON   Not in their idol-worship, but by labor
    Honest and lawful to deserve my food
    Of those who have me in their civil power.
  CHORUS   Where the heart joins not, outward acts defile not.
  SAMSON   Where outward force constrains, the sentence holds:[6]
1370   But who constrains me to the temple of Dagon,
    Not dragging? The Philistian lords command:
    Commands are no constraints. If I obey them,
    I do it freely, venturing to displease
    God for the fear of man, and man prefer,
1375   Set God behind; which, in his jealousy,
    Shall never, unrepented, find forgiveness.
    Yet that he may dispense with me, or thee,
    Present in temples at idolatrous rites
    For some important cause,[7] thou need'st not doubt.
1380   CHORUS   How thou wilt here come off surmounts my reach.
  SAMSON   Be of good courage; I begin to feel
    Some rousing motions in me which dispose
    To something extraordinary my thoughts.
    I with this messenger will go along—
1385   Nothing to do, be sure, that may dishonor
    Our Law or stain my vow of Nazarite.
    If there be aught of presage in the mind,
    This day will be remarkable in my life
    By some great act, or of my days the last.[8]
1390   CHORUS   In time thou hast resolved: the man returns.
  OFFICER   Samson, this second message from our lords
    To thee I am bid say: Art thou our slave,
    Our captive, at the public mill our drudge,
    And dar'st thou, at our sending and command,
1395   Dispute thy coming? Come without delay;
    Or we shall find such engines to assail
    And hamper thee, as thou shalt come of force,
    Though thou wert firmlier fastened than a rock.
  SAMSON   I could be well content to try their art,
1400   Which to no few of them would prove pernicious;
    Yet, knowing their advantages too many,
    Because° they shall not trail me through their streets   *so that*
    Like a wild beast, I am content to go.
    Masters' commands come with a power resistless
1405   To such as owe them absolute subjection;

---

6. I.e., where outward force constrains, your maxim is right.
7. God will make a special dispensation for Samson to attend idolatrous ceremonies "for some important cause," which Samson cannot yet define but which he intuits.
8. By a classic device of dramatic irony, Samson proposes as alternatives two events that will both simultaneously come true. "Presage": premonition, presight.

And for a life who will not change his purpose?
(So mutable are all the ways of men!)
Yet this be sure, in nothing to comply
Scandalous or forbidden in our Law.
OFFICER I praise thy resolution. Doff these links:[9]
By this compliance thou wilt win the lords
To favor, and perhaps to set thee free.
SAMSON Brethren, farewell. Your company along
I will not wish, lest it perhaps offend them
To see me girt with friends; and how the sight
Of me, as of a common enemy,
So dreaded once, may now exasperate them
I know not. Lords are lordliest in their wine;
And the well-feasted priest then soonest fired
With zeal, if aught religion seem concerned;[1]
No less the people, on their holy-days,
Impetuous, insolent, unquenchable.
Happen what may, of me expect to hear
Nothing dishonorable, impure, unworthy
Our God, our Law, my nation, or myself;
The last of me or no I cannot warrant.
CHORUS Go, and the Holy One
Of Israel be thy guide
To what may serve his glory best, and spread his name
Great among the heathen round;
Send thee the angel of thy birth, to stand
Fast by thy side, who from thy father's field
Rode up in flames after his message told
Of thy conception, and be now a shield
Of fire; that Spirit that first rushed on thee
In the camp of Dan,
Be efficacious in thee now at need![2]
For never was from Heaven imparted
Measure of strength so great to mortal seed
As in thy wondrous actions hath been seen.
But wherefore comes old Manoa in such haste
With youthful steps? Much livelier than erewhile
He seems: supposing here to find his son,
Or of him bringing to us some glad news?
MANOA Peace with you, brethren! My inducement hither
Was not at present here to find my son,
By order of the lords new parted hence
To come and play before them at their feast.
I heard all as I came; the city rings,
And numbers thither flock: I had no will,
Lest I should see him forced to things unseemly.
But that which moved my coming now was chiefly

---

9. Take off these chains. "Resolution": decision.
1. Milton's animus against paid priests, whom he considered particularly likely to contaminate the Word of God with their own private interests

and worldly desires, comes out plainly here.
2. As a Nazarite (specially consecrated person), Samson had been frequently inspired by the "Spirit of the Lord."

To give ye part with me[3] what hope I have
With good success to work his liberty.
1455 CHORUS   That hope would much rejoice us to partake
With thee. Say, reverend sire; we thirst to hear.
MANOA   I have attempted, one by one, the lords,
Either at home, or through the high street passing,
With supplication prone and father's tears,
1460 To accept of ransom for my son, their prisoner.
Some much averse I found, and wondrous harsh,
Contemptuous, proud, set on revenge and spite;
That part most reverenced Dagon and his priests:
Others more moderate seeming, but their aim
1465 Private reward, for which both God and State
They easily would set to sale: a third
More generous far and civil, who confessed
They had enough revenged, having reduced
Their foe to misery beneath their fears;
1470 The rest was magnanimity to remit,
If some convenient ransom were proposed.[4]
What noise or shout was that? It tore the sky.
CHORUS   Doubtless the people shouting to behold
Their once great dread, captive and blind before them,
1475 Or at some proof of strength before them shown.
MANOA   His ransom, if my whole inheritance
May compass it, shall willingly be paid
And numbered down. Much rather I shall choose
To live the poorest in my tribe, than richest
1480 And he in that calamitous prison left.
No, I am fixed not to part hence without him.
For his redemption all my patrimony,
If need be, I am ready to forgo
And quit. Not wanting him, I shall want nothing.
1485 CHORUS   Fathers are wont to lay up for their sons:
Thou for thy son art bent to lay out all;
Sons wont to nurse their parents in old age:
Thou in old age car'st how to nurse thy son,
Made older than thy age through eyesight lost.
1490 MANOA   It shall be my delight to tend his eyes,
And view him sitting in the house, ennobled
With all those high exploits by him achieved,
And on his shoulders waving down those locks
That of a nation armed the strength contained.
1495 And I persuade me God hath not permitted
His strength again to grow up with his hair
Garrisoned round about him like a camp
Of faithful soldiery, were not his purpose
To use him further yet in some great service—
1500 Not to sit idle with so great a gift

3. I.e., to impart to you.
4. The three parties are in effect bigots, swindlers, and gentlemen—types common enough in

Restoration England, with whom Milton and the
defeated Puritans had frequently to deal.

Useless, and thence ridiculous, about him.[5]
And since his strength with eyesight was not lost,
God will restore him eyesight to° his strength.   *in proportion to*
CHORUS   Thy hopes are not ill-founded, nor seem vain,
1505   Of his delivery, and thy joy thereon
Conceived, agreeable to a father's love;
In both which we, as next,° participate.   *as kinsmen*
MANOA   I know your friendly minds, and—O what noise!
Mercy of Heaven! what hideous noise was that?
1510   Horribly loud, unlike the former shout.
CHORUS   Noise call you it, or universal groan,
As if the whole inhabitation perished?
Blood, death, and deathful deeds are in that noise,
Ruin,[6] destruction at the utmost point.
1515   MANOA   Of ruin indeed methought I heard the noise.
Oh! it continues; they have slain my son.
CHORUS   Thy son is rather slaying them; that outcry
From slaughter of one foe could not ascend.
MANOA   Some dismal accident it needs must be.
1520   What shall we do, stay here, or run and see?
CHORUS   Best keep together here, lest running thither
We unawares run into danger's mouth.
This evil on the Philistines is fallen:
From whom could else a general cry be heard?
1525   The sufferers then will scarce molest us here;
From other hands we need not much to fear.
What if, his eyesight (for to Israel's God
Nothing is hard) by miracle restored,
He now be dealing dole[7] among his foes,
1530   And over heaps of slaughtered walk his way?
MANOA   That were a joy presumptuous to be thought.
CHORUS   Yet God hath wrought things as incredible
For his people of old; what hinders now?
MANOA   He can, I know, but doubt to think he will;
1535   Yet hope would fain subscribe, and tempts belief.
A little stay will bring some notice hither.
CHORUS   Of good or bad so great, of bad the sooner;
For evil news rides post, while good news baits.[8]
And to our wish I see one hither speeding—
1540   An Hebrew, as I guess, and of our tribe.
MESSENGER[9]   O whither shall I run, or which way fly
The sight of this so horrid spectacle,
Which erst° my eyes beheld, and yet behold?   *just now*
For dire imagination still pursues me.

5. Much of the play deals with the concept of relevance and irrelevance; outward weapons and outward strength are often beside the point ("ridiculous") in the face of inward and spiritual powers.
6. From Latin *ruina*, downfall.
7. Grief, pain, with perhaps a pun on "dole," that which is handed out.
8. Pauses to renew ("bait") the horses.
9. Greek tragedy forbade the representation on stage of actual bloodshed; a messenger is, therefore, a frequent figure at the end of these plays, arriving posthaste from the scene of the final catastrophe, to deliver in a long set speech a descriptive report.

1545   But providence or instinct of nature seems,
       Or reason, though disturbed, and scarce consulted,
       To have guided me aright, I know not how,
       To thee first, reverend Manoa, and to these
       My countrymen, whom here I knew remaining,
1550   As at some distance from the place of horror,
       So[1] in the sad event too much concerned.
       MANOA   The accident was loud, and here before thee
       With rueful cry; yet what it was we hear not.
       No preface needs; thou seest we long to know.
1555   MESSENGER   It would burst forth; but I recover breath,
       And sense distract, to know well what I utter.
       MANOA   Tell us the sum; the circumstance defer.
       MESSENGER   Gaza yet stands; but all her sons are fallen,
       All in a moment overwhelmed and fallen.
1560   MANOA   Sad, but thou know'st to Israelites not saddest,
       The desolation of a hostile city.
       MESSENGER   Feed on that first; there may in grief be surfeit.[2]
       MANOA   Relate by whom.
       MESSENGER   By Samson.
       MANOA   That still lessens
       The sorrow, and converts it nigh to joy.
1565   MESSENGER   Ah! Manoa, I refrain too suddenly
       To utter what will come at last too soon,
       Lest evil tidings, with too rude irruption
       Hitting thy agèd ear, should pierce too deep.
       MANOA   Suspense in news is torture; speak them out.
1570   MESSENGER   Then take the worst in brief: Samson is dead.
       MANOA   The worst indeed! O all my hope's defeated
       To free him hence! but Death who sets all free
       Hath paid his ransom now and full discharge.
       What windy° joy this day had I conceived,   *empty, talky*
1575   Hopeful of his delivery, which now proves
       Abortive as the first-born bloom of spring
       Nipped with the lagging rear of winter's frost!
       Yet ere I give the reins to grief, say first
       How died he; death to life is crown or shame.
1580   All by him fell, thou say'st; by whom fell he?
       What glorious hand gave Samson his death's wound?
       MESSENGER   Unwounded of his enemies he fell.
       MANOA   Wearied with slaughter, then, or how? Explain.
       MESSENGER   By his own hands.
       MANOA   Self-violence! What cause
1585   Brought him so soon at variance with himself
       Among his foes?
       MESSENGER   Inevitable cause
       At once both to destroy and be destroyed.
       The edifice, where all were met to see him,
       Upon their heads and on his own he pulled.

---

1. The construction "as . . . so . . . ." is equivalent to "though . . . yet. . . ."
2. I.e., there may be all too much grief to follow.

1590 MANOA O lastly over-strong against thyself!
A dreadful way thou took'st to thy revenge.
More than enough we know; but while things yet
Are in confusion, give us, if thou canst,
Eyewitness of what first or last was done,
1595 Relation more particular and distinct.
MESSENGER Occasions drew me early to this city;
And as the gates I entered with sunrise,
The morning trumpets festival proclaimed
Through each high street. Little I had dispatched,
1600 When all abroad was rumored that this day
Samson should be brought forth, to show the people
Proof of his mighty strength in feats and games.
I sorrowed at his captive state, but minded
Not to be absent at that spectacle.
1605 The building was a spacious theater,
Half round on two main pillars vaulted high,
With seats where all the lords, and each degree
Of sort,° might sit in order to behold;   *of rank*
The other side was open, where the throng
1610 On banks and scaffolds under sky might stand:[4]
I among these aloof obscurely stood.
The feast and noon grew high, and sacrifice
Had filled their hearts with mirth, high cheer, and wine,
When to their sports they turned. Immediately
1615 Was Samson as a public servant brought,
In their state livery clad: before him pipes
And timbrels;° on each side went armèd guards;   *tambourines*
Both horse and foot before him and behind,
Archers and slingers, cataphracts[5] and spears.
1620 At sight of him the people with a shout
Rifted the air, clamoring their god with praise,
Who had made their dreadful enemy their thrall.
He, patient but undaunted, where they led him,
Came to the place; and what was set before him,
1625 Which without help of eye might be essayed,
To heave, pull, draw, or break, he still performed
All with incredible, stupendous force,
None daring to appear antagonist.
At length for intermission sake they led him
1630 Between the pillars; he his guide requested
(For so from such as nearer stood we heard),
As over-tired, to let him lean a while
With both his arms on those two massy pillars,
That to the archèd roof gave main support.
1635 He unsuspicious led him; which when Samson
Felt in his arms, with head a while inclined,
And eyes fast fixed he stood, as one who prayed,

---

4. The temple at Gaza comprised a covered pavilion or shell for the gentry, semicircular in shape
and supported at the center of the semicircle by
two pillars; on the open side, under the hot sun,
and behind the stage, as it were, stood the common people.
5. Armored horsemen on armored horses.

Or some great matter in his mind revolved:
At last, with head erect, thus cried aloud:
1640 "Hitherto, Lords, what your commands imposed
I have performed, as reason was, obeying,
Not without wonder or delight beheld;
Now of my own accord such other trial
I mean to show you of my strength yet greater
1645 As with amaze shall strike all who behold."
This uttered, straining all his nerves,° he bowed;   muscles
As with the force of winds and waters pent
When mountains tremble,[6] those two massy pillars
With horrible convulsion to and fro
1650 He tugged, he shook, till down they came, and drew
The whole roof after them with burst of thunder
Upon the heads of all who sat beneath,
Lords, ladies, captains, counselors, or priests,
Their choice nobility and flower, not only
1655 Of this, but each Philistian city round,
Met from all parts to solemnize this feast.
Samson, with these immixed, inevitably
Pulled down the same destruction on himself;
The vulgar° only 'scaped, who stood without.   common people
1660 CHORUS   O dearly bought revenge, yet glorious!
Living or dying thou hast fulfilled
The work for which thou wast foretold
To Israel, and now li'st victorious
Among thy slain self-killed;
1665 Not willingly, but tangled in the fold
Of dire Necessity,[7] whose law in death conjoined
Thee with thy slaughtered foes, in number more
Than all thy life had slain before.
SEMICHORUS[8]   While their hearts were jocund and sublime,
1670 Drunk with idolatry, drunk with wine
And fat regorged[9] of bulls and goats,
Chaunting their idol, and preferring
Before our living Dread, who dwells
In Silo, his bright sanctuary,[1]
1675 Among them he a spirit of frenzy sent,
Who hurt their minds,
And urged them on with mad desire
To call in haste for their destroyer.
They, only set on sport and play,
1680 Unweetingly° importuned   unwittingly
Their own destruction to come speedy upon them.
So fond are mortal men,
Fallen into wrath divine,
As their own ruin on themselves to invite,

6. Earthquakes in Milton's day were supposed to be caused by escaping winds and waters imprisoned ("pent") beneath the earth.
7. Samson must not be supposed guilty of suicide (see lines 1586–87).
8. In classical theater a chorus was commonly split in two parts, their speeches to be recited alternately.
9. Greedily devoured. "Jocund and sublime": joyous and exalted.
1. Shiloh, where the Israelites established their tabernacle (Joshua 18.1).

1685 Insensate left, or to sense reprobate,
And with blindness internal[2] struck.
SEMICHORUS   But he, though blind of sight,
Despised, and thought extinguished quite,
With inward eyes illuminated,
1690 His fiery virtue roused
From under ashes into sudden flame,
And as an evening dragon[3] came,
Assailant on the perchèd roosts
And nests in order ranged
1695 Of tame villatic[4] fowl, but as an eagle
His cloudless thunder bolted on their heads.
So Virtue, given for lost,[5]
Depressed and overthrown, as seemed,
Like that self-begotten bird,[6]
1700 In the Arabian woods°   *enclosed, hidden*
That no second knows nor third,
And lay erewhile a holocaust,[7]
From out her ashy womb now teemed,
Revives, reflourishes, then vigorous most
1705 When most unactive deemed;
And, though her body die, her fame survives,
A secular[8] bird, ages of lives.
MANOA   Come, come; no time for lamentation now,
Nor much more cause. Samson hath quit° himself   *acquitted*
1710 Like Samson, and heroicly hath finished
A life heroic, on his enemies
Fully revenged; hath left them years of mourning
And lamentation to the sons of Caphtor[9]
Through all Philistian bounds; to Israel
1715 Honor hath left and freedom, let but them
Find courage to lay hold on this occasion;
To himself and father's house eternal fame;
And, which is best and happiest yet, all this
With God not parted from him, as was feared,
1720 But favoring and assisting to the end.
Nothing is here for tears, nothing to wail
Or knock the breast; no weakness, no contempt,
Dispraise, or blame; nothing but well and fair,
And what may quiet us in a death so noble.
1725 Let us go find the body where it lies
Soaked in his enemies' blood, and from the stream
With lavers° pure and cleansing herbs wash off   *basins*
The clotted gore. I, with what speed the while[1]
(Gaza is not in plight to say us nay),

2. The play accomplishes itself by showing the internal blindness of the Philistines at the very moment of Samson's spiritual illumination.
3. Serpent (from Latin *draco*).
4. Farmyard (from Latin *villaticus*).
5. Given up for lost. "Bolted": cast as a thunderbolt.
6. The mythical phoenix begets itself out of its own ashes; it is unique, in that there is only one phoenix alive at any one time, and it lives in the scrubland of Arabia.
7. A sacrifice burned whole on the altar.
8. Living through the centuries (Latin *saecula*).
9. In Amos 9.7 the Philistines are described as immigrants from Caphtor (perhaps Crete).
1. I.e., with what speed (I may) in the meanwhile.

1730 Will send for all my kindred, all my friends,
To fetch him hence and solemnly attend,
With silent obsequy and funeral train,
Home to his father's house. There will I build him
A monument, and plant it round with shade
1735 Of laurel ever green and branching palm,[2]
With all his trophies hung, and acts enrolled
In copious legend, or sweet lyric song.
Thither shall all the valiant youth resort,
And from his memory inflame their breasts
1740 To matchless valor and adventures high;
The virgins also shall, on feastful days,
Visit his tomb with flowers, only bewailing
His lot unfortunate in nuptial choice,
From whence captivity and loss of eyes.
1745 CHORUS[3]   All is best, though we oft doubt
What th' unsearchable dispose°   *disposition*
Of Highest Wisdom brings about,
And ever best found in the close.
Oft he seems to hide his face,
1750 But unexpectedly returns,
And to his faithful champion hath in place[4]
Bore witness gloriously; whence Gaza mourns,
And all that band them to resist
His uncontrollable intent.
1755 His servants he, with new acquist°   *acquisition*
Of true experience from this great event,
With peace and consolation hath dismissed,
And calm of mind, all passion spent.

1671

---

2. Leaves of laurel were worn by civic conquerors on triumphal occasions; wreaths of palm were given to victors in the Olympic games. Samson, as both an athletic victor in his *agon* and the savior of his people, gets both.
3. The final chorus of the play is cast in the rhyme pattern of a sonnet.
4. On this very spot, at this very instant.

APPENDIXES

General Bibliography

This bibliography consists of a list of suggested general readings on English literature. Bibliographies for the authors in *The Norton Anthology of English Literature* are available online in the NAEL Archive (digital.wwnorton.com/englishlit10abc and digital.wwnorton.com/englishlit10def).

Suggested General Readings

Histories of England and of English Literature

Even the most distinguished of the comprehensive general histories written in past generations have come to seem outmoded. Innovative research in social, cultural, and political history has made it difficult to write a single coherent account of England from the Middle Ages to the present, let alone to accommodate in a unified narrative the complex histories of Scotland, Ireland, Wales, and the other nations where writing in English has flourished. Readers who wish to explore the historical matrix out of which the works of literature collected in this anthology emerged are advised to consult the studies of particular periods listed in the appropriate sections of this bibliography. The multivolume *Oxford History of England* and *New Oxford History of England* are useful, as are the three-volume *Peoples of the British Isles: A New History*, ed. Stanford Lehmberg, 1992; the nine-volume *Cambridge Cultural History of Britain*, ed. Boris Ford, 1992; the three-volume *Cambridge Social History of Britain, 1750–1950*, ed. F. M. L. Thompson, 1992; and the multivolume *Penguin History of Britain*, gen. ed. David Cannadine, 1996–. For Britain's imperial history, readers can consult the five-volume *Oxford History of the British Empire*, ed. Roger Louis, 1998–99, as well as *Gender and Empire*, ed. Philippa Levine, 2004. Given the cultural centrality of London, readers may find particular interest in *The London Encyclopaedia*, ed. Ben Weinreb et al., 3rd ed., 2008; Roy Porter, *London: A Social History*, 1994; and Jerry White, *London in the Nineteenth Century: "A Human Awful Wonder of God,"* 2007, and *London in the Twentieth Century: A City and Its People*, 2001.

Similar observations may be made about literary history. In the light of such initiatives as women's studies, new historicism, and postcolonialism, the range of authors deemed significant has expanded, along with the geographical and conceptual boundaries of literature in English. Attempts to capture in a unified account the great sweep of literature from *Beowulf* to the early twenty-first century have largely given way to studies of individual genres, carefully delimited time periods, and specific authors. For these more focused accounts, see the listings by period. Among the large-scale literary surveys, *The Cambridge Guide to Literature in English*, 3rd ed., 2006, is useful, as is the nine-volume *Penguin History of Literature*, 1993–94. *The Feminist Companion to Literature in English*, ed. Virginia Blain, Isobel Grundy, and Patricia Clements, 1990, is an important resource, and the editorial materials in *The Norton Anthology of Literature by Women*, 3rd ed., 2007, eds. Sandra M. Gilbert and Susan Gubar, constitute a concise history and set of biographies of women authors since the Middle Ages. *Annals of English Literature, 1475–1950*, rev. 1961, lists important publications year by year, together with the significant literary events for each year. Six volumes have been published in the *Oxford English Literary History*, gen. ed. Jonathan Bate, 2002–: Laura Ashe, *1000–1350: Conquest and Transformation;*

James Simpson, *1350–1547: Reform and Cultural Revolution*; Philip Davis, *1830–1880: The Victorians*; Chris Baldick, *1830–1880: The Modern Movement*; Randall Stevenson, *1960–2000: The Last of England?*; and Bruce King, *1948–2000: The Internationalization of English Literature*. See also *The Cambridge History of Medieval English Literature*, ed. David Wallace, 1999; *The Cambridge History of Early Medieval English Literature*, ed. Clare E. Lees, 2012; *The Cambridge History of Early Modern English Literature*, ed. David Loewenstein and Janel Mueller, 2003; *The Cambridge History of English Literature, 1660–1780*, ed. John Richetti, 2005; *The Cambridge History of English Romantic Literature*, ed. James Chandler, 2009; *The Cambridge History of Victorian Literature*, ed. Kate Flint, 2012; and *The Cambridge History of Twentieth-Century English Literature*, ed. Laura Marcus and Peter Nicholls, 2005.

Helpful treatments and surveys of English meter, rhyme, and stanza forms are Paul Fussell Jr., *Poetic Meter and Poetic Form*, rev. 1979; Donald Wesling, *The Chances of Rhyme: Device and Modernity*, 1980; Charles O. Hartman, *Free Verse: An Essay in Prosody*, 1983; John Hollander, *Rhyme's Reason: A Guide to English Verse*, rev. 1989; Derek Attridge, *Poetic Rhythm: An Introduction*, 1995; Robert Pinsky, *The Sounds of Poetry: A Brief Guide*, 1998; Mark Strand and Eavan Boland, eds., *The Making of a Poem: A Norton Anthology of Poetic Forms*, 2000; Helen Vendler, *Poems, Poets, Poetry*, 3rd ed., 2010; Virginia Jackson and Yopie Prins, eds., *The Lyric Theory Reader*, 2013; and Jonathan Culler, *Theory of the Lyric*, 2015.

On the development and functioning of the novel as a form, see Ian Watt, *The Rise of the Novel*, 1957; Gérard Genette, *Narrative Discourse: An Essay in Method*, 1980; *Theory of the Novel: A Historical Approach*, ed. Michael McKeon, 2000; McKeon, *The Origins of the English Novel, 1600–1740*, 15th anniversary ed., 2002; and *The Novel*, ed. Franco Moretti, 2 vols., 2006–07. *The Cambridge History of the English Novel*, eds. Robert L. Caserio and Clement Hawes, 2012; *A Companion to the English Novel*, eds. Stephen Arata et al., 2015; eight volumes have been published from *The Oxford History of the Novel in English*, 2011–16. On women novelists and readers, see Nancy Armstrong, *Desire and Domestic Fiction: A Political History of the Novel*, 1987; and Catherine Gallagher, *Nobody's Story: The Vanishing Acts of Women Writers in the Marketplace, 1670–1820*, 1994.

On the history of playhouse design, see Richard Leacroft, *The Development of the English Playhouse: An Illustrated Survey of Theatre Building in England from Medieval to Modern Times*, 1988. For a survey of the plays that have appeared on these and other stages, see Allardyce Nicoll, *British Drama*, rev. 1962; the eight-volume *Revels History of Drama in English*, gen. eds. Clifford Leech and T. W. Craik, 1975–83; and Alfred Harbage, *Annals of English Drama, 975–1700*, 3rd ed., 1989, rev. S. Schoenbaum and Sylvia Wagonheim; and the three volumes of *The Cambridge History of British Theatre*, eds. Jane Milling, Peter Thomson, and Joseph Donohue, 2004.

On some of the key intellectual currents that are at once reflected in and shaped by literature and contemporary literary criticism, Arthur O. Lovejoy's classic studies *The Great Chain of Being*, 1936, and *Essays in the History of Ideas*, 1948, remain valuable, along with such works as Georg Simmel, *The Philosophy of Money*, 1907; Lovejoy and George Boas, *Primitivism and Related Ideas in Antiquity*, 1935; Norbert Elias, *The Civilizing Process*, orig. pub. 1939, English trans. 1969; Simone de Beauvoir, *The Second Sex*, 1949; Frantz Fanon, *Black Skin, White Masks*, 1952, new trans. 2008; Ernst Cassirer, *The Philosophy of Symbolic Forms*, 4 vols., 1953–96; Ernst Kantorowicz, *The King's Two Bodies: A Study in Medieval Political Theology*, 1957, new ed. 1997; Hannah Arendt, *The Human Condition*, 1958; Richard Popkin, *The History of Skepticism from Erasmus to Descartes*, 1960; M. H. Abrams, *Natural Supernaturalism: Tradition and Revolution in Romantic Literature*, 1971; Michel Foucault, *Madness and Civilization: A History of Insanity in the Age of Reason*, Eng.

trans. 1965, and *The Order of Things: An Archaeology of the Human Sciences*, Eng. trans. 1970; Gaston Bachelard, *The Poetics of Space*, Eng. trans. 1969; Martin Jay, *The Dialectical Imagination: A History of the Frankfurt School and the Institute of Social Research, 1923–1950*, 1973, new ed. 1996; Hayden White, *Metahistory*, 1973; Roland Barthes, *The Pleasure of the Text*, Eng. trans. 1975; Jacques Derrida, *Of Grammatology*, Eng. trans. 1976, and *Dissemination*, Eng. trans. 1981; Richard Rorty, *Philosophy and the Mirror of Nature*, 1979; Gilles Deleuze and Félix Guattari, *A Thousand Plateaus*, 1980; Raymond Williams, *Keywords: A Vocabulary of Culture and Society*, rev. 1983; Pierre Bourdieu, *Distinction: A Social Critique of the Judgment of Taste*, Eng. trans. 1984; Michel de Certeau, *The Practice of Everyday Life*, Eng. trans. 1984; Hans Blumenberg, *The Legitimacy of the Modern Age*, Eng. trans. 1985; Jürgen Habermas, *The Philosophical Discourse of Modernity*, Eng. trans, 1987; Slavoj Žižek, *The Sublime Object of Ideology*, 1989; Homi Bhabha, *The Location of Culture*, 1994; Judith Butler, *The Psychic Life of Power: Theories in Subjection*, 1997; and Sigmund Freud, *Writings on Art and Literature*, ed. Neil Hertz, 1997.

Reference Works

The single most important tool for the study of literature in English is the *Oxford English Dictionary*, 2nd ed. 1989, 3rd ed. in process. The most current edition is available online to subscribers. The *OED* is written on historical principles: that is, it attempts not only to describe current word use but also to record the history and development of the language from its origins before the Norman conquest to the present. It thus provides, for familiar as well as archaic and obscure words, the widest possible range of meanings and uses, organized chronologically and illustrated with quotations. The *OED* can be searched as a conventional dictionary arranged a–z and also by subject, usage, region, origin, and timeline (the first appearance of a word). Beyond the *OED* there are many other valuable dictionaries, such as *The American Heritage Dictionary* (5th ed., 2016), *The Oxford Dictionary of Abbreviations*, *The Concise Oxford Dictionary of English Etymology*, *The Oxford Dictionary of English Grammar*, *A New Dictionary of Eponyms*, *The Oxford Essential Dictionary of Foreign Terms in English*, *The Oxford Dictionary of Idioms*, *The Concise Oxford Dictionary of Linguistics*, *The Oxford Guide to World English*, and *The Concise Oxford Dictionary of Proverbs*. Other valuable reference works include *The Cambridge Encyclopedia of the English Language*, 2nd ed., ed. David Crystal, 2003; *The Concise Oxford Companion to the English Language*; *Pocket Fowler's Modern English Usage*; and the numerous guides to specialized vocabularies, slang, regional dialects, and the like.

There is a steady flow of new editions of most major and many minor writers in English, along with a ceaseless outpouring of critical appraisals and scholarship. James L. Harner's *Literary Research Guide: An Annotated List of Reference Sources in English Literary Studies* (6th ed., 2009; online ed. available to subscribers at www.mlalrg.org/public) offers thorough, evaluative annotations of a wide range of sources. For the historical record of scholarship and critical discussion, *The New Cambridge Bibliography of English Literature*, ed. George Watson, 5 vols. (1969–77) and *The Cambridge Bibliography of English Literature*, 3rd ed., 5 vols. (1941–2000) are useful. The *MLA International Bibliography* (also online) is a key resource for following critical discussion of literatures in English. Ranging from 1926 to the present; it includes journal articles, essays, chapters from collections, books, and dissertations, and covers folklore, linguistics, and film. The *Annual Bibliography of English Language and Literature* (*ABELL*), compiled by the Modern Humanities Research Association, lists monographs, periodical articles, critical editions of literary works, book reviews, and collections of essays published anywhere in the world; unpublished doctoral dissertations are covered for the period 1920–99 (available online to subscribers and as part of Literature Online, http://literature.proquest.com/marketing/index.jsp).

For compact biographies of English authors, see the multivolume *Oxford Dictionary of National Biography* (*DNB*), ed. H. C. G. Matthew and Brian Harrison, 2004; since 2004 the *DNB* has been extended online with three annual updates. Handy reference books of authors, works, and various literary terms and allusions include many volumes in the *Cambridge Companion* and *Oxford Companion* series (e.g., *The Cambridge Companion to Narrative*, ed David Herman, 2007; *The Oxford Companion to English Literature*, ed. Dinah Birch, rev. 2016; *The Cambridge Companion to Allegory*, ed. Rita Copeland and Peter Struck, 2010; etc.). Likewise, *The Princeton Encyclopedia of Poetry and Poetics*, ed. Roland Greene and others, 4th ed., is available online to subscribers in ProQuest Ebook Central. Handbooks that define and illustrate literary concepts and terms are *The Penguin Dictionary of Literary Terms and Literary Theory*, ed. J. A. Cuddon and M. A. R. Habib, 5th ed., 2015; William Harmon, *A Handbook to Literature*, 12th ed., 2011; *Critical Terms for Literary Study*, ed. Frank Lentricchia and Thomas McLaughlin, rev. 1995; and M. H. Abrams and Geoffrey Harpham, *A Glossary of Literary Terms*, 11th ed., 2014. Also useful are Richard Lanham, *A Handlist of Rhetorical Terms*, 2nd ed., 2012; Arthur Quinn, *Figures of Speech: 60 Ways to Turn a Phrase*, 1995; and the *Barnhart Concise Dictionary of Etymology*, ed. Robert K. Barnhart, 1995; and George Kennedy, *A New History of Classical Rhetoric*, 2009.

On the Greek and Roman backgrounds, see *The Cambridge History of Classical Literature* (vol. 1: *Greek Literature*, 1982; vol. 2: *Latin Literature*, 1989), both available online; *The Oxford Companion to Classical Literature*, ed. M. C. Howatson, 3rd ed., 2011; Gian Biagio Conte, *Latin Literature: A History*, 1994; *The Oxford Classical Dictionary*, 4th ed., 2012; Richard Rutherford, *Classical Literature: A Concise History*, 2005; and Mark P. O. Morford, Robert J. Lenardon, and Michael Sham, *Classical Mythology*, 10th ed., 2013. The Loeb Classical Library of Greek and Roman texts is now available online to subscribers at www.loebclassics.com.

Digital resources in the humanities have vastly proliferated since the previous edition of *The Norton Anthology of English Literature* and are continuing to grow rapidly. The NAEL Archive (accessed at digital.wwnorton.com/englishlit10abc and digital.wwnorton.com/englishlit10def) is the gateway to an extensive array of annotated texts, images, and other materials especially gathered for the readers of this anthology. Among other useful electronic resources for the study of English literature are enormous digital archives, available to subscribers: Early English Books Online (EEBO), http://eebo.chadwyck.com/home; Literature Online, http://literature.proquest.com/marketing/index.jsp; and Eighteenth Century Collections Online (ECCO), www.gale.com/primary-sources/eighteenth-century-collections-online. There are also numerous free sites of variable quality. Many of the best of these are period or author specific and hence are listed in the period/author bibiliographies in the NAEL Archive. Among the general sites, one of the most useful and wide-ranging is Voice of the Shuttle (http://vos.ucsb.edu), which includes in its aggregation links to Bartleby.com and Project Gutenberg.

Literary Criticism and Theory

Nine volumes of the *Cambridge History of Literary Criticism* have been published, 1989– : *Classical Criticism*, ed. George A. Kennedy; *The Middle Ages*, ed. Alastair Minnis and Ian Johnson; *The Renaissance*, ed. Glyn P. Norton; *The Eighteenth Century*, ed. H. B. Nisbet and Claude Rawson; *Romanticism*, ed. Marshall Brown; *The Nineteenth Century ca. 1830–1914*, ed. M. A. R. Habib; *Modernism and the New Criticism*, ed. A. Walton Litz, Louis Menand, and Lawrence Rainey; *From Formalism to Poststructuralism*, ed. Raman Selden; and *Twentieth-Century Historical, Philosoph-*

ical, and Psychological Perspectives, ed. Christa Knellwolf and Christopher Norris. See also M. H. Abrams, *The Mirror and the Lamp: Romantic Theory and the Critical Tradition*, 1953; William K. Wimsatt and Cleanth Brooks, *Literary Criticism: A Short History*, 1957; René Wellek, *A History of Modern Criticism: 1750–1950*, 9 vols., 1955–93; Frank Lentricchia, *After the New Criticism*, 1980; and J. Hillis Miller, *On Literature*, 2002. Raman Selden, Peter Widdowson, and Peter Brooker have written *A Reader's Guide to Contemporary Literary Theory*, 5th ed., 2015. Other useful resources include *The Johns Hopkins Guide to Literary Theory and Criticism*, 2nd ed., 2004; *Literary Theory, an Anthology*, eds. Julie Rivkin and Michael Ryan, 1998; and *The Norton Anthology of Theory and Criticism*, 3rd ed., gen. ed. Vincent Leitch, 2018.

Modern approaches to English literature and literary theory were shaped by certain landmark works: William Empson, *Seven Types of Ambiguity*, 1930, 3rd ed. 1953, *Some Versions of Pastoral*, 1935, and *The Structure of Complex Words*, 1951; F. R. Leavis, *Revaluation*, 1936, and *The Great Tradition*, 1948; Lionel Trilling, *The Liberal Imagination*, 1950; T. S. Eliot, *Selected Essays*, 3rd ed. 1951, and *On Poetry and Poets*, 1957; Erich Auerbach, *Mimesis: The Representation of Reality in Western Literature*, 1953; William K. Wimsatt, *The Verbal Icon*, 1954; Northrop Frye, *Anatomy of Criticism*, 1957; Wayne C. Booth, *The Rhetoric of Fiction*, 1961, rev. ed. 1983; and W. J. Bate, *The Burden of the Past and the English Poet*, 1970. René Wellek and Austin Warren, *Theory of Literature*, rev. 1970, is a useful introduction to the variety of scholarly and critical approaches to literature up to the time of its publication. Jonathan Culler's *Literary Theory: A Very Short Introduction*, 1997, discusses recurrent issues and debates.

Beginning in the late 1960s, there was a significant intensification of interest in literary theory as a specific field. Certain forms of literary study had already been influenced by the work of the Russian linguist Roman Jakobson and the Russian formalist Viktor Shklovsky and, still more, by conceptions that derived or claimed to derive from Marx and Engels, but the full impact of these theories was not felt until what became known as the "theory revolution" of the 1970s and '80s. For Marxist literary criticism, see Georg Lukács, *Theory of the Novel*, 1920, trans. 1971; *The Historical Novel*, 1937, trans. 1983; and *Studies in European Realism*, trans. 1964; Walter Benjamin's essays from the 1920s and '30s represented in *Illuminations*, trans. 1986, and *Reflections*, trans. 1986; Mikhail Bakhtin's essays from the 1930s represented in *The Dialogic Imagination*, trans. 1981, and *Rabelais and His World*, 1941, trans. 1968; *Selections from the Prison Notebooks of Antonio Gramsci*, ed. and trans. Quintin Hoare and Geoffrey Smith, 1971; Raymond Williams, *Marxism and Literature*, 1977; Tony Bennett, *Formalism and Marxism*, 1979; Fredric Jameson, *The Political Unconscious: Narrative as a Socially Symbolic Act*, 1981; and Terry Eagleton, *Literary Theory: An Introduction*, 3rd ed., 2008, and *The Ideology of the Aesthetic*, 1990.

Structural linguistics and anthropology gave rise to a flowering of structuralist literary criticism; convenient introductions include Robert Scholes, *Structuralism in Literature: An Introduction*, 1974, and Jonathan Culler, *Structuralist Poetics*, 1975. Poststructuralist challenges to this approach are epitomized in such influential works as Jacques Derrida, *Writing and Difference*, 1967, trans. 1978, and Paul de Man, *Blindness and Insight: Essays in the Rhetoric of Contemporary Criticism*, 1971, 2nd ed., 1983. Poststructuralism is discussed in Jonathan Culler, *On Deconstruction*, 1982; Slavoj Žižek, *The Sublime Object of Ideology*, 1989; Fredric Jameson, *Postmodernism; or the Cultural Logic of Late Capitalism*, 1991; John McGowan, *Postmodernism and Its Critics*, 1991; and *Beyond Structuralism*, ed. Wendell Harris, 1996. A figure who greatly influenced both structuralism and poststructuralism is Roland Barthes, in *Mythologies*, trans. 1972, and *S/Z*, trans. 1974. Among other influential contributions to literary theory are the psychoanalytic approach in Harold Bloom, *The Anxiety of*

Influence, 1973; and the reader-response approach in Stanley Fish, *Is There a Text in This Class?: The Authority of Interpretive Communities*, 1980. For a retrospect on the theory decades, see Terry Eagleton, *After Theory*, 2003.

Influenced by these theoretical currents but not restricted to them, modern feminist literary criticism was fashioned by such works as Patricia Meyer Spacks, *The Female Imagination*, 1975; Ellen Moers, *Literary Women*, 1976; Elaine Showalter, *A Literature of Their Own*, 1977; and Sandra Gilbert and Susan Gubar, *The Madwoman in the Attic*, 1979. Subsequent studies include Jane Gallop, *The Daughter's Seduction: Feminism and Psychoanalysis*, 1982; Luce Irigaray, *This Sex Which Is Not One*, trans. 1985; Gayatri Chakravorty Spivak, *In Other Worlds: Essays in Cultural Politics*, 1987; Sandra Gilbert and Susan Gubar, *No Man's Land: The Place of the Woman Writer in the Twentieth Century*, 3 vols., 1988–94; Barbara Johnson, *A World of Difference*, 1989; Judith Butler, *Gender Trouble*, 1990; and the critical views sampled in Elaine Showalter, *The New Feminist Criticism*, 1985; *The Hélène Cixous Reader*, ed. Susan Sellers, 1994; *Feminist Literary Theory: A Reader*, ed. Mary Eagleton, 3rd ed., 2010; and *Feminisms: An Anthology of Literary Theory and Criticism*, eds. Robyn R. Warhol and Diane Price Herndl, 2nd ed., 1997; *The Cambridge Companion to Feminist Literary Theory*, ed. Ellen Rooney, 2006; *Feminist Literary Theory and Criticism*, ed. Sandra Gilbert and Susan Gubar, 2007; and *Feminist Literary Theory: A Reader*, ed. Mary Eagleton, 3rd ed., 2011.

Just as feminist critics used poststructuralist and psychoanalytic methods to place literature in conversation with gender theory, a new school emerged placing literature in conversation with critical race theory. Comprehensive introductions include *Critical Race Theory: The Key Writings That Formed the Movement*, eds. Kimberlé Crenshaw et al.; *The Routledge Companion to Race and Ethnicity*, ed. Stephen Caliendo and Charlton McIlwain, 2010; and *Critical Race Theory: An Introduction*, ed. Richard Delgado and Jean Stefancic, 3rd ed., 2017. For an important precursor in cultural studies, see Stuart Hall et al., *Policing the Crisis*, 1978. Seminal works include Henry Louis Gates, Jr., *The Signifying Monkey: A Theory of African-American Literature*, 1988; Patricia Williams, *The Alchemy of Race and Rights*, 1991; Toni Morrison, *Playing the Dark: Whiteness and the Literary Imagination*, 1992; Cornel West, *Race Matters*, 2001; and Gene Andrew Jarrett, *Representing the Race: A New Political History of African American Literature*, 2011. Helpful anthologies and collections of essays have emerged in recent decades, such as *The Oxford Companion to African American Literature*, eds., William L. Andrews, Frances Smith Foster, and Trudier Harris, 1997; also their *Concise Companion*, 2001; *The Cambridge Companion to Jewish American Literature*, eds. Hana Wirth-Nesher and Michael P. Kramer, 2003; *The Routledge Companion to Anglophone Caribbean Literature*, eds. Michael A. Bucknor and Alison Donnell, 2011; *The Routledge Companion to Latino/a Literature*, eds. Suzanne Bost and Frances R. Aparicio, 2013; *A Companion to African American Literature*, ed. Gene Andrew Jarrett, 2013; *The Routledge Companion to Asian American and Pacific Islander Literature*, ed. Rachel Lee, 2014; *The Cambridge Companion to Asian American Literature*, eds. Crystal Parikh and Daniel Y. Kim, 2015; and *The Cambridge Companion to British Black and Asian Literature (1945–2010)*, ed. Deirdre Osborne, 2016.

Gay literature and queer studies are represented in *Inside/Out: Lesbian Theories, Gay Theories*, ed. Diana Fuss, 1991; *The Lesbian and Gay Studies Reader*, eds. Henry Abelove, Michele Barale, and David Halperin, 1993; *The Columbia Anthology of Gay Literature: Readings from Western Antiquity to the Present Day*, ed. Byrne R. S. Fone, 1998; and by such books as Eve Sedgwick, *Between Men: English Literature and Male Homosocial Desire*, 1985, and *Epistemology of the Closet*, 1990; Diana Fuss, *Essentially Speaking: Feminism, Nature, and Difference*, 1989; Terry Castle, *The Apparitional Lesbian: Female Homosexuality and Modern Culture*, 1993; Leo Bersani, *Homos*, 1995; Gregory Woods, *A History of Gay Literature: The Male Tradition*,

1998; David Halperin, *How to Do the History of Homosexuality*, 2002; Judith Halberstam, *In a Queer Time and Place: Transgender Bodies, Subcultural Lives*, 2005; Heather Love, *Feeling Backward: Loss and the Politics of Queer History*, 2009; *The Cambridge History of Gay and Lesbian Literature*, eds. E. L. McCallum and Mikko Tuhkanen, 2014; and *The Cambridge Companion to Lesbian Literature*, ed. Jodie Medd, 2015.

New historicism is represented in Stephen Greenblatt, *Learning to Curse*, 1990; in the essays collected in *The New Historicism Reader*, ed. Harold Veeser, 1993; in *New Historical Literary Study: Essays on Reproducing Texts, Representing History*, eds. Jeffrey N. Cox and Larry J. Reynolds, 1993; and in Catherine Gallagher and Stephen Greenblatt, *Practicing New Historicism*, 2000. The related social and historical dimension of texts is discussed in Jerome McGann, *Critique of Modern Textual Criticism*, 1983; and *Scholarly Editing: A Guide to Research*, ed. D. C. Greetham, 1995. Characteristic of new historicism is an expansion of the field of literary interpretation still further in cultural studies; for a broad sampling of the range of interests, see Lawrence Grossberg, Cary Nelson, and Paula Treichler, eds., *Cultural Studies*, 1992; *The Cultural Studies Reader*, ed. Simon During, 3rd ed., 2007; and *A Cultural Studies Reader: History, Theory, Practice*, eds. Jessica Munns and Gita Rajan, 1996.

This expansion of the field is similarly reflected in postcolonial studies: see Frantz Fanon, *Black Skin, White Masks*, 1952, new trans. 2008, and *The Wretched of the Earth*, 1961, new trans. 2004; Edward Said, *Orientalism*, 1978, and *Culture and Imperialism*, 1993; *The Post-Colonial Studies Reader*, 2nd ed., 2006; and such influential books as Homi Bhabha, ed., *Nation and Narration*, 1990, and *The Location of Culture*, 1994; Robert J. C. Young, *Postcolonialism: An Historical Introduction*, 2001; Bill Ashcroft, Gareth Griffiths, and Helen Tiffin, *The Empire Writes Back: Theory and Practice in Post-Colonial Literatures*, 2nd ed. 2002; Elleke Boehmer, *Colonial and Postcolonial Literature*, 2nd ed. 2005; and *The Cambridge History of Postcolonial Literature*, ed. Ato Quayson, 2011; *The Cambridge Companion to the Postcolonial Novel*, ed. Ato Quayson, 2015; and *The Cambridge Companion to Postcolonial Poetry*, ed. Jahan Ramazani, 2017.

In the wake of the theory revolution, critics have focused on a wide array of topics, which can only be briefly surveyed here. One current of work, focusing on the history of emotion, is represented in Brian Massumi, *Parables for the Virtual*, 2002; Sianne Ngai, *Ugly Feelings*, 2005; *The Affect Theory Reader*, eds. Melissa Gregg and Gregory J. Seigworth, 2010; and Judith Butler, *Senses of the Subject*, 2015. A somewhat related current, examining the special role of traumatic memory in literature, is exemplified in Cathy Caruth, *Trauma: Explorations in Memory*, 1995; and Dominic LaCapra, *Writing History, Writing Trauma*, 2000. Work on the literary implications of cognitive science may be glimpsed in *Introduction to Cognitive Cultural Studies*, ed. Lisa Zunshine, 2010. Interest in quantitative approaches to literature was sparked by Franco Moretti, *Graphs, Maps, Trees: Abstract Models for Literary History*, 2005. For the growing field of digital humanities, see also Moretti, *Distant Reading*, 2013; *Defining Digital Humanities: A Reader*, eds. Melissa Terras, Julianne Nyhan, and Edward Vanhoutte, 2014; and *A New Companion to Digital Humanities*, eds. Susan Schreibman, Ray Siemens, and John Unsworth, 2nd ed., 2016. There has also been a flourishing of ecocriticism, or studies of literature and the environment, including *The Ecocriticism Reader: Landmarks in Literary Ecology*, eds. Cheryll Glotfelty and Harold Fromm, 1996; *Writing the Environment*, eds. Richard Kerridge and Neil Sammells, 1998; Jonathan Bate, *The Song of the Earth*, 2002; Lawrence Buell, *The Future of Environmental Criticism: Environmental Crisis and Literary Imagination*, 2005; Timothy Morton, *Ecology Without Nature*, 2009; and *The Oxford Handbook of Ecocriticism*, ed. Greg Garrard, 2014. Related are the emerging fields of animal studies and posthumanism, where key works include

Bruno Latour, *We Have Never Been Modern*, 1993; Steve Baker, *Postmodern Animal*, 2000; Jacques Derrida, *The Animal That Therefore I Am*, trans. 2008; Cary Wolfe, *Animal Rites: American Culture, the Discourse of Species, and Posthumanist Theory*, 2003, and *What is Posthumanism?* 2009; Kari Weil, *Thinking Animals: Why Animal Studies Now?* 2012; and Aaron Gross and Anne Vallely, eds. *Animals and the Human Imagination: A Companion to Animal Studies*, 2012; and *Critical Animal Studies: Thinking the Unthinkable*, ed. John Sorenson, 2014. The relationship between literature and law is central to such works as *Interpreting Law and Literature: A Hermeneutic Reader*, eds. Sanford Levinson and Steven Mailloux, 1988; *Law's Stories: Narrative and Rhetoric in the Law*, eds. Peter Brooks and Paul Gerwertz, 1998; and *Literature and Legal Problem Solving: Law and Literature as Ethical Discourse*, Paul J. Heald, 1998. Ethical questions in literature have been usefully explored by, among others, Geoffrey Galt Harpham in *Getting It Right: Language, Literature, and Ethics*, 1997, and Derek Attridge in *The Singularity of Literature*, 2004. Finally, approaches to literature, such as formalism and literary biography, that seemed superseded in the theoretical ferment of the late twentieth century, have had a powerful resurgence. A renewed interest in form is evident in Susan Stewart, *Poetry and the Fate of the Senses*, 2002; *Reading for Form*, eds. Susan J. Wolfson and Marshall Brown, 2007; and Caroline Levine, *Forms: Whole, Rhythm, Hierarchy, Network*, 2015. Interest in the history of the book was spearheaded by D. F. McKenzie's *Bibliography and the Sociology of Texts*, 1986; Jerome McGann's *The Textual Condition*, 1991; and Roger Chartier's *The Order of Books: Readers, Authors, and Libraries in Europe Between the Fourteenth and Eighteenth Centuries*, 1994. See also *The Cambridge History of the Book in Britain*, 7 vols., 1998–2017; and *The Practice and Representation of Reading in England*, eds. James Raven, Helen Small, and Naomi Tadmor, 2007; *The Book History Reader*, eds. David Finkelstein and Alistair McCleery, 2nd ed., 2006; and *The Cambridge Companion to the History of the Book*, ed. Leslie Howsam, 2014.

Anthologies representing a range of recent approaches include *Modern Criticism and Theory*, ed. David Lodge, 1988; *Contemporary Literary Criticism*, ed. Robert Con Davis and Ronald Schlieffer, 4th ed., 1998; and *The Norton Anthology of Theory and Criticism*, gen. ed. Vincent Leitch, 3rd ed., 2018.

Literary Terminology*

Using simple technical terms can sharpen our understanding and streamline our discussion of literary works. Some terms, such as the ones in section A, help us address the internal style, structure, form, and kind of works. Other terms, such as those in section B, provide insight into the material forms in which literary works have been produced.

In analyzing what they called "rhetoric," ancient Greek and Roman writers determined the elements of what we call "style" and "structure." Our literary terms are derived, via medieval and Renaissance intermediaries, from the Greek and Latin sources. In the definitions that follow, the etymology, or root, of the word is given when it helps illuminate the word's current usage.

Most of the examples are drawn from texts in this anthology.

Words **boldfaced** within definitions are themselves defined in this appendix. Some terms are defined within definitions; such words are *italicized*.

A. Terms of Style, Structure, Form, and Kind

accent (synonym "stress"): a term of **rhythm.** The special force devoted to the voicing of one syllable in a word over others. In the noun "accent," for example, the accent, or stress, is on the first syllable.

act: the major subdivision of a play, usually divided into **scenes.**

aesthetics (from Greek, "to feel, apprehend by the senses"): the philosophy of artistic meaning as a distinct mode of apprehending untranslatable truth, defined as an alternative to rational enquiry, which is purely abstract. Developed in the late eighteenth century by the German philosopher Immanuel Kant especially.

Alexandrine: a term of **meter.** In French verse a line of twelve syllables, and, by analogy, in English verse a line of six stresses. See **hexameter.**

allegory (Greek "saying otherwise"): saying one thing (the "vehicle" of the allegory) and meaning another (the allegory's "tenor"). Allegories may be momentary aspects of a work, as in **metaphor** ("John is a lion"), or, through extended metaphor, may constitute the basis of narrative, as in Bunyan's *Pilgrim's Progress*: this second meaning is the dominant one. See also **symbol** and **type.** Allegory is one of the most significant **figures of thought.**

alliteration (from Latin "litera," alphabetic letter): a **figure of speech.** The repetition of an initial consonant sound or consonant cluster in consecutive or closely positioned words. This pattern is often an inseparable part of the meter in Germanic languages, where the tonic, or accented **syllable,** is usually the first syllable. Thus all Old English poetry and some varieties of Middle English poetry use alliteration as part of their basic metrical practice. *Sir Gawain and the Green Knight*, line 1: "Sithen the sege and the assaut was sesed at Troye" (see vol. A, p. 204). Otherwise used for local effects; Stevie Smith, "Pretty," lines 4–5: "And in the pretty pool the pike stalks / He stalks his prey . . ." (see vol. F, p. 733).

*This appendix was devised and compiled by James Simpson with the collaboration of all the editors. We especially thank Professor Lara Bovilsky of the University of Oregon at Eugene, for her help.

allusion: Literary allusion is a passing but illuminating reference within a literary text to another, well-known text (often biblical or **classical**). Topical allusions are also, of course, common in certain modes, especially **satire.**

anagnorisis (Greek "recognition"): the moment of **protagonist's** recognition in a narrative, which is also often the moment of moral understanding.

anapest: a term of **rhythm.** A three-syllable foot following the rhythmic pattern, in English verse, of two unstressed (uu) syllables followed by one stressed (/). Thus, for example, "Illinois."

anaphora (Greek "carrying back"): a **figure of speech.** The repetition of words or groups of words at the beginning of consecutive sentences, clauses, or phrases. Blake, "London," lines 5–8: "In every cry of every Man, / In every Infant's cry of fear, / In every voice, in every ban . . ." (see vol. D, p. 141); Louise Bennett, "Jamaica Oman," lines 17–20: "Some backa man a push, some side-a / Man a hole him han, / Some a lick sense eena him head, / Some a guide him pon him plan!" (see vol. F, p. 860).

animal fable: a **genre.** A short narrative of speaking animals, followed by moralizing comment, written in a low style and gathered into a collection. Robert Henryson, "The Preaching of the Swallow" (see vol. A, p. 523).

antithesis (Greek "placing against"): a **figure of thought.** The juxtaposition of opposed terms in clauses or sentences that are next to or near each other. Milton, *Paradise Lost* 1.777–80: "They but now who seemed / In bigness to surpass Earth's giant sons / Now less than smallest dwarfs, in narrow room / Throng numberless" (see vol. B, p. 1514).

apostrophe (from Greek "turning away"): a **figure of thought.** An address, often to an absent person, a force, or a quality. For example, a poet makes an apostrophe to a Muse when invoking her for inspiration.

apposition: a term of **syntax.** The repetition of elements serving an identical grammatical function in one sentence. The effect of this repetition is to arrest the flow of the sentence, but in doing so to add extra semantic nuance to repeated elements. This is an especially important feature of Old English poetic style. See, for example, Caedmon's *Hymn* (vol. A, p. 31), where the phrases "heaven-kingdom's Guardian," "the Measurer's might," "his mind-plans," and "the work of the Glory-Father" each serve an identical syntactic function as the direct objects of "praise."

assonance (Latin "sounding to"): a **figure of speech.** The repetition of identical or near identical stressed vowel sounds in words whose final consonants differ, producing half-rhyme. Tennyson, "The Lady of Shalott," line 100: "His broad clear brow in sunlight glowed" (see vol. E, p. 149).

aubade (originally from Spanish "alba," dawn): a **genre.** A lover's dawn song or lyric bewailing the arrival of the day and the necessary separation of the lovers; Donne, "The Sun Rising" (see vol. B, p. 926). Larkin recasts the genre in "Aubade" (see vol. F, p. 930).

autobiography (Greek "self-life writing"): a **genre.** A narrative of a life written by the subject; Wordsworth, *The Prelude* (see vol. D, p. 362). There are subgenres, such as the spiritual autobiography, narrating the author's path to conversion and subsequent spiritual trials, as in Bunyan's *Grace Abounding*.

ballad stanza: a **verse form.** Usually a **quatrain** in alternating **iambic tetrameter** and **iambic trimeter** lines, rhyming abcb. See "Sir Patrick Spens" (vol. D, p. 36); Louise Bennett's poems (vol. F, pp. 857–61); Eliot, "Sweeney among the Nightingales" (vol. F, p. 657); Larkin, "This Be The Verse" (vol. F, p. 930).

ballade: a **verse form.** A form consisting usually of three stanzas followed by a four-line envoi (French, "send off"). The last line of the first stanza establishes a **refrain,** which is repeated, or subtly varied, as the last line of each stanza. The form was derived from French medieval poetry; English poets, from the fourteenth to the sixteenth centuries especially, used it with varying stanza forms. Chaucer, "Complaint to His Purse" (see vol. A, p. 363).

bathos (Greek "depth"): a **figure of thought.** A sudden and sometimes ridiculous descent of tone; Pope, *The Rape of the Lock* 3.157–58: "Not louder shrieks to pitying heaven are cast, / When husbands, or when lapdogs breathe their last" (see vol. C, p. 518).

beast epic: a **genre.** A continuous, unmoralized narrative, in prose or verse, relating the victories of the wholly unscrupulous but brilliant strategist Reynard the Fox over all adversaries. Chaucer arouses, only to deflate, expectations of the genre in *The Nun's Priest's Tale* (see vol. A, p. 344).

biography (Greek "life-writing"): a **genre.** A life as the subject of an extended narrative. Thus Izaak Walton, *The Life of Dr. Donne* (see vol. B, p. 976).

blank verse: a **verse form.** Unrhymed **iambic pentameter** lines. Blank verse has no stanzas, but is broken up into uneven units (verse paragraphs) determined by sense rather than form. First devised in English by Henry Howard, earl of Surrey, in his translation of two books of Virgil's *Aeneid* (see vol. B, p. 141), this very flexible verse type became the standard form for dramatic poetry in the seventeenth century, as in most of Shakespeare's plays. Milton and Wordsworth, among many others, also used it to create an English equivalent to **classical epic.**

blazon: strictly, a heraldic shield; in rhetorical usage, a **topos** whereby the individual elements of a beloved's face and body are singled out for **hyperbolic** admiration. Spenser, *Epithalamion*, lines 167–84 (see vol. B, p. 495). For an inversion of the **topos,** see Shakespeare, Sonnet 130 (vol. B, p. 736).

burlesque (French and Italian "mocking"): a work that adopts the **conventions** of a genre with the aim less of comically mocking the genre than of satirically mocking the society so represented (see **satire**). Thus Pope's *Rape of the Lock* (see vol. C, p. 507) does not mock **classical epic** so much as contemporary mores.

caesura (Latin "cut") (plural "caesurae"): a term of **meter.** A pause or breathing space within a line of verse, generally occurring between syntactic units; Louise Bennett, "Colonization in Reverse," lines 5–8: "By de hundred, by de tousan, / From country an from town, / By de ship-load, by de plane-load, / Jamaica is Englan boun" (see vol. F, p. 858), where the caesurae occur in lines 5 and 7.

canon (Greek "rule"): the group of texts regarded as worthy of special respect or attention by a given institution. Also, the group of texts regarded as definitely having been written by a certain author.

catastrophe (Greek "overturning"): the decisive turn in **tragedy** by which the plot is resolved and, usually, the **protagonist** dies.

catharsis (Greek "cleansing"): According to Aristotle, the effect of **tragedy** on its audience, through their experience of pity and terror, was a kind of spiritual cleansing, or catharsis.

character (Greek "stamp, impression"): a person, personified animal, or other figure represented in a literary work, especially in narrative and drama. The more a character seems to generate the action of a narrative, and the less he or she seems merely to serve a preordained narrative pattern, the "fuller," or more "rounded," a character is said to be. A "stock" character, common particularly in many comic genres, will perform a predictable function in different works of a given genre.

chiasmus (Greek "crosswise"): a **figure of speech.** The inversion of an already established sequence. This can involve verbal echoes: Pope, "Eloisa to Abelard," line 104, "The crime was common, common be the pain" (see vol. C, p. 529); or it can be purely a matter of syntactic inversion: Pope, *Epistle to Dr. Arbuthnot*, line 8: "They pierce my thickets, through my grot they glide" (see vol. C, p. 544).

classical, classicism, classic: Each term can be widely applied, but in English literary discourse, "classical" primarily describes the works of either Greek or Roman antiquity. "Classicism" denotes the practice of art forms inspired by classical antiquity, in particular the observance of rhetorical norms of **decorum** and balance, as opposed to following the dictates of untutored inspiration, as in Romanticism. "Classic" denotes an especially famous work within a given **canon.**

climax (Greek "ladder"): a moment of great intensity and structural change, especially in drama. Also a **figure of speech** whereby a sequence of verbally linked clauses is made, in which each successive clause is of greater consequence than its predecessor. Bacon, *Of Studies*: "Studies serve for pastimes, for ornaments, and for abilities. Their chief use for pastimes is in privateness and retiring; for ornament, is in discourse; and for ability, is in judgement" (see vol. B, p. 1223–24).

comedy: a **genre.** A term primarily applied to drama, and derived from ancient drama, in opposition to **tragedy.** Comedy deals with humorously confusing, sometimes ridiculous situations in which the ending is, nevertheless, happy. A comedy often ends in one or more marriages. Shakespeare, *Twelfth Night* (see vol. B, p. 741).

comic mode: Many genres (e.g., **romance, fabliau, comedy**) involve a happy ending in which justice is done, the ravages of time are arrested, and that which is lost is found. Such genres participate in a comic mode.

connotation: To understand connotation, we need to understand **denotation.** While many words can denote the same concept—that is, have the same basic meaning—those words can evoke different associations, or connotations. Contrast, for example, the clinical-sounding term "depression" and the more colorful, musical, even poetic phrase "the blues."

consonance (Latin "sounding with"): a **figure of speech.** The repetition of final consonants in words or stressed syllables whose vowel sounds are different. Herbert, "Easter," line 13: "Consort, both heart and lute . . ." (see vol. B, p. 1258).

convention: a repeatedly recurring feature (in either form or content) of works, occurring in combination with other recurring formal features, which constitutes a convention of a particular genre.

couplet: a **verse form.** In English verse two consecutive, rhyming lines usually containing the same number of stresses. Chaucer first introduced the **iambic pentameter** couplet into English (*Canterbury Tales*); the form was later used in many types of writing, including drama; imitations and translations of **classical epic** (thus *heroic couplet*); essays; and **satire** (see Dryden and Pope). The *distich* (Greek "two lines") is a couplet usually making complete sense; Aemilia Lanyer, *Salve Deus Rex Judaeorum*, lines 5–6: "Read it fair queen, though it defective be, / Your excellence can grace both it and me" (see vol. B, p. 981).

dactyl (Greek "finger," because of the finger's three joints): a term of **rhythm.** A three-syllable foot following the rhythmic pattern, in English verse, of one stressed followed by two unstressed syllables. Thus, for example, "Oregon."

decorum (Latin "that which is fitting"): a rhetorical principle whereby each formal aspect of a work should be in keeping with its subject matter and/or audience.

deixis (Greek "pointing"): relevant to **point of view**. Every work has, implicitly or explicitly, a "here" and a "now" from which it is narrated. Words that refer to or imply this point from which the voice of the work is projected (such as "here," "there," "this," "that," "now," "then") are examples of deixis, or "deictics." This technique is especially important in drama, where it is used to create a sense of the events happening as the spectator witnesses them.

denotation: A word has a basic, "prosaic" (factual) meaning prior to the associations it connotes (see **connotation**). The word "steed," for example, might call to mind a horse fitted with battle gear, to be ridden by a warrior, but its denotation is simply "horse."

denouement (French "unknotting"): the point at which a narrative can be resolved and so ended.

dialogue (Greek "conversation"): a **genre.** Dialogue is a feature of many genres, especially in both the **novel** and drama. As a genre itself, dialogue is used in philosophical traditions especially (most famously in Plato's *Dialogues*), as the representation of a conversation in which a philosophical question is pursued among various speakers.

diction, or **"lexis"** (from, respectively, Latin *dictio* and Greek *lexis*, each meaning "word"): the actual words used in any utterance—speech, writing, and, for our purposes here, literary works. The choice of words contributes significantly to the style of a given work.

didactic mode (Greek "teaching mode"): **Genres** in a didactic mode are designed to instruct or teach, sometimes explicitly (e.g., sermons, philosophical **discourses, georgic**), and sometimes through the medium of fiction (e.g., **animal fable, parable**).

diegesis (Greek for "narration"): a term that simply means "narration," but is used in literary criticism to distinguish one kind of story from another. In a *mimetic* story, the events are played out before us (see **mimesis**), whereas in diegesis someone recounts the story to us. Drama is for the most part *mimetic*, whereas the novel is for the most part diegetic. In novels the narrator is not, usually, part of the action of the narrative; s/he is therefore extradiegetic.

dimeter (Greek "two measure"): a term of **meter.** A two-stress line, rarely used as the meter of whole poems, though used with great frequency in single poems by Skelton, e.g., "The Tunning of Elinour Rumming" (see vol. B, p. 39). Otherwise used for single lines, as in Herbert, "Discipline," line 3: "O my God" (see vol. B, p. 1274).

discourse (Latin "running to and fro"): broadly, any nonfictional speech or writing; as a more specific genre, a philosophical meditation on a set theme. Thus Newman, *The Idea of a University* (see vol. E, p. 64).

dramatic irony: a feature of narrative and drama, whereby the audience knows that the outcome of an action will be the opposite of that intended by a **character.**

dramatic monologue (Greek "single speaking"): a **genre.** A poem in which the voice of a historical or fictional **character** speaks, unmediated by any narrator, to an implied though silent audience. See Tennyson, "Ulysses" (vol. E, p. 156); Browning, "The Bishop Orders His Tomb" (vol. E, p. 332); Eliot, "The Love Song of J. Alfred Prufrock" (vol. F, p. 654); Carol Ann Duffy, "Medusa" and "Mrs Lazarus" (vol. F, pp. 1211–13).

ecphrasis (Greek "speaking out"): a **topos** whereby a work of visual art is represented in a literary work. Auden, "Musée des Beaux Arts" (see vol. F, p. 815).

elegy: a **genre.** In **classical** literature elegy was a form written in elegiac **couplets** (a **hexameter** followed by a **pentameter**) devoted to many possible topics. In Ovidian elegy a lover meditates on the trials of erotic desire (e.g., Ovid's *Amores*). The **sonnet** sequences of both Sidney and Shakespeare exploit this genre, and, while it was still practiced in classical tradition by Donne ("On His Mistress" [see vol. B, p. 942]), by the later seventeenth century the term came to denote the poetry of loss, especially through the death of a loved person. See Tennyson, *In Memoriam* (vol. E, p. 173); Yeats, "In Memory of Major Robert Gregory" (vol. F, p. 223); Auden, "In Memory of W. B. Yeats" (see vol. F, p. 815); Heaney, "Clearances" (vol. F, p. 1104).

emblem (Greek "an insertion"): a **figure of thought.** A picture allegorically expressing a moral, or a verbal picture open to such interpretation. Donne, "A Hymn to Christ," lines 1–2: "In what torn ship soever I embark, / That ship shall be my emblem of thy ark" (see vol. B, p. 966).

end-stopping: the placement of a complete syntactic unit within a complete poetic line, fulfilling the metrical pattern; Auden, "In Memory of W. B. Yeats," line 42: "Earth, receive an honoured guest" (see vol. F, p. 817). Compare **enjambment.**

enjambment (French "striding," encroaching): The opposite of **end-stopping,** enjambment occurs when the syntactic unit does not end with the end of the poetic line and the fulfillment of the metrical pattern. When the sense of the line overflows its meter and, therefore, the line break, we have enjambment; Auden, "In Memory of W. B. Yeats," lines 44–45: "Let the Irish vessel lie / Emptied of its poetry" (see vol. F, p. 817).

epic (synonym, *heroic poetry*): a **genre.** An extended narrative poem celebrating martial heroes, invoking divine inspiration, beginning in medias res (see **order**), written in a high style (including the deployment of **epic similes;** on high style, see **register**), and divided into long narrative sequences. Homer's *Iliad* and Virgil's *Aeneid* were the prime models for English writers of epic verse. Thus Milton, *Paradise Lost* (see vol. B, p. 1495); Wordsworth, *The Prelude* (see vol. D, p. 362); and Walcott, *Omeros* (see vol. F, p. 947). With its precise repertoire of stylistic resources, epic lent itself easily to **parodic** and **burlesque** forms, known as **mock epic;** thus Pope, *The Rape of the Lock* (see vol. C, p. 507).

epigram: a **genre.** A short, pithy poem wittily expressed, often with wounding intent. See Jonson, *Epigrams* (see vol. B, p. 1089).

epigraph (Greek "inscription"): a **genre.** Any formal statement inscribed on stone; also the brief formulation on a book's title page, or a quotation at the beginning of a poem, introducing the work's themes in the most compressed form possible.

epistle (Latin "letter"): a **genre.** The letter can be shaped as a literary form, involving an intimate address often between equals. The *Epistles* of Horace provided a model for English writers from the sixteenth century. Thus Wyatt, "Mine own John Poins" (see vol. B, p. 131), or Pope, "An Epistle to a Lady" (vol. C, p. 655). Letters can be shaped to form the matter of an extended fiction, as the eighteenth-century epistolary **novel** (e.g., Samuel Richardson's *Pamela*).

epitaph: a **genre.** A pithy formulation to be inscribed on a funeral monument. Thus Ralegh, "The Author's Epitaph, Made by Himself" (see vol. B, p. 532).

epithalamion (Greek "concerning the bridal chamber"): a **genre.** A wedding poem, celebrating the marriage and wishing the couple good fortune. Thus Spenser, *Epithalamion* (see vol. B, p. 491).

epyllion (plural "epyllia") (Greek: "little epic"): a **genre.** A relatively short poem in the meter of epic poetry. See, for example, Marlowe, *Hero and Leander* (vol. B, p 660).

essay (French "trial, attempt"): a **genre**. An informal philosophical meditation, usually in prose and sometimes in verse. The journalistic periodical essay was developed in the early eighteenth century. Thus Addison and Steele, periodical essays (see vol. C, p. 462); Pope, *An Essay on Criticism* (see vol. C, p. 490).

euphemism (Greek "sweet saying"): a **figure of thought**. The figure by which something distasteful is described in alternative, less repugnant terms (e.g., "he passed away").

exegesis (Greek "leading out"): interpretation, traditionally of the biblical text, but, by transference, of any text.

exemplum (Latin "example"): an example inserted into a usually nonfictional writing (e.g., sermon or **essay**) to give extra force to an abstract thesis. Thus Johnson's example of "Sober" in his essay "On Idleness" (see vol. C, p. 732).

fabliau (French "little story," plural *fabliaux*): a **genre**. A short, funny, often bawdy narrative in low style (see **register**) imitated and developed from French models, most subtly by Chaucer; see *The Miller's Prologue and Tale* (vol. A, p. 282).

farce (French "stuffing"): a **genre**. A play designed to provoke laughter through the often humiliating antics of stock **characters**. Congreve's *The Way of the World* (see vol. C, p. 188) draws on this tradition.

figures of speech: Literary language often employs patterns perceptible to the eye and/or to the ear. Such patterns are called "figures of speech"; in classical rhetoric they were called "schemes" (from Greek *schema*, meaning "form, figure").

figures of thought: Language can also be patterned conceptually, even outside the rules that normally govern it. Literary language in particular exploits this licensed linguistic irregularity. Synonyms for figures of thought are "trope" (Greek "twisting," referring to the irregularity of use) and "conceit" (Latin "concept," referring to the fact that these figures are perceptible only to the mind). Be careful not to confuse **trope** with **topos** (a common error).

first-person narration: relevant to **point of view,** a narrative in which the voice narrating refers to itself with forms of the first-person pronoun ("I," "me," "my," etc., or possibly "we," "us," "our"), and in which the narrative is determined by the limitations of that voice. Thus Mary Wollstonecraft Shelley, *Frankenstein*.

frame narrative: Some narratives, particularly collections of narratives, involve a frame narrative that explains the genesis of, and/or gives a perspective on, the main narrative or narratives to follow. Thus Chaucer, *Canterbury Tales*; Mary Wollstonecraft Shelley, *Frankenstein*; or Conrad, *Heart of Darkness*.

free indirect style: relevant to **point of view,** a narratorial voice that manages, without explicit reference, to imply, and often implicitly to comment on, the voice of a **character** in the narrative itself. Virginia Woolf, "A Sketch of the Past," where the voice, although strictly that of the adult narrator, manages to convey the child's manner of perception: "—I begin: the first memory. This was of red and purple flowers on a black background—my mother's dress."

genre and mode: The **style**, structure, and, often, length of a work, when coupled with a certain subject matter, raise expectations that a literary work conforms to a certain **genre** (French "kind"). Good writers might upset these expectations, but they remain aware of the expectations and thwart them purposefully. Works in different genres may nevertheless participate in the same **mode,** a broader category designating the fundamental perspectives governing various genres of writing. For mode, see **tragic, comic, satiric,** and **didactic modes.** Genres are fluid, sometimes very fluid (e.g., the **novel**); the word "usually" should be added to almost every account of the characteristics of a given genre!

georgic (Greek "farming"): a **genre.** Virgil's *Georgics* treat agricultural and occasionally scientific subjects, giving instructions on the proper management of farms. Unlike **pastoral,** which treats the countryside as a place of recreational idleness among shepherds, the georgic treats it as a place of productive labor. For an English poem that critiques both genres, see Crabbe, "The Village" (vol. C, p. 1019).

hermeneutics (from the Greek god Hermes, messenger between the gods and humankind): the science of interpretation, first formulated as such by the German philosophical theologian Friedrich Schleiermacher in the early nineteenth century.

heroic poetry: see **epic.**

hexameter (Greek "six measure"): a term of **meter.** The hexameter line (a six-stress line) is the meter of **classical** Latin **epic;** while not imitated in that form for epic verse in English, some instances of the hexameter exist. See, for example, the last line of a Spenserian stanza, *Faerie Queene* 1.1.2: "O help thou my weake wit, and sharpen my dull tong" (vol. B, p. 253), or Yeats, "The Lake Isle of Innisfree," line 1: "I will arise and go now, and go to Innisfree" (vol. F, p. 215).

homily (Greek "discourse"): a **genre.** A sermon, to be preached in church; *Book of Homilies* (see vol. B, p. 165). Writers of literary fiction sometimes exploit the homily, or sermon, as in Chaucer, *The Pardoner's Tale* (see vol. A, p. 329).

homophone (Greek "same sound"): a **figure of speech.** A word that sounds identical to another word but has a different meaning ("bear" / "bare").

hyperbaton (Greek "overstepping"): a term of **syntax.** The rearrangement, or inversion, of the expected word order in a sentence or clause. Gray, "Elegy Written in a Country Churchyard," line 38: "If Memory o'er their tomb no trophies raise" (vol. C, p. 999). Poets can suspend the expected syntax over many lines, as in the first sentences of the *Canterbury Tales* (vol. A, p. 261) and of *Paradise Lost* (vol. B, p. 1495).

hyperbole (Greek "throwing over"): a **figure of thought.** Overstatement, exaggeration; Marvell, "To His Coy Mistress," lines 11–12: "My vegetable love should grow / Vaster than empires, and more slow" (see vol. B, p. 1347); Auden, "As I Walked Out One Evening," lines 9–12: "'I'll love you, dear, I'll love you / Till China and Africa meet / And the river jumps over the mountain / And the salmon sing in the street" (see vol. F, p. 813).

hypermetrical (adj.; Greek "over measured"): a term of **meter;** the word describes a breaking of the expected metrical pattern by at least one extra syllable.

hypotaxis, or **subordination** (respectively Greek and Latin "ordering under"): a term of **syntax.** The subordination, by the use of subordinate clauses, of different elements of a sentence to a single main verb. Milton, *Paradise Lost* 9.513–15: "As when a ship by skillful steersman wrought / Nigh river's mouth or foreland, where the wind / Veers oft, as oft so steers, and shifts her sail; So varied he" (vol. B, p. 1654). The contrary principle to **parataxis.**

iamb: a term of **rhythm.** The basic foot of English verse; two syllables following the rhythmic pattern of unstressed followed by stressed and producing a rising effect. Thus, for example, "Vermont."

imitation: the practice whereby writers strive ideally to reproduce and yet renew the **conventions** of an older form, often derived from **classical** civilization. Such a practice will be praised in periods of classicism (e.g., the eighteenth century) and repudiated in periods dominated by a model of inspiration (e.g., Romanticism).

irony (Greek "dissimulation"): a **figure of thought.** In broad usage, irony designates the result of inconsistency between a statement and a context that undermines the statement. "It's a beautiful day" is unironic if it's a beautiful day; if, however, the weather is terrible, then the inconsistency between statement and context is ironic. The effect is often amusing; the need to be ironic is sometimes produced by censorship of one kind or another. Strictly, irony is a subset of allegory: whereas allegory says one thing and means another, irony says one thing and means its opposite. For an extended example of irony, see Swift's "Modest Proposal." See also **dramatic irony.**

journal (French "daily"): a **genre.** A diary, or daily record of ephemeral experience, whose perspectives are concentrated on, and limited by, the experiences of single days. Thus Pepys, *Diary* (see vol. C, p. 86).

lai: a **genre.** A short narrative, often characterized by images of great intensity; a French term, and a form practiced by Marie de France (see vol. A, p. 160).

legend (Latin "requiring to be read"): a **genre.** A narrative of a celebrated, possibly historical, but mortal **protagonist.** To be distinguished from **myth.** Thus the "Arthurian legend" but the "myth of Proserpine."

lexical set: Words that habitually recur together (e.g., January, February, March, etc.; or red, white, and blue) form a lexical set.

litotes (from Greek "smooth"): a **figure of thought.** Strictly, understatement by denying the contrary; More, *Utopia*: "differences of no slight import" (see vol. B, p. 47). More loosely, understatement; Swift, "A Tale of a Tub": "Last week I saw a woman flayed, and you will hardly believe how much it altered her person for the worse" (see vol. C, p. 274). Stevie Smith, "Sunt Leones," lines 11–12: "And if the Christians felt a little blue— / Well people being eaten often do" (see vol. F, p. 729).

lullaby: a **genre.** A bedtime, sleep-inducing song for children, in simple and regular meter. Adapted by Auden, "Lullaby" (see vol. F, p. 809).

lyric (from Greek "lyre"): Initially meaning a song, "lyric" refers to a short poetic form, without restriction of meter, in which the expression of personal emotion, often by a voice in the first person, is given primacy over narrative sequence. Thus "The Wife's Lament" (see vol. A, p. 123); Yeats, "The Wild Swans at Coole" (see vol. F, p. 223).

masque: a **genre.** Costly entertainments of the Stuart court, involving dance, song, speech, and elaborate stage effects, in which courtiers themselves participated.

metaphor (Greek "carrying across," etymologically parallel to Latin "translation"): One of the most significant **figures of thought,** metaphor designates identification or implicit identification of one thing with another with which it is not literally identifiable. Blake, "London," lines 11–12: "And the hapless Soldier's sigh / Runs in blood down Palace walls" (see vol. D, p. 141).

meter: Verse (from Latin *versus,* turned) is distinguished from prose (from Latin *prorsus,* "straightforward") as a more compressed form of expression, shaped by metrical norms. **Meter** (Greek "measure") refers to the regularly recurring sound pattern of verse lines. The means of producing sound patterns across lines differ in different poetic traditions. Verse may be **quantitative,** or determined by the quantities of syllables (set patterns of long and short syllables), as in Latin and Greek poetry. It may be **syllabic,** determined by fixed numbers of syllables in the line, as in the verse of Romance languages (e.g., French and Italian). It may be **accentual,** determined by the number of accents, or stresses in the line, with variable numbers of syllables, as in Old English and some varieties of Middle English alliterative verse. Or it may be **accentual-syllabic,** determined by the numbers of accents, but possessing a regular pattern of stressed and unstressed syllables, so as to produce regular numbers of syllables per line. Since Chaucer, English verse has worked primarily within the many possibilities of accentual-syllabic meter. The unit of meter is the **foot.** In English verse the number of feet per line corresponds to the number of accents in a line. For the types and examples of different meters, see **monometer, dimeter, trimester, tetrameter, pentameter,** and **hexameter.** In the definitions below, "u" designates one unstressed syllable, and "/" one stressed syllable.

metonymy (Greek "change of name"): one of the most significant **figures of thought.** Using a word to **denote** another concept or other concepts, by virtue of habitual association. Thus "The Press," designating printed news media. Fictional names often work by associations of this kind. Closely related to **synecdoche.**

mimesis (Greek for "imitation"): A central function of literature and drama has been to provide a plausible imitation of the reality of the world beyond the literary work; mimesis is the representation and imitation of what is taken to be reality.

mise-en-abyme (French for "cast into the abyss"): Some works of art represent themselves in themselves; if they do so effectively, the represented artifact also represents itself, and so ad infinitum. The effect achieved is called *"mise-en-abyme."* Hoccleve's *Complaint,* for example, represents a depressed man reading about a depressed man. This sequence threatens to become a *mise-en-abyme.*

monometer (Greek "one measure"): a term of **meter.** An entire line with just one stress; *Sir Gawain and the Green Knight,* line 15, "most (u) grand (/)" (see vol. A, p. 204).

myth: a **genre.** The narrative of **protagonists** with, or subject to, superhuman powers. A myth expresses some profound foundational truth, often by accounting for the origin of natural phenomena. To be distinguished from **legend.** Thus the "Arthurian legend" but the "myth of Proserpine."

novel: an extremely flexible **genre** in both form and subject matter. Usually in prose, giving high priority to narration of events, with a certain expectation of length, novels are preponderantly rooted in a specific, and often complex, social world; sensitive to the realities of material life; and often focused on one **character** or a small circle of central characters. By contrast with chivalric **romance** (the main European narrative genre prior to the novel), novels tend to eschew the marvelous in favor of a recognizable social world and credible action. The novel's openness allows it to participate in all modes, and to be co-opted for a huge variety of subgenres. In English literature the novel dates from the late seventeenth century and has been astonishingly successful in appealing to a huge readership, particularly in the nineteenth and twentieth centuries. The English and Irish tradition of the novel includes, for example, Fielding, Austen, the Brontë sisters, Dickens, George Eliot, Conrad, Woolf, Lawrence, and Joyce, to name but a few very great exponents of the genre.

novella: a **genre.** A short **novel,** often characterized by imagistic intensity. Conrad, *Heart of Darkness* (see vol. F, p. 73).

occupatio (Latin "taking possession"): a **figure of thought.** Denying that one will discuss a subject while actually discussing it; also known as "praeteritio" (Latin "passing by"). See Chaucer, *Nun's Priest's Tale,* lines 414–32 (see vol. A, p. 353).

ode (Greek "song"): a **genre.** A **lyric** poem in elevated, or high style (see **register**), often addressed to a natural force, a person, or an abstract quality. The Pindaric ode in English is made up of **stanzas** of unequal length, while the Horatian ode has stanzas of equal length. For examples of both types, see, respectively, Wordsworth, "Ode: Intimations of Immortality" (vol. D, p. 348); and Marvell, "An Horatian Ode" (vol. B, p. 1356), or Keats, "Ode on Melancholy" (vol. D, p. 981). For a fuller discussion, see the headnote to Jonson's "Ode on Cary and Morison" (vol. B, p. 1102).

omniscient narrator (Latin "all-knowing narrator"): relevant to **point of view.** A narrator who, in the fiction of the narrative, has complete access to both the deeds and the thoughts of all **characters** in the narrative. Thus Thomas Hardy, "On the Western Circuit" (see vol. F, p. 36).

onomatopoeia (Greek "name making"): a **figure of speech.** Verbal sounds that imitate and evoke the sounds they denote. Hopkins, "Binsey Poplars," lines 10–12 (about some felled trees): "O if we but knew what we do / When we delve [dig] or hew— / Hack and rack the growing green!" (see vol. E, p. 598).

order: A story may be told in different narrative orders. A narrator might use the sequence of events as they happened, and thereby follow what **classical** rhetoricians called the *natural order*; alternatively, the narrator might reorder the sequence of events, beginning the narration either in the middle or at the end of the sequence of events, thereby following an *artificial order.* If a narrator begins in the middle of events, he or she is said to begin *in medias res* (Latin "in the middle of the matter"). For a brief discussion of these concepts, see Spenser, *Faerie Queene*, "A Letter of the Authors" (vol. B, p. 249). Modern narratology makes a related distinction, between *histoire* (French "story") for the natural order that readers mentally reconstruct, and *discours* (French, here "narration") for the narrative as presented. See also **plot** and **story.**

ottava rima: a **verse form.** An eight-line stanza form, rhyming abababcc, using **iambic pentameter;** Yeats, "Sailing to Byzantium" (see vol. F, p. 230). Derived from the Italian poet Boccaccio, an eight-line stanza was used by fifteenth-century English poets for inset passages (e.g., Christ's speech from the Cross in Lydgate's *Testament*, lines 754–897). The form in this rhyme scheme was used in English poetry for long narrative by, for example, Byron (*Don Juan*; see vol. D, p. 669).

oxymoron (Greek "sharp blunt"): a **figure of thought.** The conjunction of normally incompatible terms; Milton, *Paradise Lost* 1.63: "darkness visible" (see vol. B, p. 1497).

panegyric: a **genre.** Demonstrative, or epideictic (Greek "showing"), rhetoric was a branch of **classical** rhetoric. Its own two main branches were the rhetoric of praise on the one hand and of vituperation on the other. Panegyric, or eulogy (Greek "sweet speaking"), or encomium (plural *encomia*), is the term used to describe the speeches or writings of praise.

parable: a **genre.** A simple story designed to provoke, and often accompanied by, **allegorical** interpretation, most famously by Christ as reported in the Gospels.

paradox (Greek "contrary to received opinion"): a **figure of thought.** An apparent contradiction that requires thought to reveal an inner consistency. Chaucer, "Troilus's Song," line 12: "O sweete harm so quainte" (see vol. A, p. 362).

parataxis, or **coordination** (respectively Greek and Latin "ordering beside"): a term of **syntax.** The coordination, by the use of coordinating conjunctions, of different main clauses in a single sentence. Malory, *Morte Darthur*: "So Sir Lancelot departed and took his sword under his arm, and so he walked in his mantel, that noble knight, and put himself in great jeopardy" (see vol. A, p. 539). The opposite principle to **hypotaxis.**

parody: a work that uses the **conventions** of a particular genre with the aim of comically mocking a **topos,** a genre, or a particular exponent of a genre. Shakespeare parodies the topos of **blazon** in Sonnet 130 (see vol. B, p. 736).

pastoral (from Latin *pastor,* "shepherd"): a **genre.** Pastoral is set among shepherds, making often refined **allusion** to other apparently unconnected subjects (sometimes politics) from the potentially idyllic world of highly literary if illiterate shepherds. Pastoral is distinguished from **georgic** by representing recreational rural idleness, whereas the georgic offers instruction on how to manage rural labor. English writers had classical models in the *Idylls* of Theocritus in Greek and Virgil's *Eclogues* in Latin. Pastoral is also called bucolic (from the Greek word for "herdsman"). Thus Spenser, *Shepheardes Calender* (see vol. B, p. 241).

pathetic fallacy: the attribution of sentiment to natural phenomena, as if they were in sympathy with human feelings. Thus Milton, *Lycidas,* lines 146–47: "With cowslips wan that hang the pensive head, / And every flower that sad embroidery wears" (see vol. B, p. 1472). For critique of the practice, see Ruskin (who coined the term), "Of the Pathetic Fallacy" (vol. E, p. 386).

pentameter (Greek "five measure"): a term of **meter.** In English verse, a five-stress line. Between the late fourteenth and the nineteenth centuries, this meter, frequently employing an iambic rhythm, was the basic line of English verse. Chaucer, Shakespeare, Milton, and Wordsworth each, for example, deployed this very flexible line as their primary resource; Milton, *Paradise Lost* 1.128: "O Prince, O Chief of many thronèd Powers" (see vol. B, p. 1499).

performative: Verbal expressions have many different functions. They can, for example, be descriptive, or constative (if they make an argument), or performative, for example. A performative utterance is one that makes something happen in the world by virtue of its utterance. "I hereby sentence you to ten years in prison," if uttered in the appropriate circumstances, itself performs an action; it makes something happen in the world. By virtue of its performing an action, it is called a "performative." See also **speech act.**

peripeteia (Greek "turning about"): the sudden reversal of fortune (in both directions) in a dramatic work.

periphrasis (Greek "declaring around"): a **figure of thought.** Circumlocution; the use of many words to express what could be expressed in few or one; Sidney, *Astrophil and Stella* 39.1–4 (vol. B, p. 593).

persona (Latin "sound through"): originally the mask worn in the Roman theater to magnify an actor's voice; in literary discourse persona (plural *personae*) refers to the narrator or speaker of a text, whose voice is coherent and whose person need have no relation to the person of the actual author of a text. Eliot, "The Love Song of J. Alfred Prufrock" (see vol. F, p. 654).

personification, or **prosopopoeia** (Greek "person making"): a **figure of thought.** The attribution of human qualities to nonhuman forces or objects; Keats, "Ode on a Grecian Urn," lines 1–2: "Thou still unvanish'd bride of quietness, / Thou foster-child of silence and slow time" (see vol. D, p. 979).

plot: the sequence of events in a story as narrated, as distinct from **story,** which refers to the sequence of events as we reconstruct them from the plot. See also **order.**

point of view: All of the many kinds of writing involve a point of view from which a text is, or seems to be, generated. The presence of such a point of view may be powerful and explicit, as in many novels, or deliberately invisible, as in much drama. In some genres, such as the **novel,** the narrator does not necessarily tell the story from a position we can predict; that is, the needs of a particular story, not the **conventions** of the genre, determine the narrator's position. In other genres, the narrator's position is fixed by convention; in certain kinds of love poetry, for example, the narrating voice is always that of a suffering lover. Not only does the point of view significantly inform the style of a work, but it also informs the structure of that work.

protagonist (Greek "first actor"): the hero or heroine of a drama or narrative.

pun: a figure of thought. A sometimes irresolvable doubleness of meaning in a single word or expression; Shakespeare, Sonnet 135, line 1: "Whoever hath her wish, thou hast thy *Will*" (see vol. B, p. 736).

quatrain: a verse form. A stanza of four lines, usually rhyming abcb, abab, or abba. Of many possible examples, see Crashaw, "On the Wounds of Our Crucified Lord" (see vol. B, p. 1296).

refrain: usually a single line repeated as the last line of consecutive stanzas, sometimes with subtly different wording and ideally with subtly different meaning as the poem progresses. See, for example, Wyatt, "Blame not my lute" (see vol. B, p. 128).

register: The register of a word is its stylistic level, which can be distinguished by degree of technicality but also by degree of formality. We choose our words from different registers according to context, that is, audience and/or environment. Thus a chemist in a laboratory will say "sodium chloride," a cook in a kitchen "salt." A formal register designates the kind of language used in polite society (e.g., "Mr. President"), while an informal or colloquial register is used in less formal or more relaxed social situations (e.g., "the boss"). In **classical** and medieval rhetoric, these registers of formality were called *high style* and *low style*. A *middle style* was defined as the style fit for narrative, not drawing attention to itself.

rhetoric: the art of verbal persuasion. Classical rhetoricians distinguished three areas of rhetoric: the forensic, to be used in law courts; the deliberative, to be used in political or philosophical deliberations; and the demonstrative, or epideictic, to be used for the purposes of public praise or blame. Rhetorical manuals covered all the skills required of a speaker, from the management of style and structure to delivery. These manuals powerfully influenced the theory of poetics as a separate branch of verbal practice, particularly in the matter of style.

rhyme: a figure of speech. The repetition of identical vowel sounds in stressed syllables whose initial consonants differ ("dead" / "head"). In poetry, rhyme often links the end of one line with another. *Masculine rhyme:* full rhyme on the final syllable of the line ("decays" / "days"). *Feminine rhyme:* full rhyme on syllables that are followed by unaccented syllables ("fountains" / "mountains"). *Internal rhyme:* full rhyme within a single line; Coleridge, *The Rime of the Ancient Mariner*, line 7: "The guests are met, the feast is set" (see vol. D, p. 448). *Rhyme riche:* rhyming on **homophones;** Chaucer, *General Prologue*, lines 17–18: "seeke" / "seke." *Off rhyme* (also known as *half rhyme, near rhyme,* or *slant rhyme*): differs from perfect rhyme in changing the vowel sound and/or the concluding consonants expected of perfect rhyme; Byron, "They say that Hope is Happiness," lines 5–7: "most" / "lost." *Pararhyme:* stressed vowel sounds differ but are flanked by identical or similar consonants; Owen, "Miners," lines 9–11: "simmer" / "summer" (see vol. F, p. 163).

rhyme royal: a verse form. A **stanza** of seven **iambic pentameter** lines, rhyming ababbcc; first introduced by Chaucer and called "royal" because the form was used by James I of Scotland for his *Kingis Quair* in the early fifteenth century. Chaucer, "Troilus's Song" (see vol. A, p. 362).

rhythm: Rhythm is not absolutely distinguishable from **meter.** One way of making a clear distinction between these terms is to say that rhythm (from the Greek "to flow") denotes the patterns of sound within the feet of verse lines and the combination of those feet. Very often a particular meter will raise expectations that a given rhythm will be used regularly through a whole line or a whole poem. Thus in English verse the pentameter regularly uses an iambic rhythm. Rhythm, however, is much more fluid than meter, and many lines within the same poem using a single meter will frequently exploit different rhythmic possibilities. For examples of different rhythms, see **iamb, trochee, anapest, spondee,** and **dactyl.**

romance: a **genre.** From the twelfth to the sixteenth century, the main form of European narrative, in either verse or prose, was that of chivalric romance. Romance, like the later **novel,** is a very fluid genre, but romances are often characterized by (i) a tripartite structure of social integration, followed by disintegration, involving moral tests and often marvelous events, itself the prelude to reintegration in a happy ending, frequently of marriage; and (ii) aristocratic social milieux. Thus *Sir Gawain and the Green Knight* (see vol. A, p. 204); Spenser's (unfinished) *Faerie Queene* (vol. B, p. 249). The immensely popular, fertile genre was absorbed, in both domesticated and undomesticated form, by the novel. For an adaptation of romance, see Chaucer, *Wife of Bath's Tale* (vol. A, p. 300).

sarcasm (Greek "flesh tearing"): a **figure of thought.** A wounding expression, often expressed ironically; Boswell, *Life of Johnson*: Johnson [asked if any man of the modern age could have written the **epic** poem *Fingal*] replied, "Yes, Sir, many men, many women, and many children" (see vol. C, p. 844).

satire (Latin for "a bowl of mixed fruits"): a **genre.** In Roman literature (e.g., Juvenal), the communication, in the form of a letter between equals, complaining of the ills of contemporary society. The genre in this form is characterized by a first-person narrator exasperated by social ills; the letter form; a high frequency of contemporary reference; and the use of invective in **low-style** language. Pope practices the genre thus in the *Epistle to Dr. Arbuthnot* (see vol. C, p. 543). Wyatt's "Mine own John Poins" (see vol. B, p. 131) draws ultimately on a gentler, Horatian model of the genre.

satiric mode: Works in a very large variety of genres are devoted to the more or less savage attack on social ills. Thus Swift's travel narrative *Gulliver's Travels* (see vol. C, p. 279), his **essay** "A Modest Proposal" (vol. C, p. 454), Pope's mock-**epic** *The Dunciad* (vol. C, p. 555), and Gay's *Beggar's Opera* (vol. C, p. 659), to look no further than the eighteenth century, are all within a satiric mode.

scene: a subdivision of an **act,** itself a subdivision of a dramatic performance and/ or text. The action of a scene usually occurs in one place.

sensibility (from Latin, "capable of being perceived by the senses"): as a literary term, an eighteenth-century concept derived from moral philosophy that stressed the social importance of fellow feeling and particularly of sympathy in social relations. The concept generated a literature of "sensibility," such as the sentimental **novel** (the most famous of which was Goethe's *Sorrows of the Young Werther* [1774]), or sentimental poetry, such as Cowper's passage on the stricken deer in *The Task* (see vol. C, p. 1024).

short story: a **genre.** Generically similar to, though shorter and more concentrated than, the **novel;** often published as part of a collection. Thus Mansfield, "The Daughters of the Late Colonel" (see vol. F, p. 698).

simile (Latin "like"): a **figure of thought.** Comparison, usually using the word "like" or "as," of one thing with another so as to produce sometimes surprising analogies. Donne, "The Storm," lines 29–30: "Sooner than you read this line did the gale, / Like shot, not feared till felt, our sails assail." Frequently used, in extended form, in **epic** poetry; Milton, *Paradise Lost* 1.338–46 (see vol. B, p. 1504).

soliloquy (Latin "single speaking"): a **topos** of drama, in which a **character,** alone or thinking to be alone on stage, speaks so as to give the audience access to his or her private thoughts. Thus Viola's soliloquy in Shakespeare, *Twelfth Night* 2.2.17– 41 (vol. B, p. 758).

sonnet: a **verse form.** A form combining a variable number of units of rhymed lines to produce a fourteen-line poem, usually in rhyming **iambic pentameter** lines. In English there are two principal varieties: the Petrarchan sonnet, formed by an octave (an eight-line stanza, often broken into two **quatrains** having the same rhyme scheme, typically abba abba) and a sestet (a six-line stanza, typically cdecde or cdcdcd); and the Shakespearean sonnet, formed by three quatrains (abab cdcd efef) and a **couplet** (gg). The declaration of a sonnet can take a sharp turn, or "volta," often at the decisive formal shift from octave to sestet in the Petrarchan sonnet, or in the final couplet of a Shakespearean sonnet, introducing a trenchant counterstatement. Derived from Italian poetry, and especially from the poetry of Petrarch, the sonnet was first introduced to English poetry by Wyatt, and initially used principally for the expression of unrequited erotic love, though later poets used the form for many other purposes. See Wyatt, "Whoso list to hunt" (vol. B, p. 121); Sidney, *Astrophil and Stella* (vol. B, p. 586); Shakespeare, *Sonnets* (vol. B, p. 723); Wordsworth, "London, 1802" (vol. D, p. 357); McKay, "If We Must Die" (vol. F, p. 854); Heaney, "Clearances" (vol. F, p. 1104).

speech act: Words and deeds are often distinguished, but words are often (perhaps always) themselves deeds. Utterances can perform different speech acts, such as promising, declaring, casting a spell, encouraging, persuading, denying, lying, and so on. See also **performative.**

Spenserian stanza: a **verse form.** The stanza developed by Spenser for *The Faerie Queene*; nine **iambic** lines, the first eight of which are **pentameters,** followed by one **hexameter,** rhyming ababbcbcc. See also, for example, Shelley, *Adonais* (vol. D, p. 856), and Keats, *The Eve of St. Agnes* (vol. D, p. 961).

spondee: a term of **meter.** A two-syllable foot following the rhythmic pattern, in English verse, of two stressed syllables. Thus, for example, "Utah."

stanza (Italian "room"): groupings of two or more lines, though "stanza" is usually reserved for groupings of at least four lines. Stanzas are often joined by rhyme, often in sequence, where each group shares the same metrical pattern and, when rhymed, rhyme scheme. Stanzas can themselves be arranged into larger groupings. Poets often invent new **verse forms,** or they may work within established forms.

story: a narrative's sequence of events, which we reconstruct from those events as they have been recounted by the narrator (i.e., the **plot**). See also **order.**

stream of consciousness: usually a **first-person** narrative that seems to give the reader access to the narrator's mind as it perceives or reflects on events, prior to organizing those perceptions into a coherent narrative. Thus (though generated from a **third-person** narrative) Joyce, *Ulysses,* "Penelope" (see vol. F, p. 604).

style (from Latin for "writing instrument"): In literary works the manner in which something is expressed contributes substantially to its meaning. The expressions "sun," "mass of helium at the center of the solar system," "heaven's golden orb" all designate "sun," but do so in different manners, or styles, which produce different meanings. The manner of a literary work is its "style," the effect of which is its "tone." We often can intuit the tone of a text; from that intuition of tone we can analyze the stylistic resources by which it was produced. We can analyze the style of literary works through consideration of different elements of style; for example, **diction, figures of thought, figures of speech, meter and rhythm, verse form, syntax, point of view.**

sublime: As a concept generating a literary movement, the sublime refers to the realm of experience beyond the measurable, and so beyond the rational, produced especially by the terrors and grandeur of natural phenomena. Derived especially from the first-century Greek treatise *On the Sublime,* sometimes attributed to Longinus, the notion of the sublime was in the later eighteenth century a spur to Romanticism.

syllable: the smallest unit of sound in a pronounced word. The syllable that receives the greatest stress is called the *tonic* syllable.

symbol (Greek "token"): a **figure of thought.** Something that stands for something else, and yet seems necessarily to evoke that other thing. In Neoplatonic, and therefore Romantic, theory, to be distinguished from **allegory** thus: whereas allegory involves connections between vehicle and tenor agreed by convention or made explicit, the meanings of a symbol are supposedly inherent to it. For discussion, see Coleridge, "On Symbol and Allegory" (vol. D, p. 507).

synecdoche (Greek "to take with something else"): a **figure of thought.** Using a part to express the whole, or vice versa; e.g., "all hands on deck." Closely related to **metonymy.**

syntax (Greek "ordering with"): Syntax designates the rules by which sentences are constructed in a given language. Discussion of meter is impossible without some reference to syntax, since the overall effect of a poem is, in part, always the product of a subtle balance of meter and sentence construction. Syntax is also essential to the understanding of prose style, since prose writers, deprived of the full shaping possibilities of meter, rely all the more heavily on syntactic resources. A working command of syntactical practice requires an understanding of the parts of speech (nouns, verbs, adjectives, adverbs, conjunctions, pronouns, prepositions, and interjections), since writers exploit syntactic possibilities by using particular combinations and concentrations of the parts of speech.

taste (from Italian "touch"): Although medieval monastic traditions used eating and tasting as a metaphor for reading, the concept of taste as a personal ideal to be cultivated by, and applied to, the appreciation and judgment of works of art in general was developed in the eighteenth century.

tercet: a **verse form.** A stanza or group of three lines, used in larger forms such as **terza rima,** the **Petrarchan sonnet,** and the **villanelle.**

terza rima: a **verse form.** A sequence of rhymed **tercets** linked by rhyme thus: aba bcb cdc, etc. first used extensively by Dante in *The Divine Comedy,* the form was adapted in English **iambic pentameters** by Wyatt and revived in the nineteenth century. See Wyatt, "Mine own John Poins" (vol. B, p. 131); Shelley, "Ode to the West Wind" (vol. D, p. 806); and Morris, "The Defence of Guinevere" (vol. E, p. 560). For modern adaptations see Eliot, lines 78–149 (though unrhymed) of "Little Gidding" (vol. F, pp. 679–81); Heaney, "Station Island" (vol. F, p. 1102); Walcott, *Omeros* (vol. F, p. 947).

tetrameter (Greek "four measure"): a term of **meter.** A line with four stresses. Coleridge, *Christabel,* line 31: "She stole along, she nothing spoke" (see vol. D, p. 468).

theme (Greek "proposition"): In literary criticism the term designates what the work is about; the theme is the concept that unifies a given work of literature.

third-person narration: relevant to **point of view.** A narration in which the narrator recounts a narrative of **characters** referred to explicitly or implicitly by third-person pronouns ("he," she," etc.), without the limitation of a **first-person narration.** Thus Johnson, *The History of Rasselas*.

topographical poem (Greek "place writing"): a **genre.** A poem devoted to the meditative description of particular places. Thus Gray, "Ode on a Distant Prospect of Eton College" (see vol. C, p. 994).

topos (Greek "place," plural *topoi*): a commonplace in the content of a given kind of literature. Originally, in **classical** rhetoric, the topoi were tried-and-tested stimuli to literary invention: lists of standard headings under which a subject might be investigated. In medieval narrative poems, for example, it was commonplace to begin with a description of spring. Writers did, of course, render the commonplace uncommon, as in Chaucer's spring scene at the opening of *The Canterbury Tales* (see vol. A, p. 261).

tradition (from Latin "passing on"): A literary tradition is whatever is passed on or revived from the past in a single literary culture, or drawn from others to enrich a writer's culture. "Tradition" is fluid in reference, ranging from small to large referents: thus it may refer to a relatively small aspect of texts (e.g., the tradition of **iambic pentameter**), or it may, at the other extreme, refer to the body of texts that constitute a **canon.**

tragedy: a **genre.** A dramatic representation of the fall of kings or nobles, beginning in happiness and ending in catastrophe. Later transferred to other social milieux. The opposite of **comedy;** thus Shakespeare, *Othello* (see vol. B, p. 806).

tragic mode: Many genres (**epic** poetry, **legend**ary chronicles, **tragedy,** the **novel**) either do or can participate in a tragic mode, by representing the fall of noble **protagonists** and the irreparable ravages of human society and history.

tragicomedy: a **genre.** A play in which potentially tragic events turn out to have a happy, or **comic,** ending. Thus Shakespeare, *Measure for Measure*.

translation (Latin "carrying across"): the rendering of a text written in one language into another.

trimeter (Greek "three measure"): a term of **meter.** A line with three stresses. Herbert, "Discipline," line 1: "Throw away thy rod" (see vol. B, p. 1274).

triplet: a **verse form.** A tercet rhyming on the same sound. Pope inserts triplets among heroic **couplets** to emphasize a particular thought; see *Essay on Criticism*, 315–17 (vol. C, p. 497).

trochee: a term of **rhythm.** A two-syllable foot following the pattern, in English verse, of stressed followed by unstressed syllable, producing a falling effect. Thus, for example, "Texas."

type (Greek "impression, figure"): a **figure of thought.** In Christian allegorical interpretation of the Old Testament, pre-Christian figures were regarded as "types," or foreshadowings, of Christ or the Christian dispensation. *Typology* has been the source of much visual and literary art in which the parallelisms between old and new are extended to nonbiblical figures; thus the virtuous plowman in *Piers Plowman* becomes a type of Christ.

unities: According to a theory supposedly derived from Aristotle's *Poetics*, the events represented in a play should have unity of time, place, and action: that the play take up no more time than the time of the play, or at most a day; that the space of action should be within a single city; and that there should be no subplot. See Johnson, *The Preface to Shakespeare* (vol. C, p. 807).

vernacular (from Latin *verna*, "servant"): the language of the people, as distinguished from learned and arcane languages. From the later Middle Ages especially, the "vernacular" languages and literatures of Europe distinguished themselves from the learned languages and literatures of Latin, Greek, and Hebrew.

verse form: The terms related to **meter** and **rhythm** describe the shape of individual lines. Lines of verse are combined to produce larger groupings, called verse forms. These larger groupings are in the first instance **stanzas**. The combination of a certain meter and stanza shape constitutes the verse form, of which there are many standard kinds.

villanelle: a **verse form**. A fixed form of usually five **tercets** and a **quatrain** employing only two rhyme sounds altogether, rhyming aba for the tercets and abaa for the quatrain, with a complex pattern of two **refrains**. Derived from a French fixed form. Thomas, "Do Not Go Gentle into That Good Night" (see vol. F, p. 833).

wit: Originally a synonym for "reason" in Old and Middle English, "wit" became a literary ideal in the Renaissance as brilliant play of the full range of mental resources. For eighteenth-century writers, the notion necessarily involved pleasing expression, as in Pope's definition of true wit as "Nature to advantage dressed, / What oft was thought, but ne'er so well expressed" (*Essay on Criticism*, lines 297–98; see vol. C, p. 496–97). See also Johnson, *Lives of the Poets*, "Cowley," on "metaphysical wit" (see vol. C, p. 817). Romantic theory of the imagination deprived wit of its full range of apprehension, whence the word came to be restricted to its modern sense, as the clever play of mind that produces laughter.

zeugma (Greek "a yoking"): a **figure of thought**. A figure whereby one word applies to two or more words in a sentence, and in which the applications are surprising, either because one is unusual, or because the applications are made in very different ways; Pope, *Rape of the Lock* 3.7–8, in which the word "take" is used in two senses: "Here thou, great Anna! whom three realms obey, / Dost sometimes counsel take— and sometimes tea" (see vol. C, p. 515).

B: Publishing History, Censorship

By the time we read texts in published books, they have already been treated—that is, changed by authors, editors, and printers—in many ways. Although there are differences across history, in each period literary works are subject to pressures of many kinds, which apply before, while, and after an author writes. The pressures might be financial, as in the relations of author and patron; commercial, as in the marketing of books; and legal, as in, during some periods, the negotiation through official and unofficial censorship. In addition, texts in all periods undergo technological processes, as they move from the material forms in which an author produced them to the forms in which they are presented to readers. Some of the terms below designate important material forms in which books were produced, disseminated, and surveyed across the historical span of this anthology. Others designate the skills developed to understand these processes. The anthology's introductions to individual periods discuss the particular forms these phenomena took in different eras.

bookseller: In England, and particularly in London, commercial bookmaking and -selling enterprises came into being in the early fourteenth century. These were loose organizations of artisans who usually lived in the same neighborhoods (around St. Paul's Cathedral in London). A bookseller or dealer would coordinate the production of hand-copied books for wealthy patrons (see **patronage**), who would order books to be custom-made. After the introduction of **printing** in the late fifteenth century, authors generally sold the rights to their work to booksellers, without any further **royalties.** Booksellers, who often had their own shops, belonged to the **Stationers' Company.** This system lasted into the eighteenth century. In 1710, however, authors were for the first time granted **copyright,** which tipped the commercial balance in their favor, against booksellers.

censorship: The term applies to any mechanism for restricting what can be published. Historically, the reasons for imposing censorship are heresy, sedition, blasphemy, libel, or obscenity. External censorship is imposed by institutions having legislative sanctions at their disposal. Thus the pre-Reformation Church imposed the Constitutions of Archbishop Arundel of 1409, aimed at repressing the Lollard "heresy." After the Reformation, some key events in the history of censorship are as follows: 1547, when anti-Lollard legislation and legislation made by Henry VIII concerning treason by writing (1534) were abolished; the Licensing Order of 1643, which legislated that works be licensed, through the Stationers' Company, prior to publication; and 1695, when the last such Act stipulating prepublication licensing lapsed. Postpublication censorship continued in different periods for different reasons. Thus, for example, British publication of D. H. Lawrence's *Lady Chatterley's Lover* (1928) was obstructed (though unsuccessfully) in 1960, under the Obscene Publications Act of 1959. Censorship can also be international: although not published in Iran, Salman Rushdie's *Satanic Verses* (1988) was censored in that country, where the leader, Ayatollah Ruhollah Khomeini, proclaimed a fatwa (religious decree) promising the author's execution. Very often censorship is not imposed externally, however: authors or publishers can censor work in anticipation of what will incur the wrath of readers or the penalties of the law. Victorian and Edwardian publishers of **novels,** for example, urged authors to remove potentially offensive material, especially for serial publication in popular magazines.

codex: the physical format of most modern books and medieval manuscripts, consisting of a series of separate leaves gathered into quires and bound together, often with a cover. In late antiquity, the codex largely replaced the scroll, the standard form of written documents in Roman culture.

copy text: the particular text of a work used by a textual editor as the basis of an edition of that work.

copyright: the legal protection afforded to authors for control of their work's publication, in an attempt to ensure due financial reward. Some key dates in the history of copyright in the United Kingdom are as follows: 1710, when a statute gave authors the exclusive right to publish their work for fourteen years, and fourteen years more if the author were still alive when the first term had expired; 1842, when the period of authorial control was extended to forty-two years; and 1911, when the term was extended yet further, to fifty years after the author's death. In 1995 the period of protection was harmonized with the laws in other European countries to be the life of the author plus seventy years. In the United States no works first published before 1923 are in copyright. Works published since 1978 are, as in the United Kingdom, protected for the life of the author plus seventy years.

folio: the leaf formed by both sides of a single page. Each folio has two sides: a *recto* (the front side of the leaf, on the right side of a double-page spread in an open codex), and a *verso* (the back side of the leaf, on the left side of a double-page spread). Modern book pagination follows the pattern 1, 2, 3, 4, while medieval manuscript pagination follows the pattern 1r, 1v, 2r, 2v. "Folio" can also designate the size of a printed book. Books come in different shapes, depending originally on the number of times a standard sheet of paper is folded. One fold produces a large volume, a *folio* book; two folds produce a *quarto*, four an *octavo*, and six a very small *duodecimo*. Generally speaking, the larger the book, the grander and more expensive. Shakespeare's plays were, for example, first printed in quartos, but were gathered into a folio edition in 1623.

foul papers: versions of a work before an author has produced, if she or he has, a final copy (a "fair copy") with all corrections removed.

incunabulum (plural "incunabula"): any printed book produced in Europe before 1501. Famous incunabula include the Gutenberg Bible, printed in 1455.

manuscript (Latin, "written by hand"): Any text written physically by hand is a manuscript. Before the introduction of **printing** with moveable type in 1476, all texts in England were produced and reproduced by hand, in manuscript. This is an extremely labor-intensive task, using expensive materials (e.g., **vellum**, or **parchment**); the cost of books produced thereby was, accordingly, very high. Even after the introduction of printing, many texts continued to be produced in manuscript. This is obviously true of letters, for example, but until the eighteenth century, poetry written within aristocratic circles was often transmitted in manuscript copies.

paleography (Greek "ancient writing"): the art of deciphering, describing, and dating forms of handwriting.

parchment: animal skin, used as the material for handwritten books before the introduction of paper. See also **vellum.**

patronage, patron (Latin "protector"): Many technological, legal, and commercial supports were necessary before professional authorship became possible. Although some playwrights (e.g., Shakespeare) made a living by writing for the theater, other authors needed, principally, the large-scale reproductive capacities of **printing** and the security of **copyright** to make a living from writing. Before these conditions obtained, many authors had another main occupation, and most authors had to rely on patronage. In different periods, institutions or individuals offered material support, or patronage, to authors. Thus in Anglo-Saxon England, monasteries afforded the conditions of writing to monastic authors. Between the twelfth and the seventeenth centuries, the main source of patronage was the royal court. Authors offered patrons prestige and ideological support in return for financial support. Even as the conditions of professional authorship came into being at the beginning of the eighteenth century, older forms of direct patronage were not altogether displaced until the middle of the century.

periodical: Whereas journalism, strictly, applies to daily writing (from French *jour*, "day"), periodical writing appears at larger, but still frequent, intervals, characteristically in the form of the **essay**. Periodicals were developed especially in the eighteenth century.

printing: Printing, or the mechanical reproduction of books using moveable type, was invented in Germany in the mid-fifteenth century by Johannes Gutenberg; it quickly spread throughout Europe. William Caxton brought printing into England from the Low Countries in 1476. Much greater powers of reproduction at much lower prices transformed every aspect of literary culture.

publisher: the person or company responsible for the commissioning and publicizing of printed matter. In the early period of **printing**, publisher, printer, and bookseller were often the same person. This trend continued in the ascendancy of the **Stationers' Company**, between the middle of the sixteenth and the end of the seventeenth centuries. Toward the end of the seventeenth century, these three functions began to separate, leading to their modern distinctions.

quire: When medieval manuscripts were assembled, a few loose sheets of parchment or paper would first be folded together and sewn along the fold. This formed a quire (also known as a "gathering" or "signature"). Folded in this way, four large sheets of parchment would produce eight smaller manuscript leaves. Multiple quires could then be bound together to form a codex.

royalties: an agreed-upon proportion of the price of each copy of a work sold, paid by the publisher to the author, or an agreed-upon fee paid to the playwright for each performance of a play.

scribe: In **manuscript** culture, the scribe is the copyist who reproduces a text by hand.

scriptorium (plural "scriptoria"): a place for producing written documents and manuscripts.

serial publication: generally referring to the practice, especially common in the nineteenth century, of publishing novels a few chapters at a time, in periodicals.

Stationers' Company: The Stationers' Company was an English guild incorporating various tradesmen, including printers, publishers, and booksellers, skilled in the production and selling of books. It was formed in 1403, received its royal charter in 1557, and served as a means both of producing and of regulating books. Authors would sell the manuscripts of their books to individual stationers, who incurred the risks and took the profits of producing and selling the books. The stationers entered their rights over given books in the Stationers' Register. They also regulated the book trade and held their monopoly by licensing books and by being empowered to seize unauthorized books and imprison resisters. This system of licensing broke down in the social unrest of the Civil War and Interregnum (1640–60), and it ended in 1695. Even after the end of licensing, the Stationers' Company continued to be an intrinsic part of the **copyright** process, since the 1710 copyright statute directed that copyright had to be registered at Stationers' Hall.

subscription: An eighteenth-century system of bookselling somewhere between direct **patronage** and impersonal sales. A subscriber paid half the cost of a book before publication and half on delivery. The author received these payments directly. The subscriber's name appeared in the prefatory pages.

textual criticism: Works in all periods often exist in many subtly or not so subtly different forms. This is especially true with regard to manuscript textual reproduction, but it also applies to printed texts. Textual criticism is the art, developed from the fifteenth century in Italy but raised to new levels of sophistication from the eighteenth century, of deciphering different historical states of texts. This art involves the analysis of textual **variants,** often with the aim of distinguishing authorial from scribal forms.

variants: differences that appear among different manuscripts or printed editions of the same text.

vellum: animal skin, used as the material for handwritten books before the introduction of paper. See also **parchment.**

watermark: the trademark of a paper manufacturer, impressed into the paper but largely invisible unless held up to light.

Geographic Nomenclature

The British Isles refers to the prominent group of islands off the northwest coast of Europe, especially to the two largest, **Great Britain** and **Ireland**. At present these comprise two sovereign states: **the Republic of Ireland**, and **the United Kingdom of Great Britain and Northern Ireland**—known for short as the **United Kingdom** or the **U.K.** Most of the smaller islands are part of the U.K. but a few, like the **Isle of Man** and the tiny **Channel Islands**, are largely independent. The U.K. is often loosely referred to as "Britain" or "Great Britain" and is sometimes called simply, if inaccurately, "England." For obvious reasons, the latter usage is rarely heard among the inhabitants of the other countries of the U.K.—**Scotland, Wales,** and **Northern Ireland** (sometimes called **Ulster**). England is by far the most populous part of the kingdom, as well as the seat of its capital, London.

From the first to the fifth century C.E. most of what is now **England** and **Wales** was a province of the Roman Empire called **Britain** (in Latin, **Britannia**). After the fall of Rome, much of the island was invaded and settled by peoples from northern Germany and Denmark speaking what we now call Old English. These peoples are collectively known as the Anglo-Saxons, and the word **England** is related to the first element of their name. By the time of the Norman Conquest (1066) most of the kingdoms founded by the Anglo-Saxons and subsequent Viking invaders had coalesced into the kingdom of **England,** which, in the latter Middle Ages, conquered and largely absorbed the neighboring Celtic kingdom of **Wales.** In 1603 James VI of **Scotland** inherited the island's other throne as James I of **England,** and for the next hundred years—except for the two decades of Puritan rule—**Scotland** (both its English-speaking **Lowlands** and its Gaelic-speaking **Highlands**) and **England** (with **Wales**) were two kingdoms under a single king. In 1707 the Act of Union welded them together as **the United Kingdom of Great Britain. Ireland,** where English rule had begun in the twelfth century and been tightened in the sixteenth, was incorporated by the 1800–1801 Act of Union into **the United Kingdom of Great Britain and Ireland**. With the division of Ireland and the establishment of **the Irish Free State** after World War I, this name was modified to its present form, and in 1949 **the Irish Free State** became **the Republic of Ireland, or Éire.** In 1999 **Scotland** elected a separate parliament it had relinquished in 1707, and **Wales** elected an assembly it lost in 1409; neither Scotland nor Wales ceased to be part of the **United Kingdom.**

The **British Isles** are further divided into counties, which in **Great Britain** are also known as shires. This word, with its vowel shortened in pronunciation, forms the suffix in the names of many counties, such as **Yorkshire, Wiltshire, Somersetshire**.

The Latin names **Britannia** (Britain), **Caledonia** (Scotland), and **Hibernia** (Ireland) are sometimes used in poetic diction; so too is **Britain's** ancient Celtic name, **Albion.** Because of its accidental resemblance to *albus* (Latin for "white"), **Albion** is especially associated with the chalk cliffs that seem to gird much of the English coast like defensive walls.

The **British Empire** took its name from **the British Isles** because it was created not only by the **English** but also by the **Irish, Scots,** and **Welsh,** as well as by civilians and servicemen from other constituent countries of the empire. Some of the empire's **overseas colonies,** or **crown colonies,** were populated largely by settlers of European origin and their descendants. These predominantly white **settler colonies,** such as **Canada, Australia,** and **New Zealand,** were allowed significant self-government in the nineteenth century and recognized as **dominions** in the early twentieth century. The **white dominions** became members of **the Commonwealth of Nations**, also called **the Commonwealth, the British Commonwealth**, and **"the Old Commonwealth"** at different times, an association of sovereign states under the symbolic leadership of the British monarch.

Other **overseas colonies** of the empire had mostly indigenous populations (or, in the Caribbean, the descendants of imported slaves, indentured servants, and others). These **colonies** were granted political independence after World War II, later than the **dominions**, and have often been referred to since as **postcolonial** nations. In South and Southeast Asia, **India** and **Pakistan** gained independence in 1947, followed by other countries including **Sri Lanka** (formerly **Ceylon**), **Burma** (now **Myanmar**), **Malaya** (now **Malaysia**), and **Singapore**. In West and East Africa, the **Gold Coast** was decolonized as **Ghana** in 1957, **Nigeria** in 1960, **Sierra Leone** in 1961, **Uganda** in 1962, **Kenya** in 1963, and so forth, while in southern Africa, the white minority government of **South Africa** was already independent in 1931, though majority rule did not come until 1994. In the Caribbean, **Jamaica** and **Trinidad and Tobago** won independence in 1962, followed by **Barbados** in 1966, and other islands of the British West Indies in the 1970s and '80s. Other regions with nations emerging out of British colonial rule included Central America (**British Honduras**, now **Belize**), South America (**British Guiana**, now **Guyana**), the Pacific islands (**Fiji**), and Europe (**Cyprus, Malta**). After decolonization, many of these nations chose to remain within a newly conceived **Commonwealth** and are sometimes referred to as **"New Commonwealth"** countries. Some nations, such as **Ireland, Pakistan**, and **South Africa,** withdrew from the **Commonwealth**, though **South Africa** and **Pakistan** eventually rejoined, and others, such as **Burma** (now **Myanmar**), gained independence outside the **Commonwealth**. Britain's last major overseas colony, **Hong Kong**, was returned to Chinese sovereignty in 1997, but while Britain retains only a handful of dependent territories, such as **Bermuda** and **Montserrat**, the scope of the **Commonwealth** remains vast, with 30 percent of the world's population.

British Money

One of the most dramatic changes to the system of British money came in 1971. In the system previously in place, the pound consisted of 20 shillings, each containing 12 pence, making 240 pence to the pound. Since 1971, British money has been calculated on the decimal system, with 100 pence to the pound. Britons' experience of paper money did not change very drastically: as before, 5- and 10-pound notes constitute the majority of bills passing through their hands (in addition, 20- and 50- pound notes have been added). But the shift necessitated a whole new way of thinking about and exchanging coins and marked the demise of the shilling, one of the fundamental units of British monetary history. Many other coins, still frequently encountered in literature, had already passed. These include the groat, worth 4 pence (the word "groat" is often used to signify a trifling sum); the angel (which depicted the archangel Michael triumphing over a dragon), valued at 10 shillings; the mark, worth in its day two-thirds of a pound or 13 shillings 4 pence; and the sovereign, a gold coin initially worth 22 shillings 6 pence, later valued at 1 pound, last circulated in 1932. One prominent older coin, the guinea, was worth a pound and a shilling; though it has not been minted since 1813, a very few quality items or prestige awards (like the purse in a horse race) may still be quoted in guineas. (The table below includes some other well-known, obsolete coins.) Colloquially, a pound was (and is) called a quid; a shilling a bob; sixpence, a tanner; a copper could refer to a penny, a half-penny, or a farthing (¼ penny).

Old Currency	New Currency
1 pound note	1 pound coin (or note in Scotland)
10 shilling (half-pound note)	50 pence
5 shilling (crown)	
2½ shilling (half crown)	20 pence
2 shilling (florin)	10 pence
1 shilling	5 pence
6 pence	
2½ pence	1 penny
2 pence	
1 penny	
½ penny	
¼ penny (farthing)	

Throughout its tenure as a member of the European Union, Britain contemplated but did not make the change to the EU's common currency, the Euro. Many Britons strongly identify their country with its rich commercial history and tend to view their currency patriotically as a national symbol. Now, with the planned withdrawal of the United Kingdom from the EU, the pound seems here to stay.

Even more challenging than sorting out the values of obsolete coins is calculating for any given period the purchasing power of money, which fluctuates over time by its very nature. At the beginning of the twentieth century, 1 pound was worth about 5 American dollars, though those bought three to four times what they now do. Now, the pound buys anywhere from $1.20 to $1.50. As difficult as it is to generalize, it is clear that money used to be worth much more than it is currently. In Anglo-Saxon times, the most valuable circulating coin was the silver penny: four would buy a sheep. Beyond long-term inflationary trends, prices varied from times of plenty to those marked by poor harvests; from peacetime to wartime; from the country to the metropolis (life in London has always been very expensive); and wages varied according to the availability of labor (wages would sharply rise, for instance, during the devastating Black Death in the fourteenth century). The following chart provides a glimpse of some actual prices of given periods and their changes across time, though all the variables mentioned above prevent them from being definitive. Even from one year to the next, an added tax on gin or tea could drastically raise prices, and a lottery ticket could cost much more the night before the drawing than just a month earlier. Still, the prices quoted below do indicate important trends, such as the disparity of incomes in British society and the costs of basic commodities. In the chart on the following page, the symbol £ is used for pound, s. for shilling, d. for a penny (from Latin *denarius*); a sum would normally be written £2.19.3, i.e., 2 pounds, 19 shillings, 3 pence. (This is Leopold Bloom's budget for the day depicted in Joyce's novel *Ulysses* [1922]; in the new currency, it would be about £2.96.)

circa	1390	1590	1650	1750	1815	1875	1950
food and drink	gallon (8 pints) of ale, 1.5d.	tankard of beer, 5d.	coffee, 1d. a dish	"drunk for a penny, dead drunk for two-pence" (gin shop sign in Hogarth print)	ounce of laudanum, 3d.	pint of beer, 3d.	pint of Guinness stout, 11d.
	gallon (8 pints) of wine, 3 to 4d.	pound of beef, 2s. 5d.	chicken, 1s. 4d.	dinner at a steakhouse, 1s.	ham and potato dinner for two, 7s.	dinner in a good hotel, 5s.	pound of beef, 2s. 2d.
	pound of cinnamon, 1 to 3s.	pound of cinnamon, 10s. 6d.	pound of tea, £3 10s.	pound of tea, 16s.	bottle of French claret, 12s.	pound of tea, 2s.	dinner on railway car, 7s. 6d.
entertainment	no cost to watch a cycle play	admission to public theater, 1 to 3d.	falcon, £11 5s.	theater tickets, 1 to 5s.	admission to Covent Garden theater, 1 to 7s.	theater tickets, 6d. to 7s.	admission to Old Vic theater, 1s. 6d. to 10s. 6d.
	contributory admission to professional troupe theater	cheap seat in private theater, 6d.	billiard table, £25	admission to Vauxhall Gardens, 1s.	annual subscription to Almack's (exclusive club), 10 guineas	admission to Madam Tussaud's waxworks, 1s.	admission to Odeon cinema, Manchester, 1s 3d.
	maintenance for royal hounds at Windsor, .75d. a day	"to see a dead Indian" (quoted in The Tempest), 1.25d. (ten "doits")	three-quarter length portrait painting, £31	lottery ticket, £20 (shares were sold)	Jane Austen's piano, 30 guineas	annual fees at a gentleman's club, 7 to 10 guineas	tropical fish tank, £4 4s.

circa	1390	1590	1650	1750	1815	1875	1950
reading	cheap romance, 1s.	play quarto, 6d.	pamphlet, 1 to 6d.	issue of The *Gentleman's Magazine*, 6d.	issue of *Edinburgh Review*, 6s.	copy of the *Times*, 3d.	copy of the *Times*, 3d.
	a Latin Bible, 2 to £4	Shakespeare's *First Folio* (1623), £1	student Bible, 6s.	cheap edition of Milton, 2s.	membership in circulating library (3rd class), £1 4s. a year	illustrated edition of *Through the Looking-glass*, 6s.	issue of *Eagle* comics, 4.5d.
	payment for illuminating a liturgical book, £22 9s.	Foxe's *Acts and Monuments*, 24s.	Hobbes's *Leviathan*, 8s.	Johnson's *Dictionary*, folio, 2 vols., £4 10s.	1st edition of Austen's *Pride and Prejudice*, 18s.	1st edition of Trollope's *The Way We Live Now*, 2 vols., £1 1s.	Orwell's *Nineteen Eighty Four*, paperback, 3s. 6d.
transportation	night's supply of hay for horse, 2d.	wherry (whole boat) across Thames, 1d.	day's journey, coach, 10s.	boat across Thames, 4d.	coach ride, outside, 2 to 3d. a mile; inside, 4 to 5d. a mile	15-minute journey in a London cab, 1s. 6d.	London tube fare, about 2d. a mile
	coach, £8	hiring a horse for a day, 12d.	coach horse, £30	coach fare, London to Edinburgh, £4 10s.	palanquin transport in Madras, 5s. a day	railway, 3rd class, London to Plymouth, 18s. 8d. (about 1d. a mile)	petrol, 3s. a gallon
	quality horse, £10	hiring a coach for a day, 10s.	fancy carriage, £170	transport to America, £5	passage, Liverpool to New York, £10	passage to India, 1st class, £50	midsize Austin sedan, £449 plus £188 4s. 2d. tax
clothes	clothing allowance for peasant, 3s. a year	shoes with buckles, 8d.	footman's frieze coat, 15s.	working woman's gown, 6s. 6d.	checked muslin, 7s. per yard	flannel for a cheap petticoat, 1s. 3d. a yard	woman's sun frock, £3 13s. 10d.

shoes for gentry wearer, 4d.	woman's gloves, £1 5s.	falconer's hat, 10s.	gentleman's suit, £8	hiring a dressmaker for a pelisse, 8s.	overcoat for an Eton schoolboy, £1 1s.	tweed sports jacket, £3 16s. 6d.
hat for gentry wearer, 10d.	fine cloak, £16	black cloth for mourning household of an earl, £100	very fine wig, £30	ladies silk stockings, 12s.	set of false teeth, £2 10s.	"Teddy boy" drape suit, £20
hiring a skilled building worker, 4d. a day	actor's daily wage during playing season, 1s.	agricultural laborer, 6s. 5d. a week	price of boy slave, £32	lowest-paid sailor on Royal Navy ship, 10s. 9d. a month	seasonal agricultural laborer, 14s. a week	minimum wage, agricultural laborer, £4 14s. per 47-hour week
wage for professional scribe, £2 3s. 4d. a year + cloak	household servant 2 to £5 a year + food, clothing	tutor to nobleman's children, £30 a year	housemaid's wage, £6 to £8 a year	contributor to *Quarterly Review*, 10 guineas per sheet	housemaid's wage, £10 to £25 a year	shorthand typist, £367 a year
minimum income to be called gentleman, £10 a year; for knighthood, 40 to £400	minimum income for eligibility for knighthood, £30 a year	Milton's salary as Secretary of Foreign Tongues, £288 a year	Boswell's allowance, £200 a year	minimum income for a "genteel" family, £100 a year	income of the "comfortable" classes, £800 and up a year	middle manager's salary, £1,480 a year
income from land of richest magnates, £3,500 a year	income from land of average earl, £4,000 a year	Earl of Bedford's income, £8,000 a year	Duke of Newcastle's income, £40,000 a year	Mr. Darcy's income, *Pride and Prejudice*, £10,000	Trollope's income, £4,000 a year	barrister's salary, £2,032 a year

labor/incomes

The British Baronage

The English monarchy is in principle hereditary, though at times during the Middle Ages the rules were subject to dispute. In general, authority passes from father to eldest surviving son, to daughters in order of seniority if there is no son, to a brother if there are no children, and in default of direct descendants to collateral lines (cousins, nephews, nieces) in order of closeness. There have been breaks in the order of succession (1066, 1399, 1688), but so far as possible the usurpers have always sought to paper over the break with a legitimate, i.e., hereditary, claim. When a queen succeeds to the throne and takes a husband, he does not become king unless he is in the line of blood succession; rather, he is named prince consort, as Albert was to Victoria. He may father kings, but is not one himself.

The original Saxon nobles were the king's thanes, ealdormen, or earls, who provided the king with military service and counsel in return for booty, gifts, or landed estates. William the Conqueror, arriving from France, where feudalism was fully developed, considerably expanded this group. In addition, as the king distributed the lands of his new kingdom, he also distributed dignities to men who became known collectively as "the baronage." "Baron" in its root meaning signifies simply "man," and barons were the king's men. As the title was common, a distinction was early made between greater and lesser barons, the former gradually assuming loftier and more impressive titles. The first English "duke" was created in 1337; the title of "marquess," or "marquis" (pronounced "markwis"), followed in 1385, and "viscount" ("vyekount") in 1440. Though "earl" is the oldest title of all, an earl now comes between a marquess and a viscount in order of dignity and precedence, and the old term "baron" now designates a rank just below viscount. "Baronets" were created in 1611 as a means of raising revenue for the crown (the title could be purchased for about £1,000); they are marginal nobility and have never sat in the House of Lords.

Kings and queens are addressed as "Your Majesty," princes and princesses as "Your Highness," the other hereditary nobility as "My Lord" or "Your Lordship." Peers receive their titles either by inheritance (like Lord Byron, the sixth baron of that line) or from the monarch (like Alfred, Lord Tennyson, created 1st Baron Tennyson by Victoria). The children, even of a duke, are commoners unless they are specifically granted some other title or inherit their father's title from him. A peerage can be forfeited by act of attainder, as for example when a lord is convicted of treason; and, when forfeited, or lapsed for lack of a successor, can be bestowed on another family. Thus in 1605 Robert Cecil was made first earl of Salisbury in the third creation, the first creation dating from 1149, the second from 1337, the title having been in abeyance since 1539. Titles descend by right of succession and do not depend on tenure of land; thus, a title does not always indicate where a lord dwells or holds power. Indeed, noble titles do not always refer to a real place at all. At Prince Edward's marriage in 1999, the queen created him earl of Wessex, although the old kingdom of Wessex has had no political existence since the Anglo-Saxon period, and the name was all but forgotten until it was resurrected by Thomas Hardy as the setting of his novels. (This is perhaps but one of many ways in which the world of the aristocracy increasingly resembles the realm of literature.)

The king and queen	(These are all of the royal line.)
Prince and princess	
Duke and duchess	(These may or may not be of the royal
Marquess and marchioness	line, but are ordinarily remote from the
Earl and countess	succession.)
Viscount and viscountess	
Baron and baroness	
Baronet and lady	

Scottish peers sat in the parliament of Scotland, as English peers did in the parliament of England, till at the Act of Union (1707) Scottish peers were granted sixteen seats in the English House of Lords, to be filled by election. (In 1963, all Scottish lords were allowed to sit.) Similarly, Irish peers, when the Irish parliament was abolished in 1801, were granted the right to elect twenty-eight of their number to the House of Lords in Westminster. (Now that the Republic of Ireland is a separate nation, this no longer applies.) Women members (peeresses) were first allowed to sit in the House as nonhereditary Life Peers in 1958 (when that status was created for members of both genders); women first sat by their own hereditary right in 1963. Today the House of Lords still retains some power to influence or delay legislation, but its future is uncertain. In 1999, the hereditary peers (then amounting to 750) were reduced to 92 temporary members elected by their fellow peers. Holders of Life Peerages remain, as do senior bishops of the Church of England and high-court judges (the "Law Lords").

Below the peerage the chief title of honor is "knight." Knighthood, which is not hereditary, is generally a reward for services rendered. A knight (Sir John Black) is addressed, using his first name, as "Sir John"; his wife, using the last name, is "Lady Black"—unless she is the daughter of an earl or nobleman of higher rank, in which case she will be "Lady Arabella." The female equivalent of a knight bears the title of "Dame." Though the word *knight* itself comes from the Anglo-Saxon *cniht*, there is some doubt as to whether knighthood amounted to much before the arrival of the Normans. The feudal system required military service as a condition of land tenure, and a man who came to serve his king at the head of an army of tenants required a title of authority and badges of identity—hence the title of knighthood and the coat of arms. During the Crusades, when men were far removed from their land (or even sold it in order to go on crusade), more elaborate forms of fealty sprang up that soon expanded into orders of knighthood. The Templars, Hospitallers, Knights of the Teutonic Order, Knights of Malta, and Knights of the Golden Fleece were but a few of these companionships; not all of them were available at all times in England.

Gradually, with the rise of centralized government and the decline of feudal tenures, military knighthood became obsolete, and the rank largely honorific; sometimes, as under James I, it degenerated into a scheme of the royal government for making money. For hundreds of years after its establishment in the fourteenth century, the Order of the Garter was the only English order of knighthood, an exclusive courtly companionship. Then, during the late seventeenth, the eighteenth, and the nineteenth centuries, a number of additional orders were created, with names such as the Thistle, Saint Patrick, the Bath, Saint Michael, and Saint George, plus a number of special Victorian and Indian orders. They retain the terminology, ceremony, and dignity of knighthood, but the military implications are vestigial.

Although the British Empire now belongs to history, appointments to the Order of the British Empire continue to be conferred for services to that empire at home or abroad. Such honors (commonly referred to as "gongs") are granted by the monarch in her New Year's and Birthday lists, but the decisions are now made by the government in power. In recent years there have been efforts to popularize and democratize the dispensation of honors, with recipients including rock stars and actors. But this does not prevent large sectors of British society from regarding both knighthood and the peerage as largely irrelevant to modern life.

The Royal Lines of England and Great Britain
England
SAXONS AND DANES

Egbert, king of Wessex	802–839
Ethelwulf, son of Egbert	839–858
Ethelbald, second son of Ethelwulf	858–860
Ethelbert, third son of Ethelwulf	860–866
Ethelred I, fourth son of Ethelwulf	866–871
Alfred the Great, fifth son of Ethelwulf	871–899
Edward the Elder, son of Alfred	899–924
Athelstan the Glorious, son of Edward	924–940
Edmund I, third son of Edward	940–946
Edred, fourth son of Edward	946–955
Edwy the Fair, son of Edmund	955–959
Edgar the Peaceful, second son of Edmund	959–975
Edward the Martyr, son of Edgar	975–978 (murdered)
Ethelred II, the Unready, second son of Edgar	978–1016
Edmund II, Ironside, son of Ethelred II	1016–1016
Canute the Dane	1016–1035
Harold I, Harefoot, natural son of Canute	1035–1040
Hardecanute, son of Canute	1040–1042
Edward the Confessor, son of Ethelred II	1042–1066
Harold II, brother-in-law of Edward	1066–1066 (died in battle)

HOUSE OF NORMANDY

William I, the Conqueror	1066–1087
William II, Rufus, third son of William I	1087–1100 (shot from ambush)
Henry I, Beauclerc, youngest son of William I	1100–1135

HOUSE OF BLOIS

Stephen, son of Adela, daughter of William I	1135–1154

HOUSE OF PLANTAGENET

Henry II, son of Geoffrey Plantagenet by Matilda, daughter of Henry I	1154–1189
Richard I, Coeur de Lion, son of Henry II	1189–1199
John Lackland, son of Henry II	1199–1216
Henry III, son of John	1216–1272
Edward I, Longshanks, son of Henry III	1272–1307
Edward II, son of Edward I	1307–1327 (deposed)
Edward III of Windsor, son of Edward II	1327–1377
Richard II, grandson of Edward III	1377–1399 (deposed)

HOUSE OF LANCASTER

Henry IV, son of John of Gaunt, son of Edward III	1399–1413
Henry V, Prince Hal, son of Henry IV	1413–1422
Henry VI, son of Henry V	1422–1461 (deposed), 1470–1471 (deposed)

HOUSE OF YORK

Edward IV, great-great-grandson of Edward III	1461–1470 (deposed), 1471–1483
Edward V, son of Edward IV	1483–1483 (murdered)
Richard III, Crookback	1483–1485 (died in battle)

HOUSE OF TUDOR

Henry VII, married daughter of Edward IV	1485–1509
Henry VIII, son of Henry VII	1509–1547
Edward VI, son of Henry VIII	1547–1553
Mary I, "Bloody," daughter of Henry VIII	1553–1558
Elizabeth I, daughter of Henry VIII	1558–1603

HOUSE OF STUART

James I (James VI of Scotland)	1603–1625
Charles I, son of James I	1625–1649 (executed)

COMMONWEALTH & PROTECTORATE

Council of State	1649–1653
Oliver Cromwell, Lord Protector	1653–1658
Richard Cromwell, son of Oliver	1658–1660 (resigned)

HOUSE OF STUART (RESTORED)

Charles II, son of Charles I   1660–1685
James II, second son of Charles I   1685–1688

(INTERREGNUM, 11 DECEMBER 1688 TO 13 FEBRUARY 1689)

HOUSE OF ORANGE-NASSAU

William III of Orange, by
   Mary, daughter of Charles I   1689–1701
   and Mary II, daughter of James II   –1694
Anne, second daughter of James II   1702–1714

Great Britain

HOUSE OF HANOVER

George I, son of Elector of Hanover and
   Sophia, granddaughter of James I   1714–1727
George II, son of George I   1727–1760
George III, grandson of George II   1760–1820
George IV, son of George III   1820–1830
William IV, third son of George III   1830–1837
Victoria, daughter of Edward, fourth son
   of George III   1837–1901

HOUSE OF SAXE-COBURG AND GOTHA

Edward VII, son of Victoria   1901–1910

HOUSE OF WINDSOR (NAME ADOPTED 17 JULY 1917)

George V, second son of Edward VII   1910–1936
Edward VIII, eldest son of George V   1936–1936 (abdicated)
George VI, second son of George V   1936–1952
Elizabeth II, daughter of George VI   1952–

Religions in Great Britain

In the late sixth century C.E., missionaries from Rome introduced Christianity to the Anglo-Saxons—actually, reintroduced it, since it had briefly flourished in the southern parts of the British Isles during the Roman occupation, and even after the Roman withdrawal had persisted in the Celtic regions of Scotland and Wales. By the time the earliest poems included in *The Norton Anthology of English Literature* were composed (i.e., the seventh century), therefore, there had been a Christian presence in the British Isles for hundreds of years. The conversion of the Germanic occupiers of England can, however, be dated only from 597. Our knowledge of the religion of pre-Christian Britain is sketchy, but it is likely that vestiges of Germanic polytheism assimilated into, or coexisted with, the practice of Christianity: fertility rites were incorporated into the celebration of Easter resurrection, rituals commemorating the dead into All-Hallows Eve and All Saints Day, and elements of winter solstice festivals into the celebration of Christmas. The most durable polytheistic remains are our days of the week, each of which except "Saturday" derives from the name of a Germanic pagan god, and the word "Easter," deriving, according to the Anglo-Saxon scholar Bede (d. 735), from the name of a Germanic pagan goddess, Eostre. In English literature such "folkloric" elements sometimes elicit romantic nostalgia. Geoffrey Chaucer's "Wife of Bath" looks back to a magical time before the arrival of Christianity in which the land was "fulfilled of fairye." Hundreds of years later, the seventeenth-century writer Robert Herrick honors the amalgamation of Christian and pagan elements in agrarian British culture in such poems as "Corinna's Gone A-Maying" and "The Hock Cart."

Medieval Christianity was fairly uniform, if complex, across Western Europe—hence called "catholic," or universally shared. The Church was composed of the so-called "regular" and "secular" orders, the regular orders being those who followed a rule in a community under an abbot or an abbess (i.e., monks, nuns, friars and canons), while the secular clergy of priests served parish communities under the governance of a bishop. In the unstable period from the sixth until the twelfth century, monasteries were the intellectual powerhouse of the Church. From the beginning of the thirteenth century, with the development of an urban Christian spirituality in Europe, friars dominated the recently invented institution of universities, as well as devoting themselves, in theory at least, to the urban poor.

The Catholic Church was also an international power structure. With its hierarchy of pope, cardinals, archbishops, and bishops, it offered a model of the centralized, bureaucratic state from the late eleventh century. That ecclesiastical power structure coexisted alongside a separate, often less centralized and feudal structure of lay authorities, with theoretically different and often competing spheres of social responsibilities. The sharing of lay and ecclesiastical authority in medieval England was sometimes a source of conflict. Chaucer's pilgrims are on their way to visit the memorial shrine to one victim of such exemplary struggle: Thomas à Becket, Archbishop of Canterbury, who opposed the policies of King Henry II, was assassinated by indirect suggestion of the king in 1170, and later made a saint. The Church, in turn, produced its own victims: Jews were subject to persecution in the late twelfth century in England, before being expelled in 1290. From the beginning of the fifteenth century, the English Church targeted Lollard heretics (see below) with capital punishment, for the first time.

As an international organization, the Church conducted its business in the universal language of Latin. Thus although in the period the largest segment of literate persons was made up of clerics, the clerical contribution to great literary writing in vernacular languages (e.g., French and English) was, so far as we know, relatively modest, with some great exceptions in the later Middle Ages (e.g., William Langland). Lay, vernacular writers of the period certainly reflect the importance of the Church as an institution and the pervasiveness of religion in the rituals that marked everyday life, as well as contesting institutional authority. From the late fourteenth century, indeed, England witnessed an active and articulate, proto-Protestant movement known as Lollardy, which attacked clerical hierarchy and promoted vernacular scriptures.

Beginning in 1517 the German monk Martin Luther, in Wittenberg, Germany, openly challenged many aspects of Catholic practice and by 1520 had completely repudiated the authority of the pope, setting in train the Protestant Reformation. Luther argued that the Roman Catholic Church had strayed far from the pattern of Christianity laid out in scripture. He rejected Catholic doctrines for which no biblical authority was to be found, such as the belief in Purgatory, and translated the Bible into German, on the grounds that the importance of scripture for all Christians made its translation into the vernacular tongue essential. Luther was not the first to advance such views— Lollard followers of the Englishman John Wycliffe had translated the Bible in the late fourteenth century. But Luther, protected by powerful German rulers, was able to speak out with impunity and convert others to his views, rather than suffer the persecution usually meted out to heretics. Soon other reformers were following in Luther's footsteps: of these, the Swiss Ulrich Zwingli and the French Jean Calvin would be especially influential for English religious thought.

At first England remained staunchly Catholic. Its king, Henry VIII, was so severe to heretics that the pope awarded him the title "Defender of the Faith," which British monarchs have retained to this day. In 1534, however, Henry rejected the authority of the pope to prevent his divorce from his queen, Catherine of Aragon, and his marriage to his mistress, Ann Boleyn. In doing so, Henry appropriated to himself ecclesiastical as well as secular authority. Thomas More, author of *Utopia*, was executed in 1535 for refusing to endorse Henry's right to govern the English church. Over the following six years, Henry consolidated his grip on the ecclesiastical establishment by dissolving the powerful, populous Catholic monasteries and redistributing their massive landholdings to his own lay followers. Yet Henry's church largely retained Catholic doctrine and liturgy. When Henry died and his young son, Edward, came to the throne in 1547, the English church embarked on a more Protestant path, a direction abruptly reversed when Edward died and his older sister Mary, the daughter of Catherine of Aragon, took the throne in 1553 and attempted to reintroduce Roman Catholicism. Mary's reign was also short, however, and her successor, Elizabeth I, the daughter of Ann Boleyn, was a Protestant. Elizabeth attempted to establish a "middle way" Christianity, compromising between Roman Catholic practices and beliefs and reformed ones.

The Church of England, though it laid claim to a national rather than pan-European authority, aspired like its predecessor to be the universal church of all English subjects. It retained the Catholic structure of parishes and dioceses and the Catholic hierarchy of bishops, though the ecclesiastical authority was now the Archbishop of Canterbury and the Church's "Supreme Governor" was the monarch. Yet disagreement and controversy persisted. Some members of the Church of England wanted to retain many of the ritual and liturgical elements of Catholicism. Others, the Puritans, advocated a more thoroughgoing reformation. Most Puritans remained within the Church of England, but a minority, the "Separatists" or "Congregationalists," split from the established church altogether. These dissenters no longer thought of the ideal church as an organization to which everybody belonged; instead, they conceived it as a more exclusive group of likeminded people, one not necessarily attached to a larger body of believers.

In the seventeenth century, the succession of the Scottish king James to the English throne produced another problem. England and Scotland were separate nations, and in the sixteenth century Scotland had developed its own national Presbyterian church, or "kirk," under the leadership of the reformer John Knox. The kirk retained fewer Catholic liturgical elements than did the Church of England, and its authorities, or "presbyters," were elected by assemblies of their fellow clerics, rather than appointed by the king. James I and his son Charles I, especially the latter, wanted to bring the Scottish kirk into conformity with Church of England practices. The Scots violently resisted these efforts, with the collaboration of many English Puritans, in a conflict that eventually developed into the English Civil War in the mid-seventeenth century. The effect of these disputes is visible in the poetry of such writers as John Milton, Robert Herrick, Henry Vaughan, and Thomas Traherne, and in the prose of Thomas Browne, Lucy Hutchinson, and Dorothy Waugh. Just as in the mid-sixteenth century, when a succession of monarchs with different religious commitments destabilized the church, so the seventeenth century endured spiritual whiplash. King Charles I's highly ritualistic Church of England was violently overturned by the Puritan victors in the Civil War—until 1660, after the death of the Puritan leader, Oliver Cromwell, when the Church of England was restored along with the monarchy.

The religious and political upheavals of the seventeenth century produced Christian sects that de-emphasized the ceremony of the established church and rejected as well its top-down authority structure. Some of these groups were ephemeral, but the Baptists (founded in 1608 in Amsterdam by the English expatriate John Smyth) and Quakers, or Society of Friends (founded by George Fox in the 1640s), flourished outside the established church, sometimes despite cruel persecution. John Bunyan, a Baptist, wrote the Christian allegory *Pilgrim's Progress* while in prison. Some dissenters, like the Baptists, shared the reformed reverence for the absolute authority of scripture but interpreted the scriptural texts differently from their fellow Protestants. Others, like the Quakers, favored, even over the authority of the Bible, the "inner light" or voice of individual conscience, which they took to be the working of the Holy Spirit in the lives of individuals.

The Protestant dissenters were not England's only religious minorities. Despite crushing fines and the threat of imprisonment, a minority of Catholics under Elizabeth and James openly refused to give their allegiance to the new church, and others remained secret adherents to the old ways. John Donne was brought up in an ardently Catholic family, and several other writers converted to Catholicism as adults—Ben Jonson for a considerable part of his career, Elizabeth Carey and Richard Crashaw permanently, and at profound personal cost. In the eighteenth century, Catholics remained objects of suspicion as possible agents of sedition, especially after the "Glorious Revolution" in 1688 deposed the Catholic James II in favor of the Protestant William and Mary. Anti-Catholic prejudice affected John Dryden, a Catholic convert, as well as the lifelong Catholic Alexander Pope. By contrast, the English colony of Ireland remained overwhelmingly Roman Catholic, the fervor of its religious commitment at least partly inspired by resistance to English occupation. Starting in the reign of Elizabeth, England shored up its own authority in Ireland by encouraging Protestant immigrants from Scotland to settle in the north of Ireland, producing a virulent religious divide the effects of which are still playing out today.

A small community of Jews had moved from France to London after 1066, when the Norman William the Conqueror came to the English throne. Although despised and persecuted by many Christians, they were allowed to remain as moneylenders to the Crown, until the thirteenth century, when the king developed alternative sources of credit. At this point, in 1290, the Jews were expelled from England. In 1655 Oliver Cromwell permitted a few to return, and in the late seventeenth and early eighteenth centuries the Jewish population slowly increased, mainly by immigration from Germany. In the mid-eighteenth century some prominent Jews had their children brought up as Christians so as to facilitate their full integration into English society: thus the nineteenth-century writer and politician Benjamin Disraeli, although he and his father were members of the Church of England, was widely considered a Jew insofar as his ancestry was Jewish.

In the late seventeenth century, as the Church of England reasserted itself, Catholics, Jews, and dissenting Protestants found themselves subject to significant legal restrictions. The Corporation Act, passed in 1661, and the Test Act, passed in 1673, excluded all who refused to take communion in the Church of England from voting, attending university, or working in government or in the professions. Members of religious minorities, as well as Church of England communicants, paid mandatory taxes in support of Church of England ministers and buildings. In 1689 the dissenters gained the right to worship in public, but Jews and Catholics were not permitted to do so.

During the eighteenth century, political, intellectual, and religious history remained closely intertwined. The Church of England came to accommodate a good deal of variety. "Low church" services resembled those of the dissenting Protestant churches, minimizing ritual and emphasizing the sermon; the "high church" retained more elaborate ritual elements, yet its prestige was under attack on several fronts. Many Enlightenment thinkers subjected the Bible to rational critique and found it wanting: the philosopher David Hume, for instance, argued that the "miracles" described therein were more probably lies or errors than real breaches of the laws of nature. Within the Church of England, the "broad church" Latitudinarians welcomed this rationalism, advocating theological openness and an emphasis on ethics rather than dogma. More radically, the Unitarian movement rejected the divinity of Christ while professing to accept his ethical teachings. Taking a different tack, the preacher John Wesley, founder of Methodism, responded to the rationalists' challenge with a newly fervent call to evangelism and personal discipline; his movement was particularly successful in Wales. Revolutions in America and France at the end of the century generated considerable millenarian excitement and fostered more new religious ideas, often in conjunction with a radical social agenda. Many important writers of the Romantic period were indebted to traditions of protestant dissent: Unitarian and rationalist protestant ideas influenced William Hazlitt, Anna Barbauld, Mary Wollstonecraft, and the young Samuel Taylor Coleridge. William Blake created a highly idiosyncratic poetic mythology loosely indebted to radical strains of Christian mysticism. Others were even more heterodox: Lord Byron and Robert Burns, brought up as Scots Presbyterians, rebelled fiercely, and Percy Shelley's writing of an atheistic pamphlet resulted in his expulsion from Oxford.

Great Britain never erected an American-style "wall of separation" between church and state, but in practice religion and secular affairs grew more and more distinct during the nineteenth century. In consequence, members of religious minorities no longer seemed to pose a threat to the commonweal. A movement to repeal the Test Act failed in the 1790s, but a renewed effort resulted in the extension of the franchise to dissenting Protestants in 1828 and to Catholics in 1829. The numbers of Roman Catholics in England were swelled by immigration from Ireland, but there were also some prominent English adherents. Among writers, the converts John Newman and Gerard Manley Hopkins are especially important. The political participation and social integration of Jews presented a thornier challenge. Lionel de Rothschild, repeatedly elected to represent London in Parliament during the 1840s and 1850s, was not permitted to take his seat there because he refused to take his oath of office "on the true faith of a Christian"; finally, in 1858, the Jewish Disabilities Act allowed him to omit these words. Only in 1871, however, were Oxford and Cambridge opened to non-Anglicans.

Meanwhile geological discoveries and Charles Darwin's evolutionary theories increasingly cast doubt on the literal truth of the Creation story, and close philological analysis of the biblical text suggested that its origins were human rather than divine. By the end of the nineteenth century, many writers were bearing witness to a world in which Christianity no longer seemed fundamentally plausible. In his poetry and prose, Thomas Hardy depicts a world devoid of benevolent providence. Matthew Arnold's poem "Dover Beach" is in part an elegy to lost spiritual assurance, as the "Sea of Faith" goes out like the tide: "But now I only hear / Its melancholy, long, withdrawing roar / Retreating." For Arnold, literature must replace religion as a source of spiritual truth, and intimacy between individuals substitute for the lost communal solidarity of the universal church.

The work of many twentieth-century writers shows the influence of a religious upbringing or a religious conversion in adulthood. T. S. Eliot and W. H. Auden embrace Anglicanism, William Butler Yeats spiritualism. James Joyce repudiates Irish Catholicism but remains obsessed with it. Yet religion, or lack of it, is a matter of individual choice and conscience, not social or legal mandate. In the past fifty years, church attendance has plummeted in Great Britain. Although 71 percent of the population still identified itself as "Christian" on the 2000 census, only about 7 percent of these regularly attend religious services of any denomination. Meanwhile, immigration from former British colonies has swelled the ranks of religions once uncommon in the British Isles—Muslim, Sikh, Hindu, Buddhist—though the numbers of adherents remain small relative to the total population.

The Universe According to Ptolemy

Ptolemy was a Roman astronomer of Greek descent, born in Egypt during the second century C.E.; for nearly fifteen hundred years after his death his account of the design of the universe was accepted as standard. During that time, the basic pattern underwent many detailed modifications and was fitted out with many astrological and pseudoscientific trappings. But in essence Ptolemy's followers portrayed the earth as the center of the universe, with the sun, planets, and fixed stars set in transparent spheres orbiting around it. In this scheme of things, as modified for Christian usage, Hell was usually placed under the earth's surface at the center of the cosmic globe, while Heaven, the abode of the blessed spirits, was in the outermost, uppermost circle, the empyrean. But in 1543 the Polish astronomer Copernicus proposed an alternative hypothesis—that the earth rotates around the sun, not vice versa; and despite theological opposition, observations with the new telescope and careful mathematical calculations insured ultimate acceptance of the new view.

The map of the Ptolemaic universe below is a simplified version of a diagram in Peter Apian's *Cosmography* (1584). In such a diagram, the Firmament is the sphere that contained the fixed stars; the Crystalline Sphere, which contained no heavenly bodies, is a late innovation, included to explain certain anomalies in the observed movement of the heavenly bodies; and the Prime Mover is the sphere that, itself put into motion by God, imparts rotation around the earth to all the other spheres.

Milton, writing in the mid-seventeenth century, used two universes. The Copernican universe, though he alludes to it, was too large, formless, and unfamiliar to be the setting for the war between Heaven and Hell in *Paradise Lost*. He therefore used the Ptolemaic cosmos, but placed Heaven well outside this smaller earth-centered universe, Hell far beneath it, and assigned the vast middle space to Chaos.

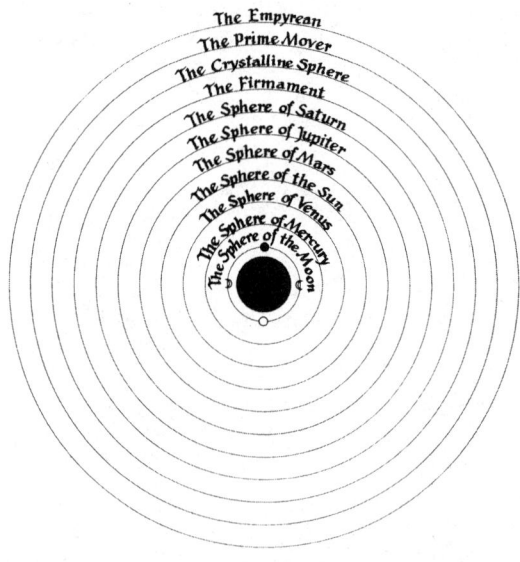

The Empyrean
The Prime Mover
The Crystalline Sphere
The Firmament
The Sphere of Saturn
The Sphere of Jupiter
The Sphere of Mars
The Sphere of the Sun
The Sphere of Venus
The Sphere of Mercury
The Sphere of the Moon

A LONDON PLAYHOUSE OF SHAKESPEARE'S TIME

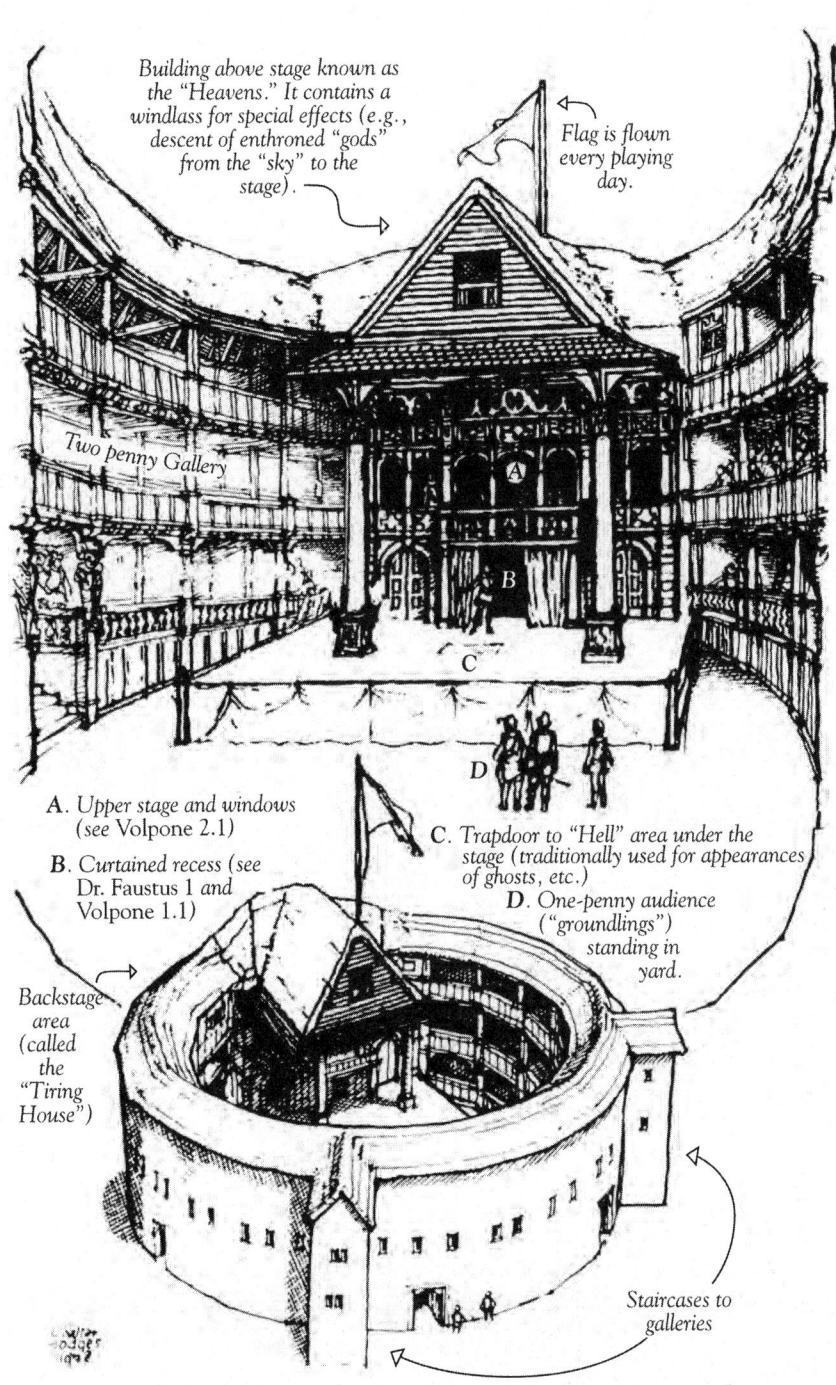

Building above stage known as the "Heavens." It contains a windlass for special effects (e.g., descent of enthroned "gods" from the "sky" to the stage).

Flag is flown every playing day.

Two penny Gallery

A. Upper stage and windows (see *Volpone* 2.1)

B. Curtained recess (see *Dr. Faustus* 1 and *Volpone* 1.1)

C. Trapdoor to "Hell" area under the stage (traditionally used for appearances of ghosts, etc.)

D. One-penny audience ("groundlings") standing in yard.

Backstage area (called the "Tiring House")

Staircases to galleries

PERMISSIONS ACKNOWLEDGMENTS

TEXT CREDITS

Margaret Lucas Cavendish: Extracts from THE BLAZING WORLD are taken from Margaret Cavendish, Duchess of Newcastle, THE DESCRIPTION OF A NEW WORLD CALLED THE BLAZING WORLD AND OTHER WRITINGS, edited by Kate Lilley (London: Pickering & Chatto 1992). Pp. 24, 132–25, 180–81, 184–86. Reprinted by permission of the publisher.

Queen Elizabeth: *On Monsieur's Departure* from THE POEMS OF QUEEN ELIZABETH I, edited by Leicester Bradner. Copyright © 1964 by Brown University. Reprinted by permission of the University Press of New England. *Letter to Sir Amyes Paulet* and *Letter to King James VI of Scotland* from THE LETTERS OF QUEEN ELIZABETH, edited by G. B. Harrison (Cassell, 1935). Reprinted by permission of David Higham Associates. *The Golden Speech* from THE PUBLIC SPEAKING OF QUEEN ELIZABETH: SELECTIONS FROM HER OFFICIAL ADDRESSES, edited by George P. Rice, Jr. (AMS Press, 1966). Reprinted with the permission of AMS Press, Inc.

Robert Herrick: *How the Roses Came Red* by Robert Herrick, from BEN JONSON AND THE CAVALIER POETS: A Norton Critical Edition by Hugh Maclean, editor. Copyright © 1974 by W. W. Norton & Company, Inc. Reprinted by permission of W. W. Norton & Company, Inc.

John Milton: Excerpts from *Areopagitica* from THE COMPLETE POETRY AND MAJOR PROSE OF MILTON, edited by Merritt Y. Hughes, copyright © 1957. Reprinted by permission of Prentice-Hall, Inc., Upper Saddle River, N.J. Complete text and endnotes from PARADISE LOST: A Norton Critical Edition, Second Edition, by John Milton, edited by Scott Elledge. Copyright © 1993, 1975 by W. W. Norton & Company, Inc. Reprinted by permission of W. W. Norton & Company, Inc.

Sir Thomas More: From UTOPIA: A Norton Critical Edition, Second Edition, by Sir Thomas More, translated by Robert M. Adams. Copyright © 1992, 1975 by W. W. Norton & Company, Inc. Used by permission of W. W. Norton & Company, Inc.

Petrarch: Reprinted by permission of the publisher from PETRARCH'S LYRIC POEMS: THE *RIME SPARSE* AND OTHER LYRICS, translated and edited by Robert M. Durling, Cambridge, Mass.: Harvard University Press, Copyright © 1976 by Robert M. Durling.

Katherine Philips: *A Married State* from NLW Orielton Collection, box 24. Courtesy of The National Library of Wales.

Richard Tottel: "Preface" from TOTTEL'S MISCELLANY: SONGS AND SONNETS OF HENRY HOWARD, EARL OF SURREY, SIR THOMAS WYATT AND OTHERS, edited by Amanda Hotlon and Tom MacFaul. Copyright © 2011 by Richard Tottel. Reprinted by permission of Penguin Random House Ltd.

Mary Wroth: From THE POEMS OF LADY MARY WROTH, edited by Josephine A. Roberts. Reprinted by permission of Louisiana State University Press.

IMAGE CREDITS

Pp. 2–3: The Granger Collection, NYC, All rights reserved; p. 8: Bridgeman Art Library; p. 10: From *Fierie Tryall of God's Saints* (1611) / Public Domain; p. 15: Woburn Abbey, Bedfordshire, UK / The Bridgeman Art Library; p. 18: University of Toronto Wenceslaus Hollar Digital Collection / Wikimedia Commons; p. 28: The Bridgeman Art Library; p. 31: Bridgeman Art Library; p. 70: The Bridgeman Art Library; p. 147: Houghton Library / Harvard; p. 161: Lambeth Palace Library, London, UK / Bridgeman Images; p. 203: Universal Images Group / Getty Images; p. 220: National Galleries of Scotland, Edinburgh / Bridgeman Images; p. 242: Private Collection / Bridgeman Images; p. 655: Culture Club / Getty Images; p. 610: Public Domain / Wikipedia; p. 621: From Cesare Vacellio's *Degli habiti* (1590) / Public Domain; p. 644: Virginia Historical Society, Richmond, Virginia, USA / Bridgeman Images; p. 720: Wikimedia Commons; p. 740: National Portrait Gallery; p. 804: Private Collection / Archives Charmet / Bridgeman Images; pp. 890–91: Galleria Borghese, Rome, Italy / Bridgeman Images; p. 897: Public Domain / Wikipedia; p. 900: Private Collection / The Bridgeman Art Library International; p. 909: Print Collector / Hulton Archive / Getty Images; p. 913: Private Collection / Bridgeman Images; p. 975: Public Domain / Wikipedia; p. 992: The Granger Collection; p. 994: *Alciato's Book of Emblems* / Wikipedia; p. 1111: Public domain / Wikipedia; p. 1199: George Wither's *Emblem Book* (1635) / Public Domain; p. 1237: Granger. All rights reserved; p. 1256: National Portrait Gallery; p. 1300: Alinari Archives / Getty Images; p. 1357: Granger. All rights reserved; p. 1408: © British Library Board / Robana / Art Resource, NY; p. 1447: Snark / Art Resource, NY.

COLOR INSERT CREDITS

C1: National Gallery London, Great Britain / Art Resource, NY; C2 (top): Frick Collection, New York; C2 (bottom): National Portrait Gallery, London, UK / Bridgeman Art Library; C3 (top): The British Museum; C3 (bottom): The Royal Collection © 2011, Her Majesty Queen Elizabeth II; C4: University of Birmingham, UK / Pictures from History / Bridgeman Images; C5 (top): National Portrait Gallery, London; C5 (bottom): National Portrait Gallery, London; C6 (top): Victoria & Albert Museum, London / Art Resource, NY; C6 (bottom): The Stapleton Collection / Bridgeman Art Library; C7: Private Collection / Bridgeman Art Library; C8: Scala / Art Resource, NY; C9: Erich Lessing / Art Resource, NY; C10 (top): Scala / Art Resource, NY; C10 (bottom): Camaraphoto / Art Resource, NY; C11: Private Collection / Bridgeman Art Library; C12: Reproduced by kind permission of Viscount De L'Isle, from his private collection at Penshurst Place; C13: Woburn Abbey, Bedfordshire, UK / Bridgeman Art Library; C14: Scala / Art Resource, NY; C15: National Gallery, London, UK / Bridgeman Art Library, NY; C16: Réunion des Musées Nationaux / Art Resource, NY.

Index

A broken A L T A R , Lord, thy servant rears, 1257

Acts and Monuments, 160, 207

Advancement of Learning, The, 1225

Affliction (1), 1260

Air and Angels, 930

Alas, 'tis true I have gone here and there, 733

Alas! so all things now do hold their peace, 136

Altar, The, 1257

A married state affords but little ease, 1334

Ambassadorial Dispatch to the Holy Roman Emperor, Charles V: The Coronation of Mary I, An, 196

Amoretti, 486

Anatomical Exercises of Dr. William Harvey Professor of Physic, and Physician to the King's Majesty, Concerning the Motion of the Heart and Blood. 1653, The, 1237

Anatomy of Melancholy, The, 1240

Anatomy of the World: The First Anniversary, An, 949

And if I did, what then? 506

And now th' art set wide ope, the spear's sad art, 1295

Another Grace for a Child, 1318

Apparition, The, 935

Areopagitica, 1479

Argument of His Book, The, 1307

Arraignment of Lewd, Idle, Froward and Unconstant Women: Or the Vanity of Them, Choose You Whether, The, 1200

As an unperfect actor on the stage, 726

Ascham, Roger, 171

As I in hoary winter's night stood shivering in the snow, 171

Askew, Anne, 156

Ask me no more where Jove bestows, 1323

Astrophil and Stella, 586

As virtuous men pass mildly away, 935

A sweet disorder in the dress, 1308

At court I met it, in clothes brave enough, 1090

At the round earth's imagined corners, blow, 961

[*Author's Epitaph, Made by Himself, The*], 532

Avenge, O Lord, thy slaughtered saints, whose bones, 1492

A ward, and still in bonds, one day, 1278

A white doe on the green grass appeared to me, 121

A woman's face with Nature's own hand painted, 725

Aye, beshrew you, by my fay, 37

Bacon, Sir Francis, 1212

Bad Season Makes the Poet Sad, The, 1315

Bait, The, 934

Barlowe, Arthur, 639

Batter my heart, three-personed God; for you, 963

Because you have thrown off your prelate lord, 1490

Bermudas, 1341

Best, George, 626

Betwixt two ridges of plowed land lay Wat, 1436

Bible, 145

    Authorized (King James), 148

    Douay-Rheims, 148

    Geneva, 146

    Tyndale, 146

Blame not my lute, 128

Blame not my lute, for he must sound, 128

Blazing World, The, 1441

Blossom, The, 939

Book of Common Prayer, 161

Book of Homilies, 164

Borde (Boorde), Andrew, 620

Brave infant of Saguntum, clear, 1102

Break of Day, 930

Brief and true report of the new-found land of Virginia, A, 643

Brief relation of my travel from the royal city of London towards the Straits of Mare Mediterraneum, A, 649

Browne, Sir Thomas, 1246

Bunch of Grapes, The, 1268

Burning Babe, The, 171

Burton, Richard, 1239

Busy old fool, unruly sun, 926

But be contented; when that fell arrest, 729

By our first strange and fatal interview, 942

Caelica, 512
Calvin, John, 153
Camden, most reverend head, to whom I owe, 1090
Campion, Thomas, 521
Can I not sin, but thou wilt be, 1318
Canonization, The, 927
Can we not force from widowed poetry, 1319
Carew, Thomas, 1318
Carmen Deo Nostro, 1297
Casket Letter Number 2 (Mary, Queen of Scots), 210
Cavendish, Margaret, 1434
Celebration of Charis in Ten Lyric Pieces, A, 1099
Centuries of Meditation, 1430
Church Monuments, 1262
Cock-Crowing, 1286
Collar, The, 1270
Come, leave the loathèd stage, 1108
Come, Madam, come, all rest my powers defy, 943
Come, my Lucasia, since we see, 1336
Come, sons of summer, by whose toil, 1312
Come live with me and be my love (Donne), 934
Come live with me and be my love (Marlowe), 678
Come we shepherds whose blest sight, 1297
Constable, Henry, 515
Corinna's Going A-Maying, 1310
Corinthians 1.13, 146
Coronet, The, 1341
Corruption, 1282
Countess of Montgomery's Urania, The, 1112
Countess of Pembroke's Arcadia, The, 541
Courtier, The, 176
Crashaw, Richard, 1290
Cromwell, our chief of men, who through a cloud, 1491

Dallam, Thomas, 649
Damon the Mower, 1351
Daniel, Samuel, 516
Davies, John, of Hereford, 520
Death, 1275
Death, be not proud, though some have callèd thee, 962
Death, thou wast once an uncouth, hideous thing, 1275
Death's Duel, 973
Defense of Poesy, The, 547
Definition of Love, The, 1348
Delia, 516
Delight in Disorder, 1308
Delights of the Muses, The, 1291
Denial, 1263
Description of Cookham, The, 986
Devotions upon Emergent Occasions, 969
Devouring Time, blunt thou the lion's paws, 725
Dialogue Between the Soul and Body, A, 1342

Dialogue Concerning Heresies, A, 151
Diana, 515
Discipline, 1274
Discovery of the large, rich, and beautiful Empire of Guiana, The, 533
Divers doth use, 124
Divers doth use, as I have heard and know, 124
Doctor Faustus, 679
Donne, John, 920
Donne, the delight of Phoebus and each Muse, 1091
Doubt of future foes, The, 230
Drayton, Michael, 517
Dreams, 1308
Drink to me only with thine eyes, 1098
Duchess of Malfi, The, 1122
Dull to myself and almost dead to these, 1315

Easter, 1258
Easter Wings, 1259
Ecstasy, The, 936
Eden, Richard, 622
Elegy 16. On His Mistress, 942
Elegy 19. To His Mistress Going to Bed, 943
Elegy upon the Death of the Dean of Paul's, Dr. John Donne, An, 1319
Elizabeth I, Queen of England, 221
Epigrams, 1089
Epitaph on S. P., a Child of Queen Elizabeth's Chapel, 1095
Epithalamion, 486, 491
Essays (Bacon), 1213
Euphues: The Anatomy of Wit, 537
Even such is time, which takes in trust, 532
Eve's Apology in Defense of Women, 983

Faerie Queene, The, 247
Farewell, false love, 530
Farewell, false love, the oracle of lies, 530
Farewell, Love, 122
Farewell, Love, and all thy laws forever, 122
Farewell, sweet Cookham, where I first obtained, 986
Farewell: thou art too dear for my possessing, 730
Farewell, thou child of my right hand, and joy, 1092
Farewell, thou thing, time-past so known, so dear, 1309
Father of lights! what sunny seed, 1286
Filmer, Robert, 1393
First Book of the Introduction of Knowledge, The, 620
First Examination of Anne Askew, The, 157
First Voyage Made to Virginia, The, 639
Flaming Heart, The, 1302
Flea, The, 923
Flower, The, 1271
Forerunners, The, 1273
Forest, The, 1096
Forget not yet, 128

Forget not yet the tried intent, 128
For God's sake hold your tongue, and let me love, 927
Fortune hath taken away my love, 233
Fourth Book of Virgil, The, 141
Foxe, John, 159
Friendship's Mystery, To My Dearest Lucasia, 1336
From fairest creatures we desire increase, 723
From the dull confines of the drooping west, 1316
From you have I been absent in the spring, 732
Full many a glorious morning have I seen, 727
Funeral, The, 938

Garden, The, 1354
Gascoigne, George, 506
Gather ye rosebuds while ye may, 1312
General history of the Turks, The, 654
Geographical History of Africa, A, 616
Get up! Get up for shame! The blooming morn, 1310
Give way, an ye be ravished by the sun, 1315
Go, smiling souls, your new-built cages break, 1295
Go, soul, the body's guest, 528
Go and catch a falling star, 924
Goe little booke: thy selfe present, 241
"*Golden Speech,*" *The,* 235
Good and great God, can I not think of thee, 1099
Good Friday, 1613. Riding Westward, 965
Good-Morrow, The, 923
Gouge, William, 1205
Grasshopper, The, 1330
Greville, Fulke, 512
Grey, Lady Jane, 199
Gut eats all day, and lechers all the night, 1095

Had we but world enough, and time, 1346
Hakluyt, Richard, 612
Halkett, Lady Anne, 1424
Happy those early days! when I, 1280
Hariot, Thomas, 643
Hark how the mower Damon sung, 1351
Harvey, William, 1236
Have ye beheld (with much delight), 1314
Having been tenant long to a rich lord, 1258
Hence loathèd Melancholy, 1459
Hence vain deluding joys, 1463
Herbert, George, 1255
Herbert, Mary (Sidney), Countess of Pembroke, 604
Here a little child I stand, 1318
Here lies, to each her parents' ruth, 1091
Here we are all, by day; by night, we're hurled, 1308
Her eyes the glowworm lend thee, 1316
Hero and Leander, 659
Herrick, Robert, 1306

Hesperides, 1307
His Farewell to Sack, 1309
His Prayer to Ben Jonson, 1315
His Return to London, 1316
History of the Rebellion, The, 1421
History of the World, The, 536
Hobbes, Thomas, 1405
Hoby, Sir Thomas, 176
Hock Cart, or Harvest Home, The, 1312
Holdfast, The, 1269
Holy Sonnets, 960
Homily Against Disobedience and Willful Rebellion, An, 165
Hooker, Richard, 167
Horatian Ode, An, 1356
Howard, Henry, Earl of Surrey, 133
How fresh, O Lord, how sweet and clean, 1271
How like an angel came I down!, 1431
How like a winter hath my absence been, 732
How oft when thou, my music, music play'st, 735
How rich, O Lord! how fresh thy visits are!, 1283
How Roses Came Red, 1314
How Soon Hath Time, 1489
How soon hath Time, the subtle thief of youth, 1489
How vainly men themselves amaze, 1354
Hunting of the Hare, The, 1436
Hutchinson, Lucy, 1418
Hyde, Edward, Earl of Clarendon, 1421
Hymn to Christ, at the Author's Last Going into Germany, A, 966
Hymn to God My God, in My Sickness, 967
Hymn to God the Father, A, 968

I am a little world made cunningly, 961
I Am the Door, 1295
I can love both fair and brown, 927
I care not for these ladies, 522
Idea, 518
I dreamed this mortal part of mine, 1308
If all the world and love were young, 527
I find no peace, 122
I find no peace, and all my war is done, 122
If I were dead, and in my place, 1277
If poisonous minerals, and if that tree, 962
If there were (oh!) an Hellespont of cream, 520
If this be love, to draw a weary breath, 516
I grieve and dare not show my discontent, 230
I have done one braver thing, 925
I have examined and do find, 1337
I have lost, and lately, these, 1307
I hope and fear, I pray and hold my peace, 514
Il Penseroso, 1463
Indifferent, The, 927
In loving thee thou know'st I am forsworn, 738
I now think Love is rather deaf than blind, 1101

Institution of Christian Religion, The, 153
In the Holy Nativity of Our Lord God: A Hymn Sung as by the Shepherds, 1297
In the nativity of time, 1332
In the old age black was not counted fair, 735
In this little urn is laid, 1317
Into these loves who but for passion looks, 518
Inviting a Friend to Supper, 1094
In what torn ship soever I embark, 966
I saw eternity the other night, 1283
I saw new worlds beneath the water lie, 1433
I sing of brooks, of blossoms, birds, and bowers, 1307
I struck the board and cried, "No more, 1270
I that have been a lover, and could show it, 1100
I think not on the state, nor am concerned, 1335
I threatened to observe the strict decree, 1269
I traveled on, seeing the hill where lay, 1268
It will be looked for, book, when some but see, 1089
I will enjoy thee now, my Celia, come, 1325
I wonder, by my troth, what thou and I, 923

Jack and Joan, they think no ill, 523
Jonson, Ben, 991
Jordan (1), 1262
Jordan (2), 1266
Joy, I did lock thee up; but some bad man, 1268

Kind pity chokes my spleen; brave scorn forbids, 945
Knolles, Richard, 654

L'Allegro, 1459
Lanyer, Aemilia, 980
Lecture upon the Shadow, A, 941
Leo Africanus, 616
Let man's soul be a sphere, and then, in this, 965
Let me not to the marriage of true minds, 734
Let me pour forth, 931
Let not my love be called idolatry, 732
Letter of the Lady Jane, Sent unto her Father, A, 205
Letter of the Lady Jane to M. H., A, 202
Letter to Elizabeth I, May 17, 1568, A (Mary, Queen of Scots), 212
Letter to Henry VIII (Mary Tutor), 195
Letter to King James VI of Scotland, February 14, 1587, A (Elizabeth I), 232
Letter to Mary, Queen of Scots, February 24, 1567, A (Elizabeth I), 229
Letter to Robert Dudley, Earl of Leicester, February 10, 1586, A (Elizabeth I), 231
Letter to Sir Amyas Paulet, August 1586, A (Elizabeth I), 232
Leviathan, 1406
Lie, The, 528

Life of Dr. John Donne, The, 976
Like as the waves make towards the pebbled shore, 728
Little think'st thou, poor flower, 939
Locke, Anne Vaughan, 505
Lodge, Thomas, 513
Lo I the man, whose Muse whilome did maske, 253
Long love that in my thought doth harbor, The, 120
Look in thy glass and tell the face thou viewest, 723
Lord, how can man preach thy eternal word?, 1263
Lord, who createdst man in wealth and store, 1259
Love (3), 1275
Love, that doth reign and live within my thought, 135
Love, who lives and reigns in my thought and keeps, 121
Love bade me welcome: yet my soul drew back, 1275
Lovelace, Richard, 1329
Love Made in the First Age. To Chloris, 1332
Lover Showeth How He Is Forsaken of Such as He Sometime Enjoyed, The, 126
Love's Alchemy, 932
Loving in truth, and fain in verse my love to show, 586
Lucasta, 1329
Lucy, you brightness of our sphere, who are, 1093
Luke 11.[27] Blessed be the paps which Thou hast sucked, 1296
Lullaby of a Lover, The, 507
Luxurious man, to bring his vice in use, 1350
Lycidas, 1467
Lyly, John, 536

Madam, withouten many words, 125
Man, 1265
Mannerly Margery Milk and Ale, 37
Mark but this flea, and mark in this, 923
Marlowe, Christopher, 658
Married State, A, 1334
Martial, the things for to attain, 141
Marvell, Andrew, 1339
Mary, Queen of Scots, 208
Mary I (Mary Tudor), 194
Meditation of a Penitent Sinner, A, 505
Meeting with Time, "Slack thing," said I, 1267
Memoirs, The (Halkett), 1425
Memoirs of the Life of Colonel John Hutchinson, 1419
Methought I Saw My Late Espousèd Saint, 1493
Methought I saw the grave where Laura lay, 531
Milton, John, 1396, 1447
Mine own John Poins, 131

Mine own John Poins, since ye delight to know, 131

Moderate, The, No. 28, 16–23 January 1649, 1386

More, Sir Thomas, 41, 151

Mower Against Gardens, The, 1350

Mower's Song, The, 1353

Mower to the Glowworms, The, 1353

Much suspected by me, 222

Music's Duel, 1291

Muzzle for Melastomus, A, 1202

My galley, 123

My galley charged with forgetfulness, 123

My God, I heard this day, 1265

My love is as a fever, longing still, 738

My Love is of a birth as rare, 1348

My lute, awake!, 127

My lute, awake! Perform the last, 127

My mind was once the true survey, 1353

My mistress' eyes are nothing like the sun, 736

My Picture Left in Scotland, 1101

My ship laden with forgetfulness passes through a harsh sea, 124

My sweetest Lesbia, 521

My sweetest Lesbia, let us live and love, 521

My tongue-tied muse in manners holds her still, 730

My worthy lord, I pray you wonder not, 508

Narrative of the Execution of the Queen of Scots, 214

Nature, that washed her hands in milk, 531

Needs must I leave, and yet needs must I love, 515

Never love unless you can, 525

New Atlantis, The, 1231

New Year's Gift Sent to the Parliament and Army, A, 1400

Night, The, 1288

Night-Piece, to Julia, The, 1316

Noble Numbers, 1318

Nocturnal upon Saint Lucy's Day, Being the Shortest Day, A, 932

No longer mourn for me when I am dead, 729

No more be grieved at that which thou hast done, 727

Not marble nor the gilded monuments, 727

Not mine own fears, nor the prophetic soul, 733

Novum Organum, 1227

Now Pontius Pilate is to judge the cause, 983

Now that the heavens and the earth and the wind are silent, 136

Now westward Sol had spent the richest beams, 1291

Now winter nights enlarge, 524

Nymph Complaining for the Death of Her Fawn, The, 1344

Nymph's Reply to the Shepherd, The, 527

O, how I faint when I of you do write, 730

O, who shall from this dungeon raise, 1342

Obedience of a Christian Man, The, 149

Ode on Cary and Morison, The, 1101

Ode to Himself, 1108

Of Domestical Duties, 1205

Of Great Place, 1216

Of man's first disobedience, and the fruit, 1496

Of Marriage and Single Life, 1214

Of Masques and Triumphs, 1222

Of Negotiating, 1221

Of Plantations, 1219

Of Studies (1597 version), 1223

Of Studies (1625 version), 1224

Of Superstition, 1218

Of the Laws of Ecclesiastical Polity, 168

Of Truth, 1213

Oh, to vex me, contraries meet in one, 965

Oh, what a lantern, what a lamp of light, 606

O happy dames, that may embrace, 140

O Lord, in me there lieth nought, 606

On Giles and Joan, 1091

On Gut, 1095

On Hellespont, guilty of true-loves' blood, 660

On Leaping over the Moon, 1433

On Lucy, Countess of Bedford, 1092

On Monsieur's Departure, 230

On My First Daughter, 1091

On My First Son, 1092

On Shakespeare, 1459

On Something, That Walks Somewhere, 1090

On the Death of My First and Dearest Child, Hector Philips, 1338

On the Late Massacre in Piedmont, 1492

On the Morning of Christ's Nativity, 1451

On the New Forcers of Conscience under the Long Parliament, 1490

On the Wounds of Our Crucified Lord, 1296

Oration of Queen Mary in the Guildhall, on the First of February, 1554, The, 198

Othello, 803

O these wakeful wounds of thine!, 1296

O thou, my lovely boy, who in thy power, 734

O thou that swing'st upon the waving hair, 1330

Pamphilia to Amphilanthus, 1116

Paradise Lost, 1493

Passage of Our Most Dread Sovereign Lady Queen Elizabeth through the City of London to Westminster on the Day before Her Coronation, The, 223

Passionate Shepherd to His Love, The, 678

Patriarcha, or The Natural Power of Kings Defended Against the Unnatural Liberty of the People, 1394

Peace I do not find, and I have no wish to make war, 123

Perfect Diurnal of Some Passages in Parliament, No. 288, A, Tuesday, January 30, 1388

Phelps, Katherine, 1333
Phyllis, 514
Picture of Little T. C. in a Prospect of Flowers,
  The, 1349
Pilgrimage, The, 1268
Pluck the fruit and taste the pleasure, 513
Poetess's Hasty Resolution, The, 1435
Poor soul, the center of my sinful earth, 737
Prayer (1), 1261
Prayer, the church's banquet; angels' age,
  1261
Prayer of the Lady Jane, A, 205
Principal Navigations, 612
Psalm 52, 605
Psalm 139, 606
Psalm 119: O, 606
Pulley, The, 1271

Queen and Huntress, 1105
Queen and huntress, chaste and fair, 1105

Ralegh, Sir Walter, 526
Rapture, A, 1325
Reading my verses, I liked them so well, 1435
Reason of Church Government Urged Against
  Prelaty, The, 1474
Redemption, 1258
Regeneration, 1278
Relation Concerning Dorothy Waugh's Cruel
  Usage by the Mayor of Carlisle, A, 1429
Relic, The, 940
Religio Medici, 1247
Renowned empress, and Great Britain's
  queen, 981
Retreat, The, 1280
Rima 134 (Petrach), 123
Rima 140 (Petrach), 121
Rima 164 (Petrach), 136
Rima 189 (Petrach), 124
Rima 190 (Petrach), 121
Rima 310 (Petrach), 135
Rise, heart, thy lord is risen. Sing his praise,
  1258
Roses at first were white, 1314

Salve Deus Rex Judaeorum, 981
Samson Agonistes, 1728
Sappho to Philaenis, 947
Sarracoll, John, 634
Satire 3, 944
Schoolmaster, The, 172, 200
Scourge of Folly, The, 520
Second Letter to Her Father, A (Lady Jane
  Grey), 207
Second voyage to Guinea, The, 622
See the chariot at hand here of Love, 1099
See with what simplicity, 1349
Shakespeare, William, 718
Shall I compare thee to a summer's day?, 724
Shepheardes Calender, The, 241
Show me, dear Christ, thy spouse so bright
  and clear, 964

Sidney, Sir Philip, 539
Silence, and Stealth of Days! 1281
Silence, and stealth of days! 'tis now, 1281
Silex Scintillans, 1278
Since brass, nor stone, nor earth, nor
  boundless sea, 728
Since I am coming to that holy room, 967
Since she whom I loved hath paid her last
  debt, 964
Sing lullaby, as women do, 507
Sin of self-love possesseth all mine eye, 728
[Sir Walter Ralegh to His Son], 528
Skelton, John, 36
So cruel prison how could betide, 137
So cruel prison how could betide, alas, 137
Some have no money, 39
Some that have deeper digged love's mine
  than I, 932
Song ("Go and catch a falling star"), 924
Song ("Sweetest love, I do not go"), 929
Song, A ("Ask me no more where Jove
  bestows"), 1323
Song: To Celia, 1098
Songs and Sonnets, 923
Songs and Sonnets, Written by the Right
  Honorable Lord Henry Howard, Late Earl
  of Surrey, and Other, 504
Song to Amoret, A, 1277
Sonnet, to the Noble Lady, the Lady Mary
  Wroth, A, 1100
Sonnets (Milton), 1489
Sonnets (Shakespeare), 723
Soote season, The, 134
So shall I live supposing thou art true, 731
Southwell, Robert, 170
Speech to a Joint Delegation of Lords and
  Commons, November 5, 1566, A, 226
Speech to the House of Commons,
  January 28, 1563, 261
Speech to the Troops at Tilbury, 234
Speght, Rachel, 1202
Spenser, Edmund, 238
Spit in my face ye Jews, and pierce my side,
  962
Stand still, and I will read to thee, 941
Stand whoso list, 129
Stand whoso list upon the slipper top, 129
Steps to the Temple, 1295
Sun Rising, The, 926
Suppose he had been tabled at thy teats,
  1296
Sure it was so. Man in those early days,
  1282
Sweet day, so cool, so calm, so bright, 1264
Sweetest love, I do not go, 929
Swetnam, Joseph, 1200

Tell me not, sweet, I am unkind, 1329
Temple, The, 1257
Tenure of Kings and Magistrates, The, 1396
Th'Assyrians' king, in peace with foul desire,
  136

That time of year thou may'st in me behold, 729

The doubt of future foes exiles my present joy, 230

The forward youth that would appear, 1356

The harbingers are come: see, *see* their mark, 1273

There is a garden in her face, 525

The soote season, that bud and bloom forth brings, 134

The wanton troopers riding by, 1344

Th' expense of spirit in a waste of shame, 735

They Are All Gone into the World of Light!, 1285

They flee from me, 125

They flee from me, that sometime did me seek, 125, 126

They that have power to hurt and will do none, 731

This is the month, and this the happy morn, 1451

This morning, timely rapt with holy fire, 1092

Thomas More to His Friend Peter Giles, Warmest Greetings, 117

Thou art not, Penshurst, built to envious show, 1096

Though frost and snow locked from mine eyes, 1323

Thou hast begun well, Roe, which stand well too, 1093

Thou hast made me, and shall thy work decay?, 960

Three things there be that prosper up apace, 528

Through that pure virgin-shrine, 1288

Throw away thy rod, 1274

Time, 1267

Tis not the work of force but skill, 1300

'Tis the year's midnight and it is the day's, 932

'Tis true, dear Ben, thy just chastising hand, 1321

'Tis true, 'tis day; what though it be?, 930

To Althea, from Prison, 1331

To Ben Jonson, 1321

To draw no envy, Shakespeare, on thy name, 1106

To Heaven, 1099

To His Book's End, 1317

To his book's end this last line he'd have placed, 1317

To His Conscience, 1318

To His Coy Mistress, 1346

To John Donne, 1091

To Lucasta, Going to the Wars, 1329

To Lucy, Countess of Bedford, with Mr. Donne's Satires, 1093

To Marigolds, 1315

To Mrs. M. A. at Parting, 1337

To My Book, 1089

Tonight, grave sir, both my poor house and I, 1094

To Penshurst, 1096

To Saxham, 1323

To Sir Thomas Roe, 1093

To the Doubtful Reader, 981

To the Immortal Memory and Friendship of That Noble Pair, Sir Lucius Cary and Sir H. Morison, 1102

To the Infant Martyrs, 1295

To the Lord General Cromwell, May 1652, 1491

To the Memory of My Beloved, The Author, Mr. William Shakespeare, and What He Hath Left Us, 1106

To The Noblest & best of Ladies, the Countess of Denbigh, 1300

To the Queen's Most Excellent Majesty, 981

To the Right Honorable Sir Francis Walsingham, 613

To the Virgins, to Make Much of Time, 1312

To the Virtuous Reader, 982

Tottel, Richard, 504

To William Camden, 1090

Traherne, Thomas, 1430

True discourse of the late voyages of discovery, A, 626

True Relation of My Birth, Breeding, and Life, A, 1438

Tudor, Mary (Mary I), 194

Tunning of Elinour Rumming, The, 39

Twelfth Night, 739

Twice forty months in wedlock I did stay, 1338

Twice or thrice had I loved thee, 930

Two loves I have of comfort and despair, 737

Tyndale, William, 149

Tyrant, why swell'st thou thus, 605

Undertaking, The, 925

Underwood, 1099

Unhappy Dido burns, and in her rage, 141

Unprofitableness, 1283

Upon Appleton House, 1361

Upon His Verses, 1316

Upon Jack and Jill. Epigram, 1314

Upon Julia's Clothes, 1317

Upon Prue, His Maid, 1317

Upon the Double Murder of King Charles, 1335

Upon the Loss of His Mistresses, 1307

Upon the Nipples of Julia's Breast, 1314

Utopia, 44

Valediction: Forbidding Mourning, A, 935

Valediction: Of Weeping, A, 931

Vaughan, Henry, 1276

Verse Exchange between Elizabeth and Sir Walter Ralegh, 233

Verses Written with a Diamond, 222

Vine, The, 1308

Virtue, 1264

Volpone, 993

Voyage set out by the right honorable the earl of Cumberland in the year 1586, The, 634

Walton, Izaak, 974
Waterfall, The, 1289
Waugh, Dorothy, 1428
Webster, John, 1157
Weep with me, all you that read, 1095
Well-meaning readers! you that come as friends, 1303
What heaven-entreated heart is this, 1300
What if this present were the world's last night?, 963
What is our life? 527
What is our life? a play of passion, 527
What needs my Shakespeare for his honored bones, 1459
What offspring other men have got, 1316
What vaileth truth? 124
What vaileth truth? or by it to take pain, 124
When, in disgrace with Fortune and men's eyes, 726
When all this All doth pass from age to age, 512
Whenas in silks my Julia goes, 1317
When by thy scorn, O murderess, I am dead, 935
When first my lines of heavenly joys made mention, 1266
When first thou didst entice to thee my heart, 1260
When for the thorns with which I long, too long, 1341
When God at first made man, 1271
When I a verse shall make, 1315
When I consider every thing that grows, 724
When I Consider How My Light Is Spent, 1492
When I do count the clock that tells the time, 724
When in the chronicle of wasted time, 733
When Jill complains to Jack for want of meat, 1314
When Love with unconfinèd wings, 1331
When my devotions could not pierce, 1263
When my grave is broke up again, 940
When my love swears that she is made of truth, 736
When night's black mantle could most darkness prove, 1116

When that rich soul which to her heaven is gone, 949
When thou must home to shades of underground, 523
When to her lute Corinna sings, 522
When to the sessions of sweet silent thought, 726
Where, like a pillow on a bed, 936
Where is that holy fire, which verse is said, 947
Where the remote Bermudas ride, 1341
While that my soul repairs to her devotion, 1262
Whoever comes to shroud me, do not harm, 938
Whoever hath her wish, thou hast thy *Will*, 736
Who list his wealth and ease retain, 130
Who says that fictions only and false hair, 1262
Who says that Giles and Joan at discord be? 1091
Whoso list to hunt, 121
Whoso list to hunt, I know where is an hind, 121
Wilt thou forgive that sin where I begun, 968
Windows, The, 1263
Winstanley, Gerrard, 1399
Within this sober frame expect, 1361
With lullay, lullay, like a child, 38
With what deep murmurs through time's silent stealth, 1289
Wonder, 1431
Woodmanship, 508
World, The, 1283
Wroth, Mary, 1110
Wyatt, Sir Thomas the Elder, 118
Wyatt resteth here, that quick could never rest, 138

Ye living lamps, by whose dear light, 1353
Yet once more, O ye laurels, and once more, 1468

Zephyrus returns and leads back the fine weather and the flowers, 135